Butterworths
UK Tax Guide 1989–90

8th edition

Consultant editor
John Tiley, MA, BCL
of the Inner Temple, Barrister;
Fellow of Queens' College, Cambridge;
Reader in the Law of Taxation, University of Cambridge

Contributors
C A Barcroft, ATII
Colin Cretton, MA, ATII
Michael D Eldridge, BD, FCA
James S MacLeod, LLM, CA, FTII
B J Sims, LLB, FTII

London
Butterworths
1989

United Kingdom	Butterworth & Co (Publishers) Ltd, 88 Kingsway, LONDON WC2B 6AB and 4 Hill Street, EDINBURGH EH2 3JZ
Australia	Butterworths Pty Ltd, SYDNEY, MELBOURNE, BRISBANE, ADELAIDE, PERTH, CANBERRA and HOBART
Canada	Butterworths Canada Ltd, TORONTO and VANCOUVER
Ireland	Butterworth (Ireland) Ltd, DUBLIN
Malaysia	Malayan Law Journal Sdn Bhd, KUALA LUMPUR
New Zealand	Butterworths of New Zealand Ltd, WELLINGTON and AUCKLAND
Singapore	Butterworth & Co (Asia) Pte Ltd, SINGAPORE
USA	Butterworth Legal Publishers, ST PAUL, Minnesota, SEATTLE, Washington, BOSTON, Massachusetts, AUSTIN, Texas and D & S Publishers, CLEARWATER, Florida

ISBN 0 406 50498-9

Typeset by CCC, printed and bound in Great Britain by
William Clowes Limited, Beccles and London

Preface

The *UK Tax Guide* is now established as an annual publication brought out as soon as possible after each year's Finance Act. Developed from John Tiley's *Revenue Law*, it is designed to be both a comprehensive tax textbook and a pointer, by means of extensive cross-referencing, to the more detailed narrative in Butterworth's looseleaf tax encyclopaedias.

For the eight edition the narrative and examples have been updated to incorporate the provisions of the Finance Act 1989 and all recent case decisions, together with relevant secondary legislation and new examples of Revenue practice; important developments since publication of the previous edition of the *Guide* are summarised on pp vii–xii.

We would like to thank Colin Cretton, James MacLeod, Michael Eldridge, Bernard Sims and Charles Barcroft for their contributions to, respectively, the sections on capital gains tax, savings, pensions and national insurance contributions, stamp duty and stamp duty reserve tax and value added tax. Our special thanks are due to John Tiley for his continuing assistance in the revision and updating of the *Guide*.

Butterworth & Co (Publishers) Ltd
August 1989

Contents

PART IV. CORPORATION TAX

PART V. SAVINGS

PART VI. ANTI-AVOIDANCE

PART VII. THE INTERNATIONAL DIMENSION

PART VIII. INHERITANCE TAX

PART IX. NATIONAL INSURANCE CONTRIBUTIONS

PART X. STAMP DUTY AND
STAMP DUTY RESERVE TAX

PART XI. VALUE ADDED TAX

TABLES AND INDEX

1989–90 Developments

Tax rates and reliefs

INCOME TAX RATES

1988–89

| Band of taxable income | | | | | |
Exceeding £	Not exceeding £	Band £	Rate %	Tax on full band £	Cumulative tax £
0	19,300	19,300	25	4,825	4,825
19,300	—	—	40	—	—

1989–90

| Band of taxable income | | | | | |
Exceeding £	Not exceeding £	Band £	Rate %	Tax on full band £	Cumulative tax £
0	20,700	20,700	25	5,175	5,175
20,700	—	—	40	—	—

Additional rate:
1988–89
Not charged on the investment income of individuals
Additional rate on income arising to trustees of discretionary trusts—10%

1989–90
Not charged on the investment income of individuals
Additional rate on income arising to trustees of discretionary trusts—10%

CORPORATION TAX RATES

	1.4.1988	1.4.1989
Financial year commencing:		
Profits (income and chargeable gains)	35%	35%
Small companies (accounting periods beginning after 16.3.87)		
Rate	25%	25%
Lower maximum profits (P)	£100,000	£150,000
Higher maximum profits (M)	£500,000	£750,000
Formula fraction (F)	1/40th	1/40th

Tax reduced by: $(M - P) \times I/P \times F$
where I = total profits on which CT is borne

	1.4.1988	1.4.1989
Capital gains:		
Fraction excluded from charge to CT	nil	nil
For authorised unit trusts and investment trusts	no charge	no charge

	1988–89	1989–90
ACT and tax credit	1/3rd	1/3rd

TABLE OF INCOME TAX RELIEFS

Year	Personal reliefs			Wife's earned income relief*	Age allowance		Widows bereavement allowance	Child relief
	Single	Married			Exempt if income not over	Liability on excess		
		Higher personal relief	Reduction per month before marriage					
1983–84	£1,785	£2,795	£84.17	maximum £1,785	M. £3,755 S. £2,360	2/3rds excess of income over £7,600	£1,010	Tax free child ben paid to the moth Each child £5.85 (£6.50 from 21.11
1984–85	£2,005	£3,155	£95.83	maximum £2,005	M. £3,955 S. £2,490	2/3rds excess of income over £8,100	£1,150	Tax free child ben paid to the moth Each child £6.50 (£6.85 from 26.11
1985–86	£2,205	£3,455	£104.17	maximum £2,205	M. £4,255 S. £2,690	2/3rds excess of income over £8,800	£1,250	Tax free child ben paid to the moth Each child £6.85 (£7.00 from 25.11
1986–87	£2,335	£3,655	£110	maximum £2,335	M. £4,505 S. £2,850	2/3rds excess of income over £9,400	£1,320	Tax free child ben paid to the moth Each child £7 p. (£7.10 from 28.7.
1987–88	£2,425	£3,795	£114.17	maximum £2,425	M. £4,675 S. £2,960 M. (80 and over) £4,845 S. (80 and over) £3,070	2/3rds excess of income over £9,800	£1,370	Tax-free child ben paid to the moth Each child £7.25 p
1988–89	£2,605	£4,095	£124.17	maximum £2,605	M. £5,035 S. £3,180 M. (80 and over) £5,205 S. (80 and over) £3,310	2/3rds excess of income over £10,600	£1,490	Tax-free child bene paid to the moth Each child £7.25 p
1989–90	£2,785	£4,375	£132.50	maximum £2,785	M. £5,385 S. £3,400 M. (75 and over) £5,565 S. (75 and over) £3,540	1/2 excess of income over £11,400	£1,590	Tax free child bene paid to the mothe Each child £7.25 p.

* Not available in year of marriage.
† 1976–77 allowances (£300, £335, £365) available for certain children living abroad.
‡ Child relief of £365 for certain students.
** Child relief at 1978–79 rates for certain students living abroad.
[1] Alternative reliefs (housekeeper/additional relief).
[2] Alternative reliefs (daughter's services/blind persons' relief).

...usekeeper relief[1]	Additional relief for children[1]	Dependent relative relief *For each dependant*	Relief for daughter's services[2]	Blind person's relief (each)[2]	Life assurance relief
r male or female housekeeper £100	£1,010	£100 Single woman, etc: £145 Dependant's income limit: basic retirement pension £1,731.00	Includes son's services £55	£360	Premium relief by deduction (15%)
r male or female housekeeper £100	£1,150	£100 Single woman, etc: £145 Dependant's income limit: basic retirement pension £1,803.85	Includes son's services £55	£360	For contracts made before 14 March 1984 *only*, given by deduction (15%). Otherwise abolished.
or male or female housekeeper £100	£1,250	£100 Single woman, etc: £145 Dependant's income limit: basic retirement pension £1,909.10	Includes son's services £55	£360	Pre 14 March 1984 contracts *only* (15%)
or male or female housekeeper £100	£1,320	£100 Single woman, etc: £145 Dependant's income limit: basic retirement pension £2,006	Includes son's services £55	£360	Pre 14 March 1984 contracts *only* (15%)
or male or female housekeeper £100	£1,370	£100 Single woman, etc: £145 Dependant's income limit: basic retirement pension £2,054	Includes son's services £55	£540	Pre 14 March 1984 contracts *only* (15%)
Abolished from 6 April 1988	£1,490	Abolished from 6 April 1988	Abolished from 6 April 1988	£540	Pre 14 March 1984 contracts *only* (15%)
Abolished from 6 April 1988	£1,590	Abolished from 6 April 1988	Abolished from 6 April 1988	£540	Pre 14 March 1984 contracts *only* (12.5%)

CAPITAL GAINS TAX RATES

1988–89

Individuals

Net gains	*Charge to tax*
£5,000 or less	Nil
excess over £5,000	income tax rates (as marginal slice of income)

(applies also to certain trusts for disabled persons)

Others (Trusts, etc.)

Net gains	*Charge to tax*
£2,500 or less	Nil
excess over £2,500	income tax rates

1989–90

Individuals

Net gains	*Charge to tax*
£5,000 or less	Nil
excess over £5,000	income tax rates (as marginal slice of income)

(applies also to certain trusts for disabled persons)

Others (Trusts, etc.)

Net gains	*Charge to tax*
£2,500 or less	Nil
excess over £2,500	income tax rates

INHERITANCE TAX RATES

15th March–5th April 1989: Death rates

Cumulative chargeable transfers (gross)	*Rate on gross*	*Tax on band*	*Cumulative tax*		*Cumulative chargeable transfers (net)*	*Rate on net fraction*
£	%	£	£		£	
0–110,000	0	0	0		0–110,000	Nil
Over 110,000	40	—	—		—	2/3

Lower rates

Cumulative chargeable transfers (gross)	*Rate on gross*	*Tax on band*	*Cumulative tax*		*Cumulative chargeable transfers (net)*	*Rate on net fraction*
£	%	£	£		£	
0–110,000	0	0	0		0–110,000	Nil
Over 110,000	20	—	—		—	1/4

Commencing on 6th April 1989: Death rates

Cumulative chargeable transfers (gross)	Rate on gross	Tax on band	Cumulative tax		Cumulative chargeable transfers (net)	Rate on net fraction
£	%	£	£		£	
0–118,000	0	0	0		0–118,000	Nil
Over 118,000	40	—	—		—	2/3

Lower rates

Cumulative chargeable transfers (gross)	Rate on gross	Tax on band	Cumulative tax		Cumulative chargeable transfers (net)	Rate on net fraction
£	%	£	£		£	
0–118,000	0	0	0		0–118,000	Nil
Over 118,000	20	—	—		—	1/4

PERSONAL PENSION SCHEMES
Maximum limits for qualifying premiums
1988–89

Age (at start of year of assessment)	Maximum percentage
Under 51	$17\frac{1}{2}$
51–55	20
56–60	$22\frac{1}{2}$
61 or over	$27\frac{1}{2}$

1989–90

Age (at start of year of assessment)	Maximum percentage
35 or less	$17\frac{1}{2}$
36–45	20
46–50	25
51–55	30
56 or over	35

From 6 April 1989, the maximum net relevant earnings to which the above percentages may be applied are £60,000

SEPARATE TAXATION OF WIFE'S EARNINGS

Tables indicating level of wife's *earnings* at which an election for separate taxation treatment of the wife's earnings is beneficial:

1988–89 Total joint income	Wife's earnings	
	Min.	Max.
Less than £28,484	Election not beneficial	
£28,484 and above	£6,579	£21,905 plus excess over £28,484

1989–90 Total joint income	Wife's earnings	
	Min.	Max.
Less than £30,510	Election not beneficial	
£30,510 and above	£7,025	£23,485 plus excess over £30,510

Notes:

The tables show figures before deduction of the single and married man's personal reliefs and the wife's earned income relief.

Before using the table any *other* personal relief due or any charges on income should be deducted from the actual total joint income (and to the extent that they would be allocated to her under separate taxation treatment, also from the wife's earnings).

The tables do not apply where either age allowance or additional relief in respect of children is due, or charges on income are paid by the wife and the couple's joint investment income, less the charges paid by the husband, exceeds the additional rate threshold.

STAMP DUTIES
Table of Ad Valorem duties

CONSIDERATION for a Conveyance or Transfer on Sale of property other than stock and marketable securities or PREMIUM for a lease

1 Consideration or Premium		2 Instrument certified at £30,000	3 Instrument not certified*	
exceeds	does not exceed			
£	£		£ p	
	50	Nil	50	
50	100	Nil	1 00	
100	150	Nil	1 50	
150	200	Nil	2 00	
200	250	Nil	2 50	
250	300	Nil	3 00	
300	350	Nil	3 50	
350	400	Nil	4 00	
400	450	Nil	4 50	
450	500	Nil	5 00	
500	30,000	Nil	1 00	per £100 or part of £100
30,000	—	—	1 00	per £100 or part of £100

*An instrument which is "certified" at a particular amount is one which contains a statement certifying that the transaction effected by the instrument does not form part of a larger transaction or series of transactions in respect of which the amount or value, or aggregate amount or value, of the consideration exceeds that amount. For the purpose of determining the amount at which an instrument is to be certified the consideration for any sale or contract or agreement for the sale of goods, wares or merchandise should be disregarded (except where the instrument is itself an actual conveyance or transfer of the goods, wares or merchandise, with or without other property).

Note
    There is no provision for the certification of transfers on sale of stock (including units under unit trust schemes) and marketable securities, or of Leases at a yearly rate of rent exceeding £300. Transfers of stock and marketable securities are chargeable with duty of 50p for every £100 or part of the consideration.

LEASE — Annual Rent (for premium see Columns 1-3)

4		5	6	7	8
Annual-Rent		Term not exceeding 7 years or indefinite	Term exceeding 7 years but not exceeding 35 years	Term exceeding 35 years but not exceeding 100 years	Term exceeding 100 years
Exceeds	does not exceed				
£	£		£ p	£ p	£ p
	5	Nil	10	60	1 20
5	10	Nil	20	1 20	2 40
10	15	Nil	30	1 80	3 60
15	20	Nil	40	2 40	4 80
20	25	Nil	50	3 00	6 00
25	50	Nil	1 00	6 00	12 00
50	75	Nil	1 50	9 00	18 00
75	100	Nil	2 00	12 00	24 00
100	150	Nil	3 00	18 00	36 00
150	200	Nil	4 00	24 00	48 00
200	250	Nil	5 00	30 00	60 00
250	300	Nil	6 00	36 00	72 00
300	350	Nil	7 00	42 00	84 00
350	400	Nil	8 00	48 00	96 00
400	450	Nil	9 00	54 00	108 00
450	500	Nil	10 00	60 00	120 00
500		50p per £50 or part of £50	£1 per £50 or part of £50	£6 per £50 or part of £50	£12 per £50 or part of £50

FURNISHED LETTINGS — A letting agreement for any definite term less than a year of any furnished dwelling house or apartment where the rent for the term exceeds £500 attracts a fixed duty of £1.

RETAIL PRICES INDEX

Year	Jan	Feb	Mar	Apr	May	June	July	Aug	Sept	Oct	Nov	Dec
1965	14.47	14.47	14.52	14.80	14.85	14.90	14.90	14.93	14.93	14.96	15.01	15.08
1966	15.11	15.11	15.13	15.34	15.44	15.49	15.41	15.51	15.49	15.51	15.61	15.64
1967	15.67	15.67	15.67	15.79	15.79	15.84	15.74	15.72	15.69	15.86	15.92	16.02
1968	16.07	16.15	16.20	16.50	16.50	16.58	16.58	16.60	16.63	16.70	16.76	16.96
1969	17.06	17.16	17.21	17.41	17.39	17.47	17.47	17.41	17.47	17.59	17.64	17.77
1970	17.90	18.00	18.10	18.38	18.43	18.48	18.63	18.61	18.71	18.91	19.04	19.16
1971	19.42	19.54	19.70	20.13	20.25	20.38	20.51	20.53	20.56	20.66	20.79	20.89
1972	21.01	21.12	21.19	21.39	21.50	21.62	21.70	21.88	22.00	22.31	22.38	22.48
1973	22.64	22.79	22.92	23.35	23.52	23.65	23.75	23.83	24.03	24.51	24.69	24.87
1974	25.35	25.78	26.01	26.89	27.28	27.55	27.81	27.83	28.14	28.69	29.20	29.63
1975	30.39	30.90	31.51	32.72	34.09	34.75	35.11	35.31	35.61	36.12	36.55	37.01
1976	37.49	37.97	38.17	38.91	39.34	39.54	39.62	40.18	40.71	41.44	42.03	42.59
1977	43.70	44.24	44.56	45.70	46.06	46.54	46.59	46.82	47.07	47.28	47.50	47.76
1978	48.04	48.31	48.62	49.33	49.61	49.99	50.22	50.54	50.75	50.98	51.33	51.76
1979	52.52	52.95	53.38	54.30	54.73	55.67	58.07	58.53	59.11	59.72	60.25	60.68
1980	62.18	63.07	63.93	66.11	66.72	67.35	67.91	68.06	68.49	68.92	69.48	69.86
1981	70.29	70.93	71.99	74.07	74.55	74.48	75.31	75.87	76.30	76.98	77.78	78.28
1982	78.73	78.76	79.44	81.04	81.62	81.85	81.88	81.90	81.85	82.26	82.66	82.51
1983	82.61	82.97	83.12	84.28	84.64	84.84	85.30	85.68	86.06	86.36	86.67	86.89
1984	86.84	87.20	87.48	88.64	88.97	89.20	89.10	89.94	90.11	90.67	90.95	90.87
1985	91.20	91.94	92.80	94.78	95.21	95.41	95.23	95.49	95.44	95.59	95.92	96.05
1986	96.25	96.60	96.73	97.67	97.85	97.79	97.52	97.82	98.30	98.45	99.29	99.62
1987	100.00	100.40	100.60	101.80	101.90	101.90	101.80	102.10	102.40	102.90	103.40	103.30
1988	103.30	103.70	104.10	105.80	106.20	106.60	106.70	107.90	108.40	109.50	110.00	110.30
1989	111.00	111.80	112.30	114.30	115.00	115.40						

Interest factor tables

These tables take into account the interest rate change in operation from 6 June 1987.

TABLE A

Repayment supplement: ready reckoner

How to use the table
The table gives the "interest factors" to apply when calculating supplement.
First work out the difference between the factors for—

the relevant date, and
the end of the tax month in which repayment or set off is due.

Then multiply the tax repayment due by the difference.

Example

Corporation Tax repayment of £2,000
Relevant date: 1 October 1981
End of month in which repayment made: 5 January 1984

Factor for 5 January 1984   2.1287
Factor for 1 October 1981   1.9020
                             ———————
                             0.2267

Supplement = £2,000 × 0.2267 = £453.40

TABLE OF INTEREST FACTORS AS AT 5TH OF MONTH

	Jan	Feb	Mar	Apr	May	Jun
1975	1.242	1.2495	1.257	1.2645	1.272	1.2795
1976	1.332	1.3395	1.347	1.3545	1.362	1.3695
1977	1.422	1.4295	1.437	1.4445	1.452	1.4595
1978	1.512	1.5195	1.527	1.5345	1.542	1.5495
1979	1.602	1.6095	1.617	1.6245	1.632	1.6395
1980	1.692	1.702	1.712	1.722	1.732	1.742
1981	1.812	1.822	1.832	1.842	1.852	1.862
1982	1.932	1.942	1.952	1.962	1.972	1.982
1983	2.0487	2.0554	2.062	2.0687	2.0754	2.082
1984	2.1287	2.1354	2.142	2.1487	2.1554	2.162
1985	2.2087	2.2154	2.222	2.2287	2.2354	2.2445
1986	2.3087	2.3178	2.3270	2.3362	2.3453	2.3545
1987	2.4098	2.4178	2.4257	2.4336	2.4411	2.4486
1988	2.4987	2.5056	2.5125	2.5193	2.5262	2.5327
1989	2.5887	2.5983	2.6079	2.6175	2.6271	2.6367
1990	2.7075	2.7177	2.7279	2.7381	2.7483	2.7585

TABLE OF INTEREST FACTORS AS AT 5TH OF MONTH (*cont*)

	Jul	Aug	Sept	Oct	Nov	Dec
1975	1.287	1.2945	1.302	1.3095	1.317	1.3245
1976	1.377	1.3845	1.392	1.3995	1.407	1.4145
1977	1.467	1.4745	1.482	1.4895	1.497	1.5045
1978	1.557	1.5645	1.572	1.5795	1.587	1.5945
1979	1.647	1.6545	1.662	1.6695	1.677	1.6845
1980	1.752	1.762	1.772	1.782	1.792	1.802
1981	1.872	1.882	1.892	1.902	1.912	1.922
1982	1.992	2.002	2.012	2.022	2.032	2.042
1983	2.0887	2.0954	2.102	2.1087	2.1154	2.122
1984	2.1687	2.1754	2.182	2.1887	2.1954	2.202
1985	2.2537	2.2628	2.2720	2.2812	2.2903	2.2995
1986	2.3637	2.3728	2.3799	2.3870	2.3940	2.4019
1987	2.4555	2.4624	2.4693	2.4768	2.4843	2.4918
1988	2.5391	2.5456	2.5537	2.5618	2.5699	2.5784
1989	2.6462	2.6564	2.6666	2.6768	2.6871	2.6973
1990	2.7687	2.7789	2.7891	2.7993	2.8095	2.8197

Rates of Repayment Supplement

To 5 December 1982	12% pa	To 5 December 1987	9% pa
To 5 May 1985	8% pa	To 5 May 1988	8.25% pa
To 5 August 1986	11% pa	To 5 August 1988	7.75% pa
To 5 November 1986	8.5% pa	To 5 October 1988	9.75% pa
To 5 April 1987	9.5% pa	To 5 January 1989	10.75% pa
To 5 June 1987	9% pa	To 5 July 1989	11.5% pa
To 5 September 1987	8.25% pa	To date	12.25% pa

If the rate changes after the operable date for this table the factors for the period from the date of change to 5 December 1989 will need amending. Please refer to the Press Release containing the revised table.

TABLE B

Investigation settlements: s 88 interest: ready reckoner

How to use the table

Find out the difference between the factors for—

the expected date of payment, and
the normal due date for payment.

The tax due is then multiplied by that difference.

Example

In a settlement for omitted interest the tax lost under Case III Schedule D for 1975–76 is £500. Payment is expected by 1 December 1985.

Factor for 1 December 1985	2.2995
Factor for 1 January 1976	1.3320
Difference	0.9675

Section 88 interest = £500 × 0.9675 = £483.75

Rates of interest

To 18 April 1967	3% pa	To 5 September 1987	8.25% pa
To 30 June 1974	4% pa	To 5 December 1987	9% pa
To 31 December 1979	9% pa	To 5 May 1988	8.25% pa
To 30 November 1982	12% pa	To 5 August 1988	7.75% pa
To 30 April 1985	8% pa	To 5 October 1988	9.75% pa
To 5 August 1986	11% pa	To 5 January 1989	10.75% pa
To 5 November 1986	8.5% pa	To 5 July 1989	11.5% pa
To 5 April 1987	9.5% pa	To date	12.25% pa

If the rate changes after the operable date for this table the factors for the period from the date of change to 1 December 1989 will need amending. Please refer to the Press Release containing the revised table.

PART 1 TABLE OF INTEREST FACTORS AS AT 1ST OF MONTH

	Jan	Feb	Mar	Apr	May	Jun
1965	0.840	0.8425	0.845	0.8475	0.850	0.8525
1966	0.870	0.8725	0.875	0.8775	0.880	0.8825
1967	0.900	0.9025	0.905	0.9075	0.910	0.9133
1968	0.9367	0.940	0.9433	0.9467	0.950	0.9533
1969	0.9767	0.980	0.9833	0.9867	0.990	0.9933
1970	1.0167	1.020	1.0233	1.0267	1.030	1.0333
1971	1.0567	1.060	1.0633	1.0667	1.070	1.0733
1972	1.0967	1.100	1.1033	1.1067	1.110	1.1133
1973	1.1367	1.140	1.1433	1.1467	1.150	1.1533
1974	1.1767	1.180	1.1833	1.1867	1.190	1.1933
1975	1.242	1.2495	1.257	1.2645	1.272	1.2795
1976	1.332	1.3395	1.347	1.3545	1.362	1.3695
1977	1.422	1.4295	1.437	1.4445	1.452	1.4595
1978	1.512	1.5195	1.527	1.5345	1.542	1.5495
1979	1.602	1.6095	1.617	1.6245	1.632	1.6395
1980	1.692	1.702	1.712	1.722	1.732	1.742
1981	1.812	1.822	1.832	1.842	1.852	1.862
1982	1.932	1.942	1.952	1.962	1.972	1.982
1983	2.0487	2.0553	2.062	2.0687	2.0753	2.082
1984	2.1287	2.1353	2.142	2.1487	2.1553	2.162
1985	2.2087	2.2153	2.222	2.2287	2.2353	2.2445
1986	2.3087	2.3178	2.3270	2.3362	2.3453	2.3545
1987	2.4098	2.4178	2.4257	2.4336	2.4411	2.4486
1988	2.4987	2.5056	2.5125	2.5193	2.5262	2.5327
1989	2.5887	2.5983	2.6079	2.6175	2.6271	2.6367
1990	2.7075	2.7177	2.7279	2.7381	2.7483	2.7585

TABLE OF INTEREST FACTORS AS AT 1ST OF MONTH (*cont*)

	Jul	Aug	Sept	Oct	Nov	Dec
1965	0.855	0.8575	0.860	0.8625	0.865	0.8675
1966	0.885	0.8875	0.890	0.8925	0.895	0.8975
1967	0.9167	0.920	0.9233	0.9267	0.930	0.9333
1968	0.9567	0.960	0.9633	0.9667	0.970	0.9733
1969	0.9967	1.000	1.0033	1.0067	1.010	1.0133
1970	1.0367	1.040	1.0433	1.0467	1.050	1.0533
1971	1.0767	1.080	1.0833	1.0867	1.090	1.0933
1972	1.1167	1.120	1.1233	1.1267	1.130	1.1333
1973	1.1567	1.160	1.1633	1.1667	1.170	1.1733
1974	1.197	1.2045	1.212	1.2195	1.227	1.2345
1975	1.287	1.2945	1.302	1.3095	1.317	1.3245
1976	1.377	1.3845	1.392	1.3995	1.407	1.4145
1977	1.467	1.4745	1.482	1.4895	1.497	1.5045
1978	1.557	1.5645	1.572	1.5795	1.587	1.5945
1979	1.647	1.6545	1.662	1.6695	1.677	1.6845
1980	1.752	1.762	1.772	1.782	1.792	1.802
1981	1.872	1.882	1.892	1.902	1.912	1.922
1982	1.992	2.002	2.012	2.022	2.032	2.042
1983	2.0887	2.0953	2.102	2.1087	2.1153	2.122
1984	2.1687	2.1753	2.182	2.1887	2.1953	2.202
1985	2.2537	2.2628	2.2720	2.2812	2.2903	2.2995
1986	2.3637	2.3728	2.3799	2.3870	2.3940	2.4019
1987	2.4555	2.4624	2.4693	2.4768	2.4843	2.4918
1988	2.5391	2.5456	2.5537	2.5618	2.5699	2.5784
1989	2.6462	2.6564	2.6666	2.6768	2.6871	2.6973
1990	2.7687	2.7789	2.7891	2.7993	2.8095	2.8197

PART 2   SUPPLEMENTARY TABLE OF INTEREST FACTORS AS AT 1ST OF MONTH

	Jan	Apr	Jul		Jan	Apr	Jul
1937	0	0.0075	0.015	1951	0.420	0.4275	0.435
1938	0.030	0.0375	0.045	1952	0.450	0.4575	0.465
1939	0.060	0.0675	0.075	1953	0.480	0.4875	0.495
1940	0.090	0.0975	0.105	1954	0.510	0.5175	0.525
1941	0.120	0.1275	0.135	1955	0.540	0.5475	0.555
1942	0.150	0.1575	0.165	1956	0.570	0.5775	0.585
1943	0.180	0.1875	0.195	1957	0.600	0.6075	0.615
1944	0.210	0.2175	0.225	1958	0.630	0.6375	0.645
1945	0.240	0.2475	0.255	1959	0.660	0.6675	0.675
1946	0.270	0.2775	0.285	1960	0.690	0.6975	0.705
1947	0.300	0.3075	0.315	1961	0.720	0.7275	0.735
1948	0.330	0.3375	0.345	1962	0.750	0.7575	0.765
1949	0.360	0.3675	0.375	1963	0.780	0.7875	0.795
1950	0.390	0.3975	0.405	1964	0.810	0.8175	0.825

Summary of main due dates

Liability	Normal due date	Exception	Notes
Schedule D and A assessments including Class 4 NIC	1 January in year of assessment	Earned income sources—tax due in 2 equal instalments on 1 January and 1 July	Where tax is payable in 2 instalments *before* 1985—the factor for the mean date of 1 April in the year of assessment may be used. Apply the difference in factors to all that tax.
Capital Gains Tax and "taxed" income assessments for 1980–81 onwards	1 December following year of assessment	—	For years up to and including 1979–80 the due date was 6 July following year of assessment. Use the factor for 1 July as this is sufficiently accurate in most cases.
Schedule E assessments for 1970–71 onwards	1 January in year of assessment	—	For years up to and including 1969–70 tax payable in 2 equal instalments. Use the factor for 1 April in year of assessment but apply the difference in factors to all that tax.
Surtax for years up to and including 1972–73	1 January following year of assessment	—	Do not use for "Special contribution" or "Special Charge".
Corporation Tax	9 months from end of chargeable accounting period	Some companies which were trading before 5/4/65. See TA 1970 s 244(1), (2) [and FA 1987, s. 36 [TA 1988, s. 478, Sch. 30]].	—
Tax under TA 1970 s 286 [TA 1988, ss. 419, 420] for periods after 5/4/73	1st day of financial year following that in which loan or advance made.	—	—

PART I. INTRODUCTION

1

1 The UK tax system

THE POWER TO TAX

1: 01   The power to levy taxes is but one manifestation of the sovereignty of
Parliament, and the Bill of Rights provides that no charge on the subject
shall be levied by pretence of prerogative without the consent of Parliament.
There is a presumption that express statutory authority is needed before a
tax can be imposed;[1] this does not apply to a charge levied for services.[2]
Within Parliament no motion requiring the expenditure of money will be
received unless a Minister can be persuaded to move a financial resolution.
Further, the powers of the House of Lords are limited in relation to a money
Bill.[3]

The power to tax extends even over a stonemason despite the fact that he
may regard his supreme authority as the Master Mason.[4]

The tax legislation distinguishes the UK from the rest of the world. The
UK includes England, Wales, Scotland and Northern Ireland—and the
Scilly Isles[5]—but not the Channel Islands nor the Isle of Man.

The EC is relevant to the power to tax in three ways.[6] First, the Treaty
limits the rights of member governments to levy taxes. Article 95 prohibits
discrimination against imports from other member States through the levy
of charges higher than those on domestic products. Article 96 prohibits
refunds on exports exceeding the actual taxation imposed on the goods.
Article 97 introduces a single tax on imports and uniform average rates of
refund on exports. Article 98 extends the principle of Article 96 to direct
taxation and prohibits member States from operating systems of compensation for the effects of direct taxation on intra-Community trade. Exemption
or, to use the correct term, derogation, is permitted with authorisation.
Article 99 requires the Commission to consider how the legislation of indirect
taxes can be harmonised. Examples of this have centred on VAT, e.g. the
Sixth Directive which provides a uniform code for VAT and which was
brought into UK law by FA 1977. Article 100 provides for the approximation
of laws by directives and it is on this basis that the Commission has tried to
achieve harmonisation of company taxes.

The second way in which the EEC is relevant to tax law is the power of
the EEC to raise taxes. As from 1975 the financial basis of the community is
entirely provided out of the revenues of the community—and consisted of
agricultural levies, customs duties and proportion of VAT equivalent to a
1.4% rate. This basis was changed by the European Council Meeting of
February 1989 which agreed a ceiling of 1.2% of Community GNP.

The third way in which the EEC is relevant to tax law is in the interpretation of statutes. As terms ought to be common to meet Article 99 so ought the interpretation of those terms; questions of difficulty can be referred to the European Court.[7]

Simon's Taxes A1.101–A1.107

[1] *A–G v Wiltshire United Dairies* (1921) 37 TLR 884. Cf. Emergency Powers (Defence) Act 1939, ss. 1(3) and 2. On (non)limitation by international law, see *Cheney v Conn* [1968] 1 All ER 779, 44 TC 217.

[2] *China Navigation Co Ltd v A-G* [1932] 2 KB 197.

[3] Parliament Act 1911, s. 1.

[4] *Lloyd v Taylor* (1970) 46 TC 539.

[5] TA 1988, Sch. 30, paras. 6(2)(*b*) and 21. See also FA 1986, s. 108 on definition of UK relating to oil taxation.

[6] See Wyatt and Dashwood *The Substantive Law of the EEC* (2nd ed) 1987 chapter 5 and Easson Tax Law and Policy in the EEC (1980), Genôt 1978 Eur Law Rev 355 and Dashwood (1982) BTR 71.See also *Hurd v Jones* [1986] STC 127, ECJ.

[7] As in *Customs and Excise Comrs v Apple and Pear Development Council* [1986] STC 192 when the House of Lords referred the interpretation of the word "consideration" to the European Court. For decision of CJEC see [1988] STC 221. For another example see *R v HM Treasury, ex p Daily Mail and General Trust plc*: 81/87 [1989] 1 All ER 328, [1988] STC 787 where the European Court held that TA 1988, s. 765 was not inconsistent with arts. 52 and 58.

The tax year and the provisional collection of taxes

1: 02 For income tax and capital gains tax, the tax year runs from 6th April to 5th April,[1] so that the year from 6th April 1986 to 5th April 1987 is known as the tax-year 1986–87. Different rules apply to corporation tax.[2] The reason for these dates[3] is that the financial year originally began on Lady Day, 25th March; this was changed in 1752 when the calendars were changed. Almost any dating is arbitrary and change now would simply substitute the apparently rational for the attractively picturesque; there are however advantages from having similar periods when calculating statistics.[3]

Since income tax is an annual tax[4] and is imposed by a charge in each year's Finance Act, difficulties arise where the Finance Act has not become law by the start of the tax year (6th April). Tax could not be levied lawfully simply on the basis of a resolution of the House of Commons.[5] However by the Provisional Collection of Taxes Act 1968 temporary statutory effect will be given to resolutions of the House of Commons. The resolutions if passed in March or April expire on 5th August next and if passed in any other month expire after four months. New taxes are expressly excluded.

Simon's Taxes A1.104, 105; Butterworths Income Tax Service A1.12, A1.13

[1] TA 1988, s. 2(2).

[2] And, before its abolition, to DLT, see DLTA 1976, s. 13.

[3] RC 1920 App 7(o).

[4] But not CGT: see also TA 1988, s. 8(6) (corporation tax), FA 1973, s. 50 (stamp duty) and VATA 1983, s. 1 (VAT).

[5] *Bowles v Bank of England* [1913] 1 Ch 57. The Finance Acts of 1909, 1910 and 1911 reached the statute book 13, 7 and 7 months after the start of the financial year. Mr Bowles was an opposition back bencher. The Chancellor of the Exchequer was Lloyd George.

Avoidance, evasion and planning

1: 03   The effectiveness of the tax base must be judged not only by its ambit and the efficiency of its administration but also by its attitude to tax avoidance. Tax avoidance, which is lawful, must be distinguished from tax evasion, which is illegal. If a person marries in order to reduce his tax burden he is practising tax avoidance; if he tells the Revenue that he is married when he is not, he is guilty of tax evasion, and may well be prosecuted. There is also an important distinction between a scheme under which no liability to tax arises—tax avoidance—and one under which a charge arises but the tax cannot be collected.[1]

Tax avoidance has now been distinguished from tax mitigation but primarily for the purpose of interpreting a general anti-avoidance provision in New Zealand law.[2] The distinction is that a tax avoidance plan does not affect the financial position of the taxpayer (other than for the costs of the plan) and the taxpayer is seeking to obtain a tax advantage without suffering the expense which Parliament intended should be suffered to qualify for the advantage. Tax mitigation occurs when that expense is suffered.

---

[1] See *Roome v Edwards* [1979] STC 546 at 561–565, [1979] BTR 261.
[2] Per Lord Templeman in *IRC v Challenge Corpn Ltd* [1986] STC 548 at 555. The New Zealand provision was Income Tax Act 1976, s. 99 renders void for tax purposes arrangements entered into for purposes of tax avoidance.

1: 04   The UK tax system has no general anti-avoidance provision. Until 1984 it could be said that the basic approach of the UK tax system was still that laid down by Lord Tomlin in *IRC v Duke of Westminster*:[1]

> "Every man is entitled if he can to arrange his affairs so that the tax attaching under the appropriate Acts is less than it otherwise would be. If he succeeds in ordering them so as to secure that result, then, however unappreciative the Commissioners of Inland Revenue or his fellow taxpayers may be of his ingenuity, he cannot be compelled to pay an increased tax."

It followed that a transaction which, on its true construction, was of a kind that would escape tax was not taxable on the ground that the same result could have been brought about by a transaction in another form which would have attracted tax.

In *IRC v Westminster* the Duke covenanted to pay an employee a sum of £1.90 per week; the covenant was to last seven years whether or not he remained in the Duke's service. The employee had a wage of £3 a week and he was told that while he would be legally entitled to the full £3 it was expected that in practice he would take only the balance of £1.10. The purpose of the scheme was to enable the Duke to deduct the payment in computing his total income for surtax.[2] The scheme succeeded; the true construction of the document showed that these sums were income of the employee not under Schedule E as an employee but under Schedule D, Case III, as an annuitant.

In reaching this conclusion the courts were entitled to look at all the circumstances of this case, including the fact that the taxpayer had received a letter containing the expectations of the Duke already referred to.[3] However the court was also entitled to look at the fact that the legal right to payment would continue even though the employment ceased. The court was not entitled to conclude that because this was a way in which money passed from employer to employee therefore it must be Schedule E income if it was, in law, income under Schedule D case III.

Simon's Taxes A1.314, 315; Butterworths Income Tax Service A7.03

[1] [1936] AC 1, 19 TC 490.

[2] Such payments are not now effective for higher rates of tax, infra § **13: 46**, nor, for new covenants, for basic rate tax, FA 1988, s. 36 introducing TA 1988, s. 347A, infra, § **13: 33**.

[3] Lord Atkin, dissenting, thought this amounted to a contractual term and not just an expectation.

1: 05 The *Westminster* doctrine is that the courts are bound by the tax result of the transaction entered into. That the courts must charge tax by reference to the facts established seems axiomatic; the problem arises when the legal form is conclusive of those facts. In 1986 the House of Lords in *Reed v Young*[1] accepted the legal form of a limited partnership and upheld a tax saving scheme based upon it.

This was sometimes expressed in the form that the court must look to the form of the transaction and not its substance. This formulation is, however, misleading. First it tends to suggest that the form of a transaction, a matter which may be within the control of the taxpayer, will be conclusive for tax purposes. Often, however, the legal form used by the parties is not conclusive and here, even before 1984 it was accepted that the court must look at the substance of the matter in order to determine the true tax consequences of the transaction in the legal form adopted by the parties. Thus by looking at the substance it could conclude that this form attracted tax just as much as another. In these instances the court was not putting upon the transaction a legal character which it did not possess but was trying to discover the true character in tax law of the transaction entered into.[2] So the court might hold that a trade is carried on by a partnership even though the only document states that there was none,[3] that a trader is still trading even though he says he is not,[4] or that the person claiming to trade is simply the means by which the trade is carried on by someone else.[5] In such contexts the documents cannot be used to deny proven facts. Where however both the facts and the legal arrangements point in the same direction, the court might not disregard them.[6]

Secondly, the name given to a transaction by the parties concerned did not necessarily decide the nature of the transaction.[7] So a description of a series of payments as an annuity or a rentcharge does not determine their character.[8]

Simon's Taxes A1.314, 315; Butterworths Income Tax Service A7.04

[1] [1986] STC 285.

[2] *Per* Sir Wilfrid Greene MR in *IRC v Mallaby-Deeley* [1938] 4 All ER 818 at 825; 23 TC 153 at 167.

[3] *Fenston v Johnstone* (1940) 23 TC 29.

[4] *J. and R. O'Kane & Co Ltd v IRC* (1922) 12 TC 303.

[5] *Firestone Tyre and Rubber Co Ltd v Lewellin* [1957] 1 All ER 561, 37 TC 111.

[6] *Ransom v Higgs* [1974] 3 All ER 949, [1974] STC 539.

[7] *Secretary of State in Council of India v Scoble* [1903] AC 299, 4 TC 618.

[8] *IRC v Land Securities Investment Trust* [1969] 2 All ER 430, 45 TC 495.

1: 06   The *Westminster* doctrine was highly regarded by the Inland Revenue, not least because it was applied in their favour when the taxpayer has carried out a transaction in manner less than wholly tax-efficient.[1] However, the doctrine was subject to limitations. First the court might conclude that the transaction was a sham, that the acts done were intended to give the appearance of creating legal rights different from those which were actually created. Such schemes still fail for the simple reason that the tax falls to be levied on the basis of the actual legal rights created. This argument although frequently advanced by the Revenue did not meet with great success. However the new approach based on the decision of the House of Lords in *Furniss v Dawson*[2] encouraged the courts to give the Revenue occasional glimpses of success. So in *Sherdley v Sherdley*[3] Sir John Donaldson, MR thought that an order to pay school fees to a school on behalf of a child and made at the suit of the parent against whom the order would have been made would be a sham. This use of the sham argument is highly questionable and probably erroneous. The decision was later reversed by the House of Lords, but without discussion of this point.[4]

Secondly, Parliament has created exceptions; it has passed a number of measures enabling the Revenue to tax transactions which are widely defined unless the taxpayer can show that there was no tax avoidance motive. See infra, e.g. § **31: 21**.

Thirdly, it is probably right to distinguish the *Westminster* doctrine just outlined from a *Westminster* approach which tended to look not too unfavourably on attempts to avoid tax; such schemes are now more likely to fail in this object as a result of the decisions in *Ramsay* and *Furniss v Dawson* even though the scope of those decisions has been checked by *Craven v White*. Finally although the courts have long recognised that tax avoidance is lawful, it is not yet a virtue and so in *Re Weston's Settlement*[5] the Court of Appeal declined to approve a variation of trust where the only advantages accruing to the beneficiaries on whose behalf they were being asked to approve the variation were financial, stemming almost exclusively from the saving of tax. Similarly in *Sherdley v Sherdley* the Court of Appeal declined to make an order for financial provision of a child when the only reason for that order would have been the tax saving; this was reversed by the House of Lords but is an indication of a general attitude.[6]

---

[1] E.g. *IRC v Fleming & Co (Machinery) Ltd* (1951) 33 TC 57 at 62.
[2] [1984] STC 153, [1984] 1 All ER 530.
[3] [1986] STC 266 at 273. Balcombe, LJ disagreed (p. 278) and Neill, LJ made no comment.
[4] [1987] STC 217.
[5] [1969] 1 Ch 223, [1968] 1 All ER 720.
[6] [1987] STC 217.

1: 07   Today the status of the *Westminster* principle is in considerable doubt. This stems from a series of House of Lords decisions beginning with *Ramsay v IRC*[1] reaching its high water mark in *Furniss v Dawson*[2] but now greatly restricted by *Craven v White*.[3]

Ramsay v IRC concerned capital gains tax. A had a large gain and wished to create an allowable loss which could be set against the gain and so remove his liability for tax. Under the scheme he bought shares in a company and proceeded to make it two loans each of £218,750 at 11%; the loans were made with the aid of the funds borrowed from a bank associated with the vendors of the scheme. A had the right once to decrease the rate of interest on one loan and make a corresponding increase on the other; this he exercised causing the rate on one loan to drop to nil and on the other to rise to 22%; the latter loan he sold for £391,481, a gain of £172,731. The other loan was repaid at par by the company but the shares in the company were sold at a large consequential loss. The narrow ratio of the House of Lords decision was that the gain on the sale of the debt was a chargeable gain because the debt was a debt on a security (a chargeable asset) and not a simple debt (a non-chargeable asset); see § **15: 06**. However the wider and more important ratio was that the court was entitled to look at the whole transaction and so to conclude that the taxpayer had suffered a loss only of some £3,000. As Lord Wilberforce said[4]

> "... [The approach for which the Crown contends] does not introduce a new principle; it would apply to new and sophisticated legal devices, the undoubted power and duty of the courts to determine their nature in law and to relate them to existing legislation. While the techniques of tax avoidance progress are technically improved, the courts are not obliged to stand still."

Simon's Taxes A1.316.
[1] [1981] 1 All ER 865, [1981] STC 174. The scheme was countered by CGTA 1979, s. 26.
[2] [1984] STC 153; the scheme was countered by what is now CGTA 1979, s. 87.
[3] [1988] 3 All ER 495, [1988] STC 476, HL.
[4] [1981] STC 174 at 181.

1: 08   After *Ramsay v IRC* it was possible to argue that the decision affected simply circular self-cancelling transactions, leaving the *Westminster* principle intact for other transactions. Doubts about this narrow view were raised by the decision of the House of Lords in *IRC v Burmah Oil Co Ltd*.[1] In this case the company, B, had transferred property to a subsidiary, S, but left the money outstanding. As the property had declined in value and was the only substantial asset held by S, it was clear that the debt was worthless. By means of a loan from a fellow subsidiary bank, SB, S was enabled to repay the original loan to B and, by means of a rights issue, attracted further money from B with which to pay off SB. S was then liquidated.[2] The effect was to substitute equity (a chargeable asset) for simple debt (a non-chargeable asset).[3]

Two further facts should be borne in mind. The first was that B still held the property so that in due course a genuine disposal of that property to an outside purchaser could give rise to an allowable loss. The second was that there were outside shareholders or creditors of S. The House of Lords, applying the *Ramsay* doctrine, refused to allow B to deduct the payments made under the rights issue in computing its loss on the shares of S when S was liquidated. There were superficial differences from *Ramsay* in that the scheme was designated just for B instead of being bought "off the shelf", and that B used its own money in making the various payments instead of borrowing it—but these differences were of no real importance.

In the course of their speeches both Lord Diplock and Lord Scarman went out of their way to emphasise "that *Ramsay's* case marks 'a significant change in the approach adopted by this House in its judicial role' towards tax avoidance schemes".[4] However, while emphasising the significance of *Ramsay's* case Lord Diplock was careful to stress that the *Duke of Westminster's* case was still law and had not been over-ruled. He distinguished that case on the grounds that it

> "was about a simple transaction entered into between two real persons, each with a mind of his own, the Duke and his gardener, even though in the 1930s and at a time of high unemployment there might be some reason to expect that the mind of the gardener would manifest some degree of subservience to that of the Duke. The kinds of tax avoidance schemes that have occupied the attention of the courts in recent years, however, involve inter-connected transactions between artificial persons, limited companies without minds of their own but directed by a single master mind."[5]

Little was said about the *Burmah* case in *Craven v White*.

Simon's Taxes A1.316.
[1] [1982] STC 30.
[2] This event triggered the tax advantage but may not have had to form part of the series of transactions; see Gammie *Strategic Tax Planning*, Part D p 17.
[3] The Commissioners had found that the steps would, almost inevitably, have been carried through.
[4] At 39 quoting Lord Diplock at 32.
[5] At 32.

1: 09   The emphasis on a new approach was reiterated, most notably by Lord Scarman in *Furniss v Dawson*.[1] In *Furniss v Dawson* a shareholder wished to sell his stake in Company A to Company C. He followed what Lord Brightman called "a simple and honest scheme which merely seeks to defer payment of tax until the taxpayer has received into his hands the gain which he has made". The shares in Company A were exchanged for shares in Company B and Company B then sold the shares in Company A to Company C. The House of Lords held that, although there was an express finding that all the steps were genuine, nonetheless the effect of the transactions for tax purposes was that the shareholder had disposed of his shares in Company A to Company C in return for consideration paid to Company B.

Lord Brightman, after stressing that no distinction was to be drawn in fact, because none existed in reality, between a series of steps carried through under a non-binding arrangement and those carried through under a contract, stated that the preconditions for the applicability of the *Ramsay* principle were:

> "First, there must be a pre-ordained series of transactions; or, if one likes, a single composite transaction. This composite transaction may or may not include the achievement of a legitimate commercial (i.e. business) end . . . Secondly, there must be steps inserted which have no commercial (business) purpose apart from the avoidance of a liability to tax—not 'no business effect'."

It followed that the courts had the power to ignore (i.e. excise) the steps inserted for no commercial purpose. So here the pre-ordained series of transactions began with the sale by the taxpayer to Company B and ended with the sale by Company B to Company C. This led to the excision of the intervening steps and therefore the whole scheme fell to be treated as a sale by the taxpayer direct to Company C in return for money paid to Company B, thereby excising Company B from this affair until the very end.

This has to be treated with care since if one simply ignores Company B one ends up with a nonsense—the taxpayers end up holding shares in Company B the very existence of which it seems, on Lord Brightman's approach, must be ignored.

Despite these reservations it is now clear, particularly after the decision in *Craven v White*, that the speech of Lord Brightman represents the ratio of the decision of the House of Lords in that case and is the basis of the "New Approach" in its present form.[1]

---

[1] [1984] 1 All ER 530, [1984] STC 153.

1: 10   Lord Bridge took a wider approach.

> "When one moves from a single transaction to a series of interdependent transactions designed to produce a given result, it is, in my opinion, perfectly legitimate to draw a distinction between the substance and the form of the composite transaction without in any way suggesting that any of the single transactions which make up the whole are other than genuine . . .".[1]

The importance of this approach is, first, that it enables one to explain the existence of company B and secondly that it is much wider and more flexible than the simple—almost mechanistic—excision approach of Lord Brightman. It also leads to a major consequence discussed below.

After the decision of the House of Lords in *Craven v White*[3] it is clear that the UK courts are not at present minded to follow Lord Bridge's approach. This may be sound. The consequences of Lord Bridge's approach would be extremely wide. Even the US tax system which Lord Bridge mentions, although not with unqualified enthusiasm, and which accepts the doctrine that the court must tax by reference to substance rather than form, finds it extremely hard to determine when the legal form of a transaction is to prevail.[2]

After *Furniss v Dawson* it was possible to argue that the law was in a highly malleable state and that the position was analogous to that of the law of negligence after *Donoghue v Stevenson* or the rule against perpetuities immediately after the *Duke of Norfolk's* case in 1681. The analogy of the rule against perpetuities has become a highly apposite one since the decision of the House of Lords in *Craven v White* and associated appeals[3] which with its insistence on following the approach of Lord Brightman can be made to look much like the developed rule against perpetuities with reasonably clear, but certainly not translucent, guidance as to when one is straying into dangerous territory.

Simon's Taxes A1.316.

[1] [1984] STC 153 at 158.

[2] For a general account of US doctrine see Bittker *Federal Taxation of Income Estates and Gifts*, especially chapter 4. For an example of scepticism see Rice, 51 Mich LR at p. 1021; see also Tiley [1987] BTR 180 and 220, [1988] BTR 63 and 108.

[3] [1988] STC 476, HL.

1:11 In *Craven v White* (and associated appeals)[1] the House of Lords had to consider the status of *Furniss v Dawson* and its application to three sets of facts.

In *IRC v Bowater Property Developments Ltd* the court was dealing with a DLT fragmentation scheme. A company which was a sister company to the taxpayer company was contemplating a sale to X. The sale did not materialise and the land was sold to the taxpayer for $97\frac{1}{2}\%$ of its market value. Subsequently, in order to take advantage of the rule that allowed each disponer, for DLT purposes, to claim an exemption on the first slice of realised development value (at that time £50,000), the taxpayer transferred the land in question to five other companies in the same group. This transfer had corporation tax consequences for the taxpayer company. A year later X reopened negotiations and, 19 months after the disposal by the taxpayer to the five companies, contracts were exchanged between the five companies and X. Could this be treated as a disposal by the taxpayer company to X, thus giving the companies only one exemption rather than five? The House of Lords unanimously said no.

In *Baylis v Gregory* the taxpayer was contemplating the sale of his company to Y; he went through a *Furniss v Dawson* operation and transferred the shares in his company to an Isle of Man company in exchange for shares in that company. However Y, unlike Wood Bastow, did not complete the sale. A year or so later a quite new company, Z, appeared and, after a further eight months, the sale to Z went through. Since the taxpayer had an intention to use the same provision as that which the taxpayers were trying to use in a *Furniss v Dawson* scheme, did it follow that the eventual sale to Z was by the taxpayer rather than by the Isle of Man company? Again, a unanimous House of Lords said no.

In *Craven v White* the taxpayer owned all the shares in Q and were advised that they should seek either a merger or a sale. As a first step the taxpayers carried through a *Furniss v Dawson* style share for share exchange with an Isle of Man company. At that time there was the prospect of either a merger with C or a sale to O. If the merger had gone through there would have been a deferral of liability under the reorganisation provisions anyway. If, however, the sale to O took place the facts were close to *Furniss v Dawson*. At the time of the share exchange the prospects for the sale to O did not look good but on the same day O asked for a further meeting. After further negotiations, including one "stormy meeting", the sale to O went through. The Commissioners rejected the taxpayers evidence that their sole intention in carrying through the exchange was to merge with C and said that the primary objective was the sale to O and that they were keeping their options open. By a bare majority the House of Lords held that the taxpayers were not to be taxed as if they had sold their shares direct to O; the entity making the disposal to O was the Isle of Man company.

Two issues faced the court. The first was whether the earlier decision in *Furniss v Dawson* should be taken as the start of the development of a general anti tax avoidance jurisprudence. On this basis the fact that when the share exchanges and the transfer of the land took place the motive of the taxpayer was to save tax should be sufficient to enable the court to undo all the later developments. This argument was quickly and decisively rejected. Amongst many matters which troubled the House, as they had troubled the Court of

Appeal, was what would be the legal status of the first transaction while one waited to see what might ensue, and, in particular, the status of any assessments to tax which might have been made on the basis of that first transaction (as might have occurred in the *Bowater* case).

The second was what degree of certainty there had to be before the steps could be said, to use Lord Brightman's word, to be "preordained". For the majority Lord Keith said that steps could be said to be preordained if, and only if, at the time the first of them was entered into the taxpayer was in a position for all practical purposes to secure that the second also is entered into. Lord Jauncey was tempted by a formulation in terms of whether there was no real likelihood that the second step would not go through but felt that this might be too rigid; the temptation to be a parliamentary draftsman was resisted.

Both the Scottish Law Lords expressly concurred in Lord Oliver's speech. Lord Oliver said that the question was whether the intermediate transfer was, at the time it was effected, so closely interconnected with the ultimate disposition that it was properly to be described as not in itself a real transaction at all but merely an element in some different and larger whole without independent effect. This was a question of fact which had to be approached within the bounds of what was logically defensible. He found that *Furniss v Dawson* only applied where there was no practical likelihood that the preplanned events would not take place in the order ordained so that the intermediate transaction was not even contemplated practically as having an independent life.

Lord Templeman and Lord Goff dissented on *Craven v White* but not on the other two appeals. For Lord Goff the matter could not be dealt with on the practical certainty test. While the interruption in *Bowater* and the unformed plan in *Baylis v Gregory* obviously dictated the conclusion in those cases, *Craven v White* was different as the sale to O was a primary purpose of the share exchange.

Lord Templeman felt that the three majority speeches went too far in narrowing *Furniss v Dawson* and would revive a surprised tax avoidance industry. He said that *Craven v White* was indistinguishable from *Furniss v Dawson*.[2] He protested that the House had not laboured in *Furniss v Dawson* to bring forth a mouse and that the limitations placed upon that case by the majority were based neither on principle nor on the speeches in that case.

Simon's Taxes A1.316; Butterworths Income Tax Service A7.08.

[1] [1988] STC 476.

[2] However it is interesting to compare his test at 490 with that of Lord Oliver at 507.

Issues and doubts

1: 12   As an example of the new approach we may take the decision of Nicholls J in *Young v Phillips* which stands as authority, even if only obiter, for the importance of the end result and for two consequential rules, that the end result, as determined by the courts after disregarding the inserted steps, cannot itself be disregarded and that it is the end result that must be subjected to the application of the tax legislation and not any of the inserted steps. This analytical approach is fully in line with that of the House of Lords in *Craven v White*.[1]

This case involved a plan by taxpayers who were resident in the UK but not domiciled here to relocate assets outside the UK so that the disposal of those assets would take place outside the UK with the result that they would be taxed only if the proceeds were remitted to the UK. The taxpayers held shares in an English company. A Jersey company was established in which the taxpayers had no interest. The English company resolved to issue preferred ordinary shares, to be paid for by capitalising accumulated profits. Renounceable letters of allotment were issued in respect of the new shares. The Jersey company then agreed to issue shares to the taxpayers for £1,364,216. The taxpayers then went to Sark, another of the Channel Islands, and there disposed of their rights under the letters of allotment to the Jersey company for £1,364,216. The taxpayers then became registered shareholders of the Jersey company.

The Revenue assessed the taxpayers to CGT on the basis that the disposal of the shares comprised in the letter of allotment was the disposal of assets located in the UK; this argument succeeded. However, the judge went on to consider what would have happened if the assets had been situated in the Channel Islands at the time of the disposal. Here the Revenue argument was that under CGTA 1979, s. 25 the taxpayers had exercised control over the company causing a loss in value and therefore there was a deemed disposal, infra, § **16: 22**. To this the answer was given that this was a share for share exchange and therefore CGTA 1979, s. 78 directed that there should be no disposal, infra, § **19: 08**. The Revenue tried to get round s. 78 in two ways. The first was to argue generally that once a scheme to avoid tax had been shown it was enough for them to show that the substance of the matter was that value had passed out of the shares they held in the English company. Nicholls J rejected this argument. The end result of the transaction after removing the inserted steps was that shares were issued by the English company to the Jersey company. That was the relevant transaction to which the tax legislation had to be applied; one cannot disregard the relevant transaction. However, the judge went on to say that the protection of s. 78 would be denied the taxpayer because of CGTA 1979, s. 87.[2]

The judge also dealt with one other argument by the Revenue. This was that as there was a composite transaction having a number of steps spread over a period of time, so the disposal of the letters of allotment had to be treated as taking place over a similar period of time and, as that period began before the taxpayers went to Sark, the disposal took place in England. This too was rejected. The argument assumed that the shares were issued to the taxpayers; this was not so as the end result of the scheme was that the shares were issued not to the taxpayers but to the Jersey companies.

---

[1] [1984] STC 520.
[2] See infra, § **19: 18**.

1: 13   A number of questions arise.

(1) Will the law accept that the presence of any commercial motive, however slight, will exclude the new rule? This is suggested by Lord

Brightman's formulation but it may be that the new principle will be excluded only if the commercial motive is the main one. This view rests on the analogy of CGTA 1979, s. 87. This issue was raised in *Craven v White*[1] where it was held that where there were two courses of action genuinely open to the taxpayer and actively being considered by him, one of which would have entitled him to use the deferral under CGTA 1979, s. 86 despite *Furniss v Dawson*,[2] and the other of which would not, the Revenue could not use *Furniss v Dawson* to deprive him of the deferral as there was a sufficient commercial motive at the time of the disposal. This aspect of the case was not developed in the House of Lords.[3] However in the speeches there are many references to transactions which have no commercial purpose other than the avoidance of tax.

---

[1] [1985] STC 531 followed in *Baylis v Gregory* [1986] STC 22, [1986] 1 All ER 289, and *IRC v Bowater Property Developments Ltd* [1985] STC 783.

[2] [1984] 1 All ER 530, [1984] STC 153.

[3] However Lord Oliver said that there was a bona fide commercial purpose ([1988] STC at 510c).

1: 14 (2) What is meant by a commercial motive? Is "commercial" simply a synonym for "non-tax" so that, for example, a wish to protect the family wealth by the creation of a protective trust will be effective even though some tax sheltering will result? Likewise, is a wish to use an Isle of Man company so as to be subject to Manx law (which permits loans to directors) a sufficient "commercial" purpose. There may be major difficulties about a case in which two partners go in for the same transaction where one is motivated purely by the thought of saving tax but the other has to raise money to pay maintenance to an ex-spouse or is motivated by some wish to preserve the business.

1: 15 (3) What taxes are protected by this new principle? So far the cases have involved CGT, income tax (or their corporate equivalent), VAT[1] and stamp duties. It has even made a surprise appearance in landlord and tenant law.[2] It can be argued that IHT is not affected as it has its own anti-avoidance provision in the associated operations rule (§ **38: 32**). This point seems doubtful since the courts appear unwilling to restrict the new principle as yet; it may, however, reappear under point (4) below. It can also be argued that stamp duties are not affected since those are taxes on instruments not transactions; however it can be countered that the new rule is ideally designed to counter avoidance schemes because it requires a broad view of the transaction which is being carried out by the instrument and this approach was adopted by Vinelott J in *Ingram v IRC*[3] (see § **58: 08**).

---

[1] *Customs and Excise Comrs v Faith Construction Ltd* [1989] STC 539 (doctrine not applied).

[2] *Gisborne v Burton* [1988] 3 All ER 760, CA.

[3] [1985] STC 835, [1986] 2 WLR 598.

1: 16 (4) What is the role of the new principle alongside an express statutory provision? Following precedents in other countries which have had to wrestle with general anti-avoidance provisions it can be argued that the courts will not allow the use of the *Ramsay* principle if the taxpayer has simply carried out a straightforward transaction falling exactly within the purpose and ambit of a provision of the tax legislation.[1] Cases such as this may fall to be dealt with as having a sufficient commercial motive or as single step transactions; see (5) below.

More difficulty will be met where the taxpayer can bring himself within an express statutory defence (e.g. TA 1988, s. 703, infra § **31: 31**). Will this exclude the new principle? It is thought that it should, a view that would presumably have commended itself to Vinelott J in *Bird v IRC*[2] where he suggested that the Revenue could not rely both on TA 1988, s. 703 and the new principle against the same taxpayer in respect of the same transaction—this leaves open the question whether the taxpayer can rely on the new principle instead of s. 703.

---

[1] As was stated by Walton J in *Reed v Nova Securities Ltd* at first instance [1982] STC 724.
[2] [1985] STC 584 at 647.

1: 17   (5) Will the new principle apply to single step transactions or only, as the cases so far suggest, to composite transactions? After *Craven v White* it appears clear that the new approach is concerned simply with the question whether two or more steps are to be taxed as one. Single step transactions are thus outside its scope[1].

---

[1] See also *Customs and Excise Comrs v Faith Construction Ltd* [1988] STC 35, upheld, on different grounds [1989] STC 539, CA.

1: 18   (6) Routing. If I wish to go from A to Z via C and on my way I detour (for tax reasons) through F the new principle will apply as if I had not made the detour. If, however, I go from A to Z via P, can I be taxed as if I had gone via C? If, as some suggest, the answer is no there is in essence a restatement of the *Westminster* principle, a principle which is much more secure after *Craven v White*. This argument may be useful to explain why, for example, I will be taxed under Schedule A on rent received if I charge rent but not on the premium received if I charge that and a reduced rent. The difficulty is to see why in that case the route chosen in *Furniss v Dawson* was disregarded.

1: 19   (7) Who can invoke the new principle? Can the taxpayer use *Ramsay*, e.g. to undo statutory absurdities such as *Ang v Parrish*?[1] See § **13: 01**). There is a suggestion in *Pattison v Marine Midland Ltd* that the courts (or at least the Master of the Rolls) will invoke *Ramsay* to counter an attempt by the Crown to "invent an artificial accounting scheme which serves no purpose and is designed solely to create a liability to tax."[2]

The matter fell to be considered in *Ewart v Taylor*[3] by Vinelott J who, in dicta, gave the taxpayer only very limited chances of success. Counsel for the Revenue had conceded that if the Revenue argued that, say, the *Ramsay* principle applied to stages 2 to 4 of a transaction, it would be open to the taxpayer to argue that the principle should apply to stages 1 to 5 but Vinelott J felt that this might be appropriate only in cases where the relevant legislation, there FA 1965, s. 42,[4] was framed in terms of "a settlement" or "arrangement". This seems very narrow and not at all in keeping with the broad approach later adopted by the House of Lords in *Furniss v Dawson*.

---

[1] [1980] STC 341, 53 TC 304.

² [1983] STC 269 at 276, CA. See also Vinelott J in *Bird v IRC* [1985] STC 584 at 647.
³ [1983] STC 721.
⁴ Later CGTA 1979, s. 17 (repealed by FA 1981, Sch. 19, Part VIII).

1: 20 (8) Can the new principle be invoked to change the timing of a transaction?[1] Thus suppose that I am about to emigrate (1st January) and wish to postpone a CGT disposal until after I have ceased to be resident in the UK—so avoiding CGT—and yet require the certainty of the sale. I therefore agree that my purchaser shall have an option to buy on any day in January and I have the right to insist on a sale during February. This agreement is made in November but the CGT timing rule will make the date of the disposal that where the contract become unconditional—see § **16: 02**. Similarly, in the days of DLT, I might have made three conditional contracts to dispose of development land in three succeeding years so as to take full advantage of the annual exemption. These are questions of fact in the light of the speech of Lord Oliver in *Craven v White*.

[1] See the discussion by Gammie in *Strategic Tax Planning* Part D p. D35.

1: 21 (9) Can the new principle be invoked to changes *where* a transaction takes place? The argument is similar to (8) and equally inconclusive.

1: 22 (10) Can the new principle be used to override the provisions of a double tax treaty in the same way as a provision of domestic law? As such treaties are in theory part of domestic law thanks to TA 1988, s. 788 there seems to be no justification for treating them differently.

1: 23 (11) Most crucially, perhaps, is the new rule one of excision (or annihilation) or reconstruction or a single matter of statutory construction? It seemed clear after *Furniss v Dawson* that whether one took the approach of Lord Brightman or that of Lord Bridge the power was one of reconstruction. Thus in *Furniss v Dawson* itself the Dawsons were to be treated as having acquired the shares in Company B in return for the consideration they provided; i.e. the value of the shares in Company A which were sold to Company C. This raises the question whether if the Revenue override a transaction for tax reasons they must do so for all tax reasons. Thus in *Cairns v MacDiarmid*[1] the taxpayer paid interest but was not allowed to claim a deduction under TA 1988, s. 353; does it follow that the recipient does not have to pay tax under Schedule D, Case III?

Here may lie the most interesting—and profitable—area for taxpayers to argue. Here too one may find the courts eventually ruling that the final stage of reconstruction must leave the facts as they exist at the end of the last transaction. In this sense the doctrine of "enduring legal effect" rejected by the House of Lords in *Furniss v Dawson* may reappear.

In *Craven v White* the whole matter was reduced to simple issue of statutory construction. When A makes a disposal to B and B makes a disposal to C, under which circumstances is this to be treated as an A–C disposal? Problems of excision and reconstruction should either be ignored or treated as reasons for concluding that there were two disposals not one.[2]

¹ [1983] STC 178, CA.
² See also *Shepherd v Lyntress Ltd* [1989] STI 570.

1: 24   Lying behind the new approach is an assumption that Parliament knew what it was doing when it passed the legislation. This is not always obvious. Thus, when relief for small profits was introduced for corporation tax (infra § **23: 13**) special rules dilute the relief by reference to the number of associated companies. By contrast, for the now repealed DLT, which had a threshold (eventually) of £75,000, there was no dilution by reference to the numbers of associated companies. Does this mean that Parliament was approving of schemes whereby a company faced with a large DLT bill would create nine subsidiary companies and divide 9/10ths of the land between them so that the threshold became £750,000? Such a scheme was upheld by Walton J in *IRC v Bowater Property Developments Ltd*¹ although not on this ground.

Similarly after the decision of the Court of Appeal in *Sherdley v Sherdley*² one had to ask why the persistent efforts of Parliament to widen the occasions on which maintenance payments could be made direct to a minor, efforts made against a background of Revenue acquiescence, should suddenly be frustrated by the invocation of the new approach.

¹ [1985] STC 783; the scheme was upheld on appeal: [1987] STC 297, but see infra, § **1: 25**.
² [1986] STC 266; reversed on appeal: [1987] STC 217.

1: 25   Conclusions may now be firmer as a result of the House of Lords decision in *Craven v White*. For the moment we have a test based on "no practical certainty" or "no real likelihood" that the second step will not follow the first. This test has now been applied in *Shepherd v Lyntress Ltd.*¹ This is a workable but limited step transaction doctrine. It is, however, consistent with transitional UK notions of the interpretation and application of tax statutes but, one suspects, not with the feeling of the House when deciding *Furniss v Dawson*.

Secondly, *Furniss v Dawson* is not to allow the taxpayer to undo transactions simply because they have a tax avoidance motive. This is consistent with a series of cases since *Furniss v Dawson*, and not cited to the House, in which tax schemes have been upheld.²

Thirdly, it is hard to resist the conclusion of Lord Templeman that this represents a major narrowing of what the House did in *Furniss v Dawson*. One can even treat it as a reassertion of the view of Vinelott J, at first instance, in *Furniss* in which he excluded from the new approach steps which had an "enduring legal effect."³ One may also note, perhaps a little cynically, that *Donoghue v Stevenson* was followed by a period of narrowing judicial decisions before being allowed to develop into the principle tort lawyers recognise today. Whether the Revenue can wait that long is another matter; they may well now feel the need for more legislation, as has occurred most recently in Canada. One other comment should be made. It is not at all clear that the decision of the majority opens the way for what Lord Brightman called the revival of a surprised tax avoidance industry. Not only has Parliament moved smartly to close up loop holes—including all those in the cases before the Lords—but there is the further risk that legislation can be and has been retrospective. Moreover insofar as much planning practice turned on the distinction between income and capital the assimilation of tax rates has done much to reduce the area of the game while the general reduction in tax rates may encourage more people not to become players. There is also the risk of further changes in the composition of the House of Lords.

Finally one may note two other points. First, the new approach being judge-made is retrospective and incapable of requiring a clearance procedure. Secondly the decision at first instance in *Coates v Arndale Properties Ltd*[3] established that when the courts are asked to determine whether a transaction has a trading character, they must answer that question yes or no and cannot invoke *Ramsay* to create an intermediate category of transactions which are trading transactions but which should be deprived of that character because of tax avoidance intentions. This aspect was not considered on appeal.

---

[1] [1989] STI 570.

[2] The list includes *Cooke v Blacklaws* [1985] STC 1 (use of foreign company to employ taxpayer), *Reed v Young* [1986] STC 285 (limited partnership scheme successful) and *Reed v Clark* [1985] STC 323 ("dropping out", infra, § **7: 44**).

[3] [1982] STC 267. However in that judgment Vinelott J held that the fact that Greenjacket held the cash received for the shares was one of enduring legal effect. This is not consistent with the decision of the House in that case or in *Craven v White* when the receipt by Greenjacket was treated as a receipt by the taxpayer.

SOURCES

Statutes

1: 26   The statute law for a particular tax is to be found in the statute which introduced it as subsequently amended. Sometimes amendments are made to the text of the original Act; at other times a new provision is introduced to exist alongside the original Act. The result might be described as a patchwork were it not for the overtones of antique cosiness that go with that word; it is better described as a shambles.

Sometimes the text relating to a particular tax is consolidated, e.g. income tax 1918, 1952, 1970 and 1988 corporation tax in 1970 and 1988, CGT in 1979, VAT 1983 and CTT 1984, but the perfection of consolidation is often marred within weeks. Consolidation of the capital allowances legislation is promised for 1990.

Income tax is an annual tax and the charge is reimposed by Parliament each year in the Finance Bill. The result is that the Tax Acts are really in the nature of an Income Tax Clauses Act and apply whenever any Act imposes an income tax.[1] The Finance Bill also amends the rules for the other taxes. The resulting combination of measures of great economic importance and matters of great technical subtlety discussed against the background of the hurly burly of Parliamentary procedure is, not surprisingly, capable of error.

---

[1] Per Atkin LJ in *Martin v Lowry* (1926) 11 TC 297 at 317.

Statutory interpretation

1: 27   A citizen is not to be taxed unless he is designated in clear terms by the taxing Act as a taxpayer and the amount of his liability is clearly defined.[1] One reason for this is that apart from statute there is no liability to pay any tax and no antecedent relationship between the taxing authority so that no reasoning founded on any such *a priori* liability or relationship can be used in the construction of the Act.[2] Other reasons may include the need to protect the individual from the state, the analogy of criminal offences and some sort of *contra proferentem* rule but these do not explain the strictness with which other tax provisions are construed against the taxpayer.

This principle of strict interpretation was well stated by Rowlatt J:[3]

> "In a taxing Act one has to look merely at what is clearly said. There is no room for any intendment. There is no equity about a tax. There is no presumption as to a tax. Nothing is to be read in, nothing is to be implied. One can only look fairly at the language used."

Since the decisions of the House of Lords in *Ramsay v IRC* and, more particularly, *Furniss v Dawson*, it may be wondered whether the doctrine that there is no equity about a tax can be maintained. However, for the moment—and particularly in the light of *Craven v White*—one should assume that the courts will at least begin with a presumption in favour of a strict or literal interpretation. This principle has two consequences. The first is that it is for the Crown to establish that the subject falls within the charge.[4] This means that if the words are ambiguous the subject is entitled to the benefit of the doubt. But the principle is not that the subject is to have the benefit if, on any argument that ingenuity can suggest, the Act does not appear perfectly accurate but only if, after careful examination of all the clauses, a judicial mind still entertains reasonable doubts as to what the legislature intended:[5] if there is no ambiguity the words must take their natural meaning.

The second consequence is that strict interpretation applies to the taxpayer just as much as to the Revenue. So if a literal interpretation produces a construction whereby hardship falls on innocent beneficiaries by the rights, monstrous or otherwise, conferred on the Inland Revenue, that interpretation must be adhered to and the hardship produced is not a relevant consideration.[6] Further where an exception from taxation is given by a statute, that exception is to be construed strictly and any ambiguity construed against the taxpayer.[7]

It is as well to recall here that support of the very highest authority can be found for general and apparently irreconcilable propositions.[8]

Simon's Taxes A1.3; Butterworths Income Tax Service A1.54

[1] Per Lord Wilberforce in *Vestey v IRC* [1980] STC 10 at 18: but contrast *Floor v Davis* [1979] 2 All ER 677, [1979] STC 379 (in which Lord Wilberforce dissented).

[2] Per Lord Cairns LC in *Pryce v Monmouthshire Canal and Rly Companies* (1879) 4 App Cas 197 at 202, 203.

[3] *Cape Brandy Syndicate v IRC* [1921] 1 KB 64 at 71, 12 TC 358 at 366.

[4] Per Parke B in *Re Micklethwaite* (1855) 11 Exch 452 at 456, approved by Lord Halsbury LC in *Tennant v Smith* [1892] AC 150 at 154.

[5] Per Kindersley V-C, in *Wilcox v Smith* (1857) 4 Drew 40 at 49.

[6] Per Danckwerts J in *Re Joynson's Will Trusts, Gaddum v IRC* [1954] Ch 567 at 573 and see *IRC v Hinchy* [1960] 1 All ER 505, 38 TC 625.

[7] Per Cohen LJ in *Littman v Barron* [1951] 2 All ER 393 at 398, 33 TC 373 at 380.

[8] Per Viscount Simonds in *A-G v Prince Ernest Augustus of Hanover* [1957] AC 436 at 464.

1: 28 However anti-avoidance provisions phrased in broad language which deliberately eschews legal terms of art have not always been strictly construed against the Revenue. As Lord Reid said in *Greenberg v IRC*:[1]

> "We seem to have travelled a long way from the general and salutary rule that the subject is not to be taxed except by plain words. But I must recognise that plain words are seldom adequate to anticipate and forestall the multiplicity of ingenious schemes which are constantly being devised to evade (sic) taxation. Parliament is very properly determined to prevent this kind of tax evasion (sic) and, if the courts find it impossible to give very wide meanings to general phrases, the only alternative may be for Parliament to do as some other countries have done, and introduce legislation of a more sweeping character which will put the ordinary well intentioned person at much greater risk than is now created by a wide interpretation of such provisions as those which we are now considering."

However words are to be given their natural meaning and are not to be given some other meaning simply because their object is to frustrate legitimate tax avoidance and it has been suggested that these words apply only to what is now TA 1988, s. 703.[2]

While the judges have wrestled with legislation of great complexity, there have been warnings that it is possible that the obscurity of an enactment or the incontrollable width of its language—or of the discretion needed to implement it—may compel a court to find that no reasonable construction is available and that the taxpayer is therefore not to be charged.[3] The House of Lords has shown itself capable on the one hand of depriving a provision of any effect[4] and on the other of imposing double taxation.[5]

Simon's Taxes A1.314.

[1] [1972] AC 109 at 137.

[2] Nourse J in *Pilkington Bros Ltd v IRC* [1981] STC 219 at 235; see also *Mangin v IRC* [1971] AC 739 at 746.

[3] *Customs and Excise Comrs v Top Ten Promotions Ltd* [1969] 3 All ER 39 at 93, HL, per Lord Donovan and at 95 per Lord Wilberforce; *Vestey v IRC* [1980] AC 1148, [1980] STC 10.

[4] *IRC v Ayrshire Employers Mutual Insurance Association Ltd* [1946] 1 All ER 637, 27 TC 331, HL.

[5] *Cleary v IRC* [1967] 2 All ER 48, 44 TC 399 infra, § **31: 22**.

1: 29 The court may look at the purpose and history of the relevant legislation and to this end reference may be made to the state of the law, and the material facts and events with which it is apparent that Parliament was dealing.[1] However it is not admissible to speculate on the probable opinions and motives of those who framed the legislation except in so far as these appear from the language of the statute.[2]

The question is not at what transaction the section is, according to some alleged general purpose, aimed but what transaction its language, according to its natural meanings, fairly and squarely hits.[3]

In *Customs and Excise Comrs v Top Ten Promotions Ltd*[4] a case concerning pool betting duty, Diplock LJ, suggested that where a new tax was introduced the courts should look for the rational basis of the new tax and bear that in mind in construing the legislation. However this approach was accepted neither by Lord Upjohn nor by Lord Wilberforce in the House of Lords[5] and is hard to reconcile with the traditional doctrine stated by Rowlatt J.

¹ See Lord Macdermott in *IRC v Rennell* [1964] AC 173 at 198 and Lord Macdermott in *Madras Electric Supply Corpn Ltd v Boarland* [1955] AC 667 at 686, 35 TC 612 at 640, [1955] 1 All ER 753 at 760.
² Viscount Haldane in *IRC v Herbert* [1913] AC 326 at 332.
³ Lord Simonds in *St Aubyn v A-G* [1952] AC 15 at 32, [1951] 2 All ER 473 at 485. See also Megarry J in *Canada Safeway Ltd v IRC* [1972] 1 All ER 666 at 671—the reasons for laying down a rule must not be confounded with the rule itself.
⁴ [1969] 3 All ER 39 at 69.
⁵ [1969] 3 All ER 39 at 80, 85, the purpose approach was reiterated by Lord Diplock in *IRC v Joiner* [1975] 3 All ER 1050, [1975] STC 657.

Some rules

1: 30   (*a*) The Act must be read as a whole. Where there is an ambiguity the scheme of the Act may resolve it.[1]

(*b*) The words of the legislation must be construed in their context. Until a person has read the whole of a document or statute he is not entitled to say that it, or any part of it, is clear and unambiguous.[2]

(*c*) The court will depart from a literal interpretation where to keep to such an interpretation would lead to a result which is so absurd that it cannot be supposed, in the absence of express words which are wholly unambiguous, to have been contemplated.[3] Likewise the courts will try to avoid highly inequitable or manifestly unfair results.[4] However it will be seen that where the words are wholly unambiguous the court is bound by its literal interpretation, however unreasonable.[5] Arguments based on competing anomalies do not find favour.[6]

(*d*) Where a statutory provision is enacted but is based upon a misconception of what the law then was, the law remains as it was and does not share the misconception of the legislature.[7]

(*e*) There is a presumption that provisions dealing with the machinery of taxation do not impose a charge.[8] The courts will not construe a machinery provision so as to defeat the charge;[9] however the absence of machinery has been used to qualify a charge.[10]

(*f*) There is a presumption that words used in the same contexts in different statutes are used in the same sense.[11]

(*g*) Where a particular interpretation would give the Revenue the power to distribute the burden of tax between taxpayers, the courts will reject it.[12]

(*h*) When interpreting a consolidated enactment, the court should not in general refer to the earlier Acts. However, the court is entitled to have regard to the fact that a subsection was later added to the original section.[13]

(*i*) The Taxes Acts[14] are equally applicable in England and Wales, Scotland and for most of them, Northern Ireland. It follows that the language which they employ ought to be construed so as to have, as far as possible, uniform effect in all four countries alike.[15]

(*j*) When the provisions are ambiguous the court may consider the effect of subsequent legislation only when the two views of the original statute are equally tenable and there are no indications favouring one rather than the other. The argument advanced on the basis of this rule is that the new provision could only have been needed if one view was held by Parliament rather than the other.[16]

[1] Per Lord Halsbury in *IRC v Priestley* [1901] AC 208 at 213.

[2] Viscount Simonds in *A-G v Prince Ernest Augustus of Hanover* [1957] AC 436 at 463.

[3] Pollock CB in *A-G v Hallett* (1857) 2 H & N 368 at 375.

[4] Per Lord Reid in *Coutts & Co v IRC* [1953] AC 267 at 281, [1953] 1 All ER 418 at 421.

[5] Per Lord Reid in *IRC v Hinchy* [1960] 1 All ER 505 at 512, 38 TC 625 at 652.

[6] Per Lord Normand in *Dale v IRC* [1953] 2 All ER 671 at 676, 34 TC 468 at 488, HL.

[7] *Davies, Jenkins & Co Ltd v Davies* [1967] 1 All ER 913 at 915, 922, 44 TC 273 at 287, HL.

[8] Per Lord Macmillan in *Straits Settlements Comr of Stamps v Oei Tjong Swan* [1933] AC 378 at 389.

[9] *IRC v Longmans Green & Co Ltd* (1932) 17 TC 272 at 282.

[10] *Colquhoun v Brooks* (1889) 14 App Cas 493 at 506, 2 TC 490 at 500.

[11] Per Lord Reid in *Gartside v IRC* [1968] AC 553 at 602, [1968] 1 All ER 121 at 131. But this is only a presumption; see Atkin LJ in *Martin v Lowry* [1926] 1 KB 550 at 561, 11 TC 297 at 315.

[12] *Vestey v IRC* [1980] AC 1148, [1980] STC 10.

[13] *IRC v Joiner* [1975] 3 All ER 1050, [1975] STC 657 but note the more restrictive approach of Lord Diplock and see the discussion by Baxter in (1976) Conv, 336 at 343.

[14] Defined TA 1988, ss. 831, 832.

[15] Viscount Simon in *I T Comrs for General Purposes (City of London) v Gibbs* [1942] 1 All ER 415 at 422, 24 TC 221 at 236, 244, HL. Hence the English courts will follow Scottish decisions— per Lord Evershed MR in *Wiseburgh v Domville* [1956] 1 All ER 754 at 758, 36 TC 527 at 538–9, CA.

[16] Per Oliver LJ in *Finch v IRC* [1985] Ch 1 at 15, [1984] STC 261 at 272, CA; and Hoffman J in *Westcott v Woolcombers Ltd* [1986] STC 182 at 191.

1: 31 The provisions can be classified in three classes.[1] First, there are those which carefully avoid legal terms.[2] Secondly, there are those in which the English term is immediately followed by the equivalent in Scots legal phraseology.[3] Thirdly, there are provisions which speak the language of the English lawyer, perhaps with some Scots legal phrases thrown in rather casually. In this third class the courts must take the meanings of the legal expression from the law of the country to which they properly belong and must then apply that meaning by analogy. This must be done even though the construction adopted may do violence to some of the best established doctrines of Scots law.[4]

[1] Per Lord Macnaghten in *IT Special Purposes Comrs v Pemsel* [1891] AC 531 at 579.

[2] E.g. IHTA 1984, s. 3(1), (2), and see Megarry J in *Sargaison v Roberts* [1969] 3 All ER 1072 at 1077, 45 TC 612 at 617.

[3] E.g. IHTA 1984, s. 199(4).

[4] Per Lord Macnaghten in *Lord Advocate v Countess of Moray* [1905] AC 531 at 540, HL.

Cases and revenue practice

1: 32 Cases are authorities in the usual way according to the rule of precedent save that tax is a UK law and so English courts will accept Scottish decisions and vice versa. However in assessing the value of a precedent in tax law special complications arise from the fact that the appeal structure in the UK allows the courts to reverse a decision of the Commissioners only for error of law or because it cannot be supported on the evidence: infra § **1: 40**.

Although previously the Revenue have resisted attempts to publish reports of the decisions of Special Commissioners on the ground that the facts are all important and therefore of little value as a guide for later cases, the Lord Chancellor may provide for publication of the reports in the procedural rules made under TMA 1970, s. 57B.[1] The Revenue have always stored reports of decisions for their own use and much so called expertise consists simply in knowing what the "Specials" have decided.

[1] Inserted by FA 1984, Sch. 22, para. 4, see [1984] STI, p. 296.

1: 33 Although not law, statements of Revenue practice are of great importance in the practical administration of the system. These statements are of different sorts.

First there are extra-statutory concessions. These are few, tightly written and almost legislative in form. One crucial difference from a statutory provision was that the Revenue could withhold the benefit of the concession if they were so minded without legal—as distinct from political or administrative—consequences. However the development of administrative law remedies suggests that an assessment made on the basis of withholding a concession could be quashed on the basis of breach of the duty to act fairly as between different taxpayers.[1] Such a situation would only arise where the taxpayer could bring himself within the scope of the concession and in this connection it is important to note that the list of concessions is prefaced with a general statement that a concession will not be given where an attempt is made to use it for tax avoidance.[2]

In a note to a new concession the Revenue stated that concessions are used "to deal with what are, on the whole, minor or transitory anomalies . . . and to read cases of hardship at the margins of the code when a statutory remedy would be difficult to devise or would run to a length out of proportion to the intrinsic importance of the matter".[3]

Secondly there are the statements of practice which are now published on a regular basis; these are only slightly less formal than the concessions. The Revenue position often prefers a broad legislative rule which can then be interpreted "liberally" or not. The disadvantages of this are that such a rule may be interpreted unevenly and there is the possibility, however unlikely, of abuse. Finally there are the statements used by the Inland Revenue for their own internal guidance. These are documents confidential to the Revenue although, of course, their contents are well known to those highly trained Inspectors who leave the service for private practice. In proceedings for judicial review the court has ordered discovery of such documents but only on the basis that the taxpayer relied on having been informed that there was a Revenue view of the correct construction of a provision and that construction was in his favour.[4]

Thirdly there are advance rulings in individual cases. There is no general scheme whereby taxpayers can obtain advance rulings on the tax consequences of a particular transaction. However in practice advice is often available provided there is a detailed scheme; the Revenue usually insist on knowing the identity of the taxpayer concerned. This practice seems both reasonable and desirable but could be expanded. The Revenue is not there to provide a free legal aid clinic, but it is in the Revenue's interests to be helpful.[5]

In certain circumstances the legislation will prescribe a clearance procedure, usually as part of broad anti-avoidance legislation.[6]

Simon's Taxes A1.309

[1] E.g. the unsuccessful applications in *R v IRC ex p J Rothschild Holdings* [1987] STC 163, *R v Inspector of Taxes, ex p Brumfield* [1989] STC 151.

[2] This general anti-avoidance statement was used by the Revenue to defeat a move to quash an assessment for breach of natural justice in *R v IRC, ex p Fulford-Dobson* [1987] STC 344.

[3] Revenue Press Release 16 February 1989, Simon's Tax Intelligence 1989, p. 74.

[4] *R v IRC, ex p J Rothschild Holdings plc* [1986] STC 410; upheld [1987] STC 163, CA.

[5] On judicial review see infra § **1: 34** n. 7.

[6] E.g. TA 1988, s. 707 but not CGTA 1979, s. 26. For an example of difficulties that arise in practice see ICAEW memorandum TP657, reprinted in *Simon's Tax Intelligence* 1987, p. 321.

ADMINISTRATION

Duties of the Board of Inland Revenue

1: 34 Responsibility for the administration of most of the taxes considered in this book is entrusted to the Board of Inland Revenue which is subject to the Treasury. The Board appoints inspectors, who carry out the work of assessment for income tax, CGT, corporation tax stamp duty and (where the charge arose before 19th March 1985) DLT, and collectors, who collect these taxes.[1] Capital transfer tax and inheritance tax are administered by the Capital Taxes Office.[2] The Board is under a duty to collect these taxes but is not guilty of an abuse of power in entering into special arrangements absolving taxpayers from liability to tax; further, a taxpayer has no sufficient interest to ask a court to investigate the tax affairs of another taxpayer.[3] In carrying out the duty laid on it the Board must act with administrative common sense.[4] However this discretion does not justify a court in construing a section so as to give the Board a discretion as to how to allocate a tax liability between different taxpayers,[4] nor does it provide a legal basis for the practice of extra statutory concessions.[5] VAT and other indirect taxes are administered by the Customs and Excise Commissioners.

Information received in the execution of duty may be disclosed to other bodies, including other government departments, only with statutory authority.[6]

As there is no estoppel against the Crown, no legal reliance may be placed on statements by officers of the Board.[7] However compensation has been obtained through the Parliamentary Commissioners for Administration and may be obtainable in tort.[8]

Simon's Taxes A2.1; Butterworths Income Tax Service A1.21–A1.24, A1.31

[1] TMA 1970, s. 1.

[2] IHTA 1984, s. 215.

[3] *IRC v National Federation of Self Employed and Small Businesses Ltd* [1981] 2 All ER 93, [1981] STC 260 (Fleet Street amnesty not illegal).

[4] Per Lord Wilberforce in *Vestey v IRC* [1980] STC 10 at 19; the Board remit tax in certain cases when the failure to collect was due to official error. Curiously the extent of this practice is governed by the circumstances of the taxpayer; Extra-statutory concession A21 (1988); **Simon's Taxes Division H2.2**.

[5] Per Lord Edmund Davies, ibid., at 35.

⁶ TMA 1970, s. 6 reinforced by FA 1989, s. 174 which comes into force on the repeal of the Official Secrets Act 1911, s. 2. See FA 1969, s. 58 as amended by F(No. 2)A 1987, s. 69.
    ⁷ *Southend on Sea Corpn v Hodgson (Wickford) Ltd* [1962] 1 QB 416, [1961] 2 All ER 46; see however *R v IRC, ex p J Rothschild Holdings plc* [1987] STC 163 where an estoppel issue was raised in judicial review proceedings but it failed on the facts. On using judicial review to protect position taken i.e. reliance on Revenue advice see *R v IRC, ex p D P Mann Underwriting Agency Ltd* [1989] STI 589, DC.
    ⁸ Wade, *Administrative Law* (6th edn pp. 381–387).

Assessment

1: 35 Most of the taxes considered in this book are assessed by the Inland Revenue. The premise of assessment by the Revenue rather than self-assessment by the taxpayer is central to the UK tax system. This premise will change under the new Pay and File system which is to be introduced for corporations, but not before 1992.[1]

.This system depends first on the gathering of information. This is done in two broad ways; first a taxpayer is under a duty to report his income source by source.[2] This is usually done on a form issued by the Revenue by which he also claims his allowances for the following year.[3] The sanctions include the withholding of those allowances and the levy of fines, however, the taxpayer has a duty to report the new source even though no return has been sent to him.[4] The penalty for failure to make a return has been increased to 100% of the tax evaded; this applies to income of the 1988–89 tax year so the penalty rule will begin on 6 April 1990. Other information is gathered from other parties; some are under a duty to supply information automatically, e.g. banks paying interest outside the composite rate scheme of more than £15,[5] while others must supply information on demand from the Revenue. There is now a general three year time limit on such calls for information.[6] There are also powers to obtain information from Government departments.[7]

The Revenue have further powers including the power to call for the documents of a taxpayer from the taxpayer or from any related person.[8] As from the passing of FA 1989, the power extends also to the furnishing of particulars and to the affairs of any other person, whether or not related.[9] From the same date there is protection for certain personal records and for journalistic material.[10] There is also power to call for the papers of any tax accountant who has been convicted of a tax-related offence[11]—again, personal records and journalistic material will be excluded after the passing of FA 1989.[12] This power is quite separate from the power of the court to order discovery of documents in the course of litigation. The falsification of documents which have been called for is now a criminal offence.[13]

There is also a power to enter and search premises for documents relating to a tax provided a warrant is obtained from a circuit judge.[14] This power is amended, for warrants issued on or after the day on which FA 1989 is passed, by confining their issue to cases of serious fraud and by the imposition on the Revenue of requirements as to detail e.g. as to number of officers who are to exercise the warrant (although they may take helpers with them) the times of day during which it is to be exercisable and whether or not a constable in uniform will be required.[15] These powers extend to taxpayers whose identities are unknown.[16]

Simon's Taxes A3.1; Butterworths Income Tax Service A1.33
 [1] See F(No. 2)A 1987, ss. 82–90 and 95 and Sch. 6.
 [2] TMA 1970, s. 7 as recast by FA 1988, s. 120; a similar rule applies to CGT, see TMA 1970, s. 11A, added by FA 1988, s. 122 and to corporation tax, see TMA 1970, s. 80 as amended by FA 1988, s. 121.
 [3] Issued under TMA 1970, s. 8; on use of substitute and computerised forms see SP5/87 and *Simon's Tax Intelligence* 1988, pp. 26 and 430. On effect of substantial delay see SP 3/88.
 [4] TMA 1970, s. 93; fines are increased by FA 1989 s. 162. On what amounts to a correct return see *Moschi v General Comrs for Kensington* [1980] STC 1.
 [5] TMA 1970, s. 17.
 [6] FA 1988, s. 123, amending TMA 1970, ss. 13, 17, 18 and 19 as from the passing of FA 1988.
 [7] FA 1988, ss. 124 and 125, introducing TMA 1970, s. 18A and amending s. 16.
 [8] TMA 1970, s. 20—subject to s. 20B. Documents include computer records (FA 1988, s. 127).
 [9] TMA 1970, s. 20(1), (2) and (3) as substituted by FA 1989 s. 142. Professional privilege is recognised by s. 20B(8) and, as from the passing of FA 1989, ss. 20(9) to (14) for auditors and tax advisers (added by FA 1989 s. 144). On scope of professional privilege of barristers see *R v Board of Inland Revenue, ex p Goldberg* [1988] STC 524.
 [10] TMA 1970, s. 20(8C) and (8D) added by FA 1989, s. 142. Personal records and journalistic material are defined by reference to the Police and Criminal Evidence Act 1984 ss. 12 and 13.
 [11] TMA 1970, s. 20A (subject to s. 20B).
 [12] TMA 1970, s. 20A(1A), added by FA 1989, s. 143.
 [13] TMA 1970, s. 20BB, introduced by FA 1989, s. 145 (as from the passing of FA 1989).
 [14] TMA 1970, s. 20C. On legality of warrants if general see *IRC v Rossminster Ltd* [1980] 1 All ER 80, [1980] STC 42.
 [15] FA 1989, s. 146 (amending s. 20C) and s. 147 (introducing new s. 20CC governing procedure to be followed once the documents are removed).
 [16] TMA 1970, s. 20 (8A), added by FA 1988, s. 126.

Making the assessment

1: 36 An assessment to income tax is made by an inspector and is "made" when the Inspector signs the certificate in the assessment book and not when notice of it is received by the taxpayer;[1] this may be made on the basis of the return but the inspector is authorised to make an assessment to the best of his judgment if dissatisfied with the return.[2] This is the basis for making assessments at figures higher than those returned and then inviting the taxpayer to appeal.

For years before 1983–84 or accounting periods ending before 1 April 1983

The normal time limit for making assessments is six years from the end of the year to which it relates;[3] so an assessment for 1983–84 must be made by 5th April 1990. If the Revenue satisfy the Commissioners that they have reasonable grounds to believe that tax has been lost due to fraud or wilful default, an assessment may be made for any year back to 1936–37.[4]

The onus of proving fraud or wilful default is on the Crown and there is no presumption of such a state of mind arising from mere proof of an omission to disclose profits, although the Commissioners are entitled to conclude that there was.[5] This is reconciled with the rule that the burden of proof of upsetting an assessment rests on the taxpayer, by imposing the burden on the taxpayer once the Revenue have established fraud or wilful default.[6] It is not necessary for the Crown to show that the profits relate to one or other source of income,[7] this being a matter which the taxpayer disputes by appealing against the assessment. Moreover it has been said that when the Crown succeeded in proving just one instance of fraud or wilful default, the

Commissioners could infer that the taxpayer had been guilty of fraud or wilful default in each of the years in issue.[8]

The test which distinguishes mere neglect from wilful default is that the latter demands knowledge or simply not caring whether the return is accurate.[9] Conscious carelessness as to whether or not one is doing one's duty is wilful default.[10] So where a husband made a return of his wife's income not knowing of a particular source, it was held that he was not guilty of fraud or wilful neglect, whereas a simple refusal to declare some of his wife's income would be wilful default.[11] On the other hand there is wilful default[12] where a person fails to make a return and simply pays the tax demanded in an estimated assessment and he knows that that sum is insufficient.

The fraud or wilful default must have been committed by the taxpayer or on his behalf. It has been held that if an agent is guilty of fraud or wilful default, that fraud or wilful default is on behalf of the principal even if he is not privy to it.[13]

Where the Revenue satisfy the Commissioners that they have reasonable grounds to believe that tax has been lost through *neglect*, they may make an assessment for a further six years back. If the neglect and loss of tax are established the Revenue can than go back to the Commissioners and seek leave to go back a further six years; this process can be repeated.[14]

These rules are modified for partnerships. Although neglect enables the Revenue to go back a further six years for all who were partners during the year of assessment, a partner not guilty of neglect may not be the subject of an additional assessment.[15]

For later years any loss of tax due to fraudulent or negligent conduct is to have a 20 year time limit. When an assessment can be made against one partner, it can be made against all.[16]

These rules are also modified after the death of a taxpayer. Normally the assessment must be made within three years instead of the usual six while assessments to recover tax lost through fraud, wilful default or neglect can only go back to a year of assessment ending within six years of the death;[17] thus if death occurs on 1st January 1990 the Revenue can go back only to recover tax lost through neglect for 1983–84 and later years.

Simon's Taxes A3.2; Butterworths Income Tax Service A1.34–A1.36

[1] *Honig v Sarsfield* [1986] STC 246, CA.

[2] TMA 1970, s. 29; see *Donnelly v Platten* [1981] STC 504; s. 29(1)(c) allows the Inspector to make an assessment during the tax year, i.e. before the income has been reported—added by FA 1988, s. 119 to reverse *Jones v O'Brien* [1988] STC 615.

[3] TMA 1970, s. 34.

[4] TMA 1970, s. 36; leave is regulated by s. 41—the taxpayer is not entitled to be heard *Pearlberg v Varty* [1972] 2 All ER 6, 48 TC 14.

[5] *Hillenbrand v IRC* (1966) 42 TC 617.

[6] *Amis v Colls* (1960) 39 TC 148.

[7] Per Pennycuick J in *Hudson v Humbles* (1965) 42 TC 380 at 387.

[8] *Nicholson v Morris* [1976] STC 269.

[9] Per Wilberforce J in *Wellington v Reynolds* (1962) 40 TC 209 at 215, but cf, Salmon LJ, in *Frederick Lack Ltd v Doggett* (1970) 46 TC 524 at 535.

[10] Cross J in *Clixby v Pountney* [1968] 1 All ER 802 at 804, 44 TC 515 at 520.

[11] *Brown v IRC* (1965) 42 TC 583 (not fraud, per Stamp J at 589).

[12] Per Cross J in *Amis v Colls* (1960) 39 TC 148 at 163.

[13] *Clixby v Pountney*, supra.

[14] TMA 1970, s. 37 defined ibid., s. 118.

15 TMA 1970, s. 38 *Harrison v Willis Bros* [1965] 3 All ER 753, 43 TC 61.

16 TMA 1970, s. 36 as revised by FA 1989 s. 149—which also repeals TMA 1970, ss. 37–39 and 41.

17 TMA 1970, s. 40.

1: 37 An assessment once made may be disturbed only by appeal, by judicial review,[1] or by agreement pending appeal[2] and so not by the unilateral act of the Inspector.[3] For this purpose an inspector is taken to have agreed to something if he accepts a computation put forward by the taxpayer since he must have directed his mind to it. This was held by the House of Lords in *Scorer v Olin Energy Systems Ltd*[4] but it must make it more difficult for the Revenue to accept computations without vigorous checking. Further, a taxpayer may claim that by reason of his error or mistake he has paid too much tax[5] although no relief can be given where the assessment was made on the basis of the practice generally prevailing when the return was made.[6]

Normally, where a claim is made the time limit will be six years from the end of the chargeable period, usually the year of assessment to which it relates,[7] but where a claim is made under the error or mistake legislation[8] the period is slightly different and the six years runs from the end of the year of assessment or accounting period in which the assessment was made.[9]

Simon's Taxes A3.2, A3.10

1 An assessment may be saved from invalidity despite errors by TMA 1970, s. 114; see *Fleming v London Produce Co Ltd* [1968] 2 All ER 975, 44 TC 582 and *Baylis v Gregory* [1987] STC 297; in the latter case the Court of Appeal held that an assessment issued for the wrong year could not be saved by s. 114 even though the taxpayer was not and could not have been misled. The conclusion seems quite ritualistic.

2 TMA 1970, s. 54; on extent of agreement see *Tod v South Essex Motors (Basildon) Ltd* [1988] STC 392.

3 *Baylis v Gregory* [1987] STC 297.

4 [1985] STC 218.

5 TMA 1970, s. 33(1).

6 TMA 1970, s. 33(2) proviso.

7 TMA 1970, s. 43(1).

8 TMA 1970, s. 33.

9 TMA 1970, s. 33(1).

1: 38 One other Revenue power should be mentioned. If an inspector "discovers" that profits have not been assessed or the assessment has become insufficient or that excessive relief has been given, he may make an additional assessment.[1] This assessment is subject to the same time rules as original assessments. The term discovery has been given a wide ambit by the courts; the words are apt to cover any case in which for any reason it newly appears that the taxpayer has been undercharged.[2] So an assessment may be made where the Revenue decide that a company should be treated as a dealing company rather than an investment company[3] or where a new inspector takes a different view of the law from his predecessor[4] or to correct an arithmetical error in the computation.[5] Since the validity of the new assessment is a question of law, the Revenue may justify it even though it refers to an incorrect provision.[5] It is open to the Revenue to issue a second (additional) assessment rather than seeking an increase in the first on appeal.[6]

Where an assessment is made under these powers, and is not to make good a loss due to fraudulent or negligent conduct, a new rule applies to claims by the taxpayer. The taxpayer may make any claim further relief for that year within one year from the end of the chargeable period in which an assessment is made.[7]

Simon's Taxes A3.246–A3.249; Butterworths Income Tax Service A1.45
  [1] See TMA 1970, s. 29(3).
  [2] Per Viscount Simonds in *Cenlon Finance Co Ltd v Ellwood* [1962] 1 All ER 854 at 859, 40 TC 176 at 204.
  [3] *Jones v Mason Investments (Luton) Ltd* (1966) 43 TC 570, [1967] BTR 75 JGM.
  [4] *Parkin v Cattell* (1971) 48 TC 462.
  [5] *Vickerman v Personal Representatives of Mason* [1984] STC 231.
  [6] *Duchy Maternity Ltd v Hodgson* [1985] STC 764.
  [7] TMA 1970, ss. 43A and 43B added by FA 1989, s 150.

Appeals

1: 39   An appeal may be made against an assessment by giving notice within thirty days of its issue.[1]

The appeal will be made either to the General Commissioners,[2] a body of lay persons assisted by a qualified clerk, or the Special Commissioners, who are highly qualified persons. The rules about Special Commissioners were altered with effect from 1st January 1985 to restrict eligibility for future appointments to persons who are legally qualified and to make it usual for a Commission to sit on his or her own.[3] Sometimes the legislation reserves particular appeal to one or other body; where this is not so the choice lies with the taxpayer. Appeal may also lie to the Lands Tribunal and to the special tribunal appointed under TA 1988, s. 706. Other methods of appeal include seeking the opinion of the court[4] and an originating summons[5] but not arbitration.[6]

The choice of tribunal as between the two sets of commissioners is governed by factors such as that the General Commissioners sit locally, are cheaper and quicker, but that the Special Commissioners are a more professional body with more time to give a complex case and perhaps a reputation for insisting on more proof from the Revenue in cases of alleged omitted profits. Costs are not awarded; legal aid is not available. Until 1985 it was usually a matter of taxpayer election as to which body to appeal to. Under the new legislation, however, this right of election may be overridden by a direction of the General Commissioners.[7] General Commissioners, however, are empowered to transfer a case to the Special Commissioners if the latter body consents and the case involves either complex matters or too much time.[8] As from 1 January 1989, where a matter is to be brought before the General Commissioners, the parties can agree in which division it should be. Failing agreement the Board may direct which division it shall be.[9]

The duty of the Commissioners was limited by Goulding J in *Wicker v Fraser*[10] when distinguishing their role from that of an inquisitorial tribunal concerned to approach the primary facts *de novo* and to perform the same office as an officer initially making an assessment.

Simon's Taxes A3.5, A3.7; Butterworths Income Tax Service A1.41, A5.27
  [1] TMA 1970, s. 31.
  [2] This system is extended to Northern Ireland by FA 1988, ss. 134 and 135.

[3] By FA 1984, Sch. 22.
[4] As in *A-G v National Provincial Bank Ltd* (1928) 14 TC 111.
[5] As in *Buxton v Public Trustee* (1962) 41 TC 235 (charitable nature of trusts) but not in *Argosam Finance Co Ltd v Oxby* [1964] 3 All ER 561, 42 TC 86 (vexatious).
[6] See Sheridan [1978] BTR 243.
[7] TMA 1970, s. 31(5A)–(5E), added by FA 1984, Sch. 22, para. 3.
[8] TMA 1970, s. 44(3A), inserted by FA 1984, Sch. 22, para. 5.
[9] TMA 1970, s. 44(1A), (1B), (2) added by FA 1988, s. 133.
[10] [1982] STC 505 at 511.

1: 40 Once an appeal is launched it can be withdrawn only with the consent of the Revenue.[1] At the hearing each party is allowed to produce any lawful evidence[2] but the onus is on the taxpayer to disprove the assessment,[3] a rule which may be rationalised on the basis that he knows all the facts and therefore should have to prove them.

A further appeal lies to the High Court by way of case stated but only on questions of law.[4] Following the changes made by FA 1984 appeals may go from the Special Commissioners direct to the Court of Appeal[5]—but still only on questions of law. The court cannot reverse a decision of the Commissioners simply because the judge would have reached a different conclusion.[6] However sometimes the facts are such that the courts are entitled to assume that there has been some error of law; it was of such a situation that Lord Radcliffe spoke in *Edwards v Bairstow and Harrison*:[7]

> ". . . I do not think it much matters whether this state of affairs is described as one in which there is no evidence to support the determination or as one in which the evidence is inconsistent with and contradictory of the determination, or as one in which the true and only reasonable conclusion contradicts the determination. Rightly understood, each phrase propounds the same test. For my part I prefer the last of the three, since I think that it is misleading to speak of there being no evidence to support a conclusion when in cases such as these many of the facts are likely to be neutral in themselves and only to take their colour from the combination of circumstances in which they are found to occur."

The question whether an issue is one of fact or law is not always easy.[8] Some matters like the construction of documents or statutes are clearly questions of law; others such as whether a document was executed on a particular date are clearly questions of fact. Difficulties arise where the Commissioners having decided the true meaning of the statute in issue have to apply that meaning to the facts. The difficulties are of two sorts. The first is the familiar problem of primary and secondary facts, the latter being inferences drawn from the former. In general such inferences are matters of fact and the courts are reluctant to substitute their own views, the more so since the Commissioners, unlike the court, have seen the witnesses. The view that secondary facts are findings of fact was emphatically restated by Lord Brightman in *Furniss v Dawson*.[9] Thus the question whether a trade is being carried on is one of fact. The Commissioners must not only decide the primary facts such as what transactions were carried on when but also form their own conclusion as to whether these activities amounted to a trade or not, a conclusion which must depend on a whole range of circumstances and impressions.[10] However the question of the meaning of trade is one of law. So the question whether an isolated transaction can come within the meaning of trade is one of law, whether this one does is one of fact. The second difficulty is that the law can be formulated in such a way as to leave more or less to the Commissioners to decide depending on the level of abstraction employed. Thus in employment cases the issue may be is it a reward for services or, more simply, is it an emolument?; clearly the latter leaves more to the Commissioners and reduces the court's power to intervene.

The procedure by way of case stated is obsolete but enduring. A distinguished practitioner had this to say of it in 1970:[11]

> "The reader may think it remarkable that the stated case procedure has survived so long. It seems to have few, if any, virtues. The Commissioners have the laborious task of compiling it; the parties have to consider and suggest amendments to—or even re-write— the Commissioners' draft; the Commissioners are naturally tempted to "slant" it in favour of their finding; it creates injustice by denying a right of appeal on an issue of fact. Here in Great Britain in the twentieth century is a system of taxes where the State assesses the liability of the citizen by estimate and provides an appeal only to a court, staffed by amateurs or by state functionaries, that meets in secret, and whose factual findings are not subject to judicial review—the whole thing could be written up as part of a totalitarian system. Injustice often occurs, and would be more frequent but for the care and objectivity usually displayed by the Commissioners.
>
> The stated case has survived so long, in spite of its clear injustice in many cases, because it suits so many of those engaged in appeals. It is irksome for the Commissioners and for the advocates to have to reveal to the gaze of the judges their notes of evidence: failure to weigh evidence and poor advocacy are both covered up by the stated case. An appeal on fact can be wearisome and embarrassing."

Appeal lies from the High Court to the Court of Appeal and House of Lords in the usual way—but still only on questions of law.

Two other ways of challenging the Commissioners' decision judicially deserve mention. One is by judicial review, a remedy equally applicable to the decision of the revenue. The most usual obstacle is that the court will not allow an applicant to use judicial review where the point should be dealt with by appeal. The second is by arguing that the assessment is ultra vires.[12] This line of argument has been used—unsuccessfully—to argue that the profits of prostitution could not be taxable since, as a matter of law, the profits of an illegal activity cannot be subject to tax. The judges will no doubt keep this use of the ultra vires doctrine under very tight control to prevent it from becoming another avenue of appeal.[13].

Simon's Taxes A3.7; Butterworths Income Tax Service A6

[1] TMA 1970, s. 54.

[2] TMA 1970, s. 52.

[3] *Norman v Golder* [1945] 1 All ER 352, 26 TC 293.

[4] In Scotland the Court of Session and in Northern Ireland the Court of Appeal (Northern Ireland). On the importance of the 30 day period in TMA 1970, s. 56(4) see *Valleybright Ltd v Richardson* [1985] STC 70.

[5] Revenue Appeals Order 1987, SI 1987, No. 1422; *Simon's Tax Intelligence* 1987, p. 636 and RSC Order 61(4) added by SI 1987, No. 1423.

[6] E.g. Du Parcq LJ, in *Bean v Doncaster Amalgamated Collieries Ltd* (1944) 27 TC 296 at 307.

[7] [1955] 3 All ER 48 at 57, 36 TC 207 at 229; see Megarry J in *Redditch Electro-Plating Co Ltd v Ferrebe* (1973) 48 TC 635 at 645; and Widgery, LJ in *Global Plant Ltd v Secretary of State for Social Services* [1972] 1 QB 139 at 154–5.

[8] See Lord Simon in *Ransom v Higgs* [1974] STC 539 at 561.

[9] [1984] STC 153 at 167.

[10] Lord Sands in *IRC v Hyndland Investment Co Ltd* (1929) 14 TC 694 at 700.

[11] Potter [1970] BTR 38 at 41.

[12] *IRC v Aken* [1988] STC 69.

[13] See also *supra*, **1: 37**.

COLLECTION

1: 41 The Revenue have a formidable battery of powers to collect tax which is due, including the power to levy distraint[1] and to sue in the magistrates court (amounts up to £250) and the county court (up to £5,000) as well as the High Court. The Revenue has also enjoyed a highly privileged position on bankruptcy.[2] With the coming into complete force on 29th December 1986 of the Insolvency Act 1986 the Crown's preferential creditor status for taxes assessed on the taxpayer has been abolished; the preferential status for taxes for which the taxpayer acts as agent for the Revenue—e.g. PAYE, payments to sub-contractors, National Insurance Contributions and VAT (for 6 months)—is retained.[3]

In addition the Revenue may deduct tax at source through the PAYE machinery[4] and direct deduction of basic rate tax under special statutory schemes e.g. that to counter "The Lump", or labour-only subcontractors not in possession of the appropriate certificate,[5] and that under which, tax is deducted from payments made to non-resident entertainers and sportsmen in respect of performances in the UK.[6]

Simon's Taxes A3.13, A3.14; Butterworths Income Tax Service A4.51

[1] TMA 1970, ss. 61–68. these rules have been recast by FA 1989 ss. 152–155.

[2] Bankruptcy Act 1914.

[3] Insolvency Act 1986, Sch. 6, paras. 1–7, **Simon's Taxes** A3.1106 et seq, Halsbury's Statutes (4th edn) BANKRUPTCY AND INSOLVENCY.

[4] TA 1988, s. 203, extended to workers supplied by agencies by TA 1988, s. 134, Sch. 29, para. 6. See *Brady v Hart* [1985] STC 498.

[5] TA 1988, ss. 559–565 as amended by F(No. 2)A 1987, s. 93.

[6] TA 1988, ss. 555–558. Much of the detail of the scheme is contained in Regulations made by the Treasury; see Income Tax (Entertainers and Sportsmen) Regulations 1987 (SI 1987, No. 530) infra, § **35: 16**.

Interest on overdue tax

1: 42 Interest runs from the date at which the tax is payable.[1] Subject to exceptions this will be either a fixed date—the due date—or 30 days from the issue of the notice of assessment—the actual due date—whichever is the later. Interest is charged at 12.25%[2] as from 6th July 1989; it is not deductible in computing income.[3] The *de minimis* exception where the interest does not exceed £30 is to be repealed as from an appointed day.[4] Concessary relief is available when the taxpayer dies before the due date.[5]

At one time once an appeal had been lodged tax could not become due until that appeal was determined; this led to appeals being made purely for delay purposes. It is therefore now provided that when the tax is subsequently found to be due interest runs not from the date of the determination of the appeal but from "the reckonable date" which will usually be six months from the due date.

Some appeals are not simply for delay. A taxpayer may therefore apply to postpone the payment of tax in dispute; the tax not in dispute is due at the normal time. If the taxpayer and the Revenue cannot agree how much is in dispute the Commissioners may determine the matter.[6] If the amount postponed as being in dispute is later found not to be due no harm is done; if the amount is found to be due interest runs from the reckonable date.[7] An exception is made if the appeal is won before the Commissioners but subsequently lost before the courts; interest will run from 30 days after the determination by the courts. If the taxpayer has elected to pay the tax but later wins his appeal the tax will be refunded. Interest runs from the due date, the actual due date or the reckonable date, whichever is the last.

EXAMPLE

The due date for capital gains tax is 1st December following the end of the year of assessment in which the gains arose: the reckonable date is the following 1st June. So if gains arose during the year 1985–86 and an assessment is made on 1st March 1987, the interest will only begin to run from 31st March 1987. If an appeal is made against the assessment, interest on the tax in dispute will (if postponed but subsequently found to be due) run from 1st June 1987. If the assessment had not been made until 1st August 1987 interest would have run only from 31st August 1987.

From 1982 the Revenue have accepted late applications to postpone the payment of tax if there is a change in the circumstances of the case which results in the appellant having grounds to believe tax has been over-charged.[8] From the same date interest is due on the postponed amount from the reckonable date and the amount which was not charged by the original assessment is treated as if it also had been postponed.[9]

EXAMPLE

A is assessed to tax under Sch. D, Case I for the year 1988–89 to the amount of £10,000. The assessment is dated 1st November 1988. A applied to postpone £2,000 of the tax due and the inspector agreed on 15th December 1988, leaving £8,000, payable in two instalments of £4,000 on 1st January 1989 and 1st July 1989. Both instalments were paid in time and the appeal was determined on 1st November 1989 in the amount of £11,000. A paid £3,000 on 5th November 1989. Although the due date of the determined balance was not until 1st December 1989 (30 days after date of the revised assessment) interest runs on this amount from 1st July 1989 because the original assessment was issued after 30th July 1988 and interest will accrue as if the tax had been charged by the original assessment. Thus the interest charge is as follows:

£3,000 for 127 days from 1st July 1989 to 5th November 1989 is 5 days at 11.5% and 122 days at 12.25% = 4.73 + 122.83 = £127.56.

Simon's Taxes A3.1308, 1309; Butterworths Income Tax Service A4.51

[1] TMA 1970, s. 86—the due date is set out in TA 1988, ss. 5, 203, etc., and CGTA 1979, s. 7. The form of s. 86 is recast by FA 1989, s. 156. As this amendment is meant to confirm the Revenue view it is retrospective to 1982. See also SP6/89, 31st July 1989 (Delay in rendering tax returns: Interest on overdue tax: TMA 1970, s. 88) and Inland Revenue Press Release 1st August 1989 (Setting Revenue rates of interest).

[2] TMA 1970, s. 89 and SI 1989/1000; the rate had been 11.5% since 6th January 1989, SI 1988, No. 2185.

[3] TMA 1970, s. 90.

[4] TMA 1970, s. 86(6) and s. 87(4) are repealed by FA 1989 s. 158(1).

[5] Extra Statutory Concession A17 (1988).

[6] TMA 1970, s. 55 is recast by FA 1989 s. 156(2)—retrospectively to 1982.

[7] TMA 1970, s. 86.

[8] FA 1982, s. 68.

[9] TMA 1970, s. 86(3A) replacing the s. 3(aa). The replacement is made by FA 1989 s. 156(1) and is retrospective to 1982.

Repayment supplement

1: 43   Where tax has been overpaid[1] and the repayment is made more than one year after the end of the year of assessment or, if later the year of assessment in which the tax was paid, the Revenue will pay a tax-free repayment supplement.[2] This applies only if the repayment would be £25 or more[3]. Repayment supplement is paid at the same rate as interest on overdue tax (see § **1: 42** above) and is 12.25% as from 6th July 1989.[4]

EXAMPLE

A is assessed to CGT for the year of 1984–85 and pays the tax on 1st December 1985; the chance of a repayment supplement will arise if repayment is not made by 6th April 1986 and interest will run from that date. Had the payment been made on 6th April 1986 interest could only run as from 6th April 1987.

As illustrated in the example above, where tax is due in April it is important to consider whether a repayment may arise and if there is such a possibility the taxpayer should be advised to pay on or before 5th April.

Tax-free treatment is also accorded to repayment supplements in respect of VAT.[5]

Simon's Taxes A3.604; Butterworths Income Tax Service A5.28

[1] See also extra statutory concession A51 (1988).
[2] TA 1988, s. 824 (F(No. 2)A 1975, s. 47); on Revenue practice see SP1/80, **Simon's Taxes, Division H3.2**.
[3] This limit is to be repealed as from an appointed day. FA 1989 s. 158.
[4] SI 1989/1000; the rate had been 11.5% since 6th January 1989, SI 1988, No. 2185.
[5] FA 1986, s. 53.

Penalties and offences

1: 44 In addition to penalties for failure to make returns and so on penalties may be imposed for fraudulently or negligently making an incorrect statement or return.[1] The penalty is not to exceed the aggregate of £50 and, if the taxpayer was negligent, the tax underpaid but, if he was fraudulent, twice that tax. For defaults after the passing of FA 1989 the maximum penalty is reduced to 100% of the tax underpaid.[2] This penalty is in addition to the tax itself. In most cases the Revenue will, if given reasonable cooperation by the taxpayer and his advisors, accept a penalty of about 25% of the tax lost in cases of pure negligence and between 50% and 75% for fraud; in the absence of cooperation the Revenue will press for maximum penalties.[3] Rules provide for a reduction in total penalties when there are two or more tax-geared penalties in respect of the same tax.[4] These are fixed in the first instance by the Commissioners or by the courts but may be agreed between the parties. In addition one who assists in preparing the return or account may be fined up to £500.[5] This sum was set in 1960 and is obviously out of date. FA 1989 therefore provides for increase to £3,000 for acts after the passing of the Act.[6] There are also increases in the penalties for delay.[6] In severe cases the Revenue may opt to press criminal charges in the criminal courts;[7] a criminal prosecution does not exclude penalties.[8] The Revenue prefer the penalty procedure to criminal prosecution because prosecution is a drastic step which ought to be reserved for really serious cases and because of practical matters such as the burden of preparing cases.

These are illustrated by a number of special rules. First, proceedings may be before the Commissioners—and so heard in private. Secondly negligence will be assumed if an error remains uncorrected.[9] Thirdly the death of the taxpayer does not end the proceedings.[10] Fourthly the Board have power to mitigate penalties even after the courts have pronounced.[11] Fifthly there are time limits for the recovery of penalties.[12] Finally there is an important rule of evidence which applies to any criminal or civil proceedings as well as those for penalties under which the Revenue may tell the taxpayer that they have the power to accept a pecuniary settlement and that the Board has a practice of being influenced by a full confession. Any statements made by the taxpayer are admissible despite the inducement;[13] the settlement gives rise to a contractual debt[14] and is not illegal.[15]

The settlement of these cases, known as back duty cases, is a skilled art. The Revenue may be tipped off as to a likely suspect or may simply disbelieve the taxpayer's return.[16] Once alerted the Revenue may require a complete statement of means and a satisfactory explanation of all sums appearing in bank accounts or supporting a luxurious lifestyle. To this end the Revenue are reported to keep records of all horse racing results.

Simon's Taxes A3.8, A3.15, A3.16; Butterworths Income Tax Service A2.27

[1] TMA 1970, ss. 95 and 98.

[2] FA 1989, s. 163.

[3] *Moores and Rowland's Yellow Tax Guide 1989–90*, under TMA 1970, s. 95.

[4] TMA 1970, s. 97B added by FA 1988, s. 129.

[5] TMA 1970, s. 99.

[6] FA 1989, ss. 162 and 164–169.

[7] E.g. Theft Act 1968, s. 32(1)(*a*); *R v Hudson* [1956] 1 All ER 814, 36 TC 561.

[8] SP 2/88.

[9] TMA 1970, s. 97.

[10] TMA 1970, s. 100A, introduced by FA 1989, s. 167.

[11] TMA 1970, s. 102.

[12] TMA 1970, s. 103. This provision is recast by FA 1989, s. 169.

[13] TMA 1970, s. 105.

[14] *A-G v Midland Bank Executor and Trustee Co Ltd* (1934) 19 TC 136.

[15] Rowlatt J described it as "a beneficial and merciful practice" in *A-G v Johnstone* (1926) 10 TC 758.

[16] Other sources include government contracts, a customer suspicious on being asked for a bearer cheque—*Rosette Franks (King Street) Ltd v Dick* (1955) 36 TC 100, and even a reported robbery *Crole v Lloyd* (1950) 31 TC 338; informers may be rewarded.

PART II. INCOME TAX

2 Income tax—general

THE SCHEDULAR SYSTEM

2: 01 Income tax is charged on the taxable income of the year of assessment. This raises the question what is income?

There is no statutory definition of income, beyond the statement that income is taxable if it falls within one or other of the Schedules of the Taxes Act 1970.[1] The Schedules are set out below.

Simon's Taxes A1.131; Butterworths Income Tax Service A1.71.
[1] TA 1988, s. 1. These provisions were Schedules to the Acts until the 1952 consolidation when they became part of the text.

Schedule A (TA 1988, s. 15)

2: 02 Schedule A taxes the annual profits or gains arising in respect of rent and similar payments from land in the United Kingdom; this includes some premiums. The tax is calculated on the balance of rents minus allowable deductions, assessed on a current year basis; and due on 1st January.[1]

Simon's Taxes A1.132; Butterworths Income Tax Service A1.72.
[1] TA 1988, s. 5(1).

Schedule B (TA 1988, s. 16)

2: 03 Schedule B taxed the occupation of woodlands in the United Kingdom managed on a commercial basis and with a view to the realisation of profits. The assessable value of that occupation was one third of the annual value (not the capital value of the land); the tax was due on 1st January.[1] The charge to tax under this Schedule is abolished with effect from 6 April 1988 subject to transitional provisions.[2]

Simon's Taxes A1.133; Butterworths Income Tax Service A1.73.
[1] TA 1988, s. 5(1).
[2] FA 1988, s. 65, Sch. 6.

Schedule C (TA 1988, s. 17)

2: 04 Schedule C taxes profits arising from public revenue dividends payable in the United Kingdom, the tax is due on a current year basis and is deducted at source.

Simon's Taxes A1.134; Butterworths Income Tax Service A1.74.

Schedule D (TA 1988, s. 18)

2: 05 Schedule D taxes annual profits or gains which fall into one or other of its six Cases:

Case I taxes profits or gains arising from any trade.

Case II taxes the profits or gains arising from a profession or vocation.

Case III taxes interest, annuities and other annual payments together with discounts and those dividends from public revenue which do not fall within Schedule C.

Case IV taxes the profits or gains arising from securities outside the United Kingdom.

Case V taxes the profits or gains arising from possessions out of the United Kingdom.

Case VI taxes any annual profits or gains not falling under any other Case or Schedule.

Generally the tax is due on a preceding year basis with special rules for opening and closing years; but for Case VI it is due on a current year basis. The tax is due on 1st January but the tax for Cases I and II is payable in two equal instalments, one on 1st January the other on 1st July.[1]

Simon's Taxes A1.135; Butterworths Income Tax Service A1.75.
[1] TA 1988, s. 5(2).

Schedule E (TA 1988, s. 19)

2: 06 Schedule E taxes emoluments from an office or employment; the tax is due on a current year basis and is usually collected by PAYE. This Schedule has three Cases according to the location of the employment.

Simon's Taxes A1.136; Butterworths Income Tax Service A1.76.

Schedule F (TA 1988, s. 20)

2: 07 Schedule F taxes distributions by companies resident in the United Kingdom, the tax is due on the dividends of the year of assessment and is in effect deducted at source.

2: 08 Higher rates are charged at the normal dates. However when such rates are charged on income which has been subject to deduction at source, such excess liability is due on 1st December following the end of the year of assessment.[1]

Whenever tax is due on a particular date, this must be taken subject to the rule that where 30 days from the issue of a notice of assessment would give a later date that date applies. On interest on overdue tax see supra, § **1: 42**.

Simon's Taxes A1.137; Butterworths Income Tax Service A1.77.
[1] TA 1988, s. 5(3) the same dates apply for the additional rate charged on accumulated income of trustees (infra, § **11: 05**).

2: 09 Where income falls within a Schedule it falls to be computed in accordance with the rules in that Schedule and no other. As Lord Radcliffe has said:[1]

> "Before you can assess a profit to tax you must be sure that you have properly identified its source or other description according to the correct Schedule; but once you have done that, it is obligatory that it should be charged, if at all, under that Schedule and strictly in accordance with the Rules that are there laid down for assessments under it. It is a necessary consequence of this conception that the sources of profit in the different Schedules are mutually exclusive."

In *Fry v Salisbury House Estate Ltd*[2] the company received rents from unfurnished offices in a building. The company also provided services for the offices such as heating and cleaning at an additional charge. The rents were chargeable under Schedule A, although the basis of assessment at that time was not simply the rents minus costs of maintenance but the annual value of the premises, which were revalued every five years, minus a statutory allowance for running costs. The company agreed that its profits from the ancillary services fell within Schedule D, Case I, but resisted the Inland Revenue's argument that it was liable to tax on the actual rent received under Schedule D, Case I rather than the notional rent under Schedule A. The Inland Revenue conceded that it would have to make an allowance in computing tax under Schedule D, Case I for the tax due under Schedule A.[3] The House of Lords found for the company. Although the company could be said to be carrying on a trade and therefore fall within Schedule D, Case I, the Schedules were mutually exclusive and each Schedule was dominant over its own subject matter. The charge under Schedule A therefore excluded the charge under Schedule D, Case I.

Simon's Taxes A1.312; Butterworths Income Tax Service A1.71.

[1] *Mitchell and Edon v Ross* [1961] 3 All ER 49 at 55, 40 TC 11 at 61.
[2] [1930] AC 432, 15TC 266. Decision reversed by FA 1940, ss. 13–18.
[3] See *Russell v Aberdeen Town and County Bank* (1888) 2 TC 321.

2: 10   Although the Schedules are mutually exclusive, it appears that the Cases within each Schedule are not; there the Revenue may choose the Case. So an insurance company may be taxed either under Schedule D, Case I, or on its investment income minus management expenses.[1] Such choices will not often arise.[2]

Income tax is one tax but each Schedule has not only its own rules for computation of income but also different dates for payment and, at one time, different administrations. Further there is no general rule that income and losses under each Schedule are aggregated so enabling a loss under one Schedule to be set off against a profit under another. Some types of loss can be set off against general income of the same or the following (but not later) years, notably Schedule D, Cases I and II; however losses under Schedule A and Schedule D, Case VI are given relief only by being rolled forward to be set off against the income of later years taxed under the same Schedule or Case.[3]

Simon's Taxes: A1.312; Butterworths Income Tax Service A1.71.

[1] Per Lord Wright in *Simpson v Grange Trust Ltd* [1935] AC 422 at 427, 19 TC 231 at 251, HL.
[2] Probably the only overlapping cases are Cases I and IV or V. An overlap of Cases I and II and Case III appears to be precluded by *Bucks v Bowers*, infra, § **4: 05** and *Cenlon v Ellwood*,

infra, § **7: 85**; but see also insurance companies, infra, § **29: 09**. Case I excludes Case VI—infra, § **10: 03**. Schedule E, Cases I or II exclude Case III, TA 1988, s. 131(2).

³ This restriction does not apply to agricultural land; TA 1988, s. 33 and has been criticised by Law Comm., Cmd. 4654, 34. Infra, §§ **5: 17**, **9: 12** and **10: 14**.

Timing

2: 11   The issue of timing is important for several obvious reasons. Income tax is charged as income of a year of assessment; it may be that the law is changed so that the tax treatment will differ according to whether the payment is income of year 1 or year 2.¹ Another reason is that a relief may be geared to a maximum percentage of a person's total income as is the case with retirement annuity premiums ($17\frac{1}{2}\%$ of net relevant earnings for that year).² A third reason is that the taxpayer is under an obligation to report his income year by year³ so that penalties may arise if he errs in the timing of a particular receipt. A fourth reason is the converse—the Revenue must generally issue assessments within six years of the end of the chargeable period to which it relates.⁴ A fifth reason is the practical matter that the effective rate of tax may vary according to the time it becomes chargeable; this is because the taxpayer's marginal rate of tax may vary from one year to the next (a matter of less importance after the reduction of rates in 1988) and because UK tax law still contains no general averaging provision. A sixth reason is that in general it will be the value at the time the income arises that is relevant for tax purposes; subsequent changes in value are in general ignored.⁵ Finally, reliefs may be available against the income of a particular year.⁶

However, the issue of timing is also relevant to a subtler matter, namely the non-correlation of the rules with regard to receipts with those for expenses. One cannot be taxed on income one does not acquire; once income has been acquired a deduction for paying it back will be allowed only if permitted by the deduction rules appropriate to the Schedule. So preventing the income from arising will avoid tax whereas a receipt followed by a disposal will not.

In *Way v Underdown (No. 2)*⁷ an insurance agent gathered in a premium and subsequently paid back to the insurer an amount equal to his commission on the premium. It was held that as there was no obligation to repay he could not deduct the sum in computing his taxable profits; he was therefore taxable on the commission. However had he simply not collected the premium in full in the first place he might well not have been taxed.

Simon's Taxes A1.126; Butterworths Income Tax Service A2.13.

¹ As in *Strick v Longsdon* (1953) 34 TC 528 (special contribution for 1947–48).

² TA 1988, s. 619.

³ TMA 1970, s. 8.

⁴ TMA 1970, s. 34; income tax seems to have been escaped in *Heasman v Jordan* [1954] 3 All ER 101, 35 TC 518. This leads to obvious avoidance whereby a special bonus would be declared for a year more than six years before the declaration, as a result the legislation had to introduce what is now TMA 1970, s. 35. Tax was also nearly escaped in part in *Grey v Tiley* (1932) 16 TC 414; at 419 and 426.

⁵ This is of crucial importance when dealing with payments in kind or payments in foreign currency; for authority in the latter instance see *Payne v Deputy Federal Comr of Taxation* [1936] AC 497, [1936] 2 All ER 793 and *Greig v Ashton* [1956] 3 All ER 123, 36 TC 581.

⁶ *Parkside Leasing Ltd v Smith* [1985] STC 63.
⁷ [1975] 2 All ER 1064, [1975] STC 425, CA; affg. [1974] 2 All ER 595, [1974] STC 293 (Pennycuick V-C).

2: 12   Timing questions are resolved in two stages. The first question is when the income arises; thus does a sum become taxable when it falls due or only when it is paid? The general answer given by the UK cases is that an assessment cannot generally be made until the payment has been received but that a payment once received may sometimes be back-dated or, to use the customary terminology, "related back" and be treated as income of the period when it became due.¹ This is subject to three main exceptions. First there are cases in which the sum is taxable even though payment has not yet occurred; the principal example here is of a sum due to a trade or profession which is taxed on an earnings basis, infra, § **7: 138**. Secondly there are some cases where the payment is not only not taxable until paid but is then treated as income of the year of receipt, summarised in the much abused dictum that "receivability without receipt is nothing". This has been applied to the payment of arrears of interest causing payments for six years to be treated as the taxable income of one² although concessionary relief is available for retrospective increases in pensions.³ Precise rules can not be stated owing to the dearth of authority. Thirdly, statute now provides that there is to be no relating back for remuneration falling within Schedule E.⁴

This principle raises the question of what amounts to receipt. Where trustees or personal representatives receive income, that receipt may be treated as receipt by the beneficiaries,⁵ as may receipt of income by an agent for a principal⁶ or by one partner for the other⁷ although it has been held that the mere receipt of a cheque is not a receipt of income.⁸ Where a taxpayer directs payment to a third party, so that the taxpayer never actually receives payment himself, the economic control shown by the direction is still sufficient to amount to receipt.⁹ The crediting of an account which act enures to the benefit of the account-owner will also be a receipt.¹⁰ A payment made direct to a third party to discharge the taxpayer's obligations to that third party¹¹ is also a receipt. Where a payer is under a duty to deduct the recipient's tax on that income, the sum withheld is treated as having been received by the taxpayer.¹²

There is a statutory definition of receipt for Schedule E.¹³

Certain foreign income is taxable not because it has accrued but because— and so only when—it is remitted to this country: see infra, §§ **6: 14** and **34: 10**.

Simon's Taxes B1.304; Butterworths Income Tax Service B1.02.
¹ This applies to payments falling within TA 1988, s. 835 see *Whitworth Park Coal Co Ltd (in liquidation) v IRC* [1959] 3 All ER 703, 38 TC 531. It used to apply to payments falling within Schedule E but see now infra, § **6: 29**.
² *Leigh v IRC* [1928] 1 KB 73, 11 TC 590 (Schedule D, Case IV).
³ Extra-statutory concession A55 (1988).
⁴ FA 1989, ss. 36–45, infra, § **6: 29**.
⁵ Infra, § **11: 07**.
⁶ E.g. infra, § **35: 08**.
⁷ *IRC v Lebus' Executors* (1946) 27 TC 136 at 147.
⁸ *Parkside Leasing Ltd v Smith* [1985] STC 63.
⁹ Lord Hansworth MR, in *Dewar v IRC* [1935] 2 KB 351 at 367, 19 TC 561 at 577.
¹⁰ *Dunmore v McGowan* [1978] 2 All ER 85, [1978] STC 217 discussed at [1982] BTR 23, the

point there taken being approved in *Macpherson v Bond* [1985] STC 678. *Dunmore v McGowan* was followed in *Peracha v Miley* [1989] STC 76 see infra, § **9: 39**.
   [11] Cf. *Salter v Minister of National Revenue* (1947) 2 DTC 918.
   [12] TA 1988, s. 349; infra, § **9: 66**.
   [13] TA 1988, s. 202B, added by FA 1989, s. 37.

Preceding year and current year

2: 13   Usually the income for the year of assessment is that arising, in the sense just discussed, within the year from 6th April to 5th April next—the current year basis.[1] However the United Kingdom system taxes some income by reference to the income from the source during the preceding year—the preceding year basis.[2] The theory is that the source is taxed on its statutory income for the year of assessment, the preceding year's income being simply the measure of that income. As Rowlatt J once put it, "You do not tax the years by which you measure; you tax the year in which you tax and you measure by the years to which you refer."[3] This rule is therefore quite different from one which uses the preceding year's figures as a preliminary basis.[4]

It follows from this principle that under the preceding year basis the income will be taxed according to the rates in force in the year of assessment and not those in the year when the income actually arises. It also follows that the amount taken as income for the year of assessment will bear no relation to the income actually arising during that period, and, where there is a sharp drop in income from the source, the tax payable during the year may even exceed the income from that source.[5]

It will be appreciated that problems will arise when a credit can be claimed for foreign income tax and the foreign system does not use a preceding year basis,[6] or where a taxpayer who has been taxed under Schedule D, Cases I or II commences Schedule E employment without ceasing the Schedule D, Case I or II work. In the latter case the previous year basis will mean that the Schedule D Case I or II earnings will be added to the Schedule E earnings and higher rates of tax will be paid even though the taxpayer has cut down on his earnings from that source in the first year of his Schedule E employment. This can be avoided by engineering a cessation, e.g. by taking on a partner, see infra §§ **7: 43** and **7: 60**.

Where partners have trading income and so are taxed on a preceding year basis, that income is allocated amongst them in accordance with their profit sharing ratio in force in the year of assessment, and not that in force in the year when income arose, infra, § **7: 49**.

The preceding year rule is reconciled with the doctrine of the source by having special rules for the opening years, when the same figure may be used for the basis of taxable income for more than one year of assessment, and the closing years, where the figure for one period is not used at all.[7] The effect is to postpone tax on the change in the level of earnings.[8] This in turn is responsible for the rule that capital allowances have to be kept distinct from normal deductions in computing profits[9] lest a major item of capital expenditure be allowed twice or not at all; a similar rule directing special treatment now applies to the enterprise allowance.[10]

¹ E.g. Schedule E and note TA 1988, s. 835 overriding the general rule for Schedule D, Case III.
² Infra, §§ **7: 40, 9: 35, 10:14, 34: 05**.
³ *Fry v Burma Corpn Ltd* (1930) 15 TC 113 at 120 followed most recently in *Moore v Austin* [1985] STC 673.
⁴ As under Schedule A—see TA 1988, s. 22, infra, § **9: 05**.
⁵ However relief of losses is on a current year as opposed to a preceding year basis. TA 1988, s. 380, infra, § **5: 02**.
⁶ Infra, § **36: 21**.
⁷ Infra, § **7: 43**.
⁸ Infra, § **7: 41**.
⁹ Infra, § **8: 05**.
¹⁰ Infra, § **7: 41**.

Non-taxable income

2: 14   The concept of income is narrowed in four main ways. First it is clear that unless a particular receipt comes within one or other of the Schedules it is not taxable income.

Secondly, although the Schedules include the wide phrase "annual profits" and contain in Schedule D, Case VI a residuary case to catch receipts not caught by the other Schedules and Cases, the courts have construed that phrase in a limited way—profits are only income if they possess a quality of recurrence[1]—and have confined that Case to profits similar to those caught by the other Schedule and Cases, § **10: 03**. In particular the courts have taken a restrictive view of what is income by drawing a line between income and capital.

Thirdly, the interpretation of the Schedules is governed by the doctrine of the source. The courts have held that every piece of income must have a source[2] and the reports abound with references to fruit and tree. The doctrine was applied to exempt certain types of income which clearly ought to have been taxed. These payments escaped tax because since income tax was an annual tax, it followed that not only must the income arise within the tax year but the source must also exist in that tax year. Hence it was decided that the post cessation receipts of a trade were not taxable.[3] Likewise where a person is taxed on a remittance basis and money is brought into this country in a year in which its source does not exist, no tax is payable. Post cessation receipts are now taxable and the remittance basis drastically reduced.[4] In *Bray v Best*[5] it has been held that payments made after an employment had ceased but for services rendered as an employee could not be retrospectively attributed to the years of service. This decision has been reversed by legislation.[6]

Although the legislature has occasionally intervened, as with premiums for leases, § **9: 17**, the proceeds of certain life assurance policies, § **28: 09** and golden handshakes, § **6: 42**, the basic distinction between income and capital is central to the system. The reason for this acceptance by the legislature is probably the high value placed by the legislature on the requirement of certainty in the sense of enforceability or practicality, even at the expense of equity. It also explains the great insistence on the system of deduction of tax at source, a system which has at one time or another covered almost all payments other than the profits of a trade or profession and short interest.

The legislature was for a long time reluctant to tax payments which could not be conveniently taxed at source.

As a consequence of these rules, non-taxable receipts include not only capital gains but also gambling winnings,[7] instalments of capital,[8] most gifts[9]—including the remission of a debt[10]—and loans.[11]

Simon's Taxes A1.121, 122.

[1] *Moss Empires Ltd v IRC* [1937] AC 785, 21 TC 264.

[2] E.g. *Brown v National Provident Institution* [1921] 2 AC 222 at 246, 8 TC at 89, per Lord Atkinson; and *Leeming v Jones* [1930] 1 K B 279 at 297, 15 TC 333 at 349–50, per Lord Hanworth. See also e.g. *Stainer's Executors v Purchase* [1951] 2 All ER 1071, 32 TC 367, *Carson v Cheyney's Executors* [1958] 3 All ER 573, 38 TC 240.

[3] TA 1988, s. 104, infra, § **7: 137**.

[4] Infra, § **34: 11**.

[5] [1989] 1 All ER 969, [1989] STC 159, HL.

[6] TA 1988, s. 19 para 4A, added by FA 1989, s. 36 (3).

[7] The gambling industry pays many taxes but the exemption for the individual winner is a remarkable exception to the principle of taxing according to ability to pay.

[8] Infra, § **9: 68**.

[9] But see §§ **6: 31**, **7: 69** and **9: 57**.

[10] But see § **7: 143**.

[11] A genuine loan is not income. It could, in theory, be treated as a receipt when received and a deduction when repaid but this would be administratively burdensome and would give rise to opportunities for income averaging for which the United Kingdom system makes little provision. This device is however used in relation to loans by close companies to participators (TA 1988, s. 419). Infra, § **27: 10**; see also *Jacobs v IRC* (1925) 10 TC 1; *Clayton v Gothorp* [1971] 2 All ER 1311, 47 TC 168; *Esdaile v IRC* (1936) 20 TC 700; and *Stoneleigh Products Ltd v Dodd* (1948) 30 TC 1.

2: 15 Fourthly, certain types of payment or persons are specifically excepted from liability to income tax:

1. Certain social security benefits escape tax, including child benefit, earnings-related supplement to unemployment benefit, invalidity benefit, mobility allowance,[1] non-contributory invalid pension, sickness benefit,[2] maternity benefit and grant, death grant, attendance allowance but not the retirement pension, unemployment benefit nor supplementary benefit to the unemployed or to those on strike (TA 1988, s. 617). On treatment of adoption allowances see extra-statutory concession A40 (1988) and one published on 16th February 1989.[3]
2. Certain pensions for disabled employees.[4]
3. War widow's pension (TA 1988, s. 318).
4. Payments under the statutory job release scheme, which closed to new applicants in 1980, had to be made to a person within one year of pensionable age (TA 1988, s. 191) (obsolete).[5]
5. Redundancy payments (TA 1988, s. 579).
6. Scholarship income arising from a scholarship held by a person receiving full time instruction at a university, college, school, or other educational establishment (TA 1988, s. 331 and see SP 4/86). Certain education allowances under the Overseas Aid Act Schemes are exempt by extra-statutory concession A44 (1988).[6]
7. Foreign service allowance for civil servants (TA 1988, s. 319).
8. Interest on damages payable for personal injuries (TA 1988, s. 329). For foreign courts see extra-statutory concession A30 (1988).[7]

9. Interest and bonuses on National Savings Certificates (TA 1988, s. 46).
10. Terminal bonuses on Save as you Earn contracts (TA 1988, s. 326).
11. Maturity bonuses on Defence Bonds, British Savings Bonds and National Development Bonds (TA 1988, s. 46).
12. Housing grants paid by local authorities (TA 1988, s. 578).
13. The first £70 of interest on Post Office Savings Bank (but not Trustee Savings Bank) deposits. Husband and wife may each claim £70 on separate accounts (TA 1988, s. 325).
14. Government securities held by non-resident central banks (TA 1988, s. 516).
15. The Issue departments of the Reserve Bank of India and the State Bank of Pakistan (TA 1988, s. 517).
16. Various Commonwealth and foreign representatives (TA 1988, ss. 320–322).
17. Various payments to members of visiting forces (TA 1988, s. 323).
18. International Maritime Satellite Organisation (TA 1988, s. 515).
19. Annuities and pensions payable to victims of National Socialist persecution under the laws of West Germany or Austria (TA 1988, s. 330).
20. Wounds and disability pensions (TA 1988, s. 315).
21. Allowances, bounties and gratuities paid for additional service in the armed forces (TA 1988, s. 316).
22. Annuities and additional pensions to holders of gallantry awards (TA 1988, s. 317).
23. Grants under the European Assembly (Pay and Pensions) Act 1979, s. 3 and certain related payments together with similar payments for Ministers and MPs. (TA 1988, s. 190).
24. Income arising under a Personal Equity Plan (TA 1988, s. 333, see infra, § **28: 22**).

The Crown is not liable to tax unless statute otherwise provides (TA 1988, s. 829); so the private estates of the Crown are subject to tax—Crown Private Estates Act 1862.

On charities see § **11: 13**; on pension funds see infra, § **30: 08** and on non-residents see § **35: 01**.

In assessing the base of the income tax a number of general points stand out despite the major changes of 1988. First, there are still a number of exemptions for payments received e.g. redundancy payments and the first £30,000 of golden handshakes infra, § **6: 42**. Secondly, there are still a number of deductions which remain sacrosanct, such as mortgage interest payments and contributions to pension funds. The reasoning behind the retention of those reliefs is presumably political as it is hard to find any other explanation for the sharply differing tax treatments of different forms of savings and investment. Thirdly, it has been the case that use could be made of trusts and companies to shelter income from the top rates of tax; these advantages have been reduced to virtual insignificance by the reduction of rates in 1988. Fourthly, the 1988 changes attack the problem of the assignment of income by covenants (infra, § **9: 34** and **13: 46**). However the new regime shows great care to preserve existing levels of relief for existing arrangements between divorced or separated spouses and for existing covenants.

Lastly there is the problem of capital gains. The 1988 changes go a long way to reducing the importance of this distinction; in particular gains are to be taxed as if they were income and so at the rates of 25% or 40%. However it is still the case that differences remain as may be seen from contrasting the treatment of an asset which is the subject of an adventure in the nature of trade (and so subject to income tax under Schedule D Case I) and a capital asset. Tax on the capital asset will be due on realisation; pre-1982 gains will be ignored; indexation relief applies and there is an annual personal exemption of £5,000. Tax on the Schedule D Case I asset will again be due on realisation although if it qualifies as trading stock and goes down in value there will be immediate relief (infra, § **7: 158**); there is no relief for increase in value before 1982; there is no indexation relief and there is no £5,000 annual exemption. There are further differences with regard to the treatment of losses. A capital loss cannot be set off against ordinary income—or vice versa. On the slightly different rules for corporations see infra, § **25: 04**.

Simon's Taxes E4.3; Butterworths Income Tax Service B1.11.

[1] Earlier payments were not taxable, see *Willows v Lewis* [1982] STC 141 and extra-statutory concession A42 (1988).

[2] Distinguish statutory sick pay, taxable by TA 1988, s. 150(1)(*c*).

[3] **Simon's Taxes, Division H2.2.**

[4] Extra-statutory concession A62 (1988), **Simon's Taxes, Division H2.2.**

[5] By concession, tax exemption is given to payments even though the recipient is not in this age group; extra-statutory concession A50 (1985) (now obsolete).

[6] **Simon's Taxes, Division H2.2.**

[7] **Simon's Taxes, Division H2.2.**

---

3 Personal reliefs and the tax unit

3: 01   UK income tax applies not only to individuals but also to entities such as trusts and partnerships. Partly for this reason the system, unlike others, does not have an initial low rate of tax nor does it automatically exempt an initial slice of taxable income.

The adjustment of the burden of income taxation is a task which is carried out by allowing deductions, known as personal reliefs, which may be claimed by individuals, including individual partners in a partnership, in computing taxable income. It also exempts from income tax certain payments coming from the social security system.

An initial problem is the choice of the taxable unit. That unit may be the individual, the husband and wife, the husband, wife and minor children, or some wider grouping. Current UK law opts for a compromise by which the normal unit is husband *and* wife but the spouses may elect to be taxed separately in respect of earned, as opposed to investment, income. The law also requires the aggregation of certain income derived by a child from its parents; from 1969–70 to 1971–72 inclusive, all investment income of children, whether or not derived from their parents had to be aggregated (FA 1968, s. 15).

The current system is to change in 1990–91. Under the new regime husbands and wives will be taxed as separate individuals. Each will have her or his own personal relief, equal to the present single person's relief. In addition a married couple will be entitled to a married couple's allowance equal to the difference between the present married man's relief and the single person's relief. This will be given to the husband but will be assignable to the wife if he is unable to use it.

The era of independent taxation which is to begin in 1990–91 has some oddities in it. First, by giving each spouse a personal relief and giving each couple the married couple's allowance they will be well off as now; this is contrary to the expectations of most people who worried about the cost of such a change. However where H has no income he will be able to assign to W only the married couple's allowance and not his personal allowance; this is as now but a long way from a system of fully transferable allowances. Finally one notes that the husband is apparently going to be allowed to assign the married couple's allowance only where he is unable to use it and not just because the wife could make better use of it—as where her rate of tax is higher. Secondly, the change will apply to all income whether investment income or earned income. This encouraged the transfer of assets between spouses to ensure that the income accrues to whichever of them has the lower tax rate; such transfers will be free of CGT consequences.[1] To counter such transfers the income arising will be treated as that of the donor unless it is an unconditional gift of both the asset and the income arising from it.[2]

---

[1] CGTA 1979, s. 44(2) and IHTA 1984, s. 18.
[2] TA 1988, ss. 685(4A) and 674A, added by FA 1989, ss. 108 and 109. See infra, Chapter 13.

Personal reliefs (see table of tax rates and reliefs at the beginning of this work).

3: 02 Personal reliefs are fixed sums, which are deductible from total income in calculating taxable income. Being *personal* reliefs they can be claimed only by individuals as opposed to, for example, trusts, and therefore are distinguishable from other deductions such as interest payments. Further they may generally be claimed only by residents. Reliefs are available only for the year of assessment; reliefs which are not used in one year cannot be rolled forward (or backwards) to another year. Reliefs may not be assigned directly (except some in the year of marriage, infra, § **3: 05**) but some may be assigned indirectly if one person can provide income for another to absorb that other's relief.

THE RELIEFS

1 Personal reliefs: s. 257

3: 03 The principal deduction or relief is provided by TA 1988, s. 257, which permits the deduction of £2,785 from total income.[1] If the claimant has his wife[2] living with him the figure is £4,375,[3] and the deduction is known as the married man's allowance. This larger figure may still be claimed by the husband if the wife, although not living with him, is wholly maintained by him *and* he is not entitled to deduct from his own income sums paid for her maintenance. In effect this means that if he is under an *obligation* to pay her the sums by way of maintenance, whether by agreement or court order (and so is entitled to deduct them in computing his own taxable income) he loses his right to the larger allowance. These reliefs apply to polygamous marriages as much as to monogamous ones.[4] So when a husband is separated from his wife but then contracts a valid (polygamous) marriage to a second wife, he is entitled to the larger allowance as the phrase "his wife" in TA 1988, s. 257(1) can be construed as meaning "a person being his wife".[4]

Simon's Taxes E2.2; Butterworths Income Tax Service B4.03.
   [1] TA 1988, s. 257(1)(*b*) and FA 1989, s. 33.
   [2] A voidable marriage is valid until annulled: Matrimonial Causes Act 1973, s. 16.
   [3] TA 1988, s. 257(1)(*a*) and FA 1989, s. 33.
   [4] *Nabi v Heaton* [1983] STC 344.

Wife's earned income relief

3: 04 If the wife earns income and the spouses do not elect for separate assessment of their earnings, the husband is entitled to the wife's earned income relief, being the amount of earned income[1] or £2,785 whichever is the less. It is given to the husband because he is the person responsible for the tax due; it does not affect the husband's claim to the married man's relief. This relief produces two curious consequences. If the wife has no earned income the relief is useless and the couple have just £4,375 of relief; yet if she earns £2,785 their combined reliefs are £7,160. Secondly, if only one of the spouses has earned income, it is better that it should be the wife since then the reliefs will be worth £7,160 whereas if it is the husband the relief will be £4,375. This anomaly will be greatly reduced when independent taxation is introduced in 1990–91.

Simon's Taxes E2.4; Butterworths Income Tax Service B4.04.
[1] FA 1989, s. 33; see TA 1988, s. 257(6) for the meaning of this phrase.

Year of marriage

3: 05   Where the claimant marries in the course of the year, the married man's personal relief is apportioned and is reduced by £132.50 for each complete month from 6th April to the date of the marriage.[1] The wife is entitled to her single person's relief in full and her income is not aggregated with that of her husband. If she continues to work after the marriage her husband may not also claim the wife's earned income relief.[2] Before 1976 this claim would have been allowed thus giving in effect double reliefs for the wife in her marriage year.

Simon's Taxes E2.206; Butterworths Income Tax Service B4.03.
[1] TA 1988, s. 257(8).
[2] FA 1976, s. 36, but the aggregation during the year of marriage is allowed so as to give the maximum effect to interest life assurance and most personal reliefs, TA 1988, s. 280; aggregation is not allowed for TA 1988, s. 259 (infra, § **3: 15**) and s. 262 (infra, § **3: 08**) reliefs.

Age allowance

3: 06   If the taxpayer or his spouse is 65 or over but less than 75 at any time in the tax year, and the total income does not exceed £11,400, a married man may claim an allowance of £5,385 and a single person £3,400.[1] Age allowance is claimed instead of the ordinary personal allowance.

If the income exceeds £11,400 the age allowance is reduced. This is achieved by reducing the excess of the age allowance over the ordinary allowance (£1,010 and £615) by one half of the excess.[2] So where a married couple's income is £11,402 the age allowance will be reduced by £1 to £5,384, so making a marginal rate of tax of 37.5%. The benefit of the age allowance disappears altogether when the total income reaches £13,420 for a married couple and £12,630 for a single person.

Age allowance may not be claimed if there is an election for separate taxation of wife's earnings in force.

In 1989–90 an enhanced age allowance was introduced where the taxpayer or his spouse is 75 or over at any time in the tax year (or would have been if he had not died during the year).[3] Before 1989–90 the age for the enhanced allowance was 80. The married man's allowance is then £5,565 (an increase of £180) and the single person's allowance is £3,540 (an increase of £140). The rules for these allowances are the same rules as those applying to persons between 65 and 74. The benefit of the enhanced allowance disappears at £13,780 for a married man and £12,910 for a single person.

Simon's Taxes E2.301, 302; Butterworths Income Tax Service B4.05, 06.
[1] TA 1988, s. 257(2) and S.I. 1989 No. 467 and FA 1989, s. 33(3).
[2] TA 1988, s. 257(5) and S.I. 1989 No. 467 and FA 1989, s. 33(3).
[3] TA 1988, s. 257(3), S.I. 1989 No. 467 and FA 1989, s. 33(3).

Changes in status

3: 07 The husband H is entitled to the married man's relief of £4,375 provided he is living with his wife at the start of the year of assessment. If H and W should separate, H will keep that relief for the rest of that year but W is treated as a separate person as from the date of separation, with the effect that she will be entitled to a single person's relief for her income arising during the rest of that year; this does not affect any claim H may have to a wife's earned income allowance for the period before the separation.

Simon's Taxes E2.204, 206; Butterworths Income Tax Service B6.06.

Death—widow's bereavement allowance

3: 08 If the husband dies during the tax year the full year's allowances, including the larger allowance and, where applicable, the wife's earned income allowance, are set against the income up to the date of death. From the date of death the widow receives a full single person's allowance; this allowance is not apportioned. In addition she receives a further allowance, the widow's bereavement allowance, of £1,590.[1] This relief is also available to her for the tax year immediately following the year of her husband's death—unless she has remarried before that year began.

This relief is additional to her single allowance. It is available whenever the husband was entitled to the larger allowance whether or not it was accepted so that it is available even though the spouses elected for separate assessments and so lost the larger allowance. It is also extra to any additional personal allowance she may be able to claim if there are children. In an extreme case the estate may be able to claim £7,160 for the period before the death and the widow £2,785 (single person's allowance), £1,590 (additional personal allowance), and £1,590 (bereavement allowance); this makes total reliefs of £13,125 for the year.

Simon's Taxes E2.207, 501; Butterworths Income Tax Service B4.09.
[1] TA 1988, s. 262.

Marriage and the tax unit

3: 09 The general rule is that a woman's income is deemed for income tax purposes to be her husband's income so far as it relates to a year of assessment at the beginning of which she is married to and living with her husband.[1] This has at present three consequences. First that their incomes must be aggregated and tax levied at the rate appropriate to that combined income. Secondly that the assessment is made on the husband who is thus primarily responsible; the wife is liable for tax on *her* income if her husband defaults.

Thirdly, the husband has to make the return in respect of his wife's income as well as his own. It is obvious that one can change the second and third rule without changing the first. However, the new system which is to begin in 1990–91 changes all three.

The prime disadvantage of aggregation is that it may subject the couple's income to higher rates of tax than if they were unmarried and so not aggregated. Opting for separate taxation, as can be done under the present law, removes this disadvantage for the wife's earnings; which leaves the only hard case, namely that in which their investment income, which cannot be disaggregated by election, is liable to higher rates. Under the new system each spouse will be taxed separately even in respect of investment income. Even under the present law, there will be some cases in which it is cheaper for the couple to be married than not, because the husband's allowance of £4,375 is greater than the single person's allowance. A further disadvantage is that the level at which the age allowance is reduced is the same for a married man as for a single person. In addition, a married couple may receive less mortgage interest relief as they are only entitled to one £30,000 exemption between them, whereas two single persons are each entitled to a £30,000 exemption. This disadvantage is to end, for the most part, as from 1 August 1988.[2]

However, not all tax consequences of aggregation are bad for the taxpayer. Life assurance relief[3] is subject to a maximum of 1/6th of the taxpayer's income;[4] aggregation may increase the income and so give fuller effect to the relief. Age allowance (supra, § **3: 06**) is given when either of the spouses is over 65. This rule will change in 1990–91, subject to transitional relief.[5]

Simon's Taxes A3.304–A3.307, A3.310, E5.101–103; Butterworths Income Tax Service B6.01.
 [1] TA 1988, s. 279; FA 1976, s. 36.
 [2] Interest on loans taken out on or after 1 August 1988 are restricted to one £30,000 exemption per residence. However, the previous position will continue for loans taken out before that date, see infra, § **5: 30**.
 [3] Given on contracts made before 14th March 1984 only.
 [4] Infra, § **28: 03**.
 [5] TA 1988, ss. 257 and 257F; the married couple's allowance will be transferrable: TA 1988. s. 257A. All these sections are added by FA 1988, s. 33.

Non aggregation

3: 10   The aggregation rule is subject to four exceptions:

(1) It does not apply to the year of marriage.

(2) It applies only where the wife is living with her husband.[1] If a wife is separated from her husband by court order or separation deed or in such circumstances that the separation is likely to be permanent, the spouses are treated as separate persons. (The husband loses his claim to a married man's allowance once he is under a legally enforceable obligation to pay her money by way of maintenance.[2] If, however, he maintains her wholly[3] and voluntarily he may keep the larger allowance even though their incomes are not aggregated.[4])

(3) If the wife is living with her husband but only one of them is resident in the United Kingdom for the year of assessment, or both of them are resident but one is and the other is not absent from the United Kingdom

throughout that year, they are to be treated as if they were separate persons, and so separately assessed and their income not aggregated; this is subject to the rule that their total tax bill must not be increased, although it may be decreased.[5]

(4) If both spouses so elect the wife is charged to tax on her earned income as if she were a single woman with no other income. The election must be made during the year of assessment or six months before or twelve months after that year.[6] An election once made continues for subsequent years. Revocation must be joint.

After such an election the husband's married man's allowance is reduced to that of a single person,[7] but the wife may claim a single person's personal relief (but not the wife's earned income allowance). The wife can claim other reliefs as if she were a single person such as premiums paid by her in respect of a life policy on the life of herself or her husband.[8] She may also claim relief for the support of a dependent relative but neither husband nor wife may claim the age allowance. Neither can claim relief under TA 1988, s. 259 infra, § **3: 15**.

Earned income in respect of which the election may be made includes all the income normally classified as earned but not social security benefits[9] nor any pension she may receive by virtue of her husband's—as opposed to her own—National Insurance contributions or his past services.[10] Deductions such as capital allowances or loss relief which would normally be set off against her earned income, as where it relates to her trade, must be so set off and cannot be used against her investment income, or any income of his. Any deductions due in respect of interest or annual payments made by her can reduce only her earnings not her investment income. Similar payments by the husband can be deducted from his income including therefore the investment income of either of them.[11] An enterprise allowance is earned income despite being taxed under Schedule D, Case VI.[12]

Simon's Taxes E5.104, 110, 115.

[1] TA 1988, ss. 279 and 282.

[2] If the wife has the children she may be able to claim relief of £1,590 under TA 1988, s. 259, infra, § **3: 15**, a sum equal to the drop in the husband's allowance.

[3] If W receives a small income in her own right but the bulk of her maintenance comes from H, his claim is in practice admitted. **Simon Taxes E5.104**.

[4] Any maintenance paid by the husband is treated as a gift and so not as the wife's income. The wife can claim her earned income allowance. See further infra, § **9: 45**.

[5] TA 1988, s. 282(2); *Gubay v Kington* [1984] STC 99.

[6] TA 1988, s. 287.

[7] TA 1988, s. 287(4)–(6).

[8] TA 1988, Sch. 14, para. 1(2).

[9] Child benefit is not taxable. The Category A retirement pension is earned income for this purpose. On invalid care allowance, see TA 1988, s. 287(2)(*b*).

[10] TA 1988, s. 287(2).

[11] TA 1988, s. 287(7).

[12] TA 1988, s. 127. See infra, § **7: 41**.

3: 11   Unless the couple have a combined income sufficient to attract tax at more than basic rate, an election for separate taxation will be disadvantageous since the husband's personal allowance is reduced. For 1989–90 an election would not generally be advantageous until the total joint income exceeds £30,511 and the separated income is at least £7,026. (The separated income may be less where the total joint income is greater.) A table is provided at the front of this work.

EXAMPLE (1989–90)

	Joint taxation	Separate taxation of wife's earnings	
		H	W
Income	£30,510	£23,485	£7,025
Deduct—personal relief	4,375	2,785	2,785
Wife's earned income relief	2,785		
	£23,350	£20,700	£4,240
Tax at 25% 20,700	5,175	5,175	1,060
Tax at 40% 2,651	1,060	—	—
	£6,235	£5,175	£1,060
		£6,235	

Separate assessment

3: 12   A wife is assessed separately from her husband in three situations:—

(1) Where she is taxed separately, supra, § **3: 10**.

(2) The husband may disclaim responsibility for any tax in respect of her income which remains unpaid at her death regardless of the year in which payment became due.[1] This places exclusive responsibility on the wife's estate so reducing its value for IHT. Notice must be served on the personal representatives.

(3) Either spouse may elect to be assessed as if they were single persons.[2] If this election is made the value of the reliefs has to be allocated between the spouses.[3] Life assurance relief (given on pre-14th March 1984 contracts) is allocated according to the premiums paid by each. This election will cease to be relevant when independent taxation begins in 1990–91.

Such an election may be made by either husband or wife in the six months before 6th July in the appropriate tax year, i.e. an election for the income tax year 1988–89 must be made by 6th July 1980. The election remains in force until it is revoked which must be done before 6th July in the tax year in question, i.e. a revocation in respect of the income tax year 1988–89 must also be made before 6th July 1988.

The election does not affect the tax payable but makes each spouse responsible for his or her share of the total tax burden. It is necessary to protect the husband who might otherwise have to pay tax in respect of his wife's income without ever receiving that income.

Under an election the procedure is as follows:

(1) calculate total tax payable on the combined income at basic and higher rates taking no account of any personal reliefs available;

(2) apportion the tax between husband and wife in the ratio of their separate incomes dealing with basic and higher rate tax in the ratio of separate total incomes;

(3) work out the tax saving which arises on the couple's personal allowances remembering that the married man's allowance is appropriate unless a separate election has been made for wife's earned income relief. These are divided between husband and wife on the basis that relief for children not of the marriage, if still available, and dependent relative relief is given to the spouse who maintains them and the remaining allowances are split in the ratio of total tax payable before allowances.

Where the normal rule applies the husband is responsible for tax in respect of his wife's income, but he is only primarily responsible. Tax attributable to the wife's income may be recovered from the wife.[4] The wife does not by this or any other procedure become responsible for tax on her husband's income. Any repayment of tax on the wife's income belongs to the wife.[5] Repayments under Schedule E are now paid direct to the wife; the repayment may be due to an overpayment by her and is due even where the repayment arises from the husband having insufficient income to absorb his personal allowances. The rule does not apply in years in which the husband is subject to higher rates of tax, or for which the wife has earnings outside Schedule E, e.g. business income.[6] This is presumably to allow the Revenue to set the repayment against other tax liabilities.[7]

A husband has to make a return of all his income where the spouses have elected for separate assessment. Separate returns may be made but the Board may seek further returns from the other spouse.[8]

Simon's Taxes E2.1118, E5.116; Butterworths Income Tax Service B6.07.
[1] TA 1988, s. 286.
[2] TA 1988, s. 283.
[3] TA 1988, s. 284.
[4] TA 1988, s. 285, and see *Johnson v IRC* [1978] 2 All ER 65, [1978] STC 196.
[5] *Re Cameron, Kingsley v IRC* [1965] 3 All ER 474, 42 TC 539.
[6] TA 1988, s. 281.
[7] Revenue Press Release dated 4th December 1979, see *Simon's Tax Intelligence* 1979, p. 498.
[8] TA 1988, ss. 284(4), 287(9) and (10).

Child allowances

3: 13 These reliefs[1] were abolished as from the start of 1979–80 following the introduction of the child benefit scheme.

The presence of children may give rise to a claim for the additional allowance under TA 1988, s. 259, infra, § **3: 15**.

Income of children is not usually aggregated with that of their parents. The only exception now is certain income derived from settlements made by the parents.[2] There is however no aggregation of income under such settlements if the income is accumulated. The consequence is that many parents with sufficient means make accumulation settlements in favour of their children.

Simon's Taxes E2.6, E5.2; Butterworths Income Tax Service B4.06.
[1] TA 1970, s. 10.
[2] Infra § **13: 32**.

Reform

3: 14   The rationale of the old tax relief for children was obscured by its meanness: the relief was little more than a gesture. The reliefs were abolished as a corollary of the introduction of the tax-free child benefit[1] towards the recognition of the expense of fulfilling a vital social role—the bringing up of children; hence the interest in using the money that might be saved by abolishing the married man's allowance to increase child benefit.

If the parents both go out to work and incur expense in looking after the children, those expenses are not deductible whether in computing general income or that from the particular source. By contrast, a quite distinct form of relief is available under American and Canadian law which allow deduction of actual costs on child care when a parent goes out to work. Such deductions are limited by a maximum figure and by the age of the children. These limits are an attempt to distinguish the expense of going out to work from mere personal expenses—the relief is designed to meet the emotional appeal of a claim by working mothers and not simply to subsidise domestic service. The precedent of the relief is important because the expense is incurred for a mixture of business and personal reasons. If the claim is allowed why should relief not be given to handicapped persons who incur expenses in riding to work by taxi or to professional people who incur expenses in obtaining qualifications or to wage earners who incur expenses in moving from job to job?[2]

---

[1] For those who pay tax there is no pecuniary difference between having £500 of his income relieved from tax and receiving a tax free state benefit equal to the tax on that amount of income. It should also be noted that child benefit payments are made to the mother.

[2] See Pechman, 8 Nat Tax Jo p. 120 and Arnold (1973) Canadian Tax Journal 176.

Additional personal allowance: TA 1988, s. 259

3: 15   TA 1988, s. 259 allows a deduction of £1,590 in respect of children resident with the claimant if the claimant is (i) a married man whose wife is totally incapacitated or (ii) a widow, widower or other person—e.g. a divorcee or a wife living apart from her husband or a relative or a foster parent—not entitled to the married man's allowance of £4,375 under s. 8. When the claimant is in class (ii) the claim can only be granted if the child resides with the claimant during that part of the year of assessment in which the claimant is not married and living with his or her spouse, a matter of importance on remarriage.

The child must be "a qualifying child"; this is a child who is under 16 or who satisfies certain conditions. Those conditions are that at the start of the tax year the child must be either (i) the claimant's or (ii) one under 18 years of age at the start of the tax year and who is maintained for the whole or part of the year by the claimant at his own expense. However, when the child is not the claimant's it is not necessary for the claimant to have custody: residence suffices. This means that a claimant may obtain relief in respect of his brother or sister if the other conditions of the relief are satisfied.

When two or more persons are entitled to claim the relief it may be split. In default of agreement apportionment is carried out according to the length of the periods of residence rather than the level of maintenance. When there are two children, one with each parent, it seems that each parent can claim this relief. When two or more children reside with an unmarried couple living together as husband and wife, each adult can claim the benefit of this allowance. However, in an effort to ensure that an unmarried couple do not obtain a tax benefit greater than that which a married couple can get, this has now ceased.[1] The practical problems of proving cohabitation, which have been daunting in the law of social security, are completely ignored.

A child whose birthday is 6th April is taken to be over the age of 16 or 18 at the start of the year beginning with his 16th or 18th birthday.[2]

This relief is not affected by the number of children nor by the level of the child's income.

This relief is of the greatest practical importance. Its level is now constant as the difference between a single person's relief and a married person's relief. Child benefit is paid to the mother. It is essential from a tax planning aspect to ensure that reliefs are not allowed to waste in one spouse's hands when they could be of use in the other's; see further, infra, § **9: 96**.

Simon's Taxes E2.502; Butterworths Income Tax Service B4.08.
  [1] FA 1988, s. 30.
  [2] TA 1988, s. 259(*a*).

Medical insurance

3: 16   As from 6th April 1990 an individual aged 60 or over and resident in the UK will be able to claim a personal relief for sums spent on medical insurance.[1] This relief will also be open to a taxpayer who pays the insurance premium for a qualifying individual, an interesting revival of a dependant relation's allowance. The relief extends only to insurance; there is no deduction for the costs of medical treatment.

  [1] FA 1989, ss. 54–57.

Blind person's relief: TA 1988, s. 265

3: 17   A registered blind person is entitled to a deduction[1] of £540. The deduction may be claimed by a married man whose wife living with him is blind. Should they both be blind the figure is £1,080. A claim under s. 264 is alternative to this. The person must be registered with a local authority for at least a part of the year; this excludes non-residents.

Simon's Taxes E2.8; Butterworths Income Tax Service B4.12.
  [1] TA 1988, s. 265; FA 1987, s. 28.

Life assurance relief

3: 18   See infra, § **28: 03**. This relief does not apply to policies taken out or amended after 13th March 1984.

Charges on income

3: 19   Reliefs take the form of deduction from total income. Where any of the claimant's income is such that he can charge the income tax on it against any other person or deduct, satisfy or retain that tax out of any payment, e.g. annuities which he pays to another, he is not entitled to relief in respect of such income.[1] Since the scheme allows for deduction of tax only at the basic rate, relief can be claimed to the extent, if any, that the relief would exceed tax at the basic rate on that income.

Simon's Taxes E1.5, E3.207.
  [1] TA 1988, s. 276 and see infra § **9: 76.**

Joint income

3: 20   Joint income (e.g. partnership income) is treated as several and divided according to the interests in it.[1]

---

  [1] TA 1988, s. 277; and see *Lewis v IRC* [1933] 2 K B 557, 18 TC 174, CA.

Non-residents

3: 21   Individuals who are not resident[1] are entitled to personal reliefs only if they fall within certain categories and then only on a special basis. The categories[2] are (i) British subject; (ii) citizen of the Republic of Ireland; (iii) a person who is or has been employed in the service of the Crown; (iv) one who is employed in the service of any missionary society; (v) one who is in the service of any territory under Her Majesty's protection; (vi) one who is resident in the Channel Islands or Isle of Man; (vii) one who has previously resided within the UK but who is compelled to live abroad for reasons of health or the health of a member of his or her family resident with him or her (viii) the widow whose late husband was in the service of the Crown. In addition some double taxation treaties provide for relief of non-residents as if they were British subjects.[3]

Non-residents are entitled to that proportion of their personal relief which their United Kingdom income bears to their world-wide income which must be declared for these purposes.[4]

This proportion is that ratio which the UK taxable income bears to world wide incomes subject, however, to a minimum amount of UK tax. This minimum is a fraction of the UK tax that would be payable if all the taxpayer's income was subject to UK tax. The fraction is A/B when A is UK taxable income and B total income. Income which is subject to a special rate of UK tax under a double tax treaty, e.g. dividends, is treated as not being UK income.[5] Where the taxpayer is married and his wife has income which is not subject to UK tax it has been held that the wife's income is not relevant to B.[6]

As from 1990–91 qualifying non-residents will receive their allowances in full and the proportion machinery will no longer apply.[7] Also, as from 1990–91 the new married couples allowance under s. 257A will be transferable by a husband to his wife if she is resident or a qualifying non-resident. However, the special transitional rules in s. 257D will not apply.

EXAMPLE
   Husband and wife are British subjects domiciled in England and Wales. In 1982 they went to live abroad in a country with the relevant clause in the UK double tax treaty and where they are both employed. In their absence from the UK they have let their house and they have some dividend income some of which arises in the UK and some abroad. Their income for 1989–90 is as follows.

	World income		UK taxable income	UK tax deducted
	£	£	£	£
Salary H		30,000		
Salary W		15,000		
Rent from house		3,250	3,250	812.50
Dividends: UK		5,000	5,000	1,250.00
overseas		3,000		
		56,250	8,250	
Personal reliefs				
Married persons allowance	4,095		4,095	
Wifes earned income relief	2,605			
		6,700		
		£49,550	£4,155	

Tax chargeable					
Basic and higher rates					
@ 25%	20,700	5,175	4,155	1,038.75	
@ 40%	28,850	11,540			
	£49,550	£16,715	£4,155	£1,038.75	£2,062.50

Tax chargeable on world income £16,715
Tax chargeable on UK taxable income £1,038.75

$$\text{Tax must not be reduced below } \frac{8,250}{56,250} \times 16,715 = £2,451$$

No repayment due for 1989–90.

Simon's Taxes E6.201–207; Butterworths Income Tax Service H1.13.
   [1] The non-residence is that of the taxpayer; the residence of dependants for whom he claims is usually irrelevant.
   [2] TA 1988, s. 278(2).
   [3] E.g. Fiji SI 1976 No. 1342, art. 23 and France S.I. 1968 No. 1869, art. 23.
   [4] TA 1988, s. 278(3).
   [5] TA 1988, s. 278(5) and (6).
   [6] *IRC v Addison* [1984] STC 540. On consequent practice see SP 7/85, **Simon's Taxes, Division H3.2**.
   [7] FA 1988, s. 31.

TAXATION AND SOCIAL SECURITY[1]

3: 22 Payments under the social security system are broadly of two sorts. The first are benefits as of right and without means test. The second are supplementary benefits. These are means tested and act as a safety net for those who fall through the primary system of benefit.

Some benefits arising are liable to tax. Retirement pensions are taxable under Schedule E[1] (i) as are widow's benefits, which consist of a widow's allowance for the first twenty six weeks of widowhood (which may be continued as the widowed mother's allowance if there are dependent children), (ii) the widow's pension which is payable if she is over 40, (iii) allowances for guardians, and (iv) the special allowance paid to the mother who looked to her divorced husband for maintenance for the dependent children, who has not remarried and whose husband has just died.

The new receipts basis for Schedule E does not apply to these benefits.[2]

---

[1] TA 1988, s. 617(1). On foreign benefits, see Extra-statutory concession A24 (1988), **Simon's Taxes, Division H2.2**.

[2] FA 1989, s. 41.

3: 23   Payments which are not taxable[1] are sickness and industrial injury benefit (save for pensions and allowances to widows and parents), invalidity benefit, attendance allowance, maternity benefit (which consists of a maternity grant to help with expenses and, for those mothers returning to work, a maternity allowance for the period they are unable to work) and death grant, a sum payable to the estate of a deceased person for funeral expenses.

Some supplementary benefits are taxable.[2] These include unemployment benefit (excluding any earnings-related supplement) supplementary benefit paid to unemployed persons (once unemployment benefit has expired) and supplementary benefit paid to strikers. Such payments will be paid gross. PAYE adjustments are made later. The benefit is earned income and a married woman's unemployment benefit will qualify for wife's earned income relief. The supplementary benefits are taxable if paid under the urgent cases regulations (save where paid to a striker). Benefits remaining non-taxable are rent and child allowances to war widows, child benefit payment, training allowances, and grants for maintaining a vehicle owned by a disabled person.

Simons Taxes E2.402; E3.202, 203; E4.104, 328, 329, 721; **Butterworths Income Tax Service B6.13.**

[1] Exemption is given by TA 1988, s. 617; this was done for reasons of practicality—most are short term.

[2] TA 1988, s. 617(1).

Reform

3: 24   The social security system has been recast by the Social Security Act 1986 but the new scheme of benefits is not to be brought into full effect until April 1988.[1] FA 1987 therefore provides for the system of exemption of some benefits and charges on others to be revised as from the date they are brought into force.[2]

The following are to be exempt from tax:

(*a*) income support (subject to an exception outlined below)

(*b*) family credit,

(*c*) housing benefit,

(*d*) child benefit, and

(*e*) various benefits at present excluded by being specifically mentioned in TA 1988, s. 617(1) and which are mentioned in § **3: 23** above.

(It should be noted that the death grant is to be abolished.) The list of payments exempt as a result of (*e*) includes maternity allowance, widow's payments, invalidity benefit, attendance allowance and mobility allowance.

Income support is to be taxable (under Schedule E) in two situations.[3] The first is that in which the claimant's right to income support depends on his being available for employment. The second is where the claimant is one of a couple, whether married or unmarried,[4] and the claimant (but not the other) is involved in a trade dispute as a result of which the income support is reduced.[5] This rule of taxability is subject to the qualification that where the income support exceeds the "taxable maximum,"[6] the excess is not taxable.[7]

One of the most important features of the new system concerns the interaction of the tax system and the social security system. By using net income rather than pre-tax income as relevant to entitlement it is hoped to avoid some of the problems of the poverty and unemployment traps.

---

[1] The principal features of the new system are explained in the Government White Paper—Reform of Social Security (Cmnd. 9691) December 1985.

[2] TA 1988, s. 617(2); on date of effectiveness see Sch. 30.

[3] TA 1988, s. 617(2).

[4] These couples are defined in Social Security Act 1986, s. 20(11).

[5] This is defined by reference to Social Security Act 1986, s. 23.

[6] Defined in TA 1988, s. 151.

[7] TA 1988, s. 151.

4 Investment income

Earned and investment income

4: 01 Until 1984 investment income was taxed more heavily than earned income.[1] This was achieved by a device known as the additional rate; in 1983–84 this was charged on so much of an individual's total income as consisted of investment income in excess of £7,100.[2]

The distinction between earned and investment income remains important for close companies, infra, § **27: 18**. It is also important in that a wife may be taxed separately from her husband (until the 1989 reforms take effect) in respect of her earned but not her investment income, supra, § **3: 11**. The distinction is also important for the wife's earned income relief and for retirement annuity calculations.

The most common types of investment income are interest, dividends and rent. FA 1984, however, made provision for income from furnished holiday accommodation to be treated as earned income with retrospective effect to 6th April 1982.[3]

The concept of the additional rate, although mostly abolished in 1984, was expressly retained for income of accumulation trusts.[4]

Simon's Taxes E1.104, E3.201, 202; Butterworths Income Tax Service B1.04, B1.05.
  [1] FA 1971, s. 32(1) (repealed by TA 1988, s. 844 and Sch. 31), and see *Ang v Parrish* [1980] 2 All ER 790, [1980] STC 341, infra, § **13: 01**.
  [2] F(No. 2)A 1983, s. 1 (repealed by TA 1988, s. 844 and Sch. 31).
  [3] TA 1988, s. 504.
  [4] TA 1988, s. 832 (1) (and the virtually obsolete development gains tax, abolished in 1985).

Definitions

4: 02 Investment income is that which is not earned income. The question whether income is earned is one of law.[1] Earned income is defined, subject to minor variations for particular contexts,[2] in TA 1988, s. 833 (4)–(7) which lists three main categories.

Simon's Taxes E3.201, 202; Butterworths Income Tax Service A1.67.
  [1] *Lawrance v Hayman* [1976] STC 227, 51 TC 376.
  [2] E.g. TA 1988, ss. 257 and 529.

(*a*) *any income arising in respect of any remuneration from any office or employment including pensions, superannuation or other allowances, deferred pay or compensation for loss of office.*

4: 03 These allowances may be in respect of the past service of the individual himself or of the individual's husband or parent or of any deceased person. Thus an allowance paid to the child of a former employee is earned income of the child. Individual includes wife unless they qualify, and elect, for separate taxation.

Income is earned within this rule if it is a reward for services. See infra, § **6: 19**. This means that any income within Schedule E will be earned. In *Dale v IRC*[1] annuity payments to a trustee "so long as he acts as trustee" were held by the House of Lords to be earned income. In that case the trustee was to receive the payments. It was said that the amount and value of the work actually done was irrelevant.[2] The Revenue argued that since a trustee was not entitled to remuneration for his services as distinct from the reimbursement of expenses, the annuity was a conditional gift. However it was held that since the condition of the annuity was compliance with the testator's condition of serving as a trustee[3] the income was earned.

The form in which the income is received is irrelevant. Hence dividends may be earned income, despite being technically within Schedule F and not E, provided they are a reward for services.

In *White v Franklin*[4] the taxpayer was assistant managing director of a company. His mother and brother settled 50% of the issued share capital to trust to pay the income to the taxpayer "so long as he shall be engaged in the management of the company," with remainder over to the mother and others. It was held that his income from the trust was earned income. The Commissioners had found that the settlement had been made as an inducement to him to remain with the company, and so the income accrued to him because, not simply while, he was an active director.[5] It was also important that the trust held a large block of shares in the employing company so that the taxpayer's work would produce direct results. These however are matters of fact to support the inference that the purpose of the settlement was to keep the taxpayer interested in the company and not simply an arrangement in a family settlement distributing income arising from family property to persons with certain qualifications.[6]

If a payment of income is not only in return for services but also for some other consideration, there can be no apportionment of the income so as to treat even a part of it as earned.[7] The question is one of the construction of the arrangement.

Simon's Taxes E3.203, E4.465; Butterworths Income Tax Service B1.04.

[1] [1953] 2 All ER 671; 34 TC 468.
[2] Per Lord Normand, ibid, at 30 and 493.
[3] Per Lord Normand, ibid, at 77 and 491.
[4] [1965] 1 All ER 692, 42 TC 283, [1965] BTR 152 (STC).
[5] Case stated: 42 TC 283 at 284.
[6] [1965] 1 All ER at 699, 42 TC at 297.
[7] *Hale v Shea* [1965] 1 All ER 155, 42 TC 260.

(*b*) *any income from any property which is attached to or forms part of the employment of any office or employment of profit held by the individual.*

4: 04   In *White v Franklin*, supra, an argument based on this provision was not pursued. The provision has remained unchanged since the days of the old Schedule A and its purpose may have been to treat as earned income the imputed income arising from beneficial occupation of property.[1] It might be needed to treat as earned income the benefit received by an employee for accommodation under TA 1988, s. 194, infra, § **6: 52**. Another example is dividend income from shares held under an employee participation scheme.[2]

Simon's Taxes E3.204; Butterworths Income Tax Service B1.04.

[1] This was introduced to protect the vicar's income from tithe rent charges on glebe land.

[2] *Recknell v IRC* [1952] 2 All ER 147, 33 TC 201.

(c) *any income which is charged under Schedule D if it is immediately derived by the individual from a trade, profession or vocation carried on by him as an individual or as a partner personally acting in the partnership.*[1]

4: 05   The trade must have been carried on by the individual. In *Fry v Shiels Trustees*[2] trustees legally owned and managed a business the income of which was held for infant beneficiaries. It was held that the income was not earned since the profits were earned by the trustees and so by individuals who certainly did not own them. A trustee-beneficiary would in such circumstances presumably be allowed to treat his income as earned and would be allowed to keep the benefit for himself.

More difficulty has come from the requirement that the profit must be derived immediately from the business, since it suggests that other profits equally taxable under one of these Schedules are not derived immediately, but only incidentally. An example is *Northend v White, Leonard and Corbin Greener*[3] where Templeman J, held that interest accruing to a solicitor on money deposited at a bank on general deposit account was investment income. The reason was that the source was not the carrying on of the profession but rather the loan deposit with the bank. This conclusion has been criticised. It rests on a statement by Pennycuick J in *Bucks v Bowers*,[4] a statement that may be only a dictum;[5] moreover the decision in that case was later reversed by statute.[6]

Income in the form of dividends cannot be earned income, under rule (c),[7] because dividends fall within Schedule F and so cannot fall within any other Schedule.

Simon's Taxes E3.205; Butterworths Income Tax Service B1.04.

[1] Cf. TA 1970, s. 122(2)(*b*) (repealed FA 1974).

[2] 1915 SC 159, 6 TC 583.

[3] [1975] STC 317, 50 TC 121, the interest belonged to the solicitor thanks to Solicitors Act 1965, s. 8(2).

[4] [1970] 2 All ER 202, 46 TC 267.

[5] The main concern seems to have been whether interest subject to deduction of tax at source could fit in with the words on s. 833(4)(*c*).

[6] FA 1971, s. 32(4) so that interest and dividends accruing to those who deal in securities and shares will be earned income if derived from stock in trade; on the significance of this reversal see the decision of the House of Lords in *Thomson v Moyse*, infra, § **34: 18**. This rule was itself repealed by FA 1984, Sch. 23.

[7] TA 1988, s. 20; Schedule F was created in 1965. This was subject to FA 1971, s. 32(4), supra n. 6.

Miscellaneous

4: 06 Certain types of income were declared to be earned income. These were income in respect of a Civil List pension, voluntary pensions,[1] maternity benefits and other social security benefits[2] and certain annuities granted under Agriculture Act 1967. Also declared to be earned income are post cessation receipts, infra, § **7: 137**, income from the sale of patent rights for an invention actually devised by the taxpayer infra, § **8: 55**, and golden handshakes, infra, § **6: 42**. Pensions to former employees are earned income, infra, § **30: 11**. Enterprise allowance payments are earned income,[3] as is income from furnished holiday lettings.[4]

Maintenance payments are investment income.[5]

Retirement income of a self employed person will generally be investment income. This is mitigated in three ways. First he may have been able to take advantage of the retirement annuity schemes, annuities payable being earned income, infra, § **30: 15**. Secondly he may take advantage of TA 1988, s. 656 and treat a part of a purchased annuity payment as the repayment of capital, infra, § **28: 20**; the portion which is treated as income is investment income. Alternatively, or in addition, he may arrange a consultant's post with his former firm.

Annuities to former partners or their widows or dependants, are treated as earned income subject to certain limits.[6] These are 50% of the partner's share of the profits over the best three years of the last seven during which he was required to devote substantially the whole of his time to the partnership and, for this purpose, the partner's share of the partnership profits for the first six years of the seven is now to be increased to reflect the increase in the retail price index (RPI) up to the month of December in the seventh year.[7] If an employee himself makes provision for the payment of an annuity should he suffer long term disability, the sums payable will be investment income. If however the employer takes out such a policy not only will he be able to deduct the premiums he pays out but the sums received by the employee will be earned income if the proceeds of the policy are paid to the employer and he makes a payment to the employee.

Simon's Taxes E3.203, 211; Butterworths Income Tax Service B1.04.

[1] TA 1988, s. 133.

[2] TA 1988, s. 617 but not for all purposes, e.g. TA 1988, s. 257 and TA 1988, s. 287(2).

[3] TA 1988, s. 127(3), § **7.41–43**.

[4] TA 1988, s. 503(1).

[5] FA 1974, s. 15 was applied only to exclude them from the additional rate.

[6] TA 1988, s. 628(1).

[7] TA 1988, s. 628(3). For RPI figures from January 1965 onwards, see the table at the beginning of this book.

5 Deductions and calculations

LOSS RELIEF

5: 01 In closely prescribed circumstances a loss may give rise to a relief from tax by being set against an equivalent amount of income and relieving that income from any liability to tax.

Simon's Taxes E1.6; Butterworths Income Tax Service B3.

Trading losses

(a) TA 1988, s. 380 : set off against general income of that and the next year

5: 02 If a person sustains a loss in his trade, profession, employment or vocation, the correct figure for his profits chargeable to tax is nil. He may then claim relief under TA 1988, s. 380 from tax of an amount of his taxable income equal to the amount of his loss.[1] If he has no other income he cannot claim relief. The loss is calculated in the same way as profits.[2]

The relief is claimed against the income taxed in that year. Income earned in a previous year but taxed in that year thanks to the preceding year basis, e.g. income of the trade, is therefore available for relief. Thus current loss may be set off against previous profit of the same source, and, by giving instant relief, the law avoids exacerbating the loss situation which would follow if in addition to financing a loss on the current year money had to be found to pay for the tax on the previous year's profit. Strictly speaking, the relief should be given on the loss accruing within the tax year but in practice the Revenue accepts a claim based on the loss of the accounting period ending within the tax year. The strict basis must be used, however, on either party's insistence and the Revenue insists on its use in (a) the first three years of a business (the first four if the assessment for the third year is on the actual basis); (b) the year of permanent discontinuance and (c) any year immediately following a year in which the strict basis is used.

Relief is given against income "of the corresponding class" before other income. The corresponding class refers to earned and investment income. So if income from the trade which has sustained the loss is, as will usually be the case, earned income, the loss must be set off against earned income[3] and only then against investment income. Where the trading income would be unearned—e.g. where the taxpayer is a sleeping partner—it will be set against investment income first.

Relief may also be set against income of the spouse and again income of the corresponding class is used first. However, three qualifications are made. First a taxpayer may elect that relief should not be set against income of the spouse.[4] Secondly, if the taxpayer with the loss is a married woman who has elected to be taxed separately in respect of her earned income, the relief may only be set against her earned income; her investment income and all her spouse's income is not available for the relief. Thirdly, where the election for separate taxation of wife's earned income is in force, the husband may not set his loss against her earned income.

Simon's Taxes E1.602; Butterworths Income Tax Service B3.11.
[1] TA 1988, s. 380(1). On loss in an opening period, see infra, § **5: 08**.
[2] TA 1988, s. 382(4).
[3] TA 1988, s. 382(2).
[4] TA 1988, s. 382(1).

5: 03   To the extent that a loss is not completely set off against general taxable income of that year it may be set off against that of the following year provided that the trade, profession, employment or vocation is carried on in that following year.[1] The legislation simply says "in" the following year and there is probably no requirement that it be carried on throughout that year. Discontinuance under TA 1988, s. 113 is ignored for this purpose provided that at least one person continues the trade.[2] Should the trade sustain a loss in that following year, the loss carried forward from the previous year is used first.

By TA 1988, s. 383 unused capital allowances are treated in the same way as losses.[3]

EXAMPLE

TA 1988, s. 380 LOSSES
A trades to the 5th April annually and he and his wife have other income. His profits for 3 years are as follows:

				Assessments	
Year to 5/4/86	Profit	£4,000	1986–87	£4,000
5/4/87	Loss	£12,000	1987–88	nil
5/4/88	Profit	£14,000	1988–89	£14,000

He has other income (interest) to be taxed as follows:

	Self	Wife
1986–87	£1,200	£3,000
1987–88	£1,300	£2,000
1988–89	£1,400	£2,500

His wife has profits from her hairdressing business to be assessed as follows:

1986–87	£2,100
1987–88	£1,700
1988–89	£2,000

If s. 380 (s. 168) is claimed the loss will be used as follows:

Loss:		£12,000

1986–87	Profits	4,000
,,	Interest self	1,200
,,	Business wife	2,100
,,	Interest wife	3,000
		£10,300

This leaves £1,700 to carry forward and offset against personal assessment for profits in 1988–89. However it has the effect of wasting personal allowances of A and his wife in 1986–87. It would be better therefore to elect not to offset the losses against the spouse's income in 1986–87 thus saving allowances and leaving more losses to be set off in 1988–89 against the larger profits. The losses would then be used as follows:

1986–87	Profits self	4,000
	Interest self	1,200
1988–89	Profits self	6,800
		£12,000

Simon's Taxes E1.604; Butterworths Income Tax Service B3.11, B3.15.
[1] TA 1988, s. 380(2). This is because of the difficulty in determining exactly when a loss item is incurred.
[2] TA 1988, s. 380(3).
[3] For unused capital allowances on cessation of business see extra-statutory concession A8 (1988), **Simon's Taxes, Division H2.2.**

(b) Restriction on TA 1988, s. 380: TA 1988, s. 117

5: 04   Where there is a limited partnership the limited partner's capital contribution (and so the amount of risk he bears) is limited. The agreement may nonetheless provide that the trading loss of the partnership should be attributed to the limited partners in full. In *Reed v Young*[1] it was held that relief could be claimed under TA 1988, s. 380 even where the loss so attributed exceeded the amount of capital at risk. TA 1988, s. 117(1)(a) limits the relief given under s. 380. The restrictions apply both to limited partnerships registered as such and to similar arrangements limiting liability.[2] Relief is limited to "the relevant sum" which is the amount of the capital contribution at "the appropriate time" which is, broadly, the end of the relevant year of assessment. These restrictions apply to reliefs under TA 1988, ss. 380 and 381 (infra, § **5: 09**), CAA 1968, s. 353 (infra, § **5: 29**) and CAA 1968, s. 71 (infra, § **8: 07**); in essence these reliefs are available only to the extent that the taxpayers capital is actually at risk and all other losses must be carried forward for relief under TA 1988, s. 385.

Simon's Taxes E5.318; Butterworths Income Tax Service C8.61.
[1] [1986] STC 285.
[2] TA 1988, s. 117(2); a Budget Press Release refers to persons participating in joint venture arrangements when liability is limited, *Simon's Tax Intelligence* 1985, p. 147; the phraseology covers, e.g., non-recourse loans. The restrictions apply to losses of periods beginning after 19th March 1985 and to losses of periods straddling that date when the limited nature of the partnership arises after that date.

(c) TA 1988, s. 385: rolling forward of trading losses

5: 05 To the extent that relief for the allowable loss has not been given against general income under s. 380 the loss may be carried forward and set off, not against the general income of subsequent years, but only against the future profits (if any) of the trade.[1] The relief must be given against the earliest profits available.[2] Where the trade has received income taxed by deduction at source such as interest or dividends the loss carried forward under s. 385 can be set off against that taxed income and a repayment claim made. This applies whenever the payment received under deduction would have been treated as trading profits but for the fact that tax had already been deducted.[3]

> **EXAMPLE**
> A makes up his accounts on a calendar year basis. His figures are as follows:

Trading year 1st Jan. to 31st Dec.	Profit for year of assessment		Loss relief	Taxable profit
1983 +6,000				
1984 +3,000	1984–85	6,000		6,000
1985 −3,000	1985–86	3,000	−3,000 (s. 380)	nil
1986 −2,000	1986–87	nil	nil	nil
1987 +5,000	1987–88	nil	−2,000	nil
	1988–89	5,000	−2,000 (B/fd s. 385)	3,000

The right to roll losses forward is available only so long as the taxpayer carries on the trade, and so is lost if there is a discontinuance of the trade. Provision is made however for two situations where the discontinuance is technical rather than commercial (infra, §§ **5.06, 07**).

Simon's Taxes E1.610–617; Butterworths Income Tax Service B3.21.
[1] TA 1988, s. 385(1); see *Gordon and Blair Ltd v IRC* (1962) 40 TC 358 and infra, § **7: 54**.
[2] TA 1988, s. 385(3).
[3] TA 1988, s. 385(4).

5: 06 *Incorporation of business.* First if the business is transferred to a company *and* the sole or main consideration is the transfer of shares of the company to the individual or his nominees, an accumulated loss may be carried forward.[1] This provision applies whether the business is incorporated or taken over by an existing company. The section does not allow the company to claim relief against the future profits of the trade but rather allows the individual to claim relief against income derived by him from the company, whether by dividend or otherwise, for example under a service agreement, but the loss must be set off against earned income before being set off against distributions. In this way the trading loss can be set against income from the company no matter how the company makes its profits, e.g. from other trades. It is not necessary that the individual or his nominees own all the shares in the company. The relief may be claimed only so long as the company carries on the business and the individual pays tax.

In addition, the individual must be beneficially entitled to the shares throughout the tax year for which he claims relief.[2] Curiously there seems to be no requirement that the beneficial ownership be unbroken, only that it last throughout the year of assessment in question. If therefore he sells the shares but then buys them back he should be able to resume his loss claim in the year subsequent to that in which he bought them back.

Simon's Taxes E1.613; Butterworths Income Tax Service B3.31.
 [1] TA 1988, s. 386.
 [2] TA 1988, s. 386(3).

5: 07 *Partnership change.* The second exception arises when there is a discontinuance under TA 1988, s. 113. It would obviously be unjust were the retirement of a partner to cause his colleagues to lose the benefit of accumulated losses. It is therefore provided that the trade shall be treated as continuing.[1] A share of the loss sustained before the notional discontinuance can be set off by the continuing partner against his share of the profits after the change. A similar treatment is accorded to his share of unrelieved capital allowances.

Simon's Taxes E1.616; Butterworths Income Tax Service B3.51.
 [1] TA 1988, s. 385(5).

(*d*)　*Losses in opening years*

5: 08　Two problems have to be resolved. The first is to explain how the reliefs already outlined apply to the opening years; the second is to explain the relief in TA 1988, s. 381.

When a trade incurs a loss in a period used as the basis for more than one year, the relief may only be claimed once. This is because the theory of loss relief is that the trade's profits are nil and relief is given by separate provision.

EXAMPLE[1]

A began to trade on 1st June 1986. He made up his accounts to 31st March 1987 and his second set of accounts to 31st March 1988. His loss for the first ten months was £610; his profit for the second year was £2,420.

His assessments will be as follows:

	Trade figures £	Schedule D Case I assessment £	Loss relief £
1986–87 (actual 1.6.86–31.3.87)	−610	nil	–
1987–88　(1st 12 months 1.6.86–31.5.87)			
1.6.86–31.3.87	−610		
1.4.87–31.5.87 $\frac{2}{12} \times £2,420$	+403		
	−207	nil	403 (aggregation)
1988–89 (Previous year basis y/e 31.3.88)	2,420		
Less s. 385 relief	−207		
		2,213	207 (s. 385)
		£2,213	£610

The figure for loss relief in 1988–89 is £207 not £207+£610=£817. The loss of £610 is thus used up as to £403 in 1987–88 and £207 in 1988–89.

Simon's Taxes E1.604, 619; Butterworths Income Tax Service B3.02.
[1] *IRC v Scott Adamson* (1933) 17 TC 679 which provides the inspiration for the figures in the example; *Westward Television Ltd v Hart* [1968] 1 All ER 303, 45 TC 1.

5: 09   *Carry-back TA 1988, s. 381.* A carry-back of a trading loss is allowed where the loss arises in the year of assessment in which the trade is first carried on or the next three years of assessment. The loss may be carried back and set off against *general* income for the three years before that in which the loss is sustained, income of an earlier year is taken first, so a loss incurred in 1988–89 can be carried back to 1985–86. When the accounting period of the business goes past the end of the year of assessment in which the trade begins the loss in that period is apportioned.

EXAMPLE

A starts a business on 1.1.1988. His income for the years of assessment from 1984–85 is as follows:

		£
Salary	1984–85	5,500
	1985–86	6,700
	1986–87	7,000
9 months to 31.12.87	1987–88	3,500
Trading loss: year to 31.12.88		6,000
year to 31.12.89		12,000

He has personal allowances and reliefs totalling £3,500 in 1987–88

A's Loss will be:

		£
1987–88	$\frac{3}{12} \times £6,000$	1,500
1988–89	$\frac{9}{12} \times £6,000$	4,500
	$\frac{3}{12} \times £12,000$	3,000
		£7,500

A will not make a claim under s. 380 for 1987–88 since his income (£3,500) is covered by personal reliefs. He can therefore claim under s. 381 in respect of the losses both 1987–88 and 1988–89. The relief given will be as follows:

	£
1984–85	
Income	5,500
Less claim under s. 381 for 1987–88	1,500
Taxable	4,000
1985–86	
Income	6,700
Less claim under s. 381 for 1988–89	6,700
Taxable	nil
1986–87	
Income	7,000
Less claim under s. 381 for 1988–89 (£7,500–6,700) ·	800
Taxable	6,200

However, A still has £9,000 of his loss in the year to 31.12.89 to use and this may be carried back to 1986–87 under s. 381.

Although the relief applies both to trades and to professions, it applies only to individuals.

If a trade is acquired from a spouse the four tax years run from the date that the spouse began to trade.[1] However this restriction applies only when the claimant acquired the trade from a spouse to whom he was then married and with whom he was then living; it follows that this restriction does not apply where he succeeds to a trade on the death of the other spouse.

The loss is computed in the same way as for TA 1988, s. 380 so capital allowances may also be carried back.[2] The loss is set off primarily against income of the corresponding class i.e. earned income before investment income and a married man can insist that the loss be set off only against his income.

Although relief may be claimed under both TA 1988, s. 380 and TA 1988, s. 381, and the claimant may decide in which order to apply the reliefs, the loss cannot be apportioned between them.[3]

The calculations involved in deciding whether or not to claim this relief must take into account other elections such as separate taxation of wife's earnings, stock relief, capital allowances and the basis of assessment for opening years, TA 1988, s. 62.

Partnership. Partners in an overseas partnership can claim the relief.

Where a partnership includes a corporate member no relief can be claimed on losses incurred in the business of leasing plant and machinery.[4]

A cessation and commencement under TA 1988, s. 113 does not enable the continuing partners to use the new relief in respect of losses in the four years after the change; however, the new partner can claim the relief.[5]

The restrictions as to losses incurred by limited partnerships apply here also.[6]

Simon's Taxes E1.619; Butterworths Income Tax Service B3.41.

[1] TA 1988, s. 381(5).
[2] TA 1988, s. 383.
[3] *Butt v Haxby* [1983] STC 239.
[4] TA 1988, s. 297(7).
[5] TA 1988, s. 381(6).
[6] TA 1988, s. 117(1), supra, § **5: 04.**

(e) *Terminal losses TA 1988, s. 388*

5: 10 Once a trade, profession or vocation has been permanently discontinued, there can ex hypothesi be no carry forward of a loss under TA 1988, s. 385. A terminal loss may however be carried *back* and set off against the profits charged under Schedule D in respect of the trade for the three years last preceding that in which the trade ends.[1] Relief is given as far as possible from the assessment of a later rather than earlier year. Assessments may thus have to be reopened.

EXAMPLE
Terminal loss relief

A trader retires at 30th September 1988. His results for the four years to 31st March 1988 and for the final six months were as follows:

Assessments

Year ended	31.3.1985	£12,000		
	31.3.1986	£11,000	1985–86	£12,000
	31.3.1987	£9,000	1986–87	£11,000
	31.3.1988	£4,000	1987–88	£9,000
Period to	30.9.1988	−£14,000	1988–89	£4,000

As 1988–89 will be revised to actual, i.e. nil under s. 63, infra, § **7.43**, s. 388 relief will be available for setting off as follows:

1987–88	£9,000 leaving nil taxable
1986–87	£5,000 leaving £6,000 taxable

£14,000

Only terminal losses can be used in this way, i.e. a loss, including unused capital allowances, sustained in the year of assessment in which the trade is permanently discontinued and in that part of the preceding year of assessment beginning twelve months before the date of discontinuance.[2]

Simon's Taxes E1.618; Butterworths Income Tax Service B3.42.
[1] TA 1988, s. 388.
[2] Normally a part of this period is omitted thanks to TA 1988, s. 63; infra, § **7: 43**.

5: 11   As with TA 1988, s. 385, dividends or interests on investments arising during any relevant period but which are excluded from the computation of profits because taxed at source may be used as profits against which the terminal loss may be set.[1] The period relevant will be that of the year in which the trade ceases or any of the three preceding years of assessment. It will be noted that the dividend or interest is taxed on an arising basis.

[1] TA 1988, s. 388(4). See *Bank Line Ltd v IRC* [1974] STC 342.

5: 12   Where payments have been made during the relevant years by the trader under deduction of tax e.g. under TA 1988, s. 348, the profits are treated as reduced by the gross amount of such payments.[1] Similarly, in computing the terminal loss the figure otherwise obtained is to be reduced by the amount of any such payments. In both instances relief has already been given. An exception is made in computing the terminal loss if the payment made under deduction of tax is treated as a loss item by s. 387.

Where a partner retires there is a discontinuance under s. 113 and a terminal loss is calculated for the retiring partner only. This loss is set off against that part of the partnership income which was included in his total income for each relevant year. His share of the loss is governed by his share of the profits at the date of discontinuance. If a continuance election is made there is no terminal loss relief for any of the partners.[2]

[1] TA 1988, s. 388(5). On ss. 348 and 349, see infra, § **9: 76**.
[2] TA 1988, s. 389(4).

What is a trading loss?

5: 13   Loss relief is important not only to the genuine trader but also to others who have used it as the basis of schemes. To claim relief the trader must have been carrying on a trade and his allowable expenses must exceed his trading receipts. In addition the trade must be carried on on a commercial basis and with a view to the realisation of profit although that the fact that the trade was being carried on so as to afford a reasonable expectation of profit is conclusive evidence that it is being carried on with a view to the realisation of profit.[1]

Further, the trade must have been carried on in a commercial way for the whole of the year of assessment whether or not there has been a change in the manner in which the trade was being carried on and whether or not there has been a change in the persons running the trade if at least one person was running it for the whole year. If the trade was set up or discontinued (or both) in a year of assessment the test is applied to those parts of the year in which the trade was in being.

By concession relief can be claimed in respect of maintenance expenses of owner occupied farms not carried on on a commercial basis,[2] a concession that also applies to the next rule.

Loss relief is restricted to trading losses as just defined. However certain expenses which do not enter into the computation of profits and losses of the trade are treated as loss items. These are capital allowances,[3] annual payments made by the trader wholly and exclusively for the purposes of the trade and which fall within TA 1988, s. 349,[4] and interest payments made for the same purposes and being payments eligible for relief.[5]

Losses on dealings in commodity futures are restricted where partnerships are involved.[6]

Simon's Taxes E1.602.
  [1] TA 1988, s. 384. See also *FA and AB Ltd v Lupton* [1971] 3 All ER 948, 47 TC 580, infra, § **7: 11** as to what is a trading transaction.
  [2] Extra-statutory concession B5 (1988), **Simon's Taxes, Division H2.2.**
  [3] TA 1988, ss. 383 and 388(6).
  [4] TA 1988, s. 387.
  [5] TA 1988, s. 390.
  [6] TA 1988, s. 399(2).

5: 14   *Hobby farming.* Where losses are sustained in a trade of farming or market gardening, relief is not available under ss. 380 or 385 if despite satisfying the test in s. 384 a loss was incurred in each of the five prior years.[1] In computing this loss capital allowances are not included. It should be remembered that all farming, but not market gardening, is treated as one trade so that a loss on one farm may be set off against the profits of another. Special provision is made for the genuine farmer who has a reasonable expectation of profit but whose business is taking longer than six years to come right.

Simon's Taxes E1.603; Butterworths Income Tax Service E4.04.
  [1] TA 1988, s. 397.

5: 15   *Woodlands.* Where a person has elected in time for assessment under Schedule D, Case I he was not assumed to be carrying on a trade. Specific mention therefore had to be made to give him relief,[1] and he was not entitled to relief under TA 1988, s. 574.

Simon's Taxes E1.602.
[1] TA 1988, ss. 380(4), 383 (12), 385 (6) and 389(8).

OTHER LOSSES

Employment losses

5: 16   Relief can be claimed under TA 1988, s. 380 only. However, although s. 380 refers to employments (but not to offices) the Revenue do not accept that a claim can ever arise—even when expenses exceed emoluments.[1]

[1] See *Taxation* 1989, p. 74.

Schedule D Case VI

5: 17   Relief can be claimed under TA 1988, s. 392 against other Case VI income of that year and then rolled forward and set against other Case VI income of later years; however the statutes which place certain types of income in Case VI often restrict their use to absorb losses. Losses on furnished holiday lettings are treated as if they were trading losses.[1]

Simon's Taxes E1.621.
[1] TA 1988, s. 503(1).

Schedule D Case V

5: 18   A loss arising from a trade or profession carried on wholly overseas can be given relief in full under TA 1988, ss. 380, 385 or 388.[1] Losses arising in 1984–85 and later years qualify for full relief. Losses sustained in 1983–84 qualify for relief only as to $87\frac{1}{2}\%$ of the actual loss; earlier losses still attract a 25% restriction.

Losses from letting of foreign property can be set off against future income from the same property.[2]

Simon's Taxes E1.641.
[1] TA 1988, s. 391(2).
[2] SP 2/80, **Simon's Taxes, Division H3.2.**

Schedule A

5: 19   See TA 1988, ss. 25–31 and § **9: 12.**

Simon's Taxes A4.108, A4.3.

Schedules C, D Cases III and IV and F

5: 20   No relief is possible.

Schedule D Cases I and II

5: 21   Pre-trading expenses can be treated as losses[1] and given relief under TA 1988, ss. 380, 381, 385 and 388; this rule extends to losses from furnished holiday lettings.[2]

Simon's Taxes B3.1204.

  [1] TA 1988, s. 401, FA 1982, s. 50.
  [2] TA 1988, s. 503(1).

Losses on unquoted shares in trading companies

5: 22   Although capital losses are the province of CGT and may not be set off against income, an exception is made by TA 1988, s. 574 where the loss arises from the disposal of unquoted shares in a trading company or member of a trading group. The relief is available only in respect of shares for which the individual or his spouse subscribed[1]—as distinct from those acquired through gift, inheritance or purchase. The shares must be ordinary share capital.[2] The company must be a "qualifying trading company". A company qualifies only if it satisfies complex criteria as to what it has been doing (e.g. trading—but not in forbidden items such as shares or land)[3] and for how long (six years if previously an investment company or a dealer in forbidden items). In addition the company must not have its shares quoted on a recognised stock exchange[4] and must be resident in the UK.

The loss is computed on CGT principles; in addition the disposal must be an arm's length sale for full consideration or a distribution on winding up or the deemed disposal which arises when shares have become of negligible value.[5] Relief is denied even for such disposals if there is a share exchange for non-commercial reasons[6] or value shifting[7] has occurred.

The relief may be claimed for the year in which the loss is realised or the following year. Any unused loss can then be set only against capital gains.

Where the taxpayer also has a loss entitled to relief under TA 1988, s. 380 or 381 the present loss is absorbed first.[8]

Further rules apply where there are mixed holdings, e.g. where some shares were acquired by subscription and others by inheritance; those rules restrict the loss to what would have been the deductible cost if mixing had not occurred. The mixing rules can be avoided by issuing different types of shares.[8] Special rules apply also to reorganisation.[9] Legislation now affirms "beyond doubt" the Revenue view that the withdrawal of funds from share accounts with Building Societies or Industrial and Provident Societies cannot give rise to this relief.[10]

Simon's Taxes E1.605; Butterworths Income Tax Service F7.21–26.

  [1] TA 1988, s. 574(4).
  [2] TA 1988, ss. 576(5) and 832(1).
  [3] TA 1988, s. 576(4) and (5), as amended by FA 1989, Sch. 12, para. 14.
  [4] A term to be adjusted by regulations as a result of the Financial Services Act 1986—see F(No. 2)A 1987, s. 73.
  [5] TA 1988, s. 575(1) and see infra, § **14: 02** and **19: 07**.
  [6] TA 1988, s. 575(2).

[7] TA 1988, s. 576(2), infra, § **15: 05**.
[8] TA 1988, s. 574(2).
[9] TA 1988, s. 575(2) and (3); mixing is the same as pooling for CGT infra, § **15: 05**.
[10] TA 1988, s. 576(5), Inland Revenue Press Release, 3 July 1987, *Simon's Tax Intelligence* [1987], p. 462.

INVESTMENT RELIEF

Business start-up scheme

5: 23 In a major shift towards an expenditure tax, a taxpayer may set against his income an amount invested by him in new corporate trades.

The first step was taken in 1981[1] with the business start-up scheme which enabled a taxpayer to set an investment in a qualifying company against his total income for that year. The relief was withdrawn if, inter alia, the shares were disposed of within five years. This scheme applied for 1981–82 and 1982–83.

Special rules apply for CGT where the relief has not been withdrawn. Where the consideration received on the disposal is less than the allowable costs, no loss relief may be claimed; this is achieved by reducing the allowable costs.[2]

Simon's Taxes E1.801–811; Butterworths Income Tax Service F7.01–F7.14.
[1] FA 1981, s. 53.
[2] FA 1981, s. 64, amended by FA 1982, s. 51(4).

Business expansion scheme

5: 24 The business expansion scheme, introduced in 1983[1] is an extension of the business start-up scheme, supra § **5: 23**. It applies to shares issued after 5 April 1983.[2] Although the expansion scheme was intended to be less restrictive than the start-up scheme, a wide variety of conditions must still be met.[3] These conditions have been frequently modified. As from 15 March 1988 there is a ceiling of £500,000 on the amount any company can raise over a twelve month period.[4]

Under the scheme a qualifying individual may claim as a deduction from his total income one half of the amount subscribed for eligible shares in that year.[5] In order to prevent too many schemes being announced towards the end of the tax year a taxpayer can elect that when shares are issued before 6th October in a year of assessment up to one half (subject to a maximum of £5,000) may be deducted for the preceding year; it is a matter of taxpayer choice—there is no obligation to carry an investment back—and affects investments after 5th April 1987.[6] The minimum investment is £500 (unless he uses an approved investment fund[7]) and the maximum is £40,000 a year[8] (which apply jointly to a husband and wife living together[9] although the limit will be applied separately as from 1990–91[10]). Investment can be through an approved investment fund.[11] The company must be a qualifying unquoted company carrying on a qualifying trade either itself or through wholly-owned subsidiaries.[12]

Simon's Taxes E1.812–822; Butterworths Income Tax Service F7.15–20.
[1] TA 1988, s. 289.
[2] TA 1988, s. 289(1).
[3] However, see *Simon's Tax Intelligence* 1983, p. 425.
[4] TA 1988, s. 290A; the period between 15th March 1988 and 6th April 1988 is covered by FA 1983, Sch. 5, para 3A. Ship chartering and the provision of private rented housing have a ceiling of £5m. On anti-avoidance see TA 1988, s. 290A(4).
[5] TA 1988, s. 289(5).
[6] TA 1988, s. 289(6).
[7] An investment fund must be approved by the Inland Revenue. The criteria for approval were published by the Revenue in July 1983, see **Simon's Taxes E1.843**.
[8] TA 1988, s. 290.
[9] TA 1988, s. 304.
[10] FA 1988, Sch. 3, para. 12.
[11] FA 1988, s. 51 (amending TA 1988, s. 311(3)).
[12] TA 1988, s. 293.

5: 25 The individual must be resident and ordinarily resident in the UK when the shares are issued, and must subscribe for shares on his own behalf. He must not be connected with the company at any time between incorporation (or two years before the issue of the shares, if later) and five years after the issue of the shares.[1] The tests used for determining whether a person is a connected person are that a person is connected with a company if he controls it, if he owns more than 30% of the voting power of the company or owns any of its loan capital, or if he or an associate is an employee, a paid director or a partner of the company. However, an overdraft from a bank is not treated as loan capital if it arose in the ordinary course of the bank's business.[2] An individual is also treated as connected with a company with which he would not otherwise be connected if he subscribes for shares as part of an arrangement under which another person subscribes for shares in a different company with which any party to the arrangement is connected.[3]

[1] TA 1988, ss. 291 and 289(12).
[2] TA 1988, s. 291(9).
[3] TA 1988, s. 291(10).

5: 26 A company is a qualifying company if it is incorporated in the UK, and for three years from the issue of the shares (or from the time it begins a qualifying trade, if later) it meets certain conditions.[1] It must be an unquoted company,[2] resident only in the UK. It must exist wholly or substantially wholly (sic) for the purpose of carrying on wholly or mainly in the UK[3] one or more qualifying trades, or its business must consist wholly of holding shares or securities in, or making loans to, one or more qualifying subsidiaries (although it also qualifies if its business consists wholly of carrying on one or more qualifying trades in the UK and of holding shares or securities, or making loans to, qualifying subsidiaries). A company carrying on research and development is a qualifying company for shares issued after 5th April 1985,[4] and, subject to certain conditions, a company carrying out oil exploration will qualify where shares are issued after 18th March 1986.[5] The share capital must not consist of shares which are not fully paid up. The company must not be controlled by, or control, alone or together with connected persons, another company, nor must it be, or own, a 51% subsidiary. However, a qualifying subsidiary is excluded from this restriction. A qualifying subsidiary is a wholly owned subsidiary resident only in the UK, which carries on a qualifying trade. A film company had to be engaged in the production of films for three years to qualify but as from 17th March 1987 this condition is relaxed to enable a company to qualify if it is engaged in production or distribution of films produced during this period.[6]

A trade is a qualifying trade if it meets certain conditions[7] e.g. it must not consist of dealing in shares, land or commodities, and hobby trades do not qualify—it must be conducted on a commercial basis with a view to profit.[8] For shares issued after 18th March 1986, property development is a qualifying trade[9] but the wider rule in TA 1988, s. 294 may make the change academic in some situations. Farming also ceased to be a non-qualifying trade in 1986 but, again, subject to s. 294.[10] Oil extraction activities may not qualify where the shares are issued after 18th March 1986.[11]

---

[1] TA 1988, s. 293. Unless within that time it is wound up or dissolved for bona fide commercial reasons ibid, sub-para. (5).

[2] Companies listed on the unlisted securities market are not treated as unquoted companies (although the Revenue will take into consideration the length of time before quotation when deciding whether to claw back relief).

[3] See SP 4/87, **Simon's Taxes Division H3.2.**

[4] TA 1988, s. 289(1)(*b*)(i).

[5] TA 1988, s. 289(1)(*d*).

[6] TA 1988, s. 297(4); the purpose is to assist the company which makes a film in less than three years and then distributes it.

[7] TA 1988, s. 297(2).

[8] TA 1988, s. 297(8).

[9] TA 1988, ss. 297(2)(*h*) and 298(5).

[10] FA 1983, Sch. 5, para. 6(2) was amended by FA 1986, Sch. 9, para. 8.

[11] See conditions in TA 1988, s. 289(1)(*d*) and (2).

5: 27   A claim for relief must be made within two years of the year of assessment in which the shares are issued or, if later, within two years and four months of the qualifying trade commencing, and must be accompanied by a certificate issued by the company and authorised by its tax inspector stating that the company has met the conditions of the scheme. A claim can not be made before the qualifying trade has been carried on for four months. Once a claim has been accepted, the relief may be given through the individual's PAYE coding.[1]

The relief is withdrawn if the individual, company or trade ceases to qualify, if the shares are disposed of within five years of issue, or if value is received from the company—even rent.[2] The tax is charged back to the year in which the relief was given but, for interest purposes, the reckonable date is the date of the event causing the withdrawal.[3]

There are also special rules for the capital gains tax consequences of a disposal of shares, information requirements and to prevent misuse of the relief.[4]

---

[1] TA 1988, s. 306.

[2] See ICAEW Memorandum TR 13 *Simon's Tax Intelligence* 1988, p. 712.

[3] TA 1988, s. 307.

[4] TA 1988, ss. 289(11), 310 and Sch. 29.

5: 28   FA 1988 contains special rules to encourage the use of the BES scheme for companies providing private rented accommodation. Various provisions have to be recast because the letting of property is not necessarily a trade. There are also a number of variations on the basic scheme. The relief applies only to shares issued after the passing of FA 1988 and before the end of 1993.[1] The relevant period is four years not three[2] and the maximum amount that can be raised is £5m not £500,000—this limit is reduced if the company is carrying on the activity in partnership, or as a joint venture, with any other company.[3]

The company must carry on qualifying activities and the company must exist wholly or substantially for the purpose of carrying on these activities. These activities are defined in terms of letting dwelling houses on qualifying tenancies, which are in turn defined as tenancies which are assured tenancies, other than assured shorthold (or short assured) tenancies, for the purposes of the Housing or the Housing (Scotland) Acts 1988. The tenancies must not be let at a premium nor may the tenant, or any associate of his have an option to purchase.[4] As assured tenancies are not expected to begin until early 1989 and the relief will not be available until the company has been carrying on a qualifying activity for four months it may be some time before this relief becomes available.[5]

There are also restrictions on the properties. They must not be expensive[6]—housing is expensive if its value is greater than £125,000 in Greater London and £85,000 elsewhere[7]—and must be fit for human habitation.[8] The house must not already be let nor may it subsequently be let on a non-qualifying tenancy.[9] The property can only qualify once—and so not in the hands of a purchaser.[10]

There are also restrictions concerning the relationship between the investor and the company. So an investor cannot use this relief if the company takes over properties he has held—directly or indirectly[11]—or if he is connected with the company.[12]

---

[1] FA 1988, s. 50(6).

[2] FA 1988, Sch. 4, para. 2(4).

[3] FA 1988, Sch. 4, para 3; provision is made for subsidiaries by FA 1988, Sch. 4, paras. 4 and 11.

[4] FA 1988, s. 50(3), (4).

[5] However, the Inland Revenue Press Release, para. 21 points out that building works will be qualifying activities.

[6] FA 1988, Sch. 4, para. 13.

[7] Detailed provisions set out the assumptions to be made—paras. 13(3) and (4).

[8] FA 1988, Sch. 4, para. 14.

[9] FA 1988, Sch. 4, para. 15—letting includes granting licences.

[10] FA 1988, Sch. 4, para. 16; the use of capital allowances has a similar disqualifying effect—para. 17.

[11] FA 1988, Sch. 4, para. 9.

[12] FA 1988, Sch. 4, para 4 (any tenancy will suffice to disqualify the individual not just a "qualifying tenancy").

INTEREST RELIEF

5: 29   Certain payments by way of interest are deductible in computing income—these are the subject of this section. In addition, interest payments may be deductible in computing income from a particular source, e.g. payments in connection with a trade.

The reason for allowing interest as a general deduction from income is that tax is levied on income and in computing income all charges on that income including interest should be deducted.

Interest payments made after 26th March 1974 may be deducted from income if [1] they are:

(i) *annual*[2] interest chargeable as income of the payee under Schedule D, Case III; or

(ii) the interest is payable in the UK[3] on a loan[4] from a bank[5] but not on an overdraft;[6] where the rate of interest exceeds a reasonable commercial rate, no relief is given for the excess.

Whether the payment comes within (i) or (ii) the loan must be for qualifying purpose.

Where only a part of a debt qualifies, relief may be given for that proportion of interest.

Simon's Taxes E1.5; Butterworths Income Tax Service B2.41.
[1] TA 1988, s. 353.
[2] On meaning of annual interest see infra, § **9: 46**.
[3] For concessionary relief for residents of the Irish Republic paying interest to Irish building societies etc see extra-statutory concession A28 (1988), **Simon's Taxes, Division H2.2**.
[4] No relief can be given for interest paid under a guarantee of another's liability—*Hendy v Hadley* [1980] 2 All ER 554, [1980] STC 292.
[5] TA 1988, s. 353(1).
[6] TA 1988, s. 353(3)(*a*); on what is an overdraft see *Walcot-Bather v Golding* [1979] STC 707.

---

1   Purchase or improvement of land

5: 30   Land includes "large caravans" (if the occupier is assessable under the General Rate Act and has paid his rates) and houseboats.[1]

Improvements are not defined except to include certain expenses of maintenance and repairs not allowable under Schedule A and certain street works.[2] Examples of "improvement" suggested by the Inland Revenue are central heating installations (including solar heating but excluding night storage heaters not fixed to a permanent spur outlet), double glazing (whether or not detachable), garden sheds, greenhouses, burglar alarms and swimming pools.[3] Relief for interest on loans for improvements is not available for loans taken out after 5th April 1988 (infra **5: 35**).

Simon's Taxes E1.535, 536; Butterworths Income Tax Service B2.42.
[1] TA 1988, ss. 354(1), (3) and 367.
[2] TA 1988, ss. 354(2) and 367.
[3] IR 11, 1985, App. 1.

Main residence rules for loans before 1st August 1988

5: 31   The land, caravan or houseboat must be used as the only or main residence of the borrower or for loans taken out before 6th April 1988 the rent-free residence of a dependent relative or of a former or separated spouse of his.[1] Whether a house is a residence is a question of fact; a house 150 miles from the accommodation provided with a job but visited frequently particularly at weekends was capable of being eligible for relief.[2] It is sufficient that the house is so used within 12 months of the date of the loan. The Revenue may extend this period.[3]

Further, relief is given only for interest on a sum not exceeding a qualifying maximum which, since 1983–84, has been £30,000[4] for each individual or married couple. There are special rules for joint borrowers, each has to fulfil the conditions and the loan is apportioned between them according to their interest payments.[5] However where a person has two qualifying houses the £30,000 limit applies to the aggregate of such loans, a problem where a husband proposes to buy a house for his (separated) wife to live in.

This may be avoided by making the ex-wife responsible for the payment of interest in respect of the house she is to live in and increasing her maintenance accordingly.

Relief is also available where the taxpayer occupies living accommodation which is job-related.[6] In the case of an employee, accommodation is job related if it fulfils criteria identical with those for exemption from FA 1977, s. 33; *infra*, § **6: 52**. Relief may be claimed for interest paid on another property, even though it is not occupied as the main residence, provided it is used by the borrower as a residence or be intended to be used in due course as his only or main residence; use and intention must exist at the time of the payment. The land must be in the UK or the Republic of Ireland.[7] There is similar relief in the case of self-employed persons who live in job-related accommodation, i.e. accommodation which they are required to occupy for the purposes of carrying on their trade under the terms of a contract entered into at arm's length.[8]

Simon's Taxes E1.538; Butterworths Income Tax Service B2.42.

[1] TA 1988, ss. 355 and 367, as amended by FA 1988, s. 44.

[2] *Frost v Feltham* [1981] 1 WLR 452, [1981] STC 115 cf *Moore v Thompson* [1986] STC 170 (CGT relief under CGTA 1979, s. 101).

[3] TA 1988, s. 354(5) and (6). On effects of temporary absence see extra-statutory concession A27 (1988) as extended for civil servants posted overseas—**Simon's Taxes, Division H2.2.**

[4] FA 1989, s. 46. From 1974–75 to 1982–83 the figure was £25,000.

[5] This enables joint borrowers other than a husband and wife each to claim up to the £30,000 exemption, but this advantage has now been restricted, see *infra*, § **5: 32**.

[6] TA 1988, s. 356.

[7] TA 1988, s. 354(1).

[8] TA 1988, s. 356(3)(*b*) and (5).

Loans on or after 1st August 1988—residence basis

5: 32   In an effort to restrict the tax advantage obtained from cohabitation as distinct from marriage and perhaps, more generally, to restrict this relief, FA 1988 contains rules which provide that for payments made on loans made on or after 1st August 1988[1] the maximum figure of £30,000 is to be applied not per person but per residence.[2] A residence is defined as a building[3] or part of a building occupied or intended to be occupied as a separate residence.[4] The temporary division of a building or part which is designed for permanent use as a single residence will be ignored.

This still leaves an advantage for the unmarried since each will be able to use the relief against a different residence—making £60,000 if they have two residences. For the married couple not only will only one relief be available, a situation that is not to change when separate taxation is introduced in 1990,[5] but an arbitrary rule directs that where each has a separate only or main residence the one first purchased is to be taken.[6] It thus becomes very dangerous for a mortgage on one property to be paid off in such circumstances.

---

[1] TA 1988, s. 356C. The Revenue view is that a loan made after 31st July 1988 is treated as made before 1st August 1988 if the offer was made before that date and was evidenced in writing by the lender before that date *and* the borrower had entered into a binding contract before 1st August to buy the property. Inland Revenue Press Release 27th July *Simon's Tax Intelligence* 1988, p. 610.

[2] TA 1988, s. 356A added by FA 1988, s. 42; the change was foreshadowed in Green Paper on Reform of Personal Taxation, Cmnd 9756 (1986).

[3] Or a caravan or a houseboat.

[4] TA 1988, s. 356D(2).

[5] FA 1988, Sch. 3, para. 14.

[6] TA 1988, s. 356B(8).

5: 33 Rules allow for the allocation and transfer of relief where more than one person is in occupation of a single residence. Where the occupants are a married couple who are not separated, qualifying interest is to be treated as paid by the husband and not by the wife.[1] If there is an election for separate taxation of wife's earnings or for separate assessment the interest can be reallocated between them as they wish but in the form and within the time limits prescribed.[2] Under the independent system of taxation to be introduced in 1990 the residence basis will be applied and, as already seen, there can only be one residence. It follows that each will be entitled to relief on one half of the limit, i.e. £15,000 under the present rule. An election will however be available to reallocate the limit between them.[3] This reallocation can be effected regardless of which of them actually pays the interest.

Where the residence is occupied by two or more people who are not married, the limit is divided equally between them so that each of three will have a limit, called the sharer's limit, of £10,000 under present rules.[4] Relief is not available to one sharer in respect of interest paid by another. Where however one sharer is unable to use his limit he is allowed to transfer the unused portion to another who can use it but only if he cannot use it and therefore not where this other can make better use of it.[5] This is so whether there is one other sharer or more.[6]

Where there are three sharers, two of whom are a married couple, the limit will be divided 2/3 to the married couple, who will then be free to reallocate it between them as they wish and regardless of which of them pays the interest, while the other 1/3 will be allocated to the stranger. Transfers between the married couple and the stranger will then take place as between unmarried sharers.[7]

[1] TA 1988, s 356B(1).
[2] TA 1988, s. 356B(4)–(7).
[3] New TA 1988, s. 356B to be applied as from 1990–91—see FA 1988, Sch. 3, para. 14.
[4] TA 1988, s. 356A(2) and (3).
[5] TA 1988, s. 356A(4) and (5).
[6] TA 1988, s. 356B(6)–(8).
[7] TA 1988, s. 356B(2) and (3).

Transitional rules

5: 34   These new rules are to apply for payments of qualifying interest on or after 1st August 1988 unless they come within transitional relief rules. These allow the old rules to continue where the payment is made under a loan made before 1st August 1988.[1] Thus loans taken out before 1st August 1988 will continue to have the limit applied per person and not per residence— provided further rules are satisfied. Thus qualifying interest must have been payable by the sharer (so that it was for example his residence and not simply an investment), that such interest has continued to be paid since 1st August 1988 and that the sharer has continued to have an interest in the property.[2] Thus, if three share the house and one leaves but the house is not sold and the leaver is not bought out, the relief will continue for the two remaining people. If a new sharer is brought in the new sharer will not be entitled to the benefit of the old rules[3] but the continuing sharers will. Only existing loans qualify for the limit.[4]

[1] TA 1988, s. 356C(1)(*a*); on evidence see s.356C(3).
[2] TA 1988, s. 356C(1); periods are defined in s. 356D(3); the notion of a point during the period is not defined—presumably because it is indefinable.
[3] He will not meet the conditions of s.356C.
[4] TA 1988, s. 356C(4).

Home improvement loans

5: 35   Revenue research showed that while much use was made of the former relief which allowed the deduction of interest for loans to improve the residence, 85% went on things like central heating or double glazing which did not extend the property, while a further 5% were for garages etc. which do not increase living accommodation.[1] Moreover one might add that the rules were very hard to police. Relief is therefore not available for a home improvement loan unless the loan was made before 6th April 1988.[2]

A loan is a home improvement loan if it is to defray money applied in improving or developing land or buildings. By itself this would withhold relief where a person builds a house on a building plot, so the definition then excludes a loan for the erection of a new building which is not part of an existing building on land which immediately before the work had no building on it. This definition raises many questions. The question whether buildings are part of an existing building may raise issues similar to the CGT relief— although here it will be the taxpayer rather than the Revenue who will be arguing for separate buildings. Equally questions may arise as to what is meant by land—if a person builds a house at the bottom of his garden, is the area needed for the building the land in question? If he uses the shell of an old windmill or oast house as the basis for his house will be really not get relief, whereas if he demolishes the old building he will qualify?

[1] Inland Revenue Press Release, 15 March 1988 *Simon's Tax Intelligence* 1988, p. 197.
[2] TA 1988, s. 355(2A) added by FA 1988, s. 43; loans made on or after that date but under an offer made before that date may qualify but writing is required—subs. (2C). On costs of clearing a site see ICAEW Memorandum TR 739 No. 15 *Simon's Tax Intelligence* 1988, p. 79.

Let property

5: 36   Relief is also given but without a £30,000 limit where the property was let at a commercial rent for more than 26 of the 52 weeks for which the interest was payable and the periods when the house was not let were either periods of occupation as a main residence as above or were prevented from being so by works of construction or repair.[1] The interest may only be set against rental income and not against general income. Any excess interest may be rolled forward to be set off against rental income from later years but only so long as the property in respect of which the interest was paid continues to satisfy these rules.[2]

Interest paid on a loan used to buy land which is occupied by a partnership for business purposes can be set against the rent received even where the landlord is one of the partners. Where the land is occupied rent free, whether by a partnership or a company of which the landlord is a director, a special practice applies in relation to accounts beginning after 4th February 1985. No relief applies where no rent is paid but special rules apply to treat interest paid by the partnership and charged in its accounts as if it were rent and so available for the set off of interest under these rules. Interest paid by the company will be a Schedule E emolument of the director[3] and not charged as rent.

Again the land must be in the UK or the Republic of Ireland.[4]

Simon's Taxes E1.531; Butterworths Income Tax Service B2.43.
[1] TA 1988, s. 355(1)(*b*).
[2] TA 1988, s. 355(4).
[3] See Statement of Practice SP 4/85, **Simon's Taxes, Division H3.2**.
[4] TA 1988, s. 354(1)—making interest on such property non-deductible unless a trade is carried on—*Ockenden v Mackley* [1982] STC 513.

Miscellaneous

5: 37   Interest on a bridging loan is deductible and each residence is treated separately for the £30,000 limit. The bridging loan may be for twelve months but this period may be extended by the Board.[1] Interest on the loan to buy the new house qualifies for relief provided it becomes the taxpayer's only or main residence within 12 months[2] while interest on the old house continues to qualify for 12 months also.[3] It is now made clear that the £30,000 limit applies to each house separately; before 1984–85 the position was that the £30,000 limit ceased to apply to the loan on the old house.[4]

There are provisions[5] to prevent a person from claiming relief where the purchase is artificial, as where the owner sells property to a spouse living with him or a connected person carries out improvements at an inflated price to a property which is let.

Where the borrower dies, relief may be claimed by his personal representative in computing the income of the estate if, assuming the deceased had not died, he could have claimed the relief and the house is used as the main or only residence of his widow or a dependent relative of his.[6]

The *method* by which basic rate tax relief is given on most loans for the purchase or improvement of land was altered from 1st April 1983 when the system of mortgage interest relief at source (MIRAS) came into operation.[7] The borrower may deduct a sum equal to basic rate tax relief from the payment of loan interest, rather than recovering the relief through his PAYE coding. Higher rate tax relief continues to be given in the usual way.

Under FA 1985 lenders may elect that loans above the £30,000 limit should be subject to the MIRAS scheme so far as the first £30,000 is concerned.[8] This will be compulsory for loans with effect from April 1987.

Simon's Taxes A3.430–434, D4.761, E1.538; Butterworths Income Tax Service B2.41, 54.

[1] TA 1988, s. 354(5). The reasons for the strictness of some of these rules are set out by the Revenue in ICAEW Memorandum TR 713—*Simon's Tax Intelligence* 1988, p. 711.

[2] TA 1988, s. 355. Failure to move in causes loss of relief, see *Hughes v Viner* [1985] STC 235 (new property found to be substantially defective).

[3] TA 1988, s. 354(6). On concessionary relief for a person moving house on marriage see extra-statutory concession A35 (1988), **Simon's Taxes, Division H2.2**.

[4] TA 1988, s. 357(4).

[5] TA 1988, s. 787.

[6] TA 1988, s. 358.

[7] TA 1988, ss. 369, 379.

[8] TA 1988, s. 373 and see *Simon's Tax Intelligence* 1985, pp. 390, 434 and 435 for further amendments to MIRAS regulations.

A trap

5: 38 The requirement that the loan be for the purchase of an estate or interest in the land gives rise to traps in the area of property adjustment on divorce or nullity. The problem arises where one spouse, usually the husband, agrees or is ordered to pay the other a lump sum and he raises that sum by way of loan. Interest payable on such a loan does not qualify for tax relief since the purpose of the loan was not the purchase of an interest in the land; this follows even if the sum is secured on land owned by the husband. The solution in such cases is either for the husband to have an interest in the house or for him to pay the wife increased maintenance out of which she pays the interest.

2 Acquisition of an interest in close company, co-operative, employee-controlled company or partnership[1]

5: 39 Interest is allowable if the loan is used to acquire a material interest (i.e. more than 5%)[2] in a close company with no capital repayment or in lending money to the company for use in its trade (or to repay an eligible loan). As from 1982 relief may be claimed if the holding is less than a material interest, but the borrower is involved in the business. Relief is still available if the company was close when the interest in the company was acquired, but is no longer close when the interest is paid. By concession, the relief will be continued even after a partnership has been incorporated or shares in one company are exchanged for shares in another provided a new loan would have satisfied all these conditions.[3] Relief is not available in respect of shares acquired after 13th March 1989 if the person acquiring them (or that person's spouse) claims business expansion scheme relief.[4]

Similar relief is available to buy an interest in a partnership or co-operative or to lend money to such a body and to purchase ordinary share capital of an employee-controlled company. The conditions applicable to the last instance were further relaxed by FA 1984.

Interest relief is not usually available if the business consists of the occupation of commercial woodlands.[5]

Simon's Taxes E1.547–551; Butterworths Income Tax Service B2.45–B2.47A.
   [1] TA 1988, ss. 360 and 361 as amended by FA 1989, Sch 12, paras 12, 13.
   [2] The definition of material interest is modified by TA 1988, s. 360(4)(a) incorporating TA 1988, Sch. 9, para. 39—shares held by trustees of approved profit sharing schemes do not qualify.
   [3] Extra-statutory concession A43 (1988), Simon's Taxes, Division H2.2.
   [4] FA 1989, s. 47.
   [5] FA 1988; Sch. 6, para. 3(3)—subject to para. 5(1).

3   Purchase of machinery or plant for partnership or employer[1]

5: 40   The partnership may claim the capital allowance but may not deduct the interest paid to the partner; in turn he is allowed to deduct the interest. This relief is available only in the year the advance is made and the next three years of assessment.

Simon's Taxes E1.533; Butterworths Income Tax Service B2.44.
   [1] TA 1988, s. 395(1)–(4).

4 Payment of CTT[1] and IHT

5: 41   For details see infra, § **12: 02**.

Simon's Taxes E1.552; Butterworths Income Tax Service B2.49.
   [1] TA 1988, s. 364.

5 Purchase of a life annuity secured on land[1]

5: 42   The conditions here are stringent. At least nine tenths of the loan must be applied in the purchase; the annuity must be a single or joint life annuity; the borrower (or each of them) must be 65 years of age at the time of the loan; the loan must be secured on land in the United Kingdom or the Republic of Ireland and the borrower must have an interest in the land. The interest must be payable by the borrower or by one of the annuitants and where the loan exceeds £30,000[2] relief is not given for the excess. Finally the borrower must be using the land as his main residence when the interest is paid. The MIRAS system applies to interest paid on this type of loan, see § **5: 32**.

Simon's Taxes E1.553; Butterworths Income Tax Service B2.50.
[1] TA 1988, s. 365.
[2] I.e. the qualifying maximum. Before 6th April 1983 the limit was £25,000.

Anti-avoidance

5: 43   (1) If a transaction is associated with the lending of money, TA 1988, s. 786 applies to deprive the transaction of its normal tax consequence. So a payment of an annuity is treated as a payment of yearly interest. Similarly the transfer of an income earning asset with a duty to sell back may result in the income of the asset being treated as that of the transferor as will the assignment, surrender or waiver of any income. But for these rules the income could be shifted to the transferee, the lender, in whose hands it would be taxable as income just as if it had been interest, but not taxable—and so in effect deductible—so far as the borrower was concerned. The need for this rule will decline in view of the alterations to the rules for new covenants after 15 March 1988.

(2) TA 1988, s. 787 denies relief under TA 1988, s. 353 in respect of interest paid after 8th June 1976 when a scheme has been made and the sole or main benefit that might be expected to accrue was the obtaining of a reduction in tax liability by means of the relief. This was particularly designed to deal with schemes whereby an individual would pay a substantial sum by way of (allowable) interest in advance and then sell the right to the capital.

(3) One should note the decision of the Court of Appeal in *Cairns v MacDiarmid*[1] that interest payable under a scheme was not interest for the purposes of a deduction under these rules.

Simon's Taxes E1.554, 555; Butterworths Income Tax Service A7.21.
[1] [1983] STC 178.

AVERAGING

5: 44   There is no general averaging procedure in the United Kingdom tax system whereby income is averaged out over a number of years. Rather the system takes the view that income tax is an annual tax and therefore taxes only the income arising in that year. Averaging is thus allowed over the year—but not beyond it.

This is unjust in a number of ways but much less unjust now that the progressive nature of the tax system has been so drastically reduced. First it is inequitable for those with fluctuating incomes.[1] Secondly it is inequitable for individuals whose income fluctuates around the bottom of the tax scale, since unused personal allowances may not be rolled forward to subsequent years. The arguments against allowing such rolling forward are largely administrative; it would also make the yield from taxes more difficult to predict.

Thirdly the absence of an averaging clause causes injustice to the individual who suddenly receives an exceptional sum which the tax system treats as income. These abnormal receipts are different from the problem of fluctuating incomes from one source not least in that the receipt may be isolated and subjected to special treatment by the tax system, see infra, § **5: 45** et seq.

---

[1] RC 1955, Cmd 9474, § 205. On reform see RC 1955, Cmd 9474, § 202; RC Canada 1966 Vol. 2, p. 253; 31 Nat Tax Jo 19 Vickrey's "Agenda for Progressive Taxation" p. 164 and Bird and Head, *Modern Fiscal Issues* (1973) p. 117.

5: 45   First, a number of receipts may be spread over a number of years:

(*a*) Copyright and public lending right—*spreading back*: sums received by an author, by way of royalty (or public lending right) within the first two years of a book's life plus sums for the assignment of copyright (or public lending right) and non-returnable advances may be spread back over the period during which he was at work on the book but with a maximum of three years.[1] This applies also to dramatic, musical and other artistic work.

(*b*) Copyright—*spreading forward*: sums received for the assignment of a copyright more than ten years after publication can be spread forward over six years.[2] This does not apply to artistic works.

(*c*) Artists' sales: The price, commission or fee for a work of art can be spread over two or three years.[3]

(*d*) Patents: *spreading forward*: a sum received in return for patent rights is taxable as income but may be spread over the year of receipt and the next five years.[4]

(*e*) Patents—*spreading back*: sums received for the use of patents over a period of at least six years may be spread back over six years.[5]

Simon's Taxes A3.421, 422, B3.801–812, B4.105–107.
[1] TA 1988, s. 534—such sums are income; *Howson v Monsell* [1950] 2 All ER 1239, 31 TC 529. The provision was extended to public lending right by TA 1988, s. 537. Public lending right was established under the Public Lending Right Act 1979.
[2] TA 1988, s. 535.
[3] TA 1988, s. 538.
[4] TA 1988, s. 524.
[5] TA 1988, s. 527.

5: 46   Secondly there is the technique of top-slicing. This applies[1] to the recapture of stock relief[2] and certain dealings with life policies[3] and government stock.[4] The technique involves taking a certain fraction of the taxable sum and then calculating the tax payable on that slice as if it were the top slice of the income of the relevant year. That rate is then applied to the whole sum. Thus, if the sum were £15,000, the slice £1,000 and the rate of tax on that slice 30%, 30% would be applied to the whole £15,000.

This technique differs from the first in that the payment is taxed only by reference to one year.

Simon's Taxes E1.407.

¹ The rules for premiums on leases, TA 1988, s. 39(3) and Sch. 2, infra, § **9: 20** were repealed by FA 1988, s. 73.
² TA 1988, Sch. 30.
³ TA 1988, s. 550, infra, § **28.12**.
⁴ TA 1988, s. 52(i), (ii).

Averaging for farmers

5: 47   Thirdly there is a system of averaging for farmers.¹ The profits of two years are compared. If the profits of either year are nil or less than 70% of the other, the profits may be equalised.²

> **EXAMPLE**
> If the profit for year 1 is £10,000 and that for year 2, £50,000, the figures are equalised at £30,000 for each year. The profit to be equalised is that chargeable for the particular year of assessment, but before deducting loss relief and capital allowances (other than those deductible in computing profits, see § **8: 07**).³
> When the profits of year 2 are compared with those of year 3, the correct figure is that for year 2 after carrying out the equalisation with year 1. So if the profits are: year 1, £60,000, year 2, £40,000 and year 3, £60,000 the claim for relief on the first two years gives revised figures of £50,000 each and so precludes averaging for years 2 and 3. The relief has to be claimed within two years of the end of the second year of assessment.

The relief must be claimed not later than two years after the end of the second year of assessment; but a further year is given if there is a further adjustment because the second year is the first year of another pair. Claims under other provisions (e.g. loss relief) can be revoked within the period.⁴

If the profit of one year is between 70% and 75% of that of the other, an adjustment is made by shifting from the higher year to the lower an amount equal to three times the difference between the two but less ¾ of the higher figure.⁵ This formula tapers the relief to nil at a 25% fluctuation.

> **EXAMPLE**
> Year 1, £7,200; year 2, £10,000. The difference is £2,800 so the amount to be shifted is (3 × 2,800) − £7,500 = £900 making the revised figures £8,100 and £9,100.

Averaging is not permitted in the first or last years of assessment.⁶ A change of partners precludes relief unless an election is made under TA 1988, s. 113 (§ **7: 49**). Corporate partners may not use the relief.

The adjustments are not made for all purposes; so it is the original and not the adjusted figures that are taken as the income for any application of TA 1988, s. 63 (§ **7: 43**).

Simon's Taxes B3.541; Butterworths Income Tax Service E4.02.
¹ TA 1988, s. 96(11). By concession farming includes intensive livestock rearing for human consumption; see extra-statutory concession A29 (1988), **Simon's Taxes, Division H2.2**.
² TA 1988, s. 96(2).
³ And stock relief for periods of account beginning before 13th March 1984; TA 1988, s. 96(7).
⁴ TA 1988, s. 96(9).
⁵ TA 1988, s. 96(3).
⁶ TA 1988, s. 96(4) and (6).

CALCULATION OF TAX

5: 48 The calculation of income tax due is complicated by a number of factors. First there is the problem of calculating the amount of income; this sometimes involves grossing up a sum received to reflect the fact that tax has been deducted at source. Secondly, there is a bewildering variety of deductions which must be distinguished. Some are deductions in computing income *from* a particular source, others are deductions *in computing* income or total income, others are deductions from particular groups of income. These must in turn be distinguished from deduction *from* income or from total income. Relief may also be given by way of relief from tax or by credit against tax. Thirdly, usually two rates of tax to be considered and each is applied to a different base; *basic rate tax* is levied on income, *higher rate tax* on an individual's total income while additional rate income tax is, from 1984–85, charged only on accumulated trust income. Fourthly, there are different methods of collecting the tax; some is deducted at source and other is levied by assessment. When calculating the amount of tax due it is necessary to distinguish the amount of tax due to the Revenue from the taxpayer from the total tax burden. Fifthly, there is the problem that income tax is paid not only by individuals but also by trusts, by estates in administration and by partnerships. What follows concentrates on the taxation of an individual. Sixthly, there may be problems stemming from the preceding year basis of assessment and from the absence of clear statutory rules of timing.

The following example will be used as the basis for the explanation which follows:

> In the tax year 1989–90 X is a married man with children aged 19 and 15; his mother-in-law is living with them and is maintained by him; her income is £8 per week. He has trading profits of £19,000 taxable under Schedule D Case I; he also receives £6,000 as director of a company. His wife has Schedule D Case I income of £5,500. He received payments of £3,187.50 by way of dividend from UK resident companies, £2,681.25 interest from a building society and £1,460 interest from a bank. He also received £4,800 by way of rent and has allowable rental expenses of £550.
>
> During the year X's mortgage interest was £2,000 gross (paid after deduction of tax relief under MIRAS). He also paid £4,000 to his ex-wife under a court order made in 1986 and £1,000 to charity under a covenant; the last figure represents a gross sum from which X deducted basic rate tax under TA 1988, s. 348, § **9: 76**. He also paid £875 in life assurance premiums (on a contract made before 14th March 1984) and £3,500 under a retirement annuity scheme. He and his wife have together paid £720 in Class 4 National Insurance contributions in 1989–90.

Calculation of total income

5: 49 Total income means the total income of that person from all sources estimated in accordance with the provisions of the Income Tax Acts: TA 1988, s. 835.

Simon's Taxes E1.4, E1.5; Butterworths Income Tax Service B1.01.

Inclusions

5: 50 (1) Income from each source according to the rule of each Schedule (TA 1988, s. 1). Sums deductible in computing income e.g. allowable expenses under Schedule A are taken into account in computing the amount of income under that Case. If the figures show a loss, the amount to be included is nil.

(2) Income subject to deduction under the PAYE scheme is included at its gross amount.

(3) Income subject to deduction at basic rate at source must be grossed up to reflect that fact; the taxpayer is then given credit for the tax withheld. Grossing up is carried out by multiplying the figure by the fraction $100/(100-BR)$ where BR is basic rate. This applies not only to annual payments within Schedule D Case III, infra, § **9: 76** but also foreign dividends under s. 123 and income under Schedule C.

(4) Bank interest and building society interest. These too must be grossed up at basic rate. However such income is not subject to basic rate tax and personal reliefs cannot be set against such income so as to give rise to a repayment.[1]

(5) Dividends under Schedule F together with the accompanying tax credit: TA 1988, s. 20(1), infra, § **24: 09**.

(6) The taxpayer's share of partnership income.

(7) Income deemed to be his under the provisions of the Act, e.g. under a settlement.

(8) Income to which he is entitled as beneficiary under a trust.

(9) Income of an unadministered residuary estate in which he has a life interest in possession or an absolute interest.

(10) Any income of another which must be treated as his, e.g. income of his wife living with him which is not the subject of separate assessment or separate taxation.

EXAMPLE

X's income:

```
 1) £19,000 (Schedule D Case I) and £4,250 (Schedule A).
 2) £6,000.
 4) £3,575 + £2,000.
 5) £4,250.
10) £5,500.
    ─────────
    £44,575
    ═════════
```

Simon's Taxes E1.4; Butterworths Income Tax Service B1.01.

[1] Building societies, banks, local authorities and other deposit takers—see TA 1988, ss. 476 and 479—pay a special "composite" rate of tax. A basic rate taxpayer has no more income tax to pay even though the composite rate is lower than the basic rate; conversely he may not claim a refund if his tax rate is lower. However, a higher rate taxpayer will find that his receipt is grossed up at the basic (not the composite) rate. The same rules apply to deposit interest paid by banks after 5th April 1985: TA 1988, s. 479. For 1989–90 the composite rate is 21.75% see SI 1988 No. 2145, *Simon's Tax Intelligence* 1988, pp. 853 and 864. For exceptions to composite rate scheme payments by building societies see *Simon's Tax Intelligence* 1987, p. 335.

Deductions

5: 51   The legislation contains a bewildering assortment of formulae.

(1) Interest allowable as under §§ **5: 29** to **5: 44**: Such interest payments can be "deducted from or set against" his income for that year of assessment (TA 1988, s. 353). Most taxpayers will receive mortgage interest relief at

basic rate by deduction from the interest payment under MIRAS; relief at higher rate is given by deduction from the tax burden.

(2) Maintenance payments and one half of the Class 4 National Insurance contributions: These are deductible in computing total income FA 1988, s. 38 (existing obligations) and TA 1988, s. 617(5).

(3) Retirement annuity premiums and contributions to approved personal pension plans are to be "deducted from or set off against" relevant earnings TA 1988, ss. 619 and 639.

(4) Loss relief: The taxpayer may claim relief from income tax on an amount of his income equal to the loss.

(5) Annuities and annual payments still payable under deduction of tax: while s. 835 permits the deduction of these items, s. 348 also allows the payer to withhold basic rate tax on making the payment. Without more this would mean that a person paying tax at 40%, who makes a payment of £100 gross under a covenant, would get a deduction of £40 and also withhold £25. In order to avoid a double deduction so far as concerns basic rate, s. 3 directs that £100 is subject to basic rate tax as the payer's income even though it has been deducted in computing his total income. The scope of these payments was greatly reduced by FA 1988—see infra, § **9: 33** et seq.

(6) Similar payments made by his wife living with him.

EXAMPLE
X's deductions:

    1) £2,000.[1]
    2)   £360.
    3) £3,325 ($17\frac{1}{2}\%$ maximum relief).
    5) £4,000 to ex wife.
       £1,000 to charity.
    ——————
    £10,685

X's total income is therefore £44,575 − £10,685 = £33,890.

Simon's Taxes A3.430–434, E1.5.
[1] Like the deductions described in item (5), tax will be charged at basic rate on the grossed-up sum of building society interest paid to ensure that relief is not given twice at the basic rate.

Credits

5: 52 Certain sums are available as credits against tax. These include not only tax paid by the trustee on trust income and the tax credit associated with Schedule F income, but also credits available under a double tax treaty or the unilateral relief under TA 1988, s. 790.

Taxable income

5: 53 Taxable income is total income minus reliefs deductible from total income. These are the personal reliefs.

EXAMPLE
X's reliefs
    Married man's allowance   £4,375

Wife's earned income relief	2,785
	£7,160
X's total (£44,575 − £10,685)	£33,890
Less reliefs	7,160
Taxable income	£26,730

X is also entitled to relief on tax of £125 in respect of his life assurance premium of £1,000; this is given effect by the payment of a net premium of £875,[1] and so is ignored for present purposes. If the contract had been made after 12th March 1984, however, no relief would be given.

---

[1] TA 1988, s. 266(5).

Basic rate liability

5: 54   A taxpayer is not liable to tax at basic rate on all items in his total income, i.e. not on sums subject only to excess liability; these items include building society interest, see supra, § **5: 50**. Further, a taxpayer is liable to basic rate tax on some items which do not form part of his total income; these are (i) annuities and annual payments made by him and subject to tax under TA 1988, s. 3 and (ii) income which is not his beneficially, such as income received as trustee or personal representative. (i) does not affect his overall tax burden since the tax will be withheld by him under TA 1988, s. 348, (ii) is in some senses quite separate from his other income since he may not use his personal allowances or other reliefs that accrue to him personally in computing this representative liability.

> **EXAMPLE**
> X is not liable to basic rate tax on the building society interest nor on the bank interest but is liable to basic rate tax (and only basic rate tax) on the covenanted sum of £1,000. The income on which he is liable *only* at basic rate is £21,700, i.e. £20,700 (base rate limit) + £1,000 which makes basic rate tax of £5,425.

Higher rate liability and excess liability

5: 55   A taxpayer is liable to higher rates of tax once his total income less reliefs exceeds a stated figure, which for 1989–90 is £20,700.[1]

A taxpayer is also subject to excess liability, i.e. to tax at the difference between the appropriate higher rate and the basic rate, on certain items; this is clearly a relic of the old surtax.

Such income is (1) building society and similar deposit taker's interest, TA 1988, ss. 476 and 479, (2) income treated as his by TA 1988, s. 683, (3) Sums received for certain restrictive covenants (TA 1988, s. 313) and (4) various gains from life policies (TA 1988, s. 547). Of these (1) will in effect have borne basic rate tax, although in fact it is the special composite rate that is charged on building societies, (2) represents a clear wish to restrict the effectiveness of income assignments by covenants; (3) and (4) represent curiosities in that Parliament appears to have taken the view that only those who are subject to higher rates should be called on to pay tax in respect of them.

EXAMPLE
X's liability to tax:
Taxable income £26,730

Tax at basic rate	£20,700	£5,175
40%	6,030	2,412
		£7,587

In addition X must pay basic rate tax on £1,000 (see § **5: 49**) which he will recover when he makes the payments to the charity. These do not therefore represent a tax burden to him.

---

[1] MIRAS only affects the mechanics of giving basic rate mortgage interest relief. Taxpayers continue to receive higher rate tax relief on their mortgage interest payments, and this is given by way of assessment or through the taxpayer's PAYE coding, see **Simon's Taxes A3.430–434**.

Allocation of rates and reliefs

5: 56 With different sources of income taxed in different ways, some at source and others by assessment and at different rates, and with different liabilities accruing at different times, rules have to be provided for regulating the order in which the various tax rates are allocated and which the various reliefs and exemption limits may be claimed.

Rates

5: 57 So far as concerns the order of allocation of tax rates, it appears to be Revenue practice to allocate these so that the earliest tax payable is charged at the lowest rates so low rates are charged first on income subject to deduction under PAYE, then on income under Schedules A and D, and then on income taxed (at basic rate) at source, for example, dividends.

Reliefs

5: 58 Deductions are allocated according to a statutory order.[1]
   (1) The general rule is that deductions are to be made in the order that will result in the greatest reduction of liability to income tax. This rule is of course subject to express provision to the contrary.[2]
   (2) Deductions for personal reliefs, that is deductions authorised by TA 1988, Part VII, Ch I,[3] are to be made after any other deductions.

---

[1] TA 1988, s. 835(3)–(5).
[2] E.g. TA 1988, s. 382(2) (loss relief) and TA 1988, s. 619 (retirement annuity premiums).
[3] Including reliefs for life assurance premiums under contracts made before 14th March 1984.

Commentary: The rate structure

5: 59 After the 1988 changes the UK income tax rate structure still presents an odd shape of marginal rates. After the personal reliefs (or zero rate band) has been exhausted then tax starts at a rate of 25%[1] with, usually, a further charge to National Insurance Contributions. The system then has a long basic rate band followed by the higher rate of 40%; however, liability to National Insurance Contributions is limited by a ceiling (for 1989–90 £325 p.w. = £16,900 p.a.) and this ceiling is reached before the end of the basic rate band. Taking both income tax and National Insurance Contributions into account together with the well known problem of the poverty trap, the system presents a pattern of high-low-high marginal rates of tax. Despite ingenious efforts such as calculating means for social security payments on a net of tax figure and then 1989 changes to the structure of NIC (2% on the first £73 and thereafter 9% up to the ceiling) it is hard to see what more can be done with the present set of concepts. The effect of this is to give most play to economic forces, such as incentives, in the middle of the income band. On economic grounds a profile that is low-high-low in terms of marginal rates has much to commend it but will be opposed on distributional grounds and rejected on political grounds.[2] A possible compromise is a system of constant marginal rates.[3]

---

[1] But the case for an introductory lower rate band is not strong—see Morris and Warren (1980) Fiscal Studies No. 3 pp. 34–43 and on the costs involved 122nd Report of Board of Inland Revenue.

[2] Meade Report c. 14.

[3] Meade Report p. 316 "the administration advantages would be incalculable".

6   Schedule E employment income

6: 01   Income tax is charged under Schedule E on the emoluments from any office or employment[1] and certain pensions.[2] Liability arises under three Cases.

Income tax under Schedule E is levied by TA 1988, s. 19(1) on emoluments from any office or employment. Emoluments "includes all salaries, fees, wages, perquisites and profits whatsoever".[3] Case law makes it clear that not all payments from employers to employees fall within this definition and that some payments from non-employers do.[4] The test is one of causation; an emolument is a payment in return for acting as or being an employee.[5]

The word emoluments covers also certain payments in kind. A payment in kind will only be taxable if in addition to being an emolument it is convertible into money, although a wider test applies to employees earning £8,500 a year or more and to directors.[6]

Income taxable under Schedule E is earned income.[7]

Expenses are deductible under Schedule E if they are incurred necessarily in the performance of the duties of this office or employment and, except in the case of travel, wholly and exclusively so incurred.[8]

Capital allowances may be claimed by the employee in respect of machinery and plant if incurred necessarily.[9]

If the expenses exceed the emoluments there will be a loss and so relief ought to be given against other income. However this is not the Revenue view.[10]

Emoluments paid by the employer are subject to a system of deduction of tax at source—the PAYE system.[11] Whether subject to that system or not, income is assessed on a current year basis. It is taxed on a receipts basis as opposed to an earnings basis—as from 1989.[12]

Simon's Taxes E4; Butterworths Income Tax Service Part D.

[1] TA 1988, s. 19, para. 1 as recast, for 1989–90 and later years by FA 1989, s. 36(2). Until 1922 Schedule E was confined to income from a *public* office or employment. A director of a company held a public office. Overseas remuneration from non-public office or employment remained in Schedule D, Case V until FA 1956, s. 10

[2] A pension is a taxable subject matter distinct from the office or employment—per Viscount Simon LC, in *Tilley v Wales* [1943] AC 386 at 392, 25 TC 136 at 149. Pensions in respect of other overseas service will come within Case IV or V if the source is foreign, infra, § **34: 05**. A reduction of 10% is applied to pensions within para. 4, TA 1988, s. 196.

[3] TA 1988, s. 131. A perquisite is merely a casual emolument additional to regular salary or wages: per Lord Guest in *Owen v Pook* [1970] AC 244 at 225, [1969] 2 All ER 1 at 5.

[4] Infra, § **6: 44**.

[5] Per Lord Radcliffe in *Hochstrasser v Mayes* [1960] AC 376 at 389, 392.

[6] TA 1988, s. 154; infra, § **6: 86**.

[7] TA 1988, s. 833(4); supra, § **4: 03**.

[8] TA 1988, s. 198; infra, § **6: 100**.

[9] FA 1971, s. 47(1).

[10] See TA 1988, s. 380; supra, §§ **5: 02** and **5: 16**.

[11] See TA 1988, s. 203; infra, § **6:114**. On who is the employer when an employee is seconded see *Caldicott v Varty* [1976] 3 All ER 329, [1976] STC 418.

[12] FA 1989, s. 36 infra, § **6: 29**.

CHARGING BASE OF SCHEDULE E[1]

6: 02   Income taxable under Schedule E: 1989–90

	Duties performed wholly in UK	Duties performed partly in UK, partly abroad	Duties performed wholly abroad
Person domiciled in the United Kingdom OR employer resident in the United Kingdom			
1. Resident in UK *and* ordinarily resident in UK	All emoluments (Case I)	(*a*) All emoluments of UK duties *plus* (*b*) All emoluments of duties abroad *unless* 365 day qualifying period —100% deduction (Case I)	All emoluments *unless* 365 day qualifying period —100% deduction (Case I)
2. Resident in UK but *not* ordinarily resident in UK	All emoluments (Case II)	*In UK* ⟵—— *Abroad* ——⟶	Remittances (Case III)
3. Not resident in UK	All emoluments (Case II)	⟵—— ——⟶	Outside scope of UK tax
Person domiciled abroad AND employer resident abroad ("foreign emoluments")			

	Duties performed wholly in UK	Duties performed partly in UK, partly abroad	Duties performed wholly abroad
4. Resident in UK *and* ordinarily resident in UK	All emoluments(Case I)	All emoluments (Case I)	Remittances (Case III)

		In UK	*Abroad*	
5. Resident in UK but *not* ordinarily resident in UK	All emoluments (Case II)	⟵	⟶	Remittances (Case III)

Person domiciled abroad AND employer resident abroad ("foreign emoluments")

		In UK	*Abroad*	
6. Not resident in UK	All emoluments (Case II)	⟵	⟶	Outside scope of UK tax

---

[1] TA 1988, s. 19.

Definitions

6: 03   (1) *Foreign emoluments.*   These are relevant to all three Cases. Emoluments are foreign only if they belong to a person not domiciled in the UK and are from a non-resident employer.[1]

(2) *Place of performance of duties.*[2]   In determining whether duties are performed wholly outside the UK, duties performed in the UK but which are purely incidental to the performance of duties abroad are ignored.[3] Certain duties are declared to be performed in the UK such as certain duties on board ships and aircraft and certain employments of a public nature under the Crown and payable out of public revenue.[4] These rules are varied when one comes to the reductions for Case 1.[5]

---

[1] TA 1988, s. 192.

[2] See *Taylor v Provan* [1974] 1 All ER 1201 at 1208, [1974] STC 168 at 175, *Barson v Airey* (1925) 10 TC 609.

[3] TA 1988, s. 132(2) cf TA 1988, s. 335, *Robson v Dixon* [1972] 3 All ER 671, [1975] BTR 466, *Taylor v Provan* [1973] 2 All ER 65 at 74.

[4] TA 1988, s. 132(4), *Graham v White* [1972] 1 All ER 1159, 48 TC 163 and extra-statutory concession A25 (1988), see **Simon's Taxes, Division H2.2**.

[5] Infra, § **6: 05**(3). TA 1988, Sch. 12, para. 5.

CASE I

6: 04   Where the employee is resident and ordinarily resident in the UK, Case I charges any emoluments arising within the chargeable period, which is the year of assessment.[1] When the duties are performed wholly in the UK, the emoluments are chargeable in full unless they are foreign emoluments. When however they are performed abroad, whether wholly or in part, a reduction may apply; see infra, § **6: 06**.

Simon's Taxes E4.111; Butterworths Income Tax Service A1.76.

[1] Infra, § **6: 29**.

Definitions

6: 05 The following rules apply for the purposes of the reductions; *not* for other Schedule E rules.

(1) *Days of absence*

These are relevant to the reductions for Case I. A person is not regarded as absent from the UK on any day unless he is absent at the end of it,[1] so the day of return is not a day of absence. The classification of the day of departure is less clear; one might infer from this rule that presence at the beginning of the day coupled with absence at the end makes the day one of absence; however if this is correct it follows that one who is absent from 23.59 to 00.01 every night is consistently absent from the UK. The Revenue view is that the day of departure is a day of absence: see Revenue leaflet IR 25 § 2: 10.

(2) *Associated employments*

These are central to the anti-avoidance provisions. Employments are associated if they are with the same person or with persons associated with each other.[2]

(3) *Place of performance—seamen and aircrew*

Special rules[3] apply to determine where these duties are performed; these rules draw a distinction between a voyage and a part of a voyage:

(i) (*a*) A voyage beginning and ending in the UK with no calls overseas; the duties are performed in the UK; but (*b*) if a part of the voyage begins and ends overseas the duties performed on that part are regarded as performed overseas.

(ii) (*a*) A voyage beginning and ending outside the UK—the duties are performed overseas; but (*b*) if a part of the voyage begins and ends in the UK, duties performed during that part are regarded as performed in the UK.

(iii) A voyage beginning in the UK and ending overseas—or vice versa—the rules are the same as for (ii).

(4) *Place of performance—incidental duties in the UK*

For the purposes of reduction 1, the rule which treats UK duties which are incidental to duties performed overseas as performed outside the UK (supra § **6: 03**) is disregarded both in deciding where duties are performed *and* whether a person is absent from the UK.[4] Insofar as the duties are treated as performed partly in the UK and partly overseas, reduction 1 may apply; the matter will also be of importance to the anti-avoidance rules although here the narrow scope given to the incidental duties seems to preclude this.

Simon's Taxes E4.113.
[1] TA 1988, Sch. 12, para. 4; on parts of a day see 3 Co Inst 53 and *Warr v Warr* [1975] Fam 25, [1975] 1 All ER 85.
[2] TA 1988, Sch. 12, para. 2(3).
[3] TA 1988, Sch. 12, para. 5. An area designated under the Continental Shelf Act 1964, is treated as part of the UK.
[4] TA 1988, s. 12, para. 6; different rules apply to actions for wrongful dismissal *Wilson v Maynard Shipbuilding Consultants AB* [1978] QB 665, [1978] 2 All ER 78.

Reduction 1: Long absences; qualifying period of 365 days—100%

6: 06   Where the duties are performed wholly or partly outside the UK the 100% deduction may apply; duties performed wholly in the UK cannot qualify for this reduction. In deciding whether the duties are performed wholly in the UK duties which are performed outside the UK but which are incidental to duties performed here are treated as performed here.[1]

The duties must be performed in the course of a qualifying period of at least 365 days. This period may be wholly or partly in the year of assessment so that a period from 1st January 1988 to 1st January 1989 may qualify. The words "in the course of" show that it is not necessary that offices or employments should exist on at least 365 days; likewise it is not necessary that there should be one employment only; further, the reason for absence from the UK is irrelevant, what matters is whether there are enough days of absence to make a qualifying period.

Simon's Taxes E4.113; Butterworths Income Tax Service H1.23.
[1] TA 1988, Sch. 12, para. 6.

Qualifying period[1]

6: 07   The rules defining a qualifying period are straightforward where the employee remains overseas throughout the period or pays only one visit to the UK during that time; but where he visits the UK more than once he may find that the effect of visits of identical total length will differ according to whether the visits are early or late in the period.

A qualifying period may consist either (*a*) entirely of days of absence or (*b*) partly of days of absence and partly of days of presence. For rule (*b*), when a period consisting entirely of days of absence, "the relevant period", comes to an end and there has been previously one or more qualifying periods, the relevant period and the (or, if more than one, the last) qualifying period together with the intervening days spent in the UK between those two periods are treated as one qualifying period provided that (*i*) there are no more than 62 intervening days; and (*ii*) the number of days in the resulting period which are not days of absence does not exceed $\frac{1}{6}$ of the total number of days in that period.[2] It will be seen that one who goes overseas for 365 days but who spends 62 days in the UK on one return visit does not qualify as 62 is greater than $\frac{1}{6} \times 365$.

EXAMPLE

A leaves the UK and returns after 153 days; he spends 60 days here and then leaves the UK for a period of 154 days. A has a qualifying period of 367 days; the relevant period is that of 154 days and it may be linked up with the earlier qualifying period of 153 days.

B leaves the UK and returns after 330 days; he spends 63 days continuously in the UK and then returns overseas for 330 days. B does not have a qualifying period of 365 days; although the number of days of presence does not exceed $\frac{1}{6}$th of the total he has a period in excess of 62 days. B could have solved his problem by going to Calais or the Channel Islands for two nights at some point during his 63 days.

For rule (*b*) the problems arise in trying to link up different periods of absence to form one qualifying period; only qualifying periods may be linked up. The question whether a period is a qualifying period must be judged at the end of the relevant period and the $\frac{1}{6}$th rule is applied at that time and not at the end of some later relevant period.

EXAMPLE

C leaves the UK and returns after 60 days; he spends 10 days in the UK; he goes abroad for 55 days and returns for 25 days; he then stays abroad for 216 days. C's first relevant period is 55 days; this can be linked up with the periods of 60 and 10 days to make one qualifying period of 125 days. C's second relevant period is 216 days; this too can be linked up with the qualifying period of 125 days to make a period of $(125 + 25 + 216)$ 366 days.

D's pattern of visits is identical with C's but for his first visit to the UK being of 25 days and his second of 10 days. D does not have a qualifying period of 366 days. D's first relevant period is 55 days but this cannot be linked up with the period of 60 days since the 25 days of presence exceeds $\frac{1}{6} \times (60 + 25 + 55)$. D's second relevant period of 216 days can be linked up with the qualifying period of 55 days and the intervening 10 days to make a qualifying period of 281 days but not with the first qualifying period of 60 days.

Days of presence can only be ignored if they are between periods of absence. A person cannot qualify for this relief by being away for 306 days and then staying in the UK.[3]

These rules are relaxed for seafarers. For earnings for a period from 6th April 1988 the qualifying period of 365 days is to be calculated by substituting $\frac{1}{4}$ for $\frac{1}{6}$ and 90 for 62.[4]

---

[1] TA 1988, Sch. 12, para. 3.
[2] TA 1988, Sch. 12, para. 3(2).
[3] *Robins v Durkin* [1988] STC 588.
[4] TA 1988, Sch. 12, para. 3(2A), added by FA 1988, s. 67.

6:08 Emoluments attributable to a period of terminal leave immediately following a qualifying period are treated as emoluments attributable to the qualifying period but not so as to change the year of assessment.[1] So if a person works overseas in Tahiti from 6th April 1985 to 6th April 1986 and on 7th April 1986 he receives an extra month's salary by way of terminal leave which he spends in Whitehaven the sum will be treated as part of his emoluments for 1986–87 but it will qualify for the 100% deduction even though paid for leave rather than services. This rule only treats the emoluments as attributable to the qualifying period; it cannot extend that period. So 364 days of work in Tahiti followed by two days of holiday in Whitehaven would not attract the 100% reduction.

Anti-avoidance

6: 09 The deduction applies to the emoluments attributable to the period of absence. However a restriction may apply where the duties are performed only partly overseas or where there is, in the same year of assessment, an associated employment the duties of which are not performed wholly overseas. The restriction is that the amount of emoluments which are to be the subject of the deduction are not to exceed such proportion of the emoluments as is reasonable having regard to the nature and time devoted to the duties performed outside and in the UK and all other relevant circumstances.[1] Here the proportion is of the aggregate of the emoluments from the overseas and related associated employments.

This restriction is intended to prevent abuse of the relief. Thus suppose that a person is employed by a UK company for two years and that he is sent overseas for one of them; his salary for his work in the UK is £5,000; his salary for his work overseas is £45,000. The onus will be on A to show that £45,000 was a reasonable proportion of £50,000. This rule applies whether the overseas employment is with the UK company itself or an overseas subsidiary since the employments will be associated.

¹ TA 1988, Sch. 12, para. 2(2).

Reduction 2: Foreign emoluments

6: 10 Where the foreign emoluments are for duties performed wholly or partly in the UK, Case I applies. At one time the amount of foreign emoluments was reduced by 50% so that a person resident and ordinarily resident was taxed on 50% of them. The reduction was only 25% if and when he had been resident here for nine of the previous ten years and was resident in that year.[1] The benefit of this reduction cannot apply for 1989–90 and later years.[2]

Simon's Taxes E4.114; Butterworths Income Tax Service H2.03.
¹ TA 1988, s. 192.
² TA 1988, s. 192(4).

Deductions for expenses

6: 11 (1) *Initial and final travel expenses.* Where the duties of the employment are carried out wholly outside the UK the general doctrine in TA 1988, s. 198 is not apt to permit the deduction of travel to take up the post and return from it since such expenses are incurred not in the performance of the duties but to enable one to carry them out or return from having carried them out.

So special legislation is needed and applies where the employee is resident and ordinarily resident in the UK and the emoluments are not foreign emoluments. The employee may deduct the costs of travel from any place in the UK to take up the employment and of travel to any place in the UK on its termination. The reference to "any place in"[1] the UK is presumably to ensure where an employee flies from Glasgow to the US via Heathrow he can deduct the costs of the flight from Glasgow to London and not just the costs of travel from the airport of departure from the UK.

(2) *Board and lodging.* Expenses of board and lodging to enable him to carry out the duties of his employment are deductible if they were met (*a*) directly by the employer or (*b*) by the employee and he was then reimbursed by the employer.[2] It will be seen that no deduction is allowed where the employee meets the expenses himself and is not reimbursed; this is presumably because in those situations in which deduction is allowed the employer will claim to deduct these sums in computing his profits and so the Revenue can check the sums claimed by the employer against the sums claimed by the employee. Where the expense is incurred partly for a non-employment purpose, s. 193 permits apportionment of those costs attributable to the employee,[3] but will allow nothing for the spouse or family.[4]

(3) *Travel between multiple employments.* Travel costs are also deductible where the employee has more than one employment the duties of at least one of which are performed wholly or partly outside the UK.[5] Travel from one job to another could not be said to be in the performance of the duties of either and so a special rule treats the expense as incurred in performing the duties of the employment to which he is going. This rule applies to journeys both from and to the UK but the employment[6] must not be such as to give rise to foreign emoluments. Apportionment is authorised where there is more than one purpose.[7]

(4) *Intermediate and family travel.* The rules so far outlined do not cover return journeys while the duties of the employment are being carried out nor do they provide for the deduction of the costs of travel by the employee's family. These matters are regulated separately—by a different and more restrictive rule.[8]

First, for the costs of family travel to qualify the employee must be absent from the UK for a continuous period of at least 60 days,[9] whether or not in the year of assessment, for the purpose of performing the duties of the employment. Secondly, the cost must be either paid or reimbursed by the employer as in the board and lodging rule.[10] Thirdly, the rule only extends to two outwards and two inwards journeys in any year of assessment. The child must not be over 17[11] at the beginning of the outwards journey.

Where the employee's travel costs are concerned the original rule limited him to two trips in each year of assessment and required a continuous period of absence of at least 60 days but these were repealed as from 1984–85. Where the duties are performed partly in and partly out of the UK they must be such that those being performed overseas can only be performed there and the journey must be wholly and exclusively for the purpose of performing those duties (in the case of an outward journey) or (in the case of an inbound journey) returning after performing such duties.[12] Where the duties are of one or more employments a similar rule applies. The employee can deduct the costs of travel for any journey from and to any place in the UK[13] provided the duties can only be performed outside the UK and the absence from the UK was occasioned wholly and exclusively for the purpose of performing the duties concerned.[14] The condition that the duties can only be performed outside the UK is relaxed for seafarers.[15]

(5) *Employees not domiciled in the UK.* Employees not domiciled in the UK but paid for duties performed here have a special rule.[16] To qualify for this rule the person must not have been resident in the UK for either of the two years preceding the year of assessment in which he arrived or must not have been in the UK for any purpose during the two years ending with the date of his arrival.[17] The special rule permits the deduction of costs of travel to and from his usual place of abode, i.e. where he normally lives.

If he is present in the UK for a continuous period of at least 60 days for the purpose of carrying out the duties of his employment the family travel rules are as for UK domiciled employees and it is necessary for the cost to be borne by the employer or reimbursed separately.[18]

Once here the employee is entitled to the benefit of these rules for a period of five years beginning with the date of arrival. There is a special commencement rule which states that where the employer is not a UK resident the five year period is not to begin before 6th April 1986.[19]

Simon's Taxes E4.115; Butterworths Income Tax Service H2.05.

[1] Added by TA 1988, s. 193(3).

[2] TA 1988, s. 193(4)(*a*).

[3] Apportionment is authorised by TA 1988, s. 193(4).

[4] Revenue Leaflet IR 25 (1977) §2:36.

[5] TA 1988, s. 193(5) (FA 1977, s. 32(4)).

[6] *Semble* the one to which he is going.

[7] TA 1988, s. 193(6).

[8] The travel may be from or to "any place in" the UK; TA 1988, s. 194(3).

[9] TA 1988, s. 194(2). On costs of travel by wife to accompany a director or employee in precarious health see extra-statutory concession A5(1) (1988), **Simon's Taxes, Division H2.2** (The phraseology of this concession is flagrantly sexist).

[10] TA 1988, s. 194(2).

[11] A person reaches 18 at the start of the day which is his 18th birthday; Family Law Reform Act 1969, s. 9.

[12] TA 1988, s. 194(3).

[13] TA 1988, s. 194(5) and (6).

[14] TA 1988, s. 194(4). On "wholly and exclusively" in a slightly different context see *Mallalieu v Drummond* [1983] STC 665, infra § **7: 89**.

[15] TA 1988, s. 194(7)–(9).

[16] TA 1988, s. 195.

[17] This rule may operate harshly, for instance, when an employee visits the UK with a view to seeing whether he wishes to come here to work.

[18] TA 1988, s. 195(6).

[19] TA 1988, s. 195(2), (3), (13).

6: 12   In addition to expenses deductible under the general rules, foreign emoluments (as defined in § **6: 10**) may attract further deductions for "corresponding payments".[1] Payments are "corresponding" if they are similar to payments which would be deductible if all the relevant elements were in the UK. Examples include alimony paid under a foreign court order, interest on a loan to purchase a sole or main residence in the employee's home country, and annual contributions to a foreign pension fund which corresponds to a UK pension fund for which relief could be given.[2]

Such payments are allowable only if made out of the foreign emoluments and, save for pension contributions, Revenue practice is to require proof that there is not sufficient overseas income (on which UK tax is not payable) to enable him to make the payments without having recourse to the foreign emoluments.[2]

---

[1] TA 1988, s. 192(3).
[2] Revenue leaflet IR 25 (1977) §§ 3: 13 and 3: 18.

CASE II

6: 13   Case II applies where the person is either not resident or, if resident, not ordinarily resident in the UK. In general he is chargeable only on such of his emoluments as are in respect of duties performed in this country. Such a person is not taxable under Case II in respect of duties wholly performed outside the UK; although he may come within Case III.

On allocation of earnings where duties are performed partly in the UK and partly outside; see SP 5/84, **Simon's Taxes, Division H3.2**.

Simon's Taxes E4.112; Butterworths Income Tax Service A1.76.

CASE III

6: 14   (*a*) Case III applies the remittance basis to three types of income if the person is resident in the UK, whether ordinarily resident or not. These are:

(i) foreign emoluments for duties performed outside the UK by one resident but *not* ordinarily resident in the UK;[1]

(ii) foreign emoluments for duties performed wholly outside the UK by one resident *and* ordinarily resident in the UK;

(iii) emoluments for duties performed outside the UK by someone resident, but not ordinarily resident, in the UK.[2]

A charge under Case I or II excludes one under Case III.[3] Where a person has some emoluments charged under Case II and others under Case III for the same employment, emoluments received in the UK are attributed to the Case II income first.[4]

On remittance basis see infra, § **34: 10**.

On allocation of earnings where duties are performed partly in the UK and partly outside see SP 5/84.

(*b*) The new timing rules for Schedule E have some effect on Case III. In determining whether a payment is chargeable under the remittance basis the new rules are to apply to the full amount received in the UK but the new definition of when a payment is to be treated as received does not apply to Case III.[5] However liability under Case III is now to arise on sums received in the UK whether or not the office or employment is still held when the emoluments are received in the UK.[6] When the person has died before the remittance, tax is charged on the personal representatives.[7]

There is a special transitional rule for sums which are emoluments for a year before 1988–89 but are received in the UK after 5th April 1989. If these would have been within Case III as it applied before 1988–89 if they had been received after 5th April 1989, they are not to be treated as emoluments of the earlier year but as income of the year of receipt. This appears to mean that if the employment had ceased before 6th April 1989 (so that they would *not* have been within charge under the old Case III) they remain free of tax. If however the source still existed at the end of 1988–89 the sums will be taxable on receipt even though the source has ceased to exist by the time of receipt.[8]

A further transitional rule concerns the opposite case where sums are received in the UK before 6th April 1989 but are emoluments of a year after 1988–89. These are deemed to be received on 6th April 1989 and so within the new Case III.[9]

Simon's Taxes E4.116; Butterworths Income Tax Service A1.76.

[1] TA 1988, s. 192(2).
[2] TA 1988, s. 19(1).
[3] TA 1988, s. 131(2).
[4] SP 5/84, see **Simon's Taxes, Division H3.2**.
[5] TA 1988, s. 202A(3).
[6] TA 1988, s. 202A(2)(*b*).
[7] TA 1988, s. 202A(3)—but no charge can arise if he died before 6th April 1989: FA 1989, s. 37(3).
[8] FA 1989, s. 37.
[9] FA 1989, s. 40(3), (4).

6: 15 Planning is important. The provision of a separate overseas contract is still advantageous; (i) it places the employee in paragraph 3 instead of 2; (ii) fixing the contract in overseas currency can produce a form of protection against UK inflation if the pound falls (iii) and overseas pay would not be affected by UK pay restraint policies.

Where a non-UK domiciled person works for a foreign employer and renders services both here and abroad it may well be worth his while to have two separate contracts of employment, the one for work in the UK (foreign emoluments) and the other for work overseas—charged on remittance basis; if the emoluments for the latter are unreasonably inflated the excess will be liable under Case I.

There is the question of taxing those who work here on a long-term basis but without acquiring UK domicile. Before 1974 these were not taxed on an arising basis on their worldwide income but only on their income arising here. This was modified in that their "foreign emoluments" would become taxable, initially as to 50% and later as to 75%. The 1984 changes have ended the favoured treatment in recognition of the fact that the general level of income tax has now fallen dramatically and is in line with rates prevailing in other countries.

One must not overlook the effect of double tax treaties on one who is not resident in the UK; these may grant exemption from Schedule E.[1]

OFFICE OR EMPLOYMENT

6: 16   Schedule E taxes emoluments from an office or employment,[1] neither of which words is further defined. An office denotes "a subsisting, permanent, substantive position which has an existence independent of the person who fills it, and which is filled in succession by successive holders".[2] Examples include a director of a company,[3] even if he has a contract of employment and owns all the shares, a trustee or executor,[4] a company auditor,[5] a National Health service consultant[6] and a local land charges registrar.[7] By contrast in *Edwards v Clinch*[8] a person appointed to act as an inspector at a public inquiry did not hold an office since the post had no existence independent of him; there was neither continuity nor permanence. The Court of Appeal in that case also held that an office and an employment were not mutually exclusive.[9]

An employment is something "more or less analogous to an office"[10] but modern cases equate employment with a contract of service. If the arrangement under which sums are paid to a taxpayer is one for services, it falls outside Schedule E. A ship's master, a chauffeur and a reporter on the staff of the newspaper are all employed under a contract of service and so come within Schedule E whereas a ship's pilot, a taxi-man and a newspaper contributor are employed (by the owner, the hirer or the newspaper) under a contract for services[11] and so do not. A consultant under the National Health service is taxed under Schedule E in respect of that employment or office whether the arrangement is whole time or part time.[12] Again, a teacher working whole time for a local education authority is taxed under Schedule E.[13] If no services are to be performed, the contract is not one of employment.[14]

North Sea divers are excluded from Schedule E.[15]

A person employed by a company is an employee; whether a person holding himself out to be an employee of a company he controls and has created is such an employee or a self-employed person is a question of fact.[16] The fact that the contract is illegal cannot of itself convert an employee into a self-employed person. Problems sometimes arise if an employee is seconded to work for another firm. Thus where the employee earns fees but is required to account to the first company for those fees there is a case for saying that the payments to him should be treated as his taxable income and so subject to PAYE. However by concession this is not required.[17] Where the employee is seconded to work for a charity on a temporary basis there is express provision allowing the employer to deduct the costs as if the employee had remained working for the employer.[18] This principle was extended in 1987 to cover the costs of secondment to an educational establishment run by a local education authority or similar bodies in Scotland and Northern Ireland.[19] Neither of these provisions states—although they apparently both assume—that the payments to the seconded employee are taxable as employment income.

Simon's Taxes E4.201, 202; Butterworths Income Tax Service D1.

[1] TA 1988, s. 19. The distinction between office and employment can be crucial. Thus by TA 1988 s. 291(2) a person is connected with a company, and so disqualified from holding shares under the BES scheme if he is an employee and not, apparently, if he holds an office. One should, however, note that a director is expressly disqualified by s. 291.

[2] Rowlatt J in *Great Western Rly Co v Bater* [1920] 3 KB 266 at 274, 8 TC 231 at 235. This is not a "complete" definition: per Lord Atkin in *McMillan v Guest* [1942] AC 561 at 564, 24 TC 190 at 201.

[3] *Lee v Lee's Air Farming Ltd* [1961] AC 12, [1960] 3 All ER 420, PC. The posts of director and managing director may be separate offices *Goodwin v Brewster* (1951) 32 TC 80.

[4] *Dale v IRC* [1951] 2 All ER 517, 34 TC 468, *A-G v Eyres* [1909] 1 KB 723.

[5] *Ellis v Lucas* [1966] 2 All ER 935, 43 TC 276.

[6] *Mitchell and Edon v Ross* [1961] 3 All ER 49, 40 TC 11.

[7] *Ministry of Housing and Local Government v Sharp* [1970] 2 QB 223, [1969] 3 All ER 225.

[8] [1981] STC 617; duties of a public nature did not necessarily make the post an office.

[9] [1980] STC 438. As might be inferred from the dictum of Lord Normand in *Dale v IRC* [1954] AC 11 at 26.

[10] Per Rowlatt J in *Davies v Braithwaite* [1931] 2 KB 628 at 635.

[11] *Stevenson, Jordan and Harrison Ltd v Macdonald and Evans* [1952] 1 TLR 101 at 111, per Lord Denning. (This case concerned copyright not tax.) On what is a contract of service, see *Ready-Mixed Concrete (South East) Ltd v Ministry of Pensions* [1968] 2 QB 497, [1968] 1 All ER 433.

[12] *Mitchell and Edon v Ross* [1959] 3 All ER 341, 40 TC 11 (Upjohn J) and [1960] 2 All ER 218, 40 TC 11, CA; [1961] 3 All ER 49, 40 TC 11, HL.

[13] *Fuge v McClelland* (1956) 36 TC 571.

[14] *Clayton v Lavender* (1965) 42 TC 607.

[15] TA 1988, s. 314, **Simon's Taxes E5.701**.

[16] *Cooke v Blacklaws* [1985] STC 1 (the illegality of the arrangement was a factor, but not a conclusive one).

[17] Extra statutory concession A37 (1988), **Simon's Taxes, Division H2.2**; if it is his taxable income it is hard to see how he can then deduct the sums when they are paid over to his employer as this is a disposition of income not the cost of earning it. It appears more correct to say obligation to account prevented the payment from having the quality of income in his hands.

[18] TA 1988, s. 86.

[19] TA 1988, s. 86(3); interestingly this clause has a "sunset" provision as it is due to expire in 1997.

An employment and a profession

6: 17   A taxpayer may have more than one source of income; the existence of a day-time employment is not however incompatible with the co-existence of a trade or profession.[1] Moreover the activity or skill which is used in the employment may be the same as that used in the trade or profession. So a doctor may be a part time employee of a Hospital Board and carry on a part time private practice, his pay under the former source will be taxed under Schedule E while that from the latter will be taxed under Schedule D, Case II.

[1] Per Rowlatt J in *Davies v Braithwaite* [1931] 2 KB 628 at 635, 18 TC 198 at 203.

Many employments or one profession?

6: 18   Where a person holds an office he can only be taxed under Schedule E so that a series of offices is just that and is not a profession.[1] However in relation to a series of employments one can discern two quite distinct approaches. In *Davies v Braithwaite*[2] the taxpayer was Miss Lilian Braithwaite, the actress. Between 1924 and 1928 she acted in the UK in a number of plays, films and wireless programmes. She also recorded for the gramophone. She had separate contracts for each play and wireless appearance. She also appeared in a play on Broadway, New York. The performance in New York being completely outside the UK, she argued that it was an employment so that she would be taxable at that time only on such sums, if any, as she remitted to the UK. The Revenue argued that it was merely one engagement in her profession as an actress, a profession carried on inside and outside the UK so that she was taxable on an arising basis under Schedule D, Case II. The Revenue won; Rowlatt J said:[3]

> "Where one finds a method of earning a livelihood which does not contemplate the obtaining of a post and staying in it, but essentially contemplates a series of engagements and moving from one to the other ... then each of those engagements could not be considered an employment, but is a mere engagement in the course of exercising a profession, and every profession and every trade does involve the making of successive engagements and successive contracts and, in one sense of the word, employments."

This test, by starting with the general scheme of the taxpayer's earnings and then seeing where a particular contract fits, is totally different from the approach of Pennycuick V-C, in *Fall v Hitchen*.[4] In this case a professional ballet dancer was held to be liable to tax under Schedule E in respect of a contract with one particular company because that contract looked at in isolation was one of service and not one for services. Pennycuick V-C, held that this concluded the matter.[5]

On this divergence two points should be noted. The first is that in *Davies v Braithwaite* neither Rowlatt J nor counsel for the Revenue seems to have been concerned with the question whether the contract was one of service or one for services.[6] The second is that the two approaches may not be quite so far apart since some cases suggest that one of the factors in determining the classification of the contract is whether that person carries on business on his own account.[7]

In determining whether a contract is one of service or one for services a useful rule of thumb is whether the taxpayer gets a salary or is paid so much an hour for work actually done. The traditional test was one of control but that is not a sufficient condition of a contract of service. One must now consider whether he provides his own equipment, or hires his own helpers, what degree of financial risk he runs, what degree of responsibility he has and how far he has an opportunity to profit from sound management.[8]

The question whether a contract is one of service or for services appears to be one of law so far as the identification of the criteria is concerned but the balancing process of applying those criteria seems to be left to the Commissioners as a question of fact.[9]

The Revenue have recently waged a campaign to bring many people within Schedule E by threatening to make the payer responsible for the payment of income tax under the PAYE system. The payer usually submits to this pressure as he has nothing to gain by resisting.[10] In 1985 the Revenue issued an explanatory booklet—IR 56.[11]

Simon's Taxes E4.203.
[1] *IRC v Brander and Cruickshank,* infra, §§ **6: 19, 6: 22**; compare *Marsh v IRC* [1943] 1 All ER 199, 29 TC 120.

² [1931] 2 K B 628, 18 TC 198. For a modern example, see *Household v Grimshaw* [1953] 2 All ER 12, 34 TC 366.

³ [1931] 2 K B 628 at 635, 18 TC 198 at 203.

⁴ [1973] 1 All ER 368, [1973] STC 66.

⁵ [1973] 1 All ER 368 at 374; the taxpayer had no other contracts at that time (unlike Miss Braithwaite), indeed, his was a full-time contract and one which prohibited him from taking on outside activities without his employer's consent.

⁶ See [1931] 2 K B 628 at 631–2. In *Mitchell and Edon v Ross* in the Court of Appeal, Lord Evershed distinguished *Davies v Braithwaite* as not involving a contract of service (!): [1960] Ch 498 at 521, 40 TC 11 at 43. Compare with *Davies v Braithwaite, Bennett v Marshall* [1938] 1 K B 591, [1938] 1 All ER 93, 22 TC 73.

⁷ *Market Investigations Ltd v Minister of Social Security* [1969] 2 QB 173 at 185.

⁸ *Ready Mixed Concrete (South East) Ltd v Minister of Pensions* [1968] 2 QB 497, [1968] 1 All ER 433. See also *Sidey v Phillips* [1987] STC 87.

⁹ *O'Kelly v Trusthouse Forte plc* [1984] QB 90, [1983] 3 All ER 456, CA, approved by Nourse LJ in *Beauchamp v F W Woolworth plc* [1988] STC 714 at 718e, CA. Cf. Lord Widgery CJ, in *Global Plant Ltd v Secretary of State for Social Services* [1972] 1 QB 139 at 154–5. See criticism by Pitt [1985] LQR 217.

¹⁰ See HC Official Report (13 July 1983) Vol. 45, cols. 384–385, [1983] STI, p. 309. Contrast the more constitutionally correct attitude of the DHSS which has power to classify certain jobs as employments.

¹¹ See [1985] STI, p. 391. See also **Simon's Taxes E4.211** for practice on particular occupations—including freelance workers in the film, television and radio industries (letter published in *Taxation* 7 February 1986).

Consequences

6: 19   The consequences of coming within Schedule E as opposed to Schedule D, Case I or II are extensive, and rest on the doctrine that the Schedules are mutually exclusive. In *IRC v Brander and Cruickshank*, Lord Donovan said that the doctrine was quite unreal and served no useful purpose. Indeed its application in that case would cause administrative chaos.¹

---

¹ [1971] 1 All ER 36 at 46–9. It seems to make Income Tax (Employments) Regulation 1973, S.I. 1973, No. 334, reg. 8(2)(*a*) quite superfluous. The concessionary relief at A37 (1988) should also be noted—tax treatment of directors fees received by partnerships and other companies.

6: 20   (1) An overseas employment may fall to be taxed on a preferential basis whereas if it is simply an incident in the carrying on of a profession within and without the United Kingdom the receipts will be taxed in full (as in *Davies v Braithwaite*, and see § **6: 03**).

6: 21   (2) Expenses incurred for an office or employment under Schedule E will only be deductible if they conform to the strict test laid down in TA1988 s. 198;¹ expenses incurred for a trade or profession will be deductible on a different and less niggardly test.²

In *Mitchell and Edon v Ross*³ the taxpayer, Ross, held an appointment as a consultant radiologist under the Birmingham Regional Hospital Board, and served at a number of hospitals under that authority. He was also in private practice as a consultant radiologist, which practice he carried on at his home in Rugby. The Revenue admitted that Ross was correctly assessed under Schedule D, Case II in respect of his private practice but argued that income accruing from the Hospital Board should be assessed—and so calculated—under Schedule E.

At first instance and in the Court of Appeal[4] the taxpayer argued unsuccessfully that the positions with the Hospital Board were not offices. He further argued that if he was correctly assessable under Schedule E, the employment should nonetheless also be seen as part of his profession under Schedule D, Case II so that the Schedule D rules for deduction of expenses should apply. This rested on a finding by the Commissioners that these employments were a necessary part of his profession as consultant radiologist and merely incidental to that profession.[5]

Only the second point was argued in the House of Lords and the taxpayer lost. If the employment was assessable under Schedule E, expenses in respect of that employment could be allowed only if they conformed to the requirements of the Schedule; the appointment could not be treated for tax purposes as part inside and part outside the Schedule.[6]

---

[1] Infra, § **6: 100**.
[2] Infra, § **6: 113**.
[3] [1961] 3 All ER 49, 40 TC 11.
[4] [1959] 3 All ER 341, 40 TC 11; and [1960] 2 All ER 218, 40 TC 11, CA.
[5] Suppl. Case stated, 40 TC 11 at 32.
[6] On concordat reached between the Revenue and the medical profession, see **Simon's Taxes E4.211**, and extra-statutory concession A9 (1988), **Simon's Taxes, Division H2.2**.

6: 22   (3) Terminal payments in connection with the ending of an office or employment may escape tax in whole or in part;[1] compensation for the loss of a trading asset will usually be a trading receipt.[2]

In *IRC v Brander and Cruickshank*[3] the House of Lords held that where a firm of Scottish advocates with a substantial general legal business also acted as secretaries and/or registrars for some 30 to 40 companies, each appointment was a separate office and therefore, thanks to the Schedule E rules, sums received on the termination of two such appointments, escaped tax.[4]

In an earlier case, *Blackburn v Close Bros Ltd*[5] the taxpayer was a merchant banking company which derived income from acting as managers, secretaries and registrars of various companies. One appointment with a particular company was terminated and Pennycuick J, held the sum paid by way of compensation to be a trading receipt within Schedule D, Case I.

In *IRC v Brander and Cruickshank*, Lord Guest,[6] with whom Lord Upjohn agreed, doubted the correctness of *Blackburn v Close Bros Ltd* but Lord Morris regarded the facts of the earlier case as being quite different[7] and thought the offices were not trading assets. Lord Donovan would have followed the earlier case if there had been a finding of fact that the taxpayer had sought the office as part and parcel of his trade or profession.[8] On such a finding Lord Donovan would have been prepared to hold that income payments fell within Schedule E and terminal payments within Schedule D. Lord Reid dismissed the appeal "for the reasons given by your Lordships".[9]

Given the logic of *Mitchell and Edon v Ross*[10] it is hard to understand any conclusion other than that of Lord Guest.[11] If an office falls exclusively within Schedule E it does not cease to be an office simply because it was sought; while if different payments from the same source can fall under two

Schedules, as Lord Donovan suggested, the selection of the applicable rules from the range offered by the two Schedules seems as arbitrary as the selection of an Easter bonnet.

By concession travelling expenses of directorships held as part of a professional practice are allowed as deductions under Schedule D.[12]

Simon's Taxes E4.211.
[1] Under TA 1988, ss. 148 and 188(4); post, § **6: 38**; and see Press Release dated 20th March 1980, [1980] STI, p. 128.
[2] But it may still escape tax as a gift or a capital payment and not a trading receipt; infra, § **7: 69**.
[3] [1971] 1 All ER 36, 46 TC 574.
[4] TA 1988, s. 148 applies when the payment is not otherwise chargeable to tax. The finding that the post was an office and so within Schedule E meant that the payment was not chargeable to tax under some other Schedule, thus enabling s. 148 to operate.
[5] (1960) 39 TC 164.
[6] [1971] 1 All ER 36 at 45, 46 TC 574 at 593.
[7] At pp. 42, 590.
[8] At pp. 47, 595.
[9] At pp. 40, 588.
[10] If the taxpayer was not carrying on a profession, the payment might have fallen within Schedule D Case VI, but this seems to be excluded by the conclusion that the post was an office and so within Schedule E.
[11] One consequence of Lord Guest's view is that a company can hold an office and so have that income computed under Schedule E.
[12] Extra-statutory concession A4 (1988), **Simon's Taxes, Division H 2.2.**

6: 23 (4) The costs of acquiring the office will not be deductible under Schedule E; they will usually be deductible under Schedule D, Cases I and II.[1]

(5) Solicitor trustees receiving annuities from the trust fund for acting as trustee have traditionally been taxed on the receipt under Schedule D, Case III with deduction at source under TA 1988, ss. 348 and 349. However, as an office, the post of trustee falls within Schedule E.[2] (**Simon's Taxes E4.212**).

(6) While partners are jointly assessed under Schedule D there is no machinery for a joint assessment under Schedule E.[3]

(7) Schedule E is assessed on a current year basis and under PAYE; Schedule D on a preceding year basis.[4]

(8) The capital allowance structure is much wider for trades than for professions and employments.

---

[1] Cf. Pennycuick J in *Blackburn v Close Bros Ltd* (1960) 39 TC 164 at 173.
[2] Supra, § **6: 16**.
[3] TA 1988, s. 111.
[4] Infra, § **7: 40**.

EMOLUMENTS

The causation test

6: 24 TA 1988, s. 19 taxes emoluments from the office or employment. The question whether a payment is from the source is one of causation. As Upjohn J said in *Hochstrasser v Mayes:*[1]

"... the payment must be made in reference to the services the employee renders by virtue of his office and it must be something in the nature of a reward for services past, present or future."

Viscount Simonds accepted this as entirely accurate subject only to the observation that the word "past" might be open to question.[2] In *Laidler v Perry* Lord Reid expressed doubts on the use of the word "reward" saying:[3]

"It is not apt to include all the cases that can fall within the statutory words. To give only one instance, it is clear that a sum given to an employee in the hope that he will produce good service in the future is taxable."

This last has been applied in two recent decisions of the House of Lords.

In *Brumby v Milner*[4] sums of money held in a profit sharing scheme were distributed when the scheme was wound up. The House held that this payment, like the previous income payments, arose from the employment and from no other source; it was therefore taxable. This decision has now been extended to situations in which the payment is made on account of services even though the employment ended some time before the payment from the trust.[5]

In *Tyrer v Smart*[6] the taxpayer applied for shares in his employing company, having preferential right of application as an employee. The House held that he was taxable on the advantage gained.

Two questions arise. The first is how to formulate the test. Despite variations, that of Upjohn J is still the starting point. The second is whether the question of whether a payment is an emolument is one of law or of fact. In *Hochstrasser v Mayes* Upjohn J took the question to be one of inference from primary fact and of legal inference at that, thus making the question one of law. In *Tyrer v Smart*, however, the inference seems to have been treated as one of fact and so within the sole jurisdiction of the Commissioners. The position is as confused as it is unfortunate; the earlier view seems preferable.

The general principle is weakened by a number of concessions. Thus there is a substantial relaxation of principle in connection with relocation expenses[7] and a published concession for payments under a suggestion scheme.[8]

Simon's Taxes E4.401; Butterworths Income Tax Service D1.21.

[1] [1959] Ch 22 at 33.

[2] See infra, § **6: 27**.

[3] [1966] AC 16 at 30, 42 TC 351 at 363.

[4] [1976] 3 All ER 636, [1976] STC 534, but distinguish *Tyrer v Smart* [1976] 3 All ER 537, [1976] STC 521.

[5] *Bray v Best* [1986] STC 96.

[6] [1979] 1 All ER 321, [1979] STC 34.

[7] Extra-statutory concession A5 (1988), **Simon's Taxes, Division H2.2**. Revenue Press Release, 28 November 1985; see also SP 1/85, **Simon's Taxes, Division H3.2**.

[8] Extra-statutory concession A57 (1988), see **Simon's Taxes, Division H2.2**.

Consequences

6: 25   Since the question is one of causation, and not consideration, the court is not confined to any expressions of consideration in any service contract. So in *Pritchard v Arundale*[1] a payment expressed in the contract of service to be in consideration of that service escaped tax. Conversely in *IRC v Duke of Westminster*, Lord Atkin would have held the payment to be an emolument notwithstanding that the service was expressed not to be the consideration.[2]

A second consequence of the rule of causation is that a payment caused by something other than services must escape tax. Even a payment to induce an employee to take up an employment with an independent employer escapes tax.[3] Moreover the onus is on the Revenue to show that the payment is an emolument.[4] A question that the courts have not yet dealt with is that of multiple causes. Where a payment is caused by service and by something else, principle would suggest an apportionment of the payment, at least where this is practicable.[5]

---

[1] Infra, § **6: 35**.
[2] [1936] AC 1; supra, § **1: 05** n. 11.
[3] *Shilton v Wilmshurst* [1989] 1 WLR 179, [1988] STC 868 it was agreed that the payment would be caught in part by TA 1988, s. 148.
[4] Per Viscount Simonds in *Hochstrasser v Mayes*, supra.
[5] See infra, § **6: 41**.

6: 26   In *Hochstrasser v Mayes*[1] the taxpayer worked for ICI Ltd, a large concern with factories in different parts of the United Kingdom. To encourage its employees to remain in the service of the company if asked to move to a different part of the country, the company would make good any loss incurred by the employee through a fall in the value of a house which the employee owned. This scheme was restricted to married employees and also to houses not exceeding £2,000 in value. On being moved from Hillhouse to Wilton, the taxpayer sold his house in Fleetwood for £1,500; it had originally cost £1,850. ICI reimbursed him this loss of £350 and the Revenue sought to assess him on the £350; they failed.

The Revenue argued that all payments by employers to their employees as such were taxable unless they were payments in return for full consideration in money or money's worth other than his services under the employment. The first difficulty with this proposition is the vagueness inherent in the notion of a payment to an employee as such. When Parker LJ, had adopted a similar approach in the Court of Appeal he would have excepted gifts to the employee in a personal capacity.[2] The second difficulty is the problem of deciding whether a payment was for full consideration or not and Viscount Simonds eschewed such a task. In the House of Lords this approach was rejected unanimously. It was not disputed that the company would not have made this payment if the taxpayer had not been an employee and it was clear that the company thought that it was going to benefit by having a more settled work force if a scheme like this were in operation. Moreover, because the taxpayer had a perfectly standard wage, it could not be said that this was disguised remuneration.

The House of Lords[3] held that the payment was not in respect of his services to the company but rather to compensate him for the loss which he had sustained, and was therefore not taxable.

The first set of difficulties concerns other possible payments. As the

Revenue's counsel put it, to be recouped a loss by someone else is plainly a profit. If these profits escaped tax, which profits would not?

It was agreed that if Mayes had suffered a bereavement and the company had seen fit to grant him something from its benevolent fund of course such payment would not have been taxable.[4] But if Mayes had been compensated for a loss on an investment on the Stock Exchange it would be a remarkable conclusion that he should not be liable to tax in respect of such a payment. Only Lord Denning gave reasons why an indemnity of the last type would be taxable.[5] Unfortunately this example was premised on the view that the indemnity would be by way of reward for services, a premise which automatically makes the sum taxable. His Lordship went on to say that the sum would be taxable because the losses were his own affair and nothing to do with his employment, but this would be equally true of the hypothetical bereavement.

The second set of difficulties concerns the case itself.[6] Other housing benefits are taxed and show how isolated the decision is. If ICI had provided him with rent free accommodation, he would have been taxable, as he would if he had gone into private rented accommodation and the employers had paid the rent; likewise if ICI had guaranteed him against any increase in rent. Perhaps if they had guaranteed him against an increase in mortgage rates such payments would have been taxable. One has also to consider the Revenue practice of permitting tax free relocation expenses.[7]

One may note that the company was getting the best of both worlds. Not only was the sum not taxable in the hands of its employee but also it was deductible by the company in computing its profits. This is legally correct but encourages planning.

However one should also note that it was not in dispute that Mayes was receiving the correct salary for the job he was doing, so that it was not a case of disguised remuneration, that he worked for a blue chip company and the scheme was restricted to houses of less than £2,000 in price so that it was not available to very senior employees;[8] quite how relevant these points are is highly debatable.

The case is authority for three important propositions:

(1) that service must be the *causa causans* and not simply the *causa sine qua non* of the payment if it is to be a taxable emolument;[9] so

(2) the categories of non-taxable payments are not closed;

(3) the onus in such cases is on the Revenue to show that the payments falls within the scope of the taxing statutes.[10]

Simon's Taxes E4.422; Butterworths Income Tax Service D1.21.

[1] [1959] Ch 22.

[2] [1959] Ch 22 at 54–55.

[3] [1960] AC 376.

[4] Per Lord Radcliffe at p. 392.

[5] At p. 396. *Quaere* if the loss were on shares of the employer company which he was obliged to sell on leaving the company; infra, § **6: 57**.

[6] Both Viscount Simonds and Lord Radcliffe thought the case was near the line (at p. 391) although the former had little doubt as to the side of the line on which it fell. In *Laidler v Perry* Lord Hodson said that *Hochstrasser v Mayes* was a decision on its peculiar facts: [1966] AC 15 at 36, 42 TC 351 at 366.

[7] See extra-statutory concession A5 and A67 (1988), **Simon's Taxes, Division H2.2** and *Simon's Tax Intelligence* 1989, p. 106.

[8] *Quaere* whether the payment would have fallen within TA 1988, s. 154, if the employee's income had exceeded (now) £8,500. In *Jennings v Kinder* [1959] Ch 22, 38 TC 673, CA the Revenue's attempt to tax it under what is now TA 1988, s. 153—as a payment in respect of expenses—failed.

[9] See [1960] AC 376, per Viscount Simonds at 389; per Lord Cohen at 395; in the vernacular Lord Radcliffe at 392. In *Brumby v Milner*, supra, § **6: 24**, Lord Simon criticised the use of these phrases and preferred to ask whether these payments arose relevantly from the employment; this, with respect, seems to get one absolutely nowhere.

[10] Per Viscount Simonds at 389.

Services past

6: 27 The liability to income tax of payments for services past was left open by Viscount Simonds in *Hochstrasser v Mayes*.[1] However it has been held that a tip to a taxi driver is taxable even though given only at the end of the service.[2] A bonus payment to an employee[3] and a payment on completion of, say, twenty five years service with the company[4] are likewise taxable although in these cases, since the employment had not yet terminated, the payments might be seen as incitements to even greater service and loyalty in the future. By concession[5] an award in the form of a tangible article or shares in the employing company is tax-free if the cost is reasonable, i.e. if it does not exceed £20 per year of service. The employee must have been in service for at least twenty years and not have received any other award within the previous ten years. This limit does not appear to apply when the employee is leaving the employment.

Such authority is only indirect since none of these cases appears to turn on the question of payment for past services but it may be taken as some authority for their liability to tax since the payments must have escaped tax had the point not been accepted.[6] The fact that past consideration is no consideration is quite irrelevant since the test is one of causation and not of consideration. The true line seems to be not one between services future and services past but between a gift for personal or other reasons and a payment for services past or future. The fact that the service is past is but one factor in enabling this line to be drawn.[7] So in *Moore v Griffiths*[8] the fact that the payment was not known about until after the services had been rendered tended to show that it was a testimonial and so not taxable. This line of reasoning seems to have been accepted in *Bray v Best*[9] when the payment was made after the employment had ceased; the court held that the payment should be retroactively attributed to the years of service.

---

[1] Supra, § **6: 24**.

[2] *Calvert v Wainwright*, infra, § **6: 32**.

[3] *Radcliffe v Holt* (1927) 11 TC 621.

[4] *Weston v Hearn* (1943) 25 TC 425.

[5] See extra-statutory concession A22 (1988), **Simon's Taxes, Division H2.2** but on long service awards to firemen see [1985] STI, p. 178.

[6] See per Evershed MR, in *Henley v Murray* [1950] 1 All ER 908, 31 TC 351 at 366—"nor was it a reward for his past service"—not taxable. Similarly Lord Warrington in *Hunter v Dewhurst* (1932) 16 TC 605 at 643.

[7] As in *Cowan v Seymour* [1920] 1 KB 500, 7 TC 372; *Denny v Reed* (1933) 18 TC 254.

[8] Infra, § **6: 33** [1972] 3 All ER 399, 48 TC 338.

[9] [1986] STC 96.

Capital

6: 28   Certain payments which have escaped TA 1988, s. 19 have been described as capital payments.[1] It is not clear whether such payments escaped s. 19 because they were capital payments, so could not be income payments and so could not come within s. 19 even if in return for services, or whether they escaped tax because not in return for services and could conveniently but irrelevantly or even inaccurately be described as capital sums. The latter view appears preferable.[2] It is axiomatic that income tax is a tax on income but since what is income is defined in each Schedule and Case it ought to follow that emoluments of an office or employment are by definition income. The decision in *Brumby v Milner*, supra, § **6: 24**, now appears to hold, although without apparent argument, that this is correct. It is, to say the least, significant that in no case has the classification of a payment as capital been the prime reason for holding that the payment is not taxable, the description capital is therefore best regarded simply as a convenient label for certain types of non-emoluments.

---

[1] E.g. Lord Denning MR in *Jarrold v Boustead* [1964] 3 All ER 76 at 81. Lord Simon in *Tilley v Wales* [1943] AC 386 at 393, 25 TC 136 at 149.

[2] Finlay LJ, in *Prendergast v Cameron* (1939) 23 TC 122 at 138.

Timing

The new rules

6: 29   The rules for determining when income arises under Schedule E have been radically revised by FA 1989. The effect of the 1989 scheme is to charge tax by reference to earnings as and when they are received. The former system made no attempt to charge tax until the taxpayer had some right to the sums in issue but would then relate those services back to the year in which the services to which they related were performed e.g. if a bonus is paid in one year for services rendered in an earlier year. For most employees there is no difference between the two systems.

Tax is charged under Schedule E Case I and II on the full amount of the emoluments received in the year in respect of the office or employment concerned.[1] In a major reversal of earlier law, including the decision of the House of Lords in *Bray v Best*,[2] it is not necessary that the employee should hold the office in the year in which the sums are received. Tax is charged under Case III on the full amount of the emoluments received in the UK in the year and again it is not necessary for the office or employment to exist in the year in which they are received in the UK; see supra, § **6: 14**.

The question what amounts to a receipt is not left to case law development but is the subject of detailed provisions. Emoluments are to be treated as received when payment is made or, if earlier when a person becomes entitled to payment.[3] These rules apply also to PAYE.[4]

In addition special rules apply if the person is a director and the emoluments relate to an office or employment with that company (whether or not that office or employment is the directorship).[5] Where sums on account of emoluments are credited in the company's accounts or records, that date is to be preferred whether or not there is any fetter on the right to draw the sum.[6] Likewise if the amount to be paid for a period is determined before the period ends, the payment will be treated as chargeable when that period ends even though no payments have yet been made. Where the amount for the period is not known until later e.g. when a bonus is finalised, the date of that determination will be taken. Where more than one of these rules, including the general rules in the previous paragraph apply, the earliest date will be taken.

These rules are not to override the special statutory timing rules for cash or non-cash vouchers, credit tokens and payments of compensation on retirement or removal from office.[7] The new rules are also excluded for the beneficial occupation rules (infra, § **6.52**), the rules governing benefits and expenses payment for directors and employees earning £8,500 pa or over (infra, §§ **6.85** et seq) and from pensions as well as from various social security benefits.[8]

In a further change of immense theoretical, and practical, interest, there is to be no deduction under Schedule D Cases I and II on account of emoluments until the emoluments would be brought into charge under Schedule E.[9]

The new rules do not apply if the employee died before 6th April 1989.[10]

Simon's Taxes E4.970, 973; Butterworths Income Tax Service D1.161–D1.165.

[1] TA 1988, s. 202A, added by FA 1989, s. 37(1).

[2] [1989] STC 159.

[3] TA 1988, s. 202B(1) added by FA 1989, s. 37(1); for origins, see Committee on Enforcement of Revenue Powers (Cmnd. 8822 the Keith Committee), pp. 141–145.

[4] FA 1989, s. 45.

[5] TA 1988, s. 202B(1) and (2); the term director is defined in sub-ss (3), (5) and (6). On problems in earlier law see ICAEW Tax Memorandum TR738—*Simon's Tax Intelligence* 1988 p. 738.

[6] TA 1988, s. 202B(4).

[7] TA 1988, s. 202B(8)–(10).

[8] FA 1989, s. 41.

[9] FA 1989, s. 43.

[10] FA 1989, s. 37(3).

The old rule

6: 29A The old rule, which applies for year of assessment before 1989–90, was very different. Emoluments were taxed on a current year basis and, generally, when they were received. However, where a payment for services was made in arrears that payment relates back to the date of the service, this was done even though there was no contractual right to the payment when the service was rendered; in *Heasman v Jordan*[1] bonus payments at the end of the Second World War were spread back over the years of work during the war and in *Inland Revenue Board v Suite*[2], a Privy Council decision on appeal from Trinidad and Tobago, arrears of salary paid to a teacher on reinstatement following a suspension were attributed to the years of suspension.

In practice arrears were usually related back only if the taxpayer asked for it. However in *Bray v Best*[3] the employment had ceased when the payments were made and the Revenue sought to have the case remitted to the Commissioners to determine the period over which they could be treated as having been made. This attempt failed in the House of Lords.

Where payment was made subject to a condition it was taxable only when the employee acquires a vested interest.[4] If he acquired such an interest and then returned it to his employer who placed it on trust under which the employer's interest was not vested the payment is an emolument when first acquired.[5] A contingent obligation to repay a sum received for services to be rendered did not prevent the sum from being an emolument when received.[6]

When payment was made in the form of a loan that payment was not income unless and until the obligation to repay is released.[7] This rule is not affected by the changes in FA 1989 since this loan is not an emolument until it is released.

These rules were unsatisfactory for a variety of reasons. A taxpayer might arrange for a payment to be related to a particular period so as to attract a lower rate of tax. Likewise he might arrange for sums to be credited to an account with the company but subject to a fetter which prevented him from having anything but a contingent right to it—and so defer tax subject only to the slight risk that the contingency might not occur.

There was also a highly dubious Revenue practice known as the accounts year basis whereby the Revenue would assess tax on the basis on the amount shown in the company's accounts for the year ending in the year of assessment even though at that time the accounts would not have been approved by the company's General Meeting.[8] This was much like the rules for Schedule D Case I (infra, § 7: 41–43) with the same income being used to measure liability to tax in more than one year to begin with, and a gap which was never so used at the end. A payment which relates to the period between the company's accounting date and 5th April 1989 will not be assessed for 1988–89 on an accounts basis. If paid before 6th April 1989, it will not be assessed on a receipts basis either.[9]

Simon's Taxes E4.970, 973; Butterworths Income Tax Service D1.161–D1.165.

[1] [1954] 3 All ER 101, 35 TC 518, following *Dracup v Radcliffe* (1946) 27 TC 188. Cases of compensation for termination of service (infra, § 6: 42), being *ex hypothesi* not for services, cannot be spread back on power to assess out of time; see TMA 1970, s. 35.

[2] [1986] STC 292.

[3] [1989] STC 159: Spreading back should not have been permitted in this case since the payments were not for services as such.

[4] *Edwards v Roberts* (1935) 19 TC 618, CA.

[5] *Smyth v Stretton* (1904) 5 TC 36; *Parkins v Warwick* (1943) 25 TC 419.

[6] *Riley v Coglan* [1968] 1 All ER 314, 44 TC 481; infra, § 6: 35.

[7] *Clayton v Gothorp* [1971] 2 All ER 1311, 47 TC 168.

[8] See *Taxation* vol. 122 p. 401.

[9] Hansard 23 May 1989, Standing Committee G, col. 186 (Mr. Lamont).

Transitional rules

6: 29B   Transitional rules are needed for two principal situations. The first concerns those payments which are received, under the terms of the new rules in 1989–90 or 1990–91, but which are also taxable as income of a previous year under the old rules e.g. a bonus declared and paid in 1989–90 in respect of the year 1988–89. Here the risk is of double taxation. Such payments are to be subject to the new regime and removed from charge for the earlier year and are made taxable in 1989–90 or whatever the year of receipt may be.[1] Any consequential adjustments are to be made.[2]

This is a matter of election; the election must be made before 6th April 1991 or such later time as the Board may allow.[3] The election may not be made if the only emoluments not paid before 6th April 1989 relate to the period from 5th March to 5th April 1989.[4]

A special rule relates to the "accounts basis", a term which is defined by reference to usage.[5] A person taxable on this basis for a period including 1987–88 is not to be allowed to revert to a strict earnings basis unless it was made in writing and before 6th April 1989.[6] The purpose is to prevent a person taking possibly undue advantage of the transitional rule.

Transitional protection for the Revenue is required if a payment would be treated as received in 1988–89 under the new rules but in 1989–90 under the old rules e.g. if a payment to a director was made subject to a fetter in the earlier year and that fetter was removed in 1989–90. Such payments are to be taxed in 1989–90 and so treated as received on 6th April 1989.[7]

The position with regard to payments under Schedule E Case III—the remittance basis—is set out at § **6.14** supra.

Simon's Taxes E4.970, 973; Butterworths Income Tax Service D1.161–D1.165.

[1] FA 1989, s. 38(2) in which case s. 38(1)(*d*) is also deferred. On employees of Lloyds underwriters, see s. 38(10) to (12).
[2] FA 1989, s. 38(3).
[3] FA 1989, s. 38(6) and (13).
[4] FA 1989, s. 38(5).
[5] FA 1989, s. 38(14).
[6] FA 1989, s. 38(7)–(9).
[7] FA 1989, s. 40.

Money's worth—discharge of employee's obligation

6: 30 Payments applied for the benefit of the taxpayer are just as much his income as moneys paid directly to him.[1] So where an employer discharges a pecuniary obligation of his employee the sum paid is treated as income of the employee even if it is income tax as in *Hartland v Diggines*.[2] This applies equally where both employer and employee are jointly liable.[3] The fact that the employer was under no obligation to make the payments was irrelevant.

A promise to pay a salary "without any deductions and taxes which will be borne by" the employer is interpreted as an agreement to pay such sums as after deduction of tax gives the net salary after deduction of tax.[4] The principle was applied in *Nicoll v Austin*[5] to future obligations. The taxpayer was life director of and had a controlling interest in his employing company. Under his contract of service he was to continue to reside in his own house but the company would pay all outgoings in respect of his house, including rates, taxes and insurance and the costs of gas, electric light and telephone and of maintaining the house and gardens[6] in proper condition, but the house remained the taxpayer's. Finlay J, reversing the Commissioners, held that the payments made by the company constituted money's worth to the taxpayer who was therefore taxable. By concession this rule does not apply to the heating, lighting, cleaning and gardening costs of certain clergymen.[7]

However the rule in *Nicoll v Austin* does not apply if after leaving the employer and before being used to discharge the liability of the employee it has become the income of someone else. In *Barclays Bank Ltd v Naylor*[8] ICI had set up a discretionary trust out of which payments could be made to assist in the cost of educating the children of employees working for overseas companies in the ICI group. Grants were made by the trust to a child of one of the employees and the sums were paid to the child's account with Barclay's Bank which as his agent sought repayment of the tax deducted at source. This claim would succeed if the payments were annual payments within Schedule D, Case III, but fail if the payments were emoluments of the child's father's employment. Cross J held that the payments had become the income of the child and the fact that income had been used to discharge the father's legal obligation to pay the school fees was insufficient to turn the income of the child into the income of the parent.

The tax avoidance possibilities thus opened up are however limited. First the payment under the trust must be a genuine payment.[9] Secondly if there is a rule that children's investment income is aggregated with that of their parents the end result may be worse for the employee.[10] Thirdly if the employee earns over £8,500 from that and connected employments or is a director, the payment will be taxable under TA 1988, s. 165[11] since, after 14th March 1983, the payment cannot be treated as exempt under TA 1988, s. 331 as scholarship income.[12]

The payment of an expense in connection with the provision of a parking place is expressly excluded.[13]

Simon's Taxes E4.402, 415.

[1] E.g. *Drummond v Collins* [1915] AC 1011, 6 TC 525.

[2] [1926] AC 289, 10 TC 247. See also *IRC v Miller* [1930] AC 222, 15 TC 25; *IRC v Leckie* (1940) 23 TC 471. An underdeduction of a director's PAYE which is accounted for to the Revenue by his employer is taxed under TA 1988, s. 158, infra, § **6: 99**.

[3] *Richardson v Worrall* [1985] STI 384 (*quaere* whether this will not be so if the primary liability and the primary benefit are the employer's).

[4] *Jaworski v Institution of Polish Engineers in Great Britain Ltd* [1951] 1 KB 768, [1950] 2 All ER 1191. But cf. *Jennings v Westwood Engineering Ltd* [1975] IRLR 245. Tax-free remuneration for directors is now prohibited by Companies Act 1985, s. 311; on definition of director see ibid s. 741; the net sum paid is to be treated as a gross sum but see **Simon's Taxes E4.453**.

[5] (1935) 19 TC 531.

[6] For a doubt about the gardens, see Lord Evershed MR, in *Wilkins v Rogerson* (1961) 39 TC 344 at 353 and infra, § **6: 47**.

[7] Extra-statutory concession A61 (1988), see **Simon's Taxes, Division H2.2**.

[8] [1960] 3 All ER 173, 39 TC 256. Under an earlier scheme an allowance was paid directly to the employee—such an allowance was taxable. See also *Constable v Federal Taxation Comr* (1952) 86 CLR 402.

[9] Cross J, emphasised that the Crown had not argued that the trust was not a genuine discretionary trust nor that the payment was not a proper exercise of the discretion. The former point, if substantiated, would presumably give rise to liability since the trust would be treated as a sham. However if the latter point was substantiated the correct result ought to be a resulting trust for the trust and so no charge on the employee.

[10] Supra, § **3: 17**. Before 6th April 1984 the income, being investment income, was liable to the investment income surcharge.

[11] Infra, § **6: 98**.

[12] Reversing the effect of the decision of the House of Lords in *Wicks v Firth* [1983] STC 25.

[13] TA 1988, s. 197A, added by FA 1988, s. 46.

EXAMPLES

Emoluments

6: 31 Payments for services include not only ordinary wages and salaries but less obvious payments such as those to mark a period of service with the employer.[1] Also included are bonus payments whether contracted for or not,[2] even if paid at Christmas.[3] A sum paid "to preserve an employer's good name and good staff relations" was held to be taxable even though it was designed to compensate staff for the withdrawal of a tax-free benefit in kind.[4]

A payment for service to an employer may be taxable even though the service was not within the scope of his duty. So in *Mudd v Collins*[5] a director who negotiated the sale of a branch of the company's business was held taxable on the sum of £1,000 granted him by the company as commission. All that had occurred was that the office had been enlarged.

However if the taxpayer can show that the payment is not for services but a testimonial[6] he will escape tax. Thus in *Cowan v Seymour*[7] a company was being wound up and the former secretary of the company acted as liquidator without remuneration. When the liquidation was nearly complete the shareholders resolved to give the liquidator £586. The Commissioners held that he was taxable in respect of that sum, as did Rowlatt J, but that decision was reversed by the Court of Appeal, where it was emphasised that the duties of the liquidator had virtually ceased[8] and that the payment was made not by the employer but the shareholders.[9] However neither of these points is conclusive.[10] The question is one of fact and the decision must today be considered doubtful.[11]

A payment by an employer to reimburse an expense incurred by the employment is not an emolument;[12] but an allowance is treated as an emolument.[13] This is so even if the employee would not have been able to deduct the expense himself under TA 1988, s. 198; however, it is assumed that this applies only to expenses incurred in connection with the employment.[14].

A gift to a savings scheme is not normally an emolument if it matches a contribution by the employee or if it is put up to ballot.[15]

Simon's Taxes E4.465.

[1] *Weston v Hearn* [1943] 2 All ER 421, 25 TC 425.

[2] *Denny v Reed* (1933) 18 TC 254. See extra-statutory concession A22 (1988), **Simon's Taxes, Division H2.2**. (Payments up to £20 for each year of service, minimum period 20 years, are not taxed.)

[3] *Laidler v Perry* [1965] 2 All ER 121, 42 TC 351. On Christmas parties see Revenue Press Release dated 26th October 1984, [1984] STI, p. 715.

[4] *Bird v Martland* [1982] STC 603. Payments for suggestion schemes are in practice governed by extra-statutory concession A57 (1988), see **Simon's Taxes, Division H2.2**.

[5] (1925) 9 TC 297; Rowlatt J. See also *Radcliffe v Holt* (1927) 11 TC 621.

[6] Infra, § **6: 33**.

[7] [1920] 1 KB 500, 7 TC 372.

[8] Per Lord Sterndale MR, at 509, 379; per Atkin LJ at 511, 381.

[9] Per Younger J at 516, 384.

[10] Supra, n. 7.

[11] *Cowan v Seymour* was distinguished in *Shipway v Skidmore* (1932) 16 TC 748 and in *Patrick v Burrows* (1954) 35 TC 138 but was, surprisingly, followed in *IRC v Morris* (1967) 44 TC 685, when the Court of Session held that there was evidence to support the Commissioners' findings.

Payments in excess of £30,000 might at first sight appear to be caught by TA 1988, ss. 148 and 188(4), but this applies only if they are "in consequence of the termination of the office" so the provision does not apply.

[12] *Owen v Pook* [1969] 2 All ER 1, 45 TC 571 but see Lord Simon (dissenting) in *Taylor v Provan* [1975] AC 194 at 218; see also *Donnelly v Williamson* [1982] STC 88. Reimbursement of car parking expenses when the parking space is at or near the place of work is not taxable—TA 1988, s. 197A (added by FA 1988, s. 46).

[13] *Perrons v Spackman* [1981] STC 739.

[14] Thus, in *Richardson v Worrall* [1985] STC 693 a reimbursement of the cost of petrol obtained for private use was taxable; but in *Donnelly v Williamson* (supra) a reimbursement of a teacher's costs for doing something outside the contract of service (attending a parents' evening) was not.

[15] See **Simon's Taxes E4.463**.

Payment for services or gifts on personal grounds

6: 32   An emolument must be distinguished from a gift which is for reasons unconnected with the employment. Thus a payment may be made to relieve poverty[1] or as a mark of personal esteem, or to mark some particular occasion such as the passing of an examination,[2] or as a reward for some service; only the last is a taxable emolument. There is now an extra statutory concession exempting from tax gifts from third parties which are emoluments up to £100 p.a.[3]

The mere fact that the donor is the employer will not suffice to make the gift an emolument, but neither is the fact that the donor is not the employer sufficient to prevent the gift from being an emolument. The question is whether the payment is made because of the services rendered by the employee in the course of his employment. On this basis Atkinson J held in *Calvert v Wainwright*[4] that a tip to a taxi driver was taxable but added that a tip of £10 would not be taxable if it was paid at Christmas or when the driver was going on holiday and was intended to acknowledge the driver's qualities and faithfulness. Such a payment would be different from one given in the ordinary way as remuneration for services rendered.[5]

In *Moorhouse v Dooland* Jenkins LJ, stated four principles:[6]

(*i*) the test of liability to tax on a voluntary payment made to the holder of an office or employment is whether, from the standpoint of the person who receives it, it accrues to him by virtue of his office or employment or, in other words, by way of remuneration for his services;

(*ii*) if the recipient's contract of employment entitled him to receive the voluntary payment that is a strong ground for holding that it accrues by virtue of the office, or, in other words is a remuneration for his services;

(*iii*) the fact that the voluntary payment is of a periodic or recurrent character affords a further, though less cogent ground for the same conclusion;

(*iv*) on the other hand, a voluntary payment may be made in circumstances which show that it is given by way of present or testimonial on grounds personal to the recipient, as for example a collection made for the particular individual who is at the time vicar of a given parish because he is in straitened circumstances, or a benefit held for a professional cricketer in recognition of his long and successful career in first class cricket. In such a case the proper conclusion is likely to be that the voluntary payment is not a profit accruing to the recipient by virtue of his office or employment but a gift to him as an individual paid and received by reason of his personal needs or by reason of his personal qualities or attainments.

These principles were stated in a case which concerned a payment by a third party. At least where the payer is the employer one should also consider the intentions of the payer.[7] The amount of the payment is also relevant.[8]

One area where the courts have had to distinguish between gifts and emoluments concerns the clergy. It was early decided that grants from a sustentation fund to supplement the incomes of clergy in poorly endowed parishes were emoluments.[9] The payments were not admittedly from their employers but they were still emoluments because they were paid for services; they were paid to the clergy by virtue of their offices. The fact that such a payment was voluntary was quite irrelevant. What mattered was that the reason for the payments was to augment stipends and not to make grants of eleemosynary nature, that is to make grants to clergy because they were poor. In *Blakiston v Cooper*[10] the House of Lords held that Easter offerings which by custom and episcopal prompting were used not for the general purposes of the church as decided by the particular parish but given to the vicar, were also taxable. It may appear startling that those who on a particular Sunday—and that one of the most significant in the Christian year—contribute to the collection in their church, should be rendering unto Caesar nearly half their contributions, but so undoubtedly it is.[11] Such payments are given to the vicar as incumbent and are therefore taxable.[12] The giving may be voluntary but it is not spontaneous and there is an element of recurrence.[13] The fact that he may get more than a previous vicar because his congregation like him better merely underlines the fact that the payment is for services. Of course not all payments to vicars by members of their congregation are emoluments. If the gift had been of an exceptional kind, such as a golden wedding present[14] or a testimonial or a contribution for a particular purpose, as to provide a holiday or a subscription due to the personal qualities of the particular clergyman, it might be a mere present.[15] On this reasoning a gift to the clergyman so that he may hire a car while on holiday might not be taxable but a gift to assist with his car costs in the parish certainly would be.

Simon's Taxes E4.467, 468; Butterworths Income Tax Service D1.52, 53.

[1] *Turton v Cooper* (1905) 5 TC 138.

[2] *Ball v Johnson* (1971) 47 TC 155 (not taxable even though the bank required the employee to take this bankers examination).

[3] Announced by Inland Revenue, 20 October 1988; *Simon's Tax Intelligence* 1988, p. 768. The limit permitted for Christmas parties is £50 per head pa (regarded as modest!).

[4] [1947] 1 All ER 282, 27 TC 475; on Revenue practice see [1984] STI, p. 187 and [1985] STI, p. 187.

[5] At pp. 529, 283, 478. The question is one of fact and degree. Christmas presents will be taxable if customary: *Wright v Boyce* [1958] 2 All ER 703, 38 TC 167, CA, or indiscriminate: *Laidler v Perry* [1966] AC 16, [1965] 2 All ER 121, 42 TC 351. A company gave each of its employees a £10 voucher at Christmas, regardless of their rate of remuneration or personal circumstances. A senior employee earning more than £2,000 a year thought the payment a charming Christmas gesture rather than as a payment for services, but this did not prevent the vouchers from being taxable under s. 19 and were taxed at £10 in view of the wide range of goods for which they could be exchanged. Among the facts which supported this conclusion were that the vouchers of the same amount were given to nearly all staff and that this pattern of giving was past its eleventh year, indeed it was only a cash equivalent for the Christmas turkey which each employee had received before a scarcity of supplies made such munificence impossible.

[6] *Moorhouse v Dooland* [1955] Ch 284, 36 TC 1.

[7] Per Lord Hodson in *Laidler v Perry* [1966] AC 16 at 35, 42 TC 351 at 366; and see Brightman J in *Moore v Griffiths* [1972] 3 All ER 399 at 411 (employer's gift; third party's gift). If the company had in return for their payment used the footballer's name to advertise their products that payment would have been taxable under Schedule D, Case VI, infra, § **10: 10**. *Quaere* whether allowing one's receipt of a gift to be used for advertisement will not also fall within Schedule D, Case VI.

[8] Thus the difference between the wage and the benefit in *Seymour v Reed* and the £10 tip in *Calvert v Wainwright*. See also Lord Denning MR in *Laidler v Perry* [1965] Ch 192 at 199, 42 TC 351 at 361.

[9] *Herbert v McQuade* [1902] 2 KB 631, 4 TC 489.

[10] [1909] AC 104, 5 TC 347.

[11] Lord Evershed in *Moorhouse v Dooland* [1955] Ch 284 at 299.

[12] So Whitsun gifts to the curate are also taxable: *Slaney v Starkey* [1931] 2 KB 148, 16 TC 45.

[13] Per Lord Phillimore in *Seymour v Reed* [1927] AC 554 at 569, 11 TC 625 at 653.

[14] Per Lawrence J in *Corbett v Duff* [1941] 1 KB 730 at 740, 23 TC 763 at 779.

[15] Per Lord Loreburn in *Blakiston v Cooper* [1909] AC 104 at 107.

Sporting achievements: bonus or appreciation

6: 33   In *Seymour v Reed*[1] Seymour, the taxpayer, was a professional cricketer employed by Kent County Cricket Club. In 1920 he was awarded a benefit season which meant inter alia that members of the club subscribed money to a fund for him and that he was to receive the gate money at one of the home matches of that season. The gate money came to £939 16s and this was held by trustees together with the subscriptions until Seymour had found a farm. The money was then paid over to him and used by him for the payment of the farm. The Revenue attempted to tax only the £939 16s and to tax it for the year when it was paid over. The attempt failed. The payment was a personal gift and not employment income. He had no right to a benefit season, the benefit would usually be towards the close of a man's career and was intended to provide an endowment on retirement; it was intended as an appreciation for services past rather than an encouragement for services to be rendered.[2]

In *Moorhouse v Dooland*[3] on the other hand the Revenue successfully claimed tax. Dooland was a professional cricketer employed by the East Lancashire Cricket Club. Under club rules he was entitled to talent money of one guinea for every time he scored 50 runs or more or took six wickets or did the hat-trick. (Until 1950 the league rules had also required collections to be taken for meritorious performances.) In the 1950 and 1951 seasons Dooland qualified for talent money and the resulting public collection, six and eleven times respectively. The Revenue successfully claimed tax in respect of the public collections. *Seymour v Reed* was distinguishable on almost every point. Dooland had a contractual right to a collection; Seymour had no such right to his benefit. Dooland had a collection whenever he performed well; Seymour had his one benefit. Dooland's payments were small compared with his salary; Seymour's were very great.

It does not follow that all collections for special feats would fall within the definition of emoluments. Thus if Dooland had no contractual right to a collection but had scored 50 runs and then taken all ten wickets in a match so that the achievement was exceptional,[4] such a collection might not be taxable. In *Moore v Griffiths*[5] payments made by the Football Association to mark England's victory in the World Cup in 1966 were held not taxable. The payment was intended to mark the association's pride in a great achievement and it would be more in keeping with the character and function of the Football Association to construe the payment as a testimonial or mark of esteem. Brightman J added darkly but presciently that the payment had no foreseeable element of recurrence.[5]

Simon's Taxes E4.469; Butterworths Income Tax Service D1.72.
 [1] [1927] AC 554, 11 TC 625.
 [2] This is a question of fact and proof—see esp. Lord Phillimore at pp. 572, 655 and see *Corbett v Duff* [1941] 1 All ER 512, 23 TC 763—footballers' benefits more frequent than once in a career and perhaps after only five years held taxable.
 [3] [1955] Ch 284, [1955] 1 All ER 93, 36 TC 12.
 [4] Per Lord Evershed MR [1955] Ch 289 at 298.
 [5] [1972] 3 All ER 399 at 411; *quaere* whether this meant that recurrence was not foreseeable for these players.

Surrender of an advantage

6: 34   A payment by way of compensation for giving up some advantage rather than by way of reward for services is not taxable as an emolument. This principle is applied even though the surrender of the advantage is a necessary consequence of taking the employment save where the advantage or right being surrendered is inseparable from the employment. Where the payment is made in return for an undertaking the effect of which is to restrict the employee as to his conduct or activities the payment may be taxable under TA 1988, s. 313.

Simon's Taxes E4.482.

(a) *Reward for services or compensation?*

6: 35   In deciding this question the Commissioners are not apparently tied to the words of the contract. There are strong policy reasons for such a line since, as Megarry J observed in *Pritchard v Arundale*,[1] the days of the skilled draftsman are not past, but the decision that the question whether a particular payment is for services or by way of compensation can be judged according to the reality and not mere words is one more qualification of the decision of the House of Lords in *IRC v Duke of Westminster*.[2]

Where an employer makes a payment to an employee at the commencement of his service it is a question of fact whether it is a payment for future services or by way of compensation for some loss. A payment does not cease to be taxable because it is a premium or other initial payment in return for entering into a contract for services. Remuneration for services is still remuneration for services even if paid in a lump sum in advance.[3] Where as it would be very difficult to demonstrate that periodical payments are anything but taxable under Schedule E, the fact that the payment is a lump sum is a factor that can be taken into account.[4]

In *Pritchard v Arundale* the taxpayer was in practice as a senior chartered accountant when a business friend of his persuaded him to leave the practice and to join him in business, as joint managing director of a company. The taxpayer received a full salary at the commercial rate but insisted upon a stake in the business. The friend who owned all but three of the 51,000 shares in the company transferred 4,000 to the taxpayer. The transfer of shares was held to be not taxable under Schedule E. Although the contract of service stated that the friend agreed to transfer the shares in consideration of the taxpayer undertaking to serve the company, a contractual expression of consideration was not conclusively determinative of causation, and anyway that expression did not mean that that was the sole consideration.[5] Other factors[6] were the date of the transfer being six months before service started, the out and out nature of the transfer, that the transferor was not technically the employer but only the principal shareholder of the employer, and that the taxpayer's surrender of his existing livelihood was expressed elsewhere in the contract. These points were emphasised by Walton J in *Glantre Engineering Ltd v Goodhand*[7] when holding that a payment to an employee who had given up an employment elsewhere was taxable. This leaves open the question of whether the distinction is between employment and self-employment or is simply one of fact; the latter is to be preferred. Where the payment is to induce the person to leave an employment the sum may be taxable under TA 1988, s. 148.

Another illustration of this principle relates to rugby league players. Once a person has joined a rugby league club he is barred from ever again playing for, or even visiting a rugby union club. If discovered on a rugby union ground as a spectator he would be asked to leave. If he signs as a professional he will be barred from competing as an amateur in, for example, amateur athletics.[8]

In *Jarrold v Boustead*[9] the taxpayer joined Hull Rugby League Club and was to receive in addition to a wage related to the team's performance, the sum of £3,000 on signing as a professional for the club. He successfully argued that the £3,000 was compensation for the loss of these various social and recreational activities, this conclusion being accepted by the Commissioners and by the Court of Appeal, leave to appeal to the House of Lords being refused.

In *Riley v Coglan*[10] however the sum was not £3,000 but £500, of which £100 was to be paid on signing professional forms and the balance on taking up residence in York. The player agreed to serve for the remainder of his playing career or for twelve years if longer. If he failed to serve the whole stipulated period a proportionate part of the £500 was to be repaid by way of ascertained and liquidated damages. The Commissioners followed *Jarrold v Boustead* but on appeal that case was distinguished by Ungoed-Thomas J, who concluded that the £500 was to be a running payment for making himself available to serve the club when required to do so.[11]

The distinction is one of fact. Coglan's contract nowhere mentioned the abandonment of amateur status, but neither did Boustead's. Boustead's contract provided for the payment of £3,000 on signing professional forms from which the court inferred that the payment was for loss; Coglan's for £500 at the same time but with the proviso that £400 was to become payable only when he took up residence in York, a factor suggesting that the payment was for services to the club. These however are minor differences. The principal distinction is that in Boustead's case no part of the £3,000 was returnable, whereas Coglan might have to return some of his £500. In *Pritchard v Arundale* the transfer was out and out.

It is significant that in *Jarrold v Boustead* the disqualification of the player from rugby union or amateur athletics was for life. On parity of reasoning if a church organist were required to give up Sunday golf as one of the conditions of his employment and was paid £500 compensation, that sum would not be taxable under s. 19.[12] If however the condition was against playing golf at those times when he ought to be playing the organ, the payment would only be a thinly disguised remuneration. More difficult is the question whether such a sum would be taxable if the disqualification against Sunday golf or against playing rugby union were binding only so long as he was church organist or played rugby league. It may be significant that in *Pritchard v Arundale* where there was nothing to prevent the taxpayer from resuming his practice as a chartered accountant on leaving his employment, Megarry J stressed the difficulties which a person of the taxpayer's age would find in building up his practice again.[13] The taxability of any such payment under TA 1988, s 313, infra, § **6: 36** has not yet been considered.

Compensation for loss of a general personal liberty such as amateur status or the playing of golf may thus be outside Schedule E. However, payment in return for the surrender of a right which is part of the employer-employee relationship, e.g. the surrender of a right to commission payments,[14] clearly falls within Schedule E. The right to join a trade union was held to fall within this second group of rights in *Hamblett v Godfrey* which concerned the surrender of rights by employees at GCHQ. Here the Court of Appeal distinguished the surrender of rights and advantages closely connected with the employment from the giving up of social advantages.[15]

Simon's Taxes E4.404; Butterworths Income Tax Service D1.22.

[1] [1971] 3 All ER 1011 at 1002.
[2] Supra, §§ **1: 04, 05.**
[3] See e.g. Lord Greene MR, in *Wales v Tilley* (1942) 25 TC 136 at 142.
[4] *Pritchard v Arundale* at 1022, followed in *Vaughan-Neil v IRC* [1979] STC 644, [1979] 3 All ER 481.
[5] At p. 1021.
[6] *Quaere* how substantial these really are.
[7] [1983] STC 1.
[8] *Jarrold v Boustead* [1964] 3 All ER 76 at 781, 41 TC 701 at 704.
[9] [1964] 3 All ER 76, 41 TC 701.
[10] [1968] 1 All ER 314, 44 TC 481.
[11] Cf. the signing on payment in *Cameron v Prendergast* [1940] AC 549, [1940] 2 All ER 35.
[12] Lord Denning MR in *Jarrold v Boustead* [1964] 3 All ER 76 at 80, 41 TC 701 at 729.
[13] [1971] 3 All ER 1011 at 1023 c. Curiously, this point was *not* emphasised in *Glantre Engineering Ltd v Goodhand* [1983] STC 1.
[14] *McGregor v Randall* [1984] STC 223, [1984] 1 All ER 1092; see infra, §6:40.
[15] [1987] STC 60, [1987] 1 All ER 916, CA.

(b) TA 1988, s. 313: restrictive covenant

6: 36   This section was introduced[1] to reverse the decision of the House of Lords in *Beak v Robson*.[2] In that case a director agreed to continue serving the company at a salary of £2,000 a year and received £7,000 in return for an agreement not to compete with the business within a radius of fifty miles for five years. The £7,000 was held not taxable. This section applies wherever consideration is provided by the employer, whether to the employee or someone else, in return for an undertaking, whether binding or not, the tenor and effect of which is to restrict the employee as to his activities. The undertaking may be given before during or after the employment. For the section to apply it must also be shown that the payment was made "in respect of" the undertaking. It has been held that this was not satisfied where the undertaking involved taking on the very duties inherent in and inseparable from the office or employment itself. In *Vaughan-Neil v IRC*[3] a barrister undertook to cease to practice at the planning bar on taking up his employment with a building contractor; the payment in return for that undertaking escaped the section.

The tax treatment of the value of the consideration, a phrase which includes consideration in kind, depends on the date on which the undertaking was given. If this occurred on or after 9 June 1988 the whole is subject to income tax at basic or higher rates in the usual way[4] and the income is to be treated as taxed for example for the purposes of TA 1988, s. 348. If, however, it occurred before this date the whole is taxed in an unusual way—it is subject only to excess liability.[5] The value of the consideration is grossed up to take account of basic rate income tax and the grossed up sum is then treated as part of his total income for the purpose of computing his excess liability. The employee then has to pay any higher rate tax due in excess of the basic rate income tax. The taxpayer cannot take advantage of the grossing up process to recover the basic rate income tax nor can he treat the sum so received as income that has already been taxed for the purposes of TA 1988, s. 348.

The reasons for the 1988 changes are a wish to remove tax advantages in the system as part of the general reduction in tax rates and also a wish to counter the tax advantages of the device under the old regime. This section enables an employer to make a tax free payment to his lower paid employees and payments free of basic rate tax to his senior employees. It may not have proved popular because of the decision of the Court of Appeal in *Associated Portland Cement Manufacturers Ltd v Kerr*[6] that the employer could not deduct such payments in computing his profits. However in that case the covenants were to last for life and it became common for employers to take covenants for shorter periods so that they could achieve a result of having the covenant taxed at a nil or low rate in the hands of the employee while being deductible by the employer. This result was not satisfactory to the Revenue. However while making the payments fully taxable to the employee, FA 1988 also makes the payment deductible by the payer—whether or not it would be deductible under normal principles even if it would be a capital payment.[7]

Simon's Taxes E4.481, 482; Butterworths Income Tax Service D4.18.

[1] FA 1950, s. 16. The purpose of backdating the section for payments within s. 34(4)(*a*) was to catch payments made to the managing directors of Austin and Morris Motor Companies. See Sabine, *A History of Income Tax*, p. 116.

[2] [1943] 1 All ER 46, 25 TC 33.

[3] [1979] 3 All ER 481, [1979] STC 644.

[4] TA 1988, s. 313(1) as substituted by FA 1988, s. 73 and FA 1988, s. 73(4).

[5] TA 1988, s. 313(2) as originally enacted.

⁶ [1946] 1 All ER 68, 27 TC 103; infra, § **7: 119**.
⁷ FA 1988, s. 73. This is achieved by directing that notwithstanding TA 1988, s. 74 any sum to which (the substituted) s. 313 applies and which is paid or treated as paid by a person carrying on a trade, profession or vocation may be deducted as an expense. This wide authorisation apparently applies not only to a payment which would otherwise be non-deductible by reason of being capital but also one for dual purposes or even one where the sole motivation by the payer was not the purposes of trade.

COMPENSATION PAYMENTS FOR CLAIMS AGAINST EMPLOYERS

1 TA 1988, s. 19

6: 37 TA 1988, s. 19 charges only payments made in return for services. It follows that sums paid by the employer where the employee has a cause of action against the employer will only be chargeable under this rule if in return for services.¹ So if an employee owns property adjoining his employer's factory sums paid by way of compensation under a claim for nuisance will not be taxable.²

Problems arise where the right being surrendered is a right under the contract of employment; in principle such payments escape tax under s. 19 unless they are made in return for services. It would have been easy for the courts to follow the line taken under Schedule D, Cases I and II and to hold that sums paid in lieu of income are themselves income;³ this however the courts have not done. The cases to be considered all turn on their own facts and, in particular, on the construction of the agreements reached, but certain principles do emerge.

Simon's Taxes E4.8; Butterworths Income Tax Service D4.23.
¹ If the compensation takes the form of annual payments it will be taxable as income under Schedule D, Case III: *Asher v London Film Productions Ltd* [1944] KB 133, [1944] 1 All ER 77. See also *Taxation Comr (Victoria) v Phillips* (1937) 55 CLR 144.
² Redundancy payments are exempt from income tax but are taken into account under s. 148: TA 1988, s. 580.
³ Infra, § **7: 74**. *Chibbett v Robinson* (1924) 9 TC 48.

6: 38 (*i*) A sum paid by way of commutation of pension rights is not within s. 19.¹ This is not technically a matter which involves the compromise of a right arising under the contract of employment since while the right may have its sources in such a contract the pension itself is a taxable entity quite distinct from the office or employment.²

¹ *Tilley v Wales* [1943] AC 386, [1943] 1 All ER 280, 25 TC 136.
² Per Viscount Simon LC [1943] AC 386 at 392, 25 TC 136 at 149.

6: 39 (*ii*) A payment by way of compensation on the termination of the contract of employment whether after judgment or by settlement is not within s. 19.¹

Payments for breach of the contract must however be distinguished from two other situations. The first is where it is agreed between employer and employee that the contract shall cease with effect from a future date and the contract is allowed to run its natural course until that date. Since the contract still exists and services are performed, sums paid under the contract are within s. 19; however a payment conditional on continued service for a short period consistent with the reasonable needs of the employer will escape s. 19.[2] Such facts must in their turn be distinguished from the situation in which the employment is to cease but the remuneration is still to be paid after the date of termination; in such circumstances the remuneration is not within s. 19.[3]

The second situation to be distinguished is that in which the contract of employment stipulates the sum to be paid in the event that the contract does not run its full course. The payment of that sum in accordance with the contract is an emolument.

In *Dale v De Soissons*[4] the company exercised its right under the contract to terminate it after one year on payment of £10,000. The payment was held to be taxable. As Lord Evershed put it,

> "The contract provided that he should serve either for three years at an annual sum or, if the company so elected, for a shorter period of two years or one year at an annual sum in respect of the two years or one year, as the case might be, plus a further sum, that is to say it was something to which he became entitled as part of the terms upon which he promised to serve".[5]

It also follows from *Dale v De Soissons* that a clear, but perhaps unfortunate, distinction arises between those who have the forethought to stipulate in advance what sums shall be due in the event of early termination of the contract, and those who are content to await events, between—to take a completely inappropriate analogy—the wise and the foolish virgins.

It should be noted that statutory redundancy payments are exempt from tax[6] and that non statutory but genuine redundancy payments are regarded as falling outside s. 19.[7]

---

[1] See *Henley v Murray* [1950] 1 All ER 908 at 909, 31 TC 351 at 363.
[2] SP 1/81, **Simon's Taxes, Division H3.2.**
[3] *Clayton v Lavender* (1965) 42 TC 607, not following *Hofman v Wadman* (1946) 27 TC 192.
[4] [1950] 2 All ER 460, 32 TC 118, CA; and see *Henry v Foster* (1931) 16 TC 605, CA and *Williams v Simmonds* [1981] STC 715. *Quaere* if the company refused to pay alleging some default by the employee, and a compromise payment was later made to the employee.
[5] [1950] 2 All ER 460 at 462, 32 TC 118 at 127.
[6] TA 1988, s. 579.
[7] SP 1/81, **Simon's Taxes, Division H3.2.**

6: 40   *(iii)* A payment for the modification of the contract of employment ought in principle to be capable of escaping s. 19 in the same way as a payment for termination. However, in practice, where the contract of employment continues, it is very difficult to persuade the courts that the payment is one for giving up a right under the contract as distinct from a payment for the services still to be rendered.

In *Hunter v Dewhurst*[1] the taxpayer wished to retire and live in Scotland but the company wished him to continue as a director, although doing less work—for less pay. This rearrangement would mean a reduction in a sum payable under a clause in the company's articles prescribing compensation of a sum equal to five years' earnings. The taxpayer agreed to continue as a director but received a lump sum of £10,000 under an agreement in which he renounced all rights to the compensation payment. The House of Lords held that this payment escaped tax, largely on the ground that it was compensation for the surrender of his contingent rights under the clause in the articles.[2]

By contrast in *Tilley v Wales*[3] the taxpayer agreed to take a reduced salary of £2,000 a year in return for a payment taken to be £20,000.[4] It was held that this was referable to the agreement to continue to serve as managing director at a reduced salary, so was advance remuneration and so within what is now s. 19.

Hunter v Dewhurst is a decision which has been more often distinguished[5] than followed[6] and it must now be taken as confined to its special facts.[7] However there does appear to be a clear distinction in principle between the surrender of rights under the contract which may after all be taken as analogous to the surrender of pension rights in *Tilley v Wales*, and a payment in consideration of refraining from resigning.

In *Holland v Geoghegan*,[8] refuse collectors had had their right to sell salvaged property lawfully terminated; they went on strike but returned to work on payment of £450 compensation for loss of earnings due to the termination of the scheme. Foster J reversing the Special Commissioners, held that as the right to sell salvaged property had been lawfully terminated the payment was not one of compensation for loss of a right but an inducement to return to work and so taxable.

In *McGregor v Randall*[9] the difficulty of persuading the court to treat compensation for variation of terms of employment was well-shown. The taxpayer had been entitled to commission on profits; he received compensation in return for the loss of this right. In all other respects the employment continued. Scott J held that s. 19 applied; he confined *Hunter v Dewhurst* to its special facts and distinguished *Tilley v Wales* and *Du Cros v Ryall*[10] on the basis that the rights lost there would not or could not be enjoyed while the employment was current.

Simon's Taxes E4.406, 805, 806.

[1] (1932) 16 TC 605. In the three courts, four judges found for the taxpayer and five for the Revenue but the taxpayer had three in the House of Lords.

[2] This is emphasised in the explanations of *Hunter v Dewhurst* in *Cameron v Prendergast* [1940] 2 All ER 35, 23 TC 122.

[3] [1943] 1 All ER 280, 25 TC 136.

[4] The sum paid was £40,000 but this was apportioned between the loss of pension rights and the reduction in salary.

[5] *Cameron v Prendergast* [1940] 2 All ER 35, 23 TC 122; *Tilley v Wales* [1943] 1 All ER 280, 25 TC 136; *Leeland v Boarland* [1946] 1 All ER 13, 27 TC 71; *Bolam v Muller* (1947) 28 TC 471; *Holland v Geogehegan* [1972] 3 All ER 333, 48 TC 482.

[6] *Duff v Barlow* (1941) 23 TC 633 and *Tilley v Wales* appear to be the only reported cases in which *Hunter v Dewhurst* has been applied but in the former *Cameron v Prendergast* [1940] 2 All ER 35, 23 TC 122 was not cited.

[7] E.g. Sir Raymond Evershed MR, in *Henley v Murray* [1950] 1 All ER 908 at 911, 31 TC 351 at 366.

[8] [1972] 3 All ER 333, 48 TC 482.

[9] [1984] STC 223, [1984] 1 All ER 1092.

[10] (1935) 19 TC 444.

6: 41   Another difficulty concerns apportionment where a payment is made for two causes, the one future services and the other compensation for loss of office or of some other right. In *Tilley v Wales* the House of Lords was relieved of the task of deciding whether an apportionment should be made because of agreement between the parties.[1] In principle apportionment is possible.[2] Whether there will be an apportionment if the sum is paid for two causes neither of which can be valued remains unclear. If one can be valued without insuperable difficulty the balance is taken as due to the other.

---

[1] [1943] AC 386 at 394, 25 TC 136 at 150.
[2] *Carter v Wadman* (1946) 28 TC 41.

---

2 TA 1988, s. 148

6: 42   Payments on retirement or removal from office or employment which are not emoluments under general principles are now subject to a special scheme of taxation. The payments caught are those made

> "directly or indirectly in consideration or in consequence of, or otherwise in connection with, the termination of the holding of the office or employment or any change[1] in its functions or emoluments, including any payment in commutation of annual or periodical payments (whether chargeable to tax or not) which would otherwise have been made as aforesaid".

Payments made in consideration of the termination are those paid by way of settlement of a suit for wrongful dismissal but the clause goes far wider. Thus periodical payments in commutation of pension rights are caught as is a resettlement allowance as a sum payable in connection with a change in the functions of the office.[2]

If the payment fits this description it is immaterial whether it is paid in pursuance of a legal obligation or not.[3] A payment is caught even if made to the executors or administrators of the holder or past holder of the office or employment,[4] and even if it is paid to the spouse or any relative or dependant of his, as is a payment on his behalf or to his order.[5] A payment in the form of valuable consideration other than money is taxed and valued at the value of the consideration at the date when it is given, so allowing the employee to keep a company car or to buy it at below market value[6] will be caught. If the payment fits the description, it is immaterial whether the payment is made by the employer or any other person.

Certain payments are excluded from the net cast deliberately wide by TA 1988, s. 148. In addition to sums already charged to income tax,[7] there are excluded, for similar reasons, any sum chargeable under TA 1988, s. 313,[8] and any benefits provided in pursuance of unapproved retirement superannuation schemes where the employee has been chargeable to tax in respect of contributions to the scheme. Certain other sums excluded from tax by other provisions are also excluded from TA 1988, s. 148,[9] such as retirement benefits for directors and employees under approved schemes, gratuity for members of Her Majesty's forces and certain payments in relation to services for a government of an overseas territory within the Commonwealth; also excluded are payments on death, disability or injury.[10]

Certain payments in respect of foreign service are reduced by 50%[11] but where the payment is made after 13th March 1984 (otherwise than one made before 1st August 1984 in pursuance of an obligation incurred before 14th March 1984) this reduction is no longer to apply where the emoluments were "foreign emoluments" (defined in § **6: 03**).[12]

If the payment is not otherwise exempt it still will escape tax if it is not more than £30,000.[13] In calculating the £30,000 one must include any redundancy payment or ex-gratia payment but not certain supplementary contributions to retirement schemes.[14] Two payments for the same employment or two payments for different employments with the same or associated employers[15] are aggregated. Payments for distinct employments with unassociated employers are not aggregated. Where payments are aggregated the aggregation is cumulative from year to year, the £30,000 exemption being applied to earlier payments before later ones.

An important point is the date on which the payment is caught. If the payment is one in commutation of annual or other periodical payments, the date is that on which the commutation is effected and in any other case will be the date on which the termination or change in the employment in respect of which the payment is made.[16]

The £30,000 exemption applies to income received after 5th April 1988.[17]

Techniques to save tax include not having other income that year and taking full relief for contributions to pension schemes.[18]

Such payments cannot count towards the final earnings relevant to the calculation of pension rights.

Simon's Taxes E4.801, 805; Butterworths Income Tax Service D4.21–32.

[1] In *Henley v Murray*, supra, Lord Evershed had distinguished the abrogation of an agreement from its modification.

[2] Cf. *Hochstrasser v Mayes*, supra, § **6: 26**.

[3] TA 1988, s. 148(2).

[4] TA 1988, s. 148(1).

[5] TA 1988, s. 148(3).

[6] *Quaere* whether market value means trade in value or the resale price, presumably the former.

[7] TA 1988, s. 148(2)—presumably this means chargeable under Schedule E since the effect of *Mitchell and Edon v Ross* is to exclude other Schedules.

[8] TA 1988, s. 188(1)(*b*); supra, § **6: 36**. This presumably refers to both the original and the substituted s. 313.

[9] TA 1988, s. 188(1)(*c*)–(*f*).

[10] TA 1988, s. 188(1)(*a*).

[11] TA 1988, s. 188(3), TA 1988, Sch. 11, para. 10—for years after 1973–74. For service in earlier years, see ibid. On cases I–III, see supra, § **6: 01**. For an example of the need to define a place of service see *Wienand v Anderton* [1977] STC 12.

[12] FA 1984, s. 30(7).

[13] TA 1988, s. 188(4) FA 1988, s. 74(1).

[14] SP 2/81, **Simon's Taxes, Division H3.2**.

[15] Defined TA 1988, s. 188(7).

[16] TA 1988, s. 148(4).

[17] On timing see TA 1988, s. 148(4), supra, n. 16. FA 1988, s. 74(2) repeals TA 1988, Sch. 11, paras. 4–7.

[18] See SP 2/81, **Simon's Taxes, Division H3.2**.

BENEFITS IN KIND—GENERAL

6: 43   The general principle that money's worth is income applies also to benefits in kind—but with difficulty. Where an employer transfers a benefit in kind to his employee any tax system has two sets of problems. The first is that of defining the benefits to be taxed. Thus the provision of a more luxurious office or of greater secretarial assistance would not at first sight give rise to a taxable benefit. To state a test in terms of causation will give rise to problems like *Hochstrasser v Mayes* while to state one in terms of a but–for test of causation then gives rise to the need to state exceptions.

The second set of problems concerns the valuation of the benefit. One basis is to tax the employee on the cost to the employer, a basis which applies in the UK where the employee earns £8,500 or more a year or is a director infra, § **6: 86**. A second basis is to tax the employee on the value to him, a test which raises very acute problems where the same benefit is conferred on employees of differing tastes and circumstances. A third basis is to take the market value of the benefit, but this is ambiguous since it could mean the price which the employee would have had to pay to acquire the asset for himself or the price which he could have obtained for the asset if he had chosen to sell it second hand. A further problem is whether to take the resulting figure or to gross it up. What follows concerns only the income tax treatment of benefits in kind; these benefits are not subject to National Insurance contributions, a point of greater importance since the changes in the contribution structure in 1985 and 1989.

Simon's Taxes E4.4; Butterworths Income Tax Service D3.

6: 44   The general principle adopted in the UK is the second variation of the third basis, the second hand value of the benefit, a principle which has the logical consequence that, if the benefit cannot be converted into money or turned to pecuniary account, it is not taxable. It is now subject to statutory modification (*a*) for higher paid employees (see § **6: 72**) and (*b*) for all employees if the benefit is provided by means of a voucher. The general principle, however remains the starting point. It was laid down by the House of Lords in *Tennant v Smith*.[1]

In *Tennant v Smith* the taxpayer was agent for the Bank of Scotland at Montrose. He was bound as part of his duty to occupy the bank house as custodian for the whole premises belonging to the Bank, and also for the transaction of any special bank business after bank hours. He was not allowed to vacate the house even for a temporary period unless with the special consent of the directors who in that case sanctioned the occupation of the house by another official of the bank during the absence of the agent. The agent, besides dealing with business after bank hours, had to lock up the bank and attend to the security of the safe. There was a night bolt from the agent's bedroom to the bank's premises. He was not allowed to sublet the bank house nor to use it for any purpose other than the bank's business. The bank house was suitable accommodation for him but as Lord Macnaghten observed, "his occupation is that of a servant and not the less so because the bank thinks proper to provide for gentlemen in his position in their service accommodation on a liberal scale".[2] His total income from other sources came to £375 and the value of his occupation of these premises was placed at £50. Where a taxpayer's income was below £400 he was entitled to an abatement.[3] The House of Lords held that he was not assessable under

Schedules D or E[4] in respect of his occupation of the premises and so was entitled to the abatement. Lord Halsbury stated that the thing sought to be taxed "is not income unless it can be turned to money".[5] The bank agent's occupation of the premises was not capable of being converted into money since he could not let it.[6]

Simon's Taxes E4.402; Butterworths Income Tax Service D1.101.

[1] [1892] AC 150, 3 TC 158, HL.

[2] At [1892] AC 150 at 162, 3 TC 158 at 169.

[3] 5 & 6 Vict. c. 35, s. 163.

[4] Nor was he assessable under Schedule A since it was not he but the Bank that was the occupier; per Lord Watson, at pp. 158, 166; per Lord Macnaghten, at pp. 162, 169.

[5] At pp. 156, 164; to the same effect Lord Watson, at pp. 159, 167; per Lord Macnaghten, at pp. 163, 170; per Lord Field, at pp. 164, 171 and per Lord Hannen, at pp. 165, 172. Lord Morris concurred.

[6] With the bank's tacit consent he used the premises for an insurance business but this was ignored. At one time it was thought that where a person was in beneficial occupation but that occupation was not convertible (into money or money's worth) then if the employer paid the Schedule A tax in respect of that occupation, the employee was not taxable in respect of that payment under Schedule E: *M'Dougall v Sutherland* (1894) 3 TC 261, but this was overruled in *IRC v Miller* [1930] AC 222, 15 TC 25.

Convertibility

6: 45 A benefit may be converted in ways other than simple sale. In *Abbott v Philbin*[1] an employee was said to be taxable in respect of the value of an option to acquire shares even though the option was expressed to be non-assignable because the employee could have turned the value of the option into money in other ways notably by raising money on the right to call for the shares.[1]

A benefit can also be turned into money by being surrendered, or by not being accepted. In *Heaton v Bell*[2] an employee was loaned a car by his employers and went on to what was called an amended wage basis. The House of Lords held that the correct construction of the agreement was that there was no change in his wage but the employers were entitled to deduct each week a sum in respect of the use of the car. It followed that tax was due on the gross wage each week with no deduction for tax purposes for the sum withheld on account of the car. Yet if the correct construction had been that the employee took a lower wage and received the free use of a car, a majority of the House would have held that he was taxable in respect of the use of the car on the amount he would have received had he surrendered that use.[3] Such statements are obiter.

It has since been held [4] that when an employee could, and did, use a non-chargeable method of obtaining a benefit, the fact that he could have chosen a different method which could have resulted in liability was enough to give rise to liability. So when an employee has a choice between an allowance and the benefit in kind it might be argued, on the basis of the dicta in the House of Lords in *Heaton v Bell*,[5] that as the employee could surrender his benefit in kind and take the (taxable) allowance in lieu he should pay tax on the value of the allowance whether he takes the benefit or the allowance.

The principle is modified by a concession allowing all agricultural workers free board and lodging to remain free of tax despite his right to take a higher cash sum in lieu.[6]

Simon's Taxes E4.401, 402; Butterworths Income Tax Service D1.103, 106.
[1] Per Lord Radcliffe [1961] AC 352 at 378–9, 39 TC 82 at 125.
[2] [1969] 2 All ER 70, 46 TC 211.
[3] Per Lord Morris of Borth-y-Gest, at 753, 84, 253 and per Lord Diplock, at pp. 767, 96, 265. To the same effect but by a different route Lord Reid, dissenting, at 746, 79, 247. While the first two Lords would have quantified the benefit as the sum subtracted each week × 52 (the number of weeks in the year) Lord Reid would have taken the same sum × 50 since two weeks notice has to be given before returning to the scheme. So while Lord Morris and Lord Diplock appear to tax the benefit foregone, Lord Reid would appear to tax the benefit that could be obtained. The latter seems more correct.
[4] *Westall v McDonald* [1985] STC 693 at p 721.
[5] [1969] 2 All ER 70, 46 TC 211.
[6] Extra-statutory concession A60 (1988), see **Simon's Taxes, Division H2.2.**

6: 46   Another problem concerns the reason why the assets may not be convertible. In *Tennant v Smith* Lord Halsbury said that a thing could be treated as money's worth where the thing was capable of being turned into money "from its own nature".[1] Yet in *Tennant v Smith* the only reason why the agent could not turn his occupation of the house into money was the *fiat* of his employer. Clearly the loopholes in the tax net will be greatly widened if it is left to the employer to decide whether a benefit is convertible and so assessable. The courts have indicated that while restrictions imposed by employers may be treated as an effective restriction[2] this will not be so if the conditions are not genuine.[3] However Lord Diplock has gone further in the defence of the Revenue and in *Heaton v Bell* said that limitations on use arising from a contract collateral to the contract of employment into which the employee entered of his own volition would not escape tax.[4] It remains to be seen whether this approach will be accepted and whether, if it is, the courts will treat a clause in a contract of employment as giving rise to a collateral contract.[5]

[1] [1892] AC 150 at 156, 3 TC 158 at 164.
[2] E.g. *Ede v Wilson and Cornwall* [1945] 1 All ER 367, 26 TC 381—shares subject to a condition that they would not be sold without employer's permission—held that valuation must take account of the restriction on effect of a term forbidding assignment of a debt see *Helstan Securities Ltd v Hertfordshire County Council* [1978] 3 All ER 262.
[3] Lord Reid in *Heaton v Bell* [1969] 2 All ER 70 at 79, 46 TC 211 at 247.
[4] At 95, 264.
[5] Cf. the test that an expense, to be deductible, must be required by the job, and not simply by the employer (§ **6: 109**).

Extent of liability

6: 47   Convertibility provides the test not only of liability but also of its extent; the employee is chargeable on the amount of money into which he could turn the benefit.[1] In *Weight v Salmon*[2] where the employee was given the right to apply for shares at less than market price he was held assessable on the difference between the market price and the price he paid.

In *Wilkins v Rogerson*[3] the employee was provided with a suit; he was held assessable on the second hand value of the suit, which was only one third of the purchase price, a fact which involved "no reflection on the tailor" because "it is notorious that the value of clothing is very much reduced the moment that it can be called second hand". Where on the other hand an employee was provided with a voucher which he could spend at a great number of stores it was held that because of the range of objects which he was enabled to buy the face value should be taken.[4] Special legislation now applies to vouchers (infra, § **6: 51**).

The value is ascertained at the date when the asset comes into charge, usually on receipt;[5] although a special rule now applies to certain share options, other options are subject to the general rule. If an asset is received in non-convertible form but later becomes convertible, there is little reason why a charge should not arise at the latter time.

Simon's Taxes E4.461, 464; Butterworths Income Tax Service D1.104.
  [1] This will relate to the way in which the benefit is convertible; see supra, § **6: 45**.
  [2] (1935) 19 TC 174.
  [3] [1961] 1 All ER 358, 39 TC 344.
  [4] *Laidler v Perry* [1965] 2 All ER 121, 42 TC 351.
  [5] *Abbott v Philbin* infra, § **6: 56**.

Anomalies and distinctions

6: 48   The test of convertibility gives rise to distinctions which mean significant variations in tax liability according to fiscal skill or simple luck. First, whereas the provision of a benefit such as a board and lodging escapes tax, the payment of an allowance in lieu of providing that benefit does not. In *Fergusson v Noble*[1] the taxpayer was a plain clothes policeman. He was allowed to buy his own clothes suitable for duty and for this purpose was given an allowance of £11.71, his choice of clothes to be approved by his superior officer. Uniformed members of the police force were provided with a uniform free of charge. It was held that the allowance was liable to tax, a money allowance being in a totally different position from the case where the employer supplies a uniform to be worn only when the man is on duty and which remains the employer's property. On similar reasoning an employee who is provided with an official house may not be taxable (but for special legislation) whereas one who is provided with an allowance is taxable,[2] a matter of great moment when the special legislation does not apply. Under reg. 50 of the Police Regulations 1979[3] the tax paid on a rent allowance is reimbursed by police authorities in the following financial year by means of a compensatory grant.[4] In principle the grant itself is taxable.

Simon's Taxes E4.421; Butterworths Income Tax Service D1.112.
  [1] 1919 SC 534, 7 TC 176. To same effect *Sanderson v Durbridge* [1955] 3 All ER 154, 36 TC 239; *Evans v Richardson* (1957) 37 TC 178.
  [2] *Corry v Robinson* [1934] 1 KB 240, 18 TC 411.
  [3] S.I. 1979 No. 1470.
  [4] HC Written Answer (31st January 1986) Vol 90 col 634, see [1986] STI, p. 40.

6: 49   Secondly one may contrast the lot of the employee who receives a salary and in addition some non-convertible benefit, such as necessaries, in respect of which extra benefit he is not taxable, with that of another taxpayer who receives a salary and has to pay out of that salary a counter amount to secure himself those necessaries.[1] The latter is assessable on the total salary and not entitled to deduct the cost of those necessaries unless he comes within the strict test laid down by TA 1988, s. 198; § **6: 100**. In *Cordy v Gordon*[2] the taxpayer was employed at an asylum and received a salary together with board, lodging, washing and uniform for which he was required to pay sums which varied according to the cost of living: he was held assessable on the gross salary.

Simon's Taxes E4.441, 442; Butterworths Income Tax Service D1.141.

[1] However, see extra-statutory concession A1 (1988)—flat rate allowances for clothes and tools and the even more extraordinary A5 (1988)—no tax on allowances paid to miners in lieu of their free coal.

[2] [1925] 2 KB 276, 9 TC 304. Also *Machon v McLoughlin* (1926) 11 TC 83; *Bruce v Hatton* [1921] 2 KB 206, 8 TC 180. Cf. *Edwards v Roberts* (1935) 19 TC 618.

6: 50   The third anomaly is the borderline between the rule in *Nicoll v Austin* and that in *Tennant v Smith*. If an employer buys each of his employees a new suit at Christmas, the employee is taxable only on the second hand value of the suit. If however the employee has already bought a suit but not yet paid for it and his employer settles the debt for him, he is taxable on the amount paid to the tailor. In *Wilkins v Rogerson*[1] the employer arranged for a tailor to provide some of its employees with clothes suitable for wear at the office, the employee to choose from a suit, overcoat or raincoat, up to a maximum cost of £15. One employee chose a suit costing £14.75 and the Revenue sought to charge him with that sum. The Court of Appeal however held that he was chargeable only on the second hand value of the suit, £5. It would appear from the reasoning of Lord Evershed MR, in that Court and of Danckwerts J at first instance that if the employer had given Rogerson a voucher with which to buy the suit he would have been taxable on the cost of the suit, £14.75, since in that case he would have acquired not a suit but a right to spend up to £15 on a suit. The reasoning of Donovan LJ, is slightly different; he rejected the Crown's argument because the employee never became liable to pay the £14.75 to the tailor. The question of whose is the liability to be discharged, rather than what right the employee acquired, is a clearer way of explaining what remains a most technical area of law. Yet its clarity leads to further anomalies. Thus would the taxpayer's liability be for £14.75 if he made the contract but only for £5 if he made the contract as agent for his employer who then gave him the suit? To escape liability a genuine agency would have to be shown. This is a question of fact; when an employee drives into a garage and begins to pump petrol into his car he may be an agent for his employer or he may be acting on his own account.[2] If the employer is an undisclosed principal the employee is personally liable on the contract so his liability may be for tax on £14.75.[3]

---

[1] [1961] 1 All ER 358, 39 TC 344.

[2] *Richardson v Worrall* [1985] STC 693.

[3] The presence of joint liability on the part of employer and employee does not *necessarily* mean that discharge by the employer will be a taxable emolument—see *Richardson v Worrall* at p 718c.

Vouchers and credit tokens

6:51 These anomalies have led to legislation concerning vouchers and credit tokens. First, a voucher that can be exchanged for cash is subject to the PAYE system.[1] Secondly a voucher, including a "cheque voucher",[2] that can be exchanged for money, goods or services—including transport—gives rise to liability on an amount equal to the cost to the employer of providing the voucher and any exchange products. As the cost to the employer is taken on the basis of charge the value of the benefit is ignored. The liability arises when the expense is incurred[3] or, if later, when the voucher is received although the appropriation of the voucher (e.g. by sticking it on a card held for him) is treated as receipt by the employee. Travel concessions for lower paid employees of passenger transport undertakings are still free of tax,[4] as are the provision of car parking at or near the place of work[5] and entertainment which is, to use broad terms, provided by someone not connected with the employer.[6] Thirdly similar rules apply to credit tokens and credit cards.[7] When the employer uses the token to obtain money, goods or services he is charged to income tax on an emolument equal to the expense involved although the costs of providing the token and of any interest charges are ignored.[8]

Relief is given when the vouchers or credit token are used to meet proper business expenses or where the employer makes good the cost involved.[9]

These rules would now catch *Wilkins v Rogerson* but only if a voucher or credit token were used. So the charge would be avoided if the employer accompanied the employee to the shop—or sent an agent, perhaps even the employee himself. For the practice where incentive award schemes are provided by way of voucher see SP 6/85, **Simon's Taxes, Division H3.2.**

Simon's Taxes E4.431–433; Butterworths Income Tax Service D3.13–15.
[1] TA 1988, s. 143 But see extra-statutory concession A2 (1988) (Meal vouchers).
[2] TA 1988, s. 141.
[3] For cheque vouchers the year is that in which the voucher is handed over in exchange for the goods etc see TA 1988, s. 141.
[4] TA 1988, s. 141(6).
[5] FA 1988, s. 46.
[6] FA 1988, ss. 47 and 48.
[7] TA 1988, s. 142. Credit token is no longer defined by reference to Consumer Credit Act 1974, s. 14.
[8] These charges were originally to give rise to liability—FA 1981, s. 71—but this was removed by FA 1982, s. 45.
[9] TA 1988, ss. 141(3) and (4), 142(2) and (3).

PARTICULAR BENEFITS: (1) LIVING ACCOMMODATION

6:52 Where living accommodation is provided for a person or for his family or household[1] by reason of his employment, he is chargeable whatever the level of his income and whether or not he is a director.[2] So if a non-domiciled person owns his house through a non-resident company, a favourite way of avoiding IHT, there will be a charge to income tax under this rule if he is a director, which he usually will be.[3] The rule is not to apply where by some other provision the accommodation is made the subject of any charge to him by way of income tax. An employee will be otherwise chargeable if he comes within the general principle of convertibility (supra, § **6: 43**): he will be chargeable on the profit which he could make by sub-letting the property or granting licences.

Whether living accommodation is provided by reason of the employment is a question of fact; however it is deemed to be so provided if it is provided by the employer. This deeming is avoided if it is shown that (*a*) the employer is an individual and he makes the provision in the normal course of his domestic, family or personal relationships or (*b*) it is provided by a local authority for an employee of theirs and on terms which are no more favourable than those for non-employees similarly circumstanced, a rule which means that a council house tenant is not to be charged with extra rent simply because he works for the council.

The terms in (*a*) are defined by reference to the rules relating to directors and higher paid employees, infra, § **6: 86**. Under this rule a secretary who fills the more personal role of mistress to her employer is able to escape tax on the flat which he provides for her. This rule only applies, however, where the employer is an individual, presumably because only an individual can have domestic family or personal relationships; this leaves open the case of a family business run by a trust, perhaps because the owner of the business has died and his estate has not yet been administered, unless one says that a trust is capable of being an individual.

If the accommodation is provided by someone other than the employer and so escapes the deeming provision, it may still give rise to tax if it is shown that the accommodation was in fact provided by reason of the employment, as may well be the case if it is provided by an associated company or trust.

This charge applies to the *provision of living accommodation*.[4] It does not apply to the provision of ancillary services; such services will not usually be capable of being turned into money and so will not give rise to any charge. However, they will give rise to a charge on directors and higher paid employees under TA 1988, s. 154, infra, § **6: 93**; when these come within the three categories of non-beneficial occupation the charge is not to exceed 10% of the total emoluments. The costs of providing living accommodation are not further defined although liability in respect of rates is not to give rise to a charge when the occupation is within the three categories of non-beneficial occupation.

From 6th April 1984, an employee who is taxable under TA 1988, s. 145 on living accommodation which cost over £75,000 to provide may be subject to an additional charge to tax under TA 1988, s. 146,[5] infra, § **6: 55**.

Simon's Taxes E4.411–415; Butterworths Income Tax Service D3.41–46.
 [1] TA 1988, s. 145(6).
 [2] TA 1988, s. 154(2).

[3] By reason of the definition in TA 1988, s. 168. The fact that the individual receives no other benefit or remuneration is irrelevant.
[4] TA 1988, s. 145(7).
[5] Added by FA 1983, s. 21.

Exceptions—non beneficial occupation

6: 53   If the accommodation is provided by reason of the employment, the cost will still not be chargeable if the taxpayer comes within any of three situations which correspond broadly with the old cases of representative occupation. These are:

(*a*) where it is necessary for the proper performance of the employee's duties that he should reside in the accommodation;

(*b*) where the employment is one of the kinds of employment in which it is customary to provide living accommodation and the accommodation is provided for the better performance of the duties of the employment;

(*c*) where, there being a special threat to his security, special security arrangements are in force and he resides in the accommodation as part of those arrangements.

Exceptions (*a*) and (*b*) are excluded so that a charge to income tax will arise if the taxpayer is a director of the company providing the accommodation unless he is a full-time working director and he does not have a material interest in the company, infra, § **6: 86**.

Those coming within (*a*) will include caretakers, the hotel manager, and other staff who are compelled to live in the hotel and the bank manager in *Tennant v Smith*;[1] for this group the necessity has to be found in the relationship between the duties and the accommodation and not in the personal exigencies of the taxpayer.[2] Group (*b*) is very wide covering farmworkers, miners and even university teachers; the requirement that it should be customary to provide the accommodation in that kind of employment is an interesting one since it is presumably a flexible one and so can take account on changes in practice and can be satisfied even though occupation is not required by the employer; the requirement that the provision be for the better performance of the duties is presumably a question of fact and is to be determined objectively paying attention to—but without being bound by—the terms of the employment and the views of the employer.

In *Vertigan v Brady*[2] the taxpayer failed to come within (*b*) because the provision of accommodation was not sufficiently common to be "customary". Among the issues considered by the court were (1) how many employers in this industry provided accommodation; (2) for how long the practice had continued; and (3) whether it had achieved general acceptance.

Simon's Taxes E4.412; Butterworths Income Tax Service D3.43.
[1] [1892] AC 150, 3 TC 158, HL.
[2] *Vertigan v Brady* [1988] STC 91.

The charge

6: 54   The charge is on the value to the employee of the accommodation for that period; a deduction is to be made for any sum made good by him to the person at whose cost the accommodation is provided. Rent paid by the employee is therefore deductible. Benefits in kind provided in return may also, in principle be taken into account but only if they clearly relate to the accommodation.[1] The value to him is the annual value calculated under TA 1988, s. 837 which is defined as

> "the rent which might reasonably be expected to be obtained on a yearly letting if the tenant undertook to pay the usual tenant's rates and taxes and the landlord undertook to pay the costs of repairs and insurance and other expenses if necessary for maintaining the subject of the valuation at that figure."

In general, the annual value is treated as being equal to the rateable value.[2] However, if those at whose cost the accommodation is provided pay rent which is higher than the annual value, that higher figure is to be taken.[3] In the absence of any provision directing otherwise it is to be assumed that in calculating the annual rent hypothetically payable account is taken of all the terms of the occupation, even those imposed in connection with the office or employment.

The employee may deduct from the value as ascertained any sums allowable under TA 1988, ss. 198 and 332.

Simon's Taxes E4.412; Butterworths Income Tax Service D3.41.

[1] *Stones v Hall* [1989] STC 138.

[2] In Scotland, an amount equal to the 1978 rates valuation figure will be used, instead of the much higher values set in the 1985 revaluation: Extra-statutory concession A56 (1988).

[3] TA 1988, s. 145(2).

The additional charge

6: 55   An employer who is taxable under TA 1988, s. 145[1] on living accommodation which cost more than £75,000 to provide is liable to an additional charge under TA 1988, s. 146.[2] The employee is taxed on the additional value to him of the accommodation, which is:

[(cost of providing accommodation) − £75,000 × appropriate %] − excess rent

The cost of providing the accommodation is the purchase price plus improvement expenditure, less any amount paid by the employee as reimbursement for the expenditure or as consideration for the tenancy. If, however, the employee first occupies the accommodation after 30th March 1983 and the person providing the accommodation has held an estate or interest in the property for the previous six years, the market value at the date on which the employee first occupies the property is substituted for the purchase price. Market value is defined.[3]

The "appropriate percentage" is the official rate of interest set for the purpose of calculating the benefit of low-interest and interest-free loans to directors and higher paid employees,[4] in force on 6th April beginning the year of assessment.

"Excess rent" is the amount by which any rent paid by the employee exceeds the value to the employee of the accommodation, supra, § **6: 54**.

EXAMPLE

A is a higher paid employee. On 6th April 1986 he begins to occupy a house provided by his employer. The house was purchased by the employer on 9th November 1982 for £196,000 and he spent £8,000 on improvements. A reimbursed £1,000 of the expenditure and pays a rent which exceeds by £2,000 the value to him of the property. The official rate of interest on 6th April 1989 was $14\frac{1}{2}\%$.

The cost to the employer of providing the property is:

$$(\text{£}196,000 + \text{£}8,000) - \text{£}1,000 = \underline{\underline{\text{£}203,000}}$$

The additional value of the property to A is:

$$[(\text{£}203,000 - \text{£}75,000) \times 14\tfrac{1}{2}\%] - \text{£}2,000 = \underline{\underline{\text{£}16,560}}$$

A is therefore taxed on an additional benefit of £16,560 in 1989–90.

If the employer had purchased the property in 1977, the market value of the property on 6th April 1986 would have been substituted for the purchase price.

Simon's Taxes E4.413; Butterworths Income Tax Service D3.42.

[1] Supra, §§ **6: 52–6: 54**.
[2] Added by FA 1983, s. 21.
[3] TA 1988, s. 146(11).
[4] Infra, § **6: 94**.

---

(2) SHARE OPTION AND INCENTIVE SCHEMES

History

6: 56 If, in return for services, an employee receives shares in his employing company he will be taxable on the value of those shares.[1] If they are ordinary shares he will be taxable on their market value on the date of receipt since he could sell them at that price. If however he receives shares subject to conditions which reduce their value, that reduction will usually be reflected in a reduction in the taxable amount.[2]

The basis of chargeability is that he is receiving a benefit by virtue of his employment. This reasoning would apply also where he is given priority in a public offer and he ends up with more shares than he would have got as a member of the public, assuming that the values at allocation exceeded the price paid. New rules apply to offers made after 22nd September 1987 to exclude the charge in such cases.[3] The maximum reserved for the priority allocation is 10% of the shares[4]: all applicants must be on level terms.[5] When the employee is allowed to buy at a discount, the effect was at first to tax both the benefit conferred by the discount and that conferred by the priority right. For offers made after 10th October 1988 only the discount right will attract tax—provided not more than 10% of the shares are offered to the employees in priority.[6] Further provision is made for the situation in which the offer to the public consists of a number of different elements, e.g. a fixed price offer and a tender offer.[7]

If he receives an option to buy shares, he is taxable only on the value of the option, which would be the difference between the price payable under the option and the market value of the shares on the date of receipt of the option.[8] In *Abbott v Philbin*[9] the employee received an option to buy shares at £3·42½ each, the market value at the date of the option, and he exercised the option in a subsequent tax year when the market value of the shares was £4·10. The House of Lords held that the emolument arose in the year the option was acquired and at that time he received no benefit from it since he was merely given an option to buy at what was then full market value. The fact that the emolument subsequently increased in value did not mean that that increase in value was an emolument.

Legislation followed in 1966 (see § **6: 57**) but this was largely avoided by the device of giving not an option to acquire shares but shares subject to restriction and not yet fully paid up. In 1978 under the Lib–Lab pact a new form of share scheme was approved, infra, § **6: 69** and another form by the Conservative government in 1980 infra, § **6: 73**. Finally, in 1984, the concept of an approved share option scheme was revived, see infra, § **6: 67**. Since that time there have been new tax incentives for profit related pay (infra, § **6: 75**) introduced in 1986 and for ESOTs (infra, § **6: 81**) introduced in 1989. In considering those rules one must also remember the possible impact of TA 1988, ss. 160 and 162 (§ **6: 94** and § **6: 96**).

---

[1] *Weight v Salmon* (1935) 19 TC 174.
[2] *Ede v Wilson and Cornwall* [1945] 1 All ER 367, 26 TC 381.
[3] FA 1988, s. 68; see *Simon's Tax Intelligence* 1987, pp. 716 and 866.
[4] *ibid.*, s. 68(2)(*a*).
[5] *ibid.*, s. 68(2)(*b*) and (3).
[6] FA 1989, s. 66; the changes have effect as from 10th October 1988—*Simon's Tax Intelligence* 1988 p. 748 and 1989 p. 106.
[7] FA 1988, s. 68(2A) and (2B), added by FA 1989, s. 66(5).
[8] [1960] 2 All ER 763, 39 TC 82.
[9] [1961] AC 352 supra, § **6: 45**.

Options to acquire shares

6: 57   (1) TA 1988, s. 135[1] provides that where a gain is realised by the *exercise* of the option, income tax is to be charged on the difference between the price paid under the option, including the price of the option,[2] and the market value of the shares acquired under the option.[3] This charge excludes any liability on the grant of the option.[4] From 19th March 1986, the receipt of consideration in money or money's worth by an employee in return for allowing an option to lapse or granting a second option or right is also treated as a taxable event.[5]

Provisions for payment by instalments apply if the option was granted before 6th April 1984.[6]

Simon's Taxes E4.503; Butterworths Income Tax Service D6.04, 05.
[1] For options granted before 3rd May 1966, see TA 1988, s. 136(4), which excepts the gain attributable to an increase in market value up to that date.
[2] This is not to include the value of the services rendered: TA 1988 s. 135(4) proviso.
[3] TA 1988, s. 135(3).
[4] TA 1988, s. 135(2) e.g. under the decision in *Weight v Salmon*.
[5] TA 1988, s. 136(6).
[6] TA 1988, s. 137.

6:58 (2) Although the effect of TA 1988, s. 135 is to charge tax on the exercise, as opposed to the grant, of an option, this was found to be unsatisfactory where long-term options were involved. Therefore TA 1988, s. 135(5) provides that if the option is capable of being exercised more than seven years after its grant, tax is chargeable at the time of the *grant* on the value of the benefit granted, any tax under s. 135(1) so charged being deducted from any tax subsequently chargeable on the exercise of the option under s. 135(1).[1] To avoid any argument based on *Abbott v Philbin*[2] the value of the benefit granted is stated to be not less than the market value at the time the right is obtained of the shares that can be acquired less the value of the consideration for which the shares are to be acquired. If the consideration is variable only its lowest value is taken.[3] Tax cannot be avoided by assigning the option to a person with whom the employee is connected nor if the assignment is otherwise than by way of bargain at arm's length; in such circumstances the assignor is chargeable in respect of the gain realised by the assignee.[4]

These charges arise when the option was granted to that person "as director or employee" a phrase which is defined as a grant by reason of the office or employment.[5] The grant may have been to that person or another. This is to prevent the obvious avoidance device of granting the option to the employee's spouse or nominee.

Simon's Taxes E4.503; Butterworths Income Tax Service D6.03.
  [1] Applied in *Williamson v Dalton* [1981] STC 753.
  [2] [1961] AC 352, 39 TC 82, supra, § **6:45**.
  [3] TA 1988, s. 135(5).
  [4] TA 1988, s. 135(6), but a special rule applies if the assignment was on bankruptcy, s. 135(7). More devious arrangements fall within s. 135(8). Exercises of the option after the employment has ceased fall within s. 140(1).
  [5] TA 1988, s. 140(1).

Planning

6:59 The effect of these rules is to make share option schemes unattractive in tax terms. So long as an option is exercisable within 7 years there will be no tax charge on the grant of the option but any gain made on the exercise of the option is treated as income under s. 135 and it may therefore be necessary for the employee to sell some of the shares to raise the money to pay the tax. The scheme also involves some dilution of equity. For these reasons so called "phantom" schemes have been devised by which, on the exercise of the option, the company pays money to a trust which then buys shares for the employee and transfers them to him—while this does not avoid s. 135 it does avoid the need to sell shares (as only the net-of-tax sum is invested) and so also reduces equity dilution.

Share purchase incentive schemes

6:60 The essence of these schemes was that they sidestepped the rules relating to share options. Instead of being given an option to buy a share for £1, the current market value of the share, which might in due course be worth

£3, the employee would be issued with a share which ordinarily would have had a current market value of £3 but which was subject to restrictions which meant that it was only worth £1. Then the restrictions would be removed. The increase in value could not be subject to the share option rules since he did not realise a gain by exercising a right to acquire shares—he owned them already. Such schemes might further involve using partly paid up shares. If the company capitalised its profits to pay them up there would be a charge on the employee on the amount so spent but this would usually be a lot less than the gain realised.

These schemes caused difficulties for the Revenue and therefore rules were introduced in 1972 (now TA 1988, s. 138)—which still apply, although in limited form, to some shares acquired before 26th October 1987.[1] Events on or after that date can still give rise to a charge under these rules in their modified form[2] (infra § **6: 61**. Shares acquired on or after that date are subject to new—and more relaxed—rules in FA 1988.[3]

The new rules differ from the old in two principal ways. First, they try to reduce the charge so that it applies only to the extent that value is being conferred by the removal of the restrictions and not to catch the general underlying increase in value attributable to the growth of the business. This represents a change of view of these schemes—from being purely a tax avoidance device to being a legitimate way of involving employees in the fate of their company. Secondly, they try to extend the new approach to companies which are subsidiaries so that employees can acquire shares in their company rather than in the head group company; this is achieved by distinguishing dependant subsidiaries from others.

In view of the wide changes of 1988 with a single higher rate of tax and an assimilation of the rates of income tax and CGT there are already calls for the repeals of these rules.[4]

---

[1] FA 1988, s. 88(1).
[2] See *Butterworths UK Tax Guide 1987–88*, § **6: 61**.
[3] FA 1988, ss. 77–89.
[4] [1988] BTR p. 249.

The 1988 scheme

6: 61   The 1988 scheme imposes three charges where shares have been acquired in pursuance of a right conferred on him or an opportunity offered to him by reason of his office or employment by that or any other company.[1] None can apply where the shares are acquired in pursuance of an offer made to the public.[2] The frequently used terms "acquisition" and "disposition" are extended to cover increases and decreases in a person's interest in the shares.[3]

The first charge to tax arises if a chargeable event occurs provided that the employee still owns or, technically, has any beneficial interest in, the shares.[4] A person who acquires the shares otherwise than under a bargain at arm's length with an unconnected person is to be deemed to continue to hold them until there is a disposal of them by a bargain at arm's length to an unconnected person. A separate set of rules applies if the company is a "dependant subsidiary";[5] (infra § **6: 62**) hence if the company is a subsidiary but not a dependant one the following rules apply.

The list of chargeable events covers the removal or variation of any restrictions[6] on the shares and the creation of rights or restrictions on them. It also covers the imposition of restrictions on other shares in the company since such events equally cause a shift in value between the groups of shares.[7] The amount to be charged is the increase in value accruing from these events[8] rather than simply the increase in value during the period of ownership, as was the case under the 1972 rules. Another difference is that there is no automatic charge at the end of seven years.

Four situations are excluded. The first is where the shareholder has not been an employee or director of that or any associated company in the last seven years.[9] The second is where the employees hold a minority of the shares whose value is increased.[10] The third is where the company is employee-controlled by virtue of the class of shares affected[11] and the fourth is where the shares affected are a single class and the company is a subsidiary which is not a dependant subsidiary.[12]

Simon's Taxes E4.581–585; Butterworths Income Tax Service D6.22–26.

[1] If he acquires the right as a person connected with a director or employee, is caught by s. 83(1); the term acquisition covers increases in a person's interest in the shares—FA 1988, s. 81.

[2] FA 1988, s. 77(3).

[3] FA 1988, s. 81.

[4] FA 1988, s. 78(1).

[5] FA 1988, s. 78(1) and 79.

[6] Widened by s. 78(7).

[7] FA 1988, s. 78(3).

[8] FA 1988, s. 78(3).

[9] FA 1988, s. 78(4); if he acquired the shares as an employee of another company he must also not have been an employee of the first company.

[10] FA 1988, s. 78(5) and (6).

[11] FA 1988, s. 78(5) and (6)(*b*); employee control is defined in s. 87(2).

[12] FA 1988, s. 78(5) and (6)(*c*).

6: 62   The second charge arises where the shares are shares in a "dependant subsidiary". The term dependant subsidiary is defined by exclusion. A subsidiary is dependant unless its business is wholly or substantially with persons who are not members of the group and there has been either no, or only a minimal, increase in the value of the company which stems from intra-group activities. The directors and auditors must certify that these conditions are satisfied.[1]

Where the company is such a subsidiary, whether at the time of the acquisition or during his ownership of the shares, rules much closer to those of 1972 apply. There will be a charge either at the end of seven years or if he ceases to own them before that time. The charge is on the increase in value over this period since acquisition.[2] The charge will be reduced if the taxpayer's interest is less than full beneficial ownership[3]; if he has to provide more consideration since acquisition in accordance with the terms of acquisition[4] or; if in accordance with the terms of the acquisition he ceases to own them by disposing of them for less than full consideration.[5]

These rules are adapted where the company was not a dependant subsidiary at the time of acquisition but became one before he ceased to own the shares.[6] Here there will be a chargeable increase if the value when the company became a dependant subsidiary is less than its value at the earliest of the following dates: (i) the passing of seven years; (ii) the person ceasing to own the shares; (iii) the company ceasing to be a dependant subsidiary.[7] There will be no charge under this head if he was not a director or employee of that or any associated company within the seven years before the company became a dependant subsidiary.[8]

The Revenue view is that these are pragmatic rules to provide the new, more generous, approach only where the subsidiary is operating more or less independently of its group.[9] In other circumstances the Revenue feel that it is just too easy for value to be shifted around the group and so into the shares of the lucky employees or directors.

---

[1] FA 1988, s. 86. On problems in defining dependant subsidiary see ICAEW Memorandum TR 739—**Simon's Tax Intelligence** 1989 p. 40.

[2] FA 1988, s. 79(2) and (3).

[3] FA 1988, s. 79(4).

[4] FA 1988, s. 79(5).

[5] FA 1988, s. 79(6).

[6] FA 1988, s. 79(1)(*b*).

[7] FA 1988, s. 79(3).

[8] FA 1988, s. 79(7); if he acquired the shares as an employee of another company he must also not have been an employee of that company.

[9] *Simon's Tax Intelligence* 1987, p. 799.

6: 63   The third charge is when the shareholder receives special benefits.[1] The benefit will be special if it does not extend to all the shares in its class or if the majority of the shares of that class are held by directors or employees of the company, or if the company is employee controlled by virtue of this class or the company is a dependant subsidiary.[2] Again the charge is excluded if the shareholder has not been a director or employee of that or any associated company within the last seven years.[3]

---

[1] This rule applies where the shares have been acquired as a person connected with a director or employee, FA 1988, s. 83(4). The same provision carries over the rule that a person who acquires the shares otherwise than under a bargain at arm's length with an unconnected person is to be deemed to continue to hold the shares until there is a disposal of them by a bargain at arm's length to an unconnected person.

[2] FA 1988, s. 70(2) and (3).

[3] FA 1988, s. 70(5); if he acquired the shares as an employee of another company he must also not have been an employee of that company.

6: 64   There are a number of ancillary provisions. Thus, rules are provided for the treatment the replacement of shares on reorganisations,[1] for the capital gains tax consequences[2] and for the provision of information.[3]

---

[1] FA 1988, s. 82.

[2] FA 1988, s. 84.

[3] FA1988, s. 85.

Transitional rules—shares acquired before 26th October 1987

6: 65 Where shares were acquired before 26th October 1987, FA 1988 attempts to ensure that if the shares would satisfy the new conditions, if they had been acquired later, the new regime can apply to them partially. Where a charge arises under the 1972 rules and the market value at that time is greater than the market value on 26th October 1987, the charge is to be calculated only by reference to the value on 26th October 1987.[1] Thus, the value on that day sets a ceiling on the liability under the 1972 rules. Naturally this ceiling cannot apply if the company is a dependant subsidiary on the day the charge arises.[2]

The new rules, with the exception of the second and third heads of charge, are to apply whatever the date of acquisition.[3] Where there is a condition that the shares are to be disposed of when the employment or office ends, the removal of that restriction is not to cause a charge under the first head of charge.[4]

Where the shares are in a dependant subsidiary the old rules apply.

For an account of the 1972 rules see *Butterworths UK Tax Guide 1987–88*, §§ **6: 60** and **6: 61**.

Simon's Taxes E4.587; Butterworths Income Tax Service D6.27.
[1] FA 1988, s. 88(2).
[2] FA 1988, s. 88(2).
[3] FA 1988, s. 88(3).
[4] FA 1988, s. 88(4).

Planning

6: 66 The effect of the pre 1988 rules was to make share purchase schemes unattractive in tax terms. Loans to trustees to enable employees to buy gave rise to taxable benefits under TA 1988, s. 160 if the loan was at a rate below the official interest rate. If an employee were allowed to leave a part of the subscription price unpaid, the unpaid part was treated as a loan. Capital gains realised were mostly made liable to income tax—e.g. the increase is the value of the shares when restrictions on those shares are removed (TA 1988, s. 138. If shares were acquired and paid for but then went down in value there was a financial risk to the employee. Further, any stop-loss provision in the scheme would also be treated as a benefit.

For these reasons there was a trend away from share schemes towards performance unit schemes which allow the employee to acquire contingent rights to bonuses; these bonuses are related to the performance of the employee's unit but, being contingent, do not become taxable until the contingency is removed (as by completing a certain number of years of service). Such schemes are free of risk to the employee and avoid cash flow problems and dilution of equity. Today these schemes are swamped by the revival of more straightforward devices such as share incentive schemes, share option schemes and profit-related pay.

Approved share option schemes

6: 67 A more generous treatment of share options is provided by the system of approving schemes introduced by TA 1988, s. 185 and Sch. 9. Where an option is granted after 5th April 1984 under an approved scheme, there is no income tax charge when the option is exercised provided that it is exercised not less than three or more than 10 years after the grant, nor within three years of a similar exercise.[1] Instead, a charge to capital gains tax arises on the *disposal of the shares*, and is charged on the difference between the full cost of the option shares and the disposal proceeds.

No tax charge arises on the grant of the option unless the sum of the consideration given for the option and the price payable under it is less than the market value of the shares at that time, when the difference is taxable under Schedule E as earned income.[2] The tax charge will be treated as allowable expenditure when the gain is calculated on the disposal of the shares.[3]

Specimen sets of rules are available from the Revenue.[4]

Simon's Taxes E4.551; Butterworths Income Tax Service D6.68–72.
  [1] TA 1988, s. 185(3). However, a participator could exercise options under several approved schemes on one day.
  [2] TA 1988, s. 185(4).
  [3] TA 1988, s. 185(7).
  [4] See [1987] STI, p. 93.

Approval of schemes

6: 68   Only full time directors or qualifying employees of the company establishing the scheme (the grantor company), or of another company covered by the group scheme, are eligible to participate.[1] However, anyone with a material interest in a company must be excluded.[2]

The value of the shares (at the time the option is granted) over which each participator may hold unexercised options is restricted to the greater of (*i*) £100,000 and (*ii*) 4 times the emoluments (for PAYE purposes, less benefits) in the year of assessment or the preceding year (or the 12 months beginning on the first day in the year of assessment for which there are such emoluments).[3] The shares must be part of the fully paid up ordinary share capital of the grantor company (or certain controlling companies)[4] and must be (*i*) quoted on a recognised stock exchange, or (*ii*) shares in a company not under the control of another company *unless* the controlling company is quoted (and is not a close company).[5] The shares must not be subject to any special restrictions,[6] other than a restriction imposed by the company's Articles requiring the employee or director to dispose of his scheme shares at the end of his employment.[7] Conditions may also be imposed in so far as they require the shares to be pledged as security for a loan to buy them or to be disposed of in repayment of such a loan.[8] The majority of the shares must not be beneficially held by persons who acquired the shares as a result of opportunities given them because of their employment or (if the shares are not quoted) held by the controlling company (or its associated company).[9] "Employee-control shares" are specifically excluded from this restriction; these are shares held by employees or directors of the company and which together confer control of the company.[10] The price paid for the shares must be stated at the time the option is granted (although there may be provision for altering it) and must not be manifestly less than their market value at the time.[11]

The transfer of rights must not be allowed under the scheme, but the exercise of the rights by personal representatives of deceased participants (within one year of death and subject to the 10 year rule) is permitted.[12]

The company establishing the scheme must apply for approval in writing (the procedure is similar to that for savings-related share option schemes). The Revenue have power to demand a wide range of information, and to withdraw approval if the conditions cease to be met (the company has power to appeal to the Special Commissioners against such a decision).[13] The company must be or be controlled by a single company.[14]

As a result of FA 1987 the scheme may now contain provisions allowing for the exchange of rights following a takeover; rights to acquire shares in the new company may be acquired.[15]

Simon's Taxes E4.552, 553, 557.

[1] TA 1988, Sch. 9 para. 27 although they may exercise the rights after the employment ends.

[2] TA 1988, Sch. 9, para. 8; on definition of material interest see TA 1988, s. 187(3) and Sch. 9, paras. 37–40; para 40 was added by FA 1989, s. 65: it excludes shares held in an employee benefit trust in the calculation of a person's holding unless caught by para. 40(3). See also FA 1989, Sch. 12, para. 9.

[3] TA 1988, Sch. 9, para. 28.

[4] TA 1988, Sch. 9, paras. 10–12. Para 10(c)(ii), relating to shares in a consortium company, was repealed by FA 1989, s. 64. The effect is to reduce the stake to be held by a member company of the consortium from 15% to 5%. The purpose is to make it easier for the consortium members shares to be used in this way.

[5] TA 1988, Sch. 9, paras. 11–12.

[6] TA 1988, Sch. 9, paras. 12–13. On effect of directors' discretion to refuse to register a transfer or to compel an employee to sell his shares on the termination of employment see Revenue Press Release of 11th June 1985: [1985] STI, p. 342.

[7] TA 1988, Sch. 9, para. 12(2)–(4). It is of particular benefit to family-run companies.

[8] TA 1988, Sch. 9, para. 13(3), added by FA 1988, s. 66—see *Simon's Tax Intelligence* 1987, p. 782. This rule does not apply to savings-related share option schemes. The rule is retroactive—FA 1984, Sch. 10, para. 10(3) is added by FA 1988, s. 69.

[9] TA 1988, Sch. 9, para. 14.

[10] TA 1988, Sch. 9, para. 14(3).

[11] TA 1988, Sch. 9, para. 29.

[12] TA 1988, Sch. 9, para. 27.

[13] TA 1988, Sch. 9, paras. 5 and 6.

[14] TA 1988, Sch. 9, para. 1(3); on concessionary relief for jointly owned companies see extra-statutory concession B27 (1988), **Simon's Taxes, Division H2.2.**

[15] TA 1988, Sch. 9, para. 15; TA 1988, Sch. 9, para. 15(7); on capital gains consequences see CGTA 1979 s. 144A, added by TA 1988, Sch. 29, para. 25.

Approved profit-sharing schemes (TA 1988, s. 186)

6: 69   Privileged tax treatment is afforded to shares appropriated to approved profit-sharing schemes. The company provides trustees with money with which they acquire shares from the company which they then appropriate to particular individuals.[1] Among the conditions for approval are (*i*) that the total initial market value appropriated to any one participant should not exceed the greater of £2,000 and 10% of the employee's salary (subject to an annual maximum of £6,000),[2] and (*ii*) that the scheme must be open on similar terms to all full time employees, and those that participate must actually do so on equal terms[3]; the scheme may provide for part-timers to be included. Other conditions are attached to the shares and the participants.

So an individual cannot have further new shares in a scheme more than 18 months after he has left his job with the employer; a person with a material interest in a closed company involved is not eligible. Companies in a group may form a group scheme, but the company must be controlled by a single company.[4] Amendments made by FA 1986 enable employee-controlled companies[5] and workers' co-operatives[6] to set up approved profit-sharing schemes.

The essence is to exclude income tax when the shares are acquired and to charge subsequent increases in value only to CGT. Income tax will however become due if the shares are disposed of within a certain period. When shares are appropriated to an individual, no charge arises on that appropriation under TA 1988, s. 19; TA 1988, ss. 154, 160 and 162, §§ **6: 88** and **6: 96** nor does any charge arise on any increase in the market value under TA 1988, s. 138(1)(*a*), § **6: 60**.[7] Dividends on scheme shares are paid over to the participant and are taxed in his hands, presumably under Schedule F, and presumably as investment income (but see § **4: 03**). The participant is treated as absolutely entitled to the shares for CGT notwithstanding many restrictions;[8] this means that he is liable to CGT at his relevant rates when he disposes of the shares.

A specimen set of scheme rules has now been published by the Revenue.[9] In 1987–88 there were 800 approval schemes. 600,000 employees had been allocated shares which had an initial market value of £450 on average; the total initial value was £270m.

Simon's Taxes E4.531–538; Butterworths Income Tax Service D6.41–52.

[1] TA 1988, s. 186 and Sch. 9.

[2] "Relevant amount" defined in TA 1988, s. 187(2), as amended by FA 1989, s. 63 for 1989–90 and later years.

[3] TA 1988, Sch. 9, paras. 8, 35 and 36.

[4] TA 1988, Sch. 9, para. 1(3) and (4); on concessionary relief for jointly owned companies see extra-statutory concession B27 (1985), **Simon's Taxes, Division H2.2.**

[5] TA 1988, Sch. 9, para. 14.

[6] Defined TA 1988, s. 187(10); see also Sch. 9, para. 12(2) and Sch. 10, para. 2.

[7] TA 1988, s. 186(2).

[8] CGTA 1979, s. 144A(1) added by TA 1988, Sch. 29, para. 25.

[9] See [1987] STI, p. 93; see also IR Leaflet IR36 (1980).

Disposal during period of retention

6: 70 The participant must be bound by contract to allow the trustees to hold his shares throughout the "period of retention" and not to dispose of his beneficial interest in that period. Certain disposals, e.g. of redeemable shares in a workers' co-operative, do not give rise to a charge.[1] The period of retention ends two years after the appropriation or earlier death or retirement by reason of injury, disability or redundancy or reaching pensionable age. A disposal of the beneficial interest during this period gives rise to a charge as if he were a disqualified person and so chargeable.[2]

---

[1] TA 1988, Sch. 9, para. 12(4).

[2] TA 1988, Sch. 10, para. 1(3).

Later disposals

6: 71   After the "period of retention" but before the "release date" the participant may at any time direct the trustees to sell his shares and to pay him the proceeds. If the participant directs the trustees to dispose of his shares he must direct them to sell at the best price. A charge to income tax under Schedule E arises on such a sale or on any disposal of his beneficial interest.[1] The release date was changed in the course of 1985–86. As from 25th July 1985 the release date is five years from the date of the appropriation, or earlier death.[2] Before this date the period was seven years from appropriation or earlier death: the charge is on a reducing proportion, called "the appropriate percentage", of the "locked-in value" of the shares. The locked-in value is the initial market value of the shares or, if lower, the actual proceeds.

Event	Percentage chargeable
During period of retention or before 4th anniversary of appropriation	100%
4th–5th anniversary	75%

Before 26th July 1985 the 100% and 75% figures applied as now but a 50% and 25% rate applied where the event occurred between the 5th and 6th anniversary, or the 6th and 7th anniversary respectively.

If he ceases to be an employee or reaches retiring age the percentage is 50%.

EXAMPLE

Shares are allocated in year 1 with a market value of £700. The shares are sold just after the fourth anniversary for £1,000. The locked in value is £700 and the relevant percentage is 75% so income tax is due on £525; CGT may be due on £1,000 − £700, i.e. £300.

If the sale had been for £500 the income tax would have been due on 75% × £500 i.e. £375.

---

[1] TA 1988, s. 186(4).
[2] TA 1988, s. 187(2).

6: 72   Adjustments have to be made if there is a capital distribution in respect of the shares. This charge arises whether the capital is received by the trustees or the participant but subject to pecuniary thresholds. Such distributions are treated as the proceeds of a percentage of the locked-in value. If this occurs the initial market value is reduced by the amount of the capital receipt.[1]

Adjustments are also made for a rights issue the consideration paid being deducted from the proceeds of the disposal.[2]

Shares are treated as disposed of on a first in-first out basis. Company reconstructions amalgamations, etc., are ignored as they are for CGT.[3] There is also provision for the PAYE machinery to apply where a charge to income tax arises.

A participant is entitled to an annual ration of £1,250 initial market value or, if greater, 10% of his salary (up to a maximum of £5,000). If this is exceeded there is a charge on 100% of the excess shares although the charge arises on disposal and not, surprisingly, on appropriation. This provision is designed for cases where it is thought inappropriate to withdraw approval of the scheme. Death and the release date bring about a deemed disposal for this purpose. A similar rule applies to shares appropriated to unauthorised persons.[4]

Sums paid over by employers for such schemes are deductible for corporation tax provided that the sums are spent on the acquisition of shares within the next nine months or are necessary to meet the reasonable expenses of the trustees.[5] Such sums are therefore tax-free investment funds. The schemes are also important for private companies since a member of the controlling family can sell shares to the trust and thus release capital without having to sell the business as used often to happen.

---

[1] TA 1988, s. 186(3).
[2] TA 1988, s. 186(7).
[3] TA 1988, Sch. 10, para. 5.
[4] TA 1988, Sch. 10, para. 6.
[5] TA 1988, Sch. 10, para. 7.

Approved savings–related share option schemes (TA 1988, s. 185)

6: 73   It is also possible to combine an approved share option scheme with an approved savings scheme so as to take advantage of the tax efficiency of the savings scheme to provide the funds to finance the exercise of the option.[1]

The savings scheme must be within TA 1988, s. 326 and approved by the Revenue for this purpose.[2] The contribution must not exceed £100 a month but this limit is to be raised to £150 from 1st September 1989.[3] The option is not normally exercisable for 5 or 7 years (i.e. the period needed to attract the bonus on maturity of the savings scheme) and the price for the shares is not to exceed the proceeds of the contract. The participants in the scheme, i.e. those eligible to participate, must include all UK resident and ordinarily resident employees or directors with at least five years' service[4] but must not include outsiders nor those with a material interest in the company if it is a close company.[5] The shares to be acquired must be ordinary share capital and must be quoted or shares in a company not controlled by another company or shares under the control of a non-close quoted company;[6] it follows from this that if a company is taken over, the existing scheme must be wound up (as approval will be withdrawn) and a new scheme, with its own five or seven year period started in relation to the new head company. The shares must be fully paid up and not redeemable—nor subject to restrictions, other than a restriction imposed by the company's Articles requiring the employee or director to dispose of his scheme shares at the end of his employment.[7] In order to make these schemes more attractive FA 1989 provides that as from 27th July 1989 the price at which the shares may be acquired is not to be manifestly less than 80% (instead of the previous 90%) of the market value at the time the option is acquired.[8]

If these conditions are met, no charge arises on the grant of the option nor on the exercise of the option[9] (so no s. 135 charge) nor is there to be any charge on the growth in value under TA 1988, s 138.[10] Special rules may apply if the company is taken over or some similar event occurs.[11] If the employee is a director or higher paid employee there may be a charge under TA 1988, s. 162.

The company must be or be controlled by a single company.[12] Schemes may now contain provisions allowing for the transfer of rights following a takeover so as to give rights to acquire shares in the new company.[13]

Specimen schemes are available from the Revenue.[14] More than 800 schemes have been approved and options have been granted to employees with an initial value in excess of £3 billion.[15]

---

[1] TA 1988, s. 185.

[2] TA 1988, Sch. 9, para. 16.

[3] TA 1988, Sch. 9, para. 24(2)(a); the increase is to be from a day to be appointed—see FA 1989, s. 62. The appointed day is 1st September; see *Simon's Tax Intelligence* 1989, p. 585.

[4] TA 1988, Sch. 9, para 26.

[5] TA 1988, Sch. 9, paras. 8 and 26.

[6] TA 1988, Sch. 9, para. 11.

[7] TA 1988, Sch. 9, paras. 12 and 13.

[8] TA 1988, Sch. 9, para. 25, as amended by FA 1989, s. 62(3).

[9] In SP 4/83 the Revenue set out the circumstances in which a participant may exercise his option when the employing company leaves a group and ceases to participate in the scheme; see **Simon's Taxes Division H3.2.**

[10] TA 1988, s. 185(3)(a).

[11] TA 1988, Sch. 9, para. 21.

[12] TA 1988, Sch. 9, para. 1(3) and (4); on concessionary relief for jointly owned companies see extra-statutory concession, B27 (1985), **Simon's Taxes, Division H2.2.**

[13] TA 1988, Sch. 9, para. 15; on capital gains consequences see CGTA 1979, s. 144A, added by TA 1988, Sch. 29, para. 25.

[14] [1986] STI, p. 10.

[15] Hansard, Standing Committee G, 6th June 1989, col. 226.

General considerations

6: 74 Share option schemes cause problems in any tax system. Most tax systems agree that the grant of an option to buy shares at a figure below the then market value is a taxable emolument; also that the gain accruing between the time of acquisition and the date of disposal should be charged as a capital gain. The problem area is that between the value at the date of the grant of the option and that at the date of its exercise.

In practice an option scheme can be the subject of many abuses and the system of approving schemes meriting certain standards was designed to prevent these. However it should not be forgotten that an option scheme is much more expensive for the employer than ordinary remuneration since its expenses are not generally deductible[1] and that the employee will usually be better off with a cash bonus of the sum which (net of corporation tax at 35% or 27% depending on the company) equals the cost of the option scheme to the company. One must therefore consider the total tax burden on both employer and employee before passing judgment.

Finally, one should note that the legislation deals only with shares; options to acquire other sorts of property, e.g. a house, therefore, remain under the general rule in *Abbott v Philbin*[2], a valuable perquisite.

Simon's Taxes E4.531–543.

[1] *Lowry v Consolidated African Selection Trust* [1940] AC 648, 23 TC 259.

[2] [1961] AC 352, 39 TC 82, supra, § **6:45.**

(3) PROFIT RELATED PAY[1]

6: 75   TA 1988, ss. 169–184 and Sch. 8 provides the legislative framework for the approval of schemes for profit related pay (PRP).[1] Where schemes are approved, one half of the profit related pay is exempt from income tax up to the lower of two limits.[2] The more complex limit is 1/5th of the sum of non-PRP and PRP; so if the non-PRP is £10,000 and the PRP is £4,000 the limit under this second rule is 1/5th of £14,000 or £2,800. The simpler limit is £4,000.[3] To continue the example, as £2,800 is the lower limit the taxpayer will be exempt from income tax on £1,400 and therefore remains fully taxable in the normal way not only on the £10,000 non-PRP but also on £2,600 of the PRP. If the PRP goes up to £14,000 making a total of £24,000 the first limit becomes 1/5th of £24,000 or £4,800; this makes the £4,000 limit the relevant one and the exemption is given only on £2,000.

Where payment of PRP is taxable it is subject to the PAYE system and is to the new receipts basis;[4] it is also subject to employer's national insurance contributions.

Simon's Taxes E4.301; Butterworths Income Tax Service D7.02.

[1] These rules follow a Green Paper (Cmnd. 9835) published in July 1986. The intellectual driving force is Martin L. Weitzman, *The Share Economy: Conquering Stagflation* (Harvard University Press 1984); the partial tax exemption is put forward in a chapter entitled "Vaccinating Capitalism Against Stagflation". See also two publications by the Employment Institute: Weitzman, *The Case for Profit-Sharing* and Estrin and Wadhwani, *Will Profit-Sharing Work?* Figures at the end of June 1989 for the number of schemes (902) and of employee participants (107,300) are given in **Simon's Tax Intelligence** 1989 p. 624.

[2] TA 1988, s. 171.

[3] TA 1988, s. 171(4), as amended by FA 1989, Sch. 4, para. 2(1)—for profit periods beginning after 31st March 1989.

[4] TA 1988, s. 170 was repealed by FA 1989, Sch. 17, Pt. V.

6: 76   There are various exclusions from the scheme. Thus if an employee gets relief for one PRP scheme he may not claim exemption in respect of any other employment for the same period.[1] Nor may exemption be claimed if there is no liability to pay the employer's national insurance contribution—although it can be claimed where the only reason for the absence of liability is that the earnings are below the earnings limit for such contributions. One situation in which the PRP would be safe from such contributions and therefore not entitled to the exemption is where it is paid through a trust.[2]

Certain employments are specifically excluded—including any employment in an office under the Crown or otherwise in the service of the Crown, or with a local authority or with a body under the control of central or local government.[3]

Simon's Taxes E4.303; Butterworths Income Tax Service D7.02–03.

[1] TA 1988, s. 172(1).

[2] Revenue Press Release, 17th March 1987, [1987] STI, p. 162, Q3.

[3] TA 1988, s. 174; the concept of control is defined in s. 174(3). Universities are not excluded employments.

6: 77   Subject to these exclusions a scheme may be established by any employer for any "employment unit". So it may cover the entire workforce of a company or a particular part of the undertaking;[1] it may not cover the employees of another company save where the parent company of a group registers a scheme for the employees of its subsidiaries.[2] Rules now allow a unit to qualify for PRP generated by the group on a whole, e.g. a headquarters or research and development unit.[3]

At the start of the profit period at least 80% of all the employees in the employment unit must be in the scheme.[4] However anyone with a material interest in the company must be excluded.[5] The scheme may also include those who work less than 20 hours a week or who have been employed with the company for less than three years.[6] For the purpose of the 80% calculation those with material interests or who are excluded from the scheme under the rules just stated are to be ignored.

Simon's Taxes E4.304; Butterworths Income Tax Service D7.04.

[1] TA 1988, Sch. 8, para. 4.
[2] TA 1988, s. 173(2); the group requirements are satisfied by 51% control—s. 174(3).
[3] TA 1988, Sch. 8, paras. 21 and 22, added by FA 1989, Sch. 4, para. 15.
[4] TA 1988, Sch. 8, para. 6.
[5] TA 1988, Sch. 8, para. 7; material interest is defined as more than 25% of the ordinary share capital or, in the case of a close company, one to whom more than 25% of the distributable assets on a notional winding up would be distributed—para. 7 as amended by FA 1989, Sch. 12, para. 8 and Sch. 4 para. 9.
[6] TA 1988, Sch. 8, para. 8.

6: 78   As the rules are concerned to allow profit to be distributed free of tax, rules have to be included in the scheme for defining the pool of profit, known as the "distributable pool" for a profit period. The profit period must be 12 months except for terminated or replacement schemes.[1]

Two methods of determining the distributable pool are offered. Method A offers a simple percentage of the profits of the employment unit for the profit period; it is no longer necessary that this pool should be a sum equal to at least 5% of the standard pay of the employment unit.[2] However a fixed percentage must be specified;[3] the term standard pay is defined but, broadly, means a reasonable estimate of the pay of the employees in the scheme.[4] This calculation involves the use of a base year which is a specified period of 12 months ending within the two years immediately before the first (or only) profit period to which the scheme relates.[5] The scheme may provide a ceiling if the percentage figure leads to an increase of more than 60% over the previous period[6] and for there to be no pool for a period if the percentage gives a figure falling below a sum specified in the scheme but which must be less than the 5%-of-standard-pay figure.[7]

Method B also contains the 5% of standard pay minimum and also contains the ceiling and floor options as in Method A.[8] However the purpose of method B is to allow the pool to vary not with the simple level of profits but with year on year *changes* in profits. So the pool in year 2 will usually be expressed as a percentage of the change in profits between year 1 and year 2.[9]

As the schemes are geared to the sharing of profits, there are rules for the ascertainment of profits for each employment unit for each period.[10] Once a particular method of calculating profit has been adopted it must not be changed save where the change alters the profits by 5% or less.[11]

Once the pool is ascertained it must be shared out to the employees in the employment unit; there can be no retentions. All employees must participate on similar terms but payments may vary according to levels of remuneration and length of service.[12]

Simon's Taxes E4.305–7; Butterworths Income Tax Service D7.05–09.

[1] TA 1988, Sch. 8, paras. 9–11; a "replacement scheme" is defined in Sch. 8, para. 10(4).

[2] TA 1988, Sch. 8, para. 13 repealed by FA 1989 Sch. 4, para. 10. See **Simon's Tax Intelligence** 1989 p. 48.

[3] TA 1988, Sch. 8, para. 13(1A), added by FA 1989, Sch. 4, para. 10(2)(*b*).

[4] TA 1988, Sch. 8, para. 13(6); what is not clear is whether pay includes PRP.

[5] TA 1988, Sch. 8, para. 13(3).

[6] TA 1988, Sch. 8, para. 13(4).

[7] TA 1988, Sch. 8, para. 13(5).

[8] TA 1988, Sch. 8, para. 14(3).

[9] The formula may contain a pre-determined percentage but may also contain a formula for limiting increases or decreases by a pre-determined fraction (not to exceed one half): TA 1988, Sch. 8, para. 14(3).

[10] TA 1988, Sch. 8, para. 19, as amended by FA 1989, Sch. 4, para. 14.

[11] TA 1988, Sch. 8, para. 20.

[12] TA 1988, Sch. 8, paras. 16–18.

6:79   There is a process of registration and rules as to what must be contained in an application.[1] Amongst these requirements is a report from an independent accountant;[2] this person must also support an annual return by the employer with a report.[3]

Registration may be cancelled if it appears to the Board that the scheme failed to meet the rules for registration or if the company fails to make annual returns.[4] The power to cancel also arises if the scheme has become incapable of administration in accordance with its terms or the statutory rules[5] or the employment becomes excluded, or if the "employment unit" runs at a loss[6] or if the employer no longer meets the minimum wage legislation requirements.[7] Cancellation may be initiated by the employer either because one of the above grounds has occurred or because he wants it cancelled.[8] A scheme need no longer lapse on the death of the employer.[9] The alteration of the terms of the scheme does not invalidate its registration[10] but may give cause for cancellation.[11] Cancellation can lead to the recovery of relief wrongly given—including recovery from persons other than the scheme employer.[12]

Appeals lie to the Special Commissioners against the refusal of the Revenue to register the scheme, against their refusal to register a change of scheme following a change of employer[13] and against their decision to cancel the scheme.[14]

Simon's Taxes E4.308; Butterworths Income Tax Service D7.11.

[1] TA 1988, ss. 175 and 176.

[2] TA 1988, s. 175(2); the term "independent accountant" is defined in TA 1988, s. 184 by

reference to the Companies Act 1985, s. 389 but subject to exclusions for persons employed by the company.

³ TA 1988, s. 180(1).

⁴ TA 1988, s. 178(2) and (3).

⁵ TA 1988, s. 178(1)(*a*), (*b*).

⁶ TA 1988, s. 178(1)(*c*) and (2)(*b*).

⁷ TA 1988, s. 178(1)(*c*) referring to TA 1988, s. 175(1)(*d*) which requires the minimum wage rules to be met without taking the PRP into account.

⁸ TA 1988, s. 178(3)–(6).

⁹ TA 1988, s. 177A added by FA 1989, Sch. 4, para. 3: the personal representatives may seek cancellation. TA 1988, s. 178 (5A).

¹⁰ TA 1988, s. 177B added by FA 1989, Sch. 4, para. 3. This has been a matter of concession since 10th October 1988; see **Simon's Tax Intelligence 1988**, p. 732. On appeals see FA 1989, Sch. 4, para. 8.

¹¹ TA 1988, s. 178(3A), added by FA 1989, Sch. 4, para. 4.

¹² TA 1988, s. 179(3) and (4), added by FA 1989, Sch. 4, para. 5.

¹³ TA 1988, s. 177(1).

¹⁴ TA 1988, s. 182.

6: 80   The PRP rules are important not only for the philosophy of incentives that lies behind it but also for the burdens placed on the employer and his independent accountant. Thus the employer is responsible for ensuring that the scheme complies with the statutory requirements, for calculating the PRP profits and the amount of PRP due to each employee and then for giving the tax relief through the PAYE scheme. The employer also has to certify the scheme in the first instance and its annual operation. The independent accountant also acts as watchdog for the Revenue. There are extensive Revenue powers to obtain information, and duties on the employer to provide it.[1] The independent accountant is also concerned to provide a report both as to the initial registrability of the scheme and that the scheme and the tax relief have been operated properly.[2]

Simon's Taxes E4.308; Butterworths Income Tax Service D7.13.

[1] TA 1988, s. 181. On penalties, see TA 1988, Sch. 29.

[2] TA 1988, ss. 175 and 181 require the independent accountant to certify that the terms of the scheme are satisfied "in his opinion".

---

(4) EMPLOYEE SHARE OWNERSHIP PLANS

6: 81   FA 1989 contains rules for a further incentive for employee share ownership schemes. Although colloquially known as ESOPs, these schemes are termed Employee Share Ownership Trusts in the legislation; (apparently the acronym ESOT is thought too bibulous in these abstemious times). In essence these arrangements combine a share participation scheme with a trust for the benefit of the employees. The new legislation is designed to ensure that the company obtains a corporation tax deduction when making its contribution to the trust.

An ESOP comes under these special rules if there is a qualifying employment share ownership trust. This is defined at length in FA 1989, Sch. 5. The trust must be established under a deed. The trust must be established by a company which is not controlled by any other company and is resident in the UK.[1] The deed must appoint the first trustees and contain various rules as to the trustees e.g. as to having a majority independent of the founding company.[2] There are rules as to beneficiaries—certain employees must be included (e.g. those working 20 hours a week or more who has been with the company or any other company within the group for at least five years) but others may be beneficiaries; those with material interests or who have worked for the company for less than one year must be excluded.[3] Thus, employees of subsidiaries can qualify. The trust deed must spell out various duties of the trustees e.g. as to their functions in receiving money from the company and investing it in the appropriate securities within the appropriate period and dealing with the securities promptly.[4] Thus they must invest the money in ordinary shares of the founding company or spend it on some other qualifying purpose within nine months;[5] they must be told not to invest if the company is then controlled by another company and that any acquisitions must be at a price at or below current market value; special restrictions on the shares are not permitted but this has to be achieved by expressly stating that the trustees may not buy shares which are subject to such restrictions.[6] The trustees are permitted to vary the basis of allocation only by reference to the basis of level of remuneration or length of service.[7] When the trust disposes of its shares it must do so either directly to the employees or to an approved profit sharing scheme under TA 1988, Sch. 9; any other transfer will be a chargeable event and this restriction must be spelt out in the trust.[8]

Apart from the acquisition of shares in the founding company the purposes for which the trustees are permitted to use the money are limited to matters such as the repayment of loans taken out to acquire the shares, the payment of interest on such loans, payments to employees and the payment of trust expenses.[9] The deed must not contain features which are not essential, or reasonably incidental, to these primary purposes.[10] A trust which ceases to satisfy some of these conditions ceases to be qualifying ESOP.

Simons Taxes D2.220.
[1] FA 1989, Sch. 5, para. 2.
[2] FA 1989, Sch. 5, para. 3.
[3] FA 1989, Sch. 5, para. 4; material interest is defined ibid, para. 16.
[4] FA 1989, Sch. 5, paras. 5–10.
[5] FA 1989, Sch. 5, para. 7.
[6] FA 1989, Sch. 5, para. 9.
[7] FA 1989, Sch. 5, para. 6.
[8] FA 1989, Sch. 5, para. 5(2)(c) and (d) the chargeable event is specified in s. 69(1) to (3).
[9] FA 1989, Sch. 5, para. 6(3).
[10] FA 1989, Sch. 5, para. 10.

The consequences

6: 82   FA 1989 contains rules allowing the company to claim a deduction for contributions to an ESOP and then provides complicated rules as to the clawback of the benefit. It will be noted that there is no CGT relief on a sale of the shares. The company may deduct a payment to the trustees if the trust is still a qualifying ESOP, at that time at least some of the employees are eligible to benefit; the company is resident in the UK a sum is spent on a qualifying purpose within nine months and a claim for relief is made.[1]

When a chargeable event occurs the benefit of the corporation tax deduction is clawed back from the trustees. The Revenue view is that this will be basic rate of tax plus the additional rate, currently 35%. The charge is under Schedule D Case VI. The company may be liable to pay if the trustees fail to pay within six months.[2]

The chargeable events are related very closely to the matters which the trustees are or are not permitted to do. So the trustees must not make a non-qualifying transfer (i.e. a transfer to someone other than a beneficiary or an approved profit sharing scheme[3] or a transfer on non-qualifying terms.[4] They must not spend the money on a non-qualifying purpose.[5] They are also barred from retaining securities for more than seven years.[6] The amount brought into charge for expenditure on a non-qualifying purpose is the sum so spent. Otherwise it is the capital gains base cost (without any allowance for indexation relief) of the security retained or transferred.[7]

In computing the sum to be charged a further adjustment is made in order to achieve the legislative object of clawing back the relief rather than simply penalising the trustee. First one adds the present sum to be charged to the total of any previous charges.[8] This is then set against the amounts deductible for corporation tax by the company (whether or not any claim for relief has actually been made). The sums to be charged is chargeable only to the extent that it exceeds the deductible amounts.

A further charge will arise in a combination of circumstances. The first is that a sum could have been charged—because it arose on a chargeable event—but it was charged because of the adjustment. The second is that at that time the trustees had borrowed money. If at any of the borrowings are subsequently repaid the trustees are chargeable under Case VI on the amount repaid.[9]

There are extensive information powers.[10]

---

[1] FA 1989, s. 67.
[2] The mechanics are set out in FA 1989, s. 68; see Hansard Standing Committee G, col. 311.
[3] FA 1989, s. 69(2) and (3).
[4] FA 1989, s. 69(4) and (6).
[5] FA 1989, s. 69(5).
[6] See FA 1989, s. 69(1)(c), (7)–(12).
[7] FA 1989, s. 70.
[8] FA 1989, s. 72(2).
[9] FA 1989, s. 71.
[10] FA 1989, s. 73.

---

(5) MEDICAL INSURANCE AND SICK PAY SCHEMES

6: 83 The cost of providing insurance against medical treatment was at one time a taxable benefit even though it cannot be converted into cash[1]—but this no longer applies from 5th April 1982.[2]

A director or higher paid employee remains taxable on medical insurance and treatment under TA 1988, s. 154 unless the need for treatment arises while he is outside the UK performing the duties of his employment, or the insurance is provided to meet such a need.[3]

Payments made to employees or their families under sick pay arrangements entered into by the employer are taxable as from 1982–83.[4]

Simon's Taxes E4.424; Butterworths Income Tax Service D3.56.
  [1] FA 1976, s. 68.
  [2] FA 1981, s. 72.
  [3] TA 1988, s. 155(6).
  [4] FA 1981, s. 30.

(6) EXEMPTION FOR TRAINING SCHEMES AND FOR SCHOLARSHIP AND APPRENTICE SCHEMES AT UNIVERSITIES AND TECHNICAL COLLEGES

6: 84   TA 1988, s. 588 provides exemption in respect of expenditure incurred by an employer in connection with training schemes; the exemption allows the employer to deduct the expenditure[1] while exempting the employee from any liability to tax under Schedule E.[2] The new rules apply to expenditure on or after 6th April 1987; previously relief was based on concessions.[3]

The exemption is given for expenditure reimbursed or incurred by the employer in connection with a qualifying course of training. The course must be attended on a full time (or substantially full time) basis; the employee must have been employed for two years and the opportunity to take the course must be available either generally to employees and former employees or to a particular class of such persons.[4] So the owner of a firm cannot use this simply to provide a child of his with a training at the state's subsidy just by taking him on to the books for a few days and then sending him off to a course. The course must be designed to impart or improve skills or knowledge relevant to and intended to be used in the course of gainful employment (including self-employment) of any description[5] and the course must be entirely devoted to the teaching and/or practical application of such skills or knowledge. In addition the course must not last more than one year and all the teaching and practical application must take place in the UK.[6]

The course must be undertaken by an employee (or former employee) with a view to retraining. This test stands as one of purpose, presumably in the light of the objective test used by the House of Lords in *Mallalieu v Drummond* (infra, § **7: 89**). However the legislation also states that the course cannot be regarded as undertaken with a view to retraining unless it is begun while employed by the employer or within one year of ceasing to be so; it is also necessary that the employee should in any event cease to be so employed within two years of the end of the course.[7] This last rule underlines the purpose of the provision. It is designed to encourage employers and employees to get retrained and then re-employed or self-employed elsewhere. Where the training is for an employee who is to be kept on the books of the employer the matter is dealt with, somewhat mysteriously and surely unnecessarily, by a combination of concession and statement of practice. Briefly an employee is not chargeable on expenses incurred by the employer on a course which is "job related" or is a course of general education for young employees.[8] Where the employee has to bear the expenses they are, by concession deductible.[9] Both concessions are limited to the costs of fees for the course and the cost of essential books. If the employee is temporarily absent from his normal place of work while attending the course allowable expenses—for both concessions—also cover additional travel costs and subsistence costs.[10] Where an employee bears the costs and seeks a deduction there are stringent conditions; thus the employer must continue to pay his full salary; the employer must require or encourage him to attend it; the course must be a full time one lasting at least four weeks, the course must take place in the UK and must not relate to a "resit".

Where the employee attends a full time course at a university or technical college payments by the employer may qualify as scholarship income under TA 1988, s. 331. A Statement of Practice sets out the conditions to be observed.[11]

Simon's Taxes E4.422; Butterworths Income Tax Service D3.101.

[1] TA 1988, s. 588(3) for deduction in computing profits and TA 1988, s. 588(4) for treatment as expense of management of investment company.

[2] TA 1988, s. 588(1).

[3] Extra-statutory concession A63 (1988), Simon's Taxes, Division H2.2.

[4] TA 1988, s. 589(3)—the two year employment condition means two years before he starts the course or ends the employment whichever is the earlier.

[5] The opportunities for intellectual philistinism in this context are legion.

[6] TA 1988, s. 589(3).

[7] TA 1988, s. 589(4); re-employment within two years is a breach of the conditions; any breach of these conditions has to be reported within 60 days of the employer coming to know of it (TA 1988, s. 588(6)) and the normal six year time limit for assessments runs from the end of the year in which the breach occurred (s. 588(5)); there are also Revenue information-gathering powers in s. 588(7).

[8] Extra-statutory concession A63 (1988), Simon's Taxes, Division H2.2; youth ends at 21 in the Revenue's eyes.

[9] Extra-statutory concession A64 (1988), Simon's Taxes, Division H2.2.

[10] This is the subject of elaborate definition for an employee bearing his own costs.

[11] SP 4/86, Simon's Taxes, Division H3.2.

EMPLOYEES EARNING £8,500 PER ANNUM OR MORE AND DIRECTORS

6: 85   One product of the rule in *Tennant v Smith*[1] was a substantial amount of tax avoidance. What would otherwise be remuneration was dressed up as an expense allowance or paid in the form of benefits in kind. Expense allowances in so far as they exceeded the sums actually spent by the recipient on behalf of his employer[2] would be taxable, but difficult to trace, while benefits in kind in so far as they could be traced would be taxable only if convertible into money or money's worth. Yet these expenses or allowances would be deductible by the employer in computing the profits of his business. For these reasons special legislation was introduced in 1948 and is now to be found in revised form in TA 1988, ss. 153–168. Special rules also apply to payments to participators in close companies—infra, § **27: 09**.

Before 1976 certain employments were exempt, notably charities and non-trading bodies such as the civil service and trade unions. The new legislation draws no such distinctions.[3]

Simon's Taxes E4.601–604; Butterworths Income Tax Service D3.21–24.

[1] [1892] AC 150, 3 TC 158, HL, supra, § **6: 44**.

[2] Such sums only escaped tax if deductible under TA 1988, ss. 198 or 201.

³ The abolition of these exemptions had been recommended by R.C. 1955 § 221; charities and non-profit making bodies are still distinct in that a director of such a body is treated as an employee and not a director. TA 1988, s. 167(5), infra, § **6: 86**; see also TA 1988, s. 145(5).

6: 86   The recipients of these expense allowances or benefits in kind who fall within the chapter are (*a*) directors[1] whatever their salary, because they can fix their own income, and (*b*) employees whose emoluments amount to £8,500.[1] By FA 1989 employees earning over £8,500 are no longer to be described as higher paid.[2] The term "director" is not restricted to directors formally appointed as such.[3]

A full time working director who does not have a material interest in the company is to be treated as an employee,[4] and so only comes within this provision if his emoluments come to £8,500 or more. His directorship is full time if he is required to devote substantially the whole of his time to the company in a managerial or technical capacity. His interest is material if he can control more than 5% of the ordinary share capital or, if the company is a close company, more than 5% of assets could be distributed to him on a notional winding up.[5]

Also excluded from the definition of director are those who are directors of non-profit making bodies and charities provided they have no material interest in the company.[6]

In computing the employee's emoluments for the £8,500 threshold sums treated as taxable by TA 1988, ss. 153 and 154 are to be included;[6] this is to prevent avoidance by means of a low salary and large expenses or benefits in kind. For a particular problem with cars see infra, § **6: 97**. More dubiously there is no deduction in making this computation for expenses allowable under ss. 198 or 201 N.B.[7] although an inspector may give a notice of nil liability[8] in respect of a benefit or allowance where he is satisfied that no extra charge to tax would arise. Such notices, however, are not issued where the effect would be to take the employee below the £8,500 threshold.[9] An expense which the employer meets directly will not be taken into account.

An employer may not avoid these rules by dividing up an employee's functions into different employments,[10] and similar rules apply if the second employment is with a controlled company. A director of a company may also be an employee but these provisions apply to him whether or not his income from the employment reaches £8,500,[11] save where he is a full time working director. If he is a director (other than a full time working director without a material interest) of one controlled company and an employee of another, these rules apply to him in respect of *both* situations.

Simon's Taxes E4.602, 603.

¹ TA 1988, s. 167(1).
² FA 1989, s. 53.
³ TA 1988, s. 168(8).
⁴ TA 1988, s. 167(5).
⁵ TA 1988, s. 168(9)–(11), as amended by FA 1989, Sch. 12, para. 8; shares held by associates are included. Participator is defined in TA 1988, s. 417(1).
⁶ TA 1988, s. 167(5).
⁷ TA 1988, s. 167(2). The Revenue claim that the purpose of this last rule is to maintain equity between one who is paid a gross salary out of which deductible expenses are met and another who receives a lower salary but separate reimbursements of deductible expenses. This claim is unsound since equity could be achieved equally well by allowing both persons to deduct their

expenses and because it creates inequity between these two and the third person who receives a lower salary but who incurs no deductible expenses because his employer meets them directly.
  [8] Under TA 1988, s. 166.
  [9] *Quaere* whether the Revenue have the power to do this.
  [10] TA 1988, s. 167(3).
  [11] TA 1988, s. 167(4).

Payments for expenses and expense allowances: TA 1988, s. 153

6: 87   Any payment[1] made by reason of the employment[2] in respect of expenses is, unless otherwise chargeable to tax, to be treated as income of the director or employee. The section applies not only to expense allowances but also to reimbursement of expenses actually incurred since here too there is payment in respect of expenses; the only expenses not caught are those which the employer meets himself. The recipient may however deduct sums actually expended if they satisfy the tests laid down in TA 1988, ss. 198, 201 or 203.[3] The section thus catches payments that would not otherwise be caught since under *Owen v Pook* the reimbursement of an expense is not an emolument;[4] further the sum must be reported as income and then claimed as an expense.

The section also applies to sums put at the employee's disposal and paid away by him.[5] So sums are caught even though the money does not at any time become the property of the employee.[6]

The employer has to report all such payments. In order to avoid too much circuity where the sum would be deductible under those sections, the inspector, having received a statement from the employer, and being satisfied that no additional tax falls to be charged under this chapter, may issue notice of nil liability directing that the chapter shall not apply.[7] The concession for the reimbursed expenses of certain living costs of members of the clergy does not apply if that member earns £8,500 p.a. or more.[8]

Simon's Taxes E4.604; Butterworths Income Tax Service D3.22.
  [1] See *Jennings v Kinder* [1958] 1 All ER 369, 38 TC 673.
  [2] All sums paid by the employer are deemed to be paid by reason of the employment, others may be; TA 1988, s. 168(5).
  [3] The burden of proof rests on the taxpayer to show that the expense comes within these provisions—*Mcleish v IRC* (1958) 38 TC 1.
  [4] RC (1955) § 226 and supra, § **6: 31**, n. 12.
  [5] TA 1988, s. 153(3).
  [6] TA 1988, s. 153(3). The effect of this extension on s. 167(2)(*b*), supra, is to make almost any employee with financial responsibility subject to the chapter.
  [7] TA 1988, s. 166 . Dispensations are not given for allowances fixed at a "round sum": IR Notes 3.
  [8] Extra-statutory concession A61 (1988), see **Simon's Taxes, Division H2.2**; is this limitation aimed at Bishops?

Benefits in kind: TA 1988, s. 154

6: 88   TA 1988, s. 154 requires there to be treated as income of the director or employee sums spent in or in connection with the provision of accommodation, other than living accommodation, of entertainment, of domestic or other services or other benefits or facilities of whatsoever nature e.g. workplace nurseries.[1] The section charges the director or employer on the cash equivalent of the benefit. This will usually be the cost of the benefit.[2] The persons providing the benefit are those at whose cost the provision is made.[3]

The section does not apply if the employee has "made good" the expense to his employer,[4] nor if apart from s. 154, the cost would be chargeable to tax as income of the director or employee—for example under *Tennant v Smith*.[5] The last exception requires elaboration. If the benefit could be converted into cash but only for less than its cost, the cost is not "otherwise chargeable to tax on income" and so comes within s. 154. If, however, the resale value is higher than cost, it appears that the Revenue can insist on the higher amount under *Tennant v Smith*.

Section 154 does not apply to income which is expressly excluded from tax by some other provision.[6]

Section 154 applies only where the benefit is provided by reason of the employment. However, all provision for an employee, or for members of his family or household, by his employer are deemed to be made by reason of the employment unless it can be shown that the employer is an individual and that the provision was made in the normal course of his domestic, family or personal relationship.[7]

A benefit is treated as provided by the employer if it is provided at his cost. In *Wicks v Firth*[8] scholarships awarded by trustees were held to be provided at the cost of the employer as the trustees used money supplied by the employer and were only performing duties imposed on them by the employer.[8]

If the deeming provision does not apply s. 154 will apply if the benefit is provided "by reason of the employment". This test may involve a *causa sine qua non*—in which case it is different from the general test of causation under Schedule E.[9]

Simon's Taxes E4.605.

[1] The Revenue view stated at [1984] STI, p. 797 was later softened, see [1985] STI, p. 246. On Christmas parties see Revenue Press Release dated 26th October 1984, [1984] STI, p. 715.

[2] TA 1988, s. 156(1).

[3] TA 1988, s. 154(3).

[4] If the employee pays a sum equal to the cost of providing the benefit he escapes s. 154 even though the market value is higher. *Quaere* whether a tenant paying a full market rent thereby "makes good" to the lessor any sums spent by the lessor even though those sums exceed the rent. See *Luke v IRC* [1963] 1 All ER 655, 40 TC 630. Lord Reid took this view at 578, 647 but contra Lord Guest at 586, 652.

[5] So the gift of an FA Cup Final ticket which he can sell to a ticket tout at a substantial profit is not within s. 154. However *quaere* whether the gift of an asset which could be sold but only for a very low value would fall within s. 154—perhaps it would because in such a case what is chargeable under general principles is not "the expense".

[6] In *Wicks v Firth* [1983] STC 25, the House of Lords held that although a scholarship awarded to the taxpayer's child by his employer was a benefit provided to the taxpayer by reason of his employment, it was exempt under TA 1988, s. 331 as scholarship income. However, the effect of this decision has been reversed by TA 1988, s. 165, infra, § **6: 98**.

[7] TA 1988, s. 168(3). *Quaere* if the business is held in a family trust so that the body of trustees is the employer.

[8] [1983] STC 25 per Lord Templeman at 31.

[9] [1982] STC 76 per Lord Denning MR at 80. This point was left open by the House of Lords; see Lord Templeman at 32.

6: 89   TA 1988, s. 154 talks simply in terms of the provision of certain services or benefits or facilities. It does not require that the employee should receive the *exclusive* benefit; so when the service benefits both employer and employee, s. 154 applies. It is quite immaterial that the employee, left to himself, would have spent less on the service.

In *Rendell v Went*[1] a company incurred expenses of £641 in the (successful) defence of one of its directors on a charge of causing death by dangerous driving. That sum was chargeable to the director under s. 154. The expense was incurred "in the provision of a benefit to" the director regardless of the fact that there might be good commercial reason for the expenditure and regardless of the fact that the director, left to himself, would have spent no more than £60 and no-one suggested that he could have received free legal aid.

Since the section talks of the provision of a service it is presumably irrelevant that no benefit accrues; so the director in *Rendell v Went* would be chargeable in respect of the £641 even if he had been found guilty and been given the maximum sentence. Likewise, where a facility is provided, it is presumably irrelevant that the employee would rather not have the benefit. Thus the cost of providing a seat in a party for the FA Cup Final would be taxable to the employee even if he detests football and would rather be at Covent Garden to attend a performance of Götterdämmerung—or vice versa.[2]

However it is presumably necessary that the employee should accept or acquiesce in the provision of the benefit. So, for Lord Reid, in *Rendell v Went* it was important that the director knew and accepted what was being done on his behalf even though he may not have realised how much it was costing and Lord Reid would express no opinion on the case of a company spending a large sum of money without the director's knowledge to procure a benefit that he did not want.[3]

Where the benefit is to the director he will presumably be aware of it and to avoid tax he has only to disclaim it.[4] However the legislation applies to benefits conferred not only on the director or employee himself but also on his spouse family, servants, dependants or guests.[5] It would seem unjustifiable to charge an employee or director with tax on sums spent in the provision of a benefit to some member of his family of which he knew nothing, whether or not he would have been pleased if he had known, and equally unjustifiable if he had known but disapproved of it, yet he appears to be taxable.

---

[1] [1964] 2 All ER 464, 41 TC 641; on apportionment see § **6: 92**.
[2] Such discrimination is ruled out by Donovan LJ in *Butter v Bennett* (1962) 40 TC 402 at 414.
[3] At 466, 655.
[4] So if he does not use his Cup Final ticket he will escape tax.
[5] TA 1988, s. 168(4). So he will be chargeable if he gives the ticket to his son.

Exceptions

6: 90   Certain payments by the employer are excluded:

(*a*) Expense incurred in the provision of accommodation supplies or services used in premises occupied by the employer[1], provided these are used by the employee solely in performing the duties of his employment. Thus a director is not chargeable on sums spent on an expensive secretary or on luxurious office furniture.[2]

(*b*) Meals served in canteens which are made available to the staff generally are excluded.[3] The provision of vouchers for use in a separated part of a restaurant run independently of the employer might well fall within this exception and although vouchers for use in any restaurant would not, those for use in a particular restaurant might well escape s. 154.

(*c*) Expenses incurred in the provision of any pension, annuity, lump sum, gratuity or other like benefit to be given to the director or employee or his spouse children or dependants on his death or retirement.[4]

(*d*) Travel warrants for H.M. forces.[5]

(*e*) Medical insurance for foreign visits and medical treatment, the need for which arises while the director or employee is abroad.[6]

(*f*) As a result of the decision of the House of Lords in *Wicks v Firth*, a provision rendering a payment non-taxable as income may also impliedly exempt the employee from liability under s. 154, whether the payment is made either to the employee or a member of his family.[7] The particular exemption in that case (TA 1988, s. 331) has now been the subject of special legislation (see infra, § **6: 98**) but the principle remains.[8]

(*g*) The provision of a car parking place at or near the employee's place of work.[9]

(*h*) The provision of entertainment by someone unconnected with his employment.[10]

(*i*) There are also concessionary exemptions for miners from coal, removal expenses, expense of a wife to accompany a husband in precarious health.[11]

Simon's Taxes E4.605.
 [1] Presumably the test of occupation is that under the pre 1977 law and not that in TA 1988, s. 145, supra, § **6: 53**—the prime difference is category (*c*).
 [2] TA 1988, s. 155(2).
 [3] TA 1988, s. 155(5).
 [4] TA 1988, s. 155(4).
 [5] TA 1988, s. 197(2).
 [6] TA 1988, s. 155(6) (supra, § **6: 71**).
 [7] [1983] STC 25, HL.
 [8] Unless the House of Lords follows its own (bad) precedent in *Thomson v Moyse*, see infra, § **34: 19**.
 [9] TA 1988, s. 155(1A), added by FA 1988, s. 46(3); this exclusion has retroactive effect when liability was settled before 15th March 1988.
 [10] TA 1988, s. 155(7), added by FA 1988, s. 49.
 [11] Extra-statutory concessions A5, A67 and A6 (1988), **Simon's Taxes, Division H2.2**.

Extent of charge

6: 91   Under TA 1988, s. 154 the measure of liability is the cash equivalent of the benefit. This is usually the expense incurred in providing the benefit;[1] no regard is had to the value of the benefit.

It follows that benefits in kind retain some value as a tax saving device. If the cost of the benefit is £100 and the taxpayer's marginal rate is 60%, he will acquire the benefit (£100) but pay tax of £60. Yet if he had had to pay for the benefit out of his own pocket his salary would have had to be increased by £250 to give him the £100 net of tax with which to acquire an equivalent benefit. The reason why s. 154 uses this technique is to preserve consistency with s. 153; the amount charged is the same whether the employee receives £100 under an expense allowance which he spends on the object or receives the object as a benefit in kind. This example can be criticised for failing to compare like with like as one is comparing tax of £40 leaving him with the benefit in kind and tax of £150 leaving him with £100 but this is not the way most employers think. There is a less contentious point that benefits in kind do not attract National Insurance Contributions.

If no expense is incurred in providing the benefit, no charge can arise under s. 154. The provision of a service at a charge lower than market value does not seem to have a cash equivalent—unless perhaps the employer could have provided the service at full cost to a stranger who was anxious to buy it. So an interest free loan does not give rise to liability; for this reason special legislation now applies, infra, § **6: 94**. A cost under s. 154 might have arisen if the employer had realised a particular asset to provide the loan and so forgone income from that asset.[2]

Where the asset remains the property of the employer, the employer is deemed to incur a cost equal to the sum of (*a*) the annual value of the asset, and (*b*) any other expense incurred in providing the asset other than the cost of producing or acquiring the asset.[3] The figure at (*a*) will be increased if the employer pays a sum by way of rent or hire which exceeds the annual value, the higher figure being taken instead.

The annual value of the asset varies according to the benefit. In the case of land TA 1988, s. 837 applies (supra, § **6: 54**); for other assets the figure is 20% of its market value at the time it was first applied by the employer for the employee.[4] So if an employer provides his employee with a cat the cash equivalent will be the sum of (*a*) 20% of the cost plus (*b*) the full cost of food and any veterinary services paid for by the employer.

The costs of acquisition or production of the asset are excluded from (*b*) presumably because they are taken into account under (*a*). Acquisition and production have been construed widely. Expenditure resulting in the replacement or renewal of the asset as distinct from its maintenance is excluded; on this basis sums spent on supplying a house with a new water main were not part of (*b*) and so escaped tax.[5]

If the asset is subsequently transferred to the employee the normal rule is to charge the employee on the market value of the asset when it is so transferred.[6] However an alternative rule will now apply if it would give rise to a higher charge. The problem arises when an asset is transferred to the employee and it has depreciated in value since it was acquired, as where an employer acquires a hi-fi system, allows the employee the use of it for two years and then transfers it to him. The cash equivalent for the first two years will be calculated on the basis of the rules already considered. The cash equivalent on the transfer to the employee is now to be the greater of (*a*) the asset's market value at that time less any price paid for it by the employee and (*b*) the market value when it was first provided but with a deduction for amounts already taxed and any sum paid for it.[7] This alternative does not apply to cars.

EXAMPLE

X provides E with a hi-fi costing £600. After two years X sells the system to E for £150, its then market value being £250. E is liable on the higher of

(a) £250 − £150 = £100 and (b) £600 − (2 × 20% × £600) − £150 = £210.

Simon's Taxes E4.606.

[1] TA 1988, s. 156.

[2] Hansard HC (18 December 1975) Vol. 902, col. 1622–3 and note TA 1988, s. 548(3)(a)(ii). But *quaere* if he sold shares which then dropped in market price would the fall in capital value be set off against the divided income forgone and when could the fall in capital value be computed. What if the share value dates increased? These speculations may suggest that income forgone is not a cost.

[3] TA 1988, s. 156(4), e.g. repair and insurance.

[4] TA 1988, s. 156(5); the percentage is 10% where the asset was first provided before 6th April 1980.

[5] *Luke v IRC* [1963] 1 All ER 655, 40 TC 630; see *infra.*

[6] TA 1988, s. 156(3).

[7] TA 1988, s. 156(4).

Apportionment

6: 92   If the expense is incurred by the employer partly to provide a benefit for the employee and partly for other purposes, TA 1988, s. 154 will tax only a proper proportion of the expense so incurred.[1] However where a particular expense confers benefits both on the employer and on the employee and no part of the expenditure is on something which benefits the employer exclusively, no apportionment can be made.

In *Westcott v Bryan*[2] the managing director wished to live in London but the company insisted that he live in a large rambling house set in two acres of garden close to the factory which lay in a rural area of North Staffordshire. He paid the company a rent of £140 pa and £500 pa for services. He paid the rates. In the tax year the company spent £1,017 on gas, electricity, water, insurance of contents, telephone, cleaning, window cleaning, gardener's wages and maintenance. The house was bigger than the taxpayer either needed or desired, but no specific area was set aside for the entertainment of the company's guests. It was held by the Court of Appeal that an apportionment under TA 1988, s. 156(2) should be made even though the expenses could not be clearly severed either on a temporal or spatial basis. The method of apportionment was not canvassed in the Court of Appeal[3] but at first instance Pennycuick J had said that it could only be done on a rough and ready basis, to determine what proportion of the total expense was fairly attributable to the use or availability for use of the house by the company.[4]

The decision is to be distinguished from that in *Rendell v Went*[5] where no apportionment could be made. In that case the employer had spent a sum of money in the provision of a benefit when the employee would have spent less, and no part of the sum was spent on something which did not benefit him.[6] In *Westcott v Bryan* the expenditure was made for two distinct purposes only one of which was of benefit to the director.

Section 156(2) directs an apportionment of the expense. Section 156(1) limits its charge to so much of the expense as is not made good by the employee. Where therefore a sum is to be apportioned and the employee makes a payment for the benefit, the question arises whether the expense is apportioned first and then the payment is set off against that apportioned figure or rather the set-off occurs first and the apportionment is then applied to that reduced figure. The former would seem more correct.[7]

[1] TA 1988, s. 156(2).
[2] [1969] 3 All ER 564, 45 TC 467.
[3] But see Sachs LJ at 571, 493.
[4] At 487.
[5] Supra, § **6: 89**.
[6] [1964] 2 All ER 464 at 467, 41 TC 641 at 659; this distinction is criticised by Kerridge [1986] BTR 36.
[7] But in *Westcott v Bryan* the latter view appears to have been accepted.

Particular benefits

(i) *Living accommodation—ancillary services, TA 1988, s. 163*

6: 93   The provision of living accommodation for a person by reason of his employment is governed by TA 1988, s. 145, supra, § **6: 52**. The exception in s. 145(4) for the first two cases of non-beneficial occupation does not apply if the taxpayer is a director of the company providing the accommodation, or of an associated company, unless (*i*) he has no material interest, i.e. one of not more than 5%, and (*ii*) the employment is either as a full-time working director or the company is a charity or non-profit making.[1]

The provision of certain ancillary services falls within TA 1988, s. 154. However, where the occupation is non-beneficial and the employee comes within the terms of the exception, supra, § **6: 53**, the amount taxable is subject to a limit. Sums in respect of (*i*) heating, lighting or cleaning the premises, (*ii*) repairs (other than structural repairs)[2] maintenance or decoration, and (*iii*) the provision of furniture or other appurtenances or effects which are normal for domestic occupation, are not to exceed 10% of the emoluments of the employment.

Where the accommodation is provided for a part of the year but the employment for longer (or shorter), the percentage is applied to the emoluments attributable to the period of occupation. Any sums made good by the employee are deducted from the 10%.

The emoluments are not to include the cost of the services notionally fixed at 10%; this avoids a circular problem. There will be included all emoluments including benefits caught by s. 154 but deduction of expenses allowable under TA 1988, s. 198 is permitted to ascertain the figure of which 10% is to be taken.

This limit does not apply where the director has a stake of more than 5% or is a part-time director of a profit-seeking concern. Nor does it apply where the ancillary services are other than those listed; liability in respect of such services is without limit. The specific exception of structural repairs is presumably because the Revenue accept the view expressed in *Luke v IRC*[3] that these are part of the cost of acquiring or producing the asset under TA 1988, s. 156(5)(*b*).[4] Costs to the owner as owner such as rates[5] and insurance and feu duty, are presumably part of the cost of providing the living accommodation and so fall within TA 1988, s. 145.[6]

Simon's Taxes E4.615.

[1] TA 1988, s. 155(3); Extra-statutory concession A61 for clergymen does not apply to higher paid clergy.

[2] Including repairs which would be the landlord's responsibility under a lease within the Landlord and Tenant Act 1985, ss. 11, 16, 36.

[3] [1963] 1 All ER 655; 40 TC 630; FA 1976, s. 62(5).

[4] This was the line taken by Lord Guest and Lord Pearce and by Lord Reid (this is a case of any port in a storm, pp. 578, 665, 646) and by Lord Dilhorne at pp. 572, 661, 643. The consequence of the repair will be an increase in the annual value of the premises. To hold that the expense of repair did not fall within TA 1988, s. 156(5) and then to increase the annual value would be a flagrant case of double taxation.

[5] Rates cannot give rise to liability under TA 1988, s. 145, where the non-beneficial occupation exception in sub-s. (4) applies.

[6] See however *Luke v IRC* on the forerunner of s. 154.

(ii) *Low interest loans: TA 1988, s. 160*

6:94 Directors and higher-paid employees are taxable on a cash equivalent of loans[1] provided by reason of their employment. A loan is a loan and so within these rules whether or not there is any other benefit or advantage to the employee.[2]

The charge is not to apply if the cash equivalent of all such loans does not exceed £200;[3] this *de minimis* exception involves all the costs of calculating the cash equivalent; a maximum amount of debt seems a less expensive but less precise limit. If this limit is exceeded the whole cash equivalent is taxable.

The charge does not apply where the loan is for a qualifying purpose i.e. where interest paid would be deductible from total income.[4] Cheap house loans therefore remain a valuable perk for those with access to such funds, although the £30,000[5] limit applies. A concession applies to bridging loans.[6] Loans for non-qualifying purposes, which therefore may give rise to liability, include loans to buy cars, shares, to assist with school or university fees or even to buy a railway season ticket.[7]

The charge will arise whether the loan is made to the employee or to a relative of his; relative is defined differently from family and means spouse, lineal ascendant or descendant, brother or sister of the employee or the spouse and the spouse of such people.[8] It is however open to the employee to show that he derived no benefit from the loan.[9]

The charge remains so long as the loan made by reason of the employment is outstanding and the borrower continues in the employment;[10] however it does end on the death of the employee.[11] It appears that a loan to an ex-employee will not be caught.

Where a loan was made otherwise than by reason of employment and, on the employment beginning, the rate of interest is reduced, no charge appears to arise; a charge would arise if new loans were made and the old loan discharged.[12]

The cash equivalent of the loan is the difference between the amount of interest that would have been paid at an official rate and any interest actually paid.[13] Loans between the same borrower and lender are aggregated; others are not—a matter of importance where different rates of interest are paid on different loans.[14] The amount of interest due at the official rate is calculated first by taking a simple average of the loan outstanding at the beginning and end of the tax year, multiplying this by the number of months of the loan in the year and divided by 12 and then applying the official rate to it.[15] However, either the taxpayer or the Revenue may elect that the interest be calculated on a day to day basis, a matter of importance where the amount of the loan fluctuates during the year.[16]

EXAMPLE

A has borrowed £10,000 from his employer just before the start of the year of assessment. On 30th June he repays £3,000 but on 3rd September he borrows another £4,000. The amount outstanding at the end of the year of assessment is £11,000. A pays £450 in interest; assume that the official rate is 12%.

(1) Simple calculation. Average amount outstanding during the year

$$\frac{£11,000+10,000}{2}=£10,500.$$ Official rate at 12% would give £1,260.

(2) More precise calculation

First period	$10,000 \times \dfrac{85}{365} \times 12\%$	£279.45
Second period	$7,000 \times \dfrac{65}{365} \times 12\%$	£149.59
Third period	$11,000 \times \dfrac{215}{365} \times 12\%$	£777.53
		£1,206.57

So cash equivalent is £1,206.57 − £450 = £756.57

As from 6th July 1989 the official rate is 15·5%.[17] In the same year it was provided that where a loan is made for a fixed period at a fixed rate, which is not less than the then official rate, s. 160 is not to apply when the official rate later rises.[18]

Simon's Taxes E4.610–612; Butterworths Income Tax Service D3.61.

[1] On practical problems see ICAEW Memorandum TR 738—*Simon's Tax Intelligence* 1988, p 738. On advances to meet expenses see SP 7/79. *Williams v Todd, Simon's Tax Intelligence* 1988, p. 538 (advance of salary held to be a loan). The charge arises regardless of the date of the loan; TA 1988, s. 160(7). In another tax context it has been held that a loan requires consensus so that a misappropriation by a director does not give rise to a loan—*Stephens v T Pittas Ltd* [1983] STC 576, infra, § **27: 11.**

[2] *Williams v Todd* [1988] STC 676.

[3] TA 1988, s. 161(1). £50 before 6th April 1980.

[4] TA 1988, Sch. 7, paras. 6–12 (FA 1976, Sch. 8, Part III).

[5] In 1983–84 and later years, if the beneficial loan is free of interest altogether, it is treated as made after any other loans on which interest qualifying for relief is payable; the £30,000 limit is only available against the beneficial loan to the extent to which it is not used up by the loans on which interest is actually payable: TA 1988, Sch. 7, para. 10(1).

[6] Extra-statutory concession A5 (1985), revised 28th November 1985, **Simon's Taxes, Division H2.2.**

[7] About 90% of City of London employers offer interest free loans for season tickets; the GLC offers loans at 4% for those who can prove a need for a car. It was estimated that 34,000 bank employees could be affected by this charge. Hansard SCE (1976) col. 1618 et seq.

[8] TA 1988, s. 160(6).

[9] TA 1988, s. 161(4).

[10] This contrasts with the charge on loan waivers, see § **6: 93**, which continues notwithstanding termination of employment.

[11] TA 1988, s. 161(6).

[12] TA 1988, s. 160(5)(*b*).

[13] TA 1988, s. 160(1).

[14] TA 1988, Sch. 7, para. 3.

[15] TA 1988, Sch. 7, para. 4.
[16] TA 1988, Sch. 7, para. 5.
[17] S.I. 1989 No. 1001, *Simon's Tax Intelligence* 1989, p. 537; it had previously been 14·5% from 6th January 1989 (S.I. 1988 No. 2186).
[18] TA 1988, s. 161(2).

(iii) *Loan waivers: TA 1988, s. 160(2)*

6: 95   Where the whole or part of a loan is released or written off, there is a charge on the amount so released or written off.[1] This applies whether or not the loan is chargeable under the previous rule; so the charge will arise even though the loan released was used for a qualifying purpose. The release of a loan to a relative comes within this rule unless the employee can show that he derived no benefit from it.[2] The charge arises even though the loan was released or written off after the employment ceased[3] but not if this is deferred until after death.[4] It appears that making a loan to a former employee with which he discharges a loan will not come within this rule nor will the gift of a sum for the same purpose.

This rule has effect for the year 1976–77 and subsequent years regardless of the date of the loan. However where arrangements have been made with a view to protecting the holder of shares from a fall in their market value, benefits received are not chargeable under this rule.[5] This is designed to protect those who acquired shares under incentive schemes which contained so called stop-loss clauses; these schemes had been approved by the Revenue and it was thought wrong to alter the tax basis upon which they had been made.

Simon's Taxes E4.610.
[1] TA 1988, s. 160(2); see also *Clayton v Gothorp*, supra, § **6: 29**.
[2] TA 1988, s. 161(4).
[3] TA 1988, s. 160(3).
[4] TA 1988, s. 161(1).
[5] TA 1988, s. 160(7).

(iv) *Share purchase schemes—deemed loans: TA 1988, s. 162*

6: 96   Where shares are acquired by a director or higher-paid employee as a right or opportunity offered by reason of his employment with that or any other company and the shares were issued at less than market price or in other than fully paid up form, the tax system decrees a notional loan of the difference between the amount paid for the shares and their then market value.[1] So long as this loan remains outstanding, interest at the official rate is treated as an emolument. Conversely any payment of a call is treated as a repayment of the loan.

When such shares are acquired on such a notional loan or on a real loan and the loan is discharged or released by any arrangement involving the disposal of the shares, the aggregate amount paid for them minus any consideration received on the disposal is compared with the market value at the time of acquisition and the amount by which the latter exceeds the former is treated as an emolument. The market value at the time of the disposal is quite irrelevant, the purpose of this provision being to catch so-called "stop loss" arrangements under which employees would offer to accept payment at current value as satisfying the debt.

. The outright purchase of shares but with time to pay was one of the few ways of granting shares to employees on favourable terms. This is now stopped for directors and higher paid employees but only for shares acquired after 6th April 1976. Any profit arising on the disposal of the shares is subject to Schedule E.

Simon's Taxes E4.614.

[1] TA 1988, s. 162. The market value ignores any restriction other than those applying to all shares of that class.

(v)   Cars and fuel: TA 1988, ss. 157 and 158

6: 97   (a) If the car is (i) one of a pool, a concept which is elaborately defined and which broadly means that the car must be genuinely available to more than one employee and not regularly garaged at an employee's house, and (ii) any private use is purely incidental to its business use, then the car is not treated as being available for the employee's use and is not a taxable emolument.[1]

(b) In other cases when the car is available for private use,[2] a special cash equivalent of the use of the car is fixed by statute and charged accordingly.[3]

A proposal to charge these to tax under PAYE has been abandoned; instead the charge is usually made by reducing the PAYE coding.

CAR BENEFITS FOR 1989–90 (FA 1989, s. 49)

TABLES A AND B
Cars with original market value up to £19,250

Cylinder capacity of car in cubic centimetres	Age of car at end of relevant year of assessment	
	Under 4 years	4 years or more
1,400 cc or less (less than £6,000)*	£1,400	£950
1,401 to 2,000 cc (£6,000–£8,500)*	£1,850	£1,250
More than 2,000 cc (£8,500–£19,250)*	£2,950	£1,950

* Where car has no cylinder capacity.

TABLE C
Cars with original market value more than £19,250

Original market value of car	Age of car at end of relevant year of assessment	
	Under 4 years	4 years or more
£19,250 or more but not more than £29,000	£3,850	£2,600
More than £29,000	£6,150	£4,100

Reductions may be made for use for part of the year or to take account of any payment by the employee, but no reduction is made to reflect the proportion of business to private use save that the cash equivalent is reduced by 50% if the car was used preponderantly for business travel, i.e. such travel amounted to at least 18,000 miles. Conversely if the business mileage is less than 2,500 miles per annum, or the car is a second car provided by the employer, the rates are increased by 50%. Subject to this the new rule is based neither on cost to the employer nor practical value to the employee. The old tax rules tried to make such an adjustment—and still apply to lower paid employees. The benefits covered by this charge are all those concerned with the provision of the car, i.e. capital cost, insurance, maintenance etc. However, the charge does not cover the costs of a chauffeur[4] and petrol[5] and car phones (unless installed and used only for business calls).[6]

A special scale charge applies where the employer provides free petrol for private motoring in company cars: anomalously there is no reduction in charge if the employee reimburses the employer a part of the cost. The general fuel scale has not been increased in 1989–90. The scale charge is reduced by 50% where business mileage exceeds 18,000 miles; however it is not increased by 50% where business mileage is less than 2,500 miles, etc.

A problem arises if an employer has, say, a salary of £8,000 and potential charge of £450; so far he is not within the charge to tax as he is below the £8,500 limit. Suppose, however, that he uses a credit card to pay for £200 of repairs. By TA 1988, s. 142 (see § 6: 51) he is taxable on £200, but on crossing the £8,500 threshold he finds that the £200 is taken out of charge again. To break this loop it is provided that car expenses that would be charged if TA 1988, s. 157 did not apply will be taken into account in determining whether an employee is higher paid; it will then be assessed either on the scale benefit or on the relevant expense as appropriate.[7]

CAR FUEL BENEFITS FOR 1989–90

TABLES A AND B

Cylinder capacity of car in cubic centimetres	Cash equivalent
Up to 1,400 cc or less (up to £6,000)*	£480
1,401 to 2,000 cc (£6,000–£8,500)*	£600
More than 2,000 cc (£8,500 or more)*	£900

* Where car has no cylinder capacity.

The sharply increased scale of charges has reduced the benefit of this perk; perhaps it is time to record the fact that most employers do not provide this benefit without reason and that in the days of a reduced public transport system the car is often an indispensable tool of business. However, it is also the case that the company car is a more widespread benefit in the UK than in other advanced economies.

(c) There is now no charge on the provision of free parking.[8]

[1] TA 1988, s. 159.
[2] TA 1988, s. 168(5)—see *Gilbert v Hemsley* [1981] STC 703 and *Gurney v Richards* [1989] STI 588.
[3] TA 1988, s. 157 and Sch. 6.
[4] TA 1988, s. 155.
[5] TA 1988, s. 157.
[6] SP5/88, **Simon's Taxes, Division H3.4.**
[7] Ring [1982] BTR 140.
[8] FA 1988, s. 46.

(vi) *Scholarships: TA 1988, s. 165*

6: 98 From 15th March 1983 the exemption from tax of scholarship income[1] is restricted to the person holding the scholarship.[2] This reverses the effect of the decision of the House of Lords in *Wicks v Firth*.[3] A director or higher paid employee will receive a taxable benefit if a scholarship is provided to a member of his family or household under arrangements made by his employer or a person connected with the employer.

No taxable benefit arises if the scholarship is awarded under a trust or scheme to a person receiving full-time education and not more than 25% of the payments made under the trust in that year would have been taxable were it not for this provision,[4] i.e. taxable as benefits in kind. For 1984–85 onwards this rule has been tightened. If the connection between the award of the scholarship and the employment is fortuitous, the 25% test will be applied so as, perhaps, to enable the award to escape tax but to ensure that, in calculating the 25%, all scholarships awarded by reason of employment are taken into account (whether or not taxable e.g. an award to the child of an employee earning less than £8,500, or the child of an overseas employee).

In deciding for this purpose whether scholarships are awarded by reason of employment, the special deeming rules are ignored.[5]

1984–85 saw a relaxation of the transitional rules. Where the scholarship was awarded before 15th March 1983 and the first payment was made before 6th April 1984, the exception will continue until the earlier of (a) the end of the scholarship, or (b) 5th April 1989, even if there is a change of educational establishment. If the scholar remains at the same establishment[6] which he attended on 15th March 1983 or, if later, the date of the first payment, the exemption will continue beyond 5th April 1989.

Simon's Taxes E4.609; Butterworths Income Tax Service D3.72.
[1] Under TA 1988, s. 331.
[2] TA 1988, s. 165.
[3] [1983] STC 25, see supra, § **6: 88**.
[4] TA 1988, s. 165(3).
[5] TA 1988, s. 165(3)(c).
[6] See [1983] STI, p. 413.

(vii) *Tax paid by employer*

6: 99   If an employer fails to deduct tax from a director's emoluments under PAYE but, after 5th April 1983, that tax is accounted for to the Revenue by someone other than the director, there is a chargeable benefit equal to the tax accounted for.[1] The benefit is reduced by the amount of any reimbursement made by the director. An amount accounted for after the employment ends is treated as a benefit of the last year of asessment in which the director was employed by the company, unless it was accounted for after the director's death.[2]

The provision applies only to directors; it does not extend to higher paid employees. It does not apply, however, if the director has no material interest in the company (i.e. not more than 5%) and he is a full-time working director or the company is non-profit making or a charity.[3]

Simon's Taxes E4.613.
[1] TA 1988, s. 164.
[2] TA 1988, s. 164(3).
[3] TA 1988, s. 164(2).

EXPENSES

6: 100   The expenses which the taxpayer may deduct in computing income under Schedule E are defined in TA 1988, s. 198:[1]

"If the holder of an office or employment is necessarily obliged to incur and defray out of the emoluments thereof the expenses of travelling in the performance of the duties of the office or employment, or of keeping and maintaining a horse[2] to enable him to perform the same, or otherwise to expend money wholly exclusively and necessarily in the performance of the said duties . . ." there may be deducted from the emoluments to be assessed the expenses so necessarily incurred and defrayed."

For the rules where a foreign element is involved, see supra, §**6.11**.
Members of Parliament have their own rules.[3]

Simon's Taxes E4.701
 [1] Introduced 1853: 16 and 17 Vict. c. 34, s. 51.
 [2] On Trojan characteristics, see Lord Reid in *Taylor v Provan* [1974] 1 All ER 1201 at 1208, [1974] STC 168 at 175.
 [3] TA 1988, s. 200 and extra-statutory concession A54 (1988) **Simon's Taxes, Division H2.2.**

Travelling expenses[1]

6: 101   Travelling expenses will be deductible only if they are incurred (*a*) in the performance of the duties of employment, and (*b*) are necessarily so incurred.

   (*a*)   Five rules may be laid down—

   (i)   The costs of travelling to work from home are in general not deductible.[2] This is because the costs are not incurred in the course of performing the duties but in order to get to the place where the duties are to be performed. This non-deductibility applied right down to the extra costs of an employee's having to travel to work by car because the car is needed for his work once he gets there.[3]
   (ii)   The costs of travel from a place of work of one employment to the place of work of a different employment are not deductible; the same applies where the first place is one where a profession is carried on.[4]
   (iii)   The costs of travelling from one's place of employment to another place where the work was to be done are generally deductible.[5] Perhaps the test to be applied is whether the employer would be vicariously liable in tort for an act of his employee.
   (iv)   Where a person has an itinerant employment, that is where there is a fixed centre of employment but is expected to travel extensively from that place, it would be quaint if his expenses of travel were deductible if he first went to his office and then to the various places as instructed by his employer, but not if he were to travel to those places directly from his home. However the absence of a fixed base may be fatal.[6] The Revenue practice for commercial travellers is to allow travel expenses while away from home. There is also an elaborate practice for construction site based employees.[7]
   (v)   TA 1988, s. 193, supra, § **6: 11**, governs travel to and from employments where services are rendered overseas.

   (*b*)   In deciding whether an expense is incurred necessarily the courts use an objective test. That stated by Lord Blanesburgh in *Ricketts v Colquhoun* was that the expense had to be one which each and every occupant of the particular office is necessarily obliged to incur.[8] Thus the necessity must emerge from the job rather than from the personal circumstances of the employee. However as the two later decisions of the House of Lords show, in determining whether the expense would be incurred by each and every occupant of the office one must look and see who could be appointed to hold the office. If the range of reasonable appointees is restricted the test must be applied in relation to such potential appointees and one must ask whether each of these persons if appointed would have to incur the expense; if the answer is yes then the expense is deductible notwithstanding that some other person, whom would not be a suitable appointee, might not have to incur it; this is *Owen v Pook*.[9] In an extreme case it may be possible to show that the taxpayer is the only person in the world who can carry out the duties; this is *Taylor v Provan*.[10]

These matters may be tested by considering the problem of the costs of travel from home. The general principle that such costs are not usually deductible is correct. It has been softened by Revenue concessions for extra travel and subsistence allowances when public transport is disrupted by strikes or other industrial action[11] when an employer has to work late[12] or is severely disabled.[13] There are also concessions for costs of transferring work to or from an offshore oil rig[14] and for workers away on qualifying external training courses.[15]

Simon's Taxes E4.708, 709.

[1] For many years the Revenue would not allow the total cost as such but would take account of the amount which the taxpayer saved by being away. The practice was defended by Rowlatt J in *Nolder v Walters* (1930) 15 TC 380 at 388. The rules are now relaxed save where the taxpayer is a single person ordinarily living in a hotel or club; see [1974] STI, p. 319. On limits, see *Collis v Hore* (1949) 31 TC 173. The present Revenue view is explained at [1985] STI, p. 312.

[2] *Cook v Knott* (1887) 2 TC 246; *Revell v Elsworthy Bros & Co Ltd* (1890) 3 TC 12; *Andrews v Astley* (1924) 8 TC 589; *Ricketts v Colquhoun* [1926] AC 1, 10 TC 118. The costs may also be disallowed under (*b*).

[3] *Burton v Rednall* (1954) 35 TC 435. It is interesting to compare the position in tort when the question is whether an employee is acting in the course of his employment—see *Smith v Stages* [1989] 1 All ER 833, [1989] 2 WLR 529, HL.

[4] *Mitchell and Edon v Ross* [1962] AC 814, [1961] 3 All ER 49, 40 TC 11. For directors of different companies in the same group (and others) see extra-statutory concession A4 (1988).

[5] *Jardine v Gillespie* (1906) 5 TC 263.

[6] This is the Revenue view of *Elderkin v Hindmarsh* [1988] STC 267. See also comment by Ward in [1989] BTR 241.

[7] **Simon's Taxes, Division H2.2.**

[8] [1926] AC 1 at 7, 10 TC 118 at 135 (cf. Lord Salmon in *Taylor v Provan* [1975] AC 194 at 227.

[9] Infra, § **6: 102**.

[10] Infra, § **6: 103**.

[11] Extra-statutory concession A58, A66 (1988), **Simon's Taxes, Division H2.2**, **Simon's Taxes, Division H2.2** (why only where the disruption is due to strikes and other industrial action?).

[11] Extra-statutory concession.

[13] Extra-statutory concession A59 (1988), **Simon's Taxes, Division H2.2**; does not the principle behind this concession lead to the deductibility of costs of spectacles and hearing aids in appropriate cases—e.g. judges?

[14] Extra-statutory concession A65 (1988), see **Simon's Taxes, Division H2.2**.

[15] Extra-statutory concession A64 (1988), see **Simon's Taxes, Division H2.2**.

Travel from home

6: 102 The cost of travel to one's place of work may sometimes be deductible. As Lord Reid pointed out in *Taylor v Provan*,[1] s. 198 states that the expense of maintaining a horse to enable one to carry out one's duties is deductible and the section must presuppose that the horse would be kept at home. The cases in which such claims have succeeded are exceptional. Both are decisions of the House of Lords—*Owen v Pook*[2] and *Taylor v Provan*[3] and both involve a finding that there was more than one place of work and that home was one of them.[4] Both involve some modification of the decision of the House of Lords in *Ricketts v Colquhoun* a case which illustrates rule (*a*) (i) above.

In *Ricketts v Colquhoun*[5] the taxpayer lived in London and was a practising member of the London bar. He was taxable under Schedule D, Case II in respect of his earnings at the bar. He was also Recorder of Portsmouth and was taxable under Schedule E in respect of his earnings from this source. He sought to deduct the costs of travelling from his home to Portsmouth. The House of Lords rejected his appeal on two main grounds. First, when travelling to his place of work he was travelling not in the course of those duties but in order to enable him to perform them.[6] His duties only began at Portsmouth. Secondly, the expenses could not be said to have been incurred necessarily.[7] Since a Recorder could have lived in Portsmouth, the costs of travel from London were not necessary. A further point was that his choice of abode in London was a personal matter and the expenses consequent on that choice were therefore personal expenses.

[1] [1974] 1 All ER 1201 at 1206, [1974] STC 168 at 172. For another view of the horse, see Pollock MR in *Ricketts v Colquhoun* [1925] 1 K B 725 at 732. See also *Elderkin v Hindmarsh* [1988] STC 267.
[2] [1969] 2 All ER 1, 45 TC 571.
[3] [1974] 1 All ER 1201, [1974] STC 168.
[4] *Pook v Owen* was distinguished in *Bhadra v Ellam* [1988] STC 239 and *Parikh v Sleeman* [1988] STC 580 (both cases concerning doctors).
[5] [1926] AC 1, 10 TC 118.
[6] Per Lord Cave, LC, at 4, 133.
[7] Per Lord Blanesburgh, at 7, 135. Cf. Lord Salmon in *Taylor v Provan* [1974] 1 All ER 1201 at 1223, [1974] STC 168 at 190.

6: 103 If however there is one employment but it has two distinct places of work, travel from one place of work to the other will be deductible. Where home is one of those places of work, it follows that travel from home to the other place of work is deductible. This is rule (*a*)(iii) above.[1] In *Owen v Pook*[2] the taxpayer was a medical practitioner who resided at Fishguard. He also held part time appointments as obstetrician and anaesthetist at Haverford-west fifteen miles away. Under these appointments he was on "stand-by duty" two weekends a month and on Monday and Friday nights, at which times he was required to be accessible by telephone. If he was called at home he would give advice by phone, sometimes set out at once and at other times await further reports. He was responsible for his patient as soon as he received the telephone call. Although he received a payment for travelling expenses this was only for the last ten of his fifteen miles. He was assessed in respect of the payments received for the ten miles and denied his claim for deduction in respect of the five miles. His appeal to the courts against this assessment was successful. Since he had two places where his duties were performed, the hospital and his residence with the telephone, the expenses of travel between the two places were deductible.

[1] There is however a problem about the cost of travel home from the place of work.
[2] [1969] 2 All ER 1, 45 TC 571.

6: 104 Exceptionally the personal qualifications of the taxpayer may supply the material to satisfy the objective test of necessity. In *Taylor v Provan*[1] the taxpayer was a Canadian citizen living in Toronto. He was the acknowledged expert in the brewing world on successful expansion by means of amalgamation and merger. He agreed to become a director of an English company which merged with others in 1958 to become United Breweries Ltd, which merged with Charringtons in 1962 which in turn merged to form Bass Charrington Ltd in 1967. The taxpayer did most of his work in connection with the English amalgamations in Canada and the Bahamas but he made frequent visits to England. He had extensive Canadian interests for which he worked from his offices in Toronto and the Bahamas. He agreed to serve as director of the companies "for reasons of prestige", although this had the unfortunate effect of bringing him within what are now TA 1988, ss. 153 and 154. He received no fees for his services since he regarded it as a business recreation, but his travelling expenses were reimbursed. The House of Lords held unanimously that the reimbursements were sums spent on behalf of the company and were taxable under TA 1988, s. 153. The House held (by 3–2) that the expenses were deductible. Of the majority Lord Morris[2] and Lord Salmon[3] held that the taxpayer's duties were performed both in the United Kingdom and in Canada so that there were at least two places of work. Travel to England could not therefore be dismissed as travel from home to a place of work and so came within rule (*a*)(iii).

Lord Reid however gave a rather different account of *Owen v Pook*:[4]

> "I think that the distinguishing fact in *Owen's* case was that there was a part-time employment, and that it was impossible for the employer to fill the post otherwise than by appointing a man with commitments that he would not give up. It was therefor necessary that whoever was appointed should incur travelling expenses."

On this approach, which goes much wider than any pronouncement in recent years and undermines both the decision of the House of Lords in *Ricketts v Colquhoun* and much of the practice of the Revenue, the expenses were deductible in *Taylor v Provan* because the taxpayer was the only person who could do this job which he was only willing to do from Canada, and that he did some of the work in Canada. It was not enough that he insisted on working in Canada (so satisfying requirement (*a*)); what was crucial was that he was the only person who could do the work (so satisfying requirement (*b*)).

The question arises whether Lord Reid's approach undermines the earlier decision in *Ricketts v Colquhoun*. No member of the majority in *Taylor v Provan* wished to question the result of that earlier decision but Ricketts' post as Recorder of Portsmouth was a part time one and anyone appointed would have had to be a member of the bar. However Ricketts was not the only member of the bar who could have been appointed and it was possible that another appointee would have lived in Portsmouth. Another explanation could be that Rickett's home was not a place of work. This would conclude the matter if as may well be the case,[5] Lord Reid's explanation of *Owen v Pook* rests on the assumption that there were two places of work.

---

[1] [1974] 1 All ER 1201, [1974] STC 168.
[2] At 1210, 177.
[3] At 1224, 191.
[4] At 1207, 174.
[5] This emerges from 1207, 174.

An alternative explanation

6: 105 Central to *Owen v Pook* and *Taylor v Provan* is a finding of a dual place of employment. When then is home a place of employment? A director's house could not become a place of employment simply because he entertained clients there, even if his employer ordered him to do so. Unless however the home is a place in which work should, as opposed to could, be done, it is hard to see when a home is a place of work. The explanation of *Owen v Pook* and *Taylor v Provan* may therefore be not that home was one of the places of work but that in each case their employment was in a sense itinerant. In *Owen v Pook* there was no reason why the employment should have been located in the taxpayer's home. What mattered was that he assumed responsibility for the patient when he received the telephone message. If he were out with friends for the evening and had given their telephone number instead of his own, that would not make his friend's house one of his places of work. The point was *when* did his duties commence rather than *where*. In the same way in *Taylor v Provan* the House of Lords seemed to be concerned with the question "was he travelling in the performance of his duties" rather than "was his office a home and, if not, did he travel from his office or from his home". On this approach one can reconcile the earlier decision of *Nolder v Walters*[1] where an airline pilot sought unsuccessfully to deduct the cost of travelling from his home to the airport. The fact that he was summoned by his employer made no difference. While travelling to the airport he was not under his employer's command. He was travelling to his office not from one office to another.

---

[1] (1930) 15 TC 380.

Amount

6: 106 The objective rule that the expenses must have been necessarily incurred is generally thought to limit the *amount* of expenditure that may be deducted. In *Marsden v IRC*[1] the taxpayer, who was an investigator in the Audit Division of the Inland Revenue, used his car for travelling on official business. There was no evidence that he could not have travelled by public transport. His claim to deduct the difference between the allowance he received, which was based on car mileage, and what he actually spent was rejected by his employers and by the courts. Pennycuick J said that the scale of expenses must be a question of fact and degree, and that the answer must turn not only on the price of transport but also such considerations as speed, convenience, the purpose of the journey, the status of the officer and so forth.[2]

However this was denied by Lord Wilberforce in *Owen v Pook*.[3] The present status of the rule is therefore uncertain.

---

[1] [1965] 2 All ER 364, 42 TC 326; see also *Perrons v Spackman* [1981] STC 739 where it was held that a mileage allowance was an emolument of the taxpayer's employment, since it included a significant contribution to the overhead costs of putting a car which was maintained for both private and official use on the road and could not be therefor a mere reimbursement of expenses actually incurred.

[2] At 367, 331. One may add that of these the status of the officer looks extremely odd and the

Revenue's own scale of allowances made to Marsden, which gave, depending upon the type of business on which he was engaged, two quite distinct allowances, 2½d and 7d, makes a nonsense of some of the arguments used by the Inland Revenue in these cases.

³ [1969] 2 All ER 1 at 12, 45 TC 571 at 596.

Other expenses

6: 107   The principles applicable to travel expenses apply with equal force to other expenses which, however, must also satisfy the test that they were wholly and exclusively incurred. The words of TA 1988, s. 198 were described by Vaisey J as:[1]

> "notoriously rigid, narrow and restricted in their operation. In order to satisfy the terms of the rule it must be shown that the expenditure incurred was not only necessarily but wholly and exclusively incurred in the performance of the relevant official duties. And it is certainly not enough merely to assert that a particular payment satisfies the requirements of the rule without specifying the detailed facts upon which the finding is based. An expenditure may be necessary for the holder of an office without being necessary to him in the performance of the duties of that office; it may be necessary in the performance of those duties without being exclusively necessary referable to those duties; it may perhaps be both necessarily and exclusively but still not wholly so referable. The words are indeed stringent and exacting; compliance with each and every one of them is obligatory if the benefit of the rule is to be claimed successfully. They are to my mind, deceptive words in the sense that when examined they are found to come to nearly nothing at all."

Simon's Taxes E4.705.
¹ *Lomax v Newton* (1953) 34 TC 558 at 561–2.

(i) *In the performance of duties*

6: 108   A sharp distinction is drawn between expenditure incurred *in the performance of* the duties of an office and expenditure incurred in order either to enable oneself to do the job initially[1] or to enable oneself to perform the duties of that office more efficiently. Thus the cost of a housekeeper to look after one's family and so enable one to go out to work is not deductible.[2]

Subscriptions to professional bodies paid by a county medical officer of health were disallowed,[3] even though the journals received from those societies enabled him to keep himself properly qualified; this has now been reversed by statute[4] and subscriptions to approved societies are now deductible.

A school teacher who attended a series of weekend lectures in history at a college for adult education for the purposes of improving his background knowledge could not deduct those expenses.[5] There is a distinction between qualifying to teach and getting background material on the one hand and preparing lectures for delivery on the other hand.[6] Likewise a clerk obliged to attend late meetings of the council and who bought himself a meal before the meeting was not allowed to deduct the cost of the meal;[7] he had been instructed to work late, not to eat. On similar grounds an employee was not allowed to deduct the costs of a record player and gramophone records which he had purchased for the purpose of providing a stimulus of good music while he worked especially late at night.[8] As Cross J drily observed, "it may well be that (he) was stimulated to work better by hearing good music, just as other people may be stimulated to work better by drink. . . ."[9]

[1] *Lupton v Potts* [1969] 3 All ER 1083, 45 TC 643; *Elderkin v Hindmarsh* [1988] STC 267.

[2] *Bowers v Harding* [1891] 1 QB 560, 3 TC 22; *Halstead v Condon* (1970) 46 TC 289.

[3] *Simpson v Tate* [1925] 2 KB 214, 9 TC 314, Rowlatt J.

[4] TA 1988, s. 201 (TA 1970, s. 192). A list of approved societies is available from the Inland Revenue for £3.50; see [1987] STI, p. 302.

[5] *Humbles v Brooks* (1962) 40 TC 500 but contrast extra-statutory concession A64, **Simon's Taxes, Division H2.2**.

[6] At 504. Even if this distinction had been ignored the expenditure might have failed on the ground of necessity since it was possible that a properly qualified history teacher could have been appointed who would not have needed to attend the course.

[7] *Sanderson v Durbidge* [1955] 3 All ER 154, 36 TC 239; nor could the Recorder in *Ricketts v Colquhoun* [1926] AC 1, 10 TC 118.

[8] *Newlin v Woods* (1966) 42 TC 649.

[9] (1966) 42 TC 649 at 658.

(ii) *Necessarily*

6: 109 The cases do not distinguish clearly the requirement that the expense be incurred in the performance of the duties of the office from the requirement that it be necessarily so incurred. It is however clear that the test of necessity is objective, as already seen.[1] Hence an employee with defective eyesight cannot recover the cost of his glasses.[2] Some softening of this objective test is discernible in *Taylor v Provan*.

The fact that the employer requires the particular expenditure is not decisive.[3] The employer will require the employee to come to work but that does not make the costs of travel to work deductible. As Donovan LJ has put it, "The test is not whether the employer imposes the expense but whether the duties do, in the sense that irrespective of what the employer may prescribe, the duties cannot be performed without incurring the particular outlay".[4] So a student assistant in the research laboratories of a company who was required to attend classes in preparation for an external degree from the University of London was not allowed to deduct his expenses,[5] any more than a soldier was obliged to share in the costs of the mess.[6]

In *Brown v Bullock*,[7] a bank manager was not allowed to deduct the cost of his subscription to a London club even though it was "virtually a condition of his employment". But in *Elwood v Utitz*[8] a director of a company in Northern Ireland who was obliged to travel to and stay in London frequently was allowed to deduct the costs of his subscription to a London club since he was buying accommodation and the fact that he chose to buy it at a club rather than a hotel was immaterial.

[1] *Ricketts v Colquhoun* [1926] AC 1 at 10; supra, § **6: 102**. But if the taxpayer is the only person capable of doing the job, different questions arise: *Taylor v Provan* supra, § **6: 104**.

[2] *Roskams v Bennett* (1950) 32 TC 129.

[3] But the fact that an employer has not sanctioned it greatly weakens the taxpayer's case; see *Owen v Burden* [1972] 1 All ER 356 at 358, and *Maclean v Trembath* (1956) 36 TC 653 at 666.

[4] *Brown v Bullock* (1961) 40 TC 1 at 10.

[5] *Blackwell v Mills* [1945] 2 All ER 655, 26 TC 468. He was not performing his duties as a laboratory assistant when he was listening to the lecture at p. 470.

[6] *Lomax v Newton* [1953] 2 All ER 801, 34 TC 558; *Griffiths v Mockler* [1953] 2 All ER 805, 35

TC 135. Major in Royal Army Pay Corps would have been subject to disciplinary action if he had not paid but mess membership not necessarily in performance of duties as an officer.
[7] [1961] 1 All ER 206, 40 TC 1. Counsel for the bank manager conceded that his client could still perform the duties of a bank manager even though he had not been a member of the club.
[8] (1965) 42 TC 482.

(iii) *Wholly and exclusively*

6: 110   Many of these cases could as easily be explained on the ground that the expenditure was not incurred wholly and exclusively for the employment. Thus in the mess cases there was some element of personal benefit[1] while in *Brown v Bullock* the bank manager derived personal benefit from the membership of the club. Unlike the test of necessity, the requirement of "wholly and exclusively" is not wholly objective.[2] Thus the expenditure may satisfy this test if its sole object is the performance of duties regardless of the fact that it may bring about some other incidental result or effect.[3]

Where a person wears ordinary clothes but of a standard required by his employer, no part of the cost is deductible. However, where a car is being used sometimes for business purposes and sometimes for personal purposes some apportionment is possible. The distinction between the two cases is that when the car is being used for business purposes it is being used only for those purposes whereas when the clothes are worn at work they have a dual purpose, part-business, part-personal.[4] So where a telephone is used partly for business calls the taxpayer can deduct the business calls but not the others and he may not deduct any part of the telephone rental.[5]

---

[1] *Griffiths v Mockler* (1953) 35 TC 135 at 137.
[2] Per Lord MacDermott CJ, in *Elwood v Utitz* (1965) 42 TC 482 at 498.
[3] Ibid, at 497, relying on cases decided under Schedule D, Case II.
[4] *Hillyer v Leake* [1976] STC 490; *Woodcock v IRC* [1977] STC 405, 121 Sol Jo 575 and *Ward v Dunn* [1979] STC 178.
[5] *Lucas v Cattell* (1972) 48 TC 353.

(iv) *Express provisions*

6: 111   On entertainment expenses see infra, § **7: 126**.

6: 112   Expenses on security assets and services are made expressly deductible by FA 1989.[1]

Payments to pension schemes are deductible under the relevant legislation—infra, chapter 30.

In a major departure from tax theory FA 1986 allowed an employee to deduct from his pre-tax pay contributions to charity under a payroll deduction scheme. The maximum amount for 1989–90 is £480 p.a. or £40 per month.[2] The scheme came into effect on 6th April 1987 and has effect both for Schedule E and for PAYE.[3]

---

[1] FA 1989, ss. 50–52; apportionment is directed where there is dual purpose; s. 48.
[2] TA 1988, s. 202 FA 1989, s. 58.
[3] TA 1988, s. 202(7); FA 1988, s. 70.

Summary

6: 113   The test of deductibility under TA 1988, s. 198 is thus strict, even severe. A particularly strong example of this is *Eagles v Levy*[1] where the employee had to sue his employer to recover wages due to him and was not allowed to deduct the costs of the action. Such costs were not incurred in the course of the performance of his duties.

The restrictive nature of the test of deductibility has often been commented upon, usually adversely,[2] and it remains true that the test is very much stricter than that laid down under Schedule D, Cases I and II where the requirement is that the expenditure be wholly and exclusively for the purposes of the business.[3]

A good example of the discrepancy is *Hamerton v Overy*[4] where a full time anaesthetist sought to deduct the cost of maintaining a telephone, a maid to take messages, his subscription to the Medical Defence Union and the excess of his car running expenses over his allowance received from his employers. All these items would have been deductible had he been in private practice under Schedule D, Case II; none were deductible under Schedule E; had he succeeded in establishing two places of work as the taxpayer did in *Owen v Pook*[5] the first and the last might well have been deductible.

The discrepancy creates tax planning problems. Thus if a trader incorporates his business, his allowable expenses will fall under Schedule E.[6] Some who fall within Schedule E try to avoid the problem by forming a management company which employs them—their own expenses remain under Schedule E but the company may in computing its profits deduct expenses not deductible by an individual employee.

However the discrepancy can be exaggerated. Many expenses disallowed under Schedule D are likewise disallowed under Schedule E. Thus travelling expenses from home to work are disallowed under both Schedules,[7] as are other expenses of a personal nature, such as living expenses. Secondly it must be noted that some expenses allowed under Schedule D may subsequently be recouped by the revenue as for example where trading stock is bought and later sold or valued at market value on discontinuance.[8] Again the cost of a home office which is allowed under Schedule E will not affect the exemption of the principal private residence from capital gains tax whereas the same allowance under Schedule D will result in a partial loss of that exemption. Thirdly there remains the crucial difference between an employment and a profession or trade, between being a servant and being an owner. If an employee incurs expense for his employer, he may ask his employer to reimburse him, a trader can only seek payment from himself. Whether the reimbursement will itself be taxable will turn on the form of reimbursement and the subtleties of taxation of benefits in kind.

One approach to the problem is to keep the present strict rule and provide exceptions for particular situations such as the child minding expenses disallowed in *Halstead v Condon*[9] or the fees payable in *Lupton v Potts*.[10] Anyway there should be made statutory some of the expenses in fact allowed by the Revenue such as the non-taxation of allowances for moving expenses[11] or those for teachers in respect of books[12] or the home study allowance.[13] The present system appears to have regional differences; such erratic administration is unfair.

Simon's Taxes E4.701.
    [1] (1934) 19 TC 23. Cf. Schedule D, Cases I and II, infra, § **7: 95** n. 1.
    [2] Rowlatt J in *Ricketts v Colquhoun* (1924) 10 TC 118 at 121; Croom Johnson J in *Bolam v Barlow* (1949) 31 TC 136 at 129; Danckwerts J in *Roskams v Bennett* (1950) 32 TC 129 at 132; Harman LJ in *Mitchell and Edon v Ross* [1960] 2 All ER 218 at 232 and 40 TC 11 at 51, [1960] Ch 498 at 532. But Cf. Lord Radcliffe in *Mitchell and Edon v Ross* [1962] AC 814 at 841, [1961] 3 All ER 49 at 56, 40 TC 11 at 62; and Rowlatt J in *Nolder v Walters* (1930) 15 TC 380 at 389.
    [3] See Lord Evershed MR in *Brown v Bullock* (1960) 40 TC 1 at 9.
    [4] (1954) 35 TC 73.
    [5] Supra, § **6: 101**.
    [6] On this, see *Maclean v Trembath* [1956] 2 All ER 113, 36 TC 653, and *Thomson v White* (1966) 43 TC 256.
    [7] Infra, § **7: 96**.
    [8] TA 1988, s. 100.
    [9] (1970) 46 TC 289.
    [10] [1969] 3 All ER 1083, 45 TC 643.
    [11] This at least is a published extra-statutory concession A5 (1988), see also extra-statutory concession A1 (1988) (flat rate allowances for costs of tools and special clothing), **Simon's Taxes, Division H2.2**. Others depend on agreements between the Revenue and various Unions, the results being made available to their members.
    [12] Supra, § **6: 98** n. 5.
    [13] This was thought to be outside s. 198 in *Roskams v Bennett* (1950) 32 TC 129, but inside in *Elwood v Utitz* (1965) 42 TC 482 at 495.

PAY AS YOU EARN[1]

6: 114   The UK has a system of withholding tax at source. Such a system, it has been said, "combines the expedient and the objectionable. It is a rough and ready system which virtually garnishees taxpayers' incomes, sometimes for debts they do not owe but subject in this event to refund. . . . It is surprising that this withholding system, to which strong objections may be raised on grounds of principle, has aroused so little comment. It has probably done more to increase the tax collecting power of central governments than any other one tax measure of any time in history."[2] The PAYE system imposes a duty on the employer[3] to account once a month for the tax that he has or ought to have deducted.[4] Interest can now be charged on late payments delayed beyond the normal end of year payment date.[5] The Revenue may in certain circumstances proceed against the employee.[6] The definition of payment is the same or under the timing rule set out at supra, § 6: 29.[7]

Simon's Taxes E4.9; Butterworths Income Tax Service A3.33ff.
    [1] For an account of the system see RC (UK) 2nd Report §§ 16–26 and 118th Report of the Board of Inland Revenue (1976), Cmnd. 6302 §§ 93–125. See now TA 1988, ss. 203, 205–207, 828 (TA 1970, s. 204–7) and Regulations, S.I. 1973, No. 334; on future see 120th Report Board of Inland Revenue Cmnd. 7092 (1978). The date from which indexed personal reliefs are implemented under the PAYE system has been amended to 18th May 1989—FA 1989, s. 32.
    [2] MacGregor, [1956] 4 Can Tax Jo 171 at 173; Carter, Study 16, p. 17.
    [3] E.g. *Glantre Engineering Ltd v Goodhand* [1983] STC 1, [1983] 1 All ER 542.
    [4] The employer is not liable if he took reasonable care to comply with the PAYE regulations and the under-deduction was made in good faith; PAYE Regulation 26(3). If the failure was wilful the sum may be recovered by the Revenue from the employee, reg. 26(3), if the latter knew of the wilful failure (PAYE Regulation 26(4)) as in *R v IRC, ex p Sims* [1987] STC 211 and *R v IRC, ex p Cook* [1987] STC 434.
    [5] Income Tax (Employments) (No. 17) Regulations (S.I. 1988/637); this will be strengthened

by FA 1988, s. 120 when implemented; the DSS are to apply a similar provision for late NIC payments.

[6] If the Revenue proceed against the employer, he may not in his turn recover from the employee: *Bernard and Shaw Ltd v Shaw* [1951] 2 All ER 267. This is because the employee is not a trustee for the employer and because the action for money had and received would not lie; however, the employer could retain the sums from later payments to the employee. Note also the very special case of *Philson & Partners Ltd v Moore* (1956) 167 Estates Gazette 92.

[7] TA 1988, s. 203A, added by FA 1989, s. 45.

6: 115   The system is one of cumulative withholding over the year. Full account is taken of the employee's income from this source and of such personal allowances as he may be entitled to. In essence he is allowed 1/52nd of his allowances each week, or 1/12th each month. At the end of any week taxable income is discovered by subtracting the accumulated 1/52nd shares of the allowances from the taxable pay to date. If the income rises over the year the tax will rise with it; if it falls, e.g. because of a change of job or a strike, a repayment may be made by the employer or lower tax paid for the rest of the year.

The system applies to all emoluments paid by an employer. Emoluments include expenses, expenses allowances and benefits in kind. Where the system does not apply, e.g. in the case of a non-resident employer, direct assessment on the employee is used.

Although the system applies to Schedule E income only it can in effect be used to collect tax in respect of other sources. This is achieved by directing that the taxpayer's allowances shall be attributed to those other sources of income, thus reducing the allowances to be set against the Schedule E income and so gathering the tax from the Schedule E source. The system can also be used to collect underpayments of tax from that or previous year as well as to refund overpayments.

The rules relating to interest on underdeducted tax are to be modified as from 20th April 1988.[1]

---

[1] TA 1988, s. 203: Inland Revenue Press Release 17th March 1987, STI 1987, p. 194; the definition of payment is to be modified as from the same date.

6: 116   The obligation on an employer to operate the PAYE system arises if he has a sufficient tax presence in the UK. For this purpose a non-resident company carrying on business in the UK through a branch agency has a sufficient presence.[1]

---

[1] *Clark v Oceanic Contractors Inc* [1983] STC 35 (where the branch was deemed to be in the UK by FA 1973, s. 38(4)).

7 Schedule D Cases I and II: trades and professions

TRADE

7: 01   Schedule D, Case I taxes the profits of a trade carried on in the UK or elsewhere.[1] This Case charges only annual profits and is therefore not a capital gains tax,[2] although the width of the definition of trade may make it appear like one at times.

---

[1] TA 1988, s. 18 (TA 1970, s. 109(2)). On "or elsewhere", see infra, § **34: 02**.
[2] On Revenue power to make alternative assessments see *Bye v Coren* [1985] STC 113.

7: 02   Trade is defined statutorily as including every trade, manufacture, adventure or concern in the nature of trade.[1] Judicial definitions of trade have been given reluctantly. However in *Erichsen v Last* Brett LJ said, "Where a person habitually does and contracts to do a thing capable of producing profit and for the purpose of producing profit, he carries on a trade or business."[2] More recently Lord Reid said in *Ransom v Higgs* that the word "is commonly used to denote operations of a commercial character by which the trader provides to customers for reward some kind of goods or services," and in the same case Lord Wilberforce said, "Trade normally involves the exchange of goods or services for reward . . . there must be something which the trade offers to provide by way of business. Trade moreover presupposes a customer".[3] Other judges have suggested that what amounts to a commercial deal is within Case I,[4] while others again have asked what the operation is if it is not trade, to which the answer that it is investment will be sufficient if that can be established.

Simon's Taxes B3.201; Butterworths Income Tax Service C1.01.
[1] TA 1988, ss. 831 and 832. On the relations between the last words and the nouns, see *Johnston v Heath* [1970] 3 All ER 915, 46 TC 463.
[2] (1881) 8 QBD 414 at 420, 4 TC 422 at 425.
[3] [1974] 3 All ER 949 at 955, per Lord Reid, and per Lord Wilberforce, at 964.

⁴ Lord Radcliffe in *Edwards v Bairstow and Harrison* [1955] 3 All ER 48 at 58, 36 TC 207 at 230.

7: 03   The question whether there is a trade, as defined, is one of fact. This means that it is for the Commissioners not only to determine the primary facts, such as what transactions were carried out, when, by whom and with what purpose, but also to conclude that the transaction was or was not a trade as defined.[1] Although this conclusion is an inference it is usually treated as one of fact. Where the findings are inconsistent it is for the court to judge.[2]

It should be remembered that it is not always to the advantage of the Revenue to argue that a particular transaction is an adventure in the nature of trade, since losses resulting from an adventure will be eligible for loss relief.[3]

Simon's Taxes B3.202; Butterworths Income Tax Service C1.01.
  ¹ *Leeming v Jones* [1930] 1 KB 279, 15 TC 333, CA; affd. sub nom. *Jones v Leeming* [1930] AC 415, 15 TC 333, HL; *Hillerns and Fowler v Murray* (1932) 17 TC 77.
  ² *Simmons v IRC* [1980] STC 350, [1980] 2 All ER 798.
  ³ *Stott v Hoddinott* (1916) 7 TC 85 but cf. *Lewis Emanuel & Son Ltd v White* (1965) 42 TC 369.

Liability—who is trading?

7: 04   The trade must be carried on by the person whom it is sought to charge; the tax is levied on the traders and not on the transactions. Hence if an individual carries out three transactions each with a different partner, it is possible to conclude that in view of the frequency of the transactions he was carrying on a trade but that his partners were not.[1]

  ¹ *Pickford v Quirke* (1927) 13 TC 251; *Marshall's Executors v Joly* [1936] 1 All ER 851, 20 TC 256.

7: 05   Where no profit accrues to the person by whom the trade is carried on no charge can be made on that person.

In *Ransom v Higgs*[1] land was owned by a company owned by H and his wife. H agreed to a scheme by which the company developed the land and paid the profits to a discretionary trust. It was held that the trade of developing the land was not carried on by H. As Lord Reid put it, "He did not deal with any person. He did not buy or sell anything. He did not provide anyone with goods or service for reward. He had no profits or gains".[2] There was no evidence that the trade carried on by the company was in fact carried on by H. H had not compelled but merely persuaded the company to conduct a trading operation and so could not be said to be the trader.

In deciding who is trading the court looks to the facts. In *Smart v Lowndes*[3] a half share in land owned by the taxpayer's wife was held to be the taxpayer's trading stock. Where a trading operation is carried out by a company there is authority for the view that the gain realised on the sale of shares in the company can be a trading receipt: *Associated London Properties Ltd v Henriksen*.[4] Although the Court of Appeal was clear that the decision turned on its facts, it is not completely clear what these facts were. If the facts had been that the new company was simply the agent of its owners so that in fact the trade was carried on by them and not by the company, the case could be treated as just a useful illustration of a general principle; however the case appears to involve a fine disregard of the separate legal personality of the company. The decision has not been much used by the Revenue despite its potentialities to counter tax avoidance.

Simon's Taxes B3.203; Butterworths Income Tax Service C1.02.

[1] [1974] STC 539, [1974] 3 All ER 949, see Twitley, [1974] BTR 335.

[2] [1974] STC 539 at 545, [1974] 3 All ER 949 at 955.

[3] [1978] STC 607 narrowing still further *Williams v Davies* [1945] 1 All ER 304, 26 TC 371.

[4] (1944) 26 TC 46, distinguished in *Fundfarms Development Ltd v Parsons* [1969] 3 All ER 1161.

PROFESSION

7: 06   Case II of Schedule D charges income tax on the profits of any profession or vocation. Neither term is defined. The term profession involves the idea of an occupation requiring either purely intellectual skill, or of manual skill controlled, as in painting and sculpture or surgery, by the intellectual skill of the operator; such an occupation is distinct from one which is substantially the production or sale or arrangements for the production or sale of commodities.[1] So a journalist and editor carries on a profession but a newspaper reporter carries on a trade.[2] The question is one of fact and degree and the crux is the degree of intellectual skill involved. So one who ran a service for taxpayers seeking to recover overpaid tax or to reduce assessments was held by the Commissioners to be carrying on a trade and the Court of Appeal felt there was no error of law.[3]

A vocation is analogous to a calling, a word of great signification meaning the way in which a man passes his life.[4] A dramatist,[5] a racing tipster[6] and a jockey[7] have all been held to be carrying on a vocation but not a perennial gambler[8] nor a film producer.[9]

Simon's Taxes B4.101, 102; Butterworths Income Tax Service C1.11.

[1] *IRC v Maxse* [1919] 1 KB 647 at 656, 12 TC 41 at 61.

[2] [1919] 1 KB 647 at 656, 12 TC 41 at 61.

[3] *Currie v IRC* [1921] 2 KB 332, 12 TC 245. Other traders include a stockbroker: *Christopher Barker & Sons v IRC* [1919] 2 KB 222; and a photographer: *Cecil v IRC* (1919) 36 TLR 164.

[4] Per Denman J in *Partridge v Mallandaine* (1886) 18 QBD 276 at 278, 2 TC 179 at 180.

[5] *Billam v Griffith* (1941) 23 TC 757.

[6] *Graham v Arnott* (1941) 24 TC 157.

[7] *Wing v O'Connell* [1927] IR 84.

[8] *Graham v Green* [1925] 2 KB 37, 9 TC 309.

[9] *Asher v London Film Productions Ltd* [1944] 1 All ER 77, [1944] KB 133.

7: 07   A profession must be distinguished from a trade because:

(a) many capital allowances are available only to traders;[1]

(b) the rule in *Sharkey v Wernher* may not apply to professions;[2]

(c) an isolated transaction may be an adventure in the nature of trade, but an isolated service cannot fall within Case II but only within Case VI;[3]

(*d*) exemption from CGT for certain damages is confined to profession and vocations;[4]

(*e*) there is some suggestion that the deduction rules are less fair for professions than for trades;[5]

(*f*) a company may not be able to carry on a profession;[6]

(*g*) the definition of a trading company for the purposes of escaping the 35% corporate tax rate on close investment companies does not refer to a profession.

---

[1] Infra, § **8: 03.**
[2] Infra, § **7: 154.**
[3] Infra, § **10: 07.**
[4] CGTA 1979, s. 19 (5).
[5] Per Lord Greene MR, in *Norman v Golder* (1944) 26 TC 293, at 297.
[6] *William Esplen, Son and Swainston Ltd v IRC* [1919] 2 K B 731 but cf. *Newstead v Frost* [1978] STC 239 at 249.

SIX PROBLEMS IN THE DEFINITION OF TRADE

1 Illegal trading

7: 08   The question whether the profits of an illegal trade are taxable has produced conflicting dicta but the answer clearly ought to be, and on balance of authority now is, yes.[1] It was decided in *Partridge v Mallandaine*[2] that a bookmaker's profits were taxable notwithstanding that wagering contracts were unlawful, and in *Lindsay, Woodward and Hiscox v IRC*[3] that profits of illegal contracts were taxable. These cases merely decide however that the profits of a contract which the law will not enforce are nonetheless taxable. No such explanation can be advanced for the decision of the Privy Council in *Minister of Finance v Smith*[4] that the profits of illegal brewing during the prohibition era were taxable. Today the true principle is that the taxpayer cannot set up the unlawful character of his act against the Revenue.[5]

There have been some suggestions that the profits of burglary would not be taxable, because crime is not a trade.[6] It is however submitted that these should not be followed.[7] Any other conclusion may lead to distinctions between acts illegal *per se* and acts which are merely incidental to the carrying on of a trade. There may be difficulty in calculating profits as there is a civil obligation to restore the goods to their owner and it should be remembered that a consistently unprofitable trade may not be a trade at all.[8]

Simon's Taxes B3.247; Butterworths Income Tax Service C1.03.
[1] *IRC v Aken* [1988] STC 69 (prostitution a trade).
[2] (1886) 18 QBD 276, 2 TC 179.
[3] (1933) 18 TC 43.
[4] [1927] AC 193.
[5] *Southern v AB* [1933] 1 K B 713, 18 TC 59; *Mann v Nash* [1932] 1 K B 752, 16 TC 523; *contra Hayes v Duggan* [1929] IR 406.
[6] E.g. per Lord Sands in *Lindsay v IRC* (1932) 18 TC 43 at 56.
[7] Fines are not deductible expenses: *IRC v Alexander von Glehn & Co Ltd* [1920] 2 K B 553, 12 TC 232.
[8] Infra, § **7: 11.**

2 Adventures in the nature of trade—scope

7: 09   The question whether there is a trade or an adventure in the nature of trade is one of fact but the question cannot be ignored for that reason. What follows is an attempt to synthesise the many cases and to indicate not only what factors the courts take into account but also the frail nature of those factors.

The Royal Commission listed six "badges of trade" (*i*) the subject-matter of the realisation, (*ii*) the length of period of ownership, (*iii*) the frequency or number of similar transactions by the same person, (*iv*) supplementary work on or in connection with the property realised, (*v*) the circumstances that were responsible for the realisation and finally (*vi*) motive. These badges are principally important in determining what is an adventure in the nature of trade. A slightly different list of badges is used in this text.

An example

7: 10   In *Wisdom v Chamberlain*[1] the taxpayer had assets worth between £150,000 and £200,000. Fearing that sterling might be devalued his accountant concluded that silver bullion would be a suitable hedge and tried to buy £200,000's worth. However the brokers would only sell £100,000 worth, a transaction which was financed on a loan from the brokers of £90,000 at 3% above bank rate. Five months later the accountant managed to get £200,000 worth of bullion from the brokers on the basis that the original purchase would be repurchased by the brokers, at a loss to the taxpayer of £3,000. The new deal was financed by loans of £160,000 from a bank and £40,000 from the brokers, both for a maximum period of one year and at high rates of interest. The brokers were under an obligation to buy back for £210,000 within a certain period. Between October 1962 and January 1963 the bullion was disposed of at a profit of £48,000 after deducting interest payment of £7,000.

The Commissioners held that this was a transaction in the nature of trade and the Court of Appeal held that they were amply justified in reaching that conclusion. For Harman LJ this was "a transaction entered into on a short term basis for the purpose of making a profit out of the purchase and sale of a commodity and if that is not an adventure in the nature of trade I do not really know what it is".[2] Salmon LJ observed that if the taxpayer had realised his other assets and used the proceeds to finance the purchase of the silver the case might have been quite different. The facts of the case however presented a trading adventure—"and a very sensible and successful one. I for my part cannot see that it is any the less a trading adventure because you describe it as something to offset the loss incurred by a fall in the value of sterling or as a hedge or insurance against devaluation".[3]

Simon's Taxes B3.211; Butterworths Income Tax Service C1.12.

[1] [1969] 1 All ER 332, 45 TC 92; cf. *Marson v Morton* [1986] STC 463.
[2] [1969] 1 All ER 332 at 336, 45 TC 92 at 106.
[3] [1969] 1 All ER 332 at 339, 45 TC 92 at 108.

Purpose of profit

7: 11   An intention to make a profit is not a necessary ingredient of a trade but its presence helps to establish a trading transaction.[1] Operations of the same kind as, and carried out in the same way, as those which characterise ordinary trading are not the less trading operations because they make a loss or there is no intention to make a profit.[2] However a scheme which inevitably involves a loss may not be a trading transaction.[3] So losses on loan transactions with no commercial element in them have been disallowed.[4]

Simon's Taxes B3.203; Butterworths Income Tax Service C1.13.
  [1] *Torbell Investments Ltd v Williams* [1986] STC 397.
  [2] See Lord Reid in *J. P. Harrison (Watford) Ltd v Griffiths* (1960) 40 TC 281; affd. sub nom. *Griffiths v J. P. Harrison (Watford) Ltd* [1962] 1 All ER 909, 40 TC 281, and cases there cited. See also *Building and Civil Engineering Holidays Scheme Management Ltd v Clark* (profit but not trading (1960) 39 TC 12. A related issue is whether a particular transaction carried out by one who clearly is trading forms part of the trade even though a loss must result.
  [3] *FA and AB Ltd v Lupton* [1971] 3 All ER 948, 47 TC 580.
  [4] *Overseas Containers Finance Ltd v Stoker* [1989] STC 364, CA.

7: 12   One must distinguish a trade from a merely charitable endeavour. In *Religious Tract and Book Society of Scotland v Forbes*,[1] the question was whether colportage, that is the sending out of colporteurs whose job was to sell Bibles and to act as cottage missionaries, was a trade. The Court of Exchequer (Scotland) ruled that the activity, which could not possibly be carried on at a profit, could not be a trade, with the result that the losses on colportage could not be set off against what were undoubtedly trading profits from the society's book shops. It would therefore appear that while the impossibility of profit will prevent the activity from being a trade, the absence of a profit motive will not.

If there is an intention to make a profit but then to apply it in some worthy way, there is a trading activity. The tax system is concerned with the acquisition and not with the distribution of profit.[2]

Simon's Taxes B3.208, C4.522, 523; Butterworths Income Tax Service C1.13.
  [1] (1896) 3 TC 415.
  [2] *Mersey Docks and Harbour Board v Lucas* (1883) 8 App Cas 891, 2 TC 25.

Motive for acquisition

7: 13   The motive attending the acquisition of an asset is a factor which, when there is doubt, is to be thrown into the balance.[1] An acquisition under a relative's last will and testament is clearly different from a purchase with a view to speedy re-sale.[2] If the taxpayer embarks on an adventure which has the characteristics of trade his purpose or object cannot prevail over it. But if his acts are equivocal his purpose or object may be very material.[3]

The acquisition of an asset with the intention of making a profit on the resale does not inevitably signify an adventure in the nature of trade since whether a person is hoping to carry out a deal or hoping to make a good investment some capital appreciation is anticipated.[4] The time at which resale is foreseen is of greater importance.

However, if the taxpayer argues that it was not his intention to make a profit through resale the onus is on him to produce some plausible explanation for his purchase, such as that he intended to enjoy the income before reselling.[5] Further, the taxpayer's assertion that he intended to buy an asset for investment purposes, whether as an investment fund for old age or as a hedge against devaluation[6] will not be allowed to stand against other facts. The Revenue thus get the best of both worlds; the taxpayer's state of mind can make up for equivocal acts while unequivocal acts cannot be distorted by intent.[7]

If there is no prospect of immediate profit through resale this may suggest that the acquisition is not an adventure in the nature of trade.[8] However, whatever the taxpayer's original intention may have been that may change.[9]

Simon's Taxes B3.203; Butterworths Income Tax Service C1.14.

[1] As in *Lucy and Sunderland Ltd v Hunt* [1961] 3 All ER 1062, 40 TC 132 and *West v Phillips* (1958) 38 TC 203.

[2] But distinguish *Pilkington v Randall* (1965) 42 TC 662 where one beneficiary bought the interest of another.

[3] Per Lord Reid in *Iswera v IRC* [1965] 1 WLR 663 at 668.

[4] *IRC v Reinhold* (1953) 34 TC 389.

[5] *Reynold's Executors v Bennett* (1943) 25 TC 401.

[6] *Wisdom v Chamberlain,* supra.

[7] E.g. *Mitchell Bros v Tomlinson* (1957) 37 TC 224.

[8] Infra, § 7: 23.

[9] Infra, § 7: 24.

7: 14　A separate question concerns companies which, as legal persons, have their capacity limited by their objects. The court, in deciding whether there is an adventure or not, may look at the objects of the company,[1] but a statement therein limiting the company's powers to investment is not conclusive against liability to tax on its income.[2] On the other hand, if a company is set up which has the power to purchase land and to turn it to account, such operations are likely to be regarded as trading operations[3] and it has been suggested that the mere setting up of a company points to a trading intention because of the implied continuity of the company.[4]

---

[1] *Cooksey and Bibbey v Rednall* (1949) 30 TC 514 at 521.

[2] *Eames v Stepnell Properties Ltd* [1967] 1 WLR 593, 43 TC 678; affd. [1967] 1 All ER 785, 43 TC 678, CA; *Emro Investments Ltd v Aller* (1954) 35 TC 305.

[3] *IRC v Reinhold* (1953) 34 TC 389 and see *IRC v Korean Syndicate Ltd* [1921] 3 KB 258, 12 TC 181 and *Ruhamuh Property Co Ltd v FCT* (1928) 41 CLR 1648; see also *Lewis Emanuel & Son Ltd v White* (1965) 42 TC 369.

[4] Per Lord Carmont in *IRC v Reinhold* (1953) 34 TC 389.

The individual

7: 15　Where a single transaction is involved and is of a nature close to, but separate from, what is undoubtedly a trade carried on by an individual, it is likely that the courts will conclude that the transaction is an adventure in the nature of a trade.[1] In *T. Beynon & Co Ltd v Ogg*[2] where the company acted as agents for the purchase of wagons and bought some on their own account, the profits on the resale of those wagons were held taxable, as they were in

Cape Brandy Syndicate v IRC[3] where South African brandy was acquired for blending and resale in this country by three persons who happened to be members of certain firms engaged in the wine trade. In these cases the taxpayer was held assessable on the profits of the adventure in the nature of trade, but the profits did not form part of his general trading activities, but rather a distinct taxable source.

The second way in which the individual may become important is if he possesses some special skill. There is some authority that if a person has a skill and makes money by it, the profit is more likely to be taxable[4] but today the absence of a skill appears to be neutral.[5]

Simon's Taxes B3.211, 214; Butterworths Income Tax Service C1.15.

[1] Per Lord Normand in *Cayzer and Irvine & Co v IRC* (1942) 24 TC 491 at 496.

[2] (1918) 7 TC 125.

[3] [1921] 2 KB 403, 12 TC 358.

[4] Per Scott LJ in *Smith Barry v Cordy* (1946) 28 TC 250 at 260 but doubts as to the correctness of this decision were raised in *Ransom v Higgs* [1974] STC 539, [1974] 3 All ER 949.

[5] Per Goff J in *Johnston v Heath* [1970] 3 All ER 915 at 921.

The subject matter

7: 16 The courts take the view that some commodities are more likely to be acquired as investments than as the subject of a deal. There are two main groups of examples. Objects recommended for investment in the light of these cases include wine, gold coins and reversionary interests. Antiques and works of art are likewise recommended provided they are retained for some time and not sold by commercial methods.

First, if the object yields income, whether in the form of rent or dividends, that object is more likely to be an investment than is one which yields no income.[1] Where the court can see some fruit, the source of the fruit is likely to be a tree. A subtle case is *Snell v Rosser Thomas & Co Ltd*[2] where the taxpayer—a developer— bought a house and $5\frac{3}{4}$ acres of land. The house produced rent from tenants but the land produced no income and was therefore stock in trade.

In determining whether or not there is income the court has looked not simply at the flow of money to the taxpayer but also at any outflow. So in *Wisdom v Chamberlain*[3] the interest payments were of importance while in *Cooke v Haddock*[4] rent of £167 a year had to be set against the £320 a year interest.

This approach was questioned in *Marson v Morton*[5] where it was said that it was no longer self-evident that unless land is producing income it cannot be an investment. The legal principle cannot change but life could. "Since the arrival of inflation and high rates of tax on income new approaches to investment have emerged putting the emphasis on the making of capital profits at the expense of income yield".[6]

Property which produces income may none the less be trading stock so that the proceeds of sale must enter a profit and loss account. The question depends on the individual circumstances of the case. Thus stocks and shares bought by a bank in order to make good use of funds in hand and subsequently disposed of in order to finance repayments to depositors are treated as trading stock of the banking business.[7] Equally a company which in addition to building ships ran a passenger service and bought and sold four ships for that service in rapid succession was held taxable on the profits from the resales of the passenger ships.[8]

Simon's Taxes B3.211, 212; Butterworths Income Tax Service C1.16.

[1] *Salt v Chamberlain* [1979] STC 750.

[2] [1968] 1 All ER 600, 44 TC 343 and consider the factory in *W. M. Robb Ltd v Page* (1971) 47 TC 465.

[3] [1969] 1 All ER 332, 45 TC 92, supra, § 7: 10.

[4] (1960) 39 TC 64.

[5] [1986] STC 463.

[6] *Marson v Morton* [1986] STC 463 per Browne-Wilkinson V-C at 472.

[7] *Punjab Co-operative Bank Ltd v Amritsar IT Comr Lahore* [1940] 4 All ER 87, [1940] AC 1055; a similar rule applies to insurance companies. *General Reinsurance Co Ltd v Tomlinson* [1970] 2 All ER 436, 48 TC 81 discussed in *General Motors Acceptance Corpn v IRC* [1985] STC 408.

[8] *J. Bolson & Son Ltd v Farrelly* (1953) 34 TC 161.

7: 17   Secondly, if the object does not yield income but can be enjoyed in kind so that there is pleasure or even pride in its possession,[1] as where a person buys a picture for purposes of aesthetic enjoyment, any profit on resale will escape income tax. Conversely, the purchase of a commodity which gives no such pleasure and which cannot be turned to account except by a process of realisation, may well give rise to a taxable profit.[2] Examples of this turn not only on the nature of the commodity, such as the railway wagons in *Gloucester Railway Carriage and Wagon Co Ltd v IRC*[3] but also on the quantity as in *Rutledge v IRC*[4] where there were one million rolls of lavatory paper; however, as always, these are questions of fact and it was important also that the taxpayer had no intention other than to resell the property at a profit.[5]

Land is another asset which can easily yield taxable profits.[6] If one owns a house and lives in it, the house is unlikely to be trading stock. However occupation is not conclusive and courts are reluctant to disturb a finding by the Commissioners that there was an adventure in the nature of trade. In *Page v Pogson*[7] the taxpayer had built a house for himself and his wife and then sold it six months after completing it. He then built another house nearby but had to sell it when his job was moved from the South to the East of England. He was held taxable on the profits of the sale of the second house and Upjohn, J. felt himself unable to reverse that finding although doubting whether he would have reached that decision himself.

Simon's Taxes B3.211, 212; Butterworths Income Tax Service C1.16.

[1] See Lord Normand in *IRC v Fraser* (1942) 24 TC 498; *quaere* how a trust can enjoy such an object—in which case one should consider the liability of pension funds which purchase pictures.

[2] Consider the tax position of unit holders in trusts which are to make investments in commodities as distinct from in companies producing commodities.

[3] [1925] AC 469, 12 TC 720.

[4] (1929) 14 TC 490 and see also *Martin v Lowry* (44 million yards of aeroplane linen), [1927] AC 312, 11 TC 297.

[5] *Mamor Sdn Bhd v Director General of Inland Revenue* [1985] STC 801 at 806, PC.

[6] Infra, § **31: 35**.

[7] (1954) 35 TC 545; cf. *Sharpless v Rees* (1940) 23 TC 361 and *Shadford v H Fairweather & Co Ltd* (1966) 43 TC 291.

Processing—supplementary work

7: 18   The alteration of the asset by the taxpayer may suggest that there is an adventure in the nature of trade. So if a purchaser were to carry through a manufacturing process which changed the character of the article, as where pig-iron is converted into steel, there is likely to be a trade, but merely to put the asset into a condition suitable for a favourable sale, such as cleaning a picture or giving a boat a general overhaul, would not suggest a trade. In the case from which these illustrations are taken *IRC v Livingston*[1] the taxpayer, a ship repairer, together with a blacksmith and a fish salesman's employee, purchased a cargo vessel which they converted into a steam drifter and then sold without themselves using it for fishing. The alterations took nearly four months and were carried out by two of the three for wages. The Court of Session held that the profit was taxable.

The mere enhancement of value, as by obtaining planning permission,[2] is not sufficient nor will be the normal use of the asset. So whereas the planting of rubber trees did not indicate a trade in *Tebrau (Johore) Rubber Syndicate Ltd v Farmer*,[3] the blending of brandy in the *Cape Brandy Syndicate* case did.[4]

Jenkinson v Freedland[5] must be regarded as a most unusual case. There the taxpayer bought two stills which were coated with a resinous substance and succeeded in removing them by a process of his own devising. It was held that there was no trade on the particular facts but this turns largely on the eventual sale of the stills by the taxpayer to his own company.

Simon's Taxes B3.231; Butterworths Income Tax Service C1.17.
[1] 1927 SC 251, 11 TC 538.
[2] *Taylor v Good* [1974] STC 148, [1974] 1 All ER 1137.
[3] (1910) 5 TC 658.
[4] [1921] 2 KB 403, 18 TC 358.
[5] (1961) 39 TC 636.

Realisation—reasons

7: 19   "Some explanation, such as a sudden emergency or opportunity calling for ready money, negatives the idea that any plan of dealing prompted the original purchase."[1] There are few reported cases in which the point has been successfully made. In *Mitchell Bros v Tomlinson*[2] a decision to sell houses originally bought for letting was motivated by changes in rent control legislation which made letting uneconomic, the rising costs of repairs and the need to realise partnership assets on the death of a partner, but the court held that the only reasonable conclusion was that the trade had commenced before the death of the partner and even before some of the houses had been bought, let alone sold. In *Stott v Hoddinott*[3] an architect was obliged as a term of a contract to take up shares in the company granting him the contract. He subsequently sold those shares in order to provide funds to take up shares under later contracts with other companies. It was held that this was a capital transaction so that he was not entitled to relief in respect of the loss which he sustained.

Simon's Taxes B3.221; Butterworths Income Tax Service C1.18.
[1] RC 1955, Cmd. 9474, § 115.
[2] (1957) 37 TC 224. See also *Page v Pogson,* supra, § **7: 17**.
[3] (1916) 7 TC 85.

Realisation—machinery

7: 20   The presence of an organisation through which the disposal of the asset is carried out is one of the hall marks of a trade, not least because the expenses of such an organisation will be deductible in computing the net profit on the deal.[1] Equally another factor in deciding whether or not a trade has been discontinued is whether the trade organisation has ceased to exist in an identifiable form.[2] However the presence or absence of an organisation is anything but conclusive in deciding whether or not there has been an adventure in the nature of trade. As Lord Wilberforce said in *Ransom v Higgs*: "Organisation as such is not a principle of taxation, or many estimable ladies throughout this country would be imperilled".[3] Thus in *West v Phillips*[4] where the taxpayer built certain houses for letting and subsequently set up an estate agency business run by a separate company for the purposes of selling the houses that action was regarded as simply a convenient method of realising investment property consisting of a large number of component parts. On the other hand, in *Hudson v Wrightson*[5] where the appellant was a retired druggist who had bought some houses and later sold them but had never had an office or staff, the Commissioners concluded that there was a trade and their decision was not reversed.

Simon's Taxes B3.221; Butterworths Income Tax Service C1.18.
[1] Lord Radcliffe in *Edwards v Bairstow and Harrison* [1955] 3 All ER 48 at 58, 36 TC 207 at 230.
[2] *Andrew v Taylor* (1965) 42 TC 557.
[3] [1974] 3 All ER 949 at 966, note extra-statutory concession C4 (1988), **Simon's Taxes, Division H2.2.**
[4] (1958) 38 TC 203 at 213; see also *Rand v Alberni Land Co* (1920) 7 TC 629.
[5] (1934) 26 TC 55. Cf. *Bradshaw v Blunden* (1956) 36 TC 397.

Realisation—the number of steps

7: 21   The number of steps taken to dispose of the asset is a fragile indicator of a trade.[1] The purchase of goods in bulk and their resale in smaller quantities is the essence of a wholesale-retail trading operation. So in *Cape Brandy Syndicate v IRC*[2] one of the factors in favour of a trade was that the brandy was disposed of in some 100 transactions spread over 18 months. On the other hand the fact that a large number of disposals of land occurred did not make them trading transactions in *Hudsons Bay Co Ltd v Stevens.*[3]

Conversely a single disposal can nonetheless amount to an adventure in the nature of trade.[4]

Simon's Taxes B3.211, 212; Butterworths Income Tax Service C1.18.
[1] Per Lord Russell in *IRC v Reinhold* (1953) 34 TC 389 at 395.

[2] [1921] 2 KB 403 at 417, 12 TC 368, at 376. For another example *Martin v Lowry* (1926) 11 TC 297 at 320.
[3] (1909) 5 TC 424.
[4] E.g. *T. Beynon & Co Ltd v Ogg* (1918) 7 TC 125.

Frequency of transactions

7: 22 The frequency of transactions is only one factor; an investor is still an investor even though he changes his investments. In *J. Bolson & Son Ltd v Farrelly* where the taxpayer company ran a passenger service but bought a large number of boats in a short time for the service and resold them after modification, Harman J agreed that the Commissioners' finding that there was a trade was inevitable. He said, "A deal done once is probably not an activity in the nature of trade, though it may be. Done three or four times it usually is. Each case must depend on its own facts."[1]

However while it is clear that repeated transactions may support the inference of a trade and that an isolated transaction many nonetheless be an adventure in the nature of trade, there is also authority that where a transaction is repeated the court may use that fact to place the label of trade on to the original transaction. In *Leach v Pogson*[2] the taxpayer had set up a driving school in early 1954; the business was incorporated. In December 1955 he transferred it to a newly formed company in return for cash and shares. He subsequently started other schools which he likewise transferred to companies. It was agreed that he was liable to income tax on the profits from the subsequent transactions but the taxpayer argued that he was not liable in respect of the profit on the first. It was held that he was so liable and that the subsequent transactions could be used to support that conclusion. It is probably of great importance that in that case, while he had no intention of embarking upon the business of establishing and selling motoring schools when the first one was set up, he did have that intention before he sold it. The case would thus appear to be correctly decided although perhaps more appropriately dealt with as a case of a change in the character of the transaction.

Simon's Taxes B3.215; Butterworths Income Tax Service C1.19.
[1] (1953) 34 TC 161 at 167. See also *Foulds v Clayton* (1953) 34 TC 382 at 388. Likewise *Pickford v Quirke* (1927) 13 TC 251.
[2] (1962) 40 TC 585 and see infra, § **7: 24**.

Duration of ownership

7: 23 A fast buck is the essence of a deal. A long period between the acquisition of an asset and its disposal may corroborate an intention to hold it as an investment.[1] Conversely, a quick sale invites a scrutiny of the evidence to see whether the acquisition was with that intent.[2] One element of an investment is that the acquirer intends to hold it at any rate for some time, with a view to obtaining either some benefit in the way of income in the meantime or obtaining some profit, but not an immediate profit by resale.[3] In *Eames v Stepnell Properties Ltd*[4] the Commissioners' finding that there was no trade was reversed by the courts. Land subject to zoning for school use in the county development plan was held by a firm of civil engineers and building contractors. The firm had agreed in principle to sell it to the council, but then sold it at its agricultural value (£2,100) to the taxpayer company which was intended to be an investment company. About that time the basis for valuation in compulsory purchase cases was altered from existing use to market value. After much delay in obtaining a ruling from the Minister as to alternative development, a matter crucial to valuation, the land was sold to the county council for £50,000. As Harman LJ put it:[5]

> "This sort of property is not of any use to a building company nor can it be described as a form of investment of any sort for as it was, and without purchase by the county council it was a mere piece of agricultural land yielding about 2% on its price. . . . This . . . was land earmarked for sale, and earmarked for sale at a profit."

However while an asset acquired on a short-term basis[6] will often be the subject of an adventure, it does not follow that this will always be so. Thus in *IRC v Reinhold*[7] the taxpayer admitted that he acquired the property with the intention of reselling it and that he had instructed his agents to sell whenever a suitable opportunity arose. The land was sold after three years. This isolated transaction escaped income tax. Much more doubtful however is the decision of Danckwerts J in *McLellan, Rawson & Co Ltd v Newall*[8] in which the Commissioners' decision that there was a taxable profit was reversed, even though the taxpayer had entered into an arrangement to sell the woodlands while he was still negotiating for their purchase.

Butterworths Income Tax Service C1.20.
[1] Per Donovan J in *Harvey v Caulcott* (1952) 33 TC 159 at 164.
[2] Per Cross J in *Turner v Last* (1965) 42 TC 517 at 522–3.
[3] Per Buckley J in *Eames v Stepnell Properties Ltd* (1966) 43 TC 678 at 692.
[4] [1967] 1 All ER 785, 43 TC 678.
[5] At 794 and 701.
[6] E.g. *Wisdom v Chamberlain*; supra, § **7: 10**.
[7] (1953) 34 TC 389.
[8] (1955) 36 TC 117.

Timing

7: 24 It is a question of fact not only whether there is an adventure in the nature of trade but also when it begins—and ends. It is also important to separate the question whether a trade has began from the question whether any income has arisen from it.[1] Where an asset is acquired and subsequently disposed of, it is open to the court to conclude from the evidence that the whole transaction was an adventure in the nature of trade. It is however open to the courts to conclude that an asset was acquired with the intention of retaining it as an investment but that trading subsequently commenced so that the profit accruing on resale will be taxable.[2] What is clear is that at any one time the asset must either be trading stock or a capital asset; it cannot be both.[3]

In computing the profit where the trade is begun subsequently to the asset being acquired, the asset must be brought into the account at its market value at that time.[4]

Butterworths Income Tax Service C1.21.
  [1] See *Eckel v Board of Inland Revenue* [1989] STC 305, PC.
  [2] *Taylor v Good* [1973] STC 383, [1973] 2 All ER 785. See also *Kirkham v Williams* [1989] STC 333.
  [3] *Simmons v IRC* [1980] STC 350, [1980] 2 All ER 798.
  [4] Ibid. This is the converse of *Sharkey v Wernher* (infra, § **7: 154**). See also CGTA 1979, s. 122, infra, § **20: 04**. Cases in which this rule should have been applied include *Leach v Pogson* (supra, § **7: 22**) and *Mitchell Bros v Tomlinson* (supra, § **7: 19**).

3 Sales by personal representatives and liquidators

7: 25 A personal representative may be empowered to carry on the deceased's business by the terms of the will, however his acts may amount to carrying on a trade for the purposes of Schedule D, Case I whether or not there is such a power.[1] If he is held to be trading this liability to tax is his and not *qua* executor.[2] As personal representative his job is to realise the assets of the estate and distribute them among the beneficiaries. There is therefore a presumption that if all he did was to realise the asset in a way advantageous to the estate then he was not carrying on a trade.[3]

Simon's Taxes B3.222; Butterworths Income Tax Service C1.31.
  [1] *Weisberg's Executrices v IRC* (1933) 17 TC 696.
  [2] *Cohan's Executors v IRC* (1924) 12 TC 602. Note Romer LJ in *Hillerns and Fowler v Murray* (1932) 17 TC 77 at 92.
  [3] Per Sargant LJ in *Cohan's Executors v IRC* (1924) 12 TC 602 at 620; approved by Greene MR in *Newbarns Syndicate v Hay* (1939) 22 TC 461 at 472.

7: 26 Whether the acts amount to carrying on a trade is a matter of degree and must depend on the nature of the trade, as two cases concerning farming show.

In *Pattullo's Trustees v IRC*[1] the taxpayers were the representatives of a tenant farmer who also carried on the trades of cattle breeder and feeder. The farm and the cattle dealing business were bequeathed specifically so that the only asset to be realised was the feeding business. The deceased died in November at which season the cattle would already be on the land of other farms feeding from it and manuring it. The trustees felt they had to complete these contracts for economic reasons. They also bought more cattle in order to consume the remaining feedstuffs on these farms. The cattle were all sold by the following June. The Commissioners held that the trustees were carrying on the business of cattle feeding and were not simply preparing the assets for sale, even though this was their motive. The Court of Session held that there was evidence to support the Commissioners.

However, in *IRC v Donaldson's Trustees*[2] the Commissioners held there was no trading and their conclusion was supported by the Court of Session. In this case the deceased was a farmer whose sole interest was a pedigree herd of Aberdeen Angus cattle. He died in March 1955 and the trustees were advised to sell the heifer calves in September 1955 and the bull calves in February 1956. This they did but had to keep the cattle alive and well in the meantime. The manager was told that the cattle were to be sold and the farm was rearranged for preparing them for sale instead of grazing and breeding.

It was held that the occupation of the farm was simply for the termination of husbandry and there was no trade.

It is thus a question of fact and degree whether the acts amount to the realisation of the asset or to trade.[3] However, if the acts are equally consistent both with the carrying on of a trade and with mere realisation, the act will be mere realisation since to hold otherwise would deprive the executors of their right *vis-à-vis* the Revenue to realise their testator's assets in the ordinary way.[4] In *Donaldson's Trustees* the personal representatives were able to show a positive change from the normal pattern of farming. In *Pattullo's Trustees* the Revenue could show, by the purchase of extra cattle, a continuation or development of the trade.

Simon's Taxes B3.222; Butterworths Income Tax Service C1.31.
[1] (1955) 36 TC 87.
[2] (1963) 41 TC 161.
[3] *Wood v Black's Executor* (1952) 33 TC 172.
[4] Per Greene MR in *Newbarns Syndicate v Hay* (1939) 22 TC 461 at 476.

7: 27 Where the deceased was carrying on a trade in partnership with others, his executors may insist that on his death the assets should be realised so that they may administer the estate. Where such assets are realised the court may hold that as far as the estate is concerned the process is one of mere realisation as in *Marshall's Executors, Hood's Executors and Rogers v Joly*;[1] it was proved that the executors did not consent to the continuation of the trade but insisted upon their share of the assets. In the absence of such a finding the court will uphold a finding by the Commissioners that there was a continuation of the trade. In *Newbarns Syndicate v Hay*[2] not only did the process of realisation take ten years but the executor attended all partnership meetings as a voting participant, something he was not entitled to do as the mere executor of a deceased member; there was thus an implied agreement to continue the trade.

Simon's Taxes B3.222; Butterworths Income Tax Service C1.31.
[1] [1936] 1 All ER 851, 20 TC 256.
[2] (1939) 22 TC 461.

Liquidation

7: 28 The liquidator's duty, like the personal representative's, is to realise the assets.[1] Here too the courts ask the question: what reason is there to suppose that the winding up was done for any purpose other than the normal carrying out of the duties of a liquidator?[2] There is a presumption that a mere disposal is not a trading operation. In *Wilson Box (Foreign Rights) Ltd v Brice*[3] the company was formed to turn patent rights to account. However no trade of dealing in patents was commenced. During liquidation certain patent rights were sold. The Special Commissioners held that there was a trading operation but the Court of Appeal held that there was no evidence to support this. On the other hand the payment to the liquidator of sums in respect of trading contracts made before the date of liquidation will be trading receipts.[4]

Simon's Taxes B3.221
[1] Per Atkin LJ in *IRC v Burrell* [1924] 2 KB 52 at 73, 9 TC 27 at 42. In these cases it is irrelevant that the assets were the trading stock of the company or represented undivided profit. The same principles apply to trustees holding on an assignment for the benefit of creditors (*Armitage v Moore* [1900] 2 QB 363, 4 TC 199, supplying steam power is trading not realising asset) and to a receiver for debenture holders (*IRC v Thompson* [1936] 2 All ER 651, 20 TC 422).

[2] *Wilson Box (Foreign Rights) Ltd v Brice* [1936] 3 All ER 728, 20 TC 736, esp. per Lawrence J at 742, and per Slesser LJ at 747; and per Ungoed Thomas J, in *John Mills Production Ltd v Mathias* (1964) 44 TC 441 at 456.

[3] [1936] 3 All ER 728, 20 TC 736.

[4] *IRC v Oban Distillery Co Ltd* (1932) 18 TC 33.

4 Retirement

7: 29   To dispose of trading stock after announcing one's retirement may well be trading, since the moment when trade ceases is a question of fact. Declarations by the trader are not of themselves decisive. In *J. and R. O'Kane Ltd v IRC*[1] the taxpayers had carried on the business of wine and spirit merchants. They announced their intention to retire in early 1916 but did not complete the disposal of their stock until late 1917, an operation which was carried out mostly in 1917 and which took the form of many small sales. The only purchases made for the business after the announcement of their retirement were under continuing contracts with distillers. The Special Commissioners held that the trade did not end in early 1916 and that the proceeds of the disposal sales were therefore taxable as the profits of the trade. The House of Lords held that there was abundant evidence for the Commissioners' findings.

On the other hand in *IRC v Nelson*[2] there was only a twelve day gap between the decision to retire and the disposal of the stock, and the whole stock was sold together with the rest of the business, the casks, the trade name and office furniture and fittings in one sale to one customer. The Commissioners held that the disposal was not by way of trade and the Court of Session held that there was evidence to support the conclusion.

Simon's Taxes B3.223, 225; Butterworths Income Tax Service C1.32.
[1] (1922) 12 TC 303.

[2] 1939 SC 689, 22 TC 716.

7: 30   Problems also arise on the completion of executory contracts entered into before retirement. In *Hillerns and Fowler v Murray*[1] the trade was run by a partnership which was dissolved by lapse of time under the terms of the partnership deed. At that time the partners held trading stock and they acquired other stock after that time under contracts entered into before the dissolution. The trading stock was used to fulfil orders placed by customers before the dissolution but no new contracts whether for purchase or sale were entered into after dissolution. The Commissioners held that there was evidence of trading after the dissolution. Although Rowlatt J reversed their decision, the Court of Appeal held that there was evidence to support their conclusion. The mere declaration by the partners that offices would remain open only for the carrying out of existing contracts could not give them immunity from the Income Tax Acts. The argument was put that this was simply the best way of realising the assets of the partnership. Romer LJ after pointing out that the realisation of the assets to best advantage might involve trading, went on "in most cases, in the winding up of a partnership it is necessary for the proper getting in of the assets and winding up of the affairs of it, to carry on the business for a short time, or to carry on the business to a limited extent".[2] So the presumption that is said to exist that a sale by an executor is a realisation of an asset and not a trading activity, does not apply.

Where however it is clear that trading has ceased, subsequent disposals will escape income tax. Thus in *Beams v Weardale Steel Coal and Coke Co Ltd*[3] the company's iron works had shut down by 1915. In 1933 they sold off some slag heaps and the Commissioners held that this was not a part of their trade. It was not suggested that this was a new trade. The Revenue's appeal was dismissed.

Simon's Taxes B3.223; Butterworths Income Tax Service C1.32.
[1] (1932) 17 TC 77.
[2] At 92, and see Lord Hanworth, at 87.
[3] (1937) 21 TC 204.

7: 31   Where a trader sells his trade to another, he ceases to trade. Whether his successor, in selling former trading stock commences to trade or simply realises assets is a matter of fact.[1] If the successor is a company which is under some obligation to hand over the whole or part of the profits of the trade to the predecessor, it may be that new owner is simply the agent of the old, so that the former owner does not cease to trade.[2] An alternative conclusion on the facts may be that the old trade has ceased but the former owner has commenced a new trade through the agency of the new owner.[3] The choice between the two solutions is not merely academic since apart from the commencement and cessation provisions there are such questions as unused loss relief and capital allowances which will be lost under the second solution.[4]

Simon's Taxes B3.3; Butterworths Income Tax Service C1.33.
[1] *Lucy and Sunderland Ltd v Hunt* [1961] 3 All ER 1062 at 1066, 40 TC 132 at 139.
[2] *Baker v Cook* [1937] 3 All ER 509, 21 TC 337.
[3] *Southern v Watson* [1940] 3 All ER 439, 23 TC 566; see also *Parker v Batty* (1941) 23 TC 739.
[4] Infra, § **7: 56**.

---

5 Mutual business

7: 32   It is necessary to distinguish a profit from a trade from an excess of contribution over expenditure. If I allow myself £10 a week for housekeeping but spend only £9, no one would contend that the £1 saved was taxable profit. The immunity of the £1 from tax rests on two principles, either of which is sufficient; the one is that no man can trade with himself and the other is that the sum does not represent a profit.

This immunity has been applied to groups of people who combine for a purpose and contribute towards expenses, as in the case of a golf club whose members pay a club subscription. Here too any excess of income from subscriptions over expenses is free from tax.[1] Each member is entitled to a share of the surplus and it is irrelevant that there is only a limited liability to contribute to any deficiency.[2] Wherever therefore there is identity[3] of contributors to the fund and the recipients from the fund, it is impossible that the contributors should derive profits from contributions made by themselves to a fund which could only be expended or returned to themselves.[4] Even if the club had a bar at which drinks were served at prices which yielded a profit there is no liability to tax since the bar is merely a part of the club, and is open only to members who thus make certain additional contributions to the fund. A different situation arises if the bar is open to the public,[5] since there is now no identity of contributors to the fund with recipients from it; profits from the bar would be taxable even if the rest of the club ran at a loss. Liability would also arise if the facts showed that the bar was a distinct trading venture separate from the rest of the club.

The mutuality principle has been used to exempt a local authority[6] from liability to tax on its rates but today its scope is limited to mutual insurance companies, institutions like the BBC[7] and members' clubs.[8]

Simon's Taxes B3.236–240.
    [1] *Carlisle and Silloth Golf Club v Smith* [1913] 3 KB 75, 6 TC 48 and 198; dist, *Carnoustie Golf Course Committee v IRC* 1929 SC 419, 14 TC 498.
    [2] *Faulconbridge v National Employers Mutual General Insurance Association Ltd* (1952) 33 TC 103.
    [3] But not equality, per Lord Macmillan in *Municipal Mutual Insurance Ltd v Hills* (1932) 16 TC 430 at 448; as long as the relationship is reasonable.
    [4] See per Lord Normand in *English and Scottish Joint Co-operative Wholesale Society Ltd v Assam Agricultural IT Comr* [1948] 2 All ER 395 at 400; [1948] AC 405 at 419. *IRC v Eccentric Club Ltd* [1924] 1 KB 390, 12 TC 657 and Finlay J in *National Association of Local Government Officers v Watkins* (1934) 18 TC 499 at 506.
    [5] *Grove v Young Men's Christian Association* (1903) 4 TC 613.
    [6] See Lord Thankerton in *IRC v Forth Conservancy Board* [1931] AC 540 at 554, 16 TC 103 at 123; contrast *IRC v Stonehaven Recreation Ground Trustees* 1930 SC 206, 15 TC 419.
    [7] *BBC v Johns* [1964] 1 All ER 923, 41 TC 471.
    [8] Originally FA 1933, s. 31.

7: 33   The principle of mutuality applies even though the contributions are made to a separate legal entity,[1] such as a company, so long as the company exists simply for the convenience of its members and as an instrument obedient to their mandate as in the case with members of a mutual insurance company.[2] Income from investments is taxable in the usual way. Any excess of premium income over liabilities will also be the income of the company. However, so long as such income is returnable to the members either in the form of bonuses or by way of reduction of premiums, that income is exempt from tax since although the company is trading[3] this sum is not a profit to its members.[4] Should a member surrender his policy he will lose his entitlement to future bonuses even though he has contributed to them. Likewise if a person becomes a member of the company by taking out a policy he may become entitled to a portion of the surplus contributed by someone else. Such possibilities do not prevent there being mutuality, since the excess of contributions must go back to the policy holders as a class even if not precisely in the proportions in which they have contributed to them.[5]

It is however essential that such companies should be mutual companies, that is one where only the policy holders are the members of the company. If the company has shareholders who do not hold life policies but who are entitled to the profits of this business the company is not a mutual company.[6] Today a body corporate—and an unincorporated association—are subject to corporation tax and TA 1988, s. 490 ensures that distributions to members will be charged to Schedule F income tax. However, this applies only to distributions out of profits chargeable to corporation tax and so the principle of mutuality remains.

---

[1] See Rowlatt J in *Thomas v Richard Evans & Co Ltd* [1927] 1 KB 33 at 47, 11 TC 790 at 823.

[2] For criticism, see RC 1955, Cmd 9474, § 22, and [1961] BTR 398.

[3] See Lord Cave in *IRC v Cornish Mutual Assurance Co Ltd* [1926] AC 281 at 286–7, 12 TC 841 at 866–7, criticising Lord Watson in the *Styles* case, at 393, 471.

[4] See e.g. Lord Macmillan in *Municipal Mutual Insurance Ltd v Hills* (1932) 16 TC 430 at 448.

[5] On position of newcomers see Upjohn J in *Faulconbridge v National Employers Mutual General Insurance Association Ltd* (1952) 33 TC 103 at 121 and 124–5.

[6] *Last v London Assurance Corpn* (1885) 10 App Cas 438, 2 TC 100, but see now TA 1988, s. 433; infra, § **29: 18**.

7: 34　The mutuality doctrine is not without its limits. First, as just indicated, it applies only to the mutual dealings between the contributors. Mutual insurance companies are taxable on the ordinary income accruing from transactions with non-members. Thus in *New York Life Insurance Co v Styles*[1] where the House of Lords held that the company was not taxable on its profits from premium income from members' participating policies, it was agreed that the company was taxable on its profits from policies for fixed sums without profits and from its general annuity business with strangers, since they were not members of the company, just as it was taxable on its investment income. Exemption is afforded not to the profits from members but to the non-profit of mutual dealings.

---

[1] (1889) 14 App Cas 381, 2 TC 460; see also *Municipal Mutual Insurance Ltd v Hills* (1932), 16 TC 430, HL.

7: 35　Secondly, the doctrine applies only if there is genuine mutuality. In *Fletcher v IT Comr*[1] a members' club owned a bathing beach in Jamaica. They permitted guests at certain hotels to use the beach on payment of an entrance fee. The club was clearly taxable on the profits of these fees since they were carrying on a trade with non-members. They then altered their arrangements, abolishing the payment of a fee by the hotel guests and making the hotels voting members of the club.[2] However, each hotel member, like each individual, held only one share. The hotels were, like the individual members, to pay a sum by way of subscription, and in addition a sum which was based on the number of its guests using the beach. The gross receipts were £1,750. The Revenue sought to tax the club on the profit element in the relevant proportion of the hotel membership subscription. Lord Wilberforce said that if mutuality was to have any meaning, although a uniform fee was not essential, "there must be a reasonable relationship, contemplated or in result, between what a member contributed and what, with due allowance for interim benefits of enjoyment, he may expect or be entitled to draw from the fund; between his liabilities and his rights".[3] The great use of the beach made by hotel guests was not sufficient allowance and so the mutuality principle did not apply.

---

[1] [1971] 3 All ER 1185, [1972] AC 414.
[2] An earlier scheme had made the hotels members but without voting rights and it had been held that this scheme failed because the hotels were not truly members.
[3] [1971] 3 All ER 1185 at 1191.

7: 36   Thirdly, as *Municipal Mutual Insurance v Hills*[1] showed, not all business between a company and its members is mutual business. A business cannot escape tax on its profits for a year simply because at the end of the year it discovers that all its business has been with its members. A mutual insurance company carries on a trade with its members but its principal function is as a mere entity for the convenience of its members.[2] The mutuality principle is satisfied because nothing belongs to the corporation which is severable from what belongs to the aggregation of individuals.[3] When a company has share capital with a chance of dividends and, to one side of that, dealings with people who happen to be the owners of the share capital affording benefits to those people one by one individually, there is no reason to ignore the incorporation. In *English and Scottish Joint Co-operative Wholesale Society Ltd v Assam Agricultural IT Comr*[4] a company was set up to own and manage a tea estate with the bulk of its produce going to its two shareholders who advanced money by way of loan to be set off against the price due for the tea supplied by the company to its shareholders. It was held that the company had earned profits from dealings with its shareholders and so was taxable. This conclusion could not have been avoided by restricting the company's business to sales to its members.[5] A different result might have been reached if the business had not been incorporated and a different practical result would have been achieved if the price paid for the tea had been fixed so that no profit would have been earned.[6]

---

[1] (1932) 16 TC 430, supra, § **7: 32**.
[2] Per Lord Normand in *English and Scottish Joint Co-operative Wholesale Society Ltd v Assam Agricultural IT Comr* [1948] 2 All ER 395 at 399, [1948] AC 405 at 417.
[3] Per Rowlatt J in *Liverpool Corn Trade Association Ltd v Monks* (1926) 10 TC 442 at 453. See also Lord Watson in *New York Life Insurance Co v Styles* (1889) 14 App Cas 381 at 393, 2 TC 460 at 471.
[4] [1948] 2 All ER 395, [1948] AC 405.
[5] [1948] 2 All ER 395 at 399, [1948] AC 405 at 417.
[6] At 421, 401 (perhaps by treating the application of profit as a discount reducing the price); see *Pope v Beaumont* [1941] 3 All ER 9, 24 TC 78.

Legislation

7: 37   An attempt was made in TA 1988, s. 486(10) and (11) to tax the profits of mutual companies from dealings with members by directing that such profits or surplus should be treated as if those transactions were transactions with non-members. Since it was the mutuality of the transaction rather than the fact that it was with a member which gave immunity from taxation, the House of Lords, in a somewhat unimaginative construction of the statute, ruled that even if the transactions had been with non-members they would be exempt from tax and thus deprived the statute of any force.[1] The section remains on the statute book although to what purpose is not clear. When such companies became the subject of profits tax the legislature was more direct and simply taxed the profits of the trade of mutual companies. This more direct approach succeeded.

---

[1] *Ayrshire Employers Mutual Insurance Association Ltd v IRC* [1946] 1 All ER 637 at 640, 27 TC 331 at 347 note comments in *Fothergill v Monarch Airlines Ltd* [1981] AC 251.

7: 38   The exemption from tax afforded by mutual dealings does not operate to prevent certain contributions being claimed as deductions in computing the taxable income of the contributor.[1] Thus a payment to a fire insurance scheme is deductible whether or not the scheme is mutual. If the mutual business then ceases there will be a repayment to the contributor of any surplus, but without any charge to tax so that he can in effect recover more than he has paid.[2] If for example, he made a contribution of £100 and has a marginal tax rate of 50%, he saves the payment of £50 in tax; if the business is wound up and he gets back £100 he is not subject to tax. Without special legislation this device could be used to build up tax free reserves. TA 1988, s. 491 now provides that where a body corporate is being wound up or dissolved and a non-taxable sum is paid to one who was allowed to deduct that payment in computing the profits or gains or losses of a trade, profession or vocation, the receipt is treated as a trading receipt of the trade or, if the trade has ceased, as a post-cessation receipt. In deciding whether the receipt is a trading one or post-cessation, technical discontinuances under ss. 113 and 337[3] are ignored. In either event the payment is treated as earned income so long as the income from the trade was earned. If it is a post-cessation receipt advantage may be taken of any unrealised losses or capital allowances.

This section applies only where the receipt is not otherwise taxable and where the receipt does not represent capital, a phrase which is very widely defined.[4] It does not apply to registered industrial and provident societies nor does it apply if the deduction has been allowed under Schedule E. It does however apply where the company is being wound up and the receipt is an asset of the corporation or is part of the consideration for the transfer of those assets as part of a scheme of amalgamation or reconstruction or a sum received for the transfer of a right to such asset or such reconstruction.

The section is confined to situations where the mutual business is carried on by a company.

---

[1] *Thomas v Richard Evans & Co Ltd* [1927] 1 KB 33, 11 TC 790.
[2] *Stafford Coal and Iron Co Ltd v Brogan* [1963] 3 All ER 227, 41 TC 305, HL.
[3] TA 1988, s. 491(3).
[4] TA 1988, s. 491(6).

---

6 Use of land and trade

7: 39   Income derived from the exploitation of property is property income rather than trading income.[1] So income from furnished lettings is taxable under Schedule A (if the land is in the UK) or Schedule D, Case V (if not).[2]

By concession, income from caravan sites where there is both trading and associated letting income can all be treated as trading income.[3]

All farming and market gardening in the UK is taxed under Schedule D, Case I[4] and all farming carried on by any particular person or partnership or body of persons is to be treated as one trade.[5]

The occupation of land for purposes other than farming or market gardening managed on a commercial basis and with a view to realisation of profits, is likewise within Schedule D, Case I[6] actual occupation is required; granting a licence to someone else to occupy is not enough.[7] Woodlands were subject to a separate regime under Schedule B.[8] Actual occupation is required for this rule; simply having a licence to fell and remove timber or clear the land for replanting is not enough.[9]

Profits from mines, quarries and other specified concerns including ferries and canals also fall within Case I.[10]

Simon's Taxes B3.4, B3.5; Butterworths Income Tax Service C1.34.

[1] *Webb v Conelee Properties Ltd* [1982] STC 913.

[2] *Gittos v Barclay* [1982] STC 390.

[3] Extra-statutory concession B29 (1988), **Simon's Taxes, Division H2.2.**

[4] TA 1988, s. 53(1). On the scope of market gardening, see *Bomford v Osborne* (1940) 23 TC 642 at 660, especially per Scott LJ. Originally farmers had been within Schedule B, infra, § **9: 29**, and remained there partly because of the difficulty farmers had in keeping accounts.

[5] TA 1988, s. 53(2)—hence if X has a farm A with accrued losses and unused capital allowances and buys farm B he may set those losses and allowances against the profits of B even if he later sells A; see *Bispham v Eardiston Farming Co (1919) Ltd* [1962] 2 All ER 376, 40 TC 322 noted [1962] BTR 255. This provision does not appear to apply to market gardening.

[6] TA 1988, s. 53(3). See *Sywell Aerodrome Ltd v Croft* [1942] 1 All ER 110, 24 TC 126. If the land is not managed on a commercial basis a charge may arise under Case VI, infra, § **10: 11**.

[7] *Webb v Conelee Properties Ltd* [1982] STC 913.

[8] TA 1988, s. 54; infra, § **9: 29**.

[9] TA 1988, s. 16(6).

[10] TA 1988, s. 55 and, on mines, infra, § **7: 87**.

BASIS OF ASSESSMENT

Preceding year basis

7: 40 Income tax is levied on the profits and gains of the trade, profession or vocation on a preceding year basis, that is on the profits of the year preceding the year of assessment.[1] In a normal business where an annual account takes place, tax is charged not on the profits of the business earned in the period from 6th April to 5th April next before the year of assessment commences, but on the profits earned in the business' accounting year ending between those dates. So if a business makes up its accounts on a calendar year basis, the profits for the year from 1st January to 31st December 1988 will be the profits or gains to be charged in the tax year 1989–90. This enables the precise liability for the tax year 1989–90 to be fixed before 1st January 1989, the date the tax becomes due.

Special rules apply if the account was not made up to a date within the preceding year or was for a period other than for 12 months. The Board may direct which period ending on a date within the preceding year of assessment of 12 months is to be taken.[2]

Special rules apply when a business first commences and when it ceases otherwise tax would not be paid until a business was well under way and would be payable sometime after it had ceased, a problem which obviously becomes more acute if the business goes bankrupt and which offends the doctrine of the source.

Simon's Taxes E1.201; Butterworths Income Tax Service C1.41.
[1] TA 1988, s. 60(1).
[2] TA 1988, s. 60(2)(*b*). See, on the Revenue's powers, *IRC v Helical Bar Ltd* [1972] 1 All ER 1205, 48 TC 253.

Commencement: TA 1988, ss. 61 and 62

7: 41   Where a trade, profession or vocation is started within a tax year, year 1, tax is charged for year 1 on the profits up to 5th April next,[1] for year 2 on the profits of the first 12 months of trading[2] and for year 3 on a preceding year basis but only if there is a complete 12 month accounting period ending in year 2. If there is not, the assessment for year 3 is again based (as is that of year 2) on the first 12 months' trading. It is clear from this that if the first accounting period falls into more than one year of assessment, the first 12 months' results will form the basis, in whole or in part, of the first three years' assessments; whereas if the first accounting period falls into one year of assessment only (i.e. year 1), year 3 will be based on the results of the 12 months ending on the regular accounting date in the second year of assessment.

It will be seen that there is no obligation to make the accounting periods of the business coincide with these tax basis periods. Where the periods do not correspond an apportionment is made.

The selection of the accounting period is important as this will affect the level of profits in the opening 12 months.

Thus a taxpayer may take a period in excess of 12 months, in which case an apportionment is made to discover the taxable profits of the 12 month period. This is of advantage when the trade is prosperous for 12 months but then has a period of decline. The device makes sure that the period of decline is properly reflected in the period taken as the measure of profits for more than one period.

As the profits of the first 12 months are usually the basis for years 1–3 it is obviously important to keep the taxable profits as low as possible, an objective that can be achieved by various devices, e.g. taking potential partners in as employees, thus having deductible wages instead of non-deductible shares of profits and borrowing starting capital rather than using one's own but repaying it after a year. Conversely, it is undesirable to have large receipts. In order to assist people leaving the unemployment register to start up in business the Manpower Services Commission pays an enterprise allowance of £40 a week over a year; to prevent this coming into the tax computation more than once, it is provided that payments are to be assessed under Schedule D, Case VI rather than Case I or II.[3]

Where profits are rising, it is advantageous to select a first accounting period straddling years 1 and 2, so that assessment of the higher profits in the second year is postponed.

EXAMPLE

C begins to trade on 1st July 1987. His tax adjusted profit month by month is as follows:

July 1987–December 1987	£750 each month
January 1988–October 1988	£900 each month
November 1988–April 1989	£1,000 each month

C decides to make up his accounts to 31st December. Accordingly, the tax adjusted profit for the 6 months to 31st December 1987 is (£750 × 6) = £4,500 and that for the year to 31st December 1988 is (£900 × 10) + (£1,000 × 2) = £11,000.

The assessments for years 1 to 3 are as follows:

1987–88 (year 1) £4,500 + £11,000 × $\frac{3}{12}$	=	£7,250
1988–89 (year 2) £4,500 + £11,000 × $\frac{6}{12}$	=	£10,000 (first 12 months)
1989–90 (year 3)		£11,000 (preceding year)
		£28,250

Suppose, however, that C had made up his accounts to 30th April. His first accounting period (of 10 months to 30th April 1988), therefore, would show a profit of £4,500 + (£900 × 4) = £8,100 and that for the year to 30th April 1989 would be (£900 × 6) + (£1,000 × 6) = £11,400.

The assessments for years 1 to 3 would now be—

1987–88 (year 1) £8,100 × $\frac{9}{10}$	=	£7,290
1988–89 (year 2) £8,100 + £11,400 × $\frac{2}{12}$	=	£10,000 (first 12 months)
1989–90 (year 3)		£10,000 (first 12 months)
		£27,290

Simon's Taxes E1.205–209; Butterworths Income Tax Service C1.42.

[1] TA 1988, s. 61(1). In computing these profits the inspector may direct an average figure to be taken for a period not exceeding the first 12 months of the business and the appropriate fraction obtained.

[2] TA 1988, s. 61(3).

[3] TA 1988, s. 127(2). The payment is still treated as earned income for the purposes of retirement annuity or personal pension plan reliefs and the wife's separate taxation of earned income election.

7: 42   Alternatively the taxpayer may elect (revocably) under TA 1988, s. 62 that for the second *and* third years of assessment, tax is levied on a current year basis;[1] the preceding year basis is then applied in the fourth year of assessment.[2]

EXAMPLE

A began to trade on 1st January 1987. He makes up his accounts on a calendar year basis and his profits are for 1985 £10,000, for 1986 £6,000 and for 1987 £9,000.

The pattern of assessments would be:

	TA 1988, s. 62		TA 1988, s. 60
1986–87	$\frac{1}{4}$ × 10,000	2,500	2,500
1987–88	$\frac{3}{4}$ × 10,000 = 7,500	9,000	10,000 (first 12 months)
	$\frac{1}{4}$ × 6,000 = 1,500		
1988–89	$\frac{3}{4}$ × 6,000 = 4,500	6,750	10,000 (preceding year)
	$\frac{1}{4}$ × 9,000 = 2,250		
1989–90	6,000	6,000	6,000 (preceding year)
Total assessable profits		24,250	28,500

---

[1] TA 1988, s. 62. He must elect for both the second *and* the third year or for neither and the election must be made within seven years of the end of the second year of assessment.

[2] Under TA 1988, s. 60(2)(*a*), supra.

Cessation: TA 1988, s. 63

7: 43   When a trade, profession or vocation is permanently discontinued the preceding year basis is abandoned. Tax for the year of assessment in which the discontinuance occurs is levied on the profits or gains of that year.[1] Tax will have been levied on the two preceding years of assessment on a preceding year basis,[2] so that if the taxpayer ceases to trade on 31st August 1989 and has made up his accounts on a calendar year basis, tax for the years 1987–88 and 1988–89 will have been levied on the profits of the business year 1986 and 1987. This will mean that the profits for the period from 1st January 1988 to 5th April 1989 will not be taxed or, more accurately, will not have been used as the measure of taxable profits, which might be regarded as a rough *quid pro quo* for the fact that the profits of the first years of the business were used more than once as a basis for assessment. However those able to arrange the discontinuance[3] of their business might be tempted to arrange for substantial profits to accrue in the period of immunity. There is therefore an alternative basis for taxation which will be applied at the Revenue's option if it would yield a higher aggregate of profits. This alternative takes the profits actually accruing during two years of assessment preceding that in which the discontinuance occurs, so that the profits for the period 6th April 1987 to 5th April 1989 may be substituted for the profits of 1986 and 1987 and the period of immunity will now be 1st January 1984 to 5th April 1985.

EXAMPLE

B ceases to trade on 31st August 1989. He makes his accounts up on a calendar year basis. His profits are as follows:

1986 £8,000   1987 £10,000   1988 £50,000   1989 £8,000

His assessments would be as follows

but instead are

				Total
1987–88	8,000	$\frac{3}{4} \times 10,000$	7,500	20,000
		$\frac{1}{4} \times 50,000$	12,500	
1988–89	10,000	$\frac{3}{4} \times 50,000$	37,500	40,500
		$\frac{3}{8} \times 8,000$	3,000	
1989–90 $\frac{3}{8} \times 8,000$	5,000		5,000	5,000
	23,000			65,500

Simon's Taxes E1.210–214; Butterworths Income Tax Service C1.43.
[1] TA 1988, s. 63(1)(*a*). However, note concessionary treatment where business passes on death of a trader to the surviving spouse; see extra-statutory concession A7 (1988), **Simon's Taxes, Division H2.2.**
[2] Under TA 1988, s. 60(1). Even if the business is of short duration so that TA 1988, ss. 61 or 62 have applied to those years, TA 1988, s. 63 will override those provisions.
[3] Especially in one of the artificial ways, e.g. new partner or sale to company.

Dropping out

7: 44   These rules apply only when the trade ceases, not where the trader simply ceases to be resident. This may be particularly attractive if he has an abnormally successful year for overseas profits. Thus suppose that C, who makes up his profits on a calendar year basis, made a profit of £10,000 in 1986. This will be the basis of his liability for 1988–89. If in 1988 C makes £100,000 this will be the liability for 1988–89 but if he can establish non-residence for 1989–90 he will escape UK income tax on that part of the profits attributable to trade outside the UK. The effectiveness of this device depends on the establishment of non-residence for 1989–90.[1]

---

[1] See *Reed v Clark* [1986] Ch 1, [1985] STC 323 and infra, § **32.03.**

When does trade commence?

7: 45   It is important to determine when a trade commenced, partly because of TA 1988, ss. 61 and 62 but also, subject to statutory amendment, because expenditure is only deductible if incurred after that time.[1] It is now provided that if an expense is incurred in the five years before trading the amount is treated as a loss incurred in the year of commencement.[2]

Preparing to commence a trade is not the same as commencing a trade. In *Birmingham and District Cattle By-Products Co Ltd v IRC*[3] the appellant company was incorporated on 20th June 1913; its directors then arranged for the installation of plant and machinery and entered into agreements for the purchase of its raw materials and the sale of its products; the raw materials were received on 6th October. The company's trade began on 6th October when they began to take the raw materials and to turn out their product. However in *Cannop Coal Co Ltd v IRC*[4] where the trade was to be the mining of coal by sinking pits in the Forest of Dean the company had since 1909 extracted a certain amount of coal from a drift nearby for use in its machines and, finding it had extracted more than it needed, sold the excess to the public, the company was held to have commenced trading when it sold the excess coal to the public and not when in 1912 coal began to emerge from the pits. That the coal company was engaged in a trade in those three years seems beyond argument and it was too fine a point to say that the trade was different from the mining of coal from the pits. Thus the mere formation of an intention to commence trading is not the moment of commencement, nor is the incurring of capital expenditure for the purpose of preparing to trade.

A difficult question concerns the use of small-scale pilot projects involving resale to the public to decide precisely what product to make. It was important in *Cannop Coal Co Ltd v IRC* that the sales were substantial[5] and it may therefore be that pilot projects are not trading.

Simon's Taxes B3.248; Butterworths Income Tax Service C1.51.
  [1] *City of London Contract Corpn Ltd v Styles* (1887) 2 TC 239.
  [2] TA 1988, s. 401 as amended, for commencements after 31 March 1989 by FA 1989, s. 114, on loss relief, see supra, § **5: 01.**
  [3] (1919) 12 TC 92 (an excess profits duty case).
  [4] (1918) 12 TC 31 (another excess profits duty case). In both instances the Revenue won.
  [5] In one year 68% of the coal was resold and in another 84%.

Commencement—new trade or development of existing one

7: 46   There is no rule of law that a person, whether or not a company, cannot carry on more than one business and it is immaterial that there is one consolidated balance sheet. The question is one of fact and degree. As Rowlatt J put it in a case where the two activities had both been bought from another company, "the real question is, was there any inter-connection, any interlacing, any interdependence, any unity at all embracing those two businesses".[1] So if a trader commences a new trade alongside his established one, the two trades are treated separately,[2] even for purposes of loss relief, capital allowances and stock relief; the sources are distinct. It is a question of fact whether a particular development is an expansion of an existing trade[3] or the commencement of a new one; it may happen that the amalgamation of two trades is to be treated as the cessation of both and the commencement of one new trade.[4]

A modern example is *Seaman v Tucketts Ltd*.[5] In 1956 control of the company was acquired by a new group. The company carried on the trade of manufacture and sale of confectionery; this included the purchase and resale of such goods from other manufacturers, which ended early in 1958. In September 1958 the two retail shops were closed and in November 1958 manufacture ceased. By April 1959 the existing stocks and the factory had been sold. The company which had previously bought sugar and cellophane for its own business now bought these for resale to the new parent company at cost plus 10%. Two years later it began to supply confectionery again. Reversing the Commissioners, Pennycuick J held that the only true and reasonable conclusion was that, at the end of 1958 when the manufacture had ceased, a new trade of sugar merchants, including the buying and selling of cellophane paper, had been commenced and the case was remitted to the Commissioners to determine whether the confectionery trade had been discontinued or had been merely quiescent.

The question is one of fact and degree. *Seaman v Tucketts Ltd* shows that not only may there be a termination of one trade and the commencement of another but there may also be a contraction of one trade and the commencement of another, even though that other deals with a commodity employed in the original trade. There is also authority that a substantial change in management policy can lead to a discontinuance and a new commencement.[6] However a barrister does not, on taking silk, start a new profession.[7]

Simon's Taxes E1.212; Butterworths Income Tax Service C1.52.
  [1] *Scales v George Thompson & Co Ltd* (1927) 13 TC 83 at 89.
  [2] *Fullwood Foundry Ltd v IRC* (1924) 9 TC 101.
  [3] *Howden Boiler and Armaments Co Ltd v Stewart* (1924) 9 TC 205 and *Cannon Industries Ltd v Edwards* (1965) 42 TC 151.
  [4] *George Humphries & Co v Cook* (1934) 19 TC 121.
  [5] (1963) 41 TC 422.
  [6] See Rowlatt J in *Kirk and Randall Ltd v Dunn* (1924) 8 TC 663 at 670.
  [7] *Seldon v Croom-Johnson* [1932] 1 KB 759, 16 TC 740.

Succession

7: 47   Problems of commencement also arise where a trade which has been carried on by one person is transferred to another; such a transfer is called a succession and must be distinguished from the mere purchase of the assets used in the trade. In the case of such a transfer there is a discontinuance by the old trader and a commencement by the new one, so that the closing years of the old trader fall within TA 1988, s. 63.

Simon's Taxes B3.3; Butterworths Income Tax Service C1.53.

Effects on new trader

7: 48   The opening years of the new trader fall within TA 1988, ss. 61 and 62[1] even though he is going to absorb the acquired trade into his existing one and even though it is in truth one business.[2] However, once TA 1988, ss. 61 and 62 are spent, the figures for the trade acquired will form part of the general profit of the trade into which it has merged.

If the new trade is not absorbed into the old but is a distinct entity then not only will the commencement provisions apply but there will be no merging once those provisions are spent.

[1] TA 1988, s. 113; infra, § **7: 59**.
[2] *Bell v National Provincial Bank* [1904] 1 KB 149, 5 TC 1; *Briton Ferry Steel Co Ltd v Barry* [1939] 4 All ER 541, 23 TC 414; if it is a separate trade it must be treated separately, *Scales v George Thomson & Co Ltd* (1927) 13 TC 83.

Effects on old trader

7: 49   Where a succession to a trade occurs, neither losses nor unused capital allowances incurred by the first trader can be used by the successor.[1]

One other point concerns the former trader. Generally, expenditure incurred shortly before a discontinuance may not be for the purposes of the continuing trade and so may not be deductible.[2] However expenditure made with a view to the trade after transfer may be incurred for the purposes of the trade and not for the purposes of the present trader and so deductible by the first trader despite the succession.[3] The reason for this departure from the general rule is that the deemed discontinuance and commencement is a statutory innovation; the older principle has only been abrogated to bring into operation ss. 61 to 63.

[1] E.g. *Rolls-Royce Motors Ltd v Bamford* [1976] STC 162.
[2] *Godden v Wilson's Stores (Holdings) Ltd* (1962) 40 TC 161, CA distinguished in *O'Keeffe v Southport Printers Ltd* [1984] STC 443.
[3] Per Lord Clyde in *IRC v Patrick Thomson Ltd* (1956) 37 TC 145 at 157.

Rules

7: 50   (1) A succession to a trade must be distinguished from the purchase of the assets of a trade. Thus where a company which had a tramp shipping business bought a ship second hand from another trader there was no succession to that person's trade, but only the purchase of a ship.[1] These are however questions of fact and it was important in that case that the purchaser acquired no list of customers along with the ship, that the ship had no special route along which and only along which she used to ply her trade and that no goodwill came with the ship.

Since the origin of the concept of succession lay in the application of the rule that profits be measured by the average of three previous years business, there had to be a "very close identity" between the business in the former proprietorship and the business in the new proprietorship.[2] A very close identity is however not the same as a complete identity. Thus a successor to a business with say fifty shops may choose to shut up some of them, make alterations in the goods that he sells, change his supplier or may cut out a particular class of customer or a particular area.[3] The question whether such changes prevent there being a succession to the business is one of fact.

There may be a succession even though there is no purchase of the entire assets.[4] In one case a circular was distributed to the former trader's customers that the new owners had acquired the "trading connection" of the former traders. The Commissioners held that there was no succession; the courts felt unable to reverse that conclusion.[4] Conversely in another case where a circular to the public described the new firm as successors, but they took over no books, no lists of customers and none of the staff except a few workpeople, they were held to be successors by the Commissioners and the courts again declined to intervene.[5]

---

[1] *Watson Bros v Lothian* (1902) 4 TC 441. Compare *Bell v National Provincial Bank of England* [1904] 1 KB 149, 5 TC 1.

[2] Per Rowlatt J in *Reynolds, Sons & Co Ltd v Ogston* (1930) 15 TC 501 at 524, approved by Lord Hanworth MR at 527.

[3] Per Sir Wilfrid Greene MR in *Laycock v Freeman, Hardy and Willis Ltd* (1938) 22 TC 288 at 297.

[4] *Reynolds, Sons & Co Ltd v Ogston* (1930) 15 TC at 524.

[5] *Thomson and Balfour v Le Page* (1923) 8 TC 541.

7:51   (2) There can be no succession to a part of a trade. However as Rowlatt J said, "I do not think that it means that if what is succeeded to is not the same extent of trade or even does not include a particular line of customers, it necessarily follows that there cannot be a successor to a trade".[1]

---

[1] *James Shipstone & Son Ltd v Morris* (1929) 14 TC 413 at 421; and see *Stockham v Wallasey UDC* (1906) 95 LT 834.

7:52   (3) There is no succession through the accidental acquisition by a trader who continues in business, of custom left by another who goes out of business. For there to be a succession there must be a transfer by one trader to another of the right to that benefit which arises from connection and reputation.[1] Thus if a trader goes out of business and his former rival captures his customers there is no succession; however if there were a transfer of the business and its goodwill to the rival, there would be.

---

[1] *Thomson and Balfour v Le Page* (1923) 8 TC 541 at 548.

7:53   (4) There is no succession if the trade has ceased before being acquired by its new owner, nor if the new owner closes it down immediately he acquires it. Thus if a business has gone bankrupt and remained in the hands of the trustee in bankruptcy for twelve months before the assets were sold, it is likely that such a sale would be treated as a sale of assets rather than of the business.[1] Indeed there is authority that where a business has been making heavy losses and practically has to sell to avoid shutting down, it is likely that there is no succession.[2] However, where a business suffered extensive fire damage and ceased to trade with the public but kept together its employees and various pieces of equipment, a delay of seventeen months between the fire and the acquisition of the business by a new owner did not prevent there being a succession.[3]

The question for the Commissioners is "whether it is true and fair to say that the business in respect of which the successor is said to be making profits is the business to which he succeeded". In *Laycock v Freeman, Hardy and Willis Ltd*[4] the respondent company bought shoes from wholesalers and resold them to the public. Some 20% to 30% of its supplies came from two subsidiary companies which it controlled. In 1935 the subsidiary companies went into voluntary liquidation and the liquidator assigned all the assets and goodwill to the respondent company which also took over all the staff. The respondent company took all the products of the factories previously owned by the subsidiary companies and sold them in their shops. It was held that there was no succession. The business of the subsidiary companies was that of wholesale manufacturing concerns; that business had ceased; manufacturing was still carried on but the business of wholesale manufacturing was not.

To be distinguished from *Laycock v Freeman, Hardy and Willis* is *Briton Ferry Steel Co Ltd v Barry*[5] where the appellant company produced steel bars which were then supplied to six wholly owned subsidiary companies, which in turn converted the bars into blackplate and tinplate. Sales were handled by another wholly owned subsidiary. In 1934 the six subsidiary companies were wound up and the conversion of the bars into blackplate and tinplate was carried on by the appellant company using the plant and workforce of the former companies. The Commissioners held that there was a succession to the trades carried on by the subsidiaries. The fact that the company through its shares already controlled them was irrelevant, as was the fact that another subsidiary company controlled their sales.[6] The Court of Appeal refused to interfere with that decision. *Laycock v Freeman, Hardy and Willis* was distinguished. In that case the business of the subsidiaries, that of making profits by wholesale sales, had ceased, and one of retail manufacturing begun. In the present case the business of the subsidiary companies, that of making profits by the conversion of steel bars into blackplate and tinplate and resale still existed, but was being carried on by someone else,[7] and the retail side was handled by a separate legal entity. The fact that someone had previously supplied the steel bars was irrelevant.

These cases produce one odd result. If there is a manufacturing concern with five distinct stages in it, each stage carried out by a separate company, it would appear that if one company takes over its neighbour, there will be a succession if the acquiring company is at an earlier stage in the process but not if it is at a later stage.

A further problem concerns the calculation of the profit of the trade acquired. In *Laycock v Freeman, Hardy and Willis* the Court of Appeal held that it was "wholly illegitimate" to invent a notional sale from the wholesale stage of the enterprise to the retail stage at a price which would yield a notional "wholesale profit".[8] But in *Briton Ferry Steel Co Ltd v Barry* the same Court, having again rejected a notional sale, directed that the transfer of the steel bars from the one artificial side of the trade to the other should be treated as carried out at the actual cost of production. This ensures that the profit from the whole operation would be attributable to the newly acquired sector of the trade.[9] One cannot help feeling that the court was being a little ingenuous.

Simon's Taxes B3.313; Butterworths Income Tax Service C1.53.
  [1] Per Greer LJ in *Reynolds, Sons & Co Ltd v Ogston* (1930) 15 TC 501 at 528.
  [2] Per Rowlatt J in *Wilson and Barlow v Chibbett* (1929) 14 TC 407 at 413.
  [3] *Wild v Madam Tussauds (1926) Ltd* (1932) 17 TC 127.
  [4] Per Sir Wilfrid Greene MR in *Laycock v Freeman, Hardy and Willis Ltd* [1938] 4 All ER 609 at 614, 22 TC 288 at 298.
  [5] [1939] 4 All ER 541, 23 TC 414, applied *IRC v Spirax Manufacturing Co Ltd* (1946) 29 TC 187.
  [6] Per Macnaghten J [1938] 4 All ER 429 at 434–5, 23 TC 414 at 431–2.
  [7] Per Sir Wilfrid Greene MR at 479, 547 and 431 of the cases cited in n. 20, supra.
  [8] Per Sir Wilfrid Greene MR [1938] 4 All ER 609 at 616, 22 TC 288 at 300.
  [9] Per Sir Wilfrid Greene MR [1939] 4 All ER 541 at 550, 23 TC 414 at 434.

Discontinuance

7: 54   There is a discontinuance if the trader ceases to carry on his trade; this will also occur if he ceases to trade in the way in which he had previously traded.[1] It is a question of fact whether the particular change is the ceasing of one trade and the commencement of another or is simply a normal development of his previous trade.

A trade does not cease if it is merely in abeyance. Thus a mere interruption in production does not cause a discontinuance[2] nor does a disposal of assets[3] nor even the appointment of a receiver.[4] Business is not confined to being busy and long periods of inactivity may occur.[5] It is however a question of fact whether a particular trade has lapsed into a period of quiescence or has ceased. A trade may be treated as permanently discontinued notwithstanding that the former trade later commences a new trade which is in all respects identical with the previous ceased trade.

Simon's Taxes E1.212; Butterworths Income Tax Service C1.54.
  [1] Supra, § 7: 46. For a deemed discontinuance to assist a person who reduces his business in order to qualify for a retirement pension under the social security system, see extra-statutory concession A20 (1988), see Simon's Taxes, Division H2.2.
  [2] *Merchiston Steamship Co Ltd v Turner* [1910] 2 KB 923, 5 TC 520.
  [3] *Aviation and Shipping Co Ltd v Murray* [1961] 2 All ER 805, 39 TC 595; see also *Watts v Hart* [1984] STC 548.
  [4] *Wadsworth Morton Ltd v Jenkinson* [1966] 3 All ER 702.
  [5] *South Behar Rly Co Ltd v IRC* [1925] AC 476, 12 TC 657; cf. *Morning Post Ltd v George* (1941) 23 TC 514.

7: 55   In *Kirk and Randall Ltd v Dunn*[1] the new owners of a trading company obtained no new contracts and tried to sell the premises; they then had their works and plant requisitioned during the First World War. However the Managing Director tried to obtain contracts overseas. Rowlatt J, reversing the Commissioners, held that the company was still trading as there was evidence of business activity resulting in expenditure and loss.

However in *J. G. Ingram & Son Ltd v Callaghan*[2] where the period was much shorter the Court of Appeal upheld the Commissioners' finding that there was not just unprofitability but inactivity and so a discontinuance. In this case the company had by May 1961 ceased to produce rubber goods, had sold off its stock and dismissed its staff, the plan being to switch to plastics. From September 1961 to June 1962 products were manufactured by another subsidiary of the owner and sold over the company's name. In this way the goodwill was kept alive but the operations of the company were confined to little more than bookkeeping and perhaps debt collecting; the trade was not kept alive between those dates. A similar conclusion was reached in *Rolls Royce Motors Ltd v Bamford*[3] where there was a discontinuance even though the company was actually reverting to its former narrow trade. This may be due to the fact that the revertor was due to a sudden crisis which the company solved by disposing of many of its activities.

---

[1] (1924) 8 TC 663. See also *Robroyston Brickworks Ltd v IRC* (1976) 51 TC 230.

[2] [1969] 1 All ER 433, 45 TC 151, CA. The same conclusion was reached in *Tryka Ltd v Newall* (1963) 41 TC 146, Ch. D, noted [1964] BTR 286, and *Goff v Osborne & Co (Sheffield) Ltd* (1953) 34 TC 441.

[3] (1976) 51 TC 319.

Effects

7: 56   When a trade, profession or vocation is permanently discontinued, the basis of assessment is determined by TA 1988, s. 63.[1] However there are special rules concerning relief for losses and capital allowances which may, contrary to the usual rule, be carried back on discontinuance.[2] Insofar as these losses or capital allowances exceed the income of the period over which they are taken back they are lost save for post-cessation receipts and cannot be used by anyone else, even a successor to the trade. Another rule directs the valuation of trading stock. By concession the discontinuance provisions in TA 1988, s. 63 are not applied on the death of a sole trader whose business passes to his surviving spouse;[3] the other discontinuance rules are applied.

Certain sums paid just before discontinuance may be non-deductible because not spent in order to keep the business in being;[4] a statutory exception is made for certain redundancy payments.[5]

---

[1] Supra, § 7: 43.

[2] Infra, § 5: 10.

[3] Extra-statutory concession A7 (1988), **Simon's Taxes, Division H2.2.** However s. 63 will be applied if this is claimed.

[4] Infra, § 7: 49.

[5] TA 1988, s. 90.

PARTNERSHIPS

7: 57   It is a question of fact whether a particular person is a partner in an enterprise or merely a senior employee. In so far as this involves a question of construing a document, it will raise questions of law. Although the receipt by a person of a share of the profits is prima facie evidence that he is a partner further evidence may be needed to establish exactly when the partnership begins to trade.[1] In *Fenston v Johnstone*[2] the appellant wished to buy some land but lacked finance. He therefore agreed with another person to share the profits and losses and to assist in the development of the land. The document said that there was no partnership and described the appellant's share of the profits as a fee for introducing the other person to the vendor. It was held that there was a partnership. On the other hand in *Pratt v Strick*[3] there was held to be no partnership where a doctor sold his practice to another but agreed as part of the sale to stay in his house with the purchaser for some three months introducing the purchaser to the patients and sharing receipts and expenses over that period. In both these cases the Commissioners were reversed.

Where there is a partnership, income tax is assessed on the profits of the trade or profession in the name of the partnership[4] although in England and Wales the partnership is not a legal entity.[5] Each partner thus becomes jointly liable for income tax on the whole of the profits.[6]

Simon's Taxes E5.301–306; Butterworths Income Tax Service C8.

[1] *Saywell v Pope* [1979] STC 824.

[2] (1940) 23 TC 29.

[3] (1932) 17 TC 459; see also *Bulloch v IRC* [1976] STC 514.

[4] TA 1988, s. 111; see also *Reed v Young* [1986] STC 285.

[5] For a consequence see *MacKinlay v Arthur Young McClelland Moores & Co* [1988] STC 116, CA, reversing [1986] STC 491, infra § **7: 93**. Contrast this position in Scotland when it is a legal person.

[6] *Stevens v Britten* [1954] 3 All ER 385.

Mixed partnership[1]

7: 58   Where a partnership includes a company, the profits of the trade are computed as if the partnership were a company and the member company's shares ascertained and subjected to corporation tax. Income tax is chargeable on the share of individual partners.[2] There is no transfer of a trade on a change of a corporate partner.

The company's share is ascertained by reference to its share of the profits in the accounting period, whereas other partners are taxed on the preceding year basis. Where there is a mixed partnership which had a bumper year, the profit ratios might be changed so that when the individuals came to be assessed on their share of the profits for that bumper year, their shares—and so their tax liability—were reduced. The Revenue are now given the power to recover the lost tax by directing that the total profits remaining after deducting the company's share is attributed to the individual partner, or if there is more than one individual, apportioned among them according to their interests; in this way any change in the profit-sharing ratios is ignored.[3]

Simon's Taxes D4.8; Butterworths Income Tax Service C8.121.
  [1] TA 1988, s. 114.
  [2] TA 1988, s. 114(3). The section fails to deal with a trust or estate which is a partner.
  [3] TA 1988, s. 115(2).

Partnerships and partnership changes[1]

7: 59 When a trade is carried on in partnership the profits will be allocated to each partner by reference to the profit sharing ratio prevailing in that year of assessment and not that applying to the accounts forming the basis of assessment.[2]

Simon's Taxes E5.311; Butterworths Income Tax Service C8.31.
  [1] TA 1988, s. 113.
  [2] *Lewis v IRC* [1933] 2 KB 557, 18 TC 174; TA 1988, s. 277.

7: 60 There is a discontinuance if the trader ceases to trade even though the trade is carried on by someone else. Since a partnership is not a legal entity, it follows that a change of partners leads to a discontinuance, and a commencement of the same trade but by different people. This is now statutory and TA 1988, s. 113 imposes a discontinuance whenever there is a change in the persons engaged in carrying on a trade. So the retirement, replacement or addition of a partner will each cause a discontinuance with the consequences that TA 1988, s. 63 operates.

Two statutory exceptions are made;[1] first, that a change in trustees or personal representatives[2] does not cause a discontinuance nor, secondly, does the entry or withdrawal of a corporate partner.[3]

Even if there is a discontinuance under TA 1988, s. 113, a continuing partner may carry forward a share of any losses and unused capital allowances arising before the notional discontinuance to set against his share of profits arising after the change.[4]

However, it is possible to elect that the trade should be regarded as continuing provided that at least one person was engaged in the trade both before and after the change[5] and provided that those engaged in the trade both before and after the change all so elect. The unanimity rule is adhered to when a partner has died, his personal representatives being authorised to elect on his behalf,[6] but relaxed in that where a company is one of the partners the consents need be only those of the individuals who are partners.[7] The election must be made within two years of the change.[8] An election once made may however be later withdrawn. If there is no unanimity the discontinuance rule will apply.

Simon's Taxes E5.312; Butterworths Income Tax Service C8.34, 41.
  [1] See also concessionary relief when partners are spouses; extra-statutory concession A7 (1988), **Simon's Taxes, Division H2.2**.
  [2] TA 1988, s. 113(7).
  [3] TA 1988, s. 114(3)(*b*).
  [4] TA 1988, s. 385(5), supra, § **5: 07**.
  [5] TA 1988, s. 113 cannot apply where A and B divide a trade between them as there can be no succession to part of a trade.
  [6] TA 1988, s. 113(6) contrary to Tucker Report 1951, Cmd. 8189 § 72(*b*). Can the deceased

anticipate the problem by giving consent in his will—and can this bind the personal representatives?

⁷ TA 1988, s. 114(3)(*b*).
⁸ For Revenue practice on out-of-time applications see [1985] STI, p. 735.

7: 61   Where there is an election to continue, the income of the year in which the change occurs is allocated between the partners as if there had been no change and apportioned as may be just.¹

If there is an election to continue and, before the end of the second year of assessment following that in which the change occurred, there is a permanent discontinuance, the rules for assessment on discontinuance contained in TA 1988, s. 63 may reach back to a period before the first change took place and in respect of which the election was made. Where this is done and the switch to current year assessment is made, one who retired at the first change may have his assessment altered.²

---

¹ TA 1988, s. 113(3)(*a*).
² TA 1988, s. 113(3)(*b*); *Osler v Hall & Co* [1933] 1 KB 720, 17 TC 68.

7: 62   If no election to continue is made, the position has been changed by FA 1985 which applies where there is a change of partnership after 19th March 1985. The position with regard to the closing years of the old partnership is as it was: TA 1988, s. 63 applies. However, with regard to the opening years of the new partnership the change from current year basis to preceding year basis is deferred for a period of two years. Thus, the year of commencement and each of the next *three* years of assessment will be charged on a current year basis.¹ The two years after that are charged on a preceding year basis although the partnership may elect to defer the charge for a further two year period.² This new rule *only* applies where no continuance election is made and one could have been made; so it does not apply where A and B sell their partnership to C and D. It is unclear whether this rule applies where a business carried on by A and B is thereafter carried on by just one of them.³

EXAMPLE

A and B trade in partnership sharing profits equally until A retires on 31st December 1985. B is joined by C on 1st January 1986 and profits are shared between them 3:1. Accounts are made up to 31st December in each year. If there were a continuance election, the allocations of the (tax adjusted) partnership profits would be as follows.

Calendar year	Adjusted profits £	A £	B £	C £
1982	25,000	12,500	12,500	
1983	28,000	14,000	14,000	
1984	30,000	15,000	15,000	
1985	27,000	13,500	13,500	
1986	26,000		19,500	6,500
1987	28,000		21,000	7,000
1988	32,000		24,000	8,000
1989	33,000		24,750	8,250
1990	40,000		30,000	10,000
1991	42,000		31,500	10,500
	311,000	55,000	205,750	50,250

If there were a continuance election, the assessments on the partners would be as follows—

Year of assessment	Basis year	Total profits £	A £	B £	C £
(A and B)					
1983–84	1982	25,000	12,500	12,500	
1984–85	1983	28,000	14,000	14,000	
1985–86	1984	22,500	11,250	11,250	
(B and C)					
1985–86	1984	7,500		5,625	1,875
1986–87	1985	27,000		20,250	6,750
1987–88	1986	26,000		19,500	6,500
1988–89	1987	28,000		21,000	7,000
1989–90	1988	32,000		24,000	8,000
1990–91	1989	33,000		24,750	8,250
1991–92	1990	40,000		30,000	10,000
1992–93	1991	42,000		31,500	10,500
		311,000	37,750	214,375	58,875

The total profits of the business for 1984 are required to be apportioned between the old and new partnerships as may be just (TA 1988, s. 113(3)(*a*). In this example a straightforward time basis has been adopted, the profits being attributed in the proportion 9:3 because the change occurred nine months into 1985–86.

If a continuance election was not made, the trade would be treated as having been permanently discontinued at 31st December 1985 and a new trade commenced on 1st January 1986. The assessments (before capital allowances) would have been as follows.

Year of assessment	Assessable profits £	A £	B £	C £
(A and B)				
1983–84* $\frac{9}{12} \times £28,000 + \frac{3}{12} \times £30,000$	28,500	14,250	14,250	
1984–85* $\frac{9}{12} \times £30,000 + \frac{3}{12} \times £27,000$	29,250	14,625	14,625	
1985–86 $\frac{9}{12} \times £27,000$	20,250	10,125	10,125	
(B and C)				
1985–86 $\frac{3}{12} \times £26,000$	6,500		4,875	1,625
1986–87 $\frac{9}{12} \times £26,000 + \frac{3}{12} \times £28,000$	26,500		19,875	6,625
1987–88 $\frac{9}{12} \times £28,000 + \frac{3}{12} \times £32,000$	29,000		21,750	7,250
1988–89 $\frac{9}{12} \times £32,000 + \frac{3}{12} \times £33,000$	32,250		24,187	8,063
Carry forward	172,250	39,000	109,687	23,563
Brought forward	172,250	39,000	109,687	23,563
1989–90*	32,000		24,000	8,000
1990–91*	33,000		24,750	8,250
1991–92	40,000		30,000	10,000
1992–93	42,000		31,500	10,500
	319,250	39,000	219,937	60,313

* The Revenue would elect to revise the assessments for 1983–84 and 1984–85 to actual profits (TA 1988, s. 63(1)). B and C would *not* elect to be taxed on actual profits for 1989–90 and 1990–91.

Where there is a discontinuance stock in trade[4] and work in progress[5] must be valued at market value and not the usual figure of the lower of cost and market value. Terminal losses must be computed and capital allowances, like these losses, spread back over the previous years.[6] Should these allowances and losses result in an excess of deductions over profits for those years the retiring partner will lose the benefit of them but it is expressly provided that the continuing partners may receive the benefit of them in the later years.[7] The unrelieved capital allowances are apportioned among the partners according to their profit sharing ratio as it stood immediately before the TA 1988, s. 113 discontinuance.[8]

The question whether or not to elect for continuance is thus one which may require careful calculation. Apart from such matters as stock in trade, work in progress, loss relief and excess capital allowances, a key matter is the effect of the change in profit sharing ratio that will result from the retirement of a partner without his being replaced. The complexities of this situation necessarily result from the preceding year basis of assessment.

Simon's Taxes E5.312; Butterworth's Income Tax Service C8.44.

[1] TA 1988, s. 61(4).

[2] TA 1988, s. 62(4) (FA 1985, s. 47(4)).

[3] Before FA 1988, it was clear that s. 61(4) did not apply but the change to the wording of s, 61(4) by FA 1988, Sch. 13, para. 2 raises a doubt.

[4] TA 1988, s. 102(2).

[5] TA 1988, s. 102(2).

[6] Supra, § **5: 10**.

[7] TA 1988, s. 380(3), s.385(6)(*a*) and s. 386(4); *Batty v Baron Schröder* [1939] 3 All ER 299, 23 TC 1.

[8] TA 1988, s. 389(4).

THE MEASURE OF INCOME

7: 63   TA 1988, s. 18 charges tax on the annual profits or gains arising or accruing from the trade, profession or vocation, while TA 1988, s. 60 adds unhelpfully that the measure is "the full amount of such profits or gains". In general the profits or gains of a period are ascertained by first computing the trading receipts of that period and then deducting the revenue expenditure. The balance is the profit (or loss) of the trade for that period. It is easier to compute the total profit or loss of a trade from its commencement to its discontinuance than it is to compute that figure for a particular artificial accounting period such as a year and so special rules apply to determine the value of trading stock and work in progress at the end of one period and the beginning of the next. All these steps however are taken subject to the provisions of the taxing acts.

Simon's Taxes B3.9; Butterworths Income Tax Service C1.61.

Accountancy principles

7: 64   One of the greatest problems in the ascertainment of the full amount of the profits or gains of the trade is the role of accountancy practice. It is clear that the aim of the accountant is in some senses the same as that of the Revenue—both are seeking to measure the income of a precise—and so an artificial—period.[1] It is also clear that the mere fact that an accountant or his employer wishes to charge a particular expense to capital or revenue will not be sufficient to determine its status at law.[2] While the ordinary principles of commercial accounting must, as far as is practicable, be observed, income tax law must not be violated.[3]

There are two distinct approaches to the relationship between questions of law and principles of accountancy. One asserts that the court should first look to see what accountancy says and then see whether any rule of law contradicts it;[4] the other that the court should first determine the question as a matter of law and then see whether accountancy gives a different answer and then determine which should prevail.[5] It will be appreciated that the former gives much greater weight to accountancy practice than the latter.

Tax law and accountancy practice conflict in a number of ways. First it is an elementary accountancy principle that capital expenditure on a depreciating asset must be written off over the lifetime of the asset. However the tax law allows the deduction of capital expenditure only if that expenditure falls within the capital allowances system (infra, chap. 8). Again prudent accountancy practice writes off abortive expenditure as a revenue expense but for tax law abortive capital expenditure is not deductible.[6] Again certain items of expenditure will be deducted by the accountants in ascertaining the income for the year but disallowed by some express provision such as business entertainment expenses[7] or Class 2 or on half of Class 4 National Insurance contributions.[8] However the courts have not confined their decisions on points of accountancy to those situations where an express statutory provision is in point. The courts have also ruled on such questions as the correct method of assessing work in progress,[9] and the correct method of valuing stock in trade,[10] matters where there is no express provision and in the latter case the courts have ruled that there is such a thing as the correct method even though accountancy knows of many methods. They have also held that the question whether an expenditure is a capital or revenue account is one of law.[11] By treating these issues as questions of law the courts have enabled themselves to keep complete residual control.

Simons's Taxes B3.906; Butterworths Income Tax Service C1.61.

[1] See Walton J in *Willingale v International Commercial Bank Ltd* [1976] STC 188 at 194–5.

[2] *Associated Portland Cement Manufacturers Ltd v Kerr* [1946] 1 All ER 68, 27 TC 103. See also *Heather v P.E. Consulting Group* [1973] 1 All ER 8, 48 TC 320.

[3] Viscount Simonds in *Ostime v Duple Motor Bodies Ltd* [1961] 2 All ER 167 at 169, 39 TC 537 at 566.

[4] E.g. Salmon J in *Odeon Associated Theatres Ltd v Jones* [1972] 1 All ER 681 at 689, 48 TC 257 at 283A and Lord Haldane in *Sun Insurance Office Ltd v Clark* [1912] AC 443 at 455, 6 TC 59 at 78; Lord Clyde in *Lothian Chemical Co Ltd v Rogers* (1926) 11 TC 508 at 520; also Tucker Report 1951, Cmd. 8189 § 135.

[5] Brightman J in *ECC Quarries Ltd v Watkis* [1975] STC 578 at 590, [1975] 3 All ER 843 at 855.

[6] Infra, § **7: 104**.

[7] TA 1988, s. 577, infra, § **7: 126**.

[8] TA 1988, s. 617(5). The significant expenses which are not deductible whether as various expenses or capital allowances are the cost of constructing commercial buildings, certain exchange losses and the costs of raising capital: TA 1988, s. 74 (*f*) and (*g*). See [1976] STI, p. 55.

[9] *Ostime v Duple Motor Bodies Ltd*.

[10] E.g. the prohibition of LIFO, infra, § **7: 160**.

[11] *Beauchamp v F W Woolworth plc* [1989] STC 510; here the tax treatment coincided with the accountancy treatment.

7: 65   A decision in which the courts made a ruling in an area where there was no one single recognised practice is *Willingale v International Commercial Bank Ltd.*[1] The taxpayer bank held a number of bills of exchange issued by borrowers all over the world and maturing over periods from one to ten years. The issue was whether the bank should bring the proceeds of such bills into the account only when the bills matured (or were disposed of) or whether, following the practice applied to the clearing banks, it should bring in a part of the expected profit each year. The House, upholding all the lower tribunals, held that although the bank had made up its accounts on the practice stated it was entitled to insist that for tax purposes the other basis should be taken as this would be in conformity with a fundamental principle that profits should not be taxed until ascertained. The division was by a bare majority and has been heavily criticised.

Simon's Taxes B3.1112; Butterworths Income Tax Service C1.61.

[1] [1978] STC 75, [1978] 1 All ER 754; see also Vinelott J in *Pattison v Marine Midland Ltd* [1981] STC 540.

TRADING RECEIPTS

(1) Trading stock

7: 66 A payment arising from the disposal of trading stock in the normal course of business is normally a trading receipt. Trading stock is not defined[1] but means (a) raw materials, (b) finished products and (c) work in progress. It does not extend to plant nor to mere utensils as distinct from raw materials nor to a source of trading stock.[2] In *Willingale v International Commercial Bank Ltd* the bills of exchange were not trading stock. It follows that the question whether an item is trading stock must depend on the nature of the trade. In *Abbott v Albion Greyhounds (Salford) Ltd*[3] a greyhound racing company argued that the dogs used in their races were trading stock.[4] This was rejected by Wrottesly J on the ground that the saleable value of the kennel was at no time a commercial picture of the company's success or failure. Had the company bought and sold dogs by way of trade the answer would have been quite different.

Simon's Taxes B3.10; Butterworths Income Tax Service C1.71.

[1] But for TA 1988, s. 100, see subs. (4); see also § 7: 72.

[2] Infra, § 7: 120.

[3] [1945] 1 All ER 308, 26 TC 390; see also *General Motors Acceptance Corpn v IRC* [1985] STC 408.

[4] And so should be valued at the end of the year; infra, § 7: 158.

Farm animals

7: 67 Special rules apply down on the farm. Generally animals kept by a farmer for the purpose of his farming are to be treated as trading stock.[1] This applies to related trades like animal breeding, dealing in cattle or milk and so on.[2] Certain animals are excluded from this treatment, namely animals kept wholly or mainly for public exhibition or for racing or for other competitive purposes,[3] and animals kept wholly or mainly for the work they do in connection with farming,[4] such as sheep dogs.

Where animals which would under this rule be treated as trading stock form part of a production herd, the farmer may instead elect[5] that the herd be treated as a capital asset. As tangible movable wasting assets such animals are exempt from CGT.[6] The rules for income tax flowing from an election for herd basis were thus summarised by the Inland Revenue:[7]

(A) The initial cost of the herd and the cost of additions

Neither the initial cost of the herd nor the cost of any animals which are added to the herd to increase its numbers (as distinct from animals which replace those which die or are taken out of the herd) will be deducted as an expense in calculating profits or losses. . . .

(B) Replacement of animals in the herd

When an animal is replaced in the herd (for example, when it dies or is culled), the sale price of the old animal, or of its carcass, will be included and the cost of the new animal will be deducted in arriving at the profit or loss, but if the new animal is of better quality than the old one, the extra cost of the new animal due to the element of improvement will not be deducted. If the new animal is home-bred, the cost of rearing it will already have been deducted as part of the expense of labour, feeding stuffs, etc., and no further deduction will be necessary. . . .

(C) Replacement of the whole herd (see also sub-para (D) below)

If a farmer sells a herd and buys another herd of the same kind, sub-paragraph (B) above will apply to the number of animals equal to the number in the smaller of the two herds, i.e., the sale price of that number of animals will be included as a receipt and the cost of that number of animals deducted as an expense (except that the extra cost of any new animals of better quality will not be deducted). If the new herd is larger than the old herd, the cost of the additional animals will not be deductible as an expense. If the new herd is smaller than the old herd, the profit or loss arising from the sale of the animals which have not been replaced will be taken into account for tax purposes. There is, however, an exception to this last rule where the new herd is *substantially* smaller than the old herd (see sub-paragraph (D) below): in that case, the profit or loss arising from the sale of the animals which have not been replaced is not taken into account for tax purposes. . . .

(D) Sale of the whole herd, or a substantial part of the herd, without replacement

If the whole of a herd is sold within a period of twelve months without replacement, any profit or loss on the sale will not be taken into account for tax purposes. Any profit or loss on the sale of a substantial part of the herd within a period of twelve months will be treated in the same way. (It will depend on the facts of the case whether a particular reduction in numbers is substantial, but the Board of Inland Revenue will normally be prepared to consider a reduction of 20 per cent or more as substantial).
[Special rules apply if a new herd is begun within five years].

(E) Sale of individual animals which are not replaced

If an animal (or a part of a herd which is not substantial) is sold out of the herd and is not replaced, any profit or loss on the sale will be taken into account.

This treatment applies only to a "production herd", which means[8] a herd of animals of the same species (not necessarily the same breed) kept wholly or mainly for the sale of their produce, e.g. a dairy herd or a flock of sheep kept for the production of wool or lambs. The term does not include cattle kept for disposal such as beef cattle, these being pure trading stock.

An immature animal is not generally treated as forming part of a production herd.[9] Where such an animal is transferred to the herd on reaching maturity, the transfer is treated as taking place at its total cost to that point. Since such an animal will have been treated previously as trading stock those expenses will have been deductible as revenue expenses; this rule provides for the recapture of those expenses before the animal passes out of the income tax net. An election for herd basis is in general irrevocable.[10]

For the valuation of shares in a stallion syndicate see **Simon's Taxes B3.1018.**

Simon's Taxes B3.515–522; Butterworths Income Tax Service E4.11–E4.13.
[1] TA 1988, Sch. 5, para 1(1).
[2] TA 1988, Sch. 5, para 9(1).
[3] TA 1988, Sch. 5, para 9(4).
[4] TA 1988, Sch. 5, para 7.
[5] The election period is extended following the abolition of stock relief to allow farmers who may have considered stock relief more advantageous to reappraise the position.
[6] Infra, § **15: 08**.
[7] Taken from Leaflet IR9 (1984) para 7.
[8] TA 1988, Sch. 5, para. 8(3).
[9] TA 1988, Sch. 5, para. 8(2).
[10] TA 1988, Sch. 5, para. 2.

(2)   Business or business assets

7: 68   By contrast sums arising from the disposal of the business itself or of a business asset is normally a capital receipt and so not a trading receipt. So in *British Borneo Petroleum Syndicate Ltd v Cropper*[1] a sum received in return for the surrender of a royalty agreement was held to be a capital receipt.

The terms on which an asset is sold may however give rise to a taxable profit. So in *Lamport and Holt Line Ltd v Langwell*,[2] A, a shipowner, sold shares in B, a company trading as fuel suppliers, to C, another company of fuel suppliers; the contract provided that A should receive a part of the commission which C should receive for supplying oil to A; these part-commissions were held to be trading receipts of A.

Simon's Taxes A1.208, B3.231; Butterworths Income Tax Service C1.72.
[1] [1969] 1 All ER 104, 45 TC 201.
[2] (1958) 38 TC 193; see also *Orchard Wine and Spirit Co v Loynes* (1952) 33 TC 97.

(3)   Payment for non-trade purposes

7: 69   While a payment in return for goods or services will normally be a trading receipt a payment made for reasons other than trade will not be a trading receipt.

A voluntary payment may be a trading receipt, e.g. the payment of an extra sum for work already paid for;[1] however, a testimonial or solatium is not. The latter, although perhaps in recognition of past services is not paid in respect of them nor for future services.[2] The question is one of fact; in deciding this issue it is the nature of the payment rather than the motive of the payer that prevails.

In *Murray v Goodhews*[3] a brewing company decided to end a number of tenancy agreements with the taxpayer and chose to make voluntary payments of some £81,000 over two years. These payments were held to be not trading receipts partly because, although an ex gratia payment had been mentioned early on in the negotiation, there was no disclosure of the basis on which the payment was calculated, there had been no subsequent negotiations between the parties on this point and the amount had not been calculated by reference to profit earned.

Payments escaping tax on this basis have included one to a firm of accountants on not being reappointed to act as auditors to a company which had changed ownership, the sum being equivalent to one year's salary, *Walker v Carnaby, Harrower, Barham and Pykett*[4] and a payment to an insurance broker on the ending of a relationship with a client when that client was taken over by another company, *Simpson v John Reynolds & Co (Insurances) Ltd.*[5] In practice, a prize awarded to an author for his literary work is not treated as taxable.[6]

On the other hand a payment to assist a taxpayer club to improve its curling facilities was held to be a trading receipt as the purpose of the payment was to enable the club to keep in business, *IRC v Falkirk Ice Rink Ltd;*[7] likewise a payment to compensate an estate agent for the loss of a fee-earning opportunity *McGowan v Brown and Cousins.*[8]

The matter is one of fact. In *Murray v Goodhews* the payment escaped tax despite the continued trading relationship between the parties, whereas in *McGowan v Brown and Cousins* the payment was taxable even though the trading relationship had ended. In *Rolfe v Nagel*[9] on the other hand, a payment was held taxable when made by one diamond broker to another because a client had transferred his business. The facts were unusual in that such a broker is unable to earn commission from a client until the client has been accepted as "an active client", a process taking a number of years. Other facts supported this conclusion; thus the two brokers agreed to accept whatever a third broker should think suitable and the sum, £15,000, was not paid until the client became "active".

The fact that a testimonial escapes tax is consistent with Schedule E.

The payment may, as a capital receipt, be liable to CGT. In practice the Revenue may treat it as a payment for goodwill and so eligible for retirement relief.

Simon's Taxes B3.901; Butterworths Income Tax Service C1.73.

[1] *Temperley v Smith* [1956] 3 All ER 92, 37 TC 18; *Isaac Holden & Sons Ltd v IRC* (1924) 12 TC 768, infra, § **7: 143** and *Australia (Commonwealth) Taxation Comr v Squatting Investment Co Ltd* [1954] 1 All ER 349, [1954] AC 182.

[2] Per Buckley LJ in *Murray v Goodhews* [1978] STC 207 at 213, [1978] 2 All ER 40 at 46.

[3] Supra, n. 2. On deduction by the brewers see *Watney Combe Reid & Co Ltd v Pike* [1982] STC 733.

[4] [1970] 1 All ER 502, 46 TC 461.

[5] [1975] STC 271, CA.

[6] [1979] STI, p. 76.

7 [1975] STC 434, 51 TC 42.
8 [1977] STC 342, [1977] 3 All ER 844.
9 [1982] STC 53.

(4) Incidental payments

7: 70 A payment arising incidentally in the course of a trade may be a trading receipt; the recurrence of the transaction will make this conclusion more likely.

(i) *Know-how*

Statute now provides that all payments in return for know-how are trading receipts if the know-how has been used in the trade and the trade is still carried on.[1] Earlier case law decided that where a trader possessed a patent or know-how sums received in return for permitting the use of these assets would be income[2] since all that was happening was that some part of the capital of the trade was being put to use in a profit earning way.[3] Where the know-how was disposed of along with other assets of a trade in a foreign country, sums received in return for the know-how were capital receipts as part of the disposal of the trade.[4] Where however the company had to supply know-how as a condition of entering into a trading arrangement in a country with which there had been no previous trade, the receipt was one on revenue account as the transaction did not materially affect the company's profit making structure.[5]

Statute also now provides that where a person disposes of a trade or part of a trade, any consideration for know-how is generally to be dealt with on both sides, as a payment for goodwill. However this is not so if the parties jointly elect otherwise or if the trade was carried on wholly outside the UK (in which latter case the old case law still applies).[6]

Simon's Taxes B3.8; Butterworths Income Tax Service C1.74.
1 TA 1988, s. 531(1).
2 See *IRC v Desoutter Bros Ltd* (1945) 29 TC 155 at 162 but cf. *IRC v Iles* (1945) 29 TC 225.
3 On patent royalties as deductions, see infra, § 7: 124. On know-how, see *Rolls Royce Ltd v Jeffrey* [1962] 1 All ER 801, 40 TC 443; *Musker v English Electric Co Ltd* (1964) 41 TC 556; infra, § 8: 54.
4 *Evans Medical Supplies Ltd v Moriarty* [1957] 3 All ER 718, 37 TC 540.
5 *Coalite and Chemical Products Ltd v Treeby* (1971) 48 TC 171 followed in *John and E. Sturge Ltd v Hessel*, [1975] STC 573, 51 TC 183, 208.
6 TA 1988, s. 531(3).

(ii) *Contracts for supply of trading stock*

7: 71 In *George Thompson & Co Ltd v IRC*[1] a shipping company found that some of its ships had been requisitioned by the Australian Government and was left with contracts for the supply of coal in excess of its needs. It therefore transferred the benefit of the contract to another company—not in the form of an assignment but a transfer of the right to take delivery at a premium first of 6s a ton and then of 10s a ton. Although they had only rarely sold coal before, Rowlatt J had no difficulty in holding that this was a revenue receipt of the trade. The coal had not been bought as capital on capital account, but as a thing which they needed to buy and use as consumable stores. The purchase of the coal had been arranged as a part of their business so that it could not be treated as a separate business.

Simon's Taxes B3.1001; Butterworths Income Tax Service C1.74.
[1] (1927) 12 TC 1091.

(iii) *Foreign currency*

7: 72   The rule that a receipt must be a receipt of that trade has had some effect where a trader invests in foreign exchange which he later realises at a gain (or loss). In *Imperial Tobacco Co (of Great Britain and Ireland) Ltd v Kelly*[1] the company bought tobacco leaf in America and to this end bought dollars over the year. With the outbreak of the Second World War the company, at the request of the Treasury, stopped buying American leaf and thereafter its dollars were acquired by the Treasury at a profit to the company. It was held that this was a profit of the trade. It did not matter that the company did not carry on the trade of dealing in foreign exchange. What mattered was that the dollars had been bought as the first step in an intended commercial transaction. One can thus view the dollars as equivalent to raw materials.

On the other hand in the earlier case of *McKinlay v H. T. Jenkins & Son Ltd*[2] a firm of builders who would shortly have to buy some marble in Italy had bought some lire for £16,500. The lira then rose in value against the pound and the holding was sold in order that a profit might be realised on the exchange.[3] The sale price was £22,870, a net profit of about £6,700. The value of the lira then fell and the firm bought the currency needed for £19,386 which sum was allowed as a deduction in computing the profits. Rowlatt J upheld the Commissioners' decision that the £6,700 was not taxable as a profit of the trade.

There was no evidence that the lire in *McKinlay v H. T. Jenkins & Son Ltd* were initially bought simply as a speculation[4] but rather, like the dollars in *Imperial Tobacco Co Ltd v Kelly*, as the first step in an intended commercial transaction. However there was evidence that the decision to sell was simply motivated by the desire for a quick profit. In *Imperial Tobacco Co Ltd v Kelly* the Court of Appeal left open the correctness of Rowlatt J's decision. Today it seems likely that the profit would be taxable, either because the case cannot stand with the later decision of the Court of Appeal or because the decision to withdraw the lire holding from the ambit of the trade would cause the rule in *Sharkey v Wernher*[5] to operate thus ensuring that the profit accruing up until the moment of the decision to withdraw should be a trading receipt, whether actually realised or not, leaving the balance of the profit on realisation to be taxed either as a capital gain[6] or as a separate adventure in the nature of trade.[7] It is however open to the trader to show that on the particular facts the money was not trading stock.

In *Davies v Shell Co of China Ltd*[7] sums deposited with the taxpayer by its agents were repaid in foreign currency which had depreciated against sterling; the resulting profit was not a trading receipt but a capital profit.

A similar problem arose in *Pattison v Marine Midland Ltd*.[8] Here a bank raised a fund of dollars by way of loan and proceeded to lend dollars in the course of its banking business. When the original funding loan was repaid the dollar had strengthened against sterling but the House of Lords held that the bank was not taxable on the sterling profit that arose on the withdrawal of the money from the bank's lending fund since the fund had never been converted into sterling and had been translated into sterling only for balance sheet (as distinct from profit and loss account) purposes. As the fund had never been converted into sterling, the money was like an asset held by the company and generating income by being hired out; the asset might be specific or, as in *Pattison v Marine Midland Ltd*, fungible. The whole question of foreign currency rate fluctuations is the subject of a major Revenue Statement of Practice—SP 1/87[9]—and a further one on investment trusts—SP1/88.[10] A further consultative document was published in 1989.

Simon's Taxes B3.1101; Butterworths Income Tax Service C1.74.

[1] [1943] 2 All ER 119, 25 TC 292; and see *Landes Bros v Simpson* (1934) 19 TC 62 and *O'Sullivan v O'Connor* [1947] IR 416.

[2] (1926) 10 TC 372.

[3] At 376.

[4] See Rowlatt J's subsequent explanation in *George Thompson & Co Ltd v IRC* (1927) 12 TC 1091.

[5] Infra, § **7: 154**.

[6] *Wisdom v Chamberlain,* supra, § **7: 10**.

[7] (1951) 32 TC 133.

[8] [1984] STC 10, HL.

[9] Replacing SP 3/85 (provisional) **Simon's Taxes, Division H3.2.** See generally Pagan, *Taxation Aspects of Currency Fluctuations* (1983) and Kay and King, IFS Report Series No 18 (1985).

[10] **Simon's Taxes, Division H3.2.**

(iv) *Investment of cash*

7: 73   Investments of spare cash on a short term basis have been held to give rise to trading receipts as part of the trade of a bank or insurance company[1] and as part of a separate trade of another sort of company.[2] Concessionary relief may apply to the lending and borrowing of securities.[3]

---

[1] *General Reinsurance Co Ltd v Tomlinson* (1970) 48 TC 81.

[2] *Cooper v C and J Clark Ltd* [1982] STC 335.

[3] Extra-statutory concession B15 (1988), **Simon's Taxes, Division H2.2.**

---

(5) Restriction of activities

7: 74   A payment received as the price for a substantial restriction on one's business or as compensation for the sterilisation of a capital asset is a capital receipt, but (6) a payment received as a surrogatum for trading profit is itself a trading receipt.

In applying these two principles the court's task is complicated by the fact that a payment may come within (5) even though the measure used by the parties to determine the level of payment is loss of profit—the measure does not determine the quality of the payment. The leading modern authority on (5) is *Higgs v Olivier*.[1] Mr Laurence Olivier (as he then was), a well-known actor, had entered into a covenant that he would not for a period of eighteen months appear as an actor in or act as producer or director of any film to be made anywhere by any other company. In return he received £15,000. The covenant was with the company which had just made the film of Henry V starring Mr Laurence Olivier. The reason for this deal appears from the Case Stated, "He was quite a popular film actor, appearing in quite the ordinary kind of films, and the company thought that if he made a more ordinary film than Henry V, the public would go to that instead". The covenant was made after the film had been completed and indeed released in England where alas it was not making much money; it was only hailed a success after its release in New York. Thus the covenant was quite separate from the original contract to make the film. The Court of Appeal held that the payment was for a restriction extending to a substantial portion of the professional activities that were open to him, and so not a trading receipt.

By contrast in *White v G and M Davies (a firm)*[2] the receipt of a premium payment by a farmer under an EEC scheme was held to be a trading receipt. In return for the payment the farmer undertook not to sell milk products for four years and to ensure that dairy cattle accounted for no more than 20% of his herd. Browne-Wilkinson J distinguished *Higgs v Olivier* on the basis that the present restrictions controlled the taxpayer as to the way in which he carried on his business whereas this had not been so in the earlier case. A similar result was reached in *IRC v Biggar*.[3]

Principle (5) was applied in *Murray v Imperial Chemical Industries Ltd*[4] where the company received a capital sum in return for agreeing not to trade in a certain country. This "keep-out" payment was made under an agreement whereby the company allowed another firm to use its patent in that country. The principle was however not applied in *Thompson v Magnesium Elektron Ltd*[5] where a company producing magnesium and therefore needing chlorine, agreed to buy chlorine from another company and agreed not to manufacture chlorine or caustic soda (a by product of the manufacture of chlorine); the company was to receive payments calculated on the amount of caustic soda it would have produced. It was held that the payments simply affected the price the company was paying for its chlorine. It would appear that if the payment had been a lump sum it would not have been a trading receipt,[6] as the form of the payment would have suggested that it was for not making caustic soda instead of for receiving chlorine.

Simon's Taxes A1.210–212; Butterworths Income Tax Service C1.81.
  [1] [1952] 1 Ch 311, 33 TC 136.
  [2] [1979] STC 415; the judge noted the unfairness of treating the payment as income of one year.
  [3] [1982] STC 677.
  [4] [1967] 2 All ER 980, 44 TC 175.
  [5] [1944] 1 All ER 126, 26 TC 1.
  [6] As in *Margerison v Tyresoles Ltd* (1942) 25 TC 59.

---

(6) Compensation payments

7: 75 A sum received in respect of trading stock is income whether it is the proceeds of sale, or damages for breach of contract or for tort, or compensation on compulsory acquisition. The occasion for the receipt is immaterial. Lord Clyde illustrated this in *Burmah Steamship Co Ltd v IRC*:[1]

"Suppose someone who chartered one of the Appellant's vessels breached the charter and exposed himself to a claim of damages . . ., there could, I imagine, be no doubt that the damages recovered would properly enter the Appellant's profit and loss account for the year. The reason would be that the breach of the charter was an injury inflicted on the Appellant's trading, making (so to speak) a hole in the Appellant's profits, and damages recovered could not be reasonably or appropriately put . . . to any other purpose than to fill that hole. Suppose on the other hand, that one of the taxpayer's vessels was negligently run down and sunk by a vessel belonging to some other shipowner, and the Appellant recovered as damages the value of the sunken vessel, I imagine that there could be no doubt that the damages so recovered could not enter the Appellant's profit and loss account because the destruction of the vessel would be an injury inflicted, not on the Appellant's trading, but on the capital assets of the Appellant's trade, making (so to speak) a hole in *them*, and the damages could therefore . . . only be used to fill that hole."

In *Burmah Steamship Co Ltd v IRC* the appellants had bought a ship which required extensive repairs before it could put to sea. The repairer was in breach of contract in that he did not complete the repairs until some five months after the due date. The appellant recovered £1,500 damages for late delivery, the sum being an estimate of the loss of profit. The sum was held to be income. The purchase price of the ship would however have been a capital item and therefore it ought to follow that had the purchaser arranged for a reduction in price that reduction would have meant a lower capital price and not a taxable income receipt.[2] So a payment for the *use* of a capital asset is a revenue receipt, but one for its realisation is a capital receipt.[3]

Simon's Taxes A1.213; Butterworths Income Tax Service C1.82.
[1] (1930) 16 TC 67 at 71–72.
[2] Per Lord Sands (1930) 16 TC 67 at 73. See also *Crabb v Blue Star Line Ltd* [1961] 2 All ER 424, 39 TC 482 (proceeds of insurance policy against late delivery held capital). On treatment of compensation payments for compulsory slaughter of farm animals, see extra-statutory concession B11 (1988), **Simon's Taxes, Division H2.2.**
[3] *Greyhound Racing Association (Liverpool) Ltd v Cooper* [1936] 2 All ER 742, 20 TC 373.

7: 76   The principle that a surrogatum for loss of profit is an income receipt has been consistently applied. It has been applied where a company which had acquired a licence to take Noel Coward's *Cavalcade* on tour in the UK received damages because a film of that show was released to the detriment of the profits of the tour,[1] where a firm who made steam ships received damages from a purchaser in return for the cancellation of an agreement to buy ships,[2] where timber which was the trading stock of a company was destroyed by fire and sums were received from an insurance company equal to the replacement value of the timber[3] and likewise where sums were payable under an insurance policy against loss of profit.[4] Slightly less obviously it has been applied where a company received a large sum under a life policy they held on one of their key employees,[5] the services of the employees being regarded as being as much part of the trading activities of the business as the goods which were its trading stock and the court noticing that sums paid to induce the resignation of a director had been held to be income expenditure.[6] More recently a company whose jetty was damaged by the negligent navigation of a tanker was held taxable on the damages received in so far as they represented damages for loss of the use of the jetty during repairs but not the much larger sum needed to repair the jetty.[7] What would have happened had there been no clear apportionment of the damages is unclear.

Where damages are received for loss of profit, the fact that the damages are used to write down certain capital expenditure incurred during the contract is irrelevant; the payment is nonetheless an income receipt.[8]

When the payment is a capital receipt, it may well give rise to capital gains tax.[9]

The principle that a surrogatum for loss of profit is an income receipt has also been applied to compensation for increased revenue expenditure.[10]

Simon's Taxes A1.213; B3.1001; Butterworths Income Tax Service C1.82.

[1] *Vaughan v Archie Parnell and Alfred Zeitlin Ltd* (1940) 23 TC 505. It follows that no deduction for tax can be made in assessing the damages. *Diamond v Campbell-Jones* [1960] 1 All ER 583, [1961] Ch 22.

[2] *Short Bros Ltd v IRC* (1927) 12 TC 955.

[3] *J. Gilksten & Son Ltd v Green* [1929] AC 381, 14 TC 364.

[4] *R v British Columbia Fir and Cedar Lumber Co Ltd* [1932] AC 441, see also *Mallandain Investments Ltd v Shadbolt* (1940) 23 TC 367.

[5] *Williams Executors v IRC* [1942] 2 All ER 266, 26 TC 23, but see Harris and Hewson, *Life Assurance and Tax Planning*, p. 102, 9–28. It appears that in general it is Revenue practice not to treat lump sum proceeds as trading receipts if no claim was made to deduct the premiums as trading expenses. But it does not follow that the company can opt to have the proceeds treated as capital by not claiming relief for the premiums. The proper tax treatment of the proceeds must be considered on its own merits.

[6] *B. W. Noble Ltd v Mitchell* (1926) 11 TC 372.

[7] *London and Thames Haven Oil Wharves Ltd v Attwooll* [1967] 2 All ER 124, 43 TC 491.

[8] *IRC v Northfleet Coal and Ballast Co Ltd* (1927) 12 TC 1102.

[9] Under CGTA 1979, s. 20; see *Lang v Rice* [1984] STC 172, CA.

[10] *Donald Fisher (Ealing) Ltd v Spencer* [1989] STC 256, CA.

7: 77   There is no relation between the measure that is used for the purpose of calculating a particular result and the quality of the figure that is arrived at by means of the application of that test. In *Glenboig Union Fireclay Co Ltd v IRC*[1] the taxpayer company held leasehold rights in certain fireclay seams with the right to remove minerals. The seam ran under the railway track of the Caledonian Railway Company. The railway company obtained an interdict to prevent the taxpayer from removing fireclay from the seam pending the hearing of their case against the company in which they claimed that although the lease granted the right to remove minerals, fireclay was not a mineral. The railway company lost its case and then exercised its powers compulsorily to prevent the fireclay company from exercising its rights. Eventually it was agreed that a large sum should be paid to the fireclay company for loss of the fireclay. The House of Lords held that the sum was a capital receipt. The case concerned excess profits duty and it was the Revenue who argued that the receipt was capital.[2] The company argued that as that seam would have been fully worked out in two and a half years the sum paid was nothing but a surrogatum for profits lost. Lord Buckmaster regarded that argument as fallacious:[3]

"In truth the sum of money is the sum paid to prevent the Fireclay Company obtaining the full benefit of the capital value of that part of the mines which they are prevented from working by the railway company. It appears to me to make no difference whether it be regarded as the sale of the asset out and out, or whether it be treated merely as a means of preventing the acquisition of profit which would otherwise be gained. In either case the capital asset of the company to that extent has been sterilised and destroyed, and it is in respect of that action that the sum . . . was paid. . . . It is now well settled that the compensation payable in such circumstances is the full value of the minerals that are left unworked, less the cost of working, and that is of course the profit that would have been obtained were they in fact worked. But there is no relation between the measure that is used for the purpose of calculating a particular result and the quality of the figure that is arrived at by means of the application of that test."

Simon's Taxes A1.211–213; Butterworths Income Tax Service C1.81.
[1] Per Lord Buckmaster (1922) 12 TC 427 at 464, HL.
[2] The higher the company's profits before 1914, the lower the excess profits duty.
[3] (1922) 12 TC 427 at 464.

7: 78   Compensation for the sterilisation of a capital asset is a capital payment (supra, § **7: 74**) but this leaves the question what is a capital asset. Goodwill is a capital asset and therefore damages payable for injury to goodwill are a capital receipt.[1] Extraction industries have always been odd for tax purposes since the process of their trade turns fixed into circulating capital.[2] Thus in *Glenboig* had the railway company accidentally destroyed the fireclay after it had been extracted it would appear that the sums payable by way of damages would have been a trading receipt.

Another question left unanswered is the duration of the restriction. In *Glenboig* the House of Lords did not have to consider a further point, namely the correct tax treatment of the damages for wrongous interdict.[3] The Court of Session held that the sum was a capital receipt on the ground that it was the reimbursement of expenditure of a capital nature—capital because it proved to be totally fruitless owing to the expropriation proceedings.[4] The parties settled this aspect of their liability before going to the House of Lords. If this payment was held to be a revenue receipt[5] one has the droll result that (*i*) the payment computed by reference to loss of profit was a capital payment while this one, not so computed, but which is for loss of profit, is a trading receipt while (*ii*) a payment relating to a period of three years would be an income payment whereas that relating to the two and half years that it would have taken to exhaust the fireclay was a capital payment.

Simon's Taxes A1.211–213; Butterworths Income Tax Service C1.81.
[1] E.g. Lord Evershed MR, in *Wiseburgh v Domville* [1956] 1 All ER 754 at 758, 36 TC 527 at 539.
[2] Per Lord Radcliffe in *Taxes Comr v Nchanga Consolidated Copper Mines Ltd* [1964] AC 948 at 964, [1964] 1 All ER 208 at 212.
[3] The amount payable to the fireclay company in respect of expenses of keeping the seam open but unused while the interdict prevented them from working it.
[4] Per Viscount Cave LC in *British Insulated and Helsby Cables Ltd v Atherton* [1926] AC 205 at 211; *Southern v Borax Consolidated Ltd* [1940] 4 All ER 412, 23 TC 597.
[5] E.g. Lord Clyde in *Burmah Steamship Co Ltd v IRC* (1930) 16 TC 67 at 72 although in the *Glenboig* case Lord Clyde had thought it a capital receipt: 12 TC at 450.

Contracts relating to structure of business

7: 79   Damages paid for breach of a contract to make good the loss of profit from that contract will usually be income under principle (6); in such instances it makes no difference what the importance of the contract is to the trade. However one must distinguish profit-earning contracts from those relating to the whole structure of the profit earning apparatus of the trade. In *Van den Berghs Ltd v Clark*[1] the appellant company entered into an agreement with a competing Dutch company in 1912. The agreement provided for the sharing of profits, the bringing in of any other margarine concerns they might acquire and the setting up of a joint committee to make arrangements with outside firms as to prices and limitation of areas of supply of margarine. The agreement was intended to last until 1926 at the earliest and later variations extended that to 1940. The outbreak of the First World War upset the arrangements of the Dutch company and eventually that company agreed in 1927 to pay the appellant company £450,000 for cancellation of the agreement. The House of Lords held that the sum was paid for loss of future rights under the agreement which was a capital asset and therefore was a capital receipt. Lord MacMillan said:[2]

> "The ... agreements which the Appellants consented to cancel were not ordinary commercial contracts made in the course of carrying on their trade; they were not contracts for the disposal of their products or for the engagement of agents or other employees necessary for the conduct of their business; nor were they merely agreements as to how their trading profits when earned should be distributed between the contracting parties. On the contrary the cancelled agreements related to the whole structure of the Appellants profit making apparatus. They regulated the Appellants' activities, defined what they might and what they might not do, and affected the whole conduct of their business. The agreements formed part of the fixed framework within which their circulating capital operated; they were not incidental to the working of their profit making machine but were essential parts of the mechanism itself. They provided the means of making profits, but they themselves did not yield profits."

Simon's Taxes A1.210; Butterworths Income Tax Service C1.84.
[1] (1935) 19 TC 390, HL.
[2] 19 TC 390 at 464.

7: 80 Sums paid on the *variation* of an agreement which relates to the whole structure of the profit-making apparatus are also capital. In *Sabine v Lockers Ltd*[1] the taxpayers held the main distributorship for the Austin motor company in the Manchester area; they were not allowed to enter into any agreement with any other manufacturer. Sums paid for variation of that contract were held capital receipts. The distributorship lasted only for one year with a right of renewal for a further year but there was reasonable prospect of further yearly renewals.

In both *Van den Bergh's Ltd v Clark* and *Sabine v Lockers Ltd* the agreements related to the framework of the company's business rather than one for the disposal of the company's products. It is less easy, but apparently not impossible,[2] for a contract of the latter type to be treated as a capital asset. However the mere fact that a trader arranges his work on the basis of a particular contract is insufficient to make that contract one relating to the structure of his business. Thus a shipbuilding company may only make a few ships a year but an order for a ship is profit yielding contract; damages for breach will therefore be an income receipt.[3] A similar result was reached on cancellation of an agreement between a film star and a company owning the right to his services.[4]

In *Glenboig* an item of fixed capital was sterilised. This must be distinguished from the prevention of the acquisition of profit.[5]

Simon's Taxes B3.911; Butterworths Income Tax Service C1.84.
[1] (1958) 38 TC 120.
[2] Note Ungoed Thomas J in *John Mills Productions Ltd v Mathias* (1964) 44 TC 441 at 453.
[3] *Short Bros Ltd v IRC* (1927) 12 TC 955.
[4] *John Mills Productions Ltd v Mathias* (1964) 44 TC 441.
[5] E.g. *Waterloo Main Colliery Co Ltd v IRC* (1947) 29 TC 235.

Agency contracts

7: 81   The restriction, even though temporary, of one's profit making apparatus is very different from the mere loss of trading opportunity such as occurs when an agency contract on commission ends and a lump sum is received for the cancellation. At first sight it would seem that such contracts, producing income, must be capital assets[1] but they are usually treated as revenue assets since their acquisition and replacement is one of the normal incidents of the business. They are disposal contracts in that the company is disposing of services. Such a contract is not a capital asset and the sum received will be taxed as a mere trading receipt. In *Shove v Dura Manufacturing Co Ltd*[2] Lawrence J gave three reasons why there was nothing of a capital nature about the contract, "No money was spent to secure it; no capital asset was acquired to carry it out; its cancellation was only an ordinary method of modifying and realising the profit to be derived from it".[3]

In *Kelsall Parsons & Co v IRC*[4] the appellants commenced business in Scotland as manufacturer's agents and engineers in 1914 when one of their two agencies was for a firm in Birmingham making electric switch gear. A series of agency agreements was made with the firm the last of which was for three years from 30th September 1932 but this was terminated by agreement on 30th September 1934 the firm agreeing to pay £1,500 compensation to the appellants. The Court of Session held that the sum was a trading receipt. It was true that the appellants had built up a considerable technical organisation to handle this particular agency agreement[5] but that was insufficient to bring the facts within the principle in *Van den Berghs Ltd v Clark*. In reaching this conclusion it was important to Lord Normand and Lord Fleming that the agreement had only one year to run, as Lord Normand put it this was not a case where "a benefit extending over a tract of future years is renounced for a payment made once and for all".[6]

Simon's Taxes B3.911; Butterworths Income Tax Service C1.85.
[1] Per Lord Evershed MR in *Anglo-French Exploration Co Ltd v Clayson* [1956] 1 All ER 762 at 766, 36 TC 545 at 557.
[2] (1941) 23 TC 779.
[3] At 783.
[4] (1938) 21 TC 608 applied in *Creed v H and M Levinson Ltd* [1981] STC 486.
[5] Case stated para. (9), 21 TC 608 at 615.
[6] 21 TC 608 at 620.

7: 82   An exceptional case the other side of the line is *Barr Crombie & Co Ltd v IRC*[1] where the appellants managed ships, 98% of its business came from an agreement with one company for a period of fifteen years from 1936 which was terminated in 1942 when the shipping company went into liquidation, and a large sum paid in respect of the eight years left of the agreement. The payment was held to be a capital receipt. Taking all the facts into account Lord Normand thought that the effect on the company's structure and character was such as to bring the facts with *Van den Berghs Ltd v Clark*.

The difficulty with *Barr Crombie & Co Ltd v IRC* is that it shows how unclear is the distinction between a contract which is merely one created in the ordinary life of the business and one which relates to its profit making structure.

These are essentially matters of degree and circumstance. One must distinguish the situation in which the rights and advantages surrendered on cancellation are such as to destroy or materially to cripple the whole structure of the recipient's profit-making apparatus, involving the serious dislocation of the normal commercial organisation and resulting perhaps in the cutting down of staff previously required, from that in which the benefit surrendered was not an enduring asset and where the structure of the recipients business is so fashioned as to absorb the shock as one of the normal incidents to be looked for and where it appears that the compensation received is no more than a surrogatum for future profits surrendered.[2] These are however only explanations and illustrations. There was no reduction in the staff employed as a result of the cancellation of the agreement in *Van den Berghs Ltd v Clark* but the fact that the work force had to be reduced after the cancellation was insufficient to turn the compensation into a capital receipt in *Elson v James G. Johnston Ltd*.[3] In *Barr Crombie* itself Lord Normand stressed that none of the factors which distinguished the case from *Kelsall, Parsons & Co v IRC* were of themselves conclusive but the combination was.[4] What *Barr Crombie* does however is to establish that compensation may be a capital receipt even though the contract is a disposal contract. However there is also authority for the proposition that a pure disposal contract will not be a capital asset no matter how big it is.[5] Therefore one must conclude that in *Barr Crombie* the contract was a capital asset primarily by reason of its duration and because the business had been built around that contract. It was not a mere disposal contract.[6] The particular agency had been the company's principal asset since the trade commenced so that it could not be said that its loss was a normal incident of the business. Further the loss of the agency necessitated the complete reorganisation of the taxpayers' business, a reduction in staff and the taking of newer and smaller premises.

Simon's Taxes A1.210, B3.910; Butterworths Income Tax Service C1.85.

[1] (1945) 26 TC 406. See also *California Oil Products Ltd v FCT* (1934) 52 CLR 28—company formed to operate one agency and liquidated following its cancellation—compensation on cancellation was a capital receipt.

[2] Per Lord Russell in *IRC v Fleming & Co (Machinery) Ltd* (1951) 33 TC 57 at 63.

[3] (1965) 42 TC 545.

[4] (1945) 26 TC 406 at 412.

[5] Per Ungoed Thomas J in *John Mills Productions Ltd v Mathias* (1964) 44 TC 441 at 456.

[6] Cf. Ungoed Thomas J 44 TC 441 at 755.

Subsidies

7: 83   Payments in the nature of a subsidy from public funds made to an entrepreneur to assist in the carrying on of his trade or business are trading receipts.[1]

When a subsidy takes the form of a payment to bring the receipt for a product up to a certain level and that product is trading stock, the payment is clearly a trading receipt.[2] Where a subsidy is paid in advance and may therefore have to be repaid, in whole or in part, the question is whether the payment is a loan or a receipt. The court looks to the business nature of such payments and treats them as trading receipts at the time of payment if they were intended to be used in the business.[3] So payments to enable the trader to meet his trading obligations are trading receipts when made but where the payments were made to assist with a specific project of a capital nature it was held that unemployment grants were not trading receipts.[4] A payment to maintain employment is neither clearly capital nor clearly revenue.[5]

The subsidy may come from another company. So in *British Commonwealth International Newsfilm Agency Ltd v Mahany* a payment to a subsidiary company as a supplement to its trading revenue and in order to preserve its trading stability was a trading receipt.[6]

Simon's Taxes B3.929; Butterworths Income Tax Service C1.83.

[1] Per Viscount Simon in *Pontypridd and Rhondda Joint Water Board v Ostime* [1946] AC 477 at 489, 28 TC 261 at 278; see also *Poulter v Gayjon Processes Ltd* [1985] STC 174. FA 1980, s. 42 expressly makes grants under the Industry Act 1972 trading receipts unless clearly capital.

[2] *Lincolnshire Sugar Co Ltd v Smart* (1935) 20 TC 643 at 667. See also *Higgs v Wrightson* (1944) 26 TC 73 (ploughing subsidies—trading receipts); *Burman v Thorn Domestic Appliances (Electrical) Ltd* [1982] STC 179.

[3] Ibid.

[4] *Seaham Harbour Dock Co v Crook* (1930) 16 TC 333 as explained in *Poulter v Gayjon Processes Ltd* [1985] STC 174.

[5] *Ryan v Crabtree Denims Ltd* [1987] STC 402; although the judgement in this case focuses on the purpose for which the payment is applied it is to be assumed that one looks first at the purpose for which the payment was made.

[6] [1963] 1 All ER 88, 40 TC 550, HL. Cf. *Moss' Empires Ltd v IRC* [1973] AC 785, 21 TC 264.

---

(7)   Property of the trader

7: 84   A receipt which has not yet become the property of the trader is not yet a trading receipt.

Where a trader receives sums of money from customers on their behalf, the receipt is not a trading receipt and so is not to be brought into account. This remains the case even though the trade is carried on by a partnership and the sums held for the customers are allocated to the partners as a domestic arrangement for book keeping purposes.[1] If however the sums originally repayable to the customers cease to be so by reason of the Limitation Act, they become trading receipts of the period when the claims are barred.[2] The question whether the money belongs to the customers or to the trader must depend on the facts. Where a sum is paid to a trader by way of part payment, it is still the customer's money whereas if the money is paid by way of deposit it immediately becomes the property of the trader and is irrecoverable by a purchaser in default; a deposit is therefore a trading receipt.[3]

Simon's Taxes B3.914; Butterworths Income Tax Service C1.86.
[1] *Morley v Tattersall* [1938] 3 All ER 296, 22 TC 51 (the limitation period did not begin to run in this case in respect of any of the payments: 29 TC 274 at 284).
[2] *IRC v Jay's the Jewellers Ltd* [1947] 2 All ER 762, 29 TC 274.
[3] *Elson v Price's Tailors Ltd* [1963] 1 All ER 231, 40 TC 671.

(8) Payment falling under different Schedule or Case

7: 85 A payment falling under some other Schedule or Case is not a trading receipt.

Income correctly taxed under some other Schedule ought not to be taxed under Schedule D, Case I and so cannot enter into the computation. Thus rental income in respect of land in the UK is assessable under Schedule A,[1] while income from government securities is usually taxed under Schedule C and, if that is done, cannot be assessed under Schedule D.[2] A line must also be drawn between trading receipts and payments falling within Schedule D, Case III; a payment which forms part of the trading activities of the recipient cannot be pure income profit in his hands and so cannot fall within Case III. So a payment incorrectly received under deduction of tax[3] must form part of his profits while one that was correctly so received cannot be a trading receipt.[4] If however a particular receipt can be taxed under Case I and another Case, it cannot be assessed to tax twice; the Revenue must choose under which Case to make the assessment.[5]

Where dividends are received by a trader dealing in investments those dividends are taxable under Schedule F, although the recipient may set off the tax credit against his liability under that Schedule.[6] Dividends cannot therefore be treated as trading receipts nor can they be earned income.[7]

Simon's Taxes B3.912; Butterworths Income Tax Service C1.87.
[1] Infra, § **9: 02**. See also *Lowe v J W Ashmore Ltd* [1971] 1 All ER 1057, 46 TC 597; sales of turf by farmer Case I not Schedule A; noted [1970] BTR 416 (PL).
[2] *Thompson v Trust and Loan Co of Canada* [1932] 1 KB 517, 16 TC 394.
[3] Under TA 1988, ss. 348–350; infra, § **9: 68**.
[4] *British Commonwealth International Newsfilm Agency Ltd v Mahany* [1963] 1 All ER 88, 40 TC 550.
[5] *Liverpool and London and Globe Insurance Co v Bennett* [1913] AC 610, 6 TC 327.
[6] Infra, § **24: 11**.
[7] Supra, § **4: 05**. On previous law, see speech of Viscount Simonds in *Cenlon Finance Ltd v Ellwood* [1962] 1 All ER 854, 40 TC 176, criticised [1962] BTR 320 (STC), [1963] BTR 133; and *F.S. Securities Ltd v IRC* [1964] 2 All ER 691, 41 TC 666, HL, noted [1964] BTR 53 and [1964] BTR 281 (Scrase).

(9) Market value

7: 86 In deciding the amount to be included as a trading receipt regard must be had to the rules substituting market value for any price agreed between the parties, especially TA 1988, s. 770 if one party controls the others infra, § **7: 152** and the rule in *Sharkey v Wernher*, infra, § **7: 154**.

(10) Mining

7: 87   Special rules apply to mining. Income from land is taxed under
Schedule A but profits from mines, quarries and other concerns are taxed
under Schedule D,[1] Case I and mining rents and royalties are charged under
the same Schedule, tax being deducted at source as if it were a royalty for use
of a patent.[2]

Owing to technological advances which have made the extraction of
minerals a much more rapid process, and because the costs were so high that
a lease in return for royalties was a better method of arranging the business
than a fixed capital sum, special rules now provide that where a person
resident or ordinarily resident in the UK is entitled to receive mineral
royalties under a mineral lease or agreement, one half of the proceeds are to
be treated as income and one half as capital gains, although basic rate income
tax is to be deducted in full under TA 1988, s. 348, infra, § **9: 66**.[3] The land
concerned may be in the UK or overseas.

Simon's Taxes B3.4.
[1] TA 1988, s. 55.
[2] TA 1988, s. 199.
[3] TA 1988, s. 122.

EXPENSES

7: 88   The right to deduct expenses in computing taxable profit rests not on
any express statutory provision but rather on the absence of any express
prohibition; the right to deduct is inferred from the fact that it is the profit,
not the receipts, of a trade that are taxed.[1]

The right to deduct is limited by a number of rules: (*a*) the expense must
have been incurred for business purposes—the principle of remoteness; (*b*) it
must have been incurred only for business purposes—the principle of duality;
(*c*) it must have been incurred for the purpose of earning profit—the rule in
Strong & Co of Romsey Ltd v Woodifield; (*d*) it must be an expense of earning
profit and not a division of profit; (*e*) it must be of an income nature as
opposed to a capital nature; it must be a revenue expense; and (*f*) it must
not be expressly barred by some statutory provision.

In answering all these questions the court has regard to established
commercial accounting principles.[2]

It is also necessary that the expense should have been incurred; this is
wider than just a matter of timing. In *Rutter v Charles Sharpe & Co Ltd*[3] the
company made payments to trustees of a fund held for the benefit of its
employees. It was held that as the company could at any time wind up the
scheme and then enforce the return of the payments, it followed that the
sums could be recalled at will by the company and so could not be allowable
deductions. For the same reason a payment will not be deductible if it can be
recouped from another person.[4]

Simon's Taxes B3.12; Butterworths Income Tax Service C2.01.
[1] TA 1988, s. 817 prohibits all deductions save those expressly authorised; TA 1988, s. 74 does

not authorise deductions but forbids them. On the difficulties in this formulation see Romer LJ in *Anglo Persian Oil Co Ltd v Dale* [1932] 1 KB 124 at 144, 16 TC 253 at 272.
[2] Per Lord Sumner in *Usher's Wiltshire Brewery Ltd v Bruce* [1915] AC 433 at 468, 6 TC 399 at 436.
[3] [1979] STC 711.
[4] *Bolton v Halpern and Woolf* [1979] STC 761 at 770; revsd for other reasons [1981] STC 14.

(a) and (b) Wholly and exclusively—remoteness and duality

7: 89 Rules (*a*) and (*b*) are derived from TA 1988, s. 74(*a*) which prohibits the deduction of expenses not being money wholly and exclusively laid ". . . for the purposes of the trade. . . ." The word "wholly" refers to the quantum of the money expended while the word "exclusively" refers to the motive or object accompanying it. The question whether the expenditure was incurred exclusively for business purposes is one of fact and purpose. However, if the sole purpose is business promotion the expenditure is not disqualified because the nature of the activity necessarily involves some other result or the attainment or furtherance of some other objective since the latter is necessarily inherent in the act.[1]

The leading case is the decision of the House of Lords in *Mallalieu v Drummond*[2] in which a lady barrister sought to deduct the cost of clothes bought for wear in court, such clothes being required by court etiquette. The undisputed evidence was that the taxpayer's expenditure was motivated solely by thoughts of court etiquette and not at all by mere human thoughts of warmth and decency. Counsel for the taxpayer disclaimed any reliance on his client's dislike of black clothing and the question was reduced to this: if clothing is purchased for use only on business occasions and such clothes are only so used (or for proceeding to and from work) is the expense deductible? The House of Lords said no. In addition to the business purpose there were the other purposes of warmth and decency. As Lord Brightman said "I reject that notion that the object of a taxpayer is inevitably limited to the particular conscious motive in mind at the moment of expenditure".

Earlier cases had decided that the courts could ignore an incidental benefit to the taxpayer. This is reformulated by Lord Brightman in his distinction between the object of the taxpayer in incurring the expenditure and the effect of the expenditure. "An expenditure may be made exclusively to serve the purposes of the business, but it may have a private advantage. The existence of that private advantage does not necessarily preclude the exclusivity of the business purpose." His Lordship gave an example of a medical consultant flying to the south of France to see a patient; if a stay in the south of France was a reason, however subordinate, no deduction could be claimed whereas if it were not a reason but an unavoidable effect the deduction could be made.

While there may be substance in what the House said there are uncomfortable questions of degree to be resolved. Thus Lord Brightman would have allowed expenditure by a self-employed nurse on clothing dictated by the practical requirements of the act of nursing and the maintenance of hygiene, and even that by a self employed waiter on the provision of "tails", this being the particular design of clothing required in order to obtain engagements. For similar reasons presumably the Revenue were disposed to concede expenditure on wig, gown and bands in the instant case.

Following *Mallalieu v Drummond* it has been held that the cost of modest lunches eaten by solicitors during office meetings was not deductible.[3]

The present position thus is that (*a*) expenditure incurred solely for a business purpose is deductible, (*b*) expenditure partly for a business purpose is not deductible, and that while for (*b*) the court will ignore a purely incidental purpose they will not ignore a merely subordinate non-business purpose, and for both (*a*) and (*b*) the test of purpose is applied subjectively but with a dash of common sense; evidence of the uppermost purposes in a person's mind is not to exclude common sense inferences as to other but unarticulated purposes.

Simon's Taxes B3.1231, 1232, 1436; Butterworths Income Tax Service C2.02.

[1] See Romer LJ in *Bentleys, Stokes and Lowless v Beeson* [1952] 2 All ER 82 at 85, 33 TC 491 at 504 and see *Dollar v Lyon* [1981] STC 333 (pocket money to children not deductible).

[2] [1983] STC 665, [1983] 2 AC 861, HL.

[3] *Watkis v Ashford Sparkes & Harward* [1985] STC 451 infra, § 7: **90**.

7: 90   *Mallalieu v Drummond*[1] also raises the problem of conference expenses. The costs of food and lodging must be incurred at least partly because one has to eat and sleep (or are these just unavoidable effects of the initial decision to attend the conference?) The problem was considered in two cases before *Mallalieu v Drummond*. In *Bowden v Russell and Russell*[2] the sole partner of a firm of solicitors attended meetings of the American Bar Association in Washington and the Empire Law Conference in Ottawa. He went in an unofficial capacity and was accompanied by his wife, although no claim was made in respect of those expenses attributable to her. He admitted that there were holiday and social purposes. He argued that his attendance was in order to maintain the firm's efficiency, to obtain new clients and to improve the office organisation. The Revenue argued that the principle of remoteness barred the deduction, the purpose of the visit being social not business and, alternatively, that, if there was a business element the deduction was barred by the principle of duality. The Revenue won.[3] On the other hand in *Edwards v Warmsley, Henshall & Co*[4] a partner in a firm of chartered accountants went to represent the firm at the International Congress of Accountants in New York. There was no evidence of any other purpose. The expenses were held deductible. In this case it was said that he had only met those whom he was meant to go and see. This however, while it may go to credibility, does not in theory affect the issue of deductibility. Had he agreed to go to the conference and while in New York decided to visit a relative in Boston simply because he was over there, this could not affect the deductibility of the expenses of travel to and from New York and it would make no difference that he had had that intention before deciding to obey the instruction of his firm. The question is one of motive and not of effect.

In *Watkis v Ashford Sparkes & Harwood*[5] Nourse J accepted the latter decision was still good law—despite *Mallalieu v Drummond*—and held that the cost of overnight accommodation at the annual conference of a firm was deductible and that no distinction could be drawn between the costs of accommodation and the costs of food and drink consumed. This was despite the fact that in the same case expenditure on meals taken at a time when the taxpayers would normally have eaten was held to be incapable of being incurred exclusively for business purposes. The moral seems to be that if one wishes to secure deduction of meal expenditure one has to have accommodation as well. The test in such cases is whether the expense is incurred as a business person or as a human being.

Simon's Taxes B3.1437, B4.203; Butterworths Income Tax Service C2.02.
[1] [1983] STC 665, [1983] 2 AC 861, HL.
[2] [1965] 2 All ER 258, 42 TC 301. See also *Knight v Parry* (1973) 48 TC 580.
[3] They agreed to allow him to deduct the conference fee but only by concession and without prejudice to the argument of remoteness.
[4] [1968] 1 All ER 1089, 44 TC 431.
[5] [1985] STC 451.

Apportionment and duality

7: 91   The duality rule prevents the deduction of expenditure for mixed purposes.[1] However it does not prevent the dissection of expenditure and subsequent deduction of that part of the expenditure which is wholly and exclusively for business purposes. Thus if a professional man uses one of his rooms in his house as an office, the expenses of that office are deductible, and this will be so even though the electricity, rates and other bills apply to the house as a whole and have to be dissected in order to discover the part attributable to the office. In these cases the sum is dissected in order to discover that part which is wholly for business purposes, wholly being a matter of quantum, and the test of exclusive business purpose is then applied to that part. This has been applied where an unreasonable amount of remuneration was paid to an employee, the court allowing the employer to deduct that part which would have been reasonable.[2] However it could not be applied in *Bowden v Russell and Russell* since one could not identify the precise point in mid-Atlantic at which the solicitor ceased to be travelling for personal reasons and began to travel for business reasons.

The present position is unsatisfactory since the Revenue do, in practice, allow an apportionment in a situation like that in *Bowden v Russell and Russell* provided that there is a genuine business element, as would be the case with the running and garage expenses of a car used partly for personal and partly for business purposes. However the present position appears to provide little scope for appeal to the Commissioners.[3]

Simon's Taxes B4.203, 1232, 1233; Butterworths Income Tax Service C2.03.
[1] *Garforth v Tankard Carpets Ltd* [1980] STC 251; for an exceptional case the other way see *Robinson v Scott Bader Co Ltd* [1980] STC 241, [1980] 2 All ER 780.
[2] *Copeman v William J. Flood & Sons Ltd* [1941] 1 KB 202, 24 TC 53.
[3] For a highly critical account of and a different view of the present law see Kerridge [1986] BTR 36.

7: 92   Expenditure for the purpose of two separate trades of one person is in theory deductible from neither[1] but it is unlikely that this absurd result would be applied by the Revenue. However this situation must be distinguished from that of two separate persons with similar trades e.g. two companies in a group.[2] Where an expense is incurred by one company for the other it is not deductible; whether it is so incurred is a question of fact. Where one company in a group takes over trading stock from another company in the group the costs of the acquisition are deductible even though the group or the other company may have motives of their own; what is important is the motive of the company making the expenditure.[3]

Where one company in a group is about to cease trading, payments to employees may be for the purpose of the orderly conduct of its trade, or for other purposes such as the interests of other companies in the group or the fulfilment of contractual or statutory duties connected with the cessation. Which it is turns on the company's purpose and so is a question of fact.[4]

The opposite problem arises where the trader purchases supplies from a subsidiary or related company and a part of the profit accruing to the other company will return to the trader. In *IRC v Europa Oil (NZ) Ltd*[5] the profit accruing would return to the trader as tax-free dividend and the price was fixed in advance to ensure the exact return to the trader. The Privy Council held that the expenditure was not incurred exclusively in the purchase of trading stock and to that extent could not be allowed. The difficulty for UK law is that there is no warrant for making an apportionment so that the whole should be disallowed. By contrast in *IRC v Europa Oil (NZ) Ltd*[6] the Privy Council held that the relations between the trader and the supplier were such that the former had no legal right to the profit and so the whole sum was allowed.

---

[1] See Walton J in *Olin Energy Systems Ltd v Scorer* [1982] STC 800.
[2] See cases cited at § 7: 91 n. 1 and *Watney Combe Reid & Co v Pike* [1982] STC 733.
[3] *Torbell Investments Ltd v Williams* [1986] STC 397.
[4] *O'Keeffe v Southport Printers Ltd* [1984] STC 443.
[5] [1971] AC 760.
[6] [1976] STC 37.

7: 93   Difficulties have also arisen in connection with partnerships. Since, in English tax law, a partnership is not a taxable entity it follows that the purposes to be investigated are those of the partners. This can seem unreal where a firm has, say, 98 partners and it is therefore tempting to equate such partnerships with companies which have separate legal personality. If such temptation is not resisted it will follow that expenditure incurred to reimburse a partner for his costs of removing his personal belongings, when moving his place of work from one part of the country to another at the request of his partners, will be deductible as has been held by the Court of Appeal in *Mackinlay v Arthur Young McClelland Moores & Co.*[1] Such a conclusion is justified on the basis that the partnership is like a company and the company could, of course, deduct such payments to an employee. Logically, however, if it is correct to say that such an expense when incurred by a sole trader cannot be deducted[2]—since it is incurred at least for dual purposes if not solely for personal purposes—it must follow that there is at least a similar element when it is incurred by the partners. If logic is rejected it would seem to make no difference whether the partners are 98 or 2 in number.

Logic does not require the non-deductibility of payments in return for goods or services supplied by the partner to the partnership. So where the partner has granted the partnership a lease of property which he owns, there is no reason why the rental payments should not be incurred wholly and exclusively for business purposes;[3] they will of course be taxed in the hands of the partner/landlord.

It would seem to be more satisfactory either to make special tax rules for partnerships equating them with companies, including subjecting them to corporation tax and NICs as employers, or to hold that such payments to partners are either not deductible or are fully taxable to the partner as being an allocation of profit not an expense of earning it (infra, § **7: 99**).

---

[1] [1988] STC 116.
[2] The Court of Appeal, however reluctantly, decided the case on this assumption.
[3] *Heastie v Veitch & Co Ltd* [1934] 1 KB 535, 18 TC 305.

7: 94 Expenditure in the form of subscriptions to charity are the generous acts of good citizens. There is therefore a duality of capacity about the payment, part as trader, part as citizen.[1] However whether the explanation is remoteness or duality they are rarely deductible.[2] The same reasoning bars payments for political purposes.[3] Gifts other than to charity also fall within TA 1988, s. 577, infra, § **7: 126**.

Subscriptions to trade associations are according to case law deductible to the extent that the expenditure by the association would have been deductible if incurred directly by the subscriber.[4] In practice however the Revenue grant complete deduction for the subscription in return for the taxability of the association.[5] Contributions to approved local enterprise agencies are now deductible.[6]

Simon's Taxes B3.1441–1444; Butterworths Income Tax Service C2.03.
[1] See Romer LJ in *Bentleys, Stokes and Lowless v Beeson* [1952] 2 All ER 82 at 85, 33 TC 491 at 505. For another reason, see infra, § **7: 99**.
[2] *Bourne and Hollingsworth Ltd v Ogden* (1929) 14 TC 349 (annual subscription to hospital used by employees deductible in practice but two special large subscriptions not deductible); *Hutchinson & Co (Publishers) Ltd v Turner* [1950] 2 All ER 633, 31 TC 495. See extra-statutory concession B7 (1988), **Simon's Taxes, Division H2.2** and concession announced in Revenue Press Release 23 September 1988 on expenses of running a payroll giving scheme.
[3] *Joseph L. Thompson Ltd v Chamberlain* (1962) 40 TC 657; cf. *Morgan v Tate and Lyle Ltd,* infra, § **7: 109**.
[4] *Lochgelly Iron and Coal Co Ltd v Crawford* (1913) 6 TC 267.
[5] See **Simon's Taxes B3.1441**. On the non-taxability of the association, see *Joseph Adamson & Co v Collins* [1938] 1 KB 477, 21 TC 400.
[6] TA 1988, s. 79.

Personal expenditure

7: 95 Expenditure for personal reasons is not deductible. One example is *Bowden v Russell and Russell* (supra). Others are (i) meals—one eats in order to live, not to work[1] and (ii) a pied à terre over the office.[2] These cases have been decided primarily under TA 1988, s. 74(*a*) although many have been argued under TA 1988, s. 74(*b*) in the alternative. There is no reported case of an expense being deductible under (*a*) but not under (*b*).

Medical expenditure is incurred primarily to put right that which is medically wrong and so not for business purposes. In *Murgatroyd v Evans-Jackson*[3] the taxpayer was a trademark agent. He fell ill and was treated in a private nursing home for five weeks, his reason for selecting private care being that he required a separate room from which to conduct his business, a facility not available under the National Health Service. He claimed only 60% of the cost, a matter which admitted duality of expenditure, but Plowman J also held that had the taxpayer claimed the whole of his costs he would still not have been able to deduct the expense since one reason for going into the nursing home was to receive treatment. However one might argue that since the choice was not between a greater and a lesser expense but between no expense at all under the National Health Service and this expense as a private patient, the whole expense was in fact for business purposes. Moreover the decision does cause some fine distinctions. Thus if he had had a bed in a room with other patients but had also rented another room as an office, the rent of that other room would have been deductible. One must distinguish from *Murgatroyd v Evans-Jackson* the case in which the operation itself is for business purposes.[4]

Payments for personal physical security, whether in the provision of an asset or a service are expressly deductible.[5]

Simon's Taxes B3.1436; Butterworths Income Tax Service C2.03.
[1] See *Caillebotte v Quinn* [1975] STC 265, [1975] 2 All ER 412.
[2] *Mason v Tyson* [1980] STC 284.
[3] [1967] 1 All ER 881, 43 TC 581, noted [1967] BTR 285 (Wallace); and see *Norman v Golder* [1945] 1 All ER 352, 26 TC 293.
[4] See Pennycuick J in *Prince v Mapp* [1970] 1 All ER 519 at 525, 46 TC 169 at 176.
[5] FA 1989, ss. 112 and 113.

Travelling expenses

7: 96   Travelling expenses will be deductible in computing the profits of the business if they are incurred wholly and exclusively for the purposes of the trade and are of a revenue as opposed to a capital nature.[1] Expenses incurred by a barrister in travelling from his home to his chambers are not deductible,[2] even though he uses his home for work and is granted a "study allowance".[3] On the other hand a solicitor with an office in two towns may deduct the cost of travel between the two offices.[4] The reason for the distinction is that although the barrister does his work in both places it is clear that he carries on his profession in his chambers; his chambers, not his home, are his base of operations and so travel from his chambers to his home in the evening is not motivated wholly and exclusively by the desire to do more work. The expense is thus at least in part a personal living expense and not a business expense.[5] Likewise the solicitor is not able to deduct the cost of travelling from his home to his office. However if the solicitor were to go to the nearer office first then to the further and then back to the nearer, he would be allowed to deduct both journeys between the offices. Such a conclusion rests on the fact that the office is a place where he carries on his profession. So where a dental surgeon visited his laboratory (L) on his way through from his home (H) to his surgery (S) he was not allowed to deduct the cost of travel from L to S.[6] The purpose of the expenditure was to get from H to S; the fact that it also enabled him to stop at L could not affect that purpose.

Where however a person's home is his base of operations different rules apply. If his travel is purely itinerant, he is allowed to deduct the cost of travel between his home and the places to which he travels as in the case of an independent contracting bricklayer.[7] However when the occupation is itinerant only within a certain area but the taxpayer lives outside that area, the costs of travel at least as far as the border of that area would not be deductible.[8]

Simon's Taxes B3.1437; Butterworths Income Tax Service C2.03.

[1] *Sargent v Eayrs* [1973] STC 50, [1973] 1 All ER 277.
[2] *Newsom v Robertson* [1952] 2 All ER 728, 33 TC 452.
[3] Under TA 1988, s. 74(c).
[4] Per Somervell LJ at 730, 462.
[5] Per Denning LJ at 731, 464.
[6] *Sargent v Barnes* [1978] STC 322, [1978] 2 All ER 737.
[7] *Horton v Young* [1971] 3 All ER 412, 47 TC 60.
[8] Per Brightman J [1971] 2 All ER at 356.

(c) The purpose of earning profits

7: 97   In *Strong & Co of Romsey Ltd v Woodifield* Lord Davey said, "It is not enough that the disbursement is made in the course of or arises out of or is connected with the trade or is made out of the profits of the trade. It must be made for the purpose of earning profits."[1] This gloss on the statute seems to have little effect in the practice of the Revenue but enables the Revenue to grant by concession that which ought to be deducted as of right.

The taxpayer company carried on the businesses of brewers and innkeepers. A chimney at one of their inns fell in and injured a guest. The guest sued and recovered damages of £1,490 which the company sought to deduct in computing its profits. In an unhappily apt phrase Lord Loreburn said that losses could not be deducted "if they fall on the trader in some character other than that of trader". So here he thought that the loss fell on the trader in its character as householder not as trader. One may suppose that one reason why this decision has not been reversed is that businesses now insure their premises, such premiums being deductible.[2] The fineness of the distinction inherent in the House of Lords approach may be seen from two examples given by Lord Loreburn: "losses sustained by a railway company in compensating passengers for accident in travelling might be deducted. On the other hand if a man kept a grocer's shop, for keeping which a house is necessary, and one of the window shutters fell upon and injured a man walking in the street the loss arising thereby ought not to be deducted".[3]

Not only are these examples unclear but they can be made to suggest that deduction should have been allowed in the instant case. First it is not clear what point is being made. On the one hand the example of the grocer's house is reasonably clear if the house is separate from the shop then there is a distinction between trading expenses and personal expenses, and the same might be true if the premises were all in one and the shutter fell off the residential part of the premises. If however the point is the distinction between trading and personal expenses then surely the expense should have been deductible in the instant case. Yet if the distinction is that between trading and householding, between at that time Schedule D, Case I and Schedule A, that suggests a very restricted scope to be given to the example of the railway company and could mean that the company could deduct if the engine was driven negligently with a resulting accident but not if injury occurred when a piece of a station platform gave way. What would happen if there were a defect in a piece of static equipment like a signal is again unclear. Lord James expressed doubts about the application of the principle to a customer within the inn but would have had no doubts about the non-deductibility of an injury to a stranger walking down the street outside the inn. Such a distinction seems today quite incredible.

Simon's Taxes B3.1221; Butterworths Income Tax Service C2.04.

[1] [1906] AC 448 at 453, 5 TC 215 at 220. This decision was based largely on what is now TA 1988, s. 74(e) (infra, § **7: 123**), but is generally treated as an authority on TA 1988, s. 74(a) e.g. *Morgan v Tate and Lyle Ltd* [1954] 2 All ER 413, 35 TC 367, infra, § **7: 106**.

[2] *Usher's Wiltshire Brewery Ltd v Bruce* [1915] AC 433, 6 TC 399.

[3] [1915] AC 433 at 452, 6 TC 399 at 419.

7: 98   Sums spent for the purpose of earning profit will be deductible even though no profit is expected that year;[1] moreover since the test is one of purpose the sums will be deductible even though no profits accrue at all.[2] Losses incurred which are incidental to the carrying out of the business are likewise deductible.[3] Damages for libel can be held deductible when the libel is published in the course of a newspaper business; such damages must be distinguished from those payable for a libel not incidental to the business[4] and from penalties imposed by a court.[5] Penalties, fines and interest charges in respect of the VAT legislation are expressly non-deductible.[6] Damages for wrongful dismissal of employees are in practice allowed although this is hard to reconcile with Lord Davey's dictum. Legal expenses are also deductible even though not for the direct purpose of earning profits provided they are incurred in the running of the business.[7]

Advertising expenses although originally in doubt,[8] are now clearly deductible,[9] as are sponsorship costs provided, in practice, that the sole purpose is to provide the sponsor with a benefit commensurate with the expenditure.[10] So wide has the principle of deductibility become that the dictum in *Strong & Co of Romsey Ltd v Woodifield* should either be repealed or be regarded as having force only in the light of the frequently quoted statement of Viscount Cave LC:

> ". . . a sum of money expended, not of necessity and with a view to a direct and immediate benefit to the trade, but voluntarily and on the grounds of commercial expediency, and in order indirectly to facilitate the carrying on of the business, may yet be expended wholly and exclusively for the purposes of the trade."[11]

However the principle can be applied. In *Knight v Parry*[12] a solicitor was not allowed to deduct the costs of defending (successfully) an action in which professional misconduct and breach of a former contract of employment were alleged. The court held that the sums were spent, at least in part, to ensure that he was not precluded from carrying on his practice and this was not the same as expenditure referable to the carrying on of his practice.

Simon's Taxes B3.1225; Butterworths Income Tax Service C2.04.
  [1] *Vallambrosa Rubber Co Ltd v Farmer* (1910) 5 TC 529; *James Snook & Co Ltd v Blasdale* (1952) 33 TC 244.
  [2] *Lunt v Wellesley* (1945) 27 TC 78.
  [3] *Golder v Great Boulder Proprietary Gold Mines Ltd* (1951) 33 TC 75.
  [4] *Fairrie v Hall* (1947) 28 TC 200.
  [5] *IRC v Von Glehn & Co Ltd* [1920] 2 KB 553, 12 TC 232.
  [6] TA 1988, s. 827(1).
  [7] See *Spofforth and Prince v Golder* [1945] 1 All ER 363, 26 TC 310.
  [8] See Kelly CB in *Watney & Co v Musgrave* (1880) 1 TC 272 at 277.
  [9] *Morley v Lawford & Co* (1928) 14 TC 229.
  [10] HL Written Answer, 26 October 1987, Vol. 489, col. 405. If the taxpayer enjoys ballooning does this enable his company to deduct the sponsorship costs of a balloon journey across the Atlantic? What if he is a sole trader?
  [11] *British Insulated and Helsby Cables Ltd v Atherton* [1926] AC 205 at 211.
  [12] [1973] STC 56, 48 TC 580.

(d) Division of profits or expense of earning profits

7: 99   A sum paid in the course of earning a profit is clearly distinct from a distribution of the profit made. A dividend by a company or a payment under a profit sharing arrangement is a distribution of profit made and not an expense of earning it;[1] by contrast a payment of interest will usually be a deductible expense. The question whether a payment is one of interest or a distribution of profits is one of substance.[2]

The principle has been applied to render non-deductible certain payments by a company purporting to be by way of remuneration to directors or employees. So remuneration based on a percentage of profits must be distinguished from a distribution of profits and while a resolution at an annual meeting to pay a bonus as an appropriation of profit will be conclusive[3] the absence of such a resolution is not conclusive the other way.[4] Excessive remuneration has generally been dealt with under the wholly and exclusively rule but this principle could have been applied instead.

Payments by a partnership to its employees will likewise be treated as deductions but the division of profits between the partners must be just that and no payment to a partner in return for services[4] can qualify as a deductible emolument.[5]

So a partnership can deduct the cost of the salary of an employee but not the share of profits accruing to a partner. However, rent paid by the partnership to a partner is deductible unless excessive.[6]

The correct treatment of a payment towards a partner's personal removal expenses awaits the decision of the House of Lords.[7] The Court of Appeal has distinguished payments for services from other payments and held that while the former are clearly non-deductible there is no reason why the latter should not be, taking the payment of rent to a partner as an example. The issue is a sharp one. The Court reluctantly accepted that a sole trader could not deduct such an expense and thus ends with a distinction between the sole trader and a partnership. This seems undesirable and yet, if one does not like the decision, one has to find a reason. The answer may lie in the fact that where the partnership pays rent to a partner it obtains value in return in the form of the use of the land or article. Where however it contributes to a partner's removal expenses it obtains no benefit other than the services of the partner in the new location and in this sense at least the payment is for his services.

Alternatively the answer may lie in an argument like that advanced—unsuccessfully—by the Revenue in *Hochstrasser v Mayes, supra,* § **6: 26**; that any payment to a partner is taxable to the partnership and thus to the partner unless it is for full consideration rendered by the partner or, perhaps, can be taxed in his hands as income under some other rule. Whether this should be rationalised on the basis that the payment is a division of profit rather than an expense or that the payment is an expense but is not incurred wholly and exclusively for business purposes is a matter the House of Lords will have to address.

A payment by a company to an approved profit-sharing scheme is an allowable deduction[8] and it is understood that in practice the Revenue will allow the deduction of a sum equal to up to 5% of profits to a non-approved scheme.

Simon's Taxes B3.1227; Butterworths Income Tax Service C2.05.

[1] See *Eyres v Finnieston Engineering Co Ltd* (1916) 7 TC 74; *Utol Ltd v IRC* [1944] 1 All ER 190; infra chap. 24 on meaning of distribution under Schedule F.

[2] *Walker v IRC* [1920] 3 KB 648.

[3] As in *Pegg and Ellam Jones Ltd v IRC* (1919) 12 TC 82.

[4] See per Lord Maughan in *Indian Radio and Cable Communications Co Ltd v IT Comr Bombay* [1937] 3 All ER 709 at 713–14, and *British Sugar Manufacturers Ltd v Harris* [1938] 2 KB 220, 21 TC 528. See also *Union Cold Storage Co Ltd v Adamson* (1931) 16 TC 293; *Overy v Ashford Dunn & Co Ltd* (1933) 17 TC 497.

[5] Salaried partners are in practice treated as employees not partners.

[6] *Heastie v Veitch & Co* [1934] 1 KB 535, 18 TC 305.

[7] *MacKinlay v Arthur Young McClelland Moores & Co* [1988] STC 116.

[8] TA 1988, s. 85.

7: 100   Reserves for future expenditure are clearly not deductible, one reason being the present rule.[1] The present rule was also applied to prevent the deduction of sums paid out of the totalisator fund to racecourse owners to assist in improving amenities at racecourses and to provide subsidies to owners and trainers.[2] The distinction inherent in the rule is a fine one but turns on the precise definition of the trade. In that case the trade was that of running totalisators at racecourses and the expenditure in question was not incurred for the purpose of that trade.

---

[1] *Edward Collins & Sons Ltd v IRC* (1925) 12 TC 773.

[2] *Young v Racecourse Betting Control Board* [1959] 3 All ER 215, 38 TC 426.

7: 101   The principle has been applied also to prevent the deduction of taxes on profits, whether imposed by the UK[1] or some foreign government.[2] However other taxes may be deductible. Thus rates[3] may be deductible, as are road licences and stamp duty[4] in all instances depending upon the actual circumstance of the case. In *Harrods (Buenos Aires) Ltd v Taylor-Gooby*[5] the taxpayer company operated in Argentina and was liable to an annual local tax levied on the capital of the company. The courts reversed the Commissioners and held that the tax was deductible since it was not a tax that depended upon the company having earned any profits but was simply an essential cost of trading in that country. The actual circumstances may show that the particular tax is a capital expense in which case it will not be deductible.[6]

Simon's Taxes B3.1451; Butterworths Income Tax Service C2.05.

[1] Lord Halsbury in *Ashton Gas Co v A-G* [1906] AC 10 at 12.

[2] *IRC v Dowdall O'Mahoney & Co Ltd* [1952] 1 All ER 531, 33 TC 259. On deduction of overseas tax, see now TA 1988, s. 811 (TA 1970, s. 516) and infra, § **36: 03**.

[3] *Smith v Lion Brewery Co Ltd* [1911] AC 150, 5 TC 568.

[4] *Semble* per Buckley J in *Harrods (Buenos Aires) Ltd v Taylor-Gooby* (1963) 41 TC 450.

[5] (1963) 41 TC 450.

[6] E.g. stamp duty on conveyance of land forming part of the fixed capital of the trade or if the payment in *Harrods (Buenos Aires) Ltd v Taylor-Gooby* had been a once only payment for the right to trade in Argentina.

7: 102   More controversially the principle has been applied to prevent the deduction of expenses incurred by a company in appealing, successfully, against an assessment to tax on profits. The expense of preparing the documents needed to be filed under the Companies Act would clearly be deductible as would the preparation of accounts for internal management.[1] However as Lord Simonds put it:[2]

> "What profit he has earned he has earned before ever the voice of the tax-gatherer is heard. He would have earned no more and no less if there was no such thing as Income Tax. His profit is no more affected by the exigibility of tax than is a man's temperature altered by the price of a thermometer, even though he starts by haggling about the price of it."

As a matter of practice the Revenue do allow the costs of preparing the income tax return.

Simon's Taxes B3.1452, 1453; Butterworths Income Tax Service C2.05.

[1] *Worsley Brewery Co Ltd v IRC* (1932) 17 TC 349 esp. per Romer LJ at 360.

[2] In *Smith's Potato Estates Ltd v Bolland* [1948] 2 All ER 367 at 374, 30 TC 267 at 293.

One criticism is that expenditure in order to preserve the company's assets is deductible; see *Morgan v Tate and Lyle,* infra, § **7: 109**. However the expense must avoid rule (d) as well as rule (e); the motive for the payment cannot turn a profit into an expense. But this reasoning seems to be contrary to that of the Court of Appeal in *Heather v PE Consulting Group Ltd* [1973] 1 All ER 8, 48 TC 320. The position cannot therefore be clearly stated.

(e) Capital expenditure

7: 103   Capital expenditure is not deductible in computing profits even though incurred wholly and exclusively for business purposes; such expenditure may qualify for relief under the capital allowance system.

The task of distinguishing revenue from capital expenditure is not easy; and the problem has been made difficult by the inevitable fact that words or formulae that have been found useful in one set of facts may be neither relevant nor significant in another.[1]

Two tests are to be discerned in the older cases, although these have now been to some extent superseded. The first distinguished fixed capital from circulating capital;[2] expenditure on the former was capital expenditure while that on the latter was not. Fixed capital is retained in the shape of assets which either produce income without further action, e.g. shares held by an investment company, or are made use of to produce income, e.g. machinery in a factory. Circulating capital is that which the company intends should be used by being temporarily parted with and circulated in the business only to return with, it is hoped, profit, e.g. money spent on trading stock.[3] The difficulty with this test is that it sometimes begs the very question at issue.[4]

The second test was enunciated by Viscount Cave in *Atherton v British Insulated and Helsby Cables Ltd* and became known as the enduring benefit test. He said:[5]

> "When an expenditure is made not only once for all, but with a view to bringing into existence an asset or advantage for the enduring benefit of a trade, I think there is very good reason (in the absence of special circumstances leading to an opposite conclusion) for treating such an expenditure as properly attributable not to revenue but to capital."

The principal difficulty with this test was that many sorts of expenditure have an enduring effect and not all of them are of a capital nature. Thus a payment to be rid of an unsatisfactory employee or agent is a revenue expense[6] but one to be rid of a term of a lease is a capital expense.[6] A payment to a trust for the benefit of certain employees where the amount and the duration of the fund were uncertain and the whole fund could be distributed at any time was held to be a revenue expense.[7]

The latest test, reinforced by the House of Lords in *Tucker v Granada Motorway Services Ltd*[8] requires first that one isolate the asset on which the sum has been spent; sums spent on an asset of a capital nature may be capital while sums spent on other things will not be. If that asset is of a capital nature, one then considers the nature of the particular expense; so sums spent on acquiring the capital asset will be capital while sums spent maintaining or repairing it will be revenue. At this point the earlier tests may reappear as in *Walker v Joint Credit Card Co Ltd*[9] and *Whitehead v Tubbs (Elastics) Ltd*.[10] This text has now been used in connection with liabilities. If the liability is on capital account, a loss, e.g. an exchange loss, incurred on repayment of the loan, will be a capital loss whereas it would have been a revenue loss if the loan had been a revenue transaction.[11]

This test is not without its difficulties. The place of the asset within the business is not usually too difficult to determine, indeed it is similar to the old distinction between fixed and circulating capital; but problems arise where the asset is not discernible as part of the assets of the business, as where one is dealing with trading arrangements with other traders or with the modification of a company's charter or articles of association. Thus is money spent in removing restrictions on a company's business a capital expense?[12] Care must also be taken in defining the asset accurately.[13] Similar problems arise with the idea of an advantage. Thus, if a taxpayer borrows money for a period does he simply receive cash or does he obtain a furtherence of the trade for the period of the loan?[14] Apart from this there remains the difficulty of deciding whether the particular expense is of a capital or a revenue nature. It would, however, be foolish to reject the asset test simply because it does not provide an answer to all cases; the danger is that it will be applied, as have its predecessors, without regard to the variety of facts or, again like its predecessors, without regard to the disclaimer of universality uttered by its formulators.

Simon's Taxes B3.911, 1241–1244; Butterworths Income Tax Service C2.11.
  [1] Per Lord Radcliffe in *Taxes Comr v Nchanga Consolidated Copper Mines Ltd* [1964] 1 All ER 208 at 212, [1964] AC 948 at 959.
  [2] The dual reference to capital is unfortunate but it refers to the capital of the company and so the source from which the expenditure is funded.
  [3] See per Swinfen Eady LJ in *Ammonia Soda Co v Chamberlain* [1918] 1 Ch 266 and per Romer LJ in *Golden Horseshoe (New) Ltd v Thurgood* [1934] 1 KB 548, 18 TC 280; *Pattison v Marine Midland Ltd* [1981] STC 540. This is not a question of pure fact per Lord Evershed MR in *Pyrah v Annis & Co Ltd* (1956) 37 TC 163 at 173.
  [4] See Lord MacMillan in *Van den Berghs Ltd v Clark* (1934) 19 TC 390 at 432.
  [5] [1926] AC 205 at 213, 10 TC 155 at 192.
  [6] See *Anglo Persian Oil Co Ltd v Dale* (1931) 16 TC 253.
  [7] *Jeffs v Ringtons Ltd* [1985] STC 809, [1986] 1 All ER 144.
  [8] [1979] STC 393, [1979] 2 All ER 801.
  [9] [1982] STC 427 at 437.
  [10] [1984] STC 1, CA.
  [11] *Beauchamp v F W Woolworth plc* [1988] STC 714 at 721c.
  [12] It was held not to be a capital expense in *IRC v Carron Co* 1968 SC 47, 45 TC 18, HL; decision reversed by HL [1989] STC 510.
  [13] See *Bolton v International Drilling Co Ltd*, infra, § **7: 109**.
  [14] See *Beauchamp v F W Woolworth plc* [1989] STC 510.

7: 104 Some other formulations may be helpful.

In *Vallambrosa Rubber Co Ltd v Farmer* Lord Dunedin said that capital expenditure was something that was going to be spent once and for all and income expenditure was a thing that was going to recur every year,[1] while in *Ounsworth v Vickers Ltd* Rowlatt J said that the distinction was between expenditure that was to meet a continuous demand and expenditure made once and for all.[2]

In *Taxes Comrs v Nchanga Consolidated Copper Mines Ltd*[3] Lord Radcliffe said that there was a demarcation between the cost of creating, acquiring or enlarging the permanent (which does not mean perpetual) structure of which the income is to be the produce or fruit and the cost of earning that income itself or performing the income earning operations; he added that this was probably as illuminating a line of distinction as the law by itself is likely to achieve.

  [1] (1910) 5 TC 529 at 536.
  [2] (1915) 6 TC 671 at 675.
  [3] [1964] 1 All ER 208, [1964] AC 948.

7: 105 In deciding these difficult questions the court's task is to determine the true profits of the business but the court is hampered by the fact that a deductible expense must be entered when the expense is incurred and therefore cannot be spread over a number of years. It follows that to allow a major item of expenditure as a deduction in one year when its benefits will be spread over many will necessarily give a distorted picture of the profitability of the company.[1] Moreover many of these cases were decided when the taxation of capital gains was not a feature of the UK tax system and it would have been anomalous to allow the deduction of an item as a revenue expense when a receipt on the disposal of the same item would not be a trading receipt.

There is no rule whereby the treatment of the expenditure in the hands of the payer predetermines its character in the hands of the payee. So an item can be a revenue expense and a capital receipt or a capital expense and a revenue receipt.[2]

Butterworths Income Tax Service C2.11.
[1] See Lord Reid in *Regent Oil Co Ltd v Strick* [1965] 3 All ER 174 at 181, 43 TC 1 at 31.
[2] *Regent Oil Co Ltd v Strick*, supra.

7: 106   *Acquisition of a business (capital) or running a business (revenue)—* The costs of acquiring a business are capital expenses. Expenses shortly after acquiring a business will not be deductible if they are part of the acquisition cost,[1] especially where the expense is the sums paid on the termination of the contract of employment of a senior employee.[2] See also supra, §§ **7: 45** and **7: 56**. The matter is however one of fact.[3]

The costs of running a business are clearly revenue expenses so payments to employees for their services are deductible. Many of these expenses will be in the form of salaries or wages[4] which will therefore be taxable as income of the employee. A director's salary is also deductible. To allow such payments to be taxable in the hands of the employee but not deductible by the employer would amount to double taxation. There is however no correlation between these two and it is possible for a payment to be deductible by the employer and not taxable to the employee,[5] as in the case of certain benefits in kind.

Deductible sums include not only salaries proper but also pensions[6] and retirement gratuities. There is no rule that to be deductible the payment must relate to services rendered in that year.[7] However lump sum payments to fund future payments tend to be capital payments.[8]

FA 1989 introduces an important timing rule for the deduction of emoluments. Broadly, these are not to be deductible for Schedule D, Case I or II until the sum is brought into charge on the employee under Schedule E.[9]

Butterworths Income Tax Service C2.12.
[1] *Royal Insurance Co v Watson* [1897] AC 1, 3 TC 500.
[2] *Bassett Enterprises Ltd v Petty* (1938) 21 TC 730.
[3] *IRC v Patrick Thomson Ltd* (1956) 37 TC 145.
[4] But not sums paid to the Revenue in respect of tax not deducted under the PAYE scheme; *Bamford v ATA Advertising Ltd* [1972] 3 All ER 535, 48 TC 359. Incentive payments are deductible even if they are to enable the workforce to buy control of the employer: *Heather v PE Consulting Group Ltd* [1973] 1 All ER 8, 48 TC 320; see the discussion of this case in *E. Bott Ltd v Price* [1987] STC 100 at 106.
[5] Supra, § **6: 23**. For the converse position, see *Weight v Salmon* (1935) 19 TC 174, supra, §§ **6: 56** and **6.57**.
[6] *Smith v Incorporated Council of Law Reporting for England and Wales* (1914) 6 TC 477.
[7] *Hancock v General Reversionary Society and Investment Co Ltd* [1919] 1 KB 25, 7 TC 358.
[8] *Rowntree & Co Ltd v Curtis* (1924) 8 TC 678; *British Insulated and Helsby Cables Ltd v Atherton* [1926] AC 205, 10 TC 155. But see TA 1988, s. 592(4) (FA 1970, s. 21(3)) *Hancock's* case, supra, and *Jeffs v Ringtons Ltd* [1985] STC 809, [1986] 1 All ER 144.
[9] FA 1989, s. 43.

Facilities for and reorganisation of business (capital)

7: 107   The facilities are clearly capital of the business so expenditure on them may be capital. Thus the building of a factory is a capital expense and there will also be so classified ancillary works such as the provision of a water supply,[1] of drainage[2] and roads.[3] Likewise the cost of sinking a mine shaft is a capital expense[4] as is the cost of reconverting an oil rig at the end of its lease period[5] or the cost of acquiring a waste tipping site.[6] Capital allowances will sometimes be available for such expenditure.

The expense of moving from one set of business premises to another is a capital expense[7] although the costs of removing trading stock are not so regarded. In practice removal costs which are forced on the trader, as on the expiration of a lease are allowed. Where however the general rule applies it prevents the deduction of ancillary costs such as conveyancing expenses.

Once for all expenditure on reorganisation may be capital. This was so in *Watney Combe Reid & Co Ltd v Pike*[7] where a brewery made *ex gratia* payments to tenants under a scheme by which separate management companies were substituted for tenants; the purpose was to make the assets more profitable[8] but it was important that the scheme involved a new corporate structure and a new way of doing business.

Facilities may be financial as well as physical. So the question whether an exchange loss on a borrowing is deductible may turn on whether the borrowing is part of the taxpayer's revenue transactions or an accretion to capital. The latter has some degree of permanence, the former is essentially short-term. A fixed five year loan was held to be on capital account—so that a foreign exchange loss on repayment was not an allowable deduction.[9]

---

[1] *Boyce v Whitwick Colliery Co Ltd* (1934) 18 TC 655.
[2] *Bean v Doncaster Amalgmated Collieries Ltd* [1944] 1 All ER 621, 27 TC 296.
[3] *Pitt v Castle Hill Warehousing Co Ltd* [1974] 3 All ER 146, [1974] STC 420. See also *Ounsworth v Vickers Ltd* [1915] 3 KB 267, 6 TC 671.
[4] *Bonner v Basset Mines Ltd* (1912) 6 TC 146.
[5] *RTZ Oil and Gas Ltd v Elliss* [1987], STC, p. 512.
[6] *Rolfe v Wimpey Waste Management Ltd* [1989] STC 454, CA (Special Commissioner reversed).
[7] *Granite Supply Association Ltd v Kitton* (1905) 5 TC 168.
[8] [1982] STC 733.
[9] *Beauchamp v F W Woolworth plc* [1989] STC 510; this was despite by the fact that the borrowing had been treated as an accretion to capital on the company's accounts.

Expansion of a business (capital) or maintenance of a business (revenue)

7: 108   The expense of an application for planning permission over land is generally capital since the land is a capital asset and this expense is more than mere maintenance.[1] Likewise the premises are capital assets and so where a brewer applies for a licence for new premises the legal cost of applying for the new licence is not deductible[2] any more than would be the legal costs of acquiring the new premises or the costs of moving his plant and stock.[3]

A licence governing the terms of one's trade is different from a tax incurred in running it. So in *Pyrah v Annis*[4] it was held that the costs of an unsuccessful application to vary an existing public carrier's licence by increasing the number of vehicles from four to seven was capital expenditure because the licence was an asset retained by the trader which produces income. However in *IRC v Carron Co* a company was entitled to deduct the legal costs of altering its charter so as to remove restrictions on ordinary business operations.[5] This distinction is somewhat fine.

Simon's Taxes B3.1331.
[1] *ECC Quarries Ltd v Watkis* [1975] STC 578, [1975] 3 All ER 843. A land developer can deduct such expenses since the land is not capital.
[2] *Morse v Stedeford* (1934) 18 TC 457.
[3] *Granite Supply Association Ltd v Kitton* (1905) 5 TC 168, see also *Pendleton v Mitchells and Butlers Ltd* [1969] 2 All ER 928, 45 TC 341.
[4] [1956] 2 All ER 858, 37 TC 163.
[5] (1968) 45 TC 18.

Preservation of capital (revenue)

7: 109   Sums paid in order to preserve the capital or capital assets of the business are revenue expenses. In *Cooke v Quick Shoe Repair Service*[1] the firm had bought a business and arranged for the vendor to settle outstanding liabilities to suppliers and employees. When he failed to do so the firm paid off the creditors and was held entitled to deduct the sums so paid because they were paid to preserve the goodwill of the business and not to buy it.

Sums paid in order to protect title to capital assets have been held to be revenue expenses. The reason for this is that the expenses are incurred in maintaining the company's capital and so are just as deductible as expenses of repair and maintenance on the fixed assets of the company.[2] The expenditure results in neither the improvement nor the acquisition of any fixed capital asset.[3] So expenses incurred in resisting an unfounded allegation of misrepresentation have been held deductible as have sums paid by way of settlement of a civil claim against the trade.[4] It is clear that sums paid by way of fines or penalty are not deductible but this is because the expense is not incurred wholly and exclusively for the purposes of trade.[5] It is however of importance since it suggests that expenditure to preserve the company's entire trading apparatus can be revenue expenditure.

However in *Bolton v International Drilling Co Ltd*,[6] where a company's sole income earning asset was originally acquired subject to another person's option to reacquire it, a sum paid for release of the option was not revenue expenditure.[6] This is because until that time the trade's right in the asset was not one of complete ownership; hence the payment did not preserve the original title but improved it.

The importance of looking at the assets is also shown by *Walker v Joint Credit Card Co Ltd* where sums paid not just to preserve goodwill, but to improve it were held to be capital expenditure.[7]

A controversial application of that principle occurred in *Morgan v Tate and Lyle Ltd*[8] where the company successfully claimed to be entitled to deduct expenses incurred in a publicity campaign to defeat the proposed nationalisation of the company. The form of nationalisation proposed for the sugar industry was not the compulsory acquisition of its shares but the compulsory acquisition of its assets and on this basis the House of Lords held that the costs of the campaign were deductible. If the company had been faced with a take-over of its business by a group of persons anxious to acquire control through the purchase of its shares it was clear that the costs of resisting such a takeover would not have been deductible, the threat in such a case being to the existing management rather than to the assets or trade of the company. Those reading the advertisements issued during the campaign might be forgiven for not appreciating that the company was resisting not nationalisation in general but merely one form of nationalisation on terms thought disadvantageous to the shareholders.

Simon's Taxes B3.1351; Butterworths Income Tax Service C2.12.
¹ (1949) 30 TC 460—"an odd case" per Walton J in *Garforth v Tankard Carpets Ltd* [1980] STC 251 at 259–260. See also *Walker v Cater Securities Ltd* [1974] STC 390, [1974] 3 All ER 63 (taxpayer owned shares in a customer-company; X had option to buy these shares; sum paid by taxpayer to X for release of option held revenue expense; this conclusion supported by Revenue evidence; payment considered in substance to be to keep an important customer, not just to acquire a capital asset—see *Bolton v International Drilling Co Ltd* [1983] STC 70 at 92).
² Distinguish *Pitt v Castle Hill Warehousing Co Ltd* [1974] STC 420, [1974] 3 All ER 146.
³ *Southern v Borax Consolidated Ltd* [1940] 4 All ER 412, 23 TC 597.
⁴ *IT Comr Bihar and Orissa v Singh* [1942] 1 All ER 362.
⁵ Supra, § 7: 98.
⁶ [1983] STC 70.
⁷ [1982] STC 427.
⁸ [1954] 2 All ER 413, 35 TC 367. Cf. *Hammond Engineering Co Ltd v IRC* [1975] STC 334.

Costs of loan capital

7: 110 The costs of raising, servicing and repaying loan capital are the subject to a mixture of case law and statute. Statute permits the deduction of incidental costs of loan finance TA 1988, s. 77 and Interest is the subject of a special set of rules—infra, § **7: 125**. This leaves the issue of the deductibility of an exchange loss on the repayment of a loan. In *Pattison v Marine Midland Ltd*¹ a bank borrowed a large sum in US dollars by way of unsecured loan stock issued to its parent, the lender. Vinelott J held that the loss was not deductible. The loan represented a long term obligation entered into for the purpose of raising money employed by the company to enable it to commence trading; the use of the funds could not alter their capital nature. This matter was not raised on the further appeals in that case.

In *Beauchamp v F W Woolworth plc*² the taxpayer company, with an annual turnover of some £300m, borrowed 50m Swiss francs for a five year period; the loan was immediately converted into sterling. The following year the taxpayer incurred a second such loan, which was also converted. In due course the loans were repaid but, owing to the decline of sterling against the Swiss franc, at a large loss. The House of Lords held that the loan was an accretion to capital and not a revenue transaction and therefore the loss was not allowable.

¹ [1981] STC 540.
² [1989] STC 510.

Examples

(1) *Ending onerous obligations and restrictions*

7: 111   A payment for getting rid of a permanent disadvantage or onerous burden may be an enduring benefit and so a capital expense. The problem here is that whereas it is well settled that a payment to dismiss an unsatisfactory employee is a revenue expense, it is equally well settled that certain other payments will be a capital expense. One starting point is to ask whether the payments made under the liability being got rid of would themselves be revenue expenses.¹ So in *Alexander Howard & Co Ltd v Bentley*² the taxpayer paid a lump sum to be rid of a contingent liability to pay an annuity to the widow of its governing director; the annuity payments would not have been deductible since not paid wholly and exclusively for trade purposes but rather as an adjunct to shares; it followed that the lump sum payment was not deductible either.

In principle an expense incurred to be rid of a revenue expense ought to be deductible; just as a surrogatum for loss of profit is a trading receipt so a commutation of deductible outlay should be a revenue expense. However, while it appears to be true that payments to get rid of liabilities which are *not* revenue expenses will be treated as not deductible, payments to get rid of revenue expenses are not always so. One must distinguish getting rid of a charge against revenue from acquiring a capital asset which enables one to get rid of such a charge. So the purchase of labour-saving machinery is a capital expense and cannot be converted into a revenue expense simply because it can be shown to reduce the wage bill.³

Whereas expenditure incurred on the maintenance of a physical asset of the company is revenue, expenditure on replacing that asset will be capital expenditure. Thus if a channel is continually being silted up and the trader decides to replace the silting channel with a concrete one, that is capital expenditure even though the costs of clearing the silt would have been a revenue expense.⁴

A payment to settle a capital liability is clearly a capital payment. So where a company had agreed to buy a ship to use in its trade a payment made on cancellation of the contract was a capital expense.⁵

Simon's Taxes B3.1353; Butterworths Income Tax Service C2.21.

¹ Per Simon LJ in *Bean v Doncaster Amalgamated Collieries Ltd* (1944) 27 TC 296 at 312.
² (1948) 30 TC 334. It does not follow that this expense was capital—simply that it was not for trading purposes and so not deductible.
³ Per Rowlatt J in *Anglo-Persian Oil Co Ltd v Dale* (1931) 16 TC 253 at 261.
⁴ Per Rowlatt J in *Mitchell v B W Noble Ltd* [1927] 1 KB 719 at 728, 11 TC 372 at 415.
⁵ *Countess Warwick SS Co Ltd v Ogg* [1924] 2 KB 292, 8 TC 652.

7: 112   Difficulties arise over payments to vary or terminate leases. These difficulties stem from the nature of the lease for tax purposes in that while payments of rent under the lease would clearly be revenue expenses, the payment of a premium would not even if paid by instalments[1] provided the lease itself formed part of the capital structure of the business. It followed that where a company had a lease of a shop for five years and the company ceased to use that shop after two years, the rent would still be deductible in computing its profits assuming, as was the case, that the trade itself was still conducted from other premises.[2]

Where the lease is a capital asset of the business a payment to vary the terms of the lease will be a capital expense. This may be because the payment rendering the lease either more advantageous or less disadvantageous improves the lease and so comes within the next example—§ 7: 114. In *Tucker v Granada Motorway Services Ltd*[3] the landlord (the Minister of Transport) was entitled to rent from the lessees of a motorway service station together with an additional rent based on takings, the latter to include an element for tobacco duty. As tobacco duty rose the lessees found it difficult to make a profit and so it was agreed to exclude the tobacco duty from the calculation in return for a lump sum. The House of Lords held that the lump sum was a capital expense; it was quite irrelevant that the purpose of the expenditure was to increase profit.

A fortiori a payment for the *surrender* of the lease in commutation of the liability to pay rent is a capital expense and not deductible.[4]

---

[1] *IRC v Adam* (1928) 14 TC 34—see Tucker Report 1951, Cmd. 8189 § 247.
[2] *IRC v Falkirk Iron Co Ltd* (1933) 17 TC 625.
[3] [1979] STC 393 [1979] 2 All ER 801.
[4] *Cowcher v Richard Mills & Co Ltd* (1927) 13 TC 216; *Mallett v Staveley Coal and Iron Co Ltd* [1928] 2 KB 405, 13 TC 772; see also *IRC v William Sharp & Son* (1959) 38 TC 341.

7: 113 Payment to be rid of a director whose continuance in office would be detrimental to the company is a revenue expense.[1] This is because the company receives no enduring advantage; one cannot point to any asset of the company which is enhanced; an employee is not a permanency and the satisfactory state of the workforce is not regarded as part of the capital of the business. In *Anglo-Persian Oil Co Ltd v Dale*[2] this was extended to allow deduction of substantial payments to agents to terminate an agency agreement with eleven years to run. This decision equates an agency with a contract of employment and rests on the statement by Lawrence LJ in the Court of Appeal that the cancellation "merely effected a change in the company business methods and internal organisation leaving its fixed capital untouched".[3]

Simon's Taxes B3.1429; Butterworths Income Tax Service C2.21.
[1] *Mitchell v B W Noble Ltd* [1927] 1 KB 719, 11 TC 372.
[2] [1932] 1 KB 124, 16 TC 253.
[3] [1932] 1 KB 124 at 141, 16 TC 253 at 272.

7: 114 In *Whitehead v Tubbs (Elastics) Ltd*[1] a payment was made to secure the release of a term in a loan agreement which had significantly limited the company's power to borrow money. This payment was held to be capital. By contrast, in *IRC v Carron Co*[2] the court had held that a payment to secure the alteration of a company's constitution was a revenue expense. This case was distinguished in *Whitehead v Tubbs (Elastics) Ltd* on the basis that the restrictions in that case were attributable not to any asset of the company but to its constitution, the alteration of which would normally have been effected as part of its day to day management; moreover in *IRC v Carron* no asset was brought into existence and nor was there any expenditure on any asset or liability of the company.

---

[1] [1984] STC 1, CA.
[2] (1968) 45 TC 18, HL.

---

(2) *Repairs (revenue) and improvements (capital)*

7: 115   TA 1988, s. 74 expressly disqualifies in para. (*d*): "any sums expended for repairs of premises occupied . . . for the purposes of the trade beyond the sum actually expended for the purpose", a provision which restricts deductions to sums actually spent and therefore prohibits the deduction of sums set aside by way of reserve for future expenditure; while para. (*g*) prohibits the deduction of any capital employed in improvements of premises occupied for the purposes of the trade profession or vocation. At first sight this paragraph would seem to be directed to the source from which the trader chooses to finance his improvements, however it is generally taken to mean that sums spent on improvements are capital payments and therefore not deductible, while sums spent on the repair of capital assets are deductible.

Improving the building of a factory is a capital cost because it is a material improvement of the land.[1] Money spent on the replacement of one kind of rail by a superior kind is not deductible, since it increases the value of the railway line.[2] Expense incurred in increasing the number of sleepers under each rail was admitted to be capital expense in *Rhodesia Railways Ltd v Bechuanaland Protectorate IT Collector*,[3] but the railway company was allowed to deduct as repairs the cost of works in renewing 74 miles of railway track by replacing rails and sleepers. This was not an improvement since it only restored the worn track to its normal condition and did not increase the capacity of the line in any way. Money spent on pulling down a chimney and building a new bigger and better chimney[4] or on renovating a factory with a higher roof line and so more space is not deductible.[5] The question whether work is a repair or an improvement is one of fact.[6]

Where an improvement is carried out no deduction may be claimed for such part of the expenditure as would have been needed to pay for mere repair. In *Thomas Wilson (Keighley) Ltd v Emmerson*,[7] Danckwerts J commented, "It seems to me to be a hardship and something which is calculated to discourage manufacturers from making the best use of their property". The theoretical reason for disallowing apportionment is clear enough but one may notice that under Schedule A the Revenue will by concession allow such part of the cost as would have been needed to carry out the repair work.[8] On the other hand if the work consists of a number of separate jobs it may be possible to distinguish between the different items thus allowing some of the expense so in *Conn v Robins Bros Ltd*[9] the construction of "a ladies toilet" was held to be an improvement but the insertion of steel joists a repair.

Simon's Taxes B3.1333, 1344; Butterworths Income Tax Service C2.22.
[1] For capital allowances, see infra, chapter 8.
[2] *Highland Rly Co v Balderston* (1889) 2 TC 485; and see *LCC v Edwards* (1909), 5 TC 383.
[3] Admitted by taxpayer [1933] AC 368 at 372; but see Lord Cooper in *Lawrie v IRC* (1952) 34 TC 20 at 25.
[4] *O'Grady v Bullcroft Main Collieries Ltd* (1932) 17 TC 93.
[5] *Thomas Wilson (Keighley) Ltd v Emmerson* (1960) 39 TC 360; *Lawrie v IRC* (1952) 34 TC 20; *Mann Crossman and Paulin Ltd v IRC* [1947] 1 All ER 742, 28 TC 410.
[6] *Conn v Robins Bros Ltd* (1966) 43 TC 266 at 274.
[7] (1960) 39 TC 360 at 366.
[8] Extra-statutory concession B4 (1988), **Simon's Taxes, Division H2.2.** infra, § **9: 12.**
[9] (1966) 43 TC 266.

7: 116   *Renewals or repairs.*—As Buckley LJ said in *Lurcott v Wakely and Wheeler*,[1] not a revenue case:[2]

> "'repair' and 'renew' are not words expressive of clear contrast . . . repair is restoration by renewal or replacement of subsidiary parts of a whole. Renewal, as distinguished from repair, is reconstruction of the entirety, meaning by the entirety not necessarily the whole but substantially the whole subject matter under discussion."

Thus the replacement of a slate on a roof[3] would be a repair, but the rebuilding of a retort house in a gas works would be a renewal.[4]

This test presupposes a satisfactory definition of the unit repaired or renewed. In *O'Grady v Bullcroft Main Collieries Ltd*[5] a chimney used to carry away fumes from a furnace had become unsafe and so the company built a new one. Rowlatt J said that in his view the chimney was not a part of the factory but an entirety. Similarly, in *Margrett v Lowestoft Water and Gas Co* the replacement of a reservoir by a new one was a renewal, not a repair. On the other hand in *Samuel Jones & Co (Devonvale) Ltd v IRC*[6] the costs of replacing an unsafe chimney at a factory were held deductible. In the Court of Session which reversed the Special Commissioners Lord Cooper said that the factory was the entirety, the chimney therefore only a part of the entirety. The court also stressed the low cost of the replacement of the chimney relatively to the insured value of the factory, a point not taken in *O'Grady v Bullcroft Main Collieries Ltd.* The distinction between a part and the entirety thus appears to be a convenient method of describing a conclusion rather than a helpful test.

The question seems to be one of the size and importance of the work. One big job may be capital whereas a combination of small jobs may be revenue. In *Phillips v Whieldon Sanitary Potteries Ltd*[7] the replacement of a barrier protecting a factory from water in a canal was held to be a renewal and so capital expenditure, the court taking into account the extent of the work, the permanent nature of the new barrier and the enduring benefit it would confer on the business by preserving a part of the fixed capital. In that case Donovan J followed the *Bullcroft* case and reversed the Commissioners.

An expenditure may be in respect of a repair as opposed to a renewal even though it is carried out some time after the need has first arisen. Thus the costs of keeping a channel dredged would be income expenditure even though the dredging was done only once every three years or so.[8] There is no need to take away every grain of sand as it comes.

[1] [1911] 1 KB 905 at 923–4 cited e.g. by Lord MacMillan in *Rhodesia Railways Ltd v Bechuanaland Protectorate IT Collector* [1933] AC 368 at 374.

[2] The case concerned the construction of a lessee's covenant to keep in thorough repair and in good condition.

[3] Per Rowlatt J in *O'Grady v Bullcroft Main Collieries Ltd* (1932) 17 TC 93 at 101.

[4] Per Donovan J in *Phillips v Whieldon Sanitary Potteries Ltd* (1952) 33 TC 213 at 219.

[5] (1932) 17 TC 93; the ratio was that the chimney was an addition, there being no evidence that the old one was pulled down, see also *Wynne-Jones v Bedale Auction Ltd* [1977] STC 50, 51 TC 426 (cattle ring, not whole complex, the relevant unit): criticised (1977) BTR 184 (Baxter).

[6] (1951) 32 TC 513; see also *Margrett v Lowestoft Water and Gas Co* (1935) 19 TC 481.

[7] (1952) 33 TC 213; contrast *Conn v Robins Bros Ltd* (1966) 43 TC 266.

[8] Per Rowlatt J in *Ounsworth v Vickers Ltd* (1915) 6 TC 671.

7: 117   *Initial repairs.*—Where a trader acquires an asset which requires extensive repairs before it is in a usable condition, the expenses of those repairs are not deductible since they are as much capital expenditure as the costs of acquiring the asset itself. Were the rule otherwise a trader could convert at least a part of the prospective capital expense into a revenue item by buying the asset in an incomplete state and finishing the work himself, perhaps by employing the person who had worked on it before its acquisition.

In *Law Shipping Co Ltd v IRC*[1] a shipping company bought a ship which was at that date ready to sail with freight booked. The Lloyds survey was then overdue but with the consent of the insurers, the ship was allowed to complete the voyage. The ship cost £97,000 and the company had to spend an extra £51,558 on repairs in order for the vessel to pass the survey. Of that sum some £12,000 was in respect of repairs caused by deterioration during the voyage and was allowed by the Revenue, the balance of £39,500 was not, correctly as the Court of Session held.

[1] 1924 SC 74, 12 TC 621 see also *IRC v Granite City Steamship Co Ltd* 1927 SC 705, 13 TC 1 and the expenditure on the branch line in *Highland Rly Co v Balderston* (1889) 2 TC 485.

7: 118   However it is not every repair incurred to put right something occurring before an asset is acquired that is disallowed. The *Law Shipping* case applies where the expenditure is required to make the asset commercially viable; a different rule applies where the asset is already so viable. In *Odeon Associated Theatres Ltd v Jones*[1] the company bought a cinema in 1945. Only small sums had been permitted to be spent in the previous five years and restrictions on repair work lasted for some time after the war. The cinema was open to the public and was a profit earning asset. The Court of Appeal held that sums spent subsequently to the acquisition in respect of the deferred repairs were deductible. The primary reason was that such would be in accordance with the normal principles of commerical accountancy, as the Commissioners had made a finding not made in the *Law Shipping* case. However there were other differences. Although in the *Law Shipping* case the ship had been permitted to complete one voyage it was clear that after that a full insurance survey would be needed and the price showed that substantial expenditure would be needed before the ship would again be a profit earning asset. By contrast the cinema was an immediate income earning asset and it appeared that the price had not been affected by the fact of disrepair. Two other facts are material. First, even if the vendors had wished to carry out the repair work before the sale they would have been unable to do so because of the restrictions. Secondly, there was no indication that the taxpayer had in fact been put to greater expense by reason of the deferred repairs. The precise extent of the case is uncertain.

Butterworths Income Tax Service C2.22.
[1] [1972] 1 All ER 681, 48 TC 257, CA. See also *Whelan v Dover Harbour Board* (1934) 18 TC 555. This decision must cast doubt on *Jackson v Laskers Home Furnishers Ltd* [1956] 3 All ER 891, 37 TC 69.

---

(3) *Allowable capital expenditure—the renewals basis*

7: 119   The distinction between repair and renewal is blurred by the Revenue practice of allowing the cost of replacing machinery and plant as a revenue expense. This practice is quite distinct from the capital allowances system. There appear to be two distinct legal bases for this practice which, confusingly, is called a renewals allowance. One is the general theory of profit which would equate a renewal with a repair and would regard both as maintaining intact the capital originally invested in the physical assets of the business. The disadvantage of the explanation is that it is quite inconsistent with the cases just considered and would presumably apply to a range of expenditures other than those on machinery and plant.[1]

The second explanation rests on TA 1988, s. 74(*d*) which disallows sums spent on the "supply, repairs or alterations of any implements, utensils or articles employed, for the purposes of a trade, profession or vocation, beyond the sum actually expended for those purposes". As drafted this simply prohibits the deduction of reserves for future expenditure and so may be taken to allow actual expenditure; further it draws no distinction between initial and replacement utensils. Moreover it would confine the allowance to implements, utensils and articles and thus not necessarily cover all types of machinery and plant.[2]

It seems best to regard this as an extra statutory concession dating from the days when there were no capital allowances. This not only avoids the problems mentioned but also justifies the Revenue's insistence that some renewals allowances are to be made only over a period of two or three years.

Where the renewals basis is adopted the allowance given is the cost of the new article (excluding additions or improvements) less the scrap or realised value of the replaced article. The cost of the new article may be greater or less than that of the old.

Successfully to claim a renewals allowance is to classify the expenditure as revenue. However this is not to prevent a later switch to the capital allowance system. The two systems of relief are alternatives.[3]

---

[1] But note Revenue Practice in relation to shop fronts: **Simon's Taxes B3.1333.**
[2] See *IRC v Great Wigston Gas Co* (1946) 29 TC 197. An item may be capital expenditure even though on utensils—see *Hinton v Maden and Ireland Ltd* [1959] 3 All ER 356, 38 TC 391.
[3] See extra-statutory concession B1 (1988), **Simon's Taxes, Division H2.2.**

(4) Trading stock—the tree and the fruit

7: 120   The purchase of trading stock is generally a deductible revenue expense. However care is needed to distinguish the purchase of trading stock from the purchase of an asset bearing trading stock.[1] Thus the purchase of a mine for extraction purposes is an item of capital expenditure and not the purchase of trading stock.[2] So in *IRC v Pilcher*[3] a fruit grower was not allowed to deduct the cost of purchasing a cherry orchard, not even that part which represented the value of the nearly ripe crop. The contract had expressly included "this year's crop" but that meant only that the vendor was not to be entitled to pick the crop ripening between contract and completion.[4] The grower had purchased an income earning asset and not two separate items namely the trees and the crop.

In these cases since one is distinguishing trading stock from capital considerable care is needed in defining the trade; thus in one case sums spent on the purchase of standing timber by a timber merchant were not deductible[5] whereas in another case the costs of standing timber bought by a dealer in standing timber were held deductible.[6]

Simon's Taxes B3.1003; Butterworths Income Tax Service C2.23.

[1] Supra, § **7: 104**.

[2] *Alianza Co Ltd v Bell* [1906] AC 18, 5 TC 172; *Stratford v Mole and Lea* (1941) 24 TC 20.

[3] [1949] 2 All ER 1097, 31 TC 314.

[4] *Quaere* how far the case turns on the distinction between *fructus naturales* and *fructus industriales*.

[5] *Hood Barrs v IRC (No. 2)* [1957] 1 All ER 832, 37 TC 188 noted [1957] BTR 174 (Silberrad); see also *Kauri Timber Co Ltd v IT Comr* [1913] AC 771; *Hopwood v C.N. Spencer Ltd* (1964) 42 TC 169 and "Taxation", vol. 79, p. 10.

[6] *Murray v IRC* (1951) 32 TC 238.

7: 121   The purchase of a business is a capital expenditure and a purchase of trading stock as part of that purchase is also capital expenditure. Normally separate entries will take care of trading stock *stricto sensu*, but this will not take care of incidental profit making sources. In *John Smith & Son v Moore*[1] the taxpayer had inherited his father's business in return for a sum which included a figure of £30,000 for specific unexpired contracts for the supply of coal. The son was not allowed to deduct this £30,000. Viscount Haldane held that the contracts formed part of his fixed capital and that it was the coal which was the circulating capital,[2] and Lord Sumner held that the business was not that of buying and selling contracts but buying and selling coal and that the price paid was the price of acquiring the business.[3]

The decision clearly needs some explanation since contracts for the supply of trading stock can lead to trading profits in ways other than taking delivery of trading stock.[4] In *Taxes Comr v Nchanga Consolidated Copper Mines Ltd.*[5] Viscount Radcliffe explained the decision as resting on two important elements in the facts of the case. One was that an aggregate price had been paid for the entire business as it stood. The other was that the son did not acquire stock in trade.[6] However the facts suggest that the son was not carrying on business on his own account before his father's death, in which case it is a simple case of pre-trading expenses and leaves the court free to dissect the price paid where the business is taken over by one already trading.

Simon's Taxes B3.1306; Butterworths Income Tax Service C2.23.
  [1] [1921] 2 AC 13, 12 TC 266.
  [2] At 20 and 282–3.
  [3] At 20 and 282–3.
  [4] *Thompson v IRC* (1927) 12 TC 1091.
  [5] [1964] 1 All ER 208, [1964] AC 948.
  [6] See *Whimster & Co v IRC* (1925) 12 TC 813; and see Lord Reid in *Regent Oil Co Ltd v Strick* [1965] 3 All ER 174 at 185, 43 TC 1 at 36.

(5) *Trading arrangements*

7: 122 Sums paid to regulate the structure of the business tend to be capital although the duration of the arrangement is of importance.[1] So a sum paid in instalments to secure a customer for ten years were held to be capital[2] as was a payment to a trade association to prevent the sale of the business of a member of the association to a non-member.[3]

Payment to a retiring employee for a covenant not to compete was held not deductible.[4] It can be argued that such expenses are made in order to preserve the business and so should be deductible; however, a significant advantage is gained and so the payment is of capital.[5] On balance it would seem that since the expense of buying up a rival business in order to suppress it is capital, the same should apply to a long term agreement to the same effect. Such arrangements relate to the commercial structure of the business. The question is however one of fact and degree. It is decisions in this area that are most open to review as a result of *Tucker v Granada Motorway Services Ltd* as it is often hard to see any identifiable business asset.

  [1] See *Taxes Comr v Nchanga Consolidated Copper Mines Ltd* [1964] 1 All ER 208, [1964] AC 948 (one year—revenue expense). Cf. Singleton J in *Henriksen v Grafton Hotel Ltd* [1942] 2 KB 184 at 196.
  [2] *United Steel Companies Ltd v Cullington* (1939) 23 TC 71.
  [3] *Collins v Joseph Adamson & Co* [1937] 4 All ER 236, 21 TC 400.
  [4] *Associated Portland Cement Manufacturers Ltd v Kerr* [1946] 1 All ER 68, 27 TC 103.
  [5] Note Lord Reid in *Regent Oil Co Ltd v Strick* [1965] 3 All ER 174 at 183, 43 TC 1 at 35.

(6) *Petrol ties*

7: 123 After 1945 the petrol trade was arranged at the retail level on the basis that a garage would sell several brands of petrol. Around 1950 however there commenced the "exclusivity war" and the petrol companies began to acquire ties over individual garages whereby the garage owner would promise to sell only that company's products and in return the company would offer to pay for minor improvements at the garage and perhaps a discount on the petrol supplied. Originally these agreements lasted for a short time with low discounts but as the war increased the garage owners demanded better terms. In *Bolam v Regent Oil Co*[1] Danckwerts J held that the expense incurred by the petrol company was still a revenue expense even though the tie was to last five years. There a round sum was paid in advance and based upon estimated sales. The expense was incurred in order to earn profits and being based upon the estimated sales was as much a revenue expense as would have been the cost of supplying the petrol at a lower cost.

The exclusivity war was not confined to the UK. In *BP (Australia) Ltd v Taxation Comr*[2] the oil company paid sums by way of a "development allowance" to garage owners in return for a five year tie, the amount being related to the estimated gallonage. The Privy Council holding that the payments were revenue expenses drew attention to the changing pattern of the petrol trade and its use of longer term arrangements and talked in terms of fixed and circulating capital. The length of the agreements was simply a matter of degree, the fact that they were to last longer than one year immaterial.

The garage owners' own tax liability was affected by these payments. In so far as they were payments for their reimbursement of capital expenditure they were capital receipts,[3] as where the petrol company paid for substantial new buildings, but in so far as they were reimbursements of revenue expenditure, for example sales promotion, they would be revenue receipts.[4] Further, if the amounts were related to gallonage they might be treated as rebates on trading stock and so revenue payments.[5] On the other hand the garage owner might successfully invoke the principle in *Glenboig Union Fireclay Co Ltd v IRC*[6] and say that the payment was in return for the restriction of his trading opportunities, an argument that succeeded in a case involving a ten year tie.[7] In order to make sure that the sums received were capital receipts there was evolved the system of the lease and lease back. The garage owner would grant a lease to the oil company which would promise to pay a nominal rent and a large premium. The company would then sub-lease the garage to the owner who would covenant to sell only the company's products, on breach of which the sub-lease would end. The premium would be a capital receipt by the garage owner, although now subject to tax in part by TA 1988, s. 34.[8] This scheme was considered by the House of Lords in *Regent Oil Co v Strick*,[9] their judgment being given on the same day as the Privy Council in *BP (Australia) Ltd v Taxation Comr* with identical judges and no mention of the one case in the other. Payments under the scheme by Regent Oil were based upon estimated gallonage and the period ranged from five years to twenty one years. It was stated that the company had 5,000 agreements in the UK, mostly of the older variety without a lease. The House of Lords unanimously held that the payments in respect of the lease arrangements were capital expenditure and so not deductible. The distinction between a five year tie of the old sort the expenditure on which was a revenue item and a five year lease, the premium on which was a capital item, means that the distinction must be sought in the nature of the asset acquired by the company. Under the lease scheme not only did the company acquire an interest in the land, but also a better security since if the owner broke the covenant they could terminate the sublease and take possession under the lease. The commercial needs of the company in a changing market which had affected the Privy Council were ignored by the House of Lords. An argument that the ties were payable out of circulating capital because they were to secure orders and would therefore come circulating back which had impressed the Privy Council was trounced by the House of Lords.

The present position is, to say the least, uncertain. A tie unaccompanied by a lease will usually be a revenue expense even if it lasts for five years. There is authority that such a tie for twenty years will not be a revenue expense since it lacks the element of recurrence, but where the line is to be drawn between five and twenty remains to be seen, although in *Bolam v Regent Oil* a six year tie had been classified as revenue. The stress in the House of Lords on the nature of the asset acquired suggests that a premium payment in respect of a lease will be a capital item. One reason for this was that the payment would be capital in the hands of the recipient, an erroneous reason made the more absurd by the subsequent decision by the legislature to tax part of the premium as income of the recipient. Whether a premium in respect of a short lease would be treated as a revenue item remains to be seen.

In *Beauchamp v F W Woolworth plc* Lord Templeman, in explaining these cases, said that where the expenditure had been held to be a revenue account it was because the petrol tie had become an integral method of trading and an ordinary incident of marketing.[10] These cases were therefore immaterial in considering the status of a five year loan.

Simon's Taxes B1.204; Butterworths Income Tax Service C2.25.

[1] (1956) 37 TC 56; for a general discussion of the cases see Whiteman [1966] BTR 115; leading cases were cited in *Rolfe v Wimpey Waste Management Ltd* [1988] STC 329.

[2] [1965] 3 All ER 209, [1966] AC 224.

[3] *IRC v Coia* (1959) 38 TC 334.

[4] *Evans v Wheatley* (1958) 38 TC 216.

[5] Ibid, *Bolam v Regent Oil* was approved only on this ground in *Regent Oil v Strick* by Lord Morris [1965] 3 All ER 174 at 191, 43 TC 1 at 43.

[6] Supra, § 7: 77.

[7] *IRC v Coia* (1959) 38 TC 334.

[8] Infra, § 9: 17.

[9] [1965] 3 All ER 174, 43 TC 1.

[10] See [1989] STC 510 at 518.

(f) Prohibited expenditure

7: 124 TA 1988, s. 74 lists many prohibited deductions. Many of these are clearly not allowable on normal accountancy principles, but the list antedates those principles and its retention was recommended in order that Inspectors of Taxes might have something in black and white to show small shopkeepers who are "among the class of persons most apt to suppose that they might charge some of their domestic expenses against their business receipts".

Section 74(*b*) prohibits the deduction of sums for the maintenance of the parties, their families in establishments or any sum expended for other domestic or private purposes distinct from the trade, profession or vocation. Whether the first limb prescribes a purely objective test is as yet unsettled. It has been held that the expression "maintenance" while not restricted to domestic maintenance is confined to the ordinary necessities of life.[1]

(*c*) prohibits the rent of domestic office and dwellinghouses.

(*d*) concerns the repair of premises and the supply, repair and alteration of articles and utensils and limits the deductions to sums actually so spent (supra, § 7: 115).

(*e*) prevents the deduction of any loss not connected with or arising out of the trade, profession or vocation. A loss is different from an expense in that it does not come from the trader's pocket but comes upon him *ab extra*. Thus money stolen from a till is a loss but money spent on legal advice is an expense or disbursement.[2] The provision also means that a loss sustained in a transaction not forming part of the trade cannot be deducted.[3]

(*f*) prohibits the deduction of any capital withdrawn from, or any sum employed or intended to be employed as capital in the trade, but with an express allowance for interest.[4] The prohibition of sums spent as capital is statutory authority for the non-deduction of capital expenses. The opening words refer particularly to capital losses in connection with loans and guarantees financing the trade. There is however a distinction between a capital loss and a revenue loss. Losses on money advanced by a consortium to a colliery company were held to be capital,[5] but losses incurred when a solicitor guaranteed a client's overdraft were held to be revenue, the distinction being that the guarantee was a normal incident of the profession.[6] Today the section operates to prohibit the deduction of a premium due on the redemption of preference shares or the repayment of loan capital. The section does not appear to apply to an exchange loss incurred on repayment of a loan in foreign currency; this section applies only to the loans themselves.[7]

(*g*) prohibits the deduction of capital employed on improvements of business premises (supra, § **7: 115**).

(*h*) prohibits any deduction for interest which might have been made if any of the sums previously mentioned had been laid out as interest. The previous mention refers to (*f*) and (*g*). This bars notional interest but not actual interest.

(*i*) concerns debts not shown to be bad (infra, § **7: 144**).

(*j*) bars any average loss beyond the actual amount of loss after adjustment and concerns insurers.

(*k*) prohibits the deduction of any sums recoverable under an insurance or indemnity. This is surprisingly limited and does not prohibit the deduction of sums recoverable for example in tort, although any sums actually recovered will be taken into account.

(*l*), (*n*) and (*o*). The rule that business expenses are deductible has to be adjusted when it comes into collision with the delicate system of deduction of tax at source which applies to annuities or other annual payments payable out of profits or gains, any royalty[8] or other sum paid in respect of the use of a patent[9] and certain mining rents.[10] That adjustment is made by providing that no deduction may be made on account of such payments when the profits are computed. This leaves the trader with the right to deduct tax when making the payment and, if the facts fall within TA 1988, s. 348 keeping the tax for himself and so recovering the tax relief in respect of the expenditure. Each category of payments must however be considered. It will be noted that payments for bona fide commercial reasons in connection with an individual's trade profession or vocation are not affected by the changes made to the scope of Schedule D, Case III in 1988.[11]

Annuities or other annual payments are not to be deductible as a business expense if, in addition to satisfying all the usual tests of such payments, they are payable out of profits or gains. This had been taken to mean that they must form a charge on the profits as opposed to being an element in computing those profits,[12] so that sums are a deductible expense if deductible in computing those profits.

Where the business consists of the grant of annuities those annuities are not payable out of profits or gains so that the payments will be deductible in computing the profits or gains.[13] On the other hand an annuity payable to the widow of a deceased partner would be payable out of profits or gains.

The phrase "any royalty or other sum paid in respect of the user of a patent", is misleadingly wide. Since the reason for the prohibition of deduction is because of the relationship with TA 1988, ss. 348 and 349, an expense will only fall within this prohibition if it has the quality of income in the hands of the recipient. Further the expense must be for the use, as distinct from the acquisition, of a patent so that for example a right to restrain the patent holder from exercising his patent in a particular area is more than a mere right of user.[14]

Simon's Taxes B3.15; Butterworths Income Tax Service C2.31.

[1] *Watkis v Ashford Sparkes & Harwood* [1985] STC 451; (*b*) was also considered briefly in *Prince v Mapp* (1970) 46 TC 169.

[2] Per Finlay J in *Allen v Farquharson Bros & Co* (1932) 17 TC 59 at 64. See also *Roebank Printing Co Ltd v IRC* (1928) 13 TC 864 and *Bamford v ATA Advertising Ltd* [1972] 3 All ER 535, 48 TC 359. Distinguish petty pilfering by an employee.

[3] E.g. *FA and AB Ltd v Lupton*, supra, § **7: 11**.

[4] This reverses *European Investment Trust Co Ltd v Jackson* (1932) 18 TC 1.

[5] *James Waldie & Sons v IRC* (1919) 12 TC 113; for a fuller example see *Beauchamp v F W Woolworth plc* [1987] STC 279 supra, § **7: 107**.

[6] *Hagart and Burn-Murdoch v IRC* [1929] AC 386, 14 TC 433, HL; *Jennings v Barfield and Barfield* [1962] 2 All ER 957, 40 TC 365.

[7] *Beauchamp v F W Woolworth plc* [1988] STC at 718c; it follows from his decision that the earlier decision in *European Investment Trust Co Ltd v Jackson* (1932) 18 TC 1, which disallowed interest under this provision, was to be explained solely on the ground that there was disregarded a concession as to the meaning of the statute—see [1988] STC at 718a. In other words the decision should be disregarded. This issue was not touched on by Lord Templeman in the House of Lords [1989] STC 510.

[8] TA 1988, ss. 74(*l*), 348, 349.

[9] TA 1988, ss. 74(*p*), 348 and 349.

[10] TA 1988, ss. 74(*q*), 119, 120, 348 and 349.

[11] TA 1988, s. 347A(2).

[12] *Paterson Engineering Co Ltd v Duff* (1943) 25 TC 43.

[13] *Gresham Life Assurance Society v Styles,* infra.

[14] Per Lord Watson in *Gresham Life Assurance Society v Styles* [1892] AC 309 at 320, 3 TC 185 at 192, supra; *British Salmson Aero Engines Ltd v IRC* [1938] 2 KB 482, 22 TC 29.

Interest

7: 125   A person carrying on a trade can, in computing the profits, deduct the interest payments he incurs in that trade. Such payments will be deductible on general accounting principles and so deductibility is distinct from the special rules in § **5: 30** but there are some special provisions.

TA 1988, s. 74(*m*) prohibits the deduction of any interest paid to a non-resident if, and so far as, it is interest at more than a reasonable commercial rate. This allows the deduction to the extent that it is reasonable, only prohibiting the deduction of the excess.

The deduction of interest paid to non-residents is further treated in TA 1988, s. 82. This section is confined to annual interest so that short interest may be ignored (see § **9: 46**). It provides that no deduction for the interest paid may be claimed unless the person making the payment has deducted income tax at the basic rate—under TA 1988, s. 349(2) —*and* has accounted for the tax to the Revenue. The gross amount paid is deductible in computing profits.

However, interest paid by a trader resident in the UK which is both payable and paid outside the UK under an obligation incurred exclusively for purposes of the trade may be paid gross and still be deductible. It is also necessary to show either that the liability was incurred for a trade carried on outside the UK or that the interest was payable in foreign currency; the purpose is to assist foreign trade or to encourage traders to borrow overseas, a policy much encouraged in the late 1960s. This exception does not apply if the borrower controls the lender or vice versa or both are under common control.

Simon's Taxes B3.1324; Butterworths Income Tax Service C2.32.

Business gifts and entertainment expenses

7: 126   The general rule that expenses incurred wholly and exclusively for the business were deductible led to particular problems in the area of business entertainment expenses, such expenses being deductible even though on a lavish scale. A famous example was the modest firm which deducted £3,600 in computing its profits of which £1,700 was on account of a grouse moor. While such expenditure might often be justified by a business purpose, there was also the chance that hospitality was offered purely in the hope that it would be reciprocated which meant that the leisure activities of senior businessmen were being subsidised by the Revenue.

TA 1988, s. 577 prohibits the deduction of expenses—including incidental expenses—incurred in providing business entertainment, a phrase defined to include hospitality of any kind;[1] s. 577 also extends to the provision of gifts,[2] subject to the de minimus exception of £10 p.a. The disallowance turns on the facts not the purpose of the trader.[3] Normally this disallowance affects computation under Schedule D or Schedule A. Where an asset is used for business entertainment purposes any capital allowance otherwise claimable is disallowed.[4]

The section extends to Schedule E. If the employer pays the employee an allowance purely for entertainment purposes, the employer may not deduct the allowance in computing his profits; the employee is taxable on the allowance but may deduct all expenditure satisfying the rule in TA 1988, s. 198 whether or not it would satisfy TA 1988, s. 577. If, however, the employer pays the employee a general allowance to cover terms which include entertainment the position is reversed. The employer may deduct the cost of the allowance, assuming that it also satisfies the other rules (e.g. TA 1988, s. 74(a)) but the employee may deduct only such entertainment costs as satisfy both ss. 198 and 577.[5]

Simon's Taxes B3.1438; Butterworths Income Tax Service C2.33.

[1] TA 1988, s. 577(5).
[2] TA 1988, s. 577(8).
[3] *Fleming v Associated Newspapers Ltd*, infra, § **7: 127.**

Exceptions to entertainment expenses rules

7: 127   (*a*) Business entertainment expenses used to be deductible if incurred in the entertainment of an overseas customer, meaning a non-resident trading overseas who might use the goods or services of the entertainer, or an agent for such a non-resident trader or overseas government or public authority, a definition to assist British exporters—not importers. In these instances the entertainment had to be of a kind and on a scale which is reasonable in all the circumstances.[1] This exception is repealed for expenditure incurred after 14th March 1988 save when it is incurred under a contract made before 15th March 1988.[2]

(*b*) Expenses incurred in the entertainment of bona fide members of staff are deductible. Curiously the requirement of reasonableness is absent here.[3] The exception does not apply when the entertainment is incidental to the provision of entertainment for outsiders.

(*c*) Expenses are deductible if they are for small gifts carrying conspicuous advertisements, such as calendars and diaries.[4]

(*d*) Expenses are deductible if (*i*) incurred in the provision of that which it is his trade to provide if it is provided by him in the course of his trade for payment or (*ii*) gratuitously if with the object of advertising to the public generally.[5] Examples of expenses within group (*i*) would be the provision of food by a restauranteur or of theatre tickets by a theatre owner and of those within group (*ii*) free samples of products or complimentary theatre tickets for the press, although not for friends.

The exception is limited to the provision of "anything which it is his trade to provide". "Anything" has been construed to mean business entertainment so that it must be his trade to supply such entertainment. Hence a newspaper man who provided drinks for potential sources of information or meals for the softening up of contributors did not fall within the exception.[6] It was his trade to produce newspapers not refreshment. It would follow that if he offered not drinks but a copy of his paper that expense might be deductible.

Another problem is whether he must supply the entertainment himself. Thus if the owner of a fried chicken shop provides business entertainment in his own shop with his own fried chicken he can clearly deduct his costs, but it is not clear whether he could deduct the costs of entertaining the same people at the Ritz. In this latter instance he is supplying that which it is his trade to supply, but one cannot help feeling that the sums would not be deductible merely because of the coincidence of the entertainment provided with his own trade. It is probable that the expense is only deductible if his trade supplies the entertainment.

(*e*) Expenses incurred in making a gift to a charity, including the Historic Buildings Commission and the National Heritage Memorial Fund are excluded from TA 1988, s. 577[7]. This leaves the taxpayer with the task of ensuring that the gift also escapes from TA 1988, s. 74(*a*).[8]

[1] TA 1988, s. 577(2), repealed by FA 1988, s. 72.
[2] FA 1988, s. 72.
[3] TA 1988, s. 577(5).
[4] TA 1988, s. 577(7). The cost to the donor must not exceed £10 per donee per year, TA 1988, s. 577(8)(*b*).
[5] TA 1988, s. 577(10).
[6] *Fleming v Associated Newspapers Ltd* [1972] 2 All ER 574, 46 TC 401.
[7] TA 1988, s. 577(*a*).
[8] Supra, § **7: 94**.

Sale and leaseback: TA 1988, s. 779 and TA 1988, s. 780

7: 128   (i) *Leasebacks of land*   Where rents in excess of the commercial rent are paid under a leaseback arrangement, the excess is not deductible.[1] Where the asset sold is a lease for a term not exceeding 50 years and it is leased back for a term of not exceeding 15 years a part of the sale consideration which would otherwise be capital is taxed as income.[2] That part is $16 - n/15$ when n is the term of the new lease. Top slicing relief used to be available[3] but this is repealed for 1989–90 and later years.[4]

Simon's Taxes B3.647; Butterworths Income Tax Service C2.34.
[1] TA 1988, s. 779.
[2] TA 1988, s. 780.
[3] TA 1988, s. 780(5).
[4] FA 1988, s. 75.

7: 129   (ii) *Leased assets other than land*   Where, before the sale and leaseback, the asset was used in the trade the allowable deduction is limited to the commerical rent.[1] Disallowed rental payments may however be rolled forward and used in later periods when the rent paid is below the commercial rent.

Where the asset was not so used and the payer, having received a tax deduction for his rent, then receives a capital sum under the lease, the deduction is clawed back to the extent of that sum;[2] the clawback is reduced when part of the rent has been disallowed. This rule applies also where the lessor's interest belongs to an associate of the payer and the associate receives a capital sum; in this case the charge is on the associate.

[1] TA 1988, s. 782.
[2] TA 1988, s. 781; capital sum includes insurance proceeds.

Other expressly prohibited deductions

7: 130   Payments of penalties, interest and surcharges under the VAT legislation are non-deductible.[1]

[1] TA 1988, s. 827.

Permitted expenditure

7: 131   Certain types of expenditure are deductible by statute. These include payments under certified and statutory redundancy schemes,[1] revenue expenditure on scientific research,[2] applications for patents,[3] any payments made by the trader to be used for the purposes of technical education related to his trade,[4] payments to superannuation funds,[5] rents paid for tied premises,[6] rents in respect of easements enjoyed in connection with a radio relay service's wires or cables,[7] employer's redundancy payments,[8] payments by market boards to reserve funds,[9] certain capital expenditure by a cemetery or cremation authority,[10] certain underwriters payments into special reserve funds—in computing excess liability,[11] deductions in computing post-cessation receipts,[12] premiums payable in respect of business premises when the landlord is chargeable[13] and certain payments under schemes for nationalising industry.[14] In addition certain payments may be deducted under the quite separate capital allowance system.[15] Payments into approved share schemes or ESOPs for employees are also deductible even though representing a division of profits,[16] as are incidental costs of loan finance,[17] contributions to approved local enterprise agencies,[18] and the costs of seconding employees to charities.[19] Incidental costs incurred by a company in obtaining the acceptance of certain bills of exchange are also deductible.[20] Payments to personal pension schemes[21], payments to an employee under a restrictive covenant under TA 1988, s. 313[22] and the costs of employees seconded to various educational bodies[23] or sent away for training are also deductible.[24]

Interestingly, the relief for National Insurance contributions[25] takes the form of a relief from total income—not an allowable deduction; this is to avoid the delay in giving relief inherent in a preceding year basis of assessment.

Simon's Taxes B3.15; Butterworths Income Tax Service C2.35.

[1] TA 1988, ss. 568 and 572.
[2] CAA 1968, s. 90.
[3] TA 1988, ss. 83 and 526.
[4] TA 1988, s. 84.
[5] TA 1988, s. 592(4).
[6] TA 1988, s. 98.
[7] TA 1988, s. 120(4)(*a*).
[8] TA 1988, s. 579(2).
[9] TA 1988, s. 509.
[10] TA 1988, s. 91.
[11] TA 1988, s. 454.
[12] TA 1988, s. 105.
[13] TA 1988, s. 87.
[14] TA 1988, s. 568.
[15] Infra, chapter 8.
[16] TA 1988, s. 85 and FA 1989, s. 67(2).
[17] TA 1988, s. 77.
[18] TA 1988, s. 400.
[19] TA 1988, s. 86.
[20] TA 1988, s. 78.
[21] TA 1988, s. 643.
[22] Substituted by FA 1988, s.73, see supra, § **6: 36**.
[23] TA 1988, s. 86(3).

EARNINGS BASIS AND CASH BASIS

7: 132   In computing the profit of the business for a particular period two main bases are used. The more normal one is the earnings basis. Sums due but not yet paid, whether debits or credits, are brought into account.[1] This is now subject to a special statutory rule for the payment of remuneration chargeable in the hands of the payee under Schedule E.[2] The other basis, the cash basis, takes into account only sums of money actually spent or received regardless of when they became due. The value of work in progress is brought into account on an earnings basis but is ignored on a cash basis. In some cases accounts are prepared on a basis intermediate between full earnings basis and simple cash basis; for example some put most figures on an earnings basis but ignore work in progress.[3]

There is no guidance in the statutes and little in the cases on whether either the Revenue or the taxpayer can insist on a particular basis although the earnings basis is preferred.[4] In practice the Revenue accept the cash basis only for certain professions and even then insist that during the first three accounting years the profits should be computed on an earnings basis—except for barristers. This insistence applies even where there is a discontinuance by reason of a change of partners. An exception is made for barristers because they have no right to sue for their fees. A barrister may now be assessed on an earnings basis if he so wishes. Persons engaging in a literary or artistic profession or vocation are not required to value work in progress.

A choice between the two methods is less obvious since the removal in 1968 of the general immunity of post-cessation receipts, an immunity which had greatly favoured the cash basis. Where a cash basis is taken the measure of profits will fluctuate more irrationally since that measure will turn not only on the level of business but also on the speed with which debts are paid and credits received, two forces which may in appropriate circumstances counteract each other. However where profits are rising, a cash basis will mean that the tax liability will be deferred, although whether that will mean more or less tax will depend upon the rates in force when those figures are taken as measuring the profits for a year of assessment. It should also be noted that there are problems of timing with a cash basis but they have not been considered in the UK. Consider the delivery of a promissory note—is that a receipt if a cash basis is used? Does it then make any difference if the note is used as security for borrowing money from a third party?

Simon's Taxes B3.9; Butterworths Income Tax Service C1.01.
[1] And see TA 1988, s. 110(3).
[2] FA 1989, s. 40 (but note adjustment permitted by s. 43(5)).
[3] Simon's Taxes B3.202.
[4] See Lord Radcliffe in *Southern Railway of Peru Ltd v Owen* [1956] 2 All ER 728 at 736, 36 TC 602 and at 640.

7: 133   Once a particular basis has been taken for a particular year, it is not open to the Revenue to make an additional assessment to gather in the extra tax chargeable if the other basis had been taken.[1] Nor is it open to the taxpayer to insist that because a particular basis was taken for a particular year no other basis may be taken for subsequent years; each year of assessment is potentially different. In *Wetton Page & Co v Attwooll*[2] the profits of a firm of accountants had been computed on a cash basis from 1932 to 1953–54 but the Revenue then insisted upon an earnings basis for the years of assessment 1954–55 to 1957–58. It was held that the Revenue could so insist, but that the taxpayers would be entitled to resist a change back to the cash basis in 1958–59.

[1] *Rankine v IRC* 1952 SC 177, 32 TC 520.
[2] [1963] 1 All ER 166, 40 TC 619.

7: 134   If a change is made from earnings basis to cash basis, receipts due in the last year of the earnings basis but paid in the first year of the cash basis will be taken into account in both years, as will expenses incurred in one year and paid in the other. This is not in theory double taxation since each year of assessment taxes by reference to the profits of a particular period and it is sufficient that those periods of time are different;[1] the methods of measuring the profits of that period is a quite separate matter.

Where however a change is made from a cash basis to an earnings basis there will be sums due in the last year of the cash basis which are not paid until the first year of the earnings basis and on parity of reasoning such sums should avoid being taken into account in measuring the profit of either period. Such sums are however now caught by the post-cessation receipt legislation;[2] relief for expenses in such instances is available.[3] Perhaps in order to discourage the use of the cash basis no provision was incorporated in that legislation to prevent the double charge where the change was from the earnings to a cash basis.

[1] *IRC v Morrison* 1932 SC 638, 17 TC 325. On amalgamation of partnership, note extra-statutory concession A18 (1985), **Simon's Taxes, Division H2.2.**
[2] TA 1988, s. 104(4); infra, § **7: 138.**
[3] TA 1988, s. 105.

Certain post-cessation receipts TA 1988, s. 103 earnings and cash basis

7: 135   Sums received by one who had previously carried on a trade, profession or vocation and relating to that business were at one time not taxable—by reason of the doctrine of the source. Thus where profits were assessed on a *cash* basis, all payments after discontinuance were free of tax. If the trader had been assessed on an *earnings* basis the sum due would have appeared as a credit item in the final account[1] so that at first sight no loss to the Revenue would accrue. However the sum owed to the trader might, in the final account, have been written off as irrecoverable in which case the subsequent unexpected payments would escape tax. Conversely the final account might have included a debt which the trader owed in respect of the trade but which debt was, after the discontinuance, released by the creditor. Again there are certain types of earnings which because of their uncertain nature cannot be included in the profits figures until they take the shape of payments. Thus in two well known cases sums of such type escaped tax because they only took the form of payments after the trade had been discontinued—in the one case a percentage of film receipts to be paid to a film actor[2] and in the other royalty payments in respect of books.[3]

Simon's Taxes B3.928; Butterworths Income Tax Service C1.102.

[1] Infra, § **7: 144**.

[2] *Stainers Executors v Purchase* [1951] 2 All ER 1071, 32 TC 367. But if not originally received in course of trade, the receipts would be, and would continue to be, taxable under Case III, *Mitchell v Rosay* (1954) 35 TC 496 at 502; the source would be the obligation not the trade.

[3] *Carson v Cheyney's Executors* [1958] 3 All ER 573, 38 TC 240.

7: 136   TA 1988, s. 103, originally introduced in 1960, makes two changes to the earnings basis. First all sums received after the discontinuance and arising from the carrying on of the trade are chargeable provided their value had not been brought into computing the profits of any period before the discontinuance. The charge arises under Schedule D, Case VI.[1]

Secondly where a debt has been allowed in the computation of the profits of a trade since discontinued and the whole or any part of the debt is later released, the amount released is treated as a sum received.[2] Presumably a covenant by the creditor not to sue, being analytically distinct from a release, will not cause a charge to tax.

Certain sums are excluded,[3] namely sums received by a person beneficially entitled thereto who is not resident in the UK representing income arising from a country or territory outside the UK; a lump sum paid to the personal representatives of the author—but not the author himself—of a work as consideration for the assignment by them of the copyright or public lending rights, wholly or in part,[4] and, finally, sums received on the transfer of trading stock or work in progress, which provision is needed to prevent an overlap with TA 1988, ss. 100 and 101[5] and to avoid depriving the exceptions in those sections from any effect.

Section 103 also charges certain post-cessation receipts of a business where that business had been assessed on a cash basis.[6] The effect is to bring into charge those sums which had just been made taxable where an earnings basis was used and to avoid widening still further the then gap between cash and earnings basis.

Simon's Taxes B4.108–110; Butterworths Income Tax Service C1.102.

[1] TA 1988, s. 103(1) and (2)(*a*).

[2] TA 1988, s. 103(4). This provision is not happily drafted; it refers to the amount released when it presumably ought to refer to the release in respect of a debt "so far as allowed as a deduction". See per Megarry J in *Simpson v Jones* [1968] 2 All ER 929 at 936, 44 TC 599 at 609.

[3] TA 1988, s. 103(3).

[4] Thus preserving the immunity from tax in the *Haig* case, infra, § **10: 08**.

[5] Infra, § **7: 168**.

[6] TA 1988, s. 103(2)(*b*).

Post-cessation receipts on cash basis: TA 1988, s. 104

7: 137   The general immunity from tax enjoyed by post-cessation receipts where the business was taxed on a cash basis was removed not by s. 103 but by s. 104, which was introduced in 1968.[1] Tax is now charged on all sums received on or after the discontinuance[2] which arise from the carrying on of the trade, profession or vocation in so far as they had not been brought into account in computing the profits or gains for any period before the discontinuance. Excluded from s. 104 are the first two payments also excluded from s. 103, i.e. sums paid to a non-resident representing income from outside the UK and lump sums paid to the personal representatives of an author in respect of copyright or public lending right. If work in progress at discontinuance is transferred, sums received by way of consideration for the transfer are brought within the charge.[3]

The sum charged is treated as earned income.[4] The sum will usually be taxed by reference to the year of receipt but it may, at the option of the taxpayer or his personal representative, be carried back to the date on which the discontinuance occurred.[5] If he so elects however he loses the right to claim any allowance or loss under s. 105.[6]

Simon's Taxes B4.109; Butterworths Income Tax Service C1.103.
   [1] FA 1968, s. 18 extra-statutory concession A18 (1985) (withdrawn for 1988–89 and later years) Simon's Taxes, Division H2.2.
   [2] Defined TA 1988, s. 110(2).
   [3] TA 1988, s. 104(6) and (7).
   [4] TA 1988, s. 107.
   [5] TA 1988, s. 108.
   [6] TA 1988, s. 109.

7: 138   TA 1988, s. 104 applies not only when the trade is discontinued but also where the trade which has been charged on a cash basis changes to being charged on an earnings basis.[1] For this reason the section also applies where there is a change of conventional basis which may result in receipts dropping out of computation.[2] The section does not apply where the discontinuance occurred before 19th March 1968 nor if there was a change to an earnings basis before that date. It is provided that any event which is to be treated as a discontinuance by TA 1988, ss. 113 or 337 is treated as a discontinuance for these sections.[3]

There is nothing in ss. 103 or 104 requiring that the payment be made to the former trader. It is however provided by s. 106 that if the right to receive the payments caught by these sections is transferred, the sale proceeds are chargeable under Case VI. A different rule applies if a trade is transferred and the transferee acquires the right to collect what would otherwise be post-cessation receipts of the former trader. No charge arises from such a transfer and the sums paid to the transferee are treated as the receipts of his trade as they are received.

Where the right to receive the payments is given away, it would appear that no tax can be charged under Case VI even if the payments are then made to a person connected with the former trader. Although ss. 103 and 104 might leave this point open it is submitted that s. 106 is only needed if there is in general no liability on the transferee.[4]

Simon's Taxes B4.111; Butterworths Income Tax Service C1.103.
  [1] TA 1988, s. 104(4), but there is no provision for immunity from double charge in the converse case.
  [2] See supra, § 7: 134.
  [3] TA 1988, s. 110(2).
  [4] TA 1988, s. 106.

The chargeable sum: post-cessation expenses and unused capital allowances

7: 139   In calculating the sum to be charged any expenses that could have been claimed if the trade had continued are deductible; a claim may also be made for any capital allowance to which he was entitled immediately before the discontinuance.[1] There are provisions for allocating these sums where charges arise under TA 1988, ss. 103 and 104 and for preventing double relief.

Simon's Taxes B4.110; Butterworths Income Tax Service C1.103.
  [1] TA 1988, s. 105.

Relief for the elderly

7: 140   A special relief from TA 1988, s. 104 but not from s. 103 is granted to individuals born before 6th April 1917.[1]

Simon's Taxes B4.112; Butterworths Income Tax Service C1.104.
  [1] TA 1988, s. 109. Special rules apply to partnerships: sub-s. (5).

TIMING—EARNINGS BASIS

7: 141   Sums due whether to or from the trade must be entered when, and only when all, the conditions precedent to earning or paying it have been fulfilled;[1] this is a question of construction of the particular contract. The leading case is *J. P. Hall & Co Ltd v IRC*.[2] In March 1914 the company made a contract to supply certain electric motors, deliveries to begin in June 1914 and end in September 1915 with payment within one month of delivery. The final delivery did not take place until July 1916. The company argued that the receipts should be taken as earned when the contract was made—in March 1914. Lord Sterndale MR, put the matter simply, "These profits were neither ascertained nor made at the time these two contracts were concluded".[3] Those profits therefore could not be anticipated.

In such cases everything turns on the construction of the agreement or statute giving rise to the payment. So in *Johnson v W. S. Try Ltd*[4] a payment for compensation for refusal of planning consent was held to date from the date of the final agreement with the council, it being open to the council until that time to change its mind and grant the consent.

A simplified view of when a profit is earned was taken by the House of Lords in *Willingale v International Commercial Bank Ltd*[5] when they held that bills of exchange owned by the bank gave rise to profit only when they were realised, whether by sale or on maturity.

Simon's Taxes B3.914, 1112; Butterworths Income Tax Service C1.111.

[1] Per Lord Greene MR in *Johnson v W. S. Try Ltd* (1946) 27 TC 167 at 185. For an exception see extra-statutory concession B6 (1988) obsolete, **Simon's Taxes, Division H2.2**; deficiency payment related to date of notification. See generally Freedman [1987] BTR 61 and 104.

[2] [1921] 3 KB 152, 12 TC 382.

[3] At 155 and 389. Their case was not strengthened by the fact that their accounts showed the receipts as brought in only after delivery.

[4] [1946] 1 All ER 532, 27 TC 167.

[5] [1978] STC 75, [1978] 1 All ER 754.

Relating back

7: 142   The general principle was stated by Viscount Simon LC in *IRC v Gardner, Mountain and D'Ambrumenil Ltd*:[1]

> "... services completely rendered or goods supplied, which are not to be paid for till a subsequent year, cannot generally be dealt with by treating the taxpayer's outlay as pure loss in the year in which it was incurred and bringing in the remuneration as pure profit in the subsequent year in which it is paid or due to be paid. In making an assessment ... the net result of the transaction, setting expenses on the one side and a figure for remuneration on the other side, ought to appear ... in the same year's profit and loss account and that year will be the year when the service was rendered or the goods delivered... This may involve ... an estimate of what the future remuneration will amount to ... (but this provisional estimate) could be corrected when the precise figure was known, by additional assessment..."

This matching principle matches receipts with the moment the services have been rendered or the goods supplied, and not with the moment that a legally enforceable right to payment arises. This has four consequences. The first is that where the goods have been delivered but payment is not to become due until some later time, that payment must be related back to the time of the delivery; meanwhile a provisional figure may have to be put into the accounts. This is shown by the decision in *IRC v Gardner, Mountain and D'Ambrumenil Ltd* itself where sums due to be paid and so paid only in 1938 in respect of underwriting services performed in 1936 were attributed to 1936.[2] The second consequence is that payments can be related back to the moment of the service even though there is no legal right to payment as in *Isaac Holden & Sons Ltd v IRC*, infra. The third is that payment cannot be related back to a time before the services were completed[3] or the goods delivered.[4]

The fourth is that a payment cannot be related back if it is not directly in return for services rendered.[5] So in *Gray v Lord Penrhyn*[6] a firm of auditors had been negligent in failing to spot defalcations by the taxpayer's employees. The firm subsequently made good the loss but the sums were not related back to the years of the defalcations or of the negligence, but were treated as trading receipts in the year of payment which was also the year in which the liability was agreed. This may also be one of the factors behind the decision of the House of Lords in *Willingale*[7] where the Revenue made no attempt to argue that the relating back principle should apply.

Simon's Taxes B3.920, 921; Butterworths Income Tax Service C1.112.
[1] (1947) 29 TC 69 at 93.
[2] On taxation of underwriters see TA 1988, ss. 452–457.
[3] *John and E Sturge Ltd v Hessel* [1975] STC 127.
[4] *J. P. Hall & Co Ltd v IRC*, supra, § 7: 37.
[5] Per Roxburgh J in *Severne v Dadswell* [1954] 3 All ER 243 at 248; 35 TC 649 at 659.
[6] [1937] 3 All ER 468, 21 TC 252.
[7] Supra, § 7: 65.

7: 143   This matching principle may lead to the reopening of accounts. The leading case is *Isaac Holden & Sons Ltd v IRC*.[1] The company was a member of a federation of companies engaged in combing wool for the Government. In July 1918 a provisional price increase of 10% was agreed between the Federation and the Government to operate from 1st January 1918 and in 1919 a total increase of 20% with effect from 1st January 1918 was agreed. The company's trading account ending 30th June 1918 had included the 10% increase but Rowlatt J directed that it should take account of the 20% increase.

The relating back of payments has been applied even though, as in *Isaac Holden* itself there was no enforceable right to the extra payment at the end of the trading period or at any later time. Moreover payments have been related back even though the trade has in the interval been discontinued.[2]

Receipts have been adjusted to take account of subsequent payments not only where services were rendered, as in the previous cases, but also where the government requisitioned trading stock,[3] where the government requisitioned a ship,[4] where payments wrongfully extracted by a government official were reimbursed[5] and where a ministry agreed to modify an agreement so as to make good a loss sustained by the taxpayer but took rather a long time to pay up.[6]

Simon's Taxes B3.920; Butterworths Income Tax Service C1.112.
[1] (1924) 12 TC 768.
[2] *Severne v Dadswell* [1954] 3 All ER 243, 35 TC 649.
[3] *IRC v Newcastle Breweries Ltd* (1927) 12 TC 927.
[4] *Ensign Shipping Co Ltd v IRC* (1928) 12 TC 1169.
[5] *English Dairies Ltd v Phillips* (1927) 11 TC 597.
[6] *Rownson, Drew and Clydesdale Ltd v IRC* (1931) 16 TC 595. In each of these four cases the effect was to increase the taxpayers liability to Excess Profits Duty.

Limitations

7: 144   The doctrine of relating back may mean the addition of a new sum or the alteration of an existing one. It is subject to two and possibly three limitations.

(i) *Default of debtor.* An adjustment for the default of a debtor is made when the default occurs and is not related back. TA 1988, s. 74(*i*) provides that "no sums can be deducted in respect of any debts [(*i*) if they are debts] except bad debts proved to be such, and doubtful debts to the extent that they are respectively estimated to be bad, and in the case of bankruptcy or insolvency of a debtor the amount which may reasonably be expected to be received on any debt shall be the value thereof". This rule simply prevents a deduction for tax purposes of a general reserve set up for bad debts; each debt must be separately justified. The practice of the Revenue is that if a debt becomes bad in a year after it first accrues, an allowance can be made in that later year with no relating back.[1] *A fortiori* where a debt is brought in no allowance can be made for the expense of collecting it in a later year—such expenses belong to the later year.[2]

It should be noted that s. 74(*i*) deals only with deductions and does not say what debts are to be brought into account nor at what value. The value of a debt, is a matter of fact and is not necessarily its face value, even if not proved to be a bad debt. In *Absalom v Talbot*[3] the taxpayer was a speculative builder. His purchasers might, after payment of a deposit and a sum borrowed from a building society, leave the balance outstanding on granting the taxpayer a second mortgage on the house, the sum to be repaid with interest over a period of twenty years.

The Revenue insisted on the face value of the debts being incorporated into the accounts until such time as it was proved to be bad, seeing no difference between the instant case and that in which the builder, having received the amount outstanding, chose to lend it out at interest. This was rejected by a bare majority in the House of Lords.

However if it is accepted that value of the debts is not their face value considerable problems of implementation are caused. One method would be to bring in the payments as they are made. The objection to that in 1944 was that payments after a discontinuance would escape tax even though the earnings basis was employed, an objection no longer valid since 1960.[4] Another method would be to value the debts, but here adjustments to take account of actual returns would be impossible.[5] Therefore Lord Atkin in *Absalom v Talbot* preferred the inclusion of the debts at their face value on one side of the account and a reserve on the other which would be calculated on the ordinary risk of bad debts but adjusted annually to take account of actual payments made or not made. Such a reserve would not be prohibited by s. 74(*i*) because that only applies to debts correctly brought in at face value.

Simon's Taxes B3.1462; Butterworths Income Tax Service C1.113.

[1] *Absalom v Talbot* [1944] 1 All ER 642, 26 TC 166. This Revenue practice was approved by Lord Atkin and by the two dissentients, Lord Simon and Lord Porter. Lord Russell of Killowen and Lord Thankerton expressed no opinion. The practice was accepted by Macnaghten J and the Court of Appeal in *Bristow v William Dickinson & Co Ltd* [1946] KB 321, 27 TC 157.
[2] *Monthly Salaries Loan Co Ltd v Furlong* (1962) 40 TC 313. The Revenue has made special arrangements for credit traders: see Goode, *Hire Purchase Law and Practice* (2nd edn), p 811.
[3] [1944] 1 All ER 642, 26 TC 166.
[4] Supra, § 7: **136**.
[5] Supra.

7: 145 (ii) *Reopening of account*. The limitation is that there can be no reopening of the account and so no relating back if the amount of the liability stated in the accounts was correctly stated as the finally agreed amount of the liability. In *British Mexican Petroleum Co Ltd v Jackson*,[1] the taxpayer company had incurred a large liability in year 1; in year 3 the creditor released a part of it. The House of Lords held that the release could not alter the amount of the liability entered for the year 1. They also held that the sum released could not be treated as a trading receipt in the year 3. The Legislature has reversed the second part of the ruling[2] and by directing the release to be treated as a trading receipt in the period of release has impliedly upheld the first part of the ruling.

The difficulty is to see just how firm this rule is, i.e. just when a figure is entered both finally and correctly if it is later shown to be inaccurate. There is no doubt that the figure originally entered can be adjusted if it has not yet been finally agreed between the Revenue and the taxpayer as a final figure,[3] and a *fortiori* where no figure appeared in the accounts at all.[4] In such instances the courts have appeared to favour the use of hindsight. Two explanations for reopening the accounts can be advanced. One is that the extra payments had never entered into the accounts at all; the other is that whenever a subsequent payment is made, the original figure cannot be regarded as having been correctly stated and therefore can be reopened notwithstanding earlier agreement between the Revenue and the taxpayer. The difficulty is that *ex hypothesi* an adjustment will usually show that the original figure was not correctly stated.[5]

In *Symons v Weeks*[6] Warner J has reasserted the authority of the principle in *British Mexican Petroleum Co Ltd v Jackson* and so weakened the force of the second explanation just given. Staged payments to architects involved a substantial element of payment in advance but the exact whole fee could not be known until the work was completed. In accordance with accounts which had been properly drawn up only a portion of the sum received in a year was shown as a trading receipt. Warner J said that *Simpson v Jones* could not apply to a case where accounts had been correctly drawn up and that it was therefore not open to the Revenue to amend the figures retrospectively and the taxpayer was right in seeking to be taxed on the figures in the accounts.

Simon's Taxes B3.919; Butterworths Income Tax Service C1.113.

[1] (1932) 16 TC 570; and see Atkinson J in *Jays the Jewellers Ltd v IRC* [1947] 2 All ER 762 at 768, 29 TC 274 at 284.

[2] TA 1988, ss. 94 and 87(4).

[3] *Bernhard v Gahan* (1928) 13 TC 723.

[4] *Simpson v Jones* [1968] 2 All ER 929, 44 TC 599.

[5] In *British Mexican Petroleum Co v Jackson* the release did not throw doubt on the correct extent of the original liability.

[6] [1983] STC 195 (Warner J pointed out that if the Revenue had not insisted on a change from cash basis to earnings basis they could have got what they wanted).

7: 146   (iii) *Harrison v John Cronk & Sons Ltd.* A third limitation might be found in the apparent decision of the House of Lords in *Harrison v John Cronk & Sons Ltd*[1] that there would be no relating back where at the end of the trading period only a guess could be made as to the correct measure of the eventual receipts. The case has since been described in the House of Lords as exceptional and as laying down no such general principle.[2] The decision may also be *per incuriam* since none of the cases on relating back were cited.

Simon's Taxes B3.628, 924; Butterworths Income Tax Service C1.113.

[1] [1936] 3 All ER 747, 20 TC 612.

[2] *IRC v Gardner, Mountain and D'Ambrumenil Ltd* (1947) 29 TC 69 at 106 per Lord Porter; per Viscount Simon, at 94. See also per Lord Simonds, at 111.

Payment in advance—relating forward?

7: 147 It ought to follow from the matching principle that where a payment is received in advance that sum should enter the account only when the service has been rendered or the goods supplied. However it appears that money which belongs to the trader will be treated as a trading receipt when received (or due) and that this overrides the matching principle at least where the sum received is final and is a trading receipt.[1] The authority is not impressive. In *Elson v Price's Tailors, Ltd*[2] the taxpayer customers would on ordering a made to measure garment be asked for a deposit. These deposits were as a matter of practice returned to customers who did not like the finished goods but some clients did not return to claim their deposits. Before the Commissioners[3] the taxpayer argued that the deposits should become trading receipts only when the customer took delivery. The Crown argued for the date the deposits became forfeitable or, alternatively, were transferred to head office. Ungoed-Thomas J, held first that the payments were truly deposits and not part payments and so were security for the completion of the purchase; the money therefore belonged to the taxpayer and the payments were trading receipts when received. He went on to reject the argument that the relating back doctrine applied where the payment preceded the performance of the contract. This seems illogical. Ungoed-Thomas J applied the decision of the House of Lords in *Smart v Lincolnshire Sugar Co Ltd*[4] where subsidies were paid by the government to farmers subject to the proviso that these were to be reduced retrospectively if the market price rose. The House held that these were receipts in the year of receipt and not the year when the contingency of repayment ceased. Although the House was obviously right to hold that these were trading receipts and it was open to the House to hold that the payments should be assigned to the year of receipt,[5] it does not follow that subsidies should be treated in the same way as payments for service.[6] Moreover in *Elson v Price's Tailors* the Crown did not apparently argue for the year of receipt but only for the date the deposits were forfeitable. The point should therefore be regarded as open, especially so far as part payments are concerned. This view is strengthened by the decision of the House of Lords in *Sun Insurance Office v Clark*,[7] not cited by Ungoed-Thomas J where premiums paid in advance for a year were not to be treated as income only of the year of receipt but a proportion was to be carried forward to the following year.

Simon's Taxes B3.914, 916; Butterworths Income Tax Service C1.114.

[1] See *Symons v Weeks* [1983] STC 195 (supra, § **7: 145**). Where the sum is not yet final it may be appropriate to defer treating it as a trading receipt even though it has been received.

[2] [1963] 1 All ER 231, 40 TC 671.

[3] The argument in the Chancery Division is not reported.

[4] [1937] 1 All ER 413, 20 TC 643.

[5] Cf. *Short Bros v IRC* (1927) 12 TC 955 when payments for the cancellation of a shipbuilding contract were attributed to the year of cancellation and not the (later) years when the ships would have been built.

[6] See also supra, § **7: 142**.

[7] [1912] AC 443, 6 TC 59.

Receipts in kind

7: 148   The only difference between a payment in money and a payment in kind is that the value of the former is more obvious. Where, therefore, a trading receipt is received otherwise than in sterling, whether in foreign currency or in kind a value must be put on the receipt at the time it becomes a trading receipt i.e. when it is delivered or, if earlier, when it is due. Subsequent changes in value should be ignored.[1]

It is no objection to such valuation that the benefit in kind cannot in fact be realised. So in *Gold Coast Selection Trusts Ltd v Humphrey*[2] the trust had sold certain rights in a gold mine concession in exchange for shares in a company and was held taxable on the value of the shares so received even though it would be quite impossible to obtain a reasonable price for them if all were sold at one go on the Stock Exchange. Where, as in this case, the shares would become part of the trading stock of the company, adjustments to their value would have to be made each year under the principle of cost or market whichever is the lower.

Where a dealing company receives shares they will be valued as trading receipts only when they represent the end of a trading transaction as opposed to a step in the course of one. The central idea was expressed by Rowlatt J:[3]

> "While an investment is going up or down for income tax purposes the Company cannot take any notice of fluctuations, but it has to take notice of them when that state of affairs comes to an end when the investment . . . ceases to figure in the company's affairs, when it is known exactly what the holding of the investment has meant, plus or minus to the Company, and then the Company starts as far as that portion of its resources is concerned with a new investment."

So in *Gold Coast Selection Trusts Ltd v Humphrey*[4] there was a realisation. In *Varty v British South Africa Co*, by contrast, where a company had an option to subscribe for shares in company C at par and decided to exercise that option, there was no realisation and so no taxable profit at the time.[5] The question in all cases is one of fact and substance, but the *Varty* case appears to be the only reported instance involving securities where the court has held there was no realisation. So even an exchange of shares under a company amalgamation scheme has constituted a realisation[6] as has the exchange of mortgage bonds against one company for debenture stock in a new one when the first company's finances were being restructured.[7] Even the exercise of an option in a Government savings scheme to convert the holding into a new Government stock was held to be a realisation.[8]

On this basis where securities—the original holding—are held as circulating capital, trading receipts arise when they are disposed of and allowable expense on their reinvestment in the new holding. If however they were held as fixed capital a form of roll-over relief might apply so postponing liability in respect of the resulting capital gain, infra, § **20: 06**. To further the policy behind the CGT relief, TA 1988, s. 473 provides that where that relief would apply if the assets were such that the proceeds of sale would not be trading receipts, then the original holding is not treated as disposed of and the new holding is treated as the same asset.

Simon's Taxes B3.924; Butterworths Income Tax Service C1.115.

[1] *Greig v Ashton* [1956] 3 All ER 123, 36 TC 581.
[2] [1948] 2 All ER 379, 30 TC 209. See [1970] BTR 150.

[3] In *Royal Insurance Co Ltd v Stephen* (1928) 14 TC 22 at 28.
[4] Supra. See also *Californian Copper Syndicate Ltd v Harris* (1904) 5 TC 159.
[5] [1965] 2 All ER 395, 42 TC 406.
[6] *Royal Insurance Co Ltd v Stephen* (1928) 14 TC 22.
[7] *Scottish and Canadian General Investment Co Ltd v Easson* (1922) 8 TC 265.
[8] *Westminster Bank Ltd v Osler* [1933] AC 139, 17 TC 381.

Timing of liabilities on an earnings basis

7: 149 On an earnings basis expenses are deductible when incurred and not when paid, but not simply because the need for that work has arisen. So in *Naval Colliery Co Ltd v IRC*[1] a company's mines were damaged during a strike which ended on 2nd July 1921; no element for the costs of reconditioning the mine could be included for the period ending 30th June 1921.

An interesting case forbidding the anticipation of a loss is *Edward Collins & Sons Ltd v IRC*.[2] Here the taxpayer had entered into contracts for the delivery of raw materials in the following year. The market price of those materials had dropped substantially by the end of his trading year. It was held that he could not anticipate his loss by deducting the excess of the contract price over current market value. Two things must be noted. First, the taxpayer did not seek to deduct the whole price due under the contract, but only the predicted loss. He was right not to claim this since the obligations to pay had not yet arisen. Secondly had the raw materials been delivered it would have become trading stock and so the loss would have become eligible for relief under the rules for valuation of trading stock.[3] These rules could not however be extended to merely executory contracts for the delivery of trading stock.

Simon's Taxes B3.917, 918; Butterworths Income Tax Service C1.116.
[1] (1928) 12 TC 1017; see also *J. Spencer & Co v IRC* (1950) 32 TC 111.
[2] 1925 SC 151, 12 TC 773; see also *Whimster & Co v IRC* 1926 SC 20, 12 TC 813 and *J H Young & Co v IRC* 1926 SC 30, 12 TC 827.
[3] Infra, § 7: 159.

Contingent liabilities
7: 150 The question whether one can make a deduction for a contingent liability must be answered first by reference to sound principles of accountancy practice. Such evidence was not forthcoming in *Peter Merchant Ltd v Stedeford*.[1] The taxpayer ran a canteen for a factory owner and was under a contractual obligation to replace utensils; owing to wartime scarcities it was not possible to replace them. The accountant recommended that the amounts owing under the liability to replace should be deducted each year. However, he had committed an error of law by construing the contract to mean that there was a liability to replace the stock each year rather than at the end of the contract; it followed that deduction could not be allowed each year.

When an obligation matures over a number of years or is contingent it is proper to make provision year by year if, and only if, reliable figures can be established. In *IRC v Titaghur Jute Factory Co Ltd*[2] a company was obliged by foreign statute to make provision for gratuities to be paid to employees on leaving the company service; the amount would depend on the final salary

308 Part II—Income tax

and the length of service. The Court of Session allowed the company to deduct a sum set aside to meet this obligation.

By contrast, in *Southern Railway of Peru Ltd v Owen*[3] the taxpayer could not justify its figures and so was not allowed any deduction. By Peruvian law it was bound to pay its employees certain sums of money on redundancy, retirement or death. The payments were to be of one month's salary for each completed year of service, the salary being computed according to the rates in force at the time of redundancy or other cause, with certain protection for employees whose salaries declined. No payments were due however if an employee on a fixed term contract resigned before the term had expired nor where an employee was dismissed for just cause. The Revenue argued that the correct method of computing profits was to deduct payments actually made during the period. The company however argued that it should charge against each year's receipts the cost of making provision for the retirement benefits that they would ultimately have to pay and conceded that as a corollary they would not be able to deduct the actual payments made each year. It was clearly impractical to regard the setting aside of these sums as provisional payments and adjust them retrospectively as each employee became entitled to his share. The House of Lords held that the company's method was far more likely to give a true picture of the company's annual profit but that this object could only be achieved if the figures were sufficiently reliable. The figures for which the company was arguing were thus explained by Lord Radcliffe, "It has calculated what sum would be required to be paid to each employee in respect of retirement benefit if he retired without forfeiture, at the close of the year". This process was defective in that it failed to take account of the length of time that would pass before the payments would become due, a factor which could be met by a discounting process, secondly in that it failed to recognise that the legislation which had created the present system could also vary it and thirdly in that there was the possibility that a certain number of employees would forfeit their rights to payments. For these reasons the figure which the company was trying to deduct, although correctly deducted in order to give a "true and fair" view of the profits, and necessarily so for the purposes of the Companies Acts, was not sufficiently precise for the Income Tax Acts.

It should be noted that the issue in *IRC v Titaghur Jute Factory Co Ltd* concerned the year in which the initial liability was imposed on the company; no attempt was made to make provision for obligations which had matured in previous years—any such obligation should have been provided for in the earlier years.

Simon's Taxes B3.916; Butterworths Income Tax Service C1.117.

[1] (1948) 30 TC 496.

[2] [1978] STC 166.

[3] [1956] 2 All ER 728, 36 TC 602 and see also the decision of Lush J, allowing the deduction of future expenses of maintaining graves: *London Cemetery Co v Barnes* [1917] 2 KB 496, 7 TC 92.

TRADING STOCK

7:151 Trading stock gives rise to a number of special rules which are dealt with together.

(1) Substitution of market value

In general, where trading stock is disposed of, the sum to be entered into the accounts will be the actual price realised on the disposal. If the goods have been given away perhaps for reasons of advertisement there will be no sum to be entered at all. Neither the Revenue nor the taxpayer are in general allowed to substitute a fair market price for that in fact obtained.[1] To this principle however there are three exceptions.

Simon's Taxes B3.927; Butterworths Income Tax Service C1.91.
[1] *Craddock v Zevo Finance Co Ltd* [1946] 1 All ER 523, 27 TC 267 at 288.

(a) Transfer-pricing: TA 1988, s. 770

7: 152 Where the parties to a sale or other transaction are such that one has control over the other and the price is less than would have been expected from a sale between independent persons,[1] then the price so expected is substituted in computing the profits of the seller. The reason for this is to prevent a transfer at a price creating a tax-deductible loss to the seller and perhaps a gain free of income tax to the buyer. For this reason the section does not apply where the buyer is a trader resident in the UK if the purchase price would be entered into his trade accounts as a deduction.[2]

Conversely if the price is higher than would have been expected there can be a similar substitution in the accounts of the buyer to prevent him from claiming an artificial loss. There is a similar exception if the seller is a resident trading in the UK and the sale price would enter his trade accounts; the exception does not apply to non-residents.[3]

The section extends to the letting and hiring of property, grants and transfer of rights, interests or licences and the giving of business facilities of whatever kind. It thus prevents the suppression of profits through manipulating the price for goods, know-how or services.[4]

This provision is limited in two respects.[5] First, it applies only where one party controls the other and so does not apply where one party has 49% of the voting power of the other, and so may have control for practical purposes. Secondly, it only enables the revenue to challenge particular transactions and cannot be used simply to reallocate the profits because trade between the two parties is carried on in an uneven manner. The former point loses some force now that the definition of control has been widened to include power held by nominees and most connected persons,[6] and the latter because of the increased powers of the Revenue to inspect books.[7] No case on the interpretation of s. 770 has yet been reported.[8]

Simon's Taxes B3.927; Butterworths Income Tax Service C1.91.
[1] Introduced FA 1951, s. 37—replacing General Rule 7 in ITA 1918 which had been confined to dealings between a resident and a non-resident.
[2] This is presumably market value.
[3] But it seems that the Revenue can use *Sharkey v Wernher* infra, § **7:154**.
[4] Infra, § **35: 07**.
[5] TA 1988, s. 773(4).
[6] TA 1988, s. 773(3).
[7] TA 1988, s. 772.

[8] See infra, § **35: 07**. It appears that the United Kingdom revenue authorities may not impute interest on interest-free loans for foreign subsidiaries if any commerical reason for such a loan can be shown; Edwardes-Ker, *International Tax Strategies*, Chapter 7 *but* see Revenue Notes [1981] STI, p. 42.

(b) Watson Bros v Hornby[1]

7: 153   Where one trader has two distinct trades[2] and transfers goods from one trade to the other the transfer must be treated as a sale and purchase at a reasonable price. In *Watson Bros v Hornby* on the transfer from a trade taxed under Schedule D, Case I, that of chicken breeder and hatcher to a farm which at that time was taxed under Schedule B, the market value was less than the cost of production and so the taxpayer succeeded in establishing a trading loss. The case was decided on the basis of a notional sale at a reasonable price.[3]

Simon's Taxes B3.926; Butterworths Income Tax Service C1.91.
  [1] [1942] 2 All ER 506, 24 TC 506; see also *Long v Belfield Poultry Products Ltd* (1937) 21 TC 221.
  [2] TA 1988, s. 770 only applies where there are two traders.
  [3] Sale of Goods Act 1893, s. 8.

(c) Sharkey v Wernher

7: 154   The Revenue turned their defeat in *Watson Bros v Hornby* to good use in *Sharkey v Wernher*.[1] Lady Zia Wernher carried on the business of a stud farm; she also rode horses for pleasure. She transferred a horse reared at the farm to her personal use and entered the costs incurred in respect of the horse until the date of its transfer as a credit item in the account of the stud farm. There was thus no attempt to take tax advantage of the deductions she had already been allowed. The Revenue successfully contended that the horse should be entered not at cost but at market value. The rule is that where a trader disposes of trading stock otherwise than in the course of trade, he is deemed to dispose of it at market value and that figure must be entered as a credit in his accounts. This principle applies whether he supplies the goods to himself or to some other person unless the disposal is a genuine commercial transaction. The value entered in the books of the transferor is also entered in the books of any trader acquiring the stock.[2]

The rule is subject to three technical objections. First the profit alleged to be made comes from a course of dealing with oneself; it is precisely because this is alleged to be impossible that no charge to tax arises from mutual dealings. In reply Viscount Simonds said that "the true proposition is not that a man cannot make a profit out of himself but that he cannot trade with himself",[3] a principle which was not to apply where trading stock was removed from the trade for a man's own use and enjoyment. However this is not consistent with other formulations of the mutuality principle.[4]

Secondly the decision appears to conflict with the fundamental principle that a person is taxed on what is actually earned and not on what he might have earned. However in *Sharkey v Wernher* the taxpayer received value; the question therefore is the figure to be entered in the accounts. Lord Radcliffe rejected the idea of taking the cost figure on the grounds that market value "gives a fairer measure of assessable trading profit" and was "better economics".[5] For a trader who was concerned with the profitability of his trade it would be better book-keeping to include market value. However the issue is not what is good book-keeping but the correct basis for taxation. In this regard it may be noted that the cost figure was in conformity with then accepted accountancy practice.[6]

Thirdly it is said that if *Sharkey v Wernher* is correctly decided there was no need for TA 1988, s. 770. There is little substance to this objection. It is now clear that *Sharkey v Wernher* applies to transactions between different persons whether or not one controls the other so that its ambit is wider than s.770;[7] further it is also clear that a transaction may be at an undervalue and still outside *Sharkey v Wernher* so that s.770 may apply.[8] In addition, s.770 applies to assets other than trading stock; it is not yet clear whether *Sharkey v Wernher* does. To make matters better still for the Revenue, it appears that *Sharkey v Wernher* can be used even though the proviso to s. 770 applies.

Simon's Taxes B3.926; Butterworths Income Tax Service C1.91.

[1] [1955] 3 All ER 493, 36 TC 275.
[2] *Ridge Securities Ltd v IRC* [1964] 1 All ER 275, 44 TC 373. See [1964] BTR 168 (Crump). This means that the transferee gets the whole profit free of tax but a double charge to tax is avoided; contrast *Skinner v Berry Head Lands Ltd* [1971] 1 All ER 222, 46 TC 377, when the transferee was fixed with the whole gain.
[3] [1955] 3 All ER 493 at 496, 36 TC 275 at 296.
[4] Supra, § 7: 22.
[5] [1955] 3 All ER 493 at 506, 36 TC 275 at 307.
[6] See Lord Oaksey (dissenting).
[7] Supra, § 7: 153.
[8] Infra.

The limits of the rule

7: 155 The most serious criticism of the decision of the House of Lords is simply that of the uncertainty as to the scope of the notional income. It would appear first that the rule is confined to Schedule D. Thus a landlord who allows himself to occupy one of his houses would not be treated as owing himself an economic rent for the property chargeable under Schedule A. Likewise a person occupying land for the purposes of a commercial woodland and who uses some timber for his own purposes would certainly incur no extra liability under Schedule B and possibly also if he had elected to be taxed under Schedule D, Case I because that election does not mean that he is trading.[1]

---

[1] *Coates v Holker Estates Co* (1961) 40 TC 75.

7: 156 It is not clear whether the rule applies to professions. In *Mason v Innes*[1] the author, Hammond Innes, had written a book called *The Doomed Oasis*. Shortly before completing the manuscript he had assigned the copyright to his father by way of gift. It was agreed that the market value of the copyright at that date was £15,425. The rule in *Sharkey v Wernher* was not applied. The effect in *Mason v Innes* was that not only did the Revenue see their share of the copyright vanish but they were still left bearing the loss of tax resulting from the deduction of expenses incurred by the author in the creation of the copyright.

Lord Denning MR, said that a professional man was different from a trader and suggested that a picture painted by an artist was somehow different from a horse produced on a stud farm. His Lordship's second reason was that this professional man was taxed on a cash basis whereas a trader was taxed on an earnings basis, a distinction which ought to be irrelevant since it goes to calculating liability to tax rather than deciding what items should be taxable. His Lordship's third reason was the set of anomalies that would result notably in contrast with the rules that allowed spreading of copyright income[2] and the taxation of post cessation receipts both of which provisions must have been passed on the basis that notional sales could not arise from the transfer of the copyright.[3] On the other hand the area is full of anomalies anyway.

A more convincing reason for the decision of the Court of Appeal is given by Potter:[4]

> "the whole point of *Sharkey v Wernher* was that some figure had to be entered in the trading account because an item of trading stock that stood in that account at cost was taken out. An author does not however enter his copyrights in his professional account. He does not deal in copyrights. His earnings are in essence fees for services, not proceeds of sale of assets. He pays tax on what he receives or is entitled to receive, no account being taken of opening or closing stock."

On this basis *Mason v Innes* was correctly decided but it may mean a closer examination of the boundary between a profession and a trade.[5] Thus an artist who sells his own pictures might be regarded as carrying on the profession of an artist and the trade of a picture dealer. In this event the value of the paintings will be entered into his trading account at their then market value.

Simon's Taxes B4.101; Butterworths Income Tax Service C1.91.

[1] [1967] 2 All ER 926, 44 TC 326; assignments of copyright may fall within TA 1988, s. 775, *infra*, § **31: 33** and be subject to CGT and IHT.
[2] TA 1988, s. 534; *supra*, § **5: 46**.
[3] TA 1988, s. 104 (TA 1970, s. 144), *supra*, § **7: 137**.
[4] [1964] BTR 438 at 442.
[5] *Supra*, § **7: 06**.

7: 157   It would also mean that the rule only applies to dispositions of trading stock and so does not extend to things which are the assets of a profession, nor to disposal of certain items in a trade. Thus the disposal of an agency at an undervalue would not be a disposal of trading stock.

The rule does not apply to a sale at a fairly negotiated price. In *Jacgilden (Weston Hall) Ltd v Castle*[1] a property developer acquired the right to buy a hotel for £72,000. He later transferred that right to a company for £72,000 although at the time the hotel was worth £155,000. He sought to have the hotel entered into the books of the company at its market price as opposed to the actual cost price—and failed. There was no question of the contract for sale being an illusory or colourable or fraudulent transaction; it was a perfectly straightforward and honest bargain between the developer and the company.

The rule may not apply to a transfer on discontinuance to one carrying on a trade in the UK and in whose accounts the cost of the stock transferred will appear as a revenue deduction.[2] The statutory rule in TA 1988, s. 100 may here exclude *Sharkey v Wernher*.

Three concluding points ought to be made. The first is that a system which provided for no figure to be entered into the accounts by way of credit on the occasion of a self-supply[3] would give the self supplier a great tax advantage. Although in *Sharkey v Wernher* the taxpayer was arguing that the figure should be cost, thus surrendering the benefit of the deductions she had been able to claim, no such surrender was offered in *Mason v Innes*.

The second is that in view of the general dislike of the rule evinced by lower courts[4] the decision may be reversed although whether this could be done through expert evidence of accountancy practice, a matter which had not weighed much with the House in *Sharkey v Wernher*, or through the exercise of the power to reverse earlier decisions remains to be seen.

The third is that these transactions may give rise not only to income tax but also to CGT and IHT. Thus in the *Jacgilden* case it would be hard for the seller to bring himself within IHTA 1984, s. 10, infra, § **38: 14** since he controlled the company; moreover CGT might well be assessed by reference to market value, infra, § **16: 20**.

Simon's Taxes B3.732; Butterworths Income Tax Service C1.91.

[1] [1969] 3 All ER 1110, 45 TC 685. In *Julius Bendit Ltd v IRC* (1945) 27 TC 44 the test seems to have been whether the deal was a bona fide trading transaction (which it was); the same result was reached in *Craddock v Zevo Finance Co Ltd* [1944] 1 All ER 566, 27 TC 267. These cases might be decided differently today but the principle which they represent is probably sound.

[2] *Moore v R J MacKenzie & Sons Ltd* [1972] 2 All ER 549, 48 TC 196.

[3] On self supply for VAT see VATA 1983, s. 3, infra § **55: 09**.

[4] The Revenue did not put the principle at risk by appealing in *Mason v Innes* (supra, § **7: 156**).

---

(2) End of year valuations

7: 158 The value of trading stock unsold at the end of the first period is entered into the account of the year as a receipt and into the account of the second period as an expense; it is thus sold from one year to the next. The figure entered is cost or market value—whichever is the lower.[1] The effect is that losses may be anticipated—but not profit—a sound conservative accounting principle.

Income tax is charged upon the profit of the trade over a particular period, usually the accounting year of the business. The true profit for the period— ignoring overheads—is not simply sums for goods sold received minus sums spent, but sums received for goods sold minus sums spent on those goods. Thus suppose that a retailer sells shoes. In the first year he spends £10,000 on shoes, and sells half of them for £10,000. The second year he sells the other half for £10,000 but buys no more stock. The naif view that the profit for his first year was nil but for his second year £10,000 would give a very distorted view of the profitability of his business. Hence the rule which takes £5,000 as a receipt for the first year and an expense of the second. Over the two year period the naif view and the correct one produce the same total profit. They differ in the methods of determining the profit of a particular artificial period during the life of the business.

Simon's Taxes B3.1010; Butterworths Income Tax Service C1.92.
[1] *Whimster & Co v IRC* (1926) 12 TC 813.

Trading stock

7: 159   The first problem is to decide the range of assets to which this valuation should apply. It clearly applies to trading stock but equally clearly does not apply to capital assets. Stock not yet delivered is not trading stock,[1] nor is it permissible to anticipate a loss on the hiring of ships on time charter,[2] since such charters are not trading stock. In *Willingale v International Commercial Bank Ltd*[3] there was no suggestion that the bills were trading stock; otherwise the Revenue would have won. Thus one may not anticipate any loss save that on trading stock proper.

Simon's Taxes B3.1001; Butterworths Income Tax Service C1.92.
[1] *Edwards Collins & Sons Ltd v IRC* (1925) 12 TC 773, supra, § **7: 149**.
[2] *Whimster & Co v IRC* (1926) 12 TC 813 and see *Scottish Investment Trust Co v Forbes* (1893) 3 TC 231 and *Lions Ltd v Gosford Furnishing Co and IRC* (1961) 40 TC 256 (future hiring receipts not stock in trade).
[3] Supra, § **7: 65**.

7: 160   The next problem is to determine what stock is to be valued. While our small shoeshop may be able to determine precisely which shoes were unsold at the end of the year, it is less practicable to expect a coal merchant to be able to say just how many tons of coal he had in stock at the end of work on the last day of his accounting period, and there is in fact no obligation on him to weigh his stock at the end of that day before resuming his business. The Revenue appear content to rely on an annual stocktaking with any adjustments necessary.

The cost of the goods is complicated if the goods are fungibles and prices alter in the course of the trading period. Three principle types of formulae are used by accountants. The first, which is the only one accepted for tax purposes, is first in first out (FIFO), i.e. last in still there. If prices are rising this means using the cheaper stock first so that the cost of the goods sold is low. The stock remaining at the end of the year, a plus item in the accounts, will therefore be the dearer items. The FIFO system has the advantage that the closing stock will be valued at the more recent prices and so, depending on the rapidity of turnover and the rate of price change, at a figure more or less close to replacement cost. It has however the converse disadvantage that it matches past costs with current receipts and thus, in an era of inflation, an over-optimistic picture of profitability.

The second formula, which was rejected for tax purposes by the Privy Council in *Minister of National Revenue v Anaconda American Brass Ltd*[1] is the opposite of the first, last in first out (LIFO). The third method—the weighted average—is a compromise. This looks at the different prices paid for the stock over the period and weights the price according to the quantity of stock bought at each price.

The different methods of determining the stock to be valued yield different results and so different profit figures for each accounting period. However over the lifetime of the business all three methods will give the same figure of profits if applied consistently since the same total amount will have been spent on stock and the same total amount received on sales and any remaining stock is valued under TA 1988, ss. 100 and 102. Aberrations will occur where there is a change in the method of valuing stock during the lifetime of the trade. For tax purposes too there will be the same total profit to be taxed although different tax rates and, for individuals, the complexities of the gaps and overlaps of the commencement and cessation period will mean that the total tax charged may well vary according to the method chosen.

---

[1] [1956] 1 All ER 20, [1956] AC 85.

Cost

7: 161   The cost is that at the original acquisition. Expenses incurred in keeping the goods in good condition are ignored;[1] these expenses properly belong to the time they were incurred since their value will not be recouped later.

Simon's Taxes B3.1011.
[1] Per Lord Reid in *Ryan v Asia Mill Ltd* (1951) 32 TC 275 at 298.

Market value

7: 162   Market value means generally net realisable value, and not replacement cost. Thus where a retail shoeshop values trading stock the correct figure for market value should be the normal retail price rather than the price the shop would have to pay wholesale to replace that item. On the other hand if the trade were that of a wholesale supplier of shoes the figure would be that which the trader would receive on a wholesale disposal.

In *BSC Footwear Ltd v Ridgway*[1] the House of Lords held that a retail shoe shop should value unsold stock by reference to the value to be expected in a sale and with a deduction for the salesperson's commission but without any allowance for the general expenses of the business for later periods of account; so no deduction could be made for the normal retail mark-up. As Lord Pearson put it:

> "The correct principle is that goods should not be written down below cost price unless there really is a loss actual or prospective. So long as the fall in prevailing prices is only such as to reduce the prospective profit the initial valuation at cost should be retained".[2]

Simon's Taxes B3.1012; Butterworths Income Tax Service C1.92.
[1] [1971] 2 All ER 534, 47 TC 495.
[2] [1971] 2 All ER 534 at 550, 47 TC 511 at 540.

The formula applied

7: 163   In applying the formula cost or market value whichever is the lower, each item may be treated separately so that one may be valued at cost and another at market value.[1] This is consistent with the idea of anticipating losses but not profits. Where stock is acquired by gift[2] the receipt is treated as being at market value. When the transfer falls within the rule in *Sharkey v Wernher* the value at which the transferor is taken to dispose of it is taken as the acquisition cost to the transferee.

Where different methods of computing the cost or market value are available the same method must be used at the end of the year as was used at the beginning.[3] However the method used at the opening of the second period need not be that used at the closing of the first.[4] Where such a change occurs there will be either a double charge or no charge at all on the difference between the closing stock of the first period and the opening stock of the second period.

Simon's Taxes B3.1012; Butterworths Income Tax Service C1.92.
   [1] *IRC v Cock Russell & Co Ltd* [1949] 2 All ER 889, 29 TC 387.
   [2] See per Lord Greene MR in *Craddock v Zevo Finance Co Ltd* [1944] 1 All ER 566, 27 TC 267.
   [3] *Steel Barrel Co Ltd v Osborne (No. 2)* (1948) 30 TC 73.
   [4] Although the Revenue will not generally allow this without good reason. The Revenue do not seem to insist upon consistency in their own behaviour, e.g. *Ostime v Duple Motor Bodies* and *BSC Footwear Ltd v Ridgway* (infra, § **7: 166** and supra, § **7: 162**).

---

(3) Ground rents and rentcharges

7: 164   Where a builder grants the house purchaser a long lease and charges both a premium and a ground rent, there is no outright realisation of the builder's interest in the land.[1] His previous freehold interest is now subject to a leasehold interest in the householder. It follows that the reversion remains part of the builder's stock and must therefore be entered each year at cost or market value, whichever is the lower.[2]

The cost of the reversion must include a part of the building cost. The formula used to ascertain that part is $A/(A+B)$ where A is the market value of the reversion (traditionally calculated as a multiple of the rent payable) and B is the premium.[3]

Very different is the situation where the builder sells the freehold interest but reserves to himself a rentcharge,[4] chief rent or, in Scotland, a ground annual.[5] Here the House of Lords has held that there is a realisation of the interest in the land for money (the price) and money's worth (the rent). The market value of the rentcharge must therefore be entered as a trading receipt in the year of sale and the rent payable will likewise be treated as a trading receipt. On the other hand the eventual disposal of the rentcharge will not give rise to a trading receipt unless the court holds that there is a trade of dealing in rent charges.

Simon's Taxes B3.629–632, 1002; Butterworths Income Tax Service C1.93.
   [1] *B G Utting & Co Ltd v Hughes* [1940] 2 All ER 76, 23 TC 174.
   [2] *Heather v G and J A Redfern & Sons* (1944) 26 TC 119.

[3] See case stated, para. V, in *J Emery & Sons Ltd v IRC* [1937] AC 91, 20 TC 213 at 219.
[4] *Broadbridge v Beattie* (1944) 26 TC 63.
[5] *J Emery & Sons Ltd v IRC*, supra.

(4) Work in progress

7: 165   Where the trader is a manufacturer and there is work in progress at the end of the accounting period as well as finished trading stock, the work in progress must be taken into account. One problem is that of determining just what is its cost—a problem of some difficulty. In *Duple Motor Bodies v Ostime*[1] the company made motor bodies and had since 1924 used the "direct cost" of ascertaining the cost of the work in progress, meaning that only the cost of materials used and labour directly employed in the manufacture were included. This gave a loss of £2,000. The Revenue argued that the cost should be computed on the "on-cost basis" meaning that there should also be included the proportion of overhead expenditure, with the effect that the profits for the year would be increased since the deductible expenses would be offset by the extra item on the credit side of the balance sheet. This gave an extra profit of £14,000. This would have the odd result that if work were slack so that the same quantity of overheads would have to be spread over fewer items, the "cost" of the work in progress would be increased so that while his receipts dropped his taxable profits in respect of work in progress would be increased. The accountancy profession was divided on the issue of which method should be adopted. The House of Lords held that the Revenue had failed to show that the "direct cost" was wrong especially in this case where it had been used for so long and dismissed the Revenue's appeal. They declined to lay down any general principle—the real question was what method best fitted the circumstances of the particular business.

Simon's Taxes B3.1017
[1] [1961] 2 All ER 167, 39 TC 537.

7: 166   A difficult question is whether the trader can anticipate a loss in respect of work in progress. The market value of work in progress is difficult to assess since the work as such is unsaleable, a point agreed on the facts in *Duple Motor Bodies v Ostime*. Where however it is clear that a loss will be incurred when the work is completed there seems at present to be no way in which that can be anticipated, although in that case Lord Reid said that there must be some way of doing it.[1]

When a firm changes its basis of valuation this may result in an extra profit which would have accrued during earlier years if the new system had been in operation. Such extra profits are taxable in the year in which they accrue which is the year in which they are revealed and are not backdated.[2]

Simon's Taxes B3.1017; Butterworths Income Tax Service C1.94.
[1] [1961] 2 All ER 167 at 175, 39 TC 537 at 572. This valuation would have avoided the problem in the case since the market value of a half-finished coach is probably less than the cost.
[2] *Pearce v Woodall-Duckham Ltd* [1978] STC 372, [1978] 2 All ER 793.

(5) **Stock relief**

7: 167   The FIFO rule means that the stock remaining at the end of the trading period and which is sold to the next period is that which was most recently bought and so, in a time of rising prices, the most expensive. This has the effect of producing paper profits on which real tax must be paid. One consequence for the businessman is that the Revenue, by taking tax on profits which has not yet accrued in cash terms, reduces his liquidity and so makes it more difficult for him to buy more stock. This phenomenon became acute in 1974 when 10% of individual traders' profits and 50% of companies' profits were attributable to stock appreciation.[1] The phenomenon was christened the Doomsday Machine.

Pending radical reform such as the introduction of LIFO special relief was given. These reliefs take the form of an arbitrary adjustment of taxable income, and at first took no account of changes in volume as distinct from value of stock; the resulting figure was remote from any concept of income. The reliefs were also criticised for giving too much relief to an expanding business and too little to one which realises cash by reducing wasteful stock levels.

The relief was abolished by FA 1984. No relief can arise for any period of account beginning after 12th March 1984 and no clawback charge can arise on a cessation or succession after that date.

Simon's Taxes B3.16.
  [1] National Income and Expenditure 1974. These figures are after allowing for depreciation; they may be compared with those for 1965—2% and 5%.

---

(6) **Valuation of trading stock on discontinuance**

7: 168   When a trade had been discontinued the general rule is that stock is entered at market value.[1] However where the stock is sold or transferred for valuable consideration to a person who carries on or intends to carry on a trade in the UK and the cost will fall to be deducted in computing that person's profits, the figure for any trading stock belonging to the trade at discontinuance is to be the sale price or the value of the consideration.[2] This exception would appear to apply where a business is incorporated.

The general rule is designed to prevent a person from discontinuing his business, bringing his stock into account at cost value and then reselling it at the much higher market value so securing to himself a large gain free of income tax, as nearly happened in *J. & R. O'Kane & Co Ltd v IRC*.[3]

The rule applies whenever a trade is discontinued including those situations made discontinuance by TA 1988, ss. 113 and 337(1). Perhaps because it is an anti-avoidance provision it does not apply where a trade carried on by a single individual is discontinued by reason of his death.[4] The market value will however be taken for CTT and IHT.

Similar rules apply to work in progress at the discontinuance of a profession. The phrase "the amount that would have been paid for a transfer as between parties at arm's length" is substituted for market value.[5] Where this amount exceeds the actual cost of the work the taxpayer may elect to pay no tax now and submit to having sums actually received later taxed as post cessation receipts under s. 103 (not s. 104).[6]

Simon's Taxes B3.1016; Butterworths Income Tax Service C1.95.
[1] TA 1988, s. 100(1)(*b*).
[2] TA 1988, s. 100(1)(*a*). See *Moore v R J Mackenzie & Sons Ltd* [1972] 2 All ER 549, 48 TC 196; supra, § **7: 157**. Trading stock is defined in s. 137(4).
[3] (1922) 12 TC 303; supra, § **7: 29**.
[4] TA 1988, s. 102(2).
[5] TA 1988, s. 101(1).
[6] TA 1988, s. 101(2), on post-cessation receipts, see supra, § **7: 135**.

8 Capital allowances

INTRODUCTION

8: 01 Expenses incurred in the acquisition of a capital asset are not deductible in computing the profits of a trade.[1] If that asset may have a limited life, its value to the business will decline. The causes of this decline may be physical, such as wear and tear on plant and machinery, or economic such as obsolescence or a change in trading policy. To anticipate the eventual loss depreciation is deductible for accounting purposes but no provision was originally made for tax purposes as the tax was thought to be temporary.

The tax system has relaxed this strict approach by making allowances for certain defined types of capital expenditure. These allowances displace the deductibility of expenditure on renewals.[2] The structure of the present system goes back to the Income Tax Act 1945. This Act defined certain types of capital expenditure which qualified for allowances. Broadly speaking the list is the same today although there have been changes in the way in which the allowances are made. The legislation is now consolidated in the Capital Allowances Act 1968 supplemented principally by the Taxes Act 1988[3] and the Finance Act 1971 but much amended by the Finance Acts 1984 to 1986.[4] A new consolidation is promised for 1990 and FA 1989 therefore contains a number of pre-consolidation amendments.

For many years the tax system enshrined the doctrine that tax allowances encouraged investment. Hence elaborate allowances were given to allow the writing off of capital expenditure far ahead of any real depreciation or obsolescence. FA 1984 and FA 1985 represented a major change in direction since they reduced the rates of allowances so making them closer to actual depreciation and compensated for this by reducing the rate of corporation tax. The aim was achieved by reductions in the rates of allowance for expenditure incurred after 13th March 1984, with further reductions for expenditure incurred after 31st March 1985 and 31st March 1986.

Simon's Taxes B2.1.

[1] *Coltness Iron Co v Black* (1881) 6 App Cas 315, 1 TC 311.
[2] Supra, § **7: 118**.
[3] For patents and knowhow, see infra, § **8: 55**.
[4] For expenditure on machinery and plant after 26th October 1970.

8: 02 Many types of capital expenditure do not qualify for any allowance. Further, apart from allowances for plant and machinery, all allowances are confined to income taxable under Schedule D, Case I, some obviously to particular trades, and do not extend to Schedule D, Case II or Schedule E.

These are all allowances and must be claimed: it is sometimes advantageous not to claim them. A claim once made cannot in theory be revised once an assessment has become final.[1]

---
[1] But see Statement of Practice A6, **Simon's Taxes Division H3.4.**

8: 03 Historically the system of allowances has provided for three[1] steps, although since 1986 it is now only (2) and (3) that are relevant for new expenditure:

(1) an initial or first year allowance of a substantial percentage of the capital expenditure; these allowances were abolished in 1986 save for certain minor exceptions.

(2) a writing down allowance during the life of the asset, an allowance that obviously does not apply if there is a 100% initial allowance;

(3) a balancing allowance or charge at the end of the trade or the life of the asset.[2] This is designed to bring the allowances into line with actual expense. If the amount so far allowed is less than the amount spent, an extra or balancing allowance is given. If however the allowance exceeds the expense, as for example if a building has been the subject of a 100% allowance but is then sold off, a sum is imposed by way of charge to recapture that part of the allowance which was not needed. The charge recovers only the amount that has been allowed, any excess being a matter for CGT. There is no provision whereby the balancing charge may be spread over the number of years for which the allowance was claimed; so an individual may pay more tax on the charge than he saved on the allowance. A balancing charge is not, technically, income.[3]

EXAMPLE

A buys an asset for £1,000 and has claimed £500 allowances when he sells it for (*i*) £600; (*ii*) £450; (*iii*) £1,200. In (*i*) there is a balancing charge of £100; in (*ii*) a balancing allowance of £50; and in (*iii*) a balancing charge of £500 the remaining £200 being left to CGT.

For expenditure after 31st March 1986 the allowances are as set out in the table below (exceptions of a minor and transitional nature e.g. under pre-14th March 1984 contracts or regional schemes are ignored).

	First year	*Initial*	*Writing-down*
Industrial buildings	—	—	4% S.L.[1]
Hotels	—	—	4% S.L.
Assured tenancies[4]	—	—	4% S.L.
Industrial and commercial buildings in enterprise zones	—	100%	25% S.L.
Machinery and plant	—	—	25% R.B.[2]
Mines/oil wells	—	—	25% or 10% R.B.
Dredging	—	—	4% S.L.
Agriculture and forestry buildings and works	—	—	4% S.L.
Scientific research	100%	—	—
Patents	—	—	25% R.B.
Knowhow	—	—	25% R.B.
Ships	Free depreciation (a)		
Miscellaneous	—	—	25% R.B.[4]

(a) extended to old ships as from 1st April 1985 (FA 1985, s. 58). This is subject to conditions—see FA 1971, Sch. 8, paras. 8 to 8C as amended by FA 1989, Sch. 13, paras. 14 and 15.

1 S.L. = Straight line reduction of percentage of initial expenditure.
2 R.B. = Reducing balance reduction of percentage of previous balance.

---

[1] In 1954 an investment allowance was introduced. This was in effect a tax free subsidy. It did not reduce the depreciable cost of the asset for other allowances nor was it taken into account for the purpose of any balancing allowance or charge; see further Cmd. 9667.
[2] But not on nationalisation: see CAA 1968, s. 80(2).
[3] *IRC v Wood Bros (Birkenhead) Ltd* [1959] AC 487, 38 TC 275 (reversed for corporation tax).
[4] Infra, § **8: 24** n. 1.

Capital expenditure and when it is incurred

8: 04   This is defined as excluding any sums allowable as deductions in computing the profits or gains of the trade profession or employment carried on by the person incurring the expense;[1] this boundary is not precise. No allowance can be claimed for sums reimbursed by others if the others can obtain capital allowances or a deduction in computing profits[2] or for subsidies from public or local authorities, save for certain grants under the Industry Acts and the Industrial Development Act 1982.[3] Provision is, however, made for allowances for contributions to the capital expenditure of others.[4] When a subsidy is made in respect of machinery and plant by a contributor for the contributor's trade, profession or vocation, a new trade is deemed to have begun. This is to accelerate the benefit of the allowance.[5]

The capital expenditure must have been incurred on the construction of the building or on the provision of the machinery and plant, etc. In *Ben-Odeco Ltd v Powlson*[6] the taxpayer was going to carry on a trade of hiring out an oil rig. In order to finance the construction of the rig it had to borrow money and for this had to pay commitment fees (£59,002) and interest (£435,988). These sums were charged to capital (correctly) in the company's accounts. However, the House of Lords held that the sums were spent not on the provision of machinery and plant but on the provision of money and so did not qualify for capital allowances. This case was distinguished in *Van Arkadie v Sterling Coated Materials Ltd*[7] where the extra (sterling) cost of a price to be paid by instalments but in foreign currency was treated as allowable expenditure.

Under CAA 1968[8] the general rule was that the date on which expenditure was incurred was that on which it became payable. For accounting or basis periods ending after 17th December 1984[9] the date is to be that on which the obligation to pay becomes unconditional.[10] The reason behind this change is to bring the capital allowance rules into line with accountancy practice (which takes this date as the one on which title normally passes). The difference is that an obligation to pay may have become unconditional even though the sum does not have to be paid until a later date.

The new rule does not apply if the due date for payment is more than four months after the obligation to pay has become unconditional[11]—here the due date for payment is taken—nor if it is being artificially exploited.[11] The new rule does not apply where the old rule deems an expenditure to be delayed e.g. capital expenditure incurred before a trade is commenced is deemed incurred on the day of commencement.[12]

Simon's Taxes B2.105, 106, 305, 307.
   [1] CAA 1968, s. 82(1), e.g. *Rose & Co (Wallpaper and Paints) v Campbell* [1968] 1 All ER 405, 44 TC 500 (pattern books of current wallpaper stock not capital expenditure).
   [2] CAA 1968, s. 84(2) and (2A); (2) was amended and (2A) added by FA 1989, Sch. 13, para. 3 as from 27th July 1989.
   [3] CAA 1968, ss. 83–85 and *Birmingham Corpn v Barnes* [1935] AC 292, 19 TC 195.
   [4] CAA 1968, s. 85, amended by the addition of professions for expenditure after 26th July 1989 by FA 1989, Sch. 13, para. 4. See also CAA 1968, Sch. 9.
   [5] FA 1989, Sch. 13, para. 5 which has effect from 27th July 1989.
   [6] [1978] STC 460, [1978] 2 All ER 1111.
   [7] [1983] STC 95.
   [8] CAA 1968, s. 82(3).
   [9] 31st March 1985 for scientific research allowances.
   [10] FA 1985, s. 56. On interaction with other training rules see FA 1985, s. 56(8) as amended by FA 1989, Sch. 13, para. 30.
   [11] FA 1985, s. 56(4).
   [12] FA 1985, s. 56(7).

The basis period

8: 05   The allowance is set against the profit of the basis period,[1] for those subject to corporation tax the accounting period, and for those subject to income tax, the year of assessment.[2] Where allowances are given against the profit of a trade and those profits are taxed on a preceding year basis, the basis period is the period on the profits of which tax falls finally to be computed. So a trader using a calendar year basis will have the calendar year 1988 taken as the basis period for the year of assessment 1989–90 and so capital expenditure in 1988 will qualify for its allowance in 1989–90. Under the preceding year system it is possible for a period of time to fall within two tax periods or none—as in the opening and closing years of the trade, or where there is a change of accounting dates. Special rules provide that despite these gaps in computing the taxable profits, all capital allowances are given once—but only once. Where there is an overlap of periods, the period common to both is treated as belonging to the first period, and where there is a gap in the basis periods the interval is treated as belonging to the second period (unless the trade is permanently discontinued in the second period in which case the interval is treated as belonging to the first).

Simon's Taxes B2.103.
   [1] CAA 1968, s. 72.
   [2] CAA 1968, s. 73.

Methods of using the allowance

8: 06   When the allowance is deductible in taxing a trade, the usual method is to set the allowance against the taxable profits of the trade profession or employment, as the case may be, when making the annual return.[1] Excess allowances may be rolled forward to be set against future profits[2] or set against general income under TA 1988, s. 383[3] or TA 1988, ss. 382, 734.[4]

Simon's Taxes B2.107, D2.206, E1.215.
[1] CAA 1968, s. 70.
[2] CAA 1968, s. 70(4), on order see s. 70(4A) added by FA 1981, s. 77.
[3] Supra, § **5: 03**.
[4] Supra, § **5: 09**.

8: 07   Other allowances e.g. for agricultural buildings or for lessors and licensors, where there is no available trade are given effect by discharge or repayment of tax on the appropriate income—e.g. rent.[1] Other instances are (i) industrial buildings allowance due to a lessor and (ii) allowances for investment and insurance companies.[2] Any excess is carried forward to the income of the same class in succeeding years. There is however a provision whereby the allowance may be set off against general income of the year of assessment for which the allowance fails to be made, or the following year.[3] Any balancing charge is claimed under Schedule D, Case VI.[4]

[1] FA 1982, s. 74; CAA 1968, s. 71; FA 1971, s. 48; see **Simon's Taxes B2.504**; on the trade of leasing see infra, § **8: 37**.
[2] TA 1970, s. 306 see **Simon's Taxes B2.356** and FA 1971, s. 47(2).
[3] CAA 1968, s. 71. See **Simon's Taxes D2.206, E1.215.**
[4] E.g. CAA 1968, s. 6(6) and s. 12(2).

8: 08   For income tax a capital allowance differs from a deductible expense in the following ways: (1) it must be an item of capital expenditure as distinct from revenue; (2) whereas a revenue expense is deductible unless statute otherwise directs, a capital allowance is only made if the statute permits; (3) whereas an allowance may be claimed in respect of expenditure incurred before a trade commences, although only when the trading begins,[1] an expense so incurred is only deductible if incurred within three years of the trade beginning; (4) an expense incurred partly for trade and partly for other purposes is not deductible whereas such duality results in an apportionment of capital expenditure;[2] (5) a revenue expense is deductible at once and in full whereas allowances are made only at specified rates and often over several years; (6) whereas an excess of expenses over receipts creates a trading loss, excess allowances are different and for the most part special provision has to be made so that they are treated like excess expenses; (7) an expense may, under the preceding year system of assessment, be deducted twice or not at all if it occurs in a period of overlap or gap; a capital allowance is made once and only once.

Where capital allowances are open to a body subject to corporation tax, the allowance is treated as a deductible expense if there is a trade;[3] otherwise by deduction from income of the specified class.[4] The allowance is to be "treated as" a trading expense rather than being an expense and so the body is under no obligation to take allowances available but has a discretion whether or not to take them.[5]

[1] CAA 1968, s. 73.
[2] E.g. *G H Chambers (Northiam Farms) Ltd v Watmough* [1956] 3 All ER 485, 36 TC 711 where an extravagant choice of motor car for personal reasons led to a reduction in the allowance.
[3] CAA 1968, s. 73.

[4] CAA 1968, s. 74.

[5] *Elliss v BP Oil Northern Ireland Refinery Ltd* [1987] STC 52, CA. (CAA 1968, s. 73 contains the word "shall" but this was interpreted in a non-mandatory sense.)

Anti-avoidance legislation

8: 09   The amount of a balancing charge or allowance clearly depends upon the amount received. The actual sale price will be taken unless either (*a*) the buyer is a body of persons[1] over whom the seller has control,[2] or vice versa or both buyer and seller are under the control of some other person or (*b*) it appears that the sole or main benefit which might have been expected to accrue was the obtaining of an allowance or deduction in which case market value is substituted unless the parties elect—as permitted for (*a*) but not for (*b*)—to take the residue of the seller's expenditure.[3] The election must now be made within two years of the sale.[4] This election is not open to a dual resident investment company.[5]

Special rules apply when the sale involves an asset in respect of which allowances have been claimed and another asset. The net proceeds of sale are to be apportioned and the Commissioners are not bound by any apportionment made by the parties.[6]

The 1985 rule as to timing also includes an anti-avoidance rule.[7]

Simon's Taxes B2.109.

[1] Defined TA 1988, s. 832(1).

[2] Defined CAA 1968, s. 87.

[3] Defined CAA 1968, s. 78 and Sch. 7. Know-how has its own provision, TA 1988, ss. 531(7) and 532(5)(*b*). Allowances under CAA 1968, s. 60 are also excluded.

[4] CAA, Sch. 7, para. 4(4) added by FA 1988, s. 91; this applies to sales after the passing of FA 1988 (29th July 1988).

[5] F(No. 2)A 1987, s. 64(1). Infra, § **32: 19.**

[6] CAA 1968, s. 77, e.g. *Fitton v Gilders and Heaton* (1955) 36 TC 233; *A Wood & Co Ltd v Provan* (1968) 44 TC 701.

[7] FA 1985, s. 56(4).

Abolition of first year and initial allowances—transitional anti-avoidance rules

8: 10   Faced with the phasing out of the first year allowances for machinery and plant taxpayers might have been tempted to incur expenditure in advance. To counter this temptation, special rules apply for this allowance as for the initial allowances for industrial buildings and for assured tenancy dwelling houses.[1]

The effect of these provisions is to spread the expenditure over the period between the date of the contract under which the expenditure was incurred and the date by which the contract is to be fully performed (or 31st March 1987, if earlier).

The provisions apply only to contracts entered into between 14th March 1984 and 31st March 1986 inclusive. They do not apply to hire purchase contracts in respect of machinery or plant where the balance of the hire purchase price is treated as incurred only when the machinery or plant is brought into use.[2]

The maximum allowable expenditure for the years commencing 1st April

1984 and 1st April 1985 respectively is defined as a fraction of the contract price.[3] The fraction for the financial year 1984 is determined by taking the number of complete months in that year in the period after the date of the contract and dividing that by the total number of complete months in the entire period from the date of the contract to the contractual completion date (or 31st March 1987 if applicable).

For the financial year 1985 the numerator of the fraction is 12 unless the contract was made during that year when the numerator will be the number of complete months between the date of the contract and 31st March 1986.

The maximum allowable expenditure, if any, for the year commencing 1st April 1984 qualifies for a first year allowance at 75%.[4] Any balance of expenditure actually incurred in that year is deemed to have been incurred in the following year and must be added to the expenditure of the latter. The total expenditure which can qualify for a first year allowance at 50%[5] is, however, restricted to the maximum allowable expenditure for that year and any balance is deemed to have been incurred in the year commencing 1st April 1986. There is, of course, no initial allowance or first year allowance for expenditure incurred on or after 1st April 1986.

EXAMPLE

M agrees on 22nd February 1985 to purchase machinery for delivery on 1st April 1986. On signing the contract he pays a deposit of £10,000, being 10% of the contract price. He pays the balance of £90,000 on 28th March 1986.

The maximum allowable expenditure which can qualify for first-year allowances at 75% is

$$1/13 \times £100,000 = £7,692$$

Of the deposit, the balance of £2,308 is treated as incurred after 31st March 1985.

The maximum allowable expenditure which can qualify for first-year allowances at 50% is

$$12/13 \times £100,000 = £92,308$$

so the balance of the deposit and the balance of the contract price will qualify at that rate.

---

[1] FA 1984, Sch. 12.
[2] See FA 1971, s. 45(1)(*b*).
[3] FA 1984, Sch. 12, para. 9.
[4] Or an initial allowance of 50% for industrial buildings and assured tenancy dwelling houses.
[5] Or an initial allowance of 25% for industrial buildings and assured tenancy dwelling houses.

Successions

8: 11   In general where a trader discontinues his trade, a balancing charge or allowance is made. Any capital allowances still unused cannot be carried forward if one trade ends and another one begins.[1] If the trade is transferred to someone else, the new trader may be able to claim allowances in respect of his own capital expenditure including that in respect of items bought from his predecessor; that expenditure may give rise to balancing charges or allowances to the vendor.

On deemed discontinuances under TA 1988, ss. 113 and 337, the new traders are to be entitled to allowances as if they had acquired the assets at market price,[2] although they are not entitled to initial, as opposed to writing down and first year allowances. Curiously perhaps these rules are not to apply to scientific research allowances.[3]

Simon's Taxes B2.111, 112.
[1] Supra, § **7: 49**; infra, § **25: 02**.
[2] CAA 1968, s. 79(1).
[3] CAA 1968, s. 79(1) proviso.

Choice of allowances

8: 12   It may happen that a particular capital expense falls within more than one category of allowance. In the absence of any express provision the taxpayer can choose the most favourable category. Special provisions do however restrict this choice in certain contexts.[1] This is recast by FA 1989 which now allows a simple (but irrevocable) choice.[2]

[1] CAA 1968, ss. 1(4), 14, 50(1), 52(1) and (2), 68, 92(5) and 93(1) and see **Simon's Taxes B2.222, 223, 224, 305, 417, 503, 708**.
[2] FA 1989, Sch. 13 para. 28. On coming into force see para 28(6).

INDUSTRIAL BUILDINGS

8: 13   Allowances are made where a person incurs capital expenditure on the construction of an industrial building or structure which is to be occupied for the purposes of a trade.[1] When the building is to be occupied by a lessee or licensee[2] it is the occupier's trade that is relevant.[3] Since the allowances are confined to the expenses of construction, the cost of the land is excluded,[4] although the costs of certain preliminary works such as cutting, levelling and tunnelling may be claimed if, but only if, they are to prepare the land for the installation of machinery or plant.[5]

The costs of repairs are allowed as if they were construction costs unless they are deductible as revenue expenses. If a building is improved or altered, the costs of that work are treated as a separate subject for allowances.[6]

Simon's Taxes B2.222; Butterworths Income Tax Service C5.01.
[1] CAA 1968, s. 1.
[2] FA 1982, s. 74. See also § **8: 16**.
[3] CAA 1968, s. 1 and see SP 4/80 (separate lettings of workshops for small businesses), **Simon's Taxes, Division H3.2**.
[4] CAA 1968, s. 17(1).
[5] CAA 1968, s. 9 "cutting" received a narrow construction in *McIntosh v Manchester Corpn* [1952] 2 All ER 444, 33 TC 428.
[6] CAA 1968, s. 8.

8: 14   The allowance may only be claimed if the building is an industrial building or structure, which is elaborately defined. The general effect of the definition is to confine allowances to productive, as opposed to distributive industries. A building in use for the purposes of a trade carried on in a mill factory or other similar premises is an industrial building as is a building for the purposes of a trade which consists in the taking and catching of fish or shellfish.[1] A building is a factory only if something is made there; so a repair depot normally cannot qualify.[2] However, a building used for the maintenance or repair of goods will qualify if the goods or materials are employed in a trade or undertaking which itself qualifies under CAA 1968, s. 7(1).[3] Other trades specified are the ploughing or cultivating of land (unless the trader occupies the land in which case he qualifies for agricultural allowances), the working of mineral deposits or a foreign plantation, transport, dock, inland navigation, water, electricity or hydraulic power undertaking, a tunnel or bridge undertaking, the manufacturing or processing of goods or materials, or subjecting goods or materials to any process,[4] the storage[5] of goods which are to be so used or the end product while it awaits delivery to a customer and the storage of goods on arrival in this country.[6] Stockists can claim allowances, provided they carry on the trade of storing goods.[7] The test is whether the building is used for the purposes of a trade which consists in the storage of the qualifying goods and not whether the building is used for the storage of such goods. An allowance can therefore be claimed for a building even though it is in part used for the storage of other goods.[8]

In *Buckingham v Securitas Properties Ltd*[9] a security firm constructed a special area in which bulk coins and notes were broken down into individual wage packets. The court held that the notes and coins were not "goods"; if they had been goods the court would have held that they were not being subjected to any process.

It is not necessary that the building be constructed in this country, indeed foreign plantations are expressly mentioned and defined. However the profits or gains of the foreign trade must be assessable under Schedule D, Case I and not Case V.[10]

This definition specifically excludes any building used as, or as part of, a dwellinghouse, retail shop, showroom, hotel or office and of any building ancillary to the purposes of those excluded.[11] In determining what is an office the courts have not been blinded by terminology. Thus a drawing office is no more an office than a machine shop is a shop.[12] It should be noted however that where an office is built in a designated enterprise zone it will qualify for special 100% initial allowances together with 25% writing down allowances as appropriate.

This allowance is extended to the provision of sports pavilions,[13] whether or not the trade falls within the qualifying list, and expenditure on safety at sports grounds.[14]

Simon's Taxes B2.203–218; Butterworths Income Tax Service C5.11.
  [1] CAA 1968, s. 7(1) see also s. 7(3) proviso and extra-statutory concession B3 (1988) now made statutory by FA 1989, Sch. 13, para. 2 adding s. 7(3A) (private road built on industrial estate), **Simon's Taxes, Division H2.2.**
  [2] *Vibroplant Ltd v Holland* [1982] STC 164.
  [3] FA 1982, s. 75. This would not have helped in the *Vibroplant* case (see note 2 above) as the trade of plant hire would not qualify under CAA 1968, s. 7(1).
  [4] For a macabre case see *Bourne v Norwich Crematorium Ltd* [1967] 2 All ER 576, 44 TC 164; this expenditure would seem now to qualify as plant (*IRC v Barclay, Curle & Co Ltd*, infra, § **8: 26**).
  [5] See *Dale v Johnson Bros* (1951) 32 TC 487.
  [6] This received a narrow construction in *Copol Clothing Co Ltd v Hindmarch* [1984] STC 33, [1984] 1 WLR 411, CA, the expression being confined to buildings in the vicinity of an airport or seaport.
  [7] This will be the case even where the stockist does not subject the materials to the industrial process himself see *Crusabridge Investments Ltd v Casings International Ltd* (1979) 54 TC 246 (a case concerning an action for breach of a covenant in a lease in which the term industrial

building was held to cover a warehouse used for the storage of tyres before they were sold for remoulding) and the Inland Revenue Press Release [1982] STI p. 145.

[8] *Saxone Lilley and Skinner (Holdings) Ltd v IRC* [1967] 1 All ER 756, 44 TC 122.
[9] [1980] STC 166.
[10] CAA 1968, s. 7(9).
[11] CAA 1968, s. 7(3).
[12] *IRC v Lambhill Ironworks Ltd* (1950) 31 TC 393 (where the office qualified because of its essentially industrial character).
[13] CAA 1968, s. 9.
[14] F (No. 2) A 1975, s. 49 and see **Simon's Taxes B2.335.**

.

8: 15   If only a part of a building qualifies for an allowance an apportionment is made save where the cost of the non-qualifying part does not exceed 25%[1] of the total cost, in which case the whole cost is allowed.[2] This raises the difficult problem of defining the building. If a building includes an office the cost of which is less than 25% an allowance is made in respect of the whole cost. If however the office is a separate building no allowance can be made even though its cost is 25% or less of the total cost of the buildings. Separate blocks which are not physically integrated do not form one building.[3]

EXAMPLE
> 30% of the area of a factory building is used as a showroom, and the capital expenditure on the showroom area is 20% of the total. The expenditure was incurred in January 1985.
> The expenditure on the showroom is less than 25% of the total cost, so no apportionment is necessary.

Simon's Taxes B2.215.
[1] From 16th March 1983; previously 10%.
[2] CAA 1968, s. 7(4) as amended by FA 1983, s. 30.
[3] *Abbott Laboratories Ltd v Carmody* [1968] 2 All ER 879, 44 TC 569.

Who can claim the allowances?

8: 16   The initial allowance is claimed by the person who incurs the cost of the building. Writing down and balancing allowances may be claimed by the person with the relevant interest.[1]

The "relevant interest" means the interest in that building to which the person who incurred the expenditure was entitled when he incurred it.[2] So if a lessee spends money improving property he can claim the allowance—but his landlord cannot. If the relevant interest is transferred, the transferee may take over the claim to allowances.[3]

If the owner of the freehold incurs the expense and later leases the building to someone else he will be able to set the allowances against his rental income.[4] It is however essential that the lessee use the building for qualifying purposes.[5]

This rigid insistence on the relevant interest could cause injustice if, for example, a pension fund (which paid no tax and therefore to which the allowance was useless) wanted to finance the construction of a building which would then be used by a tenant under a long lease. So, as from 15th February 1978, where a long lease is granted and both lessor and lessee so elect, the lessee is to be able to claim the allowances even though the expenditure was incurred by the lessor. The mechanism for this change is that the newly created lease is designated the relevant interest in place of the reversionary interest.[6] The same applies where a long sub-lease is created out of a lease. Any capital sum paid by the lessee (or sub-lessee) becomes the sum in respect of which the allowance can be claimed. It follows that the grant of such a lease may cause a balancing allowance or charge to accrue to the lessor.

A long lease is defined as one exceeding 50 years; the rules in TA 1988, s. 34 (infra, § **9: 19**) apply.[7]

This rule does not apply where lessor and lessee are connected persons, although an exception is made where the lessor is a body discharging statutory functions and the lessee is a body over which it has control.[8]

The rule is also excluded if it appears that the sole or main benefit which might be expected to accrue is the obtaining of a balancing allowance.[9] It appears that the sole object of obtaining a balancing charge, perhaps to soak up other reliefs, does not prevent the rule from operating.

If the building has not been used before the lease is granted, the lessee may claim not only the writing down allowance but also the initial allowance. This is of particular importance where the lessor is an exempt person such as a local authority, or charity since it is only the lessee who will have taxable income against which to set the allowance.

If the relevant interest is a lease, the holder of that interest is entitled to the allowances even after his lease has ended if he holds over with the consent of his landlord[10] or takes a new lease in pursuance of an option in the first lease.[11]

Where the lease is surrendered and so becomes merged in another interest that other interest becomes the relevant interest so that the right to the allowance is not lost;[12] likewise if the lessee acquires the reversionary interest.

If the relevant interest is a lease and the lease ends but the landlord pays the lessee a sum, e.g. for improvements carried out by the lessee, matters are treated as if the lease had been surrendered.[13] So also if the landlord grants a new lease to a different person and the new lessee pays a sum to the first lessee then the leases are treated as one and the same so that the new lessee has the "relevant interest".[14] This scheme makes no allowance for the situation in which the new lease is granted to the original lessee otherwise than under a right in the original lease. In this situation a balancing allowance or charge is made.

Injustice also occurred where industrial property was not let but instead occupied by someone for the purposes of his trade under a license as he has no property interest and so no industrial buildings allowances could be claimed. A license is particularly useful to those starting-up small workshops and businesses as the obligations of a licensee are normally less than those of a lessee, an important consideration where there are cash problems, so the legislation has been extended and where an owner or a lessee grants a license his interest will be treated as if it is subject to a lease thus allowing him to claim the allowances.[15] Claims for allowances can also be made where the premises are occupied by more than one licensee so long as all the licensees are carrying on industrial businesses within the terms of CAA 1968, s. 7(1).[16]

Simon's Taxes B2.219–221.

[1] CAA 1968, s. 2(1)(c) and 3(1)(a). On the situation where the expense is shared, see CAA 1968, s. 85, subject to FA 1976, s. 42.

[2] CAA 1968, s. 11.
[3] Infra, § **8: 20**.
[4] Under CAA 1968 ss. 6, 71 and 74 (corporation tax) supra, § **8: 07**.
[5] CAA 1968, s. 1.
[6] FA 1978, s. 37. Claims must be made within two years of the date the lease takes effect, s. 37(3).
[7] But CAA 1968 s. 13(3) is ignored.
[8] FA 1978, s. 37, TA 1988, s. 839.
[9] FA 1978, s. 37(6).
[10] CAA 1968, s. 13(2).
[11] CAA 1968, s. 13(3).
[12] CAA 1968, s. 11(3).
[13] CAA 1968, s. 13(4).
[14] CAA 1968, s. 13(5).
[15] FA 1982, s. 74(1) and (2) for licences granted after 9th March 1982.
[16] FA 1982, s. 74(3).

Initial allowance

8: 17 These have been repealed. On rules governing the spreading of early expenditure under contracts made before the repeal took effect see supra, § **8: 10**.

Writing down allowance

8: 18 Writing down allowances are made to the person entitled to the relevant interest provided that the building is used as "an industrial building" at the end of the chargeable period.[1] The allowance is 4% of the cost. These may be made during periods of temporary disuse.[2]

EXAMPLE

T, a toy manufacturer, bought land for the construction of an additional factory in 1980 for £50,000. The factory was constructed for a total cost of £125,000, payable: £25,000 on 4th June 1983, £60,000 on 6th June 1984, £20,000 on 9th May 1985 and £20,000 on 1st August 1986. No grant is made towards the cost of the construction. On completion (31st July 1986) the factory is brought into use by T.

T makes up his accounts to 31st August.

No capital allowance is given for the expenditure on the land (CAA 1968, s. 17(1)).

Initial allowances are available as follows—

Year of assessment	Basis period	Expenditure incurred	Rate of allowance	Amount
1984–85	y.e. 31.8.83	£25,000	75%	£18,750
1985–86	y.e. 31.8.84	£60,000	50%	£30,000
1986–87	y.e. 31.8.85	£20,000	25%	£5,000
1987–88	y.e. 31.8.86	£20,000	—	—
		£125,000		£53,750

The 4% writing down allowance cannot be claimed until the building is brought into use, which occurs in the year ending 31st August 1986. From 1987–88, therefore, a writing down allowance of £125,000 × 4% = £5,000 will be given, provided the qualifying conditions continue to be met, until the outstanding expenditure has been written off.

Simon's Taxes B2.225, 231; Butterworths Income Tax Service C5.42.
[1] CAA 1968, s. 2(1).
[2] CAA 1968, s. 12.

Balancing allowance—and charge

8: 19   A balancing allowance or charge arises if within 25[1] years of the building being first used, the relevant interest is sold or the building is demolished or destroyed or altogether ceases to be used. No such allowance or charge arises merely because the building ceases to be used for the purpose of a qualifying trade. An adjustment will, however, be made on a subsequent sale or demolition, etc.;[2] meanwhile the writing down allowance ceases unless the cessation of use is purely temporary.[3]

A balance is also struck if within 25 years of the building being first used, the relevant interest ends and is not deemed to continue[4]—as where the interest merges in the reversionary interest. It is also struck if the relevant interest depends upon a foreign concession which ends.

The charge or allowance depends upon the "residue of expenditure" which is the original cost minus the allowances made,[5] whether initial or writing down. This residue is set against any sale, insurance compensation or salvage monies.[6] Should the residue exceed those sums, the difference is the subject of the balancing allowance. Should these sums exceed the allowance the difference is the subject of the balancing charge subject to the rule that the charge may not exceed the allowances made.[7] In making these calculations any periods during which the relevant interest was held by the Crown, or by someone outside, the charge to UK tax are treated as if any allowances that could have been claimed by an ordinary taxpayer had been claimed.[8]

> **EXAMPLE 1**
> A building cost £100,000 in year 1 but is destroyed in year 3. The total allowances so far will be £75,000 initial allowance (assumed to be before 14th March 1984) and £8,000 writing down allowances, making a residue of expenditure of £100,000—(£75,000 + £8,000) = £17,000. If compensation equals £15,000 there will be a balancing allowance of £2,000. If the compensation equals £20,000 there will be a balancing charge of £3,000.

If the building has not been used for a qualifying trade throughout the period, the balancing adjustment must reflect this fact; allowances or charges are made by reference to the adjusted net cost of the building which is the excess of capital expenditure over the proceeds, reduced in the proportion that the period of qualifying use bears to the whole period.

> **EXAMPLE 2**
> Suppose that an industrial building was constructed for £20,000, was used for a qualifying purpose for two years, then as an office (a non-qualifying purpose) for one year and then reverted to a qualifying use for the fourth year. The building is sold in year 5 for £17,000.
> The balancing adjustment is calculated as follows:
> First calculate the net cost of the building to the taxpayer (£3,000) then the proportion of that figure which is attributable to qualifying use (£2,250). Then calculate the allowances given (£17,400, assuming a 75% initial allowance) and deduct the net cost applicable to the qualifying use. This gives a balancing charge of £15,150 (£17,400–£2,250). This means that the allowances given will equal the proportion of the net cost attributable to the periods of qualifying use (£2,250). In turn this will enable the purchaser to claim his allowances on the residue of expenditure before sale of £1,800 plus the balancing charge of £15,150, i.e. £16,950.

It will be noted that although no writing down allowance is given for the year of non-qualifying use, nonetheless that allowance is taken into account in calculating the residue of expenditure (£1,800) but not the allowances given (£17,400).

Simon's Taxes B2.226, 227, 228.
[1] CAA 1968, s. 3(1) proviso. On balancing charge after cessation of trade see extra-statutory concession B19 (1988), **Simon's Taxes, Division H2.2** extra-statutory concession.
[2] FA 1981 s. 75.
[3] CAA 1968, s. 4(5).
[4] CAA 1968, s. 3(1).
[5] CAA 1968, s. 4.
[6] Defined, CAA 1968, s. 86.
[7] CAA 1968, s. 6.
[8] CAA 1968, ss. 12 and 13 added by FA 1988, s. 90; s. 13 applies to sales after the passing of FA 1988 (29th July 1988).

The purchaser

8: 20   The purchaser is entitled to an allowance provided he uses the building for a qualifying purpose. He is entitled to a writing down allowance based on the residue of expenditure, i.e. the remaining unrelieved expenditure of his vendor plus any balancing charge (or minus a balancing allowance).[1] This sum is spread evenly over the remaining 25 year period—and is not in any way tied to a 4% figure. In § **8: 19**, example 2, above, the purchaser would be entitled to an allowance of $\frac{16,950}{25-4}$ =£807. The sharp contrasts for both parties—between a disposal after 24 years and 364 days and one three days later are striking whether they are sensible is a very different matter.[2]

As seen in § **8: 19** the residue of expenditure is calculated by taking account of any reliefs that could have been claimed but were not because the relevant interest was held by the Crown or by an exempt person. This is important when the building is sold for less than its original cost.[3]

These balancing adjustments do not apply when the sale is between connected persons and they elect for the building to be transferred at its written down value. Here the residue of expenditure is carried through to the purchaser save where there is a tax avoidance motive when market value is taken.[4]

Simon's Taxes B2.225.
[1] On concessionary relief when vendor's expense was on revenue account—see extra-statutory concession B20 (1988) (sale by property developer of buildings which have been let), **Simon's Taxes, Division H2.2**. This relief is now statutory—FA 1989, Sch. 13, para. 1, inserting CAA 1968, s. 5A.
[2] Thus if the parties try to avoid a sale within the period by the device of a lease plus an option to buy after the 25 year period has expired the parties run the risk of any premium for the lease being treated in part as income.
[3] See FA 1988, s. 91; the saving in tax is estimated at £150m in 1991–92. *Simon's Tax Intelligence* 1988, p. 225.
[4] FA 1981, s. 76.

Hotel buildings and extensions

8: 21   Hotels do not qualify for industrial buildings allowances since a hotel does not come within the list of trades permitted.[1] There is an annual writing down allowance of 4% on a straight line basis.[2] Subsequent holders of the relevant interest may write off the residue of the expenditure over the balance of the 25 year period.[3]

For these purposes, expenditure is not treated as incurred later than it is in fact incurred (as it would be under CAA 1968, s. 1(6)) solely because it is pre-trading expenditure.[4] Where a person buys a qualifying hotel unused, he is treated, under CAA 1968, s. 5(1)(*b*), as having incurred expenditure on its construction when the purchase price becomes payable.[5] For the purposes of determining whether or not the initial allowance is available, however, the purchaser will be deemed to have incurred his expenditure on the last date on which any of the actual construction expenditure was incurred.

EXAMPLE

Y builds a qualifying hotel, on which the last block of expenditure is incurred on 25th March 1986. Two months later, he sells it unused to Z, who pays the entire purchase price on 1st June 1986. Z is treated as having incurred construction expenditure on the hotel on 25th March 1986, and hence is still entitled to the 20% initial allowance.

The hotel must be a "qualifying hotel", a concept which is elaborately defined;[6] The hotel may be outside the UK but the trade must be taxed under Schedule D, Case I. The costs of dwelling accommodation for the owner are not allowable but such costs would be allowable if the trade were incorporated and the accommodation were for a director or employee.

Capital allowances for fire safety and thermal insulation fall under the rules for machinery and plant, see § **8: 23**, n. 1.

Simon's Taxes B2.241–244; Butterworths Income Tax Service C5.73.

[1] See § **8: 13**.

[2] FA 1978, s. 38 and Sch. 6; there was previously a 20% initial allowance but this was repealed by FA 1985, s. 66 as from 1st April 1986.

[3] Under CAA 1968, s. 2(3).

[4] FA 1978, s. 38(8) as amended by FA 1985, s. 66.

[5] FA 1985, s. 66(2).

[6] FA 1978, s. 38(3); on need to offer breakfast and dinner see SP 9/87.

Enterprise zones

8: 22   100% initial allowances are given for capital expenditure on industrial *or* commercial buildings in enterprise zones.[1] If the owner of the relevant interest wishes he may take only a part of the initial allowance in which case the balance will be written off at 25% of the cost a year on a straight line basis; thus if he elects for a 40% initial allowance the writing down allowance will be 25%, 25% and 10%. Balancing adjustments will be made if the building is sold within 25 years.

As this relief is part of a package to stimulate development in enterprise zones it is to be available only on expenditure incurred during the first ten years of the zone's life. However it is to be available not only for industrial buildings and hotels but also for all other commercial buildings used for trading or professional purposes—other than dwelling houses.

Simon's Taxes B2.238; Butterworths Income Tax Service C5.72.

[1] FA 1980, s. 74 and Sch. 13; on enterprise zone property unit trusts see *Simon's Tax Intelligence* 1988, p. 88. On treatment of machinery or plant which becomes an integral part of the building see extra-statutory concession B31 (1988), **Simon's Taxes, Division H2.2.**

Dwelling houses—assured tenancies

8: 23   Allowances may be given for the costs of construction of[1] "qualifying dwelling houses" which broadly speaking must be let on assured tenancies within the meaning of the Housing Act 1980, s. 56 or its successor in Part I of the Housing Act 1988.[2] Although it is not necessary for the landlord to be a company for the purposes of the assured tenancy scheme, from (in general) 5 May 1983, the landlord must be a company if capital allowances are claimed under these provisions.[3] Expenditure will qualify for this allowance if the company was committed to it before 15th March 1988 and the purpose was to provide dwellings let on the terms of the 1980 Act.[4]

Where a dwelling house has qualified it remains a qualifying dwelling house even if the landlord is no longer an approved body so long as it is subject to a regulated tenancy or a housing association tenancy.[5] A dwelling house will not qualify if the landlord and tenant are connected persons, if the tenant is a director of a company which is, or is connected with, the landlord, if the landlord is a close company and the tenant is a participator or associate of a participator, or if there is an arrangement between landlords or owners whereby one landlord grants a tenancy which would prevent the dwelling house qualifying if it was granted by the other.[6] It is not possible for a co-operative housing association[7], or a self build society within the Housing Associations Act 1985 to qualify.[8] The allowance is available on the first £40,000 (£60,000 in Greater London) of such expenditure only.[9] Where a building contains one or more qualifying dwelling houses the cost must be apportioned to each unit and the cost of the communal parts can be apportioned but this can not exceed one tenth of the apportioned cost of the dwelling house.[10]

A writing down allowance of 4% per annum is given[11] and balancing allowances and charges apply as appropriate.[12] Expenditure for which capital allowances have been given under these provisions is not deductible when computing any allowable loss for CGT purposes on the disposal of the building.[13]

Entitlement to the old initial allowance was extended to cover not just newly constructed properties but also certain substantially repaired or improved properties: the extension applies to lettings made on or after 7th January 1987 although the improvements can have been incurred in the two years preceding the letting.[14] The provision applied to expenditure incurred before 1st April 1986; claims had to have been made before 1st April 1988.

Simon's Taxes B2.251

  [1] F(No. 2)A 1987, s. 72 and Sch. 12, as amended by FA 1988, s. 95, keeping alive FA 1982, s. 76 and Sch. 12 until 1992. The rate of the *initial* allowance was 75% for expenditure incurred after 9th March 1982 and before 14th March 1984, 50% for expenditure incurred after 13th March 1984 and before 1st April 1985 and 25% from them until 31st March 1986. As with the initial allowance for industrial buildings, this allowance was phased out by 1986. There was special rules to reallocate expenditure incurred in advance; see supra, § **8: 10**.

  [2] FA 1982, Sch. 12, para. 3(1).

  [3] FA 1982, Sch. 12, para. 3(3)(*a*) as amended by F (No. 2) A 1983, s. 6.

  [4] FA 1988, s. 95. This is needed because the Housing Act 1988 introduces a new "assured shorthold tenancy" which is to be outside the scope of this allowance—s. 95(4). The Housing Act 1988 received the Royal Assent on 15th November 1988.

  [5] FA 1982, Sch. 12, para. 3(2).

  [6] FA 1982, Sch. 12, para. 3(3).

[7] See TA 1988, s. 488.

[8] FA 1982, Sch. 12, para. 3(3)(*b*).

[9] FA 1982, Sch. 12, para. 1.

[10] FA 1982, Sch. 12, para. 1.

[11] FA 1982, Sch. 12, para. 2.

[12] FA 1982, Sch. 12, paras. 4–6 as amended by FA 1989, Sch. 13 para. 20.

[13] CGTA 1979, s. 34(4) as amended by F (No. 2) A 1983, s. 6.

[14] F(No. 2)A 1987, s. 72(2). Revenue Press Release 17th March 1987, *Simon's Tax Intelligence* 1987, p. 199.

MACHINERY AND PLANT[1]

8: 24   The present scheme of capital allowances applies to expenditure incurred after 26th October 1970 but has been revised by FA 1984 and FA 1985. For expenditure incurred after 31st March 1985 and before 1st April 1986 there was a first year allowance[2] of 50% and a writing down allowance[3] of 25% although it was not possible to claim both the first year and writing down allowances in the same year.[4] Expenditure incurred after 31st March 1986 will not qualify for an initial allowance leaving only the writing down allowance (see § **8: 29**).

Under the original rules in FA 1971 allowances were given when the machinery or plant was brought into use. For corporation tax accounting periods and income tax basis periods ending after 31st March 1985 the rule is to be that allowances will be given by reference to when the expenditure is incurred (in line with the other allowances, see supra, § **8: 04**).

The allowances apply to trades, professions, vocations, employments and offices and to the occupation of woodlands if tax is assessed under Schedule D, Case I.[5] As from 1st April 1985 the expenditure must be on machinery and plant *wholly and exclusively* for the purposes of the trade.[6] This change brings in the rules discussed in connection with trading expenditure (see § **7: 89**) with regard to the nature of purpose (on which see *Mallalieu v Drummond*)[7] but there is no bar on expenditure incurred for dual purposes.[8]

Where the allowance is claimed under Schedule E it must also be shown that the machinery and plant was *necessarily* provided for use in the performance of the duties of the office or employment.[9] The term "necessarily" is interpreted as under TA 1988, s. 198 so that a finding that another holder of the office could have performed his duties without incurring this expense is fatal to the claim for the allowance.[10]

Special rules apply to sales between connected persons. Thus writing down allowances are given to the purchaser by reference to the disposal value of the vendor.[11] This applies also to agreements for sale, sale and leaseback etc.[12] As from the passing of FA 1989 a similar rule applies when a trader brings into use an asset which has been given to him.[13]

The asset must belong to the person in consequence of the payment. The word "belong" was interpreted narrowly in *Stokes v Costain Property Investments Ltd*[14] where plant (lifts) which was installed by a tenant and immediately became the property of the landlord under general land law principles, did not qualify as it did not belong to the tenant. This case is no authority on fixtures which remain the property of the tenant nor, presumably, where the property is a tenant's fixture, i.e. where the property becomes the property of the landlord but the tenant has the right to remove it at the end of the lease. The words "in consequence of" were held to be satisfied where a payment was made by the taxpayer to induce the holder of an option to reacquire the property to release that option.[15]

The situation resulting from *Stokes v Costain Property Investments Ltd* was seen to be unjust and FA 1985 now provides a new scheme for expenditure incurred after 11th July 1984 (unless under a contract entered into before 12th July 1984 or under a lease entered into before 12th July 1984).[16] The fixture is now to be treated as belonging to the lessee (or similar person) who incurred the expenditure in providing the machinery or plant for the purposes of a trade carried on by him (or for leasing otherwise than in the course of a trade) if the machinery or plant becomes in law a part of this land and at that time he has an interest in the relevant land.[17] The rules also cover the case where the plant becomes a fixture before the capital expenditure is incurred. The lessee's allowance excludes the lessor's but a lessor who contributes to the expenditure is not excluded.[18] There are special provisions to deal with disputes as to whether the item is a fixture,[19] for expenditure (and disposals) by equipment lessors[20] and for the transfer of the right to an allowance to a lessee.[21] There are also rules applying where an interest in the land is sold and the price is referable to the fixture[22] and when the fixture ceases to belong to a particular person.[23]

This relief was also used for works on authorised quarantine kennels[24] but this has now been repealed—with transitional relief for expenditure incurred after 15th March 1988 and before 1st April 1989 under a contract extended into on or before 15th March 1988.[25]

Simon's Taxes B2.3; Butterworths Income Tax Service C6.01.
[1] Equivalent relief is given for expenditure on security precautions (FA 1989, ss. 117 and 118; on timing see FA 1989, Sch. 13, para. 29) as from 6th April 1989; for fire safety precautions FA 1974, s. 17, for thermal insulation FA 1975, s. 14, for safety certificate work at sports *stadia*, an expression now replaced by sports *grounds* for expenditure on or after 1st January 1988. (FA 1988, s. 93, F(No. 2)A 1975, s. 49 and FA 1978, s. 40) and, as from 1st January 1989, expenditure on stands at sports grounds (FA 1989, s. 119). See **Simon's Taxes B2.304, 335, 336**. See also extra-statutory concession B16 (1988) concerning expenditure on fire safety in Northern Ireland on lessors. However, while these attract capital allowances they do not give rise to balancing charges.
[2] FA 1971, s. 41.
[3] FA 1971, s. 44.
[4] FA 1971 s 44(4)(*a*)(ii); this explains the difference of terminology between an initial allowance (as for industrial buildings) and a first year allowance.
[5] FA 1971, s. 47; CAA 1968, s. 47. Furnished holiday lettings also qualify, TA 1988, s. 503.
[6] FA 1985, s. 55(1).
[7] [1983] STC 665, HL.
[8] FA 1971, Sch. 8, para. 5 still applies although it is amended by FA 1985 s. 55, Sch. 14.
[9] On Case III see TA 1988, s. 198(2).
[10] *White v Higginbotham* [1983] STC 143.
[11] FA 1971, Sch. 8, para. 3, modified by FA 1972, s. 68(4), and FA 1989, Sch. 13, para. 17.
[12] FA 1971, Sch. 8, para. 3(2), (3).
[13] FA 1971, Sch. 8, para. 13 as amended by FA 1989, Sch. 13, para. 13; previously the market value at the time of the gift was used.
[14] [1984] STC 204, [1984] 1 All ER 849, CA; contrast the "relevant interest" rules for industrial buildings, supra, § **8: 16**.
[15] *Bolton v International Drilling Ltd* [1983] STC 70.
[16] FA 1985, s. 59 and Sch. 17.
[17] Defined in FA 1985, Sch. 17, para. 1.

[18] Under CAA 1968, s. 59(8).
[19] FA 1985, s. 59(4). On disposal value see FA 1985, Sch. 15, para. 9 as amended by FA 1989, Sch. 13, para. 23.
[20] FA 1985, Sch. 17, paras. 3 and 8.
[21] FA 1985, Sch. 17, para. 5 and where the lessee would be entitled to the allowance but the lessor not, Sch. 17, para. 6.
[22] FA 1985, Sch. 17, para. 4.
[23] FA 1985, Sch. 17, para. 7.
[24] FA 1980, s. 71.
[25] FA 1988, s. 94.

What is machinery or plant?

8: 25   Neither machinery nor plant is defined in the Act, and the question whether an item is plant or machinery depends on the facts of the case. It is clear that an expenditure may qualify for both the plant and machinery and industrial building allowances[1] but in such an event it is likely that only the former will be claimed.[2]

Different definitions have been suggested for specific instances. In *Yarmouth v France*[3] a claim was brought by a workman under the Employers' Liability Act 1880 for damages for injuries sustained due to a defect in his employer's plant, in that case a vicious horse. Lindley LJ said:[4]

"in its ordinary sense (plant) includes whatever apparatus is used by a business man for carrying on his business—not his stock-in-trade, which he buys or makes for sale; but all goods and chattels, fixed or movable, live or dead, which he keeps for permanent employment in his business."

This test has been found helpful,[5] but not exclusive in capital allowance cases.

This test is viewed by the Revenue as covering fixtures and fittings of a durable nature. So railway locomotives and carriages[6] and tramway rails[7] have been held to be plant as have knives and lasts used in the manufacture of shoes,[8] but not the bed of a harbour[9] nor stallions for stud purposes.[10]

It is now clear that machinery and plant is not confined to things used physically[11] but extends to the intellectual storehouse of the trade or profession e.g. the purchase of law books by a barrister.[12] Whether plant can include things lacking physical manifestation (e.g. computer software) is still unclear. It is not however necessary that the object be active; although a passive object may be less obviously plant.[13]

Simon's Taxes B2.304; Butterworths Income Tax Service C6.11.
 [1] *IRC v Barclay Curle & Co Ltd* (infra, § **8: 26**); however, the area of overlap will be reduced if the reasoning in *Wimpy International Ltd v Warland* [1989] STC 273, CA is upheld.
 [2] Double allowances are excluded by CAA 1968, s. 14.
 [3] (1887) 19 QBD 647.
 [4] (1887) 19 QBD 647 at 658.
 [5] Lord Donovan in *IRC v Barclay Curle & Co Ltd* [1969] 1 All ER 732 at 751, 45 TC 221 at 249.
 [6] *Caledonian Rly Co v Banks* (1880) 1 TC 487.
 [7] *LCC v Edwards* (1909) 5 TC 383.
 [8] *Hinton v Maden and Ireland Ltd* [1959] 3 All ER 356, 38 TC 391 (expected to last only three years): noted [1959] BTR 454.
 [9] *Dumbarton Harbour Board v Cox* (1918) 7 TC 147.
 [10] *Earl of Derby v Aylmer* [1915] 3 KB 374, 6 TC 665.

[11] Per Cross J in *McVeigh v Arthur Sanderson & Sons Ltd* [1969] 2 All ER 771 at 775, noted [1969] BTR 130.
[12] *Munby v Furlong* [1977] STC 232, [1977] 2 All ER 953.
[13] *Jarrold v John Good & Sons Ltd* [1963] 1 All ER 141, 40 TC 681.

8: 26   Plant does not include the place where the business is carried on; "plant" is that with which the trade is carried on as opposed to the "setting or premises" in which it is carried on[1] but these categories are not necessarily mutually exclusive and the different rates of allowance make correct classification of great practical importance. So it has been held that special partitioning used by shipping agents to sub-divide floor space to accommodate fluctuating office accommodation requirements were plant. Some stress was laid on the fact that office flexibility was needed.[2] Today, something which becomes part of the premises, as opposed to merely embellishing them, is not plant save where the premises are themselves plant,[3] as in *IRC v Barclay, Curle & Co Ltd.*[4]

While there is a clear distinction between the shell of a building and the machinery currently used in it, there are considerable difficulties where a large and durable structure is created for a specific purpose. This occurred in the leading case of *IRC v Barclay, Curle & Co Ltd.*[5] The taxpayer had constructed a dry dock, a process requiring the excavation of the site and the construction of a concrete lining. The Revenue agreed that such expenditure as that incurred on the dock gate and operating gear, the cast iron keel blocks and the electrical and pumping installations related to plant, but argued that while the expenses of excavation and concreting might relate to industrial building they did not relate to plant and machinery. The Revenue lost.

The expenditure on the concrete lining was held to be in respect of plant because it could not be regarded as the mere setting in which the trade was carried on but was an integral part of the means required for the trading operation. Hence a structure which fulfils the function of plant is, *prima facie*, plant.[6]

The costs of excavation were likewise held to be incurred in the provision of plant because what was indubitably plant, namely the dock itself, could not have been made before the excavation had taken place. This "but for" test is not however without limits and, by analogy with the express provision in relation to industrial buildings, costs incurred on the acquisition of the land could not fall within the allowance.

Where capital expenditure is incurred on alterations to an existing building incidental to the installation of machinery or plant for the purposes of trade, allowances may be claimed in respect of such expenditure just as if the works formed part of the machinery or plant. This would appear to follow from the decision of the House of Lords but is expressly provided in CAA 1968, s. 45. This provision was thought by the members of the majority to be merely for the avoidance of doubt.

The problem of the distinction between setting and plant, a problem exacerbated by the fact that the terms are not mutually exclusive,[7] depends in part upon the degree of sophistication to be employed in the concept of a setting.[8] The problem is acute when electrical apparatus and wiring are concerned. The matter has to be resolved by the use of the functional test and so, for example, lighting will not usually be plant unless it is of a specialised nature,[9] as where it is designed to provide a particular atmosphere in a hotel; this must be judged by reference to the intended market.[10] The Revenue have consistently refused to treat wiring leading to such apparatus as plant.[11]

In cases such as these it is often crucial whether the various items are taken separately or treated as one installation. This is a question of fact, and so for the Commissioners to decide.[12]

---

[1] Per Pearson LJ in *Jarrold v John Good & Sons Ltd* [1963] 1 All ER 141, 40 TC 681 at 696.

[2] *Jarrold v John Good & Sons Ltd* (supra). The decision of the Commissioners was left intact. If a new agency were taken on, a new department would have to be created.

[3] Per Fox LJ in *Wimpy International Ltd v Warland* [1989] STC 273 at 279e, CA.

[4] [1969] 1 All ER 732, 45 TC 221.

[5] Ibid.

[6] Lord Reid, [1969] 1 All ER 732 at 740, 45 TC 221 at 239.

[7] Supra n. 3.

[8] *Imperial Chemical Industries of Australia and New Zealand v Taxation Comr of the Commonwealth of Australia* (1970) 120 CLR 396.

[9] *Cole Bros Ltd v Phillips* [1982] STC 307, HL; note that the light fitting was allowed in *Wimpy International Ltd v Warland* [1988] STC 149 at 176.

[10] *IRC v Scottish and Newcastle Breweries Ltd* [1982] STC 296 distinguished in *Wimpy International Ltd v Warland* [1989] STC 273, CA.

[11] They rely strongly on *J. Lyons & Co Ltd v A-G* [1944] Ch 281, [1944] 1 All ER 477.

[12] *Cole Bros Ltd v Phillips* [1982] STC 307, HL.

8: 27   The distinction between buildings and apparatus is thus indistinct. Recent cases have shown that a prefabricated building at a school used to accommodate a chemical laboratory[1] and a canopy over a petrol station[2] (although this has since been doubted)[3] a false ceiling in a restaurant[4] an inflatable cover over a tennis court[5] and a floating ship used as a restaurant,[6] were not plant since they performed no function in the trade; further a support for plant is not necessarily plant. On the other hand it has been held that a silo used in the trade of grain importing was not simply part of the setting and could not be considered separately from the machinery and other equipment within it.[7] Likewise a swimming pool at a caravan site was held to be plant since it was part of the apparatus of the business,[8] as were decorative screens placed in the windows of a building society's offices as the screens were not the structure within which the business was carried on.[9] Particular problems have arisen on expenditure on items designed to attract customers. So, in one case murals were held to be plant[10] and, more recently, facia boards, wall panels, suspended ceilings, cold water piping and water tanks, decorative brickwork, murals, built in storage units and dispensers installed in a fast food restaurant.[11] However, in the same case the Court of Appeal refused to hold that the Commissioners had been wrong to reject claims for *inter alia* glass shop fronts, raised floors, floor tiles, a suspended ceiling and light fittings. Lloyd LJ said that the court should not look too critically at the language used by the Commissioners. These cases prove the old law that an ounce of evidence (before the Commissioners) is worth a ton of law.

Simon's Taxes B2.304.

[1] *St. John's School (Mountford and Knibbs) v Ward* [1974] STC 69; on appeal [1975] STC 7 (note the astonishingly harsh refusal by Templeman J to allow an apportionment between the building and the equipment).

[2] *Dixon v Fitch's Garage Ltd* [1975] STC 480, [1975] 3 All ER 455.
[3] *Cole Bros Ltd v Phillips* [1982] STC 307 per Lord Hailsham at 311 but see the pointed comment of Walton J in *Thomas v Reynolds* [1987] STC 135 at 140.
[4] *Hampton v Forte Autogrill Ltd* [1980] STC 80.
[5] *Thomas v Reynolds* [1987] STC 135.
[6] *Benson v Yard Arm Club Ltd* [1979] STC 266, [1979] 2 All ER 336.
[7] *Schofield v R. and H. Hall Ltd* [1975] STC 353.
[8] *Cooke v Beach Station Caravans Ltd* [1974] STC 402, [1974] 3 All ER 159.
[9] *Leeds Permanent Building Society v Proctor* [1982] STC 821.
[10] *IRC v Scottish and Newcastle Breweries Ltd* [1982] STC 296, HL.
[11] *Wimpy International Ltd v Warland* [1989] STC 273, CA.

First year allowances

8: 28   These were abolished as from 1st April 1986, save for expenditure incurred before 1st April 1987 under a contract entered into before 14th March 1984.

Writing down allowance

8: 29   This allowance, which is given on a 25% reducing balance basis, now applies where the person incurs[1] capital expenditure on the provision of machinery and plant wholly and exclusively[2] for the purposes of the trade. In consequence of the expenditure the asset must belong to him.[3] It is no longer necessary that the asset should have been brought into use in the trade.[4]

Where an asset is acquired partly for business purposes and partly for other purposes the allowance is reduced to such extent as is just and reasonable in the circumstances; particular attention is directed to the use to which the asset is put.[5] Rules are provided for an asset originally acquired solely for business purposes being used partly for non-business purposes and vice versa. Generally all plant and machinery used in the trade is placed in one pool and the writing down allowance is applied to the value of the pool.[6] However certain items *must* be pooled separately; these are (*a*) assets used partly for non-business purposes,[7] (*b*) assets for leasing outside the UK,[8] (*c*) certain road vehicles[9] and (*d*) ships[10] (here the law allows deferments of writing down allowances at will), FA 1985 also allows certain items to be pooled separately if the taxpayer so elects.[11]

Writing down allowances may be claimed in part by an individual and, for accounting periods ending after 13th March 1984, by a company.[12]

Simon's Taxes B2.311; Butterworths Income Tax Service C6.22.
[1] For accounting periods and basis periods ending after 31st March 1985 FA 1985, s. 55 and Sch. 14. On date see supra, § **8: 04** and FA 1971, s. 50(4), FA 1985, s. 56.
[2] Words added by FA 1985, s. 55(1).
[3] See supra, § **8: 24** and FA 1971, s. 45(1) (hire purchase) s. 46(2) (leased assets).
[4] FA 1985, s. 55(2).
[5] FA 1971, Sch. 8, para. 5 as recast by FA 1985, Sch. 14, para. 6.
[6] FA 1971, s. 44(2).
[7] FA 1971, Sch. 8, para. 5.
[8] FA 1980, s. 65(2)(*b*)—infra, § **8: 36**.
[9] FA 1971, Sch. 8, para. 10, infra, § **8: 39**.

[10] FA 1971, Sch. 8, paras. 8A, 8B and 8C added by FA 1985, Sch. 16.
[11] FA 1985, s. 57, see infra, § **8: 38**
[12] FA 1971, s. 44(2), (2A); FA 1984, s. 59.

8: 30   No writing down allowance may be claimed for the period during which permanent discontinuance takes place; only a balancing allowance (or charge) is made.[1] If the base period is less than one year an appropriate proportion of the allowance is given.

[1] FA 1971, s. 44(2)(*b*).

8: 31   The writing down allowance is given at 25% of the balance of the pool each year.

EXAMPLE

If an asset cost £1,000, and it was the only asset in the pool, the allowance would be £250 in the first year, but 25% of (1,000 − 250) i.e. £187.50 in the second.

Suppose that an asset was bought in year 1 for £1,000, that a second asset was bought in year 2 for £9,250, and that in year 3 the first asset was sold for £1,000. The allowances would be year 1 £250 and year 2 £2,500. At the start of year 3 the qualifying expenditure would be 10,250 − (250 + 2,500) or £7,500. This must be reduced by the £1,000 disposal so that in year 3 the allowance will be 25% of (7,500 − 1,000) = £1,625.

Where more items come into the pool, the writing down allowance is 25% of the excess of sums spent over sums so far allowed whether under a first year allowance or a writing down allowance plus disposal value.

Disposal value becomes relevant when (*a*) the asset ceases to belong to the claimant,[1] (*b*) if he loses possession of it in circumstances in which it is reasonable to assume the loss is permanent, (*c*) the asset ceases to exist as such (as a result of destruction, dismantling or otherwise, (*d*) the asset begins to be used wholly or partly[2] for purposes other than those of the trade or (*e*) the trade is permanently discontinued. If the qualifying expenditure exceeds the disposal value, the writing down allowance of 25% of the excess may be claimed. If the disposal value exceeds the qualifying expenditure, a balancing charge equal to that excess is made; however, a balancing allowance will be given only when the trade ceases.

The pool will be reduced if subsidies for wear and tear are received.[3]

[1] FA 1971, s. 45(5) as amended by FA 1985, s. 55, Sch. 14, para. 3.
[2] Or partly ceasing to be so used see FA 1971, s. 49, Sch. 8, para. 5 as amended by FA 1985, s. 55, Sch. 14, para. 6.
[3] FA 1971, s. 49, Sch. 8, para. 6.

8: 32   The disposal value to be brought into account depends upon the event by reason of which it falls to be taken into account,[1] but it cannot exceed the capital expenditure incurred on that item, any such excess being subject to capital gains legislation. The disposal value to be deducted from the pool is not to exceed the cost of the plant to the person disposing of it. However when the plant was acquired as a result of a transaction or series of transactions between connected persons the greatest acquisition expenditure incurred in any of the transactions concerned is the maximum disposal value;[2] this rule applies not only on a disposal to a connected person or to an acquisition from a connected person but extends to an acquisition as a result of some transaction between connected persons, with whom the disposer need not be connected.[3] If the asset has been sold,[4] the proceeds of sale are taken and if that sale has been affected by some event, for example, if the asset has been damaged, account is also taken of any insurance or compensation money received. Market value will, if greater, be substituted for the proceeds of sale unless there is a charge to tax under Schedule E or the buyer can in turn claim a capital allowance in respect of machinery or plant or a scientific research allowance.[5] The reason for the latter exemptions is that the low sale price will give rise in turn to low allowances. However the functional definition of plant and machinery may prevent this matching, as where the asset was plant and machinery of the vendor but is an industrial building to the purchaser, there market value will be taken for the disposal value while the purchaser's capital allowance will be geared to the actual price. There is also a bar on taking an undervalue if the buyer is a dual resident investment company—as part of the general drive against such companies.[6]

If the event is the demolition or destruction of the asset the disposal value is the sums received for the remains together with any insurance or compensation, and in other instances of permanent loss, for example theft, is simply any insurance or compensation. In all other cases market value is taken.

If the event is the permanent discontinuance of the trade and that is followed by the sale, demolition, destruction or permanent loss of the asset the disposal value on discontinuance is that specified for the event although a special election may apply if there is a succession to a trade by a connected person.[7] The predecessor's written down value overrides other provisions referring to market value.[8] No election may be made if the buyer is a dual resident investment company.[9] As from 29th July 1988 the right to elect is restricted to cases where both parties are within the charge to UK tax on the profits of the trade and is subject to a time limit of two years starting with the date of the transaction.[10] The election can be made by a partnership.[11] In all other cases market value is taken. For the period in which permanent discontinuance occurs neither first year nor writing down allowances are given, everything being settled by the balancing allowance or charge.

Simon's Taxes B2.311.
[1] FA 1971, s. 44(6).
[2] FA 1971, s. 44(7).
[3] FA 1976, s. 40.
[4] See *IRC v West* (1950) 31 TC 402.
[5] FA 1971 s 44(6)(*b*).
[6] F(No. 2)A 1987, s. 64(5).
[7] FA 1971, Sch. 8, para. 13.
[8] FA 1971, Sch. 8, para. 13(3A), added by FA 1989, Sch. 13, para. 14, as from 27th July 1989. The provisions overridden are CAA 1968, s. 48(1) and FA 1980, s. 65(5).
[9] F(No. 2)A 1987, s. 64(6).
[10] FA 1971, Sch. 8, para. 13 as recast by FA 1988, s. 92(1).
[11] FA 1971, Sch. 8, para. 13(5) as added by FA 1988, s. 92(1).

8: 33   As a result of the 1985 changes, allowances can be given for an asset which has not been brought into use. Where a first year allowance has been made for such an asset and it is disposed of in the same period, the writing down allowance can be claimed.

EXAMPLE

D Ltd has accounting periods ending on 30th June. For the period beginning 1st July 1985, it has qualifying expenditure brought forward in its general pool of £24,000. During the year to 30th June 1986, its only acquisition is a £5,000 microcomputer, purchased on 1st August 1985. Before it can be brought into use, D Ltd decides it has become obsolete and sells it at arm's length on 20th June 1986 for £1,500. There are no other acquisitions or disposals. D Ltd's capital allowance computation for the year to 30th June 1986 is as follows—

		Qualifying expenditure £	Allowances £
Balance brought forward		24,000	
Additions—			
	£		
microcomputer	5,000		
First year allowance @ 50%	(2,500)		£2,500
		2,500	
		£26,500	£2,500
Less: disposal values—			
microcomputer		1,500	
		25,000	
Writing down allowance @ 25%		(6,250)	6,250
Allowances for period			£8,750
Qualifying expenditure carried forward		£18,750	

Short life assets: the non-pooling option

8: 34   The effect of the writing down allowance is that thanks to its reducing balance basis about 90% of the cost will be written off over eight years. Because some assets have a shorter life expectancy the rules have been amended to allow such assets to be kept out of the general pool. One advantage is that if the asset is disposed of any balancing allowance is given immediately instead of waiting for the overall effect on a pool—but only if it is disposed of within, approximately, five years.

This applies *only* to assets acquired after *31st March 1986,*[1] i.e. after the abolition of the first year allowance. The asset will be kept in a pool of its own and the normal 25% writing down allowance applied on a reducing basis.[2] The (irrevocable) election must be made within two years of the year of acquisition.[3]

The asset remains in its pool for five years beginning with the year of acquisition. If the asset still belongs to the taxpayer at the end of that period the unrelieved balance of the expenditure is transferred to the general pool.[4] Special rules apply to disposals before the end of the period to connected persons etc[5] and to notional disposals where a leased asset ceases to be used for a qualifying purpose.[6]

The election is only open to those assets in respect of which first year allowances were available and which are not required to be pooled separately anyway.[7]

On practice, see SP 1/86.[8]

---

[1] FA 1985, s. 57(1) but not for assets which can claim first year allowances under the transitional rules.
[2] FA 1985, s. 57(3).
[3] FA 1985, s. 57(2).
[4] FA 1985, s. 57(5).
[5] FA 1985, s. 57(7)–(9).
[6] FA 1985, s. 57(6). This is now confined to short term assets used for leasing—FA 1989, Sch. 13, para. 21.
[7] The list is in FA 1985, Sch. 15.
[8] **Simon's Taxes, Division H3.4.**

Hire purchase

8: 35   Where machinery or plant is purchased on hire purchase or conditional sale contracts after 26th October 1970 first year and writing down allowances may be claimed in respect of the capital element.[1]

The machinery or plant is treated as belonging to him and not to any other person[2] while he is entitled to the benefit of the contract; capital expenditure to be incurred by him under the contract after the machinery or plant has been brought into use in the trade is treated as incurred by him at that time; he is thus treated as incurring the full capital cost at that time.

There are special provisions when the option under the contract is not exercised.[3]

Simon's Taxes B2.317.
[1] FA 1971, s. 45.
[2] See FA 1989, Sch. 13, para. 10 for expenditure incurred after 26th July 1989.
[3] FA 1971, s. 45(2).

Leasing

8: 36   Where a person leases out an asset in the course of a trade he is entitled to capital allowances in the usual way. As owner of the goods leased, he is entitled to allowances. This will not be so if the lease is a contract of hire purchase (see § **8: 35**, supra). There may also be difficulties in showing that the asset "belongs to" him if he has granted an option to the lessee to purchase the asset but this point has not yet been explored by the judges.[1] It is also provided that he may claim allowances where he lets the asset out otherwise than in the course of a trade and whether or not it is used by the lessee for the purpose of a trade carried on by him.[2] The asset is treated as part of a separate notional trade (and therefore is pooled separately for writing down allowances). The question whether the asset is provided wholly and exclusively for the notional trade is determined according to the actual purpose.[3]

The overall position is as follows. If B buys an asset for the purposes of his trade he may qualify for a first year allowance. If he leases it from A he will be able to deduct the rent paid as a revenue expense and A will be able to claim an allowance instead. If A were carrying on the trade of leasing he could set this allowance against his general income whether or not B were a trader;[4] equally if A were not carrying on such a trade he could claim the relief by way of discharge of tax.[5]

With the very generous first year allowances then prevailing this gave rise to much tax planning and so changes were made in 1980 with the result that A was entitled to the first year allowance *only* where the asset is used for a qualifying purpose for the requisite period.[6] The most common case of a qualifying purpose is where B would have qualified for the allowance if he had incurred the expense himself, as where he carries on business in the UK and is subject to tax under Schedule D Case I. Other purposes include use by A for the purpose of a non-leasing trade or use by B for the purpose of short term leasing to others, whether or not as a trade. The requisite period is four years. Where the uses and periods are satisfied the allowance is available to A whether or not he is carrying on the trade of leasing, although this is relevant to how he can make use of the relief.

These rules do not apply to a landlord's fixed plant in buildings, to cars leased to the disabled, or, in certain circumstances (see infra, § **8: 41**) to ships, aircraft and containers.

Where the first year allowance was not available, e.g. B's trade is carried on wholly outside the UK or B is a tax exempt body, such as a local authority, or does not trade at all but simply leases a car or television on a long term basis as a private individual, the expenditure gave A a 25% writing down allowance only. All such expenditure went into a separate pool but with the virtually final abolition of first year allowances in 1986 it is no longer necessary for new expenditure on these assets to be pooled separately.[7] Broadly, expenditure is new if it is incurred after 31st March 1986. However it is not new if it is under a pre-14th March 1984 contract[8], if it qualifies for transitional regional relief project treatment,[9] if the asset was acquired from a connected person in circumstances which treat it as still belonging to the previous owner,[10] or if the special spreading rules apply.[11] Special transitional rules applicable to teletext and viewdata receivers extend first year allowances for those assets to expenditure incurred before 1st June 1986 and therefore must be pooled separately.[12]

If the asset ceases to be used for a qualifying purpose within the requisite period the 25% allowances are substituted, the whole matter being dealt with when the non-qualifying use begins.[13] This rule is repealed for new expenditure as being unnecessary, as first year allowances are now abolished.[14]

Further provisions were introduced in FA 1982 to deal with assets leased overseas, ships and aircraft let on charter by UK residents and the leasing of films, tapes and discs. Transitional relief was provided in respect of leases of teletext and viewdata receivers and adaptors, infra, §§ **8: 40–43**.

Simon's Taxes B2.318–324.

[1] The effect of an option thus needs to be considered very carefully. It appears that in practice the lessee can be given much the same economic benefit by reducing the leasing charge or extending the period of the lease.

[2] FA 1971, s. 46(1); on cessation of leasing see s. 46(1)(*b*) adapted by FA 1985, s. 55, Sch. 14, para. 4. On meaning of lease (to include an agreement for a lease, but not a mortgage) see FA 1989, Sch. 13, para. 11, inserting FA 1971, s. 46(2A).

[3] FA 1971, s. 46(1A) added by FA 1985, s. 55, Sch. 14, para. 1.
[4] Supra, § **8: 06**.
[5] FA 1971, s. 46 and supra, § **8: 07**.
[6] FA 1980, s. 65. See also FA 1971, s. 73(5), as amended by FA 1989, Sch. 13, para. 18.
[7] FA 1986, s. 57.
[8] FA 1984, Sch. 12, para. 2; FA 1986, s. 57(2).
[9] FA 1984, Sch. 12, para. 4; FA 1986, s. 57(2)(*b*).
[10] FA 1980, s. 64(*a*); FA 1986, s. 57(3).
[11] FA 1984, Sch. 12, para. 2; FA 1986, s. 57(2), supra, § **8: 10**.
[12] FA 1984, Sch. 12, para. 7; FA 1986, s. 57(2).
[13] FA 1980, s. 66.
[14] FA 1986, Sch. 16, para. 3.

Restrictions on use of allowances—leasing

8: 37   There are other restrictions on using the allowances whether first year allowances or writing down allowances. First for income tax, although not for corporation tax, losses arising from leasing, whether from first year or writing down allowances, can only be set against general (i.e. non-leasing) income if the lessor carries on a trade of leasing, does so for at least six months, and devotes substantially the whole of his time to it.[1] The effect of this is to make equipment leasing an unattractive proposition, save when it is a full-time business.

Secondly, since 1976 there has been a restriction where a leasing partnership was involved. For example X, Y and Z Ltd. are partners who buy plant and claim allowances. X and Y then withdraw from the partnership leaving Z to face the balancing charge, but Z is a non-resident company. Relief under TA 1988, ss. 380 and 381 is now denied where a scheme has been entered into with a company partner in prospect. This applies to allowances:

(1) granted to an individual when the plant concerned was acquired for leasing in the course of a trade carried on by the individual *and*, at the time of incurring expenditure on the plant, he was carrying on the trade in partnership with a company, or arrangements had been or were later made for him to do so; or

(2) given (i) in connection with a trade carried on by a partnership (either at the time the expenditure was incurred or later) or transferred to a person connected with the individual otherwise entitled to the relief; or (ii) in respect of an asset later transferred by the individual either at undervalue or to a person connected with him; *and* in both (i) and (ii) it is apparent that, as a result of arrangements made either then or later, the sole benefit that the individual is likely to receive as a result of the acquisition of the plant is a reduction in his tax liability.[2]

When a non trading company claims capital allowances on plant leased to a non-trader, the allowances can only be set against income from letting plant.[3] Group relief is not available in such circumstances.[4]

Simon's Taxes B2.321.
[1] TA 1988, s. 384(6)–(8).
[2] FA 1976, s. 41.
[3] FA 1971, s. 48(4).

[4] FA 1971, s. 48(4A), added by FA 1989, Sch. 13, para. 12, for accounting periods ending after 26th July 1989.

Machinery and plant on lease—lessee's expenditure

8: 38   A special provision deals with capital expenditure by a lessee on the provision of machinery or plant for the purposes of his trade under the terms of his lease.[1] The asset is treated as belonging to the lessee so long as his trade continues. The asset in fact belongs to the lessor and as from the determination of the lease the rules as to disposal value and balancing charges are applied as if the original expenditure had been incurred by the lessor. Thus the allowance is given to the lessee but any balancing charge may be levied on the lessor. As a result of the 1985 rules stemming from *Stokes v Costain Property Investments Ltd*[2] this does not now apply to machinery and plant that becomes part of a building on other land.[3]

[1] FA 1971, s. 46(2).
[2] [1984] STC 204, [1984] 1 All ER 849, CA.
[3] FA 1985, s. 59(5).

Motor vehicles

8: 39   First year allowances could only be claimed in respect of certain types of mechanically propelled road vehicles. This category remains important since the reduction of first year allowances as expenditure on other vehicles must be pooled separately for the writing down allowance.

The favoured vehicles are[1] (*a*) goods vehicles of a construction primarily suited to the carriage of goods or burden of any description (*b*) vehicles of a type not commonly used as private vehicles and unsuitable to be so used, for example works buses and minivans[2] and (*c*) vehicles provided wholly or mainly for hire to, or for the carriage of members of the public in the ordinary course of a trade.[3] Shooting brakes are thought to fall outside this favoured group.

Group (*c*) was modified in 1979 so as to restrict the first year allowance to vehicles for which the number of consecutive days for which it was on hire to or used for the carriage of the same person would normally be less than thirty and the total number of days in any period of twelve months will normally be less than ninety. The vehicle is also favoured if it is hired to a person who will himself use it wholly or mainly for hire to members of the public in this way. This was an effort to distinguish the ordinary car rental business from the increasingly common leasing arrangement whereby a (new) car is leased to a person for two or three years. The latter gave rise only to the writing down allowance of 25% on a reducing balance. An exception is made on cars leased to persons receiving mobility allowance.[4]

When a car costing more than £8,000 is leased special rules apply to restrict the relief given for hiring charges; such a car is also excluded from the favoured group.[5] The amount paid by way of rent is to be reduced in the proportion which the £8,000 plus half the amount by which the retail price of the vehicle when new exceeds £8,000, bears to that retail price. Thus suppose that the car cost £12,000 new and that the rent is £4,200, the amount claimable for tax is:

$$\frac{8,000+(12,000-8,000)/2}{12,000} \quad \text{or} \quad \frac{5}{6} \times £4,200 = £3,500.$$

Similarly motivated rules restrict allowances where a car costing more than £8,000 is bought. Each such car is pooled separately and the allowance is limited to 25% of a maximum sum, now £8,000[6] so that the maximum allowance in anyone year is now £2,000.

As from 1980 expenditure on cars costing less than £8,000 is to be pooled separately from other assets. This applies to all vehicles other than those qualifying for the first year allowance.

The following example given by the Revenue illustrates why expenditure qualifying at 25% needs to be kept in a separate pool from expenditure qualifying for the first year allowance.

EXAMPLE

A company has no pool of unallowed expenditure on plant and machinery brought forward. It spends £5m on new equipment qualifying for 100% first year allowance i.e. before 13th March 1984; and £½m on cars costing less than £8,000. It receives sale proceeds of £1m on equipment sold.

Its capital allowances computation is as follows:

100% first year allowances		£5,000,000
pool brought forward	nil	
disposals	−£1,000,000	
expenditure on cars	£500,000	
balancing charge		−£500,000
net allowances due		£4,500,000

Had the company not spent £½m on cars, its allowances would have been £4m (£5m−£1m disposals). Its allowances have increased by £½m, the full amount of the expenditure on cars. In these circumstances it effectively receives 100% allowances on its expenditure on cars, although that expenditure should only qualify for writing down allowances at 25%.

Simon's Taxes B2.313, 314; Butterworths Income Tax Service C6.33.

[1] FA 1980, s. 69 as amended by FA 1986, Sch. 16, para. 11.
[2] *Roberts v Granada TV Rental Ltd* [1970] 2 All ER 764, 46 TC 295.
[3] FA 1971, s. 43.
[4] A category widened by FA 1984, s. 61.
[5] FA 1971, Sch. 8, para. 12, as amended by F(No 2)A 1979, s. 14(5); on effect of rebate of hire charge, see extra-statutory concession B28 (1988), **Simon's Taxes, Division H2.2.**
[6] FA 1971, Sch. 8, paras. 10 and 11 as amended by F(No 2)A 1979, s. 14.

Assets leased overseas

8: 40   The 25% per annum allowance for assets leased outside the UK was a favourable rate and often used to subsidise deals which had no real connection with the UK. As a result, from 10th March 1982, the allowances available with respect to expenditure on the provision of machinery and for leasing to persons who are not resident in the UK and do not use the machinery or plant for the purposes of a trade carried on in the UK or for earning profits or gains which are taxed in the UK, have been reduced to 10%.[1] This does not apply to short term leasing nor to the leasing of a ship, aircraft or transport container used for a qualifying purpose.[2]

Since the relief is capable of lasting over a period of ten years the period during which the first year allowances might be recaptured was extended from four to ten years[3] but this rule is now repealed for new expenditure as being obsolete; a similar provision now applies for the recovery of excess writing-down relief.[4] It is also possible for a first year allowance to be withdrawn if the asset is subsequently leased to a non-qualifying person during the ten years following the date on which it was first brought into use by the lessor.[5] Where the lease could be for more than thirteen years, or consecutive payments are more than a year apart or of varying amounts or collateral payments are made, or payments connected to the value of the machinery or plant at the expiry of the lease there could be possibilities for tax avoidance and no allowances are given.[6] There are transitional provisions for certain arrangements which were entered into before 10th March 1982 provided that the asset came into use before 1st April 1984.[7]

Expenditure on these assets is pooled separately.[8]

Rules about joint leases and information which had previously been part of the general rules on leasing are now to be found in the legislation concerning these leases.[9]

Simon's Taxes B2.326.

[1] FA 1982, s. 70 and Sch. 11. For transitional relief, see FA 1982, s. 70(10)(*h*), as extended by extra-statutory concession B26 (1988), **Simon's Taxes, Division H2.2.**
[2] FA 1982, s. 70(1), as amended by FA 1986, Sch. 16, para. 5.
[3] FA 1982, s. 70(3) repealed by FA 1986, Sch. 16, para. 5(3).
[4] FA 1986, Sch. 16, para. 8.
[5] FA 1982, s. 70(5).
[6] FA 1982, s. 70(4).
[7] FA 1982, s. 70(12).
[8] FA 1986, s. 57(4).
[9] FA 1986, Sch. 16, paras. 9 and 10.

Ships and aircraft leased on charter

8: 41   When the new provisions for leased assets were introduced in 1980 it was necessary to protect shipping and aircraft transactions to some extent because of the large sums involved. Thus where UK residents purchased ships or aircraft to be let out on charter, the capital allowance was preserved[1] even though the charter was with an overseas company, if the UK company was responsible for the ship's navigation and management. This saving provision led to abuse and the 100% allowance is not available in these circumstances for expenditure incurred from 10th March 1982, if the main object, or one of the main objects, for letting the ship or aircraft on charter was to obtain a first year allowance in respect of the expenditure, whether by the lessor or by some other person. This restriction also applies to a series of transactions including a letting on charter if these were aimed at obtaining a first year allowance.[2] There were transitional reliefs.[3]

Simon's Taxes B2.320.
 ¹ FA 1980, s. 64.
 ² FA 1982, s. 71.
 ³ FA 1982, s. 71(3).

Films, tapes and discs

8: 42   The rules relating to expenditure on master copies of films, tapes and discs were radically altered by FA 1982, s. 72. Previously, investment in such master copies had qualified for 100% first year allowances. Expenditure incurred after 10th March 1982[1] is now treated as a normal expense, but written off over the life of the film, tape or disc. FA 1984 gives a taxpayer the right to allocate additional expenditure to a particular period.[2] These provisions do not apply where the film etc would in any event be treated as trading stock under the general law—see supra, § **7: 151**. Sums received from the disposal of the film, etc will be treated as receipts of a revenue nature.[3]

Simon's Taxes B3.1307; Butterworths Income Tax Service C6.37.
 ¹ FA 1982, s. 72. Capital allowances continue to be available for certain British films, FA 1982, s. 72(7) and (8) as amended by FA 1983, s. 32 and FA 1984, s. 62.
 ² FA 1982, s. 72(4A), (4B); FA 1984, s. 62(3).
 ³ FA 1982, s. 72(6); see SP 2/83 and SP 2/85, **Simon's Taxes, Division H3.2.**

Teletext receivers and teletext and viewdata adaptors

8: 43   Television rental companies were badly hit by the introduction of the leasing rules for capital allowances in FA 1980 and transitional provisions were introduced so that television sets purchased by traders for rental qualified for 100% first year allowances[1] but these have now been phased out[2] and both television sets and teletext receivers and adaptors qualify for the 25% writing down allowance in the usual way.

Simon's Taxes B2.325.
 ¹ FA 1980, Sch. 12.
 ² FA 1982, s. 77.

Pre-1970 acquisitions

8: 44   Any expenditure on assets acquired before 27th October 1970 and still unallowed is brought into the pool and will attract the normal 25% writing down allowance but, of course, not first year allowance. Balancing allowances and charges will likewise be given under the new system.[1] The taxpayer may elect to be charged under the old rules.[2]

Certain categories of machinery and plant cannot be brought into the new system and so remain under the old rules. See *Butterworths UK Tax Guide 1984–85* § **8: 41**.

Simon's Taxes B2.346 and B2.356–358 for the old system.
 ¹ FA 1976, s. 39(4).
 ² FA 1976, s. 39(4)(*e*).

MINING

Old rules

8: 45   United Kingdom companies operating abroad tend to derive their money from mining metals and petroleum; those operating within the United Kingdom have been mining building materials, notably sand and gravel,[1] china clay and slate. The history of capital allowances has been erratic to say the least and different rules apply according to the place being mined. The new rules apply to new expenditure, i.e. expenditure after 31st March 1986 but in certain circumstances 31st March 1987. The old but still sometimes applicable rules are considered in previous editions of this work.

Simon's Taxes B2.4.
[1] Coal and now oil being nationalised.

New rules

8: 46   The rules for capital allowances for mines and oil wells are changed as from 1st April 1986[1] but an election may be made to defer the change until 1st April 1987.[2] Where an accounting period straddles the relevant date, the period is split into an old and a new one;[3] a similar split is effected in the basis period for income tax. Where an expense is incurred before trading begins, it is treated as incurred when the trade begins.

The principal changes under the new regime are (*a*) the replacement of generous initial and writing down allowances by a new writing down allowance based on a percentage of a reducing balance of qualifying expenditure; (*b*) the relief to start when the trade begins rather than when the working or output of the mine begins; (*c*) the exclusion of the value of the land; and (*d*) the extension of the scheme to the search for geothermal energy.

Simon's Taxes Division B2.4.
[1] FA 1986, s. 55 and Sch. 13.
[2] FA 1986, Sch. 14, para. 2.
[3] FA 1986, s. 55(3).

Qualifying expenditure

8: 47   Qualifying expenditure is defined both by inclusion[1] and exclusion.[2] Thus the expense of an abortive application for planning permission is allowed[3] but that on the acquisition of a site on which expense qualifying for relief will be carried out will not.[4] Expenditure on machinery and plant is usually left to the machinery and plant system of allowances but this will not work where the expense is a pre-trading expense and the asset is disposed of before the trade begins; such expense may therefore be qualifying expenditure.[5] There is a similar rule for pre-trading exploration expenditure.[6] Also included are certain payments by mining concerns for site comfort and development outside the UK.[7] Expenditure on restoring a site at the end of the operation also qualifies.[8] A source of mineral deposits is widened to include a source of geothermal energy.[9]

Simon's Taxes Division B2.4.
¹ FA 1986, Sch. 13, para. 4(1).
² FA 1986, Sch. 13, para. 4(5).
³ FA 1986, Sch. 13, para. 4(6).
⁴ FA 1986, Sch. 13, para. 4(5)(a).
⁵ FA 1986, Sch. 13, para. 5; otherwise the machinery and plant rules apply—para. 4(4).
⁶ FA 1986, Sch. 13, para. 6.
⁷ FA 1986, Sch. 13, para. 7; where the building is in the UK the industrial buildings allowance may apply—e.g. CAA 1968, s. 7(3).
⁸ FA 1986, Sch. 13, para. 8 (but only if the work is carried out within three years of the termination; the cost is treated as incurred when the trade ends).
⁹ FA 1986, Sch. 13, para. 1(1).

The allowance

8: 48   When qualifying expenditure is incurred for the purposes of the trade of mineral extraction, a writing down allowance is given by reference to the amount by which the qualifying expenditure exceeds any disposal proceeds received during the period. The scheme is a simple reducing balance so that previous allowances reduce the qualifying expenditure. For pre-trading expenditure on machinery and plant disposed of before the trade begins and pre-trading exploration expenditure, the figure is 10%; for other qualifying expenditure it is 25%.[1] The allowance is given in taxing the trade.[2]

Disposal proceeds include the disposal value of an asset which ceases permanently to be used for the trade of mineral extraction. Capital sums reasonably attributable to qualifying expenditure must be brought into account.[3]

Where allowances and disposal proceeds exceed expenditure, there is a balancing charge equal to the excess but this is not to lead to a charge greater than the allowances already given.[4] Balancing allowances may arise principally in the period when the trade of mineral extraction ends and there are special rules for situations in which work on a particular mining deposit ceases and when disposal proceeds arise.[5] Pre-trading expenses on machinery and plant and exploration are treated as balancing allowances.[6] Balancing allowances may also arise where an asset is lost, ceases to exist or begins to be used for a purpose other than mineral extraction (in whole or in part).[7] Expenditure on mineral exploration and access is treated as incurred for the purpose of the trade[8] and demolition costs are to be added to qualifying expenditure when the asset in question may give rise to a balancing allowance or charge.[9]

Simon's Taxes Division B2.4.
¹ FA 1986, Sch. 13, para. 9.
² FA 1986, Sch. 13, para. 15.
³ FA 1986, Sch. 13, para. 10.
⁴ FA 1986, Sch. 13, para. 11.
⁵ FA 1986, Sch. 13, para. 12(1), (2) and (3).
⁶ FA 1986, Sch. 13, para. 12(4).
⁷ FA 1986, Sch. 13, para. 12(5) and (6).
⁸ FA 1986, Sch. 13, para. 13.
⁹ FA 1986, Sch. 13, para. 14.

Limitations of qualifying expenditure

8: 49   FA 1986, Sch. 13, Pt. IV contains a number of rules restricting the amount of expenditure that would otherwise qualify for the relief. First the cost of land is excluded; the valuation is carried out by assuming no source of mineral deposits and only existing or authorised use allowed.[1] There is a similar valuation for calculating the disposal proceeds.[2]

Where the expenditure is incurred in the purchase of an asset which has already been used by a previous trader in the mineral extraction business, the purchaser is usually required to take over the previous trader's position even if the purchase is not directly from that person. So where the previous trader was not entitled to any relief it is the previous trader's qualifying expenditure that is taken rather than the price paid by the taxpayer[3] and where an allowance or charge has already been made to or on the previous trader, that too must be taken into account.[4]

Where the purchase is of mineral deposits and part is attributable to exploration and access, an apportionment is directed.[5] For similar reasons, expenditure on Petroleum Act licences must be restricted to the price paid by the original licensee[6] and where a mineral asset is transferred within a group it is the transferor's qualifying expenditure that matters.[7]

Where a person incurs expenditure on mineral exploration and access and he sells assets representing that expenditure but does not himself carry on a mineral extraction trade, the qualifying expenditure is not the price paid to him by the purchaser but his expenditure.[8]

Simon's Taxes Division B2.4.
[1] FA 1986, Sch. 13, para. 16.
[2] FA 1986, Sch. 13, para. 18.
[3] FA 1986, Sch. 13, paras. 19 and 20.
[4] FA 1986, Sch. 13, para. 20(3).
[5] FA 1986, Sch. 13, para. 21.
[6] FA 1986, Sch. 13, para. 22.
[7] FA 1986, Sch. 13, para. 23.
[8] FA 1986, Sch. 13, para. 24.

Transitional

8: 50   The transition from the old code to the new is effected by treating any outstanding balances under the old rules as if they were new qualifying expenditure incurred on 1st April 1986[1] (or 1987 if the party so elects). If all the expenditure has already been relieved under the old rule the new code deems an allowance equal to those sums to have been given under the new code and so as potentially available for a balancing charge.[2] Expenditure on mineral exploration and access[3] and on the acquisition of a mineral asset[4] can also be brought within the new code by being treated as incurred on the relevant day. Where charges arise under the new code, any allowances given under the old code must be taken into account.[5]

Simon's Taxes Division B2.4.
[1] FA 1986, Sch. 14, para. 3.
[2] FA 1986, Sch. 14, para. 4.
[3] FA 1986, Sch. 14, para. 5.
[4] FA 1986, Sch. 14, para. 6.
[5] FA 1986, Sch. 14, para. 8.

DREDGING

8: 51   Allowances are given in respect of capital expenditure incurred on dredging if the trade consists of the maintenance or improvement of the navigation of a harbour, estuary or waterway or the dredging is for the benefit of vessels coming to, leaving or using any dock or other premises occupied for the purpose of the trade.[1] Dredging refers only to acts done in the interests of navigation.[2] In general the allowance is similar to that for industrial buildings.

The allowance is made in taxing the trade.[3] The initial allowance was 15%;[4] the straight line writing down allowance is 4%. If the trade is permanently discontinued before the expenditure has been written off there is an immediate write-off of the balance.[5] There is no balancing charge. Initial allowances were reduced to zero as from 1st April 1986. The old rules remain for expenditure incurred before 1st April 1987 under a contract entered into before 13th March 1984.[6]

Simon's Taxes B2.8.
[1] CAA s. 67(1) undoing *Dumbarton Harbour Board v Cox* (1918) 7 TC 147.
[2] CAA 1968, s. 67(10).
[3] CAA 1968, s. 67(4).
[4] CAA 1968, s. 67(1)(*a*).
[5] CAA 1968, s. 67(2).
[6] FA 1985, s. 61.

AGRICULTURAL AND FORESTRY LAND

8: 52   An allowance may be claimed by a person with a major interest in agricultural or forestry land who incurs capital expenditure on the construction of farmhouses, farm or forestry buildings, cottages, fences and other works, e.g. drainage.[1] Allowances for forestry land are abolished for chargeable periods beginning on or after 20th June 1989.[2] The allowance takes the form of a writing down allowance over 25 years, i.e. 4% p.a.

However, expenditure incurred before 1st April 1987 under a contract entered into before 14th March 1984 by the person incurring the expenditure may be eligible for allowances under the previous rules,[3] as follows. An initial allowance of 20% may be claimed and then a straight line writing down allowance of the remaining 80% over the next eight years. The initial allowance may be waived in which case the writing down allowances are spread over ten years. A person other than a company may reduce the initial allowance in which case the balance is written down over the appropriate fraction of 10 years—so if 15% is claimed instead of 20% the remaining 85%

can be written off over 8½ years. In the first year the person may claim both an initial allowance and the writing down allowance, a maximum of 30%. The initial allowance may only be claimed by the person incurring the expenditure but an incoming tenant or, if there is none, the immediate reversioner can take over the writing down allowance.

Under the 1986 rules, the allowance is set primarily against agricultural or forestry income and is not available under Schedule B.[4] The quite separate industrial buildings allowance may sometimes be available.[5]

The expenditure must have been incurred for the purposes of husbandry[6] or forestry on the agricultural or forestry land but an apportionment is made where the expenditure is only partly for that purpose.[7] Where the expenditure is on a farmhouse, one third is allowable and a smaller proportion being substituted if the accommodation and amenities of the farmhouse are out of due relation to the nature and extent of the farm.[8] A farmhouse is a building used by the person running the farm as a farmhouse.[9] In *Lindsay v IRC* the only house on a sheep farm was occupied by a shepherd and the owner resided in the United States but it remained the farmhouse. In *IRC v John M Whiteford & Son*[10] the fact that the occupier was one of the partners running the farm did not mean that his house was necessarily a farmhouse; rather it could be an agricultural cottage and so entitled to the full allowance. The proper criterion is not the status of the occupant but the purpose of the occupation of the premises.[11] In that case there was evidence that the farm was run from the house of the other partner. In both cases the decision of the Commissioners was upheld. If it is of a scale extravagantly large for the purpose for which it was being used, it might be entitled to no allowance whatsoever.[12]

Simon's Taxes B2.5.

[1] FA 1986, Sch. 15, para. 1; "major interest" is defined in para. 1(3) and includes an owner in fee simple and a lessee and the Scottish equivalent; the mortgagor holds the major interest rather than the mortgagee—para. 1(4). CAA 1968, Sch. 9, concerning contributions under s. 85 applies to agricultural allowances as from 27th July 1989—FA 1989, Sch. 13, para. 6.

[2] FA 1989, s. 120.

[3] CAA 1968, s. 68.

[4] FA 1986, Sch. 15, para. 11.

[5] CAA 1968, s. 7(1)(*h*).

[6] Defined CAA 1968, s. 69 (as amended by FA 1986, s. 56(3)) to include intensive rearing of livestock or fish.

[7] FA 1986, Sch. 15, para. 2.

[8] FA 1986, Sch. 15, para. 2(2).

[9] Per Lord Carmont in *Lindsay v IRC* (1952) 34 TC 289 at 292.

[10] (1962) 40 TC 379.

[11] Per Lord Clyde, at p. 384.

[12] Per Lord Clyde, at p. 384.

8:53   By FA 1986 the details of the allowance are made similar to those for industrial buildings. So expenditure on the acquisition of land or rights over land is excluded[1] and an allowance given for a building which is not later brought into use for husbandry or forestry is withdrawn.[2] On a transfer of the relevant interest the purchaser takes over the right to writing down allowances but for the balance of the original 25 year period.[3] There are provisions to govern the partial disposal of the relevant interest and for the merger and termination of leasehold interests. Where the building is bought unused any allowance given to the vendor is withdrawn and the purchaser is treated as the person incurring the allowable expenditure.[4]

Unlike the previous system the 1986 rules contain provisions for balancing allowances or charges on the happening of a "balancing event" which is defined as arising when the relevant interest is transferred and where the building is demolished, destroyed or otherwise ceases to exist.[5] However there will only be a balancing event if an election is made not more than two years from the end of the chargeable period in which the event occurred. On a transfer of the relevant interest the vendor and purchaser must make the election; in the other events it is the former owner of the building.[6]

The anti-avoidance provisions with regard to sales where one party has control over the other, they are under common control, or are connected persons, or the object of the disposal is to get a deduction or allowance, are adopted for this allowance but with the omission of the right to elect to substitute market value for the price agreed by the parties.[7] There is also a rule directing the adjustment of the proceeds of sale where the relevant interest is disposed of subject to a subordinate interest; the value of the subordinate interest may not be ignored.[8]

---

[1] FA 1986, Sch. 15, para. 8. The provisions in CAA 1968, ss. 70–89 are brought into effect by FA 1989, Sch. 23, para. 25.

[2] FA 1986, Sch. 15, para. 1(2).

[3] FA 1986, Sch. 15, para. 4.

[4] FA 1986, Sch. 15, para. 5.

[5] FA 1986, Sch. 15, paras. 6 and 7; para. 7(3) is amended by FA 1989, Sch. 13, para. 26.

[6] FA 1986, Sch. 15, para. 7(2) and (5).

[7] FA 1986, Sch. 15, para. 9, adopting CAA 1968, Sch. 7.

[8] FA 1986, Sch. 15, para. 10.

OTHER ALLOWANCES

8: 54   Scientific research allowances are available for capital expenditure on scientific research, provided it is related to the trade carried on (or to be carried on).[1] The research may be carried on by someone other than the trader provided it is on behalf of the trader, an expression which requires something close to agency.[2] The allowance does not extend to the costs of creating a training centre since research is confined to natural or applied science for the advancement of knowledge.[3] Costs in acquiring rights in scientific research are not allowed. No allowance can be claimed for expenditure incurred after 31st March 1985 on the acquisition of land or rights over land (as distinct from buildings) or on the acquisition of a dwelling, although apportionment is permitted.[4] Apportionment of expenditure is permitted.[5]

The allowance is 100% of the cost. The rate of allowance is not to be reduced as from 1st April 1986. There are balancing allowances and charges but only if the asset ceases to be used for scientific research and is then (or later) sold (or destroyed).[6]

For expenditure incurred after 31st March 1985[7] these allowances and charges arise when the asset ceases to belong to the person whether through sale, destruction or any other event.[8]

Sums paid to approved research associations, universities and institutions may be deductible as if they were revenue expenditure.[9]

Simon's Taxes B2.7.

[1] CAA 1968, s. 91; revenue expense may be deductible under ibid. s. 90(*a*) and s 521, as amended by FA 1989, Sch. 13, para. 27 (for acquisitions from a connected person).

[2] CAA 1968, s. 91; *Gaspet Ltd v Elliss* [1985] STC 572.

[3] CAA 1968, s. 94. On meaning of when an asset is sold, see CAA 1968, s. 94(4A), added by FA 1989, Sch. 13, para. 9.

[4] CAA 1968, s. 91(1A), (1B), added by FA 1985, s. 63; the old rules remain for expenditure incurred before 1st April 1987 under a contract entered into before 13th March 1985.

[5] CAA 1968, s. 91(1C), added by FA 1989, Sch. 13, para. 7.

[6] CAA 1968, s. 92.

[7] FA 1985, s. 63; the old rules remain for expenditure incurred before that date and for expenditure incurred after that date but before 1st April 1987 under a contract entered into before 13th March 1984.

[8] On values to be taken see CAA 1968, s. 92(3A), inserted by FA 1985, s. 63. On meaning of relevant date, see FA 1989, Sch. 13, para. 8.

[9] Under CAA 1968, s. 90(*b*) and (*c*); on meaning of research for a class of trade see s. 94(1).

Patents and knowhow

8: 55   Since 1945 there has been a special regime to treat sums derived from the disposal of patents as income and conversely to allow expenditure on acquiring patent rights. The capital cost of purchasing patent rights was, broadly speaking, allowed by equal annual instalments over 17 years.[1] For expenditure incurred on or after 1st April 1986, this is replaced by an annual writing down allowance of 25% (reducing balance basis[2]). There are balancing allowances and charges if the rights come to an end or are disposed of.[3] Royalties payable under a patent agreement to a non-resident are subject to deduction at source under TA 1988, s. 349.

Capital payments received for the disposal of patent rights are taxed as income and spread over six years. If the individual dies before the six year period ends any remaining instalments may be spread back; similar rules apply on discontinuance or on the winding up of a company.[4]

Writing down allowances for the cost of acquiring know-how were previously given over 6 years.[5]

Simon's Taxes B2.6.

[1] TA 1988, s. 522.

[2] TA 1988, s. 520.

[3] TA 1988, s. 523. On special rules if sale by inventor to a company controlled by him, see extra-statutory concession B17 (1988), **Simon's Taxes, Division H2.2.**

[4] TA 1988, s. 524.

[5] TA 1988, s. 528.

9 Property income: Schedules A, B, C, and D, Case III

SCHEDULE A

9: 01 Income tax is charged under Schedule A by TA 1988, s. 15 on the annual profits or gains arising in respect of land in the UK, or, more precisely, arising in respect of:

(*a*) rents under leases[1] of land in the UK;

(*b*) rentcharges, ground annuals, feu duties and other annual payments reserved in respect of or charged on or issuing out of such land; and

(*c*) other receipts arising to a person from or by virtue of his ownership of an estate or interest in or right over such land or incorporeal hereditament or incorporeal heritable subject in the UK.

Where land is let and services are provided, payment in respect of those services will not fall within Schedule A but may fall within Schedule D, Case I or Case VI.[2] Among many differences

(*i*) income under Schedule A is investment income;[3] and

(*ii*) Schedule A is assessed on a current year basis.

Simon's Taxes A4.101; Butterworths Income Tax Service F1.

[1] Defined by TA 1988, s. 24(1) as including an agreement for a lease or any tenancy, but not a mortgage. Land includes buildings and rights over land—Interpretation Act 1978, Sch. 1.

[2] *Fry v Salisbury House Estate Ltd* [1930] AC 432, 15 TC 266. In this case it was admitted that the profits derived from the provision of lighting, cleaning, caretaking and other services fell within Schedule D; supra, § **2: 09**. On treatment of caravan sites, see extra-statutory concession B29 (1988) and supra, § **7: 39**.

[3] But close company legislation regards it as estate income; infra, § **27: 18** and special rules apply to furnished holiday lettings; TA 1988, s. 504, infra, § **9: 09**.

9: 02 Rent is not defined for tax purposes. Its general meaning[1] is a payment due from a tenant to his (land)lord by reason of tenure; it must be reserved as rent. However, it has been held that a payment can be rent even though there is no right to distrain for it.[2] The rent is a sum payable for the lease and the obligation to pay passes to an assignee; the payment of a premium in instalments is not rent.[3]

Payments falling within (*c*), above, include such items as licence fees for advertisement hoardings, parking fees and service charges which are not reserved as rent and are not in respect of services constituting a trade.[4] Thus a separate charge for meals would fall within Schedule D, Case I, whereas if a lease provides for the provision of a service for which no separate payment is made, e.g. heating, the rent comes under Schedule A and the cost of heating is an allowable expense. Where payments were made by an employer to an employee for the use of an employee's garage to store samples and stock for use in the employee's work, the payments were held to fall within Schedule E, not Schedule A.[5] Some situations will be impossible to classify. Where a farmer sold turf from his land he was held taxable under heading (*c*) but also, in the alternative, under Schedule D, Case I.[6] By concession, rental income from caravan sites may be amalgamated with associated trading income.[7]

Damages for trespass to land and loss of rent are not liable to income tax as rent.[8] Some such payments have, in another jurisdiction, been held to be income under general principles[9] in which case they may be taxable under Schedule A under heading (*c*). If the payments are not taxable at all it follows that in assessing damages the court will take account of the tax which the plaintiff has not had to pay and grant only the net sum under the rule in *British Transport Commission v Gourley*.[10] This situation must be distinguished from that in which an action is brought for arrears of rent since such sums are within Schedule A.

One may also note the generous practice whereby a trader, who lets a part of the building in which he carried on a business, may treat the rents as trading income.[11]

Simon's Taxes A4.104, 105; Butterworths Income Tax Service F1.04.

[1] On general meaning see Gray, *Elements of Land Law*, pp. 441–443.
[2] *T and E Homes Ltd v Robinson* [1979] STC 351.
[3] But it may be taxed as if it were rent: TA 1988, s. 35; infra, § **9: 17**.
[4] George, *Taxation of Property Transactions* (3rd edn), p. 48. For an excellent example of the problem see the Revenue note on the taxation of caravan sites in [1984] STI, p. 386.
[5] *Beecham Group Ltd v Fair* [1984] STC 15.
[6] *Lowe v Ashmore Ltd* (1970) 46 TC 597; see also supra, § **7: 39**.
[7] Extra-statutory concession B29 (1988).
[8] *Hall & Co v Pearlberg* [1956] 1 All ER 297n, [1956] 1 WLR 244.
[9] *Raja's Commercial College v Gian Singh & Co Ltd* [1976] STC 282, [1976] 2 All ER 801, PC (damages for almost six years; occupation after end of lease, damages equal to excess of market rent over rent under former lease).
[10] [1955] 3 All ER 796, [1956] AC 185. In *Hall v Pearlberg* the rate of tax used was that at the time of the judgment but this appears to be wrong since the rates of tax for the years in issue were known.
[11] Revenue publication IR 27 (1984), § 17 (but not where the business consists of rendering services to the tenants, § 107).

9: 03   Specifically *excluded* from Schedule A are:

(*a*) any yearly interest;[1]

(*b*) any profits or gains charged to tax under Schedule D, Case I, by TA 1988, s. 55 (which concerns mines, quarries and sand and gravel), or under Schedule D, Case III by TA 1988, ss. 119 and 120 (which concern mining and other royalties);[2]

(*c*) rent under a lease which includes the use of furniture; this is chargeable wholly under Schedule D, Case VI, unless the landlord elects to be taxed in part under Schedule A;[3]

(*d*) profits of tied premises.[4]

(*e*) profits arising from the occupation of woodlands managed on a commercial basis.[5]

Income tax is charged under Schedule A if the source, the land, is in the UK. Income from foreign land will be taxed to a UK resident under Schedule D, Cases IV or V.[6]

Simon's Taxes A4.105; Butterworths Income Tax Service F1.03.

[1] Infra, § **9: 44**.
[2] The Law Commission recommended that these should not be restored to Schedule A: 1971 Cmnd. 4654 § 63.
[3] Infra, § **9: 07**.
[4] TA 1988, s. 98.
[5] TA 1988, s. 67(1)(*aa*), added by FA 1988, Sch. 6, para. 6(2).
[6] Infra, § **34: 05**.

9: 04 Tax under Schedule A is still a tax on income and not on capital gains[1] as is shown by the phrase "annual profits or gains" in TA 1988, s. 15. A premium accruing on the grant of a lease giving possession of premises would, but for special legislation in TA 1988, ss. 34 to 36, fall outside Schedule A. Still however, a gain accruing from the assignment, as distinct from the grant of a lease,[2] or the grant of a lease of shooting rights, is a matter for CGT, not Schedule A. Likewise a sum payable in return for the grant or release of an easement would normally escape Schedule A as has a one-off payment for allowing a motorway contractor to tip sub-soil onto the taxpayer's land.[3]

---

[1] See, for example, the arguments raised (unsuccessfully) in *Jeffries v Stevens* [1982] STC 639 and *Lowe v J W Ashmore Ltd* [1970] 46 TC 597.
[2] Unless the original lease is granted at an undervalue: TA 1988, s. 35; infra, § **9: 24**.
[3] *McClure v Petre* [1988] STC 749.

Basis of assessment—timing

9: 05 Income tax under Schedule A is charged by reference to the sums to which a person becomes entitled in the chargeable period. It follows that rent due and received in year 1 in respect of a period which includes a part of year 2 is taxable in full in year 1; equally rent due in year 1 is taxable in year 1 whether or not received, although relief in respect of rent not received is permitted by TA 1988, s. 41, this relief extending to premiums taxed by ss. 34 to 36. The Revenue practice is to allow expenditure on an accounts basis.[1]

Section 41 allows the taxpayer to reopen assessments for the relevant year if the non-payment was attributable to the default of the person by whom it was payable or if he waived payment of the rent, the waiver being for no consideration and, within reason, to avoid hardship. In practice the Revenue will accept as a valid waiver a mere concurrence in the non-payment of rent if the element of hardship is present.[2] If rent is recovered after relief has been given, the taxpayer must give notice within six months and the assessment will be reopened.[3] If the waiver is in advance of the rent becoming due and in effective legal form it would appear to prevent the income from arising in the first place so that no income tax could be charged on the landlord whether not there was hardship.

Tax is levied on a current year basis and is due on 1st January of the year of assessment but, in order to avoid the difficulty that one will not know the precise profits until after the end of the tax year, a provisional assessment is made on the basis of the previous year's profits.[4] If the taxpayer has more than one source of Schedule A income he may have as many assessments as sources.[5]

Simon's Taxes A4.107; Butterworths Income Tax Service F1.71.

[1] IR 27 (1984) § 102–104.
[2] Simon's Taxes A4.401.
[3] TA 1988, s. 47(1). See Revenue publication IR 27 (1984) §§ 56, 57. Companies on an accounts basis may write off lost rents for the year in which they are written off: **Simon's Taxes A4.401.**
[4] The legal basis for this practice is now TMA 1970, s. 29(1)(c), added by FA 1988, s. 119. But excluding any premiums treated as rent: TA 1988, s. 34(7). Status quo approved by Law Commission: 1971 Cmnd. 4654 § 55.
[5] TA 1988, s. 22.

Accountability—agents and tenants

9: 06   Tax is charged on the person receiving or entitled to the profits or gains to be taxed. If the rent is paid to any person on behalf of another the Revenue may require the agent to hand over to the Revenue sums received on behalf of the principal on account of rent or receipts from the land until liability in respect of the tax has been satisfied.[1] Failure by the agent to pay the tax carries the risk of fines as well as of personal accountability.

The Revenue may also, by notice, intercept payments of rent from any person whose interest is derived from that of the person in default.[2] So a sub-lessee can be given notice in respect of a default by the head landlord; in turn the sub-lessee can withhold from the head landlord.

Should the derivative lessee default, he remains liable for the tax to the extent of the rent due from him. If the sub-lessee deducts the tax, the lessee is the loser. He in turn is therefore allowed to deduct from the rent he pays the landlord and he may recover any net loss from the Revenue.

Simon's Taxes A4.5; Butterworths Income Tax Service F1.72.

[1] TA 1988, s. 23(7) and (8).
[2] TA 1988, s. 23(1)–(6).

9: 07   Where the rent is payable directly to one whose usual place of abode is outside the UK, the payer *must* deduct tax under TA 1988, s. 349 and account to the Revenue for such deduction.[1] This duty extends to premiums and to payments to third parties but is limited to basic rate income tax.[2] The duty does not apply where the rent or other payment is made to a resident agent.[3] This procedure does not require notice to the tenant on whom is therefore cast the duty of knowing his landlord's usual place of abode.

Simon's Taxes A4.503.

¹ TA 1988, s. 43, excluding TMA 1970, s. 78. A similar rule applied to DLT.
² Infra, § **9: 79**.
³ Here TMA 1970, s. 78 applies.

Furnished lettings

9: 08   The landlord may elect to have the rent for the occupation of the
property charged under Schedule A and that for the furniture under Schedule
D, Case VI; otherwise the total rent is chargeable under Case VI.[1] The point
of an election will generally be to take Schedule D, Case VI income across to
Schedule A to absorb a loss on some other Schedule A source, TA 1988, s. 43
applies to furnished lettings.

Such income is not usually trading income.[2]

Simon's Taxes B7.206; Butterworths Income Tax Service F1.07, F5.42.
¹ Infra, § **10: 14**. The Law Commission rejected a proposal to move rent from furnished
lettings into Schedule A partly because the variable amounts from such furnished lettings make
the Schedule A machinery less appropriate: 1971 Cmnd. 4654 § 61.
² *Gittos v Barclay* [1982] STC 390.

Furnished holiday lettings

9: 09   The special rules applicable to furnished holiday lettings are contained
in TA 1988, ss. 503–504. The special rules are that while the income is not
moved to Schedule D Case I but remains under Schedule D Case VI the
following rules (otherwise applicable only to trades) apply:[1]

(*a*) tax is to be paid in two equal instalments on 1st January and 1st July;

(*b*) loss relief rules apply as for trades (§ **5: 17**);

(*c*) retirement annuity contract rules apply (§ **30: 15**);

(*d*) the income is to be treated as earned income (§ **4: 05**);

(*e*) capital allowances are to be available (§ **8: 24**);

(*f*) roll-over relief for CGT (§ **20: 06**);

(*g*) retirement relief for CGT (§ **20: 10**);

(*h*) CGT relief for gifts of business assets (§ **20: 18**);

(*i*) bad debt relief for loans to traders (§ **15: 06**) and

(*j*) relief for pre-trading expenditure (§ **5: 21**).

The three year carry back rule for losses in the first three years of a trade is
(TA 1988, s. 381) adapted.[2]

Expenditure is to be deductible as if the letting were a trade.[3] The CGT
rules in (*f*) to (*i*) apply as if the "trade" were carried on throughout the year
and the property used only for such purposes save where the accommodation
is neither let commercially nor available to be so let (unless prevented by
works of construction or repair).[4] The purpose of this rule is to withhold the
relief if there is any period of owner-occupation. Provision is also made for
the situation in which the house being replaced was eligible for exemption as
an only or main residence.[5]

The rules are intended to bring a measure of certainty to these areas.
Where the taxpayer does not fulfil the stringent conditions laid down it will

still be open to him to argue that he is carrying on a trade and so comes within Schedule D Case I rather than Case VI.

The rules may be seen as a recognition of the artificial nature of the division between property income and trading income; it remains to be seen whether other instances of this artificiality will also be amended.

There are stringent conditions to be satisfied before letting is treated as a furnished holiday letting. The property must be in the United Kingdom, the letting must be on a commercial basis and with a view to the realisation of profit and the tenant must be entitled to the use of the furniture. The property must be available for letting to the general public during the season, must be available for not less than 140 days, must be let for at least 70 days and, for a period of at least seven months it must not normally be in the same occupation for continuous periods exceeding 31 days. Where these conditions are fulfilled in relation to one property but not another the taxpayer may elect to have the properties averaged. Thus if property 1 is let for 80 days and property 2 for 68 days, an averaging election will make both properties let for 74 days and so both qualify.

These conditions have to be satisfied by reference to periods of twelve months, being the year of assessment for an individual and the accounting period of a company. Special rules apply where the accommodation was not within these rules in the previous year—the twelve months period runs from the date of the first letting; in the converse situation the period begins on the last date of letting.

Simon's Taxes B7.206; Butterworths Income Tax Service F5.42.
[1] TA 1988, s. 503(1). On start of rules, see FA 1984, s. 49(8).
[2] TA 1988, s. 503(2)–(4).
[3] TA 1988, s. 503(5).
[4] FA 1984, Sch. 11, para. 4.
[5] FA 1984, Sch. 11, para. 5.

Deductions

9: 10   A sum may only be deducted if spent by the person chargeable and, even then, may not be deducted if payment has been or will be covered by insurance or recovered from any other person, such as a tortfeasor;[1] this does not apply if the amount so recovered will be brought into the Schedule A charge by the person receiving it.[2] Deduction is also forbidden if the payment is made by the person chargeable under Schedule A under deduction of tax[3] since relief is given in other ways.[4] A sum may not be deducted more than once nor if it has already been allowed as a deduction in computing any person's tax liability.[5] Should the deductions exceed the rents, the taxpayer may choose which items to deduct immediately and he may roll the other items forward under the appropriate loss claim.[6]

Simon's Taxes A4.301; Butterworths Income Tax Service F1.21.
[1] Defined by TA 1988, s. 31(2) as including any sums deductible under TA 1988, ss. 25 to 30 and Sch. 1.
[2] TA 1988, s. 31(5)(*a*).
[3] TA 1988, s. 31(5)(*b*).

From rents under a lease

9: 11 Deductions from rents under a lease are authorised by TA 1988, s. 25. This applies where the lease confers a right, as against the person whose interest is subject to the lease, to the possession of the premises. So a licence or a lease of an incorporeal hereditament, for example shooting rights,[1] falls outside TA 1988, s. 25.

The person chargeable may deduct sums spent:

(*a*) in respect of maintenance, repairs, insurance[2] or management; for example commission to an agent for looking after the property; repairs and maintenance must be distinguished from improvements, replacements and additions (supra, § **7: 113**);

(*b*) sums spent in respect of any services provided by him otherwise than by way of maintenance or repairs being services which he was obliged to provide[3] but in respect of which he has received no separate consideration;[4] for example, the provision of heat;

(*c*) sums spent in respect of rates or other charges which the person chargeable was obliged to defray; for example where the landlord pays the water rates;

(*d*) sums spent in respect of any rent, rentcharge, ground annual, feu duty or other periodical payment reserved in respect of or charged on or issuing out of land, so where a lessee receives rent under a sub lease he may deduct the sums he himself pays under his lease. Likewise a husband who has charged maintenance payments in favour of his wife on that piece of land may deduct those payments from his rent. However the payment of rent must be of an income nature so that payments of a rentcharge to pay for the purchase of the freehold reversion were not deductible even though income in the hands of the payee.[5]

No deduction may be claimed under s. 25 for interest payments. Deduction may be claimed under other rules as a deduction from income.[6]

If the landlord retains a part of the premises, for example the stairways and roof of a block of flats, and that part is used in common by the persons occupying the various flats, expenses incurred by the landlord in respect of the part retained may be deducted as if incurred in respect of the flats, the sums being apportioned as necessary.[7]

Where properties are owned by a company as an investment, that company may deduct management expenses under TA 1988, s. 75; management expenses for that section are so defined as to exclude expenses deductible under Schedule A. Those deductible under Schedule A are concerned with the expenses of managing the property; those deductible under s. 75 with the expenses of managing the company. The former are not confined to the fabric of the buildings or to the land itself but can extend to the business of owning land[8] and so include the cost of employing a factor to look after the property and any costs in having the estate accounts properly kept, in collecting the rents and in making the necessary disbursements.[9]

Simon's Taxes A4.303, 304; Butterworths Income Tax Service F1.22.

[1] Technically the lessee of a sporting right is entitled to possession: see *Nicholls v Ely Beet Sugar Factory* [1936] Ch 343 but *quaere* whether he is entitled to possession *of the premises*. Fishing rights are outside Schedule A: TA 1988, s. 55; other sporting rights are clearly intended to fall outside s. 25.

[2] This means the expense of insuring the continued existence of the premises against loss by fire and in other ways and does not extend to a leasehold redemption policy: *Pearce v Doulton* [1947] 1 All ER 378, 27 TC 405.

[3] In practice this means obliged as a matter of commercial practice and not just legal obligation.

[4] If there is separate consideration the payment may fall within Schedule D, Case VI.

[5] *IRC v Land Securities Investment Trust Ltd* [1969] 2 All ER 430, 45 TC 495, HL. Although this case was decided on Schedule D, Case I principles it is thought relevant here.

[6] Supra, § **5: 37**.

[7] TA 1988, s. 25(8).

[8] Per Lawrence J in *Southern v Aldwych Property Trust Ltd* [1940] 2 KB 266, 23 TC 707.

[9] Per Lord Clyde in *IRC v Wilson's Executors* (1934) 18 TC 465 at 473. See also leaflet IR 27 (1984) App I.

Using the deduction

9: 12   The rules that follow severely limit the right to set off expenditure in one period against that in another and that on one source against that on another.

The basic rule in TA 1988, s. 25(3) and (4) is that sums spent on allowable expenditure[1] are deductible from the rents receivable during the chargeable period in respect of those premises or subsequent periods so long as the same lease continues. Further, the expenditure must be incurred during the lease; in the case of repair costs the dilapidation must be attributable to a period falling within the currency of that particular lease or since the person chargeable became the landlord if that is shorter. So no allowance can be claimed for sums spent to cover dilapidations occurring prior to the lease or the taxpayer's becoming the landlord.[2] Where expenditure on maintenance and repairs, which would have been allowable, is obviated by an expenditure on improvement which is not allowable, the Revenue, by concession, allow the estimated cost of the maintenance saved as a deduction.[3]

Simon's Taxes A4.305–312; Butterworths Income Tax Service F1.22.

[1] Interest on sums spent on allowable expenditure is probably deductible as allowable expenditure; but if the expenditure is not allowable under Schedule A it may still be deducted under TA 1988, s. 354(2).

[2] For the position under Schedule D, Case I, see supra, § **7: 117**, and see Law Commission, 1971, Cmnd. 4654 § 31. Pre-acquisition expenses are allowed if the acquisition was by a surviving spouse on the death of the other spouse; the expenses allowed are those incurred by that other, extra-statutory concession A21 (1988), see **Simon's Taxes, Division H2.2**.

[3] Extra-statutory concession B4 (1988), see **Simon's Taxes, Division H2.2**—but not where the works amount to reconstruction of the property or there is a change of use which would have made the repairs unnecessary.

9: 13   *Same property—other periods.* TA 1988, s. 25(5) and (6) allow the deduction of expenditure incurred during a previous qualifying period provided there is no intervening non-qualifying period. The two sorts of qualifying period are:

(*a*) where the person chargeable was the landlord in relation to a previous lease at full rent;

(*b*) a void period, that is one in which the landlord was entitled to possession but did not go into occupation.[1] The void period is only a qualifying period if it begins with the termination of a previous lease at full rent or with the acquisition by the landlord of the interest giving him the right to occupy.

Accumulated losses from an earlier lease at full rent may thus be carried forward to another lease at full rent whether the new lease follows immediately or a void period intervenes. Likewise, expenditure during the void period and attributable to it, may be set against subsequent full rent if it is between two leases at full rent or begins with the acquisition of the source by the landlord; it may also be set against the rent of the previous lease payable during the year of assessment.

A period of owner occupation[2] or a letting at less than full rent, being non-qualifying intervening periods wipe out accumulated expenditures. A lease is "at full rent" if the rent reserved (including any premium) will be sufficient, taking one year with another, to defray the cost to the lessor of meeting his obligations under the lease and the expenses of maintenance, repairs, insurance and management which fall to be borne by him.[3]

EXAMPLE

L owns a house let at a full rent to T1. The lease ends on 31st December 1985 and a new lease at full rent, in favour of T2, begins on 1st June 1986. Expenditure incurred during the lease to T1 may be rolled forward and set off against the lease to T2 if the period from 1st January 1986 to 31st May 1986 is a void period. Expenditure on repairs incurred during that void period may also be set off against the later rent whether the dilapidation was attributable to the void period or the earlier period. Expenditure incurred before 6th April 1986 may be set off against the rent accruing since 5th April 1985.

Butterworths Income Tax Service F1.22.

[1] TA 1988, s. 25(2).

[2] *Quaere* the effect of allowing a friend to use the house for an overnight stay; is this occupation on behalf of the owner so as to end the void period or is it occupation by the friend in his own right—and so perhaps a lease at less than full rent—with the same result. Can the status of the void period be preserved by granting a licence as opposed to a lease?

[3] TA 1988, s. 24(7).

9: 14   *Other properties.* TA 1988, s. 25(7) allows a taxpayer to set an excess of expenditure over rent on a lease at full rent (including a tenant's repairing lease[1]) against rent from another lease also at full rent provided that it is not a tenant's repairing lease.[2] A tenant's repairing lease is one under which the lessee is under an obligation to maintain and repair the whole or substantially the whole of the premises leased.

EXAMPLE

X has 3 properties let unfurnished. All are let at full rent and C is a tenant's repairing lease.

Incomes and expenses for the year to 5th April 1987 are as follows:

	A		B		C	
	£		£		£	
Rent received		1,000		650		480
Rates	500		375		290	
Repairs	370		425		—	
Insurances	20	890	20	820	20	310
Profit (loss)		110		(170)		170
Offset		110		(110)		—
Losses c/f		—		(60)		—
Assessable		—		—		170

If C had had an excess of expenditure that excess would have been set against any profits from A and B but because C is a tenant's repairing lease the excess remaining on lease B cannot be set against the profit from C. This would also be the case if C was not let at full rent. However, if C was not let at a full rent any excess of expenditure could not be set against rent on A and B either.

The taxpayer must also show that he would be allowed to deduct such sums from the rent in respect of the property on which they were incurred or, if there is a void period, would have been allowed such deduction had the lease continued until the end of the chargeable period. This causes problems if an excess of expenditure has accrued, is rolled forward to a subsequent year and in the meantime the property has ceased to be let at full rent, as where it has been sold. Such expenditure is simply lost for tax purposes.[3]

A further rule allows the pooling of certain rents and expenses of properties which were managed as one estate in 1962–63[4] if the taxpayer so elects.[5]

Simon's Taxes A4.313–317; Butterworths Income Tax Service F1.34.

[1] Defined TA 1988, s. 24(6).

[2] The general pooling of expenditures under these two types of commercial lease is recommended by Law Commission, 1971, Cmnd. 4654 § 13.

[3] The Law Commission has recommended the abolition of this distinction: 1971 Cmnd. 4654 § 17. The expenditure may not be used by the landlord under Schedule A and will increase the chargeable gain, it not being an allowable deduction for capital gains tax. If the purchaser incurs the expenditure he will not be able to deduct it either as it will be a pre-acquisition expense.

[4] Leaflet IR 27 (1984) §§ 82–87.

[5] TA 1988, s. 26(3)(c).

Deduction from other receipts

9: 15 Deductions from receipts other than rents under a lease are governed by TA 1988, s. 28. The person chargeable may deduct sums which are expenses of the transaction giving rise to the receipts and which are paid in respect of maintenance, repairs, insurance or management of the premises to which the sums relate. He may also deduct any rent, rentcharge, ground annual, feu duty or other periodical or non-capital payment paid for the property, *if* it is an expense of the transaction.[1] Thus if a landowner grants his neighbour an easement for a term of years at a rent, he may deduct the costs of any extra insurance cover incurred.

EXAMPLE

T leases a field from X at a rent of £200 a year and later allows a neighbour to graze his horse for a year in the field in return for £240; the rent under the lease is not deductible and he is taxable on £240. If however he used the land *only* to profit from allowing others to graze their horses, the rent would be deductible.[2]

An excess of allowable expenditure can be set off against income from any like transaction of that or any later chargeable period.[3]

Simon's Taxes A4.322, 323; Butterworths Income Tax Service F1.41.
[1] For a relaxation for sporting rights, see TA 1988, s. 26(1).
[2] *Semble* that if he fenced off a small area for the neighbour's horse an apportioned part of the £200 would have been deductible. For other examples, see IR 27 (1984) § 96.
[3] TA 1988, s. 28(2)(*d*).

Other expenses

9: 16   Three special forms of relief should be mentioned. First expenditure incurred in repairing sea walls, etc., is spread over the next 21 years.[1] Secondly, capital allowances for machinery and plant used in estate management may be claimed just as if they were used for a trade.[2] Thirdly, if the land is agricultural any excess maintenance expenditure or excess allowance for plant and machinery, which cannot be deducted owing to insufficient rents or receipts (after other deductions have been claimed), can be treated as if it were the amount of an allowance falling to be made under the CAA 1968 by way of discharge or repayment of tax.[3] Thus unlike other sources within Schedule A a loss can be set off against income generally.

---

[1] TA 1988, s. 30; see **Simon's Taxes A4.324.**
[2] TA 1988, s. 32; see **Simon's Taxes A4.303.**
[3] TA 1988, s. 33; see **Simon's Taxes A4.407–412.**

TAXATION OF PREMIUMS AS INCOME

9: 17   Since Schedule A taxes only the annual profits and not the capital gains arising from land, the payment of a premium by a tenant to his landlord would escape Schedule A[1] even though this resulted in a lower rent and so a lower income for the landlord. Premiums on leases not exceeding 50 years are now taxed, but in a special way, by TA 1988, ss. 34 to 39.

Simon's Taxes A4.201; Butterworths Income Tax Service F1.51.
[1] *O'Connor v Hume* [1954] 2 All ER 301, [1954] 1 WLR 824. Conversely payment of the premium by the lessee was a capital expense: *Green v Favourite Cinemas Ltd* (1930) 15 TC 390.

A premium

9: 18   A premium is defined[1] as "including any like sum whether payable to the immediate or superior landlord or to a person connected[2] with such landlord". Thus a payment required by a landlord on the grant of a lease to a tenant would fall within this rule but a payment required by the tenant on the assignment of his interest would not. A payment exacted by the tenant on the grant of a sub-lease would be caught.

The sum need not be mentioned in the lease document. A sum paid in or in connection with the granting of a lease e.g. key money is presumed to be a premium but it is open to the taxpayer to show some reason for the payment other than the grant.[3]

Butterworths Income Tax Service F1.51.

[1] TA 1988, s. 24(1). On pre-1963 leases, see s. 39(1).

[2] Defined in TA 1988, s. 839. The Revenue view is that a payment to a third party other than a connected person is a premium, see Revenue publication IR 27 (1984) § 46 and discussion in George, *Taxation of Property Transactions* (3rd edn), p. 69; such a payment is a premium for the Landlord and Tenant (Rent Control) Act 1949: *Elmdene Estates Ltd v White* [1960] AC 528, [1960] 1 All ER 306. A premium in non-monetary form is caught: TA 1988, s. 24(4).

[3] TA 1988, s. 24(2). *Quaere* whether payment by the lessee of the lessor's legal costs is a premium—semble not.

Duration of lease

9: 19   These rules apply only where the duration of the lease does not exceed fifty years.[1] The definition of a 50 year lease takes full account of the commercial realities.[2] Thus if a tenant has a 40 year lease with an option to extend it for a further 20 years, account may be taken of the circumstances making it likely that the lease will be so extended. Likewise if a tenant, or a person connected with him, has the right not to extend the existing lease but instead has the right to a further lease of the same premises or part of them, the term may be treated as not expiring before the end of the further lease. Both these provisions, by lengthening the lease, favour the landlord but another rule does not. This provides that if any of the terms of the lease (whether relating to forfeiture or to any other matter) or any other circumstances render it unlikely that the lease will continue beyond a date falling short of the expiry of the term of the lease, the lease shall be treated as if it ended not later than that date, provided that the premium would not have been substantially greater had the lease been expected to run its full term.[2] Thus a 51 year lease with an option to the landlord to terminate it after five years would be treated as a five year lease, as would one which provided that after five years the rent, originally a full commercial rent, should be quintupled.

The question of what is unlikely is judged at the time the lease is granted.[3] The rule by focussing on what is likely or unlikely means that a lease for lives can fall within these rules if the life is unlikely to last more than 50 years despite the imposition of a 99 year lease by virtue of the Law of Property Act 1925, s. 149.

Simon's Taxes A4.203; Butterworths Income Tax Service F1.51.

[1] TA 1988, s. 34(1).

[2] TA 1988, s. 38. These rules apply only to leases granted after 24th August 1971.

[3] TA 1988, s. 38(2).

Taxing the premium

9: 20   A premium payable in respect of a lease not exceeding 50 years is treated as payable by way of rent and falls within Schedule A;[1] if it is payable to someone other than the landlord it falls under Schedule D, Case VI as that person's income.[2] The landlord or other person is treated as becoming entitled when the lease is granted.[3]

Without modification this rule could first cause a sharp distinction between a 49 year lease and a 51 year lease and secondly could result in a substantial sum which is really attributable to the number of years the lease is expected to run being treated as the income of one year.

The first problem is solved by the fractional reduction of the premium that fraction being related to the duration of the lease, as defined; the longer the lease the less the chargeable sum.[4] The premium is reduced by $\frac{1}{50}$ for each complete period of twelve months (other than the first) comprised in the duration of the lease.[5] Only complete years are taken into account so that a premium on a lease for two years less a day would be chargeable in full. The sum by which the premium is reduced is not taxable in any subsequent year.[6]

The second problem is regarded as no longer causing any difficulty in view of the sharp reduction in tax rates. The earlier top-slicing relief has no effect for 1988–89 and later years and the provisions are repealed.[7]

If the premium is payable by instalments the taxpayer may, if he satisfies the Revenue that he would otherwise suffer undue hardship, spread the taxable fraction of the premiums over a period allowed by the Revenue. This period is not to exceed eight years or until the last instalment of the premium becomes due, if shorter.[8]

Simon's Taxes A4.202; Butterworths Income Tax Service F1.52, F1.62.

[1] TA 1988, s. 34(1).

[2] TA 1988, s. 34(6); there can be no loss relief, TA 1988, s. 392(4).

[3] *Quaere* how one grants an agreement for a lease; see further *City Permanent Building Society v Miller* [1952] Ch 840 at 853, [1952] 2 All ER 621 at 628.

[4] TA 1988, s. 34(1).

[5] This could have been more elegantly expressed by saying the fraction chargeable shall be 50 minus the number of years of the lease plus one over 50.

[6] The part not taxed as a premium may nonetheless be liable to income tax under Schedule D, Case I, if the lessor deals in land, or to CGT.

[7] FA 1988, s. 75 and Sch. 14, Part IV.

[8] TA 1988, s. 34(8).

Anti-avoidance provisions—piercing the disguise

Improvements

9: 21 TA 1988, s. 34(2) provides that if the terms subject to which the lease is granted impose on the tenant an obligation to carry out any work on the premises[1] then the amount by which the value of the landlord's estate immediately after the commencement of the lease exceeds the value which it would have had if no such obligation had been imposed on the tenant, is treated as a premium. The measure of liability is the benefit received, not the cost incurred—a matter of particular importance if the landlord is a lessee and his lease ends shortly after the sub-lease. Since the provision applies whenever there is an obligation to carry out work, there is a specific exclusion where the works are such that the costs would be deductible by the landlord if he had to do them, for example works of maintenance.

Butterworths Income Tax Service F1.53.

[1] This premium does not extend to work on other property belonging to the landlord; nor does it apply when the tenant does work under an obligation outside the lease.

Commutation of rent or surrender of lease

9: 22   TA 1988, s. 34(4) treats as a premium any sums which become payable by the tenant in lieu of rent *or* as consideration for the surrender of the lease but only if these sums are payable under the terms of the lease. A payment in lieu of rent is attributed to the period covered by the payment. So if there is a ten year lease under which the tenant is to pay rent of £700 p.a. but with the right at any time after the first year to pay £5,000 and a rent of only £200 p.a. and the right is exercised, the £5,000 would be treated as a premium.

In calculating the charge to tax on sums in lieu of rent the duration of the lease is the period for which the payment is being made. Thus, if the right in the previous example is exercised when there are eight years left, the calculations assume an eight year lease.

Butterworths Income Tax Service F1.54.

Variations and waivers

9: 23   A sum payable by a tenant on the surrender of a lease, where that sum is not stipulated in the original lease, will not fall within TA 1988, s. 34(4)[1] but may come within s. 34(5) which catches payments payable by the tenant as consideration for the variation or waiver of any terms of the lease. A waiver means the abandonment of a right in such a way that the other party is entitled to plead the abandonment by way of confession and avoidance if the right is later asserted. It is not confined to total abandonment of the right. So when a tenant's option to renew a lease had lapsed, a sum paid to the landlord for the reinstatement of the option was a payment for the variation or waiver of a term of the lease,[2] whether such sums were stipulated in the lease or not. Payments within this section are treated as becoming due when the contract of variation is entered into[3] and not, as under s. 34(4), when it becomes payable by the tenant.[4] Further, payments within s. 34(5) if paid to someone other than the landlord are only chargeable if paid to a person connected with the landlord, there being no such restriction for payments within s. 34(4).[5] Pre-1963 leases are also caught.[6]

Simon's Taxes A4.204–206; Butterworths Income Tax Service F1.55.
   [1] Nor does it catch payments due on expiration of the term of forfeiture. *Quaere* a clause which allows the tenant to break the lease on payment.
   [2] *Banning v Wright* [1972] 2 All ER 987, 48 TC 421, HL where the option lapsed owing to a breach of covenant by the lessee.
   [3] TA 1988, s. 34(5)(*b*).
   [4] TA 1988, s. 34(4)(*b*).
   [5] TA 1988, s. 34(7).
   [6] TA 1988, s. 39(2).

9: 24   *Assignment of a lease granted at an undervalue.* Although in general payments by an assignee of the lease to the assignor escape tax, this will not be so if the lease was granted to the assignor or some predecessor in title at an undervalue.[1] If A grants a lease to B at a rent plus a premium, the provisions already discussed will charge the premium to income tax. If A grants the lease to X who assigns it to B and X is obliged to pay A money for the privilege of assignment, the sum will be taxed to A under TA 1988, s. 34(4) or (5). If X is not obliged to pay A money for the privilege, the economic benefit may still accrue to A if, for example, X is a connected person or a family company. It is therefore provided in s. 35 that (i) if the original[2] grant of the lease was at an undervalue so that a sum could have been charged by way of premium—"the amount foregone"—then that sum shall be computed and, (ii) if the lessee subsequently assigns the lease, then any consideration payable on the assignment can be taxed to X the assignor under Schedule D, Case VI, as if it had been a premium[3] under the lease, but only to the extent of the amount forgone.[4] This rule cannot be avoided by X assigning to Y without permission who then assigns to B at a premium, since TA 1988, s. 35 applies to *any* assignment of the lease. So Y would be liable to tax under Schedule D, Case VI on the excess of the premium paid to him by B over any premium paid by him to X. This process continues until the amount that has been rendered chargeable equals the amount forgone.

The amount chargeable is that before the percentage reduction; the reduction is calculated by reference to the initial duration of the lease and so remains constant.

EXAMPLE

In 1979 A granted B a lease for 26 years at a premium of £1,000 and a peppercorn rent; the lease is worth £80,000. A is chargeable under Schedule A on £1,000 less 50% = £500.

In 1981 B assigned the lease to C for £10,000. B is chargeable under Schedule D, Case VI on £10,000 less £1,000 already charged, less 50% = £4,500.

In 1983 C assigns the lease to D for £9,000. C is not chargeable as the premium he receives is less than the one he paid.

In 1985 D assigns the lease to E for £200,000, its current market value. D is chargeable on £80,000 original value less £1,000 charged to A and £9,000 charged to B, less 50% = £35,000.

It will be seen that the charge is on the assignor, not the grantor, but that it applies whenever the original grant was at an undervalue and that it is not confined to situations where the lessee is a person connected with the grantor. The section applies when the sum is payable to a person other than the assignor although the charge will still fall on the assignor.

Simon's Taxes A4.209; Butterworths Income Tax Service F1.58.

[1] Nor if he takes a short lease back: TA 1988, s. 34; there may be a IHT liability if the assignment takes place before 18th March 1986.

[2] And only the original grant. If the original grant was for full value the fact that a subsequent assignment was not for full value does not create a potential charge under TA 1988, s. 35.

[3] The fractional reduction and top slicing rules apply.

[4] Any excess may be liable to CGT.

9: 25 *Sale with right of reconveyance.* Despite TA 1988, ss. 34 and 35 it would still be possible to exact the equivalent of a premium from a "tenant" by the device of conveying to him not a lease but the entire interest of the vendor and reserving to the vendor a right to reacquire the property at some future date. Thus instead of giving B a seven year lease for £4,000, A might convey the land to B for £6,000 and reserve a right to buy it back from B for £2,000 after seven years. Section 36 is designed to cure this. It applies when the terms subject to which an estate or interest is sold provide that it shall be or may be required to be reconveyed to the grantor or to a person connected with him.[1] The amount by which the sale price exceeds the repurchase price is charged to the vendor—not the connected person—under Schedule D, Case VI, the amount being assessed at the time of the sale and not of the repurchase. The sum so charged is not described as a premium, but the fractional reduction for the length of the "lease" will apply and thus reduces the amount chargeable by $\frac{1}{50}$ for each complete year after the first between the sale and the reconveyance.[2] If the sale does not fix the date of the reconveyance but does fix the price, it is assumed that the reconveyance will occur at the earliest possible date.[3] If the sale does not fix the date of the reconveyance and the price varies with the date, the sum to be taxed is computed on the assumption that the price on reconveyance shall be the lowest obtainable.[4]

Should the terms of the sale provide that the purchaser is to lease the property back to the vendor, rather than reconvey it, a notional premium may arise. If the lease is later, then the grant of the lease back is treated as a conveyance of the property at a price equivalent to the sum of the amount of the premium (if any) for the lease back and the value at the date of the sale of the right to receive a conveyance of the reversion immediately after the lease begins to run. Thus one deducts from the original sale price not only the value of the reversion on the lease but also any premium paid.[5]

No notional premium arises if the lease is granted and begins to run within one month after the sale, a provision to protect the normal commercial transaction of the lease and lease back.

Simon's Taxes A4.210; Butterworths Income Tax Service F1.59.
[1] Defined in TA 1988, s. 839.
[2] TA 1988, s. 36(1). This provision causes difficulty in the common case where a landowner sells mineral rights but with an option to buy back at the land's agricultural value.
[3] TA 1988, s. 36(1).
[4] TA 1988, s. 36(2)(*a*).
[5] TA 1988, s. 36(3).

Franking the premium on a sublease

9: 26   If a charge to tax has arisen on a payment within TA 1988, ss. 34 or 35 but not 36, that payment can be used to frank in whole or in part a similar charge arising from a dealing with the interest granted. This is designed to prevent a double charge to tax. Thus if A grants a lease for 46 years to X, and X pays a premium of say £10,000 that premium will be caught for tax by s. 34(1), the amount chargeable being £1,000. If X assigns the lease to Y, normally[1] no charge will arise, but if X grants Y a sublease for, say, nine years and exacts a premium of, say, £1,200, he is liable to be taxed on £1,008 under s. 34(1). Relief is given for the sublease premium.[2] The amount chargeable on the grant by A to X, £1,000, is called "the amount chargeable on the superior interest" and the amount chargeable on the grant by X to Y, £1,008, is referred to as "the later chargeable amount". The amount charged to X on the grant of the sublease is the excess if any of "the later chargeable amount" over the appropriate fraction of the amount chargeable on the superior interest.[3] The numerator of the appropriate fraction is the period in respect of which the later chargeable amount arose (nine years) and the denominator is the period in respect of which the earlier amount arose (46 years)[4] so that the fraction will be $\frac{9}{46}$ of £1,000 = £196. The excess of the later chargeable amount is therefore £1,008 − 196 = £812 and X's chargeable amount is reduced to £812.

If the second sum, that payable by Y to X, is payable by instalments X's relief will be to treat those instalments as rent.

The purpose of the relief is presumably to avoid a double charge to tax and preserve the tax neutrality between an assignment of a lease and the grant of a sub-lease. Thus the longer the sublease the greater the appropriate fraction of the first sum chargeable that can be set off against the new charge.

This procedure is no longer available for sums charged under s. 36. Schemes were entered into specifically so as to create large sums deductible under ss. 37 or 87. An interest in land would be sold off with a provision for reconveyance at a reduced price. Now where a vendor is assessed under s. 36 on the notional extra rent, the purchaser can no longer set that off against any tax he has to pay on the grant of a sublease (s. 37)—nor may he deduct the notional rent under s. 87.

Simon's Taxes A4.320.
[1] See TA 1988, s. 35 (lease at undervalue), supra, § **9: 24**.
[2] TA 1988, s. 37(2).
[3] TA 1988, s. 37(5).
[4] TA 1988, s. 37(7).

Set off of premium against rent

9: 27 If a tenant grants a sublease he is taxable in respect of the rent received under that sublease but may deduct the rent he himself pays under his lease. If he paid a premium charged under TA 1988, ss. 34 or 35 but not s. 36—he is allowed to deduct a part of that from the rent derived from the sublease.[1]

> EXAMPLE
> If A grants B a lease for 25 years paying a premium of £10,000 and B sublets to C for £600 a year, B is allowed to deduct from his receipts the sum of $1/25 \times £10,000 \times (50-24)/50$ = 5,200/25 or £208 plus any rent paid to A. The set-off is thus limited to that part which is taxable in A's hands. If B assigns the lease to X, X may also use the £208 each year. Where the sub-lease is also at a premium, B may deduct the taxable element of the premium paid to A from the taxable element of the premium which he receives from C. Where the sublease is at a premium and a rent, the part of the premium paid to A is set off against the taxable element of the premium in priority to the rent.

Simon's Taxes A4.320; Butterworths Income Tax Service F1.61.
[1] TA 1988, s. 37(4).

Interaction with Schedule D Case I

9: 28 (1) Where the tenant can deduct the rent paid in computing the profits of his business, whether because the lease is of business premises or is trading stock, he may deduct the proportion of any premium charged under TA 1988, ss. 34 or 35.[1] That proportion is spread over the duration of the lease.

(2) Rental income accruing to a dealer in land ought to be charged under Schedule A but if small in relation to other income, is treated as part of the computation under Schedule D, Case I.[2]

(3) Where a dealer in land receives a payment which is taxable as a premium under s. 34(1), (4) or (5) or s. 35 or s. 36 and a part is chargeable under those sections,[3] that part is so charged and only the excess is treated as trading income. Where an individual trades in land therefore he will be entitled to top slicing relief to the extent of the fractionally reduced sum, but is taxable in full on the amount of the reduction.

---

[1] TA 1988, s. 87.
[2] Law Commission 1971, Cmnd. 4654 § 69.
[3] TA 1988, s. 99(2) and (3). But note the qualification on s. 36(2)(b) in s. 99(3).

SCHEDULE B

Woodlands occupied on a commercial basis

9: 29   Schedule B[1] is abolished as from 6 April 1988.[2] This was a charge on the value of land used for commercial forestry; this value worked out at about 15p per acre. The basis was applied throughout the occupation of the land by the taxpayer.

The tax advantage of this Schedule lay in the interaction with Schedule D, Case I. A person could elect to be taxed under Schedule D, Case I in the early years when outgoings were high, so creating a trading loss, and then switch to Schedule B as the trees—and thinnings—became valuable. There was no formal right to elect, indeed the election for Schedule D, Case I was stated to be irrevocable, but as this lasted only while the same person was in occupation it was possible to change the occupier, e.g. by gift or by a transfer to a company, and so bring about the right to change to Schedule B.

The 1988 reforms also abolish the right to elect for Schedule D, Case I treatment;[3] there are corresponding changes to abolish the right to deduct interest on loans to acquire interests in businesses or companies with interests in commercial woodlands.[4]

The 1988 reforms allow certain people to continue to be taxed under Schedule D, Case I and so set their expenses against general income as a trading loss until 5 April 1993.[5] These people must be in occupation of commercial woodlands on 15th March 1988, whether or not they had yet elected to be taxed under Schedule D, Case I, or became occupiers as a result of commitments entered into before 15th March 1988; the commitments must be evidenced in writing.[6] Those who had applied for a grant under the Forestry Commission scheme in force on 15th March 1988 and whose application had been received by the Commission before 15th March 1988 also qualify[7] unless the grant is made under the new scheme.[8] If such a person disposes of the interest in the woodland before 1993 the successor may not take the benefit of the Schedule D basis[9] unless the succession is on death.[10] Where a person has validly elected for DI treatment but receives a grant under the new scheme during the period, the DI treatment will not be available in the following period.[11] For the period in which the grant is made only those expenses not covered by the grant will be allowed under DI.[12] It will be possible to divide timber holdings by sector for this purpose.[13]

The transitional rules will extend to capital expenditure, but there will be no balancing charge at 5 April 1993.[14] The costs of clearing damage caused by the 1987 storms will be allowed as will those of consequent replanting unless paid out under the new and more generous grant scheme.[15]

A typical timber area will take 57 years from acquisition to felling. During the early years there will be costs, apart from those of actual acquisition, in preparation of the ground, fencing, draining planting and around the halfway point the construction of a road for harvesting. Income will accrue through thinning but the big return comes on felling.

Simon's Taxes A5.103; Butterworths Income Tax Service F2.01–F2.04.
[1] TA 1988, s. 91.
[2] FA 1988, s. 63 and Sch. 6, para. 2; a company's accounting period which straddles this date is split to achieve this end.
[3] FA 1988, Sch. 6, para. 3.
[4] FA 1988, Sch. 6, para. 3(3)–(5).
[5] FA 1988, Sch. 6, para. 4(7).
[6] FA 1988, Sch. 6, para. 4(2).
[7] FA 1988, Sch. 6, para. 4(3).
[8] FA 1988, Sch. 6, para. 4—the new scheme was first published after 15th March 1988 and is more generous—to compensate for the withdrawal of the tax advantages!
[9] FA 1988, Sch. 6, para. 4(4)(*b*).
[10] FA 1988, Sch. 6, para. 4(1)(*b*), including, presumably one who acquires the property under a variation or disclaimer falling under IHTA 1984, s. 142.
[11] FA 1988, Sch. 6, para. 4(5).
[12] FA 1988, Sch. 6, para. 5.
[13] FA 1988, Sch. 6, para. 4(6).
[14] FA 1988, Sch. 6, para. 6(1).
[15] Inland Revenue Press Release 15th March 1988; *Simon's Tax Intelligence* 1988, p. 195, para. 9.

Income outside Schedule B

9: 30   The 1988 rules[1] exclude from tax the occupier's liability in respect of the value of his occupation of the woodlands. Profits arising otherwise may be taxable under some other Schedule. Thus if the occupier grants a lease of shooting rights[2] the rent payable will fall within Schedule A. Again if the occupier cuts the timber and turns the timber into furniture, profits from the trade of making furniture will be caught by Schedule D, Case I.[3] In *Collins v Fraser*[4] it was held that the payment under Schedule B extended so long as all that was done to the timber was done in order to make the produce of the soil marketable in some shape or form. This may well, in usual circumstances, go as far as turning the timber into planks. At that point trade would take over and the timber would be entered into the accounts of the trade at the then market value, thus ensuring that all "profits" up to that time would be outside the charge to income tax. Profits derived after that point from the making of crates were held taxable.

Simon's Taxes A5.105; Butterworths Income Tax Service F2.06.
[1] For history, see **Simon's Taxes A5.101** and Scott LJ in *Bamford v Osborne* [1940] 1 All ER 91 at 94, 23 TC 642 at 651.

[2] Schedule A, supra, § **9: 01**, although liability will be limited to the excess of Schedule A profit over 1/3 annual value: TA 1988, s. 15(3).

[3] *IRC v Williamson Bros* (1949) 31 TC 370 at 377.

[4] [1969] 3 All ER 524, 46 TC 143 (Megarry J). Similar problems arose over the extent of farming when that fell within Schedule B, see e.g. *Back v Daniels* [1925] 1 KB 526, 9 TC 183 (a cheese factory would be outside Schedule B, per Scrutton LJ at 203), *Long v Belfield Poultry Products Ltd* (1937) 21 TC 221 (profits from hatching out eggs not arising as profits from the occupation of land so outside Schedule B).

The occupier

9: 31   The question whether a person has the use of lands and so is an occupier is one of fact. Thus one who occupies land at the discretion of the owner may be an occupier[1] although this permission must extend to allowing him to cut the timber if he is to be said to be managing the woodlands.[2]

In *Russell v Hird*[3] the court stated that regard must be had both to legal rights and to what was done; a licensee with a right to enter the land and fell timber for four years was held to be the permanent occupier as against the owner.

This has now been reversed for any use commencing after 13th March 1984. A person who has the use of woodlands wholly or mainly for the purpose of felling, processing or removing timber or clearing (or otherwise preparing the land) for replanting is not to be treated as an occupier.[4]

Simon's Taxes A5.201; Butterworths Income Tax Service F2.03.

[1] *Lord Tollemache v IRC* (1926) 11 TC 277. Two persons may be occupiers for Schedule B— *Back v Daniels* [1925] 1 KB 526, 9 TC 183.

[2] *IRC v Anderson* 1922 SC 284, 8 TC 279, TA 1970, s. 67(3).

[3] [1983] STC 541.

[4] TA 1988, s. 16(5).

SCHEDULE C

9: 32   Tax is charged under Schedule C on certain dividends—usually interest—payable out of any public revenue,[1] whether of the UK or another state. The charge is on a current year basis and tax is deducted at source. The justification for having these payments treated in their own Schedule is primarily one of administrative machinery.[2] The Treasury may direct that certain securities, all of which are UK government securities, shall be taxed under Schedule D, Case III, and not Schedule C;[3] such payments are made without deduction of tax. The Treasury may also direct that the income shall not be liable to UK tax if beneficially owned by someone not ordinarily resident in the UK;[4] where stock is held by trustees it is the ordinary residence of the beneficiary that governs.[5]

When gilt edged stock is bought through the Post Office, tax is charged under Schedule D, Case III. This is because the stock is held by the National Debt Commissioners; interest on such stock is paid gross since Schedule C does not apply.[6]

Dividends paid after 25th July 1986 (the passing of FA 1986) and which are out of any public revenue other than UK public revenue are excluded from Schedule C if the securities are held "in a recognised clearing system";[7] recognition is the same as for Eurobond interest[8] but there is now no need to clear Eurobonds.[9] Collecting agents must now deduct tax on coupons if the securities are held in any recognised clearing system (whether in the UK or not), or the payment is not made by a UK paying agent.[10]

Simon's Taxes A6; Butterworths Income Tax Service F3.
[1] Defined TA 1988, s. 45. The provisions of Schedule C are extended to funding bonds of foreign governments, public authorities and institutions by TA 1988, s. 582.
[2] Basic rate tax is collected by—and from—the person entrusted with payment or the person realising the coupon if payment is made against such a coupon. See TA 1988, Sch. 3.
[3] TA 1988, ss. 17(1), paras. 5 and 50 (small payments are made gross).
[4] TA 1988, s. 47; see also s. 48 on foreign government stock for a similar, but not identical, exemption. An indirect charge could not be raised by treating them as trading receipts. *Hughes v Bank of New Zealand Ltd* [1938] 1 All ER 778, 21 TC 472, decided under what is now TA 1988, s. 123(4). This case further held that the non-resident could deduct the cost of obtaining the capital invested in this way but by FA 1940, s. 60(1) the Treasury were given power to issue securities on conditions which undid this aspect of the decision—see 84th Report of Commissioners of Inland Revenue 1945–46 Cmd. 6770, § 24.
[5] TA 1988, s. 47(3).
[6] TA 1988, s. 49.
[7] TA 1988, s. 48(4).
[8] TA 1988, s. 124, infra, § **25: 16**.
[9] FA 1988, s. 76(4), (5).
[10] FA 1988, s. 76.

SCHEDULE D, CASE III

9: 33   Tax is levied under Case III by TA 1988, s. 18[1] on

   (*a*) interest on money, whether yearly or otherwise, or any annuity or other annual payment falling outside TA 1988, s. 347A or 347B whether such payment is payable within or outside the UK, either as a charge on property of the person paying the same by virtue of any deed or will or otherwise, or as a reservation out of it, or as a personal debt or obligation by virtue of any contract, or whether the same is received and payable half yearly or at any shorter or more distant periods but not including any payment chargeable under Schedule A;

   (*b*) discounts, except, thanks to TA 1988, s. 126, Treasury Bills, relevant deep discount securities and deep gain securities (which are taxed in a special way);

   (*c*) income, except income charged under Schedule C, from securities bearing interest payable out of public revenue, unless charged under Schedule C.

   No deductions can be made.[2]

   The recipient of these income payments thus becomes liable to income tax which will generally be by direct assessment under Case III. However if the payment is an annuity or other annual payment, basic rate income tax is not directly assessed on the recipient but is deducted by the person making the payment, the scheme being regulated by TA 1988, ss. 348 and 349, infra, § **9: 82**.

   The scope of Schedule D, Case III has been substantially reduced by FA

1988 which introduced TA 1988, ss. 347A and 347B. The effect of these provisions is to make a radical change to an integral part of this scheme. Under the previous law, which remains in force for existing arrangements, an integral part of this scheme was that annuities and annual payments were in effect deductible in computing the total income of the payer by being treated as a charge on income; this allowed assignments of income by deed of covenant. The reasons that this was allowed were largely historical. Income could be assigned to charity or a mistress although special rules prevent such assignment to one's infant child, infra, § **13: 32** or lawful spouse supra, § **3: 09**, and generally confined the effect of such assignments to basic rate income tax infra, § **13: 46**. The device has been defended not least on the ground that it enabled gifts to be made by those without capital; it was the income-earner's sole tax planning device to assist him to support his widowed mother. The scale of these covenants, particularly those by grandparents for grandchildren's school fees and by parents to support their adult children at university or polytechnic grew greatly[3]; such covenants are examples of tax mitigation rather than avoidance.[4].

Under the 1988 reforms there is, in general, no right of deduction for non-charitable covenants made by individuals on or after 15th March 1988.[5] It follows that there is no deduction for new covenants in favour of a mistress or, under the system of independent taxation to begin in 1990, of one's spouse.[6] Similarly, new covenants in favour of students or by grandparents in favour of grandchildren will be of no effect. At the same time there have been major reforms for the tax rules for maintenance payments which have the effect of greatly reducing the tax subsidies granted to divorced or separated spouses.

To compensate for the removal of the right to deduct these payments, the payments, although previously being income under Schedule D, Case III, will no longer be so if the deed is made after 14th March 1988. This major reform greatly reduces the importance of Schedule D, Case III in the personal sector. However, the concepts and, regrettably, the machinery in TA 1988, s. 348 remain of importance where either (*a*) the payment is of a type specifically excluded from the new scheme or (*b*) the payer is a person other than an individual (so again the new rules do not apply), or (*c*) the payment is made under an existing obligation.

The reform package, while immensely important, does little to reduce the conceptual junkheap of the tax system.

Simon's Taxes B5.102; Butterworths Income Tax Service F4.01.
[1] Other provisions cause income to be taxed under Case III—e.g. TA 1988, ss. 119 and 554. For list see **Simon's Taxes B5.103**.
[2] See TA 1988, s. 64 and *Soul v Caillebotte* (1964) 43 TC 657.
[3] See Revenue leaflet IR74.
[4] Lord Templeman in *IRC v Challenge Corpn Ltd* [1986] STC 548 at 554f.
[5] FA 1988, s. 36(3)—this section applies to any payment falling due on or after 15th March 1988 unless in pursuance of an existing obligation.
[6] A matter reinforced by FA 1988, Sch. 3, para. 32.

9: 34   To give effect to the new regime FA 1988 introduces two new provisions—TA 1988, s. 347A and s. 347B. Section 347A provides that an annual payment which would otherwise be within Schedule D, Case III and which is not specifically excluded is to be neither deductible as an allowable charge on the income of the payer *nor taxable income of the payee*. The specific exclusions are (i) a payment of interest; (ii) a covenanted payment to charity;[1] (iii) a payment made for bona fide commercial reasons in connection with the individual's trade, profession or vocation e.g., partnership retirement annuities;[2] and (iv) a payment within TA 1988, s. 125(1); infra, § **13: 47**. Also outside the new regime are all those payments which come within Schedule D, Case III but which are made not by individuals but by other entities, i.e. companies (which have their own rules as to deduction of basic rate income tax and deductibility for corporation tax) and trusts.[3]

Section 347B provides a new regime for "qualifying maintenance payments", the effect of which is that the payments are not deductible by the payer nor are they chargeable income of the payee. Qualifying maintenance payments differ from the payments dealt with by s. 347A in two ways—they may give rise to a special deduction for the payer and they have their own special transitional rules. See further § **9: 96** et seq.

---

[1] ICAEW Memorandum (TR 738) *Simon's Tax Intelligence* 1989, p. 78.
[2] As defined by TA 1988, s. 660(3) and therefore excluding payments made for consideration in money or money's worth; see [1988] BTR, p. 231.
[3] On Scottish partnerships, see TA 1988, s. 347(6).

Transitional rules

9: 35   TA 1988 applies only as from the beginning of the tax year 1988–89. The new regime applies to any payment falling due after 14th March 1988 unless it is made in pursuance of an existing obligation.[1]

Two questions arise. The first is—when is a payment made "under an existing obligation"? This is defined as a binding obligation of any of four sorts. One is an obligation under a court order made[2] before 15th March 1988 or before the end of June 1988 on an application made on or before 15th March 1988. Another is an obligation under a deed or written agreement[2] executed or made before 15th March 1988 and received by the inspector before the end of June 1988. The third is an oral agreement made and communicated to the inspector on the same time scale. The last is a court order or written agreement[3] which replaces, varies or supplements one of the first three. If an agreement made, say, in 1986 was varied in 1988–89 (e.g., by court order) some subtle points have been taken by the Revenue. Thus, if the variation includes a child as a payee for the first time, this is treated as a new arrangement, not the variation of an existing one. However, if the child is deleted and the payments to the wife increased, this is simply a variation.

The second question is—what happens to an existing obligation? The answer is that ss. 347A and 347B do not apply to such payments. Therefore, tax at basic rate will still be deducted at source under TA 1988, ss. 348 and 349 and the payer will still be entitled to a deduction under TA 1988, s. 835 subject to the rules in Chapter 13. Payments outside s. 347B, which carries its own special rules for qualifying maintenance payments, but which are under ss. 348 or 349 will remain deductible each year in this way to so long as they continue to be made "under an existing obligation". If therefore the covenant is to pay a sum determined by a formula, and the effect of the formula is to cause the level of payment to rise, there is no reason why the payer should not claim a deduction for the increased payment. This is in marked contrast with the position for maintenance payments, infra, § **9: 93**.

[1] FA 1988, s. 36(3). Payments between 14th March 1988 and 6th April 1988 are governed by FA 1988, s. 36(2).
[2] An order is made when it is entered into the records of the court.
[3] It will be seen that an oral agreement is not sufficient.

Basis of assessment

9: 36   The traditional basis of assessment prescribed by TA 1988, s. 64, is that the taxpayer is assessed on the amount of income arising in the preceding year. However, this is subject to many exceptions. A current year basis is applied to maintenance payments under existing obligations from 1989–90,[1] interest on composite rate deposits and building society interest.[2] Where tax is deducted at basic rate under TA 1988, ss. 348 and 349 and the taxpayer is liable to pay at a higher rate, both basic and higher rate tax are assessed on a current year basis.[3]

Simon's Taxes E1.221–E1.231; Butterworths Income Tax Service F4.02.
[1] FA 1988, s. 38(2)(*b*); this is a change of form not substance. Previously, such payments come within ss. 348, 349 and 835, and are therefore taxed on a current year basis.
[2] TA 1988, ss. 351(4), 476 and 479.
[3] TA 1988, s. 835(6)(*a*).

Opening years, TA 1988, s. 66.

9: 37   Tax for the year in which the income first arises is charged on the income of that year. Tax for the second year is charged on the income of that second year. Tax for the third year is then charged on the amount of income that arose in the second, the switch from current to preceding year being thus accomplished.[1]

These simple rules are however subject to two exceptions. First, where the income first arises on 6th April, the first day of the year of assessment, the switch to the preceding year basis will be made in the second and not the third year, the reasoning being that the switch occurs as soon as there has been one full year's income. Secondly the taxpayer may elect to postpone the switch to the preceding year basis by one year.[2] If the income in the third year is lower than that in the second, it will be advantageous to elect to be taxed for that year on an arising basis.

Butterworths Income Tax Service F4.03.
[1] TA 1988, s. 66(1)(*a*) and (*b*).
[2] TA 1988, s. 66(1)(*c*).

Closing years, TA 1988, s. 67.

9: 38   When a person ceases to possess the source of income, tax for that year is charged on a current year basis.[1] Tax for the penultimate year will have been charged on a preceding year basis but tax for that year is to be reassessed on a current year basis if that would give a higher figure.

These rules can be used to advantage. Thus if the amount of interest in the second and third years is higher than that in the fourth, one can effect an artificial discontinuance, i.e. close the account and reopen it one week later in the fifth year. This will mean that the tax for the fourth year will be based on an arising basis instead of the preceding year basis. Such devices reflect little credit on the system. The scope for such devices has been greatly reduced by the composite rate rules for interest from deposits introduced by FA 1984.

EXAMPLE

	Actual income	Taxable income on normal rules (s. 67)	Taxable income with cessation in year 4
Year 1	300	300	300
Year 2	400	400	400
Year 3	500	400	500
Year 4	100	500	100

These terminal provisions apply where the person ceases to possess the source. If he ceases to possess that source but during the last two years of his possession no income arose therefrom, he may have his income assessed as if he ceased to possess the source when it ceased to produce income.[2] A similar rule applies when although the taxpayer has not ceased to possess the source it has produced no income for six years.[3] No assessment can be made for a year subsequent to that in which he ceases to possess the source.[4]

If a person dies there is a mandatory cessation. However, his personal representatives may claim the benefit of any of the rules in this section even though they retain the source.[5]

Where a deposit comes within the composite rate scheme there is a deemed cessation.[6]

---

[1] TA 1988, s. 67(1) see *Cull v Cowcher* (1934) 18 TC 449.
[2] TA 1988, s. 67(1)(*c*).
[3] TA 1988, s. 67(3).
[4] *Brown v National Provident Institution* [1919] 2 KB 497, 8 TC 57.
[5] TA 1988, s. 67(5).
[6] TA 1988, s. 480.

When does income arise?

9: 39 The commencement rules apply when income "first arises" from a source.[1] Generally income arises not when it is due but only when it is received or enures for a person's benefit.[2] For this purpose it has been held that payment by cheque is not income when the cheque is received but, probably, only when the proceeds of the cheque are received whether as cash or being credited to the account of the payee.[3]

The question when a payment enures to the advantage of a taxpayer has been explored in cases concerning guarantees. In *Dunmore v McGowan*[4] the taxpayer had money in a bank account. The bank credited his account with interest on that account but, in accordance with an agreement with the bank, that sum (and the balance of the account) was not to be withdrawn while the taxpayer was under a liability to the bank in respect of a guarantee. The Court of Appeal held that the interest income was taxable to the taxpayer as it arose each year. This case, which at first sight seems to be wrong in that a promise by a debtor to pay is not usually regarded as a receipt of income, can be justified on the basis that it was not a case of non-receipt by the taxpayer but of positive appropriation by him under the agreement (supra, § **2: 12**). The court rejected an argument that the arrangement amounted to a trust since there was no evidence to support it. Had a trust been established the income could not be said to have accrued to the taxpayer even though he would gain some incidental advantage from it. This was followed in *Peracha v Miley*[5] where interest was credited to the taxpayer but retained by the bank as security under a guarantee. This decision was reached even though it was highly unlikely that the taxpayer would ever see any of his interest.

Dunmore v McGowan was distinguished in *Macpherson v Bond.*[6] Here the taxpayer had charged money in a bank account to a bank to secure the debts of a third party. Vinelott J held that on the facts the crediting of the money to the taxpayer's account did not reduce any personal liability on the part of the taxpayer to the bank under a guarantee to the bank because no guarantee had been given. This case was distinguished in *Peracha v Miley* because in the later case there was on the facts a reduction in the amount of the taxpayer's personal liability.

If a taxpayer possesses a source which produces no income in its first or second year then no income arises and the charge will only commence when income begins to flow so that TA 1988, s. 66 applies to year 3. Likewise if the taxpayer acquires an interest bearing source in January 1988 but interest is not credited until July 1987 the first year for s. 66 is 1988–89. However once income begins to flow the fact that for one reason or another it is not taxable does not alter the fact that income has arisen.[7] The cherished doctrine that income due in year 1 but paid in year 2, is income of year 2, is to receive a further statutory qualification. Maintenance payments under existing obligations which are due in year 1 are to be taxed as income of year 1 as from 1989–90.[8]

If the taxpayer acquires a new source of income, the commencement provisions apply to the income from that source.[9] Thus the purchase of a block of debentures, the opening of an interest bearing deposit account with a bank and the acquisition of a life interest under a settlement[10] would be three distinct sources of income. In *Hart v Sangster,*[11] the taxpayer had a bank deposit account and then added money to that account. It was held that each addition was a separate source, to which the commencement provisions applied. The source was the deposit of the money on terms agreed between the banker and the depositor, i.e. each deposit was therefore a separate source. In *Hart v Sangster* the account formerly held £20,496 and the addition came to £2m. However the principle applies to all additions to existing accounts. In practice no adjustment is made unless the annual deposits or withdrawals fluctuate considerably. Once the source is ascertained additional income from that source is not an addition to the source.

In *Inchyra v Jennings*[12] a will created two rights in favour of one beneficiary, namely an annuity and a vested interest in remainder. Pennycuick J held that the source was the will and not each clause of the will so that there was only one source. Pennycuick J further observed that even if this were not so, it would appear that both sources would be acquired when the testator died.[13] However the strict words of s. 66 concerning Case III require that the commencement provisions only apply when income "arises" from the source, a phrase which suggests that those provisions should apply only when the interest vests in possession.

Since these provisions apply only where a direct assessment is made on the recipient under Case III and not when payment is made under deduction of tax, it is provided that where interest is payable on a debt under deduction of tax but the tax ceases to be deductible, a charge is levied under Case III as if the debt were a new source.[14] A converse provision prescribes the cessation rules when the tax becomes deductible.[15]

Simon's Taxes E1.225; Butterworths Income Tax Service F4.11–F4.13.

[1] TA 1988, s. 66(1). This provision does not contain the words "from a source" but these words are found in subs. (3) and are inherent in the nature of income.

[2] *Dunmore v McGowan* [1978] STC 217, [1978] 2 All ER 85; see also *Whitworth Park Coal Co Ltd v IRC* [1959] 3 All ER 703.

[3] *Parkside Leasing Ltd v Smith* [1985] STC 63 (at 69d; if the crediting is conditional one assumes that income is not received until the crediting has become unconditional).

[4] [1978] STC 217, [1978] 2 All ER 85.

[5] [1989] STC 76.

[6] [1985] STC 678.

[7] *Fry v Burma Corpn Ltd* [1930] AC 321, 15 TC 113 a decision on Case V, infra, § **34: 06**.

[8] FA 1988, s. 38(2): this is largely a change of form not substance; one area which may be changed in substance is discussed at § **9: 84**, infra. See also TA 1988, s. 4(2).

[9] TA 1988, s. 66(3).

[10] *Inchyra v Jennings*, infra.

[11] [1957] 2 All ER 208, 37 TC 231; on *when* interest is paid see *Momm v Barclays Bank International Ltd* [1976] 3 All ER 588.

[12] *Inchyra v Jennings*, [1965] 2 All ER 714, 42 TC 388.

[13] So *quaere* if the taxpayer had acquired one of the interests by assignment (or devolution).

[14] TA 1988, s. 66(4).

[15] TA 1988, s. 66(2).

Interest

9: 40 There is no statutory definition of interest. In *Bennett v Ogston*, Rowlatt J defined it as "payment by time for the use of money".[1] *Halsbury* defines it as "the return or compensation for the use or retention by one person of a sum of money belonging to, or owed to, another".[2] Thus a payment on a loan may be interest but a dividend on a share is not. The use of the word "interest" is not conclusive; so where the "interest" was due shortly after the loan and exceeded the principal sum, the court had little difficulty in holding that the payment was not interest.[3] The courts have stressed that the payment must be just recompense and so held that an excessive payment could not be interest.[4]

Compensation for delay in payment must be distinguished from compensation for delay in performing some other obligation, and payments by time for the use of money from payments by time for non-performance of obligations—the fact that time is used to measure a payment does not suffice to make the payment interest when there is no principal debt.[5] So, suppose that A buys whisky in bond for £100 and A then gives B an option to buy that whisky at any time within six months for £100 plus "interest" at the rate of 12% per annum from the time A bought the whisky until B exercises the option. If B exercises the option after three months and pays £103 this would be a simple purchase for £103 and not a purchase for £100 plus £3 interest.[6]

It is unclear whether a payment by a guarantor in respect of interest due from the principal debtor is itself interest,[7] but a payment under a contract of indemnity is.[8]

The question whether a payment is interest is relevant to the payee in determining his income and to the payer in determining his claim to a deduction see § **5: 29**. In *Cairns v MacDiarmid* the Court of Appeal used the *Ramsay* principle to disallow a claim for deduction whether or not the payment was technically one of interest under these rules.[9]

Simon's Taxes B5.201–203; Butterworths Income Tax Service F4.21.

[1] (1930) 15 TC 374 at 379.

[2] Halsbury's Laws of England (4th edn), vol. 32, para. 106.

[3] *Ridge Securities Ltd v IRC* [1964] 1 All ER 275, 44 TC 373; cf. *Chevron Petroleum (UK) Ltd v BP Development Ltd* [1981] STC 689.

[4] *Cairns v MacDiarmid* [1982] STC 226 but on appeal Sir John Donaldson MR thought that on the facts the payment might be just; [1983] STC 178.

[5] *Re Euro Hotel (Belgravia) Ltd* [1975] STC 682, [1975] 3 All ER 1075.

[6] Sir Robert Megarry VC in *Chevron Petroleum (UK) Ltd v BP Development Ltd* [1981] STC 689 at 695j.

[7] See *Westminster Bank Executor and Trustee Co (Channel Islands) Ltd v National Bank of Greece SA* (1970) 46 TC 472 at 485 (CA saying it was) but cf. 494 (point left open by HL).

[8] *Re Hawkins, Hawkins v Hawkins* [1972] Ch 714, [1972] 3 All ER 386 (this is different from the question whether the payment is interest "on a loan", a matter of importance for deduction under TA 1988, s. 353, supra, chapter 5.

[9] [1983] STC 178 (*semble* that the payment could be income of the payee but this point was not raised).

9: 41 If A lends B money for a fixed period, A may insist not only on the current general rate of interest but also on some extra payment. He might charge extra interest or he might ask for a larger sum to be paid back than was lent, *viz.* a premium. Alternatively, he might issue promissory notes but sell them for less than their face value—a discount. Where a company issues debentures at less than face value the Revenue have never argued that the difference between the issued price and the price at which the debenture is redeemed is an interest payment.[1] However if a lender offers a loan of £90 without interest on condition that the borrower pays £100 in twelve months, the extra £10 will be interest. Moreover if interest is charged but at an unreasonably low rate and the extra sum is geared to the length of the loan, the courts have held the extra sum to be interest even though the parties called it a premium.[2] This does not breach the "form versus substance" rule since the court is saying that the description given by the parties is not conclusive of its legal form and the test is whether £10 or the extra sum represents payment by time for the use of money.

In *Davies v Premier Investment Co Ltd*[3] a company issued unsecured promissory notes at par without interest but offered to redeem them at a premium of 30% after six years with the alternative of a premium calculated at 5% p.a. should the company redeem the notes or go into voluntary liquidation before six years. The premium was held to be interest though this conclusion might not have been reached had the premium been 30% regardless of when the notes were redeemed.

Where normal commercial rates of interest are charged the question whether any "premium" or discount is taxed as interest is determined according to the following rules laid down in *Lomax v Peter Dixon*:[4]

(*a*) if interest is charged at a rate that would be reasonably commercial on a reasonably sound security there is no presumption that a "discount" or a "premium" is interest,

(*b*) the true nature of the payment is a matter of fact rather than of law,

(*c*) among the factors relevant will be, the contract itself, the term of the loan, the rate of interest expressly stipulated for, the nature of the capital risk, the extent to which, if at all, the parties expressly took or may reasonably be expected to have taken the capital risk into account in fixing the terms of the contract.

In such cases the court is trying to distinguish payment for the use of money from insurance against the risk of loss of capital; one may wonder whether there is a real distinction here. One should also note that in *Lomax* the payments were made by a foreign company and under the foreign law the payments probably were interest (and so deductible under that law).

Simon's Taxes B5.201–203; Butterworths Income Tax Service F4.24.
[1] See per Lord Greene MR in *Lomax v Peter Dixon & Son Ltd* [1943] 2 All ER 255 at 259, 25 TC 353 at 363.
[2] *IRC v Thomas Nelson & Sons Ltd* (1938) 22 TC 175.
[3] *Davies v Premier Investment Co Ltd* [1945] 2 All ER 681, 27 TC 27.
[4] Supra n. 1 at 262 and 367.

Interest and damages

9: 42   The notion that interest is a sort of service charge for the use of money may explain the initial reluctance of the judges to treat as interest for income tax purposes sums awarded by them by way of interest when awarding damages—such sums were treated as extra damages.[1] In *Riches v Westminster Bank Ltd*[2] however this approach was held to be wrong. In that case the taxpayer successfully sued a business partner for his share of the profit on a transaction (£36,255) which the partner had concealed. The judge also awarded him £10,028 as interest at 4% since the original deception, exercising his discretion under the Law Reform (Miscellaneous Provisions) Act 1934, s. 3. It was held by the House of Lords that the £10,028 was interest. As Lord Simon put it, "It is not capital. It is rather the accumulated fruit of a tree which the tree produces regularly until payment."[3]

Simon's Taxes B5.206; Butterworths Income Tax Service F4.25.
[1] E.g. *IRC v Ballantine* (1924) 8 TC 595.
[2] (1947) 28 TC 159, [1947] 1 All ER 469.
[3] (1947) 28 TC 159 at 188, [1947] 1 All ER 469 at 471.

Accrued interest—general position before 1986

9: 43   Interest accrues from day to day even if payable only at intervals and is therefore apportionable in point of time between persons entitled in succession to the principal.[1] However if a person owning a security sells that security with the right to any accrued interest, the price received for the security is just that and cannot be dissected into an element representing the principal and another element representing the unpaid but accrued interest;[2] it follows that the purchaser is liable to tax on the whole of the interest paid.[3] These rules gave rise to the sale of gilts before these stocks go ex-div and the consequent conversion of income into capital gain.

The theoretical analysis devised by the courts was carried further when the courts held that the right to the interest could be sold separately from the securities themselves and the purchase price would be for the sale of a right and not an interest payment even though the date for payment had arrived before the sale.[4] Legislation to counter these decisions in certain tax saving situations is considered in §§ **31:09** et seq.

Simon's Taxes B5.204; Butterworths Income Tax Service F4.26.
  [1] Halsbury's Laws of England (4th edn), vol. 32, para. 106.
  [2] *Wigmore v Thomas Summerson & Sons Ltd* [1926] 1 KB 131, 9 TC 577.
  [3] *Schaffer v Cattermole* [1980] STC 650.
  [4] *IRC v Paget* [1938] 1 All ER 392, 21 TC 677, infra, § **31:09**.

Accrued interest—disposals after 27th February 1986

9:44   The provisions outlined at § **31:09–31:17** were not effective to counter the practice of bond washing. For a long time the Treasury, presumably anxious to do nothing to inhibit the sale of gilts, were content with the large revenue loss that stemmed from the freedom to convert accrued income into capital gain even though the purchaser might be a tax free pension fund and the vendor safe from CGT by reason of the annual exemption or having held the securities for at least 12 months. This changed for disposals after 27th February 1986: presumably the Treasury is now confident about its ability to sell gilts and is therefore more able to proclaim its belief in tax neutrality. The new rules exclude liability under TA 1970, ss. 30 which was later repealed and TA 1988, s. 29; infra, § **31:10** and **31:11**.

In essence the scheme is simple. Where securities are disposed of after 27th February 1986 and the securities carry interest the tax system will treat the interest as accruing from day to day. Therefore on the sale of such securities cum-div the vendor will have to pay tax on the interest that accrues to that date and the purchaser will deduct that amount from the interest payment he receives so that only the interest accruing after the purchase will be charged to tax. When the purchase is made ex div the converse rules apply.

Securities are defined[1] widely and include any loan stock at a fixed or variable rate of interest[2] whether issued by a public body, a company or any other body. There are specific exclusions for ordinary or preference shares, national and war savings certificates, bills of exchange and other bills and certificates of deposit.

On a transfer[3] with accrued interest the transferor is treated as entitled to a sum equal to the "accrued amount" which is a time apportioned part of the later interest payment, although this will be overridden by the actual payment when the transferee accounts separately for the interest and the capital.[4] For the purposes of the time apportionment, the transferor is treated as entitled to interest accruing for the number of days up to and including the date of settlement.[5] An interest period is not to exceed 12 months.[6]

The accrued proportion of the interest on the securities payable for the period is $A \div B$ where A is the number of days in the interest period up to and including settlement day and B is the number of days in the interest period.

EXAMPLE

A security has interest payment dates of 15th January and 15th July. It is quoted ex-div on 28th December and 27th June. The six monthly interest payment is £500.

If X sells the security cum-div in a period ending with settlement day on 15th December he will not actually receive the interest payment due on 15th January, but for tax purposes he is treated as receiving:

$$\frac{153}{184} \times 500 = £415{\cdot}76$$

On a transfer without accrued interest the transferor is treated as entitled to relief on the "rebate amount" and the transferee is treated as entitled to that amount.[7] The rebate amount is calculated in a similar way to the accrued amount but is of course the converse figure.[8]

The figures conform to the words of the legislation but not to Stock Exchange practice; this is to take the number of days from the last interest payment to the date of the settlement date and divide it by 365 (366 in a leap year). This factor is then applied to the year as a whole. It is understood that these figures, which are shown on contract notes, are accepted by the Revenue.

If in the previous example X had sold ex-div with a settlement day on 2nd January he would have received the whole interest payment on 15th January but would be entitled to treat a fraction of it as capital; the fraction would have been $\dfrac{(184-171)}{184}$ which applied to £500 gives a rebate of £35·33.

Where under these rules a person is treated as entitled to a sum, he is treated as receiving that amount by way of income on the last day of the interest period.[9] The charge is under Schedule D, Case VI.[10] An interest period is a period ending with an interest payment day[11] but any period in excess of 12 months is divided so that no period can exceed 12 months;[12] in this way an interest period can end without an interest payment day.

It is central to the scheme that the party not treated as receiving income is granted relief. The relief is set against any sums he is treated as receiving under these rules[13] and is then set against the sums actually received by way of interest during the interest period.[14] Where the interest period does not end with an interest payment day and there is no deemed income under these rules the relief may be rolled forward to the next interest period.[15]

---

[1] TA 1988, ss. 710 and 713.
[2] The term "interest" is defined in TA 1988, s. 711(9).
[3] Defined TA 1988, s. 710(5) as including sale, exchange and gift.
[4] TA 1988, s. 713.
[5] Defined TA 1988, s. 712.
[6] See TA 1988, s. 711(4).
[7] TA 1988, s. 713(3).
[8] TA 1988, s. 713(5).
[9] TA 1988, s. 714(1).

[10] TA 1988, s. 714(2).
[11] TA 1988, s. 711(3).
[12] TA 1988, s. 711(4) the tax treatment is governed by s 711(8).
[13] TA 1988, s. 714(3).
[14] TA 1988, s. 714(5).
[15] TA 1988, s. 714(6).

9: 45   These rules are excluded in a number of situations. Where this occurs there will be no deemed income for the one party. The exceptions are:[1]

(*a*) where the transferor is trading and the transfer is taken into account in computing his profits;

(*b*) where the transferor is an individual[2] and on no day in the year of assessment in which the interest period ends (or the previous year) does the *nominal*[3] value of securities held by him exceed £5,000 (for this rule, when income from the securities is deemed to be the income of another person, the securities are treated as belonging to *both*[4]);

(*c*) a provision similar to (*b*) for estates in administration;

(*d*) a provision similar to (*b*) for a trust for a disabled person;[5]

(*e*) the transferor is not resident in the UK for any part of the chargeable period nor ordinarily resident for that period and is not a non-resident UK trader;[6]

(*f*) the transferor is not ordinarily resident in the UK and he would be entitled to exemption from income tax on any income actually received by virtue of TA 1988, s. 47;[7]

(*g*) the securities were originally issued free of tax for residents abroad;[8]

(*h*) where the transferor is an individual entitled to the remittance[9] basis and any interest in the year of transfer would be taxed on that basis under Schedule D, Case IV or V;

(*i*) stock lending transactions.[10]

The relief provisions are similarly drafted but separate.[11] It follows that the exclusion of the transferor from tax on an accrued amount in respect of a sale cum-div does not in itself deny the transferee relief for that amount.

There are special rules for nominees and trusts,[12] for situations where foreign currency is involved,[13] for delayed remittances,[14] for death[15] (there is a deemed transfer with accrued interest to the personal representatives), for appropriations to and from trading stock,[16] for conversion of securities[17] and for a transfer which carries a right to receive the interest on a payment day falling before the settlement day (such interest is called "unrealised interest")[18] for variable rate securities[19] and for situations in which the interest is in default.[20] There are special provisions dealing with insurance companies,[21] underwriters,[22] charities,[23] retirement schemes[24] and building societies.[25]

Finally, there are rules concerning the effect of these charges on CGT and double taxation relief. On a sale cum div where an accrued amount is treated as a person's income, the disposal consideration is reduced by an equal amount to avoid a dual charge. Similarly, the effect of a relief is to increase the consideration to avoid a double loss.[26] If the accrued income scheme is excluded (e.g. by reason of exemption) there is no adjustment for that party for CGT purposes.

DTR for any foreign tax is given by way of credit if the income falls or would have fallen within Schedule D, Case IV and V. When an actual payment of interest is reduced for tax purposes by a relief under these rules any foreign tax credit may also be reduced.[27] Provision is made for the interaction of the new scheme with TA 1988, s. 739.[28]

---

[1] TA 1988, s. 715. To prevent tax-payers from "washing their hands" before the new rules came into force a special forestalling charge was introduced for the period 28th February 1985 to 27th February 1986; see FA 1985, s. 76 and Sch. 22 and *UK Tax Guide* 1986–87, § **31: 21**.
[2] Husband and wife living together are one person.
[3] Defined TA 1988, s. 710(11) as the value by reference to which the interest is calculated or the original issue price.
[4] TA 1988, s. 710(9).
[5] Defined by reference to CGTA 1979, Sch. 1, para. 5.
[6] Defined by TA 1988, s. 715(5).
[7] TA 1988, s. 715(1)(*f*).
[8] TA 1988, s. 715(1)(*g*).
[9] See infra, § **34: 09** et seq.
[10] TA 1988, ss. 129, 727, 828 and Sch. 29.
[11] TA 1988, s. 715(2).
[12] TA 1988, ss.711(6) and 720. On common investment fund, note TA 1988, s. 382(2)–(4).
[13] E.g. for calculating the amount of interest or the nominal value of TA 1988, s. 713.
[14] TA 1988, s. 723.
[15] TA 1988, s. 721(1)–(4).
[16] TA 1988, ss. 711(6) and 720.
[17] TA 1988, ss. 710(13) and 711(6).
[18] TA 1988, s. 716.
[19] TA 1988, s. 717.
[20] TA 1988, s. 718.
[21] TA 1988, s. 724.
[22] TA 1988, ss. 710(14), 721(5) and (6), 725 and 452(9).
[23] TA 1988, s. 715(1)–(3).
[24] TA 1988, s. 715(1), (2).
[25] TA 1988, s. 726 (FA 1985, Sch. 23, paras. 32A and 32B.
[26] TA 1988, Sch. 29.
[27] TA 1988, s. 807.
[28] TA 1988, s. 742(4)–(7).

Yearly interest

9: 46   It is sometimes necessary to distinguish yearly or annual interest from other interest.[1] Yearly interest, which presumably means the same as annual interest, is not defined in the statutes. The distinction between yearly and short interest depends on the intention of the parties.[2] If a banker makes a loan to a customer to be repaid at the end of three months the interest payable is not annual.[3] If on the other hand a mortgagor executes the usual form of mortgage, under which he becomes liable at law to pay the amount borrowed at the end of six months, the interest payable is nonetheless annual.[4] A technical explanation for this distinction may be that in the bank loan the contract specifies that the repayment of capital with interest is to be on a fixed day and there is no law which, without a new contract by the parties, says that interest is payable thereafter as a matter of right.[5] A simpler explanation is commercial reality. Mortgages are not usually repaid at the end of six months. Both parties envisage that the mortgage may well last longer than twelve months and thus the loan is in the nature of an investment as opposed to a short loan on moneys presently payable but held over.[6]

In determining whether interest is yearly, the courts have regard to substance so that a three month loan does not carry yearly interest merely because the rate is expressed in annual terms.[7] A loan of no fixed term carries yearly interest even though that interest is payable half yearly, quarterly or weekly.[8] Following the same approach, interest may be yearly even though the principal is payable after less than a year[9] or even on demand.[10] Interest may be yearly even though the amount borrowed and the rate of interest both fluctuate.[11] It will also be yearly if the period of the loan is expressed and intended to be one year only.[12]

It is hard to see why, given the above approach, interest awarded on damages should be yearly[13] or why interest payable by a purchaser on an outstanding contract[14] should be yearly, at least in the absence of some positive intention on the part of the vendor to treat the outstanding amount as an investment rather than a nuisance. These are, however, examples of yearly interest.

It therefore appears that interest payable on loans or other sums which are expressed or intended to last twelve months or longer is yearly interest, while interest on loans both expressed and intended to last less than twelve months is not.

Simon's Taxes A3.409; Butterworths Income Tax Service F4.27.

[1] See e.g. TA 1988, ss. 15, 82, 338(3)(a), 349(2).

[2] *Cairns v MacDiarmid* [1983] STC 178 at 181, CA.

[3] *Goslings and Sharpe v Blake* (1889) 23 QBD 324, 2 TC 450.

[4] *Re Craven's Mortgage, Davies v Craven* [1907] 2 Ch 448.

[5] Per Lord Esher in *Goslings and Sharpe v Blake*, supra at 328, 454.

[6] Per Rollatt J in *Garston Overseers v Carlisle* [1915] 3 KB 381, 6 TC 659.

[7] *Goslings and Sharpe v Blake*, supra. See also *Cairns v MacDiarmid* [1982] STC 226.

[8] *Re Janes' Settlement, Wasmuth v Janes* [1918] 2 Ch 54.

[9] As in a mortgage.

[10] *Corinthian Securities Ltd v Cato* [1969] 3 All ER 1168, 46 TC 93, noted [1970] BTR 144.

[11] *IRC v Hay* (1924) 8 TC 636.

[12] *Ward v Anglo-American Oil Co Ltd* (1934) 19 TC 94 (*quaere* if repayable in 365 days).

[13] *Jefford v Gee* [1970] 2 QB 130 at 149, [1970] 1 All ER 1202 at 1210; the facts were unusual in that the sale was deferred for more than twelve months.

[14] *Bebb v Bunny* (1854) 1 K & J 216. On practical problems, e.g. under s. 349(2)(c), see [1971] BTR 333.

Interest on composite rate deposits

9: 47   Interest on composite rate deposits is taxed on a special basis by TA 1988, s. 479. Interest at a composite rate is charged on the deposit holder, the bank.[1] This rate is the same as that for building societies (21.75% for 1989–90).[2] The person entitled to the interest is treated as receiving a sum on which basic rate income tax has been paid. For purposes of total income calculation the sum received is grossed up at 25%.[3] If the recipient is entitled to pay tax at less than 25% e.g. because of personal reliefs or loss relief, *no* repayment claim may be made. The sum received is treated as having been taxed for the purposes of TA 1988, ss. 348–350.[4] The rules are the same as for building society interest.[5]

These rules apply to interest on "relevant deposits" made with a "deposit taker". "Deposit taker" is, broadly, any bank.[6] A deposit is "relevant" if the person beneficially entitled to it is an individual (provision is made for concurrent interests) or a personal representative as such.[7] Thus the scheme does not apply to payments to companies nor to trusts (at least when no individual is entitled to the current income, see infra, § **11:07**). There then follows a long list of deposits which are not to be considered "relevant".[8] The list includes general client account deposits and a premium trust fund of a Lloyds underwriter[9] as well as a debt on a security,[10] a debenture, foreign accounts for non-residents and certain large deposits (£50,000) for a minimum period of 28 days.[11] Every deposit is to be assumed to be a relevant deposit until the deposit taker has satisfied himself that it is not;[12] this is an unusual example where a taxpayer, rather than the Board, has to be satisfied. These rules apply as from 6th April 1985 save that for a deposit denominated in a foreign currency the date is put back to 6th April 1986.[13]

As stated above in § **9:37**, the date on which a deposit becomes a composite rate deposit sees a cessation of the old deposit.[14] An example is the assignment of a deposit from a discretionary trust to an individual.

The effect of these rules and TA 1988, s. 476 is that the only small normal UK deposit accounts that will pay interest gross will be National Savings Accounts and National Savings bonds, an interesting example of fiscal neutrality.

Simon's Taxes D4.704; Butterworths Income Tax Service F4.06–F4.08.
[1] TA 1988, s. 479.
[2] S.I. 1988/2145; *Simon's Tax Intelligence* 1988, p. 864.
[3] TA 1988, s. 479(2).
[4] TA 1988, s. 349(3)(*d*).
[5] TA 1988, s. 476.
[6] The list is set out in TA 1988, s. 481 but TA 1988, s. 482(6) contains exceptionally wide powers enabling the Treasury to designate persons as deposit takers see also TA 1988, s. 481(2)(*d*).
[7] TA 1988, s. 481(4); on Scottish partnerships see TA 1988, s. 481(4)(*b*).
[8] TA 1988, s. 481(5).
[9] Added by TA 1988, s. 481(5)(*f*).
[10] CGTA 1979, s. 134; infra, § **15: 06**.
[11] This exception is applied also to payments by building societies—*Simon's Tax Intelligence* 1987, p. 335.
[12] TA 1988, s. 482(5).
[13] FA 1984, Sch. 8, para. 6(1).
[14] TA 1988, s. 480.

Interest: TA 1988, s. 349(2)

9: 48 Until 1968 payments of yearly interest, as opposed to short interest, were within the scheme of deduction at source. Short interest payments were always gross.[1] Now, however, only certain payments of yearly interest fall within the scheme and these are governed by TA 1988, s. 349(2). Payments of yearly interest are now made under deduction only if paid (*a*) by a company[2] or local authority otherwise than in a fiduciary or representative capacity, or (*b*) by or on behalf of a partnership of which a company is a member. This is because of the special tax regime applicable to companies.

Further, (c) tax must be deducted by any person if yearly interest is paid to another person whose usual place of abode is outside the UK (a form of withholding tax).

Even if the payment satisfies these criteria, it must be paid gross if it is interest payable in the UK on an advance from a bank carrying on a bona fide banking business[3] in the UK[4] or the interest is paid by such a bank in the ordinary course of its business.

Where the interest payment is to be made subject to deduction, the payer must account for the tax to the Revenue, the procedure in s. 349(2) being adopted, complete with the obligation to provide a certificate of deduction. A further sanction is provided by TA 1988, s. 82(1)–(5) to deal with the payment of yearly interest[5] by a person carrying on a trade or profession to a person not resident[6] in the UK. The sanction is that in computing the profits of the trade or profession no deduction can be made on account of interest payments unless (i) the procedure laid down by s. 349(2) has been followed, including the duty to account for the tax to the Revenue; or (ii) the interest satisfies the test in s. 82, supra § **7: 122.**

Simon's Taxes A3.405; Butterworths Income Tax Service A3.52, A3.54.

[1] And were not deductible under s. 835. *IRC v Frere* [1964] 1 All ER 73, 42 TC 125, an example of s. 835's domineering role.

[2] On what the company does with the tax deducted, see TA 1988, Sch. 16, esp. paras. 5 and 6; infra, § **25: 09.** A company is defined in TA 1988, s. 831.

[3] See *United Dominions Trust Ltd v Kirkwood* [1966] 1 QB 783, [1965] 2 All ER 992.

[4] *Hafton Properties Ltd v McHugh* [1987] STC 16.

[5] TA 1988, s. 82 uses the word "annual".

[6] Confusingly s. 82 is couched in terms of residence; s. 349 in terms of abode.

Discounts

9: 49   Under a Treasury Bill, the Government borrows the money paid for the bill for a certain period and pays a larger sum at the end of the period. The extra is a profit or a discount and is taxable on receipt.[1] Taxable discounts may arise on bills other than Treasury Bills. If there is a regular business of discounting, the assessment is made instead under Case I as in *Willingale v International Commercial Bank Ltd.*[2]

The discount on a Treasury Bill just described looks very like an interest payment. The distinction between a debt of £x with a discount of £y and a debt of £x − y with a premium of y is a fine one; in each case the total sum eventually paid is £x. However:

> "In the interest account, interest upon the amount is charged upon each bill until it is actually paid; but when a bill is discounted, the interest to be deducted is calculated up to the time when it becomes due and for no longer period."[3]

Liability arises when the income is realised, that is when the bill reaches maturity or when it is sold prior to maturity. In *Ditchfield v Sharp*[4] trustees bought an interest free promissory note with a guarantee from the vendor that they would receive not less than 75% of the face value. The profit accruing on maturity was held liable to tax under Schedule D, Case III as this was an income receipt from a discounting transaction. In that case the taxpayers were not allowed to argue that, as the notes were long term, the profit could be capital; such a point should have been taken before the Commissioners.

In *Ditchfield v Sharp*, the Court of Appeal said that if the whole gain could be liable to tax as arising from a discount [the whole gain should be so taxed], notwithstanding that, on another analysis, at least a part of the gain could be said to be interest.[5]

Simon's Taxes B5.4; Butterworths Income Tax Service F4.31.
[1] Per Lord Haldane in *Brown v National Provident Institution* [1921] 2 AC 222 at 232, 8 TC 80 at 83.
[2] [1978] STC 75.
[3] Per Holroyd J in *Thompson v Giles* (1824) 2 B & C 422 at 432; and see *Torrens v IRC* (1933) 18 TC 262.
[4] [1982] STC 124, upheld on appeal [1983] STC 590, CA.
[5] *Quaere* the payer's legal position if he ought to withhold tax on an interest payment.

9: 50   The traditional way in which discounts are taxed is not immediately obvious. Suppose a company issues bonds at £70 and promises to redeem them in three years' time at £100. As far as the company is concerned there will be a loss of £30 and the tax system, while allowing the company to claim that loss, does so only when the loss is realised—i.e. when the bonds are redeemed for £100. The tax system aims at symmetry of treatment for the bond holder. So if X buys the bond on issue at £70 he is taxed on the income gain arising from the transaction when in three years' time the bond is redeemed at £100. If, however, towards the end of year 2 X sells the bond to Y for, say, £92 X's gain of £22 is not treated as an income profit of £22 but as a capital gain of that amount while, when at the end of the third year, Y receives £100 he is then treated as receiving income not of £8 but of £30. Such a system lasted because the structure of the tax system ensured that there were always knowledgeable vendors and purchasers with widely differing tax circumstances. Thus, if Y had reliefs which he could not otherwise use he might pay no tax on the gain of £8 which he actually made on the £30 which the tax system treated him as receiving.

These remain the rules for taxing some discounts but special rules now apply to deep discount securities, relevant deep discount securities and deep gain securities.[1]

---

[1] See infra, § **9: 51–53**.

Deep discount securities: TA 1988, Sch. 4 rules

9: 51   Deep discount securities have been known to the tax system since 1984.[1] Relevant deep discount securities are created by FA 1989 by glossing and amending the previous law;[2] deep gain securities are also created by FA 1989 but are a brand new creation.[3] The purpose of the 1989 changes is to extend the 1984 rules to new types of security which will become possible following the abolition of the new issues queue.[4] None of the changes affect the taxation of gilts issued before 14th March 1989 or even of further tranches of gilts issued after that date but under a prospectus already used for an issue before that date.[5] Subject to qualifications the new rules apply to all disposals after 13th March 1989.[6]

Specific rules apply to certain deep discounted securities *issued* after 13th March 1984. A security comes within these rules if it is a redeemable security issued by a company other than a share, index linked stock or any security the whole or part of which is treated as a distribution under the rules in TA 1988, s. 209(2)(c) (i.e. bonus redeemable securities—see § **24: 04**).[7]

In deciding whether a discount is deep one has to look at the amount payable on redemption, an expression which excludes any payment by way of interest.[7] Subject to this a discount is deep if it represents more than 15% of the amount payable on redemption or, if it is 15% or less but exceeds $\frac{1}{2}$Y% when Y is the number of complete years between issue and redemption.[7] So a discount of 5% is deep if the life of this security is less than 10 years. In the previous example the discount of 30% is clearly deep and would be even if the period until redemption exceeded 60 years.

A security is issued when it is comprised in a letter of allotment; if the rights are conditional on acceptance the date of acceptance is taken instead.[8] The redemption date is that on which the holder has an absolute right to require redemption.[9] Where new securities are issued after 13th March 1984 in exchange for old, the new securities are to be treated as old securities if there is no extension of the period of redemption nor any increase in the amount payable on redemption and the old securities would not have been deep discount securities under the new rules.[10]

Under these rules the holder is treated as receiving income if he holds the bond until redemption (the same as under the old rules) or disposes of it before redemption (a change from the old rules).[11] The income he is treated as receiving is that which has accrued until the date of disposal[12] for this purpose income is treated as accruing evenly day by day during the period between the dates on which interest becomes payable. The income element is complex to calculate as there is an element of compounding.

Simon's Taxes B5.404, D2.215; Butterworths Income Tax Service F4.31b.

[1] Now TA 1988, s. 57, introducing Sch. 4.

[2] FA 1989, Sch. 10, introducing TA 1988, Sch. 4, para. 1(1)(*dd*) and other changes; see § **9: 54**, infra.

[3] FA 1989, Sch. 11; see § **9: 56**, infra.

[4] Revenue Press Release, 14th March 1989; *Simon's Tax Intelligence* 1989, p. 193.

[5] This is the purport of TA 1988, Sch. 4, para. 1(5), (6) and (7) and FA 1989, Sch. 11, para. 1(4) and (5). For the position if no securities have been issued before 14th March 1989 see TA 1988 Sch. 4, para. 19 and FA 1989, Sch. 11, para. 20.

[6] TA 1988, Sch. 4, para. 4(7).

[7] TA 1988, Sch. 4, para. 1(1).

[8] TA 1988, Sch. 4, para. 1(3).

[9] This is the Revenue view of TA 1988, Sch. 4, para. 1(1). [1984] STI, p. 496.

[10] TA 1988, Sch. 4, para. 1(2).

[11] TA 1988, Sch. 4, para. 4. Extra-statutory concession B13 (1988) may apply to limit the liability of a non-resident to situations where the UK tax can be recovered by being set off against a relief.

[12] Defined in TA 1988, Sch. 4, para. 4(2)–(4).

Relevant deep discount security

9: 52   Relevant deep discount securities form an extra category of securities. They are any redeemable security which has been issued by a public body at a deep discount.[1] The depth of the discount is determined as before. The category is restricted by the exclusion of index linked securities.[2] Also excluded is a non-gilt security issued under a prospectus under which other securities have already been issued and which were not deep discount securities.[3]

Simon's Taxes B5.404, 405; D2.215; Butterworths Income Tax Service F4.31a–e.

[1] TA 1988, s. 126(3), added by FA 1989, s. 95; this refers to TA 1988, Sch. 4, para. 1(1) (*dd*), as amended by FA 1989.

[2] TA 1988, Sch. 4, para. 1(1)(*d*)(ii).

[3] TA 1988, Sch. 4, para. 1(7); see also para. 20.

Deep gain securities

9: 53   Deep gain securities are a new category and are defined largely by exclusion. In essence these are variable securities which could vary so much as to become deep discounts; they might be called variable deep discounted securities. More formally they are redeemable securities whenever issued the sum payable on the redemption of which *might* be deep. The question whether a discount might be deep is judged at the time when the security is issued. If more than one date for redemption is set, the test must be applied to each of them.[1] The question whether a gain is deep is determined according to the same formula as that used for deep discounts.[2]

The legislation then goes on to exclude items such as a share in a company, a qualifying indexed security[3], a convertible security[4] and items which are already deep discount securities.[5] Also excluded are securities other than gilts which were issued later but under the same prospectus as another security which was not a deep gain security and which was issued first.[6] A charge to tax under the accrued income scheme will exclude a charge under these rules but a charge under these rules will exclude the normal charge under TA 1988, s. 123 and the withholding machinery in TA 1988, ss. 348 to 350.

---

[1] FA 1989, Sch. 11, para. 1(2); on definition of redemption see ibid., para. 1(3).

[2] FA 1989, Sch. 11, para. 1(9).

[3] Defined in FA 1989, Sch. 11, para. 3; the Treasury has power to modify the terms of para. 2—see para. 23. On variations by the parties, see para. 22.

[4] FA 1989, Sch 11, paras. 1(4) and 3.

[5] FA 1989, Sch. 11, para. 1(3).

[6] FA 1989, Sch. 11, para. 1(6).

9: 54   On a disposal of a deep discount security, whether relevant or not, the income chargeable to tax under Schedule D Case III or IV is the accrued income attributable to the period of ownership.[1] A definition is made for any amounts already brought into charge during the same period of ownership. This is the sum of the *income elements* for each or partial *income period* in the period of ownership.[2]

The length of the *income period* depends upon the terms of the security. Where interest is payable, it will be any period to which a payment of interest is attributable. Thus, if interest is paid every six months, the income period will be the six months ending with the date of payment. Where there is no right to interest (e.g. if the security is a "zero coupon" security), the income period is a year ending immediately before the anniversary of the issue date or a period of less than a year, beginning on an anniversary and ending on the redemption date.

> **EXAMPLE**
> A deep discount security carrying no interest is issued on 15th November 1988. Redemption is fixed for 31st December 1990. The relevant income periods are: (1) the year ending 14th November 1989; (2) the year ending 14th November 1990 and (3) the period 15th November–31st December 1990.

In order to calculate the *income element* for any income period, it is necessary to know the yield to maturity of the security. This is the percentage rate at which the issue price would have to grow on a compound basis over each income period to equal the redemption price at the date of redemption, subtracting the amount of any interest attributable to any income period after applying the rate.

The income element for any income period is found by applying the formula—

$$\left(\frac{A \times B}{100} \right) - C$$

where A is the "adjusted issue price" (i.e. the sum of the issue price adjusted by the addition of the income elements for all previous income periods), B is the yield to maturity and C the amount of interest attributable to that income period.[3]

> **EXAMPLE**
> A deep discount is issued at 60, with a yield to maturity of 12%. Interest of 3% is payable every six months. The income element for the first income period will be—
>
> $$\left(\frac{60 \times 12}{100} \right) - 3 = 4 \cdot 2.$$
>
> and that for the second income period—
>
> $$\left(\frac{64 \cdot 2 \times 12}{100} \right) - 3 = 4 \cdot 704$$
>
> and so on.

Where it is necessary to determine the income element for a period falling within an income period (as, for example, would be necessary if a disposal took place in the middle of an income period), the income element is treated as accruing evenly over the income period.[4]

> **EXAMPLE**
> If the length of the income period is 180 days and the disposal takes place on day 120 of that period, the income element up to the time of disposal is $120 \div 180$ or $2/3$ of the income element for the complete period.

Tax will not be deducted at source under either the rules of TA 1988, ss. 348, 349(2) or of TA 1988, s. 123 (foreign dividends) on so much of the redemption proceeds as represents income chargeable under Schedule D, Case III or IV.[5]

Simon's Taxes B5.404, D2.215; Butterworths Income Tax Service F4.31b.
[1] TA 1988, Sch. 4, para. 4(1).

² TA 1988, Sch. 4, para. 4(2). TA 1988, Sch. 4, para. 13 imposes a duty on the issuing company or body to supply the information.
³ TA 1988, Sch. 4, para. 4(3); the terms are defined in para. 1(1).
⁴ TA 1988, Sch. 4, para. 4(4).
⁵ TA 1988, Sch. 4, para. 4(7).

9: 55 A charge to tax will likewise arise on the transfer or redemption of a deep gain security.[1] The charge will be under Schedule D Case III, for a UK security, or Case IV for a foreign security. There is a deemed transfer at market value not only on death but also if the transfer is between connected persons.[2] There are special rules for underwriters and trustees.[3] There is even a rule as to the translation for a gain in foreign currency.[4] The remittance basis is available.[5]

[1] FA 1989, Sch. 11, para. 5 (charge on transfer), para. 4 (definition of transfer) and para. 6 (redemption).
[2] FA 1989, Sch. 11, para. 7–9; the tax paid is deductible for IHTA 1984, s. 174(1)(*b*).
[3] FA 1989, Sch. 11, paras. 10 and 11.
[4] FA 1989, Sch. 11, para. 12.
[5] FA 1989, Sch. 11, para. 13.

9: 56 As the new rules involve the concept of disposal it is not surprising to find many CGT rules adopted or half adopted. Thus, while the general concept of disposal is taken from CGT it is expressly provided that liability to income tax will arise on death[1] or on amalgamation and reconstruction[2] save where there is no extension to the period of redemption and no new consideration is provided.[3] Likewise a charge to income tax arises where, for CGT, the disposal would be for such consideration that neither gain nor loss arises.[4] Other rules are set out. Thus, although the charge arises under Schedule D Case III or, in appropriate facts, Case IV. Liability is on a current year basis;[5] the remittance basis applies to Case IV where relevant.[6]

The rules as to identification of securities disposed of are those for CGT.[7]

There is an exemption for charities.[8]

FA 1989 introduces further exemptions for both deep discount securities (whether relevant or not) and deep discount gains. There are exclusions for retirement benefit schemes,[9] for stock lending[10] and there is to be no charge on trust within TA 1988, s. 469.[11]

Any amount payable on the death of a holder is deductible for CTT and IHT purposes.[12]

There are also provisions for the early redemption of securities.[13]

On the position of the company issuing the deep discounted stock see § **25: 16**.

There is no obligation to deduct tax from the discount where the discount profit is realised on redemption.

Simon's Taxes B5.404, D2.215; Butterworths Income Tax Service F4.31b.
[1] TA 1988, Sch. 4, para. 7(1), (2); FA 1989, Sch. 11, para. 7.
[2] TA 1988, Sch. 4, para. 7(3), (4).
[3] TA 1988, Sch. 4, para. 11(3)(*a*)—here the amount of accrued income attributable in the period of his ownership of the old securities is added to that attributable to the new.
[4] TA 1988, Sch. 29.

[5] TA 1988, Sch. 4, para. 4(1)(*b*); FA 1989, Sch. 11, para. 19.
[6] TA 1988, Sch. 4, para. 4(5).
[7] TA 1988, Sch. 4, para. 12.
[8] TA 1988, Sch. 4, para. 14; FA 1989, Sch. 11, para. 15.
[9] TA 1988, Sch. 4, para. 15; FA 1989, Sch. 11, para. 14.
[10] TA 1988, Sch. 4, para. 16, FA 1989, Sch. 11, para. 16.
[11] TA 1988, Sch. 4, para. 17(2) and FA 1989, Sch. 11, para. 11(2).
[12] IHTA 1984, s. 174(1)(*b*).
[13] TA 1988, Sch. 4, paras. 11 and 11A.

Interaction with capital gains tax

9: 57   Amounts chargeable to income tax are normally excluded from the disposal consideration when computing the gain chargeable to capital gains tax.[1] This rule is to be disregarded for deep discount securities but the accrued income element of the disposal proceeds will be deducted from the total.[2] Owing to changes in the general level of interest rates it may well be that the gain actually made by the holder is different from the income element as just calculated. When this occurs the difference is treated as a matter for CGT, the amount subject to income tax being deducted from the actual gain to give the relevant gain or loss for CGT.

EXAMPLE

A buys £5,000 of deep discount stock when it is issued at 70; i.e. the total cost is £3,500. He sells it to B some time later for £4,000 when the accrued income is 4·56.

The capital gains computation is as follows—

	£	£
Disposal consideration	4,000	
Deduct: accrued income		
$£5,000 \times \dfrac{4\cdot56}{100}$	228	
		3,772
Deduct: cost		3,500
Gross gain (subject to indexation)		£272

A will pay income tax on the accrued income of £228.

EXAMPLE

B buys £1,000 of deep discount stock at 65; i.e. at a cost of £650 but when the adjusted issue price is 62·80. He sells it for 72 when the adjusted issue price is 73·50.

The Capital gains computation is as follows—

	£	£
Disposal consideration		
$£1,000 \times \dfrac{72}{100}$	720	
Deduct: accrued income		
$£1,000 \times \dfrac{(73\cdot50 - 62\cdot80)}{100}$	107	
		613
Deduct: cost		650
Allowable loss (subject to indexation)		£37

Where the accrued income element exceeds the disposal proceeds, the excess is to be treated as additional expenditure incurred on the security immediately before the disposal.[3]

Simon's Taxes B5.404, D2.215; Butterworths Income Tax Service F4.31c.
[1] CGTA 1979, s. 31 infra, § **21: 02**.
[2] CGTA 1979, s. 132A(1)(*a*).
[3] CGTA 1979, s. 132A(1)(*b*).

9: 58   If an attempt is made to defer tax by use of a coupon stripping operation, the investor may be chargeable to tax on the interest as it *accrues*, under the provisions of TA 1988, Sch. 4, paras. 1–3. This only applies if the deep discount securities were issued after 18th March 1985. The legislation sets out certain situations[1] in which the person holding the deep discount securities will be taxed on the interest before disposal or redemption. In general terms, the provisions apply where immediately before the issue of the deep discount securities, or at any time during the first income period, at least 75% of the issuing company's assets consist of "relevant securities", i.e. securities other than shares, UK corporate bonds, national savings certificates, certificates of deposit, bills of exchange, Treasury and local authority bills and other instruments.[2] They also apply where the company issuing deep discount securities indirectly invests by investing in UK corporate bonds issued by another company which in its turn invests in "relevant securities". In addition, the provisions apply where deep discount securities, issued in the circumstances described above, are exchanged for new deep discount securities so that the new securities would be treated as the same asset as the old for capital gains tax purposes.[3] In these situations, the deep discount securities are "chargeable securities".[4]

The holder of a chargeable security is taxable under Schedule D, Case III (or IV, if relevant) on the income element of the discount for each income period of the security which ends during his period of ownership. The charge arises at the end of the period. Where the security is purchased during the income period, the income element is apportioned.[5] Amounts charged in this way are deductible when calculating chargeable income on disposal or redemption.

Simon's Taxes B5.404, D2.215; Butterworths Income Tax Service F4.31b.
[1] TA 1988, Sch. 4, para. 1(2).
[2] TA 1988, Sch. 4, para. 2(5).
[3] Under CGTA 1979, s. 82.
[4] The certificate in respect of the security must state that tax is chargeable under these provisions.
[5] TA 1988, Sch. 4, para. 3.

ANNUITIES AND ANNUAL PAYMENTS

Annuity

9: 59   Annuity is not defined. It has been judicially described as meaning "where an income is purchased with a sum of money and the capital has gone and has ceased to exist, the principal having been converted into an annuity".[1] The precise boundary between an annuity and an annual payment is one which the courts have not had to mark out. The 1988 legislation[2] assumes that an annuity payable by an individual is an annual payment. The scope of these rules will be greatly reduced in due course.

An annuity must be distinguished from the payments of a debt by instalments.[3] In an annuity the capital has gone and, in the normal annuity contract, payments will continue so long as the annuitant lives; an annuity is thus an insurance against outliving capital. On the other hand, where a debt is being paid by instalments, the debt remains and liability is not usually affected by the death of either party.

Simon's Taxes B5.301, 310; Butterworths Income Tax Service F4.32.
  [1] Per Watson B in *Foley v Fletcher and Rose* (1858) 3 H & N 769 at 784. Purchased annuities are now dissected. TA 1988, s. 656; infra, § **28: 19.**
  [2] Supra, § **9: 33** et seq.
  [3] Infra, § **9: 69** et seq.

Annuities and advances

9: 60   Where a person goes to an annuity office and buys an annuity with cash it is clear that he receives an annuity and that tax is due on the payments he receives. Several cases have been concerned with attempts to get payments of the same economic value as an annuity out of an annuity company while making sure that the payments are not themselves annuities. The crux is that under an annuity the principal sum is liquidated.

In *Perrin v Dickson*[1] the taxpayer paid premiums under a policy of assurance to an assurance society for six years from 1912 to 1917 and the company undertook to pay an "annuity" for seven years from 1920 to 1927 to the taxpayer's son if he should so long live. If the son did not live until 1927, the total amount paid by the taxpayer was to be returned to him without interest although less any amount paid out under the annuity. Rowlatt J and the Court of Appeal, held that, since the taxpayer could not possibly lose his money, the transaction was one of deposit rather than annuity so that the payments under the "annuity", which included an increment for interest, should be dissected into interest and capital.

The opposite result was reached on different facts in *Sothern-Smith v Clancy*.[2] Here, in return for a single premium of $65,243 the company agreed to pay an annuity of $6,510 but promised that if he should die before the amount repaid reached the amount invested, the society would continue to pay out to specified beneficiaries until full repayment had been made. The purchaser died when $39,203 remained outstanding and this sum was paid to his sister who argued that she should not pay tax. The sum was held to be an annuity. *Perrin v Dickson* was distinguished on appeal on the ground that that case was really one of the investment of capital, the fruits of which were to come out only if the payments fell to be made to the son and so were not wholly income payments.

These cases have been described as very special and the reasoning of the first as hard to follow.[3] Another decision treated sums borrowed as loans not annuities[4]; this has been reversed by rather narrow legislation.[5] The first has had its particular purposes defeated by the rule that income from a settlement by a parent on an infant must be treated as that of the parent.[6] All one can say is that every case must be determined on its own facts. Many advances by insurance companies are now taxed.[7]

Simon's Taxes B5.309, 313; Butterworths Income Tax Service F4.33.
[1] [1930] 1 KB 107, 14 TC 608.
[2] [1941] 1 All ER 111, 24 TC 1 cited in *IRC v Plummer* [1979] STC 793 at 798.
[3] By Lord Greene MR in *IRC v Wesleyan and General Assurance Society* [1948] 1 All ER 555, 30 TC 11.
[4] *IRC v Wesleyan and General Assurance Society.*
[5] TA 1988, s. 554.
[6] TA 1988, s. 663; infra, § **13: 32**.
[7] Infra, § **28: 15** and **28: 16**.

Other annual payment[1]

9: 61   TA 1988, s. 18 elaborates the words annuity or other annual payment by saying

"whether such payment is payable within or without the United Kingdom, either as a charge on any property of the person paying the same by virtue of any deed or will or otherwise, or as a reservation out of it, or as a personal debt or obligation by virtue of any contract, or whether the same is received and payable half yearly or at any shorter or more distant periods . . ."

These words limit the otherwise broad notion of annual payment; annual payment must be construed eiusdem generis with annuities or yearly interest of money.[2] For this reason a rent of land is not an annual payment.[3]

Although the legislation talks of "payments", payments in kind fall within Schedule D, Case III.[4]

The criteria for establishing whether or not a payment is an annual payment—

(*i*) there must be some legal obligation to pay the sum

(*ii*) the payment must possess the essential quality of recurrence implied by the description annual

(*iii*) the payment must be pure income profit in his hands.

(*iv*) the income must belong to the payee

(*v*) the payment must form part of the income of the payee as opposed to being a capital payment to him

(*vi*) the payment must be a division of the profits of the payer. Rule (*vi*) is dubious.

Simon's Taxes B5.302; Butterworths Income Tax Service F4.35.
[1] By concession, sickness benefit payments arranged by an individual, as distinct from his employer, are only taxed if they continue for at least a year before the year of assessment: extra-statutory concession A26 (1988), see **Simon's Taxes, Division H2.2**.
[2] Per Jenkins LJ in *IRC v Whitworth Park Coal Co Ltd* [1958] 2 All ER 91 at 102, 38 TC 531 at 548.
[3] *Hill v Gregory* [1912] 2 KB 61, 6 TC 39, see now TA 1988, s. 18.
[4] Presumably the machinery in TA 1988, ss. 348 and 349 does not apply; infra, § **9: 73**.

(i) *The obligation*

9: 62   Such an annual payment must be due under an enforceable obligation; the obligation is the source. This is quite distinct from the question whether or not the obligation is created for valuable and sufficient consideration.[1]

A series of voluntary gifts cannot be an annual payment; nor can ultra vires payments by a company.[2] For this reason a voluntary tax allowance paid by a husband to his wife cannot be charged to tax under Schedule D, Case III. Hence also the rule that the husband does not lose his married man's personal allowance if he is under no legal obligation to pay her.[3] On the other hand an enforceable agreement by a husband to pay his separated wife weekly sums by way of maintenance does create income within Case III unless it is specifically taken out by the new regime; infra § **9: 92**.[4] Dividend payments by companies are not annual payments, since a company is under no obligation to pay a dividend.[5]

The obligation may be involuntary e.g. a court order or a statute.[6]

Where trustees have an express discretion to make payments to an object, sums paid under that discretion to objects of the trust[7] are not regarded as voluntary. In *Drummond v Collins*[8] trustees exercised a power of maintenance in respect of children who had a contingent interest in the trust capital. Although the children had no enforceable right to the payments, Lord Loreburn said that they were not "voluntary in any relevant sense. They were payments made in fulfilment of a testamentary disposition for the benefit of the children in the exercise of a discretion conferred by the will."[9] This principle has since been applied where, under a will, trustees exercised their discretion to give a surtax payer a voluntary allowance of £600 a month,[10] and where trustees had a discretion to have recourse to capital in order to maintain the value of an annuity.[11] In these cases the payee was an object of the trust, either in the sense that he had a vested right under the trust[12] as well as being a potential beneficiary under the discretion, or that as such a potential beneficiary the trustees were under a duty at least to consider whether or not to exercise that discretion in his favour.[13] Payments by trusts are not within the new regime and therefore remain Schedule D, Case III income of the recipient.[14]

This requirement is easily satisfied. In *Dealler v Bruce*[15] the taxpayer's mother had bequeathed shares to trustees and directed that they should pay an annuity to the taxpayer's sister out of the income. The trustees were given the power to sell the shares in order to raise funds sufficient for the annuity but the taxpayer who was a director of the company was given the right to have all the dividends paid to him if and so long as he should pay the annuity himself anyway. As it turned out, the dividends yielded no income but he paid the annuity. It was held that the payment of the annuity to the sister was not voluntary. He obtained good consideration in that he made sure that the shares were not sold.

This conclusion seems hard to justify since this advantage showed why the taxpayer acted as he did but did not impose any legal obligation on him to act.

Simon's Taxes B5.306; Butterworths Income Tax Service F4.35.
    [1] *Smith v Smith* [1923] P 191 at 197, per Lord Sterndale and at 202, per Warrington LJ.

[2] *Ridge Securities Ltd v IRC* [1964] 1 All ER 275, 44 TC 373.
[3] Supra, § 3: 07.
[4] *Smith v Smith*, supra; *Clack v Clack* [1935] 2 KB 109.
[5] *Canadian Eagle Oil Co Ltd v R* (1945) 27 TC 205 at 245, [1945] 2 All ER 499 at 504.
[6] See n. 4, supra.
[7] A payment by a charitable trust would however be regarded as voluntary since the beneficiary under the trusts is charity and not the person benefited: per Romer LJ in *Stedeford v Beloe* [1931] 2 KB 610 at 626.
[8] [1915] AC 1011, 6 TC 525 (a decision on Case V).
[9] [1915] AC 1011 at 1017, 6 TC 525 at 539.
[10] *Lord Tollemache v IRC* (1926) 11 TC 277 (Rowlatt J).
[11] *Lindus and Hortin v IRC* (1933) 17 TC 442 (Finlay J); *Cunard's Trustees v IRC* [1946] 1 All ER 159, 27 TC 122.
[12] Distinguish *Stedeford v Beloe* [1932] AC 388, 16 TC 505, where the object of the trust was the school, not the individual headmaster. Cf. *Duncan's Executors v Farmer* (1909) 5 TC 417.
[13] Per Lord Greene MR in *Cunard's Trustees v IRC* [1946] 1 All ER 159 at 163, 27 TC 122 at 133 and Finlay J in *Lindus and Horton v IRC* (1933) 17 TC 442 at 448. Voluntary pensions are now taxable under TA 1988, s. 133, Sch. E.
[14] TA 1988, s. 347A(2) is confined to individuals.
[15] (1934) 19 TC 1.

(ii) *Recurrence*

9: 63   It is the word "annual" which indicates that a payment which falls within Case III must, like interest on money or an annuity, have the quality of being recurrent or being capable of recurrence.[1] For this reason an obligation which cannot last longer than twelve months cannot create an annual payment.[2] On the other hand if the obligation can endure so long, it is quite irrelevant that the payment is expressed as a variable sum. It is irrelevant that the sum paid may vary; so payment of such a sum as after tax at the basic rate in force in the year of payment shall equal £5 is an "annual payment". It is also irrelevant that the obligation is contingent so that no sum may be payable under the obligation at all. For example, a guarantee that one will provide funds to enable a company to pay a fixed dividend should the company have insufficient profits, will create a liability to make annual payments even though in any year the company may have sufficient profits so that no sums become payable under the guarantee.[3] The purpose of the rule seems to be to exclude payments which are casual and temporary and therefore fall more easily into Case VI than into Case III.[4] Case VI has no requirement of recurrence.

Weekly payments are "annual". The annual payment in this case is the weekly sum multiplied by the number of weeks in the year, which may be 52 or 53 depending upon the day of the week on which the obligation falls.[5]

Simon's Taxes B5.305; Butterworths Income Tax Service F4.36.
[1] Per Lord Maugham in *Moss Empires Ltd v IRC* [1937] AC 785 at 795, 21 TC 264 at 299.
[2] Per Lord Sterndale in *Smith v Smith* [1923] P 191 at 196.
[3] *Moss Empires Ltd v IRC*, supra.
[4] Per Lord Radcliffe in *Whitworth Park Coal Co Ltd v IRC* [1959] 3 All ER 703 at 716, 38 TC 531 at 575.
[5] *Re Janes' Settlement, Wasmuth v Janes* [1918] 2 Ch 54.

(iii) *Pure income profit*

9: 64   It is inconsistent with the scheme of deduction at source that Schedule D, Case III, should contain payments that are likely to be *gross* receipts of the payee and not his pure income.[1] It follows that if the payee is entitled to deduct expenses from the receipt as where he promises to provide the payer with goods or services in return for the income, the payment should not fall within Case III, an idea expressed in the requirement that the payment should be pure income profit[2] in the hands of the payee.

Simon's Taxes B5.304; Butterworths Income Tax Service F4.37.

[1] Per Lord Radcliffe, in *Whitworth Park Coal Co Ltd v IRC* [1959] 3 All ER 703 at 715, 38 TC 531 at 575.

[2] In *IRC v London Corpn* (*as Conservators of Epping Forest*) Lord Normand said that the formula would lose nothing by the omissions of the words "pure" and "profit": [1953] 1 All ER 1075 at 1081, 34 TC 293 at 320.

9: 65   (*a*) *A trading receipt cannot be an annual payment*—Scrutton LJ provided a famous example in *Howe v IRC*:[1]

> "If a man agrees to pay a motor garage £500 a year for five years for the hire and upkeep of a car, no one suggests the person paying can deduct income tax from each yearly payment. So if he contracted with a butcher for an annual sum to supply all his meat for a year, the annual instalment would not be subject to tax as a whole in the hands of the payee, but only that part of it which was profits."

In these instances the trader would be entitled—and bound—in computing his profits to deduct the cost to him of the car or of the meat, so it could not be said that the payment was pure income.

In *Howe v IRC* the taxpayer had mortgaged his life estate in certain properties and had to mortgage also a life assurance policy. He sought to deduct the premiums which he was legally obliged to pay in computing his income for surtax, but failed. The payment was not pure income in the hands of the insurance company but merely a receipt which would be taken into account in computing its profits. The quality of the payment is not however determined by its place in the accounts. The question is whether it is a trading receipt or an annual payment.

Simon's Taxes B5.302; Butterworths Income Tax Service F4.38.

[1] [1919] 2 KB 336 at 352, 7 TC 296 at 303, see also *Re Hanbury, Comiskey v Hanbury* (1939) 38 TC 588.

9: 66   (*b*) In the same way a *payment which is a receipt of the payee's profession will not be an annual payment within Case III.* Here too expenses may be written off against the sum received so that it is not all income. So where a solicitor trustee was entitled to charge for his services under a charging clause, such payments were not within Case III even though by agreement with the beneficiaries and other trustees they took the form of a percentage of the trust income.[1] On the other hand an annuity of £100 for a trustee for acting as trustee has been held to be an annual payment.[2] Both payments are acts of bounty on the part of the settlor, the trustee having no right to charge for his time and trouble but only a quite independent indemnity for his expenses which is unaffected by the annuity; however the former is ex hypothesi a receipt of the firm for services rendered whereas the latter is not. More recently it has been held that such an annuity is earned income,[3] a finding which throws doubt upon the annuity's status as an annual payment although the point was expressly left open and the Revenue do not appear to have pressed it. Likewise any annuities or annual profits and gains which are charged under Schedule A, B, C or E fall outside Schedule D, Case III.[4]

Simon's Taxes B5.302; Butterworths Income Tax Service F4.39.
[1] *Jones v Wright* (1927) 13 TC 221.
[2] *Baxendale v Murphy* [1924] 2 K B 494, 9 TC 76.
[3] *Dale v IRC* [1953] 2 All ER 671 at 676, 34 TC 468 at 493.
[4] TA 1988, s. 18 (TA 1970, s. 108).

9: 67   (*c*) *Other payments.* "One must determine in the light of all the relevant facts, whether the payment is a taxable receipt in the hands of the recipient without any deduction for expenses or the like, or is simply gross revenue in the recipient's hands, out of which a taxable income will emerge only after his outgoings have been deducted".[1]

When a non-trading body is concerned, the presence of some counter-stipulation may deprive the payment of its character of pure income benefit. The difficulty is to know where precisely this line is to be drawn. At one time it was thought that the presence of any counter-stipulation or condition would be fatal[2] but this view was rejected by the House of Lords in *Campbell v IRC*.[1]

Today the presence of a counter-stipulation or condition deprives the payment of a quality of pure bounty but not necessarily of its character as pure income profit. Thus the purchaser of an annuity from an insurance company has to pay for his annuity; again where a person sold the right to use a secret process in return for a percentage of the profits those payments had the quality of pure income[3] as they did when an employee gave up all existing rights to remuneration in return for a percentage of the profits of a particular film.[4] In *Campbell v IRC* Lord Denning MR put the following case "Suppose a man gives a covenant for seven years to his old school and in return there is a private understanding that his son, who is a dunce, will be given a place".[5] In the Court of Appeal, Lord Denning, acting on the old view that a counter-stipulation would be fatal, held that such a payment would not be pure income, but in the House of Lords both Lord Hodson and Lord Donovan[6] thought that such payment would fall within Case III, although Lord Donovan added what was probably implicit in Lord Hodson's speech, that the full fees would be payable for the dunce son. In all these examples the consideration was executed before the annual payments began but Lord Donovan pointed out that in *Westminster v IRC* Lord Macmillan had said that if, in return for the annuity, the employee had promised to work for lower wages the payments would still be within Schedule D, Case III, a view with which Lord Wright had agreed.[7]

These problems have been discussed in connection with covenants in favour of charities, which sometimes offer inducements in order to obtain those covenants. The fact that the payee is a charity cannot affect the question whether the covenant is an annual payment.[8] In *IRC v National*

Book League[9] the charity provided a central lending library, arranged exhibitions, ran a book information service and made available to members various rooms at its headquarters such as sitting rooms, a restaurant and a cocktail bar. Payments under covenants in its favour were held not to be pure income profit. The correct basis of the decision is that the covenants were simply a club subscription in return for the annual provisions of goods and services.[10] The question of what inducements can be offered remains therefore a matter of doubt.

The provision of such facilities as private viewing days for Friends of a particular museum or priority booking for certain performances by a theatre or opera company is probably not sufficient to prevent the payments from being the pure income profit of the charity. The offer of seats at reduced prices was fatal in one first instance decision decided before, and not commented upon in, *Campbell v IRC*.[11] However, whether they prevent the payments being covenanted payments to charity is a separate question.[12] This separate question has now been clarified by FA 1989, s. 59, but only for charities for the preservation of property or the conservation of wildlife for the public benefit.[13]

Simon's Taxes B5.304; Butterworths Income Tax Service F4.40.

[1] Per Lord Donovan in *Campbell v IRC* (1968) 45 TC 427 at 475, [1968] 3 All ER 588 at 606; and see [1969] BTR 68.

[2] E.g. the judgments of the Court of appeal in *IRC v National Book League* [1957] 2 All ER 644, 37 TC 455 and in *Campbell v IRC* [1967] 2 All ER 625, 45 TC 427.

[3] *Delage v Nuggett Polish Co Ltd* (1905) 92 LT 682.

[4] *Asher v London Film Productions Ltd* [1944] K B 133, [1944] 1 All ER 77.

[5] [1967] 2 All ER 625 at 629, 45 TC 427 at 447; see also *Essex County Council v Ellam* [1989] STC 317, CA.

[6] [1968] 3 All ER 588 at 599, 45 TC 427 at 467.

[7] [1968] 3 All ER 588 at 606, 45 TC 427 at 474.

[8] *Campbell v IRC*, supra.

[9] 37 TC 455, [1957] 2 All ER 644.

[10] *Campbell v IRC* [1968] 3 All ER 588 at 594, 45 TC 427 at 462 and per Morris LJ in *IRC v National Book League* (supra), at 475, 652.

[11] *Taw and Torridge Festival Society Ltd v IRC* (1959) 38 TC 603, [1960] BTR 61.

[12] See [1988] BTR, p. 231.

[13] Bodies listed in TA 1988, s. 507 quality.

(iv) *Income of the payee*

9: 68   The payment must be income of the payee and not that of someone else; it will not be his income if he is under a legally enforceable obligation to hand it on to someone else.

In *Campbell v IRC* a payment by A to B under a covenant of a sum equal to 80%[1] of net profits which B had to pay to C, who paid it back to A was not income of B. The scheme was to enable B, a charity, to acquire the goodwill of A's business.

The scheme failed because the legally enforceable obligation to use the same amount of money to pay for the goodwill, deprived the payment of the character of pure income profit,[2] and/or because the payments were capital in B's hands, a conclusion resting on the need to look at the quality of the payment in the hands of the recipient and not the payer. The second view expressed by Lords Dilhorne, Hodson, Guest and Upjohn,[3] was that the legally enforceable obligation to use the same amount of money to pay for the goodwill deprived the payment of its character of pure income profit. Lords Hodson and Upjohn expressly left open this opinion of what would have happened if the obligation had not been legally enforceable.[4]

A similar principle was applied in *McBurnie v Tacey* where Peter Gibson J held that where a wife received supplementary benefit for a child and the husband was ordered to pay sums to the Secretary of State for Social Services; the payments by the husband were not small maintenance payments to the wife and so were not deductible by him. The Secretary of State was not like B in the *Campbell* case.[5]

Simon's Taxes B5.304; Butterworths Income Tax Service F4.43.
[1] 80% was chosen because the covenant was not deductible for profits tax and 20% was needed to pay that tax.
[2] Lord Upjohn [1970] AC 77 at 108, [1968] 3 All ER 588 at 603 and 45 TC 427 at 472. *Quaere* if there had been no legally enforceable obligation.
[3] Lord Dilhorne ibid at 99, 595, 463; Lord Donovan at 110, 604 and 473; Lord Hodson at 102, 598 and 466; Lord Guest at 104, 600 and 468.
[4] 45 TC at 466D and 470A.
[5] [1984] STC 347. An ancillary reason was that TA 1988, s. 617 prevented the payments to the wife from being taxable income in her hands; quaeri whether the "new approach" could lead to a different result, making this payment taxable income of the wife and deductible by the husband

---

(v) *Capital or income—or some of each*

9: 69 An annual payment is taxable within Case III only if it is income. Where, therefore, a series of payments is made, the law has to decide whether the payments are the income of the recipient or merely a payment of capital by instalments. If the former, each payment is an annual payment; if the latter, each is capital and so not an annual payment. Sometimes the answer is that the payment is partly income and partly capital but in this instance the income element is not an annual payment but rather one of interest.

The question for the court is the true legal nature of the transaction which the parties have entered into.[1] In answering that question evidence dehors the contract is admissible, particularly in order to explain that which the contract often does not explain, namely the quality of the sums in question.[2]

The test is whether, as a matter of substance, the payments are instalments of the purchase price or pure income payments.[3] This is not regarded as breaking the principle laid down in *Duke of Westminster v IRC*[4] because the test does not involve putting upon a transaction between parties a character which in law it does not possess, but rather involves discovering what is the true character in law of the transaction which was entered into.[5]

Simon's Taxes B5.309; Butterworths Income Tax Service F4.45–F4.48.
[1] *IRC v Church Comrs for England* [1976] STC 339, [1976] 2 All ER 1037. An agreement may contain two different types of payment, as in *IRC v British Salmson Aero Engines Ltd* [1938] 3 All ER 283, 22 TC 29.
[2] Per Lord Wilberforce in *IRC v Church Comrs for England* [1976] 2 All ER 1037 at 1044.
[3] *Brodie's Will Trustees v IRC* (1933) 17 TC 432 at 440.

410   *Part II—Income tax*

Supra, § 1: 05.
Per Sir Wilfrid Greene MR in *Mallaby-Deeley v IRC* [1938] 4 All ER 818 at 825, 23 TC 153 at 167.

9: 70   Certain matters are clear although they tend to add to the confusion. *First* the fact that a payment is made out of capital in no way affects the question whether the payment is income of the recipient. Therefore annuity payments are taxable even though under the terms of the will or settlement giving rise to it the trustees are empowered to have recourse to capital in order to pay the sum and the trustees exercise the power.[1] For the same reason an investment of capital in the purchase of an annuity gives rise to payments which are pure income, although here special legislation now provides that the payments are mixed capital and income if the annuitant and the purchaser are the same individual.[2]

Secondly the label which the parties choose to give to the payment is not conclusive. Thus an "annuity" payment has been held to be capital,[3] and the payment of a purchase price by instalments has been held not to create pure capital payments.[4]

Thirdly, the courts have stressed that the question in every case is one of the true legal nature of the transaction[5] and that every case is to be decided on its own facts. A particular fact may have been the dominating factor in a case but that is not the same as a conclusive test.[6]

Fourthly, the courts have said that they cannot regard the conduct of the parties as conclusive but that they may draw comfort from discovering that the decision of the court corresponds with that conduct.[7] When the Revenue are parties to the litigation the courts tend to look at what the parties have done; whether they have, by deducting tax or not, shown that they regarded the payments as income or capital.

Simon's Taxes B5.309; Butterworths Income Tax Service F4.45–F4.48.
[1] Supra, § 7: 72.
[2] TA 1988, s. 656; infra, § **28: 20**.
[3] *Secretary of State in Council of India v Scoble* [1903] AC 299, 4 TC 618.
[4] *Vestey v IRC* [1961] 3 All ER 978, 40 TC 112.
[5] *IRC v Church Comrs for England*, infra, § **9: 74**.
[6] *Dott v Brown* [1936] 1 All ER 543.
[7] Per Lord Normand in *IRC v Hogarth* (1940) 23 TC 491 at 500.

Principles

9: 71   (1) Where a definite sum of money is due and the payment of that sum in one lump would be a capital receipt of the payee, as where it is in return for an asset, the same quality attaches to the payment even though it is paid by instalments; so they will not be annual payments.

In *Foley v Fletcher and Rose*,[1] the taxpayer was one of two tenants in common of certain lands who agreed to sell the land for £99,000.[2] £6,770 was paid immediately and it was agreed that the balance of £92,230 was to be paid in half yearly instalments of £1,537 16s. over the next 30 years. The payer's claim to deduct tax in respect of each instalment as being a payment of an annuity was rejected by the Court of Exchequer.

Some judges thought that there was no method by which these payments could be dissected into capital and income elements,[3] but this is not correct today. Another view was that this was not a contract to pay an annuity but to pay a principal sum of money;[4] an annuity arises where the income is purchased with a sum of money and the capital has gone and has ceased to exist.[5] A further view was that these payments were not profits derived from property but the price of it. The fact that a part of the instalments could be regarded as the price of the inconvenience of getting the payment postponed, and thus perhaps a profit, did not mean that the whole payment thereby became a profit.[6]

In *Mallaby-Deeley v IRC*[7] an individual had undertaken to pay £33,000 to assist in the publication of Burke's Complete Peerage and to pay by equal quarterly instalments. He then made a covenant in which he was to make larger instalment payments in the earlier years and smaller payments in the later years. These payments were held to be capital.

The same result may be reached even though no fixed sum is agreed when the instalments commence, provided a formula for ascertaining the amount is fixed.

In *Ramsay v IRC*[8] the taxpayer had agreed to buy a dental practice. A primary price of £15,000 was agreed but the taxpayer agreed to pay it in the form of £5,000 at once and then to pay each year for ten years a sum equal to 25% of the net profits of that year. These were described as capital payments and no interest was payable. It was held that the payments were not annual payments but capital instalments so that the taxpayer could not deduct income tax when making the payments.

It is probably also relevant that this decision involving the Revenue corresponded with the conduct of the parties.

Simon's Taxes B5.309–312; Butterworths Income Tax Service F4.45.
  [1] (1858) 3 H & N 769.
  [2] The total amount is probably about double the sums which would have been paid if paid at once: per Bramwell B at p. 782.
  [3] Semble, per Pollock CB at 769; per Bramwell B at 783 and per Watson B at 784, but contra Channell LJ at 788.
  [4] Per Pollock CB at 779.
  [5] Per Watson B at 784.
  [6] Per Pollock CP at 779.
  [7] [1938] 4 All ER 818, 23 TC 153.
  [8] (1935) 20 TC 79.

9: 72   (2) However, where the bargain was always thought of in income terms, and was concluded in income terms, and there is nothing in the documents to give the transaction a capital character, the payments will be pure income. This is even more likely to be the case where the payments are expressed in terms strongly suggestive of income, such as a rentcharge.

In *IRC v Church Comrs for England*,[1] a charity sold a reversion on a lease to the tenant in consideration of rentcharges payable annually for ten years and amounting in aggregate to £96,000 each year. It was clear that at no time was the purchaser willing to purchase for a single lump sum. The House of Lords held that these payments were pure income and could not be dissected into capital and interest payments.

Simon's Taxes B5.309–311; Butterworths Income Tax Service F4.46.
[1] [1976] STC 339, [1976] 2 All ER 1037. This case may be taken as an *a fortiori* example of principle (3) since the calculation of the sum involved a wish to maintain an income equivalent to the rent for the remainder of the lease and to establish a fund which could then yield that sum in perpetuity.

9: 73   (3) Where, despite principle (1), a series of payments are made in exchange for a right to income payments, the payments are likely to be pure income.

In *IRC v Hogarth*[1] the partners agreed to pay one of them who was retiring not only his share of the capital account and assets of the firm but also a sum equal to one fourteenth part of the net profits of the business for the three years ending 31st December 1937, 1938 and 1939, under deduction of tax. The partners making this payment sought to deduct these sums from their income for surtax purposes, something they could only do if the payments were income of the recipient. The Court of Session held that they were income, first because a statement that the payments were to be made under deduction of tax indicated it, and secondly because the payments were in satisfaction of a claim to annual profits or gains.

In *Chadwick v Pearl Life Insurance Co.*[2] the plaintiff owned a lease which had ten years to run. The total income from the sublease was £1,925 p.a. and the rent payable under the lease was £300, leaving a rental income of £1,625. The plaintiff sold his interest to the defendant for £1,000 and a covenant by the defendant to pay £1,625 p.a. for ten years. No sum was fixed as the total amount due on the sale, although that total sum could clearly have been ascertained (£17,250). Since the intention of the transaction was that the plaintiff should continue to receive as income to the end of the term the same amount that he had previously received as rent Walton J concluded that the payments were income, although he observed that the distinction was a fine one.

Simon's Taxes B5.309, 313; Butterworths Income Tax Service F4.47.
[1] (1940) 23 TC 491; see also *Jones v IRC* [1920] 1 KB 711, 7 TC 310, doubted by Scott LJ in *Dott v Brown* [1936] 1 All ER 543.
[2] [1905] 2 KB 507.

9: 74   (4) If the payment is not pure income, it may be dissected into capital and interest. This will be done if the parties, who are buying and selling a capital asset, having agreed on a price then make provision for payment of that price by instalments, the amount of which is so calculated, and shown to be so calculated, as to include an interest element.[1]

In *Secretary of State in Council of India v Scoble*[2] the East India Company bought a railway from a company and was empowered to pay outright or in instalments over a period of 46 years; the instalments, although called an annuity, were dissected. The only question in this case was whether the payments were pure income or could be dissected.

Where no lump sum purchase price has been agreed upon the power to dissect is debatable. However, the question whether a lump sum is involved is to be decided after looking at the transaction as a whole. This may explain the most extreme example of dissection—*Vestey v IRC*.[3] The taxpayer sold shares worth £2m for £5½m, the sum to be paid in 125 yearly instalments of £44,000. The agreement stated that the price of £5½m was to be without interest. The Revenue sought to charge the taxpayer to surtax either on the whole payment as an annuity or on a part of it as interest. Cross J upheld the second claim. However, the enthusiasm with which Cross J preferred the second approach to the first is not to be found in the decision of the House of Lords in *IRC v Church Comrs for England*.[4] The facts of that case fell on the other side of the line principally because the transaction was thought of throughout in income tax terms, see principle (2), and because there was no evidence that the parties had ever settled on a firm lump sum price. Yet Lord Wilberforce accepted the *Vestey* decision as correct despite the fact that the only figure agreed on by the parties was the overall price of £5½m.[5]

Today it is likely that, when the parties have agreed on a fixed sum, the sum will be dissected and will not be pure capital unless the period is short and the contract in a common form. Dissection into interest and principal was directed in *Vestey* where the period was 125 years, but not in *Ramsay* where the period was ten years and the contract was for the disposal of a business, the price being ascertained on a common and reasonable basis. In *Foley v Fletcher and Rose* the period was thirty years but today it seems inconceivable that there would be no dissection on such facts.

Simon's Taxes B5.309–311; Butterworths Income Tax Service F4.48.
[1] Per Lord Wilberforce in *IRC v Church Comrs for England* [1976] STC 339 at 345, [1976] 2 All ER 1037 at 1043.
[2] [1903] AC 299, 4 TC 623.
[3] [1961] 3 All ER 978, 40 TC 112, (Phillips).
[4] [1976] 2 All ER 1037, esp. per Lord Wilberforce at 1043.
[5] Actuarial report made to the trustees referred to in the case stated in *Vestey* at (1961) 40 TC 112 at 115.

(vi) *Division of profits—a doubtful rule*

9: 75 The rule that the payment must be pure income profit rule (iii) concentrates on the payee; the rule that the payment must be a division of profits as opposed to spending profits concentrates on the payer. The status of this rule is therefore most uncertain.

The rule stems, like the preceding one, from the deduction machinery in TA 1988, s. 348, which enables the payer to retain the basic rate income tax which he deducts and thus in effect to deduct annual payments in computing taxable income. The essence of payments falling within TA 1988, s. 348 is that they are assignments of income and that a division of profits must therefore be distinguished from a spending of profits.[1]

This concentration on the payer seems quite out of place when the issue is whether certain payments are income of the payee and gives a quite disproportionate effect to s. 348 which is a machinery section and not a charging section. A payment that is not an annual payment and so outside s. 348 cannot then be directly assessed under Schedule D, Case III. To pay attention to the position of the payer might suggest that an annual payment cannot be such if it was an item of capital expenditure by the payer; this however is not the case.[2]

414   *Part II—Income tax*

Simon's Taxes B5.309; Butterworths Income Tax Service F4.50.
[1] Per Rowlatt J in *Jones v Wright* (1927) 13 TC 221 at 226 and see Lord Hanworth MR in *Westminster v IRC* (1935) 19 TC 490 at 505.
[2] See Lord Donovan in *IRC v Land Securities Investment Trust Ltd* [1969] 2 All ER 430 at 434, 45 TC 495 at 517. This case dealt with the deductibility of the covenanted sums for *profits tax*, which tax knew nothing of annual payments and s. 348. In Lord Donovan said that the fact that the deduction for income tax was in effect allowed by s. 348 was not relevant; it was just anomalous.

Machinery—Deduction at source—TA 1988, ss. 348 and 349

9: 76   When A makes a payment to B out of income which has been brought into charge to income tax and the payment is an annuity or annual payment, and so B's income within Schedule D Case III, A has a right to deduct basic rate tax. So if A is due to pay B £100 he will deduct £25 and pay only £75. The authority for this is TA 1988, s. 348. Payments which are removed from Schedule D, Case III by FA 1988 are not subject to this rule. See further § 9: 78.

The deduction is treated as income tax paid by B.[1] It follows that if B's marginal rate of tax is 25% there is nothing more to be done. If however B's rate is 0% he may recover the £25 by making a repayment claim to the Revenue; if his rate is 40% he has only another £15 to pay. Quite anomalously, while there is a duty on the payer to supply a certificate to show that tax has been deducted,[2] there is no penalty for non-compliance, a matter of considerable practical importance.

However s. 348 not only allows A to act as tax collector for B, it also allows him to keep the £25 for himself. This is the mechanism whereby A's payment to B is treated as an assignment of A's income to B with result that it is deductible—or not taxable in A's hands.

The scheme thus has two functions. The first is to make a provisional assessment on B by allowing A to deduct basic rate tax at source; this may be called the withholding function. The second is to give effect to A's right to deduct this payment in computing total income by first making A pay tax at basic rate on this part of his income and then permitting A to recoup that tax on making this payment;[3] this may be called the relief function.

This scheme applies where payment is made out of income that has been brought into charge to income tax. If the tax has not yet been paid, TA 1988, s. 3 ensures that an assessment will be made. That provision also directs that, subject to other provisions of the Act, the rate of tax to be paid by A will be basic rate—and only basic rate. This means that he is not liable to higher rate tax.

It will not be forgotten that A is not entitled to personal relief on that slice of his income which has been assigned to B;[4] it follows that he will pay tax at 25% on that slice and then recoup that tax under s. 348.

Simon's Taxes A3.402, 403; Butterworths Income Tax Service A3.52.
[1] TA 1988, s. 348(1)(*d*).
[2] TMA 1970, s. 106(1).
[3] TA 1988, s. 3.
[4] TA 1988, s. 276; supra, § **6: 36**.

TA 1988, s. 349(1)

9: 77   If A's total income is less than £100 TA 1988, s. 348 does not apply. Originally A was expected to make the payment in full but this might be inconvenient since A might not know what his final tax liability would be when he made the payment. Therefore A is obliged by s. 349 to deduct the £25; he must account for that sum to the Revenue.

EXAMPLES
In each case A is to make an annual payment to B of £100.
(1) A's total income is £10,000; s. 348 applies. A pays B £75.
(2) A's total income is £100,000; s. 348 applies. A pays B £75; s. 348 only authorises deduction at basic rate. If A can deduct this payment in computing A's total income any deduction in respect of higher rates i.e. for excess liability will be given effect when the higher rate liability is calculated. This is usually achieved by lengthening the band of A's income subject to basic rate and so reducing the amount subject to higher rates. (As with X's covenant of £1,000 in the example supra, § **5: 54**.)
(3) A's total income is £1,000; s. 348 applies. A would normally pay no tax as his total income is more than offset by the personal relief. However, A must pay basic rate tax on £100 of his income under s. 3 and may then recoup that tax by withholding under s. 348.
(4) A's total income is nil; s. 349 applies A pays B £75 and the Revenue £25.
(5) A's total income is £60; s. 349(1) applies; s. 349(1) requires A to pay B £75; A is liable to basic rate tax of £15 on £60 and s. 349 requires him first to account to the Revenue for basic rate tax on £40.

Simon's Taxes A3.404; Butterworths Income Tax Service A3.54.

Payments within the scheme

9: 78   Annuities and other annual payments come within this scheme provided they are taxable as B's income under Schedule D Case III and so are not removed by the 1988 changes. Annuities and other annual payments *not* within the scheme are (*a*) such payments charged on land—chargeable under Schedule A,[1] (*b*) such payments made under a source sited outside the UK—chargeable under Schedule D Case IV, (*c*) such payments from a source sited inside the UK but in favour of a non-resident and exempt under a double tax treaty.[2]

The scheme is *extended* to:

(*i*)   any royalty or other sum paid in respect of the use of a patent, TA 1988, ss. 348 and 349;
(*ii*) certain payments in the nature of rents and royalties by a mining or quarrying concern[3] (TA 1988, s. 119); and
(*iii*) electric line wayleaves (TA 1988, s. 120).

The scheme of deduction at source originally applied not only to annuities and annual payments but also to payments of yearly interest and in effect to dividends.[4] Today, most interest payments are outside the scheme[5] and dividends are the subject of a special regime under Schedule F; attempts to convert interest payments into annuities are frustrated by TA 1988, s. 786, supra, § **5: 43**.

As a result of the 1988 changes new maintenance payments are removed from TA 1988, s. 348 as are new covenanted payments. Existing maintenance payments are removed for 1989–90 and later years. In each instance the payments are entirely removed from Schedule D, Case III and not just from s. 348. New covenanted payments which remain within Schedule D, Case III, i.e. payments by trusts, covenanted donations to charities and payments for bona fide commercial purposes e.g., partnership retirement annuities,[6] remain subject to ss. 348 and 349.

Simon's Taxes A3.408, 409; Butterworths Income Tax Service A3.52, A3.54.

[1] Supra, § **9: 01.**
[2] E.g. S.I. 1970, No. 488.
[3] See list in TA 1988, s. 55.
[4] Income Tax Act 1918—All Schedules Rule 20.
[5] But see TA 1988, s. 350; supra, § **9: 48** and infra, § **25: 14.**
[6] ICAEW Memorandum (TR739) *Simon's Tax Intelligence* 1989, p. 78.

The payer

9: 79   Under TA 1988, s. 348, the person making the payment is entitled to deduct income tax when making the payment,[1] but only at the basic rate.[2] If the payments are made late, the rate of tax to be deducted is that in force when the payment falls due.[3]

"On making the payment" includes payment by cheque, by transfer of a marketable security or by the making of credit entries in books of account.[4] There must however be some effective[5] act by the payer which transfers the right to the money[5] so that the mere capitalisation of unpaid interest by the lender is not payment of interest by the borrower.[6] Where the payee is also a debtor of the payer, payment may be made by the payee extinguishing the payer's liability.[7]

Under s. 349(1), the person making the payment is obliged to deduct "a sum representing the amount of income tax on the payment"[8] and he is accountable to the Revenue for tax at the basic rate[9] on the whole sum or, where the payment is partly from taxed income, on that part not paid from taxed income, in which case he can keep the balance of the deduction; he is accountable whether or not he makes that deduction.[10]

Under s. 349(1) the duty to deduct is imposed on the person "by or through whom" it is made. Where therefore solicitors held funds for one obliged to make a payment falling within s. 349(1) the solicitors were held accountable.[11] If therefore in *Stokes v Bennett*, infra, § **9: 80**, the husband had remitted the sums to his solicitors in England to be paid over to the wife, the solicitors would have been assessable had they received the sums gross and then failed to deduct.[12] The words "through whom" are apt to cover any agent even a bank.

Simon's Taxes A3.410; Butterworths Income Tax Service A3.52, A3.54.

[1] TA 1988, s. 348(1)(*b*).
[2] TA 1988, s. 4.
[3] *IRC v Crawley* [1987] STC 147.
[4] Per Lord Wright MR, in *Rhokana Corpn Ltd v IRC* [1937] 1 KB 788 at 808; on appeal [1938] 2 All ER 51, 21 TC 552 at 573; see also *IRC v Plummer* [1979] STC 793, [1979] 3 All ER 775.
[5] See also *Re Vernon, Edwards v Vernon* (1946) 175 LT 421, and *Momm v Barclays Bank International* [1976] 3 All ER 588.
[6] *IRC v Oswald* [1945] 1 All ER 641, 26 TC 448.
[7] *Butler v Butler* [1961] P 33, [1961] 1 All ER 810.

[8] TA 1988, s. 349(1).
[9] TA 1988, s. 4.
[10] TA 1988, s. 350(1).
[11] *Rye and Eyre v IRC* [1935] AC 274, 19 TC 164 and see *Howells v IRC* [1939] 3 All ER 144, 22 TC 501.
[12] *Quaere* whether they would have been assessable if the husband had remitted to them only the net sum—semble not.

Tax deducted—immunity of payee from basic rate liability

9: 80   Under TA 1988, s. 348, the payee is treated as having paid the amount of income tax which has been deducted.[1]

Under s. 349(1), if the payer has deducted tax the payee is regarded as having paid basic rate income tax and so is safe from direct assessment whether or not the payer accounts for the tax to the Revenue.[2] In *Stokes v Bennett*,[3] a man resident in Brazil was under a liability to pay his former wife sums under an order made on their divorce by an English court. The husband made the payments but deducted tax. Having no UK income he was within s. 349(1) but did not account to the Revenue for the tax deducted. Upjohn J held that no direct assessment could be made on the wife as she had already suffered tax. Had the payment been under an order of a foreign court the payments would have fallen within Schedule D, Case V,[4] and s. 349 would not have applied. Such a payment might also fall within Case III[5] but since the Revenue may elect under which Case to charge, a direct assessment might be made on the payee under Case V.

Simon's Taxes A3.416; Butterworths Income Tax Service A3.52, A3.54.
[1] TA 1988, s. 348(1)(*d*).
[2] On the position where the payer fails to deduct, see infra.
[3] [1953] 2 All ER 313, 34 TC 337.
[4] *Chamney v Lewis* (1932) 17 TC 318 and infra, § **34: 07**.
[5] *National Bank of Greece SA v Westminster Bank Executor and Trustee Co (Channel Islands) Ltd* [1971] 1 All ER 233, 46 TC 491 suggests that this is unlikely and that Case III is to be confined to obligations arising in the UK. TA 1988, s. 18 is not so confined but cf. *Colquhoun v Brooks*; infra, § **34: 02**.

Failure to deduct—the Revenue and the parties

9: 81   Under TA 1988, s. 348 the payer is entitled but not obliged to deduct tax. An obligation to do so may however arise in some other way. In *Re Sharp, Rickett v Rickett*,[1] trustees of a settlement failed to deduct tax when paying certain annuities. This was a breach of trust because they had overpaid the annuitant at the expense of the other beneficiaries and were therefore compelled to make good the loss.

The deduction is to be treated as income tax paid by the person to whom the payment is made.[2] Therefore if no deduction is made, no tax can be treated as having been paid. It seems to follow that if tax is not deducted a direct assessment may therefore be made under Schedule D, Case III on the payee.[3] The Revenue view is that no repayment claim can be made by the payee but this is subject to concessionary relief for maintenance payments which takes the odd form of allowing the payer to deduct the payment in computing his income.[4]

It is clear that if s. 349(1) applies and tax is not deducted, the Revenue may make a direct assessment on the payee.[5] However the payer is obliged, not entitled, to deduct tax, and to account for it to the Revenue; he therefore remains liable.[6] The amount on which the payer is assessable is the amount payable. If he makes a covenanted payment of £100 but fails to deduct the £25 tax, he may be charged with the tax of £25. There is no rule which treats him as having paid the £100 *net* of tax so as to cause that figure actually paid to be grossed up to £133.33.[7]

Simon's Taxes A3.406, 416; Butterworths Income Tax Service A3.55.

[1] [1906] 1 Ch 793.

[2] TA 1988, s. 348(1)(*d*).

[3] TA 1970, s. 52(1)(*a*) precluded any direct assessment on the payee but in 1973 this was replaced by what is now s. 348(1)(*d*). Direct assessment on the payer is now possible and is common where the payee is subject to higher rate liability, whether or not the payee deducts basic rate tax under s. 348.

[4] Extra-statutory concession, A52 (1988), see **Simon's Taxes, Division H2.2**; for a critical comment see [1985] BTR 329.

[5] *Grosvenor Place Estates Ltd v Roberts* [1961] 1 All ER 341, 39 TC 433 (JGM).

[6] TA 1970, s. 53(2); *Lord Advocate v Edinburgh Corpn* 1905 7 F (Ct of Sess) 1972.

[7] *IRC v Watson* (1943) 25 TC 25.

Failure to deduct: the parties inter se

9: 82   If the payer fails to deduct tax under s. 348, and so pays more than he need, the general rule is that there is no obligation on the payee to refund the overpayment so long as the payer's mistake is one of law. The payer is treated as making a gift which, being complete, cannot be undone. It follows that no action will lie against the overpaid payee for recovery of the sum and that payer has no right to withhold later payments to reimburse himself.[1] It has also been held that if the payment is one of a series of payments within the tax year and some of those payments remain to be made, he may not make good his loss by making the deduction from one of the later payments.[2] To make matters worse for the payer it has also been held that where a sum has been paid and the payer did not then notify the payee of any deduction, he is treated as having failed to deduct tax.[3]

However, the payer may be able to take some comfort under one or more of the following qualifications:

(*i*) A failure to deduct in respect of a past payment does not prejudice his right to deduct in respect of later ones.

(*ii*) The general rule applies to payments that have been made; it follows that he may deduct in respect of payments to be made even though the due date for payment has passed.[4] Further it may be that a payment made "on account" or expressed to be made provisionally would not be treated as having been made and so as entitling the payer to adjust the account when making later payments.[5]

(*iii*) The general rule does not apply to payments made under a mistake of fact. So when a deduction system applied under Schedule A and the tenant failed to deduct income tax in respect of rent because he thought the lease was for ten years—and so outside the deduction system—when it was in fact for 99 years, the court held that his mistake was one of fact and permitted him to recover his loss.[6] In such instances it is a matter for the payer whether he recovers the sums from the payee or withholds from subsequent payments under the general principles of set-off.

(*iv*) Where payments are made by personal representatives under a mistake of law they may—contrary to the general rule—deduct the amount of tax which they should have deducted from earlier payments from later ones and thus make good the loss to the estate. This is on the ground that in the administration of an estate the court will wherever possible correct errors of account between the estate and the beneficiaries.[7] The position may be different if the trustee is the beneficiary who has been underpaid.[8] It is in any case doubtful whether the loss can be made good by recovery from the beneficiary directly,[9] save where property can be traced into his hands, he is a constructive trustee of the property or an action lies under the principle in *Ministry of Health v Simpson.*[10]

(*v*) Where the failure to deduct was due to the fact that the rate of tax had not then been fixed, s. 348 expressly allows the payer to make good the deficiency on making later payments; if there are no more payments to be made he can recover the sum by action.

(*vi*) Failure to deduct basic rate tax cannot effect the payer's right to deduct the payments in computing his total income for purposes of higher and additional rate liabilities.

Simon's Taxes A3.416; Butterworths Income Tax Service A3.55.
[1] *Warren v Warren* (1895) 72 LT 628 applied in *Re Hatch, Hatch v Hatch* [1919] 1 Ch 351.
[2] *Johnson v Johnson* [1946] P 205, [1946] 1 All ER 573.
[3] *Hemsworth v Hemsworth* [1946] 1 KB 431, [1946] 2 All ER 117.
[4] See cases at n. 1 supra and *Taylor v Taylor* [1937] 3 All ER 571, [1938] 1 KB 320.
[5] Perhaps payments to be made in instalments might come within this principle too.
[6] *Turvey v Dentons (1923) Ltd* [1952] 2 All ER 1025, [1953] 1 QB 218.
[7] *Re Musgrave, Machell v Parry* [1916] 2 Ch 417.
[8] *Re Horne, Wilson v Cox Sinclair* [1905] 1 Ch 76; see also *Re Ainsworth, Finch v Smith* [1915] 2 Ch 96.
[9] *Re Robinson, McLaren v Public Trustee* [1911] 1 Ch 502.
[10] [1951] AC 251, [1950] 2 All ER 1137.

Which section?

9: 83   S. 348 applies when the payment is payable wholly out of profits or gains brought into charge to income tax; s 349(1) applies when the payment is not wholly payable out of profits so charged. If the payment is partly payable out of such profits, s. 349 applies but the payer is accountable only for so much of the payment as is not made out of the profits already taxed. If the payer has income which has itself been subject to deduction at source, that income is treated as having been charged to income tax.[1]

In deciding whether income has been taxed one looks at income of that year, taking account of the preceding year basis, rather than the income actually arising.[2]

EXAMPLE

Suppose that A is under an obligation to pay an annuity of £900 and he has employment income which is exactly cancelled out by his personal allowances but he also has a Schedule D, Case III income from established sources which in the year ending 5th April 1989 produces £1,000 and in the year ending 5th April 1990 produces £800. A's taxable income for the year 1989–90 will be £1,000 and for the year 1990–91 will be £800. The annuity payment made in 1989–90 will therefore fall within s. 348 while that made in 1990–91 will fall within s. 349(1).

Simon's Taxes A3.404, 414, 415; Butterworths Income Tax Service A3.52, A3.54.
[1] TA 1988, s. 348(1)(*b*).
[2] Per Lord Simon in *Allchin v Coulthard* [1943] 2 All ER 352 at 357, 25 TC 445 at 463.

9: 84   Another question arises if a payment was payable in year 1 in which there was sufficient taxable income of the payer for the payment to fall within TA 1988, s. 348, but payment was actually made in year 2 when there was not sufficient income. Since the right to deduct under s. 348 only arises on "making" the payment, and since in general the income is treated as taxable to the recipient under Schedule D, Case III only in the year in which it is received, it would appear that the date, upon which the question of which section should apply depends, should be determined by reference to the date of the payment. However, the general gearing of s. 348 to the date the payment becomes due, the repetition of that in s. 835 and the provision that tax is to be deducted at the rate in force when the payment became due,[1] suggest that on balance the better view is that s. 348 should apply.

The Revenue opinion is that the former view is correct. However, by concession the payer may take a credit for the sum he could have deducted under s. 348 and set that against his liability under s. 349(1).[2] If the Revenue view is correct and year 1 is the s. 349(1) year and year 2 is the s. 348 year, no liability appears to arise at all. There is much to be said against the Revenue view.

Simon's Taxes A3.411.
[1] TA 1988, s. 4 applied in *IRC v Crawley* [1987] STC 147. If the payment is not made at all there is no liability to tax, *Woodhouse v IRC* [1936] 20 TC 673.
[2] Extra-statutory concession A16 (1988), see **Simon's Taxes, Division H2.2**.

9: 85   The rule that for TA 1988, s. 348 the payment must be wholly payable out of profits means that the tax must have been borne in the year of the payment. If there is insufficient income in that year, the payer cannot bring himself within s. 348 by pointing to excess income from previous years[1] any more than if he is forced to make the payment out of capital[2] or out of money borrowed.[3] Similarly, the payer falls within s. 349(1), and not s. 348, if he is himself exempt from income tax[4] or is not subject to income tax,[5] or if the profits of that year escape income tax because losses from previous years are rolled forward so as to relieve those profits from tax.[6] The same result follows if the payer has been allowed to deduct the payment already in computing his profits for the year, and it is apparently immaterial whether the allowance was correct or not.[7]

In general, the question out of what cash resources the payment was made is irrelevant. As Lord Wilberforce said in *IRC v Plummer*:

"What is significant . . . is not the actual source out of which the money is paid, nor even the way in which the taxpayer for his own purposes keeps his accounts, if indeed he keeps any, but the status of a notional account between himself and the Revenue. He is entitled, in respect of any tax year, to set down on one side his taxed income and on the other the amount of the annual payments he has made and if the latter is equal to or less than the former, to claim the benefit of the section."[8]

This view echoes the decision of Wilberforce J in *Postlethwaite v IRC*[9] dealing with an annuity payable by trustees and holding that it was open to the taxpayer to claim that the payment had been made out of that portion of the trust fund which yielded the most favourable result for the purposes of taxation. The learned judge went on to hold that the fact that there might not have been sufficient cash to make the gross, as opposed to the net, payment[10] was irrelevant.

A sum received by way of interest from a composite rate deposit is treated as having borne tax.[11]

Simon's Taxes A3.408, 413; Butterworths Income Tax Service A3.52, A3.54.
[1] *Luipaards Vlei Estate and Gold Mining Co Ltd v IRC* [1930] 1 KB 593, 15 TC 573.
[2] *Brodie's Will Trustees v IRC* (1933) 17 TC 432.
[3] *Dickson v Hampstead Borough Council* (1927) 11 TC 691.
[4] *Duncan's Executors v Farmer* (1909) 5 TC 417; as where the payer is subject to corporation tax, infra, § 25: 04.
[5] Ibid.
[6] *Trinidad Petroleum Development Co Ltd v IRC* [1937] 1 KB 408, 21 TC 1.
[7] *Muller & Co Ltd v IRC* (1928) 14 TC 116; *Renfrew Town Council v IRC* (1934) 19 TC 13.
[8] *IRC v Plummer* [1979] STC 793 esp. at 799 (Lord Wilberforce) see also Lord Morris, in *Chancery Lane Safe Deposit Co Ltd v IRC* [1966] 1 All ER 1 at 12, 43 TC 83 at 112.
[9] (1963) 41 TC 224.
[10] (1963) 41 TC 224 at 232.
[11] TA 1988, s. 479(2)(c).

9: 86   If the taxpayer makes a deliberate decision to charge the payment to capital and that payment has some practical effect such as entitling the taxpayer to a larger subsidy as in *Birmingham Corpn v IRC*[1] or, in the case of a company before 1965, leaving a fund of profit out of which a dividend could be paid, as in *BW Nobes & Co Ltd v IRC*,[2] the payment is governed by TA 1988, s. 349, not s. 348. However, in *Chancery Lane Safe Deposit Co Ltd v IRC*[3] the House of Lords held that s. 348 would not apply where a particular payment had been charged to capital, not as a matter of mere domestic accounting but as the result of a deliberate decision, even though the company had ample funds out of which to meet both the interest payments and dividends. The practical effect of creating a fund out of which larger or later dividends could be paid was sufficient to exclude s. 348.

There is much to be said for the dissenting view trenchantly expressed by Lords Reid and Upjohn. First there was no previous authority compelling the House to that conclusion; earlier cases had proceeded on the assumption that funds were not sufficient to meet both the dividends and the interest payments and were obviously correct. The Revenue had now discovered that in one case[4] there were in fact funds sufficient for both these purposes but, as Lord Upjohn observed, "We are not bound to follow a case merely because it is indistinguishable upon the facts. A decision even in your Lordships' House is binding on your Lordships only because it lays down some principle of law or for reasoning on some particular facts".[5] Secondly it would not be easy to distinguish mere domestic accounting from a deliberate decision and thirdly because in this case it would lead to effective double taxation.[6]

In view of the reaffirmation of this decision in *Fitzleet Estates Ltd v Cherry*[7] it is as well that the decision is of much less practical importance today. The reason for this is that ss. 348 and 349 no longer apply to yearly interest; further, companies are now subject to corporation tax and, although that tax prevents the deductibility of charges on income where a payment is charged to capital,[8] this no longer applies to interest.[9] Outside the corporate sphere it is hard to see what effect it may have in income tax save where one is dealing with a trader of eccentric taste.[10]

Simon's Taxes A3.415; Butterworths Income Tax Service A3.52, A3.54.

[1] [1930] AC 307, 15 TC 172.
[2] [1964] 2 All ER 140, 43 TC 133.
[3] [1966] 1 All ER 1, 43 TC 83.
[4] *Central London Rly Co v IRC* [1936] 2 All ER 375, 20 TC 102.
[5] At 128 and 122.
[6] The company paid tax on its profits but could not recoup that tax by withholding under s. 348.
[7] [1977] STC 397, [1977] 3 All ER 996, HL.
[8] TA 1988, s. 338(6) infra, § **25: 12**.
[9] TA 1988, s. 338. Property companies avoided this problem by charging interest to revenue but taking power in the memorandum and articles to allow surpluses as revaluation to be distributed as dividend.
[10] See Lord Wilberforce in *IRC v Plummer*, supra, § **9: 85**.

Commentary

9: 87   The scope of the scheme contained in TA 1988, ss. 348 and 349 has been greatly reduced (see supra, § **9: 33**) but outright abolition might have been better.[1] The same result could be achieved by scrapping the deduction at source and simply allowing A to deduct these items in computing total income. The disadvantages of the present scheme are many. It is complex in itself, is responsible for other complexities and opens the door to odd devices giving rise to planning and anomalies. The complexities of the system include not only the border between the two provisions and problems of timing but also the problem of the relationship between s. 348 and the charging provisions in Schedule D, thus does deductibility under s. 348 determine whether a payment falls within Schedule D, Case III or is it the other way round?[2] Among the complexities for which it is responsible are not only the many rules which need to say whether a particular piece of specially taxed income is to be treated as taxed for s. 348[3] but also the case law rule that income within Case III cannot be a trading receipt and also some of the tortuous provisions in ss. 660–685 and the decision in *Ang v Parrish*.[4] The planning opportunities are revealed by the *Church Commissioners* case and the anomalies by the boundary between an obligation to pay cash (within s. 348 and so deductible in computing income) and one to deliver in kind (not within s. 348 and so not deductible) or that between a UK court order to make periodical payments (deductible) and a foreign court order (not deductible).[5] Further, in what is probably the most common area of its application, i.e. sums paid by way of maintenance to a spouse, s. 348 causes considerable cash flow problems to the recipient.

[1] See generally [1981] BTR 263.
[2] See *IRC v Frere* [1964] 3 All ER 796, 42 TC 125 and *IRC v Whitworth Park Coal Co Ltd* [1959] 3 All ER 703, 38 TC 531. See also *McBurnie v Tacey* [1984] STC 347.
[3] E.g. TA 1988, ss. 313, 421, 476, 547, 233 and 426(1)(*d*).
[4] Infra, § **13: 01**.
[5] *Bingham v IRC* [1955] 3 All ER 321, 36 TC 254 because s. 348 and s. 835 apply only when the income of the payee is taxable under Schedule D Case III and a foreign court order is a source within Schedule D Case V. See also *Keiner v Keiner* [1952] 1 All ER 643, 34 TC 346.

Payments "free of tax"

(1) *Validity of agreements*

9: 88 By TMA 1970, s. 106(2) any *agreement* for the payment of interest, rent or other annual payment in full without allowing the deduction of income tax shall be void. This invalidates the part relating to non-deduction and not the whole agreement.[1] So if P agrees to pay Q £100 a year without deduction, P is nonetheless entitled to deduct tax under s. 348 or bound to do so under s. 349. It applies only to agreements,[2] not to wills nor to orders of the court.[3] In appropriate cases the court will rectify an agreement to avoid s. 106(2).[4]

Where there is an agreement that P shall pay Q £100 "free of tax", the House of Lords held in *Ferguson v IRC*, overriding a long line of authority, that P must pay Q such sums as after deduction of income tax leaves £100;[5] such a construction means that the agreement does not fall foul of s. 106(2). However, it also means that Q is entitled to £100 free of his marginal rate of tax; if that rate is 25%, he will be entitled to £133.33 gross i.e. £100 net. It is not clear whether the decision of the House of Lords means that the agreement is to pay free of such higher rates as Q may be liable to or only basic rate; the point was not in issue. The decision brings the rule of construction for agreements into line with that for court orders.[6]

Simon's Taxes E3.314.
[1] *Booth v Booth* [1922] 1 K B 66.
[2] *Re Goodson's Settlement, Goodson v Goodson* [1943] Ch 101, [1943] 1 All ER 201.
[3] An agreement to carry out an order of the court is subject to s. 106(2). *Blount v Blount* [1916] 1 K B 230; the converse is not; *Massey v Massey* [1949] W N 422.
[4] *Burroughes v Abbott* [1922] 1 Ch 86, distinguished in *Whiteside v Whiteside* [1950] Ch 65, [1949] 2 All ER 913.
[5] [1969] 1 All ER 1025, 46 TC 15.
[6] Infra, § **9: 90**.

(2) *The rule in Re Petitt*

9: 89 Where P is to pay Q £100 "free of tax", P will make a payment of £100; this is equivalent to £133.33 gross and Q's income is therefore taken to include not £100 but £133.33.

If Q has no other income he will be able to reclaim £33.33 from the Revenue on account of his personal reliefs. If he were allowed to keep the sum, he would have benefited to the tune of £133.33 and not £100 as undertaken by P; Q is therefore directed by the rule in *Re Pettit, Le Fevre v Pettit*[1] to hold the sum recovered from the Revenue on trust for P. Q is therefore under an obligation to make the repayment claim.[2]

If Q has other income, the value of the personal reliefs has to be shared between the annuity and the other income. It follows that the rule applies to that proportion of the reliefs which the gross amount of the annuity bears to Q's total income. So if Q is entitled to a personal relief of £2,605 and has other UK dividend income of £1,000 gross or £750 net Q will have a repayment claim for £283.33 of which 133.33/1,133.33 or 33.33 will be refunded to P. This matter becomes important where Q's total income moves above the level of his personal reliefs.

In every reported case Q has been entitled to a repayment of tax. However, the principle should apply wherever Q is entitled to set a relief from tax against his annuity income in whole or in part—and not simply when he makes a repayment claim. Any other conclusion would mean that the rule would apply where for example Q's other income was dividend income of £2,000 falling within Schedule F but not if it fell within Schedule E.

Q is obliged to account for relief from tax not only in respect of personal allowances but also for loss relief claimed under TA 1988, s. 380.[3] Although Q is under a duty to make the claim for a repayment when it is due it would appear that he is not obliged to claim relief under TA 1988, s. 380 rather than under TA 1988, s. 385.

The obligation to account causes problems in adjusting the total income of P and Q; thus is the sum due to be handed back as annual payment to P by Q so that s. 348 (or 349) applies and the gross sum treated as P's income? To make matters yet more complex one need only recall that Q would not be entitled to claim personal reliefs on that part of his income which he is under a duty to pay over.[4] It has been held that the liability to repay does not affect Q's total income nor his repayment claim.[5] The Revenue are therefore not entitled to refuse repayment simply because Q is bound to hand it over. No authority exists on the effect on P but the Revenue practice is to treat him as entitled to additional income equivalent to the grossed up sum he is repaid.[6]

The rule in *Re Pettit* is one of trust law and applies whenever the construction of the agreement, trust or will requires it. The question is whether the agreement is that Q should benefit to the extent of £100, and only that sum, in which case the rule applies or whether Q is to receive £100 net from P regardless of the actual tax Q may have to pay, if any.[7] The rule therefore applies whenever there is a fixed increase in Q's spendable income. There is thus a clear distinction between £100 "free of tax" to which the rule applies and "such sum as after deducting tax at the current rate shall leave £100"—known as a formula deduction covenant—to which the rule does not apply; the former indicates the extent to which Q is to benefit while the latter does not. Where the annuity is free of tax the annuitant is assured of a constant net sum and the payer of a constantly fluctuating liability; where the deduction formula applies, the payer is assured of a constant net outflow and the payee of constantly fluctuating net receipts. Where the annuity is free of tax, the liability of the payer will vary according to the financial position of the payee; where the deduction formula is used the benefit to the payee varies with his financial position. The rule in *Re Pettit* applies to free of tax clauses but not to a deduction formula covenant.

The rule has not been applied where Q was to receive "a clear annuity of" £100 nor £100 "free of all deductions";[8] on the other hand it was applied where Q was to receive "such sum as would leave in her hands" £100.[9]

The rule applies to agreements, estates and trusts. However, its status in Scotland is unclear. Illogically the rule does not apply to court orders[10] with the result that the same words will have one effect in an agreement and a different one in an order.

Simon's Taxes E2.1119–1128; Butterworths Income Tax Service J2.23.

[1] [1922] 2 Ch 765.

[2] *Re Kingcome, Hickley v Kingcome* [1936] 1 All ER 173, [1936] Ch 566. On position of non-residents see *Re Jubb, Neilson v King* (1941) 20 ATC 297. In *Re Batty, Public Trustee v Bell* [1952] 1 All ER 425, [1952] Ch 280. Vaisey J held that a wife could be made to elect for separate assessment so as to be compelled to make the repayment claim; on appeal it was held that the rule in *Re Pettit* did not apply so this issue was not discussed; however if the husband holds any repayment on trust for the wife (*Re Cameron* supra, § 3: 12) it ought to follow that the payer can compel the wife to compel the husband to make the claim. See also *Re Tatham, National Bank Ltd and Mathews v Mackenzie* [1945] Ch 34, [1945] 1 All ER 29.

[3] *Re Lyons, Barclays Bank Ltd v Jones* [1952] Ch 129, [1952] 1 All ER 34.

[4] Supra, § 5: 54.

[5] *IRC v Cook* [1945] 2 All ER 377, 26 TC 489.

[6] On the effect on P when P is an estate see *Re Twiss, Barclays Bank Ltd v Pratt* [1941] Ch 141, [1941] 1 All ER 93.

[7] *Re Batley, Public Trustee v Hert (No 2)* [1952] Ch 781, [1952] 2 All ER 562.

[8] *Re Skinner, Milbourne v Skinner* [1942] Ch 82, [1942] 1 All ER 32.

[9] *Re Maclennan, Few v Byrne* [1939] Ch 750, [1939] 3 All ER 81. See also *Re Jones, Jones v Jones* [1933] Ch 842 and *Re Eves, Midland Bank Executor and Trustee Co Ltd v Eves* [1939] Ch 969.

[10] *Jefferson v Jefferson* [1956] 1 All ER 31, [1956] P 136.

---

(3) *Construction of court orders*

9: 90   Since TMA 1970, s. 106(2) does not apply to court orders, the courts have long felt able to construe an order to pay £x "free of tax" as an order to pay such sum as after deduction of income tax at the basic rate leaves £x.[1] If the order is to pay "£x less tax," it is construed as an order to deduct basic rate tax on £x under TA 1988, ss. 348 or 349 and to pay the balance; the words "less tax" simply show that the order is not a small maintenance order and that tax will have to be deducted by the payer from the amount specified—hence the practice of not mentioning tax in small maintenance orders.[2]

Simon's Taxes E5.106; Butterworths Income Tax Service J2.28.

[1] *Spilsbury v Spofforth* [1937] 4 All ER 487, 21 TC 247.

[2] *Jefferson v Jefferson* [1956] P 136, [1956] 1 All ER 31.

---

(4) *Pre-war tax free annuities*

9: 91   The special rule for these annuities has been repealed.[1]

---

[1] TA 1970, s. 422(5) repealed by FA 1987, Sch. 16, Part VII.

Maintenance payments—new arrangements

9:92   Payments under arrangements made on or after 15th March 1988 are subject to a new regime.This new regime is highly restrictive and removes most of the tax planning devices currently in use. It is hard to tell whether the thinking behind the new rules and, in particular, the abolition of the right to deduct maintenance payments in computing the income of the payer, is due to a belief that a deduction is not justified in view of the general reduction in tax rates or to a wish to restore family values by increasing the costs of supporting separated families.

Under the new regime qualifying maintenance payments will not be subject to income tax in the hands of the recipient;[1] conversely, they will not be deductible by the payer subject, however, to the availability of the new but limited maintenance deduction.[2] Such payments will therefore be outside Schedule D, Case III; they will not be subject to deduction of tax under TA 1988, ss. 348 or 349; they will not be relevant to s. 835, nor will they be charged to tax under s. 3, nor will they exclude the availability of personal reliefs thanks to s. 277. Payments will therefore be made gross.

In order to recognise in part the cost of such things the payer will be entitled to a deduction, referred to here as the "maintenance deduction", of a sum equal to the difference between the single and the married man's allowance—£1,590 for 1989–90.[3] This deduction is available in respect of sums—including payments of household bills—which the payer is legally obliged to pay. Special mention is made of various payments which are not to count towards the £1,590 limit. These are: (i) voluntary payments, (ii) capital payments and lump sums, (iii) payments for which the taxpayer already gets relief in some other way and(iv) payments under a foreign court order.

This limit applies to the payer regardless of how many payees there may be. It therefore applies whether the payee has one ex-spouse or two.

The maintenance deduction is only available in respect of sums payable to the other or former spouse and so not for payments to the children; the deduction ceases once the payee remarries. Where a person makes payments to the child they will have no tax effect; the payments will not be income of the child nor will they be deductible by the payer.

In the year of separation the married man's allowance is available and the husband will also get the maintenance deduction up to £1,590 for the part of the year in which he is separated or divorced. If it is the wife who is making the payments she will get relief for payments made after the separation. In later years he will not be able to claim both the maintenance deduction and the married man's allowance.[4]

---

[1] TA 1988, s. 347A(1).

[2] TA 1988, s. 347B(2); FA 1988, s. 36(6) also excludes any right to deduct under TA 1988, s. 351.

[3] TA 1988, s. 347B(2); the amount is set by s. 347B(3); the formula is to change when separate taxation comes in in 1990–91—see Sch. 3, para. 13.

[4] Since he can only claim the maintenance deduction if there is an obligation to pay and that obligation will exclude his right to the married man's allowance.

Maintenance payments under existing obligations

9: 93   Payments under existing obligations fall outside s. 347B and also s. 347A. They therefore remain under a modified form of the present rules for 1988–89 and a severely modified form for later years. Payments are made under an existing obligation if the arrangements are in force on 15th March 1988, i.e. made before that day, or under a court order applied for on or before 15th March 1988 and made by 30th June.[1] Payments are also made under existing obligation if they are made under agreements reached on or before 15th March 1988 provided a copy of the agreement has been received by the Inspector of Taxes by 30th June 1988. Court orders or agreements made on or after 15th March which vary or replace such orders or agreements also qualify.

For 1988–89 the payee was entitled to exclude from income a sum equal to £1,490 or, if less, the sums chargeable to tax; this is referred to here as the "maintenance exclusion".[2] This only applied where the sums, if not under an existing obligation, would have been qualifying maintenance payments;[3] so the sums payable direct to a child could not qualify. The deduction by the payee is in addition to the right of the payer to deduct the sums by treating them as a charge on income; TA 1988, ss. 348 and 349 remained applicable to payments to the spouse and to payments to a child alike.

For 1989–90 and later years the payer loses the right to deduct these payments by treating them as a charge on his income,[4] and must make such payments gross—the deduction machinery under ss. 348 and 349 no longer applies.[5] This is to some extent a change of form, although a welcome one, rather than of substance since the payer is given a new statutory right to deduct these sums. The substantial element in the change is that the statutory deduction is capped—the maximum deduction is the amount due in 1988–89.[6] There is a further restriction in that, to count towards the maximum, the payments must also form part of the payee's income in that year.[7] This may bring into sharp focus the rules about the timing of income under Schedule D Case III.

The amount which is deductible by the payer will be treated as the income of the payee. However, if the payee is the other spouse that spouse will be entitled to have the chargeable payments reduced by an amount equal to the difference between the married man's allowance and the single person's allowance.[8] This carries over to later years the deduction allowed by FA 1988 for 1988–89; this is referred to in the examples as the "maintenance exclusion".

---

[1] FA 1988, s. 36(4).
[2] FA 1988, s. 37.
[3] Compare FA 1988, s. 37(1) with TA 1988 s. 347B(1).
[4] FA 1988, s. 38(2).
[5] FA 1988, s. 38(7).
[6] FA 1988, s. 38(3); on Revenue view of the meaning of due in 1988–89, see infra, § **9: 98**.
[7] FA 1988, s. 38(4).
[8] FA 1988, s. 38(6) to be recast in 1990–91 by Sch. 3, para. 33.

9: 94   If the payer[1] wishes, he may elect to move from the rules for existing obligations to the new system. This is likely to be of value only where the payments in 1988–89 are below the level of the new maintenance deduction for the payer but the liability to pay increases in later years (e.g. because of the terms of the order or agreement or because the order of agreement is varied). An election to change to the new regime can be made at any time during the year of assessment or up to twelve months after that year.[2]

The insistence on so much turning on the level of reliefs and payments in 1988–89 may raise some interesting timing problems e.g. a payment is due in 1987–88 but is made in 1988–89, does it count for relief in 1988–89? Equally, a payment due in 1988–89 is paid late (perhaps because of an error by a bank)—does this reduce the relief permanently? Conversely a payment is due in 1989–90 but is paid early in 1988–89—does this increase the relief? The answer to many of these problems lies in the rule that what matters is whether the payment is *due* in 1988–89[3] and, moreover must be due under, and therefore presumably under the terms of, an existing obligation. One issue that might arise is where the existing obligation refers to a formula and the facts specified in the formula can be manipulated; e.g. the father is to pay school fees and the school changes the date for payment so as to bring the payment for the summer term 1989 into the 1988–89 tax year. This might be challenged by the Revenue,[4] at least where the father and the school agree to the change.

[1] The consent of the payee is not required.
[2] FA 1988, s. 39.
[3] FA 1988, s. 37(1) and 38(2).
[4] See infra, § **9: 98**.

Small maintenance payments: existing obligations TA 1988, s. 351

9: 95   This provision has been repealed save for certain information powers from 1989–90.[1]

Simon's Taxes E1.514; E5.106; Butterworths Income Tax Service B2.22.
[1] FA 1988, Sch. 14, Part IV.

MAINTENANCE ORDERS

Planning points

9: 96   It is time to consider how the 1988 changes affect the use of a number of planning devices.

(1) Should the payments be made under a voluntary agreement or under an enforceable arrangement?

Under the pre 1988 rules, and under the new rules for existing arrangements, there was often an advantage in using an enforceable arrangement. Income was shifted from the payer to the payee and thus use could be made of the payee's personal reliefs and, if relevant, lower marginal rate of tax. The price to be paid for this was that if the payer were the husband, he would lose his married man's allowance and have only the ordinary single person's allowance; in the 1989–90 figures this would mean a drop from £4,375 to

£2,785 or £1,590 which at 25% is worth £397.50 (£7.64 p.w.) and at 40% is worth £636 (£12.23 p.w.). This larger allowance is, however, only available if he were maintaining her not only voluntarily but also wholly; hence if she has sufficient other income (supra, § **3: 10**) he will not be able to use the larger allowance anyway.

Under the rules for new orders for 1988–89 and later years the tax treatment of payments under a voluntary agreement turns on the fact that since they are not periodical payments they cannot be "qualifying maintenance payments". It follows that payments under a voluntary agreement will be treated as previously; they will not be taxable income of the payee so that the payee's reliefs and lower marginal rate will not be available. If the payer is the husband he will still be entitled to the married man's allowance.[1] However when the new regime for separate taxation starts in 1990–91 he will not be able to claim the new allowance under TA 1988, s. 257A although he may be able to claim transitional relief.[2] The payer will not be entitled to the maintenance deduction.

By contrast payments under enforceable agreements will be qualifying maintenance payments. The husband will not be able to claim the married man's allowance but the payer will be able to claim the maintenance deduction. However voluntary agreements and enforceable arrangements are made alike in that in neither event will payments qualify as income of the payee.

Payments under existing court orders or existing enforceable agreements will be treated as previously; a choice between voluntary and enforceable payments will have been made. It is now too late to make an agreement to change a voluntary payment into an enforceable one and retain the benefits of the old system unless, which is unlikely, the Revenue accept that an agreement to make a voluntary payment is an "agreement" which can be varied.[3]

Payments under enforceable agreements were not investment income for the purposes of the additional rate charge (abolished in 1984) but were for other purposes. So if payments are made to the wife for a child and the wife remarries the sums will not be earned income for the purposes of her earned income relief or separate taxation of her earned income.

Sums which a husband is ordered to pay to the Secretary of State for Social Services under the Social Security Acts are not deductible under the old rules—or the new rules for existing orders.[4]

(2) Should payments be made all to the other spouse or should some payments be made direct to a child?

One reason for the new rules is the criticism of the old arrangements by the House of Lords in *Sherdley v Sherdley*.[5] Under those arrangements it was advantageous in suitable cases for some of the payments to be made direct to a child. These advantages did not accrue if the payment was made to the wife for the child since such payments were treated as income of the wife— unless the settlement provisions applied in which case they would be treated as income of the husband. The advantages arose because the income would be treated as that of the child so that while the payer could still deduct the payments use could be made of the child's personal reliefs. These effects are maintained for existing orders subject to the general rule restricting relief for later years by a ceiling equal to the amounts due in 1988–89.

Under the rules for new orders a payment direct to a child cannot be a qualifying maintenance payment. It follows that the payer cannot claim any deduction for such a payment. The payment will not qualify as a charge on the payer's income as a periodical payment because of TA 1988, s. 347A (supra, § **9: 34**). The maintenance deduction is not available in respect of it.[6]

Where payments are made direct to a child under an existing order it is essential that the payments escape TA 1988, s. 663. If the payment falls foul of s. 663 the tax consequences may be worse than if the payment is to the wife for the child since, in the former case it will be treated as the income of H, while, in the latter, it will at least be treated as the income of W. The exclusion of payments made direct to the child, otherwise than under a court order, from s. 663 has, for long, rested on Revenue practice.

In *Harvey v Sivyer*[7] the practice was upheld on the basis that where a parent makes a covenant in favour of a child the parent is acting not only because of parental obligation to make a payment for the maintenance of the child but also because of natural concern and therefore there had to be an element of bounty. If this presumption of concern is irrebuttable we have a fiction worthy of the middle ages; if it is rebuttable there is a tax advantage for parents who can honestly say they have no concern for their children. Neither solution provides a satisfactory explanation for the distinction between separation agreements and separation orders.

The Revenue also take the view that a consent order or an order giving the parties leave to implement an agreement is not necessarily an order for the purpose of this practice.

Where s.663 is safely avoided the consequences of making the payments direct to the child, still assuming that there is an existing obligation, are:

(*i*) Relief under TA 1988, s. 259 is not affected whether the payment is made to the child or to W, supra, § **3: 15**.

(*ii*) Child's personal relief under s. 257 can be used; if the payment is made to W it is not then the child's income so relief may be lost.

(*iii*) Small maintenance orders can be made for the child and for W separately, thus improving the cash flow.

(*iv*) Neither arrangement has any effect on child benefit payments.

(*v*) If payments are to W for the child, H can deduct payments for excess liability and escapes TA 1970, s. 457 by virtue of s. 683(1)(*c*). Payments direct to the child are not saved by s. 683(1)(*c*) but escape s. 683 on the basis that there is no settlement.

For comparison the consequences under the new system are:

(i) as now, the parent's claim to relief under TA 1988, s. 259 is not affected,

(ii) unlike previously, the child's personal relief under TA 1988, s. 257 cannot be used; but in turn this means that the whole of that relief will be available to be set against other income of the child;

(iii) all payments are to be made gross whether or not they would be small maintenance orders;

(iv) as now there is no effect on child benefit;

(v) H cannot deduct the payments at all—and cannot set his maintenance deduction against payments to a child as distinct from payments to a spouse.

The financial consequences are illustrated in the examples which follow at the end of this Chapter.

[1] Under TA 1988, s. 257(1).
[2] Under TA 1988, s. 257F.
[3] See FA 1988, s. 36(4)(*d*).
[4] *McBurnie v Tacey* [1984] STC 347.
[5] [1987] STC 217.
[6] TA 1988, s. 347B(2).
[7] [1986] Ch 119, [1985] STC 434.

School fees

9: 97   Under the old system payments made to a school on behalf of a child to discharge the child's contractual liability to the school could be treated as income of the child.[1] This meant that school fees for a child of separated or divorced parent could be deducted from tax whereas those for the child of a continuing family could not. This anomaly was much criticised by the House of Lords in *Sherdley v Sherdley*.[2] However the House of Lords, while upholding the power of the courts to make such orders, did not determine whether they could be struck down under the new approach.

Under the new system new orders for the payment of school fees will not qualify for this treatment since they will not be qualifying maintenance payments and so will not be taxable income of the payee nor deductible by the payer. Payments under existing obligations will continue under the old system and so will be taxable income of the payee and deductible by the payer. However it is perhaps in this area that the application of the ceiling for later years by reference to the payments due in 1988–89 will most quickly be felt—as the second set of examples (see below) is designed to show.

[1] The practice was set out in *Practice Direction* [1983] 2 All ER 679 and SP 15/80.
[2] [1987] STC 217.

Could anything have been done in 1988–89?

9: 98   Assuming that any court orders applied for before 15th March 1988 were made by the end of June 1988, there seemed to be little left to be done. However, when existing obligations are in force a variation, whether by court order or new agreement, could have been effected to increase the amounts due in 1988–89 and so the ceiling for later years. Whether this will be effective is another matter. The Revenue view is that the ceiling is the amount the level of revised in 1988–89 which is different from the "amount based on payments agreed during 1988–89". Variation after 1988–89 will be ineffective to increase the ceiling.[2] On possible variation of school fees, see supra, § **9: 95**.

[1] ICAEW Memorandum (TR739) *Simon's Tax Intelligence* 1989, p. 79.
[2] On non-retroactivity of court orders see *Morley-Clark v Jones* [1985] STC 660, [1985] 3 All ER 193, CA but Revenue practice is to allow backdating to date of application for order; see SP6/81, **Simon's Taxes, Division H3.2.**

EXAMPLE

H and W have agreed to separate, W agreeing to look after their two children.

PROBLEM A

H earns £12,300; W has no other income. H offers W £6,500.

1. *New order 1989–90:*

		H		W
Income		£12,300.00		—
Less personal reliefs	£2,785		£2,785	
additional relief	—		1,590	
maintenance deduction	1,590			
(TA 1988, s. 347B(2))		4,375.00		4,095.00
Taxable income		7,925.00		—
Tax		1,981.25		—
Net income		£10,318.75		—

The result is the same if the sums are paid to the children.

2. *Existing (i.e., pre-March 1988) order 1989–90:*

		H		W
Income		£12,300.00		£6,500.00
Less personal reliefs	£2,785		£2,785	
additional relief	—		1,590	
maintenance deduction	6,500			
(FA 1988, s. 38(2)(*a*))				
maintenance exclusion			1,590	
(FA 1988, s. 38(2)(*b*), (5))		9,285.00		5,965.00
Taxable income		3,015.00		535.00
Tax		£753.75		£133.75

TA 1988, ss. 348, 349 do not apply; the payments are made gross (FA 1988, s. 38(7)).
Total combined net incomes: £11,412.50.

3. *Existing (i.e., pre-March 1988) court order 1989–90; £2,000 to each child and £2,500 to W:*

		H		W		C
Income		£12,300.00		£2,500		£2,000
Less personal reliefs	£2,785		£2,785		£2,785	
additional relief	—		1,590			
maintenance deduction	6,500					
(FA 1988, s. 38(2)(*a*))						
maintenance exclusion			1,590			
(FA 1988, s. 38(2)(*b*), (5))		9,285.00		5,965.00		£2,785.00
Taxable income		3,015.00		—		—
Tax		753.75		—		—
Net income		£5,046.25		2,500		2,000

Combined net incomes = £11,546.25
Again, payments are made gross (FA 1988, s. 38(7)).

PROBLEM B

H earns £33,600; W earns £5,600. H offers W £5,600 plus school fees of £3,500 p.a. for each child. The school fees are to be paid direct to the school for the children.

1. *New order 1988–89:*

		H		W
Income		£33,600.00		£5,600.00
Less personal reliefs	£2,785		£2,785	
additional relief	—		1,590	
maintenance deduction	1,590		—	
(FA 1988, s. 347B(2))		4,385.00		4,385.00
Taxable income		29,215.00		1,215.00
Tax 20,700 @ 25%	5,175			
8,515 @ 40%	3,406	8,581.00		303.75
Net income after tax		£25,019.00		£5,296.25

Combined net of tax incomes = £30,315.25.
Incomes net of tax and school fees = £23,315.25.

2. *Existing order 1989–90; school fees due in 1989–90 rise to £4,000 as compared with £3,500 in 1988–89:*

		H		W		C
Income		£33,600.00		£11,200.00		£3,500.00
Less personal reliefs	£2,785		£2,785		£2,785	
additional relief	—		1,590			
maintenance deduction	12,600					
(FA 1988, s. 38(2)(*a*))						
maintenance exclusion			1,590			
(FA 1988, s. 38(2)(*b*), (5))		15,385.00		5,965.00		2,785.00
Taxable income		18,215.00		5,235.00		715.00
Tax		4,553.75		1,308.75		178.75
Net income		£16,446.25		£9,891.25		£3,321.25

Combined net of tax incomes = £32,980.
Combined net incomes net of tax and school fees = £24,980.00.
Note.—No relief for extra £1,000 of school fees; payments to be made gross.

10 Schedule D, Case VI

10: 01 Income tax is charged under Schedule D, Case VI on any annual profits or gains not falling under any other Case of Schedule D and not charged by virtue of Schedules A, B, C, E,[1] and F.[2] It is thus the residual case in the residual Schedule. In addition the Taxes Acts often direct that a particular type of payment which is brought into charge to income tax is to be charged under Schedule D, Case VI.[3]

Four principles may be laid down. (1) The profit must be annual, (2) it must be of an income nature, (3) must not be gratuitous and (4) must be analogous to some other head of Schedule D.

Simon's Taxes B7.101, 102; Butterworths Income Tax Service F5.01.
[1] TA 1988, s. 18.
[2] TA 1988, s. 20(1), (2).
[3] For a list see Simon's Taxes B7.102.

---

(1) Annual profits

10: 02 Annual does not mean recurrent.[1] Casual profits may therefore be caught but only if they are of an income, as opposed to a capital, nature.[2] As Rowlatt J observed, "Annual can only mean calculated in any one year and . . . 'annual profits or gains' means 'profits or gains in any year as the succession of years comes round'".[3] The word does not therefore add very much by way of definition. This is not however surprising since the other cases of Schedule D all tax annual profits or gains and Case VI is analogous to them.

Simon's Taxes B7.201, 202; Butterworths Income Tax Service F5.02.
[1] Per Viscount Dunedin in *Jones v Leeming* [1930] AC 415 at 422, 15 TC 333 at 359; see also Rowlatt J in *Townsend v Grundy* (1933) 18 TC 140 at 148.
[2] *Jones v Leeming*, supra; for a complex example see *Black Nominees Ltd v Nicol* [1975] STC 372.
[3] In *Ryall v Hoare* [1923] 2 KB 447 at 455; also "the plant is not annual—it is the sowing that is annual" (at 454). The mere fact that the profit arises within the course of one calendar year only and does not recur is not sufficient to exclude it from the category of annual profits,": per Lord Warrington in *Jones v Leeming* [1930] AC 415 at 425, 15 TC 333 at 361; and see Lord Inglis in *Scottish Provident Institution v Farmer* (1912) 6 TC 34 at 38: "There is nothing said in the Act about a gain being necessarily within the year of assessment."

---

(2) (3) and (4) Income eiusdem generis

10: 03 To fall within Case VI a receipt must be of an income nature, must not be gratuitous and must be analogous to those profits or gains caught by the preceding Cases of Schedule D.[1] A profit derived from the sale of an asset will either be income from an adventure in the nature of trade and so taxable under Schedule D, Case I or be of a capital nature and so outside both Case I and Case VI.[2]

To be of the nature of income a receipt must have a source and be distinct from that source. Hence a mere gift, the finding of a thing or mere gambling winnings do not fall to be taxed as income under Case VI any more than does a capital gain. On the other hand a receipt in return for services rendered will be caught by Case VI if not by some other case. In such an instance the effort made in rendering the service is regarded as the source.

Simon's Taxes B7.208; Butterworths Income Tax Service F5.02.
[1] Per Lord Dunedin, in *Jones v Leeming* [1930] AC 415 at 422, 15 TC 333 at 359.
[2] *Jones v Leeming*, supra.

Gambling and distinguishable transactions

10: 04   Profits arising from gambling transactions do not fall within Case VI.[1] Such transactions are merely irrational agreements. The event which entitles the gambler to his winnings does not of itself produce the profit. There is no increment, no service, but merely an acquisition.[2] This has to be distinguished from an organised seeking after profits which may create a trade and so a subject matter which bears fruit in the shape of profits or gains. Hence it has been held that while gambling may be a way of life—indeed in *Graham v Green* it was the taxpayer's sole means of livelihood—it is not a trade and so its winnings escape Cases I, II[3] and VI. Such views however do not prevent courts from holding that a bookmaker is carrying on a vocation and is therefore taxable under Case II, the distinction being that a bookmaker has an organisation.[4]

Also to be distinguished from mere gambling winnings are winnings incidental to a taxable activity. Thus in *Norman v Evans*[5] the taxpayer leased horses bred at his stud to other persons to be raced by them and would receive one half of all sums received in respect of the horses' winnings. The Revenue did not argue that he was carrying on the trade of racing horses. Hence if he had raced these horses himself (as a hobby) any winnings would have been non-taxable. Yet it was held that his one half of the winnings were taxable. On the other hand where a bet is on professional skill it is still a bet and therefore not taxable. A borderline case is *Down v Compston*[6] where a golf professional taxable under what is now Schedule E was held not taxable in respect of money won on bets with other persons with whom he played golf. This decision should be contrasted with certain Commonwealth cases in which gains from betting which is associated with other taxable horse racing activity have been subjected to income tax as part of that other activity—by a horse owner,[7] by a horse trainer,[8] by a registered bookmaker[9] and even by a horse owner who leased racehorses and had a stud farm for breeding horses.[10] The question must be one of fact. *Down v Compston* was distinguished in *Burdge v Pyne*[11] when the proprietor of a gambling club was held taxable on the profits of his gambling at his club under Schedule D, Case I.

Also to be distinguished from mere gambling is speculation. Thus a person who buys shares on the stock exchange or cotton futures[12] in the hope of an increase in capital value is a speculator and not a gambler—the distinction being that the contract to buy or sell the cotton is a very real one from the point of view of the vendor and gives rise to very real contractual rights whereas in a gambling transaction both parties regard the matter as a mere wager.[13] Thus the profits of speculation in commodity futures may be taxable if there is a sufficient substratum of activity to give rise to the finding that there is a trade and so a source taxable under Case I.

Also to be distinguished are payments for the provision of services. So a professional tipster is taxed under Schedule D, Case II.[14]

Simon's Taxes B7.204, 212; Butterworths Income Tax Service F5.11–F5.13.
[1] *Graham v Green* [1925] 2 KB 37, 9 TC 309.
[2] See per Rowlatt J at 39; 312 who draws a parallel with finding and gift.
[3] The Revenue argued in favour of liability under Case II in *Graham v Green*, n. 1, supra.
[4] *Partridge v Mallandaine* (1886) 18 QBD 276, and *Graham v Green* (n. 1, supra), at pp. 42, 314.
[5] [1965] 1 All ER 372, 42 TC 188 (Buckley J) (but what if the contract had provided for him to receive one half of the side bets made by the lessees?).
[6] [1937] 2 All ER 475, 21 TC 60 (Lawrence J).
[7] *Knight v Taxation Comr* (1928) 28 SR NSW 523.
[8] *Holt v Federal Taxation Comr* (1929) 3 ALJ 68.
[9] *Vandenberg v Taxation Comr New South Wales* (1933) 2 ATD 343.
[10] *Trautwein v Federal Taxation Comr* (1936) 56 CLR 196.
[11] [1969] 1 All ER 467, 45 TC 320.
[12] *Cooper v Stubbs* [1925] 2 KB 753, 10 TC 29, followed in *Townsend v Grundy* (1933) 18 TC 140.
[13] Per Warrington LJ at 769, 52 and per Atkin LJ at 770–771; 53–54.
[14] *Graham v Arnott* (1941) 24 TC 157. *Semble* therefore that an occasional tipster falls within Case VI; infra, § **10: 10**.

TAXABLE PROFITS

Profits analogous to trading profits

10: 05   Given the width of the judicial definition of trade and the statutory notion of an adventure in the nature of trade,[1] it might appear that there was little scope for Case VI. Indeed as already seen[2] it is clear that in relation to an isolated transaction where a profit arises on resale of an object there is no scope for Case VI.

Where however regular as opposed to isolated transactions are concerned there is some authority for a charge under Case VI. Case law shows that profits from stud fees are taxed under Case VI rather than under Case I.[3] Thus where a taxpayer owned and raced a horse for pleasure and not as a trading activity and, to that end, bred his own horses, he would not be trading. If in addition he allowed his stallion to serve dams belonging to other people in return for fees he would be taxable on the profits[4] so earned under Case VI, such activities being clearly separable from his horse racing. In *Earl Derby v Bassom*[5] on the other hand, where a farmer had a bull which he used principally for his own animal breeding but occasionally sold its services to other farmers in return for fees, it was held that such fees were part of the income from the farm and so were not taxable under Case VI. At that time farmers were charged under Schedule B rather than Schedule D,

Case I[6] so that the fees escaped tax. The decision to charge farmers under Case I rather than Schedule B has removed most, but not all, of the tax advantages derived by the taxpayer from not being charged under Case VI. However it remains odd that fees received for the services of a horse used for recreation should be taxable under Case VI while those received for the services of a bull used for farming should be taxable under Case I.[7] It seems likely in the light of the cases on income derived from property and from services that even very occasional fees will be taxable.[8]

Simon's Taxes B7.205; Butterworths Income Tax Service F5.21.
[1] TA 1988, s. 832(1), supra, § **7: 01.**
[2] Per Lord Buckmaster in *Jones v Leeming* [1930] AC 415 at 420, 15 TC 333 at 357.
[3] Although why is not quite clear.
[4] For computation, see infra, § **10: 14.**
[5] (1926) 10 TC 357 at 371.
[6] Ibid. Farmers now fall within Schedule D, Case I: TA 1988, s. 53(1).
[7] Assessments under Case I were upheld in *Malcolm v Lockhart* [1919] AC 463, 7 TC 99; *McLaughlin v Bailey* (1920) 7 TC 508.
[8] Infra, § **10: 11.**

10: 06   Liability under Schedule D, Case I differs from that under Case VI in a number of respects:

(*i*) generally liability under Case I is on a preceding year basis, that under Case VI may be, but is not always, on a current year basis;[1]
(*ii*) capital allowances may be claimed under Case I but not under Case VI;[2]
(*iii*) income under Case I may be earned but not all income under Case VI will be so treated;[3]
(*iv*) losses suffered under Case I may be set off against general income of that and the next year but then only against later profits of the same trade; losses under Case VI may only be set off against other Case VI income but can be rolled forward against all such income of later years;[4]
(*v*) profits are generally computed under Case I on an earnings basis; those under Case VI on a cash basis;[5]
(*vi*) the income of a charity under Case I is exempt from tax if certain conditions are met; there is no exemption for the income of a charity under Case VI;[6]

The contrast may be illustrated by the plight of the owners of stately homes who open their homes to visitors. If this is done on a commerical basis, liability arises under Case I; if not then under Case VI. Under Case VI the only costs allowable will be those involved in showing the house, such as those on the wages of guides, additional cleaning, advertising and the purchase of souvenirs; if however the matter comes within Case I one will be able to deduct these items and the costs of upkeep of the building and its gardens, the wages of caretakers, gardeners, heating, lighting and insurance. Allowances may also be claimed for expenditure on car parks, and plumbing, refreshment rooms and access roads. In practice it is difficult to bring oneself within Case I without heavy capital expenditure; yet it is only if one is sure to be within Case I that one can (perhaps) afford the expenditure.

Simon's Taxes B7.301, 302; Butterworths Income Tax Service F5.22.
¹ TA 1988, ss. 60 and 69.
² Supra, Chapter 8.
³ See definition section: TA 1988, s. 833(4)(*c*) and supra, § **4: 05**. Income analogous to a trade may be earned income; see **Simon's Taxes B7.206**. In *Hale v Shea* [1965] 1 All ER 155, 42 TC 260. Buckley J appears to have thought the question whether income was earned was independent of the question whether liability arose under Case VI.
⁴ TA 1988, ss. 380, 383 and 392; supra, § **5: 16**.
⁵ *Pearn v Miller* (1927) 11 TC 610 at 614; *Grey v Tiley* (1932) 16 TC 414.
⁶ TA 1988, s. 505 and infra, § **11: 13**.

Activities analogous to a vocation

10: 07   There is no concept in Schedule D, Case II equivalent to an adventure in the nature of trade under Case I. Where therefore a taxpayer receives profits in return for services which are not sufficiently regular to amount to a vocation,[1] he may not be taxed under Schedule D, Case II but only Case VI. Again however care must be taken to distinguish income in return for services from capital receipts for the disposal of property.

¹ Supra, § **7: 06**.

(a) Casual authorship

10: 08   In *Hobbs v Hussey*[1] the taxpayer, a solicitor's clerk who had not carried on the profession of author, agreed to write his memoirs and to assign the copyright in return for payment and was held taxable on the proceeds under Case VI.

In *Earl Haig's Trustees v IRC*[2] however trustees who held the copyright in certain diaries and who allowed an author to use the materials in those diaries "so far as the public interest permitted" in return for a half share in the profits of the book, were held not taxable. The Court of Session there held that the sums were capital payments in return for the partial realisation of assets and so escaped income tax and not, as the Special Commissioner had held, remuneration for the use of and access to the diaries by the author, and so taxable under Case VI as being income derived from property. The question is whether the transaction is really a sale of property or the performance of services. A transaction may be one for the performance of services even though it may involve some subsidiary sale of property e.g. dentures supplied by a dentist.[3] Hence in *Hobbs v Hussey* the payments were held to be income even though as part of the contract the taxpayer transferred his copyright in the articles. So also, in *Alloway v Phillips*[4] where memoirs were ghosted, the fact that she promised not to write for any other publisher was not sufficient to take the matter out of Case VI as this restriction was simply an adjunct of the main contract.

It has not been easy for taxpayers to place themselves on the *Haig* side of the line, which is of course inherently vague. Thus when in *Housden v Marshall*[5] a jockey agreed to make available to a reporter his reminiscences and supporting documents together with the right to use a facsimile of his signature, payments to the jockey were held taxable. The situation is complicated by two further factors. First, the test of what is income as opposed to capital seems to be different under Case VI from that prevailing under Case II where sums received for the sale of copyright have been held to be income receipts.[6] Secondly the Solicitor-General commented in *Hobbs v Hussey*[7] that he was not to be taken as admitting that the *Haig* case was rightly decided. However it would appear to follow from the present authorities that had Hobbs and Marshall written their reminiscences first and then allowed them to be published, sums received in return for the sale would have escaped tax under Schedule D, Case VI.[8] What was fatal to their case was that under the contract they agreed to perform services, in the one case to write his memoirs and in the other to supply information.

If a charge under Case VI is to arise it is probably necessary that the activities analogous to a profession be concurrent with the sale.[9] It is not sufficient that they were carried on at some time in the past. Thus where there has been a discontinuance of a profession so that Case II is inapplicable, a subsequent sale will not be caught by Case VI if there have been no activities analogous to a profession after discontinuance.[10]

Simon's Taxes B7.203, 209; Butterworths Income Tax Service F5.32

[1] [1942] 1 All ER 445, 24 TC 153.

[2] (1939) 22 TC 725.

[3] See Lawrence J in *Hobbs v Hussey* (supra, n. 1), at 446, 156. For the converse case where the court disregarded a trifling service, see *Bradbury v Arnold* (1957) 37 TC 665 and the *Earl Haig* case, supra, n. 2.

[4] [1980] STC 490, [1980] 3 All ER 138.

[5] [1958] 3 All ER 639, 38 TC 233, where Harman J reversed the Special Commissioners.

[6] *Howson v Monsell* [1950] 2 All ER 1239, 31 TC 529 (Schedule D, Case II). Cf. *Beare v Carter* [1940] 2 KB 187, 23 TC 353 (Schedule D, Case VI).

[7] [1942] 1 KB 491 at 495, 24 TC 153 at 155.

[8] But on capital gains tax liability, see infra, § **16: 10**.

[9] *Beare v Carter* [1940] 2 KB 187, 23 TC 353, where the advance to an author for a new edition of a work published many years previously was held to be a capital sum which was not assessable.

[10] *Withers v Nethersole* (1948) 28 TC 501, HL.

(b) Introduction fees

10: 09   One who introduces a potential purchaser to a vendor may expect some appreciation in pecuniary form. If the introducer has a right to sue for these sums he will be taxable under Schedule D, Case VI, should he escape Cases I and II. If however he has no right to sue then it was held in *Dickinson v Abel*[1] the sums escape tax just like any other gifts, the law not concerning itself with the motive of a donor.

On the other hand in *Brocklesbry v Merricks*[2] the taxpayer, an architect, met at a social occasion a landowner who expressed interest in selling his land. Later the taxpayer arranged a meeting between the landowner and a developer who then arranged to buy the land. The taxpayer then agreed with the developer to endeavour to dispose of the land and to assist in negotiations in return for one fourth of the net profit of the sale. The Court of Appeal held that the taxpayer was chargeable under Case VI on the share of the profit received.

The agreement to act in the negotiation for resale was fatal to the taxpayer's case. Yet had he been content with a cash payment from the developer for the introduction to the landowner he might well have escaped tax. Further, as *Scott v Ricketts* suggests, if he had been offered a sum for the introduction and then commuted it into a share of the profits after the developer had bought the land, and had he taken this share of profits as his introduction fee rather than for his work on the negotiations on the resale, he would presumably have escaped tax.[3]

In *Scott v Ricketts*[4] an estate agent was paid £39,000 in consideration of his withdrawing any claim he might have to participate in a development scheme. The Court of Appeal held that although the payment was made under a contract there was no liability under Case VI (*a*) because the original scheme was not a legally enforceable agreement and (*b*) because the payment was made in settlement of a moral claim or for the sale of an asset and neither gives rise to a profit within Schedule D, Case VI. It is highly questionable whether the sum was paid under a contract since a moral claim does not amount to good consideration.

Simon's Taxes B7.203, 208, 211; Butterworths Income Tax Service F5.33.
[1] [1969] 1 All ER 484, 45 TC 353.
[2] (1934) 18 TC 576. The possibility of a charge under Schedule D, Case II was reserved by the Crown. See also *Bloom v Kinder* (1958) 38 TC 77.
[3] The usual rate appears to be $1\frac{1}{2}\%$ of the purchase price. In *Brocklesbry v Merricks,* supra, the sum agreed was 25% of the *profit.*
[4] [1967] 2 All ER 1009, 44 TC 303.

(*c*) *Miscellaneous*

10: 10 Commission payments received by a director for guaranteeing the company's bank overdraft have been held taxable under Case VI because they were received by virtue of services which had been rendered.[1] The same result followed when a solicitor guaranteed an overdraft of a third party for the commission was earned by the pledging of credit.[2] In each case there was a contractual right to the payment. Whether such sums should be taxed under Case II or Case VI is one of fact. Such receipts are held taxable and are not treated as capital payments because the source from which the income flows is not the service but the individual's efforts and those efforts are capable of recurring.[3]

There was some doubt whether a prostitute was taxable under Case II or Case VI or not at all. It appears that where the Revenue is aware of the source of income a charge is made under Case VI.[4] However a charge under Case I has now been upheld.[5]

Simon's Taxes B7.203; Butterworths Income Tax Service F5.34.
[1] *Ryall v Hoare* [1923] 2 KB 447, 8 TC 521. See 1977 Can. Tax Jo. 26.
[2] *Sherwin v Barnes* (1931) 16 TC 278; but cf. *Trenchard v Bennet* (1933) 17 TC 420 where in reality shares received were not for the guarantee but in order to gain control of a company—a capital asset—and so were not taxable.
[3] *Whyte v Clancy* [1936] 2 All ER 735, 20 TC 679.
[4] (1973) Times, 19th May.
[5] *IRC v Aken* [1988] STC 69.

The analogy of income from property

10: 11   Schedule D in addition to taxing the annual profits of a trade or a profession or vocation also taxes the annual profits or gains arising or accruing from any kind of property whatsoever. Although the cases under Case VI have not always been decided expressly on this analogy, it would appear that many of the cases can be so rationalised and indeed that much of the talk of a "source" is an implicit recognition of the analogy. Thus stud fees received for the services of a stallion[1] could be caught on this analogy. Sums derived from the sale of a right to nominate a particular dam for whom the stallion should stand are taxed, the analogy of the sale of property being specifically rejected.[2] Again sums received for the use as distinct from the disposal of information,[3] or for the display of property such as Earl Haig's diaries[4] or the pledging of one's credit[5] or leasing a horse[6] could all fall intelligibly within this analogy, which has the further advantage of focusing attention on the sums earned by the property which would be income as distinct from the sums received on the disposal of the property which would be capital.

Where land is owned rent received is usually taxable under Schedule A. However, not all income from the use of land falls within that Schedule,[7] so that for example sums received for car parking or visitors' green fees at a golf club[8] will normally be taxed under Schedule D, Case VI, as will income derived from the furnished letting of a house[9] which being in return for the use of the furniture as well as for the use of the land is not all within Schedule A.

On the treatment of furnished holiday letting income see § **9: 09**, supra.

Income which might fall within Case VI as derived from commodity and financial futures and traded options is now removed to CGT by FA 1985. This change does not affect income arising from dealing in assets in such a way as to give rise to liability under Case I.[10]

---

[1] As in *Earl of Derby v Bassom* (1926) 10 TC 357.
[2] *Benson v Counsell* [1942] 1 All ER 435, 24 TC 178.
[3] As in *Housden v Marshall* [1958] 3 All ER 639, 38 TC 233.
[4] See Lord Normand in *Earl Haig's Trustees v IRC* 1939 SC 676 at 682, 22 TC 725 at 732.
[5] E.g. *Wilson v Mannooch* [1937] 3 All ER 120, 21 TC 178.
[6] E.g. *Norman v Evans* [1965] 1 All ER 372, 42 TC 188.
[7] *Carlisle and Silloth Golf Club v Smith* [1913] 3 KB 75, 6 TC 198.
[8] *Coman v Rotunda Hospital (Governor) Dublin* [1921] 1 AC 1, esp. at 12–14, 7 TC 517, at 559–560. See also *Forth Conservancy Board v IRC* [1931] AC 540, 16 TC 103.
[9] Furnished letting is not usually a trade—see *Gittos v Barclay* [1982] STC 390.
[10] TA 1988, s. 128.

FOREIGN QUESTIONS: CASES IV, V AND VI

10: 12   In accordance with the general principles of the tax system, gains accruing to those not resident and which would be taxable under Case VI are presumably so taxable where the source is in the UK.[1]

In *Alloway v Phillips*[2] a person resident in Canada who agreed to provide information in Canada about her life as the wife of one of the Great Train

Robbers was held taxable under Case VI because the contract was made, was enforceable, and provided for payment in England by a person resident in England.

Where the source is outside the UK but the income arises in favour of a UK resident the charge will presumably arise under Case V rather than under Case VI.[3] Any other conclusion would remove the remittance basis[4] from any income within Case VI while leaving it intact for income within other Cases.

[1] As in *Curtis-Brown Ltd v Jarvis* (1929) 14 TC 744.
[2] [1980] STC 490, [1980] 3 All ER 138.
[3] *Colquhoun v Brooks,* infra, § **34: 02** and note *Lilley v Harrison* (1952) 33 TC 344, CA.
[4] TA 1988, s. 65(4), infra, § **34: 11**.

Offshore income gains

10: 13   An offshore income gain is assessable under Schedule D, Case VI, see infra, § **34: 43**.

COMPUTATION

10: 14   Tax is chargeable under Case VI in respect of annual profits and gains and not simply on receipts. Sums spent in earning the receipts may therefore be deducted in computing the taxable profits—or losses. On the other hand no deduction has been permitted for the landlord's costs of obtaining alternative accommodation for himself since these are in the nature of personal expenditure.[1]

EXAMPLE
Furnished Lettings Assessment 1989–90 (not furnished holiday lettings)
Year ended 5th April 1990

Rent received		£3,500
Less allowable expenses		
Rates	£560	
Water rates	£80	
Insurance	£300	
Repairs to property	£500	
Wear and tear	£286	
(10% of rent received allowed as a deduction)		
Accountancy	£600	£2,326
Profit		£1,174

Note: Revenue practice is to limit the 10% deduction to the figure for rent net of rates and other expenses normally borne by tenants Statement of Practice A19 (see **Simon's Taxes, Division H3.4**).
The Revenue practice of making this assessment during 1989–90 is given statutory authority by TMA 1970, s. 29(1)(c), added by FA 1988, s. 119.

Simon's Taxes B7.206; Butterworths Income Tax Service F5.51.
[1] *Wylie v Eccott* (1913) 6 TC 128.

Machinery

10: 15 Tax is charged under Case VI on a current year basis unless otherwise directed by the Inspector.[1] Where the Inspector so directs it is no answer to the assessment that whereas there were profits in the preceding period there are none in the current year.[2] Any loss under a transaction[3] falling within Case VI may be set off against income from any other transaction within Case VI of that or any later year,[4] subject however to express statutory direction as in transactions involving house premiums.[5] Case VI losses may not be set off against income under another Case of the same year.

Income is chargeable under Case VI when it is received. This emerges from the unsatisfactory case of *Grey v Tiley*[6] where counsel for the Crown conceded that the taxpayer could not be taxed in respect of the year when the money became due to him.

Simon's Taxes B7.301, D2.410, E1.621; Butterworths Income Tax Service F5.51.

[1] TA 1988, s. 69.

[2] TA 1988, s. 71.

[3] On meaning of transaction, see *Barron v Littman* [1951] 2 All ER 393, 33 TC 373.

[4] TA 1988, s. 392.

[5] TA 1988, ss. 40(5) and 392(4).

[6] (1932) 16 TC 414, where the court felt bound by *Leigh v IRC* [1928] 1 KB 73, 11 TC 590 (Case IV).

11 Trusts

INTRODUCTION

11: 01   A trust is a financial intermediary which causes considerable difficulty in any tax system. Where trustees receive income, the law might charge the trustees to income tax as agents of the beneficiary taking into account all the personal circumstances of the beneficiary, including his personal allowances and any other taxable income he might have. Alternatively it might treat the trust as an independent entity like a company which was fit to be taxed in its own right. If it adopts the second approach it can choose between a system that gives credit at the beneficiary level for the tax paid by the trustees and one which allows the trustees to deduct those parts of the trust income which become income of the beneficiary.

   The UK opts for the second approach but contains both systems—trustees are liable to basic rate tax on income arising during the administration of the trust; sometimes they are also liable to additional rate (infra, § **11: 05**). When we are not concerned with additional rate problems a credit system is used. The beneficiaries can claim a credit for the tax paid by the trustees. Were this two tier procedure not available, taxpayers would run into obvious temptations when there is no beneficiary currently entitled to the trust income as where it is accumulated, there being no deemed distribution of income not in fact distributed. These temptations have been reduced but not abolished by the reduction in rates in 1988. When the additional rate applies a deduction system is used.

   Exceptionally trustees for a person under incapacity are taxed as agent for that person.[1]

---

[1] TMA 1970, s. 72; *IRC v McIntosh* (1955) 36 TC 334.

THE TRUSTEE

11: 02   The basis for the liability of the trustee to basic rate income tax under the UK system must be sought in the present legislation and in history. Schedule A income tax is charged on the person receiving or entitled to the profits so charged,[1] that under Schedule D is charged on the person receiving or entitled to the income in respect of which it is charged[2] and under Schedule F the tax credit is available to the person receiving the distribution.[3] Trustees come within each of these rules even though they are not entitled to the income beneficially; they are entitled to the income in that they can sue for it and they may be said to receive it. Moreover this approach of taxing the person in receipt is fully consistent with the original notion of income tax as a flat rate tax largely deducted at source.

The trustees are assessable to income tax regardless of the personal tax circumstances of the beneficiary or of themselves. They are assessable and chargeable not as agent for the beneficiary nor as trustee as such but simply because they receive income.[4] This is so even if there is only one beneficiary and he is *sui iuris*.[5]

However if the circumstances of the trustees (or those of them whom it is sought to tax) are such as to take them out of the charge to tax they cannot be taxed. In *Dawson v IRC*[6] there was a discretionary trust and no beneficiary was entitled to the income. The administration of the trust was carried on outside the UK and the principal beneficiaries were resident outside the UK. No income was remitted to the UK. There were three trustees only one of whom was resident in the UK. The Revenue attempted to tax the single UK resident trustee; this failed as they could not show that the trustee had sufficient control[7] over the income for it to be said that the income had accrued to him. This decision rejected an established Revenue practice and is now reversed by legislation.[8]

In calculating the total income of the trustees and so of their personal tax liability, the trust income is not added to their personal incomes; conversely their personal incomes are ignored in computing their liability as trustees.

The trust may not claim any personal reliefs of the trustees; nor, since it is not an "individual",[9] may it claim any personal reliefs for itself. On the other hand it may be entitled to various reliefs which are available to "persons", such as loss relief or deductions on account of interest. Likewise it may deduct and retain income tax on making a payment falling within TA 1988, s. 348, and the trustees may be guilty of a breach of trust if they fail to deduct.[10]

In computing the taxable income of the trust liable to basic rate income tax no deduction may be made for trust expenses incurred in the administration, any more than an individual with investment income can deduct his expenses.[11] So if a trustee has £100 of income and £10 of expenses, income tax for 1988–89 will be 25% of £100 i.e. £25. On the other hand a trust which includes a trade is only taxable on the profits of that trade and any expenses incurred in earning those profits may be deducted according to normal principles. Such profits are not earned income.[12]

Most trust income will be investment income arising under Schedule D, Case III or Schedule F and so often subject to taxation by deduction at source. In other instances, for example where the trustees carry on a trade, a direct assessment is made.

Simon's Taxes C4.202–206; Butterworths Income Tax Service J1.01.

[1] TA 1988, s. 21(1).

[2] TA 1988, s. 59.

[3] TA 1988, s. 44.

[4] Per Viscount Cave in *Williams v Singer* [1921] 1 AC 65 at 71, 7 TC 387 at 411. See also *Reid's Trustees v IRC* 1929 SC 439, 14 TC 512; trustees assessable under Schedule D because they are receiving or entitled to the income within what is now TA 1988, s. 59.

[5] *Hamilton Russell's Executors v IRC* (1943) 25 TC 200.

⁶ [1989] STC 473, HL. In the Court of Appeal [1988] 3 All ER 753, [1988] STC 684 considerable emphasis was placed on the joint nature of the title and responsibility of trustees.

⁷ There was a negative control in that the trustee's consent was needed before the discretions could be exercised but this was held not to be sufficient.

⁸ One should note that none of the income accrued to the trustees from sources in the UK. The decision is of importance for its insistence on finding a basis for liability in the words of the taxing statutes (i.e. TA 1988, ss. 18 and 59 rather than in established practice. The amending legislation is FA 1989, s. 110—see infra, § **35: 25**.

⁹ It is very difficult to find authority for this rule: but it is generally accepted.

¹⁰ *Re Sharp, Rickett v Rickett* [1906] 1 Ch 793.

¹¹ *Aikin v Macdonald's Trustees* (1894) 3 TC 306.

¹² *Fry v Shiel's Trustees* 1915 SC 159, 6 TC 583; supra, § **4: 05**.

Exceptions to general liability of trustees

(i) *Income accruing to beneficiary*

11: 03   Since the trustee is assessable simply because income accrues to him, it follows that where income accrues not to him but directly to the beneficiary, the trustee is not assessable. In *Williams v Singer*¹ income from investments held in the United States was, at the direction of the trustees, who were resident in the UK, paid directly to the beneficiary who was domiciled and resident outside the UK. The beneficiary, if taxable at all, would only have been taxed on a remittance basis and since no income was remitted to this country no tax was due from her. The Revenue tried to charge tax on the trustees. The attempt failed. The trustees had not themselves received any income and were not assessable. They were not "in actual receipt and control" of the income.²

By TMA 1970, s. 76 a trustee who has authorised the receipt of profits by the person entitled thereto or his agent is only required to make a return of the name, address and the profits of that person. This was relied on in the House of Lords in *Williams v Singer* as negativing any further liability on the trustees,² but in fact is completely immaterial since the section is concerned only with the trustee's duty to supply information with regard to the assessment *of the beneficiary*.

Conversely, when foreign income accrued to a non-resident trustee, by whom it was accumulated, there was no liability on a resident beneficiary who was chargeable only on a remittance basis since it was not his income.³

Simon's Taxes A3.329, C4.202, E1.351; Butterworths Income Tax Service J1.01.

¹ [1921] 1 AC 65, 7 TC 387. See also *Dawson v IRC* [1988] 3 All ER 753, [1988] STC 684, CA.

² At 71, 411.

³ *Drummond v Collins*, infra, § **11: 10**.

(ii) *Beneficiary not liable to income tax*

11: 04   Where trustees receive income, they may not be assessed if the income accrues beneficially to a cestui que trust in whose hands it is not liable to income tax.¹ This is a second explanation of *Williams v Singer* (supra).² It can apply only where the link between the income and the beneficiary is established; it cannot apply to absolve the trustee when for example income is accumulated contingently for a beneficiary.³

This exception cannot be said to be firmly grounded since it blurs the nature of the trustees' liability confusing the liability of the trustee with that of the beneficiary.[4] What is here under consideration is the tax liability of the trustee in that capacity. This exception comes close to saying that the trustee is not liable to income tax when there is a beneficiary with a vested life interest[5] (infra).

If the exception is sound it is very limited. It applies only where the income is not liable to income tax in the hands of the beneficiary, as where he is non-resident, but not where the income is liable to tax but no income tax will be due perhaps by reason of the personal allowances due to the beneficiary.

Simon's Taxes C4.402.

[1] Lord Clyde in *Reid's Trustees v IRC* 1929 SC 439, 14 TC 512 at 525.

[2] Per Viscount Cave 7 TC at 412.

[3] Such income does not belong to the beneficiary: *Stanley v IRC* [1944] 1 All ER 230, 26 TC 12 *sed quaere* if the beneficiaries are non-resident; see *Kelly v Rogers* [1935] 2 KB 446 at 468, 19 TC 692 at 714.

[4] The position is further complicated by the rule that a trustee may be liable for tax due from a non-resident beneficiary under TMA 1970, s. 78 (non-residents).

[5] It is clear that the beneficiary is liable: *IRC v Hamilton Russell's Executors* [1943] 1 All ER 474, 25 TC 200; as are the trustees, supra, n. 1.

Rates of tax

11: 05 The higher rate of tax does not apply to trustees since they are not "an individual".[1]

Although the additional rate no longer applies to individuals TA 1988, s. 686 provides that the trustees are liable at the additional rate where the income is to be accumulated or is payable at the discretion of the trustees or any other person (whether or not there is a power to accumulate). The rate of tax used to be set by reference to the second band of higher rate tax;[2] however, under the 1988 reforms it is set at 10%.[3] It is interesting that this when added to basic rate is below the higher rate of income tax and is the same as corporation tax. This applies not only to discretionary trusts but also where beneficiaries have contingent interests and Trustee Act 1925, s. 31 empowers the trustees to apply income for their maintenance. It applies also to income which the trustees have power to withhold—as when they exercise a power to accumulate under a protective trust where the discretionary trust has arisen.[4]

Sums which are income of a person before being distributed i.e. income of a beneficiary with a vested interest in the income or of an annuitant or which has to be treated as income of the settlor are to be deducted as are sums spent on expenses and properly chargeable to income.[5] This permits the deduction of any expense which the trustee is authorised to incur provided it is properly chargeable to income, a question to be determined according to general trust law, any express provision in the instrument permitting the charge of the expense against income being ignored.[6]

The purpose of this provision is to increase the cost of accumulation and discretionary trusts which have significant tax advantages as shelters in which income can be generated but taxed only at the rates appropriate to trustees rather than the marginal rates of the individual beneficiaries. The rule applies to all income after 5th April 1973. Many small accumulation trusts for children have been set up in recent years under unit trust schemes. Paradoxically the tax bill will now often be lower if the parent is entitled to some interest under the settlement so that the income is to be treated as his.

The surcharge is not to apply to income of an estate of a deceased person during administration nor arising under a trust established for charitable purposes only nor to occupational pension schemes. The surcharge does however apply to income of a close company which is treated as the income of the trustees under an apportionment.

Non-resident trustees are liable to additional rate under s. 16 even though they are not liable to basic rate tax on that income.[7]

The tax is due on 1st December following the end of the year of assessment in which it arose.[8]

Simon's Taxes C4.202, 203 Butterworths Income Tax Service J1.02.

[1] TA 1988, s. 1(2). Before 1973 trusts were not entitled to earned income relief so this change can be exaggerated.

[2] TA 1988, s. 1(2).

[3] FA 1988, s. 24(4) amending TA 1988, s. 832(1).

[4] *IRC v Berrill* [1981] STC 784.

[5] TA 1988, s. 686(2)(*d*) express provisions of the trust are ignored in deciding what is properly chargeable.

[6] *Carver v Duncan* [1985] AC 1082, [1985] STC 356, HL (life insurance premiums and fees for investment advice not deductible—*quaere* whether they were "expenses" anyway).

[7] *IRC v Regent Trust Co Ltd* [1980] STC 140; this is odd because the credit for s. 686 tax against s. 687 liability is not available on a literal interpretation of s. 687(3)(*a*).

[8] TA 1988, s. 5(4).

THE BENEFICIARY

Is the beneficiary taxable?

11: 06   Where the trustees have paid the tax and administration expenses and the balance belongs to a beneficiary as income, as where he has a vested life interest in the income, that income is liable to income tax in his hands. The amount received is grossed up at basic rate to take account of the basic rate tax paid by the trustees. So a receipt of £65 will be grossed up to £86.66. If the beneficiary's rate of tax is nil he will recover £21.66 from the Revenue. While this is clear the underlying theory is not.

Where a beneficiary is currently entitled to the income under the trust the result of the decision of the House of Lords in *Baker v Archer-Shee*[1] is that he is entitled to—and so taxable on—the income as and when it arises, whether or not he receives it from the trustee. This may have the further consequence that he will be taxable under the Schedule and Case appropriate to the income as it arises.[2] Different principles apply where there is an annuity under the trust, the annuitant in this instance being chargeable under Schedule D, Case III although an assessment under that Schedule will usually be precluded—as far as basic rate is concerned—by the prior deduction of basic rate income tax by the trustees under TA 1988, ss. 348 and 349.[3] Different principles also apply where the beneficiary is entitled to an interest in the residue of an estate in the course of administration, it being well settled that *Baker v Archer-Shee* does not apply in such an instance and so special rules apply.[4]

Simon's Taxes C4.220, 221, 225, 403.
[1] [1927] AC 844, 11 TC 749. For facts, see infra, § **34: 09**. The facts of this case were most favourable to the Revenue's contentions. Not only was the beneficiary sole life tenant but she had also been given the power to nominate trustees and was herself involved with the management of the fund to the extent that her consent was needed for any change of investments. The majority decision may be criticised for failing to distinguish between an active from a passive trust and it may be suggested that the decision does not apply to an active trust. See also the explanations in *Reid's Trustees v IRC* 1929 SC 439, 14 TC 512. On the question of whether the tenant for life is entitled to capital allowances see Venables, *Tax Planning Through Trusts*, § 20: 20.
[2] However in determining whether the income is earned or investment income, the question is whether it was earned by the beneficiary and not whether it was earned by the trustees, see supra, § **4: 05**.
[3] Supra, § **9: 76**.
[4] Infra, § **12: 03**.

---

(1) *Vested rights in income*

11: 07   A beneficiary is currently entitled to the trust income if the trustees are under a duty to pay the income to the beneficiary and he is then absolutely entitled to it or is entitled to have income applied for his benefit.[1] Benefits in kind are caught and questions whether the benefit is convertible into money are completely irrelevant.[2] If the beneficiary's title to the income is contingent or vested subject to being divested,[3] it is not taxable as his income.

Where a trustee receives income from investments held for a tenant for life each sum received is the income of the tenant for life as soon as it is received and regardless of the date on which it is paid over to the beneficiary. This is because the income is immediately under the beneficiary's control.[4]

Simon's Taxes C4.221, 222; Butterworths Income Tax Service J1.21.
[1] *Tollemache v IRC* (1926) 11 TC 277; *Miller v IRC* [1930] AC 222, 15 TC 25.
[2] *Lindus and Hortin v IRC* (1933) 17 TC 442.
[3] *Stanley v IRC* [1944] 1 All ER 230, 26 TC 12; *Brotherton v IRC* [1977] STC 73.
[4] Per Megarry J in *Spens v IRC* [1970] 3 All ER 295 at 299, 46 TC 276 at 285, citing *Hamilton Russell's Executors v IRC* (1943) 25 TC 200 at 207–8, and *Dreyfus v IRC* (1963) 41 TC 441 at 448. See also *Stern v IRC* (1930) 15 TC 148, HL.

11: 08   Sums received by the beneficiary are grossed up to reflect the basic rate tax paid by the trustees. However this grossed up income will not necessarily be the same as the trustee's income. This is because of *Macfarlane v IRC*[1] which is authority for the rule that while trust expenses are non-deductible in computing the trustees' income,[2] such expenses are deductible in computing that of the beneficiary.

Suppose that a trust has income of £100 and expenses of £10. For 1989–90 income tax on the trustees will, as already seen (supra, § **11: 02**), be £25 i.e. 25% of £100. However the beneficiary receives £65 and it is this figure which is grossed up to £86.66. The beneficiary thus gets credit for tax of £21.66. He cannot claim credit for the whole £25 tax paid by the trustees.

One may wonder whether this rule is correct; certainly the basis of the rule is suspect. *Macfarlane v IRC* rests on an earlier case[3] in 1926 in which the Court of Session held further that the beneficiary's income was the sum received net of tax paid by the trustees and then minus expenses, making a sum of £55 in our example. The reasoning on this point was destroyed by the decision of the House of Lords in *Baker v Archer-Shee* but on the main point was reaffirmed by *Macfarlane v IRC*.[4] The reason given for deduction was that the expenses were incurred before the beneficiary received the money and not by anyone she employed but rather by the trustees appointed by the settlor.[5] This is inconsistent with the notion that the income is the beneficiary's as soon as it is received by the trustee.[6] The anomaly may be the prohibition on allowing the trustees to deduct their expenses.[7]

Simon's Taxes C4.225; Butterworths Income Tax Service J1.21, 22.
[1] 1929 SC 453, 14 TC 532.
[2] Supra, § **11: 02**.
[3] *Murray v IRC* (1926) 11 TC 133.
[4] Cited with approval by Lord Blanesburgh in *Baker v Archer-Shee* (1926) 11 TC 749 at 786.
[5] Per Lord Sands at 138.
[6] Cf. Lord Sands in *Macfarlane v IRC* (1929) 14 TC 532 at 540.
[7] These expenses are deductible in computing the trust's liability to additional rate: TA 1988, s. 686(2)(*d*).

---

(2) *No vested right in income—accumulations*

11: 09   Income will only be treated as the income of a beneficiary if he has a vested and indefeasible interest in that income; his rights in capital may be different. In *Stanley v IRC*[1] the appellant had a vested life interest in certain property but the trustees had a power under Trustee Act 1925, s. 31 to accumulate the income during his minority. This power was exercised until the appellant reached the age of majority, when he became entitled to the accumulated income. When the appellant reached that age, the Revenue sought to levy additional assessments to cover the years in which the income had been accumulated. Trustee Act 1925, s. 31 provided that when a person died before reaching the age of majority,[2] the accumulated income was to be paid not to that person's estate, as would be the case if his title to that income was absolute, but was to be added to capital. It followed that although the infant beneficiary had a vested life interest he only had a contingent right to the income or, at best, a right that was vested subject to being divested if he failed to reach the age of majority. Since there would be no guarantee that he would reach that age and so no certainty that he would be entitled to the income it could not be said that the income was his in the years as it arose.

The case also shows that when the beneficiary under an accumulation trust reaches the age of majority, or whatever event is specified in the trust, and so becomes entitled to the accumulated income, that income cannot be taxed as his in the year of receipt because it is then a capital payment to him and not the income of that year.

The advantages of the accumulation trust for the wealthy used to be substantial and turned on the difference between the 45% or so charged on trust income and the top rate of individual tax. After the 1988 reforms there is only the difference between the 35% tax on accumulated income and the single higher rate of 40%. When the settlement is made on children the income is, thanks to the Trustee Act 1925, s. 31, available if needed.[3] Such a settlement can be made even by a parent in favour of his own child without the income being treated as that of the settlor so long as it is actually accumulated.[4] Further there are IHT advantages, infra, § **42: 27**.

Simon's Taxes C4.235, 236; Butterworths Income Tax Service J1.02, 21.

[1] [1944] 1 All ER 230, 26 TC 12.
[2] Now 18 for settlements made and wills executed after 31st December 1969: Family Law Reform Act 1969, s. 1.
[3] TA 1988, s. 686, infra, § **11: 05**.
[4] TA 1988, s. 664(2), infra, § **13: 32**.

11: 10   Today, the tax liability of the beneficiary depends on the nature of his right in the income. First, if this interest is vested, he will be taxed like any other beneficiary with such an interest. The income—less trust expenses—is taxed as the beneficiary's income even though it is in fact accumulating in the hands of the trustees. Moreover the fact that he has such a right will mean that the trustees do not have to pay the additional rate.[1] This will occur when a contingent beneficiary reaches the age of majority since s. 31 gives him a right to subsequent income even though his interest in capital remains contingent.

Secondly, if his interest is contingent as when he is still under 18 the income cannot be treated as his unless and until actually made his e.g. under a power.[2] It will be remembered that income which is advanced is to be grossed up at the basic and additional rates in force in the year of the payment and the resulting figure enters the beneficiary's total income.

Simon's Taxes C4.236, 237; Butterworths Income Tax Service J1.21.

[1] Because it is his income *before* it is distributed TA 1988, s. 686(2)(*b*).
[2] *Drummond v Collins* [1915] AC 1011, 6 TC 525.

Additional rate complications

11: 11   When the trustees make any payment to the beneficiary[1] TA 1988, s. 687 requires them to treat the payment as one net of both basic and additional rate. This deduction applies whether or not there is trust income available—TA 1988, ss. 348 and 349 are excluded—in that year and the tax can be collected from the trustees.[2] This tax is due on 1 December following the end of the year in which it arose.[3] However the trustees can set against this liability under TA 1988, s. 687 certain amounts, including any liability arising under s. 686.

EXAMPLE

Trustees have income of £7,500 net of tax from investments and have expenses of £600. They have to pay an annuity of £1,000 gross to X, and choose to make an advance of £1,950 to pay school fees of a beneficiary, A, with a contingent interest in income.

Assuming that they actually pay over £1,950 this must be grossed up at basic rate and additional rate, giving a gross sum of £3,000. A is therefore liable to tax on £3,000 at his rates. If he has no other income he will deduct his personal allowance of £2,605 leaving taxable income of £395 and a tax liability of £98.75.

Part II—Income tax

Under s. 687 the trustees are assessable to tax at 35% on £3,000 i.e. £1,050. They may set against this sum the tax charged on them, under s. 16 i.e. the tax due under s. 16 on £3,000. This leaves the trustees with a liability to basic rate tax on £10,000 i.e. £2,500 (of which they will recoup £250 on making the payment to X). They also have to pay additional rate on £10,000 minus £600 (expenses) and £1,000 (gross annuity) leaving £8,400 or tax of £840. The tax due under s. 687 is reduced to nil by £300, the tax chargeable under s. 686.

The trustees are allowed to make use of their s. 686 payment as a set-off against their s. 687 liability even if the s. 686 tax was paid in a previous year of assessment. When the rates change complications arise. Thus, if the trust accumulates income in year 1 when the rate is, say, 35% (25 + 10) but makes the distribution in year 2 when the rate is 50% (35 + 15), the trust will have to pay at 35% in year 1 under s. 686 but can use that tax only against the tax due at 50% under s. 687 in year 2 causing an extra 15% to be due. The beneficiary's income is grossed up at the rates for year 2.

If, on the other hand, the rate drops from 50% to 35% it seems that the extra 15% already paid is lost. Further, if the liability under s. 687 is in a year previous to that in which the liability arises under s. 686, it seems that no relief can be given either.

Provision is made for undistributed income on hand when the new regime was introduced in 1973. Tax levied on such income can be set off against liability arising under s. 687 and the amount of such tax is taken to be $\frac{2}{3}$ of the net amount of that income.[3] So if the income arose in the year 1972–73 when the rate was 38.75%, the tax is taken to be $\frac{2}{3} \times 100 - 38.75 = 40.83\%$.

An exception arises where income of a close company which is apportioned to the trustees has been taxed under s. 686 but there then follows an actual distribution by the company.[4]

These rules only apply where the receipt by the beneficiary properly falls to be treated as his income and so not where it is a capital payment. Where therefore the trustees make a loan to a beneficiary eligible for the receipt of income, the receipt cannot be treated as his income, and no tax will be due. However where the trustees have no power to make the loan the courts have treated the payments as income.[5] Further, whether a payment is a loan or income is a question of fact.[6]

Complications arise if, as will often be the case, the trust income includes building society or bank deposit account interest. These complications arise from the fact that such interest is not liable to basic rate tax (supra, § 5: 45) but must be grossed up at basic rate to determine any higher or additional rate liability of the lender. Only additional rate concerns the trust. It would be wrong to give the trust credit for the tax due on the payment to X if basic rate had not been paid. The rule, therefore, is that credit is given only if a certificate is produced stating that tax at basic rate will be accounted for.[7] This result is harsh since it appears that in calculating tax at the basic rate no allowance can be made for tax at the composite rate which the building society or bank will in fact have paid.

A non-resident beneficiary receiving income under a discretionary trust is not entitled to repayment of the tax borne by the trustees but in practice the Revenue "look through" to the underlying income and may grant any relief, including double taxation relief under the applicable agreement, which could have been available if the income had been paid direct.[8]

11   Trusts   453

Simon's Taxes C4.226; Butterworths Income Tax Service J1.23, 24.

[1] On the Revenue view as to when a payment is made see Tolley: Practical Tax 1987 p. 202.

[2] TA 1988, s. 687(2). Note extra statutory concession B18 (1988), **Simon's Taxes, Divison H2.2**, where income would escape UK tax if paid direct to the beneficiary instead of through a trust. On concession for employee trusts, see extra-statutory concession A68 (1988), **Simon's Taxes, Division H2.2**.

[3] TA 1988, s. 5(4).

[4] TA 1988, s. 687(3); there is also provision for the obsolete development gains tax.

[5] *Esdaile v IRC* (1936) 20 TC 700; the lack of power could not be cured by agreement between the trustees and some only of the beneficiaries.

[6] *Williamson v Ough* [1936] AC 384, 20 TC 194. Cf. *Peirse-Duncombe Trustees v IRC* (1940) 23 TC 199.

[7] TA 1988, s. 687(3) proviso.

[8] SP 3/86; see **Simon's Taxes, Division H3.2**.

Capital as income

11: 12   Where trustees hold property on trust but have to pay an annuity, or other annual payment, the annuitant's liability falls to be determined under Schedule D, Case III and the trustees are under a duty to deduct tax under TA 1988, ss. 348 and 349.[1] Thus duty survives the 1988 changes since those only apply to annual payments made by individuals.[2]

Whether the payments are to be regarded as an annuity or as a series of payments of capital depends upon the rights of the recipient and not on the source of the payments. In *Brodie's Will Trustees v IRC*[1] the annuity was charged on both income and capital so that the trustees were under a *duty* to have recourse to capital. The payments were annuities and so wholly taxable as income of the recipient. In *Lindus and Hortin v IRC*[3] the trustees had a *discretion* to have recourse to capital to make good any shortfall in the trust income, and the payments were still annuities. This principle was then applied in *Cunard's Trustees v IRC*[4] where the trustees had power to use capital to supplement the income of the tenant for life. In all these cases there was a series of recurrent payments over a substantial period of time.

These cases were taken by the Revenue to justify the position that any payment out of the capital of a trust fund which is intended to be used by a beneficiary for an income purpose (e.g. payment of school fees) is income of the beneficiary.[5] However this approach was rejected by the Court of Appeal in *Stevenson v Wishart*[6] who held that payments made in exercise of a power over capital[7] were not payments of income and could not be turned into income simply because it was applied to an income purpose. Where trustees have a discretion to resort to capital, the effect of exercising that discretion may be to cause the payment to fall within TA 1988, s. 687 since the sum is received by the annuitant as income and was not his income before the discretion was exercised.

A similar result had earlier been reached in *Lawson v Rolfe*.[8] There a tenant for life was under the law applicable to the settlement entitled to all bonus shares issued by corporations in which the trust held shares. Issues of such shares were not infrequent and the Revenue argued that the frequency of these payments meant that they should be treated as income payments and so taxable in the hands of the beneficiary. This argument was rejected by Foster J. There was all the difference in the world between a series of payment by the trustees under the terms of the will and these distributions by companies which so far as the trust was concerned was purely fortuitous and unplanned.

Simon's Taxes C4.223, 224.
[1] (1933) 17 TC 432.
[2] TA 1988, s. 347A(2).
[3] (1933) 17 TC 442.
[4] [1946] 1 All ER 159, 27 TC 122.
[5] See Venables, *Tax Planning Through Trusts*, § 20: 19.
[6] [1987] STC 266, [1987] 2 All ER 428.
[7] This is a strong case as the beneficiary was also an income beneficiary.
[8] [1970] 1 All ER 761, 46 TC 199.

CHARITIES

Reliefs: general

11: 13   Income and capital gains[1] accruing to charities[2] receive privileged treatment. First, various types of income are exempt from income tax.[3] These are:

(*a*) rents and profits (taxable under Schedules A or D) of any lands belonging to a hospital,[4] public school[5] or almshouse[6] or vested in trustees for charitable purposes so far as they are applied to charitable purposes only.[7]

(*b*) income chargeable under Schedule B in respect of any lands occupied by a charity;

(*c*) income under Schedule C (interest, annuities, dividends or shares of annuities), Schedule D[8] (deep discounts,[9] yearly interest[10] or other annual payment[11]) and Schedule F (distributions) if belonging to a charity or which is applicable to charitable purposes only and is so applied;

(*d*) income under Schedule C for what may broadly be termed restoration of ecclesiastical buildings;

(*e*) certain trading income (below); and

(*f*) offshore income gains.[12]

This list does not exhaust the range of taxable income and so the charity is chargeable on any income it may receive, for example such as falls within Schedule E, or which falls within Schedule D and is not yearly interest or other annual payments. (*a*), (*c*), (*e*) and (*f*) apply only where the income is actually applied for charitable purposes only; this gives the Revenue a policing role. There are also wider exemptions for certain specified public charities.[13]

Secondly there are reliefs which assist or encourage the donor. Thus where income of the charity takes the form of annual payments the trust may recover the basic rate income tax which the payer will have deducted at source;[14] such payments are safe from TA 1988, s. 660 (TA 1970, s. 434) only if capable of lasting four years or more (for other covenants the period is seven years). Further, covenants for a now unlimited sum each year are deductible in computing income for higher rates; covenanted donations to charity remain effective despite the general bar on deductions for covenants.[15]

FA 1986 introduces a payroll deduction scheme (to apply from 1987–88)[16] and a scheme whereby companies may treat as charges on income donations to charities of an amount equal to up to 3% of the dividends paid on ordinary share capital in that period.[17] Earlier legislation had provided for the deduction in computing trading income of costs incurred in sending employees to work for charities[18] and had removed the application of TA 1970, s. 411 (but not other rules such as s. 130(a)) from gifts to charities.[19] CGT is not charged on gains accruing on a disposal to a charity,[20] a rule quite distinct from the exemptions given to a gain arising on a disposal by a charity.[21] On inheritance tax exemptions see infra, § **44: 10**.

Simon's Taxes C4.518–525; Butterworths Income Tax Service J4.03–15.

[1] CGTA 1979, s. 145. If the charity is incorporated and so liable to corporation tax, similar relief is provided; TA 1988, s. 9(4).

[2] Defined as any body of persons or trust established for charitable purposes only. On this meaning of charitable purposes see Pettit, *Equity and the Law of Trusts* (5th edn), chapter 13; the English law of charities is to be applied in Scotland: *IRC v City of Glasgow Police Athletic Association* [1953] 1 All ER 747, 34 TC 76. On position of contemplative orders see extra-statutory concession B10 (1988), **Simon's Taxes, Division H2.2.**

[3] TA 1988, s. 505(1) and corporation tax TA 1988, s. 9(4) on capital gains tax see, infra, § **14: 09**, on inheritance tax see, infra, § **44: 09**. There are also reliefs from rates under General Rate Act 1967, s. 40(1), VATA 1983, Sch. 5, Group 16 from VAT, stamp duty and national insurance contributions FA 1977, s. 57.

[4] See *Royal Antediluvian Order of Buffaloes v Owens* [1928] 1 KB 446, 13 TC 176.

[5] See *Girls Public Day School Trust Ltd v Ereaut* [1931] AC 12, 15 TC 529.

[6] See *Mary Clark Home Trustees v Anderson* [1904] 2 KB 645, 5 TC 48.

[7] On application for charitable purposes, see *IRC v Helen Slater Charitable Trust Ltd* [1981] STC 471, CA; the scope of that decision is however greatly restricted by the new rules outlined infra, § **11: 16**.

[8] Any Case—even IV and V.

[9] TA 1988, Sch. 4, para. 14.

[10] Non-yearly bank and building society interest received by charities see extra-statutory concession B9 (1988), **Simon's Taxes, Division H2.2.** Trading profits are not annual payments: *Trustees of Psalms and Hymns v Whitwell* (1890) 3 TC 7, but distinguish *R v IT Special Comrs, ex p Shaftesbury Home and Arethusa Training Ship* [1923] 1 KB 393, 8 TC 367; obligation to pay surplus profits creates annual payments.

[11] The Revenue will not normally seek to challenge a claim for relief when a loan or other advance payment is made to a charity to satisfy the terms of a deed of covenant drawn up in favour of the charity at the same time; see [1985] STI p. 572.

[12] TA 1988, s. 761.

[13] TA 1988, s. 507 as amended by FA 1989, s. 60.

[14] Supra, § **9: 84**; for payments by corporations, see TA 1988, s. 339, infra, § **25: 12**. In 1985–86, the total tax cost of the exceptions, i.e. the loss of income and corporation tax was estimated at £200m; see Inland Revenue Statistics 1986.

[15] TA 1988, s. 683(3) amended by FA 1986, s. 32(1).

[16] TA 1988, s. 202. The figure is £480 p.a. or £40 per month; FA 1989, s. 58.

[17] TA 1988, s. 339(5); see infra, § **25: 13**.

[18] TA 1988, s. 86.

[19] TA 1988, s. 577.

[20] CGTA 1979, s. 145(2).

[21] CGTA 1979, s. 145(1).

Trading income

11: 14   If a charity carries on a trade, it will be exempt from the tax on the profits of that trade only if (*i*) the profits are applied solely for the purposes of the charity and (*ii*) either (*a*) the trade is exercised in the course of the actual carrying out of a primary purpose of the charity or (*b*) the work in connection with the trade is mainly carried out by beneficiaries of the charity.[1]

In considering whether money is applied for charitable purposes, the court looks to see how the money has been applied. If it has been applied to charitable purposes it does not matter that the charity was obliged to apply it that way, nor probably is it relevant what reason or motive the trustees may have had, nor that they may confer some incidental benefit upon some third person.[2] However, if a charity established for the public benefit gives all its income to the children of employees of a particular firm which is connected with the managers of the charity, this requirement is not met.[3]

Requirement (*ii*)(*a*) is that the trade is exercised in the course of the actual carrying out of a primary purpose of the charity. So if a charity runs a law surgery and one of its objects is the provision of lectures and general legal education, the profits of conferences for solicitors escape tax. Likewise, if a school or college carries on the trade of education and charges fees, or presumably an old people's home charges for its services, the trade is exercised in the course of the actual carrying out of a primary purpose of the charity. Requirement (*ii*)(*b*) contemplates "the basket factory of a blind asylum, the blind inmates being the beneficiaries by whose work the trade of manufacturing baskets for sale mainly, is carried on".[4] However, it has been extended to a charitable association which organised a competitive music festival, the competitors being treated as the beneficiaries.[5] More obviously the profits of a school run by nuns have been held exempt, the nuns, and not just the pupils, being regarded as the beneficiaries.[6] But it does not follow that ordinary school masters are beneficiaries.[7]

Simon's Taxes C4.522, 523; Butterworths Income Tax Service J4.15.

[1] TA 1988, s. 505(1)(*e*). Introduced by FA 1920, s. 30(1)(*c*) to reverse *Coman v Governors of the Rotunda Hospital* [1921] 1 AC 1.

[2] Per Buckley J in *Campbell v IRC* (1966) 45 TC 427 at 443–4.

[3] *IRC v Educational Grants Association* [1967] 2 All ER 893, 44 TC 93.

[4] Per Lord Clyde in *IRC v Glasgow Musical Festival Association* (1926) 11 TC 154 at 163.

[5] Ibid.

[6] *Brighton Convent of the Blessed Sacrament v IRC* (1933) 18 TC 76.

[7] Per Lord Buckmaster in *Brighton College v Marriott* [1926] AC 192 at 203, 10 TC 213 at 234.

11: 15   It will be seen that commercially orientated trading such as the sale of Christmas cards or the organisation of the sales of gifts give rise to taxable, not exempt profits, such sales not being integral parts of the charity's purposes. However, by concession the profits from bazaars or jumble sales run by voluntary organisations are not generally charged to tax.[1] A result similar to complete exemption of trading income from income tax can be achieved by the device of letting the trade be carried on by a company whose shares are held by the charity and which then covenants to make the payments to the charity equal to its profits; such payments are charges on income and so in effect deductible, infra, § **25: 12**. Theoretically such arrangements are vulnerable to attack under the *Ramsay* principle, especially in the light of *Furniss v Dawson* but the Revenue have indicated that such schemes will not usually be challenged provided no circularity is involved such as when the charity provides an interest-free loan to the trading entity or the trader effectively controls the charity using it as a tax free money box.[2]

Where a charity incurs expense and so a loss on its charitable but non trading activities, it cannot set that loss off against its profits from a taxable trade.[3] However, if a charity carries on two trades one exempt, on which it makes a loss, and the other taxable, on which it makes a profit, it may be that the loss, can be relieved.[4] This view seems doubtful but has not been tested in the courts. The charity would in any case have to surmount TA 1988, s. 384 first.[5] On the other hand, it is perfectly permissible for a loss on a taxable trade to be set off against the profit of another taxable trade.

Simon's Taxes C4.522, 523; Butterworths Income Tax Service J4.15.
[1] Extra-statutory concession C4 (1988), Simon's Taxes, Division H2.2.
[2] [1985] STI, 572. Of course the company must comply with the requirements of TA 1988, Sch. 16.
[3] *Religious Tract and Book Society of Scotland v Forbes* (1896) 3 TC 415.
[4] Under TA 1988, s. 380, supra, § 5: 02, or s. 393, infra, § 25: 21; Whiteman and Wheatcroft (2nd edn), § 21–15.
[5] Supra, § 5: 13.

Restriction of exemptions

11: 16 In certain circumstances, the tax exemptions available to a charity may be restricted under provisions in respect of chargeable periods ending after 11th June 1986.[1]

In general, the restrictions apply only if, in the chargeable period concerned, the charity has "relevant income and gains" of £10,000 or more.[2] "Relevant income and gains" means income which would be taxable but for the exemptions provided by TA 1988, s. 505 (supra, §§ 11: 13, 14) together with income which is taxable regardless of TA 1988, s. 505(1), and gains which would be taxable but for CGTA 1979, s. 145 (see infra, § 14: 09), together with chargeable gains falling outside that provision.[3] The provisions may be applied to charities with relevant income and gains below that figure, however, if it appears to the Board that two or more charities are acting in concert, with the avoidance of tax (whether by the charities or by another person) as one of their main aims. The Board must serve notice in writing on the charities, which have the right to appeal against the Board's decision.[4]

The tax exemptions to which the charity is entitled are restricted if any expenditure by the charity during the chargeable period is incurred otherwise than for exclusively charitable purposes. Expenditure which is not incurred for charitable purposes only is referred to as "non-qualifying expenditure", and "qualifying expenditure" is expenditure incurred for charitable purposes only. A payment made to a body outside the UK is treated as non-qualifying expenditure unless the charity has taken such steps as are reasonable in the circumstances to ensure that the payment will be used for charitable purposes only.[5] Loans and investments are also treated as non-qualifying expenditure unless they fall within the categories of qualifying loans and qualifying investments set out.[6]

The following are treated as "qualifying loans":[7]

(*a*) a loan made to another charity for charitable purposes only;

(*b*) a loan to a beneficiary of the charity made in the course of its charitable activities;

(*c*) money placed in a current account with a bank (unless this forms part of an arrangement under which the bank makes a loan to another person).

"Qualifying investments" are elaborately defined.[8]

A special rule ensures that if a non-qualifying investment is made and realised, or loan made and repaid, during the same chargeable period, the reinvestment of the proceeds during that chargeable period is left out of account when calculating the amount of "non-qualifying expenditure" incurred by the charity.[9]

Tax relief under both TA 1988, s. 505 and CGTA 1979, s. 145 is withheld from the amount by which a charity "relevant income and gains" exceeds its "qualifying expenditure" to the extent that this amount does not exceed the "non-qualifying expenditure" incurred by the charity in that chargeable period.[10] The charity may specify the items of relevant income and gains which are to be treated as attributable to the non-exempt amount.[11]

If the charity's total expenditure in a chargeable period exceeds its relevant income and gains so that part of the non-qualifying expenditure has not been taken into account under these provisions, that part may be attributed to earlier chargeable periods.[12]

Where exemptions are restricted under these provisions, higher rate tax relief on covenants to the charity may also be restricted.[13]

Simon's Taxes, C4.528.

[1] TA 1988, ss. 505 and 506. The purpose is to prevent schemes such as those behind *IRC v Helen Slater Charitable Trust Ltd* [1981] STC 471, CA. On transitional relief see FA 1986, s. 31(10).

[2] TA 1988, s. 505(3)(*a*).

[3] TA 1988, s. 505(5).

[4] TA 1988, s. 505(7).

[5] TA 1988, s. 506(1).

[6] In TA 1988, s. 506.

[7] FA 1986, Sch. 7, Part III.

[8] FA 1986, Sch. 7, Part II.

[9] TA 1988, s. 506(5).

[10] TA 1988, s. 505(3).

[11] TA 1988, s. 505(7).

[12] TA 1988, s. 506(6).

[13] TA 1988, s. 683(4).

12 Estates in the course of administration

DECEASED'S INCOME

12: 01   Estates have to settle the liability of the deceased person to income tax on the income that accrued to him during his lifetime.[1] In computing this liability the personal reliefs of the deceased are allowed in full—there is no reduction for dying before 5th April. If the deceased was carrying on a trade his death will involve a discontinuance and so a reopening of the accounts for the previous years.[2]

Income payable after, but in respect of a period before, the death of the deceased is treated as that of the estate, not of the deceased.[3] However the income is apportioned for CTT and IHT purposes, so that the payment may both be charged with CTT or IHT as the deceased's income and income tax as the income of the estate—and of the beneficiary. TA 1988, s. 699 provides that in computing the beneficiary's income for excess liability, the residuary income of the estate is to be reduced by the amount of CTT or IHT payable in respect of that income.

Simon's Taxes C4.102; Butterworths Income Tax Service J3.01.
[1] TMA 1970, s. 74 and note s. 40(1), supra, § **1: 36**.
[2] Supra, **7: 43**.
[3] *IRC v Henderson's Executors* (1931) 16 TC 282 distinguish the situation in which the dividend is payable before, but is paid after, the death *Potel v IRC* [1971] 2 All ER 504, 46 TC 658.

INCOME ARISING AFTER DEATH

The liability of the personal representatives

12: 02   Like trustees, personal representatives are assessable to income tax at the basic rate[1] and not the higher rate.[2] They may not use any personal allowances of the deceased which were not absorbed by his income. They may however claim relief in respect of interest payments or in respect of any loss which *they* incur in running a business. Interest in respect of unpaid CTT or IHT is not deductible,[3] but interest on a loan to pay CTT or IHT is if the loan is made to the representatives and relates to tax payable on personalty before the grant of representation. Only interest on the first year of the loan is deductible; excess interest can be carried back and then forward.[4]

On liability to tax on trading income, see § **7: 25**.

Simon's Taxes C4.101, 102; Butterworths Income Tax Service J3.02.
[1] There is no liability to additional rate: TA 1988, s. 686(6).

[2] *IRC v Countess of Longford* [1927] 1 KB 594, 13 TC 573.
[3] *Lord Inverclyde's Trustees v Millar* (1924) 9 TC 14.
[4] TA 1988, s. 364 (FA 1974, Sch. 1 para. 17–21).

The beneficiary

12: 03   Until the administration is complete no beneficiary has any rights in the property of the estate or to the income from it;[1] it follows that no beneficiary is liable to income tax on the income of the estate.[2] The question whether administration is complete is a matter of fact, the issue being whether the residue has been ascertained.[3] A prolonged administration can see a fund administered with expertise but taxed only at the basic rate of tax; conversely if the prospective beneficiaries had low incomes and so unused personal allowances the administration might be expedited.

Simon's Taxes C4.103; Butterworths Income Tax Service J3.03.
[1] *Stamp Duties Comr (Queensland) v Livingston* [1964] 3 All ER 692, [1965] AC 694.
[2] *R v IT Special Purposes Comrs, ex p Dr Barnardo's Homes National Incorporated Association* [1920] 1 KB 26, 7 TC 646; *Corbett v IRC* [1937] 4 All ER 700, 21 TC 449; see also *Prest v Bettinson* [1980] STC 607 and SP 7/80, but contrast extra-statutory concession A14 (1988), **Simon's Taxes Division H2.2.**
[3] *George Attenborough & Son v Solomon* [1913] AC 76.

Non-residuary beneficiaries

12: 04   Where a personal representative vests a specific legacy in the legatee intermediate income accruing during the administration is related back and so assessed on the beneficiary as at the times that income had accrued to the property.[1]

Where a legacy carries interest, the beneficiary is liable to tax on that interest under Schedule D, Case III if it has become his income. An attempt to disclaim the interest failed where a sum had been set aside to pay the legacy.[2] From this it should follow that where no sums have been set aside, the legatee may have a right to interest but is not taxable in respect of it. When he receives the legacy with its interest, it is an open question whether the payment relates back.

Simon's Taxes C4.120, 121; Butterworths Income Tax Service J3.07.
[1] *IRC v Hawley* [1928] 1 KB 578, 13 TC 327.
[2] *Spens v IRC* [1970] 3 All ER 295, 46 TC 276; cf. *Dewar v IRC* [1935] 2 KB 351, 19 TC 561.

Residuary beneficiaries

(1) *Limited interest; TA 1988, s. 695*

12: 05   The rules which follow distinguish a UK estate from a foreign estate.

A person has a limited interest[1] if he would have a right to income if administration were complete. It is an open question whether a person whose interest is vested subject to being divested is entitled to the income.[2]

Any sums which are paid[3] in respect of the limited interest are grossed up[4] at basic rate and treated as his income for the year of assessment in which the sum was paid or, if the interest has ceased, as income for the year of assessment in which it ceased.[5] Income from a foreign estate is grossed up only to reflect the UK tax paid.[6]

When the administration is completed the total sums paid before or payable on the completion are then aggregated and apportioned on a day to day basis, any adjustments being then made.[7] This basis completely supersedes the original assessments based on the date of receipt.

The income on which the beneficiary is taxed may, and almost certainly will, bear no relation to the actual income of the estate in respect of which the personal representatives are chargeable. This is partly because administration expenses are deductible in computing the beneficiary's income, but not in computing the estate income, but also because the fluctuation in rates of tax and the variation in the estate income mean that the estate income will not have an even day to day flow.

Income of a legatee who is not resident or not ordinarily resident in the UK may, by concession, be treated as if it arose directly from the various sources, even though the estate is a UK estate (e.g. sole assets are UK government securities: supra, § **9: 32**).[8]

Simon's Taxes C4.107, 108, 111; Butterworths Income Tax Service J3.05.

[1] TA 1988, s. 701(2).
[2] The doubts stem from *Stanley v IRC*, supra, § **13: 20**.
[3] Widely defined—TA 1988, s. 701(12).
[4] Benefits in kind must be grossed up: *IRC v Mardon* (1956) 36 TC 565.
[5] TA 1988, s. 695(2).
[6] TA 1988, s. 695(5).
[7] TA 1988, s. 695(3). **Simon's Taxes C4.110, 113.**
[8] Extra-statutory concession A14 (1988), **Simon's Taxes, Division H2.2.**

---

(2) *Absolute interests; TA 1988, s. 696*

12: 06   A beneficiary has an absolute interest in residue if, on the hypothesis that the administration were then complete, he would be entitled to the capital or a part of it in his own right.[1] It is unclear whether a person entitled to capital but subject to the payment of an annuity is entitled to it "in his own right".[2]

Sums actually paid[3] are grossed up at basic rate and treated as his income.[4] As however he is also entitled to capital, this treatment applies only to the extent that there is residuary income available;[5] any excess is treated as capital. Income from a foreign estate is grossed up only to reflect the UK tax actually paid.[6]

When administration is complete the residuary beneficiary is treated as having received each year the amount of the residuary income of that year, grossed up as necessary.[7] Any assessments already made on the basis of sums received are re-opened and adjusted.[8] This does not undo the possible tax advantages of prolonged administration and is designed to tax income of years in which he received less than his share of the income and to treat such payments as income of those years.

Where on completion of administration the aggregate of benefits received, grossed up as necessary,[9] turns out to be less than the residuary income—or his share of it—that income is reduced to the level of that aggregate.[10]

Where the residuary beneficiary is exempt from income tax, he will be entitled to a repayment. Where the residuary income includes building society income, a repayment can be obtained in spite of TA 1988, s. 476(5)(*b*). This is because the Revenue does not look through to the underlying source.[11]

Concessionary treatment of income of a non-resident from a UK estate which is dealt with at § **12: 05** applies here also.

Simon's Taxes C4.107, 109–111, 113; Butterworths Income Tax Service J3.04.

[1] TA 1988, s. 701(2).
[2] See Simon's Taxes C4.107.
[3] Widely defined TA 1988, s. 701(12).
[4] TA 1988, s. 696(3).
[5] Defined TA 1988, s. 701(7).
[6] TA 1988, s. 696(6).
[7] TA 1988, s. 696(4) on allocation of expenses see extra-statutory concession A13 (1988), Simon's Taxes, Division H2.2.
[8] TA 1988, s. 700.
[9] *IRC v Mardon* (1956) 36 TC 565.
[10] TA 1988, s. 697(2).
[11] SP 7/80; Simon's Taxes, Division H3.2.

---

(3) *Other*

12: 07   If the residue is held on discretionary trusts, neither of the provisions so far considered applies, since there are neither absolute nor limited interests. It is therefore provided that the scheme used for limited interests applies.[1]

Provision is also made for the possibility that the beneficiary himself dies before administration is complete. If the beneficiary had an absolute interest, that interest passes to his personal representatives and the income of the first estate will now form part of the beneficiary's estate; the personal representatives are treated as succeeding to the absolute interest despite their representative status.[2] Payments during the administration period of the first estate are, regardless of their actual time of payment, treated as being made to the now deceased beneficiary until such time as they reach the total residuary income up to the date of his death; only thereafter will the payments be treated as the income of his estate.[3] If the beneficiary had a limited interest, payments made until the date of death are treated as his income but his tax liability is adjusted on a day to day basis when administration is complete.[4]

Simon's Taxes C4.114, 115; Butterworths Income Tax Service J3.06.

[1] TA 1988, s. 698(3).
[2] TA 1988, s. 698(1).
[3] TA 1988, s. 698(2).
[4] TA 1988, s. 698(3)(*a*).

13 Anti-avoidance: settlements and arrangements

INTRODUCTION

13: 01 TA 1988, Part XV contains a series of provisions designed for three ends. The first is to restrict the use of other taxable entities, particularly trusts, as piggy banks, in which income can be taxed at the rates appropriate to that entity, rather than at the settlor's marginal rates, and so grow more rapidly before being passed back for the settlor or his spouse to enjoy. The second is to restrict the income splitting opportunities within the family as between parents and minor children. The third is to restrict the income assignment possibilities created by the system for taxing covenants supra, § : 73; these provisions remain in place despite the abolition of the general right to deduct sums paid under new covenants.

These provisions were not introduced at one time and in consequence do not form a single code; gaps and overlaps result. They do not apply to funds for the maintenance of heritage property.[1]

The technique used by the legislature is to provide that where one of these arrangements, usually described as a settlement, but sometimes as a disposition, is made, the income arising under the arrangement instead of being the income of the entity in whose hands it arises, shall instead be treated as the income of the person who made the arrangement, the settlor. Sometimes, but not always, the settlor is given a right to recover the tax from the entity concerned. Some affect income arising,[2] others only income which is accumulated.[3] Some treat the income as that of the settlor for all purposes but one only for excess liability.[4]

When income is treated as that of the settlor under one of these rules, the correct legal analysis is that the income arises first in the hands of the entity and then is transferred back to the settlor by parliamentary transfer.

In *Ang v Parrish*[5] the taxpayer made a covenant in favour of his parents in law which fell foul of TA 1988, s. 683. The taxpayer only had earned income out of which to make the payments. Walton J held that the payment came back to him as investment income and so were subject to the additional rate, this even though the payment was originally made out of earned income.

This rather silly decision left the taxpayer's final state worse than the first. It is one more example of the folly of the system of deduction at source now, thankfully, greatly reduced. A rational system of taxation would have prescribed deductions e.g. payments under covenants, and then listed the circumstances in which deduction was not permitted.

A study of these rules might leave one with the impression that a trust is never effective for tax purposes. This is quite untrue. Income may be accumulated or distributed and the settlor may specify relatives, other than his wife or infant children as objects of the trust without any adverse income tax consequences under these rules. Indeed he may even be a trustee and himself control the selection of beneficiaries, again other than his wife or infant children, under a discretionary trust or a power of appointment.

Simon's Taxes C4.301, 304, 367; Butterworths Income Tax Service J1.11–16, J2.02–12.
¹ TA 1988, s. 691.
² TA 1988, ss. 663, 672, 674 and 683.
³ TA 1988, ss. 673 and 677.
⁴ TA 1988, s. 683.
⁵ [1980] STC 341, [1980] 2 All ER 790.

SETTLEMENTS

13: 02   It is unfortunate that Part XV is entitled "Settlements", with its overtones of the ladies of Jane Austen. The law would look remarkably foolish if it took the view that income splitting should be countered only where it took place behind devices akin to the strict settlement and the law does not take such a view.

A settlement "includes any disposition, trust, covenant, agreement or arrangement".¹ In relation to settlement on infant children the term also includes a transfer of assets.²

The word "settlement" is not a dominating word which colours the others and the word arrangement is not a term of art.³ Many acts have been held to be settlements, including the setting up of corporate structures (an arrangement) and the disclaimer of an interest by a remainderman (a disposition) as the following cases show. The limiting factor is that a transaction can only be a settlement if it contains an element of bounty.⁴

It remains to be seen how far the principle in *IRC v Ramsay* and *Furniss v Dawson* can or will be invoked to expand the concept of "settlement". The principle may well be relevant in determining its scope.⁵

Simon's Taxes C4.330; Butterworths Income Tax Service J1.11.
¹ TA 1988, s. 681(4).
² TA 1988, s. 670.
³ Greene MR in *IRC v Payne* (1940) 23 TC 610 at 626. Cf. *Shop and Store Developments Ltd v IRC* [1967] 1 All ER 42, [1967] 1 AC 472 (stamp duty).
⁴ *IRC v Plummer* [1979] STC 793, [1979] 3 All ER 775; *Chinn v Collins* [1981] STC 1.
⁵ *Ewart v Taylor* [1983] STC 721.

Two cases

13: 03   In *IRC v Mills*¹ the taxpayer was a child film star. In order to make sure that her earnings were "legally protected", her father formed a company and settled the shares of that company on trust for the taxpayer with various contingent remainders over. The taxpayer then signed a service contract with the company giving the company the right to her exclusive services for a period of five years at a salary of £400 a year. The company received large sums for the films she made and distributed those sums in the form of dividend to the trustees. Since the trustees did not distribute the income the question arose whether the income accumulated by the trust could be treated as hers. The House of Lords held that there was a settlement, that she was the settlor and that the source of the dividends was the money paid for her work so that she had by her work provided the settlement with income indirectly. The result was that income accumulated by the trustees was deemed to be hers by TA 1988, s. 673, infra, § **13: 11**.

---

[1] [1974] 1 All ER 722, [1974] STC 130. Note TA 1988, s. 775, infra, § **31: 37**. Where a stranger provides trustees with advice as a result of which the income of the fund is increased it appears that this section cannot apply since the stranger provides advice not funds, see *Mills v IRC* 49 TC 367 per Viscount Dilhorne at 408.

13: 04   In *IRC v Buchanan*[1] property was settled by X on A for life with remainder to B for life on protective trusts with remainder to B's children. The settlement also provided that if B should disclaim her life interest, the property should be administered at the moment when B's interest would have fallen into possession as if B were dead, thus avoiding the discretionary trusts that would otherwise have arisen on A's death following the disclaimer. B disclaimed her interest and the next day A released his interest. The Court of Appeal held that the destruction of an interest was a disposition. B had a disposable interest in that she had the right to income after A's death and could end that entitlement or not as she chose. The result was that the disclaimer was a settlement and so income arising in favour of B's infant children was deemed to be hers under TA 1988, s. 663, infra, § **13: 32**.

---

[1] [1957] 2 All ER 400, 37 TC 365.

13: 05   If there is no element of bounty the transaction is not a settlement; this follows even if the transaction is not carried out for commercial reasons.

So in *IRC v Levy*[1] an interest-free loan by a taxpayer to a company wholly owned by him, a transaction which the Commissioners had found to contain no element of bounty, was not a settlement. As Nourse J said:[2]

> "A commercial transaction devoid of any element of bounty is not within this definition. The absence of any correlative obligation on the part of him who is on the receiving end of the transaction may be material, but is not conclusive in determining whether it contains an element of bounty or not."

In *IRC v Plummer*[3] a charity paid £2,480 to the taxpayer who covenanted to pay the charity a sum which net of tax at basic rate would amount to £500 each year for five years. The purpose of the scheme was to enable the taxpayer to reduce his liability to surtax. The payments were annual payments being income of the charity under Schedule D, Case III and, in consequence, deductible under s. 835. The difference between £500 grossed up at basic rate and £500 were thus relieved from surtax thus enabling the taxpayer to keep the benefit of the tax relief himself. Despite the fact that the arrangement was made solely to obtain the tax advantage the House of Lords held that as there was no bounty as between the parties it was not a settlement. Such reverse annuity schemes have now been stopped by statute; infra, § **13: 47**. In the new era of *IRC v Ramsay* and *Furniss v Dawson* such a scheme would surely fail but whether this would be through a revised view of what is a settlement[4] or, more simply, the refusal of the deduction under s. 835 on the basis that the flow of money was a self cancelling transaction and so not an annual payment[5] remains to be seen.

One may doubt the validity of the bounty test. If X settles property for two years upon trust for X absolutely if X survives the period and, if not, for Y and Y provides full consideration for his interest, *IRC v Plummer* seems to say there is no settlement and yet this is the very type of avoidance at which provisions like s. 673 are aimed.[6]

In applying the test the courts look at the transaction as a whole. In *Chinn v Collins*[7] trustees exercised a power of appointment in favour of a beneficiary who later assigned his contingent interest under that exercise as part of a scheme to avoid tax. It was argued that there was no element of bounty about the appointment or the subsequent transaction. However the House of Lords held that the appointment and the subsequent activities made an arrangement and that the benefit accrued to the taxpayer as a result of the original act of bounty by the settlor in creating the settlement; the settlor's bounty remained incomplete until the appointment was made and the trustees then conferred bounty on the beneficiary.

More recently the test of bounty was applied in *Butler v Wildin*.[8] Parents who were architects had worked for a company without fee. They had arranged for shares to be held by their infant children. Vinelott J, reversing the Special Commissioner, held that there was a settlement. The children had contributed nothing of substance and were not exposed to any risk. Income arising from the company in the form of dividends was therefore not the income of the children and the claim for repayment of income tax because they had unused personal allowances failed.

Simon's Taxes C4.307, 330, 352; Butterworths Income Tax Service J1.11.

[1] [1982] STC 442.

[2] [1982] STC 442 at 457.

[3] [1979] STC 793, [1979] 3 All ER 775.

[4] The Revenue refused to concede relief to the taxpayer for any year other than the one in issue; liability for the later years has, apparently, been determined in favour of the Revenue by the Special Commissioners—see Gillard, *In The Name of Charity* (1987) p. 282.

[5] This involves only a small extension of the decision in *Campbell v IRC* (supra, § **9: 63**) from cases where the payment is under a legally enforceable obligation to one where the payment is one of a pre-ordained series of steps.

[6] Venables, *Tax Planning Through Trusts* § 20: 26.

[7] [1981] STC 1, [1981] 1 All ER 189 and see discussion in *IRC v Levy*, supra, n. 1.

[8] [1989] STC 22.

13: 06   The term settlement is so widely defined that the more crucial question[1] is to determine what property is comprised in the settlement. In *Chamberlain v IRC*[2] the settlor transferred assets to a company which he controlled and trustees acquired ordinary shares issued by the company. The trustees paid for the shares with money given them by the settlor. The settlor later gave them more money with which to buy further shares. It was held that the property comprised in the settlement was the money given by the settlor and the shares purchased with that money. The assets of the company did not constitute the settled property.

Simon's Taxes C4.343.
[1] Per Lord Thankerton in *Chamberlain v IRC* [1943] 2 All ER 200 at 203, 25 TC 317 at 329.
[2] Supra, n. 1.

13: 07   In *Wachtel v IRC* the arrangement embraced not only the sum of £1,000 transferred by the settlor but also the sum then borrowed from the bank by the trustees and guaranteed by the settlor, and the Revenue relied on the creation of the deposit account as part of the provision of the trust funds. However they did not argue that the deposit account formed part of the settled property because no interests in favour of the beneficiaries were charged on it or created out of it.

SETTLOR

13: 08   A settlor is defined[1] as any person by whom the settlement was made, whether directly or indirectly; so in *IRC v Buchanan* B made the settlement when she disclaimed her interest. It is however widened to cover (*i*) one who has provided or undertaken to provide funds, directly or indirectly, for the settlement as with the film star in *IRC v Mills* and (*ii*) one who has made a reciprocal arrangement with another person for that other to make or enter into the settlement. The purpose of class (*ii*) is to catch the obvious device whereby A makes a settlement on B's children and in return B makes a settlement on A's children; in such instances there must be a reciprocal arrangement.[2]

A person makes a settlement if he carries out any steps of that settlement. So where the taxpayer had carried out one step and later a scheme was devised and carried out by his solicitors and accountants, it was held to be part of his settlement even though he was not consulted or present at any meetings.[3] An infant can make a settlement.[4]

Where funds are provided for a settlement a very strong inference is to be drawn that they are provided for that purpose,[5] an inference which will be rebutted if it is established that they were provided for another purpose. So in *IRC v Mills* the infant provided funds for the purposes of a settlement even if unconsciously.

Simon's Taxes C4.331.
[1] TA 1988, ss. 681(4) and 670 (TA 1970, ss. 454(3) and 444(2)).
[2] E.g. *Hood Barrs v IRC* [1946] 2 All ER 768, 27 TC 385.
[3] *Crossland v Hawkins* [1961] 2 All ER 812, 39 TC 493.
[4] *Semble*—in *IRC v Mills* no argument was raised by the infant to have the arrangement set aside on the grounds of its invalidity by reason of her infancy.
[5] *IRC v Mills* [1974] 1 All ER 722 at 727, [1974] STC 130 at 135.

Whose income?

13: 09   The breadth of the definition of settlement and of settlor means that more than one person may be a settlor in relation to a particular settlement.[1] Two issues arise: (i) are these two settlors (ii) if so what are the consequences?

The first issue is resolved by looking at the section to be construed. Where the relevant provision talks of income arising a settlor is responsible only for the income originating from him.[2] The statute also provides that in determining how much of the income arising under a settlement has been distributed, any sums paid partly out of income originating from the settlor and partly out of other income must be apportioned evenly over all that income.[3]

In *IRC v Mills*[4] it was held that while the father was clearly a settlor, so also was the taxpayer and, since it was the taxpayer's services which supplied the company with funds from which to pay dividends to the trust, she indirectly provided the income for the settlement; hence all the income originated from her. The problem of the two settlors did not therefore arise in relation to the taxpayer and her father, and what would happen in such a case was left undecided by the House of Lords. In the Court of Appeal, Orr LJ suggested that this was simply a case in which it is left to the Revenue authorities to act reasonably:[5] a solution which may be illustrated by *IRC v Buchanan*.[6] In that case the Revenue argued that the income accrued to B's children in consequence of her disposition. Yet if A had not released his interest no income would actually have accrued to the children. The Revenue won but did not make any assessment for any year before that in which A died. One should note that the Court of Appeal treated X as not being a settlor for this purpose, a conclusion difficult (but not impossible) to reconcile with *Chinn v Collins*.[7]

This decision was followed in *d'Abreu v IRC*.[8] In simplified terms, property had been settled by P on his daughters J and A; each moiety was held for life with remainders over to children in default of appointment and in default of children the moiety was to pass to the other. In 1959 J, who never married, released her power to appoint in favour of any husband she might marry; A then released and assigned her contingent interest in J's moiety to the trustees of her moiety and then exercised the power of appointment in favour of her children. The result was that when J died in 1963 the income from her moiety accrued to A's children who were still infants.

Oliver J held that, as in *Buchanan*, the whole of the income accruing to A's children did so in consequence of A's acts and so fell within TA 1988, s. 663. However, he went on to say that even if J were also a settlor s. 668 directed that s. 663 was to apply to each settlor as if he were the only settlor; all the income therefore originated from A and one could not apportion on the basis of an actuarial valuation of their interests in 1959.

Two comments may be made. First the decision draws a sharp and so unfortunate distinction between successive and other interests. Thus if A and J had under the Variation of Trusts Act extracted capital sums which they had then jointly settled on A's children it is at least arguable that the income from J's fund would not fall within s. 663. Secondly even within s. 663 difficulties remain. Thus, suppose that there are successive life interests for H and W and they both release their interests in favour of their infant children. One could not say that they were both settlors and so tax the income twice. It is no answer to say that W's income is treated as H's since this does not stop the income being potentially liable twice and in any case the issue arises again if the spouses separate. The appropriate answer would be to apportion on the basis of actuarial valuation of their interests but this was rejected in *d'Abreu*.

To treat the matter as turning on the reasonableness of the Revenue is to make liability turn on administrative discretion, the very view rejected by the House of Lords in *Vestey v IRC*[9]. It is therefore to be hoped that *d'Abreu* is not the last word.

Simon's Taxes C4.319.
[1] Defined TA 1988, s. 679(5)–(7).
[2] TA 1988, s. 679(3).
[3] But contrast TA 1988, s. 668(4)(c) settlements on children.
[4] [1974] STC 130, [1974] 1 All ER 722, 49 TC 367.
[5] [1973] STC 1 at 22, [1972] 3 All ER 977 at 998.
[6] [1957] 2 All ER 400, 37 TC 365.
[7] [1981] STC 1, [1981] 1 All ER 189.
[8] [1978] STC 538.
[9] [1980] STC 10, [1980] AC 1148.

CHARGE ON INCOME ARISING

Income arising

13: 10   Income arising under a settlement includes any income chargeable to income tax, whether by deduction or otherwise.[1] It also includes any income which would have been so chargeable if it had been received in the UK by a person domiciled, resident and ordinarily resident in the UK. This creates a hypothetical remittance to a hypothetical resident and so catches all income wherever it arises.[2] An exception has therefore to be made and this is where the settlor is not domiciled or resident or ordinarily resident in the UK and the settlor would by reason of that not be chargeable to UK tax on that income.[3]

Also to be included is any income of any body corporate that has been apportioned under the close company legislation to the trustees or any beneficiary,[4] as is the income of such a body which could have been apportioned if the body had been incorporated and is resident and ordinarily resident in any part of the UK.[5]

Simon's Taxes C4.332.
[1] TA 1988, s. 681(1).
[2] Reversing *Astor v Perry* [1935] AC 398, 19 TC 255.
[3] TA 1988, s. 681(1) proviso; s. 670 contains no such restriction; since s. 663 it restricted to cases where the settlor is resident in the UK—s. 663(5).
[4] TA 1988, s. 681(3).
[5] TA 1988, s. 681(2)—but not s. 670. Income apportioned to an overseas company in which the settlor held shares escaped s. 672 in *Lord Howard de Walden v IRC* (1948) 30 TC 345.

Revocable settlements allowing reversion to settlor: TA 1988, s. 672

13: 11   If a settlement can be revoked and, on that revocation, the property reverts to the settlor or to his wife (or husband) then income arising under the trust is treated as that of the settlor from the very beginning. If, on revocation, only a part of the property will so revert, only that part of the trust income arising is treated as the settlor's income.

The power to revoke may be immediate or future but it is provided, on the partial analogy of the rule concerning covenants, that if the power cannot be exercised for at least six years,[1] the income will not be treated as that of the settlor until the power becomes exercisable. The settlor need not become entitled to the property immediately the power is exercised; it is sufficient that he may eventually become entitled to it.[2]

A power to advance the whole of the settled capital is a power to revoke the settlement.[3] A power to diminish the property comprised in the settlement or the income people other than the settlor or his wife receive from it, is treated as a power to revoke.[4]

It is immaterial whether it is the settlor or some other person who has the power to revoke. It is likewise immaterial whether the power to revoke is exercisable with or without the consent of any other person.

Simon's Taxes C4.338–345; Butterworths Income Tax Service J1.14.
[1] A supplemental deed is not retroactive—*Taylor v IRC* [1946] 1 All ER 488n, 27 TC 93.
[2] *Barr's Trustees v IRC* (1943) 25 TC 72 (a case on s. 673; see **Simon's Taxes C4.344**.
[3] *Kenmare v IRC* [1957] 3 All ER 33, 37 TC 383.
[4] TA 1988, s. 672(2), revsg. *IRC v Saunders* [1957] 3 All ER 43, 37 TC 416.

13: 12   However it is not every chance of the reduction in the trust that may give rise to s. 672, but only a power to be found in the settlement and derived directly therefrom. In *IRC v Wolfson*[1] the settlement was of shares in a company which was controlled by the settlor. He was thus in a position to deprive the trust of its income. This was held not to amount to a power of revocation. However, if the company had been set up as part of the scheme of settlement a different result might have followed and it would have been permissible to look at the structure of the company to determine whether there was a power of revocation.[2] So if a settlement is expressed to endure only so long as the company exists, and the settlor has the power to cause the company to go into liquidation, he may have a power to revoke.[3]

When property is in the United Kingdom, s. 672 can operate regardless of the fact that the settlor and the trustees are non-resident.[4]

Simon's Taxes C4.338, 339.
[1] [1949] 1 All ER 865, 31 TC 158.
[2] But note Lord Simonds at 868, 169.
[3] *IRC v Payne* (1940) 23 TC 610. Cf. *Chamberlain v IRC* [1943] 2 All ER 200, 25 TC 317.
[4] *Kenmare v IRC*, supra, § **13: 11** n. 3.

Wife or husband

13: 13   As a result of *IRC v Tennant*[1] s. 672 will apply where the person becoming entitled on revocation is the *then* wife or husband of the settlor, i.e. any possible future husband or wife is included. This must in the case of a male settlor, include practically any female in the world.[2] In practice therefore the Revenue give a more restricted definition to wife or husband.[3] Where the settlor is unmarried *IRC v Tennant* applies only where (*a*) the settlor is unmarried and the terms of the settlement are such that a benefit may be conferred on practically any person who may become the spouse of the settlor in the future; or (*b*) where the terms indicate a specific intention to benefit a future spouse.

An ex-wife or husband is not a wife or husband,[4] nor is a widow or widower.

Simon's Taxes C4.333.
[1] (1942) 24 TC 215.
[2] The only limitation would appear to be the law of consanguinity and affinity.
[3] Statement of Practice A30, **Simon's Taxes Division H3.4.**
[4] *Lord Vestey's Executors v IRC* [1949] 1 All ER 1108, 31 TC 1.

The charge

13: 14 Where a charge is made on the settlor under s. 672 it is made under Schedule D, Case VI[1] and is deemed to be the top slice of his income.[2] Since the settlor will not himself have derived any benefit from the income deemed to be his, he is given a right to recover the amount paid by way of tax from the trustees.[3]

If the settlor has personal reliefs that would otherwise be unused, he may claim them but if he obtains repayment of a sum which he would have been unable to claim back had the trust income not been deemed to be his, he must hand that excess over to the trust.[4]

> **EXAMPLE**
> Suppose that S, a settlor, has personal allowances of £3,000 but that his income is only £1,000. The trustees receive income of £4,000 gross which is required to be treated as that of S.
>
> > S's total income is £1,000 + £4,000 = £5,000
> > Deduct personal allowances = £3,000
> > So tax is due @ 25% on £2,000 = £500
>
> The trustees will have received this income under deduction of tax and so will have paid tax at 25% on £4,000 = £1,000. S may reclaim the tax already paid on the income which is deemed to be his. The correct tax is £500 so he recovers £500. For this he must account to the trustees.

Simon's Taxes C4.304, 310, 322, 355.
[1] TA 1988, s. 675(1). These rules apply also to ss. 673 and 674.
[2] TA 1988, s. 675(5).
[3] TA 1988, s. 675(3).
[4] TA 1988, s. 675(4).

Discretionary power for possible benefit of settlor: TA 1988, s. 674

13: 15   There are a number of situations in which the settlor has not effectively alienated the settled property from himself. These are when the settlor's wife is an object of a discretionary trust or is an alternative beneficiary under a deed of covenant or the funds can be used for the indirect benefit of the settlor as by reducing his overdraft.[1] Since 1958 there has been a charge on the settlor.

   This charge applies if and so long as the terms of any settlement (whenever made) are such that any person has, or may have, the power, whether immediately or in the future, and whether with or without the consent of any person to pay the whole or part of the income to the settlor or the wife or husband of the settlor or to secure the payment for the benefit of that person, wife or husband of the income or the property. If only a part of the income or property can be paid or applied under the power only a part of the income is attributed to the settlor.

   By s. 674 a discretionary trust or any other settlement containing a power to benefit the settlor or his spouse is assimilated to a revocable settlement caught by s. 672.[2] As under that section there is an exclusion if the discretionary power cannot arise for six years until such time as the power actually arises. However there is an analogy with s. 673 in that interests excepted from s. 673 are also excepted from s. 674.[3]

Simon's Taxes C4.354; Butterworths Income Tax Service J1.16.
   [1] This list is taken from Butterworth's Annotated Statutes. Many of these situations would fall within the wide definition of interest to be found in s. 673 but, while s. 673 treats accumulated income as that of the settlor, s. 664 so treats income arising.
   [2] Supra, § **13: 11**
   [3] Infra, § **13: 22**.

Other provisions, including especially TA 1988, s. 674A

13: 16   If the settlor has not divested himself absolutely there may be excess liability under TA 1988, s. 683. If the settlement is incapable of lasting more than six years, liability may arise under s. 660.

   TA 1988, s. 674A is designed to counter a number of devices which owed their existence to the scrapping of the system of annuities and other annual payments in 1988. S. 683 (infra, § **13: 29**) had rendered such schemes ineffective for higher rates of tax since 1965 but this left basic rate liability to be determined by reference to the circumstance of the beneficiary. If the beneficiary were a person with a zero marginal rate of tax, e.g. due to unused personal allowances, income tax at basic rate could be reclaimed by the beneficiary. This was the basis of the extensive use of covenants for students at universities and polytechnics. Following the removal of the effectiveness of new covenants by FA 1988, those taxpayers who could afford to do so resorted to short term settlements of capital. These were not affected by the 1988 changes and were effective for basic and zero rates of tax because they were not touched by s. 663. For settlements made on or after 14th March

1989 the schemes fail at once; for earlier settlements the new rules are to apply as from the start of 1990–91.[1]

Under the new rule (TA 1988, s. 674A) all income arising under a settlement is to be treated as that of the settlor for all purposes unless it comes within one or more of a favoured group. The group consists of those settlements that are excluded from TA 1988, s. 683 (infra, **13: 29**) and therefore comprises:

(*a*) annual payments made under a partnership agreement to a former partner or the widow or dependant of a partner;[2]

(*b*) similar payments due under the terms on which a business was acquired;[3]

(*c*) payments under a divorce (or nullity) settlement to a former spouse or under a separation agreement to a spouse;

(*d*) income from property of which the settlor has divested himself absolutely;

(*e*) covenanted payments to charity as defined in s. 660(3);

(*f*) as from 1990–91 income from an outright gift by one spouse to another.[4] The effect will be to prevent taxpayers from transferring assets to their spouses while retaining control of the capital but allowing their partner to benefit from the income. It is also to make clear that income arising from an outright gift will be treated as income of the donee.

The provisions ancillary to s. 683 dealing with such matters as when a person is to be taken to have divested himself absolutely of any property apply here also.[5]

Two mysteries are raised by this provision. The first is the appropriate definition of the term "settlement." By appearing in the middle of Part XV Chapter III it must be taken to be found in s. 681, a provision used also by s. 683.[6] This definition includes the word disposition but not the term "transfer of assets", which is found in s. 670 (children's settlements). However too much excitement should not be derived from this since a straightforward definition of the word disposition will suffice to catch many schemes. Problems might arise if the courts were to define disposition in such a way as to exclude a transfer of assets.[7] Meanwhile we are left with the rule that if there is a disposition and income arises under that disposition, that income will be treated as that of the settlor unless it comes within one of the favoured categories or the disposition is not a settlement.

The second is to wonder why it is that so all-embracing a provision is not accompanied by the repeal of many of its neighbours.

---

[1] TA 1988, s. 674A(5).

[2] TA 1988, s. 683(1)(*a*)—amplified by sub-ss. (8)–(10).

[3] TA 1988, s. 683(6) and (7).

[4] TA 1988, s. 685(4A) referred to in TA 1988, s. 674A(3). See Hansard, 13th June 1989, Standing Committee G cols. 398 et seq.

[5] TA 1988, s. 674A(3) added by FA 1989, s. 110, all other inter-spousal transfers will be caught.

[6] TA 1988, s. 685(4).

[7] See the discussion of the phrase "transfer of assets" by Lord Greene MR in *Hood Barrs v IRC* (1946) 27 TC 385 at 400–401 and by Lord Morton in *Thomas v Marshall* (1953) 34 TC 178 at 200 et seq.

CHARGE ON UNDISTRIBUTED INCOME

Undistributed income

13: 17   Undistributed income means total income less (*a*) payments made to persons by way of income and (*b*) any expenses properly chargeable to income[1]

(*a*) is modified by the exclusion of interest payments and of capital sums treated as the settlor's income by s. 677 and by the inclusion of sums paid over to a company connected with the settlement or another settlement made by the same settlor.

Interest is excluded from (*a*) because it is the subject of a special rule as a result of the restriction on the right to deduct interest imposed in 1972; interest paid to the settlor or his spouse is ignored as this will be taxed anyway. Other interest will normally be a trust expense and so within (*b*) above. However, a proportion of that interest is disallowed.[2] It is easier to say that a proportion is allowed, that being B/A where A is the income arising minus the sums at (*b*) and B is the sums within (*a*) paid to someone other than the settlor or his spouse. In effect the proportion allowed is that which the income actually distributed to the beneficiaries bears to the income available for distribution.

Simon's Taxes C4.349, 350.
[1] TA 1988, s. 682(1).
[2] TA 1988, s. 682(2)–(6).

Interest retained: s. 673[1]

13: 18   If the settlor retains an interest whether in the income arising under or in the property comprised in a settlement, any income arising and which is distributed will, under general principles, be charged to the beneficiaries, including the settlor, to the extent of the income benefits they receive. The tax system regards such a settlement with indifference. However any income which is not distributed will be treated as that of the settlor.[2] The extent to which that undistributed income is treated as his depends on the extent of his interest in the income or the capital.[3] If he is entitled to one half of the income or one half of the capital one half of that undistributed income is treated as his. Were he entitled to one half of the income *and* one half of the capital it would appear that the whole income can be treated as his unless presumably his claim to the income arose by virtue of his share of the capital.

Simon's Taxes C4.351; Butterworths Income Tax Service J2.05.
[1] For an unsuccessful attempt to get rid of a retained interest, see *IRC v Cookson* [1977] STC 140, [1977] 2 All ER 331.
[2] TA 1988, s. 673.
[3] TA 1988, s. 673(1) proviso (*a*).

13: 19   The circumstances in which a settlor retains an interest are defined in typically wide words, but these are followed by certain exceptions.

The settlor retains an interest if, in any circumstances whatsoever, any income or property which may at any time arise under or be comprised in that settlement is, or will or may become, payable to or applicable for the benefit of the settlor or the wife or husband of the settlor. These words are wide extending as they do to possible and not simply to actual payments and to capital as well as to income payments. Moreover although it does not contain the word "indirectly" it does apply to payments applicable for the benefit of the settlor.[1]

Simon's Taxes C4.352; Butterworths Income Tax Service J2.05.
[1] Cf. TA 1988, s. 677, infra, § **13: 24**.

13: 20   Some possible benefits clearly fall within the ambit of s. 673. Thus the failure to transfer the settlor's entire beneficial interest with a consequent resulting trust causes s. 673 to operate.[1] The same will occur if the settlor retains a general power of appointment or a special power of which he is one of the objects. This was carried further in *Glyn v IRC*[2] where the power was to be exercised jointly by the settlor and his son. Although the Revenue admitted that the section would not have applied if the power had been vested in the son alone, the court held that the settlor was subject to s. 673. This conclusion seems surprising in view of the fact the son's concurrence was needed for the exercise of the power, but it may be regarded as realistic; after all no appointment could be made without the settlor's consent who could thereby determine whether or not the income was accumulated. It is unclear whether the fact that the settlement itself was brought about by a joint arrangement with the son forms part of the ratio; it certainly provides a means of distinction.

If the property may only come back to the settlor through the independent act of a third party,[3] as where the son exercises the power of appointment in the settlor's favour, the section does not apply. The same holds good where the son leaves the property by will. However where the settlor's position as heir gives him the right to succeed not as beneficiary under his son's will or intestacy but because the remainder is given by the settlement to those falling within the class, s. 673 applies.[4]

Simon's Taxes C4.352; Butterworths Income Tax Service J2.05.
[1] *Hannay's Executors v IRC* (1956) 37 TC 217, as nearly happened in *IRC v Bernstein* [1961] 1 All ER 320, 39 TC 391, and *Pilkington v IRC* [1962] 3 All ER 622, 40 TC 416.
[2] [1948] 2 All ER 419, 30 TC 321.
[3] Today, TA 1988, s. 674, supra, § **13: 17** would apply.
[4] *Barr's Trustees v IRC* (1943) 25 TC 72.

13: 21   Some limits have been placed on the scope of this phrase.

First it has been held that where the power of the settlor over the assets is fiduciary rather than beneficial, no interest is retained. So in *Lord Vestey's Executors v IRC*[1] a power to direct investments granted to the settlor and another and not to the trustees did not cause s. 673 to operate. Likewise the possibility that the settlor may become a trustee of another settlement to which the first settlement transfers funds should not have that effect.

Secondly the reservation of an interest to a wife or husband is to be construed strictly and a benefit to a widow or widower or presumably an ex-wife or ex-husband, does not count.[2]

Thirdly, Pennycuick J has said that although s. 673 is in very wide terms it must be confined to cases where income or property will or may become payable to or applicable for the benefit of the settlor *either* under the trusts of the settlement itself *or* under some collateral arrangement having legal force.[3] So the possibility that a beneficiary to whom funds are properly paid may then decide to make a gift to the settlor should not be taken into account.

In *IRC v Wachtel*[4] that possibility arose under the terms of the trust. The settlor transferred £1,000 to trustees. The trustees then bought shares at a cost of £7,691. The extra money needed was borrowed from a bank on the basis that the settlor guaranteed the debt. As part of the arrangement the settlor deposited an amount equal to the sums borrowed with the bank. Interest on the trust overdraft was limited to 1% and no interest was payable to the settlor on his deposit. The trustees were to use the trust income to discharge the debt and as the debt was discharged so the settlor's deposit was freed. The Court of Appeal held that there was an arrangement and so a settlement. Further that arrangement embraced not only the £1,000 but also the sum borrowed from the bank by the trustees and guaranteed by the settlor. The Revenue relied on the creation of the deposit account as part of the provision of funds but did not argue that the deposit account formed part of the settled property because no interests were charged on it or created out of it in favour of the beneficiaries. The Court then held that the arrangement fell within s. 673 so that the undistributed income was to be treated as the settlor's.[5]

Fourthly the possibility that the property will come back to the settlor's estate and not during his lifetime is too remote.[6]

Fifthly, in *Muir v IRC* Pennycuick J said that the mere fact that there was some present doubt about the validity of the trust could not cause the section to apply.[7] Eventually the doubt would be resolved one way or the other and then the issue could be determined. Unfortunately this may cause a problem for the Revenue since by the time the doubt is resolved it may be too late to make an assessment. A different problem might arise under the wait-and-see rule for perpetuities since the validity of the remainder will not be resolved until some future date. It is presumed that the statutory direction[8] that the gift is to fail only when it becomes clear that vesting cannot occur within the perpetuity period and that the gift is to be treated as valid until that time is effective for tax purposes, thus excluding s. 673.

Sixthly the possibility that the settlor may derive some incidental benefit in the course of a commercial transaction should be ignored.[9] This contains many difficulties, not the least of which is the distinction of the situation where the benefit of the interest is incidental to the commercial transaction of the loan from that where the commercial rate of interest is incidental to the benefit of obtaining a loan.

Finally one should presumably ignore the possibility of subsequent legislation or the migration of the trust to a country which would regard the trust (or part of it) as invalid.[10]

The Revenue originally took the view that a settlor retained an interest if the trustees could—or had the power to—pay the CTT (now IHT) due on the transfer. This was because the property in the settlement could be used to meet a liability that was his—even though jointly. This view has now been abandoned.[11]

Simon's Taxes C4.352.
[1] [1949] 1 All ER 1108, 31 TC 1.
[2] Ibid.
[3] In *Muir v IRC* [1966] 1 All ER 295 at 305, 43 TC 367 at 381.
[4] [1971] 1 All ER 271 at 280, 46 TC 543 at 556.
[5] In *Jenkins v IRC* [1944] 2 All ER 491, 26 TC 265, the discharge by the trustees of an interest free loan made by the settlor was held to fall within s. 673 because the power to discharge the loan was contained in the settlement.
[6] *IRC v Gaunt* [1941] 2 All ER 82, 24 TC 69. It is unclear whether now his wife must also predecease the return of the asset to his estate—*semble* not since she will benefit, if at all, only through his generosity in leaving her an interest in his estate.
[7] See supra, n. 3.
[8] Perpetuities and Accumulations Act 1964, s. 3(1). Halsbury's Statutes (4th edn) PERPETUITIES.
[9] See *Wachtel v IRC*; and note Lord Morton in *Lord Vestey's Executors v IRC* (1949) 31 TC 1 at 114, who said that while a loan at a commercial rate of interest might benefit a person by tiding him over a difficult period, it was not money lent "for the benefit of" the debtor within s. 447.
[10] *Quaere* if the trust contained an express power to migrate to a country with such a rule.
[11] SP 1/82 (for years 1981–82 and following); **Simon's Taxes, Division H3.2.**

Permitted interests

13: 22   Certain types of interest may however be retained by the settlor without causing a charge under TA 1988, s. 673 and these are specified in s. 673(3). No charge arises if the capital or income can only become payable or applicable in the event of

(*a*)   (*i*) the bankruptcy of some beneficiary; or

   (*ii*) any assignment of or charge on that income or property by a beneficiary; or

   (*iii*) in the case of a marriage settlement, the death of both the parties to the marriage and of all or any of the children of the marriage; or

   (*iv*) the death under the age of 25 or some lower age of some person who would be beneficially entitled to that income or property on attaining that age.

(*b*)   No charge arises "if and so long as some person is alive and under the age of 25 during whose life that income or property cannot become payable or applicable as aforesaid except in the event of that person becoming bankrupt or assigning or charging his interest in that income or property."

The difference between (*a*) and (*b*) is important because s. 683 has exceptions for (*a*) but no mention of (*b*).

The difference between the two provisions is that the four events listed in (*a*) are alternatives but those in (*b*) are not. Thus a settlement on trust to accumulate the income until X reaches the age of 25 and then for X for life determinable on X's bankruptcy and then to revert to the settlor, will not satisfy (*a*) but will satisfy (*b*). Had the accumulations been directed to end at 28, not 25, the accumulated income would have been treated as that of the settlor only in the years after X reached 25.

The charge

13: 23   Undistributed income is treated as that of the settlor in the same way as income arising under TA 1988, s. 672.[1] However the charge under s. 671 or s. 672 excludes that under s. 673.[2]

Simon's Taxes C4.310, 353, 355.
[1] Supra, § **13: 14**.
[2] TA 1988, s. 673(1)(*b*). Curiously there is no mention of s. 663.

Sums paid to the settlor otherwise than as income: TA 1988, s. 677

13: 24   If income has been accumulated and a capital sum is paid by the trustees directly or indirectly to the settlor, that sum is under TA 1988, s. 677 treated as the income of the settlor if it was not paid for full consideration in money or money's worth.[1] This applies whenever there is "available income"[2] in the trust, i.e. both when accumulated income exists in the fund when the sum is paid and, subject to limits, when the accumulation arises subsequently.

In one instance however sums paid for full consideration cause a charge. If the trustees lend money to the settlor or his spouse there would be a promise to repay and so full consideration and yet also the risk that the repayment terms might not be enforced at least so long as the settlor was alive. In this way a settlor could create a fund which would be taxed only at basic and additional rates and yet enjoy what was once his money at the same time. The section therefore defines capital sum as any sum paid by way of a loan and goes on to extend this to any sum paid (by the trustees to the settlor or the settlor's wife) by way of repayment of a loan.[3]

A capital sum does not cause s. 677 to apply if it could not have become payable to the settlor except in one of the events specified in the proviso to s. 673(3).[4]

As drafted the section did not catch payments to third parties to whom the settlor owed money.[5] This and other loopholes are now sealed, the term capital sum extending to (*a*) any sum paid to the settlor (or the spouse of the settlor) jointly with another person; (*b*) any sum paid to a third party at the settlor's direction; (*c*) any sum paid to a third party by virtue of the assignment by him of his right to receive it and (*d*) any sum otherwise paid or applied by the trustees for the benefit of the settlor.[6] The section applies to capital payments made directly or indirectly to the settlor.[7]

Simon's Taxes C4.358; Butterworths Income Tax Service J1.15.
[1] TA 1988, s. 677(9)(ii).
[2] Defined in TA 1988, s. 677(2).
[3] TA 1988, s. 677(9)(ii).
[4] Supra, § **13: 22**.
[5] *IRC v Potts* [1951] 1 All ER 76, 32 TC 211.
[6] TA 1988, s. 677(10).
[7] TA 1988, s. 677(1)—*quaere* whether these words add anything; *IRC v Wachtel* [1971] 1 All ER 271, 46 TC 543.

Loans and repayments

13: 25   The concept of "loan" is central to TA 1988, s. 677 yet the term is not further defined. Case law shows that it is not confined to the common law relationship of debtor and creditor and applies equally where there is an equitable right to reimbursement.[1] A loan need not be in cash and a secured loan is still a loan. A loan is a loan even though the person giving it may view the transaction as an investment.[2]

Under rules introduced in 1981 once the loan is repaid it ceases to be subject to s. 677 for years subsequent to that in which the repayment takes place.[3] So if a loan was made in 1985–86, is repaid in 1988–89 and income is accumulated for the first time in 1988–89, s. 677 will have no effect. Furthermore, if the settlor receives a loan of say £5,000 which he then repays only to take a further loan of £5,000 he will be liable to a charge only on £5,000.

Section 677 applies also where a loan by the settlor to the trustees is repaid.[4] Analogous mitigating rules apply. So where the loan has been repaid but the settlor then makes a further loan of an amount not less than the original loan, s. 677 does not apply.[5] This provision is curious in that it applies only where the original loan has been completely repaid; there is no proportionate relief for a partial repayment. However while the rule requires complete repayment this does not necessarily mean repayment in full; an agreement by a settlor to accept a lesser sum in complete discharge of the original loan will presumably suffice.

Simon's Taxes C4.358, 361; Butterworths Income Tax Service J1.15.
[1] *De Vigier v IRC* infra, § **13: 30**.
[2] *McCrone v IRC* (1967) 44 TC 142.
[3] TA 1988, s. 677(4).
[4] See *Piratin v IRC* [1981] STC 441.
[5] TA 1988, s. 677(5).

The charge

13: 26   Since a capital sum is here in issue, and since the whole purpose of the legislation is to prevent a settlor from deriving benefit for himself from property the income of which may be taxed at a lower rate than if it were still his, TA 1988, s. 677 only applies to the extent that the payment could have been made from income, that is to the extent that the income arising under the trust since it was created[1] is greater than the sums distributed or which although not distributed, have already been treated as his together with the tax on these payments.[2] Perhaps because the payment is made to the settlor himself he is given no statutory right to be reimbursed out of the trust funds, in respect of the tax; for the same reason, any repayment of tax by reason of the settlor's personal relief may be retained by him.[3] These acts of apparent generosity are however more than offset by the fact that there is no way of refunding the tax when the settlor, or his estate, repay the loan.[4]

Simon's Taxes C4.360; Butterworths Income Tax Service J1.15.
[1] Or since the year 1937–38 if shorter.

[2] TA 1988, s. 677(1) and (2).
[3] TA 1988, s. 677(8). Cf. supra, § **13: 24**.
[4] Cf. TA 1988, s. 419(4); infra, § **27: 10**.

13: 27   The section applies with equal vigour to a capital sum received by the settlor from a body corporate connected with the settlement, e.g. a loan from the company.[1] A body corporate is connected with a settlement if it is at any time in the year either (i) a close company (or only not a close company because it is not resident in the UK) and the participators then include the trustees of the settlement, or (ii) controlled by such a company.[2]

Partly because of the habit of using accumulation trusts to receive dividend income from private companies which income was not needed by the family owners, TA 1988, s. 677 was a lethal trap whenever the settlor would think of making a loan to the company, or vice versa. In order therefore to limit the operation of s. 677 to those situations in which it could fairly be said that the settlor was deriving some benefit from the accumulation, s. 678 provides that s. 677 shall apply only where there has been an "associated payment", that is a payment by the trustees to the company in a period of five years ending or beginning with the date on which the payment is made to the settlor. Further, s. 677 is not to apply if the loan is repaid within twelve months and the period for which loans are outstanding in any five year period does not exceed twelve months.

Simon's Taxes C4.359; Butterworths Income Tax Service J1.15.
[1] TA 1988, s. 678. For reason, see Lord Reid, infra, § **13: 29** n.1.
[2] TA 1988, s. 681(5). This means that whenever a trust has shares in a family company the settlor must beware, s. 677 and s. 419 infra, § **27: 10**, whenever he takes or makes a loan.

13: 28   The sum which is charged on the settlor—under Schedule D, Case VI—is the undistributed income grossed up at the basic rate plus the additional rate.[1] Credit is given for such tax as has been charged on the trust.[2] Trustees who have made payments to the settlor which fall within TA 1988, s. 677 must therefore be anxious to distribute all the trust income each year until the settlor dies or the 11 year period, see § **13: 29**, expires.

If the settlor emigrates it would appear that, the source being within the UK, the charge to tax remains although if he has little other UK income his tax bill may be reduced.

A further problem is that the sum is treated as the income of the settlor in the year of payment notwithstanding that it may have been accumulated over many years. It is small wonder that most trusts now contain a clause making it a breach of trust to pay any capital sum to the settlor or his spouse; this is simply a reminder to trustees since if payments are made they will fall within s. 677 even though in breach of trust.

Simon's Taxes C4.359.
[1] TA 1988, s. 677(6) and (7).
[2] TA 1988, s. 677(7).

13: 29   Should the capital sum paid exceed the undistributed income, the excess is carried forward and charged to the settlor in the next year to the extent that there is undistributed income available up to the end of that year, and so on for succeeding years subject to a maximum of 11 years. There is no 11 year maximum to the carry-back rule where the income has been accumulated before the capital sum is paid. An allowance is made for sums already charged under TA 1988, s. 677.[1]

Simon's Taxes C4.360; Butterworths Income Tax Service J1.15.
[1] On previous law see Lord Reid in *Bates v IRC* [1967] 1 All ER 84 at 90, 44 TC 225 at 261.

13: 30   The capricious nature of the section has caused much adverse comment as when an innocent transaction is caught by the section. In *De Vigier v IRC*[1] trustees held property for two infant children contingently upon their attaining the age of 25 years, with a power to accumulate and maintain. The trustees had wished to take advantage of a rights issue by a company whose shares they held but they had no money and no power to borrow. The trustees were the settlor's wife and a solicitor. The settlor's wife therefore paid £7,000 into the trust bank account to pay for the shares and within nine months that sum had been repaid in two equal instalments. The settlor was held taxable on the grossed up equivalent of £7,000, £12,174 at that time. It was a sum paid by way of repayment of a loan. The fact that her right to the repayment arose from the equitable right of an indemnity given to a trustee who incurs expenses on behalf of the trust rather than the common law claim on a contract of loan made no difference. Yet had the trust had the power to borrow and had she merely guaranteed that loan, no charge would have arisen.[2]

In the Court of Appeal Russell LJ, suggested that had she been a sole trustee there could have been no loan. However in the House of Lords Lord Upjohn said "the mere fact that under the old forms of pleading, in the circumstances of this case, an action of debt for return of a loan would not lie does not prevent the transaction being properly described as a loan".[3] The point was that an advance of money was made to the trust upon the terms that it was to be repaid out of the trust fund. That was a loan.

Simon's Taxes C4.361.
[1] [1964] 2 All ER 907, 42 TC 24.
[2] Per Russell LJ, 42 TC 24 at 33, CA.
[3] [1964] 2 All ER 907 at 915, 24 TC 24 at 41.

CHARGE TO EXCESS LIABILITY ON INCOME ARISING

TA 1988, s. 683

13: 31   Where, during the life of the settlor, income arises from property of which the settlor has not divested himself absolutely it is to be treated as the income of the settlor for the purposes of computing any excess liability.[1] This is not to apply to a matrimonial settlement[2] nor if the income is treated as that of the settlor under some other provision.[3]

The circumstances in which the settlor is deemed not to have divested himself of the property are very widely defined.[4] He is so treated if that property or any income therefrom or any property directly or indirectly representing proceeds of or income from that property or any income therefrom is, or will, or may become payable to or applicable for the benefit of the settlor or the wife or husband of the settlor in any circumstances whatsoever. This is subject to four exceptions considered above.[5] Wife or husband presumably does not extend to widow or widower.[6] A resulting trust for the settlor means that he has not completely divested himself of the property.[7]

Simon's Taxes C4.367; Butterworths Income Tax Service J1.16.

[1] On pre 1965 settlements see s. 684 and Simon's Taxes C4.366.
[2] TA 1988, s. 683(1)(c), infra, § **13: 46**.
[3] TA 1988, s. 683(1)(e).
[4] TA 1988, s. 685.
[5] Under s. 673, supra, § **13: 22**.
[6] *Lord Vestey's Executors v IRC* [1949] 1 All ER 1108, 31 TC 1.
[7] *Vandervell v IRC* [1967] 1 All ER 1, 43 TC 519. A resulting trust for the settlor may be negatived by the rule in *Lassence v Tierney* (1849) 1 Mac & G 551, as in *Watson v Holland* [1984] STC 372.

PARENTAL SETTLEMENTS ON INFANT CHILDREN

13: 32   Originally the UK income tax system did not aggregate the income of a child with that of his parent. Since 1936 an exception has been made to prevent income splitting when the income is derived from the parent. Such income is attributed to the parent but only so long as the child is unmarried and under the age of majority, now eighteen, so that dispositions in favour of adult children escape this rule.[1]

The general rule contained in TA 1988, s. 663 is that any income paid by the trustees during the life of the settlor to or for the benefit of such a child of the settlor by virtue or in consequence of any settlement to which the section applies, is treated as that of the settlor.

There is a de minimis exception of £5 from all sources within this chapter of the Taxes Act[2]; this figure has remained unchanged since it was introduced in 1936.[3]

"Child" is defined as "including a stepchild, an adopted child and an illegitimate child".[4] Whether this includes a foster child remains to be seen although this seems unlikely since the three examples in the definition are precise legal relationships. If payments are made to or for a natural child who has since the date of the settlement been adopted by someone else, the correct construction of s. 663 would suggest that the beneficiary must be a child of the settlor in the year of assessment and it is not sufficient that he was a child of the settlor at the date of the settlement so that the section would not apply.

---

[1] TA 1988, s. 663(1). For pre-1936 settlements, see TA 1988, Sch. 30, para. 10 and **Simon's Taxes** C4.317; for differences from certain other parts of this chapter of the legislation see § **13: 09** n. 3 and § **13: 10** n. 5.
[2] TA 1988, s. 663(4).
[3] FA 1936, s. 21(4).

[4] TA 1988, s. 670.

Settlement

13: 33   The law is anxious to prevent any income from being treated as that of a child if it originates from the parent. The definition of settlement is therefore widened to include a transfer of assets.[1] So a settlement has included not only a formal accumulation trust but also an outright gift of money by a father where money was paid into a savings bank account.[2] It is important to remember that it was not the sum given by the father that was treated as his income but only the income derived from the gift.

It follows from this that a court order directing a father to make payments to his child or to a person on trust for his child would be a settlement so that the income would be treated as the father's and not the child's as long as the father was alive.[3] This position was accepted by the Revenue although a sharp distinction was drawn between an order and any agreement. The importance of this practice will decline under the new regime for maintenance payments.[4] Payments to a mother for the children will not of themselves create any rights in the children and the income for tax purposes is that of the mother[4] and so not a settlement on the children. In Scotland payment to a wife as tutrix for the child makes the income that of the child rather than of the wife.[5]

The settlor is given an indemnity against the trustees.[6] If he has surplus allowances resulting in a repayment of tax in respect of settlement income, he must account to the trustees for it.[7]

Simon's Taxes C4.319; Butterworths Income Tax Service J1.13.
[1] TA 1988, s. 670.
[2] *Thomas v Marshall* [1953] 1 All ER 1102, 34 TC 178.
[3] Supra, § 9: 89 et seq.
[4] *Yates v Starkey* [1951] 1 All ER 732, 32 TC 38; *Stevens v Tirard* [1939] 4 All ER 186, 23 TC 321.
[5] *Finnie v Finnie* [1984] STC 598.
[6] TA 1988, s. 667—*quaere* whether he made a transfer of value for CTT or IHT if he fails to exercise it (semble yes).
[7] TA 1988, s. 669—supra, § 13: 14.

Accumulation settlements

13: 34   Any income under a settlement which will, or may, become payable or applicable to or for the benefit of a child of the settlor, is deemed to be paid to or for the benefit of the child.[1] If the income is not required by the settlement to be allocated to any particular child or children, it is treated as accruing to them equally. While these words are clearly sufficient to deem income of an accumulation settlement for the settlor's children to be that of the settlor, TA 1988, s. 664(2) provides this shall *not* apply to income from an *irrevocable* settlement of *capital*.

If sums are actually paid to or for a child from an accumulation settlement, whether irrevocable or not, they are presumed to be payments of income to the child (and so are treated as income of the settlor if the child at the date of the payment is unmarried and under eighteen).[2] This presumption will however be displaced if the total sums actually paid out exceed the trust income which could have been paid out to the children of the settlor.[3]

The charge on income actually paid to or for the benefit of a child of the settlor applies also where the income is so dealt with that it or assets representing it will or may become payable or applicable to or for the benefit of the child in the future. However *income* arising under discretionary trusts may be allocated to a child upon contingent trusts with a power of accumulation without such income being treated as the settlor's, so long as it is accumulated. Any income arising from such accumulated income will be treated as that of the child thanks to s. 664(1)(*a*) and not that of the settlor under s. 663(1).

When the class of beneficiaries contains both children and strangers the same principles are applied, a task which is easier if the shares of the children are precisely defined. If however there is a discretion to allocate income among children and strangers it seems that any income which is accumulated under a revocable settlement is treated as payable to the children.

When income is received by trustees in year 1 and paid out to an infant beneficiary in year 2, s. 664 will treat the income as that of the settlor in year 1. It is understood that the Revenue will treat the payment in year 2 as falling within s. 687 for year 2.

Simon's Taxes C4.320; Butterworths Income Tax Service J1.13.
  [1] TA 1988, s. 664(1).
  [2] TA 1988, s. 664(2)(*b*).
  [3] TA 1988, s. 664(3).

Revocability

13: 35   The question of revocability is determined first according to general principles but any settlement which is so irrevocable must then satisfy the tests in TA 1988, s. 665 which lays down three exceptions and then some exceptions to those exceptions.

13: 36   (i) *General principle.* The term "revocable" has a technical conveyancing meaning[1] as a power to terminate the trusts; this meaning is applied here. There is a distinction between revoking the trust and destroying it. So where a settlor had settled shares in a company which he controlled it was held that the power which he had of putting the companies into liquidation while it might destroy the trust fund would not revoke the trust.[2] On the other hand if the settlement can be revoked it is quite immaterial whether the power is in the hands of the settlor or some complete stranger.[3] A power to diminish a settlement in part, it has been held, is not a power to revoke it[4] and while this decision has been statutorily reversed in TA 1978, s. 672, that reversal has not been extended to s. 665.

Simon's Taxes C4.321; Butterworths Income Tax Service J1.13.
  [1] Greene MR in *Jenkins v IRC* [1944] 2 All ER 491, 26 TC 265. Note also that while s. 672, supra, talks of "revoking or otherwise determining, the settlement", s. 665 talks simply of "a revocable settlement". However such a settlement may fall within s. 672 so that the income arising may be deemed to be the settlor's under that provision.
  [2] *IRC v Wolfson*, supra, § **13: 12**.
  [3] *IRC v Warden* (1939) 22 TC 416.
  [4] *IRC v Saunders* [1957] 3 All ER 43, 37 TC 416.

13: 37   (ii)   *Three extensions of TA 1988, s. 663.* Despite being "irrevocable" in the sense just described, an accumulation settlement on children of the settlor will not be treated as irrevocable if:

(*a*) in any circumstances whatsoever the terms of the settlement provide that any income or assets should be payable to or for the benefit of the settlor or his wife (or husband).[1] This however is not to apply to a period only after the death of the child;[2]

(*b*) if the settlement contains terms which provide for the determination of the settlement by the act or on the default of any person.[3] Thus if the settlement is to end if some third person ceases to be a UK resident, that person could not strictly be said to have a power to revoke the settlement, but the same effect is achieved by this express direction. However an exception is made if on the determination of the settlement no benefit arises to the settlor or his wife (or husband) during the lifetime of any child of the settlor;[4]

(*c*) if its terms provide for the payment of any penalty by the settlor in the event of his failing to comply with the provisions of the settlement.[5] This phrase is found in other sections of this part of the Act[6] but is usually concerned with covenants of income. Since income under such a covenant must be treated as that of the settlor whether or not it is accumulated, its presence in TA 1988, s. 665 presents something of a mystery.

Simon's Taxes C4.321; Butterworths Income Tax Service J1.13.
  [1] TA 1988, s. 665(1)(*a*), as where there is a power of appointment in favour of a group including the settlor or his spouse. Such a clause causes complete attribution of the trust income to the settlor.
  [2] TA 1988, s. 665(1)(*a*).
  [3] TA 1988, s. 665(1)(*b*).
  [4] TA 1988, s. 665(2)(*b*).
  [5] TA 1988, s. 665(1)(*c*).
  [6] TA 1988, s. 671(1)(*b*).

13: 38   (iii)   *Exceptions to the extensions*[1]

(1) If any income or assets which may become payable to or for the settlor or his wife (or husband) only becomes so payable or available (*i*) on the bankruptcy of the child or (*ii*) because of a charge or assignment of those assets by the child.[2] Thus trusts motivated by prudent parental concern do not have to provide for the gift over to someone other than the settlor.

(2) If the trust falls within Trustee Act 1925, s. 33[3] such a trust would fall within (1) but it is dealt with separately because the legislature wished to restrict the availability of this exception by directing that income *is* attributable to the parent if either the trust period is less than the life of the child or the trust specifies some event in addition to those in s. 33 which will bring the protective trusts into operation.

Simon's Taxes C4.321; Butterworths Income Tax Service J1.13.
  [1] The third exception applies to one only of the three exceptions and has been mentioned above in § **13: 37**.
  [2] TA 1988, s. 665(2)(*a*).
  [3] TA 1988, s. 665(2)(*c*).

SETTLEMENTS OF INCOME: COVENANTS

13: 39   Under the 1988 regime many new covenants will be ineffective for tax purposes. However the following principles remain relevant for existing covenants and for covenants outside the new regime. The wide definition of settlement is quite sufficient to catch a covenant to make annual payments or annuities. Where a covenant breaks one of the rules to be described the income payable will be treated as that of the settlor and not of the payee. However TA 1988, ss. 348 and 349 apply as the income goes across to the covenantee before coming back to the settlor.[1]

---

[1] Supra, § **13: 01**.

TA 1988, s. 660

13: 40   The basic rule is that any income payable under a "disposition" to or for the benefit of another person is treated as the income of the payer and not the payee if the sums are payable for a period which cannot exceed six years. A disposition is defined as including any trust, covenant, agreement or arrangement. A trust under which the settlor settles capital on persons by way of absolute gift is obviously capable of exceeding six years. The section is thus concerned primarily with income assignments but a settlement of capital expressly limited to last five years would also be caught. There is a further distinction although it is unclear whether this is anything but a formal point. The general rule in s. 660 speaks of a period which cannot exceed six years; the special rule excludes covenants for charities for a period which may exceed three years and is not capable of earlier termination under any power exercisable without the consent of the payees.

The income attribution rule does not apply if the settlor has died, nor does it apply if the disposition was made for valuable and sufficient consideration,[1] and so is primarily concerned with the voluntary assignments of income during the life of the settlor. In *IRC v Plummer* the consideration was sufficient only if one took account of the tax saving; this the House of Lords allowed.[2]

If the covenant is capable of exceeding six years it is irrelevant that it may end before then. Thus a covenant to pay for the life of some person escapes this rule. Likewise the fact that the two parties could by agreement terminate the covenant is not sufficient to bring it within s. 660. If the covenant were expressed to last eight years but to be terminable by the settlor at any time, still the covenant would escape s. 660 although it would fall within s. 671 and so would give the settlor no tax advantage.

The period of six years, which means calendar years and not years of assessment, is that during which the income is payable and not the period during which the deed is effective.

These points are illustrated by *IRC v St. Luke's Hostel Trustees.*[3] On 3rd February 1927 X covenanted that he would during the term of seven years from 6th April 1926 or during his lifetime, whichever was the shorter, pay to the funds of the hostel each year the sum of £8 after deduction of tax, the first annual payment to be made on 31st December 1926 and subsequent annual payments to be made on 31st December each year. The last payment would fall due on 31st December 1932 which was less than six years after the date of the deed. The court has to assume that the payer will perform his obligations on the due date and so could not rely on the possibility that the final payment might be delayed.[4] The period could not begin before there was an obligation and so the six years began to run on 3rd February 1927.

Although s. 660 talks only of a period that cannot exceed six years it is customary to talk of seven year covenants. This is because the payments must be made each year and the period must be capable of exceeding six years, not of being six years precisely. There must therefore be at least seven payments.[5]

Simon's Taxes C4.307, 308; Butterworths Income Tax Service J2.02.

[1] TA 1988, s. 660. *Quaere* whether a deed replacing a voluntary deed is made for valuable consideration, a question left open in *IRC v Mallaby-Deeley* [1938] 3 All ER 463, 28 TC 153. On the effect of subsequent deeds see *Taylor v IRC* [1945] 1 All ER 488n, 26 TC 93.

[2] [1979] STC 793, [1979] 3 All ER 775; consideration excludes s. 660 whether or not there is bounty.

[3] (1930) 15 TC 682.

[4] (1930) 15 TC 682. Per Lord Hanworth, at 689.

[5] On the construction of "during a period of seven years", see *IRC v Verdon-Roe* (1962) 40 TC 541.

13: 41   If the payments are to fluctuate they are still annual payments within Schedule D, Case III but in applying TA 1988, s. 660 the courts have insisted that there must be some constant element. So if a person covenants to pay £50 a year for the first three years and £110 a year for the next four the payments in excess of £50 will be treated as his by s. 660.[1] However the employment of a constant formula seems to satisfy the requirement of a constant element,[2] so that the promise to pay £50 a month after deduction of tax at the basic rate then in force will escape s. 660 even though the basic rate may well change.

Although usually the settlor will have a marginal rate higher than that of the payee, it may happen that the reverse is the case and in that event s. 660, which directs the income to be treated as that of the settlor, may actually reduce the amount of tax otherwise payable. However there are limits. In *Becker v Wright*[3] the payee was resident in the UK but her father-in-law, the payer, was resident in Trinidad. The covenant was to last only three years and the payee's husband was assessed to tax under Schedule D, Case V. He argued that the effect of s. 660 was to deem the income to be the payer's "for all the purposes of the Income Tax Acts", and so not his. Stamp J however accepted the Crown's argument that this effect of s. 660 would deem there to be income of a non-resident arising outside the UK which was contrary to the general principles of the tax system. Such a person cannot have such income "for the purposes of the Income Tax Acts". No assessment could be made on the payer under Schedule D, Case V nor did s. 660 as such create any power to assess.

Simon's Taxes C4.309; Butterworths Income Tax Service J2.02.

[1] *D'Ambrumenil v IRC* [1940] 2 All ER 71, 23 TC 440, *IRC v Prince-Smith* [1943] 1 All ER 434, 25 TC 84.

[2] *D'Ambrumenil v IRC*, supra, *IRC v Black* [1940] 4 All ER 445, 23 TC 715.

[3] [1966] 1 All ER 565, 42 TC 591.

Other provisions

13: 42   TA 1988, s. 660 is backed up by various provisions designed to prevent abuse of covenants which can exceed six years.

First, TA 1988, s. 663[1] is wide enough to catch covenants in favour of the covenantor's children; income consisting of annual payments by the settlor is deemed to be his even if accumulated for the children under irrevocable trusts.[2]

Simon's Taxes C4.319; Butterworths Income Tax Service J2.03.
[1] Supra, § **13: 32**.
[2] TA 1988, s. 664(2)(*a*).

13: 43   *Secondly*, TA 1988, s. 671 deems the annual payments to be the income of the settlor if the obligation, although capable of exceeding six years may be "revoked or otherwise determined" and on that revocation the liability of the settlor ceases. It is irrelevant whether it is the settlor or some third person who has the power, whether the power requires the consent of some third person, and whether it is exercisable immediately or in the future. The power must arise under the terms of the settlement so that the power of the parties to terminate the covenant by mutual agreement will not cause s. 671 to apply. Revocation bears its ordinary meaning but is widened to include any power to diminish the income.[1]

If the settlement prescribes that the liability to make the payments shall end when the settlor does a certain thing it would appear that since he has a power to do the thing stated he has a power to revoke or otherwise determine the liability. However it has been doubted whether a liability until the settlor marries would be revocable.

The exercise of the power must result in the termination of the liability. In *IRC v Rainsford-Hannay*[2] the payer had assumed a liability to make payments to a controlled company. It was held that while the settlor could, by her control of the company, terminate the settlement if she were to liquidate the company, nonetheless the liability would not end and therefore s. 671 did not apply. This may be contrasted with *IRC v Payne*[3] when the liability was during the settlor's lifetime or until the company went into liquidation and s. 671 applied.

An exception is made if the power to revoke or otherwise determine the settlement cannot be exercised within six years of the first of the annual payments becoming payable.[4]

Although the effect of s. 660 is to undo those covenants which cannot exceed six years it is no objection to a covenant that it could be terminated by the mutual agreement of payer and payee. The same is true of s. 671. If however, the settlement itself provides that the payer's liability shall cease, on the payment of a penalty, s. 671(1)(*b*) directs that the payments shall be treated as those of the settlor. This consequence follows even if the right to terminate on penalty cannot arise for at least six years.

Tax is charged on the settlor under Schedule D, Case VI who can recover the tax from the trustee or other person to whom the income arises in the usual way.[5]

Simon's Taxes C4.339–341; Butterworths Income Tax Service J2.04.
[1] TA 1988, s. 671(3). TA 1988, s. 665 (supra, § **13: 35**) does not apply.
[2] (1941) 24 TC 273.
[3] (1940) 23 TC 610.
[4] TA 1988, s. 671(2) proviso.
[5] TA 1988, s. 675; supra, § **13: 14**.

13: 44   *Thirdly,* TA 1988, s. 673 applies so that any undistributed income of the settlement will be treated as that of the settlor if he retains an interest in it. This provision is needed to stop the obvious device of a person covenanting to make annual payments to trustees giving them a power to accumulate the income and designating the settlor as beneficiary. To allow him to set up his own investment pool free of higher rate tax liability would be most inequitable. Again the charge is under Schedule D, Case VI and there is an indemnity for the settlor.[1]

Simon's Taxes C4.351; Butterworths Income Tax Service J2.05.
[1] TA 1988, s. 675.

13: 45   *Fourthly,* TA 1988, s. 676 is at once more sweeping and more restricted. It applies where there is undistributed income of any settlement, whether or not the settlor or his spouse[1] retains an interest and whether or not the settlement is revocable. It is however restricted in that it applies only where the settlor makes payments to the trustees or to a body corporate connected with the settlement[2] which would otherwise be deductible in computing his total income for the year. Thus it prohibits the deduction of these payments for the purposes of computing his excess liability. It leaves untouched his right to deduct and retain tax at basic rate under TA 1988, s. 348.

This section is of limited use in view of s. 683. However its practical effect is that the settlor may not escape excess liability on the sums paid under the covenant to the extent that they exceed income which has in fact been distributed (and so charged to tax as the income of the beneficiaries).

Simon's Taxes C4.357; Butterworths Income Tax Service J2.06.
[1] Supra, § **13: 13**; presumably an ex spouse is not a spouse.
[2] Defined TA 1988, s. 681.

13: 46   *Fifthly,* TA 1988, s. 683[1] disallows all annual payments in computing excess liability—but not basic rate—unless it comes within certain exceptions namely:

(*a*) payments under a partnership agreement to a former member or the widow or dependant of a former member provided that the liability is incurred for full consideration;

(*b*) payments in favour of similar people by an individual in connection with the acquisition of a business;

(*c*) payments by one party to a marriage for the other where the marriage has been dissolved or annulled or where they are separated and the separation is likely to be permanent—such payments must be by way of provision for the other spouse and so do not include payments for the children, which will usually fall foul of s. 663 anyway. However, under Revenue practice, payments under a court order are not treated as made under a settlement[2] and so escape s. 683 also.

(*d*) payments which are already treated as the income of the settlor by some other provision.

(*e*) covenanted payments to charities.[3]

Where an individual pays at least £1,000 under covenant to a charity in a year of assessment, and relief on that payment is denied to the charity under TA 1988, s. 505(3) (supra, § **11: 16**), higher rate relief will also be denied.[4] Provision is made for apportionment of such payments where the charity receives a number of covenanted payments and relief is restricted in respect of only part of the total sum received.[5]

(*f*) annuities for former partners widows or dependants which although not for full consideration (and so within (*a*)) nonetheless are treated as earned income of the recipient under the rule at § **4: 06**, supra; sums in excess of those limits are subject to s. 683 to the extent of that excess.[6]

Subject to these exceptions therefore no deduction may be made in computing total income even if made for full consideration although deduction is still permitted in so far as basic rate of tax is concerned under s. 348.

---

[1] Pre 1965 covenants fall within s. 684. **Simon's Taxes C4.366; Butterworths Income Tax Service J2.07.**
[2] Supra, § **13: 33**.
[3] TA 1988, s. 683(3).
[4] TA 1988, s. 683(4).
[5] TA 1988, s. 683(5).
[6] TA 1988, s. 628.

13: 47   *Sixthly*, legislation was introduced in 1977 to deal with "reverse annuities".[1] Where the annuity or annual payment is made under a liability incurred for money or money's worth not all of which is required to be brought into account in computing the income of the person making the payment, the payments are not deductible in computing total income; ss. 348 and 349 are also excluded. Payments falling within the provision are specifically excluded from the new regime for annual payments.[2]

The rule applies whenever the payment is made under a liability incurred for money or money's worth and so does not affect purely voluntary covenants; nor does it affect the purchase of annuities from insurance companies since the sums paid by the individual will enter into the profits of the company. Also excluded are (*i*) payments in connection with partnership agreements,[3] maintenance agreements[4] (supra) and transfers of business[5] (*ii*) payments on the surrender of a life interest to a remainderman (*iii*) annuities granted in the ordinary course of granting annuities and (*iv*) annuities charged on an interest in settled property and granted before 30th March 1977 to a company dealing in interests in settled property or then carrying on life assurance business in the UK.

Simon's Taxes E1.503; Butterworths Income Tax Service J2.48.

[1] TA 1988, s. 125 reversing *IRC v Plummer* [1979] STC 793, [1979] 3 All ER 775, supra, § **13: 06**.

[2] TA 1988, s. 347A(2)(*d*).

[3] Within TA 1988, s. 683(1)(*a*).

[4] Within TA 1988, s. 683(1)(*c*).

[5] Within TA 1988, s. 683(6).

PART III. CAPITAL GAINS TAX

14 Introduction

OUTLINE

14: 01 Capital gains tax (CGT) is charged on chargeable gains accruing to, that is realised by, a person, other than a company, during a year of assessment.[1] The tax is due on 1st December following the end of that year or, if later, 30 days after the issue of the notice of assessment.[2]

Chargeable gains accrue only on chargeable disposals of chargeable assets. Certain events are treated as disposals, e.g. the complete loss or destruction of an asset.[3]

CGT is a tax separate from income tax, although a number of the machinery provisions relating to assessments, appeals and so on, are common. This is still the case, notwithstanding the unification of the rates of CGT and income tax from 1988–89.[4] Any gain liable to income tax is excluded from CGT[5] and losses available for set off against income are not allowable losses for CGT. Conversely, an excess of capital losses cannot be set off against income liable to income tax.[6] Further, deductions that are or would be allowable for income tax are not allowable for CGT.[7]

The tax was introduced in 1965 and applies only to gains accruing since 5th April 1965. For disposals on or after 6th April 1988, CGT is effectively imposed only on gains accruing since 31st March 1982, subject to certain restrictions.[8] The application of these restrictions involves computing the gain under the pre-6th April 1988 rules, including the special assumptions made in order to calculate gains in respect of assets owned on 6th April 1965.[9] The restrictions may be disapplied if the taxpayer elects.[10]

Reliefs take the form of exemption from liability or the deferment of liability until the following disposal; the latter is usually effected by adjusting the cost base. Since 1982 there has been indexation relief in the form of a further deduction after the unindexed gain has been arrived at (see infra, § **21: 20**) to take account of inflation since 1982. Account is taken of inflation before 1st April 1982 by the rebasing of CGT to 31st March 1982 values.

Simon's Taxes C1.101; Sumption CGT A1.01.
[1] CGTA 1979, s. 1. On the taxation of offshore income gains see infra, § **34: 38**.
[2] CGTA 1979, s. 7.
[3] CGTA 1979, s. 22(1), see infra, § **14: 02**.
[4] See infra, § **14: 05**.
[5] CGTA 1979, s. 31.
[6] No statute allows it: therefore it is not allowable.
[7] CGTA 1979, s. 33.
[8] FA 1988, s. 96, see infra, § **22: 02**.
[9] See infra, § **22: 01**.

¹⁰ See infra, § **22: 04**.

14: 02   Losses are computed in the same way as gains. If a disposal can give rise to a chargeable gain it can also give rise to an allowable loss; whereas if it gives rise to a non-chargeable gain it cannot give rise to an allowable loss.¹ Exceptions mar this symmetry in that there are disposals which can give rise to chargeable gains but not allowable losses.² Special rules apply to wasting assets. These rules restrict the deductible expenditure so that any loss is limited or becomes a gain, see § **21: 16**.

A disposal is deemed to occur in the event of the entire loss, destruction, dissipation or extinction of the asset.³ If the asset becomes of negligible value and the inspector is satisfied of this there is a deemed disposal³—strictly when the inspector is so satisfied and not before, although the Revenue practice of relating this back to the date of the claim has been approved.⁴ The Revenue have now made it clear that the negligible value condition must also be satisfied at the date of the claim.⁵ Since the asset still exists it is deemed to be reacquired and any subsequent gain is taxable. A building and its site can be treated as separate assets for this rule although, since the land is also treated as having been disposed of and reacquired at market value, the benefit is limited.⁶

EXAMPLE

C purchased a country cottage in 1983 for £25,000. Late in 1988, it is burned down but as C's insurance policy had lapsed, the loss was not covered. The value of the site after the building is destroyed is £30,000. The values of the building and site on acquisition are £15,000 and £10,000 respectively.

Assumed indexation factor: 0.3

(*a*) Disposal of building		
Disposal proceeds		nil
Allowable cost	£15,000	
Indexation (0.3)	4,500	19,500
Allowable loss		£19,500
(*b*) Deemed disposal of land		
Disposal proceeds		£30,000
Allowable cost	£10,000	
Indexation (0.3)	3,000	13,000
Chargeable gain		£17,000
Net allowable loss		£2,500

Losses must be set off against capital gains of the same year.⁷ Unrelieved losses may be carried forward to later years⁸ but not back to previous years save on death, infra, § **17: 08**. For this reason it is generally preferable to realise losses sooner rather than later. Quoted shares and securities may easily be sold on one day and bought back the next, a process known as the bed and breakfast trade. This provides a relatively simple method of realising accrued losses just before the end of the year of assessment, although the effects on indexation (see infra, § **21: 20**) may not always be favourable. Bed and breakfast transactions by companies may be rendered ineffective by anti-avoidance legislation, infra, § **25: 06**.

On losses and £6,000 chattels exemption see infra, § **15: 09**; on losses and wasting chattels see infra, § **15: 08**, on disposals to a connected person, infra, § **16: 25**.

Simon's Taxes C1.108, 120; Sumption CGT A1.03.
[1] CGTA 1979, s. 29(2).
[2] E.g. CGTA 1979, s. 134(4).
[3] CGTA 1979, s. 22. On Rolls Royce shares, see [1975] STI, p. 47. In practice, this can operate very harshly on securities in private companies, the Revenue generally not being willing to countenance a claim before full liquidation without any dividend.
[4] *Williams v Bullivant* [1983] STC 107, followed in *Larner v Warrington* [1985] STC 442.
[5] Extra-statutory concession D28 (1988), **Simon's Taxes, Division H2.2.**
[6] CGTA 1979, s. 22(3).
[7] CGTA 1979, s. 4(1)(*a*).
[8] CGTA 1979, s. 4(1)(*b*).

14: 03   Normally CGT is due on 1st December following the end of the year of assessment, or 30 days after the assessment notice is issued, if later.[1] However, the tax may be paid by instalments if the consideration is payable by instalments over a period exceeding 18 months and the taxpayer satisfies the Board that he would otherwise suffer undue hardship.[2] The tax is to be paid by such instalments as the Board shall direct over a period not exceeding eight years.[3] Where a vendor sells an asset but does not immediately receive the full price it is a question of fact whether there is a sale by instalments or a sale for the full price but with a loan to the purchaser.[4]

Payment of tax by instalments is also permitted in certain instances of disposals by gift or of settled property on or after 14th March 1989.[5] The facility for payment by instalments was reintroduced following the withdrawal of holdover relief for gifts etc., subject to certain exceptions, from the same date, infra, § **16: 21**.

CGT is payable by instalments in respect of a gift of the following assets, where holdover is not available or only partly available:

(*a*)   land or an estate or interest in land;
(*b*)   shares or securities giving the donor control of the company concerned;
(*c*)   shares or securities not within (*b*) which are unquoted (and not traded on the USM).

Interest on each instalment runs from the original reckonable date for the CGT due and is added to each instalment. However, interest runs only from the date of each instalment if the asset is agricultural property for IHT purposes: infra, § **45: 12**. If the donor and donee are connected persons, and the asset is disposed of in a subsequent disposal for valuable consideration, the whole of the CGT becomes payable immediately.

Simon's Taxes C1.109; Sumption CGT A24.08.
[1] CGTA 1979, s. 7.
[2] It appears that "undue hardship" is measured only by reference to the funds arising under the transaction concerned. Generally, the Revenue would not expect more than 50% of each instalment to be used to pay the tax arising.
[3] CGTA 1979, s. 40(1).
[4] *Coren v Keighley* (1972) 48 TC 370.
[5] CGTA 1979, s. 7A.

PERSONS CHARGEABLE

14: 04   CGT is charged on chargeable gains accruing to a person in a year of assessment during any part of which he is resident in the UK, or during which he is ordinarily resident in the UK.[1]

Non resident persons are subject to CGT in respect of UK assets used for the purposes of a trade carried on in the UK through a branch, or UK assets held for the purposes of the branch.[2]

Each partner is liable for the tax on his share of the gains realised by the partnership.[3]

Trustees and personal representatives are chargeable in respect of gains realised on a disposal, whether actual or deemed, in the course of administration.

A body subject to corporation tax has its gains charged to that tax and not to CGT. Shareholders are liable to CGT on the disposal of their shares, assuming that they are not corporations. Corporation tax paid by the corporation is not automatically imputed to the shareholder even though it be shown that the latter's gain is attributable entirely to the gain already taxed in the company. This can lead to double taxation of gains—and double relief for losses. However, if the capital gain is distributed by the company to the shareholder, the corporation tax paid may wholly or partially be imputed by virtue of the tax credit attaching to the distribution, infra, § **24: 09**. Undistributed capital gains of a non-resident close company may be attributed to the participators.[4]

Unit trusts and investment trusts are exempt from tax on capital gains.[5]

Sumption CGT A24.03.

[1] CGTA 1979, s. 2; in *R v IRC, ex p Fulford-Dobson* [1987] STC 344 an attempt by a taxpayer to get round this rule by a scheme using extra-statutory concession D2 failed (supra, § **1: 32**).
[2] CGTA 1979, s. 12; infra, § **20: 23**.
[3] Infra, § **20: 19**.
[4] Infra, §§ **23: 06, 34: 55** and **35: 01**.
[5] FA 1980, s. 81.

RATES OF TAX

14: 05   When originally introduced, the rate of CGT was a flat 30%. This rate applied until 1987–88. From 1988–89 onwards, chargeable gains are taxed at income tax rates. An individual's net chargeable gains for the year of assessment are treated as the top slice of income in computing the CGT liability.[1] Nevertheless, the tax charged remains CGT, not income tax. Chargeable gains realised by companies are now chargeable to the full corporation tax rate of 35%;[2] this applies to disposals after 16th March 1987.

There is now a simple annual exemption for gains accruing to individuals; for 1989–90 the figure is £5,000. This annual exemption is index linked.[3] When spouses are living together only one relief is given, allocated between them pro rata to their net gains. On trusts see § **18: 08** and on estates see § **17: 03**.

Simon's Taxes C1.113; Sumption CGT A1.01, 14; A5.02.

[1] FA 1988, s. 98. As to married couples, see § **14: 06**, infra; as to trusts, see § **18: 08** and as to estates, § **17: 03**.
[2] F(No. 2)A 1987, s. 74; this was so also between 1965 and 1973. Between 1973 and 1987 the

effective rate of corporation tax on chargeable gains was 30%, an effect achieved by including only a prescribed fraction of chargeable gains in profits subject to corporation tax.
[3] FA 1982, s. 80. The 1989–90 figure is set by FA 1989, s. 122. Indexation was disapplied for 1989–90.

HUSBAND AND WIFE

14: 06 Following the income tax rule, a husband is assessable and chargeable with the gains accruing to his wife if, during the whole or part of the year of assessment beginning on 6th April she is living with him;[1] it follows that this does not apply for the year in which they marry. For 1989–90, the rate of tax on the wife's net chargeable gains is found by treating them as the top slice of her husband's income (after including his chargeable gains, if any).[2] Either of them may elect to be assessed separately. On separate assessment applying, the total CGT liability is apportioned between the husband and wife pro rata to their net chargeable gains.[3] The Revenue have the power to proceed against the wife and the husband has the right to disclaim liability in respect of his deceased wife's liability. The spouses are entitled to one annual exemption between them. The exemption is allocated pro rata to each spouse's net chargeable gains, except that, where either has losses brought forward, the exemption can be allocated as they choose.[4]

Either spouse may set off the one's gains against the other's losses, but they may elect that this set-off shall not apply.[5] The election is effective only for the year of assessment for which it is made, but it may be made again and again. Once the election is made, the gains will be taxed in full and the losses will be carried forward to be set off against the subsequent gains of that spouse only. The election may be useful if one spouse is resident and the other not, or if neither spouse is resident but the one runs a business through a branch or agency here. In the absence of an election, allowable losses of the spouse subject to CGT would still have to be set off against chargeable gains of the spouse not so subject.

Simon's Taxes C1.120, 204; Sumption CGT A24.03.
[1] CGTA 1979, s. 45, and see *Aspden v Hildesley* [1982] STC 206.
[2] FA 1988, s. 99(1). This applied for 1988–89 also.
[3] FA 1988, s. 99(3).
[4] CGTA 1979, Sch. 1, para. 2(1).
[5] CGTA 1979, s. 4(2); tax recovered by H as a result of using W's loss presumably belongs to W—*Re Cameron, Kingsley v IRC* [1967] Ch 1, [1965] 3 All ER 474, 42 TC 539.

14: 07 The provisions outlined in § **14: 06**, supra cease to apply after 1989–90. From 1990–91 onwards, when a married couple will be subject to separate taxation of income, chargeable gains will also be taxed separately.[1] The rate of CGT on each spouse's net gains will be found by treating the gains as the top slice of their income. Each spouse will have a separate annual exempt amount which will not be transferable to the other spouse if not fully utilised. The allowable losses of one spouse will not be available for offset against the other spouse's gains.

Simon's Taxes C1.120.
[1] FA 1988, s. 104.

Inter-spousal transfers

14: 08   If husband and wife are living together[1] any disposal by one to the other is treated as if the consideration were such that neither a gain nor a loss would accrue to the disposer.[2] This rule will continue to apply after 1989–90 when separate taxation applies for CGT. The effect is to increase the acquisition cost to take account of any allowable expenses subsequent to the acquisition by the disposer including the incidental costs of the present disposal. Further, the acquirer's acquisition is treated as taking place when the other acquired it, where the asset was originally acquired before 1st April 1982.[3] Any indexation allowance available to the transferor is also taken into account.[4]

The no gain/no loss rule does not apply to appropriations to or from trading stock, market value being taken instead to preserve the integrity of the rules concerning the interaction of income and capital gains tax.[5] Nor does it apply to *donatio mortis causa*, the purpose here being consistency with the exemption from CGT of assets passing on death.[6]

When spouses separate or are treated as separated they are no longer living together,[7] a matter which affects the annual exemption (each is entitled to an exemption on that sum),[8] the set-off of losses,[9] accountability,[10] the exemption for principal private residence[11] and the inter-spousal transfer rule. In principle, these matters are affected as from the date of separation, not the end of the year in which they separate. However, for the year of separation, the wife shares the husband's annual exemption for the part of the year up to the separation, but is entitled a full annual exemption in her own right for the remainder of that year.[12] A husband is liable for CGT on his wife's gains which accrued before the separation. It follows that if there is an inter-spousal transfer before the separation any accrued but unrealised gains will become the liability of the recipient, a matter of considerable importance if what has previously been the spouses' second house becomes the principal residence of one of them. However, they remain connected persons.[13] In addition, each spouse may claim exemption in respect of a residence provided for a dependent relative of the other as that relative's principal residence,[14] despite the fact of the separation.

Simon's Taxes C1.120, 204; Sumption CGT A5.04–A5.11.
[1] Or are treated as living together by TA 1988, s. 282 (TA 1970, s. 42)—see *Gubay v Kington* [1984] STC 99, [1984] 1 All ER 513—however in this case the House of Lords applied the proviso to s. 42(2) to ensure that the tax otherwise arising was not increased as a result of the deemed living together. If the spouses are not living together the normal rules apply but a concession applies where after breakdown one spouse transfers an interest in the matrimonial home to the other, extra-statutory concession D6 (1988), **Simon's Taxes, Division H2.2,** infra, § **15: 15,** n. 2.
[2] CGTA 1979, s. 44; on part disposal computation see CGTA 1979, s. 35(5).
[3] FA 1988, Sch. 8, para. 1.
[4] FA 1982, Sch. 13, paras. 2 and 3.
[5] Infra, § **21: 04**.
[6] Infra, § **17: 02**.
[7] Supra, § **3: 10**.
[8] CGTA 1979, Sch. 1, para. 2.

⁹ CGTA 1979, s. 4.
¹⁰ CGTA 1979, s. 45.
¹¹ CGTA 1979, s. 101(6).
¹² CGTA 1979, Sch. 1, para. 2(2).
¹³ Infra, § **16: 24**.
¹⁴ CGTA 1979, s. 105(5). Note the restrictions on this exemption for disposals on or after 6th April 1988 : see § **15.16**, infra.

CHARITIES

14: 09   A gain accruing to a charity and which is both applicable to and applied for charitable purposes is not a chargeable gain.[1] If property is held on charitable trusts but then ceases to be so held, there is a deemed disposal and reacquisition at market value and any gain so accruing is chargeable.[2] There is thus no immunity for unrealised capital gains built up behind the screen of charity.

A further benefit for charities is the rule that the disposal of property to charities or certain listed bodies otherwise than under a bargain at arm's length will be treated as being made for such consideration that neither gain nor loss accrues,[3] thus transferring the liability to unrealised gains to the charity where immunity may reasonably be expected. This applies whether the transfer is by way of gift or sale; however where the sale is at a figure above the disposer's cost base (excluding indexation) the excess is deducted from the gain eligible for exemption. A similar exemption is given when there is a deemed disposal under CGTA 1979, s. 54 or 55 and the property then passes to a charity or listed body.[4]

Simon's Taxes C1.235, 428; Sumption CGT A22.02.
¹ CGTA 1979, s. 145(1) and TA 1970, s. 360(2); there is no requirement that the gain be applied for charitable purposes *only*; cf. TA 1988, s. 505(1) (TA 1970, s. 360(1)), infra, § **15: 16**, but note definition of charity in TA 1988, s. 506(1) (s. 360(3)). For chargeable periods ending after 11th June 1986, restrictions are placed on the exemption where the charity has non-qualifying expenditure in the period: TA 1988, s. 505 (FA 1986, s. 31), supra, § **11:13**.
² CGTA 1979, s. 145(2).
³ CGTA 1979, s. 146.
⁴ CGTA 1979, s. 146(2).

15 Assets, exemptions and reliefs

ASSETS

15: 01 All forms of property are assets whether situated in the UK or not.[1] Property is not further defined. Assets are however stated to include (*a*) options, debts and incorporeal property[2] generally (*b*) any currency other than sterling[3] and (*c*) any form of property created by the person disposing of it, or otherwise coming to be owned without being acquired. Property owned without being acquired covers items such as goodwill[4] and property which is found. Property created includes not only such items as paintings but also copyrights, patents and crops.

This definition leaves uncertain the scope of incorporeal property. It is not confined to interests in or over other property since the statutory words contain no such limitation. Hence rights under contractual licences or rights of registration under the Matrimonial Homes Act 1983 may equally be "property" and sums received on the redemption of a rentcharge, the release of a covenant and for the release of a right to occupy the matrimonial home may all give rise to CGT.[5]

The meaning of asset was considered by the House of Lords in *O'Brien v Benson's Hosiery (Holdings) Ltd.*[6] It was held that the series of rights of an employer under a service agreement was an asset for CGT so that a sum received to secure the release of the employee was derived from that asset and so liable to CGT. The fact that the rights could not be assigned by the employer was irrelevant. It was sufficient that they could be "turned to account". This may indicate a wide view of the concept; however the right was, like the others already mentioned, legally enforceable in some way or other. More recently it has been held that a right to bring an action to enforce a claim that is neither frivolous nor vexatious and which could be settled on payment of a capital sum can be an asset for CGT and, moreover, that is an asset in its own right quite distinct from the property to which it relates.[7] Unenforceable promises probably do not qualify.[8] The position of statute barred rights is obscure but on balance such rights would appear to be assets since they can be revived by acknowledgement and may be enforced indirectly.[9] The problems raised by doubtful rights are likewise ignored by the legislature.[10]

Simon's Taxes C1.401, 404; Sumption CGT A1.04.

[1] CGTA 1979, s. 19(1). For the taxation of a gain arising on the disposal of a material interest in an offshore fund, see infra, § **34: 43**.

[2] Semble that amateur status is not an asset. See *Jarrold v Boustead*, supra, § **6:35**.

[3] Distinguish a holding of foreign currency from a debt expressed in foreign currency which will generally be an exempt asset, infra, § **15: 06** (for a limited exception, see CGTA 1979, Sch. 6, paras. 17 and 18). On this definition, note also *Greig v Ashton* [1956] 3 All ER 123, 36 TC 581.

[4] And see TA 1988, s. 531(2) (TA 1970, s. 386(3)).

[5] Under CGTA 1979, s. 20, infra, § **16: 09**.

[6] [1979] STC 735, [1980] AC 562, [1979] 3 All ER 652, but cf. *Cleveleys Investment Trust Co v IRC* [1975] STC 457 (rights acquired by guarantor against debtor company on discharge of debt to third party not assets for CGT).

[7] *Zim Properties Ltd v Procter* [1985] STC 90.

[8] See the valuable discussion in *Emmet on Title* (16th edn), p. 1043 who raises the problem of *A-G v Murray* [1904] 1 KB 165—void insurance policy forming part of deceased's estate for estate duty.

[9] See Emmet, *loc. cit.*, citing *Leroux v Brown* (1852) 12 CB 801 and *Holmes v Cowcher* [1970] 1 All ER 1224.

[10] Emmet, *loc. cit.*, suggests that they are not assets until proved to be well founded. The issue in this and the previous note is important in view of CGTA 1979, s. 20, infra, § **16: 24**. *Quaere* whether the receipt of money shows that the right was well founded.

Pooling of assets

15: 02 In general each asset is treated as a distinct item so that tax only arises on the disposal of that asset and is then computed in the light of the expenditure on that asset. Shares or securities of a company being of the same class and held by one person in one capacity are regarded as indistinguishable parts of a single asset—a holding—so that the sale of a part of the holding is treated as a part disposal.[1] This treatment does not apply to shares held on 6th April 1965, except for quoted shares where an election has been made, infra, § **22: 12**.

Special rules apply to shares acquired before 6th April 1982 and after 5th April 1965. Such shares from a pool separate from the pool containing shares acquired on or after 6th April 1982.[2] For disposals before 6th April 1985, shares acquired on or after 6th April 1982 were not pooled.[3] Under rules introduced in 1983 a company could elect for what was called parallel pooling,[4] see, infra, § **19: 05** although for disposals on or after 1st April 1985, parallel pooling no longer applies.[5]

Simon's Taxes C2.401; Sumption CGT A12.03, 08.

[1] FA 1985, Sch. 19, para. 9(2).

[2] FA 1985, Sch. 19, para. 9(1).

[3] FA 1982, s. 88.

[4] FA 1983, s. 34 and Sch. 6.

[5] FA 1985, Sch. 19, para. 21.

Securities: pooling and non-pooling (identification)

15: 03 Where shares have been acquired at different times for different prices and some of them are now disposed of, special rules are required to calculate the relevant acquisition cost, so as to compute the gain or loss and any indexation allowance. The necessity for special rules simply reflects the fact that shares and securities are fungible assets, like commodities and foreign currency.

Before the indexation allowance was introduced in 1982 the general rule was one of pooling. Any number of shares or securities of a company were treated as indistinguishable parts of a single asset, called a holding, if the shares were of the same class and held by one person in one capacity.[1] Hence a disposal of some of the shares was a part disposal of the holding.[2] The pooling principle is effectively reinstated for shares acquired after 5th April 1982, in relation to disposals after 5th April 1985.[3]

This basic rule of pooling applies to any other assets which are of such a nature that they can be dealt in without identifying the particular assets disposed of or acquired,[4] such as commodities.

Special rules apply to shares under the business expansion scheme.[5] Shares issued to an employee on restrictive terms are pooled separately for as long as the restrictions remained.[6] Shares held at 6th April 1982 form a separate pool to which no further additions can be made.[7] Shares acquired before 6th April 1965 are not pooled unless an election is made, whereupon they are added to the 6th April 1982 pool as if they had been acquired on 6th April 1965 at their market value on that day.[8] This election applies only to quoted securities. Shares disposed of on or before the day of acquisition are identified in priority to pooled shares.[9] Other securities subject to CGT, such as corporate bonds acquired before 13th March 1984, are not pooled and the pre 6th April 1985 identification rules apply instead.[10]

From 6th April 1982 to 5th April 1985, different rules identifying the particular shares disposed of replaced the basic pooling rule for shares; previous acquisitions remained pooled but with special rules for shares acquired between 6th April 1981 and 5th April 1982 (inclusive).

---

[1] CGTA 1979, s. 65(2) now superseded by FA 1985, Sch. 19.
[2] CGTA 1979, s. 65(3).
[3] FA 1985, s. 68 and Sch. 19.
[4] FA 1985, s. 68(9).
[5] CGTA 1979, s. 149C.
[6] FA 1985, Sch. 19, para. 8(2).
[7] FA 1985, Sch. 19, para. 7.
[8] FA 1985, Sch. 19, para. 6(3).
[9] CGTA 1979, s. 66.
[10] FA 1985, s. 68(9).

Exempt assets

15: 04   Neither chargeable gain nor allowable loss accrues on the disposal of a non-chargeable asset. Such assets include:

(1) Motor cars, defined as mechanically propelled road vehicles constructed or adapted for the carriage of passengers, unless of a type not commonly used as a private vehicle and unsuitable to be so used. The definition is similar to that for capital allowances supra, § **8: 39**.[1] The exclusion covers vintage cars bought as an investment, as well as the family car, but not an ambulance, a steam roller or a bus.

(2) Savings certificates and non-marketable securities issued under the National Loans Act 1939.[2]

(3) Gambling winnings.[3]

(4) Gains from foreign currency acquired by an individual for the personal expenditure outside the UK of himself or his family or dependants. Expenditure on the maintenance of any residence outside the UK is personal.[4] The exemption extends to gains on foreign currency bank accounts representing currency acquired for personal expenditure whilst abroad.[5]

(5) Gains accruing on the disposal by a person (not just an individual) of a decoration awarded for valour or gallant conduct which he acquired otherwise than for consideration in money or money's worth.[6] Thus in the uncommon case where a decoration was sold for more than £6,000, the person honoured and his legatee would still be exempt from CGT.

(6) The rights of the insurer under a policy of insurance do not constitute chargeable assets but the rights of the insured do in so far as the insurance relates to chargeable assets. Thus, the insurer cannot claim a loss, whilst the insured is liable on a disposal of his rights if they relate, for example, to buildings cover.[7]

(7) Rights under a life assurance policy do not give rise to chargeable gains unless acquired for money or money's worth by someone other than the original beneficial owner.[8]

Other exclusions from the tax base are:

(8) debts and covenants, infra, § **15: 06**.

(9) wasting chattels, infra, § **15: 08**.

(10) chattels disposed of for less than £6,000, infra, § **15: 09**.

(11) only or main private residence, infra, § **15: 12**.

(12) gilt edged stock, infra, § **15: 18** and qualifying corporate bonds § **15: 19**.

(13) works of art, infra, § **15: 20**.

(14) gifts to charities, supra, § **14: 09**.

(15) gains accruing on death, infra, § **17: 02**.

(16) exempt persons—charities, superannuation funds, friendly societies, trade unions and other bodies (CGTA 1979, ss. 144, 145 and TA 1988, ss. 320, 459, 467, 507(2), 508, 514, Sch. 29).

Simon's Taxes C1.402, 701, 702; C3.101–107, 302, 413, 415, 504–511, 601–603, 605; C4.228; Sumption CGT A1.05.
[1] CGTA 1979, s. 130.
[2] CGTA 1979, s. 71.
[3] CGTA 1979, s. 19(4).
[4] CGTA 1979, s. 133.
[5] CGTA 1979, s. 135(2).
[6] CGTA 1979, s. 131.
[7] CGTA 1979, s. 140, nullifying *IRC v Montgomery* [1975] STC 182, [1975] 1 All ER 664.
[8] CGTA 1979, s. 143.

Anti-avoidance—value shifting

15: 05   The existence of exempt assets enabled tax avoidance schemes to be developed which moved value from chargeable to non-chargeable assets in order to create a loss or remove a gain. Thus in *Eilbeck v Rawling*[1] the taxpayer arranged to shift value from a purchased interest in settled property to an interest in another settlement which had not been purchased and was exempt fom CGT. On the sale of the two interests, there arose an allowable loss on the purchased reversionary interest and an equal but non-chargeable gain on the other.[2] The scheme failed because the House of Lords treated the various acts as one whole transaction (supra, § **1: 06**).

Nevertheless, specific anti-avoidance legislation[3] was introduced to counter value shifting. It applies where:

(*i*) there is a disposal other than between spouses or by a personal representative to a legatee;

(*ii*) there is a scheme or arrangements whereby,

(*iii*) the value of an asset has been materially reduced, and

(*iv*) a tax-free benefit has been or will be conferred on any person.

Condition (*iii*) is amplified to ensure that where the disposal precedes the acquisition the reference to reduction includes an increase. Both benefit and tax free are defined in the widest possible way for condition (*iv*). There is some minor relief in that if the benefit is conferred on a person other than the disposer or one connected with him, the provision is excluded if it is shown that the avoidance of tax was not a purpose of the scheme or arrangements in question.

Where the provisions apply, the Inspector may recalculate any allowable loss or chargeable gain on whatever basis appears to him to be just and reasonable; he may then do whatever is just and reasonable to adjust the base cost of the assets concerned for the following disposal.

The value-shifting rules can apply to transactions far removed in spirit from the artificiality of *Eilbeck v Rawling* and a similar case, *W T Ramsay Ltd v IRC* (supra, § **1.08**), but there is no formal clearance procedure.

The section does not generally apply to a reduction in the value of shares arising from an intra-group dividend or from an intra-group disposal but there are exceptions in relation to disposals on or after 14th March 1989.[4]

Simon's Taxes C1.438; Sumption CGT A2.07, A2.08.

[1] [1981] STC 174, [1981] 1 All ER 865.
[2] Infra, § **18: 17**.
[3] CGTA 1979, s. 26.
[4] FA 1989, ss. 135–137; infra, § **26: 25A–F**.

EXEMPTIONS AND RELIEFS

Debts and covenants

15: 06   No chargeable gain or allowable loss accrues to the original creditor or his personal representatives or legatee on the disposal of a debt, except in the case of a debt on a security.[1] In general, creditors will be denied relief for losses, although there is also exemption for gains arising on foreign currency debts (other than foreign currency bank accounts[2]). There are provisions designed to counter the creation of losses on debts transferred between connected persons.[3] The courts take a narrow view of a debt; there must be a liability to pay a sum which is at that point in time ascertained or capable of ascertainment.[4] The nature of the obligation is settled at the start of its life; an uncertain obligation does not become entitled to exemption as a debt just because it becomes certain.[5]

There are two major exceptions. First, the rule does not apply to a debt on a security. It appears that a debt on a security does not have to be constituted or evidenced by a document[6] but it must be marketable and be capable if necessary of being converted into shares or other securities. In *W T Ramsay Ltd v IRC* among the factors indicating to Lord Fraser that the debt was one on a security were the following (*a*) there was a long fixed term, (*b*) the terms as to early repayment of the debt were unusual save where loan stock was involved and (*c*) the debt bore interest.[7] (Many schemes were designed to convert non-allowable losses on debts into allowable losses on debts on securities.[8])

Secondly, relief may be given for loss on loans to traders[9], provided that the borrower uses the loan for trading purposes (including setting up the trade) and that he is resident in the UK.

Relief is not available if (*i*) the claimant has assigned his rights to recover the debt; (*ii*) if the claimant and the borrower are spouses living together; (*iii*) if the claimant and borrower are members of the same group of companies. For (*ii*) and (*iii*) the test is applied at the time of the loan and any subsequent time. It is also necessary that the irrecoverability of the loan should not arise from any act or omission on the part of the lender nor from the terms of any arrangement of which the loan forms part. If the loan is repaid, in whole or in part, the relief may be recaptured; the same applies where the lender receives any money or money's worth in satisfaction of his rights or if he assigns his rights in return for money or money's worth; provision is made for the substitution of market value if the assignment is not a bargain at arm's length. Similar relief (and restrictions thereon) applies to sums paid by a guarantor. The Revenue view is that this relief applies to guarantees of bank overdrafts but not hire purchase agreements.

Simon's Taxes C1.401, 404; Division C3.7; Sumption CGT A1.05, A19.01, 04.
[1] CGTA 1979, 134.
[2] CGTA 1979, s. 135(1).
[3] CGTA 1979, s. 134(4).
[4] Slade J in *Marren v Ingles* [1979] STC 58 at 70 (who left open whether it had to be a present liability); this case was reversed on appeal [1979] STC 637, CA; affd. [1980] STC 500, HL. See also *Marson v Marriage* [1980] STC 177.
[5] *Marren v Ingles* [1980] STC 500, [1980] 3 All ER 95, HL.
[6] Lord Wilberforce in *W T Ramsay Ltd v IRC* [1981] STC 174 at 184. See also *Cleveleys Investment Trust Co Ltd v IRC* (1971) 47 TC 300 and *Aberdeen Construction Group Ltd v IRC* [1978] STC 127, [1978] 1 All ER 962.
[7] At 188.
[8] E.g. *Harrison v Nairn Williamson Ltd* [1978] STC 67, [1978] 1 All ER 608 infra, § **16: 23**; *IRC v Burmah Oil Co Ltd* [1982] STC 30.
[9] CGTA 1979, s. 136 including a profession. See SP3/83 and furnished lettings, TA 1988, s. 503(1) (FA 1984, Sch. 11, para. 1).

15: 07 No chargeable gain accrues on the disposal of a right to or to a part of annual payments due under a covenant made by any person and which was not secured on any property.[1] In *Rank Xerox Ltd v Lane*[2] the House of Lords held that this rule was confined to situations where there was a gratuitous promise to make the payments and the promise was enforceable only because of its form; in that case the taxpayer was held liable on the gain arising from the disposal to its shareholders of a right to receive royalty payments.

Simon's Taxes C1.702; Sumption CGT A21.04.
[1] CGTA 1979, s. 144(*c*).
[2] [1979] STC 740.

Tangible movable property—wasting assets

15: 08   No chargeable gain accrues on the disposal of tangible movable property or an interest in such property, which is also a wasting asset.[1] A wasting asset is defined as an asset having a predictable life of 50 years or less.[2] Plant and machinery is always assumed to have a life of less than 50 years.[3] However, the exemption for wasting chattels does not apply to assets in respect of which capital allowances were or could have been claimed, nor to commodities dealt with on a terminal market.[4]

Simon's Taxes C2.136; C3.601; Sumption CGT A17.04.
  [1] CGTA 1979, s. 127(1).
  [2] CGTA 1979, s. 37 applied by s. 127(5).
  [3] CGTA 1979, s. 37(1)(*c*).
  [4] CGTA 1979, s. 127(2) and (3) infra, § **20: 03**.

Chattels sold[1] for £6,000 or less

15: 09   If an asset which is tangible movable property is disposed of and the amount or value of the consideration does not exceed £6,000, there is no chargeable gain.[2] The consideration taken into account is the gross amount, before any expenses of disposal.

If the asset is sold for more than £6,000 any gain is computed in the normal way. However, there is marginal relief whereby the gain is limited to 5/3rds of the difference between the consideration and £6,000.[3]

> **EXAMPLE**
> M sells a chattel for £6,400, which he had purchased for £800. The indexation factor is 0.255.

		£6,400
Disposal consideration		£6,400
Allowable cost	800	
Indexation allowance: 800 × 0.255	204	1,004
Chargeable gain		£5,396
Gain is limited to $\frac{5}{3} \times (6,400{-}6,000)$		£667

Loss relief is restricted where a chattel is disposed of for less than £6,000.[4] The allowable loss is computed on the assumption that the consideration was £6,000.

> **EXAMPLE**
> N acquired an antique object for £7,000 but sells it, in a falling market, for £5,200. The indexation factor is 0.360.

		£6,000
Deemed consideration for disposal		£6,000
Allowable cost	7,000	
Indexation allowance: 7,000 × 0.360	2,520	9,520
Allowable loss		£3,520

The relief does not apply to commodities in a terminal market or currency of any description.[5]

Simon's Taxes C3.603, 604; Sumption CGT A17.03.
  [1] This is the word used in the heading of the section but the section itself applies to any disposal and not just sale.

² CGTA 1979, s. 128(1). For disposals before 6th April 1989, the limit was £3,000.
³ CGTA 1979, s. 128(2).
⁴ CGTA 1979, s. 128(3).
⁵ CGTA 1979, s. 128(6); the relief being only for tangible movable property means that it is not available for fixtures before severance.

Anti-avoidance provisions—part disposal

15: 10   There are provisions to counter exploitation of the chattel exemption by successive disposals of part-interests in a chattel worth more than £6,000. Where there is a disposal of a right or interest in or over tangible movable property, the consideration for the disposal is treated as the aggregate of the sum received for the interest disposed of *and* the market value of the remainder.[1] Any marginal relief is calculated as already described (§ **15: 09**) by reference to the deemed consideration for the disposal, and the relief is then allocated pro rata to the actual disposal consideration.

EXAMPLE
Q sells a one-third share in a watercolour for £2,500. The value of the remainder is £5,000. The watercolour cost £900 and the indexation factor is 0.138.

(*a*) The disposal consideration is deemed to be £7,500, so that the chattel exemption is not available.

(*b*) The gain is calculated as follows:

Disposal consideration (actual)		£2,500
Allowable cost: $900 \times \dfrac{2,500}{2,500+5,000} =$	300	
Indexation allowance: 300×0.138	41	341
Gain		£2,159

(*c*) Marginal relief:

Gain is limited to $\frac{5}{3} \times (7,500 - 6,000) =$	£2,500
Allocate pro rata to interest disposed of:	
$2,500 \times \dfrac{2,500}{7,500}$	£833
Relief given: £2,159 − £833 =	£1,326

This principle is applied also to the loss restriction.

EXAMPLE
If, in the preceding example, Q had purchased the picture for £8,400, and had sold a ⅓ share for £1,500 (value of remainder £3,000), the position would be as follows:

Allowable loss without restriction		
Actual proceeds		£1,500
Allowable cost: $£8,400 \times \dfrac{1,500}{1,500+3,000} =$	£2,800	
Indexation allowance: $2,800 \times 0.138$	387	3,187
Allowable loss		£1,687
Deemed disposal proceeds		£6,000
Allowable cost	£8,400	
Indexation allowance: $8,400 \times 0.138$	1,160	9,560
Allowable loss		£3,560
Allowable loss on ⅓ sold restricted to		£1,187

There may be still an advantage in making a series of part disposals so as to take advantage of the annual exemption.

Sumption CGT A17.03.
[1] CGTA 1979, s. 128(5).

15: 11 Different provisions apply to a set of articles where the owner can make a disposition of one of the items in the set rather than, in the case of a single object, making a part disposal of it. The disposal of one item of the set is not treated as a part disposal of the set. However, special rules apply if there is a disposal of more than one item either to the same person or to persons who are acting in concert or to persons who are connected with each other (but not necessarily connected with the disposer).

Whether the disposals take place on the same or different occasions the two or more transactions are treated as a single transaction disposing of a single asset with any necessary apportionments of marginal relief and in restriction of losses.[1] The apportionment is made by reference to the consideration received for each of the items concerned. If disposals of parts of a set are made over a period of years, it appears that marginal relief or loss restriction for earlier years may be affected, although there is no extension of the normal six-year time limit for assessment or repayment claims.

> **EXAMPLE**
> G purchased a set of six antique dining chairs for £5,400 in 1987. On 1st April 1990, he sells three of them to a dealer for £4,200 and the remaining three to the same dealer for £4,200 on 6th April 1990. (Assumed indexation factor for the disposals is 0.281).
>
> | | | |
> |---|---:|---:|
> | Disposal proceeds per chair | | £1,400 |
> | Allowable cost | £900 | |
> | Indexation (0.281 × £900) | 253 | 1,153 |
> | Chargeable gain | | £247 |
>
> | | | |
> |---|---|---:|
> | Marginal relief: | | |
> | Deemed transaction value | | £8,400 |
> | Chargeable gain limited to $\frac{2}{3}$ × (£8,400 − £6,000) = | | £4,000 |
> | Chargeable gain limit per chair: $\frac{1}{6}$ × £4,000 = | | £667 |
>
> Marginal relief is therefore inapplicable.
> Total chargeable gains: 1989–90   £741
> 1990–91   £741

There is no definition of a set although the Revenue seem to take the view that just two items cannot constitute a set. The statute requires that they should all have been owned at one time by one person and that they are disposed of by that person. The provisions do not apply where the set is owned by connected persons.

Simon's Taxes C3.605; Sumption CGT A17.03.
[1] CGTA 1979, s. 128(4). *Quaere* when the recipients must be acting in concert or connected persons; is it the time of the first disposal or the subsequent one or both?

Only or main residence

15: 12 Any gain is wholly or partly exempt if it is attributable to[1] the disposal of or of an interest[1] in a dwelling-house which is or has been the owner's only or main residence. It is sufficient that the house was the owner's residence *at any time* during the period of ownership, however long ago the period of owner occupation ended.

There is no requirement that the residence should be in the UK. It is, however, necessary that it is a dwelling house; this is a question of fact—even a caravan has qualified.[2] It has also been held that a separate bungalow adjacent to but within the curtilage of a dwelling house was part of the dwelling house even though the bungalow was occupied by a part-time caretaker.[3]

The disposal may be of an interest in the dwelling house. This covers not only a freehold whether or not held on trust for sale but also a lease so that a sum paid by a landlord to secure the surrender of a lease would qualify.[4]

As well as the actual site of the dwelling house, land is included in the exemption if the owner has it as the garden or grounds of the dwelling house, for his own occupation and enjoyment. There is no express requirement that the house and garden be adjacent. If the garden or grounds exceed one acre, the exemption applies only if the Commissioners are satisfied that the larger area was, having regard to the size and character of the house, required for the reasonable enjoyment as a residence.

The sale of a garden separate from the rest of the house causes difficulties. To be exempt the garden must be occupied as such, with the house, at the time of the disposal. Where the house is sold with part of the garden and the remainder of the garden is sold later, the subsequent sale is not entitled to the exemption.[5] If the order of sales were reversed both sales would qualify.[6] The point is taken by the Revenue only where the garden has development value.[7]

A further problem of separate sales is that, where the garden is in excess of one acre, it may weaken the plea that the garden was required for the reasonable enjoyment of the house.

The exemption is lost if the acquisition of the house was wholly or partly for the purpose of making a gain from its disposal.[8] Likewise where expenditure is incurred in carrying out improvements or in acquiring additional land with that purpose of gain, then there will be a charge on the proportion of the gain attributable to that expenditure. A mere hope of making a gain is probably insufficient to lose the exemption.[9]

Simon's Taxes C3.503; Sumption CGT A16.52.

[1] CGTA 1979, s. 128(4). Disposals of assets other than interests in the dwelling house are therefore not exempt. Presumably an interest in the proceeds of sale will be exempt. In practice difficulty is often met when the house is owned through a housing association, the Revenue harshly and probably wrongly denying relief here.

[2] *Makins v Elson* [1977] STC 46, [1977] 1 All ER 572 on the degree of residence required see *Moore v Thompson* [1986] STC 170.

[3] *Batey v Wakefield* [1981] STC 521 distinguished on facts in *Green v IRC* [1982] STC 485; see also *Markey v Sanders* [1987] STC 256 and doubts on analysis used in that case in *Williams v Merrylees* [1987] STC 445, when the Commissioners' decision in favour of the taxpayer was set aside and the matter remitted for a new hearing.

[4] Quaere, however if he receives compensation for agreeing not to seek a new lease since the interest is disposed of.

[5] *Varty v Lynes* [1976] STC 508, [1976] 3 All ER 447.

[6] But not, strictly, if the sales are simultaneous but the taxpayer ceases to occupy the dwelling house one month before the sale takes effect.

[7] CCAB, June 1976, *Moores & Rowland's Yellow Tax Guide 1989–90*, Appendix 1.

[8] CGTA 1979, s. 103(3). *Semble* the onus of proof is on the Revenue. *Quaere* if the exemption is lost where an intending vendor of a leasehold interest acquires the freehold reversion (under the Leasehold Reform Act 1967) in order to obtain a larger price, see Revenue leaflet CGT 8 (1980), para. 76.

[9] Cf. TA 1988, s. 776.

Apportionment

15: 13 Full exemption applies where the dwelling-house has been used throughout the period of ownership as the owner's main residence.[1] The last twenty-four months of ownership are treated as a period of owner occupation, whether so occupied or not, provided that the house has at some time been the only or main residence. Where the house was so used for only a part of the period of ownership, partial exemption applies, and is given by apportionment of the overall gain rateably to the period of owner occupation as a main residence.[2] For disposals on or after 6th April 1988, only periods of ownership after 31st March 1982 are relevant in making the time apportionment.[3] Where the individual has held different interests in the property, the period of ownership is treated as commencing with the acquisition of the first interest in respect of which allowable expenditure was incurred.[4] There is no provision whereby an owner who has used his house as his main private residence, but intends to do so no longer, can have its then value taken and be liable only for any subsequent gain—the apportionment rule is mandatory.

Apportionment will also take place if a part of the house has been used exclusively for business purposes e.g. a surgery attached to a doctor's residence.[5]

EXAMPLE

J purchased a house as his main residence for £20,000 on 1st March 1973 and occupied it as such until 31st May 1982. From then until its sale on 1st October 1988, the house was occupied rent-free by J's son and daughter in law. The net proceeds of sale are £150,000. (Value at 31st March 1982: £80,000; indexation factor 0.378.)

Disposal consideration		£150,000
Allowable cost	£80,000	
Indexation allowance: 0.378 × £80,000	30,240	110,240
Gain		39,760
Exempt: $\dfrac{\frac{2}{12}+2}{6\frac{6}{12}} \times £39,760$		13,253
Chargeable gain		£26,507

Gains attributable to a period of letting are partially or wholly exempt.[6] This additional relief is available on a letting either of the whole dwelling house or of part of it. The gain which becomes chargeable as a result of the letting is reduced by the smaller of (*a*) the gain attributable to owner-occupation and (*b*) (for disposals on or after 6th April 1983) £20,000.[7] It seems that, in a case where chargeable gains arise as a result of letting and also for some other reason, e.g. house left unoccupied, or partial use for business, the gain resulting from the letting needs to be identified separately. However, there are no provisions setting out how this is to be done.

EXAMPLE

A sells his house on 31st January 1989 for £170,000. The cost on 1st June 1971 was £12,000. The house was let until 30th June 1984, when A occupied it as his private residence. The market value of the house on 31st March 1982 was £67,000 and the indexation factor to January 1989 is 0.397.

Disposal consideration		£170,000
Allowable cost	£67,000	
Indexation allowance: £67,000 × 0.397	26,599	93,599
Gain		76,401
Exempt:		
(*a*) owner occupation		
$£76,401 \times \dfrac{4\frac{7}{12}}{6\frac{10}{12}}$	£51,245	
(*b*) letting (maximum)	20,000	71,245
Chargeable gain		£5,156

Simon's Taxes C3.507; Sumption CGT A16.54.

[1] CGTA 1979, s. 101. The legislation does not say that the ownership must be of the land and it is therefore arguable that the period of ownership is that of the dwellinghouse, a matter of importance where land is bought and a house later built on it.

[2] CGTA 1979, s. 102(2).

[3] CGTA 1979, s. 102(4), as amended by FA 1988, Sch. 8, para. 8. Previously the time apportionment took account of periods falling after 5th April 1965.

[4] CGTA 1979, s. 101(7).

[5] CGTA 1979, s. 103(1); no relief is lost if a room is used exclusively for employment purposes or partly for business purposes and partly for personal use.

[6] FA 1980, s. 80. Distinguish a lodger living as a member of the owner's family, see SP14/80. The letting must be as residential occupation i.e. the persons to whom the accommodation is let must use it as their home. Hotel accommodation does not qualify (*Owen v Elliott* [1989] STC 44).

[7] FA 1984, s. 63. The monetary limit was £10,000 for disposal before 6th April 1983.

15: 14   Certain periods of non-occupation are treated specially, in effect as periods of residence. First, the period of 24 months immediately before disposal is treated as a period of owner occupation.[1] This may benefit owners who move elsewhere but experience difficulty in selling the house. In practice a 12 month period before occupation is also treated as owner occupation if the owner cannot take up residence because the house is being built or repaired.[2]

Certain other periods are treated as periods of residence, provided they are both preceded and followed by periods of occupation[3] and no other residence is eligible for relief during the period of absence. These periods, which may all be claimed in aggregate, are:

(*a*) any period of up to three years,

(*b*) any period of overseas employment[4], and

(*c*) any period not exceeding four years during which the owner could not occupy the house by reason of his place of work or a reasonable condition imposed by his employer that he should reside elsewhere.[5]

Where the period of absence under (*a*) or (*b*) is exceeded, only the excess (not the whole period) is treated as giving rise to a chargeable gain.[6]

Where a person (either an employee or, from 6th April 1983,[7] a self-employed person) lives in job related accommodation, he may claim another house as his residence, provided he intends in due course to occupy it as his only or main residence.[8] In the case of employees, this rule applies to periods after 31 July 1978.

Simon's Taxes C3.504, 507; Sumption CGT A16.53.
[1] CGTA 1979, s. 102(1).
[2] Statement of Practice D4, **Simon's Taxes, Division H3.4.**
[3] Periods of occupation need not *immediately* precede and follow the period of absence, but they must be periods of *actual* occupation, not other qualifying periods of absence. Where on a person's return he is not able to resume occupation because the terms of his employment require him to live elsewhere this condition is treated as satisfied, extra-statutory concession D4 (1988), **Simon's Taxes, Division H2.2.**
[4] Where the house belongs to one spouse and the other is required to go overseas, the condition is treated as satisfied, extra-statutory concession D3 (1988), **Simon's Taxes, Division H2.2.**
[5] CGTA 1979, s. 102(3).
[6] [1983] STI, p. 116, para. 13, and confirmed by the Inland Revenue Technical Division.
[7] FA 1984, s. 25.
[8] CGTA 1979, s. 101(8) amended by FA 1984, s. 25. For earlier periods see less generous Revenue Press Release, 27th September 1973 but note interest deduction case of *Frost v Feltham* [1981] STC 115, supra, § **5: 30**.

15: 15   An individual may only have one exempt residence. If he has more, he may elect which is to be exempt,[1] but only if they are both residences. Thus he could not select a house which he always lets to tenants, although an occasional letting is probably not inconsistent with his residence. Any such election can take effect for a period beginning up to two years before the election is made.[2]

Where a husband and wife live together they are entitled to only one private residence exemption between them and they must jointly make any election.[3] Whether or not the spouses have more than one house a spouse may in determining liability, take advantage of any period during which the house was the main residence of the other.[4] Thus, if the husband dies and devises the main residence to his wife, who does not occupy the house but sells it, say, three years later, she will not be taxed in full on the whole gain since the death, but only on a proportion which takes account of her husband's period of occupation—whether or not she was also in occupation.[4]

Simon's Taxes C3.503, 505; Sumption CGT A16.52.
[1] CGTA 1979, s. 101(5). On relaxation of two year time limit when the interest is of negligible value, see extra-statutory concession D21 (1988), **Simon's Taxes, Division H2.2.**
[2] CGTA 1979, s. 101(5)(*a*). Although the wording of the provision seems clear enough, especially in view of the option to vary an election, the views of inspectors of taxes seem to be that an election is not competent unless made within two years of the date of coming to own a second property.
[3] CGTA 1979, s. 101(6). On separated couples, see extra-statutory concession D6 (1988)— disposal by one spouse of interest in former matrimonial home is treated as falling within CGTA 1979, s. 29 provided the other has continued to live in the house *and* the one has not elected that some other house should be treated as his main residence for this period. The concession is very narrow, and since it encourages the spouses to rearrange their property interests before separation (so that the husband may make an election for some other house) also encourages the taking of hostile acts. This runs counter to much recent family law legislation and contrasts with the CTT and IHT exemption for transfers between spouses.
[4] CGTA 1979, s. 101(7).

Related reliefs

15: 16 An individual or married couple living together may also claim exemption in respect of one private residence which is provided for a dependent relative and without any consideration of any sort rent free.[1] The strictness of the last condition is considerably relaxed by concession.[2] However, for disposals on or after 6th April 1988, the exemption is withdrawn except where the property was the sole residence of a dependent relative on 5th April 1988 or at some earlier time.[3] Where a dependent relative has ceased to occupy the residence, but it is later reoccupied (after 5th April 1988) by that or another dependent relative of the owner, the subsequent period of occupation is ignored in computing the exempt gain. This should not affect disposals prior to 6th April 1990, since the last 24 months will in any event be treated as qualifying occupation.

[1] CGTA 1979, s. 105; on dependent relative see supra, § **3: 21**.
[2] Extra-statutory concession D20 (1988), **Simon's Taxes, Division H2.2**.
[3] FA 1988, s. 111.

15: 17 An exemption may be claimed by trustees if the dwelling house is owned by them[1] and has been the main private residence of one entitled to occupy it under the terms of the trust, or who is allowed by the trustees to occupy it and would be entitled to the income from the house or from the proceeds of sale. When trustees of a discretionary trust in exercise of their discretion allow an object of the trust to occupy the house, the object is entitled to occupy the house under the terms of the trust since he has a right to remain in occupation until asked to leave by the trustees.[2]

By concession the relief applies also to property held by personal representatives but occupied both before and after the death by an individual entitled to an absolute or a limited interest in the proceeds of sale.[3]

Simon's Taxes C3.506.
[1] CGTA 1979, s. 104.
[2] *Sansom v Peay* [1976] STC 494, [1976] 3 All ER 375.
[3] Extra-statutory concession D5 (1988), **Simon's Taxes, Division H2.2**.

Government securities

15: 18 Disposals on or after 2nd July 1986 of listed government securities, or of options or contracts to dispose of or acquire such securities, are exempt from CGT;[1] the accrued income scheme outlined in Chapter 31 applies to most disposals. Between 28th February and 2nd July 1986, the accrued income provisions took priority over CGT.

For disposals before 2nd July 1986, gains on listed government securities were subject to CGT only where the disposal occurred within twelve months of acquisition, but not if the person disposing of them acquired them as legatee or by devolution on death or, if they had been settled property, by becoming absolutely entitled as against the trustee.[2] There was no exemption for options and contracts.

Securities disposed of were identified on a first in, first out basis subject to the securities being identified primarily with those acquired within the twelve months preceding the disposal, rather than with others; within the twelve month period however the first in first out rule applied.[3]

EXAMPLE

On 1st February 1985, X buys £1,000 stock. On 25th February he buys £500 and on 10th March he buys £1,000. On 10th February 1986 he sells £1,000 and on 1st March he sells £500.

(a) Disposal on 10th February 1986:

Identify as follows: (i) £500 with stock acquired on 25th February 1985
(ii) £500 with £500 of stock acquired on 10th March 1985

(b) Disposal on 1st March 1986

Identify as follows: £500 with £500 of stock acquired on 10th March 1985

Subject to the accrued income scheme, both disposals can give rise to chargeable gains or allowable losses.

When a person disposed of a holding of gilt-edged securities and sustained a loss, but then acquired the same securities in the same capacity within one month, the loss was not deductible, save against any chargeable gain accruing on the disposal of the acquired securities.[4] This rule prevented bed and breakfast deals in relation to such securities and was also modified to counter double banking—buying the same amount of the securities and then disposing of the original holding one day later.[5]

The abolition of the twelve month waiting period for indexation relief did not apply to government securities.[6]

Simon's Taxes C2.414; Sumption CGT A10.12, A12.16.

[1] CGTA 1979, s. 67 as substituted by FA 1986, s. 59.

[2] CGTA 1979, s. 67 as originally enacted (there was no exemption from Schedule D, Case VII).

[3] CGTA 1979, s. 68; on disposal to spouse see s. 69.

[4] Six months, if the reacquisition was not through a stock exchange.

[5] CGTA 1979, s. 70.

[6] FA 1985, s. 68(2).

Qualifying corporate bonds

15: 19   Qualifying corporate bonds disposed of on or after 2nd July 1986 are not subject to CGT, and neither chargeable gains nor allowable losses arise.[1] The gain arising on the disposal of an option or contract to acquire or dispose of such securities is also exempt from that date.[2] The accrued income scheme applied to such securities with effect from 28th February 1986.[3]

The CGT rules applicable to gilt-edged securities were extended to qualifying corporate bonds acquired after 13th March 1984—even if issued before that date.[4] As with gilts, the exemption applied only where the securities had been held for more than 12 months or acquired on death or from a settlement.

A qualifying corporate bond is a bond, debenture, debenture stock or loan stock; it may be secured or unsecured. For disposals before 14th March 1989, either the bond itself had to be quoted on a recognised stock exchange in the UK or dealt in on the Unlisted Securities Market or some of the shares or securities of the body making the issue had to be so quoted or dealt in.[5] The bond must be expressed in sterling and there must be no provision for conversion or redemption in any other currency.[6] In addition the debt must represent a normal commercial loan; for this purpose the debt does not qualify if the stock etc is convertible into shares or securities of any different description, or confers the right to acquire further shares or securities, or the rate of interest is linked to the results of the company, business or the value of its assets, or if the amount repayable exceeds the amount lent and is more than is reasonable by comparison with securities in The Stock Exchange Official List.

Where a security falls to be treated as a deep gain security, it is also a qualifying corporate bond, without regard to the date of issue.[7]

The CGT rules as to identification of securities disposed of before 2nd July 1986 are as for gilts.

The CGT exemption did not apply to securities issued by a group company to another member of the group; for this purpose the test of a group is that in TA 1970, s. 272 (see § **26: 19**).

The exemption was restricted to CGT and therefore did not exclude liability to tax on income if the holder is a dealer in securities or if the accrued income scheme in Chapter 31 applies.

Special rules apply for company reorganisations; these cover the situation in which as a result of the reorganisation the bonds become or cease to be qualifying corporate bonds.

The abolition of the 12 month waiting period for indexation relief did not apply to qualifying corporate bonds.[8]

Simon's Taxes C2.419; Sumption CGT A12.17.
[1] FA 1984, s. 64 and Sch 13.
[2] CGTA 1979, s. 67 as substituted by FA 1986, s. 59.
[3] TA 1988, s. 713 (FA 1985, s. 73).
[4] FA 1984, s. 64(4).
[5] The quotation requirement was removed by FA 1989, s. 139(2).
[6] FA 1984 s. 64(2).
[7] FA 1984, s. 64(3A)–(3C), (5A)–(5C).
[8] FA 1985, s. 68(2).

CGT, works of art and maintenance funds

15: 20   Where a transfer qualifies for conditional exemption from IHT infra § **45: 20** there is a similar conditional exemption for CGT; this takes the familiar form of a roll over.[1] This is confined to gifts and certain deemed disposals by trusts.

If the conditional exemption is lost not only will the original CGT become due but there is also a deemed disposal of that and any associated assets at the time of the loss of exemption.[2] The special relief for deferred gains (infra, § **22: 05**) does not apply.

Complete exemption applies to transfers to various approved bodies (e.g. certain museums) and to the Board of Inland Revenue if property is accepted in lieu of tax.[3]

Similar reliefs applied when property was settled on approved maintenance funds;[4] such reliefs were repealed for disposals after 5th April 1984 on the ground that the general right to elect to hold over under FA 1980, s. 79 made them redundant.[5]

Simon's Taxes C3.413–415; Sumption CGT A22.04–06.
  [1] CGTA 1979, s. 147(3) and (4).
  [2] CGTA 1979, s. 147(5).
  [3] CGTA 1979, s. 147(1) and (2).
  [4] CGTA 1979, s. 148.
  [5] FA 1984, s. 68.

Timber

15: 21   No CGT charge arises on the disposal of trees or saleable underwood in respect of woodlands managed by the occupier on a commercial basis and with a view to the realisation of profits.[1] Further, on a disposal of any woodland, such part of acquisition cost—or the disposal consideration—as is attributable to the trees and underwood is disregarded for CGT. This exclusion prevents a taxpayer from buying land, cutting the timber and then claiming a loss due to the decline in value due to the felling.

Simon's Taxes C2.121; Sumption CGT A16.34.
  [1] CGTA 1979, s. 113. Prior to 6th April 1988, the exemption for the disposal of standing timber was applied to woodlands within Schedule B for income tax purposes.

16 Disposal

16: 01 The central concept of disposal is not defined,[1] but nor has it yet caused much reported litigation. It has been suggested that any form of transfer or alienation of the beneficial title to an asset (whether legal or equitable) from one person to another involves a disposal by the one and an acquisition by the other.[2] A disposal by a trustee of shares in the course of administration is clearly a disposal on this definition since beneficial title passes to the purchaser and the fact that the disposer is not himself beneficially entitled is quite irrelevant. A disclaimer appears not to be a disposal since it operates by way of avoidance not disposal.[3]

An exchange of assets is a disposal of each asset involved. An example is the surrender of a lease in exchange for a new one; in order to avoid CGT it is common to grant the new lease subject to the existing lease and perhaps increasing the rent under the existing lease.[4]

There is no general exclusion for involuntary disposals.[5]

On partnership assets see, infra, § **20: 19**.

The concept of disposal is extended to certain deemed disposals and by treating certain shifts of economic value as disposals even though no asset is disposed of—see infra, § **16: 22**.

In deciding what is the subject matter of a disposal undertaken in steps as part of a scheme, it is permissible to look at the effect of the whole scheme.[6] So in *Furniss v Dawson*[7] a disposal by X of shares in Company A to Company B, followed by a disposal by Company B to Company C of the same shares, was treated as a disposal by X to Company C in return for consideration paid to Company B (see § **1.09**). The fiscal effects of the intermediate transfer are suppressed because the transfer was made purely to avoid tax.

Simon's Taxes C1.107; Sumption CGT A1.06.

[1] Contrast TA 1988, s. 776(4) and TA 1988, s. 777(2), (3). See *Turner v Follet* [1973] STC 148, 48 TC 614, where the CA made extremely heavy weather of the point if the definition in the text is right. A loan is not a disposal but a loan must be distinguished from a gift, see *Dewar v Dewar* [1975] 2 All ER 728. On switching between different unit trusts in a multi-portfolio see F(No. 2)A 1987, s. 78 and Inland Revenue Press Release 17th March 1987, STI, p. 200.

[2] The Revenue definition is "An asset is disposed of whenever its ownership changes or whenever the owner divests himself of his rights or interests over that asset, for example, by sale, exchange or gift". CGT 8 § 108.

[3] *Re Paradise Motor Co Ltd* [1968] 2 All ER 625.

⁴ On problems see *Bayley v Rogers* [1980] STC 544.
⁵ But note CGTA 1979, s. 61 (bankruptcy not a disposal but acts of trustee treated as acts of bankrupt) and ss. 110 and 111 (compulsory purchase-disposal).
⁶ *W T Ramsay Ltd v IRC* [1981] STC 174, [1981] 1 All ER 865, particularly so far as it approves dicta of Eveleigh LJ in *Floor v Davis* [1978] STC 436, [1978] 2 All ER 1079.
⁷ [1984] STC 153, [1984] 1 All ER 530, HL.

TIMING—CONTRACTS AND COMPULSORY PURCHASE

16: 02   Where an asset is disposed of and acquired under a contract, the time at which the disposal and acquisition take place is the time the contract is made and not, if different, the date of conveyance.¹ Thus the usual time will be that at which the acceptance reaches the offeror, subject to the rules as to postal acceptance. The general rule applies only when the disposal takes place *under* the contract; whether this is so is a question of fact.²

The contract is conditional then the disposal occurs when the condition is satisfied; condition here means something on which the existence of the contract depends rather than a major contractual term.³

The rule just stated deals with the timing of the disposal when an asset is transferred under a contract and does not answer the question whether the contract itself is the disposal. This question is of importance for three reasons. First, the rule applies only when the asset is conveyed or transferred and so does not expressly deal with the contract which is not completed. Where a deposit is forfeited the forfeiture is not treated as the disposal of an asset⁴ but the contract itself will be treated as a part disposal of the asset if it creates an interest in or right over the asset,⁵ a matter which presumably turns on whether equity could order specific performance of the contract. If however the specifically enforceable contract is itself the disposal then the Revenue may be able to ignore the subsequent ending of the contract and so charge CGT both on the original part disposal and the subsequent ending of the equitable interest. This, however, is unlikely. Secondly, there is the problem of when the tax is due. Thus if in 1988 A made a contract to sell with completion in 1993 can the Revenue demand payment of the gains tax in 1988? If the contract itself is not the disposal then presumably the Revenue may argue that they are entitled to treat the 1988 transaction as a part disposal and then when the contract is completed in 1993 relate the completion back to 1988. This, however, is only partly sound. The postponed completion date does not render the contract conditional so the completed contract will give rise to gains chargeable in 1988 but the postponement means that equity could not order specific performance so that there can be no part disposal in 1988.⁶ If however the contract is itself the disposal then the Revenue can insist that there is a chargeable disposal in 1988 and so demand its tax.⁷ Thirdly, the rule is not retroactive.⁸

In view of the practical difficulties raised it seems preferable to reject the notion that the contract is itself a disposal whether or not the contract is specifically enforceable. It follows that when property is disposed of under an unconditional contract of sale, the disposition takes place under the contract and that when the contract is not followed by a disposal it is not open to anyone to treat the contract itself as a part disposal.⁹

Simon's Taxes C1.412; Sumption CGT A1.10.
[1] CGTA 1979, s. 27 even if the contract is unenforceable—*Thompson v Salah* [1972] 1 All ER 530, 47 TC 559 (Schedule D, Case VII).

[2] *Magnavox Electronics Co Ltd v Hall* [1986] STC 561, CA; see also the discussion of the phrase "in pursuance of" in *IRC v Mobil North Sea Ltd* [1987] STC 458.

[3] As in *Pym v Campbell* (1806) 6 E & B 370. The phraseology does not obviously apply to a condition subsequent—*semble* that such a contract would give rise to a disposal only when it is clear that the condition cannot occur, see also *Eastham v Leigh, London and Provincial Properties Ltd* [1971] Ch 871, [1971] 2 All ER 887 (Schedule D, Case VII). On difficulties see *Lipmans Wallpaper Ltd v Mason and Hodghton Ltd* [1969] 1 Ch 20, [1968] 1 All ER 1123.

[4] CGTA 1979, s. 137(8).

[5] CGTA 1979 s. 19(2).

[6] The forfeited deposit will be taxed neither on forfeiture nor on the grant of the option.

[7] Generally it will be the Revenue insisting on the disposal being treated as taking place as early as possible but this will not always be so—e.g. there might be a loss on the transaction which can therefore be rolled forward to 1989 but not back from 1993 supra, § **14: 02**.

[8] *Johnson v Edwards* [1981] STC 660.

[9] Cf. forfeiture of a deposit, s. 137(8).

Hire purchase

16: 03 Where a person acquires an asset under a contract of hire purchase, the transaction is treated as if it amounted to an entire disposal of the asset to that person at the beginning.[1] If the period terminates, but the property in the asset does not pass to him, all necessary adjustments are made. The implication appears to be that the disposal and acquisition deemed to have occurred at the outset are then treated as not having taken place, so that the hirer is not treated as disposing of the asset when his interest terminates. However, he may be treated as having disposed of his rights under the contract, depending upon the circumstances.

The legislation does not say how the disposal consideration is to be valued. However, the Revenue practice in hire purchase cases is to divide the total of the rent and purchase price into capital and interest elements, and tax only the latter as income. If this is followed, the capital element will be the purchase price rather than the sum payable under the option.[2] In practice the asset will probably either be a car,[3] a wasting chattel or a chattel whose cost is less than £6,000, so that the problem may not arise often.

Sumption CGT A18.01.
[1] CGTA 1979, s. 24.

[2] Infra, § **16: 15**.

[3] As in *Lyon v Pettigrew* [1985] STC 369 where the vehicle was a taxi but a chargeable gain arose in respect of consideration paid for the licence.

Compulsory purchase

16: 04 When land is acquired under compulsory purchase powers, the disposal and acquisition are treated as taking place when the compensation for the acquisition is agreed or otherwise determined (variations on appeal being disregarded for this purpose) or, if earlier, the time when the authority enter on the land in pursuance of their powers.[1] This general rule does not apply if the purchase is made under a contract, the normal contract rule applying here.

On treatment of compensation see SP 8/79.[2] Where land is disposed of by being compulsorily purchased after 5th April 1982, any gain realised on the disposal may be rolled over and deducted from the acquisition cost of replacement land.[3] If the rollover occurred before 6th April 1988, there is relief for the deferred gain (see § **22: 06**, infra).

The relief applies where the disposal consideration is spent on the purchase of land and the compulsory purchase was truly compulsory.[4] Relief is not available if, at any time within the next six years, the new land or any part of it qualifies for exemption from CGT under the rules for only or main residence of the owner or a dependent relative.[5] If only a part of the proceeds are reinvested, the relief is available only to the extent that the part not reinvested is less than the gain, i.e. to the extent that the gain element has to be used.[6] The reinvestment must be within a period of four years beginning twelve months before the disposal.[7]

If the payment includes compensation for severance or injurious affectation to other land which is retained, there may be a part disposal under s. 110(2). Roll over relief under s. 111A excludes gains arising on a part disposal under s. 110.[8]

If the new interest is a depreciatory asset, the rules in CGTA 1979, s. 117 apply.[9]

Sumption CGT A16.41–47.
[1] CGTA 1979, ss. 110 and 111.
[2] Simon's Taxes, Division H3.2.
[3] CGTA 1979, s. 111A as inserted by FA 1982, s.83.
[4] CGTA 1979, s. 111A(1)(b).
[5] CGTA 1979, s. 111B as inserted by FA 1982, s. 83.
[6] CGTA 1979, s. 111A(3).
[7] CGTA 1979, s. 111A(5).
[8] CGTA 1979, s. 111A(6).
[9] CGTA 1979, s. 111B(3).

Exchange of joint interests

16: 05   Where A and B are joint beneficial owners of a piece of land and they exchange their interests so that each becomes sole owner of part, a strict analysis said that each had made a disposal to the other of his interest in the part, the other now owned solely.[1] By concession the provisions just outlined with regard to roll-over or compulsory purchase apply in this situation also. The concession also applies where a number of separate holdings of land are held jointly and each person becomes sole owner of one or more holdings.[2] The concession applies to exchanges after 19th December 1984.

Where the property is a dwelling house and so the only or main residence exemption may apply, the concession will only be given if each individual accepts that he acquires the other person's interest at its original base cost and on the original date of acquisition.

---

[1] Doubt may have been cast on this analysis by the judgment in *Jenkins v Brown* [1989] STI 436, where a disposal was held not to have occurred on a distribution of land holdings out of a

pool held by trustees. It was held that the measure of the beneficial interests of the settlors was unaffected by the trust.

[2] [1984] STI, p. 793. The calculations are complex.

DISPOSAL WITHOUT ACQUISITION

16: 06   There may be a disposal of assets by their owner even though no asset is acquired by anyone else, for example, if the owner of the asset receives a capital sum which is derived from the asset.[1] This rule is stated to apply "in particular" to four types of capital sum. It follows that these four are not exhaustive of the general principle and may have effect whether or not the general principle applies.[2] However, the rule does require that the asset should have been owned by the person treated as disposing of them.[2] A mere spes cannot be owned, and so cannot be an asset.

On a sale of shares for a cash sum plus the right to receive a further sum to be computed by reference to future, unpredictable events, the right to receive the future sum is itself an asset.[3] Such a right is not a debt (supra, § **15: 06**). When the events occur and the further sum is paid that sum is derived from the right to receive the sum and so there is a disposal of that asset. This is so whether or not the person paying the capital sum acquires any asset.[4]

The requirement that the capital[5] sum must be derived from an asset applies to each of the four types; a sum derived from some other source is not caught by these rules.[6] So sums payable under the Agricultural Holdings Act 1986 to an agricultural tenant for disturbance on the surrender of his tenancy[6] or under the Landlord and Tenant Act 1954 to a business tenant for like loss,[7] are not subject to CGT, because the sums are payable under the Acts by way of compensation for various types of loss and expense and are not sums derived from the lease. Compensation under an Order in Council for expropriation of an asset by a foreign government has been held liable to CGT[8] because, inter alia, the right to compensation was an independent property right whereas the right under the Agricultural Holdings Act was a claim against the pocket of the landlord for expense which the tenant was deemed already to have met.

Where a person received a capital sum in settlement of an action for negligence against solicitors in relation to a conveyancing matter concerning particular properties, it was held that the charge to CGT stemmed from the right to sue and not from the properties concerned and thus was not a part disposal of those properties.[9]

A sum received for entering into a restrictive covenant, in connection with the sale of shares in subsidiary companies, has been held not to be as such a capital sum derived from an asset, because the freedom to engage in the activities concerned is not an asset.[10] However, on appeal, it was held that the sum in question was received in part for agreeing not to exploit the goodwill attaching to the group.[11]

Compensation for the release of an option to participate in a development has been held taxable under this head.[12] The fact that another provision[13] states that the abandonment of an option is not the disposal of an asset was irrelevant.

Simon's Taxes C1.404; Sumption CGT A1.09.
¹ CGTA 1979, s. 20.
² *Davenport v Chilver* [1983] STC 426.
³ *Marren v Ingles* [1980] STC 500, [1980] 3 All ER 95.
⁴ Reversing *IRC v Montgomery* [1975] STC 182 at 189. As to "earn-out" sales where the deferred consideration takes the form of shares, see § **19: 17**, infra.
⁵ *Lang v Rice* [1984] STC 172.
⁶ *Davies v Powell* [1977] STC 32, [1977] 1 All ER 471.
⁷ *Drummond v Austin Brown* [1984] STC 321; this distinguished at 325 a sum paid by a landlord in return for the surrender of the "fag end" of a lease. It was also important that the landlord was entitled to possession. *Quaere* whether the sum was a trading receipt, see supra, § **7: 75**.
⁸ *Davenport v Chilver* [1983] STC 426, although in this case liability was virtually escaped because the new right was deemed to have been acquired for market value. The position would now be different as a result of CGTA 1979, s. 29A, infra, § **16: 23**.
⁹ *Zim Properties Ltd v Procter* [1985] STC 90.
¹⁰ *Kirby v Thorn EMI plc* [1986] STC 200.
¹¹ [1987] STC 621.
¹² *Powlson v Welbeck Securities Ltd* [1986] STC 423; affd. [1987] STI, p. 425, CA.
¹³ CGTA 1979, s. 137(4).

(a) and (b) Compensation and insurance payments

16: 07   If capital sums are received by way of compensation for any kind of damage or injury to or loss of or depreciation of assets, there is a disposal of those assets, and so a consequent gain or loss by reference to the acquisition cost of those assets. These words are of wide effect and are not limited to physical damage.¹ A similar rule applies to sums received under a policy of insurance of the risk of any kind of damage or injury to, or the loss or depreciation of, assets. Thus, if a trader loses a capital asset by fire and recovers under his insurance policy, there is a disposal of the asset even though the insurance company does not acquire it.

This rule applies only where the sum is a capital as opposed to an income payment.

Compensation or damages received as the result of a Court action, or by negotiated settlement of such an action, is a disposal of the right of action and is subject to CGT.² In most cases, the base cost of the rights will be nil where they came into being on or after 10th March 1981.³ This is so even if the compensation or damages relates to an underlying asset. However, the Revenue have issued a concession under which compensation or damages will be treated as relating to the underlying asset where the right of action arises because of total or partial loss of or damage to the asset.⁴ Thus, the base cost of the asset will be available to compute any chargeable gain, and the various replacement and reinstatement reliefs may be claimed. Where there is no underlying asset, e.g. in a case involving damages for professional negligence resulting in expense to the plaintiff, any gain is by concession treated as exempt. Payments made under a contractual warranty or indemnity are not regarded as affected by the *Zim Properties* case and will reduce the purchaser's acquisition cost.

Sums obtained by way of compensation or damages for any wrong or injury suffered by an individual in their person or in their profession or vocation are not chargeable gains.⁵

A problem arises if the assets are destroyed, and not just damaged, in that whilst the receipt of the capital sum is treated as a disposal, the destruction of the asset is also treated as a disposal.[6] The logical result is that if the destruction should occur in one year and the receipt in the next year, loss relief should be given immediately and there should be a taxable sum accruing on receipt. The Revenue view is that if no sum is received the disposal occurs at the time of the destruction but that if a payment subsequently accrues the disposal takes place at the time of the receipt.[7]

On loss of value as a disposal, see supra, § **14: 02**.

Simon's Taxes C1.404, 407; Sumption CGT A1.09.
[1] *Davenport v Chilver* [1983] STC 426.
[2] *Zim Properties Ltd v Procter* [1985] STC 90.
[3] CGTA 1979, s. 29A(2); infra, § **16: 23**.
[4] Statement of Practice SP 1/89; **Simon's Taxes, Division H3.2.**
[5] CGTA 1979, s. 21.
[6] CGTA 1979, s. 22.
[7] IR Leaflet CGT 8 (1980), § 230 (now withdrawn). Compare *Williams v Bullivant* supra, § **14.02.**

Restoration and replacement reliefs

16: 08   In the absence of special provisions, compensation or insurance payments for damage to assets would be treated for CGT as part disposals. However, if the sum is wholly (or all but a small sum which is not needed for the purpose) applied in restoring the asset, the receipt is not to be treated as a disposal.[1] If the restored asset is later disposed of, the sums received are deducted from the allowable expenditure. If only a part of the sum is so used that part will be deducted from allowable expenditure on a subsequent disposal but the remainder will be treated as consideration for a part disposal of the asset.[2]

> EXAMPLE
> A picture cost T £6,000 in 1977. In 1988 the picture, then worth £20,000 was damaged in a fire and T incurred £1,200 in restoration costs. T received £1,200 under his insurance policy. This can be treated as a disposal of the asset; however A may instead claim that it should not be so treated, in which case the allowable expenditure on the picture (which includes the cost of restoration) will be reduced by £1,200 if he later sells the picture or otherwise disposes of it. If, however, he recovers £2,500 the part spent in restoration (£1,200) will be treated as just outlined while the balance of £1,300 will be taxed at once.

If the asset is lost or destroyed, there is relief from CGT on replacement. The compensation or insurance payment received must be applied in acquiring a replacement asset within one year of the receipt or such longer period as the Inspector may allow.[3] The consideration for the disposal is then treated as such that neither gain nor loss accrues. The acquisition cost of the new asset is then reduced by the excess of the compensation (plus scrap value, if any) over the deemed consideration for disposal of the old asset. The reduction can be greater than the chargeable gain where not all of the gain would have been chargeable.

> EXAMPLE
> A acquired an asset for £10,000. He spent a further £2,000 on it. It was destroyed in an accident caused by B's negligence and has a scrap value of £500. B pays £15,000 damages. The replacement asset costs £16,000. The disposal is treated as taking place at £12,000

(ignoring indexation). The new asset is treated as being acquired at £16,000 less £15,000 − (£10,000 + £2,000); i.e. £3,000 and less the scrap value giving a revised cost of £12,500.

If the asset is lost and only a part of the sum is used to replace it, there is some relief, provided the part unspent is less than the amount of the gain.[4] In other words, postponement of tax liability is available only to the extent that it is necessary to make use of the gain in the replacement. Relief may be available in respect of compensation applied in replacement or partial replacement before 6th April 1988 (see § **22: 05**, infra).

Three items of warning. First, this relief in effect allows the taxpayer to postpone his tax liability, not escape it, unless perhaps he can later take advantage of an exemption such as that on retirement. Secondly, these rules do not apply to wasting assets.[5] Thirdly, the relief is expressed to be limited to an owner of property.[6]

When a building is destroyed or irreparably damaged, it is by concession treated as an asset separate from the land.[7]

Simon's Taxes C1.404, 407; Sumption CGT A21.06.

[1] CGTA 1979, s. 21(1).
[2] CGTA 1979, s. 21(3).
[3] CGTA 1979, s. 21(4).
[4] CGTA 1979, s. 21(5).
[5] CGTA 1979, s. 21(7).
[6] Insurance proceeds received by the lessee of land are by concession exempt if accepted by the lessee in discharging an obligation to restore damage to property; extra-statutory concession D1(1985), **Simon's Taxes, Division H2.2**.
[7] Extra-statutory concession, D19(1988), **Simon's Taxes, Division H2.2**.

(c) Forfeiture or surrender of rights

16: 09   Capital sums received by a person in return for forfeiture or surrender of rights e.g. the surrender of a lease, or for refraining from exercising rights are taxable. Thus a sum received for the release of a restrictive covenant or for an agreement not to sue on a contract would be chargeable events. It has been said that it is not possible to use s. 20 to widen the scope of the term "assets".[1] So, according to this view, no charge arises when a sum is received for the surrender of something which is not an asset; e.g. the right to play amateur rugby as in *Jarrold v Boustead*, supra, § **6: 35**. Nor does a charge arise when the asset surrendered is an exempt asset; e.g. a life interest under a settlement, or a debt. However, uncertainty has been revived as a result of the decision of Nourse J in *Davenport v Chilver*[2] to the effect that the individual heads (*a*)–(*d*) in s. 20 can apply whether or not the general words at the beginning of s. 20 are satisfied. Following this view, it is enough to show that a sum has been derived from the forfeiture or surrender of a right and it follows that the term "right" must be defined by reference to things which can be surrendered, forfeited or not exercised, but again the failure of the draftsman to be precise causes difficulty. Thus the right to play amateur rugby is such a right and so, on this basis, the sums paid in *Jarrold v Boustead* could be taxable as a capital gain and, since the acquisition cost was presumably nil, the whole sum appears to be chargeable. However the freedom to engage in business has been held not to be an asset for s. 20.[3]

It should not be forgotten that if the owner of a right over an asset releases it, there is a disposal even though he receives no consideration.[4]

Simon's Taxes C1.403, 404; Sumption CGT A1.09.
[1] *O'Brien v Benson's Hosiery (Holdings) Ltd* [1978] 3 All ER 1057, [1978] STC 549, CA.
[2] [1983] STC 426.
[3] *Kirby v Thorn EMI plc* [1986] STC 200. This judgment was overturned on appeal, [1987] STC 621, but the Court of Appeal affirmed that freedom to engage in business is not an asset for CGT purposes.
[4] The disposal will be treated as taking place at market value if done gratuitously, infra, § **16: 22**.

(d) Use of assets

16: 10 Capital sums received for the use or exploitation of assets are also caught. Thus a sum received in return for the right to exploit a copyright or to use the goodwill created by that person would be caught, including perhaps the part disposal resulting from a restriction on one's trading activities as in *Higgs v Olivier*.[1]

Simon's Taxes C1.404.
[1] Supra, § **7: 74**.

MORTGAGES AND BANKRUPTCY

16: 11 A mortgage is in essence a security for a debt so neither a conveyance or transfer by way of security nor a retransfer on redemption of the security is treated as involving any acquisition or disposal.[1]

Any dealing with the asset by the mortgagee for the purpose of giving effect to the security is treated as an act by a nominee of the mortgagor. So a sale by him will be a disposal by the mortgagor.[2]

An asset is treated as passing free of the security. When an asset is acquired subject to a security, the value of any liability taken over by the acquirer is treated as part of the consideration; a converse rule applies on disposal.[3] So if X buys an asset for £3,000, subject to a mortgage of £7,000, he is treated as buying it for £10,000 and if he sells it for £5,000 still subject to the mortgage and not having reduced that mortgage, his consideration on disposal will be £12,000—a gain of £2,000.

When a vendor disposes of land, grants a mortgage to the purchaser and later recovers possession on default by the purchaser, the original disposal is, by concession, undone.[4]

Simon's Taxes C1.418; Sumption CGT A1.14.
[1] CGTA 1979, s. 23(1). On what is a mortgage, see *Beattie v Jenkinson* [1971] 3 All ER 495, 47 TC 121 (a decision on Case VII). Since 1925 a mortgage of freehold land does not end by retransfer but by cesser of the mortgagee's leasehold interest. One must presume that the draftsman's error would be corrected by any court.
[2] CGTA 1979, s. 23(2).
[3] CGTA 1979, s. 23(3). This rule is stated to apply where the liability is assumed by the acquirer. Emmet, *op. cit.*, points out that an assignee of a mortgagor does not *assume* the liability,

Waring v Ward (1802) 7 Ves 332; however, technical arguments have not found great favour with the courts, e.g. *Pexton v Bell* infra, § **18: 13**.
   [4] Extra-statutory concession, D18(1988), **Simon's Taxes, Division H2.2**.

16: 12   Just as the mortgagee's acts are treated as those of the mortgagor, so the acts of a trustee in bankruptcy are treated as those of the bankrupt.[1] However, the trustee in bankruptcy is assessable for the tax.[2]

Sumption CGT A8.01.
   [1] CGTA 1979, s. 61.
   [2] *Re McMeekin* [1974] STC 429, 48 TC 725 (QBD, NI).

PART DISPOSALS

16: 13   There is a part disposal where, on a person making the disposal, any description of property derived from the asset remains undisposed of.[1] This very wide definition presumably refers only to beneficial property so that a declaration of trust over an asset would give rise to a total rather than a part disposal. There is a part disposal when an interest or right in or over an asset is created by the disposal, as well as where it subsists before the disposal. For example, a sum derived from the grant of an easement is a part disposal. The grant of a contractual licence does not appear to give any interest or right in or over the land, but the grant of a licence is equated with the grant of a lease[2] and is presumably a part disposal.

A general problem is the relationship between a part disposal and a complete disposal. Thus the grant of an option is a total disposal of the option,[3] but it may also be a part disposal of the asset over which the option is created if this creates a property right in the holder of this option, e.g. an estate contract. The matter is of importance since the basis of computing the gain are quite different. However, it has now been held that the grant of an option over land is not treated as a part disposal since, although the option creates an interest in land, special computational rules apply—infra, § **16: 18**. Technically, the grant of an option in such cases is a part disposal but the only practical consequence (the rule of computation) is excluded.[4]

Another unresolved problem is that of the sale and leaseback. It is quite unclear whether this is to be treated as two disposals or as one part disposal; on balance the former seems preferable.

Simon's Taxes C1.413; Sumption CGT A1.07.
   [1] CGTA 1979, s. 19(2).
   [2] CGTA 1979, Sch. 3, para. 10.
   [3] CGTA 1979, s. 137(1).
   [4] *Strange v Openshaw* [1983] STC 416.

16: 14   If there is a part disposal, the proportion of the acquisition cost attributable to the part disposed of is $A/(A + B)$, where A is the consideration for the disposal and B is the market value of the remainder.[1]

EXAMPLE

X purchased a house and grounds for £20,000 in 1972. He occupied the house as a holiday home but in November 1988, he sold part of the grounds for development, receiving £100,000. The market value of the house and remaining land is then £180,000. The market value of the whole at 31st March 1982 was £60,000 (indexation factor 0.385).

Disposal consideration	£100,000
Allowable cost:	

$$£60,000 \times \frac{£100,000}{£100,000 + £180,000} = £21,429$$

Indexation allowance:		
0.385 × £21,429	=	8,250 29,679
Chargeable gain		£70,321

The incidental costs of the part disposal are attributable solely to the part disposed of. It should also be borne in mind that the formula is applied only to those costs common to the part disposed of and the part retained. There is no apportionment of expenditure which, on the facts, is wholly attributable to either the part disposed of or that retained.[2] In practice the formula is not strictly applied on the disposal of quoted shares in a pool, the costs being apportioned simply pro rata to the number of shares disposed of.[3]

In the case of a part disposal before 6th April 1988 of an asset owned on 31st March 1982, the expenditure apportioned under the formula would be the original expenditure or, where relevant the market value at 6th April 1965. If a further disposal or part disposal of the remaining asset occurs on or after 6th April 1988, the expenditure treated as relating to the remainder at the date of the first part disposal is recomputed by reference to the 31st March 1982 market value of the whole asset.[4] This is not necessarily the same result as rebasing the part undisposed of to its separate value at 31st March 1982.

Simon's Taxes C2.134; Sumption CGT A4.09.
[1] CGTA 1979, s. 35.
[2] CGTA 1979, s. 35(4).
[3] IR Leaflet CGT 8 (1980) para 152 (now withdrawn).
[4] FA 1988, Sch. 8, para. 4.

16: 15 The practical disadvantage of the part-disposal rule is that market value needs to be determined. Particularly in the case of land, this may be a very expensive process. However, where it is possible for a disposal out of a land holding to be treated as a separate asset, in practice any fair and reasonable method of attributing a part of the total cost to it will be accepted.[1]

In addition there are two statutory provisions. First, if there is a part disposal of land to an authority with compulsory powers and the amount or value of the consideration is small in comparison with the market value of the remainder,[2] there is deemed to be no disposal but the sum received will be treated as arising on the occasion of some subsequent disposal of the land. The effect is to defer liability until the next disposal. Secondly, the same postponement of tax is allowed if the taxpayer so wishes when the consideration for the part disposal of land, is no more than 20% of the market value of the total holding, no matter who the acquirer is, provided that the total consideration received for the part disposal or from any other disposal (part or total) of land does not exceed, for disposals on or after 6th April 1983, £20,000.[3]

It is also necessary to distinguish a part disposal from a total disposal when dealing with assets acquired before 6th April 1965. An election for market value on that date on the occasion of a part disposal is binding on a subsequent disposal of the remainder whereas an election in regard to one asset does not affect the position on another, separate asset.[4]

Simon's Taxes C1.414; C3.803; Sumption CGT A16.46.

[1] Statement of Practice D1, **Simon's Taxes, Division H3.4.**

[2] CGTA 1979, s. 108. "Small" is in practice treated as meaning 5% or less. (CCAB Press Release, June 1965).

[3] CGTA 1979, s. 107; FA 1984, s. 63(2) and FA 1986, s. 60. For disposals before 6th April 1986, the consideration had to be small compared to the value of the retained land (see footnote 2, supra).

[4] CGTA 1979, Sch. 5, para. 12(4). The ability to make an election for 6th April 1965 value has not been removed by the rebasing of CGT to 31st March 1982, since the gain or loss has still to be computed under the former rules: see § **22: 02, 09,** infra.

16: 16   The question whether there is a part disposal or a total disposal of a separate asset is one of fact. According to the Revenue, a single acquisition normally continues to be regarded as a single asset although this presumption can be displaced. Where a block of small let properties is acquired, of a size which can conveniently be held as an investment, it normally continues to be regarded as a single asset although in practice the Revenue will allow the taxpayer to treat a disposal of one (or more) houses as separate disposals so that the cost can be attributed according to the available evidence rather than according to the formula.[1]

Simon's Taxes C1.413.

[1] Revenue Statement of Practice **Simon's Taxes, Division D1, H3.4.**

Part disposals and leases

16: 17   A number of events are treated as part disposals. These include the charge of a premium on the granting of a lease,[1] the payment of sums on the commutation of rent or the surrender of a lease[2] (provided the sums are payable under the terms of the lease) and payments by a tenant on the variation or waiver of any terms of the lease.[3] These events are defined in terms similar to TA 1988, s. 34(1), (4) and (5) (see supra, §§ **9: 18, 9: 22** and **9: 23**). It will be seen that there is no part disposal where the event falls within TA 1988, s. 34(2). A premium is also treated as paid where the landowner develops land and receives payments in respect of building costs from a person entering into a lease of the land.[4] On computation see infra, § **21: 16**.

Simon's Taxes C1.413; C2.601, 609; Sumption CGT A18.03.

[1] CGTA 1979, Sch. 3, para 2; on assets other than land see para 9.

[2] CGTA 1979, Sch. 3, para. 3(2).

[3] CGTA 1979, Sch. 3, para. 3(3).

[4] *Clarke v United Real (Moorgate) Ltd* [1988] STC 273.

OPTIONS

16: 18   An option is an asset for CGT. Although, on general principles, the grant of an option may be a part disposal,[1] this is overridden by a special rule providing that the grant is a disposal of the option.[2] Further, where the option is exercised, the grant and the exercise are treated as one transaction;[3] the disposal is treated as taking place when the option is exercised.[4] The term option includes the right binding the grantor to grant a lease at a premium or any other transaction other than a sale.[5] The *expressio unius* rule of construction suggests that an option to grant a lease at a rack rent is not within the general rules.

If the contract binds the grantor to sell, the sum paid by the grantee to the grantor for that option will be added to the sums paid on exercise of the option, to ascertain the consideration for the transaction. The exercise of the option is not a disposal of the option.[6] Conversely, if the contract binds the grantor to *buy*, any sums paid to the grantor for the option will be deducted from the sum paid under the option. The rule also means that a sale cannot be carried out in two stages by option and exercise so as to take advantage of the annual exemption. However, for the purposes of the indexation allowance,[7] the cost of the option is treated as an expense separate from the price paid for the option.

If the option is abandoned, the grant of the option will stand as a disposal and any sums received by the grantor will be a capital gain.[8] As regards the grantee, the abandonment is not a disposal and no allowable loss can arise. Exceptions allow loss relief if the option is to acquire business assets or is a traded option[9] (whether quoted on a recognised stock exchange or on the London International Financial Futures Exchange or purchased over the counter[10]). Although abandonment is not a disposal, other events (not involving exercise) can be disposals, e.g. where the grantee receives a sum for the surrender of the option,[11] and a gain or loss can arise accordingly.

Where a deposit has been paid in contemplation of a proposed purchase but it is later forfeited, the matter is treated as the grant and abandonment of an option to purchase, thus making the recipient liable to CGT but the payer unable to claim a loss.[12] This applies even where the article which is subject to the option is an exempt asset. The legislation does not appear to cope with the problems that arise when the option is exercised but the consequent contract is not completed.

Simon's Taxes C2.202, 501, 505, 506; Sumption CGT A20.
   [1] *Strange v Openshaw* [1983] STC 416, supra, § **16: 13**.
   [2] CGTA 1979, s. 137(1).
   [3] CGTA 1979, s. 137(2).
   [4] CGTA 1979, s. 27(2) but special rules apply for indexation allowance, see FA 1982, Sch. 13, para. 7 and FA 1985, Sch. 19, para. 15.
   [5] CGTA 1979, s. 137(7). *Quaere* a right of pre-emption as in *Thomas v Rose* [1968] 3 All ER 765, [1968] 1 WLR 1797.
   [6] CGTA 1979, s. 137(3).
   [7] Infra, § **21: 26**.
   [8] CGTA 1979, s. 137(1). On deductions, see infra, § **21: 03**.
   [9] CGTA 1979, s. 137(4) and FA 1984, s. 65. This rule also applies to options on the FT–SE 100 Index ([1984] STI, p. 387). The term traded option includes a quoted option to subscribe for shares so that s. 137(4)(*a*) is now otiose. Financial options are included by F(No. 2)A 1987, s. 81(5) from a date to be fixed by statutory instrument.

[10] F(No. 2)A 1987, s. 73.
[11] *Golding v Kaufman* [1985] STC 152. See also *Welbeck Securities Ltd v Powlson* [1987] STC 468, CA, where a capital gain was held to arise on the receipt of consideration for agreeing to abandon an option.
[12] CGTA 1979, s. 137(8). Does this apply to land?—Baxter, *loc. cit.* at p. 248.

16: 19   An option is a wasting asset and the rules restricting the deduction of expenditure apply. The costs are written off over the life of the option, which means the period during which the option is exercisable, or, if sooner, until it becomes valueless. This restricts the amount of loss deductible. If the option is exercised, it appears that the full amount paid for the grant is added to (or deducted from) the amount payable on exercise, without writing off any amount up to the date of exercise. These wasting rules do not, however, apply to options to acquire business assets nor to traded options.[1] A quoted option to subscribe for shares can be treated as part of the new holding if it follows a reorganisation, reduction, conversion or amalgamation.[2]

Simon's Taxes C2.507–511; Sumption CGT A20.03.
[1] CGTA 1979, s. 138 and supra, § **15: 08** on scope of "traded options" see supra, § **16: 18**, n. 9.
[2] CGTA 1979, s. 139.

GIFTS, BARGAINS NOT AT ARM'S LENGTH AND OTHER GRATUITOUS TRANSACTIONS

16: 20   The CGT legislation sometimes talks of gifts, and sometimes of bargains not at arm's length; it also refers to disposals to a connected person. If the term gift is used it is a question of construction whether a sale at a price below market value is included.

A gift is a disposal.[1] Further, when a person acquires an asset otherwise than by way of a bargain made at arm's length and in particular where he acquires it by way of gift or on a transfer into a settlement, he is deemed to acquire it at market value.[2] For situations in which market value is not to be taken see infra, § **16: 23**.

Where the tax due was not paid by the donor it can be recovered from the donee.[3]

A bargain at arm's length is not defined; it may be that the presence of any non-commercial factor, ulterior motive or object may be a bargain otherwise than at arm's length, perhaps even a contract at a price dictated by one party's tax position or even moral obligation.[4]

Simon's Taxes C1.205, 428; Sumption CGT A1.12.
[1] *Turner v Follett* [1973] STC 148, 48 TC 614; a disposal by donatio mortis causa is exempt-CGTA 1979, s. 49(5).
[2] CGTA 1979, s. 29A, replacing CGTA 1979, s. 19(3) for acquisitions after 9th March 1981.
[3] CGTA 1979, s. 59.
[4] See Goulding J in *Clark v Follett* (1973) 48 TC 677 at 702–4; *quaere* whether the sale in *Jacgilden*, supra, § **7: 157**, would come within this rule.

Holding over

16: 21 CGT on a gift may be deferred in certain circumstances if the transferor and transferee so elect. If both parties agree, the chargeable gain otherwise accruing to the transferor is reduced by the amount of the "held over gain".[1] The reduction also reduces the donee's acquisition cost. This relief applies to bargains not at arms length and not just to gifts stricto sensu; where the consideration paid exceeds the transferor's base cost the held-over gain is reduced by that excess.

> **EXAMPLE**
>
> A owns land which cost £10,000 in 1978. The value on 31st March 1982 was £15,000. A gives the land to his daughter B in 1988 when its value is £125,000 (indexation factor assumed to be 0.375).
>
> A and B elect for holdover.
>
> | | | |
> |---|---:|---:|
> | Disposal consideration | | £125,000 |
> | Allowable cost | £15,000 | |
> | Indexation allowance: 0.375 × £15,000 = | 5,625 | 20,625 |
> | Chargeable gain | | £104,375 |

The effect of the holdover election is to reduce A's deemed disposal consideration to £20,625, and to reduce B's base cost of the land by £104,375. B's base cost is then £125,000 less £104,375, i.e. £20,625 (subject to expenses).

For disposals on or after 14th March 1989[2], holdover relief may be claimed only where:

(*a*) the assets concerned are business assets, as defined;[3] or

(*b*) the transfer is a chargeable transfer for IHT purposes, other than a potentially exempt transfer;[4] or

(*c*) the transfer is an exempt transfer by trustees of an accumulation and maintenance settlement;[5] or

(*d*) the transfer is a specified type of exempt transfer for IHT purposes e.g. transfer for public benefit.[6]

In any other case, or where CGT is only partly held over because there is consideration in excess of base cost, the tax may be paid by instalments for certain types of asset.[7] Thus, except for business asset transfers or specified types of exempt transfers for IHT, CGT holdover is now available only in very limited circumstances. The main instance is likely to be a transfer by an individual to trustees of a discretionary settlement or vice versa, which is not a potentially exempt transfer (PET).[8] It is not necessary for IHT actually to be payable, e.g. where the transfer is within the nil rate band. In the case of CGT paid on a PET, there is no relief if the transfer becomes a chargeable transfer by virtue of the death of the transferor within 7 years of the date the transfer is made, so that IHT becomes payable in respect of the original gift.[9] However, if the donee pays any CGT arising on the gift, the value transferred is correspondingly reduced in computing the IHT liability.[10]

Where a disposal made prior to 1st April 1982 was the subject of a holdover election, the rebasing to 31st March 1982 valuation effectively eliminated the held over gain. However, a holdover made after 31st March 1982 but before 6th April 1988 will not be affected by the rebasing, even though the transferor owned the asset on that date. In these circumstances, there is relief on a subsequent disposal on or after 6th April 1988, equal to one-half of the reduction in the donee's acquisition cost (see § **22: 06**, infra).[11]

Where the gain arising would otherwise have been reduced by the annual exemption or by allowable losses, there is a disadvantage, since there is no provision for electing a partial holdover. However, where retirement relief is also due on the asset, that relief is given first, and only the balance of chargeable gain is deducted from the transferee's base cost.[12]

If the asset is a dwelling house and it is not the donor's only or main residence but becomes the donee's only or main residence, it is possible for the donee to take the donor's base cost and then claim exemption under the rule at § **15: 12** on the subsequent disposal of the house. This is applicable also to gifts to trustees, where the house is occupied as a main residence by one of the beneficiaries, in accordance with the terms of the trust. In the converse case, when the asset has been the donor's only or main residence throughout, then there will be no holding over since chargeable gains will not arise.

The holdover facility applies to a transfer between individuals who so elect, to a transfer by an individual to trustees and to a transfer by trustees to other trustees. In the case of trustee transferees, only the transferor need elect that there should be a holding over.[13] In addition both parties must be resident in the UK. Where the transferee becomes non-resident within six years of the transfer, the held over gain is deemed to accrue immediately before that event.[14] The transferor may be made liable for any tax.[15] In the case of trustee transferees, the six year time limit does not apply.

Anti-avoidance provisions introduced by FA 1986 prevent an election being made in respect of gifts into dual resident trusts made after 17 March 1986 and provide for a charge to tax in respect of earlier gifts if the trust attains dual residence status after that date.[16]

Simon's Taxes C3.401, 402; Sumption CGT A5.13.
[1] FA 1980, s. 79.
[2] FA 1989, s. 124.
[3] CGTA 1979, s. 126; infra, § **20: 18**.
[4] Infra, § **38: 02**.
[5] Infra, § **42: 27**.
[6] Infra, § **44: 07**.
[7] CGTA 1979, s. 7A; supra, § **14: 03**.
[8] Infra, § **41: 06, 42: 15**.
[9] Infra, § **38: 02**.
[10] Infra, § **46: 27**.
[11] FA 1988, Sch. 9, para. 2.
[12] FA 1980, s. 79(3).
[13] FA 1981, s. 78 (for disposals after 5th April 1981) and FA 1982, s. 82.
[14] FA 1981, s. 79.
[15] FA 1981, s. 79(2).
[16] FA 1986, s. 58.

Gratuitous transfers of value[1]

16: 22   The term disposal is widened to catch three types of transaction. In all three, the market value which would be payable by the acquirer under a bargain at arm's length is to be taken as the consideration. The first of these transactions is where a person has control of a company and exercises that control so that value passes out of shares in the company owned by him, or by a person with whom he is connected, and passes into other shares in or rights over the company. A controlling shareholder using his voting power to pass a resolution increasing the rights of a particular type of share at the expense of his own is clearly shifting value to the other shareholders, although no particular piece of property has been disposed of. Despite the fact that the singular "person" is referred to, it has been held that the section applies where two or more persons control the company.[2] It has also been held that control was exercised when under a pre-arranged scheme a winding up resolution was passed even though the taxpayer himself did not vote on the motion.[3] Outside the context of a scheme the taxpayer must presumably vote in order to exercise control.

The second type of transaction caught is where, after a transaction whereby the owner of any property has become the lessee of the property, there is an adjustment of the rights and liabilities of the lease which is as a whole favourable to the lessor.

The third is where there is an asset which is subject to a right or restriction and there is a transaction whereby that right or restriction is extinguished or abrogated in whole or in part. Here the figure to be taken is the value accruing to the owner of the property from which the restriction falls.

Simon's Taxes C1.435; Sumption CGT A2.07.
[1] CGTA 1979, s. 25.
[2] *Floor v Davis* [1979] STC 379, [1979] 2 All ER 677.
[3] In the light of the decision in *W T Ramsay Ltd v IRC* [1981] STC 174, [1981] 1 All ER 865 it would appear that the same result would have been reached if, as part of a scheme, they had voted against the resolution.

Exclusion of market value rule

16: 23 The market value rule does not apply where there is an acquisition of an asset without a disposal and the consideration is either non-existent or is less than the market value.[1] In these circumstances the acquisition consideration will be nil or the actual value as appropriate. The purpose of this rule is to defeat schemes known as "reverse *Nairn Williamson* schemes". Under such schemes, shares were issued to shareholders (so being acquired by them without being disposed of by the issuing company). Although a relatively small amount might be subscribed (especially if the issued share capital was not substantial), the shares acquired were valued at market value thus giving the shareholders a substantial uplift in the base cost of their holding. Such schemes would now probably fall foul of the *Ramsay* principle anyway.[2]

The former exception to the market value rule for disposals by excluded persons, such as non residents, was withdrawn for disposals after 5th April 1983, subject to transitional rules for disposals before 6th April 1985.

Simon's Taxes C1.415, 416; Sumption CGT A1.12.
[1] CGTA 1979, s. 29A—for acquisition and disposals on or after 10th March 1981.
[2] Goldberg (1982) BTR 13 at 16.

CONNECTED PERSONS

16: 24   An individual is connected[1] with his husband or wife, with his relatives, with the husband or wife of his relatives, and with the relatives of his husband or wife. An ex-husband or widower is not a husband and an ex-wife or widow is not a wife. Relative means brother, sister, ancestor or lineal descendant. So one's mother is a relative, but one's uncle is not, nor is one's mother-in-law (although she is a connected person as a relative of one's spouse). However, the fact that A is connected with B does not necessarily mean that A is also connected with all those persons connected with B.

The category of connected persons is widened to cover trusts, partners and companies. In his capacity as trustee of a settlement, a person is connected with (1) the settlor (if he is an individual), (2) with any person connected with the individual-settlor and (3) with a body corporate which is deemed to be connected with the settlement. The terms settlement and settlor have the wide income tax sense of any arrangement containing an element of bounty.[2]

A partner is connected with his partner, and with the spouse or relative of his partner. Even so, he is not treated as being so connected if the disposal is of partnership assets pursuant to bona fide commercial arrangements.[3]

A person is connected with a company if he, or he with others with whom he is connected, control it. Where two or more persons act together to secure or exercise control of a company, then they are treated as connected with each other and with any person acting on their directions, but they are so treated only in relation to the company.

One company is connected with another if they are under the control of the same person, or under the control of that person and others with whom he is connected, or the one is controlled by one person and the other is controlled by persons with whom that one person is connected. The same result follows if a group of two or more persons has control of each company and either the group consists of the same persons or the groups could be regarded as consisting of the same persons by treating (in one or more cases) a member of either group as replaced by a person with whom he is connected.

Simon's Taxes C1.423, 424; Sumption CGT A2.01–05.
[1] CGTA 1979, s. 63.
[2] TA 1988, s. 681, supra, § **13: 05**.
[3] CGTA 1979, s. 63(4).

Disposals between connected persons

16: 25   Where the person making the disposal is connected with the person acquiring, they are treated as parties to a transaction otherwise than at arm's length.[1] Hence in particular the disposal will be deemed to have taken place at market value.[2]

Where a person disposes of an asset to a connected person, and a loss accrues, then, even though the loss occurs after the application of the rule that the consideration for the transaction is deemed to be market value, that loss can *only* be set off against gains accruing from some other disposal to that person.[3] Further, the other disposal must be at a time when they are connected persons.

Special rules apply to the valuation of assets when a connected person has a right over that asset.[4]

Simon's Taxes C1.423; Sumption CGT A2.06.
[1] CGTA 1979, s. 62.
[2] CGTA 1979, s. 29A.
[3] CGTA 1979, s. 62(3).
[4] CGTA 1979, s. 62(5) and (6).

Disposal in a series of transactions

16: 26   In estimating the market value of an asset for CGT, regard is normally had only to that asset in isolation, in contrast to the "loss to estate" principle adopted for IHT. However, the value may be increased where a disposal forms one of a series of linked transactions. This special rule applies where, by two or more transactions, one person disposes of assets to another person with whom he is connected, or to two or more persons with each of whom he is connected. Connected person status is vital and there must be connection with a common disponor (not necessarily between each disponee).[1] For the special rule to apply to a particular transaction in the series, the original market value[2] of the assets transferred by that transaction must be less than the appropriate portion[3] of the aggregate market value[4] of the assets disposed of by all the transactions in the series. The original market value is simply the market value determined without regard to the linked transactions rule. The aggregate market value used to determine the uplifted transaction value is the value of the transferred assets in aggregate, determined as at the time of the transaction in question. Transactions are not linked unless they occur within six years of each other. Once a value for a given transaction has been adjusted, it may still be adjusted again if there is a further linked transaction in the series, within the six years time limit.

The linked transactions rule does not override the normal rule as to valuation on a disposal between spouses living together.[5] There are certain special provisions for assets passed down chains which include intra group transfers.[6]

EXAMPLE
F owns 80% of the issued share capital on XYZ Ltd, a private investment company. In October 1986, F gives 2,000 shares—one-quarter of his holding—to G, his son. In June 1987, he gives a further 2,000 shares to H, G's wife. F gives a further 2,000 shares to G in December 1989, and the remaining 2,000 to H in November 1992. The values of the shareholdings are as follows—

	Shareholding of		
	2,000	4,000	6,000
October 1986	£80,000	£300,000	£600,000
June 1987	90,000	340,000	700,000
December 1989	120,000	450,000	900,000
November 1992	150,000	550,000	1,150,000

(*a*) *October 1986 disposal*
(i) Initial consideration for disposal   £80,000
(ii) Following the June 1987 disposal, the consideration is increased to

$$£300,000 \times \frac{2,000}{4,000} = \qquad £150,000$$

(iii) Following the December 1989 disposal, the consideration is increased to

$$£600,000 \times \frac{2,000}{6,000} = \qquad £200,000$$

(iv) The November 1992 disposal does not affect the disposal consideration any further, because it occurs more than 6 years after the October 1986 disposal and is not therefore linked with it.

(*b*) *June 1987 disposal*

(i) Initial consideration: £340,000 × $\dfrac{2,000}{4,000}$ = £170,000

(ii) Following the December 1989 disposal, the consideration is increased to

$$£700,000 \times \frac{2,000}{6,000} =$$ £233,333

(iii) There is no further adjustment following the November 1992 disposal, since at that time the October 1986 disposal is no longer linked and the aggregate under consideration is still 6,000 shares.

(*c*) *December 1989 disposal*

(i) Initial consideration: £900,000 × $\dfrac{2,000}{6,000}$ = £300,000

(ii) Following the November 1992 disposal, there is no further adjustment, since the October 1986 disposal is no longer linked and the aggregate under consideration is still 6,000 shares.

(*d*) *November 1992 disposal*

Consideration: £1,150,000 × $\dfrac{2,000}{6,000}$ = £383,333

The linked transactions rule applies to transactions after 19th March 1985. For disposals on or before that date, a different rule applied.[7] Whereas the new rule seeks to counter avoidance of CGT by fragmentation of assets, such as holdings of unquoted shares, the old rule seemed concerned to penalise the assembly of such assets in the hands of a transferee. The old rule applied where a person was given assets, or acquired them from two or more persons with whom he was connected, and the total value of the assets taken together was greater than the total value of each asset taken separately. The value of each asset was to be the apportionable part of the total market value, the apportionment presumably being according to the value of each asset taken separately. This formula proved difficult to apply in practice. A particular difficulty arose because there was no express time limit within which the later acquisition should take place although the Revenue accepted that the rule could apply only to transactions occurring within a two year period preceding the latest transaction in the series.[8]

Transactions occurring since 19th March 1983 may form part of a series of transactions after 19th March 1985 if they would fall within both the old and new rules.[9] To be linked in this way the transaction must be within two years of the first transaction after 19th March 1985. Transactions after 19th March 1985 cannot fall under the old rule.[10]

Simon's Taxes A1.316; Sumption CGT A2.09; A23.05.
[1] FA 1985, s. 71(1).
[2] Defined FA 1985, Sch. 21, para. 2.
[3] Defined FA 1985, Sch. 21, paras. 3(1)(*a*) and 4.
[4] Defined FA 1985, Sch. 21, paras. 3(1)(*b*) and 4.
[5] FA 1985, s. 71(2).
[6] FA 1985, s. 71(6) and (7).
[7] CGTA 1979, s. 151.
[8] HC (Written Answer) dated 27th December 1985, [1985] STI, p. 2.
[9] FA 1985, s. 71(8).
[10] FA 1985, s. 71(5).

17 Death

17: 01 There is no charge to CGT on the estate of a deceased person by virtue of a deemed disposal on death.[1] The estate on death is subject to inheritance tax (IHT, formerly CTT). From 1965 until 1971 the United Kingdom position was that both taxes were payable, the CGT being a deduction in computing the value of the estate for estate duty purposes; since 1971 only estate duty, now IHT, has been charged.

---

[1] Death is an occasion of charge under the system of taxing offshore income gains, see TA 1988, s. 757 (FA 1984, s. 92), infra, § **34: 43** and can give rise to tax on a gain held over when property was settled, see infra, § **18: 15**.

Acquisition at market value on death

17: 02 Where the deceased had property of which he was competent to dispose, the personal representatives, or other person on whom it devolves, are deemed to acquire it at market value at the date of death.[1] However, there is no deemed disposal by the deceased. Any potential liability in respect of unrealised gains is extinguished—as are any potential allowable losses.

The deceased was competent to dispose of[2] any assets which he could, if of full age and capacity, have disposed of by his will. This includes any severable beneficial share in joint property, but not entailed property nor property over which he had a power of appointment.

The value at the date of death is taken even though no IHT may actually be payable, as when the value of the estate is not high enough to attract IHT.

Where the value of an asset has been ascertained for IHT that value is taken for CGT;[3] this may not be the same as the value on which IHT is charged. So if farm land is valued at £200,000 the actual value transferred for IHT purposes may be reduced to £100,000 by reason of agricultural relief, infra, § **45: 12**; the value for the CGT acquisition will be £200,000.

Where a gift was made before 27th March 1974 and the donor died after 12th March 1975 but within seven years of the gift only a fraction of the value of the gift was liable to CTT. It follows that only that same fraction was valued at the date of death.[4]

A donatio mortis causa is not subject to CGT when made; the donee takes at the market value at the date of the death.[5] On a gift with reservation, which is treated as remaining part of the donor's estate on death for IHT, the market value for CGT is determined as of the date of the gift if the gift is a disposal for CGT. In the case of a potentially exempt transfer, which becomes a chargeable transfer for IHT if the donor dies within seven years of the date the transfer is made, the CGT treatment of the gift is undisturbed.

This is because the gift is not treated as included in the transferor's estate on death.

On the death of a life tenant of settled property see, § **18: 15**.

Simon's Taxes C1.211; Sumption CGT A7.01.
[1] CGTA 1979, s. 49(1).
[2] CGTA 1979, s. 49(10).
[3] CGTA 1979, s. 153.
[4] CGTA 1979, Sch. 6, para. 15.
[5] CGTA 1979, ss. 49(5) and 47(2).

DISPOSALS DURING ADMINISTRATION

17: 03   Any disposal by the personal representatives during administration otherwise than to a legatee may give rise to CGT in the usual way; this is so even if the purpose of the disposal is to raise money to pay tax or to pay the proceeds to the beneficiaries—unless they can prove that they are absolutely entitled (infra, § **18: 04**) as against the personal representatives.[1] The personal representatives are treated as a single body of persons but having the same residence, ordinary residence and domicile as the deceased at the time of his death.[2] So if he was non-resident there will be no CGT liability on the personal representatives even if they are resident.

The personal representatives are not to be treated as an individual.[3] Thus, CGT on any chargeable gains accruing to them will be assessed only at the basic rate of income tax, for 1988–89 onwards.[4] However, they are entitled to the annual exemption on the first £5,000 of net chargeable gains for the year in which the deceased died (this is in addition to the same exemption for the deceased himself) and for the next two years of assessment.[5] Despite this relief the selection of which assets to sell and which to retain for transmission in specie to the legatees is of great practical importance.

The deductible expenditure will include the costs of obtaining probate.[6]

Simon's Taxes C1.113; C4.126; Sumption CGT A7.05.
[1] *Prest v Bettinson* [1980] STC 607.
[2] CGTA 1979, s. 49(3). As to who is liable to assessment see s. 48(1).
[3] CGTA 1979, s. 48(2).
[4] FA 1988, s. 98(1). For 1987–88 and earlier years, the flat 30% rate applied.
[5] CGTA 1979, Sch. 1, para. 4.
[6] *IRC v Richards' Executors* [1971] 1 All ER 785, 46 TC 626.

DISPOSAL TO LEGATEE

17: 04   When the estate is administered, the personal representatives will dispose of the property to the specific and residuary legatees. If the property has been turned into money in the course of administration, an actual disposal will have occurred and there can be no further capital gains liability when the money so acquired is handed over to the beneficiary.

Where chargeable assets are passed to the beneficiary there would be an actual disposal. However, on a person acquiring any asset as legatee (*a*) no chargeable gain accrues to the personal representatives and (*b*) the legatee is treated as if the personal representatives' acquisition of the asset had been his acquisition of it.[1] Thus if there is a specific legacy of a piece of furniture which cost the deceased £1,500 and which was worth £2,500 when he dies, leaving the piece specifically to A, A will be taken to have acquired it at £2,500, even though when he eventually receives it, it is worth £3,000 or £2,000. Rule (*b*) has the consequence that where some of the assets have accrued gains and other losses and there are two legatees, one resident in the UK and the other non-resident, it will be advantageous to transfer the assets with the losses to the UK resident (so that he may take advantage of them in due course) and the other assets to the non-resident so that they will escape UK CGT.

Simon's Taxes C1.211; Sumption CGT A7.04.
[1] CGTA 1979, s. 49(4); on a subsequent disposal by the legatee he may include any expenses incurred by him or the representatives on the transfer to him; CGTA 1979, s. 47(1).

17: 05   A person acquires an asset "as legatee" if he takes it under a testamentary disposition, or on an intestacy and the phrase includes any asset appropriated by the personal representatives in or towards satisfaction of a pecuniary legacy or any other interest or share in the property devolving under the disposition or intestacy.[1] So a pecuniary legatee takes as legatee as does a residuary or a specific legatee. A creditor, on the other hand, does not.[2] A person claiming under the Inheritance (Provision for Family and Dependants) Act 1975 takes as legatee.[3] The position of a person entitled to a part of the estate and who buys from the personal representatives an asset in satisfaction of that claim but for a price greater than the value of that claim, by paying the difference, is obscure.[4]

It is presumably irrelevant that the asset was acquired by the personal representatives after the death. It is also likely that a person acquiring an asset by exercising an option to buy that asset granted to him by the will also takes as a legatee, but this question cannot be regarded as settled.

Simon's Taxes C1.211.
[1] CGTA 1979, s. 47(2).
[2] *Quaere* if the equitable doctrines of performance and satisfaction applied.
[3] Under s. 19(1) of that Act. See also IHTA 1984, ss. 146, 236(2).
[4] In *Passant v Jackson* [1985] STC 133 the reasoning of Vinelott J suggests that such an acquisition is not "as legatee"; appeal dismissed [1986] STC 164, CA.

17: 06   If, within a two year period from the date of death, there is a variation or disclaimer by an instrument in writing the variation or disclaimer is not a disposal (so there can be no CGT) and the CGT rules apply as if the new scheme had been made by the deceased.[1] This rule is confined to property of which the deceased was competent to dispose and does not apply where the variation or disclaimer is in return for extraneous consideration. The two year time limit is important, the more so when an application has to be made to a court; e.g. under the Variation of Trusts Act 1958. However, only one of the elections need be made on a variation, if this is more beneficial; for example, if some of the legatees are not UK resident.

Simon's Taxes C1.211; Sumption CGT A7.06.
[1] CGTA 1979, s. 49(6); the relief should be claimed within 6 months of the instrument of variation. The time limit for election can be extended at the discretion of the Revenue, but the two year period for making the variation etc. cannot.

17: 07   Technically, when a clear residue has been ascertained, the personal representatives become trustees. Where the asset is transferred to the beneficiary before administration is complete he takes as legatee; if he acquires the asset subsequently he will usually have been absolutely entitled as against the representatives at the moment they became trustees; there will, therefore, be no disposal by the trustees to the beneficiary. Where property is transferred to the trustees they presumably take as legatees. This metamorphosis should not of itself prevent any subsequent disposal by them to the residuary legatee from being to him as legatee. Different questions of course arise if the residue is to be held on trust.[1]

Whatever view one takes on this last point, there is no significant tax disadvantage on those who delay the distribution of the estate, as compared with those who are entitled under trusts. Indeed, the relatively low rate of CGT on personal representatives may make it beneficial for them to sell assets and distribute the proceeds, rather than to distribute the assets in specie, for the legatees to dispose of. In practice, the result will depend on whether assets appreciate or decline in value after the date of death.

[1] If the trustees are not the same as the personal representatives they presumably take "as legatees".

LOSSES

17: 08   If, in the year of assessment in which he dies, an individual has allowable losses, in excess of chargeable gains, they may be rolled backwards for the preceding three years of assessment, taking later years first.[1] The relief does not apply to an excess of allowable losses in the year before that of death, since they are set off against gains *after* allowable losses for the year.[2] Any liability in respect of CGT due from the deceased is deductible in computing the value of his estate for IHT purposes.

Simon's Taxes C1.211, C2.106; Sumption CGT A7.02.
[1] CGTA 1979, s. 49(2).
[2] CGTA 1979, s. 4(1).

18 Settled property

INTRODUCTION

18: 01 A charge to CGT may arise (1) on the creation of the settlement; (2) on gains accruing to trustees during the settlement, and (3) on the occurrence of certain events which are deemed to be disposals of the trust assets. In (2) and (3) the general principle is to charge the tax on the trustees, who are treated as a single and continuing body of persons.[1] This is so even if the property is held by different sets of trustees.[2] The trustee is not liable where—
(1) he is a bare trustee (infra, § **18: 04**)
(2) a trust gain accruing to a non-resident trustee is attributed to a beneficiary (infra, § **34: 53**).

The disposal of a beneficial interest in settled property is exempt, thereby avoiding effective double taxation of trust gains. The exemption does not apply if the disposal is by a person who has acquired the interest for a consideration in money or money's worth[3] or if the trustees are not resident in the UK.[4]

Since trustees are not regarded as individuals for CGT purposes,[5] they are subject to CGT on chargeable gains at the basic rate of income tax, but not at higher rates.[6] However, if the trust is an accumulation or discretionary settlement (see § **11: 05**), the rate of CGT is the sum of the basic rate and the additional rate; this is 35% for 1989–90.[7] In addition, where the settlor or his spouse retains an interest in the settled property, chargeable gains of the trust are treated as accruing to the settlor and taxed at his marginal rate of income tax.[8] The settlor is entitled to recover from the trustees any CGT paid on trust gains. However, if the trustees have net allowable losses for the year, the benefit of the losses does not pass to the settlor in that year, but they are carried forward for offset against trust gains of the following year.

The settlor retains an interest if the settled property, or income arising to the trustees, may be applied for his benefit or for that of his spouse, or if either of them enjoys any direct or indirect benefit from the property or the income.[9] Thus the settlor has an interest if he is merely a member of a class of discretionary beneficiaries, or if the settled property reverts to him on the happening of certain contingent events. However, there are exclusions in cases where the settlor can benefit only in the event of the bankruptcy of a beneficiary or on the attempted assignment or mortgaging of trust property by a beneficiary. The settlor is also not treated as having an interest in a marriage settlement if he benefits only after the death of both parties to the marriage and the children of the marriage. There are provisions excluding trust gains of the year in which the settlor dies, or, if the settlor's spouse has an interest, of the year in which they die or the couple separate. The term "settlor" is defined so that a person is a settlor if the settlement concerned includes property which originated from that person, being provided for the purposes of that settlement.[10]

There is an annual exemption for the first £2,500 of gains.[11] The annual exemption does not apply where the settlor or his spouse retains an interest, since the gains are not then the trustees' gains. Settlements made after 6th June 1978 by the same settlor are grouped together for this purpose and each settlement is entitled to a fraction of the annual exemption so that if there were two each would get an exemption of £1,250; however, there is a minimum exemption of one-tenth of the amount available to individuals i.e. £500. The figure of £2,500 is index linked;[12] it is increased to £5,000 for trusts for the disabled.[13]

Simon's Taxes C4.207; Sumption CGT A6.01.
[1] CGTA 1979, s. 52(1).
[2] CGTA 1979, s. 52(3).
[3] CGTA 1979, s. 58.
[4] FA 1981, s. 88.
[5] CGTA 1979, s. 48(2).
[6] FA 1988, s. 98(1).
[7] FA 1988, s. 100. The additional rate is 10%, unless raised by Parliament: TA 1988, s. 832(1). There are provisions to catch trusts where the trust would be an accumulation or discretionary settlement, but for the income being treated as the settlor's income, or there being no income for the year of assessment.
[8] FA 1988, s. 109 and Sch. 10. The provisions apply to *all* settlements, whenever they were created, unless the settlor and his spouse are both deceased.
[9] FA 1988, Sch. 10, para. 2(1).
[10] FA 1988, Sch. 10, para. 6.
[11] CGTA 1979, Sch. 1, paras. 5 and 6; FA 1989, s. 122.
[12] FA 1982, s. 80(2). Index linking was disapplied for 1989–90.
[13] CGTA 1979, Sch. 1, para. 5 as amended by FA 1982, s. 80(3).

18: 02   Property is declared to be settled if it is held in trust and it is not a bare trust, infra, § **18: 04**.[1] Property being administered as part of deceased's estate is not settled property;[2] nor is property vested in a trustee in bankruptcy.[3] Since various events cause a deemed disposal of the settled property it is important to know exactly what property is subject to the settlement concerned.[4] Three situations must be considered. First, where trustees exercise a power to subject property to further trusts, it is a question of fact whether the particular new trusts are part of the main settlement or a new one. This is to be decided by invoking practical common sense in the light of established legal doctrine. In a case where a part of the main fund was held by separate trustees on separate trusts, it was held that the property remained subject to one settlement.[5] This had two consequences; (*a*) there was no deemed disposal just because the power to create new trusts was exercised and (*b*) less attractively, as the trustees were one continuing body, disposal by the trustees of one part of the fund gave rise to a liability in tax which could be collected from the trustees of the other part.[6] In another case, it was held that property remained part of the first settlement even though appointed on exhaustive trusts because the power under which the appointment was made did not authorise the trustees to remove the property from the trusts altogether.[7] As Slade LJ said, it would be surprising if the CGT rules were different from the general legal rules applying to trusts.[8]

Secondly, the question may arise whether a single disposition creates two or more settlements. The creation of distinct but undivided shares in one asset gives rise to one settlement even though the shares are held on different trusts.[9] However a different answer may be reached if there are distinct assets as well as different trusts; this will be especially the case where more than one settlor is involved.

Thirdly, where property is added to an existing settlement, the presumption is that no new settlement is created although special factors such as distinct trustees or an independent trust instrument may lead to a different conclusion.

If there is one settlement and the property is in the hands of different trustees, they are treated as a single body of trustees.[10] An example would be where a part of the land held under the Settled Land Act has been sold so that the proceeds of the sale will be in the hands of the trustees while the remaining land will be in the hands of the tenant for life.

Simon's Taxes C4.207; Sumption CGT A6.02.

[1] CGTA 1979, s. 51 subject also s. 93 (unit trusts).

[2] Supra, § **17:03**.

[3] CGTA 1979, s. 61.

[4] It is also important for other reasons, e.g. the annual exemption, the residence of trustees and whether trustees of one fund are liable for tax arising as a gain arising from another part.

[5] *Roome v Edwards* [1981] STC 96, [1981] 1 All ER 736; See also *Ewart v Taylor* [1983] STC 721.

[6] The solution seems to be either to ensure that the appointed fund is truly separate and to pay the tax resulting from the deemed disposal of the assets appointed—or to retain control of the subsidiary part by having joint trustees. See also SP 7/84 superseding SP 9/81, **Simon's Taxes, Division H3.2.**

[7] *Bond v Pickford* [1983] STC 517.

[8] At 527.

[9] *Crowe v Appleby* [1976] STC 301, [1976] 2 All ER 914.

[10] CGTA 1979, s. 52(3).

A TRANSFER INTO SETTLEMENT

18:03 A transfer into settlement whether revocable or irrevocable is a disposal of the entire property thereby becoming settled property.[1] The provision directs that the disposal shall be total and not partial even though the settlor has some interest under the settlement.[2] This rule is quite different from that for IHT, infra, § **41:07**.

The rule applies even where there is consideration.[3]

There is, however, a disposal only of the property settled. If therefore the settlor has a piece of property but settles only a part of that property there will be a part disposal of the property. If S declares himself trustee of shares for A for life, but does not expressly grant a remainder the question whether there is a settlement of the shares or of a life interest in the shares must be answered by studying the wording and intention of the settlement.[4]

The provision probably is superfluous to the extent that it states that there is to be a total disposal even though the settlor is a trustee or the sole trustee of the settlement, since, if this is the only link remaining between settlor and the property settled, it would appear that there has in fact been a total disposal.

Any gain or loss on the disposal is computed by taking the consideration to be the market value of the assets concerned, since the gift is a transaction other than by way of a bargain at arm's length. Since the settlor is connected with the trustees, any allowable loss arising on the gift into settlement will be capable of offset only against chargeable gains arising on subsequent disposals to the trustees.

If the transfer is not a potentially exempt transfer, or if the assets transferred are defined business assets, the settlor may elect that any gain accruing on the transfer should be held over provided that the settlor and the trustees are resident in the UK; the consent of the trustees is not required.[5] The main opportunity for making a holdover claim where business assets are not involved is now likely to be on the transfer of assets to trustees of a discretionary settlement.

Simon's Taxes C4.207; Sumption CGT A6.06.
[1] CGTA 1979, s. 53.
[2] The trust cannot set any of the settlor's losses against trust gains; or vice versa. Contrast at the end of the trust CGTA 1979, s. 54(2).
[3] FA 1981, s. 86.
[4] *Berry v Warnett* [1982] STC 396 (a decision concerned with the earlier formulation of s. 53 which spoke of a gift in settlement and where the settlor argued that he had settled the remainder but not the life interest).
[5] FA 1981, s. 78. See supra, § **16: 21**.

BARE TRUST

18: 04 Where assets are held by a trustee for another person who is absolutely entitled as against the trustee, or for two or more persons who are so entitled, the property is not settled and the acts of the trustee are treated as the acts of the beneficiary and disposals between them are disregarded.[1] All gains and losses and consequent liability concern the beneficiary and not the trustee.

Simon's Taxes C4.207; Sumption CGT A6.02.
[1] CGTA 1979, s. 46(1). The same also applies to Lloyd's Underwriters: CGTA 1979, s. 142. So if A transfers property to T to hold on trust for A absolutely there is no chargeable disposal.

The power of the beneficiary

18: 05 The beneficiary is absolutely entitled if he has the exclusive right, subject only to satisfying any outstanding charge, lien or other right[1] of the trustee to resort to the asset for the payment of duty, taxes, costs or other outgoings,[2] to direct how that asset shall be dealt with.[3] Other outgoings are construed *eiusdem generis* with rates and taxes and so do not include an annuity.[4] This definition sits oddly with the trust doctrine that a beneficiary who is absolutely entitled has the right to end the trust but no power to direct the trustee how his discretion shall be exercised.

It appears that a right to call for the conveyance of the trust asset to the beneficiary meets this test even though the beneficiary cannot control the trustee in other ways.

It was held that, where the taxpayer and members of his family pooled their shares in a family company behind a trust so as to retain effective control, the shares were not settled property.[5] Each beneficiary could direct the trustees how to exercise the voting rights attached to the shares; the trust could be ended by majority vote and each beneficiary could sell his interest subject to a right of pre-emption. The beneficiaries had it in their power to end the trust notwithstanding any powers or discretions conferred on the trustees.[6]

If the test is whether the beneficiary can call upon the trustees for the transfer of the trust property, the answer may well turn on the nature of the trust property. Thus, a co-owner of land has no right to call for the land itself because of the trust for sale. Similar problems arise with certain shares in a private company and to mortgage debts.[7] However, it appears likely that such technical points will not be accepted by the courts and that therefore such property is not settled.[8]

Simon's Taxes C4.208; Sumption CGT A6.07.

[1] These words refer to some personal right of indemnity and are not apt to cover another beneficial interest arising under the same instrument: per Walton J in *Stephenson v Barclays Bank Trust Co Ltd* [1975] 1 All ER 625 at 636. Charges are included in this list because of the estate and powers of the mortgagee: per Goff J in *Crowe v Appleby* [1975] STC 502 at 510.

[2] This is mentioned because otherwise a very small right could lead to the postponement of tax otherwise payable under s. 54: per Walton J in *Stephenson v Barclays Bank Trust Co Ltd* at 638.

[3] CGTA 1979, s. 46(2). See Walton J in *Stephenson v Barclays Bank Trust Co Ltd* at 637 and see *Crowe v Appleby* [1975] STC 502, [1975] 3 All ER 529.

[4] *Stephenson v Barclays Bank Trust Co Ltd* (supra) (the property ceased to be settled property when specific assets were appropriated to satisfy the annuity, that appropriation causing a deemed disposal under s. 54).

[5] *Booth v Ellard* [1980] STC 555, [1980] 3 All ER 569.

[6] Per Buckley LJ at p. 559g.

[7] See comments of Walton J in *Stephenson v Barclays Bank Trust Co Ltd* [1975] STC 151 at 163 who said that one of several co-owners would, in these circumstances, have to wait until the property was sold before being entitled to call for the transfer of his or her share. In relation to shares note the special circumstances in *Booth v Ellard*, supra.

[8] See *Jenkins v Brown* [1989] STI 436, where land comprised in a pool held by trustees was conveyed to beneficiaries according to their interests prior to the trust being created.

Co-owners

18: 06   Another area of difficulty concerns the extension of the bare trust concept to co-owners. In cases where there is more than one beneficiary, the rule applies when the beneficiaries are entitled against the trustees absolutely and "jointly". The word "jointly", although not a term of art,[1] is not the same as "joint tenants". Therefore, there is a bare trust whether the owners hold as joint tenants or as tenants in common.

It has been held that for there to be a bare trust the interests must be co-existent and of the same quality;[2] the word jointly is not the same as "together". Where two persons are entitled to succession, e.g. to A for life remainder to B, it might be argued that there is a bare trust, since together they are entitled, if of full age, to terminate the trust.[3] However, it has been held that the property is clearly settled.[4] Were there a bare trust, it is unclear how those gains would be apportioned. Under the trust only B is entitled to the capital and yet A would not normally consent to the ending of the trust unless the capital were divided between them. The Revenue would therefore either attribute the whole gain to B or divide it between A and B in accordance with some quite arbitrary assumptions of life expectancy and willingness, thus making A chargeable with a gains liability in respect of capital which may never be his.[5]

Fortunately, it is now clear that there can be a bare trust only when the beneficiaries' interests are qualitatively the same.[6] This is true of tenants in common but not of those entitled to succession nor when one beneficiary holds subject to the rights of an annuitant.

It has been held that a residuary legatee does not hold absolutely as against the personal representatives during the administration of the estate. Disposals by personal representatives to pay debts and pecuniary legacies cannot therefore be attributed to the legatee. This is because those assets never formed part of the residue to which he was entitled.[7]

Simon's Taxes C4.207; Sumption CGT A6.03.
[1] *Kidson v Macdonald* [1974] STC 54, [1974] 1 All ER 849.
[2] *Booth v Ellard* [1980] STC 555 at 559.
[3] Under the rule in *Saunders v Vautier* (1841) Cr & Ph 240.
[4] "It is clearly settled property" per Foster J in *Kidson v Macdonald* [1974] 1 All ER 849 at 858.
[5] But cf CGTA 1979, s. 17.
[6] *Stephenson v Barclays Bank Trust Co Ltd* [1974] STC 151, [1975] 1 All ER 625.
[7] *Cochrane v IRC* [1974] STC 335, 49 TC 299; see also *Prest v Bettinson* [1980] STC 607.

18: 07   There is a bare trust not only where the person is absolutely entitled as against the trustee, but also where he would be so entitled but for being an infant or other person under a disability. However this must be the only reason for his not being absolutely entitled. Where property was held "for such of the beneficiaries as shall attain the age of 21 years or marry under that age" (21 was then the age of majority), the beneficiary, even if he had not been an infant, would not have been absolutely entitled, since his interest was contingent upon attaining his majority (or marrying before that time).[1] A further reason was that the interests of the beneficiaries might be defeasible *pro tanto* if other children were born so that it could not be said that these infants had "vested indefeasible interests in possession". The result was that a gain realised by the trustees during the administration (infra, § **18: 09**) was a disposal by the trustees and so chargeable at 30% and could not be attributed to the beneficiaries, in which case the rate would have been nil.

Simon's Taxes C4.208; Sumption CGT A6.03.
[1] *Tomlinson v Glyn's Executor and Trustee Co* [1970] 1 All ER 381, 45 TC 607. What would have happened if the beneficiary had married and so satisfied the condition precedent while still an infant? *Semble* that there is a disposal under s. 54, infra, § **18: 10**.

DISPOSALS DURING ADMINISTRATION

18: 08 Gains or losses will accrue to the trustees on the disposal of assets in the course of administration, as where the trustees sell some of the trust investments to buy new ones. The trustees are chargeable on their chargeable gains less allowable losses for the year of assessment in the same way as individuals. The annual exempt amount is £2,500; £5,000 if the trust is for the disabled.[1] In cases where the settlor retains an interest in the settled property, the net chargeable gains are his, and not those of the trustees.

A problem not cleared up in the legislation is that of the incidence of the tax as between the beneficiaries. Where the property disposed of forms part of the capital of the trust, any CGT accruing will fall on the capital. If however the trust document or some right were to provide that all the produce of a particular source, even a capital gain, was to be paid to a life tenant it would seem that the tax should fall on that life tenant rather than on the general capital.

Simon's Taxes C1.114.
[1] CGTA 1979, s. 5 and Sch. 1, paras. 5 and 6 as amended FA 1988, s. 108.

DEEMED DISPOSALS

18: 09 In addition to the actual disposals that arise in the course of the administration of the trust, there are deemed disposals on two principal occasions[1] although only one will give rise to a chargeable gain. It is Revenue practice usually to allow roll over relief on deemed disposals where a gain would arise, although strictly it is uncertain that a rollover election is competent. For deemed disposals on or after 14th March 1989,[2] rollover is in any case limited to:

(*a*) transfers of business assets; or
(*b*) transfers chargeable to IHT; or
(*c*) certain exempt transfers by trustees of accumulation and maintenance settlements.

Under (*b*), transfers of assets by trustees of discretionary settlements should be included.

Simon's Taxes C4.208–213; Sumption CGT A6.07, 08.
[1] There is also a deemed disposal where property subject to charitable trusts ceases to be so, CGTA 1979, s. 145(2).
[2] FA 1989, s. 124; supra, § **16: 21**.

1 Property ceasing to be settled: CGTA 1979, s. 54

18: 10 When a person becomes absolutely entitled to any settled property as against the trustee, whether because the trust itself ends or the property leaves the settlement through the exercise of a power of advancement, the trustees are deemed to dispose at their market value of all the assets forming part of the settled property to which the beneficiary becomes entitled and immediately to re-acquire them at the same value.[1] The deemed disposal in effect ends the capital gains regime of the trust and commences that of the recipient under a bare trust,[2] even though the assets themselves remain vested in the trustees. It follows that any gains or losses arising on the deemed disposal will be those of the trust whilst any later gains or losses arising on the assets concerned will be those of the beneficiary. The deemed disposal occurs also if the person would be absolutely entitled as against the trustee but for being an infant or other person under disability.[3]

Where the property ceases to be settled on the death of the life tenant there is a deemed disposal but no chargeable gain or allowable loss[4]—save where a chargeable gain was held over when the settlement was created against assets still held by the trustees at the date of death of the life tenant.[5] The earlier held over gain is then chargeable.[6] Where the life interest extends to only a part of the property, a chargeable gain or allowable loss will arise in respect of the part not represented by the deceased's interest.[7]

The disposal is of those assets to which the person becomes entitled. Where a beneficiary assigned his interest to X who became entitled to a holding in a company but who was then obliged to sell a similar holding to the beneficiary, it was held that the beneficiary became entitled to the shares received from X.[8]

Should the trustees have any allowable loss, whether from the notional disposal or some earlier disposal (even in a previous year), the beneficiary may take over the entitlement to the loss provided two conditions are satisfied.[9] The first condition is that the loss arose in respect of the property now ceasing to be settled (or in respect of other property represented by the property now ceasing to be settled). The second is that there are not enough chargeable gains accruing to the trustee in that year, but before the deemed disposal, to absorb the losses. Where the beneficiary and the trustees are connected persons,[10] it is unclear whether the rule restricting the set-off of losses on such transfers[11] effectively prevents the beneficiary taking over the loss.

If the trustees and the disponee so elect the gain otherwise accruing may in limited circumstances be held over—provided the disponee is resident in the UK.[12]

Simon's Taxes C4.208; Sumption CGT A6.07.

[1] CGTA 1979, s. 54; on deductible expenditure note s. 47(1). On hysterectomy and castration as events causing the disposal see [1968] BTR 56 (J.G.M.).

[2] Supra, § **18: 08**.

[3] FA 1981, s. 87.

[4] CGTA 1979, s. 56.

[5] CGTA 1979, s. 56A.

[6] Presumably this gain may itself be held over under FA 1982, s. 82.

[7] CGTA 1979, s. 56(1A) and s. 56A(3)—on effect of earlier holding over; see § **18: 15**.

[8] *Chinn v Collins* [1981] STC 1, [1981] 1 All ER 189.

[9] CGTA 1979, s. 54(2).

[10] By virtue of the beneficiary being connected with the settlor, if he is still living; supra, § **16: 24**.

[11] CGTA 1979, s. 62(3); supra, § **16: 25**.

[12] Supra, § **16: 21**. But where the disponee is another trust, a charge will arise if the disponee-trust later becomes non-resident; there is no six year limit to such a charge.

18: 11   The property will cease to be settled if it ceases to be subject to the settlement even though it may become subject to another trust. This is because it is necessary only for the person to be entitled absolutely as against the trustee; he need not be entitled beneficially. For example, property may be settled on A for life with remainder to B, and B predeceases A leaving his residuary estate to X and Y on various trusts. If A then releases his life interest, there will be a deemed disposal since X and Y are entitled as against the trustees of the settlement to call for the property. Clearly, the property will not be the subject of a deemed disposal if it remains in the same settlement.[1]

When a trust is varied under the Variation of Trusts Act the variation itself is probably not a disposal but if the terms of the variation provide for any actual or deemed disposal, then there will be such a disposal.[2] Since the better view is that it is the order of the court rather than the arrangement which is the variation,[3] the date of the disposal will be that of the order. Where some of the beneficiaries are *sui iuris* and the court's consent is sought on behalf of those not *sui iuris* the agreement among the former group is presumably in the nature of a conditional contract, supra, § **16: 02**. Where the property reverts to the settlor on the death of a life tenant the disposal and reacquisition takes place not at the value on the death but at the trustee's adjusted base cost.[4]

Simon's Taxes C4.208; Sumption CGT A6.08.
[1] *Roome v Edwards*, supra, § **18: 02**. See SP 7/78; Simon's Taxes, Division H3.2.
[2] But note CGTA 1979, s. 58(2) and *Hoare Trustees v Gardner* [1978] STC 89.
[3] See Lord Reid and Lord Wilberforce in *IRC v Holmden* [1968] AC 685 at 701, 702, 710, 713.
[4] CGTA 1979, s. 56(1)(*b*).

---

2 Termination of a life interest in possession on death

18: 12   There is a deemed disposal and reacquisition by the trustees when a life interest in possession terminates on the death of the person beneficially entitled to the interest.[1] This deemed disposal will relate to property remaining subject to the settlement; property leaving the settlement will be deemed to be disposed of under the rules already set out, supra, § **18: 10**. If, for example, property is settled on A for life or until marriage, with remainder to B for life with remainder to C absolutely, then on A's death there will be a deemed disposal of the settled property at market value. However, consistent with general principles, no chargeable gain or allowable loss arises,[2] save where a chargeable gain was held over on the disposal of the assets to the trustees; the gain originally held over becomes chargeable on the occasion of the death[3] (see § **18: 15**). Similar principles apply where the person entitled to the life interest dies but the interest itself continues—on the death of a tenant *pur autre vie*.[4] Since 5th April 1982 there has been no deemed disposal when the life interest terminates otherwise than on the death of the life tenant; thus the trustees' acquisition cost is unchanged.

Sumption CGT A6.01, 08.
[1] CGTA 1979, s. 55(1)(*a*).
[2] CGTA 1979, s. 55(1)(*b*).

³ CGTA 1979, s. 56A(2)—only a part of the held over gain is chargeable if the interest extends only to a part—s. 56A(3). When a charge arises it may presumably be held over under FA 1982, s. 82.
⁴ CGTA 1979, s. 55(3).

Life interest in possession

18: 13   Life interest as such is not defined so that it must be taken to bear its usual conveyancing meaning and the distinctions between a lease and a life estate must be observed. However, statute declares that life interest is to include a right under the settlement to the income of, or to the use or occupation of, settled property for the life of a person other than the person entitled to the right so that a life interest *pur autre vie* is included.¹ The term also includes a right to income under the settlement for lives. A lease for lives does not fall within the provision since settled property is defined as any property held in trust and lease for lives does not operate behind a trust.²

There is excluded from the definition of a life interest any right which is contingent on the exercise of the discretion of the trustee or the discretion of some other person.³ In view of the further requirement that the life interest be in possession, and of the principle that the objects of a discretionary trust do not have any interest in the trust property,⁴ this provision may appear superfluous.

An interest in possession is not further defined. Generally, an interest is in possession if it gives an immediate entitlement to the income as it arises. A duty or power to withhold the income negatives possession. Thus, a power to accumulate the income negatives possession save where the accumulation is for the person with the interest. A power to revoke the entitlement or to appoint another does not affect the immediate entitlement to the income since until the power is exercised the income belongs to the beneficiary.⁵

On practice, where a tenant for life releases part of his interest to the remainderman, see Statement of Practice D10.⁶

Simon's Taxes C4.209; Sumption CGT A6.08.
¹ CGTA 1979, s. 55(4).
² LPA 1925, s. 149.
³ CGTA 1979, s. 55(4).
⁴ *Gartside v IRC* [1968] AC 553, [1968] 1 All ER 121.
⁵ See infra, § **41: 08**. Can trustees make a binding decision to appoint income to someone before it has arisen?
⁶ **Simon's Taxes, Division H3.4.**

Parts

18: 14   There is deemed disposal on the death of the life tenant whether the life interest in possession is all or any part of settled property. Where his interest relates only to a part of the property, there is a deemed disposal only of a corresponding part of the property. On the termination of a life interest on an occasion other than death of the life tenant there is now no disposal under these rules.

A life interest which is a right to a part of the income of settled property is treated as an interest in a corresponding part of the property.¹ Thus if property is held on trust for A and B for their lives with remainders over, A's death will cause a deemed disposal of one-half of each of the assets forming part of the settled property. If however two settlements had been created the one with life interest to A, the other with life interest to B, there would have been a deemed disposal of all the assets forming part of A's settlement.

If there is a life interest in income from a part of the settled property and no right of recourse to, or to the income of, the remainder of the settled property, that part is treated as a separate settlement. A part in this context means a fraction and not necessarily a separated piece so that four one-quarter shares of the income for life[2] create four separate settlements.[3]

Normally an annuity is not treated as a life interest notwithstanding that it is payable out of or charged on settled property or the income of settled property.[4] However, it will be so treated if it is created by the settlement *and* some or all of the settled property is appropriated by the trustees as the exclusive fund out of which the annuity is payable.[5] The fund so appropriated is treated as a separate settlement.

Simon's Taxes C4.211; Sumption CGT A6.03.
  [1] CGTA 1979, s. 55, see *Pexton v Bell* [1976] STC 301, [1976] 2 All ER 914, noted [1976] BTR 257 (Milne).
  [2] Assuming they are not *joint* tenants, yet the wording of s. 55(6) stresses that there must be no right of recourse to the income. What of the future right of recourse by virtue of survivorship?
  [3] *Pexton v Bell* supra; *Allison v Murray* [1975] STC 524, [1975] 3 All ER 561, hence the termination of one share causes a deemed disposal of that quarter share only and not of the whole settled property.
  [4] CGTA 1979, s. 54(4).
  [5] CGTA 1979, s. 54(5).

Earlier holding-over

18: 15 Where a gain was held over on the creation of the settlement of the property deemed disposed of, the death of the life tenant may result in a chargeable gain arising to the extent of the gain so held over,[1] where the property remains in the settlement, as well as where it leaves the settlement.

EXAMPLE
    S transfers assets valued at £15,000 to trustees in trust for L for life and then to B absolutely. S's acquisition cost was £10,000 and he elects to roll over the gains of £5,000 deemed to accrue on his disposal of the assets to the trustees. The trustees' acquisition cost of the assets is therefore £10,000. L dies; the settled assets are then valued at £21,000. A gain of £11,000 accrues to the trustees on the deemed disposal but the chargeable gain is restricted to £5,000, the amount of the rolled-over gain.
    If the gain accruing to the trustees on the deemed disposal had been £4,000, the whole of this would have been chargeable as it is less than the rolled-over gain.
    The new acquisition cost of the settled assets to which B is now absolutely entitled as against the trustees is £21,000, the value thereof at L's death.

Simon's Taxes C4.208.
  [1] FA 1982, s. 82; CGTA 1979, s. 56A.

Discretionary trusts

18: 16 There is no deemed disposal on the termination of a beneficiary's rights under a discretionary trust since he does not have a life interest in possession. There will however be gains or losses arising when the trustees dispose of trust property in the course of administration or when they exercise their powers over capital to cause settled property to cease to be settled.

Market value

18: 17   The value at which the deemed disposal takes place is the market value of the trust assets on the date of disposal. Hypothetical costs of such a disposal and acquisition are excluded, but actual costs are not.[1]

Where property was held on trust for A for life with remainder to B contingent on B surviving A and with remainder to C if B predeceased A, an order was made under the Variation of Trusts Act. The capital was to be divided 40% to A, and 60% to B but with a condition that B take out an insurance policy to cover C's contingent interest. This was a deemed disposal and so a later disposal by the trustees fell to be treated as a disposal by bare trustees.[2] One issue was whether the premium was deductible. It was held that the premium paid for the purchase not of the *trust* assets but of C's interest.[3] Further, the statute said what the consideration was to be and that could not be glossed so as to being in value paid as part of an arrangement whereby a larger interest was acquired under the settlement.

Simon's Taxes C2.122.
[1] Infra, § 21: 04.
[2] *Allison v Murray* [1975] STC 524, [1975] 3 All ER 561. A died one year later so the scheme to save estate duty failed.
[3] So not deductible under CGTA 1979, s. 32(1)(*a*).

BENEFICIAL INTERESTS

18: 18   Two principal rules apply. (1) An interest created by the settlement may be disposed of in the same way as any other asset but a chargeable gain can accrue *only* if the interest was acquired by the disposer or by the person from whom the disposer derives his title by assignment for money or money's worth. In these circumstances there is no chargeable disposal by the person for whose benefit the interest was created.[1] Neither is there any chargeable disposal by the assignee unless he acquired the interest for a consideration in money or money's worth; even then there is no chargeable gain if the consideration consisted of another interest under the settlement. (2) Where a person has acquired an interest in settled property and then becomes absolutely entitled as against the trustee to any settled property, he is treated as disposing of the interest in return for the property to which he becomes entitled, the latter being valued at current market value.[2]

> **EXAMPLE**
> Property is held on trust for A for life remainder to B and X bought B's reversionary interest ten years ago and A now dies. X is treated as disposing of the reversionary interest so that a CGT liability may accrue. In computing his gain X is allowed to deduct the acquisition consideration he paid to B. If X, having bought the reversionary interest had given it to Y there could have been a charge to CGT at that time by reference to the then market value.

A life interest in settled property is a wasting asset and the costs of acquisition must be written down.[3]

Variation of trusts involving the transfers of beneficial interests will not therefore cause a disposal of those interests, so long as they are all interests under the same settlement and none was acquired for money or money's worth. If however an interest under one settlement is used as consideration for the acquisition of a beneficial interest under another, very different results may follow. There may moreover be a deemed disposal by the trustees.

The exemption for interests in settled property does not apply if the trustees are non-resident. Moreover, where an interest in a resident settlement has been disposed of subject to the exemption, the trustees may be deemed to realise chargeable gains if the settlement subsequently becomes non-resident.[4]

Simon's Taxes C4.228; Sumption CGT A6.12.
[1] CGTA 1979, s. 58(1) but for non-resident settlements, infra, § **34: 52**; the IHT position is quite different, infra, § **41: 15**.
[2] CGTA 1979, s. 58(2).
[3] CGTA 1979, s. 37.
[4] FA 1981, s. 88 infra, § **34: 52**.

19 Shares and companies

SECURITIES: POOLING AND IDENTIFICATION

19: 01   In determining which securities are disposed of on a particular disposal, special rules apply. These rules are relevant not only for indexation relief purposes but whenever allowable expenditure has to be ascertained. In general, all shares or securities of the same class, held by the same person in the same capacity, are pooled. This pooling rule is subject to a number of exceptions and qualifications.

(1) Certain securities are subject to special identification rules linking particular disposals with particular acquisitions.[1] These are:

(a) gilt-edged securities, on a disposal before 1st July 1986 (supra, § **15: 18**);[2]

(b) shares issued before 19th March 1986 in business expansion schemes, when relief has not been withdrawn. The identification rule was that shares disposed of were identified first with shares which qualified for relief under the business start-up scheme, then with shares qualifying under the business expansion scheme, on a first-in, first-out basis in each case;[3]

(c) loan stock and similar securities subject to the accrued income scheme;[4]

(d) deep discount securities;[5]

(e) securities comprising a material interest in a non-qualifying offshore fund.[6]

Securities under headings (c) to (e) are covered by the rules (infra, § **19: 03**) which applied to securities generally before 6th April 1985.

(2) Certain securities outside the prescribed list in (1) are not pooled. These are securities disposed of on or before the day of acquisition[7] and shares disposed of within 10 days after acquisition.[8] There is also the special rule for companies, infra, § **25: 06**.

(3) Other securities of the same class which are held by one person in one capacity are pooled and treated as a single asset.[9] The pooling rule applies notwithstanding that one can or one intends to transfer particular identifiable securities.

The pooling rule is also modified according to the dates on which the securities were acquired.

(a) *Acquisition before 6th April 1965*   Where no pooling election has been made these remain separate assets. A right to elect for pooling is given.[10] Where an election has been made they form part of the 1982 pool (see (*b*)).

(*b*) *Acquisitions before 6th April 1982*[11]   These form a pool of their own[12] distinct from later acquisitions. Where the shares were acquired after 5th April 1981[13] but before 6th April 1982[11] the rules in force before 6th April 1985 required that to the extent that they represented a net increase in the holding they should be treated as separate assets (infra, § **19: 03**). Such segregated shares are added to the 1982 pool with effect from 6th April 1985.[14]

(*c*) *Acquisitions since 5th April 1982*[13]   Those which have been acquired since that date and not disposed of before 6th April 1985[11] are now treated as a single asset. The pool will henceforward grow or diminish as shares are acquired or disposed of[15] and anything short of a disposal of all the shares in the pool will be a part disposal.

Shares which are issued on terms restricting the holder's right to dispose, e.g. to an employee, are pooled separately so long as the restrictions remain.[16] The effects of rebasing CGT to 31st March 1982 are clearly limited only to categories (*a*) and (*b*). However, because of the continuing requirement to compare gains or losses computed on the new basis with the result of applying the former rules,[17] categories (*a*) and (*b*) still cannot be consolidated in relation to disposals after 5th April 1988 unless the shareholder has elected under FA 1988, s. 96(5) (see § **22: 04**, infra).

Rules for the interaction of (*a*), (*b*) and (*c*) are also provided where, as may occur, a holding includes pre-1965 acquisitions, a pre-1982 pool and a current pool. The shares disposed of are treated as coming first from the current pool, then from the pre-1982 pool and finally from pre-1965 acquisitions which have not been pooled—such shares are treated as disposed of on a last in first out basis.[18] As with the general pooling rule these rules cannot be overridden by any designation by the parties or the disposal itself. The rules are, however, subject to the special rules for identifying shares bought on the same or later day or within the previous 10 days.[19]

Simon's Taxes C2.401; Sumption CGT A12.04, 08, 13.
[1] FA 1982, s. 88 as amended by FA 1985, Sch. 19, para. 3.
[2] Rules in CGTA 1979, s. 68 apply.
[3] CGTA 1979, s. 149C and TA 1988, s. 299.
[4] Defined FA 1984, s. 72 and Sch. 19; FA 1982, s. 88 as amended by FA 1985, Sch. 19, para. 3 applies.
[5] Defined FA 1984, s. 36, see supra, § **9: 49**; FA 1982, s. 88 as amended by FA 1985, Sch. 19, para. 3 applies. See also FA 1984, Sch. 9, para. 11.
[6] Defined FA 1984, ss. 92–95: FA 1982, s. 88 as amended by FA 1985, Sch. 19, para. 3 applies.
[7] CGTA 1979, s. 66 revived by FA 1985, Sch. 19, para. 17.
[8] FA 1985, Sch. 19, para. 18.
[9] FA 1985, Sch. 19, Part III replacing CGTA 1979, s. 65; see FA 1985, Sch. 19, para. 17.
[10] FA 1985, Sch. 19, para. 6(3).
[11] 1st April for corporation tax.
[12] FA 1985, Sch. 19, para. 6(1).
[13] 31st March for corporation tax.
[14] FA 1985, Sch. 19, para. 6(2).
[15] FA 1985, Sch. 19, para. 9.
[16] FA 1985, Sch. 19, para. 8(2).
[17] FA 1988, s. 96(3). See, infra, § **22: 02**.

[18] FA 1985, Sch. 19, para. 19.
[19] FA 1985, Sch. 19, para. 19; presumably the reference in para. 19 to CGTA 1979, s. 66 is surplus in view of para. 17(1)(*a*).

Share pooling and indexation[1]

19: 02   The basic principle of pooling under the post 5th April 1985 rules is that, in addition to the allowable cost of the pool, an indexed cost must also be calculated.[1]

Where an event occurs which increases or reduces the qualifying expenditure, an event called an operative event, the "indexed rise" in the value of the pool since the last such event is computed and is added to the indexed cost of the pool.[2] If the operative event is an increase in qualifying expenditure, e.g. more shares are acquired, the acquisition cost is added to both the unindexed and indexed pools (in the latter case, after computing the indexed rise).[3] If there is a decrease in the qualifying expenditure because there is a disposal, the indexed pool is reduced in the same *proportion* as the unindexed pool.[4] If there is a decrease in the expenditure but no disposal, e.g. on receipt of a small capital distribution, infra, § **19: 13**, the indexed pool is reduced by the same amount as the reduction in qualifying expenditure.[5]

When the holding consists of shares held on 6th April 1985 and acquired since 5th April 1982 the indexed pool consists of the qualifying expenditure plus any indexation allowance due to it down to 6th April 1985.[6]

In the case of any other new holding, i.e. shares acquired after 5th April 1985, the indexed pool begins when the holding begins[7] and consists of the qualifying expenditure at that time.

The indexed rise is calculated by multiplying the value of the indexed pool immediately before the operative event by the fraction $\dfrac{RE - RL}{RL}$, expressed as a decimal.[8] RE is the retail prices index for the month in which the operative event occurs and RL is the figure for the month in which the last operative event occurred, or, if there is none, the pool began. If the index drops over this period the indexed rise is nil.[9]

On a disposal of the whole holding, the indexation allowance is simply the difference between the indexed and unindexed pools.[10] Where there is a part disposal the qualifying expenditure in the unindexed pool is attributed to the part disposal in accordance with the part disposal formula, $\dfrac{A}{A+B}$ (see § **16: 14**). For securities which are quoted on the Stock Exchange, the apportionment is made according to the number of shares involved.[11] The indexation allowance is then the amount by which the portion of the indexed pool attributed to the part disposal exceeds the portion of qualifying expenditure so attributed.[12]

EXAMPLE

AB made the following transactions in ordinary shares of ER Co plc. He held no such shares before 6th April 1982.

1st June 1983	Bought 1,500: cost £2,750
30th September 1984	Bought 3,500: cost £7,250
15th May 1985	Bought 2,000: cost £4,100
30th September 1985	Sold 1,000: proceeds £2,050

21st March 1986   Sold 6,000: proceeds £10,000

Relevant values of the retail prices index are as follows—

June 1983	334·7
September 1984	355·5
April 1985	373·9
May 1985	375·6
September 1985	376·5
March 1986	381·7

	Shares	Unindexed pool £	£	Indexed pool £
June 1983 acquisition	1,500	2,750	2,750	
$\dfrac{373\cdot9 - 334\cdot7}{334\cdot7} \times £2,750$			322	3,072
September 1984 acquisition	3,500	7,250	7,250	
$\dfrac{373\cdot9 - 355\cdot5}{355\cdot5} \times £7,250$			375	7,625
April 1985 holding	5,000	10,000		10,697
$\dfrac{375\cdot6 - 373\cdot9}{373\cdot9} \times £10,697$				49
May 1985 acquisition	2,000	4,100		4,100
May 1985 holding	7,000	14,100		14,846
$\dfrac{376\cdot5 - 375\cdot6}{375\cdot6} \times £14,846$				36
				14,882
September 1985 disposal	(1,000)	(2,014)		(2,126)
September 1985 holding	6,000	12,086		12,756
$\dfrac{381\cdot7 - 376\cdot5}{376\cdot5} \times £12,756$				176
				12,932
March 1986 disposal	(6,000)	(12,086)		(12,932)

(a) September 1985 disposal   £2,050
Disposal proceeds
Allowable cost   £2,014
Indexation allowance: £2,126 − £2,014   112   2,126

Allowable loss   £(76)

(b) March 1986 disposal   £10,000
Disposal proceeds
Allowable cost   £12,086
Indexation allowance: £12,932 − £12,086   846   12,932

Allowable loss   £(2,932)

Special provisions apply where shares are acquired under an option.[13] The cost of the option is a separate item of expenditure but it is not added to the pool unless and until it is exercised to acquire shares, when the option cost becomes part of the share cost.[14] The indexed rise then takes account of the period during which the option was held prior to exercise.

Simon's Taxes C2.401; Sumption CGT A12.08.

[1] FA 1985, Sch. 19, paras. 11–14.
[2] FA 1985, Sch. 19, para. 13(5)(*a*).
[3] FA 1985, Sch. 19, para. 13(5)(*b*).
[4] FA 1985, Sch. 19, para. 13(5)(*c*).
[5] FA 1985, Sch. 19, para. 13(5)(*d*).
[6] FA 1985, Sch. 19, para. 13(2).
[7] FA 1985, Sch. 19, para. 13(3).
[8] FA 1985, Sch. 19, para. 14. It is unclear why the fraction should be expressed as a decimal, since there is no rounding to a specified number of decimal places; contrast FA 1982, s. 87(4) in relation to the calculation of indexation factors.
[9] FA 1985, Sch. 19, para. 14(2).
[10] FA 1985, Sch. 19, para. 11(3).
[11] See Revenue booklet CGT 8 (1980), para. 152 (now withdrawn).
[12] FA 1985, Sch. 19, para. 11(2).
[13] FA 1985, Sch. 19, para. 15.
[14] CGTA 1979, s. 137(3).

Identifying the pool of 6th April 1985

19: 03   In order to calculate which shares are in the pool on 6th April 1985 it may be necessary to consider what has happened to the shares before that date. In particular, the rules as to identification which operated between 1982 and 1985 will have to be taken into account.

For disposals after 5th April 1982 and before 6th April 1985 the rules are as follows. On disposal, shares are to be considered for identification in order of disposal, the earliest disposal being identified first. Shares disposed of must (if quoted) first be identified with any concurrent or later acquisitions in the same Stock Exchange period of account.[1]

Once shares purchased in the same Stock Exchange account have been identified, shares disposed of must be identified first with shares acquired in the previous twelve months, on a first in first out basis, and then with shares acquired more than twelve months before the disposal, on a last in first out basis.[2] Any balance of shares still not identified are then matched with the pre 6th April 1982 pool (infra, § **19: 04**) and then with pre 6th April 1965 acquisitions (if not pooled) on a last in first out basis (infra, § **22: 11**).

> EXAMPLE
> A made the following acquisitions and disposals of ordinary shares in PQR plc:
> On 6th April 1983   Acquired 2,000
> On 6th May 1983   Acquired 1,000
> On 6th July 1983   Acquired 1,000
> On 6th October 1983   Acquired 3,000
> On 6th June 1984   Sold 2,000
> On 6th August 1984   Sold 3,000
> (*a*) Disposal on 6th June 1984
>   (i) 1,000 identified with the 1,000 acquired on 6th July 1983
>   (ii) 1,000 identified with 1,000 of the 3,000 acquired on 6th October 1983
> (*b*) Disposal on 6th August 1984
>   (i) 2,000 identified with 2,000 of the 3,000 acquired on 6th October 1983
>   (ii) 1,000 identified with the 1,000 acquired on 6th May 1983
> A's remaining holding therefore consists of the 2,000 shares acquired on 6th April 1983.

Where shares are acquired for delivery on a specified date (or account) and, under the same bargain, are disposed of for delivery on a later date (or account), the acquisition and disposal are identified with each other, notwithstanding the general rules.[3] Such bargains ("contangos") could otherwise have been used to exploit the pre 6th April 1985 indexation rules.

There are rules to prevent indexation allowances being claimed where shares have been acquired both within the twelve month period and before it and it is sought to transfer the shares bought within the twelve month period to a spouse or group company so that the indexation allowance can be claimed on the subsequent sale to a third party.[4] This is countered by deeming the order of the transfers to be reversed.

Simon's Taxes C2.401; Sumption CGT A12.05.
[1] FA 1982, s. 88(4).
[2] FA 1982, s. 88(5).
[3] FA 1982, s. 88(7).
[4] FA 1982, s. 89.

Pre 6th April 1982 acquisitions

19: 04   The position with regard to shares held on 6th April 1982 is that, similarly to the present rules, shares of the same class held by the same person in the same capacity are pooled. Disposals before 6th April 1982 were treated in the same way as disposals from a 1985 pool,[1] but clearly without any special adjustments regarding indexation. However, disposals were identified with shares acquired before 6th April 1965 on a first in, first out basis, not last in, first out as at present.[2] For disposals on or after 6th April 1982 but before 6th April 1985, special rules applied to adjust the indexation allowance where there was a net addition of shares to the pool during 1981–82, in view of the then 12 months waiting period for indexation. Any acquisitions segregated from the 1982 pool and which remain undisposed of at 6th April 1985 are added back to the 1982 pool for disposals on or after that date,[3] following the abolition of the 12 month waiting period.

For disposals on or after 6th April 1988, the pool cost is recomputed to include any additions on or before 31st March 1982 at their market value on that date.[4] Additions to the pool on or after 1st April 1982 but before 6th April 1982 are included at cost. It is not clear how to identify these two elements of the 1982 pool where there have been disposals out of the pool before 6th April 1988, since no rules are provided for this purpose.

Simon's Taxes C2.404; Sumption CGT A12.04.
[1] FA 1982, Sch. 13, para. 8.
[2] FA 1982, Sch 13, para 9.
[3] FA 1985, Sch. 19, para. 12.
[4] FA 1988, s. 96. See, infra, § **22: 02**.

Parallel pooling

19: 05   As an alternative to the identification rules described in §§ **19: 03–04**, a modified version of the former pooling provisions,[1] was introduced by FA 1983,[2] and was intended to assist companies with computerised records of large share portfolios subject to rapid turnover. The election for parallel pooling, which was originally irrevocable, was able to be revoked not later than 31st March 1987.[3] In any event, the election ceases to have effect for disposals on or after 1st April 1985, and the Treasury has issued regulations to facilitate the application of the present rules to holdings still covered by a parallel pooling election.[4]

For an outline of the indexation rules as they applied to disposals before 6th April 1985 to shares held in this way see Butterworths *UK Tax Guide 1984–85* § **19: 15, 16.**

Simon's Taxes C2.405; Sumption CGT A12.10.

[1] Supra, § **15: 02.**

[2] FA 1983, s. 34 and Sch. 6.

[3] FA 1985, Sch. 19, para. 20. It appears that an election will have effect only from 1st April 1985, so that the holdings concerned will then fall to be treated as part of the 1985 pool. However, the reference to adjustments falling to be made on revocation suggests that the effect might be retroactive.

[4] FA 1985, Sch. 19, para. 21; Capital Gains Tax (Parallel Pooling) Regulations 1986, S.I. 387, No. 1986.

CAPITAL DISTRIBUTIONS

19: 06   A company makes a capital distribution if it makes any distribution in money or money's worth which would not be treated as income in the hands of the recipient for purposes of income tax.[1] A capital distribution is a disposal or part disposal of the shares held, the consideration being the amount received by the shareholder.[2] However, there is relief from tax where the capital distribution consists of shares or securities issued as part of a capital reorganisation (such as a scrip or rights issue) or, on election, where the capital distribution is "small" (infra, § **19: 13**). Taxable capital distributions commonly include distributions in liquidation,[3] repayment of share capital,[4] repurchase by a company of its own share capital,[5] and certain capital distributions by foreign companies.[6] For relief on demergers, see infra, § **26: 27.**

Simon's Taxes C2.425; Sumption CGT A10.14.

[1] CGTA 1979, s. 72(5)(*b*).

[2] CGTA 1979, s. 72(1).

[3] Per TA 1988, s. 209(1).

[4] Per TA 1988, s. 209(2)(*b*).

[5] Per TA 1988, s. 219.

[6] Infra, § **34.08.**

Reorganisations

19: 07   A reorganisation is not treated as a disposal of a shareholding.[1] There is a reorganisation if there is a reorganisation or reduction of share capital; this is stated to include (*a*) the allotment of shares or debentures in proportion to shareholdings and (*b*) any alteration of share rights—assuming that there are at least two classes.[2] Although a reduction in share capital is a reorganisation, both the paying off of redeemable share capital and the redemption of shares other than by the issue of new shares or debentures are excluded.[3] The reorganisation rules do not apply to the extent that the shareholder receives consideration other than the new holding (such as a cash payment) from the company, or any consideration from the other shareholders.[4]

Simon's Taxes C2.421; Sumption CGT A10.01; A13.02.
[1] CGTA 1979, s. 78.
[2] CGTA 1979, s. 77; an allotment to debenture holders does not qualify. The guiding principle appears to be that there is continued identity of the shareholders, holding their shares in the same proportions: *Dunstan v Young Austen Young Ltd* [1989] STC 69.
[3] CGTA 1979, s. 77(3).
[4] CGTA 1979, s. 79(2).

Bonus (scrip) issues

19: 08 Where new shares or securities are allotted to shareholders without consideration, the new shares or debentures are treated as forming one combined asset with the shares previously held, and make a new holding but with the old date of acquisition and acquisition cost.[1] Where the original shares were acquired before 1st April 1982, the rebasing to 31st March 1982 value applies to the whole shareholding, including the bonus shares issued. There is neither acquisition of the new shares or debentures nor disposal of the original shares. So, on a bonus issue of shares of the same class as the original holding, the bonus shares are simply added to those already held. On any subsequent disposal of a part of the holding, gains or losses are computed by taking the appropriate proportion of the cost of the original shares, supra, § **19: 02**.

Simon's Taxes C2.423; Sumption CGT A13.02.
[1] CGTA 1979, s. 78. Special rules apply to shares issued as stock dividends (as they are income). They are treated as acquired for the appropriate amount of cash (infra, § **24: 15**, ss. 89 and 90). Special rules also apply to shares acquired as an employee, s. 76.

Rights issues

19: 09 If the person provides consideration for the new shares or debentures, as on a rights issue, again the holding forms a single asset but the consideration paid is added to the expenditure incurred on the holding.[1] For a pre 1st April 1982 holding, the consideration paid is added to the value of the holding at 31st March 1982. However, for the purposes of the indexation allowance, the consideration paid is treated as a separate item of relevant expenditure incurred when it is actually incurred and not as having been incurred on the acquisition date of the original shares.[2]

EXAMPLE
V purchased 1,000 ordinary shares in XYZ Ltd in 1979, for £5,800. In May 1983, there was a rights issue of one ordinary share for every five held, at £9.50 per share. In March 1986, V sold his entire holding of 1,200 shares for £15,000.

Disposal consideration		£15,000
Allowable cost:		
Original holding	£5,800	
Rights issue	1,900	7,700
Gain		7,300
Indexation allowance:		
Original holding: 0.218 × 5,800 =	1,264	
Rights issue: 0.065 × 1,900 =	124	1,388
Chargeable gain		£5,912

The consideration will not be so added if it originates from the shares themselves rather than from the shareholder, for example if it consists of the surrender, cancellation or alteration of the original shares, nor if the new shares are paid up out of the assets of the company or out of a dividend or any other distribution declared—but not made—out of the company's assets. This is to prevent an uplift in the base cost by the use of the company's assets.

On a reorganisation after 9th March 1981 any new consideration, e.g. that payable under a rights issue, forms part of the allowable cost of the shares only to the extent that the reorganised shareholding is more valuable than the original.[3] This restriction counters schemes intended to secure relief for losses on loans.[4] There could be difficulties for a minority shareholder in an unquoted company subscribing for a rights issue since the value of his minority holding is unlikely to increase by as much.

Simon's Taxes C2.423; Sumption CGT A13.02.
[1] CGTA 1979, s. 79(1).
[2] FA 1982, Sch. 13, para. 5.
[3] CGTA 1979, s. 79(1), proviso, added by FA 1981, s. 91.
[4] See *IRC v Burmah Oil Co Ltd* [1980] STC 731; revsd. [1982] STC 30.

Computation

19: 10   Where a reorganisation involves the issue of shares of a different class, or of debentures, the new securities cannot be pooled with the old for computing the allowable cost on a part disposal out of the new holding. Instead, the original consideration and any new consideration are both apportioned between the different classes of securities in the new holding. If any of the classes is listed on a recognised stock exchange, the allowable costs are apportioned pro rata to the market values of each element on the first day of market quotation.[1]

EXAMPLE

Y purchased 5,000 ordinary shares in Z plc for £4,000 in January 1981. In May 1984, Y took up a rights issue in Z plc, of one convertible preference share per four ordinary shares, at £1.04 per share. In February 1986, Y sold 1,000 of the ordinary shares for £4,500. Relevant values of the shares on the first day of listing after the reorganisation.

Ordinary   £2.10
Preference   £1.08

(a) *Allocate costs*:
Ordinary shares:

(i) Original cost $£4,000 \times \dfrac{10,500}{10,500+1,350} =$ £3,544

(ii) Rights $£1,300 \times \dfrac{10,500}{10,500+1,350} =$ £1,152

Preference shares:
(i) Original cost £4,000 − £3,544   £456
(ii) Rights   £1,300 − £1,152   £148

(b) *Computation of gain*
Disposal consideration   £4,500
Allowable costs:
$£3,544 \times \dfrac{1,000}{5,000}$ £709

$£1,152 \times \dfrac{1,000}{5,000}$	230	939	
Indexation allowance:			
£709 × 0.216	153		
£230 × 0.086	20	173	1,112
Chargeable gain			£3,388

In other cases, where none of the elements of the new holding is quoted, the apportionment of costs is made pro rata to market values at the date of disposal.[2]

Simon's Taxes C2.423; Sumption CGT A12.03.
[1] CGTA 1979, s. 81.
[2] CGTA 1979, s. 80(1). This provision relates only to the cost of the original shares not to the cost of the rights issue; this is difficult to reconcile with the 'one asset' principle of the reorganisation rules.

19: 11   Where there are unpaid calls in respect of any of the shares or securities in the new holding, adjustments may be required when apportioning allowable costs. The amounts unpaid are treated as part of the allowable costs to be apportioned, but the market values used in the apportionment are similarly increased.[1] For indexation purposes, calls paid are treated as expenditure incurred when the shares are acquired, unless payable more than 12 months after that date.[2]

EXAMPLE
   P inherited 10,000 ordinary "A" shares in Q plc from his father in 1972. Probate value was £3,500. In December 1982, Q plc made a rights issue of one ordinary "B" share for each 10 "A" shares held at 90p per share part paid. A further 30p is payable in June 1983. In December 1985, P sold 500 of his "B" shares for £1,500. Relevant market values on the first day of listing are:

"A" shares	200p
"B" shares (part paid)	95p

(*a*) *Allocate costs*:
   "A" shares:

(i) Original cost $£3,500 \times \dfrac{20,000}{20,000+1,250} =$	£3,294
(ii) Rights $£1,200 \times \dfrac{20,000}{20,000+1,250} =$	£1,129

   "B" shares:

(i) Original cost £3,500 − £3,294	£206
(ii) Rights £1,200 − £1,129	£71

(*b*) *Computation of gain*

Disposal consideration		£1,500
Allowable costs:		
$£206 \times \dfrac{500}{1,000}$	£103	

$$£71 \times \frac{500}{1,000} \qquad \underline{35} \qquad 138$$

Indexation allowance:

£103 × 0.209	22		
£71 × 0.164	12	34	172

Chargeable gain   £1,328

Simon's Taxes C2.423; Sumption CGT A12.03.
[1] CGTA 1979, ss. 80(1), 81(2).
[2] FA 1982, Sch. 13, para. 6.

Other capital distributions

(1) Rights issue—sale of rights

19: 12   A sale of rights under a rights issue is an example of a taxable capital distribution. The distribution is not a new holding; instead the shareholder is treated as having disposed of an interest in his holding[1] and as having received consideration equal to the market value of the distribution.[2] The sale of rights under a rights issue will be treated as a part disposal.[3] There will similarly be a part disposal if, on a bonus or rights issue, the company sells fractional entitlements on the market and allocates the cash to shareholders.

EXAMPLE

    S bought 5,000 ordinary shares in T plc for £8,500 in December 1984. In March 1986, S was allotted rights on a 2 for 5 rights issue of ordinary shares. He immediately sold the rights nil paid for £1,500. The value of T plc ordinary shares is £3.30 ex rights.

Disposal consideration		£1,500
Allowable cost		
$£8,500 \times \dfrac{1,500}{1,500+16,500}$	£708	
Indexation allowance		
£708 × 0.064	45	753
Chargeable gain		£747

Simon's Taxes C2.427; Sumption CGT A12.23.
[1] CGTA 1979, s. 72.
[2] CGTA 1979, s. 29A(1)(a).
[3] CGTA 1979, s. 73. Whether or not company has made a provisional allotment; a relaxed valuation rule applies to disposal of rights.

19: 13   *Small distributions.* An exception is made for small distributions. The amount of the distribution is compared with the value of the shares in respect of which the distribution is made.[1] In practice it is treated as small if the distribution amounts to less than 5% of the value of the shares,[2] valued after the distribution is made. If the inspector of taxes so directs, the amount received is deducted from the allowable expenditure. Where the gain exceeds the allowable expenditure, the excess remains chargeable. There is provision for appeal against a refusal by the inspector to apply the provision.[3] In

practice, the shareholder can choose to apply the normal rules if it would be
to his benefit, e.g. if the gain is covered by the annual exemption.

Simon's Taxes C2.428; Sumption CGT A12.23.
[1] CGTA 1979, s. 72(2) and (5).
[2] IR Booklet, CGT 8 (1980), § 125 (now withdrawn).
[3] CGTA 1979, s. 72(3).

---

(2) *Liquidation*

19: 14   If a liquidator makes a distribution of the entire assets of the
company to the shareholders, there is a disposition of their shares, for a
consideration equal to the value of the assets so distributed.[1] More usually
however the liquidator will make a number of successive distributions to the
shareholders. Since each distribution is a part disposal of the shares, great
practical difficulties arise because of the need to find the market value of the
shareholding after each such distribution. Where unquoted shares are
concerned the Board[2] accept the taxpayer's valuation provided it appears
reasonable and the winding-up is expected to be completed within two years,
and is in fact completed only shortly beyond that time. There is no need to
discount for deferment. If, as will usually be the case, the final distributions
are made before the assessments, the market value is ascertained by reference
to the sums actually received in the later distributions.

A more fundamental problem is whether there is a notional disposal by the
company when winding-up commences. The point here is that the company
ceases to be beneficially entitled at that point and a trust arises in favour of
creditors and contributories; accordingly it is unclear whether beneficial
ownership is in suspense[3] or passes to the shareholders.[4] If the latter is
correct, then the holders become entitled to receive the assets so that there is
a disposal by the company to the shareholders when winding-up commences.
The former view seems to be more correct. In practice the Revenue treat the
shareholders as making a part disposal as and when cash or other property is
received.

Simon's Taxes C2.425.
[1] This is also a disposal by the liquidator on behalf of the company; infra, § 25: 04.
[2] Inland Revenue Press Release, 20th January 1972.
[3] *IRC v Olive Mill Ltd* [1963] 2 All ER 130, 41 TC 77.
[4] See Court of Appeal in *Ayerst v C & K (Construction) Ltd* [1975] STC 1, [1975] 1 All ER 162;
affd. by the House of Lords on other grounds [1975] STC 345, [1975] 2 All ER 537.

CONVERSION OF SECURITIES

19: 15   The technique of treating the original and the new holding as the
same asset is applied to the conversion of securities. These transactions are
dealt with separately in the legislation since securities are distinct from share
capital. There is no disposal where debentures are converted into shares or
into other securities whether or not the taxpayer could have those securities
redeemed for cash as an alternative to conversion.[1] There is, however, a part
disposal when the person also receives a premium in addition to new
securities—unless the consideration is small i.e. less than 5% of the value of
the securities.[2] Government stock acquired as compensation on nationalisa-

tion is not treated as a conversion.[3] The old shares are treated as being sold at a consideration equal to the market value of the Government securities at the date of issue. Any chargeable gain or allowable loss crystallises only when the Government securities are themselves disposed of. For disposals after 5th April 1988 of Government securities acquired as compensation stock before 1st April 1982, no gain or loss crystallises.[4]

Simon's Taxes C2.422, 423; Sumption CGT A13.03.
[1] CGTA 1979, s 82(1). On the meaning of "securities" see *Cleveleys Investment Trust Co v IRC* (1971) 47 TC 300.
[2] CGTA 1979, s. 83.
[3] CGTA 1979, s. 84; certain disposals are ignored—sub-s. (5).
[4] FA 1989, Sch. 15, para. 1.

COMPANY RECONSTRUCTIONS AND AMALGAMATIONS

Exchange of securities

19: 16   The issue of shares or debentures in exchange for shares or debentures in another company is treated as if the two companies were the same and the exchange was a reorganisation of the share capital.[1] In other words, the shares in the offeror company are treated as having been acquired by the shareholder at the same time, and for the same consideration, as the shares in the company taken over. If cash forms part of the consideration received by the shareholder, then to that extent there is a part disposal, supra, § **19: 06**. The acquiring company must either have or acquire by the exchange more than 25% of the ordinary share capital of the other company[2] or the transaction must be part of a general offer seeking control (i.e. 51%) of that capital (notwithstanding that the offer may subsequently be made unconditional).

Where shares have been exchanged prior to 1st April 1982, any gains which would otherwise have accrued at that time are now effectively eliminated. This is because the new holding is deemed to have been acquired when the original shares were acquired, so that the holding is rebased to its value at 31st March 1982.[3] A share exchange after that date does not necessarily benefit from the rebasing, and any accrued gain at the time of the takeover remains, subject to subsequent movements in the share value. There is no relief for the deferred gain, in contrast with the position in other rollover or holdovers.

Simon's Taxes C2.429; Sumption CGT A13.05.
[1] CGTA 1979, s. 87.
[2] Defined, TA 1988, s. 832(1).
[3] FA 1988, s. 96. See, infra, § **22: 02**.

19: 17   It is not uncommon for a company acquisition to involve the payment of deferred consideration, the quantum of which is related to future results of the target company. The treatment of deferred consideration generally is discussed, supra, § **16: 06**. Where the deferred consideration takes the form of shares in or debentures of the acquiring company, it is doubtful that the target company shareholders are entitled to the tax-free treatment described, supra, § **19: 16**, since the immediate consideration is a right to receive the deferred consideration. The Inland Revenue have issued an Extra-Statutory Concession indicating that tax-free treatment will in practice be extended to such transactions, and setting out the conditions which must be met for this practice to apply.[1]

---

[1] Extra-Statutory Concession D27 (1988); **Simon's Taxes, Division H2.2.**

Schemes of reconstruction

19: 18 The rules relating to reorganisations of capital are also adapted to cover schemes of reconstruction or amalgamation where shares are issued by a company to the shareholders of another, but there is no exchange of shares. Instead, the original shares are either retained, perhaps with altered rights, or cancelled. In this case, the original shares are treated as having been exchanged for the new shares, so that the provisions in § **19: 16** apply.[1] Generally, the new company must carry on substantially the same business as the old, and have substantially the same members. In practice, the split of a company's business between different sets of shareholders is treated as a reconstruction if it is carried out for bona fide commercial reasons.[2] A mere segregation of assets would not be so treated.

Simon's Taxes C2.429; Sumption CGT A13.06.
[1] CGTA 1979, s. 86. Debentures are covered as well as shares.
[2] Statement of Practice SP5/85 incorporating Statement of Practice D14; see **Simon's Taxes, Division H3.2.**

Anti-avoidance

19: 19 The reliefs outlined in §§ **19: 16** and **19: 18** are available only if two conditions are satisfied:[1]

(*a*) that the transaction is effected for bona fide commercial reasons; *and*

(*b*) that it does not form part of a scheme or arrangements of which the main purpose, or one of the main purposes, is avoidance of liability to CGT or corporation tax.

These conditions do not apply—so relief is always available—to a shareholder holding not more than 5% of, or 5% of any class of,the shares in or debentures of the original company. In calculating this 5%, shares or debentures held by connected persons are treated as held by him.

There is a clearance procedure under which it is possible to establish in advance whether or not conditions (*a*) and (*b*) are regarded by the Revenue as satisfied.[2] There is also provision for the recovery of tax remaining unpaid after six months; tax is recovered from the person holding the shares unless there has been an intervening disposal other than one between spouses or members of a group of companies.

Condition (*b*) does not state which of the parties must have this purpose in mind. Commonsense suggests that the purpose should be that of the disposer since he is the person otherwise liable to an immediate charge to CGT;

however caution suggests that the purpose is to be found in the scheme and so perhaps in the minds of all or any of the parties to it.

Simon's Taxes C2.429; Sumption CGT A13.05, 06.
  [1] CGTA 1979, s. 87.
  [2] CGTA 1979, s. 88.

MISCELLANEOUS

19: 20   A company does not own its shares so the issue of shares is not a chargeable disposal by the company. The figure at which the shares are issued, a matter of importance in calculating acquisition cost, is governed by CGTA 1979, s. 29A; see § **16: 23**.

Alterations in share rights may be chargeable disposals (supra, § **16: 22**). On the position of the company's liability to gains, see infra, § **25: 04**.

The gain arising on the disposal of a material interest in an offshore fund (an offshore income gain) is charged to income tax or corporation tax under the provisions of TA 1988, ss. 757–764 and Sch. 27 and 28, see infra, § **34: 43**.

20   Business and partnerships

CAPITAL ALLOWANCES

20: 01   Where a capital allowance is given, the trader is allowed to write off the cost of an asset against the profits of his trade. If he sells the asset at more than the written down value there will be a balancing charge. However, the balancing charge does no more than recover income or corporation tax allowances already given, and does not tax any profit which the trader makes by selling the asset for more than he paid for it. Consequently, any balancing charge does not fall to be excluded from the consideration for disposal, notwithstanding the general exclusion for sums chargeable to income tax or corporation tax as income.[1]

Simon's Taxes C2.120; Sumption CGT A4.08.
   [1] CGTA 1979, s. 31(2).

20: 02   Where assets are sold and a net gain accrues, the fact that capital allowances have been claimed does not prevent the historic cost from being claimed as allowable expenditure;[1] this is because such allowances will have been recaptured by the balancing charge.

Where however a loss arises on disposal of an asset on which allowances have been granted, the allowable expenditure is reduced by the amount of the allowance.[2] Allowances include any balancing allowance on disposal, but are net of any balancing charge on disposal. It may still be possible for an allowable loss to arise in these circumstances, by virtue of the indexation allowance. If the asset has been deemed, for capital allowances purposes, to have been acquired by the disponer at its written down value then account must also be taken of any allowances made to the previous transferor.[3]

Following the rebasing of CGT to 31st March 1982, capital allowances given in respect of the actual expenditure incurred are treated as given in respect of the deemed acquisition cost on 31st March 1982.[4]

Similarly if the asset was acquired before 6th April 1965 and the taxpayer elects to take the value on 6th April 1965 instead of the time apportionment rule, adjustments are made only for allowances after that date.[5]

EXAMPLE

S carries on a trade. In 1981, he purchased an item of equipment for use in the trade, at a cost of £7,500. S claimed first year allowances on the plant, at 100% In February 1986, the equipment is sold for £5,000. The indexation factor is 0.216

			£5,000
Disposal consideration			£5,000
Allowable cost	£7,500		
Net allowances given	2,500	£5,000	
Indexation allowance: 0.216 × 5,000		1,080	6,080
Allowable loss			£1,080

Simon's Taxes C2.107, 323; Sumption CGT A4.08.
[1] CGTA 1979, s. 34(1).
[2] CGTA 1979, s. 34—allowances include the renewals allowance (sub-s. 4) whether or not the allowance is claimed.
[3] CGTA 1979, s. 34(3).
[4] FA 1988, Sch. 8, para. 3.
[5] CGTA 1979, Sch. 5, para. 15.

Wasting assets

20: 03   Although tangible movable property which is a wasting asset is normally exempt from CGT,[1] the exemption does not apply to assets used for the purposes of a trade or profession, where capital allowances were or could have been claimed.[2] Appropriate apportionments are made if the asset is used only in part for trade or professional purposes. Similarly, the provisions for straight line restriction of allowable expenditure on wasting assets do not apply to assets used in a trade or profession.[3] The £6,000 exemption limit for tangible, movable property does however apply to such assets, as does the limitation on losses for assets sold for less than £6,000.[4]

Simon's Taxes C2.136; Sumption CGT A4.11.
[1] CGTA 1979, s. 127(1).
[2] CGTA 1979, s. 127(2). Capital allowances are capable of being claimed if the expenditure concerned is of a qualifying kind, notwithstanding that the asset is sold before being brought into use so that no allowances are due: *Burman v Westminster Press Ltd* [1987] STC 669.
[3] CGTA 1979, s. 38.
[4] CGTA 1979, s. 128; supra, § **15:09**.

TRADING STOCK

20: 04   On the appropriation of capital assets of the trade to trading stock, there is a deemed disposal at market value if there would be a chargeable gain or allowable loss.[1] The exemptions for wasting chattels (subject to the capital allowance restriction) and chattels where the consideration does not exceed £6,000 are of importance here. Where a trader is assessable to income tax under Schedule D, Case I, as opposed, for instance, to Case V,[2] he may elect that the figure at which the trading stock is entered is reduced by the amount of any gain or increased by the amount of any loss, leaving income tax to be levied in due course on the profit derived from the disposal in the course of trade. However, in order to qualify as an appropriation to trading stock there must be a genuine trading purpose in mind, and not simply a wish to gain a tax advantage.[3] Thus, the asset must not only be of a kind sold in the ordinary course of the trade but also acquired with a view to resale at a profit.[4]

Where an asset which has been trading stock is appropriated by the trader for any other purpose or is retained on the ending of the trade it is deemed to be acquired for CGT at the figure entered in the accounts of the trade.[5] This presumably refers to the amount relevant for income tax purposes whether under the rule in *Sharkey v Wernher* or under TA 1988, s. 100.[6]

Simon's Taxes C1.420; Sumption CGT A10.05, A14.07.
[1] CGTA 1979, s. 122.
[2] Infra, § **34: 02**.
[3] *Coates v Arndale Properties Ltd* [1984] STC 637; *Reed v Nova Securities* [1985] STC 124, CA.
[4] Per Lord Templeman in *Reed v Nova Securities Ltd* [1985] STC 124 at 130f.
[5] The logic of *Reed v Nova Securities* is very difficult to apply in this situation.
[6] On a death s. 100 will not apply but market value will be imposed by CGTA 1979, s. 49: on transfer within groups see TA 1970, s. 274.

TRANSFER OF A BUSINESS TO A COMPANY

20: 05 The transfer of a business to a company is a disposal of the assets of the business and so can give rise to chargeable gains and allowable losses. However a roll over relief applies where shares are received in exchange for the business.[1] This applies where the business,[2] and not merely the assets of a business, is transferred to a company as a going concern;[3] all the business assets (other than cash) must be assigned. In practice, the assumption of liabilities by the company is not required.[4] The gain is computed and then allocated to the shares and any other consideration received in return. The assumption of liabilities by the company is not in practice treated as consideration for the transfer.[4] The gain allocated to the other consideration is chargeable immediately. When the shares are themselves disposed of, the amount by which the gain has been reduced and which escaped tax before must be deducted from the cost of the shares and so becomes chargeable.

As in other cases where rollover relief is given, the rebasing of CGT to 31st March 1982 arbitrarily eliminates gains rolled over against shares before 1st April 1982, but not gains rolled over on or after that date. In the latter case, one-half of the gain rolled over is exempt on a subsequent disposal of the shares (infra, § **22: 06**).[5]

Where a person controls a close company through shares which he acquired before 7th April 1965, there is a restriction on the application of time apportionment on disposal of the shares if assets have been transferred to the company by him.[6]

Simon's Taxes C3.201; Sumption CGT A14.08.
[1] CGTA 1979, s. 123. (Cf. TA 1988, s. 386, supra, § **5: 05**.)
[2] Quaere the meaning of business as distinct from trade or profession—see *American Leaf Blending Co Sdn Bhd v Director-General of Inland Revenue* [1978] STC 561, [1978] 3 All ER 1185.
[3] Semble there is no succession to the trade if the company wishes to close it down (supra, § **7: 47**). As a going concern in context refers only to the transferor.

⁴ Extra-statutory concession 20th October 1988, **Simon's Taxes Division H2.2.**
⁵ FA 1988, Sch. 9, para. 2.
⁶ CGTA 1979, Sch. 5, para. 16.

REPLACEMENT OF BUSINESS ASSETS

20: 06   A trader who disposes of assets used for the purposes of his trade throughout the period of ownership may elect to defer any liability to CGT by means of roll-over relief.¹ Other qualifying assets must be acquired within a prescribed period before or after the date of the disposal (see infra, § **20: 07**). The deferral is until such time as he disposes of the new assets or interest in the new assets; however, because the deferral simply takes the form of an adjustment of the cost of the new assets the deferred charge does not crystallise just because the trade is discontinued. Alternatively, the new assets may be disposed of at a loss, or some other relief, e.g. retirement relief may be available.

If the relief is claimed, the disposal is treated as made for a consideration such that neither gain nor loss accrues. The purchaser of the old asset is, however, unaffected by the claim. The chargeable gain that would otherwise have arisen to the vendor is deducted from the base cost of the new assets. Full rollover is available provided that the acquisition cost of the new assets equals or exceeds the actual disposal proceeds of the old asset.

EXAMPLE
In December 1985, K sold for £100,000 a workshop which he had purchased in 1974, realising a chargeable gain of £54,000. In April 1986, he exchanges contracts on new business premises which cost £130,000. K claims rollover relief.

(*a*) Disposal consideration	£100,000
Chargeable gain	54,000
Deemed consideration	£46,000
(*b*) Cost of new property	£130,000
Chargeable gain rolled over	54,000
Base cost deemed to be	£76,000

Where a gain is rolled over against more than one item of qualifying expenditure, there is no prescribed method of apportioning the gain.²

For disposals after 31st March 1982 where a chargeable gain was rolled over, the rebasing of CGT to that date has no effect. Relief is given by deducting one-half of the rolled over gain then computing gains on a subsequent disposal.³ The position is unclear if the gain was rolled back against pre 1st April 1982 expenditure. For disposals prior to 1st April 1982, the gain will effectively be eliminated if rolled over against expenditure prior to that date.

Simon's Taxes C3.101; Sumption CGT A14.01–06.
¹ CGTA 1979, s. 115.
² The Revenue favour apportionment pro rata to the amount of the expenditure.
³ FA 1988, Sch. 9, para. 2.

Partial rollover

20: 07 If the acquisition cost of the new assets is less than the disposal proceeds of the old asset, only partial rollover is available. Relief is available only to the extent that the gain element has to be used in acquiring the new asset.

The chargeable gain is in such a case limited to the difference between the disposal proceeds of the old asset and the acquisition cost of the new assets.[1] The balance of the chargeable gain is rolled over against the cost of the new assets. Where the gain is only partly chargeable, e.g. because of time apportionment, the gain rolled over is scaled down rateably.

EXAMPLE 1

N disposes of a qualifying business asset for £75,000, realising a chargeable gain of £25,000. He acquires a replacement asset for £60,000 and claims rollover relief.

Gain remaining chargeable: £75,000 − £60,000 = £15,000
Gain eligible for rollover: £25,000 − £15,000 = £10,000
Adjusted base cost of new asset: £60,000 − £10,000 = £50,000

EXAMPLE 2

In 1987, J sells a business asset which has been owned since 1960. The sale price is £120,000 and the gain is £90,000. After time apportionment, the chargeable gain is £70,000. J buys a new asset for £100,000 and claims rollover relief.

Gain not reinvested: £120,000 − £100,000   = £20,000

Chargeable gain deemed not reinvested: $\dfrac{70,000}{90,000} \times £20,000$ = £15,555

Chargeable gain rolled over: £70,000 − £15,555   = £54,445

Adjusted base cost of new asset: £100,000 − £54,445   = £45,555

Relief is also restricted where the old asset was not used for trade purposes throughout the period of ownership,[2] or—in the case of buildings—a distinguishable part was used for non-trade purposes.[3] The restriction in the former case is on a time basis. For disposals before 6th April 1988, the whole period of ownership, including periods before 6th April 1965, is relevant in computing the restriction.[4] For disposals after 5th April 1988, only periods after the new base date of 31st March 1982 are relevant in the time apportionment calculation.[5] Where the taxpayer carries on a trade in partnership, gains on his share of partnership assets can be rolled over only against his share of the consideration for the new assets.[6]

Simon's Taxes C3.105; Sumption CGT A14.04.
  [1] CGTA 1979, s. 116.
  [2] CGTA 1979, s. 115(6).
  [3] CGTA 1979, s. 115(5).
  [4] *Richart v J Lyons & Co Ltd* [1989] STC 8.
  [5] CGTA 1979, s. 115(7A).
  [6] *Tod v Mudd* [1987] STC 141.

Conditions of the relief

20: 08 Rollover relief is available to persons carrying on a trade, profession, vocation or employment or occupying woodlands on a commercial basis and with a view to the realisation of profits.[1] It is also available to public authorities, to certain clubs and societies run on non-commercial lines, to certain bodies concerned with trade protection and in respect of furnished holiday letting property.[2]

The old asset must have been used throughout the period of ownership only for the purposes of the trade. Mere intention to use an asset for trade purposes is not sufficient. For example, visits to a site coupled with an intention to build do not amount to using and occupying land.[3] The new asset must not only be taken into use in the trade,[4] but must be acquired solely for that purpose and not, wholly or partly, for the purpose of realising a gain on their disposal.[5]

If there was trade use only for a part of the period of ownership an apportionment is made.[6] An asset used only partly for trade purposes does not qualify although this rule is relaxed for buildings.[7] A person carrying on two trades, whether successively or concurrently, is treated as carrying on one trade.[8] Hence relief can be claimed where the old asset belonged to trade A and the new one to trade B. The artificial discontinuance of a trade for income tax purposes under TA 1988, s. 113 is disregarded.[9]

The relief is available only for certain types of asset as follows:[10]

(*a*) Any building or part of a building and any permanent or semi-permanent structure in the nature of a building, occupied (as well as used) only for the purposes of the trade.

(*b*) Any land occupied (as well as used) only for the purposes of the trade.

(*c*) Fixed plant or machinery which does not form part of a building or of a permanent or semi-permanent structure in the nature of a building.[11]

(*d*) Ships, aircraft and hovercraft ("hovercraft" having the same meaning as in the Hovercraft Act 1968).

(*e*) Goodwill.

(*f*) Satellites, space stations and space vehicles (including launch vehicles).[12]

(*g*) milk quotas and potato quotas.[13]

Under (*b*), land does not qualify if it is occupied for the purposes of a trade of dealing in or developing land, unless the profit on sale of such land would not be a profit of the trade.[14]

It is not necessary for the old and new assets to be of the same type, provided that both old and new fall within one or other of the classes (*a*)–(*g*).

The requirement that a new asset be acquired is substantially relaxed in practice. The Revenue have stated that the relief applies where a partnership asset, whether land or any other qualifying asset, is partitioned on the dissolution of the partnership.[15] The relief is also available where the disposal proceeds are used to enhance an existing asset used for the purposes of the trade rather than acquiring a new asset,[16] or where the proceeds are spent acquiring a further interest in an asset already used for the trade.[17] The rules are also relaxed where the new asset is not brought immediately into use but work is done on it and it is then brought into use; for example, where land is bought and a building is built or reconstructed. The land must not be used for any non-trade purpose nor let during this period of work.[18]

The new acquisition must take place within a period beginning 12 months before and ending three years after the date of disposal or such other time as the Board may by notice in writing allow.[19] However if an unconditional contract for the acquisition has been entered into, provisional roll-over relief may be given at once and any adjustments made later such as would be necessary if for example the contract were cancelled.

The legislation requires that the proceeds be applied in acquiring the new asset; this does not appear to carry too literal an interpretation. In practice, it is sufficient to match disposal proceeds with one or more items of qualifying expenditure, regardless of how that expenditure was in fact financed.

Where the trade is carried on by a family company but the person owning and replacing the asset is an individual, relief may be claimed, provided the company is his family company.[20] This provision does not apply where the asset is held by another company nor if the company owns the asset and the individual carries on the trade. The old and new assets must both be used either for a trade of the individual or for a trade of the company. It is not possible to roll over gains realised by the individual against expenditure incurred by the company, or vice versa.

Simon's Taxes C3.102–109; Sumption CGT A14.04.

[1] CGTA 1979, ss. 115 and 121.

[2] FA 1984, Sch. 11, para. 1(2)(*f*) (for disposals on or after 6th April 1982).

[3] *Temperley v Visibell Ltd* [1974] STC 64, 49 TC 129; on occupation see *Anderton v Lamb* [1981] STC 43.

[4] CGTA 1979, s. 115(1).

[5] CGTA 1979, s. 115(4).

[6] CGTA 1979, s. 115(6).

[7] CGTA 1979, s. 115(5).

[8] CGTA 1979, s. 115(7). It does not appear material whether there was a delay between ceasing to carry on one trade and beginning to carry on another.

[9] CGTA 1979, s. 121(2).

[10] CGTA 1979, ss. 115(1) and 118. Under (*e*), goodwill is not regarded by the Revenue as including trademarks.

[11] "Fixed" applies to both plant and machinery—*Williams v Evans* [1982] STC 498.

[12] FA 1988, s. 112, in relation to disposals or acquisitions after 27th July 1987.

[13] FA 1988, s. 112, in relation to disposals or acquisitions after 29th October 1987.

[14] CGTA 1979, s. 119.

[15] Extra-statutory concession D23 (1988), **Simon's Taxes, Division H2.2.**

[16] Extra-statutory concession D22 (1988), **Simon's Taxes, Division H2.2.**

[17] Extra-statutory concession D25 (1988), **Simon's Taxes, Division H2.2.**

[18] Extra-statutory concession D24 (1988), **Simon's Taxes, Division H2.2.**

[19] CGTA 1979, s. 115(3).

[20] CGTA 1979, s. 120; "family company" is defined as for s. 124, infra, § **15: 09**.

20: 09   The relief is modified where the new asset is a depreciating asset, that is a wasting asset or one which will become a wasting asset within ten years.[1] The gain is not deductible from the cost of the new asset but instead is held over until

(*i*) the new asset is disposed of, or

(*ii*) the new asset ceases to be used for the purposes of the trade, or

(*iii*) ten years have expired,

whichever first occurs.

If a third asset is acquired, which is not a depreciating asset, the held over gain can be rolled over to the new acquisition and deducted from its acquisition cost in the usual way. The new acquisition need not occur within the usual period beginning on the disposal of the first asset but must occur before one of the events (*i*)–(*iii*) has occurred.

Part of the held over gain may be rolled over if the expenditure on the non depreciating asset is insufficient for full rollover.[2]

The rebasing of CGT to 31st March 1982 did not initially have any effect in relation to gains held over against depreciating assets prior to 1st April 1982. However, with effect retroactively to 6th April 1988, gains arising on disposals prior to 1st April 1982 are not brought back into charge if held over against depreciating assets.[3] In addition, where a held over gain is attributable to the disposal before 6th April 1988 of an asset acquired before 31st March 1982, one half of the gain is excluded from charge on the occurrence of the relevant event[3] (infra, § **22: 06**).

Simon's Taxes C3.110; Sumption CGT A14.04.
[1] CGTA 1979, s. 117.
[2] CGTA 1979, s. 117(5).
[3] FA 1989, Sch. 15, para. 1.
[4] FA 1988, Sch. 9, para. 3.

DISPOSALS ON RETIREMENT FROM FAMILY BUSINESSES AND RELATED RELIEFS

20: 10   Relief is available for an individual who makes a "material disposal" of business assets and who has either attained the age of 60 or has retired on grounds of ill health below that age.[1] A person who has retired on grounds of ill health must submit medical evidence to the Revenue.[2] There is no appeal specifically against a Revenue refusal to accept evidence of ill health, although this could form part of the subject matter of an appeal against a CGT assessment on the gains concerned.

Although this relief is often referred to as retirement relief it is not necessary that the person should go into retirement save when he is under 60. It suffices that he is disposing of the business or part of it or of business assets in the way defined.

For this relief to apply the disposal must be of business assets as defined.[3] This definition includes:

(*a*) a disposal of the whole or part of a business, or

(*b*) one or more assets which, at the time at which the business ceased to be carried on, were in use in the business.

The effect of (*b*) is to extend the relief to disposals after the trade has ceased of assets used in the business. However, it is necessary to distinguish the sale of a part of a business from the sale of an asset used in the business.[4]

The question whether an activity amounts to a business is one of fact. A finding by the Commissioners that the management of property was not a business was not disturbed by the Courts.[5] Retirement relief is also available for furnished holiday lettings.[6]

Simon's Taxes Division C3.3; Sumption CGT A15.
[1] FA 1985, s. 69.

[2] FA 1985, Sch. 20, para. 3.
[3] FA 1985, s. 69(2).
[4] *McGregor v Adcock* [1977] STC 206, [1977] 3 All ER 65 (sale of five acres of a 35 acre farm; nothing to suggest scale of business significantly altered by the sale: no relief). It is clear that any change in the scale of activities following a sale of assets must be directly attributable to the sale if a claim is to be sustained: *Atkinson v Dancer, Mannion v Johnston* [1988] STC 758.
[5] *Harthan v Mason* [1980] STC 94.
[6] FA 1984, Sch. 11, para. 1(2)(*g*).

20: 11   The disposal of a business or part of it is a material disposal if the business is owned by an individual for at least one year ending with the date of the disposal[1] and on or before the date the business ceased the individual has reached 60 or retired through ill-health.[2] For disposals of business assets after the business has ceased, the disposal should take place within one year of the ceasing of the business (or such longer time as the Revenue may, in writing, allow).[3]

The date of disposal for these, and indeed all, purposes of retirement relief may be taken as the date of completion where the business activities continue beyond the date of unconditional contract, pending completion.[4]

The rules relating to businesses owned by an individual extend to partnerships.[5]

The relief applies only to gains arising on any disposal[6] of chargeable business assets comprised in the disposal of the business. A chargeable business asset is defined[7] as an asset (including goodwill but not shares or securities or other assets held as investments) which is, or is an interest in, an asset used for the purposes of the trade carried on by the individual. An asset is not a chargeable business asset unless any gain arising would be a chargeable gain.[8] Thus an exempt asset, such as an item of plant valued at less than £6,000, is not a chargeable business asset. An asset used in a business carried on by a partnership of which the individual is a member can be a chargeable business asset[9] and there is a similar extension for assets used for the trade of a family company or subsidiary of a family holding company.

If the disposal also involves assets which give rise to allowable losses, those losses are set against the gains arising from the chargeable business assets; it is not necessary that the loss should be from a chargeable business asset.[10] The balance of gains as so reduced is available for the relief.

[1] FA 1985, s. 69(3).
[2] FA 1985, s. 69(4).
[3] FA 1985, s. 69(4) and Sch. 20, para. 1.
[4] Extra-statutory concession 20th October 1988, **Simon's Taxes, Division H2.2.**
[5] FA 1985, s. 69(8).
[6] No longer just sale or gift.
[7] FA 1985, Sch. 20, para. 12(2).
[8] FA 1985, Sch. 20, para. 12(3).
[9] FA 1985, Sch. 20, para. 12(2)(*d*). The disposal of an asset owned by a partner but made available to the partnership may qualify as an associated disposal, infra, § **20:13**, although relief may be restricted where a rent is charged: FA 1985, Sch. 20, para. 10(1)(*c*).
[10] FA 1985, Sch. 20, paras. 6 and 12(1)(*b*).

20: 12   For disposals after 5th April 1988 relief is available on net chargeable gains of up to £500,000.[1] The first £125,000 of gains is wholly exempt from CGT. Of the next £375,000, one-half is exempt and the whole of any excess over £500,000 is taxable. Where the qualifying conditions have been satisfied for less than ten years, these maxima are abated pro rata to the length of the qualifying period. The minimum relief, for a qualifying period of exactly one year, is £12,500 complete exemption, plus one-half of the next £37,500 exempt. The qualifying period applies to ownership of the business, not ownership of the asset. There is no variation in the relief according to the age of the individual.

EXAMPLE

MJ has carried on a mail order business since being made redundant on 1st January 1982. At the age of 60, on 31st March 1989, he sells the business as a going concern to an unconnected company. Gains and losses are as follows:

Goodwill	£150,000
Lease of office	50,000
Office equipment	(5,000)
Shares in supplier	8,000

Gains eligible for relief: £200,000 − £5,000 = £195,000
Retirement relief available:

$\dfrac{7\frac{3}{12}}{10} \times £125,000$	90,625	
$\dfrac{1}{2} \times £(195,000 - 90,625)$	52,188*	142,813
		52,187
Gains not eligible for relief		8,000
Chargeable gains on disposal		£60,187

$$* \text{ Maximum marginal relief} \frac{1}{2} \times \frac{7\frac{3}{12}}{10} \times £375,000 = £135,938$$

---

[1] FA 1985, Sch. 20, para. 13 as amended by FA 1988, s. 110: previously, relief was available on gains up to £125,000 (£100,000 before 6th April 1987).

20: 13   The length of the qualifying period, and so the percentage available for relief, may be increased by reference to other businesses owned in the ten year period,[1] to businesses owned by the disponor's spouse (if an election is made)[2] and to businesses run by the individual's family company or a subsidiary of the family holding company, as well as by periods relevant for the related reliefs.[3]

Where retirement relief has been given on one or more earlier disposals, the maximum relief available is reduced.[4] This is done as follows:

(*a*) compute the gains qualifying for relief;
(*b*) add the "underlying" gains relieved on all earlier disposals;
(*c*) add together the qualifying periods for all the disposals (excluding any overlaps);
(*d*) compute the amount available for relief;
(*e*) deduct the relief already given.

If all the earlier disposals occurred before 6th April 1988, the "underlying" gains are simply the gains relieved from tax. If there was just one earlier disposal, after 5th April 1988, the "underlying" gains are the sum of the exempt gain within the £125,000 limit (scaled down as appropriate) plus twice the gain exempted within the marginal band. In other cases, where there have been two or more earlier disposals, one or more of which occurred after 5th April 1988, the amount under (*d*) above is ascertained for the last such disposal. Then, taking the notional qualifying period for that disposal, (*c*) above, the gains relieved under

(*i*) the £125,000 limit, and
(*ii*) the marginal limit,

respectively, are computed. The underlying gains for the present disposal are then the sum of (*i*) plus twice (*ii*).

---

[1] FA 1985, Sch. 20, para. 14; short breaks of up to two years are ignored but do not count towards the ten year period, para. 14(5).
[2] FA 1985, Sch. 20, para. 16; the transferee must take the whole of the spouse's interest but may do so by inter vivos gift as well as on death. On an inter vivos gift, the relief is not due unless it would have been due by reference to the transferor spouse's age, e.g. when a woman of 58 gives her interest to her husband aged 60.
[3] FA 1985, Sch. 20, para. 14(3).
[4] FA 1985, Sch. 20, para. 15 as amended by FA 1988, s 110.

20: 14 Relief is also available when the disposal is of shares in a company owning the business and the company is a trading company which is either:

(*a*) that individual's family company or
(*b*) a member of a trading group of which the holding company is that individual's family company.[1]

The individual must be a full time working director[2] of the company or, if the company is a member of a group[3] or commercial association[4] of companies, a full time working director[5] of one or more companies in that group or association. The purpose of the concept of commercial association is to bring within the relief companies which, whilst closely related, lack a group structure, but the concept is tightly defined.

Relief is thus available whether the trade is carried on by a subsidiary of the holding company or a sub-subsidiary so long as the group requirements are met.

A family company is a company[6] the voting rights of which are either exerciseable by the individual as to 25%, or as to 5% if he and a member or members of his family have control, i.e. more than 50% of the voting power.[7] It has been held that a voting right which a person chooses not to exercise is still a voting right.[8] Voting rights held by trustees of a family settlement can be included.[9]

---

[1] FA 1985, s. 69(2)(*c*) including the deemed disposal on a capital distribution within CGTA 1979, s. 72; on computation see FA 1985, Sch. 20, para. 11.
[2] Defined FA 1985, Sch. 20, para. 1.
[3] Defined as a company with one or more 51% subsidiaries together with those subsidiaries.
[4] FA 1985, Sch. 20, para. 1.
[5] Defined FA 1985, Sch. 20, para. 1.
[6] FA 1985, Sch. 20, para. 1.
[7] Defined as spouse, brother, sister, ancestor or lineal descendant of the individual or the spouse: FA 1985, Sch. 20, para. 1.
[8] *Hepworth v William Smith Group* [1981] STC 354.
[9] FA 1985, Sch. 20, para. 1(3) and (4).

20: 15   As where the individual disposes of the business itself, the percentage of the £125,000 and £500,000 available by way of relief is related to the length of the qualifying period. This period must be at least one year. The period ends on the "operative date" which is usually the date of the disposal concerned.[1] The date on which the company ceases to be a trading company or a member of the trading group is instead the operative date if the disponor was then (or previously) 60 or had retired through ill health.[2] The disposal of the shares must then be within one year of the operative date (or such longer period as the Revenue may allow). Provision is also made for the situation in which the disponer had ceased to be a full time working director before the disposal, but has continued in part-time work of at least ten hours a week (on average);[3] here the operative date is that on which he ceased to be a full-time working director.

The disposal will qualify for relief (subject to adjustment for the length of the qualifying period) if, throughout a period of at least the one year ending with the operative date:

(a) the individual owns the business which at the date of the disposal is owned by the company, or

(b) the individual is a full time working director of the company or of any member of the group and the company is the individual's family company and within a trading company or the holding company of a trading group.[4]

The length of the qualifying period may be increased by reference to earlier business periods[5] and to a spouse's interest in the business.[6]

---

[1] FA 1985, s. 69(5).
[2] FA 1985, s. 69(6).
[3] FA 1985, s. 69(7).
[4] FA 1985, s. 69(5).
[5] FA 1985, Sch. 20, para. 14.
[6] FA 1985, Sch. 20, para. 16.

20: 16   On a share disposal, the chargeable gain eligible for relief is limited to that proportion of the overall chargeable gain which the chargeable business assets[1] bears to the chargeable assets of the company. This limitation is relatively easy to apply to a trading company which is not a member of a group.[2] Only assets in the company at the operative date are taken into account, even if the date of disposal is later and the nature and values of the company's assets are then different. Thus, assets disposed of in anticipation of a liquidation need not affect the relief.[3] When the company has no chargeable assets the appropriate proportion is the whole.[4] Special, and more complex, rules have to apply to the disposal of shares or securities in a holding company[5] where account is taken of the chargeable assets and chargeable business assets of the trading group as a whole.

EXAMPLE
    PQ owns 60% of the shares in BNM Ltd, a trading company of which he is the full time managing director. PQ acquired his shares on 1st January 1980 on the death of his father. In December 1988, PQ suffers severe injuries in a car accident and is forced to retire. After a period during which he works two days a week for the company, PQ sells his shares in

June 1989, realising a gain of £200,000. The value of the company's assets at the date of PQ's retirement from full time work are as follows:

Freehold workshops	£260,000
Goodwill	500,000
Plant and equipment(i)	100,000
Shares held as trade investments	50,000
Trading stock	200,000
Debtors	160,000
Cash	20,000
Total chargeable business assets	£860,000
Total chargeable assets	£910,000

Gains eligible for relief:

$$\frac{860,000}{910,000} \times £200,000 \qquad £189,011$$

Retirement relief:

$$\frac{8}{10} \times £125,000 \qquad £100,000$$

$$\frac{1}{2} \times £(189,011 - 100,000) \qquad 44,506\text{(ii)} \quad 144,506$$

		44,505
Gains not eligible for relief		10,989
Chargeable gains		£55,494

Notes: (i) Items valued at more than £6,000 each
(ii) Maximum marginal relief: $\frac{1}{2} \times \frac{8}{10} \times £375,000 =$ £150,000

Where the disposal is a deemed disposal on a company reorganisation the taxpayer may elect that the normal rule treating the new shares as representing the old should not apply. This will enable him to set the relief against the gains arising on the reorganisation.[6]

---

[1] Defined in FA 1985, Sch. 20, para. 7(3) so as to include assets in respect of which an allowable loss would arise.
[2] FA 1985, Sch. 20, para. 7.
[3] FA 1985, Sch. 20, para. 7(2). The liquidation must still occur within the one year permitted period after the cessation of trading.
[4] FA 1985, Sch. 20, para. 7(2).
[5] FA 1985, Sch. 20, para. 8.
[6] FA 1985, Sch. 20, para. 2.

20: 17 There are three extensions of retirement relief.

First, relief is available on the disposal of an asset by an employee where the asset is provided or held by him for the purposes of his employment.[1] Employment as a company director does not count if the company is the individual's family company or a member of a trading group of which his family company is the holding company.[2] At the time of disposal or, if earlier, the end of his employment, the person must be 60 or over, or have retired through ill health.[2] The employment must have been full time.

Secondly, relief is available to trustees of a settlement on the disposal out of the settled property of shares or securities in a company or of assets used for a business.[3] The conditions which, in the case of unsettled property, apply to the disponer are here adapted to apply to a beneficiary with an interest in

592   Part III—Capital gains tax

possession.[4] Thus, the asset must have been used for a business carried on by the beneficiary; in the case of shares or securities the beneficiary must be a full time working director, the company must be his family company and the beneficiary must have reached 60 or retired through ill health.[5] Where the beneficiary involved is not the only beneficiary with an interest in possession the relief may be reduced.[6]

The cumulative limits of £125,000 and £500,000 are applied by reference to the qualifying beneficiary, so that if he has already qualified for relief in his own right, the amount available for the trustees' disposal to reduced.[7] Similarly relief given on the trustees' disposal will reduce the maximum relief available to the beneficiary on subsequent disposals in his own right. Where on the same day there is a disposal by the beneficiary and a disposal by the trustees the relief is given to the beneficiary's disposal first.

Thirdly, relief is available for "associated disposals". A disposal is associated if it takes place as part of withdrawal of the individual from the business carried on by a partnership or a company fulfilling the conditions for the principal relief.[8] The asset must have been in use in the business immediately before that withdrawal and must have been used by that business or a similar qualifying business during the whole or part of the period.[8] For the relief to apply it is still necessary that the asset should be a qualifying business asset. The gain eligible for relief is reduced where rent is charged, or the asset is not used for a business throughout the period, or the individual is not actively involved in the business (as partner or full-time working director) throughout the period.[9] This extension of relief applies where a person has allowed a partnership or family company to use the asset free of charge; where a rent below market value has been charged, relief is restricted. The individual must have reached 60 or have retired through ill health.[10]

---

[1] FA 1985, s. 70(1).
[2] FA 1985, s. 70(2).
[3] FA 1985, s. 70(3).
[4] Defined as excluding an interest for a fixed term.
[5] FA 1985, s. 70(4)—these conditions are analogous to those for the relief at § **20: 14**.
[6] FA 1985, Sch. 20, para. 9.
[7] FA 1985, Sch. 20, para. 13(3).
[8] FA 1985, s. 70(7).
[9] FA 1985, Sch. 20, para. 10.
[10] Only then is the disposal material. See FA 1985, ss. 69(1) and 70(8).

GIFTS OF BUSINESS ASSETS—HOLDING OVER

20: 18   Where an individual transfers business assets by gift or sale at less than market value to a UK resident the chargeable gain otherwise accruing may be held over.[1] As it is only the chargeable gain that is held over, any retirement relief is given first and only the balance held over to reduce the acquisition cost.[2] In view of the withdrawal of general holdover on gifts from 14th March 1989, this relief is a valuable one. Previously, gifts of business assets to individuals or trustees were subject to the general relief, with a separate holdover relief for gifts to other persons such as trustees.

An individual must dispose otherwise than under a bargain at arm's length (see § **16: 18**) of:

(*i*) an asset (or an interest in an asset) used in his trade profession or vocation, or

(*ii*) an asset (or an interest in an asset) used in his family company's trade profession or vocation (or that of a member of the same trading group), or

(*iii*) unquoted shares or securities in a trading company (or holding company of a trading group) which is his family company.[3]

This relief extends to commercially managed woodlands[4] and to furnished holiday lettings.[5]

"Family company", "holding company" and "trading company" are defined as for retirement relief, supra, § **20: 14**.[6]

The relief is available only on a disposal to a person who is resident and ordinarily resident in the UK.[7] As in the case of the general gifts relief, there is recapture of the held over gains in the event that the transferee ceases to be UK resident.[8] There are various anti-avoidance provisions relating to the transfer of assets to UK companies controlled by non resident trustees, or to dual residents who could claim exemption under a double tax treaty.[9]

The relief must be claimed jointly by the transferor and transferee unless the transferee is a trust, in which case the transferor alone may elect.[10]

Apportionments are made where only a part of the asset has been used for business purposes,[11] or where there has not been business use throughout the period of ownership.[12] Where the disposal is of shares in a family company, the proportion entitled to relief is that which the chargeable business assets bear to all chargeable assets of the company, but only where the transferor could exercise at least 25% of the voting power at any time within the preceding 12 months or, if the transferor is an individual, the company was his family company at any time within that period.[13]

On a disposal before 6th April 1988 of business assets acquired before 31st March 1982, one half of the gain held over is excluded on a subsequent disposal on or after 6th April 1988 (infra, § **22: 06**).[14]

Where the assets or the shares are held by trustees and there is a deemed disposal e.g. on the termination of the settlement, relief may be claimed provided the business is carried on either by the trustees or by a relevant beneficiary or by a company in which the trustees hold at least 25% of the voting rights.[15] This would apply in the less usual case where a company was the life tenant under the settlement. The relevant beneficiary is the one who had an interest in possession immediately before the deemed disposal.

In contrast with the position for gifts not subject to holdover, any IHT becoming payable if the gift proves to be a chargeable transfer is allowable as a deduction to the transferee when he disposes of the asset.[16]

Simon's Taxes C3.401, 405–410; Sumption CGT A14.09.

[1] CGTA 1979, s. 126 as amended by FA 1989, Sch. 14, para. 1.
[2] By implication from FA 1985, Sch. 20, para. 6; gains eligible for retirement relief are not chargeable gains.
[3] CGTA 1979, s. 126(1).
[4] CGTA 1979, s. 126(8).
[5] FA 1984, Sch. 11, para. 1(*h*).
[6] CGTA 1979, s. 126(7).

[7] CGTA 1979, s. 126A(1).
[8] FA 1981, s. 79(1)(*a*), as amended.
[9] CGTA 1979, ss. 126A, 126B and 126C.
[10] CGTA 1979, s. 126(1)(*b*).
[11] CGTA 1979, Sch. 4, para. 6. The restriction does not apply if the asset qualifies for the 50% business relief for IHT purposes.
[12] CGTA 1979, Sch. 4, para. 5. The restriction does not apply if the asset qualifies for the 50% business relief for IHT purposes.
[13] CGTA 1979, Sch. 4, para. 7.
[14] FA 1988, Sch. 9, para. 2.
[15] CGTA 1979, Sch. 4, para. 2.
[16] CGTA 1979, s. 126(9).

PARTNERSHIP

20:19 The application of CGT to partnership transactions is complex because, whilst the legislation does not clearly distinguish the partnership property from the partners' shares, nor does it wholly identify them with one another. Because a strict legal analysis can produce over-complex results a practical approach has been developed by the Inland Revenue, and is set out in a lengthy Statement of Practice.[1]

The statutory guidance is brief. Partnership dealings are treated as made by the partners and not by the firm as such[2], although returns are made by the firm.[3] Partners are assessed individually, not jointly, to CGT.

The Revenue practice is to treat each partner as owning a fractional share of each of the partnership assets, so that disposals and acquisitions of those assets by the firm are treated accordingly. A partner's fractional share is taken as his share in any surplus on dissolution of the partnership, although in the absence of provision for such sharing, the ordinary profit-sharing ratio is taken.[4]

EXAMPLE

C, G and T practice in partnership as estate agents. They share profits as follows:

C	$\frac{1}{2}$
G	$\frac{1}{4}$
T	$\frac{1}{4}$

In 1987, the firm purchased a property as a speculative investment, for £40,000. In April 1989, they sell the property for £200,000. [Indexation factor: 0.124]

C:	Disposal consideration	$\frac{1}{2}$ × £200,000		£100,000
	Allowable cost	$\frac{1}{2}$ × £40,000	£20,000	
	Indexation allowance	£20,000 × 0.124	2,480	22,480
	Chargeable gain			£77,520
G & T:	Disposal consideration	$\frac{1}{4}$ × £200,000		£50,000
	Allowable cost	$\frac{1}{4}$ × £40,000	£10,000	
	Indexation allowance	£10,000 × 0.124	1,240	11,240
	Chargeable gain			£38,760

Simon's Taxes C1.215, 413; E5.331, 332; Sumption CGT A9.01.
[1] Inland Revenue Statement D12, **Simon's Taxes, Division H3.4.**
[2] CGTA 1979, s. 60.
[3] TMA 1970, s. 12(4).

20: 20   The general CGT principles relating to disposal are substantially modified under the Revenue practice statement where the disposal results from a transaction between the partners. A change in profit sharing ratios, including that occurring on the admission of a new partner, involves disposal by some partners of fractional interests in partnership assets, and corresponding acquisition by other partners. Since the partners are connected with one another other than in relation to acquisitions or disposals of partnership assets pursuant to bona fide commercial arrangements,[1] market value in strictness should be substituted for any actual consideration passing. However, the disposal will in general be treated as taking place at a consideration which gives rise to neither gain nor loss.[2] This will result in a reduction in the base cost of a partner whose share is reduced and an increase for one whose share is increased. Moreover, a simple fractional basis replaces the usual part disposal formula. The treatment of indexation allowance has not been clarified, but for consistency it would appear that indexation should be applied in arriving at the deemed consideration.[3]

> **EXAMPLE**
>
> F, H and W trade in partnership as building contractors, sharing profits equally. The firm's only chargeable asset is a freehold store, office and yard, purchased for £300,000 in December 1984. In December 1985, F reduced his involvement in the business and, by agreement, his profit share became $\frac{1}{10}$th with effect from 1st January 1988. [Indexation factor: 0.137]

F:	Share of acquisition cost of land: $\frac{1}{3} \times$ £300,000	£100,000
	Cost of interest disposed of: $(\frac{1}{3} - \frac{1}{10}) \times$ £300,000	70,000
	Base cost of remaining interest	£30,000
	Cost of interest disposed of:	£70,000
	Indexation allowance: £70,000 × 0.137	9,590
	Deemed disposal consideration	£79,590
H & W:	Share of acquisition cost of land:	£100,000
	Cost of additional share: $\frac{1}{2} \times$ £79,590	£39,795

This general rule is subject to three exceptions. First, the Revenue may substitute market value as the disposal consideration where the partners are connected persons, other than by virtue of being partners, e.g. they are relatives. However, market value is not substituted if the consideration passing is not less than the amount that would have been paid between the parties if they had been at arm's length.[4]

Market value may also be substituted where the consideration cannot be valued, whether or not the parties are at arm's length.[5] This would apparently authorise the use of market value where one partner gives another a larger share of the assets in return for the other shouldering a greater burden of the work. This would, however, be inconsistent with the general practice on changes in partnership shares.

Secondly, gains or losses may arise if there has previously been an adjustment through the accounts in respect of partnership assets, such as a revaluation. On a subsequent change in profit sharing, the partners are treated as disposing of fractional shares for a consideration equal to their share of the revalued amount, which will be more or less than the original base cost.[6] A revaluation of partnership assets is not itself a disposal.

EXAMPLE

J and K trade in partnership as antique dealers sharing profits equally. They took over a previous trade, paying £50,000 for goodwill in 1982. In 1987, goodwill was revalued to £80,000 in their accounts. In 1988, J and K take in L as a partner, sharing profits J $\frac{2}{5}$ths; K $\frac{2}{5}$ths; L $\frac{1}{5}$th. [Indexation factor: 0.250]

J & K:	Disposal of fractional share in goodwill: $(\frac{1}{2} - \frac{2}{5}) \times £80,000$		£8,000
	Allowable cost: $(\frac{1}{2} - \frac{2}{5}) \times £50,000$	£5,000	
	Indexation allowance: £5,000 × 0.250	1,250	6,250
	Chargeable gain		£1,750
L:	Acquisition cost of share in goodwill: $\frac{1}{5} \times £80,000$		£16,000

The third exception arises where there is a payment outside the framework of the accounts, e.g. payments for goodwill not included in the balance sheet. Such payments are private matters between the partners but do give rise to CGT.[7]

Simon's Taxes C1.215, 413; E5.331, 332; Sumption CGT A9.03–06.

[1] CGTA 1979, s. 63(4).

[2] Inland Revenue Statement D12, para. 4; **Simon's Taxes Division H3.4**. The disposal is also treated as a no gain/no loss deposit for the purposes of rebasing: Statement of Practice SP 1/89, **Simon's Taxes, Division H3.2**. See infra, § 22: 05.

[3] FA 1985, Sch. 13, para. 2 refers only to no gain, no loss disposals which occur by virtue of any *enactment*. The implications of the indexation allowance also have an impact upon the pooling of fractional shares acquired at different times: Inland Revenue Statement D12, para. 10. Presumably a form of parallel pooling would give a consistent result.

[4] Inland Revenue Statement D12, para. 7.

[5] CGTA 1979, s. 29A(1)(*b*).

[6] Inland Revenue Statement D12, para. 5.

[7] Inland Revenue Statement D12, para. 6.

20: 21 Sometimes, e.g. on the retirement of a partner where the assets are not revalued, an annuity may accrue to a retiring partner. Where the capitalised value of the annuity is consideration received by the retiring partner for the value of his share,[1] it could give rise to a chargeable gain even though the rest of the transaction was carried through at cost. In practice, however, the Revenue treat the annuity value as consideration only where it goes beyond reasonable recognition of the past contribution of work and effort. An annuity is regarded as reasonable recognition if it does not exceed $\frac{2}{3}$ of the average of the best three of the last seven years share of profits whilst a full time partner.[2] The $\frac{2}{3}$ fraction is reduced if the individual has been a partner for less than 10 years. Where further payments are made outside the accounts in the way described, e.g. for goodwill (which is usually entered in the balance sheet at nil) that will be further consideration for the disposal.[3]

If a retiring partner receives a lump sum from the continuing partners (or any one else) for his share in the partnership, there will be a disposal of his interest in the assets in return for cash and so, potentially, a charge to CGT.

Simon's Taxes C1.215, 413; E5.331, 332; Sumption CGT A9.06.

[1] However, this arises only when the annuity is in return for the disposal; usually it will be part of the wider partnership agreement.

[2] Inland Revenue Statement D12, para. 8. The practice may also apply where a lump sum is paid in addition to the annuity (but not so as to exclude the lump sum): SP1/79, **Simon's Taxes, Division H3.2.**
[3] Inland Revenue Statement D12, para. 6.

20: 22 Various CGT reliefs apply to partners as they would apply to other individuals carrying on a business:

(*a*) Holding over the gain on a gift or sale below market value; this relief applies to a transfer of business assets between individuals as well as other assets; see § **16: 16**.

(*b*) The relief for transfers of business assets otherwise than between individuals; see § **20: 18**.

(*c*) Retirement relief; see § **20: 10**.

(*d*) Rollover relief; see § **20: 06**. Chargeable gains realised by partners on qualifying business assets may be rolled over against their shares of expenditure on new qualifying assets, either within the partnership or in relation to other trades carried on by the partners.

(*e*) Incorporation relief; see § **20: 05**. It would appear that the relief applies only where the partnership as a whole transfers all or part of its business to a company, but not where a partner transfers his share of the business.

NON RESIDENTS TRADING IN THE UK

20: 23 Non-residents are subject to CGT if they carry on a trade (or from 14th March 1989, a profession or vocation)[1] in the UK through a branch or agency.[2] Gains or losses are within the scope of CGT if they arise in respect of UK assets:

(*a*) used for the purposes of the branch trade etc or

(*b*) held for the purposes of the branch.

The allowable costs of such assets are established in the normal way.[3] There are a number of anti-avoidance provisions to counter the transfer of such assets outside the CGT net, namely:

(1) transfer of assets abroad prior to disposal;[4]
(2) disposal after cessation of UK trade;[5]
(3) rollover of gains against non-UK assets;[6]
(4) use of tax treaty relief by persons resident both in the UK and in another country.[7]

Simon's Taxes C1.202.
[1] CGTA 1979, s. 12(2A), inserted by FA 1989, s. 126.
[2] CGTA 1979, s. 12.
[3] Even if acquired from another non-resident, but subject to CGTA 1979, s. 29A if the non-residents are connected persons: supra, § **16: 23**. UK branches of non-resident professions or vocations in existence at 14th March 1989 are deemed to have disposed of and reacquired the branch assets at market value on that date.

⁴ FA 1989, s. 127(1).
⁵ FA 1989, s. 127(3).
⁶ FA 1989, s. 129(1).
⁷ FA 1989, s. 129(3).

21 Computation

21: 01 CGT is imposed on gains computed in accordance with Part II, Chapter II of the Capital Gains Tax Act 1979.[1] These rules do not in fact say how gains and losses are to be computed but instead direct what adjustments are to be made to the consideration and to the deductible costs. It is implicit therefore that gains and losses are primarily computed according to the normal convention of deducting the cost of an asset from the proceeds on disposal.

Simon's Taxes C2.101; Sumption CGT Div A4.
[1] CGTA 1979, s. 28(1).

CONSIDERATION

21: 02 The disposal consideration will usually be the sums paid by the acquirer.[1] Sums paid in foreign currency are to be converted to a sterling equivalent by reference to the exchange rate for the date of incurring the expenditure.[2] Where payment is in kind, it will be the market value of the asset received by the disposer. The gain becomes chargeable on the date of the disposal so that questions of earnings or cash basis do not arise. No discount is to be made for the risk that the consideration may not be received in full, although if the inspector is satisfied that it is irrecoverable, adjustments are to be made.[3]

In valuing the consideration there is to be excluded any money or money's worth which is chargeable as income of the disposer, whether to income tax or corporation tax, or which enters into the computation of profits for those taxes.[4] An exception is made where the payment is taken into account for the purposes of a balancing charge (supra, § **20: 01**). However, the capitalised value of a rentcharge or a right to any other income is expressly included as consideration, notwithstanding that the income receipts will themselves be subject to income tax or corporation tax.[5] In practice, it will sometimes be necessary to determine whether the receipts are in fact income, or instalments of a capital sum.[6] Where there is a disposal for a consideration which includes a rental, the capitalised value of the rental is excluded as consideration although it is relevant in applying the part disposal formula (infra, § **21: 19**).

Simon's Taxes C2.101; Sumption CGT A4.02.
  [1] CGTA 1979, s. 40(2); on connected persons, see note, § **16: 24**, supra.
  [2] *Bentley v Pike* [1981] STC 360, 53 TC 590.
  [3] CGTA 1979, s. 40.
  [4] CGTA 1979, s. 31(1). This prevents any CGT liability on payments falling within TA 1988, s. 148.
  [5] CGTA 1979, s. 31(2). Note that in such cases the capital element in the annuity which is exempt from income tax under TA 1988, ss. 656, 657, infra, § **28: 20**, is not the same as the capitalised value.
  [6] See, for example, *IRC v Adam* (1928) 14 TC 34.

Allowance for liabilities

21: 03   Certain contingent liabilities assumed by the vendor are to be ignored in valuing the consideration received by him. They are:

(a) in the case of a lease, any liability contingent upon default by the assignee in relation to his obligations under the lease;

(b) any contingent liability in relation to a covenant for quiet enjoyment or any other obligation assumed as a vendor of land or of any estate or interest in land or as lessor;

(c) any contingent liability in respect of a warranty or representation made on a disposal by sale or lease of property other than land.[1]

If such a liability has become enforceable, and is in fact enforced, appropriate adjustments are then made to the original assessment.

Any contingent liability other than one referred to above is taken into account in valuing consideration,[2] although practically speaking valuation may be difficult in such cases. Moreover, there is then no statutory basis for the making of subsequent adjustments where the contingent liability becomes enforceable.

Where the vendor assumes an actual liability on the disposal of an asset, it seems clear that the liability must be deducted from any consideration received, although the position in practice will depend upon the terms agreed between the parties. However, any liability in respect of the asset disposed of which remains with the transferor is not deductible from the consideration received.[3]

Simon's Taxes C2.128, 140; Sumption CGT A4.05.
  [1] CGTA 1979, s. 41.
  [2] *Randall v Plumb* [1975] STC 191, 50 TC 392, [1975] 1 All ER 734.
  [3] This seems to follow from the judgment in *Coren v Keighley* [1972] 1 WLR 1556, 48 TC 370.

Market value

21: 04   In a number of circumstances, the market value of the assets is required to be substituted for any actual consideration passing.[1] Market value means the price at which the assets might reasonably be expected to fetch in a sale on the open market.[2] In making that estimate, no reduction is to be made because the whole of the assets are to be hypothetically placed on the market at one time.[3] The legislation seems to assume that the price paid in the open market would be a capital sum. However, it is debatable whether the market consideration for a lease granted at undervalue is the premium otherwise obtainable for a lease at that rent, or instead a rack rent with no premium.

The value to be taken for quoted shares and securities is taken from the Stock Exchange Official Daily List.[4] It is either the lower of the two prices shown in the quotations plus one-quarter of the difference between the two figures, or halfway between the highest and lowest prices at which bargains, other than bargaining done at special prices, were recorded for the relevant date. Where both figures are available it is the lower figure which is used.

This formula does not apply if special circumstances exist to make the market price an incorrect method of valuation, where special means unusual or uncommon. This does not mean that the stock market figure can be taken only when all information known to the directors is known also to the Stock Exchange, and the normal market value has been applied even where take over negotiations were under way.[5] Probably, however, special circumstances would obtain if information which ought to have been made public had not been.[6]

Unquoted shares must be valued in the hypothetical open market. As in inheritance tax, account must be taken of information which although secret would be divulged to a prudent purchaser buying by private tender and at arm's length.[7] This assumption will usually result in a higher value but it applies only to disposals after 5th July 1973. Special rules apply where the acquisition was before that date and had to be valued at market value.[8]

Simon's Taxes C2.110–115; Sumption CGT Div A23.
 [1] CGTA 1979, s. 29A; supra, § **16: 20**.
 [2] CGTA 1979, s. 150.
 [3] CGTA 1979, s. 150(2).
 [4] CGTA 1979, s. 150(3).
 [5] *Crabtree v Hinchcliffe* [1971] 3 All ER 967, 47 TC 419.
 [6] Lord Dilhorne at 983, 450–1.
 [7] CGTA 1979, s. 152.
 [8] CGTA 1979, Sch. 6.

ALLOWABLE EXPENDITURE

21: 05   From the disposal consideration (as adjusted or substituted) there is to be deducted

 (1) the value of the consideration provided when the asset was acquired;
 (2) the incidental costs of the acquisition;
 (3) any expenditure enhancing the value of the asset;
 (4) costs incurred in protecting rights over the asset and
 (5) the incidental costs of the disposal.[1]

These five categories are considered below; § **21: 08** et seq. In addition there is to be deducted the indexation allowance; see infra, § **21: 27**. Any expenditure incurred in foreign currency is translated into sterling at the rate prevailing at the date the expenditure is incurred.[2]

The burden of proving expenditure lies on the taxpayer in accordance with the general rule that the taxpayer has to disprove the assessment.[3]

Simon's Taxes C2.126; Sumption CGT A4.06
¹ CGTA 1979, s. 32.
² *Bentley v Pike* [1981] STC 360, 53 TC 590.
³ *Neely v Rourke* [1987] STC 30.

General restrictions

21: 06   Expenditure falling within these categories is nonetheless not deductible if

(1) it has been or is to be met out of public money whether of the Crown or any Government anywhere or any local authority anywhere;[1]

(2) it consists of premiums or other payments made under a policy of insurance of the risk of any kind of damage or injury to or loss or depreciation of, the asset;[2]

(3) it is a payment of interest,[3]

No deduction may be made more than once,[4] and any allowable expenditure must be incurred. No allowance can be made for the value or purely notional cost of work carried out by the owner himself.[5]

On a deemed disposal and reacquisition only actual expenses may be deducted, but not expenses that would have been incurred had the disposal actually been made.[6] Where legal and other fees were incurred on the preparation of a deed of variation under which funds would be divided between a tenant for life and the remainderman, the variation being a deemed disposal, those expenses were deductible.[7]

Simon's Taxes C2.128, 131, 133; Sumption CGT A4.07.
¹ CGTA 1979, s. 42.
² CGTA 1979, s. 141.
³ CGTA 1979, s. 32(3). Cf. TA 1970, s. 269.
⁴ CGTA 1979, s. 43(1).
⁵ *Oram v Johnson* [1980] STC 222, [1980] 2 All ER 1.
⁶ CGTA 1979, s. 32(4).
⁷ *IRC v Chubb's Settlement Trustees* (1971) 47 TC 353.

Revenue expenditure

21: 07   In the same way that sums taken into account in computing income are excluded from the consideration for CGT (supra, § **21:02**), revenue expenditure is disallowed in computing chargeable gains. First, a sum is not allowable expenditure for CGT if it is allowable as a deduction in computing the profits or losses of a trade, profession or vocation for purposes of income tax, or as a deduction in computing any other income for the purposes of the Income Tax Acts.[1] This exclusion is extended to sums which would be deductible in computing losses but for the fact that there are insufficient profits against which the losses may be offset.

There is a second, more stringent, limitation on the deduction of expenses. Expenditure is not deductible for CGT if, on the hypothesis that the asset were employed as a fixed asset of a trade, the expenditure would be deductible in computing the profits of that trade for income tax purposes.[2]

For assets such as land and buildings, this restriction denies relief for maintenance expenditure, even where the property is not let. It is important to bear in mind that even extensive expenditure on rehabilitating an asset may be deductible for income tax, unless it can be shown that the dilapidations requiring attention depressed the price paid for the asset.[3]

Simon's Taxes C2.129, 130; Sumption CGT A4.06.
[1] CGTA 1979, s. 33(1).
[2] CGTA 1979, s. 33(2).
[3] *Odeon Associated Theatres Ltd v Jones* [1973] Ch 288, [1972] 1 All ER 681, 48 TC 257, supra, § **7: 117.**

Acquisition cost

21: 08   The allowable expenditure on acquisition is the amount or value of the consideration paid on the acquisition—or costs incidental thereto—in money or money's worth, given by the person making the disposal or on his behalf wholly and exclusively for the acquisition of the asset.[1] For an asset not acquired, such as the goodwill of a new business, the allowable expenditure refers to sums incurred to provide the asset. The exclusion of revenue expenditure is likely to limit sums allowable in this context. Costs incidental to the acquisition may only be deducted if they are incurred by the acquirer.

What constitutes consideration is a question of the correct construction of any agreement. Where assets were acquired in return for a stated sum to be satisfied by the issue of shares, the House of Lords held that the consideration was that sum and not the market value of the shares at the time of issue since the agreement was honestly reached and by way of bargain at arm's length.[2]

Where the asset was acquired other than by way of a bargain at arm's length, e.g. by gift, the allowable expenditure is the market value at the date of acquisition,[3] and similarly in other cases where market value is to be substituted for actual consideration.

For disposals on or after 6th April 1988 of assets owned at 31st March 1982, the consideration deemed to be given is the asset's open market value on the latter date (see infra, § **22: 02**).[4]

Simon's Taxes C2.126; Sumption CGT A4.06.
[1] CGTA 1979, s. 32(1)(*a*) note the decision of Goff J in *Allison v Murray* [1975] STC 524, [1975] 3 All ER 561; supra, § **18: 16**. On the actual costs of acquiring certain overseas assets before 19th November 1967 (the date of devaluation), see CGTA 1979, Sch 6, paras 17 and 18. In *Cleveleys Investment Trust Co v IRC* [1975] STC 457 the Court of Session disallowed sums not paid wholly and exclusively *for the purpose* of acquiring certain rights—italics supplied; this reference to purpose is not in the legislation and introduces an unwelcome subjective element.
[2] *Stanton v Drayton Commercial Investment Co Ltd* [1982] STC 525.
[3] CGTA 1979, s. 29A.
[4] FA 1988, s. 96.

Incidental costs of acquisition

21: 09   Incidental costs must have been incurred by the person making the disposal, wholly and exclusively for the purposes of the acquisition. Such costs are expressly limited to fees, commission or remuneration paid for the professional services of any surveyor or valuer, or auctioneer, or accountant or agent or legal adviser and the costs of transfer or conveyance (including stamp duty) together with the costs of advertising to find a seller.[1] Fees for the services on acquisition must be distinguished from the fees payable for investment advice, which are not allowable.[2]

Other costs, such as expenses of travel to inspect property with a view to purchase, are not allowable, even if the property is in fact acquired.

Simon's Taxes C2.126; Sumption CGT A4.06.
[1] CGTA 1979, s. 32(2).
[2] Revenue Leaflet CGT (1980) 8 § 146 (now withdrawn).

Improvements

21: 10   Expenditure wholly and exclusively incurred on the asset by the person making the disposal or on his behalf is allowable if it is for the purpose of enhancing the value of the asset.[1]

Such expenditure must be reflected in the state or nature of the asset at the time of the disposal. If the expenditure is so reflected, no matter in how small a way, it is deductible in full. It also appears that the expenditure must make an identifiable change in the state or nature of the asset.[2] It follows that a payment to a valuer to determine the authenticity of a painting or other work of art is not deductible—whatever his verdict. This rule also excludes an advance payment to a builder who goes bankrupt before beginning the work. When the disposal is by contract followed by conveyance it is unclear how far, if at all, the improvements must be reflected in the state or nature of the asset at the time of the conveyance.[3]

Simon's Taxes C2.126; Sumption CGT A4.06.
[1] CGTA 1979, s. 32(1)(*b*). In *Emmerson v Computer Time International Ltd* the company owed rent to its landlord. The landlord agreed to consent to an assignment of the lease on condition that the rent arrears were paid. The Court of Appeal held that the payments of the arrears were not deductible under this rule; [1977] STC 170, 50 TC 628, [1977] 2 All ER 545.
[2] *Aberdeen Construction Group Ltd v IRC* [1977] STC 302 (Court of Session); the point was not raised in the House of Lords.
[3] *Chaney v Watkis* [1986] STC 89.

21: 11   The three categories referred to above allow the deduction of expenditure incurred on behalf of the disposer, as well as that incurred by him. This phrase is apt to cover expenditure incurred by a person such as a trustee or mortgagee whose acts are treated as those of the owner. If any other person pays for the improvements, e.g. by way of gift to the owner the position is less clear. It is not necessary that the owner ultimately bears the cost, but it does seem that there should be a contractual relationship between the owner and the person incurring the expenditure, of the nature of an agency.[1]

Particular problems arise in the case of joint tenancies, where one of them incurs expenditure on the asset but the other subsequently becomes solely entitled. Property law suggests that the whole should be allowable since each joint tenant has an interest in the whole property. However, it is unclear that one joint tenant necessarily incurs expenditure on behalf of the other, in the absence of any additional agreement between them. On a death of one of the joint tenants, his severable share will be deemed acquired by the other at its market value,[2] so that any expenditure incurred by the deceased prior to death will no longer be relevant.

Simon's Taxes C2.126.
[1] *Gaspet Ltd v Ellis* [1985] STC 572, [1985] 1 WLR 1214, a case concerning scientific research allowances under CAA 1968, s. 91.
[2] CGTA 1979, s. 49(10).

Preservation of title

21: 12   A further category of allowable expenditure includes the costs wholly and exclusively incurred by the owner (but not on his behalf), in establishing, preserving or defending his title to, or to a right over, the asset.[1] This category must be distinguished from acquisition costs (supra, § **21: 08**) and operates narrowly. First, the word "establishing" is to be read *eiusdem generis* with "preserving" and "defending". In a case involving a settlement, a beneficiary secured the agreement of the trustees to vest the trust funds in her absolutely.[2] She was, however, required to take out a single premium policy on her life, written in favour of the trustees, to indemnify them against her predeceasing another beneficiary having a contingent interest. It was held that the payment of the premium was not to establish the beneficiary's defeasible interest in the fund, since that was not in dispute, but to acquire something greater namely the absolute interest. Hence, the costs could only be deducted if they came within the category of acquisition costs.[3]

The main obstacle in the way of claiming allowable expenditure under this heading is the exclusion of expenditure which would be deductible as a revenue expense if the asset were a fixed asset in a trade, and the income tax rule that money spent on defending title to a capital asset is a revenue expense (supra, § **21: 07**).[4] For example, a sum paid by a liquidator in respect of arrears of rent, even if it had been spent in preserving the asset (a leasehold interest) would not have been deductible.[5] However, the incidental costs of valuing shares and securities for estate duty purposes has been held to be allowable for CGT under this category, on the grounds that the main purpose is to obtain probate of the will, which establishes the title of the executors to the assets.[6] The Revenue allow such expenses in practice on the basis of a fixed scale according to the value of the estate.[7]

Simon's Taxes C2.126; Sumption CGT A4.06.
[1] CGTA 1979, s. 32(1)(*b*).
[2] *Allison v Murray* [1975] STC 524, [1975] 3 All ER 561, supra, § **18: 16**.
[3] The expense did not come within the first category since it was not consideration for the acquisition of absolute title but to acquire the other beneficiary's contingent interest.
[4] Supra, § **7: 107**.
[5] *Emmerson v Computer Time International Ltd* [1976] STC 111, [1976] 2 All ER 131.
[6] *IRC v Richards' Executors* [1971] 1 All ER 785, 46 TC 626; but see also *Passant v Jackson* [1986] STC 164.
[7] Statement of Practice SP7/81, **Simon's Taxes, Division H3.2.**

Incidental costs of disposal

21: 13   The incidental costs of disposal[1] are defined in the same way as the incidental costs of acquisition, and cover legal fees and the costs of advertising to find a buyer.[2] There is also express mention of costs reasonably incurred in making any valuation or apportionment required for the computation of CGT and including in particular the costs of ascertaining the market value where required. The costs of drafting the CGT computation, agreeing it with the Revenue and appealing any assessment are not included and in consequence are not allowable. Moreover, the costs of taking advice regarding valuation etc are deductible only if they relate to a disposal of the asset, and not if the advice is taken for another purpose.

Simon's Taxes C2.126; Sumption CGT A4.06.
[1] CGTA 1979, s. 32(1)(*c*).
[2] CGTA 1979, s. 32(2).

Apportionment of expenditure

21: 14   The categories of allowable expenditure all require that the costs be incurred "wholly and exclusively" for acquisition etc., although in practice this phrase is not interpreted restrictively. Expenditure incurred on valuing stocks and shares both for the probate and for estate duty has been held to be allowable notwithstanding the apparent dual purpose.[1] This may however simply be because the estate duty payment was incidental to the main purpose of obtaining probate. It is clear that where the main purpose is allowable, expenditure is deductible in full even though there is some subsidiary or incidental purpose which is not allowable. Conversely no sum is deductible at all if the allowable purpose is purely incidental.[2] This leaves open the question whether an apportionment can be made where there are two main purposes only one of which is allowable.[3]

Where a taxpayer carried out a scheme designed to avoid CGT the expenses of the scheme were deductible, even though it could be argued that one of the purposes of the expenditure was to avoid tax.[4]

Where a sum has been spent on two or more assets the expenditure must be apportioned.[5] The issue in such cases is the correct construction of the agreement; once the parties have paid one part of the consideration for one asset and another part for another, they cannot subsequently seek to reallocate that consideration for tax purposes.

Where, under an agreement, a sum was paid for shares, the vendor was in addition to be entitled to a sum in respect of a debt due to it.[6] That sum was much less than the debt but it was not open to the parties to treat the amount paid for the shares as reduced by the amount of the shortfall.

Simon's Taxes C2.126; Sumption CGT A4.06.
[1] *IRC v Richards' Executors* [1971] 1 All ER 785, 46 TC 626.
[2] *Cleveleys Investment Trust v IRC* [1975] STC 457.
[3] The point was not directly faced in *IRC v Richards' Executors* but compare Lord Reid, at 790, 635 with Lord Guest, at 798, 644.
[4] *Eilbeck v Rawling* [1980] STC 192, [1980] 2 All ER 12 not affected by [1981] STC 174, [1981] 1 All ER 865, HL.

[5] CGTA 1979, s. 43(4).

[6] *E V Booth (Holdings) Ltd v Buckwell* [1980] STC 578, distinguishing *Aberdeen Construction Group Ltd v IRC* [1978] STC 127, [1978] 1 All ER 962, HL.

FOREIGN TAX

21: 15 Any foreign tax for which relief is not available by way of credit may be deducted in computing the gain.[1]

Simon's Taxes C1.502.
[1] CGTA 1979, s. 11.

WASTING ASSETS

21: 16 On the disposal of a wasting asset[1] (supra, § **15: 07**) special rules restrict the allowable expenditure; these rules do not apply to assets in respect of which capital allowances have been or could have been claimed (supra, § **20: 02**). Any residual or scrap value of the asset is deducted from the costs of acquisition and the resulting figure is written-off on a straight line basis over the life of the asset remaining unexpired at the date of acquisition.[2]

Similarly, where enhancement expenditure is incurred, it is written off on a straight line basis over the life of the asset still unexpired at the time the expenditure is first reflected in the asset.[3] If the enhancement expenditure alters the residual or scrap value, then the writing off of acquisition costs is altered accordingly.

The exemption from CGT of wasting chattels (supra, § **15: 08**), and the exclusion for chattels where capital allowances may be claimed, mean that the straight line wasting formula applies primarily to intangible property such as leases, options (supra, § **16: 18**) and life interests in settled property. Straight line wasting does not apply to leases of land; see infra, § **21: 18** for the special rules applying.

EXAMPLE

GH purchased an option to acquire the film rights of a novel, for £5,000 on 1st January 1983. On 30th March 1988, he assigned the option without exercising it, for £40,000. The option, originally granted by the copyright owner on 1st January 1980, expires on 31st December 1990. (Indexation factor: 0.260)

Disposal consideration		£40,000
Allowable cost	£5,000	
Wasted: $\dfrac{5\frac{3}{12}}{8} \times £5,000$	3,281	
	1,719	
Indexation allowance:		
$0.260 \times £1,719$	447	2,166
Chargeable gain		£37,834

There is no provision for altering the period taken as the predictable life of the wasting asset, which is to be determined solely on the basis of information ascertainable at the time of acquisition.[4] However, a person acquiring a wasting asset need not take as the predictable life the period assumed by the previous owner, if circumstances have changed in some relevant respect since his acquisition.

The position where a wasting asset ceases to be a wasting asset is not explicitly covered by the legislation. Since the asset will have changed its nature, allowable expenditure on the original asset should be capable of being traced through. In practice, the Revenue appear to require that the expenditure on the original asset be wasted down to the date it ceased to be a wasting asset. The balance is then added to the allowable cost of the new asset in relation to a subsequent disposal. However, the exercise of a wasting option to acquire an asset results simply in the addition of the cost of the option to the cost of the asset.[5]

Simon's Taxes C2.136; Sumption CGT A4.11.
[1] CGTA 1979, s. 37; a quoted option to subscribe for shares, a traded option and a financial option are not wasting assets, CGTA 1979, s. 138; the inclusion of financial options is by F(No. 2)A 1987, s. 81(6)—from a date to be set by statutory instrument.
[2] CGTA 1979, s. 38.
[3] CGTA 1979, s. 38(2)(*b*).
[4] CGTA 1979, s. 37(3).
[5] CGTA 1979, s. 137(3).

LEASES

21: 17 A lease with an unexpired term of 50 years or less is a wasting asset.[1] Any lease of movable property which is a wasting asset is treated as expiring no later than the end of the life of that asset,[2] and so will always be itself a wasting asset. Expenditure on a lease which qualifies for capital allowances will not be subject to the wasting asset rules.[3] On grant of a lease for a premium, there is a part disposal of the asset in respect of which the lease is granted.[4] The normal part disposal rule applies for computing the allowable expenditure, except that the market value of the asset remaining undisposed of is to include the capitalised value of rentals due under the lease.[5] On the grant of a sublease out of a lease, there is also a disposal if the sublease is granted for a premium, and the part disposal formula takes account of the capitalised value of rentals under the sublease. However, if the lease is a wasting asset, then the allowable expenditure on the part disposal is not computed by reference to the $\dfrac{A}{A+B}$ formula, but is instead equal to the expenditure in respect of the head lease that wastes over the term of the sub lease.[6]

Simon's Taxes C2.609, 610; Sumption CGT A4.11.
[1] CGTA 1979, s. 37(1).
[2] CGTA 1979, Sch. 3, para. 9(3).
[3] CGTA 1979, s. 38.
[4] CGTA 1979, Sch. 3, para. 2(1).
[5] CGTA 1979, Sch. 3, para. 2(2)
[6] CGTA 1979, Sch. 3, para. 4.

Leases of land

21: 18   The general rules for leases in § **21: 17**, above, apply to leases of land with appropriate modifications. Thus, a lease of land is a wasting asset if its unexpired term is 50 years or less,[1] although not during the term of a sub lease at less than a rack rent.[2] However, the expenditure in respect of a wasting lease of land is not written off on a straight line basis. Instead, it is written off according to statutory percentage tables,[3] which give a gradual depreciation in the early years of the lease, accelerating towards the end of the term. Of the acquisition cost of the lease, the fraction $\dfrac{P(1)-P(3)}{P(1)}$ is written off to the date of disposal, where

P(1) = percentage applicable to unexpired term at date of acquisition
P(3) = percentage applicable to unexpired term at date of disposal.

Similarly, enhancement expenditure written off is $\dfrac{P(2)-P(3)}{P(2)}$, where P(2) is the percentage applicable at the date the expenditure was reflected in the lease. Expenditure qualifying for capital allowances e.g. on a lease of an industrial building is not written off[4] and apportionments may be necessary.

EXAMPLE
XY acquired a lease of a block of flats on 31st May 1984 for £105,000. The lease was for 99 years from 1st January 1923. On 1st March 1988, XY assigned the lease for £500,000. (Indexation factor: 0.170).
Unexpired term at date of acquisition: 37 years 7 months
Percentage P(1): 93.901
Unexpired term at date of disposal: 33 years 10 months
Percentage P(3): 91.010

Fraction of expenditure written off:
$$\frac{93.901-91.010}{93.901}=0.031$$

Disposal consideration		£500,000
Allowable cost	£105,000	
Wasted: 0.031 × £105,000	3,255	
	101,745	
Indexation: 0.170 × £101,745	17,297	119,042
Chargeable gain		£380,958

Simon's Taxes C2.604; Sumption CGT A16.02, 03.
[1] CGTA 1979, Sch. 3, para. 1(1).
[2] CGTA 1979, Sch. 3, para. 1(2).
[3] CGTA 1979, Sch. 3, para. 1(3).
[4] CGTA 1979, Sch. 3, para. 1(6).

21: 19   On the grant of a lease for a premium, either out of an unencumbered freehold or out of a lease, there is a part disposal taking into account, in valuing the interest subject to the sublease, the rentals due thereunder.[1]

EXAMPLE

BC purchased a freehold factory for £180,000 in May 1984. After occupying it for the purposes of his own business, he grants a 15 year lease to a company for £50,000 with effect from 1st December 1987. The capitalised value of rentals under the lease is £150,000 and the freehold reversion is worth £200,000. (Indexation factor: 0.161).

Disposal consideration		£50,000
Allowable expenditure		
$£180,000 \times \dfrac{50,000}{50,000+200,000+150,000}$	£22,500	
Indexation allowance: $0.161 \times £22,500$	3,623	26,123
Chargeable gain		£23,877

If the lease is granted out of a short lease, the allowable expenditure is the amount which will have wasted over the term of the sublease,[2] given by the fraction $\dfrac{P(4)-P(5)}{P(1)}$, where

$P(1)$ = percentage applicable to unexpired term of headlease at date of acquisition

$P(4)$ = percentage applicable to unexpired term of headlease at date sub lease is granted

$P(5)$ = percentage applicable to unexpired term of headlease at date sub lease expires.

On the grant of a lease for a term of less than 50 years, any premium may be subject in part to income tax, supra § 9: 17. If the lease has been granted out of a freehold or long lease, the premium subject to CGT is reduced by the amount subject to income tax.[3] However, the reduced premium is substituted only in the numerator, not in the denominator, of the $\dfrac{A}{A+B}$ formula for apportioning allowable expenditure. In the case of a short lease granted out of a short lease, the CGT computation follows the normal format and the amount of the premium subject to income tax is then deducted from the chargeable gain.[4] An allowable loss cannot be produced by this deduction, however.

Simon's Taxes C2.609, 615; Sumption CGT A16.03.
[1] CGTA 1979, Sch. 3, para. 2(2).
[2] CGTA 1979, Sch. 3, para. 4.
[3] CGTA 1979, Sch. 3, para. 5(1).
[4] CGTA 1979, Sch. 3, para. 5(2).

INDEXATION ALLOWANCE

21: 20   On the disposal of an asset, an indexation allowance is given, equal to the allowable expenditure multiplied by the fraction $\dfrac{RD-RI}{RI}$ where RD is the retail prices index figure for the month in which the disposal occurs and RI that for the month in which the expenditure is incurred.[1] If RI exceeds RD, the indexation allowance is nil.[2]

The fraction has to be expressed as a decimal, taken to the nearest three decimal places.[3] Where there are several items of allowable expenditure incurred at different times, the indexed rise is calculated separately for each, and the aggregate is then the indexation allowance. However, indexation applies only to items of relevant allowable expenditure, broadly the cost of acquisition and any expenditure on enhancement or preservation of title (supra, § **21: 08–12**).[4] It does not apply to other deductions e.g. for IHT on a gift (infra, § **46: 25**) or foreign tax which is not creditable (supra, § **21: 15**). No indexation allowance is due on the disposal on or after 4th July 1987 of a share in a building society or a registered industrial and provident society.[5] The indexation allowance is treated as a deduction from the gain or loss computed under general CGT rules. It may reduce a gain, turn a gain into a loss or increase a loss. The gain or loss prior to deduction of indexation allowance are termed the "unindexed gain or loss".[6]

Where an asset was acquired before 1st April 1982 and is disposed of after 5th April 1988 the allowance is calculated by reference to the market value on 31st March 1982 rather than the various items of expenditure incurred before that date, if this gives a result favourable to the taxpayer.[7] However, the 31st March 1982 value must be used to compute the indexation allowance if the taxpayer has elected under FA 1988, s. 96(5) (infra, § **22: 04**). Provision is made for changes in the state of the asset since 31st March 1982.[8] For disposals before 6th April 1988, but after 5th April 1985, the use of the 31st March 1982 value for indexation purposes was elective.

EXAMPLE

A bought a house for investment purposes in 1976. The costs of acquisition were £18,000. In 1980 he incurred improvement costs of £6,000.

On 31st March 1982 the value of the property was £40,000. He sells it in February 1986 for £50,000.

Proceeds of sale	£50,000
Deduct Allowable costs	24,000
Unindexed gain	26,000
Indexation allowance	

$$\frac{RD-RI}{RI} = \frac{381.1-313.4}{313.4} = 0.216$$

£40,000 × 0.216	8,640
Chargeable gain	£17,360

(The election for 31st March 1982 value is clearly favourable in this case.)

Simon's Taxes C2.201, 202; Sumption CGT A4.17.
[1] FA 1982, s. 88(2) as amended by FA 1985, Sch. 19, para. 2.
[2] FA 1982, s. 87(3)(*b*).
[3] FA 1982, s. 87(4).
[4] FA 1982, s. 86(2)(*b*).
[5] FA 1988, s. 113.
[6] FA 1982, s. 86(2)(*a*) as amended by FA 1985, Sch. 19, para. 1.
[7] FA 1985, s. 68(4) and (5), as amended by FA 1988, Sch. 8, para. 11.
[8] FA 1985, s. 68(6).

21: 21 On a part disposal the deductible expenditure in respect of the whole asset must be apportioned before the indexation allowance is calculated. The indexation allowance on the part disposal applies only to that part of each item of expenditure which is to be taken into account on the disposal.[1]

Where an element of expenditure falls to be reduced (the most obvious example concerns the reduction of expenditure on leased property), increased or excluded, the indexed rise is to apply only to the expenditure as reduced, increased or excluded.[2]

Simon's Taxes C2.203, 207; Sumption CGT A4.17.
[1] FA 1982, Sch. 13, para. 1.
[2] FA 1982, s. 86(3).

Special situations

(1) *No gain/no loss*

21: 22 Certain CGT provisions apply a no-gain/no-loss rule on certain types of disposal, for example on a transfer of an asset between member companies in groups (see § **26: 22**) and on a gift by an individual where both donor and donee so elect; § **16: 20**. For a disposal of this kind after 5th April 1985, the consideration for the disposal will simply take account of any indexation allowance due to the transferor.[1]

However, for assets transferred under such a disposal before 6th April 1985 but after 5th April 1982, the rules were somewhat different.[2]

Where a person acquired an asset after 31st March 1982 by a no gain, no loss disposal and any earlier disposal of the asset after that date was also such a disposal,[3] he is treated as having held the asset on 31st March 1982 and so is eligible to take 31st March 1982 as the base date value for indexation relief. Any indexation relief already claimed must be brought into account.[4] This special rule for indexation purposes is now mirrored by the general rule for computing gains or losses on assets held on 31st March 1982.[5]

Simon's Taxes C2.204; Sumption CGT A4.18; A12.10.
[1] FA 1982, Sch. 13, para. 2.
[2] FA 1982, Sch. 13, para. 3 repealed by FA 1985, Sch. 19, para. 5(3). See *Butterworths UK Tax Guide 1985–86*, § **21: 18** for an explanation of the earlier rules.
[3] Defined in FA 1985, s. 68(7).
[4] FA 1985, s. 68(8).
[5] FA 1988, s. 96; see § **22: 01**, post.

Relevant receipts

21: 23 The receipts of certain sums are treated as not giving rise to a disposal, but rather as reducing the base cost of the asset. For example, on a rights issue if the shareholder sells his "rights", the amount received is not treated as a chargeable disposal if the proceeds amount to less than 5% of the value of his shareholding ex-rights.[1] The proceeds are instead deducted from the acquisition cost of the shares. Here, the indexation allowance on a disposal of the shares takes account of the reduction in allowable expenditure but only from the date of the receipt.[2]

Simon's Taxes C2.202; Sumption CGT A4.17.
[1] Supra, § **19: 13**.
[2] FA 1982, Sch. 13, para. 4.

Reorganisations, etc.

21: 24 Where, on a reorganisation of a company or an amalgamation, new shares are acquired, they are generally treated as if the original acquisition were still in existence. If new consideration is provided, it is treated as new relevant allowable expenditure.[1] The indexed rise on the expenditure is therefore calculated by reference to the date the new consideration was provided, not by reference to the date the allowable expenditure on the original shareholding was incurred.

Simon's Taxes C2.205; Sumption CGT A4.17.
[1] FA 1982, Sch. 13, para. 5.

Calls on shares, etc.

21: 25 Unpaid calls due in respect of the shares are treated as having been paid when the shares were acquired provided they are paid within 12 months of that date.[1] This applies even though the contract gives the right to pay by instalments. Calls paid outside the twelve month period are treated as separate items of expenditure incurred when paid, and the indexation allowance on disposal of shares is calculated accordingly.

Simon's Taxes C2.205; Sumption CGT A4.17.
[1] FA 1982, Sch. 13, para. 6(1)(*b*).

Options

21: 26 Special rules apply to options. The acquisition of property under an option is treated as an acquisition when the option is exercised but, in computing the indexed rise, the sums paid for the option are treated as separate items of expenditure incurred when the option was acquired.[1]

Simon's Taxes C2.202; Sumption CGT A12.10; A20.07.
[1] FA 1982, Sch. 13, para. 7. On treatment of sums paid for shares under the 1985 rules see FA 1985, Sch. 19, para. 15.

Before 6th April 1985

21: 27 Up to April 1982 no account was taken of inflation in calculating capital gains although often the only gain involved was an inflationary gain. For disposals from April 1982 until April 1985, however, relief was given on the basis of the following principles:[1]

(1) only changes due to inflation after March 1982 were taken into account;

(2) no relief was given for changes due to inflation occurring during the first twelve months of ownership, thus excluding relief whether the asset was disposed of within those twelve months or not;

(3) the relief could only reduce (or eliminate) a gain.

Companies could elect for the separate system of pooling, known as "parallel pooling" (see supra, § **19: 05**).

The indexation allowance was determined by applying the fraction $\frac{RD-RI}{RI}$ (expressed as a decimal figure rounded to the nearest third decimal place) to the cost. RI is the retail prices index (RPI) figure for the base month, and RD is the RPI figure for the month in which the disposal is made. The base month is the later of March 1982 or the month which is the twelfth month after which the expenditure is incurred.[2] To qualify for an indexation allowance the disposal must have been made on or after 6th April 1982 (1st April 1982 for companies) and more than 12 months after the acquisition of the asset disposed of.[3]

EXAMPLE

A purchases a painting for £30,000 in May 1981. The RPI figure for May 1982 (12 months after the purchase) is 322. He sells the painting in February 1985 for £45,000 when the RPI is 362·7. The chargeable gain is as follows:

		£
Consideration		45,000
Less cost		30,000
Gross gain		15,000
Indexation allowance		

$$\frac{RD-RI}{RI} = \frac{362\cdot7-322}{322} = 0.126$$

£30,000 × 0.126		3,780
		£11,220

If the painting was sold for £37,000 in April 1982 there would have been no indexation allowance available as the asset would not have been held for the qualifying period of twelve months.

Under these rules the indexation allowance did not apply if no gain actually accrued to the transferor on the disposal.[4] Nor could it be used to turn a gain into a loss; if on a disposal the expenditure as increased by the allowance exceeded the disposal proceeds there was neither gain nor loss.[5] The indexation allowance was nil if the expenditure was incurred less than 13 months before the month in which disposal occurred.[6]

Simon's Taxes C2.201, 202; Sumption CGT A4.17.
 [1] FA 1982, s. 86.
 [2] FA 1982, s. 87(2).
 [3] FA 1982, s. 86(1)(*a*).
 [4] FA 1982, s. 86(5)(*b*).
 [5] FA 1982, s. 86(5)(*b*).
 [6] FA 1982, s. 87(3)(*b*).

22   Assets held on 31st March 1982

22: 01   One premise of the original CGT legislation was to exclude gains which had accrued but were not realised until after CGT came into force i.e after 6th April 1965. As a corollary accrued losses were likewise excluded. The method by which the limitation is effected is explained infra, § **22: 09– 16**.

22: 02   In 1982, indexation was introduced to eliminate purely inflationary increases in the values of assets, as measured by the RPI. However, no adjustment was made to exclude inflationary gains accruing between 1965 and 1982. The modifications made to indexation in 1985 also left this problem largely untouched, although the indexation allowance itself was computed on the value of the asset held at 31st March 1982, if the taxpayer so elected. For disposals on or after 6th April 1988, relief is given for pre 1982 inflation by treating assets held on 31st March 1982 as having been disposed of and immediately reacquired on that date at their then market value.[1] There is no option to use time apportionment. Chargeable gains or allowable losses are computed accordingly, with the indexation allowance being based upon the higher of 31st March 1982 value or original cost.[2] There is nevertheless an overall restriction on the 1982 rebasing, in that it can serve only to reduce gains or losses by comparison with the rules applying before 6th April 1988. If the rebasing produces a higher gain or a higher loss, the old rules apply instead. Where the new rules produce a gain, but the old rules produce a loss (or vice-versa), the disposal is treated as giving rise neither to a gain nor to a loss. For all practical purposes, therefore, the former rules continue in existence. However, a taxpayer can elect that gains and losses are computed on the basis of 31st March 1982 value, without reference to original cost (infra, § **22: 04**).[3]

Simon's Taxes C2.101, 126, 301.
[1] FA 1988, s. 96.
[2] FA 1985, s 68(5), as substituted by FA 1988, Sch. 8, para. 11.
[3] FA 1988, s. 96(5).

22: 03   The steps in the CGT computation are therefore as follows:

(1) Compute the gain or loss under the old rules. If the result is no gain/no loss, this result stands.[1]

(2) Compute the gain or loss under the new rules.

(3) If (1) gives a gain and (2) gives a greater gain, the result of (1) stands; similarly for losses.[2]

(4) If (1) gives a gain and (2) gives a smaller gain, the result of (2) stands; similarly for losses.

(5) If (1) gives a gain, and (2) a loss (or vice-versa), the result is no gain/no loss.[3]

It is not entirely clear from the legislation whether the comparison is to be made between indexed or unindexed gains and losses, although the intention appears to be the former and this interpretation is adopted by the Revenue.[4]

EXAMPLE

D purchased an acre of land for £12,000 in 1979. The value of the land on 31st March 1982 was £100,000. In June 1988, D sold the land for development, netting £450,000. Assumed indexation factor = 0.325.

	£	£
Disposal proceeds	450,000	450,000
Cost	(12,000)	
Value at 31st March 1982		(100,000)
Indexation: £100,000 × 0.325	(32,500)	(32,500)
Gain	£405,500	£317,500
Chargeable gain	£317,500	

---

[1] FA 1988, s. 96(3)(*c*).
[2] FA 1988, s. 96(3)(*a*), (*b*).
[3] FA 1988, s. 96(3)(*a*), (*b*).
[4] FA 1988, s. 96(2) refers to computing the gain or loss "for the purpose of capital gains tax". In FA 1982, s. 86(4), the gain or loss after the deduction of the indexation allowance is the gain or loss "for the purposes of the Capital Gains Tax Act 1979".

22: 04   The taxpayer may elect that the restrictions on rebasing by reference to the former rules do not apply.[1] Any such election must be made within two years of the end of the year of assessment in which the first disposal to which it applies is made. In strictness, the first relevant disposal would be a disposal of any asset, even if the asset or the gain was exempt. The Revenue have indicated that in practice they propose to disregard certain exempt disposals for this purpose.[2] The election, which is irrevocable, applies to all disposals, including those made prior to the election, to which rebasing applies. Thus the election is all or nothing and does not permit the taxpayer to disapply the restrictions only where this would be of benefit. In the case of assets acquired from a spouse (supra, § **14: 08**) or from another member of a group of companies (infra, § **26: 18**), where the transferor has already made the election, the transferee's disposal of the asset is also covered by that election, whether or not the transferee has made such an election.[3] An election under these provisions does not cover—

(*a*) plant or machinery;
(*b*) assets used in connection with a trade of working mineral deposits;
(*c*) oil exploration licences;

but, under (*a*) or (*b*), only where capital allowances were or could have been claimed on the asset concerned.[4]

Simon's Taxes C1.307; C2.107.
[1] FA 1988, s. 96(5).
[2] Statement of Practice SP 2/89, **Simon's Taxes, Division H3.2**. It is understood that this would include a disposal of a chattel for £6,000 or less (£3,000 or less before 6th April 1989).

³ FA 1988, Sch. 8, para. 2.
⁴ FA 1988, Sch. 8, para. 12.

22: 05   Although the rebasing of CGT to 31st March 1982 affects only disposals made on or after 6th April 1988, it does have important implications for certain prior transactions. In particular, gains which were realised before 1st April 1982 but which were rolled over against acquisition expenditure will generally be "washed". The main types of rollover affected are:

(*a*)   replacement of assets lost or destroyed (§ **16: 08**, supra);
(*b*)   compulsory acquisition of land (§ **16: 04**, supra);
(*c*)   replacement of business assets (§ **20:06**, supra);
(*d*)   transfer of business to a company (§ **20: 05**, supra);
(*e*)   transfer of business assets (§ **20: 14**, supra);
(*f*)   gifts and other transfers by individuals or trustees (§ **16: 21**, supra).

Capital reorganisations in respect of shares, mergers and reconstructions before 1st April 1982 also result in a rebasing to the value of the new shareholding at 31st March 1982.

However, reliefs which involve merely the holding over of a gain until the occurrence of a certain event are unaffected, so that the new asset falls to be rebased to 31st March 1982, ignoring the held over gain, which is not "washed". The chief instances are:

(i)   replacement of business assets with depreciating assets (§ **20: 09**, supra);
(ii)   certain share disposals on nationalisation (§ **19: 15**, supra).
(iii)   depreciating assets acquired on compulsory acquisition of land (§ **16: 04**, supra).
(iv)   domestication of foreign branch of UK company[2].

It is therefore specifically provided that these recaptures are not to apply in consequence of events occurring on or after 6th April 1988, where their application is directly attributable to a disposal which occurred before 1st April 1982.[1]

¹ FA 1989, Sch. 15, para. 1.
² TA 1970, s. 268A.

22: 06   Relief is given in a number of the above circumstances where rolled over or held over gains arose after 31st March 1982 but before 6th April 1988. Where the relief applies, the chargeable gain concerned is halved; this broad brush approach avoids having to compute how much of the gain on such disposals arose prior to 31st March 1982. In cases where there was a roll over in the sense that the chargeable gain was deducted from allowable expenditure, the amount of the deduction is reduced by one half in relation to disposals of the assets concerned on or after 6th April 1988.[1] The deduction must have been wholly or partly attributable, directly or indirectly, to gains accruing on the disposal before 6th April 1988 of assets acquired before 31st March 1982. The reduction can apply only once, which leaves it unclear whether a part disposal has the effect of denying relief on a subsequent disposal of the asset retained. The qualifying rollovers are:

(a) replacement of assets lost or destroyed (CGTA 1979, s. 21(4), (5));
(b) compulsory acquisition of land (CGTA 1979, s. 111A);
(c) replacement of business assets (CGTA 1979, s. 115);
(d) incorporation of business (CGTA 1979, s. 123);
(e) gifts of business assets (CGTA 1979, s. 126);
(f) gifts (FA 1980, s. 79).[2]

In cases where gains are held over without being deducted from allowable expenditure, the deferred gain is reduced by one-half. Qualifying holdovers are:

(a) domestication of foreign branch (TA 1970, s. 268A);
(b) degrouping (TA 1970, s. 278(3));
(c) compensation stock on nationalisation(CGTA 1979, s. 84);
(d) compulsory acquisition of land—depreciating asset acquired (CGTA 1979, s. 111B(3));
(e) replacement of business assets—depreciating asset required (CGTA 1979, s. 117(2));
(f) emigration of donee after gifts holdover (FA 1981, s. 79);
(g) reorganisation involving qualifying corporate bonds (FA 1984, Sch. 13, para. 10).[3]

Simon's Taxes C3.401, 402, 407.
[1] FA 1988, Sch. 9, para. 1.
[2] FA 1988, Sch. 9, para. 2.
[3] FA 1988, Sch. 9, para. 3.

22: 07   Relief for pre-6th April 1988 charges is due only if claimed within two years of the end of the year of assessment in which the asset concerned is disposed of after 5th April 1988.[1] Claims must be supported by all necessary particulars, which presumably includes a computation of the gain arising on the earlier disposal, where this has not already been produced. There are provisions for tracing through a series of no gain/no loss disposals, as defined (infra, § **22: 08**),[2] and for assets derived from other assets acquired before 31st March 1982.[3]

Simon's Taxes C3.401, 402, 407.
[1] FA 1988, Sch. 9, para. 8.
[2] FA 1988, Sch. 9, paras. 4, 5.
[3] FA 1988, Sch. 9, para. 7.

22: 07A   Where chargeable gains were reduced before 6th April 1988 on receipt of compensation etc, by the deduction of the receipt from allowable expenditure, the rebasing to 31st March 1982 could have the effect of eliminating such a reduction. For disposals on or after 6th April 1989, the pre-6th April 1988 reduction is deducted from the actual allowable expenditure i.e. historic cost *or* 31st March 1982 value.[1] The restriction applies to:

(a) compensation or insurance receipt for loss or damage
(b) capital distributions
(c) premium on conversion of securities

(*d*) small part disposal of land.

[1] FA 1989, Sch. 15, para. 3. The restriction is necessary only in cases where the receipt exceeds allowable expenditure at the date of the receipt. In other cases, the amount of the receipt is deducted from allowable expenditure available at the time of subsequent disposal, and no special adjustment is required to cope with rebasing.

22: 08   Where an asset was not owned at 31st March 1982, it may still be traced back to that date for the purposes of rebasing. This is done if the asset was acquired by means of a defined no gain/no loss transaction and either the transferor held it at 31st March 1982 or it was acquired through one or more disposals after that date which were all no gain/no loss transactions.[1] The main types of no gain/no loss disposals covered are:

(*a*)   between spouses living together (§ **14: 07**, supra);
(*b*)   settled property passing on the death of the life tenant (§ **18: 12**, supra);
(*c*)   between members of a group of companies (§ **26: 18**, infra).

Where the asset concerned consists of shares, and the transferee held shares of the same class in his own right at 31st March 1982, the value of the combined holding must be determined at that date. The allowable cost on a disposal is determined on a simple pro rata basis.[2] There is also provision for rebasing where an asset is derived from another asset held on 31st March 1982;[3] for example, an undivided interest in land formerly held as joint tenant. Where an asset was held at 31st March 1982 and there was then a part disposal before 6th April 1988, the allowable expenditure attributable to the part remaining is the amount relating to the whole asset less the fraction allocated to the part disposed of.[4] The effect of rebasing is not to value the retained part separately at 31st March 1982 but to recompute the allowable expenditure taking the cost of the whole asset as its value at that date.[5]

[1] FA 1988, Sch. 8, para. 1.
[2] Inland Revenue Statement of Practice SP 5/89.
[3] FA 1988, Sch. 8, para. 5.
[4] CGTA 1979, s. 35; see § **16: 14**, supra.
[5] FA 1988, Sch. 8, para 4.

ASSETS HELD ON 6TH APRIL 1965

22: 09   Despite the rebasing of CGT to 31st March 1982, it is still necessary to retain the rules relating to assets held on 6th April 1965, since, except where an election has been made, the rebasing applies only if the effect is to reduce a gain or a loss. In the case of 6th April 1965 assets, it is clear that the comparison to be made involves the rebased gain or loss and the gain or loss after applying the time-apportionment or 6th April 1965 valuation.[1] Thus the taxpayer retains the right to elect for such a valuation in appropriate cases.

[1] FA 1988, Sch. 8, para. 10.

Quoted securities

22: 10   Securities quoted on the Stock Exchange on 6th April 1965 or in the previous six years and units in unit trusts, whose prices are published regularly by the managers, are treated as sold and immediately reacquired on 6th April 1965; there is no time apportionment.[1]

The usual rules as to valuation, supra, § **21: 04**, are slightly modified. The value is whichever is the higher of a figure halfway (not $\frac{1}{4}$) up from the lower of the two figures quoted or halfway between highest and lowest prices. Unit trusts are valued halfway between offer and bid prices. The 6th April 1965 value of quoted securities is readily ascertainable from listings such as Extel.

Simon's Taxes C2.113; Sumption CGT A12.11.
[1] CGTA 1979, Sch. 5, para. 1.

22: 11   There is a restriction of any gain or loss to the actual gain or loss computed by reference to historic cost, without any time apportionment.[1] Thus, if the 6th April 1965 value results in a gain, but by reference to historic cost there is a smaller gain, the latter prevails, and similarly for a loss. If, however, the 6th April 1965 value results in a gain, and the historic cost in a loss (or vice-versa), then neither gain nor loss is deemed to arise on the disposal. In this case, rebasing to 31st March 1982 does not apply and the no gain/no loss position stands.[2] In all cases, the comparison is made before deducting any indexation allowance.[3]

EXAMPLE

MT purchased ordinary shares in BJ plc on 1st January 1960. He sold them in April 1986.

Cost	£2,000	
Value at 6th April 1965	£1,500	
Value at 31st March 1982	£5,000	
Sale proceeds	£7,000	
(Indexation factor 0.229)		

Sale proceeds	£7,000	£7,000
Allowable cost:		
(*a*) 6.4.65 value	1,500	
(*b*) Cost		2.000
Gain	5,500	5,000
Indexation: 0.229 × £5,000		1,145
Chargeable gain		£3,855

EXAMPLE

JP purchased ordinary shares in LS plc in 1963 for £10,000. He sold them in December 1985 for £8,000. On 6th April 1965, the shares were valued at £7,000; on 31st March 1982, at £7,500. (Indexation factor: 0.209)

Sales proceeds	£8,000	£8,000
Allowable cost		
(a) 6.4.65 value	7,000	
(b) Cost		10,000
Gain/(loss)	1,000	(2,000)
Unindexed gain/loss	—	
Indexation allowance: 0.209 × £7,500	£1,568	
Allowable loss	£1,568	

These rules are applied on each disposal. There is no pooling of the shares disposed of after 19th March 1968 and the actual shares disposed of are discovered by the last in first out principle.[4] This is of particular importance where shares of the same company are acquired both before and after 6th April 1965 or where shares in that company have been acquired at different prices whether before or after that date.

Simon's Taxes C2.305; Sumption CGT A12.12.
  [1] CGTA 1979, Sch. 5, para. 2.
  [2] FA 1988, s. 96(3)(c).
  [3] This is in contrast to the comparison under FA 1988, s. 96(2), supra, § **22: 03**. However, the wording in CGTA 1979, Sch. 5, para. 2 is reasonably clear in referring to the gain or loss "computed in accordance with Chapter II of Part II" which, per FA 1982, s. 86(2)(a), as amended, is the unindexed gain or loss.
  [4] CGTA 1979, Sch. 5, para. 2(2). A new pooling election is offered by FA 1985, Sch. 19, para. 6(3) and (4), applying CGTA 1979, Sch. 5, paras. 4–8, but with modifications.

22: 12   The rules regarding quoted securities require the ascertainment of the initial purchase price and involve time and expense in making the calculations. The taxpayer may therefore elect to take the value on 6th April 1965 as an alternative.[1] His election will bind either all his fixed interest securities, including preference shares, or all his ordinary shares, including units in unit trusts, or both, and must be made within two years of the end of the year of assessment in which the first such disposal after 19th March 1968 occurs. Although for most taxpayers it is no longer possible to make that election, a new pooling election, is available for disposals after 5th April 1985.[2] Separate elections are needed for husband and wife. The election will mean that all the shares covered will be pooled with those acquired later but before 6th April 1982.[3] Clearly the decision whether or not to elect is one that requires complicated calculations and difficult speculations as to the price at which later disposals may take place.

Simon's Taxes C2.310–314; Sumption CGT A9.09; A12.11.
  [1] CGTA 1979, Sch. 5, para. 4.
  [2] FA 1985, Sch. 19, para. 6.
  [3] See § **19: 01**.

Indexation allowances

22: 13   For quoted securities held on 6th April 1965, the indexation allowance is given after any restriction of gains or losses as referred to above, § **22: 11**.[1] If a pooling election is made, the indexation allowance will be computed in the normal way on the cost of the 1982 pool[2] or, on election on the value of the pool at 31st March 1982.[3]

Simon's Taxes Division C2.2.
[1] By implication from FA 1982, s. 86(2)(*a*) and CGTA 1979, Sch. 5, para. 2(1)(*a*).
[2] FA 1985, Sch. 19, para. 7.
[3] FA 1985, Sch. 19, s. 68(4).

Land with development value

22: 14   Where land was acquired before 6th April 1965 but is disposed of after that date at a price in excess of current use value, the land is deemed to have been disposed of and immediately reacquired on 6th April 1965.[1] This rule also applies if the land has been subject to material development since 17th December 1973. The disposal and reacquisition are deemed to take place at market value on that date. Current use value is determined on the basis that the land is permanently incapable of being developed, and cannot reflect any hope value. The existence of hope value must reflect a possibility of development for other than current use.[2] This rule therefore applies even though no planning permission was in force on that date.[3] As with quoted securities actual cost must be substituted if this would produce a smaller gain or loss.

This rule prevents CGT on the development value being calculated on a simple time apportionment basis even where the land was acquired before 1965 by way of a gift.[4]

Simon's Taxes C2.317; Sumption CGT A16.12.
[1] CGTA 1979, Sch. 5, para. 9; allowance can be claimed for betterment levy, para. 10.
[2] *Morgan v Gibson* [1989] STI 416.
[3] *Watkins v Kidson* [1979] STC 464, [1979] 2 All ER 1157.
[4] *Mashiter v Pearmain* [1985] STC 165.

Other assets

22: 15   For other assets the gain is apportioned over the period of ownership,[1] unless the taxpayer elects for valuation on 6th April 1965.[2] The gain is presumed to grow evenly from the date of acquisition or the 6th April 1945 whichever is the later.[3] However, expenditure incurred before 6th April 1945 is taken into account in computing the gain. The Revenue have taken the view that the indexation allowance is deducted before the time apportionment fraction is applied. However, a decision by the Special Commissioners on this point has found that the time-apportioned gain is computed first, and the indexation allowance is then deducted. Where expenditure is incurred after the asset is acquired (but before 6th April 1965), the gain attributable to that expenditure is treated as accruing at an even rate from the date when the expenditure was first reflected in the value of the asset, and not from the date of acquisition. The total gain is allocated between the original acquisition expenditure and the subsequent expenditure according to the amounts of each.[4] Each element is then time apportioned as appropriate, but gains attributable to expenditure incurred after 5th April 1965 are not adjusted. However, the gain will be divided according to the value actually attributable to each and not the costs incurred if there is no expenditure on acquisition, or if that initial expenditure was disproportionately small compared with any item of subsequent expenditure, having regard to the value of the asset immediately before that subsequent expenditure.[5] The rebasing of CGT to 31st March 1982 should eliminate some of the practical difficulties arising from the application of these provisions, particularly in the case of land and buildings acquired many years ago, before the rapid property price inflation since the early 1970s.

EXAMPLE

On 1st April 1958, DB purchased land for £5,000. On 30th September 1970, the construction of a building on the land was completed at a cost of £20,000. The building was let until 1984; on 1st January 1986 DB sold the building with vacant possession for £250,000. (Value of land and building at 31st March 1982: £100,000; indexation factor 0.212)

Disposal consideration	£250,000
Allowable costs (£5,000 + £20,000)	25,000
Gain	£225,000

(a) Apportion:

Acquisition cost: $\dfrac{5,000}{25,000} \times £225,000$ £45,000 (A)

Building cost: $\dfrac{20,000}{25,000} \times £225,000$ £180,000 (B)

(b) Time apportion:

(A) $£45,000 \times \dfrac{20\frac{9}{12}}{27\frac{9}{12}}$ £33,648

(B) (time apportionment inapplicable) £163,040

Unindexed gain	196,688
Indexation allowance: 0.212 × £100,000	21,200
Chargeable gain	£175,488

Special provisions apply to part disposals; in essence, the whole of the remainder is deemed disposed of at open market value.[6] On a part disposal before 6th April 1965, the effect is that time apportionment on subsequent disposals on or after that date runs from the date of the earlier part disposal. On a part disposal after 5th April 1965, the time apportionment ends on the date of the part disposal and subsequent gains on the remainder are brought in without reduction.

Where part of a gain arising from a dwelling house acquired before 6th April 1965 is chargeable, the time apportionment rule is applied first and then the appropriate fraction (supra, § **15: 13**).[7]

Where one asset is derived from another the new asset is treated as if it had been acquired at the same time as the other.[8]

As an alternative to the time apportionment rule the taxpayer may elect to take the market value on 6th April 1965.[9] However, as with quoted securities, the election may not increase the loss nor turn a gain into a loss; in such circumstances neither gain nor loss accrues.[10]

The no gain/no loss rule applies only if an election has been made.[11]

The election is irrevocable; there is no chance of returning to the time apportionment formula if the alternative proves to be unfavourable.[12] If a part disposal of an asset occurs after 6th April 1965 an election must be made at that time and if it is not then made it cannot be made on a later disposal of that asset.[13] The possibility of making such an election still arises for disposals on or after 6th April 1988, but in many cases, where the value of the asset was considerably greater at 31st March 1982 than the original cost, there will clearly be little purpose in considering the 6th April 1965 value.

Simon's Taxes C2.318, 319; Sumption CGT A4.14, 15.
1 CGTA 1979, Sch. 5, para. 11.
2 CGTA 1979, Sch. 5, para. 12; see *Butler v Evans* [1980] STC 613.
3 CGTA 1979, Sch. 5, para. 11(6).
4 CGTA 1979, Sch. 5, para. 11(4).
5 CGTA 1979, Sch. 5, para. 11(5).
6 CGTA 1979, Sch. 5, para. 11(7).
7 CGTA 1979, Sch. 5, para. 11(10).
8 CGTA 1979, Sch. 5, para. 11(9); see also *Bayley v Rogers* [1980] STC 544.
9 CGTA 1979, Sch. 5, para. 12.
10 CGTA 1979, Sch. 5, para. 12(2).
11 *Whitaker v Cameron* [1982] STC 665.
12 CGTA 1979, Sch. 5, para. 12(4).
13 CGTA 1979, Sch. 5, para. 12(5).

Special rules

22: 16 Unquoted securities held at 6th April 1965 are not pooled but are treated as being disposed of on a last in first out basis.[1] For each separate disposal, the taxpayer may therefore elect whether to take market value on 6th April 1965 rather than apply time apportionment. If the shares are required to be valued at 31st March 1982, all the shares held at that date are treated as part of a single holding and the value of part disposals is determined pro rata.[2] The same rule applies to other assets of such a nature that they can be dealt with without identifying the particular assets disposed of or acquired.[3] Special rules apply also to re-organisations of share capital.[4]

There are also special rules concerning capital allowances,[5] and the transfer of assets to a close company[6] which are discussed elsewhere.

Simon's Taxes C2.320; Sumption CGT A12.13.
1 CGTA 1979, Sch. 5, para. 13(3), as amended by FA 1982, Sch. 13, para. 11.
2 Inland Revenue Extra-Statutory Concession 25th May 1989, **Simon's Taxes, Division H2.2**.
3 CGTA 1979, Sch. 5, para. 13(6).
4 CGTA 1979, Sch. 5, para. 14. See also extra-statutory concession D10 (1988) on meaning of reorganisation see *IRC v Beveridge* [1979] STC 592 and SP 14/79, **Simon's Taxes, Division H3.2**.
5 Supra, § **20: 02**.
6 Supra, § **20: 05**.

PART IV. CORPORATION TAX

23 Introduction

23: 01 Corporations resident in the UK are subject to corporation tax (CT) on their profits, the term profits covering both income and capital gains.[1] There is a single rate of CT although there is a special regime for corporations with profits below £750,000.[2] This single rate is charged whether the company distributes or retains its profits. The tax was introduced in 1965. Before that time corporations were subject to income tax, but not surtax, on their income[3] with further taxes, profits taxes,[4] also charged on their income to make up for the absence of surtax.

Since 1965 shareholders of corporations to whom qualifying distributions, such as dividends, are made have been liable to income tax under Schedule F on those distributions.[5] Between 1965 and 1973 the income tax under Schedule F was entirely separate from CT on the profits. This was based on a view that corporations should be encouraged to retain their profits rather than distribute them to their shareholders.[6] Since 1973 a different philosophy has prevailed which emphasises the close relationship between the shareholder and the corporation and which allows the shareholder to use a part of the CT paid by the company to offset his own liability to Schedule F income tax. The mechanism imputes a part of the company's tax liability to the shareholder and so is known as the imputation system.[7] However, in order to ensure that this represents tax actually paid by the corporation, the corporation must, when paying the dividend (or any other qualifying distribution (QD)) pay advance corporation tax (ACT).[8] To avoid a situation in which the shareholder could recover the tax paid through claiming the benefit of his tax credit even though the company pays no CT, ACT must be paid when the dividend is paid whether or not the company is liable to pay CT, e.g. through lack of profits. The ACT is set against the company's liability to CT.

The rate of ACT is tied to the basic rate of income tax (BR) and can be expressed algebraically as $BR/(100-BR)$. This is applied to the value of the qualifying distribution (QD); QD + ACT gives the shareholder's income for tax purposes. The tax credit, if available, is the same amount as the ACT. The algebraic formulation is now statutory.[9]

EXAMPLE

Company income	£100
Less CT @ 35%	35
	£65
Dividend	65.00
Tax credit, i.e. 25/75 × £65	21.66
	£86.66

The taxpayer receives £65 in payment but is treated as receiving dividend income of

£86.66 (i.e. the sum of the dividend and the credit) which after deduction of tax at 25% leaves a net dividend of £65; dividend income is taxable under Schedule F.[10] He will be liable to income tax at his appropriate rate on £86.66; if that rate is nil he will recover £21.66 from the Revenue; if it is 40% so that the tax bill will be £40.06, he will pay an extra £13.00.

The company will pay ACT of £21.66 and can set this off against its CT liability of £35[11] leaving it with a bill of £13.34.

The effect of this is that the shareholder is treated as receiving taxable income of £86.66 which will be subject to his full rate of income tax when the company decides to distribute £100 of its pre-tax income. There is thus an underlying tax (in the financial year 1989) of 13.34% on the company income; this is sometimes called mainstream corporation tax (MCT). However, when the company pays tax at the lower rate (see infra, § **23: 13**) there will be no mainstream corporation tax at all. This is because the lower rate of corporation tax now moves in line with the basic rate of income tax which, in turn, dictates the level of ACT.

Some subtleties should be noted for future reference. First, a matter now of largely historical importance. Until 1987 ACT could only be used against the company's liability to CT on its income (not to capital gains).[12] Secondly, ACT is due only on qualifying distributions (QD); not all distributions are qualifying distributions.[13] Thirdly, not all taxpayers are entitled to a tax credit.[14]

Corporation tax is charged by financial years (see infra, § **23: 07**); the financial year 1989 runs from 1st April 1989 to 31st March 1990.[15] Until FA 1984 the rate of CT was fixed in arrears; however that Act set the rate not only for the financial year 1983 (at 50%) but also for 1984 (45%), 1985 (40%) and 1986 (35%); the rate since then has been 35% but is 40% on certain profits of close investment-holding companies, supra § **27: 32**.[16] This reduction in the corporate tax rates represents a major change in tax structure and is offset by the abolition of stock relief and the phasing out of initial capital allowances, also in 1984. The rate of ACT is now fixed by reference to the basic rate of income tax and for the financial year.[17] In previous years when the rate of CT was fixed in arrears it was provided that in order to avoid delays in winding up, the CT rate for the previous year may be used.[18] The previous year's rates may also be used as the basis for provisional assessments when the company is not in its final year.[19]

Simon's Taxes D2.101–105, 108.

[1] TA 1988, s. 6(1) and (4); on non-resident corporations see TA 1988, s. 11 and infra, § **23: 06**.
[2] Infra, § **23: 13**.
[3] Dividends fell within the system of deduction at source now to be found in TA 1988, ss. 348 and 349; however the precise way in which dividends fitted in with the Schedular system was unclear, see Heyworth Talbot [1962] BTR 394.
[4] Originally the National Defence Contribution introduced in 1937; as the tax was not an income tax a shareholder could not reclaim it under what is now TA 1988, ss. 348 and 349. Profits tax could be used to levy tax at different rates on retained and distributed earnings and was so used between 1947 and 1958. There were precedents for the tax not only in the excess profits tax during the first World War but also in the general corporation profits tax introduced in 1920 and repealed in 1924. On profits tax see RC (1955) Cmd. 9474 Chapter 20.
[5] TA 1988, s. 20.
[6] The flavour of the debate can be gathered from Whittington's Lecture to the Institute for Fiscal Studies in June 1974 (IFS Lecture Series No. 1). See also Chown Reform of Corporation Tax (IFS).

[7] TA 1988, ss. 6–16, 239–253 and Sch. 19; on the reasons for selecting this rather than a two rate system of CT—one rate for retained and the other for distributed profits—see Chown *op. cit.* Report of Select Committee on Corporation Tax H.C. 1970–71 No. 622 and [1972] BTR 15 (Prest).

[8] TA 1988, s. 14.

[9] TA 1988, s. 14(3). Where the basic rate has not been set the previous year's ACT rate is to be used up to 5 August: TA 1988, s. 246(2).

[10] TA 1988, s. 20.

[11] TA 1988, s. 239.

[12] Infra, § **24: 15**.

[13] Infra, § **24: 07**.

[14] Infra, § **24: 11**.

[15] TA 1988, s. 834.

[16] FA 1989, s. 34; (FA 1984, s. 18, FA 1987, s. 21, FA 1988, s. 26).

[17] TA 1988, s. 14(3).

[18] TA 1988, s. 342(2), (7), 8(5). If the winding-up is completed late in the year, the rates proposed by the Budget resolution for that (and not the preceding) year are used: TA 1988, s. 342(3).

[19] TA 1988, s. 8(4), (5).

The charge

23: 02   Corporation tax is chargeable on the profits of companies. Profits means income and chargeable capital gains.[1] From 1973 to 1987 only a certain fraction (6/7ths for the financial year 1986) of capital gains was included in the computation.[2] This meant, in effect, a lower rate of tax on capital gains but avoided the inelegance of two rates.[3] For gains realised after 16th March 1987, a different regime applies and the same rate of tax is now charged on all profits, whether income or capital gain.

The charge to corporation tax excludes any charge to income tax and capital gains tax.[4] There is no charge to corporation tax where profits accrue to a company in a representative or fiduciary capacity[5] or in the form of a distribution by a company resident in the UK (known as franked investment income (FII): see § **24: 18**). Where profits accrue in the course of winding up, corporation tax is payable notwithstanding the fact that fiduciary obligations are owed to the shareholders. Where profits accrue to the company under a trust or partnership the company is chargeable to corporation tax.[6]

The tax is payable nine months after the end of the accounting period or one month after the issuing of the notice of assessment, whichever is the later.[7] So a company whose accounting period ends on 31st December cannot be made to pay its MCT before 1st October following.

Interest runs from the reckonable date but, for ACT and certain income tax, from the date that tax became due and payable; i.e. within fourteen days of the end of the quarter.[8]

For accounting periods beginning before 17th March 1987, a company which was trading before the introduction of CT on 1st April 1965 can preserve the interval it had under the income tax preceding year basis.[9] For later accounting periods the general nine month interval is to apply subject however to a two year transitional period.

For periods beginning before 17th March 1987, the tax is due from such companies after the same interval as fell between the end of the basis period for 1965–66 and 1st January 1966 or, if later, one month after the notice of assessment is issued. This makes for a maximum interval of 21 months. So a company with a period ending on 31st December 1986 does not have to pay its CT until 1st January 1988. This rule does not apply if the interval is less than nine months, since this is the time interval for other companies anyway.[10] Since, these days, so much attention is paid to what happens in the USA one should note that under their system most corporations pay their corporate tax on a current year basis and pay 25% of a provisional estimate of their tax every quarter.[11]

This advantage, a matter of some significance in a time of high interest rates, applies to the company so long as the trade remains within the charge to CT; it therefore applies to all trades—and other sources—of the company even if these are begun or acquired after 31st March 1965. It is not lost simply because there is a change in the ownership of the shares in the company[12] nor if there is only a change of accounting date nor if there is a change in the way the trade is carried on which falls short of the conclusion that the trade has ceased. However the advantage is lost if the trade ceases[13] or is transferred to a company which did not have a trade on 1st April 1965—this is so even if the transfer takes place under the provisions in TA 1988, s.343.[14]

Where a group of companies is concerned each company is considered separately; there is no rule allowing a company with a pre-1965 trade to pass the benefit to other companies in the group simply because of group status. It may however be possible for the companies to use the group rules so as to ensure that the profits accrue in the hands of the member with the most favourable payment date.

Where the accounting period begins on or after 17th March 1987 this privilege is abolished.[15] Provided that the company was entitled to the benefit of the old rule as respects the last accounting period ending before that date, the company may use a transitional rule. For the first accounting period the gap between the time for payment under the old rule and the nine month interval is reduced by $\frac{1}{3}$rd;[16] for the second by a further $\frac{1}{3}$rd;[17] thus leaving the third accounting period at the nine month interval. Thus if the time gap for payment was 18 months it will be reduced to 15 months for the accounting period beginning on or after 17th March 1987 and to 12 months for that beginning on or after 17th March 1988. There are further provisions for accounting periods of less than twelve months the effect of which is to spread the process of reduction evenly over the same period.[18] There are consequential amendments for the calculation of interest and the repayment supplement.[19]

Simon's Taxes D2.104–107, 111.

[1] TA 1988, s. 6(4).

[2] Infra, § **25: 04**.

[3] However trading losses could be set off against the chargeable portion of capital gains: TA 1988, s. 393(2).

[4] TA 1988, s. 6(2) and (3). But a company may be accountable for income tax of another: TA 1988, Sch. 16, infra, § **25: 09**.

[5] TA 1988, s. 8(2).

[6] TA 1988, s. 8(2), infra, § **25: 01**.

[7] TA 1988, s. 10(1). Distinguish ACT which must be paid when a qualifying distribution is made and is accounted for on a quarterly basis (TA 1988, Sch. 13, para. 3; infra, § **24: 15**) and payments in respect of which the company is accountable for income tax; see TA 1988, Sch. 16, para. 4; infra, § **25: 09**.

⁸ TMA 1970, s. 87; TA 1988, Sch. 13, paras. 1 and 3 and TA 1988, Sch. 16, paras. 4 and 10.
⁹ TA 1970, s. 244 (repealed by FA 1987, s. 36); when the company has (and had on 1st April 1965) two trades with different basis periods, the period ending first is taken (subs. (2)); for building societies, see TA 1988, s. 478.
¹⁰ TA 1988, s. 10(1).
¹¹ Internal Revenue Code §6154; this was introduced in 1970. Before then the tax was due in four quarterly instalments in the 12 month period following the end of the accounting period—a shorter period than in the UK even then.
¹² Contrast the restriction on loss relief in TA 1988, s. 768.
¹³ On which see supra, § 7: 60.
¹⁴ This is because TA 1988, s. 343 (infra, § 25: 27) directs that the cesser is to be ignored only for certain reasons and this provision is not one of those listed.
¹⁵ TA 1988, s. 8(i); there are special rules for building societies some of which now have time intervals of less than nine months—they also are to be standardised.
¹⁶ TA 1988, Sch. 30, para. 1.
¹⁷ TA 1988, Sch. 30, para. 1.
¹⁸ TA 1988, Sch. 30, para. 1.
¹⁹ TA 1988, Sch. 30, para. 1.

A company

23: 03   A company means¹ any body corporate or unincorporated association,² but does not include a partnership, a local authority or a local authority association. Individuals who invest a joint account; e.g. as members of an investment club, are not treated as a company carrying on business together.

In *Conservative and Unionist Central Office v Burrell*³ Lawton LJ defined an unincorporated association as meaning (*a*) two or more persons bound together for one or more common purposes, not being business purposes, by mutual undertakings, (*b*) each having mutual duties and obligations, (*c*) in an organisation which had rules which identified in whom control of it and its funds rested and on what terms and (*d*) which can be joined or left at will. He went on to hold that the structure of the Conservative Party was such that it lacked elements (*b*) and (*c*); rather it was, as it described itself, an amorphous combination of elements, with the result that the party was not liable to corporation tax on its investment income. The Revenue had accepted that the party's "Central Office" was not an unincorporated association but argued that the party was such an association and comprised all the individual members of the local constituency associations and the Parliamentary party. The case does not hold that the individual constituency associations are not unincorporated associations.

Authorised unit trusts are treated as if they were companies.⁴ A charitable company will be entitled to exemption on so much of its profits as satisfy the income tax or capital gains tax rules for charities.⁵ There are also exemptions for registered and unregistered friendly societies, for trade unions, for scientific research associations and for some more esoteric bodies.⁶

This definition of a company applies for the purposes of CT.⁷ Special rules apply to certain nationalised industries,⁸ miscellaneous housing bodies,⁹ various marketing boards,¹⁰ the Passenger, Transport Executive,¹¹ and London Transport Executive.¹²

Simon's Taxes D2.104.
¹ TA 1988, s. 832(1) and (2). On charitable bazaars, see Extra-statutory concession C4 (1988)

and on thrift funds and holiday funds, see Extra-statutory concession C3 (1988), **Simon's Taxes, Division H2.2**.

[2] See *Frampton (Trustees of the Worthing Rugby Football Club) v IRC* [1987] STC 273 and *Blackpool Marton Rotary Club v Martin* [1988] STC 823. On liability of officers, see TMA 1970, s. 108(2) and (3).

[3] [1982] STC 317, CA.

[4] TA 1988, s. 468.

[5] TA 1988, s. 9(4).

[6] TA 1988, ss. 459, 460, 467, 508, 516 and 517.

[7] And for income tax.

[8] TA 1988, s. 511; CAA 1968, s. 80.

[9] TA 1988, s. 488.

[10] TA 1988, s. 509.

[11] Transport Act 1968, s. 13.

[12] Transport (London) Act 1969, s. 3.

Associated companies[1]

23:04 Companies are associated if at the relevant time, or at any time within one year previously, one has control of the other or both are under the control of the same person or persons.[2] A person has control if he exercises or is able to exercise or is entitled to acquire control over the company's affairs, a phrase which could mean (*i*) the power to carry a resolution at a general meeting, including the power to elect the board of directors; or (*ii*), more narrowly, the power to run the company's affairs, that is power at the director level, the point being that the general meeting cannot usually tell its directors how to manage the day to day affairs of the company. The correct meaning is uncertain. Control is however declared[3] to exist in defined circumstances although these are without prejudice to the broad principle. These circumstances are where one possesses or is entitled to acquire (*a*) the greater part of the share capital or issued share capital of the company or of the voting power of the company; or (*b*) such part of the share capital as would entitle him to the greater part of the income of the company were it all distributed ignoring any loan capital; or (*c*) such rights as would entitle him in the event of the winding up of the company to the greater part of the assets of the company. Where two persons together satisfy any of these tests they are taken to have control of the company.[4]

EXAMPLE

So if L and M each have 50% of the shares of A Ltd, they have control of A Ltd. If they also have control of B Ltd, then A Ltd and B Ltd are associated.

If L and M each have 50% of the shares of A Ltd but each has 25% of the shares in C Ltd, these two companies are not associated since L and M do not have control of C Ltd.

If the remaining 50% are divided equally between N and P and N transfers his 25% to L, the companies now become associated since L and M together have 75% of the shares in C Ltd. The fact that M might vote with P and block L is irrelevant. If however M then transferred his 25% holding in C Ltd to P the companies would cease to be associated since while L and M control A Ltd, they do not have control of C Ltd.

A nice question arises if L and M still have 50% of the shares in A Ltd and L obtains 75% of the shares in C Ltd. If the remaining 25% of the shares in C Ltd are held by M the companies will be associated. If however the remaining 25% are held by P the companies would appear not to be associated since although L had control of C Ltd he does not have control of A Ltd for in regard to this company he must rely on M's holding.[5]

Simon's Taxes D2.601–603.
[1] A matter relevant to TA 1988, ss. 774 and 13 and Sch. 4, para. 9. (A different definition applies to close companies in TA 1988, Sch. 19, para. 2(4).
[2] TA 1988, s. 416(1). On shareholdings by different trusts with common trustees, see *IRC v Lithgows* (1960) 39 TC 270 and, for close companies, Statement of Practice C4, Simon's Taxes, Division H3.4.
[3] TA 1988, s. 416(2).
[4] TA 1988, s. 416(3).
[5] Extra-statutory concession C9 (1988), Simon's Taxes, Division H2.2.

23: 05   In applying these rules there is to be attributed to a person any rights held by a nominee for him[1] and also the rights held by any associate[2] of his, a wide term[3] including any relative[4] or partner. There may also be attributed to him all the powers of any company of which he has control whether by himself or with associates.[2]

Despite these attributions it is possible for companies not to be associated. Thus if L controls A Ltd and M controls B Ltd the companies are not, without more, associated and in practice this is so even if L controls A Ltd and L and M together control B Ltd.[5] If the companies agree to pool their profits or a percentage of them they will still not be associated unless the Revenue succeed in arguing that they have become partners. Yet if they were to put themselves under a holding company they would become associated since they would each be controlled by the holding company.

Simon's Taxes D2.109.
[1] TA 1988, s. 416(5).
[2] TA 1988, s. 416(6).
[3] TA 1988, s. 417(3).
[4] Relatives other than spouse and minor children are generally ignored, see extra-statutory concession C9 (1988), see Simon's Taxes, Division H2.2.
[5] See Simon's Taxes D2.109.

Non-resident companies

23: 06   Non-resident companies are only subject to corporation tax if they are carrying on a trade through a branch or agency in the UK but, if so, are taxable on all its chargeable profits wherever arising.[1] This is a deceptively wide statement since chargeable profits are then defined[2] as (i) trading income from the branch, (ii) income from property or rights held by the branch e.g. royalties on a patent held by the branch and profits on the realisation of assets held on a short-term basis and funded by an insurance company's surpluses[3] and (iii) gains accruing from the disposal of assets within the UK in the circumstances in which a non-resident individual would be liable to capital gains tax.[4]

EXAMPLE

X Ltd, a non-resident company carries on a trade in the UK through a branch. The branch has a UK trading income of £750,000 and sells UK property from its trade realising a capital gain of £60,000; it also sells overseas property realising a gain of £75,000. UK CT (in the financial year 1988) will be

Trading income	£750,000
Chargeable gains (infra, § **25: 04**)	£60,000
Chargeable profits	£810,000
Corporation tax at 35%	£283,500

If the company carries on a trade here otherwise than through a branch or agency, it pays income tax on its profits as it would on any other UK source income.

If a resident company ceases to be resident or ceases to be liable to UK tax there is a deemed disposal of its capital assets.[5] However, there is no deemed disposal of assets which remain in a branch or agency in the UK and so within the charge to corporation tax.[6]

When the disposal occurs on or after 14th March 1989 and the company fails to pay the tax within six months from its becoming payable, the tax may be collected from others.[7] Those others are any other group company and the controlling director of that or any other group company at the relevant time.[8]

Simon's Taxes D4.122, 123.

[1] TA 1988, s. 11(1); on mode of assessment, see TMA 1970, ss. 85, 78 and 79; branch or agency defined in s. 118; infra, § **35: 08**. On place of trade see infra, § **35: 02**, for an example see *IRC v Brackett* [1986] STC 521.

[2] TA 1988, s. 11(2).

[3] *General Reinsurance Co Ltd v Tomlinson* (1970) 48 TC 81.

[4] Infra, § **34: 44**.

[5] FA 1988, s. 105; there are special rules when the migrating company is a 75% subsidiary of a company which is not migrating: s. 107; a company can cease to be liable to UK tax through the application of a double tax treaty (see infra § **32: 13**).

[6] FA 1988, s. 105(4).

[7] FA 1989, s. 134(1).

[8] FA 1989, s. 134(4)–(8). On special capital gains rules for dual resident investment companies see infra, § **32: 20**.

Financial years—accounting periods and periods of account

23: 07   CT is not troubled by the preceding year basis of assessment; the tax is charged on the profits of the corporation during the financial year. However, assessments are made by reference to accounting periods.[1] Where the accounting period does not correspond with the financial year the profits of the period are apportioned. Where the rate changes from one financial year to the next, each rate is applied to that portion of the accounting period falling within it.

EXAMPLE

In financial year 1985 the rate is 40%; in financial year 1986, 35%. The company makes up its accounts to 30th June and the total profit for the accounting period ending on 30th June 1986 amounts to £612,000. CT will be:

$$\frac{9}{12} \times £612,000 \times 40\% = £183,600$$

$$\frac{3}{12} \times £612,000 \times 35\% = \quad 53,550$$

Total	£237,150

The financial year is relevant only to the rate of tax. If the method of computing income or capital gains and so corporate profits changes from one year to the next, the accounting period is treated as if it were a year of assessment.[2]

Simon's Taxes D2.106–108.
 [1] TA 1988, s. 8(3).
 [2] TA 1988, s. 9(1).

23: 08   Accounting periods will usually be the successive periods for which the company makes up its accounts. An accounting period cannot exceed twelve months. A period of account is simply the period taken by the company in computing its accounts.[1] Where the period of account exceeds twelve months the accounting period will end after twelve months and a new one begin. Thus if the period of account is sixteen months there will be an accounting period of twelve months followed by one of four months the profits will be allocated $\frac{3}{4}$ to the first period and $\frac{1}{4}$ to the second.

Where one set of accounts covers more than one period, an apportionment may be made on a time basis unless a more accurate method can be established.[2]

Simon's Taxes D2.109, 110.
 [1] On the position where a company makes its accounts up both yearly and six-monthly, see *Jenkins Productions Ltd v IRC* [1943] 2 All ER 786, 29 TC 142 and extra-statutory concession C12 (1988) for retail co-operative societies; see **Simon's Taxes Division H2.2.** On accounts for an unauthorised period, see *BFP Holdings Ltd v IRC* (1942) 24 TC 483.
 [2] TA 1988, s. 72; *Marshall Hus & Partners Ltd v Bolton* [1981] STC 18.

23: 09   An accounting period begins because the previous accounting period has ended and the company remains subject to charge or if the company, not then being within the charge to corporation tax, comes within it, whether by the company becoming resident or acquiring a source of income.[1] A UK resident company not within the charge to corporation tax because, for example, its only income is franked investment income, is treated as coming into charge when it commences business.[2]

Simon's Taxes D2.107.
 [1] TA 1988, s. 12(2).
 [2] TA 1988, s. 12(4).

23: 10   An accounting period ends[1] on the expiration of twelve months from its beginning or, if earlier, any of the following:

(*i*) the end of the company's period of account;

(*ii*) if there is a period during which no accounts have been taken at the end of that period;

(*iii*) the company begins or ceases to trade or to be within the charge to corporation tax in respect of the trade, as where a non-resident company continues to trade but no longer through a branch or agency here; if the company carries on more than one trade the charge to tax must cease in respect of all of them if the period is to end;

(*iv*) the company begins or ceases to be resident; or

(*v*) the company ceases to be within the charge to corporation tax.

Simon's Taxes D2.107.
[1] TA 1988, s. 12(3).

23: 11 The scheme of tax is designed so that the period of account will usually coincide with the accounting period and is designed to interfere as little as possible with the freedom of the company to take whatever period of account it likes. If the company has two trades and each trade has a separate period of account and the company does not make up accounts for the company as a whole, the Board can determine which accounting date to take for tax purposes and the profits of the other trade will have to be apportioned.[1] This emphasises the point that the taxable person is the corporation and not the trade.

An accounting period ends and a new one begins when the winding up of a company commences.[2] Thereafter the accounting period will end every twelve months until the winding up is complete.

A company might wish to extend its period of account. For example, at a time falling under the pre-1984 system of capital allowances, in month 13 a large sum is spent on an item in respect of which 100% capital allowance was available; the effect of extending the normal twelve month period would be to have an accounting period of twelve months followed by one of one month. The almost inevitable loss in the second period could then be carried back to the first period and thus improve the cash flow.[3]

Simon's Taxes D2.208.
[1] TA 1988, s. 12(5).
[2] TA 1988, s. 12(7); on effect of an uncertain date, see TA 1988, s. 12(8).
[3] TA 1988, s. 393(4). There may be company law obstacles—see Companies Act 1985, ss. 225, 226; further, allowances can only be carried back to periods beginning within two years before the current accounting period. On groups see Companies Act 1985, s. 227.

23: 12 It is perfectly possible for there to be gaps between accounting periods as when the company ceases to trade and then starts again. This gives rise to a problem should a capital gain accrue during this period of quiescence. It is therefore provided that an accounting period is to commence when the chargeable gain or allowable loss accrues to the company.[1] Should the company subsequently begin to trade again the deemed period will end and a new one begin.

If despite these rules the beginning or end of a period is uncertain the inspector may make an assessment for such periods not exceeding twelve months as seems to him appropriate.[2]

If the company is a member of a partnership, its share of the profits is ascertained as an ordinary person and then allocated to its corresponding accounting period making any apportionments that may be necessary.[3]

Simon's Taxes D2.107.
[1] TA 1988, s. 12(6).
[2] TA 1988, s. 12(8).
[3] TA 1988, s. 114(2).

Small profits relief[1]

23: 13   A special lower rate is imposed where the company's profits do not exceed £150,000; for the financial year 1989, this rate is 25%[2] the same as the basic rate of income tax and so related to the rate of ACT: in turn this gives rise to full imputation of CT to the dividend, For the purposes of this relief "profits" includes income, capital gains and franked investment income but, not group income.[3] Loan interest is deductible. Capital gains accruing before 17th March 1987 did not qualify for small profits relief.[4]

This rate applies to companies resident in the UK (other than close-investment-holding companies; see infra, § 27: 32) and not to non-resident companies with a UK branch.[5] The Revenue, however, interpret a non-discrimination clause in an applicable double tax agreement as entitling the non-resident company to this rate.

Simon's Taxes D2.109.
[1] TA 1988, s. 13.
[2] FA 1989, s. 35(1)(a).
[3] TA 1988, s. 13(7), FII is also excluded if it would have been group income if an election under TA 1988, s. 247 had been made.
[4] However, after 1973 but before 1987 they were taxed at 30%; only for the financial year 1986 was the small profits rate lower than 30%; see infra, § **25: 04**.
[5] However, a non-resident company may be an associated company.

23: 14   Marginal relief applies when the profits exceed £150,000 but not £750,000. This relief does not take the form of automatically charging the first £150,000 of any company's income at the low rate. Instead the CT due at the full rate of 35% is calculated and then reduced by a sum determined by a complex formula. The reduction declines until the figure reaches £750,000 at which point it vanishes; it provides a smooth graduation of liability from 25% to the full rate of CT; this gives a marginal tax rate of 36·66%. The figures of £150,000 and £750,000 are not index-linked and were last increased in 1989.[1]

The deduction is calculated[2] by subtracting the profits[3] of the company from £750,000; then multiplying that sum by a fraction whose denominator is the profits of the company during that accounting period and whose numerator is the amount of basic profits[4] (i.e. the figure for profits including capital gains but not franked investment income) and then multiplying the resulting figure by another fraction, fixed by Parliament, which for the financial year 1987 was 1/50th and for 1988 and 1989 is 1/40th[5]. For this purpose the figure for capital gains is before the deduction for charges on income which can be set off against more than one sort of profit. The distinction between profits and basic profits is as follows. "Profits" is the total of profits on which corporation tax falls finally to be borne, i.e. both income and capital gains, together with FII; however group income, and FII which would have been group income if the elections had been made, is not included.[6] "Basic profits" consist of income and capital gains, i.e. profits minus the FII.[7] The reference to tax falling finally to be borne indicates that any charges on income or allowable losses must be taken into account first.

EXAMPLE
   A Ltd has for the financial year 1989 trading income of £222,000, capital gains of £30,000 (realised in June 1989) and franked investment income of £25,000.

Profits will be	
Income	222,000
Capital gain	30,000
Franked investment income	25,000
	277,000

As franked investment income is exempt from CT, normal CT at 35% would be £88,200. The reduction is:

$$(\pounds 750,000 - \pounds 277,000) \times \frac{252,000}{277,000} \times \frac{1}{40} = \pounds 10,758$$

which makes final CT of £77,442.

This relief is described in the statute as mitigation of corporation tax liability for small companies. This is a complete misnomer since the relief is available wherever there are small profits regardless of the size of the company and regardless of the size of profits retained in previous years.
   If the company makes a qualifying distribution it must pay ACT; the recipient will be entitled to the full amount of the credit and the ACT is available to the company in the usual way.
   If the accountancy period straddles the end of the financial year, a new period is treated as starting on the first day of the new year. The new rates and bands apply only to the profits (appropriately calculated) of the new year.[7] The limits of £150,000 and £750,000 are proportionately reduced for periods of less than 12 months.[8]

EXAMPLE
   B Ltd has an accounting period ending 30th June. Its profits (consisting entirely of CT income) for the year ended 30th June 1988 are £230,200. The upper and lower limits for 1988 were £500,000 and £100,000 respectively and the fraction set by Parliament was 1/40.

	Proportion of profit £	Proportion of upper limit £	Proportion of lower limit £
1.7.88–31.3.89	172,650	375,000	75,000
1.4.89–30.6.89	57,550	187,500	37,500

   In each period the proportion of the profits exceed the proportion of the lower limit. Marginal relief applies and CT is calculated as follows:

1.7.88–31.3.89	£172,650 at 35%	£60,427	
	Less 1/40 × (£375,000 – 172,650)	5,059	
			£55,368
1.4.89–30.6.89	£57,550 at 35%	£20,143	
	Less 1/40 × (£187,500 – 57,550)	3,249	
			16,894
Corporation tax payable for period 1.7.88–30.6.89			£72,262

Simon's Taxes D2.109.
[1] FA 1989, s. 33(2) amending TA 1988, s. 13(3); when the company's accounting period straddles the financial year, apportionments are to be made—s. 33(3)—see example at end of § **23: 14.**
[2] TA 1988, s. 13(2).
[3] Supra § **23: 13.**
[4] Defined TA 1988, s. 13(8); previously, the relief has only applied to "income". Capital gains are included only for periods beginning after 16th March 1987, but the straddle period is split: F(No. 2)A 1987, Sch. 5, para. 2(3), (5).
[5] FA 1989, s. 35(1)(*b*).
[6] TA 1988, s. 13(7).
[7] TA 1988, s. 13(8).
[8] TA 1988, s. 13(6).

Associated companies

23: 15   But for express provision, it would be easy to exploit the relief by dividing a business between many companies. It is therefore provided that when the company has one or more associated companies in the accounting period the figures of £150,000 and £750,000 shall be divided by the total number of companies which are associated with each other.[1] This technique of crude division by the number of companies rather than division according to the size of profits, has the effect that two associated companies each with a profit of £150,000 will together pay less tax than if one had profits of £299,000 and the other of £1,000. It arises, however, because company A may be associated with companies B and C without B being associated with C.

In computing the reduced relief it is immaterial that the other company was associated for only a part of the accounting period or that it was not resident. However it will be disregarded if it was not carrying on any trade or business at any time during the period of association or the accounting period whichever is the shorter.[2]

Particular problems may arise where a person with substantial interests in one company joins in a new venture under the business expansion scheme (see § **5: 24**). If the two companies are associated the limits for the relief will have to be divided between the two companies, something the other members of the new venture may not have expected.

Simon's Taxes D2.109.
[1] TA 1988, s. 13(3). On associated status when fixed rate preference shares are involved see extra-statutory concession C9 (1988), **Simon's Taxes Division H2.2.**
[2] TA 1988, s. 13(4).

Incorporation of a business

23: 16 The consequences of incorporation are varied. The first and obvious difference is that the profits of the trade will now be charged to CT instead of income tax. The rate of CT tax will depend on the level of profits; directors remuneration is deductible[1] so that although the company is not entitled to personal allowances enough can be paid out to ensure that the personal allowances of the incorporators and their bands of income liable to basic rate income tax are all used up.

Assuming that the company's profit was substantial and that the director's marginal rate of income tax exceeds 35%, the company appears to be a tax shelter in that 35% is the maximum rate of tax on the company's profits. This appears to be a significant advantage over an unincorporated business if the business is looking to internal sources of finance for growth and has become more marked as the general rate of CT has dropped to 35% in 1986. However, the taxpayer will, presumably, eventually wish to get his capital out of the company and this means selling shares, so incurring CGT or taking dividends and paying income tax. A dividend is a dividend even if it is a capital dividend. Today the use of the rules relating to demergers or to the purchase by the company of its own shares for its own trading purposes are ways of avoiding dividend treatment, but here again practice is being turned on its head. If a taxpayer receives a dividend he can use the tax credit (and the company can use the ACT). If he sells and realises a capital gain his tax may be the same but there will be no credit. The incorporated business is not so often a useful tax shelter in the climate of lower rates of tax now prevailing—see infra, § **27: 01**.

From the director's point of view there are advantages and disadvantages. First, he becomes liable to Schedule E tax and so to the PAYE system and, secondly, he becomes liable to the stringent rules surrounding benefits derived from the company, § **6: 91**. Against this he may find that the benefit rules are not as strict as may appear at first sight. Further, he will be substantially better off as far as pensions are concerned. As a director he can have a pension of up to $\frac{2}{3}$ of final salary; as a self-employed person he may put up to $17\frac{1}{2}\%$ of his trading income into a retirement annuity and even more into a personal pension plan but unless the taxpayer is young and has taken maximum advantage of this entitlement throughout his working life he cannot hope to build up so large a fund. Income distributed as salary to the employee/director is fully deductible by the company; income distributed as dividend is in effect (but not in theory) deductible provided there is ACT against which to set the dividend. However National Insurance contributions are charged on the salary but not on a dividend.

It should also be noted that the company is a separate legal person so that its trading or capital losses cannot be set off against the shareholder's income or gains—or vice versa.

Other matters are that gains made by the company are in effect subject to double taxation, infra, § **25: 05**; that a company may need Treasury consent for some of its international transactions, infra, § **32: 23**; that TA 1988, s. 703 hangs over the problem of extracting reserves from the company otherwise than by dividend or straightforward liquidation, infra, § **31: 21**; and that companies pay on a current year basis. A CGT catch is that retirement relief

666   *Part IV—Corporation tax*

can only be claimed by a full time working director. Once a company is established it is possible to use the annual £3,000 exemption for IHT to make gifts of shares to trusts for children or others. More generally it is easier to pass a share in an incorporated business to a child than a portion of an unincorporated business.

On the other hand individuals exporting a business to a non-resident may run into TA 1988, s. 739, infra, § **34: 24** and as self-employed persons they have to pay Class 2 and Class 4 national insurance contributions.

When the business is incorporated, the shift from income tax Schedule D, Case I (or II) to corporation tax is made by discontinuing the trade for income tax with consequent assessments under TA 1988, s. 63 (supra, § **7: 62**). However, loss relief may be preserved (supra, § **5: 06**) and roll-over relief is granted for CGT, § **20: 05** provided *all* the assets are transferred to the company if in return for shares.

This list has concentrated on the tax aspects of incorporation. However, the non-tax aspects are of great importance. These include the costs of running the paperwork of a company—not less than £200 a year; the fact of limited liability, although this will be qualified by the insistence of collateral personal liability at least in the early stages and the significant change in status, when more than one person is involved, on moving from equal partner to minority shareholder. Further, company law requirements seem to be becoming more stringent and some professions do not allow incorporation. One should also note that a company may find it easier to raise finance since, unlike an individual, it can create a floating charge and see **Simon's Taxes D2.114** for a comparison with partnerships. In the United States certain closely-held corporations can be taxed as if they were partnerships—an election that lies with the relevant taxpayers.

The Inland Revenue are currently reviewing the tax consequences of disincorporation.[2]

---

[1] Such part of it as is reasonable.
[2] *Simon's Tax Intelligence* 1987, p. 456.

24 Distributions—Schedule F and ACT

ACT—uses and surpluses 675
Stock dividends 678
Franked investment income 679
Purchase by company of own shares 681

24: 01 When a distribution is made by a company resident in the UK, the recipient is assessable to income tax under Schedule F.[1] If the distribution is also a "qualifying distribution" ACT is payable at that time by the company;[2] in the definition which follows, only (c) § **24: 04** is not a qualifying distribution. Distributions, whether qualifying or not, are not deductible in computing the profits of the company.[3] On use of ACT see, infra § **24: 15**. On stock dividends see, infra § **24: 16**.

ACT is payable fourteen days after the end of the quarter in which payment is made and there is no need for an assessment;[4] so payment of a dividend on 31st December will result in instant liability whereas one on 1st January will give a further three months. The rate is fixed in advance by reference to the financial year.

Distributions in respect of share capital in a winding up,[5] including surplus assets distributed, are not distributions within Schedule F nor within any other Schedule.[6] They are simply treated as the return of capital[7] and perhaps as giving rise to chargeable capital gains or allowable losses. This is so even if the payments represent arrears of undeclared cumulative preference dividends.[8]

Other payments which are not distributions are covenanted donations to charity,[9] and certain payments by an industrial provident society,[10] building society[11] or a mutual trading society[12] as well as certain group payments (infra, § **26: 05**).

If the distribution falls within Schedule F, it must be taxed under that Schedule and is not chargeable under any other provision of the Income Tax Acts.[13] The purpose of this rule which was introduced in 1972 is not immediately clear. It cannot be to keep the device of the tax credit intact since that is expressed to be dependent upon the payment of ACT and not upon liability under Schedule F. Its effect may be seen on a share dealer company which will now have its profits on its dealing taxed under Schedule D.[14] It also has the effect that income charged under Schedule F cannot come within the term earned income which has the curious consequence that while the profits on the share deals may be earned income the income from the investments may not be.

Simon's Taxes D1.102–105.
[1] TA 1988, s. 20. Distributions by industrial and provident societies are not treated as such: TA 1988, s. 486. Special rules also apply to building societies: TA 1988, s. 476 and money and loan societies extra-statutory concession C2 (1988), Simon's Taxes, Division H2.2. On distribution under rights created before 1973 see TA 1988, s. 255; infra § **24: 02**.
[2] TA 1988, s. 14.

667

3 TA 1988, ss. 337(2).
4 TA 1988, Sch. 13; on distributions in kind and doubtful distributions see para. 7.
5 By concession this includes dissolution under the Companies Act 1985, s. 652, where the Registrar strikes off a defunct company. The company must have ceased to trade and paid off its creditors: extra-statutory concession C16 (1988), **Simon's Taxes, Division H2.2.**
6 TA 1988, s. 209(1); *IRC v Burrell* [1924] 2 KB 52, 9 TC 27. This exclusion applies, by concession, to the winding up of social or recreational unincorporated associations, provided that the distributions are small: extra-statutory concession C15 (1988), **Simon's Taxes, Division H2.2.**
7 CGTA 1979, s. 72, supra, § **19: 12.**
8 *Re Dominion Tar and Chemical Co Ltd* [1929] 2 Ch 387.
9 TA 1988, s. 339(6), (7).
10 TA 1988, s. 486(10) and (11).
11 TA 1988, s. 476.
12 TA 1988, s. 486(5), (9).
13 TA 1988, s. 20(2).
14 Supra, § **7: 83.**

Definition

24: 02 *(a) Dividends, including a capital dividend.* A dividend is regarded as paid when it becomes due and payable,[1] that is when it becomes an enforceable debt, not necessarily the date of the resolution. A final dividend is, in the absence of any other date in the resolution, *prima facie* due when declared and so creates an immediate debt; the directors have power to stipulate the date and if this power is exercised the debt arises only when that date is reached. An interim dividend resolved upon by the directors may be reviewed by them and so does not create an immediate debt.[2]

A dividend which has been waived in advance will be effective to prevent the income from accruing to the shareholder.[3] The amount by which ACT is calculated is the amount of the dividend. The amount on which the recipient will be taxed depends on whether he is entitled to a tax credit; if he is so entitled his income will be the sum of the dividend and the credit and, if not so entitled, the amount of the dividend (see § **24: 09**, infra). The amount of the dividend is thus crucial. For the most part this is easy to determine but statute intervenes in one situation—where the dividend is expressed to be a gross amount and arises under a right or obligation created before 6th April 1973. Under the pre-1973 law, which embodied the classical system of corporate tax, the charge on the dividend was on the gross amount of the dividend—and there was no tax credit device. So a dividend of £10 taxed at 30% would carry tax of £3 leaving a net sum of £7; under the post-1972 law a dividend of £7 carries a tax credit of £3 and this gives tax of £3 at 30% while a dividend of £10 would carry a credit of £4.28 giving income of £14.28. In order to prevent dividends of £10 gross under the old system from being converted into dividends of £10 net or £14.28 gross under the new system it was provided that the right to the dividend at the gross amount should be converted into a right to a dividend to which should be added a figure for ACT to reach the original gross figure.[4] So the old gross dividend of £10 was reduced to a right to a dividend of £7.50. After some litigation, legislation now provides that this is a once for all adjustment by reference to the rate of ACT in 1973, so the dividend becomes £7 notwithstanding that the rate of ACT and so the tax credit and so the income to be attributed to the shareholder for Schedule F may vary.[6] Thus if the rate of income tax is 25% the dividend will attract ACT of £2.33 and so income of £9.33.[7]

Simon's Taxes D1.102, 105.
[1] TA 1988, s. 834(3).
[2] *Potel v IRC* [1971] 2 All ER 504, 46 TC 658.
[3] On IHT consequences see infra, § **38: 20** (4).
[4] TA 1988, s. 255.
[5] Apparently whether the recipient was entitled to a tax credit or not.
[6] TA 1988, s. 255 reversing *Sime Darby London Ltd v Sime Darby Holdings Ltd* [1975] STC 562.
[7] This fluctuation in rate does not prevent the dividend from being "at a fixed rate" for the purposes of the definition of ordinary share capital in TA 1988, s. 832(1) see *Tilcon Ltd v Holland* [1981] STC 365, 54 TC 464.

24: 03   (*b*) Any other distribution out of the assets of the company, in cash or otherwise, made in respect of shares,[1] e.g. a distribution by A Ltd to its shareholders of shares held by A Ltd in X Ltd.

A payment will not be within this category if it represents a repayment of capital on the share nor if, and to the extent that, new consideration is received by the company for the distribution.[2] Consideration is new if it is external to the company, that is, it is not provided directly or indirectly by the company itself.[3] So a bonus issue is not a distribution since there is no cost to the company; nor is a rights issue since the consideration is new.

Simon's Taxes D1.102, 105.
[1] On timing see *John Paterson (Motors) Ltd v IRC* [1978] STC 59, decision of Special Commissioners that date of approval of balance sheet was correct date upheld.
[2] TA 1988, s. 209(2)(*b*), but note TA 1988, s. 209(6).
[3] TA 1988, s. 254(1).

24: 04   (*c*) The issue of any *redeemable* share capital or any security issued by the company in respect of shares or securities is a distribution (but not a qualifying distribution) unless it is wholly or in part for new consideration.[1] Where part of the amount issued is not referable to the new consideration the excess is treated as a distribution. Thus the issue of bonus redeemable preference shares, or debentures or loan stock in A Ltd by A Ltd are all treated as distributions. This definition[2] does not cover the non-redeemable bonus share; the mere prospect of an eventual return of capital on a winding up does not make an ordinary share redeemable. Bonus securities on the other hand are in their nature redeemable and therefore fall within the term distribution.

The issue of bonus securities or bonus redeemable share capital is not a qualifying distribution. It is now provided that a redemption of these securities shall be treated as a qualifying distribution.[3]

Simon's Taxes D1.102, 105.
[1] Defined TA 1988, s. 254(1).
[2] TA 1988, s. 254(1).
[3] TA 1988, ss. 210 and 211; infra, § **24: 08**.

24: 05   (*d*) Also within the definition is any excess in the market value of an asset transferred by a company to its members or of a liability transferred to a company over any new consideration given. Consideration is new if it is external to the company, that is, it is not provided directly or indirectly by the company.[1] Special rules apply to transfers by subsidiary companies to parents.[2]

Simon's Taxes D1.102, 105.
[1] TA 1988, s. 209(4).
[2] TA 1988, s. 209(6) and FA 1972, Sch. 22, para. 4.

24: 06   (*e*) Although interest payments on debentures are not within the term distribution, and therefore are deductible in computing profits, there are rules designed to equate debenture interest payments with dividends where the debenture is more like a share than a genuine debenture.[1] So if the debentures had themselves been distributions, any interest or other distribution of assets in respect of those securities are treated as distributions. Also, payments of interest on securities which are convertible directly or indirectly into shares of the company are distributions unless the securities are quoted on the Stock Exchange or are on terms comparable with those of quoted securities. Interest payments in respect of securities under which the consideration given by the company for the use of the principal secured is to any extent dependent on the result of the company's business used to be distributions; they are now only so treated where the return is at more than a reasonable commercial rate, see infra § **25: 11**. Another type of interest payment caught is that where the securities are issued by a company but held by a non-resident company. Finally interest on certain securities "connected with" shares of the company is caught.

(*f*) Repayment of bonus shares (infra, § **24: 08**.)

Simon's Taxes D1.102, 105.
[1] TA 1988, s. 209(2)(*e*).

Qualifying distribution

24: 07   This term is defined by exclusion. All distributions but two are qualifying distributions. These two are (i) the issue of bonus redeemable shares and bonus securities, (ii) the issue of any share capital or security which the company making the distribution has directly or indirectly received from another company in the form of bonus redeemable shares or securities.[1] Thus, distributions resulting in immediate distribution of reserves are qualifying distributions whereas those causing only a potential claim on profits are non-qualifying distributions. A company only has to pay ACT on the former;[2] equally the tax credit is only available in respect of the former.

Simon's Taxes D1.105.
[1] TA 1988, s. 14(2) referring to TA 1988, s. 209(2)(*c*); on duty to report see TA 1988, s. 234(5)–(9).
[2] TA 1988, s. 14(1).

Repayment of share capital and issue of bonus shares

24: 08 The rule that a distribution out of the capital of the company in respect of shares is a qualifying distribution (supra, § **24: 03**) expressly excludes a repayment of capital. TA 1988 goes on to provide two important qualifications of this rule. The first is TA 1988, s. 211 which applies where a company has issued (or paid up) any share capital after 6th April otherwise than for new consideration, and the amount so paid up was not a qualifying distribution at that time. In such circumstances a subsequent distribution in respect of the capital is not to be treated as a repayment of capital; it will therefore be treated as a qualifying distribution with the usual consequences for the Schedule F or FII income status of the receipt and the paying company's liability for ACT.

Since neither a bonus issue of paid up irredeemable shares nor the repayment of share capital are distributions avoidance could be rife. Thus, if a company had £10,000 to distribute it would be unwise for the Revenue— from their point of view—to allow the company to capitalise the reserve and distribute it by way of bonus shares and then repay the bonus capital without at any stage falling foul of Schedule F. The effect of TA 1988, s. 211 is that if a company has made a bonus issue which was not treated as a qualifying distribution, repayments of such share capital are so treated to the extent to which those repayments of capital exceed the amount paid up on the share.[1] So if the company had an issued share capital of 20,000 £1 shares and it distributed by way of bonus 10,000 fully paid up £1 shares and it then made a reduction of capital of 50p per share on all 30,000 issued shares, the payments to shareholders would amount to £15,000 of which £10,000 would be treated as distribution and £5,000 as repayment of capital. So one can say that to the extent that money has been distributed by way of non-distributions, subsequent repayments of capital will be treated as distributions. In applying this rule any new previous repayments are brought into account.[2]

There are special rules for premiums. A premium paid on the redemption is not treated as a return of capital.[3] If the share was issued at a premium which represented new consideration, the amount of the premium is to be treated as part of the share capital and so the repayment of the premium will fall outside TA 1988, s. 211.[4] This exception does not apply where the premium has been applied in paying up share capital.[5]

The ambit of TA 1988, s. 211 is subject to a time limit. A distribution in respect of a share originally issued as a bonus which is made more than ten years after the issue will escape s. 211 provided the company is not closely controlled.[6]

Where a reduction in capital is followed by or concurrent with the distribution of bonus shares, it is provided that although the reduction in capital will not be treated as a distribution, the issue of the bonus shares will be so treated to the extent of the earlier payments.[7]

The second provision is TA 1988, s. 210. This is essentially an anti-avoidance provision. The amount treated as a distribution is the amount paid up on the new shares or the amount repaid on the old shares whichever is the lower.

EXAMPLE

A Ltd repaid 50p per £ on its £20,000 ordinary stock on 1st June 1985; the nominal value of the stock is reduced to £10,000. This stock was originally issued wholly for new consideration so no distribution arose on the repayment. Two years later A Ltd capitalises its reserves and makes a distribution of stock on the basis of 1 for every £5 stock held. The amount paid up is £2,000. As this is less than the amount repaid (£10,000), the whole £2,000 will be a qualifying distribution.

This rule is modified in two important ways. First there is an exception for preference shares issued before 6th April 1965 or issued after that time but for new consideration.[8] Secondly, as with TA 1988, s. 211, there is a time limit. Where the new shares are irredeemable bonus shares issued more than ten years after the reduction in share capital, TA 1988, s. 210 applies only where the company is closely controlled.[9]

Simon's Taxes D1.102.

[1] TA 1988, s. 211.

[2] TA 1988, s. 211(3).

[3] TA 1988, s. 211(7).

[4] TA 1988, s. 211(5).

[5] TA 1988, s. 211(6); the share capital may have been paid up under Companies Act 1985, s. 130.

[6] TA 1988, s. 211(2). The definition of control is by reference to TA 1988, s. 704 (infra, § **31: 29**) which refers to TA 1988, s. 416 (infra, § **27: 03**).

[7] TA 1988, s. 210.

[8] TA 1988, s. 210(2).

[9] TA 1988, s. 210(3); control is defined by reference to TA 1988, s. 704, on which see infra, § **31: 29** which in turn refers to TA 1988, s. 416, infra, § **27: 03**.

Income tax on distributions—Schedule F

(1) UK resident individuals—and others entitled to the tax credit

24: 09   The amount charged to tax is the amount of the qualifying distribution plus the amount of the credit.[1] The amount of the credit is the amount of the ACT. An individual can set the credit against his total income. Where the credit exceeds the tax he may claim to have the excess paid to him although this is subject to restriction for distribution by a close investment company.[2] Special restrictions apply to distributions by close investment-holding companies.[3]

EXAMPLE

S receives a net dividend of £750 from a UK company. Assuming a basic rate income tax of 25% S will be assessable under Schedule F on the £750 plus the attached tax credit of 25/75ths of £750, i.e. £250, in total £1,000. Assuming S is subject to basic rate income tax only, his liability of 25% on £1,000 i.e. £250 will be exactly offset by the tax credit received.

Simon's Taxes D1.108, 109.

[1] TA 1988, s. 20(2) and s. 231(3A); see infra, § **27: 35**.

[2] TA 1988, s. 231(3).

[3] FA 1989, s. 106, infra, § **27: 35**.

24: 10   *The tax credit.*   There is no tax credit in respect of a distribution by a non-resident company for the simple reason that such a company is not liable to pay ACT[1] but there is an express provision to this effect.[2]

The tax credit is generally available only to residents;[3] however credit may be claimed by a non-resident who is entitled to personal reliefs[4] or under a double tax treaty[5] or the recipient is a colonial pension fund, a sovereign state or an international organisation.[6] So under the UK–US double tax treaty the US resident is entitled to a repayment of the tax which exceeds 15% of the sum of the dividend and the credit. So if, in the previous example, S had been a US resident, he would have been entitled to a repayment of £100.[7]

When a non-resident is entitled to a tax credit he is chargeable on the sum of the dividend and the credit as UK source income but the liability will be restricted in the appropriate treaty to a fixed percentage known as withholding tax. This does not affect the rate of ACT. If a qualifying distribution is made to a trust, the trustees are entitled to the tax credit if no one else is treated as receiving the distribution.[8]

Simon's Taxes D1.108, 110, 213.
   [1] TA 1988, s. 14(1).
   [2] TA 1988, s. 231(1).
   [3] TA 1988, s. 231.
   [4] Under TA 1988, s. 232(1), supra, § **3: 19**.
   [5] The company may pay the credit direct to the shareholder; this discharges the company's liability to advance corporation tax: SI 1973, No. 317.
   [6] TA 1988, s. 232.
   [7] See UK–US Treaty, art. 10(2)(*a*)(ii). The withholding of this credit in certain circumstances is authorised by TA 1988, s. 812; the provision has not yet been implemented and may invite retaliatory action under the US Internal Revenue Code § 891.
   [8] TA 1988, s 231(4).

24: 11 *Non-qualifying distributions.* As already seen two types of distribution are not qualifying distributions. These are the issue of bonus redeemable shares and securities and the issue of any share capital or security which the company making the distribution has received from another company in such form. The tax treatment of non-qualifying distributions differs from that of qualifying distributions in that no ACT is due and, in consequence no tax credit is available.

Tax on the recipient of a non-qualifying distribution is determined in the same way as for any other recipient of a distribution in respect of which he is not entitled to a tax credit[1]—the amount of the distribution is subject to excess liability. There is no liability to basic rate income tax and the payment does not count as income which has borne tax for the purpose of TA 1988, ss. 348 and 349. Tax is due on the nominal value of the distribution plus any premium stated to be due on redemption. There is no grossing up of the amount received.[2] Since 1972 the payment of sums on the redemption of such stock or securities has been a qualifying distribution; special rules are therefore required to prevent double taxation.

The redemption of these two types of distribution is a qualifying distribution by TA 1988, s. 211. On redemption ACT will be payable by the company and a tax credit and further liability under Schedule F apply to the taxpayer. However tax paid on the issue of the securities[3] can be set off against any excess liability on redemption. If he is now paying tax only at basic rate or less he can use the tax credit on redemption but cannot recover the tax paid on issue.[4]

EXAMPLE

X Ltd makes a bonus issue of redeemable preference shares. S receives shares whose redemption value is £250, assume that he pays £17.50 income tax by way of excess liability under TA 1988, s. 233.

On redemption of the shares there is deemed to be a qualifying distribution. Assume that S is now liable to higher rate tax of 40%.

$$£250 \text{ net represent} \qquad \frac{£250}{0.75} \text{ gross, i.e. } £333.33$$

Tax at 40% gives	£133.33
Less	
Basic rate credit of (25% on £333.33)	83.33
Income tax payable	£50.00
Deduct tax already paid	17.50
	£32.50

In addition X Ltd on the repayment has an ACT liability of 25/75 of £250, i.e. £83.33.

---

[1] TA 1988, s. 233.

[2] This is simply because no provision directs it; contrast, for a qualifying distribution, the clear words of TA 1988, s. 20 and, for stock dividends, TA 1988, s. 249(4).

[3] The legislation does not state how this is to be calculated but it is assumed that the tax is the top slice of the person's income; an alternative is to use the average rate; another alternative is to treat it as the bottom slice.

[4] The person receiving the sum on redemption must be the same as the one who paid the tax on the issue: TA 1988, s. 233.

---

(2) Non-residents—not entitled to tax credit

24: 12   When a company makes a distribution to a non-resident who is not entitled to a tax credit, ACT is nonetheless due from the company.[1] The non-resident is liable to income tax on the distribution under Schedule F. Where no credit is available there is no liability to income tax at basic rate.[2] If excess liability arises he is assessed only on the actual amount of the distribution; there is no grossing up to take account of the non-existent credit. Such a distribution cannot cover an annual payment within TA 1988, s. 348 or even in part under TA 1988, s. 349(1).

EXAMPLE

There is a qualifying distribution of £750 to a non-resident subject to the higher rate of tax. He is liable to income tax under Schedule F at (40–25)% on £750. He is therefore liable to pay £112.50. The Revenue will have collected £250 ACT so the total tax taken is £362.50.

If the distribution had been to a resident he would have had to pay tax on income of £1,000 but with a credit for £250. He would therefore have had to pay £150; the ACT would have been the same and the total tax taken would have been £400.

Simon's Taxes D1.110, 114, 213.

[1] TA 1988, s. 14(1).

[2] TA 1988, s. 233.

---

(3) Companies resident in the UK

24: 13   When the recipient is another company resident in the UK the qualifying distribution plus the credit is franked investment income.[1] A non-qualifying distribution is not franked investment income nor will it be liable to CT.[2] If the receiving company in turn passes it to its own shareholders there is no ACT liability and the shareholders are deemed to have received a non-qualifying distribution.

Simon's Taxes D1.112.
[1] TA 1988, s. 238(1), infra, § **24: 18**.
[2] TA 1988, s. 208.

(4) Non-resident companies

24: 14   If the recipient is a non-resident company it is not franked investment income but simply Schedule F income of that company and will be dealt with as under (1) or (2) as appropriate.

This will, however, be subject to the provisions of any relevant double tax treaty. So when the recipient is a US corporation which controls 10% of the paying UK company, the US corporation is entitled to a repayment of one half the tax credit but with a withholding tax of 5% of the sum of the dividend and the repayment. So if £7,500 was paid and ACT was £2,500, the US corporation is entitled to repayment of £1,250 but with a withholding tax of 5% of £8,750, i.e. £437.50 which makes total receipts of £8,312.50.[1]

Simon's Taxes D1.110.
[1] UK-US Treaty, art. 10(2)(*a*)(i). On interpretation see FA 1989, s. 115, comprehensively and retrospectively, reversing *Union Texas Petroleum Corpn v Critchley* [1988] STC 691; see Revenue Press Release 25th October 1988, *Simon's Tax Intelligence* 1988, p. 784. For the proposed withdrawal of certain treaty benefits from companies present in a "unitary state" (directed at unitary taxation in California) see supra, § **24: 10**, n. 7.

ACT—USES AND SURPLUSES

24: 15   The ACT paid by a company when it makes a qualifying distribution can be set off against its liability to CT;[1] for gains realised after 16th March 1987 ACT can be set off against CT payable in respect of capital gains[2] and charges can be set off against capital gains.[3] For earlier gains this set off was restricted in that the company could only apply it against its liability to CT in respect of its *income*—and so not capital gains. Where a company had a large capital gain which it used to finance its dividend payment the result might be that the company had ACT which it could not set off against its liability to CT—this is known as surplus ACT. The risk of this occurring was exacerbated by the rule that charges on income and other deductions made in arriving at the company's profits were to be set against income rather than capital gains.[4] The risk could be reduced in practice by transferring the asset to a 51% subsidiary so enabling it to make the disposal;[5] however there must be a risk that the new approach, even after *Craven v White*, would apply in blatant cases.

The amount of ACT that may be set off is not to exceed that which would have been payable had the whole income been divided between a notional distribution and the ACT thereby notionally payable.[6] For accounting periods ending after 31st March 1984 the ACT may be set against only that part of the CT on that income which remains after the crediting of any foreign tax (see § **36: 25**).

EXAMPLE

A Ltd has trading income and capital gains totalling £500,000. It makes a dividend payment of £450,000 and pays ACT of £150,000. The ACT available for set-off is restricted to 25% of £500,000 (£125,000), leaving surplus ACT of £25,000.

For an example of the effect of capital gains, see § **25: 04**.

Surplus ACT arises where the ACT paid exceeds the company's mainstream liability. At first this arose most frequently when large capital profits were distributed but in recent years the combination of reduced profits, deduction for stock relief and capital allowances and maintained dividends have made this problem a common one. Corporation Tax (Cmnd. 8456 1982) para. 14.7 states that in 1980 40% of the leading listed companies were paying dividends not fully covered by current CCA profits and that the surplus ACT was estimated to average £600m annually. Since that time the general revival of profitability coupled with the reduction in the rates of capital allowances and the abolition of stock relief and the 1987 decision to allow the set-off of ACT against CT on chargeable gains have done much to reduce the scale of this problem.

Where the surplus arises in an accounting period ending after 31st March 1984, a claim may be made that it be carried back and set off against the tax liability of accounting periods beginning within the six years preceding the period in which the surplus arose.[7] (Where the surplus arose in an accounting period ending before 1st April 1984, the carry-back period was limited to two years.) These steps may bring about repayment where earlier years have seen distributions of amounts less than income.

EXAMPLE

D Ltd makes up its accounts to 31st March. In January 1988, i.e. in the financial year 1987, it made a distribution of £21,900 and paid ACT of £8,100. In its accounting period ending 31st March 1988 it made a loss. It also made losses in the periods ending in 1986, 1984 and 1982. Its profits, adjusted for corporation tax, were—

Year ended	£
31st March 1987	24,000
31st March 1985	3,000
31st March 1983	5,000

If D Ltd so elects by 30th March 1990, the surplus ACT may be set off thus—

Year ended	Profits	Tax at small companies rate		Set off
	£		£	£
31st March 1988	—		—	—
31st March 1987	24,000	29%	6,960	6,960
31st March 1985	3,000	30%	900	900 (restricted)
31st March 1983	5,000	38%	1,900	240
				8,100

It will be seen that a decision may have to be made whether or not to pay a dividend to prevent the loss of surplus ACT through the expiry of the six year period.

The six year set-off period is subject to one restriction. Where surplus ACT can be set against profits of an accounting period ending before 1st April 1984 only because of the extended six-year set-off period, the set-off is restricted to ACT in respect of distributions actually made in the accounting period in which the surplus arose and so not on one treated as made in that period through being brought forward from an earlier period.[8]

Should the surplus still not be relieved, it may be rolled forward indefinitely to later accounting periods and be used to frank payments in those years.[9]

A surplus which cannot be relieved by being carried back may be surrendered to a subsidiary rather than being carried forward.[10]

A further restriction arises from the rule that when surplus ACT is carried back over the six year period, ACT of later years is taken before that of earlier years. This may mean that by the time the tax of the earlier year could be relieved it will be outside the six year period and so too late. A practical difficulty arises where surplus ACT has arisen in two different years, say years seven and nine, and it is desired to carry these back to offset CT in two different earlier years, say years one and four. If a claim is made first in respect of year nine, this will relieve year four and open the way for a subsequent claim for year seven to be carried back to year one. If however the first claim were in respect of year seven that would have to be set off against year four and so mean that the later claim for year nine would have to be set off against the tax for year one and so be blocked by the six year period.

The right to roll the surplus forward is restricted where within any three year period (*a*) there have been both a change in the ownership of the company and a major change in the company's trade; or (*b*) after the trade has become small or negligible and before it revives there is a change in ownership.[11]

The definitions of a change in ownership and of a change in trade follow those in relation to losses.[12] But a "major" change is here widened to include a change whereby a trading company becomes an investment company or an investment company makes a major change in its investments. Where the change in ownership occurs during an accounting period, that period is split at that date; ACT may not be carried forward beyond it, although it may be carried back over it.

The change of ownership is specified to be within the three year period so that it may either precede or follow it. As a result any major reorganisation of a trade may imperil the carry forward of ACT should a change of ownership occur within the following three years; this is a common risk where there is a reorganisation of businesses within a group.

For changes of ownership after 13th March 1989 further rules apply. First the restriction is to apply where a company surrenders ACT to a subsidiary and both companies pass into the same ownership and there is a major change in the business of the company which made the surrender.[13] The reasoning here is that if the ACT had not been surrendered to the subsidiary, the surrendering company would have been barred from carrying the ACT forward by s. 245—the same should apply to the subsidiary. This is to apply if there is a major change in the business within the period of six years beginning three years before the change of ownership (i.e. three years either side of the change of ownership).

The second does not involve a change in the company's business but an acquisition falling within TA 1970, s. 275(1). It applies where there has been a change in the ownership of a company (C), and C has unused ACT which it is carrying forward from a period before the change in ownership. Suppose that C acquires an asset after the change from another group company at base cost thanks to TA 1970, s. 273 and that within the three years following the change of ownership, C disposes of the asset, so realising a chargeable gain. What C is doing here is receiving a chargeable gain so as to make use of the ACT. Under the new provision the ACT that can be set off is not to include the amount of ACT that would be attributable to a distribution of the amount of the chargeable gain or, if less, the surplus ACT carried forward. It will be noted that there need have been no change in any company's business for this restriction to apply. The new rule applies to changes of ownership after 13th March 1989.

Simon's Taxes D1.102–105, D2.141–144.

[1] TA 1988, s. 239(1).

[2] TA 1988, s. 239(2).

[3] F(No. 2)A 1987, Sch. 5.

[4] FA 1972, s. 85(1).

[5] And perhaps assigning to it the liability to pay any charges that would otherwise reduce the parent's income.

[6] TA 1988, s. 239(2). On the problem where the rate of ACT changes during an accounting period, see TA 1988, s. 246(5).

[7] TA 1988, s. 239(3). On difficulties of establishing amount of surplus ACT, a matter of practical difficulty under the two year limit, see *Procter & Gamble Ltd v Taylerson* [1988] STC 854. On repayment when ACT was paid in an earlier quarter of the same accounting period, see TA 1988, Sch. 13, para. 4. For repayment supplement purposes the CT being repaid is treated as tax of the period in which the surplus ACT arose. TA 1988, s. 825(4)(a).

[8] Under TA 1988, s. 239(4).

[9] TA 1988, s. 239(4); the authority for this is the phrase "(including any further application of this subsection)".

[10] Infra, § **26: 10**.

[11] TA 1988, s. 245. The restriction does not apply to carrying the surplus backwards.

[12] TA 1988, s. 768 (infra, § **25: 28**).

[13] TA 1988, s. 245A, added by FA 1988, s. 99(1).

[14] TA 1988, s. 245B, added by FA 1989, s. 98(1).

STOCK DIVIDENDS

24: 16   When a person has an option[1] to receive either a dividend or additional share capital, special rules treat the share capital so issued as giving rise to a charge to tax on the recipient. The payment, however, is not a distribution and therefore, although the recipient may be liable to higher rates of tax, there is no ACT due from the company. There is no liability to basic rate income tax[2] but no repayment of basic rate tax may be made and the payment is not taxed income for TA 1988, s. 348. Payments to other companies are not income of the recipient.[3] These rules also apply if the shareholder has shares which carry the right to receive bonus share capital[4] and that right is conferred by the terms on which the shares were issued (or later varied if bonus share capital is then issued). It is inherent in every share that it carries the right to any scrip issue, the right arising from the articles of association, but it seems likely that the provision will not be given so wide a scope.[5]

Such distributions of share capital were previously valuable to companies since, not being qualifying distributions, no ACT was due and, since most shareholders would elect to take the shares rather than the dividend, the company could declare a dividend[6] without serious damage to its liquidity position.[7] No income tax was due from the shareholders.

These rules apply only to stock dividends paid by companies resident in the UK.

Simon's Taxes D1.111.
[1] Defined in TA 1988, s. 251(1)(*c*). The failure to exercise a right is taken to be the exercise of the option.
[2] It was not subject to lower rate income tax in 1978–79 and 1979–80: FA 1978, Sch. 2, para. 19.
[3] TA 1988, ss. 249–251. Such dividends were also caught by FA 1968, s. 32, repealed FA 1972, s. 106.
[4] Meaning share capital issued otherwise than wholly for new consideration: TA 1988, s. 251(1)(*a*).
[5] Hansard, 18th July 1975, vol. 895, col. 1881.
[6] Thus perhaps keeping its status as a trustee investment.
[7] *Quaere* the valuation for CGT.

24: 17 Liability is based on "the appropriate amount in cash," usually the dividend forgone.[1] The market value of the shares is substituted where the dividend is substantially greater or smaller[2] than that or the number of shares issued is not related to any cash dividend.

The "appropriate amount in cash" is grossed up at the basic rate of income tax in force at the date of issue and forms part of his total income.[3] Liability to higher rates of tax may arise but basic rate tax is treated as having been paid. As already seen, basic rate tax cannot be recovered, nor can the receipt be treated as income charged to income tax for TA 1988, ss. 348 and 349.[4]

Simon's Taxes D1.111.
[1] TA 1988, s. 251(2). On trusts and estates see TA 1988, s. 249(5), (6).
[2] In the Revenue's view about 15% is substantial, Statement of Practice A8, **Simon's Taxes, Division H3.4.**
[3] The section specifies no Schedule.
[4] TA 1988, s. 249(4).

FRANKED INVESTMENT INCOME

24: 18 By TA 1988, s. 208, qualifying distributions received by a company resident in the UK are not subject to corporation tax. The purpose of this rule is to secure tax neutrality between distributions to individual shareholders and distributions to corporate shareholders. It also means that so long as money stays within the UK resident corporate sector only one charge to ACT will be made.

If Company A, resident in the UK, makes a qualifying distribution to Company B, also resident in the UK, Company A will, on making the distribution, pay ACT. The qualifying distribution received by B together with the amount of the credit is called franked investment income[1] so a receipt of a dividend of £150,000 accompanied by a tax credit of £50,000 amounts to the receipt of £200,000 of FII. The credit can be reclaimed from the Revenue by direct payment only if (*a*) the company is wholly exempt from corporation tax or is only not so exempt in respect of its trading income or (*b*) the distribution is one in relation to which express exemption (otherwise than by TA 1988, s. 208) is given, whether specifically or by virtue of a more general exemption from tax, under the provisions of the Taxes Act.[2]

B may use the franked investment income to frank its own qualifying distributions known as franked payments, so that it does not have to pay ACT on them. If B now distributes £150,000 it would normally have to pay ACT of £50,000. However, it may instead use the £50,000 credit on the dividend from A and set that off against its own ACT liability, reducing it to nil. It will be seen that the amount of a franked payment, like that of FII, is a gross amount made up of the amount of the distribution and the accompanying ACT liability (for a franked payment) and tax credit (for FII). This means that a company may distribute its franked investment income without additional tax cost. However it also means that there may be no ACT to set against mainstream CT in due course. Where B distributes a sum greater than the dividend element in its FII it will have some ACT liability. Where it has both FII and a liability to ACT the liability to ACT will arise only to the extent that the amount of the franked payment exceeds its FII.[3] The amount by which the franked payment exceeds the FII is split into dividend and accompanying ACT liability.[4]

EXAMPLE 1
In year 1 a company has trading income of £500,000 and FII of £100,000. It declares a dividend of £300,000, making ACT of £100,000. It can set against this the credit element of £25,000 in the £100,000 FII, making an ACT payment of £75,000.
If the company had trading income of £100,000 and FII of £500,000 the ACT of £100,000 would have been completely absorbed by the credit element in £400,000 FII leaving £100,000 as surplus FII to carry forward to the next year.

EXAMPLE 2
A Ltd makes a qualifying distribution to X, one of its individual shareholders of £1,500 in respect of which it will pay ACT of £500. It makes another to Y, another individual, of £750 on which it will pay ACT of £250 and to B Ltd of £750 on which it will also pay ACT of £250. B Ltd now has franked investment income of £750 + £250 = £1,000. If B Ltd now makes a qualifying distribution to one of its shareholders of £750 it ought to pay £250 by way of ACT. However it is making a franked payment of £750 + £250 and so nothing will be payable by way of ACT. If however B Ltd makes a qualifying distribution of £1,500, that is a sum on which it will have to pay ACT of £500. The excess of that sum plus ACT (£1,500 + £500 = £2,000) over the franked investment income is £1,000. This sum must now be divided to ascertain the sum which, paid as a qualifying distribution, would, when added to the ACT, add up to £1,000. That figure is £750 and the ACT is £250. So that the ACT collected in the two stages from A Ltd and B Ltd is £250 + £250 which is the same as that due on the qualifying distribution by A Ltd direct to X, its own individual shareholder.

These rules as to franking apply only when the distribution by B is on the same accounting period as the receipt of the franked investment income. When the distribution by B preceded the receipt from A, but is the same accounting period, the tax credit takes the form of the repayment of the ACT paid by B in respect of the qualifying distribution.[5]

If the franked investment income exceeds its franked payments, the company has a surplus of franked investment income.[6] This surplus may be rolled forward to frank payments in the following and subsequent accounting periods.[7] Alternatively trading losses and certain unrelieved expenditure of the same accounting period may be given relief against it—see infra, § **25: 36**. On demergers see § **26: 32**.

Simon's Taxes D1.112, 113.
[1] TA 1988, s. 238(1).
[2] TA 1988, s. 231(3). If a repayment can be claimed under TA 1988, s. 231(3) the franked investment income cannot be used to frank the distribution: TA 1988, s. 241(5).
[3] TA 1988, s. 241(1).
[4] TA 1988, s. 241(2). On special rules for building society interest, see TA 1988, s. 476(3).
[5] TA 1988; Sch. 13.
[6] See infra, § **25: 33**.
[7] TA 1988, s. 241(3).

PURCHASE BY COMPANY OF OWN SHARES

24: 19 Provision was made in the Companies Act 1981, ss. 45 and 46[1] for a company to issue redeemable equity shares and to purchase its own shares, subject to authorisation in the company's memorandum and articles of association and to various conditions imposed by the Act.[2] These provisions came into force on 15 June 1982.[3]

Under existing tax law, any excess of the redemption proceeds or purchase consideration over the amount subscribed for the shares would constitute a qualifying distribution and is treated in the same way as a dividend. In such circumstances there is also a disposal for capital gains purposes.[4] If the recipient is an individual it would, before 1988 usually be to that person's advantage to take the receipt by way of capital gain rather than income. For a company, however, it may be advantageous to take the payment as a dividend and so as FII which is exempt from CT in its hands and comes with a tax credit which it can use to frank its own dividend payments and offset against its own ACT liability. Charging the shareholder to tax on income in these circumstances was inconsistent with the policy behind the Companies Act and so the tax effects have been amended by rules clearly derived from s. 302 of the US Internal Revenue Code. FA 1982 directs that the distribution rules are not to apply to a payment made by a company after 5th April 1982 for the redemption, repayment or purchase of its own shares provided the conditions (see **24: 20** to **24: 26**, infra) there laid down are satisfied. The purpose of these conditions is to confine the favourable treatment to situations in which the purchase is effected to meet the business requirements of the trade or to pay a charge to CTT or IHT on death.

Simon's Taxes D1.130, D2.507–512.
[1] Now Companies Act 1985, ss. 159–162.
[2] Companies Act 1981, ss. 45, 46(3) and 54–58.
[3] Companies Act 1981 (Commencement No. 4) Order 1982 (S.I. 1982 No. 672).
[4] On computation of capital gains where shareholder is a company, see Inland Revenue Press Release 19th April 1989, *Simon's Tax Intelligence* 1989, p. 371.

24: 20 The company buying its own shares must be an unquoted company; the exclusion of quoted companies is based on the belief that a ready market exists for the disposal of shares in such companies. The company is unquoted if its shares are not listed on the official list of a stock exchange;[1] shares dealt in on the Unlisted Securities Market qualify as unquoted shares.[2] A company which is a 51% subsidiary of a quoted company is a quoted company.[3]

Simon's Taxes D2.507–512.
[1] TA 1988, s. 229(1)(*a*).
[2] See SP 18/80, **Simon's Taxes, Division H3.2.**
[3] TA 1988, s. 229.
[4] On computation of capital gains where shareholder is a company, see Inland Revenue PRess Release 19th April 1989, *Simon's Tax Intelligence* 1989, p. 371.

24: 21 The company must be a trading company or a holding company of a trading group. For these purposes a holding company is one whose main business (apart from any trading activities of its own) is to hold shares in one or more 75% subsidiaries.[1] A trading group will consist of a holding company or one or more 75% subsidiaries where the main business of the members taken together is the carrying on of the trade or trades. For these purposes dealing in shares land or futures does not qualify.[2]

Simon's Taxes D2.507–512.
[1] TA 1988, s. 229.
[2] TA 1988, s. 229.

24: 22 Unless the sale is needed to pay CTT or IHT on a death the purchase of shares must be made wholly or mainly to benefit the trade of the company concerned or of any of its 75% subsidiaries.[1] The Revenue view is that the benefit to the trade is to be contrasted with a benefit to the vending shareholder (although he will usually also benefit) or some wider commercial purpose to which he may put the payment he receives or a business purpose of the company which is not itself a trade such as an investment activity it may carry on.[2] The Revenue Statement of Practice gives as reasons which would benefit the trade a disagreement at boardroom level,[3] an outside shareholder who has provided equity finance now wishing to withdraw, the proprietor retiring to make way for new management and the death of a shareholder the beneficiaries of whose estate do not wish to keep the shares. The interaction of this rule with the rules as to the minimum reduction in the vendor's shareholding is considered below.

In addition to directing that the purchase must be to benefit a trade of the company, the legislation provides that the purchase must not form part of a scheme or arrangement, a main purpose of which is either to avoid tax or to enable the shareholder to share in the company's profits otherwise than by receiving a dividend.[4]

Simon's Taxes D2.507–512.
[1] TA 1988, s. 219(1).
[2] See SP 2/82, para. 2, **Simon's Taxes, Division H3.2.**
[3] However not all disagreements will qualify; SP 2/82, para. 3, rules out disagreements as to whether or not to cease trading and become an investment company—where the shareholder being bought out wanted the trade to continue.
[4] TA 1988, s. 219(1)(*a*).

24: 23 The vendor must meet certain residence requirements.[1] A shareholder whose shares are purchased must be resident and ordinarily resident in the

UK in the year of assessment in which the shares are purchased. In the case of a company it is not necessary to be ordinarily resident. If the shares are held by a nominee both the nominee and the beneficial owner must be resident and ordinarily resident. The residence status of a personal representative is taken to be that of the deceased immediately before his death. The residence and ordinary residence of trustees is determined as for CGT.

Simon's Taxes D2.507–512.
[1] TA 1988, s. 220; the reference to CGT is CGTA 1979, s. 52.

24: 24 There are minimum holding period requirements for the vendor.[1] First, he must have owned the shares for at least five years at the time they are purchased by the company; however if the shareholder acquired the shares from his spouse, the spouse's period of ownership will be counted towards the five year condition—provided the transferor was then living with the vendor and was then the vendor's spouse.[2] Where different shares are acquired at different times, a first in first out rule is applied.[3]

If the vendor became entitled to the shares on an intestacy or under the will of the previous owner, he may bring in both the period of ownership of the testator or intestate and that of the personal representatives; moreover the period is reduced to three years.[4] Where the vendor is the personal representative of a deceased owner, he may bring in the deceased's period of ownership; again the period is reduced to three years.[5]

Bonus share and other shares acquired on a company reconstruction, reorganisation or amalgamation are treated as acquired at the same time as the original holding in respect of which they are issued. However, this favourable treatment is not extended to rights issues or stock dividends.[6]

Simon's Taxes D2.507–512.
[1] TA 1988, s. 220(5).
[2] TA 1988, s. 220(6); however the period may not be added if the spouse is still alive at the date of the purchase but no longer the vendor's spouse living with him, i.e. they are divorced or separated.
[3] TA 1988, s. 220(8).
[4] TA 1988, s. 220(7).
[5] TA 1988, s. 220(7).
[6] TA 1988, s. 220(9).

24: 25 The vendor's interest in the company must either be completely eliminated or be substantially reduced as a result of the purchase of the shares by the company.[1] A reduction is not substantial if it is less than 25%.[2] If the company is a member of a 51% group it is the shareholder's interest in the group that must be reduced by at least 25%.[3] For these purposes the holdings of associates can be taken into account.[4] It is also necessary that there should be a corresponding reduction in shareholders' entitlement to profits.[5] If the shareholder sells all his shares to the company and does not retain shares in any company which is a member of the same group the 25% condition does not have to be fulfilled.[6]

Where the vendor's holding is not eliminated he may be in difficulty meeting the requirement that the purchase must be for the sole or main purpose of benefiting the company's trade. Where his continuing presence is regarded as a danger to the trade the interest ought to be eliminated completely and the Revenue have indicated a firm line on this; their view is that the requirement will only[7] be satisfied if the interest retained was minimal or for sentimental reasons or, where the intention is to terminate the interest but this has to be achieved by more than one transaction (for example because the company cannot afford to buy all his shares at one time).[8] This last example is interesting since it raises the question whether a series of purchases by the company can be linked together so as to achieve the 25% reduction where no individual purchase meets that condition; such a linkage is allowed in the USA under their step transaction doctrine but the doctrine has also had this effect where the taxpayer sells some shares and gives others away provided it is all part of the one plan; at this stage it is thought unlikely that the UK courts would accede to such an argument.

Simon's Taxes D2.507–512.
[1] TA 1988, s. 221.
[2] TA 1988, s. 221(4).
[3] TA 1988, s. 222(6).
[4] TA 1988, s. 221(2). The combined holdings of the vendor and the associate have to be reduced by at least 25% (TA 1988, s. 222(3) which extends the rule in TA 1988, s. 222(2) to the situation in which groups are involved) and TA 1988, s. 224 (which provides that where the conditions are satisfied as to the combined holdings of the vendor and the associate and the vendor joined in to help the associate meet those conditions in all the conditions in TA 1988, ss. 221 to 223 are to be treated as satisfied for both of them); for the definition of associate, see TA 1988, s. 227.
[5] TA 1988, s. 221(5) to (8).
[6] TA 1988, s. 221.
[7] There is some evidence that a more lenient attitude is adopted where the shares were acquired under an approved share option scheme since here the Revenue do not insist that the vendor should cease to be an employee. **Simon's Taxes D2.508.**
[8] SP 2/82 para. 5, **Simon's Taxes, Division H3.2.**

24: 26 The purchase must not be part of a scheme or arrangement which is designed or likely to result in the vendor or any associate having an interest in the company such that if he had that interest immediately after the purchase any of the previous conditions would not be satisfied.[1] There is a conclusive presumption that transactions within one year of each other are part of such a scheme.[2]

Simon's Taxes D2.507–512.
[1] TA 1988, s. 223(2).
[2] However succession to property on death is not regarded as a "transaction" for this purpose; see SP 2/82, para. 8.

24: 27 The vendor must not immediately after the purchase be connected with the company or any other member of the group.[1]

Simon's Taxes D2.507–512.
[1] TA 1988, s. 223(1); on the definition of "connected", see TA 1988, s. 228.

24: 28 This special treatment is also available if the purchase is not for the benefit of the trade but the vendor needs the funds to discharge a CTT or IHT liability arising on death. In these circumstances it is not necessary for conditions in **24: 22** to **24: 27** to be met. The whole or substantially the whole—a phrase taken by the Revenue to mean almost all[1]—of the payment must be paid in respect of the liability to CTT or IHT falling on the shareholder as a result of a death; this rule is applied after taking out the funds needed to pay any CGT liability consequent upon the purchase. The CTT or IHT payment must be made within two years of death and it must be shown that the liability could not have been met without undue hardship otherwise than through the purchase.[2]

Simon's Taxes D2.507–512.
[1] SP 2/82, para. 6.
[2] TA 1988, s. 219(2).

24: 29 If the conditions outlined above are complied with the transaction will be treated as a disposal by the shareholder for CGT purposes and not as a distribution. If the shareholder is a dealer in securities the transaction will be treated as a trading transaction not a distribution.[1]

The company may apply to the Revenue for advance clearance as to the treatment of any payment made by it for the purchase of shares. The procedure is available whether the purchase is for the benefit of the trade or is needed to pay CTT or IHT. The application must be made in writing to the Board giving full particulars of the transactions proposed. Within 30 days the Board must either request further particulars or give a decision on the application.[2]

Simon's Taxes D2.507–512.
[1] TA 1988, s. 95.
[2] TA 1988, s. 225.

24: 30 The whole purpose behind these rules has been largely undermined by the 1988 changes assimilating the rates of tax on income and capital gains. Income treatment is now preferable since the availability of tax credit means that if he receives £75 and pays income tax at 40% he only has to find an extra £15 (20% of £75). By contrast he may have to pay £30 (40% of £75) if CGT treatment is directed.

25 Computation

Income 686
Capital gains 688
Charges on income 691
Losses 700
Surplus franked investment income 708

25: 01 The profits of the company, which include both income and chargeable gains,[1] are computed broadly according to the principles used for income tax and CGT. Profits accruing for the benefit of the company under a trust or partnership are taxable as if they had accrued directly.[2] The company is also chargeable on profits accruing during winding up but "not *otherwise* on profits accruing to it in a fiduciary or representative capacity except as respects its own beneficial interest (if any) in those profits". This could be made to suggest that both corporation tax and income tax could be chargeable on income arising to the company as trustee during the period of winding up.[3] Income arising to a company as trustee is chargeable to income tax even though the beneficiary is a company.

Simon's Taxes D2.201, 202.
[1] TA 1988, s. 6(4). The company may spread payments under TA 1988, s. 524(4).
[2] TA 1988, s. 8(2). On overseas profits, see TA 1988, s. 70; on profits in course of winding-up see TA 1988, s. 8(2); on profits from building societies, see TA 1988, s. 476.
[3] On the liability of the liquidator see *Re Mesco Properties Ltd* [1979] STC 788.

INCOME

25: 02 The amount of income is in general computed according to income tax principles.[1] Where those principles change in the course of an accounting period, those in force at the end of that period are applied.[2] It follows that income is computed under the Schedules and Cases applicable to income tax. It follows that a company whose business is to let real property or to make investments is not regarded as trading for tax purposes[3] and so its income will be assessed under the rules relevant to Schedules A, C, D, Case III, IV and V and Schedule F rather than Schedule D, Case I. The question whether interest is deductible from rental income according to ordinary commercial principles is a question of fact.[4] A company is not entitled to any personal reliefs since it is not an individual and because reliefs apply to income tax and not to corporation tax.

Some minor qualifications should be noted. First the company which begins or ceases to be within the charge to corporation tax in respect of a trade, is treated for the purposes of computing its income as if it in fact began or ceased to trade. Thus a company which ceases to be resident is treated as ceasing to trade whether or not the trade ends.[5] Secondly, neither the preceding year nor remittance bases of taxation apply for corporation tax.[6] Thirdly, neither franked investment income,[7] infra, § **24: 18** nor group income (infra, § **26: 05**) are subject to corporation tax.[8] Fourthly, while, not surprisingly, there are no deductions for payments in respect of dividends or other distributions,[9] this applies also to certain rents, royalties and annuities or other annual payments;[10] the reason for this is that they qualify as charges on income and are treated differently—infra, § **25: 08**. Fifthly, there are now express timing rules for payments of interest between associated companies.[11] Special arrangements are also made for management expenses of investment companies, minor capital allowances and for trading losses.

Simon's Taxes D2.202–208.
[1] TA 1988, s. 9(1); any exemption from income tax applies to corporation tax: TA 1988, s. 9(4).
[2] TA 1988, s. 9(2).
[3] *Webb v Conelee Properties Ltd* [1982] STC 913.
[4] *Wilcock v Frigate Investments Ltd* [1982] STC 198.
[5] TA 1988, s. 9(1).
[6] TA 1988, s. 70 and infra, § **34: 11**, so neither did the reduced income basis; infra, § **34: 21** (TA 1988, s. 65(3)), a matter relevant to losses.
[7] TA 1988, s. 238 infra, § **25: 35**.
[8] TA 1988, s. 208.
[9] TA 1988, s. 9(2).
[10] TA 1988, s. 9(2) and (3) and Statement C5, **Simon's Taxes, Division H3.4.**
[11] TA 1988, s. 341.

Transactions between a dealing and an associated non-dealing company: TA 1988, s. 774

25: 03   The rule that an expense may be a revenue expense of the payer but a capital receipt of the payee, with consequent leakage of tax, is modified where one company is a dealing company and the other an associated[1] non-dealing company. A dealing company is one dealing in securities, land or buildings. Section 774 applies if the dealing company becomes entitled to a deduction on account of the depreciation of any right against the other company or makes any deductible payment to the other, and the depreciation or payment is not brought into account in computing the profits or gains of the other, s. 774 makes the latter chargeable on an amount equal to the deduction[2] either under Case VI or if it carries on a trade as a trading receipt of such of its trades as it selects. A purchaser of the non-dealing company may thus find an unexpected liability.

An example[3] of a device at which TA 1988, s. 774 is aimed is where a dealing company A waives a loan which it has made to the non-dealing company B; A might get relief for the loan and, but for s. 774, B would keep the money tax-free; s. 774 makes B liable to tax on the amount waived.

Simon's Taxes D2.512.
[1] See *IRC v Lithgows Ltd* (1960) 39 TC 270.
[2] Subs. (3) excludes s. 774 if the non-dealing company has incurred a non-allowable capital loss as a result of the loan or payment being used as abortive expenditure.
[3] See also *Alherma Investments Ltd v Tomlinson* [1970] 2 All ER 436, 48 TC 81.

CAPITAL GAINS

25: 04   Corporation tax is levied on the "profits" of companies and "profits" include chargeable gains. Corporations are not subject to capital gains tax but only to corporation tax; however from 1973 to 1987 this distinction was a matter of statutory convenience rather than substance. Gains are computed in the same way for both taxes.[1] The acts of a liquidator are treated as the acts of the company so as to bring them on to the corporation tax side of the line and to ignore disposals between company and liquidator. However gains are treated differently from income.

Since 1987 the importance of the distinction between capital gains and ordinary income has been greatly reduced. Not only is the same rate of tax to be charged on both types of profit but a number of technical rules have been relaxed.

(1) General rate of corporation tax. For gains realised after 16th March 1987[2] the rule is that the same rate of tax, 35% for the financial year 1988, is to apply to both ordinary income and capital gains. For gains realised before 17th March 1987[3] only a fraction of the net chargeable gains were to be brought into the net and charged at the current corporation tax rate; the effect of the fraction was to make the effective rate of corporation tax on capital gains 30%, the same as the capital gains tax rate.[4]

(2) Reduced rate of corporation tax. Gains realised after 16th March 1987 can benefit from the lower rate of tax, 25% for the financial year 1989, where the company's profits do not exceed £150,000. Gains realised before 17th March 1987 are not so eligible.

(3) Set off of ACT. ACT can be set off against corporation tax due in respect of both ordinary income and capital gains realised after 16th March 1987. Before 16th March 1987 the rule was that the maximum ACT that could be set off against CT was that equal to the ACT element in an amount of FII equalling the ordinary income.

EXAMPLE—for financial year 1986.
X Ltd has trading income of £180,000. It pays net dividends to shareholders of £142,000. X Ltd also has chargeable gains of £539,000.
Profits subject to corporation tax:

Trading income	£180,000
Chargeable gains ($\frac{6}{7}$ × £539,000)	462,000
	£642,000

Corporation tax due is 35% of £642,000 i.e. £224,700.
ACT due is 29/71 × 142,000, i.e. £58,000
Net mainstream corporation tax payable is given by:

35% of £180,000	£63,000
Less 29% of £180,000 (ACT)	£52,200
	£10,800
35% of £462,000	£161,700
Net corporation tax payable	£172,500

Surplus ACT is £58,000 − £52,200 = £5,800.
(Note that as the profits exceed £500,000, the small companies rate did not apply; in 1986 the CT rate was 35%.)

ACT can now be set off against corporation tax due on profits, whether income or capital gains. So if today X makes a distribution of £150,000 and pays ACT of £50,000 there will be no surplus ACT.

(4) Set off of losses. It has long been the rule that trading losses can be set off against all the profits of the same or the previous accounting period.[5] The term profits includes chargeable gains or, more accurately for gains realised before 17th March 1987, the chargeable fraction of chargeable gains.

Despite these changes the distinction still remains of importance.

(*a*) Where a trading loss is carried forward to a later accounting period it may only be set off against trading income—and not capital gains—of that trade of that period.[6]

(*b*) A terminal trading loss can be carried back and set off against trading income—and not capital gains—of that trade in previous accounting periods.[7]

(*c*) A capital loss cannot be set off against ordinary income—even income of the same accounting period.

(*d*) A capital loss, unlike a trading loss, cannot be passed to other members of a group under the group relief rules.

There remain also the fundamental differences outlined supra, § **2: 15** and the differences for gains realised before 17th March 1987.

Simon's Taxes D2.109, 301.

[1] TA 1988, s. 345.

[2] Where an accounting period straddles the date there is a notional end of one accounting period and an equally notional start of a new period simply in order to bring the change into effect straight away and not wait for the end of current accounting periods.

[3] But after 31st March 1973—FA 1972, s. 93 as originally enacted.

[4] Thus if the corporate tax rate was 35% only 6/7 of the gains would be brought into charge.

[5] TA 1988, s. 393(2).

[6] TA 1988, s. 393(1).

[7] TA 1988, s. 394(1).

The company and the shareholder—general

25: 05   Until 1987 there was no imputation of the company's liability to corporation tax on its realised capital gains to the shareholder in respect of a dividend paid out to the shareholder. This is still the case for gains realised before 17th March 1987 but for later realised gains imputation is allowed (supra, § **24: 15**). This alters—but does not altogether remove—the problem of the double charge to tax on capital gains. A double charge can arise if (*i*) the gain was realised before 17th March 1987 or (*ii*) the gain is realised but for some reason the profits are not distributed to the shareholders. In such circumstances there will have been a full charge to tax on the gain in the hands of the company and a further charge on the shareholder when the shares are sold. This leads to double taxation where there is a profit and double relief where there is a loss. The problem can be exaggerated—it arises also when the company makes a trading profit, retains some or all of that profit and the shareholder later sells his shares.

Two major avoidance techniques have been used[1] particularly when small companies are concerned. The first is to ensure that any appreciating assets are held by the individual shareholder rather than the company. The second is to transfer the asset at full value to a wholly owned subsidiary. This transfer will not give rise to a chargeable gain.[2] The disposal of the shares in the subsidiary after six years will be a chargeable disposal by the shareholder[3] but the liability in respect of the gain accruing before the transfer to the subsidiary will have been avoided. A shareholder may be liable for CT on gains accruing to the company if the shareholder is connected[4] with the company and then received a capital distribution from the company.[5]

Simon's Taxes D2.302, 621–623, 630–632.

[1] This may however risk the loss of roll-over relief under CGTA 1979, s. 115, supra, § **20: 06**.

[2] TA 1970, s. 273, infra, § **26: 18**.

[3] The transfer must be later than six years after the acquisition to avoid TA 1970, s. 278 infra, § **26: 23**.

[4] Defined by TA 1988, s. 839.

[5] TA 1988, s. 346.

Special rules

25: 06 (1) Special rules apply to deny the benefit of loss relief on bed and breakfast deals by companies when the holding disposed of is reacquired within one month and constitutes at least 2% of the issued share capital of that kind.[1]

(2) The charge arising on the disposal of an overseas trade plus its assets[2] to a non-resident company[3] in return for shares may be deferred provided the transferor company ends up with at least 25% of the ordinary share capital of the transferee company.[4] It is postponed until (*i*) the transferor company disposes of all or any of the shares or (*ii*) the transferee company disposes of all or some of the assets; however the charge under (*ii*) only arises if the disposal is within six years.[5] Where only a part of the consideration received is in the form of shares or loan stock then only a proportionate part of the charge is postponed. The purpose of the rule is to acknowledge that the gain is primarily a paper gain and to give the company time to find the cash; the technique used is a form of rollover. Section 268A is a matter of taxpayer election; it has the effect of deferring losses as well as gains and so the alternative of electing for CGTA 1979, s. 115 roll-over should be considered. The fact that foreign tax may have been paid and so is available for credit relief may make both of these elections superfluous or inadvisable.

(3) Although a matter for the holder rather than for the issuing company one should note the special exemption from CGT now offered to qualifying corporate bonds.[6]

(4) If a company ceases to be resident or subject to tax in the UK there may be a deemed disposal of its assets.[7] There is no deemed disposal by an individual who ceases to be resident.

Simon's Taxes D2.305, 309.

[1] F (No. 2) A 1975, s. 58 and FA 1982, s. 88(1)(*a*). Repurchases on the same day are caught by CGTA 1979, s. 66; the period is one month through ARIEL or the Stock Exchange and six months in other cases.

[2] But not if the assets consist wholly of cash.

[3] Treasury consent is needed for the transfer: TA 1988, s. 765.

[4] TA 1970, s. 268A the present version applies to transfers taking effect after 19 April 1977; the original version, s. 268, was introduced by FA 1969, Sch. 18, para. 19, apparently to assist in the Dunlop/Pirelli merger. Ordinary share capital is defined in TA 1988 s 832(1).

[5] Other than by a group transfer within TA 1970, s. 273; the non-residence bars in s. 272 are ignored for (*ii*).

[6] FA 1984, s. 64.

[7] FA 1988, ss. 105 and 106; infra § **32: 13**.

Transfer of Asset on Company reconstruction: TA 1970, s. 267

25: 07   If a company's business is transferred to another company,[1] the transfer will normally involve the transfer, and so the disposal, of chargeable assets. This result will be mitigated for assets other than trading stock[2] in that neither gain nor loss accrues to the company making the disposal[3] provided (*i*) the scheme involves the transfer of the *business* in whole or in part, as opposed simply to the transfer of assets,[4] (*ii*) that both companies are UK resident[5] and (*iii*) the transferor receives no consideration other than the transferee taking over of any liabilities from the transferor. This rule is similar in intent to those which apply on the incorporation or takeover of a business; where the rule applies the disponee takes over the base cost of the disponor.

If the main purpose, or one of the main purposes, is the avoidance of liability to CT, CGT or income tax, the section does not apply and the normal rules applicable to a disposal will apply;[6] any CT due can be recovered from the disponee if the disponor has not paid within six months of the tax becoming payable.[7] A scheme for the reconstruction of an investment company to avoid the double charge to tax in capital gains may well escape this provision.

The term reconstruction has been construed by the courts to require a degree of continuity of common ownership.[8] On this view the section would not apply when a business is split between two different groups of shareholders but the Revenue take a more generous position.[9]

Simon's Taxes D2.303.

[1] But not to a unit trust or an investment trust. TA 1970, s. 267(3), FA 1980, s. 81.

[2] Trading stock of the transferor will be valued under TA 1988, s. 100 for computing income and so is excluded.

[3] TA 1970, s. 267.

[4] Cf. *McGregor v Adcock* [1977] STC 206 § **20: 10**.

[5] On transfer to a non-resident s. 268A may apply.

[6] TA 1970, s. 267(3A).

[7] On clearance procedure, etc., see supra, § **19: 19**.

[8] *Brooklands Selangor Holdings Ltd v IRC* [1970] 2 All ER 76.

[9] Statement of Practice SP5/85, **Simon's Taxes, Division H3.2.**

CHARGES ON INCOME

25: 08   Charges on income are defined[1] as

(*a*) any yearly interest, annuity or other annual payment and any other payments such as is mentioned in TA 1988, s. 348 (such as patent royalties, mining rents and royalties and payments for easements) but not including sums which are, or but for any exemption would be, chargeable under Schedule A,[2] and

(b) any other[3] interest payable in the UK on an advance from a bona fide banking business[4] or from a member of the Stock Exchange or a discount house. A payment which is deductible in computing profits, e.g. interest qualifying as a business expense, is not to be treated as a charge on income.[5]

The line between a charge on income and a deductible expense is important, first because some items, e.g. patents and mining royalties can only be treated as charges, secondly because charges are deducted when made, relief is not available on an accruals basis:[6] the latter means that a charge may be paid at the due date or early or late with consequent effect and thirdly because an expense deductible in computing income affects trading income and so trading losses whereas a charge on income can be set off against all types of income.

Given the importance of this distinction the position of interest is peculiar and unsettled. Revenue practice is always to treat yearly interest as a charge unless paid to a UK bank but when advantageous it ought to be possible to treat it as an expense.[7] *Wilcock v Frigate Investments Ltd*[8] establishes that a sum deductible in computing trading income cannot be a charge on income by reason of TA 1988, s. 338(2)—and so in that case could not be set off against rental income.

Simon's Taxes D2.209, 210.

[1] TA 1988, s. 338(3). Interest payments under schemes to avoid tax may well fall foul of TA 1988, s. 787.

[2] Supra, § 9: 83. A rent is an allowable deduction as a business expense.

[3] I.e. non-yearly.

[4] By concession this applies to UK customers of foreign banks. See *United Dominions Trust Ltd v Kirkwood* [1966] 1 QB 783, [1965] 2 All ER 992. On application of s. 349 see *Hafton Properties Ltd v McHugh* [1987] STC 16.

[5] TA 1988, s. 338(2).

[6] TA 1988, s. 338(1); bank interest is treated as paid when the account is debited TA 1988, s. 338(3). On timing of interest payments when parties are related companies, see TA 1988, s. 341.

[7] TA 1988, s. 338(3)(*a*) appears to treat it as a charge but TA 1988, s. 82 implies that it may be an expense. TA 1988, s. 337 may be taken to give *sub silentio* support to the Revenue view.

[8] [1982] STC 198.

The payer—deduction of income tax

25: 09   These payments are income of the payee and so fall within the TA 1988, s. 349.[1] The company must therefore deduct income tax at the basic rate when making the payment and must account to the Revenue for the sums deducted.[2] The deduction must be made even though the recipient is another company liable to pay corporation tax and so not income tax. In such circumstances the payee company is entitled to set off the amount deducted by way of income tax against its own liability to account for income tax deducted on any payments it makes during the period;[3] otherwise it may set the income tax off against its corporation tax liability. If the income tax deducted exceeds the corporation tax payable the company is entitled to a refund.[4] These sums are subject to corporation tax like any other income.[5]

Simon's Taxes D1.208–210.
[1] Supra, § **9: 81**.
[2] These deductions are accounted for quarterly at the same time as but separately from ACT by TA 1988, Sch. 16 as distinct from TA 1988, Sch. 13.
[3] TA 1988, Sch. 16, para 5.
[4] TA 1988, s. 7(2).
[5] TA 1988, s. 8(1).

The payer—deduction of charges from profits

25: 10 The company may deduct these charges on income against its total profits for the period.[1] This latter deduction applies to payments made—not payments due.[2]

EXAMPLE

X Ltd has the following income in the financial year 1989:

Trading profit	£150,000
Bank interest	£15,000
Chargeable gains	£166,667
Rents received	£25,000

X Ltd pays debenture interest of £45,000 (gross), royalties of £20,000 (gross) and bank interest of £10,000.

Profits subject to corporation tax given by:

Trading profit	£150,000	
Less: Bank interest	£10,000	
		£140,000
Rents received		£25,000
Chargeable gains		£166,667
Bank interest received		£15,000
Gross profit		£346,667
Less:		
Charges on income of:		
Debenture interest	£45,000	
Royalties	£20,000	
		£65,000
Profits subject to corporation tax		£281,667

Simon's Taxes D2.208–211.
[1] TA 1988, s. 338(1), as reduced by any relief other than group relief on use of excess charges as trading losses see TA 1988, s. 393(9) infra, § **25: 25**.
[2] Save for interest which is deductible when debited to the company in the books of the payee: TA 1988, s. 338(3); the position where the payment is creditable to the account of the payee is obscure. See Simon's Taxes D2.109.

25: 11 TA 1988, s. 209(2)(*e*)(*iii*) which treats certain payments of interest by a company as distributions was used by company-borrowers whose tax position was such that they would receive no immediate benefit from being able to deduct the interest for corporation tax purposes: a small part of the consideration for the loan was made dependent on the results of the company's business so that the interest was treated as a distribution by the company. The lender thereby received the interest as franked investment income instead of as profits liable to corporation tax: the benefit of this was then shared with the borrower by charging a lower rate of interest.

With effect from 9th March 1982 (or 1st April 1983 in respect of loans made before 9th March 1982) interest on such a loan which is paid to a company within the charge to corporation tax is no longer treated as a distribution unless the recipient would anyway be exempt from tax thereon.[1] The same applies to interest or distributions in respect of redeemable shares and certain unquoted convertible stock issued by the company as well as securities connected with corresponding shareholdings in the company. Where the consideration for the loan exceeds a reasonable commercial return for the use of the principal sum, the interest is treated as a distribution to the extent only of the excess.

---

[1] TA 1988, s. 212.

25: 12   Bearing this system in mind the tax structure restricts the notion of charges on income. *First*, the deduction of payments within class (*a*) at **25: 08** above to a person not resident in the UK is only permitted if the pay*er* company is resident in the UK[1] and the payment satisfies any one of four tests:

(*i*) the payer deducts[2] income tax under the machinery laid down in TA 1988, s. 349; or

(*ii*) the payment is one payable out of income brought into charge under Case IV or V, that is wholly overseas income.[3] There is no need for such restrictions in class (*b*) since the payee must necessarily be resident or be carrying on a business here; or

(*iii*) the payment is of interest and falls within TA 1988, s. 340 (infra, § **25: 14**); or

(*iv*) the payment is of interest on a quoted Eurobond[4] and, as a result, no deduction of tax need be made under TA 1988, s. 349(2) (infra, § **25: 16**).

Secondly, no deduction is permitted if the payment is a distribution, whether qualifying or not.[5] This is axiomatic. So interest on debentures is deductible but preference dividends are not.

Thirdly, the payment is not to be treated as a charge on income if it could be dealt with as a deduction in computing income or gains.[6]

Fourthly, no deduction is permitted if the payment is not ultimately borne by the company as where the company is ultimately reimbursed, presumably whether or not there is a legal right to reimbursement nor, save for interest, if it is charged to capital.[7]

Fifthly, the payments will not be deductible unless it is made under a liability incurred for valuable and sufficient consideration. Value and sufficiency are determined when the liability is incurred and "incurred" means "in return for" rather than "with a view to" so that an expected business advantage is not sufficient.[8] The consideration must represent a fair equivalent of the company's liability.[9]

Sixthly, if the payer is a non-resident company the liability must also have been incurred wholly and exclusively for the purposes of the trade carried on through the branch or agency in the UK.

Simon's Taxes D2.209–214.

[1] TA 1988, s. 338(4). However, a branch of a non-resident company may deduct interest as a charge if there is a non-discrimination clause in the applicable double tax treaty.

[2] Or is absolved by the Inspector of Foreign Dividends; see S.I. 1970 No. 488, reg. 6. Tax may also be eliminated or reduced by Double Tax Treaty, e.g. UK/US Treaty Act 11(2). It is not uncommon for the borrower to insist on payment gross. This frequently occurred on the Eurobond Market and led to the introduction of TA 1988, s. 124 which enables interest on Eurobonds to be paid gross (supra, § **25: 16**).

[3] It used to be possible to create overseas income. So as not to impede UK companies overseas investment programmes, loopholes existed here with the tacit consent of the Revenue. The process was known as the Swiss roundabout. The UK company borrowed money on the European money market and then lent it to a Swiss subsidiary company (perhaps specially created) at a rate of interest sufficient to give it income to cover its interest commitments on the loan. The interest from the Swiss subsidiary was within Case IV. There were snags which make this operation more expensive for the UK company. The Revenue has conceded that this device is not affected by the new approach but has said that interest paid by a UK borrower is necessarily Case III income and so is subject to s. 349.

[4] TA 1988, s. 124. Payments after 31st March 1989 to certain Netherlands Antilles subsidiaries also qualify—FA 1989, s. 116; the provision is needed as a result of the abrogation of the Treaty.

[5] TA 1988, s. 338(2).

[6] The status of yearly interest paid to a UK bank is anomalous supra, § **25: 08**; in practice the Revenue used to allow either method; but see now *Wilcock v Frigate Investments Ltd* [1982] STC 198.

[7] TA 1988, s. 338(5). If the realisation of capital asset gives rise to a chargeable capital gain and this is used to finance the payments such a payment is not "charged to capital". It is payable "out of" profits even though only a fraction of those profits is chargeable.

[8] *Ball v National and Grindlay's Bank Ltd* [1971] 3 All ER 485, 47 TC 287. The case turns on a provision reversed by TA 1988, s. 338(2). Today the payment might be deductible as a business expense.

[9] On the problem of the provision for past employees, see BTE 1–248/1.

25: 13   To the fifth and sixth rules there is an exception where the payment is a *covenanted* donation to charity, a phrase which is defined as a payment under a disposition or covenant made in favour of a body of persons[1] or trust established for charitable purposes only, whereby the like annual payments (of which the donation is one) become payable for a period which may exceed three years and is not capable of earlier termination under any power exercisable without the consent of the persons for the time being entitled to the payments. This is broadly the same definition as that which allows an individual to deduct charitable covenants in computing his liability to income tax at basic rate.[2] If the donation satisfied this test it cannot be a distribution.[3] Hence the company may deduct payments to a charity even though they are variable with its profits.

A company may claim relief for a *qualifying* donation to a charity. This applies to payments after 31st March 1986. It is designed to encourage companies to give to charity without having to tie themselves to a four-year covenant. A payment cannot fall into this category if it is a covenanted donation or a deductible expense. The payment is treated as a charge but tax must be deducted at source. There is a limit equal to 3% of the dividends paid on the company's ordinary share capital; covenanted donations and deductible expenses are not included for this calculation.[4] The company must be resident in the UK and not a close company.

Simon's Taxes D2.210, 213, 214.

[1] Defined TA 1988, s. 832(1) to include corporations.

² Supra, § **13: 40** and **13: 47**.
³ TA 1988, s. 339(6).
⁴ TA 1988, s. 339.

25: 14   Two special rules apply to interest payments. First, the payments of interest must satisfy the further test of coming within one of the favoured purposes of trade, or the payment must exist wholly or mainly for the purposes of trade, or the payment must be wholly and exclusively laid out or expended for the purposes of a trade carried on by the company, or the company must be an investment company, or the interest would have been deductible by an individual.¹

Secondly, if the payment is made to a non-resident it will rank as a charge on income if it comes within TA 1988, s. 340 even if it does not come within the rules (i) and (ii) mentioned under the first part of § **25: 12**. Section 340 was designed to deny relief unless the liability was incurred for foreign trade or payable in foreign exchange.

The test which must be passed in order to satisfy s. 340 is complicated; three conditions must be met one of these being in the alternative. First, under the terms of the contract under which the interest is payable, the interest may be required to be paid outside the UK (TA 1988, s. 340(1)(*a*)). Secondly, the interest must in fact be paid outside the UK (TA 1988, s. 340(1)(*b*)). Thirdly,² either (*i*) the liability to pay the interest must be incurred wholly or mainly for the purposes of activities of the company's trade carried on outside the UK, or (*ii*) if the interest is payable in a non-sterling currency, the liability to pay the interest must be incurred wholly or mainly for the purposes of activities of the company's trade wherever carried on (TA 1988, s. 340(1)(*c*)).

It should be noted that under TA 1988, s. 340(2)(*a*) or (*b*) or (*c*), if the interest paid is in a foreign currency and is paid outside the UK, then it will not be allowed as a charge on income if the trade referred to in TA 1988, s. 340(1)(*c*)(*ii*):

> "(*a*) is carried on by a body of persons over whom the person entitled to the interest has control, or
> (*b*) the person entitled to the interest is a body of persons over whom the person carrying on the trade has control, or
> (*c*) the person carrying on the trade and the person entitled to the interest are both bodies of persons, and some other person has control over both of them.
> In this subsection the references to a body of persons include references to a partnership and 'control' has the meaning assigned to it by section 534 of this Act [TA 1988, s. 840]."

In other words, interest paid by a UK subsidiary to its parent in a foreign currency would not qualify as a charge on income under TA 1988, s. 340(1)(*c*)(*ii*), since condition (*a*) above is violated. However, it might be eligible as a charge under TA 1988, s. 340(1)(*c*)(*i*).

Excluding relief under a double tax agreement, any gross interest paid to a non-resident would not be allowed as a charge on income if the borrowed money was used to acquire shares in a subsidiary wherever resident. This is so since neither TA 1988, s. 340(1)(*c*)(i) nor (ii) is satisfied.

On the other hand, interest paid gross on a foreign borrowing by a UK company to finance an overseas branch would be eligible as a charge under either TA 1988, s. 340(1)(*c*)(*i*) or (*ii*).

Excess charges which are made wholly and exclusively for the purposes of the company's trade are treated as trading losses and so can be rolled forward to be set against future trading profits.[3] Surplus charges not so made can be used for a group relief claim (infra, § **26: 16**) or be set against surplus franked investment income (infra, § **25: 36**).

Simon's Taxes D2.214.
[1] TA 1988, s. 338(6).
[2] This condition cannot be satisfied where a UK company decides to make an overseas borrowing for an acquisition overseas since it will not be used for the UK company's trade; this led to the Swiss roundabout (supra, § **25: 12**, footnote 3).
[3] TA 1988, s. 338(6) and see supra, Chapter 5.

25: 15 If the non-resident wishes to receive the interest without deduction of tax[1] and the payer is still to be entitled to claim a deduction the payment must be covered by a double tax treaty, or payable out of overseas income[2] or meet either condition of TA 1988, s. 340(1)(*c*).

Simon's Taxes D2.214.
[1] On duty to account when tax is deducted see TA 1988, Sch. 16.
[2] TA 1988, s. 338(4)(*d*).

25: 16 Special provision is made for the deduction by a company[1] of interest paid gross on a quoted Eurobond where the payment is made by either:[2]

(*a*) a person outside the UK (this means the subsidiary paying agent where the funds for paying the interest are transferred to him from the company through a principal paying agent[3]), or

(*b*) a person in the UK (which will again include a subsidiary paying agent), provided that one of the following conditions is met: (*i*) the beneficial owner of the bond or the person whose income the interest is deemed to be under the Tax Acts (if different) is not resident in the UK,[4] or (*ii*) the bond is held in a recognised clearing system.

A claim under (*b*)(*i*) is similar to that made in respect of foreign dividends and a declaration of non-residence (made by way of affidavit) has to be supplied.[5] The person paying the interest is under a duty to make returns— to the Inspector of Foreign Dividends in the case of payments within (*b*)(*i*),[5] and to the Revenue in any case where the payment falls within (*b*).[6] Payments of interest to certain Netherlands Antilles subsidiaries are to be treated in the same way.[7]

Simon's Taxes A3.405, D2.213.
[1] TA 1988, s. 338(4)(*b*).
[2] TA 1988, s. 124(1), (2).
[3] Statement of Practice SP 8/84, **Simon's Taxes Division H3.2.**
[4] TA 1988, s. 124(2), (5).

⁵ TA 1988, s. 124(2), (*a*), Statement of Practice SP 8/84, **Simon's Taxes Division H3.2.**
⁶ TA 1988, s. 124(3).
⁷ FA 1989, s. 116.

Discounts

25: 17   Where a discounted bill of exchange drawn by a company becomes payable after 31st March 1983, the company may deduct from its total profits an amount equal to the discount.[1] Incidental costs incurred in obtaining acceptance of the bill are deductible in computing the company's Schedule D, Case I profits (or management expenses).[2]

Simon's Taxes B3.1321.
¹ TA 1988, s. 78.
² TA 1988, s. 78(4).

Deep discount securities

25: 18   The rules for determining what is a deep discount and what is the income element arising on a disposal of the security are set out at § **9: 51**. When the new rules apply the issuing company no longer has to wait until the redemption of the security before claiming a deduction, but may deduct the income element for any income period (see supra, § **9: 51**) ending in its accounting period from its total profits for that period. This is achieved by treating the income element as a charge on income.[1] The deduction is from total profits as reduced by any relief other than group relief.

The right to make the deduction is subject to certain conditions at least one of which must be satisfied.

(*i*) The company must be a trading company (i.e. exist wholly or mainly for the purposes of a trade).

(*ii*) The stock must have been issued wholly and exclusively for the purposes of a trade the company carries on.

(*iii*) The company is an investment company within TA 1988, s. 130.

The deduction may not be made if the cost of the discount is not ultimately borne by the company.

A deduction under these provisions is not made if it may already be made under any other provision.

If any part of the amount payable on redemption represents a distribution by virtue of TA 1988, s. 209(2)(*d*) and (*e*) no deduction may be made in respect of any income element of that security.

If at any time the issue of the security has been linked to a tax avoidance scheme (a scheme or arrangement of which the sole or main benefit is a reduction in the company's tax liability) relief is to be denied under any provision of the Tax Acts in respect of any income element of that security. Where group relief is being claimed, the circumstances of both the claimant and the surrendering company are to be taken into account.

Special provisions[2] attempt to counteract coupon stripping operations, infra, § **25: 22**.

Any incidental costs of issuing deep discounted securities is brought within

TA 1988, s. 77 if it would not be deductible under that rule or general principles.

The right to deduct on an accruals basis is denied, i.e. the deduction may only be taken on redemption, if the securities are held by an associated company or a fellow group company of the issuing company.[3] Associated companies are defined by TA 1988, s. 416 (see supra, § **23: 04**) and groups on a 51% subsidiary test. A similar restriction applies when the company is a close company and the security is held by a participator, the associate of a participator or a company controlled by a participator.[4]

Simon's Taxes D2.215.
[1] TA 1988, Sch 4, para. 5.
[2] TA 1988, Sch. 4, paras. 1–4.
[3] TA 1988, Sch. 4, para. 9.
[4] TA 1988, Sch. 4, para. 10 (but note definition of participator in TA 1988, Sch. 4, para. 10(4).

Early redemption

25: 19 If a deep discount security is redeemed early, there are adjustments to both the accrued income charged on the investor and the issuing company's relief. Early redemption is redemption before the redemption date.[1]

Simon's Taxes D2.215.
[1] TA 1988, Sch. 4, para. 11.

(a) The investor

25: 20 The accrued income attributable to the person who was the beneficial owner of the security immediately before early redemption is to be the amount payable on redemption less the adjusted issue price at the time of his acquisition.

Simon's Taxes B5.404.

(b) The issuing company

25: 21 The deduction to be allowed to the issuing company in the accounting period in which the early redemption takes place is to be the amount payable on redemption less the adjusted issue price as at the beginning of the first income period to end within the accounting period in which the redemption takes place. Any linked income elements (i.e. sums only deductible on redemption by reason of group, company or close company status) must be deducted from that adjusted issue price.

Where the adjusted issue price exceeds the amount paid on early redemption, the smaller of—

(a) the excess and
(b) the adjusted issue price less the original issue price—that is, the sum of the income elements attributable to all the income periods from the issue

of the security to the last period to end in the accounting period preceding the redemption

is treated as the company's income arising in the accounting period in which redemption takes place. It is charged under Schedule D, Case VI.

> **EXAMPLE**
> A deep discount security is issued at 50 by a company whose accounting periods end on 31st December. The adjusted issue price at the end of income periods 8, 9 and 10 is—
>
> | | |
> |---|---|
> | period 8 (ended 30.11.88) | 73·08 |
> | period 9 (ended 30.5.89) | 76·89 |
> | period 10 (ended 30.11.89) | 80·95 |
>
> The security is redeemed early on 1st December 1989 for 72.
> The accounting period in which redemption takes places—year ended 31.12.89.
> The first income period to end in that period—period 9 (6 months ended 30.5.89)
> Adjusted issue price at beginning of period 9—73·08
> Excess over amount paid on redemption = 73·08 − 72 = 1·08(A)
> Adjusted issue price less original issue price = 73·08 − 50 = 23·08(B)
> Smaller of A and B = 1·08
> This is the amount charged to tax under Schedule D, Case VI in the year ended 31st December 1989.

Simon's Taxes D2.215.

Coupon stripping

25: 22   Companies were able to take advantage of the deep discount security provisions by issuing deep discount stock (e.g. zero coupon bonds bearing no interest) and making a related acquisition of interest-bearing securities with the intention of offsetting the deductions available in respect of the discount against the interest received. The holder of the deep discount securities would not be liable to tax on the interest, of course, until the securities were disposed of or redeemed. A significant deferral of tax could therefore be achieved by the holder.

Legislation[1] was therefore introduced to bring the tax charge forward in this type of situation. The legislation sets out certain situations in which the person holding the deep discount securities will be taxed on the interest before disposal or redemption: supra, § **9: 58.**

Simon's Taxes B5.404, D2.215.
   [1] TA 1988, Sch. 4, paras. 1–4 (applying to deep discount securities issued after 18th March 1985 i.e. from Budget Day 1985).

LOSSES

Trading loss

25: 23   Where a company incurs a loss on its trade[1] (including woodlands if it has elected to come within Schedule D, Case I) during an accounting period TA 1988, s. 393 allows various forms of relief. These rules may have little commercial merit and ignore the fact that the company's business is commercially a single activity.[2] So in one case income generated by investments financed by funds set aside for the eventual replacement of the company's fixed assets was held to be investment income and so not eligible for offset of trading loss under rule (i).[3]

The rules for a company with a trading loss are as follows.

(*i*) The company may roll the loss forward to be set off against the trading income[4] from the trade of succeeding accounting periods, the loss being set off against the earliest available profits.

(*ii*) Alternatively, it may set the trading loss off against other profits of the same period[5] including (before 17th March 1987 the chargeable fraction of) capital gains.

(*iii*) Continuing the analogy with trading losses under income tax, the loss may be set off against the profits from all sources of the previous accounting period[6] provided the company was then carrying on the trade. Where the previous accounting period was of a different length from that in which the loss was sustained, the loss may be set off against the profits of a period equal to that of the period in which the loss occurred, making such apportionments as may be necessary.[7]

(*iv*) A trading loss may be carried back three years if and to the extent that the reason why the loss was not relieved is that first year capital allowances were claimed in respect of machinery and plant. For accounting periods ending after 13th March 1984, the amount carried back is limited to the amount of the first year allowances for the loss making period.[8]

EXAMPLE

X Ltd has produced the following results:

12 months to 31st December 1985	Profit	£14,000
12 months to 31st December 1986	Loss	£5,000
12 months to 31st December 1987	Profit	£10,400
8 months to 31st August 1988	Loss	£7,800
12 months to 31st August 1989	Profit	£9,500

Assessments to corporation tax:

Year to 31st December 1985	£14,000	
Less:		
TA 1988, s. 393(2) carry back	£5,000	
		£9,000
Year to 31st December 1986		Nil
Year to 31st December 1987	£10,400	
Less:		
TA 1988, s. 393(2) carry back *but* limited to 8/12 × £10,400	£6,933	£3,467
8 months to 31st August 1988		Nil
Year to 31st August 1989	£9,500	
Less:		
Unrelieved loss brought forward of £867 (£7,800 − £6,933)	£867	£8,633

Simon's Taxes D2.401–408.

[1] Supra, § **5: 12**.
[2] CBI Submission on Corporation Tax, p. 24.
[3] *Bank Line Ltd v IRC* [1974] STC 342.
[4] Defined TA 1988, s. 393(8) but modified for industrial and provident societies by extra-statutory concession C5 (1988), **Simon's Taxes Division H2.2.**

⁵ TA 1988, s. 393(2).
⁶ TA 1988, s. 393(2).
⁷ TA 1988, s. 393(3). The claim must be made within two years: TA 1988, s. 393(11).
⁸ TA 1988, s. 393(4).

Non-allowable trading losses

25: 24   The privilege of loss relief does not apply to trades falling within Schedule D, Case V[1] nor to dealings in commodity futures.[2] The restrictions on loss relief applied to persons in respect of farming and market gardening apply here also.[3] Further, the trade whether or not connected with farming must either have been carried on (*i*) under some enactment or (*ii*) on a commercial basis and with a view to the relation to gain whether in itself or as part of a larger undertaking of which the trade formed part. A reasonable expectation of gain at the end of the period will satisfy this test.[4]

Simon's Taxes D2.401–408.
  ¹ TA 1988, s. 393(5) but see SP2/80, **Simon's Taxes, Division H3.2.**
  ² TA 1988, s. 399(2)–(4).
  ³ TA 1988, s. 397, supra, § **5: 13**.
  ⁴ TA 1988, s. 393(6).

Charges on income as losses

25: 25   Where charges on income consisting of payments made wholly and exclusively for the purposes of a trade carried on by the company, and those and other charges on income exceed the profits of that period against which they are deductible, then whichever is the smaller of those payments or the excess, is treated as a trading expense[1] and so becomes entitled to loss relief. Where the company carries on two trades, the excess interest which falls to be treated as an allowable loss may only be set off against future income of the trade for which the loan was raised; the fact that there are individual (beneficial) side effects for the other trade is irrelevant.[2]

This excess may be rolled forward against subsequent trading income. Where a loss has been so rolled forward but the profits of that period chargeable under Schedule D, Case I or V are insufficient to absorb it, account may be taken of any interest or dividends which would have been within these Cases but for falling within another Case[3]—Schedule D, Case III or IV for interest and Schedule F for dividends and other distributions. In this way franked and other investment income[4] can be used to absorb a loss from an earlier period, but this is confined to those situations where it would be trading income.

Simon's Taxes D2.403.
  ¹ TA 1988, s. 393(9); on management expenses of an investment company see TA 1988, s. 75(3).
  ² *Olin Energy Systems Ltd v Scorer* [1982] STC 800.
  ³ TA 1988, s. 393(8).
  ⁴ Infra, § **25: 37**.

Terminal trading loss

25: 26   A terminal loss is one incurred in any accounting period falling wholly or partly within the twelve months before the company ceases to carry on the trade. When that period straddles the twelve months, an apportionment is made. Such losses can be carried back and set off against trading income of accounting periods falling wholly or partly within the three years preceding those last twelve months.[1] The section states that the relief takes the form of reducing the trading income of "any of those periods" by the amount of the loss "or by so much as cannot be relieved under this subsection against income of a later accounting period."[2] These closing words mean that the company must set the loss against the profits of later periods before earlier ones, a matter of importance when the rates of tax change from year to year—as recently.   This rule carries a proviso that relief is not to be given under it in respect of any loss in so far as it can be taken into account in other ways. This presumably refers to rules such as that allowing the loss to be set off against other income of the same accounting period. It is unlikely that this proviso extends to the rules allowing the loss of one subsidiary to be set off against the profits of another.

EXAMPLE
   X Ltd makes up its accounts to 30th April but it ceased to trade on 31st August 1989. Trading results were as follows:

12 months to 30th April 1989	Loss	£10,500
4 months to 31st August 1989	Profit	£5,000

Terminal loss given by:

4 months to 31.8.89	Profit	£5,000
8 months to 30.4.89	Loss	£7,000
(i.e. 31.8.88 to 30.4.89)		
Terminal loss		(£2,000)

The terminal loss of £2,000 may be relieved against trading income arising any time after 31st August 1985, i.e. during three years preceding last twelve months, namely, 1st September 1988 to 31st August 1989.

Simon's Taxes D2.407.
   [1] TA 1988, s. 394, this extends to excess charges and management expenses; TA 1988, s. 394(5).
   [2] TA 1988, s. 394(1).

Restrictions

(i)   Company reconstruction without change of ownership: TA 1988, s. 343

25: 27   Where a company transfers a trade or part of a trade to another company, and there is no change of ownership, the change is ignored for the granting of allowances under the Capital Allowances Act 1968[1] and any trading loss may be rolled forward[2] to be set off against the subsequent trading income subject only to the first company's right to set the loss against other profits.[3] There is no terminal loss relief.[4] Assets qualifying for capital allowances will be transferred at the written down value;[4] there will therefore be no balancing charges (or allowances) nor any first year allowance. Where a company ceases to trade or to carry on a part of a trade after 18th March 1986[5] restrictions apply if the transferring company is insolvent. The amount of the loss that may be taken over is reduced by the amount by which the transferor company's "relevant liabilities"[6] exceed its "relevant assets".[7]

If a company wishes to separate a particular business and place it in a subsidiary, often called a hive-down, TA 1988, s. 343 will be invoked; TA 1970, s. 273 (infra, § **26: 18**) will be used for assets with potential capital gains liability. The Revenue has indicated that where a receiver intending to sell off a company, trade, or part of it effects a hivedown, the *Ramsay* approach will not normally be considered relevant provided the entire trade (or part) and its assets are transferred with a view to its being carried on in other hands.[8]

These are the only purposes for which the change is ignored. Therefore the successor company cannot use any Schedule D, Case VI nor capital losses of its predecessor.[9] This is scarcely unreasonable since, for this rule to apply, it is only necessary that the predecessor company cease to trade. It is not necessary that the company should cease to exist; such losses will be relieved by being set against subsequent Schedule D, Case VI gains or capital gains of the predecessor company. Further the provision does not allow the transfer of surplus FII or unused ACT.

There is regarded as being no change of ownership if on, or at any time within two years of, the ending of the trade by the predecessor, the trade or an interest amounting to not less than a $\frac{3}{4}$ share in it should belong to the same persons as the trade or such interest belonged to within a year before the event. It is also necessary that the trade should be carried on by companies which are within the charge to corporation tax.[10]

If the successor company itself ceases to carry on the trade within four years and is entitled to more terminal loss relief than it can use, the relief may be carried back to the original transferor.[11] Another relief is available if the cesser occurs within one year in that the predecessor can claim terminal loss relief for any loss *it* has sustained in the 12 months up to the date on which the successor ceases to trade.[12] Provision is also made for the situation in which the successor company transfers its trade to a new owner.[13] Where the first successor company does not satisfy the common control test but the second one does (in comparison with the original transferor) the losses may be used by the second successor—provided it is within the four year period.[14]

Simon's Taxes D2.501, 502.

[1] TA 1988, s. 343(2). E.g. *Blower v Langworthy Bros (Drills) Ltd* (1968) 44 TC 543. This did *not* enable the successor company to use their predecessor's date for payment under TA 1970, s. 244; supra, § **23: 02**.

[2] Under TA 1988, s. 393(1).

[3] Under TA 1988, s. 393(2).

[4] TA 1988, s. 343(3).

[5] TA 1988, s. 343(4).

[6] A liability assumed by the transferee company cannot be a relevant liability; TA 1988, s. 344(6).

[7] TA 1988, s. 343(4) proviso. "Relevant assets" are defined in TA 1988, s. 344(5) and "relevant liabilities" in TA 1988, s. 344(6).

[8] See a letter sent by the Revenue to the Institute of Chartered Accountants for England and Wales, [1985] STI p. 568; but the Revenue would not give an assurance that the new approach would never be relevant.

[9] Infra, § **25: 32**.
[10] TA 1988, s. 343(1).
[11] TA 1988, s. 343(6)(*a*).
[12] TA 1988, s. 343(6)(*b*).
[13] TA 1988, s. 343(7).
[14] On the restriction where the transferor is insolvent see TA 1988, s. 343(4).

25: 28   In determining whether the trade belongs to the same persons, the law pierces not only the veil of any company but also that of any trust identifying shareholders and beneficiaries as the people with the interest in each case.[1] Persons who are relatives or who are entitled to the income of the trust are treated as being one person.[2] If shares in company A Ltd are held on trust for L, M, N and P, and the company transfers the trade to a company whose shares are held on trust for L, M, N, P and Q it would appear that there has been a change in ownership since although less than ¾ of the interest has been changed, each body of beneficiaries is treated as a single person. In determining the extent of a person's interest in a trade one looks to the extent of his entitlement to share in the profits.[3]

Simon's Taxes D2.501, 502.
[1] TA 1988, s. 344(1). On ownership where there is a conditional contract of sale, see *Wood Preservation Ltd v Prior* [1969] 1 All ER 364, 45 TC 112; because the controlling company had accepted the conditional offer, it was no longer the beneficial owner of the shares needed to entitle it to set off the loss, but if the condition had then failed, would the failure have been retroactive?
[2] TA 1988, s. 344(4).
[3] TA 1988, s. 344(1).

(ii)   Change in ownership of company and change in trade: TA 1988, s. 768

25: 29   The converse case arises when the control of the trade passes to other people but the identity of the person trading remains the same. The right to roll losses forward is excluded if either

(*a*)   within any period of three years there is *both* a change in the ownership of the company *and* (either earlier or later or simultaneously) a major change in the nature or conduct of a trade carried on by the company or

(*b*)   there is a change in the ownership of the company at any time—and not just within a three-year period—after the scale of the activities in a trade carried on by a company has become small or negligible, and before any considerable revival of the trade.

Where these conditions are satisfied, losses accruing up to date of the change in ownership are not capable of being carried forward. These provisions were introduced in 1969 to stop the sale of companies simply for their tax losses. The going rate was then 10p for £1 of loss. Some companies were only kept in existence for their losses—hence (*b*). This provision does not apply to capital losses.

The rules for ascertaining the change in ownership are complex.[1] These rules are amended by FA 1989.[2] The first change concerns the definition of 75% subsidiary for the purposes of s. 769(5). Section 769(5) provides that a change of ownership is to be disregarded if before and after the change the company is a 75% subsidiary of another company. This provision is aimed at the situation in which the company ceases to be the directly owned 75%

subsidiary of another company but remains within the same ultimate ownership. The definitions of 75% ownership in sub-ss. 7(*b*) and (*c*), which are exclusively in terms of ownership of ordinary share capital, are repealed and new tests in terms of entitlement to profits and to assets on winding up are substituted (by new sub-s. 6B). These rules are already in place for group loss relief and so it is not surprising to find that TA 1988, Sch. 18 is to apply to s. 769 also (sub-s. 6C).

The second change concerns s. 769(6). At present this provides that a change in the ownership of a company which has a 75% subsidiary (whether owned directly or indirectly) automatically brings about a change in the ownership of the 75% subsidiary (unless, of course, s.769(5) applies). Sub-sections (6) and (6A) widen this deemed change of ownership to cover the situation where a subsidiary is a 60% subsidiary of one company within a group and the 40% subsidiary of another such company—or the 50% subsidiary of each. At present the sale of the 60% holding and of the 40% holding to the same purchaser would not bring about a change in the ownership of the subsidiary for the purpose of s.769; this is to change for all changes of ownership on or after 14th March 1989.

For (*a*) there must be a major change in the trade. This is further defined[3] by "including" a major change in the property dealt in, services or facilities provided or in the customers, outlets or markets. Moreover where the change has been a gradual process it may be treated as a change even though it took more than three years. Since it is almost inevitable that a person taking over a loss-making business will want to make some changes the courts will have some nice questions to decide. However in *Willis v Peeters Picture Frames Ltd*[4] it was emphasised that these are essentially matters of fact. There the taxpayer company was taken over by a group and its sales to its former customers were divided through distribution companies in the same group; this reorganisation was held by the Commissioners to be not a major change and the court declined to interfere with that decision. In *Purchase v Tesco Stores Ltd* it was said that the word 'major' imported something more than significant but less than fundamental; the effects of the change should be considered.[5]

There are technical provisions to treat a company reconstruction without a change in ownership as concerning only one company[6] and for allowing for intra group transfers to take place without raising TA 1988, s. 768.[7]

Where the loss is due to an unused capital allowance, provisions ensure that no balancing charge[8] applies to the extent that the charge reflects the unallowable loss.

Simon's Taxes D2.410.

[1] TA 1988, s. 769.

[2] FA 1989, s. 100.

[3] TA 1988, s. 768(4). Of course if the change in trade was sufficiently great, losses could not be carried forward, whether the trader was an individual or a company, by virtue of the rules as to discontinuance of a trade, supra, § 7: 46.

[4] [1983] STC 453.

[5] [1984] STC 304; see also *Pobjoy Mint Ltd v Lane* [1985] STC 314, CA (both cases on stock relief under FA 1976, Sch 5, para 23).

[6] TA 1988, s. 768(5).

[7] TA 1988, s. 768(6).

[8] TA 1988, s. 768(7).

(iii) Successor companies—groups—machinery and plant: TA 1988, ss. 395 and 116

25: 30   A further restriction applies where two companies are concerned and where either they are connected companies,[1] or there is a company reconstruction without change of ownership as defined by TA 1988, s. 343. If a company incurs expenditure on machinery and plant which it leases to another person and there are arrangements[2] whereby a successor company will be able to carry on any part of that company's trade which includes that lease, the first company can set that loss off only against the profits of the leasing contract, the contract being thus treated in effect as a separate trade.[3] But for this special provision, the first company would be able to create a loss to set off against its profits while giving the successor company profits to set off against its losses, and thus in effect permit the assignment of the generous capital allowances provided for machinery and plant.

A similar rule applies where a company is a member of a partnership and arrangements exist whereby the company's share of profits or losses is adjusted for a consideration in money or money's worth. Here too, in broad terms, the company's shares in the partnership loss may be set off against the profits of the firm.[4]

Simon's Taxes D2.409.
[1] Under TA 1988, s. 839.
[2] TA 1988, s. 116. On meaning see *Pilkington Bros Ltd v IRC* [1982] STC 103.
[3] TA 1988, s. 395.
[4] TA 1988, s. 116.

Other losses

25: 31   Case VI losses may be set off against other Case VI losses for that or any subsequent accounting periods.[1] Schedule A losses are given relief in the same way as income tax.[2]

Another problem arises with post-trading expenses where a company has ceased trading and is in the process of selling up its assets, it may receive investment income on its funds. Reliefs for the incidental expenses will not be available since it is not a trading company any longer and was not set up as an investment company. Unrelieved trading losses from its trading days cannot be used since the company is no longer trading.

Simon's Taxes D2.412.
[1] TA 1988, s. 396.
[2] TA 1988, s. 25; supra, § **9: 11**.

Capital losses

25: 32   Allowable capital losses may be set off against chargeable gains of that or any later accounting period[1] but not against income. Such losses are not affected by TA 1988, s. 768 (above). Group relief does not extend to capital losses.

Simon's Taxes D2.415.
¹ TA 1988, s. 345(1).

SURPLUS FRANKED INVESTMENT INCOME (FII)

Releasing the credit: TA 1988, s. 242

25: 33   Dividends and other distributions by a company resident in the UK are exempt from CT[1] as having been taxed already. When they are received by a company accompanied by an income tax credit they are called franked investment income (FII); this is the sum of the distribution and the credit. The company can use the credit only in certain ways.[2] The company cannot generally claim to have the income tax repaid, supra, § **24: 18**.

The prime use of the credit is to frank qualifying distributions by the recipient company and so to be set against the company's liability to pay ACT. Any surplus FII, i.e. the amount left after franking the distributions, can be rolled forward to subsequent accounting periods.

Simon's Taxes D2.413.
¹ TA 1988, ss. 208 and 238(1); supra, § **23: 01**.
² A company cannot use the procedure in TA 1988, s. 231 unless it is wholly exempt from corporation tax (or on all but trading income) or the distribution itself is exempt otherwise than under TA 1988, s. 208.

25: 34   However for certain purposes any surplus franked investment income can be made to release its tax credit for immediate use.

The purposes for which this can be done are

(*i*)   the setting off of trading losses,[1]
(*ii*)   the deduction of charges on income,[2]
(*iii*)   the deduction of the expenses of management of investment[3] companies and
(*iv*)   the granting of certain minor capital allowances.[4]

These items can be set off against the surplus FII of the same accounting period. The technique used is to treat the surplus as if it were profits chargeable to corporation tax and on which tax has, to the extent of the credit, already been paid.[5]

> **EXAMPLE**
> A Ltd has a trading loss of £6,000. It has received qualifying distributions from other companies of £7,500 on which there is a tax credit of £2,500, making franked investment income of £10,000. The company pays a dividend of £3,750 and would have to pay ACT of £1,250 but uses £5,000 of its FII to frank the payment to avoid having to pay ACT, thus leaving surplus franked investment income of £5,000. The loss of £6,000 can be set off against the surplus franked investment income and the credit of £1,250 will be *repaid* to the company. This will leave a loss of only £1,000 to be carried forward to the next year.

This releases the tax credit comprised in the FII and reduces that FII. At first sight this appears disadvantageous in that both the surplus FII and the funding loss which might have been given relief at 35% later on are reduced.[6]

However relief is at hand to enable the trading loss to be reinstated. Thus, if, in a later accounting period there is an excess of franked payments over FII, the excess is treated as a loss available for CT relief to the extent that the excess is less than the amount of the loss used to generate the relief under s. 242(1).[7] To achieve this the loss is treated as occurring in the accounting period next before that in which the excess arises. The company must still be carrying on the trade and be within the charge to corporation tax. The statute thus tries to make provision for those untidy companies that cannot balance their distributions, their profits and their FII income within each neat but artificial accounting period. It is likely to be of most use to those companies with income profits in addition to FII since they are more likely to be able to make distributions in excess of franked investment income in later years. A claim under TA 1988, s. 242 is in practice particularly useful to sharedealing companies which can make sufficient future profit to ensure that in a later year its franked payments exceed its FII. A TA 1988, s. 242 claim necessarily involves a judgment as to the future.

EXAMPLE

Year 1:	Trading loss	£700,000
	Surplus FII (s. 242)	200,000
	Trading loss carried forward	£500,000
	Credit released and repaid to the company	50,000

Year 2:	(Excess of franked payments over FII = £300,000)		
	Trading profit		1,200,000
	Loss brought forward		500,000
			£700,000
	Less lower of s. 242 relief (£200,000) and excess		
	of franked payments (£300,000)		
			200,000
			£500,000

ACT payable on £300,000	£75,000		
ACT to be set off against CT			
ACT paid		75,000	
Less credit repaid (s. 244)		50,000	
		25,000	
CT at 35%			175,000
Less ACT set off			25,000
CT			£150,000

Relief may not be claimed both under these rules and under the normal set of rules. So when a claim under these rules is made the surplus FII is reduced.[8] There is also to be a reduction from any ACT.[9]

Simon's Taxes D2.413.

[1] TA 1988, s. 242(2) referring to TA 1988, s. 393(2).
[2] TA 1988, s. 242(2) referring to TA 1988, s. 338.
[3] TA 1988, s. 242(2) referring to TA 1988, ss. 75, 76.
[4] CAA 1968, s. 74(3).
[5] TA 1988, s. 242(1).
[6] TA 1988, ss. 242(1), 244(2).
[7] TA 1988, s. 242(5)–(7), 243(4).

  [8] TA 1988, s. 242(1).
  [9] TA 1988, s. 244(2).

25: 35   The taxpayer is not obliged to use his surplus FII. If the relief is claimed any losses must first be set off against any profits normally chargeable to corporation tax[1] including of course capital gains[2] and foreign income on which a lower rate of tax may have been paid because of double taxation relief,[3] and only then against surplus franked investment income.

Simon's Taxes D2.413.
  [1] TA 1988, s. 242(3).
  [2] TA 1988, ss. 393(2) and 6(4).
  [3] Infra, § **36: 25**.

Carry back of losses and capital allowances

25: 36   Losses and capital allowances may be set off against the general profits of a previous accounting period.[1] They may also be set off against the surplus franked investment income of that previous period.[2] If that previous accounting period is longer than that in which the loss or allowance accrues, only a proportion of the profits of that period is available for relief and so only a proportion of the surplus franked investment income of that period. This carry back does not extend to charges on income nor to management expenses.

Simon's Taxes D2.413.
  [1] TA 1988, s. 393(2).
  [2] TA 1988, s. 242(4).

Carry forward of FII (TA 1988, s. 393) and of losses to FII (TA 1988, s. 243)

25: 37   FII still surplus may be rolled forward to the next accounting period where it may be used to frank qualifying distributions or, as just outlined, losses or capital allowances of that next period. For later periods however it may be used *only* to frank qualifying distributions.

Losses, a term which includes capital allowances and certain charges on income,[1] may be rolled forward to be set off against the profits of a later period but only of that trade. The rigid division between FII and trading profits is however softened where the income would be trading income but for being designated FII,[2] as commonly happens to banks and discount houses and investment dealing companies, and losses can be set off against this sort of surplus FII of later accounting periods.

A yet wider use can be made of such surplus FII i.e. FII that would otherwise be trading income. Under TA 1988, s. 393(1) trading losses may be rolled forward to be set off against trading income of subsequent accounting periods. For this purpose such surplus FII can be treated as profits of the later period and the loss set off against them.[3] The same applies to the carrying back of terminal losses.[4] The relief is additional to that already outlined and has the same effects of releasing the tax credit immediately but allowing the loss to be carried over, under TA 1988, s. 393(1) to other years only to the extent that distributions then exceed FII. The claim is much like a claim under TA 1988, s. 242. Finance companies may find this particularly useful since they are likely to be able to distribute more than they receive by way of FII.

Simon's Taxes D2.413.
  [1] TA 1988, s. 393(9).
  [2] TA 1988, s. 393(8).
  [3] TA 1988, s. 243.
  [4] TA 1988, s. 243.

Periods

25: 38   The election whether to put surplus franked investment income to relieve these debit items must be made within two or sometimes six years of the end of the accounting period.[1] In the meantime the surplus may have been used to frank a qualifying distribution and so avoid the payment of ACT. This too is regulated.[2]

Simon's Taxes D2.413.
  [1] Compare TA 1988, s. 242(8)(*a*) (loss relief—2 years) with (*b*) (charges on income and management expenses—6 years).
  [2] TA 1988, s. 242(5).

26   Groups and consortia

26: 01   A group consists of a parent company and its subsidiaries which may in turn have subsidiaries. Broadly, a company is a subsidiary if the other company owns the relevant percentage of its ordinary share capital[1]—more than 50% (commonly called a 51% subsidiary), 75% or more, 90% or more and even 100%.

Ordinary share capital means "all issued share capital (by whatever name called) of the company, other than capital the holders whereof have a right to a dividend at a fixed rate . . . but have no other right to share in the profits of the company".[2] So loan stock and non-participating preference shares are not treated as ordinary share capital unless convertible into, or giving an option to acquire, shares or securities carrying a right greater than that of a dividend at a fixed rate. Conversely, however, shares can be ordinary share capital even if they carry no voting rights.

Ownership must be beneficial[3] but may be direct or indirect. It will be seen that the parent must be a company. If, an individual, P owns all the shares in X Ltd and all the shares in Y Ltd, X Ltd and Y Ltd do not form a group. If a company buys shares in return for £1 the purchaser becomes beneficially entitled to the shares; it is not necessary to prove that the £1 was paid as failure to pay entitles only the vendor (not the Revenue) to set the transfer aside for failure of consideration.[4] Conversely, if a company contracts to sell its shares it is thereafter precluded from disposing of the shares or receiving a dividend or bonus on them as it ceases to be the beneficial owner.[5]

In most instances the share capital owned directly must be held as an investment (not as a trading asset[6]) and the companies must be resident in the UK; if the shares are held indirectly the intermediate companies must hold the assets as investments (and be resident in the UK).

EXAMPLE

A Ltd owns 80% of the ordinary share capital of B Ltd. B Ltd owns 70% of such share capital of C Ltd. B Ltd also owns 30% of D Ltd. A Ltd also owns 25% of D Ltd. A owns 10% of E Ltd which in turn owns 20% of D Ltd.

Since both direct and indirect holdings are aggregated, D is a 51% subsidiary of A Ltd.

A Ltd's direct holdings in D Ltd	25%
A Ltd's indirect holdings in D are:	
B Ltd owns 30% of D Ltd, A Ltd. owns 80% of B Ltd = 80% of 30% =	24%
E Ltd owns 20% of D Ltd, A Ltd owns 10% of E Ltd = 10% of 20% =	2%
A's total holdings in D	51%

For some of the rules that follow[7] these percentages must also be satisfied, as to profits available for distribution and the division of assets available on winding up. The list of rules insisting on these further qualifications has been widened by FA 1989.[8]

Simon's Taxes D2.601–603.

[1] TA 1988, s. 838(1).

[2] TA 1988, s. 832(1); *semble* that a preference share with a fixed rate of dividend but a right to share in surplus assets as a winding up is ordinary share capital as the surplus assets are from profits of the company; see also *Tilcon Ltd v Holland* [1981] STC 365.

[3] TA 1988, s. 838(3); *semble* that beneficial ownership of some only of the rights of ownership may suffice; *Wood Preservation Ltd v Prior* (1968) 45 TC 112—see also SP5/80, **Simon's Taxes, Division H3.2.**

[4] *Irving v Tesco Stores (Holdings) Ltd* [1982] STC 881.

[5] *Semble* that beneficial owneship of some only of the rights of ownership may suffice to retain beneficial ownership but this seems odd if it means that both vendor and purchaser may be entitled to beneficial ownership; *Wood Preservation Ltd v Prior* (1968) 45 TC 112—see also SP 5/80, **Simon's Taxes Division H3.2**, and *J H & S (Timber) Ltd v Quirk* [1973] STC 111.

[6] Note *Cooper v C & J Clark Ltd* [1982] STC 335

[7] On reasons for the change, see infra, § **26: 14**. Other rules involving groups include CGTA 1979, Sch. 5, paras. 3–8, TA 1970, ss. 268A and 270, TA 1988, s. 502(3) and TA 1988, s. 341 (although not confined to groups of resident companies).

[8] FA 1989, s. 99 (dividends and charges).

26: 02   Consortia are particularly common in advanced technology projects and the extension of group income and group relief concepts to them allows for the pooling of resources and of risks. The definition of a consortium varies (infra, §§ **26: 07** and **26: 15**).

Simon's Taxes D2.601–603.

ONE COMPANY OR A GROUP?

26: 03   If a company's trading activities are divided up between different companies, the premise of UK tax law is that each company is a separate entity with separate profits and therefore separate corporation tax liability. There is no simple charging of the group as a whole on its group profits. However this premise is relaxed by rules (1)–(6) which follow.[1] One should note also the restriction on the deduction of the accrued income element on a deep discount security if the security is held by another group member.[2]

---

[1] A seventh, dealing with the treatment of a surrender of a company tax refund within a group, will come into force in 1992 (at the earliest), FA 1989, s. 102.

[2] TA 1988, Sch. 4, para. 9 supra, § **25: 18**.

26: 04   The decision whether to run a business through one company or through a group of companies depends upon many factors, not all concerned with taxation. It appears that in practice the activities of a single company will be regarded as one trade unless they are widely different. This has tax advantages in that expenditure incurred for dual purposes is non-deductible unless they are regarded as one trade; one may also avoid the problem of the non-deductibility of pre-commencement and post cessation expenses.[1]

Further, sales within the group will give rise to immediate profits whereas in a single company profits will not accrue until the sale is made to an outsider. By concession the existence of separate companies is ignored for certain rules concerning directors.[2] A further problem is that the trading income of the subsidiary will be investment income of the parent if passed to it as dividend or interest. Where a company is proposing to dispose of a subsidiary it may wish to reduce its potential capital gains liability by causing the subsidiary to declare a (large) dividend. The Revenue has indicated that it will not normally regard the *Ramsay* approach as applicable to such a distribution.[3]

Simon's Taxes D2.661–662.

[1] A payment by Company A for the purposes of its subsidiary, B, or for the purpose of both A and B, is not deductible by A *Garforth v Tankard Carpets Ltd* [1980] STC 251; distinguish *Robinson v Scott Bader Co Ltd* [1981] STC 436 and see supra § 7: 92.

[2] See extra-statutory concession A4 (1988), Simon's Taxes, Division H2.2.

[3] See a letter from the Revenue to the Institute of Chartered Accountants for England and Wales [1985] STI p. 568.

(1) INTRA GROUP DIVIDENDS—GROUP INCOME

26: 05   If a parent company has a subsidiary which carries on a trade, the subsidiary company may wish to pass its profit to its parent. If this is done by dividend ACT will be due and the parent receives franked investment income. This cumbersome method could be a check on the normal business practice of operating through separate companies, so if both payer and payee elect,[1] the payment is excluded from the ACT system.

Simon's Taxes D2.611, 613.

[1] On procedure see TA 1988, s. 247(3) and [1979] STI p. 199.

26: 06   The payer must be a 51% subsidiary of the payee, which means that dividends from a subsidiary to a parent may be paid gross—but not vice versa. In calculating the 51% of the shares owned beneficially by the parent one does not include shares in a non-resident company nor shares owned indirectly if profit on the sale would be a trading receipt of the direct owners.

As from the passing of FA 1989 dividends will only qualify for group income treatment if the 51% test is met as to profits available for distribution or assets on a winding up as well as ownership of ordinary share capital.[1]

Simon's Taxes D2.602, 603, 615.

[1] TA 1988, s. 247(8A) added by FA 1989, s. 99(4).

The consortium

26: 07   The regime also applies where the payer is a trading or holding company[1] owned by a consortium the members of which include the company receiving the dividend. For this purpose the company is owned by the consortium if the member companies[2] are UK-resident and own at least 75% of the company's ordinary share capital (none owning less than 5%). As from the passing of FA 1989, the 5% must also be satisfied as to distribution of profits and of assets on a notional winding-up.[3]

Simon's Taxes D2.612.
[1] A trading or holding company is either one whose business consists wholly or mainly of the carrying on of a trade or trades (a trading company) or one whose business consists wholly or mainly in the holding of shares or securities of trading companies which are its 90% subsidiaries.
[2] TA 1988, s. 413(6). For payments made before 31st December 1984 the maximum number of consortium members was restricted to five.
[3] New TA 1988, s. 247(9)(c) added by FA 1989, s. 99(5).

Group income: TA 1988, s. 247

26: 08 Dividends paid and received in this way are "group income" and are not subject to ACT; they are neither franked payments of the payer nor FII of the payee. They are not subject to CT in the hands of the payee. The payer may, despite the election, nonetheless pay ACT when paying the dividend. This may be useful since the parent cannot use its subsidiary's FII to frank its own distributions.

The regime applies only if *both* companies elect in writing and in advance.[1] Either party may revoke an election and the company paying the dividend may by notice waive that election in relation to any amount of dividend specified in the notice.

EXAMPLE

X Ltd has a wholly owned subsidiary, Y Ltd. The following are the results for the period ending in the financial year 1989 with ACT at $\frac{27}{33}$ and the CT rate at 35%:

	X Ltd.	Y Ltd.
Trading profit	£500,000	£300,000
Dividends paid (net)	£187,500	£112,500

Without TA 1988, s. 247 the dividend paid by Y to X is subject to ACT and is FII in the hands of X.
CT liability will be:

X Ltd CT at 35%		£175,000
Less ACT on dividends	£62,500	
Less credit on FII	37,500	25,000
MCT		£150,000
Y Ltd CT at 35%		£105,000
Less ACT on dividend		37,500
MCT		£67,500

With TA 1988, s. 247 no ACT is due when the dividend is paid by Y; the payment becomes group income—not FII—of X and cannot relieve X's ACT liability.

X Ltd CT at 35%	£175,000
Less ACT on dividends	62,500
MCT	£112,500
Y Ltd CT at 35%	105,000
Less ACT on dividend	nil
MCT	£105,000

It will be seen that in this simple example TA 1988, s. 247 makes no difference to the overall amount of CT £280,000, ACT £62,500 or MCT £217,500; what it does however is to reallocate the burden of ACT and MCT as between X and Y. The importance of the provision is as follows:

(i) convenience—if TA 1988, s. 247 is invoked X and Y avoid the administrative costs of making the ACT payment and claiming the FII credit;

(ii) cash-flow—ACT is accounted for quarterly; if Y pays its dividend in the first quarter and X in the last quarter there is a cash flow advantage in the ACT being paid in the fourth quarter.

(iii) ACT and FII—if TA 1988, s. 247 is not invoked Y might find itself with surplus ACT and X with surplus FII; if there is to be surplus ACT it is best located in the parent since the parent can pass it to its subsidiary but not vice versa (see, § **26: 10**); further, group income can only flow in the opposite direction, that is from the subsidiary to the parent.

Where both X and Y are trading companies it is usual for the election to be made. However if X is an investment company it will need sufficient FII against which to set its management expenses. If the subsidiary has FII of its own it may prefer not to invoke TA 1988, s. 247 so as to ensure that it is not left with surplus FII.

The election can only refer to dividends and not to other distributions. It is further necessary that the payee should be beneficially entitled to the income. Income received by some other persons on behalf of or in trust for the company qualifies as group income.[2] The election does not apply when the receiving company would be entitled to claim repayment of the tax credits by being exempted.[3]

Simon's Taxes D2.611.
[1] For details, see TA 1988, ss. 247 and 248.
[2] TA 1988, s. 247(10).
[3] TA 1988, s. 247(5)—or would be so exempt but for TA 1988, ss. 235 and 237.

(2) TRANSFER PAYMENTS—CHARGES ON INCOME (51% SUBSIDIARIES)

26: 09 A joint election procedure is available when one company makes a payment which qualifies as a charge on its income. This is available when the companies are in the same relationship as that for group income or where the recipient is a 51% subsidiary of the other. Again the tests have been tightened for payments after the passing of FA 1989.[1] Thus whereas group dividends flow up, charges on income may flow up or down. The payment may flow from one subsidiary to another only if both payer and payee are subsidiaries of a parent company and all three are resident.

If the election is made, the company on making the payment does not deduct income tax but makes the payment gross—TA 1988, s. 349 and 350 are excluded.[2] It appears that once the election is made all subsequent payments must be made gross. There is no room for selection as there is for dividends. These charges are still deductible by the payer, and are income of the payee.

A covenanted donation to a charity made after 18th March 1986 will be a charge only if paid after deduction of tax.[3]

A payment of interest is treated as received on the same date as that on which the paying company is treated as paying it. This rule applies to all payments on interest between related companies and not just when a TA 1988, s. 247 election can be made.[4]

Simon's Taxes D2.613.
[1] TA 1988, s. 247(8A) and 9(*c*) added by FA 1989, s. 99.
[2] TA 1988, s. 247(4).
[3] TA 1988, s. 339(7), inserted by FA 1986, s. 30(2).
[4] TA 1988, s. 341. Companies are related if one controls the other or they are under common control. The rule is not confined to resident companies.

(3) SURRENDER OF ACT[1] (51% subsidiaries)

26: 10 A parent company which has paid ACT on dividends in an accounting period may surrender all or part of that ACT to any company or companies which are its 51% subsidiaries throughout the accounting period, although not up to a parent.[1] Surrender to a company which is a fellow-subsidiary of a third company is now permitted.[2] There is no relief for a consortium. The subsidiary is treated as paying the ACT surrendered to it on the day the parent made the distribution giving rise to the ACT; where the parent made more than one payment at different times the subsidiary's ACT is attributed rateably to the different dates.[3] Surrender is permitted even though the ACT is not surplus to the transferor.[4]

The ACT must have been payable in respect of a dividend as opposed to any other form of distribution[5] and it must not have been carried back from another year.[6] The ACT so taken over by the subsidiary may not be carried back to any of its previous periods and may not itself be surrendered. However for the period in respect of which the surrender takes place the surrendered ACT is used before the company's own ACT thus freeing that to be carried back.[7] The surrender may be claimed up to six years after the end of the accounting period to which it relates.[8]

The subsidiary must be a 51% subsidiary as for group income but the parent must be beneficially entitled to more than 50% both of the income and of the assets on a winding up[9] and there must be no arrangements for transfer of control of the subsidiary separate from that of the parent.[10] In determining the 51% holdings it does not qualify if a profit or sale by the direct owner would be a holding receipt, nor if they are in non-resident companies[11].

One advantage of the power to surrender concerns companies whose subsidiaries trade overseas. When the foreign tax burdens of the subsidiaries are finally settled, ACT can be passed to the companies with the lowest foreign and so the highest UK taxes.

Any payment to the surrendering company up to the amount of the ACT made in return for the surrender is ignored in computing the profits of both payer and payee.[12]

The normal practice is for the parent of the group to pay all ACT on dividends, any dividends for subsidiaries being paid without ACT under the rules outlined at § **26: 08**. The parent then surrenders to the subsidiary such ACT as is needed to offset the subsidiary's CT liability.

On planning one should note first the rule that the subsidiary may not carry back the surrendered ACT to previous years; this means that when the subsidiary will wish to carry ACT back it should make its dividend to its parent subject to ACT in the usual way and so not elect for group income treatment under § **26: 08**. Secondly, the rule that the subsidiary must have been a 51% subsidiary throughout the whole of the parent's account period means that care must be taken when a company joins or leaves a group; the subsidiary can of course use its own ACT in the usual way; once again care is needed on deciding whether or not to elect for group income treatment as well as in setting the dates for the periods of account; this is reinforced by the related rule that the subsidiary may set the surrendered ACT only against its corporation tax liability for those periods throughout which it was a 51% subsidiary.[13] In appropriate cases this may mean consideration should be given to changing the period of account of either the subsidiary or the parent. Where a company leaves a group the Revenue view is that any ACT which has been surrendered to it and has not yet been used is no longer available for set off; here too the problem may be avoided by opting out of the group income scheme and allowing the subsidiary to pay and use its own ACT.

When several subsidiaries are involved it may prove more useful to spread the ACT around rather than give it all to one subsidiary; this is especially so if there is a risk that the favoured subsidiary would not be able to carry the surrendered ACT back but only forward.

Simon's Taxes D2.655.
[1] Perhaps because much the same can be achieved by a group income election under TA 1988, s. 247(1). The previous relief enables a parent to pay advance corporation tax to a subsidiary even though in respect of a dividend originally flowing as group income from the subsidiary to the parent.
[2] TA 1988, s. 240(5) as amended by FA 1989, s. 97 for accounting periods ending after 13th March 1989.
[3] TA 1988, s. 240(2).
[4] TA 1988, s. 240.
[5] But see TA 1988, s. 240(9) on purchase of own shares by company.
[6] TA 1988, s. 240(7).
[7] TA 1988, s. 240(4).
[8] TA 1988, s. 240(6).
[9] TA 1988, s. 240(10).
[10] TA 1988, s. 240(11).
[11] TA 1988, s. 240(10).
[12] TA 1988, s. 240(8).
[13] TA 1988, s. 240(6).

---

(4) DISTRIBUTIONS

26: 11   The transfer of an asset at an undervalue is normally to be treated as a distribution. However, this does not apply when both transferor and recipient are resident in the UK and one is a 51% subsidiary of the other or both are 51% subsidiaries of another resident company.[1] In determining whether the company is a 51% subsidiary of the other, holdings, whether direct or indirect, do not qualify if a profit on the sale would be a trading receipt or if the company is non-resident.[2]

In other respects the definition of distribution is unchanged save that a distribution made by one company out of its assets but in respect of shares or securities of another company in the same 90% group is treated as a distribution if all other conditions are satisfied.[3] This is primarily concerned to extend to groups another provision dealing with distribution by two or more companies to each other's members; such avoidance schemes do not work.[4]

Simon's Taxes D1.106.
[1] TA 1988, s. 209(5).
[2] TA 1988, s. 209(7).
[3] TA 1988, s. 254(1)–(4).
[4] TA 1988, s. 254(8).

(5) GROUP RELIEF (75% SUBSIDIARIES AND CONSORTIA)

26:12 Group relief enables current trading losses, capital allowances, excess management expenses of investment companies and excess charges on income to be surrendered by one company (the surrendering company) to another (the claimant company) enabling the latter to put the other company's loss etc. against its total profits. Both companies must satisfy the group or consortium tests throughout their respective accounting period and need not be members of the same group or consortium when the claim is made.[1]

If Company A makes a loss and surrenders that relief to Company B, Company A may insist upon receiving some payment. This will be particularly so if it is not a wholly owned subsidiary so that there will be different minority interests as well as different creditors. If the amount paid is due under a legally enforceable[2] agreement and does not exceed the amount surrendered the payment is ignored in computing the profits and losses of either company and is treated neither as a distribution nor as a charge on income.

This device is of particular use when for example a company with foreign income is already relieved from CT by the foreign tax credit or where the surrendering company is entitled to the reduced rate of 25% and the claimant is not.

The Revenue has indicated that where a UK holding company is interposed between UK resident companies and a non-resident parent the device will not normally be regarded as falling foul of the *Ramsay* approach.[3] This is equally true where the owner is an individual or his family.[3] In these instances the purpose of the holding company is to obtain or maximise group relief.

Simon's Taxes D2.641–650.
[1] *A W Chapman Ltd v Hennessey* [1982] STC 214. On form of claim see *Gallic Leasing Ltd v Coburn* [1989] STC 354.
[2] *Haddock v Wilmot Breeden Ltd* [1975] STC 255.
[3] See a letter from the Revenue to the Institute of Chartered Accountants for England and Wales, *Simon's Tax Intelligence* 1985, p. 568.

The group[1]

26:13 Two companies are members of the same group for group relief purposes if one is a 75% subsidiary of the other or both are 75% subsidiaries of a third company. For this purpose only a body corporate resident in the UK qualifies. So the presence of a non-resident company with a 26% holding disqualifies group relief for a resident UK company with a 74% holding. One must ignore any share capital owned directly or indirectly in a non-resident company and any share capital owned directly or indirectly if a profit on sale would be a trading receipt of the direct owners.

Simon's Taxes D2.642.
[1] TA 1988, s. 413(5).

26: 14   In addition, the parent must be entitled to not less than 75% of any profits available for distribution to equity holders of the subsidiary company and to not less than 75% of any of its assets available for distribution to its equity holders on a winding up.[1] The purpose of these rules is to confine the passing of the reliefs, especially capital allowance, to parents who were such in commercial as well as legal terms at some time during the accounting period in which the loss arises. It is also necessary, for similar reasons, to show that there are no arrangements in existence for transfer of control of the surrendering company without also transferring control of the claimant company.[2] The term "arrangements" is broadly construed.[3] If such arrangements are anticipated it may be desirable to end the accounting period before the arrangements are made. Without some such rule an outside company could buy participation preference shares to establish 75% control and later the shares would be redeemed or sold back to the parent; in this way the loss could be sold to an outsider.

Simon's Taxes D2.642.
[1] TA 1988, s. 413(7)–(10) and Sch. 18.
[2] TA 1988, s. 410(1)–(6) (extra-statutory concession C10 (1988) on effect of first refusal agreement between consortium members) and SP 5/80, **Simon's Taxes, Division H3.2**. See also ICAEW Memorandum (TR 713—No 16) *Simon's Tax Intelligence* 1988, p. 714 N.
[3] *Pilkington Bros Ltd v IRC* [1982] STC 103; *Irving v Tesco Stores (Holdings) Ltd* [1982] STC 881.

Consortium

26: 15   Group relief may also be claimed by members of a consortium in respect of losses and other debit items incurred by companies which the consortium owns.[1] A consortium owns a company if 75% of the ordinary share capital of that company is directly and beneficially owned between the consortium members, each owning at least 5%.[2] All the companies must be resident.[3] The requirements of entitlement to divisible income and to assets on a winding up applied to groups apply also to consortia.[4]

The group relief may be claimed by members of the consortium in three situations:

(*a*) if the surrendering company (*i*) is owned by the consortium, (*ii*) is not a 75% subsidiary of any company but (*iii*) is a trading company.

(*b*) if the surrendering company (*i*) is a 90% subsidiary of a holding company which is owned by the consortium, (*ii*) is not a 75% subsidiary of any other company but (*iii*) is a trading company, and (*c*) if the surrendering company (*i*) is a holding company which is owned by the consortium but (*ii*) is not a 75% subsidiary of that company.

The relief may be claimed by the member of the consortium and not by the holding company. As with ordinary group relief the relief may not be claimed by a member company if a receipt on the disposal of that member's shares in the trading or holding company is nil for that accounting period.

Group relief within a consortium may pass in either direction.[5] Each member may claim only that part of the loss which is proportionate to its share in the consortium. Where a member surrenders downwards to a trading company that amount can only be set against a similar proportion of the trading company's profits.[5] There is no surrender to the intermediate holding company but that company may claim group relief proper. There is no objection to finding a group within a group or a group within a consortium.

Simon's Taxes D2.642.

[1] TA 1988, s. 402(3).

[2] TA 1988, s. 413(6). Before 27th July 1984 100% of the ordinary share capital had to be held by the consortium, the maximum number of member companies was 5, and there was no requirement of a 5% holding by each company. There was transitional relief to 31st March 1986 where the 5% condition *only* was not met.

[3] TA 1988, s. 258(8). So the membership of one non-resident company is fatal to group relief for the other members. In such circumstances assets are commonly owned by the non-resident company and leased by the company owned by the consortium—of which of course the non-resident is not a member.

[4] TA 1988, s. 413(8).

[5] TA 1988, s. 402(2); a surrender downwards may affect that company's ability to surrender further losses within its group (TA 1988, s. 411(9)).

Groups and consortia

26: 16 For accounting periods beginning after 31st July 1985, it is possible for consortium relief to "flow through" a consortium member to and from other companies in the same group.[1] The maximum relief which may be claimed through a consortium member is restricted,[2] and it is essential that the company claiming the relief was a member of the group throughout the accounting period(s) in which the consortium member could have claimed the relief, or the accounting period in which the loss was incurred.[3]

It is also possible to surrender part of the available relief to a group company and part to a consortium company, subject to restrictions on the amount available for relief.[4]

Simon's Taxes Division D2.642.

[1] TA 1988, s. 406.

[2] TA 1988, s. 406(4) and (8).

[3] TA 1988, s. 406(2) and (9).

[4] TA 1988, ss. 405 and 411(9).

Reliefs

26: 17 Four reliefs may be surrendered to the claimant company.

(1) Trading losses as computed under TA 1988, s. 393, may be set off

against the total profits of the claimant company for its corresponding accounting period.[1] The trading loss of a consortium-owned company must, as far as possible, be set off against the company's other profits of the same accounting period and only the balance is available for set off against the profits of consortium member companies.[2]

(2) Minor capital allowances in excess of income of the relevant class arising in that accounting period;[3] these are allowances which attract relief through the discharge of tax rather than being treated as a trading expense (supra § **8: 07**). These can be surrendered to the extent that they exceed income of the relevant class. Again the set off is against total profits of the claimant company for its corresponding accounting period.

(3) Management expenses[4] in excess of the company's profits may be set off against the total profits of the claimant company (whether or not itself an investment company) for the corresponding accounting period of the claimant company.[5] The total profits of the surrendering company means profits before deduction of any losses or allowances of other periods and before deduction of the expenses of management.[6]

(4) The amount paid by way of charges on income of the surrendering company and exceeding the profits of that company for that period may be surrendered to be set off against the total profits of the claimant company for the corresponding accounting period.[7] The profits of the surrendering company are computed before the deduction of losses or allowances of any other period and before the deduction of expenses of management rolled forward from a previous period.[8] This means that if charges are carried forward from a previous period they cannot be used to free current reliefs for grouping; such charges can therefore become locked into the company. A problem has arisen over these charges since the Revenue sometimes argue that excess charges can be surrendered only if incurred wholly and exclusively for the purpose of the trade of the surrendering company; on this reasoning no relief could be given where a loan is raised to finance the acquisition of a subsidiary. There seems to be nothing in TA 1988, s. 403(7) to justify this approach.

Reliefs, (3) and (4), unlike (1) or (2), must be set off against other profits of the company and only the resulting balance surrendered. Both (3) and (4) may be permanently lost if the company's income bears only foreign as opposed to UK tax since neither can be rolled forward.

In these four instances there are references to the total profits of the claimant company for the corresponding accounting period. Where the accounting periods of the two companies do not coincide, an apportionment is made. Where the two companies are not "grouped" or "consorted" throughout the accounting periods—as where a company joins a group—an apportionment may be made.[9]

Special rules apply when companies join or leave the group or consortium and elaborate provisions are designed to ensure that relief is given only once.[10]

The surrendering company is not of course obliged to give up its loss relief and it may, if it wishes, surrender only part of the loss. Further the relief may be claimed by more than one company in the group or member of the consortium.

The relief if claimed is taken as exhausting profits of the accounting period in which it is claimed in priority to other reliefs that may be brought back into that period from future ones.[11]

Simon's Taxes **D2.643**.
[1] TA 1988, s. 403(1).
[2] TA 1988, s. 403(10), (11).
[3] TA 1988, s. 403(3).
[4] Infra, § **29: 02**.
[5] TA 1988, s. 403(4) but not insurance companies: subs. (6) ((5)).
[6] TA 1988, s. 403(5).
[7] TA 1988, s. 403(6), but note TA 1988, s. 787.
[8] TA 1988, s. 403(8).
[9] TA 1988, s. 408(2).
[10] TA 1988, ss. 409 and 411.
[11] TA 1988, s. 407. Terminal loss relief can only be given against trading income whereas group relief can be given against total profits—hence group relief should be claimed against non-trading income and chargeable gains if terminal loss relief is foreseen.

---

(6) INTRA-GROUP TRANSFERS OF CAPITAL ASSETS (75% SUBSIDIARIES)

Tax neutrality TA 1970, s. 273

26: 18   The transfer of a chargeable asset between two members of a group takes place at such figure as ensures there is neither chargeable gain nor allowable loss.[1] The effect is to postpone any capital gains liability until the asset is disposed of outside the group. This is a matter of law, not of election and overrides the normal rule that bargains otherwise than at arm's length are to be treated as taking place at market value.[2]

The general rule is excluded in certain situations; what these have in common is that value is being received by one company but the capital gains structure, for reasons of its own, treats the receipt as being in exchange for an asset. The first situation is where a debt is disposed of by one group member to another and the debt is disposed of by being satisfied in whole or in part. This rule contains the interesting idea that there is a disposal of a debt when it is satisfied—as distinct from the disposal of the property being transferred to satisfy the debt. There is also the point that except for a debt on a security no chargeable gain can arise on the disposal of a debt. One is therefore left with the idea that s. 273 is excluded where a debt on a security is satisfied—as where one member company pays off a debenture and another member company receives a payment in respect of it; the overall effect being presumably to allow the claim of a loss or, occasionally, to tax a gain—as where a debt is acquired for less than face value and afterwards settled in full.[3]

The second is where redeemable shares are disposed of on redemption. So a gain on redemption will be taxable notwithstanding that there is a disposal of the shares in exchange for the consideration received on redemption.

The third is a disposal by or to an investment trust.[4]

The fourth is the deemed disposal which arises on a capital distribution by a member company in which it holds shares; there will still be a disposal by the company making the capital distribution and this *will* fall within s. 273.[5]

Where the asset is disposed of by destruction and compensation is payable, the disposal is deemed to be to the person who ultimately bears the burden of paying the compensation money, e.g. an insurance company.[6]

The principle applies when it is a disposal or deemed disposal and an acquisition. It was held that it also applied where statute directed that there should be neither an acquisition nor a disposal.[7] However, this has been reversed for disposals after 14th March 1988 which come within the capital gains reorganisation provisions.[8]

These postponement provisions do not apply to transfers between subsidiary and a parent in liquidation since, once liquidation of the parent has begun, the shares in the subsidiary are not held by the parent beneficially but on trust for its own members.[9] The effect of a voluntary winding up is less clear.[10] Distributions by a subsidiary in liquidation are likewise taxed immediately. These problems can be overcome by arranging for transfers and distributions by or to the parent before liquidation.

As there is no group relief for capital losses it is common to use one company to make all disposals outside the group of all chargeable assets. This ensures that the allowable losses can be set against the chargeable gains.[11]

The Revenue view is that the routing of assets through a company which has allowable capital losses is safe unless the assets were acquired after the losses had arisen. The Revenue's concern is that, where the assets were acquired after the losses had arisen, the taxpayers may be trying to transfer a loss from one group to another. Even here however it is unlikely that the new approach will be used "where losses were a relatively insubstantial element in the acquisition, as evidenced by the circumstances in which they were utilised and the commerciality of the circumstances surrounding the acquisition".[12]

Simon's Taxes D2.623.

[1] TA 1970, s. 273.

[2] CGTA 1979, s. 29A. S. 273 applies "notwithstanding any provision in CGTA fixing the amount of the consideration deemed to be received." It might be argued that if a sale takes place at market value s. 273 should not apply as there is nothing "deemed" about the consideration however this seems unlikely to succeed.

[3] As in the example of a loan account—**Simon's Taxes D2.623.**

[4] TA 1970, s. 273(2)(c) added by FA 1980, s. 81.

[5] *Innocent v Whaddon Estates Ltd* [1982] STC 115.

[6] TA 1970, s. 273(3).

[7] As in CGTA 1979, s. 78 *Westcott v Woolcombers Ltd* [1986] STC 182; see London [1986] BTR 117.

[8] FA 1988, s. 115 adding s. 273(2A): the corporate reorganisation provisions are CGTA 1979, ss. 78 and 85, *supra*, § **19: 07** et seq.

[9] *Ayerst v C & K (Construction) Ltd* [1975] STC 345, [1975] 2 All ER 537. The House of Lords decided only that the company ceased to be beneficial owner of its assets. The Court of Appeal had held that the ownership was in suspense [1975] STC 1, [1975] 1 All ER 162.

[10] *Wadsworth Morton Ltd v Jenkinson* [1966] 3 All ER 702, 43 TC 479.

[11] *Moores & Rowland's Yellow Tax Guide 1985-6* p. 152 which points out that the Revenue do not seek to use s. 776 to prevent this when land is involved.

[12] [1985] STI p. 568 at 570.

The group[1]

26: 19 A group comprises a principal company and all its 75% subsidiaries, all of which must be resident. The 75% is applied to the beneficial ownership of shares; unlike group income this relief is available even though the shares are held otherwise than as investments. A company owns shares beneficially if it is free to dispose of them as it wishes; it is irrelevant that the shares may not be owned very long.[2]

The mere passing of a winding-up resolution or order is not sufficient to end group membership.[3] Further, the group remains the same group so long as the same company remains the principal company. If the principal company becomes a 75% subsidiary of another company the group is regarded as expanded rather than ended and refounded.

FA 1989 s. 138 makes major changes in the definition of a group. The purpose behind the changes is to counter the use of "bridge" companies. These are arrangements which use a company with special classes of share; in turn these enable the commercial control of companies to pass to a company outside the group while allowing the company to remain within the group structure for tax purposes and so avoiding the triggering of charges that would otherwise arise on the company ceasing to be a member of the group. This has led to the avoidance of tax on the capital gains that would otherwise arise on the sale of a subsidiary or the sale of an asset.[5]

Under the new rules the group is still made up of the principal company and its 75% subsidiaries, including 75% subsidiaries of those subsidiaries and so on. However, two major changes are made. First a subsidiary which is not an effective 51% subsidiary is excluded.[6] A company is an effective 51% subsidiary only if the parent is beneficially entitled to more than 50% of any profits available for distribution or of any assets on a winding up.[7]

The second change is that in future a company can only be a principal company if it is at the head of the corporate chain. So a company cannot be a principal company if it is a 75% subsidiary of another company.[8] There is an exception if the company does not form part of a group because it is not an effective 51% subsidiary.[9] To reinforce this policy it is provided that a company may not be a member of more than one group; to carry this policy through the legislation contains a descending order of tests.[10] To prevent a charge from arising unexpectedly as a result of this change TA 1988, s. 273(3) is also amended so as to provide that where a principal company subsequently becomes a 75% subsidiary of another company, thereby bringing two groups together, the two are regarded as being the same group for these purposes. These purposes include the question whether a company has ceased to be a member of another group.[11] Thus a charge under TA 1988 s. 278 is not triggered simply by such an event. It is also provided that the winding up of a company in the group does not result in either that company or any other company in the group being treated as ceasing to be a member of the group.[12]

Simon's Taxes D2.622, 623.

[1] TA 1970, s. 272.

[2] *Burman v Hedges and Butler Ltd* [1979] STC 136.

[3] TA 1970, s. 272(4).

[4] The former TA 1970, s. 272(1)(*b*) and (*c*) are repealed and subs. 272(1A) to (1F) are added; there is also a consequential change for IHT—s. 138(6) amending IHTA 1984, s. 97. These rules are further backed up by a cross reference to TA 1988, Sch. 18.
[5] *Simon's Tax Intelligence* 1989, p. 222. Hansard Standing Committee G, col. 597.
[6] TA 1988, s. 272(1A)(*a*).
[7] TA 1970, s. 272(1E).
[8] TA 1970, s. 272(1B).
[9] TA 1970, s. 272(1C).
[10] TA 1970, s. 272(1D).
[11] TA 1970, s. 272(3); as amended by FA 1989, s. 138(3).
[12] TA 1970, s. 272(4); as amended by FA 1989, s. 138(4).

Trading stock (TA 1970 s. 274)

26: 20 Where one company transfers a capital asset to another company in the group and the recipient company appropriates the asset to trading stock, the rule that the disposal should be at such a figure that neither gain nor loss accrues collides with the principle that the asset should enter the trading stock at market value.[1] The legislation therefore provides that the recipient company should receive the asset as a capital asset and then transfer the asset to trading stock at market value. This gives the recipient the right to choose between an immediate chargeable gain and a later Schedule D, Case I profit. Where the asset transferred was trading stock of the transferring company, but is received as a capital asset by the recipient, it is treated as having ceased to be trading stock before the transfer; the consequence is that for capital gains purposes the transferor is treated as having disposed of the asset to himself at whatever figure is entered in the books of the trade in respect of the asset.[2]

Simon's Taxes D2.624.
[1] TA 1970, s. 274(1) referring to CGTA 1979, s. 122; supra, § **20: 04**.
[2] TA 1970, s. 274(2) refers to CGTA 1979, s. 122(2) which treats the disposal as being at such figure as is entered in the computation of trading profit; this will usually be current market value because of *Sharkey v Wernher*.

Disposal outside the group (TA 1970 s. 275)

26: 21 Once the asset is disposed of to a person outside the group the normal liability to corporation tax in respect of the capital gain will follow.[1] If an asset has been acquired under an intra-group transfer and is later disposed of outside the group, provision has to be made to reflect the group's ownership of the asset. So the disposing company is treated as having acquired the asset when it was originally acquired by a group member.[2] Provision is made for recognising the previous ownership by another group member both for pre-1965 acquisitions[3] and for capital allowances so account must be taken of any capital allowances made to previous group owners.[4] The tax may be recovered from the principal member at the time the gain accrues and from any previous owner.[5]

Simon's Taxes D2.625.
[1] FA 1972, s. 93.
[2] TA 1970, s. 275(1); however this does not apply to a disposal to or by an investment trust after 31st March 1980; see s. 275(3) added by FA 1980, s. 81.

³ TA 1970, s. 275(2).
⁴ TA 1970, s. 275(1).
⁵ TA 1988, s. 347.

Business assets—roll-over relief[1] (TA 1970 s. 276)

26: 22 Another way in which the group is recognised as the relevant owner concerns the roll-over provisions for business assets. All the trades of the member companies are treated as being one trade so that if X Co sells an asset and buys another for use by Y Co, its subsidiary, roll-over may be claimed. If Y Co buys the assets for its own use relief will be available if the group requirements are satisfied when Y buys the asset even though it did not satisfy them when X sold.[2]

Where the asset disposed of was acquired before the disposer became a group member, it is understood that the Revenue view is that rollover relief is not available for the gain attributable to the period before X joined the group. However this point is not taken where X's joining the group was a genuine commercial arrangement.

This rule does not apply if the acquisition by Y is itself a transfer within the group. Without such a rule X could make a disposal outside the group and realise a gain which could then be rolled over by a shuffling of assets within the group. The rule is also excluded if X's disposal is a transfer within the group—presumably this simply reinforces the no gain no loss rule in s. 273.

For the purposes of the rule restricting rollover relief where the replacement asset is a depreciating asset, not only are all the trades treated as one but that trade is deemed to be carried on by one person.[3] Where an event occurs giving rise to a chargeable gain that gain accrues to the member holding the replacement asset at that time.

Simon's Taxes D2.626.
[1] TA 1970, s. 276. On position of a non-trading member, see [1971] BTR 268.
[2] This is the Revenue view, Statement of Practice D19, **Simon's Taxes, Division H3.3.**
[3] TA 1970, s. 276(2).

Anti-avoidance

(1) Company leaving the group: TA 1970, s. 278

26:23 The privilege of postponing tax liability on transfers within the group was in addition to the basic rule that there could be no charge without a disposal of the asset. So an asset would be transferred to another company within the group in exchange for shares which would then be sold to a stranger company without giving rise to a chargeable gain.

This situation is now regulated by TA 1970, s. 278. This does not prescribe a deemed disposal when the company ceases to be a member of the group but instead directs that if a company leaves a group[1] (the departing company) and it then holds a chargeable asset which it has acquired from another member of the group within the previous six years, the departing member is treated as having disposed of the asset and reacquired it at its market value at the time of its *acquisition*.[2] The effect of this is to remove retrospectively the immunity enjoyed by the intra group acquisition, but to impose the charge primarily on the company then acquiring the asset. There is power to recover the unpaid tax from the principal member of the group and from the company which formerly owned the asset.[3] This provision will apply where an asset is transferred to a subsidiary and the subsidiary later leaves the group through the parent selling its shares; in logic but probably not in practice it applies equally clearly where the asset is transferred by the subsidiary to the parent and the parent leaves the group through the sale of its shares in the subsiduary.[4]

These rules are modified as a result of the changes made by FA 1989. First, it is expressly provided that where a principal company subsequently becomes a 75% subsidiary of another company, thereby bringing two groups together, the two are regarded as being the same group so that this event will not of itself cause a company to cease to be a member of the group.[5] The winding up of a company is not to have such an effect either.[6]

A new s. 278(3B) applies that where s. 278(3) would be triggered in respect of a company deemed to leave the group only by reason of the principal company becoming a member of another group. In such circumstances a deemed sale of assets previously transferred under s. 273 to the company leaving the group, will be deemed to occur if within six years of the company leaving the group, it ceases to satisfy certain conditions.[7] Those conditions are.[8]

(i) that the company remain a 75% subsidiary of one of the members of the group; and

(ii) that the company remain an effective 51% subsidiary.[9] The chargeable gain or allowable loss arises at the time the conditions cease to be satisfied.[10] In calculating the gain or loss s. 278(3F) requires that CGTA 1979, s. 26 shall apply.

Where on the commencement of the new definitions of a group, a company would cease to be a member of a group and s. 278(3) would apply, the company is not to be treated as selling the asset unless under the old definition it would cease to be a member of the group and this occurs within six years.[11]

TA 1988, as originally enacted but still in force, provides that these rules are to apply whether the company on leaving the group owns the original asset or another in respect of which replacement roll-over relief has been obtained under CGTA 1979, s. 115.[12] The relief under s. 115 could not be claimed when the new company leaves the group since it applies only when a new asset is acquired. An asset owned by the chargeable company when it leaves the group is also treated as being the same as the asset acquired from the other group member if it derives its value in whole or in part from the first asset;[13] this rather delphic rule is stated to apply specifically where the first asset was a leasehold interest and the second asset is the freehold the lessee having in the meantime acquired the reversionary interest.[14]

Where two or more companies leave the group at the same time and together they form a group the rules do not apply to acquisitions which had taken place between companies within the newly independent group.[15] Also outside the rules are certain types of merger, provided that they do not have the avoidance of tax as one of their main objects, and demergers, infra, **§ 26: 28**.[16]

The section is also excluded where the company ceases to be a member of the group by being wound up or dissolved or in consequence of another member being wound up or dissolved.[17] The Revenue currently hold the view that a distribution of shares in a subsidiary company by a parent which is in liquidation is a liquidator's distribution in the course of winding up rather than one in consequence of winding up—and so s. 278 applies.

EXAMPLE

A has a subsidiary, B. In 1982 it transferred to B an asset with a base cost of £10,000 but with a current value of £15,000. TA 1970, s. 273 ensures that the base cost to B is £10,000 and that no chargeable gain arises in 1982.

If, in 1986, A sells its shareholding in B, B will be treated as receiving a chargeable gain of £5,000 but this will be treated as part of its corporation tax profits for 1982—not 1986. If in 1984 B had sold the asset to an independent purchaser for £18,000 and replaced it with another asset which cost £18,000 the rollover relief in CGTA 1979, s. 115 will then have treated the disposal as being for £10,000. When s. 278 is applied in 1986 B will be treated as notionally disposing of the replacement asset at £15,000—again with consequences for its 1982 profit figure—and with consequent adjustment to its cost base. If rollover relief had not been claimed s. 278 will not apply—because the capital gains liability would not have been discharged in 1984.

Simon's Taxes D2.630.

[1] Including 272(3).

[2] TA 1970, s. 278(1) and (3). *Note.* On extension of time limit for election in respect of pre-1965 assets, see SP D21, **Simon's Taxes, Division H3.1.**

[3] TA 1970, s. 278(5).

[4] It is understood that the Revenue do not currently view this as falling within s. 278.

[5] TA 1970, s. 272(3), as amended by FA 1989, s. 138(3).

[6] TA 1970, s. 272(4) as amended by FA 1989, s. 138(4).

[7] TA 1970, s. 278(3C).

[8] TA 1970, s. 278(3D).

[9] It is not clear whether s. 278(3B) is necessary since under the amended s. 272(3) a company will not be treated as leaving a group by virtue of the principal company ceasing to be a principal company.

[10] TA 1970, s. 278(3E); on commencement see FA 1989, s. 138(7).

[11] FA 1989, s. 138(8) and (9).

[12] TA 1970, s. 278(1).

[13] TA 1970, s. 278(4)(*b*).

[14] TA 1970, s. 278(4)(*c*).

[15] TA 1970, s. 278(2).

[16] TA 1970, s. 278A (introduced by FA 1970, s. 27).

[17] TA 1970, s. 278(1).

---

(2) Shares in a subsidiary leaving the group following reconstruction: TA 1970, s. 279

26: 24 This provision, which applied if the company should leave the group within the six years following the reconstruction, only applies to reconstructions before 20th April 1977; it therefore ceased to have effect after 19th April 1983.[1] The prevention of such abuse is now left to CGTA 1979, ss. 87 and 88.

Simon's Taxes D2.632.

[1] CGTA 1979, s. 157(2)–(4) and Sch. 7, para. 2(4).

(3) Losses attributable to depreciatory transactions: TA 1970, ss. 280 and 281 and FA 1989

26: 25   If there is a disposal[1] by one group member to another of an asset at a nominal figure, neither gain nor loss arises (s. 273); this may cause a decline in the value of the former company. Losses resulting from such depreciatory transactions[2] and realised on a subsequent disposal of the shares or securities are disallowed by s. 280. The disallowance is limited to the under-value of the transaction. If there is a later disposal of the shares in the acquiring company the previously disallowed loss can reduce the gain. Section 280 restricts losses; it does not create or increase gains.[3] (CGTA 1979, s. 25, supra, § **15: 05**, does not apply to intra-group transfers.)

Section 281 deals with dividend stripping. The payment of accumulated profits by means of an intra group dividend can be treated as giving rise to a depreciatory transaction and any resulting capital loss disallowed by s. 280.

This was introduced in 1969 as a companion to TA 1988, s. 736 (infra, § **31: 00**) which deals with share-dealing companies.

EXAMPLE

X buys the share capital of Y for £100,000. A dividend of £60,000 is then declared by Y which is then liquidated. The distribution to X on the liquidation of Y is £40,000. Although X has a capital loss of £60,000 on its investment in Y, s. 281 empowers the Inspector to disallow that loss to the extent of the dividend received (£60,000).

This section deals only with the disallowance of losses it does not apply to the reduction of gains. It follows that the common practice of a subsidiary making a distribution shortly before it is sold—so reducing the gain on the sale of those shares—is not caught by this provision.

Simon's Taxes D2.633.

[1] TA 1970, s. 280(8) includes a claim under CGTA 1979, s. 22(2), that the value of shares or securities has become negligible.

[2] Defined TA 1970, s. 280(3) as including the cancellation of securities under Companies Act 1985, s. 135; it is odd that there should be no mention of the Companies Act 1985, s. 425.

[3] Defined TA 1970, s. 280(7). CGTA 1979, s. 25, supra, § **15: 05** does not aply to intra-group transfers.

26: 25A   By 1989 the practice of reducing the value of subsidiary companies prior to disposal of those companies outside the group was in danger of becoming a standard feature of UK tax practice. The basic scheme, according to the Government, involved stripping out of a subsidiary unrealised gains in the value of its chargeable assets by means of a tax free intra group dividend out of artificially created profits. In this way the group would shelter from tax that would otherwise be, and effectively were, realised gains in the sale of the subsidiary. That could even mean a group lending money to one subsidiary to buy an asset from another.[1]

This scheme was not stopped by CGTA 1979, s. 26 because s. 26(7) specifically excluded the shifting of value arising from the payment of dividends between members of a group of companies within the meaning of TA 1970, s. 272 and the disposal of assets between them within TA 1970, s. 273. Section 26(7) is now recast so as to ensure that s. 26 does apply in the prescribed circumstances.

The closing of this loophole was announced at the time of the 1989 Budget and were enacted as FA 1989, ss. 135–138. In attacking those devices the legislation safeguards ordinary dividend payments within a group and tries not to penalise a group for extracting profits from a subsidiary before sale by a dividend payment where the profits supporting that dividend have borne tax. The target is the extraction of gains from profits that have not borne tax.[2] Not surprisingly, in seeking to target on a specific type of abuse the provisions are extremely detailed and complex. (On changes in the definition of a group see supra, **§ 26: 19** and on changes to s. 278 see supra, **§ 26:23**). Where the new rules apply, the chargeable gains on the sale of the subsidiary are increased (or the allowable losses reduced) by an amount which appears to the inspector or on appeal the Commissioners, to be just and reasonable. The legislation refers to associated companies but this means simply that they are members of the same group.[3]

Simon's Taxes D2.621.
[1] Hansard Standing Committee G col. 598 (Mr. Lamont).
[2] Hansard Standing Committee G col. 598 (Mr. Lamont).
[3] CGTA 1979, s. 26C(9); groups are defined by reference to s. 272 sub-s (10).

26: 25B   The new CGTA 1979, s. 26(7) provides that s. 26 shall apply to the sale of shares owned by one company in another company in the circumstances prescribed by the new ss. 26A–26C.

Section 26(1) is then expanded to include the reduction in the value of a relevant asset.[1] A reduction in the value of the relevant asset is only relevant if the conditions in (1A)(*a*) to (*c*) are satisfied. This is designed to counter variations of a technique for avoiding CGTA 1979, s. 26 whereby the asset that is reduced in value is subsequently transferred to another company, X, and it is the shares in company X which are disposed of.[2]

---

[1] A term defined in the new sub-s. 26(1A); see also s. 26C(7).
[2] Inland Revenue Press Release *Simon's Tax Intelligence* 1989 p. 221, para. 10.

Distributions within a group followed by a disposal of shares

26: 25C   FA 1989, s. 136 introduces CGTA 1979, s. 26A. This brings within the value shifting provisions of s. 26, by excluding them from the exclusion provision in s. 26(7), reductions in the value of the subsidiary to be sold arising from the payment of dividends generated by chargeable profits. It is the disposal of the shares which is the disposal for s. 26 purposes. Consistent with its policy, s. 26(7) is only to apply to a reduction attributable to the payment of a dividend by company A to company B, at a time when A and B are associated, to the extent (if any) that the dividend is attributable to chargeable profits of company A.

Section 26A counters the drain out dividend. Thus company A, the subsidiary to be sold, sells an asset containing unrealised capital gains to company B, or other members of the group, at market value. Thanks to TA 1970 s. 273, the transaction is taken for tax purposes at such figure that neither gain nor loss accrues. The value of A is then reduced by A declaring a dividend of the realised but untaxed capital gain. A number of variations on this general framework were possible. A similar result would be achieved by the use of CGTA 1979, s. 85, or, in certain circumstances, a straightforward revaluation of the asset in the accounting records of the company.[1]

The section excludes dividends paid out of chargeable profits. These are distributable profits which satisfy the conditions of s. 26A plus distributions received from another company to the extent that they contain chargeable profits.[2] Distributable profits are those able to be distributed after allowing for tax.[3]

Profits targeted by the section are those satisfying each of the three conditions.[4] Broadly, the distributing company, company A, must have:

(1) disposed of the asset under TA 1970, s. 273 or entered into a share exchange within s. 85 (2) or (3) or revalued an asset.[5]

(2) that asset must not have subsequently been the subject of any CGT disposal other than a s. 273 disposal,[6] and

(3) the asset must, immediately after the s. 26 disposal (i.e. the disposal of the shares in A) be owned by a person other than the distributing company or by any company associated with it.[7] Where A disposed of the asset to B and A was later disposed of this condition is obviously satisfied.

There is an exclusion of s. 26A if, at the time of the disposal, share exchange or revaluation, the company or, if appropriate, its associate, carries on a trade and the profit would form part of its trading profits. Section 26A is also excluded if the asset is not subject to CGT provisions and therefore no abuse occurs.[8] Allowance is also to be made for a dividend by B.[9]

There are rules for the calculation of chargeable profits. All losses are to be set first against profits other than chargeable profits. However the provisions only apply where distributions exceed profits other than chargeable profits.[10] Thus the Revenue try to achieve their aim of not seeking to stop a pre-sale dividend reducing the value of the subsidiary if the dividend comes out of profits which have been taxed.[11]

Chargeable profits are attributed to any person in receipt of a distribution in the same proportion as chargeable gains bear to totals distributions.[12]

---

[1] *Simon's Tax Intelligence* 1989, p. 220 para 2.
[2] CGTA 1979, s. 26A (3).
[3] CGTA 1979, s. 26A (4).
[4] CGTA 1979, s. 26A (5); the conditions are in sub-s. (6) to (8).
[5] CGTA 1979, s. 26A (6).
[6] CGTA 1979, s. 26A (7); on disposal and other terms see s. 26C.
[7] CGTA 1979, s. 26A (8); *Simon's Tax Intelligence* 1989, p. 221 para 3; on the meaning of disposal and other terms in s. 26A(8) see s. 26C.
[8] CGTA 1979, s. 26A (9); on the meaning of disposal see s. 26C.
[9] CGTA 1979, s. 26C (8).
[10] CGTA 1979, s. 26A (3) and (10).
[11] Hansard Standing Committee G, col. 598.
[12] CGTA 1979, s. 26A (11).

Disposals within a group followed by a disposal of shares

25: 26D CGTA 1979, s. 26B tackles the avoidance of capital gains on the sale of a subsidiary by transferring assets from the subsidiary to other members of the group at a price below market value and cost price. The policy behind s. 273 does not require a deferral in such circumstances. Section 26C therefore is a logical extension of s. 280 (supra, §**26: 25**).

So s. 26(7) does not apply (so that s. 26 will apply) if there is a reduction attributable to a s. 273 disposal of an asset ("the underlying asset") by company A at a time when it and company B are associated, if the actual consideration for the underlying asset is, as already stated, less than the market value and the cost.[1]

The new provision does not apply where the subsidiary ceases to be a member of the group by virtue of being wound up. It is also excluded if there is a bona fide commercial reason for the disposal and does not form party of any scheme or arrangements of which the main purpose—or one of them— is the avoidance of tax.[2]

---

[1] CGTA 1979, s. 26B (2); cost is defined in sub-s. (3) and makes no allowance for any indexation relief.

[2] CGTA 1979, s. 26B (2).

26: 25E FA 1989, s. 137 introduces CGTA 1979, s. 26D. This applies where s. 26 would apply but for the reorganisation provisions in CGTA 1979, ss. 78 and 85 (3). In such circumstances the company selling the shares in the subsidiary is to be treated for the purposes of s. 79 (2) as receiving an amount that would have been calculated by applying s. 26. This withholds the normal deferral on a reorganisation to the extent that s. 26 would apply.

Commencement of the new provisions

26: 25F In general the changes contained in ss. 135–138 apply as from 14th March 1989.[1] However there is a special rule where two companies would have formed a group under the old rules but fail the new test because one is not an effective 51% subsidiary. Where this has arisen under a compromise or arrangement entered into before 14th March 1989 in pursuance of Companies Act 1985, s. 425, and sanctioned by the court, the commencement date is six months from the date of the arrangement or, if earlier, the date on which the company ceases to be a member under the old rules.[2]

---

[1] FA 1989, ss. 136 (2), 137 (2) and 138 (7); s. 278 (3E) has its special rule—see ibid.

[2] FA 1989, s. 138 (10) and (11).

---

(4) Losses due to indexation relief on debt transactions between linked companies: FA 1988, s. 114 and Sch. 11

26: 26 If one company lends another money and receives payment no loss results. This is true also whether the debt takes the form of a simple loan or of a debt on a security. However, since the indexation rules were relaxed to permit the creation of a loss, a tax saving opportunity arises—since the loss may be due solely to the indexation. To counter this, special rules withhold the benefit of indexation where the parties are "linked", a term which broadly means under common control or one controlling the other but which also covers members of a 51% group.[1]

The rules apply where there is a disposal of the debt or a repayment and in analogous situations. Thus they apply where there is a disposal of the debt owed by any person and the debt was incurred by the person as part of arrangements involving another company being put in funds.[2] They also apply to redeemable preference shares.[3] They apply to other types of share if the companies were linked when the shares were acquired, the acquisition was wholly or substantially financed by an intra-group loan[4] and the sole or main benefit which might have been expected to accrue was an indexation allowance on an eventual disposal of the shares.[5]

Simon's Taxes D2.633.
[1] FA 1988, Sch. 11, para. 4.
[2] FA 1988, Sch. 11, para. 2
[3] FA 1988, Sch. 11, para. 3(1)(*a*)(i).
[4] Or by an "indexed company subscription"—defined in para. 3(4).
[5] FA 1988, Sch. 11, para. 3.

DEMERGERS

26: 27   Until 1980 it was difficult—but not impossible—to split a group up. The difficulty was that the transfer of the piece being split off would cause the value received by the shareholder to be treated as a qualifying distribution supra, § **24: 02**; in addition there were capital gains and DLT (now repealed) and stamp duty problems when a company or assets left the group. As part of a campaign to free British industry from unnecessary constraints Parliament included certain provisions in TA 1988—ss. 213–218—to encourage the process of "demerging" by removing some of the obstacles.[1]

There are three types of demerger provided by the Act. These are (i) where a company spins off a subsidiary directly to its shareholders i.e. where it distributes shares in a subsidiary to its shareholders so that those shareholders control the former subsidiary directly and no longer through the distributing company—the conditions are discussed at infra, § **26: 28**; (ii) where a company spins off a subsidiary indirectly to its shareholders, i.e. where it transfers shares in a subsidiary to another company in exchange for shares but the shares are not held by the subsidiary but distributed to the shareholders of the parent—see infra, § **26: 30**—and (iii) where a company spins off a trade to its shareholders but indirectly i.e. where it transfers a trade to another company in exchange for shares and those shares are not held by the parent but distributed to its shareholders—see infra, § **26: 31**. One situation not covered by these alternatives arises when the company has a trade which it wishes to transfer to its shareholders directly, i.e. by transferring ownership of the trade itself rather than having to use a company to hold the trade and transferring shares in the company. It is presumably thought that such a situation would involve the trade leaving the corporate sector entirely and therefore not an occasion for relief.

Certain conditions are common to all of them. First there must be a transaction which would otherwise be a distribution of income under TA 1988, s. 209.[2] This means amongst other things that the new reliefs cannot apply to a demerger in the course of a liquidation. Also, under TA 1988,

s. 209, a distribution other than a dividend, e.g. a distribution of shares, is not a distribution if it represents a repayment of capital.[3]

Secondly, the company making the distribution must, at the time of the distribution, be a trading company[4] (or a member of a trading group—a phrase which will not be repeated); certain trades notably those dealing in shares, land and commodity futures are excluded.[5]

Thirdly the transaction must be wholly or mainly to benefit some or all of the trading activities involved in the demerger.[6] This test is a narrow one. A demerger will not qualify simply because there are bona fide commercial reasons for it. It is probably sufficient that the benefit should be either to the retained or the transferred trade and not to both but this is not absolutely clear.

The combination of these two conditions means that relief is available only where trade is being demerged from trade and so not, for example, to the demerger of trade from investment. In many instances the exact status of the secondary business of an unlisted company may be in doubt; such doubts need to be resolved before a demerger is embarked upon.

Fourthly it is intended that the newly demerged trade should be left free to operate under its new independent management—quite separate from the former parent. To this end it is provided that where the company distributes shares in its subsidiary to its members (type (i) above) those shares must not be redeemable and must represent the whole or substantially the whole of the distributing company's interest.[7] If the transfer is of a trade to another company (type (ii)) the distributing company is not to retain anything more than a minor interest in the trade[8] while if it is of shares in a subsidiary (type (iii)) the shares must not be redeemable and must represent the whole or substantially the whole of the distributing company's interest.[9]

Fifthly all the companies involved must be resident in the UK at the time of the distribution.[10]

Finally one should note that there are elaborate anti-avoidance provisions which may disqualify the scheme altogether. Thus the demerger must not be part of a scheme or arrangement for the avoidance of tax, for the making of a chargeable payment,[11] for the acquisition of control of any company involved by a third person nor for the cessation of a trade or its sale after demerger. The purpose of the demerger provisions is to encourage the hiving off of active businesses so that they may thrive on their own; so the provisions are designed to ensure that assets remain within the corporate sector and not used to get tax advantages on what is really the sale of a business; hence a passing of control to another company in return for shares which flow back to the shareholders in the previous owners is essential. Intra-group transfers cannot qualify for this treatment.

Simon's Taxes D1.124–129

[1] See [1980] STI, pp. 171 and 418 and SP 13/80, **Simon's Taxes, Division H3.2.**
[2] SP 13/80.
[3] Supra, § **24: 01**.
[4] TA 1988, s. 213(5); the terms are defined in para. 23.
[5] TA 1988, s. 218(1)—"trading".
[6] TA 1988, s. 213(10).
[7] TA 1988, s. 213(6).
[8] TA 1988, s. 213(8)(*a*).

736 Part IV—Corporation tax

9 TA 1988, s. 213(8)(b).

10 TA 1988, s. 213(4).

11 TA 1988, s. 213(11).

Demergers of subsidiaries

26: 28   The first type of demerger allowed arises where one company, X, transfers to all or any of its members, i.e. ordinary shareholders[1] shares in a directly owned 75% subsidiary, Z.[2] This allows a simple spinning off of the distinct business run by Z which is already a separate entity and takes the form of a simple distribution in specie. The insistence on a 75% holding in Z is to be noted. The transfer must be to X's shareholders and not simply to another conglomerate.

The conditions for the relief require *inter alia* that Z must be a trading company[3], that its shares must not be redeemable[4] and that the shares distributed must constitute substantially the whole of X's holding in Z and also confer on them substantially the whole of X's voting rights.[5] The Revenue view is that "substantially the whole" represents at least 90%. These demerger provisions are intended to operate only where the control passes from X to the shareholders. It will also be noted that the conditions insist that the transfer should be of the *ordinary* shares in Z and to the *ordinary* shareholders of X.[6] It follows that preference shareholders of X may not benefit from these distributions although, of course, they may be in a position, by virtue of their voting rights, to exact a high price for their concurrence in any demerger scheme.

There are also conditions to ensure that X should not only have been a trading company before the spin off[7] but continues as a trading entity after the demerger[8] save where it is disposing of all its net assets and at least two companies such as Z are involved.[9] This is to prevent the use of the demerger rules on what is really a simple cessation.

A transfer of shares by X of this sort would normally cause a number of tax consequences; some of these are modified. First, the distribution is to be exempt.[10] It follows that there will be no Schedule F income tax, no franked investment income and, just as important, no ACT. Neither will there be a capital distribution to the shareholders which might otherwise cause capital gains consequences under CGTA 1979 s. 72[11] (capital gains liability is thus deferred until the shares are disposed of). Further as Z is leaving the group, there might be a charge under TA 1970, ss. 278 and the now obsolete 279[12] on assets acquired from other members of the group within the last six years[13]; this too is removed as is any similar liability to the now repealed development land tax.[14]

Yet some tax consequences remain. Since Z ceases to be a member of the group it will not in future be entitled to group privileges such as, for example, the surrender of surplus ACT. Secondly the change in control of Z will mean that the restrictions on loss relief in TA 1988, s. 768 and on the carry forward of surplus ACT under TA 1988, s. 252 may have to be noted should a change in Z's trade be contemplated; however the Revenue has indicated sympathetic treatment here by treating the underlying ownership as remaining unchanged.[15] Thirdly where close companies are involved there may be CTT and IHT implications.

Another very important tax consequence is that X will be disposing of its holding in Z, a disposal that may give rise to substantial liability on the gains involved. This cost may be reduced if either the gains are minimal or X has unrelieved capital losses. Where this is not so it may be possible to reduce the value of the shares in Z by paying a dividend. However, the more unusual the steps taken the greater the risk that the scheme will fall into the anti-avoidance provisions on the ground that it forms part of a scheme one of the main purposes of which is the avoidance of tax. This very high tax cost may inhibit many schemes of demerger under these rules.

To assist the process in some respects it is possible to apply to the Revenue for clearance and thus obtain their binding agreement that the proposed distribution is indeed within these rules. Details of the information required are set out in the Revenue statement of practice SP13/80, see **Simon's Taxes, Division H3.2.**

---

[1] TA 1988, s. 218(1).
[2] TA 1988, s. 213(3)(*a*).
[3] TA 1988, s. 213(6).
[4] TA 1988, s. 213(6)(*a*).
[5] SP 13/80.
[6] Supra note 1.
[7] TA 1988, s. 213(5).
[8] TA 1988, s. 213(6)(*b*); this rule does not apply when the distributing company is the 75% subsidiary of another company—TA 1988, s. 213(12).
[9] TA 1988, s. 213(7) and see extra-statutory concession C11 (1988) (**Simon's Taxes Division H2.2**) (company may return funds to meet costs of liquidation provided excess is negligible).
[10] TA 1988, s. 213(2).
[11] FA 1980, Sch. 18, para. 9.
[12] CGTA 1979, s. 157(2)–(4) and Sch. 7, para. 2(4) mean that after 19 April 1983 the Revenue have to use CGTA 1979, ss. 87 and 88 instead.
[13] FA 1980, Sch. 18, para. 10; however the receipt of a chargeable payment within five years would revive such a charge; see para. 15.
[14] FA 1980, Sch. 18, para. 11; on the receipt of a chargeable payment, see para. 16.
[15] SP 13/80.

Three party demergers

26: 29 The *second* type of demerger arises when X disposes of a trade to Y and, in exchange, Y issues shares not to X but to the ordinary shareholders of X. In this way the trade is hived off from the rest of X's activities and thus demerged and X's ordinary shareholders receive shares in Y.[1] The legislation refers simply to the transfer of a trade. The Revenue take a broad view of this requirement and will regard it as satisfied when what is received by Y is a trade. Hence what is transferred may be only a part of X's trade e.g. the retail end of a combined manufacturing/retailing trade. Or the assets transferred may be being assembled for the first time from one or more trades carried on by X—or by other members of the group. It may even be that some of the assets have not previously been used in any trade—e.g. land held by an investment company. What matters, according to the Revenue, is that there should be a division of trading activities and that the assets transferred should be transferred to be used in a trade carried on by Y and should be so used. Relief is not denied solely because some minor asset is transferred which is linked with a trading asset e.g. a flat over a shop.[2]

The conditions for relief here require that X itself should after the demerger hold only a minor interest in the transferred trade.[3] The term interest is not defined but in the Revenue's view it must be given a wide meaning; it therefore covers not only an interest in the trade giving rise to a right to profits or an asset of the trade but also less obvious rights such as an entitlement to be a main supplier or customer.[4] The Revenue view is that common management may "possibly" amount to such a right. In these less obvious cases the Revenue would normally concede that the interest was a minor one unless the interest gave control of the trade or its assets or a material influence on the profits or their destination. In general the term "minor" is regarded as the corollary of "substantial" and therefore as being, in those circumstances where quantification is possible, 10% or less.[5]

It is also necessary that Y's only or main activity is to be the transferred trade.[6] Further, control must be shifted to X's ordinary shareholders from X, so Y's shares must not be redeemable[7] and must constitute in the Revenue's view at least 90% of the issued ordinary share capital and carry 90% of the voting rights.[8]

Other provisions relate to X. So there are also provisions to ensure that X continues as a trading entity[9] save where it is transferring all its net assets and at least two companies in Y's position are involved.[10]

Normally such a distribution by X of its assets would be treated as a distribution but as with the first type of demerger it is provided that the distribution is to be exempt and so gives rise neither to ACT nor to income tax.[11] In addition, TA 1970, s. 278 and the now obsolete s. 279 are also excluded.[12] The legislature has not thought it necessary to exclude any charge under CGTA 1979, s. 72 in these circumstances, presumably because in these circumstances it is Y rather than X that is making the distribution to X's shareholders; in the light of the new approach this assumption becomes debatable. However, the rules make no provision for other consequences. Thus X is disposing of the trade, one of its capital assets, and its shareholders are receiving an amount with capital gains implications; these consequences can be avoided by ensuring that the scheme is a company reconstruction and so making use of the provisions of TA 1970, s. 267 and CGTA 1979 s. 86. Another set of consequences will flow from the fact that X ceases to carry on this trade and that Y begins to carry it on; this will give rise to all the usual problems of discontinuance and commencement with restrictions on losses, unused capital allowances and possible stock relief recapture not to mention possible changes of accounting date, a matter of some, but dwindling, importance if X was a pre-1965 company.

---

[1] TA 1988, s. 213(3)(*b*).

[2] This is taken almost verbatim from SP 13/80; although the UK demerger provisions are very different in some ways from the US provision (see Internal Revenue Code § 355). This passage in SP 13/80 shows clear signs of having been written in the light of the US experience.

[3] TA 1988, s. 213(8)(*a*).

[4] Here the emphasis must be on the word "entitlement".

[5] SP 13/80.

[6] TA 1988, s. 213(8)(*c*); this condition must be met both at the time of the distribution and thereafter, a phrase which is interpreted by the Revenue as meaning not forever thereafter but simply sufficient to show a bona fide trade by Y; see SP 13/80.

[7] TA 1988, s. 213(8)(*d*).
[8] TA 1988, s. 213(8)(*b*).
[9] TA 1988, s. 213(8)(*b*).
[10] TA 1988, s. 213(9); as in note 6 this does not mean forever thereafter.
[11] TA 1988, s. 213(2).
[12] FA 1980, Sch. 18, para. 10; however the receipt of a chargeable payment within five years will revive the liability under these rules, FA 1980, Sch. 18, para. 15.

26: 30   The *third* type of demerger is a mixture of the first two. Here X transfers shares in its 75% subsidiary Z to Y and Y in turn issues shares in Y to the ordinary shareholders of X.

The conditions for relief are similar to those for the first two. So Z must be a trading company[1] and the shares transferred by X to Y must be at least 90% of X's holding of the ordinary shares capital and voting power of Z[2] and Z must be a 75% subsidiary of X.[3] Y's only or main activity must be to hold the shares in Z.[4] The shares issued by Y must not be redeemable and must constitute at least 90% of its issued share capital[5] and a similar percentage of its voting power. Again after the demerger X must continue to be a trading company or dispose of all its net assets with two or more X companies being transferred to two or more Y companies.[6]

The tax consequences are a similar mixture of the first and the second. As with the first the distribution of the shares in Y is to be an exempt distribution[7] with the result that there is no Schedule F income tax, franked investment income nor ACT. Z leaves the group controlled by X but there is exemption from TA 1970, s. 278 and the now obsolete s. 279[8] as in the first type of demerger. X's disposal of the shares in Z may give rise to chargeable gains but those can be avoided by using a reconstruction; and same device will save the shareholders in X from liability. As the control of Z passes from X there will be matters to be noted with regard to losses and loss of group benefits as already set out under the first type. Where this type of demerger scores over the first is in the matter of the tax cost arising from the realisation of any gains on the disposal of the shares in Z.

[1] TA 1988, s. 213(5) as must X.
[2] TA 1988, s. 213(8)(*b*).
[3] TA 1988, s. 213(8)(*b*)(ii).
[4] TA 1988, s. 213(8)(*c*).
[5] TA 1988, s. 213(8)(*d*).
[6] TA 1988, s. 213(8)(*e*).
[7] TA 1988, s. 213(2).
[8] FA 1980, Sch. 18, para. 10; this is subject to the receipt of a chargeable payment in the next five years. On the now obsolete DLT see paras. 11 and 16.

Groups

26: 31   The 1980 scheme is not designed to assist intra-group demergers. Where therefore there is a chain of companies it will be necessary to demerge the group from the bottom up.

Anti-avoidance-subsequent payments

26: 32   Although a demerger under these rules may have been successfully carried through, a subsequent "chargeable payment" during any of the next five years may have serious consequences.

A chargeable payment is any payment which is not itself a distribution (or an exempt distribution) made otherwise than for a bona fide commercial reason, or forming part of a scheme or arrangement for the avoidance of tax and made between companies or between a company and a shareholder in a company in the demerger; the payment must have been made in connection with the shares of the company.[1] Only intra-group payments are saved from the ambit of this definition[2] which is widened yet further when dealing with unquoted companies.[3]

The effect of such a payment within the five year period is that it will itself be treated as income of the recipient and so is liable to tax under Schedule D, Case VI.[4] No deduction for the payment can be made in computing profits chargeable to corporation tax.[5] Further the capital gains (and, formerly, development land tax reliefs) are withdrawn,[6] i.e. the exemption from TA 1970, ss. 278 and 279 and from DLTA 1976, s. 21.[7]

An example of a situation in which this will arise is where a company demerges a subsidiary by transferring shares to its members and then buys them back. The repurchase price would normally be a capital receipt but is instead to be taxed as income of the shareholder. This device is preferred to the alternative of retrospectively withdrawing exemption from the distribution.

---

[1] TA 1988, s. 214(2).

[2] TA 1988, s. 214(2)(*c*).

[3] TA 1988, s. 214(3).

[4] TA 1988, s. 214(1)(*a*); TA 1988, s. 349(1) applies unless the payment is a transfer of money's worth—ibid. TA 1988, s. 214(1)(*b*).

[5] TA 1988, s. 214(1)(*c*); nor is it a repayment of capital within TA 1988, ss. 210, 211, see TA 1988, s. 214(1)(*d*).

[6] FA 1980, Sch. 18, para. 15.

[7] FA 1980, Sch. 18, para. 16.

27 Close companies

27: 01 The present taxation of close companies differs from that of other companies in three major respects.[1] First the law takes a wider view of what amounts to a distribution, with the result that not only are such payments not deductible in computing profits of the close company, but also ACT will be payable. Secondly, where the company makes a loan to a participator a payment equivalent to ACT must be made to the Revenue. Thirdly, for accounting periods beginning before 1st April 1989 the law specifies a certain amount of profit, which could be distributed (see infra § **27: 13**). The sum by which actual distributions fall short of that amount is apportioned among the participators.[2] The income tax due from the participators on these notional distributions can be recovered from the company. The purpose of this rule is to prevent the use of companies as incorporated piggy-banks in which profits could be taxed at company rates instead of individual rates, the latter sometimes reaching 98%; the retained profits might then be realised as capital gains and so, before 1965, free of further tax. With the reduction in 1979 in top rates of tax on earned income to 60% there was no tax advantage in retaining profits in the company and so the power to apportion trading income of trading companies was abolished; since that time it has remained for non-trading income of such companies and for all income of non-trading companies. Meanwhile one should note that the apportionment is avoided if the company is open at the beginning or end of the accounting period.[3] For accounting periods beginning after 31st March 1989 a quite different—and simpler—system applies. In broad terms the profits of an investment company cannot qualify for the reduced rate of corporation tax and the normal right to a repayment of the tax credit may be restricted. See § **27: 32** et seq, infra.

In so far as the shareholders envisage an eventual sale of the company they may find that their expected capital gains tax liability is turned into an income tax liability by TA 1988, s. 703,[4] a provision which naturally applies particularly to small companies although it is not so confined. The 1988 assimilation of CGT and income tax rates may undermine this point in part but substantial differences, especially the exemption of pre-1982 gains remain.

---

[1] See also §**27: 31** (deep discount securities) and TA 1988, ss. 210(3) and 211(2).

² Between 1965 and 1973 the classical system of taxation meant that the participator could not claim credit for basic rate income tax paid by the company. Hence participators were liable to basic rate tax as well as excess liability when an apportionment was made. The same fact led to special rules for restrictive covenants (TA 1970, s. 288) and certain annual payments (TA 1988, s. 418); these rules were repealed on the introduction of the imputation system. Between 1965 and 1969 there were special restrictions on the level of director's remuneration (FA 1965, s. 74); these were abolished because they were too complicated. When excessive remuneration to a director is disallowed under the rules for Schedule D, Case I or TA 1988, s. 75 the excess will be treated as a distribution unless it is refunded—on which see Statement of Practice C4, para. 4, **Simon's Taxes, Division H3.4**.

³ The wording of TA 1988, s. 423(1)(*a*) suggests that the company must have been a close company throughout the accounting period if an apportionment is to be made but the previous practice was as stated in the text and see *CHW (Huddersfield) Ltd v IRC* [1963] 2 All ER 952, 41 TC 92.

⁴ Esp. TA 1988, s. 704 D; infra, § **31: 29**.

CLOSE COMPANIES

The tests

27: 02   A company will be designated a close company if it satisfies any of three tests. There are exceptions discussed below. The tests are (*i*) that it is controlled by five or fewer participators, (*ii*) that it is controlled by its directors,[1] (*iii*) that, if it were a close company and its relevant income therefore apportionable, more than one-half of that income could—on any of the methods of apportionment permitted—be apportioned among participants who were directors or who numbered five or fewer.[2] If one of the participators is itself a close company, a sub-appointment must be made among the participators of that company. Test (iii) is then applied by reference to those amongst whom the amount falls finally to be apportioned. For accounting periods beginning after 31st March 1989 this test has to be reformulated. It now turns on entitlement to assets on a notional winding up.

A non-resident company, even if controlled by a resident company, cannot be a close company.

EXAMPLES

(1) The share capital of X Ltd (a private company) is owned as to 25% by three directors and the 75% balance by ten individuals, no five of which own over 50%. X Ltd is not a close company.

(2) The directors of X Ltd, numbering 12, own 51% of the ordinary share capital. X Ltd is a close company.

(3) The directors of Z Ltd, numbering 3, own 45% of the ordinary share capital. Two other unconnected individuals own 8%. Since five persons own 53% of the share capital of Z Ltd, it is a close company.

The Revenue have extensive information gathering powers.[3]

Simon's Taxes D3.102.
¹ TA 1988, s. 414(1).
² TA 1988, s. 414(2) as amended by FA 1989, s. 104.
³ FA 1989, Sch. 12, paras. 1–4.

Control[1]

27: 03   This element is central to the first two tests but it can be satisfied in many, sometimes overlapping ways. A person is taken to control a company if he exercises or is able to exercise now or as of right in the future, or is entitled to acquire (now or as of right in the future) control over the company's affairs. "Control over the company's affairs" is not defined and may mean control at a general meeting or control of those matters which are within the discretion of the directors. Precise analysis is probably unnecessary since the statute gives certain instances which are however not to detract from the generality of the principle:

(*a*) the greater part of the share capital or of the issued share capital, or

(*b*) the greater part of the voting power of the company, or

(*c*) such part of the share capital as would entitle him to receive the greater part of the income of the company if, ignoring the rights of loan creditors, it were all distributed among the participators, or

(*d*) such rights as would enable him to receive the greater part of the assets of the company in the event of a winding up or in any other circumstances.

Simon's Taxes D3.107–109.
[1] TA 1988, s. 416(2).

Who has control?

27:04 Having ascertained the meaning of control one then looks to see who, and how many, have got it. If two or more persons together satisfy the test of control they are taken together to control it.[1]

In assessing the extent of a person's control all rights and powers held by him or by nominees are of course included.[2] Less obviously but equally crucial in establishing the extent of a person's control is the attribution to a person of all the rights and powers held by an associate.[3] An associate means[4] any relative—which means spouse,[5] direct ancestor or issue, or brother or sister[5]—or partner and any trustee of a settlement[6] of which he, or any relative, as previously defined, is the settlor. The definition of associate has been altered as from 6th April 1986.[7] Where the participator is interested in any shares or obligations of a company which are subject to any trust, the trust or trustees of the settlement concerned are associates.[8] Likewise if the participator is a company and is interested in shares held on trust, any other company interested in those shares or obligations is an associate.[9] These rules apply also where shares are held as part of the estate of a deceased person. The effect is to make the trustees associates rather than the beneficiaries, as had previously been the case, save where the beneficiary is another company. The term "interested" is not defined; it is unclear whether being an object of a discretion is sufficient to make one "interested".[10] The previous provision[11] went on to exclude individuals who were interested in trusts which were exempt approved pension schemes or for the benefit of employees; with the shift to the trustees as the associated persons this part of the section becomes redundant and is repealed; trustees of such scheme are now associates as are corporate beneficiaries.

If our participator has control of another company, the power of that company and of any other he may control are attributed to him as are powers of companies controlled by him and his associates.[12] While the powers of

744   Part IV—Corporation tax

nominees of associates are to be attributed to the participator, those of
associates of associates are not so the rights of a sister-in-law would be
ignored.

Simon's Taxes D3.103, 104.
[1] TA 1988, s. 416(3).
[2] TA 1988, s. 416(5). The Revenue has no really effective means of discovering whether a
shareholder is a nominee. TMA 1970, s. 26 is in practice insufficient.
[3] TA 1988, s. 416(6).
[4] TA 1988, s. 417(3).
[5] TA 1988, s. 417(4). But in practice relatives other than spouse and minor children are usually
ignored see Revenue Statement of Practice C4, para. 2, Simon's Taxes Division H3.4.
[6] Defined in TA 1988, s. 681(4); supra, § 13: 02. There are exceptions for certain funds for
employees. TA 1988, s. 417(3). A will is not a settlement: *Willingale v Islington Green Investment
Co* [1972] 1 All ER 199, 48 TC 547.
[7] By TA 1988, s. 417(3)(c).
[8] TA 1988, s. 417(3)(c)(i).
[9] TA 1988, s. 417(3)(c)(ii).
[10] The term was part of the previous TA 1970, s. 303(3)(c); it was then held that an executor
was interested in shares held as part of an incompletely administered estate—*Willingale v
Islington Green Investment Co* [1972] 1 All ER 199, 48 TC 547.
[11] TA 1970, s. 303(3)(c), proviso.
[12] TA 1988, s. 417(6).

Test (1) Control by directors[1]

27: 05 A company controlled by its directors is a close company no matter
how many directors there are. Persons listed as directors are any persons
occupying the position of director by whatsoever name called, and any
person in accordance with whose wishes the directors are accustomed to act.
Also qualifying as a director is any person who is a manager or otherwise
concerned with the management of the company's trade or business and who
controls (or is able to control) 20% of the ordinary share capital of the
company. There is the customary attribution of the control of associates and
intermediate companies even if the manager himself has no shares at all.

Simon's Taxes D3.106.
[1] TA 1988, s. 417(5).

Test (2) Control by participators[1]

27: 06 If control does not rest in the directors, the company will still be
close if control rests in five or fewer participators.

A participator is defined as any person with a share or interest in the
capital or income of the company and in particular (*i*) one with or who is
entitled to acquire share capital or voting rights, or (*ii*) entitled to secure that
income or assets (present or future) will be applied directly or indirectly for
his benefit, or (*iii*) entitled to receive or participate in distributions of the
company or entitled to any amounts payable by the company in cash or in
kind by way of premium on redemption, or (*iv*) certain loan creditors,[2] a term
defined to include one who has a beneficial interest in the debt. A creditor of
a nearly insolvent company might well be entitled to the greater part of the
company's assets and thus could find himself to be a participator with the

result that the company would be a close company. To avoid such complications bona fide commercial loans, salvage operations and business loans made by a person carrying on a banking business are ignored. A person may be a director although not a participator.

Simon's Taxes D3.103, 105.
[1] TA 1988, s. 417(1).
[2] Defined TA 1988, s. 417(7)–(9). This is omitted for IHT, infra, § **43: 03**. Recognised money brokers are excluded: extra-statutory concession C8 (1988), **Simon's Taxes, Division H2.2**.

Exceptions

27: 07 Certain companies cannot be close companies even though they satisfy one or other of these tests e.g. a non-resident company[1] or one controlled by the Crown.[2]

Further, a company is not a close company if it is controlled by one (or more) open companies *and* it cannot be treated as close except by taking an open company as one of its five or fewer participators.[3] Thus the subsidiary of a non-close company is not close any more than a company set up by two or three such companies. However if another test of control would result in its being a close company, the company would be close.

Also excluded and therefore not close is a company which is only close because it has one or more open companies as loan creditors with control[4] under that rule which gives control to one entitled to the greater share of the assets on a winding-up.

In looking at these cases of control by non-close companies, a non-resident company which would be a close company if it were resident is treated as if it were close.[5]

Where a close company is resident in the UK but 90% or more of its ordinary share capital is held by non-residents the Revenue will often not use their power to apportion income.[6]

Simon's Taxes D3.111.
[1] TA 1988, s. 414(1), see also TA 1988, s. 486(9).
[2] TA 1988, s. 414(4).
[3] TA 1988, s. 414(5)(*a*).
[4] TA 1988, s. 414(5)(*b*).
[5] TA 1988, s. 416(2)(*c*).
[6] Extra-statutory concession B22 (1988), **Simon's Taxes, Division H2.2**.

The 35% rule

27: 08 A quoted company is not a close company if shares carrying 35% or more of the voting power[1] of the company have been allotted unconditionally to or acquired unconditionally by and are at the time beneficially held by members of the public.[2]

Shares entitled to a fixed rate of dividend do not count towards the 35% but they do towards the 100%. This applies even though they carry voting rights and participate in profits.

Shares are not treated as held by the public if they are owned by (*i*) a principal member (i.e. the top five[3] of those with more than 5% of the voting power other than an approved pension scheme or a non-close company), (*ii*) any director or his associate (*iii*) any company controlled by (*ii*), (*iv*) any associated company and (*v*) any fund (e.g. a pension fund) for the benefit of any employee or director of the company or of a company within (*iii*) or (*iv*).

This exception does not apply if the voting power possessed by all its principal members is more than 85%. At first sight, since shares held in a principal member's holding cannot be held by the public, it is hard to see how a company with 35% of its shares held by the public could have 85% of its shares held by principal members. However shares held by open companies or approved superannuation funds are treated as owned by the public even if the company or fund is a principal member. Therefore, where one of the principal members is an open company with, say, 25% of the voting power and together the principal members control 80% of the voting power, the company so controlled is an open company under the 35% rule. If however the principal members had controlled 86%, it would have been a close company.

Simon's Taxes D3.112.
  [1] Thus the surrender of voting shares for non-voting shares may enable a company to come within this rule. Where the public owns less than 35% only for a short period which unhappily straddles the end of the accounting period, the Revenue promises "sympathetic treatment": Statement of Practice C4, para. 9, **Simon's Taxes, Division H3.4**.
  [2] TA 1988, s. 415.
  [3] TA 1988, s. 415(6)(*a*): if there are two or more with equal percentages five may be increased to six or more.

DISTRIBUTION

Expense on participators or their associates: TA 1988, s. 418

27: 09   The definition of distribution is widened in the case of a close company to cover expenses incurred by the company for the benefit of a participator. When a company has incurred expenses in providing a participator, including one who is a participator in a controlling company or who is an associate of a participator,[1] with the provision of living or other accommodation, of entertainment, of domestic or other services, or other benefits or facilities of whatsoever nature, TA 1988, s. 418 directs that expense so incurred is to be treated as a distribution.[2] The analogy is with TA 1988, s. 154[3] and s. 418 is excluded if the participator comes within s. 154.[4] The rules there laid down for valuation are incorporated into s. 418.[5] There is no grossing up of the expense and there is a deduction for sums made good by the participator. Curiously perhaps s. 418 fails to incorporate the exceptions listed in s. 155. This is easily overcome if the participator falls within s. 154 and, in practice, the Revenue would not seek to charge the expense.

The section does not apply to expenses incurred in the provision of living accommodation provided by reason of the employment or of benefits on death or retirement for the participator or his dependants.[6] It is also excluded if the participator is another close company and one is the subsidiary of the other or both are subsidiaries of a third company and the benefit arises on the transfer of assets or liabilities by or to the company.[7]

Attempts might be made to avoid s. 418 where one has a participator in one close company but not in another close company by the companies agreeing that the other pays or should provide the facilities for that person. In such circumstances the payment is treated as coming from the company in which he is a participator.[8]

The payment is declared to be a distribution. Since it is not stated to be a non-qualifying distribution, it is a qualifying distribution and ACT is therefore due.

Simon's Taxes D3.201, 204.
[1] TA 1988, s. 418(8).
[2] TA 1988, s. 418(2).
[3] Supra, § **6: 94**.
[4] TA 1988, s. 418(3).
[5] TA 1988, s. 418(4).
[6] TA 1988, s. 418(3).
[7] TA 1988, s. 418(5). Subsidiary is defined in subs. (6).
[8] TA 1988, s. 418(7).

QUASI-DISTRIBUTIONS—LOANS TO PARTICIPATORS: TA 1988, s. 419

27: 10 Where a loan is made to a participator a sum equal to the ACT payable if it were a distribution is due from the company by way of corporation tax when the loan is made. This advance payment cannot be set off against the company's own liability to corporation tax on its profits. It is a payment equal to ACT, not ACT itself. The reason for this non-deduction may be the rule that as the loan is repaid the tax is refunded to the company.[1] Thus the rule requires in effect the payment of a special refundable deposit. Without some rule governing loans to participators and their associates, it would be easy for the company to avoid the widened definition of distribution and still enable the participators to enjoy the untaxed capital reserves of the company.[2]

The sum due as if it was ACT is due even though the loan is repaid before the notional ACT charge is levied, although relief is given by repayment of the tax.[3] Without this rule it would be easy to avoid s. 419 by making a loan, repaying it before the ACT charge became due and then making a further loan.[4]

If the loan is at a low rate of interest, the borrower may incur liability under TA 1988, s. 160, see supra, § **6: 94**.

When the loan is made neither by the close company, A, nor by another close company which A controls but by a non-close company which A controls,[5] TA 1988, s. 422 makes s. 419 apply. To catch obvious avoidance devices, loans existing when A acquires control are treated as being made after that control was acquired thus falling within TA 1988, s. 422.

The section is aimed at schemes to avoid s. 419 and therefore provides an exception when

"it is shown that no person has made any arrangements (otherwise than in the ordinary course of a business carried on by him) as a result of which there is a connection (*a*) between the making of the loan and the acquisition of control; or (*b*) between the making of the loan and the provision by the close company of funds for the company making the loan; and the close company shall be regarded as providing funds as aforesaid if it directly or indirectly makes any payment or transfers any property to or realises or satisfies (in whole or in part) a liability of, the company making the loan".[6]

The onus of establishing that the loan was in the ordinary course of business or that there was no arrangement is thus placed on the taxpayer.

Simon's Taxes D3.401–404.
[1] TA 1988, s. 419(4).
[2] See *Jacobs v IRC* (1925) 10 TC 1.
[3] TA 1988, s. 419(3) clarifying the position for loans and repayments made after 18th March 1986; the position before that date was unclear.
[4] Although the general step transaction or sham doctrine might apply to prevent this.
[5] TA 1988, s. 419(4). When two or more companies control the lender the company is treated as controlled by each—but the loan is apportioned between them: TA 1988, s. 419(5).
[6] TA 1988, s. 422(4).

27: 11   The statute gives a wide definition of loan.[1] Despite this it was held that there has to be some consensual element so that money due to a company by way of restitution of sums misappropriated by a director was not within s. 419;[2] however, it is also provided that a company is to be regarded as making a loan when a person "incurs a debt" to the close company and the liability to make good the misappropriation has been held to be a loan for this purpose.[3] If the borrower is a full time worker for, and does not have a material interest in the company or an associated company, he is excluded from s. 419 provided that total loan outstanding does not exceed £15,000.[4] In computing the amount of the loan there are to be included loans made to the spouse of the director or employee, but not to other associates. Provision is made for the possibility of acquiring a material interest after the date of the loan by deeming a new loan on that happy occasion. A participator who is neither a director nor an employee is not entitled to those exceptions.

Exceptions are also made for ordinary trade credit (subject to a six month maximum period) and for certain loans made to certain directors or employees of that or an associated company.[5]

Simon's Taxes D3.401, 402.
[1] TA 1988, s. 419(2).
[2] *Stephens v T Pittas Ltd* [1983] STC 576.
[3] This was held by the Special Commissioners in *Stephens v T Pittas Ltd* but was not the subject of an appeal to the High Court. The issue raises interesting questions about the meaning of the word "debt". The provision is TA 1988, s 419(2); s. 419(2) also covers the assignment of a debt due from the participator to another person by that person to the close company.
[4] A special rule applies for pre 1971 housing loans—TA 1988, s. 420(2).
[5] TA 1988, s. 420(2).

Release as distribution

27: 12   Should a loan falling within s. 419 later be released or written off in whole or in part, the person to whom it was made is treated as receiving an amount grossed up by the amount of income tax at basic rate which would have been payable had it been a distribution. The grossing up is to achieve parity with distributions proper but only has an effect if the person thereby becomes liable to higher rate tax. No repayment of income tax can be claimed and the income is not treated as having been taxed for the purposes of TA 1988, ss. 348 and 349.[1]

If the loan is repaid, so causing a repayment of tax, that repayment is calculated by reference to the rate of ACT prevailing when the loan was made. However, when a loan is released the amount released is grossed up at the rate prevailing at that time. So if in 1976 a company made a loan of £33,000 within s. 419, the company would at that time have had to pay a sum of £17,000 as the ACT rate then was 34/66ths. If in July 1989 the loan is repaid in half, the other half being released, the company will recover tax on £16,500 at 1976 rates i.e. £8,500 but the participator's £16,500 will be grossed up at 25% to give a total of £22,000 which will be added to his income.

For repayment supplement purposes, the repayment is treated as being of ACT paid in the repayment period[2]—i.e. the supplement, if any, is not calculated by reference to the date of the original payment to the Revenue under s. 419.

Simon's Taxes D3.405, 406.
[1] TA 1988, s. 421.
[2] TA 1988, s. 825(4)(*h*).

APPORTIONMENT OF RELEVANT INCOME—ACCOUNTING PERIODS BEGINNING BEFORE 1st APRIL 1989

27: 13   If the close company fails to distribute what is called its relevant income, the Inspector was previously empowered but is now directed[1] to act as if the company had distributed that income and thus to tax the participators on income which they have not in fact received. This only applies to the extent that the relevant income exceeds the actual distributions for the same accounting period.[2] If one of the participators is itself a close company, a sub-apportionment takes place. Since, under the imputation system, basic rate income tax is treated as having already been paid, an apportionment only causes problems of excess liability.

In general it is undesirable for companies to allow these apportionments to arise since the only advantage is the availability of retained funds as sources of finance and this can be achieved by making the distribution and then taking the money back under a loan or in exchange for new shares. It seems particularly pointless for shareholders to have the company's retained income apportioned and then have to pay CGT on the disposal of the shares.

An apportionment is not made on a trading company or member of a trading group in respect of its trading income, nor on other income unless the excess of relevant income over actual distributions exceeds £1,000.[3] By concession, no apportionment is made on a property investment company where the excess is less than £250.[4]

If tax on an actual distribution would be exempt under or limited by a double tax treaty an apportionment is not made.[5]

The Inspector may apportion the whole of the relevant income of a *non-trading* company even if there is no excess of relevant income over actual distributions.[6] This means that he is empowered to substitute a deemed distribution among the participators of the company for the actual distributions made by the company save only that he may not thus apportion sums which the company could not by law distribute.[7]

Simon's Taxes D3.322.
[1] TA 1988, s. 423(1).
[2] TA 1988, s. 423(3).
[3] TA 1988, s. 424(1)(*b*) and Sch. 19, para. 1(1).
[4] TA 1988, s. 424(1); extra-statutory concession C6 (1988).
[5] Extra-statutory concession B22 (1988), Simon's Taxes, Division H2.2.
[6] TA 1988, s. 424(2); thus remaining a power for the Inspector "if he sees fit" and is not affected by F(No. 2)A 1987.
[7] TA 1988, Sch. 19, paras. 10(4) and 11(2).

Apportionment of charges and interest

27: 14 In computing the profits and so the distributable income of the company, certain charges on income are deductible.[1] Often such charges are not deductible by an individual in computing his total income, that is they are only allowable against basic rate income tax.[2] A process of un-deduction is directed whereby these amounts which have been deducted in computing the profits of the company can be apportioned among the participators, if either they would not have been deductible by an individual in computing his total income or would not have been deductible at all. This is additional to the apportionment already described and the limits of £1,000 and £250[3] do not apply. Payments made wholly and exclusively for the company's trade are excluded from this process. For periods beginning before 17th March 1987 the inspector is under no obligation to apportion charges and interest under this rule,[4] perhaps this conclusion is odd as the legislation gives no guidance as to the matters an inspector should consider in exercising his discretion. For later accounting periods the discretion is removed.[5]

A close company may not treat a qualifying donation to a charity as a charge.[6]

Simon's Taxes D3.324.
[1] Supra, § **25: 08**.
[2] TA 1988, s. 683; supra, § **13: 46**.
[3] TA 1988, s. 423.
[4] *R v HM Inspector of Taxes, ex p Lansing Bagnall Ltd* [1986] STC 453 (notice issued by inspector on assumption he had no discretion quashed); on practice, see SP2/87.
[5] TA 1988, s. 423(3).
[6] TA 1988, s. 339(2); on qualifying donations see supra, § **25: 13**.

27: 15 For similar reasons[1] interest payments made by close companies are attributable to the participators.[2] This does not apply to interest wholly and exclusively laid out for the purposes of a trade carried on by the company, nor interest eligible for relief in the case of an individual.[3] The rule applies to payments by non-trading companies.[4] If apportionable interest[5] is paid to a participator, that payment reduces any amount apportionable to the participator.[6]

Like the apportionment of charges on income, this power to apportion is quite separate from that over income and so may be exercised whether or not the relevant income of the company exceeds its distributions.[7]

As a result of the rules for deep discounts (see § **9: 29** and § **25: 18**) any amount deducted by the company on the redemption of the security is to be treated as interest and so as potentially apportionable under this rule.[8]

Simon's Taxes D3.325.
[1] Supra, § **5: 30**.
[2] TA 1988, s. 423(1)(c); FA 1974, Sch. 1, para. 26.
[3] TA 1988, s. 424(6)—on eligible interest, see supra, § **5: 31**.
[4] TA 1988, s. 424(4).
[5] Defined TA 1988, s. 424(5).
[6] TA 1988, s. 423(4).
[7] TA 1988, s. 423(2).
[8] TA 1988, Sch. 4, para. 10.

Method of apportionment

27: 16 The basic principle is that the relevant income should be apportioned among the participators according to their respective interests in the company.[1] The various definitions of participators clearly leaves the Inspector with wide powers as to the method of apportionment, and he is expressly authorised to apportion to each according to the interests they would have in the assets of the company available for distribution in the event of a winding up, a matter of importance if shares are preferential as to capital on winding up but not as to dividend, or "in any other circumstances".[2] Thus the apportionment may be according to interest in income or interests in capital.[3]

A loan creditor may be a participator but does not technically have an interest in the company. In relation to a non-trading company such a person is to be treated as if he had an interest and the extent of his interest is related to the amount of the income which is to be apportioned, which has been spent or is available to be spent in the redemption repayment or discharge of the loan capital or debt.[4]

The Inspector may disregard the actual pattern of distribution of the relevant income of a non-trading company. However, he must choose one only of these methods and may not apply each method to $\frac{1}{2}$ of the relevant income.

The apportionment can only be made on one who was a participator on the last day of the accounting period.[5]

Simon's Taxes D3.326.
[1] TA 1988, s. 425(1).
[2] TA 1988, s. 425(2).
[3] *Lothbury Investment Corpn v IRC* [1979] STC 772.
[4] TA 1988, s. 425(3).
[5] *Semble—CHW (Huddersfield) Ltd v IRC* [1963] 2 All ER 952, 41 TC 92, HL.

The sum to be apportioned: Method (1) Excess relevant income

27: 17 The first method by which the apportionable sum is calculated takes the form of a complex mathematical calculation which determines the maximum amount that may be taken. This is the company's distributable investment income plus 50% of the estate or trading income for the period.[1] This rule is adapted when dealing with a trading company or a member of a trading group it being provided that the trading income of such a company is to be ignored.[2] These rules give the figure for relevant income. This figure is then compared with the distributions to see if there is excess relevant income.

The steps taken are set out in the following paragraphs.

Simon's Taxes D3.312.
[1] TA 1988, Sch. 19, para. 2(1).
[2] TA 1988, Sch. 19, para. 2(2).

27: 18   (1) *Classifying the company.* A "trading company"[1] is one which exists wholly or mainly[2] for the purposes of carrying on a trade or whose income does not consist wholly or mainly of investment income. In deciding what is investment income the test used is that for determining earned income for an individual.[3] Any income which is apportioned must be treated as investment income whether or not it was trading income in the hands of the company.

The advantages of being a trading company or a member of a trading group[4] are (*i*) that it is not liable to apportionment on its trading income; (*ii*) that it is not liable to the alternative method of apportionment, supra, § **27: 16**; (*iii*) that it may benefit from the first business loan rule, infra, § **27: 25** and (*iv*) that it may benefit from the abatements; (*iv*) applies only to a trading company not to a member of a trading group.

[1] TA 1988, Sch. 19, para. 7.
[2] This provides great scope for argument—it may mean almost entirely or more than half.
[3] Supra, § **24: 09**.
[4] Defined TA 1988, Sch. 19, para. 7. On Revenue practice, see SP 8/87.

27: 19   (2) *Classifying the income.* Estate income: income chargeable under Schedule A and B or income chargeable under Schedule D which arises from the ownership or occupation of land or from the furnished letting of a building but with the exclusion of yearly or other interest.[1]

Trading income: income which (*i*) would not be investment income if accruing to an individual or (*ii*) accruing incidentally to a trade provided the company's activities consist wholly or mainly of the carrying on of the trade and that trade if financial, including share dealing.[2] (*ii*) is designed to cover such matters as dividends received by shares dealing companies.

[1] TA 1988, Sch. 19, para. 5(2).
[2] TA 1988, Sch. 19, para. 5(3) and 5(4); on enterprise allowances, see TA 1988, s. 127(3).

27: 20   (3) *Determining what is distributable.* Distributable income is the amount of distributable profits (which are defined as excluding that attributable to chargeable gains) after all allowable deductions, such as interest and less corporation tax. Included are group income[1] and franked investment income (but net of the tax credit); however FII relieved under TA 1988, ss. 242 and 243 (supra, §§ **25: 33** and **25: 37**) is not included. In deciding what is distributable a restriction imposed by law must be taken into account.[2] In *Noble v Laygate Investments Ltd* Oliver J held that restrictions imposed by the articles which the company could remove by altering the articles were not imposed by law but by the company.[3]

Distributable investment income is distributable income less estate or trading income.

---

[1] TA 1988, Sch. 19, para. 4(1); on receipt of stock dividends see TA 1988, Sch. 19, para. 12.
[2] TA 1988, Sch. 19, para. 11. Money in a share premium account is not available: *Shearer v Bercain Ltd* [1980] STC 359.
[3] [1978] STC 430, [1978] 2 All ER 1067 (query if the company was bound by contract not to alter its articles.

27: 21 (4) *Deductions.* Charges on income, expenses of management and other sums which can be deducted from profits of more than one description are treated as reducing first income charged to corporation tax other than estate or trading income, secondly the estate or trading income, and thirdly, the amount included in the profits in respect of chargeable gains.[1] Expenses attributable only to one source must be deducted from that source.

---

[1] TA 1988, Sch. 19, para. 6(2).

27: 22 (5) *Abatements.* (*a*) Estate income abatement for trading companies[1] (but not members of a trading group). This is best explained historically. Originally the abatement was for estate or trading income of such companies; if such income were less than £25,000 it was ignored; if between £25,000 and £75,000 it was reduced by one half of the difference between £75,000 and that income. Owing to the abolition of apportionment of trading income this now applies only to estate income but trading income remains relevant to this abatement since the figures of £25,000 and £75,000 are reduced in the proportion that the estate income bears to the total estate and trading income.

Legislation was needed to prevent abuse of this relief by the creating of associated companies and this need is met, the figures £25,000 and £75,000 being divided equally among the associated companies concerned.[2] An association which exists for only a part of the year enjoys no relief even though an association is subseqently found with another company so that two of the companies were not associated with the close company at the same time.

(*b*) Investment income abatement:[3] One must deduct the lesser of (*i*) 10% of the estate and trading income (after tax) and (*ii*) £1,000. This applies to all types of company save that for a trading company or a member of a trading group the figure of £1,000 is increased to £3,000.[4]

---

[1] TA 1988, Sch. 19, para. 2(2).
[2] TA 1988, Sch. 19, para. 2(4).
[3] TA 1988, Sch. 19, para. 4(2).
[4] TA 1988, Sch. 19, para. 4(2)(*b*).

27: 23   (6) *Calculating distributions.* Distributions include all dividends declared in respect of the period and paid within a reasonable time thereafter—in practice 18 months is reasonable[1]; any other distributions are taken into account strictly by reference to the time they are made.

Sums which would have been distributions but for being exempted by the legislation dealing with demergers or the acquisition by a company of its own shares are to be treated as distributions, and so removed from the risk of apportionment.[2]

EXAMPLE (1) (trading company) (financial year 1988)

Trading income	£30,000	£30,000
Estate income	£40,000	40,000
FII	£ 3,000	
		70,000
Corporation tax at 25%		17,500
		£52,500

Calculation of abatement of estate income (see (5)(*a*) above)
Trading income $\frac{3}{4}$ Estate income $\frac{4}{7}$
So figures of £75,000 and £25,000
are reduced to £42,857 and £14,285
Estate income abatement:

$\frac{1}{2}$ (£42,857 − £30,000 i.e. estate income net of CT) = $\dfrac{12,857}{2}$ = £6,428.

Investment income abatement (see (5)(b) above)
Deduct the lesser of (i) 10% of £52,500
    or (ii) £3,000   i.e. £3,000
∴ Investment income reduced to nil

∴ Maximum relevant income = $\frac{1}{2}$ (30,000 − 6,428) = $\dfrac{23,572}{2}$ =   £11,786

EXAMPLE (2) (A non-trading company) (financial year 1988)

Capital gains	£175,000	150,000
FII	50,000	
Interest	27,000	27,000
Rents	340,000	340,000
Interest paid	8,000	
Trading profit	50,000	50,000
		567,000
Less charges		8,000
		559,000
Corporation Tax @ 35%		195,650
		363,350

Income available for distribution			
Investment income net of tax credit	37,500	Estate income (net of CT)	221,000
Interest less charges (all net of CT)	12,350	Trading income (net of CT)	32,500
	49,850		£253,500
Abatement	1,000		
	48,850		

Maximum relevant income = £47,850 + $\dfrac{£253,500^3}{2}$ = £174,600

---

[1] 18 months was the original statutory period; see statement of Practice C3, **Simon's Taxes, Division H3.4.**
[2] TA 1988, Sch. 19, para. 8(4).
[3] There is no abatement of estate income as it exceeds £75,000.

The sum to be apportioned: Method (2)   Business requirements

27: 24   The second method rests on the rule that for a trading company or member of a trading group, relevant income is to include only so much of the company's distributable income,[1] whether estate or investment income, as can be distributed without prejudice to the company's business and an analogous provision applies to other companies with estate or trading income[2] and which have a business. In looking at the requirements of the business regard is to be had to the current requirements and such as may be necessary or advisable for the maintenance and development of the business. The term business extends to a new business which the company is starting up alongside its existing business;[3] the test requires consideration of anything that is genuinely in the contemplation of the company at the relevant date as being then required for the future maintenance and development of the business in whatever form the company might think desirable.

The circumstances of the company and its business requirements are to be considered at the date when the accounts are approved by the directors and they judge whether or not to pay a dividend.[4]

In assessing the liquidity position at that time one must take account of sums that will be noticed through the payment of debts and the disposal of stock.[5] One may take into account such matters as the length of time the company has been trading, the type of business, the general economic position and seriously considered plans for expansion.[6] Where the close company is in a group regard may be had to the needs of other companies in the group when appropriate, e.g. when there are trading links.

Simon's Taxes D3.319.

[1] Income means profits so payments which are deductible in computing profits are not made out of income: *Hanstead Investments Ltd v IRC* [1975] STC 419, [1975] 2 All ER 1066, noted [1976] BTR 124 (Trevett).

[2] TA 1988, Sch. 19, paras. 1(2) and 8.

[3] *Wilson and Garden Ltd v IRC* [1982] STC 597 per Lord Roskill at 601.

[4] *IRC v Thompson Bros (London) Ltd* [1974] STC 16, 49 TC 110.

[5] *MacTaggart Scott & Co Ltd v IRC* [1973] STC 180, 48 TC 708.

[6] The Revenue give sympathetic treatment to certain situations—see statement of practice C4, para. 1, **Simon's Taxes, Division H3.4.**

27: 25   Certain sums are regarded as not having been spent on the company's business and so as being available for distribution.[1] These are (*i*) sums spent in redeeming or repaying any share or loan capital issued otherwise than for adequate consideration; (*ii*) sums spent on any fictitious or artificial transaction; (*iii*) if the company is not a trading company or a member of a trading group, (a) sums spent repaying loan capital or on acquiring land or buildings and (b) sums spent repaying loans to acquire the first business, undertaking or property of a substantial character (commonly known as first business loans). (*iii*)(b) is extended to cover sums spent repaying share or loan capital issued to finance these first purchases or any other obligation in respect of such items. The deduction of first business loan repayments by a trading company or a member of a trading group is now permitted.[2] Income used by a company to purchase its own shares is treated as income spent on the redemption or repayment of share capital.[3]

The rationale behind the privileged treatment of trading companies ceases to apply if the company goes into liquidation or for some other reason ceases to trade. Hence the relevant income for the accounting period in which this occurs or any other period ending within the previous twelve months is all treated as relevant income;[4] an exception for trading income[4] is made if the cessation is part of a company reconstruction. In view of the abolition of apportionment of trading income of trading companies and members of trading groups it is further provided that for these companies trading income is to be excluded from the calculation for accounting periods ending after 26th March 1980 even though within twelve months of cessation. The practical effect is that if there is a risk of apportionment, e.g. the company has non-trading income or is not a trading company or member of a trading group a cessation should take place just after rather than just before the end of an accounting period. In working out what is available for distribution the company is not required to distribute sums which could only be distributed to the prejudice of creditors. However not all creditors are treated equally; participators and their associates are ignored unless the debt is an ordinary business debt which arose in the ordinary course of the creditor's business or the sum is remuneration chargeable under Schedule E or is normal rent for the use of tangible property or copyright.[5]

Since a payment to a shareholder in the course of a liquidation is made non-deductible by this rule and so subject to apportionment but is also a capital payment for CGT purposes a concession is made so as to enable the shareholder to treat the CGT as a credit against the income tax apportionment.

Simon's Taxes D3.320
  [1] TA 1988, Sch. 19, paras. 1(2) and 8; the onus is on the Revenue, *IRC v White Bros Ltd* (1956) 36 TC 587.
  [2] TA 1988, Sch. 19, paras. 1(3) and 9 although it has been indicated that the Revenue do not regard first business loan repayments by a non-trading member of a trading group as deductible. Their authority for such a contention is unclear.
  [3] TA 1988, Sch. 19, para. 8(4).
  [4] TA 1988, Sch. 19, para. 10.
  [5] TA 1988, Sch. 19, para. 10(3).

CONSEQUENCES

Income tax[1]

27: 26   Where an apportionment takes place, the participator is liable to pay income tax provided the amount to which he is assessable is at least £1,000 (for accounting periods ending on or after 6th April 1984) or 5% of the sum apportioned, whichever is the less.[2] The income is his investment income even though it may be estate or trading income of the company.

If the participator is an individual, the sum is treated as income received at the end of the accounting period to which the apportionment relates and is deemed to be the highest part of his income.[3] Because of the imputation system he is treated as having already paid income tax at the basic rate so that only the excess over basic rate attributable to the higher rate tax will be due.[4] However he may not claim repayment under the credit scheme[5] and the deemed distribution is treated as income not brought into charge to income tax for the purposes of TA 1988, ss. 348 and 349.[6] On the other hand a deduction may be made for any deductions which could be made in computing total income, e.g. any annual payments. Where a covenanted payment to charity is apportioned, the sum added to the individual's total income is reduced by the amount by which his covenanted payments to charity in that year fall to be treated as his income for excess liability[7].

The sums which are treated as being added to the individual's income must be grossed up to reflect the amount that would have been paid by way of ACT in respect of that distribution.[8] The rate of ACT is that prevailing at the time of the deemed distribution—the end of the accounting period.[9]

EXAMPLE
> X owns 50% of the shares in A Ltd. In 1988 the relevant income is £36,000. £18,000 is apportioned to X who is treated as receiving £24,000 (£18,000 grossed up at 25%). If his marginal tax rate is 40% he will pay £3,600 (i.e. £9,600 − £6,000) (basic rate).

Simon's Taxes D3.311, E1.101–104.
[1] TA 1988, s. 426. On apportionment to non-residents see extra-statutory concession B22 (1988), **Simon's Taxes, Division H2.2.**
[2] TA 1988, s. 427(1).
[3] TA 1988, s. 426(2)(*a*).
[4] TA 1988, s. 426(2)(*b*).
[5] TA 1988, s. 426(2)(*c*).
[6] TA 1988, s. 426(2)(*d*).
[7] TA 1988, s. 427(3).
[8] There is no grossing up for advance corporation tax if that which is being apportioned is an annual payment or interest within TA 1988, ss. 423, 427(5): TA 1988, s. 428(1).
[9] TA 1988, s. 428(2).

27: 27 Since the relevant income which is being apportioned is computed after the deduction of sums actually distributed, there is no further deduction for such amounts but a specific rule is needed to preserve that effect when an inspector exercises his power to apportion the income of a non-trading company.[1]

Sums apportioned to trustees are treated as if they had been apportioned to individuals,[2] so that the trustees may be liable to the investment surcharge where the trust is discretionary, supra, § **11: 05**.

---

[1] TA 1988, s. 427(2).
[2] TA 1988, s. 686(4) and note set off in TA 1988, s. 687(2), supra, § **11: 10**. On estates see TA 1988, s. 426(3).

Subsequent distributions

27: 28 A problem arises if a company's income, having been apportioned under a deemed distribution, is subsequently distributed and in that period the sum distributed by the company exceeds its relevant income. To avoid double taxation, it is provided that if an individual has already been charged to tax on the deemed distribution a certain amount of the actual distribution is deemed not to be a distribution.[1] The amount is a fraction of the income distributed in the second period or, if less, the excess of the distribution over relevant income; the fraction is whichever is the less of (*i*) the fraction of the apportioned income under the deemed distribution and (*ii*) the fraction to which he is entitled on the subsequent distribution. It will be seen not only that the first part refers to the pattern of the deemed distribution, a matter resting with the Inspector, and which may not have been based upon his rights in income, but also that the same individual must be concerned.

> **EXAMPLE**—assuming ACT rate of $\frac{25}{75}$ for all relevant periods
>
> X, to whom £24,000 was apportioned in the previous example, reduces his 50% holding to a 30% holding by selling the balance to Y in the following period. In the following year the company has net relevant income of £39,000 and it decides to distribute that along with the £36,000 from the previous year, making a total of £75,000 on which ACT of $\frac{25}{75}$ = £25,000 will be paid. X receives 30% of this, £22,500, which would give him Schedule F income of £30,000.
>
> However, the distribution in year 2 (£75,000), exceeds the relevant income for year 2 (£39,000) by £36,000, so X is entitled to a reduction. The fraction is applied to the lesser of £75,000 and £36,000 = £36,000, the fraction is 50% or 30% and again the lesser is taken. X is treated as not receiving 30% of £36,000 = £10,800. This reduces his distribution from £22,250 to £11,450 and the Schedule F income from £30,000 to £15,267.
>
> It will be seen that X forfeits the balance of his credit from the previous year (£24,000 − £15,267 = £8,733). Since he does not receive 50% of the later distribution this may be seen as just but this is no comfort to Y and does increase the total tax take. X is deemed not to receive this income only for the purposes of excess liability; he is therefore treated as receiving £30,000 for other purposes, e.g., TA 1988, s. 348.

Simon's Taxes D3.329.
[1] TA 1988, s. 427(4).

Advance corporation tax

27: 29   One difference between an actual distribution and a deemed one is that in the former case there will be ACT which can of course be set off against the mainstream CT liability. Certain rules are designed to prevent the close company from deriving a cash flow advantage from not making actual distributions.

The company is assessed to CT on an amount equal to the ACT it would have had to pay if it had distributed its excess relevant income.[1] In making this calculation account must be taken of any FII which the company could have used to frank the notional distribution. This amount is reduced by the amount of ACT that could have been set against the company's liability to CT of that period or which could have been carried back to previous periods under the rules discussed supra, § **24: 16**. The resulting hypothetical ACT must be paid but can then be set against CT liabilities in later periods.

More fully, these rules are designed to prevent the close company from deriving a cash flow advantage from not making actual distributions. They deal with "the apportioned amount" which is the amount apportioned together with the advance corporation tax hypothetically payable in respect of it.[2] One advantage might be that if the distribution of the relevant income had occurred, any surplus FII might have been absorbed by the ACT instead of being used in other ways; the other advantage is that the ACT might not all have been absorbed in the payment of mainstream corporation tax. The problems are thus surplus FII and surplus ACT and to ensure, hypothetically, that these problems exist.

The apportioned amount is manipulated in three ways.

(1) If the company has surplus franked investment income which has not been used in a s. 242 claim or to frank actual distributions in that period, then that surplus is reduced or extinguished by the apportioned amount.[3] This prevents the company from using the surplus franked investment income to frank its own distributions or to relieve charges on income in some *later* accounting period.

EXAMPLE 1—assuming ACT rate of $\frac{2}{3}$

A Ltd has estate income of £20,000, FII of £6,000 net (£8,000 gross) and makes a distribution of £2,000 net (£2,667 gross). Surplus FII = £8,000 − £2,667 = £5,333. Assuming that the relevant income is £10,000, the amount apportioned is £13,333 (£10,000 grossed up at 25%). The surplus FII is extinguished leaving £13,333 − £5,333 = £8,000 of the amount apportioned of which £2,000 is the hypothetical ACT element.

Rules (2) and (3) apply only if some of the apportioned amount remains after Rule (1) has been applied. These deal only with the advance corporation tax element in the apportioned amount.

(2) This rule restricts the company's right to carry surplus advance corporation tax—that is advance corporation tax in excess of the actual corporation tax liability[4]—of later periods back to the accounting periods over the previous two years. The rule directs the hypothetical advance corporation tax in those earlier periods to be set off against the corporation tax liability and only allows the carryback from later periods to the extent that there remains any unrelieved liability for those periods.[5] The company may of course carry the surplus forward.[6]

(3) This rule provides that where in the accounting period the amount of hypothetical advance corporation tax exceeds the mainstream corporation tax then it may be gathered from the company by direct assessment.[7] This only applies after that surplus has been carried back to be set against the mainstream liability of earlier periods of the previous two years. Such advance corporation tax may be carried forward to subsequent accounting periods[8] but the purpose of the rule, to discourage any cash flow advantage, has been achieved.

EXAMPLE 2

	1	2	3	4	5
		£	£	£	
Interest		45,000	45,000	90,000	
FII		15,000	12,000	10,000	
Distributions made		40,000	40,000	50,000	nil

Notes

(1) The excess problem arises in year 4, not year 5. This is because distributions are to be deducted from the period *in respect of* which they are made; this is quite different from ACT which is charged on deductions as they are made. The distributions shown as made in years 2, 3 and 4 were made in respect of the previous years.

(2) The figures shown do not include capital gains; these will be needed in order to finance the various distributions but they are not relevant in computing relevant income (supra, § **27: 23**).

The excess of relevant income for year 4:

The relevant income will be £90,000 net of tax at 35% = £58,500 plus £7,500 (FII net) = £66,000.

Hypothetical ACT at ⅔ would be	£22,000
Maximum set off would be 25% of £90,000	£22,500
Less: actual set off ⅔ (£50,000 – 10,000)	£13,333
	£9,167

One must then deduct set off for years 2 and 3.

Year 3

Maximum ACT set off 25% of £45,000	£11,250	
Less: Actual set off ⅔ × (£40,000 – £12,000)	£9,333	£1,917
		£7,250

Year 2

Maximum set off 25% of £45,000	£11,250	
Less: Actual set off ⅔ × (£40,000 – £15,000)	£8,333	£2,917
Real assessment to hypothetical ACT		£4,333

Simon's Taxes D3.330.

[1] TA 1988, s. 430.

[2] TA 1988, s. 430(1). When there has been a stock dividend the apportioned income is reduced by the appropriate amount in cash: TA 1988, s. 430(2); see supra, § **9: 45**.

[3] TA 1988, s. 430(3). Franked investment income is defined ibid, s. 238 and is also grossed up.

[4] TA 1988, s. 239(3).

[5] TA 1988, s. 430(5).

[6] TA 1988, s. 239(4).

[7] TA 1988, s. 430(7).

[8] Under TA 1988, s. 239(4).

Capital gains tax

27: 30 Although the charge to income tax is made on the participator, the company is also accountable for this tax and in practice usually pays the tax. If the shareholder pays, he is allowed to treat the tax so paid as a deduction for any subsequent CGT liability on the disposal of shares in the company (except in so far as relief has been allowed on a subsequent distribution).[1] There is no mechanism whereby shareholders can avoid CGT liability in respect of accrued profits even though these have been the subject of apportionment.

When the company has gone into liquidation so that a participator may have to pay both CGT, on the deemed disposal of the shares, and income tax under these rules, concessionary relief prevents a double charge.[2]

Simon's Taxes C2.127.

[1] CGTA 1979, s. 74 extended by extra-statutory concession D12 (1988), see **Simon's Taxes, Division H2.2**.

[2] Extra-statutory concession A36 (1988), **Simon's Taxes, Division H2.2**.

Deep discount securities

27: 31 One should note the restriction which requires a close company which has issued qualifying deep discount securities to claim a deduction only on redemption for such periods as the securities are held by a participator, the associate of a participator or a company controlled by a participator.[1]

---

[1] TA 1988, Sch. 4, para. 10; see §§ **9: 51, 25: 18.**

CLOSE INVESTMENT HOLDING COMPANIES—ACCOUNTING PERIODS BEGINNING AFTER 31st MARCH 1989

27: 32 The latest stage in the saga of close companies is the decision to scrap the system of attribution of relevant income to participators altogether. This is carried out for accounting periods beginning after 31st March 1989.[1] It is unclear whether companies will shorten their accounting periods in order to come within the new regime.

As published, the 1989 Finance Bill proposed that close investment companies should be subjected to corporation tax at the top rate of income tax (40%) but the final Act opts instead for a system under which the income of such companies cannot use the reduced rate (of 25%) and must instead bear the normal corporation tax rate of 35%.[2] However some of the flavour of the old apportionment rules lingers on in that the Act also contains provisions restricting the amount of tax credit available if the actual pattern of distributions by the company is unusual.

Where a distribution is made to a participator after 31st March 1989 out of profits which were made before then and so subject to the old attribution regime, the old relief recognising the tax already paid continues to apply—but only for distributions made before 1st April 1992.[3]

Simon's Taxes D3.101, 102, 121, 201, 204, 205.
[1] FA 1989, s. 103.
[2] TA 1988, s. 13A, introduced by FA 1989, s. 105.
[3] TA 1988, s. 427 (4) preserved by FA 1989, s. 103 (2).

Defining a close investment-holding company

27: 33 A company is a close investment-holding company if it is a close company and fails to satisfy a long statutory test. The definition of close company set out at §§ **27: 02–27: 08** applies for the present purpose.[1]

The long statutory test allows the company to escape designation as an investment holding company if, throughout the relevant accounting period, it exists wholly or mainly for any one or more of six purposes of which the first two are the most important. In practice the Revenue accept more than 50% as being "mainly". The effect of the list is to exclude trading companies, property investment companies which are part of a group and the main purpose of those group companies is to support the trading or property investment activities of the group.[2]

The first qualifying purpose is carrying on a trade or trades on a commercial basis.[3] This definition does not extend to professions. The second purpose is that of making investments in land where the land is, or is intended to be, let to unconnected persons.[4]

The remaining qualifying purposes embroider the first two. Thus a company will escape close investment company status if its purpose is to hold shares in and securities of or making loans to a qualifying company[5] or to co-ordinate the administration of two or more qualifying companies.[6] It may also exist for the purposes either (i) of a trade carried on, on a commercial basis, by a company which controls it or by a qualifying company, or (ii) of making investments by a company which controls it or by another qualifying company. There is a special provision for companies in the course of a winding up.[7]

---

[1] FA 1989, s. 104, replaces TA 1988, s. 414(2) by ss. 414(2)–(2D).
[2] Hansard Standing Committee G, 22 June 1989, col. 587.
[3] TA 1988, s. 13A (2) (*a*), added by FA 1989 s. 105 (2).
[4] TA 1988, s. 13A (2) (*b*), added by FA 1989 s. 105 (2).
[5] TA 1988, s. 13A (2) (*c*), added by FA 1989 s. 105 (2); on definition of qualifying company, see TA 1988, s. 13A (3).
[6] TA 1988, s. 13A (2) (*d*), added by FA 1989 s. 105 (2).
[7] TA 1988, s. 13A (4), added by FA 1989 s. 105 (2).

Consequences for the company

27: 34 If the company is a close investment-holding company, a matter determined by reference to the company's purpose throughout the accounting period, the reduced rate of corporation tax is not applicable and all profits will be charged at 35% regardless of the overall level of the profits of the company.[1] The profits of the company will be calculated in the usual way, with the normal deduction of expenses and interest payments.

---

[1] TA 1988, s. 13A (1), added by FA 1989, s. 105.

Consequences for the shareholder

27: 35 Any actual distribution by the company will carry with it a tax credit under TA 1988, s. 231 in the usual way. However where there is a repayment of the tax credit element due that repayment will be made only if the hurdle set by FA 1989, s. 106 is cleared. This starts by giving the inspector a power to restrict the credit if there appear to him to be arrangements relating to the distribution of profits and their main purpose is to enable payments of the credit to be made.[1] This applies where the person making the repayment claim has received a qualifying distribution consisting of the redemption, repayment or purchase of its own shares; where the distribution consists of a dividend, the power exists only if the amount of value of the distribution is greater that might in all the circumstances have been expected but for the arrangements.[2]

This power is however excluded if throughout the period the company's ordinary share capital consisted only of one class of shares and no person waived his entitlement to any dividend becoming payable by the company in the period or failed to receive any dividend which had become due and payable to him by the company in that period.[3]

The purpose of this restriction is to deter those controlling the company from distributing its profits disproportionately to others whose marginal tax rates might be lower, e.g. a child with unused personal allowances or a relative with losses. Waiver of dividends and issuing more than one class of ordinary share capital are two ways of achieving such uneven distributions.[4]

Where this hurdle is not cleared the company will pay tax at 35% and when the remaining 65% is distributed, ACT of £21.66 will fall due, there being a tax credit of £21.66. A taxpayer with a marginal rate of 40% will be able to use this credit as will one with 25%; however one who would be entitled to a repayment will find that the Inspector has power to restrict the repayment to such extent as appears to the inspector to be just and reasonable.

---

[1] TA 1988, s. 231(3A)(*a*).
[2] TA 1988, s. 231(3A)(b)
[3] TA 1988, s. 231(3B.
[4] Hansard Standing Committee, G 22 June 1989, col. 591.

PART V. SAVINGS

28 Savings

INTRODUCTION

28: 01 Savings enjoy a range of privileges under UK income tax law. First, exemption from tax is given to certain forms of saving, viz:

National savings:
    (*i*) National savings certificates: interest.[1]
    (*ii*) Premium bonds: prizes.
    (*iii*) Save as you Earn: bonuses.
    (*iv*) British savings bonds: bonuses (but not interest).
    (*v*) National Savings Bank interest up to £75, other than on deposit accounts.[2]

Secondly, various privileges are granted to other types of saving. Thus:

    (*vi*) Government stock: capital gains are exempt from capital gains tax if held for at least one year (supra, § **15: 18**).
    (*vii*) Building societies and banks: interest is "tax paid" for basic rate taxpayers; this is paid by the institutions at a special composite rate (21·75% for 1989–90)[3] but where the taxpayer's tax rate is zero no repayment claim can be made.[4]
    (*viii*) Pension schemes contributions are exempt from tax while no tax is levied on the fund either, while similar relief is given for retirement annuity premiums.
    (*ix*) Limited relief is given to life insurance premiums on contracts entered into before 14th March 1984.
    (*x*) Investment relief is given under the business start-up and the business expansion schemes.
    (*xi*) relief from income and capital gains tax will be given to investments held under a "personal equity plan".

---

[1] TA 1988, s. 46. On concessionary relief for accumulated interest on Ulster savings certificates following the death of the holder see extra-statutory concession A34 (1988).
[2] S.I. 1988 No. 2145; *Simon's Tax Intelligence* 1988, p. 864.
[3] TA 1988, s. 325.
[4] See generally TA 1988, s. 476.

LIFE ASSURANCE POLICIES

28: 02 The UK tax system accorded special treatment to the life insurance industry. Until 1984 there was income tax relief on premiums.[1] A special system of taxing income and gains applies to insurance companies;[2] in addition the proceeds of a policy are exempt from CGT unless the policy was acquired for money or money's worth.[3] These privileges and reliefs were granted to encourage savings so that people would be encouraged to provide for their old age and for their dependants and the wide range of taxpayers concerned. However in recent years these advantages have been used to promote tax avoidance schemes which probably push the concessions to or even beyond the reasonable limit; many restrictions now apply to policies qualifying for relief. These culminated in the decision embodied in FA 1984, to withhold relief from insurance policies taken out after 13th March 1984. However, the relief remains intact for policies taken out before that date; hence the following exposition retains the present tense.

---

[1] Infra, § **28: 03**.
[2] Infra, § **29: 16–29: 25**.
[3] Infra, § **15: 03**.

Income tax relief on pre-14th March 1984 policies

28: 03 The claimant is entitled to deduct from the premium which he pays a sum equal to 12·5% of the premium;[1] thus if the premium is £100 he actually pays £87·50. This is not a deduction from total income. The limit of relief on premiums is £1,500 or ⅙th total income whichever is the greater.[2] When a person receives the commission in respect of his policy he may only claim to deduct from the net sum.[3] The claim is not affected by a wife's earnings election.[4]

The policy of life insurance or contract for a deferred annuity must be with one of the bodies listed[5] and the policy must have been made by and the premium paid by the taxpayer or his spouse.[6] No relief can be given for sums due but not paid. To agree that the premium be deducted from the proceeds of the policy is not to pay the premium.[7] If a bonus is used to reduce the premium, the premium and so the relief is likewise reduced.[8] However, a premium is paid where the payer borrows the money to pay it, even if the lender is the insurer.[9]

Simon's Taxes E2.1031, 1032; Butterworths Income Tax Service B4.21, Division F8.
[1] TA 1988, s. 266. The same rules now apply to pre-1916 life policies, FA 1988, s. 29.
[2] TA 1988, s. 274.
[3] CCAB Press Release 26 April 1977; see *Simon's Tax Intelligence* 1977, p. 97.
[4] TA 1988, Sch. 14, para. 1(2).
[5] TA 1988, s. 266(2).
[6] TA 1988, s. 266(1) and (2)(*c*).
[7] *Hunter v R* [1904] AC 161, 5 TC 13.
[8] *Watkins v Jones* (1928) 14 TC 94.
[9] Certain borrowings may be treated as income: TA 1988, s. 554; infra, § **28: 17**.

28: 04 There are conditions which the policy must meet. First it must be a policy on the life of the claimant or his wife or on their joint lives.[1] A joint policy on the life of the claimant and someone other than his wife is not eligible.[2] The policy may be a term assurance or an endowment assurance,[3] but the policy must secure a capital sum payable on death, whether or not in connection with other benefits so that a temporary term policy is not eligible.[4] No relief is given during a period of deferment in respect of a policy of deferred insurance.[5] The policy must be a qualifying policy.

Simon's Taxes E2.1032; Butterworths Income Tax Service F8.11.

[1] TA 1988, s. 266(2)(b). On year of marriage see TA 1988, s. 280.

[2] Wilson v Simpson [1926] 2 KB 500, 10 TC 753.

[3] Gould v Curtis [1913] 3 KB 84, 6 TC 293 at 302.

[4] TA 1988, s. 266(3)(a) but note exceptions, ibid.

[5] TA 1988, s. 266(3)(d). Policies taken out before 20th March 1968 are subject to different rules. On date of variation, note IRC v Anderson (1971) 47 TC 145.

A qualifying policy

28: 05   Since 1968[1] relief will only be given if the policy is a "qualifying policy", i.e. it satisfies the conditions in TA 1988, Sch. 15.[2] For endowment assurances the term must be at least ten years. The premiums must be payable at yearly or shorter intervals or until the event specified, whether death or disability. The premiums may be payable for a period of at least ten years. The total premiums payable under the policy in any period of twelve months must not exceed twice the amount payable in any other twelve month period or one-eighth of the total premiums payable if the policy were to run for the specified term.

As from 1975 further conditions must be satisfied. The policy must guarantee that the sum payable on death will be at least 75%[3] of the total premiums payable if the policy were to run its term. Where a new policy is issued for an old one there is to be ignored that part of the premiums which is attributable to the old policy;[4] this is to enable the 75% rule to be applied fairly. Where a policy includes one or more options, the policy must be tested on each option and will only "qualify" if it meets the conditions on every such test.[5] A policy may make provision for total or partial surrender without ceasing to qualify,[6] but if an option in a qualifying policy is exercised after 13th March 1984, and either extends the term of the policy or increases the benefits payable under it, the policy ceases to qualify.[7]

Broadly similar principles apply to whole life and term assurances.[8] A temporary assurance for a period of not more than ten years may be a qualifying policy but only if the surrender value is not to exceed the total premiums previously paid. A term policy of less than twelve months cannot be a qualifying policy.[9]

The purpose of these conditions is to prevent too great an abuse of the tax privileges accorded to life assurance by ensuring that the premiums are paid each year and with a reasonably even spread. If the policy is not a qualifying policy no relief may be claimed in respect of the premiums. A policy issued in connection with another policy cannot qualify if either policy provides unreasonable benefits.[10]

In order to prevent clawback of relief (§ **28: 06**) and any excess liability charge (§ **28: 15**) TA 1988, Sch. 15, para. 20 provides that where one qualifying policy replaces another as a result of a change in the life assured, the change is, in effect, treated as a mere variation of the policy so that neither charge arises.[11] Premiums payable under a policy varied after 13th March 1984 will continue to qualify for relief only if the original policy was made before 14th March 1984 and the benefits remain substantially the same after variation.[12]

Simon's Taxes E2.1036–1041; Butterworths Income Tax Service F8.11–16.

[1] Policies taken out before 20th March 1968 are exempt from these conditions unless they are varied after that date: TA 1988, Sch. 14, para. 8.

[2] TA 1988, Sch. 15, para. 15. On industrial assurance policies, note TA 1988, Sch. 15, paras. 7, 8.

[3] There is a 2% reduction for every year by which the person exceeds 55: TA 1988, Sch. 15, para. 2(1)(*d*)(i). The conditions imposed by FA 1975 apply to policies issued after the appointed day, 1st April 1976.

[4] TA 1988, Sch. 15, para. 17(4) and TA 1988, Sch. 15, para. 17(2); see also extra-statutory concession A45 (1988), **Simon's Taxes, Division H2.2.**

[5] TA 1988, Sch. 15, para. 19. For policies issued before "the appointed day", the test ignores the options until one is in fact exercised and then the policy is tested on its new form (ibid).

[6] TA 1988, Sch. 15, para. 2(1)(*e*) and for other policies, TA 1988, Sch. 15, para. 1(7)(*b*).

[7] On Revenue view of what amounts to a variation see Press Release 27 January 1988, *Simon's Tax Intelligence* 1988, p. 35.

[8] No relaxation for those over 55 including the 75% rule, unless the policy makes no provision for payment on surrender and the term does not run beyond age 75. Where the capital sum may be taken as a single sum or a series of sums, the 75% rule is applied to the smallest sum that can be taken—an obvious anti-avoidance measure: TA 1988, Sch. 15, para. 1(9).

[9] TA 1988, Sch. 15, para. 10(1).

[10] TA 1988, Sch. 15, para. 14.

[11] See also *Simon's Tax Intelligence* 1982, p. 143.

[12] TA 1988, Sch. 15, para. 8(6).

Clawback of relief

28: 06 Relief in respect of premiums paid under qualifying life policies is clawed back[1] if the policy was issued after 26th March 1974 but before 14th March 1984, and is surrendered or converted soon after issue. Otherwise the taxpayer could be left with a profit due simply to tax relief obtained.

---

[1] TA 1988, ss. 268–270.

The first four years

28: 07 If a policy is surrendered (in whole or in part) converted into a paid up policy or there is any payment by way of bonuses or participation in profits on the policy otherwise than on death within four years, the following rules apply.[1]

There is to be clawed back—from the insurance company—the lesser of (*a*) the "appropriate percentage" of the premiums payable under the policy up to the happening of the event and (*b*) the surrender value of the policy minus the "complementary percentage". The complementary percentage is 100 minus the appropriate percentage.

The appropriate percentage is found by first doubling the rate of relief in force for the year in which the event happens[2] and then taking a fraction of that sum: $\frac{3}{6}$ in years 1 and 2, $\frac{2}{6}$ in year 3 and $\frac{1}{6}$ in year 4. So if the event occurs in 1983–84 the relief of 15% is doubled to 30% and the fraction then applied giving (*a*) percentages of 15%, 15%, 10% and 5% of the premium paid and (*b*) the surrender value of the policy minus 85, 85, 90 and 95. The function of the (*b*) limit is to try to restrict the liability to the relief received—but without account for inflation, a matter for once in the taxpayer's favour.

> **EXAMPLE**
>
> Qualifying policy, issued on 1st April 1981 with monthly premiums of £10 payable on 1st of each month, is surrendered for £300 on 25th October 1983. The appropriate percentage would be $\frac{2}{6}$ of 30% = 10%. Clawbacks will be lesser of:
>
> (*a*)　10% of 310 = £31.
>
> (*b*)　$300 - \dfrac{90}{100} \times 310 = \pounds 21.$

When the event is the *partial* surrender or its conversion into a *partly* paid up policy the clawback is not to exceed the surrender value of the policy and, when it is any payment by way of participation in profits, the amount so received.[3]

Provision is also made for more than one event in the four year period,[4] the technique being broadly to treat the amount clawed back on the first event as a deduction on the occasion of the second.

Since the rules are designed to attack events within the first four years, any increase of more than 25% in the premiums payable is treated as the start of a new policy.[5]

Simon's Taxes E2.1051; Butterworths Income Tax Service F8.05.

[1] TA 1988, s. 268(1)—events occurring in connection with the winding up of a life office are excluded.

[2] Since the rate of relief changes and the clawback is calculated by reference to the rates at the time of the event exact correlation between the benefit and the clawback does not occur. However $\frac{2}{6}$ or $\frac{1}{2}$ is the exact value of the relief, if there is no change in rates.

[3] TA 1988, s. 268(3).

[4] TA 1988, s. 268(4).

[5] TA 1988, s. 268(6) and see TA 1988, s. 269(4).

After four years

28: 08　Events more than four years after the issue of the policy only give rise to clawback if two conditions are satisfied:[1]

(*i*) that the event is (*a*) the surrender of the whole or part of the rights conferred by the policy or (*b*) the falling due (other than on death or maturity) of a sum payable in pursuance of a right conferred by the policy to participants in profits;

(*ii*) that either of these events has happened already, whether more or less than four years after the issue of the policy.

The presence of the second condition is meant to provide relief for a "genuine" non-tax avoidance arrangement; one is only expected to make one such arrangement. Its purpose is to stop the payment of premiums out of the proceeds of periodic partial surrenders.[2]

The sum clawed back is the applicable percentage of (*a*) the total premiums payable during the year of assessment and (*b*) the sums payable on surrender or otherwise falling due.[3] If more than one event occurs during the year, the sums payable are aggregated for (*b*), above, and the total amount of clawback is not to exceed the applicable percentage of of (*a*).[4]

Simon's Taxes E2.1052; Butterworths Income Tax Service F8.05.
[1] TA 1988, s. 269.
[2] Inland Revenue Press Release, 10th December 1974; see *Simon's Tax Intelligence* 1974, p. 518.
[3] TA 1988, s. 269(2).
[4] TA 1988, s. 269(3).

Insurance policies issued outside the UK

28: 09   FA 1984, Sch. 15 altered the treatment of policies issued outside the UK. Policies issued after 17th November 1983 (new non-resident policies) are treated as non-qualifying and the gain arising from such a policy is chargeable at the basic rate under Schedule D, Case VI[1] (in addition to the higher rate charge). The gains of offshore capital redemption policies issued after 17th November 1983 are also subject to the basic rate charge. As a result, modifications are made to the chargeable events provisions, see infra §§ **28: 13, 14**.

Nevertheless, in certain circumstances new non-resident policies may qualify if they conform to a standard form prescribed by the Revenue[2] and meet one of two sets of conditions:[3]

(*a*) (*i*) the issuing company is lawfully carrying on life assurance business in the UK; (*ii*) the premiums are payable through a UK branch through which the company carries on its business; and (*iii*) the premiums form part of the company's business receipts arising through that branch; or alternatively

(*b*) (*i*) the policy holder is resident in the UK; and (*ii*) under TA 1988, s. 446, the issuing company's income from the investments of its life assurance fund is charged to corporation tax under Schedule D, Case III.

Special rules apply to determine whether a policy is a qualifying policy where one policy is substituted for another, or the terms of a policy are varied.[4]

Simon's Taxes Division E2.10; Butterworths Income Tax Service F8.19.
[1] TA 1988, Sch. 15, para. 24.
[2] TA 1988, Sch. 15, para. 21(1)(*b*).
[3] TA 1988, Sch. 15, para. 24.
[4] TA 1988, Sch. 15, Part III.

Excess liability charge

(i) *Non-qualifying policies*

28: 10   If the policy is a non-qualifying policy a special charge to income tax may arise on the occurrence of a chargeable event as defined for CGT and, if the taxpayer is liable to the higher rates of tax (or, before 1984–85, investment income surcharge), a proportion of the proceeds will be taxable, the familiar top slicing process being used.[1] Examples of such policies are the single premium policy property bond and policies issued outside the UK after 17th November 1983 (new non-resident policies).[2] These rules do not apply to mortgage protection policies, retirement annuity policies nor policies forming part of pension scheme.

Where a new non-resident policy is created the charge is limited to the period for which the policy holder is resident in the UK. However, where a resident policy holder transfers the policy to non-resident trustees after 19th March 1985 this limitation does not apply[3] so that the full charge remains.

Simon's Taxes E3.415; Butterworths Income Tax Service F8.22.
[1] TA 1988, s. 541.
[2] TA 1988, Sch. 15, Part III.
[3] TA 1988, s. 553(5).

28: 11   *Chargeable events.* The events are:

   (*i*) death giving rise to benefits under the policy;

   (*ii*) the maturity of the policy;[1]

   (*iii*) the total surrender[2] of the rights under the policy including a bonus[3] and

   (*iv*) the assignment of the rights for money or money's worth.[4]

Once such an assignment had occurred, and the rights were not at the time of the event held by the original beneficial owner, the original rule was that no later event could be a chargeable event.[5] An assignment between spouses was ignored as was an assignment by way of security for a debt or the discharge of a debt secured by the rights under the policy.[6]

The original rule was the basis of avoidance in that the owner would not take out a policy but would take an assignment of the policy—the so called second-hand bond. TA 1988, s. 544 therefore provides that the old rule is to apply only to policies made before 26th June 1982 and then only if the assignment was also made before that date.[7] It follows that events subsequent to an assignment for money or money's worth can be chargeable events if the policy was made on or after 26th June 1982. Despite the old rule certain events occurring after 23rd August 1982 are to give rise to tax even though the policy was issued and an assignment made before 26th June 1982.[8] These events are (*a*) a further assignment of the rights under the policy (with exceptions for (*i*) assignment as security of a debt, (*ii*) reassignment on the discharge of a debt secured by the policy, and (*iii*) a transfer between spouses); (*b*) the payment of a premium or capital sum in respect of the policy, and (*c*) certain loans.

Simon's Taxes E3.415; Butterworths Income Tax Service F8.18.
[1] But note TA 1988, s. 540(2). No chargeable event arises where a qualifying policy substituted for a new non-resident policy, see TA 1988, Sch. 15, para. 24.
[2] On partial surrender, see infra.
[3] Payment of a bonus may be treated as a surrender: TA 1988, s. 539(4)—and so may loans (infra, § **28: 17**).
[4] TA 1988, s. 540(1).
[5] TA 1988, s. 540(3). Such matters fall within capital gains tax: CGTA 1979, s. 143, supra, § **15: 04**.
[6] TA 1988, s. 540(3).
[7] TA 1988, s. 544.
[8] TA 1988, s. 544.

28: 12 *The gain.* For death the gain is the amount by which the surrender value immediately before the death plus the "relevant capital payments", such as bonuses, exceeds the total amount paid by way of premiums, plus any sums already treated as gains on partial surrender or assignment.

On maturity or surrender in whole, the gain is the excess of the proceeds including bonuses over the premiums paid with adjustments for sums treated as gains on earlier partial surrender or assignment.

On assignment the gain is the excess of the consideration received (except for connected persons when market value is substituted[1]) plus the amount or value of any relevant capital payments over the total amount of premiums paid with adjustments for the assignment.[2]

Partial surrenders[3] and partial assignment are also chargeable events. Many modern policies allow partial surrenders at frequent intervals and such surrenders gave rise to complex calculations. In an attempt to reduce the work involved, both for life offices and the Revenue, a different system of determining both whether there has been a gain and its extent applies.[4]

The chargeable amount is defined as an excess of "reckonable aggregate value" over "allowable aggregate amount".[5] The former term is the sum of all the values of surrender and assignments not brought into account.[6] The latter term is the sum of all appropriate portions of premiums paid.[7] Each year there is an allowance of (*a*) 5% of any premium paid up to the end of the year, and (*b*) 5% of any premiums on which an allowance has been due in previous years, up to a maximum of $\frac{20}{20}$th. So a premium payment only gets a full allowance 20 years after payment. Allowances not used will be carried forward accumulatively. The effect of this is to allow withdrawals of up to 5% of premiums paid without attracting any charge.

If the gain arises in respect of a new non-resident policy or a new offshore capital redemption policy, it is reduced to take account of periods of residence outside the UK.[8] The gain is reduced by the fraction:

$$\frac{\text{number of days for which the policy ran (up to the chargeable event) in which the holder was UK resident}}{\text{total number of days for which the policy ran up to the chargeable event}}$$

Simon's Taxes E3.414; Butterworths Income Tax Service F8.21–25.
[1] TA 1988, s. 541(3).
[2] TA 1988, s. 541(1).
[3] Payment of a bonus may be treated as a surrender: TA 1988, s. 339(4)—and so may loans (infra, § **28: 17**).
[4] Inland Revenue Press Release, 10th December 1974; see *Simon's Tax Intelligence* 1974, p. 518.
[5] TA 1988, s. 540(1)(*a*)(v).
[6] TA 1988, s. 546(2).
[7] TA 1988, s. 546(3).
[8] TA 1988, s. 553(3).

28: 13 *The slice of the gain.* Individuals may claim top slicing relief, a process which requires first the calculation of the slice of the gain.[1] To do this one spreads the gain back over a number of years by multiplying it by 1 over the number of complete years (*i*) on the first chargeable event—back to the start of the policy, (*ii*) on any later chargeable event other than final termination—back to the previous chargeable event; (*iii*) on final termination—the number of whole years from the start of the policy. In calculating the top-slicing relief for a gain on a new non-resident policy or a new offshore capital redemption policy, the number of complete years is, in each case, reduced by the number of complete years during which the holder was non-resident.[2]

The slice of the gain is then added to the taxpayer's other income to discover the amount of extra tax payable by reason of its addition. If the addition of that sum does not give rise to anything but tax at the basic rate, no tax is payable.[3] If however extra tax is payable, the amount of that tax is then calculated. The average of that tax rate is then ascertained, the basic rate deducted and the resulting rate applied to the whole gain.[4] Although a policy gain is not liable to basic rate income tax, the amount is income for age relief purposes and may restrict the amount of that relief.[5] This relief is not affected by the abolition of top-slicing relief by FA 1988, s. 75.

When there is a chargeable event through death or maturity and there is a loss, an individual may deduct that loss from total income so far as it does not exceed gains taxed in earlier partial surrender or assignments.[6] Thus the tax on gains made earlier may be recovered. The relief does not apply to losses on assignments nor does it make any allowance for inflation.

Simon's Taxes E3.428; Butterworths Income Tax Service F8.22.
  [1] TA 1988, s. 550.
  [2] TA 1988, s. 541(1).
  [3] However, if the effect is to cause the withdrawal of age relief some liability may arise.
  [4] TA 1988, s. 541(1).
  [5] See Simon's Taxes E2.303.
  [6] TA 1988, s. 549.

(ii) *Qualifying policies*

28: 14 It would be easy to create a qualifying policy, to convert it and then to realise it in an attempt to avoid these rules. Hence the charge applies also to qualifying policies if any of these events occur provided that the policy is dealt with within its first ten years or first three-quarters of its term if this is shorter. Thus if the policy is converted into a paid up policy and then the death occurs or the policy matures before the expiry of ten years from the making of the insurance or, if sooner, 75% of the term of the policy, or if it is surrendered or assigned for money or money's worth within that time, a charge accrues.[1] No charge would have arisen for a qualifying policy simply because the death occurred within ten years—a dealing is also needed.

Simon's Taxes E3.415; Butterworths Income Tax Service F8.18.
  [1] TA 1988, s. 340(1)(*b*).

28: 15 *Trusts and companies.* Where a non-qualifying policy is held by trustees, the charge to tax falls on the settlor, if he is alive, although there is an indemnity against the trustees.[1] If the settlor is dead, there is no tax charge. A close investment company must treat as income, chargeable under

Schedule 6 Case VI, any gain arising on a non-qualifying policy,[2] or if the policy was issued before 14th March 1989, and has not been varied or extended since that date on a qualifying policy where the gain is of a kind described in § **28: 14**, infra. For policies issued to a company, close or otherwise, after 13th March 1989, or existing policies which are varied or extended after that date, the entire gain, that is, the excess of the surrender value of the policy over premiums paid, is treated as income taxable under Schedule D Case VI. A company is similarily liable in respect of a policy which secures a debt owed by the company, as well as a policy settled by the company on trust.

Simon's Taxes E3.427; Butterworths Income Tax Service F8.23.
[1] TA 1988, s. 551, but see TA 1988, s. 547(1)(*a*).
[2] TA 1988, s. 547(1)(*b*).

Loans as surrenders

28: 16 If money were withdrawn in the form of loans instead of by the normal surrender of policy rights, these rules might be frustrated. It is therefore provided that loans are in general equivalent to surrender of rights[1] but with exceptions for loans at a commercial rate on qualifying policies.[2] Any repayment of the loan is treated as a premium.[3] This counters the common borrow-all arrangement under which the policyholder paid the first few premiums out of his own resources and then borrowed from the insurance company—at interest—to pay subsequent premiums.

Simon's Taxes E3.419.
[1] For determining any excess charge and any clawback.
[2] TA 1988, s. 548. There is also an exception for house loans to full time employees of the body issuing the policy: TA 1988, s. 548(3)(*a*) (extended by extra-statutory concession A47 (1988) to employees of certain insurance associations; **Simon's Taxes, Division H2.2**) and for certain loan annuity contracts made by the elderly: TA 1988, s. 271(2)(*b*).
[3] TA 1988, s. 548(2).

Loans—other rules

28: 17 Special rules once restricted the deductibility of interest on loans used to pay premiums. In view of the general restrictions on the deduction of interest these have been repealed.[1]

More importantly, TA 1988, s. 554 treats certain borrowings against life policies as income taxable under Schedule D Case III unless the Revenue is satisfied that the borrowings do not amount to disguised annuity payments.[2]

Simon's Taxes B5.103.
[1] TA 1970, s. 403 and 404 (repealed by FA 1987, Sch. 16, Pt. VII.
[2] Reversing *IRC v Wesleyan and General Assurance Society* [1948] 1 All ER 555, 30 TC 11.

Life annuity contracts

28: 18 The rules prescribing excess liability on chargeable events in relation to endowment policies are adapted to the surrender of life annuity contracts.[1]

Special rules apply to guaranteed income bonds; a charge to basic rate income tax is made.[2]

Simon's Taxes E3.416, 421.
[1] By TA 1988, ss. 542, 543 and 544.
[2] TA 1988, s. 547(6).

PURCHASED ANNUITIES

28: 19   The investment of one's capital in the purchase of an annuity meant that one was buying income with capital and that income tax was therefore due on the whole of each payment received, even though in commercial reality one was receiving back each year a part of one's capital together with interest. A number of ways around this rule were devised. The first, which lasted until 1949, provided for an advance by way of interest-free loan each month which was to be extinguished by set off against a capital sum due under the contract on his death.[1] The Revenue's argument that these were in substance annual payments was rejected. Such loans are now treated as income.[2] A second way, which still survives, applies to an annuity certain, that is an annuity payable for a stated number of years, not depending on the survival of the annuitant. Here the Court of Appeal held that tax was chargeable only on so much of the payment as represented interest and not on the whole sum.[3] This split treatment was not accorded to normal annuities which terminated on the death of the annuitant and so companies would issue "split annuities", meaning an annuity certain for a stated number of years to be followed by a deferred annuity. The payments under the former annuity would be divided into capital and interest and while the latter would be taxable in full it was arranged that the sum payable under the contract would be higher and in any case the cost of it would be lower in view of the more advanced age.

---

[1] *IRC v Wesleyan and General Assurance Society* (1946) 30 TC 11, supra, § **32: 17**.
[2] TA 1988, s. 554.
[3] *Perrin v Dickson* [1930] 1 KB 107, 14 TC 608; but doubted in *Sothern-Smith v Clancey* [1941] 1 All ER 111, 24 TC 1, supra, § **9: 68**.

28: 20   Purchased annuities are now divided by TA 1988, s. 656 so that the part which represents the estimated capital content is exempt from tax and only the balance is income. The section does not however apply where the annuity is already given some relief or is not purchased by the annuitant. An annuity is not split if, apart from TA 1988, s. 656, it is treated as having a capital element, or if it qualifies for relief in respect of the premiums paid under TA 1988, ss. 266, 273 or 623. Also taxable in full are annuities purchased or provided for under a will or settlement, out of income of property disposed of by the will or settlement (whether with or without resort to capital) or provided under a sponsored superannuation scheme.[1] Tax is deducted in respect of the income element by the payer.

The method of apportionment between income and capital is carried out by dividing the sum spent by the normal expectation of life according to

Government mortality tables, regardless of the individual.² The sum so ascertained is the capital element and this remains constant and is not revised to take account of the length of time the annuitant actually survived. The actuarial value is computed as at the date when the first payment begins to accrue.³ If there are contingencies other than the ending of a human life, the capital element is such as may be just having regard to the contingency.⁴ Annuities may be geared to inflation; the Revenue practice is to fix the capital content at the start of the annuity so making all increases wholly taxable.

Simon's Taxes B5.314; Butterworths Income Tax Service G2.73.
¹ TA 1988, s. 657.
² The tables are authorised under TA 1988, s. 658. They must be obeyed: *Rose v Trigg* (1963) 41 TC 365. This is hard since a person with lower than average life expectancy may get special terms from a company.
³ TA 1988, s. 656(3)(*c*). It is usually paid half yearly in arrear.
⁴ TA 1988, s. 656(3)(*d*). Where the amount (and not just the term) is to vary, see TA 1988, s. 656(2), (3)(*e*).

REGISTERED FRIENDLY SOCIETIES

28: 21 Friendly societies are exempt on the profits of certain life and annuity business, particularly where the sum assured is a gross sum of not more than £750 or an annual amount not exceeding £156,¹ but also other business.² For contracts made on or after 1st September 1987 an annual premium of £100 is to be substituted for the gross sum of £750—with a certain rounding of the edges where the premiums are paid more frequently than annually so as to enable policies to be written at £2 a week or £9 a month.³ The policy may be tax-exempt as well as being a qualifying policy for terms longer than 10 years; if the policy is a non-qualifying policy any gain will attract a basic rate charge. Following changes made by FA 1984 it was discovered that a number of policies had accidentally become disqualified and of doubtful validity, a matter rectified by the Friendly Societies Act 1984. FA 1985⁴ made a number of changes designed to assimilate the treatment of friendly societies with that of insurance companies. So the surrender of an annuity contract made after 31st May 1984 is to be a chargeable event,⁵ breach of the limits by a policy invalidates the policy instead of disqualifying the society⁶ (and so all policies issued by it) and societies are empowered to issue policies to all adults⁷ and not just to those with spouses or dependent children. The old rules drawing a distinction between older and newer societies were also revised so as to reduce the differences and in particular to allow newer societies to write endowment as well as whole life policies.⁸

¹ TA 1988, s. 460; on unregistered societies see TA 1988, s. 459.
² TA 1988, s. 460(2)(*d*).
³ TA 1988, s. 460(2)(*c*)(i).
⁴ TA 1988, s. 464, Schs. 15 and 29.
⁵ TA 1988, s. 539(3).
⁶ TA 1988, Sch. 15, paras. 3–6.
⁷ TA 1988, Sch. 15, paras. 3, 4.
⁸ FA 1985, s. 41(3).

PERSONAL EQUITY PLANS

28: 22 Personal equity plans (PEPs), which came into operation on 1st January 1987,[1] are intended to encourage direct investment by individuals in UK companies through the granting of tax reliefs. Provided the conditions of the scheme are satisfied, gains from the sale of shares within a plan, and withdrawals of capital from a plan, will be free of capital gains tax, and dividends, and interest from cash holdings, are exempt from income tax if they are reinvested in a plan. Regulations governing the operation of the scheme and setting out the conditions have now been issued.[2]

The scheme is open to individuals aged 18 and over who are resident and ordinarily resident in the UK. The maximum annual investment for 1989–90 is £4,800 of which up to one half may be held in unit trusts. The rule that the investment must be held for the whole of the calendar year following that in which it entered the PEP is repealed as from the start of 1989–90.

Qualifying investments under a PEP are restricted to ordinary shares in UK companies quoted on The Stock Exchange, and investments in authorised unit trusts or approved investment trusts (although the initial investment in unit or investment trusts is limited). There are restrictions on the nature of reinvestments: the proceeds of share disposals may only be reinvested in other shares; the proceeds of disposal of trust holdings may be reinvested in shares or other trust holdings, but if reinvested in shares it may not later be switched back to trusts. Provision is also made for cash holdings; interest on the holding is paid gross.

The plan must be run by an authorised manager who will carry out all transactions and holds the investments on behalf of the investors (who nevertheless retain beneficial ownership and voting rights, etc). The manager must make any repayment claims and is responsible for keeping records and submitting an annual return. If for any reason (eg loss of PEP status) tax becomes payable, the manager must account for it to the Revenue.

Detailed administration rules for PEPs are contained in The Personal Equity Plan Regulations 1989, which came into force on 5th April 1989.

Simon's Taxes Division E1.9.

[1] TA 1988, s. 333.

[2] S.I. 1986 No. 1948.

[3] The rules were relaxed as from 1 January 1988; see *Simon's Tax Intelligence* 1987, p. 795 and S.I. 1987 No. 2128.

---

29 Investment intermediaries

INVESTMENT COMPANIES

29: 01   Most revenue expenses incurred in earning profits assessable under Schedule D, Cases I and II, or income from property assessable under Schedule A, are deductible from gross receipts in arriving at the net income assessable. No relief is normally given, however, for expenses incurred in earning investment income, such as company dividends, and interest. But since 1915,[1] investment companies have been entitled to set their expenses of management against total profits, thus reducing the profits assessable, or entitling the company to a repayment of tax deducted at source from income received. The relevant legislation is now contained in TA 1988, s. 75.

Simon's Taxes D4.401.
[1] FA 1915, s. 14, later ITA 1918, s. 33.

29: 02   At first, the legislation restricted the deductible expenses by providing that the total taxable income was not to fall below that which would have been taxable under Schedule D, Case I. But in *Simpson v Grange Trust Ltd*,[1] it was shown that that restriction had no application to investment companies. It has now been repealed, except for life insurance companies.

[1] 19 TC 231.

29: 03   An "investment company", eligible for relief for its expenses of management, is any company whose business consists wholly or mainly of the making of investments, and the principal part of whose income is derived therefrom.[1] The term includes savings banks or other banks for savings, investment trusts and unit trusts.[2] In *IRC v Tyre Investment Trust Ltd*,[3] the phrase "the making of investments" was held to mean "investing". It is not necessary for an investment company to buy and sell investments regularly, provided that it takes some active interest in the investments which it has made. It follows, therefore, that a holding company formed to hold shares in subsidiary companies will normally qualify as an investment company. On the other hand, a trading company deriving income from the investment of large amounts of surplus cash will not be an investment company until it can establish that the main part of its business consists in the making of investments, and the principal part of its income is derived therefrom.

815

Simon's Taxes D4.401.
[1] TA 1988, s. 130.
[2] Ibid.
[3] 12 TC 646.

Expenses of management

29: 04   Viscount Simonds has said in *Sun Life Assurance Society v Davidson*[1] that the term "expenses of management" is "insusceptible of precise definition". It is clearly wider than the expenses to which the managers are put, but does not extend to all expenses incurred in running the company's business. In *Sun Life*, the House of Lords held that all revenue expenses incurred by a company in managing its business qualify for relief. These expenses will include (*a*) staff costs, including wages, salaries, pension contributions, and the cost of staff training and welfare; (*b*) other indirect costs, including stationery, printing, advertising, repairs to equipment, legal and other professional fees, and unrelieved value added tax; and (*c*) property maintenance costs, including rents, rates, maintenance and repairs of premises occupied for business purposes. In addition, certain expenses qualify for relief by statute. The cost of maintaining let property is not a management expense, but is deductible from income assessable under Schedule A.[2] Sums paid to purchase investments are not management expenses, and, moreover, in *Sun Life*, it was held that expenses necessarily incurred in acquiring investments were part of the costs of the investments, and not management expenses. Thus stamp duty and brokerage on the acquisition or sale of investments are not management expenses, and likewise legal expenses incurred in the acquisition of heritable property in an investment are not deductible. Relief is available, however, for expenditure incurred in evaluating an investment, such as the legal costs of investigating title, as well as for expenditure on an abortive investment. Relief is given for expenses incurred but not paid at the end of an accounting period, although wages and salaries accrued at the end of the accounting period do not qualify for relief unless paid within nine months of the end of the accounting period.[3]

Simon's Taxes D4.408.
[1] [1958] AC 184 at 196; 37 TC 330 at 354.
[2] TA 1988, s. 75(1), (2).
[3] FA 1989, s. 87.

29: 05   Among the expenses which do not qualify for relief are (*a*) capital expenditure on plant and equipment, vehicles, fixtures and fittings, (*b*) entertainment expenditure, (*c*) losses on the disposal of investments, except that relief may be given for certain losses on the disposal of shares in unquoted trading companies,[1] (*d*) exchange losses.[2]

Simon's Taxes D4.408.
¹ TA 1988, s. 573.
² *Bennett v Underground Railways Co of London* [1923] 2 KB 535, 8 TC 475.

29: 06 In the view of the Revenue, interest is not an expense of management.¹ In practice, this restriction is often of little importance, because all interest payable to a bank carrying on business in the UK, and all annual interest payable otherwise into a UK bank, is treated as a charge, deductible from total profits. So the restriction would seem to apply only to short interest, paid other than to a bank, although in practice this is often allowed as a management expense.

¹ Apparently on the authority of *Bennett v Underground Railway* [1923] 2 KB 535, 8 TC 475.

29: 07 The term "expenses of management" includes commissions.¹ In *Hoechst Finance Ltd v Gumbrell*,² however, commissions paid by a company to its parent company for guaranteeing of loans to other subsidiaries of the parent were held not to be deductible; although the taxpayer's business was the provision of finance to those companies, the costs of the commission could not be severed from the other costs of raising capital.

Simon's Taxes D4.408.
¹ TA 1988, s. 75.
² [1983] STC 150.

29: 08 To qualify for relief, expenses must be "disbursed for" an accounting period. Accrued expenditure is deductible, but expenditure which is never "disbursed", that is, paid out, cannot qualify for relief.¹ On the other hand there is no requirement that expenses must be "wholly and exclusively" incurred for the purposes of the company's business. Apportionment of expenditure is therefore possible. In particular, if expenditure is excessive, only amounts reasonably incurred will qualify as expenses of management.²

¹ *North British & Mercantile Insurance Co v Easson* (1919) 7 TC 463.
² *L G Berry Investment Ltd v Attwooll* [1964] 2 All ER 126, 41 TC 547 see also *Fragmap Developments Ltd v Cooper* (1967) 44 TC 366.

29: 09 No relief is available for depreciation, since that is an accounting allowance, and not a disbursement. However, since 1953 investment companies have been entitled to claim capital allowances. Allowances for expenditure on qualifying assets, insofar as they cannot be set against income from any other source, can be added to the expenses of management for the year, with any balancing charges being brought in as income.¹ Alternatively, allowance for expenditure on plant, etc. may be claimed on a renewals basis.

Simon's Taxes D4.405.
¹ TA 1988, s. 75(4).

The relief

29: 10   Relief under TA 1988, s. 75 is given by first deducting expenses of management from income not otherwise charged to tax, other than franked investment income, group income, and regional development grants. The balance of expenses remaining is then deducted from other income and chargeable gains of the company. Any expenses not so used can be set against franked investment income of the same year under TA 1988, s. 242 which may result in a release of ACT and a repayment of tax. The excess cannot be set against franked investment income of later years, since that relief applies only to trading companies. Expenditure still unrelieved can be carried forward, without time limit, against future income, from whatever source, of the company,[1] or it can be relieved by way of group relief.[2] Excess management expenses, unlike trading losses, cannot be carried back to previous accounting periods.

Simon's Taxes D4.403.
 [1] TA 1988, s. 75(3).
 [2] TA 1988, s. 403(4), (5).

INVESTMENT TRUSTS

29: 11   An investment trust is an investment company which by complying with TA 1988, s. 842 is exempt from tax on its chargeable gains.[1] This exemption enables the company to switch investments tax-free. All other income of the company, however, is taxed in the usual way. The exemption for capital gains tax does not extend to shareholders. To obtain relief, the company must comply with the conditions in TA 1988, s. 842 *for*, that is throughout, its accounting period although there are extra-statutory concessions for the accounting period in which a company first seeks to qualify as an investment trust and for the accounting period in which an investment trust is wound up. The conditions in TA 1988, s. 842 are as follows:

(*a*) The company must be UK resident; it must not be a "close" company; and every class of its ordinary share capital must be quoted on a recognised stock exchange.

(*b*) The company's income must be derived wholly or mainly from shares or securities. The Revenue regard this condition as satisfied if 70% of gross income, before expenses, is so derived.[2]

(*c*) The company's Memorandum and Articles of Association must prohibit the distribution by way of dividend of surpluses arising on the realisation of investments.

(*d*) The company must not retain, for any accounting period, more than 15% of the income it derives from shares and securities.

(*e*) No holding of shares and securities in a company must represent more than 15% by value of the investing company's investments. This condition does not apply (1) where a holding, when it was acquired, was worth no more than 15% of the then value of the investing company's investments and (2) to shares held in a company which is itself an investment trust, or would be an investment trust if its ordinary share capital was quoted on a stock exchange. Where an investment trust adds to an existing holding by acquiring other shares or securities for a consideration, the entire holding must be revalued at the date of the latest acquisition, to see whether the 15% test is satisfied. The word "holding" means all the shares and securities in one company. Where an investment trust has two or more subsidiary companies, all its subsidiaries are treated as a single company.

Simon's Taxes D4.422.
[1] FA 1980, s. 81(1). The definition of "investment trust" is amended by FA 1988, s.117.
[2] By agreement with the Association of Investment Trust Companies.

UNIT TRUSTS

29: 12 Unit trusts are trusts in the strict legal sense of the word, and operate in accordance with the terms of their trust deed. The trustee is usually a bank or insurance company, but the management of the trust is carried on by a separate management company. The unit holders are simply beneficiaries under the trust whose rights are regulated by the trust deed. A unit holder disposes of his units by selling them to the trust manager at a price equal to asset value, less a small discount. The manager may either hold the units for sale to an investor, or it may sell them back to the trustee, when they are cancelled.

Simon's Taxes D4.413–417.

29: 13 An authorised unit trust is treated, for tax purposes, as though it were a UK resident company, and as if the units were shares in the company.[1] An authorised unit trust is therefore liable to corporation tax on its income, and may make a claim for relief for its expenses of management.[2] As from 1st January 1990 certified unit trusts, a phrase which will cover most UK authorised unit trusts, will pay corporation tax at the lower rate of 25%.[3] These trusts will continue to get relief on their expenses of management. This charge facilitates the repeal of special provisions for gilt unit trusts.[4] Authorised unit trusts are not, however, liable to corporation tax on their chargeable gains.[5] Thus the tax treatment of an authorised unit trust is the same as that of an investment trust.

Unit trusts, however, are often preferred to investment trusts as investment vehicles because the value of units is directly linked to the value of the unit trust's underlying investments. Shares in an investment trust, on the other hand, are subject to normal market forces. If investment performance is poor, and in particular at times of high interest rates and investment yields, the quoted prices of investment trust company shares might stand at a substantial discount to the underlying asset value of the company.

Simon's Taxes D4.414.
[1] TA 1988, s. 468. On new definition as from 29 April 1988, see *Simon's Tax Intelligence* 1988, p. 359.
[2] TA 1988, s. 468(4).
[3] TA 1988, ss. 468A, 468B and 468C inserted by FA 1989, s. 78. Trusts are certified if they

comply with the conditions in the EC Directive of 20th December 1985 No 85/611/EEC. The Direction covers only trusts investing in transferable securities; trusts investing e.g. in property remain subject to tax at 35%.
⁴ TA 1988, s. 468(5) is repealed by FA 1989, s. 80.
⁵ FA 1980, s. 81(1).

29: 14   FA 1989[1] introduced a new sub-class of authorised unit trust, the certified units trust. This is an authorised unit trust which invests only in "transferable securities" and which obtains the benefits conferred by the EC Directive relating to undertakings for collective investments in transferable securities (the UCITS Directive). To obtain the benefits of the Directive, the authorised unit trust must comply with conditions contained in the Financial Services Act 1986, s. 78. Where an authorised unit trust is a certified investment trust throughout an accounting period beginning on or after 1st January 1990, its rate of corporation tax is limited to the basic rate of income tax. Capital gains are, of course, tax free. Transitional provisions apply to accounting periods which begin before, and end after, 1st January 1990. A distribution made by a certified unit trust from income arising on or after 1st January 1990 is no longer treated as a dividend for corporation tax purposes. Instead, it is treated as an annual payment, in the hands of the recipient, from which income tax at 25% has been deducted at source. This does not affect the income tax position of a unit holder who is an individual or a trustee—such a unit holder is treated as having paid income tax by deduction, at the basic rate. But the new rules will have an adverse effect where a unit holder is a company, because distributions cease to be franked investment income, so that the distributions may be liable to corporation tax at up to 35%, with a credit for the income tax at 25% suffered by deduction at source.

---

¹ FA 1989, s. 78.

29: 15   A unit trust scheme which is not an authorised unit trust is treated as a trust.[1] In the first instance, income received is taxed, not as income of the unit holders, but as the income of the trustees, who are liable to income tax on it in the usual way. Income distributions to unit holders are deemed to have been paid under deduction of income tax at the basic rate, any income not actually distributed at the end of the accounting period being treated as having been distributed on that date.[2] The trustees are also liable to capital gains tax on trust capital gains, except where, throughout the year of assessment, all the unit holders are themselves exempt from tax on capital gains (otherwise than by reason of residence) in which case trust capital gains are not chargeable to tax.[3] When the distribution exceeds the trust income of that year use can be made of surplus income from earlier periods.[4]

---

¹ TA 1988, s. 469.
² TA 1988, s. 469(3).
³ CGTA 1979, s. 96.
⁴ TA 1988, s. 469(5A)–(5D), added by FA 1988, s. 71.

INSURANCE COMPANIES

29: 16   The taxation of insurance companies is complex, and the following paragraphs contain no more than a broad outline of the main principles. Readers are referred to *Simon's Taxes* **Division D4.5** for more detailed treatment.

29: 17   The Insurance Companies Act 1982 divides insurance business into two main categories, long term insurance business, including life assurance business, industrial assurance, annuity and pension business; and general business, including accident, sickness, marine, transport, property, and general liability insurance.[1] An insurance company is classified as a "life" or a "general" insurance company depending on the class of business carried on. If the company carries on both classes of business, it is known as a "composite" company. Some UK insurance companies are organised as mutual societies, with all profits held for the benefit of policyholders. Companies with shareholders are known as proprietary companies.

Simon's Taxes D4.501, 502.
[1] Insurance Companies Act 1982, Schs. 1, 2.

Life insurance taxation

29: 18   The principles of life insurance taxation are derived, in part, from legal decisions around the turn of the century, and in part from legislation originally introduced in 1923, and substantially amended by FA 1989. The present position may be summarised as follows:

(1) Where an insurance company carries on life insurance business together with general insurance business, the profits of the life business must be calculated, and taxed, separately.[1]

(2) Where a life insurance company carries on both ordinary life insurance business and industrial life insurance business, each must be treated as a separate business.[2] The important point here is that excess expenses cannot be transferred from one business to another.

(3) Life insurance is a trade within Schedule D Case I[3]. But a contract of life insurance has special features. First, it is a long term contract, in terms of which the liability of the insurance company, which is contingent on human mortality, may not crystallise until many years after the policy contract was issued. Second, a contract of life insurance is, in a sense, a mutual contract, whereby the insurance company collects premiums from a policyholder, which are then invested for his benefit, and returned to him when the policy matures. The law recognises the first of these special features by permitting the actuarial liability of the company to its policyholders to be deducted in arriving at its Schedule D Case I profits.[3] The law recognises the second feature of the contract by treating, as an expense deductible from Schedule D Case I profits, amounts expended on behalf of policyholders and annuitants, and amounts allocated to them by way of bonus payments, together with the present value of the cost of reversionary bonuses. In addition, if, at the end of an accounting period, the company shows a surplus

calculated according to actuarial principles, it may set aside, tax free, any part of that surplus which it can show is required to meet the expectations of policyholders as regards bonuses or other benefits payable under the policies.[4]

Simon's Taxes D4.503.
[1] TA 1988, s. 432(1).
[2] TA 1988, s. 432(2). Industrial insurance is defined in the Industrial Assurance Act 1923, s. 1.
[3] *Scottish Union and National Insurance Co v Smiles*; *Northern Assurance Co v Russell* (1889) 2 TC 551.
[4] FA 1989, s. 82.

29: 19   In practice, a mutual insurance company cannot be assessed on its total profits under Schedule D Case I, since profits from mutual trading are not Case I profits. But although it is perfectly possible for a proprietary insurance company, that is, a company with shareholders, to be within the charge to tax under Schedule D Case I on its total profits, such a charge to tax is rare. The reason is that the deduction of actuarial liabilities normally means that a life insurance company sustains a Schedules D Case I loss, and as a result, it is unlikely that such a company will ever pay tax. At an early stage in the development of the law, the courts decided that (*a*) investment income, and gains and losses arising on the disposal of investments, form part of the trading receipts of an insurance company but that (*b*) since the cases of Schedule D are not mutually exclusive, the Revenue can elect either to tax an insurance company on its Schedule D Case I profits, or to tax it on its investment income and capital gains.[1] Where a company is taxed on its investment income, and not on its Schedule D Case I profits—

(1) there is no deduction for actuarial liabilities or amounts reserved for policyholders;

(2) premiums received, and claims paid, are ignored;[2]

(3) gains and losses on the realisation of investments are taxed according to capital gains tax rules;

(4) investment income and capital gains held for policyholders are taxed at the basic rate of income tax of 25%;[3] and

(5) the company is entitled to relief for its expenses of management.[4]

The taxation of an insurance company on its investment income and capital gains less management expenses is known as the "I–E" basis of assessment. It is the basis which is always used for mutual insurance companies, and it is the basis usually preferred by the Revenue for proprietary companies, since there, the taxable income emerging is usually higher than that which would emerge if profits were computed along Schedule D Case I lines.

Simon's Taxes D4.505.
[1] *Liverpool and London and Globe Insurance Co v Bennett* [1913] AC 610, 6 TC 327, HL.
[2] TC 321.
[3] FA 1989, s. 88.
[4] TA 1988, s. 76.

29: 20   Although life insurance business includes pension business and general annuity business, separate taxation provisions have been applied to these two classes of business since 1956.[1] These provisions were amended by

FA 1989.[2] Profits from general annuity business and pension business must be calculated, separately, according to the rules of Schedule D Case I, although the assessments are made under Schedule D Case VI.[3] Any Schedule D Case VI loss emerging cannot be set against other Schedule D Case VI income, but may be carried forward against future profits from the same source.[4] The computation of general annuity and pension fund profits is somewhat complex. Broadly, income consists of premiums received and gains, less losses, on the realisation of investments attributable to each class of business. Investment income attributable to general annuity business is excluded from the Schedule D Case VI computation, and instead falls into the main "I–E" computation.[5] Investment income attributable to pension business is exempt from tax as such, any tax paid by deduction being repaid.[6] But the gross amount of such income must still be brought into the pension fund business computation, to determine whether any Schedule D Case VI profit arises.[7] Pension annuities paid by the company are deductible in the pension fund Schedule D Case VI computation. Annuities other than pension annuities are treated as charges in the main "I–E" computation, up to the amount of the investment income received.[8] If the general annuities paid exceed investment income, the excess is deductible in the general annuity Schedule D Case VI computation. Bonus allocations, and other amounts expended on behalf of policyholders, including an appropriate proportion of the general trading expenses of the company, are deducted from the profits, and it may be possible for the company to reserve, tax free, a proportion of the emerging profits if (*a*) there is an overall surplus and (*b*) the company can justify further reservations to meet the reasonable expectations of policyholders.[9]

Simon's Taxes D4.507.
  [1] TA 1988, s. 436.
  [2] FA 1989, ss. 84–89, Sch. 8.
  [3] TA 1988, s. 436(1) and (2).
  [4] TA 1988, s. 436(4).
  [5] TA 1988, s. 437(2)(*a*).
  [6] TA 1988, s. 438(1).
  [7] TA 1988, s. 437(2).
  [8] TA 1988, s. 437(1).
  [9] FA 1989, s. 82.

29: 21   It will be evident that investment income and capital gains received by a life insurance company must be apportioned between basic life insurance business, general annuity business, and pension business. These apportionments are normally made on the basis of the insurance funds attributable to each class of business, or by reference to the actuarial liabilities of each class.

29: 22   It follows, therefore, that the components of the main I–E computaton consist of (*a*) investment income and gains attributable to basic life insurance business, less expenses of management attributable to that business, plus, (*b*) general annuity fund Schedule D Case VI profits, plus, (*c*) pension business fund Case VI profits. The treatment of expenses of management, however, is subject to the following three restrictions:

(1) First, the expenses are confined to items attributable to basic life insurance business.[1] If, in any year, expenses exceed investment income and gains attributable to that class of business, the excess can only be carried forward. Since expenses attributable to general annuity fund and pension business fund business can only be set against profits from these sources,[2] the result is to introduce a "ring fence" round each of the three classes of business carried on by a life insurance company, thus preventing excess expenses from one class being set against profits from another.

(2) Expenses, including commissions, attributable to obtaining new basic life insurance business are further restricted, in that relief is spread forward over seven years.[3]

(3) The final restriction applies, in practice, only to proprietary life insurance companies. Where, on a claim for relief for management expenses in respect of basic life assurance business, the emerging taxable profit on the I–E basis is less than it would have been if the company had been assesssed under Schedule D Case I on its total profits, the taxable profits from I–E must be increased to the Schedule D Case I profits, by restricting the management expenses allowable.[4] Any expenses so restricted may be carried forward to future years. This means that an insurance company taxed on the I–E basis must nevertheless prepare a Schedule D Case I computation to determine whether management expenses should be restricted. The computation is usually referred to as the "notional Case I computation". The practice hitherto adopted by life assurance companies in calculating the notional Case I liabilities is likely to be changed as a result of FA 1989. In particular, surplus which has not been paid or allocated to policyholders by way of bonus forms part of the Case I profits. Previously, such amounts were treated as having been reserved for policyholders, and were, under previous legislation, deductible from profits.

Simon's Taxes D4.503.
  [1] FA 1989, s. 87.
  [2] FA 1989, s. 87.
  [3] TA 1988, s. 76(2).
  [4] FA 1989, s. 87.

29: 23   Where a life insurance company carries on business abroad through a foreign branch, foreign income and capital gains attributable to the foreign branch are not liable to UK tax except to the extent that they are remitted here.[1] This is known as "foreign life fund relief". Certain UK government securities have been issued on the basis that they are free of all taxation so long as held by non-residents. Where foreign life fund income or gains are remitted to the UK and invested in these securities, the foreign income and gains continue to enjoy exemption from UK tax.[2] A UK insurance company with a foreign life fund is denied relief for a proportion of its management expenses, attributable to its foreign branch.[3]

Simon's Taxes D4.512.
  [1] TA 1988, s. 441(1), (7).
  [2] TA 1988, s. 441(2).
  [3] TA 1988, s. 441(5).

29: 24   Where a foreign insurance company carries on business in the UK through a branch or agency, the proportion of its total income which its UK life insurance fund bears to its world life insurance fund is liable to UK tax under Schedule D, Case III.[1] In addition, it is liable to UK tax on the Case VI profit from its UK and general annuity and pension business.

Simon's Taxes D4.525.
[1] TA 1988, s. 445.

General insurance business

29: 25   General insurance business is a trade, and profits from it are computed along normal Schedule D, Case I lines. There are, however, a number of special points of which the main ones are:

(*a*) Income within Schedule D, Cases III–VI and gains and losses arising on the disposal of investments are normally treated as incidents of the insurance trade, and brought in as trading receipts.

(*b*) General insurance premiums are normally payable in advance. At the end of an accounting period, therefore, the company will still be "on risk" in respect of insurance contracts for which premiums have already been received. The company can therefore defer a proportion of its premiums to the next accounting period.

(*c*) At the end of each accounting period, the company can make provision for known claims. Experience shows, however, that there will be claims attributable to an accounting period which are not intimated until after the end of it. The Revenue, therefore, will usually permit an estimated deduction to be made in respect of these claims, the deduction being based on the statistical evidence of past experience.

Simon's Taxes D4.527, 528.

30 Pensions

THE WIDENED CHOICE

30:01 "The changes proposed here in our system of pension provision are fundamental. They are intended to achieve a new partnership between state and personal provision in which the provision by the state and by the private sector are complementary rather than in competition. They will ensure that eventually every employee is able to contribute to his own additional pension to augment the basic state pension".[1]

This comment refers to the recommendations made in the Green Paper "Reform of Social Security" presented to Parliament in June 1985 following a major review by Government of the social security system. The reforms proposed were not confined to the future shape of the state pension scheme but touched the wider question of the relationship between state and private pension provision: there were therefore important consequences for the existing system of tax reliefs supporting private pension arrangements.

As a result a number of significant changes have been made to the tax provisions covering pension arrangements. The principal changes were legislated for in F(No 2)A 1987 and are as follows:

(*a*) Introduction of new approved personal pension schemes in place of approved retirement annuity contracts. These became available to all employees as well as the self-employed as from 1st July 1988. Previously it was intended that personal pension schemes should become available on 4th January 1988 but the date of introduction had to be postponed because of delays in setting up the investor protection rules required under the Financial Services Act 1986.

(*b*) Provision for new "freestanding" AVC schemes in which the employee can invest his additional contributions in a scheme of his own choice. These became available as from 26th October 1987.

(*c*) Introduction of new controls to prevent abuse of the tax privileges enjoyed by approved occupational pension schemes.

(*d*) Provisions to allow free transfer from one kind of approved pension arrangement to another.

Many of the provisions are supplemented by statutory instruments which set out the detailed rules.

In addition under the existing legislation the Revenue has made available two kinds of new simplified occupational pension scheme which are granted automatic approval provided the standard documentation is used.

The changes made in 1987 essentially achieved the Government's aim of enabling employees to make additional pension provision in a form of their own choice. But additional encouragement was given to the setting up of personal pension schemes by a provision in FA 1988 which allows employees, while remaining members of an occupational scheme, to contract out of the state earnings related pension scheme (SERPS) simply by having the contracted-out rebate and incentive payment contributed to a personal pension scheme which can only receive such payments.

In his 1989 Budget statement the Chancellor introduced certain further changes which, he indicated, completed the pension measures introduced in his 1987 Budget.[2] The change which was of most significance and which has accordingly provoked controversy is the setting of an earnings cap of £60,000 (to be price inflation-linked) on final salary for the purpose of fixing maximum approvable benefits than can be paid from an occupational scheme: this means that the maximum pension a tax-approved scheme will be able to pay is £40,000 a year and the maximum lump sum commutation payment will be £90,000. The intention is to limit the extent to which very highly paid individuals can obtain pensions through a scheme enjoying generous tax treatments. The move is part of a world-wide trend to widen the income tax base at the same time as reducing tax rates.[3] Several other developed countries have applied this process to pension schemes, in particular New Zealand and Australia.

At the same time the Government has made changes which make it easier, though at greater cost, for employers to make additional pension provision for very highly paid employees by means of unapproved "top-up" schemes.

The new restrictions only apply to schemes established on or after 14th March 1989 and in the case of schemes already in existence before that day to employees who join after 31st May 1989.

A parallel change has been made to the tax regime governing personal pensions. As from 6th April 1989 an earnings cap of £60,000 (to be price inflation-linked) is placed on the net relevant earnings on which maximum contributions are made but at the same time higher contribution limits have been brought in for individuals aged 36 or over.

These and a number of associated changes are described more fully below.

Simon's Taxes E7.1; Butterworths Income Tax Service G1

[1] Green Paper "Reform of Social Security" Cmnd. 9517 para. 7.19.
[2] Hansard Vol 149 No. 69 Col. 304.
[3] OECD Report 1988: The Taxation of Fringe Benefits, para. 28.

Earlier developments

30: 02   The tax changes which have recently been made are the outcome of developments in the pensions field which have been taking place for some years. Of particular significance are the following matters:

1 Preservation

When an employee leaves an occupational pension scheme the retirement benefits earned by pensionable service to date must be preserved. This may be achieved in various ways. The Social Security Act 1985 introduced a new alternative: the cash equivalent of the accrued pension entitlement may be applied towards "other types of pension arrangements that meet prescribed conditions" i.e. as a contribution to a personal pensions scheme set up by the employee when these became possible as from 1st July 1988.

2 Early leaver's disability

The preservation requirements only secure pension entitlement earned by service up to the point of leaving the scheme. Thus in a typical final salary scheme providing a pension of 40/60ths of final salary an employer who leaves after 20 years service is entitled to a deferred pension of 20/60ths of final salary at the date of leaving the scheme, not final salary prior to eventual retirement.

An employee whose career development may entail several job changes is thus at a particular disadvantage when pension is provided by final salary schemes.

Some alleviation for those now at the start of their careers was made by a provision in the Social Security Act 1985 requiring an early leaver's accrued pension entitlement to be revalued by cost of living increases (up to a maximum increase of 5% per year) for pensionable service after 31st December 1984.

But the main response by Government to this problem has been to encourage adoption of money-purchase schemes. A money purchase scheme is one where the employee or employer (or both) make defined contributions to a fund and the ultimate pension depends on the size of the fund when the employee retires. With such an arrangement the employee on changing jobs takes with him the part of the fund that represents contributions made by or for him and the income and gains thereon.

A personal pension scheme is a money-purchase arrangement set up by the employee which is not dependent on a particular employment. The employer may however contribute to such a scheme.

A significant change made in the Social Security Act 1986 made it unlawful from 6th April 1988 for a contract of employment to require compulsory membership of the employer's occupational scheme. It is therefore possible for employees from that date to elect not to belong to the employer's scheme and if they wish, to have a personal pension scheme instead.

3 Increasing cost of the state scheme

It has been calculated that by the year 2035 each pensioner will be supported by only 1.6 persons in employment as against 2.3 persons in 1985.[1] This is the result of changes in the birth rate and an increased life expectancy of those now coming up to pensionable age.

This anticipated trend has serious implications for the financing of the state pension scheme especially the second tier known as the state earnings related pensions scheme (SERPS). SERPS provides for a supplementary earnings-related component to be added to the basic flat-rate pension provided increased graduated national insurance contributions have been paid by the employer and employee.

Because the state scheme including SERPS is not funded and benefits are paid out of current contributions, the increasing number of pensioners will cause heavy costs to fall on those in employment in the coming decades.

The Social Security Act 1986 made a number of modifications to SERPS intended to limit future costs. In addition the following provisions have been made to encourage "contracting out" of SERPS.

(1) Individuals will be able to contract out of SERPS by setting up an "appropriate" personal pension scheme i.e. one which satisfies conditions prescribed in the relevant regulations.[2]

(2) The condition which must normally be met for an employee to be contracted out is that the private scheme provides not less than a "guaranteed minimum pension" i.e. broadly the additional state pension payable if the employee continued to participate in SERPS.

As from 6th April 1988 an alternative money-purchase test has been made available i.e. contracting out is now possible if the contributions to be made to a money-purchase scheme are no less than the increased national insurance contributions payable under SERPS.

(3) As an incentive to setting up personal pension schemes and new occupational pension schemes an addition to the contracted-out rebate of 2% of earnings between the upper and lower earnings limits (the "incentive payment") is to be paid by the Department of Social Security into such schemes until 5th April 1993. Notwithstanding that an appropriate personal pension scheme could not be set up until 1st July 1988, such a scheme could be used to enable the employee to contract out of SERPS as from 6th April 1987, rather than 6th April 1988 provided the prescribed notice was given before 6th April 1989. In that event the incentive payment became available as from 6th April 1987. Where, however, an employee had previously belonged to a contracted-out occupational scheme for at least 2 years ending after 5th April 1988 but voluntarily left the scheme while remaining in the same employment to set up an appropriate personal pension scheme, the scheme did not qualify for the incentive payment for any year.[3]

Simon's Taxes E7.104–106; Butterworths Income Tax Service Part G1.02.

[1] Green Paper "Reform of Social Security" Cmnd. 9517 para 5.4.
[2] S.I. 1988, No. 137.
[3] S.I. 1987, No. 1115, reg. 2 and S.I. 1987, No. 1933, reg. 4.

The schemes available

30: 03 The main tax-favoured pension arrangements now available are summarised below:

(*a*) *Occupational pension schemes approved under the "new code" rules.*

(*b*) *AVC arrangements.* Under these an employee covered by an occupational scheme makes additional provision within the overall limits allowed. The additional contribution may be made to the employer's scheme or as from 26th October 1987 to a "freestanding" scheme established by the employee.

(*c*) *Simplified occupational pension schemes.* These are "off the peg" schemes to which new code approval will be granted automatically if they are adopted without variation. They are intended for smaller employers for whom the costs of establishing a tailor-made scheme could be a deterrent. They are of two kinds:

(i) Simplified final salary schemes. With these, only basic pension benefits can be provided and the limits of maximum benefits are more restrictive than under normal exempt approved schemes.

(ii) Simplified money purchase schemes. With these no limits apply to the benefits that arise but there is a limit on the contributions made to such schemes similar to that applying to personal pension schemes.

(*d*) *Approved retirement annuity contracts.* The existing rules but subject to a new scale of contribution limits for older individuals will continue to apply to schemes which were established before 1st July 1988 (except where a new member joins an established trust scheme and first makes contributions after that date).

(*e*) *Approved personal pension schemes.* These schemes take the place of approved retirement annuity contracts and are more widely available. They did not come into operation until 1st July 1988. The rules are based on those for retirement annuity contracts.

(*f*) *Unapproved "top-up" schemes.* These are schemes made possible by FA 1989. They are intended to be used in cases where the earnings cap of £60,000 restricts the maximum pension to £40,000 and the maximum lump sum commutation payment to £90,000 and the employer wishes to make additional pension provision on an unapproved basis. Previously the rules in respect of unapproved schemes could in certain cases result in a double charge to tax. Moreover, the existence of an unapproved scheme could also prejudice an approved scheme covering the same employees because the benefits provided by all the schemes, including the unapproved arrangement, had to be taken into account in determining approvable limits. These deterrents have now been removed. (See infra, §§ **30: 06** and **30: 07**).

These various arrangements are discussed in more detail in the following paragraphs.

APPROVED OCCUPATIONAL SCHEMES

The "new code" of approval

30: 04   The modern approved occupational scheme owes a great deal to the Civil Service schemes which were established during the 19th century. This is in part because the railway companies and certain other large commercial concerns of the time modelled their own arrangements on those of the Civil Service but more importantly because when the "old code" of approval was brought in by FA 1921 the Revenue in exercising their discretionary power to approve schemes looked to the rules of the state schemes in deciding what could be accepted: hence such rules as the maximum pension payable being 40/60ths of final salary became part of the code.

The "old code" remained in being until 1970 but did not cover all forms of occupational scheme. As a result there were inconsistencies between the tax treatments applying to different kinds of scheme. Certain staff assurance schemes, for example, did not qualify for tax exemption of the income generated by the amounts subscribed. Again under "old code" approved schemes it was not possible for the member to commute part of his pension into a tax-free lump sum whereas this had long been allowed under statutory schemes and certain other arrangements requiring a more limited form of approval.

The "new code" of approval was established in 1970 to replace the "old code": it provides a simple and uniform framework of rules and practices applying to all occupational pension schemes. The relevant legislation is TA 1988, ss. 590–612 and Schs 22 and 23.

Under the transitional arrangements occupational schemes approved under the old code had to be re-approved under the new code by 5th April 1980 in order to retain their privileges.[1]

The main consequences of obtaining new code approval are:

(a) Employer contributions are allowable tax deductions to the extent that they are ordinary annual contributions.

(b) Employee contributions are deductible from earnings subject to an overall limit of 15% of annual remuneration.

(c) The employer's contributions are not taxable emoluments of the employee.

(d) The income and capital gains arising on fund investments are exempt from tax.

(e) Pensions paid during retirement are taxable on the members as earned income under Schedule E.

These points are considered in more detail in the succeeding paragraphs. They only apply to schemes which obtain full approval and are thus "exempt approved schemes". A more limited form of approval only secures the advantage in (c) i.e. avoidance of the employer's contributions being taxed on the employee.

Many different kinds of scheme may qualify as exempt approved schemes. They include:

(a) Employer-sponsored schemes which provide for defined benefits e.g. a pension payable by reference to final salary. The employee's contributions, if the scheme is a contributory one, will normally be fixed e.g. a percentage of annual earnings and the employer must bear the responsibility for seeing that the fund is sufficient to meet the pension benefits which must eventually be provided. The vast majority of occupational schemes are of this kind.

(b) Employer-sponsored schemes under which defined contributions by both employer and employee are made i.e. "money purchase" schemes. Here the pension benefits ultimately made available depend on the build-up of the fund representing the contributions made.

Hitherto such an arrangement has been uncommon in occupational schemes but as explained in **30: 02** some encouragement is being given to setting up schemes of this kind.

(c) Schemes popularly known as "top hat" schemes where the employer has some discretion over the amount of benefit provided.

(d) The trustees of approved schemes may secure pensions through insurance contracts or through making direct investments. In practice the Revenue insists that small occupational schemes be run through insurers unless they qualify under a special regime for small self-administered schemes.

(e) The statutory schemes for public sector employees are strictly outside the scope of the "new code" but their tax rules have been brought closely into line with those of exempt approved schemes.[2]

Simon's Taxes E7.102, E7.211; Butterworths Income Tax Service Part G1.03.

[1] For the position of frozen s. 208 schemes which did not apply for approval under the new code, see Simon's Taxes E7.251.

[2] TA 1988, s. 594.

Meaning of "retirement benefits scheme"

30: 05 The new code makes it possible for approval to be given to "any retirement benefits scheme". Such a scheme is one which provides for "relevant benefits". These are very widely defined.[1] The Revenue regards the definition as including any type of financial benefit given in connection with the termination of an employee's service with a particular employer but in practice it does not treat a single ex gratia lump sum or a voluntary pension as constituting a retirement benefits scheme.[2] Benefits provided solely for disablement or death by accident during though not necessarily arising out of service are specifically excluded.[3]

Schemes providing relevant benefits may relate to only a small number of employees or even one and they may provide for the pension to start immediately.[4] Provision of relevant benefits or a pension includes provision by means of a contract with a third party e.g. an insurance contract.[5]

The Revenue may divide a retirement benefits scheme into two or more schemes relating to different classes of employee such as employees of different group companies.[6] This procedure is commonly followed where approval is sought for the UK section of a world-wide scheme set up by a multinational group.

Simon's Taxes E7.203; Butterworths Income Tax Service G2.01.

[1] TA 1988, s. 612(1).
[2] IR 12 (1979), paras. 2.1 and 2.2.
[3] TA 1988, s. 612(1).
[4] TA 1988, s. 611(2).
[5] TA 1988, s. 612(2).
[6] TA 1988, s. 611(3), (4).

Consequences of non-approval

30: 06 If a scheme or arrangement is a retirement benefits scheme by virtue of the wide definition considered above but is not an approved scheme (not necessarily an exempt approved scheme), the main consequence will be that any sum paid by the employer with a view to the provision of relevant benefits is treated as income of the employee.[1]

This is a severe sanction: it derives from an anti-avoidance provision in FA 1947, s. 19 to counter the practice of an employer making pension provision for an employee out of all proportion to his current salary, part of which could be commuted into a tax-free lump sum.

If the unapproved scheme is not funded, the position before FA 1989 was passed was that a notional cost of securing the provision of the benefits was treated as income of the employee. Any pension paid (unless commuted into a lump sum payment) would also be taxed on the employee, so resulting in a double charge to tax.

This rule is changed as from 27th July 1989; in future in an unfunded scheme the employee will not be taxed on the employer's notional cost but will be subject to tax under Schedule E on any benefit received from the scheme, including a lump sum payment.[2] If the benefit is received by a person other than an individual, the scheme administrator is to be charged to tax under Schedule D Case VI on the amount received or the cash equivalent of the benefit.[3] In the case of a funded unapproved scheme, lump sum payments (but not pension payments) to the employee are tax-free so long as the payments can be attributed to employer contributions which have been taxed on the employee.[4]

If the scheme is not approved, neither can it be an exempt approved scheme and hence the tax privileges enjoyed by such schemes, e.g. exemption for income and gains on investments held by the fund, will not be available.

Simon's Taxes E7.221; Butterworths Income Tax Service G2.261.
[1] TA 1988, s. 595(1).
[2] TA 1988, s. 596A(1), (2).
[3] TA 1988 s. 596A(3), (4) and s. 596B.
[4] TA 1988, s. 596A(8).

Conditions for approval

30: 07   Approval of a scheme rests with the Board of Inland Revenue[1] although this must be given if the scheme satisfies all the "prescribed conditions" in TA 1988, s. 590(2) and (3): this is known as mandatory approval. However, the Board is empowered to approve schemes which do not satisfy these prescribed conditions on a discretionary basis: this is normally referred to as discretionary approval.

Mandatory approval.

The prescribed conditions to qualify for mandatory approval are first, in TA 1988, s. 590(2) that:

(*a*) the scheme is bona fide established for the sole purpose of providing relevant benefits in respect of service as an employee. These may be paid to the employee, his personal representative, his widow, children or dependants, the last word being undefined;

(*b*) the scheme is recognised by employer and employee and that written particulars are given to every employee eligible to belong;

(*c*) there must be a person resident in the UK to fulfil the duties of an administrator, in particular to make the necessary returns to the Revenue;

(*d*) the employer must be a contributor;

(*e*) the scheme must be in connection with some trade or undertaking carried on in (not with) the UK by a person resident in the UK; and

(*f*) in no circumstances can any repayment of contributions be made to the employee.

Of these conditions (*e*) and (*f*) are in practice relaxed.[2]

These conditions simply lay down a framework. To be assured of automatic approval a scheme must further satisfy the conditions in TA 1988, s. 590(3) which are:

(*i*) the benefit is a pension on retirement at an age between 55 for a woman, 60 for a man and 70 in both instances, and that the pension must not exceed x/60 of the employee's final remuneration, meaning the average annual remuneration over the previous three years where x is the number of years of service but may not exceed 40, a maximum of $\frac{2}{3}$;

(*ii*) any pension to the employee's widow is to commence on the employee's death after retirement and must not exceed $\frac{2}{3}$ of the employee's pension;

(*iii*) no other benefits are payable under the scheme; and

(*iv*) no pension can be surrendered, commuted or assigned save that the scheme may allow a lump sum of up to 3x/80 of the final remuneration, where x is the number of years of service, but may not exceed 40—a maximum lump sum of $1\frac{1}{2}$ times the final remuneration. This has an impact on (*i*) in that it must be converted into a pension equivalent and added to the figure in (*i*) in calculating the maximum benefit.

For schemes for which mandatory approval was applied for on or after 17th March 1987 final remuneration for the purpose of condition (iv) was confined to a "permitted maximum" of £100,000 per annum. This had the effect of limiting the maximum lump sum commutation payment to £150,000.

For a scheme which is not approved until on or after 27th July 1989 and as regards employees who on after 31st May 1989 become members of a scheme which came into existence before 14th March 1989, the foregoing restriction is removed and replaced by a rule which limits final remuneration to £60,000 for the purpose of determining both pension benefit and the maximum lump sum commutation payment.[3] The £60,000 figure applies for 1988/89 and 1989/90 but thereafter the figure may be increased by Treasury order under a formula which reflects price inflation per the retail price index.[4] There are special rules which apply the restriction on an aggregated basis in cases where the employee belongs to a scheme through having "relevant associated employments" or the scheme to which the employee belongs is "connected with" another approved scheme.[5]

Very few schemes will satisfy all these conditions. In particular, condition (*iii*) prevents automatic approval of any scheme with a death-in-service benefit.

Discretionary approval

The Board are allowed to approve schemes that do not meet these conditions, a process known as discretionary approval.[6] They are in particular empowered to approve schemes providing for higher pensions, death in service pensions for widows, pensions for children and dependants, lump sum death-in-service benefits of up to four times the final remuneration exclusive of any refund of contributions, pensions within ten years of retirement age, or earlier incapacity, the refund of contributions and pensions which relate to a trade carried on only partly in the UK and by a non-resident.[7]

The Revenue's booklet IR 12 (1979) sets out detailed practice notes applied by the Revenue in exercising their discretion. Within the parameters indicated schemes may be approved even though they fall substantially short of the conditions laid down for mandatory approval. The practice notes have to be read in conjunction with subsequent memoranda issued by the Joint Office of the Occupational Pensions Board and the Inland Revenue Superannuation Funds Office.

In some cases the practice notes are superseded by subsequent legislation. In particular F(No 2)A 1987 amended the interpretation provision (TA 1988, s. 612(1)) so that for all purposes of the new code the definition of remuneration must exclude amounts assessable under Schedule E in respect of the acquisition and disposal of shares or from rights to acquire shares or in respect of payments on termination or variation of employment charged by virtue of TA 1988, s. 148.

Discretionary approval subject to F(No 2)A 1987 changes

For schemes which obtained discretionary approval before 23rd July 1987 F(No 2)A 1987 introduced the following new rules which if necessary override the scheme's own rules. These rules, which are now in TA 1988, Sch 23, are as follows:

(*a*) Where a late entrant joins the approved scheme on or after 17th March 1987, a new "accelerated accrual" scale applies in relation to pension entitlement. The maximum rate of accrual allowed is 1/30th of the "relevant annual remuneration", i.e. normally final remuneration, for each year of service up to a maximum of 20. A late entrant will therefore need to complete 20 years pensionable service with the new employer in order to obtain a full 2/3rds final salary pension. Previously under what is known as the uplifted 60ths scale only 10 years pensionable service was required.

(*b*) If the employee becomes a member of the approved scheme on or after 17th March 1987, the provisions of the scheme allowing for commutation of part of the pension into a lump sum are to be modified as follows:

(i) If the pension before commutation is not subject to accelerated accrual i.e. it is calculated at the rate of 1/60th of relevant annual remuneration for each year of service up to a maximum of 40, no accelerated accrual can be applied to the lump sum commutation payment allowed i.e. that payment is limited to 3/80ths of relevant annual remuneration for each year of service up to a maximum of 40. This rule counteracts the practice that was previously possible of applying accelerated accrual to the lump sum when the pension itself was not subject to accelerated accrual, so enabling a disproportionately high tax-free lump sum to be obtained.

(ii) If the pension before commutation results from application of the new accelerated accrual scale for pension entitlement (1/30th for each year of service up to a maximum of 20), the existing uplifted 80ths scale of accelerated accrual (which permits a maximum lump sum of $1\frac{1}{2}$ times final salary to be obtained after 20 years service) can still be applied to the calculation of the lump sum commutation payment.

(iii) If the pension before commutation reflects some measure of accelerated accrual but is less than one produced by the new scale of 1/30th of relevant annual remuneration for each year of service up to a maximum of 20, accelerated accrual based on the uplifted 80ths scale can still be applied to the lump sum to be taken in commutation but only to the extent to which accelerated accrual is applied to the calculation of pension benefit.

For schemes set up on or after 14th March 1989 and, in relation to schemes set up before that day, for members who join after 31st May 1989, the foregoing provisions are replaced by a simpler and often more favourable rule (see below under *Discretionary approval subject to FA 1989 changes*).

(*c*) For members who retire on or after 17th March 1987, pension benefits are to be calculated using the amended definition of remuneration (see above) which excludes amounts assessed under Schedule E in respect of the acquisition and disposal of shares, rights to acquire shares and payments on termination and variation of employment.

(*d*) Where retirement takes place on or after 17th March 1987 the following additional classes of employee must have their final salary based on the highest average annual remuneration for any period of three or more years ending within the last 10 years before retirement:

(i) an employee who at any time in the last 10 years of service was a controlling director of the employer company;

(ii) an employee whose relevant annual remuneration exceeds £100,000 per annum.

This restriction already applies to controlling directors and the purpose of (i) is to prevent controlling directors from resigning shortly before retirement in order to adopt the basis which only has regard to remuneration for any single year in the last five before retirement.

(*e*) Where an employee becomes a member on or after 17th March 1987 of a scheme approved before 23rd July 1987 and the scheme rules allow for a lump sum to be taken in commutation of pension benefit calculated by reference to relevant annual remuneration, that remuneration is to be limited to the permitted maximum i.e. £100,000, so restricting the maximum tax free lump sum payment to £150,000.

For schemes set up on or after 14th March 1989 and, in relation to schemes set up before that day, for members who join after 31st May 1989, this restriction is displaced by the earnings cap of £60,000 (price inflation-linked) which is relevant to all benefits, not simply the maximum lump sum commutation payment (see below under *Discretionary approval subject to FA 1989 changes*).

Discretionary approval subject to FA 1989 changes

As with the changes made by F(No. 2)A 1987, FA 1989 applies certain statutory overriding provisions to the rules of certain schemes. In general these provisions only apply to schemes which come into existence on or after 14th March 1989 and, in the case of schemes which were already in existence before that day, to employees who join the schemes after 31st May 1989. In the case of a centralised scheme, i.e. one covering numerous unrelated employers in a particular industry or sector, the provisions apply if the employer in question began to participate in the scheme on or after 14th March 1989.[8] The main changes made are:

(*a*) For the purpose of calculating maximum benefits e.g. pension benefit, lump sum commutation payment, death-in-service benefit etc, final remuneration is limited to £60,000.[9] This figure applies to 1988–89 and 1989–90 but for subsequent years the figure is to be increased by Treasury order to reflect price inflation in the same way as the £60,000 earnings cap introduced into the conditions for mandatory approval (see above).

(*b*) If the employee is a member of a scheme through having two or more "relevant associated employments", the earnings cap described in (*a*) is applied on an aggregated basis.;[10] There is a similar aggregation in applying the restriction in a case where the scheme to which the employee belongs is "connected with" another approved scheme.[11]

(*c*) A simpler rule has to be applied for calculating accelerated accrual of the lump sum commutation payment. Under the new rule the maximum lump sum commutation payment is to be the greater of

(i) 3/80ths of final remuneration for each year of service up to a maximum of 40, and

(ii) the pension (before commutation) for the first year in which it is payable multiplied by 2.25.[12]

(*d*) Because the new rule on accelerated accrual of the lump sum benefit will often be more favourable than the corresponding statutory over-ride made by F(No. 2)A 1987 (see above), a member who joined the scheme on or after 17th March 1987 but before 1st June 1989 is given the right to elect to be treated as if he became a member on 1st June 1989.[13] This will result in his being subject to the new rule on accelerated accrual but he will also have to accept the other statutory over-rides made by FA 1989, in particular the £60,000 earnings cap for calculating maximum benefits. This restriction applies for 1989–90 onwards but regulations are to be introduced prescribing cases where the restriction is not to apply.[14] The intention is that where the scheme was established before Budget Day (14th March 1989) the restriction will not apply to members who joined before 1 June 1989.[15]

(*e*) In applying the 15% of remuneration limit on permitted employee contributions (see § **30: 10**, infra), remuneration is limited to £60,000 for 1989–90 so that the maximum contributions which an employer can pay becomes £9,000.[16] The £60,000 figure is to be increased for subsequent years in line with price inflation as in (*a*).

This particular restriction unlike the other changes indicated above applies for 1989–90 onwards to all members of schemes approved before 27th July 1989 regardless of when they became members.

For schemes for which discretionary approval is applied for in the future, parallel changes to those set out above will be made to the practice notes regulating discretionary approval.

It will in future be possible in discretionary approved schemes to provide early retirement benefits of 1/30th for each year of service but as a corollary increases for late retirement will then be limited to N/30ths or by taking final salary at actual retirement[17]. The practice notes are to provide this alternative. Schemes set up after 13th March 1989 may adopt this alternative but there is no compulsion to do so.[18] It seems likely that the decision will have to be taken for the scheme as a whole and not in relation to individual members but this awaits classification. As with the election in (*d*) above, if the alternative is adopted, the new earnings cap of £60,000 in relation to maximum approvable benefits will also have to be accepted.

Because the adoption of the alternative basis for early retirement benefits is voluntary, no statutory over-riding provision is needed to cover existing schemes.

Transitional arrangements

It will be seen that both F(No. 2)A 1987 and FA 1989 introduced a number of sweeping changes to the regime governing approval of occupational schemes. In both cases members who already belonged to existing schemes were protected from some but not all of the new restrictions. In each case a distinction is made between an existing scheme under which those who were already members could enjoy such protection and a new scheme which must be completely subject to the new regime.

However, it was appreciated that what constitutes a new scheme is not always clear and that in practice there could be hard cases. Accordingly, the Board was enabled to introduce regulations modifying or disapplying the statutory provisions.[19] The regulations that were made in relation to the F(No. 2)A 1987 changes[20] specified a number of situations in which the employee was not to be treated as joining a new scheme, in particular—

(*a*) on changing to another scheme of the same or an associated employer;

(*b*) on rejoining the scheme after a temporary absence or secondment or posting;

(*c*) on joining a supplementary scheme while remaining a member of the existing scheme.

It is intended that similar regulations should be introduced in relation to the FA 1989 changes. They will also cover the situation where the employee joins a scheme following a merger or acquisition.[21]

Aggregation

Before FA 1989 was passed the Revenue, in dealing with an application for approval of a particular scheme, had to consider the scheme in conjunction with all other schemes covering the same class or description of employees. If taking all the schemes together the conditions were not satisfied, none of the schemes could be approved.[22]

This rule would have meant that the grafting of an unapproved "top-up" scheme on to an approved scheme would have caused approval of the latter scheme to be withdrawn. To remove this obstacle FA 1989 amends the relevant rule so that the other schemes which have to be taken into account when considering approval are confined to other approved schemes, schemes for which approval has been applied, frozen old code schemes and statutory schemes.[23]

For schemes for which discretionary approval is applied for after 22nd July 1987, parallel changes to those set out above have been made in the practice notes governing discretionary approval. Thus for such schemes to obtain discretionary approval the scheme rules will have to incorporate the foregoing restrictions. Because the restrictions can be built into the scheme before discretionary approval is applied for, there is no need in this situation to bring in statutory restrictions which if necessary override the scheme rules.

F(No 2)A 1987 also made provision (in what is now TA 1988, Sch 23, para 1) for regulations to be introduced by means of the statutory instrument procedure which would to some extent limit the Revenue's power to grant discretionary approval in that the Revenue would have to exercise their discretion in a manner consistent with the regulations. While the scope of the regulations which can be made is very wide, it is understood that the intended regulations will be confined to the approval of small self-administered schemes (see supra, § **30: 03**). Hitherto such approval has been given entirely on the basis of Revenue practice as set out in Memorandum 58.

Simon's Taxes E7.212; Butterworths Income Tax Service G2.02.

[1] In fact with the Superannuation Funds Office.

[2] They are empowered to do this by TA 1988, s. 591(2). For relaxation of (*e*) see IR 12 Part 17, for (*f*), see §§ **13: 12** et seq.

[3] TA 1988, s. 590C(1).

[4] TA 1988, s. 590C(2)–(6).

[5] TA 1988, ss. 590A, 590B.

[6] TA 1988, s. 591(1).

[7] TA 1988, s. 591(2).

[8] FA 1989, Sch. 6, para. 28.

[9] FA 1989, Sch. 6, para. 20.

[10] FA 1989, Sch. 6, para. 25.

[11] FA 1989, Sch. 6, para. 26.

[12] FA 1989, Sch. 6, para. 23.

[13] FA 1989, Sch. 6, para. 29.

[14] FA 1989, Sch. 6, para. 21.

[15] FA 1989, Sch. 6, para. 18(4).

[16] Hansard, Standing Committee G. 8 June 1989 col. 342.

[17] Memorandum 99, paras. 23 to 25.

[18] Memorandum 99, para. 25.

[19] TA 1988 Sch. 23, para. 1(2).

[20] The Occupational Pension Schemes (Transitional Provisions) Regulations, S.I. 1988 No. 1436.

[21] Memorandum 99, paras. 13–16.

[22] TA 1988, s. 590(7).

[23] FA 1989, Sch. 6 para. 3(4).

Exempt approved schemes

30: 08 Obtaining Revenue approval of a scheme, whether on a mandatory or discretionary basis, only secures exemption from the charge to tax on the employee in respect of employer contributions (see § **30: 06**, supra).

For the tax privileges described in the following paragraphs to apply, the scheme must not only be approved but must also be an "exempt approved scheme". An exempt approved scheme is defined as:

(a) any approved scheme which is shown to the satisfaction of the Board to be established under irrevocable trusts, or

(b) any other approved scheme which the Board, having regard to any special circumstances directs shall be an exempt approved scheme.[1]

In practice the Revenue does not insist on a formal trust deed provided that the fund or policy is held in a fiduciary capacity and that the disposal of assets is governed by the approved terms of the scheme.[2]

Simon's Taxes E7.214; Butterworths Income Tax Service G2.04.
[1] TA 1988, s. 592(1).
[2] IR 12 (1979), para. 2.4.

Employer's contribution-deduction

30: 09   Where an employer makes contributions to a retirements benefits scheme, the amounts may be deductible on general principles i.e. as expenses incurred in order to obtain the services of the employees in question. Contributions to provide the initial funding of the scheme or to provide an enhanced level of benefits could, however, be disallowed on the grounds that they constitute capital expenditure.[1]

If the scheme is an exempt approved scheme, a specific provision gives allowance for employer contributions either as an expense of the trade or as a management expense.[2] The deduction is given for ordinary annual contributions and to the extent that a contribution falls outside this category, the Revenue may require the contribution to be spread over an agreed period of years.[3] An initial contribution on setting up a scheme to provide benefits for back service, a special contribution to provide improved benefits and an additional contribution to make good an actuarial deficiency would not be ordinary annual contributions. But additional contributions to meet cost of living increases to the pensions paid to existing pensioners are allowed as ordinary annual contributions and so not subject to spreading.

For unapproved schemes FA 1989 has introduced a new statutory rule governing the allowability or otherwise of employer contributions or in the case of an unfunded scheme pension or lump sum payments made by the employer. It is expressly provided that unless the employee is chargeable to income tax on the sums paid by the employer, the employer may not deduct the expense in computing business profits or if the employer is an investment company the sums may not be treated as management expenses.[4] This rule is intended to ensure that employees are charged to tax on the sums in question.

Simon's Taxes E7.218; Butterworths Income Tax Service G2.32.
[1] *Atherton v British Insulated andHelsby Cables Ltd*, supra, § 7: 103; but cf. *Hancock v General Reversionary and Investment Co Ltd* [1919] 1 KB 25, 7 TC 358, supra, § 7: 106. See also *Lowe v Peter Walker (Warrington) and Robert Cain & Sons Ltd* (1935) 20 TC 25 and *Samuel Dracup & Sons Ltd v Dakin* (1957) 37 TC 377.
[2] TA 1988, s. 592(4).
[3] TA 1988, s. 592(6). For the main rules on spreading see IR 12 (1979), para. 5.5.
[4] FA 1989, s. 76(1).

Employee's contribution-deduction

30: 10   For employee contributions paid on or after 6th April 1987, FA (No 2) 1987 amended the statutory rule giving relief for employee contributions to an exempt approved scheme.[1] The maximum deduction for contributions paid by an employee in a year of assessment is not to exceed 15% of his remuneration for that year.[2] This limit applies to all contributions to exempt approved schemes including AVC schemes whether set up by the employer or the employee (see § **30: 16**, infra). The statutory rule allows for the limit to be increased to "such higher percentage as the Board may in a particular case prescribe". It is understood that this power will be exercised in strictly limited circumstances, one case being where scheme benefits have been improved subsequent to an employee joining the scheme and the employee has the opportunity to participate in the improvements through making additional contributions.

The previous position was effectively the same. The statutory rule gave relief for "ordinary annual contributions" and the Revenue practice notes imposed the 15% of remuneration limit in setting out what was regarded as an ordinary annual contribution.[3]

Following the statutory amendment there is now no distinction between "ordinary annual" and "special" contributions, and it seems that non-recurring once-for-all contributions will be allowed in full subject to the 15% of remuneration limit whether or not they are paid by instalments (as was required under previous Revenue practice). Accordingly the decision in *Kneen v Ashton* (1950) 31 TC 343, under which "back contributions" on late entry into a scheme were held to be special contributions and so not deductible, has been overruled by legislative amendment.

For 1989–90 and subsequent years, the statutory rule is amended so that the annual remuneration subject to the 15 per cent limit is restricted to £60,000 (to be price inflation-linked).[4] Where the employee has more than one employment, the restriction is applied to each employment in turn.[5]

Simon's Taxes E7.218; Butterworths Income Tax Service G2.33.
[1] TA 1988, s. 592(7).
[2] TA 1988, s. 592 (8).
[3] IR 12 (1979), para. 4.5.
[4] FA 1989, Sch. 6 para 5(4).
[5] FA 1989, Sch. 6 para 5(3).

Taxation of the fund

30: 11   An exempt approved scheme enjoys certain specific tax exemptions. The basic exemption is that income from the investments and deposits held for the purposes of the scheme is exempt from income tax.[1] Gains from disposals of investments (but not deposits) held for the purposes of the scheme are exempt from capital gains tax.[2]

Because the management of investments has become more sophisticated, pension funds will often carry out investment-related transactions which were not anticipated in the original legislation. To deal with new situations further exemptions have been added to cover:

(*a*) underwriting commissions applied for the purposes of the scheme which otherwise would be taxed under Schedule D Case VI.[3]

(*b*) gains from the disposal of certificates of deposit unless treated as trading profits,[4] and

(*c*) gains on financial futures or traded options.[5]

At present there are no special rules dealing with currency hedging arrangements made by exempt approved funds to protect income flows fixed in foreign currency or to cover the exchange risk in holding investments realisable in foreign currencies but it is considered that these transactions should enjoy the same exemptions from tax as the investments to which they relate.

Dealing in securities and other forms of trading are outside the scope of these exemptions and so are liable to tax. The distinction between making investments and dealing in them is sometimes hard to draw and the Revenue have set up a Special Office based in Sheffield to review cases where non-exempt transactions by exempt approved schemes are suspected. However following discussions with the National Association of Pension Funds the Revenue have written to them concluding that "in general it seemed highly unlikely that purchase and sale of securities would be shown to be trading in cases where the fund has been run solely in accordance with the normal guidelines to investment managers".[6] Particular areas of difficulty include the buying of certificates of deposit and selling them before maturity and sub-underwriting where the volume and frequency of the transactions may be an indication of trading.

In the case of an insured scheme, the insurance company is granted exemption from corporation tax on income and capital gains in respect of investments and deposits referrable to its "pension business".[7] Such business includes contracts with persons having the management of an exempt approved scheme.[8]

Simon's Taxes E7.216; Butterworths Income Tax Service G2.04
[1] TA 1988, s. 592(2).
[2] TA 1988, Sch. 29, para. 26.
[3] TA 1988, s. 592(3).
[4] TA 1988, s. 56(1)–(3).
[5] TA 1988, s. 659.
[6] NAPF Information Bulletin (July 1988) p. 5; see *Pensions World*, July 1988.
[7] TA 1988, s. 438.
[8] TA 1988, s. 431(4).

Taxation of pensions

30: 12   There are certain general provisions which charge pension payments to tax under Schedule E whether or not paid by an approved fund. The primary rule is TA 1988, s. 19(1) which charges emoluments and "any pension which is paid otherwise than by or on behalf of a person outside the UK". The term pension is not defined but TA 1988, s. 133 states "for the avoidance of doubt" that the word pension includes a pension which is paid voluntarily or is capable of being discontinued.

Whether a payment is by way of pension is one of fact. If the payment is of an income nature and made after the employment has ceased and paid on account of services rendered during the employment it is probably a pension but not if some other reason can be given for the payment. In *McMann v Shaw*[1] the taxpayer had worked as Borough Treasurer at Southall. When that borough was abolished under the London Government reorganisation, he was transferred to Ealing as a consultant, but after two years that work ended and he was awarded compensation for loss of emoluments[2] until he became entitled to his pension. It was held that these payments were compensation for loss of office and not payments for services past or present. The fact that the payments were quantified by reference to his previous salary did not turn them into a pension. It followed that since the payments satisfied the requirements of annual payments,[3] they fell to be taxed under Schedule D, Case III as unearned income and not under Schedule E.

However where the payment is a pension payable under the rules of an approved scheme (not necessarily an exempt approved scheme) there is a specific statutory rule that the pensions shall be charged to tax under Schedule E.[4]

In the case of foreign pensions chargeable under Schedule D Case IV or V the remittance basis is not to apply but the income to be charged is reduced by 10 per cent. The same reduction also applies to certain Commonwealth government pensions chargeable under Schedule E para. 4.[5]

Simon's Taxes E7.206; Butterworths Income Tax Service G2.73
  [1] [1972] 3 All ER 732, 48 TC 330.
  [2] Statutory redundancy payments are exempt: TA 1988, s. 579.
  [3] Supra, § **9: 69**.
  [4] TA 1988, s. 597(1).
  [5] TA 1988, s. 65(2).

Lump sums

30: 13   Under the new Civil Service superannuation arrangements introduced in 1973, the lump sum gratuity which had previously been discretionary was made payable as of right and it was thought desirable to declare by TA 1988, s. 189 that lump sums payable on retirement were not taxable whether payable as of right or not. In this way the lump sum was assimilated to the proceeds of a life assurance policy.

This exemption is not unrestricted. First, it does not apply to an unjustified payment of compensation for early retirement unless due to ill health; such a payment falls within TA 1988, s. 148. A payment is justified if it is properly regarded as a benefit earned by past service.[1] Secondly, it does not apply to unauthorised payments from a fund nor to a payment after the cessation of tax exemptions.[2] Thirdly, it does not apply unless the scheme in question is an approved scheme, a statutory scheme or a foreign Government scheme[3] or, alternatively, is an unapproved retirement benefits scheme, so that the person to whom the lump sum is paid has been charged to tax on employer contributions to the scheme.[4]

In the case of an approved scheme the maximum lump sum that can be paid in commutation of pension is subject to the rules under which approval is given and normally (but subject to accelerated accrual) must not exceed 3/

80ths of final salary for each year of service up to 40. (For the detailed rules see supra, § **30: 07.**)

Other types of lump sum are subject to special rules of taxation. Thus the consideration paid for a restrictive covenant given in connection with an office or employment past or present or future is liable to tax at the higher rate.[5] Secondly sums payable for termination of the office are chargeable to tax under TA 1988, s. 148 to the extent that they exceed £30,000.[6] If they do exceed that figure however they will still be exempt if they come from exempt approved schemes and are within the limits allowed for such schemes.

Simon's Taxes E4.807; Butterworths Income Tax Service D4.22.
  [1] TA 1988, s. 188(2).
  [2] TA 1988, s. 600.
  [3] TA 1988, s. 189.
  [4] TA 1988, s. 189.
  [5] TA 1988, s. 313, § **6: 39**, supra.
  [6] Supra, § **6: 45**.

Refunds of employee contributions and special commutation payments

30: 14   Where an employee's contributions are refunded to him there is a special tax of 20% levied on the trustees.[1] Further, where the scheme rules allow in special circumstances a lump sum payment in commutation of the entire pension, there will be a charge to income tax on the amount by which the sum paid exceeds the greater of (*i*) a sum equal to $\frac{3}{80}$ths of the final remuneration multiplied by the number of years' service, and (*ii*) the sum payable under certain special rules.[2] For payments made on or after 17th March 1987 (except to employees who became members of an approved scheme before that date) final remuneration for this purpose is limited to the permitted maximum of £100,000 per annum.[3] For payments made on or after 14th March 1989 (except where the scheme was in existence before that day and the employee became a member before 1st June 1989) final remuneration for this purpose is limited to £60,000 for 1988–89 and 1989–90 (to be increased for subsequent years by reference to price inflation).[4] This tax is also at the rate of 20% and applies to any approved scheme whether exempt or not.

Simon's Taxes E7.218; Butterworths Income Tax Service D4.22.
  [1] TA 1988, s. 598(2). The rate of tax was increased from 10% to 20% for payments made on or after 6th April 1988; S.I. 1988 No. 504. This may be deducted from the payment made. On effect of deduction of tax, see *Lord Advocate v Hay* (1924) 21 ATC 146 and *Bridge v Watterson* [1952] 2 All ER 910, 34 TC 47.
  [2] TA 1988, s. 599. The scheme may have been approved at any time—or be a statutory scheme.
  [3] TA 1988, Sch. 23, para 6.
  [4] FA 1989, Sch. 6 para 11.

Correction of surpluses

30: 15   As a result of a sustained appreciation in stock market prices over a number of years up to and including 1986 it was not unusual for a pension scheme to hold assets of a value beyond that required to meet future obligations. The precise position depended on the method of actuarial valuation which was consistently followed.

The problem of overfunding received Government attention when certain schemes applied for permission to make refunds to employers of past contributions. Hitherto when an approved scheme became overfunded the Revenue under certain practice rules only permitted a refund of employer contributions as a last resort after all other steps to deal with the surplus, e.g. providing for a contribution holiday for up to 5 years, had been taken.[1]

The Government took the view that it was no longer appropriate for such a question to be determined by Revenue practice and in FA 1986, now TA 1988, ss. 601–603 and Sch. 22, introduced "clear and objective rules" for identifying and remedying pension scheme surpluses. Subject to transitional provisions covering the period 19th March 1987 to 5th April 1987, these rules took full effect from 6th April 1987; they only apply to exempt approved schemes. Many of the substantive rules are in supporting regulations dealing with valuation and administration respectively.[2]

The key feature of these rules is that an actuarial valuation on a prescribed basis must be periodically submitted to the Revenue.[3] The prescribed basis of actuarial valuation is "the projected accrued benefit method"; this takes account of accrued service to the date of valuation and projected salary increases to retirement attributable both to inflation and career progression. The various assumptions to be made in applying this method are set out in the regulations dealing with valuation.[4]

An actuarial valuation on this basis must be provided whenever a valuation of the scheme assets and liabilities is made. Such a valuation will therefore be an additional valuation where the valuation for the purpose of the scheme rules is on a different basis. The interval between successive valuations on the prescribed basis must not exceed 3 years and 6 months (5 years in the case of public service schemes) as measured by reference to the dates taken for the purposes of such valuations.[5]

As an alternative to submitting an actuarial valuation on the prescribed basis, the scheme administrator may submit a certificate indicating whether on the prescribed basis a surplus does or does not exceed the permitted limit but where such a certificate is given the Revenue is entitled to call for a valuation on the prescribed basis in support.

If the valuation on the prescribed basis shows a surplus of scheme assets in excess of liabilities by more than 5%, the scheme administrator is required to submit proposals for reducing the surplus to that level by one or more of certain "permitted ways".[6] These are:

(*a*) returning contributions to the employer;
(*b*) suspending or reducing employer's contributions for up to 5 years;
(*c*) suspending or reducing employees' contributions for up to 5 years;
(*d*) improving scheme benefits;
(*e*) providing additional benefits;
(*f*) other methods that may be prescribed by regulations.

These methods may be used singly or in combination. Unlike the Revenue practice which previously regulated the correction of surpluses, no order of priority is laid down. Contributions may be returned to the employer without first using the other methods if that is desired, although in that case the new charge to tax on payments to employers will apply as explained below. If this particular course is chosen the surplus must not be reduced to below 5% of the scheme liabilities.[7]

If the scheme administrator does not submit proposals, or the proposals are not approved by the Revenue, or the proposals are approved but not carried out in the time allowed, the Revenue may restrict the tax exemptions enjoyed by the scheme to the proportion A/B where A is the Revenue's estimate of the scheme liabilities as increased by a specified percentage and B is its estimate of the scheme assets.[8]

If one of the permitted ways used to reduce the surplus is to return contributions to the employer, a new freestanding tax charge of 40% applies.[9] The tax payable cannot be reduced by loss reliefs or set offs and is not available for set off of other tax.[10] The charge applies to all payments by the scheme to the employer except for certain "excluded payments" which include reimbursements of expenditure incurred by the employer relating to the administration of the scheme and loans to the employer provided the interest produced is a reasonable commercial return.[11]

The charge applies to payments to the employer made on or after 19th March 1986 (not 6th April 1987) unless permission to make the refund was applied for before 19th March 1986 and not subsequently withdrawn or the payment was one made in the course of winding up where the winding up commenced before 19th March 1986.[12] In these two cases and where the payment was made prior to 19th March 1986 the payment to the employer was charged to tax as a receipt of the employer's trade, profession or vocation or if the scheme did not relate to such a trade etc, the payment was charged to tax under Schedule D Case VI.[13]

Where the new freestanding tax charge at 40% applies, the scheme administrator is required to deduct the tax at source when making the payment to the employer and to file a return within 14 days of making the payment.[14] The tax deducted has to be paid to the Revenue when the return is made.[15] If this procedure is not followed, the Revenue may recover the tax due in respect of the payment by an assessment on the administrator in the name of the employer and where the administrator then pays the tax he is entitled to recover it from the employer.[16]

Simon's Taxes E7.232–235; Butterworths Income Tax Service G2.32.
[1] See Simon's Taxes E7.233.
[2] S.I. 1987/412 and S.I. 1987/352.
[3] TA 1988, Sch. 22, para. 2.
[4] S.I. 1987/412, regs. 5 to 8.
[5] S.I. 1987/412, reg. 4.
[6] TA 1988, Sch. 22, para. 3.
[7] TA 1988, Sch. 22, para. 3(2)(b).
[8] TA 1988, Sch. 22, para. 7.
[9] TA 1988, s. 601
[10] TA 1988, s. 602(4).
[11] S.I. 1987/352, reg. 4.
[12] TA 1988, s. 601(3).
[13] TA 1988, s. 601(5).
[14] S.I. 1987/352, reg. 3.
[15] S.I. 1987/352, reg. 5.
[16] S.I. 1987/352, reg. 6.

ADDITIONAL VOLUNTARY CONTRIBUTIONS

30: 16 As explained in § **30: 10** the maximum contribution to an exempt approved scheme which an employee can make and obtain deduction for is normally limited to 15% of his annual remuneration, such remuneration being limited for 1989–90 onwards to £60,000. For members of schemes set up on or after 14th March 1989 or in the case of schemes already in existence before that day, for members who joined after 31st May 1989. In fact even in contributory schemes the employee's contributions would normally be fixed at a much lower rate and in any event remuneration for the purpose of the limit includes commissions, bonuses and taxable benefits charged under Schedule E (apart from those specifically excluded by FA (No 2) 1987 i.e. in respect of share incentive schemes, termination payments etc—see § **30: 07**) whereas employee contributions required under the scheme rules are normally based on salary alone.

Consequently many employees are able to make additional contributions to those required under the scheme rules without exceeding the 15% of remuneration limit. Such contributions are termed "additional voluntary contributions" or AVCs.

For many years the majority of exempt approved schemes have offered the employee the facility of making AVCs and the Social Security Act 1986, s. 12 makes it mandatory for members to be given this opportunity as of right from 6th April 1988.

However hitherto AVCs have had to be made to a scheme operated by the employer and commonly the terms are that the contributions are accumulated within the scheme, interest being credited at a rate related to that charged by building societies, but subject to a guaranteed minimum rate. This type of scheme secures income but not capital appreciation.

While this kind of arrangement is often appropriate for older members whose retirement is not far off, the lack of possible capital appreciation taken with the long-term erosion of money values resulting from even modest inflation may make such an arrangement unattractive to the younger member wishing to make additional provision for his retirement.

The Government as part of its overall policy of giving employees greater freedom of choice in how they provide for their retirement has taken steps to enable employees to make AVCs to new freestanding schemes. Such schemes are governed by supplementary practice notes[1] and first became available as from 26th October 1987.

A freestanding AVC scheme is one which is established by the employee and is completely separate from the employer's scheme. Pension providers may include banks, building societies, insurance companies and unit trusts and it is intended that a wide range of schemes should be available to meet individual requirements. An employee must not contribute to more than one freestanding scheme in respect of the same employment in any one tax year: he may however change the scheme to which he contributes in a subsequent year.

A freestanding AVC scheme is a form of exempt approved scheme: a distinguishing feature is that only the employee (and if the scheme is used for contracting out of SERPS, the Department of Health and Social Security) can make contributions. Previously an occupational pension scheme could not obtain discretionary approval unless the employer contributed to the scheme but F(No. 2)A 1987 made an amendment to enable a freestanding AVC scheme to come into a category of scheme for which the Revenue can grant discretionary approval.[2]

Previously, for the AVCs to be deductible from the employee's earnings the payments once begun had to be continued on a uniform basis for at least 5 years unless the employee's circumstances so changed that to continue paying the AVCs would involve financial hardship.[2] The Chancellor of the Exchequer in his 1987 Budget statement indicated that this rule would be relaxed so that members would be free to vary the amount and timing of AVC payments. A parliamentary statement by a Treasury minister on 7th April 1987[3] made it clear that this change would take effect from that day. The change of practice applies to arrangements whether made before or after 7th April where the AVCs are paid into the employer's scheme and also to the new freestanding AVC schemes which were made available from 26th October 1987.

The 1987 Budget statement indicated that one feature of the new freestanding AVC schemes would be that the employee would not be permitted to commute any part of the pension secured by the AVCs into a tax-free lump sum. The Treasury Minister's statement of 7th April 1987 made it clear that this restriction would also apply to new arrangements made after that day under which AVCs are paid into an employer's scheme. The restriction was given legislative effect by F(No 2)A 1987.[4]

This rule is rather less restrictive than at first appears. The maximum lump sum commutation payment can still be calculated by reference to the total pension benefits including those produced by the AVC payments and therefore the maximum lump sum will not normally be reduced. All that the rule does is to require the lump sum to be taken exclusively out of the pension provided by the main scheme.

If a freestanding AVC arrangement is made it is possible that despite the "headroom checks" under the administrative procedures the additional benefits provided together with the benefits provided by the main occupational scheme will in total exceed approvable limits. It was originally stipulated that in this eventuality the benefits provided by the main scheme had to be cut back; this would mean that part of the benefit derived from the AVC arrangement would be wasted so far as the employee in question was concerned.

To prevent this inequity, a different way of dealing with the situation is laid down in FA 1989. Any excess benefits are now to be corrected by a return of surplus funds to the member from the AVC scheme. Because the employee's contributions attracted tax relief when they were made the refund is to be subject to a special tax charge at the rate of 35%.[5] The rate may be increased or decreased by Treasury order.[6] This special charge operates in the following way.

The scheme administrator is charged to income tax under Schedule D Case VI on the grossed-up equivalent of the amount paid to the member or to his personal representatives. The member on the other hand is treated as having received an amount of income which has suffered tax at the basic rate, not the special rate of 35%. If the member is only liable to tax at the basic rate there is no further tax to pay but if the member is a higher rate taxpayer he will be liable to higher rate tax on the amount received grossed-up at the basic rate.

EXAMPLE

The scheme administrator returns a surplus of AVC funds of £1,000.

Tax charge on the administrator

Surplus	1,000
Less: tax at 35%	350
Payable to member	£650

Tax charge on the member
(assume a higher rate taxpayer)

Net received	£650
Grossed-up at basic rate (25%)	£866·66
Tax at 40%	346·66
Less: Credit for basic rate tax (866·66–650·00)	216·66
Additional tax to pay	£130·00

Although the amount received by the member has to be grossed-up at the basic rate, it will not be possible for the member or his personal representatives to make an income tax repayment claim in respect of the grossing up addition.[7]

It has also been made possible in an integrated AVC scheme, i.e. one where the AVC facility is supplementary to the main scheme, for the scheme administrator to refund a surplus to a member in the situation where additional benefits would have been provided by the voluntary arrangement if the benefits provided by the principal provisions, i.e. those which the AVC arrangement supplements, had been less.[8] A surplus refunded in this situation is likewise subject to the special tax charge at the rate of 35%.

If a freestanding AVC scheme is established for the purpose of contracting out of SERPS, the "minimum contributions", i.e. the contracted-out rebate and incentive payment where applicable will be paid direct into the scheme in the following tax year by the Department of Social Security. These contributions are disregarded in applying the 15 per cent of remuneration limit to the total contributions which an employee can make to all the employer's schemes and the freestanding scheme in any year.[6]

However, unlike the position with a personal pension, in a freestanding AVC scheme the employee's share of the contracted-out rebate does not qualify for tax relief. To make contracting out more attractive to an employee whose interests are better served by staying with his employer's scheme, the Government has made it possible for such an employee to contract out of SERPS and yet also stay in the employer's scheme through setting up a personal pension scheme which can only accept DHSS minimum contributions (see § **30: 20**, infra). As a result it is unlikely that freestanding AVC schemes will be used for the purpose of contracting out of SERPS though they may be used as a means of making equity-based additional pension provision.

Simon's Taxes E7.222. Butterworths Income Tax Service G2.33.
[1] IR12 (1979) Supplement, 2/88 (2nd edn); see also Memorandum 89.
[2] TA 1988, s. 591(2)(*h*) is the outcome of this amendment.
[3] Revenue Press Release, dated 7th April 1987.

SIMPLIFIED OCCUPATIONAL SCHEMES

30: 17　In 1983 some 11 million employees belonged to occupational pension schemes: that figure represented just over half the total national workforce, including the public sector. That proportion has remained virtually static since the early 1960s. Of those who belong to occupational schemes about half are employed in the public sector; in the private sector there are certain industries where coverage by occupational schemes is low and has not been increasing, in particular agriculture, construction and distribution.[1]

One aim of Government in the pensions field has been to extend the coverage of occupational schemes. Two of the problems which have to be overcome are that for many smaller employers the costs of setting up a tailor-made scheme for their employees can be discouragingly high while many such employers would also regard it as imprudent in their circumstances to take on the open-ended commitment implicit in a final salary scheme. Moreover in certain industries movement from job to job is endemic, making it impractical for individual employers to set up their own schemes.

Proposals to deal with these problems were put forward in the Consultative Document "Improving the pensions choice" published by the Revenue in November 1986. For employers who wish to avoid the complications entailed by having a scheme tailored to their particular circumstances and are prepared instead to accept a scheme providing "no frills" benefits, certain simplified schemes have now been made available which if accepted as they stand will obtain Revenue approval without negotiation.

The simplified schemes are of two kinds:

(*a*)　A simplified final salary scheme;
(*b*)　A new "money purchase" scheme.

The simplified final salary scheme has the following features:

(i)　Pension benefits will accrue at a maximum of 1/80th of final salary for each year of service up to 80.

(ii)　The maximum tax-free lump sum that can be taken is 3/120ths of final salary for each year of service up to 40.

(iii)　Additional voluntary contributions can be paid by the employer or employee to bring the pension benefit accrual rate up to 1/60th for total benefits and 3/80ths for commutation into a lump sum.

(iv)　No accelerated accrual is permitted for late entrants either as regards pension benefits or the lump sum commutation payment.

(v)　Members cannot be members of any other approved scheme, including a freestanding AVC scheme, except a scheme providing only death in service or widow's or dependant's benefits.

(vi)　The scheme may not be self-administered; all premiums must be applied as premiums under an insurance contract.

The new "money purchase" occupational scheme is similar to the new personal pension schemes (see infra § **30: 19**) except that this is an employer-sponsored scheme. The main features are:

(i) Contributions by employer and employee taken together must not exceed 17.5% of the employee's earnings; the employer must make some contributions and the employee's contributions must not exceed 15% of his earnings.

(ii) There is no limit on retirement benefits;

(iii) A lump sum commutation payment can be taken up to 25% of the total value of the benefits.

(iv) Death benefits can be provided on the same basis as for personal pensions.

(v) The employee may in addition contribute to a freestanding AVC scheme but within the limit indicated in (i) above.

(vi) Part-time employees may be members.

(vii) A normal retirement age does not have to be specified; benefits can be taken from age 50 but not later than age 70.

(viii) Contributions may be invested in a building society, bank or authorised unit trust as well as being applied as premiums under an insurance contract.

The new "money purchase" test in relation to contracting out of SERPS is available for this kind of occupational scheme (see supra § **30: 02**). If the scheme is contracted out on this basis, it is possible for the scheme to be self-administered. Where a simplified money purchase scheme is used in order to contract out of SERPS the employer and the employee pay the reduced national insurance contributions appropriate to being contracted out. The incentive payment where applicable is paid by the Department of Social Security direct into the scheme and this payment will count as a contribution in applying the 17.5 per cent of employee's earnings limit.[2]

Hitherto in those few cases where exempt approved schemes have been "money purchase" arrangements, the normal Revenue limits which are more appropriate to final salary schemes have applied e.g. maximum pension limited to 40/60ths of final salary etc. This will still be the position for new "money purchase" schemes not conforming to the simplified scheme to be made available and which therefore will require separate negotiation with the Revenue.

Where such non-simplified money purchase schemes are used for the purpose of contracting out of SERPS, the practice notes have been supplemented by detailed rules[3] which require total contributions to be restricted if benefits are likely to exceed the normal Revenue limits and which apply the rules dealing with the correction of surpluses subject to modifications made to preserve "protected rights" i.e. benefits secured by the incentive payments where made and by the employer's "minimum payments"— the equivalent of the contracted-out rebate.

With both simplified and non-simplified contracted-out money purchase schemes, the employee's share of the minimum payments ie the part representing the employee's share of the contracted out rebate is eligible for tax relief to the employee, so long as that share together with his other contributions are within the 15 per cent. of remuneration limit. The scheme documentation must clearly require the employee's share to be contributed to the scheme so that tax relief can be given by deduction under the nett pay system.

The new kinds of simplified scheme are available for adoption on an industry-wide basis as well as by single employers.

In an industry-wide scheme a job change between employers who each participate in the scheme does not involve the employee leaving the scheme and thus the need to provide a deferred pension, negotiate a transfer value etc does not arise.

The Revenue have made available model documents for both types of scheme. Because these models have to be used as they stand, they have been kept very simple and not all the features which can be adopted by simplified schemes have been included. However it is possible for pension providers to prepare their own standard documents incorporating other permitted features and schemes resulting from such documents will receive immediate Revenue approval so long as the standard documents have been cleared in advance.

These new arrangements have not required any legislative changes to be made. The Revenue have simply used the discretionary power conferred by TA 1988, s. 591 in relation to the new and more straightforward schemes introduced. Two appendices to the practice notes dealing with discretionary approval have been issued which cover the new simplified arrangements.[4]

Simon's Taxes E7.223.

[1] These statistics are taken from Green Paper "Reform of Social Security" Cmnd. 9517 Ch. 7.
[2] IR12 (1979) Supplement 2/88, Appendix II, para. 4.1.
[3] In Memorandum 96, Part I.
[4] IR12 (1979) Supplement 2/88, Appendices I and II.

RETIREMENT ANNUITIES

The present framework

30: 18   In a report presented in 1954 the Millard Tucker Committee, which had been set up by the Government to review the tax law relating to retirement provision generally, recommended that premiums paid under retirement annuity contracts should be deductible from an individual's earnings. Until then only life assurance relief had been allowed. The intention was to provide tax reliefs for retirement provision by individuals comparable with those enjoyed by occupational schemes.

The recommendations envisaged approval of the contracts by the Revenue, a limit to the premiums to be deducted based on a percentage of the individual's earnings from a trade, profession or employment and exemption from tax for income earned by the annuity fund.

These recommendations were put into effect by FA 1956. The provisions were subsequently made more favourable; in particular following FA 1971 it became possible to commute part of the pension benefit into a tax-free lump sum to an extent similar to that permitted in an approved occupational scheme.

This tax framework has remained with its main features intact up to the present time. A key feature of the rules for retirement annuity contracts is that only the self-employed and those employees who are not covered by occupational schemes are able to take advantage of the provisions. As explained in § **30: 02** it will no longer be possible for employers to require employees to belong to employer-sponsored occupational schemes. If employees elect not to belong to such schemes they then have the choice of being contracted in to SERPS or, alternatively, of contracting out by setting up an "appropriate" personal pension scheme. The new rules covering personal pension schemes enable the employee to obtain relief for contributions to such schemes.

The tax rules for personal pensions are closely modelled on those which have hitherto regulated retirement annuities. Indeed, subject to transitional provisions, the rules dealing with personal pensions will also cover pension provision made by the self-employed, the Government having taken the view that there should be a single tax regime covering all forms of pension arrangements made by individuals, whether employees or self-employed.[1]

Under the transitional provisions[2] the old rules will continue to apply to premiums paid on or after 1st July 1988 under retirement annuity contracts made before that date. They will also apply to contributions paid under a trust scheme on or after that date if the trust scheme was established before that date and the individual had paid his first contribution before that date. Thus, in a number of cases the old rules will still be in operation for some time to come.

Because the rules for personal pensions follow the same basic pattern as those for retirement annuity contracts, an outline of the main features now follows.

---

[1] "Improving the pensions choice", Consultative document published by the Board of Inland Revenue in November 1986, para. 4.3.
[2] TA 1988, s. 618.

Main features

30: 19   The following features of the rules relating to retirement annuity contracts are maintained in those covering personal pensions:

(1) An upper limit is imposed on the amount which can be deducted in a tax year from the individual's "relevant earnings" in respect of premiums under approved retirement annuity contracts or contributions to approved personal pension schemes as the case may be. This upper limit in each case is 17·5% of the individual's "net relevant earnings".

For older individuals, i.e. those whose retirement is drawing close, higher upper limits apply. For the years 1982–83 to 1986–87 there was a scale of increased limits based on the individual's year of birth. For 1987–88 and 1988–89, the following scale based on age at the beginning of the tax year applied:

51 to 55	20%
56 to 60	22·5%
61 or older	27·5%

For 1989–90 onwards, for personal pension schemes but not for retirement annuity contracts this scale is replaced by the following which allows higher contributions to start in earlier age ranges[1]:

36 to 45	20%
46 to 50	25%
51 to 55	30%
56 or older	35%

(2) Relevant earnings are in the case of an employee the emoluments chargeable under Schedule E including taxable benefits together with any income from property forming part of the emoluments of the employment. In the case of a self-employed person relevant earnings cover mainly income chargeable under Schedule D which is immediately derived from carrying on a trade, profession or vocation. If the income is derived from a partnership, the individual must be "acting personally" in the partnership: this rule excludes profits allocated to sleeping partners and limited partners in limited partnerships. Relevant earnings also include income from patent rights treated as earned income under TA 1988, s. 529.

A wife's relevant earnings are not treated as her husband's relevant earnings, notwithstanding that for income tax purposes generally her income is treated as his income. Accordingly both husband and wife can claim relief up to the 17.5% limit against their respective relevant earnings.

For the purposes of relief for retirement annuity premiums, relevant earnings could not include income from a pensionable office or employment i.e. one to which a "sponsored superannuation scheme" relates. A sponsored superannuation scheme is widely defined but is essentially an occupational scheme to which some person other than the employee e.g. the employer contributes. If the employee has the right to participate in an employer-sponsored scheme but does not do so, the employment is not for that reason pensionable service.

There are corresponding provisions for personal pensions: in particular if the individual does not participate in a relevant superannuation scheme related to his employment the earnings are not treated as arising from a pensionable employment and may therefore be included in relevant earnings. A relevant superannuation scheme is one intended to provide "relevant benefits" (see supra, § **30: 05**) and which is established by a person other than the individual e.g. the employer.[2] Thus normally if an employee continues to participate in the employer's scheme, his earnings from the employment will not be relevant earnings and he will not be able to establish a personal pension scheme. A limited exception is the case where the only benefits provided by the employer's scheme comprise a widow's or widower's pension and/or a death in service lump sum.[3] FA 1988 introduced a further exception to this rule. It is now possible for an employee who belongs to a contracted-in employer's scheme to contract out of SERPS by establishing a personal pension scheme into which only minimum contributions from the DSS can be made.[4]

(3) Net relevant earnings are relevant earnings less certain items which must be specifically deducted therefrom. The main items are:

(*a*) stock relief for periods of account beginning before 13th March 1984;

(*b*) losses and capital allowances in respect of activities the profits or gains of which would be included in computing the individual's relevant earnings or those of his spouse;

(c) "business charges".

Business charges are deductions which could be made in computing profits of the trade, profession or vocation but for the express prohibitions in TA 1988, s. 74(*m*), (*p*) and (*q*), i.e. annual payments other than interest, patent royalties, and mining rents and royalties. In practice such charges do not have to be deducted to the extent that they can be set off against income other than relevant earnings.

For personal pension schemes but not retirement annuity contracts, the net relevant earnings as so found are restricted to £60,000 for 1989–90 and for subsequent years. The figure of £60,000 is to be increased to reflect price inflation in the same way as the earnings cap on final remuneration in occupational pension schemes (see supra, § **30: 07**). This limit, being applied to net relevant earnings, effectively restricts the contributions which the individual can pay to all personal pension schemes in a particular tax year to the percentage (for his age range) of £60,000.

If an individual has one or more pensionable employments and one or more non-pensionable employments and the employers are associated, the remuneration payable in respect of the pensionable employments has to be taken into account in arriving at the earnings from the non-pensionable employments which can be included in relevant earnings for the purposes of making contributions to a personal pension scheme. If the remuneration from the pensionable employments is £60,000 or more, the earnings from the associated non-pensionable employments have to be excluded from relevant earnings.[5] If the remuneration from the pensionable employments is less than £60,000, the earnings from the non-pensionable employments to be included in relevant earnings must not exceed the shortfall.[6] These provisions are designed to prevent the fragmentation of an employment so that one part is covered by an occupational scheme subject to its £60,000 earnings cap and another part is covered by a personal pension scheme subject to an additional £60,000 earnings cap.

Employers are associated for this purpose if one is under the control of the other or both are under the control of a third person, the test of control in the case of close companies being that in TA 1988 s. 416, otherwise that in TA 1988 s. 840.[7]

(4) Where the amounts paid in the tax year fall short of the 17·5% of net relevant earnings limit (or higher maximum allowed for older individuals) the shortfall called unused relief can be carried forward for up to six years. This means that the individual can make payments in subsequent tax years in excess of the 17·5% (or other relevant) limit and obtain allowance for the excess to the extent that it absorbs any unused relief being carried forward. Unused relief for an earlier year must be used before that of a later year.

In cases where an assessment become final and conclusive more than six years after the end of the year of assessments and as a result further relief could be claimed but for the six year time limit having expired, an express provision permits an additional payment to be made to absorb the unused relief provided the additional payment is made within six months of the assessment becoming final and conclusive.

(5) It is also possible for the individual to elect for a qualifying premium

or contribution to a personal pension scheme to be treated as paid in the year of assessment preceding that in which the payment is made or if there were no relevant earnings in that preceding year, for it to be treated as paid in the year of assessment before that. Where such an election is made the payment carried back is treated as paid in the earlier year for all purposes, so that this provision effectively extends the time allowed for carrying forward unused relief to seven years or even eight if there are no net relevant earnings in the seventh year.

(6) In the case of retirement annuity contracts made with an insurance company, the premiums are treated as in respect of "pension business" carried on by the insurance company and the company is granted exemption from corporation tax in respect of income and chargeable gains from investments and deposits referable to such business. Premiums payable under approved personal pension arrangements are treated in the same way. However with personal pensions, the pension provider is not confined to an insurance company but could be a bank, building society or other qualifying institution. In these cases a specific provision[8] makes income from investments and deposits held for the purposes of the scheme exempt from income tax; likewise gains from the disposal of investments held for that purpose are exempt from capital gains tax. (This corresponds to the present provision covering the position where contributions are made to an approved trust scheme set up to provide retirement annuities: the income and gains in respect of investments of the fund maintained for this purpose are similarly protected).

(7) The annuity payable under the retirement annuity contract or personal pension scheme is treated as earned income in the hands of the original annuitant.

(8) A part of the annuity provided by the arrangement may be commuted into a tax-free lump sum. Under retirement annuity contracts, the lump sum may not be more than 3 times the value of the annual annuity which remains after the part has been commuted. For personal pension schemes, the maximum lump sum must not exceed one quarter of the total value of the benefits provided by the scheme at the time the commutation is made. For 1989–90 onwards benefits for this purpose include benefits for widows and other dependants but protected rights have to be excluded; previously the former were excluded but the latter were included. The rule applicable to retirement annuity contracts, being based on the residual annuity value, will often produce the larger commutation payment. In addition, in the case of a retirement annuity contract made after 16th March 1987, there is an upper limit of £150,000 on the maximum lump sum that can be taken. This restriction applies separately to each retirement annuity contract set up by the individual and not to such schemes in aggregate. The same restriction originally applied to personal pension schemes but with the introduction of the £60,000 limit on net relevant earnings for 1989–90 onwards (see above) the restriction has been made unnecessary and has been removed.

(9) The kind of arrangement to which the foregoing treatments apply is one which provides essentially for an annuity to be paid for the life of the annuitant but commencing after a certain specific age—between 60 and 75 in the case of retirement annuity contracts and 50 and 75 in the case of personal pension scheme. Payment of the annuity can begin earlier if it is

payable on the individual becoming incapable through infirmity of body or mind of doing his job or a similar one, or if the occupation is one in which it is customary to retire at an earlier age. The Revenue has published a list of occupations where an earlier retirement age is accepted.

With both retirement annuity contracts and personal pension schemes provision can also be made for the payment of an annuity after the individual's death to a surviving spouse or to dependants.

In addition, under the rules for retirement annuity contracts only, approval can be given for the following kinds of separate contract:

(1) One the sole object of which is to provide for the payment of a lump sum on the death of the individual, providing he dies before reaching the age of 75.

(2) An arrangement the main object of which is to provide for an annuity commencing after the individual's death to a surviving spouse or a dependant. This annuity must normally be payable for the life of the annuitant.[9]

Under the rules dealing with retirement annuity contracts, deductible premiums in respect of both (1) and (2) cannot taken together exceed 5% of the individual's net relevant earnings.[10] The total amount paid within that limit forms part of and is not an addition to the 17·5% maximum of net relevant earnings applying to qualifying premiums generally. For personal pensions the position is different: any provision of an annuity for a surviving spouse or dependants has to be part of the personal pension scheme, not a separate arrangement, and accordingly there is no separate limit relating to this benefit. Any provision for payment of a lump sum on death before the age of 75 must also be part of the personal pension scheme but in this case there is a separate 5% of net relevant earnings limit to be applied within the overall 17·5% limit. This new 5% limit is therefore narrower in coverage than the corresponding limit applying to separate contracts under the retirement annuity premium rules.

There is also a difference in the basis on which approval is given. For retirement annuity contracts, if certain stringent conditions were fully met, Revenue approval was automatic;[11] where the conditions were not satisfied in all respects the Revenue had a discretionary power to grant approval in certain defined circumstances.[12] For personal pension schemes Revenue approval is always to be given on a discretionary basis and the relevant statutory provisions restrict the circumstances in which this discretion can be exercised.

Simon's Taxes E7.3. Butterworths Income Tax Service Division G3.
[1] FA 1989, Sch. 7, para. 3(1); TA 1988, s. 640(2).
[2] TA 1988, s. 645(3).
[3] TA 1988, s. 645(4).
[4] TA 1988, s. 638(8), inserted by FA 1988, s. 55(2).
[5] FA 1989, Sch. 7, para. 8(1); TA 1988, s. 646A(2).
[6] FA 1989, Sch. 7, para. 8(1); TA 1988, s. 646A(3).
[7] FA 1989, Sch. 7, para. 8(1); TA 1988, s. 646A(5).
[8] TA 1988, s. 643(2).
[9] TA 1988, s. 621.
[10] TA 1988, s. 619(3).
[11] TA 1988, s. 620(2).
[12] TA 1988, s. 620(4).

PERSONAL PENSIONS

30: 20   Personal pensions have been made available from 1st July 1988. Contracts made or schemes set up on or after that date by individuals making private pension arrangements will be subject to the tax rules dealing with personal pensions. These rules will also apply to persons who first make contributions after that date to trust schemes established before that date.

As explained in § **30: 19** these rules closely follow those relating to retirement annuity contracts. The main differences arise out of the broader scope of personal pensions and are as follows:

(1) As from 6th April 1988 employees can no longer be compelled by their terms of employment to belong to an employer-sponsored scheme and thus if the employee does not in fact participate in the employer's scheme, the earnings from the employment are relevant earnings so allowing a personal pension scheme to be set up.[1]

(2) It will be possible for the employer to make contributions to the personal pension scheme set up by the employee.[2] In that case such contributions are not to be treated as taxable emoluments of the employee[3] but they must be aggregated with the employee's contributions in applying the 17·5% of net relevant earnings limit.[4]

(3) "Appropriate" personal pension schemes can be contracted out of SERPS. In this case the employer and employee will continue to pay national insurance contributions on the same basis as if the employee was contracted in but the Department of Social Security (DSS) will pay the contracted-out rebate directly into the personal pension scheme. The part of the contracted-out rebate attributable to the employee's contributions will be grossed up at the basic rate of income tax[5] and the DSS will recover the grossing up addition from the Revenue under a deficiency claims procedure.[6] The DSS will also pay into the personal pension scheme the incentive payment paid in addition to the contracted-out rebate until 6th April 1993. Entitlement to the incentive payment, where available, can be backdated to 6th April 1987 (see supra, § **30: 02**).

The amounts paid by the DSS into a personal pension scheme (together termed "minimum contributions") do not have to be taken into account in applying the 17·5% of net relevant earnings limit.[7]

As a result of an amendment made by FA 1988, an employee who belongs to an employer's contracted-in scheme can set up a personal pension scheme to contract out of SERPS without having to leave the employer's scheme. A condition is that so long as the individual remains in pensionable employment the personal pension scheme may only accept minimum contributions from the DHSS: contributions from the individual or the employer must not be accepted.[8] The employee's share of the contracted-out rebate will be grossed up as described above, so effectively giving the employee tax relief. With this arrangement, the pension secured by the minimum contributions (termed a "protected rights pension") stands outside the limits on the pension benefits which can be provided by the employer's occupational scheme.

(4) Pension providers are not confined to life assurance companies and friendly societies. Certain other financial institutions e.g. banks and their subsidiaries, authorised building societies and their associated pension companies and authorised unit trusts may also operate personal pension

schemes.[9] They will however mainly be concerned with designing the scheme and stewarding the build-up of the funds invested. When the individual retires an annuity will have to be purchased from an insurance company.[10] If a personal pension scheme is to be an "appropriate" scheme for the purpose of contracting-out (see § **30: 02**, supra), the arrangement if not in the form of an insurance or deferred annuity contract must be in the form of a unit trust scheme or interest-bearing account with a building society, bank or licensed deposit-taker.

It is proposed to widen the investment choice available in a personal pension scheme by enlarging the categories of pension providers and allowing members a degree of individual choice over how the funds are invested as between stocks and shares quoted on the U.K. Stock Exchange, stocks and shares traded on an overseas stock exchange, unit trusts, insurance company managed funds and deposit accounts.[11] These matters will be dealt with in a forthcoming Memorandum.[12]

(5) In the case of employees, but not the self-employed, regulations have been made to enable the individual to obtain tax relief for his contributions by deduction of tax at source.[13]

(6) As discussed in § **30: 19**, the rules for determining the relief for contributions are similar to those applying to retirement annuity contracts but as noted the 5% limit within the overall 17·5% limit is confined to contributions to secure payment of a lump sum on the individual's death before the age of 75.[14] Again, as noted, approval of personal pension schemes is always to be given on a discretionary basis.[15] Discretionary approval is to be operated by reference to the practice notes set out in Revenue publication IR76.

(7) There is free transferability between personal pension schemes and the other kinds of retirement schemes. In particular the regulations[16] require a personal pension scheme to accept a transfer payment from an approved occupational scheme, a statutory scheme, another personal pension scheme or a retirement annuity contract or trust scheme.[17] The only restriction applies where the individual at any time during the ten years before the right to a cash equivalent arose was a controlling director or had an annual remuneration of £100,000 or more. In these cases the transfer payment to be accepted is restricted to the cash equivalent of benefits under the paying scheme calculated (in accordance with stipulated actuarial rules) by reference to the maximum benefits which could have been provided at retirement by the paying scheme and the proportion of potential service under that scheme which the individual actually served.[18] Service under a previous scheme is to be taken into account where the paying scheme itself accepted a transfer payment.

(8) As from 6th April 1989, controlling directors (as defined for this purpose) are prevented from taking early retirement benefits from an occupational scheme and subsequently making contributions to a personal pension scheme on the basis of earnings from the same or an associated employer.[19]

Simon's Taxes E7.4; Butterworths Income Tax Service G4.
 [1] Social Security Act 1986, s. 15.
 [2] TA 1988, s. 638(6).

3 TA 1988, s. 643.
4 TA 1988, s. 640(4).
5 TA 1988, s. 649(1).
6 TA 1988, s. 649(4).
7 TA 1988, s. 640(5).
8 TA 1988, s. 638(8), inserted by FA 1988, s. 55(2).
9 TA 1988, s. 632.
10 TA 1988, ss. 634(1), 636(1). The individual may choose the insurance company to be used, if the scheme rules permit.
11 Memorandum 99, para. 58.
12 Memorandum 99, para. 63.
13 TA 1988, s. 639(2)–(5), S.I. 1988, No. 1013.
14 TA 1988, s. 640(3).
15 TA 1988, s. 631(2).
16 S.I. 1988, No. 1014 made under TA 1988, s. 638(2).
17 S.I. 1988, No. 1014, reg. 5.
18 S.I. 1988, No. 1014, reg. 6.
19 FA 1989, Sch. 7 para. 5.

PART VI. ANTI-AVOIDANCE

31   Anti-avoidance legislation

INTRODUCTION

31:01   Unlike many countries, the UK has no general provision that schemes which save tax shall be void against the Revenue. Further, the doctrine laid down by the House of Lords in *IRC v Duke of Westminster* prevented the courts from going behind the legal effect of a transaction and taxing it as if the transaction had some different legal effect. The problems raised by this rule for the Revenue were compounded by the judicial approach to the interpretation of tax legislation which placed on the Revenue the burden of showing that the taxpayer fairly fell within the scope of the charge.[1] To this one could add the judicial neutrality observed by those judges who saw nothing inherently evil in tax avoidance as distinct from tax evasion.[2] Much might have been changed as a result of the decision of the House of Lords in *Furniss v Dawson*[3] but none of the many specific anti-avoidance provisions have as yet been repealed on the basis that they are unnecessary and the decision in *Craven v White*[4] rejects any possible wide scope of the New Approach in favour of a narrowly defined step transaction doctrine.

---

[1] Contrast Lord Sumner in *IRC v Fisher* [1926] AC 395 at 412 and in *Levene v IRC* [1928] AC 217 at 227 and Lord Clyde in *Ayrshire Pullman Motor Services and Ritchie v IRC* (1929) 14 TC 754 at 763 with the wartime utterings of Lord Simon in *Latilla v IRC* [1943] AC 377 at 381 and Sir Wilfred Greene MR in *Lord Howard de Walden v IRC* [1942] 1 KB 389 at 397. See also Lord Simon in *Ransom v Higgs* (1974) 50 TC 1 at 94. "For the Courts to try to stretch the law to meet hard cases (whether the hardship appears to bear on the individual taxpayer or on the general body of taxpayers as represented by the Inland Revenue) is not merely to make bad law but to run the risk of subverting the rule of law itself."

[2] On dividend stripping compare Upjohn LJ in *J. P. Harrison (Watford) Ltd v Griffiths* (1961) 40 TC 281 at 290 with Lord Morris in *Bishop v Finsbury Securities Ltd* [1966] 3 All ER 105 at 110; 43 TC 591 at 625.

[3] [1984] STC 153.

[4] [1988] STC 476; see supra, § **1:11.**

31:02   To counter the problems so raised the Revenue in this and other countries have adopted various solutions which were classified by the Carter Commission in four groups.[1]

(1) The sniper approach, which contemplates the enactment of specific provisions which identify with precision the type of transaction to be dealt with and prescribes with precision the tax consequences of such a transaction.

This has been the traditional pattern of UK legislation. One example is the rule for business entertainment expenses.[2]

---

[1] Carter Report, vol. 3, App. A at p. 552.
[2] TA 1988, s. 577, supra, § **7: 126**.

31: 03   (2) The shotgun approach, which contemplates the enactment of some general provision which imposes tax on transactions which are defined in a general way. The difference from the sniper approach lies in its conscious rejection of certainty. Of this TA 1988, s. 703 probably represents the most obvious example, but others are TA 1988, ss. 775 and 776. All these sections create penumbral areas although the areas are circumscribed.

31: 04   (3) The transaction not at arms length approach, which provides that the tax consequences shall be different from what they would be by treating the transaction as if it had taken place between parties at arm's length. Typical examples are the rules substituting market value for the price if any actually received for disposal of capital assets[1] and sales between associated persons for income tax.[2] Technically this is a means of carrying out one of the other approaches rather than a separate approach since the circumstances in which the technique is to be applied can be described with more or less precision.

---

[1] Supra, § **16: 22**.
[2] Infra, § **35: 07**, CGTA 1979, s. 19(3). TA 1988, s. 770 and TA 1988, s. 541(3).

31: 05   (4) The "administrative control approach" which contemplates the grant of wide powers to an official or an administrative tribunal in order to counteract tax avoidance transactions. There is no such provision in UK law. Such a provision was included in the Excess Profits Tax during the Second World War.[1] However, that scheme was less than fully effective.

---

[1] FA 1941, s. 35 For an example of its application see *Crown Bedding Co Ltd v IRC* [1946] 1 All ER 452, 34 TC 107, CA.

31: 06   If one rejects the case for a general anti-avoidance provision, and one accepts the case for a sniper as distinct from the shotgun approach, one has to accept all the consequences of that approach. If the argument is based on the Rule of Law, the concept of certainty and the rejection of official discretion, then one must also reject any discretion in the Revenue to soften the application of a particular rule in hard circumstances. All too often critics of the Revenue really want the best of both worlds, a Revenue bound hand and foot by red tape in its efforts to get taxes but with unfettered power to waive tax due.

SPECIFIC PROVISIONS RELATING TO SHARES

Introduction

31:07   Since a company is a legal entity distinct from its shareholders tax advantages accrue. Thus an individual trader will be liable to tax on his profits as they accrue; whereas, if he trades through a company, he may accumulate profits in the company and then withdraw as appropriate, either in the income form of dividends or management fees or in the capital form of further shares treated as paid up out of the profits, which shares he can then sell and thus realise a capital gain, or through the eventual winding-up or outright disposal of the concern. The basic distinction between the company and its shareholders has been accepted by UK tax law, although some manoeuvres are checked in the general interest of equity. Two such practices are dividend stripping and bond washing.

Dividend stripping

31:08   When a taxpayer transfers shares in a company, the tax system is normally content to accept that income payments made by the company after a sale of shares must be taxed according to the tax circumstances of the new owner of the shares, and the fact that the previous owner had a higher marginal tax rate does not entitle the Revenue to tax the new owner at his predecessor's rates. However, if the new owner is able to extract all the surplus cash in the company without incurring any liability to tax, to strip the company of its cash, the Revenue have caused the legislature to come to their aid.

This stripping can be achieved in the following way. A has shares in company X. A sells those shares to B. B uses his voting power to compel the company to pay a large dividend to B. B then sells the shares back to A or to someone else. At first sight there is nothing inequitable about this. If B's marginal rate is simply lower than that of A there is a loss of tax. This lower rate may be achieved if B is either an exempt person or is simply less well off than A. If however B is a dealer in securities he may claim that, while the dividend paid out is undoubtedly his income, that must be set off against the loss he incurs when the shares he had bought are resold, the loss being due to the payment out of the cash reserve of the company. The effect is that the payment will have been drawn out free of tax, while A has received a sum which reflects the value of those cash reserves and that sum will be treated as a capital payment only.

Attempts to obstruct these schemes have been ineffective unless drastic. Thus it was not clear whether the courts would hold that the transaction of buying in order to resell at a loss was a trading transaction.[1] If it was not a trading transaction, no relief could be given in respect of the loss and the scheme would fail. However, the UK courts at first accepted the arguments on behalf of B and so allowed the whole dividend stripping industry to get under way.

Some legislation was designed to prevent the accumulations from arising in the first place, this being the purpose of the close company legislation. Then the Revenue tried by a quite separate avenue to undo the tax advantages of stripping. Such devices however have always been subject to exceptions which exemplify the ambivalent attitudes of Government to small, and therefore largely unregulated businesses. At first legislation was designed to interfere with the sales to security dealers and exempt persons but in 1960 the legislature aimed at transactions in securities generally.

Simon's Taxes B3.732.
 [1] This is not a happy field for believers in precedents. The final view seems to be that this is not a trading transaction—see *FA and AB Ltd v Lupton* [1971] 3 All ER 948, 47 TC 580 but earlier cases especially *Griffiths v J P Harrison (Watford) Ltd* [1962] 1 All ER 909, 40 TC 281, were distinguished not overruled and the whole area was examined in *Coates v Arndale Properties Ltd* [1984] STC 124, CA, where the *Harrison* case was distinguished.

Bond washing

31: 09   Dividends and interest payments only become income when they are due and payable[1] and there is no apportionment of that dividend over the period in respect of which it is declared.[2] Further, time usually elapses between the announcement of a proposed dividend by the company and its becoming payable. If during this time a high rate taxpayer sells his securities to one paying tax at a lower rate, the purchase price which he receives, although reflecting the value of the impending payment, cannot be segregated into an amount on account of capital and another amount on account of the dividend so as to tax the latter.[3]

This is still the law although legislation has been passed to prevent too blatant abuses; serious anti-avoidance legislation now applies, see supra, §§ **9: 43** et seq. One abuse is where the vendor sells the shares to his purchaser who collects the dividend taxed at his lower rate and who then sells them back to the original purchaser, all this being planned under the original agreement. In this way the bond or shares are said to be washed of their dividend.

Simon's Taxes B3.725.
 [1] Supra, §§ **24: 01** and **9: 39**.
 [2] *Wigmore v Thomas Summerson & Sons Ltd* [1926] 1 KB 131, 9 TC 577.
 [3] *Thompson v Trust and Loan Co of Canada* [1932] 1 KB 517, 16 TC 394.

TA 1970, s. 30

31: 10   This provision has been repealed.[1]

 [1] FA 1985, Sch. 23, para. 40 and Sch. 27, Part VIII.

TA 1988, ss. 729 and 730

31: 11   In 1937[1] a more serious attempt was made to counteract one type of tax avoidance. This applied where a high rate taxpayer agreed to transfer securities[2] and either in the same or a collateral[3] agreement he agreed to buy back, or acquired an option to buy back those or similar securities.[4] If the result of such a transaction was that any interest, a term defined to include a dividend, became payable in respect of the securities and was receivable by someone other than the vendor, it was deemed to be the vendor's income.

Thus the legislation was primarily intended to nullify any advantage to the vendor.

It was further provided that where the purchaser carried on a trade consisting wholly or partly in dealing with securities, the transaction was to be ignored in computing his profits. This applies not only where the vendor had a right to reacquire the shares, but also where the purchaser had a right— under the same or some collateral agreement—to sell them back to the vendor.[5] This was the only part of the provision to deal with the purchaser and was designed to prevent him from using the loss that would almost inevitably result from buying cum-div and selling ex-div. It is thus the first anti-stripping provision. This provision is excluded where the more powerful rules in FA 1985 apply.[6]

In 1986 it was decreed that s. 729 shall not apply to transactions in Eurobonds or overseas government stocks denominated in foreign currency— provided both parties are dealers in securities.[7] This has retroactive effect (to 1937).

Section 729 no longer applies to securities within the accrued interest scheme.[8]

Simon's Taxes B3.725; Butterworths Income Tax Service A7.52.

[1] FA 1937, s. 12.
[2] TA 1988, s. 729.
[3] See *Re Athill, Athill v Athill* (1880) 16 Ch D 211 at 222.
[4] Defined TA 1988, s. 729(2)(c).
[5] Defined TA 1988, s. 729(4).
[6] TA 1988, s. 729(6).
[7] TA 1988, s. 729(7) and (8) (see Revenue Press Release 13th December 1985, [1985] STI, p. 733).
[8] The change takes place as from 9 June 1988: see *Simon's Tax Intelligence* 1988, p. 480. On accrued interest scheme see § **9: 44**.

31: 12   Curiously TA 1988, s. 729 failed to cover the situation where the vendor sold not the shares but simply the right to the dividend. In *Paget v IRC*[1] the taxpayer held Hungarian bonds which carried the right to interest payable in sterling in London. Hungarian legislation altered the terms of the bonds making the interest payable in pengos through the Hungarian National Bank in London but the money could be spent only for certain limited purposes in Hungary. It was held that the fact that the pengos were on deposit for Miss Paget in London did not constitute the receipt of interest since the bank was not acting as agent for her and that she was not taxable on the purchase price received by her when she sold the coupons to a coupon dealer.

What is now TA 1988, s. 730 was therefore passed in 1938[2] to catch the sale of the right to receive any interest payable in respect of securities without selling or transferring the securities themselves. The interest is deemed to be that of the vendor.

Simon's Taxes B3.726; Butterworths Income Tax Service A7.53.

[1] [1938] 2 K B 25, 21 TC 677.
[2] FA 1938, s. 24.

TA 1988, ss. 731-734

31: 13   TA 1988, s. 729 applied to disallow the purchaser's loss where he was under a duty or had the right to resell to the original vendor and so did not apply where there was a right to resell to some other person. Nor did it restrict the rights of persons other than traders. A series of provisions was introduced in 1959, now TA 1988, ss. 731-734, to widen the net but these rules are excluded by the more powerful accrued income scheme's introduced by FA 1985.[1] If however a dealer in securities is involved and the facts fall within TA 1988, s. 729, these sections do not apply.[2] This is to the advantage of the Revenue since while TA 1988, s. 732 disallows only a proportion of the loss, TA 1988, s. 729 disallows it completely.

These provisions extend to three main groups of persons, dealers in securities, persons entitled to exemption from income tax such as charities, and persons other than dealers in securities who, having trading losses, are close to being exempt persons. The purpose of the provisions is to prevent the purchase of shares cum dividend to persons in these three groups who would receive the dividends subject to deduction of tax and then having resold them ex-dividend, recover the tax already paid. For dealers the difference between the price cum-div and that ex-div is a trading loss and the tax system is not otherwise able to take account of the fact that the gap between the two prices may be virtually bridged by the net dividend. Thus is set up a "purely technical loss" which is available for relief by way of repayment of the tax deducted from the dividend. An exempt person would recover the tax deducted as would any other person with unrelieved losses. The Revenue's worry about these last two categories is that their tax advantages might attract the attention of high rate taxpayers who might agree to sell to those in these two categories at special prices so as to share the financial advantages flowing from the purchaser's immunity from tax. The basic scheme of the legislation for exempt persons and those with losses is to try to apportion the sums between capital and income and treat as interest entitled to relief only that part attributable to the period during which the exempt person held the shares. For a dealer the technique used is to reduce his acquisition price.

TA 1988, s. 732 has never applied to Eurobond dealers.[3]

Simon's Taxes B3.727, 729; Butterworths Income Tax Service A7.61.
[1] TA 1988, s. 731(9) (for purchase transactions after 18th March 1986). On exclusion of TA 1988, s. 734 when securities are purchased after 28th February 1986 see FA 1985, Sch. 23, para. 42 (repealed by FA 1986, Sch. 23, Part VIII).
[2] TA 1988, s. 732(3).
[3] TA 1988, s. 732(5); see also FA 1986, Sch. 18, para 1.

31: 14   The provisions apply where a person in the appropriate category buys securities and subsequently sells or acquires an option to sell them within a period of six months or less,[1] having received a payment of interest in between.[2] Provision is made for the purchase of one set of securities and the sale of similar securities,[3] a first in, first out rule being adopted for more than one purchase or disposition. In order not to impede the market too much it is provided that a sale of more than one month after purchase shall escape the provision if it is shown to the satisfaction of the Board that both purchase and sale were at current market price and that the sale was not effected in pursuance of an agreement or arrangement made before or at the time of the purchase.[4]

Simon's Taxes B3.727.

[1] TA 1988, s. 731(1)–(3). For options, see TA 1988, s. 731(4).
[2] TA 1988, s. 731(9).
[3] TA 1988, s. 731(5).
[4] TA 1988, s. 731(3).

31: 15   In computing the profits of a dealer in securities, TA 1988, s. 732 directs that the price paid by him for the securities is reduced by "the appropriate amount in respect of interest", thus reducing his loss on the deal. This does not apply to overseas securities purchased on a stock exchange outside the UK if he elects not to take the tax credit provided for double taxation relief under TA 1988, ss. 788 or 790, and the interest is brought into account in computing profits.[1] Also exempt are bona fide discount houses in the UK and those performing jobbing, or, from 1986, market-making,[2] functions on the Stock Exchange, since in each case the purchase of stock is a part of the function they fulfil in the market.[3]

Simon's Taxes B3.727; Butterworths Income Tax Service A7.61, 62.

[1] TA 1988, s. 732(4).
[2] TA 1988, s. 732(2) and 738(1); the market-making exemption may be extended by statutory instrument.
[3] TA 1988, s. 732(2).

31: 16   Exempt persons are required by TA 1988, s. 733 to deduct "the appropriate amount" before claiming their exemption and other taxpayers claiming loss relief under TA 1988, s. 380 must by TA 1988, s. 734, leave out "the appropriate amount".

The formula for computing "the appropriate amount" is in TA 1988, s. 735 and involves a fraction. The numerator is the number of days starting with the date when the securities were first quoted on the London Stock Exchange "ex-div" that div being the payment previous to the one received by the buyer and ending with the day before that on which the buyer bought the securities. The denominator is the number of days beginning on the same date and ending with the date on which the securities are quoted "ex-div" next after the purchase, the div being the payment received by the buyer.[1] Thus if shares were first quoted "ex-div" on 2nd January and then as excluding the next dividend on 1st July and the buyer buys them on 1st June, the fraction will be $\dfrac{150}{180}$

EXAMPLE 1

Suppose a dealer buys shares for £4,000 cum-div and sells them for £3,000 ex-div having received a net dividend of £750. This *prima facie* establishes a trading loss of £1,000. However, assuming dates to be as above, the purchase price of £4,000 must be reduced by $\dfrac{150}{180} \times £750 = £625$ giving a revised purchase price of £3,375 and a loss of £375.

EXAMPLE 2

If however the purchaser is a charity the formula is applied to the gross amount corresponding with the appropriate portion of the net interest so that when he makes his claim for a repayment of £250 on account of the tax credit on a gross payment of £1,000, and his exempt status, his claim will be restricted and he will be entitled to reclaim only the credit on

$$£1,000 - \left(£625 \times \frac{100}{75}\right) = £167 \text{ which gives a repayment of £41.75}$$

Provision is made for new issues which have not previously been quoted ex-div, although allowances are made for payments of capital amounts in respect of securities.[2] Provision is also made for unquoted securities.[3]

Simon's Taxes B3.728; Butterworths Income Tax Service A7.62.
[1] TA 1988, s. 735(3).
[2] TA 1988, s. 735(4).
[3] TA 1988, s. 735(5).

Manufactured dividends—TA 1988, s. 737

31: 17   This deals with something "which the ordinary layman could fairly describe as a swindle at the expense of the honest taxpayer—not a criminal conspiracy but a racket".[1] Briefly, a vendor would sell a stock on the Stock Exchange "cum-div" but would not buy the stock until later, when it had gone ex-div. He would then hand over to the purchaser the stock together with a net amount of the dividend and a voucher showing the tax deducted. Thus the purchaser would receive the dividend net of income tax which he might be able to reclaim. Yet no tax would have reached the Treasury since the operator was not required to account for the tax[2] and he would make a profit since the difference between the price cum-div and price ex-div would be more than the net amount of dividend after tax had been deducted. To counter this TA 1988, s. 737 requires the vendor to account for tax deducted unless he can produce a bona fide voucher showing that he was in fact entitled to the taxed dividend when he sold. As originally enacted the section only applied when the vendor had to account to the purchaser for the interest but this was widened in 1986 to cover the situation in which the purchaser accounts to the vendor and it is the purchaser who manufactures the dividend.[3]

This section now applies to certain securities issued by building societies.[4]

Simon's Taxes B3.731; Butterworths Income Tax Service A7.65.
[1] Hansard, vol. 624, col. 451 (Sir Edward Boyle). On interaction with Accrued Income Scheme, see TA 1988, s. 715(6).
[2] The situation is complicated by the presence of the jobber; exemption is given to transactions by jobbers and this is to be extended to other "market-makers": TA 1988, s. 737(3) and (6).
[3] TA 1988, s. 737(4).
[4] TA 1988, s. 737(2).

OTHER PROVISIONS

1   TA 1988, s. 736

31: 18   Where a company dealing in securities obtains a holding of more than 10% in another company and then there is one or more distributions by that other company the net effect of which is materially to reduce the value of the holding, TA 1988, s. 736 directs that the reduction in the value of the holding is to be added to the value of the security.[1] The purpose of this is to counteract the tax advantage obtained in a typical dividend strip by simply wiping out the loss on the shares which the dealing company would hope to put against the distribution. It appears however that the Revenue are today using the powers in TA 1988, s. 703 in preference to TA 1988, s. 736, a course which is scarcely surprising.

Simon's Taxes B3.730.
[1] Cf. TA 1970, s. 281, supra, § **26: 25**.

2   TA 1988, s. 235

31: 19   This applies to charities or exempt funds in an attempt to cancel the advantages to them of dividend stripping. Where the fund holds at least 10% in another company which then makes a distribution which materially reduces the value of the holding, then the fund is not entitled to collect the money due on its tax credit, is subject to a further charge of 15% and cannot treat the payment as one in respect of which tax has been paid for the purpose of TA 1988, s. 348. The reason for the further charge of 15% is to reduce still further the tax gap between the fund and the other party to the typical strip operation. Since the purpose of the section is to restrict distributions out of profits before the charity acquired its holding, relief is provided where the profits were earned subsequently.[1]

Simon's Taxes B3.734, D2.615.
[1] TA 1988, s. 236.

3   TA 1988, s. 237

31: 20   Certain bonus issues are treated as distributions.[1] These may not give rise to repayment claims in respect of the tax credit if the recipient is an exempt person; it may not be used for loss relief by a trader, nor is it available for TA 1988, ss. 348 and 349.

Simon's Taxes B3.735, D2.615.
[1] Under TA 1988, ss. 210 and 211.

CANCELLATION OF TAX ADVANTAGES—TRANSACTIONS IN SECURITIES—TA 1988, ss. 703–709

31: 21   The technique used in these sections is to allow the Revenue to issue a notice counteracting tax advantages gained in certain circumstances prescribed in language of uncertain scope.[1] The effect of the notice is to undo the transaction but only for tax purposes. Briefly, (*i*) the tax advantage must have been obtained as a result of a transaction in securities and (*ii*) it must fall within one of the five sets of circumstances set out in TA 1988, s. 704. It is however open to the taxpayer to show that the transaction was carried out either for bona fide commercial reasons or in the ordinary course of making or managing investments and, in either event, not with the obtaining of a tax advantage as its main or one of its main objects. In *Bird v IRC*[2] Vinelott J said that it was not open to the Revenue to rely on *Furniss v Dawson* and TA 1988, s. 704 in the same transaction. In the same case the Court of Appeal held that the taxpayer could not use the new approach to disregard a step which TA 1988, s. 703 said had to be taken into account.[3] This comes close to saying that TA 1988, s. 703 cannot be excluded.

These provisions which follow are among the most difficult in the UK tax law. They are, generally speaking, the most obscure, the penalties for infringing them are the most severe, and they are barely touched upon by published statements of Revenue Practice.[4] A further difficulty is the absence of any provision governing the interaction with CGT. Where the proceeds of sale of shares fall within TA 1988, s. 703, Revenue practice is to allow the tax under TA 1988, s. 703 as a credit against CGT.[5] There is a clearance procedure.[6]

One example is *IRC v Wiggins*.[7] A company restored and sold picture frames. One frame was found to contain a valuable painting, The Holy Family, by Poussin.[8] Rather than simply sell the painting and distribute the profits as dividend the company sold initially all its other stock to one company after which another company bought the shares of the first company for £45,000. The courts held that the £45,000 represented the value of trading stock so that para. D applied, and the £45,000 could be treated as income of those who had sold their shares.

Simon's Taxes B3.701, 708, 716–725; Butterworths Income Tax Service A7.31.

[1] However, the Revenue are under a duty to exercise their power fairly: *R v IRC, ex p Preston* [1983] STC 257.

[2] [1985] STC 584.

[3] [1987] STC 168; the point was not taken in the House of Lords; [1988] STC 312.

[4] Nolan, IFS Conference (28th June 1974), p. 25, para. 3.

[5] See *IRC v Garvin* [1981] STC 344 at 349 and 353.

[6] TA 1988, s. 707; see *Balen v IRC* [1978] STC 420 and SP 3/80.

[7] [1979] STC 244, [1979] 2 All ER 245.

[8] The frame was bought in 1955 for £50; the picture was found to be by Poussin ten years later—value £130,000.

A tax advantage

31: 22   This is defined in TA 1988, s. 709 as (*i*) a relief or increased relief from or a repayment or increased repayment of tax or (*ii*) the avoidance or reduction of an assessment to tax or the avoidance of a possible assessment thereto, whether the avoidance or reduction is effected by receipts accruing in such a way that the recipient does not pay or bear tax on them or by a deduction in computing profits or gains. A husband is assessable in respect of a tax advantage accruing to his wife.[1]

Curiously the word "tax" is undefined. When the provision was first introduced there was no CGT[2] so presumably that is excluded as is corporation tax in respect of the capital gains of companies. However, the tax system has changed in other respects since 1960 so that this must be open to question.

The definition of tax advantage suggests that there must be a contrast of the actual case where there is an accrual in a non-taxable way with a possible accrual in a taxable way.[3] So where a company had issued and later redeemed bonus debentures there was an avoidance of tax in that had the money been distributed as dividends it would have been taxable.[4] However whether it is the issue or the redemption that constitutes the tax advantage is still unclear.[5] In *Cleary v IRC*[6] it was argued that the words "avoidance of a possible assessment thereto" indicated that Parliament had in mind the reduction of profits available for dividends and not the reduction of physical assets for that purpose, so that there would be no tax advantage if a company simply used its cash resources to buy shares in another company. However, this view was rejected by the House of Lords. In the case two sisters owned the shares of two companies and they extracted the cash from one company by allowing that company to buy their shares in the other. They thus avoided the possible assessment that would have arisen if the cash had been paid out by way of dividend.[7] The fact that this would have been the worst possible procedure, and so unlikely to happen, did not matter. This case is disturbing since, when the purchasing company in turn made its distribution no credit could be claimed for the tax already exacted.[8]

Similarly in *Emery v IRC*[9] where a company had made a large trading profit the taxpayer was held to have derived a tax advantage when he sold his shares because he could have got the company to declare a dividend or go into liquidation.

In *Bird v IRC*[10] it was held that the quantum of the advantage was ascertained by contrasting the non-taxable receipt with a similar receipt that might have accrued in some other, taxable, way. Further, the House of Lords held that in determining what should be done to counter such an advantage there was an obligation to make an accurate measure of the tax advantage obtained. When the taxpayer had to make good the liability of another person that should reduce the tax advantage obtained.

Simon's Taxes B3.702; Butterworths Income Tax Service A7.34, 39.

[1] TA 1988, s. 703(7); *Green v IRC* [1975] STC 633, CA.

[2] On overlap with CGT see *IRC v Garvin* [1981] STC 344 especially per Lord Wilberforce at 349.

[3] Per Lord Wilberforce in *IRC v Parker* [1966] AC 141 at 178–9.

[4] *IRC v Parker* [1966] 1 All ER 399, 43 TC 396; cf. *Anysz v IRC* [1978] STC 296.

[5] Infra, § **31: 23**, n. 5.

[6] [1967] 2 All ER 48, 44 TC 399.

[7] See *Hague v IRC* [1968] 2 All ER 1252, 44 TC 619. In a judgment not easy to reconcile with *IRC v Parker* or *Cleary v IRC*, the Court of Appeal refused to accept as a possible assessment one that would arise if spouses opted for separate assessments, a possibility scarcely more fanciful than that envisaged by the House of Lords in *Cleary v IRC*. This has since been reversed—TA 1988, s. 703(7).

[8] In the Court of Appeal Lord Denning said that "the courts are well able to take care of that contingency". However there is no legislation analogous to TA 1988, s. 419(4) or TA 1988, s. 427(4). It is therefore hard to see what his Lordship had in mind.

[9] [1981] STC 150.

[10] [1988] STC 312 at 317 per Lord Keith.

Transaction

31: 23   Transaction is defined in TA 1988, s. 709(2) as including transactions of whatever description relating to securities and in particular, (*i*) the purchase, sale or exchange of securities, (*ii*) the issuing or securing the issue of or applying for or subscribing for new securities and (*iii*) the altering or securing the alteration of the rights attached to securities. This wide statement is not qualified in any way.[1] Hence repayment of share capital as a reduction is a transaction[2] as is the payment of the purchase price for shares by instalments, at least when the instalments were related to dividends,[3] and perhaps even if not so related.[4] However, TA 1988, s. 703(2) is based on the premise that the liquidation of a company is not a transaction in securities.[5] The combination of a transaction with a liquidation will give rise to a charge.[6]

Simon's Taxes B3.703; Butterworths Income Tax Service A7.37.
  [1] Per Lord Guest in *IRC v Parker* [1966] AC 141 at 172–3.
  [2] *IRC v Brebner* [1967] 1 All ER 779, 43 TC 705.
  [3] *Greenberg v IRC* [1972] AC 109, [1971] BTR 1319.
  [4] *Greenberg v IRC* per Lord Reid at p. 137.
  [5] This view was accepted by Lords Dilhorne and Diplock in *IRC v Joiner* [1975] 3 All ER 1050 at 1057 and 1060.
  [6] *IRC v Joiner* [1975] 3 All ER 1050.

Securities

31: 24   This is defined to include shares and stock and, in relation to a company not limited by shares (whether or not it has a share capital) includes a reference to the interest of a member of the company as such. Thus debentures and securities are included and their redemption is a transaction in securities. A loan note even though unsecured is a security;[1] likewise the receipt of a loan from and repayable to a controlled company is a transaction in securities.[2]

Simon's Taxes B3.703.
  [1] Per Lord Wilberforce in *IRC v Joiner* [1975] 3 All ER 1050 at 1056. What if in *Cleary v IRC*, the assets sold had been buttons not shares?
  [2] *Williams v IRC* [1980] 3 All ER 321, [1980] STC 535, HL.

The five sets of circumstances

31: 25   A. The first concerns abnormally high dividends where:

in connection with the distribution of profits of a company or in connection with the sale or purchase of securities followed by the purchase or sale of the same or other securities, the person in question, being entitled by reason of

(*a*)   any exemption from tax,
(*b*)   the setting-off of losses against profits or income,
(*c*)   the giving of group relief, to recover tax in respect of dividends received by him,

(*d*) the application of franked investment income in calculating a company's liability to pay ACT,

(*e*) the application of a surplus of franked investment income under TA 1988, ss. 242 and 243,

(*f*) the computation of profits or gains out of which are made payments within TA 1988, ss. 348 and 349 and

(*g*) the deduction for interest,

receives an abnormal amount by way of dividend.

A dividend is regarded as abnormal[1] if (*i*) it substantially exceeds a normal return on the consideration provided paid for securities or (*ii*) it is a dividend at a fixed rate and substantially exceeds the amount which the recipient would have received if the dividend had accrued from day to day and he had been entitled only to so much of the dividend as accrued while he held the securities. This special rule applies only if he sells or acquires a right to sell those or similar securities within six months.

The word profit is defined to include income, reserves or other assets. This is unfortunate when compared with standard accountancy definitions, but indicates the wide scope of the section.[2]

Simon's Taxes B3.705; Butterworths Income Tax Service A7.32.

[1] TA 1988, s. 709(4).

[2] Cf. Lord Upjohn in *Cleary v IRC*.

31: 26   B. This concerns the drop in the value of securities as a result of the dividend and:

> that in connection with the distribution of profits of a company or in connection with the sale or purchase of securities being a sale or purchase followed by purchase or sale of the same or other securities, the person in question becomes entitled (*a*) in respect of securities held or sold by him or (*b*) in respect of securities formerly held by him (whether sold or not) to a deduction in computing profits or gains by reason of the fall in the value of securities resulting from the payment of a dividend thereon or from any other dealing with any assets of the company.

This extends to allowances to another company through group relief[1].

The purpose here is to catch the stripper who does not receive an abnormal dividend but who simply claims a loss. In *IRC v Kleinwort Benson Ltd*[2] a dealing company bought debentures on which interest was in arrears; subsequently, that interest was paid off and the debentures redeemed on the same day—and by one cheque, it was held that there was no "fall in the value of the debentures" by reason of the payment of the interest and so no liability under TA 1988, s. 703; rather the stock had simply ceased to exist. But had the interest been paid off even one day before there would have been such a fall in value since the market price would have fallen.

Simon's Taxes B3.706; Butterworths Income Tax Service A7.33.

[1] TA 1988, s. 704 B. (2).

[2] [1969] 2 All ER 737, 45 TC 369.

31: 27   C. This deals with the opposite side of the transaction from that covered by A and B:

that where the person in question receives consideration in consequence of a transaction whereby any other person (*a*) subsequently receives or has received an abnormal amount by way of dividend or (*b*) subsequently becomes entitled or has become entitled to a deduction as mentioned in B and that consideration either (*i*) is, or represents, the value of assets which are (or apart from anything done by the company in question would have been) available for distribution by way of dividend or (*ii*) is received in respect of future receipts of the company or (*iii*) is, or represents, the value of trading stock of the company, and the said person so receives that consideration that he does not pay or bear tax on it as his income.

"Available for distribution by way of dividend" means legally available, not commercially available.[1]

In the ordinary dividend strip or bond washing operation it was not to be supposed that all the economic advantage would be confined to the purchaser. Thus in one instance[2] a company had 15,000 unclassified £1 shares. These were converted into 300,000 5p shares and a once for all dividend of £2.37½ was declared. These shares were sold to superannuation funds and to charities at £3.37½ which then reclaimed the tax paid on the dividend. After the dividend the shares were worth about 15p each. The funds and charities had paid £3.37½ for shares worth only about £2.37½, an operation that only made sense on the basis that they collected tax of about £1.50 per share thanks to their exempt status. Thus the vendor collected £1 and the funds 50p per share—free of tax. Hence paragraph C.

Simon's Taxes B3.707; Butterworths Income Tax Service A7.34.

[1] TA 1988, s. 704(3); *IRC v Brown* [1971] 3 All ER 502, 47 TC 236—even though current liabilities exceed current assets. See now Companies Act 1985, ss. 263 and 275.

[2] HC Deb., vol. 624, col. 626 (Sir Edward Boyle).

31: 28   This paragraph also catches two other devices, known as forward stripping and "scissors" or stock stripping. Forward stripping occurred when a company was about to make a large profit.[1] Special shares were created carrying a high rate of dividend and these would be sold to a dealing company for a capital sum. The dealer would then set off the loss on resale against the predicted dividend that had subsequently accrued.

Stock stripping occurs when a company has stock on its books at the correct conservative figure of cost or market value whichever is the lower. Should the stock be realised there would be a considerable income receipt. Enter the finance company which also deals in stock. The company buys both stock and shares at book value. The increased price obtained by sale at market value is offset by the drop in the value of the shares. Thanks to (*iii*) above the original company, if it is allowed its loss, will be subject to tax as having obtained a tax advantage.

For para. C to apply the Revenue must not only establish each element but also show that the transaction and the abnormal dividend or whatever it may be are causally linked; this flows from the word "whereby".[2] In deciding the scope of the transaction the court may take a broad view and is not limited to the immediate cause of the dividend but still the causal connection must be shown.[3] Where, as is usually the case, more than one step is involved this causal connection can be established even though the taxpayer does not take part in each one.[4] It has also been decided that the causal link can be found in the purpose and design of those who, for a fee and instructed by the taxpayers, controlled the operation of the schemes.[5]

Simon's Taxes B3.707; Butterworths Income Tax Service A7.34.
[1] See *Greenberg v IRC* [1972] AC 109, [1971] 3 All ER 136, 47 TC 240, HL.
[2] *Bird v IRC* [1985] STC 584.
[3] *IRC v Garvin* [1981] STC 344.
[4] *Emery v IRC* [1981] STC 150.
[5] *Bird v IRC* [1985] STC 584.

31: 29   D. This has given the courts the most difficulty:

> that in connection with the distribution of profits of a company to which this paragraph applies, the person in question so receives as is mentioned in paragraph C (*i*), (*ii*) or (*iii*) such a consideration as is therein mentioned.

This superb example of legislation by reference was, when the Finance Bill 1960 was first presented, originally a part of C; hence perhaps the reference. The companies in question are those under the control[1] of five or fewer persons and all unquoted companies, unless under the control of a quoted company. Like C it applies to the vendor rather than the purchaser, but unlike C there is no requirement that conditions A or B should also be present. Moreover, there is no requirement that the amount of any dividend should be abnormal. These matters give para D its wide ambit.

The phrase "distribution of profits" is very widely defined; thus profits include references to income, reserves or other assets and references to distribution include references to transfer or realisation including an application in discharge of liabilities. Thus the capitalisation of undistributed profits followed by a reduction in capital is a distribution for this purpose,[2] as are a reduction in capital followed by capitalisation,[3] an issue and redemption of debentures,[4] and even the purchase of one company's shares by another.[5] There may be a distribution of profits without diminution of assets.[5]

Control must be shown to exist. This will trigger liability whether it exists at the time the asset is realised or at the time of the subsequent distribution but it is not enough for the Revenue simply to prove control when the sum is received.[6]

Para. D requires that the sum be received "in connection with" the distribution of profits, this imposes a less definite causal link than the word whereby in para. C.[7]

IRC v Wiggins, supra, § **31: 21**, is an example of para. D. The purchase price paid for the shares in the company owning the picture represented the value of that company's trading stock so that the taxpayer received consideration of the proscribed type; the company was controlled, a tax advantage obtained and there was a transaction in securities.

Simon's Taxes B3.708; Butterworths Income Tax Service A7.35.
[1] Defined by reference to TA 1988, s. 416(2)–(6), supra, § **27: 03**.
[2] *Hague v IRC* [1968] 2 All ER 1252, 44 TC 619.
[3] *IRC v Horrocks* [1968] 3 All ER 296, 44 TC 645.
[4] *IRC v Parker* [1966] 1 All ER 399, 43 TC 396.
[5] *Cleary v IRC* [1967] 2 All ER 48, 44 TC 399.
[6] *IRC v Garvin* [1981] STC 344.

31: 30 E. This paragraph was added in 1966 and applies where there are two or more paragraph D. companies and where the taxpayer receives non-taxable consideration in the form of share capital or a security issued by a paragraph D. company and does so "in connection with the transfer directly or indirectly of assets" of one paragraph D. company to another such company, and the consideration is or represents the value of assets available for distribution by such a company. If the consideration is non-redeemable share capital the liability arises when the share capital is repaid. If it takes any other form, liability arises upon receipt. It is very unclear whether this adds anything to the other paragraphs. In *Williams v IRC* the Court of Appeal held that where a transaction falls within both D and E, paragraph E should apply. This point was not taken in the House of Lords.

Simon's Taxes B3.709; Butterworths Income Tax Service A7.36.

Defences

31: 31 TA 1988, s. 703 does not apply if the taxpayer shows[1] that the transaction was carried out for bona fide commercial reasons, or in the ordinary course of making or managing investments, and that no transaction had as its main object or one of its main objects to enable tax advantages to be obtained.[2] It is perhaps interesting, in view of the decision of the House of Lords in *FA and AB Ltd v Lupton*,[3] to note that this defence presupposes that a transaction whose main object was the obtaining of a tax advantage could be in the ordinary course of making investments or have bona fide commercial reasons.

Perhaps correctly, this is the only part of the legislation in which the courts have shown any sympathy for the taxpayer. In determining what are bona fide commercial reasons, the word commercial includes non-financial reasons. Hence a view that to retain family control of a company is important for the future prosperity of the company, whether in the context of company–customer or employer–employee relationships can be good commercial reasons so that steps taken to preserve that control will escape TA 1988, s. 703.[4]

In deciding whether there are commercial reasons it is not necessary for the taxpayer to show that those reasons are connected with the company concerned. So in *Clark v IRC*[5] the taxpayer, a farmer, decided to sell shares in a controlled company in order to raise money with which to buy another farm; his claim to use this defence was upheld. When the Revenue invoke TA 1988, s. 703 it may be that they may not also invoke the decision in *Furniss v Dawson*.[6]

Simon's Taxes B3.710; Butterworths Income Tax Service A7.40.

[1] On the importance of onus of proof note *Hasloch v IRC* (1971) 47 TC 50 where the transaction was instituted by a board of directors of which he was not a member. The transaction was the redemption of certain preference shares, a move which would improve the capital structure of the company but also confer a tax advantage on the taxpayer who failed to persuade the

commissioners that the latter was not an object. The case also shows that TA 1988, s. 703 applies even though the intention to mitigate tax exists only for some of the time.

2 TA 1988, s. 703(1).
3 [1971] 3 All ER 948, 47 TC 580, supra, § 7: 11.
4 *IRC v Goodwin* [1976] STC 28, HL.
5 [1978] STC 614, [1979] 1 All ER 385; the Special Commissioners had ruled that there was a bona fide commercial motive but that it had to be intrinsic to the transaction.
6 The question was left open by Vinelott J in *Bird v IRC* [1985] STC 584 at 647.

31: 32   Most litigants have argued that the obtaining of a tax advantage was not one of the main objects. The test is subjective and the question is one of fact.[1] If a business operation is carried out in two distinct phases, one of which is purely commercial and the other of which had the tax advantage as one of its main objects, it is a question of fact for the Commissioners whether there was one transaction or two. The House of Lords has commended a "broad common sense view" to the Commissioners.[2]

In *IRC v Brebner*[3] the respondent and his colleagues were resisting a takeover bid and so made a counter offer for the shares. This was financed by a loan from a bank on terms requiring early repayment. After two unsuccessful attempts to persuade the minority interests to sell out, the original counter offer was accepted by a majority of the shareholders. The company then resolved first to increase its capital by £75,000 by capitalising its reserves and then reducing them by the same amount thus causing £75,000 to come out of the company to the new shareholders who used them to pay off the loans from the bank. The Commissioners held that the whole was one transaction and that it did not have as one of its main objects the obtaining of a tax advantage. A notice to counteract the advantage therefore failed. The House of Lords held that there was ample evidence to support the findings. Lord Upjohn said that a choice of a method which carried less tax than another did not necessarily mean that one of its main objects was to obtain a tax advantage.[4]

It has also been said that a charity does not have a tax advantage as one of its main objects simply because, in reaching a decision, it is influenced by its privileged tax status.[5]

Other defences were that the transaction was effected before 6th April 1960[6] and that the assessment was made out of time.[7]

Simon's Taxes B3.710, 713–715; Butterworths Income Tax Service A7.40.
1 *IRC v Brebner* [1967] 2 AC 18 at 30 (Lord Upjohn); [1967] 1 All ER 779 at 784, 43 TC 705 at 718 and Lord Pearce at 26, 781, 715. In all five reported cases the Commissioners' decision on fact has (eventually) been upheld—*IRC v Brebner, IRC v Hague* [1968] 2 All ER 1252, 44 TC 619; *Hasloch v IRC* (1971) 47 TC 50 (supra), *IRC v Goodwin* (supra) and *Clark v IRC* (supra).
2 Lord Pearce in *IRC v Brebner,* supra, *loc. cit.*
3 *Supra.*
4 *Loc. cit.,* supra.
5 Per Cross J in *IRC v Kleinwort Benson Ltd* [1969] 2 All ER 737 at 743, 45 TC 369 at 382. If this is correct there is still some scope for TA 1988, s. 729, supra, § **31: 13**.
6 TA 1970, s. 468(1) on which see *IRC v Brebner,* supra. This was repealed in 1987 as a pre-consolidation amendment presumably for obsolescence.
7 TA 1988, s. 709(1).

SALE BY INDIVIDUAL OF INCOME DERIVED FROM HIS
PERSONAL ACTIVITIES—TA 1988, s. 775

31: 33   This is the famous Beatles or constellation clause which was
introduced in 1969[1] to prevent one form of converting future taxable income
into present untaxable capital. This form was the sale of the right to an
individual's future services to a company in return for shares or an option
over shares, a practice particularly prevalent in the entertainment industry,
whose practitioners of course were more likely than others to suffer from the
absence of any proper averaging clause in the UK tax system. Suppose that
a film is about to be made and that £1m is available for the star's services. A
company acquires his services in return for option to take shares. It would
pay him say £50,000 by way of living allowance so as to cover his expenses,
these being taxable to the individual under Schedule E but deductible by the
company. The company would sell the star's services to the film company in
return for £1m, would receive that sum and would suffer corporation tax.
Likewise if a company was formed to promote the career of a potential star
over a number of years. Again the company would acquire exclusive rights
for a number of years; then, when the star was well launched, he would sell
out his shares in the company to another company at a large capital gain.
Before the sale the company would be a close one[2] but would argue the need
to retain earnings for the future in a highly uncertain trade.

Simon's Taxes E1.701; Butterworths Income Tax Service A7.91.
  [1] FA 1969, s. 31 and Sch. 16.
  [2] At that time the rules for close companies were stricter than they are now—supra, chap. 27.
The effect of the schemes was to reduce tax from 91.25% (income tax) to something like 60%
(corporation tax and capital gains tax)—[1970] BTR 84 (Potter). The tax payable on the
emoluments received would be corporation tax and income tax, and often higher than 60%. For
example of such schemes see *Crossland v Hawkins* [1961] 2 All ER 812, 39 TC 493, supra, § **13: 08**
and *IRC v Mills* [1974] STC 130; [1974] 1 All ER 722, supra, § **13: 03** and *Black Nominees Ltd v
Nicol* [1975] STC 372 at 411. These schemes were unsuccessful on other grounds.

31: 34   The scope of TA 1988, s. 775 as drafted is much wider than the
covering of these devices in the entertainment industry. It applies where (*i*)
arrangements are made to exploit the earning capacity of an individual by
putting some other person (e.g. the company) into a position to receive the
income from his activities, and (*ii*) as part of the arrangement the individual
or any other receives a capital amount, provided (*iii*) that the main object or
one of the main objects was the avoidance of tax.[1] Since the purpose of the
provision appears to be to stop rather than to regulate this kind of contract,
the whole capital sum is made taxable under Schedule D, Case VI and there
is no provision for top-slicing or any other form of relief although it is treated
as earned income. Further the section applies to all persons regardless of
their residence provided that the occupation is carried on in whole or in part
in the UK,[2] and to any indirect methods of enhancing the value of property.[3]
    The section does not apply to a capital amount obtained in respect of the
disposal of assets (including any goodwill) of a profession or vocation or
shares in a company so far as the value is attributable to the value of the
business as a going concern.[4] However an exception is made where the value

of the business as a going concern is derived to a material extent from the individual's activities and for which he does not get full consideration.

The definition of capital amount is very wide and vague. It means any amount in money or money's worth which would not otherwise fall to be included in any computation of income for the purpose of the Tax Acts.[5] The justification for this legislation must turn on the way in which the Revenue apply it.

Simon's Taxes E1.702–710; Butterworths Income Tax Service A7.92.

[1] Presumably this has a subjective meaning—cf. TA 1988, s. 703, supra, § **31: 32**. It was added at Report Stage but in TA 1988, s. 775 the onus is on the Revenue.

[2] TA 1988, s. 775(9).

[3] TA 1988, s. 777(2).

[4] TA 1988, s. 777(4). This too was added at Report Stage.

[5] TA 1988, s. 777(13). Consider unremitted partnership profits when the remittance basis applies. Is there a charge at once under TA 1988, s. 775 and again under TA 1988, s. 65(4) when the profits are remitted?

ARTIFICIAL TRANSACTIONS IN LAND—TA 1988, s. 776

31: 35   This provision was also introduced in 1969[1] to charge to income tax certain gains of a capital nature arising from the disposal of land. The purpose is to charge profits that escape Schedule D Case I and to charge the prime mover in schemes such as *Ransom v Higgs*, supra, § **7: 05** rather than the person making the trading profit.

TA 1988, s. 776 says that the section applies wherever:

(*a*) land, or any property deriving its value from land, is acquired with the sole or main object of realising a gain from disposing of the land, or

(*b*) land is held as trading stock, or

(*c*) land is developed with the sole or main object of realising a gain from disposing of the land when developed,

and any gain of a capital nature is obtained from the disposal of the land—

(*i*) by the person acquiring, holding or developing the land, or by any connected person, or

(*ii*) where any arrangement or scheme is effected as respects the land which enables a gain to be realised by any indirect method, or by any series of transactions, by any person who is a party to, or concerned in, the arrangement or scheme;

and this subsection applies whether any such person obtains the gain for himself or for any other person.

Thus the section applies only to the gain arising on an actual disposal of the land which had been so acquired, held or developed. It has, however, been observed that the rule that the gain of a capital nature must be derived *from* the disposal of land may have to be treated differently when para (*c*) is involved from situations where para (*a*) and (*b*) are involved. Differently probably means more widely. So in *Page v Lowther*[2] X granted a lease of land to Y and, in accordance with an arrangement between X and Y, Y arranged for payments due on the grants of subleases to be made to X by the sublessee. Y having developed the land, the court held that X was liable under s. 776(2)(*c*) as X had arranged for a gain to be realised by X by an indirect method—getting Y to make the sublessee make the payments to X.

It should be noted that the section is not confined to "artificial transactions" in land i.e. to transactions entered into for the purpose of tax avoidance.[3]

The charge arises under Schedule D, Case VI and is generally made under s. 776(3)(*b*) on the person realizing the gain. However s. 776(8) provides that:

> if all or any part of the gain accruing to any person is derived from value, or an opportunity of realising a gain, provided directly or indirectly by some other person, whether or not put at the disposal of the first-mentioned person, subsection (3)(*b*) of this section shall apply to the gain, or that part of it, with the substitution of that other person for the person by whom the gain was realised.

So when A provides B with an opportunity of realizing a gain the gain which B makes can be taxed as the income of A: A is given an indemnity against B.[4]

The charge is on the whole of the gain and is made for the year in which the gain is obtained but TA 1988, s. 777(13) provides that an amount in money or money's worth shall not be regarded as receivable by some person until that person can effectively enjoy or dispose of it. So A's liability does not arise until B can effectively enjoy or dispose of the gain. The income must be treated as investment income since no provision directs that it be treated as earned income.

The charge arises regardless of the residence of the taxpayer if all or any part of the land is situated in the UK.[5]

Simon's Taxes B3.636; Butterworths Income Tax Service A7.101.

[1] FA 1969, s. 32; it does not apply to gains realised before 15th April 1969. On validity of alternative assessments see *Lord Advocate v McKenna* [1989] STC 485.

[2] [1983] STC 799, CA.

[3] *Page v Lowther* [1983] STC 799, CA. The taxpayer argued unsuccessfully that the heading of TA 1988, Part XVII (in which s. 776 occurs), "Tax Avoidance", and the side heading of TA 1988, s. 776, "Artificial transactions in land" restricted the scope of the section.

[4] TA 1988, s. 777(8); B is treated as having paid income tax for the purposes of CGT, ibid, TA 1988, s. 777(12).

[5] TA 1988, s. 776(14); in the case of a non-resident the Board may direct the deduction of income tax at basic rate—TA 1988, s. 777(9).

The three situations

(*a*) *Where land or property deriving its value from land, is acquired with the sole or main object of realising a gain from disposing of the land*

31: 36   *Land or property*. Land includes references to all or any part of the land and includes buildings and any estate or interest in land or buildings.[1] So a disposal of the benefit of a contract to buy land or the grant of a lease are covered. The interest may be legal or equitable.[2] Property deriving its value from land includes any shareholding in a company or any partnership or interest or any interest in settled property deriving its value directly or indirectly from land and any option consent or embargo affecting the disposition of land; so the right to insist that a sale should take place only with A's consent gives A the necessary property deriving its value from the land.

Simon's Taxes B3.636, 637; Butterworths Income Tax Service A7.102.
[1] TA 1988, s. 776(13), see also TA 1988, s. 777(5).
[2] *Winterton v Edwards* [1980] STC 206, [1980] 2 All ER 56.

31: 37 *Disposal.* The property is disposed of if (*i*) the property in the land or (*ii*) the property deriving its value from the land or, (*iii*) control over the land is effectually disposed of.[1]

The word effectually prevents too much legalism. Thus the grant of a long lease for a premium will not permanently dispose of control of the land but presumably a suitably long lease with wide powers in the tenant would deprive the nominal landlord of effectual control. In appropriate circumstances the Revenue might argue that that portion of a premium on a lease which escaped tax under Schedule A by reason of the fractional reduction would fall within this charge. Disposal of a majority shareholding in a company holding land would come within (*iii*); on the other hand the disposal of a minority shareholding does not come within (*iii*) but instead comes within (*ii*).

These words are widened still further by TA 1988, s. 777 which provides:

> (2) . . . account shall be taken of any method, however indirect, by which—
>
> (*a*) any property or right is transferred or transmitted, or
> (*b*) the value of any property or right is enhanced or diminished, and accordingly the occasion of the transfer or transmission of any property or right, however indirect, and the occasion when the value of any property or right is enhanced, may be an occasion when, under the principal sections, tax becomes chargeable.
>
> (3) Subsection (2) above applies in particular—
>
> (*a*) to sales, contracts and other transactions made otherwise than for full consideration or for more than full consideration, and
> (*b*) to any method by which any property or right, or the control of any property or right, is transferred or transmitted by assigning share capital or other rights in a company or any partnership or interest in settled property and
> (*c*) to the creation of any option or consent or embargo affecting the disposition of any property or right, and to the consideration given for the option, or for the giving of the consent or the release of the embargo, and
> (*d*) to the disposal of any property or right on the winding up, dissolution or termination of any company, partnership or trust.

Further, TA 1988, s. 776(5) allows any number of transactions to be treated as one disposal.

[1] TA 1988, s. 776(4).

31: 38 *Object.* The principal practical problems concern the requirements that the sole or main object should be the realising of a gain from disposing of the land and that this should be the object at the time of acquisition.[1] In choosing the word object rather than intention or purpose the legislature has presumably left it for the courts to infer as a matter of fact regardless of any document stating the powers and objects of any company partnership or trust. An intention to hold the land as a source of income will not prevent a charge from arising if there was also the object of making a gain from disposing of the land, provided that object was the main one. If the two objects were equal it would appear to follow that TA 1988, s. 776 cannot apply. If land is acquired with this object, a subsequent change of mind is irrelevant.

Objects other than making a gain include deriving income from it, preservation of visual or other amenity value of existing land, the provision of accommodation for a relative and in the case of a company retention of family control. One must not forget that for TA 1988, s. 776 to apply the object of gain must relate to the property acquired and not some other land.

The rule that the property must be acquired with the object of making a gain has on the not dissimilar Australian legislation been held not to include property acquired under a testamentary gift;[2] however buying the land from executors in satisfaction of a pecuniary legacy is clearly distinguishable.

---

[1] E.g. *Sugarwhite v Budd* [1988] STC 533, CA.

[2] *McClelland v Taxation Comr of Australian Commonwealth* [1971] 1 All ER 969.

(b)   Where land is held as trading stock

31: 39   When land held as a trading stock is disposed of the profits would normally enter a computation under Schedule D, Case I and as such would be outside TA 1988, s. 776. The purpose of (b) in conjunction with s. 776(8) is to catch the indirect disposals which might otherwise give rise to income accruing to others. This charge does not extend to property deriving its value from land.

Simon's Taxes B3.636; Butterworths Income Tax Service A7.103.

(c)   Where land is developed with the sole or main object of realising a gain from disposing of land when developed

31: 40   If land is acquired without the object of realising a gain from disposing of the land (a) does not apply. Where however land is developed with that object a charge arises under this provision. Development is not defined. The object of realising a gain on disposal must presumably exist at the moment of development but it is unclear whether it is necessary that the object should be to dispose of the land immediately the land is developed. The fact that it is envisaged that the land should be used as a source of, say, rental income for a few years before its final effectual disposal should be only one factor in deciding whether the sole or main object of the development was to realise the gain. Conversely if the object is to use the property developed as a source of rental income but, after development, a change of mind occurs, no charge under TA 1988, s. 776 can arise. What happens when the change of mind occurs during the development is less clear since (c) simply states that the land is to be developed with the object of realising a gain. Such words would appear apt to cover any development in the course of which there was at any time such a sole or main object.

Where (c) applies so much of the gain as is attributable to the period before the intention to develop is formed is excluded.[1]

This provision was successfully invoked by the Revenue in *Page v Lowther*.[2]

Simon's Taxes B3.636; Butterworths Income Tax Service A7.104.
[1] TA 1988, s. 776(7) makes the facts satisfy (*a*) or (*b*) although in such circumstances the charge is apparently made under (*c*). This slice is chargeable to CGT. Presumably the existing use value is taken as the figure at which the charge for capital gain to taxable income occurs.
[2] [1983] STC 799; see § **31: 35.**

Exceptions

31: 41   The charge does not apply to a gain accruing on the disposal of the taxpayer's principal private residence, as defined for capital gains tax purpose. However, such a residence which was bought partly with a view to gain while not exempt from capital gains tax is not liable to a charge under TA 1988, s. 776.[1]

The charge does not apply where there is a disposal of shares in a company which holds land as trading stock or in a company that is a dealing company not an investment company which owns directly or indirectly 90% or more of the ordinary share capital of another company which holds land as trading stock provided that all the land so held is disposed of in the normal course of trade, and so that all opportunity of profit accrues to the company.[2] This exclusion applies to the straightforward disposition of the shares but does not apply if a scheme or arrangement enabling a gain to be achieved by indirect means.

When the land is held by a company it may be in the company's interest to escape TA 1988, s. 776 since not only will the tax paid be lower but also the company may be able to use roll over relief.[3] Apparently some companies avoid s. 776 by not disposing of the land but revaluing the property and then distributing a capital profit dividend.[4]

Simon's Taxes B3.636; Butterworths Income Tax Service A7.105.
[1] TA 1988, s. 776(9), supra, § **15: 12.**
[2] TA 1988, s. 776(10); in practice the Revenue confine this provision to companies already dealing in land.
[3] Supra, § **20: 06** and § **26: 22.**
[4] This may cause difficulties with advance corporation tax; supra, § **24: 16.**

Computation and clearance—and losses

31: 42   The computation of the gain is defined in very broad terms, the statute merely directing that there shall be used such method as is just and reasonable in the circumstances, taking into account the value obtained for the land, but allowing only such expenses as are attributable to the land disposed of. This broadness may assist the taxpayer. If he submits a computation based on Schedule D Case I principles it appears that in practice it will be for the Revenue to show that the computation is not just and reasonable, it is not enough for them to show that another method is also just and reasonable.

Because of the vague and broad nature of the charge there is a clearance procedure. However, taxpayers seldom apply for clearance and when they do they are usually refused.

TA 1988, s. 776 makes no mention of losses. It appears therefore that other

Schedule D Case VI losses can be set off against TA 1988, s. 776 income and vice versa.[1]

Simon's Taxes B3.636 and see also B3.638–646; Butterworths Income Tax Service A7.106, 111, 114.
    [1] TA 1988, s. 392 is sub silentio authority for this: it puts an express ban on TA 1988, ss. 34–36 but does not mention TA 1988, s. 776.

An example—Yuill v Wilson[1]

31: 43   The taxpayer and connected settlements controlled company X which owned two pieces of land. He set up a non-resident trust which controlled two other non-resident companies C and M which proceeded each to buy a property from X for full market value. The trust then disposed of its shares in C and M to an overseas company in which neither the taxpayer nor his family had any interest, the consideration due to C and M was to be paid in instalments on the happening of certain contingencies.

The House of Lords held that TA 1988, s. 776(2) applies to the gains realised by C and M. The gains had been obtained for the companies either directly or through his companies and with the aid of the trustees and the taxpayer remained liable notwithstanding his subsequent sale of his shares in C and M to the overseas company. The House also held that a right to money which could not be said to be effectively enjoyed was not yet taxable; it followed that as yet there was no liability in respect of the unpaid conditional instalments.[2]

Simon's Taxes B3.636.
    [1] [1980] STC 460, [1980] 3 All ER 7. For another recent example see *Chilcott v IRC* [1982] STC 1.
    [2] The taxpayer unsuccessfully appealed again on the grounds that the contingent rights of the companies to the instalments were "money's worth", capable of being valued and sold within a year of the contract. Following *Yuill v Wilson*, however, the gains were realised only when the instalments were received and ceased to be subject to restriction: *Yuill v Fletcher* [1984] STC 401.

PART VII. THE INTERNATIONAL DIMENSION

32 Connecting factors

INTRODUCTION

32: 01   In general a UK resident is taxable in respect of all income no matter where it arises; a non-resident is taxable on income arising from sources within the UK.[1] The former is taxed because, whether he be a British subject or not, he enjoys the benefit of our laws for the protection of his property; the latter because in respect of his property in the UK he enjoys the benefit of our law for the protection of that property.[2]

The UK regards citizenship[3] as a suitable test of the jurisdiction to execute a person but not of that to tax him. Citizenship does however have some tax consequences.[4]

Even if all foreign systems of taxation accepted these principles there would be occasions on which a particular piece of income would be taxed in two countries—a non-resident with a source of income in the UK would be taxed both here and at home while a UK resident with a foreign source would be taxed both in the country of source and in this country. These problems are exacerbated by the different bases used by different countries; thus one country may tax by residence, another by domicile and a third by citizenship.

---

[1] On definition of United Kingdom, see supra, § **1: 01** for an example of this fundamental principle see *Becker v Wright*, supra, § **13: 41**.

[2] Per Lord Wrenbury in *Whitney v IRC* [1926] AC 37, 10 TC 88 at 112.

[3] A company incorporated abroad is a subject of that country—*Janson v Driefontein Consolidated Mines* [1902] AC 484.

[4] E.g. TA 1988, s. 65(4) remittance basis if not ordinarily resident; this matter is also relevant to tax treaties.

INDIVIDUAL'S RESIDENCE

32: 02   There is no statutory definition of residence although in practice much turns on the Revenue code.[1] The basis for this code is uncertain since the cases on which they rest are for the most part illustrations of the principle that since residence is a question of fact the courts cannot reverse a finding by the Commissioners simply because they would not reach the same conclusion. The Revenue practice is based on decisions in favour of the Revenue and conveniently ignores those in favour of the taxpayer.

Residence is distinct from domicile in its legal nature and purpose. The tax system asks whether a person is resident in the UK not whether he is resident in this country or another; the conflict of laws asks where a person has his domicile. Hence a person may have two residences but not two domiciles.[2] Equally he may have no residence but must have a domicile.[3]

In the one context where it is important to determine whether an individual is resident in this country or that country, namely that of double tax treaties, each treaty will generally contain its own code for determining residence, which code has nothing to do with common law residence.[4]

Simon's Taxes E6.101, 301; Butterworths Income Tax Service H1.03, H1.04.
[1] Leaflet IR 20.
[2] *A-G v Coote* (1817) 4 Price 183, 2 TC 385; *Lloyd v Sulley* (1885) 2 TC 37.
[3] *Bell v Kennedy* (1868) LR 1 Sc & Div 307 at 320.
[4] Infra, § **36: 09**.

32: 03 Certain rules may be laid down:

(1) A person need not be physically present during the tax year to be resident. This was decided by Nicholls J in *Reed v Clark*;[1] the question is one of fact and the issue is not beyond doubt[2]. For some persons a clear rule is laid down by TA 1988, s. 334 which applies to a British subject or citizen of the Republic of Ireland whose ordinary residence has been in the UK. Such a person is taxed as if he were actually resident if he has left the UK for the purpose only of occasional residence[3] abroad. So a master mariner whose wife and family lived in the UK throughout the tax year while he was absent, was taxed as if still resident in the UK.[4] However, in *Reed v Clark* it was held that a person who was absent from the UK for the whole of a tax year and who set himself up in another country in such a way as to acquire residence there was not within TA 1988, s. 334, as he was not in the other country for the purpose of "occasional" residence. A person can thus escape s. 334 even though his time abroad is limited and he always intends to return.[5]

(2) A place of residence is not essential. In the normal case residence means "the place where one dwells permanently or for a considerable time, where one has one's settled or usual abode or the particular place at which one lives",[6] but "resident" indicates a quality of the person to be charged not of his property.[7] A vagrant is not the less resident in the UK for preferring a different hedgerow or doss house each night nor is a person with a place of abode abroad incapable of being also resident in the UK,[8] even though he should lack such a place here.

(3) A person may be resident here notwithstanding the absence of any element of intention or desire. An intention to depart at any moment is no hindrance to residence.[9] Thus a person may be resident here if his presence is compelled by reasons of business,[10] military service,[11] attendance at school[12] or even ill health.[13] A foreigner compelled to spend time here in prison[14] is presumably also resident here.

Among the factors that the courts look at are past[15] and present habits of life,[16] the frequency, regularity and duration of visits to the UK,[17] possibly the purpose of such visits,[18] ties with this country,[19] nationality[20] and whether or not a place of abode is maintained in this country.[21]

In considering this test however it is essential to bear in mind that "residence is not a term of invariable elements, all of which must be satisfied in each instance. It is quite impossible to give it a precise and inclusive definition. It is highly flexible and its many shades of meaning vary not only in the contexts of different matters but also in different aspects of the same matter."[22]

Simon's Taxes E6.102–107; Butterworths Income Tax Service H1.04.

[1] [1986] Ch 1, [1985] STC 323.

[2] *Iveagh v IRC* [1930] IR 386 is to the contrary and most of the (few) cases relied on could be and maybe were decided on the basis of the rule in TA 1988, s. 334.

[3] See per Lord President Clyde in *IRC v Combe* (1932) 17 TC 405.

[4] *Rogers v IRC* (1879) 1 TC 225. Contrast *Turnbull v Foster* (1904) 6 TC 206 where the merchant had not previously been ordinarily resident in the UK and so was held not resident.

[5] *Reed v Clark* [1986] Ch 1, [1985] STC 323.

[6] Per Viscount Cave LC in *Levene v IRC* [1928] AC 217 at 222, 13 TC 486 at 505.

[7] Per Lord Sumner in *IRC v Lysaght* [1928] AC 234, 13 TC 511.

[8] *IRC v Lysaght,* supra.

[9] *Brown v Burt* (1911) 5 TC 667 (yacht in tidal water—resident).

[10] *IRC v Lysaght* [1928] AC 234 at 248.

[11] *Inchiquin v IRC* (1948) 31 TC 125.

[12] *Miesagaes v IRC* (1957) 37 TC 493.

[13] *Re MacKenzie* [1941] Ch 69, [1940] 4 All ER 310.

[14] Viscount Sumner in *Egyptian Delta Land and Investment Co Ltd v Todd* [1929] AC 1 at 12, 14 TC 119 at 140.

[15] *Levene v IRC* [1928] AC 217 at 227, 13 TC 486 at 501, Viscount Sumner.

[16] *Levene v IRC,* supra.

[17] *Levene v IRC,* supra; *IRC v Brown* (1926) 11 TC 292 and *IRC v Zorab* (1926) 11 TC 289.

[18] In *Lysaght v IRC,* it was stressed that volition was not necessary. Intention is relevant for TA 1988, ss. 334 and 336.

[19] *IRC v Lysaght* [1928] AC 234; *Kinloch v IRC* (1929) 14 TC 736.

[20] *Levene v IRC* [1928] AC 217 at 224, 13 TC 486 at 506, and TA 1988, s. 334.

[21] *Cooper v Cadwalader* (1904) 5 TC 101.

[22] Per Rand J in *Thomson v Minister of National Revenue* [1946] SCR 209 at 224.

Revenue Rule (1). Six months actual residence—extended presence as residence

32: 04   One who has actually resided in the UK, a confusing statutory phrase, for a period equal in the whole to six months in any year of assessment is treated as resident.

The phrase "actually resides" causes some difficulty since it may simply mean "is physically present" or it may be wider so that a visitor with a short lease on a house might be treated as "actually resident" even during a week's visit to France if he left his wife and family in the house. The former meaning seems preferable yet it means that, while he may be a non-resident, his wife and children may be residents.

The word "months" is ambiguous. In *Wilkie v IRC*[1] the respondent arrived in the UK at 2 p.m. on 2nd June 1947 intending to leave at the end of November. Events conspired against him and not only did he have to undergo an operation which compelled him to select a flight out of the UK at the last possible moment, but his arrangement to fly on 30th November was cancelled by the airline. He finally left at 10 a.m. on 2nd December, 182 days and 20 hours after his arrival. The court rejected the idea that "months" meant lunar months not calendar months, and the respondent escaped a tax charge of £6,000. The court also held that parts of a day (20 hours) could be taken into account although a part of a day does not count as a whole day.

The six months need not be continuous. Under the code six months is equated with 183 days ignoring the days of arrival and departure, and whether or not it is a leap year.[2] However, it is presumably open to one who is present for six of the months of 31 days (with intervals abroad during the short months) to argue that he was present for only six months even though his actual presence was 186 days.

The six months must be in the year of assessment. Therefore one who arrives on 6th April can, on the view taken in the code, only stay 183 days in the next twelve months whereas one who arrives on 5th October may stay all but twelve months and still not be resident.

TA 1988, s. 336 contains the corollary that one who has not actually resided in the UK for six months is not treated as resident if he is in the UK for some temporary purpose only and not with any view or intent of establishing residence. "The meaning of it is this, if a foreigner comes here for merely temporary purposes connected with business or pleasure, or something else, and does not remain for a period altogether within the year of six months, he shall not be liable for a certain portion of taxation . . . He would have been liable but for this exemption."[3] This rule applies to exempt from tax income within Schedule D, Cases IV and V and to state a special residence rule for Schedule E (supra, § **6: 03**). It does not affect other aspects of residence.

Simon's Taxes E6.102, 110–112.
[1] [1952] 1 All ER 92, 32 TC 495.
[2] Leaflet IR 20 § 8.
[3] Per Lord Inglis in *Lloyd v Sulley* (1884) 2 TC 37 at 42.

Revenue Rule (2). The place of abode

32: 05   Under the code if a visitor has accommodation available here and does not work full time abroad he is regarded as resident no matter how short his visit.[1] The question turns on whether he has accommodation available for his use, which is a matter of fact rather than of legal rights. Hence he does not have to own or rent the property if it is in fact available for his use. A parent's home would presumably not be "available accommodation". The case on which this ruling appears to be based is *Cooper v Cadwalader*[2] where an American who was resident in New York, leased a shooting box in Scotland where he spent two months each year. The court held that since his occupation of the shooting box was neither casual nor temporary and his visits were in pursuance of his regular habits of life in conjunction with the maintenance of his establishment in Scotland, he was resident here.

The decision in *Cooper v Cadwalader* scarcely seems to support the Revenue view that any visit of whatever nature and duration will give rise to residence. In particular if there is also a place of abode in the UK it would appear to be necessary that the visit should include a period of occupation of the place of abode; this, however, is not in the code.

The reason for the reference to full time work abroad is that TA 1988, s. 335 provides that the question of a person's residence is to be decided without regard to the existence—as distinct from the occupation—of any place of abode maintained in the UK if a person works full time at a trade, profession or vocation and no part of that is carried on inside the UK. The same rule applies to an office or employment where the duties of that post are performed outside the UK. Duties that have to be performed in the UK, but which are merely incidental to the main duties, are ignored. Examples of incidental duties given by the Royal Commission[3] were returning to report or to collect samples. Duties may be slight yet more than incidental. In *Robson v Dixon*[4] the taxpayer was a pilot with a Dutch airline whose duties always commenced in Amsterdam but whose planes would sometimes land at Heathrow airport en route to Amsterdam. It was held that such landings were co-ordinate with and not merely incidental to comparable duties performed elsewhere. A single landing might be disregarded under the *de minimis* rule, as would landings due to an emergency or a diversion.[5] The Act does not say whether the full-time work abroad must be carried on throughout the year; it is likely that this would be necessary before s. 335 can apply.

Simon's Taxes E6.104, 110–112.
[1] Leaflet IR 20 §§ 20–21; cf. *Loewenstein v de Salis* (1926) 10 TC 424.
[2] (1904) 5 TC 101.
[3] RC 1955 (Cmd. 9474), p. 300. On Revenue practice see IR 20 §§ 37 to 39.
[4] [1972] 3 All ER 671.
[5] At pp. 677 and 678.

Revenue Rule (3). Habitual and substantial visits

32: 06   A visitor who does not have a place of abode is normally regarded as resident here if his visits are substantial and habitual, substantial meaning that the average annual period or periods amount to three months and habitual meaning that they are regarded as becoming habitual, and so the taxpayer becomes resident, after four years. If he intends to follow this pattern from the beginning he is treated as resident from the beginning. These are however only rules for normal cases.[1]

The bases for this rule are the decisions of the House of Lords in *Levene v IRC*[2] and *IRC v Lysaght*,[3] each of which concerns a claim by a resident to have given up residence.

In *Levene v IRC* the taxpayer had been resident in this country in previous years but had left the country in 1919. He did not set up a place of abode overseas. From 1919 to 1925 he spent about five months in each year in the UK but had no fixed abode in this country. He was "a bird of passage of almost mechanical regularity".[4] The reasons for his visits were the obtaining of medical advice, visiting his relatives, taking part in certain religious observances and dealing with his income tax affairs. The Commissioners held that he was resident here, a decision not reversed by the House of Lords.

Simon's Taxes E6.105; Butterworths Income Tax Service H1.04.
[1] Leaflet IR 20 § 21 and see SP 3/81, **Simon's Taxes, Division H3.2.**
[2] [1928] AC 217, 13 TC 486.
[3] [1928] AC 234, 13 TC 511.
[4] Per Viscount Sumner, at pp. 226, 501.

32: 07   In *IRC v Lysaght* the taxpayer had resided in England where he lived with his family and was managing director of the family business. In 1919 he went to live permanently in Ireland and set up a home there. He retained a seat on the board of the company, visited England once a month for meetings but for no other purposes. On such visits he was not accompanied by his wife and he usually stayed at a hotel. The Commissioners held that he was still resident in the UK. The House of Lords could find no reason for holding that there was no evidence to support that finding and therefore dismissed the appeal. For Viscount Sumner the crucial point appeared to be that the taxpayer was obliged to come to this country, that that obligation was continuous and the sequence of the visits excluded the element of chance and occasion.[1] For Lord Buckmaster with whom Lord Atkinson agreed the matter was one of fact and degree and so pre-eminently one of fact.[2] Lord Warrington was not sure that he would have taken the same view as the Commissioners.[3] Viscount Cave dissented, arguing that the matter was one of mixed fact and law and so could be interfered with and, if it was a matter of fact, that there was no evidence to support the conclusion reached by the Commissioners.[4]

IRC v Lysaght has generally been looked upon as marking the most extreme frontier of residence. However, the case concerned the two years immediately after the move to Ireland. The taxpayer was still involved in the running of the English business and he had no business interests in Ireland. He remained a member of a London club and had a bank account in Bristol. Moreover his visits, although only for company meetings once a month, lasted on average a week and meant that he was physically present in England for 94 days in the one year and 101 days in the other. The fact that he had found a permanent home outside the jurisdiction is only one factor to be weighed against these.

The importance of recognising that in *IRC v Lysaght* the House of Lords merely declined to interfere with a finding of fact by the Commissioners is shown by a comparison of that case with *IRC v Brown*[5] where the taxpayer's usual habit was to spend seven months in Mentone, two months in Switzerland or at the Italian lakes and three months in the UK.[6] The Special Commissioners held that he was not resident. Rowlatt J held that he could not interfere with that finding. The same judge later held that he could not interfere with the finding of fact by the Commissioners in *IRC v Lysaght*. Yet it is the *Lysaght* case, despite the doubts on the facts expressed in the House of Lords, which is taken as the basis of current Revenue practice under the code.

Simon's Taxes E6.106, 107, 110–112.
[1] [1928] AC 234, 13 TC 511, per Viscount Sumner, at 245, 529.
[2] Ibid, at 247, 534.
[3] Ibid, at 251, 537.
[4] Ibid, at 241, 533.
[5] (1926) 11 TC 292.
[6] Case stated, para. 3 (4). One difference from *Levene* is that *Brown* had no business interests here. This difference is not reflected in the code.

Change of residence during tax year

32: 08   Not all persons acquiring residence do so on 6th April and the Tax Acts make no provision for splitting a tax year so as to tax the new resident only for that part of the year which he was resident.[1] By concession however a split is carried out where an individual, who has not prior to his arrival been ordinarily resident in the UK, comes to the UK to take up permanent residence, or to stay at least three years, or to enter to take up employment that is expected to last at least two years.[2] The time of departure or arrival can make a significant difference to total tax liability since personal reliefs are not apportioned by reference to the duration of residence. This concession is withheld if the taxpayer is using it for tax avoidance.[3]

Simon's Taxes E6.114; Butterworths Income Tax Service H1.04.
  [1] See *Neubergh v IRC* [1978] STC 181.
  [2] Extra-statutory concessions A11 (1988) and D2 (1988), **Simon's Taxes Division H2.2**. This has only a limited application to Eire and does not apply to IHT or CTT—nor to trusts. See also IR 20 § 11.
  [3] *R v IRC, ex p Fulford-Dobson* [1987] STC 344.

Giving up residence

32: 09   Under the Code if a person has accommodation available to him in the UK, he is regarded as resident here if he pays a visit to the UK during the tax year and as ordinarily resident if he comes here in most years. If he has no such accommodation here, he is regarded as remaining both resident and ordinarily resident if he returns for periods which amount to an average of three months a year. If he claims that he has ceased to be resident and ordinarily resident here and can produce some evidence for this (for example that he has sold his house here and set up a permanent home abroad) his claim is usually admitted provisionally with effect from the date following his departure. Normally this provisional ruling is confirmed after he has remained abroad for a period which includes a complete tax year and during which his visits to this country have not amounted to an annual average of three months. If he cannot produce such evidence, he will be assessed on the provisional basis that he is still resident here and a decision made after three years in the light of what actually happens in that period. If he is found to have lost his residence, his liability is reassessed on that basis.

Where residence is given up during a tax year in order to take up permanent residence abroad, an individual is by concession charged only by reference to the actual period of residence.

Simon's Taxes E6.112.

ORDINARY RESIDENCE

32: 10   The Tax Acts also talk of "ordinary residence".[1] Common sense would suggest that ordinary residence is narrower than residence. In *IRC v Lysaght* Viscount Sumner said, "I think the converse to ordinarily is extraordinarily and that part of the regular order of a man's life, adopted voluntarily and for settled purposes, is not extraordinary."[2] A person is ordinarily resident in the UK if he habitually and normally resided lawfully in the UK from choice and for a settled purpose throughout the relevant period apart from temporary or occasional absences. A specific limited purpose, such as education, can be a settled purpose; it is irrelevant that his real house was outside the UK or that his future intention and occupation might be to him outside the UK[3].

On this view those who are resident within Rule 1 above clearly would not be ordinarily resident, those within Rule 3 clearly would be ordinarily resident and those within Rule 2 are probably not. The Revenue view ordinarily resident as "broadly equivalent to habitually resident".[4] Both Mr Levene and Mr Lysaght were held to be ordinarily resident in the UK. It would appear that presence, although necessary for residence is not necessary for ordinary residence. It may also be that ordinary residence, unlike residence, at least for an adult,[5] is a voluntary matter, but it might be that a foreigner imprisoned for life would be treated as ordinarily resident.

Simon's Taxes E6.108; Butterworths Income Tax Service H1.04.

[1] E.g. TA 1988, ss. 334, 65(4) and 19 Case II.
[2] [1928] AC 234 at 243, 13 TC 511 at 528.
[3] *Shah v Barnet London Borough Council* [1983] 1 All ER 226.
[4] IR note on Finance Bill 1974—[1974] STI, p. 225, para. 3.
[5] *Miesagaes v IRC* (1957) 37 TC 493 supra, § **32: 03**, involved an infant and see **Simon's Taxes E6.120** for the treatment of spouses and children.

32: 11   CGTA 1979, s. 2 contemplates the possibility of a person being ordinarily resident but not resident. One who has been resident here but who is absent from the jurisdiction for the purpose only of occasional residence abroad is treated as actually resident by TA 1988, s. 334. However, this rule only applies to one who is a British subject or citizen of the Republic of Ireland so that one who does not fall within those categories but who has been resident here and who has gone abroad for the purpose only of occasional residence, perhaps retaining a place of abode here, is ordinarily resident but not resident.

Simon's Taxes E6.119.

DOMICILE

32: 12   A person is domiciled[1] where he has or is deemed by law to have his permanent home. He must have a domicile; but may not have more than one domicile. The test of domicile is that developed by the general rules of the conflict of laws.

For tax purposes the question is whether or not a person is domiciled in the UK.[2] For general conflict of law purposes the question will be whether a person is domiciled in England and Wales, or Scotland or some other separate jurisdiction. Although generally a person domiciled in the UK will be domiciled in one of its constituent parts this is not necessarily so since a person with a domicile of origin in France who decides to live in the UK but is undecided as between Scotland and England may have a UK domicile for UK tax purposes and a French domicile for conflict of laws purposes. However it is understood that the Revenue do not take this point and would treat the person as still domiciled in France.

Simon's Taxes E6.301–307; Butterworths Income Tax Service H1.03.
[1] For a recent example, see *Re Clore (No 2), Official Solicitor v Clore* [1984] STC 609. For a discussion of possible reform and of some of the recent case law see Fentiman, *Oxford Journal of Legal Studies* 1986 Vol. 6, p. 353.
[2] E.g. TA 1988, ss. 65(4), 19(1) and 739.

RESIDENCE OF CORPORATIONS

32: 13 Since income tax originally applied both to individuals and to companies it was perhaps inevitable that residence would be taken as the basis of taxation of companies. The test of residence was laid down by Lord Loreburn in *De Beers Consolidated Mines Ltd v Howe* "... a company resides, for the purpose of income tax, where its real business is carried on ... and the real business is carried on where central management and control actually resides".[1] As Lord Radcliffe has remarked, "this judgment must be treated today as if the test which it laid down was as precise and unequivocal as a positive statutory injunction".[2] Under this test a company is resident where its controlling board meets rather than where its directors are resident.[3]

In the *De Beers* case the company was registered in South Africa where also were the mines whose diamonds the company marketed, its head office, and the venue of its shareholders meetings. The diamonds were sold through a London syndicate. Directors meetings were held both in South Africa and London but it was in London that the majority of the directors resided. The Commissioners held that London was the place from which the directors controlled and managed the chief operations of the company. In challenging this conclusion, the company took as a point of law the proposition that being incorporated and registered in South Africa it must be resident in South Africa. That proposition was rejected by the House of Lords.

32.14 There is now a second test. Following extensive consultations, FA 1988 provides that as from 15th March 1988 a company which is incorporated in the UK is resident here for tax purposes; such a company is not also resident where its central management and control exists.[4] This major change brings the UK tax system into line with many others.

An exception is provided where immediately before 15th March 1988 the company was carrying on business and was not then resident in the UK and has ceased to be so resident in pursuance of Treasury consent under TA 1988, ss. 765–767 or its predecessors. If that consent was a general one it was also necessary that the company should have been taxable in a territory outside the UK.[5] If the company ceases to carry on business or to be taxable then the new rule as to corporate residence is to apply as from that time or, if later, 15th March 1993.[6] If it becomes resident in the UK it becomes subject to this rule at once.[7]

A further exception applies where the company was resident here on 15th

March 1988[8] but ceases to be so in pursuance of a consent at some later time. Such companies are free to depart even though they were incorporated here. However if they cease to do business the new rule is to apply as from that time or, if later, 15th March 1993. Similarly if the company becomes resident in the UK it becomes subject to this rule at once.[9]

There are two transitional exceptions. If at any time before 15th March 1988 a company whose central control and management is carried on outside the UK and so is not resident here under the old rule but which was incorporated here before, and carried on business before, 15th March 1988 will become resident here under this rule as from 15th March 1993—thus enjoying a five year holiday.[10] This holiday will be curtailed and the company will become subject to the new rule if it becomes resident in the UK before then.[11] This might be triggered by some unexpected event such as the appointment of a UK liquidator.[12] This 1993 rule applies also to companies which fall outside the second exception above but cease to be resident under present UK rules with the appropriate Treasury consents on or after 15th March 1988.[13]

This change does not mean the abolition of the old case law test that a company is resident where its central management and control are to be found. This old test will remain particularly important in two situations, (i) where the company is incorporated abroad, (ii) where the company was incorporated in the UK before 15th March 1988 and the issue arises before 15th March 1993.

A company which ceases to carry on any business or which is being wound up is treated as retaining its prior resident.[14]

Simon's Taxes D4.101, 103.

[1] [1906] AC 455 at 458, 5 TC 198 at 212.

[2] In *Unit Construction Co Ltd v Bullock* [1960] AC 351 at 366, 38 TC 712 at 738. The test has been adopted by the legislature TA 1988, s. 967(1), and was approved by RC 1st Report § 11, and is present in e.g. the UK—USA Double Tax Treaty Art II (1)(*f*). The UK–Netherlands Treaty uses the phrase "effective management"—Art 4(3). On the extent to which the parent company can interfere note Statement of Practice C8, **Simon's Taxes, Division H3.4.**

[3] *John Hood & Co Ltd v Magee* (1918) 7 TC 327.

[4] FA 1988, s. 66(1).

[5] FA 1988, Sch. 7, para. 1(1); this presumably refers to being taxable immediately before 15 March 1988.

[6] FA 1988, Sch. 7, para. 1(2).

[7] FA 1988, Sch. 7, para. 1(3).

[8] And was carrying on business both immediately before 15th March 1988 and after ceasing to be resident.

[9] FA 1988, Sch. 7, para. 2.

[10] FA 1988, Sch. 7, para. 3(1).

[11] FA 1988, Sch. 7, para. 3(2); presumably this refers to a company incorporated here which is currently controlled abroad but which subsequently ceases to be so controlled.

[12] ICAEW Memorandum TR 739, para. 28; *Simon's Tax Intelligence* 1989, p. 80.

[13] FA 1988, Sch. 7, para. 4.

[14] FA 1988, s. 66(2).

32: 15   It was not clear whether Lord Loreburn's test meant that a company could have only one residence. This was discussed in the difficult and unfortunate decision of *Swedish Central Rly Co Ltd v Thompson*.[2] The company had been set up in England to obtain the concession for and then build a railway line in Sweden. The company had in 1900 leased the railway to a Swedish company in return for an annual rent of £33,500. In 1920 the articles of the company were altered to remove the central management and control of the company to Stockholm and the Revenue admitted that the company was now controlled and managed from Sweden, so as to cease being liable to tax under Schedule D, Case I. If however the company was still resident in England it would be liable to tax under Schedule D, Case V.[3] The Special Commissioners observed that Lord Loreburn's test was laid down in a case concerning a foreign company,[4] and concluded that the company was resident in the UK. The conclusion that a company could have two residences was upheld by Rowlatt J by the Court of Appeal[5] (Atkin LJ dissenting) and by the House of Lords (Lord Atkinson dissenting); what is less clear is the reasoning on which that conclusion was applied to the facts.

The sole question for the House of Lords was whether as a matter of law a company which was resident in Sweden could also be resident in the UK. If so, the question whether this company was resident in the UK was one of fact, and therefore one for the Commissioners. Lord Cave, with whom Lord Dunedin agreed was not prepared to say that registration in the UK would itself be sufficient proof of residence here but was satisfied that registration plus the other circumstances were sufficient to enable the Commissioners to arrive at their finding.[6] Lord Sumner concurred in the decision. Lord Buckmaster thought that as there was a real and not merely a nominal residence here the company's appeal failed.[7]

In view of the decision it is useful to set out precisely what was done in the two countries. In Sweden, in addition to central control and management were meetings of shareholders and directors, dividends declared and the company's bank account. London, in addition to being the place of incorporation and registered office, was the location of the secretary's residence, the company seal, the share register and transfers, the accounts were made up and audited, and dividends for UK shareholders were paid from funds in London, further share certificates were made out, and a committee of directors met to deal with share transfers, to attach the company seal to appropriate documents and to sign cheques.

Simon's Taxes D4.105.
   [1] It is now clear that the test is the same for all companies, infra, § **32: 17**. However in practice the Revenue tend to rely on TA 1988, s. 739 to tax individuals who clearly are resident rather than make direct assessments on companies incorporated abroad.
   [2] [1925] AC 495, 9 TC 342. The Swedish Central Railway opened up the Bergslagen Region— a remote forested area. The track was 62¼ miles long with, in 1920, four passenger trains a day taking an average of five hours for the journey. (Bradshaw's Continental Railway Guide 1920.)
   [3] This minimal activity was still a trade—see *IRC v South Behar Rly Co Ltd* (1925) 12 TC 657.
   [4] Case stated, para. 17. 9 TC 342 at 347.
   [5] [1924] 2 KB 255, 9 TC 342.
   [6] [1925] AC 495 at 505, 9 TC 342 at 375.
   [7] [1925] AC 495 at 519, 9 TC 342 at 386.

32: 16   The major difficulty lies in reconciling the case with the decision of the House of Lords four years later in *Egyptian Delta Land and Investment Co Ltd v Todd*.[1] The company was incorporated in 1904 in England for the purpose of dealing in and developing land in Egypt; in 1907 most of its functions were transferred to Egypt. All that remained in London was required by the Companies Act—a registered office, which meant simply an address rather than a specific amount of floor area, a register of members and a register of bearer warrants. There was a London secretary of the company who dealt with occasional correspondence and filed the annual returns, a job he did for many other companies.

The company contended, that the mere satisfaction of the requirements of the Companies' Acts could not constitute residence.[2] The Revenue on the other hand contended that if management and control were not the sole test of residence there were carried on in the UK acts of sufficient importance to justify a finding of residence.[3] The Special Commissioners decided that the *Swedish Railway* case was distinguishable on its facts.[4] Rowlatt J reversing the Commissioners held that the duties which the law imposed on the company fulfilled the idea of residence. The Court of Appeal decided unanimously for the Crown. The company's appeal to the House of Lords was allowed unanimously. The mere satisfaction of the requirements of the Companies Acts could not be sufficient residence otherwise all English companies would be resident here while foreign companies might also be held to be resident here on the *De Beers* principle. The Crown could not have it both ways. In reliance on the *De Beers* principle many English companies had shifted their management overseas to escape UK taxation.[5] Moreover Parliament in 1915 had legislated on a tax point by charging "a non-resident person ... not being a British company ...,"[6] thereby displaying an assumption that a British company could be a non-resident person, a point not taken in *Swedish Central Rly Co*, but repeated by the two other members of the House to deliver reasoned speeches.[7]

Simon's Taxes D4.104, 108.
[1] [1929] AC 1, 14 TC 119.
[2] Ibid, case stated § 8.
[3] Ibid, case stated § 9.
[4] Case stated § 10.
[5] [1929] AC 1 at 34, 14 TC 119 at 157.
[6] F (No. 2) A 1915; 1918 Income Tax Act 1918, Sch. 1, General Rule 7.
[7] Lord Buckmaster, at 37, 159 and Lord Warrington at 40, 162.

32: 17   The reconciliation of these two cases is not easy but if however the cases are reconciled one can take them as authority for three propositions (1) that the test of residence laid down in the *De Beers* case applies to all corporations regardless of the place of registration or incorporation; (2) that a company may be resident in two places; and (3) that a finding of dual residence is not to be made unless the control of the general affairs of the company is not centrally placed in one country but is divided among two or more. It is also clear that residence may be in one country and the company's sole trade carried on in another,[1] and conversely that the mere carrying on of trade in the UK is not sufficient to establish residence here.[2]

Where the 1988 rules apply and a company is resident here through incorporation a dual residence problem cannot arise, since incorporation is the only test.[3] However, dual residence problems will arise when this test does not apply.

[1] E.g. *San Paulo (Brazilian) Rly Co v Carter* [1896] AC 31, 3 TC 407. *New Zealand Shipping Co Ltd v Thew* (1922) 8 TC 208, HL.
[2] *A-G v Alexander* (1874) LR 10 Exch 20.
[3] FA 1988, s. 66(1).

Relevant control

32: 18   The control which is important, at least for a company under an English type of company law, is that of the directors rather than the shareholders.[1] The shareholders can by virtue of their votes control the corporation; they can compel the directors to do their will[2] but it does not follow that the corporators are managing the corporation. However the mere fact that English company law takes this view is not conclusive. The question is one of the control of the business and under a foreign system of company law a different conclusion might be justified.

The place of control and management means that of actual control and not merely the place where control should properly be exercised. In *Unit Construction Co Ltd v Bullock*[3] three subsidiary companies had been incorporated and registered in Kenya. Their articles of association placed the management and control of the business in the hands of directors and provided that meetings might be held anywhere outside the UK. The purpose of this scheme was to use the profits for development in Africa without becoming liable to UK taxation, and to forestall possible difficulties in the event of African nationalisation. Two years later the Kenya companies had incurred substantial losses and the parent company took over the management and control of the subsidiaries in an attempt to save its investment. All decisions of major importance and many of minor importance were thereafter taken by the parent company.

The House of Lords held that despite the admission by the Kenya companies that they were resident in Kenya they were in fact resident in the UK. As Viscount Simonds put it, "The business is not the less managed in London because it ought to be managed in Kenya."[4]

The consequences of this decision have not yet become clear. The constitution of the company remains an important factor in determining where control is exercised, and it remains to be seen how far back in the decision making process the courts will go. If major decisions are taken by a company only after consultations with a principal shareholder who lives in another jurisdiction, where is the company resident? One possible result of the decision will be an increase in the number of corporations which have more than one residence, although *Unit Construction Co Ltd v Bullock* is not itself such a case.

[1] *American Thread Co v Joyce* (1911) 6 TC 1 at 32–3 of *John Hood & Co Ltd v Magee* (1918) 7 TC 327 at 351, 353, 358.
[2] But only by dismissal—*Automatic Self Cleansing Filter Syndicate Co Ltd v Cunninghame* [1906] 2 Ch 34.
[3] [1960] AC 351, 38 TC 712.
[4] Ibid, at 363, 736.

Company residence

32: 19   The Revenue have issued the following Statement of Practice[1] on residence of companies under the case law test. It is rumoured that a new statement is being prepared.

(1)–(3) . . .

Place of "central management and control"

(4)   In determining whether or not an individual company is resident in the UK, it thus becomes necessary to locate its place of "central management and control". The case law concept of central management and control is, in broad terms, directed at the highest level of control of the business of a company. It is to be distinguished from the place where the main operations of a business are to be found, though those two places may often coincide. Moreover, the exercise of control does not necessarily demand any minimum standard of active involvement: it may, in appropriate circumstances, be exercised tacitly through passive oversight.

(5)   Successive decided cases have emphasised that the place of central management and control is wholly a question of fact. For example, Lord Radcliffe in *Unit Construction* said that "the question where control and management abide must be treated as one of fact or 'actuality'" (p. 741). It follows that factors which together are decisive in one instance may individually carry little weight in another. Nevertheless the decided cases do give some pointers. In particular a series of decisions has attached importance to the place where the company's board of directors meet. There are very many cases in which the board meets in the same country as that in which the business operations take place, and central management and control is clearly located in that one place. In other cases central management and control may be exercised by directors in one country though the actual business operations may, perhaps under the immediate management of local directors, take place elsewhere.

(6)   But the location of board meetings, although important in the normal case, is not necessarily conclusive. Lord Radcliffe in *Unit Construction* pointed out (p. 738) that the site of the meetings of the directors' board had *not* been chosen as "*the* test" of company residence. In some cases, e.g. central management and control is exercised by a single individual. This may happen when a chairman or managing director exercises powers formally conferred by the company's Articles and the other board members are little more than cyphers, or by reason of a dominant shareholding or for some other reason. In those cases the residence of the company is where the controlling individual exercises his powers.

(7)   In general the place of directors' meetings is significant only in so far as those meetings constitute the medium through which central management and control is exercised. If, for example, the directors of a company were engaged together actively in the UK in the complete running of a business which was wholly in the UK, the company would not be regarded as resident outside the UK merely because the directors held formal board meetings outside the UK. While it is possible to identify extreme situations in which central management and control plainly is, or is not, exercised by directors in formal meetings, the conclusion in any case is wholly one of fact depending on the relative weight to be given to various factors. Any attempt to lay down rigid guidelines would only be misleading.

(8)   Generally, however, where doubts arise about a particular company's residence status, the Revenue adopt the following approach—

   (i) They first try to ascertain whether the directors of the company in fact exercise central management and control.

   (ii) If so, they seek to determine where the directors exercise this central management and control (which is not necessarily where they meet).

   (iii) In cases where the directors apparently do *not* exercise central management and control of the company, the Revenue then look to establish where and by whom it is exercised.

Parent/subsidiary relationship

(9)   It is particularly difficult to apply the "central management and control" test in the situation where a subsidiary company and its parent operate in different territories. In this situation, the parent will normally influence, to a greater or lesser extent, the actions of the subsidiary. Where that influence is exerted by the parent exercising the powers which a sole or majority shareholder has in general meetings of the subsidiary, for example to appoint and dismiss members of the board of the subsidiary and to initiate or approve alterations to its financial structure, the Revenue would not seek to argue that central management and control of the subsidiary is located where the parent company is resident. However, in cases where the parent usurps the functions of the board of the subsidiary (such as *Unit Construction* itself) or where that board merely rubber stamps the parent company's decisions without giving them any independent consideration of its own, the Revenue draw the conclusion that the subsidiary has the same residence for tax purposes as its parent.

(10) The Revenue recognise that there may be many cases where a company is a member of a group having its ultimate holding company in another country which will not fall readily into either of the categories referred to above. In considering whether the board of such a subsidiary company exercises central management and control of the subsidiary's business, they have regard to the degree of autonomy which those directors have in conducting the company's business. Matters (among others) that may be taken into account are the extent to which the directors of the subsidiary take decisions on their own authority as to investment, production, marketing and procurement without reference to the parent.

Double taxation agreements

(11), (12) . . .

(13) . . . It is now considered that effective management may, in some cases, be found at a place different from the place of central management and control. This could happen, for example, where a company is run by executives based abroad, but the final directing power rests with non-executive directors who meet in the UK. In such circumstances the company's place of effective management might well be abroad but, depending on the precise powers of the non-executive directors, it might be centrally managed and controlled (and therefore resident) in the UK.

Conclusion

(14) In outlining factors relevant to the application of the case law test, this statement assumes that they exist for genuine commercial reasons. Where, however, as may happen, it appears that a major objective underlying the existence of certain factors is the obtaining of tax benefits from residence or non-residence, the Revenue examines the facts particularly closely in order to see whether there has been an attempt to create the appearance of central management and control in a particular place without the reality.

(15) The test examined in this statement is not always easy to apply in present day circumstances. The last relevant case was decided over 20 years ago, and there have been many developments in communications since then, which in particular may enable a company to be controlled from a place far distant from where the day-to-day management is carried on. As the statement makes clear, while the general principle has been laid down by the Courts, its application must depend on the precise facts.

---

[1] SP 6/83.

Dual resident investing companies: TA 1988, s. 404

32: 20 F(No. 2)A 1987 contained provisions restricting the availability of certain reliefs where a company is resident under the domestic tax systems of the UK and another country.[1] The problem may be illustrated simply.

When a company is incorporated in the USA, but has its central management and control in the UK, it will be treated as resident in the USA under US rules and in the UK under UK rules. Such a company is able to use many UK reliefs, such as loss relief and capital allowances on the basis that it is a UK resident company and will be able to pass the benefit of those reliefs to other companies within its group notwithstanding that it is also resident in the USA and so able to claim reliefs under that tax system as well. Particular problems arise from the payment of interest. The dual resident company can pass the benefit of such a payment to other companies in the

US and UK groups and so get relief twice. Where the borrowing is from another company within the multinational's structure the recipient of the interest will perhaps pay tax once but this will be more than off set by the double relief.

Restrictions now apply only where the accounting period in which the relief arose begins on or after 1st April 1987.[2] Further they apply only where the company is a "dual resident investment company".[3] The process of defining an investment company is tortuous; it begins with a rule of exclusion—an investment company is one which is not a trading company; however the term trading company is itself defined so as to exclude a company whose main function is to carry on all or any of various activities such as acquiring and holding shares in dual resident companies or raising finance; this is backed up by the exclusion of other companies carrying on such activities to an extent which does not appear to be justified by any trade it does carry on or for a purpose which does not appear to be appropriate to any such trade.[4]

The reliefs restricted are those relevant to group relief, i.e. losses, excess capital allowances, expenses of management and charges on income.[5] However there are further provisions dealing with certain intra group transactions for capital allowances purposes.[6] There are also restrictions on the operation of TA 1988, s. 343 (supra, § **25: 27**), TA 1970, s. 273 (supra, § **26: 18**) and TA 1970, s. 276 (supra, § **26: 22**).[7]

These rules are seen as complementary to the US 1986 provisions.[8] The effect is to ban relief under the rules of both systems where a dual resident company makes the payment and so to encourage the group to ensure that deductible payments are in future made only by companies which are resident in only one jurisdiction.

Simon's Taxes D4.109.

[1] The proposal to restrict these reliefs goes back to a consultative document issued by the Revenue in November 1984; the provisions in F(No. 2)A 1987 are based on draft clauses published in December 1986.

[2] TA 1988, s. 404(2).

[3] TA 1988, s. 404(1).

[4] TA 1988, s. 404(6); there is also a special rule for companies whose main activity is the paying of charges on deep discount securities.

[5] TA 1988, s. 404(2).

[6] F(No. 2)A 1987, s. 64(1), (4) and (5); the provisions affected are CAA 1968, Sch. 7, para. 4(3) and FA 1971, s. 44(6) and Sch. 8, para. 13; all these provisions are concerned with a right to take a price other than market value as the basis for capital allowances. On timing of the new rules see s. 64(6).

[7] TA 1988, s. 343(2), F(No. 2)A 1987, s. 64(3) amending TA 1970, s. 273 and F(No. 2)A 1987, s. 64(4) amending TA 1970, s. 276. On timing of the new rules see F(No. 2)A 1987, s. 64(7).

[8] IRC § 1503(*d*) introduced by Tax Reform Act 1986, § 1249; for a comparison of the two sets of rules see *Law Society's Gazette* 11th March 1987, pp. 713–14.

Ordinary residence

32: 21   No point seems to turn now on the distinction between residence and ordinary residence of corporations. It was apparently admitted in *Union Corpn v IRC*[1] that residence and ordinary residence of companies were coextensive but it has been suggested that in cases of dual residence, ordinary residence is linked with the registered office.

Simon's Taxes D4.110.
  [1] [1952] 1 All ER 646.

Corporation—domicile

32: 22   The law of domicile can only be applied to corporations,[1] "with a certain sense of strain". A corporation is domiciled in its place of corporation.[2] It would appear to follow that its domicile cannot change save for some quite exceptional circumstance such as a private Act of Parliament.

Simon's Taxes D4.111.
  [1] The concept is very rarely relevant; see e.g. TA 1988, ss. 47 and 739, TA 1988, s. 740 and TA 1988, ss. 761 and 762.
  [2] *Gasque v IRC* [1940] 2 K B 80, 23 TC 210.

Tax presence

32: 23   In *Clark v Oceanic Contractors Inc*[1] the House of Lords invented a new connecting factor-tax presence. This is a presence sufficient to make the PAYE system applicable; see § **6: 117**.

  [1] [1983] STC 35.

Change of residence; TA 1988, ss. 765–767

32: 24   As a result of the 1988 changes it will not be possible for a company incorporated here after 14 March 1988 to change its residence simply by changing the place of its central management and control. A company incorporated here but resident abroad under previous rules will remain abroad until 1993. Special rules are needed to prevent companies moving too much out of the reach of the tax authorities.

If a body corporate which is resident in the UK wishes to cause or permit its non-resident subsidiary to create or issue any shares or debentures, it must obtain the consent of the UK Treasury.[1] A similar consent is needed if the resident body corporate wishes to transfer shares or debentures of its non-resident subsidiary; this consent is only needed if the resident body owns or has an interest in the shares or debentures and is not needed if the transfer is for the purpose of enabling a person to be qualified to act as a director.[2] This is all that remains of a wider power;[3] under that provision Treasury consent was needed for a company to cease to be resident in the UK.[4] The sanction for breach is criminal rather than treating the acts as if they were acts of the parent; apparently no prosecution has even been brought.

If the resident company transfers its business to a non-resident company,[5] there will be a normal capital gains charge.[6] If the company wishes to cease to be resident, it must make suitable arrangements for paying tax before it leaves.[7] That tax must include any due in respect of a deemed realisation of its assets on migration.[8] This deemed disposal does not apply to assets of a branch or agency which remains here since those will remain within the charge to corporation tax.[9] It is also possible to defer the charge if a subsidiary company migrates but the principal company remains resident here.

A similar deemed disposal rule applies where the company remains resident in the UK under normal UK rules but becomes resident abroad under a double taxation agreement and thanks to the rules of that agreement, will not be subject to UK tax on gains realised on "prescribed assets".[10] For disposals on or after 14th March 1989 this deemed disposal is extended to cover the situation in which an asset held by a dual-resident company becomes a prescribed asset.[11] With effect from the same date there are new rules withholding rollover relief on the disposal of a non-prescribed asset and the acquistion of a prescribed one.[12]

---

[1] TA 1988, s. 765(1)(c).

[2] TA 1988, s. 765(1)(d).

[3] Sub-ss. 1(a) and (b) were repealed by FA 1988, Sch 14, Part IV. On procedure see Revenue Press Release 20 September 1988, *Simon's Tax Intelligence* 1988, p. 702.

[4] The validity of this control was upheld by the European Court—*R v H. M. Treasury, ex p Daily Mail and General Trust plc* [1988] STC 787— neither Art. 52 nor Art. 58 were breached.

[5] A matter previously falling within sub-s. (1)(b).

[6] TA 1970, s. 273 cannot apply if the transferee is non-resident.

[7] FA 1988, s. 130; this provision does not apply to a company ceasing to be resident under the now-repealed TA 1988, s. 765(1)(a). On Revenue practice see Press Release 4th August 1988, *Simon's Tax Intelligence* 1988, p. 637.

[8] FA 1988, s. 105.

[9] FA 1988, s. 107.

[10] FA 1988, s. 106.

[11] FA 1989, s. 132.

[12] FA 1989, s. 133.

Other bodies

32: 25   Trading partnerships are resident when the control and management of the trade is situate[1] regardless of the residence of the partners.[2] Other partnerships are presumably not treated as entities separate from their partners and each partner is liable according to his own residence or non-residence. There is no reported case on other unincorporated bodies.

The position with regard to trustees is now governed by legislation. For CGT it has long been established that the trust is non-resident if the majority of the trustees are non-resident and the trust is ordinarily administered overseas.[3] However there was no direct provision for income tax. The Revenue view was that the residence of one trustee within the UK was enough to make the whole trust liable to UK income tax on the basis of residence. However this view was rejected by the House of Lords in *Dawson v IRC*.[4] The Government responded by introducing new provisions in FA 1989 s 110.

The new provision applies only where one of the trustees is resident in the UK and another is not. It has no application where all the trustees are resident or non-resident. Where trustees have mixed residence they will be treated as UK residents if the settlor was resident, ordinarily resident or domiciled in the UK at any time when he put funds into the settlement.[5] In the case of a testamentary trust the critical time is the date of death. The effect of these rules is that a settlement with a UK settlor will be taxed on its foreign income so long as there is at least one UK resident trustee. Conversely a foreign settlor will be able to appoint UK trustees and preserve non-resident status for the trust by ensuring that he retains at least one non-resident trustee.[6] As a non-resident body the provisions of TA 1988, ss. 739–746 may fall to be considered.

The new provision applies for 1989–90 and later years but contains some degree of transitional relief. For the year 1989–90 if none of the trustees was resident in the UK at any time between 1st October 1989 and 5th April 1990 (inclusive) then the residence, ordinary residence and domicile of the settlor is ignored.[7] This enables trustees who would otherwise be caught by the new rule to establish non-resident status by ensuring that all their trustees are non-resident by 1st October. Of course if the trustees remain of mixed residence they will be subject to the new rule.

There are further transitional rules to ensure that ss. 739 and 740 do not apply to income payable and benefits received before 15th June 1989, the day on which the proposals were announced.[8] For s. 740, where liability is restricted to the amount of "relevant income" received by the beneficiary, income received before 1989–90 can still be relevant income. This is because it restores the pre-*Dawson* position.

FA 1989, s. 111 introduces equivalent provisions for mixed residence personal representatives.

Simon's Taxes E6.122, D4.808.
  [1] TA 1988, s. 112. On CGT see Wheatcroft and Whiteman, §§ 3–23 and 3–24.
  [2] This view was reasserted in *Padmore v IRC* [1989] STC 493, CA when the decision of the Special Commissioner that the individual partner carried on this trade was reversed.
  [3] CGTA 1979, s. 52(1) and (2), infra, § **34: 53**.
  [4] [1989] STC 473.
  [5] FA 1989, s. 110(2) and (3); there is a wide definition of settlor in subs. (4).
  [6] Hansard Standing Committee G 22nd June 1989 cols 609 and 610. *Quaere* whether any action could lie against the non-resident trustee if he were to become a UK resident e.g. by staying in the UK for more than six months in a year of assessment.
  [7] FA 1989, s. 110(6) and (7).
  [8] FA 1989, s. 110(8) and (9).

TAX HAVENS

32: 26   A tax haven is simply a place with a favourable tax climate. Among the favourites are the Channel Islands,[1] the Isle of Man or, with greater tax advantages, the Bahamas, the Turks and Caicos Islands, the Cayman Islands and Liechtenstein. All depend on the local rules with regard to tax, trust and company law. Even the UK has tax advantages for foreigners. One country's tax incentive causes another country to brand it as a tax haven. Some countries need overseas earnings and may accept it in fees for financial services rather than the profits of polluting plant and machinery. If other countries tax so highly as to encourage the flight of fiscal refugees they have to take the consequences.

Some tax havens are used as suitable places in which to make profits arising through manipulation of transfer prices between different companies and countries. Such arrangements appear to be effective despite legislation in those other countries. However in an effort to counter such activities new rules have been introduced in the UK by TA 1988, s. 747 to deal with controlled foreign companies; see §§ **34: 57–34: 67**.

Spitz Tax Havens Encyclopaedia
  [1] The Jersey income tax is a flat 20% but foreign controlled companies pay only £200. There are said to be 26 banks on a waiting list to get into the 45 square miles of Jersey (population 75,000). Apparently much of the money deposited in the islands is promptly placed on the British securities market.

33 Enforcement of foreign revenue laws

33: 01 United Kingdom courts decline to exercise jurisdiction to entertain a suit for the enforcement of the revenue law of another country;[1] nor can a foreign judgment for a sum payable in respect of taxes be registered under the Foreign Judgments (Reciprocal Enforcement) Act 1933.[2] Where a foreign government had successfully sued in its own courts for tax due to it and recovered the tax but not the costs, it was not able to sue for the costs in the UK since no separate claim lies for costs under English or Scottish law.[3] What is a revenue law is a matter for the *lex fori*. It has extended to compulsory contributions to a state insurance scheme since a compulsory contribution levied by a state organisation is a revenue matter.[4] A payment for services supplied by the state would however seem to fall outside this definition, at least where there is some choice over whether to accept the services.

---

[1] *Government of India v Taylor* [1955] AC 491, [1955] 1 All ER 292; noted 3 ICLQ 161 & 465; 4 ICLQ 564. See also *Re State of Norway's Application* [1989] 1 All ER 745, [1989] 2 WLR 458, HL.

[2] Section 1(2)(*b*).

[3] *A-G for Canada v William Schulze & Co* 1901 9 SLT 4.

[4] *Metal Industries (Salvage) Ltd v ST Harle (Owners)* 1962 SLT 114 (employer's contribution). But not to matters of exchange control. *Kahler v Midland Bank Ltd* [1950] AC 24, [1949] 2 All ER 621.

33: 02 The principle probably originates in a dictum of Lord Mansfield in 1775[1] when, upholding a vendor's claim for the purchase money due on goods sold in France and which the purchaser intended, to the vendor's knowledge, to smuggle into England, he said that "no country ever takes notice of the revenue laws of another". The proper law of the contract being French, English law was irrelevant.

The principle extends to an indirect attempt to enforce a foreign revenue law as is shown by the Irish decision in *Peter Buchanan Ltd and MacHarg v McVey*.[2] The taxpayer, a director of a Scottish company, had disposed of his shares in two other companies and, after full disclosure to the UK Inland Revenue, was assured that the deal did not involve excess profits levy. Subsequently the levy was retrospectively applied to the taxpayer. He therefore arranged to transfer his stock of whisky and his private assets to safe hands in Ireland, followed his wealth to Ireland and thought that "he might safely snap his hands in the face of the disgruntled Scottish Revenue". The liquidator of Peter Buchanan Ltd, a man admittedly chosen by the Revenue because of his potentialities as a financial Sherlock Holmes, then sued in the Irish courts on the ground that the stripping of the company's assets was *ultra vires* the company and a breach of his duty as director. The action was dismissed on the ground that it was in substance an indirect attempt to enforce the revenue laws of another country. At first instance

Kingsmill Moore J placed some weight on the fact that the Inland Revenue was the only unpaid creditor but this point was not touched on by the Supreme Court of Eire.

---

[1] *Holman v Johnson* (1775) 1 Cowp 341.
[2] [1954] IR 89.

33: 03   The result of the rule is to permit a person to avoid his tax liability to a foreign country by bringing himself and his wealth within the UK. However the rule is that UK courts will not enforce a foreign revenue law not that they will not recognise it. Thus in *Regazzoni v KC Sethia (1944) Ltd* Viscount Simonds said: "It does not follow from the fact that today the court will not enforce a revenue law at the suit of a foreign state that today it will enforce a contract which requires the doing of an act in a foreign country which violates the Revenue laws of that country,"[1] a statement which may limit the initial decision of Lord Mansfield.

More recently the courts have distinguished enforcing the foreign revenue law from enforcing the consequences of that revenue law.

In *Brokaw v Seatrain UK Ltd*[2] household goods were on the high seas on a US ship sailing from Baltimore to England when the US Treasury served a notice of levy on the shipowner and demanded the surrender of all property in their possession. When the ship reached England the US Government claimed possession and the consignees of the goods sued the shipowners in detinue. It was held that the service of the notice of levy was insufficient to reduce the goods into the possession of the US Government and therefore that Government has to rely upon its revenue law to support its claim to possession.

If however the notice of the levy had been sufficient, under English conflict of law rules, to reduce goods into the possession of the US Government, that claim would have been enforced because the English courts would then be enforcing an actual possessory title and not a revenue law.[3] How this can be reconciled with those cases in which the courts have refused indirectly to enforce a revenue law is a difficult matter.[4] Perhaps a proprietary claim cannot be an indirect enforcement whereas a personal claim may be.[5]

The English courts have also held that a person can be extradited for an offence of fraud falling within the relevant treaty even though the fraud relates to a tax matter.[6]

---

[1] [1957] 3 All ER 286 at 292.
[2] [1971] 2 QB 476, [1971] 2 All ER 98.
[3] *Brokaw v Seatrain UK Ltd* 100, 482. Cf. *Singh v Ali* [1960] AC 167, [1960] 1 All ER 269.
[4] *Peter Buchanan Ltd v McVey*, supra, § **34: 02**; see also *Jones v Borland* (1969) 4 SA 29 and *Rossano v Manufacturer's Life Insurance Co Ltd* [1962] 2 All ER 214, [1963] 2 QB 352. If a foreign court made a person bankrupt for non-payment of tax, how far would the UK courts go in deciding the consequences of that status.
[5] Thus if a foreign country holds X liable for Y's tax (cf. TMA 1970, s. 78) can X bring an action on an indemnity against Y in the UK courts? Such a claim succeeded in *Re Reid* (1970) 17 DLR (3d) 199.
[6] *R v Chief Metropolitan Stipendiary Magistrate, ex p Secretary of State for the Home Department* [1989] 1 All ER 151, [1988] 1 WLR 1204, DC.

33: 04 Since a foreign tax law cannot be enforced in the UK courts it follows that it gives rise to no legally enforceable obligation, and it ought in turn to follow that for a trustee to pay such a tax would be a breach of trust. However, in deciding such issues the court must pay attention to the consequences for the trust of non-payment. These points emerge from *Re Lord Cable's Will Trusts, Garret v Waters*.[1] The issue was whether the court should grant an injunction to prevent the passing of money from the UK to trustees in India given that the primary purpose of the payment was to enable the trustees to make payments due under the Indian exchange control legislation. If the payment was not made the trustees were liable to imprisonment and to a penalty of up to five times the sum involved. Slade J refused to grant an injunction.

This leaves various questions open. First, would the position be the same for a tax as for exchange control? The answer appears to be yes, since Slade J went on to consider obiter the position of payments of Indian estate duty.[2] Secondly, would it be a breach of trust for the trustees to pay? The refusal of an injunction to prevent the trustees from paying is not conclusive of this issue; however, Slade J, said that the reimbursement of the trustees from the trust funds in respect of estate duty so paid would be a proper payment.[3] Thirdly, would it be a breach of trust not to pay? The effects for the trust fund would be so drastic that it would appear that the trustee's general duty to preserve the trust fund would require him to pay and so would make it a breach of trust not to pay. However both in relation to this and the second point it must be remembered that this was a case of an Indian trust with funds and trustees in India; had there been no such connection with the country asserting a claim against the trust funds, a different result might have followed as indeed might have been the case if the consequences of non-payment had been minimal.

Other problems arise when a foreign country will regard payment of UK tax as a breach of trust and the present UK trustees are trying to export the trust to that other country.

---

[1] [1976] 3 All ER 417.
[2] At 435–6.
[3] *Loc. cit.*, citing *Re Reid* (1970) 17 DLR (3d) 199 (Canada) and explaining dicta of Lord Robertson in *Scottish National Orchestra Society Ltd v Thomson's Executors* 1969 SLT 325 at 330. This would distinguish the payment of a foreign tax from the payment of a statute barred debt.

Exceptions

33: 05 Under European Community law various levies are now charged by the authorities of the community rather than by the member states.[1] The Commission and the Intervention Board for Agricultural Produce are now given the right to sue in the UK courts.[2] The taxes concerned are[3] (*i*) refunds, interventions and other payments forming part of the European Agriculture Guidance and Guarantee Fund (*ii*) agricultural levies (*iii*) customs duties.

---

[1] See Decision 70/243 (OJ L94/19 1970) and Lipstein, *The Law of the European Economic Communitites*, p. 82.
[2] FA 1977, s. 11.
[3] See Article 128 of the Art of Accession and Directive 76/308 (15 March 1976 OJ L73/18).

33: 06 Most double tax treaties attempt to counter some evasion techniques by providing for the exchange of information. Some treaties, although none involving the UK, actually make provision for the mutual enforcement of tax claims.[1]

---

[1] The experience has not been happy—see 50 Col. L.R. 490. There is no such clause in the UK-US Treaty.

34   Foreign income and capital gains of residents

34: 01   Those resident in the UK may find themselves taxable on overseas income under the following provisions but the extent of liability may be affected by other connecting factors:

Schedule C—securities of foreign states (TA 1988, s. 17).

Schedule D, Case IV—securities outside the UK other than those charged under Schedule C (TA 1988, s. 18).

Case V—possessions out of the UK (TA 1988, s. 18). A special reduction formerly applied if the source was a trade. Where the income is a foreign dividend, TA 1988, s. 123 imposes a system of deduction at source on persons handling the dividend in the UK, e.g. banks but this has been removed if the underlying securities are held in a "recognised clearing system" (TA 1988, s. 123(1)(*b*)).[1]

Case VI—(supra, § **10: 12**) and offshore income gains (infra, § **34: 38**).

Schedule E—(supra, § **6: 03**).

UK residents may be liable to income tax on certain foreign income accruing to non-residents (TA 1988, s. 739), infra, § **34: 24** and TA 1988, s. 775, supra, § **31: 33**).

Corporation tax is levied on the income of the corporation as computed for Schedule D, Cases I to VI on all income arising within the period (TA 1988, s. 70(1)); trading income under Case V is computed under the principles applicable to Case I, that is with no remittance basis and no percentage reductions (TA 1988, s. 70(2)).

Capital gains tax is levied on all gains accruing to a person resident or ordinarily resident in the UK regardless of the location of the asset (CGTA 1979, ss. 2 and 14 infra, § **34: 55**, with a remittance basis for those not domiciled in UK).

---

[1] The conditions for being a recognised clearing system are relaxed by FA 1988, s. 76 (no need to clear Eurobonds). The same provision amends TA 1988, s. 123 and makes UK collecting agents liable to deduct tax on interest or dividends on securities in any recognised clearing system, whether in the UK or not, or when the payment is not made by a UK paying agent.

PLACE OF TRADE—CASE I OR CASE V

34: 02　Profits of a trade carried on wholly overseas are taxable under Schedule D, Case V;[1] profits of a trade carried on partly overseas are taxable under Schedule D, Case I. It is immaterial whether the taxpayer is a sleeping or an active partner in the firm. In *Sulley v A-G*[2] the taxpayer bought goods in the UK for export to America where they were resold by his partners; the trade was carried on wholly overseas, and so was within Case V, not Case I.

It will be more difficult for a sole trader to establish that his trade is carried on wholly overseas. In *Ogilvie v Kitton*[3] the taxpayer who was resident in Aberdeen was the sole owner of a business of woollen warehousemen carried on by his employees in Toronto. He had the sole right to manage and control his business and although that right was not exercised, it could have been. The trade was therefore not wholly overseas.

Where a company wishes to trade overseas, it may do so by direct exporting, by a licensing system or by establishing a branch in the foreign country, or by establishing a foreign subsidiary company.[4] In such instances, the profits will flow back to the UK in the form of dividends, interest,[5] royalty payments and in other forms such as payments for services. The flow can be reversed by loans. The company can thus become an overseas incorporated pocket book.

Simon's Taxes B3.106; B6.221; D4.122.

[1] *Colquhoun v Brooks* (1889) 14 App Cas 493, 2 TC 490, but note explanation by Lord Watson in *San Paulo (Brazilian) Rly Co v Carter* (1895) 3 TC 407 at 411.

[2] (1860) 5 H & N 711, 2 TC 149, n.

[3] (1908) 5 TC 338.

[4] Conversion of a branch into a subsidiary falls within TA 1988, s. 765 and requires Treasury consent; it may also cause a taxable gain to arise (but see TA 1970, s. 268, supra, § **25: 06**).

[5] Loans to overseas subsidiaries have advantages over direct equity investment in that interest, unlike a dividend is generally deductible in computing profits (but note TA 1988, s. 340, supra, § **25: 14**) and it is in general easier to reduce investment by repaying capital than by re-exporting it.

34: 03　Where the resident company sets up a wholly owned subsidiary in the foreign country to carry on a trade there, it is a question of fact whether that subsidiary is carrying on its own trade or is simply acting as agent for its parent's trade.[1] The question is however not concluded by saying that the overseas company is a wholly owned subsidiary[2] and one may not argue that "in substance" the trade is for the parent and so is the parent's trade.[3] The question depends on who manages the trade and not on who owns the shares.[4]

Simon's Taxes B3.107.

[1] *Apthorpe v Peter Schoenhofen Brewing Co Ltd* (1899) 4 TC 41.

[2] *Gramophone and Typewriter Ltd v Stanley* [1908] 2 KB 89, 5 TC 358; and see *Watson v Sandie and Hull* [1898] 1 QB 326, 3 TC 611.

[3] *IRC v Duke of Westminster* [1936] AC 1, 19 TC 490, supra, § **1: 05**.

[4] *Kodak Ltd v Clark* [1903] 1 KB 505, 4 TC 549.

34: 04　A corporation is resident in the UK because its central management and control abides in the UK where it might appear to follow that it cannot trade wholly overseas.[1] In *San Paulo (Brazilian) Rly Co v Carter*,[2] Lord Halsbury said that the place of trade was not the place where the subject matter of the trade was, in that case a railway in Brazil, but where the conduct and management, the head and the brain of the trading adventure was to be found.[3] Despite this the House of Lords held in *Mitchell v Egyptian Hotels Ltd*[4] that a company resident in the UK could be trading wholly abroad. The company was resident in England and carried on the business of hotel proprietors. They so amended their articles of association as to provide for the carrying on of their Egyptian business by a local board[5] in that country which was to be wholly independent of the London board or any other part of the company. The only way in which the London board could have influenced their activities was by controlling the remuneration of the directors in Egypt. The Court of Appeal held that the company was carrying on a trade wholly outside the UK and an evenly divided House of Lords could not reverse that decision.[6] This case must be confined to its special facts. Other cases[7] have shown that regular oversight of the foreign trade will prevent it from being one carried on wholly overseas. It is important that in the facts of the case there was no power directly to control the Egyptian trade. In *Mitchell v B. W. Noble Ltd*[8] control was shared between London and Paris, and it was held that the trade did not fall within Case V.

Where a trade or business is carried on by a partnership and the control and management is abroad, it is deemed to be carried on by a person resident outside the UK.[9] If the partnership trades in, as opposed to with, the UK tax will become due in respect of the profits of that trade as with any other non-resident person, and an assessment can be made on the partnership in the name of any partner resident here.

Simon's Taxes B3.102, 106; B6.221.
  [1] E.g. per Hamilton J in *American Thread Co v Joyce* (1911) 6 TC 1 at 18.
  [2] [1896] AC 31, 3 TC 407.
  [3] Ibid, at 38, 410.
  [4] [1915] AC 1022, 6 TC 542. For a similar result in relation to a trust see *Ferguson v Donovan* [1929] IR 489.
  [5] The Egyptian Board controlled only the Egyptian business per Viscount Cave LC in *Swedish Central Rly Co Ltd v Thompson* [1925] AC 495 at 523–4.
  [6] Mere oversight regularly exercised is sufficient control but merely to have the right to intervene and not to exercise that right is not—per Lord Sumner in *Mitchell v Egyptian Hotels Ltd* [1915] AC 1022 at 1040, 6 TC 542 at 551.
  [7] *San Paulo Brazilian Rly Co v Carter* supra.
  [8] [1927] 1 KB 719, 11 TC 372.
  [9] TA 1988, s. 112 (but not for mixed partnership: TA 1988, s. 115(4)).

SCHEDULE D, CASE IV AND CASE V

34: 05 In general, assessments are made on a preceding year basis, that is on the full amount of the income arising in the year preceding the year of assessment. Interest due but unpaid is neither received, nor accrued and is therefore not taxable[1] so that a payment in respect of several years but made in one year is all income of that year,[2] although concessionary relief is available for retrospective grants or increases in pensions.[3] All income within either of these Cases may be assessed in one sum,[4] where the sum is taxed on a remittance basis the sum remitted in 1988-89 will be used as the measure of taxable income in 1989-90.

Simon's Taxes E1.302, 304; Butterworths Income Tax Service H1.41.
[1] *St Lucia Usines v Taxes Comrs* [1924] AC 508, 4 ATC 112.
[2] *Leigh v IRC* [1925] 1 KB 673, 11 TC 590.
[3] Extra-statutory concession, A55 (1988), **Simon's Taxes, Division H2.2.**
[4] TA 1988, s. 65(4). Before 1926 Case IV was charged on a current year basis and Case V on a three year average, see RC 1955 § 785. An amalgamation of the two Cases now seems a natural development.

34: 06   When income first arises from a source,[1] tax is charged in the same way as for Case III,[2] supra, § **9: 36.**

Income first arises when it arises and not when it first becomes taxable in the UK[3] so that where a person, who has had an overseas source for a number of years, becomes resident in the UK and so liable to income tax on that source, he is not subject to the commencement provisions.

When the source ceases he is chargeable in the year of cessation on the actual income. His income for the year before cessation will be the income arising either in that year or in the preceding year, whichever is the greater.[4]

Where no income accrues from a source in its final two years the cessation provisions are applied, if the taxpayer so elects, to the year in which the income last arose.[5] This has been explained on the basis that the taxpayer is thus relieved of the duty to pay tax in a year in which he receives no income; it is more correctly seen as a device whereby the Revenue, having, when the income first arose, taken the second year's income as the basis for two years, make a realistic adjustment at the end.

The rule just considered required that the source actually cease. A separate rule provides that if the source still exists but no income has arisen for the last six years, there is in effect a deemed cessation in the year when income last arose.[6] A new source is deemed acquired at the end of those six years— just in case income begins to flow again.

Simon's Taxes E1.304–309; Butterworths Income Tax Service H1.43.
[1] TA 1988, s. 66.
[2] This is so even if the foreign source is a trade—there is nothing analogous to TA 1988, s. 60(2)(a), supra.
[3] *Fry v Burma Corpn Ltd* [1930] AC 321, 15 TC 113. *Back v Whitlock* [1932] 1 KB 747, 16 TC 723. On what is a source note *Inchyra v Jennings* [1965] 2 All ER 714, 42 TC 388, cf. supra, § **9: 39.**
[4] TA 1988, s. 67. There will be a deemed cessation if the person previously chargeable under Case IV or V comes within TA 1988, s. 123.
[5] TA 1988, s. 67(1)(c).
[6] TA 1988, s. 67(5).

The Cases

34: 07   Schedule D, Case IV charges income from securities. "Securities" means a debt or claim the payment of which is in some way secured, e.g. a debenture,[1] but the term has been held to extend to a personal guarantee,[2] but not to stocks and shares.

Schedule D, Case V charges income from possessions, a phrase which it has been held includes any source of income,[3] presumably other than securities. A payment under a discretionary trust becomes a possession at least once the trustees have exercised their discretion.[4] A foreign trade is also a possession. So an alimony order by a foreign court is a foreign possession,[5] whereas such an order under a UK court is not foreign even if the payer is now not resident in the UK and pays only out of income not subject to UK tax.[6] Maintenance payments which have a foreign source[7] were taxable income under Schedule D Case V. However the 1988 changes now exclude such a charge.[8] This is regardless of the treatment of the payment under the foreign tax system, i.e. whether or not the payment is taxable to the payee or deductible by the payer. A foreign pension falls within Case V but a foreign employment falls within Schedule E.[9] Certain borrowing on life policies falls within Case V.[10] Interest on a loan to a UK resident to buy property overseas may not be set against the rental income derived from it.[11]

The one remaining difference between Cases IV and V appears to be that expenses are deductible under Case V if they would have been deductible had the source fallen within Case I, but are never deductible under Case IV.[12]

On losses, see extra-statutory concession B25 (1988).[13]

Simon's Taxes B6.201–208; Butterworths Income Tax Service H1.41.

[1] Viscount Cave LC *Singer v Williams* [1921] 1 AC 41 at 49, 7 TC 419 at 431.

[2] *Westminster Bank Executor and Trustee Co (Channel Islands) Ltd v National Bank of Greece* [1971] 1 All ER 233, 46 TC 491, [1969] BTR 415.

[3] *Colquhoun v Brooks* (1889) 14 App Cas 493 at 508 (Lord Herschell) and 514 (Lord MacNaghten). In *IRC v Reid's Trustees* [1949] AC 361 at 371 Lord Simmonds suggested that "income" for Case V might be wider than income for the rest of the Taxes Acts. This seems doubtful but in that case a dividend from a foreign company was held taxable even though a dividend in similar circumstances under the then UK law would have escaped tax. Such a payment is now no income for UK tax law: TA 1988, s. 209, supra, § **24: 02**. *Reid* was applied by the Privy Council in *Bicber v IT Comrs* [1962] 3 All ER 294.

[4] Per Horridge J in *Drummond v Collins* [1913] 3 KB 583 at 594, 6 TC 525 at 532.

[5] *IRC v Anderström* (1928) 13 TC 482; even an agreement to pay. *Chamney v Lewis* (1932) 17 TC 318. On concessional double taxation relief, see extra-statutory concession A12 (1988), **Simon's Taxes Division H2.2.**

[6] *Stokes v Bennett* [1953] 2 All ER 313, 34 TC 337.

[7] The question whether a payment had a foreign source was one of some nicety, however TA 1988, s. 347B directs that a payment is to be a "qualifying maintenance payment" only if it is made by a court in the UK or under a written agreement the proper law of which is the law of a part of the UK.

[8] TA 1988, s. 347A(4).

[9] TA 1988, s. 19.

[10] TA 1988, s. 554(1).

[11] *Ockenden v Mackley* [1982] STC 513.

[12] TA 1988, s. 65(5)(*b*). This is expressed to apply only to the remittance basis; if the arising basis applies, the only guide is TA 1988, s. 65(4) which is less than helpful. Thus if the source is land do the deduction rules under Schedule A or Schedule D, Case I apply? *Quaere* the meaning, if any, to be attached to "abatement", which seems to be a throwback to the 1918 Act. On non-deduction of interest paid as a loan to buy a property for letting; see *Ockenden v Mackley* [1982] STC 513.

[13] **Simon's Taxes Division H2.2.**

Travel expenses

34: 08   An individual who carries on a trade, profession or vocation wholly outside the UK and who therefore falls under Schedule D, Case V but who is not taxable on a remittance basis may claim the deduction of certain travel costs as from 6th April 1984.[1] The allowable expenses are those for travel by the businessman from any place in the UK to any place where the business is carried on or from any such place to any place in the UK and for board and lodging.[2] These rules are similar to those introduced, also by FA 1986, for Schedule E.[3] The similarity is taken further in that the Schedule D, Case V rules allow also for the deduction of the costs of travel for a spouse and child under 18.[4] In these cases the taxpayer's absence from the UK must be wholly and exclusively for the purpose of performing the function of the trade, profession or vocation or those of some other business, with apportionment between the different businesses.

Where there are two or more overseas locations the taxpayer may deduct the cost of travel from one to the other; of the two at least one must satisfy the rules, i.e. be a Schedule D, Case V source in respect of which an arising basis of assessment is used.[5] The absence from the UK must still be wholly and exclusively for the purpose of performing the functions of both activities and he must actually perform those functions at each location. The deduction is put against the trade carried on at the destination unless it is outside these rules in which case the place of departure is taken instead. Where there are two businesses at the place of destination or departure apportionment is carried out.

---

[1] TA 1988, s. 80.
[2] TA 1988, s. 80(2).
[3] Supra, § **6: 11** but not identical, e.g. there is no need for separate reimbursement (there is no one to do the reimbursing).
[4] TA 1988, s. 80(5)–(8).
[5] TA 1988, s. 81.

Is it income?—The role of foreign law

34: 09   The question whether a particular payment is income arising from security or possession is a question for UK tax law but that question must be determined according to the legal nature of the rights arising from the security or possession under the foreign law. In *Archer-Shee v Garland*[1] a tenant for life was entitled under a New York trust and the issue was whether money to which the taxpayer was entitled, was income "from stock and securities",[2] the alternative view being that a tenant for life had only a right to see that the property was correctly administered by the trustees. By English law the former had already been held to be correct[3] but, on evidence being presented that by New York law the latter was correct, the House of Lords held that the rights of the beneficiary could not be said to be income arising "from stocks and shares". Since the UK tax liability turned on the nature of that foreign right, foreign law was relevant in determining that right.

The quality of the receipt must be determined according to the legal rights of the taxpayer, but UK tax rules must then be applied to those rights. So in

Rae v Lazard Investment Co Ltd[4] a distribution in partial liquidation, a process known to Maryland law but not to UK company laws was a payment of capital.[5] By contrast in *Inchyra v Jennings*[6] a direction in an American trust that a beneficiary should receive 1% of the trust capital each year was held to create annual payments[7] and so income for UK tax law.

Simon's Taxes B6.203, 208; E1.315; Butterworths Income Tax Service H1.41.
[1] [1931] AC 212, 15 TC 693.
[2] See Income Tax Act 1918, Schedule D, Case IV, Rule 1.
[3] *Baker v Archer-Shee* [1927] AC 844, 11 TC 749, supra, § **11: 06**.
[4] (1963) 41 TC 1, noted [1963] BTR 121 (JGM).
[5] To the same effect *Courtaulds Investments Ltd v Fleming* [1969] 3 All ER 1281, 46 TC 111.
[6] [1965] 2 All ER 714, 42 TC 388.
[7] Supra, § **11: 12**. Cf. *Lawson v Rolfe* [1970] 1 All ER 761, 46 TC 199, [1970] BTR 142 (JGM).

THE REMITTANCE BASIS

34: 10   If income is taxed on a remittance basis it is taxed not as it arises but only as it is received by the taxpayer in the UK and then on the preceding year basis. Before 1914[1] all income accruing to a resident from a foreign source, that is one wholly outside the UK, was taxed on a remittance basis. In 1914 the arising basis was applied to income from stocks, shares and rents and this was extended in 1940[2] to a few remaining categories of investment income such as income on foreign bank deposits and income arising to beneficiaries under foreign trusts.[3] In 1974 the remittance basis was effectively abolished for residents although it remains of importance to those who are not domiciled in the UK or who, being British subjects or citizens of the Republic of Ireland are not ordinarily resident here. Further, even the remittance may be exempt from UK tax under a double tax treaty.[4]

The remittance basis does not apply to trading income of corporations.[5] However if a foreign trade is run through a subsidiary company resident in that other country, the profits will not be taxed in the UK until they are transferred to this country as dividends, interest or royalty payments.[6]

Simon's Taxes E1.312; Butterworths Income Tax Service H1.51.
[1] FA 1914, s. 5.
[2] FA 1940, s. 19—as recommended by RC 1920 § 27.
[3] Thus undoing *Archer-Shee v Garland,* supra, § **34: 09**.
[4] *Lord Strathalmond v IRC* [1972] 3 All ER 715, 48 TC 537.
[5] TA 1988 s. 70(2).
[6] Debt is usually easier to repatriate than equity—see Edwardes-Ker, *International Tax Strategy,* chap. 21, p. 7.

34: 11   Other systems showed special favour to overseas profits by perhaps exempting them in whole or in part, for example France and Eire, or by arranging their double taxation treaties so that overseas profits were taxable only in the country where they arose. Since 1974 in those situations in which the remittance basis has been abolished, that is for residents, the UK system has gone for percentage reductions, 100%, 50%, 25% or 10% in the amount falling to be taxed but these reductions have been largely removed as a result of the general lowering of tax rates.

Where the remittance basis applies the sum received must be received as the income of the recipient in the UK that is it must be income according to UK tax law, it must be received in the UK, by the taxpayer. In deciding whether it is income it is essential that the source of the income should still exist.

The remittance basis only applies to certain types of person and to certain types of income. It applies to income within Schedule D, Cases IV and V only if the taxpayer satisfies the Board that he is not domiciled in the UK or, that being a British subject or a citizen of the Republic of Ireland he is not ordinarily resident in the UK,[1] but it does not apply to sources in Eire.[2] It also applies to Schedule E, Case III, supra, § **6: 14**.

Simon's Taxes E1.312.
[1] TA 1988, s. 65(4).
[2] TA 1988, s. 68.

What is a remittance?

34: 12   There is no uniform definition of a remittance. Where the remittance basis applies, income tax is levied under Schedule D, Case IV, on the full amount of the sums received in the UK.[1] No deductions are allowed under Case IV.

Where the remittance basis applies and tax is levied under Schedule D, Case V, tax is levied not only on actual sums received from remittances payable in the UK but also actual sums received from property imported or from money or value arising from property not imported or from money or value so received on credit or on account in respect of any such remittances, property, money or value brought or to be brought into the UK.[2] Like Case IV, Case V requires that actual sums be received in the UK.[3] It follows that if foreign income were converted into a car which was then brought into the UK, no liability would arise under the remittance basis. If, however, the car were then sold, the proceeds might be taxable.[4] If by that time the source has been extinguished, or he had given the car to someone else, the proceeds will not be taxable.[5] For income falling within Schedule E, Case III, it is provided[6] that emoluments shall be treated as received in the UK if they are paid, used or enjoyed in or in any manner or form transmitted or brought to the UK. It is clearly contemplated that this would be parallel to TA 1988, s. 65(5) since TA 1988, s. 123(5) also provides that s. 65(6)–(9) shall apply to s. 123(5) as it applies for the purposes of s. 65(5). However the wording is much wider and s. 123(5) clearly contemplates the possibility of transmission in kind while s. 65(5) does not. Nor can s. 123(5) be confined to emoluments received in kind but which have not altered their form. The point remains untested by litigation. The position under Schedule E Case III is now that the ending of the source will not preclude liability.[7]

Simon's Taxes E1.315, 316; Butterworths Income Tax Service H1.52.
[1] TA 1988, s. 65(5)(*a*). On valuation and the time at which the exchange rate should be applied see *Magraw v Lewis* (1933) 18 TC 222 and *Payne v Deputy Federal Comr of Taxation* [1936] AC

497, [1936] 2 All ER 793. On negligence liability of intermediaries see *Schioler v Westminster Bank Ltd* [1970] 2 QB 719, [1970] 3 All ER 177.
[2] These instances are illustrations and are *not* exhaustive *per* Lord Radcliffe in *Thomson v Moyse* [1960] 3 All ER 684 at 692, 39 TC 291 at 335.
[3] TA 1988, s. 65(5)(*b*).
[4] In the year in which the car was sold. *Scottish Provident Institution v Farmer* (1912), 6 TC 34.
[5] *Bray v Best* [1989] 1 All ER 969, [1989] STC 159, HL.
[6] TA 1988, s. 132(5). This was a decision under Schedule E Case I and involved no international element. It has since been reversed by legislation—FA 1929 s. 36(3).
[7] FA 1989 s. 36(3); on transitional relief see s. 39.

Income of the taxpayer

34: 13   To be taxable the money must have the character of income of the taxpayer when it is remitted to this country. The mere arrival of the money will not be sufficient if it has been the subject of a complete and irrevocable gift to someone else before it arrives. In *Carter v Sharon*,[1] the taxpayer arranged for a banker's draft to be sent to her daughter from California. It was shown that by Californian law the gift was complete not later than when the draft was posted; the money therefore was not a remittance of income to the taxpayer. Had the mother simply sent her daughter a cheque drawn on her California bank account the money when it arrived in England would still have been the taxpayer's since she could have revoked the cheque.[2] The question of the effectiveness of the gift is judged according to the foreign law.

[1] [1936] 1 All ER 720, 20 TC 229. Cf. *Thomson v Bensted* (1918) 7 TC 137.
[2] As in *Timpson's Executors v Yerbury* [1936] 1 All ER 186, 20 TC 155.

34: 14   Another situation in which income altered its character before it arrived in this country was *Timbrell v Lord Aldenham's Executors*[1] where a London firm was a partner in a firm in Australia and in another firm in Chile. The Australian firm had made a profit and the Chilean firm a loss which the London firm had to meet. Money due to the London firm from the Australian profits was transmitted to Chile to discharge the debt of the Chilean firm to the London firm, a process involving the eventual arrival of the money in London. It was held that what arrived was not income from Australia but the payment of a debt from Chile.

[1] (1947) 28 TC 293.

34: 15   If the taxpayer has both capital and income abroad and remits only capital, there will be no charge to tax.[1] The same result follows if he has both taxed and untaxed income abroad[2] (taxed meaning either that the income is taxed on an arising basis or that in some other way UK tax has been paid) and only the taxed income is remitted. One major problem is that of proof. There is no rule that if there is foreign income and remittances from abroad then the Revenue can tax the foreign income by assuming that the remittances are of income.[3] It is a question of fact in every case. The mere fact that the taxpayer's foreign bank account is overdrawn is not sufficient to show that money remitted from the account is capital.[4] In *Walsh v Randall*[2] it was held that a taxpayer could not convert what was undoubtedly income into capital simply by investing it. If he sells his investment and then remits the proceeds to this country he is treated as remitting income[5] even though by the tax law of the foreign country he is taxable in respect of a capital gain.

Simon's Taxes E1.315.
[1] *Kneen v Martin* [1935] 1 KB 499, 19 TC 33 (separate accounts in USA for income and capital).
[2] *Walsh v Randall* (1940) 23 TC 55 at 56, para. 3; p. 57, para. 7 of the Case Stated. For another example but in a different context see *IRC v McNaught's Executors* (1964) 42 TC 71.
[3] *Kneen v Martin* supra, per Finlay J at 43. The point was not even argued in CA, but cf. capital gains tax, infra, § **34: 52.**
[4] *Fellowes-Gordon v IRC* (1935) 19 TC 683.
[5] *Patuck v Lloyd* (1944) 26 TC 284.

Remittance of money

34: 16 Considerable difficulty has been experienced in deciding what is a remittance of money. Clearly it is not necessary to have a receipt of coins; equally the mere entry of a sum of money in a balance sheet is not generally a remittance if the actual funds remain outside the UK.[1]

If sums received here are derived from the application of income overseas which is taxable on a remittance basis, there is a remittance.[2] This may take the form of a loan. So there was a remittance in *Harmel v Wright*[3] where the taxpayer had funds overseas with which he bought shares in a company which he controlled, that company made an interest free loan to an independent company which in turn made a loan to the taxpayer in the UK. It was important in that case that the sums could be quite clearly traced through the different transactions.

Simon's Taxes E1.316.
[1] *Gresham Life Assurance Society v Bishop* [1902] AC 287, 4 TC 464.
[2] Per Lord Radcliffe in *Thomson v Moyse* [1960] 3 All ER 684 at 688 and 39 TC 291 at 331.
[3] [1974] STC 88, [1974] 1 All ER 945.

34: 17 Particular difficulty was experienced when a taxpayer with funds overseas taxable on a remittance basis borrowed money in the UK and the loan was then repaid from the fund overseas. The problem is whether the economic value accruing to the taxpayer results from the receipt of income in the UK or the export of a debt from the UK. There has been statutory intervention to widen or render certain the scope of remittance when the taxpayer is ordinarily resident in the UK,[1] but taxpayers who are not ordinarily resident must rely on the old case law. The cause of the difficulty has been a confusion of two distinct questions, has there been a remittance and has there been a remittance of income, but this has been compounded by a basic uncertainty in applying the physical notion of a receipt to the metaphysical notion of money.

In *IRC v Gordon*[2] the taxpayer, a partner in a firm carrying on business in Ceylon, had an account with the Colombo branch of a bank which had its head office in London. He came to the UK and opened an account at the head office. He was allowed to overdraw his account and the overdrafts were transferred to Colombo as they reached £500. At the Colombo branch the overdrafts were converted into rupees and were satisfied by periodic payments into the account from the Ceylon firm. The House of Lords held that there was no remittance payable in the UK; no property had been imported here and there had been no receipt in the UK of sums from money or value arising from property not imported. Lord Cohen summarised the case, "It is plain that the income receipts of the respondent were all received in Ceylon. It is plain that the monies he received in London were advances of capital. There is no finding that the advances were made on credit or on account or in respect of income in Ceylon which it was intended should be brought to London."[3]

Simon's Taxes E1.316.

[1] TA 1988, s. 65(6)–(9).
[2] [1952] 1 All ER 866, 33 TC 226 and see *Hall v Marians* (1935) 19 TC 582.
[3] [1952] 1 All ER 866 at 874, 33 TC 226 at 242.

34: 18   Legislation was enacted in 1953, now TA 1988, s. 65(6) to (9), to counteract the decision in *IRC v Gordon*. This provided that income arising from securities or possessions outside the UK which was applied outside the UK in or towards the satisfaction of a debt for money lent in the UK or of a debt for money lent out of the UK but received in or brought to the UK should be treated as received in the UK. The same result is to follow if a loan is made outside the UK and the debt is discharged before the money is brought in or received here.[1] What is received is the amount applied in the discharge of the debt. The date will be the date of discharge or, where the loan is discharged first, the date on which the money is received or brought into the UK.

There is also a remittance if income of the debtor is held by the creditor and is available for payment of the debt or reducing it by set-off. But for this provision it might be argued that such money was not "applied by" the taxpayer in discharging the debt. The rule only applies when there is some relation between the loan and the holding.

This complex provision is confined to those ordinarily resident in the UK. In general it does not treat the loan itself as the remittance but only its discharge; purchase money left outstanding is not spent.

In *Thomson v Moyse*[2] the taxpayer had income in a New York bank account which had arisen from a family trust. He drew a cheque on that account in favour of a bank in the UK. This was treated as the sale of the cheque to the UK bank. Under the Exchange Control Act the bank then sold the cheque to the Bank of England and received the sterling equivalent. The Bank of England then transmitted the cheque to New York where it was cleared and the proceeds credited to the account of the Bank of England with the Federal Reserve Bank of the US. The House of Lords held that the sterling equivalents received by the taxpayer in London were assessable under Case IV as sums received in the UK and under Case V as actual sums received in the UK from money or value arising from property not imported.[3]

For Lord Radcliffe income was brought into this country not only if dollar notes were physically brought within the jurisdiction but also by the effecting of its transmission from one country to another by whatever means the agencies of commerce or finance may make available for that purpose.[4] The fact that the person to whom the taxpayer gave the cheque would take it to

New York for clearing was therefore irrelevant. The case was analogous to that of one who having foreign income turned that income into property, brought the property to this country and sold it here.[5]

Simon's Taxes E1.316.
[1] TA 1988, s. 65(7); as where UK debts are paid abroad with a foreign credit card.
[2] [1960] 3 All ER 684, 39 TC 291.
[3] TA 1988, s. 65(5)(*b*).
[4] [1960] 3 All ER at 690, 39 TC at 333.
[5] Ibid, and per Walton J in *IRC v Montgomery* [1975] STC 182 at 188.

34: 19   It is not at all clear whether *IRC v Gordon* can now be relied upon. In *Thomson v Moyse* Lord Cohen, who had given the leading speech in *IRC v Gordon*, distinguished that case.[1] In *Gordon* monies received by the taxpayer in London were advances of capital. There was no nexus between the loan and the income receipt in Ceylon. There had been no finding of fact that the payments were made on credit or on account or in respect of the income in Ceylon. In the present case by contrast when the taxpayer drew a cheque on his New York account and sold it to his bank there was a remittance of income. Lord Radcliffe after doubting the findings of fact in *Gordon* and stating that the legislature had intervened to reverse the decision, opined that "it would be a mistake to build any principles upon the basis of [that decision]".[2] Lord Denning thought that he need not say much since the decisions had been reversed by Parliament, and they could no longer be regarded as of binding authority nor could the reasons on which they were based.[3] For Lord Reid too the cases would have caused considerable difficulty were it not for the fact that by reason of legislation they were no longer good law.[4] He added however that the cases were distinguishable although without explaining this comment.

These reasons are in certain respects shocking. At a time when the House was bound by its own decisions, the members felt that they could disregard their earlier decision because of the subsequent legislation even though the statute in question related only to years of assessment subsequent to that with which they were dealing. One of the distinctions between the judiciary and the legislature is the right of the legislature to overrule prospectively,[5] a power not shared by the judiciary. Yet the House turned a prospective provision of the legislature into a retrospective decree of the judiciary. Even this might have been forgivable if the House had not been in fundamental error in supposing that the legislation did in all cases reverse *IRC v Gordon* whereas in truth the reversal only affected those ordinarily resident in the UK.

Simon's Taxes E1.316.
[1] [1960] 3 All ER at 688, 39 TC at 339.
[2] [1960] 3 All ER at 694, 39 TC, at 337 (with whom Viscount Simonds agreed).
[3] [1960] 3 All ER at 699, 39 TC at 342.
[4] [1960] 3 All ER at 688, 39 TC at 331.
[5] Cf. Viscount Simonds in *John Hudson & Co Ltd v Kirkness* [1955] AC 696 at 713, 36 TC 28 at 63, and Upjohn J in *Jennings v Kinder* [1958] 1 All ER 369 at 376 E.

Avoiding remittance liability

34: 20   Avoidance methods are many. Obviously the money can be used abroad free of income tax, for example to finance overseas holidays. A change of employment will mean the ending of a source and so the avoidance of tax if the money is brought in the following year.

Thus if a taxpayer domiciled abroad earns $10,000 overseas and brings it back with him into the UK, he will be held to have remitted the income and so be taxable. If, however, he makes a gift of that income to his wife before they return to the UK, the money will not be taxable since none of his income is remitted and what is remitted is not his income.

A loan taken out before arrival in the UK will escape TA 1988, ss. 65(6)–(9) and 123(5) if paid off after leaving this country. An employer may perhaps guarantee the loan.[1]

Simon's Taxes E1.316; Butterworths Income Tax Service H1.52.
[1] See *Newstead v Frost* [1980] STC 123, [1980] 1 All ER 363.

Foreign trade or profession

34: 21   A trade or profession carried on partly in the UK and partly overseas is taxable under Schedule D, Case I or II. From 1978–79 to 1983–84 a reduction of 25% was made in computing taxable profits but this only applied to that proportion of the profits which could be attributed to the foreign part of the business.[1] In 1984–85 the reduction was $12\frac{1}{2}\%$ and for 1985–86 and later years this reduction is abolished.[2] The rules remain of importance for 1985–86 and later years because trading losses, capital allowances and stock relief arising between 1978–79 and 1983–84 were also restricted by 25% or $12\frac{1}{2}\%$ and only those losses as so reduced are available for loss relief.[3] There is no restriction for losses sustained after 5th April 1984.[4]

Simon's Taxes E1.346; Butterworths Income Tax Service H1.31–H1.33.
[1] FA 1978, s. 27 and Sch. 4.
[2] FA 1984, s. 30.
[3] TA 1988, Schs. 29 and 30 (preserving FA 1974, s. 23(2), (3) and FA 1981, Sch. 9, para 35 as amended by FA 1984, s. 30(4) and (5) respectively).
[4] Ibid.

RELIEF FOR UNREMITTABLE FOREIGN INCOME

34: 22   Tax is postponed where income taxed on an arising basis, whether in full or on a reduced sum, cannot be remitted, whether because of laws, executive action or the impossibility of obtaining foreign currency, and the taxpayer has not realised the income outside the territory for a consideration either in sterling or in a currency which could be convered into sterling.[1] The export to this country of an object paid for with the foreign currency will not end the relief at least until it is sold; nor apparently will the spending of the income within the foreign country. The taxpayer must show to the satisfaction of the Board[2] that he could not remit it despite reasonable endeavours on his part. When this can no longer be shown he, or his estate, is assessable to income tax, which will be assessed by reference to the year it first arose.

Simon's Taxes E1.311; Butterworths Income Tax Service H1.53.
[1] FA 1953, s. 21; TA 1988, s. 584; see RC 1952 Cmd. 8761 1st Report. Distinguish the situation where the income although due has not been paid.
[2] Appeal lies to the Special Commissioners.

34: 23 Where the unremittable foreign income is taxable on a remittance basis, a different question arises. The tax liability is inevitably postponed until the income is actually remitted but then the tax may be much higher by reason of the sudden remittance of the income of several years. When the income becomes remittable it is chargeable, if the taxpayer so elects, by reference to the year it *arose*. If for some reason no liability is incurred in the year the income arose, as where the taxpayer was not then resident, no tax is due.[1]

Simon's Taxes E1.313.
[1] TA 1988, s. 585(3), (4).

TRANSFERS OF ASSETS ABROAD—ATTRIBUTION OF INCOME

TA 1988, ss. 739 and 740

34: 24 The taxation of residents coupled with the non-taxation of non-residents might encourage residents to arrange for income which would otherwise come to them to be held by non-residents and especially by such artificial entities as trusts[1] and companies. Most Schedules take account of such obvious devices as employing a non-resident to act as trustee for a resident.[2] However a further provision was introduced in 1936 (now TA 1988, s. 739) to counter devices whereby assets would be transferred to persons resident or domiciled outside the UK in whose hands the income would either not be taxed at all by the UK or would be taxed only on a remittance basis, and some benefit of that income would or might accrue to the original resident. In practice, TA 1988, s. 739 has not been used where large public companies are involved. Where income accrued to the foreign person that income can be attributed to the transferor if he has a power to enjoy the income—TA 1988, s. 739(2)—or receives a capital sum—s. 739(3). The question whether a transfer has been made by a particular person is one of fact.[3]

Where the person with the power to enjoy or in receipt of the capital sum is not the transferor or his spouse s. 739 does not apply. This was held by the House of Lords in *Vestey v IRC*[4] the primary reason being the absence of any provision in the section whereby the income of the foreign entity could be appropriately attributed to the beneficiaries and a reluctance on the part of the court to allow that attribution to be carried out simply by revenue discretion. So in *IRC v Pratt*[5] the court held that s. 739 did not apply to multiple transfers if the respective interests of the assets transferred could not be separated and clearly identified.

TA 1988, s. 740 (see § **34: 37**) is designed to fill the resulting gap by making persons other than the transferor or his spouse liable when and to the extent that they receive a benefit which is not otherwise chargeable to income tax.

Simon's Taxes E1.751, 752; Butterworths Income Tax Service A7.71, 72, 77.
    [1] E.g. *Astor v Perry* [1935] AC 398, 19 TC 255.
    [2] E.g. TA 1988, ss. 47(1) and 48(2).
    [3] *IRC v Pratt* [1982] STC 756, 57 TC 1.
    [4] [1980] AC 1148, [1980] STC 10, reversing the earlier House of Lords decision in *Congreve v IRC* [1948] 1 All ER 948, 30 TC 163.
    [5] [1982] STC 756.

34: 25   TA 1988, s. 739(2) applies where there has been a transfer of assets, and charges any individual[1] who has, by virtue of the transfer or any associated operations, the power to enjoy income which in consequence of the transfer becomes that of a person resident or domiciled outside the UK. Such income is deemed to be that of the person with the power to enjoy and is taxed under Schedule D, Case VI. The concept of income becoming payable to a non-resident is wide enough to include the profits of a non-resident trader.[2]

Simon's Taxes E1.753; Butterworths Income Tax Service A7.72.
    [1] I.e. the transferor or his spouse TA 1988, s. 742(9); but not a widow: *Vestey's Executors v IRC* [1949] 1 All ER 1108, 31 TC 1.
    [2] *IRC v Brackett* [1986] STC 521.

34: 26   TA 1988, s. 739(3) applies where there is a transfer of assets and whether before or after the transfer an individual ordinarily resident in the UK receives a capital sum. This sum must be connected with the transfer and be either (1) a sum paid or payable by way of loan[1] or (2) any other sum paid or payable otherwise than as income and which is not paid or payable for full consideration in money or money's worth. Thus this does not apply where a resident simply sells assets for full market value to a non-resident.

The term capital sum is widened to cover sums paid to third parties at the direction of the individual or by assignment from him and sums received jointly.[2] Where however there is a capital sum as defined, the income accruing from the assets to the person outside the UK is deemed to be that of the individual who received the capital sums; this is narrower than s. 739(1). This is so whether or not he has the "power to enjoy" since in economic terms he already has that power thanks to the capital sum. It will be noticed that tax under this section is not limited to the capital sum[3] but goes on for ever— or at least for the duration of the life of the individual or so long as income accrues to the non-resident.

Simon's Taxes E1.754; Butterworths Income Tax Service A7.75.
    [1] Unless wholly repaid before the beginning of the year; TA 1988, s. 739(6). Leaving money outstanding on a purchase is not a loan: *Ramsden v IRC* (1957) 37 TC 619.
    [2] TA 1988, s. 739(5).
    [3] *Vestey v IRC* [1980] AC 1148, [1980] STC 10.

Defences

34: 27   Neither of these provisions will apply if the individual shows[1] to the satisfaction of the Board that (1) the purpose of avoiding tax liability was not the purpose or one of the purposes[2] for which the transfer or associated operations were made or (2) that the transfer was a bona fide commercial transaction and not designed for the purpose of avoiding liability to taxation.[3] This was one of the first legislative attempts at an anti-avoidance clause; later clauses prefer references to objects over those to purposes.[4] The defence in (1) will not apply if one among many purposes was the saving of tax.[5] Today this seems very hard to satisfy as judges have come to expect taxpayers to take tax matters into account, supra, § 31: 32; moreover where someone other than the transferor is involved it may be very difficult to establish what the purposes of the perhaps now deceased transferor were.[6] Further the meaning of "avoidance" is unclear[7] although the courts have applied s. 739 despite a plea by the taxpayer that he would be taxed on the income eventually.[8] The test of purpose is to be applied only to the transfer in question; it is not clear whether a subsequent tax-induced associated operation may infect the initial transfer.[9] Taxation includes taxes other than income tax, e.g. death duties[10] but, it appears, not foreign taxes.[11] The burden is on the taxpayer to bring himself within the defence. There is no formal clearance procedure.

Simon's Taxes E1.753.

[1] On importance of burden of proof on the taxpayer, see *Philippi v IRC* [1971] 3 All ER 61, 47 TC 75.

[2] The 1936 test was one of the main purposes but this was amended in 1938; contrast e.g. TA 1988, s. 703 and CGTA 1979, s. 26.

[3] TA 1988, s. 741.

[4] E.g. TA 1988, s. 776(2). Cf. cases on TA 1988, s. 703, supra, § 31: 31.

[5] *Cottinghams's Executors v IRC* [1938] 3 All ER 560, 22 TC 344.

[6] *MacDonald v IRC* [1940] 1 K B 802, 23 TC 449.

[7] See *Page v Lowther* [1983] STC 799.

[8] Such difficulties did not hinder the court unduly in *Philippi v IRC*, supra.

[9] But, *semble*, not—*IRC v Herdman* [1969] 1 All ER 495, 45 TC 394. On the other hand note Salmon LJ in *Philippi v IRC* (1971) 47 TC 75 at 113–114.

[10] *Sassoon v IRC* (1943) 25 TC 154.

[11] *IRC v Herdman*, supra.

Elements

34: 28   (1) For both provisions there must be a transfer of assets or operations associated with the transfer. Further the income accruing to the non-resident must accrue by virtue of or in consequence of that transfer or those operations.[1] It is not necessary that the income should come from the transferred assets. The situs of the assets is unimportant. The term asset is defined to include property or rights of any kind[2] and has been construed in a way similar to that for CGT (supra, § 15: 01). It therefore includes rights under a contract of employment.[3] The term transfer is defined to include the creation of rights or property.[4]

¹ See *Vestey's Executors v IRC* [1949] 1 All ER 1108, 31 TC 1 and infra, § **34: 31**.
² TA 1988, s. 742(9)(*b*).
³ *IRC v Brackett* [1986] STC 521.
⁴ TA 1988, s. 742(9)(*b*).

34: 29   (2) For both provisions the transferee must be either not resident or not domiciled in the UK when the income accrues, regardless of his residence when the transfer is made.¹ Whether they apply if the transferor becomes ordinarily resident only after the transfer is not completely clear, but it is unlikely that they apply.²

Simon's Taxes E1.755; Butterworths Income Tax Service A7.73.
¹ *Congreve v IRC* [1946] 2 All ER 170, 30 TC 163.
² But in pre-*Vestey* days a person within s. 739(2) who acquired UK ordinary residence after the transfer was caught. *IRC v Herdman* [1969] 1 All ER 495, 45 TC 394.

34: 30   (3) For both provisions the associated operations may be by the transferor or the transferee or any other person.¹ The scope of an "associated operation" is very widely defined in s. 742(1), as operations of any kind effected by any person in relation to any of the assets, or income or assets representing those assets or that income. Thus the transfer of shares or a partnership to a company,² taking up residence or domicile overseas,³ an exchange of debentures⁴ and the making of a will have all been held to be associated operations, but not the death of a testator.⁵ Whether debentures are associated is a question of fact.⁶

Simon's Taxes E1.754; Butterworths Income Tax Service A7.72, 73.
¹ E.g. *Lord Chetwode v IRC* [1977] STC 64, [1977] 1 All ER 638.
² *Latilla v IRC* [1943] 1 All ER 265, 25 TC 107.
³ *Congreve v IRC* [1946] 2 All ER 170, 30 TC 163.
⁴ *Earl Beatty's Executors v IRC* (1940) 23 TC 574.
⁵ *Bambridge v IRC* [1955] 3 All ER 812, 36 TC 313 (intestate succession).
⁶ *Corbett's Executrices v IRC* [1943] 2 All ER 218, 25 TC 305.

34: 31   (4) For s. 739(2) there has to be a power to enjoy income. This requirement is satisfied if any of the following sets of circumstances exist.¹

(*a*) The income is in fact so dealt with by any person as to be calculated, at some point of time and whether in the form of income or not, to enure for the benefit of the individual.
"So dealt with" denotes activity.²

(*b*) The receipt or accrual of the income operates to increase the value to the individual of assets held by him or for his benefit.³

The income need not be received by the transferor; but it must increase the value of his assets, as where an individual resident transferred assets to a non-resident company in return for promissory notes, income subsequently accruing to the company increased the value of the notes.³ Moreover where a vendor transferred shares to a company but left the purchase money outstanding it was held that he had the power to enjoy the income accruing to the company in the form of dividends since the income of the company increased by the value of the right to recover the debt.⁴ This seems open to question at least where the company could always meet its obligations—but s. 742(3) directs attention to substance not form.

(c) The individual receives or is entitled to receive, at any time any benefit provided or to be provided out of that income or out of moneys that are or will be available for the purpose by reason of the effect or successive effects of the associated operations on that income and on any assets which directly or indirectly represent that income.

This turns on actual receipt or entitlement to receipt by the transferor. The possession of shares in a company gives a right to any dividends that may be declared.[5] There is some doubt whether loans fall within (c).[6]

In *IRC v Brackett*[7] the benefits provided included the provision of liquidity through the purchase of assets he could not otherwise dispose of easily, the provision of money for repairs he could not otherwise afford and the payment of money in discharge of his moral obligations. These were held sufficient for (c).

(d) The individual may, in the event of the exercise or successive exercise of one or more powers by whomsoever exercisable and whether with or without the consent of any other persons, become entitled to the beneficial enjoyment of the income.

This provision is designed to apply where foreign trustees of a discretionary trust own shares in an overseas company controlled by persons other than the trustees.[8] The term "power" is undefined—and therefore unlimited.

(e) The individual is able in any manner whatsoever, and whether directly or indirectly, to control the application of the income.

For this, it will be noted, he need not control the application for his own benefit! A right to control investments is not a right to control the application of the income. Control of a company gives control over income through control over the directors.[9] However the donee of a special power of appointment among a defined and ascertainable group of persons does not have the power required for this head,[10] a decision since extended to the donee of an intermediate power, that is a power to appoint among the whole world subject to the exclusion of a defined class of persons which included the donee.[11] Where a settlor has a power to appoint and remove trustees it should not be assumed that the trustees will disregard their fiduciary duties and simply act as the settlor directs.

As if these provisions (a)–(e) were not wide enough it is further provided that, when these tests are applied, regard is to be had to the substantial results and effects of the transfer or the operations and all benefits accruing as a result of the transfer are to be taken into account regardless of the nature or form of the benefits and whether or not he had any rights.[12] This clause was intended to counteract the Cayman Islands legislation[13] reducing the legal character of interests of beneficiaries under trusts subject to Cayman Island law to that of mere *spes*.

Simon's Taxes E1.755–757; Butterworths Income Tax Service A7.74.
  [1] TA 1988, s. 742(2).
  [2] Per Lord Simonds in *Lord Vestey's Executors v IRC* [1949] 1 All ER 1108, 31 TC 1 at 68.

³ See *Lord Howard de Walden v IRC* [1942] 1 KB 389, 25 TC 121.
⁴ *Ramsden v IRC* (1957) 37 TC 619; *Earl Beatty's Executors v IRC* (1940) 23 TC 574.
⁵ *Lee v IRC* (1941) 24 TC 207.
⁶ See Lord Normand in *Lord Vestey's Executors v IRC* (1949) 31 TC 1 at 90. Another problem concerns s. 743(4) which directs that the individual within s. 742(2)(c) is to be charged on the whole of the amount or value of the benefit received save in so far as he has already been charged to tax for that on a previous year of assessment. *Quaere* whether this extends to accumulations of income—the reason against liability being that no liability would accrue if the transaction had no foreign element. But for liability it may be argued that (1) income of an English accumulation trust is charged to income tax and (2) income has been taxed within Schedule D, Case V even though domestic equivalents would have escaped—see *Reid v IRC* (1926) 10 TC 673.
⁷ [1986] STC 521.
⁸ IHTA 1984 s.204(5).
⁹ *Lee v IRC* (1941) 24 TC 207.
¹⁰ *Vestey's Executors v IRC* [1949] 1 All ER 1108.
¹¹ *IRC v Schroder* [1983] STC 480.
¹² TA 1988, s. 472(3).
¹³ Cayman Islands Trust Act 1967, s. 75(3)—all rights were vested in the Registrar of Trusts.

34: 32   (5) The fact that the resident has no power to enjoy the income of the transferee is not conclusive; the section asks whether he has the power to enjoy any income of any person; so control over the transferee is sufficient.[1]

¹ *Earl Beatty's Executors v IRC* (1940) 23 TC 574 at 590.

34: 33   (6) The Board has the most extensive power to demand information[1] in applying this section both from the transferor and any other person. There is some protection for solicitors[2] and bankers.[3]

Simon's Taxes E1.766; Butterworths Income Tax Service A7.79–A7.81.
¹ TA 1988, s. 745(1)—e.g. *Clinch v IRC* [1973] 1 All ER 977, 49 TC 52.
² TA 1988, s. 745(3).
³ TA 1988, s. 745(4). Strictly construed in *Royal Bank of Canada v IRC* [1972] 1 All ER 225, 47 TC 565.

The charge

34: 34   Under TA 1988, s. 739(2) the whole of the income of the non-resident person may be treated as that of the transferor, and this even though the "power to enjoy" does not extend so far.[1] In logic this should extend to all income, whether or not from the assets transferred but in practice the Revenue appears to take a less exacting line. Under TA 1988, s. 739(3) the Revenue treat only the income of the non-resident derived from the transfer or associated operations as taxable.

Where the individual is not domiciled in the UK a remittance basis is used.[2]

Simon's Taxes E1.756; Butterworths Income Tax Service A7.76.
¹ The Revenue view derives some support from *Congreve v IRC* [1948] 1 All ER 948, 30 TC 163; at 954 and 199 per Cohen LJ.
² TA 1988, s. 739(5).

34: 35   The income caught is that "which becomes payable" to the non-resident, and the House of Lords has held that deduction may not be made for the non-resident's management charges.[1] Expenses of collection are allowable as are deductions and reliefs that would be allowed if the income belonged to the individual.[2]

When the income of the non-resident is in the form of a dividend from a UK company that person will, as a non-resident,[3] not be entitled to the tax credit. However the resident whose income it is deemed to be is presumably so entitled. In the heyday of offshore funds it appears that the UK tax authorities were not very active in using s. 739 even to charge a UK resident on his proportionate share of the income, apparently because these funds had a favourable effect on the UK balance of payments.

Simon's Taxes E1.756; Butterworths Income Tax Service A7.73.
[1] *Lord Chetwode v IRC* [1977] STC 64, [1977] 1 All ER 638; on the meaning of payable see also *Latilla v IRC* [1943] 1 All ER 265, 25 TC 107.
[2] TA 1988, s. 743(2).
[3] TA 1988, s. 231(1).

Limitations

34: 36   TA 1988, s. 739 is not completely unlimited. First, it applies only where the power to enjoy income or the receipt of a capital sum rests in or accrues to an individual. Intermediaries such as UK trusts and companies are not individuals although of course transfers by such bodies may be associated with earlier or later transfers by individuals.

Secondly, the income must accrue to the non-resident person *in consequence* of the transfer or the associated operations. In *Fynn v IRC*[1] an individual had a right to demand repayment of a loan from a foreign company which he had set up. He also had a charge on the company's assets. It was held that he had no power to enjoy the income accruing to the company in consequence of the charging of the assets of the company.

Thirdly, the section applies only where the individual is ordinarily resident in the UK; non-residence short of ordinary residence does not suffice.

Fourthly, both ss. 739(2) and 739(3) are limited to situations where income accrues to the non-resident person. Investment of assets transferred abroad so that no income is produced therefore avoids both provisions.[2] The question whether a particular receipt is income is presumably to be decided by UK tax law in the light of the rights and duties arising under the foreign law.[3] Techniques used include (1) the transfer of assets to a non-resident company which in turn is owned by a non-resident trust, the income being retained in the company and not allowed to slip up to the trust[4] and (2) the interposition of a trust between holdings in an accumulate offshore fund.

Simon's Taxes E1.754; Butterworths Income Tax Service A7.72, 73.
[1] [1958] 1 All ER 270, 37 TC 629.
[2] For CGT anti-avoidance provisions, see infra, § **34: 49** and **34: 52**.
[3] Supra, § **34: 09**.
[4] But the beneficiaries must beware *Butt v Kelsen* [1952] Ch 197, [1952] 1 All ER 167.

TA 1988, s. 740

34: 37   As already seen this provision is designed to charge a person other than the transferor who receives a benefit supra, § **34: 24**. Like TA 1988, s. 739 there must be an initial transfer of assets either alone or in conjunction with associated operations and as a result income must become payable to a person resident or domiciled outside the UK; further the person chargeable must be an individual ordinarily resident in the UK. Also like s. 739 the charge if any is made under Schedule D, Case VI and various supporting provisions, including s. 745 on information powers are made expressly applicable. In addition, the general defences supra, § **34: 27** apply to s. 740. The payment may also include a capital gains element; on interaction see infra, § **34: 53**.

TA 1988, s. 740 charges on a different basis—by reference to the benefit received to the extent that it falls within relevant income.[1] Relevant income is income accruing after 9 March 1981 to a person resident or domiciled outside the UK and which can by virtue or in consequence of the transfer or associated operations be used directly or indirectly for providing a benefit for the individual or enabling a benefit to be provided for him.[2]

Section 740 then proceeds along lines similar to s. 677 supra, § **13: 24**. To the extent that the benefit falls within the amount of relevant income up to and including that year it is taxable as income of the individual. If the benefit should exceed that income it is carried forward and can be made liable to tax in later years by reason of the existence of relevant income in those later years.[3]

Where the person is not domiciled in the UK a remittance basis is applied.[4] There is no charge if the benefit is not received in the UK. On a literal interpretation a benefit received abroad and later brought to the UK escapes charge as it is not received in the UK.

To prevent double charges TA 1988, s. 745 provides that no amount of income may be charged more than once under TA 1988, ss. 739 and 740. It may happen that the transferor has a power to enjoy or has received a benefit. In such circumstances the Revenue are to attribute the income as appears to them just and reasonable, a decision made reviewable by the Special Commissioners.

Simon's Taxes E1.764; Butterworths Income Tax Service A7.77.
[1] TA 1988, s. 740(2).
[2] TA 1988, s. 740(3).
[3] TA 1988, s. 740(2).
[4] TA 1988, s. 740(5).

OFFSHORE INCOME GAINS

34: 38   TA 1988, ss. 757–764 and Schs. 27 and 28 impose a charge to income tax or corporation tax (under Schedule D, Case VI[1]) on the offshore income gain which arises to an investor disposing of material interests[2] in any offshore fund which is, or has at any material time been, a non-qualifying offshore fund[3]. In general, the provisions relate to disposals after 31 December 1983.[4]

Simon's Taxes C1.511–514; D4.431–436; Butterworths Income Tax Service A7.108–A7.110a.
[1] TA 1988, s. 761(1).
[2] TA 1988, ss. 757(1), 759.
[3] TA 1988, ss. 757(1), 760, Sch. 27.
[4] TA 1988, s. 757(1) (a). There are transitional provisions in s. 757(1)(b), relating to certain types of disposal.

Disposals

34: 39 The capital gains tax definition of disposal[1] applies, with two amendments. First, death is an occasion of charge, the gain being calculated by reference to the market value of the deceased's interest in the fund,[2] and secondly the provisions covering exchange of securities (on take-overs, reconstructions and amalgamations, for instance)[3] are modified.[4]

Simon's Taxes C1.512; Butterworths Income Tax Service A7.108.
[1] TA 1988, s. 757(2).
[2] TA 1988, s. 757(3).
[3] CGTA 1979, ss. 85, 86.
[4] TA 1988, s. 757(5), (6).

Material interests

34: 40 Interests caught by the rules are interests in non-resident companies or in unit trusts with non-resident trustees. Arrangements which, under the laws of a foreign territory, create rights in the nature of co-ownership are also included.[1]

An interest is a material interest if, when it was acquired, it was reasonable to suppose that the value of the interest could be realised within the next seven years.[2] A person is deemed to be able to realise the value of his interest if he can realise an amount which is approximately equal to the proportion of the underlying assets of the company (or assets subject to the unit trust scheme or arrangements) which his interest represents.[3] Realisation of the amount can be in money or in assets of that value.[4]

Certain interests are excluded from the definition of material interests.[5] They include an interest in respect of loan capital or other debt incurred for money lent in the ordinary course of a banking business,[6] and rights under an insurance policy. Special rules apply to exclude shares in overseas *companies*,[7] provided that four conditions are met:

(1) the shares are held by the company because it is necessary or desirable for the maintenance and development of the trade carried on by that company or an associated company;

(2) the shares must confer at least 10% of the voting rights in the overseas company and also a right, in winding up, to at least 10% of the residual assets after all prior liabilities have been discharged;[8]

(3) the maximum number of persons holding shares in the company is ten

and all the shares must confer both voting rights and a right to participate in the assets in the event of a winding up;

(4) at the time the shares were acquired, the company must have reasonably expected that the holder would be able to realise their value in only one, or both, of the following circumstances: (*a*) under an arrangement whereby, at some time within seven years, the company could require other participators to purchase the shares; or (*b*) because of an agreement between the participators under which the company will be wound up within a period which is or is reasonably expected to be, less than seven years.

Simon's Taxes C1.512; Butterworths Income Tax Service A7.108.
¹ TA 1988, s. 759(1).
² TA 1988, s. 759(2); see also SP 2/86, para. 2, Simon's Taxes Division H3.2.
³ TA 1988, s. 759(3); see also SP 2/86, para. 4, Simon's Taxes Division H3.2.
⁴ TA 1988, s. 759(4).
⁵ TA 1988, s. 759(5), (6).
⁶ See SP 2/86, para. 3, Simon's Taxes Division H3.2.
⁷ TA 1988, s. 759(6).
⁸ TA 1988, s. 759(6).

Distributing funds and non-qualifying offshore funds

34: 41   The charge only arises if the fund is, or has at any material time been, a non-qualifying offshore fund, see supra, §**34: 38**. The material time is a time after 1st January 1984 or, if later, the earliest date on which relevant consideration is given for the asset, ("relevant consideration" being consideration which, under the normal capital gains rules, would be taken into account in computing the gain or loss on the disposal).[1]

An offshore fund is a non-qualifying fund except during those account periods[2] for which the Board has certified the fund as a distributing fund.[3] A fund will only be so certified if it has a full distribution policy during the period.[4] The conditions are set out in detail in TA 1988, Sch. 27, but in general the following must be met;[5]

(1) a distribution must be made for the account period or for some other period which falls, in whole or in part, within the account period;

(2) the amount of the distribution made to holders of material and other interests in the fund must equal at least 85% of the fund's income for the period, and be not less than 85% of the funds' UK equivalent profits for the period;

(3) the distribution must be made during the account period, or within the following six months or, as a result of F(No. 2)A 1987, such longer periods as the Board may allow;[6]

(4) the distribution must be in such a form that any sum forming it would, if received by a UK resident, be chargeable under Schedule D Case IV or V.

In (2) above, about one-half of any income of an offshore fund which is derived from dealing in commodities is left out of account in determining the distributable income of an offshore fund, or in calculating the fund's UK equivalent profits.[7] The fund's UK equivalent profits are the total profits of the fund upon which, after deductions, corporation tax would be chargeable, but for this purpose profits *exclude* chargeable gains.[8]

The general rules are modified where the assets of a fund include interests in other offshore funds[9] or an interest in a trading company,[10] and where the fund has a wholly-owned subsidiary company whose business consists wholly or mainly of dealing in commodities.[11] In particular, rule (4) above is relaxed to enable funds operating equalisation arrangements, under which some of their income is distributed in capital form, to obtain distributor status.[12]

Simon's Taxes C1.512; D4.432–434; Butterworths Income Tax Service A7.109.

[1] TA 1988, s. 757(7).
[2] TA 1988, s. 760(8)–(10).
[3] TA 1988, s. 760(1).
[4] TA 1988, s. 760(2).
[5] TA 1988, Sch. 27, para. 1; see also SP 2/86, para. 5, Simon's Taxes Division H3.2.
[6] TA 1988, Sch. 27, para. 14; thus applies for accounting periods ending after the passing of F(No. 2)A 1987.
[7] TA 1988, Sch. 27, para. 4.
[8] TA 1988, Sch. 27, paras. 5, 8–11 and SP 2/86, Simon's Taxes Division H3.2.
[9] TA 1988, Sch. 27, paras. 6–9.
[10] TA 1988, Sch. 27, paras. 7 and 10 and SP 2/86, and see SP 2/86, para. 7, Simon's Taxes Division H3.2.
[11] TA 1988, Sch. 27, para 11.
[12] TA 1988, s. 758 and Sch. 27, para. 2. Section s 758(6) is amended by FA 1989, s 81.

34:42   A fund will not be certified as a distributing fund in an account period if any of the prescribed circumstances apply at any time during the period[1] although the Revenue now has the power to disregard inadvertent breaches. The circumstances are:

(a) if more than 5% of the value of assets of the fund comprise interests in other offshore funds;

(b) if more than 10% of the value of the assets of the fund comprise interests in a single company;[2]

(c) if the assets of the fund include more than 10% of the issued share capital of any company or of any class of that share capital;[2]

(d) if there is more than one class of material interest in the offshore fund and they do not all receive proper distribution benefits.

However, the following classes of holding can be ignored:

(1) those held by persons concerned in the management of the fund's assets;

(2) those carrying no right to participate in the profits of the fund;

(3) those which, in the event of winding up or redemption, entitle the holder to no more than the original purchase price.

An application for certification, which must be made to the Board within six months of the end of the account period,[3] must be accompanied by the accounts and any other relevant information.[4] A fund will automatically be treated as not pursuing a full distribution policy in an account period for which no accounts are made up.[5]

The fund has the right of appeal against the Board's decision, and if no application for certification has been made, a person assessed to tax has the right to require the Board to determine whether the fund should be certified, and can apply for postponement of the tax while this is done.[6]

Simon's Taxes C1.513; D4.435; Butterworths Income Tax Service A7.109.
[1] TA 1988, s. 760(3); the Revenue's power is in TA 1988, Sch. 27, para. 14.
[2] Modified if the interest is in certain types of company—see TA 1988, Sch. 27, Part II, § **34: 41** and Statement of Practice SP 2/86, para. 6, **Simon's Taxes Division H3.2.**
[3] TA 1988, Sch. 27, para. 15. There is a transitional period for applications up to 1 January 1985.
[4] TA 1988, Sch. 27, para. 15(1).
[5] TA 1988, Sch. 27, para. 1(3).
[6] TA 1988, Sch. 27, paras. 16–20.

The charge to tax

34: 43   If a disposal gives rise to an offshore income gain, the gain is treated as arising at the time of the disposal and is assessable under Schedule D Case VI.[1]

The rules for calculating the gain are set out in TA 1988, Sch. 28. Except where the disposal involves an equalisation element,[2] it is necessary to calculate the unindexed gain on the disposal, ignoring the charge to income tax or corporation tax. If the gain or loss has to be calculated in a way which takes account of the indexation allowance on an earlier no gain/no loss disposal (e.g. transfers between spouses) the unindexed gain is calculated on the basis that no indexation allowance was available on the earlier disposal. The general relief for gifts, and roll-over relief on the transfer of a business, are not available. If the computation produces a loss, the unindexed gain is deemed to be nil and there is no material disposal.

If the interest disposed of was acquired, or is deemed to have been acquired, before 1st January 1984, the interest is deemed to have been sold and immediately reacquired on 1st January 1984 at its then market value. The unindexed gain is calculated using that value, unless that method produces a larger gain. An interest required after 1st January 1984 on a no gain/no loss basis must be traced back to its original acquisition, the last no gain/no loss disposal before 1st January 1984, or to the last material disposal.[3]

If the material disposal also gives rise to a charge to capital gains tax, the consideration taken into account for capital gains tax is reduced by the offshore income gain.[4]

Special rules apply to persons resident and domiciled abroad,[5] insurance companies[6] and trustees.[7] Charities are exempt.[8]

Simon's Taxes C1.513; Butterworths Income Tax Service A7.110.
[1] TA 1988, s. 761(1).
[2] See TA 1988, Sch. 28, Part II.
[3] TA 1988, Sch. 28, paras. 2–5.
[4] TA 1988, s. 763.
[5] TA 1988, s. 762.
[6] TA 1988, s. 441(8).
[7] TA 1988, s. 764. See also TA 1988, ss. 663(2) and 687(3).
[8] TA 1988, s. 761(6).

CAPITAL GAINS TAX

34: 44   A person is chargeable to CGT if he is resident or ordinarily resident in the UK for at least a part of the year of assessment.[1] If he is not so resident he is chargeable only if he is carrying on a trade through a branch or agency and the asset was both situated in the UK and either used in or for the trade when or before the gain accrued or used by or for the branch or agency at or before the gain accrued.[2] This potential charge has now been extended from trades to professions.[3] The extension affects all disposals after 13th March 1989. In order to implement the new system there is a deemed disposal of these assets at current market value immediately before 14th March 1989.[4] These rules preserve the basic premise that a person is taxable either because he is resident or because the source is here, but curiously restricts the source to the one type—through a branch or agency. Thus a non-resident without such a trade or profession bears no capital gains tax even though he buys an asset in the UK. Equally, a resident with a substantial liability to capital gains tax can go overseas, lose both his UK residence and ordinary residence, and then dispose of his assets free of all UK tax.

However in some respects the system is gradually being tightened up. Thus companies are, broadly, treated as making a deemed disposal of assets on ceasing to reside—supra, § 32.24—and under the provisions of FA 1989 a non-resident who has chargeable assets in the UK, as with a trade or profession, will be treated as making a disposal of them when the assets cease to be chargeable assets by being removed from the UK after 13th March 1989.[5] Curiously, as if to underline the timidity of the approach, this charge does not apply if the non-resident is also ceasing, contemporaneously, to carry on the trade or profession through a branch or agency here or if the asset is an exploration or exploitation asset.[6] There is a similar charge if the asset ceases to be a chargeable asset because he ceases, after 13th March 1989, to carry on his trade or profession in the UK through a branch or agency.[7] So there is no deemed disposal if the asset remains a chargeable asset.

Residence and ordinary residence are to have the same meanings as for income tax,[8] and one who is in the UK for some temporary purpose and not with a view to establishing his residence here, is treated as resident only if his period of residence in the UK exceeds six months.[9]

Where an asset is acquired and disposed of in foreign currency acquisition cost and disposal proceeds are calculated at the exchange rates prevailing at the acquisition and disposal.[10] On foreign currency as a chargeable or exempt asset see § **15: 04**(4).

The extended scope of the charge has led to the introduction of special rules with regard to rollover relief for non-residents. The general rule, applicable to disposals and acquisitions after 13th March 1989, is that rollover relief is not permitted if the old assets are "chargeable assets in relation to a person" at the time of the disposal unless the new assets are similarly related immediately after the time of acquisition.[11] The expression "chargeable assets in relation to a person" is defined as referring to assets in relation to which a non-resident would be subject to tax under TA 1988, s. 11(2)(b) in the case of a non-resident company and CGTA 1979, s. 12 in relation to a non-resident with a branch or agency.[12]

This exclusion of rollover relief does not apply if the person acquiring the new asset had come within the UK tax net by reason of his personal status, i.e. by becoming resident or ordinarily resident in the UK, when the asset was acquired.[13] However this (logical) generosity is withheld (logically) from dual residents in whose hands the assets are safe from the UK tax charge by reason of a double tax agreement.[14]

Simon's Taxes C1.102, 201–203, 501; Sumption CGT A3.01.
  [1] CGTA 1979, s. 2. On residence for year of commencement or cessation see extra statutory concession D2 (1988) (as modified by Revenue Press Release 6th April 1989); see **Simon's Taxes Division H2.2.**
  [2] CGTA 1979, s. 12; he may also be exempt by treaty, ibid, and infra, § **36: 04**. On post-cessation disposals see CGTA 1979, s. 12(1A) added by FA 1989, s. 128.
  [3] CGTA 1979, s. 12(2A), added by FA 1989, s. 126(2).
  [4] FA 1989, s. 126(3).
  [5] FA 1989, s. 127(1) and (7).
  [6] FA 1989, s. 127(2). Exploration and exploitation assets are defined by s. 130; the relevant deemed disposal is governed by s. 131.
  [7] FA 1989, s. 127(3) and (8).
  [8] CGTA 1979, s. 18(1). On residence of partners, see CGTA 1979, s. 60 and TA 1988, s. 112.
  [9] CGTA 1979, s. 18(3).
  [10] *Bentley v Pike* [1981] STC 360, 53 TC 590.
  [11] FA 1989, s. 129(1) and (4).
  [12] FA 1989, s. 129(6).
  [13] FA 1989, s. 129(2).
  [14] FA 1989, s. 129(3).

Remittance basis

34: 45   If the person is an individual resident or ordinarily resident, but not domiciled, in the UK then the charge to tax on gains accruing from the disposal of an asset outside the UK is on the amount received in this country in respect of those gains.[1] In computing the amount of the gain any liability to foreign tax is deductible in full.[2] Where the proceeds of the disposal are remitted to the UK and exceed the gain, the Revenue adopt an apportionment principle when deciding how much of the remittance is in respect of the gain.[3]

The availability of the remittance basis is thus governed by the status of the person rather than simply by the location of the asset. The rule is analogous to the treatment of investment income. One consequence of the rule is that a disposal for less than acquisition cost, for example, a gift, cannot be charged in this country. Another is that little use can be made of losses, although the shrewd operator will make sure that his loss item is brought within the UK before disposal.

Simon's Taxes C1.102; Sumption CGT A3.05.
  [1] CGTA 1979, s. 14. Since the remittance basis applies only to individuals why does s. 49(3) treat the personal representatives as domiciled where the deceased was domiciled?
  [2] CGTA 1979, s. 11—unless relief is given under s. 10.
  [3] The apportionment principle was adopted by the Revenue in 1971.

34: 46   However, whereas under income tax it is open to a person to prove that the particular remittance to the UK does not represent income but capital,[1] the Revenue appear to take a different view on CGT. This may be supported by the wider language of the CGT rule.[2] In particular they hold that where a sum is remitted to this country, and it is less than the total proceeds of the disposal, it will be treated as being composed first of the amount of the gains and only the balance is to represent the original expenditure. Thus if the asset cost £1,000 and is sold for £1,500, the remittance of £1,000 will be treated as being £500 gain and the balance as non-taxable. Yet one may argue with equal cogency either that the sum received being $\frac{2}{3}$ of the proceeds, it should be treated as $\frac{2}{3}$ of the gain and $\frac{2}{3}$ of the expenditure or that it should be treated as the return of the original expenditure. One might further argue that if one had another asset which had cost £1,500 but which was sold for £1,000 then if one remitted £1,000 one was remitting the proceeds of the second sale; if one remitted £2,500 it is presumably open to argue that the loss should be set off against the gain. In the absence of authority, it is hard to anticipate how the courts will resolve these problems. However, the present solution, which makes it possible for the individual to specify the nature of his receipt, by splitting the proceeds while still in the foreign country, or using separate bank accounts is simply to place one more advantage in the hands of the skilled and one more trap for the innocent.

Simon's Taxes C1.503; Sumption CGT A3.05.
 [1] Supra, § **34: 15**.
 [2] CGTA 1979, s. 14 not only incorporates TA 1988, s. 65(6) to (9), supra § **34:18** but adds that "all amounts paid used or enjoyed in or in any form transmitted or brought to" the UK are to be treated as received in the UK.

34: 47   The remittance basis *only* applies to foreign assets. The rules as to the location of assets are:[1]

(*a*) the situation of rights or interests (otherwise than by way of security) in or over immovable property is that of the immovable property,

(*b*) subject to the following provisions of this subsection, the situation of rights or interests (otherwise than by way of security) in or over tangible movable property is that of the tangible movable property,

(*c*) subject to the following provisions of this subsection, a debt, secured or unsecured, is situated in the UK if and only if the creditor is resident in the UK,

(*d*) shares or securities issued by any municipal or governmental authority, or by any body created by such an authority, are situated in the country of that authority,

(*e*) subject to paragraph (*d*) above, registered shares or securities are situated where they are registered and, if registered in more than one register, where the principal register is situated,

(*f*) a ship or aircraft is situated in the UK if and only if the owner is then resident in the UK, and an interest or right in or over a ship or aircraft is situated in the UK and if and only if the person entitled to the interest or right is resident in the UK,

(*g*) the situation of goodwill as a trade, business or professional asset is at the place where the trade, business or profession is carried on,

(*h*) patents, trade-marks and designs are situated where they are registered, and if registered in more than one register, where each register is situated, and copyright, franchises, rights and licences to use any copyright material, patent, trade-mark or design are situated in the UK if they, or any rights derived from them, are exercisable in the UK,

   (*i*) a judgment debt is situated where the judgment is recorded,

   (*j*) from 6th April 1983 a non-sterling bank account is situated outside the UK unless the branch at which it is maintained is in the UK[2].

Simon's Taxes C1.501; Sumption CGT A3.10.
   [1] CGTA 1979, s. 18(4).
   [2] FA 1984, s. 69.

Delayed remittances

34: 48   If a person is chargeable to tax on a gain accruing from the disposal of an asset situated overseas, but is unable to remit that gain to the UK then, if he makes a claim and is not chargeable on a remittance basis, he, or his personal representative,[1] is not assessed to tax on those gains as they arise, on conditions analogous to income tax relief, supra, § **34: 22**. Since tax is levied as soon as the conditions cease it may happen that gains accruing over several years will come into charge at one time. In such circumstances, unlike income tax, there is no charge by reference to the years in which the gain accrued. This may mean the loss of the annual exemption for the years in which the gains actually arose. Similar Revenue reasoning means that this relief does not apply where the taxpayer is chargeable on a remittance basis.

   The gain deemed to accrue under CGTA 1979, s. 15 (infra, § **34: 49**) may not take advantage of the present rule for delayed remittances.[2] This is because the inability of the taxpayer to remit the gain arose from his position as a minority shareholder and s. 15 disregarded that difficulty.

Simon's Taxes C1.503; Sumption CGT A3.04.
   [1] CGTA 1979, s. 13.
   [2] *Van Arkadie v Plunket* [1983] STC 54, 56 TC 310.

Non-resident companies

34: 49   Gains accruing to a company are not usually attributable to their shareholders, but an exception is made by CGTA 1979, s. 15 where the company would be close company but for being non-resident. The gain will be attributed to a shareholder who is either resident or ordinarily resident and, if an individual, is domiciled in the UK. Further he must have a shareholding of at least 5% in the company, his portion being ascertained by reference to his share of the assets on a hypothetical liquidation. The charge cannot be avoided by placing another company between the shareholder and the company to which the gain accrues since the Revenue are given power to attribute the gain down through any number of intervening companies to the real shareholders.[1]

   EXAMPLE
      X Ltd is a non-resident company. Smith buys 25% of the share capital in X Ltd. X Ltd realises a gain of £10,000; £2,500 is attributed to Smith making a tax liability (but for any exemption) of £750. If Smith later sells his shares realising, say, a gain of £1,000 that gain will be reduced by the £750 to £250.

Simon's Taxes C1.311; Sumption CGT A3.06.
   [1] CGTA 1979, s. 15(9).

34: 50   Since the section only applies where "chargeable gains accrue to the company" it is possible that it has only a very restricted operation, being confined to those gains which are chargeable to the company, and since the company is non-resident these will be very few. However the section does not apply to such gains so that it is more likely that "chargeable gains" means any gains that would be chargeable if the company were resident. On this construction the purpose of the section is simply to prevent abuse of the exemption of non-resident companies. The section does not apply[1] to the amount of any gain which is distributed within two years of the gain accruing to the company nor to gains accruing on the disposal of tangible property or foreign currency, used and only used in the foreign trade. Further the amount of CGT paid by the shareholder is deductible in computing any later gain accruing on the disposal of the shares, unless that tax is re-imbursed by the company,[2] always assuming however that there is a chargeable gain on such disposal.[3] Losses can be attributed only to cover attributable gains.[4]

Simon's Taxes C1.311; Sumption CGT A3.06.
[1] CGTA 1979, s. 15(5).
[2] Such a reimbursement is exempt from tax; CGTA 1979, s. 15(10).
[3] CGTA 1979, s. 15(7).
[4] CGTA 1979, s. 15(8).

34: 51   The section carries the very real risk that a taxpayer will be liable to CGT without being able to secure the payment or get his hands on any of the gain. Relief for unremittable gains[1] does not extend to gains which he cannot get out simply because of his status as a minority as opposed to a majority shareholder.[2]

The section applies only when the company is, or would, if resident, be, a close company. It does not apply to individuals domiciled abroad nor when the part to be attributed is less than 5% of the whole.[3] Further losses accruing to the company can be brought in.[4]

Simon's Taxes C1.311; Sumption CGT A3.06.
[1] CGTA 1979, s. 13, supra, § **34: 48**.
[2] One solution may be to sell the shares in the non-resident company before the company disposes of the asset.
[3] CGTA 1979, s. 15(4).
[4] CGTA 1979, s. 15(8).

Groups

34: 52   Special provision is made for non-resident groups—CGTA 1979, s. 16.

Simon's Taxes C1.311; D2.621; Sumption CGT A3.07.

International trusts

34: 53   Trustees do not take over the residence of their settlor; they are treated as resident and ordinarily resident in the UK unless the majority of them are not so resident and the general administration of the trust is ordinarily carried on overseas.[1] The assessment may be made on all the trustees or on those resident in the UK.[2] In *Roome v Edwards*[3] an assessment on UK trustees of a part of the fund was upheld even though the gain accrued to the trustees of another part all those trustees being non-resident.

Trustees may cease to be resident in the UK but the concession allowing individuals to be treated as non-resident for the remainder of the year in which they migrate does not apply to trustees in their capacity as trustees.[4] A migration within six years of the creation of the settlement may cause the tax held over on the creation of the settlement to fall due.[5]

A further difference is that if the trustees are non-resident the disposal of a beneficial interest may be a chargeable disposal.[6]

Many of these rules apply only as from 1981. Before then the trustees would use a contingent appointment scheme to avoid CGT. The trustees would appoint to A contingently on A surviving a few days. They would become non-resident. A would then sell his interest to B, a non-resident. The sale by A was exempt under s. 58;[7] the vesting in B was exempt as neither the trustees nor the beneficiaries were resident.[8]

Simon's Taxes C4.412–416, 420–424; Sumption CGT A3.08.
   [1] CGTA 1979, s. 52(2); the rule is relaxed for professional trustees of a trust created by a person resident and domiciled outside the UK.
   [2] CGTA 1979, s. 48.
   [3] [1981] STC 96, [1981] 1 All ER 736, HL.
   [4] Extra-statutory concession A11 (1988), **Simon's Taxes Division H2.2**.
   [5] FA 1981, s. 79.
   [6] FA 1981, s. 88.
   [7] Supra, § **18: 17**.
   [8] These schemes did not always work. In *Chinn v Collins* [1981] STC 1, [1981] 1 All ER 189 the property was reacquired by A under a pre-existing contractual scheme. Most such schemes now fall within the scope of *Ramsay v IRC*.

34: 54   Special rules apply to settlements created by a settlor who was at the time of making the settlement domiciled and resident (or ordinarily resident) in the UK.[1] As gains accrue to non-resident trustees they are cumulated as "trust gains".[2] Capital payments received by the beneficiaries are then attributed to the trust gains which become chargeable gains in the hand of the beneficiaries.[3] This applies only to beneficiaries who are domiciled in the UK, and resident or ordinarily resident at some time during the year.[4] When a capital payment is made to a beneficiary in one year and a trust gain arises in a later year, a charge may arise in that later year. Relief may be claimed for trust losses.[5]

The gains are attributed to beneficiaries in proportion to the capital payment received by them, but are not to exceed those payments. This obscure provision seems to mean that if the only payments made to the beneficiaries are made to A, then A can be assessed for all the gains accruing to the non-resident trustees up to the amount he has received; he is thus at risk for up to 40% of the entire sum received.

This provision attempts to regulate the use of non-resident trusts as devices in which gains can be accumulated free of CGT outside the jurisdiction.[6] The present limitation of liability to payments actually made to a beneficiary is in line with the new income tax rule following the decision of the House of Lords in *Vestey v IRC*, supra, § **34: 24**.

For this purpose the term settlement receives not its narrow CGT meaning but the wide income tax meaning of arrangement.[7]

A capital payment is defined as one which is not chargeable to income tax. The term covers the transfer of an asset, a loan, and various indirect payments.[8]

Provision is made for the migration of settlements. Where a trust migrates to the UK complete with trust gains capital payments subsequent to the distribution are treated as chargeable gains of the beneficiaries.[9] This appears to be in addition to any liability that may arise under s. 54.

When a trust migrates from the UK payments made before it ceases to be resident are only treated as capital payments (thus causing a liability in respect of subsequent gains) if made in anticipation of a disposal by the trustees in the non-resident period.[10]

Provision is also made for the transfer of settled property to other trusts, whether or not the latter were made by the original settlor; the infection of "trust gains" will be transferred with the property so far as not already attributed to the beneficiaries and so far as not made for a consideration in money or money's worth.[11]

As from 1984–85 discretionary capital payments received by a beneficiary are taxable under s. 80 even though the gains arose before 6th April 1981.[12]

Simon's Taxes C4.412–416; Sumption CGT A3.08.

[1] FA 1981, s. 80; the expressions settlement and settlor are to have the same meaning as for TA 1988, s. 681(4), see supra, § **13: 02** et seq and even applies to a settlement on death (e.g. by will or intestacy FA 1984, s. 71) as from 1984–85 onwards.

[2] I.e. Such gains as would have been chargeable if they had been resident or ordinarily resident in the UK.

[3] FA 1981, s. 80(3).

[4] FA 1981, s. 80(6).

[5] FA 1981, s. 83(6).

[6] Chargeable gains accruing to trustees before 6th April 1981 are ignored as are capital payments received by beneficiaries before 10th March 1981 s. 76(5). The primary rule was CGTA 1979, s. 17. See also *Leedale v Lewis* [1980] STC 679.

[7] FA 1981, s. 83(7).

[8] FA 1981, ss. 83(2) and 83(5).

[9] FA 1981, s. 81(2).

[10] FA 1981, s. 81(1).

[11] FA 1981, s. 82.

[12] FA 1984, s. 70.

34: 55 Where a payment falling within TA 1988, s. 740 (supra, § **34: 37**) exceeds the then relevant income, the excess may be taxed in future years under s. 740 should relevant income arise; however, it may also be taxed straight away under FA 1980, s. 80. When this occurs the excess reduces the amount liable to be taxed under s. 740 in later years, i.e. the charge under FA 1980, s. 80 excludes the subsequent charge under s. 740.[1]

Simon's Taxes C4.412–416; Sumption CGT A3.08A.
¹ TA 1988, s. 740(6).

34: 56 FA 1984 contains one other provision of interest. This concerns liabilities to tax arising under CGTA 1979, s. 17, which, as interpreted by the House of Lords in *Leedale v Lewis*, allowed the Revenue to charge a beneficiary with tax on a gain made by the trustees even though he had received nothing. The new provision allows the beneficiary to defer the liability to tax on any assessment made before 1984–85 and which had not been paid before 29th March 1983.¹

Simon's Taxes C4.421; Sumption CGT A3.08A.
¹ FA 1984, s. 70, Sch. 14.

CONTROLLED FOREIGN COMPANIES RESIDENT IN LOW TAX AREAS

34: 57 As from 6th April 1984¹ if the Board of Inland Revenue have reason to believe that in any accounting period a company is "resident"² outside the UK but is controlled by persons resident in the UK and that the company is subject to a lower level of taxation in that country of residence, the Board may invoke special powers.

These special powers enable the Board to apportion the total *income* profits of the foreign company computed as for UK corporation tax (its chargeable profits) and any creditable tax among all the persons who had an *interest* in the company during the accounting period to which the direction relates.

The persons amongst whom the profits can be apportioned in this way may be resident or non-resident and corporations or individuals. However, these rules apply only to enable corporation tax to be assessed on a company resident in the UK and then only if 10% of the total chargeable profits of the foreign company can be apportioned to it or to connected or associated persons.³ So if a company is resident outside the UK but has 30% non-UK shareholders, 40% UK corporate shareholders and 30% UK individual shareholders, the company is controlled by persons resident in the UK, and these rules can apply to the 40% UK corporate shareholders. Where profits are apportioned to a UK company in this way it may happen that a charge may also appear to arise under TA 1988, s. 739. When TA 1988, s. 739 applies to treat the profits of the controlled foreign company attributed to the UK resident shareholders as the profits of an individual, the s. 739 charge is excluded.⁴ In order to prevent the avoidance of the 10% minimum by fragmentation of share ownership, it is provided that shares held by connected or associated persons are to be taken into account in calculating the extent of the interest. This does not mean that the connected or associated persons are liable to tax under these rules, nor that the amounts apportioned to them are taxable in the hands of the UK-resident taxpayer.

The 1984 rules allow the Board to charge a UK resident company to a sum equal to UK corporation tax. They do not allow the Board to go further and to attribute the UK resident company profits amongst those with interests in the UK company.

Tax on the amount apportioned to, and assessable on, a UK company is attributed to the accounting period of the UK company in which the relevant accounting period of the controlled foreign company ends.[5]

If the Revenue consider that a particular company is a controlled foreign company it may require any UK resident company which is a controlling company (as defined) in relation to that foreign company to supply certain specified information about the foreign company within a prescribed period not being less than 30 days.[6] This power is limited to information relevant to these rules and relating to the affairs of the controlling company, the foreign subsidiary or any connected or associated company.

Simon's Taxes D4.131–152.
[1] FA 1984, s. 91(4). See generally Arnold, *The Taxation of Foreign Controlled Companies: An International Comparison* (1986).
[2] As defined in TA 1988, s. 749(1).
[3] TA 1988, s. 747(5).
[4] TA 1988, s. 747(4)(*b*).
[5] TA 1988, s. 754.
[6] TA 1988, s. 755.

Definitions

34: 58   Control is determined as for close companies[1] supra, § **27: 03**. However, there is no requirement that control be in the hands of five or fewer participators. The rules include both indirect control and attributed ownership provisions.[2] A company is regarded as resident in any territory in which throughout the relevant accounting period it is liable to tax (whether or not it actually pays any) by reason of its domicile, residence or place of management.[3] Presumably this question is determined by reference to the foreign tax law,[4] although the question whether it is a company is presumably decided by UK tax law. There are further rules for determining the residence of a company when it is liable to tax in more than one country.[5] Those rules make residence turn on (1) place of effective management, failing which (2) situs of majority of assets, failing which (3) the country specified in the Board's direction.

Whether a person has an interest in a company is determined as for close companies,[6] (supra, § **27: 06**) although there is a simple Revenue discretion in the case of a loan creditor.[7] Where a person's entitlement to secure the application of a company's income or assets for his benefit is contingent upon a default of the company under any agreement, this is an interest in the company only if the default has occurred.[8]

Accounting periods are defined broadly as for corporation tax although such a period is made to begin when a company comes under the control of UK residents and to end when it ceases to be so.[9]

Creditable tax is defined to comprise:

(*a*) any double taxation relief which would be available if the foreign company's chargeable profits were liable to corporation tax, in respect of any foreign tax attributable to income comprised in those chargeable profits;

(*b*) income tax deducted at source from income received by the company which could be set off against such corporation tax; and

(c) income or corporation tax actually charged on or borne by the chargeable profits and not repayable.[10]

A trading company is one whose business consists wholly or mainly of the carrying on of a trade or trades.[11] Companies dealing in shares, securities, land, trade or commodity, or financial futures are therefore classed as trading companies, a matter relevant to the acceptable distribution test (see § **34: 62**) although other issues arise in connection with this exempt activities test[12] (see infra, § **34: 64**).

Simon's Taxes D4.133, 134, 145.

[1] TA 1988, s. 756(3).
[2] These rules are important where these relatives etc are not UK residents.
[3] TA 1988, s. 749(1).
[4] This raises a problem if the foreign law taxes on the basis of incorporation and does not equate incorporation with domicile.
[5] TA 1988, s. 749(2).
[6] TA 1988, s. 749(5).
[7] TA 1988, s. 749(7)—on rights of appeal see s. 753(4)(c).
[8] TA 1988, s. 749(6).
[9] TA 1988, s. 751(1)–(5).
[10] TA 1988, s. 751(6).
[11] TA 1988, s. 756(1).
[12] TA 1988, Sch. 25 para 9.

The apportionment process and its assumptions

Interests

34: 59   The Board is empowered to apportion the chargeable profits of the foreign company and then to charge a sum equal to corporation tax on the apportioned amount of profits less the portion of the foreign company's creditable tax.

The chargeable profits, and any creditable tax, of the foreign company is to be apportioned among the persons having an interest in the company at any time during the accounting period in question according to their respective interests at any time during the accounting period.[1] An apportionment to a person with an interest held for only part of the period will only be made however to the extent that it is just and reasonable and this will be subject to review by the Special Commissioners on appeal. Because the concept of an interest is wide, the rules are complex and give the Revenue a wide discretion.

In determining the respective interests, the Board may attribute to any person an interest corresponding to his interest in the assets of the company available for distribution on a winding up.

In the case of a non-trading company the Board may treat a loan creditor as having an interest to the extent that income of the company has been or is available to be applied in repayment of his loan capital or debt.

Apportionment among persons who have held shares of the same class throughout the accounting period is to be made in direct proportion to the number of shares held by them. Similar principles apply for other persons holding interests of the same description.

Where the same interest in a controlled foreign company is held directly by one person and indirectly by another or others, the Board may treat the interest as held solely by one of them; and if only one of them is resident in the UK they may treat that person alone as holding the interest. Special rules apply, where more than one UK resident company is involved, the broad effect of which is to charge the first UK resident company one comes across as one goes up the chain while making other UK companies liable for the tax in default by that one.[2]

Any interest held in a fiduciary or representative capacity may be treated as held by the person or persons for whose benefit it is held.[3]

Simon's Taxes D4.146.
  [1] TA 1988, s. 752.
  [2] TA 1988, s. 754(6)–(8).
  [3] TA 1988 s. 752(7).

34: 60   The assumptions to be made in computing the chargeable profits, the creditable tax and the corresponding UK tax are many. First,[1] the controlled foreign company is to be deemed resident in the UK. The company's income is computed under the rules appropriate to Schedule D, Cases IV and V (though there may be occasional exceptions where the company trades in the UK through a branch or agency, or has other UK-source income) with the result that TA 1988, s. 338 applies.

To allow certain reliefs and allowances to be carried forward there are rules to ensure the continuation of assumed UK residence over a number of accounting periods. The assumed residence begins with the first accounting period for which the Board has made a direction and continues until the company is no longer under UK control, whether or not a direction is made. For the purposes of carry forward of loss relief the chargeable profits and corresponding UK tax are assumed to have been computed for each accounting period since that for which the first direction was made, even if no directions have been made for subsequent periods. Losses incurred during any of the six years before the first period for which a direction is made (e.g. pre-1984 losses) can be used.[2] Because capital gains are not attributed, capital losses are not allowed.

The company, despite its deemed UK residence, is not deemed to be a close company.

Secondly,[3] it is assumed that the company has claimed or is to be given the maximum amount available of those reliefs which have to be claimed and allowances which are given automatically but which can be disclaimed in whole or part, unless any UK company or companies holding a majority interest disclaim any such relief or claim a smaller amount.[4]

However, not all reliefs are available. Thus, group relief and related provisions are excluded for the purposes of computing chargeable profits. Accordingly the foreign company is not treated as a member of a UK group or consortium. Such a company may not make any election under the group income provisions, TA 1988, s. 247 and ACT cannot be surrendered to it by a UK company.

TA 1988, s. 343 does not apply on the transfer of a trade by another company to the foreign company. Relief may however be available on the transfer of a trade by the foreign company to a UK company.

In computing the profits of the foreign company for the accounting period for which the first direction is made (the starting period) and subsequent accounting periods, trading losses incurred by that company in the previous six years will be taken into account if a claim is made to do so.

Thirdly,[5] the full range of capital allowances, including scientific research allowances, are treated as available. However, initial allowances on industrial buildings or first year allowances on plant and machinery (before 1 April 1986) were not given if the sole or main purpose of the transaction whereby the asset was acquired was to secure an allowance which would reduce the company's chargeable profits or the corresponding UK tax.

Fourthly,[6] relief may be given for unremittable foreign income under TA 1988, s. 584 (see supra, § **34: 22**).

When profits are apportioned to a UK company, there are further rules indicating the reliefs available to it. These include excess relevant allowances[7] (e.g. loss relief) and surplus ACT.[8]

In addition relief has to be given when the UK company receives a dividend from the foreign company.[9] Where a dividend is paid by the controlled foreign company out of profits from which the apportioned chargeable profits are derived, the gross amount of UK tax charged on UK companies in respect of those profits (the gross attributed tax) is treated as tax paid in respect of the profits concerned and accordingly as underlying tax for the purposes of double taxation relief under TA 1988, Pt XVIII. The full amount of gross attributed tax qualifies for relief, even though some or all of that tax may have been reduced following a claim in respect of relevant allowances or ACT. This rule only applies where the dividend comes from the profits which have been charged under these rules.

Any excess tax (such as a withholding tax but exclusive of underlying tax) qualifying for tax credit relief may be set against the gross amount of tax assessed on the UK resident companies. On a claim by any of those companies, the amount of tax assessed on the claimant in respect of the chargeable profits of the company is to be reduced and, where necessary, tax repaid.

Relief for underlying tax is generally confined, under the terms of a double taxation agreement or the unilateral relief provisions in TA 1988, s. 790(4), to UK resident companies that have a particular degree of control (normally 10% or more of the voting power) in the foreign company. This condition is deemed to be satisfied in considering whether any such company is entitled to the relief in respect of any of the gross attributed tax.

Gross attributed tax is not, to be added to the amount of the dividend in determining the liability to tax of the person who receives that dividend. The effect is that when the UK company owns all the shares in the foreign company, UK tax on the dividends received should be completely offset by the tax already paid under these rules; subsequent dividends thus become tax free. Naturally, more complex results ensue when there is more than one person with an interest in the foreign company.

There are special rules to deal with dividends paid otherwise than out of specified profits in cases where only part of the chargeable profits of the foreign company are apportioned to UK resident companies that are liable for tax thereon. In these circumstances, the gross attributed tax is regarded as attributable to a corresponding proportion of the chargeable profits of the controlled foreign company (the taxed profits) and so much of the dividend as is received by, or by a successor in title of, any such UK resident company is to be regarded as paid primarily out of taxed profits. For this purpose, a person can be a successor in title in respect of the whole or any part of the interest held by a UK resident company in the controlled foreign company by virtue of which an amount of its chargeable profits was apportioned to that company.

There are also rules to provide relief against any capital gains charge in respect of tax paid under these provisions when shares in the foreign company are subsequently disposed of.[10]

Simon's Taxes D4.144.
  [1] TA 1988, Sch. 24, paras. 1–4.
  [2] But only in accordance with the rules in TA 1988 Sch. 24, para. 9.
  [3] TA 1988, Sch. 24, paras. 5–9.
  [4] The time limit is 60 days but may be extended: TA 1988, Sch. 24, paras. 4(2) and 9(4).
  [5] TA 1988, Sch. 24, paras. 10–11; special rules apply where plant and machinery was acquired before the first year for which the direction is given under the 1984 rules. Allowances preventing the making of a direction are deemed to have been given.
  [6] TA 1988, Sch. 24, para. 12.
  [7] TA 1988, Sch. 26, para. 1.
  [8] TA 1988, Sch. 26, para. 2.
  [9] TA 1988, Sch. 26, para. 4.
  [10] TA 1988, Sch. 26, paras. 3 and 6.

Exclusion from direction making power

34: 61   (1) *Territories with a lower level of taxation.*[1] A company is subject to a lower level of taxation only if the local tax paid is less than one-half of the corresponding UK tax. The effect of the reduction in UK tax rates will be dramatic.

The corresponding UK tax is the hypothetical corporation tax on the chargeable profits of the foreign company computed on the assumptions described in Sch. 24. UK income or corporation tax actually charged on chargeable profits is deducted from the corresponding UK tax. Double taxation relief attributable to the local tax is not taken into account.

The local tax is confined to tax paid under the law of the controlled foreign company's territory of residence and does not include tax paid or suffered in a third territory. Since the controlled foreign company is assumed to be resident in the UK for the purposes of computing its chargeable profits, third territory taxes are taken into account under the normal double taxation relief rules in computing the corresponding UK tax with which the local tax is being compared.

The local tax paid by the controlled foreign company excludes those taxes which are computed on some basis other than profits.

A list of those territories not regarded by the Revenue as low tax countries was published[2] in 1984. This list now has a different role, infra § **34: 66**.

When a company is not resident in the UK and is not liable to tax by reason of domicile, residence or place of management in any territory outside the UK it is deemed subject to a lower level of taxation.[3]

Simon's Taxes D4.136.
¹ TA 1988, s. 750.
² See [1985] STI, p. 469.
³ TA 1988, s. 749(3).

34: 62   (2) *Acceptable distribution policy*. The Board has no power to invoke these rules if the foreign company follows an acceptable distribution policy. The conditions which must be met to satisfy this test are:[1]

(*a*) a dividend, which is not paid out of specified profits, is paid for the accounting period in question or for some other period falling wholly or partly within that accounting period;

(*b*) it is paid during or within 18 months after the period for which it is paid (the Revenue may extend the time allowed for this); and

(*c*) a trading company distributes by way of dividend at least 50% of its available profits for the accounting period to UK residents and any other company distributes by way of dividend at least 90% of its available profits to UK residents. Where there is only one class of shares and all the interests are share interests held by UK residents,[2] only 50% (or 90%) of profits attributable to the UK shareholders must be distributed. There is a similar relief if one class is voting shares and the other is non-voting fixed rate preference shares.

Detailed rules attribute dividends to particular periods (and so to particular profits). There are also rules dealing with payments through intermediate companies, the avoidance of double counting and others countering the avoidance of liability through the manipulation of accounting periods.

The parallel with domestic close companies is obvious but the rationale behind this exception is obscure. The thought probably was that the dividend would be subject to UK tax on its receipt by the shareholders. Unfortunately this objective could be thwarted if the company had become a UK resident by the time it made its dividend distribution since it would be franked investment income of the corporate shareholder. Where a dividend is paid on or after 17th March 1987 it will be relevant only if the company was then not resident in the UK (whether or not it was a controlled foreign company).[3]

Simon's Taxes D4.138.
¹ TA 1988, Sch. 25, paras. 1–4.
² TA 1988, Sch. 25, para 2(4) does not apply as 2(4)(*b*) is not satisfied.
³ TA 1988, Sch. 25, para. 2(1)(*c*).

34: 63   (3) *The public quotation condition*. Pursuing the analogy of domestic close companies, yet further, the legislation, through a late amendment, provides that those powers are not to apply if the controlled foreign company fulfils a public quotation condition closely modelled on TA 1988, s. 415 (see supra, § **27: 08**). Then not less than 35% of the voting power must be held by "the public" and there is a bar if more than 85% of that power is at any time within the period possessed by all the company's principal members. The shares must have been the subject of dealings on a recognised stock exchange situated in the territory in which the company is resident, these dealings must have taken place within the twelve month period ending with the end of the accounting period and the shares must have been quoted on the official list of that stock exchange.[1]

Simon's Taxes D4.140.
[1] TA 1988, Sch. 25, Part III.

34: 64   (4) *Exempt activities.*[1] The objective of this test is to exclude automatically from the charge those foreign companies which, because of the nature of their activities in their territories of residence, can reasonably be regarded as not being used with the object of reducing UK tax.

A foreign company is outside the charge if it satisfies four conditions. These are:

(a) that it has a real presence i.e. a business establishment with an effective management[2] in its territory of residence, sufficient and local staff, not merely a formal presence such as just a registered address in the territory;

(b) that its main activity is not leasing, dealing in securities or the receipt of income such as dividends, interest, or royalties and is not such that the company may be used as an invoicing route;

(c) that its business is not primarily with associates in those trades which frequently involve cross-frontier transactions;

(d) that the company does not receive a significant amount of dividends from controlled foreign companies except where the exemption for holding companies applies.[3]

There are special rules for holding companies (which inter alia can separate out their own exempt activities) and it is made clear that banks are not barred from this exclusion on the ground that they carry on an investment business.

The purpose of the legislation is also shown by the further rule that, if the company is engaged mainly in wholesale, distributive or financial business,[4] less than 50% of its gross trading receipts must be derived from connected persons. The legislation is then also aimed at transfer pricing and similar devices such as captive insurance companies.

Simon's Taxes D4.139.
[1] TA 1988, Sch. 25, paras. 5–12.
[2] TA 1988, Sch. 25, paras. 7–8.
[3] TA 1988, Sch. 25, paras. 6(4) and 12.
[4] Defined TA 1988, Sch. 25, para. 11.

34: 65   (5) *Motive test.* A company which fails to satisfy either the acceptable distribution policy or exempt activities tests will nevertheless escape the charge if it meets the requirements of the motive test.

No direction will be made for an accounting period in so far as,[1] any of the transactions the results of which are reflected in the profits arising in the accounting period, or any two or more of those transactions taken together achieved a reduction in UK tax which was no more than minimal or it was not a main purpose of any of those transactions (either alone or taken together) to achieve that reduction, and a reduction in UK tax by the diversion of profits from the UK was not a main reason for the company's existence in that accounting period.

A transaction achieves a *reduction in UK tax*[2] (meaning income tax, corporation tax or CGT[3]) if any person would have been liable for more tax or would have been entitled to less relief or a smaller repayment if the transaction had not taken place. A "transaction" for this purpose may comprise one or more transactions which are reflected in the company's profits in any accounting period.

The purpose in question in this test is that of the foreign company and any person who had an interest in that company in the relevant accounting period.

A reduction in UK tax by a diversion of profits[4] from the UK is achieved by the existence of a company if the whole or a substantial part of the receipts making up the foreign company's profits in that period could reasonably have been expected to be received by a UK resident and been subject to UK tax without any relief had it not been for the existence of the foreign company in question or another foreign company connected or associated with it and capable of fulfilling the same functions relative to any UK resident company. Companies are only meant to fall foul of this test if the diversions achieve a loss of UK tax and are a main reason for the existence of the company.

Simon's Taxes D4.142.
[1] TA 1988, s. 748(3).
[2] TA 1988, Sch. 25, para. 16.
[3] TA 1988, Sch. 25, para 17(2)—the inclusion of CGT is noteworthy as capital gains are excluded from the CFC attribution process.
[4] TA 1988, Sch. 25, para. 19.

34: 66   The Revenue publish a list of countries which are regarded as either wholly or completely outside these rules.[1] A company which is resident in and carrying on business in a country in Part I of the list is outside these rules while a similar relief is given for a country in Part II of the list only if it does not benefit from one of the reliefs specified. A company is regarded as carrying on a business in a country if 90% of its commercially quantified income is local source income.

This is not a list of countries which are regarded as not having a low level of taxation. The basis for the exclusion of the rules must be sought in the motive test. The point is explained by Arnold thus, "the reason . . . appears to be that low taxation is determined only for the country in which the company is resident. By adding the requirement that a company derive at least 90% of its income from the country, the list permits inclusion of high tax countries (such as France) that exempt foreign income."[2]

¹ See Revenue Press Release 20th October 1988, *Simon's Tax Intelligence* 1988, p. 771; however the list may be revised prospectively, e.g. *Simon's Tax Intelligence* 1988, p. 60.
² [1985] BTR 302.

34: 67 (6) *Limits—a summary.*

(a) The powers apply only to income profits of the foreign company—not capital gains; TA 1988, s. 747(6).

(b) The charge applies only to bodies subject to UK corporation tax—not income tax.

(c) no charge is made unless the amounts apportioned to the entitiy (or any associates) equals or exceeds 10% of the total chargeable profits of the foreign company; TA 1988, s. 747(5).

(d) no charge is made unless the chargeable profits of the foreign company exceed £20,000; TA 1988, s. 748(1)(d).

(e) no charge is made unless the foreign company is resident in a country in which there is a lower level of taxation.

(f) no charge is made if the foreign company follows an acceptable distribution policy.

(g) no charge is made if the company fulfils the public quotation condition.

(h) no charge is made if the foreign company's activities are exempt.

(i) no charge is made if the transactions generating the profits were carried out for reasons other than reducing UK tax.

35 The foreign taxpayer and the United Kingdom tax system

35: 01 Income tax is charged on sources within the UK[1] and so to non-residents by the following provisions:

Schedule A—land in the UK (TA 1988, s. 15).

Schedule C—public revenue dividends payable in the UK but certain special rules exempt non-residents (TA 1988, ss. 17, 47 and 48).

Schedule D, Cases I and II—profit from any trade or profession carried on within the UK to the extent of the profits there arising (TA 1988, s. 18(1)(*a*)(iii).[2]

Case III—from any property—as defined—within the UK (TA 1988, s. 18(1)(*a*)(iii).

Case VI—any annual profits or gains not falling under any other Case or Schedule.

Schedule E—Cases I, II and III (TA 1988, s. 19), supra, § **6: 01**.

Schedule F—distributions by companies resident in the UK (TA 1988, s. 20).

Corporation tax is charged on non-resident companies trading through a branch or agency in the UK (TA 1988, ss. 6 and 11), supra, § **23: 06**; the profits of a trade carried on in the UK but without a branch or agency are subject to income tax.

CGT is charged on the trade assets of non-residents trading through a branch or agency supra, § **34: 44**.

A review of the principles applicable in this area has resulted in the decision not to make any general change.[3]

EXAMPLE
Smith is neither resident nor ordinarily resident in the UK, nor has he a UK domicile. His UK sources of income assessable for 1989–90 are as follows:

Rent from UK property	£3,000
Dividends from UK companies	£10,000 net
Duties performed outside UK as part of employment with non-resident employer	£10,000
Duties performed in UK under employment with a non-UK employer	£2,500
Interest in the following UK government stocks:	
$3\frac{1}{2}\%$ War Loan	£3,500
6% Funding Loan	£1,200

Assessment on Smith to UK tax would be as follows:

Rents (Schedule A)	£3,000
Dividends (Schedule F)	£10,000 (excluding tax credit)
UK Schedule E duties	£2,500
	£15,500

Notes

(1) Assuming that Smith does not satisfy any of the conditions in TA 1988, s. 278 he is not entitled to claim any personal reliefs, supra, § 3: 21.

(2) Smith is not subject to UK tax on UK Schedule E earnings paid by non-UK employer for work performed outside the UK.

(3) Interest on certain UK Government securities to non-residents is tax free, supra, § 9: 33.

(4) Assuming no double taxation treaty and since Smith is not entitled to personal reliefs, he is not entitled to claim credit on UK company dividends. The sum distributed is not grossed up to include the credit since he is not entitled to use it, supra, § 24: 12.

---

[1] A UK patent is a UK source, TA 1988, s. 524(2); but see extra-statutory concession B8 (1988), **Simon's Taxes, Division H2.2.**

[2] On generous practice with regard to certain types of interest see extra-statutory concession B13 (1988), **Simon's Taxes Division H2.2.**

[3] [1985] STI, p. 741.

PLACE OF TRADE

35: 02   A non-resident is taxable under Schedule D, Case I on his profits from a trade *within* as opposed to one *with* the UK.[1] On the other hand, the presence of an administrative office or perhaps a representative office supplying information in London will not give rise to tax so long as the office does not trade. United Kingdom practice appears to be generous, especially in the banking and finance fields. A company may of course have both a representative office and a separate trading branch.

It was decided early on that the mere purchase of goods in this country for export and resale abroad was not enough to amount for trading here.[2] Trading here was defined by Brett LJ in *Erichsen v Last*:[3]

> "Wherever profitable contracts are habitually made in England by or for a foreigner with persons in England because those persons are in England, to do something for or to supply something to those persons, such foreigners are exercising a profitable trade in England even though everything done or supplied by those persons in order to fulfil the contract is done abroad."

Hence the running of a cabled message service sending messages overseas and the running of a shipping company[4] are trades within the UK.

Simon's Taxes B3.108, 109; Butterworths Income Tax Service C8.101, H2.01, 02.

[1] TA 1988, s. 18(1)(*a*)(iii).

[2] *Sulley v AG* (1860) 5 H & N 711, 2 TC 149n; cf. *Greenwood v F. L. Smidth & Co* [1922] 1 AC 417, 8 TC 205 where the goods were sold in England and *Taxation Comrs v Kirk* [1900] AC 588, PC where the goods were manufactured here for export and not simply bought. The danger in

the rule in *Sulley v AG* is that a foreigner may employ an agent here to buy goods and yet the agent may have an undisclosed interest in the business. This may lead to evasion especially when the agent is a relative of the principal.

[3] (1881) QBD 414, 4 TC 422 at 425.
[4] *Neilsen, Andersen & Co v Collins* [1928] AC 34, 13 TC 91.

35: 03 Most of the cases have been concerned with the sale of goods by a non-resident to someone in the UK, and the basic test has been that the trade is carried on where the contracts of sale are made.[1] The place of a contract is determined according to English domestic law and this is the place at which the acceptance of an offer is communicated. It follows that an acceptance by post completes the contract at the place of posting whereas an acceptance by telex completes the contract at the place of receipt. This principle is comparatively simple to apply when the foreigner deals directly with the customer but difficult questions of fact arise when an intermediary is employed. The fact that the foreigner uses an agent or stations an employee[2] in England is not sufficient to create a trade within as distinct from with the UK. Here too great attention is paid to the place of the contract.[3]

Simon's Taxes B3.109.
[1] E.g. *Maclaine & Co v Eccott* [1926] AC 424, 10 TC 481. On importance of place of delivery see Wills J in *Thomas Turner (Leicester) Ltd v Rickman* (1898) 4 TC 25 at 34, but cf. Lord Cave in *Maclaine & Co v Eccott* at 432, 575.
[2] As in *Greenwood v F L Smidth & Co* [1922] 1 AC 417, 8 TC 205.
[3] E.g. per Will J in *Thomas Turner (Leicester) Ltd v Rickman* (1898) 4 TC 25 at 34.

35: 04 Where a contract is made through an agent, the normal principles of offer and acceptance must be applied to determine where the contract is made. Where an agent merely has to consult his foreign principal before accepting contracts the trade is carried on here. If however his sole function is to pass the offer to head office which communicates directly with the customer, the foreigner is trading with and not within the UK.

In *Grainger & Son v Gough*[1] Louis Roederer canvassed orders for champagne in the UK through the firm of Grainger and Son, who would pass on all orders and money received from the customers in the UK to Rheims from where Roederer would despatch the champagne. The contracts for the sale of wine being made in France and both the property and the risk passing to the purchasers in France, the House of Lords held, reversing the Commissioners, that Roederer was not trading in but with the UK. There being no liability on Roederer, Grainger and Son were not accountable for tax as agents of Roederer.

The place of the contract distinguished *Grainger v Gough* from the earlier cases in which the courts had held that a trade was carried on in the UK. In *Pommery and Greno v Apthorpe*,[2] the London agents of Pommery held stocks of wine in London which were used for all save orders for "considerable quantities" and paid monies received into Pommery's London bank account. The court had little difficulty upholding the Commissioners' finding that the trade was carried on in England. The fact that Pommery had a principal establishment outside the UK and that their sales in the UK amounted to only a small part of their total trade was irrelevant.

Simon's Taxes B3.110.
[1] [1896] AC 325, 3 TC 462.
[2] (1886) 2 TC 182; cf. *Werle & Co v Colquhoun* (1888) 20 QBD 753, 2 TC 402.

35: 05   The notion that the place of the contract determines the place of the trade is a very English notion since it combines the obsession with sale as the paradigm contract with the doctrine of the source. As Esher MR, put it in *Werle & Co v Colquhoun*, "the contract is the very foundation of the trade. It is the trade really"[1] or, as Rowlatt J, put it, until the sale is effected the trade is incomplete.[2] There has to be some practical limit saying how far the courts are to go back in locating profits. The question is where the profits are made and not why. So the courts do not go beyond the business operations from which the profits derive.

The cases also show that the place of the contract is not a touchstone. In *Maclaine & Co v Eccott* while describing the place of the contract as the most important and indeed the crucial question, Lord Cave listed other factors such as the place where payment is to be made for the goods sold, and the place where the goods are to be delivered, and disclaimed any exhaustive test.[3] The place of contract has been further downgraded by Lord Radcliffe[4]— "It cannot mean more than that the law requires that great importance should be attached to the place of sale. It follows that the place of sale will not be the determining factor if there are other circumstances present that outweigh its importance." The formulation generally preferred is that of Atkin LJ—"Where do the operations take place from which the profits in substance arise".[5] So in *IRC v Brackett*[6] a non-resident company was held to be trading in the UK where its agent carried on its activities in the UK, these being the essential operations of the company's trade.

Simon's Taxes B3.107–117.
[1] 2 TC 402 at 410 and [1908] AC 46 PC.
[2] *F. L. Smidth & Co v Greenwood* (1920) 8 TC 193 at 199.
[3] [1926] AC 424 at 432. To the same effect Scrutton LJ in *Belfour v Mace* (1928) 13 TC 539 at 558.
[4] *Firestone Tyre and Rubber Co v Lewellin* [1957] 1 All ER 561, 37 TC 111 at 142.
[5] *F. L. Smidth & Co v Greenwood* [1921] 3 KB 583 at 593, 8 TC 193.
[6] [1986] STC 521 the case concerned the services of a property consultant working for a Jersey company created by a settlement of which he was the settlor. The settlor was held assessable under TA 1988, s. 739 (supra, § **34: 24**) on his own account and on behalf of the company under TMA 1970, s. 79 (infra, § **35: 08**).

35: 06   The place of contract, although useful as a test in the area of simple sale, is less happy in the manufacturing sphere.[1] Atkin LJ said that it was perfectly possible for a manufacturing business to be carried on here even though the contracts for the sale of goods are made abroad. "The contracts in this case were made abroad. But I am not prepared to hold that this test is decisive. I can imagine cases where the contract of resale is made abroad and yet the manufacture of the goods, some negotiation of the terms and complete execution of the contract take place here under such circumstances that the trade was in truth exercised here. I think the question is where do the operations take place from which the profits in substance arise."[2] In *Firestone Tyre and Rubber Co Ltd v Lewellin*[3] the UK subsidiary—Brentford—of a US parent—Akron—made tyres in the UK and supplied them to foreign subsidiaries at cost plus 5%. The court held that the US parent was trading in the UK—as was the UK subsidiary and that the location of the master agreement governing the trade between the parent and its subsidiaries was not conclusive.

The operations, the supply of the tyres and delivery alongside ship in a UK port, took place in England, constituted the carrying on of a trade in England and that trade, the Commissioners had correctly held, was the trade of Akron not Brentford.[4] The obligation on Brentford to account to Akron for any profit in excess of 5% was of crucial importance here. It followed that Brentford as the regular agents of Akron could be assessed to the tax due from Akron.

Simon's Taxes B3.118.
[1] Cf. Lord Salvesen in *Crookston Bros v Furtado* (1910) 5 TC 602 at 623.
[2] Cf. Lord Esher in *Grainger & Son v Gough* (1896) 3 TC 311 at 317.
[3] [1957] 1 All ER 561, 37 TC 111.
[4] Per Lord Radcliffe at 143.

COMPUTATION OF PROFITS—TRANSFER PRICING

35: 07   Profits of a trade carried on within the country will be computed according to the normal principles applicable to Schedule D, Case I. TA 1988, s. 770 enables the Revenue to counteract the efforts of a trader with concerns in several countries who seeks to prevent profits arising in this country through the manipulation of prices. In such circumstances the Board may direct that face market value be taken.[1] The proviso, preventing the substitution of market value when the price enters into the accounts of the other party, is no obstacle to the Revenue since it applies only where that other party is resident in the UK. Other ways of reducing profits are to establish in the UK other aspects of business of an inherently loss making character such as administration or research. These are not necessarily harmful to the UK even though induced by thoughts of tax saving.

When it appears to the inspector that the true amount of the profits cannot be readily ascertained, he may instead assess on a percentage of the turnover of the business done between the non-resident and his branch or agent.[2]

EXAMPLE
X Ltd is a non-UK resident company with a branch operation "B" trading within the UK. The world-wide profits of X Ltd amount to £20 million. Total turnover amounts to £200 million of which £25 million is said to be attributable to B. The UK Revenue authorities having failed to ascertain the true amount of the profits of B assign 12½% (i.e. £25 million as a percentage of £200 million) of the worldwide profits to B, namely, £2.5 million (i.e. 12½% of £20 million).

Some relief is provided when the trade is carried on inside the UK but the goods or produce are manufactured or produced outside the UK, as when a foreign car manufacturer sells cars in the UK. Then the person in whose name the non-resident person is chargeable may elect to be charged not in respect of the whole profit but only in respect of that part which arises from the sale as distinct from the manufacture of the goods.[3] This rule establishes neutrality between the manufacturer who sells in this country and one who establishes a separate distributing company here. If this election is made, the basis of taxation is what an agent might reasonably have earned; the use of a separate agency company forces the Revenue to use TA 1988, s. 770. This notional dividing up of the trade does not apply where a resident manufactures goods in the UK for resale abroad. He must set up his subsidiary companies overseas with any necessary Treasury consent.[4] Nor does it apply where an agent manufactures goods in the UK for export to the non-resident for resale.[5]

The issue of transfer pricing has become highly topical. The problem arises in various contexts. In connection with the sale of goods the problems mostly concern the method by which the goods are to be priced. In some situations there will be an actual market in which identical goods are dealt in at arm's length. Where this is not so another method must be sought. Sometimes a figure which will give a profit similar to that of the other companies in the same sector may be suitable and at others the yield on the capital involved may be employed. However, both these methods make a series of assumptions which may be quite misplaced and the more usual methods are either cost plus or resale price, the latter being more correctly described as price minus. Cost plus involves taking the cost of production and adding an appropriate percentage. This involves many problems in determining cost and the appropriate mark-up.[6] It may however be useful where semi-finished goods are sold or when the subsidiary is in essence a sub-contractor. The resale price method begins with the price at which the goods are sold on to an independent purchaser and then reduces that price by a percentage to reflect the vendor's profit.[7] Here there are problems about the appropriate mark-up save where the goods are sold on very quickly with little risk to the person reselling and without having been subjected to any intermediate process.

Problems also arise in connection with royalty and trade-mark licence payments,[8] with the allocation of research and development costs[9] and of head office and other central administration costs.[10] There are also many problems in connection with banking enterprises.[11] However, one of the principal current problems is the effect of a loan by one company to another within the same group but usually, although not necessarily, in different jurisdictions. The current Revenue view is that where the debt-equity ratio of the borrower company is greater than 1:1 any interest paid on the loan is not really interest but a dividend with the result that not only is the sum not deductible as a charge on income but it is a qualifying distribution with ACT consequences. This is known as the thin capitalisation problem.

Where problems of this nature arise there will be obvious difficulties in negotiating with the Revenue to see whether TA 1988, s. 770 should apply, and if so how it should be applied. There are, however, even more substantial problems where the Revenue may take one view but the revenue authorities in another jurisdiction—or even the Customs and Excise— may take a different view. Where double tax treaties apply it may be possible to use the mutual agreement and competent authority provisions to resolve these problems to avoid double taxation but the time taken can be substantial. In 1977 there was an EEC draft Directive to give the taxpayer a right to take the matter to independent arbitration which would set the figure for all the interested systems. It says much about the European ideal that even this proposal has got nowhere—despite its favourable reception by the European Parliament.[12]

Simon's Taxes B3.119, 120, 927; Butterworths Income Tax Service C1.91.

[1] TA 1988, s. 770(1) and (2)(*d*). On Revenue practice see [1981] STI, p. 42. On whether this can be widened by a double tax treaty see [1970] BTR 388 (Oliver) at 396. Cf. Belgian Tax Code, Art. 146(1) and OECD Model Treaty, Art. 9. For a depressing example see UK Monopolies Report on the Supply of Chlordiazepoxide and Diazepam, paras. 138 and 162 and an earlier use see [1977] BTR 493. The allocation of group research costs and overheads made the company's profits vary from £5,000 to £263,000 but the Monopolies Commission added back excess transfer prices and made additional profit of £1,700,000 to £1,930,000. There was no record of TA 1988, ss. 770, 773 having been used, however the Inland Revenue later extracted extra taxes of £1.85m.

[2] TMA 1970, s. 80 (appeal on the percentage lies to the Commissioners and from there to the Board of Referees). The RC (1920) § 50 recommended that turnover to be fixed by reference to the results shown by British resident traders in the same class of business.

[3] TMA 1970, s. 81.

[4] Under TA 1988, s. 765.

[5] See RC 1920 § 54 and *Taxation Comrs v Kirk* [1900] AC 588.

[6] See OECD Report 1979, pp. 63–69.

[7] Ibid, pp. 56–62.

[8] Ibid, Chapter III.

[9] Ibid, pp. 102–104.

[10] Ibid, Chapter IV and OECD Report 1984, pp 73–91.

[11] OECD Report 1984, pp. 45–70.

[12] Ibid, p. 21, § **42**.

Collecting the tax[1]

35: 08   It is one thing to charge the non-resident who trades in the UK and another thing to collect the tax. Until 1915 an agent could be charged with his non-resident principal's tax but only if the profits or gains of the trade passed through the hands of the agent. This charge was avoided by devices which made sure that the agent received nothing, as where the proceeds were paid to a foreign agent or to the principal direct. Hence in 1915 it was provided that a non-resident should be chargeable in the name of any branch or agent whether in receipt of gains or not. This now forms part of TMA 1970, s. 78. In 1915 it was also provided by what is now TMA 1970, s. 79 that "A non-resident person shall be assessable and chargeable to income tax in respect of any profits or gains arising, whether directly or indirectly, through or from any branch or agency[2] and shall be so assessable and chargeable in the name of the branch or agent".[3] It is not clear whether s. 79 adds anything to s. 78.[4] The only possible difference lies in the use of the word indirectly in s. 79. However it is clear that neither s. 78 nor s. 79 are charging sections; they are simply machinery sections which make the agent liable only in those circumstances in which the non-resident is liable.[5] TMA 1970, s. 79 is frequently used by the Revenue.[6]

Simon's Taxes B3.118; Butterworths Income Tax Service A5.07, H1.12.

[1] See also S.I. 1970, No. 488, and TA 1988, s. 536 on which see *IRC v Longmans Green* (1932) 17 TC 272.

[2] "Branch or agency" is defined in TMA 1970, s. 118.

[3] F (No. 2) A 1915, s. 31 heavily attacked in submissions to the RC (1920).

[4] Probably it adds nothing—Lord Sterndale MR in *F L Smidth v Greenwood* [1921] 3 KB 581

974   Part VII—The international dimension

at 591, 8 TC 193 at 202. The problem seems to be that, s. 31(1) stated a purpose which sub-s. (2) carried it into effect, but these were separated in ITA 1918 (General Rules 5 & 6).
⁵ Greenwood v F L Smidth & Co [1922] 1 AC 417, 8 TC 193.
⁶ As in IRC v Brackett [1986] STC 521.

Independent agents

35: 09   Not all intermediaries are liable to tax on the profits of their principals. First, a broker is not liable for tax on the profits of those non-residents for whom he acts provided he is carrying on a bona fide brokerage business in the UK and he receives at least the customary rate of remuneration for the transaction. If these conditions are satisfied the broker is not liable even though he acts regularly for the non-resident.[1]

Simon's Taxes B3.119.
¹ TMA 1970, s. 82(1). A broker, unlike an agent, acts for both sides (per Bankes LJ in Wilcock v Pinto & Co [1925] 1 KB 30 at 42, 9 TC 111 at 130).

35: 10   Secondly the term "broker" includes a "general commission agent". This term must be construed eiusdem generis with broker.[1] Such an agent holds himself out as willing to act for others;[1] further he generally negotiates for commission so that in one case he was held not to be a general commission agent when he paid for the goods as soon as he received them instead of waiting to pay the principal out of the proceeds of sale.[2]

¹ Per Megarry J in Fleming v London Produce Co Ltd [1968] 2 All ER 975 at 985–6.
² T L Boyd & Sons Ltd v Stephen (1926) 10 TC 698 at 746.

35: 11   Thirdly an agent is not liable unless he is an authorised person carrying on the regular agency of the non-resident as Brentford did for Akron in the Firestone case. These words are however "apparently very vague".[1]

¹ Per Rowlatt J in T L Boyd & Sons Ltd v Stephen (1926) 10 TC 698 at 747.

35: 12   Fourthly the fact that a non-resident person executes sales or carries out transactions with other non-residents which would make him chargeable in the name of a resident, e.g. an agent, is not of itself to make the agent liable.[1] This "two foreigner" provision is apparently designed to protect the entrepot trade.[2] Where neither the goods nor the parties are within the jurisdiction it would be wrong to make the agent liable to tax on his principal's profits, and the agent is therefore not liable. It would seem that the agent will not be liable for his principal's tax even if he does receive the profits.[3]

Simon's Taxes B3.123.
¹ TMA 1970, s. 82(2).
² RC 1920 § 52.

³ *Contra* Lord Cave LC in *Maclaine & Co v Eccott* [1926] AC 424 at 435. While Lord Cave's view may have been good law before 1915 there is nothing in Part VIII of the TMA 1970 to make liability turn on receipt of profit.

35: 13   Fifthly, TMA 1970, s. 78 is excluded for profits arising from investment transactions carried out by investment managers acting for non-residents provided they are not connected persons, there is no offshore fund involved (as in § **34: 38**) and the managers' remuneration is reasonable.¹

Investment transactions are defined as transactions on a Stock Exchange or a recognised futures exchange or the placing of money at interest. If the investment business is part of a larger business it is treated as a separate trade. This applies for 1985–86 and later years.

Simon Taxes B3.118; Butterworths Income Tax Service H1.12.
¹ FA 1985, s. 50 following a consultative document issued by the Inland Revenue December 1984, see [1984] STI, p. 789.

35: 14   Sixthly, by concession, when agents do not have management and control of interest paid through them to non-residents, no claim is made under TMA 1970, s. 78.¹ If the principal does not have a branch in this country over which he has control he may be treated as exempt from UK tax in respect of the interest.

¹ Extra-statutory concession B13 (1988); **Simon's Taxes Division H2.2.**

Deduction at source

35: 15   One should note also the various provisions which require deduction by the person making the payment where the payee is non-resident; e.g. rent, (TA 1988, s. 43), interest (TA 1988, ss. 82 and 349) and public lending rights and copyright royalties (TA 1988, s. 536) as does the ACT scheme applicable when a UK resident company makes a qualifying distribution.

35: 16   TA 1988, s. 555 provides for the deduction of tax from payments to a person who is an entertainer or sportsman of a prescribed description who performs an activity of a prescribed description in the UK and the person is not resident in the UK in the year of assessment in which the activity is performed.¹ The task of prescribing and refining is carried out by regulations published on 26 March 1987;² the obligation to deduct begins with payments on or after 1st May 1987.³ The Revenue accept that the obligation to deduct is subject to the provisions of the relevant double taxation agreement; thus the UK–US convention grants an exemption where the gross receipts of the person do not exceed $15,000 in the tax year concerned.⁴

The regulations contain considerable scope for problems of interpretation and timing but their main thrust is clear and they are widely drawn. Among matters to be noted is the rule that while the maximum amount to be withheld is the basic rate of tax, now 25%, the amount paid can be treated by the revenue as a net sum thus causing the sums to be grossed up, a process which makes the effective rate of tax on the net sum one of 33.33%.⁵ There is also provision for covering payments to persons other than the entertainer, a rule which uses the concepts to be found in TA 1988, s. 681.[6]

---

[1] TA 1988, s. 555.

[2] Income Tax (Entertainers and Sportsmen) Regulations 1987, SI 1987, No. 530, [1987] STI, p. 283.

[3] SI 1987 No. 530, para. 1.

[4] HC Written Answer 25 March 1987, Vol. 113, col. 212; [1987] STI, p. 274.

[5] SI 1987, No. 530, para. 17.

[6] Cf supra, §§ **13: 02** et seq. Interestingly the definition of settlement is taken from s. 670 which is wider than s. 681.

---

36 Double taxation relief

INTRODUCTION

36: 01 The UK taxes income if it arises here or if the person entitled to it is resident here. This leaves untaxed only foreign income[1] arising to a non-resident. Since other countries too adopt a generous view of their own taxing powers it is inevitable that some income will be taxed twice.

Such double taxation is thought to be objectionable since, by making overseas profits more expensive than domestic profits, it discourages a person from trading overseas and so interferes with international trade. The ideal situation would be one in which there was neutrality both between the tax burdens of a person trading at home and abroad and between a resident and a non-resident trading in the same country. Until however there is one tax system common to all countries it will be impossible to achieve both these objectives.

---

[1] On concessionary double taxation relief for two types of UK income see extra-statutory concession A12 (1988)—maintenance payable under UK court order—and B8 (1988)—royalties due under UK patent etc; **Simon's Taxes Division H2.2.**

Methods

36: 02 A tax system could achieve the avoidance of double taxation in a number of ways. Thus it could simply decide not to tax overseas income, either generally or of a particular sort. Such was in effect the case when the remittance basis was at its height, before 1914,[1] and until 1974 when the remittance basis was available to UK residents in respect of income earned overseas. The special status afforded to overseas trade corporations whereby they were exempt on trading income reinvested overseas was another instance.[2] Many countries give substantial exemptions for overseas trade in an attempt to assist their own balance of trade and general level of economic activity.[3]

---

[1] FA 1914, s. 5. For history see RC (1953) 1st Report Cmnd. 8761, §§ 15–20.
[2] Supra, § **34: 10.**
[3] See RC (1953) 1st Report, § 23 and Final Report 1955, App. III and see supra, § **34: 11.**

36: 03 Short therefore of abandoning the taxation of overseas income, the government has three options. First, it can enter into a double taxation agreement with the other country, a process authorised by TA 1988, s. 788. Treaty relief may exempt some income from tax in one country and give credit for foreign taxes on other income. Secondly it can unilaterally allow the foreign tax paid as a credit against the UK tax liability. This is permitted by TA 1988, s. 790. Thirdly it can decide that the foreign tax shall be deductible in computing the profits of the business, thus treating the foreign tax like any other business expense. This is permitted by TA 1988, s. 811; such foreign tax may not be deducted in respect of income charged on a remittance basis.

A person may elect not to take the credit relief.[1] This he will usually do if to treat the foreign tax as a deduction in computing income from that source will yield tax advantages. This may lead an excess of foreign tax to form part of a loss allowable against general income of that year.

Conversely as country of source, it may wish to levy income tax on income accruing to a non-resident. Here it may either not tax at all (e.g. Schedule C, supra, § **9: 32**) or may give credit for tax paid in the country of residence (not a feature of the UK tax system) or it may under treaty levy a reduced rate of tax, called withholding tax, leaving the other country to give credit if it wishes.

Similar provisions apply to CGT[2] and to corporation tax[3] on capital gains.

The basic pattern is for UK treaties to follow that laid down in successive model treaties devised by the OECD in 1946, 1963 and 1977. This pattern has been criticised for its bias in favour of the country of residence over the country of source. This bias may have been acceptable to West European governments anxious for foreign, particularly American, involvement but has caused great difficulties for less developed countries.[4]

Butterworths Tax Treaties/Simon's Taxes: F1.101–113, 131–151; Butterworths Income Tax Service H3.03.

[1] TA 1988, s. 805.
[2] CGTA 1979, ss. 10 and 11 on which see SP 6/88; **Simon's Taxes Division H3.2.**
[3] TA 1988, s. 797.
[4] See Irish, 1974 ICLQ p. 292; Atchabahian, 1971 JBIFD p. 451 and Caroll, *International Lawyer*, vol. 2, p. 692. Other models have been drawn up in Mexico (1943) and by the Andean States.

UNITED KINGDOM TREATY RELIEF

36: 04　The UK today has treaties with 91 countries[1] including (separately), the Isle of Man, Jersey, and Guernsey (including Alderney). There are treaties with nearly all Western European countries with most members of the Commonwealth and with countries such as Japan and Israel. However there are no treaties with many of the Arab countries such as Saudi Arabia, nor with tax havens such as the Cayman Islands and Liechtenstein. Arrangements with some countries are limited to transport profits and employees, e.g. Argentina, Brazil, Ethiopia and Iran.

Butterworths Tax Treaties/Simon's Taxes: F4.101, 102; Butterworths Income Tax Service H3.13.
[1] More correctly "territories" since the Crown is authorised to make treaties with any "territory". TA 1988, s. 788.

Effect

36: 05   A double taxation treaty provision being made under statutory authority and so becoming part of municipal law may override the normal rules of UK tax law,[1] but whether it does so or not is a matter of construction.[2]

Where a treaty assigns a tax exclusively to the UK this is not a direction that the UK shall tax, but rather the recognition of a power to tax. An appropriately drafted treaty might be interpreted as a direction to tax, but it is unclear whether this would override the normal domestic tax law.

[1] It follows that where the text of the order in council does not agree with that of the treaty, the former prevails. See [1970] BTR 388 (Oliver), at 398–400.

[2] *IRC v Collco Dealings Ltd* [1961] 1 All ER 762, 39 TC 509, and see *Ostime v Australian Mutual Provident Society* [1960] AC 459, 38 TC 492 (TA 1988 s. 445 excluded by treaty).

Relief by exemption

36: 06   This simply provides that income of the type stated shall be exempt in one country.[1] Whether and to what extent it will be taxable in the other country is a matter for the revenue law of that other country. For example income earned overseas by a visiting teacher there for temporary purposes, is sometimes exempt from tax in the country of service but is taxed in the country of residence.[2] If that employment lasts more than 365 days and the teacher is continuously absent from the UK for that period, no UK tax will be payable either.[3] A more common form of exemption will exempt a person from tax in the country where the income arises if he is subject to tax in respect of the income in the other country. It appears to be the generous practice of some foreign countries to regard income taxed in the UK on preferential reduced or remittance bases as being "subject to tax" in the UK and so not liable to the foreign tax.

Examples of income which is often given exemption in either of these forms include, trading profits arising otherwise than through a permanent establishment, pensions and salaries paid by governments.

Butterworths Tax Treaties/Simon's Taxes: F1.112; Butterworths Income Tax Service H3.03.
[1] Receipts by a non-resident carrying on a banking, insurance or share-dealing business in the UK, although exempt from UK tax, are not to be excluded in computing the profits of that business so as to give rise to a loss under TA 1988, s. 393 or s. 436: TA 1988, s. 808. This ends a "fascinating anomaly" by which UK branches of US banks and insurance companies could claim treaty exemption on US source interest without restriction on the right to offset interest paid on the corresponding borrowing against their other UK income.

[2] E.g. 1975 UK–US Treaty, Art. 20.

[3] TA 1988, s. 193 and Sch. 12, para. 3, supra, § **6: 06**.

Discrimination

36: 07   The model agreement[1] prohibits the Government from discriminating against citizens of the other countries with sources in the first country. This does not prevent the first from raising or lowering its own tax rates but only from discriminating against non-residents. The purpose of this clause is to prevent discriminatory legislation—not to prevent unfairness.[2] The UK Inland Revenue allow taxpayers to invoke such a provision only sparingly; for examples see §§ **23: 13** and **25: 12**.

Treaties also contain a mutual agreement procedure to resolve any remaining difficulties.[3] The taxpayer may thus become the pawn in a battle between two revenue machines.

Butterworths Tax Treaties/Simon's Taxes: F1.261, 263.
[1] OECD Model Treaty, Art. 24; [1981] BTR 47.
[2] *Sun Life Assurance Co of Canada v Pearson* [1984] STI, p. 364.
[3] OECD Model Treaty, Art. 25, e.g. under transfer-pricing, supra, § **35: 07**.

Changes

36: 08   Double tax treaties are not immutable. The usual method of change adopted is renegotiation, a process which may be accelerated by announcing that a particular country will no longer be bound by its present treaties after a certain date.[1] Changes in the domestic tax law are not inhibited by the presence of a treaty[2] and some changes may have the effect of altering completely the basis of a treaty, e.g. the adoption of the imputation system of corporate taxation.

An interesting example of this process is TA 1988, s. 112(4), (5) which was designed to reverse the decision in *Padmore v IRC*.[3] That case held that where a partnership was resident in Jersey the effect of the UK–Jersey treaty was that not only was the Jersey Partnership as such exempt from UK tax on its profits but, more surprisingly, that a UK resident individual partner was exempt from UK income tax on his share of the profits. The new provision reverses this decision by amending TA 1988, s. 112 with retroactive effect[4] and states that the treaty is not to affect any liability to tax in respect of the resident partner's share of any income or capital gains of the partnership.[5]

Butterworths Tax Treaties/Simon's Taxes: F1.102, 111.
[1] E.g. Kenya.
[2] Whether the new domestic law is excluded by the treaty is a question of construction—*IRC v Collco Dealings Ltd* [1961] 1 All ER 762, 39 TC 509.
[3] [1989] STC 493, CA.
[4] The new provision is deemed always to have been made save that it is not to affect any court decision before 17th March 1987 or the law to be applied by an appellate court where the judgment of the High Court or Court of Session was given before that date—one infers that no litigation was concluded in Northern Ireland. FA 1989, s. 115 purports to affect the construction of a treaty, an altogether different matter, but also retrospectively.
[5] Such a formula had been employed in other treaties e.g. Art II(3) of the UK–Switzerland Treaty of 1955.

TYPICAL CLAUSES

Residence

36: 09   The most important interpretation section will define the connecting factors, principally residence, so as to avoid the situation in which income is taxed in the country of residence and yet the taxpayer is resident in both countries according to those countries' definitions of residence. These definitions displace the normal rules of residence but, save where this would deprive a provision of any force, only for the purposes of the treaty.[1]

The Revenue now accept that "effective management" may be located elsewhere than central management and control, see SP6/83, *supra*, § **32: 19**.

Butterworths Tax Treaties/Simon's Taxes: F1.205; Butterworths Income Tax Service H3.23.

[1] *IRC v Exxon Corpn* [1982] STC 356. For an example of the importance of such definitions see *Lord Strathalmond v IRC* [1972] 3 All ER 715, 48 TC 537 and compare *Avery Jones v IRC* [1976] STC 290, [1976] 2 All ER 898.

(i) *A trader*

36: 10   If a trader is resident in the UK and carries on a trade partly inside and partly outside the UK he will be taxable under Schedule D, Case I on his profits as they arise.[1] Whether he is taxable in the foreign country depends first on that country's tax law. If no foreign tax is payable no double tax problem arises. If, however, foreign tax is payable, the next step is to look at the treaty which will probably permit the foreign country to tax the industrial and commercial profits allocable to the enterprise's "permanent establishment" in that state. This last term is separately defined in each treaty but generally includes,[2] a branch, place of management,[3] factory or other fixed place of business but not an agency (unless the agent has and habitually exercises a general power[4] to negotiate and conclude contracts on behalf of his principal), nor a bona fide broker nor a general commission agent.[5] Often treaties will also state that certain activities such as the display of goods are not to amount to having a permanent establishment.[6] The foreign state will usually be allowed to tax only so much of the investment income and profits as are attributable to the permanent establishment[7] and the treaty may say how the profits are to be allocated to that establishment.

Butterworths Tax Treaties/Simon's Taxes: F1.206.

[1] TA 1988, s. 18(3), *supra*, § **34: 02**.

[2] See 1977 OECD Model Treaty, Art. 5.

[3] This derives from the United Kingdom test of residence. A person may have a permanent establishment in the United Kingdom and yet not be resident here—e.g. *Greenwood v F L Smidth & Co Ltd* [1922] 1 AC 417, 8 TC 193.

[4] A permanent establishment in the foreign country will also give rise to tax on capital gains and it may result in a heavier tax on dividends from that country if the business is incorporated there.

[5] See *American Wheelabrator and Equipment Corpn v Minister of National Revenue* (1951) 51 DTC 285.

[6] 1977 OECD Model Treaty, Art. 5(4).

[7] E.g. 1977 OECD Model Treaty, Art. 7. At one time more drastic tax consequences followed the presence of a permanent establishment giving rise almost to residence.

(ii) *A foreign trader*

36: 11   Where a business is carried on through a permanent establishment in a foreign country business profits earned by that permanent establishment are taxable in the country of source.[1] Profits earned otherwise than by the establishment are taxable in the country of residence. If the trader decides to set up a subsidiary company in the country of source, the profits of that company will be taxable in that country and there will be no immediate double tax problem. It is however possible to make sure, for example by fixing the prices at which goods are sold between different subsidiaries of the same multinational group, that the profits made in particular countries are not spectacular.[2] Moreover charges can be made for interest. Double tax problems arise when interest payments are made to the parent company and when the profits earned by the subsidiary leave that country in the form of dividends.

The model agreement provides for a withholding tax of a maximum of 10% on payments of interest[3] and of 15% on dividends save where the recipient is a company holding at least 25% of the shares in the paying company when the rate is 5%.[4] Royalty payments are taxable only in the country of residence save where there is an effective connection between the permanent establishment in the source country and the property giving rise to royalties.[5] By contrast the Mexico model gave the taxation of dividends to the place where the capital was invested,[6] of interest to the place of indebtedness[7] and of royalties to the place of exploitation[8]—that is the country of source. Many of these provisions in the OECD model, particularly those relating to dividends are simply unacceptable to less developed countries.

Butterworths Tax Treaties/Simon's Taxes: F1.212, 215–223; Butterworths Income Tax Service H3.25, 26.
  [1] 1977 Model Treaty, Art. 7(1).
  [2] Note Model Treaty, Art. 7(2).
  [3] Model Treaty, Art. 11. Uruguay levies a withholding rate of 44%. Some treaties exempt interest on normal intra-group loans.
  [4] Model Treaty, Art. 10.
  [5] Model Treaty, Art. 12.
  [6] Article IX.
  [7] Article II.
  [8] Article X (copyright royalties were excluded).

(iii) *An employee*

36: 12   A UK resident goes to work for a foreign company overseas. He may or may not be taxable in whole or in part under UK tax rules on foreign earnings.[1] Under the treaty he may well be declared to be taxable only in the country of his residence and not in the country of the employment if the employment is exercised there, which will probably be defined. Some treaties tax in the country of source only if the taxpayer spends a certain number of days in that country.[2]

Butterworths Tax Treaties/Simon's Taxes: F1.228; Butterworths Income Tax Service H3.27.
  [1] Supra, § 8: 09.
  [2] E.g. US–Belgium—90 days.

(iv) *Professional services*

36: 13   The OECD treaty grants the exclusive right to tax to the country of residence unless there is a "fixed base" in the other contracting state, in which even so much of the profit as is attributable to that fixed base is taxed there;[1] but this is modified for artistes and athletes.[2]

Butterworths Tax Treaties/Simon's Taxes: F1.227, 230; Butterworths Income Tax Service H3.25.
[1] 1977 OECD Model Treaty, Art. 14.
[2] 1977 OECD Model Treaty, Art. 17.

TREATY RELIEF BY CREDIT

36: 14   Where a treaty provides for relief by way of credit for the foreign tax paid, the way of giving relief is a matter for UK law and the rules are stated in TA 1988, ss. 792–806.[1]

Butterworths Tax Treaties/Simon's Taxes: F1.113; Butterworths Income Tax Service H3.03.
[1] TA 1988, s. 788(2). See TA 1988, s. 812–815 for the proposed withdrawal of certain treaty benefits from companies present in a "unitary state" (directed at unitary taxation in California and other states); for the current UK position see *Simon's Tax Intelligence* 1989, p. 283.

---

1 Residence

36: 15   The taxpayer must have been resident in the UK—whether or not also resident in another country—for the chargeable period.[1] This requires that he has been a resident throughout the period. Residence is defined by UK law—not by the code in the treaty.

Butterworths Tax Treaties/Simon's Taxes: F1.118.
[1] TA 1988, s. 794 see further, infra, § **36: 32**, for unilateral relief in two cases where taxpayer not resident. See also TA 1988, s. 794 which extends relief to UK branches of non-resident banks. For earlier periods relief was by extra-statutory concession C14 (1985) (obsolete), **Simon's Taxes, Division H2.2.**

---

2 The foreign tax

36: 16   The foreign tax is defined as the tax chargeable under the laws of the foreign territory.[1] The treaty making power is limited to relief for income tax or corporation tax and any taxes of a similar character imposed by the laws of that territory.[2] It is usual for the treaty to state precisely the taxes which may be claimed for credit.

The foreign tax is that chargeable rather than that paid so that credit is given only to the extent of the tax properly payable to the foreign country.[3]

Butterworths Tax Treaties/Simon's Taxes: F1.117; Butterworths Income Tax Service H3.04.
[1] TA 1988, s. 792(1). On adjustments to foreign tax by reason of change in exchange rate, see

Greig v Ashton (1956) 36 TC 581. In some treaties, although none involving the UK, the credit may exceed the local tax charged e.g. Argentine–West Germany 1966, which allowed a 15% credit although the Argentine tax was then 8%.

² TA 1988, s. 788(1). The Revenue often declares that taxes are similar, e.g. [1980] BTR 606.

³ On method of calculation see Revenue Press Release [1979] BTR 459.

Pioneer relief or tax sparing

36: 17 The logic of the tax credit scheme of relief means that concessions whereby the country of source lowers its tax rates are cancelled out since it results simply in a lower credit to set against the tax liability in the country of residence. Since 1961¹ provisions allow the taxpayer to treat the amount in respect of which the relief was given by the foreign country as if that tax had been paid. So far treaties containing such clauses have been made with Barbados, Israel, Malaysia, Malta, Jamaica, Pakistan, Portugal, Singapore and Trinidad and Tobago.²

The device of tax-sparing has been heavily criticised in and scarcely used by the US. The main objection to it is that by giving a positive advantage to the citizen trading overseas it breaks the fundamental principle underlying the notion of the tax credit which is neutrality between citizens trading abroad and those trading at home. Other objections are that it gives the largest tax benefits to the countries with the highest nominal tax rates³ without any necessary relationship to the fundamental economic needs of the country. It should not however be inferred that the US ignores the problem; it gives relief in a different way by in effect granting capital allowances in respect of expenditure outside the US, something permitted only under the UK capital allowance system if the trade falls within Schedule D, Case I.

Butterworths Tax Treaties/Simon's Taxes: F1.161.

¹ FA 1961, s. 17, now TA 1988, s. 788(3); s. 17 was amended in 1976.

² The UK's 100% tax allowances for machinery and plant (supra, § **8: 23**) placed the UK in a similar position *vis à vis* foreign countries whose capital this country is anxious to attract.

³ Counter-measures taken by developing countries include conditional withholding tax (Jamaica) and the raising of the tax level (Panama).

3 United Kingdom income

36: 18 In order to calculate the UK tax against which the foreign tax is to be set as a credit, one must first calculate the income to be taxed under UK law.

Income which is taxed on a remittance basis is grossed up to include the foreign tax payable. One cannot remit a sum net of tax and ask to have the foreign credit set against the UK tax on the net sum.

Income taxed on an arising basis is taken gross, that is without any deduction for the foreign tax. Where the income is a dividend and credit relief is due for the corporation tax underlying it, the sum must be grossed up to take account of the underlying tax, infra, § **36: 26**.

4   United Kingdom tax

36: 19   The UK tax on the income taxable is now calculated. A problem arises if the foreign territory allows the writing-off of capital expenditure more slowly than the UK. In order to prevent possible anomalies TA 1988, s. 810[1] allows the taxpayer to postpone his claim for UK allowance.[2] The maximum sum which may be postponed is that by which the UK allowance in that year exceeds the foreign allowance. The right to postpone UK allowances applies to all capital allowances except those for expenditure on machinery and plant incurred after 27th October 1970.[2]

Butterworths Tax Treaties/Simon's Taxes: F1.136.
[1] There is no provision for the converse case when the foreign allowance exceeds the UK allowance—this is in line with the general rule of charging UK tax at full rate save to the extent that foreign *tax* is payable. By concession this relief applies to trades under Schedule D, Case V [1981] STI, p. 201.
[2] TA 1988, s. 810(4)(*b*).

---

5   The credit

36: 20   Where credit is to be allowed against any of the UK taxes chargeable in respect of any income, the amount of the UK taxes so chargeable shall be reduced by the amount of the credit.[1] This simple rule masks many problems.

---

[1] TA 1988, s. 793(1). On credit for banks see TA 1988, s. 794.

Different basis periods

36: 21   It may happen that foreign tax is charged by reference to one period and UK tax by reference to another, e.g. where the UK uses a preceding year basis and the foreign system a current year basis. The Revenue view was that one should set the tax on the foreign income against the UK tax when that income came to be taxed; so if the foreign tax was paid in 1982–83 on current year basis it would be set against UK tax in 1983–84. This view has received statutory recognition for unilateral relief[1] but for treaty relief that view was rejected by the House of Lords in *Duckering v Gollan*[2] where owing to a change in the foreign country (New Zealand) from a preceding year to a current year no foreign tax had been paid in respect of the income taxed later in the UK and the Revenue therefore sought unsuccessfully to refuse any relief at all.

The decision of the House was based on the construction of what is now TA 1988, s. 793 and on the terms of the agreement with New Zealand which spoke of UK tax "in respect of" the foreign income. Since that time treaties falling to be renegotiated have adopted a different formula and credit is now allowed against any UK tax computed "by reference to the same profits".[3] Thus the decision in *Duckering v Gollan* has been reversed where the new formula has been adopted. While this may cause hardship in a case such as *Duckering v Gollan* where it could lead to the loss of relief, it is far more sensible to compare the two amounts of tax calculated by reference to the same figure. The House of Lords view could lead to serious discrepancies and perhaps loss of relief where the income from the source fluctuates from year to year.

Butterworths Tax Treaties/Simon's Taxes: F1.117.
[1] TA 1988, s. 790.
[2] [1965] 2 All ER 115, 42 TC 333.
[3] E.g. UK–NZ Agreement (1966), Art. XVIII(1)(a). However some treaties have not yet been renegotiated on this point.

36: 22   A further problem arises where as with opening years the same period is taken as the basis of assessment for more than one year. The Revenue view meant that once the foreign tax credit charged on the opening year had been used it could not be used against the income of later years; this was upheld in *Imperial Chemical Industries Ltd v Caro*[1] where the tax paid in the first period could not be also set against tax for the second. This is now reversed and additional relief given by TA 1988, s. 804 subject to an overall limit.

EXAMPLE

A, resident in the UK, makes up the profits of his trade on a calendar year basis. On 1st January 1987 he opened a new trade in Ruritania. His profits from Ruritania for the period to 31st December 1987 were £2,000, on which he paid Ruritanian tax of £500.

A's assessment to UK tax on the Ruritanian profits will be:

	Basis	Profits	Credit
1986–87	actual to 5/4/85	500	125
1986–87	first twelve months	2,000	500
1987–88	preceding year	2,000	500
			£1,125

The rule stated in s. 804 and which is applied in the example requires the adjustment of the overseas tax where the number of UK periods of assessment (here $2\frac{1}{4}$) exceeds the number of foreign periods of assessment (1); i.e. £500 is inflated by $2\frac{1}{4}$ to £1,125. By s. 804(3) the credit is adjusted in the proportion which the number of UK periods of assessment bears to the number of foreign periods; parts of periods are entered at their true fractional value. This is the total credit allowable. The additional credit to be given for any year is not to exceed the difference between the total credit allowable for the period of $2\frac{1}{4}$ years and the credit already given in previous years.

A complication arises on the cessation of the source since under UK tax law some periods, here called non-basis periods, will provide no figure for the UK assessment, even though foreign tax is paid during those periods. Section 804(5) goes on to provide that one is to add the foreign tax paid during those non-base periods to the basic credit for the opening period (in our example £500) and compare that sum with the total tax credit in fact allowed (£1,125). If the latter exceeds the sum of the former two figures then the excess is to be assessed to income tax under Schedule D, Case VI—the excess relief is clawed back. There is no provision whereby excess foreign tax paid during the non-base period can be allowed as a credit.

Butterworths Tax Treaties/Simon's Taxes: F1.117.
[1] [1961] 1 All ER 658, 39 TC 374.

36: 23   A question arises whether TA 1988, s. 804 applies to treaties in the new form¹ which direct that credit is to be allowed where the UK tax is computed by reference to the profits taxed in the foreign country. It is an open question whether *Imperial Chemical Industries v Caro* would apply to such a treaty. This is of importance since relief under s. 804 for the opening years has to be claimed and the clawback under s. 804(5) is only applied where relief has been given under s. 804(1).

Butterworths Tax Treaties/Simon's Taxes: F3.2.
¹ Many treaties are still in the old form—e.g. Burma and Greece.

6 The relief

Income tax and capital gains tax

36: 24   Once the amount of the credit has been ascertained, it is set against the UK tax chargeable and the latter is reduced by the amount of the credit. However the amount of the credit is not to exceed the difference between (1) the amount of income tax which would be borne by the taxpayer if he were charged to income tax on his total income from all sources, including the foreign income grossed up as necessary and (2) the tax borne by him on his total income but minus the foreign income as computed.¹ The effect of this rather inelegant formula is to treat the income as the top slice of his income thus treating the UK tax against which the foreign tax is to be credited as his top slice rate and not his average rate.

Where more than one foreign source is involved, each is treated separately but in order, the order being at the taxpayer's option.² In such circumstances it obviously pays to take the income taxed at the highest foreign rates first.

In any event the total tax credit is not to exceed the total income tax payable.³

Equivalent relief is given for CGT⁴.

Butterworths Tax Treaties/Simon's Taxes: F1.121; F3.104; Butterworths Income Tax Service H3.05.
¹ TA 1988, s. 796(1).
² TA 1988, s. 796(2).
³ TA 1988, s. 796(3).
⁴ CGTA 1979, s. 10 and see SP6/88; see **Simon's Taxes, Division H3.2**.

Corporation tax

36: 25   Where the income is subject to corporation tax, the amount of credit is not to exceed the corporation tax attributable to that income.¹ The difference from the income tax rule is that all the income chargeable is charged at one rate. This leads to companies with high overseas income from countries with high rates of tax deciding to expand their UK operations.

Where a company has overseas income and domestic income it is necessary to allocate such items as charges on income and ACT among the different sources so as to calculate the amount of UK corporation tax attributable to that foreign income. For accounting periods ending on or before 31st March

1984 the generally accepted and certainly the Revenue view was that foreign tax could be deducted only *after* any available ACT. However the Revenue view has been rejected.[2]

From the Revenue's viewpoint, if the corporation tax (net of ACT) is less than the foreign tax, the excess is lost, especially as unused DTR may not be carried forward. Hence, for such periods it will usually pay a company to attribute charges and ACT to domestic sources thus increasing the tax attributable to the foreign sources and so obtain the maximum amount of credit.[3]

For accounting periods ending after 31st March 1984 the legislation is amended to ensure that the foreign tax credit is deductible before the ACT.[4] As a result, it has ceased to be necessary to set ACT against domestic source income rather than foreign source income.

However, it was suggested[5] that the amount of ACT available for set off by a company which had income in respect of which a foreign tax credit was available was limited only by reference to a company's total income, including the full amount of the foreign income reduced by the credit. So if a company's foreign tax credit equalled its UK tax liability on that income it could still use all its ACT against its liability to UK tax on the remaining income. Equally, if it had two sources of foreign income, one with low foreign tax, it could use the ACT which was not used up against the higher foreign source liability to reduce its liability to UK tax on this source. These devices struck at the root of the system taking each source separately for DTR purposes. So by TA 1988, s. 797(5) it is provided that for accounting periods ending after 2nd June 1986, the amount of ACT which may be set against the company's CT liability in respect of foreign income from which DTR has been deducted is limited to the lesser of:

(*a*) the ACT limit calculated as if that foreign income were the company's only income for the relevant accounting period; and

(*b*) the amount of CT which, after deducting the foreign tax credit, the company is liable to pay in respect of that income.

In addition, the company's right to allocate ACT against the CT on its various sources of income is removed. Surplus ACT may be carried forward or backwards.[6]

It remains the case that when loss relief is available it will be applied first, thus cancelling the tax credit for DTR.

Butterworths Tax Treaties/Simon's Taxes: F1.122; F2.103.

[1] TA 1988, s. 797.
[2] *Collard v Mining and Industrial Holdings Ltd* [1989] STC 384, HL.
[3] TA 1988, s. 797(2)–(4).
[4] TA 1988, s. 797(4).
[5] *Collard v Mining and Industrial Holdings Ltd* [1989] STC 384, HL.
[6] TA 1988, s. 239(3), (4).

Dividends and underlying tax

36: 26 Where a UK resident receives a dividend from a non-resident company, he is liable to income tax under Schedule D, Case V or, if a company, to corporation tax.[1] The tax deducted in the country of source will have been a withholding tax, probably at the rate of 5 or 15%[2] if there is a treaty and the full local income tax rate if there is none. These taxes may be taken as credits against the UK tax due, whether income tax or corporation tax. Where however the foreign tax system has charged a separate tax on the profits of the company, it would be equitable to allow credit not only for the income tax charged on the dividend but also for at least a proportion of the tax levied on the profits of the company which underlie the dividend.

EXAMPLE

Y Ltd, a UK resident company, has trading profits of £400,000 and receives a dividend of £864,000 net (960,000 gross) from one of its overseas subsidiaries. Foreign tax and local withholding tax on dividends paid are 40% and 10% respectively. Y Ltd. pays dividends (net) of £750,000 to its shareholders.

	UK source income (£)	Foreign source income (£)
Profits	400,000	1,600,000 (1)
UK CT @ 35%*	140,000	560,000
DTR		736,000 (2)
Actual UK CT		nil
Allowable ACT*	100,000 (3)	nil (3)
MCT	140,000	nil

(1) £1,600,000 represents the underlying gross foreign source profits out of which £864,000 net dividend was paid to X Ltd, i.e. £864,000 + £96,000 withholding tax grossed up at 40% local tax. The gross dividend was £960,000.
(2) Foreign tax is 40% of £1,600,000 + 10% of £960,000 or £736,000.
(3) ACT at 25/75 on £750,000 is £250,000. On UK profits maximum ACT set off is £100,000, i.e. 25% of £400,000. On foreign source profits maximum ACT set off is nil (the CT after deduction of DTR). Total ACT allowed is £100,000, so surplus ACT is £150,000.

Recent treaties provide[3] that relief for the underlying tax is to be given only if the UK resident is a *company* which either (*a*) controls directly or indirectly or (*b*) is a subsidiary of a company which so controls at least 10% of the voting power in the overseas company. A company is a subsidiary of another if that other control directly or indirectly not less than 50% of the voting power in the first company.[4] So where a parent has such control over the foreign dividend paying company, relief for the underlying tax may be claimed by the parent *and* by any of its 51% subsidiaries receiving dividends.

These restrictions apply also to unilateral relief[5] but provision is made for the preservation of this relief where a 10% holding is reduced by dilution.[6] Existing treaty relief may be granted on the terms of general UK tax law or on some special basis.[7]

---

[1] The payment is not franked investment income (and so exempt from corporation tax) as the payer is a non-resident, TA 1988, s. 7(1) and the payment therefore falls outside the scheme.
[2] Supra, § **36: 03**.
[3] See Revenue Leaflet IR 6 § 1. The problem with wider relief is one of proof—see RC (1955) § 708. Formerly relief could be claimed without such control and this survives in some treaties. The change in policy occurred in FA 1966, s. 40.
[4] TA 1988, s. 792.
[5] TA 1988, s. 790(3) and (4) and 800.

⁶ TA 1988, s. 790(6)–(10).
⁷ E.g. UK–Canada, Art. 21; UK–USA, Art. 10; UK–Netherlands, Art. 11. See also extra-statutory concession C1 (1988), **Simon's Taxes, Division H3.4**.

36: 27   Where relief for the underlying tax is given, the next step is to ascertain the profits underlying the dividend, the rate of tax available for credit depending on a comparison of the tax paid with the profits.

The relevant profits are (*a*) if the dividend is paid for a specified period, the profits of that period, (*b*) if the dividend is not specified for a period, but is stated to come out of specified profits, those profits and (*c*) if the dividend is neither for a specified period nor from a specified source, the last complete internal accounting period of the company before the payment. If under rules (*a*) or (*c*) the dividend exceeds the profits, profits from previous years may underly the dividend unless they have already done so.[1] The profits are those appearing in the company's accounts, and not those which are the basis upon which the foreign tax is assessed.[2] If distributable profits are restricted, the average rate of foreign tax payable will be increased.

Where treaty relief applies only to certain classes of dividend, e.g. ordinary shares, unilateral relief for the underlying tax may be claimed for other classes, e.g. preference dividends.[3]

In the standard situation, the first company, resident in the UK, has the 10% stake in the second company resident overseas. However that company may in turn be related to another company, the third company, and so on down a chain.[4] Since 1971 the first company has been able to claim credit relief in respect of the tax borne by the third company on its profits when those profits are passed back up the chain in the form of dividends. It is necessary that the general UK conditions for tax relief would have been satisfied at each stage up the chain.[5] It is also necessary that the appropriate degree of relationship exists at each link stage. The relationship requires that either the second company control, directly or indirectly, not less than 10% of the voting power of the third company, or that is a subsidiary of a company which controls 10% of that voting power.[6] Where the company has had 10% voting power and that percentage then drops below 10% in a way which it could not reasonably prevent and which was not foreseeable, the relief is not lost.[7]

The third company may be resident in some third country or even in the UK. In the former case relief will probably be unilateral. Where any company in the chain is resident in the UK the tax on its profits for which relief is claimed is not to include income tax paid in respect of dividends received by that company from other companies resident in the UK.[8]

On company with overseas insurance business see TA 1988, s. 802.

On relief for foreign tax when a close company apportionment is made see extra-statutory concession B22 (1988), **Simon's Taxes, Division H2.2**.

Butterworths Tax Treaties/Simon's Taxes: F1.134; F2.107–112.
¹ TA 1988, s. 799. Where under the tax law in a foreign country, a dividend is increased for tax purposes by an amount which may be set against his own tax liability (or, if in excess thereof, paid to him) then any such increase is to be subtracted from the underlying tax: TA 1988, ss. 788, 799, 808. It is thus clear that foreign imputation credit is excluded from the calculation of credit relief for underlying tax.
² *Bowater Paper Corpn Ltd v Murgatroyd* [1969] 3 All ER 111, 46 TC 37.

[3] TA 1988, s. 800.
[4] TA 1988, s. 801(1).
[5] TA 1988, s. 801(2).
[6] TA 1988, s. 801(5).
[7] TA 1988, s. 790(6)–(10), e.g. nationalisation.
[8] TA 1988, s. 801(4).

Shipping and aviation and agencies

36: 28   TA 1970, s. 514 authorised the Crown to enter into agreements relating to profits from these sources. This provision was repealed in 1987—except one relating to shipping with Iceland.[1] The reason for the repeal was that the forerunner of s. 514 was enacted in 1923,[2] before what is now TA 1988, s. 788, which was first enacted in 1945.[3] The reason for the preservation of Iceland was that the agreement with Iceland was the only agreement still depending on the 1923 power.

[1] FA 1987, Sch. 16, Part VII.
[2] FA 1923, s. 18; see also FA 1924, s. 31.
[3] F(No. 2)A 1945, s. 51(1).

Banks and loan interest

36: 29   The credit available to banks for foreign taxes on interest received is restricted to the lesser of the actual tax withheld (or spared) by the overseas company and 15% of the gross interest. There were parallel restrictions on relief for underlying tax.[1] Previously, relief had been particularly valuable as banks could claim full credit for the foreign tax paid on gross interest although liable to UK tax only on the profit actually made.[2]

These provisions were tightened by F(No. 2)A 1987 which applies to interest payable on or after 1st April 1987 but with two years' delay where the loan was made before that date.[3] The 1987 rules amend both s. 65 and s. 66 of the 1982 Act (now TA 1988, ss. 798 and 803) by limiting the right to credit relief by allowing the foreign tax to be credited only against the tax payable on the profit of the particular loan in respect of which the foreign tax was paid.[4] The explanation for the new rule is the Revenue view that the rules as amended in 1982, by allowing the bank to set overseas withholding taxes on interest to be set against corporation tax on profits from unrelated business, encouraged the banks to make overseas loans and to do so at reduced rates of interest.[5] The new rules are designed to reduce such subsidies. It seems only yesterday that balance of trade problems made overseas lending desirable in the national interest. Although the rules restricting relief for the underlying tax reflecting interest on loans[6] applies only to banks or a company connected with a bank, the more general rule applies to "any person".[7] The Board has a regulation-making power under s. 798.[8]

[1] TA 1988, ss. 798 and 803.
[2] See [1982] STI, pp. 108, 254.
[3] TA 1988, s. 798(11).
[4] TA 1988, s. 798(5)(*b*).

[5] Inland Revenue Press Release, 17th March 1987, p. 196.
[6] TA 1988, s. 803.
[7] TA 1988, s. 803.
[8] TA 1988, s. 798(9). For the regulations (S.I. 1988/88) see *Simon's Tax Intelligence* 1988 p. 43.

UNILATERAL TAX CREDIT

36: 30   The unilateral tax credit was introduced into the UK in 1950. At first the credit was to be for $\frac{3}{4}$ of Commonwealth taxes and $\frac{1}{2}$ of foreign taxes. This may have been because of the notion of imperial preference or because to give full credit unilaterally would weaken the hand of the UK negotiators as they worked towards a full set of bilateral arrangements. The pace of negotiation was slow and in 1953 these limits on credit were abolished.[1]

The credit is of use today in two main situations, first where there is no double tax treaty with the country of source[2] and secondly where there is but it does not cover this particular tax.[3]

Treaty relief takes precedence because it is to apply "notwithstanding anything in any enactment".[4] However the legislation goes on to limit the extent to which the treaty applies to the extent that it provides relief. It may therefore be argued that where a less generous treaty relief appears to supersede a unilateral relief, the latter relief may still be claimed.

Butterworths Tax Treaties/Simon's Taxes: F1.145–F1.151.
[1] FA 1950, s. 36.
[2] As recommended by RC (1953) 1st Report §§ 40–42.
[3] TA 1988, s. 790(6) extends unilateral relief to taxes levied by municipalities or other local bodies.
[4] TA 1988, s. 788(3).

36: 31   The credit is for the amount of taxes paid under the foreign law and computed by reference to income arising within the foreign territory.[1] That sum is allowed by way of credit against any UK tax computed by reference to that income. This means that foreign income taxes on the income from the foreign source are allowed against the UK tax charged on the income from that source. In *George Wimpey International Ltd v Rolfe*[2] the taxpayer company made profits in three countries and paid local tax on them but made an overall trading profit of nil. However the company had other sources of income which gave rise to profits chargeable to UK tax. Hoffman J, upholding the decision of the Special Commissioner, held that the taxpayer company was not entitled to double taxation relief. He reached this decision in reliance on the doctrine of the source and the Schedular system.

[1] TA 1988, s. 790(4).
[2] [1989] STI 511.

36: 32   Unilateral relief differs from treaty relief in three ways, all related to the obvious general difference that in treaty relief one looks first to the terms of the treaty.

(1) Although treaty relief is available only to one resident in the UK

throughout the year, unilateral relief is given (*a*) for tax paid under the law of the Isle of Man or the Channel Islands if the person is resident in the UK *or* the Isle of Man or the Channel Islands and (*b*) for tax paid under a foreign law computed by reference to income from an office or employment the duties of which are performed wholly or mainly in that territory, against UK income tax chargeable under Schedule E, whether the person is resident here or in that country.[1]

(2) In deciding whether the tax paid in this country is related to tax paid in the foreign country the formula is that the foreign tax is a credit against UK tax if the latter is computed "by reference to" that income.[2]

(3) Relief for underlying tax is governed by TA 1988, ss. 800, 801 which states the rules now sought when treaties are renegotiated. The relief is as stated supra, § **36: 26**.[3]

---

[1] TA 1988, s. 794.
[2] TA 1988, s. 790(4).
[3] TA 1988, s. 790(5)(*c*).

Capital gains

36: 33   The provisions in TA 1988, ss. 788–806 are extended to CGT[1] including the unilateral tax credit and the power to make treaties to give relief for foreign tax charged on the same disposal. Where credit relief is not available, or not available in full, the unused foreign tax may be treated as an allowable deduction.

Owing to the variety of systems of taxing gains this relief may be lost. Thus, different events may give rise to a tax liability in respect of what is in substance the same gain. For example, a capital asset in a foreign branch may incur a tax charge in that country if, without being sold, it is written up in the books, and the foreign country charges tax on the unrealised gain. If, in a later year, the asset is sold and UK CGT liability arises it seems that DTR should not be available in respect of the earlier foreign disposal; however in practice a generous approach is adopted.[2]

---

[1] CGTA 1979, s. 10.
[2] See SP 6/88, **Simon's Taxes Division H3.2**.

REFORM AND PLANNING

1 General

36: 34   The foreign tax credit—whether by treaty or unilateral—at first sight appears fair and reasonable. If the foreign tax is lower than the domestic tax, as will usually be the case, (since the domestic tax rate reflect the person's total income from all sources as opposed to his income from one country where he is not resident) the effect is to deprive the country of residence of a part of its tax but to enable it to preserve equality of tax rates between the person with foreign income and his fellow resident with only domestic income (unless the foreign rate exceeds the UK rate). However the tax credit has some increasingly debated consequences particularly where the profits of incorporated business are concerned. Historically the extensive use of the tax credit by the US has had two consequences. First it has encouraged other countries to put a tax on the profits of companies, at a time when in the US the wisdom of taxing such profits was coming increasingly into question. Secondly it encouraged the countries of source to pitch their corporate tax rates as high as the US since this would simply increase their share of the tax which the company had to pay anyway thus causing a loss to the US Revenue without any disincentive for the company.[1]

One alternative would be to extend the relief to indirect taxes—a course which has some attractions for those who believe that an indirect tax on the turnover of companies is to be preferred to a direct tax on their profits. Other courses of action would be simply to abolish the credit, thereby penalising the resident with foreign income, or at the other extreme, to abolish the taxation of foreign income, thereby penalising the stay-at-home. Another possibility would be differential tax rates. Other devices include deferment of tax in the country of residence until the income has been repatriated (an extension of the remittance basis) and the use of investment credits.[2]

---

[1] E.g. Panama.
[2] See e.g. Atchabahian, 1971 JBIFD 451 at 461.

---

2 Particular[1]

36: 35 (1) The band of taxes against which the tax credit works, income and corporation taxes[2] and CGT and foreign taxes similar in character,[3] is narrow. Indirect taxes are regarded traditionally as deductible in computing the profits[4] and so as a part of the costs of the enterprise. A different explanation for the restriction may be that historically the demand was for relief against the double taxation of income. This causes trouble where the country of source, seeing that it can only levy low withholding rates of tax on dividends and interest, decides to levy taxation by means of royalties, or devices such as the famous Middle Eastern posted prices for oil[5] which charge local tax on an inflated price. The argument against this extension would be that to allow relief now would simply encourage the source countries to raise their rates of indirect tax.

---

[1] See Shelburne (1957) BTR 48 and 143.
[2] TA 1988, s. 790(6).
[3] CGTA 1979, s. 10.
[4] Supra, § **7: 101**.
[5] See Public Accounts Committee 1972–73. First Report §§ 14 and 57. There are no full double tax treaties with these countries.

36: 36 (2) The credit itself is narrow. It may be used only against the UK tax on that source. If the foreign tax is higher, that excess may not be set off against other income, not even against UK tax on other foreign income. There is thus no pooling of foreign income for credit-relief[1]—nor may it be carried forward to the next year against income from the same or any other source. The credit is thus quite distinct from an expense item or a trading loss. There is of course no reason why the UK Revenue should refund tax collected by another country, unless it be to encourage exports and for this there may be more efficient methods. The UK does recognise the excess as a deduction in computing the extent of foreign income for such purposes as determining the profits of a close company for distribution, but some relaxation of the present rules may seem desirable.

[1] Criticised by CBI—Select Committee on Corporation Tax (1971) p. 149, § 11; see also RC (1955), § 732; contrast US Internal Revenue Code, s. 904(*a*)(2). One avoidance device is to interpose an overseas holding company from which alone the foreign profits (and credits) are channelled to the UK.

36: 37   (3) There are problems over differences between the fiscal concepts used in different systems. One example is that under Australian law that part of a director's fees in excess of reasonable remuneration may be treated as dividend. The tax paid on this notional dividend would be ineligible for relief in the UK where, if tax were levied, the whole of the director's fees would be taxable as such.[1]

[1] Shelburne, *loc. cit.*, p. 53.

36: 38   (4) There are problems where a third country enters the scene since treaties are bilateral arrangements and very few lay down how each party is to give credit for taxes paid in a third country. While the UK may give unilateral relief or even treaty relief under an arrangement between this country and the third country,[1] such rules do not solve the interaction of the relief with the third country and the relief with the second.

[1] E.g. UK–Denmark, Art. XVII, para. 4 and RC 1955, § 759.

36: 39   (5) The present tax treaties often frustrate the domestic purposes of the source country. Thus if a UK company operated a mine in the US before 1963 it found that its American depletion allowances were cancelled out by the UK tax, the US not being one of the underdeveloped countries with which we have treaties allowing for pioneer relief. The obvious tax planning answer in such circumstances is that a separate company should be formed in the US.

36: 40   (6) There are the complications and nonsenses surrounding the preceding[1] year of assessment and the inequities surrounding the operation of TA 1988, s. 804.

[1] Supra, § **36: 22**. RC (1955), § 789 recommended a current year basis.

PART VIII. INHERITANCE TAX

37 Introduction

37:01 Inheritance tax (IHT) is a direct tax on transfers of capital. It applies to transfers on or after 18th March 1986. Unlike the capital transfer tax (CTT) which preceded it, IHT is designed to operate primarily as a tax on transfers which occur on death. In order to prevent too obvious avoidance the tax also charges retrospectively certain gifts made within the previous seven years. Gifts which are potentially liable to IHT if the transferor should die within this period are known as "potentially exempt transfers". There is no tax on such gifts when they are made but if the donor dies within seven years the potential exemption is lost. The scheme of the tax is further strengthened by the inclusion of gifts made outside the seven year period but from which the deceased has not been entirely excluded for the past seven years, known as gifts with reservation. As a result of the 1986 scheme and the 1987 amendment most gifts are potentially exempt. However others are not and as in the days of CTT these are known as chargeable transfers and are chargeable immediately—whether or not the transferor dies within seven years; one does not wait for the death of the transferor.

The legislation for the new tax takes the form of extensive amendment of the CTT legislation. However the tax is to be known by its own name.

IHT is thus a direct tax on transfers of capital. There is a cumulative charge on chargeable transfers made over any seven year period during his lifetime and on death. Unlike the old estate duty it otherwise so greatly resembles, it does charge certain transfers *inter vivos* immediately. Unlike CTT, it does not tax immediately most types of *inter vivos* transfers and it has an unfortunate willingness to look to the moment of the death of the donor not only to see whether a potentially exempt transfer has become chargeable but also whether certain conditions for relief are still satisfied. Unlike succession duty, and despite its name, it is charged by reference to the circumstances of the transferor and not those of the transferee. Unlike CGT it is a charge on the whole of the value transferred; some transfers will give rise to both taxes with the liability to the inheritance tax only becoming clear on the deceased's death. Unlike a wealth tax it is charged on moving and not stationary wealth.

37:02 Duties imposed on capital are either of a mutation character, that is, charged according to the value of the property changing hands, regardless of its destination, or of an acquisition character, that is, charged on the benefits acquired by those who acquire them.

The mutation duties which have from time to time been chargeable under English law are, in chronological order, probate duty, account duty, temporary estate duty, estate duty, settlement estate duty, CTT and now

IHT. The acquisition duties are legacy duty and succession duty. Of all these duties only IHT is now in force. Estate duty and CTT may still be payable if they arose in respect of a death or a transfer occurring when the relevant tax was in force, and has not been paid, but any outstanding liability to the other duties has been abolished.

Foster's Capital Taxes A1.

AN OUTLINE OF IHT

Occasion of charge

37: 03 IHT is charged whenever there is a chargeable transfer of value which is defined as a disposition causing loss to a person's estate which is not an exempt transfer, see (1) below. In addition IHT is charged in certain other situations, see (2)–(5) below. These other situations are treated as transfers of value[1] but they are not deemed to be dispositions.

Foster's Capital Taxes A1.17, 18
[1] IHTA 1984, s. 3(4).

37: 04 (1) IHT is payable on a transfer of value. A transfer of value is any disposition by which the value of a person's estate is reduced. The tax is levied at one of two rates on the transferor, either 0% or 20% in the case of a lifetime transfer. The effect is a mixture of proportional and progressive features; i.e. the more transfers of value he makes the higher his average tax liability is likely to be.[1] If the transfer is made on or after 18th March 1986, it is cumulated with all chargeable transfers made by him in the previous seven years.

A transfer *inter vivos* (for example, a gift) will be a transfer of value unless the transfer is exempt or potentially exempt. Where the transfer is for consideration the consideration received will enter into the computation of the value transferred, only the balance being chargeable. However, commercial transactions are not treated as transfers of value, nor are certain other dispositions.[2]

With the change from CTT to IHT, it has become necessary to divide transfers of value into those which are immediately chargeable and those which are only potentially chargeable, which the Act chooses to call potentially exempt. Chargeable transfers enter the cumulative total of transfers made by the transferors at once and, if the total goes over the nil rate band, will give rise to tax straight away. Potentially exempt transfers by contrast do not give rise to tax straight away and do not enter the transferor's cumulative total of transfers unless and until the donor dies within a period of seven years from the date of the transfer, whereupon they become chargeable as lifetime transfers but at death rates, with reductions if the donor dies more than three years after the gift. Most types of gift are potentially exempt transfers.

37: 05   (2) On a person's death there is a transfer of all the property to which he was beneficially entitled immediately before his death; the transfer on death is accumulated with *inter vivos* transfers whether originally chargeable or having become chargeable by reason of the loss of their potentially exempt status made up to seven years before, see **Chapter 39**.

The death charge differs from the *inter vivos* in three ways. First, the rate is higher on death than on chargeable *inter vivos* transfers at − 0% and 40%. The higher rate is applied retrospectively to *inter vivos* transfers made within seven years of death (there is some tapering relief for transfers between four and seven years before the death). Secondly some of the exemptions are confined to *inter vivos* transfers and others are confined to transfers on death.

Thirdly while chargeable *inter vivos* transfers must be grossed up to ascertain the loss to the transferor's estate where the burden of IHT falls on the transferor, there is usually no need to gross up on death for the simple reason that the benefits eventually distributed out of the estate will necessarily be net of IHT. For similar reasons there is no grossing up of potentially exempt transfers should tax become payable. There are also minor differences in administration; one such was the rate of interest on overdue IHT (which used to be 11% for transfers *inter vivos* and 9% for transfers on death, but which was standardised at 9% for all unpaid IHT with effect from 6th October 1988.[1]). It now stands at 11% as from 6 July 1989.[2]

In certain cases, events after death may affect IHT charged.

37: 06   (3) There is a transfer of value not only where the transferor makes a chargeable transfer, but also where he is treated as making one. This may occur if he is beneficially entitled to an interest in possession in settled property because, for IHT, he is treated as being beneficially entitled not to the value of his interest in it but to the value of the settled property underlying it. For example, if he is entitled to the whole of the income of a fund worth £50,000, he is taken to be beneficially entitled to £50,000. He is, therefore, treated as making a transfer of value of £50,000 if he dies, or disposes of the interest, or if the interest ends. This is cumulated and, where appropriate, aggregated with his own property, see **Chapter 41**. If he gives away his life interest more than seven years before he dies the gift can, under the 1987 rules, qualify as a potentially exempt transfer here.

37: 07   (4) Where there is no interest in possession in settled property different rules apply.[1] In general there is a charge every ten years at a special rate on the property held in the settlement on such trusts. There is also a partial charge if property ceases to be subject to the discretionary trusts between such anniversaries or before the first one, see **Chapter 42**.

37: 08   (5) A company is not liable to IHT when it makes a disposition reducing the value of its estate because that charge is restricted to dispositions by individuals.[1] A company may, in certain circumstances, be entitled to a beneficial interest in possession in settled property but, unless the company's business consists of the acquisition of interests in settled property, the settlement will be taxed as if there were no interest in possession.

Where a *close* company makes a transfer of value the transfer of value may however be attributed to its individual participators and be treated as having been made by them.[2] There may also be a charge on the trustee participators, depending upon the type of trust. There is also a deemed transfer of value when a person's rights in the company are reduced in value as a result of an alteration in the rights of his shares.

---

[1] Infra, **Chapter 47**; IHTA 1984, s. 2(1).
[2] Infra, § **47: 03**.

Exemptions and reliefs

37: 09   Exemptions and reliefs take various forms. Some direct that a particular transfer shall be exempt up to a certain limit. Others direct that a transfer shall be exempt in full. Others give relief by a special basis for valuation, or a reduction in the value transferred. Yet others take the form of a reduction in the tax otherwise payable so that the value transferred must be cumulated in full and the tax normally payable ascertained before relief can be given. Reliefs may also take the form of an exemption in whole or in part from aggregation. In addition some dispositions are not "transfers of value"; this means that they have no effect for IHT if made inter vivos. The same transfer may, however, be chargeable if made on death.

CALCULATION OF TAX

Progression—and how to gross up

37: 10   The amount of tax chargeable depends on three principles, progression, aggregation and cumulation; the first can be seen in the rate structure, although this has been greatly reduced since 1988.

An obvious feature to be noted from the table of rates is the difference between the lifetime rates and those on death, the former being half those of the latter. Although the former are no longer referred to in the legislation as "lifetime" rates, it is convenient to retain the expression but it must be understood that when potentially exempt transfers become chargeable on the death of the donor within seven years, it is the death rates that are relevant. For transfers after 5th April 1989 there are only three rates. There is a long zero rate band (£118,000) and then a single rate of 40% which is also the top rate of income tax and CGT. The third rate is the 20% lifetime rate.

The columns headed "rate on net fraction" refer to the rate needed in grossing up a net transfer. Thus if A who has already made chargeable transfers of £118,000 makes a further chargeable transfer of £10,000 gross, this gives rise to IHT of £2,000 at lifetime rates. The same result follows if he makes a net transfer of £8,000; this will be grossed up at 100/(100 − 20) which is equivalent to adding tax at $\frac{1}{4}$ (20/80) of the net amount.

Normally one is concerned with grossing up only on *inter vivos* transfers which are chargeable as distinct from potentially exempt, but there are some situations where one has to gross up a net transfer on death, infra, § **44: 14.**

37: 11   Rates

Inheritance Tax Rates—after 5th April 1989

Scale on death				Half-rate scale				
Cumulative chargeable transfers (gross)	Rate	Cumulative tax	Rate on net fraction	Rate on gross	Tax on Band	Cumulative tax	Cumulative chargeable transfers (net)	Rate on net fraction
£	%	£		%	£	£	£	
0—118,000	0	nil	nil	0	nil	nil	0—118,000	nil
Over 118,000	40	—	$\frac{2}{3}$	20	—	—	over 118,000	$\frac{1}{4}$

Foster's Capital Taxes: Calculation Tables.
Rates are index linked; IHTA 1984, s. 8(4). The rates as from 6th April 1989 are set by SI 1989/468; [1989] STI, p. 278.

Aggregation

37: 12   Where more than one piece of property is the subject of one chargeable transfer, the tax chargeable on the total or aggregate value transferred is attributed to the properties in the proportion which they bear to the aggregate.[1] The most obvious example is a transfer on death. Here there will be a transfer of all the pieces of property which form part of the deceased's estate, as defined.

The principle of aggregation will also be relevant to *inter vivos* transfers. Thus if S settles property which includes some land and some shares the burden of the tax will be shared rateably between the different pieces of property transferred, and thus affect the extent of the Inland Revenue charge on each piece.

When different funds pass in different directions, the rate of tax which has to be borne by each fund is increased by reason of the existence of other funds passing elsewhere. Thus if the deceased had made no chargeable transfers during his life but immediately before his death had free estate of £55,000 and a life interest in a fund worth £100,000, the tax due on a transfer of £165,000 would be divided between the free estate (55/165ths) and the settled property (100/165ths).

Foster's Capital Taxes B1.41; C4.12; D1.02.
[1] IHTA 1984, s. 265 but for a minor qualification see infra, § **41:35** n. 5

Exemptions from aggregation

37: 13   Transfers which are exempt from liability are exempt also from aggregation. For the same reason transfers which are conditionally exempt, such as works of art, § **39: 21** and, but only on death, timber, § **39: 21**, are also exempt from aggregation.

The payment of premiums in respect of certain life policies issued before 29th March 1968 gives rise to an exemption from aggregation.

Transfers on same day

37: 14 All chargeable transfers, including potentially exempt transfers which have become chargeable, made on the same day are aggregated regardless of the actual order in which they are made, save that an *inter vivos* gift made on the day of death is treated as taking place before that on death.[1]

However in calculating the amount of tax they are assumed to be made in the order which results in the lowest value chargeable, a matter of importance where one gift bears its own tax while another does not; the lower the figure at which grossing up is to be carried out the less the tax. As potentially exempt transfers always bear their own tax this rule has little importance for them.

EXAMPLE

A whose cumulative total stands at £68,000 makes two gifts in settlement each of £50,000 and each on discretionary trusts on the same day, 4th July 1989. The gift to trust X is to bear its own tax; that for trust Y is to be borne by A.

If the gift to trust X is made first the tax on it will be nil; this will exhaust the zero lifetime rate band so that trust Y will have its tax assessed on the basis that £50,000 has to be grossed up at 20% making tax of £12,500. Total tax on the two trusts will be £12,500 and A's cumulative total will be £180,500.

If, however, the gift to trust Y is made first, tax on it will be nil and tax on trust X will be £10,000 making total tax of £10,000 and leaving A's cumulative total at £178,000.

It follows that the second method will be used. The total tax of £10,000 is divided between the trusts in the proportion 50,000:60,000 making the tax on trust X £4,545.5 and that on trust Y £5,454.5.

Foster's Capital Taxes C2.30.
[1] IHTA 1984, s. 266(1).

Cumulation

37: 15 Cumulation requires that the tax on the present transfer must take account of chargeable transfers already made by the transferor and which remain chargeable—including those made in the days of CTT. As from 1981 chargeable transfers made more than ten years previously ceased to be cumulated and as from 18th March 1986, the period was reduced to seven years.[1]

EXAMPLE

In 1972 A gave B £100,000; in January 1976 he gave C £100,000 leaving C to pay the CTT. In June 1981 he married as a result of which his life interest in a fund worth £100,000 ceased. In May 1987 he makes a chargeable transfer to D of £50,000.

The first gift is not chargeable as it was made before CTT was introduced.

The second gift is chargeable and C would have paid the tax at the rates prevailing in 1976. A's cumulative total becomes £100,000.

In 1981 the trust would pay the tax as on a transfer by A of £100,000, ascertained by deducting the tax on £100,000 using 1981 rates—from that on £200,000. £39,750 − £9,500 = £30,250. A's cumulative total now stands at £200,000.

In January 1986 the cumulative total dropped back to £100,000 as the gift to C ceased to be cumulated.

In May 1987 A's chargeable transfer to D would be taxed at the rates then prevailing by reference to A's then cumulative total of £100,000. If it were a potentially exempt transfer which became chargeable later by reason of A's death, in, say, 1989, tax on the 1987 transfer would be calculated by using the 1989 rates.

In June 1988, the 1981 transfer of value would cease to be cumulated.

It is important to grasp that when a transfer ceases to be cumulated that is all that happens; there is no question of repaying the tax charged.

Foster's Capital Taxes B1.41.
[1] IHTA 1984, s. 7(1).

37: 16   The transfers which are cumulated are those which are the chargeable transfers of this transferor. Exempt transfers are not cumulated; nor are conditionally exempt transfers until a chargeable event has occurred; nor are potentially exempt transfers unless and until the donor dies within the seven year period[1] nor are the transfers which are made by others. Transfers which are of settled property but which are treated as made by him, for example when his beneficial life interest in possession terminates, must be cumulated.

If a person makes a chargeable transfer in December 1989, matters affecting the cumulative total will include all chargeable transfers made in the previous seven years. These will include all chargeable transfers made since 17th March 1986, the date of the introduction of IHT (but not potentially exempt transfers), and also those transfers of value made before 18th March 1986 but after December 1982 which were chargeable transfers when made, i.e. under the rules then in force, and so including those gifts which if made after 17th March 1986 would have been potentially exempt transfers.

The values to be cumulated are those transferred by chargeable transfers. Where a particular relief takes the form of a reduction in the value of the property and so in the value transferred, such as agricultural relief or relief for business assets, it is the value so reduced which is cumulated. Where however the relief takes the form of a reduction in tax, such as quick succession relief or double taxation relief by credit, the whole value transferred must be cumulated both to ascertain the amount of tax which is to be reduced and to ascertain the value transferred for subsequent transfers.

---

[1] IHTA 1984, s.3A(5) but then with retroactive effect.

Taxation of potentially exempt transfers

37: 17   A potentially exempt transfer remains potentially exempt until the passage of seven years, in which case it becomes exempt,[1] or the death of the transferor in that period, in which case it becomes chargeable. It is to be assumed that the transfer will reach total exemption by the passing of seven years until this is disproved,[2] hence no tax will become due at the time of the gift. If the transferor dies within that period, the transfer has its potentially exempt status retrospectively removed and it falls to be taxed as if it had been a chargeable transfer when made; thus the transfer is not treated as taking place immediately before he died and so as forming part of the general transfer on death. This will have consequences where the donor makes a potentially exempt transfer within the seven year period but later makes a chargeable transfer; here the tax on the chargeable transfer will have been calculated on the basis that the previous transfer is exempt; this has to be corrected. The amount of tax will be determined by reference to the cumulative total of chargeable transfers in the previous seven years prior to the date of the potentially exempt transfer—not the date of the death. The removal of the exempt status is however not completely retrospective since the rates to be applied will be those in force at the date of death with a reduction if the transfer was made more than three years before the death. The rate of tax will be reduced by a tapering relief if the donor dies more than three years after making the potentially exempt transfer.

EXAMPLE (assuming that only IHT (and not CTT) is relevant).
D dies in year 20.
In year 11, D settled £100,000 on discretionary trusts, the tax to be paid by the trust; this is a chargeable transfer.
In year 16 D gave D £58,000; this is a potentially exempt transfer.
On the death of D in year 20, the gift to A will cease to be potentially exempt and will become chargeable. The rates used will be those in force at the death of D but there will be a 20% reduction in the tax because D died four years after the gift. In calculating the tax D will be assumed to have a cumulative total of £100,000.
Tax using the 1989–90 rates will therefore be—

Tax on £158,000 (£16,000) less tax on £100,000 (nil) = £16,000 reduced by 20% = £12,800.

On D's death he is treated as making a transfer of his remaining estate. This will be charged on the basis that his cumulative total for lifetime transfers will be £50,000. This is because the gift in year 16 is relevant as it is now chargeable but that in year 11 is not relevant as it was made more than seven years before the death and therefore ceases to be cumulated. It follows that if he had died in year 17 that cumulative total would have been £158,000.
If the transfer in year 11 had been an outright gift to B, it would have been a potentially exempt transfer which would have achieved exempt status in year 18. It would have been ignored in calculating the tax on the gift in year 16 and the tax due in respect of that gift would therefore have been nil thanks to the nil rate band of £118,000 in the 1989 rates.

It might seem that where a transferor has made no previous transfers but proposes to dispose of a large amount of wealth, it would usually be advantageous for the chargeable transfer to precede the potentially exempt one so as to enable the former to use the transferor's nil rate band. However whereas the tax payable on the death in respect of a potentially exempt transfer is always determined *de novo*, this is not true of the chargeable transfer. So where the tax paid in respect of the chargeable transfer on that occasion is higher than that which would be payable on such a transfer on the death, there is no refund of the tax already paid and that this gives rise to a greater total burden of tax.[3]

Foster's Capital Taxes C4.12; D4.11.
[1] IHTA 1984, s. 3A(4) added by FA 1986, Sch. 19, para. 1. The definition of potentially exempt transfers is discussed infra § **38.02**.
[2] IHTA 1984, s. 3A(5) added by FA 1986, Sch. 19, para. 1.
[3] See the discussion in Tolley's Estate Planning pp. 29–30.

SOME DEFINITIONS

Estate

37: 18   The notion of an estate is important because a disposition only gives rise to IHT if it causes a reduction in the value of the transferor's estate[1] and also because on death a person is treated as having made a transfer of value equal to the value of his estate immediately before death.[2]

A person's estate is the aggregate of all the property to which he is beneficially entitled. Allowable deductions should also be made.[3] Property which he holds in a fiduciary capacity is not included. Property is widely defined as "including rights and interests of any description". It will therefore cover not only tangible property, but also equitable rights, debts and other choses in action, and indeed any rights capable of being reduced to a money value. So on death a person's estate will include a share of property held in common and a severable share of property held on joint tenancy. It would also have included any right to claim damages for loss of expectation of life in respect of a tort causing death, for which an action lay at the suit of the personal representatives under the Law Reform (Miscellaneous Provisions) Act 1934 (repealed 1977), but not damages obtainable under the Fatal Accidents Act in respect of a wrongful act causing death since these belong to the deceased's dependants and not to him.

A mere spes is presumably not a "right" even "of any description"; however a completed payment stemming from such a spes is not a mere spes. Gratuities payable as of right do form part of an estate even though no precise amount can be placed upon them.[4] Sums paid by trustees of a superannuation scheme in the exercise of a discretion to pay a lump sum death benefit to a member's dependant do not form part of the member's estate. Property to which a person is entitled as a corporation sole is not included.[5] "Excluded property" does not form part of a person's estate immediately before death (see infra § **38: 10** for other transfers).

A person beneficially entitled to an interest in possession in settled property is treated as beneficially entitled to the property in which the interest subsists and not to the interest itself.[6] Thus the tenant for life of a fund worth £100,000 whose free estate is worth £10,000 will on death make a chargeable transfer of £110,000.

A person's estate will include property (other than settled property) over which he has a general power which enables him, or would if he were *sui iuris* enable him, to dispose of it; he is treated as beneficially entitled to the property. If he has a general power to charge money on such unsettled property he is treated as beneficially entitled to the money. "General power" is defined as "a power or authority enabling the person by whom it is exercisable to appoint or dispose of property as he thinks fit".[7] The scope of this rule is not completely certain. Where a person makes an incomplete gift there will be no disposition since the title has not passed and so there is no reduction in the value of the transferor's estate. This will still be so even though the title is eventually perfected under the rule in *Strong v Bird* (1874) since here the title is not perfected until death and the transfer on death is treated as taking place immediately before death.

Where A makes a revocable gift of personalty to B, the property appears to form part of the estate of both of them. It forms part of the estate of A since there are no restrictions on the right to revoke; A can therefore revoke the gift and dispose of the property as he thinks fit. It forms part of the estate of B since B gets good title subject to A's right to revoke.[8] A power of appointment will not fall within this rule since such a power will only form part of a settlement and the present rule is restricted to unsettled property.

Where a person has a general but fiduciary[9] power over property, for example an agent duly authorised to sell on behalf of the owner, it would appear that the property ought not to form part of his estate. It is however arguable that the rule could be used to reverse this conclusion. The rule defines a general power as one to dispose of the property as he thinks fit and is not expressly confined to one which carries with it the beneficial right to the proceeds of sale. Such a conclusion would have the odd result that the property will at once form part of the estate of the vendor and of the agent and so is most unlikely.[10] One answer to this is to say that the agent has a power to sell, not a power to give and so no power to dispose as he thinks fit; this leaves open the case of a power of attorney.

There is no rule which prevents an asset from being in two estates at the same time. This is likely to be more common as a result of the rules treating a gift subject to reservation as remaining chargeable on the donor's death.

A person's estate is reduced by allowable liabilities; infra, § **38: 03**.

Foster's Capital Taxes B3.01.
[1] IHTA 1984, s. 3(1).
[2] IHTA 1984, s. 4(1).
[3] IHTA 1984, s. 5(1).
[4] *A-G v Quixley* (1929) 98 LJKB 652, CA.
[5] IHTA 1984, s. 271.
[6] IHTA 1984, s. 49(1).
[7] IHTA 1984, s. 5(2).
[8] Semble that A's right to revoke will be taken into account in valuing B's right.
[9] IHTA 1984, s. 5(2) declares that the person with a general power is to be treated as beneficially entitled to it so that the fiduciary quality of the power is irrelevant.
[10] See Standing Committee A, 4th February 1975, cols. 629, 630.

Connected persons

37: 19   Persons are connected with each other in the same way as for CGT but with the addition of uncle, aunt, nephew and niece.[1]

Foster's Capital Taxes C1.21.
[1] CGTA 1979, s. 63; supra, § **16: 23** incorporated and adapted by IHTA 1984, s. 270.

Excluded property[1]

37: 20   The following is excluded property:
(1) Property, other than settled property, situate outside the UK provided the person beneficially entitled to it is an individual domiciled outside the UK;[2]

(2) Settled property situate outside the UK provided the settlor was domiciled outside the UK when the settlement was made;[3]

(3) A reversionary interest in settled property provided the person beneficially entitled to it is not domiciled in the UK;[4]

(4) Certain other reversionary interests[5] in settled property.

(5) Certain types of property situated in the UK owned by persons domiciled elsewhere—infra, § **49: 10**

Foster's Capital Taxes J3.11.

[1] On effects see IHTA 1984, ss. 3(2), 5(1); infra, § **38: 10** and IHTA 1984, ss. 53(1), 82; infra, § **41: 20**.

[2] IHTA 1984, s. 6(1); infra, § **49: 13**.

[3] IHTA 1984, s. 48(3); infra, § **49: 15**.

[4] IHTA 1984, s. 6(1); infra, § **49: 17**.

[5] IHTA 1984, s. 48(1); as amended—infra, § **41: 32**.

Exempt persons

37: 21   Although not excluded property, property of the following persons escapes IHT (*i*) foreign diplomats (Diplomatic Privileges Act 1964), (*ii*) members of International Organisations (International Organisations Act 1968), and (*iii*) consular officers (Consular Relations Act 1968).

Foster's Capital Taxes J3.27.

38 Transfers of value by disposition

38: 01   Whether one is dealing with a transfer which has been chargeable *ab initio* or one which was originally potentially exempt but which has become chargeable by reason of the death of the donor within seven years, the central concept is the transfer of value; IHT is charged on the value transferred by a chargeable transfer.[1]

A transfer of value is any disposition made by a person (the transferor) as a result of which the value of his estate immediately after the disposition is less than it would be but for the disposition.[2] However the statute may direct otherwise. So if it is shown that the transfer was not intended to confer any gratuitous benefit on any person and, either it was made in a transaction at arm's length between persons not connected with each other or was such as might be expected to be made in such a transaction no charge arises, it being declared not to be a transfer of value.[3]

A chargeable transfer is any transfer of value made by an individual after 26th March 1974 other than an exempt transfer[4] or a potentially exempt transfer made after 17th March 1986.[5]

At a technical level it is necessary to distinguish (i) the value transferred by a transfer of value from (ii) the value transferred by a chargeable transfer. This is because (i) is calculated ignoring the exempt transfer rules and without regard to grossing up (on which see infra, § 38: 09). The technical niceties are important when considering the application of reliefs such as business relief.

Foster's Capital Taxes C1.01.
[1] IHTA 1984, s. 1.
[2] IHTA 1984, s. 3(2).
[3] IHTA 1984, s. 10; infra, § **40: 01**.
[4] IHTA 1984, s. 2(1). On partly exempt transfers see IHTA 1984, s. 2(2) and infra, § **44: 14, 49: 01**.
[5] IHTA 1984, s. 3A(1) added by FA 1986, Sch. 19, para. 1.

POTENTIALLY EXEMPT TRANSFERS

38: 02   The key concept in the shift from CTT to IHT is the potentially exempt transfer. This has three elements.[1] First, it must be a transfer of value made by an individual on or after 18th March 1986; transfers before that date remain chargeable or not according to the law then in force.[2] Secondly, it must otherwise be a chargeable transfer (in whole or in part). So if the transfer is exempt under existing rules it remains fully exempt and is not made potentially chargeable. Thirdly it must be either a gift to another individual or a gift into an accumulation and maintenance trust.[4] As from 17th March 1987, certain transfers into settlements in which there is a beneficial interest in possession also qualify as potentially exempt transfers. The method of taxing potentially exempt transfers is discussed at § **37: 17** supra.

The third condition is the subject of statutory elaboration. Two preliminary issues arise. The first is whether the definition which follows is intended to be exhaustive; it is thought that this is so but the conclusion is not crystal clear.[5] The second is what weight to put on the meaning of the word gift. Since one is only talking about transfers of value it cannot widen the scope of the tax but the question is whether it is to be taken literally so that a sale at an undervalue might not count as a potentially exempt transfer. It is thought that to adopt such a meaning would lead to an unjustified narrowing of the scope of potentially exempt transfers and that in any event a sale at an undervalue can be treated as a gift of the part of the price foregone.

A gift is to an individual to the extent that the value is attributable to property which, by virtue of the transfer becomes comprised in the estate of the other individual; as from 17th March 1987 it does not matter whether it becomes so comprised as settled property or unsettled property. This form of words would seem to ensure that where the disposition causes a loss to the transferor's estate greater than the benefit to the estate of the donee the whole transfer is potentially exempt and not just to the extent of the value of the property disposed of. Thus to take the usual example, if D has 60 of the 100 shares in a company and gives A 20, the loss of D's estate reflects the loss of control. If this is all to be treated as a gift to A it will be potentially exempt. In turn this means that if D wishes to give A 20 but to settle the other 40 on discretionary trusts he will be well advised to make to gift to A first, so ensuring that the loss of control will be the subject of a potentially exempt transfer and not an immediately chargeable transfer.[6]

Where the value is not attributable to property becoming comprised in the estate of another person it is treated as being to an individual to the extent that, by virtue of the transfer, the estate of that person is increased; again as from 17th March 1987 it does not matter that the increase is in the value of settled property comprised in his estate. This rule is designed to cover situations in which there is a transfer of value but no property becomes part of the transferee's estate as where the donor pays off some debts of the donee or pays a premium on a life policy belonging to him or allows an option to buy on advantageous terms to lapse. However it contains something of a trap since the opening words[7] refer to the situation where the value is not attributable to property becoming comprised in the estate of another *person* (not individual). So a gift to a company which has the incidental effect of increasing the value of the estates of its participators cannot be a potentially exempt transfer.[8]

What both rules have in common is a requirement that there should be an increase in the value of the estate of an individual; from this it follows that if there is no such increase the transfer cannot be a potentially exempt transfer. One situation in which this would seem to occur is where a grandparent pays the school fees of a grandchild; here there is no increase in the value of the grandchild's estate.

Where under the provisions of the Act tax is charged "as if" a transfer of value had been made, the transfer cannot be a potentially exempt transfer.[9] So a transfer of value by a close company is not a potentially exempt transfer. Before 17th March 1987 the termination of an interest in possession in settled property could not be potentially exempt but this is now changed by the exclusion of any charge arising from IHTA 1984, s. 52 from the list of disqualified transfers. The scheme of charging settled property in which there is no interest in possession no longer uses the concept of a transfer of value and thus is also outside the new category.

In addition various situations have been specifically excluded from being potentially exempt transfers. So where there is an alteration in the rights in a close company falling within s. 98 the transfer of value cannot be potentially exempt.[10] Any transfer of value arising on the purchase of an interest in possession before 17th March 1987 is excluded[11] as is the transfer of value that can arise where—before the same date—a person with an interest in settled property purchased an interest in reversion expectant on it.[12] Finally there is a transitional provision dealing with timber and stemming from the days of estate duty.[13]

Foster's Capital Taxes Division C4

[1] IHTA 1984, s. 3A(1) added by FA 1986, Sch. 9, para. 1 and amended to apply to interest in possession settled property after 16th March 1987 by F(No. 2)A 1987, s. 96.

[2] FA 1986, Sch. 19, para. 40.

[3] As defined in IHTA 1984, s. 71.

[4] As defined in IHTA 1984, s. 89.

[5] Venables *Inheritance Tax Planning*, 2.1.2.8.

[6] Venables *op cit* 2.1.2.11.

[7] IHTA 1984, s. 3A(2)(*b*).

[8] Venables *op cit* 2.1.4 who however points out that where the donor simply allows an option to lapse which has the effect of increasing the value of the company's assets and so the estates of the participators, the gift *can* be a potentially exempt transfer since the words at the start of this rule exclude it only where no *property* becomes part of the estate of another person.

[9] IHTA 1984, s. 3A(6).

[10] IHTA 1984, s. 98(3) added by FA 1986, Sch. 19, para. 20; infra, § **43: 07**.

[11] IHTA 1984, s. 49(3) added by FA 1986, Sch. 19, para. 14.

[12] IHTA 1984, s. 55(2) amended by FA 1986, Sch. 19, para. 15; infra, § **41: 32**.

[13] FA 1986, Sch. 19, para. 46; infra, § **45: 27**.

DISPOSITION

38: 03   The word disposition is not defined in the legislation[1] although it is stated to include a disposition effected by associated operations. The word disposition is not the same as the word disposal used in CGT—and in the definition of a gift with reservation for IHT. A disposition need not be of any existing property[2] so that distinctions between the creation and the disposition of interests are quite immaterial; all that is required is some act or, in some situations, an omission, which results in a loss in value to a person's estate. From this it might appear to follow that deliberately to destroy an asset, for example a picture or stamp, would be a disposition as would an accidental destruction, although the absence of an intent to confer a benefit will usually prevent a charge arising. The notion of a transfer, however, suggests the need for a transferee so that one could argue that even deliberate destruction could not be a disposition.[3] Against this one may point out that the word "transferee" was almost completely removed in the 1984 consolidation[4] and that the word to be construed is disposition, not transfer. Moreover, to suggest that the destruction of an interest, as where a lessee surrenders his lease to his landlord, is not a transfer of value, would open the door to avoidance. The position is obscure.

If one wishes to say that the destruction of a picture is not a transfer of value[5] whereas the surrender of a lease is, there are several ways of justifying one's distinction. The first is to say that in the case of a surrender there may be a *scintilla temporis* during which the landlord holds the tenant's interest before it is destroyed by merger; the picture case is therefore distinguishable. The second is to say that the loss must be to the transferor's estate and an estate consists of *rights*; the surrender of the lease is a transfer of the rights to the landlord whereas the destruction of the asset is not. A third is to say that, whether or not the estate consists of rights, there is a transfer of property by an act of the lessee in surrendering his lease; one difficulty here is that an act whereby the lessee forfeits his lease cannot be treated in the same way.[6]

The incurring of a liability will result in a reduction of a person's estate and so be a disposition provided the liability is deductible in computing the value of his estate under the relevant rules (§ **46: 18**). Where the liability is not deductible there is no reduction in the transferor's estate and so no value is transferred. Thus if I agree to guarantee my son's overdraft, there will be no reduction in the value of my estate since a liability incurred otherwise than for consideration is only deductible if and to the extent that it is incurred for consideration in money or money's worth.[7] Should I have to pay sums under the guarantee such payments will be transfers of value.

On the discharge of a non-deductible liability in respect of a loan as a transfer of value see infra, § **46: 24**.

---

[1] Contrast estate duty—FA 1939, s. 30(3).

[2] It must however be of property as defined supra, § **37: 18**, so that a disposition of services would not cause a charge to tax whereas the disposition of a right to be paid for services would.

[3] Destruction of an asset by disclaimer was held to be a disposition in *IRC v Buchanan* [1957] 2 All ER 400, 37 TC 365 (TA 1988, s. 663 (TA 1970, s. 437), see supra, § **13: 04**. See also Venables, *Tax Planning Through Trusts* § 11: 03).

[4] Removed from e.g. IHTA 1984, s. 199(1)(*a*).

[5] But suppose that A has a valuable stamp and his son B has another copy of the same stamp and that these are the only two copies known to exist in private hands; each stamp is worth £20,000 but if A destroys his stamp B's will be worth £60,000. A destroys his stamp.

[6] Does the forfeiture count as an omission under IHTA 1984, s. 3(3)—probably not; see infra, § **38: 05**.

[7] One must distinguish a liability from a contract with proprietary effect. Thus if A contracts to sell land to B, B acquires an estate contract—an incumbrance against that land; the loss to A's estate therefore arises at the time of the contract.

TIMING

38: 04   The use of a concept of a disposition causing loss to an estate rather than a transfer of property means that where a person transfers shares to his son by way of gift, there will be a transfer of value as soon as the estate suffers loss, i.e. when the transferor has done all in his power to effect the transfer rather than the time when the transfer is entered in the books of the company.[1] Similarly, where there is a sale at an undervalue the transfer of value will take place when the property in the goods passes to the purchaser.

It also follows that subsequent changes in the value of the thing disposed of are ignored. So it is advantageous to retain things whose value will remain static or even fall and to give away things which will appreciate.

Foster's Capital Taxes B3.12; C2.11
[1] *Re Rose, Midland Bank Executor and Trustee Co Ltd v Rose* [1949] Ch 78, [1948] 2 All ER 971.

OMISSION TO EXERCISE A RIGHT

38: 05   IHTA 1984, s. 3(3) states: ". . . [w]here the value of a person's estate is diminished and that of another person's estate is increased by the first-mentioned person's omission to exercise a right he shall be treated as having made a disposition at the time, or the latest time, when he could have exercised the right, unless it is shown that the omission was not deliberate."

This is one of the rare instances in which an increase in the other person's estate is relevant; however the measure of value is still the loss to the transferor not the benefit to the transferee. It follows that if the omission does not increase another person's estate, no tax is due. Where a benefit to the other person's estate occurs, the transfer may be potentially exempt since s. 3(3) treats the omission as a disposition and not simply as an event to be taxed as it it were a transfer of value.

The failure of a landlord to exercise a rent review clause, thus increasing the value of the lessee's interest, would fall within this provision; as would the failure on the part of a shareholder to exercise his rights under a rights issue, a course of action which might increase the value of shares taken up, especially where control of a company is involved, or allowing an option to purchase a property at a favourable price to lapse. The Revenue have invoked IHTA 1984, s. 3(3) where a settlor, chargeable to income tax on income of a settlement under the rules considered in **Chapter 13**, supra, failed to exercise his right of indemnity against the trust.

It must not however be forgotten that this rule only declares that the omission will be treated as a disposition and it is therefore open to the person to bring himself within one of the rules excluding liability, particularly that for *bona fide* deals without donative intent in IHTA 1984, s. 10.

IHTA 1984, s. 3(3) applies only on the omission to exercise a right. "Right" is not defined but presumably means a legal right. Thus if a tenant commits an act as a result of which his lease is forfeited, it may well be that the section cannot be used to charge him on the ground that he omitted to exercise his "right" not to commit the act.[1]

Foster's Capital Taxes C1.12.

[1] Normally it would be hard to argue that such an act is a disposition. *Quaere*, however, where the forfeiture results not from an act but from a failure to act.

VALUE TRANSFERRED

38: 06   The value transferred is not simply the amount which the transferee receives but rather is the amount by which the value of the transferor's estate is reduced.[1] This has three major consequences for calculating the value transferred.

---

[1] IHTA 1984, s. 3(1).

38: 07   (1) The estate concerned is that of the transferor; that of the transferee is not relevant in determining whether there is a transfer of value, although it is relevant in determining whether the transfer is potentially exempt. So if a particular disposition results in a greater loss to the transferor than benefit to the transferee it is that greater loss which is taken into account for tax. For example if A has 60% of the shares in a company[1] and B has 40%, the transfer by A to C of one-third of his holding (20% of the shares of the company) will give C simply a minority holding in the company. On the other hand A will have lost control of the company so that the loss he sustains will be greater than the value of the benefit received by C; it is A's loss which is used to measure the value of the transfer for tax. Again, suppose that G pays the school fees of his grandson J; the value transferred is the loss to G, the amount spent by him, and the issue of how to value the benefit received by J does not arise;[2] however as no property passes to J and it is impossible to see that J's estate is increased, it follows that the transfer cannot be potentially exempt. The converse of this consequence is equally true. Where a particular disposition results in a greater benefit to the transferee than loss to the transferor only that loss is taxed.[3] On whether this affects the status of the gift as a potentially exempt transfer see supra, § **38: 02**.

The loss to the transferor's estate will depend on the extent of his estate. Where A gives B a fur coat or a painting it is clear that there is a transfer of the coat or the painting and the value of that object grossed up as necessary will be the measure of the transferor's loss and so the chargeable amount. More complicated questions may however arise where A buys the object for B. Suppose that A sees a picture for sale in an antique shop for £50 but knows that it is really by a famous artist and worth £50,000. If A buys the picture and takes it home where he gives it to B, that will be a net chargeable transfer by A of £50,000. If, however, he is in the shop with B and pays £50 to B with which to buy the picture or perhaps himself pays over the £50 instructing the antique dealer to deliver the picture to B, then so long as the picture did not become part of A's estate there will be a net chargeable transfer of only £50.[4] The question of the precise subject-matter of the gift is also relevant to gifts with reservation since the rules as to tracing property do not apply if the property given is a sum of money in sterling or any other currency.

Where A's transfer to B is void, there is no loss to A's estate and so no chargeable transfer. Where the transfer is voidable the same result should follow since A's right to rescind the transfer and recover the property is part of his estate; there may be a transfer when the right to rescind is lost. However, IHTA 1984, s. 150, is premised on the assumption that a voidable transfer is effective despite the existence of the right to rescind. Similarly a gift subject to a condition precedent causes no loss to the estate until the condition occurs; a gift subject to a condition subsequent is analogous to a voidable transfer when the right to rescind has not yet become exercisable.

Foster's Capital Taxes C2.22.
[1] If A had 80% and he gave 20% to C he would still have voting control of the company but would have lost the power to wind up the company (which requires 75%).
[2] Under the estate duty rules it was Revenue practice that education could not be valued and so its value was nil.
[3] IHTA 1984, s. 3(3); see also IHTA 1984, ss. 148(2)(a) and 149(5)(a).
[4] Cf. Goff J in *Ralli Bros Trustee Co Ltd v IRC* [1967] 3 All ER 811 at 820.

38: 08 (2) Any consideration provided in return for the property is automatically taken into account. Thus if A sells a piece of property worth £1,000 to his son B for £400, there will be a transfer of value of £600. Where the consideration provided in return is full but is paid to someone other than the vendor there will also be a transfer of value. So when A sells the property worth £1,000 to a dealer and directs him to pay the price to A's son B, then there will be a transfer of value by A of £1,000, the subject matter of the transfer.

38: 09 (3) *Grossing up.* Suppose that A has made transfers of £140,000 when he makes an immediately chargeable transfer of £10,000 to a trust. If A bears the burden of the tax the amount of the gift must be grossed up at 20% to take account of the tax due; the loss sustained by him will be the amount transferred by him plus the tax due (a total of £12,500) since this is the total amount of the loss to his estate. A is thus taken now to have made transfers of £152,500. If on the other hand the trust bears the burden of the tax there is no grossing up and the total loss to A's estate is only £10,000; see supra, §37: 11. Grossing up has no role in potentially exempt transfers since the primary liability rests on the donee.

This strengthens rather than weakens the logical structure of the tax as IHT charges the reduction in the value of the estate. The grossing up rule has the further strength that it avoids differences of principle between chargeable transfers *inter vivos* and those on death. On death there is a transfer of all the property to which the transferor was beneficially entitled, whether actually or notionally. On transfers on death it will only be the sums net of tax that reach the beneficiaries. One is used to thinking of transfers on death in gross terms. There is no reason why this should not apply to transfers *inter vivos* as well.

The grossing up principle applies to the value transferred, i.e. the loss to the estate. Where A settles shares on trust there may also be incidental costs and even CGT. Where these costs are borne by A they are not grossed up; where they are borne by the trust they reduce the value transferred, infra, § **46: 26**.

Foster's Capital Taxes C2.23, 24.

DISPOSITION OF EXCLUDED PROPERTY

38: 10   A person's estate is the aggregate of all the property to which he is beneficially entitled, except that the estate of a person immediately before his death does not include excluded property.[1] It follows from this that excluded property does form part of a person's estate at other times. However it is further provided that no account is to be taken of the value of excluded property which ceases to form part of a person's estate as a result of a disposition.[2] It follows from this that while a transfer of excluded property will not give rise to liability in respect of the property transferred, liability will accrue if the transfer of non-excluded property causes a loss to the excluded property.

> **EXAMPLE**
> A, a person domiciled outside the United Kingdom, owns 40% of the shares in X Ltd, an English company. Another 30% of the shares are held by Y Ltd, a foreign company. A owns 75% of the shares in Y Ltd so that he has control of X Ltd by virtue of the two holdings of 40% and 30%. If A makes a transfer of his 40% holding in X Ltd, there will be a transfer of value, whether chargeable or potentially exempt. There is a chargeable transfer since those shares are not excluded property.
> The value transferred is the loss to A's estate and this will therefore take account of the loss of control notwithstanding that control is achieved only by the inclusion of excluded property.

Liability may also arise if the transfer of excluded property causes a loss to other property forming part of the estate. So if A had transferred the holding in Y Ltd first there would again have been a loss to his estate, perhaps a loss of control. It might be argued that since no account is taken of the value of the excluded property transferred and since that property gave A control it ought to follow that the loss of control will escape tax. However, it may be replied that the "value of the excluded property" is to be valued on its own and so without reference to the power it gave A over X Ltd, so that the difference between the loss of control and the value of the excluded property on its own is taxable; the position is not completely clear but on balance liability seems to arise.

A yet more absurd situation is where A has control of a company through shares which are all excluded property, e.g. a 55% holding, and he then gives a 10% holding to B. It cannot be supposed that a charge to tax arises here and yet the gift of the 10% causes a loss to A's estate reflecting the loss of control.

One reason for the rule is to prevent a charge to tax from arising where A sells non-excluded property and invests the proceeds in excluded property.

Foster's Capital Taxes B3.15; C2.26.
[1] IHTA 1984, s. 5(1).
[2] IHTA 1984, s. 3(2).

FREE USE OF PROPERTY

38: 11   If A agrees to lend B an asset for a period of say five years without charge it will be possible to calculate the loss to A's estate, by reference to income foregone and other matters under general principles. Where the loan is for a period which is not fixed there used to be special provisions to calculate the loss;[1] these were scrapped in 1981, presumably leaving the matter to general principles and so giving rise, perhaps, to chargeable or potentially exempt transfers; where the property can be recalled at will the loss appears to be negligible.

[1] FA 1976, ss. 115–117 and see **Foster's Capital Taxes C1.13, 14.**

MUTUAL TRANSFERS

38: 12   With the change from CTT to IHT, the rules providing relief where A makes a transfer of value to B and B later makes a transfer of value to A are repealed; they do not apply if B's transfer is made after 18th March 1986.[1] These are no longer generally needed since the only dispositions by A and B that will qualify for relief are now potentially exempt transfers rather than chargeable transfers. However, the Board of Inland Revenue is empowered to make regulations to avoid a double charge where a potentially exempt transfer by A to B proves to be a chargeable transfer and, immediately before A's death his estate includes property acquired by him from B otherwise than for full consideration. These regulations apply for transfers or other events occurring on or after 18th March 1986.[2] It has been suggested that the reason behind the repeal is to prevent the undoing of previous chargeable transfers to enable potentially exempt transfers to be made instead.[3]

Foster's Capital Taxes C2.51.
[1] FA 1986, Sch. 19, para. 25.
[2] FA 1986, s. 104(1)(*a*); see **39: 24** et seq.
[3] McCutcheon's *Capital Transfer Tax*, § 2: 07.

VOIDABLE TRANSFERS

38: 13   IHTA 1984, s. 150 provides that where by virtue of any enactment or rule of law the whole or any part of a transfer has been set aside as voidable or otherwise defeasible, a claim may be made and (*i*) any tax[1] due shall cease to be due; (*ii*) any tax[1] already paid in respect of that or any other chargeable transfer[2] made before the claim that would not have been payable if the transfer had been void *ab initio* can be reclaimed; (*iii*) where the transferor has subsequently made other transfers, the rates of tax are determined as if the first transfer had been void.[3] (*iii*) is different from—and more generous than—the rule for mutual transfers. Examples include bankruptcy[4] and gifts made under undue influence.

The provision, although well intentioned, is not without its difficulties. First, it applies not just where the transfer is voidable but also where it is otherwise defeasible. Hence perhaps a subsequent condition which defeats the grant of an interest may come within this rule. However a transfer subject to a condition precedent which has not yet occurred would appear to be ineffective and so not to fall within this rule even though it should come about that the condition can never occur.

Secondly, it applies only where the transfer has been set aside and so not where the parties elect or the court directs that the transferor shall receive damages in lieu of the setting aside. Such matters ought technically to be treated as mutual transfers.

Thirdly, it assumes that a voidable transfer is an effective transfer yet, in theory, the reduction in the value of the estate should be exactly offset by the value of the right to recover the property.

Foster's Capital Taxes C2.55.

[1] And any interest due, IHTA 1984, s. 150(2); interest paid to the taxpayer is tax free IHTA 1984, s. 236(3).

[2] As when the voidable transfer was exempt under IHTA 1984, s. 19 and the second would have been if the first had not been made.

[3] IHTA 1984, s. 150(1).

[4] Insolvency Act 1986, ss. 339, 340, 423.

MATTERS WHICH ARE NOT TRANSFERS OF VALUE

Transactions with no intent to give (IHTA 1984, s. 10)

38: 14   IHT is intended to be a tax on gratuitous transfers of value. IHTA 1984, s. 10 therefore provides that if the transferor shows (*a*) that the transfer was made (*i*) in a transaction at arm's length between persons not connected with each other[1] or (*ii*) if they are so connected, that the transfer was such as might be expected to be made in a transaction at arm's length; and (*b*) that the transfer was not intended and was not made in a transaction intended to confer a gratuitous benefit on *any* person then it is not a transfer of value. Not only is intention to be judged according to the normal legal rule that a person is taken to intend the natural and probable consequences of his acts[2] (or omissions) but there is the further point that the onus is placed on the transferor to show that this intention was not present.

EXAMPLES

(1) G, a grandfather, pays £20,000 to a school fees scheme for his grandson. This does not escape tax since although the purchase is an arm's length transaction, G intends to

confer a gratuitous benefit on his grandson. Moreover it may well be an immediate chargeable transfer rather than a potentially exempt one.

(2) G sells a picture for £10,000; unknown to him the picture is worth £100,000. Assuming that these facts are established, IHTA 1984, s. 10 prevents there being a transfer of value despite the loss to G's estate.

(3) F grants his son S the protected tenancy of a dwelling house. Although S pays the maximum fair rent the Revenue may treat the grant of the lease as subject to tax, as it is clearly a disposal causing loss to F's estate, and deny the availability of IHTA 1984, s. 10 on the ground that persons dealing at arm's length do not usually grant protected tenancies. A similar argument arose out of the grant of tenancies of agricultural land but there special legislation now applies, infra, § **38. 20** (6). Returning to the grant of a protected tenancy one may perhaps distinguish the parent who grants a tenancy of the only property he has other than his own home from one who regularly lets property to protected tenants and who treats his son in the same way as any other tenant. As always the question is one of fact. Since the lease is an asset of S's estate, the grant would seem to be capable of being a potentially exempt transfer rather than an immediately chargeable one.

IHTA 1984, s. 10 does not apply to (*i*) a sale of unquoted shares or debentures[3] unless it is shown that the sale was at a price freely negotiated at the time of the sale; even then the requirements of IHTA 1984, s. 10(1) must presumably, also be met;[4] (*ii*) certain reversionary interests, IHTA 1984, s. 55, infra, § **41: 32**. IHTA 1984, s. 10 applies to transactions; transactions include a series of transactions and any associated operations.

For IHTA 1984, s. 10 the expression "transaction" is expressly stated to include a series of transactions and any associated operations.

Foster's Capital Taxes C1.21.

[1] An example would be an employer making ex gratia payments to his employees.

[2] See *Cunliffe v Goodman* [1950] 2 K B 237 at 253.

[3] On meaning of quoted and unquoted shares see IHTA 1984, s. 272 as amended by FA 1987, Sch. 8, para. 1; shares listed on the USM are now quoted securities.

[4] However the Revenue may argue that when the vendor has a 75% holding the sale of a 33% holding is only freely negotiated if the purchaser pays a price equal to $\frac{33}{75}$ths of the value of the 75% holding.

Dispositions for maintenance of family (IHTA 1984, s. 11)

38: 15   Certain dispositions for the maintenance of one's family are not transfers of value (not even potentially exempt ones).

(1) *Spouse and ex-spouse*. A disposition made by one party to a marriage in favour of the other party is not a transfer of value if it is for the maintenance of the other party. Further, "marriage" is defined in relation to a disposition made on the occasion of the dissolution of annulment of a marriage, and in relation to a disposition varying a disposition so made, as including a former marriage.[1]

The exemption is necessary because the general exemption for transfers between spouses (infra, § **44: 01**) is limited to £55,000[2] where the transferor is, but the transferee is not, domiciled in the UK, and does not apply to former spouses.

The scope of this relief is uncertain in a number of respects. First, there is the problem of the precise meaning of the word disposition. This is apt to cover a transfer within IHTA 1984, s. 2 and is expressly stated to cover the termination of an interest in possession in settled property under IHTA 1984, s. 51(1).[3] This leaves open those matters which are treated as transfers of value. Thus a deemed transfer by participators in a close company under IHTA 1984, s. 98(5); infra, § **43: 07**, is treated as being a disposition by them; when a person dies he is treated as having made a transfer of value; infra, § **39: 10**, but this is not expressly stated to be by way of disposition although other provisions assume that he does make a disposition.[4]

The Revenue view is that a transfer on death is not capable of coming within IHTA 1984, s. 11. The correct view is probably that IHTA 1984, s. 11 applies only where the transfer is by disposition or in circumstances in which the legislation in its charging provisions treats the transfer as made by disposition. On this view transfers under IHTA 1984, s. 98 would fall within IHTA 1984, s. 11 but those on death or under IHTA 1984, s. 94 and payments ceasing to be relevant property under IHTA 1984, s. 65 would not. The status of transfers of value under IHTA 1984, s. 52(1), (3) and (4) has become much clearer since the consolidation which enacts the Revenue view that IHTA 1984, s. 11 does not apply. This is harsh, hard to justify and in need of reform. One should also recall that a deemed transfer of value otherwise than by disposition cannot be a potentially exempt transfer.

The second difficulty is that the transfer must be "in favour of" the other spouse. This is sufficient to cover payments direct to the other spouse or to trustees for the spouse absolutely and probably also a transfer to a trust to hold on trust for the spouse for life[5] but may not extend to the creation of a discretionary trust of which the spouse is to be one of the objects. If a transfer to a trust under which the spouse takes a life interest is completely exempt it may follow that a transfer to a trust under which the spouse takes a reversionary interest is taxable in full.

The third difficulty is that the section is confined to transfers for the maintenance of the other spouse. Matrimonial legislation on divorce moved from the concept of maintenance to that of financial provision on 1st January 1971. Presumably, IHTA 1984, s. 11 should be construed in this light.[6]

Certain practical problems arise over the implementation of agreements or court orders on divorce or annulment. If the carrying out of the agreement or order is deferred until after decree absolute the transfer is presumably made "on the occasion of" the dissolution or annulment and so qualifies for relief; moreover a transfer is defined in terms of the date of the loss to the transferor's estate and so presumably the date of the transfer is that on which the agreement or order was made. Such transfers ought therefore to be safe whether carried out before or after decree absolute. Subsequent transfers in favour of the ex-spouse will however only be exempt if they vary the disposition made on the divorce or annulment; such transfers should therefore be expressed to be by way of such variation. Whether a completely new agreement can be by way of variation of the old is unclear.[7]

It is unclear whether transfers which simply implement orders made by the court can ever have any tax consequences. It can be argued that these are not 'dispositions' so long as there is no consensual element in them, or that they are protected from tax by IHTA 1984, s. 10.

Foster's Capital Taxes C1.22.
[1] IHTA 1984, s. 11(6).
[2] IHTA 1984, s. 51(2).
[3] IHTA 1984, s. 18(1).

⁴ IHTA 1984, ss. 18(1) and 147 also Administration of Estates Act 1925, s. 1.
⁵ See Revenue Consultative document, [1980] STI, p. 581.
⁶ Infra, § **41: 09**.
⁷ Cf. the cases in Variation of Trusts Act 1958, especially *Re Ball's Settlement* [1968] 2 All ER 438.

38: 16 (2) *A child of either party to a marriage.* A disposition by one party to a marriage in favour of a child of either party for the maintenance, education or training of the child for a period ending in the year in which the child attains the age of 18 or, if later, ceases to undergo full-time education or training is not a transfer of value. Child includes a step child and an adopted child. The word training is undefined; presumably solicitors articles provide training.

The rule enables a parent, but not a grandparent, to make transfers free of tax. The transfer may be in favour of the child. There is no need for the transfer to be on the occasion of a divorce and the provision is presumably designed to exempt a parent from liability to tax in respect of private school fees.

Where a child resumes full-time education or training after attaining 18, a literal reading suggests that later transfers may not come within the provision.

Another problem is that where a husband covenants to pay his wife annual sums for a child until he reaches 21 the payments will presumably be treated as made year by year, each year being a period. If however he hands over a lump sum for the maintenance of the child until he reaches 21 regardless of whether or not the child receives full time education after reaching the age of 18 the transfer would appear to fall outside the relief.

38: 17 (3) *A child not in the care of his parent.* Where the child is not in the care of a parent a disposition—by anyone—for his maintenance, education or training is not a transfer of value if (*i*) it is for a period ending not later than the year in which he attains the age of 18 or, (*ii*) if the child has for substantial periods been in the custody of the transferor, the year in which he ceases to undergo full time education or training.

38: 18 (4) *Illegitimate child of the transferor.* A disposition in favour of an illegitimate child of the transferor is not a transfer of value. The disposition must be for the maintenance, education or benefit of the child and for the same period as for other children.

38: 19 (5) *Dependent relative.* A disposition in favour of a dependent relative is not a transfer of value provided it is a reasonable provision for his care or maintenance. The notion of a dependent relative is narrowly defined as (1) any relative of the transferor or his spouse who is incapacitated by old age or infirmity from maintaining himself, the term relative not being further defined, and (2) the mother of the transferor or his spouse if widowed or living apart from her husband or, in consequence of dissolution or annulment of the marriage, a single woman.[1] By concession this extends to a gift by a child to his unmarried mother.[2]

Foster's Capital Taxes C1.23, 24.
[1] The same as TA 1988, s. 263 (TA 1970, s. 16) now repealed by FA 1988, s. 25 and CGTA 1979, s. 104; supra, §§ **3: 15** and **15: 16**.
[2] Extra-statutory concession F12 (1988).

Other transfers not transfers of value

38: 20 (1) A disposition which is allowable in computing the transferor's profits or gains for income tax or corporation tax is not a transfer of value. The same applies where the sum would be so allowable if the profits or gains were sufficient and fell to be so computed.[1]

(2) A disposition which is a contribution to an approved retirement benefits scheme or personal pension plan and provides benefits in respect of service with the transferor is not a transfer of value.[2] The same applies to one made so as to provide benefits on or after retirement for an employee who is not connected with the transferor or for the widow or dependants of such a person if the benefits do not exceed those that would have been provided under an approved scheme. For this purpose the right to occupy a dwelling rent free or at a rent below market value is treated as a pension equal to the amount of rent forgone.

(3) A waiver or repayment of remuneration is not a transfer of value if (*i*) it would have been chargeable to income tax under Schedule E and (*ii*) the sum, if not waived, would have been deductible in computing the profits of the payer and, by reason of repayment or the waiver, is not allowed or is brought back into charge.[3]

(4) A waiver of any dividend on shares of a company within twelve months before—but not after—any right to dividend has accrued is not a transfer of value;[4] the right accrues when the dividend is declared, not when it becomes enforceable.[5] It will be noted that there is no provision dealing with the waiver of interest or rent.

(5) Transfer to trustees for employees[6] by a close company; a similar transfer by an individual is an exempt transfer[7] and qualifies for exemption only if the trust has control.

(6) The grant of an agricultural tenancy is declared not to be a transfer of value if it is made for full consideration in money or money's worth.[8] The reason for this is that the grant of such a lease inevitably reduces the value of an estate owing to the different values of freehold and tenanted land and the system of control of agricultural rents. But for such a provision a landlord would find himself liable to tax on granting a lease to his son even though the terms were the best he could obtain from any third party.[9]

Foster's Capital Taxes C1.25–29.
[1] IHTA 1984, s. 12. The wording is wide enough to cover a trade which in fact makes a loss or which is not within the charge to UK tax, e.g. a foreign trade.
[2] IHTA 1984, s. 12(2) as amended by F(No. 2)A 1987, s. 98(2).
[3] IHTA 1984, s. 14. Remuneration is not defined—*quaere* whether it extends to any payment falling within Sch. E. An example of a payment falling within (*ii*) is *White v Franklin*; supra, § **8: 05**.
[4] IHTA 1984, s. 15.
[5] Long-term waiver may cause liability to tax under IHTA 1984, s. 98; infra, § **43: 07** and to tax under CGTA 1979, s. 25.

⁶ IHTA 1984, s. 30 (note restriction of rights of participators to income only).
⁷ IHTA 1984, s. 28.
⁸ IHTA 1984, s. 16.
⁹ IHTA 1984, s. 10 would not apply as, in the Revenue view, no-one in his right mind would grant a lease of such land anyway and therefore there must have been an intention to confer a gratuitous benefit.

EXEMPT GIFTS

Transfers not exceeding £3,000 (IHTA 1984, s. 19)

38: 21   Each tax year a person may make transfers of value up to £3,000 without incurring any liability to tax.

Where several transfers are made in one year, the exemption is given according to the date of the transfer, the earlier transfers enjoying the exemption. Where two transfers are made on the same day, the exemption is apportioned between them in proportion to the values transferred, this is so even though one knows the order in which the transfers were made.¹

To the extent that transfers in one year fall short of £3,000 the amount by which they fall short may be rolled forward to the next year and used to exempt gifts in that year.² Any shortfall unused at the end of the second year is lost.

This exemption applies to all dispositions *inter vivos* to the termination of a life interest in possession³ and to sums apportioned under IHTA 1984, s. 94 (close companies).⁴ However it does not apply on death.

> **EXAMPLE**
> On 10th June year 1 A transfers £2,826 to B. He makes no other transfers in that year. In year 2 A makes the following transfers–
>
> | 10th May | £1,400 (C) |
> | 11th May | £1,000 (D) and £1,500 (E) |
> | 12th May | £3,000 (F) |
>
> A can roll forward £174 of the £3,000 exemption from year 1 to year 2.
> In year 2, transfer C is exempt. Transfers D and E are partly exempt, the remaining exemption (£1,600 + £174) being apportioned ⅖ to D (£710) and ⅗ to E (£1,064) i.e. £290 of transfer D and £436 of transfer E are chargeable. The whole of transfer F is chargeable.

Where there is a potentially exempt transfer in the year, the annual exemption is set first against any chargeable transfers even if made after the potentially exempt transfer.⁵ If it later becomes a chargeable transfer it is treated, for this purpose only, as made after the other transfers in that year.⁶

> **EXAMPLE**
> In year 1, D makes a potentially exempt transfer of £3,000. In year 2, D makes a chargeable transfer of £6,000. Originally the whole of the transfer in year 2 would be exempt. However if D dies within seven years of the transfer of £3,000 the year 1 exemption will be switched from year 2 to year 1.⁷

A gift with reservation cannot use this exemption.⁸

Foster's Capital Taxes C3.01, 02.
¹ IHTA 1984, s. 19(3).
² IHTA 1984, s. 19(2).
³ IHTA 1984, s. 19(5).

⁴ IHTA 1984, s. 94(5).
⁵ IHTA 1984, s. 19(3A)(*a*).
⁶ IHTA 1984, s. 19(3A)(*b*).
⁷ IHTA 1984, s. 19(3A) allows the potentially exempt transfer to be left out of account only for the year in which it was made.
⁸ FA 1986, s. 102(5).

Small gifts to the same person (IHTA 1984, s. 20)

38: 22   Transfers of value made by a transferor in any one year by outright gifts to any one person are exempt to the extent that the values transferred, without grossing up, do not exceed £250. There is no rollover of any unused portion of £250. This is intended as a de minimis exception and so cannot be used to exempt the first £250 of a larger transfer.

The restriction to "outright gifts" bars *inter alia* a transfer to trustees to hold on trusts unless perhaps to hold on bare trusts for one or more of full age and capacity.¹ The phrase would appear to exclude a transfer at an undervalue, and sums apportioned under IHTA 1984, s. 94² (close companies).

A free loan is treated as an outright gift.³

A gift with reservation cannot use this exemption.⁴

Foster's Capital Taxes C3.03.
¹ In practice the reservation of an interest is ignored.
² Compare IHTA 1984, s. 20(3) with IHTA 1984, s. 79(5).
³ IHTA 1984, s. 29(3).
⁴ FA 1986, s. 102(5).

Normal expenditure out of income (IHTA 1984, s. 21)

38: 23   A transfer is exempt to the extent¹ that it is shown that (*i*) it was made as part of the normal expenditure of the transferor and (*ii*) that taking one year with another it was made out of income, and (*iii*) that after allowing for all transfers forming part of his normal expenditure, the transferor was left with sufficient income (after tax) to maintain his usual standard of living.² The capital repayment element in a purchased life annuity is declared not to form part of the transferor's income for this purpose unless purchased before 13th November 1974.³

Whether a gift forms part of the deceased's normal expenditure is a question of fact.⁴ A single transfer is unlikely to qualify unless presumably it is part of his normal pattern of expenditure to make isolated gifts. A single first payment when there is a continuing obligation will qualify, for example, an assurance premium⁵ or a payment under a deed of covenant unless death was imminent.⁶

This exemption applies to any disposition *inter vivos*, including payments to a settlement but not to a gift with reservation.⁷

Foster's Capital Taxes C3.04.
¹ Where the transfer exceeds this limit, only the excess is chargeable.
² IHTA 1984, s. 21(1).
³ IHTA 1984, s. 21(3).

⁴ *A-G for Northern Ireland v Heron* [1959] TR 1.
⁵ Provided it was capable of continuing for at least three years.
⁶ IHTA 1984, s. 21 does not use the phrase outright gift but does exclude IHTA 1984, s. 3(4). The usefulness of deeds of covenant is greatly restricted by TA 1988, s. 347A.
⁷ FA 1986, s. 102(5).

Marriage gifts (IHTA 1984, s. 22)

38: 24   Three rules apply (*a*) The first £5,000 of a transfer of value made by · gift made in consideration of marriage by the parent of either party to the marriage is exempt from tax.¹ (*b*) Where the transferor is a remoter ancestor or is a party to the marriage, the first £2,500 is exempt.² For (*a*) and (*b*) the gift may be an outright gift or the property settled by the gift—subject to further rules set out below. (*c*) The first £1,000 of a marriage gift made by a person other than a party to the marriage or his or her parent or remoter ancestor, is also exempt; for rule (*c*) only an outright gift will suffice, a gift in settlement will not. The net effect is that the four parents can between them make exempt transfers of £20,000 to the couple—but not to each of them. If a single donor makes more than one gift in consideration of the same marriage, the exemption is applied to the gifts rateably according to their respective values.³ An event causing a charge on settled property when there is a beneficial interest in possession, as where a power of appointment or advancement is exercised, can come within these rules provided notice is given to the trustees of the availability of this exemption;⁴ a gift with reservation is also eligible.⁵ Property which ceases to be settled property is treated as an outright gift; property remaining settled is treated as property becoming settled.

There is no qualification to these exemptions where the gift is an outright gift to one or other of the parties to the marriage,⁵ but where the gift is by way of settlement, exemption will be given only if the settlement is primarily for the benefit of the parties to the marriage, their issue (including legitimated and adopted issue) and the spouses of their issue.

It must also be shown that the gift, including its extended sense relating to settled property, is in consideration of marriage. Neither a gift made on the occasion of a marriage, nor one made conditional upon the marriage taking place, is necessarily made in consideration of marriage. The question is one of fact, and where the gift is in settlement the solution may lie in the terms of the settlement in the light of the surrounding circumstances.⁶ If therefore the settlor's prime motive was to save IHT and so benefit his family as a whole rather than the individual who was getting married, the gift is not in consideration of marriage; but it appears that an absolute disposition in favour of a party to their marriage cannot be attacked on this ground.⁷ Subject to this it is irrelevant to the question whether a gift is made for such consideration that there are beneficiaries outside the marriage consideration.

Foster's Capital Taxes C3.05.
¹ IHTA 1984, s. 21(1)(*a*). Where the gift is to a child, child includes an illegitimate child, an adopted child and a step child, IHTA 1984, s. 22(2).
² IHTA 1984, s. 22(1)(*b*).
³ IHTA 1984, s. 22(1).
⁴ IHTA 1984, ss. 22(6) and 57(2).

[5] FA 1986, s. 102(5).
[6] IHTA 1984, s. 22(4). Free loans are treated as outright gifts—IHTA 1984, s. 29(3).
[7] Per Lord Guest in *Rennell v IRC* [1964] AC 173 at 209, [1963] 1 All ER 803 at 817.
[8] *Re Park, IRC v Park (No. 2)* [1972] Ch 385, [1972] 1 All ER 394.

Miscellaneous trusts

38: 25 A transfer by an individual to an employee trust[1] is an exempt transfer if it meets the full requirements of IHTA 1984, s. 28, in particular that the trustees have then or within one year, control of the company.[2]

A transfer to a maintenance fund for heritage property is an exempt transfer.[3]

[1] As defined by IHTA 1984, s. 86.
[2] IHTA 1984, s. 28(2); contrast IHTA 1984, s. 13.
[3] IHTA 1984, s. 27 and Sch. 4.

DISPOSITION BY ASSOCIATED OPERATIONS (IHTA 1984, s. 268)

38: 26 A disposition is defined as including one made by associated operations.[1] Further, IHTA 1984, s. 10 provides that a transaction includes a series of transactions and any associated operations.[2] Such operations are elided; all are treated as made at the time of the last. Broadly such operations are either two or more affecting one piece of property or one paving the way for another. More precisely, they are defined[3] as—

> "any two or more operations of any kind whether effected by the same person or by different persons and whether or not simultaneous being (*a*) operations which affect the same property or one of which affects some property and the other or others affect property which represents, directly or indirectly, that property or income arising from that property or any property representing accumulations of such income or (*b*) any two operations of which one is effected with reference to the other or with a view to enabling the other to be effected or facilitating its being effected and any further operations having a like relation to any of those two and so on . . .".

The word "operation" is not defined save that it is to include omission.[4] An operation effected after 26th March 1974 is not to be associated with one effected before that date.

[1] IHTA 1984, s. 272.
[2] *Macpherson v IRC* [1988] STC 362, [1988] 2 All ER 753, HL.
[3] IHTA 1984, s. 268(1).
[4] A statutory reversal of *Nichols v IRC* [1975] STC 278, [1975] 2 All ER 120.

38: 27   An example of (*a*) would be the grant of a lease followed by the gift of the reversion to the lessee. However, where a lease is granted for full consideration in money or money's worth the lease is not taken as associated with any operation effected more than three years after its grant.[1]

EXAMPLE
Suppose that A has a house worth £50,000 and on 1st January 1987 he grants B, his son, a lease at full rent. The effect is to reduce the value of A's interest to £40,000. On 1st January 1987 when the house would have been worth £70,000 with vacant possession A gives B the reversion then worth £55,000.
The grant of the lease is not a transfer of value since it comes within IHTA 1984, s. 10[1] but the gift of the reversion is so that there would be transfer of £55,000. However the operations affect the same property and are therefore associated; they are therefore treated as one transfer of property worth £70,000 taking place on 1st January 1989. This will almost certainly be a potentialy exempt transfer but the point is that it is a potentially exempt transfer of property worth £70,000 not, £55,000.
If the gift of the reversion had taken place on 1st January 1991 over three years would have elapsed since the grant of the lease. The grant and the reversion would therefore not have been associated operations.

Another example of (*a*) would be the transfer of the fee simple followed by a lease back.

---

[1] The Revenue might argue that IHTA 1984, s. 10 does not apply as no-one would deliberately create the possibility of a protected tenancy unless he wished to confer a gratuitous benefit on the lessee. There is much sense in this view—see supra, § **40: 01** Example (3).

38: 28   (*b*) is directed particularly at persons trying to use exemptions, as where A, faced with a serious illness and so the real possibility that a potentially exempt transfer will become a chargeable one, transfers £3,000 to his son and the same sum to his wife so that she may pass that same sum to his son, in an attempt to knit together the exemption of the first £3,000 of otherwise chargeable transfers and that of transfers between spouses. These are sometimes called channelling operations. The Revenue regard such operations as safe from the new approach provided the gift to the spouse is, as a matter of substance, genuine[1].

It has been suggested[2] that in order for operations to be associated, the prime reasons for *each* of them taking place must be that the other will take place or has already done so. On this basis channelling operations would not necessarily be associated. However where T holds 51% of the shares in a company, transfers 2% to X, a stranger, for value and then transfers 20% to each of his two sons, the transfers to X and his sons might well be associated operations; equally the transfer of all one's UK assets to a non-resident company in return for shares in the company followed by the acquisition of a foreign domicile might also be associated operations.

---

[1] [1985] STI, p. 571.
[2] *Law Society's Gazette*, April 1976, p. 350.

38: 29   The consequences of operations being associated are complex but fall into three distinct parts. First, there is a timing rule. Where a transfer of value is carried out by associated operations at different times, it is treated as made at the time of the last one. This may increase the rate of tax payable on earlier transfers not only because there may have been other transfers in the interval raising the rate of tax but also because the last happens within three years of the transferor's death thus triggering the higher rates of tax. So the grant of the lease and the gift of the reversion may be treated as a transfer of the fee simple made at the time of the gift of the reversion. Likewise where A gave £250 to X and another £250 to Y for transmission to X, the scheme will be treated as being a disposal by A to X of £500 and so chargeable in full, supra, § **38: 15**. It also affects the date for valuing the property involved.

Secondly, there is a rule requiring that earlier transfers of value be taken into account. Where two transactions are carried out by the same person the value transferred by the earlier operation is treated as reducing the value transferred by all the operations taken together. This is to prevent a double charge to tax. Presumably, however, this could lead to a repayment of tax if the effect of the first rule is to bring the earlier transfer into a period of lower (or even nil) rates.

So if in the example supra, § **38: 27** A had granted the lease at a nominal rent so that there was a reduction in the value of A's estate of, say £10,000, and a consequent charge in 1986–87, this in turn would have reduced the later transfer from £70,000 to £60,000.

This affects not only the value of the property transferred but also the rate which any grossing up is carried out. It also seems to follow that where there have been intermediate transfers the tax on those transfers may have to be reopened; this is because the first transfer is now treated as taking place at the time of the last of the associated transfers by IHTA 1984, ss. 268(1)(*b*) and 272.

Thirdly, the second rule is subject to one important exception. This reduction does not apply to the extent that the transfer constituted by the earlier operations, but not that made by the operations taken together, is exempt as a transfer between spouses. So where A transferred £3,000 to his son and another £2,500 to his wife for transmission to the son the transfer will be treated as one of £5,500 to the son.

It will be noticed that there is no prohibition on the reduction where the earlier transfer is exempt by reason of some other provision. So if C gives his daughter D shares worth £10,000 in five equal instalments and makes no other transfers each year, the transfers will be associated operations and so will be treated as being of £10,000 in year 5 but reduced by the aggregate of the annual exemptions for each of years 1–4. Lest potential Cs should be carried away it should be remembered that if in year 5 the value of the shares rises sharply to £20,000, that increase will determine the value transferred.

Effects

38: 30   The practical effect of this provision must depend on Revenue practice. It appears that where H gives W property on condition that she pass it on to the real object of H's benevolence, such transactions will be treated as associated. Likewise the subject matter of the transaction may invite the attention of the Revenue as where H, having a 60% holding, transfers 35% to his son, having previously tranferred 25% to his wife who later transfers that holding to the son. The Revenue in such an instance might wish to ensure that the value of a controlling holding was taxed.[1]

Another consequence of the transactions being associated is that IHTA 1984, s. 10 must be applied to the single transaction. So if A grants B a lease at full rent and then sells him the reversion for full market value there may still be a chargeable transfer if the grant of the lease caused a drop in market value.[2]

One matter which IHTA 1984, s. 268 does not resolve is just who is to be treated as making the reconstructed transfer. Thus if A uses the spouse exemption to channel a controlling interest to his son is the whole transfer to be treated as made by A or is the value to be allocated between A and Mrs. A? The latter will at first sight avoid problems if A has died before the associated transfer is made by Mrs. A but this will not avoid the problem of reopening the transfer by A to give it a different value.

Where parents sell property to children but leave the purchase price outstanding to be released year by year using the annual exemption, the Revenue regard the operations as associated. However, the gift of an asset to a child, the child to pay the IHT, followed by gifts within the annual exemption limit to fund the IHT are not so regarded.[3]

Foster's Capital Taxes C1.11, 25.

[1] See Hansard Standing Committee A, 13th February, vol. 1596 and 10th March, col. 55. Yet the loss of control will be taxed, thanks to the related property rules, § **46: 07**; however, the later transfer by the wife will not be caught by those rules.

[2] But on agricultural land see IHTA 1984, s. 16.

[3] *Law Society's Gazette*, 1st March 1978.

38: 31   The effect of the recent decisions of the House of Lords stemming from that in *Furniss v Dawson*[1] is at present hard to assess (see § **1: 09**). It may be that the rule in IHTA 1984, s. 268 will be treated as excluding the new doctrine, but this is an unsafe assumption and is not the Revenue view[2].

A number of distinct problems arise. First, if the operations are associated under IHTA 1984, s. 268, will the courts allow the Revenue to use *Furniss v Dawson*? On balance this seems unlikely since the courts will presumably allow the detailed provisions in IHTA 1984, s. 268(3) as to the effects of operations being associated to apply. This is of particular importance where IHTA 1984, s. 268(3) determines the timing of a transaction.

Secondly, if the only reason why the operations are not associated is the applicability of the exclusion in IHTA 1984, s. 268(2) will the courts allow the Revenue to use *Furniss v Dawson*. Again it is thought that this is unlikely; the exclusion from IHTA 1984, s. 268 is an implied direction that the matters must be treated as separate transactions for tax purposes.

Thirdly, if IHTA 1984, s. 268 does not apply because the operations do not fall within the definition in IHTA 1984, s. 268(1) will the courts allow the Revenue to use *Furniss v Dawson*? This seems much harder to predict and there is nothing in the reasoning in the cases so far to suggest that the answer will be, or should be, "no".

Fourthly, if the answer to the previous question is yes, will the courts require the Revenue to proceed by analogy with IHTA 1984, s. 268(3) in reconstructing the transaction? There would seem to be good sense in such a requirement but the Revenue may find the timing rule in particular to be unnecessarily constraining and again, it would appear that there is nothing in the reasoning in the cases to limit the applicability of the new approach in this way.

---

[1] [1984] STC 153, HL.

[2] [1985] STI, p. 571. See moreover the decision of a Special Commissioner reported in *Taxation* 8th April 1988 p. 268.

---

39 Death

INTRODUCTION

Lifetime transfers

39: 01 Lifetime transfers other than gifts with reservation are not treated as taking place on death. However the subsequent death of the transferor may affect lifetime transfers in the following ways.

(1) *Loss of complete exemption*

39: 02 Transfers to political parties on death or within one year of death and made before 14th March 1988 are exempt only to the extent of the first £100,000, infra, § **44: 11**. Such transfers made after 14th March 1988 are now completely exempt. A similar, but different, limit also applied to transfers to charity made before 15th March 1983, infra, § **44: 10**.

(2) *Transfer undone*

39: 03 Where a transfer of value is undone by an order made under Inheritance (Provision for Family and Dependants) Act 1975, s. 10 any tax paid is to be repaid or, if unpaid, to cease to be payable; the transfer on death is charged as if the previous transfer had not been made but the money or property recovered does form part of the estate for the purpose of the transfer on death.[1]

Foster's Capital Taxes D2.03, 04; D5.31, 32.
[1] IHTA 1984, s. 146.

---

(3) *Death within seven years: loss of potential exemption*

39: 04 Transfers which are potentially exempt will become chargeable if the donor dies within seven years. The amount of tax will be determined by using the death rates prevailing at the time of the death, although the transfer is for most purposes treated as having taken place when it actually occurred.

Where the donor dies more than three years after the transfer the amount of tax, as distinct from the amount of value transferred, is reduced by 20%

for each complete year survived. Thus if the donor died five and a half years after the transfer, having made a potentially exempt transfer of £50,000 the death rate of, one assumes, 40%, i.e. tax of £20,000 is to be reduced to 40% of that rate i.e. 16% or £8,000.

The tax due under this rule is due from the donee and so there is no grossing up to be carried out.

Where a potentially exempt transfer becomes chargeable in this way it is treated as a chargeable transfer as of the date at which it actually took place. This may mean that tax in respect of the later chargeable transfer will have been understated. It may also mean an adjustment in the total of chargeable transfers made by the deceased in the seven years before he established a trust without an interest in possession, (see infra, § **42: 10**).

Foster's Capital Taxes D4.11.

---

(4) Death within seven years: additional tax on chargeable transfers

39: 05   If the transferor has made a chargeable transfer tax will have been paid at that time. However, if he dies within seven years additional tax may become due since the transfer falls to be taxed at death rates instead of lifetime rates;[1] although a tapering rule ensures that additional tax is unlikely to arise after the fifth year. The transferee is primarily liable,[2] a rule which avoids the problem of re-grossing up. The donor may provide that the additional liability is to be met from his estate or the donee may take out an insurance policy to cover the risk. Where the death was due to some tort, the additional tax may be recoverable by way of damages.[3]

When the death is not more than three years after the transfer, the full death rates will apply but with credit for the tax already paid. When the death is more than three but not more than four years later, there is a 20% reduction in the tax given by the death rate figure and a further 20% reduction for each of the next three years.[4] When the death rate figure would be less than the lifetime rate tax already charged, the lifetime tax is left to stand.[5]

Where the rates of tax have changed between the date of the transfer and that of the death, the additional tax is calculated on the rates prevailing at the time of death but with full credit for the lifetime tax actually paid.[6] Where the lifetime tax on the original value exceeds the tax at death rates on the value as reduced, no additional tax is due but there is no repayment of *inter vivos* tax.

> **EXAMPLE**
> A whose cumulative total stood at £317,000 in July 1989, then settled on discretionary trusts shares worth £80,000. A agreeing to pay the tax. At 1989–90 rates this would be grossed up at 20% to make a gross transfer of £100,000 and tax of £20,000.
> (*a*) If A had died one month later the additional tax would have been calculated using death rates on a transfer of £100,000 i.e. at 40% giving tax of £40,000 making the additional tax payable £20,000 (i.e. after allowing for the £20,000 already payable).
> (*b*) If A had died in May 1990, the additional tax would have been calculated using the 1990–91 death rates.
> (*c*) If A died in August 1992 the additional tax would have been calculated using the 1992–93 rates but with a 20% reduction.

As tapering relief reduces the amount of tax payable on the death to 40%

or even 20% of the tax otherwise due and the lifetime rates, which will have been charged on the chargeable transfer, are half the death rates, it may be wondered how the tax charged under such tapered rates can ever exceed the tax charged at the lifetime rate. The answer lies in the fact that the death tax may be charged on a different value.[7] This is most likely to occur where the property qualified for business or agricultural relief at the time of the lifetime transfer but does not qualify at the time of the death transfer (infra, §§ **45: 11** and **45: 19**). The situation may also arise if the donor made a potentially exempt transfer before the chargeable transfer and which was therefore ignored when that transfer was made.

Foster's Capital Taxes D4.11; H1.01.
  [1] IHTA 1984, s. 7(2) as amended by FA 1986, Sch. 19, para. 2.
  [2] IHTA 1984, s. 199(2).
  [3] *Davies v Whiteways Cyder Co Ltd* [1975] QB 262.
  [4] IHTA 1984, s. 7(4) added by FA 1986, Sch. 19, para. 2.
  [5] IHTA 1984, s. 7(5) added by FA 1986, Sch. 19, para. 2.
  [6] IHTA 1984, Sch. 2, para. 2.
  [7] Another possibility is that the rates in force at the time of the death may be higher than those in force at the lifetime transfer.

---

(5) Relief for decline in value

39: 06   Where tax (under § **39: 04** on potentially exempt transfers) and additional tax (under § **39: 05** on chargeable transfers) becomes due because the transferor dies within seven years, that tax is generally calculated by reference to the value actually transferred so that the extent of liability (potential or actual) crystallises at the date of the transfer and later changes in value are ignored. However this will not necessarily be so if the property has (*i*) since the transfer been held continuously by the transferee or his spouse or (*ii*) been the subject of a qualifying sale. In (*i*) if the market value at the time of death is less than the market value at the time of the transfer, the value transferred is reduced by the decline in value for the tax or additional tax.[1] For property attracting agricultural or business relief the reduction is that remaining after applying these reliefs.[2] There is no provision requiring a higher value to be taken when the asset has increased in value since the transfer. In (*ii*) the same applies save that the market value at the date of the qualifying sale is taken rather than that at the time of death.[3] A sale is a qualifying sale if (*a*) it is at arm's length for a price freely negotiated at the time of the sale; and (*b*) no person concerned as vendor (or having an interest in the proceeds of the sale) is the same as or connected with any person concerned as purchaser (or as having an interest in the purchase); and (*c*) no provision is made, in, or in connection with the agreement for the sale, that the vendor (or any person having an interest in the proceeds of sale) is to have any right to acquire some or all of the property sold or some interest in or created out of it. This relief does not apply to tangible movable property which is a wasting asset.[4]

  EXAMPLE
   If the shares, originally worth £80,000 (see example supra, § **39:05**) had declined in value to £60,000 when A died in August 1989, the additional tax is calculated as if the value

transferred (£100,000) were reduced by £20,000 to £80,000. This would make the tax due only £32,000 so that additional tax would be £12,000.

It will be noted that there is no recalculation of the value transferred so as to gross up from a figure of £60,000 rather than £80,000. This seems to follow from the form of the legislation.

Foster's Capital Taxes D4.03.
[1] IHTA 1984, s. 131. This does not affect the value for tax on the original transfer. Market value is defined by IHTA 1984, s. 140(2).
[2] IHTA 1984, s. 131(2A) added by FA 1986, Sch. 19, para. 23.
[3] IHTA 1984, s. 131(3). These restrictions are the same as IHTA 1984, s. 176; infra, § **46: 08**.
[4] IHTA 1984, s. 132.

39: 07   Special rules are needed to deal with the application of the relief just outlined where the property changes between the transfer and the death or sale as the case may be.[1]

(1) *Shares.* Capital payments to which the transferee or his spouse becomes entitled in respect of the shares, for example bonus issues, have to be brought into account and are added to the market value at the date of the death or sale,[2] conversely a reduction is to be made if any calls have been made.[3] The transferee or his spouse are treated as retaining their shares notwithstanding certain alterations such as reorganisation or amalgamation or takeover.[4]

Where the shares are an alleviation in the rights attached to any unquoted shares or unquoted debentures and so a deemed transfer in a close company and there has been a transfer of value by the company under IHTA 1984, s. 94(1)[5] or by the participators under IHTA 1984, s. 98(1) the market value at the relevant date is treated as increased; the amount of the increase being the reduction in value attributable to the transfer under IHTA 1984, s. 94(1) or s. 98(1) assuming it had occurred *before* the transfer now subject to additional tax.[6] So if A gave B shares and later value flows out of these shares to C, that decrease must be added back. This hypothetically timed increase is to be reduced by any increase in the value of the estate of the transferor or his spouse[7] and is not to affect the value of the shares at the time of the chargeable transfer.[8]

Foster's Capital Taxes D4.05, 06.
[1] IHTA 1984, s. 131.
[2] IHTA 1984, s. 133(1).
[3] IHTA 1984, s. 134.
[4] IHTA 1984, s. 85, referring to CGTA 1979, ss. 77–86, supra, **Chapter 23**. Allowance is made where value is paid or received on the changeover.
[5] IHTA 1984, s. 136; on meaning of quoted and unquoted see IHTA 1984, s. 272 as amended by FA 1987, Sch. 8, para. 17; securities listed on the USM are now treated as quoted.
[6] IHTA 1984, s. 136(2).
[7] IHTA 1984, s. 136(3).
[8] IHTA 1984, s. 136(4).

39: 08   (2) *Land.* If the interest in land is not at both critical dates the same in all respects and with the same incidents and/or the land is not in the same state and with the same incidents, the market value is increased or reduced to take account of what its value would have been if it had remained unaltered.[1]

If the interest was worth £12,000 but has become subject to a restrictive covenant which reduces its value to £10,000 and, at the relevant time, the land freed from the covenant would be worth £13,000 but subject to it is worth £10,500, then the market value for this relief is £13,000 and since that exceeds the original market value of £12,000 the relief does not apply.

If compensation is received under some enactment for a reduction in the value of the interest, that sum is added to the market value at the relevant time just as bonus issues are added in the case of shares.[2]

Leases which, at the time of the chargeable transfer had no more than 50 years to run are subject to a special rule to offset the inevitable reduction in value due to the passing of time. The market value is increased by the amount by which the value of the lease is treated as having wasted between the two dates, the percentage table from CGT being used.[3]

Foster's Capital Taxes D4.07, 08.
[1] IHTA 1984, s. 137.
[2] IHTA 1984, s. 137(2).
[3] IHTA 1984, s. 138, CGTA 1979, Sch. 3, para. 1, supra, § **21: 16**.

39: 09 (3) *Other property.* Where the property is not in all respects the same at the time of the chargeable transfer and the relevant date the market value is ascertained as if the change had not occurred.[1] Where benefits in money or money's worth have been derived from the property and those benefits are in excess of a reasonable return on its value at the time of the chargeable transfer, the excess is added back and any effect of those benefits on the transferred property is ignored.[2]

Foster's Capital Taxes D4.09.
[1] IHTA 1984, s. 139.
[2] IHTA 1984, s. 139(4).

DEATH TRANSFER

39: 10 By IHTA 1984, s. 4 on the death of any person[1] tax is to be charged as if, immediately before his death, he had made a transfer of value and the value transferred by it had been equal to the value of his estate immediately before his death; this will include any gifts with reservation when the reservation exists down to the donor's death.

The rate(s) at which IHT is charged will be determined both by the value now transferred and by the deceased's cumulative total of chargeable transfers (including potentially exempt transfers which have become chargeable by reason of the donor's death within seven years) over the last seven years. The value transferred is simply that of the estate; there is no need to gross up since after distribution there will be no estate left—the transfer on death is necessarily gross. The amount of tax, but not the chargeable value, may be reduced by the availability of quick succession relief see, infra, § **39: 23**. On liability for tax see infra, § **47: 04**.

Foster's Capital Taxes D1.01.
[1] On events after 12th March 1975 but relating to estates of persons dying earlier see IHTA 1984, Sch. 6, para. 1.

Transfer immediately before death

39: 11   The rule that the transfer of value is treated as taking place immediately before the death gives rise to the problem that it is not clear to whom the transfer is then made: a matter of importance if the estate is left to a spouse. In practice the Revenue treat the transfer on the death as if it were made immediately before the death and so avoid the problem. The rule means that domicile can be ascertained immediately before the death thus avoiding the need to investigate problems of theology and uncertainty as to the degree of optimism to be applied. Despite this general rule the valuation is made immediately *after* the death; infra, § **39: 15**.

Posthumous acquisition

39: 12   The general rule in IHTA 1984, s. 4 means that property accruing to the estate after the death will not be subject to tax. This is of importance in one situation and was in another. The first is *commorientes*. Where it cannot be known which of two or more deceased persons survived the other or others, they are assumed to have died at the same instant.[1]

> EXAMPLE
> Suppose A left his residuary estate to his son B and they are both killed outright in a road accident, tax will be chargeable on the transfers made on their deaths by A and B. However since A and B are deemed to have died simultaneously the property passing from A to B will be taxed on A's death as property forming part of his estate immediately before his death, but not on B's since the property did not form part of his estate at that time but only later.

This rule applies only where it cannot be known which of A and B died first. Where the order of deaths is known and B survives A there will be a transfer by A to B and then one by B, although the latter may qualify for quick succession relief.

The second situation is where a legacy is preserved from lapse. If before 1st January 1983 in the previous example B had predeceased A but had left issue alive at A's death the legacy to B would have been saved from lapse by Wills Act 1837, s. 33. The property will be the subject of a transfer by A but, since it did not form part of B's estate immediately before his death, not by B. With effect, in general, from 1st January 1983 the saving of a gift from lapse in such a case by virtue of the Administration of Justice Act 1982, s. 19, has different consequences: the property goes to B's issue, not to B, and so never forms part of B's estate.

Foster's Capital Taxes D1.01.
[1] IHTA 1984, s. 4(2).

Exemption—members of armed forces

39: 13   IHT is not chargeable on the death of a person dying from a wound inflicted, an accident occurring or a disease contracted or aggravated while a member of the armed forces of the Crown, if the deceased was on active service or on service of a warlike nature or involving the same risks.[1] Service in Northern Ireland is currently regarded as coming within this exemption[2] as was active service in the Falkland Islands.[3]

A person dies "from" a wound if he dies earlier than he otherwise would have done.[4]

The exemption applies only on death but covers all property transferred on death under IHTA 1984, s. 4 such as settled property in which he had a life interest.

Foster's Capital Taxes D2.05.
[1] IHTA 1984, s. 154(1).
[2] See also extra-statutory concession F5 (1985); Foster's Capital Taxes, Division U2.
[3] [1982] STI, p. 271.
[4] *Barty-King v Ministry of Defence* [1979] STC 218, [1979] 2 All ER 80 (23 years after being wounded).

Estate—exclusions

39: 14   The general notion of an estate is modified on death in the following ways:

(1) *Excluded property.* Excluded property does not form part of the estate immediately before the death.[1] This is of significance since the value of non-excluded property will not take account of the value of excluded property: **Foster's Capital Taxes C2.26**.

(2) *Cash options under approved annuity schemes.* Where on a person's death a pension becomes payable to his widow or dependant and, under the terms of the contract or scheme, a sum of money might at his option be payable instead to his personal representatives, the mere fact that the sum could be so paid—so that he could be said to have a general power over it—is not sufficient to cause it to form part of his estate.[2] However where the option is exercised and the sum is paid it will form part of the estate. This exception is stated to apply only where the scheme is approved or is an approved personal pension plan[3]; where the scheme is not so approved therefore the sum of money will form part of the estate whether or not the option is exercised:[4] **Foster's Capital Taxes B3.15**.

(3) *Overseas pensions.* In valuing a person's estate there is to be left out of account any pensions payable under a fund falling within the Government of India Act 1935, s. 273 or the Overseas Pensions Act 1973, s. 2. Sums payable to his estate on his death are exempt from tax.[5]

Further, pensions payable under certain schemes, including sums payable on death and returned contributions, are to be treated as paid by the government of the country in which the colonial service was performed even though the obligation to pay them has been assumed by a fund in this country.[6] The effect is simply to alter the *situs* of the pensions and so, where the deceased was not domiciled here, to bring them into the category of excluded property under IHTA 1984, s. 6(1): **Foster's Capital Taxes D1.20.**[7]

(4) *Reverter to settlor.* Settled property reverting on the death to the settlor but during the settlor's lifetime is not taken into account[8] unless the settlor acquired the reversion for money or money's worth;[9] infra, §§ **41: 21–41: 22.** The exclusion does not apply, so tax will be due, if the reversionary interest has itself been settled after[10] March 1981 and this is how it comes to revert to the settlor: **Foster's Capital Taxes E2.22; E6.24.**

(5) *Reverter to settlor's spouse.* Settled property reverting on the death to the settlor's spouse is not taken into account unless the spouse was not domiciled in the UK at the time of death. The spouse must become beneficially entitled to the property on the death a requirement which is satisfied whether the entitlement is absolute or to a beneficial interest in possession in property remaining settled. Spouse includes widow or widower if the settlor died less than two years before the deceased; infra, §§ **41: 21–41: 22.** The special restrictions on settled and purchased reversionary interests apply here also: **Foster's Capital Taxes E2.23; E6.24.**[11]

(6) *Trustee's annuity.* An interest in possession which the deceased had in settled property and to which he was entitled as remuneration for his services as trustee is not taken into account to the extent that it represents a reasonable amount of remuneration;[12] supra, §§ **36: 18–36: 30. Foster's Capital Taxes E2.26.**

(7) *Pension and annuity.* If the deceased had an interest in various types of superannuation or under funds or schemes, that interest is left out of account provided it does not result from the application of any benefit provided otherwise than by way of a pension or an annuity (e.g. a lump sum[13]); **Foster's Capital Taxes D1.19.**

(8) *Conditional exemption.* Works of art, any other objects and land may enjoy conditional exemption on a transfer on death; if they qualify they are left out of account; infra, § **45: 18: Foster's Capital Taxes G5.11–15; K1.22.**

(9) *Timber.* The value of timber may be left out of account until such time as the timber is sold; it is then restored to the estate unless there has been another transfer on death in the meantime; infra, § **45: 26: Foster's Capital Taxes Division G4.**

(10) *Already earned surviving spouse relief.* Under estate duty law if property was left by one spouse to the other and the other was not competent to dispose of the property, as for example where she had only a life interest, the property was exempt from estate duty on the death of the surviving spouse. Where the first death occurred before 13th November 1974, the settled property is to be exempt from IHT on the death of the surviving spouse:[14] **Foster's Capital Taxes M1.05.**

(11) *Exempt transfers.* Transfers to a surviving spouse, to certain heritage bodies to charity and to political parties, are exempt transfers on death; infra **Chapter 43.** Values which are the subject of exempt transfers do not form part of the estate on death. Other exempt transfers, most notably £3,000 of value transferred in one year, do not apply on death: **Foster's Capital Taxes D1.02, 18.**

(12) *Survivorship clauses.* Property left to a person contingently upon his surviving a period of time may be treated as not forming part of his estate if he fails to survive that period—see infra, § **41: 08.** This avoids the second

charge that would arise on the death of the beneficiary, a form of complete quick succession relief built in by the testator.

(13) *Not transfers of value.* Certain transfers by way of disposition are declared not to be transfers of value. As the transfer on death is not deemed to be a disposition these exclusions do not apply,[15] supra, §§ **38: 14** et seq.

---

[1] IHTA 1984, s. 5(1) unless, presumably, the latter is related property.
[2] IHTA 1984, s. 152 as amended by F(No. 2)A 1987, s. 98(5).
[3] Approval is given under TA 1988, ss. 619–621 or predecessors such as FA 1956, s. 22. Personal Pension plans are authorised by TA 1988, ss. 630–655.
[4] See supra, § **37: 18**.
[5] IHTA 1984, s. 153.
[6] IHTA 1984, s. 153(2).
[7] Infra, § **49: 13**.
[8] IHTA 1984, s. 54(1).
[9] IHTA 1984, s. 53(3).
[10] IHTA 1984, s. 54(2).
[11] IHTA 1984, ss. 54(3), 53(5).
[12] IHTA 1984, s. 90.
[13] IHTA 1984, s. 151(2); see also F(No. 2)A 1987, s. 98(4).
[14] IHTA 1984, Sch. 6, para. 2.
[15] However, a waiver of remuneration or dividends (supra, § **38: 20**) does not have to be by disposition; quaere whether these are therefore exempt on death if effected by will.

VALUATION OF ESTATE ON DEATH

39: 15   The rule that on death a person is deemed to make a transfer of all the value of his estate immediately before the death[1] is substantially modified when it comes to valuation. Changes in the value of the estate which have occurred by reason of the death are taken into account as if they had occurred before the death.[2] Such changes are (*i*) additions to the property comprised in the estate, such as lump sums payable under pension schemes and (*ii*) any increase or decrease of the value of the property in the estate. Thus the death of a proprietor of or a partner in a business frequently causes loss of goodwill, and this is a factor to be taken into account in valuing his business or partnership share. An example of an increase in value is life assurance; the proceeds of life assurance policies are higher than the surrender value immediately before the death.

However it is also provided that "the termination on the death of any interest or the passing of any interest by survivorship" does not fall within this special valuation rule. On the death of a joint tenant his interest passes to the surviving joint tenants; in valuing the right of the deceased joint tenant the fact of his death is to be ignored otherwise the value would be nil.[3] This provision may also be meant to ensure that life interests in settled property are valued in full.

Foster's Capital Taxes D1.03.
[1] IHTA 1984, s. 4. For the general valuation rules see **Chapter 46**, post.
[2] IHTA 1984, s. 171.
[3] Problems arise if an option expires on the death of an option holder.

Reliefs—changes in valuation

39: 16   Although property is valued at the date of death, relief is available where the property is realised for a lower value within a certain period from the death; the lower value being substituted. This relief applies only to certain securities—one year, infra, § **46: 11**; and interests in land—three years, infra, § **46: 14**. Relief is also available where property is valued by reference to related property and is later sold; here the related property valuation may be undone if the sale is within three years; infra, § **46: 08**.

EVENTS AFTER DEATH

(1) Disclaimers and rearrangements

39: 17   Where within two years of a death the disposition on death is varied or a benefit disclaimed, neither the variation nor the disclaimer is a transfer of value. The variation is treated as if made by the deceased, the disclaimer as though the benefit had never been conferred.[1] However, in *Russell v IRC* it was held that a further deed varying a prior deed was not entitled to this treatment even though expressed to be supplemental to the prior deed and fulfilling the other requirements of this section.[2] Knox J. stressed that the second deed substantially altered the beneficiaries' rights under the first and did not merely increase them.[3]

In order to take advantage of this the variation must be within two years of the death and must be carried out by an instrument in writing made by the beneficiaries affected. In an important change of practice the Revenue now accepts that the document does not have to be expressed to be by way of variation of the will provided it identifies the disposition to be varied and varies it. A variation is treated as irrevocable so that a variation of a variation is not entitled to the protection of IHTA 1984, s. 142.[4] Written notice must be given to the Board within six months of the instrument. The election should be by the persons making the instrument and, where the variation results in additional tax, the personal representatives; however the latter may only refuse to join in if they have not sufficient assets to meet the tax.

The rule applies to all property in the deceased's estate immediately before his death e.g. property in which the deceased had a joint interest, save that excluded property is included while settled property in which the deceased had an interest in possession and gifts subject to a reservation where the reservation still exists at the death are not.[5]

A beneficiary may claim the protection of this provisions notwithstanding that he has taken some benefit under the succession. However, this will not be so if consideration other than another right in the succession is provided.[6] So a variation in return for £15,000 would not be within these rules whereas a variation in return for an interest under the will worth £15,000 would be. A transfer to the deceased's widow in return for property already owned by her would not be within these rules and it is at this arrangement that the provision is aimed.

Where a variation results in property being held in trust for a person for a period ending within two years of the death that person's interest is disregarded.[7] So if property is held under the variation of D's will for A for life with remainder to B and A dies or releases his interest within two years of D's death the property is treated as if it had passed direct from D to B. This result applies only where the parties have elected to treat the variation as made by D.

A similar rules applies to CGT (supra, § **17.06**) but curiously there is no provision in relation to TA 1988, s. 663; so if a parent varies the grandparent's will in favour of the parent's infant children, the variation will be effective for IHT and CGT but may not be for income tax.

The Finance Bill 1989 contained proposals to alter this relief drastically but the proposals were dropped.

Foster's Capital Taxes D5.42–43.
[1] IHTA 1984, ss. 17, 142.
[2] *Russell v IRC* [1988] STC 195, [1988] 2 All ER 405.
[3] [1988] STC 195.
[4] *Law Society's Gazette*, 22nd May 1985, p. 1454; [1985] STI, p. 298.
[5] IHTA 1984, s. 142(5), FA 1986, Sch. 19, para. 24.
[6] IHTA 1984, s. 142(3).
[7] IHTA 1984, s. 142(4).

(2) *Election by surviving spouse to redeem life interest*

39: 18   Where a surviving spouse elects to redeem the life interest given him under the intestacy legislation and the election is under those rules, the consequent ending of that life interest is not treated as a transfer of value.[1] The normal effect of the termination of the interest is that there is a transfer of value equal to the value of the settled property save and to the extent that the person entitled to the interest in possession now becomes entitled to the capital.[2] This exception makes sure that there is no transfer of value even though the surviving spouse does not become entitled to the whole of the settled property.

Foster's Capital Taxes D5.05.
[1] IHTA 1984, ss. 17, 145.
[2] IHTA 1984, s. 53(2), infra, § **40: 34**.

(3) *Payment out of property settled by will on trusts with no interest in possession*

39: 19   Where the property was settled by the will and no interest in possession has yet vested in the property; tax is not chargeable. Instead tax applies as if the payment out of the trust had been made by the testator in his will.[1] As originally drafted, this rule was inconsistent with that in §**39: 11** in that, while that rule applied to a variation or disclaimer which could not otherwise give rise to a charge, this rule did not; i.e. this rule did not apply to exempt distributions. This is now amended for *deaths* after 12th March 1984 so that it is now clear that a distribution to charity is given exemption on the death.

Foster's Capital Taxes D5.11.
[1] IHTA 1984, s. 144.

(4) *Carrying out the testator's wishes*

39: 20   A testator may express a wish that the legatee should transfer the property to someone else. If that wish is legally binding the transfer to that other is a transfer by the testator; if however it is not legally binding there would be a transfer by the testator followed by a transfer by the legatee. To avoid a double charge to tax the transfer is treated as made by the testator provided the transfer by the legatee is within two years of the death.[1]

Foster's Capital Taxes D5.44.
[1] IHTA 1984, ss. 17, 143.

(5) *Inheritance (Provision for Family and Dependants) Act 1975*

39: 21   Where an order is made by a court under this Act, IHT is charged as if the property had devolved on the death in accordance with the order.[1]

Foster's Capital Taxes D5.31, 32.
[1] IHTA 1984, s. 146; see also IHTA 1984, s. 236(2) and (3).

(6) *Legitim*

39: 22   Under Scots law a child is entitled to certain fixed rights in his parent's estate even against the surviving spouse, but cannot renounce those rights while still a minor. When the bequest to the spouse reduces the child's rights the executors may assume either that full rights of legitim will be claimed thus reducing the spouse's share (and increasing the IHT) or that the will will be allowed to stand. Any adjustments due when the child reaches 18 must be made.[1] If the person renounces his or her claim to legitim, tax is repaid to the estate with (non-taxable) interest.[2]

Foster's Capital Taxes D5.64.
[1] IHTA 1984, s. 147.
[2] IHTA 1984, s. 236(4).

QUICK SUCCESSION RELIEF

39: 23   Where a person's estate is increased by a chargeable transfer—the first transfer—and he then dies within five years, the tax chargeable on his death—the second transfer—is reduced by a percentage of the tax paid in respect of the first.[1] The percentage is 100% for death within the first year and then drops by 20% a year.

The tax paid on the first transfer only qualifies for use later if, and to the extent that, it relates to the amount of increase in the estate.

> **EXAMPLE**
>   In year 1 A makes a chargeable transfer to B of an asset worth £24,000; suppose tax is payable by A at a rate of 20% making a gross transfer of £30,000 including tax of £6,000.
>   If B then dies two and a half years later the amount available by way of credit on B's death will be 60% of tax at 20% on £24,000 (the increase in B's estate) i.e. £2,880.[2]

This credit is available regardless of any change in the value of the asset given. It applies whenever there is an increase in B's estate and so whether what is given is an identifiable asset or cash.

In determining whether a person's estate has been increased excluded property is to be left out of account. So if D died leaving property to A for life with remainder to B and then B predeceased A, no quick succession relief would be available on B's death for any IHT paid on D's death.

Foster's Capital Taxes E2.41, 42.
    [1] IHTA 1984, s. 141.
    [2] There is no case for relief on the tax on £30,000 since B's estate was only increased by £24,000 and that is what he is now paying tax on.

RELIEFS FOR EARLIER TRANSFERS OF THE SAME PROPERTY BY THE SAME TRANSFEROR

39: 24   With IHT reaching back to catch events that happened before death there was the risk of a dual charge to tax in certain circumstances. By FA 1986 the Inland Revenue were empowered to make regulations to cover three defined situations—and any similar ones. These regulations, which apply to events after 17th March 1986, have now come into force.[1]

The new regulations differ from the old CTT rules for mutual transfers which had been part of that tax code from its early days.[2] A makes a gift of property to B; one month later B transfers the property back to A. At first sight there should be a CTT charge on the gift by A to B and another when B makes the gift to A; however it was provided that, assuming no change in the value of the property, B's transfer to A should be exempt and that A should be allowed to undo the transfer to B and recover any tax paid.[3] The old CTT rules for mutual transfers were repealed for deaths and other transfers after 17th March 1986.[4] The new IHT rules apply only where the second of the two transfers comes about on the death of the transferor (A).

Foster's Capital Taxes D4.31–34.
[1] Inheritance Tax (Double Charges Relief) Regulations 1987, SI 1987 No. 1130. See [1987] *Simon's Tax Intelligence* pp 506, 602.
[2] But not the earliest as the rules were introduced by FA 1976, ss. 87 and 88.
[3] The rules were complex—see *UK Tax Guide* 1985–86 §§ **38: 11** to **38: 15**.
[4] The old rules were CTTA 1984, ss. 148 and 149; repeal was effected by FA 1986, Sch. 23, Part X, and the preservation of the old rules where the donee's transfer was before 18th March 1986 was by FA 1986, Sch. 19, para. 40.

Potentially exempt transfers and death transfers of same property

39: 25   The first situation is where A makes a potentially exempt transfer[1] which proves to be a chargeable transfer and, immediately before his death, A's estate includes property acquired by A from B otherwise than for full consideration in money or money's worth.[2] A's death within seven years makes the A–B transfer chargeable instead of potentially exempt while the property returned forms part of A's estate and so is chargeable under IHTA 1984, s. 4.

The property transferred by B may be the original property given or property which directly or indirectly represents that property.[3] It is hard to know whether to insist on giving these words meaning;[4] if A gives B a painting, must B give the identical one back? If A gives B money, must B give A money or will any property do—and must B be able to show that the money could in some way have been channelled into the property given to A?

The rules then demand that two calculations of the total tax chargeable as a consequence of the death of A should be made. The first requires that in calculating the tax on the potentially exempt transfer one should disregard the value of the property given by A to B and then restored, so leaving it to be part of the death transfer. The second requires that one should disregard the same value in calculating the tax on the transfer on death, so leaving it to be taxed as an originally potentially exempt but now chargeable transfer.[5] Put more simply, one calculates the tax assuming that the value restored forms part of one transfer only. Where this results in two different figures the lower one is reduced to nil and the higher is taken; if the two figures are the same the transfer is treated as being part of the death transfer and not a potentially exempt transfer.[6]

> EXAMPLE
> This example is based on that issued by the Revenue as part of the Regulations but the material is rearranged.
> The facts.
> July 1987. A makes a potentially exempt transfer of £100,000 to B.
> January 1988. A makes a chargeable transfer of £95,000—and pays IHT of £750.
> February 1988. A makes a further chargeable transfer of £45,000 and pays tax (still at 1987–88 rates) of £6,750.
> January 1990. B dies and the 1987 potentially exempt transfer returns to A.
> December 1990. A dies. His estate (value £300,000) includes the property restored to him in 1990 (still worth £100,000).

First calculation assumes that the £100,000 forms part of A's death estate and is not chargeable as a potentially exempt transfer. A therefore has an estate on death of £300,000 but a lifetime cumulative total of £140,000. Tax on the death estate (ignoring quick succession relief under IHTA 1984, s. 141) will be £120,000 which, when added to the additional tax due on the chargeable transfers because A dies within seven years (nil and £2,050 (using 1989–90 rates) due to the charging of death rather than lifetime rates), makes a total of £122,050.

Second calculation charges the £100,000 as a potentially exempt transfer (but with taper relief[7]) and reduces the estate on death to £200,000. Tax on the potentially exempt transfer will be nil. Tax at death rates on an estate of £200,000 with a lifetime cumulative total of £240,000 will give tax on the death of £80,000 but when the additional tax on the chargeable transfers is included (£30,050 and £11,250—higher figures attributable to higher cumulative total to take account of the potentially exempt transfer) gives a total for tax on death of £121,300.

As the first calculation gives the greater amount of tax it is preferred and tax is calculated for all purposes as if the potentially exempt transfer were reduced to nil. This has major consequences for the calculation of the additional tax due on the chargeable transfers in 1988.

Foster's Capital Taxes **D4.32.**
[1] By definition therefore, but also expressly, the transfer must be on or after 18th March 1986.
[2] FA 1986, s. 104(1)(*a*); SI 1987 No. 1130, reg. 4.
[3] The term property is defined as including part of any property; SI 1987 No. 1130, reg. 4.
[4] Contrast the care lying behind the formulation in FA 1986, s. 103.
[5] SI 1987 No. 1130, reg. 4(4).
[6] Ibid, reg. 8.
[7] Although the potentially exempt transfer qualifies for taper relief of 20% this does not affect the calculations since (i) the tax is nil anyway and (ii) the reduction would be a reduction in tax and not in the value transferred.

Chargeable transfer and death transfer of same property

39: 26   The second situation is that in which A makes a chargeable transfer to B but dies within seven years and the property forms part of A's estate on his death having been returned by B.[1] The difference from the first situation is that the A–B transfer is a chargeable transfer not a potentially exempt transfer. As the A–B transfer must be made after 17th March 1986[2] the scope of this rule is not great.

Here the same principles are applied as in § **39: 25** with credit being given for the tax already paid in respect of the A–B transfer. If this leads to a reduction in the value transferred by the A–B chargeable transfer, there is nonetheless to be no change to A's cumulative total for the purpose of any discretionary trust charges under the rules outlined at §§ **42: 08** et seq. In making these calculations credit is to be given for tax paid before the death.[3]

EXAMPLE
Again this uses the Revenue example which forms part of the regulations but sets the material out differently and follows rather than reproduces that example. In view of the uncertainty about tax rates in 1993 it has been decided to continue using the 1987–88 rates

for that year rather than assuming that the 1989–90 rates will apply. This will facilitate checking against the Revenue text which is difficult to understand.

The facts.

May 1986. S makes a gross transfer of £150,000 on discretionary trusts; tax at 1986–87 rates £13,750.

October 1986. S settles shares worth £85,000 on T for life; under the rules then in force this a chargeable transfer (would have been a potentially exempt transfer if made a year later) tax due under 1986–87 rates £19,500.

January 1991. S makes a potentially exempt transfer to R of £20,000.

December 1992. T dies; shares revert to S—no charge to tax § **39: 21** (4).

August 1993. S dies. His estate includes the shares (now worth £75,000); his other property is worth £144,000.

First calculation treating the shares as part of the death estate. May 1986 transfer now more than seven years passed so no additional tax (but remains chargeable and cumulative for seven years i.e. until May 1993). October 1986 gift is ignored[4]—no adjustment to tax already paid. January 1991 potentially exempt transfer attracts tax of £8,000.[5] Death estate is £219,000.[6] Cumulative total of chargeable transfers in last seven years is £20,000 so tax would be £56,500 but this is reduced for the purpose of this calculation by £19,350 to £37,150 to take account of the lifetime tax already paid in respect of the shares.[7] This makes the total tax on death £45,150.

The second calculation treats the shares as settled on T in October 1986 and not part of the estate on death. May 1986 transfer is treated as in the first calculation. October 1986 chargeable transfer is followed by death within seven years but there is no additional tax.[8] January 1991 potentially exempt transfer attracts tax of £10,000 (potentially exempt transfer of £20,000 by person with pre-potentially exempt cumulative total of £235,000). Death estate is now £144,000 by person with cumulative lifetime total over last seven years of £105,000 (£85,000 and £20,000); this makes tax of £57,000 and so total tax of £65,000 due on death. In this instance no credit can be given for the inter vivos tax since it is restricted to the amount of tax paid on the death and as that amount is nil there is no credit.

The second calculation gives the higher figure and so is taken.

Foster's Capital Taxes D4.32.

[1] This is treated in the regulations as the fourth situation as it is not expressly listed in FA 1986, s. 104 but relies on the "similar situations" power in s. 104(1)(*d*).

[2] The position of A–B transfers made before 18th March 1986 is obscure. They are, by definition, chargeable rather than potentially exempt transfers. They are unable to use IHTA 1984, s. 147 and 148 if the B–A transfer is on or after that date and yet are not covered by these Regulations.

[3] The credit is authorised by reg. 7(5)(*b*); the example which follows assumes that the credit rules are relevant in determining the amounts under reg. 7(4) since this is what the Revenue example assumes also. However a case can be made for saying that the credit is not relevant to the calculations under para. (4) and only comes into play when applying reg. 7(5).

[4] It will be noted that although A gave B shares worth £85,000 and the value of the property on return is only £75,000 one ignores the whole of the A–B transfer and does not seek to treat £10,000 of it as still chargeable. Presumably this is because what was restored by B was the entire holding.

[5] Tax at 1987–88 rates (deemed to be in force) on transfer of £20,000 by person with cumulative total of £150,000.

[6] I.e. (£144,000 + £75,000).

[7] The figure of £19,350 is the amount of the death tax which is attributable to the shares i.e. £75,000/£219,000 × £56,500. The amount of lifetime tax was £19,500 but as the proportion of death tax attributable to the shares is less, that lesser figure is taken by way of credit.

[8] Tax, after taper relief, would be £7,100 but as this is less than the tax already paid (£19,500), no additional tax is due.

Transfer and gift with reservation of same property

39: 27   The third situation covered by the Regulations[1] is that in which there is a transfer of value which is also a gift with reservation under FA 1986, s. 102 (supra, § **40: 01**) but the property also forms part of the estate of the donor on death; an example is where A makes a gift to a discretionary trust of which he is a potential beneficiary and dies within seven years.[2] Here A's rights (or hopes) under the trust will bring him within s. 102, as the property does not otherwise form part of his estate immediately before his death; the property was also the subject of a (chargeable) transfer when it was settled; the risk of a dual charge is therefore present. This situation is illustrated by the example in the Regulations. The regulation also embraces the situation in which the gift with reservation ceases to be subject to a reservation in circumstances amounting to a potentially exempt transfer but the donor dies within seven years.[3]

As in the other Regulations, calculations are made on the alternative assumptions that the s. 102 charge applies or the charge on the original property applies and whichever assumption gives the higher tax is taken as the basis of liability. Where this leads to a reduction of the original inter vivos transfer the reduction is not to affect any discretionary trust charges arising before A's death if the transfer was chargeable when made.[4] Provision is also made for credit to be given for tax already paid on the original transfer to be set against the tax now charged on the assumption that the earlier transfer is to be ignored (or reduced).[5]

Foster's Capital Taxes D4.33.
[1] Regulation 5 stemming from FA 1986, s. 104(1)(*b*).
[2] E.g. A gives a house to B but takes a life interest in it in circumstances which do not permit A to argue that A only gave B the reversion this is not a situation in which a double charge can arise since s. 102 only applies if the property which is the subject of the gift with reservation would not otherwise be chargeable on death.
[3] And so a charge arises under FA 1986, s. 102(4).
[4] SI 1987 No. 1130, reg. 5(4)(b).
[5] SI 1987 No. 1130, reg. 5(4)(a).

Transfer and liability disallowed under FA 1986 s. 103

39: 28   Finally, the Regulations provide for the situation in which A's estate is subject to a liability in favour of B but A's estate is unable to deduct that liability because of FA 1986, s. 103 (see infra, §§ **46: 22** et seq). Broadly this rule applies where A makes a gift to B but B later lends the property (or equivalent wealth) back to A; the liability to repay is clearly for money's worth but s. 102 bars the deduction.[1] This could lead to a double charge if the original gift is also chargeable, whether because it was a chargeable transfer all along or has become one because A dies within seven years. The usual alternative calculations are made—the one on the basis of disallowing the debt and ignoring the transfer, the other on the basis of charging the transfer but allowing the debt. Section 102 only applies where the loan is made after 17th March 1986;[2] the regulation only applies where the original transfer occurs after the same date.[3]

Foster's Capital Taxes D4.34.
  [1] SI 1987 No. 1130, reg. 6.
  [2] FA 1986, s. 103(6).
  [3] SI 1987 No. 1130, reg. 6(2); this therefore leaves without any relief against dual charges any case where the loan is after 17th March 1986 but the gift was a chargeable transfer made before 18th March 1986. There is also no relief in any case where the loan is repaid within seven years of death and there is a charge under s. 103(5).

ABATEMENT OF EXEMPTIONS ON DEATH

39: 29   The exemptions in ss. 18 and 23 to 28[1] are subject to a rule of abatement applying to deaths occurring after 26th July 1989.

The abatement applies where a transfer of value would be exempt but the beneficiary under the exempt transfer, known as the exempt beneficiary,[2] disposes of property not derived from the exempt transfer of value to settle of the whole or part of a claim against the estate.[3] The abatement does not apply if the claim being settled is a liability which would be deductible in computing the value of the estate.[4]

Thus suppose that an estate worth £200,000 is left to the deceased's widow and that the deceased has made chargeable lifetime transfers equal to the nil rate band. Suppose also that D had made a covenant in favour of his son that he would pay him £100,000. Under the normal rules of administration of estates a payment would be made out of the estate to the son in satisfaction of his claim, which is a valid contractual claim even though not deductible in computing the value of D's Estate for IHT. The property remaining in the estate after satisfying the son's claim and the tax in respect of it would pass to the widow and be exempt but, as just seen, IHT would have been paid on the value needed to finance the payment to the son.

This result would, but for the abatement rule, be avoided if the widow were to pay the £100,000 out of her own money. The whole £200,000 would pass to her free of tax and her payment of £100,000 would be a PET. Whichever of these two ways of paying the son would be more advantageous in tax terms would presumably be taken by the widow.

To counter this choice of tax liabilities, IHTA 1984, s. 29A provides that the reduction in the value of the exempt beneficiary's estate by the payment or, if less, the legacy to her,[5] is to be treated as a chargeable specific gift[6]; to this extent the exemption is abated.

In determining the value of the exempt beneficiary's estate for this purpose, no deduction is to be made for the claim.[7] Moreover neither agricultural nor business reliefs are to be available for the property she transfers and no deduction is to be made for any tax borne by her.[8]

The term "claim" is not defined.

Foster's Capital Taxes B2.61
[1] IHTA 1984, s. 29A(10) defines exempt gift; where the exemption extends up to a certain figure these rules apply only to the extent that the transfer is exempt.
[2] Defined in IHTA 1984, s. 29A(10).
[3] IHTA 1984, s. 29A(1).
[4] IHTA 1984, s. 168(5).
[5] IHTA 1984, s. 29A(2).
[6] IHTA 1984, s. 29A(3).
[7] IHTA 1984, s. 29A(4)(i).
[8] IHTA 1984, s. 29A(4)(ii).

40   Gifts with reservations

40: 01   FA 1986, s. 102 directs that property which the transferor gave[2] away in his lifetime shall be treated as forming part of his estate immediately before his death, if the transferor reserved a benefit out of the property given, no matter how long ago the gift was made (subject to the important proviso that the rule applies only to gifts on or after 18th March 1986).[3] The object of the provision is to counter avoidance devices that might otherwise escape the new potentially exempt transfer rules and, in particular, to charge inheritance trusts and similar devices which had proliferated since the advent of CTT and which enabled a person to give property away while deriving benefit from it for the remainder of his or her lifetime.[4] While the rule treats the property as forming part of the estate on death—and is therefore valued at that time—the initial gift may also have been a transfer of value whether chargeable or potentially exempt. Regulations provide for any tax paid on a chargeable inter vivos transfer to be credited on death, supra, § 39: 27.

Foster's Capital Taxes Division B5.
[1] See generally, Whitehouse, *Tolley's Practical Tax* 1988, p. 33.
[2] Presumably this includes a sale at an undervalue.
[3] FA 1986, s. 102(1).
[4] Revenue Press Release, 18th March 1986: [1986] STI, p. 193.

What is a gift with reservation?

40: 02   FA 1986, s. 102, following the old estate duty definition,[1] applies where an individual disposes of property and either (*a*) possession and enjoyment of the property is not bona fide assumed by the donee at or before the beginning of the relevant period; or (*b*) at any time in the relevant period, the property is not enjoyed to the entire exclusion, or virtually the entire exclusion,[2] of the donor and of any benefit to him by contract or otherwise. The relevant period is the seven year period ending with the donor's death.[3] The section expressly contemplates the possibility that a gift may be made subject to a reservation and the reservation itself end at a later time.

If the gift is to escape IHT on the ground that it was made outside the statutory period, the first essential is that possession or enjoyment must have been assumed by the donee outside the relevant period. In turn therefore the gift must have effectively deprived the donor of his rights in the property before that time, a problem to be resolved by looking at the rules relevant to the transfer of the particular type of property involved. Possession and enjoyment must then satisfy rule (*b*) which contains two distinct limbs, there must be both (i) the entire exclusion of the donor and (ii) the entire exclusion of any benefit to him by contract or otherwise.

The first limb requires total exclusion of the donor both in law and in fact, subject to three statutory qualifications. Two cases illustrate the severity of this rule. In *Stamp Duties Comr of New South Wales v Permanent Trustee Co of New South Wales*[4] the donor had settled property on his daughter contingently on her attaining the age of 30; he retained no benefit and was

1056

entirely excluded. Fourteen years later, shortly before the daughter reached 30, he arranged with the daughter to borrow some of the income of the trust fund. He later died within the relevant period beginning with the date of the loan. The property was included in his estate as he had not been entirely excluded from it. So the rule may apply not only where the donee is obliged to allow the donor to continue to use the property, but also where there is an "honourable understanding" to this effect and even where there is no such understanding but simply an application of the property for the benefit of the donor at some later time.[5]

Chick v Stamp Duties Comr[6] is similar. In 1934, a father made an absolute gift of grazing land to his son. A year later the son brought the land into a farming partnership with his father and another brother. The partnership was an arm's length arrangement and yet the Privy Council held that the son had not retained possession and enjoyment of the land to the entire exclusion of the donor, so that when the father died some 18 years after the original gift, the land was charged with estate duty.

Foster's Capital Taxes B5.02.

[1] FA 1984, s. 2(1)(*c*), incorporating Customs and Inland Revenue Act 1881, s. 38(2) and Customs and Inland Revenue Act 1889, s. 11.

[2] Not part of the estate duty legislation; for a practice favourable to tax approved pension schemes see SP 10/86.

[3] FA 1986, s. 102(1).

[4] [1956] AC 512, [1956] 2 All ER 512, PC.

[5] Taken from Beattie's *Elements of Estate Duty*, 8th edn., p. 99.

[6] [1958] AC 435, [1958] 2 All ER 623, PC.

40: 03 This severe rule is subject to three statutory qualifications apart from the important transitional rule that gifts before 18th March 1986 are ignored. The first is the *de minimis* qualification, not to be found in the estate duty rule, which requires entire or "virtually" the entire exclusion of the donor. While these words are obviously apt to cover such matters as social visits paid by the donor to the donee at the property, their precise ambit is inevitably obscure; one wonders why the legislation retains the words "entire exclusion" if "virtually entire exclusion" will do.

The second was introduced for estate duty as a result of the *Chick* case. In the case of property which is an interest in land or a chattel, retention or assumption by the donor of actual occupation of the land or actual enjoyment of an incorporeal right over the land, or actual possession of the chattel shall be disregarded if it is for full consideration in money or money's worth.[1] So where a donor makes a gift of a house to a donee and continues to reside in it under a lease providing for payment of a full rent, presumably the maximum allowed by law, there is no gift with reservation. Similarly if a donor gives land to his son but later is given a right to fish, there will be a gift with reservation unless full payment is made. One must also note that this qualification applies only to land and chattels and that the only types of enjoyment ignored are actual occupation and enjoyment. Thus the rule has no mitigating effect in a situation such as the *New South Wales* case or trusts of insurance policies.

This was the subject of elaboration in the following statement in the course of the debate on the 1986 Finance Bill "Elderly parents make unconditional gifts of undivided shares in their house to their children and the parents and the children occupy the property as their family home, each owner bearing his or her share of the running costs. In these circumstances, the parents' occupation or enjoyment of the part of the house they have given away is in return for similar enjoyment of the children of the other part of the property. Thus the donor's occupation is for full consideration"[2].

The third qualification is a new provision[3] which says that where the property is an interest in land, any occupation by the donor can be ignored if it was unforeseen, was not brought about by the donor to receive the benefit of the rule, occurs when the donor is unable to maintain himself through old age, infirmity or otherwise and it represents a reasonable provision for the care and maintenance of the donor. The donee must also be a relative of the donor or his spouse.

Foster's Capital Taxes B5.16.
  [1] FA 1986, Sch. 20, para. 6(1)(*a*).
  [2] 3 HC Official Report, Finance Act 1986, Standing Committee G, 10 June 1986, col 425. Emphasis was placed on the fullness of the consideration.
  [3] FA 1986, Sch. 20, para. 6(1)(*b*).

40: 04   It will have been noted that the two cases mentioned above in § **38: 15** concern situations in which the donor first gave away the property and then received some benefit from it. Thus suppose that in the *Chick* case the formation of the partnership and the transfer of the land to the son had occurred at the same time. Could not one argue that the gift to the son was not a complete gift of the grazing land, but rather a gift of the land subject to the rights of the partnership, with the result that there would have been no gift with reservation? This matter has been discussed in connection with the second limb, the entire exclusion of the donor from any benefit by contract or otherwise but it is equally applicable to the first. The current view is as stated by Lord Simonds in *St Aubyn v A-G.*[1] By retaining "[S]omething which he has never given, a donor does not bring himself within the mischief of [the statutory provisions] . . . In the simplest analysis, if A gives B all his estates in Wiltshire except Blackacre, he does not except Blackacre out of what he has given; he just does not give Blackacre."[2]

In *Munro v Stamp Duties Comr*[3] a father, the donor, owned freehold land which was farmed by a partnership of himself and his six children. In 1913 he gave the land to the children but he continued as a partner in the business until his death in 1929. The Privy Council held that the property given was not the land but his interest in the land subject to the rights of the partnership. There seems little justification for the different result reached in *Chick* and the distinction that in *Chick* the father's interest was taken back out of property that had already been given has been described as "so fine as to be almost beyond perception."[4] The distinction gives rise to much planning, known as "shearing", and is apparently accepted by the Revenue.[5]

More recently in *Nichols v IRC*[6] the Court of Appeal held that where a donor made a gift of property subject to an obligation on the donee to grant a lease back to the donor the property given was the land subject to the obligation and not the land unfettered. However the charge to estate duty was not escaped in that case since certain benefits were then reserved to the donor.

Foster's Capital Taxes B5.15.
[1] [1952] AC 15, [1951] 2 All ER 473, HL.
[2] [1952] AC 15 at 29, [1951] 2 All ER 473 at 483, HL.
[3] [1934] AC 61, 103 LJPC 18.
[4] Beattie's *Elements of Estate Duty*, 8th edn., p. 101.
[5] Law Society Gazette, 1988, p. 50.
[6] [1975] STC 278, [1975] 2 All ER 120, CA.

40: 05   Assuming that the property given has been identified it should then be possible to tell whether the transferor has retained any benefit by contract or otherwise. To fall foul of this rule however "it is not necessary that the benefit should be reserved out of the property itself; it suffices that it trenches on the possession and enjoyment of the property given".[1] So a covenant by the donee to pay the donor an annuity, even though not charged on the property given, has been held sufficient,[2] as has a right to remuneration as a trustee.[3] Similarly where an annuity is charged on the whole of the property given, the whole property given will be a gift with reservation, however small a percentage of the property's income the annuity may represent.[4] These points are reinforced by the rule that a benefit obtained by virtue of any associated operations, as defined in IHTA 1984, s. 268, of which the disposal by way of gift is one shall be treated as property comprised in the gift.[5]

The meaning of "or otherwise" in the expression "by contract or otherwise" has not been settled by the courts. In *A-G v Seccombe*[6] the donor made a gift of a farm to his great nephew who resided with him and who had taken over the management of the farm the previous year. Until his death outside the relevant period the donor continued to reside in the farmhouse and was, from the date of the gift, maintained by the donee. The donor no longer sat at the head of the table but at the side. There was no enforceable agreement, nor any arrangement, that the donor should continue to reside there. It was held that the donee had assumed possession and enjoyment of the property to the entire exclusion of the donor and of any benefit to him by contract or otherwise. The court said that "or otherwise" should be construed *eiusdem generis* with contract and so required an enforceable obligation. If it is correct to conclude that the presence or absence of a legal right is irrelevant in determining whether the donor has been entirely excluded from the property, one wonders why a different rule should apply for the second limb; and one wonders why *A-G v Seccombe* did not fall within the first limb anyway. Today it can hardly be contended that the extensive privileges enjoyed by the donor were such as to amount to his virtual exclusion from the property and there must be some doubt about the correctness of the decision.

Foster's Capital Taxes B5.14.
[1] Beattie's *Elements of Estate Duty*, 8th edn., p. 100.
[2] *A-G v Worrall* [1985] 1 QB 99, 64 LJQB 141, CA.
[3] *Oakes v Stamp Duties Comr of New South Wales* [1954] AC 57, [1953] 2 All ER 1563, PC.
[4] *Earl Grey v A-G* [1900] AC 124, 69 LJQB 308, HL.
[5] FA 1986, Sch. 20, para. 6(1)(c).
[6] [1911] 2 KB 688.

40: 06   Two cases have concerned settled property. In *Stamp Duties Comr of New South Wales v Perpetual Trustee Co Ltd*[1] a father settled property on his infant son but failed to direct what should happen to the property in the event that the son should fail to reach 21. The Privy Council held that the property given was not the entire settled property but rather that property minus the settlor's remainder interest. In this way, the charge to estate duty was avoided. In *Oakes v Stamp Duties Comr of New South Wales*[2] the deceased had been a trustee of the settlement and, as such, entitled to remuneration as trustee; this right was held to constitute a benefit. Today the right to remuneration as trustee might be held to be like the remainder in the previous case, at least where he was a trustee from the time the settlement was created, or it might come within the *de minimis* exception.

Foster's Capital Taxes B5.15.
[1] [1943] AC 425, [1943] 1 All ER 525, PC.
[2] [1954] AC 57, [1953] 2 All ER 1563, PC.

Consequences

40: 07   Where a gift with reservation is made and the reservation continues until the time of the donor's death the property is to be treated as property to which he was still beneficially entitled immediately before his death and so as part of his estate for IHT.[1] Where at some time before the end of the relevant period, which is the donor's death, the property ceases to be subject to a reservation, the donor is treated as if he had at that time made a disposition of property by a disposition which is a potentially exempt transfer,[2] and so one waits a further seven years to see whether it becomes an exempt transfer.

However, it may be that the original gift with reservation is itself a fully chargeable transfer, as where it is a settlement. In such circumstances regulations will be made to prevent a double charge to tax.[3] Where a settlor settles property but is not entirely excluded from it and he later releases his rights there will, it is assumed, be a chargeable transfer on the occasion of the settlement and it is hard to see why there should also be a potentially chargeable transfer on the occasion of the release.

Further rules prevent any use being made of IHTA 1984, s. 142 (alteration of disposition within two years of the death)[4] and direct that the donee is primarily liable for the tax.[5]

This complex of rules does not apply where the transfer would be an exempt transfer (save for the annual exemption and the small expenditure out of income exemption).[6] Gifts made after 17th March 1986 under the terms of regular premium insurance policies made before 18th March 1986 and not altered since then are excluded from these rules by FA 1986, s. 102(6), and (7).

The rules are designed to bring into the estate the value of the property immediately before the donor's death and not its original value at the time of the gift. Where the reservation ceases at an earlier time but still within the relevant period it is the value at that time which is taken. Rules therefore have to be provided to determine how far one may trace the property between the date of the gift and the subsequent cesser of the reservation or death. These are less sweeping than the estate duty rules of 1957.[7] The first set of rules is designed to trace the value of the gift made with reservation into property substituted for the gift and into all accretions to the property.[8] Where an accretion involves expenditure by the donee, e.g. rights issues, any consideration provided for the accretion is deductible.[9] Where the donee dies before the donor it is the donee's personal representatives that take over and tracing continues into their acts.[10]

The tracing rules do not apply where the property is settled (there are separate rules for these) or where the property given is a sum of money in sterling or any other currency[11] (the value of this gift is fixed for all time in the case of sterling; for foreign currency it is unclear whether one uses exchange rates appropriate to the date of the gift rather than the death.)

Where the donee gives the property away, other than to the donor, or otherwise than for consideration in money or money's worth not less than the value of the property at that time, he is treated as continuing to have the possession or enjoyment of the property.[12] This is presumably because the basic rule is defined in terms of the donee assuming possession and enjoyment of the property to the exclusion of the donee.

The rules as to settled property[13] require that the property in the settlement should be taken as representing the original property. If the settlement comes to an end, in whole or in part, before the reservation ends then the property ceasing to be settled is treated as the given property but with a deduction for property becoming property of the donor and with an addition of any money the donor pays at that time. Where the property is not originally settled but is settled by the donee these rules apply. Although income which is accumulated becomes part of the settled property this is not to apply to income accumulated after the date of the ending of the reservation.

Foster's Capital Taxes B5.21–24.
  [1] FA 1986, s. 102(3).
  [2] FA 1986, s. 102(4).
  [3] FA 1986, s. 102(1)(*b*).
  [4] IHTA 1984, Sch. 19, para. 24.
  [5] IHTA 1984, s. 204(9) added by FA 1986, Sch. 19, para. 28.
  [6] FA 1986, s. 102(5); gifts to charities are subject to their own reservation of benefit rules—see IHTA 1984, s. 23(4).
  [7] FA 1957, s. 38.
  [8] FA 1986, Sch. 20, para. 2.
  [9] FA 1986, Sch. 20, para. 3.
  [10] FA 1986, Sch. 20, para. 4.
  [11] FA 1986, Sch. 20, para. 2(2).
  [12] FA 1986, Sch. 20, para. 2(4); on "voluntary" see para. 2(5).
  [13] FA 1986, Sch. 20, para. 4.

41 Settled property

41: 01 Where property is comprised in a settlement, tax is chargeable in circumstances defined in IHTA 1984, Part III. This Schedule provides one regime for settlements in which there is an interest in possession and another, more complex one, for settlements in which there is no such interest. These rules were originally virtually unchanged despite the introduction of IHT in place of CTT but in 1987 a major change was made when transfers of beneficial interests in possession were made potentially exempt transfers.[1] This treatment is subject to anti-avoidance provisions contained in F(No. 2)A 1987.[2]

---

[1] F(No. 2)A 1987, s. 96.
[2] F(No. 2)A 1987, Sch. 7.

SETTLEMENTS

41: 02 A settlement is defined[1] as:

> Any disposition or dispositions of property, whether effected by instrument, by parol or by operation of law, or partly in one way and partly in another, whereby the property is for the time being—
> (a) held in trust for persons in succession or for any person subject to a contingency; or
> (b) held by trustees on trust to accumulate the whole or any part of any income of the property or with power to make payments out of that income at the discretion of the trustees or some other person, with or without power to accumulate surplus income; or
> (c) charged or burdened (otherwise than for full consideration in money or money's worth paid for his own use or benefit to the person making the disposition), with the payment of an annuity or other periodical payment payable for a life or any other limited or terminable period;
> or would be so held charged or burdened if the disposition or dispositions were regulated by the law of any part of the UK; or whereby, under the law of any other country, the administration of the property is for the time being governed by provisions equivalent in effect to those which would apply if the property were so held, charged or burdened.

Property is settled whether or not the settlement was created for value[2]—except for head (c).

Head (a) is sufficient to cover entailed interests, life interests and contingent interests, but not purely concurrent interests, while head (b) catches discretionary and accumulation trusts.

Head (*c*) deals only with annuities or other periodical payments which are charged on property. Annuities payable under a personal obligation only do not create settlements. The phrase "or other periodical payments" is presumably to be construed *eiusdem generis* with annuity and so does not cover instalments of capital.[3] The obligation must be for life or any other limited or terminable period so that while a rent charge for a limited period will give rise to a settlement unless for full consideration, a perpetual rentcharge will not. When full consideration is in issue, it does not matter who provides it.[4]

The concluding words of the section are aimed at foreign devices such as *stiftungen*. They had no counterpart in estate duty legislation. The words are also needed because these rules extends to property outside the UK if the settlor was domiciled in the UK at the time the settlement was made.[5]

The definition is adapted for Northern Ireland;[6] Scotland has its own definition.[7]

Partnership assurance schemes were often arranged on the basis that each partner effected a policy on his own life in trust for the other partners. Such arrangements usually create settlements. However by concession policies effected before 15th September 1976 are not treated as settlements provided (*i*) there is no variation after that date and (*ii*) the premium payments fall within IHTA 1984, s. 10.[8]

Foster's Capital Taxes E1.11, 15, 16.
[1] IHTA 1984, s. 43(1).
[2] The question whether the creation of the trust is a chargeable transfer is quite distinct.
[3] Supra, § **11: 12**.
[4] *A-G v Boden* [1912] 1 KB 539.
[5] IHTA 1984, s. 48(3), infra, § **49: 14**.
[6] IHTA 1984, s. 43(5).
[7] IHTA 1984, s. 43(4).
[8] Extra-statutory concession F10 (1985); **Foster's Capital Taxes, Division U2**.

41: 03   As for CGT supra, § **18: 02** it is often important to know whether property is part of an existing settlement or subject to a separate settlement. Where two documents create one compound settlement there is just one settlement; equally however one document may create two settlements as where a will creates a trust of a specific legacy and separate trusts or residue. what is not so clear is whether the addition of property by someone other than the original settlor creates a new settlement or merely adds to an existing one;[1] trust law distinguishes an accretion to a settlement from a new referential settlement.[2] The official position seems obscure.

Where a power of appointment over property is exercised so that the property does not vest in an object absolutely the question whether the property remains subject to the original settlement is one of construction, supra, § **18: 02**. However for the purposes of the provisions covered in **Chapter 42** it is provided that the property is to be treated as remaining subject to the first settlement.[3]

Foster's Capital Taxes E1.12.
[1] IHTA 1984, s. 44(2) says that they may be treated as separate settlements where the circumstances so require subject to exceptions in IHTA 1984, ss. 48(4)–(6).
[2] E.g. *Re Rydon's Settlement* [1955] Ch 1. *Re Gooch* [1929] 1 Ch 740.

[3] IHTA 1984, s. 81.

Lease for lives

41: 04   A lease[1] for lives does not usually create a settlement since LPA 1925, s. 149(6) provides that the lease falls outside the Settled Land Act if it is in consideration of a fine or at a rent. However a lease of property for lives, or for a period ascertainable only by reference to a death—for example, a lease to end ten days after A's death—is to be treated as a settlement for IHT unless granted for full consideration in money or money's worth. The same applies where the lease is for a term of years but is terminable on or at a date ascertainable by reference to a death.[2] However, if the lessee is expected to live 10 years, a lease for 10 or 15 years is not a lease for lives.

Where a lease for lives is a settlement, it is not the lease which is the settled property but the interest out of which the lease was created. The landlord has a reversion.[3]

By LPA 1925 a lease terminable on marriage is likewise converted into a 90 year lease if granted in consideration of a fine or at a rent. Such leases do not create settlements for this tax.

Foster's Capital Taxes E1.13, 14.

[1] *Quaere* whether an agreement for a lease is a lease—*semble* not, see *City Permanent Building Society v Miller* [1952] 2 All ER 621, [1952] Ch 840. In respect of Northern Ireland references to property held in trust for persons are to include references to property standing limited to persons and as if the lease treated as a settlement under IHTA 1984, s. 43(3) above did not include a lease in perpetuity within s. 1 of the renewable Leasehold Conversion Act 1849 or a lease to which s. 37 of that Act applies: IHTA 1984, s. 43(5).

[2] IHTA 1984, s. 43(3).

[3] On valuation see IHTA 1984, s. 170; the rules for reversionary interests, infra, § **41: 33** et seq, do not apply: IHTA 1984, s. 48(1)(*c*).

Settlor and trustees

41: 05   The "settlor" is not exhaustively defined but the term is stated to include any person by whom the settlement was made directly or indirectly and, in particular, (but without prejudice to the generality of the preceding words) includes any person who has provided funds directly or indirectly for the purpose of, or in connection with, the settlement or has made with any other person a reciprocal arrangement for that other person to make the settlement.[1]

The trustees of a settlement will normally be easily ascertained but in the rare cases where there would otherwise be no trustees "trustees" are defined as any persons in whom the settled property or its management is for the time being vested.[2] This ensures that there will always be some trustee as an accounting party liable for payment of IHT in respect of settled property.[3]

Foster's Capital Taxes E1.21, 22.

[1] IHTA 1984, s. 44(1); this is very similar to TA 1988, s. 681(4) (TA 1970, s. 454(3)) on which see supra, § **13: 02** et seq but not like TA 1988, s. 679(2) (TA 1970, s. 452(2)).

[2] IHTA 1984, s. 45. This may affect the settlor's liability to pay the tax under IHTA 1984, s. 201(1)(*d*).

[3] IHTA 1984, ss. 199(4), 200(4), 201(1), 204(2), 216(1)(*b*).

CREATION OF A SETTLEMENT

41: 06 The creation of a settlement, whether by will or *inter vivos* will often be a chargeable transfer and so give rise to tax under IHTA 1984, s. 2 or s. 4; however, if it was made after 16th March 1987 and creates an interest in possession so that the holder of that interest has his estate increased, the gift will be potentially exempt.[1] Moreover, the creation of the trust will be a potentially exempt transfer if it occurred after 17 March 1986 but was an accumulation and maintenance settlement (see infra, § **42: 27**) or for disabled persons (see infra, § **42: 34**).[2] When the settlor makes a settlement with an interest in possession in favour of someone else and dies more than seven years after the creation of that settlement no IHT will arise as it will be a potentially (but not actually) exempt transfer.[3]

The making of a settlement will not be a transfer of value if there is no loss to the transferor's estate. This will arise if the settlor settled property on himself for life since a person beneficially entitled to an interest in possession is treated as beneficially entitled to the property in which the interest subsists.[4]

Where the settlor declares himself trustee of property for others, there will, unless the arrangement falls within the previous paragraph, be a transfer of value since there is a reduction in the value of his estate. It appears that the settlor must pay on the grossed-up value of the settlement and that he cannot *qua* trustee pay tax on the net transfer; it would be open for him to specify that the beneficiaries should pay the tax.

While the declaration of trust will be a disposition and so a transfer of value, a covenant to settle which has effect simply in contract will not cause a transfer of value. This follows from the rule that while liabilities are deductible in computing the value of a person's estate and so in determining whether there has been a loss in value, no deduction may be made for a liability except to the extent that it was incurred for a consideration in money or money's worth.[5] If the covenant to settle is construed as a completely constituted trust of a chose in action, the same result will follow since it is a completely constituted trust of a liability.

Foster's Capital Taxes E1.21. On interaction with income tax see **Simon's Taxes C4.344, 352, 361**, and Statement of Practice SP1/82 reproduced in **Simon's Taxes Division H3.2**.

[1] IHTA 1984, s. 3A(2) added by FA 1986, Sch. 19, para. 1.
[2] IHTA 1984, s. 3A(1)(*c*).
[3] F(No. 2)A 1987, s. 96(2) and (3).
[4] IHTA 1984, s. 49(1).
[5] IHTA 1984, s. 5(5).

Interest in possession

41: 07 Where there is an interest in possession, tax is charged on the trust in accordance with IHTA 1984, ss. 49–57, infra, §§ **41: 13–41: 34**; when however there is no interest in possession, a very different regime applies— infra, **Chapter 42**. The expression is also crucial in that potential exemption may now be given to a trust with an interest in possession but not to one without. It is therefore surprising that the term interest in possession is not defined.[1] In ordinary property law the term is used to distinguish present interests from future interests, such as remainder or reversions. In ordinary property law therefore a gift to A for life but with power to pay the income over to someone else is an interest in possession notwithstanding its defeasibility.[2]

In *Pearson v IRC*[3] property was held on trust for specified beneficiaries subject to a power in the trustees to accumulate income for 21 years. The House of Lords held that this power prevented the beneficiaries from having an interest in possession. The basis for the view of the (bare) majority was that an interest in possession was one which gave a present right to present enjoyment.[4] The beneficiaries had agreed that if there had been a *duty* to accumulate they would not have had a right to present enjoyment. The Revenue argued—successfully—that there was no difference between a duty to accumulate and a power, since the exercise of that power by the trustees would prevent the beneficiaries from having anything to enjoy.

The case is authority for two other propositions. The first is that a power to advance capital to a remainderman would not have prevented the beneficiaries from having an interest in possession. This turns not, as one might have thought, on the need for the life tenant to give his consent to the exercise of the power, but on the distinction between a power to terminate a present right to present enjoyment (e.g. the power of advancement) and a power to prevent a present right of present enjoyment from arising (e.g. the power to accumulate).

The second proposition is that a power in the trustees to apply income to meet trust expenses etc does not prevent the life tenant from having an interest in possession. Although that power could be said to prevent a present right to present enjoyment it does not have that effect since it is an administrative power as distinct from a dispositive power. This distinction is stated rather than explored in the speeches. More recently the Court of Session, in holding that a power to make a payment out of income in order to meet the depreciation of capital value was an administrative power, said that this was because it was not a power to increase the capital value by diverting the income to those in right of capital.[5]

If A has a life interest and there is no power to withhold income from him short of depriving him of capital, he has an interest in possession notwithstanding that no income may in fact arise.[6]

Where there is a duty to distribute the income amongst a class and, at the relevant time, there is only one person in the class but there is a chance that others may be added to it as the class is not closed, the one person does not have an interest in possession.[7] When trustees appoint property to a beneficiary but resolve to make the payment only after receiving an indemnity from the appointee, it is a question of construction whether the interest in possession arises at the time of the resolution or on receipt of the indemnity.[8]

Foster's Capital Taxes E1.31–38.
  [1] In respect of Scotland "any reference to an interest in possession in settled property is a reference to an interest of any kind under a settlement actually being enjoyed by the person in right of that interest and the person in right of such an interest at any time shall be deemed to be entitled to a corresponding interest in the whole or any part of the property comprised in the settlement": IHTA 1984, s. 46.

[2] He has a right to the income once the period for the trustees to exercise their discretion has expired—*Re Allen-Meyrick's Will Trusts, Mangnall v Allen-Meyrick* [1966] 1 All ER 740.
[3] [1980] STC 318, [1980] 2 All ER 479.
[4] So a right to income under the Trustee Act 1925, s. 31(1)(ii) suffices for there to be an interest in possession, *Swales v IRC* [1984] STC 413.
[5] *Miller v IRC* [1987] STC 108.
[6] On effect of a power to allow a beneficiary to occupy a dwelling house see SP 10/79; **Foster's Capital Taxes, Division W3.**
[7] *Moore and Osborne v IRC* [1984] STC 236.
[8] *Stenhouse's Trustees v Lord Advocate* [1984] STC 195.

ESTATES IN ADMINISTRATION AND SURVIVORSHIP CLAUSES

41: 08   A person having an interest in possession in the residuary estate of a testator which is still being administered does not have an interest in the property but only a right of action against the executor to ensure due administration.[1] However for the purposes of this tax the residuary estate is to be treated as if it had been administered. The interest is deemed to exist from the date when he became entitled to income from the residue which will usually be the date of death.[2]

The position of one entitled to an interest in a specific or pecuniary legacy is unclear in theory;[3] there is no special IHT provision.

Where property is held for a person conditional upon his surviving the testator for a certain period, a settlement might be created by reason of the condition.[4] It is therefore provided that if the period does not exceed six months, the resulting disposition which takes effect, whether on his surviving the six months or his prior death, is treated as having had effect from the beginning of the period.[5] However this is not to affect the application of tax to any distribution or application of property before the disposition takes effect.

Foster's Capital Taxes E1.51, 61.
[1] *Stamp Duties Comr (Queensland) v Livingston* [1965] AC 694, [1964] 3 All ER 692.
[2] IHTA 1984, s. 91.
[3] See *Re Leigh's Will Trusts, Handyside v Durbridge* [1970] Ch 277, [1969] 3 All ER 432, 86 LQR 20 (PVB).
[4] Because the arrangement comes within (*a*) at § **41: 02**, supra.
[5] IHTA 1984, s. 92.

INTEREST IN POSSESSION—ENTITLEMENT TRUSTS

Extent of entitlement

41: 09   A person beneficially entitled[1] to an interest in possession in settled property is treated as beneficially entitled to the property in which the interest subsists.[2] It follows that if B dies leaving a free estate of £50,000 and was also life tenant of a fund whose value was £30,000, he is treated as beneficially entitled to the whole of the property comprised in the settlement at his death, making a total transfer of property worth £80,000.

Where a person is entitled to part only of the income his interest is treated as subsisting in that part of the property comprised in the settlement which corresponds with his share of the income.[3] So a half share in the income gives rise to a half share in the capital.

Where the part of the income is a specified amount, for example an annuity of £100, or the whole income less a specified amount, for example to B for life subject to the payment of an annuity of £100 to A, the interest corresponds with that part of the property which produces that income.[4]

Where the annuity is fixed and the income of the fund is constant, no difficulty will be encountered in discovering the shares of capital. However where the income fluctuates the shares of A and B will vary from time to time.

If A were old or critically ill it would be in the interests of the trust to increase the income of the trust substantially so as to reduce the proportion of trust income needed to pay A's annuity; the opposite would arise if B were old or critically ill. In order to counter such arrangements, the Treasury prescribe higher and lower rates by statutory instrument.[5] The higher or maximum rate is applied in relation to A and IHT is charged as if the rate of return were that maximum rate.

EXAMPLE 1
    Under a settlement worth £200,000 A receives an annuity of £2,000 p.a. whilst B receives the balance of income. Out of the £40,000 income A receives £2,000 and B £38,000. If A's interest terminates when the higher rate is 15% A's share will not be taken as 2,000/40,000 of £200,000 = £10,000. The higher rate of 15% only allows a notional income of £30,000 instead of the actual £40,000 income. So A's share is taken as 2,000/30,000 of £200,000 = £13,333.

It is expressly provided that the value taken as a result of this rule is not to exceed 100% of the settled property.

EXAMPLE 2
    Under a settlement worth £200,000 A receives an annuity of £32,000 p.a. whilst B receives the balance of income. Out of the £40,000 income A receives his £32,000 and B £8,000. If A's interest terminates when the higher rate is 15% A's share will not be taken as 32,000/40,000 of £200,000 = £160,000. On applying the higher rate of 15% as the maximum allowable yield a notional £30,000 income only is allowed, but 32,000/30,000 of £200,000 would result in a chargeable value of £213,333 which is £13,333 more than the whole capital value. Accordingly A's share is treated as no greater than the whole capital value of £200,000.

The lower or minimum rate is applied in relation to B.

EXAMPLE 3
    Under a settlement worth £200,000 A receives an annuity of £2,000 p.a. and B receives the balance of income. Out of the £6,000 income B thus receives £4,000. If B's interest terminates when the lower rate is 5% B's share will not be taken as 4,000/6,000 of £200,000 = £133,333. The lower rate of 5% treats a notional income of £10,000 to have arisen instead of the actual £6,000 income. So B's share is taken as 8,000/10,000 of £200,000 = £160,000.

However neither of these rates is to apply where the chargeable transfers are made simultaneously and the tax is chargeable by reference to the interests of both A and B as where both interests end on the death of X and the property then vests in C. In such circumstances the Revenue will collect tax on 100% anyway.

The higher rate is the yield on the FT Actuaries Share Index for irredeemable gilts; the lower rate is the gross dividend yield of the All-Share Index.[6] The relevant rates are those for the date of the transfer.

Foster's Capital Taxes E2.01–03.

[1] If property is settled on X for life remainder to Y and X declares himself trustee of his interest for P and Q, P and Q are beneficially entitled to the interest in the settled property.
[2] IHTA 1984, s. 49(1).
[3] IHTA 1984, s. 50(1).
[4] IHTA 1984, s. 50(2).
[5] IHTA 1984, s. 50(3).
[6] CTT (Settled Property Income Yield) Order, SI 1980, No. 1000; see **Foster's Capital Taxes Division T2**.

41: 10   Although the legislation does not define how income is to be computed, one presumably looks at the income of the trust after the deduction of trust expenses but ignoring income tax and one compares this with the rights of A and B again before income tax; However there are other possibilities.

Where the person entitled to the interest in possession is not entitled to any income but is entitled jointly or in common with one or more others to the use and enjoyment of the property, his interest is that proportion which the annual value of his interest bears to the aggregate of all their interests.[1] This applies only where the person is not entitled to the income; this is presumably because if he could turn his enjoyment into income, as by selling the asset and taking income from the proceeds of sale or by leasing it,[2] the matter would fall within previous rules. For the same reason someone solely entitled to the use of property is not within this rule. Where the rule applies, annual value is presumably to be determined by reference to actual enjoyment of the property but this is unclear.[3]

---

[1] IHTA 1984, s. 50(5).
[2] E.g. by virtue of the powers conferred on the tenant for life under a strict settlement within SLA 1925.
[3] If A and B are entitled to a picture and B allows A to have the whole use of it, does A have a 100% interest or do A and B each have 50%?

Lease for lives

41: 11   Where a lease related to a life is treated as a settlement,[1] the lessor is treated as retaining a beneficial interest in part of the leased property, such interest being the proportion that the value of the consideration at the time the lease was granted bears to the then value of a full consideration: the tenant is treated as having a beneficial interest in the rest.[2] Thus if property is let to T for life at one-tenth of the then full market rent the lessor is treated as owning one-tenth of the property and T is treated as owning nine-tenths of the property.

This only applies to a lease for lives. If S grants himself a lease for 20 years

and gives away the reversion there is no settlement even though his life
expectancy is 20 years and he does what is expected.[3]

Foster's Capital Taxes E1.13, 14; E2.05.
[1] IHTA 1984, s. 43(3).
[2] IHTA 1984, ss. 50(6), 150.
[3] For this reason the gift of a reversion expectant on a lease set to last 10 years longer than life
expectancy is a way of reducing IHT—provided the gift with reservation rules are avoided.

Unadministered estate

41: 12   A charge may arise if, before administration is complete, the person
with the potential interest in possession dies or disposes of his interest.[1] To
ascertain the residue allowance has to be made for specific dispositions,[2]
annuities,[3] general and demonstrative legacies, statutory legacies on an
intestacy, funeral, testamentary and administration expenses, debts and
liabilities, and any apportionment required between capital and income.[4]

Foster's Capital Taxes E1.51.
[1] IHTA 1984, s. 91.
[2] TA 1988, s. 701(5) (TA 1970, s. 432(5)).
[3] TA 1988, s. 701(6) (TA 1970, s. 432(6)).
[4] E.g. *Allhusen v Whittell* (1867) LR 4 Eq 295 (apportionments).

TRANSFERS OF SETTLED PROPERTY

41: 13   Certain events are treated as lifetime transfers of value by the person
beneficially entitled to the interest in possession;[1] such events on or after
17th March 1987 are now mostly potentially exempt transfers.[2] If he dies
within seven years his circumstances therefore determine the rate of tax
payable and whether any exemptions or reliefs apply. If the transfer is
immediately chargeable the total transferred is added to his lifetime total of
chargeable transfers for the purpose of determining liability on any
subsequent transfer. However there is no grossing up. The title by which he
has become entitled is quite irrelevant: he may be the designated life tenant
or have acquired it by assignment: all that matters is that he is entitled to
that interest and that his entitlement is beneficial.[3]

Foster's Capital Taxes E2.11.
[1] IHTA 1984, ss. 51, 52.
[2] IHTA 1984, s. 3A(6) as amended by F(No. 2)A 1987, s. 96(2).
[3] Property is held on trust for A for life with remainder to B. A settles his life interest on X to
hold on trust for C for life with remainder to D. *Semble* C's entitlement is beneficial and X's is
not.

---

(1) *Death*

41: 14   On the death of a person beneficially entitled to an interest in
possession the settled property or, where appropriate the relevant portion of
that property, is treated as forming part of his estate under IHTA 1984, s. 4.[1]

Such a transfer is not a potentially exempt transfer and normal death rates will apply.

Foster's Capital Taxes E2.15.
[1] Supra, § **39: 15.**

---

(2) *Termination*

41: 15 Where at any time during the life of a person beneficially entitled to an interest in possession the interest comes to an end, tax is charged under IHTA 1984, s. 52 as if he had then made a transfer of an amount corresponding to the value of the property in which his interest subsisted; the transfer will be a potentially exempt transfer if the property becomes part of the estate of another person.[1]

> **EXAMPLES**
> (1) Property is held on trust for C for the life of X with remainder to B. C dies; X dies. On C's death there is a transfer by C under IHTA 1984, s. 4. On X's death there is a transfer under IHTA 1984, s. 52 by the person then entitled to the interest in possession but it will be a potentially exempt transfer as it goes into the estate of B.
> (2) Property is held on trust for A for life with remainder to B for life with remainder to C. B dies; A dies. On B's death there is no charge on the settled property since B was not entitled in possession; on A's death there is a charge under IHTA 1984, s. 4.
> (3) Property is held on trust for A for life or until remarriage, with remainder on discretionary trusts. A remarries. There is a charge under s. 52 and it cannot be a potentially exempt transfer.

Foster's Capital Taxes E2.13.
[1] If on or after 17th March 1987 IHTA 1984, s. 3A(6) as amended by F(No. 2)A 1987, s 96(2)(*c*).

---

(3) *Disposal*

41: 16 Where the person beneficially entitled to an interest in possession disposes of his interest, that disposal is not to be treated as a transfer of value equal to the actuarial value of his interest; rather it is treated by IHTA 1984, s. 51 as the termination of the interest thus causing a transfer under s. 52 and so from 17th March 1987 a potentially exempt transfer[1] equal to the value of the property in which his interest subsisted. The disposal of the interest may be by assignment or, perhaps by surrender, it may be voluntary or involuntary. If it results in the destruction of the interest, as on surrender, it is probably also an actual termination of the interest and comes within the previous charge.[2]

Where the disposal is for a consideration in money or money's worth, tax is charged as if the value transferred were reduced by the amount of the consideration.[3] However in determining the value of that consideration the value of any reversionary interest in the property or of any interest[4] in any other property comprised in the same settlement is left out of account. So if property is settled on A for life with remainder to B and there is a partition of the property, the value of B's interest is not treated as consideration for the disposal of the life interest; hence there is a deemed transfer of value of the property allotted to B but not that allotted to A because of the rule in § **41: 20**.

If B provides A not with an interest under the settlement but with full market value in cash, there will inevitably be a charge since the market value of A's life interest must be less than the full value of the settled property. However, B is also treated as making a transfer of value if he pays a sum equal to the value of the underlying settled property.[5] Such a purchase can now be a potentially exempt transfer.[6]

Foster's Capital Taxes E2.12, 14.
 [1] IHTA 1984, s. 3A(2) amended by F(No. 2)A 1987, s. 96(2)(*c*).
 [2] This is of importance in connection with the exemption in IHTA 1984, s. 51(2).
 [3] IHTA 1984, s. 52(2).
 [4] Presumably not just reversionary interests but also, e.g. a life interest in another part of the settlement.
 [5] IHTA 1984, s. 49(2).
 [6] IHTA 1984, s. 49(3) added by FA 1986, Sch. 19, para. 14 but repealed by F(No. 2)A 1987, s. 96(4).

---

(4) *Depreciatory transactions*

41: 17   A charge arises where a depreciatory transaction is entered into between (1) the trustees and (2) any beneficiary or potential beneficiary or any person connected therewith. For example, under an express authorisation in the trust instrument trustees might sell property at an undervalue or lease at a low rent, e.g. by allowing a beneficiary to occupy a house under a lease at less than the rack rent, or lend money for a fixed period at well below market rates without being in breach of trust. To the extent that such a transaction reduces the value of the settled property which will be chargeable to tax at some future date partial termination of the interest in possession in the property is deemed by IHTA 1984, s. 52(3) the beneficiary with such interest being the transferor in respect of this transfer of value.[1] However, the transaction will not constitute a notional termination where it would not constitute a transfer of value if the trustees were beneficially entitled, e.g. where the transaction was not intended to confer any gratuitous benefit and was such as might be expected to be made in a transaction at arm's length between persons not connected with each other.[2] A capital payment falls within (2) rather than the present charge.[3]

Foster's Capital Taxes E2.16.
 [1] IHTA 1984, s. 3(4).
 [2] IHTA 1984, ss. 52(3) and 10.
 [3] E.g. the exercise of a power to augment income from capital—*Law Society's Gazette*, 5th November 1975.

---

(5) *Close companies*

41: 18   Transfers of value by close companies may be apportioned to the participators. Where the participator is a settlement, the transfer may be apportioned to the person with the beneficial interest in possession infra, § **43: 08**. Such a transfer cannot be a potentially exempt transfer.

(6)   Deemed transfer by participators in a close company

41: 19   Where there is a variation in the rights attached to securities in a close company and this is treated as a deemed disposal by the participators, the loss in value will be treated, where there is an interest in possession, as though that interest had come to an end to the extent of that loss[1] infra, § **43: 08**. Such a transfer cannot be a potentially exempt transfer.

Foster's Capital Taxes E2.17, 18.
[1] IHTA 1984, s. 101.

Exceptions

(1)   Where the beneficiary becomes entitled to the property or to an other interest in possession in the property[1]

41: 20   This exception is dictated by the logic of the charge on interests in possession. If property is held on trust for A for life, he is treated as beneficially entitled to the whole property; if the settlement adds, "but to A absolutely if he reaches the age of 25", it would be contrary to all sense to direct a transfer by A on his 25th birthday when the property then becomes part of his free estate. It is not necessary that the new interest should arise under the terms of the settlement so no charge arises whether the property is appointed to A under a power in the settlement or he partitions the property with the remainderman and becomes entitled to a capital sum absolutely. Equally the exercise of a power to augment the tenant for life's income from capital causes no charge to this tax.

The section also applies where the person with the interest in possession becomes entitled not absolutely but to another interest in possession. So when a tenant in tail's interest is reduced to a life interest on a resettlement this exception applies.

A restriction applies in that if the value of the property to which he becomes entitled is less than the value on which tax would otherwise be chargeable, tax is chargeable on the difference.[2] Thus if A is entitled to a life interest in the whole of the property until marriage but that interest is to be reduced to ⅔ on marriage, there will, in the event of marriage, be a transfer of ⅓ of the settled property. Likewise when A, the life tenant partitions the property with B, the remainderman, there will be a charge on that part of the property which becomes the property of B.

> **EXAMPLE**
> In July 1985 S, who has made chargeable transfers of £50,000 settled £10,000 on A for life with remainder to B, and directed the trustees to pay the tax on the transfer. Five years later the fund is worth £10,000. A and B agree to divide it equally. A has made previous transfers of £20,000, B of £1 million. When S created the settlement he made a chargeable transfer of £10,000; his total then rose to £60,000. When A and B divide the fund there is a termination of A's interest in £10,000 (IHTA 1984, s. 52) but tax is not chargeable on the half which he takes; he therefore makes a potentially exempt transfer of the other half, i.e. £5,000, so that his total remains at £20,000. IHT will become due if A dies within seven years.

Foster's Capital Taxes E2.21.
[1] IHTA 1984, s. 53(2).

(2) *Where the property reverts to the settlor*

41: 21   If the interest comes to an end during the settlor's life and on the same occasion reverts to the settlor, tax is not chargeable.¹ The purpose of this relief is to enable persons to provide life interests for relatives without charge to tax; however this relief is not confined to such transfers and does not preclude a charge on the creation of the settlement.

The exception applies only where the reverter is during the life of the settlor; however it applies even though the settlor takes a beneficial life interest in possession.²

The exception is lost if the settlor acquired a reversionary interest in the property for money or money's worth.³ Thus if the property was settled on B for life with remainder to C absolutely, the exception would not apply on the ending of B's interest in possession if S, the settlor, had bought C's remainder. However if S had acquired the remainder by way of gift from C, the exception would apply. It appears that the purchase of any reversionary interest is fatal. If B's life interest had been preceded by a life interest to A and S had then bought B's interest and been given C's interest, the exception would have been lost even though B predeceased A without his interest ever vesting in possession.

The exception is also lost if the reversionary interest has itself been settled after 9th March 1981.⁴ Property could be settled on A for life, remainder to B. B would then settle the remainder on C for life with remainder to B. While there would be a charge when A died there would not be when B created the settlement as the subject matter was excluded property (rule (10) below), nor when C died, thus leaving C free to enjoy the income after A; death without risk of IHT after the creation of the settlement. The 1981 charge creates a charge on C's death.

¹ IHTA 1984, s. 53(3).
² This was not so under the old estate duty exemption and is not obvious but appears to be the Revenue view. **Foster's Capital Taxes E2.22; E6.24**.
³ IHTA 1984, s. 53(5)(*a*).
⁴ IHTA 1984, s. 53(5)(*b*).

(3) *Transfer on termination to the settlor's spouse*

41: 22   Since a reversion to the settlor is the subject of one exception and a transfer between spouses is exempt, the legislation also provides that tax is not chargeable if when the interest comes to an end and on the same occasion the settlor's spouse becomes beneficially entitled to the settled property.¹

This exception does not apply if the settlor or the spouse acquired a reversionary interest for consideration in money or money's worth; nor does it apply if the spouse was not at the relevant time domiciled in the UK. However it applies for a limited period after the death of the settlor in that the term spouse is to include widow or widower if the settlor has died less than two years before the interest ends.

The restriction on settled reversionary interests applicable to (2) applies here also.[2]

Foster's Capital Taxes E2.23; E6.24.
[1] IHTA 1984, s. 53(4).
[2] IHTA 1984, s. 53(5).

---

(4) *Disposition to provide family maintenance*

41: 23 Where a disposition for the maintenance of one's family satisfied the conditions of IHTA 1984, s. 11 but amounts to the disposal of an interest in possession, and so would be treated as a termination, the interest is not to be treated as coming to an end.[1] This applies to partial terminations as well as to total terminations as where a father tenant for life consents to an advance of capital to enable the outright purchase of an annuity to cover his son's future public school fees.

Foster's Capital Taxes E2.32.
[1] IHTA 1984, s. 51(2); supra, § **41: 20**.

---

(5) *Disclaimer*

41: 24 On a disclaimer made otherwise than for consideration in money or money's worth, the person disclaiming is treated as never having become entitled to the interest.[1] A disclaimer cannot be made once the gift has been accepted; a surrender is not a disclaimer.

Foster's Capital Taxes E2.24.
[1] IHTA 1984, s. 93; *Re Sharman's Will Trusts, Public Trustee v Sharman* [1942] Ch 311, [1942] 2 All ER 74. *Variation* relating to settled property are excluded from IHTA 1984, s. 142 by s. 142(5).

---

(6) *Trustee's annuities*

41: 25 Where a person is entitled to an interest in settled property as remuneration for his services as trustee, tax is not charged on the termination of that interest to the extent that it represents a reasonable amount of remuneration.[1] This exclusion does not apply if the trustee disposes of the right. In valuing the interest of the beneficiary it is presumably possible to make allowance for that proportion of the trust income needed for the annuity.

---

[1] IHTA 1984, s. 90.

---

(7) *Order under the Inheritance (Provision for Family and Dependants) Act 1975*

41: 26 An order under this Act terminating an interest in possession gives rise to no charge.[1]

Foster's Capital Taxes E2.27.
[1] IHTA 1984, s. 146(6).

(8) *Redemption of life interest on intestacy*

41: 27   Where the surviving spouse of an intestate has a life interest in possession and exercises her statutory right to redeem her life interest for a capital sum she is to be treated as always having been entitled to the capital sum and so not as having been entitled to the interest in possession.[1]

[1] IHTA 1984, s. 145. The right arises under the Administration of Estates Act 1925, s. 47A; presumably this exemption applies only if the redemption takes place under this Act so that a simple partition will be exempt only if it comes within the previous exception.

(9) *Excluded property*

41: 28   Tax is not charged under IHTA 1984, s. 52 if the settled property is excluded property.[1]

[1] IHTA 1984, s. 53(1).

(10) *Exempt transfers*

41: 29   Transfers to spouses, charities, political parties and public bodies are exempt;[1] see § **44: 01** et seq.

EXAMPLE
Property is held on trust for H for life with remainder to J. H transfers his life interest to Mrs. H. Mrs. H consents to the power of advancement being exercised in favour of J. H's disposal of his life interest in possession is not a chargeable transfer, IHTA 1984, s. 53(4), (5). When Mrs. H consents to the advancement there is a termination of her interest and so a charge under IHTA 1984, s. 52 to the extent that of the property advanced.

The £3,000 annual exemption is available—provided notice is given by the transferor to the trustees within six months.[2] The marriage exemption is also available.[3]

Another rule concerns a transfer to a maintenance fund for heritage buildings.[4] There is however no relief under IHTA 1984, s. 20, nor under IHTA 1984, s. 11.

Foster's Capital Taxes E2.31.
[1] IHTA 1984, ss. 18, 23–27, 56.
[2] IHTA 1984, s. 57(1).
[3] IHTA 1984, s. 57(5).
[4] IHTA 1984, ss. 27 and 57(5) see, infra, § **45: 20**.

(11) *Transitional*

41: 30   Earned Surviving Spouse Relief. Where a person died before 13th November 1974 and left property to his spouse for life in circumstances qualifying for the old estate duty exemption and the surviving spouse's interest terminates, no tax is chargeable. This applies whether the termination is on death or otherwise.[1]

---

[1] IHTA 1984, Sch. 6, para. 2.

Quick succession relief

41: 31   This relief is given on the same basis as at supra, § **39: 23**,[1] whether or not the transfer is on death provided it is settled property in which the transferor had an interest in possession and provided that the first transfer was either the creation of the settlement or some subsequent event.

> **EXAMPLE**
> Property is inherited by S in year 1; in year 2 he settles it on P for life with remainder to Q; in year 3 P surrenders the life interest; in year 4 Q gives to the property to R.
>   No credit is available on the transfer in year 2 as it is an inter vivos transfer. In year 3 credit is available but only for the tax from year 2—not that from year 1 as that was prior to the creation of the settlement. No credit is available in year 4 as the transfer is not then of settled property in which Q had an interest in possession.

If the whole of the credit is not used on the first subsequent transfer it may be rolled on to the next and so on in sequence. The credit is used to the extent to which it is covered by the relief given. If £10,000 credit is available and £4,000 relief is given on tax of £5,000 in year 2 (i.e. 80% of £5,000) only £5,000 remains to be rolled forward—and to be subject to further percentage reductions.

Foster's Capital Taxes E2.42.
[1] IHTA 1984, s. 141.

REVERSIONARY INTERESTS

41: 32   A reversionary interest[1] is a future interest under a settlement, whether vested or contingent (including an interest expectant on the termination of a lease treated as a settlement, e.g. a lease for life at a nominal rent).[2] A future interest must be distinguished from a mere *spes*. So where property is settled on A for life with remainder to Y, but with overriding power for the trustees to appoint capital to such of B to X as they see fit, then B merely has a *spes* whilst Y has a reversionary interest.

In general, a reversionary interest is excluded property.[3] Thus, if property was settled on A for life with remainder to B and B died before A there would be no transfer on B's death of the interest in the settled property, the Revenue being content to wait and to tax the transfer of the property on the termination of A's interest. This prevents overcharging to IHT.

Since the general immunity of reversionary interests is open to exploitation IHTA 1984, s. 48(1) provides that a reversionary interest in settled property in the UK is not excluded property (*i*) if it has *at any time* been acquired (whether by the person entitled to it or by a person previously entitled to it) for a consideration in money or money's worth or (*ii*) it is one to which either the settlor or his spouse is or has been entitled under a settlement or (*iii*) if it is the interest expectant on the termination of a lease treated as a settlement, i.e. a lease for life at a nominal rent.[4] Further IHTA 1984, s. 55(1) provides that where a person entitled to an interest (whether in possession or not) in any settled property acquires a reversionary interest expectant (whether immediately or not) on that interest, the reversionary interest is not treated as part of that person's estate.

The effect of these rules is not immediately obvious but is to be discerned from the avoidance of tax. If property worth £130,000 is held on trust for A for life, with remainder to B, and A has free estate worth £50,000 there will on A's death be a transfer of £180,000. If A buys B's remainder for £40,000 the property will cease to be settled but there will be no transfer of value in that event because although A's life interest in the property terminates he becomes on the same occasion absolutely entitled to it. When A dies the formerly settled property will pass as his free estate. The avoidance consists in the fact that A purchases B's remainder for full consideration of £40,000. This has the effect of reducing the value of A's free estate by £40,000 so that on A's death the total value of the property transferred will only be £140,000 and not £180,000. Thus A has depleted his free estate by a payment which, is not itself a transfer of value and has replaced it with property which would have been chargeable in any event.

The legislative solution is to treat A's purchase of B's remainder as a transfer of value by A of the amount of the purchase price notwithstanding that full value has been given for the remainder. This is achieved by IHTA 1984, s. 55(1) which directs that A's estate is not increased by the reversion with the result that the money passing to B is pure loss to A's estate and so chargeable (s. 55 also specifically excludes IHTA 1984, s. 10). If the purchase is effected after 16th March 1987 it is a potentially exempt transfer.[5]

IHTA 1984, s. 55(1) is also useful where A has both a life interest and a purchased remainder. Thus suppose that property is settled on A for life, remainder to X for life, remainder to Y absolutely. On a purchase by A of Y's remainder A will be deemed to make a gift to Y of the consideration he gives Y. However, owing to the purchase, the reversionary interest no longer ranks as excluded property and so forms part of A's estate in which the value of the settled property is already represented owing to A's life interest in possession. Since A has already been charged with IHT in respect of the value of the reversionary interest, IHTA 1984, s. 55(1) excludes the reversion from A's estates. A is thus deemed to have acquired nothing, so on a subsequent transfer of the reversion by A e.g. on A's death no transfer of value can arise since there can be no loss in the value of A's estate.

Rule (*ii*) has the effect of treating a reversion falling within it as non-excluded property. If S settles property, say £100,000, on X for life with remainder to himself, the transfer by S is not of £100,000 but only of that sum *less* the then actuarial value of the reversion. It follows that if S then gives away the reversion there may be a charge to IHT; equally it follows that if S sells it for full market value there will not.

In 1981 the rule was extended to cover the situation in which S, or his spouse, had at any time been entitled to the reversionary interest. Under the previous rule the interest would, as now, not be excluded property while S was alive; he could then leave the interest to his spouse free of CTT. However as a widow is not a spouse the interest became excluded property on reaching her. The new rule makes sure that the reversion remains chargeable.

Foster's Capital Taxes Division E6.
[1] IHTA 1984, s. 47.
[2] IHTA 1984, s. 43(3), see, supra, § **40: 04**.
[3] IHTA 1984, s. 48(1).
[4] IHTA 1984, s. 48(1). On reversionary interests belonging to a person domiciled abroad see infra, § **49: 16**.
[5] IHTA 1984, s. 55(2); words at end added by FA 1986, Sch. 19, para. 15 but repealed by F(No. 2)A 1987, s. 96(5).

Purchasers

41: 33   Special provision was made to prevent purchasers or mortgagees of reversionary interests before 27th March 1974 being caught out by the then new CTT provisions. The tax payable by such persons when the reversionary interest falls into possession is not to exceed the amount of estate duty that would have been payable: any tax which thereby becomes payable by the mortgagor instead of the mortgagee is to rank as a charge subsequent to that of the mortgagee.[1] This applies also to IHT.

Foster's Capital Taxes M1.06.
[1] IHTA 1984, Sch. 6, para. 3.

POTENTIALLY EXEMPT TRANSFERS: SPECIAL RATE OF CHARGE

Special rate of charge on chargeable transfer of settled property following potentially exempt transfer creating settlement

41:34   As a consequence of the introduction of the potentially exempt transfer rule into the area of settled property a special rate of charge may apply.[1] This will apply where an interest in possession comes to an end on its termination under s. 52 or the person beneficially entitled dies;[2] this formulation is presumably wide enough to cover deemed terminations of interest such as a disposition of the interest in possession or a depreciatory transaction.

The reason behind the rule is apparently to prevent a settlor (S) from gaining an advantage by creating a discretionary trust subject to an initial life interest in favour, say, of A as distinct from creating one immediately. The advantage would be that S could avoid his personal aggregation being used to calculate the tax on the chargeable (not potentially exempt) transfer arising on the announcement of the discretionary trusts by settling the property on trusts such that, before the discretionary trusts arise, there is a short interest in possession in favour of a person who has made no previous chargeable transfers by the time that the interest in possession terminates and the discretionary trusts arise. Tax will be due if S dies within seven years as potentially exempt status will be lost; there is the further risk of extra tax when A's interest ends—whether or not within the seven year period.

The five conditions which trigger this charge are cumulative.[3] First the creation of the settlement must have been a potentially exempt transfer—as distinct from a chargeable or exempt one. So the settlement of property on a spouse for life with a discretionary trust over will not cause this charge to apply. Equally it cannot apply unless the trust is created after 16th March 1987.[4] Provision is made for the situation in which only a part of the transfer was potentially exempt.[5] Secondly, the ending of the interest in possession or death of the life tenant must occur within seven years of the potentially exempt transfer by which the settlement was made. Thirdly, the settlor must be alive at the time of the ending of the interest or the death of the life tenant.

Fourthly, on that termination or death the property must become settled property in which no qualifying interest in possession[6] subsists (other than an accumulation and maintenance settlement). So the charge applies where property is settled by S on A for life with remainder over on discretionary trusts and A dies within seven years or releases the life interest. There will be a chargeable transfer in either of these events; it cannot be a potentially exempt transfer by A since the property does not become part of the estate of any other person.

Fifthly, the property must not have become settled property in which an interest in possession subsists or which is an accumulation and maintenance settlement or become property to which an individual is beneficially entitled within six months of the termination. This rule, added late in the legislative process, gives the trust six months to escape from the special rate.

Tax would apart from these special rules be chargeable by reference to the circumstances of A in these events, and as S is still alive and the creation of the settlement was potentially exempt there would not be any charge on S. The alternative charge under the special rules is by reference to S's personal circumstances, and applies if—and only if—it results in more tax being chargeable. There is assumed a hypothetical transfer by a person with a cumulative total of chargeable transfers equal to that of S's cumulative total at the time the settlement was created; this total is to include any sums already caught by these rules,[7] and lifetime rates are applied.[8] Thus one calculates the amount of tax that would have been due if the original transfer in trust had been chargeable and not potentially exempt, although using the current and not the original value of the settled property. If this tax would be greater the greater amount is due now[9]—it is primarily due from the trustees of the settlement.[10]

The charge applies only where S is still alive. If S should die later but within seven years of the settlement extra tax may be due from the settlement.[11] Conversely if A's interest ends but A dies within seven years additional tax may also be due.[12] These deaths are to be ignored in determining the sum initially due under these rules.

Foster's Capital Taxes C4.13.
    [1] IHTA 1984, s. 54A added by F(No. 2)A 1987, Sch. 7.
    [2] IHTA 1984, s. 54A(1).
    [3] IHTA 1984, s. 54A(2).
    [4] The rules cannot apply where there was a settlement before that date on a disabled person as s. 54(2)(*a*) is specific as to the date; moreover the charge cannot apply where the trust is initially an accumulation and maintenance settlement since there is no initial interest in possession—this raises questions as to the policy behind the rule.

5 By use of the concept of "special rate property"—IHTA 1984, s. 54B(3). The burden of the tax falls exclusively on this part of the settled property F(No. 2)A 1987, Sch. 7, para. 5 amending IHTA 1984, s. 265.

6 See infra, § **42:02**.

7 IHTA 1984, s. 54B(4) to (6).

8 IHTA 1984, s. 54A(6).

9 IHTA 1984, s. 54A(5).

10 IHTA 1984, s. 54B(3).

11 IHTA 1984, s. 54B(1).

12 IHTA 1984, s. 54B(2).

42 Discretionary trusts

42:01 Special rules apply where property is settled but no qualifying interest in possession subsists in it, as in the case of discretionary trusts. These rules apply only to "relevant property", a term used to exclude certain situations which would otherwise come within the scope of these rules. However, they apply whether the trust was created before or after 27th March 1974. These rules apply to events on or after 9th March 1982 although changes have been made by FA 1986 as from 18th March 1986 to take account of the reduction of the basic cumulation period for transfers by individuals from ten years to seven.

Definitions

A qualifying interest in possession

42:02 The meaning of the term interest in possession was considered at § **41:07** supra. Such an interest is a qualifying interest if it is one to which the person entitled is either an individual or a special type of company;[1] such a company is one whose business consists wholly or mainly in the acquisition of interests in settled property but in order that the interest should be a qualifying interest it is also necessary that the company should have acquired it for consideration in money or money's worth from an individual who was beneficially entitled to it.[2] The effect is that a trust does not shift from the rules in the previous chapter just because a beneficiary sells his interest to such a company. If the interest was acquired before 14th March 1975 the company need not have acquired the interest for consideration from the person beneficially entitled to it and may simply be a company authorised to carry on long term insurance. However where any other sort of company or interest is involved, the rules in this chapter apply even though the company's interest is one in possession.

Foster's Capital Taxes E1.41.
[1] IHTA 1984, s. 59.
[2] IHTA 1984, s. 59(2).

Related settlements

42:03 Settlements are related if they are made by the same settlor on the same day; a settlement which would be related by this rule is not related if immediately after the settlement commenced the property was held for charitable purposes only and without limit of time.[1]

¹ IHTA 1984, s. 62; when part of the income is to be applied to such purposes a corresponding part is treated as held for charitable purposes; IHTA 1984, s. 84.

Settlements—property moving between settlements

42: 04   The definition of settlement and who is a settlor are the same as for the rules in the previous chapter.

Where property moves between settlements it is provided that the property is to be treated as remaining in the first settlement.[1] The purpose here is probably to prevent a charge from arising. However, this rule does not apply if in the meantime any person becomes beneficially entitled to the property (as distinct from becoming entitled to an interest in possession in the property).

This rule applies only if the property ceases to be subject to one settlement after 10th December 1981 but a similar rule applies where the cesser occurred after 26th March 1974 but before 10th December 1981.[2] As originally drafted this rule which is wider than its predecessor[3] had the effect that if a reversionary interest arising under a settlement was settled on trusts of another settlement fell into possession, the property would have to be treated as remaining in the first settlement. This is not to apply to events occurring after 14th March 1983 if the reversion was settled before 10th December 1981 and the reversion is expectant on the termination of a qualifying interest in possession the purpose of the change is to restore the law to the position which was expected when the reversion was settled.[4]

Foster's Capital Taxes E4.52.
¹ IHTA 1984, s. 81; on conditions for status as excluded property see IHTA 1984, ss. 48(3) and 82.
² IHTA 1984, s. 81(2).
³ FA 1975, Sch. 5, para. 11(4).
⁴ IHTA 1984, s. 81(3).

Commencement of settlement

42: 05   In deciding when a settlement commences the rule is that one looks to the time when property first becomes comprised in it.[1] However, a special rule applies if the settlement begins with an interest in possession in the settlor or his spouse infra, § **42: 22.**

Relevant property—the exclusions

42: 06   The property is not relevant property—and so these rules do not apply—if, although no qualifying interest in possession subsists in the settled property, the property is held on certain special trusts.[2] These are:

(*a*)   property held for charitable purposes only, whether for a limited time or otherwise
(*b*)   property held as maintenance funds for historic buildings, etc.
(*c*)   property held on accumulation and maintenance settlements
(*d*)   property held on approved superannuation schemes

(e) property held on trusts for employees or the special newspaper trusts
(f) property held on the discretionary trusts arising under a protective trust and arising before 12th April 1978
(g) property held on trusts for disabled persons and settled before 10th March 1981
(h) property held on a trade or professional compensation fund; and
(i) excluded property.

A charge to tax may, nonetheless, arise in relation to these trusts; see § **42: 24** et seq.
On effect of presence of works of art, see infra, § **45: 20**.

Foster's Capital Taxes E4.01–05.
[1] IHTA 1984, s. 60.
[2] IHTA 1984, s. 58.

PRINCIPAL OCCASION OF CHARGE

The ten year anniversary: IHTA 1984, s. 64

42: 07   Where, immediately before a ten year anniversary, all or any of the property comprised in a settlement is relevant property, tax is charged on the value of that relevant property at that time.[1] As it is the value of this relevant property that is taken there is no grossing up. After the 1986 changes the periodic charge continues to arise at ten-yearly intervals notwithstanding the reduction in the general cumulation period from ten years to seven; but the hypothetical cumulative total used in calculating the charge assumes a cumulative period of seven years, see infra, § **42: 10**.

It is first necessary to define the ten year anniversary. Generally this means the tenth anniversary of the date on which the settlement commenced and subsequent ten year anniversaries.[2] However no date falling before 1st April 1983 can be a ten year anniversary.[3] So if a settlement was created on 1st May 1976 the first occasion for this charge will be 1st May 1986 while if the settlement had been created on 1st March 1973 the first occasion of charge would not arise until 1st March 1993.

A further special rule provides that if the anniversary would be after 31st March 1983 but before 1st April 1984 and during that year there is a payment out of the settlement which could not have been made without an application to a court, the first ten year anniversary shall be taken to be 1st April 1984 with the result that the principal charge to tax will not affect that property; however this is not to affect later ten year anniversary dates.[4]

It will be noted that the ten year period runs from the date of the creation of the settlement. This is not necessarily the same as that on which the property became relevant property. So if the settlement created on 1st May 1976 began with a life interest in possession, the first ten year anniversary would still be 1st May 1986, although no charge would then arise unless the property had then become relevant property, i.e. no qualifying interest in possession then subsisted in it.

Special rules apply if the settlement begins with an interest in possession in the settlor or his spouse.[5]

The value of the property will be reduced if the property is entitled to agricultural or business relief.

The severity of this charge is mitigated where the property, although relevant property on the anniversary, has not been so throughout the period. This may be because it was not "relevant" or because it was not comprised in the settlement at all. The mitigation takes the form of a reduction in the rate at which the tax is to be charged.[6]

If a part periodic charge has been paid under the 1975 rules, that payment can be used as a credit against any liability arising under the 1982 rules.[7]

Foster's Capital Taxes E4.11.
[1] IHTA 1984, s. 64.
[2] IHTA 1984, s. 61.
[3] IHTA 1984, s. 61(3).
[4] IHTA 1984, s. 61(4).
[5] IHTA 1984, s. 80; infra, § **42: 22**.
[6] IHTA 1984, s. 66(2).
[7] IHTA 1984, s. 85.

Rate of tax on the principal occasion of charge: IHTA 1984, s. 66

Trusts created after 26th March 1974

42: 08 The rate at which tax is charged is to be 30% of "the effective rate". In making these calculations only the lifetime rates of tax are used. With the top applicable rate of tax reduced to 20% this makes the maximum rate on a 10 year charge $30\% \times 20\% = 6\%$

The effective rate is the tax chargeable, using lifetime rates, expressed as a percentage of the amount on which it is charged. The tax chargeable depends on a calculation of a hypothetical value to be taxed and a hypothetical point from which that value is to start. It is inherent in these rules that a particular figure should not enter both hypothetical parts.

These rules give rise to the important planning points that where a settlor proposes to make a "discretionary trust" and another "fixed trust", (i) they should be created on different days, and (ii) the discretionary trust should be created first; (i) avoids the related property rules in § **42: 09** while (ii) ensures a lower starting point by reducing figure a) in § **42: 10**.

(i) *The hypothetical value transferred, IHTA 1984, s. 66(4)*

42: 09 The value deemed to be transferred for this purpose is the aggregate of (*a*) the value charged under IHTA 1984, s. 66(4), (*b*) the value, immediately after the settlement was created, of any part of the property then comprised in the settlement which has not then and has not since become relevant property (e.g. a life interest which still subsists), and (*c*) the value immediately after a related settlement commenced of the property then comprised in it.

EXAMPLE

On 10th April 1979 S, whose cumulative total of transfers stood at £68,000 made two settlements. No. 1 was of £100,000 and was to be held on discretionary trusts subject to a life interest in half the income in favour of A. No. 2 was to be held only on discretionary trusts of £70,000. On the ten year anniversary the value of No. 1 is £320,000 and that of No. 2 is £90,000; A is still alive; £10,000 was advanced to a beneficiary from No. 2 on 1st May 1984.

The hypothetical value transferred for settlement No. 1 is:
   (a) £160,000, i.e. the half of the £320,000 that is relevant property, (b) £50,000, i.e. the initial value of the property in which A has a life interest, and (c) £70,000 i.e. the initial value of the related property settlement = £280,000.

The hypothetical value transferred for Settlement No. 2 is:
   (a) £90,000, (b) nil and (c) £100,000 = £190,000.

It will be noted that the sum charged under s. 64 on a previous ten year anniversary is ignored. On the second ten year anniversary in 1999 the hypothetical value of settlement No. 1 will, assuming the value of fund No. 1 to be £500,000 and that A is still alive, be the sum of (a) £250,000 (b) £50,000 and (c) £70,000 i.e. £370,000.

(ii) *The starting point—the hypothetical cumulative total, IHTA 1984, s. 66(5)*

42: 10   The rules suppose a transferor who has in the preceding seven[1] years made aggregate total transfers of,

   (a) all chargeable transfers made by the settlor in the seven year period ending with the date the settlement was made, but disregarding transfers made on that day, and

   (b) the amounts on the appropriate fractions of which any charges to tax arose under IHTA 1984, s. 65 within the previous seven years in respect of the settlement, i.e. any amount which has been the subject of a fractional charge under the rules to be considered at infra, § **42: 21**.

EXAMPLE (supra, § **42: 09** *cont*)
Settlement No. 1
   On 10th April 1989 the hypothetical starting point will be:
   (a) 68,000 + (b) nil = £68,000
   So, putting (i) and (ii) together one calculates the IHT at lifetime rates of a transfer of £280,000 by a person with a cumulative total of £68,000.
   The tax will be:

Tax at lifetime rates on £(68,000 + 280,000)	£46,000
less tax at lifetime rates on £68,000	Nil
	£46,000

   Tax of £46,000 on £280,000 would give an effective rate of 16·43% so the rate of charge is 30% of that, i.e. 4·93% and this is applied to £160,000 to give total tax of £7,885·71.

Settlement No. 2
   The hypothetical starting point is:
   (a) 68,000 + (b) 10,000 (the sum advanced to A) = £78,000 so one calculates IHT at lifetime rates of a transfer of £190,000 by a person with a cumulative total of £78,000.

Tax at lifetime rates on (78,000 + 190,000)	£30,000
less tax at lifetime rates on £78,000	Nil
	£30,000

   Tax of £30,000 on £190,000 would give an effective rate of 15·79% so the rate of charge is 30% of that, i.e. 4·74% and this is applied to £90,000 to give total tax of £4,263·15.

One effect of IHTA 1984, s. 66(4) and (5) is that any tax paid by the settlor on the creation of the settlement is ignored.

On effect of purchase of a work of art, see infra, § **45: 20**.

One consequence of the introduction of the potentially exempt transfer should be noted. Such a transfer becomes chargeable if the donor dies within seven years but is treated as having taken place at the time of the transfer not the time of death. If the settlor has made such a transfer, then settles this property on discretionary trusts, and then dies within seven years of the potentially exempt transfer, there may be additional tax to pay on the creation of the settlement but there is also an increase in the total of chargeable transfers in the seven years ending with the date of the settlement.[2]

Foster's Capital Taxes E4.45.
[1] Seven years was substituted for ten in IHTA 1984, s. 66(3) by FA 1986, Sch. 19, para. 16. This applies to anniversaries on or after 18th March 1986.
[2] The extra tax is due six months from the death of the settlor; IHTA 1984, s. 226(3B) added by FA 1986, Sch. 19, para. 30(2). Instalment relief may be available; IHTA 1984, s.236(1A) added by FA 1986, Sch. 19, para. 33(2).

Trusts created before 27th March 1974

42: 11 For settlements created before 27th March 1974 a simpler regime applies. First, the hypothetical value transferred consists simply of the value charged under IHTA 1984, s. 64, i.e. the value of the relevant property on the anniversary. Secondly, for the first ten year anniversary the hypothetical cumulative total consists simply of distribution payments[1] made after 26th March 1974 but before 9th March 1982 and within the ten year period together with any sums charged since 9th March 1982 under IHTA 1984, s. 65. For subsequent anniversaries the hypothetical cumulative total consists simply of sums charged under IHTA 1984, s. 66. As one is dealing with a pre-1974 settlement, there will be no chargeable transfer made by the settlor before the settlement.

Foster's Capital Taxes E4.41.
[1] On definition see Tiley, *Revenue Law* (3rd edn.), § 45: 02 and note *IRC v Sir John Aird's Settlement Trustees (No. 2)* [1984] STC 81.

Property relevant property for only part of the period

42: 12 Where the property to be charged under IHTA 1984, s. 66, although relevant property on the anniversary, has not been so throughout the period a reduced rate applies. The reduction is 1/40th for each quarter in that period which expired before the property became or last became relevant property comprised in the settlement.

EXAMPLE
  On the tenth anniversary the fund is worth £200,000. A died half-way through the ten year period. For the first five years one half of the income of the fund was paid to A by reason of a life interest. A's one half of the property was not relevant property throughout the ten year period; the rate otherwise due on that part, £100,000, is therefore reduced by 20/40ths. There will have been an occasion of charge on the ending of A's life interest but under the rules discussed in the previous chapter.

While the principle behind the mitigation is clear, it is anything but clear how the rules should be applied where the property was not relevant property by reason of some annuity since it is difficult to see exactly what part of the property is to be reduced by the 40ths formula.

Added property etc.

42: 13   Special provision has to be made for the situation in which value is added to the settlement after 8th March 1982, but at a time during the ten years before the anniversary on which the principal charge arises.[1] The risk of an increase in the hypothetical cumulative total stemming from even the slightest addition to the settlement is a major point in tax planning for such trusts. These rules apply whenever the settlor makes a chargeable[2] transfer in that time as a result of which the property in the settlement is increased in value; it is not necessary that there should have been any increase in the property in the settlement. Thus these rules will apply when the settlor makes an omission which results in an increase in the value of the settlement and so is a chargeable transfer by him; however an exception is made when the transfer was not primarily intended to increase the value of the settled property and the increase in the value of the settled property was not more than 5%.[3]

Where value is added in this way these rules provide for an adjustment of the starting point, i.e. the hypothetical cumulative total from which to begin the calculation of the effective rate. The rule is that instead of the values transferred by chargeable transfers by the settlor in the period, as from 18th March 1986, of seven (previously ten) years before the day on which the settlement was made there shall, if greater, be taken the aggregate of values transferred by chargeable transfers by the settlor in the ten years ending with the day on which the addition occurred, but disregarding the transfers made on that day.[4]

If the settlor has made more than one addition the highest figure is taken. If, as is likely, the seven year period brings in the sum originally settled that sum is excluded. This is because it will be brought into account in other parts of the IHTA 1984, s. 66 calculation. For similar reasons property which has ceased to be settled and on that account is part of the hypothetical starting point is also excluded.[5]

EXAMPLE
In 1976 S made a chargeable transfer of £60,000.
In 1980 S made two settlements on discretionary trusts on the same day; No. 1 of £110,000 and No. 2 of £90,000.
In 1982 S made a chargeable transfer of £40,000.
In 1988 S adds £50,000 to settlement No. 1 and £20,000 to settlement No. 2.
In 1990 the first ten year anniversary comes round. The cumulative total will be the greater of (a) £60,000 and (b) £60,000 + 40,000—i.e. (b). If the chargeable transfer of £40,000 had taken place in 1987 not 1982, the figures would have been (a) £60,000 and (b) £40,000 so (a) would have been taken.
It will be noticed that for settlement No. 1 the £20,000 is ignored—as being a transfer made on the same day as the value added to settlement No. 1—as are the sums of £90,000—taken in as the initial value of a related settlement in calculating the amount to be used in calculating the value used to find the effective rate—and the £50,000 itself.

Where the settlement was made before 27th March 1974 but an addition is made after 8th March 1982 the hypothetical cumulative total (or starting point) is the aggregate of the settlor's chargeable transfers made in the seven years before the addition.[6]

Foster's Capital Taxes E4.45.
[1] IHTA 1984, s. 67.
[2] An exempt transfer is not a chargeable transfer nor is a potentially exempt transfer unless the donor dies within seven years.
[3] IHTA 1984, s. 67(2).
[4] IHTA 1984, s. 67(3).
[5] IHTA 1984, s. 67(5).
[6] IHTA 1984, s. 67(4) seven years substituted for ten for period after 17th March 1986 by FA 1986, Sch. 19, para. 17.

42: 14 If property ceases to be relevant property through, say, being appointed to A for life, and is then subject to a charge under IHTA 1984, s. 65, but the property later comes back into the category of relevant property (because, say, A dies) also within the ten year period, the sum charged under IHTA 1984, s. 65 would feature in both hypothetical parts. A reduction in the hypothetical cumulative total is therefore directed. The reduction is by the lesser of (*a*) the amount on which the tax was charged (ignoring the fractions and any grossing up) and (*b*) the hypothetical value chargeable.[1] Where only part of the property is involved, apportionments are made. It will be noted that only sums subject to the exit charge are taken into account—not capital distributions under the pre-1982 rules.[2]

---

[1] IHTA 1984, s. 67(6).
[2] IHTA 1984, s. 67(4).

OTHER OCCASIONS OF CHARGE

Ceasing to be relevant property—the exit charge; IHTA 1984, s. 65

42: 15 A charge to tax arises where the property ceases to be relevant property,[1] unless this occurs in a quarter beginning with the day on which the settlement commenced or with a ten year anniversary—this is to avoid very small charges.[2] Compared with the 1975 rules three points stand out. First, the rate of charge is reduced; secondly, a number of exceptions in the 1975 rules (e.g. reverter to settlor) are not part of the 1982 scheme. The reason for these is the same—the 1982 exit charge is a proportionate ten year anniversary charge designed to compensate the Revenue for the fact that this property will not be relevant property when the next ten year anniversary comes round. The third difference is the change to basing liability on loss to the trust.

The first situation covered by this rule is that in which the property ceases to be comprised in the settlement. In this connection the rule treating property moving to a different settlement as remaining comprised in the first settlement[3] must not be overlooked. Property transferred to a beneficiary under a power of appointment or of advancement or simply distributed from the discretionary settlement could give rise to a charge under this rule. Where the property is transferred to an individual absolutely it is to be presumed that the transfer is chargeable and cannot be potentially exempt.

The second situation is that in which the property remains comprised in the settlement but ceases to be relevant property, as where the beneficiary is given a life interest in a fund. There will be a charge under the present rule. If the property is still held for the beneficiary when the ten year anniversary comes round, that part cannot be charged under the principal charge as it is not then relevant property—hence the present charge.

Another way in which the property ceases to be relevant property is where there is still no qualifying interest in possession but the trust falls within the list of excluded trusts—above. One example would be when an accumulation and maintenance settlement arises.

Exceptions are made where the property (i) is a payment of costs and expenses properly attributable to the relevant property and (ii) if the payment is income of any person for the purposes of UK income tax (or would be if he were resident in the UK).[4]

The amount to be taxed under IHTA 1984, s. 65 is the reduction in the value of the property in the settlement. So if the trust had a 60% shareholding in a company and the trustees granted A a 15% holding, the loss of control would be taken into account.

If the tax is paid out of other relevant property remaining comprised in the settlement, the sum otherwise chargeable must be grossed up.

If a part periodic charge was paid under the 1975 rules, that payment can be used as a credit against any liability arising under the 1982 rules.[5]

For exit charges between ten year anniversaries after 17th March 1986, where the last ten year anniversary was before 18th March 1986, the rate of tax must be recalculated to take account of the reduction from ten years to seven for which chargeable transfers by the settlor before the creation of the settlement are taken into account but no other changes of substance are made by FA 1986.[6]

Foster's Capital Taxes E4.12.
[1] IHTA 1984, s. 65(1)(a).
[2] IHTA 1984, s. 65(4).
[3] IHTA 1984, s. 81.
[4] IHTA 1984, s. 65(5).
[5] IHTA 1984, s. 125.
[6] FA 1986, Sch. 19, para. 43.

Disposition by the trustees—loss to the trust

42: 16   There is also a charge under IHTA 1984, s. 65 if the case does not fall within the previous rule but the trustees make a disposition as a result of which the value of the relevant property comprised in the settlement is less than it would be but for the disposition.[1]

As with the previous rule no charge arises if it occurs within three months of the creation of the settlement or a ten year anniversary.[2] Equally there is no charge if the disposition is a payment by way of expenses or costs fairly attributable to the relevant property or the payment would be income of the recipient (or would be if he were resident in the UK).[3]

This head of charge is similar in formulation to the general rule applying to dispositions by individuals[4] and the rules relating to transfers by omissions[5] are therefore adapted as is the defence in IHTA 1984, s. 10 where no gratuitous benefit is intended.[6]

Foster's Capital Taxes E4.13.
[1] IHTA 1984, s. 65(1)(*b*).
[2] IHTA 1984, s. 65(4).
[3] IHTA 1984, s. 65(5).
[4] IHTA 1984, s. 3(1).
[5] IHTA 1984, s. 3(3).
[6] IHTA 1984, s. 65(6).

Foreign element

42: 17 Where the settlement was created by a settlor who was not then domiciled in the UK, there will be no charge where the property becomes excluded property (and so ceases to be relevant property—thus causing a drop in the value of the relevant property)[1] or, if the beneficiaries are also foreign, where the trustees acquire gilt edged securities (which qualifies as excluded property).[2]

Foster's Capital Taxes E4.24.
[1] IHTA 1984, s. 65(7).
[2] IHTA 1984, ss. 65(8) and 267.

Other exclusions

42: 18 No charge arises if the property becomes settled on certain favoured trusts or by certain bodies; these are permanent trusts for charitable purposes, a political party within IHTA 1984, s. 24, a national body within IHTA 1984, s. 25 or a body not established or conducted for profit.[1] There are also exceptions where property becomes the property of maintenance funds for heritage property[2], and for shares or securities of a company becoming held on employee trusts.[3] If the amount chargeable but for the exception exceeds the value of the property subject to most of these favoured trusts or bodies, the excess is chargeable.[4]

Foster's Capital Taxes E4.25–27.
[1] IHTA 1984, s. 76.
[2] IHTA 1984, s. 77 and Sch. 4.
[3] IHTA 1984, s. 75.
[4] IHTA 1984, s. 76(3) and Sch. 4.

Before the first ten year anniversary

Trusts created after 26th March 1974

42: 19 Where a charge arises under IHTA 1984, s. 65 before the first ten year anniversary, the tax is charged at a special rate, which is the "appropriate fraction" of the effective rate on a hypothetical transfer.[1]

The "appropriate fraction" is 3/10 multiplied by so many fortieths as there are complete successive quarters in the period beginning with the day on which the settlement commenced and ending with the day before the occasion of charge—so the greater the number of quarters, the higher the appropriate fraction.[2]

EXAMPLE (supra, § **42: 09** *cont*)
In relation to the £10,000 advanced on 1 May 1984 from settlement No. 2 the number of completed quarters would be 20 and the fraction therefore 3/10 × 20/40.

Adjustments are made to the number of quarters for chargeable property which was either not comprised in the settlement at all throughout these quarters—as when it was added later—or was not relevant property throughout these quarters—as where there was a life interest in possession which ended before the charge under IHTA 1984, s. 65 arose. Quarters expiring before the property became (or last became) relevant property are excluded; conversely the quarter then in progress is included.[3]

The hypothetical value[4] to be transferred is the sum of (*a*) the value immediately after the settlement commenced of the property then comprised in it; (*b*) the similar value of any related settlement and (*c*) the initial value of any property later added to the settlement (whether or not it remained in the settlement). There is no grossing up at this point.

The hypothetical starting point[5] is the sum of any chargeable transfers made by this settlor in the period of seven years ending with the day on which the settlement commenced, disregarding transfers made on that day.

EXAMPLE (supra, §**42: 09** *cont*)
Settlement No. 2. When £10,000 leaves the settlement on 1st May 1984 the hypothetical starting point is £68,000 and the hypothetical value to be transferred is (*a*) 70,000 (*b*) 100,000 (*c*) nil = £170,000

Tax at 1984 lifetime rates on 170,000 + 68,000	£36,700
less tax at 1984 lifetime rates on £68,000	£ 600
	£36,100

The charge is therefore $\frac{36,100}{170,000} \times \frac{3}{10} \times \frac{20}{40} \times 10,000 = £318·53$

As £10,000 is the gross sum, the beneficiary got £9,681·47.

Foster's Capital Taxes E4.44.
[1] IHTA 1984, s. 68(1).
[2] IHTA 1984, s. 68(2).
[3] IHTA 1984, s. 68(3).
[4] IHTA 1984, s. 68(5).
[5] IHTA 1984, s. 68(4). Seven substituted for ten as from 18th March 1986 by FA 1986, Sch. 19, para. 18.

Trusts created before 27th March 1974

42: 20   If the trust began before 27th March 1974 the property to be charged is taxed in the following way. The hypothetical starting point is the sum of (*a*) any amounts previously taxed under IHTA 1984, s. 65 and (*b*) any distribution payments made before 9th March 1982 but after 26th March 1974 and which were made within the ten years prior to the present chargeable event, the values being determined under the 1975 rules.[1]

The value hypothetically to be taxed is the same as that actually to be taxed, i.e. the reduction in value. The amount of hypothetical tax is then calculated using lifetime rates and grossing up if necessary (i.e. if the tax is paid out of other property which remains relevant property). This amount of tax is expressed as a percentage of the value and gives the effective rate. Tax is then charged at 30% of the effective rate.

The rate to be applied to settlements commencing before 27th March 1974 was 20% instead of 30% of the effective rate if the charge arose before 1st April 1983 (or 1st April 1984 in the case of an event that could not have occurred except as a result of court proceedings).[2] However this rate was available only if "a qualifying person" became entitled to the property (or to an interest in possession in it) or the trust became an accumulation and maintenance settlement when each of the beneficiaries was such a person. A qualifying person was an individual who was domiciled (deemed or actual) in the UK who had not acquired an interest under the settlement for a consideration in money or money's worth (this restriction is the same as under the 1975 transitional rate rules).

The effect is similar to that under the 1975 scheme with the trust having its own cumulative total starting in 1974.[3]

Foster's Capital Taxes E4.41.
[1] IHTA 1984, s. 68(6).
[2] FA 1982, Sch. 15, para. 4.
[3] On transitional right to elect see FA 1982, Sch. 15, Part II.

Between the tax year anniversaries

42: 21 When the charge under IHTA 1984, s. 65 arises between ten year anniversaries this tax is charged. The rate is the appropriate fraction of the rate used for IHTA 1984, s. 64 on the most recent anniversary. Where this rate was further reduced for certain property which was not relevant property throughout the previous ten years, those further reductions are ignored.[1] The rate used on the most recent anniversary is recalculated if there has been a reduction in the rates of tax since the anniversary.[2] Further, if the anniversary was before 18th March 1986, and the exit charge arises on or after that date, the rate may have to be recalculated to take account of the reduction from ten years to seven in the period during which chargeable transfers by the settlor before the creation of the settlement are relevant.[3]

The appropriate fraction is determined as for IHTA 1984, s. 65 save that the quarters begin with the last ten year anniversary.[4]

> **EXAMPLE** (supra, § **42: 09** *cont*)
> In Settlement No. 1 (supra, §**42: 10**) the trustees advance £25,000 to a beneficiary, the beneficiary to pay the tax. The advance is made on 1st June 1991, 2 years 2 months after the first ten year anniversary.
> The amount to be charged is £25,000.
> The appropriate fraction is $\dfrac{8}{40}$.
>
> The tax at 1989–90 rates $\dfrac{8}{40} \times \dfrac{3}{10} \times \dfrac{46,000}{280,000} \times 25,000 = £246.43$

Adjustments are made to the rate to take account of property becoming relevant property since the last ten year anniversary and so not taken into account in computing the last ten year charge. Property which has become comprised in this settlement and which either (*a*) became relevant property straight away or (*b*) was not and has not become relevant property is taken at its value when joining the settlement; i.e. its central value.[5] The rate is that which would have been charged on the anniversary if the property had been relevant property at that time; it will be noted that this applies whether or not the property has ever become relevant property. Other added property is taken at the value when it became (or last became) relevant property.

Property which was comprised in the settlement at the anniversary but was not then relevant property is likewise taken into account if it has since become relevant property by being added to the sum to be charged at the last ten year anniversary; for this purpose then it is valued as at the date it became (or last became) relevant property.[6]

EXAMPLE

Suppose that in settlement No. 1 (supra, § **42: 09**) A had died one year after the anniversary and that the value of the fund at that time was £400,000. The effect of A's death would be that half the fund, £200,000 would become relevant property but that figure of £200,000, would be reduced by the tax payable on A's death to, say, £110,000. Suppose again that £25,000 is advanced 2 years and 2 months after the anniversary.

This leads to a recalculation of the rate charged under IHTA 1984, s. 66 (supra §**42: 10**). The hypothetical value is now (*a*) £160,000+£110,000+(*b*) £nil+(c) £70,000=£340,000; the hypothetical starting point is unchanged at £68,000.

Assuming 1989–90 rates still apply, the tax would be:

Tax at lifetime rates on £(68,000+340,000)	£58,000
less tax at lifetime rates on £68,000	nil
	£58,000

The effective rate is therefore $\dfrac{58,000}{340,000} = 17.06\%$

of which 30% is taken i.e. 5.12%.

The £25,000 is advanced to a beneficiary one year and two months after A's death i.e. 2 years and two months after the ten year anniversary, the appropriate fraction is $\frac{8}{40}$ so the tax is

$$\frac{8}{40} \times \frac{3}{10} \times \frac{58,000}{340,000} \times £25,000 = £255.88$$

This applies unless the property to be charged under IHTA 1984, s. 69 is the property coming in on A's death. In that event the rate of tax is further reduced. This may mean some difficulty in trust administration since it may not be clear where B's money comes from.

If the rate of tax has been reduced by legislation since the last ten year anniversary, these figures are calculated as if the lower rates now applying had been in force at the time of the anniversary.[7]

Foster's Capital Taxes E4.46.
[1] IHTA 1984, s. 69(1).
[2] IHTA 1984, Sch. 2, para. 3.
[3] FA 1986, Sch. 19, para. 43.
[4] IHTA 1984, s. 69(4).
[5] IHTA 1984, s. 69(2) and (3).
[6] IHTA 1984, s. 69(2)(*b*) and (3).
[7] IHTA 1984, Sch. 2, para. 3.

Initial interest of settlor or spouse

42: 22   A special provision applies where the settlor or his spouse, a term which includes widow or widower, is beneficially entitled to an interest in possession in the settled property immediately after the settlement is set up.[1] Such property is not treated as having become comprised in a settlement at that time.

When such property later becomes held on trusts such that neither the settlor nor his spouse is so entitled, the property is treated as becoming comprised in a separate settlement made at the time by the person ceasing or last ceasing to be beneficially entitled. The consequences of this rule are to be found in the rules for calculating the effective rate of tax. However, the ten year anniversaries are determined by reference to the date of the original settlement.[2]

> **EXAMPLE**
> H settled property on trust for W for life with remainder on discretionary trusts under s. 120. Such property does not become comprised in a settlement until W dies (or for some other reason her interest ends); on such occasion the settlement is treated as made by W at that time with consequent results in calculating the effective rate.
> If W had been entitled to a life interest in one third of the settled property, two thirds is treated as subject to the rules set out above on the basis that H is the settlor, while the remaining third will become subject to those rules when W's interest ends, but as a settlement made by W.

These rules apply whether the property became settled before or after March 1982—but not if before 27th March 1974.

Foster's Capital Taxes E4.51.
[1] IHTA 1984, s. 80; on conditions for status as excluded property see IHTA 1984, s. 82.
[2] IHTA 1984, s. 6(2).

Planning

42: 23   The 1982 rules for discretionary trusts are so much more generous than the 1975 rules that planners bold enough to anticipate a long life for the 1982 rules have taken a close interest in such trusts. Among the points to bear in mind are the following:

(a) If the settlor's cumulative total on the making of the trust is low enough it may well be that no tax will be paid on a modest discretionary trust at all.

(b) If the settlor wishes also to make non-discretionary trusts these should be done by a separate settlement.

(c) If the settlor wishes to make both a discretionary and a non-discretionary trust, he should make the discretionary trust first.

(d) The settlor should avoid making two settlements on the same day.

(e) It is better to make several small discretionary trusts rather than one big one.

(f) It is better to create a new discretionary trust than to add to an existing one.

(*g*) If a discretionary trust has been set up since March 1974 it is usually better to make any distribution before rather than after the ten year anniversary.

SPECIALLY FAVOURED TRUSTS

42: 24   Certain types of trust in which there is no qualifying interest in possession are not subject to the ten year and intermediate charges as the property comprised in the settlement is excluded from being relevant property; see § **42: 02**. If the conditions entitling the trust to this special treatment cease to apply a special tapered charge applies to compensate for the tax that has not been collected previously.

The exceptions outlined at § **42: 18** apply here also. Where the charge arises before 1st April 1983 (or 1984 if court proceedings are involved) the old pre 1982 rules may be applied instead.[1]

---

[1] FA 1982, Sch. 15, paras. 6–9.

The tapered charge

42: 25   The amount on which the tapered charge is levied is the amount of the reduction in the value of the settled property as a result of the event. If the tax is paid out of the settled property subject to the charge, the value has to be grossed up.[1]

The rate at which the tax is charged reflects the length of time the property has been in the favoured settlement. The rate for the first forty successive quarters in the relevant period is 0·25% each, i.e. 10% after the first ten years. The figures for subsequent decades are 0·20% (8%), 0·15% (6%), 0·10% (4%) and 0·05% (2%).[2] The relevant period begins with the date on which the property first fulfilled the conditions entitling it to special treatment subject to the important proviso that the start cannot be taken back beyond 13th March 1975.[3] Years during which the property was excluded property are to be ignored[4] (e.g. property situated abroad by a settlor not domiciled in the UK) for events occurring on or after 9th March 1982. The effect of these rules is that the maximum applicable rate is 30% and that cannot be applied until the year 2025. So a charge arising in October 1989 under a trust which has been in existence since February 1978 will have the reduction in value taxed at 40 (the number of quarters) × 0·25%, i.e. 10% plus 6 at 0·20% i.e. 11·20% total.

A special rule applies where the property was relevant property immediately before 10th December 1981 and then became entitled to special treatment before 9th March 1982. In such circumstances the relevant period begins on the date the property became relevant property (or, if later 13th March 1975).[5]

Certain other rules are common to these occasions of charge. The first is that a tax is not charged if the property involved is a payment of costs or expenses fairly attributable to the property concerned or is a payment which is income of the recipient (or would be if he were resident in the UK).[6]

Secondly where the trustees make a disposition reducing the value of the settled property, the trustees can invoke IHTA 1984, s. 10 or s. 16 as a defence.[7]

Thirdly the trustees are to be treated as making a disposition if they do so by omission, by analogy with IHTA 1984, s. 3(3).[8]

Foster's Capital Taxes E5.01–03.
[1] IHTA 1984, s. 70(5)(*b*).
[2] IHTA 1984, s. 70(6).
[3] IHTA 1984, s. 70(8).
[4] IHTA 1984, s. 70(2).
[5] IHTA 1984, s. 70(9).
[6] IHTA 1984, s. 70(3).
[7] IHTA 1984, s. 70(4).
[8] IHTA 1984, s. 70(10).

The favoured trust and their charges

(1) *Temporary charitable trusts*

42: 26 Where property is held for charitable purposes—and only for such purposes—and the property is so held for a period (whether defined by a date or in some other way such, perhaps, as someone's life) the property is not relevant property and so the normal charges cannot arise.[1] However the tapered charge will apply in the way outlined as if settled property ceases to be property fulfilling this description (apart from being applied for charitable purposes), or if the trustees make a disposition reducing the value of the settled property.[2] One should note that while a temporary charitable trust is favoured in this way, a gift to such a trust will not be an exempt transfer (see § **44: 10**).

Foster's Capital Taxes E5.38.
[1] IHTA 1984, s. 58; where a part of the income is to be so used a corresponding part is subject to these rules; IHTA 1984, s. 84.
[2] IHTA 1984, s. 70(2).

(2) *Accumulation and maintenance settlements*

42: 27 The conditions entitling these trusts to special treatment are as under the pre-1982 scheme (see infra, § **42: 28**).

So long as the trust satisfies these conditions the property is not relevant property and so the normal charges cannot arise.[1] In addition the legislation provides that there is to be no charge where the beneficiary becomes beneficially entitled to, or to an interest in possession in, settled property on or before attaining the specified age; similarly there is to be no charge on the death of a beneficiary before attaining the specified age.[2] Unlike transfers into most other trusts, a transfer to an accumulation and maintenance trust by an individual has been a potentially exempt transfer since the beginning of IHT.[3]

In the event of death between 18 and attaining the specified age there may be a charge under IHTA 1984, s. 4 if he has an interest in possession thanks to Trustee Act 1925, s. 31.[4] The result is similar where such a beneficiary has such an interest and another member of the class comes into existence thus causing a reduction in the first beneficiary's share; in this case the charge arises under IHTA 1984, s. 52.

However, subject to the previous paragraph, there is a charge, using the tapered charge basis, if the property ceases to satisfy the conditions entitling it to this special treatment or if the trustees make a disposition reducing the value of the settled property.[5]

Foster's Capital Taxes E5.21, 22.
[1] IHTA 1984, s. 58.
[2] IHTA 1984, s. 71(4).
[3] IHTA 1984, s. 3A(3) added by FA 1986, Sch. 19, para. 1.
[4] E.g. *Swales v IRC* [1984] STC 413.
[5] IHTA 1984, s. 71(3).

42: 28   These trusts receive favoured treatment. They are narrowly defined as settlements where:

(*a*) one or more persons (in this paragraph referred to as beneficiaries) will, on or before attaining a specified age not exceeding 25, become entitled to, or to an interest in possession in, the settled property or part of it;

(*b*) no interest in possession subsists in the settled property or part and the income from it is to be accumulated so far as not applied for the maintenance, education or benefit of a beneficiary; and

(*c*)[1] either (*i*) not more than 25 years have elapsed since the day on which the settlement was made or, if it was later, since the time (or latest time) when the conditions stated in paragraphs (*a*) and (*b*) above became satisfied with respect to the property[2] (i.e. 25 years since the settlement was created or it became an accumulation and maintenance settlement) or (*ii*) all the persons who are or have been beneficiaries are or were either grandchildren of a common grandparent or children,[3] widows or widowers of such grandchildren who were themselves beneficiaries but died before the time when, had they survived, they would have become entitled as mentioned in paragraph (*a*) above.

Condition (*a*) causes one to be wary of wide powers of appointment and of their exercise. Thus in *Inglewood v IRC*[4] the fact that the appointment in favour of a beneficiary could be revoked and resettled on trusts outside these rules meant that it was not certain that he would become entitled and so the reliefs did not apply.

Now that transfers to such settlements can be potentially exempt transfers it is possible to settle property on A for life and get potentially exempt treatment if A is 24 but not if he is 25.

Condition (*b*) demands a duty to accumulate surplus income rather than a mere power.

The reasoning behind condition (*c*) is the wish to prevent relief from being rolled forward from one generation to the next under settlements containing a power to substitute successive generations for the present one. Condition (*c*)(*ii*)—known as the common grandparent condition—is needed as an alternative to (c)(i) since the class may include unborn children, in which case the 25-year rule cannot easily be satisfied. This definition is apt to cover the simple case where income is accumulated and the capital plus accumulations are to pass to beneficiaries contingent upon them attaining the age of 21 or 25 as the case may be. Where the condition is attaining an age greater than 25, the trust will still satisfy these conditions if Trustee Act 1925, s. 31 gives the contingent beneficiary a right to intermediate income and so an interest in possession.[5] The definition is however a narrow one as the following examples issued by the Inland Revenue will show:

The examples set out below are used on a settlement for the children of X contingently on attaining 25, the trustees being required to accumulate the income so far as it is not applied for the maintenance of X's children.

A. The settlement was made on X's marriage and he has yet no children.

[IHTA 1984, s. 71] will not apply until a child is born and that event will give rise to a charge for tax under [IHTA 1984, s. 65(1)(a)].

B. The trustees have power to apply income for the benefit of X's unmarried sister.

[IHTA 1984, s. 71] does not apply because the condition of [IHTA 1984, s. 71(1)(b)] is not met.

C. The trustees have power to apply capital for the benefit of X's unmarried sister.

[IHTA 1984, s. 71] does not apply because the condition of [IHTA 1984, s. 71(1)(a)] is not met.

D. X has power to appoint the capital not only among his children but also among his remoter issue.

E. The trustees have an overriding power of appointment in favour of other persons.

[IHTA 1984, s. 71] does not apply (unless the power can be exercised only in the favour of persons who would thereby acquire interests in possession on or before attaining 25). A release of the disqualifying power would give rise to a charge for tax under [IHTA 1984, s. 65(1)(a)]. Its exercise would also give rise to a charge under [IHTA 1984, s. 65(1)(a)].

F. The settled property has been revocably appointed to one of the children contingently on his attaining 25 and the appointment is now made irrevocable.

If the power to revoke prevents [IHTA 1984, s. 71] from applying (as it would, for example, if the property thereby became subject to a power of appointment as at D or E) tax will be chargeable under [IHTA 1984, s. 65(1)(a)] when the appointment is made irrevocable.

G. The trust to accumulate income is expressed to be during the life of the settlor.

As the settlor may live beyond the 25th birthday or any of his children, the trust does not satisfy the condition in [IHTA 1984, s. 71(1)(a)] and the paragraph does not apply.

Foster's Capital Taxes E5.11–20.

[1] IHTA 1984, s. 71(2). Settlements in existence on 15th April 1976 are subject to transitional rules.

[2] This will have caused a charge under FA 1975, Sch. 5, para. 15(3) if after 12th March 1975 and under IHTA 1984, s. 65 if after 8th March 1982.

[3] Defined IHTA 1984, s. 76(8) as including illegitimate children, adopted children and stepchildren.

[4] [1983] STC 133, however some relaxation may be seen in extra-statutory concession F8 (1988); **Foster's Capital Taxes, Division U2.**

[5] Extra-statutory concession F8.

Some problems

42: 29   *Condition (a).* Where S settles property to be accumulated with the capital and accumulations to pass to such of his grandchildren as attain 25 but with an overriding power in the trustees to appoint the income and capital to such of his children and grandchildren as they think fit, the settlement is outside IHTA 1984, s. 71. The children are not the beneficiaries in (a) and their presence means that it cannot be said that "the income is to be accumulated so far as not applied for the maintenance, education or benefit of a beneficiary", i.e. a grandchild.

Even if the children are deleted from the overriding power of appointment it would seem that the trust still does not come within IHTA 1984, s. 71 since the overriding power of appointment could be exercised so as to enable one of the older grandchildren to become entitled to, or to an interest in possession in, the settled property or part of it well after attaining the age of 25 so preventing requirement (a) from being satisfied, since it will not be the case that the beneficiaries between them will, on or before attaining 25, become entitled to the settled property or to an interest therein. IHTA 1984, s. 71, it seems, will only be satisfied if the overriding power is exercisable only in favour of grandchildren who have not attained 25 and only so as to confer an absolute interest or an interest in possession in such grandchildren. If the power could be exercised so as to appoint the capital to trustees upon discretionary trusts for the grandchildren or to trustees for the grandchildren upon attaining 30 it could not be said that the grandchildren *will* before attaining 25 become *entitled* to, or to an interest in possession in, the property.

42: 30   *Condition (b).* First, a literal interpretation might require that the income be capable of being applied for the maintenance, education or benefit of the beneficiary.[1] On such a construction a trust from which the statutory powers of maintenance and advancement were excluded would not satisfy IHTA 1984, s. 71. This result might be avoided where the court has an inherent power to order maintenance even in the face of an express clause.

Secondly, problems arise if the settlement, although for grandchildren contingent upon their attaining the age of 25, contains an express[2] power of advancement on discretionary trusts for the grandchildren since this power might be exercised so as to give the grandchild an interest contingent upon reaching an age greater than 25.[3]

Thirdly, the requirement in IHTA 1984, s. 71(1) that income "is to be accumulated so far as not applied for the maintenance education or benefit of a beneficiary" raises particular dangers where the accumulation period expires before the attainment of a specified age such as 25. This will be the case where no express accumulation period exists so that accumulation is only under the trust contained in the Trustee Act 1925, s. 31(2) so that accumulation must cease when the beneficiary in question attains 18 in a post-1969 settlement or 21 in a pre-1970 settlement. Thus, if property is settled on A and B upon attaining 25 the trust to accumulate will cease when the younger attains 18 or 21 as the case may be and the favoured treatment accorded to the settlement will then cease although the tax consequences of this will depend on what trusts of income then follow. In many cases A and B will then have interests in possession under Trustee Act 1925, s. 31(1)(ii).

[1] Pettit, *Equity and the Law of Trusts*, (5th edn.) pp. 392–403.
[2] This would be *ultra vires* the statutory power—*Pilkington v IRC* [1962] 3 All ER 622, 40 TC 416.
[3] Perhaps the reasoning in *Blausten v IRC* [1972] 1 All ER 41, 47 TC 542 could be used to limit the power so as not to fall outside IHTA 1984, s. 71(1)(*b*).

42: 31 *Condition* (*c*), IHTA 1984, s. 71(2). This too has its dangers. Alternative (*i*) requires that the beneficiaries must actually become entitled in the 25 year period. This may well be difficult in the case of a settlement on a class which is not yet closed. It may therefore be necessary for the trustees to use their powers of advancement or appointment over the whole trust fund; they should also be given the power to accelerate interests in possession in favour of minors.

Alternative (*ii*) requires particular care where substitutional clauses are involved. It appears that if the clause comes into operation after the testator's death condition (*c*) is satisfied but if before that death it will not be; this anomaly appears to be quite nonsensical.

Care should also be taken to ensure that the clause is restricted to situations in which the beneficiary dies before attaining an interest in possession rather than attaining a specified age, say of 25. While the mere possibility that such a clause might operate in this way may not prevent (*ii*) from being satisfied, it appears that the actual operation of that clause in that way will.

One may note that condition (*c*) was added in 1976, and that where the trust existed on 1st April 1976 and satisfied condition (*a*) and (*b*) condition (*c*)(i) needs only 25 years from that date and (*c*)(ii) is also relaxed.

Employee trusts and newspaper trusts: IHTA 1984, ss. 86 and 87

42: 32 Settled property satisfying the rules in IHTA 1984, ss. 86 and 87 are also favoured. Property held on such trusts is not relevant property. Further, property becoming comprised in such trusts but coming from a discretionary trust and so ceasing to be relevant property is exempt from a charge under IHTA 1984, s. 65.[1] There may, however, be a tapered charge on property when property leaves the trust.[2] In addition, any interest in possession is disregarded if it is less than 5% of the whole.[3]

Foster's Capital Taxes E5.37, 40.
[1] IHTA 1984, s. 75.
[2] IHTA 1984, s. 72.
[3] IHTA 1984, s. 86(4)(*b*).

Funds for maintenance of heritage property

42: 33 These are favoured trusts and there is a charge when property leaves such trusts other than for its favoured purposes: IHTA 1984, Sch. 4, para. 8. The calculation of the rate of tax is not always the same as that outlined in § **42: 25**. The rules distinguish situations in which the property extends the maintenance fund from a discretionary trust from other situations. In the former the relevant period begins on the latest of (i) the last five year anniversary of the discretionary trust, (ii) the day on which the property became relevant property (i.e. entered the discretionary trust), and (iii) 13th March 1975. The rules at § **42: 25** are then applied. However in other situations one takes the higher of two rates. The first rate is similar to that in § **42: 25**, taking the period the property was held on approved maintenance trusts, while the second is the rate that would be charged on the settlor (if he is still alive) or would be charged if it were added to his estate (if he is dead). If the settlor has died lifetime rates are used unless the settlement was made on death. When more than one settlor is involved the Revenue can pick the relevant settlor. There is also provision when the second rate is used and another charge has arisen in the previous ten years.[1]

Where the property went into the maintenance fund on the death of a person entitled to an interest in possession (or is treated as doing so through being so placed within two years of the death of such a person) the rules are now modified.[2] In particular the charge will be based on the cumulated lifetime chargeable transfers of the life tenant rather than the settlor.

Foster's Capital Taxes G5.41–45.
[1] IHTA 1984, Sch. 4, paras. 11–13.
[2] IHTA 1984, Sch. 4, para. 15A added by FA 1987, Sch. 9, para. 3 for occasions of charge falling after 16th March 1987.

Protective trusts

42: 34   Although under Trustee Act 1925, s. 33 a discretionary trust will arise on the bankruptcy of the principal beneficiary and will endure for the remainder of his life, this trust is ignored and his original interest is treated as still subsisting. It follows that sums paid to other objects to the discretionary trust will be treated as transfers by him, but that there will be no charge on the arising of discretionary trust, even though his interest ceases under s. 33. Another consequence is that if on his death, the property devolves on his widow the spouse exemption may apply.[1]

To achieve these results the statute says that "the failure or determination" of the life interests is to be disregarded. This was given a restrictive interpretation in *Cholmondley v IRC*[2] so that one could not disregard property which left the settlement under the exercise of an overriding power and which did not bring about the forfeiture of the life interest.

Foster's Capital Taxes E5.34–36.
[1] IHTA 1984, s. 88; see *Egerton v IRC* [1982] STC 520.
[2] [1986] STC 384; this case is also important as a scheme case. Property was appointed on protective trusts which were ended within 24 hours by the use of the overriding power. Scott J said that there never had been intention to hold the property on protective trusts.

Trusts for disabled people

42: 35   Trusts for disabled persons are treated similarly so that payments to that person are free of tax; moreover a gift by an individual to such a trust has been capable of being a potentially exempt transfer since the beginning of IHT.[1]

43 Special occasions of charge

FUTURE PAYMENTS: IHTA 1984, s. 262

43: 01   Where there is a transfer of value by disposition and payments are to be made or assets transferred by the transferor more than 12 months after the disposition, each payment or transfer is taxed separately. However tax is charged on that fraction of the payment or transfer represented by the fraction A/B where A is the original value transferred (the gift element) and B the total value of the payments made or assets transferred calculated at the time of the disposition.

This provision is more complex than at first appears since it applies only where the assets are transferred by the transferor more than one year after the disposition. Thus it does not apply simply because A sells an asset to B at a figure below market value and B is to pay by instalments—in such a case B may be paying by instalments but B is not making a transfer of value—A is. So the section does apply where A agrees to transfer an asset in stages to B.

> **EXAMPLE**
> A agrees to sell B 10,000 shares worth £60,000 for £18,000,[1] the shares to be transferred in tranches of 2,000 shares over five years.
> Tax will be charged on fraction (60,000 − 18,000)/60,000 = 7/10ths making the transfer in the first year 7/10 × £12,000 or £8,400.
> The importance of this fraction is considerable. By spreading the value over the five years s. 40 may enable A to use his annual £3,000 exemption. On the other hand there may have been intervening transfers having the effect of increasing the rates of tax. However the important point is that this fraction is applied to the value of the shares at the time each transfer is made. So if the shares double in value the chargeable transfer of the next tranche will be 7/10 × £24,000 or £16,800.[2]

The section applies only where the disposition is for a consideration in money or money's worth. It would therefore not apply if A simply made a covenant to transfer the shares over five years.

Foster's Capital Taxes C2.31.
[1] £18,000 might be a single cash payment; if however B agreed to pay £25,000 over 5 years it would be necessary to discount this figure £25,000 and one might again have £18,000.
[2] Note that the fraction does not increase to 8·5/10.

TRANSFERS REPORTED LATE

43: 02   The cumulative principle requires that transfers be correctly and promptly reported. Where a transfer is reported late and in the meantime a later transfer has been taxed, that tax may not have been correctly calculated.

Where there is a seven year gap between the transfers there is no problem owing to the rule that gifts cease to be cumulated after seven years; tax (plus interest) will be due on the unreported transfer at the rates prevailing at the date of the transfer and not at later (and, most probably, lower) rates. Where the gap is less than seven years the earlier transfer used to be treated as taking place after the later one thus putting the extra tax on the earlier transfer. Now a different rule applies; the tax on the earlier transfer is charged as at the rates appropriate to its actual date; the extra tax which should have been collected from the second transfer is then added to the tax charged on the earlier one; interest is charged on the tax which should have been paid on the earlier transfer in the normal way, but interest on the additional tax relating to the later transfer (but charged on the earlier transfer) runs only from six months from discovery of the earlier transfer.[1]

Where there are two unreported transfers the extra tax is apportioned by reference to the values transferred.[2] This rule is modified if tax has been settled in respect of one of the earlier transfers; no further tax is due in respect of the settled transfer but this does not reduce the liability of the unsettled transfer.[3] Provision is also made for the situation in which the transfer is itself an earlier transfer in relation to another later transfer.[4]

EXAMPLE

In November 1984 A made a gift of £10,000 having used his annual exemptions earlier in the year. His cumulative total before making the gift was £80,000 and consisted of chargeable transfers made in August 1983. He fails to report the November 1984 gift.

In June 1989 A makes a chargeable transfer of £78,000 gross.

The IHT paid on the 1989 gift was	
Tax at lifetime rates on £158,000	£8,000
Less tax at lifetime rates on £80,000	nil
	£8,000

Subsequently the November 1984 transfer is discovered. A must pay—

(a) The CTT that should have been paid on the earlier transfer using 1984–85 rates	£1,625
(b) The additional IHT on the June 1989 transfer using 1988–90 rates	2,000

If, instead of making one transfer of £10,000 in 1984, A had made one of £4,000 in May 1981 and one of £6,000 in June 1981, the additional tax of £2,000 would be divided between them in the proportions $\frac{4}{10}$ (£800) and $\frac{6}{10}$ (£1,200).

If the later transfer were in June 1991 instead of June 1989 more than seven years would have elapsed since the 1983 gift. This will not affect A's liability to pay CTT at the 1984–85 rates on the transfer in November 1984 i.e. £1,625. However, the tax, IHT, on the 1991 transfer will be calculated on the basis that A's cumulative total of chargeable transfers was only £10,000. Hence no IHT would be due on the 1991 transfer but A's cumulative total in June 1991 would be £88,000.

Foster's Capital Taxes C2.41, 42.
[1] IHTA 1984, s. 264(6).
[2] IHTA 1984, s. 264(3).
[3] IHTA 1984, s. 264(4).
[4] IHTA 1984, s. 264(5).

CLOSE COMPANIES

43: 03   Although transfers by companies do not generally give rise to IHT an exception is made by IHTA 1984, s. 94(1) for a transfer by a close company; otherwise property could be transferred to a tame company in return for shares only for the company then to give the property to the intended donee.

The value transferred is charged as if each participant had made a transfer of value, an expression which ensures that it cannot be a potentially exempt transfer.[1] The value transferred is apportioned among the participators in the company by reference to their rights immediately before the transfer. The transfer is treated as made by each participator; where that amount is less than 5% of the value transferred it is not cumulated. When the participator is itself a close company sub-apportionments are made until the individual participators are discovered.

The amount apportioned is reduced by the amount by which the value of the participator's estate is increased. In making this calculation the value of his rights in the company is ignored; so the Revenue cannot use any loss in the value of the shares to reduce the increase to his estate.

   EXAMPLE
   X Ltd is valued at £150,000 and is owned equally by A and B. X Ltd gives A £18,000 and B's daughter £24,000. The values transferred are apportioned to A and B equally. Of the £18,000, £9,000 is attributed to B and none to A (as the increase in his estate is set off against it). The £24,000 is attributed equally to A and B and must be grossed up at their respective rates.

For this purpose the corporation tax definition of a close company is adopted supra, § **27: 02** save that it is extended to cover non-resident companies. The definition of participator is also adopted save that loan creditors are ignored.

   [1] IHTA 1984, s. 3A(6) and s. 94(1).

Liability

43: 04   The primary liability rests on the company but those liable to apportionment or to whom the transfer is made are also liable;[1] this secondary liability is limited to the amount apportioned or the increase in value as appropriate. An exception is made in that a person to whom not more than 5% of the value transferred is apportioned is not liable, leaving the company solely liable.

   [1] IHTA 1984, s. 202(1).

Exemptions

43: 05   If there is a transfer of value to a participator's spouse the spouse exemption will apply. Other exemptions available are the participator's annual £3,000 exemption and those for charities, political parties and other public benefit. The small gifts and marriage gifts rules do not apply and potential exemption treatment is not available.

There is also a specific exception for payments that fall to be taken into account in computing the recipient's profits or gains or losses for income or corporation tax[1]—e.g. a dividend.[2] There is also an exception where the person to whom the transfer would be apportioned is domiciled outside the UK and the apportionment is attributable to property situated outside the UK. Further exceptions apply to the surrender of ACT or group relief.

---

[1] Or would do so but for TA 1988, s. 208 (TA 1970, s. 239).
[2] Another example would be where the transfer is caught by CGTA 1979, s. 25 as a transfer at an under-value causing a reduction in the acquisition value of the shares for CGT.

43: 06 In order to prevent over-nice calculation there are further rules where the transfer of value has only a small effect on the value of preference shares; provision is also made for transfers between members of a group or between close companies in both of which the participators has an interest, the purpose here being to get the right value.[1]

---

[1] IHTA 1984, ss. 95–97.

Alteration in share rights

43: 07 Under IHTA 1984, s. 98(1) there is a deemed disposition when there is an alteration to the company's unquoted share or loan capital or any alteration in the rights attached to the unquoted shares or unquoted debentures of the company. Alteration includes extinguishment. The effect is to charge the participators on the value shifted even though nothing emerges from the company; without some such rule wealth could be shifted by juggling share rights. Although IHTA treats this as a disposition, it also makes it clear that this cannot be a potentially exempt transfer.[1] This provision does not apply to alterations in the rights of quoted securities.[2]

The company is not liable for tax under IHTA 1984, s. 98(1).

EXAMPLE

Y Ltd has an issued share capital of 100 ordinary shares of £1 owned equally by C and D; the value of each holding is £40,000. If the company now issues 75 such shares each at par to C's son (CS) and D's daughter (DD) the parents' holdings will drop in value. Suppose the value of each parent's holding after the issue of the new shares is £13,000.

Hence, after the new shares are issued, the position is as follows—

	Holding	*Value*
C	50	£13,000
D	50	13,000
CS	75	27,000
DD	75	27,000
		£80,000

C and D have each made a transfer of value of £40,000 − £13,000 = £27,000.

In order to prevent schemes to reduce tax by removing rights from shares on death it is provided that a decrease in value occurring on death and resulting from an alteration coming within IHTA 1984, s. 98(1) is not to affect the valuation of the shares for the purposes of the transfer on death.

---

[1] IHTA 1984, s. 98(3) added by FA 1986, Sch. 19, para. 20.
[2] On meaning of unquoted see IHTA 1984, s. 272 as amended by FA 1987, Sch. 8, para. 17; securities listed on the USM are now treated as quoted.

Settled property trustees as participators

43: 08   A transfer under IHTA 1984, s. 94 or s. 98 can be apportioned to trustee-participators. In such an event there is a deemed coming to an end of a qualifying interest in possession: the value concerned is that apportioned to the participators less any increase in the value of the settled property (other than the value of rights in the company). Any person who is beneficially entitled to a qualifying interest in possession under the settlement is treated as the participator in place of the trustees.[1]

If there is no qualifying interest in possession, as with a discretionary trust, the trustees are treated as having made a disposition reducing the value of the settled property by a similar amount and so giving rise to an exit charge under IHTA 1984, s. 65.

---

[1] IHTA 1984, ss. 99 and 100 as amended by FA 1987, Sch. 8, para. 3.

Close company as beneficiary

43: 09   Where a close company is entitled to an interest in possession those who are participators in relation to the company are treated as entitled to the interest for all purposes other than in relation to acquired reversions and IHTA 1984, s. 10.[1]

---

[1] IHTA 1984, s. 101(1).

---

44   Exempt transferees

TRANSFERS BETWEEN SPOUSES (IHTA 1984, s. 18)

44: 01   A transfer of value by one spouse is an exempt transfer (*i*) to the extent that the value transferred is attributable to[1] property which becomes comprised in the estate of the other spouse,[2] or (*ii*) so far as the value transferred is not so attributable, to the extent that that estate is increased.[3] The reason for this formulation lies in the wide range of chargeable transfers. (*i*) makes it clear that the transfer is exempt in full even though the loss to the transferor is greater than the benefit to the transferee, as might happen when a husband gave his wife a chair which broke up a set belonging to the husband. (*ii*) is designed to deal with situations in which there would otherwise be a chargeable transfer but no asset becomes the property of the other spouse as where a husband pays his wife's debts or he pays a premium on a life policy belonging to her.

Foster's Capital Taxes B2.01.
 [1] This means that the relief is not confined to the value received by the transferee.
 [2] A problem arises on death since the transfer is treated as taking place immediately before the death and the property does not vest in the beneficiaries (and then retrospectively) until the death; supra, § **40: 02**.
 [3] IHTA 1984, s. 18; this formula is also used in IHTA 1984, s. 3A(1).

Conditions

44: 02   The transfer will only be exempt if it satisfies certain rules.
   (*i*) The disposition by which the transfer of value takes effect must not take effect on the termination after the transfer of any interest or period.[1] The phrase "takes effect" is not defined but presumably means takes effect in possession. So if D left his property to his widow for life with remainder to A, the transfer on D's death to his widow would be free of tax; however if he had left his property to A for life with the remainder to his (D's) widow, the transfer on D's death would not be exempt unless A predeceased D.

Foster's Capital Taxes B2.01.
 [1] IHTA 1984, s. 18(3)(*a*).

44: 03   (*ii*) The exemption does not apply if the disposition by which the property is given depends on a condition which is not satisfied within 12 months after the transfer.[1] A legacy to a surviving spouse conditional on surviving nine months will be exempt under this rule if she survives; if, however, she does not survive, her estate will not be entitled to the survivorship clause exemption supra, § **41: 08** as the period exceeds six months.

Foster's Capital Taxes B2.01.
[1] IHTA 1984, s. 18(3)(*b*).

44: 04   (*iii*) *Reversionary interests.* While the exemption will apply when, on the termination of an interest, the property passes to the previous life tenant's spouse, this is not so if that spouse purchased the reversionary interest for a consideration in money or money's worth.[1] This is to prevent abuse of the relief. For example if A wishes to benefit his son B, he could settle property on himself for life with remainder to B. On A's death there would be a transfer of value under IHTA 1984, s. 52; however if on A's death the property passed to A's widow the transfer would be exempt. If therefore A's widow bought B's remainder, the exemption on A's death would arise. It is true that the sum paid might well be a chargeable transfer but this would be a transfer by the spouse and not by A, and the sum paid by the spouse would reflect the fact that the transfer by A would become exempt. If the life interest ends after 16th March 1987, the exemption will, after all, apply if B *gives* the remainder to A's spouse.[2]

A similar restriction applies in relation to property given in return for a purchased reversionary interest.[3]

Foster's Capital Taxes E3.31.
[1] IHTA 1984, s. 56(2).
[2] F(No. 2)A 1987, Sch. 7, para. 2.
[3] IHTA 1984, s. 56(1); a reversionary interest is purchased if it falls within IHTA 1984, s. 55(1).

Spouses with separate domiciles and transferor spouse domiciled in UK

44: 05   Where, immediately before the transfer, the transferor was domiciled in the UK but the spouse was not, the exemption is limited. Such a transfer is exempt to the extent only that it does not exceed £55,000 less any amount previously taken into account for the purposes of the exemption;[1] once the £55,000 total has been exceeded the exemption is lost. The reason for this restriction is that foreign property will be excluded property in the hands of the transferee—infra, § **49: 13**. Previous transfers are included whenever made; there is no 10 or 7 year cut off period. Originally the value of this exemption moved in line with the threshhold for tax, but it has not been increased since 1982.[2]

EXAMPLE
In December 1977 H, who is domiciled in England and Wales gives W, his wife who is domiciled in the United States, a gift of £10,000. The gift is exempt.
In 1979 H makes a further gift of £20,000. The cumulative total for this exemption is £30,000 and the exemption was then £25,000 so that there is a chargeable transfer of £5,000.
If H makes a further gift of £40,000 in December 1989 the amount of the transfer would be £10,000; this would be a potentially exempt transfer because although the cumulative total for this exemption stood at £70,000 only £25,000 had previously been taken into

account for the exemption leaving £30,000 free to exempt this transfer under this rule leaving the balance of £10,000 as potentially exempt.

Foster's Capital Taxes B2.01.
[1] IHTA 1984, s. 18(2).
[2] FA 1982, s. 92(1), (3) substituted £55,000 with effect for transfers of value made after 8th March 1982.

Spouse

44: 06 The legislation does not find it necessary to define spouse. It is however important to remember that an ex-spouse is not a spouse, that a decree of divorce does not become effective until it is made absolute and that a decree of nullity in relation to a voidable marriage has the same effect as a decree of divorce.[1] On the other hand a void marriage, however innocent the parties, is not a marriage. A polygamous marriage will presumably be recognised. Fiancés are not spouses; however when a man wishes to buy a house before his marriage and to give his future wife a half share he can achieve his object by making her a loan with which she buys her half share and then releasing the debt after marriage.

Foster's Capital Taxes B2.01.
[1] Matrimonial Causes Act 1973, s. 16.

GIFTS FOR PUBLIC PURPOSES

44: 07 This group of exempt transfers covers gifts to charities, to political parties, for the public benefit and for national and similar purposes.

Conditions[1]

44: 08 Such gifts must all satisfy certain conditions designed to prevent abuse of the exemptions given. The first two are the same as for transfers to a spouse.

(1) The disposition must not take effect on the termination after the transfer of value of any interest or period. Unlike the transfer to spouse but for self-evident reasons, there is no relaxation of this condition for a period of survivorship.[2]

(2) The disposition must not depend on a condition which is not satisfied within twelve months of the transfer.[3]

(3) A transfer to these bodies or for these purposes will not be exempt if the disposition is defeasible.[4] Any disposition which has not been defeated twelve months after the transfer and is not defeasible thereafter is treated as indefeasible even though it was defeasible when made or at some time during the twelve month period.[5]

(4) The transfer will not be exempt if the property or any part of it may become applicable for purposes other than charitable purposes or those of a body mentioned in the exemptions; this is to prevent finite charitable trusts.[6]

(5) The transfer will not be exempt if the disposition is of an interest in

property and that interest is less than the donor's or the property is given for a limited period.[7] This question is to be decided as at a time twelve months after the transfer of value. This rule is relaxed to allow the donor to give the benefit of an agreement restricting the use of land which he retains to bodies specified in IHTA 1984, Sch. 3, see infra, § **44: 12**.

> EXAMPLE
>
> If D leaves property by will to A for life with remainder to charity and A dies two years after D, the property will not be exempt from tax on D's death since it breaks both the rules (1) and (5). If A had died after six months the gift would have broken (1) but not (5). Therefore whether A died two years or six months after D's death there is a chargeable transfer on D's death. However, there will be an exempt transfer on A's death.

Foster's Capital Taxes C3.12–15.
¹ IHTA 1984, s. 23(2)(*a*).
² IHTA 1984, s. 23(2)(*b*).
³ IHTA 1984, s. 23(2).
⁴ IHTA 1984, s. 23(2)(*c*).
⁵ IHTA 1984, s. 23(2).
⁶ IHTA 1984, s. 23(5).
⁷ IHTA 1984, s. 23(3).

Settled property, and reserved rights

44: 09   Further rules apply to prevent the avoidance of tax through this relief. The transfer is not exempt if—

(1) the property is an interest in possession in settled property and the settlement does not come to an end in relation to that settled property on the making of the transfer;[1]
(2) the property is land or a building but subject to an interest reserved or created by the donor which entitles him, his spouse or any person connected with him to possession of, or to occupy, the whole or part of the land or building rent free or at a rent less than might be expected to be obtained in a transaction at arm's length between persons not connected with each other,
(3) the property is not land or building and is given subject to an interest reserved or created by the donor other than—
   (*a*) an interest created by him for full consideration in money or money's worth; or
   (*b*) an interest which does not substantially affect the enjoyment of the property by the person or body by whom it is given.[2]

Further a special rule applies to reversionary interests. Where a person or body acquires a reversionary interest in any settled property for a consideration in money or money's worth, this relief does not apply to the property when it becomes the property of that person or body on the termination of the interest to which the reversionary interest is expectant.[3]

The purpose of rule (*i*) is to prevent avoidance through the gift of a life interest in possession. A would create a settlement on himself for life with remainder to his son B and would then assign the life interest to a charity; the charity would then be used as an intermediary and the benefit would pass to B.

Rule (*i*) prevents the transfer to charity from enjoying relief. However if the settlement had been on A for life with remainder to charity the transfer to charity occurring on the ending of A's interest would be exempt. Here however the special rule comes in. If the settlement had originally been on A for life with remainder to B and the charity had bought B's interest, the price naturally reflecting the immunity from IHT that would result on the termination of A's interest, then the exemption is not to apply on that termination.

Rules (*ii*) and (*iii*) are designed to deal with arrangements similar to this covered by (*i*) but which are not technically settlements.

Foster's Capital Taxes C3.13–15.
[1] IHTA 1984, s. 56(3).
[2] IHTA 1984, s. 23(4). These apply to transfers of value made after 15th April 1976 but not to certain payments out of discretionary trusts.
[3] IHTA 1984, s. 56(2).

Charities (IHTA 1984, s. 23)

44: 10   Transfers to charities are exempt transfers. A transfer is to charity if it becomes the property of charities or is held on trust for charitable purposes only.[1]

Foster's Capital Taxes D2.04.
[1] IHTA 1984, s. 23(1) and (6).

Political parties (IHTA 1984, s. 24)

44: 11   Gifts to political parties are now[1] wholly exempt from IHT. If however they were made before 15th March 1988 and on or within one year of death only the first £100,000 was exempt. The burden of any tax fell on the donee exclusively.

Political parties qualify only if at the general election preceding the transfer they secured two seats or one seat and not less than 150,000 votes.[2]

Foster's Capital Taxes B2.03; D2.05.
[1] FA 1988, s. 137, amending IHTA 1984, s. 24.
[2] For a list of qualifying parties see [1988] STI p. 375.

Specified bodies (IHTA 1984, ss. 24A, 25 and Sch. 3)

44: 12   Gifts to certain bodies are exempt whether on death or *inter vivos.* The bodies listed in IHTA 1984, Sch. 3 include the National Gallery, the British Museum, the Historic Buildings and Monuments Commission for England, any local authority, any government department and any university or university college in the UK. Oxford and Cambridge colleges are regarded as being on the list. Gifts of land to a registered housing association are also exempt.[1]

Foster's Capital Taxes B2.03A; D2.06.
[1] IHTA 1984, s. 24A added by FA 1989 *s. 171.* For transfers on or after 14th March 1989.

Property given for public benefit (IHTA 1984, s. 26)

44: 13   Land, buildings, contents of buildings, maintenance funds and any work of art or scientific collection given for the public benefit to a body not established or conducted for profit is exempt from tax if the Treasury agree.

Foster's Capital Taxes D2.07.

PARTLY EXEMPT TRANSFERS—ALLOCATION OF RELIEF

44: 14   Where a transfer includes a gift to a spouse and the transfer is exempt only as to a part of the value whether because the limit of £55,000 is exceeded, because the gifts do not meet the conditions at § **44: 07** in relation to all the property, or because the transfer also contains gifts to others, special rules apply. The purpose of these rules is to ensure that the benefit of the exemption accrues primarily to the gifts which are exempt. These rules do not apply where the transfer is wholly chargeable nor where it is wholly exempt.

These problems will usually arise on death, but may arise on transfers *inter vivos*. Moreover the gifts may be made separately out of separate funds as where A holds free estate of which he is to leave a substantial part to a political party and also holds a life interest in possession in settled property which on his death is to pass at least in part to a political party. Where this occurs the rules which follow are to be applied separately to the gifts taking effect out of each fund, with the necessary adjustments of values and amounts referred to in those provisions.[1]

The practical (i.e. arithmetical) difficulties in this area have been greatly reduced by the advent of a single rate of IHT. However, problems still arise.

Foster's Capital Taxes D2.11.
[1] IHTA 1984, s. 40.

Definitions

44: 15   *Gift* is widely defined and means the benefit of any disposition or any rule of law by which, on the making of a transfer, any property becomes the property of any person or applicable for any purpose or would do so if it were not abated.[1] So the benefit of a disposition *inter vivos*, or by will or on an intestacy all qualify as a gift. A surviving joint tenant obtains the benefit of the rule of law known as the *ius accrescendi* whereby the interest of the deceased joint tenant is extinguished; however the interest of the deceased joint tenant does not "become" the property of the survivor so it is doubtful whether such a transfer comes technically within this definition.

Although these rules use the word gift and require these gifts to be valued they do not state how this valuation is to be carried out. Presumably all must be valued as at the time of the transfer; since the transfer on death is treated as occurring immediately before death any expenses of administration must be left out in valuing the estate as must any gains or losses realised in the course of administration save perhaps in so far as they are the subject of later relief.[2]

Foster's Capital Taxes D2.11.
[1] IHTA 1984, s. 42(1).
[2] Supra, § **44: 13**.

44: 16 *Specific gift.* These rules distinguish gifts of residue, which must necessarily bear their own tax, from other gifts. Gifts which are not of residue or of a share in residue are specific gifts.[1] A liability which is not deductible in computing the value of the estate is treated as a specific gift for this purpose[2] including one not deductible by FA 1986, s. 103. Legal rights in Scotland are also treated as specific gifts.[3]

Foster's Capital Taxes D2.13.
[1] IHTA 1984, s. 42(1) see also *Russell v IRC* [1988] STC 195, [1988] 2 All ER 405.
[2] IHTA 1984, s. 38(6), as amended by FA 1986, Sch. 19, para. 13.
[2] IHTA 1984, s. 42(4).

44: 17 *Bearing its own tax.* A gift bears its own tax if the tax attributable to it falls on the person who becomes entitled to the property given or if the tax is payable out of property applicable for the purposes for which the property given becomes applicable.[1] The direction that the tax must fall on the person suggests that the mere presence of an Inland Revenue charge will not be sufficient to make the gift bear its own tax. The same direction also suggests that if the tax is in fact paid by someone else the gift does not bear its own tax; presumably the draftsman intended to indicate that the tax should fall on the beneficiary rather than on some other part of the estate but this is not what he has said.

Foster's Capital Taxes D2.13–20.
[1] IHTA 1984, s. 42(2).

44: 18 Where the value transferred or part of it is attributable to property which is the subject of two or more gifts and the aggregate value of the property so given is less than the value transferred, the value of each gift is the proportion of the value transferred or part of it which the value of the property given by it bears to the aggregate.[1] So if a 90% share holding is left to two people equally, each is treated as obtaining half the value of a 90% holding—not that of a 45% holding.

Foster's Capital Taxes D2.13–20.
[1] IHTA 1984, s. 42(3).

44: 19 First one must calculate the values which are exempt and so discover both the value of residue and the tax due on the transfer. The major problem is the calculation of the value of specific gifts (IHTA 1984, s. 38). The residue is whatever is left after the valuation of the specific gifts (IHTA 1984, s. 39).

44: 20   *Situation 1.* Where the only gifts are specific gifts which bear their own tax or which are wholly exempt: here a simple rule applies—the face value is taken.

> **EXAMPLE**
>   D who has made chargeable lifetime transfers of £98,000 dies on 1st December 1989 leaving an estate of £150,000 and a legacy of £40,000 to his son on condition that he pays the tax and the residue to his widow.
>   Tax due will be £8,000 being the tax due on a gross transfer on death of £40,000 by one who has already made transfers of £98,000. This tax will fall on the son.

44: 21   *Situation 2.* Where there are specific gifts bearing their own tax and only a *part* of the residue is exempt. Here again life is relatively simple; there is no grossing up.

> **EXAMPLE**
>   D, who has made chargeable lifetime transfers of £98,000 dies on 1st December 1989 leaving an estate of £150,000. He leaves a legacy of £40,000 to his son on condition that he pays the tax and the residue to be divided between his widow and his sister.
>   The value attributable to the legacy to the son is £40,000, the residue is therefore £110,000 and the ½ share in the residue is worth £55,000. Tax is therefore due on £95,000 at death rates for one who has already transferred £98,000 i.e. £30,000. The son will therefore pay 40/95 × £30,000 = £12,631.58 and the sister will pay 55/95 × £30,000 = £17,368.42.

44: 22   *Situation 3.* Where the only gifts with respect to which the transfer might be chargeable are specific gifts which do *not* bear their own tax a grossing up process is carried out. The amount to be attributed to the specific gifts is the aggregate of (*a*) the sum of the value of those gifts and (*b*) the amount of tax chargeable if the value transferred equalled that aggregate.[1] The grossing-up process is thus geared to the tax applicable if the transfer consisted only of these free-of-tax gifts. This grossing up process tends to induce numbing terror; however it is really quite logical once one remembers that one does not usually have to gross up on death and realises that that is what is unusual about it. The purpose of this rule is to ensure that the tax should be the same whether the legacy is at the grossed up figure bearing its own tax or at the net figure but not bearing its own tax.

> **EXAMPLE**
>   D who has made chargeable lifetime transfers of £98,000 dies on 1st December 1989 leaving an estate of £150,000 bequeathing a legacy of £40,000 to his son and the residue to his widow.
>   The calculation requires care since one must gross up from a net figure when all the previous calculations have involved gross figures.
>   The previous cumulative total of £98,000 is equivalent at death rates to £98,000 net as the IHT is nil. D is treated as having made a *net* transfer on death of £40,000 on top of a *net* cumulative total of £98,000.

	Net £	Tax £	Gross £
Previous cumulative total	98,000	0	98,000
Legacy	40,000 (at *net* rates on death)	13,333	53,333
	138,000	13,333	151,333

The grossed up value of the legacy is £53,333 and the tax borne by the estate is £13,333.

Foster's Capital Taxes D2.13–20.
  [1] IHTA 1984, s. 38(3).

44: 23   *Situation 4.* Where the specific gifts not bearing their own tax are not the only gifts with respect to which the transfer is or might be chargeable. This will arise if there is a specific legacy not bearing its own tax and a division of residue between exempt and non-exempt transferees; there may also be other specific gifts some exempt others not. Here the non-exempt specific gifts are grossed up at "the assumed rate" which is[1]—

"(a) the rate found by dividing the assumed amount of tax by that part of the value transferred with respect to which the transfer would be chargeable on the hypothesis that

    (i) the amount corresponding to the value of specific gifts not bearing their own tax [grossed up as in situation 3 above], and

    (ii) the parts of the value transferred attributable to specific gifts and to gifts of residue and shares in residue are determined accordingly; and

"(b) the assumed amount of tax is the amount that would be charged on the value transferred on the hypothesis mentioned in (a)."

EXAMPLE

The facts are as in the previous example save that D leaves one half of the residue to his daughter. If there had been no other taxable gift the grossed up legacy to the son would be £53,333.

This is taken as the initial gross value of the legacy in order to determine the value of the non-exempt share of residue which will be $\frac{1}{2} \times (£150,000 - £53,333) = £48,333$. The total chargeable transfer based on these initial values would be—

Gross legacy	£53,333	(a(i))
Non-exempt residue	48,333	(a(ii))
	£101,666	

The tax which would be chargeable on a transfer of this amount is calculated, to give the assumed rate for the purposes of the revised grossing up of the legacy.

	Gross £	Tax £
Previous cumulative total	98,000	0
Gross transfer on death	101,666	32,666
	199,666	32,666

The assumed rate is 32,666/101,666.

The net legacy of £40,000 is now grossed up at the assumed rate—

$$£40,000 \times \frac{101,666}{101,666 - 32,666} = £58,936$$

The revised gross value of the legacy is higher than the earlier gross value as it reflects the fact that one half of the residue is also chargeable to tax.

The total chargeable transfer on death is re-calculated using the revised gross value of the legacy—

Gross legacy	£58,936
Non-exempt residue	
$\frac{1}{2} \times (£150,000 - £58,936)$	45,532
	£104,468

The actual tax borne by the estate is charged on this amount.

	Gross £	Tax £
Previous cumulative total	98,000	0
Gross transfer on death	104,468	33,787
	202,468	33,787

The tax on the estate is £33,787.

It is possible to create more complex examples where there are (*i*) exempt specific gifts, (*ii*) non-exempt specific gifts bearing their own tax, (*iii*) non-exempt specific gifts not bearing their own tax, (*iv*) exempt shares in residue, and (*v*) non-exempt shares in residue. In such instances the gifts in (*iii*) are first grossed up using the calculation in situation 3, and then all the non-exempt gifts in (*ii*) at probate value, (*iii*) at probate value but as just grossed up, and (*v*), are aggregated to discover the assumed rate. This assumed rate is then again applied to (*iii*) to give the revised grossed up value. It will be seen that both in this example and the worked example the only gift requiring to be grossed up is the non-exempt gift not bearing its own duty and this is done at the assumed rate, which however takes account of the previous grossing up. There are therefore two grossing up steps to be taken. The purpose of the calculation is simply to put a value on the specific gift not bearing its own duty. The assumed rate is not the rate applied to the chargeable portion of the estate.

Foster's Capital Taxes D2.13–20.
[1] IHTA 1984, s. 38(4) and (5).

44: 24   Where two or more specific gifts are exempt but exempt only up to a limit, two rules apply: (*a*) the excess is attributed to gifts not bearing their own tax before gifts which do bear their own tax; and (*b*) subject to rule (*a*) the excess is attributed to the gifts in proportion to their value.[1]

EXAMPLE
B dies on 1st December 1987. He leaves three legacies to political parties as follows—

(*a*) Scottish National Party	£90,000
(*b*) Plaid Cymru	£60,000
(*c*) Mebyon Kernow	£20,000

The residue of his estate he leaves to charity. At the date of B's death Mebyon Kernow does not qualify for the exemption for gifts to political parties under IHTA 1984, s. 24. Legacies (*a*) and (*b*) are exempt up to £100,000 (this limit has been repealed for transfers after 14 March 1988). The tax on each of the legacies is to be borne by the party concerned. The residue is exempt.
The chargeable estate is—

	£
Legacy (*a*)	90,000
Legacy (*b*)	60,000
	150,000
Less exempt	100,000
	50,000
Legacy (*c*)	20,000
	70,000

Since both (*a*) and (*b*) bear their own tax, the excess over the exemption limit must be apportioned between them, so the chargeable amounts of the legacies are—

(*a*) £50,000 × $\frac{90}{150}$	£30,000
(*b*) £50,000 × $\frac{60}{150}$	20,000
(*c*) Wholly chargeable	20,000
	£70,000

Foster's Capital Taxes D2.13–20.
[1] IHTA 1984, s. 38(2).

Abatement

44: 25   Where a gift would be abated owing to an insufficiency of assets but ignoring tax, the gift must be abated before the rules for valuation of specific gifts are applied.[1] Those rules are then applied.

A separate problem arises where the grossing up process in paragraph 19 leads to the value exceeding the total value transferred. Here the gift is to be treated as reduced to the extent necessary to reduce their value to that of the value transferred. The reduction is made in the order in which under the terms of the relevant disposition or any rule of law, it would fall on a distribution of assets.[2]

Foster's Capital Taxes D2.13–20.
[1] IHTA 1984, s. 37(1).
[2] IHTA 1984, s. 37(2).

Burden of tax

44: 26   IHTA 1984, s. 41 lays down that:

"Notwithstanding the terms of any disposition
"(*a*) none of the tax on the value transferred shall fall on any specific gift if or to the extent that the transfer is exempt with regard to the gift; and
"(*b*) none of the tax attributable to the value of the property comprised in residue shall fall on any gift of a share of residue if or to the extent that the transfer is exempt with regard to the gift."

This significant restriction on the testator's freedom of testamentary disposition is clearly needed to prevent the subversion of the policy underlying the preceding rules, as well as to enable the calculations to be carried out. Where therefore there is a non-exempt specific legacy not bearing its own tax, the tax due will not fall on an exempt specific legacy but on residue; it will fall on residue whether the residue is exempt or not. However tax in respect of non-exempt shares in residue must fall on the non-exempt parts.

EXAMPLE

Taking the facts of the example in § **44: 23**, the tax due on the estate was £33,787. The tax attributable to the legacy will be borne equally by the exempt and non-exempt shares of residue; but the tax attributable to the non-exempt share of residue must be borne entirely by that share. Suppose the administration costs of the estate were £2,213. The total residue is—

		£
Estate		150,000
Less		
Legacy	£40,000	
Tax	33,787	
Costs	2,213	76,000
		74,000

The tax attributable to the legacy is considered (see below) to be—

$$\frac{58,936}{104,468} \times £33,787 = £19,061$$

The shares of residue are calculated as follows—

	£	£
Total for distribution	74,000	74,000
Tax on non-exempt share £33,787 − £19,061	14,726	
	88,726	

	£	£
		44,363
Exempt share ½ × £88,726		
Non-exempt share ½ × £88,726	44,363	
Less tax thereon	14,726	29,637
		74,000

Since the tax was charged on the basis of the legacy grossed up at the assumed rate it is to be presumed that the proportion of tax attributable to the legacy will also be calculated on that gross value although this problem is treated with complete disdain by the legislation.

Foster's Capital Taxes D2.19.

Planning

44: 27 Particular care is needed when a part of the property is entitled to a relief such as business or agricultural relief. If such property is left to the exempt person and other property to a chargeable person the benefit of the relief is lost; if the gifts were reversed, the property going to the exempt person would attract no tax while the other gift would be reduced in chargeable value.

Agricultural and business reliefs

44: 28 For transfers after 17th March 1986, statute provides rules for the interaction of the reliefs for agricultural and business property and the rules for partly exempt transfers.[1]

The first rule is that the value of specific gifts of business or agricultural property are to be taken to be their value as reduced by the relevant reliefs.[2] The second rule is more complex and directs that the value of any other specific gifts shall be "the appropriate fraction" of their value.[3] The numerator of the appropriate fraction is the difference between the value transferred and the value of any specific gifts of business or agricultural property as reduced after the application of the first rule and the denominator is the difference between the unreduced value transferred and the value, before the reduction, of property falling within the first rule.[4]

EXAMPLE

D dies leaving a total estate of £600,000. Of this £280,000 is attributable to agricultural property, £120,000 to business property and the rest to other property. He leaves the business property to his son but on terms requiring him to pay the tax concerned, a pecuniary legacy of £100,000 to his widow and the residue to his daughter.

The total value of the estate is £600,000. Of this amount £400,000 is attributable property which is assumed to attract the full 50% reliefs. After applying these reliefs the value transferred is £400,000. The gift to the son falls within the first rule and so the value attributed to it is £60,000.

The gift to the widow is the "appropriate fraction" of their value. The numerator is the value transferred (£400,000) less the property within the first rule (£60,000), giving a figure of £340,000. The denominator is the pre-relief value of the estate (£600,000) less the pre-relief value of the property within the first rule (£120,000) giving a figure of £480,000. The fraction is thus—

$$\frac{340,000}{480,000}$$

and this is applied to the pecuniary legacy of £100,000 to give a figure of £70,833. The consequence is that the part entitled to the spouse exemption is £70,833 and the remainder of the value transferred (£400,000 less £70,833 = £329,167) is chargeable.

In essence what the rule is trying to do is to provide a formula whereby a part of the benefit of the agricultural and business reliefs is attributed to the exempt transfer even though the effect is that the estate loses the value of part of the relief. It will thus no longer be possible to have the chargeable part of the estate reduced by the full amount of the reliefs even though the property goes, or is treated as going, in part, to an exempt beneficiary.

It is further provided that in calculating the value of the specific gift of agricultural or business property any pecuniary legacy which is charged on that property must be deducted before these rules are applied.[5] The pecuniary legacy will then come within the second rule.

Foster's Capital Taxes D2.16A.
[1] IHTA 1984, s. 39A added by FA 1986, s. 105.
[2] IHTA, s. 39A(2).
[3] IHTA, s. 39A(3).
[4] IHTA, s. 39A(4).
[5] IHTA, s. 39A(5).

45 Particular types of property

LIFE POLICIES

General

45: 01 (1) On the death of the life assured, the proceeds of the policy will be payable to the person owning the policy. If that person is the life assured, the proceeds will be paid to his personal representatives, will form part of his estate and so will be the subject of the transfer of value he is deemed to have made immediately before death. Since the value of the policy after death, the proceeds, will be greater than that immediately before death, its then surrender value, the higher value is taken. If that person is not the life assured the proceeds do not form part of the estate of the life assured.

(2) On the death of a beneficial owner of the policy, being a person other than the life assured, the policy will form part of his estate and must be valued at that time.

(3) On an *inter vivos* transfer of the policy the special valuation rule infra, § **45: 03** may apply.

(4) A further new provision is aimed at insurance based IHT unification schemes. In determining the value of a person's estate immediately before his death no account is taken of any liability under or in connection with a life insurance policy made on or after 1st July 1986 unless the whole of the sum assured is part of the estate.[1] So if the deceased made a contract with the company that on his death the company would pay out a sum to a named person in return for a premium to be paid out of his estate on his death, the liability to the company is not deductible.

Foster's Capital Taxes D1.23, 24; D4.22.
[1] FA 1986, s. 103(7).

Premiums as transfers of value

45: 02 Where a life policy has been taken out by the life assured who assigns the policy but pays the premiums, each premium payment will be a transfer of value, being the amount paid in respect of the premiums, grossed up as necessary. There is no provision deeming the transferor to have transferred a proportion of the policy proceeds as opposed to the amount of the premium.

Where a person pays a premium on a policy owned by another, that payment, although a transfer of value, may fall within one of the exemptions, in particular the exemption for normal and reasonable gifts out of income; see § **38: 31**.[1] None of these rules is affected by the 1986 change to IHT. However the rules relating to gifts with reservation and deduction of debts are designed to ensure that the policy proceeds will be included in the donor's estate if any interest is retained in the policy or any benefit enjoyed from it and that if they are not included in the donor's estate any borrowing in connection with the policy is not deductible.

Foster's Capital Taxes C3.04; D1.03.
[1] IHTA 1984, s. 21.

Valuation

45: 03   Where there is a transfer otherwise than on the death of the life assured, the normal market valuation rule would be the surrender value of the policy. However, IHTA 1984, s. 167 provides that there shall be taken instead, if greater than the market value,

> "the total of premiums paid under the policy transferred or earlier policy for which it has been substituted less previous payments under the policy or in consideration of or the surrender of rights under the policy or any earlier policy for which it has been substituted".

Examples of sums which may be deducted are payments under partial surrender and cash bonuses. Such sums will have formed part of the payee's estate and so be taken into account anyway.

The purpose of the rule is to prevent avoidance by the payment of high premiums but on terms which give a low value when transferred *inter vivos*. Its effect is harsh as the net cost is often higher than the surrender value.

This rule applies to life policies and annuity contracts.

> **EXAMPLE**
> A took out a policy on the life of D. Before D died A gave the policy to B having paid £1,200 by way of premiums and received £150 as a cash bonus. The surrender value of the policy at the time of the gift was £750. The value under IHTA 1984, s. 167 is £1,200 − £150 = £1,050.

Exceptions and modifications

45: 04   (1) This rule of valuation does not apply to term assurance policies where the indemnity period exceeds three years and the premiums are paid at normal intervals.[1]

(2) *Unit linked policies.* Where the benefit secured is expressed in units the value of which is published and subject to fluctuation and the payment of each premium secures the allocation of a specified number of units to the policy and the value of the units is less than when they were first allocated to the policy, the reduction is taken into account.[2] Thus any investment loss on these unit-linked policies is to be deducted from the premiums paid in applying the market value or total premium rule of valuation.

(3) The rule does not apply to a transfer on death.

(4) The rule does not apply where the transfer in value does not result in the policy ceasing to be part of his estate.[3] This was introduced to counter avoidance schemes centred on the high value imposed by s. 167. A would

pay a large single premium on a policy which would mature only if he reached say 100 years; he would also take out a policy in favour of B which would mature on A's death before 100 years but which would carry only a small premium. The second policy would contain a clause allowing surrender in return for the premium within seven days—a device which prevented there being a substantial transfer to B. The right would not be exercised; this omission would not give rise to a charge under IHTA 1984, s. 3(3) since the value of the policy was taken to be the premium; on A's death the charge would be limited to the value of the first policy. Effecting the second policy would often be exempt by reason of the smallness of the premium. To counter this s. 167 is excluded so that the drop in value of the policy is brought into charge when the right to surrender lapses.

Foster's Capital Taxes H3.75.
[1] IHTA 1984, s. 167(3).
[2] IHTA 1984, s. 167(4).
[3] IHTA 1984, s. 167(2)(*b*).

Associated operations

45: 05   Annuities on wealthy persons' lives coupled with life assurance policies on those lives in the hands of relatives were long useful in avoiding estate duty. Such devices may fall foul of IHTA 1984, s. 263. This applies in the following terms—

Where—
   (*a*) a policy of life insurance is issued in respect of an insurance made on or after 27th March 1974 or is on or after that date varied or substituted for an earlier policy; and
   (*b*) at the time the insurance is made or at any earlier or later date an annuity on the life of the insured is purchased; and
   (*c*) the benefit of the policy is vested in a person other than the person who purchased the annuity;
then, unless it can be shown that the purchase of the annuity and the making of the insurance (or, as the case may be, the substitution or variation) were not associated operations, the person who purchased the annuity shall be treated as having made a transfer of value by a disposition made at the time the benefit of the policy became so vested (to the exclusion of any transfer of value which, apart from this section, he might have made as a result of the vesting or of the purchase and the vesting being associated operations).

In practice operations will only be regarded as associated if the life policy has been issued on terms different from those which would have applied if the annuity had not been taken out or if there are exceptional circumstances, such as a very short life expectancy whether due to bad health or advanced age or the payer is very old and dies before the second payment is made. In essence the life policy must be issued on normal underwriting terms.

   When the life policy and the annuity are regarded as associated operations, not only will the exemption for normal and reasonable gifts be lost, but the two transfers will be elided and treated as a transfer of the total sums spent by the person purchasing the annuity.

   EXAMPLE
   M, an elderly millionaire on his death-bed, spends his £1m (without having a medical examination) with the L Assurance Co Ltd of the Bahamas on an annuity of £100,000 p.a. for the rest of his life. M could give this annuity to his only son, S, who could then assure

M's life (without a medical examination) with the L Assurance Co Ltd for £960,000 with a first premium payable of £101,000; this could virtually be paid for out of the first annuity payment. If M then died, his estate shortly before his death will have been diminished by the value of the annuity given to S: but this diminution would have been small since the value of the annuity lost by him would have been small in view of his terminal state of health. S would receive £960,000 under the life assurance policy.

M is regarded as making a transfer of value to S. The transfer is treated as taking place when the benefit is so vested, so that the rule cannot be avoided by vesting the benefit of the policy in M who later assigns the policy. It will be seen that the rule does not require that benefit to be vested in that person beneficially.

The value thus transferred is whichever is the lesser of (*a*) the consideration given for the annuity *and* any premium paid or other consideration given for the policy on or before but not after, the transfer (£1,101,000) and (*b*) the value of the greatest benefit capable of being conferred at any time by the policy, calculated as if that time were the date of the transfer (£960,000); by taking the lower figure the legislation recognises the cost to M.

The value of the benefit of the policy is that of the greatest benefit capable of being conferred *at any time* by the policy, so that if the benefit should vary under the terms of the policy, only the highest benefit will be taken; great practical problems arise over the valuation of with profits policies and unit-linked policies. There would appear to be no discounting of that value even though the sum is not payable until a future event, the death of the life assured.

Foster's Capital Taxes C1.15.

BUSINESS PROPERTY

45: 06   A reduced value of as much as 50% is applied to transfers of certain business property provided (*i*) the asset is relevant business property (*ii*) the business is a qualifying business (*iii*) the asset has been held for the minimum period of ownership, and (*iv*) the asset is not an excepted asset. A legacy that can only be satisfied by resort to an identified asset which is subject to business property relief is entitled to this relief.[1] The percentage is applied to the value transferred, not the chargeable transfer and not the property.[2] It is therefore applied before other relief, e.g. for CGT borne by the donee. Where the property is the subject of a chargeable transfer but the donor dies within seven years (so that additional tax may be due) or is the subject of a potentially exempt transfer (so that tax may become due) the benefit of the relief may, in those terms, be clawed back unless further conditions (set out infra, § **45: 11**) are satisfied at the time of the death.

There are six categories of relevant business property:[3]

(*a*) property consisting of a business or interest in a business e.g. reserve funds of a Name at Lloyd's;

(*b*) shares in or securities of a company which (either by themselves or together with other such shares or securities owned by the transferor) gave him control of the company immediately before the transfer;

(*bb*) for transfers on or after 17th March 1987, unquoted shares in a company not falling within (*b*) which (either by themselves or together with other shares or securities owned by him) gave him 25% of the voting power; this category is subject to special conditions considered below;

(c) unquoted shares in a company not falling within (b) or (bb);

(d) any land or building, machinery or plant which, immediately before the transfer, was used wholly or mainly for the purposes of a business carried on by a company of which the transferor then had control or by a partnership of which he was then a partner;

(e) land or buildings used for the purposes of a business carried on by the transferor where the property is settled but the transferor had a beneficial interest in possession at the time of the transfer.[4]

Category (d) is restricted in that it will only qualify if the transferor's interest in the business or shares or securities of the company carrying on the business fulfils the conditions of relevant business property under (a), (b) or (c).[5] Thus category (a) deals with an unincorporated business whether run by a sole trader or a partnership, (b) with a controlling interest in any company, (bb) with a major minority interest in any company, (c) with a minority interest in an unquoted company and (d) with assets held other than by a sole trader. Property within (a), (b) or (bb) qualifies for 50% relief, other property for 30%.

EXAMPLE
On 1st April 1986 A, who has made no previous transfers settles a controlling interest in the family company on trust; this is a chargeable transfer. The interest is valued at £134,000. The 50% relief will reduce the value transferred to £67,000.

The control needed for (b) is defined by reference to voting power; related property and settled property in which the transferor has an interest in possession can be included.[6] Category (bb) was introduced in 1987 and is subject to the condition that the shares should give the transferor control of more than 25% of the votes on all questions concerning the company as a whole.[7] In computing the 25% voting power needed one can include, as one could for (b), any related property[8] and any settled property in which the person has an interest in possession.[9]

The question arises whether category (bb) displaces either (b) or (c). Since (bb) requires only 25% against the 50% needed for (b) it appears, at first sight, to make (b) redundant. This however is not so. For (bb) to apply the transferor must have had the 25% control not only at the time of the transfer but also throughout the preceding two years;[10] this condition does not apply to (b) where it suffices that he meets the general rule that he should have held the property being transferred throughout that period[11]—a rule which applies also to (bb).

EXAMPLE
A had a 20% holding on 1 January 1985. On 1 December 1985 he acquires a 35% holding. In July 1987 A settles a 10% holding on trust. This will fall within (b) but not (bb).

Further, while (b) applies to all shares or securities, (bb) only applies to unquoted shares or securities. This leaves only (b) to apply to shares quoted on the full list of the Stock Exchange but also, since 1987, on the unlisted securities market.[12] Finally, (bb) does not displace (c) since (c) will continue to give 30% relief for unquoted holdings in companies which are below 25% or which fail to meet the condition as to 25% throughout the previous two years.

The relief is designed to alleviate the tax consequences of the transfer of a business. For this reason the transfer of property subject to a binding contract for sale is not relevant business property save where the property is a business or an interest in a business the sale is to a company which is to carry on that business and is made in consideration wholly or mainly of shares or securities in that company.[13] For similar reasons a sale of shares or securities for the purpose of reconstruction or amalgamation is ignored.

While business includes a business carried on in the exercise of a profession or vocation,[14] it does not include a business carried on otherwise than for gain.[15] Further, if the business consists wholly or mainly of dealing in securities, stocks, or shares or land or buildings or the making or holding of investments, it does not qualify for relief. Here however exceptions are made in that the relief will be available where (*i*) the business is that of a jobber[16] (or "market maker") or discount house and is carried on in the UK, and (*ii*) the company is a holding company at least one of whose subsidiaries has a business outside these disqualified areas. Subject to this the business need not be in the UK, nor in manufacturing industry.

Foster's Capital Taxes G1.01–11.
[1] *Russell v IRC* [1988] STC 195, [1988] 2 All ER 405.
[2] IHTA 1984, ss. 103–104; on payment by instalments see infra, § **47: 15**.
[3] IHTA 1984, s. 105(1).
[4] For the previous position see *Fetherstonhaugh v IRC* [1984] STC 261.
[5] IHTA 1984, s. 105(6).
[6] IHTA 1984, s. 269 referring to s. 161.
[7] FA 1987, Sch. 8, paras. 4–7 and IHTA 1984, s. 105(1A).
[8] But not if the related property valuation is undone by IHTA 1984, s. 176—see s. 105(2A).
[9] IHTA 1984, s. 105(1A) referring to s. 161.
[10] IHTA 1984, s. 109A; this is softened where s. 108 or s. 109 enables a shorter period to be taken.
[11] IHTA 1984, s. 106 infra, § **45: 07**.
[12] IHTA 1984, s. 272 as amended by FA 1987, Sch. 8, para. 17.
[13] IHTA 1984, s. 113.
[14] IHTA 1984, s. 105(3). Thus while an adventure in the nature of trade qualifies for relief, casual services taxed under Case VI might not; supra, § **10: 07**. If a strict approach is taken a business whose income is taxed under Schedule A would not qualify; consider also a business which lets land (Schedule A) and supplies services Schedule D, Case I; see [1985] STI, p. 316 (anomaly No. 23).
[15] Ibid, contrast more detailed wording of TA 1988, s. 384 (TA 1970, s. 170); supra, § **5: 13**.
[16] IHTA 1984, s. 105(4)(*a*) referring to TA 1988, s. 737(6) (TA 1970, s. 477(6)); "market maker" is defined in IHTA 1984, s. 105(7) inserted by FA 1986, s. 106.

Period of ownership

45: 07   The property must have been owned by the transferor throughout the two years immediately preceding the transfer.[1] Alternatively it must have replaced other property and it, the other property and any property directly or indirectly replaced by the other property must have been owned by the transferor for periods which together comprised at least two years falling within the five years immediately preceding the transfer of value.[2] For the alternative rule it is further necessary that any replaced property should have fulfilled all the conditions of relevant business property other than the minimum period of ownership. The number of replacements is not limited;

nor is there any need when one business replaces another for the two businesses to be related in any way.

Where the transferor became entitled to the property on the death of another person, the period of his ownership is taken back to the date of death and if the deceased was his spouse he may also use any of the spouse's periods of ownership.[3]

Where property has been replaced and the new property has not been owned for two years, the relief is not to exceed what it would have been had the replacement not been made. This is designed to prevent a person from obtaining relief through death-bed purchases of extra business property. This purpose is achieved by comparing the values at the time the property is replaced, but this is difficult to reconcile with a literal interpretation of the rule. Changes resulting from the formation, alteration or dissolution of a partnership and from the incorporation of a business into a close company are to be ignored for this rule.

Where there is an IHT charge under the gift with reservation rules, on the death of the donor or the cesser of the reservation within seven years of his death, there are special provisions directing that the question whether the property qualifies for business relief is to be determined as if the transfer were one by the donee so far as it is attributable to property comprised in the gift. However, as from 17th March 1987, in determining whether the property qualifies for the 50% relief under (*b*) or (*bb*), the transfer is to be treated as if it were by the donor—so enabling the donor's other holdings (including related and settled property) to be taken into account.[4]

Foster's Capital Taxes G1.13.
[1] IHTA 1984, s. 106.
[2] IHTA 1984, s. 107.
[3] IHTA 1984, s. 108.
[4] FA 1986, Sch. 20, para. 8 as amended by FA 1987, Sch. 8, para. 18; previously the *donee*'s property was considered.

Succession

45: 08   Where A transfers the property to B (T1) and within two years B transfers the property to C (T2) the minimum period of ownership cannot be complied with. However the relief can still be obtained provided:

(*i*) either T1 or T2 was a transfer on death,
(*ii*) the property fulfilled the conditions for relief at T1—including the minimum period of ownership,
(*iii*) the property transferred under T1 had become the property of B or B's spouse,
(*iv*) the property would have been relevant business property but for the minimum period of ownership rule.[1]

Where only a part of the property under T1 qualified for relief whether because some of the assets were excepted assets (infra, § **45: 09**) or there was some replacement element in the T1 transfer only that same part qualifies for relief on T2.

EXAMPLE
In year 5 A who had owned the relevant business property for 5 years sold it to B; the property was then worth £60,000 but the sale was for £20,000. In year 6 B died leaving the property to C, the property then being worth £75,000. Both A and B fulfilled all the conditions for relief apart from the period of B's ownership. The relief is available on B's death.

---

[1] IHTA 1984, s. 109.

Excepted assets

45: 09 Any value attributable to an excepted asset is to be left out of account. This is to prevent private assets from being disguised as business assets. An asset, if not relevant business property by virtue of category (*d*) only, is excepted if it was not either used wholly or mainly for the purposes of the business concerned throughout the whole or the last two years of the relevant period or required at the time of the transfer for future use for those purposes.[1] The relevant period is that immediately preceding the transfer during which the asset was owned by the transferor or his company. An asset which is used wholly or mainly for the personal benefit of the transferor or of any person connected with him is deemed not to be used wholly or mainly for the purposes of the business and so is an excepted asset.[2]

Where the asset is relevant business property by virtue of category (*d*) only, the rule is adjusted to take account of replacements. In order that the property be treated as relevant business property it must be shown that the asset was used wholly or mainly for the purposes of the business concerned throughout the two years immediately preceding the transfer or it replaced another asset so used and the periods of such use together with those of any other assets replaced comprised at least two of the last five years immediately preceding the transfer. It will be seen that assets not so used are not technically excepted assets but rather do not qualify as relevant business property.

Where a part of any land or building is used exclusively for business purposes but the land or building would be an excepted asset, the two parts may be treated as separate assets and the value of the part used exclusively for business will qualify for relief;[3] so a surgery attached to a doctor's home will qualify for relief. However the benefit of this rule does not extend to machinery or plant.

Foster's Capital Taxes G1.19.
[1] IHTA 1984, s. 112.
[2] IHTA 1984, s. 112(6).
[3] IHTA 1984, s. 112(4).

Companies—special rules

45: 10 Where the relevant business property consists of shares in or securities of a company, the transferor must have control of the company to qualify for the 50% relief. Control is determined as for agricultural relief.[1]

With regard to excepted assets, where the company is a member of a group, use by another company within the group is treated as use for the purposes of the business provided the other company was a member of the group both at the time of the use and immediately before the transfer and the other company was not excluded by the next rule.[2]

Where the company is a member of a group and another company in the group has a non-qualifying business, the shares and securities in the company are to be valued as if the non-qualifying company was not a member of the group.[3] An exception is made where the business consists wholly or mainly in the holding of land or buildings wholly or mainly occupied by members of the group with qualifying businesses.

No relief can be given if the company is in liquidation.[4]

Foster's Capital Taxes G1.21–32.
[1] IHTA 1984, s. 269.
[2] IHTA 1984, ss. 112(2) and (5).
[3] IHTA 1984, s. 111.
[4] IHTA 1984, s. 105(5).

45: 11   In the days of CTT the qualification of the property for business property relief was determined exclusively by reference to facts known at the date of the transfer. With the shift to IHT a more complicated regime applies.

Where a donor makes a potentially exempt transfer and dies within seven years, tax will not have been due at the time of the transfer but may become due on the death. Business relief is available on that death only if further conditions are fulfilled as at the date of that death.[1] Similarly, where a chargeable transfer has taken place, additional tax may become due by reason of the transferor's death within seven years; here nothing affects the tax due on the original transfer but the additonal tax now due[2] may be calculated on the basis that business property relief is not available this time.[3] Although it is convenient to refer to this as clawing back the earlier relief, the rule does not take that form. The original tax, if any, remains unaffected; only the additional tax falling due on death may have to be calculated on the basis that the business relief does not apply.

The first condition is that the original property must have been owned by the transferee from the time of the original transfer down to the death of the transferor or, if earlier, that of the transferee.[4] As expressed, this condition is absolute so that even a transfer by way of gift to a spouse, something which in terms of the theory of IHT (and CTT) is meant to be a tax-free event, will bring about the potential loss of the relief. The legislation provides that where the property is settled on trusts with no interest in possession the trustees are to be treated as the owners and transferees.[5] This leaves open the situation in which the property is settled on trusts with an interest in possession although it is thought that the person with the interest in possession will, under the general principles of IHT, be treated as the transferee. Where the property is settled on discretionary trusts and the trustees then appoint that property to someone absolutely, the condition is presumably not satisfied. In determining what is the original property a change of shares on a reorganisation of a company is ignored as is a transfer of a business in exchange for shares.[6]

The second condition supposes a hypothetical transfer by the transferee on the death of the transferor (or, if earlier, the death of the transferee) and requires that the property should be "relevant business property" at that time.[7] It is not necessary that the property should be relevant business property of the same type. Where only a part of the property meets these conditions, relief is available only in part.[8]

This condition is severe. Thus if the gift is of shares in a company which, at the date of the death of the transferor but since the date of the transfer has been admitted to the Unlisted Securities Market (USM) (or, *a fortiori*, the full Stock Exchange) relief would not be available in calculating the tax or additional tax. However this condition is subject to some relaxation in FA 1987. It is now provided that where the transfer is out of a controlling shareholding which was in a quoted company it will suffice that the transferee retains ownership of the property given until the death; it will not be necessary that the property should still be relevant business property at that time.[9] Where the transfer is out of an unquoted holding it will suffice that the transferee retained ownership and the shares remained unquoted.[10]

This condition is relaxed in one other way. In determining whether the property is relevant business property at the time of the notional transfer on the death the condition as to two year's ownership is to be ignored.[11] This presumably refers to the situation in which the transferee dies within two years of the transfer to him.

Since the transferee may legitimately (i.e. for business reasons) wish to replace the actual property given provision is made for the wider problem of replacement property.[12] In essence the property given and the property replacing it must be the subject of arm's length transactions, the whole of the proceeds must be applied in acquiring the replacement property and the replacement must occur within 12 months after the disposal.[13] The conditions are then adapted for the two properties. Provision is also made for the situation in which the transferor dies before the transferee but the transferee has disposed of the property by that time; he is allowed to replace it within 12 months of his disposal.[14] The rules are adapted for the situation in which the transferee predeceases the transferor.[15] They also apply where only part of the property is replaced.

One transitional rule should be noted resulting from the 1987 changes— particularly the shift of USM securities to the category of quoted securities as from 17th March 1987. Where tax or extra tax becomes due in respect of the death within seven years of a transfer made after 17th March 1986 but before 17th March 1987 the 1987 changes are to be disregarded in determining whether the property would be relevant business property.[16]

Foster's Capital Taxes G1.91.

[1] IHTA 1984, s. 113A, added by FA 1986, Sch. 18, para. 14.

[2] This presumably means the additional tax in respect of the transfer of the business property. However, since the effect of withdrawing the benefit of the relief is that the original value has to be increased there may be a knock-on effect on later chargeable transfers so that more tax may be due from them by reason of a higher cumulative total—see Venables *Inheritance Tax Planning* p. 31.

[3] This explains why the additional tax can be greater than the original tax even though the original tax was calculated at lifetime rates whereas the additional tax is charged at 40% or 20% of the death rates in force at the time of the death.

[4] IHTA 1984, s. 113A(3)(*a*) and (4), added by FA 1986, Sch. 19, para. 21.

[5] IHTA 1984, s. 113A(8), added by FA 1986, Sch. 19, para. 21.

⁶ IHTA 1984, s. 113A(6), added by FA 1986, Sch. 19, para. 21; the reorganisation rules are defined by reference to CGTA 1979, ss. 77–86.
⁷ IHTA 1984, s. 113A(3)(*b*) and (4), added by FA 1986, Sch. 19, para. 21.
⁸ IHTA 1984, s. 113A(5).
⁹ A holding in a quoted company can only be relevant business property if the holding gives control.
¹⁰ FA 1987, Sch. 8, para. 8.
¹¹ IHTA 1984, s. 113A(3)(*b*).
¹² IHTA 1984, s. 113B added by FA 1986, Sch. 19, para. 21.
¹³ These rules are much stricter than for rollover relief under CGTA 1979, s. 115; thus no provision is made for the situation in which the replacement property is acquired before the disposal.
¹⁴ IHTA 1984, s. 113B(5).
¹⁵ IHTA 1984, s. 113B(4).
¹⁶ FA 1987, s. 58(3).

AGRICULTURAL PROPERTY

45: 12   A special reduction applies to the agricultural value element in transfers of agricultural property in the UK,¹ the Channel Islands or the Isle of Man. The relief applies also to controlling interests in farming companies.² It applies whether the transfer is *inter vivos*, on death or relates to settled property.

The reduction applies to the agricultural value of the land so there is no reduction for the value attributable to non-agricultural purposes, e.g. land with development value.

Agricultural property is agricultural land or pasture and includes the woodlands (as distinct from the timber) and buildings for intensive fish-farming or livestock-rearing if occupied with such land or pasture; stud farms now qualify.³ Sport is not agriculture.⁴ Such property also includes such cottages, farm buildings and farm houses as are of a character appropriate to the property.

Relief is lost if the transferor has entered into a binding contract of sale at the time of the transfer. An exception is made where this property is being sold to a company which the transfer or controls.⁵

The form of the relief is a reduction in the "transfer of value" and not as previously the chargeable transfer. It does not have to be claimed. The relief is now very similar to that for business property.

Foster's Capital Taxes G3.01.
¹ IHTA 1984, s. 115(1).
² IHTA 1984, s. 122.
³ IHTA 1984, s. 115(4).
⁴ *Earl of Normanton v Giles* [1980] 1 WLR 28.
⁵ IHTA 1984, s. 24.

45: 13   The rate of relief is 50% if the transferor has vacant possession of the property or the right to obtain it within twelve months.¹ Joint tenants and tenants in common satisfy this requirement if the aggregate of their interests carry the right to vacant possession.² The rate is also 50% if the transferor has been beneficially entitled to the interest since before 10th

March 1981 and he would have been entitled to the relief under the pre-1981 rules in FA 1975, Sch. 8 but has no right to vacant possession e.g. the transferor was a "working farmer" but the tenant was an employer or a relative who had occupied the farm since the transferor retired or a transfer to a company which the taxpayer controlled or a partnership of which he was a member. Such a person not only preserves his 50% relief but has previously been able to reduce the value of his estate, without liability, by creating the lease.

In most other instances, e.g. where the transferor is the landlord of tenanted land the reduction is 30%.[3]

The original limits on relief of 1,000 acres and £250,000 value no longer apply.[4]

The reduction applies to the value before the exemptions but before any grossing up;[5] it is excluded by business relief where that applies.

Foster's Capital Taxes G3.02, 04.
[1] IHTA 1984, s. 116(2)(*a*).
[2] IHTA 1984, s. 116(6).
[3] IHTA 1984, s. 116(2)(*b*).
[4] Save where the 50% reduction is claimed under the transitional rule.
[5] IHTA 1984, s. 116(7).

45: 14 Generally a person can claim the 50% transitional relief only if he has held the interest since before 10th March 1981. However he can also make the claim if he succeeded to the property on the death of his spouse on or after 9th March 1981 and that spouse would have been entitled to the relief. He is deemed to have been beneficially entitled to the interest to which his spouse was so entitled. The condition barring the relief if the taxpayer could have obtained vacant possession is applied to both spouses.[1]

[1] IHTA 1984, s. 120(2).

Two conditions

45: 15 To qualify for the relief, whether 50% or 30%, the transferor must either (*i*) have occupied the property for agricultural purposes throughout the last two years; or (*ii*) have owned the land throughout the last seven years provided in this instance that the land has been occupied by himself or another for agricultural purposes.[1] The purpose behind (ii) is to prevent short term investment in land simply for tax purposes.

Foster's Capital Taxes G3.11, 21.
[1] IHTA 1984, s. 117.

45: 16 Various rules apply to determine the period in special cases. Thus if he became entitled to the property on a death his ownership or occupation run from the date of death.[1] If the death was that of a spouse that spouse's ownership or occupation may be taken over.[2] Occupation by a controlled company or by a Scottish partnership is attributed to the controller or partners.[3] It is not necessary that the main business of the company should be farming in the UK.[4]

Where there is an IHT charge under the gift with reservation rules there are special provisions enabling the donee's ownership and occupation to be taken into account for the purposes of agricultural relief on the property subject to the charge.[5] The donor's ownership and occupation are included as if it were the donee's to see if this two year minimum ownership rule is satisfied.

Foster's Capital Taxes G3.11, 21.
[1] IHTA 1984, s. 120(1).
[2] IHTA 1984, s. 120(2).
[3] IHTA 1984, s. 119; on control see IHTA 1984, s. 209 infra, § **47: 16**.
[4] On valuation, see IHTA 1984, s. 122.
[5] FA 1986, Sch. 20, para. 8.

45: 17   Provision is also made for replacement farms so that the ownership or occupation of the previous farm can be counted. Thus the period of occupation is satisfied by including the occupation of a previous farm within the last five years and that of ownership by seven of the last ten years.[1] Where these farms differ in value only the lowest agricultural value qualifies, although special rules apply to partnership changes.

Foster's Capital Taxes G3.13, 22.
[1] IHTA 1984, s. 118(1).

45: 18   Provision is also made for relief where the conditions as to length of occupation or ownership are not satisfied but the farm was acquired on a previous transfer which did qualify for relief. It is further necessary that it should be only these conditions which prevent relief on this occasion and that one of the transfers should be on death.[1] Provision is made for the replacement of property between the two transfers; as with the general replacement rule relief is restricted to the lower of the agricultural values of the replaced and present farms.[2] Where on the previous transfer only a part of the value qualified for relief as where the earlier transfer was a part purchase, only a like part can be reduced on the present transfer.[3]

Foster's Capital Taxes G3.14, 15, 23, 24.
[1] IHTA 1984, s. 121.
[2] IHTA 1984, s. 121(2).
[3] IHTA 1984, s. 121(3).

45: 19   Where a donor makes a potentially exempt transfer and dies within seven years, tax may become due; similarly where a chargeable transfer takes place, additional tax may become due by reason of a prior potentially exempt transfer which has become chargeable. The problem—and the legislative solution—is the same as that for business relief see supra, § **45: 11**.

As with business relief the first condition is that the original property transferred must be owned by the transferee from the time of the transfer down to the death of the transferor or the earlier death of the transferee.[1]

There is a similar definition of transferee which provides that where property is settled on trusts in which there is no interest in possession the trustees are to be treated as the transferee.[2] One presumes that where the property is settled on trusts which give a person a beneficial interest in possession that person is the transferee. The condition means that a gift to a spouse results in loss of relief.

The second condition is that the original property should be agricultural property immediately before the death (of the transferor or, if earlier, that of the transferee) and should have been occupied by the transferee (or another) for the purpose of agriculture throughout the relevant period.[3] This condition is obviously inapplicable where the original property consists of shares in a farming company and so in this instance it will suffice that the company owned the land and the farm was occupied for the purposes of agriculture throughout the period.[4]

The insistence on the property being the original property is relaxed where there has been a reorganisation of share capital or where the property held at the date of the death consists of shares for which the original property was exchanged.[5] In the 1986 version the shares were to be treated as if they were the original property; this was not effective and so in 1987 the wording was amended to provide that ownership of the shares is deemed to be that of the original agricultural land—as from 17th March 1987.

As with business relief there is a further section to cover the situation in which the agricultural property is replaced.[7] As with the other relief the rule can apply only where both the disposal of the original property and the acquisition of the replacement are made in a bargain at arm's length or on such terms as would be contained in such a bargain.[8] The time limit of twelve months is also the same. The conditions for the relief are then applied to the original and replacement property so that the transferee must have owned the original property down to the date of the disposal and the replacement as from the date of the acquisition. The properties must have been occupied for purposes of agriculture during these times and the replacement property must be agricultural property immediately before the death.[9] The rules are also adapted where the transferor dies before the transferee but the replacement process is not then complete as the new property has not yet been acquired by the transferee.[10]

---

[1] IHTA 1984, s. 124A(3)(*a*) and (4).
[2] IHTA 1984, s. 124A(8).
[3] IHTA 1984, s. 124A(3)(*b*).
[4] IHTA 1984, s. 124A(3)(*c*).
[5] IHTA 1984, s. 124A(6).
[6] FA 1987, Sch. 8, para. 9, amending FA 1986, s. 124A(6) as from 17th March 1987.
[7] IHTA 1984, s. 124B.
[8] IHTA 1984, s. 124B(2).
[9] IHTA 1984, s. 124B(3).
[10] IHTA 1984, s. 124B(5).

WORKS OF ART AND OTHER HERITAGE PROPERTY

45: 20   Two quite distinct exemptions apply:
   (1) Transfers of certain objects or land to approved non-profit making bodies[1] or to the Revenue in satisfaction of tax are exempt transfers.[2]

(2) When the transfer of value is of a "designated" object and certain undertakings are given to the Treasury, the transfer may be treated as conditionally exempt.[3]

Conditional exemption is given to (*i*) any transfer on death and (*ii*) any other transfer of value provided

(*a*) the transferor or his spouse, or the transferor and his spouse between them, have been beneficially entitled to the property throughout the six years ending with the transfer; or

(*b*) the transferor acquired the property on death and the property was then the subject of a conditionally exempt transfer.[4]

In the case of a potentially exempt transfer of heritage property, no claim for conditional exemption can be made until the death of the transferor, and no claim at all can be made if the property has been sold before then.[5] However, if the property has, between the transfer and the death, been sold by private treaty or given to an exempt public body specified in IHTA 1984, Sch. 3, or transferred to the Government in satisfaction of IHT under IHTA 1984, s. 230, the transfer becomes exempt.[6]

A similar exemption applies where there is an occasion giving rise to tax in relation to property held on discretionary trusts.[7] Exemption may be claimed both in respect of the ten year charge[8] and the exit charge under IHTA 1984, s. 65. Exemption from the ten year charge is complete if there was a conditionally exempt transfer of the asset or a capital gains tax roll-over on or before the occasion on which it became settled. In other situations a subsequent chargeable event gives rise to a charge similar to that outlined at § **42: 27** where privileged tax treatment of favoured discretionary trust ceases.[9] If the trustees buy a "designated object" it enters the cumulative hypothetical total for IHTA 1984, s. 66(5).[10]

Foster's Capital Taxes G5.11; K1.22.

[1] IHTA 1984, s. 26.
[2] IHTA 1984, s. 230. On present problems see [1985] STI, p. 175.
[3] For post 1976 transfers see IHTA 1984, s. 30; on transitional rules see IHTA 1984, s. 35. The conditional exemption will yield to the general spousal exemption where applicable.
[4] IHTA 1984, s. 30(3).
[5] IHTA 1984, ss. 3A to 3C added by FA 1986, Sch. 19, para. 7.
[6] IHTA 1984, s. 26A added by FA 1986, Sch. 19, para. 6.
[7] IHTA 1984, s. 78.
[8] IHTA 1984, s. 79.
[9] IHTA 1984, s. 79(3)–(8).
[10] IHTA 1984, s. 79(9), (10).

Designated objects

45: 21   The exemption from IHT is conferred in respect of pictures, prints, books, manuscripts, works of art or scientific collections or other things not yielding income appearing to the Treasury to be of national, scientific, historic or artistic interest.[1] National interest includes interest within any part of the UK.[2] When the thing so appears to the Treasury it is designated by the Treasury.

Undertakings must be given to keep the object permanently in the UK (save for a purpose and a period approved by the Treasury), and to take reasonable steps for its preservation and to give reasonable facilities for its examination to make sure that it is being preserved, or for purposes of research, by persons approved by the Treasury, although the Treasury may here allow a reasonable degree of confidentiality.

The exemption is conditional in that a charge will arise if the Treasury are satisfied that the undertakings are broken in a material respect,[3] or if the object is disposed of, whether by sale or otherwise or on death. Presumably the word disposal receives its ordinary meaning and does not extend to situations where there is a deemed disposal for CGT, as where the object is accidentally destroyed by fire and insurance proceeds are received.[4] The case of deliberate destruction seems less clear.

A disposal will not cause a charge if the object is sold by private treaty to a public body listed in IHTA 1984, Sch. 3 (supra, § **44: 11**[5]) or if it is disposed of otherwise than by sale and fresh undertakings are accepted.[6] Acceptance of the object by way of payment of tax likewise causes no charge.[7]

Foster's Capital Taxes G5.12.
[1] IHTA 1984, s. 31.
[2] IHTA 1984, s. 31(5).
[3] IHTA 1984, s. 32; the burden of the tax is governed by IHTA 1984, s. 207.
[4] CGTA 1979, ss. 20–22.
[5] IHTA 1984, s. 32(4).
[6] IHTA 1984, s. 32(5).
[7] IHTA 1984, ss. 32(4) and 230.

Land

45: 22 Conditional exemption is also provided for land.[1] The land must be of outstanding scenic or historic interest, or adjoin a building of outstanding historic or architectural interest. In relation to events after 19th March 1985 the latter category is widened to include land which, although not adjoining the building, is nonetheless essential for the protection of the character and amenities of the building.[2] The exemption is conditional on undertakings being given.[3] The conditions relate to the maintenance of the land, the preservation of its character, the repair and preservation of other property and keeping objects associated with a building with the building concerned and to reasonable access for the public. The only significant difference seems to be that a chargeable event with regard to a part of the property is treated as a chargeable event relating to the whole and any associated property unless the Treasury otherwise directs.

Foster's Capital Taxes G5.11, 12; K1.22.
[1] IHTA 1984, s. 31(1)(*b*)–(*e*).
[2] FA 1985, s. 94, Sch. 26.
[3] IHTA 1984, s. 31(4).

The charge

45: 23 When a chargeable event occurs and the conditional exemption ceases, tax is charged on an amount equal to the value of the property at the time of the chargeable event.[1] The value will be measured by the sale proceeds or market value as appropriate.[2]

The tax is calculated by reference to the circumstances of the "relevant person". This will be the person who made the last conditionally exempt transfer, save that where there have been two or more such transfers within the last thirty years, the Revenue may select whichever of the transferors they choose.[3] For these purposes the Revenue may not go back beyond a chargeable event.[4]

> EXAMPLE
> A makes a conditionally exempt transfer to B in 1978.
> B makes a conditionally exempt transfer to Y (A's son) in 1983.
> Y gives the property to Z, his son, in 1985. At the time of the transfer in 1985, A has a cumulative total of £130,000 and B has a cumulative total of £40,000. The Revenue are entitled to select A as the relevant person and charge tax at the rate appropriate to his cumulative total of chargeable transfers.

The rate of tax is, if the relevant person is still alive, the lifetime rate. The tax is calculated as on a transfer made by the relevant person at the time of the chargeable event.[5] If the relevant person has died, tax is charged as if it had been added to the value transferred on his death and had formed the highest part of that value.[6] The lifetime rate is used even where the transfer was within three years of the death; the death rates are used if the transfer was on death.[7]

> EXAMPLE
> C makes conditionally exempt lifetime transfers to P and Q.
> P makes a conditionally exempt lifetime transfer to V.
> C dies; his cumulative total of chargeable transfers (including the value of his estate immediately before his death) is £155,000.
> On 22nd April 1988 Q sells his property for £65,000 and this is a chargeable event (event 1). The rate of tax is 20% (the lifetime rate on the top £65,000 slice of an estate of £220,000 (£155,000+£65,000).
> On 3rd December 1988 V sells his property for £30,000 and this is a chargeable event (event 2). C is nominated as relevant person. The rate of tax is 20% (the lifetime rate on the top £30,000 slice of an estate of £250,000.

It should be emphasised that the only function of the relevant person is the calculation of tax. He is not liable for the tax.

Where the asset is transferred in circumstances which do not qualify for conditional exemption, it may well happen that not only will tax be due but also that the conditional exemption on the previous transfer will be lost so that two lots of tax are due. In such cases the tax on the present transfer is available as a credit against the tax due in respect of the earlier transfer; this is a credit of tax against tax. If the chargeable transfer is not a chargeable event, the tax paid will be available as a credit against liability when the conditional exemption is lost.[8]

There are similar arrangements for crediting the tax on a chargeable event against the tax on a potentially exempt transfer which becomes chargeable and which was made after the conditionally exempt transfer to which the chargeable event relates.[9]

Foster's Capital Taxes G5.13, 14; K1.22.
  [1] IHTA 1984, s. 33(1)(a) on calculation of estate duty clawback charge see SP 11/84 Press Release 3rd May 1984, STI 1984, p. 359 and 1987, p. 518.
  [2] IHTA 1984, s. 33(3).

³ IHTA 1984, s. 33(5); the object is to prevent the use of a man of straw to make the fateful transfer.
⁴ IHTA 1984, s. 33(6).
⁵ IHTA 1984, s. 33(1)(*b*)(i).
⁶ IHTA 1984, s. 33(1)(*b*)(ii).
⁷ IHTA 1984, s. 33(2).
⁸ IHTA 1984, s. 33(7).
⁹ IHTA 1984, s. 33(8).

The transferor's cumulative total

45: 24 Where there has been a chargeable event so that the conditional exemption is lost, the cumulative total of the person making that conditionally exempt disposal is adjusted; this is done whether or not he is the relevant transferor. If he is still alive the amount chargeable is added to his total as at the time of the chargeable event and so affects rates of tax on chargeable transfers made after that event.[1]

If however he has died and he is the relevant transferor and is so in relation to more than one chargeable event, the amounts liable to IHT are added to the value of the estate in chronological order.[2]

A special rule applies to settlements. If within the previous five years the property was comprised in a settlement made within the previous 30 years, and the person who made the last conditionally exempt transfer is not the relevant transferor, the previous rules are applied to the estate of the *settlor* if he made a conditionally exempt transfer of the property within the thirty years.[3] Thus suppose that in year 1 S settled property on A for life, remainder to B and that the transfer was conditionally exempt as was the transfer on A's death in year 21. If in year 25 a chargeable event occurs, the Revenue may select S as the relevant transferor and can alter *his* total. The total of the person who made the last conditionally exempt transfer is not affected where this rule applies. For this rule any conditionally exempt transfer by the settlor prior to a chargeable event relating to the property is ignored as are transfers prior to an event which is declared not to be a chargeable event because it is a disposal to an approved body or in payment of tax.[4]

If a chargeable event follows "a conditionally exempt occasion", the relevant person is the settlor or, if more than one, whichever the Board selects.[5] The rule assumes a further transfer by that person; the sum is added to his cumulative total if he is still alive; otherwise it is added to his estate. Death rates are used only if the trust was established by his will. The rate is then reduced to 30% if there has been no ten year anniversaries while the asset was comprised in the settlement and to 60% if there had been just one.

Foster's Capital Taxes G5.15.
¹ IHTA 1984, s. 34(1).
² IHTA 1984, s. 34(2).
³ IHTA 1984, s. 34(3).
⁴ IHTA 1984, s. 34(4).
⁵ IHTA 1984, ss. 33(5), (6), 78(3).

Maintenance funds for historic buildings, etc.

45: 25 Special rules apply also to funds set up for the maintenance of these types of property. Broadly such funds are exempt from income tax, CGT and

IHT. Transfers to such funds are exempt transfers.[1] After an initial six year period the asset may be returned to the settlor or applied for non approved purposes but should this occur there will be a charge to income tax and capital gains tax designed to put the settlor back in the tax position he would have been if he had simply maintained the property out of his new post tax income.[2] There is also a charge to IHT[3] see infra, § **42: 33**.

These reliefs are extended by FA 1987. For deaths of a person with an interest in possession in settled property after 16th March 1987 relief will be available for any property going into a maintenance fund within two years of the death; this period is extended to three years if a court order is needed, e.g. under the Variation of Trusts Act 1958.[4]

Foster's Capital Taxes G5.41–43.
[1] IHTA 1984, s. 27.
[2] IHTA 1984, s. 77 and Sch. 4, FA 1980 s. 82 (CGT) and FA 1977, s. 38 and TA 1988, s. 694 (FA 1980, s. 52) (income tax).
[3] IHTA 1984, Sch. 4, paras. 16–18.
[4] IHTA 1984, s. 57(A), introduced by FA 1987, Sch. 9, para. 1.

TIMBER[1]

45: 26 A special relief is available in respect of growing timber if certain conditions are satisfied, the person liable so elects[2] and the value is transferred on death. Tax may be deferred until the timber is disposed of or until the value is transferred on another death. In the former case the tax becomes due on the net proceeds or value. In the latter case no IHT will ever become due in respect of the first death. It does not apply to *inter vivos* transfers, nor to land outside the UK. The relief applies to the timber and not to the land.

The deceased must have been beneficially entitled to the land or to an interest in possession in the land[3] throughout the five years immediately preceding his death *or* became beneficially entitled to it otherwise than for consideration in money or money's worth. Hence, one who inherits timber land and dies after only three years of beneficial entitlement may use the relief, but one who buys may not. This condition is aimed at deathbed purchases of timber. Beneficial ownership of shares in a company which is entitled to possession of the land does not suffice.[4]

The refusal to extend this treatment to *inter vivos* transfers or to discretionary trusts seems odd.

Foster's Capital Taxes G4.01–03, 07.
[1] IHTA 1984, s. 125.
[2] *Semble* that he can elect for different areas of woodland.
[3] IHTA 1984, s. 49(1).
[4] However this may qualify for agricultural or business relief IHTA 1984, ss. 115(2), 103, see also IHTA 1984, s. 127(2).

The relief

45: 27 The relief provided is that the value of the timber may be left out of account in determining the value transferred on death if the person liable so elects within two years of death or such longer period as the Board may allow.[1] The relief applies only to the trees or underwood; it does not apply to the value of the land itself which however may qualify for agricultural or business relief.

Where the person liable has elected to take the relief, the tax will nonetheless become payable if the timber should be disposed of before the next death, whether by sale for full consideration or not. Since the tax has merely been deferred since death, the tax will become payable on a subsequent disposal whether or not that disposal is itself a chargeable transfer. The only exception is that a disposal by a person to his spouse will not cause the provisional exemption to be lost.[2]

Where the disposal is itself a chargeable transfer so that two sets of liability to tax will arise, the first by reference to the previous death, the second by reference to the disposal, it is provided that in computing the value transferred on the second transfer a deduction is made for the tax chargeable on the first.[3] The deduction is simply in valuing the transfer. It is not a credit of tax against tax. Where the second transfer is an occasion for business relief, the reduction under that relief is applied to the value as reduced by the tax paid in respect of the first death.[4]

This regime for timber is still highly favourable but not as favourable as that under estate duty. Under that tax the value of the timber was excluded from the estate and the proceeds of sale of the timber were taxed at the rate which had applied to the estate; this was the basis upon which the proceeds were charged until the next death when the process would be resumed using the new deceased person's estate rate. Where a person died under the estate duty regime this option was preserved notwithstanding the introduction of CTT; however it was provided that the period during which this potential charge to tax was calculated on this basis should end not only on the death of that person but on any prior chargeable transfer.[5] This remains the case with the rider that such a transfer after 30th June 1986 is not to be treated as a potentially exempt transfer.[6]

Foster's Capital Taxes G4.02.
  [1] IHTA 1984, s. 125(1).
  [2] IHTA 1984, s. 126.
  [3] IHTA 1984, s. 127.
  [4] IHTA 1984, s. 114(2).
  [5] FA 1975, s. 49(4).
  [6] FA 1986, Sch. 19, para. 46.

45: 28   If the timber is sold for full consideration in money or money's worth, tax becomes payable on the net proceeds of sale. The person exclusively liable is the person who is or would be entitled to the proceeds. In any case other than sale for full consideration in money or money's worth, tax is payable on the net value of the trees or underwood valued at the time of the chargeable event, not the date of death;[1] however plantings since the death are ignored.[2] It will be seen that the tax payable is tax; any liability to income tax under Schedule D, Case I or Schedule B is quite irrelevant. The proceeds are therefore aggregated with the rest of the property transferred on the previous death. There is however no retrospective increase in the amount of tax payable in respect of all the other items in the estate, the whole burden of the marginal rate of tax thus falling on the timber. It will also be seen that the proceeds caught are the *net* proceeds of sale or the *net* value. For the net proceeds of sale one must deduct from the proceeds certain expenses, namely those incurred in the disposal, in replanting within three years or such longer time as the Board may allow,[3] and in replanting to replace earlier disposals so far as not allowable on those previous disposals.[4] These deductions however are not allowed if they are allowable for income tax, a phrase which presumably means theoretically allowable, and so excludes deduction for IHT whether or not there is sufficient income to absorb its expense. The net value is the value of the timber after allowing for these deductions.

When rates of IHT change the tax is charged at the death rates prevailing at the time of the sale;[5] it may be inferred that this is because it is presumed that the increase in rates simply reflects the change in values due to inflation, a presumption that is usually quite untrue.

EXAMPLE

D made inter vivos chargeable transfers of £90,000 and left E his entire estate which, after omitting the timber, came to £100,000. After D's death E sold one parcel for £5,000 on 2nd May 1988 and another for £15,000 on 1st July 1989 these being the net proceeds of sale. IHT is due at 40% on the disposals, so that the tax will be £2,000 and £6,000 respectively.

If E had given the second parcel, still worth £15,000 to his son, F, this would again trigger IHT liability of £6,000 as regards D's death. However the tax is deducted to leave £9,000 as the value of the property in calculating such tax as might arise on the potentially exempt transfer to F if E should die within seven years.

Foster's Capital Taxes G4.04–06.
[1] IHTA 1984, s. 130.
[2] IHTA 1984, s. 126(1).
[3] This power is needed because planning permission can take substantially more than three years.
[4] IHTA 1984, s. 128.
[5] IHTA 1984, Sch. 2, para. 4.

Scottish agricultural tenancies

45: 29   Prior to 1981 the value of a person's estate immediately before his death was increased by the value of any interest in agricultural property in Scotland which was an interest held by virtue of Tacit Relocation. FA 1981, s. 99 and Sch. 15 were introduced with the intention of relieving property held in his manner by leaving it out of account in determining the value transferred on death. The provisions were not wholly successful and have been re-enacted.[1] Scottish agricultural property held by virtue of tacit relocation is now left out of account in determining the value transferred on death if the deceased had been a tenant for at least two years before his death or had acquired the tenancy by succession. The value left out of account is not to include any rights in respect of compensation for tenants' improvements.[2]

Foster's Capital Taxes G3.61–69.
[1] IHTA 1984, s. 177.
[2] IHTA 1984, s. 177(4).

46 Valuation

46: 01   Where property has to be valued the general rule is that the value is the price which it might reasonably be expected to fetch if sold on the open market[1] at the relevant time; the costs of such a sale are ignored. The price is not to be reduced on the ground that the whole property is placed on the market at the same time.

This rule means that a higher value may be placed on the property than could be obtained if it were sold in the open market. Thus if the whole property is placed on the market at the same time and the transferor's son pays the full market price for the property bearing in mind that it is in fact lower than the IHT value because if the whole property being sold at one time, the value of the property transferred will be greater than the price which he paid for it. In such a case since the sale will be one which might be expected to be made in a transaction between persons not connected with each. Such sales may save tax since there is no transfer of value so long as he pays that price.[2]

Foster's Capital Taxes H2.01.
   [1] IHTA 1984, s. 160.
   [2] IHTA 1984, s. 10. However if he pays less than the full market price, the amount chargeable will not be the amount by which it falls short of that amount but that by which it falls short of the value assuming that it was not sold in one lot.

EFFECTS OF SALE

46: 02   The price realised on a sale of property in the open market after a transfer provides some evidence of the value of that property at the time of the transfer. In the absence of special circumstances, either the Board or the accountable parties may require the valuation to be adjusted to the sale price, if the sale takes place reasonably soon, say up to two years, after the transfer.

Relief may be claimed when the transfer was on death, the property consisted of shares (§ **46: 10**) or land (§ **46: 14**) and the sale was within three years and at a lower value.

THE SPECIAL PURCHASER

46: 03   In computing market value it would seem that account is to be taken of the possibility of an offer from any person who may be specially interested in the purchase of the property.[1] The true value lies somewhat between normal market value and the highest price which the special purchaser would pay.

The problem of the special purchaser frequently arises in the case of shares in a private company. The other shareholders may be particularly anxious to acquire the deceased's shares, in order to prevent them going to the public or to strangers.

In one case of shares in a private company decided by the House of Lords,[2] the argument that a higher valuation should be put on the shares because they were a kind of investment which was particularly attractive to a trust corporation was rejected by at least one of the law lords. But this decision cannot be treated as a binding authority for the view that the existence of a special purchaser should be disregarded, because in that particular case restrictions in the company's articles would have discouraged an acquisition by a trust corporation.

Foster's Capital Taxes H2.04, 08.

[1] *IRC v Clay, IRC v Buchanan* [1914] 3 K B 466 (an increment duty case). *Glass v IRC* 1915 SC 449.

[2] *IRC v Crossman, IRC v Mann* [1937] AC 26, [1936] 1 All ER 762.

RESTRICTIONS ON SALE

46: 04   The fact that the property cannot be sold, or can be sold only to certain persons or at a certain price, or otherwise subject to restrictions, does not preclude the finding of an open market value. The value has to be found on the assumption that the property can be offered freely in the market. Nevertheless, the effect of any restrictions on sale, if they will persist when the property reaches other hands, is not nugatory. The value is to be found on the assumption that the purchaser, buying freely in the market, will be subject, after he has become the purchaser, to the same restrictions on sale as those affecting the vendor.[1] Accordingly, the market price, although found on the assumption of a free market, will be lower than it would have been had no restrictions existed. Although this view has been widely held, it has been denied recently by the Revenue where the property concerned was a lease containing a covenant against assignment. The Revenue position, which requires the covenant to be disregarded and the asset to be treated as simply any other assignable leasehold, seems to be wrong,[2] but future legislation will no doubt confirm the matter.

Foster's Capital Taxes H2.03.

[1] *IRC v Crossman, IRC v Mann* [1937] AC 26, [1936] 1 All ER 762; *Lynall v IRC* [1971] 3 All ER 914, 47 TC 375.

[2] There is no question of IHTA 1984, s. 163 applying.

46: 05 The rule that one must take account of a restriction on the right to dispose of the property could provide an easy way of saving tax. A restriction would be created by contract, the value of the property would fall and on a subsequent transfer only the reduced value would be transferred. To counter this it is provided that where a restriction or exclusion has been placed upon the right to dispose, then on the occasion of the next relevant event, i.e. chargeable transfer of the property, that restriction or exclusion is to be taken into account only to the extent that consideration in money or money's worth was given for it.[1]

EXAMPLE
A grants B an option to buy Blackacre for £40,000 at any time in the next three years, its then market value. After two years when Blackacre's value ignoring the option is £80,000 A gives the land to B.
In calculating the value transferred when A gives the land to B the option is to be taken into account only to the value of the consideration given. If B paid £4,000, the then market value of the option, the value of Blackacre would be reduced to £76,000.
It will be seen that the option is ignored only on the next chargeable transfer, so if A had given the land to C the option would have been taken into account only to this limited extent. If C later gave the land to D the option would now be taken into account in full.
If the next transfer is not a chargeable one, e.g. because A gives the land to Mrs A, the rule would still apply to the next chargeable transfer of the land by Mrs A.

It will be seen that this rule applies even though the option is granted for full consideration. In effect the issue of whether or not there is a chargeable transfer and if so its extent is left in suspense until the next chargeable transfer.

Where the grant of the option is itself a chargeable transfer of value, a different rule applies—to avoid a double charge. An allowance is to be made on the next chargeable transfer for the value already transferred, ignoring any grossing up, or for so much of it as is attributable to the restriction.

EXAMPLE
P grants Q an option to buy Whiteacre at any time in the next three years for £50,000 its current market value. If Q paid nothing for the option which had a value of £5,000 that sum perhaps grossed up would have been chargeable on that occasion. If P later gave the land to Q when it was worth £90,000 there would be a deduction for the £5,000, making the value of the property £85,000. This would be so whether the original £5,000 were grossed up or were reduced by the annual exemption.

Foster's Capital Taxes H2.31.
[1] IHTA 1984, s. 163.

RELATED PROPERTY

46: 06 Where (*a*) there is a transfer of property and (*b*) other property is related to it, and (*c*) the value of the property transferred is less than the value of the "appropriate portion" of that plus the related property, the value of the property transferred is that portion.[1] In determining the appropriate portion, the general rule is that the value of each property is taken as if it did not form part of the aggregate; however this rule does not affect the calculation of the aggregate value.[2] Where shares of the same class are concerned, the appropriate proportion will be found by taking simply the number of shares.[3]

Foster's Capital Taxes H2.41.
[1] IHTA 1984, s. 161.
[2] IHTA 1984, s. 161(3); this is not crystal clear, but is (undoubtedly) the official view.
[3] IHTA 1984, s. 161(4). On definition of the same class see IHTA 1984, s. 161(5).

46: 07   Property is related if (*i*) it forms part of the estate[1] of his spouse or (*ii*) it is property which has within the preceding five years been the property of a charity or other exempt body under an exempt transfer made by the transferor or his spouse after 15th April 1976.[2] Under (*ii*) the property remains related property, despite being disposed of by the trust or body, for a period of five years after that disposal.

The purpose of this rule is to prevent the avoidance of IHT through the use of exempt transfers. Thus if A holds 800 of the 1,000 shares of a family company and he transfers 350 of them to his son, there will be a transfer of value which will take account of the loss of control of the company.[3] However if he transfers them to his wife the transfer will be exempt.[4] If he then gives a further 350 to his son he will be reducing a 45% holding to a 10% holding and so there will be no loss of control. This rule therefore provides that as the value of the property transferred—35%—is less than the appropriate portion of the aggregate of the holdings of A and Mrs A—35/80ths of an 80% holding, the value of the property transferred[5] will be 35/80 × the value of their combined holdings. It will be seen that this rule applies whether it is A or Mrs A who makes the transfer to the son. However a subsequent transfer of her 35% holding by Mrs A to make the son's total up to 70% will only be a transfer of 35/45ths of a 45% holding so that IHT may be reduced by this procedure.

The purpose of group (*ii*) is to prevent the loss of IHT arising on an exempt transfer which results in a loss of control. Thus if A holds 51% of the shares in a company and gives 2% to charity, he will have lost control of the company and perhaps reduced the value of the holding by 50%.

Although shares in a family company are the most likely objects of these rules, other assets caught will be collections and sets of valuable objects, property held jointly or by a partnership. It has been suggested that if a wife holds a lease and her husband the reversion, these rules do not apply. This seems to be doubtful.

Foster's Capital Taxes H2.42.
[1] IHTA 1984, s. 161. Note the wide definition of estate—excluded property is included.
[2] Transfers before 16th April 1976 are exempt.
[3] Supra, § **38: 27**.
[4] Supra, § **44: 01**.
[5] The actual value transferred will depend on who bears the tax.

Undoing related property valuation after death

46: 08   Where within three years of the death the executors or beneficiaries sell property which has been valued as related property, the value for IHT purposes can be recalculated as if the related property rules did not apply. This is needed to achieve fairness where for example shares are left to beneficiaries who are not related to the spouse.[1]

Thus if A had 80% of the shares in a company and transferred 35% to his wife, the transfer would be exempt and no IHT would be payable notwithstanding that A had lost control of the company. If A died his 45% holding would be valued as the appropriate portion (45/80ths) of the 80% holding. If however A's executors sold the 45% for the market value of a 45% holding the related property rule would be excluded; this does not necessarily mean taking the sale proceeds instead but rather the recalculation of the value at death.

To qualify for this relief the sale must be an arm's length sale for a price freely negotiated and not in conjunction with a sale of any of the related or other property to which the relief applies; there must be no provision for reacquisition and no person concerned as vendor (or having an interest in the proceeds of sale) may be the same as or connected with any person concerned as purchaser (or having an interest in the purchase). Further the vendors must be the deceased's personal representatives or those in whom the property vested immediately after the death.

An alteration in the company's share or loan capital or rights attached to shares or securities of a close company will disqualify the property from this relief if the effect of that alteration is to reduce the value of the property by more than 5%.

Quasi related property
46: 09 This relief applies also whenever property falls to be valued in conjunction with property which was also comprised in the deceased's estate but has not at any time since the death been vested in the vendors,[2] as where D held a 60% holding in a company and left half to A and half to B and A now sells his half.

Foster's Capital Taxes D3.21–24.
[1] IHTA 1984, s. 176(1)(*a*) but only for deaths after 6th April 1976. There are risks in electing for relief since one may lose agricultural (supra, § **45: 12**) or business relief (supra, § **45: 06**) if the farm or business is incorporated.
[2] IHTA 1984, s. 176(1)(*b*).

VALUATION OF PARTICULAR ASSETS

Stocks and shares

46: 10 In the case of stocks and shares the CGT quarter up rule is used.[1]

Stocks and shares which are not quoted or dealt in on a stock exchange must be valued on an estimate of market worth. This involves a consideration of the value of the company's assets as at the date of death, and its earning power and dividend record for several years, perhaps three, up to the date of death. Dividend record is usually the most important factor. But in those cases where the directors, being substantially the same persons as the shareholders, took out the company's profits in the form of director's fees rather than dividends, the earnings yield is more important. The same applies in those cases where for special reasons the shareholders preferred to keep profits within the company rather than to take them out in dividends. The value of assets may become the dominating factor if liquidation was imminent at the date of death.

Where unquoted shares and unquoted securities are valued, an important factor will be the amount of information which the hypothetical purchaser will have. The rule now is that there is available to the purchaser all the information which a prudent prospective purchaser might reasonably require if he were proposing to purchase from a willing vendor by private treaty and at arm's length.[2]

The hypothetical sale takes place in an open market but must take account of the fact that the hypothetical purchase will be selling in a restricted market.[3]

Foster's Capital Taxes H3.01, 11–19.
  [1] CGTA 1979, s. 150(3).
  [2] IHTA 1984, s. 168 reversing *Lynall v IRC* [1971] 3 All ER 914, 47 TC 375; on meaning of quoted and unquoted see IHTA 1984, s. 272, as amended by FA 1987, Sch. 8, para. 17; securities listed on the USM are now treated as quoted.
  [3] *IRC v Crossman* [1937] AC 26, [1936] 1 All ER 762.

Relief for sales of shares at a loss following transfer on death[1]

46: 11   Where investments are the subject of a transfer on death the general rule is that for IHT they carry the value they bore immediately before the death. If however qualifying investments are sold at a lower value within twelve months of the death, the lower value may be used instead.[2]

Where the sale is preceded by a contract, the date of sale is that of the contract.[3] If it results from the exercise of an option, the critical date is that of the grant of the option.

The relief applies to any shares forming part of his estate on death, whether free estate or settled property, save for shares held by a company in which he had a controlling interest.

The relief applies only to qualifying investments[4] i.e. broadly, quoted shares and securities and units in authorised unit trusts.

Foster's Capital Taxes D3.01.
  [1] IHTA 1984, Part VI, Chapter III.
  [2] IHTA 1984, s. 179(1).
  [3] IHTA 1984, s. 189.
  [4] IHTA 1984, s. 178; on suspended shares, see IHTA 1984, s. 161(2); on meaning of quoted and unquoted see IHTA 1984, s. 272, as amended by FA 1987, Sch. 8, para. 17; securities listed on the USM are now treated as quoted.

46: 12   Where more than one sale of qualifying investments takes place within the 12-month period, all such sums received must be aggregated to determine the relief. If the sum is less than the principal value at the date of death, the difference, called the loss on sale, is deducted from the value at death.[1] So if an estate includes eight blocks of shares, each worth £1,000 at the date of death, and in the next 12 months three blocks are sold at £700, £900 and £1,050 respectively, the loss on sale is £3,000−£2,650=£350 and the value will be reduced to £7,650.

In making these calculations the Revenue may substitute for the actual sale price the best consideration which could reasonably have been obtained.[2] Any commission or stamp duty[3] and, in accordance with general principles,[4] any expenses of sale and any capital gains liability are all ignored. There are rules for bringing into account both capital sums received[5] and calls made[6] in respect of the investments between the death and the sale.

Under no circumstances can any investment be treated as being sold at a loss greater than its basic value at the date of death.[7] This might occur if calls were made and the shares then sold for a low price.

Foster's Capital Taxes D3.02, 03.

[1] IHTA 1984, s. 179; on effect of sale of part of a holding, see IHTA 1984, s. 186.
[2] IHTA 1984, s. 179.
[3] IHTA 1984, s. 178(5).
[4] See infra, § **46: 23**.
[5] IHTA 1984, s. 181.
[6] IHTA 1984, s. 182.
[7] IHTA 1984, s. 188.

46: 13 The sale must have been carried out by the appropriate person.[1] This is the person liable for the tax in respect of the investments,[2] that is the executors, trustees or the beneficiary. If only one of them is paying the tax he is the appropriate person. For this purpose the personal representatives of the estate and the trustees of a settlement are each treated as a single and continuing body of persons.[3] The very fact that a person holds property subject to a charge for the tax is sufficient to make him—as well as the property—liable and so he is an appropriate person.[4]

Foster's Capital Taxes D3.01.

[1] IHTA 1984, s. 179(1).
[2] IHTA 1984, s. 178.
[3] IHTA 1984, s. 178(4).
[4] IHTA 1984, s. 200(1)(c).

46: 14 The primary reason for the relief was to provide for the case where securities having been valued at death had then to be sold in order to pay the tax and were sold at a loss. The relief is not confined to such sales. Relief may be claimed simply because of a change in investments. However where new shares or securities are bought the relief may be extinguished or reduced.[1] This will occur if the purchases take place within the period beginning at the date of death and ending two months after the last sale within the 12 month period. Where the purchase is by a personal representative or trustee then all the purchases of qualifying investments are aggregated. This forms the numerator of a fraction whose denominator is the total sales figure for the qualifying investments sold since the death, taking actual price obtained or the best consideration that could have been obtained as above. This fraction is then applied to the loss on sale and only the proportion of that loss remaining after the taking away the fraction is eligible for relief. Thus suppose that the proceeds of sale come to £3,000 giving a loss on sale of £600 and that £1,000 is then reinvested. The fraction will be 1,000/3,000. The relief will therefore be reduced by one-third to £400.

If the reinvestment is carried out by someone other than a trustee or personal representative, the loss claim will be reduced only if the purchase is of the same description as the investments sold.[2] Investments are not of the same description if they are quoted separately on a recognised stock exchange or dealt in separately on the Unlisted Securities Market, nor if they are different authorised unit trusts.[3] A person selling Lloyds Bank shares could therefore purchase Midland Bank shares the next day without imperilling his claim for relief.

Where shares or securities are exchanged for other property and the market value of the investments at the time of the exchange is greater than their value on death, that market value is taken into account.[4]

Special rules apply to ignore certain transactions which relate more to the form than the substance of an investment, for example a reorganisation or reduction of the share capital or the conversion of securities.[5] These transactions are only partly ignored if the appropriate person has to give new consideration for the new holding. If the new holding is itself sold within 12 months of the death, the sale is treated in the normal way.

Foster's Capital Taxes D3.04–09.
[1] IHTA 1984, s. 180(1) distinguish subscribing for new shares *Re VGM Holdings Ltd* [1942] Ch 235, [1942] 1 All ER 224.
[2] IHTA 1984, s. 180(1).
[3] IHTA 1984, s. 180(3) as amended by FA 1987, Sch. 8, para. 14.
[4] IHTA 1984, s. 184.
[5] IHTA 1984, s. 183.

LAND

Relief for sales at a loss following transfer on death

46: 15   Where an interest in land was included in a person's estate immediately before his death and was later sold within three years of the death and the sale price was less than the value at the date of death, the sale price can be substituted if the "appropriate person" so claims.[1] This recognition of a decline in value after the death applies only where the sale is by the appropriate person, is not to a beneficiary of the estate or one of his near relatives and the vendor has no right to repurchase the interest sold or any other interest in the same land.[2] The sale price is not necessarily conclusive since the Revenue will substitute the best consideration that could reasonably have been obtained for it at the time of the sale, if this would be greater. This relief is not to apply if the decline in the value of the interest is £1,000 or 5% of the value at death, whichever is the lower; however a drop of £1,001 will be recognised in full.

An interest in land is not defined. While an interest in the proceeds of sale is in practice treated as an interest in land, neither an interest in a company owning land nor an interest in unadministered residue appear to qualify.

In deciding whether the sale is within three years of the death the critical date is that of the contract to sell; if the sale results from the exercise of an option to sell, the date will be the exercise of the option unless the exercise was within six months of the grant in which case the date of grant is preferred.[3] A notice of compulsory purchase delivered within the three-year period will bring the eventual conveyance within relief whatever the date of completion.[4]

All sales within the period must be brought into account to determine the overall loss.

EXAMPLE
A died in June 1989. His estate included four pieces of land, two of which were sold in November 1989 and two in January 1990.

	Value at date of death £	Sale value £	Profit or loss £
Property 1	10,500	7,750	(2,750)
Property 2	16,000	16,200	200
Property 3	18,000	17,850	(150)
Property 4	23,000	23,900	900
	67,500	65,700	(1,800)

Although the total loss is £1,800, the gain on property 2 (£200) and the loss on property 3 (£150) are ignored because they are neither £1,000 nor 5% of the value of the properties at death. The adjusted overall loss is therefore increased to £1,850.

Foster's Capital Taxes D3.11, 12.
[1] IHTA 1984, s. 191. The costs of sale are ignored—IHTA 1984, s. 190(4).
[2] IHTA 1984, s. 191.
[3] IHTA 1984, s. 198.
[4] IHTA 1984, s. 197.

Adjustments and restrictions

46: 16   In comparing the sale price with the value at date of death a number of adjustments may have to be made:

(*i*) Any change in the interest in land arising between the death and the sale must be taken into account;[1] likewise, if the interest is a lease with less than 50 years to run, the value is increased to take account of the inevitable loss due to the passage of time.[2] This is to ensure that the two values are compared on the same basis.

(*ii*) Where on the death other interests, whether in the same or other land, were taken into account, as for example occurs where the other interest is related property, the excess attributable to that other value must be brought into account again by being added to the sale price.[3]

(*iii*) Where other interests in land in the estate are sold by claimant in the same capacity, that is as personal representative or as beneficiary, any gains on such sales must be set off against the loss. If the claim relates to more than one interest, the gains are apportioned between the interests. The same applies to a sale to a connected person.[4]

(*iv*) If the claimant reinvests in land, that is if he buys other land within the period beginning with the death and ending four months after the last sale in respect of which relief is claimed, then, if the aggregate of the purchase prices (A) exceeds the aggregate of the sales (B) no relief may be claimed. If A does not exceed B the fraction A/B is applied to the sale price and the resulting sum is added to it.[5]

If in consequence of all or any of these rules the sale price should be reduced, that reduction must be carried out.[6]

Foster's Capital Taxes D3.14–19.
[1] IHTA 1984, s. 193.
[2] IHTA 1984, s. 194.
[3] IHTA 1984, s. 195.
[4] IHTA 1984, s. 196.
[5] IHTA 1984, s. 192.
[6] IHTA 1984, s. 192(4).

DEBTS DUE TO THE TRANSFEROR

46: 17   In valuing the debt it is assumed that the debt will be paid in full unless and to the extent that recovery of the sum is impossible or not reasonably practicable. Even then recovery will be assumed if the non-recoverability is due to any act or omission on his part.[1]

Where a debt thought at the death of the creditor to be irrecoverable is subsequently paid, the debt will on payment become part of the deceased's estate and so will be added to it.

Foster's Capital Taxes H3.72.
[1] IHTA 1984, s. 166.

ACCRUED INCOME TO DATE OF TRANSFER

46: 18   Every estate presumably[1] includes all income upon the property included therein down to and outstanding at the relevant date, usually the death of the transferor.

In the case of quoted securities, which are not ex-dividend, the accrued income is included in the valuation and does not have to be accounted for separately. In all other cases, such as land producing rents, income which is accruing due at the date of transfer must be apportioned, and the proportion (less income tax, if deductible) up to the relevant date included in the estate.

[1] There is no express provision similar to FA 1894, s. 6(5) which applied for estate duty; however if this income were not included there would have been no need for FA 1975, Sch. 12, para. 16(2) amending TA 1970, s. 430 (now TA 1988, s. 699); supra, § **12: 01**.

LIABILITIES

46: 19   Liabilities fall to be taken into account[1] and valued either to determine the overall value of an estate, whether of the transferor or someone else, or to determine the loss to that estate when a liability is incurred.

Foster's Capital Taxes B3.21, 24.
[1] IHTA 1984, s. 5(3).

Liabilities incurred by the transferor

46: 20 These are in general allowable deductions provided that, and then only to the extent that, they were incurred for a consideration in money or money's worth.[1] This proviso does not apply to liabilities imposed by law.

It is not sufficient to show that payment is made under a legal obligation of the transferor, e.g. by reason of the covenant being under seal; the subsequent discharge of the obligation will be the chargeable transfer. Deduction is excluded, because the consideration was not money or money's worth.

Payments by a husband to his wife under a valid deed of separation may continue during the life of the wife, whether or not the husband predeceases her. On the death of the husband, the wife being still alive, future covenanted payments are a debt of his estate. The payments are for full consideration in money or money's worth, since he would have had to pay larger amounts during his lifetime had he not entered into a covenant binding on his executors.

Where the liability is incurred for a consideration in money or money's worth it is not necessary that that consideration should move to the transferor. Thus if A agrees to sell a chair worth £500 for that sum on condition that the proceeds of sale are paid to B, but dies before making delivery, the liability to transfer the chair is an allowable deduction in valuing A's estate. Equally of course the direction to pay £500 to B would, if discharged before A's death, itself have been a separate transfer of value.

In these instances however deduction is allowed only to the extent of the consideration in money or money's worth. Suppose therefore that A has agreed to buy a chair worth £500 from B for £800. The liability to pay £800 is deductible only to the extent of £500 and so not allowable as to £300.

Foster's Capital Taxes B3.21, 24.
[1] IHTA 1984, s. 5(5).

Incumbrances created by the transferor

46: 21 A liability which is an incumbrance[1] on any property is as far as possible taken to reduce the value of that property.[2] If a husband leaves the matrimonial home to his widow subject to a mortgage, the transfer to the widow is exempt and the debt to the lender is taken as reducing the value of the property transferred to the widow and so will be ignored in computing the value of the rest of the estate unless the debt is greater than the value of the house. It will be seen that the rule talks of a liability which is an incumbrance. The husband in our example is liable to the building society for the sum owed and this liability is personal as well as being an incumbrance on the house itself. It is not open to him to deduct his personal debt as distinct from the sum secured by the incumbrance since there is only one liability and that is an incumbrance on the property.

The rule is also important when one comes to liability for the tax. Property

1154   *Part VIII—Inheritance tax*

bearing its own tax may find the burden greatly reduced and the Inland Revenue charge will be for a lower sum.

It is to be assumed that where the debt is properly payable out of more than one item of property, the person liable to pay the debt must apportion the liability.

Foster's Capital Taxes B3.21.
[1] Defined IHTA 1984, s. 272.
[2] IHTA 1984, s. 162(4).

The estate immediately before death

46: 22   With the introduction of IHT as from 18th March 1986 it became necessary to revive certain estate duty rules for determining the value of a person's estate immediately before death. A debt or incumbrance incurred or made after 17th March 1986[1] is to be disallowed to the extent to which the consideration given for it is property derived from the transferor.[2] This rule is widened to cover the situation in which the consideration is given not for the very property derived from the deceased but from the economic value which that property represents. So the provision also applies to disallow the deduction where there is consideration given by any person who was at any time entitled to property derived from the deceased or among whose resources such property was at any time to be found.[3]

This rule is aimed at the simple device of a loanback.[4] Two examples may be given. First a father gives money to his son; some time later the son lends it back to his father; when the father dies the loan would, but for this rule, be an allowable deduction. Secondly, the same father wishes to give his son some property but wishes at the same time to keep control of it and retain the income from it. If he makes a gift of the property on these terms there will be a gift with reservation. If, however, he gives the property to his son and then buys it back and leaves the purchase price outstanding, the value of the property, which would still form part of his estate as property to which he is beneficially entitled would, but for this rule, be reduced by the amount of the debt. The prohibition on the deduction of debts incurred otherwise than for full consideration (supra, § **46: 20**) would not apply as there would be full consideration. In these two examples, therefore, deduction of the debt is disallowed by this rule.

The expression "property derived from the deceased" is defined widely to cover property which was the subject matter of a disposition by the deceased whether by him alone or in concert with others whether directly or indirectly and including any property which represented the subject matter of such a disposition.[5] The term disposition includes disposition by associated operations.[6]

This wide definition of property derived from the deceased is not without its difficulties. Thus if the father gives his son a house which the son sells and the son then uses the proceeds to buy shares[7] it appears that there are three sets of property ready to trigger this rule should the father buy them and not have paid the debt before he dies viz. the house, the price and the shares.

There is nothing in the legislation to state that only the house is to be taken as the property derived from the father or that it is replaced by the shares.

This very wide definition is then narrowed by a provision that it cannot apply to a disposition which is not a transfer of value.[8]

So if the father gives the property to the son as in the previous example the deduction will be disallowed but if he sells the property for full value and later buys it back and the price is left outstanding, the debt will be an allowable deduction. It will be seen that if the initial sale by the father is at an undervalue the rule will apply.

Foster's Capital Taxes D1.23.

[1] FA 1986, s. 103(6).

[2] FA 1986, s. 103(1)(*a*); the provision re-enacts FA 1939, s. 31.

[3] FA 1986, s. 103(1)(*b*); it is most unclear what is added by the idea of property "found" amongst his resources.

[4] See McCutcheon § 2–177 et seq.; the so called "inheritance trust" is a further example popular in the days of CTT. F would lend money to trustees of a trust for his children; the trustees would buy a single premium insurance bond; they would withdraw 5% p.a. as allowed as tax free return of capital (see supra, § **28: 12**) and pay this to the father; thus the capital would enure to the children with no CTT other than that (if any) due on the creation of the trust and the father would enjoy a tax free 5% return until the debt was paid off.

[5] FA 1986, s. 103(3); the term "subject matter" is defined in s. 103(6) to include annual or periodical payments due under the disposition.

[6] IHTA 1984, s. 272.

[7] The problem is raised by Venables *Inheritance Tax Planning* § 2.4.4.6. Presumably the problem will arise whether the father buys back the house from the son or buys it from someone else.

[8] FA 1986, s. 103(4); it is also necessary that the disposition should not be part of associated operations designed to circumvent this rule.

46: 23 It will be recalled that the liability is also disallowed if the consideration for the debt was given by any person who was then entitled to any property derived from the deceased or among whose resources the property was at any time to be found. The formula for determining the disallowance involves an abatement of the liability otherwise deductible to an extent proportionate to the value of any consideration given which consists of the property derived directly or indirectly from the transferor.[1] This is needed for situations in which the amount of the debt and that of the consideration do not correspond.

So if the father gives the son a house and the son does not sell the house but lends the father money this rule applies to the extent that the father's liability to repay falls within the value of the house;[2] so if the house is worth £50,000 and the son lends the father £40,000 there is no deduction for the liability to repay in calculating the value of the father's estate; if the loan is for £60,000 there is a disallowance to the extent of £50,000.

One matter not addressed in the legislation is the problem of timing. Where the property in respect of which the liability arises is the same as that received under the original transfer of value, i.e. when the first rule applies, there is no problem and the change in the value of the property will have to be taken into account. What is not clear is how matters will be treated under the second rule. Thus in the example just considered what is to happen if the house was worth £50,000 at the time of the transfer but is worth £60,000 when the son makes the loan back? In applying this rule one is to exclude such property which is not derived from the deceased (but only brought in under the wider formula) "as to which it is shown that the disposition of which it, or the property which it represented, was the subject matter was not made with reference to, or with a view to enabling or facilitating, the giving of the consideration or the recoupment in any manner of the cost thereof."[3] So, to continue with the same generous father, let us suppose that the father gives his son a house and some shares and the son later sells his father the shares and some other property and the sums due have not been paid at the time the father dies. The general rule will apply in relation to the debt due in respect of the shares[4] but in relation to the other property the present exclusion rule will exclude the liability (i.e. permit its deduction after all) if it can be shown that the gift of the house was not made to enable the other property to be sold to the father; if this cannot be shown then the liability in respect of the other property will be non-deductible subject to an upper limit equal to the value of the house.

This rule will also be relevant if the son should sell the house to a stranger and the father should subsequently buy property from that stranger and die with the liability still outstanding. However it appears that this rule has no relevance if the father should buy the house from the stranger and leave the liability outstanding when he dies.[5]

Foster's Capital Taxes D1.23.

[1] FA 1986, s. 103(2); no "abatement" i.e. disallowance is made to the extent that the father's liability to repay exceeds the value of the property.

[2] It will be noted that what is at issue is the value of the property derived by the son from the father; this may be a quite different value from that of the loss of the father's estate.

[3] FA 1986, s. 103(2)(*b*).

[4] FA 1986, s. 103(2)(*a*).

[5] Because of FA 1986, s. 103(2)(*a*).

46: 24   To reinforce this legislative strategy it is provided that the *repayment* of a loan which is non-deductible by reason of the rules just outlined is to be treated as a transfer of value; the only relief is that the transfer is to be treated as potentially exempt and so will not cause a charge if the payment occurs more than seven years before the payer's death.[1] To continue the example of father and son, suppose that the father gives the property to the son and buys it back leaving the purchase price outstanding but later pays off the debt. The son is better off to the extent of the payment of the debt and the father has reduced his estate by a similar amount. If the father dies within seven years IHT may become due.

This rule causes some surprises. Thus if the father gives a house to his son who sells it to a stranger and the father later buys it from the stranger and dies without paying the debt there will, as already seen, be no deduction for the liability. What this rule seems to say is that if the liability is paid off there will be a chargeable transfer if the father should die within seven years.[2]

This rule is also difficult in that it fails to define when there is a liability, a matter of some importance as it applies only where there is a liability which is discharged. The intention is to reinforce the rule barring the deduction of a liability remaining unpaid at the date of death. If therefore no liability is created the rule cannot apply. So if the father buys the property back from the son and does not leave the money outstanding but pays the price at the same time as—or before—the date of performance it appears that this rule cannot apply. One wonders whether a few days delay in settling the debt will be enough to trigger the present rule or whether some clear intention to allow time to pay will be required.

Foster's Capital Taxes D1.23.
  [1] FA 1986, s. 103(5).
  [2] See Venables *Inheritance Tax Planning*, § 2.4.4.10.

Other debts and incumbrances

46: 25   In the case of debts which were not incurred, and incumbrances which were not created, by the transferor himself, but for which he or the property is liable, allowance is made whether or not the debts were incurred or the incumbrances created for consideration. Thus, if the deceased had acquired property subject to a mortgage, the mortgage money would be deductible even if the mortgagee received his mortgage as a gift from the previous owner of the property. Future liabilities must be discounted.[1]

Foster's Capital Taxes B3.25.
  [1] IHTA 1984, s. 162(3).

Non-deductible debts

46: 26   If neither the executor nor anyone else is liable to pay the debt, nor is it charged on any property, then no deduction is allowed.

In *Re Barnes*,[1] the deceased had made gifts inter vivos within the statutory period before death rendering them liable to estate duty, amounting to £185,000. He died leaving assets worth £12 and debts and funeral expenses amounting to £90,000. It was held that estate duty was payable on the value of the gifts inter vivos without deduction of the debts and funeral expenses, because those liabilities were neither chargeable on the gifts nor payable by the donees. It was immaterial that the donees in fact paid the debts.

For the same reason, debts which are unenforceable, such as gaming debts, debts under illegal contracts, and debts of which evidence in writing required by statute is absent, are not allowable. Statute-barred debts, which an executor may pay if he chooses, are not apparently allowable if actually paid.[2]

No allowance is to be made for any debt in respect whereof there is a right to reimbursement from any other estate or person, unless such reimbursement cannot reasonably be expected to be obtained.[3]

Debts incurred or incumbrances created by the executor, such as administration expenses, not being debts of the deceased, are not deductible.

Foster's Capital Taxes B3.23.
  [1] [1939] 1 K B 316, [1938] 4 All ER 870.
  [2] *Norton v Frecker* (1737) 1 Atk 524.
  [3] IHTA 1984, s. 162(1).

Interaction of taxes and other matters

46: 27   Where A makes a chargeable transfer of property to B both IHT and CGT may arise. The following rules should be borne in mind. In deciding whether the IHT should be borne by A or by B one should also note that IHT may be paid by instalments if B pays this tax infra, § **47: 15**.

(*a*) Where the IHT is borne by A it may have to be grossed up. This is because the transferor's liability to tax resulting from the transfer is to be taken into account in determining the value of his estate immediately after the transfer.[1] Where the tax is borne by B there is no grossing up. In potentially exempt transfers there is no grossing up.

(*b*) Where CGT falls due, as where no election is made under FA 1980, s. 79, and is borne by A, no deduction can be made on account of the CGT in calculating the value for IHT.[2] So where the transfer gives rise to a liability to CGT (*i*) the value transferred is the value of the asset grossed up as necessary to take account of the IHT but not the CGT but (*ii*) equally the amount payable by way of CGT is not deductible in computing the value transferred. The reason for (*i*) is self-evident. The reason for (*ii*) is to prevent anomalies. If A transfers an asset worth £5,000 on which there is a capital gains liability of £1,000, his liability to CGT and IHT should be the same as where he sells the asset for £5,000 and then transfers the proceeds of sale. It should be noticed that the liability to CGT is ignored only in determining the value of the estate immediately after the transfer. So if A should die the day after making the transfer his liability to CGT on the previous transfer would be deductible in computing the value of his estate.

Quite different rules apply when the tax is borne by B; there the tax paid by B is deductible in computing the value transferred. It should be noted that this is deductible whether it is A or B who actually pays the IHT.

Similar rules apply to the payment of incidental expenses; they are deductible only if borne by B.[3]

(*c*) Where the CGT arises but an election was made under the now repealed FA 1980, s. 79[4] and IHT also arises, the IHT will be deductible in computing the chargeable gain on a subsequent disposal by B but only to the extent of wiping out a chargeable gain; the IHT cannot be used to create a loss. This applies even though the IHT is borne by A; in this instance the IHT is that due after the grossing up rules have been applied. If the IHT is subsequently increased through A dying within seven (in practice not more than five) years of the gift adjustments are made to the CGT to give effect to the extra deduction now due. A similar rule applies where the transfer is potentially exempt but tax becomes due because the donor dies within 7 years.

Foster's Capital Taxes C2.24, 25.
    [1] IHTA 1984, s. 5(4) On settled property, see IHTA 1984, s. 165.
    [2] IHTA 1984, s. 165.
    [3] IHTA 1984, s. 164.
    [4] Repealed by FA 1989 Sch 17 Part VII but effect preserved for disposals before 14th March 1989.

Other taxes

46: 28   Income and other taxes due from and repayments of such taxes due to the estate must be taken into account.[1]

An outstanding liability to pay tax on an earlier transfer tax (whether CTT or IHT) is deductible on death only if actually paid out of the estate.[2]

Foreign taxes are generally allowed only as deductions from foreign property.[3]

---

[1] On complications of repayments to a married man see *Re Ward, Harrison v Ward* [1922] 1 Ch 517.
[2] IHTA 1984, s. 174(2).
[3] Because not enforceable in the UK, infra, § **49: 22**.

Valuation of debts due from the estate

46: 29   There is no statutory provision stating how debts owing by the transferor are to be valued. It is, therefore, a matter of finding how much money was really owing at the date of transfer, or, in the case of liabilities of uncertain amounts and contingent liabilities, of estimating the value of the debt as at the date of transfer in the light of circumstances which then exist.[1] In the case of a certain liability which is not to mature until a future date, the amount will have to be discounted according to the time which is to elapse before maturity.[1]

Any payments in advance, which fell due before the transfer, but are unpaid at the transfer, are proper deductions. The value obtained by advance payment is not taxable as an asset of the estate, unless it is capable of being turned into money. For example, if rates on the house occupied by the deceased were payable in advance before the date of death, the amount (if not paid) would be a proper deduction from his estate. The value to the estate of the rates paid in advance would not be included unless the executors were reasonably able to obtain a cash advantage therefrom by arrangements with an incoming occupier.

Foster's Capital Taxes D1.03.
[1] IHTA 1984, s. 162(2).

Funeral expenses

46: 30   In determining the value of the estate immediately before death allowance is made for reasonable funeral expenses.[1]

The cost of mourning is not part of the funeral expenses but under a concession a reasonable amount for mourning for the family and servants was allowed.[2] The cost of a tombstone is now allowed.[3]

Foster's Capital Taxes D1.12.
[1] IHTA 1984, s. 172 .
[2] Extra-statutory concession F1 (1988); **Foster's Capital Taxes, Division U2**.
[3] SP 7/87 **Foster's Capital Taxes, Division W3**.

47 Accountability and administration

47: 01 Accountability means the liability of a person to account to the Revenue for the tax due; the questions who should report the transfer and who bears the burden of the tax, incidence, are separate.

Accountability of persons is supplemented by the Inland Revenue charge which enables the Revenue to obtain payment out of the property itself, whether or not the owner is accountable.

LIABILITY TO THE REVENUE FOR TAX

Lifetime transfers

47: 02 Those liable are

(a) the transferor;

(b) the transferee;

(c) any person in whom the property is vested whether beneficially or not;

(d) any person beneficially entitled to an interest in possession in the property;

(e) where the property has become settled property as a result of the transfer any person for whose benefit the property or income is applied;[1] and

(f) the transferor's spouse who has been the recipient of a transfer of value from (a) since 26th March 1974 and was his spouse at the time of each transfer.[2]

(g) in the case of a potentially exempt transfer the transferor's personal representatives. This rule also applies to any additional tax due in respect of other chargeable transfers[3] including tax due in respect of a gift with reservation.

Liability under (f) may not exceed the market value of the property at the time of the subsequent transfer (or, if already sold, market value at the time of sale);[4] this rule is confined to falls in value. References to property in these rules (a)–(e) include references to property directly or indirectly representing that property.[5]

For the tax due in respect of chargeable transfers the primary liability rests on (a)[6] and the others become liable only if the tax remains unpaid after the due date; they have the further advantage that they are not to be liable to a greater extent than if the transfer had been gross rather than net, i.e. for no more than the tax due if the transfer had not been grossed up.[7] If a transferee bears the tax in this way it is presumably not open to the Revenue to collect the balance of tax due to the grossing up from the transferor unless perhaps the transferor reimburses the transferee.

Making anyone other than the transferee liable for the additional tax due in respect of a chargeable transfer where the transferor dies within seven years is a major change from the days of CTT. Presumably this was to bring matters in to line with the rules of potentially exempt transfers. In both these instances the primary liability remains that of the transferee and the liability of the personal representatives is limited. For potentially exempt transfers it appears[8] that personal representatives are liable only after all other possible candidates or the tax remains unpaid 12 months after the end of the month in which the death occurred and then subject to the limit of the assets.[9] A similar rule applies to gifts with reservation.[10] For all these transfers and gifts the primary liability is on the donees.

Foster's Capital Taxes K1.11.
[1] IHTA 1984, s. 199(1).
[2] IHTA 1984, s. 203(1).
[3] IHTA 1984, s. 199(2) as amended by FA 1986, Sch. 19, para. 26.
[4] IHTA 1984, s. 203(1)—this limitation does not apply to tangible movable property.
[5] IHTA 1984, s. 199(5).
[6] IHTA 1984, s. 204(6).
[7] IHTA 1984, s. 204(5).
[8] The wording of IHTA 1984, s. 204(7) and (8) is extremely obscure—see Venables *Inheritance Tax Planning* p. 22.
[9] IHTA 1984, s. 204(8) added by FA 1986, Sch. 19, para. 28.
[10] IHTA 1984, s. 204(9) added by FA 1986, Sch. 19, para. 28.

Settled property

47: 03   Those primarily liable are the trustees.[1] In addition tax can be collected from (*b*) any person entitled to an interest in possession in the settled property whether beneficially or not, e.g. the trustees of a subsequent settlement, (*c*) any person for whose benefit the property or income is applied, e.g. a discretionary beneficiary, and (*d*) the settlor, provided (*i*) the settlement was made in his lifetime, and (*ii*) the trustees are not for the time being resident in the UK. Head (*d*) does not apply if the settlement was made before 11th December 1974 and the trustees having been resident in the UK when the settlement was made have been non-resident from 10th December 1974 to the date of the transfer.[2] Head (*d*) is also excluded in relation to any additional tax that becomes due by reason of the settlor's death within seven years.[3] Similar rules apply to potentially exempt transfers. Head (*d*) is further restricted where there is a potentially exempt transfer on the termination of an interest in possession. Here the trustees are primarily liable but the settlor will be liable under head (*d*) unless the settlement was made before 17th March 1987, the trustees were initially resident in the UK but had become non-resident by that day and remained so until the death of the transferor.[4]

Foster's Capital Taxes K1.13, 14.
[1] IHTA 1984, s. 201 defined IHTA 1984, s. 199(4) and see *IRC v Stype Investments (Jersey) Ltd* [1981] STC 310 and subsequently [1982] STC 625.
[2] IHTA 1984, s. 201(3)
[3] IHTA 1984, s. 201(2) as amended by FA 1986, Sch. 19, para. 27.

4 IHTA 1984, s. 201(3A) added by F(No. 2)A 1987, Sch. 7, para. 3.

Death

47: 04   Here liability is concurrent among (*a*) the personal representatives—so far as the property[1] is not settled unless it is settled land in the UK which devolves on them; (*b*) trustees—so far as concerns property settled immediately before death; (*c*) the beneficiaries, or any other person in whom the property is vested after the death e.g. the trustees of a settlement created by the will and (*d*) where property was settled at the time of the death—any person for whose benefit property or income is applied e.g. a person benefitting under a trust which became discretionary on the death of the life tenant. As far as the personal representatives are concerned it should be noted that there is no immunity from liability simply because the person is not resident in the UK and that the liability is personal (not simply representative).[2]

The tax may be due on delivery of the account, infra, § **47: 10**; the due date i.e. that from which interest runs may be different, infra, § **47: 13**. A further rule may give rise to penalties if the account is not delivered within twelve months, infra, § **47: 12**.

Foster's Capital Taxes K1.12.
1 Defined IHTA 1984, s. 200 and see *IRC v Stype Investments (Jersey) Ltd* [1981] STC 310, [1981] 2 All ER 394 and subsequently [1982] STC 625; liability on foreign assets may be deferred if the foreign government imposes restrictions—extra-statutory concession F6 (1985); **Foster's Capital Taxes, Division U2**.
2 *IRC v Stannard* [1984] STC 245.

Limitations of liability

47: 05   A purchaser is liable if and to the extent that the property is subject to an Inland Revenue charge (infra, § **47: 07**).[1] So if F gives property to S who sells it to X, X may escape liability notwithstanding that he is a person in whom the property is vested (supra, §§ **47: 02** and **47: 04**, groups (*c*)).

Personal representatives are liable only to the extent of the assets they received or would have received but for their own neglect or default.[2] A similar rule applies to limit their liability to tax on UK settled land devolving on them. Trustees are only liable to the extent of the property available to them as trustee or which they have actually received or disposed of or they have become liable to account for to the beneficiaries;[3] the property here means the property in relation to which the charge arises.

Those liable as having possession of or a beneficial interest in property have their liability limited to the extent of that property.[4] This limitation does not mean that they are liable only to the extent that the tax is attributable to that property; the value of the whole property can be taken.

Those liable as receiving benefits under a discretionary trust cannot be made liable beyond the amount received (less income tax).[5]

On limits of liability of personal representatives in relation to potentially exempt transfers and gifts with reservation, see, supra, § **47: 02**.

Foster's Capital Taxes K1.11, 12, 25.
[1] IHTA 1984, s. 200.
[2] IHTA 1984, s. 204(1).
[3] IHTA 1984, s. 204(2).
[4] IHTA 1984, s. 204(3).
[5] IHTA 1984, s. 204(5).

Special cases

47: 06   Special rules apply to limit those accountable as follows:

(1) Transfers within seven years of death. Any tax or additional tax may be collected from any of those set out above at §§ **47: 02** and **47: 03** and settled property with the exception of the transferor, the transferor's spouse and if the property was settled the settlor.[1] This is not a charge on the transferor's estate. Liability is limited where the person liable is not entitled to the property beneficially; his liability is limited to the value of the property still vested in him at the death or which he handled as trustee after the death.[2]

(2) Designated objects—loss of conditional exemption. Those liable are: (*a*) those who disposed of the object and (*b*) those for whose benefit the object was disposed.[3]

(3) Timber. Those liable for tax deferred from death are those entitled to the proceeds of sale or who would be if there were a sale.[4]

(4) Political parties. Where the £100,000 limit was exceeded, the tax due in respect of transfers before the death was collected from the party.[5] (This also applied where the £250,000 limit which applied to transfers to charities before 15th March 1983 was exceeded).

(5) Close companies—see supra, § **43: 04**.[6]

Foster's Capital Taxes K1.12, 25; L1.04.
[1] IHTA 1984, ss. 199(2), 201(2) (amended by FA 1986, Sch. 19, para. 27).
[2] IHTA 1984, s. 204(4).
[3] IHTA 1984, s. 207.
[4] IHTA 1984, s. 208.
[5] IHTA 1984, s. 209. This limit of £100,000 was repealed for transfers after 14th March 1988 by FA 1988, s. 137.
[6] IHTA 1984, s. 202(3).

Inland Revenue charge

47: 07   Where tax is not paid on the due date in respect of a transfer of property, a charge for the unpaid tax arises;[1] in the case of settled property this extends to all the property comprised in the settlement.

The charge does not apply to most property in the UK which was beneficially owned by the deceased immediately before his death and which vests in his personal representatives; however this charge does apply to land. The charge does not apply to heritable property in Scotland.

The charge covers property, moveable or immoveable, outside the UK, real property, joint personal property which has accrued to a surviving joint owner and personal property nominated under a general power to dispose (e.g. under a power to nominate benefits under a superannuation fund[2]) unless the general power is contained in a settlement (when the trustees are liable for the tax, though it is a charge on the settled property).[3] In all these instances the personal representatives, even though they have transferred the property to the beneficiary, can still recover from him the tax that they have paid, though there will be obvious practical difficulties in the case of property situated outside the UK if the foreign executors and the beneficiary are out of the jurisdiction.

The charge takes effect subject to existing incumbrances. If the property is land in England, Wales or Northern Ireland and the charge is not registered a purchaser takes clear of the charge, which is transferred to the proceeds of sale. In other cases a purchaser will take clear of the charge if he had no notice of it. He will also escape the charge if the Revenue have issued a certificate of discharge and he is not aware of any grounds that would invalidate it or by the effluxion of time—six years from the date the tax became due or the delivery of the account whichever is the later.

The charge applies to property subject to a potentially exempt transfer when that property is still retained by the transferee at the transferor's death.[4] However, when that property is sold before the transferor's death the charge is placed instead on the property received in its place. Property which is disposed of by the donee, otherwise than by sale, is subject to the charge.[5]

Foster's Capital Taxes Division L6.
[1] IHTA 1984, ss. 237 and 238.
[2] IHTA 1984, s. 151(4); *O'Grady v Wilmot* [1916] 2 AC 231.
[3] IHTA 1984, s. 237.
[4] IHTA 1984, s. 237(3A)(*a*) added by FA 1986, Sch. 19, para. 34.
[5] IHTA 1984, s. 237(3A)(*b*) added by FA 1986, Sch. 19, para. 34.

Certificate of discharge

47: 08   A person liable for tax may apply for a certificate of discharge. The certificate discharges all persons from any further claim for tax on the transfer and extinguishes the Inland Revenue charge.[1] It may also be given to discharge specific property from the charge when it is being acquired by a purchaser.

No application for a certificate may be made in respect of property subject to a conditionally exempt transfer until two years after the donor's death.[2]

Foster's Capital Taxes L4.13, 14.
[1] IHTA 1984, s. 239.
[2] IHTA 1984, s. 239(2A) added by FA 1986, Sch. 19, para. 35.

ACCOUNT—REPORTING THE TRANSFER

Lifetime dispositions and trusts

47: 09   In the case of a chargeable transfer a transferor must give an account of all such transfers unless some other person liable for the tax, e.g. the transferee, has already done so.[1] An account is required of all chargeable transfers on which tax falls due to that there is no obligation to report transfers within the nil rate band or which fall within one or other of the exemptions.[2] The account must be delivered within twelve months or, if later, three months from the date on which he first becomes liable for the tax.

Similar rules apply to trustees.[3]

Where the transfer is a potentially exempt transfer it is the transferee's duty to report it.[4] The same applies to gifts with reservation.[5] In each case the account must be delivered not later than 12 months after the end of the month in which death occurred.[6] A similar rule applies when the termination of an interest in possession is a potentially exempt transfer.[7]

Foster's Capital Taxes L2.11.
[1] IHTA 1984, s. 216.
[2] See [1984] STI, p. 520.
[3] See *Re Clore (No.3), IRC v Stype Trustees (Jersey) Ltd* [1985] STC 394.
[4] IHTA 1984, s. 216(1)(*bb*) added by FA 1986, Sch. 19, para. 29(1).
[5] IHTA 1984, s. 216 (*bc*) added by FA 1986, Sch. 19, para. 29(1).
[6] IHTA 1984, s. 216(6)(*aa*), (*ab*) added by FA 1986, Sch. 19, para. 29(3).
[7] IHTA 1984, s. 216 (*bd*) added by F(No. 2)A 1987, Sch. 7, para. 4.

Death

47: 10 Personal representatives must make an account of the property forming the estate of the deceased person.[1] This account must be delivered before the grant of representation can be obtained; sometimes the tax must also be paid (infra, § **47: 13**). They may make a provisional account where the exact value of the property cannot be ascertained.

This rule creates a practical problem in that the personal representatives have to pay the tax but, not yet having the grant of probate, cannot prove title to a purchaser. Tax may therefore be funded by a loan from the beneficiaries, or the sale of assets for which probate need not be produced, or the appropriate use of a life policy (i.e. one not belonging to the deceased's estate) or, if necessary, a loan from a bank.[2]

Where no UK grant of representation has been obtained within 12 months of the death those in whom the property is vested (at the time of death or since) or those beneficially entitled to an interest in possession are under a duty to account; this extends to the actual beneficiaries of a discretionary trust.[3]

The Board now has power by regulation to amend these rules[4] and has ended the duty to account for persons dying on or after 1st April 1989 where the estate is "excepted" i.e. when the gross value of the property is less than £100,000, there is no settled property, not more than £15,000 value out of the £100,000 is outside the UK and the deceased died domiciled in the UK having made no lifetime gifts chargeable to IHT or CTT (and therefore no potentially exempt transfers within the last seven years).[5]

As to the duty to account for potentially exempt transfers which became chargeable and for gifts with reservation see supra, § **47: 09**.

Foster's Capital Taxes L1.03; L2.12, 31.
[1] IHTA 1984, s. 216.
[2] On relief from interest see supra, § **12: 02**.

³ IHTA 1984, s. 216(2).
⁴ IHTA 1984, s. 216(3).
⁵ Inheritance Tax (Delivery of Accounts) Regulations, SI 1989 Nos. 1078, 1079 (Scotland) and 1080 (Northern Ireland) (amending SI 1981 Nos. 880, 881 and 1441).

Revenue procedure and appeals

47: 11   The account is delivered to the Capital Taxes Office which determines the tax payable and then issues a notice of determination.[1] Appeals lie to the Special Commissioners and from there to the High Court, Court of Session etc. on points of law by way of case stated.[2] Appeals on value of land go to the Lands Tribunal rather than the Special Commissioners. With agreement the parties may appeal direct to the High Court etc. thus leapfrogging the Special Commissioners.

Foster's Capital Taxes Division L3.
  [1] IHTA 1984, s. 221.
  [2] IHTA 1984, ss. 222–225.

REVENUE POWERS

47: 12   The Revenue have power to take proceedings for the recovery of tax[1] and to accept property in satisfaction of a liability to tax and interest.[2] The value may be taken either at the day the property is offered or that on which it is accepted. If the former is chosen, the interest is due after that date.[3]

The Revenue have extensive powers to obtain information. The normal privilege given to communications between a solicitor and his client is respected but the solicitor may be required to disclose the name and address of his client and, where that client is a non-resident involved in forming companies or making settlements, that client's clients.[4] There is further power where a person (other than a barrister) is concerned in making an *inter vivos* settlement with a UK domiciled settlor but non-resident trustees; such a person must inform the Revenue of the names and addresses of the settlor and the trustees within three months of the settlement being made.[5]

Penalties may be incurred for failing to deliver an account, failing to make a return, failing to comply with a notice seeking information and any fraud or negligence in connection with the supply of accounts or information. There may also be criminal liability. The penalty for fraud by an accountable person is £50 plus twice the amount of tax that would have been lost—this is in addition to a liability for the tax.[6]

A person who discovers that he has supplied incorrect information is under a duty to correct it, failure to correct it is treated as negligence.[7]

There are also penalties for failing to comply with a notice issued by the Special Commissioners.[8]

Foster's Capital Taxes L2.21, 31; L4.09.
  [1] IHTA 1984, s. 242.
  [2] IHTA 1984, s. 230.

³ IHTA 1984, s. 233(1A), SP 6/87; Press Release 8th April 1987, STI, p. 302—for acceptance for IHT after 16th March 1987; this has been extended to CTT and estate duty by F(No. 2)A 1987, s. 97.
⁴ IHTA 1984, s. 219.
⁵ IHTA 1984, s. 218.
⁶ IHTA 1984, ss. 247, 249–253.
⁷ IHTA 1984, s. 248.
⁸ IHTA 1984, s. 247.

Due date for payment

47: 13 Tax is in general due six months after the end of the month in which the transfer takes place; for potentially exempt transfers six months after the month in which death occurred.[1] However, tax due on a chargeable lifetime transfer made between 6th April and 30th September is not due until the end of April in the following year.[2]

Tax due from personal representatives[3] as a prerequisite to obtaining probate must be paid on delivery of the account to the Probate Registry. This does not apply to tax on instalment property or on property for tax on which the personal representatives are not primarily liable, e.g. potentially exempt transfers.

Interest runs from these dates whether or not a notice of determination has been issued. Tax may therefore be paid on account.

Foster's Capital Taxes L1.01–03.
¹ IHTA 1984, s. 226(3A) added by FA 1986, Sch. 19, para. 30(2).
² IHTA 1984, s. 226(1).
³ IHTA 1984, s. 226(2); supra, § **47: 10**.

Interest

47: 14 Unpaid tax carries interest at 11% on all transfers.[1] This runs from the date the tax fell due and is not generally affected by changes in rates. The death rates are used also for extra tax becoming due by reason of the transferor's death within seven years or where gifts to charity or political parties become liable because of the transferor's death within 1 year.

If tax is overpaid interest is paid on the repayments; interest is calculated from the date of payment to the date of repayment—a more generous rule than for income tax. Such interest is not taxable as income of the recipient. The rate is the same as that for underpayment.

Interest can cease to run from the offer date where property is accepted in satisfaction of tax on the basis of an offer date valuation: see supra, § **47: 12**.

Foster's Capital Taxes L4.05.
¹ IHTA 1984, s. 233 amended by SI 1989, No. 1002 with effect from 6th July 1989. See *Simon's Tax Intelligence* 1989, pp 510 and 537; see also Inland Revenue Press Release 1st August 1989 (setting Revenue rates of interest).

Payment by instalments

47: 15 IHT may be paid by instalments if it is attributable to certain types of property and the transfer is either (i) on death, or (ii) is a lifetime transfer with the donee paying the tax or (iii) the charge relates to settled property and either (*a*) the property remains settled (e.g. it passes to another life tenant) or (*b*) the tax is borne by the beneficiary.[1] The taxpayer must elect in writing. The tax is payable by ten equal yearly instalments. The first instalment is due when the whole of the tax would otherwise have been payable; in the case of a transfer on death six months after the end of the month in which death occurred.

The taxpayer may at any time pay off the outstanding tax and must do so if the property is sold or, in the case of a partnership he receives a sum in satisfaction of his interest, in the case of a lifetime transfer if there is a further lifetime chargeable transfer of the property or in the case of settled property it ceases to be comprised in the settlement. Where only a part of the property is sold or transferred only a proportionate part of the tax becomes due.

The property qualifying for this treatment is (*i*) land and buildings situated in or out of the UK, (*ii*) certain shares and securities, (*iii*) the net value of a business or an interest in a business provided it is carried on for gain (i.e. not as a hobby)[2] and (*iv*) timber.[3]

The instalment method is available to tax on potentially exempt transfers which become chargeable because the transferor dies within seven years and to the additional tax due because the transferor of a chargeable transfer dies within seven years only if certain conditions are satisfied.[4] First the transferee[5] must own the property, whether land or shares,[6] throughout the period from the date of the transfer down to the date of the death of the transferor (or his own earlier death); alternatively the property must have been replaced by property falling within the replacement rules for business or agricultural property reliefs.[7]

Foster's Capital Taxes Division L5.
[1] IHTA 1984, s. 227.
[2] IHTA 1984, s. 228.
[3] IHTA 1984, s. 229.
[4] IHTA 1984, s. 227(1A), amended by FA 1987, Sch. 8, para. 15.
[5] Defined in IHTA 1984, s. 227(1B).
[6] IHTA 1984, s. 228(3A), added by FA 1987, Sch. 8, para. 16.
[7] IHTA 1984, ss. 113B or 124B.

47: 16   Shares and securities qualify[1] if:

(*a*) they gave control of the company immediately before the transfer. Control means having a majority of the votes on all issues affecting the company as a whole; at one time it sufficed to have a majority on any particular question affecting the company as a whole but this gave rise to avoidance devices. Where husband and wife have shares or securities each is deemed to have control if they have control together.

(*b*) if they are unquoted and do not give control but undue hardship would otherwise result; this is extended—and no hardship need be shown—where the transfer is on death and the person liable for the tax shows that at least 20% of the tax for which he is liable is attributable to unquoted shares or securities or other property in respect of which instalment relief is available).

(*c*) if they are unquoted shares (but not other securities) and the value transferred is more than £20,000 and the shares constitute at least 10% of the nominal value of all the shares then issued by the company or they are ordinary shares and their nominal value is at least 10% of all the ordinary shares then issued.

Foster's Capital Taxes L5.11–14.
[1] IHTA 1984, s. 228.

Interest on instalments

47: 17 For property falling within (*i*) interest is payable on instalments from the date the first instalment fell due.[1] However for other property interest runs only from the date the instalment falls into arrears so that tax on each instalment is interest free if paid on time. At one time there was a ceiling of £250,000 but this has now been repealed.

Certain types of investment companies may qualify for instalment relief as businesses but not for interest free instalment relief.[2]

Foster's Capital Taxes L5.31–32.
[1] IHTA 1984, s. 234.
[2] By virtue of IHTA 1984, s. 234(2). IHTA 1984, s. 234(3) provides exceptions to this exception and the list is modified by FA 1986, s. 107 to substitute "market maker" for "jobber".

48 Incidence

48: 01 The law relating to incidence determines on which beneficial interests the ultimate burden of IHT shall fall. The special rules for partly exempt transfers are considered supra, § **44: 14**.

POSITION OF ACCOUNTING PARTIES

Transferors

48: 02 If the transferor has accounted for the tax, he has no right to raise the tax out of the property under IHTA 1984, s. 212(1) nor to recover it from the transferee unless the transferee has expressly agreed to pay it.[1] In such a case it would seem that since the transferor has an enforceable right to reimbursement in respect of liability to tax this liability should be ignored in determining the loss in value of the transferor's estate so that the transferor should pay tax on the net and not the gross value of the transfer.

Foster's Capital Taxes K1.11; L2.11.
[1] IHTA 1984, s. 162(3).

Transferees

48: 03 If the beneficial transferee pays the tax, he has no right to recover it from the transferor unless by deed under seal[1] the transferor has expressly agreed to pay it. The transferee will pay tax on the net value of the transfer; any transfer of the amount of this tax to him later on by the transferor will be a further transfer of value.[2] He may raise this tax out of the property under IHTA 1984, s. 212(1).

Foster's Capital Taxes K1.11; L2.11
[1] Or by contract outside IHTA 1984, s. 10.
[2] IHTA 1984, s. 5(5); but taxable only if not exempt.

Trustees

48: 04 If trustees pay the tax they may recover the amount out of any money in the settlement held on the same trusts as the property in respect of which the tax was payable.[1] Whether or not the property in respect of which they have paid tax is vested in them (as will usually be the case), they have power to raise the amount of the tax by sale or mortgage of the property under IHTA 1984, s. 212(1).

Foster's Capital Taxes K1.16; L2.13, 21.
[1] IHTA 1984, s. 212(1).

Limited owners

48: 05   A person having a limited interest in property (e.g. a life tenant or an annuitant or a remainderman) who pays the tax in respect of the property is entitled to the same charge as if the money had been raised by a mortgage to him.[1] This charge arises automatically[2] and, being equitable, is registrable as a Class C (ii) land charge, if the land is unregistered, or protectible by entry of a notice or caution, if the land is registered, assuming the land is in England or Wales.

Foster's Capital Taxes K1.16.
[1] IHTA 1984, s. 212(2). Presumably, the fact of reimbursing personal representatives tax paid by them should enable a person to fall within IHTA 1984, s. 212(2) as a person who "pays the tax attributable to" the property.
[2] *Lord Advocate v Countess of Moray* [1905] AC 531 at 539.

Discretionary beneficiaries

48: 06   A beneficiary under a discretionary trust or the object of a power of appointment who pays the tax has power, even though the property in respect of which he has paid the tax is not vested in him, to raise the amount of the tax by sale or mortgage of the property under IHTA 1984, s. 212(1). The power may be used for the purpose of paying the tax in the first place. The power, is indeed, available for any person liable to pay the tax except a transferor or a spouse of his who is accountable under IHTA 1984, s. 203 to the extent of property received from him.

Foster's Capital Taxes K1.16.

Personal representatives

48: 07   Where personal representatives have paid IHT in respect of a chargeable transfer on death and the tax is not a testamentary expense (see infra, § **48: 08**) the personal representatives have a right to repayment by the person in whom the property is vested, property including any property directly or indirectly representing the original property.[1]

They also have an indemnity where settled land[2] or formerly settled land[3] vests in them.[4] A similar rule exists for heritable property in Scotland.[5]

An official certificate, specifying the tax paid, can be obtained from the Revenue.[6] Repayments are made to the person producing the certificate.

If the person who has paid the tax could have paid it by instalments, the other persons can insist upon reimbursing him by instalments.[7]

Foster's Capital Taxes K1.16; L2.12
[1] IHTA 1984, s. 211(3).
[2] Administration of Estates Act 1925, s. 22(1); Supreme Court Act 1981, s. 116.
[3] *Re Bridgett and Hayes Contract* [1928] Ch 163.

4 IHTA 1984, ss. 211(1) and 237.
5 IHTA 1984, ss. 237(4) and 211(1)(*b*).
6 IHTA 1984, s. 214.
7 IHTA 1984, s. 213.

POSITION OF BENEFICIARIES

Estates of deceased persons

48: 08   Where, under the rules outlined at §§ **47: 06** and **48: 07**, personal representatives are liable for tax, the tax is treated as part of the general testamentary and administration expenses of the estate.[1] The effect is to cause the incidence of the tax to fall on the assets of the estate in the order set out in the Administration of Estates Act 1925, Sch. 1, Part II or as varied by the testator.[2]

This broad rule does not apply to all types of property which are treated as disposed of on the death, but only to property in the UK which vests in the personal representatives and was not immediately before the death comprised in a settlement. The rule is further narrowed by the right of the testator to express a contrary intention in his will.[3]

The broad rule draws no distinction between real and personal property. This marks a change not only from the old law of estate duty but also from the original CTT provision as it was thought it should be construed. However in *Re Dougal*[4] what is now the broad rule was accepted by a Scottish court; the rule was made statutory in 1983.[5]

When property does not fall under this general rule, whether because the rule does not, in terms, apply or because it is excluded by the testator, it bears its own tax. If, nonetheless, the personal representatives have paid tax, as may have been necessary in order to obtain probate, the amount of tax is to be repaid by the person in whom the property is vested.

Foster's Capital Taxes K2.01.
1 IHTA 1984, s. 211(1).
2 Administration of Estates Act 1925, s. 34(3) and Sch. 1, para. 8.
3 IHTA 1984, s. 211(2).
4 [1981] STC 514.
5 But only for deaths after 25th July 1983.

48: 09   The burden of deferred tax on works of art etc falls on those entitled to the proceeds of sale[1] not the estate; for other special cases see supra, § **47: 06**.

Foster's Capital Taxes K1.11.
1 IHTA 1984, s. 207.

Apportionment of tax

48: 10   Where tax is payable as a testamentary expense, the general rule is that the tax exhausts each category of property available for payment of testamentary expenses and, to the extent that a particular category of property is only partially reduced, the partial reduction is borne rateably by all those interested in that particular category of property.

Where personal representatives have a right to recover the tax under IHTA 1984, s. 212 no problems arise if the beneficiaries are absolutely entitled between them to the property: the tax is simply divided between them according to their appropriate interests in the property.

If property is left on trust for A for life with remainder to B the tax charged in respect of it comes out of the capital of the settled property, though interest should come out of income.[1] A bears his proportion of IHT by suffering a reduction of income through diminution of the capital.

A pecuniary legacy will always bear the tax when it has to be paid out of property in respect of which personal representatives have a right of recovery, as where T bequeaths foreign property subject to payment of legacies thereout or where legacies have to be paid thereout in due cause of administration.

Foster's Capital Taxes K1.12.
[1] IHTA 1984, s. 212.

48: 11   If there is *no* express direction for payment of legacies out of property but in due course of administration it is necessary to pay legacies out of e.g. foreign property then to the extent that they are so paid they must bear the tax.

Annuitant and remainderman

48: 12   If real property is left on trust for A for life and after his death on trust to pay an annuity to X for life and subject thereto to hold the property on trust for B absolutely the tax is payable out of the capital of the settled property.[1] However, when A dies, thereby causing IHT to fall on the settled property even if it is personal property, X, the annuitant, and B, the residuary legatee, bear the tax on the property in respect of A's death rateably according to the value of their respective interests.[2] X will bear his share by way of a reduction in the amount of his annuity and not by a lump sum payment of a part of the tax. The tax will be paid out of the capital of the property, being raised by way of sale, mortgage or otherwise.

Foster's Capital Taxes D5.21–26.
[1] IHTA 1984, s. 212.
[2] IHTA 1984, s. 212 *Re McNeill, Royal Bank of Scotland v Macpherson* [1958] Ch 259, [1957] 3 All ER 508.

48: 13   The difficulty lies in determining the amount by which the annuity is to be reduced. In simple cases it will no doubt be a sufficient approximation to reduce the annuity by the percentage equal to the over-all effective rate of capital transfer tax. But if greater accuracy is necessary, the method laid down in *Re Parker–Jervis, Salt v Locker*[1] may perhaps be followed. Calculate the "slice" of capital supporting the annuity according to the income yield of the estate; notionally apportion the tax between this "slice" of capital and the rest of the estate; and charge the annuitant, in reduction of the annuity, with interest on the tax so apportioned to the "slice" of capital. The interest should be charged at the rate at which interest is payable on tax until payment of the tax, and thereafter at the rate at which the amount of the tax can be raised by mortgage of the property.

This method is not satisfactory when the yield is abnormally high or low.[2] In such cases the "slice" of capital should perhaps be found by reference to the mean between the gross dividend yield appearing in the Financial Times Actuaries Share Index and the yield obtained irredeemable gifts as revealed by the same Index.[3]

---

[1] [1898] 2 Ch 643.
[2] *Re Viscount Portman, Portman v Portman* [1924] 2 Ch 6.
[3] These are the low and high yields used etc, see supra, § **41: 09**.

48: 14   These problems of valuation arise also on the death of the annuitant,[1] as where property is settled on trust to pay an annuity of £2,000 a year to X and on X's death a similar annuity to A and subject to these for B absolutely. On X's death the burden must be shared between A and B on the basis of one of the methods just outlined.

Foster's Capital Taxes H3.75.
    [1] Cf. *Re Palmer, Palmer v Palmer* [1916] 2 Ch 391; *Re Weigall's Will Trusts, Midland Bank Executor and Trustee Co Ltd v Weigall* [1956] Ch 424, [1956] 2 All ER 312.

Death of life tenant of part

48: 15   If a life tenant of part of settled property dies the loss of income arising from the payment of the tax is to be borne solely by those who become entitled to the income of the deceased's share and the loss of capital by those who eventually take the deceased's share, and not at all by the other beneficiaries.[1] This will arise if T leaves property on trust to pay the income equally between X, Y and Z during their respective lives and on the death of each of them to pay his share of income to his children during their lives and X dies. The distinctive feature of this kind of case is that what is charged to tax on the death of X is an aliquot share of the property to which X's children succeed. The reduction of income to be suffered by the children can be calculated at current mortgage interest rates on the amount of IHT payable as in *Re Parker–Jervis* unless the fund is physically divided following the death.

---

[1] Cf. *Betts Brown's Trustees v Whately Smith* 1941 SC 69.

Person exercising option

48: 16   If T by his will gives B an option to purchase foreign property at a price below its probate value and B exercises the option, B must bear the proportion of tax attributable to the excess of the value of the property above the option price. Essentially, B is obtaining a pecuniary legacy of the excess value and to the extent that it is paid out of property in respect of which personal representatives have a right or recovery of tax it will bear a proportion of that tax.[1] Thus if foreign property worth £21,000 is purchased under an option for £14,000 then B will have to bear one-third of the tax payable in respect of the foreign property. The position is otherwise if the option were to purchase some of the deceased's property in the UK for in such a case the personal representatives have no right of recovery: the tax in respect of such property is a testamentary expense and such property subject to an option at an undervalue is the last category of property available for payment of testamentary expenses, debts and liabilities.[2]

Foster's Capital Taxes H2.31.
[1] Cf. *Re Lander, Lander v Lander* [1951] Ch 546, [1951] 1 All ER 622.
[2] *Re Eve, National Provincial Bank Ltd v Eve* [1956] Ch 479, [1956] 2 All ER 321.

Variation of incidence by will or other document

48: 17 A clause in a will or settlement varying the ordinary rules of incidence must be interpreted in accordance with the precise words of the will or settlement. The only case law concerns estate duty.[1] The general approach of the courts where there has been any ambiguity has been to presume that "free of estate duty" clauses have altered the ordinary rules of incidence as little as possible. It seems that such a clause in a will should be interpreted as conferring only freedom from tax payable in respect of a testator's death.[2] Thus if a testator gives foreign property free of tax to A for life, with remainder to B it will be presumed (rebuttably)[3] that the clause refers only to IHT payable in respect of the testator's death and not A's death or on an earlier disposal of A's interest, so that B will bear the tax on A's death or on the earlier disposal of A's interest. This facilitates the administration of the testator's estate for it is most inconvenient if the executors have to retain a significant part of the residuary estate to meet the tax claim that will arise if A disposes of his life interest or when A dies.

Foster's Capital Taxes D5.21–26.
[1] Free of estate duty includes free of CTT or IHT; free of CTT includes free of IHT: IHTA 1984, Sch. 6, para. 1 and FA 1986, s. 100(1)(*b*), the use of expressions like "clear of all deductions" or "net sum" will probably be regarded as importing freedom from CTT and IHT: *Re Sebright, Public Trustee v Sebright* [1944] Ch 287, [1944] 2 All ER 547; *Re Saunders, Saunders v Gore* [1898] 1 Ch 17.
[2] *Re Shepherd, Public Trustee v Henderson* [1949] Ch 116, [1948] 2 All ER 932; *Re Embleton's Will Trusts, Sodeau v Nelson* [1965] 1 All ER 771.
[3] *Re Paterson's Will Trusts, Lawson v Payn* [1963] 1 All ER 114.

48: 18 It is likely that a similar approach will prevail in respect of "free of inheritance tax" clauses in a settlement though not quite so severely since the executor's convenience rationale is absent.

It would seem that a direction to pay "testamentary expenses" out of residue would be construed as a direction to pay thereout only such IHT which ranks as a testamentary expense,[1] and so not tax on foreign property.

Where a testator directs the payment of tax out of residue this will usually be construed as freeing from tax any property in respect of which IHT does not rank as a testamentary expense.[2] But if in such a case the will contains not only a general clause for payment of tax out of residue but also clauses specially freeing certain devises and bequests from IHT, the general provisions for payment of tax out of residue will not necessarily be construed as referring to tax on gifts of foreign property which are not specially freed from IHT[3] although in some cases it may be, depending upon the context of the particular will.[4]

A bequest free of IHT of designated works of art etc. on which tax is not payable until they are sold or until certain conditions are broken will relieve only the beneficiary under the will. If such a beneficiary gives the articles away, and the donee sells them, thereby attracting IHT the donee will not be able to take advantage of the clause, and will have to bear the tax himself.[5]

---

[1] *Re Owers* [1941] Ch 17, [1940] 4 All ER 225.
[2] *Re Pimm, Sharpe v Hodgson* [1904] 2 Ch 345.
[3] *Re King, Barclays Bank Ltd v King* [1942] Ch 413, [1942] 2 All ER 182.
[4] *Re Neeld, Carpenter v Inigo-Jones* [1964] 2 All ER 952n at 953.
[5] *Re Oppenheimer, Tyser v Oppenheimer* [1948] Ch 721.

49 Foreign element

TERRITORIAL LIMITS

49: 01   The provisions of IHTA 1984 relating to IHT operate as law in England, Wales, Scotland and Northern Ireland. They do not extend to the Channel Islands nor to the Isle of Man. Transfers of foreign property may be subject to IHT. Broadly, where the transferor is domiciled, or deemed so, in the UK, a charge to IHT arises regardless of the location of the asset; if he is not so domiciled the charge arises only if the asset is located in the UK. The rules are thus very different from those for CGT. The rules may be overridden by double tax agreement.[1]

When a charge is imposed on foreign property it does not follow that the Revenue will be able to collect the tax. The Revenue may find themselves unable to sue in the foreign court.[2] In such circumstances the liability of persons within this country for tax on property outside assumes great importance.[3]

Foster's Capital Taxes J1.01.
[1] IHTA 1984, s. 158; and see extra-statutory concession F6 (1985); **Foster's Capital Taxes, Division U2.**
[2] Supra, § **33: 01.**
[3] Infra, § **49: 23** and **Chapter 47.**

LOCATION OF ASSETS

49: 02   This is determined by reference to English, Scottish or N. Ireland laws; foreign law rules are irrelevant save for double taxation relief.

Foster's Capital Taxes J4.01.

Land

49: 03   Land is located in the country in which it is physically situated.

Mortgages of land, even if they take the English form of a lease for 3,000 years, are not treated as land but as debts, except in the one case where they are a charge on land only, not accompanied by any personal obligation of the mortgagor to repay.

Exceptionally, a Scottish heritable bond is treated in the same way as land.

Foster's Capital Taxes J4.61, 71.

Debts

49: 04   A simple contract debt is in general situated in the country where the debtor resides, that being the country where the debt can be recovered.

A specialty debt, e.g. one payable by virtue of a document under seal, is located in the country where the document evidencing the debt is physically situated. Different rules apply under Scottish Law.

A judgment debt is located in the country where the judgment is recorded.

Foster's Capital Taxes J4.21–25.

Stocks, shares and other securities

49: 05   A bearer security is located in the country where the document of title is physically situated.

Registered or inscribed securities are located in the country in which the register ought to be kept. This rule extends to debenture stock, but not apparently to a debenture, which, if under seal, is to be regarded as a specialty debt.

Stocks and shares in a company registered under the Companies Acts are therefore generally situated in the UK, even though the entire business of the company, and even its residence, may be abroad. So while dividends may be treated as income from a foreign source, the shares themselves may be treated as located in the UK for IHT. Rights under renouncable letters of allotment have been held to be situated where the company resides or is registered since this is where the rights are enforceable. For an instrument to be treated as analogous to a chattel more is required than mere transferability of title by delivery. What is required is a market for these rights.[1]

Companies incorporated abroad cause problems, especially when securities are entered on two principal registers, one in the UK and one abroad. The rational approach is to ask where the transferor dealt, or, for a transfer on death, would have dealt, with the shares in the ordinary course of affairs.[2] Physical presence of the share certificate in the one country[3] may be sufficient to turn the scales in favour of that country.

Foster's Capital Taxes J4.11, 12.
[1] *Young v Phillips* [1984] STC 520.
[2] *Standard Chartered Bank Ltd v IRC* [1978] STC 272, [1978] 3 All ER 644.
[3] *R v Williams* [1942] AC 541, [1942] 2 All ER 95.

Miscellaneous

49: 06 Tangible property, such as furniture, coins or bank notes, is located in the country of physical situation, so a yacht berthed in an English harbour was situated in the UK even though it was registered in Jersey.[1]

Business assets, including goodwill, or a share in a partnership firm, are located in the country where the business is carried on. This does not however determine the situs of the beneficiary's interest save where a beneficiary with a valid interest in possession is treated as having a right in rem in the trust assets. A reversionary interest under a trust for sale has been treated as a chose in action and so as located where the trustees are resident;[2] an exception is made for immovable property, the situs being preferred.[3] In the confused state of the authorities it is safe to say only that the chose in action treatment is given where there is a trust for sale *and* more than one beneficiary, or the trust may be varied.[4]

A share in the unadministered estate of a deceased person is located in the country which is the forum of administration.[5]

The location of property held in trust is found according to the rules applying to the particular property, without regard to the proper law of the trust or the residence of the trustees.

Currency is located in the country of physical situation, without regard to the country by which the currency was issued.

A bank account is located in the country in which the branch of the bank at which the money is payable is situated.

Certain pensions in respect of service overseas are treated as payable outside the UK even though the United Kingdom Government may have become liable to pay them. Life assurance policies are regarded simply as debts.

A cause of action in tort is probably located where it arose.

Foster's Capital Taxes J4.71, 81, 91.
[1] *Trustees Executors and Agency Co Ltd v IRC* [1973] Ch 254, [1973] 1 All ER 562.
[2] *Re Smyth, Leach v Leach* [1898] 1 Ch 89.
[3] *Dymond's Death Duties* (15th edn) p. 1319.
[4] Foster's Capital Taxes J4.31.
[5] *Stamp Duties Comr (Queensland) v Livingston* [1965] AC 694, [1964] 3 All ER 692.

Deemed domicile

49: 07 The notion of domicile supra, § **32: 12** is extended by IHTA 1984, s. 267 in two ways. These rules may however be overridden by a double tax treaty[1] and are excluded by particular rules.[2]

(1) A person is treated as domiciled in the UK and not elsewhere[3] if he was so domiciled on or after 10th December 1974 and within three years immediately preceding the relevant time. The three-year period begins to run only from the date on which the new domicile is acquired. So where a person previously domiciled in the UK establishes a domicile overseas, any transfer he makes within the succeeding three years will be caught regardless of the *situs* of the asset. This highly questionable rule appears to be based on the practice of the Inland Revenue for income tax under which a person is

treated as remaining resident in this country for the following three years supra, § **32: 09.** However there is an essential difference in that the income tax practice is simply a provisional matter and if residence is not resumed within three years the taxpayer is reassessed for those three years as if he had not been resident. There is no such provisional character about the rule for IHT.

Foster's Capital Taxes J2.06.
[1] IHTA 1984, s. 267(2).
[2] IHTA 1984, ss. 6(2), (3) and 48(4).
[3] IHTA 1984, s. 267(1).

49: 08   (2) A person is treated as domiciled in the UK and not elsewhere[1] if he was *resident* in the UK on or after 10th December 1974 and in not less than 17 of the 20 years of assessment ending with the year of assessment in which the relevant time falls. In deciding whether a person is resident no regard is had to any dwelling house available in the UK for his use.[2] This is far more justifiable than the first rule in that a person resident here for 17 of the previous 20 years might be said to have a substantial connection with this country and it is only the very permanent tie required for the UK notion of domicile that prevents such a person as being treated as domiciled here. One should however note the wide scope of residence which is taken by UK tax law, the effect of which is to make it relatively difficult to get rid of a UK residence once acquired.

[1] IHTA 1984, s. 267(1)(*b*).
[2] IHTA 1984, s. 267(4).

49: 09   (3) In relation to transfers of value made and for events occurring before 15th March 1983,[1] a person was treated as domiciled in the UK if he had, since 10th December 1974, become and had retained domicile in the Channel Islands or the Isle of Man[2] and, immediately before becoming domiciled there he had been domiciled in the UK. A person falling within this third rule was treated as domiciled in the UK however long he remained domiciled in the Channel Islands or Isle of Man.

Foster's Capital Taxes J2.06,11.
[1] F(No. 2)A 1983, s. 12.
[2] FA 1975, s. 45 (1) actually says "the Islands" which are thus defined as the Channel Islands *and* the Isle of Man. Since one cannot be domiciled in both places at once it has been suggested that the section is nugatory; however such a construction seems, to say the least, unlikely.

PROPERTY IN THE UNITED KINGDOM

49: 10   As a general rule property in the UK, whether real or personal, which is the subject of a chargeable transfer is liable to tax whatever foreign elements may be concerned in the passing. For example, if an Arab sheik domiciled and resident in a Middle Eastern country owns a house in London and some shares on the register of a company incorporated in England and he gives these to his son, IHT is payable on the house and the shares, assuming these to be or to become chargeable transfers. The value of these gifts will be aggregated with previous chargeable transfers to ascertain the rate of tax and will thus raise the rate of tax payable on subsequent transfers.[1]

There are however some exceptions to this general rule.

(1) Property may be deemed to be located abroad under a double tax treaty; such property is therefore foreign property.[2]

(2) Certain pensions payable in respect of colonial service do not form part of a person's estate for the purposes of the transfer on death.[3]

(3) National Savings and other "small" savings held by persons actually (as opposed to deemed) domiciled in the Channel Islands or Isle of Man are treated as excluded property.[4]

(4) Property of members of visiting forces or of staff of allied headquarters is also excluded property.[5]

(5) Certain international securities are exempt.[6]

(6) Certain British government securities are excluded property if owned by persons neither domiciled[7] nor ordinarily resident in the UK.[8] A transfer of such stock by such a person is therefore a transfer of excluded property. The power to issue securities on such terms was granted in 1915.[9]

Where the securities are settled property, the securities are excluded property so long as the person beneficially entitled to an interest in possession in them is neither domiciled nor ordinarily resident.[10] On the other hand there is some doubt as to the position where there are two or more persons entitled to interests in possession, for example joint life tenants, only some of whom are ordinarily resident and domiciled outside the UK. In such a situation it would appear that since there is a deemed transfer of only a part of the settled property and the legislation speaks only of "an interest" as opposed to "the interest" in possession, it will be sufficient that the conditions are fulfilled with regard to the one person who is making the deemed transfer and the property will not be excluded on the occasion of a deemed transfer by one who did not fulfil those conditions.

Foster's Capital Taxes J3.21–28.

[1] On the other hand transfers by the same person of property situated outside the UK will be transfers of excluded property and so will not be aggregated.

[2] IHTA 1984, s. 158; infra, § **49: 19**.

[3] IHTA 1984, s. 153.

[4] IHTA 1984, s. 6(3); deemed domicile is excluded by IHTA 1984, s. 267(2).

[5] IHTA 1984, s. 155.

[6] E.g. FA 1976, s. 131.

[7] Deemed domicile is ignored, IHTA 1984, s. 267(2).

[8] IHTA 1984, s. 6(2).

[9] Because of the sharp increase in tax rates due to war; F (No. 2) A 1915, s. 47; the power lapsed in 1922 but was revived by FA 1931, s. 22; see also TA 1970, s. 99 and supra, § **9: 33**.

[10] IHTA 1984, s. 48(4).

49: 11   Where the securities are settled property and no qualifying interest in possession subsists in them, IHTA 1984, s. 48(4)(b) provides that they are excluded property only if it can be shown that all known persons for whose benefit the settled property or the income from it has been or might be applied or who might become beneficially entitled to an interest in possession in it are persons neither domiciled nor ordinarily resident in the UK. This extraordinarily wide list was narrowed slightly by the decision of the Court of Appeal in *Von Ernst & Cie SA v IRC*[1] that an unincorporated association or company established only for charitable purposes cannot become beneficially entitled nor have property or income applied for it. It followed that where the beneficiaries comprised UK resident charities and non-resident non-domiciled individuals the relief applied.

This case also held that the test as to the list of beneficiaries and their residence must be answered on the facts as they are immediately before the relevant event. In *Minden Trust (Cayman) Ltd v IRC*[2], government securities were bought by trustees of the A settlement; they resolved to advance these to be held on trust for the B settlement; the trustees of the B settlement then appointed the property in favour of X, a non-resident. The court held that in applying para. 3 the expression "the settled property" referred to the property which had been in the A settlement and which was advanced to the B settlement; it followed that that property was excluded property.

If property moved from one settlement to another between 19th April 1978 and 10th December 1981 (exclusive) or moved from the first settlement to the second after December 1981 without any person having in the meantime become beneficially entitled to the property (and not merely to an interest in possession in it) these conditions had to be satisfied by the beneficiaries of both settlements.[3] This rule is now to be relaxed for events occurring after 14th May 1983 if a qualifying reversionary interest arising under the first settlement was settled on the trusts of the second before 10th December 1981; only the beneficiaries under the second settlement need to be considered in relation to that second settlement.[4]

---

[1] [1980] STC 111, [1980] 1 All ER 677.
[2] [1985] STC 758.
[3] IHTA 1984, s. 48(5).
[4] IHTA 1984, s. 48(6).

49: 12   Non resident's bank accounts do not form part of a person's estate for the purpose of the transfer immediately before death. The person must not be domiciled in the UK nor may he be resident or ordinarily resident here at the time of death. The account must not be denominated in Sterling.[1]

Similar rules apply to bank accounts held by trustees of settled property in which the deceased had a beneficial interest in possession, although the exclusion will be lost if the settlor was domiciled in the UK when he made the settlement or if the trustees were domiciled resident or ordinarily resident in the UK immediately before the beneficiary's death.[2] These rules apply to deaths after 8th March 1982.

Foster's Capital Taxes Division J3.
[1] IHTA 1984, s. 157(1)(*a*).
[2] IHTA 1984, s. 157(1)(*b*).

FOREIGN PROPERTY

49: 13   Property other than settled property situated outside the UK will be excluded property if the person beneficially entitled to it is an individual domiciled outside the UK.[1] The individual in question is the transferor not the transferee and generally the question must be answered by reference to the facts at the time of the transfer.

Foster's Capital Taxes J3.01.
[1] IHTA 1984, s. 6.

Settled property

49: 14 Where property is settled a very different approach prevails. The key elements are the domicile of the settlor at the time of the settlement and the situs of the asset. The status of the trustees and even of the beneficiaries is ignored. The rule is that where property is situated outside the UK, the property (but not a reversionary interest in that property) is excluded property unless the settlor was domiciled in the UK at the time the settlement was made.[1] This rule applies whether or not there is an interest in possession. The settlor's domicile at the time of the settlement fixes liability to the tax on the settlement regardless of his subsequent changes of domicile. If the property became comprised in a settlement before 10th December 1974 domicile has its ordinary and not its extended meaning.

Excluded property held on discretionary trusts is not relevant property and so is not subject to the ten year or intermediate charges—supra, **Chapter 42**. Where the property is situated in the UK it will not be excluded property and so can be relevant property; however no charge arises under IHTA 1984, s. 65 simply because the property ceases to be situate in the UK or is invested in Government securities and so becomes, in either case, excluded property.[2]

Collection of the tax will be a separate matter but it must not be forgotten that the settlor will be liable for the tax on a chargeable transfer, for example the death of a life tenant, occurs during his life and the trustees are not resident in the UK.[3]

Foster's Capital Taxes J3.26, 32, 33.
[1] IHTA 1984, s. 48(3). The rule is framed in terms of exemption for the property comprised in the settlement; however changes of investments by the trustees after the settlor has become domiciled in the UK do not deprive the settled property of its status as excluded property—*Law Society's Gazette*, 3rd December 1975.
[2] IHTA 1984, ss. 65(7), (8) and 267(3).
[3] IHTA 1984, s. 201(1)(*d*), supra, § **47: 03**.

49: 15 *The Islands.* If a person became domiciled in the Islands after 10th December 1974 but was deemed domiciled in the UK by virtue of the rule mentioned at § **49: 09**, and he then made a settlement, he is presumably to be treated as having UK domicile for events before 15th March 1983 but a non-UK domicile for events thereafter, but this is not completely clear.

Reversionary interests in foreign property

49: 16 A reversionary interest in settled property does not come under the settled property[1] rule but under the general rule: so it is excluded property if the person beneficially entitled to it is an individual domiciled outside the

UK and it is situated outside the UK; the situs of the reversionary interest is not necessary that of the settled property.[2] Where the settled property is itself a reversionary interest the settled property rule applies to it.

EXAMPLES

(*a*) X dies domiciled in England, leaving land abroad and shares in companies whose registers of shareholders are abroad. The land abroad and the shares are liable to IHT.

(*b*) X dies domiciled abroad, leaving land abroad and shares in companies whose registers of shareholders are abroad. The land and shares are excluded property and so not liable to IHT.

(*c*) X, domiciled in Canada, gives Y domiciled in the UK £1,000 in Toronto; the gift is of excluded property.

(*d*) X, domiciled in Canada wishes to give Y, domiciled in the UK, £1,000 and does so by sending Y a cheque drawn on X's account in London; the gift is not of excluded property.

(*e*) In 1980 A, domiciled in the UK, settled English property on B for life with remainder to C, both of whom were domiciled in the UK. In 1983 B emigrated to Canada and established domicile there. C remained in the UK and died in 1989. B died of frostbite in 1990. On B's death there will be a charge by reason of the location of the property in the UK and A's domicile in 1980. There will be no charge on the reversionary interest on C's death in 1989.

(*f*) In 1980 X domiciled in Canada settled Canadian property on Y for life with remainder to Z, both of whom were then domiciled in Canada. In 1983 Y and Z migrated to and established domicile in the UK. Z died of sunstroke in 1989. Y died in 1990. On Y's death there will be no charge since the property was situated outside the UK and the settlor was not domiciled here when the settlement was made. There will be a charge on the reversionary interest on Z's death.

(*g*) A testator dies domiciled in England, leaving foreign land and shares on trust for X for life. X dies domiciled abroad. The shares and the land are liable to IHT on the death of the testator and in theory on the later death of X but the testator's estate is not liable for the IHT on X's death.

(*h*) A testator dies domiciled abroad, leaving foreign property on trust for X for life. X dies domiciled in England, and at his death the trust fund consists of foreign land and shares. There is no charge to IHT on the death of the testator, nor on that of X.

Foster's Capital Taxes J3.41.
[1] IHTA 1984, s. 48(3) applying IHTA 1984, s. 6(1).
[2] IHTA 1984, s. 6(1).

DOUBLE TAXATION RELIEF

49: 17   Where tax is payable in both countries it is generally on the basis of the location of the property in one country and the domicile of the transferor in the other. The law of the UK (and of many foreign countries) makes provision for relief in respect of such double taxation in certain circumstances. What follows is concerned with relief granted by the law of the UK; for relief granted by the laws of a foreign country, reference must be made to those laws.

Double tax treaties were made in relation to estate duty between the UK and various overseas countries. These conventions remain in force but only for transfers of value on death.[1] Fresh conventions are being made for transfers *inter vivos* and these are being adapted for IHT,[2] because some transfers *inter vivos* remain chargeable.

Foster's Capital Taxes Division J5; Division R4.
[1] IHTA 1984, s. 158(6).
[2] E.g., Double Taxation Relief (Taxes on Estates of Deceased Persons and Inheritances and on Gifts) (Sweden) Order 1989, SI 1989 No. 986.

49: 18   Two sorts of arrangement were made for estate duty and apply to IHT on death:[1]

(1) Arrangements under F (No. 2) A 1945, s. 54. These contain codes for determining the *situs* of certain kinds of property, which may in certain cases lead to property which is situate in the UK being treated as situate in the other country, and so excluded property. In other situations one tax can be used as a credit against the other; the effect is that the transfer will not bear tax in excess of the larger amount due to each country separately. The difference between the two reliefs is substantial. Not only will transfer within the first relief escape UK tax completely and usually only partly under the latter, but the transfer under the former relief will be of excluded property and so exempt from aggregation whereas under the latter the value transferred must be aggregated with any other value transferred and cumulated. These treaties often also contain tests for the resolution of dual domicile problems and are now in force with France, India, Italy and Pakistan. In addition, treaties have also been negotiated with Denmark, France and Italy, although these are not yet in force. The OECD has produced a new model convention. The pattern of the new treaties, and this model, is to allow states the primary right to tax on the basis of situs if the property is immovable or is a business based there and otherwise to grant the (primary) right to tax to the country of fiscal domicile, a concept loosely defined as almost any connecting factor on which a state may wish to tax but with a tie breaker clause like the dual residence provision mentioned at § **36.09**.

Foster's Capital Taxes, J5.04.
[1] However, new treaties applying both on death and inter vivos have been made with Ireland, Netherlands, South Africa, Sweden and USA. That with Sweden now covers IHT–see supra, § **49: 17**.

49: 19   (2) Conventions were made under the Finance Act 1948, s. 77 with countries which did not have a duty similar to estate duty. Their effect is limited; they merely contain a *situs* code, which may in certain circumstances lead to exemption as excluded property. Conventions were made with the Netherlands and Switzerland, the latter remaining in force. The Swiss Convention applies only on death[1] and has no dual fiscal domicile provision. It applies only where the deceased was fiscally domiciled in one country but not in the other; on fiscal domicile, see supra, §**49.18**.

Foster's Capital Taxes J5.03, 04.
[1] IHTA 1984, Sch. 6, para. 1.

Unilateral relief

49: 20   Unilateral relief is available[1] against any amount of tax chargeable by reason of any disposition or event provided (*i*) the tax is similar in character to IHT or is chargeable on or by reference to death or gifts *inter vivos* and (*ii*) the IHT chargeable is attributable to the value of that property. This relief is by way of credit so that the transfer remains nonetheless a chargeable transfer and must be cumulated in the usual way. Unilateral relief may be claimed even if there is a double tax agreement provided it exceeds the relief under the agreement.[2]

Foster's Capital Taxes J5.02.
[1] IHTA 1984, s. 159.
[2] IHTA 1984, s. 159(7).

The credit

49: 21   (1) *Single situs:* Where the asset is situated in the foreign country the credit is for the full amount of the foreign tax on the property.[1] This credit concedes priority of taxation to the country of *situs*.

(2) *Dual situs:* Where the property is situate in both (or neither) of the UK[2] and the foreign country, credit is determined by the formula $\dfrac{A}{A+B} \times C$ where A is the IHT, B is the overseas tax and C is whichever is the smaller of A and B.[3] This form of relief is used in some double tax agreements[4] and is often more advantageous than that in other agreements. The relief has the curious effect that the greater the foreign tax the less credit is available; this is understandable where, as in a treaty, the other country uses the same formula but is very odd in unilateral relief.

(3) *A third country taxes:* Where three countries are involved B becomes the aggregate of the foreign taxes and C the aggregate of A and B minus the largest single charge.[5]

(4) *Effect of foreign credit:* Where relief by credit is available, whether by convention or unilaterally, and rule 2 or 3 applies, any credit under the $\dfrac{A}{A+B} \times C$ formula is calculated by treating A as the tax as reduced by any credit relief due in respect of tax in another country; equally B is to be reduced by any credit available under the foreign law.[6]

EXAMPLES

(1) A dies domiciled in the UK but some of the assets are in another country, Q. Suppose that the charge to tax is £5,000 and Q charges tax of £3,000. Assuming that under UK rules the assets are in Q, the IHT liability will be £2,000.

(2) If however Q says the assets are in Q and the UK says the assets are in the UK, the formula will be applied:

$$\frac{5,000}{5,000+3,000} \times 3,000 = £1,875$$

so IHT liability would be £5,000 − 1,875 = £3,125.

The same would result if both the UK and Q regarded the property as located in a third country, R, assuming that R charged no tax.

Assuming that Q uses the same formula the credit there will be

$$\frac{3,000}{8,000} \times 3,000 = £1,125,$$

making a tax liability in Q of £1,875. The aggregate of the liabilities in the UK and Q will be £5,000. If however Q has no treaty the total tax liability may be as much as £(3,000 + 3,125).

(3) If R also charged tax on the property say of £1,000 the credit against tax would for the tax charged in Q and R be

$$\frac{5,000}{5,000+(3,000+1,000)} \times (3,000+1,000) = £2,222.$$

(4) If however UK and Q gave credit for the tax of £1,000 in R the credit against IHT is adjusted and the formula gives the following credit for the tax levied in Q

$$\frac{5,000-1,000}{(5,000-1,000)+(3,000+1,000-1,000)} \times (3,000-1,000) = £1,143.$$

Foster's Capital Taxes J5.02.
[1] IHTA 1984, s. 159(2).
[2] Presumably *situs* is determined according to the law of each country and not just by the law of the UK; this is the official view—Thus if UK law says the *situs* is X and X says the *situs* is the UK, or vice versa, relief is available. However there appears to be a gap if UK law says that the *situs* is X while X says the *situs* is Y.
[3] IHTA 1984, s. 159(3).
[4] USA, South Africa, India and Pakistan.
[5] IHTA 1984, s. 159(4).
[6] IHTA 1984, s. 159(5).

MISCELLANEOUS

Foreign debts and administration expenses

49: 22 A liability to a person resident outside the UK is allowable as a deduction in computing the value of the estate provided it satisfies the general rules at supra, § **46: 19**. However where the liability falls to be discharged outside the UK and is not an incumbrance on property inside the UK, the liability is, so far as possible, taken to reduce the value of property outside the UK.[1] One reason for this rule is that a person not domiciled in the UK is liable to IHT only on property in the UK and it would be giving him an undue advantage to allow him to deduct all his overseas liabilities while taxing him only on some of his property. Such a person can avoid the problem by making his creditors reside in the UK or creating an incumbrance on his UK property. Another reason for the rule concerns persons domiciled in the UK. Such persons pay tax on their foreign property but there may be double tax relief by way of allowing a credit for the foreign tax payable in respect of the property. Foreign liabilities must be set off against the value of overseas property so far as possible. If therefore the particular asset is exempt from tax under the double tax treaty the benefit of that exemption may be cancelled by the disallowance of the liability.

Additional expenses of administering foreign property, incurred by reason of its being situate abroad, may be allowed as a deduction from the value of the property for the purpose of capital transfer tax, but not exceeding 5% of the value of the property.[2]

Foster's Capital Taxes J1.22.
[1] IHTA 1984, s. 162(5).
[2] IHTA 1984, s. 173.

Liability and incidence

49: 23   A foreign resident may become liable for tax or liable to indemnify English executors or others who have paid tax which falls to be borne by him.[1] However personal liability of a foreign resident cannot be enforced by legal process in the UK unless he is personally present in, or has assets situate in the UK or unless the foreign courts permit enforcement. A charge of duty on foreign property cannot be enforced, unless the property, or the proceeds of sale thereof, is brought to this country or unless the foreign courts permit enforcement. The reason for these difficulties is that, by international law, the courts of one country will not usually enforce the revenue laws of another (see **Chapter 33**).

---

[1] As the property is outside the UK, IHTA 1984, s. 211(1) (supra, § **48: 08**) does not apply and IHTA 1984, s. 211(3) preserves the personal liability of the holder of the property to indemnify the personal representatives.

PART IX. NATIONAL INSURANCE CONTRIBUTIONS

50 The contributory scheme

INTRODUCTION

50: 01   The inclusion of national insurance among the subjects covered in a publication dealing with UK taxation calls for some explanation.

Contributions under the national insurance scheme go into a separate fund and help to pay for social security benefits; strictly they do not form part of the central Government's revenue. Moreover, on the face of it there would seem to be no choice but to pay the contributions due and no control over the amounts required and if there are no opportunities for planning is there any point in studying a multitude of detailed rules?

For the reasons explained below, it will be found that national insurance has some of the characteristics of a tax system and requires consideration as such. From the detailed treatment of the subject, it will become apparent that choices are available and that substantial sums can be involved. For this reason, throughout this part attention is drawn to the relevant planning considerations.

Certainly, in concept, the British national insurance scheme is wholly different from a tax régime. Beveridge sharply distinguished taxation from insurance contributions in the following words:

> "The distinction between taxation and insurance contribution is that taxation is or should be related to assumed capacity to pay rather than to the value of what the payer may expect to receive, while insurance contributions are or should be related to the value of the benefits and not to the capacity to pay".[1]

The national insurance system which was set up in 1946,[2] to implement the proposals of the Beveridge Report, was based on a view of social security which enjoyed widespread support at the time. Beveridge expressed this view thus:

> "The plan is not for giving to everybody something for nothing and without trouble or something that will free the recipients for ever thereafter from personal responsibilities. The plan is to secure income for subsistence on condition of service and contribution and in order to make and keep men fit for service."[3]

The means adopted was to apply, on a unified and comprehensive basis, the form of national insurance first introduced in this country by Lloyd George to provide sickness benefit and, in some industries, unemployment benefit and which was administered through approved friendly societies.[4] This scheme was inspired by the system of social security which was well established in Germany by the end of the 19th century. It involved a tripartite system of contributions under which the employee, the employer and the state respectively made contributions into a designated fund at prescribed rates.

At the heart of the Beveridge plan was what is known as the contributory principle. That this principle is very much alive is evident from a comment made by the Chancellor of the Exchequer in his 1989 Budget statement. In describing why a low-paid employee earning just slightly above the threshold for starting to pay national insurance contributions should pay 86p per week on the first £43 of his earnings, the Chancellor explained:

> "The step which has always existed at the lower earnings limit, where people first come into the national insurance system, is the entry ticket to the full array of contributory benefits. As such it is an essential feature of the contributory principle".[5]

What is the contributory principle and why is it so important? When a senior official gave a sombre and reasoned explanation of this principle to a House of Commons subcommittee he was asked:

"Do you agree that it is mumbo-jumbo?".[6]

But for Beveridge the contributory principle was quite clear and entirely appropriate. It was the principle "that a material part of the total cost of maintaining income under the plan should be met from monies contributed by citizens as insured persons".[7] It was only by adopting this principle that Beveridge considered benefits could be made available without a means test, against which then, as probably now, there was strong popular objections on the ground that those who had put by savings against a rainy day were penalised.[8] Hence, the Beveridge plan was intended to be "first and foremost a plan of insurance—of giving in return for contributions, benefits up to subsistence level, as of right and without means test".[9]

But despite the theory the connection between contributions and benefits has always been tenuous and in recent years, certainly in relation to retirement pensions, there has been an increasing awareness that "the working generation today basically pays for the pensions of the generation that has now retired".[10] It is, however, worth restating what is meant by the contributory principle and the motivation behind it, particularly since social security is again a topic of public debate and there have been two recent studies proposing a replacement of the present arrangements by a system of tax credits for all those whose income is below a basic standard.[11]

Attitudes to the contributory principle will of course vary according to the social philosphies espoused but in any event it has to be accepted that the national insurance system which we have at present has departed from Beveridge's principle in a number of important respects, in particular:

(1) For Beveridge the plan of insurance proposed involved a pooling of risks on a community-wide basis as opposed to adjusting premiums according to the level of risk for different categories of insured persons.[12] On this basis contributions were to be at a flat rate and likewise benefits, "each individual paying the same contribution for the same rate of benefit".[13]

However in 1959 the graduated pension scheme was superimposed on the 1946 arrangements. This required employees to pay additional contributions at 4% of their earnings between £9 and £18 a week in return for a very small increase in retirement pension related to the additional contributions paid. The contributory principle followed here was a different one; enhanced benefits in return for additional contributions, though in fact the extra pension secured was not commensurate with the additional contribution.

With all party agreement the graduated pension scheme was replaced in 1975[14] by the system of national insurance which is still in operation. The principle of graduated contributions dependent on the level of earnings between the lower and upper earnings limits was now incorporated in the basic scheme. A supplement to the basic retirement pension was provided by the State Earnings Related Pension Scheme (SERPS) but for those many employees who were contracted out[15] of this scheme, as a result of belonging to employer-sponsored occupational schemes providing benefits at least equivalent to those under SERPS, both employee and employer contributions (after deduction of the contracted-out rebate) varied according to the level of the employer's earnings. However, the basic state pension for contracted-out employees does not vary according to earnings and thus the direct relationship between contributions and benefits was breached in this situation.

(2) Self-employed persons were not included in SERPS but the introduction of graduated contributions in respect of employed persons into the main contributory scheme meant that a wide divergence opened up between the contributions required from an employed person with earnings at or above the upper earnings limit and those payable by a self-employed person with the same level of earnings: these were still at a flat rate. This was considered inequitable notwithstanding that the self-employed person could only expect the basic state pension and was not (and still is not) entitled to unemployment benefit. In order to correct the divergence, a new class of contributions—Class 4—was imposed on those carrying on a trade, profession or vocation on their own account. Class 4 contributions are payable on the contributor's business profits as assessed for income tax and secure no additional benefits. They therefore represent a further departure from the Beveridge principle of "benefit in return for contributions".[16]

(3) Until 1985 both employee and employer contributions reached a maximum where the employee's earnings passed above the upper earnings limit. But in 1985 this ceiling was removed for employer contributions. Accordingly once earnings are above a certain lower threshold (for 1989–90 £8,850 pa) employer contributions are payable at 10·45% on the employee's earnings without upper limit. From the outset the employer contributions could be seen as "a direct tax on employment"[17] since the employer gains little from the payment of the contributions but since 1985 the employer contributions have borne no relationship at all to benefits provided by the scheme and represent nothing more than a payroll tax.

(4) In the social security scheme envisaged by Beveridge, virtually all benefits were to be contributory, non-means tested benefits. Only for "the limited number of cases of need not covered by social insurance" would "national assistance subject to a uniform means test" be made available.[18]

But the last 40 years have seen a continuous growth in the range of non-contributory benefits, many of which such as child benefit, one parent benefit and the disability benefits are not means tested. As a result many who are only entitled to limited contributory benefits have their income is supplemented by non-contributory benefits. This tends to reduce the distinctiveness of the contributory scheme and the practical importance of the contributory principle.

The introduction of graduated contributions and the removal of the upper limit on employer contributions and for self-employed persons, the introduction of Class 4 contributions have all eroded the contributory principle and made national insurance progressively more like a tax.

Considered as a tax, national insurance is a source of revenue second only to income tax: in 1988–89 the yield is likely to be over £30,000 million, of which more than half represents employer contributions based on the earnings of their employees.

In view of the character of the contributory system and the size of the figures involved, it will now be clear why treatment of this subject is appropriate in a comprehensive account of UK taxation

¹ Social Insurances and Allied Services (Cmd 6404 (Beveridge Report) para. 272).
² By the National Insurance Act 1946. This came into effect in 1948.
³ Beveridge Report, para. 455.
⁴ The arrangement established by the National Insurance Act 1907.
⁵ Hansard 14 March 1989, Vol 149, col. 308.
⁶ Minutes of evidence, Subcommittee of the House of Commons Treasury and Civil Service Committee, (Session 1982–83) 'The Structure of Personal Income Taxation and Income Support', para. 840.
⁷ Beveridge Report, para. 273.
⁸ Beveridge Report, para. 21.
⁹ Beveridge Report, para. 10.
¹⁰ The structure of Personal Income Taxation and Income Support, supra, para. 841.
¹¹ Institute of Fiscal Studies Report 1984 The Reform of Social Security (authors A W Dilnot, J A Kay and C N Morris; Stepping Stones to Independence; national insurance after 1990, Brandon Rhys Williams (ed Hermione Parker, Aberdeen University Press).
¹² Beveridge Report, para. 25.
¹³ Beveridge Report, para. 273.
¹⁴ As a result of Social Security Act 1975 and Social Security Pensions Act 1975.
¹⁵ For contracting-out, see further § 30: 02.
¹⁶ Beveridge Report, para. 21.
¹⁷ Beveridge Report, para. 276.
¹⁸ Beveridge Report, para. 11.

THE NATIONAL INSURANCE FUND

50: 02   Because the national insurance system is founded on the conception that the members of the community provide against risks on a community-wide basis, an essential feature is that all contributions should be held in a separate fund and that benefits or claims should be met out of that fund. That separate fund is the National Insurance Fund which was first set up in 1948. Originally there were in addition two separate funds, the National Insurance (Reserve) Fund and the Industrial Injuries Fund, but these funds were absorbed into the National Insurance Fund in 1975.

Contributions from employees (primary Class 1 contributions) and contributions from employers (secondary Class 1 contributions) form the main receipts of the fund, together accounting for receipts of about £23,600 million in 1987–88, the last year for which accounts have been made up. To those contributions must be added the contributions which self-employed persons have to make (Class 2 and Class 4) which in 1987–88 together came to £660 million and the state's own contribution, called the Treasury

Supplement, of £2,135 million. This is arrived at by taking a percentage of the total contributions from all four classes but after deducting the national health service allocation (see below).[1] The percentage applied is subject to re-rating by means of statutory instrument (up or down by up to two percentage points)[2] or by legislative change. For many years the percentage remained the same at 18% but since 1981–82 the percentage has progressively been reduced until for 1987–88 it was 7%, for 1988–89 only 5% and for 1989–90 it has been reduced to nil. This reflects the current buoyancey of the fund.

The main outgoings are the contributory benefits, including statutory sick pay and statutory maternity pay where responsibility for payment is placed on the employer who then recoups the payments from contributions due. In 1987–88 these benefits in total amounted to £25,800 million. The National Health Service is not part of the contributory scheme—medical treatment does not depend on a contribution record—and the cost is met primarily out of government revenues, but from the inception in 1948 of the present national insurance system a small allocation of contribution receipts has been made towards the costs of the National Health Service. The only other outgoing involving a substantial figure is the administration of the fund itself, i.e. mainly the administrative costs of the Department of Social Security (DSS) in so far as they relate to the contributory system. In 1987–88 these costs amounted to £802 million.

The contributory system is not funded on insurance principles at all, i.e. there is no attempt to relate contributions to future obligations nor are contributions invested to any appreciable extent, so producing investment income and capital appreciation to go towards meeting the liabilities as they mature. Instead the National Insurance Fund is run on the "pay as you go" principle, that is, receipts and outgoings are required to balance year by year. The balance of the Fund is quite small; some £1,600 million at the end of 1987–88.

Because the Fund operates on a finely balanced basis, the Government Actuary is required every five years to review the state of the fund having regard to current and expected contribution yields, demographic trends and the future demands expected to be made on the fund.[3] The Government Actuary is also required to make an annual report in connection with the changes which the Secretary of State makes to the contribution rates and the earnings brackets on which they depend.[4] These changes which are made under the statutory order procedure result from and annual review which the Secretary of State is required to make of contributions and benefits having regard to movements in general earnings levels and other matters which appear to him to be relevant.[5] Such changes are normally announced in November and take effect from the following 6th April.

[1] SSA 1975, s. 1(5).
[2] SSA 1975, s. 1(5A).
[3] SSA 1975, s. 137 and s. 4(6F).
[4] SSA 1975, s. 121 and s. 4(6HH).
[5] SSA 1975, s. 120.

THE CONTRIBUTION CLASSES

50: 03   Contributions to the contributory scheme fall into four classes.

Class 1

These are due in respect of the earnings of "employed earners" as defined[1] which are broadly employees and office holders.

(1) Primary contributions. These are due (normally by deduction under the PAYE system) from the employed earner on the total earnings if they exceed the lower earnings limit but insofar as they exceed the upper earnings limit primary contributions are not due on the excess.

(2) Secondary contributions. These are due from the "secondary contributor" i.e. the employer or government department, public authority etc. paying the office holder.[2]

They are payable on the total earnings of the employed earner if they exceed the lower earnings limit. If the total earnings exceed the upper earnings limit secondary contributions continue to be payable on the total earnings. Since 6th October 1985 there has been no ceiling on secondary contributions.

Within the lower earnings limit and the upper earnings limit there are prescribed earnings brackets. When earnings exceed the upper limit for each earnings bracket, the rate of contribution which applies to total earnings is that for the next earnings bracket. By this mechanism, the rate applying to all earnings is stepped up as earnings pass prescribed thresholds.

Class 2

There are modest flat rate contributions payable by all self-employed earners. They secure sickness and invalidity benefits and long term benefits, mainly retirement pension and widows benefits.

Class 3

These are voluntary contributions which can only be paid by those not otherwise securing benefits through contributions and secure only the long-term benefits.

Class 4

These are payable on business profits between a lower and upper threshold which are immediately derived by an individual from carrying on a trade, profession or vocation. They are thus payable by the majority of self-employed earners who also pay Class 2 contributions.

Business profits for this purpose are ascertained as for income tax and collection is through the income tax system i.e. the Class 4 contributions are treated as amounts payable under the Schedule D Case I or Case II assessment.

Contribution liability under the four classes is described in detail in the succeeding sections.

---

[1] SSA 1975, s. 2(1)(a).
[2] SSA 1975, s. 4(4).

RELEVANT LAW

50: 05   The primary legislation relating to contribution liability is contained in the Social Security Act 1975 and Social Security Pensions Act 1975. These Acts have been supplemented by subsequent Social Security Acts including those of 1986 and 1989. All the primary legislation is to be consolidated in due course. There is in addition a vast body of secondary legislation including regulations dealing with categorisation, contributions, credits, earnings factors, adjudication and certain other specific issues. The secondary legislation includes a number of reciprocal social security agreements which the UK has made with certain other countries. Finally it should be borne in mind that certain European Community legislation touches social security questions and is binding on the UK.

This publication does not deal with the law relating to social security benefits except in general terms but it should be appreciated that each benefit has its own régime, normally found in regulations dealing with conditions of entitlement, calculation of the benefit, claims and manner of payment.

51　The employed earner

CATEGORISATION

51: 01　One of Beveridge's six principles of social insurance was that there should be different insurance classes corresponding to different sections of the community and their needs;[1] in particular a sharp distinction has always been made between employees (Class 1) and self-employed persons (Class 2).

The process by which persons were allocated to different classes was originally called "classification" but in the scheme at present in operation the term used is "categorisation". However, more than a change of name has occurred. In the original scheme persons had to be classified either as employed or self-employed whereas now it is particular kinds of employment that are categorised and give rise to appropriate contribution liability. So, for example, an individual may have one employment in which he is an employee and so pays Class 1 contributions and at the same time be in business on his own account and be liable as a self-employed person to Class 2 contributions and, since 1975, Class 4 contributions.

The two kinds of employment are termed in the legislation those of an "employed earner" and of a "self-employed earner" respectively. An employed earner is defined as "a person who is gainfully employed in Great Britain either under a contract of service or in an office (including elective office) with emoluments chargeable to income tax under Schedule E".[2] By contrast, a self-employed earner is "a person who is gainfully employed in Great Britain otherwise than in employed earner's employment (whether or not he is also employed in such employment)".[3] The qualifying adverb "gainfully" is significant in relation to the definition of self-employed earner (see infra, § 54: 01) but is redundant in the definition of employed earner since contribution liability depends on there being earnings in excess of the lower earnings limit.

It will be noted that an employed earner either has a contract of service or holds an office. An office involves "a degree of continuance (not necessarily continuity) and of independent existence; it must connote a post to which a person can be appointed, which he can vacate and to which a successor can be appointed".[4] So a person appointed to hold a public inquiry on a temporary ad hoc basis was held not to hold an office. Salaries, fees etc arising from an office fall within the charge of Schedule E.[5]

A contract of service has to be distinguished from a contract for services; an individual having a contract of service is an employed earner but not one performing a contract for services. This important distinction is considered further below (see infra, § 51: 03).

[1] Beveridge Report para. 309.
[2] SSA 1975, s. 2(1)(*a*).
[3] SSA 1975, s. 2(1)(*b*).
[4] *Edwards v Clinch* [1981] STC 617, [1981] 3 All ER 543, HL.
[5] TA 1988, s. 19.

EMPLOYEE OR SELF-EMPLOYED?

51: 02   There is a substantial divergence between the contributions payable by a self-employed person and those payable on the earnings of an employee.

EXAMPLE
    Both A and B are public relations consultants with annual earnings of £50,000: A is employed by a company but B works on a freelance basis.
    Contributions in 1989–90:

    A

    Primary Class 1 contributions—restricted to earnings at upper
        earnings limit (£16,900)[1]   1,442·29
    Secondary Class 1 contributions: £50,000 at 10·45%   5,225·00

                                                                               £6,667·29

    B
    Class 2 contributions: 52 at £4·25   221·00
    Class 4 maximum[1]   746·55

                                                                               £967·55

Consequently self-employed status holds out attractions so far as contribution liability is concerned and throughout the last 40 years, that is since the inception of the national insurance scheme, many who might otherwise be employees have attempted to become self-employed and the DSS has constantly challenged such attempts.

How are such questions resolved and on what grounds?

It must be emphasised at the outset that a question involving the categorisation of an employment is a "principal question" to be determined by the Secretary of State for Social Security acting in his judicial capacity (see infra, § **57: 05** for the adjudication procedure). Consequently if the DSS and the individual concerned or his alleged employer cannot reach agreement, the question can be referred to the Secretary of State either by application from an interested person or through the DSS suing for unpaid contributions and the Court having to refer the question to the Secretary of State.

It is possible to make an appeal against the determination of the Secretary of State to the High Court (Court of Session in Scotland) but only on a point of law. The decision of that Court is then final; there is no right of appeal to a higher Court.

The Secretary of State will need to apply the legislation, in particular the statutory definitions, to the particular facts. However, in many cases the question as to whether the individual is an employed earner or a self-employed earner is essentially a matter of fact and degree rather than a question of law. The Secretary of State is a tribunal of fact and it is not possible to challenge the primary facts found. It is however possible to challenge inferences from the primary facts, even though they themselves may be findings of fact, in a case where "the facts found are such that no person acting judicially and properly instructed as to the relevant law could have come to the determination".[2] That is a question of law on which an appeal to the High Court can be made.

Certain determinations made by the Secretary of State in the 1950s were once published[3] and the decisions reported still provide useful guidance. However, on the ground of confidentiality it is no longer the practice to publish determinations. When an appeal from a determination is heard by the High Court, the case is reported in the usual way and there have been several such appeals on categorisation questions in recent years.

[1] See example in § **54: 03**, infra for details.

[2] *Edwards v Bairstow and Harrison* [1956] AC 14, 36 TC 229, HL.

[3] "Selected Decisions of the Minister on Questions of Classification and Insurability"; each decision is given a reference beginning with M and followed by a number.

The case law

51: 03   In applying the statutory definitions to the particular facts, regard must be had to the case law bearing on the terms. One of the key terms in the definition of an employed earner is "contract of service". The distinction between a contract of service and a contract for services is often difficult to draw and has given rise to a substantial body of case law. It should be appreciated that the question also has to be considered in contexts other than contribution liability; it determines in employment law whether employer obligations to the employee and to third parties arise and in relation to income tax whether income is assessed under Schedule E or Schedule D Case I or Case II. The general consensus now is that cases decided in these other areas of law are equally relevant to the meaning of the term in relation to contribution liability. Moreover the courts will expect a position taken by the parties in, for example an employment law context to be followed for income tax and national insurance.[1]

The test which originally was regarded as decisive was whether the individual was placed under the control and supervision of the person to whom service was rendered as in a master and servant relationship: "a servant is a person subject to the command of his master as to the manner in which he shall do his work".[2] In many instances this test can be applied easily and settles the matter. Thus "a ship's master, a chauffeur, and a reporter on the staff of a newspaper are all employed under a contract of service; but a ship's pilot, a taxi-man and a newspaper contributor are employed under a contract for services".[3]

But there are many situations where the control test alone is inadequate to determine the position. For example, professional and highly skilled people use their own judgement as to how they perform their tasks whether they are employees or in business on their own account. For this reason, a further test has been developed alongside the control test which is known as the integration test. This was introduced by Lord Denning who declared: "In this connection I would observe the test of being a servant does not nowadays rest on submission to orders. It depends on whether the person is part and parcel of the organisation".[4] In another case he expressed the test as whether the individual was "employed as part of the business and his work is done as an integral part of the business".[5] Thus in *Cassidy v Ministry of Health*[6] a consultant surgeon appointed by a hospital board was held to be a servant of the board because the operations he performed were an integral part of the work of the hospital.

A still further supplementary test which has been adopted by the courts, here taking a lead from the US Supreme Court, is the economic reality test— essentially whether the individual is in business on his own account. This test was first applied in *Market Investigations Ltd v Minister of Social Security*.[7] It is decided by such factors as whether the individual is at financial risk, or responsible for the management of the work and stands to gain or lose according to how well the work is managed, whether he can directly employ others to assist and whether he provides substantial equipment.

In certain recent cases an increased emphasis has been placed on the control test. Thus in a Privy Council decision on an appeal from Australia it was held that "in most cases the decisive criterion is the extent to which the person, whose status as employee or independent contractor is at issue, is under the direction and control of the other party to the contract with regard to the manner in which he does his work under it".[8] Again in a Court of Appeal case in 1984, the view that the economic reality test was "the fundamental test" was rejected, it being regarded as "no more than a useful test".[9]

In certain of the cases a further test has been debated. This addresses the preliminary question of whether there are sufficient mutual obligations on each side to create a contract of service. However, while it has been held that there has to be "an irreducible minimum of obligation"[10] to create such a contrct, little more is required than the payment of remuneration in return for work:

"There must be a wage or other remuneration. Otherwise there will be no consideration, and without consideration no contract of any kind. The servant must be obliged to provide his own work and skill".[11]

In two cases concerning outworkers[12] the finding that the employer had no obligation to supply any work and that employees were under no obligation to accept any work was not regarded as precluding the existence of a contract of service which could be inferred from a course of dealing extending over several years. This test is therefore not normally decisive, though in one case concerning casual workers at a hotel it was found that there was no mutuality of obligation and the casual workers were not working under any overall contract of employment.[13]

A recent tendency has been to pay increased attention to the actual contractual terms to determine the nature of the contract, particularly if the relationship is ambiguous, though the court will not accept a written contract which deliberately sets out a contractor/client relationship because that is what the parties want, when in reality there is a master/servant relationship.[14]

Since several different tests may be applied and none in particular can be regarded as fundamental, it may be wondered whether a decision on an individual's employment status can only be reached in a somewhat arbitrary manner. The approach taken by the industrial tribunal in one of the relevant cases was to:

"consider all aspects of the relationship, no single factor being in itself decisive and each of which may vary in weight and direction, and having given such balance to the factors as seems appropriate, to determine whether the person was carrying on business on his own account".[15]

The Court of Appeal approved this procedure as wholly correct in law and considered that it could only interfere if the determination made on the basis of such evaluation of the factors was "perverse" i.e. one which a person acting judicially and properly instructed in the law could not have reached from the primary factors found—the principle established in *Edwards v Bairstow and Harrison.*[16]

Both the Revenue and the DSS have issued an identical leaflet setting out certain practical tests applied in distinguishing employment from self-employment.[17] The leaflet does not purport to represent a comprehensive summary of the relevant case law and in fact is too influenced by the economic reality test as expounded in the *Market Investigations Ltd* case. Since 6th April 1987 the two departments have co-ordinated their approach; each Tax District and local social security office have a designated officer responsible for enquiries and decisions on employment status and where a decision is made by one of the departments it will be accepted by the other so long as there has been no change in the circumstances.[18]

---

[1] *Young & Woods Ltd v West* [1980] 1 RLR 201, CA.

[2] *Yewens v Noakes* (1880) 6 QBD 530, 1 TC 260, CA.

[3] *Stevenson, Jordan and Harrison Ltd v Macdonald and Evans* [1952] 1 TLR 101, CA.

[4] *Bank voor Handel en Scheepvaart NV v Administrator of Hungarian Property* [1954] AC 584, 35 TC 311, HL.

[5] *Stevenson, Jordan and Harrison Ltd v Macdonald and Evans* [1952] 1 TLR 101, CA.

[6] [1951] 1 All ER 574, [1952] 2 KB 343.

[7] [1969] 2 QB 173, [1969] 3 All ER 732.

[8] *Narich Pty Ltd v Pay-roll Tax Comr* [1983] ICR 286, PC.

[9] *Nethermere (St Neots) Ltd v Gardiner* [1984] ICR 612, CA.

[10] *Nethermere (St Neots) Ltd v Gardiner* [1984] ICR 612.

[11] *Ready-Mixed Concrete (South East) Ltd v Ministry of Pensions* [1968] 2 QB 497, [1968] 1 All ER 433.

[12] *Airfix Footwear Ltd v Cope* [1978] ICR 1210; *Nethermere (St Neots) Ltd v Gardiner* [1984] ICR 612.

[13] *O'Kelly v Trusthouse Forte plc* [1984] QB 90, [1983] 3 All ER 456, CA.

[14] *BSM (1257) Ltd v Secretary of State for Social Services* [1978] ICR 894; *Narich Pty Ltd v Pay-roll Tax Comr* [1983] ICR 286, PC; *Davies v Presbyterian Church of Wales* [1986] 1 All ER 705, [1986] 1 WLR 323, HL.

[15] *O'Kelly v Trusthouse Forte plc* [1984] QB 90, [1983] 3 All ER 456, CA.

[16] [1956] AC 14, 36 TC 207, HL; see supra. § **51: 02**.

[17] Revenue Publication IR 56; DSS leaflet NI 39

[18] Revenue press release, 19 March 1987.

CATEGORISATION BY REGULATION

51: 04 There are certain occupations where it is often difficult to determine whether the individual is an employee or self-employed, for example actors, musicians, part-time lecturers and teachers, and because the arrangements differ according to the particular case there can be—indeed have been— many disputed rulings often resulting in determinations by the Secretary of State and appeals to the court. For this reason the Secretary of State is authorised to introduce regulations which will treat persons in prescribed occupations as either employed earners or self-employed earners as the case may be, whether or not they would be so categorised on the basis of the particular facts and relevant law.[1] Such regulations may also provide for persons in prescribed occupations to be treated as non-earners and so free from any contribution liability.[2]

Regulations have been made under these provisions; these are known as the "Categorisation Regulations".[3] Under these regulations the following employments must always be categorised as employed earners whether or not they have contracts of service or hold offices with emoluments chargeable to income tax under Schedule E:

(1) office cleaners;
(2) agency workers;
(3) employment by spouse for the purpose of the spouse's employment;
(4) lecturers, teachers and instructors;
(5) ministers of religion remunerated mainly by stipend or salary.[4]

The rules defining agency workers are framed in similar language to that in the corresponding rules for income tax purposes.[5] An agency worker is defined as a person who is required to render personal service and is subject to supervision, direction or control as to the manner of rendering the service. The agency worker must be supplied by a third person (the agency) and the earnings for the service either have to be paid for on the basis of accounts submitted by the agency or other arrangement made with the agency or there must be payments (other than to the agency worker) made by way of fees, commission etc which relate to the agency worker's continued employment. The wording is deliberately wide; for example it matters not whether it is the agency or the person receiving the personal service (the client) which exercises the direction, supervision or control.

Certain kinds of agency workers are excepted from this rule and may therefore still be treated as self-employed depending on the particular facts; they are certain homeworkers, actors, singers, musicians and other entertainers, fashion, photographic and artist's models, and those who are merely introduced to the client and as a result become employees of the client and the agency has no direct financial interest in the continuation of the employment. Lecturers etc who give instruction for no more than three days in three consecutive months or who only deliver public lectures are excepted from the rule and may therefore in appropriate circumstances be treated as self-employed.

The only case where the occupation must always be categorised as self-employed earner's employment is that of examiners, moderators, invigilators etc and those engaged to set examination questions, so long as the contract for the work has to be performed in less than 12 months.[6]

In the following cases the employment is to be regarded as non-earner's employment and so disregarded for contribution purposes:

(1) employment by spouse otherwise than for the purpose of the spouse's employment;
(2) employment by certain close relatives for domestic purposes;
(3) employment as a self-employed earner where the earner is not ordinarily so employed (see infra, § **54: 02**);
(4) employment as a returning officer or counting officer;

(5) employment as a member of a visiting force or as a civilian employee of such force or as a member of an international headquarters or defence organisation.[7]

Where the Secretary of State makes a determination on a categorisation question from which there is an appeal to the High Court and the determination is overruled, the Secretary of State may direct that the employment status which he determined shall apply up to the date of the decision of the High Court if it appears to him that this would be in the interests of the contributor or any person claiming benefit on the basis of the contributions.[8] This power is normally only exercised where the individual was categorised as an employed earner under the Secretary of State's determination and the High Court decides that he is self-employed.

---

[1] SSA 1975, s. 2(2)(*b*).
[2] SSA 1975, s. 2(2)(*a*).
[3] Social Security (Categorisation of Earners) Regulations 1978, SI 1978 No. 1689.
[4] SI 1978 No. 1689, Sch. 1, Part I.
[5] TA 1988, s. 134.
[6] SI 1978 No. 1689. Sch. 1, Part II.
[7] SI 1978 No. 1689, Sch 1, Part III.
[8] SI 1978 No. 1689, reg. 4.

Secondary contributors

51: 05 If a person is categorised as an employed earner, a corollary is that there must be an employer or equivalent, called in the legislation the "secondary contributor". Where the employed earner is employed under a contract of service, the secondary contributor is the employer.[1] Where the employed earner holds an office with emoluments, the secondary contributor is either the government department, public authority or body responsible for paying the emoluments or a person specifically prescribed by regulations.[2]

The "Categorisation Regulations" set out various situations where a prescribed person is to be treated as the secondary contributor; in these situations the foregoing general rules are displaced. Thus, in the case of office cleaners, the supply agency will be the secondary contributor if the cleaner is remunerated by the agency but where there is no agency or the agency does not remunerate the cleaner, the client is the secondary contributor. Where lecturers etc are treated as employed earners, the educational establishment providing the education is the secondary contributor. Where a person is employed by a company in voluntary liquidation, the liquidator is to be treated as the secondary contributor. Where a person is employed in chambers as a barrister's clerk, the head of the chambers is to be treated as the secondary contributor.[3]

The general rule regarding agency workers (for definition see supra, § **51: 04**) is that the agency is to be treated as the secondary contributor[4] but where the agency does not meet the residence conditions for contribution liability, the client company i.e. the person to whom the agency worker is supplied, is to be treated as the secondary contributor[5] (see infra, § **56: 05** for the possible significance of this point in relation to certain overseas companies having expatriate staff in this country.)

Where an employed earner works under the general control or management of a person other than the immediate employer (i.e. in circumstances where reg. 3 of the PAYE Regulations operates,[6] the Secretary of State may introduce regulations which prescribe which person is to be treated as the secondary contributor.[7] The Categorisation Regulations are made in part on the basis of this enabling power.[8] Schedule 1 of the Contribution Regulations deals with the collection of contributions under PAYE and incorporates reg. 3 of the PAYE regulations: the better view would seem to be that the effect is to make the principal employer the secondary contributor only for collection purposes and so the provision only operates where the immediate employer is already liable for secondary contributions.[9]

[1] SSA 1975, s. 4(*a*).
[2] SSA 1975, s. 4(*b*).
[3] SI 1978 No. 1689, Sch. 3.
[4] SI 1978 No. 1689, Sch. 3, Col. (B), para. 2(*a*), (*b*).
[5] SI 1978 No. 1689, Sch. 3, Col. (B), para. 2(*c*).
[6] Income Tax (Employments) Regulations 1973, SI 1973 No. 334.
[7] SSA 1975, s. 4(5).
[8] SI 1978 No. 1689, foreword and reg. 5.
[9] Social Security (Contributions) Regulations 1979, SI 1979 No. 591, Sch. 1, para. 3.

PERSONAL SERVICE COMPANIES

51: 06   In certain fields, notably among computer software programmers, it is common for the individuals concerned to provide their services not as self-employed persons but through personal service companies. With such an arrangement the individual owns the majority of the shares in the personal service company but is also an employee of the company; the personal service company makes the services of the individual available in consideration for a fee or time charge. This can be attractive so far as contribution liability is concerned because although primary and secondary Class 1 contributions will be payable in respect of the individual's remuneration from employment with the personal service company, such remuneration can be kept fairly low, in which case a net profit may result so allowing a dividend to be paid to the individual in his capacity as majority shareholder. A dividend is not earnings from the employment and should not require contributions to be paid. By this means contribution liability can be held to a modest level.

The DSS appears to be happy to accept the arrangement in cases where, as in the computer service industry, work assignments tend to be fairly short-term e.g. not usually exceeding six months and the client does not wish to assume the employer obligations which would arise from having a contract of employment. But in a case where in the ordinary way the individual would clearly be an employee of the company using his services and self-employed status would be very difficult to achieve, some caution must be advised over the possible use of a personal service company and areas of vulnerability would need careful evaluation.

It should be appreciated that the personal service company arrangement has a variety of implications in other areas e.g. the timing of payment and recovery of ACT, the overall level of tax on income derived in the form of dividend—this will not be greater than that applying to equivalent salary so long as corporation tax is only payable at the small companies rate, the build up of value in the company with capital gains and inheritance tax implications and possible restriction of pension entitlement because of salary being kept at a low level.

52 Employment earnings

MEANING OF EARNINGS

52: 01   The basic definition of earnings for contribution (as well as benefit) purposes is that "earnings includes any remuneration or profit derived from an employment".[1] There have been no legal decisions on the meaning of earnings for contribution purposes but it is generally accepted that "remuneration" covers wages, salaries, fees etc and "profit" other items of gain or benefit arising out of the employment e.g. benefits in kind in so far as not taken out by specific exclusion (see below). The profit must however be derived from the employment and therefore the income tax cases which consider whether or not a payment to the employee arises out of the employment are highly relevant. In the leading case of *Hochstrasser v Mayes*, Upjohn J in the High Court summarised the authorities thus: "in my judgment not every payment made to an employee is necessarily made to him as a profit arising from his employment. Indeed in my judgment the authorities show that to be a profit arising from the employment, the payment must be made in reference to the services the employee renders by virtue of his office and it must be in the nature of a reward for services past, present or future".[2] When the case came before the House of Lords, Viscount Simonds considered the summary could not be improved upon, except for the reference to past services which was open to question.

In another House of Lords judgment Lord Radcliffe laid down the following test for determining whether the payment arises from the office or employment: "while it is not sufficient to render a payment assessable that an employee would not have received it unless he had been an employee, it is assessable if it has been paid to him in return for acting or being an employee".[3]

The latter passage has frequently been cited as the main ground for the decision and was relied on in the more recent case of *Hamblett v Godfrey*.[4] Here attention was focussed on the final phrase "or being an employee" and it was held that because a payment to an employee at the Cheltenham GCHQ in recompense for withdrawing her right to belong to a trade union could only have been made because she was an employee, the source of the payment was the employment and the payment must be a profit arising from the employment. The DSS is known to have considered this decision and taken legal advice on its implications in relation to contribution liability.

But although emoluments chargeable under Schedule E and earnings for contribution purposes will often be arrived at under the same principles the two expressions do not converge and have precisely the same scope.

Notwithstanding that Class 1 contributions are collected through the PAYE system, the distinction is maintained in the provisions dealing with collection machinery. For that purpose emoluments are defined as "so much of a person's remuneration or profit derived from the employed earner's employment as constitutes earnings for the purposes of the Act".[5] Emoluments for Schedule E purposes are therefore not the same as earnings for contribution purposes.

The distinction is necessary because until the change made by FA 1989, income taxable under Schedule E was taken on the earnings basis and earnings for contribution purposes always refers to actual payments, including in some cases payments made in advance. Secondly, certain income tax rules allowing specific deductions have no application to contribution liability. Finally, for contribution purposes only, certain specified payments have to be excluded from the gross earnings.[6]

These matters are considered further at infra, § **52: 02, 03**.

---

[1] SSA 1975, s. 3(1).
[2] (1957) 38 TC 673 at 705.
[3] (1959) 38 TC 673 at 707.
[4] [1987] STC 60.
[5] SI 1979 No. 591, Sch. 1, para. 2(1).
[6] SI 1979 No. 591, reg. 19.

Deductions not allowed

52: 02   The following deductions which can be made from emoluments taxed under Schedule E have no application to earnings for contribution purposes:

1. Employee's expenses wholly exclusively and necessarily incurred in the performance of the duties (TA 1988, ss. 198, 199, 200 and 332(3)). There is, however, a special rule covering reimbursement of expenses (see infra, § **52: 04**).
2. Fees and subscriptions to professional bodies (TA 1988, s. 201).
3. Charitable donations under the payroll deduction scheme (TA 1988, s. 202).
4. Employee contributions under approved pension arrangements (TA 1988, ss. 592(8), 619 and 639).
5. The exempt sum (£30,000) in the case of certain termination payments (TA 1988, s. 188(4)).
6. The 100% deduction from earnings where there are overseas duties and a qualifying period of absence of at least 365 days (TA 1988, s. 193).
7. The one half of profit-related pay which is exempt from income tax (TA 1988, s. 171(1)).

Payments excluded from earnings

52: 03   The contribution regulations require the following payments to be excluded from earnings:[1]

1. Payments of amounts previously included in earnings.

2. Holiday pay from a centralised fund operated by a number of employers and not under the management and control of any one employer.
3. Tips or gratuities which are either paid directly to the employee by the customer or if pooled are shared out among the employees without the employer's involvement. Shares of service charges, however, are always to be included in earnings.
4. Payments in kind.
5. Pension payments.
6. Fees paid to ministers of religion not forming part of their stipend or salary.
7. Home to work travelling expenses paid to disabled persons under the Disabled Persons (Employment) Act 1944.
8. Allocation of shares made under an approved profit-sharing scheme.[2]
9. Employer contributions to an approved personal pension scheme providing they are within the permitted maximum and so do not fall to be treated as emoluments of the employee.[3]
10. Sickness payments out of a fund representing contributions by the employee.
11. VAT on remuneration for the supply of goods or services e.g. where an office is accepted in the course of practising a profession or vocation.[4]
12. Redundancy payments.
13. Specific reimbursement of expenses actually incurred by the employee in carrying out the employment.
14. Discretionary payments made before 6th April 1990 by the trustees of certain discretionary trusts created before 6th April 1985 or which succeeded such trusts.

The kind of holiday pay scheme which would fall within 2. are those found in the construction and allied industries e.g. the Building and Civil Engineers Industries Holiday Pay Scheme. In such schemes the employer purchases special stamps to build up holiday pay entitlement for the employees and the amounts spent on these stamps (following DSS guidance) do not have to be included in earnings.[5] Thus, provision of holiday pay in this way completely escapes contribution liability.

Holiday pay normally falls to be included in earnings when paid unless it represents sums previously set aside with the earner's consent and which were treated as earnings at that time.

The sickness payments that can be excluded under 10. are those payable under a private scheme. Statutory sick pay and statutory maternity pay have to be included in earnings for contributions purposes, just as they do for Schedule E purposes.

Certain of the other items are considered further at infra, § **52: 04, 05, 06.**

---

[1] The exclusions are set out in SI 1979 No. 591, reg. 19.
[2] TA 1988, ss. 186, 187.
[3] TA 1988, ss. 640, 643.
[4] See VATA 1983, s. 47(4).
[5] DSS leaflet NI 269, p. 60.

REIMBURSEMENTS

52: 04 The Contribution Regulations permit exclusion from earnings of "any specific and distinct payment of, or contribution towards expenses actually incurred by an employed earner in carrying out his employment.[1] This rule is made "for the avoidance of doubt" and in the absence of such a rule, it could still be argued that a reimbursement of expenses incurred in carrying out the employment was not a profit derived from the employment and should not therefore be included in earnings (see supra, § **52: 01**).

One consequence of the rule is that according to DSS guidance round sum allowances have to be included in earnings, even though intended to be used entirely for business purposes.[2] However, if specific business expenses which are met out of the allowance can be identified these may be excluded from earnings and only the balance of the round sum allowance treated as earnings. The DSS refers to this balance as the profit element[3] but where in fact the allowance is used to meet business expenses but these cannot be identified and listed in a cost-effective manner, the employee will not have derived a profit in respect of that part of the reimbursement at all.

Realising the inequity of a simplistic differentiation between specific reimbursements on the one hand and all other reimbursements on the other, the DSS in the Employer's Manual, which takes effect from 6th April 1989, has recognised a third class of reimbursement—one where the reimbursement represents a reasonable estimate of the expenses likely to be incurred but the employee is not required to list and claim specific items. Relocation allowances and subsistence allowances often follow this basis. For the DSS to accept such an arrangement it must satisfy the following conditions:

(*a*) the payments are based on an accurate survey of the costs involved;
(*b*) the scheme is designed to allow for movements in prices;
(*c*) the payments are reasonable in relation to the payment involved;
(*d*) the scheme has no overall profit element; and
(*e*) the employee makes a claim for the allowance (not the specific items of expense).[4]

It is important to note that exclusion from earnings for contribution purposes depends simply on the expenses being incurred by the employee in carrying out the employment. This is a less restrictive test than that which applies for deduction of expenses from income chargeable under Schedule E where "the employee must be obliged to expend the money wholly, exclusively and necessarily in the performance of the duties of the office or employment".[5] This means that where duality of purpose lies behind the expenditure and deduction from emoluments chargeable under Schedule E would not be possible, the expense reimbursement may nevertheless be excluded from earnings for contribution purposes; thus in the case of an overseas visit combining both sight-seeing and business duties, it seems clear that reimbursement of the expenses should be excluded from earnings for contribution purposes, though no deduction can be made from the income assessable under Schedule E.[6]

On the other hand it is essential that there is a reimbursement by the employer. The terms of the exclusion are not met if the employee incurs an expense in carrying out the employment and bears it on his own account.

Finally it should be remembered that Revenue concessionary treatments such as those set out in Extra-Statutory Concession A5 (1988)[7] in relation to removal expenses have no relevance to contribution liability. This can cut both ways. If the DSS conditions regarding estimated allowances are not met, the allowances will have to be included in earnings except in so far as specific items can be identified. On the other hand if the reimbursement is entirely in respect of specific items, it can be excluded for contribution purposes even if the total reimbursement exceeds the current Revenue limits.

Reimbursement of home to work travel expenses (except in the case of certain disabled persons) cannot be excluded from earnings. This is because the individual is not "necessarily obliged to incur" the expenses in the performance of the duties (as decided in *Ricketts v Colquoun*)[8] and the income tax test is similar to the one for exclusion from earnings in this instance.

---

[1] SI 1979 No. 591, reg. 19(4).
[2] DSS leaflet NI 269, p. 62, para. (80).
[3] DSS leaflet NI 269, p. 62, para. (80).
[4] DSS leaflet NI 269, p. 58 and p. 62, paras. (77) and (88).
[5] TA 1988, s. 198(1).
[6] *Thomson v White* (1966) 43 TC 256.
[7] See **Simon's Taxes Division H2.2**.
[8] [1926] AC 1, 10 TC 118, HL.

TERMINATION PAYMENTS ETC

52: 05   There is a specific exclusion from earnings for redundancy pay.[1] Payments in lieu of notice are similarly excluded in practice.[2] Payments for accrued holiday pay and in respect of a back-dated pay award which are made after the employment has ended have to be included in earnings because they stem from the employment.[3]

Where a lump sum is payable in respect of the remuneration, it is necessary to determine whether the payment represents on the one hand compensation payable under the terms of the employment contract or an agreed payment in settlement of any claims under the contract e.g. in respect of premature termination or whether on the other hand it is a true ex gratia payment i.e. one to which the employee has no entitlement. Only in the latter case can the payment be excluded from earnings for contribution purposes. This follows from the application of the income tax principles determining whether a termination payment is taxable under Schedule E in the ordinary way or under the special provisions of TA 1988, s. 148.[4]

Income tax principles are also applied to determine the nature of golden hellos, golden handcuffs etc made at the start of the employment.[5] If the payment is linked to the services to be performed it will arise from the employment and so be earnings for contribution purposes as well as emoluments for Schedule E purposes but not if it represents solely compensation for an irrevocable loss of status.[6]

---

[1] SI 1979 No. 591, reg. 19(4)(a).
[2] DSS Leaflet NI 269, p. 61, para. (62).
[3] DSS Leaflet NI 269, p. 59, para. (4).

⁴ See **Simon's Tax Division E4.8**.
⁵ See **Simon's Taxes E4.404**.
⁶ *Pritchard v Arundale* [1972] Ch 229, 47 TC 680 but contrast *Glantre Engineering Ltd v Goodhand* [1983] STC 1.

PAYMENTS IN KIND

52: 06   Because earnings are defined as including any "profit derived from the employment" benefits in kind are in general brought into the scope of the term but the specific exclusion for "any payment in kind" will take many benefits out again. The exclusion of payments in kind is the principle cause of earnings for contribution purposes diverging markedly from income as assessable under Schedule E.

The fringe benefits frequently provided with a job e.g. company car, private medical insurance, club memberships, magazine subscriptions etc will, in the case of directors and higher-paid employees, be charged to tax under Schedule E under special provisions[1] but so long as certain precautions are taken these will constitute payments in kind and so not be earnings for contribution purposes.

Remunerating employees through provision of benefits is therefore attractive from a national insurance point of view, particularly in the case of employees already earning above the upper earnings limit since in their case maximum employee contributions are being paid and it is only employer contributions which are being reduced so that benefit entitlement is not impaired in any way. For this reason there has been a tendency to provide more than the customary fringe benefits, particularly as a means of paying bonuses or other special awards. So, for example, expensive holidays, kitchen or bathroom refurbishments, suites of furniture, the use of yachts or overseas apartments may all be encountered. In some cases vouchers which can be used to buy such items are provided but as explained below these must not be exchangeable for cash.

Until May 1988 many employers awarded bonuses in the form of short-dated gilt-edged securities. With this type of security price fluctuations are minimal and there is a narrow bid/offer spread; the asset provided was thus almost equivalent to cash. A substantial amount of contribution revenue was being lost to the national insurance fund as a result of widespread use of this device and in May 1988 a statutory instrument was laid[2] which introduced a new regulation into Categorisation Regulations.[3]

This blocking measure is remarkably specific; it simply lays down that securities (as defined) and derivative instruments (also as defined) are not to be treated as payments in kind for the purpose of exclusion from earnings. The securities indicated are debentures, loan stock, certificates of deposit—in fact all instruments evidencing indebtedness—whether issued by a government (not necessarily the British Government), local authority or a company or an individual. Derivative instruments are widely defined but there has to be a security in the first place; they include options over securities and warrants to subscribe for securities.

The new regulation indicates two exceptions which are outside its scope and may therefore continue to be used for payment in kind. These are:

1. Shares in a company.
2. Units in an authorised trust.

Naturally payment in such forms has received considerable attention, though if payment takes the form of shares it appears that these will have to be excluded from relevant earnings and thus contributions to a personal pension scheme will be restricted.[4]

The provision of an asset other than cash however does not necessarily constitute a payment in kind, even if the asset is outside the scope of the blocking measure. In the following cases in particular, the list is not exhaustive, there will not be a payment in kind such as to be excluded from earnings for contribution purposes:

(1) *If the asset can be surrendered and exchanged for cash.* In this case the DSS consider that the employee is in effect being provided with cash, whether or not an actual surrender takes place. The DSS guidance distinguishes items which can be turned into cash if sold from those which can be turned into cash by surrender and instances premium bonds and national savings certificates as examples of the latter kind.[5]

The precise legal grounds for this rule are unclear and it should be appreciated that there is very little case law on the meaning of payment in kind and none at all in the context of contribution liability. Nevertheless it would be foolish in practice to disregard the rule. It is for this reason that if vouchers are provided for the purchase of goods, there must be no possibility of the recipient being able to obtain cash e.g. on the return of faulty goods.

(2) *If the employee already has an entitlement to a cash sum.* In this situation the remuneration is treated as paid at the point the entitlement arises and the asset provided merely discharges the cash sum due.

This follows from the principle established in *Garforth v Newsmith Stainless Ltd,*[6] in which it was held in the case of directors that payment of remuneration is made at the time sums are placed unreservedly at their disposal. Thus, if the resolution or other form of consent of the shareholders authorising the directors' remuneration[7] does not specify that it must be taken in kind, the directors will be treated as having a cash sum placed at their disposal.

(3) *If a liability of the employee is discharged by the employer.* In *Hartland v Diggines*[8] a Schedule E case, it was held that payment by the employer of a liability due from the employee—in that case income tax due on his salary—constituted an emolument of the employment. On similar reasoning such payment is regarded as earnings for contribution purposes. This means that if the employee himself makes the contract for the supply of the goods or services in question and is reimbursed by the employer, the reimbursement becomes a payment of remuneration in cash. The point is well known in connection with telephone charges; the employer must be the subscriber if payment for private telephone use is to be excluded from earnings.[9]

The new Employer's Manual which applies as from 6th April 1989 has caused some controversy by its comments on the provision of petrol. It requires the purchase of petrol by use of a company credit card to be included in earnings unless business use can be identified.[10] The unstated basis for this guidance is that in *Richardson v Worrall*[11] it was held that a contract for the purchase of petrol was made at the pump when it was put into the car and that the employee did not enter into the contract as agent of the employer. Hence use of the company credit card discharged the employee's liability.

The pre-existence of this oral contract, "the forecourt arrangement" was recognised in *Re Charge Card Services Ltd*,[12] where the legal consequences of the service station subsequently accepting payment by credit card were considered.

However, the DSS is expected to issue some further guidance in the form of a supplement to the Employer's Manual and it is understood that this will contain relaxations on certain points.

---

[1] TA 1988, Pt. V, Ch. II.
[2] SI 1988 No. 1860.
[3] SI 1979 No. 591, reg. 19C.
[4] TA 1988, s. 644(4)(*a*).
[5] DSS leaflet NI 269, p. 61, para. (60).
[6] [1979] STC 129.
[7] For other forms of shareholders' consent, see *Re Dvomatic Ltd* [1969] 2 Ch 365, [1969] 1 All ER 161.
[8] [1926] AC 289, 10 TC 247, HL.
[9] DSS leaflet NI 269, p. 63, paras. (93), (94) and (95).
[10] DSS leaflet NI 269, p. 61, para. (68).
[11] [1985] STC 693.
[12] [1988] 3 All ER 702, [1988] 3 WLR 764, CA.

53 Employer and employee contributions

CLASS 1 CONTRIBUTIONS

53:01 Where an employment is categorised as an employed earner's employment, both the employee ie the employed earner, and the employer ie the secondary contributor, are normally required to pay respectively primary and secondary Class 1 contributions. If the employee is under 16, neither employee nor employer have this obligation until the employee reaches the age of 16[1] after which earnings paid to him may become liable to both primary and secondary contributions. Where the employee reaches pensionable age (currently 65 for a man and 60 for a woman) liability for primary contributions on earnings paid to him or her after that date ceases, unless the earnings would normally fall to be paid before that date.[2] Conversely, if earnings are paid before the date but in the tax year in which pensionable age is reached and those earnings would normally be paid in a following tax year those earnings do not give rise to primary contributions.[3] The employer is still required to pay secondary contributions in respect of the employee's earnings after pensionable age is reached.[4]

No primary or secondary contribution liability arises unless the employee's weekly earnings exceed a threshold termed the lower earnings limit[5] but if earnings do exceed that threshold contributions are payable on the earnings up to as well as above that limit. In the case of primary contributions, the maximum liablity is reached when earnings are at or above a further threshold, the upper earnings limit; earnings above that limit do not attract primary contributions.[6] However, since 6th October 1985 that limit is not relevant to secondary contributions; since there is no upper limit to the earnings on which the employer must pay such contributions.

---

[1] SSA 1975, s. 4(2)(*a*).
[2] SSPA 1975, s. 4(1); SI 1979 No. 591, reg. 20A.
[3] SI 1979 No. 591, reg. 20.
[4] SSPA 1975, s. 4(1).
[5] SSA 1975, s. 4(1)(*a*) and (2)(*b*).
[6] SSA 1975, s. 4(6).

EARNINGS LIMITS: EARNINGS BRACKETS: RATES

53: 02   Both the lower and upper earnings limits are tied to the basic Category A retirement pension. The lower earnings limit must be a figure very close to the Category A retirement pension, the margin allowed being up to 99p. The retirement pension is revalued each year by reference to price inflation, the revised amounts payable from the following April being usually announced in the Autumn. Increases made by any Act or more usually statutory order before the beginning of a tax year must be taken into account in fixing the lower earnings limit for that year so long as the increases take effect before 6th May in that year.[1] In this way the lower earnings limit is revised annually in tandem with the basic retirement pension.

The upper earnings limit has to be a figure approximately equal to seven times the basic retirement pension but subject to a margin of half the amount of the basic pension.[2]

Whereas fixing the earnings limits determines the level of earnings at which contribution liability begins (but then by reference to total earnings) and for employees the level of earnings at which maximum liability is reached, the rates at which contributions are payable have to be reviewed annually and must be set so as to result in contributions paid into and benefits paid out of the national insurance fund being approximately in balance in each tax year. The changes which result from the review are normally announced in November and apply as from the following 6th April.

Since 6th October 1985 there has been a graduated series of rates dependent on the level of earnings for both employee and employer contributions. The rates change when earnings exceed stipulated figures. The figures are found from prescribed earnings brackets.[3] During 1989–90 this scheme is being modified for employee contributions so that after 5th October no regard is to be had to earnings brackets in calculating primary contributions and instead there is one rate applying to earnings above the lower earnings limit—the main primary percentage—and another rate which is very low (the initial primary percentage) applying to earnings below the lower earnings limit where total earnings exceed that limit.[4] This reform prevents employees suffering the net reduction in pay which a small pay increase used to cause by bringing earnings into the next earnings bracket.

For 1989–90 the lower earnings limit has been set at £43 per week and the upper earnings limit at £325 per week. The earnings brackets are as shown in the following tables.

The standard rates for primary and secondary Class 1 contributions in 1989–90 are as follows:

Standard rates from 6th April 1989 to 4th October 1989

Primary contributions	*Percentage on all earnings*
Where earnings are:	
between £43 and £74.99 per week	5
between £75 and £114.99 per week	7
between £115 and £325 per week	9

No contributions are payable on earnings in excess of £325 per week.

Secondary contributions

Percentage on all
earnings

Where earnings are:
between £43 and £74.99 per week   5
between £75 and £114.99 per week   7
between £115 and £164.99 per week   9
above £165 per week   10.45

Standard rates from 5th October 1989 to 5th April 1990

Primary contributions   %

Where earnings are between £43 and £325 per week
initial primary percentage on first £43   2
main primary percentage on earnings above £43 9

No contributions are payable on earnings in excess of £325 per week.

Secondary contributions

Percentage on all
earnings

Where earnings are:
between £43 and £74.99 per week   5
between £75 and £114.99 per week   7
between £115 and £164.99 per week   9
above £165 per week   10.45

From an employer's point of view there will still be some advantage to be gained from keeping earnings below the start of next earnings bracket e.g. by making payments in kind in lieu of increases to cash wages.

The above tables show the rates for standard contributions. There are two other sets of rates—contracted out rates and the reduced rate.

The contracted out rates apply where the employee belongs to an occupational pension scheme which has received a contracting out certificate from the Occupational Pensions Board. For the conditions which need to be fulfilled to obtain such a certificate see supra, § **30: 02**. Because as a result of being contracted out the employee will not be entitled to the additional pension based on earnings related contributions provided by SERPS, both employee and employer contributions are payable at a reduced rate on earnings between the lower and upper earnings limit. The reduction in rate results from the application of a rebate to compensate for the loss of entitlement to additional pension under SERPS. The rebate is fixed following reviews made every five years by the Controller and Auditor General. The total rebate is allocated between employer and employee contributions as the Secretary of State decides.

For 1989–90 the rebate is 5.8% in total, 2% being allocated to employee contributions and 3.8% per cent to employer contributions[5]. Where the rebate applies, earnings below the lower earnings limit still attract contributions at the standard rate and likewise employer contributions on earnings above the upper earnings limit remain at the standard rate.

As a result of applying the rebate the contracted out primary and secondary Class 1 contributions in 1989–90 are as follows:

Contracted out rates from 6th April 1989 to 4th October 1989

Primary contributions	On first £43 %	On balance of earnings %
Where earnings are:		
between £43 and £74.99 per week	5	3
between £75 and £114.99 per week	7	5
between £115 and £325 per week	9	7

No contributions are payable on earnings in excess of £325 per week.

Secondary contributions	%	%
Where earnings are:		
between £43 and £74.99 per week	5	1.2
between £75 and £114.99 per week	7	3.2
between £115 and £164.99 per week	9	5.2
between £165 and £325 per week	10.45	6.65
above £325 per week	10.45	6.65 on earnings up to £325 pw; 10.45 on earnings in excess of £325 pw.

Contracted out rates from 5th October 1989 to 5th April 1990

Primary contributions	%
Where earnings are between £43 and £325 per week	
initial primary percentage on first £43	2
main primary percentage on earnings above £43	7

No contributions are payable on earnings in excess of £325 per week.

Secondary contributions	On first £43 %	On balance of earnings %
Where earnings are:		
between £43 and £74.99 per week	5	1.2
between £75 and £114.99 per week	7	3.2
between £115 and £164.99 per week	9	5.2
between £165 and £325 per week	10.45	6.65
above £325 per week	10.45	6.65 on earnings up to £325 pw; 10.45 on earnings in excess of £325 pw.

The reduced rate applies in the case of certain married women and widows who prior to 12th May 1977 had elected to pay reduced contributions[6] into the scheme and have not subsequently revoked the election[7] or lost the right to pay reduced contributions. The woman will lose this right if her marriage ceases otherwise than through the death of her husband, if on becoming a widow she subsequently remarries or otherwise ceases to be a qualifying widow, if there is a consecutive period of two tax years in which she has no earnings on which any primary Class 1 contributions would be payable and in which she was not at any time a self-employed earner and in certain other circumstances.[8]

The reduced rate contributions secure no entitlement to benefits and in consequence are very low—for 1989–90 they are payable at the rate of 3.85% on earnings up to £325 per week so long as the earnings exceed the lower earnings limit of £43 per week.

It will be noted that the earnings limits and the earnings brackets are expressed in terms of earnings per week. This is because the legislation assumes that normally the earnings period i.e. the interval at which earnings are regularly paid (see § **53: 04**, infra) will be one week. But earnings periods can be for longer periods and in such cases there are rules for converting the weekly figures to equivalent amounts for the longer period. For both earnings limits and earnings brackets the rules are similar; they are:

1. Where the earnings period is a multiple of a week, multiply the weekly amount by the multiple in question.
2. Where the earnings period is a month, multiply the weekly amount by $4\frac{1}{3}$.
3. Where the earnings period is a multiple of a month, multiply the weekly amount by $4\frac{1}{3}$ and then multiply the result by the multiple.
4. In any other case divide the weekly amount by 7 and multiply the result by the number of days in the earnings period.[9]

---

[1] SSPA 1975, s 1(2).
[2] SSPA 1975, s 1(3).
[3] SSA 1975, s 4(6B) and (6E).
[4] SSA 1989, s. 1(1).
[5] SSPA 1975, s 27(2).
[6] SI 1979 No. 591, reg. 100(1), (4).
[7] SI 1979 No. 591, reg. 100(5), (6).
[8] SI 1979 No. 591, reg. 101(1).
[9] SI 1979 No. 591, regs. 8 and 8A.

EARNINGS PERIOD

53: 03   The earnings period is the period taken for the purpose of calculating contribution liability. Where earnings are normally paid at regular intervals, the earnings period will normally be the length of the period between each pay date e.g. if earnings are paid weekly, one week, if they are paid monthly one month.[1] A regular interval in this connection means the interval at which under the express or implied agreement between the employer and the employee the earnings are normally paid, each interval being of substantially equal length.[2] Where earnings are normally paid at a regular interval e.g. every Friday but occasionally a payment is made at another time e.g. because of public holidays, such a payment is to be treated as made at the regular interval.[3]

There are certain other circumstances in which earnings are to be treated as paid at regular intervals:

1. Where there is a succession of periods of equal length i.e. consisting of the same number of days, weeks or calendar months, and one and only one payment is made in each period the payments are to be treated as made at the end of such period.[4] This covers such cases as where weekly pay is

paid on either Thursday or Friday depending on the time taken to prepare the payroll or where monthly pay is paid on the last Friday in each month.

2. Where the earnings are payable at regular intervals but the payments are not in fact made at such regular intervals the payments are to be treated as made at the end of each such interval.[5]

However, these deeming provisions are not to have the effect of causing a payment of earnings made in one tax year to fall in another tax year.[6]

Where a payment of earnings (but not on termination of the employment) includes holiday pay which under the deeming provisions would be treated as paid at a regular interval of a week or a multiple of weeks, the earnings period may be the length of the period in respect of which the payment is made.[7] This is optional; otherwise the holiday pay is treated as pay in the week or weeks in question.

The following rules cover further cases where earnings are paid or treated as paid at regular intervals:

1. The employee may have earnings payable at one regular interval and other earnings payable at different regular intervals e.g. basic pay paid weekly, overtime paid monthly and commissions paid quarterly. In this situation the earnings period is based on the shortest interval,[8] in this case one week, subject to a possible exception indicated below.
2. If the regular interval at which earnings are paid is less than seven days, the earnings period will be one week. This will also be the case where earnings are payable at different regular intervals, each of which is less than seven days.[9]
3. Where earnings are being paid at different regular intervals and some intervals are seven days or more and others are less than seven days, the earnings period will be one week.[10]

The importance of the earnings period can be seen from the following example.

EXAMPLE

Alice is a shop manager. She receives basic pay of £200 per week and in addition is entitled to a bonus related to sales targets which is paid at the end of the following month. Her bonus for April 1989 was £700.

Her primary contributions in May are as follows:

Week ending	Basic Pay	Bonus	Primary Class I Contributions (at 9%)
12th May	200		18.00
19th May	200		18.00
26th May	200		18.00
2nd June	200	700	29.25 (on £325 max.)
	£800	£700	£83.25

If Alice's employer decides to pay all her earnings monthly by bank transfer the position becomes—

Month ending	Earnings	Primary Class 1 Contributions (at 9%)
31st May	£1,500	£126.81 (on £1,409 max)

Increase £ 43.56

The reason for the increase is that when an earnings period of one month is taken the excess of earnings over the upper earnings limit is reduced.

Because where earnings are paid at differing regular intervals it is possible to reduce contribution liability by increasing earnings payable at longer intervals at the expense of earnings paid at the shortest interval there is an anti-avoidance rule. If the greater part of the total earnings is normally (ie this implies a regular practice) paid at intervals of greater length than the shorter or shortest interval as the case may be, the earnings period is to be the longer or longest interval.[11] This provision is brought into operation by the Secretary of State giving notice to the employer and the employee, indicating the date from which the new earnings period is to be adopted.

Thus, if in the above example Alice's bonuses normally exceeded her basic pay, the Secretary of State could issue a notice making the earnings period one month. If the longer or longest interval is one year and the Secretary of State under this provision makes the earnings period one year, the change only takes effect so as to make the remainder of the tax year after the change the earnings period.[12]

Earnings periods, whether a week, month or other period, must always begin on the first day of the tax year and follow in sucession from that date.[13] Earnings periods of one week and one month respectively will therefore correspond to the tax weeks and months used for operating PAYE. Where, however, the earnings period is of some other length, there may be a gap between the end of the last full earnings period in the tax year and the end of that year: in that case the period covering the gap is to be treated as an earnings period of normal length.[14]

Where the earnings are paid at irregular intervals and the rules for deeming the payments to be made at regular intervals do not apply, the earnings period is to be the length of the period for which the earnings are paid or a week whichever is the longer.[15] If it is not reasonably practicable to determine that period, the earnings period is the period from the last payment of earnings (or if none the commencement of the employment) until the date of the payment but in any case no less than a week.[16] If the payment is made before the employment begins or after it ends, the earnings period is to be one week.[17]

There are special rules for determining the earnings period in the case of payments under the employments protection legislation.[18]

If there is a change in the regular intervals at which earnings are paid and the new earnings period is longer than the old, a payment of earnings made at the old interval may fall within the first new earnings period. In that case the contributions payable on payments made after the date of change are limited to those which would be payable if all payments made during the first new earnings period had been paid at the new interval.[19]

---

[1] SI 1979 No. 591, reg. 3(1)(*a*)(i).
[2] SI 1979 No. 591, reg. 1(2).
[3] SI 1979 No. 591, reg. 6(1)(*a*).
[4] SI 1978 No. 1689, reg. 6(1)(*b*) and (2).
[5] SI 1978 No. 1689, reg. 6(1)(*c*) and (2).
[6] SI 1978 No. 1689, reg. 6(3).
[7] SI 1979 No. 591, reg. 15.
[8] SI 1979 No. 591, reg. 3(1)(*a*)(ii).

9 SI 1979 No. 591, reg. 3(1)(a)(iii).
10 SI 1979 No. 591, reg. 3(1)(a)(iv).
11 SI 1979 No. 591, reg. 3(2).
12 SI 1979 No. 591, reg. 3(2A).
13 SI 1979 No. 591, reg. 3(1)(b).
14 SI 1979 No. 591, reg. 3(3).
15 SI 1979 No. 591, reg. 4(a).
16 SI 1979 No. 591, reg. 4(b)(i).
17 SI 1979 No. 591, reg. 4(b)(ii).
18 SI 1979 No. 591, reg. 5.
19 SI 1979 No. 591, reg. 14.

COMPANY DIRECTORS

53:04   Where the employed earner is a company director there are special rules for determining the earnings period. If the individual was a company director at the beginning of the tax year, the earnings period is that year, even if he does not remain a director for the rest of the year.[1] If the person is appointed a director during the course of a tax year, the earnings period is the remainder of the tax year beginning with the week in which he is appointed.[2]

There is also a special rule as to the earnings which are to be treated as paid to a company director; any payment to or for the benefit of a director which is made on account of or by way of an advance of remuneration is to be treated as a payment of earnings for contribution purposes, if it would not otherwise be so treated.[3] These rules were introduced in 1983 to frustrate widespread exploitation of the earnings period rules on the part of directors. The term "director" is not defined for the purpose of these rules but the term "company" is: "company" in the Contribution Regulations means a company within the meaning of Companies Act 1985, s. 735(1) or a body corporate to which any provision of that Act applies by virtue of s. 718.[4] The DSS has made it clear that a director of a building society is not a company director.[5]

Where a person ceases to be a director and in a subsequent tax year he is paid earnings which relate to a period in which he was a director e.g. a deferred bonus, the earnings are not to be aggregated with any other earnings and the earnings period is to be the tax year in which they are paid.[6]

In certain professions it is common for members of partnerships to hold directorships; likewise it is common for companies which have substantial shareholdings in other companies or in certain other situations to nominate directors to those companies. As from 6th January 1988 fees and other payments received by such directors can be excluded from their earnings from such offices if the individual has to account for such fees to the partnership or company appointing him and the fees are brought into the accounts of the partnership or company and charged to tax. Where a partnership is concerned, this rule only applies if the director is a partner in the firm concerned and the payment received forms an insubstantial part of the gross income of the firm.[7]

1 SI 1979 No. 591, reg. 6A(3).
2 SI 1979 No. 591, reg. 6A(2).

³ SI 1979 No. 591, reg. 17A.
⁴ SI 1979 No. 591, reg. 1(2).
⁵ DSS Leaflet NI35, para. 2.
⁶ SI 1979 No. 591, reg. 6A(5).
⁷ SI 1979 No. 591, reg. 19B.

ANTI-AVOIDANCE RULES

53: 05   There are regulations which enable the Secretary of State to counter practices which avoid or reduce the payment of Class 1 contributions. One deals with abnormal pay practices;[1] the other with irregular or unequal payments of earnings.[2] An abnormal pay practice is described as one which is followed in the payment of earnings and is abnormal for the employment in question.[3] If the Secretary of State has reason to believe that such a practice has been or is being followed, he may make a determination on any question regarding contribution liability on the basis that the abnormal practice is ignored and that the practices normal for the employment in question apply.[4] This is a determination of a "principal question" (see infra, § 57: 05) but whereas under the adjudication procedure such a question has to be referred to the Secretary of State, in this case exceptionally such a referral is not necessary; the Secretary of State can make the determination as if an application had been made.[5]

The determination can apply retrospectively to the tax year before that in which the decision is given.[6] If additional primary contributions become payable for the previous year, the employer will not be able to recover them from the employee.[7] This particular power is rarely invoked. In recent years the DSS have countered avoidance by the introduction of new regulations e.g. those dealing with company directors in 1983, those dealing with discretionary employee trusts in 1987 and those dealing with certain securities used for payment in kind in 1988.

A possible limitation on the scope of the power lies in the fact that it can only be exercised where the secondary contributor has followed the abnormal pay practice in the payment of earnings. So it could be argued that where the payment falls within one of the specific exclusions from earnings e.g. it is a payment kind, the power cannot be used. This is, however, open to question: a practice of, for example, paying some remuneration in kind leaving cash earnings reduced could well be seen as a practice followed in paying the latter earnings. Although the DSS has never in fact sought to use this provision to counter unused payments in kind, the provision, it would seem, gives the Department a formidable reserve power which should be treated with respect.

The Secretary of State's power to counter an abnormal pay practice requires resort to the formal procedure of making a determination of a principal question. There could be an appeal from such a determination to the High Court (or Court of Session in Scotland) on a point of law. No such formalities are required to counter a practice involving irregular or unequal payments of earnings. Here the Secretary of State may simply give a direction.[8] The practice in this case is one involving the payment of earnings under which the incidence of contributions is avoided or reduced. The provision clearly has in view the manipulation of earnings periods; where a direction is made it is to the effect that contribution liability is to be calculated as if the practice in question was not being followed.

---

[1] SI 1979 No. 591, reg. 21.
[2] SI 1979 No. 591, reg. 22.
[3] SI 1979 No. 591, reg. 21(2).
[4] SI 1979 No. 591, reg. 21(2).
[5] SI 1979 No. 591, reg. 21(3).
[6] SI 1979 No. 591, reg. 21(1).
[7] SI 1979 No. 591, Sch. 1, para. 13(2A)(*a*).
[8] SI 1979 No. 591, reg. 22.

MORE THAN ONE EMPLOYMENT

53: 06   If an individual is an employee under more than one employment with the same employer, the primary rule is that the earnings paid in the week or other earnings period in respect of each employment have to be aggregated and treated as a single payment of earnings in respect of one employment only.[1] The DSS has confirmed to the Institute of Chartered Accountants in England and Wales that associated companies in the same group do not represent the same employer but divisions of a company do. This rule is necessary to prevent a fragmentation of an essentially single employment with the earnings under some of the resulting employments being below the lower earnings limits and so escaping contribution liability.

An exception from this rule is made to cover the case where the aggregation is "not reasonably practicable because the earnings in the respective employments are separately calculated".[2] The DSS regards this condition as met if the employer works out earnings at different paying points e.g. where employees are paid locally at different branches.[3] Where the employments are dealt with under separate PAYE schemes, the test is also likely to be met.

There is another primary rule that concerns the case where the individual has more than one employment but with different employers. Again in this case also the earnings paid in the week or other earnings period from each of the employments have to be aggregated and treated as a single payment of earnings from one employment but in this case only in prescribed circumstances.[4]

The circumstances where aggregation is required are where:

(*a*) the different employers carry on business in association with each other, or

(*b*) there are different employers but one of them is treated as the secondary contributor under the categorisation rules (see supra, § **51: 05**) in respect of each of the employments, or

(*c*) the earnings are paid by various persons for whom the work is performed and some other person is treated as the secondary contributor under the categorisation rules.[5]

In these cases there is also an exception for the case where it is not reasonably practicable to aggregate the earnings: but there is no requirement in this case that the earnings should be separately calculated.[6]

No indication is given in the regulations as to what is meant by employers carrying on business in association with each other but the DSS guidance adds "that is, they share profits or losses, or to a large extent resources".[7] In applying this test it is understood that the DSS look for some degree of common purpose, substantiated by, for example, the sharing of facilities, personnel, accommodation, customers etc. Sharing of profits or losses can cover cases such as where the costs of staff or premises are divided among different companies. Whether employer companies belong to the same group is not of itself decisive, though ordinarily in such a case the required degree of interdependence will be found.

Where earnings from two or more employments (whether with the same or different employers) have to be aggregated and the earnings periods for the various employments when considered separately are of different lengths, special rules determine the earnings period to be taken for the combined earnings:

1. If there are both contracted-out and non-contracted-out employments, the earnings period is that for the contracted-out employment or if there is more than one such employment that for the one having the shorter or shortest earnings period.[8]
2. Otherwise, the earnings period is the shorter or shortest period for all the employments.[9]
3. But if in the case of any of the employments the earnings period rules for directors have been applied, the earnings period so found or the longer or longest such period must be taken as the earnings period for the combined earnings.[10]

Where earnings from contracted-out and non-contracted-out employments are aggregated, the calculation of the Class 1 contributions is subject to special rules.[11] These require that the calculation of both primary and secondary contributions is on the basis that the earnings from the contracted-out employment or employments form the first part of total earnings and therefore non-contracted-out rates apply to the remainder (except in the case of primary contributions to the extent that they do not exceed the upper earnings limit).

---

[1] SSA 1975, Sch. 1, para. 1(1)(*a*).
[2] SI 1978 No. 1689, reg. 11.
[3] DSS Leaflet NI269, p. 34, para 91.
[4] SSA 1975, Sch. 1, para, 1(1)(*b*).
[5] SI 1979 No. 591, reg. 12(1).
[6] SI 1979 No. 591, reg. 12(1) proviso.
[7] DSS Leaflet NI269, p. 34, para. 90.
[8] SI 1979 No. 591, reg. 5A(2)(*a*).
[9] SI 1979 No. 591, reg. 5A(2)(*b*).
[10] SI 1979 No. 591, reg. 6A(4).
[11] SSA 1975, Sch. 1, para. 1(1A), (1B), (1C) and (1D).

ANNUAL MAXIMUM CONTRIBUTIONS

53: 07   There may be cases where an individual has employments with different employers which are not aggregated e.g. because the different employers do not carry on business in association with each other. In such cases contribution liability will be calculated separately for each employment, and the upper earnings limit applied in each case without reference to the other employments. So, for example, if Dizzy has earnings of £400 per week from employment with Roller Ltd and £300 per week from employment with Coaster Ltd, a wholly independent company, earnings of £(325 plus £300) i.e. £625 will be subject to primary contributions as opposed to £325 if the earnings had been aggregated.

Similarly where an individual in the same tax year has earnings both as a self-employed person and as an employee, his total contributions could be much higher than if all his earnings arose from being an employee.

For these reasons annual limits have been placed on the total contributions payable. There are two rules to consider. The first rule limits the total primary Class 1 and Class 2 contributions payable to 53 primary Class 1 contributions at the maximum weekly standard rate[1] i.e. for 1989–90

$$26 \times (9\% \times £325) + 27 \times (2\% \times £43 + 9\% \times £325 - 43) = £1,468.98.$$

Because this maximum is set in terms of contributions at non-contracted-out rates, if the individual has actually paid contributions in respect of a contracted-out employment these have to be converted to contributions at the standard rate for the purpose of seeing whether the maximum has been exceeded.[2] But if it has been exceeded and a repayment is therefore due, the amount to be repaid is based on the actual contributions paid i.e. overpaid standard rate contributions are converted back to the rates at which they were paid. Contributions paid at the reduced rate are similarly converted to standard rate contributions in applying the maximum but any repayment is based on the actual contributions paid.

It should be noted that the maximum applies only to employee and self-employed contributions. Because the upper earnings limit is not relevant to secondary Class 1 contributions, non-aggregation of earnings does not result in excess employer contributions being paid.

The other rule applies in the case where Class 4 contributions are payable in addition to primary Class 1 and Class 2 contributions. In this situation the Class 4 contributions are not to exceed A–B, where

A is 53 Class 2 contributions, i.e. in 1989–90 53 × £4.25	225.25
Plus the maximum Class 4 contributions, in 1989–90 6.3% × £(16.900 − 5,050)	746.55
	£971.80

and B is the aggregate of the primary Class 1 and Class 2 contributions paid.[3] For this purpose also Class 1 contributions paid at contracted-out rates or at the reduced rate are converted to standard rate contributions.[4]

EXAMPLE
Ruby works as a cook in a restaurant at £150 per week; in 1989–90 she earned £7,800 from

this employment. She is also in business on her own account, providing catering at wedding receptions, business functions etc; in 1989–90 she earns £11,000 after expenses from this business.

Her contribution liabilities for 1989–90 before application of the annual maxima will be—

Class 1

26 weeks at £150 × 9%	351.00	
26 weeks at £43 × 2%	22.36	
and £(150 − 43) × 9%	250.38	
		272.74
		623.74

Class 2

52 weeks at £4.25		221.00
		844.74

Class 4

£(11,000 − 5,050) × 6.3%		374.85
		£1,219.59

Restrictions

The total Class 1 and Class 2 contributions (£844.74) are less than 53 Class 1 contributions at the maximum weekly standard rate (i.e. £1,468.98—see above). The Class 1 and Class 2 contributions are therefore not restricted.

But the Class 4 contributions (£311.85 are restricted to:

A (see above)	971.80
Less: B (the total Class 1 and Class 2 contributions paid)	844.74
	£127.06

Where through application of these limits, contributions have been overpaid, or where contributions have been paid in error, there are complex rules for dealing with a return of contributions: these establish an order of priority for refunding different kinds of contribution.[5] Broadly, any overpaid Class 4 contributions are repayable first, then primary Class 1 contributions at the reduced rate, followed by Class 2 contributions and then primary Class 1 contributions at the standard rate on non-contracted-out employments. Last to be repaid are primary Class 1 contributions in respect of contracted-out employments where there are further rules governing the repayment of amounts paid at non-contracted-out rates and contracted-out rates respectively.[6] Where it is anticipated that the annual maximum limits will be exceeded, it is advisable to apply for deferment of contributions before the start of the tax year for which deferment of liability is sought.

There are two kinds of deferment available. One covers the case where the individual in a tax year will have earnings from two or more employments and is expected to pay, in respect of one of the employments, contributions equal to 52 primary Class 1 contributions at the rate applicable to earnings at the upper earnings limit. In such a case deferment will be granted in respect of the other employments.[7] The other kind of deferment covers the case where the individual is both an employee and self-employed in a tax year. It is necessary to show that the annual maximum which limits the total primary Class 1 and Class 2 contributions to 53 primary Class 1 contributions at the maximum standard rate (see above) is likely to apply. In that case a deferment arrangement in respect of the Class 2 contributions may be made.[8] Similarly if it can be shown that the annual maximum restricting Class 4 contributions described above is likely to apply, a deferment of liability for Class 4 contributions may be granted.[9] In all cases of deferment, the position is reviewed after the end of the tax year and any unpaid contributions are then payable by means of direct collection.

---

¹ SI 1979 No. 591, reg. 17(1), (3).
² SI 1979 No. 591, reg. 17(2).
³ SI 1979 No. 591, reg. 67(1).
⁴ SI 1979 No. 591, reg. 67(2).
⁵ SI 1979 No. 591, reg. 32.
⁶ SI 1979 No. 591, reg. 33.
⁷ SI 1979 No. 591, regs. 47, 48, 49.
⁸ SI 1979 No. 591, reg. 54.
⁹ SI 1979 No. 591, regs. 62, 63, 64.

COLLECTION OF CLASS 1 CONTRIBUTIONS

53: 08 Class 1 contributions are normally payable under the PAYE system i.e. the employer must account for the primary contributions deducted from pay and for the secondary contributions, for which he is liable to the Collector of Taxes, within 14 days from the end of each tax month. The Revenue in due course surrenders the contributions collected to the DSS for payment into the national insurance fund.

To enable this procedure to operate, the PAYE regulations (subject to some modification) have been incorporated into the Contribution Regulations.[1] The following points should be noted—

1. The employer i.e. the secondary contributor is liable both for his own contributions and for the employee's primary contributions[2] but he is entitled to recover the primary contributions by deduction from the employee's earnings.[3] Where an under-deduction occurs, the right to recover the shortfall is restricted to earnings subsequently paid in the same tax year[4] but with the further restriction that any additional deduction must not exceed the amount deductible from the payment of earnings in the ordinary way, i.e. the normal deduction can be doubled but no more.[5]

2. Under the present arrangements for statutory sick pay and statutory maternity pay, the employer is required to pay these benefits to employees entitled to them but has the right to recover the payments from contributions which he is liable to pay to the Collector of Taxes.[6]

3. Because statutory sick pay and statutory maternity pay are treated as earnings for contribution purposes, it follows that the employer has to pay secondary contributions on these benefits. However the employer is entitled to compensation. The compensation is not for the precise amount of secondary contributions to which the actual benefits paid by the employer in question give rise, but rather a notional amount, arrived at by applying a percentage to the amounts of statutory sick pay and statutory maternity pay paid to employees.[7] The percentage is currently 7%; this rate is derived from estimates made by the Secretary of State

of the total statutory sick pay and statutory maternity pay paid by all employers and the total secondary Class 1 contributions paid by all employers on that total.

The compensation as so calculated is to be deducted from contributions which the secondary contributor is liable to pay to the Collector of Taxes.

Although collection through the PAYE machinery is the normal procedure, ther is also provision for arrangements to be made to recover Class I contributions by means of direct collection.[8] This can occur in the following circumstances:

(a) a deferment of Class I contributions has been granted (see supra, § **53: 08**) and the employee has agreed to pay any primary Class I contributions that may ultimately become due,[9]

(b) the secondary contributor has failed to account for primary Class I contributions and the failure is due to an act or default on the part of the employee and not to any negligence on the part of the secondary contributor,[10]

(c) the collection provisions cannot be enforced against the secondary contributor because protection is afforded by an international treaty or convention and the secondary contributory is unwilling to pay primary contributions on behalf of the employee,[11]

(d) the employer does not fulfill the conditions as to residence, presence or having a place of business in Great Britain so as to become liable as the secondary contributor to account for primary contributions.[12]

---

[1] SI 1979 No. 591, Sch. 1.

[2] SSA 1975, Sch. 1, para. 3(1).

[3] SSA 1975, Sch. 1, para. 3(3).

[4] SI 1979 No. 591, Sch. 1, para. 13 (2A)(a).

[5] SI 1979 No. 591 Sch. 1, para. 13(3A).

[6] SI 1979 No. 591, Sch. 1, para. 26(1); Statutory Sick Pay (Compensation of Employers) and Miscellaneous Provisions Regulations 1983, reg. 2; Statutory Maternity Pay (Compensation of Employer's) Regulations 1987, reg. 2.

[7] Statutory Sick Pay Additional (Compensation of Employer's and Consequential Amendments) Regulations 1985, reg. 3; Statutory Maternity Pay (Compensation of Employers) (Amendment) Regulations 1988, reg. 2.

[8] SI 1979 No. 591, reg. 47.

[9] SI 1979 No. 591, reg. 48(1).

[10] SI 1979 No. 591, reg. 50(1)(a).

[11] SI 1979 No. 591, reg. 50(1)(b).

[12] SI 1979 No. 591, reg. 119(1)(b); Sch. 1, para. 50(1).

54   The self-employed earner

Class 2 contributions   1241
Class 4 contributions   1243

CLASS 2 CONTRIBUTIONS

54: 01   Every self-employed earner[1] is required to pay Class 2 contributions from age 16 onward until reaching pensionable age.[2] Liability, however, is confined to such contribution weeks during any part of which he is treated as such a self-employed earner.[3]

Whether a person is a self-employed earner or an employed earner[4] is a matter of categorisation which is often difficult to determine.[5] Whether a person falls into the category of self-employed earner depends, inter alia, on whether he is ordinarily employed in employment as a self-employed earner,[6] and where he has been treated as falling into that category, he will continue to be so treated unless and until he is no longer ordinarily employed.[7]

The effect of these rules is that if a person is treated as ordinarily employed in self-employed earner's employment, liability for Class 2 contributions will continue during weeks of holiday or other inactivity. When, however, the individual ceases to be so ordinarily employed there is to be no such liability even if the previous activity produces a continuing source of income e.g. licence-royalties from devices which an inventor has patented.

Because to be a self-employed earner, a person must be "gainfully employed",[9] certain activities by themselves will not give rise to Class 2 contribution liability, e.g. the receipt of investment income, the letting of property, the receipt by a sleeping partner of a share of a firm's profits.

Class 2 contributions, where payable, are at a small flat rate (for 1989–90 £4.25 a week). The rate is slightly above that for Class 3 contributions and in addition to securing entitlement to long-term benefits (as do Class 3 contributions) Class 2 contributions also enable sickness and invalidity benefits to be claimed.

Payment is made either by purchase of special stamps from the Post Office which are affixed to a contribution card or alternatively contributions may be paid by direct bank debit.

Class 2 contributions cannot be deducted as an allowable business expense for income tax purposes.[10]

---

[1] SSA 1975, s. 2(1)(b).
[2] SSA 1975, s. 7(1); SSPA 1975, s. 4(2).
[3] SSA 1975, s. 2(5).
[4] SSA 1975, s. 2(1)(c).
[5] See supra, § **51: 02**.
[6] S.I. 1978 No. 1689, Sch. 1, para. 9.
[7] S.I. 1978 No. 1689, Sch. 2.
[8] SSA 1975, s. 2(1)(b).
[9] SSA 1975, s. 2(1)(b).
[10] TA 1988, s. 617(3)(a).

Exceptions from Class 2 liability

54: 02   There are a number of exceptions from liability to pay Class 2 contributions. The most important of these is normally referred to as "the small earnings exception".

It applies where the self-employed earner can show that his earnings do not exceed a specified figure for the tax year for which application for the exception to apply is made.[1] This can be met best by showing either that for that year the earnings are likely to be less than the specified amount or that for the preceding year the earnings were less than the amount specified for that year and that since then there has been no material change of circumstances.[2]

The specified figure for 1989–90 is £2,350. The figure is revised each year and is maintained at a small margin above the lower earnings limit for Class 1 contribution purposes.

The exception does not apply unless the self-employed earner makes an application for a certificate of exception.[3] This has to be in a prescribed form;[4] the DSS require form CF10 to be used: this can be found as part of DSS leaflet N1 27A. The applicant has to provide information and evidence relating to his earnings as the Secretary of State may require.[5] The DSS normally require accounts or tax computations for a recent tax year together with estimates for the tax year for which the application is made or the preceding year.

The earnings to take into account are the applicant's net earnings from employment as a self-employed earner.[6] No detailed rules are laid down as to how such earnings are to be computed.

The certificate when granted relates to such period as may be specified:[7] normally this is for the whole of a tax year (if application is made in advance) or for part of the current tax year. The Secretary of State is allowed at his discretion to backdate the certificate for no more than 13 weeks before the date on which the application was filed.[8]

Frequently those starting a new business will find it difficult to provide evidence that their expected earnings will be below the specified limit. The DSS now waives the requirement to provide evidence in the case of all new traders who apply for certificates of exception.[9]

Where a certificate is issued, the self-employed earner is relieved of the obligation to pay Class 2 contributions for the period covered, but is entitled to pay such contributions if he wishes.[20] This would improve his contribution record in relation to claims for long-term benefits and has the advantage over paying Class 3 contributions of also securing entitlement to sickness and invalidity benefits.

There are other exceptions from liability to pay Class 2 contributions, including:

(1) *The spare time employment exception*

This applies where the individual has a substantial regular job as an employed earner and the income from the self-employed activity is below a threshold set by the DSS, which currently is £800 pa.

The basis of this exception is that in these circumstances the individual will not be regarded as ordinarily employed in a self-employed earner's employment (see supra, § **54: 01**). The threshold figure has no legislative authority; it is simply an element in an administrative practice applied by the DSS.

(2) Exceptions for receipt of benefits etc

If in any contribution week, the self-employed earner is in receipt of sickness benefit or invalidity benefit, or maternity allowance, or is incapable of work or in prison or legal custody, or in receipt of unemployability supplement or invalid car allowance, he or she will be excepted from liability to pay Class 2 contributions.[10] Such a person is nevertheless entitled to pay such contributions if he or she so wishes.[11]

---

[1] SSA 1975, s. 7(5).
[2] S.I. 1979 No. 591, reg. 25(1).
[3] S.I. 1979 No. 591, reg. 24(1).
[4] S.I. 1979 No. 591, reg. 24(2).
[5] S.I. 1979 No. 591, reg. 24(3).
[6] S.I. 1979 No. 591, reg. 25(2).
[7] S.I. 1979 No. 591, reg. 24(4).
[8] S.I. 1979 No. 591, reg. 24(5)(*b*).
[9] DSS Leaflet N127A.
[10] S.I. 1979 No. 591, reg. 23(1).
[11] S.I. 1979 No. 591, reg. 23(3).

CLASS 4 CONTRIBUTIONS

54: 03 Prior to 1975 the flat-rate principle favoured by Beveridge[1] was still much in evidence in the contributory system: both the self-employed and the employee paid flat-rate contributions although the latter also paid additional graduated contributions in exchange for additional pension entitlement under the graduated pension scheme introduced in 1959. With the replacement of the scheme by SERPS and the introduction of graduated rates for primary and secondary Class 1 contribution rates with effect from 6 April 1975, a substantial difference opened up between the still flat-rate contributions payable by a self-employed person with earnings at or above the upper earnings limit and those payable by an employee with the same earnings.

Unlike the employee, the self-employed person had no entitlement to the additional pension provided by SERPS but the differential was considered inequitable. One solution would have been to increase sharply the level of flat-rate contributions for all self-employed persons but this would have borne hardly on those with modest earnings but not covered by the small earnings exception. Instead, the solution adopted was to impose a new class of contribution, Class 4, payable on business profits as assessed for income tax under Schedule D, Case I or Case II. In this way the self-employed were subjected to an additional separate contribution dependent on the level of business profits.

Because no additional benefit entitlement is obtained by payment of

Class 4 contributions many saw the introduction of the new class as no more than a tax which discriminated against the self-employed. There was fierce opposition at the time and an architect even challenged Parliament's right to introduce such a measure on the ground that during the second reading of the Social Security Act 1975 all MPs had changed their status from being self-employed to employees and this, he argued made them employees holding offices for profit under the Crown and so disqualified them from passing any Act of Parliament, including the Social Security Act 1975. The attempt failed.[2]

Nowadays, the Class 4 contributions are accepted without demur and because employer contributions (which since 6th October 1985 have no upper limit) do not attach to the earnings of a self-employed earner, self-employed status is still very advantageous.[3]

Class 4 contributions are payable at a prescribed rate on a band of profits between a lower limit and an upper limit. The lower limit is set well above the lower earnings limit for Class 1 contribution purposes but the upper limit is set at or about the same level as the upper earnings limit. Both upper and lower limits are revised annually: for 1989–90 the lower limit is £5,050 and the upper limit is £16,900. The prescribed rate is intended to be maintained year by year—each tax year since 1983–84 including 1989–90 the rate has been 6.3%—but the Secretary of State is given an enabling power to alter the rate but not to more than 8.25%.[4]

Although the intention behind the introduction of Class 4 contributions was to put the self-employed person with high earnings on a similar footing to an employed person with similar earnings, there is in fact still a differential.

EXAMPLE

Employed earner with earnings at upper earnings limit (£16,900)
Primary Class 1 contributions in 1989–90

$26 \times £325 \times 9\%$	760.05
$26 \times £43$ at 2%	22.36
$26 \times £(325 - 43) \times 9\%$	659.88
	£1,442.29

Self-employed earnings with earnings at upper earnings limit (£16,900)
Class 2

$52 \times £4.25$	221.00
Class 4	
$6.3\% \times £(16,900 - 5050)$	746.55
	£967.55

Class 4 contributions are collected through inclusion in the Schedule D Case I or Case II assessment and payment is made to the Collector of Taxes. The income tax appeal provisions apply to the determination of Class 4 contribution liability but not to any question of exception from liability or deferment of liability.[5] When the assessment becomes final and conclusive for income tax purposes, it also becomes final and conclusive as regards the Class 4 contribution liability.[6] The income tax provisions for charging interest on overdue tax do not apply to Class 4 contribution liabilities except in the case of an assessment to make good a loss of tax due to fraud, wilful default or neglect on the part of any person.[7] The repayment supplement is not available in respect of overpaid Class 4 contributions.[8]

It is possible to recover overpaid Class 4 contributions either through the income tax provisions under which an assessment can be adjusted[9] or through direct application for repayment to the DSS either within six years of the tax year in respect of which the contributions were paid or within two years of the tax year in which payment was made.[10]

Where the Schedule D Case I or II assessment is a joint assessment on a partnership, the Class 4 contributions due from each partner are normally aggregated and collected through the joint assessment. There is also provision for separate assessment of the individual partner but this will only be appropriate if the individual has other sources of business profits[11].

Class 4 contributions are payable with a few exceptions by all self-employed persons below pensionable age[12] whose business income exceeds the lower limit. However the charging provision[13] bases liability not on persons but on "all annual profits or gains immediately derived from the carrying on" of a trade profession, or vocation. Because the profits have to be immediately derived from carrying on the profession etc, the share of profits allocated to a sleeping partner will not give rise to Class 4 contributions. There are also exceptions from liability for:

(a) Persons not resident in the UK in the tax year in question.[14]

(b) Divers and diving supervisors.[15]

(c) Persons under the age of 16 (but an application has to be made for this exception to apply).[16]

(d) Trustees, guardians etc of incapacitated persons.[17]

(e) Trustees who are charged to tax under TA 1988, s. 59 on the income of others.

For the position of persons who are treated as employed earners but who receive income taxed under Schedule D Case I or Case II see infra, § **54: 05**.

---

[1] See supra, § **50: 02**.
[2] *Martin v O'Sullivan* [1984] STC 258n, CA.
[3] See supra, § **51: 02**.
[4] SSA 1975, s. 122(1)(d) and 6(b).
[5] SSA 1975, Sch. 2, para. 9.
[6] SSA 1975, Sch. 2, para. 8.
[7] SSA 1975, Sch. 2, para. 7.
[8] SI 1979 No 591, reg. 70.
[9] SSA 1975, Sch. 2, para. 8.
[10] SI 1979 No. 591, reg. 69.
[11] SSA 1975, Sch. 2, para. 5.
[12] SI 1979 No. 591, reg. 58(a).
[13] SSA 1975, s. 9(1).
[14] SI 1979 No. 591, reg. 58(b).
[15] SI 1979 No. 591, reg. 59.
[16] SI 1979 No. 591, reg. 60.
[17] SSA 1975, Sch. 2, para. 6(a).

Computation of profits for Class 4

54: 04   The charging provision[1] requires the annual profits or gains on which Class 4 contributions are payable to be those which are "chargeable to income tax under Case I or Case II of Schedule D".[2] This means that the profits as adjusted for Schedule D Case I or II form the basis of the amount on which Class 4 contributions are payable i.e. the same adjustments for depreciation/capital allowances and balancing changes, disallowable entertaining expenses etc. are made.

There are however, certain special rules which enable certain losses and similar items which are not deductible as expenses in arriving at the profits for Schedule D Case I or Case II purposes to be deducted from the profits for Class 4 contribution purposes.

These items are:

(a) Capital allowances given primarily against a specific source of income and given by way of discharges or repayment of tax so long as they relate to the relevant trade or profession.[3]

(b) Interest, annuities and other annual payments deductible from total income for income tax purposes so far as incurred exclusively for the purpose of the trade, profession or vocation.[4]

(c) Trading losses brought forward from an earlier year under TA 1988, s. 385[5] or in the case of terminal losses carried back under TA 1988, s. 388 or 389.[6]

(d) Trading losses and excess capital allowances over trading income which can be set off against general income under TA 1988, ss. 380, 381 and 383.[7]

The losses in (d), being available against general income for the current or succeeding tax year, normally reduce taxable income from sources other than the trade or profession in which they arise. The fact that such losses thereby become used up against other source income for income tax purposes is irrelevant in relation to Class 4 contributions: in calculating contributions such losses are regarded as unused and can be carried forward for deduction from Schedule D Case I or Case II profits for a later period.[8] This means that in the subsequent period the profits for Class 4 purposes will be lower than for income tax purposes. It is very easy to overlook this point when considering the position for the subsequent year.

The following items, however, are not deductible from the profits on which Class 4 contributions are payable:

(a) Personal reliefs.[9]

(b) Retirement annuity contract premiums.[10]

(c) Interest payments for which relief is given under TA 1988, s. 353.[11]

(d) Taxed annual payments carried forward as losses under TA 1988, s. 387.[12]

(e) Interest treated as a loss for the purposes of carry-forward or carry-back under TA 1988, s. 390.[13]

(f) The relief which is given for income tax purposes for Class 4 contributions.[14]

As to (f), it should be appreciated that in computing total income for income tax purposes one half of the Class 4 contributions is deductible.[15]

---

[1] SSA 1975, s. 9(1).
[2] SSA 1975, s. 9(1).
[3] SSA 1975, Sch. 2 para. 2(a)(ii).

⁴ SSA 1975, Sch. 2, para. 3(4).
⁵ SSA 1975, Sch. 2, para. 3(1)(c).
⁶ SSA 1975, Sch. 2, para. 3(1)(d).
⁷ SSA 1975, Sch. 2, para. 3(1)(a) and (b).
⁸ SSA 1975, Sch. 2, para. 3(3).
⁹ SSA 1975, Sch. 2, para. 3(2)(a).
¹⁰ SSA 1975, Sch. 2, para. 3(2)(b).
¹¹ SSA 1975, Sch. 2, para. 3(2)(c).
¹² SSA 1975, Sch. 2, para. 3(2)(d).
¹³ SSA 1975, Sch. 2, para. 3(2)(e).
¹⁴ SSA 1975, Sch. 2, para. 3(2)(f).
¹⁵ TA 1988, s. 617(5).

Individual both employed and self-employed

54: 05   It will sometimes be the case that a person is categorised as an employed earner (as will always be the case for e.g. office cleaners, and certain lecturers, teachers and instructors), for contribution purposes and so pays Class 1 contributions for contribution purposes but the earnings are taxed under Schedule D Case I or Case II for income tax purposes. Again it is common in certain professions, e.g. solicitors and accountants for practitioners to hold offices such as directorships where the fees are brought into their accounts and assessed to income tax under Schedule D Case I or II but the earnings are subject to Class 1 contributions.

In such cases the earnings on which Class 1 contributions have been paid would also create a liability for Class 4 contributions in the absence of any special rule. It is however possible to apply in such cases for exception from Class 4 contribution liability.¹ The exception will in effect cover the amount of the earner's profits which have been subject to Class 1 contributions. Two steps are required to arrive at this amount:

(1) Take the amount of the business profits which exceed the lower limit for Class 4 purposes but do not exceed the upper limit.

(2) Quantify the earnings on which Class 1 contributions have been paid by reference to the number of contributions and the rates at which they have been paid, distinguishing between standard, contracted-out and reduced rates.

The amount to be excepted is that arrived at in (2) so far as it does not exceed that found in (1).

EXAMPLE
In 1989–90 W, a sole practitioner, is assessed under Schedule D Case II on £10,500 being the adjusted profits for the year to 31 December 1989. In December 1989 W receives a gross fee of £6,000 as a director of Omicron Ltd under deduction of standard rate Class 1 contributions.

Earnings on which Class 1 contributions paid	£6,000
(there is an annual earnings period but the fee is above the lower earnings limit and below the upper earnings limit for 1989–90)	
Business profits otherwise subject to Class 4 contributions	
£10,500 – £5,050	£5,450
Earnings subject to exception	£5,450

This exception will not be available unless the individual makes an application for it. The application should be made before the tax year to which the exception is to apply or such later date as may be allowed.[2] Because it is not possible to know in advance the Class 1 contributions which the individual will pay nor the level of his business profits, the amount to be excepted cannot normally be calculated until after the end of that tax year and consequently in practice a certificate of deferment of Class 4 contribution liability is issued in response to such an application.[3]

Where a person whose earnings are taxed under Schedule E is, under the categorisation regulations, treated as a self-employed earner and the earnings in the tax year exceed the lower limit for Class 4 purposes, special Class 4 contributions are payable at the normal rate (currently 6.3%) on the earnings in excess of the lower limit but not exceeding the upper limit for Class 4 purposes.[4] The earnings are arrived at for this purpose as if earnings-related Class 1 contributions were payable.[5]

[1] SI 1979 No. 591, reg. 61(1).
[2] SI 1979 No. 591, reg. 61(2).
[3] SI 1979 No. 591, reg. 61(4).
[4] SI 1979 No. 591, reg. 71.
[5] SI 1979 No. 591, reg. 73.

55 Interaction with benefits

Earnings factors   1249
Credits   1250
Voluntary contributions   1251

EARNINGS FACTORS

55: 01   This publication does not attempt to deal with the circumstances in which the various contributory and non-contributory benefits can be claimed and the conditions which have to be fulfilled. However, it should not be forgotten that under the contributory scheme there is an essential link between contributions paid and benefits claimable and therefore a brief review of this link is appropriate.

It is difficult to summarise the contribution requirements for the different kinds of contributory benefits since each has its own set of rules. But at the risk of oversimplification, it is useful to draw a distinction between short-term and long-term benefits. Examples of short-term benefits are unemployment benefit and sickness benefit. The main long-term benefits are retirement pensions, in Category A or Category B, widow's pension and related benefits.

With both short-term and long-term benefits entitlement depends on both an entrance fee requirement, i.e. the payment of sufficient contributions to be regarded as eligible for benefit, and a continuing membership record. In the case of the entrance fee only, contributions which are actually paid count but in the case of the membership record, credits (see below) can be taken into account. The difference between the two classes of benefit is that for the long-term benefits, the membership record or, more precisely, the extent to which contributions have been maintained over the claimant's working life is the critical test and directly affects the level at which the benefit is payable. Thus, to qualify for the maximum basic rate retirement pension, the claimant must have paid or be credited with contributions for nine out of every 10 years from age 16 until pensionable age (65 for a man, 60 for a woman).

In the form of contributory system that was in force before 1975 contributions were at a flat rate and the contribution requirement could be expressed simply in terms of the number of weekly contributions that had to be paid in a year. Because since 1975 Class 1 contributions have been payable at graduated rates, depending on the level of earnings, it has become necessary to use a mechanism which gives due weight to contributions payable at higher rates when considering whether the contribution requirement has been satisfied. This mechanism consists of expressing contribution requirements and contributions paid or credited in terms of "earnings factors". An earnings factor is a notional amount of earnings derived from the contributions paid.

Thus so far as entitlement to retirement pension is concerned, an individual is only treated as having paid contributions for a particular tax year if the contributions paid or credited are equivalent to 52 weeks contributions at the lowest rate i.e. as if his earnings were continuously at the lower earnings limit. The qualifying earnings factor in this case is thus 52 weeks of earnings at the lower earnings limit.

The individual's earnings factor is then compared with this requirement. For years before 1987–88 very complicated calculations are required to arrive at an individual's earnings factor but for 1987–88 onwards all that is necessary is take the earnings on which Class 1 contributions have been paid (or treated as paid) i.e. ignoring earnings in earnings periods which were below the lower earnings limit or if they were above the upper earnings limit, ignoring the excess, and to add in earnings credited e.g. in relation to periods of unemployment or sickness (see below).[1]

If the individual was self-employed for part or all of the year in question or has paid Class 3 contributions in respect of that year, the Class 2 and Class 3 contributions paid produce earnings factors at a weekly rate equivalent to the lower earnings limit.[1]

The earnings factors produced by Class 1 contributions and credits and Class 2 and Class 3 contributions are aggregated. In a case where Class 1 contributions have been paid or treated as paid (but disregarding credits) and the total of the earnings factors falls short of the required sum (qualifying earnings factor) or the "standard level" (50 weeks at the lower earnings limit) by a relatively small amount (as specified) the shortfall is added to the total earnings factors.[3]

---

[1] Social Security (Earnings Factor) Regulations 1979, SI 1979 No. 676, as amended, Sch. 1, para. 2(1).
[2] SI 1979 No. 676, Sch. 1, para. 8.
[3] SI 1979 No. 676, Sch. 1, para. 6.

CREDITS

55: 02　Reference has already been made to credits. A credit is an amount of deemed earnings which an individual is allowed to bring into the calculation of his total earnings factors (see supra § **55: 01**). Credits are given in certain, but not all, situations where the individual will not normally be able to pay contributions. In the following situations credits are given for the purpose of claiming any benefit:

(a) Unemployment or sickness

An earnings credit is given for each week of unemployment or incapacity. Where the benefit being claimed is itself unemployment or sickness benefit, the credit is dependent on fulfilment of certain other conditions.

(b) Other non-working periods

Credits are also given for weeks in respect of which an individual receives an invalid care allowance, or for which maternity pay was paid or for which the individual's earnings fall below the lower earnings limit as a result of jury service in part or all of the week in question.

(c) Education and training

Earnings credits are given to those who already have a contribution record and who, after reaching the age of 18 undertake an approved full-time course not intended to last for more than 12 months and not related to the individual's employment.

(d) Retirement at 60

Pensionable age for a man under the State scheme is 65. If he retires earlier, he is entitled to earnings credits for contribution years in which he is not working beginning with the year in which he reaches 60.

If the individual is self-employed and therefore has a liability to pay Class 2 contributions, he must still pay such contributions and any Class 4 contributions due for weeks in which he is actually at work even after he is 60 though not when he has reached 65.

For the purpose of claiming certain benefits, credits are also given in other circumstances. For example, in the case of unemployment and sickness benefits termination credits are given to women whose marriage has terminated and to an individual who has completed an approved course of full-time education begun before reaching the age of 21.

For the purpose of entitlement to long-term benefits only i.e. principally retirement pension, persons under 18 are credited with Class 3 contributions for the years in which the 16th and 17th and 18th birthday falls.

VOLUNTARY CONTRIBUTIONS

55: 03   To enable individuals to improve deficient contribution records, the possibility of paying Class 3 contributions has been provided. These are voluntary contributions of a small amount per week (for 1989–90 £4·14 a week) which produce an earnings factor at a rate per week equal to the lower earnings limit. They count for the purpose of the long term benefits e.g. Category A and Category B retirement pensions, widow's pension etc but not for short-term benefits such as unemployment benefit, sickness benefit or invalidity benefit.

Class 3 contributions can only be paid if the total of contributions already paid for the year in question plus any earnings credits fall short of the qualifying earnings factor, that is 52 times the weekly lower earnings limit for the year in question.[1] There are a number of situations set out in the contribution regulations[2] where the individual is debarred from paying Class 3 contributions. The purpose of these rules is to prevent an individual paying Class 3 contributions in circumstances where no advantage would result.

Class 3 contributions can be paid in respect of a particular tax year within the following six years.[3] Whether or not it is desirable to pay Class 3 contributions depends on the particular circumstances, but the following points should be noted.

(1) Most young people who go on to higher education after leaving school at about age 18 will have up to a three year gap in their contribution record

for long term benefit purposes. This means that if any further break occurs during their working lives (which is not covered by credits) their retirement pension will be eroded unless either the earlier or subsequent gaps is made good by voluntary contributions.

(2) It is particularly important for a married man to maintain a good contribution record. This is because if he dies the widow's pension will be based on that record dependent on the normal time limits it will be possible for the widow herself to make good missing years. If the man dies at a very early age, any contribution gap will have a disproportionate effect on the entitlement to widow's pension.

(3) In relation to retirement pension, it is necessary to consider whether the man's or the wife's contribution record is the more important. For example if the wife has been in paid work for only, say, 15 years before reaching pensionable age, she would have to pay Class 3 contributions for nine years before the pension she could claim in her own right would equal the additional pension payable on the husband's contribution record (60% of the pension for an unmarried person) assuming that record is sound. If, however, there are substantial gaps in the husband's contribution record, it would be better in such a case for the husband to pay Class 3 contributions to improve his record.

However, if the wife has held a job for 24 years or more and thus will be able to claim a substantial pension on her own contribution record, it would be worthwhile for her to pay Class 3 contributions to cover missing years and bring her pension entitlement up to the maximum so that both husband and wife can each then have full retirement pensions as payable for unmarried persons.

---

[1] SSPA 1975, s. 5.
[2] SI 1979 No. 591, regs. 28(1), 105.
[3] SI 1979 No. 591, reg. 27(3).

56　The international dimension

TERRITORIAL SCOPE

56:01　The national insurance system described in this Chapter is of application only to Great Britain. There is a virtually identical system for Northern Ireland. Great Britain comprises mainland England, Wales and Scotland and off lying islands such as the Isle of Wight and the Hebrides, but not the Isle of Man or the Channel Islands which though having the same Sovereign are separate jurisdictions. For this reason the social security legislation when referring to the home territory consistently indicates Great Britain. In a few provisions the term UK is used: this expression covers both Great Britain and Northern Ireland. The territorial scope of the legislation is important in relation to contribution liability. A person is not liable to pay Class 1 or Class 2 contributions unless prescribed conditions of residence or presence in Great Britain are fulfilled.[1] Similarly a person is not entitled to pay Class 3 contributions unless such conditions are fulfilled.[2]

The prescribed conditions are set out in the contribution regulations.[3] The conditions make use of a number of terms, the meaning of which must be considered before proceeding further. They are described below.

Residence

The question of what constitutes residence has been considered in a number of decided cases, including such leading cases as *Lloyd v Sulley*[4], *Reid v IRC*[5] and *Lysaght v IRC*.[6] These cases were decided in the context of potential income tax liabilities, but their application is general and they are therefore relevant to the interpretation of the contribution regulations.

The Revenue has developed certain practices for settling questions of residence which are set out in Revenue publication IR 20 (1986). These practices are intended to give practical effect to the decided cases and in so far as they properly reflect those authorities will also determine the position for national insurance purposes, though it must be emphasised that these practices are not binding on the DSS.

Presence

This term usually occasions no difficulty; it is normally simply a question of fact whether or not a person is present in Great Britain.

Directors of British registered companies who live abroad may be present in Great Britain through attending board meetings. The DSS will however ignore such visits if the visits are only to attend board meetings in this country and no more than 10 board meetings are attended in a year so long as no single attendance last for more than two nights at a time and attendance at consecutive board meetings does not exceed two weeks.[7]

Ordinary residence

There is similarly a body of case law concerning the meaning of ordinary residence. This term is encountered in certain income tax legislation and again the Revenue has developed certain practices for determining the question. However, here the DSS take a different approach and their practice is to regard an individual as continuing to be ordinarily resident in Great Britain where he is absent from Great Britain for up to five years but during that time has not abandoned the intention to return.[8] It follows that it is very difficult to shake off ordinary residence for national insurance purposes.

Place of business

The question of where the employer has a place of business is important in several provisions. The DSS regards a place of business as being any place from which a person can, as of right, conduct his business, or from which his agent has power to conduct business on his behalf. A company incorporated under the Companies Act 1985 is normally regarded as having a place of business in Great Britain. Whether an overseas company has such a place of business depends on the facts and the case law on whether an overseas company is required to file particulars under what is now Companies Act 1985, s. 69(1) will be relevant: that question turns on whether the company has established a place of business in the UK.

A UK resident subsidiary of an overseas company will not be regarded as a fixed place of business of such a company but an overseas company which carries on business through a branch in Great Britain will without question have a place of business here.

It is now possible to state the residence conditions for contribution liability for the respective classes of contribution as follows:

Primary Class 1. The employed earner must be resident or subject to any temporary absence, present in Great Britain at the time of the employment or be ordinarily resident in Great Britain at such times.[9]

Secondary Class 1. The secondary contributor must be resident or present in Great Britain when the secondary contributions become payable or must have a place of business in Great Britain at that time.[10]

Class 2. The self-employed earner must be ordinarily resident in Great Britain in the period for which the contributions are due, or if not, so ordinarily resident, then before that period he must have been resident in Great Britain for a period at least 26 out of the immediately preceding 52 contribution weeks.[11]

There are also residence rules as regards entitlement to pay contributions which are not obligatory. Thus the secondary Class 1 contributor is permitted to pay the secondary contributions even though the normal residence conditions are not met.[12] A self-employed person covered by the small earnings exemption is entitled to pay Class 2 contributions for any contribution week in which he is present in Great Britain.[13] Class 3 contributions, which are always voluntary, can normally only be paid for a contribution year during the course of which the individual is resident in Great Britain.[14] There are special rules enabling Class 2 and Class 3[15] contributions to be paid where the individual spends periods abroad.[15]

---

[1] SSA 1975, s. 1(6)(*a*).
[2] SSA 1975, s. 1(6)(*b*).
[3] SI 1979 No. 591, reg. 119.
[4] (1884) 2 TC 37.
[5] (1926) 10 TC 673.
[6] (1928) 13 TC 511.
[7] DSS Leaflet NI 35, para. 42, as subsequently clarrified.
[8] DSS Leaflet NI 38, p 6.
[9] SI 1979 No. 591, reg. 119(1)(*a*).
[10] SI 1979 No. 591, reg. 119(1)(*b*).
[11] SI 1979 No. 591, reg. 119(2)(*d*).
[12] SI 1979 No. 591, reg. 119(1)(*b*).
[13] SI 1979 No. 591, reg. 119(1)(*c*).
[14] SI 1979 No. 591, reg. 119(1)(*e*).
[15] SI 1979 No. 591, reg. 120(2)(*b*), regs. 121 and 122.

Special rules for continental shelf workers, airmen and mariners

56: 02 Certain kinds of workers have activities which take them physically outside Great Britain for most of their working time. In the absence of special rules such workers might escape contribution liability and hence benefit entitlement through not being gainfully employed in Great Britain[1] or through not meeting the conditions as to residence or presence in Great Britain.[2] However special rules have been laid down to cover the cases of continental shelf workers, airmen and mariners.[3]

The special rules which deal with airmen and mariners only apply to those having a contract of service i.e. employees. The rules for continental shelf workers apply whether the person is employed under a contract of service or not i.e. they apply equally to self-employed persons as to employees.[4] Subject to these rules are those workers whose employment relates to any of certain specified exploration and exploitation activities,[5] and who carry out their employment in any designated area of the continental shelf i.e. specific areas outside the three mile limit but within the areas of the continental shelf over which the UK has jurisdiction under international agreement.[6] Where the rules operate, the designated area is treated as being in Great Britain and thus the continental shelf worker is made subject to contribution liability, notwithstanding that he may not otherwise satisfy the residence or presence conditions.[7]

An airman for the purposes of the special rules is a person employed under a contract of service on board an aircraft as a pilot, commander, navigator or other crew member or in any other capacity related to the aircraft, its crew, passengers, cargo or mail, where the contract has been entered into in the UK with a view to its performance (in whole or in part) while the aircraft is in flight.[8]

In the following situations an airman as so defined, is to be treated as an employed earner and so subject to contribution liability notwithstanding that he is not gainfully employed in Great Britain or does not fulfill the residence or presence requirements.[9] The situations are where the employer or the person who pays the airman his earnings (whether or not as agent for the employer) or the person (if different from the employer) under whose directions the terms of the employment (this suggests the fixing of duty rosters etc) and the calculation of the earnings to be paid are determined, has:

(a) in the case of aircraft being a British aircraft a place of business in Great Britain or

(b) where the aircraft is not a British aircraft, his principal place of business in Great Britain.[10]

A British aircraft in this context means an aircraft belonging to the Crown or an aircraft registered in the UK and having an owner or managing owner (if more than one owner) who resides or has his principal place of business in Great Britain. Where an aircraft has been leased, the owner for this purpose is the person having possession and control over the aircraft.[11]

But the foregoing rule will not apply if the airman in question is neither domiciled nor has a place of residence (a more concrete test than that of being resident) in Great Britain.[12] In such a case unless a reciprocal social security agreement (see infra § **56: 04**) provides otherwise the airman will not be treated as an employed earner subject to British contribution liability.[13]

A mariner for the purose of the special rules is a person employed under a contract of service either as a master or member of the crew of any ship or vessel or in any other capacity on board any ship or vessel for the purpose of the ship or vessel or crew or passengers or cargo or mails, where the contract is entered into in the UK with a view to its performance (in whole or in part) while the ship or vessel is on her voyage.[14] Those who serve "in any other capacity" would include supernumeraries such as hairdressers, shop keepers etc. The term does not include members of the forces.

The special rules for mariners displace the normal conditions as to residence or presence in Great Britain but subject to any reciprocal social security agreement, for contribution liability to arise the mariner must be domiciled or resident in Great Britain and for secondary contributions to be payable the secondary contributor must be resident or have a place of business in Great Britain.[15]

Under these rules a mariner is treated as an employed earner subject to contribution liability in the following situations:

(a) the employment is on board a British ship, the mariner is employed as the master or member of the crew and the person paying the mariner's earnings or the owner (or the managing owner if more than one) has a place of business in Great Britain;

(b) the employment is under a contract entered into in the UK with a view to its performance (in whole or in part) while the vessel is on her voyage and the person paying the mariner's earnings has a place of business in Great Britain;

(c) neither (a) nor (b) applies but the mariner is employed as a master, member of the crew or radio officer (but not as a supernumerary) on board any ship or vessel, the contract is not entered in the UK and the employer or the person paying the earnings has his principal place of business in Great Britain;

(*d*) neither (*a*) nor (*b*) applies but the mariner is employed as a radio officer, the contract in this case is entered into in the UK and the employer or person paying the radio officer his earnings has a place of business in Great Britain.[16]

A British ship for this purpose means a ship or vessel belonging to the Crown or registered in Great Britain[17].

In the case of mariners there are special rules for the ascertainment of earnings,[18] the determination of earnings periods[19] and calculation of contributions;[20] there are also provisions for treating the person paying the earnings as the secondary contributor[21] and allowing for a small reduction in secondary contributions.[22] Share fishermen are subject to a separate regime under which they are treated as self-employed for contribution purposes but because they are entitled to unemployment benefit they must pay Class 2 contributions at a higher rate.[23]

---

[1] SSA 1975, s. 2(1)(*a*).
[2] SI 1979, No. 591, reg. 119(1)(*a*).
[3] SI 1979, No. 591, Part VIII, Cases A, B and C.
[4] SI 1979, No. 591, reg. 85(1).
[5] As set out in Oil and Gas (Enterprise) Act 1982, s. 23(2).
[6] Continental Shelf Act 1964, s. 1(7) provides for such designation.
[7] SI 1979, No. 591, reg 85(2).
[8] SI 1979, No. 591, reg 81.
[9] SI 1979, No. 591, reg 82(1).
[10] SI 1979, No. 591, reg 82(1).
[11] SI 1979, No. 591, reg 81.
[12] SI 1979, No. 591, reg 82(2).
[13] SI 1979, No. 591, reg 82(3).
[14] SI 1979, No. 591, reg 86.
[15] SI 1979, No. 591, reg 87.
[16] SI 1979, No. 591, reg 88.
[17] SI 1979, No. 591, reg 86.
[18] SI 1979, No. 591, reg 94.
[19] SI 1979, No. 591, reg 90.
[20] SI 1979, No. 591, reg 91.
[21] SI 1979, No. 591, reg 93.
[22] SI 1979, No. 591, reg 89.
[23] SI 1979, No. 591, reg 98.

Coming to and going from Great Britain

56: 03   There are special rules to cover respectively the case where a non-UK resident is temporarily employed in Great Britain and the case where a person previously resident in Great Britain is posted abroad. Each of these rules is hedged round by a multitude of conditions but where they apply they respectively provide a 52 week contribution holiday for the employee sent to Great Britain and impose a 52 week continuation of contribution liability on the employee sent overseas. The rule for incoming employees is an unbroken sentence of 172 words.[1] It may be summarised as follows:

Where the employee:

(*a*) is not ordinarily resident in the UK, and

(*b*) is not ordinarily employed in the UK i.e. apart from the temporary posting, and

(*c*) the posting is in the course of an employment mainly outside the UK and *the employer* sending him,

has his place of business, i.e. the principal place of business, outside the UK—he may also have other places of business in the UK—*and the employment* is "for a time" in Great Britain,

Then:

no primary or secondary contributions will be payable on the employee's earnings from the date of the employee's coming to Great Britain (the last entry into Great Britain) and his having been resident in Great Britain for a continuous period of 52 contribution weeks, starting with the beginning of the contribution week following that in which his "last entry" fell.

It will be noticed that this is one of the provisions where there are references to UK (because it is intended that a truly foreign connection should be established) as well to Great Britain (which is relevant to contribution liability).

The provision gives some temporary relief from British contribution liability in a case where a foreign employer sends a foreign employee to Great Britain on a temporary assignment. What is meant by a temporary assignment is simply indicated by the expression "for a time" and no limitation is specified for the duration of this period. However if it became too long, the condition that the employment should be mainly outside the UK would not be fulfilled. It should be noted that the relief is not given where the foreign employee takes up a new employment in Great Britain e.g. with a UK subsidiary under a new contract of employment. A secondment arrangement under which the employer is still employed by the overseas employer, but his services are made available to the UK subsidiary, may however enable the contribution holiday to be obtained.

The converse rule which imposes a continuation of contribution liability for 52 weeks is easier to state. Where the employee is employed outside Great Britain, and,

(*a*) the employer has a place of business in Great Britain, and

(*b*) the employee is ordinarily resident in Great Britain, and

(*c*) immediately before the overseas employment began, the employee was resident in Great Britain,

then, primary and secondary Class 1 contributions are payable on the employee's earnings for the 52 contribution weeks beginning with the contribution weeks in which the employment outside Great Britain begins to the same extent as if the employment had been in Great Britain.[2]

This continuation of contribution liability can be avoided if the overseas employment is with a separate, albeit affiliated employer, which does not have a place of business in Great Britain. However this course has a number of other implications (see § **56: 05**, infra).

---

[1] SI 1979 No. 591, reg. 119(2).

RECIPROCAL AGREEMENTS

56: 04   As explained above, when an employee previously resident in Great Britain takes up an overseas employment and the employee has a place of business in Great Britain, British contribution liability will normally continue for 52 weeks. But for part or all of that period the employee may also be required to pay social security contributions in the overseas country where he is employed. The employee will therefore be obliged to pay contributions in two countries at the same time.

Some countries, e.g. the USA, have a social security system which requires contributions to be maintained indefinitely during periods of working abroad. So, for example, if an American is sent by his employer for a tour of duty in the UK for three years, he would be liable to pay British national insurance contributions as well as FICA payments after the first 52 weeks of his employment in the UK but for there being some special arrangement. It is to prevent such cases of dual liability that the UK has made reciprocal social security agreements with certain countries which contain rules. which fix contribution liability in one only of the two countries and according to the circumstances determine which country that should be.

The countries with which the UK has concluded reciprocal agreements containing contribution liability provisions are as follows: Austria, Bermuda, Cyprus, Finland, Iceland, Israel, Jamaica, Malta, Mauritius, Norway, Sweden, Switzerland, Turkey, USA, Yugoslavia.

The UK has also made reciprocal social security agreements with a number of other countries which only deal with the reciprocation of benefits.

The general pattern of a reciprocal agreement containing contribution liability provisions is that the primary rule is that an employee is only liable to pay contributions in the country in which he is actually employed but this may be over-ridden by an important exception covering a temporary assignment from the employee's home country to the other country. The exception applies where the employee is employed by an employer based in his home country who sends him to work in the other country for not longer than a specified maximum period. Where the exception applies, the employee continues to be subject only to contribution liability in the home country.

A necessary condition is that prior to the temporary assignment the employee was already subject to contribution liability in the home country. It is essential that during the temporary assignment the employee remains an employee based in the home country. The maximum period allowed for a temporary assignment varies from agreement to agreement. In the majority of the agreements it is one year; with Austria and Switzerland two years are specified; in the case of Cyprus the period is three years. Untypical in this respect is the agreement with the USA which specifies five years as the limit for a temporary assignment. Should the actual assignment last longer than originally expected, the agreement normally allows for an application to be made for an extension of the time allowed: this would require mutual agreement by the special security authorities in both countries.

Reciprocal social security agreements dealing with contribution liability normally also contain provisions regarding the self-employed and for mariners, air crews, government employees, and members of the armed forces.

EC LAW

56: 05   Prior to the UK's accession to the Treaty of Rome in 1973 by which it became a member of the European Community, the UK had already concluded reciprocal social security agreements with the countries which then constituted the Community, though only those with Italy and Luxembourg covered contribution liability. The UK also made reciprocal agreements with contribution provisions with Spain and Portugal which later joined the Community. All these agreements have been superseded by a Regulation made by the European Council in 1971 which is binding on all the member states. This Regulation,[1] which is supplemented by a further Regulation,[2] which only deals with implementation, is in effect a reciprocal agreement covering not two countries, but all the countries of the Community. However, unlike the normal reciprocal agreement which forms part of the secondary social security legislation of the UK, the Council Regulation takes precedence over the national law of member states and where necessary over-rides inconsistent provisions in that law. The Regulation covers both social security benefits[3] and contribution liability. Articles 13 to 17 contain the rules for determining which country's contribution law shall apply. The principle on which these rules are based is that a person shall be subject to the legislation of a single member state only.[4] For a person who is an employee, this principle is given effect by a primary rule that if the employee is employed in the territory of one member state he is to be subject to that state's contribution legislation even though he may be resident in another member state or the employer may have its registered office or place of business in another member state.[5] But, as with reciprocal agreements generally, this rule is displaced where an employee is sent to work in another member state or a temporary posting. In this case contribution liability continues in the home country for the duration of the assignment. The conditions to be met for this rule to apply are:

(*a*) the person must immediately prior to the assignment be employed in the home country by an undertaking to which he is normally attached,
(*b*) the posting to the other member state must be made by that undertaking,
(*c*) the employee must perform work in the other member state for that undertaking,
(*d*) the anticipated duration of the assignment must not exceed 12 months, and
(*e*) the assignment must not be a replacement posting i.e. the employee must not be sent to replace another person who has completed his posting.[6]

In order to operate this provision, the employer should apply to the social security authority of the home country for a certificate of coverage on form

E101. The certificate will satisfy the authority in the country where the employer is posted that contributions in that country are not required.

The DSS in considering such applications will not issue a certificate if the employee is not already paying British contributions. The employee does not have to be already working for the UK employer which posts him to the other member state but in a case where a person is recruited in the UK for an immediate posting in the other country the UK employer must directly employ the individual in activities which the employee would normally carry out in the UK. If, owing to unforeseen circumstances, the duration of the work extends beyond that originally anticipated and exceeds 12 months, there is provision for home country contribution liability to be extended but this requires the agreement of the social security authority in the member state where the employee is posted. An application for an extension must be made before the expiry of the 12 month period and under this provision the extension cannot be given for more than a further 12 months.[7]

However in some cases it is possible to obtain an agreement from the two authorities that home country contribution liability should be continued for a longer period e.g. three years. This is because there is provision[8] for the authorities of the two member states concerned to make by common agreement exceptions from the strict application of the rules. This procedure can be resorted to when a person is posted overseas and charged with a specific assignment which only he or she is qualified or suited to carry out. A specific application setting out the circumstances will need to be made to the social security authority in the home country.[9] Where home country contribution liability no longer continues e.g. because of expiry of the period allowed for a temporary posting, the employer will become liable to primary contributions in the member state where the employment is carried out. However, the employer, i.e. the secondary contributor, often in such a case will not be resident in that country and consequently that country may find it difficult to collect secondary contributions. In the UK, for example, the claim of a foreign government to payment of contributions due under its own law will not be recognised.[10] The Regulation accordingly allows member states to make agreements for the mutual recovery of contributions.[11] The United Kingdom, however, has not so far made such an agreement with any member state and therefore the other member states will not be able to recover secondary contributions from UK resident employers in a UK court and likewise the DSS will normally be unable to recover secondary contributions from employers in the other member states.

There may be situations where a person is employed in more than one member state at the same time with the same or different employers. The Regulation deals with these situations by fixing contribution liability in the country where the individual resides if that is one of the countries where he is employed or if he is attached to several undertakings or several employers with registered offices or places of business in different member states.[12] If the individual does not reside in any of the member states where he works, he is to be subject to contribution liability of the member state in which the employer has its registered office or place of business.[13] In this context the country where a person resides is that in which he habitually resides and where the habitual centre of his interest lies.[14] There are special rules for the situation where the employer is an undertaking which straddles a frontier between two member states.[15]

There are also special rules for diplomatic staff.[16]

Workers in international transport undertakings are subject to the following rules. An international transport undertaking is one which operates services for passengers or goods by rail, road, air or inland waterway.[17] A person who belongs to the travelling or flying personnel of such an undertaking is liable for contributions in the member state where the undertaking has its registered office or place of business but subject to the following exceptions:

(*a*) if the undertaking has a branch or permanent representation in another member state any person employed by such branch or permanent representation is liable for contributions in that other state, and

(*b*) if a person is employed principally in the member state in which he resides he is liable for contributions in that state even if the undertaking has no registered office, place of business, branch or permanent representation in that state.[18]

Mariners are subject to the following rules. The primary rule is that a person who is employed on board a vessel flying the flag of a member state is to be liable to contributions in that state.[19] But this is subject to the following exceptions:

(*a*) If a person is normally employed on board a vessel flying the flag of one member state or otherwise employed in the territory of that state and the undertaking to which he is normally attached posts him to work on board a vessel flying the flag of another member state, he is to remain subject to contribution liability in the former member state.[20]

(*b*) If a person is not normally employed at sea but performs work in the territorial waters or in a port of one member state on a vessel flying the flag of another member state but is not a member of the crew of that vessel, he is to be subject to contribution liability in the former member state.[21]

(*c*) If a person is employed on board a vessel flying the flag of one member state but is remunerated by an undertaking having a registered office or place of business in another member state and the person is resident in the territory of that state, he is to be subject to contribution liability in the latter state.[22]

The Regulation deals with self-employed persons in the following way. A person who is normally self-employed in one member state and who performs work in another member state will continue to be subject to contribution liablity in the member state where he normally works provided the anticipated duration of the work in the other state does not exceed 12 months.[23] There is provision for an extension of home country contribution liability for a further 12 months in a case where due to unforeseen circumstances the work in the other state extends beyond the duration originally anticipated.[24] If a person is normally self-employed in two or more member states he is to be subject to contribution liability in the member state where he resides if that is one of the states where he pursues any part of his activity.[25] If he does not pursue any activity in the member state where he resides, he is to be subject to contribution liablity in the member state where he pursues his main activity.[26] However these two later rules will be over-ruled if the result would be that the individual could not even on a voluntary basis join a (state) pension scheme: in that event the position apart from these provisions will apply and if the legislation of two or more member states would then apply, the member states concerned will have to decide on which should apply by mutual agreement.[27]

There may be cases where a person is at one and the same time self-employed in one member state and working as an employee in another member state. In such a case he will be subject to contribution liability in the member state where he works as an employee in paid employment[28] except in certain specified instances where he will be simultaneously subject to contribution liability in two member states.[29]

---

[1] Regulation 1408/71/EEC.
[2] Regulation 574/72/EEC.
[3] Art. 4.
[4] Art. 13(1).
[5] Art. 13(2)(*a*).
[6] Art. 14(1)(*a*).
[7] Art. 14(1)(*b*).
[8] Art. 17.
[9] See DSS Leaflet, SA 29.
[10] *Metal Industries (Salvage) Ltd v Owners of the ST Harle* 1962 SLT 114.
[11] Art 92.
[12] Art. 14(2)(*b*)(i).
[13] Art. 14(2)(*b*)(ii).
[14] Case 76/76: *Di Paolo v Office National de l'Emploi* [1977] ECR 315, [1977] 2 CMLR 59, ECJ.
[15] Art. 14(3).
[16] Art. 16.
[17] Art. 14b.
[18] Art. 16.
[19] Art. 13(2)(*c*).
[20] Art. 14b(1).
[21] Art. 14b(3).
[22] Art. 14b(4).
[23] Art. 14a(1)(*a*).
[24] Art. 14(1)(*b*).
[25] Art. 14a(2).
[26] Art. 14a(2).
[27] Art. 14a(4).
[28] Art. 14c(1)(*a*).
[29] Art. 14c(1)(*b*) and Annex VII.

PLANNING CONSIDERATIONS

56: 06   It will be evident that whether the Contribution Regulations, a reciprocal agreement or the EC Council Regulation is relevant, a number of planning opportunities open up wherever an expatriate is assigned to the UK or a British resident is posted abroad. There are choices available as to duration of the assignment and the form of the employment arrangements. For example, if the posting is made the subject of a new contract of employment, continuation of home country liability will normally not apply and the employer will become liable for contributions in the country where he is assigned.

It is difficult to give general guidance as to the best course to follow since the objectives of different employees and their employers will vary. For example the minimisation of contribution liabilities will not always be the aim since in some countries benefits, such as retirement pension, may be very significant and preservation of entitlement to full benefits may be the prime concern.

There are however two common planning areas where comment is appropriate:

(1) When a UK company sends British employees to countries which are not members of the European Community and with which there is no reciprocal agreement having contribution provisions, liability for both primary and secondary contributions will normally continue for a further 52 weeks (see supra, § **56: 02**). This liability could be avoided by the assignment overseas being made the subject of a new contract of employment with a company which does not have a place of business in Great Britain.

It will however be necessary to consider all the other implications, including those affecting the corporation tax position, the individual's personal tax position and the pension arrangements made for him.

(2) If an employer in a non EC country which has no reciprocal agreement with the UK sends employees to the UK, primary Class 1 contributions will become payable after the first 52 weeks (see supra, § **56: 02**). However, secondary Class 1 contributions will normally only become payable at that time if the non-resident company has a place of business in Great Britain (see supra, § **56: 01**).

It might therefore be concluded that secondary contribution liability can be avoided by the simple expedient of the overseas company ensuring that it does not have a place of business in Great Britain. However a substantial amount of contribution revenue is being lost in this way and the DSS is known to be seeking to prevent this loss. Two approaches are being followed:

(1) to establish where possible that despite the precautions taken the overseas company does in fact have some form of presence which constitutes a place of business in Great Britain, and
(2) to seek to apply the part of the Categorisation Regulations which relate to agency workers[1] to the situation so that a UK resident affiliate is thereby made the secondary contributor and secondary contributions can then be collected without difficulty. These rules may possibly have this effect[2] being very wide-embracing.

This is currently a highly contentious area and cases in dispute are not yet resolved.

---

[1] See supra, § **51: 04**.
[2] See supra, § **51: 05**.

57 Administration

THE DEPARTMENT OF SOCIAL SECURITY

57: 01 The national insurance system is administered by the Department of Social Security (DSS). It is responsible for the operation of the contributory scheme, both as regards contributions and benefits, and also administers the payment of non-contributory benefits made available under social security legislation.

Prior to 26th July 1988 the DSS was part of a larger department, the Department of Health and Social Security, which in addition administered the national health service.

The DSS is a highly decentralised Government department which has headquarters both in London (Alexander Fleming House, Elephant and Castle, London SE1 6BY) and Newcastle (Central Office, Newcastle-upon-Tyne, NE98 1YU; tel. 091–857111). Most policy questions are handled by specialist sections at Newcastle e.g. Headquarters branch (earnings, directors etc.), Class 4 group (the self-employed, mixed self-employed and employed earner situations), Overseas Branch (contribution liability as affected by overseas factors), Mariners Section (liability of mariners) etc. But policy questions on matters of categorisation are dealt with by a separate London department (Friar's House, 157–168 Blackfriar's Road, London SE1 8EU; tel. 01–703 6380) and there is also in London the International Relations Division (151 Great Titchfield Street, London W1P 8AD; tel. 01–636 1696) which handles questions arising from reciprocal agreements and the relationships between the other country's schemes and the UK scheme.

The DSS deals with employers, employees, the self-employed and other contributors through a network of local offices for which a series of regional offices is responsible. Each local office is run by a Manager who is in charge of a team of Inspectors.

The Employer's Manual and other DSS publications

57: 02 The DSS publishes a number of free leaflets giving guidance on contribution and benefits questions. They deal with specific topics and most are quite short e.g. NI 48 Unpaid and Late Paid Contributions, NI 32 National Insurance Contributions on Tips and Service Charges, SA 33 Social Security Agreement with the USA.

A particularly important publication is the Employer's Manual (Green Book 1) (NI 269) which is issued to all employers. The current version is sufficiently large for a key (Yellow Book) to be produced also: the key sets out the general rules and the Green Book gives detailed guidance. It applies for the tax year beginning 6th April 1989 and replaces NP 15 The Employer's Guide which applied to 1988–89 and in various editions to earlier years. While no departmental publication purports to represent an authoritative statement of the law on the subject covered, the Employer's Manual (and its predecessors) does set out the DSS interpretation of the relevant provisions and in cases of doubt the employer is asked to consult the local DSS office.[1] With the passing of the years, the guidance has become increasingly detailed and focussed on specific topics. So, for example, the edition of NP 15 which applied for 1987–88 and 1988–89 gave for the first time detailed guidance on the contribution liability under the various possible ways in which the employer can deal with home telephone charges. The Employer's Manual (NI 269) gives similar detailed guidance for the first time on a variety of topics including "essential car users allowances, use of credit cards and provision of petrol".

The significance of such detailed guidance is that it puts the employer on notice of how the DSS consider the item in question should be treated. If the employer has treated the item differently in the past, the DSS do not in practice require adjustments to be made for tax years prior to that to which the new edition or version of the guide first applies. Thereafter if the employer disagrees with the guidance, e.g. because there are special circumstances or there is reason to question the legal basis of the guidance, it is generally desirable to take up the issue with the DSS as soon as possible. If the employer fails to account for national insurance contributions on the basis of the guidance given and the matter subsequently comes to light in the course of a PAYE audit, the employer's negotiating position is weakened. In the event of the employer and the DSS not being able to come to an agreement on the treatment to be followed, the employer must either concede or apply for a determination by the Secretary of State (§ **57: 06**, infra).

---

[1] See for example NI 269, p. 58.

POWERS OF SECRETARY OF STATE TO INTRODUCE SECONDARY LEGISLATION

57: 03   In charge of the DSS is the Secretary of State for Social Security. The social security legislation gives him very wide powers to introduce regulations by means of the statutory instrument. However, before any such regulations can be laid before Parliament, they must be submitted in draft for review by the Social Security Advisory Committee.[1] The committee is required to make a report and when laying the regulations before Parliament, the Secretary of State must include a statement indicating the extent to which the committee's recommendations have been adopted and where not adopted his reasons for not accepting them.[2] This procedure is intended to provide a safeguard against arbitrary legislation which might otherwise escape Parliamentary scrutiny. If the Secretary of State by reason of the urgency of the matter considers it inexpedient to refer the regulations to the committee, this requirement is waived[3] but if the regulations are given Parliamentary approval, the Secretary of State must as soon as practicable refer them to the committee which must then make a report, which may include recommendations, to be laid before each House of Parliament.[4]

Apart from vetting proposed regulations the committee is an advisory body giving advice and assistance to the Secretary of State on the discharge of his functions under the social security legislation.[5] The Secretary of State must supply the committee with such information as it may reasonably require to discharge its functions.[6]

The committee is appointed by the Secretary of State and comprises the Chairman and between 10 and 13 other members.[7] One member must be appointed after consultation with organisations which represent employers, another after consultation with organisations which represent workers and a third after consultation with the head of the Northern Ireland Department of Social Security. The committee must include at least one person with experience of work among the chronically sick and disabled and preferably the person appointed should also be chronically sick and disabled.[8]

---

[1] SSA 1980, s. 10(1).
[2] SSA 1980, s. 10(3) and (4).
[3] SSA 1980, s. 10(2)(*a*).
[4] SSA 1980, s. 10(7).
[5] SSA 1980, s. 9(1).
[6] SSA 1980, s. 9(4).
[7] SSA 1980, Sch. 3, para. 1.
[8] SSA 1980, Sch. 3, para. 3.

ENFORCEMENT POWERS

57: 04 Most national insurance contributions are collected through the PAYE system or in the case of Class 4 contributions through Schedule D Case I or Case II assessments. It follows therefore that the Revenue and the DSS have a common interest in ensuring compliance in certain areas.

The assessment and collection of Class 4 contributions is an adjunct to the income tax system and is dealt with by the Revenue. But as regards the PAYE system which is the collection mechanism for both Schedule E income tax and Class 1 primary and secondary contributions both Departments have staff engaged in visiting employers premises and carrying out inspections. The PAYE auditors and DSS Inspectors used to operate independently but following a pilot scheme conducted in 1983–84 and a decision to apply it nationally taken in December 1985, there is close co-ordination between the two departments and though the inspection will be carried out by only one of the departments, it is also conducted on behalf of the other, so avoiding the need for separate visits.

If the following such inspections, irregularities come to light, the Revenue, or the DSS as the case may be will require recovery of arrears, normally for the tax year in which the inspection takes place and for the preceding six years. This approach to recovery treats the unpaid contributions in the same way as unpaid PAYE and rests on the regulation which requires Class 1 contributions to be paid, accounted for and recovered in like manner as income tax is deducted under PAYE.[1]

However, as an alternative, the DSS is entitled to require payment of Class I contributions by means of direct collection. Moreover the remedies available for recovery of unpaid contributions are not confined to those available in respect of unpaid PAYE.[2] In fact the DSS may pursue two other remedies:

(1) *Prosecution in a magistrates' court*

This procedure requires that as a first step a person is prosecuted in a magistrates' court for failure to pay contributions.

The non-payment of contributions at the due time is an offence under contribution laws but on summary conviction only a modest fine can be imposed i.e. at level 3 on the standard scale—currently £400.[3] Where the offence has been committed by a limited company or other body corporate which involved the consent or connivance of a director, manager, secretary or other similar officer or which resulted from the neglect of any such person, each individual concerned will be treated as guilty of the offence and on conviction be subject to such a fine.[4]

The proceedings for an offence of non-payment of contributions have to be begun within three months from the date on which evidence sufficient in the opinion of the Secretary of State to justify a prosecution came to his knowledge or within a period of twelve months from the commission of the offence, whichever period last expires.[5] The evidence of non-payment required may consist of a certificate from a collector of taxes that contributions for which a person is liable have not been paid.[6] For the DSS to establish that an offence has been committed it is only necessary to demonstrate that contributions which the person was liable to pay have not been paid: thus non-payment as a result of an incorrect understanding of the collection procedures is no defence.[7] If there is disagreement over whether contributions are in fact due, that is a "principal question" which must be resolved by the adjudication process (see infra, § **57: 05**) before the recovery proceedings can continue.

Under these proceedings the DSS customarily brings a charge for a specimen offence in respect of a recent non-payment of contributions with a view to securing a summary conviction. Once such a conviction is obtained, the unpaid contributions subject to the charge can be recovered as a penalty.[8] In addition, on providing evidence of previous failure to pay contributions, unpaid contributions which should have been paid during the two years up to the date of the offence can also be recovered.[9]

If directors or similar officers are convicted of the offence of non-payment, the unpaid contributions (subject to the charge and for the two preceding years) can also be recovered frm them personally, though the DSS is not known to have pursued this course.[10] Before 1985 there was another provision under which directors could become peresonally liable for unpaid contributions[11] but the Government considered that the existence of this power placed an unduly heavy burden on directors and the relevant provision was repealed in 1985.[12]

(2) *Recovery proceedings in the High Court*

Under this procedure there is no need to establish an offence under contribution law as the first step. The action brought is for the recovery of the unpaid contributions as a debt due to the Crown. The Limitation Act 1980 does not apply to such a debt and there is no time limit on the commencement of recovery proceedings in the High Court. If the DSS follows this course, unpaid contributions cannot be recovered from directors implicated in their non-payment; they can be recovered only from the employer company.

Although information relating to a taxpayer's affairs must normally be treated as confidential and not divulged to others, the Revenue is permitted to disclose to the DSS information obtained or held in connection with the assessment on collection of income tax.[13] In the case of self-employed persons who carry on a trade, profession or vocation, the profits from which are assessable under Schedule D Case I or II the information which can be passed on is limited to particulars about the commencement or cessation of the business and those relating to employees engaged in such a business.[14]

---

[1] SI 1979 No. 591, reg. 46; Sch. 1, para. 28(1).
[2] SI 1979 No. 591, reg. 47.
[3] SSA 1975, s. 146(1).
[4] SSA 1986, s. 57(1).
[5] SSA 1986, s. 56(2).
[6] SSA 1975, s. 149(2).
[7] *R v Highbury Corner Stipendiary Magistrate, ex p Department of Health and Social Security* (1987) Times, 4 February, DC.
[8] SSA 1975, ss. 150(1), 152(5).
[9] SSA 1975, s. 151(3).
[10] SSA 1986, s. 57(1); SSA 1975, s. 150(1).
[11] SSA 1975, s. 152(4).
[12] Insolvency Act 1985, s. 216, Sch. 10, Pt. IV; SI 1986 No. 463, Sch. 2.
[13] SSA 1986, s. 59(1), as amended by SSA 1989, s. 20(*a*).
[14] SSA 1986, s. 59(2), as amended by SSA 1989, s. 20(*b*).

ADJUDICATION BY SECRETARY OF STATE

57: 05   The Secretary of State for Social Security is given jurisdiction over the following questions:

(*a*) whether a person is an earner and, if he is, as to the category of earner in which he is to be included, and

(*b*) whether the contribution conditions for any benefit are satisfied or *otherwise relating* to a person's contributions or his earnings factor.[1]

These are described as "principal questions". They relate to categorisation and because of the "otherwise relating" in (*b*) to virtually the whole field of contribution law. The main exception concerns Class 4 contributions. While the question as to whether a person is excepted from liability for Class 4 contributions or his liability is deferred is specifically brought under the jurisdiction of the Secretary of State as are certain collection questions;[2] Class 4 liability, being essentially an income tax liability, is subject to application for determination by the General or Special Commissioners from whose decision an appeal may be made to the Court on a point of law.

It may seem strange that the Secretary of State should be given power to determine questions in which his own department, the DSS, is normally an interested if not contending party. However, he is empowered to appoint a person to hold an inquiry into the question at issue and in practice such inquiries are held by senior officials of the DSS Solicitors Office. Moreover though not obliged to do so, the Secretary of State will normally accept the result of the inquiry even when it overturns previous departmental practice.[3]

The jurisdiction of the Secretary of State over the principal questions is exclusive. If, for example, it is necessary in the course of Court proceedings, for say recovery of arrears of contributions, for a categorisation question to be determined, that question must be referred to the Secretary of State.[4]

Any "person interested"[5] in the question at issue may apply for a determination by the Secretary of State though Social Security Act 1989 allows regulations to be introduced which restrict the persons who may apply.[6] The DSS itself however is not able to make an application and therefore if the other parties are unwilling to apply the DSS must begin recovery proceedings so that the Court is compelled to refer the contribution question to the Secretary of State for determination. However where the Secretary of State has reason to believe that an abnormal pay practice is being followed he is given power to determine the question without the need for any application to made to him.[7]

Neither the report of the inquiry nor the decision of the Secretary of State is published, though between 1950 and 1958 a selection of decisions on categorisation questions was published.[8] The Secretary of State must however give written notice of the decision to the applicant and to any persons appearing to the Secretary to be interested in the decision.[9] The notice will do no more than indicate the decision itself but the applicant and other persons receiving the notice have the right to request a statement of the grounds of the decision such as will enable them to determine whether any question of law has arisen on which an appeal may be made to the High Court.[10] If the applicant is dissatisfied with the decision, the following courses are open to him:

1. An application can be made to the Secretary of State to set aside the decision on any of the following grounds:

(*a*) relevant documents were not sent or received in time;
(*b*) a party to the proceedings was not present or represented at the inquiry;
(*c*) the interests of justice so require.[11]

2. An application can be made to the Secretary of State for a review of the decision on the grounds that:

(*a*) new facts are brought to his notice, or
(*b*) the decision was given in ignorance of some material fact or based on a mistake of some material fact or erroneous in point of law,[12]

3. An appeal may be made to the High Court (in Scotland, the Court of Session) on a question of law by any person aggrieved with the decision.[13]

However unlike tax appeals, the decision of the High Court (or Court of Session) is final: there is no right of appeal from the High Court to the Court of Appeal or from there to the House of Lords. The number of questions for which application is made to the Secretary of State for determination is very small and consequently appeals to the High Court on questions of law are few and far between.

For completion, two other means of recourse available to those dissatisfied with the handling of contribution issues should be mentioned:

(1) Application can be made to the Court for a judicial review.

(2) Application can be made through an MP for the Parliamentary Commissioner for Administration (Ombudsman) to review the Department's handling of the matter.

In recent years the DSS have preferred to introduce blocking regulations to counter abuse rather than to cause a principal question to be referred to the Secretary of State with the possibility of a question of law then being settled in the High Court. For example in October 1987 the use of discretionary employee trusts to make payments to employees free of contribution liability was closed by amending regulations. Again in May 1988 the payment of remuneration in the form of gilt-edged securities was prevented from being treated as payment in kind by the introduction of a new regulation. However, the DSS is known to be currently taking legal advice on a number of contentious issues and it must not be assumed that it will always proceed in this way. A blocking regulation is not retrospective and therefore leaves previously completed transactions unscathed. That does not mean that if a completed transaction is vulnerable in certain respects, e.g. where the the procedures followed for making a payment in kind are defective, the DSS are precluded from challenging the particular arrangements. Where very substantial amounts of contribution revenue are at stake, it is always possible that the DSS will prefer to use the adjudication procedure.

---

[1] SSA 1975, s. 93(1)(*a*) and (*b*).
[2] SSA 1975, s. 93(2).
[3] See National Insurance Advisory Committee Report (Cmnd. 8117).
[4] SSA 1975, s. 148(2).
[5] Social Security (Adjudication) Regulations 1986, SI 1986 No. 2218, reg. 13.
[6] SSA 1989, Sch. 3, para. 1(1).
[7] SI 1979 No. 591, reg. 21(3).
[8] Selected Decisions of the Minister on Questions of Classification and Insurability.
[9] SI 1986 No. 2218, reg. 16(1).
[10] SI 1986 No. 2218, reg. 16(2).
[11] SI 1986 No. 2218, reg. 11.
[12] SSA 1975, s. 96(1).
[13] SSA 1975, s. 94(3).

PART X. STAMP DUTY AND STAMP DUTY RESERVE TAX

58 Stamp duty—general

INTRODUCTION

Introduction

58: 01 Stamp duties are one of the country's oldest taxes. They were originally introduced in 1694. Strictly, they are taxes on documents[1] and not on transactions or persons and are now governed by the Stamp Act 1891 and the Stamp Duties Management Act 1891 as amended by the Finance Acts and by various Revenue Acts. The basic structure has changed little over the years but a consultative document has been issued[2] with a view to reforming and modernising the stamp duties and some progress has been made. In addition, a number of regulations have been made. Stamp duties bring in a modest but not insignificant amount of revenue a year[3] and the tax is relatively cheap to administer and collect.

FA 1986 introduced stamp duty reserve tax. It is a separate tax from stamp duty (see infra, § **63: 01**).

Sergeant and Sims, pp. 5–16 and Supplement.
[1] See Stamp Duty Act 1694 Will & Mary c 21.
[2] *The scope of reforming stamp duties*, 21st March 1983.
[3] See Inland Revenue Statistics 1988.

Form of stamp duties

58: 02 The law of stamp duties is governed solely by statute and no document can be charged with stamp duty unless it comes within the clear words of an Act of Parliament.[1] The general rules for the construction of taxing statutes apply (see supra, § **1: 27–1: 32**) and there is a special rule to deal with the situation where a document would have been taxable under a particular head of charge which has been repealed.[2] In these cases the instrument will not be charged under an unrepealed general head.

The Stamp Act 1891 is divided into three parts. Part I consists of a number of general provisions and contains the charging section[3] which imposes the stamp duties specified in the first schedule to the Act on the documents set out in that schedule. These are arranged in alphabetical order and are called the *heads of charge*. Each head of charge may be divided into several subheads. Part II consists of a number of explanatory sections which relate to and supplement the various heads of charge. Part III contains supplementary provisions relating to stamp duties. The duties specified in the First Schedule are of two kinds, fixed and ad valorem. Fixed duties do not vary with the consideration for the document whereas the ad valorem duties vary with the amount of the consideration and in accordance with the scales stated in the schedule as amended by subsequent Finance Acts.

Sergeant and Sims, pp. 16–18 and Supplement.
[1] *Morley v Hall* (1834) 2 Dowl 494 per Taunton J at 497.
[2] *A-G v Lamplough* (1878) 3 Ex D 214.
[3] SA 1891, s. 1.

Rates of duty

58: 03   The present ad valorem stamp duties[1] are:

Agreement for lease	**59: 28**	Exchange or partition	**59: 38**
Bearer instrument	**59: 31**	Leases—rent and premium	**59: 23**
Bond, covenant (rent increases)	**59: 33**	Life insurance policies	**59: 39**
Conveyance or transfer on sale	**59: 02**	Life insurance policies—abolition of duty	**59: 39**

The current rates can be found in the table of tax rates and reliefs, supra.

The current fixed duties are:

		Amount
Conveyance or transfer (unless certified as exempt)— miscellaneous	**59: 19**	50p
Declaration of trust	**59: 35**	50p
Duplicate or counterpart[2]	**59: 37**	50p
Exchange or partition[3]	**59: 38**	50p
Leases—small furnished letting	**59: 23**	£1
—miscellaneous	**59: 23**	£2
Release or renunciation	**59: 45**	50p
Surrender	**59: 46**	50p

The former fixed duties

FA 1985, s. 86 and Sch. 24 repealed the fixed duties payable under the following heads of charge:

	Amount
Agreement pursuant to the Highways Acts	5p
Appointment	50p
Covenant	50p
Deeds not liable to other duties	50p
Letter or Power of Attorney	50p
Procuration	50p
Revocation	50p

	Amount
Warrant of Attorney	50p
and in Scotland	
Charter of Resignation	25p
Precept of Clare Constat	25p
Resignation	25p
Seisin and Notarial Instruments	25p
Writ	25p

The repeals apply to instruments executed on or after 19th March 1985. Instruments that required stamping before 26th March continue to attract the former fixed duty.

FA 1985, s. 87 contains an enabling power under which the Board of Inland Revenue is able to require that documents remaining liable to a fixed duty shall be certified in a form prescribed by the Board. FA 1985, s. 89 contains an enabling provision under which the Treasury is able to exempt specified documents from the requirements of a produced stamp. Regulations have now been made under the Stamp Duty (Exempt Instruments) Regulations 1985.[4]

Sergeant and Sims, Division A, Part 2 and Supplement.

[1] The duty on contract notes and voluntary dispositions were repealed by FA 1985, s. 82 and FA 1987, s. 49 and FA 1985, s. 86.

[2] Or less: SA 1891, Sch. 1; FA 1974, Sch. 11, para. 9.

[3] Unless relating to real property and the value of any equalisation payment exceeds £100.

[4] S.I. No. 1688. (See infra, §§ **58: 21**).

(a) Exempt Instruments—certification

58: 04   Under the Stamp Duty (Exempt Instruments) Regulations 1987, SI 1987 No. 516 which came into force on 1st May 1987, many instruments formerly liable to a nominal 50p fixed duty are now exempt if executed on or after 1st May 1987, subject to certification.[1] The instruments exempted under the regulations, are listed in the Schedule to the Order which is reproduced below. Furthermore, an instrument which is certified in accordance with the Regulations and executed on or after 1st May 1987 is no longer required under FA 1985, s. 82 (abolition of ad valorem duty on gifts inter vivos) or s. 84 (variations on death and appropriations) to be adjudicated.

Once certified, exempted instruments should not be sent to Stamp Offices but to the registrar or other person who needs to act upon them.

SCHEDULE

An instrument which effects any one or more of the following transactions only is an instrument specified for the purposes of regulation 2—

A. The vesting of property subject to a trust in the trustees of the trust on the appointment of a new trustee, or in the continuing trustees on the retirement of a trustee.

B. The conveyance or transfer of property the subject of a specific devise or legacy to the beneficiary named in the will (or his nominee).

C. The conveyance or transfer of property which forms part of an intestate's estate to the person entitled on intestacy (or his nominee).

D. The appropriation of property within section 84(4) of the Finance Act 1985 (death: appropriation in satisfaction of a general legacy of money) or section 84(5) or (7) of that Act (death: appropriation in satisfaction of any interest of surviving spouse and in Scotland also of any interest of issue).

E. The conveyance or transfer of property which forms part of the residuary estate of a testator to a beneficiary (or his nominee) entitled solely by virtue of his entitlement under the will.

F. The conveyance or transfer of property out of a settlement in or towards satisfaction of a beneficiary's interest, not being an interest acquired for money or money's worth, being a conveyance or transfer constituting a distribution of property in accordance with the provisions of the settlement.

G. The conveyance or transfer of property on and in consideration only of marriage to a party to the marriage (or his nominee) or to trustees to be held on the terms of a settlement made in consideration only of the marriage.

H. The conveyance or transfer of property within section 83(1) of the Finance Act 1985 (transfers in connection with divorce etc.).

I. The conveyance or transfer by the liquidator of property which formed part of the assets of the company in liquidation to a shareholder of that company (or his nominee) in or towards satisfaction of the shareholder's rights on a winding-up.

J. The grant in fee simple of an easement in or over land for no consideration in money or money's worth.

K. The grant of a servitude for no consideration in money or money's worth.

L. The conveyance or transfer of property operating as a voluntary disposition inter vivos for no consideration in money or money's worth nor any consideration referred to in section 57 of the Stamp Act 1891 (conveyance in consideration of a debt etc.).

M. The conveyance or transfer of property by an instrument within section 84(1) of the Finance Act 1985 (death: varying disposition).

THE CERTIFICATE

The certificate should:

● be—
—included as part of the document or—
—endorsed upon the document or—
—firmly attached to the document (if prepared separately);
● include—
—the category into which the document falls and—
—a sufficient description of the document where the certificate is separate but physically attached.
● be signed by the transferor or grantor, or by a solicitor on his behalf. (An authorised agent of the transferor or grantor who is not a solicitor may also sign provided he states the capacity in which he signs, confirms that he is authorised and that he has knowledge of the facts of the transaction.)

A suggested form of words is:

"I/We hereby certify that this instrument falls within category . . .† in the Schedule to the Stamp Duty (Exempt Instruments) Regulations 1987".
† Insert the letter opposite the category concerned.

(b) Practical problems

Although the Regulations and Technical Note seem clear and straightforward, it is apparent that they give rise to practical difficulties and some uncertainty in relation to the stamping of settlements themselves and the instruments required for the vesting of settled property in the trustees. Broadly, the position seems to be as follows. The basic principle is that an instrument which effects a gift qualifies for the appropriate certificate under the Regulations and, if certified, is exempt from duty and need not be sent to the Stamp Office for adjudication; but an instrument which serves merely to transfer the legal interest in settled property does not qualify for a certificate and must be stamped 50p.

It seems to follow that:

(a) if the settlement is stated to be executed before the transfers (so that it is the latter which effect the gift), the settlement must be stamped 50p and must not be certified, and the transfers require to be certified and then attract no duty (but if not certified attract 50p and require adjudication), and,

(b) if the settlement is stated to be executed after the transfers (or if there is no evidence as to the order of execution, in which case this will be presumed to be the position) then,

(i) subject to (ii) below, the settlement has to be certified and then attracts no duty (but if not certified attracts 50p duty and requires adjudication), and the transfers attract 50p duty,

(ii) but if the settlement "contains provision for future additions to the Trust Fund" it too requires a 50p stamp whether or not it contains a certificate (but then would not require to be adjudicated).

As regards this type of case the argument seems to be:

(a) that if a settlement makes no provision for further additions, the trustees have no power to accept them;

(b) that the charge to 50p duty in respect of such a provision is justified by *Ansell v IRC* [1929] 1 KB 608 and by the Stamp Act 1891, s. 4.

Sergeant and Sims, pp. 111, 349–352 and Supplement.
[1] The Stamp Office has issued further guidance in the form of a Technical Note (June 1987) obtainable from any Stamp Office. See also *Law Society's Gazette*, 3 February 1988 p. 11 and letter from R. T Oerton and his interesting comments.

The administration of stamp duty

58: 05   Stamp duty is managed by the Commissioners of Inland Revenue[1] and administered in England and Wales by the Controller of Stamps and in Scotland, by the Controller (Stamps) Scotland. The Provisional Collection of Taxes Act 1968 (see supra, § **1: 02**) does not apply but similar legislation was introduced by FA 1973, s. 50.[2] The Stamp Act 1891, s. 1 charges the duties specified in the First Schedule on the instruments specified in the said Schedule; this is the only section of the Act which imposes directly any obligation to stamp any instrument.[3] The process of determining formally the correct duty is by adjudication. An instrument must be sent to the Commissioners of Inland Revenue for adjudication and an appeal lies from their decision by way of case stated to the Chancery Division in England and Wales, in Scotland to the Court of Session, in Northern Ireland to the High Court, with further rights of appeal as for income tax cases (see § **1: 32** and § **1: 40**). For the procedure and requirements generally, see infra, § **58: 18**. The provisions forbidding disclosure of information in FA 1989, s. 182 apply to stamp duty.

Sergeant and Sims, pp. 21–24 and Supplement.

[1] SDMA 1891 and Inland Revenue Regulation Act 1890.

[2] The legislation is not identical since the duty must be final—income tax can be adjusted later; for this reason the rate approved in the resolution is binding for the period stated.

[3] Fletcher Moulton LJ in *Maple & Co (Paris) Ltd v IRC* [1906] 1 KB 834 at 843; this judgment contains a useful analysis of the Stamp Act 1891.

Territorial limits

58: 06   The territorial limits of SA 1891 are defined incidentally in SA 1891, s. 14(4) which lays down the rules of inadmissibility of unstamped documents. Such documents are barred if the instrument is executed in the UK or relates to property in the UK. Stamp duty applies in Scotland as well as England and Wales.

Until 1974 there was separate legislation for Northern Ireland passed by the Northern Ireland Government; since that time changes in stamp duties have been made by Parliament at Westminster.

Sergeant and Sims, pp. 21–22 and Supplement.

BASIC PRINCIPLES

Stamp duties are duties on documents

58: 07   Stamp duties are duties basically on instruments[1] and for the purposes of stamp duty an instrument is defined to include every written document.[2] If a transaction is effected orally or arises solely from the conduct of the parties so that there is no document to stamp, then, generally there can be no duty. So on a transfer of ownership of chattels by delivery no duty arises but if the ownership is transferred by bill of sale duty must be paid on that instrument.[3]

It is sometimes possible to structure transactions so that they are not effected by documents and this may be done in one of three main ways; by delivery or conduct, by operation of law or orally. Delivery or conduct can be used to make gifts or to accept contracts. Operation of law will apply where by statute or common law a particular action gives rise to a particular legal consequence without any, or any further, documentation e.g. (i) where not complying with the terms of a lease can be treated as a surrender of the lease;[4] or (ii) where property vests in a trustee on his appointment as a trustee,[5] or (iii) a *donatio mortis causa*,[6] or (iv) an oral declaration of trust.[7]

For stamp duty saving purposes advantage has been taken of this rule wherever it is possible to effect a transaction without using an instrument, but in the case of securities this facility is now severely restricted by the imposition of the new stamp duty reserve tax introduced in FA 1986 Part IV (see infra, § **63: 02** for further details).

A contract need not be in writing, so one of the issues in the well known case of *Carlill v Carbolic Smoke Ball Co*[8] was whether evidence could be given of the contract because the document issued by the defendants was not stamped. It was held that the contract was made by acceptance and, as that was not in writing, no stamp was needed. It should, however, be borne in mind that some transactions must be in writing if they are to be valid. Examples of such transactions include the creation or disposition of a legal estate in land for which a deed is required[9] and the disposition of an existing equitable interest by the beneficial owner,[10] while a declaration of trust relating to land may be made orally but must be evidenced in writing.[11]

Problems of evidence may arise where there is no document to act as evidence of a transaction and there are other risks inherent in disposing of the need for a document, in particular where assignments are involved because an oral assignment will, in most cases, be an equitable assignment and not the more favourable legal assignment. In some cases this will not matter, where for example the two parties are connected as where a debt owed by a subsidiary company is assigned to the parent company. Here the parent company can enforce payment by its subsidiary so it is possible to ensure that the debt is paid to the assignee.

Situations where it might be possible to save stamp duty by utilising the fact that the transaction does not have to be in writing or evidenced in writing include severing fixtures when land is sold so that they pass by delivery rather than conveyance of the land itself and allowing title to chattels to pass by delivery when a business is sold. It is difficult to create oral trusts for this purpose because a prior oral transaction and its subsequent written record can be treated as one transaction[12] but as there is no exemption for stamp duty in relation to transactions between spouses an oral declaration of trust could be used to pass property between spouses. There could be a problem where the property was land because such a trust must be evidenced in writing signed by the settlor[13] but it seems that the statutory declaration, which is merely a formal record of evidence, is not stampable as it does not create or dispose of rights or interests in property.

Sergeant and Sims, pp. 25–37 and Supplement.
[1] SA 1891, s. 1.
[2] SA 1891, s. 122(1).
[3] SA 1891, Sch. 1 and s. 41.
[4] *Foster v Robinson* [1951] 1 KB 149.
[5] Trustee Act 1925, s. 40.
[6] *Birch v Treasury Solicitor* [1951] Ch 298.
[7] This is the common position and the Law of Property Act 1925 sets out the circumstances in which writing is required.
[8] [1892] 2 QB 484.
[9] Law of Property Act 1925, s. 52(1).

¹⁰ Law of Property Act 1925, s. 53(1)(*c*).
¹¹ Law of Property Act, 1925, s. 53(1)(*b*).
¹² *Cohen and Moore v IRC* [1933] 2 KB 126.
¹³ Law of Property Act 1925, s. 53(1)(*b*).

Documents are stamped according to their legal effect¹

58: 08   If because of a misapprehension an appointment of new trustees is made by the wrong person, the document has no legal effect and does not attract stamp duty. The legal effect of an instrument depends on its substance so in *Eastern National Omnibus Co Ltd v IRC*² an agreement to discontinue business in a specified area, to assist their successors to obtain the necessary licences and not to compete, made by a public motor service company was held to be an agreement for the sale of goodwill even though it was not recorded in that manner.

As to the doctrine of form and substance in tax matters generally see now §§ **1: 04–1: 25** following the decision in *Furniss v Dawson* [1984] STC 153, HL. It certainly seems that the principle of that case is applicable in some situations to stamp duty.⁴

Duty paid on an instrument which fails to carry out a transaction may be recovered.³

Sergeant and Sims, pp. 30–37 and Supplement.
¹ See *Oughtred v IRC* [1958] Ch 678 per Lord Evershed MR at 688; affd on appeal [1960] AC 206.
² [1939] 1 KB 161.
³ SDMA 1891, s. 9(7).
⁴ See *Ingram v IRC* [1985] STC 835.

Time of execution governs (complete and incomplete documents)

58: 09   The original theory of the Stamp Act was that liability was determined as the instrument was prepared and before it was executed;¹ hence the practice of preparing an instrument on stamped paper. This can be seen in SA 1891, s. 15(1) which imposes certain penalties on instruments stamped after execution (§ **58: 26** infra) and in the provisions relating to wasted stamps (§ **58: 23** infra). Today this theory bears little relation to practice since it is clear that there is no obligation to stamp an instrument at all, although the consequences of not stamping it may compel one to do so, and that, in practice, the Revenue do not insist on the strict interpretation of s. 15(1), there being a general period of grace of 30 days following the date of execution.

The principle that the time of execution governs means, as the House of Lords held in *Wm Cory & Son Ltd v IRC*,² that the liability of an instrument to stamp duty arises when it is executed and that the character of an instrument is ascertained by reference to its legal effect at that date and not by what use was made of it later. This does not prevent the courts from looking at later events to discover the true position when the instrument was executed.

An incomplete document does not need a stamp. It follows that it can be produced in evidence unstamped[3] but it also follows that if the rate of stamp duty changes before the document is complete it will be the later rate of duty that applies.[4]

The true test is probably that a document is complete when it has been executed by the last party to execute whose execution is necessary to make it an effective document, and this is the date which should be inserted in the document. So a transfer by way of gift is complete in equity when the donor has done all in his power to perfect the gift;[5] if, however, the transfer requires registration before it is complete the instrument is not complete until executed by all the parties necessary for registration.[6]

A deed will normally take effect, i.e. be complete, on delivery. A deed which has been signed and sealed but not delivered, is not yet complete and so not yet liable to stamp duty. The same rule now applies to a deed delivered in escrow, i.e. one that has been delivered but which is to take effect only on the satisfaction of some condition.

In *Terrapin International Ltd v IRC*[7] a deed of exchange was delivered in escrow and stated that, subject to satisfactory land searches being obtained by one party, the exchange would take place on 30th April 1974. Owing to delay in the Land Registry, completion did not take place until 8th May 1974. It was held that the deed was complete only when the conditions were satisfied and the rate of stamp duty was therefore that applying on 8th May; the rate had been doubled for documents executed after 30th April 1974.

It is perhaps curious that the Stamp Act does not go on to define the term "executed"[8] except for documents not under seal: such documents are executed when they are signed. This raises the question whether a deed which has been signed and sealed, but not yet delivered, needs a stamp. Here one has to observe the distinction already made between a document which is complete and one which is incomplete. The curious position appears to emerge that a document may be incomplete—and so not yet need a stamp— and yet be beyond the date of execution mentioned in s. 15. The practical solution to this problem is the one adopted by the Revenue which is to calculate the period of 30 days for s. 15(2) from the date inserted in the instrument and to say that the date to be inserted should be that on which it became complete.

Sergeant and Sims, pp. 27, 83–84 and Supplement.

[1] Per Dixon J in *Stamp Duties Comr (Queensland) v Hopkins* (1945) 71 CLR 351 at 379.

[2] [1965] AC 1088 especially per Lord Reid at 1105; this loophole has now been closed. For a case when this principle operated against the taxpayer see *Western United Investment Co Ltd v IRC* [1958] Ch 392.

[3] *Sinclair v IRC* (1942) 24 TC 432 at 442.

[4] *Terrapin International Ltd v IRC* [1976] 2 All ER 461; see also *Crane Fruehauf Ltd v IRC* [1975] 1 All ER 429 (document not under seal but subject to condition; date of instrument was date condition satisfied).

[5] See *Re Rose* [1952] Ch 499 at 515.

[6] *Sinclair v IRC* (1942) 24 TC 432 at 444.

[7] [1976] 2 All ER 461.

[8] Contrast the position in Australia under Stamps Act 1958 (Victoria) s. 3—execution for instruments under seal means signature and sealing and so delivery is not necessary.

Overlapping heads of charge

58: 10   If an instrument is chargeable under more than one head, the Crown may choose the head but may not charge under both heads.[1] This situation should be distinguished from that in which one document carries out separate transactions and is therefore liable to duty as separate instruments.

Sergeant and Sims, p. 26 and Supplement.
 [1] *Speyer Bros v IRC* [1908] AC 92 (instrument both a promissory note and a marketable security, both duties now repealed; *Anderson v IRC* [1939] 1 KB 341.

Leading and principal object

58: 11   The leading and principal object rule directs that an instrument's liability to duty is determined by its leading and principal object, so, if that object does not give rise to duty, no duty is due merely because there is a subsidiary clause with a different object; and vice versa.[1] If an instrument is stamped in respect of the leading and principal object there is no need to stamp it for matters which are merely accessory,[2] but the problem is deciding when the second matter is merely accessory and when it is not. The test appears to be whether the second contract can "stand on its own feet".[3] Thus a policy of accident insurance was not also taxable as a life policy merely because the agreement provided for the return of the premium on death without a claim.

This point arises in connection with the conveyance of land where covenants in the conveyance do not give rise to further duty unless they clearly amount to further consideration.

Sergeant and Sims, p. 25 and Supplement.
 [1] *Deddington SS Co Ltd v IRC* [1911] 2 KB 1001.
 [2] *Limmer Asphalte Paving Co Ltd v IRC* (1872) LR 7 Exch 211 per Martin B at 217.
 [3] *General Accident Assurance Corpn Ltd v IRC* 1906 8F (Ct of Sess) 477 per Lord Dunedin at 482.

One instrument—two instruments (alterations)

58: 12   If more than one instrument is written on the same piece of paper each instrument must be stamped separately e.g. an endorsement postponing the completion of a contract of sale, the contract being a chargeable instrument.[1] Hence, if an instrument is executed and subsequently altered to a substantial degree, further stamp duty may be required.[2] This does not apply if the first document was only a draft and so not executed; so a stamp on an incomplete document will cover a subsequent alteration.[3] The alteration of an instrument after execution may make a new stamp necessary either because it is a new instrument or because it increases the amount of duty payable on the other instrument.[4]

Sergeant and Sims, p. 57 and Supplement.
 [1] SA 1891, s. 3(2); *Bacon v Simpson* (1837) 3 M & W 78.
 [2] *Prudential Assurance Co Ltd v IRC* [1935] 1 KB 101 (Memorandum) correcting age of life assured held to require a fresh stamp but see infra § **59: 23**.

³ *Matson v Booth* (1816) 5 M & S 223.

⁴ *London and Brighton Rly Co v Fairclough* (1841) 2 Man & G 674; *Bambro (No 2) Pty Ltd v Stamp Duties Comr* (1964) 8 WN (NSW) 1142.

One instrument—two or more matters

58: 13   Where one matter is ancillary to the other, the general principle of the leading and principal object ensures that only one stamp is required.

SA 1891, s. 4 provides that, subject to the provisions of the Stamp Acts,[1] an instrument containing or relating to several distinct matters is to be separately and distinctly charged as if it were a separate instrument with duty in respect of each of the matters.

It follows that an instrument passing property of two different classes for stamp duty must be stamped in respect of each.[2] So an instrument which both appoints new trustees and vests property in them is liable both to appointment duty and to deed duty.[3] An instrument vesting property in separate persons requires a stamp for the transfer to each person;[4] so also an instrument effecting both a sale and a sub-sale of shares requires more than one stamp.[5] However it is possible for persons to transfer interests by one instrument when they act jointly. So in *Wills v Bridge*[6] several shareholders transferred their holdings to a common purchaser by one instrument and the single *ad valorem* stamp was held sufficient. So also a lease to joint tenants requires only one stamp.[7]

The word "matters" is not defined in s. 4 and it is not clear whether it means matters in respect of which duty is chargeable or any transaction whether or not within a head of charge.

Sergeant and Sims, pp. 26, 57 and Supplement.

[1] E.g. SA 1891, s. 77 (leases) and see FA 1989, s. 173(2) (insurance policies).

[2] *Ansell v IRC* [1929] 1 K B 608.

[3] *Hadgett v IRC* (1877) 3 Ex D 46.

[4] *Freeman v IRC* (1871) LR 6 Exch 101, 40 LJ Ex 85.

[5] *Fitch Lovell Ltd v IRC* [1962] 3 All ER 685.

[6] (1849) 4 Exch 193.

[7] *Cooper v Flynn* (1841) 3 ILR 472. In *Baker v Jardine* (1784) 13 East 235 n. an assignment of prize money by several seamen out of one fund required only one stamp.

One instrument—two or more considerations

58: 14   Section 4 then provides that an instrument made for any consideration in respect whereof it is chargeable with ad valorem duty, and also for any further or other valuable consideration or considerations, is to be separately and distinctly charged, as if it were a separate instrument, with duty in respect of each of the considerations.[1]

An example would be a lease granted in return for a premium and a rent but this must be distinguished from the situation in which the lessee promises to pay rent and to look after the property, the latter promise being clearly ancillary to the leading object and so not separately chargeable.

Sergeant and Sims, pp. 26, 57 and Supplement.

[1] SA 1891, s. 4(*b*).

Two instruments—one transaction

58: 15   A transaction may well take more than one instrument. It is a general rule that ad valorem duty is not paid more than once. So where there are several conveyances for completing title to property sold, the principal conveyance only is charged with ad valorem stamp duty. This is in accordance with Revenue practice and statutory provision as regards conveyances.[1]

Sergeant and Sims, p. 27 and Supplement.
[1] E.g. SA 1891, s. 58(3).

The contingency principle—consideration of uncertain value

58: 16   On a transfer or sale ad valorem duty is chargeable on the value of the consideration.[1] If that value is uncertain special rules apply:

(a) if neither a maximum nor a minimum figure can be placed upon it, no ad valorem duty may be charged;[2] however a figure that may be varied up or down may itself be taken;[3]

(b) if a definite minimum figure can be set, ad valorem duty is charged on that figure and, in addition, fixed duty of 50p is charged on the possibility of the larger sum;[4]

(c) if a definite maximum figure can be set ad valorem duty is charged on that figure notwithstanding that the actual consideration finally paid may be much less;[5]

(d) It follows that if both a maximum and a minimum figure can be set duty is chargeable on the maximum.

EXAMPLE
So if A is liable to pay £10,000 and, contingently, another £20,000, ad valorem duty is due on £30,000; if however, he is liable to pay £10,000 and then a royalty which has neither a minimum nor a maximum element in it, ad valorem duty is due on only £10,000.

The effect of uncertainty as to amount may be further illustrated by the decision of the House of Lords in *Independent Television Authority and Associated Rediffusion Ltd v IRC*.[6] In this case a series of payments was due but the sum would be varied (up or down) by reference to the retail prices index. It was held that the sum dutiable was that stated in the agreement notwithstanding the possibility of later variation.

Most of the reported cases concern bond covenant duty which has now been largely repealed. However a modern instance of this principle is an insurance policy where the sum charged is the sum assured together with any guaranteed or specified bonuses but not merely the normal promise of the chance of a bonus since it is too uncertain (see infra, § **59: 39**).

Sergeant and Sims, p. 28 and Supplement.
[1] A sum payable only on breach of a term of the contract is not consideration—*Western United Investment Co Ltd v IRC* [1958] Ch 392.
[2] *Underground Electric Railways v IRC* [1916] 1 KB 306, CA; fixed duty may be due, but this is not related to the consideration.

³ See n. 6.
⁴ *Underground Electric Railways v IRC* [1916] 1 KB 306, CA; *Jones v IRC* [1895] 1 QB 484; SA 1891, s. 4(*b*).
⁵ *Underground Electric Railways v IRC* [1906] AC 21.
⁶ [1961] AC 427. Contrast *Clifford v IRC* [1896] 2 QB 187. The charging provision in the case (bond covenant duty) was repealed by FA 1971, s. 64.

ADMINISTRATION

Methods of stamping

58: 17   Instruments are presented at one of the stamp offices¹ and are then impressed with a die stamp. Postage stamps are no longer acceptable.² The duty to set out all the facts and circumstances affecting the liability to duty of any instrument should be noted.³

¹ For addresses see **Sergeant and Sims, p. lvii.** The telephone number of the Birmingham Office has been changed to 021 200 2616.
² They were only acceptable for heads of charge which have now been repealed.
³ SA 1891, s. 5.

Adjudication and adjudication stamp

58: 18   The special nature of stamp duties is illustrated by the adjudication process which enables the correct amount of duty to be determined—usually conclusively—by the Revenue. Any person may require the Commissioners to express their opinion on the liability to duty or the amount due. Following such an opinion the instrument *may* be stamped with the amount of duty determined and a further stamp—the adjudication stamp—denoting that it is duly stamped or with a stamp to show that it is not chargeable. There is, however, no obligation to pay that duty and generally the only consequence is that the document is not adjudicated and duly stamped (see § **58: 25**). The instrument for adjudication must be delivered to the Stamp Office together with any information the office may require.¹

In some instances adjudication is compulsory:

(*a*) conveyance in contemplation of sale;²
(*b*) orders made under the Variation of Trusts Act 1958;³ and
(*c*) orders made under the Companies Act 1985, s. 427.⁴

It is also required when relief or exemption is claimed under:

(*a*) FA 1930, s. 42 (transfer between associated companies);
(*b*) FA 1980, s. 98 (maintenance funds for historic buildings);
(*c*) FA 1980, s. 102 (conveyances in consideration of a debt);
(*d*) FA 1982, s. 129 and FA 1983, s. 46 (for conveyances, transfers or leases to charities or the National Heritage Memorial Fund or the Historic Buildings and Monuments Commission for England);
(*e*) FA 1986, ss. 75, 76, 77 (reconstruction of a company).

Under the Stamp Duty (Exempt Instruments) Regulations 1987, SI 1987 No. 516 adjudication is no longer required for instruments under FA 1985, s. 82 or s. 84 if duly certified.

Apart from satisfying statutory requirements the main advantages in requesting adjudication is that the instrument is—if duly stamped under the adjudication process—admissible for all purposes notwithstanding any objection relating to duty;[5] thus it is the most that can be done to convince third parties. The process is also the first step in disputing the Stamp Office's view of the correct amount of duty.

The adjudication process is normally conclusive of the amount of duty but here too there are exceptions:

(*a*) some instruments also require a produced stamp (infra, § **58: 21**);

(*b*) if the document requires two stamps, adjudication of one is not conclusive of duty on the other;[6]

(*c*) bearer instruments require a stamp under FA 1963, s. 60(3);

(*d*) the court can probably go behind the adjudication stamp if it was obtained by misrepresentation or without full disclosure of the material facts.[7]

Sergeant and Sims, pp. 24, 64 and Supplement.
[1] SA 1891, s. 12(2) and see Official notes indicating information required in certain common situations which is reproduced in Sergeant and Sims, pp. 53–55.
[2] FA 1965, s. 90 and see **Sergeant and Sims, pp. 67, 68, 236.**
[3] See *Practice Note* [1966] 1 All ER 672.
[4] **Sergeant and Sims, p. 73.**
[5] SA 1891, s. 12(5).
[6] *Fitch Lovell Ltd v IRC* [1962] 1 WLR 1325 at 1363.
[7] SA 1891, ss. 5 and 12(2).

Limits of adjudication

58: 19   The process of adjudication is not without its limits. Thus the process cannot authorise the stamping after the execution thereof of any instrument which by law cannot be stamped after execution.[1] Moreover if a court has ruled that an instrument is not duly stamped, subsequent adjudication cannot retrospectively make it duly stamped;[2] for the same reason the process cannot prejudice rights that have been asserted and relied upon prior to adjudication. As Brightman J (as he then was) has said:

> "Suppose a vendor of land requires the purchaser to accept a title deed which is not properly stamped. The purchaser declines. The vendor serves a notice to complete. The purchaser does not complete. The vendor forfeits his deposit. Suppose that this purchaser was right in law in his assessment of the stamp duty liability. It would be absurd to suppose in that case that the purchaser loses his deposit merely because the vendor between rescission and trial succeeds in getting the instrument in question erroneously adjudicated as not liable to duty".[3]

Sergeant and Sims, p. 73 and Supplement.
[1] SA 1891, s. 12(6)(*b*).
[2] *Prudential Mutual Assurance Investment and Loan Association v Curzon* (1852) 8 Ex 97.
[3] *Marx v Estates and General Investments Ltd* [1976] 1 WLR 380 at 387 per Brightman J.

Denoting stamp

58: 20   The amount of ad valorem duty due may depend on whether another instrument has been duly stamped. So no ad valorem duty will be due on a conveyance on sale if it carries out an agreement for sale which has itself borne ad valorem duty.[1] In such an instance the conveyance will carry a stamp showing—or denoting—the amount of duty paid on the agreement.

Such a stamp does not guarantee that the stamp on the agreement is sufficient; such a guarantee requires adjudication. The denoting stamp is usually impressed only when both the original and the new instruments are presented at the same time.[2]

Other instances of denoting stamps are:

On the transfer or conveyance of a freehold or leasehold interest or the grant of a lease for a term exceeding 35 years (which is not directly enforceable against any intermediate interest in the land) the duty paid on the agreement must be denoted on the conveyance, transfer or lease.[3]

(*i*) substituted bearer instruments when the original has been duly stamped,[4] and

(*ii*) on duplicates or counterparts.[5]

Sometimes, denoting stamps are also used in other situations even though they do not denote duty paid on another instrument; viz. before an inland bearer instrument is issued.[6]

Sergeant and Sims, p. 62 and Supplement.
 [1] SA 1891, s. 59(3).
 [2] SA 1891, s. 11.
 [3] FA 1984, s. 111(2), (3).
 [4] FA 1963, s. 59(1), para (4) and s. 60(8) duty of only 10p is due.
 [5] SA 1891, s. 72.
 [6] FA 1963, s. 60(3) infra, § **61: 16**.

Produced stamp—Particulars Delivered form

58: 21   FA 1931, s. 28 requires purchasers to produce to the Stamp Office, whether or not duty is payable, the conveyancing document together with a form (the so called Particulars Delivered form) which summarises the details of the transaction.[1] The document is stamped with a "produced stamp" in addition to any ad valorem duty stamp. Without the produced stamp the document is not duly stamped. Failure to produce also carries a fine. In England, Wales and Northern Ireland all conveyancing documents, subject to certain exceptions, had to be submitted to the Stamp Office and also, in the case of land subject to the compulsory registration requirement, to the Land Registry.

Now, however, in England and Wales the majority of conveyances of registered land where the sale price is below the stamp duty threshold (currently £30,000) go direct to the Land Registry together with the Particulars Delivered form. The necessary enabling legislation is contained in FA 1985, s. 89 and the Stamp Duty (Exempt Instruments) Regulations 1985.[2] The date from which the new arrangements took effect was 1st January 1986.

The arrangements apply to:

(*i*) transfers on sales of commercial premises as well as land and houses; and

(*ii*) on assignment or surrender of an existing lease.

They do not, however, apply to:

(*i*) transfers on sales of property which attract stamp duty (the threshold is £30,000);

(*ii*) transfer on sales which do not fall to be registered with the Land Registry;

(*iii*) the grant of a new lease.

In Scotland arrangements already exist for non-dutiable dispositions of property to be sent direct to the Keeper of the Registers of Scotland. No change is at present proposed to the arrangements that apply in Northern Ireland.

It will be seen that there is no obligation to produce a voluntary conveyance; there is also no need to produce an instrument relating solely to incorporeal hereditaments, a grave, a right of burial or the transfer of a mining lease.

Sergeant and Sims, p. 197 and Supplement.
[1] The particulars required are to be found in FA 1931, Sch. 2, as amended and FA 1985, s. 89 and the Stamp Duty (Exempt Instruments) Regulations 1985, S.I. 1985, No. 1688. In Scotland, Form LV(A) is used for leases.
[2] S.I. 1985 No. 1688.

Appeals following adjudication and judicial review

58: 22 An appeal lies to the High Court by way of case stated but only after an adjudication[1] and payment of the duty.[2] The appeal must be made within 21 days of assessment. The Commissioners of Inland Revenue must state a case and deliver it to the appellant who may then within seven days set it down for hearing. The legislation, remarkably, gives the Commissioners the right to state the case and thus to determine the facts on the basis of which the appeal will be heard in the first instance. However not only is oral evidence admissible to supplement the case stated,[2] but, in practice, the case is submitted to the appellant in draft form.[3]

If the appeal is successful, overpaid duty can be repaid with such interest as this court may determine.[4] The Revenue may not sue to recover the excess of any higher duty the court may determine; in such circumstances the instrument is simply not duly stamped unless the excess is paid.

An application for judicial review is open to a taxpayer in appropriate circumstances, but for an unsuccessful application, see *J Rothschild Holdings plc v IRC*[5].

Sergeant and Sims, p. 77 and Supplement.
[1] However there may be an appeal without there having been an assessment—see FA 1973, s. 47. In Scotland the case stated goes to the Court of Session.
[2] E.g. *Holmleigh (Holdings) Ltd v IRC* (1958) 46 TC 435.
[3] Sergeant and Sims, p. 77.
[4] FA 1965, s. 91. In *Clarke Chapman-John Thompson Ltd v IRC* [1976] Ch 91 interest was awarded at back rate for the time being: interest cannot be awarded under Law Reform (Miscellaneous Provisions) Act 1934, *Western United Investment Co Ltd v IRC* [1958] Ch 392.
[5] [1989] STC 435, CA.

Spoiled stamps

58: 23 By SDMA 1891, s. 9 an allowance is made for spoiled stamps in certain defined circumstances, including an instrument if executed but

(a) found to be void *ab initio*, or

(b) found to be unfit, by reason of error or mistake therein, for the purpose originally intended, or

(c) which fails by reason of the inability or refusal or some other person to sign it or complete the transaction, or

(d) which fails by reason of the inability or refusal of some other person to act under it or for want of enrolment or registration within a time limit, or

(e) which is inadvertently and undesignedly spoilt and another substituting instrument has been executed (and duly stamped) or which has become useless in consequence of another instrument being executed (and duly stamped) effecting the same transaction.

This relief is limited in that there is a two year time limit for claiming the allowance and no legal proceeding must have been commenced in which the instrument *could* be offered in evidence. It is also limited in that the conditions do not cover instruments failing for non-fulfilment of a condition precedent or relating to transactions which are voidable. This point is less troublesome if one considers that the transaction was initially valid and therefore the document should have been stamped; this however must be balanced by the fact that if the instrument had not been stamped no-one could be any the worse off and that these restrictions do not apply to the wider relief for duty on a conveyance on sale in SA 1891, s. 59. It is also a condition of the relief that the instrument must be given up to be cancelled: where the document has been lost the allowance is given by Extra-statutory concession G2 (1988).

There is also relief where a person has inadvertently used a stamp of greater value than was necessary.[1]

Sergeant and Sims, p. 44 and Supplement.
[1] SDMA 1891, s. 10.

Lost instruments

58: 24 When an instrument is lost there is a presumption that it was duly stamped; however if it can be shown that the instrument had not been stamped the presumption is that it remained unstamped.[1] This gives rise to a nice problem. An instrument which is not lost can be presented for stamping out of time on payment of penalties: a lost instrument obviously cannot be so presented nor—since it was unstamped—can secondary evidence of its contents be given.[2]

When an instrument which was duly stamped has been lost, a replica may, by concession, be stamped free or, if a replica has been stamped, the original duty repaid. The rate of duty is that in force at the time of the original.[3]

Sergeant and Sims, pp. 29, 48 and Supplement.
[1] *Marine Investment Co v Haviside* (1872) LR 5 HL 624.
[2] See **Sergeant and Sims, p. 80 and Supplement** for authorities and discussion.

INSTRUMENTS NOT PROPERLY STAMPED

Admissibility

58: 25   An instrument which is not properly stamped is nevertheless effective,[1] the failure to stamp a document (unlike a failure to pay income tax) is not an offence and, in general, the Crown cannot sue for duty on an unstamped instrument; however the Stamp Acts provide a number of sanctions against non-stamping.

An instrument which is not duly stamped in accordance with the law in force at the time when it was first executed "shall not, except in criminal proceedings, be given in evidence, or be available for any purpose whatsoever ..." (SA 1891, s. 14(4)). This cannot be remedied by the consent of the parties.[2] The instrument is not admissible whether directly or for a collateral purpose;[3] nor is secondary evidence of the instrument admissible;[4] cross-examination upon an unstamped document is not allowed[5] but unstamped instruments are admissible to refresh a witness's memory[6] and to prove fraud[7] or an act of bankruptcy.[8] It has also been held that a plaintiff need not stamp an instrument when he was trying to prevent the transaction from being implemented and was arguing that the agreement was void.[9] The prohibition on admissibility does not extend to criminal proceedings, nor apparently, to rent tribunals[10] since these are not courts of law. This reasoning could be extended to proceedings before the Commissioners[11] but not to the High Court on appeal by way of case stated. The Inland Revenue will refuse to give effect to unstamped instruments, presumably because an action will then have to be brought against them and the fact of inadmissibility forced before the courts. The effect of the general rule as to late stamping on payment of a penalty (infra, § **58: 26**) is that the defect of non-stamping is inherently remediable. One consequence of this is that it is unprofessional for counsel to object to the admissibility of the document for non-stamping unless the case is a revenue case or the defect goes to the validity of the document.[12] Counsel may however take the stamp point if this would unfairly prejudice his client after the trial; so counsel for a purchaser of land may take the point that a document of title is not stamped.

However, it *is* the duty of the court, arbitrator or referee to take the stamp objection itself;[13] when this is done the legislation prescribes the method to be adopted but in practice the unstamped instrument is admitted subject to all undertaking by the conducting solicitor to have the instrument stamped.[14] The court's decision is final.[15]

Sergeant and Sims, pp. 80–85 and Supplement.

¹ See Isaacs J in *Dent v Moore* [1919] CLR 316 at 324; contrary dicta by Eve J in *Re Indo China Steam Navigation Co* [1917] 2 Ch 100 at 106 are generally thought to be incorrect. **Sergeant and Sims, p. 93**. For a statutory exception see SA 1891, s. 118. See also infra, § **59: 39**.

² *Nixon v Albion Marine Insurance Co* (1867) LR 2 Exch 338.

³ *Fengl v Fengl* [1914] P 274 although the position in Scotland is unclear—*Watson v Watson* 1934 SC 374 at 379. See **Sergeant and Sims, p. 84**.

⁴ *Hamilton Finance Co Ltd v Coverley Westray Waltaum & Toseti Ltd* [1969] LI R 53.

[5] *Baker v Dale* (1858) 1 F & F 271.

[6] *Birchall v Bullough* [1896] 1 QB 325.

[7] *Re Shaw* (1920) 90 LJ KB 204.

[8] *Re Gunsbourg* (1919) 88 LJ KB 562.

[9] *Mason v Motor Traction Co* [1905] 1 Ch 419.

[10] See *R v Fulham etc Rent Tribunal* [1951] 2 KB 1 at 7–8.

[11] See *Sinclair v IRC* (1942) 24 TC at 432 at 444 and Vaisey J in *Lamport and Holt Line Ltd v Langwell* (1958) 38 TC 193 at 198. However this is unlikely. A decision of the commissioners can be reversed for error of law: the admission of inadmissible evidence is an error of law: it could be certain if a document could be relied on before the commissioners but not, an appeal, before the High Court. See also *A-G v BBC* [1979] 3 All ER 45 on meaning of court for contempt rule.

[12] Boulton, *Conduct and Etiquette at the Bar* (6th edn) p. 70; see also *Skandinavia Reinsurance Co of Copenhagen v Da Costa* [1911] 1 KB 137 when the successful objector was deprived of costs.

[13] SA 1891, s. 14(1) but only when the point is clear—*Don Francesco v De Meo* 1908 SC 7; in practice doubtful points are covered by requiring an undertaking that the instrument will be submitted for adjudication. If the form of the undertaking cannot be agreed upon it would appear that the document will not be admitted.

[14] E.g. *Parkfield Trust Ltd v Dent* [1931] 2 KB 579 at 582, this seems to rest on the status of the solicitor as an officer of this court—an undertaking by a barrister would therefore not suffice.

[15] RSC Ord. 59, r. 11(5); but an appeal is possible; see *The Belfort* (1884) 9 PD 215.

Penalties for late stamping

58: 26   The failure to stamp an instrument is not a criminal offence but SA 1891 provides a tariff of penalties for late stamping. The general rule (SA 1891, s. 15(1)) is that the person presenting the instrument for stamping after the date of execution[1] must pay the unpaid duty, a penalty of £10 and a further penalty, if the unpaid duty exceeds £10, of interest on such duty at 5% p.a. from the day upon which the instrument was first executed up to the time when such interest is equal in amount to the unpaid duty. The effect of the closing words is to limit the amount of interest to the amount of unpaid duty.

Different penalty rates apply to some, but not all, instruments liable to ad valorem duty; here, SA 1891, s. 15(2) prescribes that in addition to the unpaid duty, the person must pay a penalty of £10 and a sum equal to the unpaid duty unless there is a reasonable excuse for the delay.

Title of instrument	Persons liable to penalty
Bond, covenant, or instrument of any kind whatsoever.	The obligee, covenantee, or other person taking the security.
Conveyance on sale	The vendee or transferee.
Lease or tack...	The lessee.
[Agreement for lease or tack chargeable under section 75][1]	[The person contracting for the lease or tack to be granted to him or another][2]

Any penalty may be mitigated or remitted by the Commissioners;[3] it is probably through this rule that penalties are not imposed under s. 15(1) on instruments, presented for stamping within 30 days following execution; this period is specifically authorised for documents within s. 15(2).

Sergeant and Sims, p. 89 and Supplement.

[1] See infra, § 59: 28 in practice the Commissioners allow late stamping without penalty if the instrument is presented within 30 days after first execution unless the instrument is liable to ad

valorem duty or is within s. 15(2). See **Sergeant and Sims, p. 75 and Supplement** and FA 1984,
s. 111(4).
  [2] FA 1984, s. 111(4).
  [3] SA 1891, s. 15(3)(*b*).

An action for recovery of duty

58: 27   Action for the recovery of stamp duty may be instituted in the High
Court as a debt due to the Crown in the case of:

(*a*) unpaid capital duty (now abolished) (see infra, § **61: 07**); and

(*b*) duty payable on the assignment of a policy of life assurance when the
policy monies have been paid to the assignee without the instrument being
stamped[1] (infra, § **59: 39**).

These are exceptions to the general principle that the Crown cannot sue for
stamp duty.

Anyone who receives money as or for any duty may also be sued.[2] This
covers not only public officials but also a solicitor who has charged his client
for the duty.[3]

Sergeant and Sims, p. 183 and Supplement.
  [1] SA 1891, s. 118(2). This section will cease to have effect as regards instruments made after
31st December 1989 (FA 1989, s. 173(4), (9)).
  [2] SDMA 1891, s. 2.
  [3] *Lord Advocate v Gordon* 1901 8 SLT 439.

Fines

58: 28   The Stamp Acts provide fines for various breaches of the Act.[1] In
particular a £10 fine is chargeable if a person executes an instrument in which
not all the facts and circumstances affecting the liability to or the amount of
duty are fully or truly set forth; the same applies to any person employed or
concerned in the preparation of the instrument. However these apply only
when there is an intent to defraud the Crown.[2]

A similar £10 fine is due if a person whose office it is to enrol, register or
enter upon any rolls, books or records, an instrument chargeable with duty,
enrols an instrument which has not been duly stamped—e.g. a company
secretary[3] who registers a share transfer which has not been duly stamped;
he may safely register a transfer stamped to the value of the market value on
the date of transfer. If the person rejects an instrument presented for
registration on stamping grounds, the instrument should be submitted for
adjudication and then re-presented.[4] A registrar may now register an
unadjudicated transfer by way of gift if appropriately certified.[5]

There is a two year limitation period in these instances.[6]

There are also various offences involving forgery;[7] in addition Stamp Duties Management Act 1891, s. 21 imposes a fine of £50 where any person practices or is concerned in any fraudulent act not specifically provided for by law with intent to defraud Her Majesty.[8]

The Keith Committee made recommendations for changes in the enforcement law relating to stamp duty but the necessary legislation has not been brought forward yet.

Sergeant and Sims, p. 24 and Supplement.

[1] The distinction between a fine and a penalty is that a fine is a personal penalty for an offence under the Act; a penalty is a price for late stamping. A fine is recovered in criminal proceedings; a penalty as a debt to the Crown. For procedure for recovery of fines see SDMA 1891, s. 26.

[2] SA 1891, s. 5.

[3] SA 1891, s. 17.

[4] *R v Registrar of Joint Stock Companies* (1888) 21 QBD 131 (rejecting an application for mandamus as the applicant had not exhausted other remedies).

[5] See supra, § **58:18**.

[6] Inland Revenue Regulation Act 1890, s. 22(2).

[7] Stamp Duties Management Act 1891, ss. 13–18. See also the Forgery and Counterfeiting Act 1981, Pt. II and Pt. III.

[8] Contrast the position in Australia with the fine of £1,000 in the Stamps Amendment Act 1977 (Victoria). On intent to defraud note *Balcombe v De Simoni* (1971–72) 126 CLR 577.

Miscellaneous

58: 29   The rights of a party acquiring property under a transaction are obviously affected by the proper stamping of any document. For this reason it has been held that a purchaser may have the instrument properly stamped and charge the amount to the vendor; this extends to all documents on which the purchaser's title depends,[1] but not to others.[2] Likewise he is entitled to repudiate the contract if the vendor refuses to stamp an unstamped instrument.[3] The onus is on the purchaser to prove improper stamping.[4] If the land is registered the title will not be registered if the documents are insufficiently stamped.[5]

These rights depend on contract; once the transaction has been completed or the purchase money has been paid, the purchaser has lost his power over the vendor. Hence in the days when receipts had to be stamped, the only penalty for non-stamping was a fine on a refusal to give a stamped receipt; the purchaser had no right to a stamped receipt.[6]

Sergeant and Sims, pp. 87, 183 and Supplement.

[1] *Whiting to Loomes* (1881) 17 Ch D 10 on specific performance see *Glessing v Green* [1975] 2 All ER 696 at 702.

[2] *Ex p Birkbeck Freehold Land Society* (1883) 24 Ch D 119.

[3] SA 1891, s. 117 invalidates conditions and agreements designed to get around this rule.

[4] *Re Weir & Pitt's Contract* (1911) 55 Sol Jo 536.

[5] Land Registration Act 1925, s. 14(3) and rules 94 and 95, but note [1962] BTR 36, 384.

[6] SA 1891, s. 103.

EXEMPTIONS

General exemptions under SA 1891, Sch. 1

58: 30   Some instruments are exempt under SA 1891; others have been removed from charge by later Acts. These exemptions may be from all stamp duties,[1] a general exemption, or from a particular stamp duty—a particular exemption. A general exemption will not apply if the matter for which it is exempt is not the primary purpose of the instrument.[2] The exemptions which follow are general exemptions, SA 1891, Sch. 1.

(1) Transfers of shares in the Government or Parliamentary stocks or funds.

(2) Instruments for the transfer of ships.[2]

(3) Instruments of apprenticeship to be served in a UK colony or possession overseas.

(4) Testaments, testamentary instruments and dispositions *mortis causa* in Scotland.

(5) Instruments made by to or with the Commissioners of Public Works for any of the purposes of the Commissioners of Works Act 1852.[3]

Sergeant and Sims, p. 187 and Supplement.
[1] The exemption is only from stamp duty and so not from other charges levied by means of a stamp; *Re Elsie Inglis Memorial Fund* [1954] 1 All ER 411.
[2] See *Deddington Steamship Co Ltd v IRC* [1911] 2 KB 1001.
[3] 15 and 6 Vict. c. 28.

Exemptions under Finance and other Acts and Orders

58: 31   The following are some of the more important exemptions—

(*a*) Merchant Shipping Act 1894, ss. 563, 721, 731—various documents.

(*b*) Insolvency Act 1986, s. 378—various instruments relating to bankruptcy.

(*c*) Land Settlement (Facilities) Act 1919, s. 21—leases of allotments unless rent exceeds 50p pa or a premium is paid.

(*d*) Land Registration Act 1925, s. 130—various documents.

(*e*) Agricultural Credits Act 1928, s. 8—agricultural charges.

(*f*) Insolvency Act 1986, s. 190—various documents in winding-up.

(*g*) FA 1949, s. 35—articles of clerkship to a solicitor and apprenticeship instruments; bonds on obtaining letters of administration; charterparties (see **Sergeant and Sims, p. 215**).

(*h*) Representation of the People Act 1983, s. 21(7)—proxies.

(*i*) County Courts Act 1984, s. 79—agreement to treat County Court decisions as final.

(*j*) FA 1963, s. 65(3)—forms relating to Legal Aid.

(*k*) FA 1964, s. 23—contracts of employment and memoranda thereof (see **Sergeant and Sims, p. 235 and Supplement**).

(*l*) FA 1985, s. 96 and European Communities (Tax Exempt Securities) Order 1985, SI 1985 No. 1172 the European Economic Community, the European Coal and Steel Community, the European Atomic Energy Community and the European Investment Bank.

(*m*) FA 1986, s. 79—transfers of loan capital (see **Sergeant and Sims, pp. 340–343 and Supplement**).

(*n*) Civil Aviation Act 1982, s. 59—certain conveyances and transfers of land.

(*o*) Conveyances, transfer and leases to charities or to the National Heritage Memorial fund (FA 1982, s. 129 or to the Historic Buildings and Monuments Commission for England (FA 1983, s. 46).

(*p*) F(No. 2)A 1983, s. 15 (as amended by FA 1985, s. 82)—conveyances and transfers between local constituency associations of political parties on reorganisation of constituencies.

(*q*) FA 1987, s. 50 as amended by F(No. 2)A 1987, s. 99—extends stamp duty exemptions that already applied to gilt edged securities and to most categories of loan stock, to options to acquire or to dispose of such stock.

(*r*) FA 1989, s. 174—transfers of units in certain authorised unit trust schemes.

Certain documents relating to local authority loans and Treasury guaranteed stock are also exempt—FA 1947, s. 57. Of the privileged savings media, Trustee Savings Bank—(Trustee Savings Bank Act 1985, s. 5) and building societies (Building Societies Act 1986, s. 109 and FA 1988, s. 145 and Sch. 12, para. 8) receive special treatment; also relevant are the Friendly Societies Act 1974, s. 105 and Loan Societies Act 1840, ss. 9 and 14.

Also exempt are certain documents relating to church lands; e.g. Sharing of Church Buildings Measure 1970, s.2 and the Consecration of Churchyards Act 1867, s. 6.

There is no general exemption for conveyances on the compulsory purchase of land but there is for nationalisation schemes (FA 1946, s. 52 and various specific later Acts, e.g. Atomic Energy Authority Act 1971, s. 22). Where property is purchased under a statutory power FA 1895, s. 12 defines the document to be stamped.

Sergeant and Sims, Division 5, pp. 418–449 and Supplement.

Crown and departmental exemptions

58: 32   FA 1987, s. 55 replaces exemptions from stamp duties granted to the Secretaries of State for the Environment and Transport (but not other Secretaries of State) with a general exemption for all Government Departments. Also exempt are various documents connected with the workings of government; e.g. instruments:

(1) relating to the business of the Social Security Act 1975 (s. 163) or Industrial Injuries Acts or War Pensions (War Pensions Act 1920, s. 10);

(2) relating to and under the Diplomatic and other Privileges Act 1971;

(3) relating to various international banking bodies e.g. IMF (Bretton Woods Agreements Act 1945);

(4) relating to barracks and camps and other needs of visiting forces: FA 1960, s. 74, or

(5) relating to conveyance to reduce the National Debt or in satisfaction of IHT (FA 1946, s. 50) or relating to National Savings.

Sergeant and Sims, pp. 56, 318 and Supplement.

Charities

58: 33   No duty is charged on conveyances or transfers on sale, voluntary dispositions and leases, made to bodies of persons or trusts established for charitable purposes only. The instrument must be adjudicated[1]. The Historic Buildings and Monuments Commission for England established under the National Heritage Act 1983 is now treated as a charity for stamp duty relief purposes.[2]

Sergeant and Sims, p. 106 and Supplement.
[1] FA 1982, s. 129.
[2] FA 1983, s. 46(3).

59 Heads of charge

Introduction

59: 01   For the main part stamp duty is charged by reference to specific heads of charge but since the duty is a duty basically on instruments (see supra, § **58: 07**), rather than transactions the same head of charge may apply to many different types of transaction. In this chapter the provisions of the more important heads of charge are dealt with; this is followed by a section dealing with specific transactions or types of transaction and indicates what heads of charge might apply, how any conflict between these is resolved and how such transactions might be arranged to save duty.

CONVEYANCE OR TRANSFER ON SALE

The charge

59: 02   One of the instruments specified in SA 1891, Sch. 1 is the conveyance or transfer on sale of any property (other than stocks and shares). Duty is charged at 1% on the value of the consideration.[1] When the consideration for property other than stocks and shares is not more than £30,000 no duty is charged. A certificate of value must be furnished to qualify for the nil rate.

Sergeant and Sims, p. 106 and Supplement.
[1] FA 1984, s. 109.

Conveyance

59: 03   SA 1891, s. 54 defines a conveyance on sale as including "every instrument, and every decree or order of any court or of any commissioners, whereby any property, or any estate or interest in any property, upon the sale thereof is transferred to or vested in a purchaser, or any other person on his behalf or by his direction". If therefore the instrument transfers property[1] and does so on sale duty will be chargeable.

This definition must be broken down into its constituent elements but three general points should be noted. First, in conformity with general principle, a transfer of property on sale which does not take the form of an instrument cannot give rise to duty under this head—e.g. a sale of goods by delivery. Secondly, it is not necessary that any beneficial interest should pass under the instrument. Thirdly, it is necessary that property be transferred by

1376

the instrument; so a letter of renunciation is not a transfer of shares[2] nor is an ineffective transfer[3]. Where property of a partnership was transferred to a company it was held that there was a transfer in return for the shares in the company so that duty was due and the fact that the partners were also the shareholders was quite irrelevant.[4]

Sergeant and Sims, p. 113 and Supplement.
[1] E.g. the direction to a company to allot shares to persons nominated by the partner in *Letts v IRC* [1956] 3 All ER 588 (an assignment of a chose on action).
[2] *Re Pool Shipping Co Ltd* [1920] 1 Ch 251.
[3] *R v Ridgwell* (1827) 6 B & C 665.
[4] *John Foster & Sons Ltd v IRC* [1894] 1 QB 516.

Instrument

59: 04 The term instrument includes every written document.[1] A court order is also included in s. 54 provided it satisfies the other elements of that definition—e.g. an order sanctioning a scheme of arrangement under Companies Act 1985, s. 425[2] and a foreclosure order.[3] An order is executed when it is drawn up, passed and entered.[2]

Where a statute vests property by way of sale in a person, that person has to present a copy of the Act for stamping.[4]

Sergeant and Sims, p. 113 and Supplement.
[1] SA 1891, s. 122.
[2] *Sun Alliance Insurance Ltd v IRC* [1972] Ch 133.
[3] FA 1898, s. 6.
[4] FA 1895, s. 12.

Property

59: 05 The term property is not defined;[1] however it has been held that it does not include the grant of a mere permission—or licence—to do something on property remaining vested in the owners.[2] It has been said that property is something which belonged to a person exclusive of others and which can be the subject of bargain and sale to another; it followed that an assignment of goodwill was a transfer of property.[3] The status of know-how is uncertain; there are dicta for and against the notion that know-how is property[4] but it can clearly be the subject of bargain and sale and can, by agreement, be enjoyed to the exclusion of others; know-how has been treated as part of goodwill for bankruptcy purposes.[5] A mere covenant to pay money is presumably not a transfer of property since no property passes under the covenant.

Items which have been held to be property include goodwill,[6] copyrights,[7] debts,[8] the benefit of a contract,[9] an option[10] and a contingent interest.[11] On the other hand a right to property which in a business sense is almost certain to arise but has not yet arisen is not property.[12]

When the property to be transferred consists partly of property for which an instrument is necessary e.g. shares or land, and partly of other property, duty is saved by ensuring that the other property is not transferred by the instrument. When the instrument merely records the transfer of the other property duty may also be saved, but there are difficulties here.[13]

Sergeant and Sims, p. 121 and Supplement.
[1] Cf. IHT supra, § **37: 17.**
[2] *Conservators of the River Thames v IRC* (1886) 18 QBD 279; it was however liable to duty as an agreement.
[3] *Potter v IRC* (1854) 10 Exch 147 at 156 (Pollock CB).
[4] E.g. *Phipps v Boardman* [1967] 2 AC 46 per Lord Cohen at and Lord Hodson at 107 but contra Lord Upjohn at 127–8: see also *Handley-Page v Butterworth* (1935) 19 TC 328 per Lord Tomlin at 372 and Lord Radcliffe in *Musker v English Electric Co Ltd* (1964) 41 TC at 585.
[5] *Re Keene* [1922] 2 Ch 475.
[6] *Eastern National Omnibus Co Ltd v IRC* [1939] 1 KB 161.
[7] *Leather Cloth Co v American Leather Cloth Co* (1865) 11 HL Cas 523.
[8] *Measures Bros Ltd v IRC* (1900) 82 LT 689.
[9] *Western Abyssinian Mining Syndicate v IRC* (1935) 16 ATC 286.
[10] *George Wimpey & Co Ltd v IRC* [1975] 2 All ER 45.
[11] *Onslow v IRC* [1891] 1 QB 239; even an equitable interest—see *Grey v IRC* [1958] Ch 690 per Lord Evershed at 707.
[12] *Re Duffy* [1949] Ch 28.
[13] *Supra*, § **58: 06** see also *Stamps Comrs v Queensland Meat Export Co Ltd* [1917] AC 624.

On sale

59: 06   The rule that the conveyance be "on sale" requires a vendor, a purchaser, property sold and a price. It is satisfied if there is a contract in existence at the time of the conveyance,[1] but a separate preceding contract is not required. A conveyance at a time where no such contract exists, even though in contemplation of a sale to a particular person, is not a conveyance on sale but is now the subject of special legislation.[2] It is not necessary that the conveyance should correspond exactly with the contract;[3] it suffices that it gives effect to that contract.

The word sale suggests money[4] but this is enlarged by SA 1891, ss. 55 and 57 which provide that a transfer of property in return for stocks or securities[5] or in satisfaction of a debt[6] is to be treated as a transfer on sale. However, these exchanges are regarded as qualifications of the general principle so that a transfer of property in exchange for property other than shares or the extinction of a debt will be an exchange and so will not generally cause the transfer to be treated as being "on sale",[7] although duty may be charged under some other head.[8]

It is necessary that the transfer be on sale but this does not mean an outright sale of the vendor's entire interest. So to grant a lease may be a transfer on sale[9] as may a declaration of trust.[10]

Some element of consensus is needed for a sale, although the cases do not draw a very clear line. Thus some early stamp duty cases suggest that a compulsory acquisition is a sale[11] and more recently it has been held that the compulsory transfer of shares following a take-over under the Companies Act 1948, s. 209 (now the Companies Act 1985, ss. 428–430) is a sale, the consent of the statutory agent supplying the necessary consent.[12] However the Revenue do not treat as a sale an election by a surviving spouse of an intestate to have the matrimonial home appropriated in satisfaction of his or her claims under the intestacy legislation.

The term sale covers a multitude of transactions. Thus on the foreclosure of a mortgage the court held that there was a conveyance by sale by reason of the original agreement of mortgage.[13] Likewise there is a transfer on sale if there is an exchange of property with a cash equalisation payment,[14] or a cash payment under a deed of family arrangement.[15] In the context of a partnership it has been held to cover the transfer of a share in the partnership in return for cash[16] but not, in practice, when the new partner brings cash into the partnership and no other partner withdraws capital on that occasion. A withdrawal of capital by a partner under the terms of the partnership agreement generally operates as a partition carrying fixed duty of 50p and not as a transfer or sale.[17] Stamp duty is also arrived at by taking the amount due to the retiring partner and then giving a receipt absolving the other partners from all liability.[18]

On the liability of a conveyance in contemplation of a sale see infra, § **59: 17**.

Sergeant and Sims, pp. 123–129 and Supplement.

[1] *Ridge Nominees v IRC* [1962] Ch 376.

[2] FA 1965, s. 90 nullifying *Wm Cory & Son Ltd v IRC* [1965] AC 1088, see infra, § **59: 17**.

[3] *A-G v Brown* (1849) 3 Exch 662.

[4] *Littlewoods Mail Order Stores Ltd v IRC* [1963] AC 135 at 152 per Viscount Simonds.

[5] SA 1891, s. 55; for an attempt to depreciate the value of shares between agreement and conveyance see *Fitch Lovell Ltd v IRC* [1962] 3 All ER 685; on valuation see *Hatrick v IRC* [1963] NZLR 641.

[6] SA 1891, s. 57. The position as to conveyances in consideration of a debt is now often regulated by FA 1980, s. 102.

[7] *Littlewoods Mail Order Stores v IRC* (*supra*). An exchange of shares has been held to come within this category of sale by reason of s. 55—*J & P Coats Ltd v IRC* [1897] 2 QB 423.

[8] E.g. exchange of realty—50p fixed duty infra, § **59: 38**.

[9] *Littlewoods Mail Order Stores Ltd v IRC* (*supra*).

[10] Such a declaration will, if oral, escape s. 54 (see *West London Syndicate Ltd v IRC* [1898] 2 QB 507 at 520)—but may be caught by s. 59 infra, § **59: 18**.

[11] E.g. *IRC v Glasgow and South Western Rly* (1887) 12 App Cas 315, but cf. *Kirkness v John Hudson & Co* [1955] AC 696. See **Sergeant and Sims, pp. 123–124 and Supplement.**

[12] *Ridge Nominees v IRC* [1962] Ch 376. See also *Sun Alliance Insurance Ltd v IRC* [1972] Ch 133 (s. 306).

[13] *Huntington v IRC* [1896] 1 QB 422 since affirmed by FA 1898, s. 6.

[14] *Littlewoods Mail Order Stores Ltd v IRC* [1963] AC 135 at 151 per Viscount Simonds.

[15] *Bristol v IRC* [1901] 2 KB 336.

[16] *Christie v IRC* (1866) LR 2 Exch 46; see also **Sergeant and Sims, pp. 14, 30 and Supplement.**

[17] *Macleod v IRC* (1885) 12 R (Ct of Sess) 105.

[18] *Garnett v IRC* (1899) 81 LT 633.

Consideration

(a)   Generally

59: 07   The duty on a transfer on sale is charged ad valorem on the amount or value of the consideration.[1] The value of cash consideration is straightforward, but it has been held that interest on the sum due is to be ignored;[2] foreign currency is valued at the current rate of exchange at the date of the instrument.[3] Quoted stocks and securities are meant to be valued at the average price on the relevant date but, in practice, the CGT rule is used.[4] Unquoted shares are valued by whatever means may be appropriate.[5]

If the consideration consists of unmarketable securities it is taken to be the amount due at the date of the conveyance for principal and interest.[6] A sum payable only on breach of a term of the agreement is not consideration.[7]

There are special provisions for reducing the consideration on the sale of houses at discount by local authorities.[8]

(b) Value added tax

FA 1989, s. 18 and Sch. 3 make important changes in the system of VAT on supplies relating to buildings and land. The question arises as to the treatment of VAT in determining consideration for the purpose of stamp duty. It affects the stamp duty on leases also. This is of considerable importance to conveyancers. The position appears to be as follows. It is, of course, subject to the important proviso that it is essential to consider the terms of any particular instrument before determining the stamp duty position. It is considered that stamp duty would be correctly chargeable in law on any VAT element in either the sale price of a new—or used—non-domestic building, or the rent charged therefor. In other words consideration for stamp duty is inclusive of VAT.

The position may be further explained thus. To take sales first, it is implicit in VATA 1983, s. 10(2) that the consideration for the "supply" is the gross amount of the consideration inclusive of VAT. So where VAT is payable, the stamp duty charge falls on the total consideration. This is of course the position already with sales of businesses or business assets subject to VAT. It follows that on the coming into effect of these changes on non-domestic construction, sales of non-domestic buildings will likewise fall into this category.

As to rent, there are two separate situations to be considered and distinguished.

The first is where the VAT actually forms part of the rental consideration. This would be the case where the rent is reserved by reference to a net amount plus VAT, producing a gross rental figure, on which it seems that stamp duty is chargeable. In the alternative case, where the VAT does not form part of the rent, it will be regarded as a separate item of consideration— but still within the charge to stamp duty. The landlord is not able to add VAT to the rent (or any increase in the rate of VAT) where the terms of the lease or tenancy specifically prevent him from passing on VAT to the lessee or tenant.

Sergeant and Sims, pp. 129–133 and Supplement.

[1] On inclusion of an offer made to the vendors by a third party see *Central and District Properties Ltd v IRC* [1966] 2 All ER 433.

[2] *Hotung v Collector of Stamp Revenue* [1965] AC 766.

[3] SA 1891, s. 6 and FA 1985, s. 88.

[4] See § **21: 04**.

[5] SA 1891, s. 6: The inheritance tax provisions in IHTA 1984, s. 168 (§ **46: 09**) do not apply.

[6] SA 1891, s. 6.

[7] *Western United Investment Co Ltd v IRC* [1958] Ch 392.

[8] FA 1981, s. 107, as amended by FA 1984, s. 110.

Periodical payments as consideration

59: 08   When the consideration consists of periodical payments, SA 1891, s. 56 provides a special set of rules. A covenant to pay a balance of purchase money in instalments comes within these rules.[1]

(*a*) Where there is a definite period of payment not exceeding 20 years so that the total can be ascertained, that total is the consideration.

(*b*) Where the period is definite but will exceed 20 years, or is in perpetuity or indefinite (but not terminable with life) the total payable during the next 20 years is taken.[2]

(*c*) Where the period is for life or lives, the amount payable for the next 12 years is taken.

It appears that a period for a certain number of years but terminable on earlier events is to be treated as being for the definite period of that number of years[3] with the result that payments for the life of A will come within rule (*c*) but payments for 20 years or until A dies whichever shall first happen will come within rule (*a*). It has also been held that money is payable periodically even though payments may be contingent.[4] In determining the amount of the consideration, the contingency principle must be borne in mind. It is the amount of consideration calculated under these rules which is relevant for determining whether the reduced rates apply.

It has been held that where a sum of money only becomes due at a particular time if the contract is broken, one should ignore that possibility.[5] So when the sums were payable in 125 annual instalments but the sums remaining would become due immediately in the event of default it was held that the chargeable amount of the consideration was the total of the first 20 scheduled payments—rule (*b*) being applied.

Sergeant and Sims, pp. 135–137 and Supplement.

[1] *Limmer Asphalte Paving Co Ltd v IRC* (1872) LR 7 Exch 211.
[2] *Blendett v IRC, Quietlece v IRC* [1984] STC 95, CA.
[3] *Earl Mount Edgecumbe v IRC* [1911] 2 KB 24.
[4] *Underground Electric Railways Ltd v IRC* [1906] AC 21; this is similar to the element of recurrence, in Schedule D, Case III, § 9: 63.
[5] *Western United Investment Co Ltd v IRC* [1958] Ch 392.

Discharge of debts and liabilities as consideration

59: 09   If A owes B £60,000 and A transfers property to B for £40,000 plus release of the debt, duty is chargeable on £100,000. This is because SA 1891, s. 57 provides that if property is conveyed in consideration of a debt due to the transferee duty is payable on the amount of the debt. The debt need not have been due from the transferor.

This section also provides that when property is conveyed subject, whether contingently or absolutely, to the payment or transfer of any money or stock, the money or stock is subject to duty. So if a mortgagor assigns his equity of redemption and the assignee assumes the liability to pay the mortgage debt, duty is due not only on the purchase price but also the amount of the liability taken over. Another example is where the purchaser agrees to pay the vendor's legal costs. The rule that it is the amount of the debt that is taken into account—not its value (so a bad debt is included at face value)[1] gave rise to uncertainty and dissatisfaction. The position is now largely regulated by FA 1980, s. 102. Where property is conveyed wholly or in part in consideration of a debt due to the transferee the duty chargeable is now limited by reference to the value of the property conveyed if this is less than the amount of the debt. However, that rule is somewhat limited in its application; see further **Sergeant and Sims, pp. 137, 291–292 and Supplement.**

Not all liabilities increase the chargeable value. On an assignment of a lease one does not take into account the liability of the assignee to pay the rent. This is because the liability to pay rent is inherent in the property, like the liability to pay a call on shares.[2] Likewise the future interest element on an assignment of a mortgage is to be ignored.

Sergeant and Sims, pp. 137, 291–292 and Supplement.

[1] *IRC v North British Rly Co* 1901 4 F (Ct of Sess) 27 but note *Huntington v IRC* [1896] 1 QB 422, where it was held that the consideration is not to exceed the value of the property.

[2] *Swayne v IRC* [1900] 1 QB 172.

Apportionment of consideration

59: 10   If there are separate conveyances for separate parts of the property, the consideration is to be apportioned among the conveyances as the parties may see fit.[1] When the different parts go to different people, as where A buys for A, B and C, the consideration must be specified in each conveyance.[2]

Where there are several instruments to complete the purchaser's title, only the principal instrument is chargeable with ad valorem duty, the others bearing such duty as may be appropriate, e.g., as miscellaneous transfers, but not so as to exceed the duty on the principal instrument.[3] It is for the parties to determine which is to be the principal instrument.[4]

Sergeant and Sims, pp. 139–142 and Supplement.

[1] SA 1891, s. 58(1).

[2] SA 1891, s. 58(2).

[3] SA 1891, s. 58(3).

[4] SA 1891, s. 61.

Sub-sales

59: 11   A common problem of sub-sale is dealt with by SA 1891, s. 58 which, as amended by FA 1984, s. 112, provides that in specified circumstances ad valorem duty need not be paid twice. So where P has contracted to purchase property from V but has not yet obtained a conveyance and he contracts to sell it to R, the conveyance from V to R is charged on the consideration due from R to P, not that due from P to V;[1] originally this applied whether the R-P consideration was more or less than the P–V consideration but now if the sub-sale was agreed after 19th March 1984 this does not apply when the consideration for the sub-sale is less than the value of the property immediately before the sub-sale was agreed (except where the sub-sale falls within FA 1981, s. 107 and FA 1984, s. 110—certain sales at a discount). For this relief to operate P must not have taken a conveyance for V. Further the property conveyed to R must be the property which P had agreed to purchase from V. It was observed in *Fitch-Lovell v IRC*,[2] that the point is, in a sense, of a metaphysical character, rather like the familiar dilemma whether a river is still the same river at different points, but he concluded that where the agreement related to shares the rights of which had changed before the transfer to R, the relief in s. 58(4) should not apply notwithstanding the fact that both contract and transfer related to ordinary shares in the company. The same case seems to exclude the relief under s. 58(4) where P's contract to sell to R precedes the contract to buy from V.

When the sub-sale is to several persons the duty is on the value of the consideration moving from the sub-purchasers subject to exceptions.[3] When there is a sub-sale of part of the property to R, the remainder being transferred to P, *Maples v IRC*[4] decides that the duty is charged on the consideration moving from R together with an apportioned part of consideration from P to V; it is *not* charged on the whole of the consideration from P to V less the sum recouped from R.

Where the sub-contract is not one of sale but rather of exchange, duty on the conveyance to R should be that on an exchange; as there is no transfer to P there can be no duty on a sale.

Sergeant and Sims, pp. **141–142** and Supplement.

[1] SA 1891, s. 58(4) as amended by FA 1984, s. 112(1); but distinguish the case when duty has been charged on the V–P contract as an agreement to sell—infra, § **59: 18**.

[2] [1962] 1 WLR 1325 at 1341–1344. There the change flowed from the creation of a class of preferred shareholders which effectively took all the distributable profit. The device of omitting to insert the transferee's name is now unlawful; FA 1963, s. 67.

[3] SA 1891, s. 58(5) as amended by FA 1984, s. 112(1).

[4] [1914] 3 K B 303.

Sale of an annuity

59: 12   The creation of an annuity by grant or conveyance in return for consideration in money or shares will attract duty as a transfer on sale. The narrow scope of this rule is extended by SA 1891, s. 60 which provides that "where upon the sale of an annuity or other right not before in existence, such annuity or other right is not created by actual grant or conveyance, but is only secured by bond, warrant of attorney, covenant, contract or otherwise, the bond or other instrument, or some one of such instruments, if there be more than one, is to be charged with the same duty as an actual grant or conveyance on sale . . ."

For this rule to apply there must be a sale as opposed to an exchange. The words "other right not before in existence" are vague but it has been held that the right must be one the sale of which can be completed by grant or conveyance.[1]

There are two exceptions. Purchased life annuities are now subject to Bond Covenant duty at a lower rate[2] and the purchase of an annuity certain for a definite number of years is now not dutiable at all.[3]

Sergeant and Sims, pp. **149–152** and Supplement.

[1] See Collins LJ in *Great Northern Rly v IRC* [1901] 1 K B 416 at 426.

[2] On instruments made before 1st January 1990, see infra, § **59: 40**.

[3] FA 1971, s. 64 repealed the only applicable sub-heads of charge.

Rates of duty and certificate of value

59: 13   The rates of duty are set out in FA 1984, s. 109 and in FA 1986, s. 64 and in the tables of rates and reliefs, supra.

For transfers of property other than stock or marketable securities where the consideration does not exceed £30,000 the duty is nil. The nil rate of duty operates only if the instrument is certified as being for a consideration not exceeding the sum of £30,000.[1] Certification requiries that the instruments contain a statement certifying that the transaction does not form part of a large transaction or series of transactions in respect of which the amount or value, or aggregate amount or value of the consideration exceeds the relevant figure.[2] The sanction against abuse of this rule is SA 1891, s. 5 supra, § **58: 28.** The section thus depends on the good faith of the parties or their advisers.

Freedom from ad valorem duty also ensures freedom from miscellaneous conveyance transfer duty.[2]

---

[1] FA 1958, s. 34; the certification must be in the instrument although the Revenue allow this to be added later. **Sergeant and Sims, p. 107 and Supplement.**

[2] *A-G v Lamplough* (1878) 3 Ex D 214.

One transaction

59: 14   The question whether the transaction forms part of a larger transaction is a complex one and one on which there is little guidance in the cases. Some guidelines based on decisions have been suggested.[1]

(1) Purchases between the same parties at public auctions in separate lots are not one transaction;[2] the reasoning that there is no contractual linkage may apply equally to purchases by private treaty but the Revenue would require strong evidence.

(2) A simultaneous related transaction which is not a sale, may be disregarded.[3]

(3) Transactions between different and non-associated persons should be disregarded even if part of one transaction.

However,

(4) all property transferred by sale should be included, whether or not by the instrument, unless statute directs otherwise. So a sum paid for fixtures should be included,[4] but on the sale of a business, goods, wares and merchandise not actually conveyed by the instrument may be omitted.[5]

(5) A succession of sales governed by a single master agreement constitutes a series of transactions and so each forms part of a larger transaction.

---

[1] **Sergeant and Sims, p. 108 and Supplement.**

[2] *A-G v Cohen* [1936] 1 KB 478 and [1937] 1 KB 478.

[3] *Kimbers & Co v IRC* [1937] 1 KB 132 and *Paul v Paul* 1936 SC 443.

[4] See further infra, § **60: 02.**

[5] Because FA 1958, s. 34(4)(*a*) is expressed so.

Criticism

59: 15   The consultative document issued by the Inland Revenue[1] highlights criticism of these rates pointing out that it produces sharp increases in duty.

This is because the present scale is a 'slab' scale i.e. the rate of duty appropriate to a given value is applied to the whole of that value, as opposed to a 'slice' scale under which the duty on a given value becomes the aggregate of the duty on the successive slices of value over which the total changeable values spreads, each slice being charged at a rate appropriate to that slice. The document made five suggestions for removing or reducing these sharp increases in duty.

One problem which would arise if a 'slice' scale is introduced is that where there is one transaction but several conveyances presented for stamping at different times each conveyance would be subject to the sliding scale. In this case the duty payable would probably have to be apportioned on the basis of a certificate of the total value of the transaction.

---

[1] Inland Revenue consultative document: *The scope for reforming stamp duties*, issued March 1983.

Exemptions

59: 16   Among transfers which are exempt from this head of duty are:

(*a*) transfers of shares in a building society;[1]
(*b*) transfers to a stock exchange nominee and other such transactions;[2]
(*c*) certain securities issued by international organisations;[3]
(*d*) securities issued by European Communities and the European Investment Bank.[4]

The exceptions for transfers forming part of company reconstruction[5] and those between associated companies[6] should also be borne in mind—as well as the general exemptions from stamp duty.[7]

Sergeant and Sims, p. 110 and Supplement.
[1] Building Societies Act 1986, s. 109. See also FA 1988, s. 145, Sch. 12, para. 8.
[2] FA 1976, s. 127 and FA 1986, s. 114 and Sch. 23, Part IX, infra, § **61: 04**.
[3] FA 1984, s. 126.
[4] FA 1985, s. 96.
[5] Infra, § **62: 06**.
[6] Infra, § **62: 01**.
[7] Supra, § **58: 30**.

Conveyance or transfer in contemplation of a sale

59: 17   Originally, a conveyance or transfer in contemplation of a sale was not charged since it was not made on sale;[1] but it is now charged as if it were on a sale (FA 1965, s. 90 as amended by FA 1985, s. 82 and Sch. 27, Part IX), the consideration being the value of the property (see further § **59: 07**, supra). It must be submitted for adjudication.[2]

If the contemplated sale does not materialise and the property is transferred back to the transferor (or his successor in title on death or bankruptcy) the duty will be repaid. If the price on the sale is less than that assessed on the original transfer, excess duty is repaid.

A sale is contemplated when both parties intend it but do not say so.[3]

Sergeant and Sims, pp. 115, 236 and Supplement.
[1] *Wm Cory & Son Ltd v IRC* [1965] AC 1088 supra.
[2] FA 1965, s. 90(3).
[3] **Sergeant and Sims, p. 302 and Supplement.**

Agreements for sale

59: 18   A contract or agreement for the sale of:

(*a*) any equitable interest in any property; or

(*b*) any estate or interest in property other than:

   (*i*) land;

   (*ii*) foreign property;

   (*iii*) goods, wares or merchandise;

   (*iv*) stock or marketable securities; or

   (*v*) ships;

is charged with the same ad valorem duty as if it were an actual conveyance on sale under SA 1891, s. 59. The section applies only if the agreement is written or under seal; oral contracts are outside its scope as are contracts made outside the UK.

This section was designed to nullify *IRC v Angus*[1] which had held that an agreement for the sale of goodwill, although specifically enforceable in equity, was not a conveyance on sale, a contract to convey being different from a conveyance. The section provides that the subsequent conveyance shall bear no duty although a sub-sale gives rise to ad valorem duty if the consideration is greater than that under the contract;[2] the conveyance carries a denoting stamp duty denoting the duty paid on the agreement.[3] Any apportionment of consideration in the event of sub-sale must be bona fide.[4]

An example of the section in operation is an agreement to hold property on trust for another in return for money or stock.[5] Where the contract was to transfer a legal estate but with an option in the vendor to declare himself a trustee for the purchaser instead it was held that this was not an agreement for the sale of an equitable interest.[6] It has also been held that an option to buy is a mere offer to sell and so not an agreement for sale under s. 59; likewise, the acquisition of an option is not the same as an agreement for the sale of an equitable interest but rather a transfer of the option and so a transfer of property which, if for consideration, is a transfer on sale.[7]

Sergeant and Sims, pp. 142–149 and Supplement.
[1] (1889) 23 QBD 579.
[2] SA 1891, s. 59(2); there is no rebate if the consideration on the sub-sale is less.
[3] SA 1891, s. 59(3).
[4] *West London Syndicate v IRC* [1898] 2 QB 507 at 526.
[5] *Chesterfield Brewery Co v IRC* [1899] 2 QB 7 at 12 per Wills J: the court also held that this was a conveyance on sale.
[6] [1898] 2 QB 507 at 512 but it was an agreement for the sale of property other than land and so chargeable under the section.
[7] *Wm Cory & Son Ltd v IRC* [1965] AC 1088 at 1107–1110.

MISCELLANEOUS FIXED CONVEYANCE OR TRANSFER DUTY

59: 19 Conveyance or transfer duty is also charged on a "conveyance or transfer of any other kind not hereinbefore described"; the duty is 50p. This head is however limited to any "instrument and every decree of any court or of any commissioners, whereby any property on any occasion, except a sale or mortgage, is transferred to or vested in any person . . ."[1] A voluntary disposition would now be chargeable under this head unless appropriately certified as exempt (see supra, § **58: 04**).

The exclusion of sale is because ad valorem duty is charged on such transfers by other provisions; mortgage duty and voluntary disposition duty were also separate charges until their abolition in 1971 and 1985 respectively. Although sale is excluded, the structure of this head of charge includes the requirements of an instrument and a transfer of property like that head; so, as with that head, there is no need for a transfer of any beneficial interest in the property.

Examples are numerous. A conveyance in consideration of service is not a sale, since there is no money passing. However, many instruments which would have attracted the fixed duty under this head are now exempt if appropriately certified (see supra, § **58: 04**). A conveyance to a residuary legatee, to a beneficiary under a settlement or under the exercise of a power of advancement or by a liquidator to a shareholder in the course of a winding up[2] are all examples of such.

Sergeant and Sims, p. 111 and Supplement.
[1] On construction note Lord Evershed in *Littlewoods Mail Order Stores Ltd v IRC* [1961] Ch 597 at 624. See also *GHR Co Ltd v IRC* [1943] K B 303.
[2] *Henty & Constable (Brewers) Ltd v IRC* [1961] 3 All ER 1146.

CONVEYANCE OR TRANSFER BY WAY OF VOLUNTARY DISPOSITION OR IN CONTEMPLATION OF A SALE

Abolition of the charge on Voluntary Dispositions

59: 20 The ad valorem stamp duty formerly chargeable by virtue of F (1909–10) A 1910, s. 74(1) (gifts inter vivos) is abolished.[1]

Conveyances or transfers by way of gift are no longer liable to the 50p fixed duty if appropriately certified (see supra, § **58: 04**). Also if appropriately certified they no longer require an adjudication stamp. FA 1985 contains a provision to enable regulations to be made to exempt voluntary dispositions from this requirement[2] and these have now been made (see supra, § **58: 04**).

Sergeant and Sims, pp. 312–313 and Supplement.
[1] FA 1985, s. 82.
[2] FA 1985, s. 87.

Conveyance or transfer

59: 21 SA 1891, s. 54 which defines a conveyance on sale (supra, § **59: 03**) applies and has received a wide construction. An appointment under a general power is a conveyance.[1] A release of an interest is a conveyance[2] but a disclaimer is thought not to be one since it operates as an avoidance and not as a disposition.[3] An order under the Variation of Trusts Acts 1958 is a conveyance.[4]

Sergeant and Sims, pp. 113–133 and Supplement.
[1] *Fuller v IRC* [1950] 2 All ER 976.
[2] *Thorn v IRC* [1976] STC 208, but not the consent by a life tenant to the exercise of the power of advancement—*Re Pauling's Settlement* [1962] 1 WLR 86 at 115.
[3] *Re Paradise Motor Co Ltd* [1968] 2 All ER 625.
[4] *Thorn v IRC* supra.

Settlements—Power to re-invest or forfeit

59: 22 The following provisions now relate only to conveyances or transfers in contemplation of a sale. The amount of ad valorem duty relates to the value of the interest transferred and difficulties of valuation are apparent. Where only a revocable interest is transferred that contingency must be taken into account in valuing the interest. This principle means that the valuation of a revocable interest must take into account the possibility of revocation.[1] This led to the use of powers of revocation followed by their release, the former being of little value, so giving rise to little duty and the latter only to fixed duty of 50p as a deed or a release. To combat this FA 1965, s. 90(5) as amended by FA 1985, s. 82(3)[2] provided that the valuation should ignore any power (in any person) to cause the property to revest in the seller or in any person on his behalf; the same applies to forfeitable annuities and life or other interests reserved out of property. The words on his behalf are not immediately clear and it is questionable whether a termination causing the property to revest in the seller's spouse or child could be caught. Likewise there must be a power to revoke; termination on an event is not caught. It is provided that duty will be refunded if the power is exercised within two years.

Sergeant and Sims, pp. 237–239, 312 and Supplement.
[1] *Stanyforth v IRC* [1930] AC 339.
[2] See also FA 1985, s. 82, Sch. 27, Part IX which repeals sub-s. (5).

LEASE OR TACK

The charge

59: 23 The principal charge under the heading "lease or tack" head (3) charges stamp duty when the lease is for a definite term of one year or more or for any indefinite term.[1] The charge is ad valorem and is on the rent or the premium or both if both are paid. The lease must be of lands, tenements or heritable subjects so that leases of chattels are excluded. The word lease, which is not defined, is construed as excluding licences so a licence of real property is not chargeable.[2] A written acknowledgment of an existing lease is not a lease[3] but an instrument withdrawing a valid notice to determine a lease is treated as a new lease.[4]

The charge arises on the grant of a lease; the assignment or surrender of a lease will give rise to conveyance on sale duty if in return for cash or marketable securities.

The other heads of charge are:

(2) for any definite term less than a year:

(a) of any furnished dwelling house or apartment when the rent for such term exceeds £500—£1.

(b) of any lands, tenements or heritable subjects except or otherwise than as aforesaid—the same duty as a lease for a year at the rent reserved for the definite term.

(4) of any other kind whatsoever not hereinbefore described £2.

Duty on the lease of a furnished dwelling house when the rent is £500 or less, and so outside (2)(a), will be nil because the table applied by (2)(b) so provides. There is no duty on a premium on such a lease.

Head (4) is presumably confined to leases of land although this is not explicitly stated. It applies when heads (2) and (3) do not as when, even after applying the contingency principle, the rent cannot be stated; the same applies when there is no certain premium. When a lease contains both an ascertainable rent and an uncertain one, duty will be chargeable under heads (2) or (3), as appropriate on the certain rent, and under head (4) on the uncertain one.

In certain cases of shared ownership transactions the lease is chargeable not under the head "Lease" but under the head "Conveyance or Transfer on Sale".[5]

As to the interaction of VAT and stamp duty following the changes to VAT on supplies relating to buildings and land under the FA 1989, s. 18 and Sch. 3 see §§ **59: 07**(b), *supra.*

Sergeant and Sims, pp. 158–164 and Supplement.

[1] SA 1891, Sch. 1 Lease or Tack (3).

[2] The Revenue place great reliance on the test in *Addiscombe Garden Estates Ltd v Crabbe* [1958] 1 QB 513 (CA).

[3] *Eagleton v Gutteridge* (1843) 11 M & W 465.

[4] *Freeman v Evans* [1922] 1 Ch 36, CA.

[5] FA 1980, s. 97.

Leases—duration

59: 24   This question is important for determining both the head of charge and the amount of duty. In deciding whether a lease is for a definite term statute provides that a lease for a fixed term and thereafter until determined should be treated as a lease for a definite term equal to the fixed term together with such further period as must elapse before the earliest date at which the lease can be determined.[1] A lease for a certain period but terminable on some event is not within this rule but, it has been held, is to be treated as a definite term for the certain period.[2] As a lease for an indefinite term, e.g.

until the end of the war,[3] is void, it appears that the phrase "indefinite term" refers to periodic tenancies like weekly and monthly tenancies and tenancies at will. A lease for x years with an option to renew for y years is treated as a lease for x years and not one for x + y years.[4]

A lease expressed to commence on a date prior to the instrument is regarded as starting on the date of execution.[5]

Sergeant and Sims, pp. 163–164 and Supplement.
[1] FA 1963, s. 56(3).
[2] *Earl Mount Edgecumbe v IRC* [1911] 2 K B 24.
[3] *Lace v Chandler* [1944] K B 368.
[4] *Hand v Hall* (1877) 2 Ex D 355.
[5] (1963) 60 *Law Society's Gazette* pp. 175–176.

Duty on rent

59: 25   The duty is charged ad valorem on the rent charged. The table reproduced in the table of rates and reliefs, supra, shows that the rate increases with the length of the lease and has an initial sliding scale. As to VAT see §§ **59: 07**(*b*), *supra*.

It will be seen from that that the rate of duty rises sharply with the duration of the lease so that a lease of 60 years will carry duty of 12% of the rent, whereas one of 30 years will carry duty of only 2%. One method of reducing the duty on a long lease is to grant an initial lease for 20 years and then a lease of the reversion for the balance of 40 years.[1] There is no rule aggregating the leases in such circumstances.[2] The first lease will carry duty at 2% and the reversionary lease will carry fixed duty of £2 under head (4).

Where the consideration is payable for a definite period exceeding 20 years the charge is limited to the amount payable during the 20 year period. This relief, however, applies only to sums "payable periodically for" the period; such sums must be payable within the period.[3]

Sergeant and Sims, pp. 162–163 and Supplement.
[1] See *Precedents for the Conveyancer*, Vol. I, p. 2910. The editor points out that the initial lease should not be for 21 years or more because of LPA 1925, s. 149(3), and that the lease can be voluntarily registered under the Land Registration Rules 1925, r. 47.
[2] Cf TA 1988, s. 38; supra, § **9: 19**.
[3] *Blendett v IRC, Quietlece v IRC* [1984] STC 95, CA.

Rents

59: 26   The term rent is not defined for stamp duty.[1] It has been defined as the recompense paid by the tenant to the landlord for the exclusive possession of the land; this payment must be reserved out of the land.[2]

The head of charge refers to the rate "or average rate" of the yearly rent. These words refer to the possibility of a varying rent level. So if a lease is at a rent of £3,000 p.a. for the first 30 years and a peppercorn for the next 15 it will be treated as a lease for 45 years at a rent of £2,000 p.a.[3]

When the rent is variable the contingency principle (supra § **58: 15**) may apply. In *Coventry City Council v IRC*[4] rent was due under a sublease from the council to a developer; that rent was expressed to be 8.142% of the total expenditure up to a maximum of £130,000. Brightman J held that stamp duty was due on a rent equal to 8.142% of £130,000 even though the actual rent might not be that percentage of that figure. If the maximum figure had not been inserted, no duty would have been payable by reason of the uncertainty of the consideration; the same reason prevented any duty from being claimed by the Crown on rent in the form of sums equal to a share of the annual rents received by the corporation from occupants of the building in excess of a certain minimum. However rent due in the form of a sum equal to that paid by the developer under the headlease was taken into account.

Any penal rent, or increased rent in the nature of a penal rent, is ignored for stamp duty.[5] A penal rent is an additional rent becoming payable if the lessee breaks a covenant in the lease.[6] However, if the lessee has a choice between paying an increased rent and doing—or not doing—some act, the increased rent is not penal.[7]

If a lease is granted for consideration, whether rent or premium, in respect of which it is chargeable with ad valorem duty and in further consideration of a covenant to improve the property, no duty is chargeable on the further consideration.[8] However this section does not apply if this covenant would be subject to ad valorem stamp duty if it were in a conveyance by itself.[9]

Where the rent or premium under a new lease is partly in consideration of the surrender or abandonment of an existing lease, no duty is chargeable in respect of that consideration. However duty may be chargeable on the surrender either as a surrender-fixed duty of 50p—or as a sale should the landlord pay money for the surrender.

Service charges will not be dutiable as part of the consideration unless they are reserved as rent; how they will then be charged depends on whether they are ascertainable.

An instrument increasing the rent under the term of the lease does not cause a surrender and regrant of the lease and so is the subject of a special rule; bond, covenant duty is due on the additional rent charged.[10]

Sergeant and Sims, pp. 160–167 and Supplement.

[1] See *Gable Construction Co Ltd v IRC* [1968] 1 WLR 1426 at 1435.

[2] For the distinction between a rent and a premium see *Hill v Booth* [1930] 1 KB 381 and *Samuel v Salmon & Gluckstein* [1946] Ch 8; on that between rent and royalties see *T and E Homes Ltd v Robinson* [1976] STC 462.

[3] The head of charge thus nullifies *Pearson v IRC* (1868) LR 3 Exch 242.

[4] [1979] Ch142, [1978] 1 All ER 1107.

[5] SA 1891, s. 77(1).

[6] E.g. he fails to follow a stipulated system of cultivation—*Fuller v Fenwick* (1846) 3 CB 705.

[7] *French v Macale* (1842) 2 Dr & War 269.

[8] SA 1891, s. 77(2), this is similar to FA 1900, s. 10 (which relates to conveyances on sale).

[9] FA 1909, s. 8 enacted to nullify *British Electric Traction v IRC* [1902] 1 KB 441, CA—the covenant would have been liable to bond covenant duty but the charge was repealed for electricity by FA 1958, s. 35(1) and the remaining heads were almost all abolished by FA 1971, s. 64.

[10] SA 1891, s. 77(5).

Duty on premium

59: 27 When the consideration or part of the consideration for the lease moves to the lessor, or some other person, and consists of money, stock or securities, duty is charged ad valorem in the same way as would be charged on a conveyance or sale. So there is a nil rate if the premium does not exceed £30,000 and the rent does not exceed £300 p.a. Otherwise it will be 1%.[1] Payment by the lessee of the lessor's legal fees on the grant of the lease is ignored;[2] however if the landlord incurs expenses before the lease at the lessor's request and the lessee reimburses the landlord those payments are taken into account as a premium.[3] A premium payable periodically is chargeable on the basis in SA 1891, s. 56.[4]

The reliefs from conveyance on sale duty in FA 1930, s. 42 do not apply to this duty.[5]

Sergeant and Sims, p. 167 and Supplement.
[1] FA 1982, s. 128.
[2] (1959) *Law Society's Gazette* p. 95.
[3] Sergeant and Sims, p. 167 and Supplement.
[4] *Blendett v IRC, Quietlece v IRC* [1984] STC 95, CA.
[5] Sergeant and Sims, p. 365 and Supplement.

Agreement for a lease

59: 28   An agreement for a lease entered into after 19th March 1984 is chargeable as if it were the actual lease irrespective of the length of the term.[1] Unlike the analogous provision for sale agreements there is no provision for re-payment of duty if the agreement is cancelled.[2]

Where the duty has been paid on an agreement for a lease, the duty payable on a lease granted pursuant to such agreement is reduced by the amount of duty already paid.[3]

Where a freehold or leasehold interest is conveyed or transferred or a lease is granted subject to an agreement for a lease for a term exceeding 35 years (which is not directly enforceable against any intermediate interest in the land) the duty paid on the agreement must be denoted on the conveyance, transfer or lease.[4]

An agreement for a lease for a term of seven years or more also requires a produced stamp; there is no need to produce the subsequent lease.[5]

Sergeant and Sims, p. 167 and Supplement.
[1] SA 1891, s. 75, as amended by FA 1984, s. 111. In Scotland a concluded contract is a lease.
[2] SA 1891, s. 75(2) as amended by FA 1984, s. 111.
[3] FA 1984, s. 111(1).
[4] FA 1984, s. 111(2).
[5] FA 1931, s. 28.

Shared ownership transactions

59: 29   FA 1987 s. 54 amends FA 1980, s. 97 and FA 1981, s. 108 which limit the duty payable on a shared ownership lease, to take account of recent changes to the shared ownership scheme. Section 54(1) amends the list of lessees to which FA 1980, s. 97 applies to include unregistered as well as registered housing associations. The Housing and Planning Act 1986 brought within the shared ownership scheme leases granted by unregistered housing associations.

FA 1987, s. 54(2) extends the reliefs provided by FA 1980, s. 97 and FA 1981, s. 108 to leases granted by a private landlord who has taken over a public housing estate. FA 1988, s. 142(1) extends relief under FA 1980, s. 97 to a housing action trust established under the Housing Act 1988, Part III. FA 1988, s. 142(2) similarly extends the relief under FA 1981, s. 107 to a housing action trust established under the Housing Act 1988, Part III. The Housing Act 1985, s. 171A inserted by the Housing and Planning Act 1986, preserves a tenant's right to be granted a shared ownership lease when an estate is privatised.

Subsection (3) defines the category of leases to which sub-s. (2) applies.

Subsection (4) provides that the section applies to leases granted on or after 1st August 1987.

See also the Local Government Reorganisation (Preservation of Right to Buy) Order 1986, SI 1986, No. 2092.

OTHER HEADS OF CHARGE

Appointment

59: 30   There is no longer a duty of 50p on an instrument appointing a new trustee or on one in execution of a power of any property, or for any use, shares or interest in any property, by an instrument not being a will, the duty having been abolished by FA 1985, s. 85 and Sch. 24.

Sergeant and Sims, pp. 289, 295 and Supplement.

Bearer instruments

59: 31   This charge which was introduced by FA 1963, s. 59 is dealt with in the section dealing with companies at infra, §§ **61: 13–61: 19**.

Bills of sale

59: 32   An absolute bill of sale is liable to ad valorem duty as a conveyance on sale; a bill of sale cannot be registered unless a duly stamped original is produced.[1]

Sergeant and Sims, p. 103 and Supplement.
[1] SA 1891, s. 41.

Bonds, covenants or instruments of any kind whatsoever

59: 33   This duty is charged on superannuation and life annuities, (but see § **59: 40**, infra) and now also on instruments increasing the rent reserved by another instrument.[1] When the amount of lease duty is less than that of the bond duty it is the amount due under the former which applies, but it is still bond duty; what happens in the converse case is unclear.[2]

Sergeant and Sims, pp. 103–105 and Supplement.
[1] FA 1971, s. 64(1)(*a*)(i); SA 1891, s. 77(5).
[2] See *Gable Construction Co Ltd v IRC* [1968] 2 All ER 968 and **Sergeant and Sims, p. 104.**

Contract notes—abolition of charge and obligation to issue

59: 34   The ad valorem duty on contract notes for the sale or purchase of any stock or marketable security is abolished by FA 1985, s. 86. However, the statutory obligation under F(1909–10)A 1910 to issue contract notes was retained until the new requirements following the Financial Services Act 1986 were introduced. FA 1987 (Commencement No. 2) Order 1988,[1] has now brought an end to the requirements under stamp duty law for contract notes to be issued for dealings in securities. The order has effect from 29th April 1988. Contract notes will still be required under rules laid down by the Securities and Investment Board.[2]

---

[1] SI 1988 No. 780.
[2] See Whittaker and Morse: *The Financial Services Act 1986.*

Declaration of trust

59: 35   A declaration of trust by any writing not being a will or instrument liable to ad valorem duty is liable to duty of 50p, see infra, § **60: 07.**

Deeds of any other kind—abolition of charge

59: 36   The fixed duty of 50p on deeds not otherwise described in the First Schedule to the Stamp Act 1891 was abolished with effect generally as regards deeds executed after 25th March 1985.[1]

Sergeant and Sims, p. 315 and Supplement.
[1] FA 1985, s. 85 and Sch. 24(*e*).

Duplicate or counterpart

59: 37   The duplicate or counterpart of any instrument chargeable with any duty is chargeable with duty of 50p or the same duty as the original instrument whichever is the less. So the duplicate of a conveyance where the consideration does not exceed £30,000 will be nil.

A duplicate or counterpart is duly stamped if it is stamped as an original or, if as a duplicate, it indicates by a denoting stamp that duty has been paid on the original.[1]

An exception provides that the counterpart of a lease does not require a denoting stamp if it is not executed by the lessor or grantor.[2]

Sergeant and Sims, pp. 155–156 and Supplement.
[1] SA 1891, s. 72; see also SA 1891, s. 11 (denoting stamp).
[2] SA 1891, s. 72.

Exchange and partition

59: 38   When property is exchanged there is no sale and no stamp duty under the head of transfer on sale. However if there is an exchange, division or partition of real or heritable property and the equality money exceeds £100, SA 1891, s. 73 provides that ad valorem duty be paid on the equality money at a rate equal to that for a transfer on sale; the same reduced and nil rates apply. This duty is charged on the principal instrument. If the equality money is less than £100 a fixed duty of 50p is charged.

When freehold land was exchanged for leasehold, it was held that real property was being exchanged for personal property and so s. 73 did not apply.[1] If, in that case, there had been equality money there would have been a conveyance on sale and so duty under that head. The position where the interest exchanged is one arising under a trust for sale is unclear.[2]

An exchange must be distinguished from an instrument which implements two contracts of sale.[3]

Sergeant and Sims, pp. 156–157.
[1] *Littlewoods Mail Order Stores Ltd v IRC* [1963] AC 135.
[2] See *Irani Finance Ltd v Singh* [1970] 3 All ER 199.
[3] *Portman v IRC* [1956] TR 353.

INSURANCE POLICIES

(a)   The position up to 31st December 1989

59: 39   A policy of life insurance is subject to a separate head of charge, which is ad valorem depending on the amount insured.[1] The amount insured is calculated according to general principles so, whereas guaranteed bonuses must be added to the sum assured, bonuses which are not guaranteed will not be.[2] Failure to stamp the policy carries liability to a fine.[3]

The policy must be one of life assurance; one which provides for payment only as death by non-natural causes is not included.[4] So an endowment policy is liable to duty under this head;[5] however an accident policy is not even though it provides for the return of provisions as death by accident;[6] this is an instance of the leading and principal object rule.

The rate of duty is as follows:

Amount insured	Rate of duty
Not exceeding £50	Nil
£50.01 to £1,000	£5 per £100 or part £100
Over £1,000	50p per £1,000 or part £1,000

A special rate of 5p is charged if the period of cover does not exceed two years. Clauses allowing extension of a policy and variation of the policy which extends the policy beyond the two years result in the loss of this relief.[7]

When a policy is duly stamped under this head, any policy of reinsurance carries duty of only 50p and then only if it is under seal.[8]

This is one of the areas in which composition arrangements are authorised. The life assurance companies account for the duty periodically and the instrument will state that duty has been and will be paid to the Commissioners of Inland Revenue.[9]

(b) The position after 31st December 1989

With effect from 1st January 1990 the head of charge is repealed and no stamp duty is to be charged on policies made on or after that date.[10] Consequentially, there will no longer be fines for failure to stamp insurance policies on payments made on unstamped policies.[11] The fine for not preparing a duly stamped policy within one month of receipt of the premium ceases to apply to premiums received after 30th November 1989. An assignment of a life policy will no longer be required to be stamped.[12] Variations made after 31st December 1989 to a short term policy (whenever made) will not attract additional duty. The provisions which required higher rates of duty to be imposed with effect from the date of variation on a life insurance policy (originally for a period not exceeding two years) which is subsequently varied will cease to operate.[13]

Following the abolition of the charge to duty on policies of life assurance and superannuation annuities there will be a repeal of a considerable number of statutory provisions as follows:[14]

	Extent of repeal
The Stamp Act 1891.	Section 91. Section 98(1). Section 100. Section 118. In Schedule 1, paragraph (3) of the heading beginning "Bond, Covenant, or Instrument of any kind whatsoever", the whole of the heading beginning "Insurance", and the whole of the heading beginning "Policy of Life Insurance".
The Finance Act 1956.	Section 38.
The Finance Act (Northern Ireland) 1956.	Section 6.
The Finance Act 1959.	In section 30(4), the words preceding paragraph (a) and the words following paragraph (c).
The Finance Act (Northern Ireland) 1959.	In section 5(4), the words preceding paragraph (a) and the words following paragraph (c).
The Finance Act 1966.	Section 47.
The Finance Act (Northern Ireland) 1966.	Section 5.

	Extent of repeal
The Finance Act 1970.	In Schedule 7, paragraphs 7(4) and 17.
The Finance Act (Northern Ireland) 1970.	In Schedule 2, paragraphs 7(4) and 17.
The Finance Act 1982.	Section 130.
The Income and Corporation Taxes Act 1988.	In Schedule 14, in paragraph 3(4) the words from "and section 100" to the end.

These repeals will have effect in accordance with FA 1989, s. 173.

Sergeant and Sims, pp. 171–175 and Supplement.
  [1] FA 1970, Sch. 7, para. 17 (see Extra-statutory concession G3 (1988) and **Sergeant and Sims**, **p. 172** on group policies).
  [2] See the Contingency Principle, supra, § **58: 16.**
  [3] SA 1891, s. 100.
  [4] SA 1891, s. 98.
  [5] *Prudential Assurance Co v IRC* [1904] 2 KB 658; see too *Gould v Curtis* [1912] 1 KB 635 and *National Mutual Life Association of Australasia Ltd v Federal Taxation Comr* (1959) 102 CLR 29 (Australian income tax case).
  [6] *General Accident Assurance Corpn v IRC* 1906 8 F (Ct of Sess) 477.
  [7] FA 1966, s. 47; FA 1970, Sch. 7, para. 17.
  [8] FA 1970, Sch. 7, para. 17(3).
  [9] FA 1956, s. 38.
  [10] FA 1989, s. 173(1), (2), (6).
  [11] FA 1989, s. 173(3), (7).
  [12] FA 1989, s. 173(4), (9).
  [13] FA 1989, s. 173(5), (10).
  [14] FA 1989, s. 187, Sch 17, Pt IX.

Superannuation and purchased life annuities

(a)   The position up to 1st January 1989

59: 40   Ad valorem duty is charged on the grant or covenant for payment of a superannuation annuity.[1] The duty is one of the last remaining examples of Bond Covenant duty;[2] and the rate of duty is 5p per £10 or part £10 of the annuity.[3] This head of duty was extended to purchased life annuities in 1956.[4] There are composition arrangements.[5]

(b)   The position after 31st December 1989

The head of duty "Bond, Covenant or Instrument of any kind whatsoever" in SA 1891, Sch. 1 (superannuation annuities) will cease to apply to instruments made after 31st December 1989.[6]

Sergeant and Sims, pp. 103–105 and Supplement.
[1] SA 1891, Sch. 1.
[2] The other is a document *increasing* rent, SA 1891, s. 77(5).
[3] FA 1956, s. 38(4).
[4] FA 1970, Sch. 7, para. 7(4); FA 1956, s. 38(1); this was when apportionment of payments under certain purchased annuities was introduced for income tax. On the scope of the phrase "purchase life annuity" see *Stevenston Securities Ltd v IRC* (1959) 38 TC 459.
[5] FA 1956, s. 38(2)–(5).
[6] FA 1989, s. 173(1)(*b*).

Assignments of life policies

(a) Assignments made before 1st January 1990

59: 41   An assignment of a policy must be stamped in order to be valid; no payment may be made under the policy if the assignment is not stamped. If payment is made, the payee is liable to the duty and penalty.[1] This represents a contrast to the normal consequences of failure to stamp. No special head of charge is applicable on the assignment, the head of transfer on sale or the fixed duty of 50p on a voluntary disposition (unless certified as nil) being used as appropriate. Ad valorem duty will be nil unless the policy has a surrender or sale value of more than £30,000.

A declaration of trust of a policy will bear duty as a declaration of trust (50p). This head applies whether the policy is one of life assurance or some other kind.

(b) Assignment of life policies after 31st December 1989

Assignments of life policies made after 31st December 1989 need not be stamped, and variations made after 31st December 1989 to a short term policy (whenever made) will not attract additional duty.[2] A declaration of trust will continue to be chargeable as a declaration of policy (50p) and this will apply whether the policy is one of life assurance or some other kind.

(c) Repeal of stamp duty provisions and superannuation annuities

Consequent upon the abolition of certain duties on stamp life policies and superannuation annuities a considerable number of statutory provisions will be repealed as follows:[3]

Sergeant and Sims, p. 172 and Supplement.
[1] SA 1891, s. 118.
[2] FA 1989, s. 169.
[3] FA 1989, s. 187, Sch. 17, Pt. IX; see § **59: 39**, supra.

Letter or power of attorney—abolition of head of charge

59: 42   The charge of 50p fixed duty under the heading "Letter or power of attorney" has been abolished (FA 1985, s. 85 and Sch. 24(*f*)).

Unit trusts

59: 43   Unit trusts are subject to stamp duty under the appropriate head of duty applicable on a transfer of units in the trust. These matters are dealt with infra, §§ **61: 20, 61: 21, 61: 23.**

Miscellaneous

Mortgage duty—abolition

59: 44   The transactions now removed from mortgage duty include the grant of the mortgage, or equitable mortgage, a collateral or substituted mortgage, the assignment of the mortgage or the security, a reconveyance of the mortgage and a release of the debt.

Sergeant and Sims, p. 170 and Supplement.

Release or renunciation

59: 45   A release or renunciation of any property or of any interest in property (e.g. an interest under a partnership) is liable to fixed duty of 50p unless it is upon a sale in which case it attracts ad valorem duty as a conveyance on sale.

Sergeant and Sims, pp. 175–176 and Supplement.

Surrender

59: 46   A surrender of any kind whatsoever, not chargeable with duty as a conveyance on sale, attracts duty of 50p.

Sergeant and Sims, p. 177 and Supplement.

60 Stamp duty in specific situations

Sale of a business

60: 01 In some cases ad valorem duty may be due under SA 1891, s. 59; however goods, wares, merchandise, stocks and marketable securities are exempt from this section; the denoting procedure is used to prevent ad valorem duty being chargeable on the subsequent conveyance.

On the sale of a business the agreement may provide for the purchaser to collect the outstanding debts as agent of the vendor and use them in discharging the debts of the vendor. This is because if the purchaser simply undertook to discharge the vendor's debts the value of those debts would have to be included in the consideration.[1]

---

[1] SA 1891, s. 57; see *E Gomme Ltd v IRC* [1964] 3 All ER 497 at 502.

LAND

Sale of land

60: 02 A contract for the sale of an interest in land is not caught by SA 1891, s. 59. However a contract for the sale of an equitable interest is caught by that provision. It follows that a contract for the sale of an option will be within s. 59; this however must be distinguished from an agreement creating the option, which comes within s. 54.

In *George Wimpey & Co Ltd v IRC*[1] the Court of Appeal held that a contract creating an option to buy a legal interest in land was within s. 54. The option was property, it was transferred to the purchaser in return for consideration in money and nothing further needed to be done to perfect title to the option. In option cases close attention is needed to determine what is sold.[2]

A question arises where the contract for sale covers both several fixtures and the land itself. It has been held in the context of the Statute of Frauds that the sale of a tenant's right to his landlord is neither a sale of goods nor of land.[3] Whether it follows that such a contract is within s. 59 is open and not decided.

The conveyance of the land on sale will attract duty under s. 54. The usual practical problem is to ensure that the value is kept to a level low enough to eliminate duty; this requires certification of value. It is common for the vendor to sever any severable chattels before the sale in the hope that a part

1400

of the consideration can be attributed to those chattels; this device ought to be successful only where the transfer of those chattels is not effected by the conveyance but by a separate transaction not involving an instrument and only when severance has taken place; fixtures which have not been severed must be included unless they are goods, wares or merchandise.[4]

Sergeant and Sims, pp. 143–149 and Supplement.
[1] [1975] 2 All ER 45.
[2] E.g. *Muller & Co's Margarine Ltd v IRC* [1900] 1 QB 310 as explained by Collins LJ in *Danubian Sugar Factories Ltd v IRC* [1901] 1 KB 245 at 251.
[3] *Lee v Gaskell* [1876] 1 QBD 700.
[4] See *Law Society Gazette*, November 1963, p. 782.

Exchanges

60: 03   At present, particularly where a new house is bought from the builder it is possible sometimes to exchange the purchaser's own house for the new one and make up the purchase price in cash. Ad valorem duty is only payable under the head of charge, conveyance or transfer on sale if the price is paid in money, stock or marketable securities or if it is a debt due to the transferor so that if the price to be paid consists of any other form of property only fixed duty of 50p is payable. However where there is an equality payment of more than £100[1] ad valorem duty is due on the cash payment. This is particularly useful when it is noted that the nil rate of duty[2] will still apply so that in the case of a new house worth £60,000 no duty will be payable if the consideration is made up of £30,000 cash and a property worth £40,000 as opposed to duty of £700 if the whole amount is paid in cash. The Inland Revenue Consultative document[3] indicates that the Revenue are in favour of abolishing this distinction between cash and property although it suggests that it may be necessary to make provisions to cover the position where the builder sells the property within a short period.[4]

Sergeant and Sims, pp. 156–157 and Supplement.
[1] SA 1891, s. 73.
[2] FA 1984, s. 109.
[3] *The scope for reforming stamp duties*, March 1983.
[4] Ibid, pp. 16–17, 49.

Covenant to improve property

60: 04   Where a purchaser covenants to improve property or where the conveyance is in consideration of his having previously improved the property, or of any covenant relating to the subject matter, the value of the covenant is ignored in calculating the duty.[1] So where V sells land to P in consideration of a sum of money and a covenant—in a separate contract—by V to build a house for P, ad valorem duty is chargeable only on the price paid by P.[2] This must be distinguished from the case where V has already built the house and then sells both the land and the house to P. This has given rise to considerable difficulty when there is a conveyance of land and a separate contract to build.[3]

Sergeant and Sims, p. 108 and Supplement.
[1] FA 1900, s. 10.
[2] *Kimbers & Co v IRC* [1936] 1 KB 132.
[3] See *Sergeant and Sims, p. 103*. See now Revenue Statement of Practice SP10/87, 22 November 1987 (1988 *Simon's Tax Intelligence* p. 9).

Conveyances and leases of building plots

60: 05   In 1957 the Revenue published a statement[1] summarising the law dealing with the stamp duty payable on conveyances and leases of building plots where, at the date of the contract, no house was built or a house was only partly built. In brief it stated that if in reality the purchaser is buying a completed house duty is payable on the total amount paid for the land and the building work, but that if there are two separate transactions (for example the purchaser makes a separate deal to build the house after buying the land) duty is payable on the price of the land only.

The Revenue are advised that the 1957 statement still accurately reflects the law on this subject. That statement has however sometimes been misconstrued or misapplied. Therefore, a new Statement of Practice[2] has been issued which restates the view the Revenue takes and, subject to the proviso that ultimately each case depends on its own facts, clarifies the position in a number of respects.

Sergeant and Sims, pp. 108–109 and Supplement.
[1] *Law Society's Gazette* (1957), p. 450.
[2] SP 10/87. See *Simon's Tax Intelligence* 1988, p. 9.

Leases—a way of reducing duty

60: 06   There is one way of reducing the stamp duty on creating a leasehold interest. It does not avoid stamp duty but may reduce it. This is done by granting a lease for not more than 35 years with options for one or more renewals. The existence of the option is not considered to make the lease one of more than 35 years[1] although further stamp duty will be payable when the options are exercised. Alternatively a 21 year lease with a 35 year reversionary lease with options can be used, in which case duty will be paid on both the 21 year lease and the reversionary lease immediately even though the reversionary lease is not a lease in possession. This allows a long lease to be granted at the more advantageous rate of £2 per cent rather than the more onerous £12 or £24 per cent.

Sergeant and Sims, pp. 163–165 and Supplement.
[1] *Hand v Hall* [1877] 2 Ex Div 355.

TRUSTS AND SETTLEMENTS

Declaration of trust

60: 07   A declaration of trust by any writing not being a will or instrument liable to ad valorem duty, is liable to duty of 50p. An ineffective transfer to trustees is not construed as a declaration of trust and therefore is not liable to this duty.

If a person declares himself trustee of personal property the trust is effective and binding save only perhaps where his interest in the property is equitable.[1] It follows that since a subsequent transfer to trustees is not a sale it will bear only miscellaneous transfer duty of 50p since no beneficial interest passes; here the decision in *Cohen & Moore v IRC* must be borne in mind.[2] A transfer direct from vendor to trustees at the direction of the purchaser/settlor attracts conveyance on sale duty and an extra 50p duty.[3]

Where a settlor agrees to sell his property to the trust the subsequent instrument of transfer will be chargeable as a disposition on sale or the agreement may be chargeable as an agreement to convey.[4]

Sergeant and Sims, pp. 153–154 and Supplement.
[1] See infra, § **60: 11**.
[2] [1933] 2 K B 126 and **Sergeant and Sims, p. 127**.
[3] See **Sergeant and Sims, pp. 128, 133**.
[4] SA 1891, s. 59 supra, § **59: 18**.

Change of trustees

60: 08   Duty (formerly 50p fixed duty) is no longer charged on the appointment of a new trustee,[1] and transfer from the old to the new trustee is exempt if appropriately certified (see supra, § **58: 04**).

---

[1] FA 1985, s. 85 and Sch. 24(*b*).

Distributions

60: 09   Distributions by the trustees in the course of administering the trust are not transfers on sales. Instruments effecting such distributions will be exempt if appropriately certified (see supra, § **58: 04**).

Revocation—repeal

60: 10   The revocation of a trust no longer attracts fixed duty of 50p.[1]

---

[1] For its repeal, see FA 1985, s. 85 and Sch. 24(*k*).

Assignment of interests under trusts

60: 11   The assignment of a beneficial interest under a trust must be in writing to satisfy the requirements of LPA 1925, s. 53(1)(*c*); it follows that there must be an instrument and so something chargeable, whether as a sale or a gift. The same conclusion is reached if the beneficiary directs the trustees to hold his interest on trust for someone else in view of the decision of the House of Lords in *Grey v IRC*.[1] The House rejected the argument that the word 'disposition' in s. 53(1)(*c*) should be equated with the words 'grant' or 'assignment' formerly found in the Statute of Frauds and did so because the

LPA 1925 consolidated not the Statute of Frauds but subsequent amending Acts so that one could not assume that no change of scope was intended; it followed that the word 'disposition' should receive its natural meaning. What is not clear is whether a declaration of trust by a beneficiary of his beneficial interest is now a disposition and so void under LPA 1925, s. 53(1)(c). What is clear is that if such a declaration—or instruction as in *Grey v IRC*—falls within s. 53(1)(c), and is not in writing, it is void and so a subsequent document confirming the transfer is itself the conveyance and so liable to duty.

If the beneficiary instructs the trustee to transfer both his equitable and the trustee's legal intent to a third person the instruction does not require writing under s. 53(1)(c)[2] but the transfer to the third person may have to be by instrument anyway.

In *Oughtred v IRC* [3] a trust held shares for A for life with remainder to B. B agreed to surrender his remainder in exchange for certain shares held by A absolutely; the effect would be to change A's life interest in the settled shares into an absolute one. The parties executed a deed of release whereby A and B released the trustees, the deed reciting that the trust shares were now held for A absolutely and that it was intended to transfer them in return for the release. A deed between A and the trustees transferred the shares to A on the same day.

The question was whether the transfer of the shares to A was subject to ad valorem duty as a transfer on sale,[4] the sale being of B's equitable interest. It was argued that the effect of the contract was that A became the beneficiary under a constructive trust so that the deed simply vested A with legal title to what was already his. By a bare majority the House of Lords rejected the argument and held that ad valorem stamp duty was chargeable. Of the majority Lord Jenkins, with whom Lord Keith agreed, held that the prior constructive trust did not prevent the subsequent transfer from being a transfer on sale. He said:

> "The parties to a transaction of sale and purchase may no doubt choose to let the matter rest in contract. But if the subject matter of a sale is such that the full title to it can only be transferred by an instrument, then any instrument they executed by way of transfer of the property sold ranks for stamp duty purposes as a conveyance on sale notwithstanding the constructive trust which arose on the conclusion of the contract."[5]

Lord Denning used wider language. He said:

> "In my opinion, every conveyance or transfer by which an agreement for sale is implemented is liable to stamp duty on the value of the consideration . . . the instrument is the means by which the parties choose to implement the bargains they have made. It is then a conveyance on transfer consequent upon the sale of the property and in implementation of it."[6]

Where an instrument transfers both an equitable interest and the related legal interest, Revenue practice does not require an additional 50p duty on the transfer of the latter.

Sergeant and Sims, pp. 113–119 and Supplement.
[1] [1960] AC 1.
[2] *Vandervell v IRC* [1967] AC 291.
[3] [1960] AC 206.
[4] The fact that the consideration was shares not money is irrelevant—see SA 1891, s. 55.

Variation of trusts

60: 12   If one beneficiary buys another beneficiary's interest for cash or shares there will be a conveyance on sale liable to ad valorem duty. If, however, the beneficiaries divide the funds according to an actuarial valuation of their interests, stamp duty will not be ad valorem since no interest passes and hence there is no sale.

If there is a danger that the transaction will be treated as one of sale and the value of the interest transferred is not above £30,000, certification is desirable to ensure freedom from duty.

Where the interest of one beneficiary is bought out by the others, the disposal of parts of his share to each of the others may with advantage be done by separate instruments if this would enable the nil duty rate to apply where they otherwise would not. It is felt that these would be separate transactions.

60: 13   The stamp duty on the creation of a trust or settlement inter vivos depends on the nature of the instrument effecting it and the nature of the assets. Where there is more than one instrument effecting it, the duty in practice is charged on what is regarded as the final instrument in the transaction. If the instrument is a declaration of trust simpliciter it will attract duty of 50p under the head 'Declaration of Trust'[1] but if the instrument also constitutes a voluntary disposition it will be exempt from duty where appropriately certified under Category L of the Stamp Duty (Exempt Instruments) Regulations 1987.[2] If not so certified it will attract 50p fixed duty as a conveyance or transfer of any other kind.

Where there is more than one instrument involved it will be necessary for ascertaining which instrument requires to be stamped to determine either by reference to the date of the instrument(s) which one of the instrument(s) was first executed to accept whether a certificate is appropriate. In the absence of any such indication the instrument creating the settlement or trust will be treated as the final instrument for stamping. Notwithstanding that the instrument has been properly certified as exempt it will still be stampable 50p as a Declaration of Trust (i) where the assets subject to the settlement or trust comprise or include cash or exempt assets e.g. Government securities, and/or (ii) where the instrument contains a provision that additional assets can be transferred into the settlement or trust.

¹ SA 1891, Sch. 1.
² SI 1987 No. 516; see § **58: 04**, supra.

WILLS AND INTESTACIES—VARIATIONS

General

60: 14   A will or testamentary instrument is exempt from stamp duty. An assent under Administration of Estates Act 1925, s. 36 is not liable to duty.

Where property is appropriated by a personal representative in or towards satisfaction of a general legacy of money no duty is now chargeable on an instrument giving effect to the appropriation.[1]

---

[1] FA 1985, s. 84(4).

Deeds of family arrangement

60: 15   *Historical note*

The use of deeds of family arrangement for IHT purposes was allowed and this gave rise to problems since such deeds were not exempt from stamp duty even though they were not liable for capital transfer tax or capital gains tax if executed within two years of the death. Such deeds were normally dutiable as voluntary dispositions and therefore were liable to ad valorem duty but in some cases a deed might also have been charged as a conveyance or transfer on sale.[1] The consultative document[2] suggested that an exemption should be made for deeds of family arrangement corresponding to that already available for IHT and CGT under CGTA 1979, s. 49(6) and IHTA 1984, s. 17.

The present position

It is now specifically provided for stamp duty that on instruments executed on or after 26th March 1985 where, within two years of a person's death, any of the dispositions (whether effected by will, under the law relating to intestacy or otherwise) of the property of which he was competent to dispose are varied by an instrument executed by the persons or any of the persons who benefit or would benefit under the dispositions, no ad valorem conveyance or transfer on sale duty is chargeable.[3]

However, this provision does not apply where the variation is made for monetary consideration other than consideration consisting of the making of a variation in respect of another of the dispositions.[4] This provision applies whether or not the administration of the estate is complete or the property has been distributed in accordance with the original dispositions.[5] All qualifying deeds of family arrangements and similar instruments are exempt from duty if appropriately certified (see supra, § **58: 04**).

Sergeant and Sims, pp. 313–314.
[1] *Oughtred v IRC* [1959] 3 All ER 623.
[2] *The scope for reforming stamp duties*: an Inland Revenue Consultative Document issued 21st March 1983.
[3] FA 1985, s. 84(1).
[4] FA 1985, s. 84(2).
[5] FA 1985, s. 84(3).

MATRIMONIAL ARRANGEMENTS

60: 16   Formerly the incidence of stamp duty on instruments executed in connection with marriage breakdowns depended on the circumstances and form and whether the conveyance or transfer was one of sale or voluntary disposition, or neither, or pursuant to or incorporated in a court order.

Transfer of property on the break-up of a marriage

A separation deed which conveys property, or the conveyance of property under an order of the Family Division of the High Court, has hitherto been normally liable to a fixed duty but formerly might have been liable to transfer on sale duty.

An exemption is now provided for those instruments formerly liable to transfer on sale duty.[1] Such instruments are exempt from 50p fixed duty also if appropriately certified (see supra § **58: 04**). The exemption from ad valorem duty applies to instruments executed after 25th March 1985.[2]

Sergeant and Sims, p. 313 and Supplement.
[1] FA 1985, s. 83(1).
[2] FA 1985, s. 83(3).

61 Companies: stamp duty

SHARE TRANSACTIONS

Company formation

61: 01   On the formation of a company no stamp duty is payable, see infra, § **61: 07**. The memorandum of association and articles of association do not bear duty.

Issue of shares

61: 02   The issue of shares on the formation of a company for cash no longer attracts duty. Where the issue is in return for assets there will be a conveyance on sale of the asset.[1]

If the shares issued are bearer shares they are liable to bearer instrument duty, infra, § **61: 15**. This duty is additional to any capital duty. When shares are issued in exchange for assets, there may be capital duty, conveyance on sale duty and also bearer instrument duty.

Sergeant and Sims, pp. 133–134 and Supplement.
[1] SA 1891, s. 55.

Other issues

61: 03   Loan capital duty was repealed in 1973 so the only duty now is conveyance or transfer on sale duty if the loan capital is issued in return for assets.

Transfer of shares

61: 04   A contract of sale of shares does not attract stamp duty.

If the shares are not represented by bearer instruments they can only be transferred by registration; this process requires a further document, a requirement with which the company may not dispense.[1] This is to protect duty on conveyance or transfer on sale. The rate of duty is the same even if there is an overseas buyer.[2]

If the transfer is of a bearer instrument no duty will be due unless another instrument is used to transfer title[3] or it is the first transfer in the UK of an overseas instrument; infra, § **61: 14**.

1408

An exchange of shares will give rise to conveyance on sale duty.[4]
For reliefs for companies, see §§ **62: 01, 06**.

Special rules apply to various transfers which are simply part of the computerised workings of the Stock Exchange.[5]

As regards the proposed system known as "TAURUS" for dealing with paperless transfers of shares, to be introduced by the International Stock Exchange, FA 1989, s. 176 enables the Revenue to make regulations for the operation of this system. So far no regulations have been made.[6]

---

[1] SA 1891, s. 17 makes a person liable to a fine if he registers an improperly stamped transfer.
[2] FA 1974, Sch. 11, paras. 20–23 has ceased to have effect (FA 1984, s. 109(2)).
[3] E.g. a deed of gift.
[4] SA 1891, s. 55; *J & P Coats Ltd v IRC* [1897] 2 QB 423.
[5] See **Sergeant and Sims, p. 407**.
[6] For further information, see "Dematerialisation of Share Certificates and Share Transfers: A Consultative Paper" issued in November 1988 by the Department of Trade and Industry HC Written Answer 14th June 1989, Vol. 154 cols. 443–444, and an article in [1989] BTR 1; see § **63: 09**, infra.

Loan capital

61: 05   For a better understanding it will be helpful to recall the history of the legislation. Clause 65 of the Finance Bill 1986 contained the Budget proposal to withdraw the exemption for transfers of certain categories of loan capital and to charge duty at 0.5%. The rate on equity-linked loans was also reduced to 0.5%. On 29th April 1986 the Chancellor announced that the Government had decided to restore the exemption for loan capital. Full details of the announcement were in an Inland Revenue Press Release of the same date.[1] Amendments to clause 65, now contained in FA 1986, s. 78, provide for it to terminate on 6th July 1986. The pre-Budget law is reinstated from 7th July 1986.

FA 1986, s. 79 provides a new regime for loan capital to apply from 1st August 1986. It re-enacts, with minor improvements, the pre-Budget exemptions. It also provides that for the period between 1st August 1986 and 27th October 1986 loan stocks which are still chargeable will pay at the 0.5% rate and not at 1%. These stocks have been paying duty at 0.5% since the Budget and the Government took the view that this rate should be restored as soon as possible. (In the period between 7th July 1986 and 1st August 1986 the 1% rate applies.) The improvements to the pre-Budget exemptions made by FA 1986, s. 79 are the inclusion within the exemption of bearer loans denominated in sterling and registered loans in a foreign currency raised by foreign Governments and foreign companies. There seemed no reason why these loans should be treated differently, and s. 79 deals with these minor anomalies.

The new regime established under FA 1986, s. 79 for loan capital (as defined):

(*i*) consolidates a number of exemptions for the issue or transfer of loan capital;

(*ii*) provides an exemption for non-sterling loans raised by foreign governments or companies;

(*iii*) provides an exemption for all bearer loan capital;

(*iv*) provides for a rate of 0.5% stamp duty on such transfers of loan capital as remain liable.

The detailed position is as follows:

(1) Section 79(1) provides for the repeal of a number of enactments, which made special provision for certain categories of loan stock and which are no longer necessary as a result of these changes. The enactments affected are:

(*a*) FA 1963, s. 62(2), (6) and FA (Northern Ireland) 1986, s. 11(2), (5) which provided a special rate of duty—broadly 0.5%—for Commonwealth Government stock;

(*b*) FA 1967, s. 29 and FA (Northern Ireland) 1967, s. 6 which exempted transfers of loan capital issued by local authorities from stamp duty;

(*c*) FA 1976, s. 126 which provided an exemption from duty for the transfers of most categories of loan stock.

(2) There is an exemption from duty for issues and transfers of loan capital in bearer form.[2]

(3) There is an exemption for transfers of loan capital issued by certain named organisations and by "designated international organisations" for which the UK is under a treaty obligation to provide an exemption.[3] The loans covered by this provision are loans raised by:

(*a*) the Organisation for Economic Co-operation and Development;

(*b*) the Inter-American Development Bank;

(*c*) the Asian Development Bank; and

(*d*) the African Development Bank.

The following bodies in respect of which the UK has a similar obligation to provide an exemption retain exemptions under other legislation:

(*a*) the International Bank of Reconstruction and Development;

(*b*) the European Economic Community;

(*c*) the European Coal & Steel Community;

(*d*) the European Atomic Energy Authority;

(*e*) the European Investment Bank.

(4) There is an exemption for transfers of loan capital other than that to which paragraphs (5) and (6) below apply.[4]

(5) There is an exception from the exemption for transfers of loan capital which is convertible into equity.[5]

(6) There is an exception from the exemption for transfers of loan capital which carries, or has carried:

(*a*) interest rights which are significantly different from what is normally expected in a commercial loan,

(*b*) interest rights which are geared to such factors as production achieved by the borrower his trading results or the price of commodities, and

(*c*) an entitlement to a premium on maturity which is unusually large by ordinary commercial standards.[6]

The exceptions in paragraphs (5) and (6) are to prevent exemptions for the kind of loan capital which is very much akin to equity capital. There were similar exceptions from the exemption that applied up to 25th March 1986.

(7) There is a provision which prevents the provisions referred to in paragraphs (6)(*a*) and (*c*) above being triggered simply because the terms of

the loan link either the interest return or the amount ultimately repayable to movements in a general domestic prices index.[7]

(8) Stamp duty at the rate of 0.5% is charged on transfers of loan capital.[8]

(9) The exemption is applied from 1st August 1986 to the issue of "inland bearers".[9]

(10) The exemption is applied from 1st August 1986 to transfers of "overseas bearers".[10]

(11) It is provided that s. 79 applies to any other instruments executed on or after 1st August 1986.[11]

(12) The following definitions apply:

"Loan capital" means:

(a) any debenture stock, corporation stock or funded debt,[12] by whatever name known, issued by a body corporate or other body of persons (which here includes a local authority and any body whether formed or established in the UK[13] or elsewhere);

(b) any capital raised by such a body if the capital is borrowed or has the character of borrowed money, and whether it is in the form of stock or any other form;

(c) stock or marketable securities issued by the government of any country or territory outside the UK.[14]

(13) "Designated international organisation" means an international organisation designated for the purposes of FA 1984, s. 126 by any order made under s. 126(1).[14]

(14) It is provided that the repeal of FA 1976, s. 126 shall not affect the construction of FA 1985, ss. 80(3), 81(3).[14] These provisions are concerned with the stamp duty treatment where stocks (defined by reference to FA 1976, s. 126) of a company being taken over are exchanged for shares in the acquiring company.

(15) The provisions of FA 1986, s. 79 apply to Northern Ireland.[14]

Sergeant and Sims, pp. 340–343 and Supplement.

[1] [1986] STI, p. 330.
[2] FA 1986, s. 79(2).
[3] FA 1986, s. 79(3).
[4] FA 1986, s. 79(4).
[5] FA 1986, s. 79(5).
[6] FA 1986, s. 79(6).
[7] FA 1986, s. 79(7).
[8] FA 1986, s. 79(8).
[9] FA 1986, s. 79(9).
[10] FA 1986, s. 79(10).
[11] FA 1986, s. 79(11).
[12] For the meaning of "funded debt" see *Reed International Ltd v IRC* [1976] AC 336.
[13] On the meaning of this phrase see *Camille and Henry Dreyfus Foundation Inc v IRC* [1956] AC 39.
[14] FA 1986, s. 78(7), (9), (10) and (14), applied by FA 1986, s. 79(12).

61: 06   Purchase by a company of its own shares

General

The Companies Act 1985, s. 161 (formerly Companies Act 1981, s. 46) enables companies to purchase their own shares. A specific exemption from ad valorem stamp duty was not provided although it was intended apparently that s. 52 of the 1981 Act (Disclosure of Particulars of Purchase and Authorised Contracts) should effectively provide for this. Doubt arose as to whether s. 52 achieved this objective. The doubt has now been resolved.

FA 1986 provides with effect from 27th October 1986 for the 0.5% rate of duty to apply to a purchase by a company of its own shares.[1] It also provides for the statutory return required under company law when a company purchases its own shares to be liable to stamp duty and to be treated as an instrument transferring the shares on sale for stamp duty purposes. This has the effect of applying the 0.5% rate to the return.[2] The provision applies to any return delivered on or after 27th October 1986 but it does not apply where the shares to which it relates were purchased under a contract entered into before 27th October 1986.[3]

Sergeant and Sims, p. 120.
[1] FA 1986, s. 66. It is considered that the provisions do not apply to a redemption by the company of its own redeemable shares.
[2] FA 1986, s. 66(2). The return is made on Company Form 169.
[3] FA 1986, s. 66(3)–(5).

CAPITAL DUTY—HISTORY—ABOLITION

Introduction

61: 07   Capital duty which was charged by FA 1973, ss. 47, 48 and Sch. 19 (now repealed) and was introduced in conformity with an EEC Directive[1] has been abolished by FA 1988, s. 141. It was in form a stamp duty and the provisions were construed as one with the Stamp Act 1891.[2] Some of the occasions of charge were, in substance, transactions rather than documents but the general principle that duty was levied on instruments and not transactions was preserved by the method of placing the charge on a statement which had to be delivered to the Commissioners within one month of a chargeable transaction by a capital company.[3] The rate of duty was 1%. The charge arose if at the time, or as a result of, the chargeable transaction (as defined)[4] relating to a capital company was either (*a*) the place of effective management of the capital company was in Great Britain or (*b*) the registered office[5] was in Great Britain but the place of effective management was outside the member states.[6]

The brief summary which follows is intended to assist in capital duty cases which may still be outstanding and the subject of outstanding enquiry and possibly appeal.

Sergeant and Sims, pp. 477–612 and Supplement.
[1] 69/335 as amended by 73/79.
[2] FA 1973, s. 59(3).
[3] FA 1973, s. 47(1) and (2).
[4] FA 1973, s. 48.
[5] For a limited partnership this was the principal place of business (s. 47(9)).
[6] FA 1973, s. 47(1) and (2).

Origins

61: 08   On joining the EEC the UK was obliged to implement an existing Directive to tax the raising of capital. The necessary legislation was included in FA 1973. It replaced stamp duty at 0.5% on nominal share capital and loan capital by a new stamp duty charge known as capital duty.

A change to the Directive in 1985 allowed reductions in the rate of duty or its abolition. The UK is the first member state to abolish this duty.

When capital duty was paid

61: 09   The main transactions[1] which could give rise to capital duty were:

(*a*) the formation of a company;
(*b*) sales of new shares to the public;
(*c*) rights issues;
(*d*) some takeovers.

When a transaction was chargeable the amount of duty was 1% of the assets contributed to the company. For example a company which raised £10 million from a public offer would pay £100,000.

---

[1] FA 1973, Sch. 19.

Method of abolition of capital duty

61: 10   The provisions of FA 1988, s. 141 abolish capital duty for all transactions occurring after 15th March 1988. This applies to:

(*a*) *chargeable transactions*, on which duty would have been payable within one month;

(*b*) *events which would cause a company to lose an exemption from capital duty for a transaction on or before 15th March 1988.* Exemption from capital duty was available in various circumstances, including for a share-for-share takeover. That exemption would be lost as a result of charges in the five years following the transaction—e.g. if the acquiring company sold the shares it acquired. Duty was then payable. No transaction or charge occurring after 15 March 1988 will give rise to a charge of this kind.

(*c*) *contributions of assets in fulfilment of undertakings made on or before 15 March 1988.* An example is where a company had issued partly paid-up shares. (Capital duty was not charged on the full price at the time of issue. It was charged as and when calls were actually made.)

Procedure following abolition of capital duty

61: 11   The Department of Trade and Industry has replaced the three forms previously required for notifying the Registrar of Companies of allotments of shares under the Companies Act 1985, s. 88(2) with a single form. The Companies (Forms) (Amendment) Regulations 1988 (SI 1988 No. 1359) came into force on 1st August 1988, introducing a new form 88(2) (revised 1988). This form is to be used instead of forms PUC2, PUC3 and the old form 88(2). Additionally forms PUC1, PUC4, PUC5 and PUC6 are no longer required. These changes do not affect the need to submit a contract for sale on form 88(3) where shares have been allotted for a consideration other than cash. Stamp duty could be payable as before, in respect of the value of certain assets. If chargeable, the duty can be paid at any stamp office.[1]

Sergeant and Sims, Supplement pp. A40A–D.
[1] See Department of Trade and Industry Press Notice 8th August 1988 (No. 88/588).

Company reconstructions and amalgamations

61: 12   There was an important exemption from capital duty if an acquiring capital company acquired either (i) at least 75% of the issued share capital of the acquired company or (ii) the whole or part of that company's undertaking.[1]

The exemption has been the subject of case law[2], notably a leading case, *J Rothschild Holdings plc (formerly Charterhouse J Rothschild plc) v IRC*.[3] The case involved an application for judicial review, referal to the European Court on interpretation of EEC Directives, and the Stamp Office practices in addition to the issue of exemption from capital duty. The company argued, in that case, that it had entered into two related transactions on the assurance of the Revenue that, under current Revenue practice, both would be exempt from capital duty. The Revenue contended that there was no Revenue practice in relation to the exemption, and that no assurance had been given to the company.

It was held by Vinelott J that each transaction was to be looked at separately. Although there was evidence as to incidents where the Revenue had given exemption from stamp duty where two or more transactions were made but noted on a single form, there was no established practice. Accordingly, there could be no estoppel on the Revenue in such circumstances and the relief asked for by the taxpayer company should be refused. The decision has been affirmed by the Court of Appeal.

---

[1] FA 1973, Sch. 19, para. 10.
[2] *National Smokeless Fuels Ltd v IRC* [1986] STC 300.
[3] [1989] STC 435, CA.

BEARER INSTRUMENT

The charge

61: 13   This charge,[1] introduced by FA 1963, s. 59 and amended by FA 1986, s 65(3) applies to bearer instruments. The rates of duty depend on the type of instrument:

(1) Inland[2] bearer instrument (other than deposit certificate for overseas stock).	Duty of an amount equal to three times the transfer duty.

(2) Overseas bearer instrument (other than deposit certificate for overseas stock or bearer instrument by usage).	Duty of an amount equal to three time the transfer duty.
(3) Instrument excepted from paragraph (1) or (2) of this heading.	Duty of 10p for every £50 or part of £50 of the market value.
(4) Inland or overseas bearer instrument given in substitution for a like instrument duly stamped *ad valorem* (whether under this heading or not).	Duty of 10p.

The high rates of duty are designed to compensate for the loss of transfer duty since these instruments are transferable by delivery. If these instruments are transferred by deed, normal transfer duty would be chargeable.

The rates of duty payable on both classes of bearer shares are now the same i.e. $1\frac{1}{2}\%$. Thus the rate of duty on the conversion of UK shares into depositary receipts and that on the issue of bearer shares is in line with each other.[3]

As to the similar position in Northern Ireland see FA 1986, s. 65(7).

Sergeant and Sims, pp. 95–101 and Supplement.

[1] See also the notes for guidance issued by the Inland Revenue and printed in **Sergeant and Sims, pp. 97–101.**

[2] As to meaning of place of issue see *Grenfell v IRC* (1876) 1 Ex D 242; *Chicago Railway Terminal Elevator Co v IRC* (1891) 75 LT 157; *Brown v IRC* (1900) 84 LT 71; *Revelstoke v IRC* [1898] AC 565 and *Canada Permanent Mortgage Corpn v IRC* 1932 SC 123.

[3] FA 1986, s. 65.

Instruments chargeable

61: 14   The instruments chargeable on issue are those which are issued in the UK (not just Great Britain) and all instruments issued by a body formed or established in Great Britain but not instruments relating to a foreign loan security.

Instruments which are not chargeable on issue are chargeable on the first transfer in Great Britain; because such instruments are transferable by delivery the rule states that the charge arises if the transfer would have been chargeable under or by reference to the head "Conveyance or Transfer on Sale" if it had been effected by an instrument of transfer.

Amount of duty

61: 15   The amount of duty in paras (1) and (2) of the head of charge is related to the amount of duty that would be chargeable if there were a transfer on sale of the instrument at market value.[1]

The market value is ascertained differently according to the transaction. On issue, if the stock was not offered for public subscription but is dealt with on the UK Stock Exchange within one month of issue, the value is that on the first day of dealing: if it was so offered (whether in registered or bearer form) within twelve months before the issue, the value is the amount subscribed; in all other cases the value immediately after issue is taken.

On the *transfer* of a bearer instrument the market value, in the case of a transfer pursuant to a contract of sale, is that on the day of the contract and, in any other case, that on the day before the day on which the instrument is presented for stamping; if it is not presented the value at the date of transfer is taken.[2]

Sergeant and Sims, pp. 95–101 and Supplement.

[1] FA 1963, s. 59(3) not face value as previously. This sub-section is amended by FA 1986, s. 65(2) apply to transfers after 27th October 1986.

[2] FA 1963, s. 61.

Procedures and penalties

61:16   On issue of a bearer instrument, duty is chargeable if it is (i) issued in Great Britain[1] or (ii) issued—anywhere—by or on behalf of a company or a body of persons, corporate or unincorporated, formed or established in Great Britain. An exception is made to (ii) if the instrument is a foreign loan security.[2] An exception is made to (i) *and* (ii) if it is expressed in any currency other than sterling or in any units of account defined by reference to more than one currency (whether or not including sterling).[3]

The duty is due on issue but the instrument should be lodged before issue; the instruments are then stamped with a denoting stamp and returned. The duty is due within six weeks of the issue, or such longer time as the Commission may allow.[4] Failure to lodge or pay at the right time carries a fine of the duty plus £50—apart from liability to pay the duty;[4] this liability is imposed on the person by whom or on whose behalf the instrument is issued as well as on the agent of these persons.

On the *transfer* of a bearer instrument the instrument must be presented for stamping. Again there are fines on the transferor and any broker or agent concerned in the transfer if the instrument is not duly stamped. However the charge on transfer arises only in respect of those instruments which were not charged as issue.

Sergeant and Sims, p. 96 and Supplement.

[1] I.e. not Northern Ireland.

[2] FA 1963, s. 69(1).

[3] FA 1967, s. 30, amended by FA 1987, s. 51.

[4] FA 1963, s. 60(3).

Bearer instruments not chargeable to duty

61:17   Certain instruments are not chargeable to duty as bearer instruments.[1] These are:

(1) Instruments which are exempt from all stamp duties under the general exemption in SA 1891, Sch. 1 or any other enactment.

(2) Instruments issued by certain designated international organisations or transfers of stock constituted or transferable by means of any instrument issued by the organisation.[2]

As to bearer letters of allotment, see FA 1986, s. 80 supra, § **61: 14** and regarding renounceable letters of allotment, see FA 1986, s. 88 infra, § **63: 03**.

(3) Instruments issued for stock expressed in a currency other than sterling or in European Currency Units (ECUs).[3]

(4) Paired shares, see FA 1988, s. 143 infra, § **61: 18**.

Sergeant and Sims, p. 95 and Supplement.

[1] FA 1963, ss. 59(1) and 65(1), as amended by FA 1985, s. 81.

[2] FA 1984, s. 126(3)(*c*) and FA 1985, s. 96.

[3] FA 1967, s. 30 is amended by FA 1987, s. 51 (which redefines foreign currency for the purposes of that section following the repeal of the Exchange Control Act 1947 and the abolition of the scheduled territories).

Paired shares

61: 18   FA 1988, ss. 143 and 144 are designed to deal with matters of stamp duty and stamp duty reserve tax respectively in relation to what are described as paired shares.

There was a Revenue Press Release[1] relating to the sale of units in Eurotunnel plc and in Eurotunnel SA. Under the terms of that offer applicants received "units", each comprising one share in the UK company paired with a share in the French company, where the component securities could not be transferred independently. Newly issued bearer shares in Eurotunnel plc were to be delivered in France and other countries, which would ordinarily have attracted UK bearer instrument duty at a rate of £1.50 per £100 or part thereof.

The Press Release announced that bearer instrument duty would not be payable on the issue of those shares (and bearer warrants) as they corresponded with Eurotunnel SA shares included in the units used in the UK. The charge to bearer instrument duty would be preserved in relation to any subsequent conversion of registered units into bearer form and on any subsequent issue of bearer units (on the value of both components). In general both for stamp duty reserve tax and for stamp duty purposes, these would be charged as if the unit was a single security.

The release stated that although the arrangements outlined therein reflected the Equity 3 offer by Eurotunnel, similar proposals would apply if the same kind of share structure was adopted in other cases.

FA 1988, s. 143 applies only where:

(*a*) a UK company's Articles of Association and the equivalent constitutional documents of a foreign incorporated company each provide that a share in one company can only be transferred as part of a unit involving a share in the other company; and

(*b*) an equal number of units are to be, or have been, offered for sale to the public both in the UK and in the country in which the foreign company is incorporated at a broadly equivalent price. The offers are required to be made at the same time.[2]

There is an exemption from bearer instrument duty[3] which applies to any bearer instrument representing shares in a UK company, or to a right of allotment of such shares or subscription therefore if issued—

(*a*) for sale (as part of units) pursuant to either the simultaneous public offerings at broadly equivalent prices referred to above or in a country other than the UK or the country of incorporation of the foreign company or

(*b*) to effect an allotment of such shares (as components of such units) as fully or partly paid bonus shares.[4]

It is provided that where bearer shares in, or bearer warrants over shares of, the foreign company are issued otherwise than pursuant to any of the public offers referred to above, bearer instrument duty will be payable as if the foreign company was formed or established in Great Britain (and the exemption from duty relating to stock in foreign currencies will not apply (FA 1967, s. 30)).[5]

Stamp duty is payable at the rate of 1.5% on transfers of relevant securities in UK companies to certain transferees under FA 1986, ss. 67 and 68 (depositary receipts) and ss. 70 and 71 (clearance services). It is provided that where a foreign company's shares are paired with those of the UK company, the foreign company will be treated as incorporated in the UK so that duty will be charged on the consideration for the unit and not just for the UK component.[6]

There is provision to alleviate the need for any bearer instrument representing shares or a right to allotment of, or to subscribe for, shares in either the UK or the foreign company, to be separately stamped as regards each security represented thereby.[7] Section 143 is to be construed as one with the Stamp Act 1891.[8]

Exemption from payment of duty on the issue of bearer shares in Eurotunnel plc is deemed to operate with effect from 1 November 1987 and the charge to bearer instrument duty on subsequent issues of Eurotunnel SA shares operates with effect from 9 December 1987.[9]

Any additional stamp duty caused by treating shares in Eurotunnel SA as if it were incorporated in the UK (in connection with depositary receipt arrangements and clearance services) applies to transfers executed on or after the enactment of FA 1988.

Sergeant and Sims, Supplement.
[1] Dated 5 November 1987, [1987] STI 825.
[2] FA 1988, s. 143(1).
[3] FA 1988, s. 143(2).
[4] FA 1988, s. 143(3).
[5] FA 1988, s. 143(4).
[6] FA 1988, s. 143(5), (6).
[7] FA 1988, s. 143(7).
[8] FA 1988, s. 143(8).
[9] FA 1988, s. 143(9).

Bearer letters of allotment, etc

61: 19   With effect from 25th March 1986 the previous exemption from bearer instrument duty for bearer letters of allotment is repealed.[1]

As regards "overseas bearer instruments", the exemption is withdrawn where the first transfer in this country of a bearer letter issued by an overseas body takes place after 24th March 1986.[2]

The provision extends to Northern Ireland.[3]

The provision is deemed to have come into force on 25th March 1986.[4]

[1] FA 1986, s. 80.
[2] FA 1986, s. 80(3).
[3] FA 1986, s. 80(4).
[4] FA 1986, s. 80(5).

UNIT TRUSTS

History

61: 20 Unit trusts have been subject to stamp duty in two principal ways. The first was unit trust instrument duty, which was charged by FA 1946 but later by FA 1962, s. 30(1), when the trust was created or added to by contribution of capital: this head of charge was abolished by FA 1988, s. 140. The second is the appropriate head of duty applicable on the transfer of units in the trust which may be a conveyance on sale or a conveyance by voluntary disposition (unless certified as exempt).

It is provided that any references to stock in stamp duty legislation includes a reference to unit trust units[1] (and sub-units);[2] among the consequences of this are that a transfer of property to trustees in exchange for units is a conveyance on sale[3] and that the nil rate of conveyance on sale duty,[4] generally applicable when the value does not exceed £30,000 and the instrument is certified, do not apply.[5] It also follows that an agreement for sale of units is not liable to duty as a conveyance under s. 59.[6]

Sergeant and Sims, pp. 177–182.
[1] FA 1946, s. 54(1).
[2] FA 1946, s. 57(1) 'unit'.
[3] SA 1891, s. 55, supra, § **61: 02**.
[4] See, supra, § **58: 03**.
[5] FA 1984, s. 109.
[6] SA 1891.

Unit trust instrument duty: history of and abolition

61: 21 As indicated unit trust instrument duty has been abolished. It was payable formerly at the rate of 0.25% on the value of property which:
  (*a*) became subject to the trust instrument which creates the unit trust, or
  (*b*) becomes trust property represented by units under the scheme.

Until 1962 there was stamp duty at 0.25% on settlements of money, stock or securities generally but in 1962 this duty was abolished, except in the case of unit trusts.

The abolition of unit trust instrument duty applies to property which became trust property on or after 16th March 1988, and will reduce the cost of creating or expanding a unit trust to the benefit of investors.

No unit trust instrument duty will be payable on property acquired on or after 16th March 1988. From that date there will be a fixed stamp duty of 50p on a trust deed or other instrument creating or recording a unit trust (as a declaration of trust).

Object of abolition

61: 22   The object of abolition of unit trust instrument duty was to:

(*a*) lower costs for companies issuing shares;

(*b*) remove a bias against risk capital as compared with debt finance and bank borrowing;

(*c*) lower costs for unit trusts (and hence for their investors);

(*d*) simplify the tax system for companies, unit trusts, their advisers and the Revenue.

Keeping of records

61: 23   The Revenue are empowered by FA 1946, s. 56(3) to make regulations regarding the records to be kept by the trustees and fund managers. These regulations are contained in SI 1946 No. 1586.

Conveyance on sale duty/on transfer of units

61: 24   The abolition of unit trust instrument duty does not affect stamp duty and stamp duty reserve tax on transfer of property to a unit trust or on transfers and agreements to transfer units in a unit trust. If a unit holder sells his units direct to another person and authorises or instructs the trustees to treat the purchaser as the person interested in the units, the instruction is treated as an instrument of sale:[1] a similar rule applies where the holder surrenders his units by instrument instructing the trustees to treat him as no longer interested.[2] If surrendered units are resold within two months, duty on the resale is limited to 50p,[3] a provision of great importance where units are surrendered and replacements issued. Other provisions apply to certain forms of resale of surrendered units, these reissues or replacements being declared to be transfers,[4] and allow a refund of duty on the surrender or extinction of certain units[5] the point being that duty due on the surrender is repaid where, in consequence, a part of the property has been realised and the unit then extinguished.

Repayment claims should be submitted to—Stamp Allowance Section, Office of the Controller of Stamps, Inland Revenue, South Block, Barrington Road, Worthing, West Sussex BN12 4SF. In Scotland claims should be submitted to Stamp Allowance Section, Inland Revenue, Controller (Stamps) Scotland, 16 Picardy Place, Edinburgh EH1 3WF.

The trustees are not permitted to register a transfer of units unless an instrument of transfer has been delivered, save when the right to the unit has been transmitted by law.[6] This rule overrides anything in the trust instrument and means that any transfer must be appropriately stamped.[7]

Sergeant and Sims, pp. 180–182 and Supplement.

[1] FA 1946, s. 57(2).

[2] FA 1946, s. 57(3). See *Arbuthnot Financial Services Ltd v IRC* [1985] STC 211.

[3] FA 1946, s. 54(3).

[4] FA 1946, s. 57(4).

[5] FA 1946, s. 54(4). For procedure, see notices issued by the Stamp Office.

[6] FA 1946, s. 56(4).

[7] SA 1891, s. 17.

Unit trust schemes

61: 25   For definitions and exceptions see the Stamp Duty and Stamp Duty Reserve Tax (Definitions of Unit Trust Scheme) Regulations 1988, SI 1988 No. 268.

These Regulations provide for certain unit trust schemes to be excepted from the definitions of unit trust scheme given by FA 1946, s. 57(1) and F(No 2)A (Northern Ireland) 1946, s. 28(1). As substituted by FA 1987, s. 48, those sections provide that "unit trust scheme" is to have the same meaning as in the Financial Services Act 1986. Two types of unit trust scheme are excepted from the definitions in FA 1946, s. 57(1) and F(No 2)A (Northern Ireland) 1946, s. 28(1) by these Regulations: limited partnership schemes and approved profit sharing schemes. In these cases the trust instrument relating to the scheme will not be liable to unit trust instrument duty and units under the scheme will not be treated as stock for transfer duty purposes or (by virtue of FA 1986, s. 99(9)) as chargeable securities for the purposes of stamp duty reserve tax.

FA 1989, s. 174 (which is substituted for FA 1980, s. 101) provides for exemption from stamp duty on certain transfers of units in an authorised trust scheme under the terms of which the funds of the trust cannot be invested in certain ways.

Sergeant and Sims, Supplement p. A33.

62 Companies: reliefs

RELIEF FROM CONVEYANCE OR TRANSFER ON SALE DUTY—TRANSFERS BETWEEN ASSOCIATED COMPANIES

The relief

62: 01 FA 1930, s. 42 provides relief from conveyance or transfer on sale duty[1] for an instrument which transfers a beneficial interest in property from one associated company to another. As with other reliefs the claim must be adjudicated. The Stamp Office, Adjudication Section, Worthing has issued a set of explanatory notes about the procedural requirements.[2]

Sergeant and Sims, pp. 362–380 and Supplement.
[1] It does not grant relief from lease or tack duty and so does not exempt leases operating as conveyances nor those involving premiums. It is considered to apply to purchases by companies of own shares (see supra, § **61: 06**).
[2] The notes are reproduced in **Sergeant and Sims, pp. 376–377.**

Associate status

62: 02 Companies are associated if (*a*) one is the beneficial owner of at least 90% of the issued share capital of the other; or (*b*) a third body corporate is the beneficial owner of both bodies corporate. So if X Ltd owns all the shares of Y Ltd and Z Ltd, X is associated with Y and with Z under rule (*a*) and Y and Z are associated with each other under rule (*b*). Indirect holdings are taken into account using a multiplication formula; so if P Ltd owns 80% of the shares in Q Ltd which holds 50% of the shares in R Ltd, P owns 40% of the shares in R Ltd.[1] The amount of issued share capital is calculated by adding up the nominal value of the shares issued without regard either to market value or to different classes of shares.[2] Shares which have not yet been registered are not issued.[3]

1422

Sergeant and Sims, p. 366 and Supplement.
[1] FA 1938, Sch. 4, added by FA 1967, s. 27(2).
[2] *Canada Safeway Ltd v IRC* [1972] 1 All ER 666.
[3] *Holmleigh (Holdings) Ltd v IRC* (1958) 46 TC 435.

Conditions

62: 03   It has been held that the condition that the instrument should transfer a beneficial interest from the one associated company to the other requires that this should be substantially the sole effect of the instrument but this is questionable.[1] It has also been held that there should be beneficial ownership of the interest in each company and that a company which has entered into an unconditional contract of sale is not the beneficial owner of the property.[2] Even a conditional contract has had this effect if the purchaser can waive the conditions[3] or where the vendor is otherwise unable to sell.[4] The courts have even held that when a company is controlled by persons who have bound themselves to procure a sale by the company, the company is not the beneficial owner.[5] A company ceases to be a beneficial owner when it is placed in liquidation.[6]

These cases are relevant also to the question of the beneficial ownership of shares needed to ensure associate status. However whereas the relief is when beneficial ownership of this interest is satisfied at the time of the contract or opposed to the conveyance, the Revenue appears to insist on the beneficial ownership test for associate status being satisfied at both dates and all dates in between.[7]

Sergeant and Sims, p. 366 and Supplement.
[1] *Escoigne Properties Ltd v IRC* [1957] 1 WLR 174; on appeal [1958] AC 549.
[2] *Parway Estates Ltd v IRC* (1958) 45 TC 135; *Baytrust Holdings Ltd v IRC* [1971] 3 All ER 76.
[3] *Wood Preservation Ltd v Prior* [1968] 2 All ER 849.
[4] *Brooklands Selangor Holdings Ltd v IRC* [1970] 2 All ER 76.
[5] *Holmleigh (Holdings) Ltd v IRC* (1958) 46 TC 435.
[6] *Ayerst v C & K (Construction) Ltd* [1976] AC 167.
[7] But cf. *Times Newspapers Ltd v IRC* [1973] Ch 155.

Restriction of relief

62: 04   Since 1967, following FA 1967, s. 27(3), it has also been necessary to show that the transfer was not effected in pursuance or in connection with any arrangement under which

(a) the consideration—or any part of it—was to be provided or received, directly or indirectly, by a person other than a body corporate which was then an associated company; or

(b) the beneficial interest was previously conveyed or transferred, directly or indirectly, by such a third party; or

(c) the transferor and transferee were to cease to be associated by reason of a change in the percentage of issued share capital of the *transferee* in the beneficial ownership of the transferor or a third body corporate.

These represent a strengthening of words of FA 1930, s. 42. Under that legislation it had been held for the predecessor of (a) that a third party "provided consideration" if the amount due was left unpaid and that person guaranteed it or otherwise intends to provide for payment,[1] or if the money is to be raised by a sale of the assets to that person.[2] It would appear that a loan from a bank on normal commercial terms does not prevent the relief.

For (b) the predecessor of the words "conveyed or transferred" have been construed widely to include the grant of a lease by the third party.[3]

It will be seen that in (c) the words process on the position of the transferee; a change in any holding by the transferor appear to be irrelevant.

The conditions in FA 1967, s. 27(3) were enacted to counter avoidance schemes.[4] The general words "in connection with" and "arrangement" are presumably to be construed widely.[5]

It is not necessary that the company be an English or Scottish company.

An example of the devices at which these rules are aimed is the "dummy bridge company". It was explained by Lord Denning in *Escoigne Properties Ltd v IRC*[6] as follows:

"They took advantage of s. 42 by forming a small company which was a puppet in their hands. It was done in this way: If company A. wished to sell property to company B. for £100,000 and avoid stamp duty, company A. would form a small 'bridge' company of 100 £1 shares in which it held all the shares. Company A. would convey the property to the 'bridge' company for £100,000 but the price would be left owing. By reason of s. 42 that conveyance would be exempt from stamp duty. Then company A. would sell the 100 shares in the 'bridge' company to company B. for £100: and stamp duty of a trifling amount would be paid on the transfer. The 'bridge' company would then convey the property to company B. for £100,000 on the terms that the £100,000 should be paid direct to company A. By reason of s. 42 no stamp duty would be payable on that conveyance. So the sale from company A. to company B. was completed without paying any stamp duty on the £100,000. ... The object of s. 50 was to put a stop to that device: and it succeeded. If any one were to resort to it after 1938 both conveyances would be liable to stamp duty. The first conveyance would be caught by subsection (1)(a). The second subsection (1)(b)" [s. 50 of the FA 1938]. These subsections were repealed in 1967 and sub-ss. (3)(a) and (3)(b), s. 27 of the FA 1967 were substituted for them.

Sergeant and Sims, pp. 365–366 and Supplement.
    [1] *Curzon Offices Ltd v IRC* [1944] 1 All ER 163 and 606.
    [2] *Metropolitan Boot Co Ltd v IRC* (1958) 46 TC 435.
    [3] *IRC v Littlewoods Mail Order Stores Ltd* [1963] AC 135; on the position where the transferee intends to grant a long lease to a third party see **Sergeant and Sims, p. 242**.
    [4] See *Shop and Store Developments Ltd v IRC* [1967] 1 AC 472 and *Times Newspapers Ltd v IRC* [1973] Ch 155.
    [5] See *Clarke Chapman-John Thompson Ltd v IRC* [1976] Ch 91.
    [6] [1958] AC 549.

RELIEFS FROM CONVEYANCE OR TRANSFER ON SALE DUTY ON COMPANY RECONSTRUCTIONS

Withdrawal of reliefs for takeovers, mergers and demergers

62: 05   With effect from 27th October 1986 (when the 0.5% rate of duty on transfer of stocks and shares commenced to apply generally) the complicated and highly technical series of reliefs for takeovers, mergers and demergers were withdrawn.[1] The following provisions were repealed at the same time:

(a) FA 1927, s. 55 and FA (Northern Ireland) 1928 (reconstructions and amalgamations);
(b) FA 1980, Sch. 18, paras. 12(1) and (1A) (demergers);
(c) FA 1985, ss. 78, 79 and 80 (takeovers and winding up).[2]

The withdrawal applied to instruments executed after 26th October 1986.[3] A new set of reliefs were introduced for company reconstructions and reorganisations by FA 1986, ss. 75, 76, 77, and are explained below.

Notwithstanding the repeal of FA 1927, s. 55 there has been important case law decided and more may be expected (in relation to transactions before the date of withdrawal) on the interpretation of expressions used in that section which may be relevant in interpreting the new provisions relating to reliefs for company reconstructions. In *IRC v Kent Process Control Ltd*[4], the expressions "issue of shares" (and the meaning of "beneficial ownership" in relation thereto) and "consideration for the acquisition" were considered and decided upon. The provisions of FA 1927, s. 55 (now repealed) are reproduced, along with commentary and reference made to the cases mentioned in the judgment, in **Sergeant and Sims (8th edn., 1982) pp. 224–239**.

Sergeant and Sims, pp. 383–384 and Supplement.
[1] FA 1986, s. 74.
[2] FA 1986, s. 74(1).
[3] FA 1986, s. 74(3).
[4] [1989] STC 245.

Acquisition reliefs

(a) Schemes of reconstruction

62: 06   There is (with effect from 25th March 1986), a new exemption for schemes of reconstruction where there is no real change of ownership.[1]

The provision applies where a company acquires the whole or part of an undertaking of another company (the target company) as part of a scheme of reconstruction.[2]

There is an exemption from stamp duty on an instrument transferring an undertaking or part of an undertaking, provided that two conditions are met.[3] Broadly these ensure that the undertaking continues to be owned by the same shareholders before and after the acquisition.

There is a requirement of adjudication where the instrument transferring the undertaking or part of an undertaking is claimed to be exempt from duty under these provisions.[4]

As regards the first of the conditions[5] to be satisfied in order to qualify for the exemption, the acquiring company must be registered in the UK, and the consideration for the transfer of the undertaking must be the issue of shares in the acquiring company to all the shareholders of the target company. There must be no other consideration apart from the assumption or discharge by the acquiring company of the target company's liabilities.

As indicated there is a second condition.[6] The undertaking must be acquired for bona fide commercial reasons and the acquisition must not form part of a scheme which has as its main purpose, or one of its main purposes, the avoidance of tax. There is also a requirement that the shares must be issued on a pro rata basis so that there is an identity of ownership of the undertaking both before and after the acquisition.

(b) Acquisition of target company's share capital

During the debate at the report stage of the Finance Bill 1986, attention was drawn to a problem which seemed to emerge from the wording of FA 1986, s. 75 outlined above. Whilst it was clear that the relief thereunder would apply where the reorganisation involved a transfer of a trading subsidiary from one group member to another, provided the consideration consisted of shares and the shares were issued to the shareholders of the target company, it appeared that they could not be issued to the target company itself. On that basis, therefore, there would be no relief where a group wished to restructure itself and put a new holding company on top of the existing group.[7] In such a situation the acquiring company would need to issue shares to the target company and not to the shareholders of the target company. The problem was recognised and accepted by the Government and a new clause to the Bill was introduced and the provisions are now contained in FA 1986, s. 77 to take into account the possiblity of placing a holding company over the top of an existing group and to grant the relief in such circumstances provided the conditions laid down therein are satisfied.[8]

The conditions[9] are that:

(a) the registered office of the acquiring company is in the UK,

(b) the transfer forms part of an arrangement by which the acquiring company acquires the whole of the issued share capital of the target company,

(c) acquisition is effected for bona fide commercial reasons and does not form part of a scheme or arrangement of which the main purpose, or one of the main purposes, is avoidance of liability to stamp duty, stamp duty reserve tax, income tax, corporation tax or capital gains tax,

(d) the consideration for the acquisition consists only of the issue of shares in the acquiring company to the shareholders of the target company,

(e) after the acquisition has been made, each person who immediately before it was made was a shareholder of the target company is a shareholder of the acquiring company,

(f) after the acquisition has been made, the shares in the acquiring company are of the same classes as were the shares in the target company immediately before the acquisition was made,

(g) after the acquisition has been made, the number of shares of any particular class in the acquiring company bears to all the shares in that company the same proportion as the number of shares of that class in the target company bore to all the shares in that company immediately before the acquisition was made, and

(h) after the acquisition has been made, the proportion of shares of any particular class in the acquiring company held by any particular shareholder is the same as the proportion of shares of that class in the target company held by him immediately before the acquisition was made.

The references to shares and to share capital in these statutory provisions include references to stock.[10]

The relief applies to any instrument executed after 31st July 1986.[11]

Sergeant and Sims, pp. 384–396 and Supplement.
[1] FA 1986, s. 75. For precedent letter of claim, see § **62: 08**.
[2] FA 1986, s. 75(1).
[3] FA 1986, s. 75(2).
[4] FA 1986, s. 75(3).
[5] FA 1986, s. 75(4).
[6] FA 1986, s. 75(5).
[7] FA 1986, s. 75(6), (7).
[8] FA 1986, s. 77(3).
[9] FA 1986, s. 77(3).
[10] FA 1986, s. 77(4).
[11] FA 1986, s. 77(5).

(c) Further relief provisions

62: 07   FA 1986, s. 76 is designed to ensure that transfers of property (as distinct from shares) exempt previously under the provisions repealed from 27th October 1986 are charged to no more than the 0.5% rate on or after 27th October 1986.

The relief applies where a company (the acquiring company) acquires the whole or part of the undertaking of another company (the target company).[1]

(a) There is provision for a special rate of duty (as set out) where an instrument is executed for the purposes of transferring an undertaking or for the transfer to the acquiring company by a creditor of "relevant debts" (as defined) by a creditor of the target company.[2]

(b) There is set out the condition to be satisfied for the 0.5% rate of duty to apply. The acquiring company must be registered in the UK; and the consideration must include the issue of shares to the target company itself or some or all of its shareholders.[3]

The only other consideration allowed is:

(i) cash (not exceeding 10% of the nominal value of the shares issued); and

(ii) the assumption or discharge by the acquiring company of the liabilities of the target company.

A duty at a rate of 0.5% is imposed where the instrument is within the terms of paragraph (a) and satisfies the condition in paragraph (b).[4]

There is a requirement of adjudication where an instrument is liable to the 0.5% rate under this provision.[5]

The expression "relevant debts" is defined as debts owed by the target company to a bank or a trade creditor or any other debt incurred not less than two years before the transfer takes place.[6]

The above provision applies to instruments executed on or after 27th October 1986. Instruments executed earlier are covered by FA 1986, s. 73.[7]

Sergeant and Sims, pp. 384–396 and Supplement.
[1] FA 1986, s. 76(1). For precedent letter of claim, sse § **62: 08**.

[2] FA 1986, s. 76(2).
[3] FA 1986, s. 76(3).
[4] FA 1986, s. 76(4).
[5] FA 1986, s. 76(5).
[6] FA 1986, s. 76(6).
[7] FA 1986, s. 76(7).

Procedure

62: 08   The Stamp Office has issued a set of explanatory notes and precedent letters of claim for relief under FA 1986, ss. 75–77 which are essential reading. The precedent letters are obtainable *only* from the Adjudication Section, Worthing.[1]

[1] The notes are reproduced in **Sergeant and Sims, p. 395** and the precedent letters are reproduced on **pp. 386–394**.

Bearer letters of allotment—withdrawal of exemption

62: 09   With effect from 25th March 1986, the exemption from bearer instrument duty for bearer letters of allotment, was withdrawn.[1]

The exemption for bearer letters of allotment has been repealed. Previously bearer letters were exempt from bearer instrument duty provided their life did not exceed six months.[2]

The exemption is withdrawn where any inland bearer letter is issued after 24th March 1986 unless it is issued by a company as a result of an offer which had become unconditional as to acceptances on or before 18th March 1986.[3]

For "overseas bearer instruments", the exemption is withdrawn where the first transfer in this country of a bearer letter issued by an overseas body takes place after 24th March 1986.[4]

The provision extends to Northern Ireland.[5]

The provision is deemed to have come into force on 25th March 1986.[6]

Sergeant and Sims, p. 343 and Supplement.
[1] FA 1986, s. 80.
[2] FA 1986, Sch. 23, Pt IX(3).
[3] FA 1986, s. 80(2).
[4] FA 1986, s. 80(3).
[5] FA 1986, s. 80(4).
[6] FA 1986, s. 80(5).

Sales to market makers

62:10   FA 1986, s. 81 provides an exemption for purchases of shares, etc. by market makers.[1] Under the Stock Exchange rules, member firms are no longer classified as "brokers" or "jobbers" according to their dealing capacity. All firms are known as "broker-dealers". Any firm is allowed to apply to The Stock Exchange Council for registration as a "market maker" in particular stocks.

It is provided that stamp duty is not to be charged on an instrument transferring stock on sale to a market maker or his nominee in the ordinary course of his business.

The instrument concerned must be stamped with a stamp denoting that the instrument is not chargeable with any duty.[2]

A market maker is defined as someone who:

(*a*) holds himself out at all normal times in compliance with the rules of The Stock Exchange as willing to buy and sell stock of that kind at a price specified by him, and

(*b*) is recognised as doing so by the council of The Stock Exchange.

Alternatively he may be a person who:

(*a*) is an authorised person under the Financial Services Act 1986, Part I, Chapter III,

(*b*) carried out the transaction in the course of his business as a dealer in investments, within the meaning of the Financial Services Act 1986, Sch. 1, para. 12,

(*c*) did not carry out the transaction in the course of any of the activities which fall within the Financial Services Act 1986, Sch. 1, paras. 14 and 16, and

(*d*) the stock was not at the time the transaction was carried out dealt in on a recognised investment exchange.[3]

A "recognised investment exchange" means an exchange within the meaning of the Financial Services Act 1986.[4]

Sergeant and Sims, pp. 344, 725 and Supplement.

[1] FA 1986, s. 81(1). See also Revenue Press Release, dated 4 November 1987.

[2] FA 1986, s. 81(2).

[3] FA 1986, s. 81(3) as substituted by the Finance Act 1986 (Stamp Duty and Stamp Duty Reserve Tax) (Amendment) Regulations, S.I. 1988/654, which came into force on 29th April 1988. For the references to the Financial Services Act 1986, see *Butterworths Financial Services Law and Practice*. See also FA 1986, s. 81(4)–(7) for the Treasury's regulatory powers.

[4] FA 1986, s. 85(5)).

Borrowing of stock by market makers

62: 11   FA 1986, s. 82 provides relief from ad valorem duty where a market maker "borrows stock".[1] Without the exemption ad valorem duty would be payable in some circumstances when the stock was returned to the lender. The relief replaces a similar relief for jobbers provided by FA 1961, s. 34.

FA 1986, s. 82(1) and (2) describe stock lending transactions which are covered by the relief.[2] The arrangements must be made to enable the borrower, i.e. the market maker (labelled A), to deliver securities he has sold. The identity of the other participants (B and C) depend on the nature of the arrangement. If A borrows directly from a lender, FA 1986, s. 82(1) applies. Circumstances may arise, however, where there is an intermediary through whom the stock lending is arranged, in which case FA 1986, s. 82(2) applies. In all cases, the stock lending arrangement must provide that the borrowed stock is replaced by securities of the same kind and amount.

There is a maximum duty of 50p on transfers back to the lender or the intermediary in the cases to which the provision applies.[3] This is the duty that would be payable if the transfer was made by the market maker direct to the lender or the intermediary.

There is a definition of market makers[4] and a regulatory power for the definition to be varied to include market makers on other recognised investment exchanges.[5] Subject to such regulations the provision applies to a transaction after the day specified therein.[6]

Sergeant and Sims, pp. 344–345 and Supplement.
[1] FA 1986, s. 82.
[2] FA 1986, s. 82(1), (2).
[3] FA 1986, s. 82(3).
[4] FA 1986, s. 82(4).
[5] FA 1986, s. 82(6) and FA 1987, s. 53.
[6] FA 1986, s. 82(5).

Composition agreements

62: 12   The Revenue is enabled to enter into composition arrangements for the payment of stamp duty with recognised clearing houses.[1] FA 1970, s. 33 already provides for this in relation to The Stock Exchange. Section 33 is amended to enable similar arrangements to be made with other clearing houses established under the regulatory regime now being provided by the Financial Services Act 1986.[2] The terms of the composition arrangement will be such as to ensure that there is no loss of duty.

The provision comes into force when appointed by the Board of Inland Revenue by statutory instrument.[3]

Sergeant and Sims, p. 345 and Supplement.
[1] FA 1986, s. 83.
[2] FA 1986, s. 83(2).
[3] FA 1986, s. 83(3).

Transfers to clearing houses

62: 13   There is an exemption for transfers of shares to a clearing house which has entered into a composition arrangement similar to that at present provided by FA 1976, s. 127 for transfers of stock to The Stock Exchange's nominee holding company.[1] Under The Stock Exchange's computerised system (TALISMAN) for settling bargains, stock "in transit" between a sale and purchase is held by a special nominee company. The exemption for transfers to the nominee company ensures that only one charge to stamp duty arises when stock etc., passes between seller and purchaser.[2] Without the exemption there would be two charges to duty—once on transfer into the nominee company's name and again on the transfer into the name of the purchaser.

There are detailed arrangements for the starting date of these provisions pursuant to an order to be made by the Inland Revenue.[3]

Sergeant and Sims, pp. 345–346 and Supplement.
[1] FA 1986, s. 84.
[2] FA 1986, s. 84(2).

Broker-dealers

62: 14   FA 1986, s. 85 amends FA 1920, s. 42 (which provides relief from ad valorem duty for transfers to jobbers, their nominees, or to certain qualified dealers) to take account of the introduction with effect from 27th October 1986 of a relief (FA 1986, s. 81) for transfers of shares to market makers. There is preserved the existing relief for qualified dealers until such time as they can qualify as market makers under the new regulatory regime now provided by the Financial Services Act 1986. The jobbers' relief for stock borrowing is also terminated.

The exemption for jobbers is removed for periods after 27th October 1986.[1]

The exemptions for stock borrowing by jobbers are disapplied after 27th October 1986.[2] The corresponding provision in Northern Ireland is also amended to the same effect.

The Treasury is given a regulatory power to bring the exemption provided by FA 1920, s. 42 to an end when dealers entitled to the relief provided by s. 42 are able to qualify for the exemption provided by FA 1986, s. 81(6), (7)).[3]

FA 1976, s. 127(2) (which treats transfers of stock out of The Stock Exchange nominee company to jobbers as sales) is repealed by FA 1986, s. 85(4) in respect of transactions after 27th October 1986.[4]

Definitions of various terms in FA 1986, ss. 81, 82 and 84 are provided.[5]

Sergeant and Sims, p. 346 and Supplement.
  [1] FA 1986, s. 85(1).
  [2] FA 1986, s. 85(2).
  [3] FA 1986, s. 85(3).
  [4] FA 1986, s. 85(4), Sch. 23, Pt. IX(4).
  [5] FA 1986, s. 85(5).

Depositary receipts

62: 15   Stamp duty at 1.5% is imposed on the consideration paid when UK shares are transferred against the issue of depositary receipts.[1] Transfers to which the 1.5% stamp duty applies are transfers to nominees which only hold shares for depositary receipt purposes. It is, however, provided that the Treasury shall have the power to extend stamp duty to other nominees if this should prove necessary to prevent avoidance of the charge.[2] There is provision to enable the Inland Revenue to obtain relevant information. It requires persons who issue depositary receipts, or who hold shares as nominees to a person who issues such receipts, or companies which find their shares are being held as depositary receipts, to notify the Inland Revenue of the fact.[3] There are detailed definitions of the terms used.[4] There are equivalent provisions for stamp duty on shares put into duty free clearance systems.[5]

Sergeant and Sims, pp. 332–338 and Supplement.
[1] FA 1986, s. 67. See also Revenue Press Release, dated 24 October 1986, reproduced in *Sergeant and Sims*, p. 463.
[2] FA 1986, s. 69.
[3] FA 1986, s. 68.
[4] FA 1986, s. 69.
[5] FA 1986, ss. 70–72 and FA 1987, s. 52.

63 Stamp duty reserve tax

INTRODUCTION

History

63: 01 (1) FA 1986 introduced a new tax; stamp duty reserve tax.[1] The tax is under the care and management of the Board of Inland Revenue.[2] The provisions of PCTA 1968 apply to the tax, thereby allowing future charges to take effect provisionally from the Budget.[3] The tax, although described as such in its introduction, is not technically stamp duty. It is a separate tax and not to be construed as one with the Stamp Act 1891. Unlike conveyance or transfer duty it is directly enforceable by the Revenue. The provisions in FA 1989, s. 182, forbidding the disclosure of information, apply to stamp duty reserve tax.

(2) The Stamp Office, in October 1986, issued a comprehensive booklet entitled *Stamp Duty Reserve Tax Notes for Guidance*. It is essential reading to an understanding of the law and practice relating to the tax. However, regrettably, it has not been updated and so reliance on some of its passages must not be made without an examination of the numerous changes of detail effected by subsequent legislation and regulations. The administrative rules for stamp duty reserve tax are provided in the Stamp Duty Reserve Tax Regulations, S.I. 1986 No. 1711 (infra § **63: 07**).

(3) FA 1987, s. 56 and Sch. 7 made a number of detailed changes to stamp duty reserve tax. These provisions relate to:

(*a*) the principal charge
(*b*) renounceable letters of allotment etc.
(*c*) market makers in options
(*d*) clearance services
(*e*) charities
(*f*) repayments

(4) F(No. 2)A 1987, s. 100 added a new section 89A to FA 1986 (exceptions for public issues).

(5) In 1988 two important sets of regulations were made by the Treasury. The first was the Finance Act 1986 (Stamp Duty and Stamp Duty Reserve Tax) (Amendment) Regulations, S.I. 1988 No. 654, which came into force on 29 April 1988. These contain a revised definition of "market maker" and extend the exemptions from stamp duty and stamp duty reserve tax to an "authorised person" under the Financial Services Act 1986, Part I, Chapter III in certain circumstances.

(6) The Stamp Duty Reserve Tax (Amendment) Regulations, S.I. 1988 No. 835, were made by the Treasury on 5 May 1988 to amend the administrative rules for stamp duty reserve tax. In particular they change the rules on who should account for tax, and the definition of a qualified dealer for the purposes of those rules. The changes took effect on 27th May 1988.

As mentioned above, the administrative rules for stamp duty reserve tax were provided in the Stamp Duty Reserve Tax Regulations, S.I. 1986 No. 1711 and new Regulations amend those rules to take account of changes flowing from the Financial Services Act 1986, and experience of operating stamp duty reserve tax (see infra, § **63: 07**).

(7) FA 1988, s. 144 deals with stamp duty reserve tax in relation to what are described as "paired shares" on the lines of the provisions for stamp duty in relation to such shares in FA 1988, s. 143 (supra § **61: 18**).

Sergeant and Sims, pp. 621, 629–630, 649–674, 685–713 and Supplement. These pages reproduce much of the relevant statutory material and regulations but the information therein must be read in the light of the changes made by FA 1988, s. 144 and the Stamp Duty Reserve Tax Regulations, S.I. 1986 No. 1711, as amended by SI 1988 Nos. 654, 835.
  [1] FA 1986, s. 86(1).
  [2] FA 1986, s. 86(2).
  [3] FA 1986, s. 86(3).

THE PRINCIPAL CHARGE

63: 02   (1) *Nature of the charge.* Under FA 1986, Part IV a charge of 0.5% (the stamp duty reserve tax) is imposed on agreements to transfer chargeable securities for a consideration. It commenced on 27th October 1986. There is no stamp duty on agreements to purchase UK shares (or other chargeable securities) where there is no change in the registered ownership of the shares. Also, no stamp duty arises if there is no transfer document. Stamp duty is not therefore payable on the purchase of shares (or other chargeable securities) registered in the name of a nominee acting both for the seller and purchaser or on most renunciations of letters of allotment.

The charge is at the rate of 0.5% on the amount of value of the consideration.[1] A valuation rule is provided where the consideration does not consist of money.[2] The charge applies to transfers made after 26th October 1986.[3] Broadly the charge does not apply to—

(*a*) any securities which are exempt from all stamp duty on transfer (for example gilt-edged securities);

(*b*) securities liable to bearer instrument (stamp duty);

(*c*) transactions in depositary receipts;

(*d*) traded options, i.e. options which are quoted on a recognised stock exchange or on a recognised futures exchange.

Also excluded are agreements to transfer connected with public issues of securities (F(No. 2)A 1987, s. 100 which adds new s. 89A to FA 1986).

There is a revised definition of the transactions within the scope of the charge. The charge applies where there is an agreement to transfer "chargeable securities" (see FA 1986, s. 99(3), (4) as substituted by FA 1988, s. 144(2) for money or money's worth.[4] Because the charge only applies to agreements to transfer securities it does not, for example, apply to a new issue of shares or the issue of an allotment letter.

(2) *Conditions to be fulfilled.* It is provided that the charge arises if certain conditions are not fulfilled within a period of two months of a specified day, "the relevant day" (see below).[5] The two month period provided is designed to give time for a stamped transfer to be produced.

The expression "the relevant day" is defined for the purposes of determining the beginning of the two month period.[6] Normally it is the day on which the agreement is made. Where, however, the agreement is conditional it is the day on which the condition is satisfied.

There is set out the first of two conditions that have to be satisfied within the two months following the relevant day if a charge is not to arise.

(i) The first condition is that there must be an instrument (or instruments) executed in pursuance of the agreement and the instrument transfers (or all the instruments between them transfer) the securities to which the agreement relates to B (one of the parties to the relevant agreement) or to B's nominee.[7]

For example, this condition will be satisfied where in connection with the purchase of shares on the Stock Exchange, a Stock Transfer Form or a TALISMAN Bought Transfer Form is produced within two months of the transfer.

(ii) The second condition is that the instrument (or instruments) transferring the securities to which the agreement relates must be duly stamped if it is chargeable to stamp duty.[8] An instrument is duly stamped if it is stamped in accordance with the law at the date of execution.

(3) FA 1987, Sch. 7, para. 2 adds new subsections ((7A) and (7B)) to FA 1986, s. 87.

(i) *Sub-sales.* The new subsection (7A) clarifies the law where shares (or other chargeable securities) are subsold and the number of shares bought exceeds the number of shares subsold. The subsection provides for s. 87 to have effect as if there were separate agreements in respect of each parcel of shares. The effect of this is that stamp duty reserve tax is only paid in respect of the shares subsold. The following example shows how this provision will operate.

A sells to B 1,000 shares in X plc for £1,500
B resells 750 of these shares to C
A transfers 750 shares to C and 250 shares to B

Subsection (7A) deems the agreement between A and B to be two separate agreements, one in respect of 750 shares and one in respect of 250 shares with the result that B incurs a reserve tax liability on the agreement to purchase 750 shares i.e. on £1,125 (75% of £1,500). The stamp duty payable on the transfer to B of the 250 shares franks the stamp duty reserve tax liability on that agreement.

On a strict construction of s. 87 there was a stamp duty reserve tax charge on the whole of the consideration paid by B to A. The Stamp Duty Reserve Tax Notes for Guidance issued by the Controller of Stamps in October 1986 indicated that tax would only be sought in respect of that part of the consideration which related to the shares subsold. The subsection puts this practice on a proper statutory basis.

(ii) *Purchase with loan.* Subsection (7B) clarifies the application of the tax where there is a transfer of chargeable securities to a person (e.g. a bank) who is providing a loan for the purchase and who is to hold the chargeable securities as security for the loan. On a strict construction of s. 87 the transaction gave rise to a double charge—stamp duty reserve tax on the purchase agreement and ad valorem stamp duty on the transfer of chargeable securities to the person who is to hold them. The transaction would not fall within the franking provisions in s. 87(4), (5), as the transfer to the bank would not be to the person who had agreed to purchase the chargeable securities or to his nominee. The subsection brings the transaction within the terms of those provisions with the result that the stamp duty reserve tax charge is removed.

Subpara. (2) deems these changes always to have had effect.

Exclusions and exceptions.

(a) *Unit trusts.* Excluded from the charge are transfers of units under a unit trust scheme to the managers of the scheme.[9]

(b) *Market makers.* Also excluded is an agreement to transfer securities if the person agreeing to purchase the securities does so in the ordinary course of his business as a market maker in securities of the kind concerned.[10]

FA 1987, Sch. 7, para. 4 provides a stamp duty reserve tax exemption for market makers in options.

Subpara. (1) adds a new subsection to FA 1986, s. 89 (exemptions for market makers etc.) which provides that the principal charge does not apply to the purchase of chargeable securities by a Stock Exchange market maker in quoted options in the ordinary course of the firm's business as a market maker in these options. The definition of "quoted options" provided will cover both traded options and traditional options.

Subpara. (2) deems the change always to have had effect.

The definition of "market maker" for the purposes of the section has been substituted by regulation 3 of the FA 1986 (Stamp Duty and Stamp Duty Reserve Tax) (Amendment) Regulations, S.I. 1988 No. 654). Now for these purposes a person is a market maker in securities of a particular kind:

(i) if he:

(1) holds himself out at all normal times in compliance with the rules of The Stock Exchange as willing to buy and sell securities of that kind at a price specified by him, and

(2) is recognised as doing so by the Council of The Stock Exchange; or

(ii) if:

(1) he is an authorised person under the Financial Services Act 1986, Part I, Chapter III,

(2) he makes the agreement in the course of his business as a dealer in investments, within the meaning of the Financial Services Act 1986, Sch. 1, para. 12, as a principal and in circumstances where that paragraph is applicable for the purposes of that Act.

(3) he does not make the agreement in the course of any activities which fall within the Financial Services Act 1986, Sch. 1, paras. 14 or 16, and

(4) the securities are not at the time the agreement is made dealt in on a recognised investment exchange within the meaning of the Financial Service Act 1986.

(*c*) *Clearance systems.* FA 1987, s. 56 and Sch. 7 para. 5 contains further provisions relating to exemptions from the charge. It widens the terms of the exemption from the principal charge for shares and other securities which attract the 1½% stamp duty or reserve tax charge when they enter a clearance system.[11] The change ensures that the exemption will apply in all such cases. It replaces FA 1986, s. 90(5) which provides this exemption, with two new subsections.[12] These exempt agreements to transfer securities held by nominees whose business is exclusively to hold securities as nominee for a clearance system whether or not the securities held are within the scope of the stamp duty reserve tax charge.[13] As the law was formerly, the exemption would only apply if the nominee held securities liable to the reserve tax.

The provision is deemed always to have had effect.[14]

(*d*) *Public issues.* There are exceptions for public issues in certain circumstances. The charge to stamp duty reserve tax does not apply as regards an agreement to transfer securities other than units under a unit trust scheme to B or B's nominee if—

(i) the agreement is part of an arrangement, entered into by B in the ordinary course of B's business as an issuing house, under which B (as principal) is to offer the securities for sale to the public,

(ii) the agreement is conditional upon the admission of the securities to the Official List of The Stock Exchange,

(iii) the consideration under the agreement for each security is the same as the price at which B is to offer the security for sale, and

(iv) B sells the securities in accordance with the arrangement referred to in paragraph (*a*) above.[15]

Also the charge does not apply as regards an agreement if the securities to which the agreement relates are newly subscribed securities other than units under a unit trust scheme and—

(i) the agreement is made in pursuance of an offer to the public made by A (as principal) under an arrangement entered into in the ordinary course of A's business as an issuing house,

(ii) a right of allotment in respect of, or to subscribe for, the securities has been acquired by A under an agreement which is part of the arrangement,

(iii) both those agreements are conditional upon the admission of the securities to the Official List of The Stock Exchange, and

(iv) the consideration for each security is the same under both agreements;

and for these purposes, "newly subscribed securities" are securities which, in pursuance of the arrangements referred to in paragraph (i) above, are issued wholly for new consideration.[16]

Also the charge does not apply as regards an agreement if the securities to which the agreement relates are registered securities other than units under a unit trust scheme and—

(i) the agreement is made in pursuance of an offer to the public made by A,

(ii) the agreement is conditional upon the admission of the securities to the Official List of The Stock Exchange, and

(iii) under the agreement A issues to B or his nominee a renounceable letter of acceptance, or similar instrument, in respect of the securities.[17]

These provisions were inserted to enable public offerings to be structured with merchant banks acting as principals without additional stamp duty reserve tax liabilities arising and to preclude certain "double charges" to stamp duty reserve tax and stamp duty arising.

The Treasury is empowered to make regulations to amend the provisions as specified.[18]

(6) *Charities, etc.* It is provided that stamp duty reserve tax is not to apply to purchases of shares etc by charities and certain analogous bodies.[19] It adds a new subsection to FA 1986, s. 90 (exemptions from stamp duty reserve tax charge). It disapplies the reserve tax charge where securities are bought by a charity, a charitable trust or certain analogous bodies.[20] These transactions may be adjudicated free of stamp duty and were treated as exempt from the reserve tax. This paragraph puts the reserve tax practice on to a statutory basis and this provision is deemed always to have had effect.[21]

Sergeant and Sims, Division C pp. 621–715.

[1] FA 1986, s. 87(6).
[2] FA 1986, s. 87(7).
[3] FA 1986, s. 87(9).
[4] FA 1986, s. 87(1).
[5] FA 1986, s. 87(2).
[6] FA 1986, s. 87(3).
[7] FA 1986, s. 87(4).
[8] FA 1986, s. 87(5).
[9] FA 1986, s. 90. See also the Stamp Duty and Stamp Duty Reserve Tax (Definitions of Unit Trust Scheme) Regulations 1988, S.I. 1988 No. 268 (see §§ **61: 25**, supra).
[10] FA 1986, s. 89, amended by FA 1987, s. 56 and Sch. 7 and substituted in part by FA 1986 (Stamp Duty and Stamp Duty Reserve Tax) (Amendment) Regulations, S.I. 1988 Nos. 654, 835.
[11] FA 1987, Sch. 7, para. 5.
[12] FA 1986, s. 90(5) as substituted.
[13] FA 1986, s. 90(6).
[14] FA 1987, Sch. 7, para. 5(2).
[15] FA 1986, s. 89A(1).
[16] FA 1986, s. 89A(2).
[17] FA 1986, s. 89A(3).
[18] FA 1986, s. 89A(4).
[19] FA 1987, Sch. 7, para. 6(1).
[20] FA 1986, s. 90(7).
[21] FA 1987, Sch. 7, para. 6(2).

Renounceable letters of allotment

63: 03   The liability of letters of allotment of shares to stamp duty reserve tax (see supra, § **63: 01**) is affected by FA 1986, s. 88 (as amended by FA 1987, Sch. 12, para. 3 with effect from 1 August 1987). Renunciations of allotment letters for value will be liable to stamp duty reserve tax. The charge arises on the date on which the agreement to transfer the allotment letter is concluded (or if later becomes unconditional): in practice generally the date on which the letter is renounced.

Sergeant and Sims, pp. 623, 631 and Supplement.

Persons liable to stamp duty reserve tax

63: 04   There are rules for determining the person on whom the liability for the stamp duty reserve tax falls.[1]

Liability to the tax falls on the transferee.[2]

The original express provision preventing the liability falling on a nominee has been repealed.[3]

Sergeant and Sims, pp. 624, 635, 707 and Supplement.
[1] FA 1986, s. 91.
[2] FA 1986, s. 91(1).
[3] F(No. 2)A 1987, s. 100(2); FA 1986, s. 91(2) is repealed by F(No. 2)A 1987, s. 104, Sch. 9, Pt. IV.

Repayment or cancellation of stamp duty reserve tax

63: 05   FA 1986, s. 92 provides principally for the repayment of the tax where stamp duty is also paid. It ensures that stamp duty and the stamp duty reserve tax should not both be paid in respect of a transaction.

Section 92 shall apply where after the two month period contemplated by s. 87(2) it is proved to the Board's satisfaction that the conditions mentioned in s. 87(4) and (5) have been fulfilled. It therefore applies where an instrument is executed and duly stamped after the two month period has expired. It also applies where the instrument is executed within the two month period but not stamped until after the two month period.[1]

Where the charge applies and a claim is made within six years of the agreement (the relevant day as mentioned in s. 87(3)) there is a provision for the tax (not the stamp duty) to be repaid with interest if the tax is not less than £25.[2]

Provision is made for the case where a charge has arisen because the conditions have not been satisfied within the two month period and the tax has not been paid. If the conditions are subsequently satisfied the tax charge is thereby cancelled.[3]

The rate of interest to be paid on repayments is laid down.[4]

The Treasury is given power to vary the rate of interest. The current rate after 5 July 1989 is 12.25%.[5]

It is provided that the Treasury order making power under the above provision is exercisable by statutory instrument and subject to a negative resolution procedure in the House of Commons.

Interest on repayments

FA 1987, Sch. 7, para. 7 exempts from income tax interest paid on repayments of reserve tax. This brings the reserve tax repayment provision into line with similar provisions for other taxes. The exemption is deemed always to have applied.

Sergeant and Sims, pp. 624, 635 and Supplement.
[1] FA 1986, s. 92(1).
[2] FA 1986, s. 92(2).
[3] FA 1986, s. 92(3).
[4] FA 1986, s. 92(4).
[5] The Stamp Duty Reserve Tax (Interest on Tax Repaid) Order, S.I. 1989/1003. The Note to the Order gives details of earlier Orders, the rates thereunder and the operative dates.

Depositary receipts and clearance systems

63: 06   Stamp duty reserve tax at 1.5% is applied to shares (or other securities) issued or transferred into, or appropriated towards satisfaction of a depositary receipt holder's right to obtain the underlying securities (usually shares) under a depositary receipt arrangement whenever the arrangement was made.[1] There is a definition of some of the terms used for the purpose of that charge.[2] The stamp duty reserve tax charge is applied to shares (or other securities) put into a clearance system.[3] There is an adaptation of the definitions used in the stamp duty reserve system to apply to clearance systems. There are supplementary provisions to ensure that where securities are purchased in instalments only the instalments will be liable for the stamp duty reserve tax.[4] Where the depositary bank which would be chargeable is not resident in the UK and has no branch or agency therein the stamp duty reserve tax may be recovered from the person to whom the shares are transferred.[5]

A clearance service is an arrangement for settling transactions in securities. Securities within the system are held in the name of a nominee company acting for the clearance system. Once in the system, securities can be traded *without* payment of stamp duty or need for a transfer document. However, there *is* a stamp duty charge (customarily at $1\frac{1}{2}\%$) *on the transfer into the settlement system.*

The Board of Inland Revenue have announced the names of nominee companies to which, on the transfer of shares to them, the $1\frac{1}{2}\%$ rate of stamp duty will apply (with effect from 27th October 1986) and changes to the list.[6]

Sergeant and Sims, pp. 325, 635–644 and Supplement.
[1] FA 1986, s. 93.
[2] FA 1986, s. 94.
[3] FA 1986, s. 96.
[4] FA 1986, s. 94(1) and s. 96(4).
[5] FA 1986, s. 93(9) and s. 96(7).
[6] Inland Revenue Press Releases dated 24th October 1986, 16th April 1987 and 14th June 1989 *Simon's Tax Intelligence* 1989, p. 502. The former two Releases are reproduced in **Sergeant and Sims, p. 463**.

ADMINISTRATION

63: 07 FA 1986, s. 98 provides regulatory powers[1] for providing the administrative machinery for the stamp duty reserve tax. Regulations which are called Stamp Duty Reserve Tax Administration Regulations 1986 came into operation on 27th October 1986 (SI 1986, No. 1711).
These regulations provide inter alia for:

(a) notices of charge to be furnished;

(b) definition of "accountable person" and "accountable date" for payment of the tax;

(c) power for the Inland Revenue to obtain information;

(d) claims for relief from liability to pay tax;

(e) a standard Inland Revenue appeals procedure (to the Special Commissioners in the first instance);

(f) recovery of tax;[2]

(g) the keeping of records and availability for inspection;

(h) tax liability to remain unaltered notwithstanding a subsequent legal decision or change of opinion;

(i) application of numerous machinery provisions with adaptations of TMA 1970;

(j) the disapplication of the Inland Revenue Regulation Act 1890, ss. 21, 22 and 35 (proceedings for fines, etc).

Further regulations called the Stamp Duty Reserve Tax (Amendment) Regulations, S.I. 1988/835 came into operation on 5th May 1988. In particular regulation 3, as revised, provides for who is responsible for giving the Revenue an account of any tax due, and for paying it over as follows:

(i) market makers and brokers and dealers are made accountable persons for tax on shares bought for themselves or for a client who is not a market maker or broker and dealer; and failing that

(ii) market makers and brokers and dealers are made accountable persons for tax on shares they sell, whether their own or a client's, to someone who is not a market maker or broker and dealer; and failing that

(iii) qualified dealers are made accountable persons for tax on shares they buy for themselves or as agents for a client who is not a qualified dealer; and failing that

(iv) qualified dealers are made accountable persons for tax on shares they sell or act as agents to sell.

(Investors now normally have to account for the tax themselves only when they buy shares privately, without the involvement of a broker or dealer.)

Regulation 6 provides a new definition of a "qualified dealer". For the purposes of administering the tax a qualified dealer will be a member of a self-regulating organisation or a person otherwise authorised under the Financial Services Act 1986, Part I, Chapter III, or a person treated as authorised under the Act's transitional provisions.

Sergeant and Sims, pp. 626, 644 and Supplement.

[1] FA 1989, s. 177 extends the powers to include provision for notices and information to be in a form prescribed by the Commissioners.

[2] See also Inland Revenue Press Release, 1st August 1989.

INTERPRETATION

63: 08   (1) FA 1986, s. 99 provides various definitions for use in connection with stamp duty reserve tax, in particular the definition of "chargeable securities". However, a revised definition of chargeable securities has now been substituted in that section.[1]

(2) FA 1988, s. 144 amends and adds to FA 1986, s. 99 extensively.

(3) Subject to the exceptions mentioned below, the expression "chargeable securities" now means

(*a*) stocks, shares or loan capital;

(*b*) interests in, or in dividends or other rights arising out of, stocks, shares or loan capital;

(*c*) rights to allotments of or to subscribe for, or options to acquire, stocks, shares or loan capital; and

(*d*) units under a unit trust scheme.[2]

(4) The expression "chargeable securities" does not include securities falling within sub-paras (*a*), (*b*) or (*c*) of paragraph (3) above which are issued or raised by a body corporate not incorporated in the United Kingdom unless:

(*a*) it is (or they are) registered in a register kept in the United Kingdom by or on behalf of the body corporate, or

(*b*) in the case of shares, they are paired with shares issued by a body corporate incorporated in the United Kingdom, or

(*c*) in the case of securities falling within paragraph (*a*), (*b*) or (*c*) of paragraph (3) above, paragraph (*a*) to (*b*) above applies to the stocks, shares or loan capital to which they relate.[3]

(5) The expression "chargeable securities" does not include:

(*a*) securities the transfer of which is exempt from all stamp duties, or

(*b*) securities falling within paragraph (*b* or (*c*) of paragraph (3) above and which relate to stocks, shares or loan capital the transfer of which is exempt from all stamp duties.[4] In particular this covers gilt-edged securities.

(6) The expression "chargeable securities" does not include interests in depositary receipts for stocks or shares.[5]
A depositary receipt for stocks or shares is an instrument acknowledging—

(*a*) the deposit of stocks or shares or of an instrument evidencing the right to receive them, and

(*b*) the entitlement of a person to rights, whether expressed as units or otherwise, in or in relation to stocks or shares of the same kind.[6]

(7) For the purposes mentioned in paragraph (4) above, shares issued by a body corporate which is not incorporated in the United Kingdom ("the foreign company") are paired with shares issued by a body corporate which is so incorporated ("the UK company") where:

(*a*) the articles of association of the UK company and the equivalent instruments governing the foreign company each provide that no share in the company to which they relate may be transferred otherwise than

as part of a unit comprising one share in that company and one share in the other, and
(b) such units have been offered for sale to the public in the United Kingdom and, at the same time, an equal number of such units have been offered for sale to the public at a broadly equivalent price in the country in which the foreign company is incorporated.[7]

(8) "Unit" and "unit trust scheme" have the same meanings as in FA 1946, Pt VII (as amended by FA 1987, s. 48).[8]

(9) An amendment to FA 1986, s. 99 by way of substitution has the effect that paragraph (4)(a) above and the reference to sub-paragraph (a) in sub-paragraph (c) is to be ignored for the purposes of the higher rate stamp duty reserve tax charge in relation to clearance services and depositary receipts.[9]

(10) In interpreting "chargeable securities" in FA 1986 ss 93 or 96 in a case where:

(a) newly subscribed shares, or
(b) securities falling within paragraph (b) or (c) of paragraph (3) above which relate to newly subscribed shares,

are issued in pursuance of an arrangement such as is mentioned in that section (or an arrangement which would be such an arrangement if the securities issued were chargeable securities), in sub-paragraph (b) of paragraph (4) above and the reference to that paragraph in sub-paragraph (c) of that paragraph is to be ignored again for the purposes of the higher rate stamp duty reserve tax charges.[10]

(11) In this connection "newly subscribed shares" means shares issued wholly for new consideration in pursuance of an offer for sale to the public."[11]

(12) FA 1988, s. 144 applies in relation to:

(a) agreements to transfer chargeable securities (within the meaning of FA 1986 s. 99 as amended by FA 1988, s. 144 made on or after 9 December 1987; and
(b) the transfer, issue or appropriation of such securities, or the issue of securities such as are mentioned in subsection (11) of that section, on or after that date in pursuance of an arrangement such as is mentioned in that subsection (whenever the arrangement was made),

and is deemed to have come into force on that date.[12]

F(No. 2)A 1987, s. 100 (for public issues) contains a definition of "newly subscribed securities" which contains exceptions from stamp duty reserve tax. For the application of these exceptions, see § **63: 02** supra.

Sergeant and Sims, pp. 626, 645 and Supplement.
[1] FA 1986, s. 99(3) as substituted by FA 1988, s. 144(2).
[2] FA 1986, s. 99(3) as substituted by FA 1988, s. 144(2).
[3] FA 1986, s. 99(4) as substituted by FA 1988, s. 144(2).
[4] FA 1986, s. 99(3) as substituted by FA 1988, s. 144(2).
[5] FA 1986, s. 99(6) as substituted by FA 1988, s. 144(2).
[6] FA 1986, s. 99(7).
[7] FA 1986, s. 99(6A) as substituted by FA 1988, s. 144(2).
[8] FA 1986, s. 99(9).
[9] FA 1986, s. 99(10) as substituted by FA 1988, s. 144(4).

[10] FA 1986, s. 99(11) inserted by FA 1988, s. 144(5).
[11] FA 1986, s. 99(12) inserted by FA 1988, s. 144(5).
[12] FA 1988, s. 144(6).

DEMATERIALISATION

63: 09   The government proposes to introduce a process of paperless share transactions technically known as "dematerialisation"[1] and established under a computerised system known as "TAURUS". As a paperless transaction, it will be necessary to provide for the imposition of stamp duty reserve tax, but avoiding a double charge to stamp duty reserve tax and stamp duty which might otherwise arise. FA 1989, ss. 176 and 177 accordingly empowers the Treasury to make regulations relating to stock exchange nominees to achieve this objective.[2]

[1] For further information, see HC Written Answer, 14th June 1989, Vol. 154, cols 443–444, *Simon's Tax Intelligence* 1989, p. 544.
[2] To date the scheme has not been introduced, nor have any regulations been made.

PART XI. VALUE ADDED TAX

64   General background

INTRODUCTION

History

64: 01   Member states of the European Economic Community (EEC) seek to achieve their treaty aims by establishing a common market and progressively harmonising their economic policies.[1] The common (or "internal") market is to be established by 31st December 1992 so as to comprise an area without internal frontiers in which the free movement of goods, persons, services and capital is ensured.[2]

The original text of EEC Treaty art. 99 required the EC Commission to consider how the legislation of the various member states concerning turnover taxes could be harmonised in the interest of the common market. The proposals submitted by the Commission under this provision ultimately led to the adoption of value added tax (VAT) as the common turnover tax of the member states from 1st January 1972.[3] The broad framework of VAT adopted at the same time[4] required further consideration both to fulfil the harmonising aims of art. 99 and to enable the system of "own resources" adopted by the member states[5] to be fully implemented, and these requirements ultimately led to the adoption of a common system of VAT from 1st January 1978.[6] A number of matters were held over for further consideration[7] and further measures have been adopted from time to time when member states reached a common position.[8] The Single European Act (1986) injected a sense of urgency into these deliberations by inserting a new art. 99. This requires provisions for the harmonisation of legislation concerning turnover taxes to be adopted by 31st December 1992 "to the extent that such harmonisation is necessary to ensure the establishment and functioning of the internal market". The Commission's proposals have largely been prepared[9] but little progress has been made—partly due to political objections raised by the UK—although signs of a compromise seem to be emerging.[10]

The United Kingdom (UK) became an EEC member state on 1st January 1973 and was obliged to introduce VAT in accordance with its Treaty obligations. In fact, the necessary legislation had already been enacted and came into force on 1st April 1973.[11] This legislation was substantially amended to comply with the EEC harmonising provisions effective from 1st January 1978[12] and was consolidated with effect from 26th October 1983.[13]

The United Kingdom (comprising England, Scotland, Wales and Northern

Ireland) and the Isle of Man are in customs union.¹⁴ The Isle of Man enacted
VAT under separate but almost identical legislation¹⁵ under the terms of the
customs union. The two countries are treated as a single area for VAT
purposes.¹⁶

De Voil: Value Added Tax A1.01–07; A2.02, 56, 57.
¹ EEC Treaty, art. 2.
² EEC Treaty, art. 8A (inserted by the Single European Act).
³ Directives 67/227/EEC (the First Directive) and 69/463/EEC (the Third Directive). This
time limit was deferred until 1 July 1972 and 1 January 1973 respectively in relation to Italy by
Directives 71/401/EEC (the Fourth Directive) and 72/250/EEC (the Fifth Directive).
⁴ Directive 67/228/EEC (the Second Directive).
⁵ Decision 70/243/ECSC, EEC, Euratom.
⁶ Directive 77/388/EEC (the Sixth Directive). This time limit was deferred until 1 January
1979 in relation to Denmark, France, Germany, Ireland, Italy, Luxembourg and the Netherlands
by Directive 78/583/EEC (the Ninth Directive).
⁷ See Directive 77/388/EEC arts 14(2), 16(3), 17(4), 17(6), 24(2), 24(9), 25(11), 28(2), 28(4),
28(5), 32 and 35.
⁸ See directives 79/1072/EEC (the Eighth Directive); 83/181/EEC, 83/182/EEC, 83/183/EEC
(regarding exemption from VAT on imported goods); 85/362/EEC (Seventeenth Directive); 86/
560/EEC (Thirteenth Directive).
⁹ See in particular COM (79) 794, COM (82) 402, COM (82) 870, COM (84) 648 final, COM
(84) 649, COM (85) 858 final, COM (86) 163 final, COM (86) 444 final, COM (87) 321 final,
COM (87) 322 final, COM (87) 324 final, COM (88) 846 final.
¹⁰ See HC Written Answers 23 May 1989 (Vol 153 cols 440–441) and 4 July 1989 (Vol 156 col
89).
¹¹ FA 1972, Part I and Schs. 1–6.
¹² FA 1977, s. 14 and Sch. 6.
¹³ Now VATA 1983.
¹⁴ The current agreement is Customs and Excise Agreement 1979, Cmnd. 7747, which is
given effect by Isle of Man Act 1979.
¹⁵ Value Added Tax and Other Taxes Act 1973 (an Act of Tynwald). The exception relates to
the taxation of gaming machine receipts: Isle of Man Act 1979, s. 1(1)(*d*).
¹⁶ Isle of Man Act 1979, s. 6; SI 1982, No. 1067; SI 1982, No. 1068.

Outline

Taxation of value added

64: 02   There are four basic methods of taxing value added: the direct
additive method, the indirect additive method, the direct subtractive method
and the indirect subtractive method. VAT, as its name implies, is a tax on
value added. However, the indirect subtractive method adopted by the EEC
tends to obscure this fact because tax liabilities for an accounting period are
calculated without ascertaining the underlying value added. The relationship
between tax liabilities and value added is further obscured by: (1) the use of
exemptions, valuation reliefs and multiple rates; (2) the fact that changes in
stock levels are disregarded; and (3) the fact that no distinction is made
between capital and revenue expenditure. The interaction of these factors
can give rise to the curious feature that a trader who has added value during
an accounting period may nevertheless receive a repayment of tax.

The indirect subtractive method acts as a tax on consumer expenditure
which is broadly based, largely neutral as regards businesses, and largely
confined to the consumption of goods and services within the UK. These
principles are discussed below.

Taxable transactions

64: 03   VAT is a broadly based tax on consumer expenditure. To be more specific, it is a tax on three classes of transaction made in the UK.

(1) *Supplies of goods and services.* VAT is charged on supplies of goods and services made in the UK by traders referred to as "taxable persons".[1] Tax is charged by the taxable person who makes the supply and he periodically pays the amounts so charged to the Commissioners.[2] This tax is known as "output tax".[3]

(2) *Events treated as a supply.* A number of events which do not amount to a supply, or do not meet the required conditions for tax to be charged on them, are treated as supplies for VAT purposes when made in the UK by taxable persons.[4] Tax is accounted for to the Commissioners in the same manner as output tax. The one difference from supplies is that the "customer" is normally the taxable person himself and in such cases there is no onward charge to a third party.

(3) *Imported goods.* VAT is charged when goods are imported into the UK.[5] The tax due on import is paid direct to the Commissioners at the same time as import duties.[6] This is normally the time when goods are entered for home use, either at the time of importation or when they are removed from a bonded warehouse or free zone.

De Voil: Value Added Tax A1.14.

[1] VATA 1983, ss. 1 and 2(1). For the charge to tax, see § **65: 01–13**.
[2] VATA 1983, ss. 2(3) and 14(1).
[3] VATA 1983, s. 14(3).
[4] VATA 1983, s. 1. For the charge to tax, see § **65: 14–28**.
[5] VATA 1983, s. 1. For the charge to tax, see § **65: 30–34**.
[6] VATA 1983, s. 2(4).

Credit mechanism

64: 04   VAT is largely removed from business costs, and thereby confined to consumer expenditure, by providing taxable persons with a credit mechanism. Subject to a number of exceptions, taxable persons are entitled to recover the VAT they have paid from the Commissioners.[1] This tax is known as "input tax" and represents: (1) tax chargeable on goods and services supplied to them by other taxable persons; (2) tax accounted for on events treated as supplies; and (3) tax paid to the Commissioners on imported goods.

VAT is removed from the business costs of overseas traders who are not taxable persons by a system of refunds. Separate schemes apply for traders carrying on business in EEC member states[2] and third countries.[3]

VAT is also removed from certain non-business expenditure. For example, certain goods and services supplied to specified persons are charged to tax at the zero-rate[4] and refunds of tax are made to do-it-yourself builders[5] and specified public bodies.[6]

VAT is also removed or reduced on certain expenditure common to both business and private consumers. For example, certain goods and services are charged to tax at the zero-rate[7], or exempted from tax[8], and VAT is chargeable on only part of the consideration passing in other cases.[9]

De Voil: Value Added Tax A1.15.
[1] VATA 1983, s. 14(2), (5).
[2] VAT (Repayment to Community Traders) Regulations, SI 1980, No. 1537.
[3] VAT (Repayments to Third Country Traders) Regulations, SI 1987, No. 2015.
[4] For charities, see VATA 1983, Sch. 5, Groups 4, 10, 14 and 16. For handicapped persons, see ibid, Group 16, For certain overseas persons, see ibid, Groups 9, 10 and 15.
[5] VATA 1983, s. 21; VAT ("Do-It-Yourself" Builders) (Relief) Regulations, SI 1975, No. 649.
[6] VATA 1983, s. 20 and orders made thereunder.
[7] For goods and services charged to tax at the zero rate, see § **69: 15–42**.
[8] For goods and services exempt from tax, see § **69: 01–14**.
[9] E.g. the margin schemes for used goods: see § **67: 08–11**.

Taxable persons

64: 05 A taxable person is someone who is, or is required to be, registered for the purposes of VAT.[1] Put another way, he is a person who makes taxable supplies in the course or furtherance of business who is liable to register because his turnover exceeds the prescribed limits[2] or who registers voluntarily in other circumstances.[3]

Taxable persons play an important role in the administration of VAT. It is they who collect output tax on behalf of the Commissioners[4] and they who are entitled to recover input tax from the Commissioners.[5]

De Voil: Value Added Tax A1.13.
[1] VATA 1983, s. 2(2) and (5).
[2] VATA 1983, Sch. 1, paras. 1, 15.
[3] VATA 1983, Sch. 1, paras. 5, 5A, 15.
[4] VATA 1983, s. 2(3).
[5] VATA 1983, s. 14(2), (3), (5).

Exports

64: 06 In very broad terms, goods and services supplied in the UK for consumption abroad are relieved from tax. A general relief is available for goods[1] and a more restricted relief for services.[2]

De Voil: Value Added Tax A1.16.
[1] VATA 1983, s. 16(6) and (7) and Sch. 5, Groups 15, 16. See § **69: 31, 32** and **35–42**.
[2] VATA 1983, s. 16(8) and Sch. 5, Groups 9, 10, 15. See § **69: 23, 24** and **29**.

ADMINISTRATION

Organisation

64: 07 The Department of Customs and Excise is administered by a Board of Commissioners who are authorised to commission officers and appoint or authorise other persons to discharge duties within their purview.[1] The Commissioners of Customs and Excise are collectively referred to in the legislation,[2] and in this Part, as "the Commissioners".

Subject to the general control of the Treasury, the Commissioners are responsible for the collection and management of customs and excise revenues and such other duties (known as "assigned matters") as may be imposed by statute.[3] One of these duties is the care and management of VAT in the UK.[4]

The Department is divided into six "directorates", each headed by a Commissioner. Two directorates are concerned with VAT: the Internal Taxation Directorate (formed by merging the Revenue Duties and VAT Administration Directorates in 1984/85) (based in London) is responsible for policy aspects of VAT, and the VAT Control Directorate (based in Southend-on-Sea) is responsible for collection of tax. In addition, a number of headquarters divisions are concerned with VAT to some extent, e.g. Computer Operations Division, Investigation Division and the Solicitor's Office.

The local administration of VAT is carried out separately from other customs and excise work. Local VAT offices (LVO) are situated in principal towns throughout the country. A typical LVO is headed by an Assistant Collector and divided into eight or ten districts, each headed by a Surveyor. Individual districts deal with internal office procedures (e.g. registration, enquiries and keeping traders' files), collection of outstanding tax, and making routine control visits to traders.

A centralised computer unit (VAT Central Unit) is responsible for issuing tax returns, receiving returns and remittances and maintaining a register of taxable persons.

De Voil: Value Added Tax A2.16–18.
[1] Customs and Excise Management Act 1979, s. 6.
[2] VATA 1983, s. 48(1).
[3] Customs and Excise Management Act 1979, s. 6. The Commissioners' principle responsibilities are: (1) collection of VAT and excise duties; (2) collection of customs duties and agricultural levies for the European Community; (3) enforcement of prohibitions and restrictions on imports and exports; and (4) tasks connected with foreign trade (e.g. trade statistics) on behalf of other government departments: 79th Annual Report, Cm 453, paras 1.2 and 11.1–4.
[4] VATA 1983, Sch. 7, para. 1(1). The Isle of Man has its own independent service.

Powers

64: 08   The Commissioners are given wide powers in carrying out their duty of care and management of VAT. These powers are largely described in relation to particular provisions, but a number of powers which defy a convenient pigeon-hole are described below.

First, the Commissioners are empowered to disclose information to the following bodies: (1) the Inland Revenue,[1] (2) the Business Statistics Office,[2] (3) "competent authorities" of other EEC member states,[3] and (4) the Isle of Man customs and excise service.[4]

Secondly, the Commissioners are empowered to take recovery proceedings in the UK courts to recover unpaid VAT due to the Isle of Man customs and excise service[5] and the appropriate authorities of EEC member states.[6] Judgments in the Manx High Court of Justice are enforceable in the UK.[7]

Thirdly, the legislation empowers the Commissioners to make directions, impose conditions and specify in a notice the records to be kept by certain traders. The appropriate directions, conditions and records are set out in the notices and leaflets issued by the Commissioners. The courts have upheld conditions laid down in relation to the export of goods,[8] and record keeping requirements in relation to the used goods schemes.[9] The Commissioners take the view that the general requirements for records set out in Notice No. 700 (October 1987) Part VIII are made under statutory authority.[10]

De Voil: Value Added Tax A2.21–24.
[1] FA 1972, s. 127. See Customs and Excise Press Notice No. 12/88 dated 8 March 1988.
[2] VATA 1983, s. 44.
[3] FA 1978, s. 77; FA 1980, s. 17; Directive 77/799/EEC.
[4] Isle of Man Act 1979, s. 10.
[5] Isle of Man Act 1979, s. 3.
[6] FA 1977, s. 11; FA 1980, s. 17; Directive 76/308/EEC.
[7] Isle of Man Act 1979, s. 4.
[8] *Henry Moss of London Ltd v Customs and Excise Comrs* [1981] STC 139, [1981] 2 All ER 86, CA.
[9] *Customs and Excise Comrs v J H Corbitt (Numismatists) Ltd* [1980] STC 231, [1980] 2 All ER 72, HL.
[10] VATA 1983, Sch. 7, para. 7(1).

Rulings

64: 09   The Commissioners stress that traders should seek guidance from their LVO in cases of doubt, and staff are available to deal with telephone enquiries, personal visits and correspondence. Although the legislation does not make provision for a formal clearance procedure, the Commissioners have made a practice of giving formal rulings on liability matters when requested to do so. These rulings serve a two-fold purpose. First, where a trader disagrees with a ruling, it represents a decision which can be taken to appeal if it falls within one or other of the matters over which a VAT tribunal has jurisdiction.[1] Secondly, a ruling provides a written record of what a trader is required to do and he is entitled to some protection if he abides by its terms.

De Voil: Value Added Tax A2.25.
[1] See VATA 1983, s. 40(1) and (6).

64: 10   The question now arises: What happens if a ruling is incorrect? There appear to be two possibilities. First, no harm is done if a new ruling is applied from a mutually convenient current date. The trader may have a right of appeal if he disagrees with the new ruling, but no tax consequences arise from previous transactions. Second, the new ruling may be backdated so that the trader suffers some detriment,[1] e.g. he is assessed for uncharged output tax which he is unable to recover from his customers. Here, the trader clearly has grounds for complaint and it is necessary to consider what remedies are available to him. There appear to be three.

1458   Part XI—Value added tax

(1) The most direct course is to apply to the Commissioners under the terms of a parliamentary statement made on 21st July 1978. VAT tribunals have no jurisdiction to decide whether the facts of an individual case fall within the terms of this statement,[2] and should not, therefore, consider or review the matter,[3] although they have occasionally done so at the request of both parties to an appeal.[4] It seems possible, however, that the courts may have jurisdiction by way of judicial review.[5] The statement reads as follows:

"Where it has been established that an officer of Customs and Excise, with the full facts before him, has given a clear and unequivocal ruling on VAT in writing, or it is established that an officer knowing the full facts has misled a trader to his detriment, the Commissioners of Customs and Excise would only raise an assessment based on the incorrect ruling from the date the error was brought to the attention of the registered person concerned."[6]

(2) The trader can appeal to a VAT tribunal and submit that the Commissioners are estopped from resiling from their earlier ruling. Most tribunal cases have failed because the trader concerned has been unable to demonstrate that a clear and unequivocal representation has been made. However, even if this hurdle can be surmounted, there is a more formidable obstacle to success. Tribunals have felt bound by authority to hold that, as a matter of public policy, the Commissioners cannot be restrained from carrying out their statutory duty to collect VAT by misrepresentations made by their officers.[7]

(3) Giving misleading or incorrect advice may amount to maladministration, and this is the province of the Parliamentary Commissioner for Administration. Complaints for investigation must be submitted through a Member of Parliament.[8] Unfortunately, the PCA has no power to enforce a remedy where he upholds a complaint: his effectiveness lies in the power of persuasion and the activities of the Parliamentary Select Committee having responsibility for his work.

De Voil: Value Added Tax A2.31–37.

[1] For the extent of "detriment", see *Rushmore Stores v Customs and Excise Comrs* LON/84/475 unreported.

[2] *Lunn (a firm) v Customs and Excise Comrs* MAN/83/157 unreported; *Farm Facilities (Fork Lift) Ltd v Customs and Excise Comrs* [1987] VATTR 80.

[3] *Farm Facilities (Fork Lift) Ltd v Customs and Excise Comrs* [1987] VATTR 80.

[4] E.g. *C and G Developments Ltd v Customs and Excise Comrs* LON/86/682 unreported.

[5] Cf *R v IRC, ex p D P Mann Underwriting Agency Ltd* [1989] STI 589 and *Animal Virus Research Institute v Customs and Excise Comrs* [1988] VATTR 56 at 62.

[6] HC Official Report, 21st July 1978, vol 161, col 426. See also Practice Note at [1978] VATTR 273 and Notice No. 748 (October 1987) para. A5.

[7] *GUS Merchandise Corpn Ltd v Customs and Excise Comrs* [1978] VATTR 28.

[8] Parliamentary Commissioner Act 1967, s. 5(1).

LEGISLATION

EEC directives

64: 11   A Directive is a legislative instrument which creates an obligation on member states to enact national legislation giving effect to a stated policy.[1] Although addressed to member states, the provisions of a Directive are capable of having direct effect,[2] i.e. they can create rights which are enforceable in national courts. In order to have direct effect, a provision must meet three tests: (1) it must be clear and precise; (2) it must be clear and unconditional; and (3) it must not allow member states any substantial latitude or discretion in implementing it.[3]

The broad framework of the common system of VAT adopted by the EEC is set out in the First, Sixth, Eighth, Tenth, Thirteenth and Seventeenth Council Directives,[4] the mutual assistance Directives[5] and the Directives concerning reliefs on imported goods.[6] As regards the UK, this framework is enacted by means of the legislation described in §64:12. However, although VAT is primarily administered in accordance with this legislation, the principle of direct effect cannot be ignored, and the Directives can be invoked in the following circumstances.

First, the courts are entitled to resort to the relevant provisions[7] and certain travaux preparatoires[8] where the UK legislation is unclear or ambiguous. A meaning which accords with a Directive is to be preferred to one which does not.[9] Where the relevant EEC provision is unclear, the court may decide the matter itself in accordance with principles laid down by, and relevant decisions of, the European Court of Justice,[10] or it may apply to the European Court of Justice for a preliminary ruling.[11]

Secondly, where an EEC provision having direct effect has not been enacted in national legislation, or the national legislation conflicts with it, the EEC provision should prevail. This is a principle of EEC law[12] which is recognised by European Communities Act 1972, s. 2(1) and applied by the courts.[13]

Thirdly, where a member state has made an authorised derogation from a Directive, national courts have a duty to determine whether the national legislation falls outside the margin of discretion allowed by the Directive and to take this into account when giving effect to the taxpayer's claim.[14] Derogations are authorised partly under rules which allow member states to apply special measures to simplify procedures or prevent avoidance[15] and partly under the specific terms of individual provisions.

The Commissioners cannot invoke direct effect[16] for to do so would result in a charge to tax which has not been approved by Parliament. Thus, although certain supplies have been exempt from tax[17] or zero-rated[18] under UK law in breach of the Sixth Directive traders could continue to exempt or zero rate those supplies until such time as the UK legislation was amended.

De Voil: Value Added Tax A2.55–57, 62.
[1] EEC Treaty, art. 189.
[2] Case 41/74 *Van Duyn v Home Office* [1975] Ch 358, [1975] 3 All ER 190, ECJ.
[3] Case 8/81 *Becker v Finanzamt Münster-Innenstadt* [1982] ECR 53, ECJ; case 51/76 *Verbond van Nederlandse Ondernemingen v Inspecteur der Invoerrechten en Accijnzen* [1977] ECR 113, ECJ. See also *Naturally Yours Cosmetics Ltd v Customs and Excise Comrs* [1987] VATTR 45.
[4] Directives 67/227/EEC, 77/388/EEC, 79/1072/EEC, 84/386/EEC, 85/362/EEC and 86/560/EEC.
[5] Directives 76/308/EEC and 77/799/EEC as applied to VAT by Directives 79/1070/EEC and 79/1071/EEC.
[6] Directives 74/651/EEC, 83/181/EEC, 83/182/EEC and 83/183/EEC.
[7] *English-speaking Union of the Commonwealth v Customs and Excise Comrs* [1980] VATTR 184. All foreign language texts should be referred to: see *British Tenpin Bowling Association v Customs and Excise Comrs* LON/87/404 unreported.
[8] *Open University v Customs and Excise Comrs* [1982] VATTR 29. The material concerned

must: (1) be public and accessible, and (2) clearly and indisputably point to a definite legislative intention.

⁹ *UFD Ltd v Customs and Excise Comrs* [1981] VATTR 199.
¹⁰ European Communities Act 1972, s. 3(1). For the principles of construction, see Lord Denning MR in *H P Bulmer Ltd v J Bollinger SA* [1974] 2 All ER 1226 at 1237, CA.
¹¹ EEC Treaty, art. 177.
¹² Case 8/81 *Becker v Finanzamt Münster-Innenstadt* [1982] ECR 53, ECJ.
¹³ See *Yoga for Health Foundation v Customs and Excise Comrs* [1984] STC 630; *Parkinson v Customs and Excise Comrs* [1985] VATTR 219 and *Merseyside Cablevision Ltd v Customs and Excise Comrs* [1987] VATTR 134.
¹⁴ Case 51/76 *Verbond van Nederlandse Ondernemingen v Inspecteur der Invoerrechten en Accijnzen* [1977] ECR 113, ECJ.
¹⁵ Directive 77/388/EEC, art. 27. For derogations under art. 27(5), see letter to the EC Commission dated 28th December 1977 reproduced in *Direct Cosmetics Ltd v Customs and Excise Comrs* [1983] VATTR 194 at 203, and subsequent proceedings [1985] STC 479, ECJ. For derogations under art. 27(1), see Decisions 84/469/EEC, 85/369/EEC (the validity of which was upheld in joined cases 138/86 and 139/86: *Direct Cosmetics Ltd and Laughtons Photographs Ltd v Customs and Excise Comrs* [1983] STC 540, ECJ), 86/356/EEC and 87/400/EEC.
¹⁶ *National Smokeless Fuels Ltd v IRC* [1986] STC 300.
¹⁷ Case 353/85: *EC Commission v United Kingdom* [1988] STC 251, ECJ.
¹⁸ Case 416/85: *EC Commission v United Kingdom* [1988] STC 456, ECJ.

Value added tax legislation

64: 12   The basic framework of VAT is enacted in VATA 1983, which came into effect on 26th October 1983, FA 1985, Part I, Chapter II, FA 1986, Part I, Chapter II, FA 1987, Part I, Chapter II, FA 1988, Part II and FA 1989 Part I Chapter II. This framework is supplemented by primary and secondary legislation derived from a number of sources.

(1) Many of the detailed provisions are set out in orders, rules and regulations made by statutory instrument.¹ The Treasury is given wide powers to make orders, usually of a policy nature, and the Commissioners are given similarly wide powers to make regulations, usually on matters of an administrative nature. The power to make rules of procedure in relation to VAT tribunals is vested in the Lord Chancellor.²

(2) Notice No. 727 and its associated leaflets are issued under statutory authority.³ However, although they set out what is, in effect, a statutory scheme, they also contain advice and recommendations which do not have statutory effect.⁴

(3) The Customs and Excise Acts⁵ apply, in a modified form⁶ as if all goods imported into the UK were liable to import duties and as if those duties included VAT chargeable on the importation of goods.⁷ Various administrative provisions specifically applied to assigned matters also apply to VAT, e.g. power to inspect computers and offences relating to computers, bribery, obstruction, untrue declarations and counterfeiting documents.⁸ Orders made under Customs and Excise Duties (General Reliefs) Act 1979, ss. 7, 13 and 13A apply to VAT by virtue of the specific provisions contained therein.⁹

(4) Isle of Man Act 1979, which gives effect to the customs union between the UK and the Isle of Man, largely applies to VAT.¹⁰ The two countries form a single area for VAT purposes, and the textual modifications to the VAT legislation required to give effect to this concept are contained in orders¹¹ made under Isle of Man Act 1979, s. 6.

(5) Certain provisions[12] of Police and Criminal Evidence Act 1984 (i.e. those relating to investigation of offences and arrest) apply to VAT in a modified form.[13]

De Voil: Value Added Tax A2.63, 65.
[1] VATA 1983, s. 45(1).
[2] VATA 1983, Sch 8, para. 9; FA 1985, s. 27(3); Finance Act 1985 (VAT Tribunal Rules) (Appointed Day) Order, SI 1986, No. 934.
[3] VAT (Supplies by Retailers) Regulations, SI 1972, No. 1148, reg. 2.
[4] Per Woolf J in *GUS Merchandise Corpn Ltd v Customs and Excise Comrs* [1980] STC 480 at 486.
[5] Comprising CEMA 1979, Customs and Excise Duties (General Reliefs) Act 1979, Alcoholic Liquor Duties Act 1979, Hydrocarbon Oil Duties Act 1979, Matches and Mechanical Lighters Duties Act 1979 and Tobacco Products Duties Act 1979 and any other enactments for the time being in force relating to customs or excise: CEMA 1979, s. 1(1).
[6] For the provisions included and excluded, see VATA 1983, s. 24, F(No. 2)A 1987, s. 103(7) and VAT (General) Regulations, SI 1985, No. 886, regs. 39, 40.
[7] VATA 1983, s. 24(1).
[8] CEMA 1979, ss. 15, 16, 167, 168; FA 1985, s. 10.
[9] VATA 1983, s. 24(1) ("where the contrary intention appears") overrides the specific exclusion in ibid, s. 24(3)(*b*).
[10] Ss. 8, 9 do not apply to VAT charged on imported goods: VATA 1983, s. 24(3)(*d*).
[11] VAT (Isle of Man) Order, SI 1982, No. 1067; VAT (Isle of Man) (No. 2) Order, SI 1982, No. 1068.
[12] Police and Criminal Evidence Act 1984 (Application to Customs and Excise) Order, SI 1985, No. 1800, art. 3(1) and Sch. 1.
[13] Ibid, arts. 3–11 and Sch. 2.

Extra-statutory concessions

64: 13   The notices and leaflets issued by the Commissioners contain a number of concessions. These concessions are not usually identified as such in the text, but are conveniently summarised and cross-referenced in a separate notice.[1]

Concessions have no legal force and a VAT tribunal consequently has no jurisdiction to interpret the terms in which they are set out.[2] It follows that a trader has no grounds for appeal should the Commissioners prevent him from applying a concession. It seems possible, however, that the courts may have jurisdiction by way of an application for judicial review.[3]

De Voil: Value Added Tax A2.64.
[1] Notice No. 748 (October 1988).
[2] *Cando 70 v Customs and Excise Comrs* [1978] VATTR 211.
[3] Cf *R v Inspector of Taxes, ex p Brumfield* [1989] STC 151.

65　The charge to tax

CHARGE I: SUPPLIES

Introduction

65: 01　VAT is charged on the supply of goods and services in the UK.[1] The legislation indicates that a number of progressive hurdles must be surmounted before a charge to tax arises. First, it is necessary to establish that a transaction amounts to a supply. Secondly, the supply must be made for a consideration. Thirdly, it must amount to either a supply of goods or a supply of services. Fourthly, it must amount to a taxable supply.

These conditions are described below. A transaction which fails to meet them all is outside the scope of VAT unless it is specifically brought within the scope of Charge II.

De Voil: Value Added Tax A5.01.
[1] VATA 1983, s. 1.

Supplies

65: 02　The legislation is singularly unhelpful in pinpointing those events which amount to a supply, and goes no further than to state that "'supply' ... includes all forms of supply ...".[1] However, a number of general conclusions can be drawn from the enigmatic words of the parliamentary draftsman, other charging provisions of the Act, and the cases concerning them.

(1) The word "supply" in its ordinary and natural sense means to furnish or serve.[2] This appears to indicate that there are two parties to a supply: the person who "furnishes or serves" goods or services and the person who receives them. Thus, in the normal case, a trader makes a supply to his customer. It seems clear that a person cannot supply himself,[3] but a partnership, for example, can supply one of the partners.[4]

(2) It is quite clear from the language of the Act that "supply" is a word of the widest import.[5] Thus, in relation to goods (presumably meaning tangible moveable property) a supply results from transferring the whole property, an undivided share, or the possession of goods.[6] In relation to other forms of transaction, "anything ... done for a consideration" amounts to a supply, including the grant, assignment or surrender of any right[7] and achieving what is to be done under a contract regardless of whether or not this gives rise to any positive activity.[8]

1462

(3) It is sometimes necessary to examine contractual arrangements with great care in order to decide whether a purchaser of goods and services has consumed them in the course of carrying on his business[9] or whether he has supplied them on to another trader.[10] Goods and services supplied through an agent acting in his own name may be treated as supplies made to and by the agent.[11]

(4) A transaction does not cease to be a supply merely because a contract of sale is void (e.g. the sale of a stolen car), and mere illegality is no bar to the imposition of VAT under UK law[12] (e.g. the sale of a prohibited article such as a flick knife) although the European Court of Justice has held otherwise in relation to the supply of prohibited narcotics.[13]

De Voil: Value Added Tax A5.02.
   [1] VATA 1983, s. 3(2)(*a*).
   [2] Per Lord Reading CJ in *Williams v Pearce* (1916) 114 LT 898 at 901 cited in *Carlton Lodge Club v Customs and Excise Comrs* [1974] STC 507, [1974] 3 All ER 798.
   [3] *Good v Customs and Excise Comrs* [1974] VATTR 256. For self-supplies, see Charge II, §§ **65: 19–23**.
   [4] *Border Flying Co v Customs and Excise Comrs* [1976] VATTR 132.
   [5] Per Griffiths J in *Customs and Excise Comrs v Oliver* [1980] STC 73 at 74.
   [6] VATA 1983, Sch 2, para. 1(1).
   [7] VATA 1983, s. 3(2)(*b*). For rights to buy and sell, see *Gardner Lohmann Ltd v Customs and Excise Comrs* [1981] VATTR 76; *W H Trace & Son Ltd v Customs and Excise Comrs* MAN/86/177 unreported.
   [8] *Landmark Cash and Carry Group Ltd v Customs and Excise Comrs* [1980] VATTR 1.
   [9] As in *Football Association Ltd v Customs and Excise Comrs* [1985] VATTR 106; *J Hopkins (Contractors) Ltd v Customs and Excise Comrs* MAN/88/50 unreported.
   [10] As in *Customs and Excise Comrs v John Willmott Housing Ltd* [1987] STC 192; *Ibstock Building Products Ltd v Customs and Excise Comrs* [1987] VATTR 1; *Northern Lawn Tennis Club v Customs and Excise Comrs* MAN/86/188 unreported.
   [11] VATA 1983 s 24(4). See *City College of Higher Education Ltd v Customs and Excise Comrs* LON/87/203 unreported.
   [12] *Customs and Excise Comrs v Oliver* [1980] STC 73, [1980] 1 All ER 353. See also *IRC v Aken* [1988] STC 69.
   [13] Case 289/86: *Vereniging Happy Family Rustenburger Straat v Inspecteur der Omzetbelasting* [1988] STI 552, ECJ.

Consideration

65: 03   In principle, a supply is outside the scope of VAT unless it is made for a consideration.[1] Consideration may comprise either money (i.e. cash), something other than money (i.e. a barter deal) or partly money and partly something else (e.g. a part exchange deal for a new motor car).[2]

It has been held that there must be a direct link between what has been provided and the consideration received.[3] Thus, a charge imposed under a statutory rather than a contractual obligation has been held not to be consideration where the payee received no more than an indirect benefit from services supplied by the statutory body concerned.[4] On the other hand, where a "gift" is made in accordance with a contract of employment, the goods or services given amount to a supply and the employee's services amount to consideration.[5]

The concepts of consideration and profit are wholly different, and the fact

1464   *Part XI—Value added tax*

that a trader does not make a profit on a supply does not mean that there is no consideration for it.[6]

The consideration for a transaction is that which is given, and this is determined objectively upon the facts of the transaction by reference to the terms agreed. Transactions should not be artificially dissected so as to demonstrate that the consideration is something less, or something different, from that which is given.[7] Thus, the fact that a trader does not obtain the best possible bargain does not mean that his forbearance to charge a higher price amounts to consideration.[8]

The determining factor is whether a consideration is due, not whether it has been received.[9] Thus, cash received for a retail sale amounts to consideration whether it is placed in the till or diverted by an employee before getting as far as the till.[10]

Whether or not a consideration is due is determined at the time when the supply is treated as taking place for the purposes of charging tax in accordance with the agreement made between the parties.[11] Thus, if goods or services are supplied gratuitously, they cannot be turned into a supply made for a consideration by a subsequent voluntary payment.[12] Similarly, a supply made for a consideration evidenced by a tax invoice cannot be turned into a supply for no consideration merely by issuing a credit note.[13]

It is necessary to draw a distinction between a step in the calculation of a consideration and a step in the calculation of a sum payable which involves offsetting two separate considerations. In the former case, VAT is chargeable by reference to the single consideration passing.[14] In the latter case, VAT is chargeable by reference to the separate considerations passing so that net sum payable is irrelevant for VAT purposes.[15]

De Voil: Value Added Tax A5.03, 08.

[1] VATA 1983, s. 3(2)(a). For the exceptions to this principle, see §§ 65: 15–18.

[2] VATA 1983, s. 10(2), (3).

[3] Case 230/87: *Naturally Yours Cosmetics Ltd v Customs and Excise Comrs* [1988] STC 879, ECJ; Case 102/86: *Apple and Pear Development Council v Customs and Excise Comrs* [1988] STC 221, ECJ. Cf Fox LJ in the same case, [1985] STC 383 at 389: "In its usage in English law the central feature of consideration is reciprocity".

[4] Case 102/86: *Apple and Pear Development Council v Customs and Excise Comrs* [1988] STC 221, ECJ.

[5] *Tarmac Construction Ltd v Customs and Excise Comrs* [1981] VATTR 35. See also *Customs and Excise Comrs v Tilling Management Services Ltd* [1979] STC 365.

[6] *Heart of Variety Ltd v Customs and Excise Comrs* [1975] VATTR 103.

[7] *Customs and Excise Comrs v Pippa-Dee Parties Ltd* [1981] STC 495.

[8] *Exeter Golf and Country Club Ltd v Customs and Excise Comrs* [1979] VATTR 70.

[9] VATA 1983, s. 14(1).

[10] *Benton v Customs and Excise Comrs* [1975] VATTR 138.

[11] *Potters Lodge Restaurant v Customs and Excise Comrs* LON/79/286, 105 Taxation 421.

[12] *Warwick Masonic Rooms Ltd v Customs and Excise Comrs* BIR/79/33, 104 Taxation 503.

[13] *British United Shoe Machinery Co Ltd v Customs and Excise Comrs* [1977] VATTR 187.

[14] See *National Coal Board v Customs and Excise Comrs* [1982] STC 863; *Goodfellow (a firm) v Customs and Excise Comrs* [1986] VATTR 119.

[15] See *Davies v Customs and Excise Comrs* [1975] STC 28; *Smith and Williamson v Customs and Excise Comrs* [1976] VATTR 215.

Supplies of goods and services

65: 04   Supplies made for a consideration can be classified under three headings: (1) supplies of goods, (2) supplies of services, and (3) neither a supply of goods nor a supply of services.[1] Since VAT is charged on supplies of goods and services,[2] it follows that supplies classified under the third heading are outside the scope of VAT.

Supplies are allocated under a particular heading in the following manner: (1) supplies relating to tangible moveable property are divided between supplies of goods and supplies of services in accordance with a statutory formula based on the interest transferred;[3] (2) certain supplies are stated to be supplies of goods regardless of whether or not they would normally be regarded as such;[4] (3) anything which does not amount to a supply of goods is stated to be a supply of services[5] and (4) anything which amounts to a supply of goods or a supply of services under the foregoing rules is nevertheless treated as neither a supply of goods nor a supply of services where a Treasury order is made to that effect[6] or where the legislation specifies that such supplies are to be disregarded for tax purposes.[7]

De Voil: Value Added Tax A5.11.
[1] VATA 1983, s. 3(3).
[2] VATA 1983, s. 1.
[3] VATA 1983, Sch. 2, para. 1.
[4] VATA 1983, Sch. 2, paras. 2–4.
[5] VATA 1983, s. 3(2)(*b*).
[6] Under VATA 1983, s. 3(3).
[7] E.g. VATA 1983, s. 29(1)(*a*).

Supplies of goods

65: 05 The following supplies amount to supplies of goods unless they are specifically excluded from this category and treated as either a supply of services or neither a supply of goods nor a supply of services.

(1) Any transfer of the whole property in goods is a supply of goods.[1] The term "whole property" appears to indicate that all rights of ownership existing in the goods must be transferred without retaining any reversionary right. A transfer of the whole property in goods from A to B is a supply of goods from A to B and cannot be a supply from A to any other person.[2] A transfer of the whole property in goods may amount to a contract for sale, in which case it amounts to a composite supply of goods,[3] or a contract for work and materials, in which case only the materials element comprises a supply of goods under this heading.[4]

(2) Although the transfer of possession in goods is normally a supply of services, it amounts to a supply of goods where possession is transferred either: (*a*) under an agreement for the sale of goods,[5] or (*b*) under an agreement which expressly contemplates that the property in goods will pass at a future time specified in the agreement,[6] e.g. a hire purchase agreement.

(3) Applying a treatment or process to another person's goods is a supply of goods.[7] It has been said that "process" is a word of very wide general meaning and must take colour from its context.[8]

(4) The supply of any form of power, heat, refrigeration or ventilation is a supply of goods.[9]

(5) The granting, assignment or surrender of a major interest in land is a supply of goods.[10] A major interest in land is the fee simple or a tenancy for

1466   *Part XI—Value added tax*

a term exceeding 21 years.[11] The Commissioners ignore break clauses and periodic rent revisions in determining the term of a lease.[12] The term of a time sharing arrangement is determined by the period of occupation, not the number of years for which the agreement is expressed to run.[13]

De Voil: Value Added Tax A5.12.
[1] VATA 1983, Sch. 2, para. 1(1).
[2] *Customs and Excise Comrs v Sooner Foods Ltd* [1983] STC 376.
[3] See *AZO-Maschinenfabrik Adolf Zimmerman GMBH v Customs and Excise Comrs* [1987] VATTR 25 (sale, installation and commissioning of a machine).
[4] See *ADP Installations (Group) Ltd v Customs and Excise Comrs* [1987] VATTR 36 (installation of custom built double glazing).
[5] VATA 1983, Sch. 2, para. 1. See *Astor v Customs and Excise Comrs* [1981] VATTR 174. See also *Customs and Excise Comrs v Oliver* [1980] STC 73, [1980] 1 All ER 353 (stolen goods) and *Excell Consumer Industries Ltd v Customs and Excise Comrs* [1983] VATTR 94 (title to goods not formally passed).
[6] VATA 1983, Sch. 2, para. 1.
[7] VATA 1983, s. 12(6) and Sch. 2, para. 2.
[8] *Nurse v Morganite Crucible Ltd* [1989] 1 All ER 113 at 117, HL. In relation to capital allowances, see *Vibroplant Ltd v Holland (Inspector of Taxes)* [1982] STC 164 at 167, CA.
[9] VATA 1983, Sch. 2, para. 3.
[10] VATA 1983, Sch. 2, para. 4.
[11] VATA 1983, s. 48(1).
[12] Notice No. 742 (November 1984) para. 23.
[13] *Cottage Holiday Associates Ltd v Customs and Excise Comrs* [1983] STC 278.

Supplies of services

65: 06   Anything done for a consideration which is not a supply of goods is a supply of services[1] unless it is specifically treated as neither a supply of goods nor a supply of services. "Anything done" includes, amongst other things, the grant, assignment or surrender of any right[1] (e.g. an option to buy a commodity[2]), and achieving what is to be done under a contract regardless of whether or not this gives rise to any positive activity.[3] It does not include functions which a trader is obliged to carry out on his own behalf.[4]

The following specific activities amount to a supply of services: (1) the transfer of any undivided share in the property of goods,[5] e.g. if A and B jointly own an asset and A sells his share to C; (2) the transfer of possession of goods,[6] e.g. the hire, lease, rental or loan of goods; (3) exchanging reconditioned articles for unserviceable articles of a similar kind when carried out by a trader who regularly offers to provide such facilities.[7]

De Voil: Value Added Tax A5.13.
[1] VATA 1983, s. 3(2)(*b*).
[2] *Gardner Lohmann Ltd v Customs and Excise Comrs* [1981] VATTR 76.
[3] *Landmark Cash and Carry Group Ltd v Customs and Excise Comrs* [1980] VATTR 1. For reverse premiums, see *Gleneagles Hotel plc v Customs and Excise Comrs* [1986] VATTR 196; *Neville Russell (a firm) v Customs and Excise Comrs* [1987] VATTR 194.
[4] *National Coal Board v Customs and Excise Comrs* [1982] STC 863.
[5] VATA 1983, Sch. 2, para. 1(1)(*a*). For the exceptions, see § **65: 05**.
[6] VATA 1983, Sch. 2, para. 1(1)(*b*). For the exceptions, see § **65: 05**.
[7] VAT (Special Provisions) Order, SI 1981, No. 1741, art. 13.

Supplies outside the scope of VAT

65: 07   The following transactions are treated as neither supplies of goods nor supplies of services and are thus outside the scope of VAT. The transactions are broadly described and are subject to conditions and exceptions set out in the relevant legislation. The transactions are—

(a) trading stamps issued by the promoter of a trading stamp scheme or given away by anyone else in connection with a supply of goods or services;[1]

(b) the sale of certain goods repossessed under a finance agreement or acquired in settlement of an insurance claim;[2]

(c) goods disposed of by a pawnbroker to the pawnor;[3]

(d) the sale of business assets where a business or part of a business is transferred as a going concern;[4]

(e) the assignment of rights under a hire purchase or conditional sale agreement to a financial institution;[5]

(f) certain supplies of dutiable goods deposited in a bonded warehouse;[6]

(g) supplies between group companies included in the same group registration;[7]

(h) goods imported temporarily or for possible sale when supplied to a person established outside the UK;[8]

(i) inland purchases by visiting forces.[9]

De Voil: Value Added Tax A5.14–18.
  [1] VAT (Treatment of Transactions) (No. 1) Order, SI 1973, No. 325.
  [2] VAT (Cars) Order, SI 1980, No. 442, art. 7(a), (b); VAT (Special Provisions) Order, SI 1981, No. 1741, art. 10.
  [3] VAT (Treatment of Transactions) Order, SI 1986, No 896, art. 3.
  [4] VAT (Special Provisions) Order, SI 1981, No. 1741, art. 12(1). See *Customs and Excise Comrs. v Dearwood Ltd* [1986] STC 327 and contrast *Hardlife Ladder Co Ltd v Customs and Excise Comrs* LON/87/218 unreported (business closed down prior to sale), *Thruxton Parachute Club Ltd v Customs and Excise Comrs* LON/84/331 unreported (business run down but not closed prior to sale), *Montrose DIY Ltd v Customs and Excise Comrs* EDN/87/98 unreported (vendor's business carried on uninterrupted by purchaser). For the self-supply made by the purchaser in certain circumstances, see § **65: 23**.
  [5] SI 1981, No. 1741, art. 12(2).
  [6] VATA 1983, s. 35(1), (2).
  [7] VATA 1983, s. 29(1)(a).
  [8] VAT (Temporarily Imported Goods) Relief Order, SI 1986, No. 989, art. 13. For the relief from tax on importation, see § **65: 29**.
  [9] Notice No. 748 (October 1988) para. A14. This extra-statutory concession is to be replaced by orders made under Customs and Excise Duties (General Reliefs) Act 1979, s. 13A. See Budget Notice BN 14/89.

Taxable supplies

65: 08   Supplies of goods and services made for a consideration can be divided into two categories for the purposes of charging tax: exempt supplies and taxable supplies.

An exempt supply is a supply of goods or services which is of a description for the time being specified in VATA 1983, Sch. 6.[1] However, the grant of an interest in, right over or licence to occupy land within Group 1 of Sch. 6 is not treated as an exempt supply if an election to waive exemption has been made in respect of the land or buildings concerned.[2] The position of an exempt supply is that no tax is charged on it.[3]

A taxable supply is a supply of goods or services which does not amount to an exempt supply.[4] A taxable supply is charged to tax if, but only if, *all* the following conditions are met: (1) it is made by a taxable person; (2) it is made in the UK; and (3) it is made in the course or furtherance of business.[5] A taxable supply which does not meet all these conditions is outside the scope of VAT.

De Voil: Value Added Tax A5.21, 22.
  [1] VATA 1983, s. 17(1). For the goods and services concerned, see § **69: 01–12A**.
  [2] VATA 1983, Sch. 6A, para. 2(1). For the exceptions to this rule, see ibid, para. 2(2)–(2C). For elections to waive exemption, see § **69: 02**.
  [3] I.e. because it does not meet the conditions of VATA 1983, s. 2(1).
  [4] VATA 1983, s. 2(2).
  [5] VATA 1983, s. 2(1).

Supplies made by a taxable person

64: 09   A taxable person is a trader who is, or is required to be, registered for the purposes of VAT.[1] This definition thus comprises: (1) traders who are required to register, and have done so; (2) traders who are *not* required to register but have done so; and (3) traders who are required to register but have *not* done so. These three classes can be subdivided into: (1) "actual traders", i.e. those who are making taxable supplies; (2) "intending traders", i.e. those who intend to make taxable supplies but have not yet done so; and (3) traders who neither make nor intend to make taxable supplies but who are nevertheless entitled to registration.

De Voil: Value Added Tax A5.23.
  [1] VATA 1983, s. 2(2) and (5).

Supplies made in the UK

65: 10   The UK comprises England, Scotland, Wales and Northern Ireland. For VAT purposes it also includes UK territorial seas[1] and, except in relation to certain removals of goods, the Isle of Man.[2] The following rules are applied in determining whether a supply of goods or services is made in the UK.

De Voil: Value Added Tax A5.24.
  [1] VATA 1983, s. 48(8). For the UK territorial seas, see Territorial Waters Order in Council 1964.
  [2] VAT (Isle of Man) Order, SI 1982, No. 1067, art. 2; VAT (Isle of Man) (No. 2) Order, SI 1982, No. 1068, art. 2.

65: 11   *Goods.* Goods situated in the UK[1] are supplied in the UK where they are either: (1) supplied to a place in the UK, or (2) they are exported to a place outside the UK. The fact that goods leave and re-enter the UK in the course of their removal from one part of the UK to another is disregarded.[2]

EXAMPLE
A wholesaler makes the following consignments of widgets from his warehouse in Cardiff.
Each is treated as being supplied in the UK—

    (i) By rail to a customer in Bristol
    (ii) By coastal steamer to a customer in Newcastle
    (iii) By air to a customer in Paris.

Goods situated outside the UK are supplied abroad where they are either[3]:
(1) supplied to a place outside the UK, or (2) imported into the UK.[4]

EXAMPLE
    An art dealer has his place of business in Birmingham. He attends an art auction in
Amsterdam and buys two works of art which he sells shortly afterwards as follows—

    (i) To an Italian art dealer for delivery to an art gallery in Turin. The goods are outside
the UK at the time of supply and are therefore supplied abroad. No charge to UK VAT
arises.
    (ii) To a British art dealer for delivery to an art gallery in Edinburgh. The goods are
outside the UK at the time of supply and are therefore supplied abroad. No charge to UK
VAT arises on the supply. (The goods will, however, be charged to UK VAT on import:
see §§ 65: 27 et seq.)

De Voil: Value Added Tax A5.24.
[1] See *AZO-Maschinenfabrik Adolf Zimmerman GMBH v Customs and Excise Comrs* [1987]
VATTR 25.
[2] VATA 1983, s. 6(2), (3), (4).
[3] VATA 1983, s. 6(2), (3).
[4] For goods imported under a contract for supply, installation and commissioning, see *AZO-Maschinenfabrik Adolf Zimmerman GMBH v Customs and Excise Comrs* [1987] VATTR 25.

65: 12 *Services.* Subject to special rules applicable to educational services[1]
and certain services supplied by tour operators[2] services are supplied in the
country where the supplier belongs.[3] Thus, if a supplier belongs in the UK,
his services are made in the UK regardless of whether or not they are
performed there. The place where a supplier belongs is determined by the
location of his business establishment or some other fixed establishment (if
he has one) or his usual place of residence (if he does not).

An establishment appears to be a "business establishment or some other
fixed establishment" only if it has "a sufficient minimum strength in the form
of the permanent presence of the human and technical resources necessary
for supplying specific services".[4] The Commissioners consider that a
"business establishment" includes an office, showroom, factory and mobile
workshop, and can comprise a hotel room or theatre in certain circumstances,
e.g. where an overseas architect conducts his business from a hotel room on
a temporary visit and where an overseas entertainer hires a theatre to give a
performance.[5] A trader carrying on a business through a branch or agency in
the UK is treated as having a business establishment here.[6]

The "usual place of residence" of a body corporate is the country where it
is legally constituted.[7] There is no statutory test for determining the usual
place of residence of an individual or unincorporated association.

A trader belongs in the UK, and therefore makes supplies of services in
the UK, if he meets one of the following statutory tests.

    (1) If his only business establishment or other fixed establishment is in the
UK.[8] Thus, a surveyor practising in Manchester who travels to Berlin to
inspect a factory supplies services in the UK.

1470   *Part XI—Value added tax*

(2) If he has establishments both in the UK and abroad, but the UK establishment is most directly concerned with the supply.[9] Thus, if a computer consultant has branches in Liverpool and Bonn, and a consultant from the Bonn office travels to Amsterdam to carry out an assignment, the Bonn office is most directly concerned with the supply and the services are supplied in Germany, not the UK.

(3) If he does not have a business establishment, either in the UK or abroad, but his usual place of residence is in the UK.[10] Thus an actor living in Plymouth who appears in a play in New York makes a supply of services in the UK because he is resident here. However, if he hired the theatre to stage the play, the theatre would amount to a business establishment and, since it is located outside the UK, the services would be performed abroad.

De Voil: Value Added Tax A5.24.

[1] VAT (Place of Supply) Order 1984, SI 1984, No. 1685, arts. 3–5.
[2] VAT (Tour Operators) Order 1987, SI 1987, No. 1806, art. 5.
[3] VATA 1983, s. 6(5).
[4] Case 168/84: *Berkholz v Finanzamt Hamburg-Mitte-Altstadt* [1985] 3 CMLR 667 at 678 ECJ.
[5] Leaflet No. 700/4/86, para. 3.
[6] VATA 1983, s. 8(5)(a).
[7] VATA 1983, s. 8(5)(b).
[8] VATA 1983, s. 8(2)(a).
[9] VATA 1983, s. 8(2)(c).
[10] VATA 1983, s. 8(2)(b).

Supplies made in the course or furtherance of business

65: 13   A business includes, among other things,[1] any trade, profession or vocation,[2] and is deemed to include: (1) a club, association or organisation providing facilities or advantages to its members for a subscription or other consideration;[3] (2) admitting persons to any premises for a consideration[4] and (3) supplies made by government departments[5] specified in a Treasury direction.[6] The term has been held to embrace activities of bodies carrying out statutory duties where supplies are made to the public[7] for a consideration.[8]

It has been said that it will never be possible or desirable to define the word exhaustively[9] and that it does not have the same meaning wherever used in the VAT legislation.[10] The case law suggests, however, that the following considerations should be taken into account in deciding whether an activity amounts to a business, although they are not principles which are conclusive in every case: (1) whether the activity is a "serious undertaking earnestly pursued" or "a serious occupation not necessarily confined to commercial or profit making undertakings"; (2) whether the activity is an occupation or function actively pursued with reasonable or recognisable continuity; (3) whether the activity has a certain measure of substance as measured by quarterly or annual value of taxable supplies made; (4) whether the activity is conducted in a regular manner and on sound and recognised business principles; (5) whether the activity is predominantly concerned with the making of taxable supplies to consumers for a consideration; and (6) whether the taxable supplies are of a kind which, subject to differences of detail, are commonly made by those who seek to profit by them.[11] Activities do not need to be carried on with the object of making a profit in order to amount to a business.[12]

The term does not include: (1) the services of employees;[13] (2) activities which are no more than an activity for pleasure and social enjoyment;[14] (3) activities which amount to no more than a voluntary service to the community,[15] (4) activities of public bodies performed exclusively for ministers or other public bodies,[16] or funded by a statutory levy which does not amount to consideration;[17] (5) the passive role of an investor hiring out an asset;[18] (6) the activities of certain bodies in the public domain;[19] and (7) the services of an office holder, other than in respect of an office held in the course of carrying on a trade, profession or vocation.[20]

Once an activity has been identified as a business, any supply made while carrying it on is likely to be made in the course or furtherance of business. No distinction is made between capital and revenue items. Thus, a supply in the course or furtherance of business includes: (1) the disposition of the assets and liabilities of a business; (2) the disposition of a business as a going concern; and (3) anything done in connection with the termination or intended termination of a business.[21] Similarly, no distinction is made between trading and investment activities. Thus, a firm of solicitors holding client's moneys on deposit receives the interest thereon in the course or furtherance of business.[22]

De Voil: Value Added Tax A4.01–13, A4.31–37; A5.24.

[1] Customs and Excise Comrs v Morrison's Academy Boarding Houses Association [1978] STC 1.

[2] VATA 1983, s. 47(1).

[3] VATA 1983, s. 47(2)(a). See Carlton Lodge Club v Customs and Excise Comrs [1974] STC 507, [1974] 3 All ER 798; Royal Ulster Constabulary Athletic Association Ltd v Customs and Excise Comrs BEL/87/10 unreported. This includes a consideration paid to a third party: Lord Advocate v Largs Golf Club [1985] STC 226. It also includes facilities or advantages provided for a consideration to non-members: Cambuslang Athletic Club v Customs and Excise Comrs EDN/82/ 39 unreported; but not those provided without consideration: British Olympic Association v Customs and Excise Comrs [1979] VATTR 122.

[4] VATA 1983, s. 47(2)(b). See Eric Taylor Deceased Testimonial Match Committee v Customs and Excise Comrs [1975] VATTR 8.

[5] As defined in VATA 1983, s. 27(4).

[6] VATA 1983, s. 27(1). For directions in force, see the London Gazette, 28th April 1989, pp. 5110–5124.

[7] National Water Council v Customs and Excise Comrs [1979] STC 157.

[8] Customs and Excise Comrs v Apple and Pear Development Council [1986] STC 192, HL.

[9] Per Lord Emslie in Customs and Excise Comrs v Morrison's Academy Boarding Houses Association [1978] STC 1 at 6.

[10] Singer & Friedlander Ltd v Customs and Excise Comrs [1989] 1 CMLR 814 (meaning in VATA 1983 s 8 differs from that given in relation to ss 14 and 15 in Customs and Excise Comrs v Apple and Pear Development Council [1986] STC 192, HL).

[11] Customs and Excise Comrs v Lord Fisher [1981] STC 238, [1981] 2 All ER 147.

[12] Customs and Excise Comrs v Morrison's Academy Boarding Houses Association [1978] STC 1.

[13] Rickarby v Customs and Excise Comrs [1973] VATTR 186. Also Lean and Rose v Customs and Excise Comrs [1974] VATTR 7. See also Nasim v Customs and Excise Comrs [1987] STC 387, where the taxpayer carried out various duties in respect of a business of which she had wholly divested herself.

[14] Customs and Excise Comrs v Lord Fisher [1981] STC 238, [1981] 2 All ER 147.

[15] Greater London Red Cross Blood Transfusion Service v Customs and Excise Comrs [1983] VATTR 241.

[16] National Water Council v Customs and Excise Comrs [1979] STC 157.

[17] Customs and Excise Comrs v Apple and Pear Development Council [1986] STC 192, HL; refd. [1988] STC 221, ECJ.

    [18] *Coleman v Customs and Excise Comrs* [1976] VATTR 24, approved in *Three H Aircraft Hire v Customs and Excise Comrs* [1982] STC 653. Cf *Walker v Customs and Excise Comrs* [1976] VATTR 10.
    [19] VATA 1983, s. 47(3). See *English Speaking Union of the Commonwealth v Customs and Excise Comrs* [1980] VATTR 184.
    [20] VATA 1983, s. 47(4). See *Hempsons (a firm) v Customs and Excise Comrs* [1977] VATTR 73.
    [21] VATA 1983, s. 47(5), (6). See *H B Mattia Ltd v Customs and Excise Comrs* [1976] VATTR 33 and *Stirling v Customs and Excise Comrs* [1985] VATTR 232.
    [22] *Hedges and Mercer v Customs and Excise Comrs* [1976] VATTR 146.

CHARGE II: EVENTS TREATED AS SUPPLIES

Introduction

65: 14   VAT is charged on anything treated as a supply of goods or services.[1] Events falling within this charge include those which would not be regarded as a supply within the ordinary meaning of that word, and those supplies which would otherwise escape the VAT net, e.g. because they are made outside the UK, made otherwise than in the course or furtherance of business, or otherwise than for a consideration.

The legislation cures these defects by deeming events to be a supply, stating that they are supplies regardless of whether or not they are made for a consideration, or treating them as if they were made in course or furtherance of business.

De Voil: Value Added Tax A6.01.
    [1] VATA 1983, s. 1.

Disposal of business assets

65: 15   Where goods forming part of the assets of a business are transferred or disposed of by or under the directions of the person carrying on a business, and the goods cease to form part of those assets, the goods are supplied regardless of the fact that there is no consideration. The goods are also supplied where an individual who carries on a business makes the transfer or disposition in favour of himself personally.[1] Thus, a licensee who drinks a pint of beer and a furnisher who furnishes his home from business stock are both deemed to make supplies of goods and must account to the Commissioners for output tax thereon. The same consequences follow when an interest in, right over or licence to occupy land forming part of the assets of a business is granted without consideration.[2] It follows that such a transfer or disposal is treated as a supply if it does not otherwise amount to a supply.

The supply is treated as taking place when the goods are transferred or disposed of or the grant is made.[3] The value of the supply for tax purposes is the cost to the person making the supply.[4] However, if the supply comprises food or beverages supplied to employees without consideration in the course of catering, the value is nil.[5]

De Voil: Value Added Tax A6.11.
  ¹ VATA 1983, Sch. 2, para. 5(1), (4)(a); see *Wimpey Group Services Ltd v Customs and Excise Comrs* [1984] VATTR 66. A supply within this description made for a consideration is charged to tax under Charge I. For private use of vehicle fuel, see § **65: 18**.
  ² VATA 1983, Sch. 2, para. 8.
  ³ VATA 1983, s. 5(7).
  ⁴ VATA 1983, Sch. 4, para. 7(b). By concession, used goods are valued at their current value: see Notice No. 748 (October 1988) para. A1(b).
  ⁵ VATA 1983, Sch. 4, para. 10.

65: 16   Three classes of gift are outside the scope of this provision, and thus outside the scope of VAT by virtue of the absence of consideration. First, a gift of goods where the cost to the donor is £10 or less, the gift is made in the course or furtherance of business, and it does not form part of a series or succession of gifts to the same person.[1] Secondly, industrial samples in a form not ordinarily available for sale to the public given to actual or potential customers.[2] Thirdly, the gift of a motor car which did not attract input tax credit when acquired or imported.[3]

De Voil: Value Added Tax A6.11.
  ¹ VATA 1983, Sch. 2, para. 5(2)(a).
  ² VATA 1983, Sch. 2, para. 5(2)(b).
  ³ VAT (Cars) Order, S.I. 1980, No. 442, art. 7(c).

Use of business assets

65: 17   A supply of services takes place regardless of the fact that no consideration is given for it where, by or under the direction of a person carrying on a business, land or goods held or used for the purposes of a business are either: (1) put to any private use, (2) used for any purpose other than a purpose of the business, or (3) made available to any person for use for any purpose other than a purpose of the business.[1] A supply also takes place where land or goods are used or made available for use personally by an individual who carries on a business.[2] It follows that such a use is treated as a supply if it does not otherwise amount to a supply. Thus, an asset is within these provisions if it is used privately by a sole trader or employee, or loaned to an associated company; in each case the owner must account for output tax on the supply deemed to be made.

The supply is treated as taking place when the land or goods are appropriated for use.[3] The value of the supply for tax purposes is the full cost of providing the services.[4] However, the value is nil if they comprise accommodation for employees in a hotel, inn, boarding house or similar establishment.[5]

De Voil: Value Added Tax A6.12.
  ¹ VATA 1983, Sch. 2, paras. 5(3), 8; see *Wimpey Group Services Ltd v Customs and Excise Comrs* [1984] VATTR 66. A supply within this description made for a consideration is charged to tax under Charge I. For private use of vehicle fuel, see § **65: 18**.
  ² VATA 1983, Sch. 2, paras. 5(4)(b), 8.
  ³ VATA 1983, s. 5(8).
  ⁴ VATA 1983, Sch. 4, para. 8(b); see *Customs and Excise Comrs v Teknequip Ltd* [1987] STC 664.

⁵ VATA 1983, Sch. 4, para. 10.

Vehicle fuel

65: 18   The non-business use of vehicle fuel can amount to either a disposal of business assets or use of business assets under the foregoing provisions.¹ For prescribed accounting periods commencing after 6th April 1987, a new method of valuation takes effect in relation to fuel put in the fuel tank of a vehicle² which is either:³ (1) a vehicle allocated to an employee or office holder;⁴ (2) an employee or office holder's own vehicle;⁵ or (3) a partner's own vehicle.⁵ In each case the valuation provisions take effect only where the fuel is provided below cost⁶ for private use and, in the case of an employee or office holder, by reason of his employment or office.⁷ The valuation provisions also apply where fuel is appropriated to a sole trader for private use in his own vehicle.⁸

A taxable person is deemed to make a supply when fuel is put in the fuel tank of a vehicle in the foregoing circumstances. The tax-inclusive consideration for all supplies made in a prescribed accounting period in respect of one vehicle is determined from the following table on the basis of:⁹ (1) the length of the prescribed accounting period, (2) the business travel¹⁰ of the individual in that period, and (3) the cubic capacity¹¹ of the vehicle. Where fuel is put in the fuel tank of two or more vehicles supplied successively to the same individual in a prescribed accounting period, the scale consideration of each vehicle is time apportioned.¹² The table is—

	Cylinder capacity of vehicle		
	1–1,400 cc	1,401–2,000 cc	2,001 cc or more
	£	£	£
Three month period			
Under 4,500 miles business travel	120	150	225
4,500 miles or more business travel	60	75	113
One month period			
Under 1,500 miles business travel	40	50	75
1,500 miles or more business travel	20	25	38

De Voil: Value Added Tax A6.56.
¹ See *Wimpey Group Services Ltd v Customs and Excise Comrs* [1984] VATTR 66.
² As defined in FA 1986, s. 9(10). A van is outside the scope of this definition by virtue of the terms of Decision 86/356/EEC: see Customs and Excise Press Notice No. 24/87 dated 25 March 1987.
³ FA 1986, s. 9(1), (3)(*a*), (6) and (10).
⁴ As defined in FA 1986, s. 9(3) (*c*) and (9).
⁵ As defined in FA 1986, s. 9(3)(*b*). This appears to include a vehicle within s. 9(9).
⁶ As defined in FA 1986, s. 9(2).
⁷ FA 1986, s. 9(1).
⁸ FA 1986, s. 9(1)(*b*). For "own vehicle", see note 5 supra.
⁹ FA 1986, s. 9(6), (7) and Sch. 6, paras. 1–3. The table may be substituted by Treasury Order: ibid, Sch. 6, para. 4.
¹⁰ As defined in FA 1986, Sch. 6, para. 3(3).
¹¹ As ascertained in accordance with FA 1986, Sch. 6, para 6.
¹² FA 1986, s. 9(8) and Sch. 6, paras. 3(2) and 5.

Self-supplies

65: 19   VAT is a neutral tax which seeks to tax consumer expenditure without creating distortions in trading patterns. The legislation therefore sets out to discourage exempt and partly exempt traders making things for themselves solely to reduce their irrecoverable input tax. The Treasury is given wide powers to make orders deeming such self-produced goods to be supplied by the trader in the course or furtherance of his business and thus give rise to a charge to tax.[1] To date, orders have been made in respect of motor cars, stationery and construction services.

The legislation also sets out to counteract tax avoidance schemes which involve transferring a business as a going concern to an exempt or partly exempt company included in a group registration. The representative member is deemed to make a self supply in specified circumstances.[2]

Traders can enter into occupation of certain buildings and civil engineering works without incurring irrecoverable input tax, i.e. because the supply made to them is exempt or zero-rated or because they recover any tax charged as input tax. These reliefs are withdrawn by way of a self-supply where a trader ceases to use a building or work for a purpose which attracted relief, where he ceases to occupy the building or work, or where he ceases to be a fully taxable person.[3]

De Voil: Value Added Tax A6.41.
[1] VATA 1983, s. 3(5), (6).
[2] VATA 1983, s. 29A, effective from 1st April 1987.
[3] VATA 1983, Sch. 6A, paras. 1(1), (4)–(6), 5 and 6.

Motor cars

65: 20   This provision applies to motor cars[1] which meet one of the following conditions: (1) it was produced by the trader otherwise than by converting another vehicle;[2] (2) it was produced by the trader by converting another vehicle on which input tax credit was obtained;[3] or (3) it was acquired from another person and input tax credit was obtained.[4]

Motor cars within the foregoing description are treated as supplied in the course or furtherance of business when they are used for the purpose of the business. However, no supply is deemed to be made if the use comprises: (1) a supply made in the course or furtherance of business, e.g. a sale or hire; (2) converting the motor car into another vehicle; or (3) (if his business is producing motor cars otherwise than by conversion) using the motor car solely for research and development.[5] Motor cars are treated as supplied when appropriated for use.[6] The value of the supply for tax purposes is the cost of the goods to the person making the supply.[7]

EXAMPLE
X, a motor dealer, buys a new motor car for resale through his showroom, and claims input tax credit. Three months later he appropriates the car for demonstration purposes. He is deemed to supply the car at that time and must account to the Commissioners for VAT thereon. In effect, the input tax previously credited is clawed back, and the trader is placed in the same position as if he had originally purchased the car for demonstration purposes, i.e., a purchase on which input tax credit is disallowed.

De Voil: Value Added Tax A6.42.
¹ As defined in VAT (Cars) Order, SI 1980, No. 442, art. 2.
² SI 1980, No. 442, art 5(1)(*a*).
³ SI 1980, No. 442, art. 5(1)(*b*), (2). For conversion, see *GA Security Systems Ltd v Customs and Excise Comrs* MAN/83/212 unreported.
⁴ SI 1980, No. 442, art. 5(1)(*c*) and (2).
⁵ SI 1980, No. 442, art. 5(3). For research and development see *Lea-Francis Cars Ltd v Customs and Excise Comrs* MAN/81/113 unreported.
⁶ VATA 1983, s. 5(6). For appropriation, see *A and B Motors (Newton-le-Willows) Ltd v Customs and Excise Comrs* [1981] VATTR 29.
⁷ VATA 1983, Sch 4, para 7(*a*).

Stationery

65: 21   This provision applies to "printed matter" (which includes stationery, but excludes anything produced by typing, duplicating or photocopying¹) produced by exempt or partly exempt traders with a value in excess of the current registration limit.² The Commissioners can direct that this provision shall not apply to a particular trader where they are satisfied that the loss of revenue would be negligible.³

Stationery produced by such traders is deemed to have been supplied by them in the course or furtherance of business provided: (1) they do not supply it to another person or incorporate it in other goods which they produce, and (2) it is used for the purposes of the business.⁴ The stationery is treated as supplied for tax purposes when it is appropriated for use.⁵ The value of the supply for tax purposes is the cost of the goods to the person making the supply.⁶

Output tax on a self supply of stationery is eligible for input tax credit.⁷

De Voil: Value Added Tax A6.43.
¹ VAT (Special Provisions) Order, SI 1981, No. 1741, art. 2.
² SI 1981, No. 1741, art. 14(2)(*a*), (*b*).
³ SI 1981, No. 1741, art. 14(2)(*c*).
⁴ SI 1981, No. 1741, art. 14(1).
⁵ VATA 1983, s. 5(6).
⁶ VATA 1983, Sch. 4, para 7(*a*). For the Commissioners' views, see Leaflet No. 706/1/87 para. 5(*c*).
⁷ The stationery is also deemed to be supplied to the trader for the purposes of his business: VAT (Special Provisions) Order, SI 1981, No. 1741, art. 14(1).

Construction services

65: 22   This provision applies to the following services:¹ (1) constructing a building or civil engineering work; (2) increasing the floor area of a building by 10% or more; and (3) demolition works carried out in connection with (1) or (2). However, a charge to tax arises only where the value of the services is £100,000 or more and they would have been charged to tax at the standard rate if supplied to a third party.²

The foregoing services are deemed to be supplied by a trader in the course or furtherance of business when he performs them for the purpose of his business and otherwise than for a consideration³, e.g. where a developer constructs a factory on his own land using in-house labour. The value of the supply is the open market value of those services performed on or after 1st April 1989.[4] The time of supply appears to be the time when the services are performed.[5]

The services are deemed to be supplied to the trader for the purpose of his business.[6]

De Voil: Value Added Tax A6.44.
[1] VAT (Self-supply of Construction Services) Order, S.I. 1989, No. 471, art. 3(1).
[2] Ibid, art. 3(2).
[3] Ibid, art. 3(1). For companies in a group registration, see ibid, art. 3(3).
[4] Ibid, art. 4.
[5] VATA 1983, s. 4(3).
[6] VAT (Self-supply of Construction Services) Order, S.I. 1989, No. 472, art. 3(1).

Business transferred as going concern to a group company

65: 23   The representative member of a group of companies[1] is treated as making a supply in the course or furtherance of business where[2]: (1) a business or part of a business carried on by a taxable person is transferred as a going concern to a group company; and (2) the supply of assets transferred is outside the scope of VAT.[3]

The supply comprises the assets which would have been charged to tax at the standard rate by the transferor if the supply were not outside the scope of VAT.[4] The supply is valued at open market value.[5]

No supply is treated as taking place if:[6] (1) the representative member is entitled to credit for all input tax in both the prescribed accounting period[7] and longer period[8] in which the assets were transferred; or (2) the Commissioners are satisfied that the assets transferred were acquired by the tranferor more than three years before the date of transfer.

Tax chargeable on the deemed supply is reduced if the Commissioners are satisfied that the transferor has not received credit for the full amount of input tax on his acquisition of the assets[9], e.g. because he is partly exempt.

De Voil: Value Added Tax A6.46.
[1] For group registration, see § **66: 26**.
[2] VATA 1983, s. 29A(1) and (4).
[3] I.e. under VAT (Special Provisions) Order, SI 1981, No. 1741, art. 12(1).
[4] VATA 1983, s. 29A(1)(*b*) and (9).
[5] VATA 1983, s. 29A(6) and (7).
[6] VATA 1983, s. 29A(2) and (3).
[7] See § **68: 01**.
[8] Defined in VAT (General) Regulations, SI 1985, No. 886, reg. 29.
[9] VATA 1983, s. 29A(8).

Building: change of use

65: 24   A person intending to use a building for a relevant residential[1] or charitable[2] purpose receives supplies zero-rated under VATA 1983, Sch. 5, Group 8[3] if: (1) he purchases the freehold; (2) he leases the building for a term exceeding 21 years; or (3) he engages a building contractor to construct the building on land in which he has a freehold, lease or licence. This provision creates a charge to tax where the building ceases to be used for its intended purpose.

A trader is deemed to supply his interest in the building in the course or furtherance of business if he ceases to use the building for a relevant residential or charitable purpose on or after 1st April 1989 and within ten years after the building was completed.[4] Part of the interest is deemed to be supplied if only part of the building ceases to be used.[5] The supply is treated as taking place on the date when the change of use occurred and its value is the aggregate value of zero-rated supplies made to the trader on or after 1st April 1989 in respect of the building. The supply is chargeable to tax at the standard rate.[6]

The interest (or part of the interest) is deemed to be supplied to the trader for the purpose of his business.[7]

De Voil: Value Added Tax A6.48.
 [1] As defined in VATA 1983, Sch. 5, Group 8, Note 3.
 [2] As defined in ibid, Note 4.
 [3] See § **69.23**.
 [4] VATA 1983, Sch. 6A, para. 1(1), (4), (5). For the time when a building is completed, see VATA 1983 Sch 6 Group 1 Note 2.
 [5] Ibid, para. 1(5)
 [6] Ibid, para. 1(1), (5), (6).
 [7] Ibid, para. 1(5).

Building or civil engineering work : disposal or occupation

65: 25   A developer[1] is deemed to supply his interest in, right over or licence to occupy a building or civil engineering work on the first occasion during the specified period when he:[2] (1) grants an interest in, right over or licence to occupy all or part of the building or work under an exempt supply; (2) occupies all or part of the building at a time when he is not a fully taxable person;[3] or (3) uses all or part of the work at a time when he is not a fully taxable person.[4] The specified period commences on the day when construction of the building or work is first planned and ends on the tenth anniversary of its completion.[5] The supply is deemed to be made in the course or furtherance of his business.[6]

A supply is not deemed to be made under this provision if:[7] (1) the building is designed as one or more dwellings[8] or is intended for use solely for a relevant residential[9] or charitable[10] purpose; (2) the work is a civil engineering work necessary for the development of a permanent park for residential caravans;[11] (3) construction of the building or work commenced before 1st August 1989; (4) the freehold of the completed building or work was acquired within three years of completion under a supply chargeable to tax at the standard rate;[12] (5) the value of the supply would be less than £100,000; or (6) the transitional reliefs apply.

The supply is deemed to be made on the later of:[13] (1) the last day of the prescribed accounting period in which the grant, occupation or use took place; or (2) the last day of the prescribed accounting period in which the building became ready for occupation or the work became ready for use.

The value of the supply is the aggregate of:[14] (1) the value of grants made or to be made to the developer in respect of the land on which the building or work is constructed (but not rents for future grants which cannot be ascertained at the time of supply); and (2) the value of standard rated construction supplies made or to be made to the developer in relation to the building or work.

The supply is deemed to be a taxable supply.[15] It is chargeable to tax at the standard rate.

The supply deemed to be made by the developer is also deemed to be made to him for the purpose of his business.[16]

De Voil: Value Added Tax A6.47, 50.
[1] As defined in VATA 1983, Sch. 6A, para. 5(5)–(7).
[2] VATA 1983, Sch. 6A, paras. 5(1), 6(1).
[3] As defined in ibid, para. 5(4).
[4] As defined in ibid, para. 5(4).
[5] VATA 1983, Sch. 6A, para. 5(1).
[6] Ibid, para. 6(1).
[7] Ibid, paras. 5(1)–(3), 6(3); FA 1989, Sch. 3 para. 13(6).
[8] As defined in VATA 1983, Sch. 5, Group 8, Note 2.
[9] As defined in ibid, Note 3.
[10] As defined in ibid, Note 4.
[11] As defined in ibid, Note 10.
[12] I.e. under VATA 1983, Sch. 6, Group 1, item 1(a)(ii)(iv).
[13] VATA 1983, Sch. 6A, para. 6(1).
[14] Ibid, para. 6(2).
[15] Ibid.
[16] Ibid, para. 6(1).

Services received from abroad

65: 26 Partly exempt traders could reduce their irrecoverable input tax by obtaining services from overseas traders (who would not charge tax on the supply) rather than UK traders (who would). This would both cause distortions in trading patterns and result in a reduction in VAT revenues. These consequences are avoided by making certain services received from abroad liable to a "reverse charge".

A trader receiving supplies of services from abroad is treated as if *he* had supplied them provided the following conditions are met: (1) the services fall within VATA 1983, Sch. 3; (2) they amount to a taxable supply; (3) they are supplied by a person who belongs in a country other than the UK; and (4) the trader who receives them: (a) belongs in the UK, and (b) uses them for the purposes of his business.[1]

The supply is treated as taking place on either: (1) the date when the supply is paid for (where there is a consideration in money); or (2) the last day of the prescribed accounting period in which the services were performed (where the consideration is not in money).[2] The value of the supply for tax purposes is the consideration (if any) for which it is made.[3] A money consideration expressed in foreign currency must be converted into sterling at the exchange rate ruling at the time of supply in accordance with EEC customs valuation rules.[4]

De Voil: Value Added Tax A6.31.
[1] VATA 1983, s. 7(1), (2). For services within ibid, Sch. 3, see Notice No. 741 (October 1986)

Part 2G. Prior to 1 April 1987, the trader receiving the supply was required to be a taxable person.
 2 VAT (General) Regulations, SI 1985, No. 886, reg. 18.
 3 VATA 1983, s. 7(4)(*a*).
 4 VATA 1983, Sch. 4, para. 11. See Notice No. 252 (January 1988).

Goods held at date of deregistration

65: 27   This provision is enacted to secure equity between traders who carry on trading after deregistration and traders who have never been registered. A trader in the former category is deemed to supply any land or goods then forming part of the assets of his business.[1] The supply is deemed to be made in the course or furtherance of business, takes place immediately before he ceases to be a taxable person[1] and is valued for tax purposes at cost.[2] In effect, therefore, input tax credits previously claimed are clawed back by the deemed supply and the trader is placed in the same position as if he had acquired them after deregistration.

There are two exceptions. First, no supply takes place in relation to goods which did not give rise to input tax credit when acquired.[3] Secondly, all goods are exempted from charge if either: (1) the business is transferred to another taxable person, (2) the taxable person has died or become bankrupt or incapacitated and the business is carried on by some other person, or (3) tax on the deemed supply does not exceed £250.[4]

De Voil: Value Added Tax A6.51.
 1 VATA 1983, Sch. 2, paras. 7(1)1, 8.
 2 VATA 1983, Sch. 4, para. 7(*c*). By concession, used goods are valued at their current value: see Notice No. 748 (October 1988) para. A1(*a*).
 3 VATA 1983, Sch. 2, para. 7(2).
 4 VATA 1983, Sch. 2, para. 7(1).

Services by holders of an office

65: 28   In principle, services supplied by the holder of an office (e.g. a company director) are outside the scope of VAT because they are not supplied in the course or furtherance of business. This situation could lead to avoidance of tax by, for example, solicitors providing legal services as directors of client companies rather than in their capacity as practising solicitors.

VATA 1983, s. 47(4) therefore provides that a person who accepts an office in the course or furtherance of his trade, profession or vocation is treated as supplying his services as holder of the office in the course or furtherance of his trade, profession or vocation.

This provision begs the question of when an office is, or is not, accepted in the course or furtherance of a trade, profession or vocation.[1] An office is personal to the person who holds it. Thus, where a partner holds an office and renders personal bills for services supplied, the question of chargeability to tax depends upon whether or not the partner (as distinct from the firm) is a taxable person.[2]

De Voil: Value Added Tax A4.53.
¹ For the Commissioners' views, see [1976] STI, p. 107.
² *Hempsons (a firm) v Customs and Excise Comrs* [1977] VATTR 73.

Transactions within VATA 1983, Sch. 5

65: 29 Where a transaction would not otherwise be a supply of goods or services, it is treated as such a supply made in the UK if it is of a description included in VATA 1983, Sch. 5 (i.e. the zero-rate schedule).¹ This provision widens the scope of VAT to include, for example, goods exported by a charity.²

De Voil: Value Added Tax A6.52.
¹ VATA 1983, s. 16 (5).
² VATA 1983, Sch. 5, Group 16, Item 3.

CHARGE III: IMPORTED GOODS

Introduction

65: 30 VAT is charged on goods imported into the UK.¹ An importation of goods does not include a movement of goods between two places within the UK where the goods leave and re-enter the UK² or, with one exception, the removal of goods from the Isle of Man to the UK.³

VAT on imported goods is charged and payable as if it were a duty of customs.⁴ For this purpose, customs legislation is applied to VAT in a modified form as if all goods imported into the UK were liable to duties of customs and as if those duties included VAT chargeable on imported goods.⁵

A detailed examination of customs procedures is inappropriate in a work of this nature, and the following broad principles are noted by way of general background: (1) goods may be legally imported only through places approved by the Commissioners; (2) the importation of certain goods is prohibited, or subject to quota restrictions or import licences; (3) a "report" must be lodged when a ship or aircraft enters the UK and a vehicle enters Northern Ireland from the Irish Republic; (4) importers must lodge an "entry" (a customs declaration) within a specified period of a report being made (this is normally accompanied by documents required for customs purposes); (5) customs officers are empowered to examine goods; and (6) import duties are either paid before goods are released from customs control or accounted for under deferred accounting arrangements.⁶

These principles are applied in a modified form to postal importations.⁷

1482   *Part XI—Value added tax*

De Voil: Value Added Tax A7.01–07, 11.
¹ VATA 1983, s. 1.
² VATA 1983, s. 6(4).
³ VAT (Isle of Man) Order, SI 1982, No. 1067, preamble and arts. 2–4.
⁴ VATA 1983, s. 2(4).
⁵ VATA 1983, s. 24(1). For the legislation concerned, see § **64: 12.**
⁶ See § **68: 05.**
⁷ See Postal Packets (Customs and Excise) Regulations, SI 1986, No. 260.

Goods charged to tax

65: 31   In principle, all imported goods are chargeable to tax.¹ Having established this principle, the legislation then goes on to provide various reliefs from this charge. The legislation concerned is: (1) the VAT legislation;² (2) customs legislation specifically applied to VAT;³ (3) customs legislation which is not specifically applied, but nevertheless applies by virtue of its subject matter;⁴ and (4) legislation concerning the UK–Isle of Man customs union.⁵

The reliefs arising can be broadly classified under the following headings: (1) goods on which no tax is chargeable, or on which the tax chargeable is not payable;⁶ (2) goods which can be removed or delivered without payment of duty subject to some condition;⁷ and (3) charge to tax by reference to a reduced value.⁸

De Voil: Value Added Tax A7.12.
¹ VATA 1983, ss. 1 and 24(1). But see Case 294/82: *Einberger v Hauptzollampt Freiburg* [1984] ECR 1177, ECJ (prohibited narcotics).
² I.e. VATA 1983 ss. 16(3), 18(3), 19 and 25 and statutory instruments made thereunder.
³ I.e. CEMA 1979 ss. 46–48; Customs and Excise Duties (General Reliefs) Act 1979, ss. 8 and 9(b); statutory instruments made thereunder.
⁴ I.e. Customs and Excise Duties (General Reliefs) Act 1979, ss. 7, 13 and 13A; statutory instruments made thereunder.
⁵ I.e. VAT (Isle of Man) Order, SI 1982, No. 1067, arts. 2–4.
⁶ See § **65: 32.**
⁷ See § **65: 33.**
⁸ See § **65: 34.**

Goods not charged to tax or relieved from payment of tax

65: 32   A wide range of goods are relieved from payment of tax on importation. The goods concerned are stated below under broad descriptive headings: the legislation imposes conditions and creates exceptions in many instances.

Relief is available for—

(a)   goods of a description for the time being specified in VATA 1983, Sch. 5 other than Groups 8 (building and civil engineering works), 12 (gold) and, with exceptions, 14 (drugs, medicines and appliances);¹

(b)   works of art acquired before 1st April 1973, antiques and collectors' items;²

(c) specific goods produced by the United Nations and UN organisations;[3]

(d) goods relieved from import duties under corresponding EEC provisions;[4]

(e) gold and gold coins imported by a central bank;[5]

(f) gifts under a specified value consigned by one private individual to another for personal use;[6]

(g) re-imported goods which had borne unrelieved VAT prior to export;[7]

(h) goods imported by a person who became entitled to them as legatee;[8]

(i) miscellaneous reliefs conferred by order[9] made under Customs and Excise Duties (General Reliefs) Act 1979, s. 13;

(j) trade samples, labels and awards for distinction;[10]

(k) goods imported for business purposes by Manx taxable persons;[11] and

(l) goods imported for diplomats, international organisations and visiting forces.[12]

De Voil: Value Added Tax A7.16, 61–67.

[1] VATA 1983, s. 16(3) and notes to the groups stated.

[2] VAT (Special Provisions) Order, SI 1981, No 1741, art. 6.

[3] VAT (Imported Goods) Relief Order SI 1984, No. 746, art. 4 and Sch. 1 implementing Directive 83/181/EEC art 79(8).

[4] VAT (Imported Goods) Relief Order, SI 1984, No. 746, arts. 5, 8 and Sch. 2, implementing Directive 83/181/EEC Titles III–XI. For corresponding reliefs, see Regulation 918/83/EEC.

[5] VAT (Imported Goods) (Relief) Order, SI 1977, No. 1790.

[6] VAT (Small Non-Commercial Consignments) Relief Order, SI 1986, No. 939.

[7] VAT (General) Regulations, SI 1985, No. 886, regs. 45 (re-importations by unregistered traders), 46 (re-importation by taxable persons) and 47 (works of art and motor cars).

[8] Customs and Excise Duties (General Reliefs) Act 1979, s. 7; Customs and Excise Duties (Relief for Imported Legacies) Order, SI 1984, No. 895.

[9] See: (1) Customs Duty (Personal Reliefs) (No. 1) Order, SI 1968, No. 1558 (as amended); (2) Customs and Excise Duties (Personal Reliefs for Goods Permanently Imported) Order, SI 1983, No. 1828.

[10] Customs and Excise Duties (General Reliefs) Act 1979, ss. 8, 9(b).

[11] VAT (Isle of Man) Order, SI 1982, No. 1067, art. 4(b).

[12] For reliefs given by way of extra-statutory concession, see Notice No. 748 (October 1988). These concessions are to be replaced by orders made under Customs and Excise Duties (General Reliefs) Act 1979, s. 13A. See Budget Notice BN 14/89.

Goods delivered or removed without payment of duty

65: 33 Goods falling under this heading may be imported without payment of VAT where conditions specified in the legislation, or imposed by the Commissioners, are met. The principal purpose of these reliefs is to assist national and international trade by creating a "tax free ring".

In broad terms, relief is available for—

(a) goods deposited in a bonded warehouse;[1]

(b) free zone goods;[2]

(c) goods temporarily imported for repair, renovation, modification or processing;[3]

(*d*) goods temporarily imported for business[4] or personal[5] use;

(*e*) specific classes of goods imported for possible sale;[6]

(*f*) goods entered for transit through the UK or transhipment with a view to re-exportation;[7]

The relief available for certain temporary importations by persons other than taxable persons ceased to apply to goods imported after 31st December 1985.[8]

De Voil: Value Added Tax A7.15 and 31–52.

[1] CEMA 1979, s. 46. For bonded warehouses, see Customs Warehousing Regulations, SI 1979, No. 207. VAT is charged when goods are removed from bond.

[2] CEMA 1979, ss. 100A–100F; Free Zone Regulations, SI 1984, No. 1177. VAT is charged when goods are removed from a free zone (other than for export or to another free zone) or used or consumed within a free zone. See Notice No. 702 (January 1988) para. 4.

[3] VAT (General) Regulations, SI 1985, No. 886, reg. 44. This relief is effective from 1st June 1985.

[4] See VAT (Temporarily Imported Goods) Relief Order, SI 1986, No. 1989, arts. 4–7 and Sch. 1. Separate reliefs are given for goods imported from EEC and non-EEC states. This Order applies without prejudice to temporary importation relief afforded under or by virtue of any other enactment: ibid, art. 3(1). Thus, relief appears to continue under Temporary Importation (Commercial Vehicles and Aircraft) Regulations, SI 1961, No. 1523. Other regulations made under CEMA 1979, s. 48 were either revoked by Customs Duties (Temporary Importation) (Revocation) Regulations, SI 1987, No. 1781 or do not apply for VAT purposes: see VAT (General) Regulations, SI 1985, No. 886, reg. 40(*a*).

[5] Customs and Excise Duties (Personal Reliefs for Goods Temporarily Imported) Order, SI 1983, No. 1829.

[6] VAT (Temporarily Imported Goods) Relief Order, SI 1986, No. 1989, art. 8 and Sch. 2.

[7] CEMA 1979, s. 47.

[8] VAT (General) Regulations, SI 1985, No. 886, reg. 42.

Valuation of imported goods

65: 34 Where the price paid on importation is the sole consideration, the value for VAT purposes is the aggregate of: (1) the price paid; and (2) so far as not already included: (*a*) all foreign taxes, duties and other charges, (*b*) all UK import duties other than VAT, and (*c*) all commission, packing, transport and insurance costs incurred outside the UK.[1] Any discount for prompt payment is deducted from this value, whether or not it is taken, unless the contract provides for payment by instalments.[2] Amounts expressed in foreign currency are converted to sterling in accordance with EEC customs rules.[3]

Where the price paid is not the sole consideration, the value for VAT purposes is the aggregate of: (1) open market value determined in accordance with EEC import rules; (2) all foreign taxes, duties and other charges; (3) all UK import duties other than VAT; and (4) all commission, packing, transport and insurance costs incurred outside the UK.[4]

The Commissioners are empowered to direct that imported goods are to be valued at open market value rather than the price paid in certain circumstances.[5]

Valuation reliefs apply in respect of: (1) goods re-imported after receiving a treatment or process abroad;[6] (2) goods which have borne unrelieved VAT in another EEC member state and which are imported for non-business purposes;[7] and (3) goods removed from the Isle of Man which, exceptionally, give rise to a charge to VAT in the UK.[8]

De Voil: Value Added Tax A7.14, 21-25.
  1 VATA 1983, s. 11(2).
  2 VATA 1983, Sch. 4, para. 5.
  3 VATA 1983, Sch. 4, para. 11. See Notice No. 252 (January 1988) section 12.
  4 VATA 1983, s. 11(3). See Notice No. 252 (January 1988) sections 2–6.
  5 VATA 1983, Sch. 4, para. 2.
  6 VAT (General) Regulations, SI 1985, No. 886, reg. 48.
  7 VAT (Goods Imported for Private Purposes) Relief Order, S.I. 1988, No. 1174. This gives effect to case 15/81 *Gaston Schul; Douane Expéditeur BV v Inspecteur der Invoerrechten en Accijnzen* [1982] 3 CMLR 229, ECJ; case 47/84 *Staatssecretaris van Financiën v Gaston Schul Douane-Expediteur BV* [1986] 1 CMLR 559, ECJ; case 39/85 *Bergeres-Becque v Head of the Interregional Customs Service, Bordeaux* [1986] 2 CMLR 143, ECJ. See *Practice Note: VAT on Imports of Private Property*, OJ C13, 21.1.86, p. 2.
  8 VAT (Isle of Man) Order, SI 1982, No. 1067, art. 3(2).

66 Taxable persons

REGISTRATION

Introduction

66: 01 Taxable persons play an important role in the administration of VAT: they collect output tax on behalf of the Commissioners[1] and are entitled to input tax credit for all or part of the tax they incur.[2]

A taxable person is someone who either: (1) makes or intends to make taxable supplies while he is or is required to be registered for the purposes of VAT;[3] or (2) does not make or intend to make taxable supplies but is registered under VATA 1983, Sch. 1, para. 5A.[4] The following general conclusions are drawn from the statutory provisions and the case law derived from them.

(1) A person who makes or intends to make taxable supplies may be compulsorily registered by reference to the value of his taxable supplies[5] if he makes such supplies and may be voluntarily registered if, not being liable to compulsory registration, he nevertheless makes or intends to make taxable supplies.[6]

(2) A taxable supply is a supply of goods or services made in the UK other than an exempt supply.[7] The foregoing provisions apply only to persons making or intending to make taxable supplies and it follows that a person who makes or intends to make nothing but exempt supplies is neither liable to compulsory registration nor eligible for voluntary registration.[8]

(3) A supply which is outside the scope of VAT does not amount to a supply of goods or services and cannot, therefore, amount to a taxable supply. The foregoing provisions apply only to persons making or intending to make taxable supplies and it follows that a person who makes or intends to make nothing but supplies which are outside the scope of VAT is neither liable to compulsory registration nor eligible for voluntary registration. However, a new form of voluntary registration is available from 15 May 1987 for traders who make or intend to make "outside the scope" supplies within either of the following classes: (a) supplies outside the UK which, if made in the UK, would be taxable supplies; or (b) supplies of warehoused goods which would be taxable supplies if not disregarded by VATA 1983, s. 35.[9]

(4) The taxable supplies counted for registration purposes are those which are made in the course or furtherance of business.[10] It follows that the trader's activities must amount to a business before he is eligible for registration,[11] or his supplies must be deemed to be made in the course or

furtherance of business so as to render him liable to registration, e.g. where a trader making exempt supplies produces his own internal stationery.[12]

(5) A trader who exceeds the registration limits is a taxable person regardless of whether or not he takes the necessary steps to register. Once non-registration is discovered, the trader's registration is backdated to the date from which he was liable to be registered and he must account for output tax from that date.[13]

(6) In England a "person" includes a body of persons corporate or unincorporate.[14] For practical purposes, it seems that a person is a natural person (i.e. an individual), a legal person (i.e. a body corporate) or a body of individuals having a recognisable identity (i.e. an unincorporated association, partnership[15] or body of trustees).

(7) It is persons, not businesses, who are liable to registration. A person is entitled to only one registration, and this includes all his businesses however diverse they may be.[16] There are two exceptions to this principle: (1) a body corporate organised in divisions may apply for separate registrations for each division;[17] and (2) limited partnerships having common partners, but different combinations of general and limited partners, are entitled to separate registrations.[18]

(8) Special provisions apply in determining whether a person is liable to register with the Commissioners under the UK legislation or with the Manx customs and excise service under the Isle of Man legislation.[19]

De Voil: Value Added Tax A3.01–03.
[1] VATA 1983, s. 2(3).
[2] VATA 1983, s. 15.
[3] VATA 1983, s. 2(2).
[4] VATA 1983, s. 2(5).
[5] VATA 1983, Sch. 1, para. 1.
[6] VATA 1983, Sch. 1, para. 5.
[7] VATA 1983, s. 2(2).
[8] See *Bramley v Customs and Excise Comrs* [1987] VATTR 72.
[9] VATA 1983, Sch. 1, para. 5A.
[10] VATA 1983, Sch. 1, para. 15.
[11] For businesses, see § **65: 13**.
[12] See § **65: 21**.
[13] *Whitehead v Customs and Excise Comrs* [1975] VATTR 152. For the position with regard to tax, interest and penalties, see § **66: 06**.
[14] Interpretation Act 1978, Sch. 1.
[15] For the strict position regarding partnerships, see *Customs and Excise Comrs v Evans* [1982] STC 342.
[16] *Customs and Excise Comrs v Glassborow* [1974] STC 142, [1974] 1 All ER 1041.
[17] VATA 1983, s. 31(1).
[18] *Saunders v Customs and Excise Comrs* [1980] VATTR 53.
[19] VAT (Isle of Man) Order, SI 1982, No. 1067, arts. 10–12.

The decision to register

66: 02   In theory, registration is always beneficial because a trader is eligible to credit for the input tax he incurs and, while he has a liability to account for output tax, he recovers the amounts concerned from his customers. At first sight, therefore, registration costs the trader nothing and can confer substantial advantages. Unfortunately, these advantages are sometimes more apparent than real and it is suggested that the following factors should be weighed before a decision to register is made.

(1) A trader must increase his prices by 15% to include VAT if his goods and services are chargeable to tax at the standard rate. This does not affect customers who are taxable persons because they recover the tax charged as input tax. It does, however, affect other customers. They are unable to recover the tax charged and may well decide to take their custom elsewhere. Thus, a trader selling to private individuals must either increase prices and risk losing business or keep prices steady and effectively bear the cost of tax accounted for to the Commissioners.

(2) Since input tax ceases to be a charge against profits, the trader may either keep prices unchanged, and thus retain the benefit himself, or decrease prices to reflect lower costs and thus pass on the benefit to his customers. The decision may well depend upon the level of input tax credits and three factors need to be considered: (*a*) many retail traders selling zero-rated goods (e.g. grocers) and service traders buying few goods (e.g. hairdressers) incur only small amounts of input tax and thus receive little financial benefit from registration; (*b*) some traders may find that input tax credit is disallowed on some of their more important purchases (e.g. a driving instructor cannot recover input tax on motor cars);[1] and (*c*) a trader making both taxable and exempt supplies may find that his input tax credits are restricted under the partial exemption provisions.[2]

(3) A trader who deregisters is deemed to supply stock and other business assets held at the date of deregistration and must account for output tax thereon.[3] There is no provision for input tax credit on this deemed supply and, in effect, input tax credits previously obtained are clawed back. A trader contemplating registration merely in order to obtain credit for intial capital equipment does not, therefore, obtain a permanent advantage.

(4) A registered trader must keep records which are sometimes more detailed than those required for normal accounting purposes (e.g. where he sells goods under the used goods schemes[4]); must submit tax returns and pay tax on a regular basis[5] under pain of penalty;[6] must keep up-to-date with constantly changing legislation which can often affect his output tax liabilities at short notice;[7] and must periodically spend time with customs officers on control visits.[8] It seems likely that a substantial tax saving should accrue before it is worthwhile incurring the administrative inconvenience associated with registration.

Having reached a conclusion regarding the desirability of registration, a trader must do something about it. In many cases the level of his taxable supplies is such that he is prima facie liable to compulsory registration. Where this is so, he must either register[9] or take steps to avoid the consequences of registration[10] depending on the conclusions he has drawn. Where he is not liable to register, he may apply for voluntary registration[11] if his conclusions point in that direction; if not, he must keep a close watch on the level of his turnover to ensure that he does not exceed the statutory limits unnoticed and thereby incur the financial disadvantages associated with unregistered taxable persons.

De Voil: Value Added Tax A20.16.
  [1] See § 67: 29–31.

² See § **67: 32–35.**
³ See § **65: 27.**
⁴ See § **67: 08–11.**
⁵ See § **68: 01, 04.**
⁶ See § **68: 16, 17.**
⁷ The exemption and zero-rate schedules can be amended by statutory instrument: VATA 1983, ss. 16(4), 17(2).
⁸ See § **68: 06–09.**
⁹ See § **66: 03–06.**
¹⁰ See § **66: 09–11.**
¹¹ See § **66: 07, 08.**

Liability to registration

66: 03   A trader is a taxable person, and is therefore required to register for the purposes of VAT, if the value of his taxable supplies exceeds one of the limits set out below.[1] Taxable supplies for this purpose means supplies other than exempt supplies made in the UK in the course or furtherance of business.[2] The value is equivalent to the consideration for those supplies since value is determined on the basis that no tax is chargeable on the supply.[3] The value of self-supplied stationery is taken into account for registration purposes only where it exceeds the registration limits.[4] A supply of goods or services made in the course or furtherance of business is disregarded for registration purposes if the items concerned are "capital assets" of the business.[5] However, the grant of an interest in, right over or licence to occupy land is not disregarded for this purpose if it is chargeable to tax at the standard rate.[6]

De Voil: Value Added Tax A3.21, A8.81–83.
¹ It includes certain deemed supplies under the reverse charge provisions: see § **65: 21, 22, 24–26.** A local authority which makes taxable supplies is liable to registration whatever the value of its supplies, VATA 1983, s. 28(1).
² VATA 1983, s. 2(2) and Sch. 1, para. 15.
³ VATA 1983, s. 10(2) and Sch. 1, para. 13.
⁴ VAT (Special Provisions) Order, SI 1981, No. 1741, art. 14(2)(*b*).
⁵ VATA 1983, Sch. 1, para. 1(5). For the nature of capital assets, cf VAT Notes (No. 2) 1982/83 para. 10.
⁶ VATA 1983, Sch. 1, para. 1(6).

Historical turnover limits

66: 04   Traders are required to calculate the value of their taxable supplies for three month periods (known as "quarters") ended on 31st March, 30th June, 30th September and 31st December each year.[1] Where a business has been taken over as a going concern, the taxable supplies taken into account include those of both vendor and purchaser.[2] Where a trader has previously been deregistered on the basis of a full disclosure of the relevant facts, the value of taxable supplies made prior to deregistration is not taken into account.[3] Traders are prima facie liable to registration if turnover exceeds either of the following limits.

First, if turnover for a quarter exceeds £8,000.[4] Thus, if Mr A has a taxable turnover of £8,750, for the quarter ended 30th September 1989 he is a taxable person liable to registration. However, a trader is not liable to registration under this provision if the Commissioners are satisfied that taxable turnover for the quarter and the next three quarters will not exceed £23,600.[5] Thus, Mr A would not be liable to registration if the Commissioners are satisfied that taxable turnover for the three quarters ending 30th June 1989 will not exceed £14,850 (ie £23,600—£8,750).

Secondly, if turnover for four consecutive quarters exceeds £23,600.[6] Thus, if Mr B's quarterly taxable turnover for the year ended 30th September 1989 is £5,450, £5,950, £5,850 and £6,450, he is a taxable person liable to register because his turnover amounts to £23,700. The fact that the quarterly turnover limits have not been exceeded in any one quarter is irrelevant. However, a trader is not liable to registration under this provision if the Commissioners are satisfied that taxable turnover in the next four quarters will not exceed £22,600.[7]

A trader liable to registration under either provision is required to notify the Commissioners of that fact not later than 30 days after the end of the quarter and he is registered with effect from the the end of the month in which the thirtieth day falls or a mutually agreed earlier date.[8] Thus, Mr A and Mr B must notify their liability to registration on or before 30th October 1989 and are registered with effect from a date not later than 1st November 1989.

A trader who considers that his estimated future taxable turnover will meet the stated limits must nevertheless notify the Commissioners of his liability to registration in the prescribed manner. They cannot be "satisfied" that these limits are met unless he does so.[9]

De Voil: Value Added Tax A3.41, 42.

[1] VATA 1983, s. 48(1) and Sch. 1, para. 1(1)(*a*).

[2] VATA 1983, s. 33(1)(*a*).

[3] VATA 1983, Sch. 1, para. 1(4). Taxable turnover is not disregarded if a trader has been deregistered on the grounds that he was neither liable nor eligible for registration on the day from which he was registered. This provision reverses *Short v Customs and Excise Comrs* [1983] VATTR 94.

[4] VATA 1983, Sch. 1, para. 1(1)(*a*)(i).

[5] VATA 1983, Sch. 1, para. 1(2).

[6] VATA 1983, Sch. 1, para. 1(1)(*a*)(ii).

[7] VATA 1983, Sch. 1, para. 1(3).

[8] VATA 1983, Sch. 1, para. 3. For the manner in which notifications are made, see VAT (General) Regulations, S.I. 1985, No. 886, reg. 4(1), (1A), (2).

[9] See *Briggs v Customs and Excise Comrs* MAN/85/41 unreported.

Future turnover limit

66: 05   The historical turnover limits are subject to an overriding future limit. If *at any time* a trader who makes taxable supplies has reasonable grounds[1] for believing that his taxable turnover for a future one year period will exceed £23,600, he is a taxable person liable to registration.[2] He must notify the Commissioners not later than the thirtieth day of the one year period concerned[3] and is registered with effect from: (1) the beginning of the one year period, if there are reasonable grounds for believing that the value of taxable supplies in the 30 day notification period will exceed £23,600;[4]

(2) the date from which a business was transferred, if a business is transferred as a going concern;[5] or (3) either the end of the thirty day registration period or such earlier date as may be mutually agreed, in other cases.[6]

An intending trader cannot be compulsorily registered under this provision because it is specifically applied to traders who *make* taxable supplies.[7] An intending trader, by definition, does not do so. He may, however, apply for voluntary registration during the setting up phase of his business.[8] Alternatively, he may, with the Commissioners' agreement, have his compulsory registration backdated once he has commenced to make taxable supplies.[9]

EXAMPLE
Mr C takes the first steps towards setting up a business on 1st January 1989 and plans to commence trading on 1st March 1989. He estimates that this first year's taxable turnover will be £40,000. He makes his first taxable supply on 1st April 1989. He cannot be compulsorily registered before 1st April 1989 because he does not commence making taxable supplies until that date. However, he must notify the Commissioners on or before 30th April 1989 and is registered from that date, unless he and the Commissioners mutually agree an earlier date.

De Voil: Value Added Tax A3.43.
[1] For the test applied, see *Optimum Personnel Evaluation (Operations) Ltd v Customs and Excise Comrs* LON/86/620 unreported.
[2] VATA 1983, Sch. 1, para. 1(1)(*b*).
[3] VATA 1983, Sch. 1, para. 4(1). For the manner in which notifications are made, see VAT (General) Regulations, S.I. 1985, No. 886, reg. 4(1), (1A), (2).
[4] VATA 1983, Sch. 1, para. 4(3).
[5] VATA 1983, s. 33(1A).
[6] VATA 1983, Sch. 1, para. 4(2).
[7] See *XL (Stevenage) Ltd v Customs and Excise Comrs* [1981] VATTR 192.
[8] See § 66: 07.
[9] VATA 1983, Sch. 1, paras. 3, 4.

Failure to notify liability to registration

66: 06   A trader who is liable to registration under either of the foregoing provisions is a taxable person whether or not he takes the necessary steps to register.[1] Where he is late in notifying liability to registration, his registration is backdated to the date from which he was liable to registration.[2] This has three consequences. First, he must account for output tax from the effective date of registration regardless of whether or not he has charged such tax to his customers.[3] Secondly, such tax may carry interest at the prescribed rate[4] if it is assessed in the absence of a return.[5] Thirdly, the trader may be liable to penalties.

Mere failure to notify liability to registration ceases to be a criminal offence from 25 July 1985.[6] However, if accompanied by some other act or omission, failure to notify may amount to dishonest conduct (i.e. an attempt to evade payment of tax) and as such may render a person liable to criminal[7] or civil[8] penalties.

Mere failure to notify liability to registration is a default giving rise to civil penalties from 25 July 1985 unless there is a reasonable excuse for the conduct or it gives rise to either of the foregoing penalties for dishonest conduct.[9] The prescribed penalty is the greater of £50 and either 10, 20 or 30 per cent of "relevant tax", according to whether the period of delay is nine months or less, between nine and 18 months, or over 18 months respectively. Relevant tax is output tax less input tax for the default period falling after 25 July 1985.[10] Penalties are assessed[11] and a right of appeal is given.[12]

The following conduct does not amount to a reasonable excuse:[13] (1) an insufficiency of funds to pay any tax due; (2) reliance on any other person to perform any task;[14] (3) any dilatoriness or inaccurancy on the part of any person relied on to perform any task; (4) ignorance of the law of registration;[15] (5) mitigating circumstances by reason of conduct subsequent of the material event; and (6) mere oversight unaccompanied by any other conduct.

The following conduct is capable of amounting to a reasonable excuse: (1) where the Commissioners fail to respond to a trader's request for form VAT 1 and such request is followed up within a reasonable time;[16] (2) where a trader posts form VAT 1 in a properly addressed envelope, it fails to arrive and the trader follows up his notification within a reasonable time;[17] (3) where liability to registration depends upon some complex point of law other than the requirement for registration;[18] (4) where the trader mistakenly believes that he is registered;[19] and (5) where the identity of the person liable to registration cannot be established within the statutory notification period.[20]

De Voil: Value Added Tax A3.33, A18.53, 61–67.

[1] VATA 1983, s. 2(2).
[2] *Whitehead v Customs and Excise Comrs* [1975] VATTR 152.
[3] Ibid.
[4] I.e. a rate to be prescribed by statutory instrument: FA 1985, s. 18(8). Interest is payable without deduction of income tax: FA 1985, s. 18(9). This provision applies from a day to be appointed by statutory instrument. No day has been appointed to date.
[5] FA 1985, s. 18(1)(*b*).
[6] FA 1985, s. 12(7).
[7] VATA 1983, s. 39(1)–(3); *R v McCarthy* [1981] STC 298, CA.
[8] FA 1985, s. 13; FA 1986, s. 14.
[9] FA 1985, s. 15(1), (4) and (5).
[10] FA 1985, s. 15(1) and (3A); *Customs and Excise Comrs v Shingleton* [1988] STC 190; *Rhodes v Customs and Excise Comrs* [1986] VATTR 72.
[11] FA 1985, s. 21(1).
[12] VATA 1983, s. 40(1)(*o*), (*p*).
[13] FA 1985, s. 33(2); *Hutchings v Customs and Excise Comrs* [1987] VATTR 58.
[14] A person giving advice does not "perform any task". Reliance on advice given by another person may therefore amount to a reasonable excuse in certain circumstances, but not in relation to the law of registration: *Noble v Customs and Excise Comrs* MAN/87/106 unreported.
[15] *Neal v Customs and Excise Comrs* [1988] STC 131. But see *Jenkinson v Customs and Excise Comrs* [1988] VATTR 45 (ignorance of detailed regulations) and *Mason v Customs and Excise Comrs* MAN/88/861 unreported (deaf trader with reading difficulties).
[16] See *Zaveri v Customs and Excise Comrs* [1986] VATTR 133. Cf. *Flearmoy v Customs and Excise Comrs* MAN/86/179 unreported.
[17] See *Selwyn v Customs and Excise Comrs* [1986] VATTR 142; *Hislop v Customs and Excise Comrs* LON/86/583 unreported.
[18] See *Neal v Customs and Excise Comrs* [1988] STC 131; *Jenkinson v Customs and Excise Comrs* [1988] VATTR 45. A reasonable excuse existed in *Davis v Customs and Excise Comrs* LON/86/174 unreported (whether trader's supplies exempt); *Geary v Customs and Excise Comrs* LON/86/395 unreported (whether trader employed or self-employed); *Dickson v Customs and Excise Comrs* MAN/87/218 unreported (whether trader principal or agent).
[19] See *Electric Tool Repair Ltd v Customs and Excise Comrs* [1986] VATTR 257; *Standoak Ltd v Customs and Excise Comrs* LON/86/500 unreported; *Jenkinson v Customs and Excise Comrs*

[1988] VATTR 45; *Dale v Customs and Excise Comrs* LON/87/562 unreported. See also *Daltry v Customs and Excise Comrs* MAN/86/261 unreported.
²⁰ See *Hutchings v Customs and Excise Comrs* [1987] VATTR 58.

Entitlement to registration

Intending and actual traders

66: 07   The Commissioners may register a trader who is not otherwise liable to registration if he so requests and he satisfies them that either: (1) he makes taxable supplies; or (2) he is carrying on a business and intends to make taxable supplies in the course or furtherance of that business. Registration takes effect from the day on which the request is made or an earlier mutually agreed date.[1]

A trader registered under these provisions is required to notify the Commissioners within 30 days if: (1) he ceases to make taxable supplies; or (2) he ceases to intend to make taxable supplies.[2] A trader is liable to penalties if he fails to make the required notification.[3] Penalties are assessed[4] and a right of appeal is given.[5]

De Voil: Value Added Tax A3.22, 51, 52.
   [1] VATA 1983, Sch. 1, para. 5. For the manner in which requests for registration are made, see VAT (General) Regulations, S.I. 1985, No. 885, reg. 4(1), (1A), (2).
   [2] VATA 1983, Sch. 1, para. 7. For the manner in which notifications are made, see VAT (General) Regulations, S.I. 1985, No. 835, reg. 4(4).
   [3] FA 1985, s. 17(1)(*a*). For the daily penalty applicable for days of default on or before 15 March 1988, see FA 1985, s. 17(1), (3) (as originally enacted) and FA 1988, s. 19(4). For days of default on or after 16 March 1988, see FA 1985, s. 17(1), (3) (as amended).
   [4] FA 1985, s. 21(1).
   [5] VATA 1983, s. 40(1)(*o*), (*p*).

Traders who do not make taxable supplies

66: 08   A trader is eligible for registration if he meets all of the following conditions.[1] First, he must either have a business establishment[2] in the UK or have his usual place of residence[3] there. Secondly, he neither makes nor intends to make taxable supplies.[4] Thirdly, he either makes supplies within either of the following classes or he carries on a business and intends to make such supplies in the course or furtherance of that business: (*a*) supplies made outside the UK which, if made in the UK, would be taxable supplies; or (*b*) supplies of warehoused goods which would be taxable supplies if they were not disregarded for the purposes of VAT.[5]

The Commissioners are required to register such a person if he so requests from the day on which the request is made or an earlier mutually agreed date.[6]

A person registered under this provision must notify the Commissioners within 30 days if he makes (or forms the intention of making) taxable supplies or if he ceases (or ceases to have the intention) of making supplies outside the UK or supplies of warehoused goods.[7] A trader is liable to penalties if he fails to make the required notification.[8] Penalties are assessed[9] and a right of appeal is given.[10]

De Voil: Value Added Tax A3.53.
    [1] VATA 1983, Sch. 1, para. 5A(1)–(3).
    [2] A person carrying on a business through a branch or agency in the UK meets this test: VATA 1983, Sch. 1, para. 5A(4)(a).
    [3] In relation to a body corporate, this means the place where it is legally constituted: VATA 1983, Sch. 1, para. 5A(4)(b).
    [4] I.e. supplies of goods and services made in the UK other than exempt supplies: VATA 1983, s. 2(2).
    [5] By VATA 1983, s. 35.
    [6] VATA 1983, Sch. 1, para 5A(1). For the manner in which requests for registration are made, see VAT (General) Regulations, S.I. 1985, No. 886, reg. 4(1), (1A), (2).
    [7] VATA 1983, Sch. 1, para. 7A. For the manner in which notification is made, see VAT (General) Regulations, S.I. 1985, No. 886, reg. 4(4).
    [8] FA 1985, s. 17(1)(a). For the daily penalty applicable for days of default on or before 15 March 1988, see FA 1985, s. 17(1), (3) (as originally enacted), and FA 1988, s. 19(4). For days of default on or after 16 March 1988, see FA 1985, s. 17(1), (3) (as amended).
    [9] FA 1985, s. 21(1).
    [10] VATA 1983, s. 40(1)(o), (p).

Exemption from registration

66: 09   A trader who is prima facie liable to compulsory registration may escape registration by either making use of the statutory exemption set out below or by reorganising his business affairs so that the statutory turnover limits do not apply.

Zero-rated turnover

66: 10   The Commissioners are empowered to exempt a trader from registration if: (1) he makes, or intends to make, taxable supplies and satisfies the Commissioners that any such supply would be zero-rated if he were a taxable person; (2) he applies for exemption; and (3) the Commissioners think fit to accept the application.[1]

The test to be applied by the Commissioners is whether exemption from registration is in the interests of the Revenue. This clearly applies where the trader is a repayment trader.[2]

A trader who is exempted from registration under this provision must notify the Commissioners of: (1) any material change in the nature of his supplies within 30 days of the day on which the change occurred or, if no such day is identifiable, within 30 days of the end of the quarter in which the change occurred;[3] and (2) any material change in the ratio of zero-rate to standard rate supplies which takes place in any quarter within 30 days of the end of the quarter in which the ratio changed.[4] Failure to do so may result in a liability to civil penalties[5] and interest.[6] Penalties and interest are assessed.[7] A right of appeal is given.[8]

De Voil: Value Added Tax A3.26.
    [1] VATA 1983, Sch. 1, para. 11(1). "Any" such supply does not mean "all" such supplies: Fong v Customs and Excise Comrs [1978] VATTR 75.
    [2] Fong v Customs and Excise Comrs [1978] VATTR 75.
    [3] VATA 1983, Sch. 1, para. 11(2).
    [4] VATA 1983, Sch. 1, para. 11(3).
    [5] FA 1985, s. 15.

⁶ FA 1985, s. 18. This provision applies from a day to be appointed by statutory instrument. No day has been appointed to date.

⁷ FA 1985, s. 21(1).

⁸ VATA 1983, s. 40(1)(o), (p).

Business splitting

66: 11   Traders prima facie liable to compulsory registration, and unable to avoid registration under the foregoing provision, can reorganise their business activities to avoid this position. This is sometimes referred to as "business splitting". The following conditions must exist before business splitting becomes a practical proposition: (1) a business with activities that can exist separately, e.g. a public house where food and drinks can be supplied independently; (2) two or more independent persons exist, e.g. Mr A trading sole, Mr and Mrs A trading in partnership, A Ltd controlled by Mr and Mrs A; and (3) one or more activities give rise to some tax advantage when excluded from a registration, e.g. a catering business buying zero-rated food which does not give rise to a loss of input tax credits but avoids a charge to output tax. Registration is avoided where an activity carried on by an independent person has a taxable turnover below the registration threshold.

The Commissioners have issued detailed guidelines for carrying on a severed business in this way.[1] It must be borne in mind that each case must necessarily be determined on its own facts and in the event of a dispute the question can be resolved by way of appeal to a VAT tribunal.[2]

The Commissioners can counteract business splitting by means of a direction under VATA 1983, Sch. 1, para. 1A if they are satisfied[3] that: (1) taxable supplies are made by two or more persons in the course of activities which, taken together, should properly be regarded as those of a single business;[4] (2) the combined value of those supplies exceed the registration limits; and (3) the activities are carried on separately wholly or mainly for the purpose of avoiding a liability to registration. The persons named in the direction or a supplementary direction are treated as both a partnership and a single taxable person. The single taxable person is liable to registration from the date of the direction or such later date as may be specified therein.[5] The consequences of a direction under this provision are described in § **66: 23**. A right of appeal is given in respect of a direction or supplementary direction.[6]

De Voil: Value Added Tax A3.24, 49; A4.23.

¹ Customs and Excise Press Notice No. 762 dated 20th September 1982.

² E.g. *Marner v Customs and Excise Comrs* MAN/77/140, 100 Taxation 187.

³ See *Chamberlain v Customs and Excise Comrs* [1989] STC 505; *South West Launderettes Ltd v Customs and Excise Comrs* LON/87/35 unreported.

⁴ See *Osman v Customs and Excise Comrs* [1989] STC 596.

⁵ VATA 1983, Sch. 1, para. 1A(1)–(4).

⁶ VATA 1983, s. 40(1)(hh) and (3A). See *South West Launderettes Ltd v Customs and Excise Comrs* LON/87/35 unreported.

Registration certificate

66: 12   A registered taxable person is provided with a registration certificate which shows, inter alia, his registration number, the date from which his registration takes effect, and the dates on which his prescribed accounting periods end.

The Commissioners maintain a centralised register of taxable persons.[1] To ensure that this is kept up to date, taxable persons are required to supply written particulars within 30 days of the following events: (1) a change in the name, constitution or ownership of the business; and (2) any other event which may necessitate variation of the register.[2] Notification must be made within 30 days where the trader ceases to make taxable supplies.[3]

De Voil: Value Added Tax A3.81–84.
[1] VATA 1983, Sch. 1, para. 15.
[2] VAT (General) Regulations, SI 1985, No. 886, reg. 4(3).
[3] VATA 1983, Sch. 1, para. 7. For the manner in which notifications are made, see VAT (General) Regulations, S.I. 1985, No. 886, reg. 4(4), (6).

DEREGISTRATION

Cessation of taxable supplies

66: 13   A registered person who ceases to make taxable supplies is required to notify the Commissioners of that fact within 30 days of doing so.[1] Such notifications are made in writing and must state the date on which taxable supplies ceased to be made.[2] Failure to make the necessary notification may result in a liability to civil penalties.[3] A trader can cease to make taxable supplies in a variety of circumstances and the options available to him differ in each case.

First, a trader's supplies may cease to be chargeable at the standard or zero-rate following a change in the legislation, i.e. where VATA 1983, Sch. 6 is amended to include the supplies he makes. Such a trader should deregister.

Secondly, a trader may close down his business, sell the assets piecemeal, and retire from business activities. Such a trader should deregister.

Thirdly, a trader may dispose of his business as a going concern and retire from business activities. Such a trader has two options: (1) he and the purchaser may jointly elect for the vendor's registration to be transferred to the purchaser; or (2) if this option is not exercised, he should deregister.

Finally, a trader may either close down his business or dispose of it as a going concern and start another business. Such a trader has a number of options: (1) since he continues to make taxable supplies, the new business is covered by his existing registration and he need merely notify the necessary changes in his registration particulars to the Commissioners; (2) if the new business has a turnover below the registration threshold, he can apply for voluntary deregistration; (3) if there is a gap between ceasing the old business and commencing the new one, it may be more convenient to deregister and subsequently re-register or, in the case of a business transferred as a going concern, transfer the existing registration to the purchaser and subsequently re-register.

De Voil: Value Added Tax A4.24–26.
[1] VATA 1983, Sch. 1, para. 7.
[2] VAT (General) Regulations, SI 1985, No. 886, reg. 4(4).

³ FA 1985, s. 17.

Deregistration

66: 14   A taxable person ceases to be liable to be registered at any time if the Commissioners are satisfied that the value of his taxable supplies in the period then beginning will be £22,600 or less.¹ A trader ceasing to make taxable supplies in the first, second or third situations supra falls within this description.

Where the Commissioners are satisfied that the trader has ceased to be liable to registration, they may cancel his registration from the day on which he ceased to be liable or a later mutually agreed date.²

De Voil: Value Added Tax A3.62.
  ¹ VATA 1983, Sch. 1, para. 2(1). See § **66: 18**.
  ² VATA 1983, Sch. 1, para. 9.

Transferring a registration

66: 15   The following conditions must be met before the transferor's registration can be transferred to the transferee: (1) the business must be transferred as a going concern; (2) the transferor ceases to be liable to be registered following the transfer but his registration has not yet been cancelled; (3) as a result of the transfer, the transferee either: (*a*) becomes liable to be registered, (*b*) becomes an intending trader and the Commissioners agree to register him, or (*c*) applies for voluntary registration and the Commissioners agree to treat him as liable to be registered; and (4) the prescribed form (VAT 68) is submitted by and on behalf of both transferor and transferee.¹

Form VAT 68 constitutes the notification which the transferor is required to give on ceasing to make taxable supplies.²

De Voil: Value Added Tax A3.37.
  ¹ VAT (General) Regulations, SI 1985, No. 886, reg. 4(5) and Sch., Form 3.
  ² SI 1985, No. 886, reg. 4(6); VATA 1983, Sch. 1, para. 7.

Continuation of registration

66: 16   A trader is required to provide full particulars of any change in the name, constitution or ownership of his business, and of any other event which may necessitate the variation or cancellation of his registration. The Commissioners must be notified in writing within 30 days of the event concerned.¹ Ceasing one business and commencing a new one clearly comes within this provision.

De Voil: Value Added Tax A3.84.
  ¹ VAT (General) Regulations, SI 1985, No. 886, reg. 4(3).

Voluntary registration

Not liable to registration

66: 17   Where a registered person satisfies the Commissioners that he is not liable to be registered, they must cancel his registration if he so requests. The registration is cancelled from the day on which the request is made or from a mutually agreed later date.[1]

De Voil: Value Added Tax A3.65.
[1] VATA 1983, Sch. 1, para. 8A(1).

Future turnover limits

66: 18   A taxable person ceases to be liable to be registered at any time if the Commissioners are satisfied that the value[1] of his taxable supplies[2] in the period of one year then beginning will be £22,600 or less and that he neither intends to cease making taxable supplies in the one year period nor intends to suspend making taxable supplies for a period of 30 days or more in the one year period.[3]

A trader must apply for deregistration under this provision. Where the Commissioners are satisfied that the trader has ceased to be liable to be registered, they are required to cancel his registration from the day on which he so ceased or a later mutually agreed date.[4]

De Voil: Value Added Tax A3.62.
[1] Determined on the basis that no tax is chargeable on the supply: VAT 1983, Sch. 1, para. 13.
[2] This includes the grant of an interest in, right over or licence to occupy land which is chargeable to tax at the standard rate: VATA 1983, Sch. 1, para. 2(4). Subject to this, it does not include goods and services which are capital assets of the business: VATA 1983, Sch. 1, para. 2(3). For the nature of capital assets, cf VAT Notes (No. 2) 1982/83, para. 10.
[3] VATA 1983, Sch. 1, para. 2(1) and (2).
[4] VATA 1983, Sch. 1, para. 8A(2) and 9.

Zero-rated turnover

66: 19   Where a taxable person who makes taxable supplies satisfies the Commissioners that any such supply is zero-rated, they may exempt him from registration if he so requests and they think fit.[1]

The test to be applied by the Commissioners is whether the cancellation of a registration is in the interests of the revenue. This clearly applies where the trader is a repayment trader.[2]

De Voil: Value Added Tax A3.76.
[1] VATA 1983, Sch. 1, para. 11(1). "Any" such supply does not mean "all" such supplies: *Fong v Customs and Excise Comrs* [1978] VATTR 75.
[2] Cf. *Fong v Customs and Excise Comrs* [1978] VATTR 75. See Customs and Excise Press Notice No. 1115 dated 11th June 1986.

Compulsory deregistration by the Commissioners

66: 20   The Commissoners are empowered to deregister a trader, whether or not he wants this to happen, in the following circumstances—

(1) Where the Commissioners are satisfied that he was neither liable to registration nor entitled to registration on the day on which he was registered;[1]

(2) Where the Commissioners determine that a trader should be registered under the Isle of Man legislation rather than under the UK legislation.[2]

(3) Where the Commissioners are satisfied that a trader has ceased to be entitled to registration.[3] A trader registered under VATA 1983, Sch. 1, paras. 5 or 5A is required to notify the Commisioners within 30 days if he ceases to be entitled to be registered[4] and is liable to penalties if he fails to do so.[5] He is deregistered from the date when he ceased to be entitled to be registered or a mutually agreed later date.[6]

De Voil: Value Added Tax A3.63, 64, 73.
  [1] VATA 1983, Sch. 1, paras. 8A(2), 9(2) and 10. The trader's registration is cancelled from the day when he was registered. Cf *Pichome Ltd v Customs and Excise Comrs* LON/83/63 unreported and *Knox-Richards v Customs and Excise Comrs* MAN/82/21 unreported.
  [2] VAT (Isle of Man) Order, SI 1982, No. 1067, art. 11(8).
  [3] VATA 1983, Sch. 1, paras. 8A(2), 9.
  [4] VATA 1983, Sch. 1, paras. 7, 7A. For the manner in which notification is made, see VAT (General) Regulations, S.I. 1985, No. 886, reg. 4(4), (6).
  [5] FA 1985, s. 17.
  [6] VATA 1983, Sch. 1, para 9(1).

SPECIAL PROVISIONS

Individuals

66: 21   When an individual registered for the purposes of VAT either dies, becomes bankrupt or becomes incapacitated, the person carrying on his business after that event is treated as a taxable person until such time as either: (1) some other person is registered in respect of the business, or (2) the incapacity ceases.[1]

De Voil: Value Added Tax A3.12.
  [1] VAT (General) Regulations, SI 1985, No. 886, reg. 11(1).

Partnerships

66: 22   The following special provisions apply to partnerships—

(1) Form VAT 2 must be annexed to a notification of liability to register. This shows the name, address and signature of each partner.[1]

(2) A partnership may be registered in the firm name.[2]

(3) For registration purposes, a partnership is treated as a continuing business, notwithstanding changes in its composition.[3] Such changes must, however, be notified to the Commissioners within 30 days.[4]

(4) A former partner is regarded as a continuing partner for VAT purposes until such time as his retirement is notified to the Commissioners.[5]

(5) Partners have a joint and several liability to make any notice required under the legislation, but a notification by one partner is sufficient compliance.[6]

(6) Separate partnerships with identical partners are not entitled to separate registrations.[7]

(7) New registrations are necessary (or a transfer of an existing registration) where either a sole trader takes on a partner or a partnership is dissolved but the business is carried on by a former partner.

De Voil: Value Added Tax A3.13.
[1] VAT (General) Regulations, SI 1985, No. 886, reg. 4(2) and Sch., Form 2.
[2] VATA 1983, s. 30(1).
[3] VATA 1983, s. 30(1). See *Customs and Excise Comrs v Evans* [1982] STC 342.
[4] VAT (General) Regulations, SI 1985, No. 886, reg. 4(3).
[5] VATA 1983, s. 30(2).
[6] VAT (General) Regulations, SI 1985, No. 886, reg. 9(1).
[7] *Customs and Excise Comrs v Glassborow* [1974] STC 142, [1974] 1 All ER 1041. But see *Saunders v Customs and Excise Comrs* [1980] VATTR 53 in relation to limited partnerships.

Deemed partnership

66: 23   The Commissioners are empowered to counteract business splitting by means of a direction or supplementary direction under VATA 1983, Sch. 1, para. 1A.[1] The separate persons carrying on the activities properly regarded as one business are treated as a partnership carrying on that business, and any question regarding its scope is determined accordingly. The persons concerned are known as "the constituent members".[2]

The following consequences flow from a direction:[3] (1) the partnership is a taxable person liable to registration with effect from the date of the direction or such later date as may be specified therein; (2) the taxable person is registered in such name as the constituent members jointly nominate[4] or, in the absence of a nomination, such name as may be specified in the direction; (3) goods and services made to or by the constituent members in the course of the single business are treated as if made to or by the taxable person; (4) a registered constituent member ceases to be liable to be registered in respect of taxable supplies made in the course of the single business from the date when the single taxable person became liable to be registered (in the case of persons named in a direction) or the date of the direction (in the case of persons named in a supplementary direction); (5) the constituent members are jointly and severally liable for any tax due from the taxable person; and (6) any failure by the taxable person to comply with any requirement of VATA 1983 is treated as a failure by each of the constituent members severally.

A constituent member ceases to be a member of the deemed partnership if it appears to the Commissioners that he should no longer be so regarded and they give notice to that effect. From the date of the notice, the constituent member ceases to be liable for tax due by the taxable person and failures to comply made by it.[5]

De Voil: Value Added Tax A3.14.
[1] See § **51.11**.
[2] VATA 1983, Sch. 1, para. 1A(6) and (7)(*e*).
[3] VATA 1983, Sch. 1, para. 1A(1), (5), (7).
[4] By written notice to the Commissioners not later than 14 days after the date of the direction.
[5] VATA 1983, Sch. 1, para. 1A(8).

Clubs, associations and organisations

66: 24   The legislation refers to "a club, association or organisation the affairs of which are managed by its members or a committee or committees of its members" and thus appears to be confined to unincorporated associations, trade unions, friendly societies and other unincorporated bodies. The following special provisions apply—

(1) A club, etc. may be registered in its own name.[1]

(2) For registration purposes, a club etc. is treated as a continuing business notwithstanding changes in its members.[1]

(3) Ultimately, every member has a joint and several responsibility for complying with the requirements imposed by the legislation, but notification by any official, committee member or member is sufficient compliance therewith.[2]

De Voil: Value Added Tax 3.15.
[1] VATA 1983, s. 31(3).
[2] VAT (General) Regulations, SI 1985, No. 886, reg. 10.

Bodies corporate

66: 25   The legislation refers to "bodies corporate", and is thus concerned with companies, industrial and provident societies, building societies and other incorporated bodies. The following special provisions apply—

(1) Where a trader issues a tax invoice in a company's name prior to its incorporation, it is he (not the company) who is liable to account to the Commissioners for the tax shown thereon.[1]

(2) A company carrying on a business in several divisions may be registered in the names of its divisions if the company so requests and the Commissioners see fit.[2]

(3) Where a company registered for the purposes of VAT goes into liquidation or receivership, or an administration order is made in respect of it, any person carrying on the business after that event may be treated as a taxable person until such time as some other person is registered in respect of the business or the receivership or administration order comes to an end.[3]

De Voil: Value Added Tax A3.17.
[1] Companies Act 1985, s. 36; *Customs and Excise Comrs v Wells* [1981] STC 588.
[2] VATA 1983, s. 31(1). See Leaflet No. 700/3/84.
[3] VAT (General) Regulations, SI 1985, No. 886, reg. 11(1), (3).

Groups of companies

66: 26 Two or more bodies corporate resident in the UK are eligible to be treated as members of a group if either: (1) one controls each of the others, or (2) one person (being either a company, an individual or two or more individuals carrying on a partnership) controls all of them.[1]

> EXAMPLE
> X is a person exercising control over A, B and C. The group can comprise either—
> (i) XABC, if X is a company
> (ii) ABC, if X is a company and decides not to be a group member
> (iii) ABC, if X is an individual or a partnership.

In broad terms, a person controls a company if he controls the composition of its board of directors or holds more than half of its equity share capital.[2] A company can also control another company if it is empowered by statute to control that company's activities.[3]

An application must be made before companies are treated as members of a group; the Commissioners may refuse an application only where it is necessary for the protection of the revenue. Once accepted, a group registration remains in force until either: (1) an application is made for further companies to be included, existing companies to be excluded, or for the companies to cease to be treated as a group; or (2) the Commissioners exclude a company from the group because the necessary degree of control no longer exists.[4]

Group registrations, and changes therein, take effect from the beginning of a prescribed accounting period. 90 days' notice is necessary, but the Commissioners have a discretion to accept shorter notice and even allow retrospective applications.[5] The forms used are non-statutory.[6]

The effects of a group registration are as follows—
(a) the VAT affairs of the group are vested in a group company known as the representative member.
(b) supplies between group companies are disregarded.
(c) group companies are jointly and severally liable for tax due from the representative member.[7]

De Voil: Value Added Tax A3.06, 18.
[1] VATA 1983, s. 29(3). For "resident in UK" see Leaflet No. 700/2/83, para. 2.
[2] VATA 1983, s. 29(8) applying Companies Act 1985, s. 736. See *Mannin Shipping Ltd v Customs and Excise Comrs* [1979] VATTR 83.
[3] VATA 1983, s. 29(8).
[4] VATA 1983, s. 29(5), (6).
[5] VATA 1983, s. 29(7). See *Customs and Excise Comrs v Save and Prosper Group Ltd* [1979] STC 205. For the refusal to grant retrospective applications, see *Blue Boar Property and Investment Co Ltd v Customs and Exise Comrs* [1984] VATTR 12 and *Legal and Contractual Services Ltd v Customs and Excise Comrs* [1984] VATTR 85. For changes in group registrations resulting from new partial exemption rules introduced with effect from 1st April 1987, see Customs and Excise Press Notice No. 33/87 dated 27th April 1987.
[6] Forms VAT 50, 51 and 56. See Leaflet No. 700/2/83.
[7] VATA 1983, ss. 29(1), (2) and 29A(4); FA 1986, s. 9(4); VAT (Cars) Order, SI 1980, No. 442, art. 5(4); VAT (Special Provisions) Order, SI 1981, No. 1741, art. 14(3); *Davis Advertising Service Ltd v Customs and Excise Comrs* [1973] VATTR 16.

AUTHORISATION FOR SPECIAL SCHEMES

Cash accounting scheme

66: 27   The cash accounting scheme[1] may be used only by traders who are authorised to use it.[2] A trader is eligible to apply for authorisation if:[3] (1) he expects the annual value of his taxable supplies to be not more than £250,000 (VAT-exclusive); (2) his returns are up to date; (3) he has paid all tax shown to be due on his returns; (4) he has paid all tax, penalties, surcharge and interest assessed; (5) he has not been convicted of a VAT offence,[4] compounded such proceedings[5] or been assessed for a penalty in respect of dishonest conduct[6] in the previous three years; and (6) he has not been expelled from the scheme within the previous three years.[7]

An application for authorisation is made on form VAT 621. It is accepted or rejected by way of a written decision.[8] An application may be rejected to protect the revenue[9] and a right of appeal is given against such a decision.[10] A successful application imposes an obligation to operate the statutory scheme in accordance with standard conditions.[11]

A trader's authorisation is terminated if: (1) he ceases to operate the scheme at his own volition;[12] (2) he ceases to be eligible to use it;[13] or (3) the Commissioners terminate his authorisation.[14] Special accounting provisions apply in such circumstances.[15]

Special accounting provisions arise, without an authorisation being terminated, in the following circumstances:[16] (1) a trader becomes insolvent and ceases to trade; (2) he ceases business; (3) he ceases to be registered; (4) he dies, becomes bankrupt or becomes incapacitated; or (5) he transfers all or part of his business as a going concern.[17]

De Voil: Value Added Tax A3.91.
[1] For computation of output tax and input tax under the scheme, see § **67: 07** and **67: 18**. For the records to be kept, see Notice No. 731 (October 1987) para. 6.
[2] VAT (Cash Accounting) Regulations, SI 1987, No. 1427, reg. 3.
[3] Ibid., reg. 4(1).
[4] I.e. under VATA 1983, s. 39.
[5] I.e. under CEMA 1979, s. 152.
[6] I.e. under FA 1985, s. 13.
[7] I.e. under SI 1987, No. 1427, reg. 10(1).
[8] Notice No. 731 (October 1987) para. 20.
[9] SI 1987, No. 1427, reg. 4(2).
[10] VATA 1983, s. 40(1)(r).
[11] SI 1987, No. 1427, reg. 3. For the conditions, see Notice No. 731 (October 1987) para. 5.
[12] SI 1987, No. 1427, reg. 7. For the procedure to be adopted, see Notice No. 731 (October 1987) para. 16.
[13] I.e. because his historical or future taxable turnover exceeds the limits in SI 1987, No. 1427, reg. 6(2). The trader is required to notify this fact within 30 days: ibid. He is liable to civil penalties if he fails to do so: FA 1985, s. 17(1)(c).
[14] I.e. on one or other of the grounds specified in SI 1987, No. 1427, reg. 10(1). A right of appeal is given in respect of such a termination: VATA 1983, s. 40(1)(r).
[15] SI 1987, No. 1427, regs. 7, 10(1), 10(2).
[16] SI 1987, No. 1427, regs. 8, 9(1), 9(2).
[17] For the purchaser's position where the vendor's registration is also transferred, see SI 1987, No. 1427, reg. 9(3) and Notice No. 731 (October 1987) para. 18.

Annual accounting scheme

66: 28   The annual accounting scheme[1] may be used only by traders who are authorised to use it.[2] A trader is eligible to apply for authorisation if:[3] (1) he has been registered for at least one year; (2) he expects the annual value of his supplies to be not more than £250,000; (3) his returns are up to date; (4) he has paid all tax shown to be due on his returns; (5) he has paid all tax, penalties, surcharge and interest assessed; (6) he was not a repayment trader in the previous year; (7) he has not been expelled from the scheme in the previous three years; and (8) if a body corporate, he has neither a group registration nor a divisional registration.

An application for authorisation is made on form VAT 600. It is accepted or rejected by way of a written decision.[4] An application may be rejected to protect the revenue.[5] A successful application is followed by an invitation to join the scheme setting out relevant accounting information for the first accounting year.[6]

A trader may leave the scheme at his own volition after operating it for at least two years.[7] His authorisation is terminated:[8] (1) if he ceases to be eligible to use the scheme;[9] (2) he becomes insolvent and ceases to trade; (3) he ceases business; (4) he ceases to be registered; (5) he dies, becomes bankrupt or becomes incapacitated; or (6) the Commissioners terminate his authorisation.[10]

De Voil: Value Added Tax A3.92.
  [1] For prescribed accounting periods under the scheme, see § **68: 01**. For payment of tax, see § **68: 04**.
  [2] VAT (Annual Accounting) Regulations, SI 1988, No. 886, reg. 3.
  [3] Ibid., reg. 4(1).
  [4] Notice No. 732, para. 17.
  [5] SI 1988, No. 886, reg. 4(2).
  [6] Notice No. 732, para. 18.
  [7] SI 1988, No. 886, regs. 5(2) and 6.
  [8] Ibid., regs. 5(2), 6, 7 and 8(1).
  [9] I.e. because his historical or future taxable turnover exceeds the limits in ibid., reg. 5(2)(*a*) or (*b*). A trader is required to notify relevant changes in future turnover within 30 days: ibid., reg. 5(*b*). He is liable to civil penalties if he fails to do so: FA 1985, s. 17(1)(*c*).
  [10] I.e. on the grounds specified in ibid., reg. 8(1)(*a*)–(*e*).

67 Output tax and input tax

Output tax   1505
Input tax   1518
Tax adjustments   1528

OUTPUT TAX

Introduction

67: 01   The tax charged on a supply within Charges I or II is known as output tax.[1] Output tax is chargeable on taxable supplies,[2] and events treated as such a supply, at one or other of two rates: the standard rate of 15%[3] or a nil rate of tax known as the zero rate.[4] Taxable supplies are charged at the zero rate if they fall within one of the descriptions outlined in Chapter 54. To the extent that they do not do so, they are charged to tax at the standard rate.

Tax is charged at the standard rate by reference to the value of the supply,[5] and becomes due at the time of supply.[6] This charge gives rise to two separate obligations: first (and subject to a number of exceptions), a liability to produce an invoice complying with specified requirements in respect of the supply; and secondly, a liability to account to the Commissioners for the tax chargeable.

Supplies made under Charge I can be classified under the following five headings, each of which have separate valuation, timing, invoicing and accounting requirements: (1) invoice basis, (2) cash accounting basis, (3) margin scheme for used goods, (4) margin scheme for tour operators, and (5) retail schemes. Supplies made under Charge II do not give rise to an invoicing requirement, and the differing valuation and timing provisions have already been described under each head of charge. The accounting requirements are considered below as a sixth heading.

Output tax liabilities under the margin and retail schemes have a common feature: they are calculated from a tax-inclusive figure. A standard rate of 15% charged on a tax exclusive value is equivalent to a fraction (known as the VAT fraction) of 3/23 of a tax-inclusive sum. Thus tax at 15% on a tax exclusive value of £100 is £15, and the total consideration is £115. The tax element of £115 is 3/23 of £115, i.e. £15.

De Voil: Value Added Tax A14.01.
[1] VATA 1983, s. 14(3). For supplies within this description, see § **65: 01–29**.
[2] I.e. a supply of goods or services other than an exempt supply: VATA 1983, s. 2(2); see § **65: 08**.
[3] VATA 1983, s. 9(1).
[4] VATA 1983, s. 16(1).
[5] VATA 1983, s. 9(1)(a).
[6] VATA 1983, s. 2(3).

Tax invoice basis

Time of supply

67: 02   VAT due on any supply of goods or services becomes due at the time of supply.[1] A supply is treated as taking place for the purposes of charging tax at a time known as the "tax point" which is determined in accordance with the following rules.

A supply is primarily treated as taking place at its "basic tax point". This is the time when goods are removed (i.e. collected or delivered) or made available to a customer[2] and the time when services are performed.[3] The basic tax point is displaced by a number of events, and in practice the time of supply is the earliest of: (1) the basic tax point; (2) the invoice date, where a tax invoice is issued before the basic tax point; (3) the date of receipt, where a payment is made before the basic tax point; or (4) the invoice date, where a tax invoice is issued within 14 days (or such longer period as may be specified in a direction to an individual trader) after the basic tax point.[4]

Goods removed on approval, sale or return, or similar terms before it becomes certain whether a supply will take place have a basic tax point comprising the earlier of: (1) the time when it becomes certain that a supply has taken place (i.e. when the goods are adopted); or (2) 12 months after the date of removal.[5] The basic tax point is displaced by two events, and in practice the time of supply is the earlier of: (1) the basic tax point; and (2) the invoice date, where a tax invoice is issued either: (*a*) before the basic tax point, or (*b*) within 14 days (or such longer period as may be specified in a direction to an individual trader) after the basic tax point.[6]

Traders may adopt a special tax point with the consent of the Commissioners, who will then issue a direction to that effect. The time of supply may be determined by reference to some specific event or the beginning or end of a "relevant working period".[7]

The legislation specifies that the following supplies are treated as taking place on the earlier of a payment being received and a tax invoice being issued: (1) rent in respect of a lease for a term exceeding 21 years;[8] (2) supplies of water, gas, power, heat, refrigeration or ventilation;[9] (3) retention payments;[10] (4) continuous supplies of services,[11] e.g. hire charges; (5) royalties and similar payments;[12] and (6) construction industry stage payments.[13] Special provision is made for goods sold under reservation of title,[14] services supplied by barristers and advocates,[15] and rents received either side of an election to waive exemption.[16]

Traders may elect for a special tax point to apply where a change takes place in either: (1) the rate of tax, i.e. where the standard rate is increased or decreased; (2) a description of exempt supplies, i.e. they become taxable supplies, or (3) a description of zero-rated supplies, i.e. they become exempt or chargeable to tax at the standard rate. Where goods or services are supplied on one side of the change (regardless of whether or not they have a basic tax point) but the tax point governing the charge to tax takes place on the other side, tax is charged by reference to the tax regime in force when the goods or services are supplied.[17] This election is not available where goods are sold in satisfaction of a debt or where a self-billing invoice is issued.[18]

EXAMPLE

X delivers goods to a customer on 1st January (the basic tax point) and issues a tax invoice on 10th January (the tax point governing the charge to tax). The rate of tax is increased on 5th January. X can elect to charge tax by reference to the rate of tax in force on 1st January.

Y hires a motor car to a customer on 1st February (no tax point arises) and is paid in arrears by standing order on the first day of each month (each payment creates a tax point). The rate of tax is increased on 15th April. X may account for tax at the old rate on one half of the 1st May payment. The other half is charged at the new rate.

For the purposes of the above rules, a tax invoice must contain all the information required to be shown on a tax invoice before it creates a tax point[19] and is issued when it is sent or given to a customer.[20] An invoice issued in respect of a zero-rated supply does not create a tax point.[21] Similarly, a payment must relate to a specific supply before it creates a tax point.[22] The recipient must demonstrate that he has received payment.[23] A recipient receives payment if the payment is made to him and he thereafter has no right to sue for payment,[24] even if he does not have complete freedom to draw on the moneys received.[25] Payments to a stakeholder do not amount to payment.[26]

Neither provision operates to create a supply where none has taken place.[27]

De Voil: Value Added Tax A5.31, 41–49.
1 VATA 1983, s. 2(3).
2 VATA 1983, s. 4(2)(a) and (b). See *West End Motors (Bodmin) Ltd v Customs and Excise Comrs* LON/81/218 unreported.
3 VATA 1983, s. 4(3).
4 VATA 1983, s. 5(1)–(4).
5 VATA 1983, s. 4(2)(c).
6 VATA 1983, s. 5(1)–(4).
7 VATA 1983, s. 5(5).
8 VAT (General) Regulations, SI 1985, No. 886, reg. 19.
9 SI 1985, No. 886, reg. 20.
10 SI 1985, No. 886, reg. 22.
11 SI 1985, No. 886, reg. 23.
12 SI 1985, No. 886, reg. 24.
13 SI 1985, No. 886, reg. 26.
14 SI 1985, No. 886, reg. 21.
15 SI 1985, No. 886, reg. 25; Leaflet No. 1/77/VMG.
16 VATA 1983, Sch. 6A, para. 4(1)–(4). For elections to waive exemption, see § **69: 02**.
17 VATA 1983, s. 41(2); SI 1985, No. 886, reg. 28.
18 VATA 1983, s. 41(5).
19 *J D Fox Ltd v Customs and Excise Comrs* [1988] 2 CMLR 875. The Commissioners may waive this requirement: SI 1985, No. 886, reg. 13(1).
20 *Customs and Excise Comrs v Woolfold Motor Co Ltd* [1983] STC 715.
21 *Double Shield Window Co Ltd v Customs and Excise Comrs* MAN/84/227 unreported.
22 *Weldons (West One) Ltd v Customs and Excise Comrs* LON/80/196, 107 Taxation 202 (advance payment for goods not yet ordered); *Old Chigwellians' Club v Customs and Excise Comrs* [1987] VATTR 66 (life membership fee paid in advance by instalments); *West Yorkshire Independent Hospial (Contract Services) Ltd v Customs and Excise Comrs* [1986] VATTR 151 (imprecise contract).
23 For inter-company current accounts see *Legal and Contractual Services Ltd v Customs and Excise Comrs* [1984] VATTR 85. For deposits see *Purshotam M Pattni & Sons v Customs and Excise Comrs* [1987] STC 1; *Bethway & Moss Ltd v Customs and Excise Comrs* [1988] 3 CMLR 44; *Regalstar Enterprises Ltd v Customs and Excise Comrs* [1989] 1 CMLR 117. A cheque payment is received when it is met by the drawer's bank: *Rampling v Customs and Excise Comrs* [1986]

VATTR 62. For loan-back schemes, see *Customs and Excise Comrs v Faith Construction Ltd* [1989] STC 539, CA.
  [24] *Customs and Excise Comrs v Faith Construction Ltd* [1989] STC 539, CA.
  [25] Ibid (funds released on presentation of architects' certificates); *Barratt Urban Construction (Northern) Ltd v Customs and Excise Comrs* MAN/87/116 unreported (netting arrangements and cross guarantees on bank overdraft facilities).
  [26] *Double Shield Window Co Ltd v Customs and Excise Comrs* MAN/84/227 unreported.
  [27] *Theotrue Holdings Ltd v Customs and Excise Comrs* [1983] VATTR 88.

Valuation of supplies

67: 03   Tax is charged by reference to the value of the goods or services supplied.[1] By implication, value for this purpose means tax-exclusive value,[2] and the consideration for a supply is therefore the value plus any tax charged thereon. In principle, there are three methods of valuation.

(1) Where the consideration for a supply is paid in money, value represents the trader's tax-exclusive selling price less the amount of any cash discount offered.[3] Thus, if A Ltd sells goods for £100 and offers a 5% cash discount for prompt payment, VAT is calculated on £95 whether or not the cash discount is taken. Where a single price is charged for two or more separable supplies, it is necessary to attribute a separate value to each supply for the purposes of charging tax,[4] e.g. by dividing the price in ratio to the cost or market value of each supply.[5]

(2) Where the consideration for a supply is something other than money (i.e. a barter deal) or partly money and partly something other than money (i.e. a part exchange deal) tax is charged by reference to open market value.[6] This is the tax-exclusive value which would be payable in an arm's length transaction.[7] The Commissioners are empowered to direct traders to account for tax by reference to open market value in relation to supplies to connected persons and supplies made to the public through unregistered intermediaries.[8] The validity of the latter provision[9] has been upheld by the European Court of Justice.[10]

(3) A special basis of valuation is provided for: (*a*) hotel accommodation;[11] (*b*) goods supplied under a trading stamp scheme;[12] (*c*) stamps, tokens and vouchers;[13] (*d*) food and accommodation supplied to employees;[14] (*e*) certain goods subject to treatment or process;[15] and (*f*) rents for the four years ending 31st July 1993 (where the tenant is a charity) or the year ending 31st July 1990 (other tenants) where an election to waive exemption is made.[16]

De Voil: Value Added Tax A6.51; A8.01–25.
  [1] VATA 1983, s. 9(1)(*a*).
  [2] Cf. VATA 1983, s. 10(2).
  [3] VATA 1983, s. 10(2) and Sch. 4, para. 4. For foreign currency, see ibid, Sch. 14, para. 11.
  [4] VATA 1983, s. 10(4); *Customs and Excise Comrs v Automobile Association* [1974] STC 192, [1974] 1 All ER 1257. For single prices which are indivisible, see *British Airports Authority v Customs and Excise Comrs* [1977] STC 36, [1977] 1 All ER 497, CA; *Rowe and Maw v Customs and Excise Comrs* [1975] STC 340, [1975] 2 All ER 444; *Customs and Excise Comrs v Scott* [1978] STC 191; *Customs and Excise Comrs v Bushby* [1979] STC 8; *British Airways plc v Customs and Excise Comrs* [1989] STC 182.
  [5] Notice No. 700 (October 1987) para. 17 and Appendix H. Also *River Barge Holidays Ltd v Customs and Excise Comrs* LON/77/345, 101 Taxation 375.
  [6] VATA 1983, s. 10(3).

[7] VATA 1983, s. 10(5). See Case 230/87: *Naturally Yours Cosmetics Ltd v Customs and Excise Comrs* [1988] STC 879, ECJ; *Churchway Crafts Ltd v Customs and Excise Comrs* LON/80/204 unreported.
[8] VATA 1983, Sch. 4, paras. 1 and 3.
[9] I.e. Decision 85/369/EEC, authorising the UK to derogate from the EEC common system of VAT under Directive 77/388/EEC, art. 27(1), in respect of VATA 1983, Sch. 4, para. 3.
[10] Joined cases 138/86 and 139/86: *Direct Cosmetics Ltd and Laughtons Photographs Ltd v Customs and Excise Comrs* [1988] STC 540, ECJ.
[11] VATA 1983, Sch. 4, para. 9.
[12] VATA 1983, s. 37; VAT (Trading Stamps) Regulations, SI 1973, No. 293.
[13] VATA 1983, Sch. 4, para. 6.
[14] VATA 1983, Sch. 4, para. 10. See *Goodfellow (a firm) v Customs and Excise Comrs* MAN/ 85/240 unreported.
[15] VATA 1983, s. 12(1)–(3).
[16] VATA 1983, Sch. 6A, para. 4(5). For elections to waive exemption, see § **69: 02**.

The obligation to issue a tax invoice

67: 04 A registered taxable person is required to issue a tax invoice when he makes a supply to another person, and must do so within 30 days (or such longer time as the Commissioners may allow) of the time when the supply is treated as taking place for the purposes of charging tax.[1] A tax invoice for this purpose includes a document provided by a person selling someone else's goods under a power, a self-billing invoice (i.e. an invoice prepared by the customer)[2] and an authenticated receipt given in respect of construction industry stage payments.[3]

The requirement to issue a tax invoice does not extend to supplies which are exempt from tax or charged to tax at the zero-rate, and the Commissioners may waive the requirement in other circumstances.[4]

Unless the Commissioners allow otherwise, a tax invoice is required to disclose the following information: (1) an identifying number; (2) the date of supply; (3) the supplier's name, address and registration number; (4) the customer's name and address; (5) the type of supply by reference to specified categories; (6) a description of the goods or services supplied; (7) for each description: (*a*) the quantity of goods or the extent of services, (*b*) the rate of tax, and (*c*) the tax-exclusive amount expressed in sterling; (8) the total tax-exclusive amount payable expressed in sterling; (9) the rate of any cash discount offered; (10) the amount of tax chargeable at each rate expressed in sterling and the rate to which it relates; and (11) the total amount of tax chargeable expressed in sterling.[5] Exempt or zero-rated supplies included on a tax invoice must be distinguished from taxable supplies and the amounts payable in respect of them stated separately.[6]

An unauthorised person[7] is liable to civil penalties[8] and interest[9] if he issues an invoice showing an amount as being tax or as including an amount attributable to tax.

De Voil: Value Added Tax A14.12–16.
[1] VAT (General) Regulations, SI 1985, No. 886, reg. 12(1) and (5).
[2] For the assessment of tax understated on a tax invoice, see FA 1988, s. 22.
[3] SI 1985, No. 886, reg. 12(2)–(4).
[4] SI 1985, No. 886, regs. 12(1) and 16(*a*).
[5] SI 1985, No. 886, reg. 13(1).
[6] SI 1985, No. 886, reg. 13(3).
[7] Defined in FA 1985, s. 15(2).

⁸ FA 1985, s. 15(1)(*b*). A statutory defence of reasonable excuse is available: see FA 1985, ss. 15(4) and 33(2).
⁹ FA 1985, s. 18(6). This provision applies from a day to be appointed by statutory instrument. No day has been appointed to date.

The ability to issue a credit note

67: 05   A credit note is valid for VAT purposes only if it is issued under statutory authority¹ or if it is issued bona fide in order to correct a genuine mistake or overcharge or to give a proper credit.² A credit note issued to cancel a bad debt is void.³ A credit note is ineffective unless it is issued to the person to whom it is addressed.⁴

By concession, the Commissioners allow credit notes to be issued when goods subject to a hire purchase agreement are repossessed from someone other than a taxable person.⁵

De Voil: Value Added Tax A14.18, 19.
¹ See VAT (General) Regulations, SI 1985, No. 886, reg. 14.
² *British United Shoe Machinery Co Ltd v Customs and Excise Comrs* [1977] VATTR 187; *Castle Associates Ltd v Customs and Excise Comrs* MAN/87/448 unreported.
³ *Cripwell & Associates v Customs and Excise Comrs* CAR/78/131, 102 Taxation 250.
⁴ *Leviss Compressors Ltd v Customs and Excise Comrs* MAN/84/36 unreported. For "issue" see *Customs and Excise Comrs v Woolfold Motor Co Ltd* [1983] STC 715.
⁵ Notice No. 748 (October 1988) para. A3. But see *Mannesman Demag Hamilton Ltd v Customs and Excise Comrs* [1983] VATTR 156.

Calculation of output tax

67: 06   The output tax for a prescribed accounting period is the difference between the tax shown on: (1) tax invoices issued for the period; and (2) credit notes validly issued in the period.

De Voil: Value Added Tax A14.20.

Cash accounting scheme

67: 07   Traders authorised to use the cash accounting scheme¹ account for output tax on the basis of payments² received during a prescribed accounting period.³ However: (1) payments relating to supplies made prior to commencing to use the scheme are excluded,⁴ since tax has already been accounted for thereon; and (2) tax on supplies made under hire purchase, conditional sale and credit sale transactions is accounted for outside the scheme.⁵

Where a trader's authorisation is terminated, he must account for outstanding VAT on supplies made while authorised on:⁶ (1) returns for the periods in which payments are received (if he voluntarily ceases to use the scheme or becomes ineligible to use it); or (2) his next return (if the Commissioners terminate his authorisation). Outstanding VAT on supplies made in the previous 12 months must be accounted for within two months if:⁷ (1) a trader becomes insolvent and ceases to trade; (2) he ceases business;

(3) he ceases to be registered; (4) he dies, becomes bankrupt or becomes incapacitated; or (5) he transfers all or part of his business as a going concern.

De Voil: Value Added Tax A14.03.
[1] For authorisation, see § **66: 27**.
[2] For the meaning of "payment", see Notice No. 731 (October 1987) para. 7.
[3] VAT (Cash Accounting) Regulations, SI 1987, No. 1427, regs. 3(a) and 12(1).
[4] Notice No. 731 (October 1987) para. 5.
[5] SI 1987, No. 1427, reg. 4(3).
[6] SI 1987, No. 1427, regs. 7, 12(2), 12(3).
[7] SI 1987, No. 1427, regs. 8, 9(1), 9(2).

Margin scheme for used goods

Introduction

67: 08   Certain durable goods may be bought and sold a number of times during their working lives and two adverse tax consequences could arise in the absence of relief. First, since they are often sold to private individuals, a charge to tax would arise on each sale by a taxable person without any corresponding input tax credit arising. This could cause distortions in the second hand value of such goods. Secondly, private individuals would naturally seek to bypass dealers and purchase such goods by private treaty in order to avoid paying VAT. This would seriously distort the second hand market.

The used goods schemes mitigate these disadvantages by broadly providing that dealers account for output tax by reference to their gross profit margin rather than the full sale price. As a consequence, tax revenue arises only where profits are made on resale.

Goods which can be sold under the scheme

67: 09   The legislation sets out four separate, but broadly similar, schemes for the following goods—

(*a*)   used motor cars;[1]
(*b*)   horses and ponies;[2]
(*c*)   goods acquired for entertainment purposes which do not give rise to input tax credit;[3]
(*d*)   antiques, scientific collections and works of art; used caravans, motor cycles, boats and outboard motors, electronic organs, aircraft, and firearms.[4]

De Voil: Value Added Tax A14.32.
[1] VAT (Cars) Order, SI 1980, No. 442, art. 6. For the meaning of "motor car", see ibid., art. 2. It is the physical attributes of a vehicle, and nothing else, which is taken into account in deciding whether it falls within this definition: *Customs and Excise Comrs v Jeynes* [1984] STC 30. A used motor car is one which has been used on the road after a retail sale or self supply: *Lincoln Street Motors (Birmingham) Ltd v Customs and Excise Comrs* [1981] VATTR 120. See *Burgess Detective Agency Ltd v Customs and Excise Comrs* MAN/87/333 unreported.
[2] VAT (Horses and Ponies) Order, SI 1983, No. 1099.
[3] VAT (Special Provisions) Order, SI 1981, No. 1741, art. 9.
[4] SI 1981, No. 1741, arts. 4 and 5. For definitions and conditions, see ibid., arts. 2, 3(*d*).

Conditions to be met

67: 10   First, and in broad terms, the goods must have been acquired in circumstances where either:[1] (1) no tax was charged, e.g. where goods are purchased from a private individual; (2) no tax invoice was issued, e.g. where goods are purchased from another dealer under the appropriate used goods scheme; (3) a tax invoice was issued but no input tax credit arose, e.g. goods purchased for entertainment purposes; or (4) the goods were self supplied but no input tax credit arose, e.g. a motor car purchased for resale and appropriated for use as a demonstration car.

Secondly, when the goods are sold:[2] (1) the supply must comprise something other than a hire; and (2) no tax invoice is issued in respect of the supply.[3]

Thirdly, the trader must keep the records prescribed in a notice published by the Commissioners or such alternative records as they may allow.[4] The prescribed records comprise: (1) special sales invoices, (2) purchase invoices and (3) a stock book.[5] Relief is denied for individual goods where the required records are incomplete[6] and tax must be accounted for on the full sale consideration in such circumstances.

De Voil: Value Added Tax A14.32, 33, 35–39.

[1] VAT (Cars) Order, SI 1980, No. 442, art. 6(2)(*b*); VAT (Horses and Ponies) Order, SI 1983, No. 1099, art. 2; VAT (Special Provisions) Order, SI 1981, No. 1741, arts. 4(2), 9(2).

[2] SI 1980, No. 442, art. 6(2)(*a*), (*c*); SI 1983, No. 1099, art. 3(*a*), (*b*); SI 1981, No. 1741, art. 4(3)(*a*), (*b*).

[3] A taxable person is not permitted to issue a tax invoice in respect of a supply under the used goods schemes: VAT (General) Regulations, SI 1985, No. 886, reg. 16(*d*).

[4] SI 1980, No. 442, art. 6(2)(d); SI 1983, No. 1099, art. 3(*c*); SI 1981, No. 1741, art. 4(3)(*c*). As regards motor cars, this requirement extends to motor dealers only. No requirements are stated in relation to goods acquired for entertainment purposes. For the retrospective approval of alternative records, see *Nixon v Customs and Excise Comrs* [1980] VATTR 66 and *Bardsley Car Sales v Customs and Excise Comrs* [1984] VATTR 171.

[5] See Notice Nos. 711, 712, 713, 720, 721, 722 and 724. A three part set which serves the same purpose is prescribed in relation to horses and ponies: Notice No. 726.

[6] *Customs and Excise Comrs v J H Corbitt (Numismatists) Ltd* [1980] STC 231, [1980] 2 All ER 72, HL. See also the dissenting judgment of Eveleigh LJ in the Court of Appeal, [1979] STC 504 at 511.

Calculation of output tax

67: 11   The tax due on any goods becomes due at the time of supply.[1] In relation to used goods, the time when a supply is treated as taking place for the purposes of charging tax is the earlier of: (1) the time when the goods are removed or made available to the customer, and (2) the time when he receives a payment in respect of them.[2]

The tax due on a supply is charged by reference to the "margin". This is the difference between: (1) the consideration for which the trader supplies the goods; and (2) the consideration for which he acquired them. No tax is charged unless the consideration in (1) exceeds the consideration in (2).[3] In relation to motor cars only, the consideration in (2) includes VAT charged on a self supply or importation.[4] No other costs are taken into account in calculating the margin of used goods.[5]

For the purposes of charging tax, the margin is treated as if it were the consideration for the supply.[6] It is thus a tax inclusive sum[7] and the output tax element of an individual supply is calculated by applying the VAT fraction.

EXAMPLE

A second hand car dealer buys a used car for £2,000, spends £150 (VAT-inclusive) in having it resprayed by a sub-contractor, and sells it for £2,230. The respraying costs are disregarded. Output tax is calculated thus—

Margin: £2,230 − £2,000 = £230

Output tax: 3/23 × £230   = £30

No tax would be chargeable if the car had been sold for £1,900. The VAT element of the sub-contractor's respraying charge is available for input tax credit.

Aggregate output tax liabilities for a prescribed accounting period are ascertained from the stock book maintained for the purposes of the scheme, or such other records as are maintained for motor cars sold by someone other than a car dealer and entertainment goods sold by anyone.

De Voil: Value Added Tax A14.34, 40.

[1] VATA 1983, s. 2(3).

[2] VATA 1983, ss. 4(2) and 5(1). Invoice dates are irrelevant because the invoices issued in respect of used goods are not tax invoices.

[3] VAT (Cars) Order, SI 1980, No. 442, art. 6(1)(*a*); VAT (Horses and Ponies) Order, SI 1983, No. 1099, art. 4; VAT (Special Provisions) Order, SI 1981, No. 1741, arts. 5, 9(2).

[4] VAT (Cars) Order, SI 1980, No. 442, art. 6(1)(*b*), (*c*).

[5] *Wyvern Shipping Co Ltd v Customs and Excise Comrs* [1979] STC 91 (boats); *Jocelyn Fielding Fine Arts Ltd v Customs and Excise Comrs* [1978] VATTR 164 (auctioneer's commission). See also Customs and Excise Press Notice No. 533 dated 20th November 1978.

[6] SI 1980, No. 442, art. 6(1)(*a*); SI 1983, No. 1099, art. 4; SI 1981, No. 1741, arts. 5, 9(2).

[7] VATA 1983, s. 10(2).

Margin scheme for tour operators

67: 12   Where a tour operator[1] supplies designated travel services[2] from a fixed establishment in the UK,[3] the value of the supply is the difference between:[4] (1) sums paid or payable to him in respect of the service; and (2) the sums paid or payable by him in respect of those services. This difference is referred to as "the margin".

Travel services which do not amount to designated travel services (i.e. because they are supplied from the tour operator's own resources rather than being bought in) are referred to as "in house" travel services.[5] The value of such supplies is determined in accordance with the normal valuation rules.[6]

A travel service may comprise: (1) wholly a designated travel service; (2) wholly an in house travel service; or (3) partly a designated travel service and partly an in house travel service. Supplies under head (2) are charged to tax under the tax invoice basis[7] and both purchases and sales are excluded from margin scheme calculations.

A travel service within heads (1) or (3) may include elements chargeable to tax at the zero rate,[8] exempt from tax,[9] or outside the scope of tax.[10] Disbursements for insurance are excluded from margin scheme calculations.[11]

A fixed proportion of the value of travel services within heads (1) and (3) is charged to tax at the standard rate. A provisional percentage is applied to all such supplies made in the current year (based on data for the previous year). Output tax for each prescribed accounting period is calculated by applying this percentage to the value of supplies having a tax point falling within that period.[12] A final percentage is calculated at the end of the current year (based on data for that year). Output tax for the prescribed accounting periods is then recalculated using the final percentage. Any difference between output tax provisionally and finally calculated is shown as an underdeclaration or overdeclaration of tax on the next tax return.[13]

Example
A tour operator's supplies within heads (1) and (3) for prescribed accounting periods ended 30 June 1988, 30 September 1988, 31 December 1988 and 31 March 1989 are £29m., £12m., £5m. and £41m. respectively.

Supplies made and costs incurred for the financial years ended 31 March 1988 and 31 March 1989 are as follows—

	Code[14]	Y/E 31.3.88 £(000)	Y/E 31.3.89 £(000)
Supplies within heads (1) and (3)	(A)	72,000	87,000
Costs relating to supplies within heads (1) and (3):			
Cost of standard rate designated travel services	(B)	27,000	32,000
Cost of zero rate designated travel services	(C)	17,000	18,000
Cost of standard rate in house travel services	(D)	11,000	14,000
Cost of zero rate in house travel services	(E)	6,000	7,000
Cost of "outside scope" in house travel services	(F)	2,000	5,000
Total costs	(G)	63,000	76,000
Margin (A)−(G)	(H)	£9,000	£11,000

The value of standard rate supplies for Y/E 31.3.88 is—

$$\text{Designated travel services:} \frac{27,000}{63,000} \times 9,000 \qquad = \qquad 3,857$$

$$\text{In house travel services:} \frac{11,000}{63,000} \times 72,000 \qquad = \qquad 12,571$$

Total value   £16,428

The provisional percentage applied for Y/E 31.3.89 is—

$$\frac{16,428}{72,000} \times 100 \qquad = \qquad 22.81\%$$

Output tax for the prescribed accounting periods is provisionally calculated thus—

		£(000)
P/E 30.6.88	$\frac{3}{23} \times 22.81\%$ of £29m.	862
P/E 30.9.88	$\frac{3}{23} \times 22.81\%$ of £12m.	357
P/E 31.12.88	$\frac{3}{23} \times 22.81\%$ of £5m.	148
P/E 31.3.89	$\frac{3}{23} \times 22.81\%$ of £41m.	1,219
		£2,586

The value of standard rate supplies for Y/E 31.3.89 is—

$$\text{Designated travel services:} \frac{32,000}{76,000} \times 11,000 \qquad = \qquad 4,631$$

$$\text{In house travel services:} \frac{14,000}{76,000} \times 87,000 \qquad = \qquad 16,026$$

Total value   £20,657

The adjustment to output tax declared is calculated thus—

Due: $\frac{3}{23} \times £20,657$	2,694
Deduct: declared on returns	2,586
Underdeclaration	£108

The provisional percentage applied for Y/E 31.3.90 is—

$$\frac{20,657}{87,000} \times 100 \qquad = \qquad \underline{23.74\%}$$

De Voil: Value Added Tax A14.91.

[1] As defined in VATA 1983, s. 37A(3).

[2] I.e. a supply of goods or services acquired for the purposes of a tour operator's business and supplied by him for the benefit of a traveller without material alteration or further processing: VAT (Tour Operators) Order, SI 1987, No. 1806, art. 3(1). For supplies excluded from this description, see ibid, arts 3(3), 3(4) and 14.

[3] SI 1987, No. 1806, art. 5(2). Supplies made from a fixed establishment in an EEC member state are taxed under national legislation of that state in accordance with Directive 77/388/EEC, art. 26. Supplies made from a fixed establishment in a third country do not amount to a designated travel service: SI 1987, No. 1806, art. 3(1). If a tour operator does not have a fixed establishment, his designated travel services are taxed in the EEC member state where he has established his business: ibid.

[4] SI 1987, No. 1806, art. 7

[5] Leaflet No. 709/5/88, para. 8.

[6] I.e. VATA 1983, s. 10 and Sch. 4. See § **67: 03**.

[7] See § **67: 02–06**.

[8] SI 1987, No. 1806, art. 10(1). For transport services, see VATA 1983, Sch. 5, Group 10. For designated travel services enjoyed outside the EEC, see ibid., Item 13 and Note 7. See Leaflet No. 709/5/88, paras. 6 and 18.

[9] SI 1987, No. 1806, art. 10(2). For insurance, see VATA 1983, Sch. 6, Group 2.

[10] For in house supplies supplied outside the UK, see SI 1987, No. 1806, art. 5(3)–(6). See Leaflet No. 709/4/88.

[11] Leaflet No. 709/5/88, para. 16.

[12] For the time of supply, see SI 1987, No. 1806, art. 4.

[13] For the detailed computation, see Leaflet No. 709/5/88, Section II. For directions to substitute open market value, see SI 1987, No. 1806, art. 8. For goods and services purchased before 1 April 1988, see ibid, art. 9.

[14] For the calculation of items (A)–(H), see Leaflet No. 790/5/88, Section II.

Retail schemes

Introduction

67: 13   A retailer is a trader whose business is classified under Group 24 (retail distribution) or Group 28 (miscellaneous services) of the VAT trade classification. Traders making both retail and non-retail sales are regarded as retailers only in respect of their retail supplies.[1]

The legislation authorises retailers to calculate their output tax by reference to any method described in a notice published by the Commissioners[2] and largely removes them from the obligation to provide customers with tax invoices.[3]

The general provisions relating to retail accounting methods are set out in Notice No. 727. The twelve standard retail schemes are each described in a separate leaflet[4] and more specialised information is contained in other leaflets.[5] These notices and leaflets set out what is, in effect, a statutory

scheme, although they also contain advice and recommendations which have
no statutory effect.[6]

De Voil: Value Added Tax A14.41.
[1] Notice No. 727 (October 1987) para. 1.
[2] VAT (Supplies by Retailers) Regulations, SI 1972, No. 1148, reg. 2.
[3] VAT (General) Regulations, SI 1985, No. 886, reg. 15(1).
[4] Leaflet Nos. 727/7/87–727/15/87.
[5] Leaflet Nos. 727/1/87 and 727/6/87.
[6] *GUS Merchandise Corpn Ltd v Customs and Excise Comrs* [1980] STC 480.

Gross takings

67: 14   The first step towards calculating output tax is to ascertain the value
of "gross takings" for the prescribed accounting period concerned. There are
two methods: (1) the standard method, which broadly comprises cash
received during the period from both cash and credit sales; and (2) the
optional method, which broadly comprises cash received during the period
from cash sales and the consideration for credit sales made during the period
regardless of whether or not cash has been received for them.[1]

The standard method must be used unless a retailer notifies the
Commissioners that he intends to use the optional method. The choice of
method, once made, is normally final.[1]

The rules for calculating gross takings are set out in Notice No. 727.[2] The
following general points are noted. First, the rules vary slightly according to
the retail scheme adopted. Secondly, exempt supplies are always excluded
from gross takings. Thirdly, cash receipts must be grossed up where
appropriate to reflect part-exchanges and sales subject to deductions,[3] e.g.
commissions. Fourthly, retail exports are included in gross takings in the
same manner as non-export sales. A separate adjustment is made when
calculating output tax. Fifthly, a deduction is made for the face value of
certain stamps, tokens and vouchers.[4]

De Voil: Value Added Tax A14.46–48.
[1] Notice No. 727 (October 1987) para. 9. But see *Customs and Excise Comrs v J Boardmans
(1980) Ltd* [1986] STC 10.
[2] Ibid, paras. 10–18.
[3] *Davies v Customs and Excise Comrs* [1975] STC 28, [1975] 1 All ER 309.
[4] For redemption vouchers, see *Boots Co plc v Customs and Excise Comrs* [1988] STC 138.

Retail schemes

67: 15   There are twelve basic retail schemes (A, B, B1, B2, C, D, E, E1, F,
G, H and J).[1] Traders may adopt one of the basic schemes or make use of the
provisions relating to mixed schemes and adaptions.[2] The following general
considerations should be borne in mind when choosing a scheme.[3] First, the
retailer should be capable of operating it. Secondly, Schemes B2, C, and D
are subject to turnover limits; scheme B has ratio limits; and Scheme C is
restricted to specified trades. Thirdly, certain schemes can overstate the
amount of output tax payable, e.g. the 1/8 uplift on Scheme G. Fourthly,

certain schemes make use of annual adjustments (Schemes B1, D and J) or require a specific adjustment when the rate of tax changes (Schemes E, H and J).

In principle, it is necessary to operate the chosen scheme for at least one year. A change may be made: (1) on an anniversary; (2) when the trader ceases to be eligible to use his chosen scheme, e.g. when he exceeds the turnover limit for Scheme C; and (3) retrospectively, in exceptional circumstances, at the Commissioners discretion.[4]

The purpose of the retail schemes is to divide gross takings between standard rate supplies and zero rate supplies. The methods adopted are briefly summarised in the following table—

Scheme	Leaflet No.	Method
A	727/7/87	Used where *all* takings are standard rated.
B	727/8/87 ⎫	Standard rate takings = total takings minus retail
B1	727/8A/87 ⎬	value of zero-rate purchases.
B2	727/8B/87	Standard rate takings = total takings minus zero-rate purchases grossed up by a fixed percentage.
C	727/9/87	Standard rate takings = cost of standard rate purchases for resale plus a fixed mark-up.
D	727/10/87	Total takings analysed in ratio to cost of standard rate and zero rate purchases for resale.
E	727/11/87 ⎫	Standard rate takings = retail value of standard rate
E1	727/11A/87 ⎬	purchases for resale.
F	727/12/87	Standard rate and zero rate takings distinguished at the point of sale and separate daily totals recorded.
G	727/13/87	Total takings analysed in ratio to cost of standard rate and zero rate purchases for resale.
H	727/14/87 ⎫	Total takings analysed in ratio to retail values of
J	727/15/87 ⎬	standard rate and zero rate purchases for resale.

Caterers apportion gross takings in accordance with an estimated ratio of standard rate and zero rate sales.[5]

De Voil: Value Added Tax A14.44, 51–70.
[1] See Notice No. 727 (October 1987) paras. 19 and 20 and Leaflet Nos. 727/7/87–727/15/87.
[2] Notice No. 727 (October 1987) paras. 19 and 20.
[3] See, generally, Leaflet No. 727/6/87.
[4] Notice No. 727 (October 1987) para. 22. Also *Withers & Gibbs (a firm) v Customs and Excise Comrs* [1983] VATTR 323. Also Customs and Excise Press Notice No. 1049 dated 12th November 1985.
[5] VAT (Supplies by Retailers) Regulations, SI 1972, No. 1148, reg. 10.

Calculation of output tax

67: 16 Output tax for a prescribed accounting period represents the tax element of standard rated gross takings calculated under the appropriate retail scheme. Where appropriate, deductions are made for: (1) export relief;[1] and (2) retail pharmacists relief.[2]

De Voil: Value Added Tax A14.56, 57.
[1] Notice No. 727 (October 1987) para. 17.
[2] Ibid, para. 21.

The obligation to issue a tax invoice

67: 17   A retailer is required to provide a tax invoice at the request of a customer who is a taxable person, but other than this he is relieved of the general obligation to issue tax invoices.[1]

The following types of invoice may be issued—

(i)   a less detailed tax invoice, where the consideration for the supply does not exceed £50;[2]

(ii)   a modified tax invoice;[3]

(iii)   a road fuel invoice;[4]

(iv)   a tax invoice.[5]

De Voil: Value Added Tax A14.45.

[1] VAT (General) Regulations, SI 1985, No. 886, reg. 15(1).

[2] SI 1985, No. 886, reg. 15(1) which sets out the details to be shown thereon.

[3] Notice No. 700 (October 1987) para. 50(*b*).

[4] Ibid, para. 51.

[5] VAT (General) Regulations, SI 1985, No. 886, regs. 12(1), 15(1). For the details to be shown thereon, see ibid, reg. 13(1).

INPUT TAX

Introduction

67: 18   A taxable person is entitled to credit for so much of his input tax as is allowable.[1] This comprises so much of his input tax as is attributable to supplies within the following classes: (1) taxable supplies; (2) supplies made outside the UK which, if made within the UK, would be taxable supplies; and (3) supplies of warehoused goods which, if not disregarded for VAT purposes, would be taxable supplies.[2] Special reliefs are available for certain statutory bodies and government departments.[3]

Input tax for the foregoing purposes may be said to comprise: (1) tax incurred in respect of specified supplies and imports, which (2) meets specified conditions, and (3) is not specifically excluded from credit. These matters are described below. The attribution of tax to supplies is dealt with separately.

De Voil: Value Added Tax A13.01.

[1] VATA 1983, s. 14(2). For allocation of input tax to prescribed accounting periods, see VAT (General) Regulations, SI 1985, No. 886, reg. 62(1). For the allocation made by traders approved under the cash accounting scheme, see VAT (Cash Accounting) Regulations, SI 1987, No. 1427 and Notice No. 731 (October 1987) paras 8–12. For approval under the scheme, see § **66: 27**.

[2] VATA 1983, s. 15(1) and (2).

[3] VATA 1983, ss. 20, 27 (as amended).

Supplies and importations concerned

67: 19   In principle, input tax is the VAT chargeable on goods and services supplied (or deemed to be supplied) to a taxable person and VAT paid or payable on goods which he imports.¹ The supplies and importations concerned are classified under the following headings.

De Voil: Value Added Tax A13.01.
¹ VATA 1983, s. 14(3). The word "chargeable" is read into ibid, s. 14(3)(*a*): *Podium Investments Ltd v Customs and Excise Comrs* [1977] VATTR 121.

1. Goods and services supplied to the trader by another taxable person¹

67: 20   A supply for this purpose means a transfer of goods or performance of a service. Case law indicates that a tax point does not create a supply where none has taken place,² and it follows, therefore, that input tax credit does not arise merely because a tax invoice is issued or a payment made. The clear wording of the legislation indicates that the supply must be made to the trader who claims credit. In strict terms, therefore, input tax credit does not arise in respect of supplies made to an employee,³ agent⁴ or sub-contractor.⁵ However, in practice the Commissioners allow credit for *exact* reimbursements made to employees,⁶ agency supplies treated otherwise than as a disbursement,⁷ and certain agency transactions involving motor cars purchased from franchised motor dealers.⁸

De Voil: Value Added Tax A13.11–13.
¹ VATA 1983, s. 14(3)(*a*). Goods and services supplied by someone other than a taxable person are not charged to tax. For supplies, see Chapter 50, Charge I.
² *Theotrue Holdings Ltd v Customs and Excise Comrs* [1983] VATTR 88; *Northern Counties Co-operative Enterprises Ltd v Customs and Excise Comrs* [1986] VATTR 250.
³ *Stirlings (Glasgow) Ltd v Customs and Excise Comrs* [1982] VATTR 116. Supplies purchased with the employer's credit card do not count: *Tarmac Construction Ltd v Customs and Excise Comrs* [1981] VATTR 35. But see Case 165/86: *Leesportefeuille "Intiem" CV v Secretary of State for Finance* (1988) OJ C90/5, ECJ.
⁴ See Notice No. 700 (October 1987) para. 73.
⁵ *Berbrooke Fashions v Customs and Excise Comrs* [1977] VATTR 168.
⁶ Notice No. 700 (October 1987) para. 37.
⁷ I.e. under VATA 1983, s. 32(4). See Notice No. 700 (October 1987) paras. 75–98.
⁸ See Customs and Excise Press Release dated 25th June 1982.

2. Goods and services which the trader is treated as supplying¹

67: 21   The following supplies are also treated as being supplied *to* the trader and the output tax accounted for is thus eligible for input tax credit: (*a*) self-supplies of stationery,² (*b*) reverse charge on services received from abroad,³ and (*c*) reverse charge made by the representative member of a group of companies when a business is transferred as a going concern to a group company;⁴ (*d*) self-supplied construction services;⁵ and (*e*) self-supplies of completed buildings and civil engineering works.⁶

De Voil: Value Added Tax A13.14, 15.
¹ See Chapter 56 Charge II.
² VAT (Special Provisions) Order, SI 1981, No. 1741, art. 14(1).
³ VATA 1983, s. 7(1).
⁴ VATA 1983, s. 29A(4).
⁵ VAT (Self-supply of Construction Services) Order, S.I. 1989, No. 472 art. 3(1).
⁶ VATA 1983, Sch. 6A, para. 6(1).

3. Goods belonging to the trader who imports them[1]

67: 22   A separate claim is made in respect of goods belonging wholly or partly to someone other than the importer which are to be used inter alia for private purposes of the importer, owner or joint owner.[2]

De Voil: Value Added Tax A14.16, 17; A15.52.
  [1] VATA 1983, ss. 14(3)(*b*), 26(1).
  [2] See § **68: 03**.

---

4. Motor mileage allowances

67: 23   By concession, VAT included in the petrol element of vehicle mileage allowances paid to employees in respect of business journeys ranks for credit.[1] A VAT tribunal has noted that this administrative practice "seems to involve concessions by the [Commissioners] which are not warranted by the terms of the act".[2]

De Voil: Value Added Tax A13.26.
  [1] Notice No. 700 (October 1987) Appendix C, para. 16(*b*).
  [2] *Stirlings (Glasgow) Ltd v Customs and Excise Comrs* [1982] VATTR 116 at 119.

Conditions to be met

1. The trader must be a taxable person

67: 24   VATA 1983, s. 14(2), (3) make it clear that input tax credit is restricted to taxable persons. Since a taxable person is a trader who is, or is required to be, registered for the purposes of VAT,[1] it follows that a right to input tax credit arises only in respect of goods and services supplied or imported on or after the date from which he is, or should have been, registered. It also follows that a right to input tax credit ceases to apply in respect of goods and services supplied after the date from which he is deregistered. These general propositions are subject to two exceptions.

First, taxable persons are authorised to count the following tax as if it were input tax in those cases where the statutory conditions are met: (1) tax incurred prior to becoming a taxable person; and (2) tax incurred prior to the incorporation of a body corporate. In broad terms, the tax relates to goods held in stock at the relevant date and services incurred in the six months prior to the relevant date.[2]

Secondly, the Commissioners are empowered to refund VAT to: (1) traders who have ceased to be taxable persons; and (2) persons who are not, and may never have been, taxable persons. The manner in which claims are made, and the goods and services to which they relate, are described in § **68: 03**.

De Voil: Value Added Tax A13.02, 21, 22.
  [1] VATA 1983, s. 2(2) and (5).
  [2] VAT (General) Regulations, SI 1985, No. 886, reg. 37(1)–(4).

---

2. The supply or importation must be supported by evidence

67: 25   Tax paid on supplies and importations is input tax only to the extent that the documentary evidence specified in regulations is available.[1] The evidence specified in the regulations or accepted by the Commissioners in lieu thereof is summarised in the following table—

Transaction	Evidence
Supply from another taxable person	(1) a tax invoice,[2] or (2) warehouse entry,[3] or (3) an entry in the accounting records for goods and services costing £10 or less comprising (*a*) business telephone calls from public or private telephones, (*b*) supplies through coin operated machines, or (*c*) taxable parking charges.[4] (4) a tax certificate in relation to gifts of goods.[5]
Self supplied stationery	None.[6]
Reverse charge on services received from abroad	An invoice from the overseas supplier.[7]
Imported goods	An import entry.[8]
Petrol element of car mileage allowances	Records showing: (*a*) mileage travelled, (*b*) type, model and engine capacity of the vehicle, (*c*) rate of allowance, (*d*) input tax element, (*e*) separate details of allowances for private or non-business journeys.[9]

Additional records in the form of a stock account and list of services are required where the goods or services concerned were supplied or imported prior to the registration of a taxable person or the incorporation of a body corporate.[10]

De Voil: Value Added Tax A13.07, 11.26.

[1] VATA 1983, s. 14(9)(*a*).

[2] VAT (General) Regulations, SI 1985, No. 886, reg. 62(1A)(*a*). Traders approved under the cash accounting scheme must keep a receipted invoice for payments made in notes or coin: VAT (Cash Accounting) Regulations, SI 1987, No. 1427, reg. 12(3). For the Commissioners' discretion to accept something less than a valid tax invoice, see *Morgan v Customs and Excise Comrs* LON/86/165 unreported (invoice addressed to another person), *Morsham Contractors Ltd v Customs and Excise Comrs* MAN/84/202 unreported and *Presman (Bullion) Ltd v Customs and Excise Comrs* [1986] VATTR 136 (false invoice), and *Read v Customs and Excise Comrs* [1982] VATTR 12 (missing invoices). For tax shown on self-billing invoices, see *Credit Ancillary Services Ltd v Customs and Excise Comrs* [1986] VATTR 204; FA 1988, s. 22.

[3] SI 1985, No. 886, reg. 62(1A)(*d*). This relates to goods produced in the UK held in a bonded warehouse. The change to VAT arises when goods are removed from bond and is levied by reference to the supply which gives rise to the removal: see VATA 1983, s. 35(2). For a list of the forms concerned, see Notice No. 702 (January 1988), para. 14.

[4] Notice No. 700 (October 1987) para. 66(*c*)(ii).

[5] Customs and Excise Press Notice No. 889 dated 1st March 1984.

⁶ For the records required to be kept in relation to the deemed supply made, see Leaflet No. 706/1/87 para. 5.
⁷ VAT (General) Regulations, SI 1985, No. 886, reg. 62(1A)(*b*).
⁸ SI 1985, No. 886, reg. 62(1A)(*c*). For a list of the forms concerned, see Notice No. 702 (January 1988), para. 14.
⁹ Notice No. 700 (October 1987) Appendix C, para. 16(*b*).
¹⁰ VAT (General) Regulations, SI 1985, No. 886, reg. 37(4).

---

3. *The goods or services are used for the purposes of the claimant's business*

67: 26   The VAT associated with a supply or importation is input tax only where the goods or services concerned are used or to be used for the purposes of any business carried on or to be carried on by the taxable person who claims credit.[1]

A subjective test is applied in deciding the purpose for which goods or services were acquired.[2] This is applied by ascertaining what was in the mind or minds of the person or persons who took the decision[3] and is adjudged at the time of supply or importation[4] (in the case of an acquisition) or in each prescribed accounting period of use[5] (in the case of continuous supplies such as rental agreements). The following purposes can be distinguished—

(1) Goods or services are used for the purposes of a business which the trader carries on. The associated VAT is clearly eligible for credit.

(2) Goods or services are used for the purposes of a business which the trader intends to carry on. As a matter of EEC law, input tax credit is available in respect of activities preparatory to the carrying on of an economic activity.[6] It has been held, as a matter of UK law, that an activity does not amount to a business until such time as it is possible to forecast making taxable supplies in the course of it in the reasonably foreseeable future[7] and the EEC relief therefore gives rise to input tax credit at an earlier stage in the business start-up process.

(3) Goods or services are used for the purposes of a business carried on or to be carried on by someone other than the trader. It would appear that the associated VAT is ineligible for credit[8] unless the trader makes an onward supply of the goods or services concerned, e.g. where he acts as a buying agent in his own name[9] or as a paymaster.[10]

(4) Goods or services are used for private or non-business purposes. The associated VAT is clearly ineligible for credit.[11] However, it would appear that input tax credit is permissible in those cases where the trader accounts for output tax on a free supply of goods to himself or an employee.[12] Tax on fuel for private use is treated as input tax and is thus available for credit, where output tax is chargeable by reference to a scale charge in relation to prescribed accounting periods commencing after 6th April 1987.[13]

(5) Goods or services are used partly for business purposes and partly for other purposes. In this situation the associated VAT is apportioned and only that part which relates to the business purpose is treated as input tax.[14]

De Voil: Value Added Tax A13.04.
¹ VATA 1983, s. 14(3). For the meaning of "business", see § **65: 13**.
² *National Water Council v Customs and Excise Comrs* [1979] STC 157.
³ *Ian Flockton Developments Ltd v Customs and Excise Comrs* [1987] STC 394. The credibility

of a witness with regard to evidence of intention may be tested by the standards and thinking of an ordinary businessman standing in the taxpayer's shoes: ibid.

[4] *Sisson v Customs and Excise Comrs* LON/80/310 unreported.

[5] *Denmor Investments Ltd v Customs and Excise Comrs* [1981] VATTR 66.

[6] Directive 77/388/EEC art 2; Case 268/83: *Rompelman and Rompelman-van-Deelen v Minister van Financiën* [1985] 3 CMLR 202, ECJ; *Merseyside Cablevision Ltd v Customs and Excise Comrs* [1987] VATTR 134.

[7] *K & K Thorogood Ltd v Customs and Excise Comrs* LON/82/318 unreported and the cases cited therein.

[8] See *Ashtree Holdings Ltd v Customs and Excise Comrs* [1979] STC 818; *Jackson (a firm) v Customs and Excise Comrs* LON/85/70 unreported; *Bird Semple & Crawford Herron v Customs and Excise Comrs* [1986] VATTR 218. See also Notice No. 700 (October 1987) paras 36 and 78.

[9] VATA 1983, s. 32(4). See also Notice No. 700 (October 1987) paras. 75 and 77.

[10] Leaflet No. 700/6/80 paras. 3 and 4.

[11] Notice No. 700 (October 1987) para. 36.

[12] I.e. under VATA 1983, Sch. 2, para. 5; see § **65: 15**. The supply is treated as if it is made in the course or furtherance of business. The cost of providing it must therefore be incurred for the purposes of a business: see *Wimpey Group Services Ltd v Customs and Excise Comrs* [1984] VATTR 66.

[13] FA 1986, s. 9(5). For the scale charge, see § **65: 18**. For input tax credit in relation to motor expenses generally, see Notice No. 700 (October 1987), Appendix C.

[14] VATA 1983, s. 14(4). For apportionments where some activities amount to a business and some do not, see *Customs and Excise Comrs v Apple and Pear Development Council* [1986] STC 192, HL and *Whitechapel Art Gallery v Customs and Excise Comrs* [1986] STC 156; see also Leaflet Nos. 701/1/87 para. 3 and 701/5/86 para. 6. For apportionment between business and private expenditure, see *Ballacmaish Farms Ltd v HM Treasury* MAN/86/86 unreported.

---

4. The charge to tax

67: 27　Input tax credit in respect of a supply of goods or services is restricted to the amount *chargeable* on the supply.[1] Three consequences follow from this principle. First, no credit is available where tax is erroneously charged on a supply, i.e. where it is outside the scope of VAT,[2] chargeable to tax at the zero rate, or exempt from tax. Secondly, where the tax due on a supply is overstated (perhaps due to an arithmetical error), input tax credit is limited to the amount which is properly due.[3] Thirdly, where the tax due is understated, input tax credit would appear to be limited to the amount charged since this is the only sum supported by documentary evidence.

The tax due on imported goods is either paid to the Commissioners on delivery of an entry or payable at a later date under the duty deferment or postponed accounting systems.[4] The amounts so paid or payable are available for credit as input tax.[5]

The tax chargeable on a supply or paid or payable on importation must comprise VAT arising under either the UK legislation or the Isle of Man legislation.[6] Tax charged under an overseas VAT system is not eligible for credit. However, subject to a number of qualifications, VAT incurred in an EEC member state may be recovered from the appropriate authority of that state.[7]

De Voil: Value Added Tax A13.01, 11, 16.

[1] The word "chargeable" is read into VATA 1983, s. 14(3)(*a*): *Podium Investments Ltd v Customs and Excise Comrs* [1977] VATTR 121.

[2] E.g. *Advanced Business Technology Ltd v Customs and Excise Comrs* LON/83/195 unreported (tax charged on assets of business sold as a going concern not eligible for credit).

[3] *Podium Investments Ltd v Customs and Excise Comrs* [1977] VATTR 121.

⁴ See § **68: 05**.

⁵ VATA 1983, s. 14(3)(*b*).

⁶ VATA 1983, s. 14(3) as read in conjunction with VAT (Isle of Man) Order, SI 1982, No. 1067, arts. 2, 7.

⁷ I.e. under national legislation enacting Directive 79/1072/EEC. See Notice No. 723. For the corresponding UK provisions, see § **68: 03**.

5. *Election to waive exemption*

67: 28   Input tax incurred in respect of land or buildings is deductible if it is attributable to a taxable supply made or to be made by the trader concerned.¹ A freehold sale or letting may amount to a taxable supply if an election to waive exemption is made in respect of the relevant land or building.² Thus, input tax incurred in respect of it is attributable to a taxable supply and is apparently deductible. However, the right to deduction is restricted if the input tax concerned was incurred before the election was made.³

In principle, deduction is allowed if either of the following conditions is met:⁴ (1) no exempt supplies were made before the election took effect; or (2) any exempt supply made was confined to the period 1st April–31st July 1989 and would have been a taxable supply if made before 1st April 1989.⁵

However, this general principle does entitle a trader to deduct input tax incurred prior to 1st August 1989. Two further conditions must be met:⁶ (1) the election must take effect from 1st August 1989; and (2) the input tax must be attributable to a grant made on or after 1st April 1989 which would have been a taxable supply if made before that date.⁷

An alternative relief is available if these conditions are not met. Input tax is deductible if:⁸ (1) the election takes effect from 1st August 1989; and (2) supplies or grants made to the trader (e.g. construction services) during the period 1st April–31st July 1989 would have been zero-rated⁹ or exempt¹⁰ if made before 1st April 1989⁹.

De Voil: Value Added Tax A13.42.

¹ VATA 1983, s. 15(1), (2). See § **67: 32**.

² VATA 1983, Sch. 6A, para. 2(1)–(3).

³ Ibid, para. 2(4).

⁴ Ibid, para. 2(5).

⁵ I.e. under VATA 1983, Sch. 5, Groups 8 or 8A as effective prior to 1st April 1989.

⁶ VATA 1983, Sch. 6A, para. 2(6).

⁷ I.e. under VATA 1983, Sch. 5, Groups 8 or 8A as effective prior to 1st April 1989.

⁸ VATA 1983, Sch. 6A, para. 2(7).

⁹ Under VATA 1983, Sch. 5, Group 8, Items 1 or 2.

¹⁰ Under VATA 1983, Sch. 6, Group 1.

Tax excluded from credit

Motor cars

67: 29   Tax charged on the supply or importation of a motor car¹ is excluded from credit unless the motor car is either:² (1) supplied by way of hire; (2) to be converted into a vehicle which is not a motor car;³ (3) unused and acquired for resale;⁴ (4) unused and acquired for research and development by a car manufacturer; or (5) unused and acquired for hire to certain disabled persons.

The exclusion from credit extends to delivery charges[5] and optional extras purchased from the person who sold the car,[6] but not those purchased from another person.[7]

De Voil: Value Added Tax A13.32.
[1] As defined in VAT (Cars) Order, SI 1980, No. 442, art. 2. It is the physical attributes of a vehicle, and nothing else, which determines whether a vehicle falls within this definition; *Customs and Excise Comrs v Jeynes* [1984] STC 30. See also *Withers of Winsford Ltd v Customs and Excise Comrs* [1988] STC 431.
[2] VAT (Cars) Order, SI 1980, No. 442, art. 4(1).
[3] Conversion connotes a degree of permanence and thus excludes work of a temporary and transient nature which enables the owner to alter its status from day to day; *GA Security Systems Ltd v Customs and Excise Comrs* MAN/83/212 unreported.
[4] For agency purchases and personal imports, see Customs and Excise Press Release dated 25th June 1982.
[5] *Wimpey Construction UK Ltd v Customs and Excise Comrs* [1979] VATTR 114.
[6] *Turmeau v Customs and Excise Comrs* LON/81/164 unreported.
[7] *Broadhead Peel & Co v Customs and Excise Comrs* [1984] VATTR 195.

Goods installed in new dwellings

67: 30 Subject to the conditions set out below, tax chargeable on goods installed in new and refurbished dwellings is restricted to:[1] (1) materials;[2] (2) builders' hardware; (3) sanitary ware; and (4) articles of a kind ordinarily installed by builders as fixtures.[3] These categories do not include certain fitted furniture, prefabricated parts, appliances and carpets.[4]

This restriction acts in three ways. First, goods must fall within the above description before they are eligible for credit. Secondly, they must be incorporated in a dwelling prior to completion.[5] Thirdly, the restriction applies only where goods are installed in any part of the building or its site which is used for the purposes of a dwelling. Thus any goods installed in commercial buildings are outside the scope of the restriction.

De Voil: Value Added Tax A13.33.
[1] VAT (Special Provisions) Order, SI 1981, No. 1741, art. 8.
[2] I.e. materials normally used for building purposes. This does not include carpets: *Customs and Excise Comrs v Westbury Developments (Worthing) Ltd* [1981] STC 72, CA.
[3] I.e. articles of a kind commonly installed by builders and of a kind ordinarily installed by builders as fixtures; see *Customs and Excise Comrs v Smitmit Design Centre Ltd* [1982] STC 525. See also *Campbell v Customs and Excise Comrs* [1981] VATTR 16 regarding "fixtures".
[4] SI 1981, No. 1741, art. 8.
[5] *University of Hull v Customs and Excise Comrs* LEE/75/31 unreported.

Business entertainment

67: 31 Business entertainment means entertainment (including hospitality of any kind) provided by a taxable person in connection with a business carried on by him.[1] It includes the provision of accommodation and meals[2] and keeping racehorses to provide prospective customers with a day at the races.[3]

Tax chargeable on goods or services acquired for the purpose of business entertainment is excluded from credit unless the entertainment is either: (1) provided for employees (unless its provision for them is incidental to its provision for others),[4] but not self-employed salesmen;[5] or (2) provided under a reciprocal arrangement.[6]

Input tax relating to a supply is disallowed if a business entertainment purpose exists to a measurable degree.[7]

De Voil: Value Added Tax A13.34.

[1] VAT (Special Provisions) Order, SI 1981, No. 1741, art. 2.

[2] *Customs and Excise Comrs v Shaklee International* [1981] STC 776, CA.

[3] *British Car Auctions Ltd v Customs and Excise Comrs* [1978] VATTR 56.

[4] SI 1981, No. 1741, art. 2.

[5] *Customs and Excise Comrs v Shaklee International* [1981] STC 776, CA. But see Notice No. 748 (October 1988) para. A7 regarding accommodation and meals for amateur sportsmen.

[6] *Celtic Football and Athletic Co Ltd v Customs and Excise Comrs* [1983] STC 470. See also *Football Association Ltd v Customs and Excise Comrs* [1985] VATTR 106; *Ibstock Building Products Ltd v Customs and Excise Comrs* [1987] VATTR 1; *Northern Lawn Tennis Club v Customs and Excise Comrs* MAN/86/183 unreported.

[7] *Woolf Management Services Ltd v Customs and Excise Comrs* MAN/82/7 unreported.

Attribution of input tax

Introduction

67: 32 Input tax which meets the tests described above is nevertheless available for credit only if it is attributable to supplies within the following classes[1]: (1) taxable supplies, (2) supplies made outside the UK which, if made within the UK, would be taxable supplies, and (3) supplies of warehoused goods which, if not disregarded for VAT purposes, would be taxable supplies. These supplies are hereafter referred to as "taxable supplies".

Input tax is attributed to taxable supplies in accordance with either: (1) the de minimis rule;[2] (2) the standard method;[3] or (3) a special method.[4] Input tax arising on self-supplies made by a trader is attributed in accordance with regulations[5] made under VATA 1983, s. 15(3)(*d*).

A provisional attribution of input tax is made in each prescribed accounting period by reference to the situation prevailing in that period. A final attribution is made by reference to the situation prevailing in a "longer period" allocated to the trader.[6] A "longer period" is a period ending on 31st March, 30th April or 31st May, according to the prescribed accounting periods allocated to the trader, or the date on which he ceases to be a taxable person.[7]

De Voil: Value Added Tax A13.41.

[1] VATA 1983, s. 15(1) and (2); VAT (General) Regulations, SI 1985, No. 886, regs. 30(1) and 30A.

² See § **67: 33**.
³ See § **67: 34**.
⁴ See § **67: 35**.
⁵ No regulations have been made to date.
⁶ VAT (General) Regulations, SI 1985, No. 886, regs. 32(2) and 33. For the exceptions, see ibid, regs. 29(3) and 33(1).
⁷ Ibid, reg. 29.

De minimis rule

67: 33   The standard and special methods work on the principle that input tax is wholly deductible in relation to importations and supplies wholly used in making taxable supplies and partly deductible in relation to importations and supplies partly used in making taxable supplies.

In principle, input tax wholly or partly attributable to exempt supplies is not deductible. However, such tax is treated as being attributable to taxable supplies, and therefore deductible, if it is less than:[1] (1) £100 per month on average; (2) both £250 per month on average and 50 per cent of all input tax; or (3) both £500 per month on average and 25 per cent of all input tax.

De Voil: Value Added Tax A13.47.
¹ VAT (General) Regulations, SI 1985, No. 886, reg. 32(1).

Standard method

67: 34   The amount of input tax attributed to taxable supplies is determined as follows—

(1) Importations by and supplies to the taxable person in the period are identified.[1]

(2) Input tax may be deducted in full in respect of importations and supplies wholly used or to be used in making[2]: (*a*) taxable supplies, (*b*) supplies outside the UK which, if made in the UK, would be taxable supplies, (*c*) supplies of warehoused goods which, if not disregarded for VAT purposes, would be taxable supplies, (*d*) exempt supplies within a defined class[3], provided the taxable person does not carry on an excluded business[4] or a business similar to such a business.

(3) Input tax may not be deducted in respect of importations and supplies wholly used or to be used in making exempt supplies.[5]

(4) Input tax may not be deducted in respect of importations and supplies wholly used or to be used in carrying on an activity which does not give rise to taxable supplies.[6]

(5) Input tax in respect of other importations and supplies is apportioned according to either:[7] (*a*) user in making taxable supplies,[8] or (*b*) the ratio of taxable supplies to total supplies.[9] The second option is available to traders who make exempt supplies where the Commissioners so allow, but not otherwise.[10]

De Voil: Value Added Tax A13.43, 46, 47.
¹ VAT (General) Regulations, SI 1985, No. 886, reg. 30(1)(*a*).
² Ibid, regs. 30(1)(*b*), 30A and 31.
³ Defined in ibid, reg. 31(1)(*a*)–(*e*).
⁴ Defined in ibid, reg. 31(2)(*a*)–(*g*).

[5] Ibid, reg. 30(1)(c). Such tax may, however, be deducted under the de minimis rule: see § **67: 33**. The exempt supplies concerned are those outside the class in para 2(d) supra. See *Customs and Excise Comrs v C H Beazer (Holdings) plc* [1989] STC 549; *Sheffield Co-operative Society Ltd v Customs and Excise Comrs* [1987] VATTR 216.

[6] Ibid, reg. 30(1)(c). The activities are those outside para 2(b) and (c) supra. Cf *Newvale Ltd v Customs and Excise Comrs* [1989] STC 395, CA; *Whitechapel Art Gallery v Customs and Excise Comrs* [1986] STC 156; *Customs and Excise Comrs v Apple and Pear Development Council* [1986] STC 192, HL.

[7] Ibid, reg. 30(1)(d) and (2).

[8] See Notice No. 706 (April 1987) para. 14.

[9] For exempt and taxable supplies disregarded for the purposes of this calculation, see ibid, reg. 30(3) and VATA 1983, ss. 7(3), 29A(5).

[10] Ibid, reg. 30(2) and 36(2).

Special method

67: 35   The Commissioners may allow use of a method other than the standard method.[1] This may be a method agreed between the Commissioners and a trade association in relation to members of the association generally, or a method agreed between the Commissioners and an individual trader.

De Voil: Value Added Tax A13.44.

[1] VAT (General) Regulations, SI 1985, No. 886, regs. 30(5) and 36(2).

TAX ADJUSTMENTS

Errors

67: 36   If a trader makes an error in accounting for tax, or in any tax return, he is required to correct it in such manner and within such time limit as the Commissioners may require.[1] A trader has a legal right to make a deduction from his current liability to VAT in respect of past overdeclarations made in error irrespective of whether the error was one of law or fact.[2] The Commissioners have indicated the errors exceeding £1,000 either way should be reported immediately to the trader's local VAT office.[3]

From a day to be appointed by Treasury order,[4] the Commissioners are liable to repay tax paid to them if:[5] (1) it was not due to them; (2) the person who made the payment makes a claim for repayment; and (3) he would not be unjustly enriched by the payment. Claims must be made in the form and manner to be prescribed by regulations[6] and may be made in respect of payments made before or after the appointed day.[7] Claims must be made within six years of discovery (in the case of mistake) or payment (in other cases).[8] A right of appeal is given in relation to claims.[9]

From a day to be appointed by Treasury order,[10] the Commissioners may make regulations with respect to the making of entries in accounts, and for making financial adjustments in connection with the making of entries in accounts, for the purpose of making adjustments, whether for the correction of errors or otherwise.[11]. No order has been made to date.

Large[12] or persistent[13] understatements of tax liabilities or overclaims can give rise to civil penalties.

De Voil: Value Added Tax A13.10; A14.06, A15.58.
[1] VAT (General) Regulations, SI 1985, No. 886, reg. 64. For the manner in which errors are corrected, see Notice No. 700 (October 1987) paras. 69(*b*) and 70.

[2] *Customs and Excise Comrs v Fine Art Developments plc* [1989] STC 85, HL. For proceedings taken against the commissioners to recover tax overpaid in error, see *Woodcock v Customs and Excise Comrs* [1989] STC 237, where judgment was, however, given before the House of Lords decision. See also Customs and Excise Press Notice No. 34/89 dated 13th April 1989.

[3] CCAB Technical Release No. 479, para. 1.

[4] Under FA 1989, s. 23(10). No order has been made to date.

[5] FA 1989, s. 24(1)–(3).

[6] FA 1989, s. 24(6). No regulations have been made to date.

[7] FA 1989, s. 24(8).

[8] FA 1989, s. 24(4), (5).

[9] VATA 1983, s. 40(1)(*s*).

[10] Under FA 1989, s. 25(5).

[11] VATA 1983, Sch. 7, para. 2(4). No regulations have been made to date. See Customs and Excise Press Notice No. 21/88 dated 15 March 1988.

[12] FA 1985, s. 14(1). This provision takes effect from a day to be appointed by statutory instrument. No such day has been appointed to date.

[13] FA 1985, s. 14A, effective from 29 July 1988. This penalty applies where a "material inaccuracy" occurs during a "penalty period" specified in a "penalty liability notice" unless there is a reasonable excuse for the inaccuracy or another penalty provision is invoked.

Other adjustments

67: 37   Partly exempt traders recalculate their input tax credits on an annual basis, and an adjustment is often necessary to amounts provisionally claimed.[1] The additional tax due to or from the Commissioners is shown respectively as an over- or under- declaration of tax on the trader's tax return.

Traders who have incurred a bad debt in respect of an insolvent customer are entitled to bad debt relief for the irrecoverable VAT element of the debt.[2] A number of stringent conditions must be met. In particular: (1) the customer must meet the statutory test of insolvency;[3] (2) the trader must prove the debt due *less* the amount claimed as bad debt relief;[4] and (3) he must obtain a formal document from the person in charge of the insolvency.[5] The bad debt relief claimed is shown as an over-declaration of tax in the trader's tax return.[6]

A number of other adjustments can arise. In particular: (1) adjustments to invoices which are not corrected by way of a credit note or additional invoice;[7] and (2) a special concessionary relief for traders who have been defrauded of goods.[8] The tax concerned is shown as an under- or over-declaration of tax on the trader's tax return.

De Voil: Value Added Tax A13.10; A14.05, 07.
[1] See § 67: 32.

[2] VATA 1983, s. 22; VAT (Bad Debt Relief) Regulations, SI 1986, No. 335. See Leaflet No. 700/18/86; Customs and Excise Press Notice No. 1088 dated 10th March 1986; HC Written Answer 7th March 1986, Vol. 93, cols. 284, 285. See also *CBS United Kingdom Ltd v Customs and Excise Comrs* [1987] VATTR 93 (payment from third party) and *Customs and Excise Comrs v TH Knitwear (Wholesale) Ltd* [1988] STC 79, CA.

[3] Set out in VATA 1983, s. 22(2), (3).

[4] For proof of debts, see VATA 1983, s. 22(5), (6); SI 1986, No. 335, reg. 11.

⁵ For documents, see SI 1986, No. 335, regs. 5–7; Administrative Receivers (Value Added Tax Certificates) Rules, SI 1986, No. 385; Administrative Receivers (Value Added Tax Certificates) (Scotland) Rules, SI 1986, No. 304.

⁶ SI 1986, No. 335, reg. 4(1). For the computation of relief, see VATA 1983, s. 22(1) and SI 1986, No. 335, regs. 8 and 9; also *A W Mawer & Co v Customs and Excise Comrs* [1986] VATTR 87. For the Commissioners' rights in the insolvency, see *Customs and Excise Comrs v T H Knitwear (Wholesale) Ltd* [1988] STC 79, CA.

⁷ See Notice No. 700 (January 1984) para. 63(*a*).

⁸ See Customs and Excise Press Notice No. 761 dated 20th September 1982.

68 Accounting and control

TAX RETURNS

Returns for prescribed accounting periods

68:01   A taxable person is required to account for and pay tax by reference to "prescribed accounting periods".[1] A prescribed accounting period is a period of one month, three months or such other period as the Commissioners may determine in particular cases.[2] In practice, one month periods are available to repayment traders other than those who register voluntarily.[3] A prescribed accounting period ends on the earliest occurrence of one of the following events: (1) a date specified in the trader's registration certificate; (2) the date when a liquidator, receiver or trustee in bankruptcy is appointed; or (3) the date from which the registration is cancelled.[4]

A taxable person authorised under the annual accounting scheme[5] has a prescribed accounting period of twelve months which commences on the date of his authorisation or an anniversary thereof.[6]

A taxable person is required to furnish a tax return on the prescribed form to the controller of VAT Central Unit (or such specified address as the Commissioners may allow or direct) in respect of each prescribed accounting period. The prescribed forms are VAT 100 (normal return) and VAT 193 (final return). A return must be furnished two calendar months after the end of the prescribed accounting period to which it relates (in the case of traders authorised under the annual accounting scheme) or one month after such period (in other cases).[7]

The following accounting information is shown on a tax return: (1) all output tax for the period; (2) all input tax for the period; (3) tax adjustments arising in or discovered in the period; and (4) the net amount of tax due to the Commissioners or repayable by them.[8] The Commissioners may allow traders to estimate part of their output tax or input tax.[9]

The Commissioners may terminate a trader's authorisation under the annual accounting scheme if he fails to furnish a return by the due date.[10] Failure to furnish a return in other circumstances results in a sequence of reminders from VAT Central Unit.[11] In the event of continued default, the Commissioners may estimate the amount of tax due to the best of their judgment and issue an assessment.[12] No right of appeal exists in respect of such an assessment.[13] The tax assessed is treated as an amount of tax due

1532   *Part XI—Value added tax*

from the trader and is thus recoverable as a debt due to the Crown.[14] A
liability to penalties or default surcharge may also arise.[15]

De Voil: Value Added Tax A15.01–06.
[1] VATA 1983, s. 14(1).
[2] VAT (General) Regulations, SI 1985, No. 886, reg. 58(1).
[3] Notice No. 700 (October 1987) para. 83(b).
[4] VAT (General) Regulations, SI 1985, No. 886, reg. 58(1), (3), (5).
[5] For authorisation under the annual accounting scheme, see § **51: 28**.
[6] VAT (Annual Accounting) Regulations, SI 1988, No. 886, reg. 2.
[7] SI 1985, No. 886, reg. 58; SI 1988, No. 886, reg. 3(b). For the time when a tax return is
furnished, see *Aikman v White* [1986] STC 1; *Hayman v Griffiths, Walker v Hanby* [1987] STC
649.
[8] SI 1985, No. 886, regs. 60(a), 62(1), 64.
[9] SI 1985, No. 886, regs. 61, 62(2).
[10] SI 1988, No. 886, reg. 8(1)(b).
[11] See Report of the Committee on Enforcement Powers of the Revenue Departments, Cmnd.
8822 para. 16.5.
[12] VATA 1983, Sch. 7, para. 4(1), (6A).
[13] VATA 1983, s. 40(1)(m).
[14] VATA 1983, Sch. 7, paras. 4(9), 6(1).
[15] See §§ **68: 16, 17**.

Return of goods sold under a power

68: 02   Where goods forming part of a trader's business assets are sold by
another person, they are deemed to be supplied in the course or furtherance
of the trader's business provided: (1) the goods are sold in satisfaction of a
debt owed by the trader, and (2) the person selling them acts under a power
exercisable by him,[1] e.g. a bailiff or a receiver acting on behalf of a debenture
holder. The same consequences follow when an interest in, right over or
licence to occupy land is granted by the person acting under a power in
relation to land forming part of the trader's business assets.[2]

The person selling the goods (or making the grant), or the auctioneer (if
any) acting on behalf of such a person, is required to render a special return
(form VAT 833) to VAT Central Unit within 21 days of the sale.[3] He is also
required to: (1) account to the Commissioners for the tax, (2) provide the
trader with a copy of the return, and (3) issue a document in lieu of a tax
invoice to the purchaser.[4]

De Voil: Value Added Tax A15.42.
[1] VATA 1983, Sch. 2, para. 6.
[2] VATA 1983, Sch. 2, para. 8.
[3] VAT (General) Regulations, SI 1985, No. 886, reg. 59.
[4] SI 1985, No. 886, regs. 12(2), 62.

Repayment claims

68: 03   The general scheme of VAT is such that only taxable persons are
allowed a credit mechanism whereby they recover all or part of the input tax
they incur. The strict application of this principle can lead to a number of
difficulties. The legislation therefore provides a limited repayment procedure

in certain situations to alleviate anomalies, avoid hardship or comply with treaty obligations.

Special claims for repayment may be made by—

(1) persons constructing their own buildings otherwise than in the course or furtherance of business[1]

(2) diplomats, international organisations and visiting forces[2]

(3) traders who have ceased to be taxable persons[3]

(4) taxable persons importing goods for non-business purposes[4]

(5) traders carrying on a business in an EEC member state other than the UK[5] or in a non-EEC member state[6]

(6) government departments,[7] local authorities[8] and public bodies[9] in respect of their non-business activities.[10]

Where the Commissioners repay tax in error under one of the foregoing provisions, they may issue an assessment to the person to whom the repayment was made.[11] The tax assessed is treated as an amount of tax due from him and is thus recoverable as a debt due to the Crown.[12]

A person who obtains a refund or repayment under (1) or (6) above is liable to civil penalties if he does any act or omits to take any action which involves an element of dishonesty.[13] Local authorities and public bodies claiming refunds under (7) above are liable to civil penalties if serious or persistent errors are made.[14] Penalties are assessed.[15] The penalty assessed is treated as an amount of tax and is recoverable as a debt due to the Crown.[16]

De Voil: Value Added Tax A15.51–65.

[1] VATA 1983, s. 21; VAT ("Do-it-Yourself" Builders) (Relief) Regulations, SI 1975, No. 649. See Notice No. 719 (April 1987) and forms VAT 431–434.

[2] Consular Relations Act 1968, s. 8; International Organisations Act 1968, Sch. 1, paras. 6, 7 and 12; Diplomatic and Other Privileges Act 1979, s. 1; CEMA 1979, Sch. 4, para. 12; FA 1972, s. 55(5). For reliefs given by extra-statutory concession, see Notice No. 748 (October 1988). These concessions are to be replaced by Customs and Excise Duties (General Reliefs) Act 1979, ss. 13A, 13B, 13C and orders to be made thereunder. See Budget Notice BN 14/89.

[3] VATA 1983, s. 14(9)(*d*); VAT (General) Regulations, SI 1985, No. 886, reg. 37(5). See Leaflet No. 700/11/87 para. 6 and form VAT 427.

[4] VATA 1983, s. 26. See Notice No. 702 (January 1988) para. 20. Applications are made by way of correspondence.

[5] VATA 1983, s. 23; VAT (Repayment to Community Traders) Regulations, SI 1980, No. 1537. See Notice No. 723 (January 1988) and forms VAT 65, 66.

[6] VAT (Repayments to Third Country Traders) Regulations, SI 1987, No. 2015. See Notice No. 723 (January 1988).

[7] Defined in VATA 1983, s. 27(4); Treasury directions dated 7th November 1984 (see *London Gazette* 14th December 1984) and 27 March 1985 (see ibid, 17 May 1985) as amended by direction dated 24 March 1986 (see ibid, 2 May 1986).

[8] Defined in VATA 1983, s. 20(6).

[9] Listed in VATA 1983, s. 20(3); VAT (Refund of Tax) Order, SI 1973, No. 522; VAT (Refund of Tax) (No. 2) Order, SI 1973, No. 2121; VAT (Refund of Tax) Order, SI 1976, No. 2028; VAT (Refund of Tax) Order, SI 1985, No. 1101; VAT (Refund of Tax) Order, SI 1986, No. 336; VAT (Refund of Tax) (No. 2) Order, SI 1986, No. 532; VAT (Refund of Tax) Order, SI 1986, No. 336; VAT (Refund of Tax) (No. 2) Order, SI 1986, No. 532.

[10] VATA 1983, ss. 20(1) and 27(2A).

[11] VATA 1983, Sch. 7, para. 4(2)(*a*).

[12] VATA 1983, Sch. 7, paras. 4(2) and 6(1).

[13] FA 1985, s. 13.

[14] FA 1985, ss. 14(5B) and 14A(4).

[15] FA 1985, s. 21.

[16] VATA 1983, Sch. 7, para. 6(1); FA 1985, s. 21(7).

PAYMENT AND REPAYMENT OF TAX

Tax returns

68: 04   A tax return furnished to VAT Central Unit may show either an amount of tax due to the Commissioners or an amount of tax due from them. Payments and repayments are made in accordance with the statutory provisions set out below.

An amount of tax due to the Commissioners is required to be paid within the same time limits applicable to tax returns, i.e. normally within one month after the end of the prescribed accounting period concerned.[1] Traders authorised to use the annual accounting scheme[2] are required to pay 90 per cent of the estimated tax for a scheme year by nine equal monthly instalments commencing on the last day of the fourth month of the year, followed by a balancing payment within two months after the end of the year.[3] Where a tax return is furnished, but the tax shown to be due is unpaid, the tax shown is an amount of tax due from the trader and is thus recoverable as a debt due to the Crown.[4]

An amount of tax due from the Commissioners is repayable by them,[5] and most repayments are made within 10 days of receiving the relevant return.[6] This general principle is subject to a number of qualifications. First, no repayment is made where the sum due is less than £1.[7] Secondly, the Commissioners are empowered to withhold payment if a tax return for a prior period is outstanding.[8] Thirdly, the Commissioners may require a trader to produce evidence of input tax credit as a condition for allowing repayment.[9] Fourthly, the Commissioners may require a trader to give such security for the amount of any payment as appears appropriate if they consider this necessary for the protection of the revenue.[9] If the Commissioners consider that the amount claimed is excessive, they may either limit their payment to the amount which they consider to be due or issue an assessment for the amount which they consider to be due from the trader.[10] Any tax assessed is recoverable as a debt due to the Crown.[11] The Commissioners may take recovery proceedings in respect of output tax shown in a trader's return without having to issue an assessment.[12]

Where the Commissioners pay tax to a trader which subsequently proves not to have been due to him, they may issue an assessment for the amount overpaid.[13] The tax assessed is treated as an amount of tax due from the trader and is thus recoverable as a debt due to the Crown.[14] Such an assessment carries interest at the prescribed rate.[15] The person may also be liable to civil penalties if the action or inaction which gave rise to the overpayment involved an element of dishonesty.[16] The penalty is assessed.[17] The penalty assessed is treated as an amount of tax and is recoverable as a debt due to the Crown.[18]

Repayment supplement is due on delayed repayments where the following conditions are met: (1) the return concerned is received not more than one month after the due date; (2) repayment is not authorised until 30 days[19] after the later of the due date and the date when the return is received; and (3) the amount shown on the tax return is not overstated by more than the greater of £250 or 5 per cent of the amount due. Supplement is the greater of £30 and 5 per cent of the amount of tax due.[20]

For the consequences of failing to pay tax shown to be due to the Commissioners by the due date, see §§ **68: 14–18**.

De Voil: Value Added Tax A15.07, 08.

[1] VAT (General) Regulations, SI 1985, No. 886, reg. 58(1) and 60(*b*).
[2] For authorisation under the annual accounting scheme, see § **51: 28**.
[3] VAT (Annual Accounting) Regulations, SI 1988, No. 886, reg. 3.
[4] VATA 1983, Sch. 7, para. 6(1).
[5] VATA 1983, s. 14(5).
[6] Report of the Committee on Enforcement Powers of the Revenue Departments, Cmnd. 8822, para. 24.5.2.
[7] VATA 1983, Sch. 7, para. 2(7).
[8] VATA 1983, s. 14(7).
[9] VATA 1983, Sch. 7, para. 5(1). See *Strangewood Ltd v Customs and Excise Comrs* LON/87/769 unreported.
[10] VATA 1983, Sch. 7, para. 4(1); *International Language Centres Ltd v Customs and Excise Comrs* [1982] VATTR 172; affd [1983] STC 394; *Potter (a firm) v Customs and Excise Comrs* [1983] VATTR 108; on appeal [1984] STC 45, CA.
[11] VATA 1983, Sch. 7, paras. 4(9) and 6(1). See *Customs and Excise Comrs v Fine Art Developments plc* [1988] STC 178, [1988] 2 All ER 70, CA.
[12] *Customs and Excise Comrs v International Language Centres Ltd* [1986] STC 279.
[13] VATA 1983, Sch. 7, para. 4(2)(*b*). See *Farm Facilities (Fork Lift) Ltd v Customs and Excise Comrs* [1987] VATTR 80.
[14] VATA 1983, Sch. 7, paras. 4(2), 6(1).
[15] FA 1985, s. 18(1). This provision applies from a day to be appointed by statutory instrument. No day has been appointed to date.
[16] FA 1985, s. 13.
[17] FA 1985, s. 21.
[18] VATA 1983, Sch. 7, para. 6(1); FA 1985, s. 21(7).
[19] For the days left out of account in determining this 30 day period see VAT (Repayment Supplement) Regulations, SI 1988, No. 1343; *Richard Costain Ltd v Customs and Excise Comrs* [1988] VATTR 111.
[20] FA 1985, s. 20; Finance Act 1985 (Repayment Supplement) (Appointed Day) Order, SI 1986, No. 970, art. 2. Repayment supplement arises in relation to returns for a prescribed accounting period ending on or after 1st October 1986.

Imported goods

68: 05   In principle, import duties (and therefore VAT[1]) are due for payment when an entry is made for customs purposes.[2] This general principle is modified in the following circumstances—

(1) where a charge to tax arises on postal imports, the amount due is either collected by the Post Office when the postal packet is delivered[3] or accounted for under the postponed accounting system;[4]

(2) where no entry is required on importation (e.g. on passenger's baggage) tax is charged when the goods physically arrive in the UK (e.g. when an airline passenger walks through the red channel in the customs hall of an airport);[5]

(3) approved importers may account for VAT by direct debit on a monthly basis under the duty deferment system;[6]

De Voil: Value Added Tax A15.11–26.
[1] VATA 1983, s. 24(1).

² CEMA 1979, s. 43(1).
³ See Postal Packet (Customs and Excise) Regulations, SI 1986, No. 260.
⁴ See VAT (General) Regulations, SI 1985, No. 886, reg. 41. Datapost packets and goods valued at £1,300 or more are excluded from this relief.
⁵ See CEMA 1979, ss. 37 and 78. For deferment, see Customs and Excise (Deferred Payment) (RAF Airfields and Offshore Installations) (No. 2) Regulations, S.I. 1988, No. 1898.
⁶ See Customs Duties (Deferred Payment) Regulations, SI 1976, No. 1223 (as amended), Excise Duties (Deferred Payment) Regulations, SI 1983, No. 947 and Excise Duty (Hydrocarbon Oils) (Deferred Payment) Regulations, SI 1985, No. 1032. See Notice No. 101.

CONTROL

Introduction

68: 06   VAT is a self-assessed tax and it is therefore not surprising that the legislation makes provision for the periodic inspection of traders' records[1] and the verification of returns. The normal method of audit is known as a "control visit".

Most control visits are made by prior appointment. However, this is a matter of courtesy rather than a statutory requirement. A person acting under the authority of the Commissioners[2] is empowered to enter any business premises at any reasonable time.[3] He is empowered to enter other premises only where he has reasonable cause to believe that they are used in connection with taxable supplies of goods and that goods held for supply are to be found on those premises.[4] Entry in any other case is normally by way of a search warrant issued by a justice of the peace.[5]

De Voil: Value Added Tax A16.11–15, 31–33.
¹ For the requirement to keep records, see VATA 1983, Sch. 7, para. 7(1) and Notice No. 700 (October 1987) paras. 61–70. For the requirement to preserve records, see VATA 1983, Sch. 7, para. 7(2). A person who fails to keep and/or preserve the required records may be liable to civil penalties under FA 1985, s 17(1)(*b*), (2).
² I.e. an authorised person; VATA 1983, s. 48(1).
³ VATA 1983, Sch. 7, para. 10(1).
⁴ VATA 1983, Sch. 7, para. 10(2).
⁵ VATA 1983, Sch. 7, para. 10(3)–(6). See *IRC v Rossminster Ltd* [1980] STC 42, [1980] 1 All ER 80, HL. Customs officers are empowered to enter and search premises (1) for the purpose of arresting a person for an arrestable offence and (2) where the premises are occupied or controlled by a person who is under arrest for an arrestable offence: Police and Criminal Evidence Act 1984, ss. 17 and 18; Police and Criminal Evidence Act 1984 (Application to Customs and Excise) Order, SI 1985, No. 1800, arts. 3(1), 7 and Schs. 1, 2. For arrestable VAT offences, see VATA 1983, s. 39(1)–(3).

Powers to obtain information

68: 07   Having gained access to the premises a customs officer has a number of powers to obtain the information he requires. He can—

(1) inspect and check the operation of a computer;[1]
(2) inspect the premises and any goods found on them if he has reasonable cause to believe that taxable supplies of goods are made from those premises;[2]
(3) demand production of documents,[3] inspect them, take copies of them, or remove them for a reasonable period;[4]

(4) demand information concerning certain matters;[5]

(5) demand assistance in inspecting and checking the operation of a computer;[6]

(6) take samples of goods to determine the rate of tax chargeable on them[7] e.g. to see whether a substance is an animal feeding stuff;[8]

(7) search premises and persons, and seize documents in prescribed circumstances, when so authorised by a search warrant issued by a justice of the peace;[9]

(8) require a gaming machine to be opened and checked;[10]

(9) obtain access to recorded information held by third parties when so authorised by an order issued by a justice of the peace;[11]

(10) require a trader to account for goods acquired or imported for the purposes of the business[12]

The Commissioners may also obtain information from the Inland Revenue[13] and competent authorities in EEC member states.[14]

De Voil: Value Added Tax A16.34–40.

[1] FA 1985, s. 10(1).

[2] VATA 1983, Sch. 7, para. 10(2).

[3] As defined in VATA 1983, s. 48(4) and Sch. 7, para. 8(2) and (4).

[4] VATA 1983, Sch. 7, para. 8(2)(*b*), (4A) and (4B). The Commissioners are required to provide copies of uplifted documents without charge where such items are reasonably required for the proper conduct of the business: ibid., para. 8(4C). For documents held by third parties, see ibid, para. 8(4); *Customs and Excise Comrs v A E Hamlin & Co* [1983] STC 780, [1983] 3 All ER 654; *EMI Records Ltd v Spillane* [1986] STC 374, [1986] 2 All ER 1016.

[5] VATA 1983, Sch. 7, para. 8(2). This power extends to documents held by third parties: ibid., para. 8(3).

[6] FA 1985, s. 10(2).

[7] VATA 1983, Sch. 7, para. 9(1).

[8] And thus zero-rated under VATA 1983, Sch. 5, Group 1, Item 2.

[9] VATA 1983, Sch. 7, para. 10(3)–(6). See *IRC v Rossminster Ltd* [1980] STC 42, [1980] 1 All ER 80, HL. For the removal of documents, and the rights of the owner or custodian, see VATA 1983, Sch. 7, paras. 10B and 10C.

[10] VATA 1983, Sch. 7, para. 9A.

[11] VATA 1983, Sch. 7, para. 10A. See *R v Epsom Justices, ex p Bell* [1989] STC 169. For the removal of documents, and the rights of the owner or custodian, see ibid, paras. 10B and 10C.

[12] VATA 1983, Sch. 4, para. 6. The Commissioners may make an assessment if he fails to do so: ibid. Such an assessment carries interest at the prescribed rate: FA 1985, s. 18. (This provision comes into effect from a day to be appointed by statutory instrument. No day has been appointed to date).

[13] FA 1972, s. 127. See Customs and Excise Press Notice No. 12/88 dated 8 March 1988.

[14] Under national legislation of the state concerned giving effect to Directive 77/799/EEC.

Powers to secure a trader's compliance

68: 08 Customs officers are trained to carry our their duties in a reasonable manner[1] and are thus more likely to politely request information than to wield the big stick. They do, however, have three reserve powers which can be used to encourage co-operation or penalise the lack of it.

First, the Commissioners are empowered to issue an assessment "where a person has failed . . . to keep any documents and afford the facilities necessary to verify such returns . . .".[2] *Quaere* does "and" mean "or".[3]

Secondly, a person is liable to civil penalties if he fails to comply with a demand for documents or information.[4]

Thirdly, the Commissioners can prosecute under a number of provisions: for example, where anyone obstructs the inspection of a computer,[5] fails to assist in the inspection of a computer when required to do so,[5] or obstructs, hinders, molests, or assaults any officer performing any duty or exercising any power.[6]

De Voil: Value Added Tax A16.15.
[1] Notice No. 700 (October 1987) para. 101.
[2] VATA 1983, Sch. 7, para. 4(1).
[3] Cf. *R v Oakes* [1959] 2 QB 350, [1959] 2 All ER 92, CCA.
[4] FA 1985, s. 17(1)(*b*).
[5] FA 1985, s. 10(4).
[6] CEMA 1979, s. 16(1)(*a*).

Under-declarations of tax

68: 09   Errors in tax returns and estimated assessments issued in lieu of a return come to light partly through routine control visits carried out by local VAT offices and partly through investigations carried out by specialist staff.[1] Some 426,000 control visits in 1986/87 led to recovery of £597m underpaid tax and repayments of £17m. Specialist investigations in the same year realised a further £4m in fines and settlements.[2]

As a matter of procedure, all under-declarations are dealt with by way of assessment. Where it appears to the Commissioners that a trader's tax return is incomplete or incorrect, they may assess the amount of tax due to the best of their judgment[3] together with interest[4] and notify it to him. The tax assessed is deemed to be an amount of tax due from him and may thus be recovered as a debt due to the Crown.[5]

Prior to the passing of FA 1985, the Commissioners found it necessary to either prepare a case for criminal prosecution (with the consequent requirement to produce evidence of fraud "beyond all reasonable doubt") or settle a case by way of assessment.[6] This stark choice has now been leavened by the introduction of civil penalties in respect of conduct involving dishonesty,[7] serious misdeclaration of tax[8] and persistent misdeclaration of tax.[9] Such cases are investigated to the civil standard of proof based on probability and are subject to administrative rather than criminal penalties.[10] Penalties are assessed[11] and the amount thereof is open to appeal.[12] The penalty assessed is deemed to be an amount of tax due from the trader and may thus be recovered as a debt due to the Crown.[13]

The Commissioners have two choices where the criminal standard of proof is met. First, they may prosecute under the relevant penalty provisions of the VAT legislation,[14] customs legislation,[15] general criminal legislation,[16] or at common law.[17] Where this is done, the collection of any fines imposed is the responsibility of the Court. Secondly, the Commissioners may compound proceedings,[18] i.e. accept a pecuniary penalty in lieu of prosecution. In this case, a debt arises under the contract made between the Commissioners and the trader and is collected as a debt due to the Crown.[19]

De Voil: Value Added Tax A16.61; A18.51, 52, 61–65.

[1] See Report of the Committee on Enforcement Powers of the Revenue Departments, Cmnd. 8822, Chapters 4 and 9.

[2] The Commissioners' 78th Report, Cm. 234.

[3] VATA 1983, Sch. 7, para. 4(1).

[4] FA 1985, ss. 18(1) and 21(1). This provision applies from a day to be appointed by statutory instrument. No day has been appointed to date.

[5] VATA 1983, Sch. 7, paras. 4(9), 6(1); FA 1985, s. 21(7).

[6] See Cmnd. 8822, op cit, Chapter 16.

[7] FA 1985, s. 13. See *Gandhi Tandoori Restaurant v Customs and Excise Comrs* LON/88/369 unreported. For mitigation of penalties, see FA 1985, s. 13(5). For the recovery of all or part of such penalties from the officers of bodies corporate, see FA 1986, s. 14.

[8] FA 1985, s. 14. This provision applies from a day to be appointed by statutory instrument. No day has been appointed to date.

[9] FA 1985, s. 14A. This provision applies from 29 July 1988.

[10] See *The Collection of Value Added Tax* (HMSO, 1984) para. 34.

[11] FA 1985, s. 21(1).

[12] VATA 1983, s. 40(1)(*o*), (*p*). For mitigation of penalties, see FA 1985, s. 13(4); FA 1986, s. 14(6) and VATA 1983, s. 40(1A).

[13] FA 1985, s. 21(7); VATA 1983, Sch. 7, para. 6(1).

[14] I.e. VATA 1983, s. 39(1)–(5). See *R v McCarthy* [1981] STC 298, CA; *R v Asif* [1985] STI 317, CA.

[15] I.e. CEMA 1979, ss. 167, 168, 171(4).

[16] E.g. under Theft Acts 1968 and 1978.

[17] I.e. cheating the public revenue. This is expressly retained as an offence by Theft Act 1968, s. 32(1)(*a*). See *R v Mavji* [1986] STC 508, CA; *R v Redford* [1988] STC 845, CA; *R v Fisher* [1989] STI 269, CA.

[18] I.e. under CEMA 1979, s. 152; VATA 1983, s. 39(9). See House of Commons Public Accounts Committee, Minutes of Evidence of 25 April 1988, Appendix I, Annex A (Session 1987–88, HC Paper 452-i). For settlements made on or after 1 June 1989, see HC Written Answer, 26 April 1989, Vol. 151, cols. 562, 563.

[19] See Cmnd. 8822, op cit, para. 16.4.2.

ASSESSMENTS

Introduction

68: 10   It will be seen from the preceding sections that assessments play an important role in collecting what is, in theory, a completely self-assessed tax. It is therefore necesary to make a number of general comments concerning them.

First, an assessment must precisely define the period of time to which it relates.[1]

Secondly, it must be notified to the trader concerned,[2] and is unenforceable until this has been done.[3] An assessment served on a partnership is deemed to be a notification to the past and present members of the firm jointly assessed.[4]

Thirdly, an assessment must be made for the right reason.[5] Thus, if £x is assessed but the reason for making the assessment is wrong in law, the assessment will fail even though £x is due. Thus, the Commissioners must make an additional assessment if they are to validly claim £x.[6]

Fourthly, where an assessment is found to be lower than the amount due, the Commissioners are entitled to issue a supplementary assessment where the period concerned is still in time.[7] A VAT tribunal may order an increase of an existing assessment in the same circumstances, thus avoiding the need to issue a supplementary assessment.[8]

De Voil: Value Added Tax A15.31, 33, 38.
[1] *Bell v Customs and Excise Comrs* [1979] VATTR 115.
[2] VATA 1983, Sch. 7, para. 4(1), (2), (6); FA 1985, s. 21(1); see also VATA 1983, s. 40(3A). For the manner of notification, see *Din v Customs and Excise Comrs* [1984] VATTR 228.
[3] *Grunwick Processing Laboratories Ltd v Customs and Excise Comrs* [1986] STC 441.
[4] VATA 1983, s. 30(3). See *Customs and Excise Comrs v Evans* [1982] STC 342; *Choudhury v Customs and Excise Comrs* LON/87/16 unreported; *Ahmed v Customs and Excise Comrs* LON/87/418 unreported.
[5] *Silvermere Golf and Equestrian Centre Ltd v Customs and Excise Comrs* [1981] VATTR 106.
[6] Cf *Customs and Excise Comrs v Sooner Foods Ltd* [1983] STC 376 as explained in *Football Association Ltd v Customs and Excise Comrs* [1985] VATTR 106.
[7] For supplementary assessments, see infra, § **68: 12**. For time limits, see infra, § **68: 13**.
[8] VATA 1983, s. 40(3A).

Best judgment

68: 11   An assessment made under VATA 1983, Sch. 7, para. 4(1) or (6) must be made to the best of the Commissioners' judgment. This means that

> "... the Commissioners will fairly consider all material placed before them and, on that material, come to a decision which is reasonable and not arbitrary as to the amount of tax which is due. As long as there is some material on which the Commissioners can reasonably act then they are not required to carry out investigations which may or may not result in further material being placed before them."[1]

The Commissioners are given a measure of flexibility in estimating the tax due for a prescribed accounting period for which no tax return has been rendered.[2]

De Voil: Value Added Tax A15.40.
[1] *Van Boeckel v Customs and Excise Comrs* [1981] STC 290 at 292, 293. See also *Schlumberger Inland Services Inc v Customs and Excise Comrs* [1987] STC 228. For an assessment not made to the Commissioners' best judgment, see *James A Gordon & Sons Ltd v Customs and Excise Comrs* EDN/87/73 unreported.
[2] VATA 1983, Sch. 7, para. 4(6A).

Further assessments

68: 12   In general, where the Commissioners have made an assessment within one of the time limits described in § **68: 13**, they may make a supplementary assessment within the same time limits if they subsequently discover that the amount assessed has been understated.[1] The one exception to this rule is where an assessment under VATA 1983, Sch. 7, para. 4(1) or (2) has been made within the time limit specified in ibid, para. 4(5)(*b*), i.e. within one year of evidence coming to the Commissioners' knowledge.[2] In such cases further evidence would have to come to the Commissioners' knowledge before a supplementary assessment could be made. The following comments apply to such assessments.

The Commissioners are allowed only one bite at the same cherry: a mere change of mind regarding evidence in their possession when making the first assessment does not constitute further evidence.[3]

A further assessment is justified in the following circumstances. First, where an investigation into a trader's affairs for one prescribed accounting period discloses underpayments in respect of two or more matters which are quantified at different times. Separate assessments may be made in respect of each matter.[4] Secondly, where two investigations are carried out at different times into the same prescribed accounting period, and each investigation produces evidence of an underpayment arising from a different cause.[5] Making a nil return does not normally amount to evidence of facts sufficient to justify making a further assessment.[6]

De Voil: Value Added Tax A15.39.

[1] FA 1985, s. 22(7). See *Bill Hennessy Associates Ltd v Customs and Excise Comrs* LON/87/640, 709 unreported.

[2] Ibid.

[3] *Jeudwine v Customs and Excise Comrs* [1977] VATTR 115; *Heyfordian Travel Ltd v Customs and Excise Comrs* [1979] VATTR 139.

[4] *Judd v Customs and Excise Comrs* LON/79/9, 104 Taxation 279.

[5] *Kismet Restaurant v Customs and Excise Comrs* MAN/80/191 unreported.

[6] *Parekh v Customs and Excise Comrs* [1984] STC 284.

Time limits

68: 13 The time limits for issuing an assessment can be classified under three headings. In each case there is an overriding condition that an assessment may not be made more than three years after an individual's death.[1] The six year time limit under each heading is increased to 20 years in specified circumstances.[2] However, if an individual dies, an assessment under those provisions may be made at any time in the three years after death if an assessment would have been in time at the date of death.[3]

First, an assessment under VATA 1983, Sch. 7, para. 4(1) or (2) must be made within either: (1) two years after the end of the prescribed accounting period concerned; or (2) one year after evidence justifying an assessment came to light.[4] However, an assessment in (2) may not be made more than six years after the prescribed accounting period concerned.[5]

Secondly, an assessment under VATA 1983, Sch. 7, para. 4(6) must be made within six years of the prescribed accounting period concerned.[6]

Thirdly, an assessment under FA 1985, s. 21 must generally be made within six years[7] of the event or prescribed accounting period which gave rise to penalties, interest or default surcharge. The assessment must be made within two years of penalties, interest or default surcharge arising under ss. 13, 14, 18 or 19 being determined.[8]

Where an assessment is made for two or more prescribed accounting periods without allocating an amount of tax to individual periods, the time limits run from the end of the earliest prescribed accounting period included in the assessment.[9]

De Voil: Value Added Tax A15.37.

[1] FA 1985, s. 22(5)(*a*).

[2] FA 1985, s. 22(4).

[3] FA 1985, s. 22(5)(*b*).

[4] VATA 1983, Sch. 7, para. 4(5). See *Launderette Investments Ltd v Customs and Excise Comrs* MAN/86/57 unreported.

[5] FA 1985, s. 22(1).

[6] Ibid.

⁷ A 20 year limit always applies in relation to penalties under FA 1985, ss. 13 and 15: ibid, s. 22(4).

⁸ FA 1985, s. 22(1)–(3).

⁹ *S J Grange Ltd v Customs and Excise Comrs* [1979] STC 183, [1979] 2 All ER 91, CA. See also *International Language Centres Ltd v Customs and Excise Comrs* [1983] STC 394.

ENFORCEMENT

Recovery proceedings

68: 14 Tax due from any person is recoverable as a debt due to the Crown.[1] Tax due for this purpose represents either: (1) tax shown to be due on a tax return furnished by a trader;[2] (2) tax, penalties, interest or default surcharge shown on an assessment issued by the Commissioners;[3] (3) penalties awarded by a VAT tribunal where a person has failed to comply with a direction or summons;[4] or (4) tax shown on an invoice issued by an unauthorised person.[5]

The VAT legislation and the general law provide the Commissioners with a comprehensive armoury with which to recover tax due to them: (1) they may distrain goods under statutory powers without having to obtain a court order;[6] (2) they may take civil recovery proceedings in the High Court or county court;[7] (3) they may make use of garnishee proceedings, attachment of earnings orders or Mareva injunctions;[8] (4) they may set off amounts due from a trader against amounts due to him;[9] (5) since unpaid VAT is a preferential debt in a bankruptcy, liquidation or receivership,[10] the Commissioners may secure their position by presenting a bankruptcy or winding-up petition in appropriate cases;[11] and (6) where a trader has removed himself from the jurisdiction of the UK courts to an EEC member state, the Commissioners may request the competent authority of the EEC state concerned to take recovery proceedings on their behalf in the national courts of that state.[12]

De Voil: Value Added Tax A15.71–75, 84.

¹ VATA 1983, Sch. 7, para. 6(1).

² VATA 1983, ss 2(3), 14(1). See *Customs and Excise Comrs v International Language Centres Ltd* [1986] STC 279 and § **68: 04**.

³ VATA 1983, Sch. 7, para. 4(9); FA 1985, s. 21(7).

⁴ VATA 1983, Sch. 8, para. 10(4).

⁵ VATA 1983, Sch. 7, para. 6(3).

⁶ VATA 1983, Sch. 7, para. 6(4); FA 1984, s. 16(2); VAT (General) Regulations, SI 1985, No. 886, reg. 65. For the penalty for breaches of a walking possession agreement, see FA 1985, s. 16.

⁷ Crown Proceedings Act 1947, ss. 13–15; FA 1972, s. 55(1). For recovery of tax confirmed by a VAT tribunal on appeal, see FA 1985, s. 29 and R.S.C.O. 45, r. 14.

⁸ See Report of the Committee on Enforcement Powers of the Revenue Departments, Cmnd. 8822, para. 24.2.19.

⁹ FA 1988, s. 21. See *R v customs and Excise Comrs, ex p Richmond* [1989] STC 429.

¹⁰ Insolvency Act 1986, ss. 386(1), 387 and Sch. 16, para. 3.

¹¹ 1,912 bankruptcy petitions and 1,584 petitions to wind up companies were presented in 1986–87: 78th Annual Report (Cm. 234), para. 7.30.

¹² I.e. under national legislation giving effect to Directives 76/308/EEC, 79/1071/EEC.

Security

68: 15 The Commissioners are empowered to call for security to protect their right to receive payment of any tax which is, or may become, due from a trader.[1] A trader faced with such a call has three options: (1) he may provide the required security, which may comprise, for example, a cash deposit or banker's guarantee; (2) he may appeal to a VAT tribunal[2] and submit that the call should be modified or withdrawn; or (3) if neither of the foregoing options succeeds, he must cease making taxable supplies: making such supplies without providing the required security is a criminal offence.[3]

A call for security has been described as a draconian provision which can effectively put a trader out of business.[4] The legislation prescribes that a call must be necessary for the protection of the revenue,[5] and to date it has largely been used to avoid bad debts arising under the so-called "phoenix syndrome"[6] and from traders previously involved in the management of an insolvent business. The tribunal should apply a supervisory test, i.e. whether the Commissioners have acted unreasonably, taken account of irrelevant matters or disregarded any matter which should have been given weight.[7]

De Voil: Value Added Tax A15.83.

[1] VATA 1983, Sch. 7, para. 5(2).

[2] VATA 1983, s. 40(1)(n). He should apply for an extension of any time limit imposed by the Commissioners when serving notice of appeal: *Gayton House Holdings Ltd v Customs and Excise Comrs* [1984] VATTR 11.

[3] VATA 1983, s. 39(5).

[4] *Evans v Customs and Excise Comrs* [1979] VATTR 194.

[5] VATA 1983, Sch. 7, para. 5(2). See *Rosabronze Ltd v Customs and Excise Comrs* LON/84/154 unreported; also *Anglo Associates (Tyres & Exhausts) Ltd v Customs and Excise Comrs* LON/84/154 unreported.

[6] See Report of the Committee on Enforcement Powers of the Revenue Departments, Cmnd. 8822, para. 24.4.

[7] *Mr Wishmore Ltd v Customs and Excise Comrs* [1988] STC 723.

Civil penalties

68: 16 Failure to furnish a return and/or pay the tax (if any) shown to be due thereon within the prescribed time limit[1] may give rise to civil penalties.[2] This provision takes effect in relation to a failure beginning on or after 1st October 1986.[3]

The prescribed penalty is equal to the "prescribed rate" multiplied by the number of days on which the failure continues (up to a maximum of 100) or, if greater, a penalty of £50.[4] The prescribed rate is determined by the number of failures to furnish returns *or* pay tax in the previous two years.[5] In relation to periods falling after 15 March 1988[6] the prescribed rate is—

Number of previous failures	*Daily penalty greater of*
None	£5 or $\frac{1}{6}$% of tax due
1	£10 or $\frac{1}{3}$% of tax due
2	£15 or $\frac{1}{2}$% of tax due

Subject to a statutory defence of reasonable excuse,[7] civil penalties are liable to assessment[8] provided a written warning has been given to the trader in the previous two years.[9] The amount assessed is treated as an amount of tax due from the trader and is thus recoverable as a debt due to the Crown.[10] A right of appeal is given in respect of any liability to penalty or the amount thereof.[11]

De Voil: Value Added Tax A18.58.
[1] For the time limits, see § **68: 01** (returns) and § **68: 04** (payment).
[2] FA 1985, s. 17(1)(c), (4), (5).
[3] FA 1985, s. 17(5); Finance Act 1985 (Breaches of Regulations) (Appointed Day) Order, SI 1986, No. 969, art. 2. The criminal penalty in VATA 1983, s. 39(8) ceased to apply from that date.
[4] FA 1985, s. 17(1).
[5] FA 1985, s. 17(3), (5).
[6] FA 1985, s. 21(4), (5).
[7] FA 1985, s. 17(9). An insufficiency of funds to pay any tax due is not a reasonable excuse: FA 1985, s. 33(2).
[8] FA 1985, s. 21(1).
[9] FA 1985, s. 21(1A).
[10] FA 1985, s. 21(7); VATA 1983, Sch. 7, para. 6(1).
[11] VATA 1983, s. 40(1)(o), (p).

Default surcharge

68: 17   Failure to furnish a tax return and/or pay the tax (if any) shown thereon to be due to the Commissioners within the prescribed time limit[1] can give rise to default surcharge. This provision takes effect in relation to a failure beginning on or after 1st October 1986.[2]

Default surcharge becomes due in respect of a failure occurring during a "surcharge period".[3] Default surcharge is the greater of £30 and a percentage of tax due,[4] the rate being governed by the number of previous failures to render returns and/or pay tax during the surcharge period.[5] The specified percentages are—

Number of previous failures	% of tax due
None	5%
1	10%
2	15%
3	20%
4	25%
5 or more	30%

Default surcharge is assessed.[6] The amount assessed is treated as an amount of tax due from the trader and is thus recoverable as a debt due to the Crown.[7] A right of appeal is given in respect of any liability to surcharge, or the amount thereof.[8]

A trader is not liable to default surcharge if he satisfies the commissioners or, on appeal, a VAT tribunal, that: (1) he did not receive a surcharge liability notice;[9] (2) he posted his return and remittance before the due date;[10] or (3) he has a reasonable excuse for the failure.[11]

The following conduct is capable of amounting to a reasonable excuse: (1) the trader is unable to furnish his return, despite taking all reasonable steps, due to illness,[12] fire[13] or computer problems;[14] (2) the trader misunderstands a concessionary treatment;[15] (3) the Commissioners withdraw the relevant surcharge liability notice.[16] An insufficiency of funds to pay any tax due does not amount to a reasonable excuse.[17]

De Voil: Value Added Tax A18.71–77.
[1] For the time limits, see § **68: 01** (returns) and § **68: 04** (payment).
[2] FA 1985, s. 19(10); Finance Act 1985 (Default Surcharge) (Commencement) Order, SI 1986, No. 968, art. 2.
[3] I.e. a period notified in, or extended by, a "surcharge liability notice" served by the Commissioners under FA 1985, s. 19(1)–(3).
[4] I.e. the tax due which is unpaid by the due date: FA 1985, s. 19(4).
[5] FA 1985, s. 19(4), (5).
[6] FA 1985, s. 21(1).
[7] FA 1985, s. 21(7); VATA 1983, Sch. 7, para. 6(1).
[8] VATA 1983, s. 40(1)(*o*), (*p*).
[9] See *Customs and Excise Comrs v Medway Draughting and Technical Services Ltd* [1989] STC 346.
[10] FA 1985, s. 19(6)(*a*). See *Kings Portable Buildings Ltd v Customs and Excise Comrs* LON/87/737 unreported; *Nazeing Glass Works Ltd v Customs and Excise Comrs* LON/88/70 unreported.
[11] FA 1985, s. 19(6)(*b*).
[12] See *B–P–Fabrications Ltd v Customs and Excise Comrs* MAN/88/31 unreported.
[13] See *Collyer v Customs and Excise Comrs* MAN/87/314 unreported.
[14] See *Lees Smith (East Anglia) Ltd v Customs and Excise Comrs* LON/87/567 unreported.
[15] See *T and H Collard Ltd v Customs and Excise Comrs* LON/87/692 unreported.
[16] See *Montreux Fabrics Ltd v Customs and Excise Comrs* [1988] VATTR 71.
[17] FA 1985, s. 33(2).

Miscellaneous

68: 18   The Commissioners are empowered to revoke an authorisation under the annual accounting scheme if a trader fails to furnish a tax return for the current year by the due date or fails to make any payment in that connection under the scheme.[1]

A VAT tribunal has no jurisdiction to entertain an appeal while tax returns are outstanding or tax due thereon unpaid.[2] Where the decision under appeal is an assessment,[3] the tribunal has no jurisdiction to entertain the appeal unless either: (1) the tax shown thereon has been paid, or (2) an application for the appeal to be heard without payment of tax has been successful.[4]

De Voil: Value Added Tax A3.92; A17.21–23.
[1] VAT (Annual Accounting) Regulations, SI 1988, No. 886, reg. 8(1)(*b*), (*c*).
[2] VATA 1983, s. 40(2); *R v Value Added Tax Tribunal, ex p Cohen* [1984] STC 361; *R v Value Added Tax Tribunal, ex p Minster Associates* [1988] STC 386; *R v London VAT Tribunal and Customs and Excise Comrs, ex p Theodorou* [1989] STC 292. An exception is made in relation to appeals against a call for security.
[3] I.e. under VATA 1983, s. 40(1)(*m*), (*o*) or (*p*).
[4] VATA 1983, s. 40(3); VAT Tribunal Rules, SI 1986, No. 590, r. 11.

69 Exemption and zero-rating

Exemption   1546
Zero-rating: general provisions   1553
Zero-rating: exported goods   1563

EXEMPTION

Introduction

69: 01   VATA 1983, s. 17(1) and Sch. 6 exempt a wide range of goods and services. Schedule 6 may be varied by statutory instrument.[1] It is divided into 12 groups, each of which is sub-divided into one or more items. These items are interpreted in accordance with the notes to each group.[2]

The provisions of Sch. 6 are briefly described under broad headings in the following paragraphs.

A person is liable to civil penalties if he gives an incorrect certificate to a supplier which results in a supply to him being improperly exempted from tax under VATA 1983, Sch. 6, Group 1.[3]

De Voil: Value Added Tax A9.01–03.
[1] VATA 1983, s. 17(2).
[2] VATA 1983, s. 48(6).
[3] VATA 1983, s. 13A.

Election to waive exemption

69: 02   The grant of an interest in, right over or licence to occupy land is excluded from exemption under VATA 1983, Sch. 6, Group 1,[1] and becomes chargeable to tax at the standard rate, if an election to waive exemption has been made in relation to the land or building concerned.[2] However, a grant remains exempt, despite an election, if:[3] (1) it is made in relation to (*a*) a building intended for use as one or more dwellings,[4] (*b*) a building intended for use solely for a relevant residential purpose,[5] or (*c*) a building intended for use solely for a relevant charitable purpose[6] other than as an office; (2) it is made to a registered housing association[7] which certifies that the land is to be used to construct one or more buildings for use as one or more dwellings[8] or for a relevant residential purpose[9]; or (3) it is made to an individual who is to use the land to construct a dwelling[10] for his own occupation.

An election may be made in relation to any specified land or any specified description of land.[11] An election made in relation to a building[12] has effect in relation to the whole building and all land within its curtilage.[13] An election made in relation to agricultural land (or a building thereon) has effect in relation to any other agricultural land unless both parcels of land are separated by either:[14] (1) land which is not agricultural land,[15] or (2) land which is in separate ownership.[16]

An election has effect from the beginning of the day on which it was made or such later day as may be specified therein. However, an election may be backdated to take effect from 1st August 1989 or such later day as may be specified therein, if the election is made no later than 31st October 1989.[17]

An election does not have effect unless it is notified to the Commissioners.[18] It must be notified within 30 days after it was made.[19] It is irrevocable.[20]

The rules relating to the time of supply, value and input tax credit are modified following the making of an election.[21] VAT may be added to the rent reserved in a lease or tenancy following the making of an election unless the agreement specifies otherwise.[22]

De Voil: Value Added Tax A9.04.
[1] See § **69: 03**.
[2] VATA 1983, Sch. 6A, para. 2(1). For the effect of an election on grants made by companies included in a group registration, see ibid, paras. 2(1) and 3(8).
[3] VATA 1983, Sch. 6A, para. 2(2), (3).
[4] As defined in VATA 1983, Sch. 5, Group 8, Note 2.
[5] As defined in ibid, Note 3.
[6] As defined in ibid, Note 4.
[7] As defined in VATA 1983, Sch. 6A, para. 3(9).
[8] As defined in VATA 1983, Sch. 5, Group 8, Note 2.
[9] As defined in ibid, Note 3.
[10] As defined in ibid, Note 2.
[11] VATA 1983, Sch. 6A, para. 3(2).
[12] The following are treated as a single building: (1) buildings linked internally or by a covered walkway; and (2) parades, precincts and complexes divided into separate units.
[13] VATA 1983, Sch. 6A, para. 3(3).
[14] Ibid, para. 3(4).
[15] As defined in ibid, para. 3(5)(*a*).
[16] As defined in ibid, para. 3(5)(*b*).
[17] Ibid, para. 3(1).
[18] An exception is made for the elections specified in Notice No. 742 (April 1989) para. 51.
[19] VATA 1983, Sch. 6A, para. 3(6), (7).
[20] Ibid, para. 3(6).
[21] See respectively § **67: 02, 03** and **27A**.
[22] VATA 1983, s. 42.

Group 1: Land

69: 03   Subject to the exceptions set out below, the grant[1] of any interest in or right over land[2] and any licence to occupy land[3] is exempt.[4]

The following supplies are excluded from exemption:[5] (1) freehold of a new[6] or partly completed[7] building[8] which is neither designed as one or more dwellings[9] nor intended for use solely for a relevant residential[10] or charitable[11] purpose; (2) freehold of a new[12] or partly completed[13] civil engineering work[14]; (3) rights to take game or fish[15]; (4) accommodation[16] in a hotel, inn, boarding house or similar establishment;[17] (5) holiday accommodation[18] in a house, flat, caravan, houseboat[19] or tent; (6) seasonal pitches[20] for caravans and facilities provided in connection with them; (7) pitches for tents and camping facilities; (8) facilities for parking a vehicle;[21] (9) rights to fell and remove standing timber; (10) facilities for housing or storing aircraft; (11) facilities for mooring or storing a ship, boat or vessel;[22] (12) rights to occupy accommodation at a place of entertainment; and (13) facilities for playing sport and participating in physical recreation.[23]

A grant may be chargeable to tax at the standard rate if an election to waive exemption has been made in respect of the land concerned.[24]

A major interest in a building or its site is zero-rated when granted by a person constructing or (in certain circumstances) substantially reconstructing a building.[25]

For the Commissioners' views, see Notice No. 742 and Leaflet Nos. 701/ 20/84, 701/24/84, 709/3/86, 742/1/86.

De Voil: Value Added Tax A9.11–13.

[1] As defined in VATA 1983, Sch. 6, Group 1, Note 1; VATA 1983, Sch. 6A, para. 7.

[2] See *Trewby v Customs and Excise Comrs* [1976] STC 122, [1976] 2 All ER 199.

[3] See *Customs and Excise Comrs v Zinn* [1988] STC 57; *Swindon Masonic Association Ltd v Customs and Excise Comrs* [1978] VATTR 200; *Tameside Metropolitan Borough Council v Customs and Excise Comrs* [1979] VATTR 93; *South Glamorgan County Council v Customs and Excise Comrs* LON/84/485 unreported; *Bullimore v Customs and Excise Comrs* MAN/86/145 unreported. Cf *Henley Picture House Ltd v Customs and Excise Comrs* BIR/79/107, 105 Taxation 243.

[4] VATA 1983, Sch. 6, Group 1, Item 1. For "land", see *Brodrick, Wright & Strong Ltd v Customs and Excise Comrs* LON/86/461 unreported.

[5] Ibid, Item 1(*a*)–(*h*) and Notes 1–5.

[6] As defined in VATA 1983, Sch. 6, Group 1, Note 4.

[7] For the time when a building is completed, see ibid, Note 2.

[8] For buildings completed before 1st April 1989, see ibid, Notes 5, 6.

[9] As defined in VATA 1983, Sch. 5, Group 8, Note 2.

[10] As defined in ibid, Note 3.

[11] As defined in ibid, Note 4.

[12] As defined in VATA 1983, Sch. 6, Group 1, Note 4.

[13] For the time when a civil engineering work is completed, see ibid, Note 2.

[14] For civil engineering works completed before 1st April 1989 see ibid, Notes 5, 6.

[15] An apportionment is made where an interest in, right over or licence to occupy land includes a valuable right to take game or fish: ibid, Note 7. See *Chalk Springs Fisheries (a firm) v Customs and Excise Comrs* LON/86/706 unreported.

[16] As defined in VATA 1983, Sch. 6, Group 1, Item 1(*c*) and Note 8. See *Enever v Customs and Excise Comrs* LON/83/220 unreported.

[17] See *McMurray (a Governor of Allen Hall) v Customs and Excise Comrs* [1973] VATTR 61; *Namecourt Ltd v Customs and Excise Comrs* [1984] VATTR 22; *Westminster City Council v Customs and Excise Comrs* LON/87/564 unreported.

[18] See *Sheppard v Customs and Excise Comrs* [1977] VATTR 272.

[19] As defined in VATA 1983, Sch. 5, Group 11, Item 2.

[20] As defined in VATA 1983, Sch. 6, Group 1, Note 11.

[21] See *Wilson v Customs and Excise Comrs* [1977] VATTR 225; *Dowse v Customs and Excise Comrs* LON/73/102, 92 Taxation 242.

[22] See *Strand Ship Building Co Ltd v Customs and Excise Comrs* LON/84/74 unreported; *Fisher v Customs and Excise Comrs* LON/75/47, 95 Taxation 391.

[23] Subject to the exceptions set out in VATA 1983, Sch. 6, Group 1, Note 13. See *Queens Park Football Club Ltd v Customs and Excise Comrs* [1988] VATTR 76.

[24] See § **69: 02**.

[25] See § **69: 23** and **24**.

Group 2: Insurance

69: 04   The provision of insurance and re-insurance by the following persons is exempt:[1] (1) persons permitted to carry on insurance business; and (2) the

Export Credits Guarantee Department. Certain overseas risks underwritten by these traders qualify for zero-rating.[2]

The following services in connection with insurance and re-insurance are exempt:[3] (1) arranging insurance or re-insurance;[4] and (2) handling insurance claims. Services in connection with the assessment of claims are excluded from exemption.[5]

For the Commissioners' views, see Leaflet No. 701/36/86.

De Voil: Value Added Tax A9.16.
[1] VATA 1983, Sch. 6, Group 2, Items 1, 2.
[2] VATA 1983, Sch. 5, Group 9, Items 6–8.
[3] VATA 1983, Sch. 6, Group 2, Items 3, 4.
[4] See *Ford v Customs and Excise Comrs* [1987] VATTR 130.
[5] Ibid, Note. Services in relation to certain overseas claims are zero-rated under VATA 1983, Sch. 5, Group 9, Items 5 and 6(a).

Group 3: Postal services

69: 05   The following postal services are exempt:[1] (1) postal packets conveyed by the post office; and (2) services supplied by the post office in connection with conveying postal packets.

De Voil: Value Added Tax A9.21.
[1] VATA 1983, Sch. 6, Group 3, Items 1, 2 and Notes 1, 2.

Group 4: Betting, gaming and lotteries

69: 06   The following services are exempt:[1] (1) providing facilities for placing bets; (2) providing facilities[2] for playing games of chance;[3] (3) granting a right to take part in a lottery;[4] and (4) granting a right to take part in a licenced competition for prizes.

For the Commissioners' views, see Leaflet Nos. 701/26/84, 701/27/84, 701/28/84.

De Voil: Value Added Tax A9.26.
[1] VATA 1983, Sch. 6, Group 4, Items 1, 2 and Notes 2, 3.
[2] Other than those set out in ibid, Notes 1(a)–(d), 4. See *J Seven Ltd v Customs and Excise Comrs* [1986] VATTR 42.
[3] See *Grantham (a firm) v Customs and Excise Comrs* MAN/79/102, 104 Taxation 566.
[4] See *McCann v Customs and Excise Comrs* [1987] VATTR 101.

Group 5: Finance

69: 07   The following services are exempt;[1] (1) transactions with money,[2] any security for money,[3] or any note or order for the payment of money; (2) making an advance or granting credit;[4] (3) providing certain instalment credit finance;[5] (4) certain option fees in connection with (3); (5) arranging transactions in (1)–(4); (6) transactions with any security or secondary security;[6] (7) underwriting certain capital issues; (8) making arrangements for certain capital issues; (9) operating any current, deposit or savings account. Coins and banknotes supplied as a collectors' piece or investment article are excluded from exemption.[7] Exemption extends to supplies made by payment card operators to retailers and other outlets accepting credit cards, etc.[8]

For the Commissioners' views, see Leaflet No. 701/29/85.

De Voil: Value Added Tax A9.31.

[1] VATA 1983, Sch. 6, Group 5, Items 1–7 and Notes 1, 3.

[2] See *British Hardware Federation v Customs and Excise Comrs* [1975] VATTR 172; *Barclays Bank plc v Customs and Excise Comrs* [1988] VATTR 23; *Customs and Excise Comrs v Diners Club Ltd* [1989] STC 407, CA.

[3] See *Dyrham Park Country Club v Customs and Excise Comrs* [1978] VATTR 244.

[4] For transactions of confirming houses, see Customs and Excise Press Notice No. 1078 dated 11th February 1986.

[5] For the zero-rating of certain supplies under this heading, see VATA 1983, Sch. 5, Group 9, Item 9.

[6] See *Singer & Friedlander Ltd v Customs and Excise Comrs* [1989] 1 CMLR 814.

[7] VATA 1983, Sch. 6, Group 5, Note 2. See *Milk Marketing Board v Customs and Excise Comrs* LON/87/495 unreported.

[8] Ibid, Note 4, effective from 1st May 1985. See *Customs and Excise Comrs v Diners Club Ltd* [1989] STC 407, CA. See also Customs and Excise Press Notice No. 1045 dated 21st October 1985.

Group 6: Education

69: 08   The following supplies made by schools, universities, polytechnics and equivalent non-profit making[1] bodies are exempt:[2] (1) providing education[3] or research; (2) goods and services incidental[4] thereto; and (3) instruction supplemental thereto.

The following supplies are exempt[5] when provided on a non-profit-making[6] basis: (1) training or re-training for any trade, profession or vocation;[7] (2) goods and services incidental thereto; and (3) instruction supplemental thereto.

The following supplies are exempt[8] when supplied under schemes arranged and paid for by the Training Commission or Department of Economic Development: (1) training or retraining for any trade, profession or vocation; and (2) goods and services essential to such training or retraining.

Educational tuition in educational (but not sporting or recreational) subjects provided on a one-to-one basis is exempt.[9]

Facilities provided by a youth club or association of youth clubs are exempt.[10]

For the Commissioners' views, see Leaflet Nos. 701/30/87, 701/35/84.

De Voil: Value Added Tax A10.36.

[1] See *Customs and Excise Comrs v Bell Concord Educational Trust Ltd* [1989] STC 264, CA. See also Customs and Excise Press Notice No. 30/39 dated 30th March 1989.

[2] VATA 1983, Sch 6, Group 6, Items 1, 2(*a*), 4, 5 and Notes 3A–6.

[3] As defined in VATA 1983, Sch. 6, Group 6, Note 1. See *Church of Scientology of California v Customs and Excise Comrs* [1977] VATTR 278; *Universities Athletic Union v Customs and Excise Comrs* [1974] VATTR 118; *Open University v Customs and Excise Comrs* [1982] VATTR 29; *Barker v Customs and Excise Comrs* [1984] VATTR 147.

[4] See *Woodward Schools (Midland Division) Ltd v Customs and Excise Comrs* [1975] VATTR 123.

[5] VATA 1983, Sch. 6, Group 6, Items 2(*b*), 4, 5 and Notes 5, 6.

⁶ See *Customs and Excise Comrs v Bell Concord Educational Trust Ltd* [1989] STC 264, CA. See also Customs and Excise Press Notice No. 30/89 dated 30th March 1989.
⁷ See *Boyd v Customs and Excise Comrs* [1982] VATTR 138; *Schlumberger Inland Services Inc v Customs and Excise Comrs* [1985] VATTR 35, affd [1987] STC 228.
⁸ VATA 1983, Sch. 6, Group 6, Item 7.
⁹ Ibid, Item 3 and Notes 2, 3.
¹⁰ Ibid, Item 6. See *World Association of Girl Guides and Girl Scouts v Customs and Excise Comrs* [1984] VATTR 28; *Hastings and Rother YMCA v Customs and Excise Comrs* LON/86/388 unreported.

Group 7: Health and Welfare

69: 09   The following services are exempt:¹ (1) services² of specified registered medical and para-medical³ practitioners; (2) services of registered pharmacists; (3) care,⁴ medical treatment or surgical treatment provided in certain hospitals and other institutions; (4) providing a doctor's deputising service; and (5) physical, mental and spiritual welfare provided by specified⁵ bodies.⁶

The following goods are exempt:⁷ (1) goods supplied in conjunction with a service in (3) or (5) supra;⁸ and (2) human blood, products derived therefrom, and human organs and tissues for specified purposes.

For the Commissioners' views, see Leaflet No. 701/31/85.

De Voil: Value Added Tax A9.41.
¹ VATA 1983, Sch. 6, Group 7, Items 1–5, 9 and Notes 1–6. See Case 353/85: *EC Commission v United Kingdom* [1988] STC 251, [1988] 2 All ER 557, ECJ for the legislation in force prior to 29th July 1988.
² For the hire of goods in connection with services, see *Aslan Imaging Ltd v Customs and Excise Comrs* LON/88/20 unreported.
³ See *Barkworth v Customs and Excise Comrs* [1988] STC 771 (osteopath); *Bennett v Customs and Excise Comrs* LON/79/231; 104 Taxation 684 (dental technician).
⁴ See *Crothall & Co Ltd v Customs and Excise Comrs* [1973] VATTR 20; *Cameron v Customs and Excise Comrs* [1973] VATTR 177; *Nuffield Nursing Homes Trust v Customs and Excise Comrs* LON/87/162 unreported.
⁵ In VATA 1983, Sch. 6, Group 7, Items 9, 10 and Note 6.
⁶ For cases decided under Directive 77/388/EEC, art 13A(1)(g), see *Yoga for Health Foundation v Customs and Excise Comrs* [1984] STC 630; *International Bible Students Association v Customs and Excise Comrs* [1988] STC 412; *Westminster City Council v Customs and Excise Comrs* LON/87/564 unreported.
⁷ VATA 1983, Sch. 6, Group 7, Items 4, 6–10 and Note 6.
⁸ Prescription goods are zero-rated under VATA 1983, Sch. 5, Group 14, Item 1. Medicinal products supplied to specific charities are zero-rated under VATA 1983, Sch. 5, Group 16, Items 9 and 10.

Group 8: Burial and cremation

69: 10   The following supplies are exempt:¹ (1) disposal of human remains;² and (2) funeral arrangements.

For the Commissioners' views, see Leaflet No. 701/32/85.

De Voil: Value Added Tax A9.46.
¹ VATA 1983, Sch. 6, Group 8, Items 1, 2.
² See *UFD Ltd v Customs and Excise Comrs* [1981] VATTR 199.

1552   *Part XI—Value added tax*

Group 9: Trade unions and professional bodies

69: 11   Subject to certain restrictions,[1] subscription income of the following non-profit making bodies is exempt:[2] (1) a trade union or similar body; (2) a professional association;[3] (3) a learned society;[4] (4) a trade association;[5] and (5) an organisation of organisations within (1)–(4).

For the Commissioners' views, see Leaflet No. 701/33/84.

De Voil: Value Added Tax A9.51.
[1] See VATA 1983, Sch. 6, Group 9, Item 1 and Note 1.
[2] VATA 1983, Sch. 6, Group 9, Item 1(a)–(d) and Notes 2–5.
[3] See *City Cabs (Edinburgh) Ltd v Customs and Excise Comrs* EDN/79/30, 105 Taxation 668; *Royal Photographic Society of Great Britain v Customs and Excise Comrs* [1978] VATTR 191; *Institute of Leisure and Amenity Management v Customs and Excise Comrs* [1988] STC 602.
[4] See *Bookmakers Protection Association (Southern Area) Ltd v Customs and Excise Comrs* [1979] VATTR 215; *Royal Photographic Society of Great Britain v Customs and Excise Comrs* [1978] VATTR 191. *Institute of Employment Consultants Ltd v Customs and Excise Comrs* LON/ 86/410 unreported; *British Organic Farmers v Customs and Excise Comrs* [1988] VATTR 64.
[5] See *Bee Farmers Association v Customs and Excise Comrs* LON/83/248 unreported.

Group 10: Sports competitions

69: 12   Certain competition[1] entry fees are exempt[2] where they are either: (1) wholly allocated towards the provision of prizes; or (2) charged by a non-profit-making body established for sport or recreation.

For the Commissioners' views, see Leaflet No. 701/34/84.

De Voil: Value Added Tax A9.56.
[1] I.e., in sport or physical recreation.
[2] VATA 1983, Sch. 6, Group 10, Items 1, 2 and Note.

Group 11: Works of art, etc.

69: 13   Certain heritage objects[1] are exempt[2] when supplied by way of private treaty sale to a heritage body,[3] or transfer to the Inland Revenue in lieu of duty, in circumstances where either: (1) no estate duty is chargeable; (2) no IHT is chargeable; or (3) any gain arising is exempt from CGT.

For the Commissioners' views, see Leaflet No. 701/12/84.

De Voil: Value Added Tax A9.61.
[1] I.e. works of art, pictures, prints, manuscripts, scientific collections and other objects which, in each case, are of national, scientific, historic or artistic interest; and objects historically associated with a building of outstanding historic or architectural interest.
[2] VATA 1983, Sch. 6, Group 11, Items 1–4.
[3] I.e. The National gallery, British Museum, Royal Scottish Museum, National Museum of Wales, Ulster Museum and certain similar bodies.

Group 12: Fund-raising events

69:14   Goods and services supplied by the following bodies in connection with a fund-raising event are exempt:[1] (1) a charity, in connection with an event organised for charitable purposes; and (2) a non-profit-making body,[2] in connection with an event organised exclusively for its own benefit.

De Voil: Value Added Tax A9.66.
[1] VATA 1983, Sch. 6, Group 12, Items 1, 2 and Notes 1, 2.
[2] As defined in ibid, Note 2.

ZERO-RATING: GENERAL PROVISIONS

Introduction

69: 15   VATA 1983, s. 16(2) and Sch. 5 zero-rate a wide range of goods and services. Additional provisions relating to terminal markets are contained in orders[1] made under s. 34(1)(*a*).

VATA 1983, Sch. 5 may be varied by statutory instrument.[2] It is divided into 18 groups, each of which is sub-divided into one or more items. These items are interpreted in accordance with the notes to each group.[3]

The provisions of VATA 1983, Sch. 5 and VAT (Terminal Markets) Order 1973 are briefly described under broad headings in the following paragraphs.

A person is liable to civil penalties if he gives an incorrect certificate to a supplier which results in a supply to him being improperly zero-rated under Groups 7, 8, 8A or FA 1989, Sch. 3, para. 13(4).[4]

De Voil: Value Added Tax A11.01–16.
[1] VAT (Terminal Markets) Order, SI 1973, No. 173 and amending orders.
[2] VATA 1983, ss. 16(4) and 48(7).
[3] VATA 1983, s. 48(7).
[4] VATA 1983, s. 13A.

Group 1: Food

69: 16   Food[1] and drink of a kind used for human consumption are zero-rated[2] unless: (1) they fall within one of the excepted items;[3] (2) they are supplied in the course of catering;[4] (3) they are sold for consumption on the premises where the supply takes place;[5] or (4) they comprise hot take-away food.[6]

Animal[7] feeding stuffs are zero rated[8] unless they comprise either: (1) pet food[9]; (2) products used in home brewing or wine making; or (3) an element in the overall service of keeping animals.[10]

Seeds and plants providing food for human consumption or use as animal feeding stuffs are zero-rated.[11]

Live animals are zero-rated[12] when they are of a kind generally used: (1) as food for human consumption (e.g. as meat); (2) to yield food for human consumption (e.g. milk); or (3) to produce food for human consumption (e.g. honey).

For the Commissioners' views, see Leaflets 701/14/89, 701/15/87, 701/25/86, 701/37/84, 701/38/84, 701/40/84, 709/1/87, 709/2/87.

De Voil: Value Added Tax A11.21–27.

[1] See *Marfleet Refining Co Ltd v Customs and Excise Comrs* [1974] VATTR 289; *Soni v Customs and Excise Comrs* [1980] VATTR 9.

[2] VATA 1983, Sch. 5, Group 1, Note 1, 3 and paras. (*a*), (*b*).

[3] As defined in ibid, Excepted Items 1–7; Items overriding the Exceptions 1–6; Notes 4–6. See *Adams Foods Ltd v Customs and Excise Comrs* [1983] VATTR 280.

[4] See *Customs and Excise Comrs v Cope* [1981] STC 532; *DCA Industries Ltd v Customs and Excise Comrs* [1983] VATTR 317.

[5] See *Customs and Excise Comrs v Cope* [1981] STC 532; *R v Customs and Excise Comrs, ex p Sims* [1988] STC 210; *Armstrong v Customs and Excise Comrs* [1984] VATTR 53; *Crownlion (Seafood) Ltd v Customs and Excise Comrs* [1985] VATTR 188; *Mylo's of Reading (Catering and Ices) Ltd v Customs and Excise Comrs* LON/86/575 unreported; *Maheboob Refreshment House v Customs and Excise Comrs* LON/83/259 unreported; *Levy v Customs and Excise Comrs* LON/85/297 unreported; *Streamline Taxis (Southampton) Ltd v Customs and Excise Comrs* LON/85/499 unreported; *Macklin Services (Vending) West Ltd v Customs and Excise Comrs* [1979] VATTR 31; *James v Customs and Excise Comrs* [1977] VATTR 155; *Spragge v Customs and Excise Comrs* [1977] VATTR 162.

[6] As defined in VATA 1983, Sch. 5, Group 1, Note 3(*b*). See *John Pimblett & Sons Ltd v Customs and Excise Comrs* [1988] STC 358, CA; *Redhead v Customs and Excise Comrs* MAN/87/167 unreported.

[7] As defined in ibid, Note 2.

[8] Ibid, Item 2 and Excepted Items 6, 7. See *Smith v Customs and Excise Comrs* MAN/87/321 unreported.

[9] See *Popes Lane Pet Food Supplies Ltd v Customs and Excise Comrs* [1986] VATTR 221.

[10] *Customs and Excise Comrs v Scott* [1978] STC 191; *Customs and Excise Comrs v Bushby* [1979] STC 8.

[11] VATA 1983, Sch. 5, Group 1, Item 3, applying Items 1 and 2 supra.

[12] Ibid, Item 4. See *Customs and Excise Comrs v Lawson-Tancred* [1988] STC 326.

Group 2: Sewerage services and water

69: 17   The following services are zero-rated:[1] (1) the reception, disposal or treatment of foul water or sewage in bulk; and (2) emptying cesspools, septic tanks and similar receptacles.

Water[2] is zero-rated[3] unless it comprises: (1) distilled water, deionised water or water of similar purity; (2) bottled water;[4] or (3) a saline solution.[5] For the Commissioners' views, see Leaflet No. 701/16/85.

De Voil: Value Added Tax A11.71.

[1] VATA 1983, Sch. 5, Group 2, Item 1. Supplies to industry made on or after 1st July 1990 cease to be zero-rated under head (2) by virtue of FA 1989 s. 19(2), (4).

[2] See *Scott-Morley v Customs and Excise Comrs* LON/80/297 unreported.

[3] VATA 1983, Sch. 5, Group 2, Item 2. See *Mander Laundries Ltd v Customs and Excise Comrs* [1973] VATTR 136. Supplies to industry made on or after 1st July 1990 cease to be zero-rated by virtue of FA 1989 s. 18(3), (4).

[4] Applying VATA 1983, Sch. 5, Group 1, Excepted Item 4.

[5] *Scott-Morley v Customs and Excise Comrs* LON/80/297 unreported.

Group 3: Books, etc.

69: 18   Supplies[1] of the following articles are zero-rated:[2] (1) books,[3] booklets, brochures,[4] pamphlets[5] and leaflets;[6] (2) newspapers, journals and periodicals;[7] (3) children's picture books and painting books; (4) sheet music; (5) maps, charts[8] and topographical plans;[9] and (6) covers, cases, etc supplied with the foregoing and not separately accounted for.[10]

For the Commissioners' views, see Leaflet No. 701/10/85.

De Voil: Value Added Tax A11.73.
[1] Including services defined in VATA 1983, Sch. 5, Group 3, Note (b).
[2] VATA 1983, Sch. 5, Group 3, Items 1–6.
[3] See *W F Graham (Northampton) Ltd v Customs and Excise Comrs* LON/79/332, 105 Taxation 452; *City Research Associates Ltd v Customs and Excise Comrs* [1984] VATTR 189; *GUS Catalogue Order Ltd v Customs and Excise Comrs* MAN/87/352 unreported.
[4] See *Betty Foster (Fashion Sewing) Ltd v Customs and Excise Comrs* [1976] VATTR 229.
[5] See *Pace Group (Communications) Ltd v Customs and Excise Comrs* MAN/77/210, 101 Taxation 81.
[6] See *Cronsvale Ltd v Customs and Excise Comrs* [1983] VATTR 313.
[7] See *Geoffrey E Snushall (a firm) v Customs and Excise Comrs* [1982] STC 537.
[8] See *Brooks Histograph Ltd v Customs and Excise Comrs* [1984] VATTR 46.
[9] Other than plans and drawings specified in VATA 1983, Sch. 5, Group 3, Note (a).
[10] See *Fabbri & Partners Ltd v Customs and Excise Comrs* [1973] VATTR 49.

Group 4: Talking books and wireless sets

69: 19   The following goods are zero-rated[1] in the stated circumstances: (1) talking books, transfer, copying and rewinding machines, recording equipment, magnetic tape, spoken recordings and accessories[2] supplied to the Royal National Institute for the Blind, the National Listening Library and similar charities; and (2) wireless receiving sets and cassette recorders supplied to a charity for an onward gratuitous loan to the blind.

For the Commissioners' views, see Leaflet No. 701/31/88.

De Voil: Value Added Tax A11.62.
[1] VATA 1983, Sch. 5, Group 4, Items 1, 2 and Note.
[2] As defined in VATA 1983, Sch. 5, Group 4, Item 1(a)–(h).

Group 5: Newspaper advertisements

69: 20   This group was repealed with effect from 1st May 1985. For the relief available to charities from 1st April 1986, see § **69: 30**.

Group 6: News services

69: 21   This group was repealed with effect from 1st April 1989.

Group 7: Fuel and power

69: 22   The following supplies are zero-rated:[1] (1) solid fuel and material for kindling fires; (2) coal gas, water gas, producer gases and similar gases other than road fuel gas;[2] (3) hydrocarbon gases other than road fuel gas; (4) fuel oil,[3] gas oil,[4] and kerosene[5] wholly or partly relieved from hydrocarbon oil duty;[6] and (5) electricity,[7] heat and air conditioning.

For the Commissioners' views, see Leaflet No. 701/19/87.

De Voil: Value Added Tax A11.77.
[1] VATA 1983, Sch. 5, Group 7, Items 1–5 and Notes 1, 2. Supplies made on or after 1st July

1990 are zero-rated only when made for domestic use or for use by a charity otherwise than in the course or furtherance of a business: see Group 7 as substituted by FA 1989 s. 21.

² As defined in Hydrocarbon Oil Duties Act 1979, s. 5.

³ As defined in VATA 1983, Sch. 5, Group 7, Notes 4, 7.

⁴ As defined in ibid, Notes 5, 7.

⁵ As defined in ibid, Notes 6, 7.

⁶ I.e. under Hydrocarbon Oil Duties Act 1979.

⁷ See *Dyrham Park Country Club v Customs and Excise Comrs* [1978] VATTR 244; *Mander Laundries v Customs and Excise Comrs* [1973] VATTR 136.

Group 8: Buildings and civil engineering works

69: 23   The grant[1] of a major interest[2] in all or any part of a building[3] or its site[4] is zero-rated[5] if: (1) the building is designed as one or more dwellings[6] or is intended to be used solely for a relevant residential[7] or charitable[8] purpose; and (2) the supply is made by the person who constructed the building.[9] A person does not construct a building for this purpose if he carries out specified works[10] to an existing building. The grant of a major interest in all or part of a building outside the foregoing descriptions may be zero-rated under transitional provisions.[11]

Services are zero-rated[12] if they are supplied in the course of constructing: (1) a building designed as one or more dwellings;[13] (2) a building intended to be used solely for a relevant residential[14] or charitable[15] purpose; or (3) a civil engineering work[16] necessary for developing a permanent park for residential caravans.[17] Services in the course of constructing buildings and civil engineering works outside these descriptions may be zero-rated under transitional provisions.[18] The following services are not zero-rated:[19] (1) services of an architect, surveyor, consultant or supervisor; (2) an undivided share in the property of goods; (3) hire of goods; (4) use of business goods for non-business purposes; or (5) carrying out specified works[20] to an existing building or civil engineering work.

Goods supplied in connection with the construction of a building or civil engineering work are zero-rated,[21] provided each of the following conditions is met: (1) the services are zero-rated; (2) the services include use or installation of the goods; (3) the goods are supplied by the person who supplies the services;[22] and (4) the goods fall within a defined class.[23]

A wider range of services is zero-rated in relation to land situated outside the UK.[24]

For the Commissioners' views, see Notice No. 742 and Leaflet No. 708/2/89.

De Voil: Value Added Tax A11.31–33, 36, 37, 39, 40.

¹ "Grant" includes assignment: VATA 1983, Sch. 5, Group 8, Note 1. A grant is deemed to be made by the person constructing a building if the consideration accrues to him: VATA 1983, Sch. 6A, para. 7.

² I.e. the fee simple or a lease for a term exceeding 21 years; VATA 1983, s. 48(1). See *Cottage Holiday Associates Ltd v Customs and Excise Comrs* [1983] STC 278.

³ See *Walle v Customs and Excise Comrs* [1976] VATTR 101.

⁴ See *Stapenhill Developments Ltd v Customs and Excise Comrs* [1984] VATTR 1.

⁵ VATA 1983, Sch. 5, Group 8, Item 1 and Notes 2–8.

⁶ As defined in ibid, Note 2 and meeting the conditions in ibid, Note 7.

⁷ As defined in ibid, Note 3 and meeting the conditions in ibid, Note 6. For the standard

rating of buildings within this description in the ten years following completion, see VATA 1983, Sch. 6A, para. 1(1)–(3).

[8] As defined in ibid, Note 4 and meeting the conditions in ibid, Note 6. For the standard rating of buildings within this description in the ten years following completion, see VATA 1983, Sch. 6A, para. 1(1)–(3).

[9] See *Hulme Trust Educational Foundation v Customs and Excise Comrs* [1978] VATTR 179.

[10] Defined in VATA 1983, Sch. 5, Group 8, Note 10. See *Wimpey Group Services Ltd v Customs and Excise Comrs* [1988] STC 625, CA.

[11] See FA 1989, Sch. 3, para. 13(1)–(3).

[12] VATA 1983, Sch. 5, Group 8, Item 2.

[13] As defined in ibid, Note 2.

[14] As defined in ibid, Note 3 and meeting the conditions in ibid, Note 6.

[15] As defined in ibid, Note 4 and meeting the conditions in ibid, Note 6.

[16] See *UFD Ltd v Customs and Excise Comrs* [1981] VATTR 199; *GKN Birwelco Ltd v Customs and Excise Comrs* [1983] VATTR 128.

[17] As defined in VATA 1983, Sch. 5, Group 8, Note 10.

[18] See FA 1989, Sch. 3, para. 13(1), (4).

[19] VATA 1983, Sch. 5, Group 8, Item 2 and Notes 9, 11.

[20] Defined in ibid, Note 9.

[21] VATA 1983, Sch. 5, Group 8, Item 3 and Note 12. These provisions also apply to goods supplied with services within VATA 1983, Sch. 5, Group 8A, Item 2. See *Customs and Excise Comrs v John Willmott Housing Ltd* [1987] STC 692.

[22] See *Shepherd v Customs and Excise Comrs* [1981] VATTR 158.

[23] See VATA 1983, Sch. 5, Group 8, Item 3(*a*), (*b*) and Note 12; *Customs and Excise Comrs v Westbury Developments (Worthing) Ltd* [1981] STC 72, CA; *Customs and Excise Comrs v Smitmit Design Centre Ltd* [1982] STC 525; *Campbell v Customs and Excise Comrs* [1981] VATTR 16; *Barratt Newcastle Ltd v Customs and Excise Comrs* MAN/82/172 unreported.

[24] VATA 1983, Sch. 5, Group 9, Item 1 and Note 1. See § **69: 25**.

Group 8A: Protected buildings

69: 24   The grant[1] of a major interest[2] in all or any part of a reconstructed listed building or scheduled monument[3] or its site[4] is zero-rated[5] if: (1) the building is designed to remain as or become one or more dwellings[6] or is intended to be used solely for a relevant residential[7] or charitable[8] purpose following the reconstruction or alteration; and (2) the supply is made by the person who substantially reconstructed[9] the building. The grant of a major interest in all or part of a building outside the foregoing descriptions may be zero-rated under transitional provisions.[10]

Services are zero-rated[11] if they are supplied in the course of carrying out an approved alteration[12] to: (1) a building designed to remain as or become one or more dwellings;[13] or (2) a building intended to be used solely for a relevant residential[14] or charitable[15] purpose. Services outside these descriptions may be zero-rated under transitional provisions[16]. The following services are not zero-rated:[17] (1) services of an architect, surveyor, consultant or supervisor; (2) constructing a separate building within the curtilage of the listed building or scheduled monument; (3) an undivided share in the property of goods; (4) hire of goods; or (5) use of goods for non-business purposes. An approved alteration does not include a work of repair or maintenance,[18] and an apportionment is necessary where the services performed include such work.[19]

Goods supplied in connection with an approved alteration are zero-rated under separate provisions.[20]

For the Commissioners' views, see Leaflet No. 708/1/85.

1558   *Part XI—Value added tax*

De Voil: Value Added Tax A11.31, 32, 34, 38, 40.
¹ As defined in VATA 1983, Sch. 5, Group 8, Note 1 and Sch. 6A, para. 7.
² I.e. the fee simple or a lease for a term exceeding 21 years: VATA 1983, s. 48(1). See *Cottage Holiday Associates Ltd v Customs and Excise Comrs* [1983] STC 278.
³ As defined in VATA 1983, Sch. 5, Group 8A, Note 1.
⁴ Cf. *Stapenhill Developments Ltd v Customs and Excise Comrs* [1984] VATTR 1.
⁵ VATA 1983, Sch. 5, Group 8A, Item 1.
⁶ As defined in VATA 1983, Sch. 5, Group 8, Note 2 and meeting the conditions in ibid, Note 7.
⁷ As defined in ibid, Note 3 and meeting the conditions in ibid, Note 6.
⁸ As defined in ibid, Note 4 and meeting the conditions in ibid, Note 6.
⁹ I.e. carried out the work which meets the tests set out in VATA 1983, Sch. 5, Group 8A, Note 2. See *Barraclough v Customs and Excise Comrs* LON/86/699 unreported.
¹⁰ FA 1989, Sch. 3, para. 13(1)–(3).
¹¹ VATA 1983, Sch. 5, Group 8A, Item 2, and Notes 1, 1A.
¹² As defined in VATA 1983, Sch. 5, Group 8A, Notes 3, 4. For alterations to ecclesiastical buildings, see the tests in *ACT Construction Ltd v Customs and Excise Comrs* [1982] STC 25, [1982] 1 All ER 84, HL; *Customs and Excise Comrs v Viva Gas Appliances Ltd* [1983] STC 819, [1984] 1 All ER 112, HL. See also *Sharman v Customs and Excise Comrs* [1983] STC 809 and *Home Protection Co v Customs and Excise Comrs* [1984] STC 278.
¹³ As defined in VATA 1983, Sch. 5, Group 8, Notes 2, 5.
¹⁴ As defined in ibid, Note 3 and meeting the conditions in ibid, Note 6.
¹⁵ As defined in ibid, Note 4 and meeting the conditions in ibid, Note 6.
¹⁶ See FA 1989, Sch. 3, para. 13(1), (4).
¹⁷ VATA 1983, Sch. 5, Group 8A, Item 2, and Notes 6A, 7.
¹⁸ See *ACT Construction Ltd v Customs and Excise Comrs* [1982] STC 25, [1982] 1 All ER 84, HL; *Sutton Housing Trust v Customs and Excise Comrs* [1984] STC 352, CA; *St Luke's Parochial Church Council v Customs and Excise Comrs* [1982] STC 856; *Bickersteth v Customs and Excise Comrs* LON/83/320 unreported.
¹⁹ VATA 1983, Sch. 5, Group 8A, Note 6.
²⁰ I.e. by VATA 1983, Sch. 5, Group 8, Item 3 and Note 12; see § **69: 23**.

Group 9: International services

69: 25   The following services are zero-rated when supplied to anyone who belongs¹ in a non-EEC country: (1) services within VATA 1983, Sch. 3 (to the extent that they do not fall within VATA 1983, Sch. 6);² (2) financial services within VATA 1983, Sch. 6, Group 5 (other than services in connection with a certificate of deposit);³ (3) insurance (other than marine, aviation and transport insurance) within VATA 1983, Sch. 6, Group 2;⁴ (4) re-insurance;⁵ (5) broking services and handling claims within VATA 1983, Sch. 6, Group 2, Items 3 and 4 supplied in connection with risks in (3) or (4) supra;⁶ (6) carrying out work on goods in the UK where the goods are subsequently exported;⁷ and (7) certain agency services.⁸

The following services are zero-rated when performed outside the UK: (1) cultural, artistic, sporting,⁹ scientific, educational and entertainment services;¹⁰ (2) exhibition services;¹¹ (3) services ancillary to services in (1) and (2) supra;¹² (4) valuing goods situated outside the UK;¹³ and (5) carrying out work on goods situated outside the UK.¹⁴

The following services in connection with goods exported to a non-EEC state are zero-rated: (1) insurance risks in connection with making advances or granting credit;¹⁵ and (2) credit finance within VATA 1983, Sch. 6, Group 5, Items 1–5 in connection with the export of specific goods or the transhipment of goods.¹⁶

The following miscellaneous services are zero rated: (1) services within VATA 1983, Sch. 3 supplied to traders who belongs in an EEC state other than the UK (to the extent that the services do not fall within VATA 1983, Sch. 6);[17] (2) marine, aviation and transport insurance supplied in connection with transport to or from a place outside the EEC;[18] (3) agency services in connection with goods exported from the UK and goods or services supplied outside the UK;[19] (4) services relating to land situated outside the UK;[20] and (5) hiring means of transport for use outside the EEC.[21]

For the Commissioners' views, see Notice No. 741 and Leaflet No. 701/36/86.

De Voil: Value Added Tax A11.41.
[1] For the place where the recipient of a supply belongs, see VATA 1983, s. 8(3)–(5); *Binder Hamlyn v Customs and Excise Comrs* [1983] VATTR 171; *Vincent Consultants Ltd v Customs and Excise Comrs* LON/88/254 unreported; *Singer & Friedlander Ltd v Customs and Excise Comrs* [1984] 1 CMLR 814.
[2] VATA 1983, Sch. 5, Group 9, Item 6(*a*) and Notes 4–6. See *Learned Information (Europe) Ltd v Customs and Excise Comrs* [1982] VATTR 125 (advertising); *Gardner Lohmann Ltd v Customs and Excise Comrs* [1981] VATTR 76 and *Culverpalm Ltd v Customs and Excise Comrs* [1984] VATTR 199 (financial services).
[3] Ibid, Item 6(*a*) and Notes 5, 6.
[4] Ibid, Item 6(*b*) and Note 5.
[5] Ibid, Item 6(*c*) and Note 5.
[6] Ibid, Item 6(*d*) and Note 5.
[7] Ibid, Item 10. See *Banstead Manor Stud Farm Ltd v Customs and Excise Comrs* [1979] VATTR 154.
[8] Ibid, Item 11(*b*) and Note 8.
[9] See *Ernest George Ltd v Customs and Excise Comrs* LON/83/354 unreported; *Patrick Eddery Ltd v Customs and Excise Comrs* [1986] VATTR 30.
[10] VATA 1983, Sch. 5, Group 9, item 3(*a*) and Note 3.
[11] Ibid, item 3(*b*) and Note 2.
[12] Ibid, Item 3(*c*) and Note 3.
[13] Ibid, Item 4 and Note 3.
[14] Ibid, Item 4 and Note 3.
[15] Ibid, Item 8.
[16] Ibid, Item 9.
[17] Ibid, Item 5 and Notes 3, 4. See *Learned Information (Europe) Ltd v Customs and Excise Comrs* [1982] VATTR 125 (advertising); *Gardner Lohmann Ltd v Customs and Excise Comrs* [1981] VATTR 76 and *Culverpalm Ltd v Customs and Excise Comrs* [1984] VATTR 199 (financial services).
[18] Ibid, Item 7.
[19] Ibid, Item 11(*a*), (*c*) and Note 8.
[20] Ibid, Item 1 and Notes 1, 3. See *Brodrick, Wright & Strong Ltd v Customs and Excise Comrs* LON/86/461 unreported.
[21] Ibid, Item 2 and Note 3. See *Oathplan Ltd v Customs and Excise Comrs* [1982] VATTR 195.

Group 10: Transport

69: 26 Supplies of aircraft[1] and ships[2] within specified categories are zero-rated. The following services in connection with them are zero-rated:[3] (1) repair or maintenance; (2) handling; (3) surveying; (4) classification for the purposes of any register; and (5) agency services.

The following services supplied to overseas traders are zero-rated:[4] (1) handling, storage and transport of imported and exported goods; (2)

1560   *Part XI—Value added tax*

handling any ship or aircraft; (3) surveying and classifying any ship or aircraft; and (4) certain agency services.

The following passenger transport[5] services are zero-rated:[6] (1) transport in a vehicle,[7] ship or aircraft designed or adapted to carry 12 or more passengers; (2) transport by the Post Office; (3) transport on any scheduled flight; (4) transport to or from a place outside the UK; (5) transport outside the UK; (6) ancillary services performed outside the UK; and (7) agency services.

The following freight transport services are zero-rated:[8] (1) transport outside the UK; (2) transport to or from a place outside the UK; (3) handling goods; (4) ancillary services performed outside the UK; and (5) agency services.

The following miscellaneous supplies are zero-rated: (1) certain supplies made to the Royal National Life-boat Institution;[9] (2) pilotage services;[10] (3) salvage or towage services;[11] and (4) designated travel services[12] to be enjoyed outside the EEC.[13]

For the Commissioners' views, see Notice No. 744 and Leaflet Nos. 700/25/86, 709/5/88.

De Voil: Value Added Tax A11.51.
[1] VATA 1983, Sch. 5, Group 10, Item 2.
[2] Ibid, Item 1.
[3] Ibid, Items 1, 2, 6, 9, 10 and Notes 1, 2, 4–6.
[4] Ibid, Items 10(*b*) and 12.
[5] See *Customs and Excise Comrs v Blackpool Pleasure Beach Co* [1974] STC 138, [1974] 1 All ER 1011 ("big dipper"); *British Railways Board v Customs and Excise Comrs* [1977] STC 221, [1977] 2 All ER 873, CA (rail cards); *Quarry Tours Ltd v Customs and Excise Comrs* [1984] VATTR 238.
[6] VATA 1983, Sch. 5, Group 10, Items 4, 5, 10, 11.
[7] See *Quarry Tours Ltd v Customs and Excise Comrs* [1984] VATTR 238; *Llandudno Cabinlift Co Ltd v Customs and Excise Comrs* [1973] VATTR 1.
[8] VATA 1983, Sch 5, Group 10, Items 5, 6, 10, 11 and Notes 4, 5.
[9] Ibid, Item 3 and Note 3.
[10] Ibid, Item 7.
[11] Ibid, Item 8.
[12] Defined in VAT (Tour Operators) Order, SI 1987, No. 1806, arts. 3, 14. For the calculation of output tax on such services, see § **67: 12**.
[13] VATA 1983, Sch. 5, Group 10, Item 13 and Note 7.

Group 11: Caravans and houseboats

69: 27   "Mobile home" caravans[1] and houseboats[2] together with certain removable contents[3] are zero-rated.[4] The following services in connection with such caravans and houseboats are zero-rated[5] to the extent that they do not amount to the provision of accommodation: (1) transferring an undivided share; (2) hire; and (3) use for private or non-business purposes.

For the Commissioners' views, see Leaflet Nos. 701/20/84, 709/2/87.

De Voil: Value Added Tax A11.79.
[1] I.e. exceeding 7 metres in length or 2.3 metres in breadth, excluding tow bars and similar attachments: VATA 1983, Sch. 5, Group 11, Item 1; Motor Vehicles (Construction and Use) Regulations, SI 1978, No. 1017.
[2] Defined in VATA 1983, Sch. 5, Group 11, Item 2.

³ Defined in ibid, Note (*a*).
⁴ Ibid, Items 1, 2 and Note (*a*).
⁵ Ibid, Item 3 and Note (*b*).

Group 12: Gold

69: 28   Gold and gold coins held in the UK are zero-rated[1] when supplied:[2] (1) by a Central Bank to another Central Bank or a member of the London Gold Market, or (2) by a Member of the London Gold Market to a Central Bank.
For the Commissioners' views, see Leaflet No. 701/21/87.

De Voil: Value Added Tax A11.81.
[1] VATA 1983, Sch. 5, Group 12, Items 1, 2 and Note 1.
[2] For supplies included, see ibid, Note 3.

Group 13: Bank notes

69: 29   A note payable to bearer on demand issued by a bank is zero rated.[1]

De Voil: Value Added Tax A11.83.
[1] VATA 1983, Sch. 5, Group 13, Item 1.

Group 14: Drugs, medicines, aids for the handicapped, etc.

69: 30   Prescriptions dispensed by a registered pharmaceutical chemist are zero-rated.[1]
The following supplies made to a chronically sick or disabled person are zero-rated:[2] (1) supplying and installing specified goods[3] for domestic or personal use; (2) adapting goods to suit his condition, including goods used therein;[4] (3) supplying and installing a vertical lift; (4) supplying an alarm system; (5) repair or maintenance to goods in (1)–(4); (6) receiving and responding to calls from an alarm system in (4); (7) specified alterations[5] to his private residence; and (8) hiring a motor vehicle in specified circumstances.[6] Similar supplies within (1)–(7) made to a charity for the benefit of a chronically sick or disabled person are also zero-rated.[7]
For the Commissioners' views, see Leaflet Nos. 701/7/86, 701/31/88.

De Voil: Value Added Tax A11.85.
[1] VATA 1983, Sch. 5, Group 14, Item 1 and Notes 2, 5. For medicinal products supplied to certain charities, see § **69.32**.
[2] Ibid, Item 2, 3, 5–8, 10–13, 15–17 and Notes 3, 5–9.
[3] Listed in ibid, Item 2(*a*)–(*h*) and Note 4. See *Princess Louise Scottish Hospital v Customs and Excise Comrs* [1983] VATTR 191; *Kirton Designs Ltd v Customs and Excise Comrs* LON/86/641 unreported.
[4] For apportionments, see ibid, Note 8.
[5] Listed in ibid, Items 8 and 10.
[6] Listed in ibid, Item 12 and Notes 6, 7. For leasing under the Motability Scheme, see Customs and Excise Press Notice No. 919 dated 5th June 1984.
[7] Ibid, Items 2, 4–7, 9, 10A, 11, 14, 16, 17 and Notes 3, 5, 8, 9.

Group 15: Imports, exports, etc.

69: 31 The following goods are zero-rated:[1] (1) imported goods supplied prior to delivery of an entry (i.e. before VAT due on import is accounted for); (2) goods supplied to or by certain bodies[2] managing international defence projects;[3] and (3) specified goods[4] supplied to specified overseas persons[5] for use in the UK solely for the manufacture of goods for export.

The following services are zero-rated:[6] services supplied to or by certain bodies[7] managing international defence projects.[8]

For the Commissioners' views, see Notice Nos. 702, 703 and Leaflet No. 701/22/84.

De Voil: Value Added Tax A11.87.
[1] VATA 1983, Sch. 5, Group 15, Items 1, 3, 4.
[2] Defined in ibid, Notes 3–5.
[3] Defined in ibid, Item 3 and Note 2.
[4] Defined in ibid, Item 4.
[5] Defined in ibid, Notes 3–6.
[6] Ibid, Item 3.
[7] Defined in ibid, Notes 3–5.
[8] Defined in ibid, Item 3 and Note 2.

Group 16: Charities etc.

69: 32 The following supplies made direct to certain bodies are zero-rated:[1] (1) goods donated to specified charities;[2] (2) certain advertising[3] supplied to any charity; (3) medicinal products[4] supplied to specified charities;[5] (4) substances[6] used in medical research supplied to a charity and (5) specified goods,[7] and certain services in connection with them,[8] supplied to specified bodies,[9] subject to limitation on the source of moneys used to pay for them.[10] Certain supplies made to charities are zero-rated under other groups.[11]

Specified goods are zero-rated when supplied to an intermediary for donation to specified bodies subject to limitation on the source of moneys used to pay for them.[12]

The following supplies made by a charity are zero-rated[13] (1) donated goods supplied by specified charities;[14] and (2) goods exported by a charity.[15] For the Commissioners' views, see 701/1/87, 701/6/86.

De Voil: Value Added Tax A11.66.
[1] VATA 1983, Sch. 5, Group 16, Items 2, 5–10 and Notes 6, 8–13.
[2] Defined in ibid, Item 1 and Notes 2, 3. See Notice No. 748 (October 1988) para. A8(*c*).
[3] Defined in ibid, Item 8.
[4] Defined in ibid, Note 12.
[5] Defined in ibid, Item 9.
[6] Defined in ibid, Note 13.
[7] Defined in ibid, Note 4, 11.
[8] Defined in ibid, Items 6, 7 and Note 9.
[9] Defined in ibid, Note 5.
[10] Ibid, Item 5 and Notes 8, 9.
[11] See Group 4 (Items 1 and 2), Group 10 (Item 3), Group 14 (Items 2, 4–7, 9, 11, 14, 16 and 17) supra.
[12] VATA 1983, Sch. 5, Group 16, Item 4 and Notes 4, 5, 7, 10, 11.
[13] Ibid, Items 1, 3 and Note 1.
[14] Defined in ibid, Item 1 and Notes 2, 3.

Group 17: Clothing and footwear

69: 33   The following supplies[1] are zero-rated:[2] (1) articles designed as clothing, headgear or footwear for young children[3] and neither suitable for older persons[4] nor (with exceptions[5]) made wholly or partly of fur skin;[6] (2) protective boots and helmets for industrial use (but not supplies to employers for use by employees); and (3) protective motor cycle helmets.

For the Commissioners' views, see Notice No. 714 and Leaflet No. 701/23/84.

De Voil: Value Added Tax A11.89.
1 Including services defined in VATA 1983, Sch 5, Group 17, Note 5.
2 Ibid, Items 1–3 and Notes 1, 2, 4.
3 See *Walter Stewart Ltd v Customs and Excise Comrs* [1974] VATTR 131; *Jeffrey Green & Co Ltd v Customs and Excise Comrs* [1974] VATTR 94; *VF Corpn (UK) Ltd v Customs and Excise Comrs* BEL/79/7, 105 Taxation 244.
4 See *Jeffrey Green & Co Ltd v Customs and Excise Comrs* [1974] VATTR 94; *Walter Stewart Ltd v Customs and Excise Comrs* [1974] VATTR 131; *Brays of Glastonbury Ltd v Customs and Excise Comrs* CAR/78/95, 102 Taxation 218.
5 Defined in VATA 1983, Sch. 5, Group 17, Note 2(*a*)–(*d*).
6 Defined in ibid, Note 3.

SI 1973/173: Terminal markets

69: 34   The following commodity transactions on specified[1] terminal markets are zero-rated:[2] (1) futures transactions (including options) to or by market members which do not lead to a delivery of the goods; (2) sales of physical goods between market members; and (3) brokerage services by market members.

For the Commissioners' views, see Leaflet No. 701/9/85.

De Voil: Value Added Tax A11.08.
1 In VAT (Terminal Markets) Order, SI 1973, No. 173, art. 2 (as amended).
2 Ibid, art. 3.

ZERO RATING: EXPORTED GOODS

Introduction

69: 35   Goods are exported if they are sent from one country to another.[1] Since a supply of goods is made in the UK if the goods are within the UK at the time of supply,[2] it follows that an export involves removing goods from a place inside the UK to a place outside the UK.

The underlying intention of the legislation is that all goods exported from the UK should be taxed at the zero-rate, regardless of whether or not they fall within a description in VATA 1983, Sch. 5.[3] In practice, the legislation goes one stage further and zero-rates certain removals of goods to a place *inside* the UK subject to stringent conditions which ensure that relief is given only where the goods are in fact exported by the customer.[4] Goods found in the UK after their supposed export under these provisions are liable to forfeiture.[5]

De Voil: Value Added Tax A12.01–08.
  [1] See *Guthrie v Customs and Excise Comrs* [1980] VATTR 152.
  [2] VATA 1983, s. 6(3).
  [3] VATA 1983, s. 16(6).
  [4] VATA 1983, s. 16(7), (8).
  [5] VATA 1983, s. 16(9).

Goods exported by the person who supplies them

69: 36   Goods are zero-rated if: (1) the Commissioners are satisfied that the person supplying them has exported them; and (2) such conditions as may be specified in regulations or imposed by the Commissioners are fulfilled.[1] It seems clear that a trader must possess some evidence of export if he is to satisfy the Commissioners that the goods have been exported. The evidence specified by the Commissioners for this purpose is set out in Notice No. 703.[2] The requirement for evidence is a condition which must be fulfilled, and it seems clear that failure to obtain this evidence is fatal to a claim for zero-rating.[3]

De Voil: Value Added Tax A12.11.
  [1] VATA 1983, s. 16(6)(*a*) (as amended by FA 1986, s. 12(1)). No regulations have been made to date.
  [2] (March 1987) paras. 22, 28, 31.
  [3] Cf *Henry Moss of London Ltd v Customs and Excise Comrs* [1981] STC 139, CA. This was not necessarily so prior to the amendment of VATA 1983, s. 16(6): see *Middlesex Textiles Ltd v Customs and Excise Comrs* [1979] VATTR 239. Cf. *Sadri v Customs and Excise Comrs* LON/78/265 unreported.

Stores for use in ships, aircraft and hovercraft

69: 37   Goods are zero-rated if: (1) the Commissioners are satisfied that the person supplying them has shipped them for use as stores or retail merchandise on a voyage or flight to a destination outside the UK; and (2) such conditions as may be specified in regulations or imposed by the Commissioners are fulfilled.[1] It seems clear that the trader must possess some evidence in order to satisfy the Commissioners, if called upon to do so, that goods have been so shipped. The evidence specified by the Commissioners for this purpose is set out in Notice No. 703.[2] The requirement for evidence is a condition which must be fulfilled, and it seems clear that failure to obtain this evidence is fatal to a claim for zero-rating.[3]

De Voil: Value Added Tax A12.22, 23.
  [1] VATA 1983, s. 16(6)(*b*) (as amended by FA 1986, s. 12(1)). No regulations have been made to date.
  [2] (March 1987) para. 36. For mess and canteen stores to HM ships, see ibid, para. 39.
  [3] Cf *Henry Moss of London Ltd v Customs and Excise Comrs* [1981] STC 139, CA.

Export of freight containers

69: 38   The supply of a container[1] is zero-rated where the Commissioners are satisfied that it is to be exported and such conditions as they may impose are met.[2] The conditions specified by the Commissioners are set out in Leaflet No. 703/1/83, para. 3.

De Voil: Value Added Tax A12.23.
[1] As defined in VAT (General) Regulations, SI 1985, No. 886, reg. 38(3).
[2] SI 1985, No. 886, reg. 50.

Supplies to export houses

69: 39   Goods supplied to an export house[1] are zero-rated[2] provided the following conditions are met: (1) the goods are delivered as specified below; (2) the goods are exported; and (3) such conditions as the Commissioners may impose are met.

The specified methods of delivery are: (1) direct to a port, customs and excise airport or approved inland clearance depot for immediate shipment; or (2) direct to an export packer for delivery direct to a port, customs and excise airport or approved inland clearance depot for immediate shipment to the order of the export house. Goods delivered to an export house in the UK do not qualify for zero-rating.[3]

The conditions imposed by the Commissioners relate to evidence of export. This varies according to the method of delivery and comprises: (1) normal export documents, (2) certificate of shipment, and (3) export packer's certificate.[4]

> EXAMPLE
> A Ltd receives an order for 1,000 widgets from B, an Italian trader. C Ltd, a widget wholesaler, consigns 1,000 widgets to Heathrow Airport for delivery to Milan. A Ltd is an export house and C Ltd may zero-rate the supply to A Ltd.

De Voil: Value Added Tax A12.24.
[1] As defined in VAT (General) Regulations, SI 1985, No. 886, reg. 38(5). See *Musani Garments Ltd v Customs and Excise Comrs* MAN/86/62 unreported.
[2] SI 1985, No. 886, reg. 49.
[3] SI 1985, No. 886, reg. 49(a).
[4] Notice No. 703 (March 1987) paras. 11, 22, 31.

Supplies to overseas persons

69: 40   Goods[1] intended for export are zero-rated[2] where the Commissioners are satisfied that: (1) the goods have been supplied to an eligible person; (2) the goods have been exported; and (3) such conditions as the Commissioners may impose have been met.

An eligible person is either: (1) a person not resident in the UK; (2) a trader who has no business establishment in the UK from which taxable supplies are made; or (3) the local, regional or central government of a country other than the UK. This class does not extend to the crew of a ship or aircraft leaving the UK.[3]

For the conditions imposed by the Commissioners, see Notice No. 703[4] and Leaflet No. 703/2/87 (sailaway boats). These conditions have been upheld by the courts.[5]

De Voil: Value Added Tax A12.26–28.
[1] Other than a motor car, motor cycle, motor scooter or motor caravan: VAT (General) Regulations, SI 1985, No. 886, reg. 38(6).
[2] SI 1985, No. 886, reg. 51(1).
[3] SI 1985, No. 886, reg. 51(1)(*a*) applying ibid, regs. 38(10) and 51(2).
[4] (March 1987) paras. 12, 15, 32.
[5] *Henry Moss of London Ltd v Customs and Excise Comrs* [1981] STC 139, [1981] 2 All ER 86, CA.

Supplies to persons leaving the UK

69: 41   Subject to the exceptions stated below, goods supplied to persons leaving the UK, whether as crew members or passengers, are zero-rated[1] provided: (1) the Commissioners are satisfied that the goods have been exported; (2) such conditions as the Commissioners impose are met; and (3) conditions specified in the legislation are met.

In broad terms, the following supplies are *excluded* from zero-rating: (1) supplies made to UK residents intending to leave the UK for less than 12 months and EEC passport holders other than crew members intending to leave the EEC bloc for less than 12 months; (2) motor vehicles;[2] and (3) boats intended to be exported under their own power.

In broad terms, the Commissioners require traders to hold certified forms VAT 407 or VAT 435 or specified alternative evidence.[3]

In broad terms, the statutory conditions comprise: (1) a requirement for goods to be delivered direct to the ship, hovercraft or aircraft in which the customer intends to depart in certain cases; (2) a requirement for goods to be produced to the proper officer at the port or airport of departure in certain cases; and (3) the consideration for the supply to exceed specified limits where goods are supplied to persons (other than certain crew members) travelling to an EEC member state.

For the Commissioners views, see Notice No. 704.

De Voil: Value Added Tax A12.31.
[1] VAT (General) Regulations, SI 1985, No. 886, regs. 52–55. For various definitions, see ibid, reg. 38.
[2] For the relief available, see § **69: 42**.
[3] Notice No. 704 (March 1985) paras. 7, 9, 18 and 21.

New motor vehicles supplied to persons leaving the UK

69: 42   Persons intending to leave the UK for at least 12 months can apply (on form VAT 410) to purchase a new motor vehicle without payment of VAT and use it in the UK for a specified period before exporting it. Subject to conditions[1] imposed by the Commissioners, manufacturers[2] who supply such vehicles may zero-rate them.[3]

For the Commissioners' views, see Notice No. 705.

De Voil: Value Added Tax A12.36.
  [1] See Notice No. 705 (January 1986).
  [2] Defined in VAT (General) Regulations, SI 1985, No. 886, reg. 38(7).
  [3] SI 1985, No. 886, regs. 56, 57.

TABLES AND INDEX

Table of statutes

Table of cases

[51]

PARA

PARA

PARA

Table of cases [71]

PARA

PARA

PARA

PARA

Index

Stamp duty—*contd.*
will, 60:14–60:15
see also CAPITAL DUTY
Stationery
value added tax, 65:21
Statutes
rules, 1:29–1:31
sources of law, as, 1:26
statutory interpretation, 1:27–1:29
Stock dividends
corporation tax, 24:16–24:17
Stock relief
abolition of, 7:167
trading stock, 7:166
Stocks, *see* SHARES
Stores
aircraft, for use in, 69:37
hovercraft, for use in, 69:37
ships, for use in, 69:37
Subsidies
trading receipts, 7:83
Succession
business property, transfer of, 45:08
capital allowances, 8:11
trade, of—
generally, 7:47
new trader, effects on, 7:48
old trader, effects on, 7:49
rules, 7:50–7:53
Superannuation annuity
stamp duty, 59:39
Supplies, *see* VALUE ADDED TAX
Survivorship clauses
inheritance, 41:08

Talking books
value added tax, 69:19
Tangible movable property
capital gains tax, exemption from, 15:08
Tapes
capital allowances, 8:42
Tax advantage
cancellation of, *see* SECURITIES
Tax avoidance
Burmah Oil case, 1:08
capital allowances, 8:09
capital gains tax, 15:05, 15:10
company—
amalgamation, 19:19
reconstruction, 19:19
corporation tax, computation, 25:11–25:16
DLT fragmentation scheme, 1:11
doubts, 1:12–1:25
evasion distinguished from, 1:03
Furniss v Dawson, 1:06–1:07, 1:09
generally, 1:03–1:10, 13:01
improvements, 9:21
interest relief, 5:38
issues, 1:12–1:25
land, artificial transactions in, *see* LAND

Tax avoidance—*contd.*
lease—
granted at undervalue, assignment of, 9:24
sale with right of reconveyance, 9:25
surrender of, 9:22
variations, 9:23
waivers, 9:23
legislation—
artificial transactions in land, *see* LAND
cancellation of tax advantages, transactions in securities, *see* SECURITIES
generally, 31:01–31:06
other provisions, 31:18–31:20
personal activities, sale by individual of income derived from, 31:33–31:34
shares, specific provisions relating to, *see* SHARES
long absences, 6:09
Ramsay principle, 1:07–1:09
rent, commutation of, 9:22
settlement, *see* SETTLEMENT
tax mitigation, distinguished from, 1:03
transactions for sole purpose of, 1:06
Westminster doctrine, 1:04–1:08
Tax evasion
avoidance distinguished from, 1:03
Tax haven
meaning, 32:26
Tax mitigation
deed of covenant, use of, 9:33–9:35
meaning, 1:03
Tax planning
agricultural relief, 44:27
Burmah Oil case, 1:08
business relief, 44:27
discretionary trust, 42:23
double taxation relief, 36:34–36:40
doubts, 1:12–1:25
Furniss v Dawson, 1:06–1:07, 1:09
generally, 1:03–1:10
issues, 1:12–1:25
Ramsay principle, 1:07–1:09
share incentive schemes, 6:66
share option schemes, 6:59
Westminster doctrine, 1:04–1:08
Tax returns
value added tax, 68:01–68:04
Tax unit
choice of, 3:01
Tax year
meaning, 1:02
Teletext
adaptor, capital allowances, 8:43
receiver, capital allowances, 8:43
Tenancy
assured, dwelling house, of, 8:23
Scottish agricultural, 45:29
Tenant
property income, 9:06–9:07